Elements of Land Law

ELEMENTS OF
LAND LAW

Kevin Gray
Fellow of Trinity College;
University Lecturer in Law, Cambridge

London
Butterworths
1987

United Kingdom	Butterworth & Co (Publishers) Ltd, 88 Kingsway, LONDON WC2B 6AB and 61A North Castle Street, EDINBURGH EH2 3LJ
Australia	Butterworths Pty Ltd, SYDNEY, MELBOURNE, BRISBANE, ADELAIDE, PERTH, CANBERRA and HOBART
Canada	Butterworths. A division of Reed Inc., TORONTO and VANCOUVER
New Zealand	Butterworths of New Zealand Ltd, WELLINGTON and AUCKLAND
Singapore	Butterworth & Co (Asia) Pte Ltd, SINGAPORE
USA	Butterworths Legal Publishers, ST PAUL, Minnesota, SEATTLE, Washington, BOSTON, Massachusetts, AUSTIN, Texas and D & S Publishers, CLEARWATER, Florida

British Library Cataloguing in Publication Data

Gray, Kevin J.
Elements of land law.
1. Real property—England
I. Title
344.2064'3   KD829

ISBN Hardcover   0 406 50160 2
ISBN Softcover   0 406 50161 0

The cover of the limp edition shows *A Scottish Lake Scene* by JMW Turner (1779–1851). It is reproduced by kind permission of the Tate Gallery, London.

Typeset by Kerrypress Ltd, Luton
Printed and bound in Great Britain by Mackays of Chatham PLC, Chatham Kent

Preface

By long tradition land law has acquired a reputation as a highly technical area which many students find both difficult and unrewarding. This book seeks to show that none of this need be true and that even quite complex problems of modern land law can be explained in simple terms which start from underlying 'elements' or first principles. Far from being an uninspiring subject of study, land law—when properly understood—emerges as one of the most exciting and fast-moving branches of contemporary English law.

It is, of course, quite true that the law of land often appears to have a strangely enduring quality. In England and Wales the modern law is still dominated by the vast corpus of legislation which came into effect on 1 January 1926. This legislation was itself the summation of the steady movement towards reform of real property law which had been set in motion almost a century earlier. Against this background it was perhaps inevitable that the structural elements of English land law, so painstakingly gathered together in the 1925 legislation, should have been destined to survive relatively intact to the present day.

This sense of stasis or permanence is, however, largely illusory: modern land law is not the slow-moving subject it is commonly supposed to be. Important developments over the last few years—both judicial and legislative—have begun to refashion even the structural features of the 1925 Acts to accord more closely with the constantly changing needs of the 1980s and 1990s. Significant elements of English land law are nowadays on the move and, as they gather a critical mass, may well push past a tipping point into an area where the law of the future suddenly appears markedly different from the law of the past. Thus, for instance, the unremitting extension of title registration has made it realistic for the first time to contemplate that unregistered land may shortly become a thing of the past. The rights of residential occupiers have been revolutionised by a veritable explosion of housing legislation which confers rights of security, rights to repair, rights to buy and even a so-called 'preserved' right to buy. A recent flurry of Law Commission reports indicates that there may soon be a wholesale reshaping of such areas as the law of leases, mortgages, covenants, and even of the registered land regime itself.

These are indeed interesting times not only for land lawyers but also for those who have any curiosity about the criteria of distributive justice. And it should not go unnoticed that land law, in so far as it allocates the rights and benefits traditionally labelled as 'property', provides an important reflection of our ideas of social justice. With such considerations in mind, it is the aim of this book, while remaining rigorously analytical, to provide a contextual and critical treatment of modern land law. The book says relatively little about the history of land law; nor does it purport to be a manual on conveyancing. It does, however, seek to describe the elements of contemporary land law against the background of the social and political implications of the subject.

The book is divided into two parts. 'The General Part' identifies the basic concepts and principles of land law and integrates them into a framework for comprehensive and systematic analysis. Primary emphasis has been given to those aspects of land law which are of greatest modern relevance—hence the substantial exclusion of such matters as the law of strict settlements and the rule against perpetuities. The second part of the book, 'Special Problems', gives a practical application to many of the concepts which are described in the first part. A number of key issues which illustrate the wider effects of land law are examined. Given that 1987 has been designated as the 'International Year of Shelter for the Homeless', it is perhaps appropriate that this portion of the book should concentrate particularly upon the sphere of residential property.

The book as a whole seeks to make extensive reference to the relevant English and comparative case law. Given the increasing welcome accorded even in English courts to the decisions of other jurisdictions, it seems quite wrong to ignore comparative material which contributes towards a richer understanding of a particular problem. The greater accessibility of unreported case law (through devices such as Lexis) has likewise thrown new light on areas which have hitherto been of somewhat low visibility. Although an attempt has been made to state the law as it existed at the end of July 1987, considerable attention has been given throughout to the reform proposals made by the Law Commission and other bodies.

Many people have contributed either practical help or encouragement towards the completion of this book. I must particularly thank Caroline Amory, Stephen Bellamy, Tim Bonyhady, Paul Finn, Gareth Jones, Kurt Lipstein, David Pearl, Paul Popplewell, John Tiley, Frances Wilson, and Tim Youdan. I am also indebted to the Squire Law Librarian, Keith McVeigh, and to his consistently cheerful and helpful staff, Clive Argent, Brian Humphreys, Trudy Young and Peter Zawada. I must likewise record my gratitude to the Libraries of the Institute for Advanced Legal Studies and the New Zealand High Commission in London. Back at Trinity Laura Cordy and John Hinch gave extremely generous help with computers and word-processors, while at Butterworths nothing was done without the efficient and patient intervention of the editorial staff. Ultimately, perhaps, my greatest debt is to a generation of law students in Cambridge and elsewhere who taught me very much more than I ever taught them.

Trinity College   Kevin Gray
11 August 1987

Contents

Preface v
Table of statutes xiii
List of cases xxix
Abbreviations lxxi

THE GENERAL PART

A.   CONCEPTS 3

Chapter 1   Property 5

1   The function of the law of property 5
2   The meaning of property 8

Chapter 2   Land 16

1   The legal definition of 'land' 16
2   Corporeal hereditaments 16
3   Incorporeal hereditaments 38

Chapter 3   Trust 39

1   Defining the trust 39
2   Relationship between law and equity 41
3   The origin and types of trust 42
4   Effect of the trust on third parties 45
5   The interest of the cestui que trust 49

Chapter 4   Tenures and estates 55

1   The doctrine of tenures 55
2   The doctrine of estates 58

B.   STRUCTURES 67

Chapter 5   Legal and equitable rights 69

1   The distinction between 'legal' and 'equitable' rights 69
2   Legal estates 71
3   The fee simple absolute in possession 71
4   The term of years absolute 78
5   Formal creation of estates 79
6   Legal interests and charges 80
7   Equitable interests 83
8   Significance of the distinction between legal and equitable rights 83

Chapter 6   Outline of the 1925 legislation   94

1   The distinction between registered and unregistered land   94
2   Alienability of land and fragmentation of benefit   96
3   Protection of purchasers of a legal title   97
4   Protection for owners of fragments of benefit   105

Chapter 7   Registration under the Land Charges Act   110

1   The basic concept of registration   110
2   Matters and interests registrable under the Land Charges Act 1972   110
3   Registration of land charges   113
4   Search of the Land Charges Register   125
5   The basic flaw of the land charges system   130
6   Categories of registrable land charge   133

Chapter 8   Registration of title   144

1   The distinction between registered and unregistered conveyancing   144
2   The basic features of registration of title   145
3   The Register   147
4   The classification of interests in registered land   151
5   Registrable interests   151
6   Minor interests   159
7   Overriding interests   170
8   Registered charges   193
9   Rectification and indemnity   193
10 Future reform of registration of title   201

Chapter 9   The conveyancing dimension   204

1   Dealings before exchange of contracts   204
2   The exchange of contracts   209
3   Completion   220
4   Priority of interests after the conveyance of a legal estate   226

C.   HOLDINGS   231

Chapter 10   Trusts   233

1   Ascertainment of beneficial ownership   233
2   Express trusts   235
3   Implied trusts   242
4   Resulting trusts   244
5   Constructive trusts   268

Chapter 11   Co-ownership   293

1   The social context of co-ownership   293
2   Types of co-ownership   295
3   Joint tenancy   295
4   Tenancy in common   302
5   Tenancy by entireties   314
6   Coparcenary   316

7   Severance 317
8   Severance by written notice 318
9   The *Williams v Hensman* methods of severance 320
10   Severance in consequence of unlawful killing 332
11   Severance by equitable intervention 336
12   Severance by merger of interests 337
13   Concurrent interests in the property legislation of 1925 337
14   Termination of co-ownership 341

Chapter 12   Trusts for sale 344

1   Origins of the trust for sale 344
2   Statutory definition of the 'trust for sale' 349
3   The respective roles of trustee and beneficiary 352
4   Protection for a purchaser from trustees for sale 354
5   The imposition of a trust for sale in all cases of co-ownership 358
6   Rights of occupation under a trust for sale 368
7   The decision to deal with co-owned land 375

Chapter 13   Proprietary estoppel 386

1   The central concern of proprietary estoppel 386
2   The general theory of proprietary estoppel 387
3   Categories in the caselaw 388
4   Operation of proprietary estoppel 396
5   The extent of the estoppel remedy 413
6   The nature of a proprietary estoppel 419

Chapter 14   Leases 427

1   Essential elements in a 'lease' or 'tenancy' 427
2   The distinction between 'lease' and 'licence' 443
3   Flexibility of leasehold arrangements 462
4   Formalities of leases and tenancies 464
5   Leasehold covenants 475
6   Termination of leases and tenancies 484
7   Landlord's remedies for breach of covenant by the tenant 490
8   Tenant's remedies for breach of covenant by the landlord 514
9   Enforceability of leasehold covenants in a legal lease 516
10   Enforceability of leasehold covenants in an equitable lease 529

Chapter 15   Licences 535

1   Bare licences 535
2   Licences coupled with the grant of an interest 539
3   Contractual licences 541

D.   INCUMBRANCES 561

Chapter 16   Mortgages 563

1   Definitions 563
2   The social significance of mortgage finance 564
3   The creation of legal mortgages 571

4   The creation of equitable mortgages   575
5   Reform of the law of mortgages   577
6   The discharge of mortgages   578
7   Protection for the mortgagor   579
8   Protection for the mortgagee   600
9   The mortgagee's right to possession   605
10   Remedies available to the legal mortgagee   613
11   Remedies available to the equitable mortgagee   630

Chapter 17   Easements and profits à prendre   632

1   Definitions and distinctions   633
2   Essential characteristics of an easement   644
3   Creation of easements and profits   665
4   Grant of easements and profits   667
5   Reservation   685
6   Extinguishment of easements and profits   686

Chapter 18   Covenants   689

1   The function of covenants in the planning of land use   689
2   Covenants at law   691
3   Covenants in equity   697

SPECIAL PROBLEMS

E.   A PROPERTY-OWNING DEMOCRACY?   723

Chapter 19   The tenant's 'right to buy'   725

1   Leasehold enfranchisement and extension   725
2   The public sector tenant's right to buy   733

Chapter 20   Adverse possession   740

1   The rationale of acquisition by adverse possession   740
2   The period of limitation   741
3   Dispossession and discontinuance of possession   743
4   The operation of the Limitation Act 1980   751
5   Recovery of possession by the paper owner   753

Chapter 21   Homelessness   760

1   General aim of the homelessness legislation   760
2   Conditions of eligibility   761
3   Duties of the housing authority   774
4   Remedies   777

F.   RESIDENTIAL SECURITY IN THE FAMILY HOME   779

Chapter 22   Rights of occupation   781

1   Rights of occupation enforceable against other family members   781
2   Rights of occupation enforceable against persons outside the family   785
3   The future of the Matrimonial Homes Act   789

Chapter 23 Family arrangements 792

1   Informal origins of family arrangements 792
2   The analytical problems raised by family arrangements 793
3   Legally ineffective relationships 794
4   Loan 796
5   Irrevocable licence 798
6   Life interest 803
7   Aliquot shares behind a trust 808
8   Property transfer order 818

Chapter 24 The decision to sell the family home 819

1   Section 30 of the Law of Property Act 1925 819
2   The collateral purpose of a trust for sale of the family home 820

Chapter 25 Dealings with the family home 829

1   The focus of the problem 829
2   The legal effect of the single trustee's dealings 831
3   The equitable effect of the single trustee's dealings 833
4   The problems left in the modern law 850
5   Proposals for reform 862

Chapter 26 Financial crisis and the owner-occupier 869

1   Enforcement of charging orders 870
2   Effects of bankruptcy 875
3   Recovery of possession by a mortgagee 887
4   Assertion of priority by a beneficial owner 897

G.   A CHARTER OF RIGHTS FOR RESIDENTIAL TENANTS 899

**Chapter 27 The environmental quality of tenanted
accommodation** 901

1   The principle of caveat emptor 902
2   The landlord's liability at common law 903
3   The landlord's liability under statute 916
4   The tenant's remedies for breach of landlord's repairing covenants 939

Chapter 28 Safety in and around the home 946

1   The landlord's liability at common law 946
2   The landlord's liability under statute 949
3   The landlord's liability in respect of crime 950
4   Protection against unlawful eviction 954

Chapter 29 Statutory protection in the private sector 961

1   History and social philosophy of the Rent Acts 961
2   Definition of a 'protected tenancy' 970
3   Express exclusion from the scope of a protected tenancy 982
4   Contractual deviations from the Rent Act 990

5   The statutory tenancy 1002
6   Security of tenure 1014
7   Restriction of rents 1031
8   Prohibition of unlawful payments by a regulated tenant 1038
9   Restriction of the right to levy distress 1039
10   Restricted contracts 1040

Chapter 30 Statutory protection in the public sector 1045

1   Definition of 'secure tenancy' 1045
2   Local authority allocation of secure tenancies 1048
3   Terms of the secure tenancy 1050
4   Security of tenure 1054
5   Disposal to the private sector 1058

Chapter 31 Statutory succession to tenancies 1059

1   Public sector tenancies 1059
2   Private sector tenancies 1062

Index 1073

Table of Statutes

References in this Table to *Statutes* are to Halsbury's Statutes of England (Fourth Edition) showing the volume and page at which the annotated text of the Act will be found.

PAGE

Administration of Estates Act 1925 (17 *Statutes* 257)
s 3(4) 297
9 485
33 348
(1) 316
45(1), (2) 316
46(3) 298
51(2), (4) 316
Administration of Justice Act 1956
s 35(1) 871
Administration of Justice Act 1970 (11 *Statutes* 615)
s 1 485
36 . . . . . .606, 609, 612, 630, 891, 892, 893, 894, 895, 896, 897
(1) 892, 893
(2) 892
39(1) 892
Sch 2 485
Administration of Justice Act 1973
s 8 893
(1) 892, 893
(2) 893
Administration of Justice Act 1985
s 6(4) 224
11(4) 225
12 225
55(2), (4) 495
139(2) 495
Agricultural Holdings Act 1948 (1 *Statutes* 714) 918, 975
Agricultural Holdings Act 1986
s 1(1) 983
2(2)(b) 444
10 24
86 133
Ancient Monuments and Archaeological Areas Act 1979
s 42(1) 36
Annuity, etc., to Duke of Marlborough (1706)
s 5 62
Annuity, etc., to Duke of Wellington (1814)
s 28 62

PAGE

Bankruptcy Act 1914 (4 *Statutes* 507) . . 887
s 22(3) 424
42(1) 887
48ff 877
108(1) 878
Bill of Rights (1688) (10 *Statutes* 44) . . 240
Bodies Corporate (Joint Tenancy) Act 1899
s 1(1), (2) 298
Building Act 1984
s 82(1)(b) 655
Building Societies Act 1986
s 10(1) 589
(5) 565
13(7) 620
Sch 4
para 1 620
2 578
Capital Gains Tax Act 1979
s 101(1) 568
Capital Transfer Tax Act 1984. See Inheritance Tax Act 1984
Charging Orders Act 1979 (22 *Statutes* 337) 160, 870, 871, 872, 873, 874
s 1(1) 870
(5) 872, 893
(a), (b) 872, 893
2(1)(a) 871
3(1) 875
(3) 870
(4) 324, 870
(5) 872
Civil Aviation Act 1982 (4 *Statutes* 144)
s 76(1), (2) 29
Coal Act 1938
s 3 26
41 170
Coal Industry Nationalisation Act 1946
s 5 170
Common Law Procedure Act 1852 (23 *Statutes* 32)
s 210 . . . . 494, 495
212 494
Companies Act 1929
s 74, 380 586

PAGE

Consumer Credit Act 1974 (11 *Statutes*
   15) 594
s 8(2) 594
   16(1), (7) 594
   137 596
      (1) 594
   138 596
      (1) 594
      (2)(a), (c) 595
      (3), (4) 595
   139 . . . . 594, 596
   140 596
   171(7) 594
Control of Pollution Act 1974
s 58 926
   (1)-(4) 926
   73(1) 926
Conveyancing Act 1882
s 3(1), (3) 89
Countryside Act 1968
s 22(6) 640
County Courts Act 1984 (11 *Statutes* 411)
s 77(6)(d) 1015
   89(1) 512
   138(2) 494
      (3)-(5), (9A) 495
   139(1) 494
Criminal Damage Act 1971 (12 *Statutes*
   557)
s 10(1)(b) 26
Criminal Injuries Act (Northern Ireland)
   1956
s 4(4) 1006
Criminal Law Act 1977 (12 *Statutes*
   742) 492, 754
s 6 756
   (1), (3) 756
   7(1), (2), (10) 754
   12(3), (4) 756
Defective Premises Act 1972 950
s 4 . . . . 923, 949
   (1) 923, 924
   (2) 924
   (3) 925
   (4), (5) 924
   6(3) 924
Distress for Rent Act 1689 (13 *Statutes* 556)
s 1 513
Distress for Rent Act 1737 (13 *Statutes* 559)
s 9 513
Domestic Violence and Matrimonial
   Proceedings Act 1976 763
s 1(1), (2) 301
   4(1) 301
Duke of Marlborough; Pension (1706)
s 4 62
Family Law Reform Act 1969 (6 *Statutes*
   213)
s 1(1) 7
Finance Act 1963 (13 *Statutes* 79) . . . 82
   Sch 14 82

PAGE

Finance Act 1972
s 75 567
Finance Act 1974
s 19 567
   Sch 1 567
Finance Act 1986
s 20 567
   Sch 19
      para 36 568
Forfeiture Act 1982 (12 *Statutes* 862)
s 1(1) 332
   2 336
      (2) 336
   5 336
Game Act 1831 (2 *Statutes* 155)
s 3 34
General Rate Act 1967
s 26(3)(a) 983
Grantees of Reversions Act 1540 . . . 521
Health and Safety at Work etc. Act 1974
   (19 *Statutes* 613)
s 4(1), (2), (4) 925
   21 . . . . 908, 925, 926
   33(1) 926
Highways Act 1980 (20 *Statutes* 135)
s 31(1) 636
   130(1) 635
   137(1), (2) 636
   139(1), (3) 637
   148(c) 637
   161(3) 636
   263 72
   328(1) 635
   329(1) 635
Housing Act 1936
s 2(1) 916
Housing Act 1957
s 6(2) 916
Housing Act 1961
s 32, 33 918
Housing Act 1969 (23 *Statutes* 283)
s 82 730
Housing Act 1974 (23 *Statutes* 287)
s 118 727
      (4) 731
   125(1) 942
   Sch 8 727
Housing Act 1980 (23 *Statutes* 308, 581) . 81,
      725, 964, 996, 1030, 1045
s 1(3)(a) 735
   27(3) 735
   48(1) 1047
   52(1) 1028
      (a)-(c) 1028
      (4) 1028
   53(1) 1028
   55(1) 1028
      (2) 1029
   60(1), (3) 1033
   61(1) 1032
   62(1) 1033

PAGE

Housing Act 1980—*contd*

s 64(1)	1014
65(1)	989
66(1), (3)	1024
(4)	1027
69(1)	1015, 1043
(2), (3)	1043
70(1)	1043
73(1)	983
(2)	1041
75(2), (3)	1023
76(1)	1062
(2)	1063
79	1039
(c)	1039
88(1), (4)	1001
89	892
(1)	1024, 1029
(2)(a)	892
(c)	1023
(d)	1043
141	727, 728
142	731
Sch 7	1024
Sch 21	
para 1	728
2	727
3	728
Sch 22	731
Sch 25	
para 40	1034

Housing Act 1985 (21 *Statutes* 29): 482, 495, 567, 733, 734, 736, 737, 760, 762, 764, 766, 767, 769, 1031, 1045, 1046

s 8(1)	1049
9(1)	1049
21(1)	945, 1049
22	1049
24(1), (2)	1051
58(1)	762
(a)-(c)	762
(2)	764
(2A)	761, 766, 928, 934
(2B)	766
(3)(a)	762, 960
(b), (c)	762
(4)	766, 960
59(1)(a), (b)	766
(c)	767
(d)	766
60(1)	767, 770
(3)	768, 770
(4)	771
61(1)(a)-(d)	773
(2)(b)	773
(3)	773
62(1)	773
(2)	774
63(1)	454, 774
64(1)-(5)	774
65	766

PAGE

Housing Act 1985—*contd*

s 65(1)	761
(2)	761, 766, 767, 774, 775
(3)(a), (b)	777
(4)	777
66	766
(2)	776, 960
(3)	777
67	766, 773
(2)	761
68	766
69(1)	766, 775, 776
(2)	775
71(1)	762
75	764, 770, 775
79(1)	1046, 1047, 1048
(3)	444, 1047
(4)	1047
80(1)	1046
81	1046, 1047
82(1), (2)	1055
(3), (4)	1055, 1057
83(1), (2)	1056
84(1)	1056
(2)(a), (b)	1056
(c)	1057
85(1), (2)	1056
86(1), (2)	1055
87	1059, 1061
(a)	1059
(b)	1060
88(1)(b)	1054, 1061
(2)	1061
89(2)(a)	1059
(b)	1062
91(1)	1051
(3) (a), (b)	1052
92(1)-(3)	1051
93(1)(a), (b)	1052
(2)	1053
94(2)	1052
(3), (5), (6)	1053
96(1)	944
97(1)	936, 1053
(2)	1053
(a)-(d)	1053
(3)	1053
98(1)	1053
(2)	1054
(4)(a), (b)	1053
99(1), (2), (4)	1054
100(1), (2)	1054
101(1)-(3)	1054
102	1050
103	1050
(3)	1050
104(1)	1050
(c)	919
(2)	1050
106(1)(a)	1049
(2)	1049
112(1)	1048

PAGE

Housing Act 1985—*contd*

s 113	734
(1)(a), (b)	1060
(2)	1060
115(1)	1048
118	153
(1)(a), (b)	734
(2)	734
119(1), (2)	735
121(1), (2)	735
122(1)	736
123(1)-(3)	734
125(4)(a), (b)	737
125A(1), (2)	737
125B(1), (2)	737
126(1)(a), (b)	736
127(1)-(3)	736
129(2)(a), (b)	736
131(2)	736
132(1)	737
139(1)	434, 737
(2)	737, 1055
142(1)(c)	737
143(1)	737
144(1)	738
145(2), (3)	738
148(1)	738
151(1)	738
(2)	1055
154(1)	153
155(1), (2)	736
156(3)	736
159(1)(b)	736
160(1)	736
171A	1062
171B(1)	739
(4)(a)	1062
173(1)	728
183(2)	734
(a), (b)	734
(3)	734
186	734
189	929, 930, 932
(1)	928, 929, 930
(3)	930
190	927, 929
(1)	930
(a), (b)	927
(2)	927
(3)	930
191(1)	930
192(1)	930
193(1), (3)	930
207	927, 930
209(a)	931
(b), (c)	932
210(1)	932
212(1)	932
(3)	933
213(1)	933

PAGE

Housing Act 1985—*contd*

s 215(1), (2), (4)	933
216(1)	933
217	933
(5)	933
220(1), (6)	933
221(2)	933
223(1)	933
227(1)	933
228(1)	933
232(2)	932
234(1)-(3)	932
237	931
239, 253	932
264(1)	929
265	766
(1)	929
268(1)	930
300(1)	929
302(c)	918
324	936
325(1)	936
(2)(a)	937
(b)	936
326(1)	937
(2)(a)	937
(3)	937
327(1)	937
329, 330	937
331(1)	937
(2)(a)-(c)	937
332(1)(b)	937
335(1)	937
336(1)	937
337(1)	937
338(1), (2)	937
340(1)	937
343	936
345	938
352ff	938
(2)	938
354(1)	938
355(2)	939
358(1)	939
365ff	938
369ff	938
(5)	938
372	938
375ff	938
379(1)	938
450A(1)	737
474(1)(a)	933
494(1)	929
508(1)	931
604(1)	928
606	928
(2)	928
(3)	927
609	703

PAGE

Housing Act 1985—*contd*
Sch 1
 para 1, 2, 4, 5, 10 1048
Sch 2 1052
 Pt I
  Grounds 1-8 1056
 Pt II
  Grounds 9-11 1056
 Pt III
  Grounds 12-16 1057
 Pt IV 1056
Sch 3 1051
 Ground 1 1051
  2-4 1052
Sch 3A
 para 2, 3, 5 1058
Sch 4
 para 1, 2, 4 735
Sch 5
 para 1 734
  2, 6-8, 11 735
Sch 6 737
 Pt I 738
  para 1 737
 Pt III 738
  para 11 734
   12 . . . . . . 434, 734, 738
   16c 737
Sch 8 738
 para 1, 2, 4, 5 738
Sch 9
 para 1 738
Sch 9A 149, 153, 159, 160, 174,
             184
 para 5, 6 739
Sch 10 . . . . 930, 933
Sch 17
 para 1 . . . . . . 609, 624, 892
  3 620
Housing and Planning Act 1986 . 183, 736,
          766, 1036
s 1 735
 2 736
 (3) 736
 4(1), (2), (4) 737
 5 737
 6 1058
 7(1) 1034
 8(1) 739, 1062
 (2) . . . 149, 153, 159, 160, 184,
             739
 14(1) 766, 775
 (2) 766, 934
 (3) 775, 776
 15 1054
 17(2) 1036
 18 983
 23(1) 731
Sch 1 1058
Sch 2 . . . . 149, 153, 159, 160, 184,
             739

PAGE

Housing and Planning Act 1986—*contd*
Sch 3 1054
Sch 4
 para 1 983
Sch 5
 para 7 1051
Housing Finance Act 1972
 s 49ff 1051
Housing (Homeless Persons) Act 1977 . 760
 s 3(4) 454
 17 767
Housing of the Working Classes Act
 1885 903
Housing of the Working Classes Act 1890
 s 75 916
Housing Rents and Subsidies Act 1975
 s 1(1) 1051
Housing, Town Planning etc. Act 1909
 s 15(1) 916
Income and Corporation Taxes Act 1970
 s 67 974
Increase of Rent and Mortgage Interest
 (Restrictions) Act 1920 963
 s 12(1)(g) 1070
Increase of Rent and Mortgage Interest
 (War Restrictions) Act 1915 . . . 961
Inheritance Act 1833 (17 *Statutes* 239)
 s 1 88
Inheritance (Provision for Family and
 Dependants) Act 1975 (17 *Statutes*
 344) 61, 297
 s 1-3 569
 9(1) 297
Inheritance Tax Act 1984
 Sch 1 568
Insolvency Act 1985
 s 215 150
Sch 8
 para 5 161
Sch 10 885
Insolvency Act 1986: 862, 876, 878, 879, 882
 s 283(1)(a) 876, 884
 (3)(a) 876, 884
 284(1) 875
 305(2) 876
 306 876
 (1) 880
 315(1) 489
 (2)(b) 489
 (3)(a) 489
 317 489
 336(1) 881
 (2) 789
 (3) 789, 881
 (4) 789, 881
 (b), (d) 881
 (5) 789, 881
 337(1) 880
 (b) 880

PAGE

Insolvency Act 1986—*contd*
s 337(2) 880
   (a) 880
   (3)(a) 880
   (5) 880
   (6) 881
339 885
339ff 887
   (1), (2) 885
   (3)(a) 885
   (b), (c) 886
340 . . . . 885, 887
   (3) 885
341(1)(a) 885, 887
   (2) 887
342(1)(a), (b), (d) 885
343(2) 594
Sch 14 887

Intestates' Estates Act 1952 (17 *Statutes* 315)
s 1(4) 298

Judgment Mortgage Act 1850 324

Judgments (Enforcement) Act (Northern Ireland) 1969
s 122 510

Land Charges Act 1972 . . . 103, 106, 107,
           110, 111, 116, 119, 159,
           425, 706, 870
s 2 . . . . 133, 160
   (1) 787
   (2) Class A 115, 133
   (3) Class B 115, 133
   (4) Class C . . . 95, 99, 113, 134, 135,
           137
     (i) 99, 115, 134
     (ii) 115, 134
     (iii) 115, 134, 135
     (iv) . . . 115, 119, 120, 125, 130,
          134, 135, 136, 137, 138
   (5) 532
    Class D 115, 139, 141
     (ii) 140, 141
     (iii) 141, 142, 143
   (6) Class E 143
   (7) 787
    Class F 115, 129, 143
3(1) 113, 131
4 . . . . 107, 112, 221
   (6) 115, 121, 122, 123, 125,
         140, 221, 474, 525, 530
   (8) 841
5(1) 111
   (7) 111, 120
   (8) 111
6(1)(a) 112, 870
   (b), (c) 112
   (4) 112
7(1), (2) 112
8 . . . . 111, 112

PAGE

Land Charges Act 1972—*contd*
s 10(1), (2) 126
   (4) 126, 127, 162
   (6) 127
11(1)-(3), (5), (6) 126
13(2) 121
17(1) 111, 115, 122, 123, 501,
           939
   (3) 126
20(8) 123

Land Compensation Act 1973 487

Land Registration Act 1925 . 95, 118, 131,
       144, 145, 146, 153, 736,
       751
s 1(1), (2) 148
2(1) 151, 152
3(i) 829
   (xi) 151
   (xv) 159
   (xvi) 170, 172
   (xviii) 178, 199
   (xx) 833
   (xxi) 167, 829
   (xxii) 193
   (xxxi) 167
4(a), (b) 152, 154
5 . . . . 154, 155
6, 7 156
8(1) 152, 155
   (2) 152
9 155
10-12 156
13(c) 154
18(1) 833
   (e) 833
19(1) 157
   (2) 157, 173, 197
20(1) 104, 160, 163, 164, 166,
       167, 179, 198, 229, 833
   (a) 647
   (4) 167
21(1) 833
22(1) 157
   (2) 157, 173
23(1) 160
   (a) 529, 532
   (b) 647
   (2) 529, 532
24(1)(b) 519
26(1) 193
27(1) 193
29 193
34(3) 628
   (4) 284, 617
47(1) 299
49(1)(f) 160
   (g) 160, 870
50(1) 529, 532
52 160

PAGE

Land Registration Act 1925—*contd*
s 53(1) 161
54 945
(1) 161
55(1) 161
57(1) 161
58(1) 159
(b) 864
(2) 160
(3) 159, 864
(5) 159
59(6) . . . 104, 163, 164, 166, 167,
229
61(1) 160
(3) 161
63(1) 149
64(1) 149, 160
(2) 149
(5) 149, 787
65 . . . . 149, 193, 605
66 576
69(1) 158, 197, 833
70 648
(1) 170, 179, 201
(a) 172, 173, 647, 648
(c) 173, 174
(f) 174, 752
(g) . . . 65, 119, 158, 172, 174,
175, 176, 177, 178, 179,
180, 181, 182, 183, 184,
185, 186, 187, 189, 190,
191, 197, 229, 385, 426,
475, 601, 604, 648, 730,
789, 846, 849, 851, 853, 860
(k) 174, 475
(3) 172
75(1) 751
(2) 752
77(1)-(3) 156
82(1) 194, 195, 196
(2) 197, 198
(3) 155, 199
83(1), (2) 199
(4) 198
(5), (11) 200
86(2) 183
106(1), (2) 193
112(1)-(3) 150
112A 150
(1) 150
112B, 112C 150
113A 148
123(1) 151, 152, 153, 154, 157
126 . . . . 147, 148
127 148
131 148

Land Registration Act 1966
s 1(2) 154

PAGE

Land Registration Act 1970 (Northern
Ireland)
Sch 5
Pt I
para 15 175
Land Registration Act 1986 152
s 1(1), (2) 156
2(5) 152
3(1) 152
4(1), (4) 174
Land Registration and Land Charges Act
1971
s 3(1) 200
Land Transfer Act 1875
s 18 175
Landlord and Tenant Act 1709 (23
Statutes 22)
s 6, 7 511
Landlord and Tenant Act 1927 (23
Statutes 55)
s 18(1) 514
19(1), (2) 480
Landlord and Tenant Act 1954 (23
Statutes 136) . . . 430, 478, 484, 508,
918, 979, 982, 983
s 23(1) 444, 976
30(1) 1038
43(1)(d) 987
Landlord and Tenant Act 1985 (23
Statutes 322)
s 1 478
(1)-(3) 478
2 478
(1) 478
3(1), (4) 478
3A 478
4(1), (2) 478
5(1) 478
(a), (b) 479
7(1) 479
8 . . . . 482, 918
(1) 916, 917, 918, 920, 928
(2) 482, 917
(4) 916, 918
(5) 916
(6)(a) 916
10 917
11 482
(1) 918, 919, 920, 921, 922,
923, 924
(a) 918
(b), (c) 919
(2)(a) 918, 920
(b) 920
(3) 923
(4) 919, 924
(6) 482
12(1), (2) 919
13(1) 918
(2)(b) 919

PAGE

Landlord and Tenant Act 1985—*contd*
s 14(3) 918
  18(1) 479
  19(1), (2) 479
  20(2) 479
    (3)(a)-(c) 479
  21(1), (6) 479
  22(2) 479
  32(1) 478
    (2) 918

Landlord and Tenant Act 1987 . . 901, 926
s 1ff 926
  21ff 926
  25ff 926
  41(2) 150
  41ff 926
  47(1) 478
  48(1), (2) 478
  50 478

Law of Distress Amendment Act 1888 (13
  Statutes 579)
s 4 512
  5 513
  7 512

Law of Distress Amendment Act 1908 (13
  Statutes 584)
s 1 . . . . 511, 512, 513

Law of Property Act 1922 (23 *Statutes*
  42) 58, 119, 364
s 1(1) 70
  3(5) 119
  10 364
  33 119
  145 436
Sch 15
  para 1, 10 436
       11 517
Sch 16
  Pt I
    para 5 175

Law of Property Act 1925 . . 97, 116, 119,
                    349, 350, 351, 359, 365,
                    374, 422, 601, 1005
s 1 . . . . 69, 70, 99, 103
  (1) 71, 80, 98, 139, 151
    (a) 71, 74, 78, 87
    (b) 78, 87, 427
  (2) 71, 80, 139, 151
    (a) 80, 85, 665
    (b) 81
    (c) 81, 82, 85, 564, 575
    (d) 82
    (e) 82, 85, 491
  (3) 71, 78, 80, 82, 83, 491
  (6) 7, 71, 263, 339, 432
  (8) 80, 83
  2(1) 100, 101, 102, 106, 134,
                  139, 221, 355, 425
    (i) 100, 806

PAGE

Law of Property Act 1925—*contd*
s 2(1)(ii) . . 100, 355, 356, 357, 358, 385,
                          601, 860
    (iii) 100, 616
    (iv) 100
  (2) 350, 357
  4(3) 73
  7(1) 74
  14 . . . . 91, 119, 385
    (8) 91
  19(1) 432
    (2) 366
    (5) 367
  23 . . . . 91, 357
  25(1) 349
    (2) 357
    (4) 349
  26(1) 357
    (3) 357, 381, 860
  27(1) 356, 602
    (2) 221, 356, 601
  28 377
    (1) 352, 353
    (3) 341
  29 . . . . 353, 354, 377
    (1) 353, 354
    (3) 354
  30 . . . . 341, 352, 353, 377,
          379, 380, 382, 385, 819, 820,
          821, 822, 823, 824, 825,
          826, 827, 862, 871, 873,
          874, 876, 877, 878, 881,
                          882, 887
  32(1) 349, 353
  34(1) 339, 362
    (2) 98, 339, 362, 363
    (3) 98, 339, 363
  35 . . . . 359, 369
  36(1) 315, 316, 360, 361, 362
    (2) 316, 318, 319, 320, 325,
                          339, 342
    (3) 315
    (4) 365
  38 672
  40 . . . . . . 210, 216, 371, 469, 576
    (1) 207, 210, 211, 212, 223
    (2) 212
  44 . . . . 114, 155, 221
    (1) 131
    (5) 114
    (8) 91
  47 220
  51(1) 64, 438
  52 221
    (1) 80, 221, 464, 466, 487
    (2) 79, 85, 221, 464
    (a) 221
    (c) 221, 487
    (d) 221, 464
    (g) 221, 464, 465

PAGE

Law of Property Act 1925—*contd*

s 53	238, 239
(1)	186
(b)	236, 237, 238, 239, 240, 250, 270
(c)	260, 291, 292, 575
(2)	237, 240, 243, 270
54(1)	221, 464
(2)	79, 85, 464
55(d)	238
56(1)	521, 691, 692
60	63
(1)	63
(3)	247
(4)	63
61(a)	485
62	18, 20, 474, 674, 675, 676, 677, 678, 710, 737
(1)	18, 24, 38, 521, 647, 675, 678
(2)	24, 675
(4)	675, 679
63(1)	602, 603
65(1), (2)	685
72(3)	433
(4)	342
73	222
(1)	222
74(1)	222
75(1)	222
76	695
(6)	695
77	519
78	711, 712
(1)	521, 694, 710, 711, 712
79	704, 711
(1)	695, 704
(2), (3)	704
84(1)	720
(a), (aa)	720
(b), (c)	720
(1A), (2)	720
85(1)	81, 564, 573, 604
(2)(a)	573
(3)	572
86(1)	81, 573, 574
(2)(a)	573
(3)	572
87(1)	87, 508, 573
(b)	574
88(1)	615, 616
(b)	616
(2)	628
89(1)	615, 616
(b)	616
(2)	628
90(1)	613, 631
91	630
(2)	629, 631
(7)	631
96(1), (2)	605

PAGE

Law of Property Act 1925—*contd*

s 99	611
(2)	608
101	614, 1024
(1)	614, 630
(i)	614, 615
(iii)	627, 631
(3), (4)	614
103	614
(i)-(iii)	614
104(1)	615
(2)	615, 617, 616
105	617
109(1)	627
(2)	627, 628
111	341
115(1)	578
130(4)	316
136	695
141(1)	141, 521, 522, 527, 529
142	525
(1)	141, 523, 524, 525, 527, 530
(2)	520
146	496, 497, 499, 500, 501, 502, 503, 506, 508, 1057
(1)	496, 497, 498, 499, 502
(a)-(c)	496
(2)	502, 503
(4)	507, 508, 1057
(7)	484
(8), (9), (11), (12)	496
147	501
148(1)	506
149(3)	434, 435
(6)	435, 436
153	490, 697
(1)	490, 697
(b)	490
(2)	697
(i), (ii)	490
(8)	490, 697
176	62
184	298
185	489
196	319, 496
198(1)	89, 107, 111, 112, 114, 115, 127, 128, 129, 131, 132, 133, 140, 221
199	843
(1)	116, 122, 865
(ii)(a)	87, 88, 89
(b)	91, 92
205(1)(ii)	83, 221, 355, 432, 474, 676
(ix)	16, 18
(xix)	77, 178, 433
(xxi)	83, 87, 122, 123, 829
(xxvii)	79, 427, 429, 435, 441
(xxix)	349, 353, 355

PAGE

Law of Property Act 1925—*contd*
Sch 1
  Pt IV 316
  Pt VI 315
Law of Property Act 1969
 s 23 . . . . . 125, 131, 132, 221
  24(1) 128
  25(1)(a) 132
    (b), (c) 133
   (2) 133
   (4) 132
  28 720
Law of Property (Amendment) Act 1924
Sch 10 304
Law of Property (Amendment) Act 1926
Schedule 74, 356
Law of Property (Joint Tenants) Act 1964
 s 1(1) 343
   (a), (b) 343
  3 343
Law Reform (Married Women and
  Tortfeasors) Act 1935 7
Leasehold Property (Repairs) Act 1938
  (23 *Statutes* 76) 500, 501
 s 1(1)-(4) 501
   (5)(a), (e) 502
  7(1) 501
Leasehold Reform Act 1967 (23 *Statutes*
  196) 480, 725, 726, 727, 728,
           731, 732, 733
 s 1(1)(a) 727, 728
   (b) 728
  2(1) 727
   (a) 727
  3(1), (4) 728
  4(1) 728
  5(5) 136, 183
  8(1) 729
  9(1) 730
   (1A) 731
  14(1) 729
  15(2)(a), (b) 730
  16(1)(a) 729
  22 729
  23(1) 727
  32 728
  Sch 3 729
   para 4 729
Legal Aid Act 1974 (24 *Statutes* 3)
 s 9(6) 133
Limitation Act 1623 740
Limitation Act 1980 (24 *Statutes* 629) . 174,
               740, 741
 s 15(1) 630, 741, 742
  16 578
  17 751
  18 741
  19 . . . . 510, 514
  20(1), (5) 613
  32(1), (3) 749

PAGE

Limitation Act 1980—*contd*
Sch 1
  para 1 741
    4 . . . . 741, 742
    5 . . . . 742, 743
    8 . . . . 741, 742, 746
    10, 11 741
Limitation Amendment Act 1980 (17
  Statutes 370)
 s 4 746
Married Women's Property Act 1870 . 7
Married Women's Property Act 1882 . 7,
              319, 824
 s 1, 5 315
  17 326
Matrimonial Causes Act 1973 . . 320, 819,
     825, 827, 873, 874, 875
 s 23 822
  24 . . . . 326, 736, 822, 826, 874
   (1) 318, 811, 818, 873
    (a) 1052
  24A 318, 326, 736
  25 . . . . 811, 822
   (1)-(4) 818
  25A 818
  39 887
Matrimonial Homes Act 1967 143,
         782, 789, 858
 s 1(9) 841
  2(7) 182
Matrimonial Homes Act 1983 . . 143, 149,
     150, 160, 763, 782, 783,
            790, 881
 s 1 880
  (1) 782, 783, 784, 786
   (a), (b) 782
  (2) 784
   (a), (b) 785
  (3) 785
  (5) 889
  (6) 1011
  (8) 783
  (10) 783, 784
  (11) 784, 836, 841
  2(4)(a), (b) 788
  (7) 788
  (8) 182
   (a) 787
   (b) 182, 789
  (9) 160, 787
  3 787
  4(1) 788
  5(1) 788
  6(1) 783, 788
  (3) 788
  8(1) 783
  (2) 895
   (a), (b) 895
  (3) 896
  9(1) 784
  10(1) 784

PAGE

Matrimonial Homes Act 1983—*contd*
 Sch 1
  Pt II
   para 3 1004
Matrimonial Homes and Property Act
  1981
 s 4(1) 787
Matrimonial Homes (Family Protection)
  (Scotland) Act 1981
 s 18 782
Matrimonial Proceedings and Property
  Act 1970 811
 s 37 . . . . 311, 809
  38 . . . . 784, 836, 841
Middlesex Registry Act 1708 123
Minors' Contracts Act 1987
 s 1 432
Money-lenders Act 1900 590
Moneylenders Act 1927 590
Munitions of War Act 1915 962
National Parks and Access to the
  Countryside Act 1949
 s 60ff 641
National Trust Act 1937
 s 8 703
Obscene Publications Act 1959 (12
  Statutes 320) 500
Occupiers' Liability Act 1957 657
 s 2(6) 536
Patents Act 1977
 s 33(1) 120
Perpetuities and Accumulations Act 1964
 s 1(1) 436
  9(2) 434
  12(1) 74
   (a) 72
Petroleum (Production) Act 1934
 s 1(1) 26
  2(1) 26
Police and Criminal Evidence Act 1984
  (12 *Statutes* 941)
 s 8(1) 537
  17(1) 537
  18(1) 537
Prescription Act 1832 (13 *Statutes* 593) . 664,
                                          684
 s 1-4 684
  7, 8 680
Prevention of Crime Act 1953 (12 *Statutes*
  263)
 s 1 954
Protection from Eviction Act 1977 (23
  Statutes 293) 486, 959
 s 1 957
  (1) 955
  (2) 956
  (3) 956, 960
  (4) 955
  (5) 957
  (6) 956
  2 . . . . 492, 954

PAGE

Protection from Eviction Act 1977—*contd*
 s 3 1015
  (1) 955, 1042
  (2A) 955, 1043
  5 486
  (1)(a), (b) 486
  6 955
Public Health Act 1936 . . . 928, 934, 936
 s 72(2) 933
  92 933
   (1)(c) 933
  93 935
  94(1), (2) 935
  96(1) 935
  99 935
  343(1) 933
Public Order Act 1986 754
 s 1-5 640
  39(1)-(3), (5) 755
Quia Emptores (1290) 57, 58, 61
Race Relations Act 1976 (6 *Statutes* 765)
 s 21 61
  (1) 75
   (a), (b) 482
  (2)(a), (b) 483
  (3) 482
  22(1), (2) 483
  24(1), (2) 483
Real Property Act 1845
 s 3 464
  5 691
Rent Act 1957 1029
Rent Act 1965 963
                                 691
 s 14 1026
  30(1), (2) 955
Rent Act 1968 963
Rent Act 1974 (23 *Statutes* 403) 963,
                                   984, 987
 s 1(1) 971
Rent Act 1977 (23 *Statutes* 405) 310,
                   417, 484, 492, 495, 728,
                   975, 985, 1002, 1059, 1061
 s 1 . . . . . . 955, 971, 973, 974, 975,
                 976, 977, 981, 982, 987,
                            1007, 1012
  2 955
  (1) 1005
   (a) 976, 1002, 1007, 1012
  (3) 1007, 1062
  3(1) 916, 1003
  (2) 1006
  4(1) 982
  5 1039
  5A(1) 738, 983
  6 983
  7(1) 985
  (2) 987
  8-11 . . . . 983, 1040
  12 . . . . . 981, 987, 988, 989, 990,
                                  1040

	PAGE
Rent Act 1977—*contd*	
s 12(1)(a)	989
(b)	988, 989, 990
(c)	990
13(1)	983
14(a)-(e)	983
15(1)	983
16	983
19(2)	1040
(4)	1041
(5)(a)-(c), (e)	1041
(6)	998, 1040
20	1040
21	1040
(a)	1041
(c)	1040
22(1)	981
24(3)	982
26(1)	983
44(1)	1032
(2)	1033
57	1033
(3)	1033
66(1)	1031
67(1)	1031
(3)	1033
68(1)	1031
69(1)	1034
(1A)	1034, 1058
(4)	1034
70(1)	1034, 1036
(a)	1035
(b), (c), (e)	1036
(2)	1036
(3)(a), (b)	1037
71(2)	1032
72	1032
73(1)(c)	1033
(1A)	1033
77(1)	1043
78(2)	1043
79(1)	1043
80(2)	1043
81(1), (3)	1043
86ff	1051
98(1)	1015, 1022
(a)	1017, 1056
(2)	1023
(4)	1017, 1056
(5)	1024
100	1022, 1023, 1040
(3), (4A), (4B)	1023
101	1031
(2)	903, 1031
103	1043
(1)	1042
104(1)	1042
(c)	1042
105	1042, 1043
106	1043

	PAGE
Rent Act 1977—*contd*	
s 106A	1043
(2)-(4)	1043
119(1)	1038
120(1)-(4)	1039
122(1), (2)	1044
123(1)	1039
125(1)	1038
126(1)	1039
128(1)	1039
(c)	1039
141	1032
147(1)	1039
152(1)	971, 976
Sch 1	
para 2	1062
3	1063, 1064
6	1063
7	1063, 1064
10	1063
13	1004
Sch 2	
para 1, 2A	990
4	989
5	990
Sch 8	1033
Sch 15	993, 1027
Pt I	1015, 1019, 1023, 1056
Cases 1-10	1019
Pt II	1015, 1029
Cases 11-20	1023, 1024
Pt III	
para 1	1022
Pt IV	1017, 1018
para 3, 5, 6	1017
Pt V	
para 2	1024, 1025, 1027
Rent (Amendment) Act 1985 (23 *Statutes* 613)	
s 1(1)	1025
Rentcharges Act 1977	
s 1	81
2(1)	73, 81
(2), (3)	81
3(1)	81
10(1)	81
Rights of Light Act 1959 (13 *Statutes* 601)	
s 2	682
Settled Land Act 1925	33, 74, 100, 183, 221, 293, 350, 363, 435, 603, 803
s 1	807
(1)	62, 804
(i)	804, 807
(ii), (iii)	803
(v)	81, 803
(7)	348
4(1)	804
9(2)	805
13	468

PAGE

Settled Land Act 1925—*contd*
s 16(1)(i) 806
18(1) 806
(a) 832
19(1) 62, 346, 417, 805
(2) 348
20(1) 62, 346, 805
27(1) 432, 468
36(4) 362
38ff 346
38 . . . . 352, 806
41 352
41ff 806
71 352
(1) 806
72(2) 134, 806
(3) 355, 806
73(1)(xi) 353
102 352
106 351
(1) 806
107(1) 806
109(1) 352
117(1)(xxxi) 362
Sex Discrimination Act 1975 (22 *Statutes* 474)
s 30(1) 75, 1049
(a), (b) 482
(2)(a), (b) 483
(3) 482
31(1), (2) 483
32(1), (2) 483
Small Dwellings Acquisition Act 1899
s 5(1) 628
Social Security and Housing Benefits Act 1982
s 28ff 1051
Solicitors Act 1974
s 1 224
22(1), (3) 224
87(1) 224
Statute of Frauds (1677) (11 *Statutes* 205) 207, 237
s 1, 2 464
7 237
9 291
Statute of Uses (1535) 44
Statute of Westminster I (1275) . . . 683
Supplementary Benefits Act 1976 . . . 310
s 34(1) 1067
Sch 1
para 3 1067
Supreme Court Act 1981 (11 *Statutes* 756)
s 35A 518
37(1) 631, 944

PAGE

Supreme Court Act 1981—*contd*
s 37(2) 631
38(1) 494
(2) 495
49 42
50 217
Supreme Court of Judicature Act 1873 . . . . 52, 69, 75, 532
25(11) 42, 471
Supreme Court of Judicature Act 1875 . . . . 52, 69, 75, 471
Supreme Court of Judicature (Consolidation) Act 1925
s 45 631
Tenures Abolition Act 1660 58
Theft Act 1968 (12 *Statutes* 514)
s 4(1) 26
(2)(b), (c) 23
(3) 26
(4) 34
Tithe Act 1936 (14 *Statutes* 1246)
s 1 82
Town and Country Planning Act 1971
s 52 702
Trustee Act 1925
s 14(1) 357
(2) 831
(a) 357
17 602
34(2) 98, 339
36(1), (7) 299
40 299
41(1) 299
43 299
Unfair Contract Terms Act 1977 (11 *Statutes* 214) 203
Usury Laws Repeal Act 1854 580
Validation of War-time Leases Act 1944
s 1(1) 435
Vendor and Purchaser Act 1874
s 1 221
Water Act 1973
s 9 32
Water Resources Act 1963 680
s 23(1) 32
24(2)(b) 32
79(3), (4) 640
Wildlife and Countryside Act 1981
s 2(2) 34
4(3) 34
10(4) 34
13(1) 26
21(3) 26
27(1) 34

Table of Foreign Enactments

PAGE

AUSTRALIA
Family Law Act 1975 791
NEW SOUTH WALES
Conveyancing Act 1919
  s 66G(1), (4) 342
    93(1) 585
Conveyancing (Strata Titles) Act 1961:   19
Strata Titles Act 1973
  s 8(1)(f)(iii) 19
QUEENSLAND
Property Law Act 1974-82
  s 85(1) 617
    180 671
    196, 197 397
SOUTH AUSTRALIA
Real Property Act 1858 146
VICTORIA
Marriage Act 1958
  s 161(4)(b) 791
Marriage (Property) Act 1962
  s 3 791
Property Law Act 1958 (No 6344)
  s 79A 709
    223 342
Transfer of Land Act 1958 (No 6399)
  s 77(1) 617
Transfer of Land (Restrictive Covenants)
  Act 1964 (No 7130) 709
CANADA
Interest Act (RSC 1970, c I-18)
  s 8(1) 593
ALBERTA
Exemptions Act (RSA 1980, c E-15)
  s 1(1)(k) 883
Land Titles Act (RSA 1980 c L-5)
  s 195 165
BRITISH COLUMBIA
Property Law Act (RSBC 1979, c 340)
  s 32 . . . . 397, 671
Residential Tenancy Act (RSBC 1980,
  c 48)
  s 13 1026
MANITOBA
Law of Property Act (RSM 1970, c L90)
  s 27 397
Mortgage Act (RSM 1970, c M200)
  s 16 628
NEW BRUNSWICK
Property Act (RSNB 1952, c 177)
  s 42(1)(a) 624

PAGE

CANADA—*contd*
NOVA SCOTIA
Matrimonial Property Act 1980
  s 21(1)(a) 267
ONTARIO
Conveyancing and Law of Property Act
  (RSO 1980, c 90)
  s 37 397
Family Law Reform Act 1978 (RSO
  1980, c 152)
  s 11(1)(a) 267
Landlord and Tenant Act (RSO 1980,
  c 232)
  s 89 515
Residential Tenancies Act (RSO 1980,
  c 452)
  s 9(1) 1039
    28(1) 907
SASKATCHEWAN
Exemption Act (RSS 1965, c 96)
  s 2(1), para 11 883
Land Titles Act (RSS 1978, c L-5)
  s 240 317
NEW ZEALAND
Joint Family Homes Act 1964 . . . 882, 883
  s 5 882
    6(1) 882
    9(1)(b) 882
      (2)(c) 315
      (d) 882
    16 882
      (1) 882
        (a) 883
    17-20 882
    22(1) 300
Land Transfer Act 1952
  s 182 165
Property Law Act 1952
  s 49 433
    64 695
    66A 323, 433
    122 644
    127 686
    129B 669
      (1)(c) 669
REPUBLIC OF IRELAND
Family Home Protection Act 1976
  s 3(3)(a) 842
    (6) 842
    7(1) 893

	PAGE
REPUBLIC OF IRELAND—*contd*	
Housing (Private Rented Dwellings) Act 1982	
s 7(2)	1065
13(2)	970
Housing (Private Rented Dwellings) (Amendment) Act 1983	970
Registration of Title Act 1964	
s 72(1)(j)	175

	PAGE
REPUBLIC OF IRELAND—*contd*	
Rent Restrictions Act 1960	970
UNITED STATES OF AMERICA	
Air Commerce Act 1926 (49 USC)	
s 171	29
1304	29
Uniform Residential Landlord and Tenant Act	
s 4.105	515

List of Cases

PAGE

ANZ Banking Corpn (NZ) Ltd v Gibson (1981) 589
ANZ Banking Group Ltd v Bangadilly Pastoral Co Pty Ltd (1978) . 620, 622, 623, 624, 625
Abbey v Lord (1955) 334
Abbey National Building Society v Maybeech Ltd (1985) . . 19, 494, 503, 508
Abbeyfield (Harpenden) Society Ltd v Woods (1968) 456, 458
Abbott (A Bankrupt), Re (1983) . . . 887
Abbott v Bob's U-Drive (1960) 521
Abdulla v Shah (1959) 219
Abela v Public Trustee (1983): 320, 325, 327, 328, 329
Abiafo v Lord (1984) 1022
Abigail v Lapin (1934) 162
Abingdon RDC v O'Gorman (1968) . . 510
Aboriginal Development Commission v Treka Aboriginal Arts & Crafts Ltd (1984) 236
Abramson v Lakewood Bank and Trust Co (1981) 626
A'Court v Cross (1825) 740
Ackroyd v Smith (1850) 644, 649
Adair v Murrell (1981) 1038
Adams v Cairns (1901) 467
Addiscombe Garden Estate Ltd v Crabbe (1958) 451, 453
Addy v Donnelly (1983) 488, 993
Adler v Blackman (1952) 465
Adult Anonymous 11, Re (1982): 1070, 1071
Afan BC v Marchant (1980) 774
Afton Band of Indians v A-G of Nova Scotia (1978) 741
Agra Bank Ltd v Barry (1874) 165
Ailion v Spiekermann (1976) 991
Al-Sabrya (Jersey) Ltd v Willis (1983) .1010, 1013, 1014
Alarm Facilities Pty Ltd v Jackson Constructions Pty Ltd (1975) . . . 216
Alden v Alden (1964) 322
Aldenburgh v Peaple (1834) 512
Aldin v Latimer Clark, Muirhead & Co (1894) 477
Aldred's (William) Case (1610) 654
Aldrich v Canada Permanent Loan & Savings Co (1897) 623
Aldrington Garages Ltd v Fielder (1978) 448, 452, 995, 999
Alec Lobb (Garages) Ltd v Total Oil (Great Britain) Ltd (1985) 588
Alefounder's Will Trusts, Re (1927) . . 62

PAGE

Alexander v Mohamadzadeh (1985) . . 1022
Alford v Vickery (1842) 510
Ali v Booth (1966) 500, 503
Ali Reza Suleyman v Knapp (1983) . .1012, 1013, 1014
Allan v Liverpool Overseers (1874) . . 455
Allcard v Skinner (1887) 597
Allen v Gomme (1840) 660, 661
Allen v Greenwood (1980) . . 654, 663, 664
Allen v Gulf Oil Refining Ltd (1981) . . 656
Allen v Roughley (1955) 753
Allen v Seckham (1879) 91
Allen v Snyder (1977) . . . 233, 239, 240, 243, 244, 246, 254, 255, 257, 258, 259, 261, 265, 266, 268, 269, 272, 273, 276, 278, 281, 282, 285, 810, 816
Allen (SJ) (South Island) Ltd v Crowe (1980) 695, 711
Alliance Building Society v Pinwill (1958): 608
Alliance Perpetual Building Society v Belrum Investments Ltd (1957) . . . 606
Allied Irish Banks Ltd v Glynn (1973) . 576
Allied Irish Banks Ltd v McWilliams (1982) 248, 252, 265, 267, 837, 842
Allied London Investments Ltd v Hambro Life Assurance Ltd (1984) . . . 518, 519
Allingham, Re (1932) 327
Alpenstow Ltd v Regalian Properties plc (1985) 114, 207, 208
Amad v Grant 437
Amalgamated Investment & Property Co Ltd v Texas Commerce International Bank Ltd (1982) . 387, 396, 404, 410, 413
American Express International Banking Corpn Ltd v Hurley (1985) . . 620, 628
American Oil Service v Hope Oil Co (1961) 306
Amoco Australian Pty Ltd v Rocca Bros Motor Engineering Co Pty Ltd (1975) 991
Amrani v Oniah (1984) . . . 957, 958, 959
Anand v Gill (1978) 858
Anchor Brewhouse Developments Ltd v Berkley House (Docklands) Development Ltd (1987) 28
Ancketill v Baylis (1882) 455
Anderson v Bostock (1976) 634
Anderson v Midland Rly Co (1861) . . 467
Anderson v Oppenheimer (1880) . . . 910
Anderson v Tooheys Ltd (1937) . . . 430

PAGE

Andrews v Colonial Mutual Life Assurance Society Ltd (1982) . . 395, 416, 443
Andrews v Parker (1973) 77
Anglia Building Society v Lewis (1982) 858, 859, 895
Angus & Co v Dalton (1877) . . . 683, 684
Annally Hotel Ltd v Bergin (1970) . . 682
Annen v Rattee (1985) 251, 256, 260, 538
Anns v Merton L B (1978) 902, 913, 948
Anon (1684) 307, 311
Antrim County Land, Building, and Investment Co Ltd v Stewart (1904): 612
Appah v Parncliffe Investments Ltd (1964) 445, 456, 950
Appleby v Cowley (1982) 236, 291, 396, 402, 405, 411, 412
Arbutus Park Estates Ltd v Fuller (1977): 719
Arcade Hotel Pty Ltd, Re (1962) . . . 709
Arden v Sullivan (1850) 467, 468
Argyle Building Society v Hammond (1985) 158, 194, 195, 196, 198, 199, 833
Aristocrat Property Investments Ltd v Harounoff (1982) 1032
Arlesford Trading Co Ltd v Servansingh (1971) 518, 523
Armstrong v Armstrong (1970) . . 439, 441, 460
Armstrong v Armstrong (1979) . . . 242
Arrowfield Finance v Kosmider (1984): 595
Arya v Leon (1983) 1022
Asco Developments Ltd v Gordon (1978): 942
Asher v Whitlock (1865) . . . 64, 752, 753
Ashgar v Armed (1984) 958, 959
Ashley v Tolhurst (1937) 541
Ashton v Sobelman (1987) 492
Assets Co Ltd v Mere Roihi (1905) . . 164
Atkins' Will Trusts, Re (1974) 350
Atkisson v Kern County Housing Authority (1976) 1020
Attersley v Blakely (1970) 748
A-G v Antrobus (1905) 641, 652
A-G v Biphosphated Guano Co (1879): 86
A-G v McCarthy (1911) 32, 33
A-G v Magdalen College, Oxford (1854): 313
A-G v PYA Quarriers Ltd (1957) . . . 640
A-G v Trustees of British Museum (1903): 37
A-G for British Columbia v A-G for Canada (1914) 31, 32
A-G of Duchy of Lancaster v GE Overton (Farms) Ltd (1981) 35, 37
A-G of Hong Kong v Humphreys Estate (Queens Gardens) Ltd (1987) . . . 208
A-G of Southern Nigeria v John Holt & Co (Liverpool) Ltd (1915) . . . 655, 656, 658, 680
A-G to the Prince of Wales v Collom (1916) 397

PAGE

Atyeo v Fardoe (1979) 1004, 1009, 1010, 1011
Auerbach v Nelson (1919) 211
Aujla v Tuffin (1981) 1001
Austerberry v Oldham Corpn (1885) . . 695
Austin (John) & Sons Ltd v Smith (1982): 25
Australian Hardwoods Pty Ltd v Comr for Railways (1961) 470
Australian Hi-Fi Publications Pty Ltd v Gehl (1979) 672
Australian Safeway Stores Pty Ltd v Toorak Village Development Pty Ltd (1974) 480
Aveling v Knipe (1815) 247
Avest Seventh Corpn v Ringelheim (1981); revsd (1982) 1071
Avon Finance Co Ltd v Bridger (1985): 599
Avondale Printers & Stationers Ltd v Haggie (1979) . 218, 243, 244, 262, 273, 274, 281, 282, 283, 289, 290, 291, 397, 398, 404, 812, 816
Axler v Chisholm (1978) 679, 681
Ayer v Benton (1967) 351
Ayres v Falkland (1697) 72

B

B v B (1976) 264
BOJ Properties Ltd v Allen's Mobile Home Park Ltd (1980) 669, 671
B & W Investments Ltd v Ulster Scottish Friendly Society (1969) . . . 652, 668
Babcock v Carr (1982) 164, 217
Backhouse v Bonomi (1861) 642
Badcock and Badcock's Marriage, Re (1979) 323, 325, 329
Badley v Badley (1983) 493, 494
Bagot's Settlement, Re (1894) . . . 369
Bailey (A Bankrupt), Re (1977) . . 877, 878
Bailey v Barnes (1894) 89, 615
Bailey v Stephens (1862) 634, 650
Bailey (CH) Ltd v Memorial Enterprises Ltd (1974) 441
Bain v Brand (1876) 20
Baird v Moore (1958) 308, 313
Baker v Biddle (1923) 583
Baker v Lewis (1947) 1021
Baker v Turner (1950) 982
Balchin v Buckle (1982) . . . 115, 701, 720
Baldock v Murray (1981) . . . 1040, 1041
Balfour v Balfour (1919) 793
Ball v Crawford (1981) 438
Ballard v Dyson (1808) 662
Ballard v Tomlinson (1885) 32
Ballard's Conveyance, Re (1937) . . . 703
Bank Negara Indonesia v Hoalim (1973): 403, 416
Bank of British Columbia v Nelson (1979): 328
Bank of Cyprus (London) Ltd v Gill (1980) 621, 622

PAGE

Bank of Ireland Finance Ltd v D J Daly
  Ltd (1978) 219, 76, 577
Bank of Montreal v Stuart (1911) . 599, 857
Bank of Montreal v Woodtown Develop-
  ments Ltd (1980) 511, 512
Bank of New Zealand v Rogers (1941) . 857
Bank of Nova Scotia v Dorval (1980) . 628
Bank of Nova Scotia v Mitz (1980) . 23, 24
Bannerman Brydone Foster & Co v
  Murray (1972) 581
Bannister v Bannister (1948) . . . 240, 269,
          271, 273, 274, 282,
         283, 284, 804, 807
Bannister v Chiene (1902) 653
Banstead Downs Golf Club, The v The
  Commissioners (1974) . . . 542, 644
Barba v Gas & Fuel Corpn of Victoria
  (1976) 668
Barcabe Ltd v Edwards (1983) 595
Barclay v Barclay (1970) 382, 383
Barclays Bank Ltd v Bird (1954) . . . 612
Barclays Bank Ltd v Taylor (1974) . . 162
Barclays Bank plc v Tennet (1984) . . 612
Bardrick v Haycock (1976) . . . 988, 989
Barker v Corpn of City of Adelaide (1900): 28
Barkshire v Grubb (1881) 669
Barnes (A Bankrupt), Re (1979) . . 258, 887
Barnes v Addy (1874) 120
Barnes v Barratt (1970) 443, 454,
              460, 973
Barnes v Gorsuch (1982) 988, 989
Barnett v Djordjevic (1984) 958
Barnett v Hassett (1981) . . 114, 787, 788
Barnhart v Greenshields (1853) . . . 89, 175
Barns v Queensland National Bank Ltd
  (1906) 618, 622
Barnwell v Harris (1809) 221
Barrett v Dalgety New Zealand Ltd
  (1979) 205
Barrett v Hilton Developments Ltd
  (1975) 114
Barrow's Case (1880) 93
Barrowcliff, Re (1927) 333
Barry v Hasseldine (1952) . . . 669, 686
Barry v LB of Newham (1980) . . . 774
Bartlett v Robinson (1980) 657
Barton v Fincham (1921) 993
Barton v Morris (1985) . . . 317, 318, 329
Barton v Raine (1981) . . . 685, 686, 687
Basham, Re (1986) . . . 387, 396, 398, 399,
        404, 405, 406, 407,
       412, 419, 420
Bass Holdings Ltd v Lewis (1986) . . 436
Bass Holdings Ltd v Morton Music Ltd
  (1987) 499
Basset Realty Ltd v Lindstrom (1980) . 948
Bassett v Fraser (1981) 1022
Bassett v Nosworthy (1673) 88
Bateman Television Ltd v Bateman and
  Thomas (1971) 247, 262
Baten's Case (1610) 28

PAGE

Bath v Bowles (1905) 520
Bathe, Re (1925) 76
Bathurst (Earl) v Fine (1974) 503
Battlespring Ltd v Gates (1983): 1015, 1016
Baumgartner v Baumgartner (1985) . . 246,
     254, 255, 258, 259, 262,
     269, 273, 281, 282, 398,
      399, 405, 406, 795
Baxendale v Instow Parish Council (1982): 33
Baxendale v North Lambeth Liberal and
  Radical Club Ltd (1902) 645
Baxter v Eckersley (1950) 991
Baxter v Four Oaks Properties Ltd
  (1965) 717, 718
Baxton v Kara (1982) . . . 470, 494, 505
Bay of Islands Electric Power Board v
  Buckland (1978) 583
Bayley v Great Western Rly Co (1884) . 672,
              674
Bayley v Marquis Conyngham (1863) . 665
Baynton v Morgan (1888) 518, 519
Beard v Wood (1980) 636
Beatty v Guggenheim Exploration Co
  (1919) 268, 812
Beauchamp v Timberland Investments
  Ltd (1984) 593
Beaudoin v Aubin (1981) 746
Beaufort (Duke) v Patrick (1853) . . . 425
Beck v Scholz (1953) 1012, 1014
Becker v IRM Corp (1985) 948
Beckerman v Durling (1981) 486
Beckett (Alfred F) Ltd v Lyons
  (1967) 633, 641
Beckford v Beckford (1774) 263
Beddington v Atlee (1887) 653
Bedford Properties Pty Ltd v Surgo Pty
  Ltd (1981) 114
Bedson v Bedson (1965) 241, 309,
        310, 315, 316, 318,
       322, 324, 329, 822
Beech v Beech (1982) 405
Beer v Bowden (1981) 443
Beesly v Hallwood Estates Ltd (1960) . 117,
     136, 395, 524, 525, 530
Beetham, Re; ex p Broderick (1887): 576, 577
Behrens v Bertram Mills Circus Ltd
  (1957) 34
Belajev, Re (1979) 437
Belfour v Weston (1786) 902
Belgravia Insurance Co Ltd v Meah
  (1964) 495
Bellew v Bellew (1982) 745
Belmont Finance Corpn Ltd v Williams
  Furniture Ltd (1979) 120
Bendall v McWhirter (1952) . 119, 785, 789
Benecke v Chadwicke (1856) 210
Benger v Drew (1721) 247
Bennet v Bennet (1879) 263, 264
Bennett v Brumfitt (1867) 222
Benton v Chapman (1953) 1020

PAGE

Beresford v Royal Insurance Co Ltd
(1938) 332
Berg v Markhill (1985) 1023
Berg (E & L) Homes Ltd v Grey (1980): 394,
399, 400, 401, 402,
404, 411, 425, 539
Berger v State of New Jersey (1976) . . 1071
Berger Bros Trading Co Pty Ltd v Bursill
Enterprises Pty Ltd (1970) 659
Berkeley Road, (88), NW9, Re (1971) . 319
Berkley v Poulett (1976) 22
Bernard v Josephs (1982): 233, 240, 241, 246,
249, 251, 252, 254, 255,
256, 259, 268, 272, 278,
288, 290, 306, 309, 310,
360, 817, 826, 827
Bernstein of Leigh (Baron) v Skyviews &
General Ltd (1978) 17, 28, 29, 30
Berry, Re (1976) 884
Berry (A Bankrupt), Re (1978) . . 264, 265
Beswick v Beswick (1966); affd (1968) . . 692
Bevan, Ex p (1803) 613
Bevington v Crawford (1974) . . 1009, 1013,
1014
Bhimji v Salih (1981) 407, 495
Bickel v Duke of Westminster (1977) . . 480
Bickford v Parson (1848) 521
Bickman v Smith Motors Ltd (1955) . . 481
Biggs v Hoddinott (1898) 586, 587
Binions v Evans (1972) 182, 268,
271, 274, 285, 417, 435,
548, 551, 552, 553, 807
Binmatt v Ali (1981) 264
Birch v Ellames (1794) 90
Birch v Wright (1786) 606
Bird v Lord Greville (1884) 904
Bird v Syme-Thomson (1979) . . . 188,
846, 853, 877
Birmingham, Re (1959) 219
Birmingham Citizens Permanent Build-
ing Society v Caunt (1962) . 606, 890, 891
Birmingham DC v Kelly (1985) . . 934, 935,
936
Birmingham, Dudley and District Bank-
ing Co v Ross (1888) 476, 672
Bishop v Moy (1963) 515
Biss v Hygate (1918) 213
Bistany v Williams (1975) 1069
Black v Black (1949) 307
Black v Oliver (1978) 1035
Blackburn v Y V Properties Pty Ltd
(1980) 244, 263
Blacklocks v J B Developments (Godal-
ming) Ltd (1982) . . . 179, 181, 197
Blackstone (David) Ltd v Burnetts (West
End) Ltd (1973) 505
Blades v Higgs (1865) 34, 35
Blake v A-G (1982) . . .966, 967, 970, 1031
Blakeney v MacDonald (1981) 745
Blathwayt v Baron Cawley (1976) . 75, 76, 77
Blewett v Blewett (1936) 496

PAGE

Blewman v Wilkinson (1979) 643
Bligh v Martin (1968) 747
Bloch v Bloch (1981) . . 236, 247, 255, 285
Blodgett, Re (1953) 324
Blok-Glowczynski and Stanga, Re (1979): 1021
Bloomfield v Johnston (1868) 641
Blumenthal v Gallery Five Ltd (1971) . 442
Blundell v Catterall (1821) . . . 32, 33
Bocardo SA v S & M Hotels Ltd (1980) . 480
Boccalatte v Bushelle (1980) . 257, 258, 272,
276, 281, 292
Bognuda v Upton & Shearer Ltd
(1972) 642, 643
Bohan, Re (1957) 633
Bohn v Miller Bros Pty Ltd (1953) . . 692
Bolton v Bolton (1879) 668
Bolton v Buckenham (1891) 613
Bolton v Puley (1983) 205
Boodle Hatfield & Co v British Films Ltd
(1986) 219, 575
Booker v Palmer (1942) 460
Booth v Thomas (1926) 910
Booth v Turle (1873) 238, 283
Borg v Rogers (1981) 1043
Borman v Griffith (1930) . 474, 653, 656, 672,
673, 674, 676
Bostock v Tacher de la Pagerie (1987) . 1021
Boswell v Crucible Steel Co (1925) . . 918
Botting v Martin (1808) 466
Bottomley v Bannister (1932) . . . 904, 911
Boulter v Boulter (1898) . . . 307, 312, 313
Bouris and Button, Re (1976) 64
Bovill v Endle (1896) 585
Bowen v Anderson (1894) 437
Boxbusher Properties Ltd v Graham
(1976) 401
Boydell v Gillespie (1970) 241
Boyer v Worbey (1953) 532
Boyle's Claim, Re (1961) 148, 175
Brace v South East Regional Housing
Association Ltd (1984) 655
Bracewell v Appleby (1975) 660
Bradburn v Lindsay (1983) 655
Bradburn v Morris (1876) 662
Bradford Corpn v Pickles (1895) . . . 643
Bradford House Pty Ltd v Leroy Fashion
Group Ltd (1982-83) 904
Bradley v Baylis (1881) 446, 455
Bradley v Carritt (1903) 586
Bradley v Chorley BC (1985) 918
Bradley v Fox (1955) 333, 334, 335
Bradley v Mann (1974); affd (1975) . . 320
Bradshaw v Baldwin-Wiseman (1985). .1022,
1023, 1027, 1029
Bradshaw v Smith (1980) 983
Brady v Superior Court (1962) . 1071, 1072
Braithwaite v Winwood (1960) . . . 891
Braithwaite & Co Ltd v Elliot (1947) . 1021
Braythwayte v Hitchcock (1842). . 466, 467
Breams Property Investment Co Ltd v
Stroulger (1948) 521

PAGE

Brent People's Housing Association Ltd
v Winsmore (1985) 458
Breskvar v Wall (1971) 158
Bretherton v Paton (1986) 454
Brett v Cumberland (1619) 519
Brickwood v Young (1905) . . 306, 311, 312,
                                313, 314
Bridges v Harrow LBC (1981) . . . 711
Bridges v Hawkesworth (1851) 36
Bridges v Mees (1957) . . . 174, 191, 219
Bridges v Smyth (1829) 510
Bridgwood v Keates (1983) 661
Brighton and Hove General Gas Co v
Hove Bungalows Ltd (1924) 32
Brikom Investments Ltd v Carr (1979) . 403,
                                424, 848
Brikom Investments Ltd v Seaford (1981): 919
Brinckman v Matley (1904) 641
Brinnand v Ewens (1987) 387, 404
Bristol and West Building Society v
Henning (1985) . 185, 401, 419, 420, 421,
                    425, 842, 859, 860
Bristol DC v Clark (1975) 1050
British American Oil Co Ltd and De Pass,
Re (1960) 433, 440, 441
British Anzani Felixstowe Ltd v Inter-
national Marine Management (UK)
Ltd (1979) 943
British Columbia Land & Investment
Agency v Ishitaka (1911) . . . 619, 622
British Land Co Ltd v Herbert Silver
(Menswear) Ltd (1958) 977
British Museum Trustees v Finnis (1833): 636
British Petroleum Pension Trust Ltd v
Behrendt (1985) 500
British Railways Board v Glass (1965) . 662
British Red Ash Collieries Ltd, Re (1920): 24
Britton v Green (1963) 306
Broadway Corpn v Alexander's Inc
(1979) 428
Brock v Wollams (1949) 1065, 1069
Brocklebank v Thompson (1903) . . . 643
Brockway's Estate v CIR (1954) . . . 295
Bromley Park Garden Estates Ltd v Moss
(1982) 480
Bromley Securities Ltd v Matthews
(1984) 1014
Brooker Settled Estates Ltd v Ayers
(1987) 455, 1000
Broome v Monck (1805) 218
Broomfield v Williams (1897) 685
Brophy v Brophy (1974) 265
Broughall v Hunt (1983) . . . 290, 417, 544,
                                545, 548, 797
Broughton v Snook (1938) 213
Brown v Alabaster (1887) 668
Brown v Board of Education (1954) . . 905
Brown v Brash and Ambrose (1948) . .1007,
                            1008, 1009, 1011
Brown v Brown (1981) 309
Brown v Cole (1845) 585

PAGE

Brown v Draper (1944) 991
Brown v Gould (1972) 137, 433,
                                442, 443
Brown v Liverpool Corpn (1969) . . . 919
Brown v Ministry of Housing and Local
Government (1953) 1003, 1006
Brown v Oakshot (1857) 329
Brown v Raindle (1796) 323
Brown v Robertson (1962) . . . 247, 365
Brown v Staniek (1969) 241
Brown v Stokes (1980) 815
Browne, Re (1954) 75
Browne v Flower (1911) 654
Browne v Pritchard (1975) 825
Browne v Ryan (1901) 581
Browning v Dann (1735) 512
Brownlee v Duggan (1976) 416
Broxhead Common, Whitehill, Hamp-
shire, Re (1977) 675
Brunker v Perpetual Trustee Co (1937) . 216
Brunner v Greenslade (1971) . . . 715, 716,
                                717
Brunner v Williams (1975) 536
Brunscher v Reagh (1958) 309
Brutan Investments Pty Ltd v Under-
writing and Insurance Ltd (1980) . . 626
Bryan and Heath, Re (1980) 330
Bryant v Foot (1867) 683
Brykiert v Jones (1981) 241, 291
Brynowen Estates Ltd v Bourne (1981) . 414
Buchanan-Wollaston's Conveyance, Re
(1939) 361, 362, 377, 379
Buchmann v May (1978) 984
Buck v Dickinson (1978) 167
Buck v Howarth (1947) 430
Buckingham v Buckingham and London
Brick Co Ltd (1978) 1004
Buckleigh v Brown (1968) 654
Buckley v SRL Investments Ltd and
Cator and Robinson (1971) . . 117, 136,
                            153, 727, 730
Budd-Scott v Daniell (1902) . . . 476, 910
Budhia v Wellington City Corpn (1976) . 220
Bull v Bull (1955) . . 247, 264, 304, 305, 309,
                    364, 374, 375, 380, 381, 382, 831
Bulstrode v Lambert (1953) 660
Bunt v Hallinan (1985) 162, 164
Burden v Rigler (1911) 639
Burfort Financial Investments Ltd v
Chotard (1976) 480
Burgchard v Holroyd Municipal Council
(1984) 19
Burgess v Rawnsley (1975) 318,
                319, 320, 323, 325, 327,
                328, 329, 330, 331, 332
Burgess v Wheate (1759) . . . 46, 48, 52, 88
Burke v Burke (1974) 824, 825
Burke v Stevens (1968) 317, 321
Burke and Arab, Re (1980); affd (1983) . 515
Burkholder v Superior Court (1979) . . 30
Burnham v Galt (1869) 628

PAGE

Burns v Burns (1984): 233, 246, 249, 253, 254,
255, 256, 257, 258, 259,
260, 272, 273, 275, 277,
280, 287, 793, 794, 811
Burr v Copp (1983) 168
Burrogh v Cranston (1840) 585
Bursill Enterprises Pty Ltd v Berger Bros
Trading Co Pty Ltd (1970) . . 19, 658,
659
Bury v Pope (1586) 17
Bushell v Hamilton (1981) 755
Buswell v Goodwin (1971) 917
Butcher v Butcher (1827) 506
Bute (Marquis) v Guest (1846) . . . 480
Butler v Craine (1986) 271, 272,
273, 287
Butler v Fairclough (1917) 164
Buttle v Saunders (1950) 206
Button v Button (1968) 260, 277
Byrne, Re (1906) 312
Byrne v Byrne (1953) 75
Byrne v Judd (1908) 642

C

C v C (1976) 255, 277, 794
C & P Haulage v Middleton (1983): 543, 545
C J Belmore Pty Ltd v AGC (General
Finance) Ltd (1976) 593
Cadd v Cadd (1909) 274
Cadogan v Dimovic (1984) . . . 507, 508
Caerphilly Concrete Products Ltd v
Owen (1972) 436
Calabar Properties Ltd v Stitcher (1984): 940
Caldwell v Fellowes (1870) 323
Caldwell v McAteer (1984) 990
Calgary and Edmonton Land Co Ltd v
Discount Bank (Overseas) Ltd (1971): 194
California v Ciraolo (1986) 31
Callard v Beeney (1930) 646
Calverley v Green (1984): 244, 245, 247, 248,
251, 252, 255, 261, 262,
265, 267, 268, 273, 285
Calwell, ex p (1828) 609
Calye's Case (1584) 952
Camden v Batterbury (1860) . . . 531, 533
Cameron v Eldorado Properties Ltd
(1981) 511, 513
Cameron v Murdoch (1983) . . . 387, 399,
403, 406, 407, 409, 410,
413, 416, 418, 423, 424
Cameron v Young (1908) 904
Campbell v Holyland (1877): 630
Campbell v Paddington Corpn (1911) . 654
Campbell v Secretary of State for Social
Services (1983) 1067
Campden Hill Towers Ltd v Gardner
(1977) 439, 920
Campion v Palmer (1896) 609
Canada Life Assurance Co v Kennedy
(1978) 313, 314, 324

PAGE

Canada Trustco Mortgage Co v McLean
(1983) 896
Canadian Long Island Petroleums Ltd
v Irving Industries Ltd (1975) . . 136, 137
Canadian Pacific Hotels Ltd and Hodges
(1979) 456
Canadian Superior Oil Ltd v Paddon-
Hughes Development Co Ltd (1969) . 401,
403
Cannock Chase DC v Kelly (1978) . . 778
Cannon v Villars (1878) 661
Canterbury City Council v Bern (1981) . 933
Cantliff v Jenkins (1978) 558
Cantor v Cox (1976) 266
Capar v Wasylowski (1983) . . . 658, 680,
681, 682
Caplan v Marden (1986) 1000
Carden v Choudhury (1984) . 444, 450, 511
Cardiothoracic Institute v Shrewdcrest
Ltd (1986) 429, 430
Carega Properties SA v Sharratt (1979): 852,
1065, 1070
Cargill v Gotts (1981) 662, 680
Carkeek v Tate-Jones (1971) . 261, 265, 313
Carley v Farrelly (1975) 118, 816
Carley v Smith (1980) 256
Carmichael v Ripley Finance Co Ltd
(1974) 710, 719
Carney v Herbert (1985) 991
Carr-Saunders v Dick McNeil Associates
Ltd (1986) 663, 664
Carringtons Ltd v Smith (1906) . . . 591
Carter v Carroll (1968) 1064
Carter v Murray (1981) 914
Carter v SU Carburetter Co (1942) . . 1001
Cartwright, Re (1889) 60
Caruso v Owen (1983) 960
Casborne v Scarfe (1738) 572
Casella's Estate, Re (1967) 321
Cash, Re (1911) 334
Cassidy v Foley (1904) 512
Castle Phillips Finance Co Ltd v Khan
(1980) 594
Castle Phillips Finance Co Ltd v Williams
(1986) 596
Caunce v Caunce (1969) . . . 90, 187, 384,
832, 835, 836, 837, 838,
839, 840, 841, 842, 852
Cavalier v Pope (1906) . . . 911, 947, 948
Cave v Cave (1880) 87, 88
Cedar Holdings Ltd v Green (1981) . . 602
Celsteel Ltd v Alton House Holdings Ltd
(1985) 173, 189, 647,
648, 662, 663
Celsteel Ltd v Alton House Holdings Ltd
(No 2) (1987) 476, 520, 523, 527
Centaploy Ltd v Matlodge Ltd (1974) . 437,
485
Central Estates (Belgravia) Ltd v Wool-
gar (No 2) (1972) 503, 505, 729

PAGE

Central Trust and Safe Deposit Co v
Snider (1916) 218
Centrax Trustees Ltd v Ross (1979): 893, 896
Centrovincial Estates plc v Bulk Storage
Ltd (1983) 518, 519
Chalmers v Pardoe (1963) . . . 412, 413
Chambers v Kingham (1878) 489
Chambers v Randall (1923) 702
Chancellor v Webster (1893) 511
Chandler v Kerley (1978) . . 540, 544, 547,
548, 550, 799
Chandler v Pocock (1880) 370
Chang v Registrar of Titles (1975-76) . 218,
219
Chaplin v Young (No 1) (1864) . . . 610
Chaplin & Co Ltd v Brammall (1908) . 599
Chapman v Smith (1907) . . . 522, 608
Chappell (Fred) Ltd v National Car
Parks Ltd (1987) 659
Charter Township of Delta v Dinolfo
(1984) 1071, 1072
Chase Manhattan Bank N A v Israel-
British Bank (London) Ltd (1981) . . 268,
556, 812
Chasemore v Richards (1859) . . . 643
Chatham Empire Theatre (1955) Ltd v
Ultrans (1961) 507
Chattock v Muller (1878) 239
Chaudhry v Chaudhry (1987) 781
Chelsea Investments Pty Ltd v Federal
Commissioner of Taxation (1966) . .1003,
1004, 1006
Cheryl Investments Ltd v Saldanha
(1978) 982
Chester v Buckingham Travel Ltd (1981): 481,
482, 492
Chesterfield (Lord) v Harris (1908) . . 634
Chetwynd v Boughey (1981) 989
Cheyenne Airport Board and City of
Cheyenne v Rogers (1985) 27
Chhokar v Chhokar (1984) . . . 188, 303,
306, 307, 309, 377, 821,
833, 834, 847, 852, 877
Child v Douglas (1854) 717
Childers v Childers (1857) 283
Chillingworth v Esche (1924) 206
Chivers & Sons Ltd v Air Ministry (1955): 173
Cholmondeley (Marquis) v Lord Clinton
(1817) 612
Chorley BC v Barratt Developments
(North West) Ltd (1979) . . . 903, 1031
Choudhury v Meah (1981) . . . 158, 981
Chowood's Registered Land, Re (1933): 200
Chowood Ltd v Lyall (No 2) (1930) . . 157,
194, 195, 196
Chrisdell v Tickner (1987) 506
Chrispen v Topham (1986) 225
Christ's Hospital v Budgin (1712) . . . 264
Christian v Christian (1981) . 276, 277, 287,
406, 419, 802
Christophedis v Cumming (1976) . . . 987

PAGE

Christophers v Sparke (1820) 609
Chronopoulos v Caltex Oil (Australia)
Pty Ltd (1982-83) 531, 533
Chrysostomou v Georgiou (1982) . 958, 1043
Chukwu v Iqbal (1985) 479, 958
Church Comrs for England v Nadjoumi
(1985) 506
Church of England Building Society v
Piskor (1954) 603, 834
Churchward v Studdy (1811) 35
City and Metropolitan Properties Ltd v
Greycroft Ltd (1987) 517
City Mutual Life Assurance Society Ltd
v Lance Creek Meat Works Pty Ltd
(1976) 608
City of Campbellton v Gray's Velvet Ice
Cream Ltd (1982) 656
City of Des Plaines v Trottner (1966) . 1071
City of London Building Society v Flegg
(1986); revsd (1987) 91, 97, 98,
119, 176, 179, 180, 185,
242, 352, 356, 362, 375,
382, 384, 385, 601, 819,
829, 861
City of London Land Tax Comrs v
Central London Rly Co (1913) . . . 32
City of Santa Barbara v Adamson (1980): 1072
City of Westminster v Mavroghenis
(1983) 938
City of White Plains v Ferraioli (1974): 1071,
1072
City Permanent Building Society v Miller
(1952) 174
Cityland and Property (Holdings) Ltd v
Dabrah (1968) 590
Civil Service Co-operative Society Ltd v
McGrigor's Trustee (1923) 498
Clancy v Whelan and Considine (1958): 683
Clapman v Edwards (1938) 653
Clarey v Principal and Council of The
Women's College (1953) 1020
Clark v Carter (1968) 321, 323
Clark v Follett (1973) 208
Clark v National Mutual Life Association
of Australasia Ltd (1966) 617
Clark v Smith (1920) 1018
Clark v UDC Finance Ltd (1985) . . . 620
Clarke v Barnes (1929) 678
Clarke v City of Edmonton (1929) . . . 32
Clarke v Ramuz (1891) 219
Clarke v Taff Ely BC (1980) . . . 924, 949
Clarke (Richard) & Co Ltd v Widnall
(1976) 491
Classic Communications Ltd v Lascar
(1985) 143, 387, 653
Clavering v Ellison (1856) 75
Clayhope Properties Ltd v Evans (1986): 945
Clays Lane Housing Co-operative Ltd v
Patrick (1985) 491
Clayton v Green (1979) . 290, 411, 418, 797
Clayton v Ramsden (1943) 75, 76

PAGE

Clayton v Sale UDC (1926) 934
Clayton v Singh (1984) 409
Clearlite Holdings Ltd v Auckland City
    Corpn (1976) 306
Cleaver v Mutual Reserve Fund Life
    Association (1892) 332
Clegg v Hands (1890) 522
Clem Smith Nominees Pty Ltd v Farrelly
    (1980) 697, 702
Clement v Jones (1909) 745, 749
Cliffe v Cooper (1985) 430
Cliffe v Standard (1982) 990
Clifford v Hoare (1874) 663
Clifford v Johnson's Personal Representa-
    tives (1979) 503
Clifton v Viscount Bury (1887) 28
Climie v Wood (1869) 24
Clippens Oil Co Ltd v Edinburgh and
    District Water Trustees (1904) . . . 679
Clooney v Clooney (1978) 252, 815
Clore v Theatrical Properties and Westby
    & Co Ltd (1936) . . . 182, 451, 542, 549
Clothier v Snell (1966) 701, 719
Coastplace Ltd v Hartley (1987) . . 521
Coatsworth v Johnson (1886) . . . 213, 217,
                                   470, 472
Cobb v Lane (1952) 446, 460
Cobstone Investments Ltd v Maxim
    (1985) 1019, 1020
Cochrane v Cochrane (1980) 342
Cockburn v Smith (1924) . . . 911, 915
Cockerill, Re (1929) 75
Cocks v Thanet DC (1983) 777
Cohen v Cohen (1929) 269
Cohen v Nessdale Ltd (1982) 207
Cohen v Popular Restaurants Ltd (1917): 522
Colchester Estates (Cardiff) v Carlton
    Industries plc (1984) 502
Coldunell Ltd v Gallon (1986) . . 598, 599
Cole v Cole (1956) 327
Cole v Kelly (1920) 429
Colebrook's Conveyances, Re (1972) . . 242
Coleman v Steinberg (1969) 947
Colin Smith Music Ltd v Ridge (1975) . 1011
Collens, Re (1983) 576
Collier v Collier (1952) 311
Collier v Stoneman (1957) 1065
Collin v Duke of Westminster (1985) . . 729
Collins v Barrow (1831) 904
Collins v Hopkins (1923) 904
Collins v Northern Ireland Housing
    Executive (1984) 909, 912, 948
Collins v Sanders (1956) 265
Collins Cartage & Storage Co Ltd and
    McDonald, Re (1981) 442
Colls v Home and Colonial Stores Ltd
    (1904) 663, 664, 684
Colton v Wade (1951) 335
Combs v Ritter (1950) 307

PAGE

Commercial and General Acceptance
    Ltd v Nixon (1981-82) . . 618, 620, 621,
                                   622, 623
Commercial Bank of Australia Ltd v
    Amadio (1982-83) 225
Commonwealth v Registrar of Titles
    (Victoria) (1918) 648, 654
Commonwealth Life (Amalgamated)
    Assurance Ltd v Anderson (1946) . . 436,
                                   437
Commonwealth of Australia v New South
    Wales (1920-23) 22, 25, 61
Compton v Compton (1981) 327
Comyns v Comyns (1871) 609
Congleton Corpn v Pattison (1808) . . 522
Congregational Christian Church v
    Iosefa Tauga (1982) 432, 435
Containercare (Ireland) Ltd v Wycherley
    (1982) 324, 855, 893
Continental Oil Co of Ireland Ltd v
    Moynihan (1977) 588
Conquest, Re (1929) 352
Convey v Regan (1952) 633
Cook, Re (1948) 342
Cook v Bath Corpn (1868) 688
Cook v Minion (1979) . . . 405, 988, 989
Cook's Mortgage, Re (1896) . . . 312, 313
Cooke, Re (1857) 262, 796
Cooke v Chilcott (1876) 700
Cooke v Head (1972) 277, 815
Cooke v Ramsay (1984) 669, 682
Coombes v Smith (1986): 394, 396, 399, 402,
                     404, 406, 408, 420, 802
Cooper v Critchley (1955) 371
Cooper v Henderson (1982) . . . 499, 500,
                                   506, 1002
Cooper v Metropolitan Police Comr
    (1985) 636, 637
Cooper v Tait (1984) 989
Coopers & Lybrand Ltd and Royal Bank
    of Canada, Re (1982) 511
Copeland v Greenhalf (1952) 658
Corbett v Hill (1869-70) 28
Cordell v Second Clanfield Properties
    Ltd (1969) 685
Cornish v Brook Green Laundry Ltd
    (1959) 470, 471
Cornish v Midland Bank plc (1985) . . 600
Costa Investments Pty Ltd v Mobil Oil
    Australia Ltd (1979) 21
Costagliola v English (1969) . 402, 674, 682,
                                   687, 688
Costley v Caromin House Inc (1981) . . 1072
Cottage Holiday Associates Ltd v Cus-
    toms and Excise Comrs (1983) . . 435, 436
Coughlan v Mayor of the City of
    Limerick (1977) 909
Country Kitchen Ltd v Wabush Enter-
    prises Ltd (1981) 511
County of Los Angeles v Berk (1980) . . 642
Coupe v Ridout (1921) 206

PAGE

Cousins v Dzosens (1981) . . 309, 310, 378
Cove v Flick (1954) 1014
Coventry (Earl) v Willes (1863) . . . 641
Coventry City Council v Doyle (1981) . 935
Coventry City Council v Quinn (1981) . 934
Coventry Permanent Economic Building
  Society v Jones (1951) 117, 119
Cowcher v Cowcher (1972) . . . 118, 236,
      237, 238, 240, 243, 244,
      247, 249, 250, 261, 263,
      269, 273, 276, 285, 290,
      291, 296, 302, 316, 360
Cowell v Rosehill Racecourse Co Ltd
  (1937) 541, 549
Cox v Bishop (1857) 531, 533
Cox v Colossal Cavern Co (1925) . . . 18
Cox v Davison (1965) 308, 311
Cox and Neve's Contract, Re (1891) . . 91
Crabb v Arun District Council (1976) . 386,
      387, 390, 392, 394, 396,
      399, 402, 405, 410, 413,
      414, 415, 416, 422, 684
Craddock v Green (1983) 637
Craig v Federal Comr of Taxation (1945): 297
Crake v Supplementary Benefits Com-
  mission (1982) 1067
Crane v Davis (1981) 262
Crane v Morris (1965) 430
Crate v Miller (1947) 485
Cray v Willis (1729) 317
Credit Valley Cable TV/FM Ltd v Peel
  Condominium Corp No 95 (1980) . . 23
Cresswell v Hodgson (1951) 1015
Cresswell v Potter (1968) 225
Crest Homes plc's Application, Re
  (1984) 718, 719
Cricklewood Property and Investment
  Trust Ltd v Leighton's Investment
  Trust Ltd (1945) 489
Crisp v Mullings (1976) . . . 233, 248, 252,
      268, 360
Croft v Lumley (1858) 505
Croft v William F Blay Ltd (1919) . 467, 468
Crofts v Beamish (1905) 75
Crooke v De Vandes (1805) . . . 317, 328
Crossley & Sons Ltd v Lightowler (1867): 687
Crossley Bros Ltd v Lee (1908) . . . 24, 512
Crow v Wood (1971) 657
Crowder v Mercer (1981) 1020
Crown Estate Comrs v Wordsworth
  (1982) 983
Crown Street (195) Pty Ltd v Hoare
  (1969) 465, 487, 518
Cruise v Terrell (1922) 1006
Cruse v Mount (1933) 904
Cubitt v Lady Caroline Maxse (1873) . 636
Cubitt v Porter (1828) 305
Cuckmere Brick Co Ltd v Mutual
  Finance Ltd (1971): 618, 619, 620, 621, 626
Cuddon v Tite (1858) 219
Cudworth v Masefield (1984) 758

PAGE

Culkin v McFie & Sons Ltd (1939) . . 636
Cullen v Cullen (1962) . . . 408, 412, 418
Culling v Tufnal (1694) 21
Cumberland Consolidated Holdings Ltd
  v Ireland (1946) 219
Cumming v Danson (1942) 1015
Cummings v Anderson (1980) . . 311, 312
Curl v Angelo (1948) 979, 980
Curl v Neilson (1946) 307
Cushley v Seale (1986) 417, 418

D

DHN Food Distributors Ltd v LB of
  Tower Hamlets (1976) 552
Daalman v Oosterdijk (1973) 439
Daiches v Bluelake Investments Ltd
  (1985) 945
Daire v Beversham (1661) 218
Dale (Rita) v Adrahill Ltd and Ali Khan
  (1982) 985, 986
Dalton v Angus & Co (1881): 642, 673, 681,
      682, 683
Dalton v Christofis (1978) . . . 260, 283
Daly v Cullen (1958) 644
Dando v Dando (1940) 297, 330
Daniel v Camplin (1845) 296
Daniell v Sinclair (1881) 613
Daniels v Trefusis (1914) 210
Darby v Harris (1841) 512
Dartstone v Cleveland Petroleum Co Ltd
  (1969) 141, 706
Daulia Ltd v Four Millbank Nominees
  Ltd (1978) 207
Davenport v R (1877) 505
Davenport Central Service Station Ltd
  v O'Connell (1975) 524
Davey v Durrant (1857) 622, 623
David v London Borough of Lewisham
  (1977) 445, 460
David v Szoke (1974) 239, 265, 266
Davies, Re (1950) 302
Davies v Beynon-Harris (1931) . . . 432
Davies v Davies (1983) . . . 318, 325, 326
Davies v Directloans Ltd (1986) . 594, 595
Davies v Du Paver (1952) 681
Davies v Hilliard (1967) 459
Davies v Marshall (1861) 687
Davies v Messner (1975) 398
Davies v Otty (No 2) (1865) 283
Davies v Stephens (1836) 662
Davies v Sweet (1962) 210, 211
Davis, Re (1954) 23
Davis v Foots (1940) 904, 911
Davis v Johnson (1979) . 301, 559, 848, 965
Davis v Lisle (1936) 536
Davis v Pearce Parking Station Pty Ltd
  (1954) 541
Davis v Town Properties Investment
  Corpn Ltd (1903) 521
Davis v Vale (1971) 253
Davis v West (1806) 502

PAGE

Davis v Whitby (1973) 680
Davison Properties Ltd v Manukau City
  Council (1980) 697
Dawson v Dyer (1833) 958
Deacon v South-Eastern Rly Co (1889): 668
Dealex Properties Ltd v Brooks (1966): 1063
Dean v Superior Court for County of
  Nevada (1973) 30
Dean and Chapter of Rochester v Pierce
  (1808) 442
Deanshaw and Deanshaw v Marshall
  (1978) 660
Dear v Newham LBC (1987) 933
De Beers Consolidated Mines Ltd v
  British South Africa Co (1912) . 587, 588
Debney, Re (1960) 317
Debtor, A, Re (1967) 879
Debtor (No 24 of 1971), A, Re (1976) . 884
Deen v Andrews (1986) 21
De Falco v Crawley Borough Council
  (1980) 762, 772
De La Cuesta v Bazzi (1941) 305
De La Warr (Earl) v Miles (1881) . 679, 680
De Lusignan v Johnson (1973): 163, 164, 168
De Luxe Confectionery Ltd v Wadding-
  ton (1958) 533
De Markozoff v Craig (1949) 1018
De Mattos v Gibson (1982) 699
Demers (Maurice) Transport Ltd v
  Fountain Tire Distributors (Edmon-
  ton) Ltd (1974) 169, 401, 407
Demuren v Seal Estates Ltd (1978) . . 451,
  452, 996, 997, 999
Denne d Bowyer v Judge (1809) . . . 322
Denning (Garry) Ltd v Vickers (1985) . 528
Dennis v McDonald (1982) . 305, 309, 310
Denny, Re (1947) 317, 329
Denny v Jensen (1977) . . . 399, 401, 402
Densham (A Bankrupt), Re (1975): 273, 292,
  877, 886, 887
Department of Natural Resources v
  Ocean City (1975) 642
Department of Transport v Egoroff
  (1986) 919
De Rocco v Young (1981) 741
De Silva v Qureshi (1984) 959
Deutsche Bank v Banque des Marchands
  de Moscou (1931) 613
Devine v Fields (1920) 239, 240
Devlin v Northern Ireland Housing
  Executive (1982) 207, 402
Dewhirst v Edwards (1983) . . . 399, 405,
  410, 412, 415,
  650, 679, 684
De Witt v San Francisco (1852) . . . 296
De Wolf v Ford (1908) 952
D'Eyncourt v Gregory (1866) 22
Dibble (H E) Ltd v Moore (1970) . . . 21
Dickeson v Lipschitz (1972) 503
Dietsch v Long (1942) 313, 314
Dikstein v Kanevsky (1947) 658

PAGE

Diligent Finance Co Ltd v Alleyne (1971): 129
Dillwyn v Llewelyn (1862) . . . 388, 389,
  416
Diment v N H Foot Ltd (1974) . . 680, 681
Dimmick v Dimmick (1962) 303
Dinefwr B C v Jones (1987) 920
Dingle v Coppen (1899) 613
Diotallevi v Diotallevi (1982) 305
Di Palma v Victoria Square Property Co
  Ltd (1984); affd (1986) . . . 491, 493,
  494, 495, 939
Diplock, Re (1948) 46
Direct Food Supplies (Victoria) Pty Ltd
  v DLV Pty Ltd (1975) 491
Divis v Middleton (1983) 730
Dixon, Re (1903) 75
Dixon v Tommis (1952) 1010
Dobie v Pinker (1983) 536
Dobson v Jones (1844) 460
Dodds v Walker (1981) 485
Dodsworth v Dodsworth (1973) . . 391, 403,
  414, 417,
  418, 801, 807
Doe d Cheny v Batten (1775) 429
Doe d Rigge v Bell (1793) 468
Doe d Warner v Browne (1807): . . . 467
Doe d Mitchinson v Carter (1798) . . 1004
Doe d Tomes v Chamberlaine (1839) . 446
Doe d Bastow v Cox (1847) 429
Doe d Lord v Crago (1848) 429
Doe d Lord Macartney v Crick (1805): . 485
Doe d Parsley v Day (1842) 606
Doe d Chippendale v Dyson (1827) . . 494
Doe d Ellerbrock v Flynn (1834) . . . 489
Doe d Groves v Groves (1847) 430
Doe d Roylance v Lightfeet (1841) . . 606
Doe d Davenish v Moffatt (1850) . . . 467
Doe d Tucker v Morse (1830) 443
Doe d Gill v Pearson (1805) 75
Doe d Flower v Peck (1830) 505
Doe d Aslin v Summersett (1830) . 296, 485
Doe d Bennett v Turner (1840) 430
Doe d Henniker v Watt (1828) 492
Doe d Martin and Jones v Watts (1797): . 467
Doe d Hanley v Wood (1819) 540
Doe d Hull v Wood (1845) 431
Doe d Ambler v Woodbridge (1829) . 506
Doherty v Allman (1878) 60
Dolan, Re (1970) 76
Dollar Land Corpn Ltd v Solomon (1963): 524
Dolphin's Conveyance, Re (1970) . . . 717
Domaschenz v Standfield Properties Pty
  Ltd (1977) 613
Domb v Isoz (1980) 215
Donald v Baldwyn (1953) 995
Donoghue v Stevenson (1932) 620
Doohan v Nelson (1973) . . . 265, 266,
  273, 274, 793, 794
Dooley v A-G (1977) 754
Doran v Willard (1873) 24
Do Rosario v Dewing (1982) 941

PAGE

Doubledown Realty Corpn v Harris
 (1985) 1064
Douglas-Scott v Scorgie (1984) . . 919, 920
Dover v Prosser (1904) 461
Dover DC v Farrar (1980) 934
Dow Chemical Co v United States
 (1986) 31
Downes v Grazebrook (1817) . . . 625
Downie v LB of Lambeth (1986) . . . 939
Drake v Gray (1936) 708
Drane v Evangelou (1978) . . . 957, 959
Draper's Conveyance, Re (1969) . . . 315,
 316, 319, 320, 325, 326
Dreger, Re (1976) 333, 334
Drury v Drury (1675) 264
Drury v Johnston (1928) 1003
D'Silva v Lister House Development Ltd
 (1971) 206
Duddy v Gresham (1878) 76
Dudley and District Benefit Building
 Society v Emerson (1949) . . . 608, 1003
Dufaur v Kenealy (1908) 532
Duggan v Kelly (1847) 76
Dukart v District of Surrey (1978) . . 648,
 650, 652
Duke v Porter (1986) 1010
Duke v Robson (1973) 616
Dullow v Dullow (1985) . . . 244, 246, 261,
 263, 264
Dumpor's Case (1603) 508
Duncan v Paki (1976) 464
Duncan v Suhy (1941) 295
Dundee Harbour Trustees v Dougall
 (1852) 740
Dunn (Harry), Re (1949) 879
Dunn v Blackdown Properties Ltd (1961): 667
Dunraven Securities Ltd v Holloway
 (1982) 497, 500, 503
Dunstan v Hell's Gate Enterprises Ltd
 (1986) 33
Dunster v Hollis (1918) 946
du Pont de Nemours (E I) & Co v
 Christopher (1970); affd (1971) . . 30
Duppa v Mayho (1669) 492, 494
Durham and Sunderland Rly Co v Wawn
 (1841) 306
Durrett v Washington National Insur-
 ance Co (1980) 626
Du Sautoy v Symes (1967) 128, 129
Dutton v Bognor Regis UDC (1972) . . 913
Dyce v Lady James Hay (1852) . . . 654
Dye v Dye (1884) 236
Dyer v Dyer (1788) 244, 263
Dyett v Pendleton (1826) 957
Dyson v Kerrier DC (1980) 772
Dyson Holdings Ltd v Fox (1976) . . .1065,
 1067

E

E I Du Pont de Nemours Powder Co v
 Masland (1917) 557

PAGE

E O N Motors Ltd v Secretary of State
 for the Environment (1981) . . . 465
E R Ives Investment Ltd v High (1967): 141,
 226, 391, 392, 407, 413,
 416, 424, 425, 647, 697
Earl v Earl (1979) 323
East India Co v Skinner (1695) . . . 512
Easterbrook v The King (1931) . . . 397
Eastern Construction Co Ltd v National
 Trust Co Ltd (1914) 25
Eastgate v Equity Trustees Executors and
 Agency Co Ltd (1963-64) 297
Eastleigh Borough Council v Betts
 (1983) 769, 773
Eastleigh BC v Walsh (1985) . . . 432, 455,
 775, 1048
Eaton v Swansea Waterworks Co
 (1851) 679, 681
Eccles v Bryant and Pollock (1948): 206, 215
Ecclesiastical Comrs for England's Con-
 veyance, Re (1936) 692
Economy Shipping Pty Ltd v ADC
 Buildings Pty Ltd and Fischer Con-
 structions Pty Ltd (1969) 643
Ecroyd v Coulthard (1898) 32
Edbrand v Dancer (1680) 263
Eden Park Estates Ltd v Longman
 (1980) 183, 523, 524
Edge v Boileau (1885) 958
Edge v Worthington (1786) 576
Edmunds v Jones (1957) 1064
Edward Street Properties Pty Ltd, Ex p
 (1977) 671
Edward Wong Finance Co Ltd v John-
 son Stokes & Master (1984) . . . 578
Edwards v Bradley (1957) 264
Edwards v Lee's Administrator (1936) . 26
Edwards v Marbyn (1980) 959
Edwards v Sims (1930) 26
Ee v Kaker (1980) 214
Effra Investments Ltd v Stergios (1982) . 731
Efstratiou, Glantschnig and Petrovic v
 Glantschnig (1972) . . 168, 247, 253, 254
Egan v Egan (1975) 782
Egerton v Esplanade Hotels, London,
 Ltd (1947) 500
Egerton v Harding (1975) 657
Egerton v Jones (1939) 503
829 Seventh Avenue Co v Reider (1986): 1066
Electrolux Ltd v Electrix Ltd (1953) . . 394
Elfassy v Sylben Investments Ltd (1979): 911
Elias v George Sahely & Co (Barbados)
 Ltd (1983) 211
Elias v Mitchell (1972) 193, 371
Eliason and Registrar, Northern Alberta
 Land Registration District, Re (1981): 33
Elite Investments Ltd v TI Bainbridge
 Silencers Ltd (1986) 502
Ellenborough Park, Re (1956) 641,
 644, 649, 650,
 651, 652, 654

PAGE

Elliot, Re (1896) 75
Elliott v Brighton BC (1981) 930
Elliot (JN) & Co (Farms) Ltd v Murga-
  troyd (1984) 418
Elliott, Re (1918) 76
Elliott v Roberts (1912) 213
Ellis v Loftus Iron Co (1874) 28
Ellis v Mayor of Bridgnorth (1863) . . 651
Ellis & Sons Amalgamated Properties
  Ltd v Sisman (1948) 1004
Ellis & Sons Fourth Amalgamated
  Properties Ltd v Southern Rent
  Assessment Panel (1984) 1035
Ellis Copp & Co v LB of Richmond upon
  Thames (1976) 929
Elliston v Reacher (1908) 716
Elmcroft Developments Ltd v
  Tankersley-Sawyer (1984) 922
Elsden v Pick (1980) 486
Elvy v Norwood (1852) 613
Elwes v Brigg Gas Co (1886) 35
Emery's Investment Trusts, Re (1959) . 266
Enfield LBC v French (1985) . . 1057, 1060
Enfield London Borough Council v
  McKeon (1986) 735
Entick v Carrington (1765) 535
Epps v Esso Petroleum Co Ltd (1973) . 154,
  189, 199
Epsom Grand Stand Association Ltd v
  Clark (1919) 974
Eriksen's Estate, Re (1983) 815
Errington v Errington and Woods
  (1952) 182, 430, 449,
  460, 547, 548,
  550, 552, 798
Essex (Earl) v Capel (1809) 34
Essex County Roman Catholic Separate
  School Board and Antaya, Re (1978) . 73
Esso Petroleum Co Ltd v Alstonbridge
  Properties Ltd (1975) 606
Esso Petroleum Co Ltd v Harper's
  Garage (Stourport) Ltd (1968) . . . 588
Essoldo (Bingo) Ltd's Underlease, Re
  (1971) 442
Estelle's Estate, Re (1979) 317, 328
Estey v Withers (1975) 680
Eton College v Bard (1983) . . . 435, 728
Euston Centre Properties Ltd v H & J
  Wilson Ltd (1982) 450, 470
Evans v Clayhope Properties Ltd (1987): 945
Evans v Engelson (1980) . . . 1002, 1021
Evans v Forsyth (1979) 536
Evans v Prothero (1852) 211
Evers' Trust, Re (1980) . 350, 359, 376, 826
Eves v Eves (1975) . . . 259, 273, 274, 275,
  277, 310, 815, 816
Eyre v Hall (1986) 1005
Ezekiel v Orakpo and Scott (1980) . 398, 408
Expert Clothing Service v Sales Ltd v
  Hillgate House Ltd (1986) . . . 496, 497,
  498, 499, 500,
  504, 505, 506

PAGE

F

FFF Estates Ltd v L B of Hackney
  (1981) 931, 932
Facchini v Bryson (1952) . . 446, 461, 995
Fadden v Deputy Federal Comr of
  Taxation (1943) 297
Fairclough v Marshall (1878) . . 609, 707
Fairclough v Swan Brewery Co Ltd
  (1912) 584, 585
Fairmaid v Otago District Land
  Registrar (1952) 883
Falcke v Scottish Imperial Insurance Co
  (1886) 397
Falconer v Falconer (1970) . . 259, 265, 279
Family Housing Association v Miah
  (1982) 1047, 1048
Fanjoy v Gaston (1982) 947
Farimani v Gates (1984) 501, 506
Farrar v Farrars Ltd (1888) . 618, 619, 621,
  624, 625
Farrell v Alexander (1977) 1038
Farrugia v Official Receiver in Bank-
  ruptcy (1982) 884
Faulkner v Willetts (1982) 536, 537
Fay v Prentice (1845) 28
Feather Supplies Ltd v Ingham (1971): 976
Federated Homes Ltd v Mill Lodge
  Properties Ltd (1980) . . . 709, 710, 711,
  712, 719
Feld v Merriam (1983) 952
Felix v Karacritos and Jachni (1986) . 1000
Felix v Lockwood (1986) 1000
Felix v Rajar and Mahindra (1986) . 1000
Fellowes v Rother District Council
  (1983) 33
Fels v Knowles (1906) 162
Ferguson v Miller (1978) . . . 305, 306
Ferguson and Lepine, Re (1983) . 397, 671
Fergusson v Fyffe (1841) 613
Ferris v Weaven (1952) 785
Fernandes v Parvardin (1982) . 1022, 1027
Festing v Costas 1018
Feyereisel v Turnidge (1952) 965
Field v Adames (1840) 512
Field v Barkworth (1986) 480
Figgis, Re (1969) 264
Filburn v People's Palace and Aquarium
  Co Ltd (1890) 34
Finch v Earl of Winchelsea (1715) . . 46
Finck v Tranter (1905) 612
Fink v McIntosh (1946) 436
Finlay v Curteis (1832) 633
Finlayson v Taylor (1983) 512
First Middlesbrough Trading and
  Mortgage Co Ltd v Cunningham
  (1974) 893
First National Bank of Denver v
  Groussman (1971) 322
First National Bank of Southglenn v
  Energy Fuels Corpn (1980) . . 317, 322
First National Securities Ltd v Bertrand
  (1980) 596

PAGE

First National Securities Ltd v Hegerty
(1985). 319, 321, 325, 602, 603,
872, 874
First National Securities Ltd v Jones
(1978) 222
Firstcross Ltd v East West (Export/
Import) Ltd (1984) 1002, 1008
Firstcross Ltd v Teasdale (1984) . 481, 1032
Fishenden v Higgs & Hill Ltd (1935) . 664
Fisher v Dixon (1845) 24
Fisher v Knowles (1982) 205
Fisher v Macpherson (1954) 1016
Fisher v Wigg (1700) 338
Fitts v Stone (1942) 317
Fitzhardinge (Lord) v Purcell (1908) . . 640
Flannigan v Wotherspoon (1953) . 327, 328
Fleischmann v Grossman Holdings Ltd
(1978) 907
Fleming v Fleming (1921) 297
Fleming v Hargreaves (1976) . . 316, 324
Fletcher v Davies (1981) 1005
Fletcher v Nokes (1897) 496
Fletcher v Storoschuk (1981) 744
Flexman v Corbett (1930) 481
Flood v Wisconsin Real Investment Trust
(1980) 953
Florent v Horez (1983) 1019, 1020
Floyd v Heska (1975) 674
Flynn v Flynn (1930) 317, 329
Flynn v Harte (1913) 663
Flynn v O'Dell (1960) 324
Flynn v United States (1953) 304
Foisy v Wyman (1973) 906
Foley v Galvin (1932) 1009
Foley's Charity Trustees v Dudley Corpn
(1910) 72, 635
Food Distributors Ltd v Tower Hamlets
LBC (1976) 421
Forbes v New South Wales Trotting Club
Ltd (1979) 538
Foreman v Beagley (1969) 1064
Formby v Barker (1903) 702, 703
Forsey and Hollebone's Contract, Re
(1927) 128
Forster v Elvet Colliery Co Ltd (1908) . 692
Forster v Hale (1798) 237, 238
Forsyth v Blundell (1972-1973) . . 615, 617,
619, 621, 622, 626
Foshee v Foshee (1962) 306
Foster, Re, ex p Foster (1883) 213
Foster v Robinson (1951) . . 487, 488, 548,
807, 992
Foster's Estate, Re (1958) 297
Fothringham v Kerr (1984) 32
Four-Maids Ltd v Dudley Marshall
(Properties) Ltd (1957) 606, 609
420 East 80th Co v Chin (1982) . . . 1071
Foxell v Mendis (1982) 505, 985,
1015, 1016, 1020
Framton v McCully (1976) 214

Francini and Canuck Properties Ltd, Re
(1982) 493, 518, 525
Francis v Cowcliffe (1977) 942
Francis Jackson Developments Ltd v
Stemp (1943) 430
Francke v Hakmi (1984) 984
Fraser v Hopewood Properties (1986) . 941
Frazer v Walker (1967) 158, 164
Fredco Estates Ltd v Bryant (1961) . . 487
Frederick v Shorman (1966) 300
Freed v Taffel (1984) 323, 325
Freeman v Wansbeck District Council
(1983) 735
Freer v Unwins Ltd (1976) 197
Freeway Mutual Pty Ltd v Taylor
(1978-79) 577
Fresno County v Kahn (1962) 327
Frewen v Relfe (1787) 327
Fridberg v Doyle and Ryan (1981) . . 1009
Fritz' Estate, Re (1933) 299
Frobisher Ltd v Canadian Pipelines &
Petroleums Ltd (1960) 136
Frodsham (Charles) & Co Ltd v Morris
(1974) 524
Frogley v Earl of Lovelace (1859) . 540, 665
Frost v Feltham (1981) 1047
Frost Ltd v Ralph (1981) . . 618, 619, 621,
622, 623
Fruin v Fruin (1983) 745, 747
Fry v Lane (1888) 225
Fryer v Brooks (1984) 381, 424
Fryer v Bunney (1982) 205, 941
Fuggle (RF) Ltd v Gadsden (1948) . . 1021
Furniss v Dawson (1984) 995
Fyfe v Smith (1975) 610

G

G A Investments Pty Ltd v Standard
Insurance Co Ltd (1964) . . . 584, 585
G & C Kreglinger v New Patagonia
Meat and Cold Storage Co Ltd
(1914) 581, 582, 583, 586, 587
GMS Syndicate Ltd v Gary Elliott Ltd
(1982) 503, 507, 508
Gadd's Land Transfer, Re (1966) . . . 703
Galasso v Del Guercio (1971) 303
Gallagher v N McDowell Ltd (1961) . 948
Galletto's Estate, Re (1946) 323
Gallo v St Cyr (1983) 481
Gammans v Ekins (1950) . . . 1066, 1069
Gandy v Jubber (1865) 437
Gardner v Hodgson's Kingston Brewery
Co Ltd (1903) . . . 679, 681, 682, 684
Gardner v Howie (1983) 669
Gardner v Rowe (1828) 237
Garland v Johnson (1982) . . . 441, 459
Gas & Fuel Corpn of Victoria v Barba
(1976) 644, 646, 667
Gascoigne v Gascoigne (1918) 266
Gasking & Co Ltd v Evans, McGeachie
and Proctor (1981) 1064, 1067

PAGE

Gateley v H & J Martin Ltd (1900) . . 642
Gatien Motor Co Ltd v Continental Oil
  Co of Ireland Ltd (1979) . 452, 459, 994
Gaul v King (1980) . 907, 917, 920, 924, 947
Gaumont v Luz (1980) 464
Gaved v Martyn (1865) 682
Gavin v Lindsay (1985) 986
Gaw v Córas Iompair Éireann (1953) . 693
Gayford v Moffatt (1868) 680
Gebert's Estate, Re (1979) 329
Gebhardt v Dempster (1914) 327
Gedye v Montrose (1858) 219
Geldhof v Bakai (1983) 397
General Credits (Finance) Pty Ltd v
  Stoyakovich (1975) 626
General Management Ltd v Locke (1980): 1063
Georgiades v Edward Wolfe & Co Ltd
  (1965) 114, 135
Gerling's Estate, Re (1957) 297
German v Chapman (1877) 701
Gerraty v McGavin (1914) 465
Gibbons, Re (1920) 804
Gibson v Death (1986) 461
Gifford v Dent (1926) 28
Gifford v Lord Yarborough (1828). . . 33
Gilbert v Spoor (1983) 720
Giles, Re (1972) 332, 334
Gilham v Breidenbach (1982) 538
Gill v Lewis (1956) 495
Gillette v Cotton (1979) 326
Gillette v Nicolls (1953) 327
Gillick v West Norfolk AHA (1986) . . 848
Gilmurray v Corr (1978) 239
Giltrap v Busby (1970) 655
Gin v Armstrong (1969) 331
Gion v City of Santa Cruz (1970) . . . 642
Gioukouros v Cadillac Fairview Corpn
  Ltd (1984) 742
Gissing v Gissing(1969); revsd (1971): . 233,
        237, 241, 243, 244, 245,
        246, 247, 249, 253, 254,
        255, 256, 257, 258, 259,
        262, 265, 270, 272, 273,
        275, 276, 277, 278, 279,
        280, 281, 287, 288, 292,
        390, 407, 409, 794, 798,
        809, 810, 813, 817, 818
Gladyric Ltd v Collinson (1983) . . . 1017
Glasgow Corpn v Johnstone (1965) . . 461
Glass v Kencakes Ltd (1966) . . . 496, 500
Glass v Patterson (1902) 527
Glastonbury Royal British Legion Club
  Ltd v Govier (1981) 993
Glenn v Federal Comr of Land Tax
  (1915) 423, 556
Glenwood Lumber Co Ltd v Phillips
  (1904) 440
Gloucestershire County Council v
  Farrow (1985) 636
Goddard v Torridge District Council
  (1981) 768

PAGE

Goding v Frazer (1967) 206
Godwin v Bedwell (1982) 241
Godwin v Schweppes Ltd (1902) . . . 647
Gofor Investments Ltd v Roberts
  (1975) 1009, 1010
Goforth v Ellis (1957) 308
Gohl v Hender (1930) 663
Goldberg v Edwards (1950) . . . 675, 677
Goldberg v Housing Authority of Newark
  (1962) 953
Goldberg v Kelly (1970) 12
Goldblatt v Town of Hempstead (1962): 26
Goldcall Nominees Pty Ltd v Network
  Finance Ltd (1983) 619, 621, 623,
        624, 625, 626
Golding v Hands, Golding and Boldt
  (1969) 321, 325
Goldsmith v Burrow Construction Co Ltd
  (1987) 681
Goldstein v Sanders (1915) . . . 472, 522
Goldsworthy v Brickell (1987) 598
Goldsworthy Mining Ltd v Federal Comr
  of Taxation (1972-73) . . . 438, 439, 449
Gonin, Re (1979) 213, 214
Gonzales v Gonzales (1968) 321
Goodfriend v Goodfriend (1972) . . 244, 245,
        263, 266
Goodhue House Co v Bernstein (1981) . 1066
Goodlet & Smith, Ex p (1983) 397
Goodman v Dolphin Square Trust Ltd
  (1979) 983
Goodman v Gallant (1986) . . . 240, 241,
        242, 247, 270, 318,
        319, 358, 360, 361
Goodman v J Eban Ltd (1954) 222
Goodman v Ross (1948) 1004
Goodright & Humphreys v Moses (1775): 87
Gordon v Phelan (1881) 512
Gordon v Selico Co Ltd (1986) . . . 902,
        904, 909, 910, 919
Gordon and Regan, Re (1985) . . 646, 660
Gordon Grant & Co Ltd v Boos (1926): . 628
Gore, Re (1972) 333, 334, 335
Gorog v Kiss (1977) 245, 264
Gosling v Woolf (1893) 529
Gotobed v Pridmore (1970) 687
Gough v Fraser (1977) 272
Gough v Kiddeys Korner Ltd (1976) . 169
Gould v Kemp (1834) 323
Governor and Company of the Bank of
  Scotland v Grimes (1985) . . . 892, 893
Gower v Public Trustee (1924) 74
Graham v KD Morris & Sons Pty Ltd
  (1974) 28
Graham v Philcox (1984) . . 647, 662, 667
Graham H Roberts Pty Ltd v Maurbeth
  Investments Pty Ltd (1974) 547
Grand Junction Co Ltd v Bates (1954): 564
Grangeside Properties Ltd v Colling-
  woods Securities Ltd (1964) 575
Grant v Edmondson (1931) 692

PAGE

Grant v Edwards (1986) 258, 270,
271, 272, 274, 275, 276,
278, 279, 280, 287, 406,
420, 803, 817
Grant v Gresham (1979) 987
Grant v Sanderson (1983) . . 280, 288, 811
Graves v Berdan (1863) 902
Graves v Dolphin (1826) 75
Graves v Interstate Power Co (1920) . 28
Gravesham BC v Secretary of State for
the Environment (1982) 972
Gray, Re (1927) 352
Gray v Gray (1980) 337
Gray v Spyer (1922) 437
Gray v Wykeham Martin (1977) . . . 746
Graystone Property Investments Ltd v
Margulies (1984) 26, 439
Greasley v Cooke (1980): 399, 403, 404, 405,
406, 407, 417, 420,
544, 800, 801, 807
Great Central Rly Co v Bates (1921) . 536
Great Western Rly Co v Smith (1876): 507
GLC v Connolly (1970) 442
GLC v Jenkins (1975) 758
GLC v LB of Tower Hamlets (1983) . 934
GLC v Minchin (1981) 430
Greaves Organisation Ltd v Stanhope
Gate Property Co Ltd (1973) . . . 181
Green v Ashco Horticulturist Ltd
(1966) 675, 677
Green v Belfast Tramways Co (1887) . 642
Green v Burns (1879) 609
Green v Eales (1841) 941
Green v Skinner (1921) 297, 298
Green v Smith (1738) 218
Green v Superior Court of City and
County of San Francisco (1974) . 906
Green (HE) & Sons v Minister of Health
(No 2) (1948) 1031
Greene v Church Comrs for England
(1974) 136
Greenfield v Greenfield (1979) . . 317, 329,
330, 332
Greenhi Builders Ltd v Allen (1979) . 111
Greenstreet v Moorchat Ltd (1982): 451, 995
Greenway v Rawlings (1952) . . . 1064
Greenwich LBC v McGrady (1983) . . 485,
487
Greenwood v Martins Bank Ltd (1933): 401
Gregg v Richards (1926) 678
Gregory v Mighell (1811) 390
Grescot v Green (1700) 527
Griffies v Griffies (1863) 304, 309
Griffiths v Band (1974) 709
Griffiths v English (1982) 989
Griffiths v Williams (1977) . . . 402, 405,
406, 408, 413, 417,
804, 807, 808, 983
Griffiths v Young (1970) 207
Griggs v Allegheny County (1962) . . 29

PAGE

Grigsby v Melville (1974); affd (1972) 18, 26,
658, 659
Grigsby's Estate, Re (1982) 301
Grime v Bartholomew (1972) . . 211, 214
Grinskis v Lahood (1971): 645, 660, 661, 662
Grocott v Ayson (1975) 643
Grosglik v Grant (1947) 437
Gross v French (1975) 242, 264,
312, 313, 402, 795
Grosvenor (Mayfair) Estates v Amberton
(1983) 975
Grosvenor Hotel Co v Hamilton (1894): 477
Group House of Port Washington Inc v
Board of Zoning etc (1978) . . 1071, 1072
Groves v Christiansen (1978) . . 264, 323
Groveside Properties Ltd v Westminster
Medical School (1983) 979
Grundt v Great Boulder Pty Gold Mines
Ltd (1937) 409
Guckian v Brennan (1981) 180
Guerin v The Queen (1983) 236
Guild v Mallory (1983) 746
Guppy v O'Donnell (1979) 988
Guppys (Bridport) Ltd v Brookling
(1984) 450, 456, 914, 959
Guppys Properties Ltd v Knott (1980): 1034
Gurasz v Gurasz (1970) 781, 783
Gurren v Casperson (1928) 952
Gwent Chief Constable v Dash (1986) . 636

H

Habib Bank Ltd v Tailor (1982) . . . 897
Hackney L B v Ezedinma (1981) . . . 939
Hadwell v Righton (1907) 636
Hagee (London) Ltd v A B Erikson and
Larson (1976) 429, 430
Haggert v Town of Brampton (1897) . 22, 23
Hahn and Kramer, Re (1980) . . . 982
Haigh v Kaye (1872) 283
Hale v Hale (1975) 1052
Halet v Wend Investment Co (1982) . 483
Halifax Building Society v Clark
(1973) 892, 893
Halifax County Pulp Co Ltd v Rutledge
(1982) 747
Hall v Busst (1960) 137
Hall v Ewin (1887) 433, 528, 702
Hall v Hall (1982) 259, 277
Hall v Warren (1804) 216
Hall's Estate, Re (1914) 332
Halliday v Nevill (1984) . . 536, 537, 538
Halsall v Brizell (1957) 142, 697
Hallwood Estates Ltd v Flack (1950) . 1008
Hamerton v Stead (1824) 467
Hamilton (Baron) v Edgar (1953) . 451, 675
Hamilton v Geraghty (1901) 393,
417, 418, 424
Hamilton v Martell Securities Ltd
(1984) 501, 502, 924
Hamilton DC v Brown (1982) . . 774, 777
Hammerton v Honey (1876) 641

PAGE

Hammond v Farrow (1904) 464
Hammond v McArthur (1947) . . . 323
Hammond v Mather (1862) 494
Hammond v Prentice Bros Ltd (1920): 645
Hamp v Bygrave (1983) . . 22, 24, 399, 403
Hamps v Darby (1948) 34
Hampshire v Wickens (1878) . . 477, 481
Hampstead Way Investments Ltd v
  Lewis-Weare (1985) . . . 972, 974, 980,
          1011, 1012, 1013
Hampstead Way Investment v Mawdsley
  (1980) 1039
Hanbury v Jenkins (1901) 646
Hancock v Austin (1863) . . . 511, 512
Hand v Hall (1877) 465
Haniotis v Dimitriou (1983) . . . 506, 507
Hankinson v Kyle (1982) 815
Hanlon, Re (1933) 76
Hanna v Pollock (1900) 680, 683
Hannaford v Selby (1976) . . 262, 278, 406,
          539, 795, 811
Hansford v Jago (1921) 674
Hanson, Re (1928) 349
Harada v Registrar of Titles (1981) . . 644,
          650, 658
Harding v IRC (1977) 433
Hardwick v Johnson (1978) . 409, 445, 550,
          793, 800, 808
Hare v Elms (1893) 508
Hargrave v Goldman (1963) 306
Hargrave v Newton (1971) . . 256, 279, 816
Hargroves, Aronson & Co v Hartopp
  (1905) 911
Harley v King (1835) 527
Harley Queen v Forsyte Kerman
  (1983) 439, 659
Harlow v Hartog (1978) . . 701, 718, 719
Harman v Glencross (1986) . . . 373, 782,
          784, 787, 870, 871,
          872, 873, 874, 875,
          877, 879, 895
Harmer v Jumbil (Nigeria) Tin Areas Ltd
  (1921) 476, 477
Harper v Aplin (1886) 609
Harper v Charlesworth (1825) 444
Harper v Joblin (1916) 583
Harper v O'Neal (1978) 305
Harrigan v Brown (1967) 217
Harrington v Croydon Corpn (1968) . 928,
          929, 933, 1003
Harris v Flower (1904) 660
Harris v Goddard (1983) . . . 316, 317,
          318, 319, 320, 321,
          325, 329, 331, 342
Harris v James (1876) 915
Harris v Plentex (1980) 728
Harris v Swick Securities Ltd (1969) . . 728
Harrison v Carswell (1976) 538
Harrison v Duke of Rutland (1893): 635, 636

PAGE

Harrison v Hammersmith and Fulham
  LBC (1981) 963, 1045, 1055
Harrogate Borough Council v Simpson
  (1984) 855, 1060, 1071
Hart v Chief Constable of Kent (1983): 537
Hart v Emelkirk Ltd (1983) 944
Hart v O'Connor (1985) 225, 226
Hart v Windsor (1843) 904
Hart's Estate, Re (1982) 335
Harvey v Harvey (1982) . . 309, 310, 827
Harvey v Pratt (1965) 433
Haskins v Lewis (1931) 979, 1010
Haslemere Estates Ltd v Baker (1982) . 111,
          396, 425
Hastings and Thanet Building Society v
  Goddard (1970) 851, 894
Hastings Minor Hockey Association v
  Pacific National Exhibition (1982) . 409
Haughabaugh v Honald (1812) . . . 330
Hawaii Housing Authority v Midkiff
  (1984) 732
Hawes v Evenden (1953) 1067
Hawkesley v May (1956) . . . 318, 325
Hawkins v Dhawan (1987) 911
Hawkins v Price (1947) 210, 211
Hawkins v Sherman (1828) 527
Hayes' Estate, Re (1920) 327
Hayward v Chaloner (1968) 742
Hayward v Giordani (1983) . . . 272, 274,
          277, 419, 813, 817
Hayward v Skinner (1981) 342
Haywood v Brunswick Permanent
  Benefit Building Society (1881) . 700, 701
Hazell v Hazell (1972) . . . 256, 279, 816
Heap v Ind Coope and Allsopp Ltd
  (1940) 914
Heath v Keys (1984) 755
Heath Estates Ltd v Burchell (1979) . . 488,
          1011, 1014
Heatley v Tasmanian Racing and
  Gaming Commission (1977) . . 538, 545
Heavey v Heavey (1977) 265
Heberley, Re (1971) 556
Hedley v Roberts (1977) 653, 659
Hedson and Hove's Contract, Re (1887): 630
Hegan v Carolan (1916) 506
Heglibiston Establishment v Heyman
  (1978) 1019, 1020
Helby v Rafferty (1979) . . 1065, 1067, 1070
Hellawell v Eastwood (1851) 22
Helton v Allen (1940) 332
Helvering v Gregory (1934) 995
Hemmings v Stoke Poges Golf Club Ltd
  (1920) 756
Henderson v Eason (1851) . . . 304, 306,
          307, 308, 309
Henderson v Law (1984) 758
Henderson v Volk (1982) . . . 681, 682
Heneghan v Davitt (1933) 86
Henry Ltd v McGlade (1926) 656

PAGE

Henry Reach (Petroleum) Pty Ltd v Credit House (Vic) Pty Ltd (1976) 617, 618, 619, 621, 622, 623
Hepworth v Hepworth (1963): 234, 261, 264
Herbert v Byrne (1964) 976
Herklots' Will Trusts, Re (1964) . . . 351
Heron v Sandwell MBC (1980) 235
Hervey v Smith (1856) 91
Herzog v Joy (1980) 1004
Heseltine v Heseltine (1971) 816
Hessling v City of Broomfield (1977) . . 1072
Heslop v Burns (1974) . . 430, 431, 446, 447, 460, 542, 973
Hewett, Re (1894) 323
Hewitt v Lewis (1986) 1025
Hewitt v Rowlands (1924) . . . 940, 1006
Hexter v Pearce (1900) 216
Heyland v Heyland (1972) 278
Heys Estate, Re (1914) 330
Heyse v Heyse (1970) 309
Heywood v BDC Properties Ltd (No 2) (1963) 114
Hick v Raymond & Reid (1893) . . . 497
Hickman v Maisey (1900) 636
Hickman v Peacey (1945) 298
Hiern v Mill (1806) 220
High Street (139) Deptford, Re, ex p British Transport Commission (1951): 155, 199
Higgins v Bank of Ireland (1947) . . . 76
Higgins v Betts (1905) 664
Higgins and Mathot, Re (1984) . . . 1025
Hill v Barclay (1810) 514, 941
Hill (Viscount) v Bullock (1897) . . . 22
Hill v Hill (1947) 211
Hill v Rochard (1983) . . 983, 1015, 1018
Hill v Tupper (1863) . . . 444, 535, 648, 649, 651, 654
Hillbank Properties Ltd v Hackney LBC (1978) 927, 929, 930
Hiller v United Dairies (London) Ltd (1984) 1001
Hilton v James Smith & Sons (Norwood) Ltd (1979) 915
Hinckley and Country Building Society v Henny (1953) 608
Hind, Re (1933) 361
Hindmarsh v Quinn (1914) . . 438, 441
Hine v Hine (1962) 268
Hink v Lhenen (1975) 405, 411
Hinman v Pacific Air Transport (1936); affd (1936) 29
Hipperson v Newbury District Electoral Registration Officer (1985) 185
Hirst v Chief Constable of West Yorkshire (1986) 636, 638
Hirst v Klomp (1981) 643
Hoare v Hoare (1982) . . 248, 252, 262, 360
Hobson v Gorringe (1897) 21, 24

PAGE

Hodgkinson v Crowe (1875) . . . 482, 492
Hodgson v Marks (1971) 178, 181, 185, 187, 190, 191, 227, 235, 239, 247, 260, 833, 841, 842, 856, 859
Hoffman v Fineberg (1949) . . . 498, 500
Hofman v Hofman (1965) 245, 840
Hogben v Hogben (1964) 791
Hogg, Re (1983) 248, 266, 267, 268
Hoggett v Hoggett (1980): 188, 487, 488, 782, 783, 995, 1009, 1010
Hohol v Hohol (1981) . . 246, 271, 272, 276
Holden v White (1982) 536, 657
Holdom and Lucas, Re (1983) 1026
Holiday Flat Co v Kuczera (1978) . . 985
Holiday Inns Inc v Broadhead (1974) . 290, 386, 405, 408, 409
Holland v Hodgson (1872) . . 21, 22, 23, 24
Halles v Wyse (1693) 593
Holley v Mt Zion Terrace Apartments, Inc (1980) 952
Holliday (A Bankrupt), Re (1981) . . 324, 822, 825, 876, 877, 878, 879
Hollington Bros Ltd v Rhodes (1951) . 117, 192, 530
Hollins v Verney (1884) 680
Holloway v Povey (1984) 1020
Holman v Johnson (1775) 794
Holmes v Cowcher (1970) 613
Holmes v Goring (1824) 669, 686
Holmes v Kennard & Son (1984) . . . 788
Holohan v Friends' Provident and Century Life Office (1966) 619
Holt, Renfrew & Co Ltd v Henry Singer Ltd (1982) 125, 164, 165, 169
Holyman, Re (1935) 311
Home Office v Dorset Yacht Co Ltd (1970) 912
Hood v Oglander (1865) 75
Hoofstetter v Rooker (1895) 576
Hopgood v Brown (1955) 142
Hopper v Liverpool Corpn (1943) . . 73
Hopwood v Cannock Chase DC (1975): 919
Horford Investments Ltd v Lambert (1976) 965, 972, 974, 976, 977
Horlock v Smith (1842) 608
Horn v Hiscock (1972) 673, 674
Hornsby v Maynard (1925) 973
Hornsby's Application, Re (1968) . . 718
Horrocks v Forray (1976) . . 541, 544, 799
Horsey Estate Ltd v Steiger (1899) . . 498
Horsford v Carnill (1951) 972
Hoskins v Hoskins (1981) 795, 800
Houghton v Butler (1791) 507
Hounslow LBC v Twickenham Garden Developments Ltd (1971) . . . 539, 540, 541, 542, 545, 546, 547, 548, 549
Household Fire and Carriage Accident Insurance Co v Grant (1879) 215

PAGE

How v Weldon and Edwards (754) . . 225
Howard v Fanshawe (1895) . 491, 494, 495
Howard v Miller (1915) 218
Howie v New South Wales Lawn Tennis
  Ground Ltd (1955-1956) 549
Hoyle, Re (1893) 210, 211
Howson v Buxton (1929) 981
Hoystead v Federal Comr of Taxation
  (1920) 53, 218, 369, 423
Hua Chaio Commercial Bank Ltd v
  Chiaphua Industries Ltd (1987) . . 183,
                        521, 522, 524
Hubbard v Pitt (1976). . 635, 636, 637, 638
Hubble v Lambeth LBC (1986) . . . 941
Hudson v Cripps (1896) 476, 715
Hudson View Properties v Weiss (1983): 1069,
                                  1071
Hughes v Griffin (1969) 745
Hughes v Metropolitan Rly Co (1877): 386
Hughes v Mulholland & McCann Ltd
  (1982) 748
Hughes v Overseers of Chatham (1843): 461
Hughes v Waite (1957) 891
Hull v Parsons (1962) . . . 439, 444, 535
Hulme v Brigham (1943) 21
Hulme v Langford (1985) . 488, 489, 1011
Hulse, Re (1905) 22, 24, 25
Humphery v Young (1903) 988
Humphrey and Ontario Housing Corpn,
  Re (1979) 487
Hunt v Allgood (1861) 467
Hunt v Luck (1901); affd (1902) . . 90, 91,
                        180, 837, 838
Hunt v Peake (1860) 642
Hunter v Schultz (1966) 308
Hurontario Management Services Ltd
  and Menechella Bros Ltd (1983) . . 493
Hurst v Picture Theatres Ltd (1915) . . 539,
                        541, 546, 548
Hussey v Palmer (1972) . . . 262, 277, 289,
                   290, 405, 418, 797, 816
Hutchins v Lee (1737) 238, 283
Hutchison v Milne (1980) 669
Hutton v Hamboro (1860) 662
Hyde Management Services Pty Ltd v
  FAI Insurances Ltd (1979) . . 584, 586

I

IAC (Finance) Pty Ltd v Courtenay
  (1963) 157
Ibbotson v Kushner (1978) 265
Ildebrando de Franco v Stengold Ltd
  (1985) 412
Inchbald v Robinson (1869) 914
Incorporated Village of Freeport v
  Association for the Help of Retarded
  Children (1977) 1071
Ind Coope & Co Ltd, Re (1911) . . . 608
Industrial Enterprises Inc v Schelstraete
  (1975) 624

PAGE

Industrial Properties (Barton Hill) Ltd v
  Associated Electrical Industries Ltd
  (1977) 472
Ingalls v Hobbs (1892) 903
Ingram v Ingram (1941) 252
IRC v Duke of Westminster (1936) . . 995
Inns, Re (1947) 351
International Tea Stores Co v Hobbs
  (1903) 652, 677
Inwards v Baker (1965) 391, 399,
                        400, 405, 413,
                        417, 425, 807
Inworth Property Co Ltd v Southwark
  LBC (1977) 929
Irani Finance Ltd v Singh (1971) . . . 371,
                                  383, 871
Irish Shell & BP Ltd v John Costello Ltd
  (1981) 450, 451, 1000
Irish Shell & BP Ltd v Ryan (1966) . . 588
Irvine v Helvering (1938) 300
Isaryk v Isaryk (1955) 312
Islington LB v Metcalfe and Peacock
  (1983) 1056
Israel v Leith (1890) 674
Issitt v London Borough of Tower
  Hamlets (1983) 924
Iveagh v Martin (1961) 636
Ivory v Palmer (1976) . . 398, 545, 547, 807

J

Jackson, Re (1887) 341
Jackson v Crosby (No 2) (1979) . . . 387,
                        389, 412, 418
Jackson v Horizon Holidays Ltd (1975): 545
Jackson v Jackson (1971) 824
Jacobs v Seward (1872) 304, 305,
                   306, 307, 308, 309
Jacobson, Re (1970) 350
James v Dean (1805) 431
James v James (1873) 631
James v Lock (1977) 434
James v Stevenson (1893) 687
James Case (1986) 732
James Jones & Sons Ltd v Earl of
  Tankerville (1909) 540
Jameson v London and Canadian Loan
  Agency Co (1897) 463
Jamieson's Tow & Salvage Ltd v Murray
  (1984) 507
Jarvis v Duke (1681) 76
Jarvis v Jarvis (1893) 23
Javins v First National Realty Corpn
  (1970) 905, 909, 952, 953
Jeffereys v Small (1683) 340
Jeffress v Piatt (1963) 306
Jeffries v Stevens (1982) . . . 246, 291, 974
Jelbert v Davis (1968) 661
Jemzura v Jemzura (1975) 304
Jenner v Turner (1880-81) 73, 76
Jennings v Northavon District Council
  (1981) 768

PAGE

Jennings v Sylvania Waters Pty Ltd (1972) 643
Jennings v Ward (1705) 586
Jess B Woodcock & Sons Ltd v Hobbs (1955) 785
Jessamine Investment Co Ltd v Schwartz (1978) 1004
Jeune v Queens Cross Properties Ltd (1974) 941
Johansen v Pelton (1970) . . 333, 334, 335
Johnnie Johnson Housing Trust Ltd v Sandon (1982) 1016, 1020
Johns' Assignment Trusts, Re (1970): . 241, 242
Johnson v Agnew (1980) 217
Johnson v Johnson (1986) 799
Johnson v Moreton (1980) . . . 14, 969, 991
Johnson v Nova Scotia Trust Co (1974): 211
Johnson v Ribbins (1975) . . . 620, 623
Johnson v Sheffield County Council (1982) 730
Johnson's Will Trusts, Re (1967) . . . 77
Johnston v Duke of Westminster (1986): 728
Johnston v Harris (1972) 952
Johnston v O'Neill (1911) 640
Johnstone, Re (1973) 326
Johnstone v Holdway (1963) . . . 667, 685
Jolliffe v Willmett & Co (1971) 536
Jolly v Arbuthnot (1859) 606
Jones, Re (1893) 312, 313, 314
Jones, Re (1898) 75
Jones v Bouffier (1911) 557
Jones v Challenger (1961) . . . 377, 378, 821, 822, 824
Jones v Chapman (1849) 506
Jones v Chappell (1875) 437, 914
Jones v Green (1925) 917
Jones v Jones (1875-76) 76
Jones (AE) v Jones (FW) (1977) . 308, 309, 379, 405, 424, 425, 823
Jones v Lipman (1962) 168
Jones v Llanrwst UDC (1911) 32
Jones v Lloyd (1981) 537
Jones v Mills (1861) 437
Jones v Price (1965) 657, 695
Jones v Pritchard (1908) 657
Jones v Smith (1841) 89
Jones v Whitehill (1950) 1065
Jones v Wrotham Park Settled Estates (1980) 730
Jones's Estate, Re (1914) 593
Joram Developments Ltd v Sharratt (1979) 1065, 1070
Jordan v Holkham (1753) 76
Jourdain v Wilson (1821) 523
Joyce v Barker Bros (Builders) Ltd (1980) 340
Julian v Furby (1981) 261, 795
Juson v Dixon (1813) 513

K

PAGE

K, Re (1985) 333, 334, 336
Kahnovsky v Kahnovsky (1941) . . . 307
Kanizaj v Brace (1954) 476
Karaggianis v Malltown Pty Ltd (1979): 907, 908
Karak Rubber Co Ltd v Burden (No 2) (1972) 120
Kater v Kater (1960) 430
Kavanagh v Lyroudias (1985) . 1011, 1012, 1013, 1017, 1070
Kay and Parkway Forest Developments, Re (1982) 504
Kearry v Pattinson (1939) 34
Keech v Sandford (1726) 40, 269
Keefe v Amor (1965) 662
Keefer v Arillotta (1977) . . 659, 745, 749
Keen v Holland (1984) 991
Keeves v Dean (1924) . . 1003, 1004, 1006
Keighley's Case (1610) 657
Kelley v Barrett (1924) 702
Kelley v Goodwin (1947) 1025
Kelly v Monklands District Council (1985) 767
Kelly v Park Hall School Ltd (1979) . . 212
Kelly v Purvis (1983) 500
Kelsen v Imperial Tobacco Co (of Great Britain and Ireland) Co (1957) . . . 28
Kelsey v Dodd (1881) 692
Kemp v Derrett (1814) 485
Kemp v The Public Curator of Queensland (1969) 333
Kempthorne, Re (1930) 370
Kendall v Baker (1852) 442
Kennaway v Thompson (1981) . . . 656
Kennedy v De Trafford (1897): 306, 308, 618
Kenny v Kingston upon Thames Royal LBC (1985) 927, 932
Kenny v Preen (1963) 476, 910
Kensington and Chelsea London Borough Council v Wells (1974) . . 754
Kent v Millmead Properties Ltd (1982): 1032
Kent v Regan (1964) 365, 808
Keppel v Wheeler (1927) 206
Keppell v Bailey (1834) 645, 698
Kerby v Harding (1851) 511
Kerns v Manning (1935) 433
Kerrigan, Re, ex p Jones (1947) . . . 261
Kerry County Council v O'Sullivan (1927) 633
Ketley (A) Ltd v Scott (1980) 596
Kevans v Joyce (1896) 591
Kidder v Birch (1983) 1021
Kidderminster Mutual Benefit Building Society v Haddock (1936) 629
Kiddle v Afoa and Afoa (1984) 264
Kileel and Kingswood Realty Ltd (1980): 687
Kilgour v Gaddes (1904) 680
Kimsey v Barnet LBC (1976) . . . 928, 929
King, Re (1963) 523

PAGE

King v David Allen and Sons, Billposting, Ltd (1916) 549
King v King (1951) 300
King v King (1980) 442
King v Liverpool City Council (1986): 912, 951
King v Smith (1843) 609
King's Estate, Re (1952) 334
King's Estate, Re (1978) 295, 315
King's Trusts, Re (1892) 73, 76
King's Motors (Oxford) Ltd v Lax (1970) 442
Kings North Trust Ltd v Bell (1986): . 599, 857
Kingsford v Ball (1852) 323
Kingsnorth Finance Co Ltd v Tizard (1986) 384, 601, 832, 836, 837, 842, 843, 850, 852, 853
Kingston v Preston (1773) 515
Kingswood Estate Co Ltd v Anderson (1963) 213
Kinlock v Harrigan (1968) 1064
Kinnaird v Trollope (1888) 628
Kirby v Cowderoy (1912) 747
Kiriri Cotton Co Ltd v Ranchhoddas Keshavji Dewani (1960) 1038
Kirkland v Briancourt (1890) . . 505, 511
Kitney v MEPC Ltd (1977) 155
Kleeman v Sheridan (1953) 297
Kline v 1500 Massachussetts Ave Apartment Corp (1970) 951
Kling v Keston Properties Ltd (1983) . 137, 171, 176, 179, 181, 189, 190, 192
Knight, Re, ex p Voisey (1882) . . 442, 464
Knight v Benett (1826) 467
Knight v Biss (1954) 264
Knight's Case (1588) 441
Knightly v Sun Life Assurance Society Ltd (1981) . . 363, 833, 858, 859, 860
Knightsbridge Estates Trust Ltd v Byrne (1939) 585, 588, 590
Knockholt Proprietary Ltd v Graff (1975) 942
Knox v Anderton (1982) 954
Kopec v Pyret (1983) 136, 137
Kovats v Corpn of Trinity House (1981): 1035
Krell v Henry (1903) 541, 543
Krishnan v LB of Hillingdon (1981) . . 771
Krocker v Midtown Mortgage & Loans Ltd (1975) 595
Kronheim v Johnson (1877) 236
Kumar v Dunning (1987) 521
Kushner v Law Society (1952) . . 464, 465
Kwaitkowski v Superior Trading Co (1981) 952
Kyriacou v Pandeli (1980) 958

L

LV Realty Co v Desommosy (1983) . .1069, 1071
Lace v Chantler (1944) . 433, 435, 438, 552

PAGE

Lacon v Laceby (1897) 480
Ladies' Hosiery & Underwear Ltd v Parker (1930) 465
Ladup Ltd v Williams & Glyn's Bank plc (1985) 495, 508, 612, 613, 631
Ladypool Road Old National School, Birmingham, Re (1985) 71
Lagar v Erickson (1936) 327
Laird v Nelms (1972) 29
Lake v Bayliss (1974) 219
Lake v Bennett (1970) 727
Lake v Craddock (1732) 340
Lake v Gibson (1729) 247
Lakhani and Weinstein, Re (1981): 717, 719
Lally v Kensington and Chelsea Royal Borough (1980) 774, 777
Lamanna and Lamanna, Re (1983) . . 323
Lamb v Camden London Borough Council (1981) 755
Lambert v Ealing LBC (1982) 772
Lambert v Roberts (1981) . . 536, 538, 539
Lambert (A) Flat Management Ltd v Lomas (1981) 926
Lambeth LBC v Stubbs (1980) 935
Lambeth London Borough Council v Udechuku (1981) 479, 486
Lancaster v Eve (1859) 20
Land Securities plc v Receiver for the Metropolitan Police District (1983) . 501
Landale v Menzies (1909): 430, 431, 445, 467
Landi, Re (1939) 369, 375
Lane v Cox (1897) 904
Langdon v Horton (1951) . . . 1065, 1066
Langford Property Co Ltd v Goldrich (1949) 972
Langford Property Co Ltd v Tureman (1949) 1012
Lapham v Orange City Council (1968): 449
Larking v Great Western (Nepean) Gravel Ltd (1940) 505, 506
La Salle Recreations Ltd v Canadian Camdex Investments Ltd (1969) . . 23
Lask v Cohen (1925) 1006
Last v Rosenfeld (1972) 212, 238, 274, 282, 283, 286, 575
Latec Investments Ltd v Hotel Terrigal Pty Ltd (1964-65) 422, 572
Latimer v Official Co-operative Society (1885) 642
Latter v McDonald (1985) 259
Lattimer v Lattimer (1978) 264
Laurie v Winch (1952) 646
Laurin v Iron Ore Co of Canada (1978): 583
Lavender v Betts (1942) 958
Law v Jones (1974) 207, 211
Lawrence v Jenkins (1873) 657
Lawrence v Lawrence (1959) 309
Lawrence v South County Freeholds Ltd (1939) 717
Lawrence Chemical Co Ltd v Rubinstein (1982) 513

PAGE

Lawton v Lawton (1743) 25
Lawton v SHEV Pty Ltd (1969) . . . 701
Layton v Martin (1986): 272, 274, 275, 277,
                        278, 398, 399, 404
Lazare v Slough Borough Council (1981): 767
Lazarus Estates Ltd v Beasley (1956) . 123
Leach, Re (1912) 72
Leake v Bruzzi (1974) 310, 311
Le Compte v Public Trustee (1983) . . 236,
                        272, 275, 279, 281
Lee v Lee (1952) 782, 785
Lee v Smith (1854) 467
Lee-Parker v Izzett (1971): 181, 515, 942, 943
Lee-Parker v Izzet (No 2) (1972) . . . 214
Leech v Schweder (1874) 647
Leech Leisure Ltd v Hotel and Catering
  Industry Training Board (1984) . . 986
Leeds Corpn v Jenkinson (1935) . . . 1051
Leek & Moorlands Building Society v
  Clark (1952) 437, 485, 487
Leeman v Stocks (1951) 211
Lees v Fleming (1980) 210
Leeward Securities Ltd v Lilyheath
  Properties Ltd (1983) . . 480, 1017, 1030
Legg v Coole and Sheaff (1978) . . . 1020
Legg v Strudwick (1709) 437
Legione v Hateley (1983) 216, 396
Leigh v Dickeson (1884-85): 307, 311, 312, 313
Leigh v Jack (1879) 744, 746, 748
Leigh v Taylor (1902) 22
Leigh's Settled Estates, Re (1926) . . . 351
Leighton's Conveyance, Re (1936): 195, 198
Leith Properties Ltd v Byrne (1983) . . 1021
Lemmon v Webb (1894); affd (1895) . 27, 28
Le Neve v Le Neve (1748) 123, 168
Leon Asper Amusements Ltd v North-
  main Carwash & Enterprises Ltd
  (1966) 651, 659
Lepel v Huthnance (1979): 412, 418, 425, 797
Lester v Foxcroft (1701) 213
Lester-Travers v City of Frankston
  (1970) 656
Lethbridge v Banin (1981) 1022
Lever Finance Ltd v LN & HM Needle-
  man's Trustee (1956) 627
Levet v Gas Light & Coke Co
  (1919) 654, 663
Levin (Mrs) Ltd v Wellington Co-
  operative Book Society (1947) . . . 435
Levy, Re (1982) 244, 263, 299
Lewen v Cox (1595) 338
Lewen v Dodd (1595) 338
Lewin v American & Colonial Distribu-
  tors Ltd (1945) 522
Lewis v Bell (1985) 440, 444, 449,
                        450, 451, 453
Lewis v Frank Lane Ltd (1961) . . . 583
Lewis v Latham (1955) 307, 311
Lewis v Meredith (1913) 675, 677
Lewis v Stephenson (1898) 465
Lewis v Weldcrest Ltd (1978) 982

PAGE

Lewisham BC v Roberts (1949) . . 431, 444
Lewvest Ltd v Scotia Towers Ltd
  (1982) 17, 28
Lichty v Voigt (1978) 23
Liford's Case (1614) 25
Lifshitz v Forest Square Apartments Ltd
  (1982) 1004
Liggins v Inge (1831) 687
Lincoln v Wright (1859) 238, 281
Lincoln Hunt Australia Pty Ltd v Wil-
  lesee (1986) 537
Linden v Wigg (1968) 1006
Lindop, Re (1942) 298
Lircata Properties Ltd v Jones (1967) . 493
Lister v Lane & Nesham (1893) . . . 922
Lister v Rickard (1969) 663
Littledale v Liverpool College (1900) . 748,
                                    749
Liverpool City Council v Irwin (1977) . 657,
                        907, 908, 909, 918,
                        919, 920, 922, 925,
                                  946, 954
Liverpool Corpn v H Coghill & Son Ltd
  (1918) 681
Llewellin v Llewellin (1985) 874
Lloyd v Banks (1868) 89
Lloyd v Grace, Smith & Co (1912) . . 950
Lloyd v Sadler (1978) . . . 1005, 1007, 1025
Lloyds and Scottish Trust Ltd v Britten
  (1982) 628
Lloyds Bank Ltd v Bundy (1975) . 597, 857
Lock v Abercester Ltd (1939) 662
Lock v Pearce (1893) 496
Locker v Stockport MBC (1984) . . . 185
Locket v Norman-Wright (1925) . . . 206
Loke Yew v Port Swettenham Rubber
  Co Ltd (1913) 169
Lockhart v Hardy (1846) 628
Lockwood v Wood (1844) 644
Lombard and Ulster Banking Ltd v
  Kennedy (1974) 21, 24, 25
London & Associated Investment Trust
  plc v Calow (1986) 462
London and Cheshire Insurance Co Ltd
  v Laplagrene Property Co Ltd (1971): 177,
                                  181, 219
London & County (A & D) Ltd v Wil-
  fred Sportsman Ltd (1971) 523
London and South of England Building
  Society v Stone (1983) 205
London and South Western Rly Co v
  Gomm (1881-82) 86, 88, 136, 700
London & Winchester Properties Ltd's
  Appeal, Re (1983) 730
London Corpn v Riggs (1880) 669
London County and Westminster Bank
  Ltd v Tompkins (1918) 564, 631
LCC v Agricultural Food Products Ltd
  (1955) 222
LCC v Allen (1914) 702, 703
LCC v Marks & Spencer Ltd (1953) . 655

PAGE

London Housing and Commercial Properties Ltd v Cowan (1977) 1033
London Housing Authority and Coulson, Re (1978) 504
London Permanent Benefit Building Society v De Baer (1969) 891
London Rent Assessment Committee v St George's Court Ltd (1984) . . . 1035
Lonergan v McCartney (1983) 136
Long v Clarke (1894) 512
Long v Dennis (1767) 76
Long v Gowlett (1923) 676
Long v Millar (1879) 211
Longfellow v Williams (1804) 211
Longrigg, Burrough & Trounson v Smith (1979) 429
Lonsdale (Earl) v A-G (1982) 26
Lonsdale (Earl) v Rigg (1856) 34
Lorch's Estate, Re (1941) 295
Lord Advocate v Lord Lovat (1880) . . 747
Louis and the Conveyancing Act, Re (1971) 702, 715, 716, 718
Lovell v Smith (1857) 687
Lovelock v Margo (1963) 494
Lovibond (John) & Sons Ltd v Vincent (1929) 1004
Low v Peers (1770) 76
Lowdens v Keaveney (1903) 639
Lowe v Adams (1901) 467
Lowe v Griffith (1835) 432
Lowe (Philip) (Chinese Restaurant) Ltd, v Sau Man Lee (1985) . . 280, 399, 404, 409, 419, 852
Lowrie (A Bankrupt), Re (1981): 876, 877, 879
Lows v Telford (1876) 506
Lowther v Carlton (1741) 92
Lowther v Heaver (1889) 473
Luby v Newcastle-under-Lyme Corpn (1965) 1051
Lucie-Smith v Gorman (1981) 219
Luciv v Filinov (1980) 822, 823
Luganda v Service Hotels Ltd (1969) . 456
Luke v Luke (1936) 309
Lund v AJA Taylor & Co Ltd (1974) . 719
Lund v Taylor (1975) 718, 719
Lundrigans Ltd and Prosper, Re (1982) 744, 747
Lyle v Smith (1909) 521
Lynch v Dolan (1973) 486
Lynes v Snaith (1899) 430, 446
Lyons v Caffery (1983) 990
Lyons v Lyons (1967) . . 320, 326, 327, 329
Lyons (J) & Co Ltd v Knowles (1943): 527
Lysaght v Edwards (1876) . . 218, 219, 220
Lyus v Prowsa Developments Ltd (1982) 147, 169, 271, 274, 275, 284, 616

M

M v M (1980) 265

PAGE

M W Investments Ltd v Kilburn Envoy Ltd (1947) 435
M & L Jacobs Inc v DelGrosso (1985): 1004, 1069
McAlinden v Bearsden and Milngavie District Council (1986) 763
McAuliffe v Moloney (1971) 947
McBlain v Cross (1871) 211
McCabe v McGonigle (1956) 1009
McCall v Abelesz (1976) . . . 910, 914, 919, 955, 956, 957
Macann v Annett (1948) 461
McCarrick v Liverpool Corpn (1947) . 917
McCarthy v Preston (1951) 980
McCarthy and Stone Ltd v Hodge & Co Ltd (1971) 227, 604
McCausland v Young (1948) 76
McConaghy v Denmark (1880) 747
McCorley v Chief Executive of Birmingham City Council (1984) . . . 933, 934
McCormick v Grogan (1869) 238
McCormick v McCormick (1921): 309, 313
McCoy & Co v Clark (1982) 941
McCullough v Ministry of Commerce for Northern Ireland (1961) . . 1003, 1006
McDonagh v Cromie (1982) 701
McDonagh v Kent AHA (1985) . . . 445, 451, 923, 925, 949
McDonald v Morley (1940) 327
McDonell v Giblin (1904) 747
MacEachern and MacIsaac, Re (1978): 748, 749
McFarlane v McFarlane (1972) . . . 255, 257, 258, 259, 267, 268, 273, 275
McGhee v LB of Hackney (1969) . . . 1035
McGill v S (1979) 257, 258, 278, 390, 415, 544, 794
McGillicuddy v Joy (1959) 239
McGowan v Harrison (1941) 911
McGrath v Hilding (1977) 815
McGreal v Wake (1984) 920, 941
McGugan and McNeill v Turner (1948): 746
McGuigan Investments Pty Ltd v Dalwood Vineyards Pty Ltd (1970) . 702
McHale v Daneham (1979) 984
Machu, Re (1882) 75
McHugh v London Borough of Islington (1984) 445, 999
McHugh v Union Bank of Canada (1913) 619
McIlwraith v Grady (1968) 660
McIntyre v Hardcastle (1948) 1021
McIntyre v Porter (1983) 687
McIvor v Donald (1984) 503
Mack and the Conveyancing Act, Re (1975) 702, 716, 717, 718
Mackay v Abrahams (1916) 536
McKee v Kratz (1922) 641
McKee and National Trust Co Ltd, Re (1975) 323, 328

PAGE

McKellar v Guthrie (1920) 662
McKeown v McKeown (1975) . . 258, 280
McKillop v McMullan (1979) 214
McKinty v Belfast Corpn (1973) . . .1003,
1004, 1006
Mackowik v Kansas City (1906) . . . 261
Maclay v Dixon (1944) 1000
Maclean v Currie (1884) 904
MacLeay, Re (1875) 75
McLorie v Oxford (1982) 537
M'Mahon v Burchell (1846) 308
McMahon v Kerry County Council
(1981) 408
McMahon v McMahon (1979): 269, 272, 273
McMahon v The Public Curator of
Queensland (1952) 313
McManus v Cooke (1887) . . . 213, 665
McMillan v Singh (1985) 958, 959
McMinn v Town of Oyster Bay (1985): 1072
McNab v Earle (1981) 320, 323
McPhail v Persons (Names Unknown)
(1973) 606, 754, 756, 757, 758
McPhee v McPhee (1980) 278
McQuaid v Lynam (1965) 433
McQuaker v Goddard (1940) 34
McTaggart v Boffo (1976) 245
Maddison v Alderson (1883) 212
Maddocks, Ex p, Re Brown (1968) . . 486
Maddox v Maddox's Administrator
(1854) 76
Mafo v Adams (1970) 558, 1003
Maguire v Browne (1913) 743
Mahony v Danis (1983) 407
Main v Main (1939) 264
Main Roads Comr v North Shore Gas
Co Ltd (1967) 644, 645
Maiorana and the Conveyancing Act, Re
(1970) 646
Makins v Elson (1977) 972
Malayan Credit Ltd v Jack Chia-MPH
Ltd (1986) 260, 302, 340, 341
Malden Farms Ltd v Nicholson (1956) . 662
Malloy and Lunt v Alexander (1982) . 958
Malone v Laskey (1907) 444, 535
Malsbury v Malsbury (1982) . . . 269, 273,
274, 275, 290
Malzy v Eichholz (1916) 476, 477
Manaton v Edwards (1985) 1022
Mancetter Developments Ltd v Gar-
manson Ltd (1986) 24
Manchester Brewery Co v Coombs
(1901) 472, 473, 530, 533
Mander v Falcke (1891) 529
Mangaroo v Mangaroo (1981) . 1021, 1022
Mangus v Miller (1975) 320
Manitoba Development Corp v Berkovits
(1980) 628
Manly Properties Pty Ltd v Castrisos
(1973) 686
Mann v Bradley (1975) 326
Mann v Cornella (1980) . . . 971, 987

PAGE

Mann v Stephens (1846) 698
Manning's (Matthew) Case (1609) . . 74
Manson v Duke of Westminster (1981): 728,
731
Manton v Parabolic Pty Ltd (1985) . . 64,
222, 223
Marchant v Capital & Counties Prop-
erty Co Ltd (1982) 655
Marchant v Charters (1977) . . . 450, 451,
454, 456
Marcroft Wagons Ltd v Smith (1951) . 411,
445, 458, 1003, 1004,
1007
Marina Point Ltd v Wolfson (1982) . . 483
Marjorie Burnett Ltd v Barclay (1981): 436
Markham v Paget (1908) 476
Markou v Da Silvaesa (1986): 440, 441, 444,
451, 452, 453, 455, 456,
459, 758, 990, 995, 997
Marks v Attallah (1966) 177
Marlborough (Duke), Re (1894) . . . 283
Marlborough (Duke) v Osborn (1864) . 443
Marples of Wallasey v Holmes (1976) . 893
Marriott v Anchor Reversionary Co
(1861) 610
Marsden v Campbell (1897) 167
Marsden v Edward Heyes Ltd (1927) . 481
Marshall v Berridge (1881) 433
Marshall v Cottingham (1982) 627
Marshall v Ulleswater Steam Navigation
Co (1871) 641
Marshall (Charles) Pty Ltd v Grimsley
(1956) 263
Marten v Flight Refuelling Ltd (1962) . 710
Martin v Davies (1952) 1001
Martin v Martin (1959) . . . 263, 264, 266
Martin v Smith (1874) 467, 468
Martins Camera Corner Pty Ltd v Hotel
Mayfair Ltd (1976) . . . 910, 911, 915
Martinson v Clowes (1882) . . . 624, 625
Masidon Investments Ltd v Ham (1983): 744,
748, 749
Mason v Clarke (1955) 438, 665
Mason v Hill (1833) 32
Mason v Skilling (1974) 1034
Massart v Blight (1951) 463
Mastad v Swedish Brethren (1901) . . 952
Mastbaum v Mastbaum (1939) 307
Mastercraft Construction Co Ltd and
Baldwin, Re (1978) 1019
Masters v Snell (1979) 686
Mastin v Mastin's Administrator (1932): 313
Mastron v Cotton (1926) 309
Matchams Park (Holdings) Ltd v Dom-
mett (1984) 448
Matthew v Bobbins (1981) . .594, 993, 1021
Matthews v Ahmed (1985) 1020
Matthews v Bucknell (1984) 1017
Matthews v Dobbins (1963) 494
Matthews v Goodday (1861) . . . 577, 631
Matthews v Smallwood (1910) 491

PAGE

Matthie v Edwards (1846) 619
Matures v Westwood (1598) 522
Maude v Thornton (1929) 686
Maughan, Re, ex p Monkhouse (1885): 473
Maurice (Leslie) & Co Ltd v Willesden
  Corpn (1953) 929
Maurice Toltz Pty Ltd v Macy's Em-
  porium Pty Ltd (1969) 667
Mavromatis v Mavromatis (1968) . 487, 488
Maxwell v Brown (1982) 454, 456
May v Belleville (1905) 665
Mayes v Mayes (1969) . 241, 242, 252, 312,
     313, 377, 802, 824, 826
Mayfield Holdings Ltd v Moana Reef
  Ltd (1973) . . . 538, 540, 541, 542, 547,
     548
Mayho v Buckhurst (1617) 522
Mayo, Re (1943) 353, 376
Mayo v Mayo (1966) 309
Maysels v Maysels (1974); affd (1976) . 266
Meade's Estate, Re (1964) 298
Meah v LB of Tower Hamlets (1986) . 941
Mee, Re (1971) 323
Meehan v Jones (1982) 214
Meier v Lucas (1986) 973
Meinhard v Salmon (1928) 269
Mellowes v Collymore (1981) . . 248, 253,
     287, 362
Melville v Grapelodge Developments Ltd
  (1979) 942
Memvale Securities Ltd's Application,
  Re (1975) 522, 714
Mens v Wilson (1973) 135
Mercer v Denne (1905) 643, 644
Mercian Housing Society Ltd's Appli-
  cation (1972) 720
Meretune Investments v Martin (1984): 486
Mesher v Mesher (1980) 875
Metcalf v Campion (1828) 610
Metrobarn Ltd v Gehring (1976) . . . 1032
Metropolitan Properties Co (FGC) Ltd
  v Barder (1968) 979
Metropolitan Properties Co Ltd v Cord-
  ery (1980) 504
Metropolitan Properties Co Ltd v Cro-
  nan (1982) 782, 1011, 1014
Metropolitan Property Holdings Ltd v
  Finegold (1975) 1036
Metropolitan Rly Co v Fowler (1893) . 18
Michael v Phillips (1924) 985
Michel v Volpe (1967) 441, 973
Micklethwait v Newlay Bridge Co
  (1886) 32
Micklethwait v Vincent (1892) 641
Midanbury Properties (Southampton)
  Ltd v Houghton (1981) 1035
Middlegate Properties Ltd v Gidlow-
  Jackson (1977) 501
Middleton v Baldock (1950) . . . 488, 993
Midland Bank Ltd v Farmpride Hatch-
  eries Ltd (1981) . . . 401, 554, 837, 859

PAGE

Midland Bank Ltd v Goodall (1983) . 857
Midland Bank plc v Dobson (1986) . . 237,
     238, 275, 280, 858
Midland Bank plc v Perry (1987) . . . 599
Midland Bank Plc v Phillips (1986) . . 598
Midland Bank Plc v Pike (1986) . 870, 871
Midland Bank Trust Co Ltd v Green
  (1980); on appeal (1981) . 86, 87, 120, 122,
     123, 124, 125, 136, 163,
     164, 168, 170, 227, 474
Midland Bank Trust Co Ltd v Green
  (No 3) (1982) 125
Midland Bank Trust Co Ltd v Hett,
  Stubbs and Kemp (1979) 125
Midland Rly Co's Agreement, Re
  (1971) 437, 485
Miles v Bull (No 2) (1969) 162
Miles v Easter (1933) . . 702, 707, 709, 714
Millennium Productions Ltd v Winter
  Garden Theatre (London) Ltd (1946): 546
Miller v Emcer Products Ltd (1956) . 659
Miller v Jackson (1977) 656
Miller v Miller (1983) 266
Miller v Prater (1937) 311
Miller v State (1984) 952
Miller and Zuchek, Re (1982) 504
Millett v Regent (1975) 213, 548
Millichamp v Jones (1982) 216
Millington v Duffy (1984) . . 957, 958, 959
Mills v Brooker (1919) 26, 28
Mills and Andrews, Re (1983) 322
Milmo v Carreras (1946) 463, 464
Milroy v Lord (1862) 388
Minay v Setongo (1983) . . 1023, 1024, 1027
Minchburn Ltd v Fernandez (1986) . . . 1018
Mines Case (1568) 26
Minishall v Donovan (1980) . . 1009, 1014
Minister v New South Wales Aerated
  Water and Confectionery Co Ltd
  (1916) 465
Minister of Health v Bellotti (1944) . . 539
Minister of State for the Army v Dalziel
  (1943-44) 59, 61, 63, 64, 549
Ministry of Housing and Local Govern-
  ment v Sharp (1970) 127
Minouk State Bank v Grassman (1982): 317
Mint v Good (1951) 914
Miscamble's Application, Re (1966) . . 709
Mitchell v Mosley (1914) 16, 18, 26
Mitchell v Rands (1982) 669
Mitchell v Wieriks, ex p Wieriks (1975): 437
Moate v Moate (1948) 265
Mobil Oil Co Ltd v Rawlinson (1982): 605,
     609, 610, 612, 890
Moham v Manning (1981) 1022
Moltan Builders Ltd v City of West-
  minster LBC (1975) 477
Monashee Enterprises Ltd and Minister
  of Recreation and Conservation for
  British Columbia (1979) 33
Monk v Cooper (1727) 902

PAGE

Monolithic Building Co, Re (1915): 124, 168
Montague v Browning (1954) 973
Montague v Long (1972) . . . 21, 142, 143
Montreuil v Ontario Asphalt Co (1922): 418
Moody v Cox & Hatt (1917) 266
Moody v Steggles (1879):18, 20, 651, 656, 679
Moorcock, The (1889) . . . . · 543
Moore, Re (1888) 72
Moore v Dimond (1929) 467
Moore v Greg (1848) 531
Moore v Hall (1878) 664
Moore v Hart (1682) 211
Moore v MacMillan (1977) . . . 444, 535
Moore v Moore (1971) 164, 168
Moore v Rawson (1824) 687, 688
Moores v Choat (1839) 531
Moran v Duffy (1982) 959
Morgan v Jeffreys (1910) 585
Morgan v Liverpool Corpn (1927) . . 917
Morgan v Marquis (1853) 324
Morgan v Murch (1970) 1064
Morgan's Case (Eliz 1) 337
Morgan's Lease, Re (1972) . . . 603, 806
Morland v Cook (1868) 700
Morley v Bird (1798) 341
Morley v Pincombe (1848) 512
Morley v Rennoldson (1843) . . . 74, 76
Morris v Beardmore (1981) 535
Morris v Duke-Cohan & Co (1975) . . 216
Morris v Edgington (1810) 652
Morris v Morris (1982) 418, 420
Morris v Pinches (1969) 745
Morrison v Coast Finance Ltd (1966) . 597
Morrison, Jones & Taylor Ltd, Re
(1914) 25
Moses v Lovegrove (1952) 748
Moses v Macferlan (1760) 812
Mosley v Hickman (1986) 731
Moss v Gallimore (1779) . . . 608, 609
Moss v McLachlan (1985) 638
Mottee, Re (1977) 879
Moule v Garrett (1872) 519
Mounsey v Ismay (1865) 652
Mount Cook National Park Board v
Mount Cook Hotels Ltd (1972) . . . 477
Mountford v Scott (1975) 226
Mowat v Federated Farmers of New Zea-
land (Waikato Provincial District) Inc
(1980) 669
Moy's Estate, Re (1963) 299
Moyse v Gyles (1700) 324, 325
Muckleston v Brown (1801) 266
Mulcahy v Curramore Pty Ltd (1974) . 742,
745, 747, 748, 751,
753
Mulhall v Haren (1981) . . . 206, 207, 208,
210, 211, 212
Muljee v Rezaul Haque (1985) . . . 958
Muller v Trafford (1901) 524
Mulley v Mulley (1983) 360
Mulliner v Midland Rly Co (1879) . . 653

PAGE

Mullins v Pine Manor College (1983) . 952
Multiservice Bookbinding Ltd v Marden
(1979) 590, 591, 593, 840
Municipality of Metropolitan Toronto v
Atkinson (1977) 485
Munroe v Carlson (1976) 325, 330
Munton v GLC (1976) 207
Murdoch and Barry, Re (1976) . . 317, 320,
321, 323, 325
Murdock v Aherne (1878) 265
Murless v Franklin (1818) 263
Murnane v Findlay (1926) 749
Murphy v Ford (1855) 430
Murphy v Murphy (1980) . . . 745, 746, 747
Murray v Devonport BC (1980) . . . 669
Murray v Hall (1849) 296
Muschamp v Bluet (1617) 75
Murray v Roty (1983) 815
Muschinski v Dodds (1985) . . . 233, 235,
243, 244, 248, 251, 261,
265, 268, 269, 273, 281
Muskett v Hill (1839) 539, 540
Mykolyshyn v Noah (1970) 1018

N

NLS Pty Ltd v Hughes (1966) 183
Nagy v Weston (1965) 636, 637
Nahhas v Pier House (Cheyne Walk)
Management Ltd (1984) 950
Naish v Curzon (1986) 1026
Najia Naim v Bemrose (1986) 1026
Nanda v Nanda (1968) 781
Napier v Light (1975) 354
Napier v Public Trustee (Western
Australia) (1980) . 247, 261, 263, 265, 274
Nash v Lucas (1867) 512
Nasti v Verderosa (1973) 304
National Carriers Ltd v Panalpina
(Northern) Ltd (1981) . . . 6, 17, 427,
434, 444, 489, 543
National City Bank of Evansville v
Bledsoe (1957) 335
National Guaranteed Manure Co Ltd v
Donald (1859) 654
National Provincial Bank Ltd v Ains-
worth (1965) . . 50, 84, 96, 180, 181, 182,
259, 422, 551, 557, 559,
567, 781, 786, 789, 840
National Provincial Bank Ltd v Hastings
Car Mart Ltd (1964) . . . 180, 181, 182,
426, 546, 551, 552, 553,
555, 557, 786, 798, 851
National Trust v Midlands Electricity
Board (1952) 703
National Trust v White (1987) . . 660, 662
National Westminster Bank Ltd v
Stockman 871
National Westminster Bank Plc v Jones
(1984) 612
National Westminster Bank Plc v Mor-
gan (1985) . . . 597, 598, 599, 600, 857

PAGE

National Westminster Group Plc, Re (1985) 151
Nationwide Building Society v Registry of Friendly Societies (1983) . . 591, 593
Neal v Neal (1971) 307
Neale v Willis (1968) 240, 276
Neesom v Clarkson (1842) 424
Neiman v Hurff (1952) 335
Nelson v Larholt (1948) 120
Nelson v Walker (1910) 672, 673
Nelthorpe v Holgate (1844) 839
Nemeth v Nemeth (1977-78) . 258, 271, 287
Neo Tai Kim v Foo Stie Wah (1982) . 267
Ness v O'Neill (1916) 628
Never-Stop Rly (Wembley) Ltd v British Empire Exhibition (1924) Inc (1926): 24
Nevill v Halliday (1983) 537
Neville v Cooper (1834) 507
New Eberhardt Co, Re (1889) 210
New Windsor Corpn v Mellor (1975) . 643
New Zealand Government Property Corpn v HM & S Ltd (1982) . . 20, 24
New Zealand Loan and Mercantile Agency Co Ltd v Wellington Corpn (1890) 683
Newbolt v Bingham (1895) 495
Newby v Alto Riviera Apartments (1976) 959
Newham v Lawson (1971) 663, 667
Newham v Patel (1978) 923
Newman v Jones (1982) 659
Newman v Powter (1978) 397
Newman v Real Estate Debenture Corpn Ltd and Flower Decorations Ltd (1940) 716
News Group Newspapers Ltd v SOGAT '82 (1986) 635, 638, 639, 640
Newton Abbot Co-operative Society Ltd v Williamson & Treadgold Ltd (1952) 700, 703, 714
Newton-King v Wilkinson (1976) . . . 211
Nicholls v Ely Beet Sugar Factory Ltd (1936) 35
Nichols v RA Gill Ltd (1975) 430
Nicholson, Re (1974) 809, 851
Nickerson v Barraclough (1980); revsd (1981) 660, 669, 670, 671
Niederberger v Memnook (1982) . 257, 794
Nielson-Jones v Fedden (1975) . 296, 317, 318, 320, 325, 326, 328, 329, 331
Nisbet and Potts' Contract, Re (1906) 85, 86, 88, 91, 700, 705, 752
Nishi Industries Ltd, Re (1979) 136
Nives v Nives (1880) 219
Noack v Noack (1959) . . . 247, 264, 312, 313, 314
Noakes & Co Ltd v Rice (1902) . 586, 587
Noble v South Herefordshire District Council (1983) 766

PAGE

Nock v Munk (1982) 1039
Nocton v Ashburton (1914) 281
Nordstrom, Re (1962) 332
Norfolk v Trinity College Cambridge (1976) 731
Norfolk (Duke) v Arbuthnot (1880) . . 683
Norfolk Capital Group Ltd v Kitway Ltd (1977) 480
North Gower Township Public School Board and Todd, Re (1968) 73
North Shore Gas Co Ltd v Comr of Stamp Duties (NSW) (1939-40) . . . 21, 23, 24
North Sydney Printing Pty Ltd v Sabemo Investment Corpn Pty Ltd (1971) . . 670
Northbourne (Lord) v Johnston & Son (1922) 704
Northern Bank Ltd v Beattie (1982) . . 258, 834, 837, 842, 862
Northern Bank Ltd v Henry (1981) . . 86, 89, 90, 267, 832, 838, 839, 842
Northern Ireland Carriers Ltd v Larne Harbour Ltd (1981) 433, 528
Northern Ireland Housing Executive v Duffin (1985) 505
Northern Ireland Housing Executive v Fox (1981) 754
Northern Ireland Housing Executive v McAuley (1974) 758
Northern Ireland Housing Executive v McCann (1979) 442
Northern Ireland Housing Executive v McGinn 505
Northern Press & Engineering Co v Shepherd (1908) 21
Norton, Re (1929) 351
Norton v Kilduff (1974) 700
Norton v Knowles (1969) 955
Norton v Williams (1939) 681
Norwich General Trust v Grierson (1984) 621
Nottingham Patent Brick and Tile Co v Butler (1885); affd (1886) . . . 92, 705, 717, 718, 719
Nova Mink Ltd v Trans-Canada Airlines (1951) 29
Noyes v Pollock (1886) 610
Nunn v Parkes & Co (1924) . . . 444, 535
Nuti v Nuti (1980) 814

O

Oak Co-operative Building Society v Blackburn (1968) 127, 129
Oak Property Co Ltd v Chapman (1947) 505
Oakley v Boston (1976) 683
Oastler v Henderson (1877) . . . 487, 511
Oates v Oates (1949) 305
O'Brien v Bean and Bean (1957) . . . 264
O'Brien v Robinson (1973) . . . 916, 920
O'Connell v Harrison (1927) 247

PAGE

O'Connor v JG Mooney & Co Ltd (1982) 507
Official Assignee v Lawford (1984): 882, 883
Official Assignee of Pannell v Pannell (1966) 882
Official Custodian for Charities v Mackey (1985) 507, 508
Official Custodian for Charities v Mackey (No 2) (1985) 517
Official Custodian of Charities v Parway Estates Developments Ltd (1984) . . 504
Ogilvie v Ryan (1976) . . 271, 276, 281, 286
O'Hara v Allied Irish Banks Ltd (1985): 600
O'Hara v Western Seven Trees Corpn Intercoast Management (1977): . . 952
O'Keeffe v Irish Motor Inns Ltd (1978): 535
O'Leary v LB of Islington (1983) . 909, 915, 951, 1020
Old & Campbell Ltd v Liverpool Victoria Friendly Society (1982) . . . 115
Old Gate Estates Ltd v Alexander (1950) 488
Old Grovebury Manor Farm Ltd v W Seymour Plant Sales and Hire Ltd (No 2) (1979) 463, 493
Oldham v Lawson (No 1) (1976) . 444, 535
O'Leary v LB of Islington (1983) . 913, 1020
Oliver v Hinton (1899) 87
Oliver v Menton (1945) 76
Oliver v United States (1984) 30
Olsson v Dyson (1968-69) 421
O'Malley v Seymour (1978) . . . 451, 994, 996, 999
Omsac Developments Ltd v Colebourne (1980) 433
O'Neill, Re (1967) 613
O'Neill v Mehain (1985) 815
Oney's Estate, Re (1982) 296
Onslow v Corrie (1817) 527
Orakpo v Manson Investments Ltd (1977) 196, 813
Orby v Trigg (1722) 583
Organ v Sandwell (1921): 238, 239, 266, 283
Orme, Re (1883) 264
O'Rourke v Hoeven (1974) 213
Osborne v Bradley (1903) 708
Osterloh's Estate v Carpenter (1960) . 295
Otto v Bolton and Norris (1936) . . 911
Ough v King (1967) 656
Oughtred v IRC (1960) 291
Owendale Pty Ltd v Anthony (1966-67): 491, 504, 505
Oxley v James (1844) 437

P

P & N Investment Corpn v Florida Ranchettes Inc (1968) 308
P T Stevens Earthmoving Pty Ltd's Caveat, Re (1975) 551
Pacific Cassiar Ltd and Esso Canada Resources Ltd (1986) 165

PAGE

Pacific Savings & Mortgage Corp and Can-Corp Development Ltd (1982) . 629
Paddington Building Society v Mendelsohn (1985) 176,184, 859, 860
Page v Barclays Bank Ltd (1980) . . . 622
Page Motors Ltd v Epsom and Ewell BC (1982) 914
Paget v Paget (1898) 884
Paine v Meller (1801) 218
Paine & Co Ltd v St Neots Gas & Coke Co (1939) 653, 658
Painter, Ex p (1895) 879
Pakwood Transport Ltd v 15 Beauchamp Place (1978) 503
Palachik v Kiss (1983) 815
Palfrey v Palfrey (1974) . 221, 488, 742, 745, 746, 993
Pallant v Morgan (1953) 239
Palmer v Barclays Bank Ltd (1972): 618, 621
Palmer v Hendrie (1859) 628
Palmer v Palmer (1942) 322
Palmer v Protrka (1970) 309
Palmer v Rich (1897) 327
Palser v Grinling (1946) . .37, 985, 986, 987
Paluszek v Wohlrab (1953) . . . 295, 296
Pamplin v Fraser (1981) 536
Pampris v Thanos (1968) 904
Papadopoulos v Goodwin (1982) . . . 667
Paradine v Jane (1647) 902
Paradise Motor Co Ltd, Re (1968) . . 263
Parceluk v Knudtson (1966) 308
Park v Brady (1976): 578, 612
Park South Associates v Daniels (1983): 1069
Parkash v Irani Finance Ltd (1970) . . 162, 163
Parker v British Airways Board (1982): 35, 36
Parker v Camden LBC (1986) . . 942, 945
Parker v McKenna (1874) . . . 219, 269
Parker v Taswell (1858) . . . 468, 470, 471
Parker v Trigg (1884) 313
Parker v Webb (1693) 522
Parker's Settled Estates, Re (1928) . . 351
Parkus v Greenwood (1950) 436
Parr v Wyre BC (1982) 775, 776
Parsons v Parsons (1983) 485
Partriche v Powlet (1740) 321, 325
Pascoe v Swan (1859) 313
Pascoe v Turner (1979) 389, 399, 405, 416, 421, 425, 818
Patel v Ali (1984) 217
Patel v Mehtab (1980) 934
Patel (Mahendrakumar) v Patel (Bharat) (1981) 1021
Patel v Patel (1983) . 540, 542, 547, 549, 554
Patel v W H Smith (Eziot) Ltd (1987) . 755
Paten v Cribb (1862) 324
Paterson v Paterson (1980) 327
Paterson Zochonis Ltd v Merfarken Packaging Ltd (1983) 912
Patman v Harland (1881) 114
Paul v Nurse (1828) 527

PAGE

Paul v Summerhayes (1878) 34
Payne v Adnams (1971) 173
Payne v Callahan (1940) 308
Payne v Cardiff RDC (1932) 614
Payne v Haine (1847) 923
Pazgate Ltd v McGrath (1984) 1015,
1016, 1021
Peabody Donation Fund (Governors) v
Grant (1982) 1059, 1060, 1064
Peabody Donation Fund (Governors) v
Higgins (1983) 463, 1052
Peach v Peach (1981) 348, 804
Peakin v Peakin (1895) 439, 460
Pearce v Pearce (1977) . . . 417, 420, 551
Pearch v Gycha (1953) 441
Pearlman v Keepers and Governors of
Harrow School (1979) 727
Pearson v Adams (1912) 75
Pearson v IRC (1981) 77
Pearson v Pearson (1961) . . 254, 263, 267,
268, 273
Pearson v Spencer (1861) 668
Peat v Chapman (1750) 338
Pechar, Re (1969) 333, 334
Peckham Mutual Building Society v
Registe (1981) . . . 607, 608, 893, 896
Peffer v Rigg (1977) . . . 147, 167, 170,
195, 199, 229, 271, 292
Pembery v Lamdin (1940) 922
Pendlebury v Colonial Mutual Life
Assurance Society Ltd (1912) . . 618,
619, 622, 623
Peninsular Maritime Ltd v Padseal Ltd
(1981) 942
Penn v Dunn (1970) 1023
Penn v Wilkins (1974) 675
Penn Central Transport Co v City of New
York (1978) 27
Pennell v Nunn (1982) 401
Pennine Raceway Ltd v Kirklees Metro-
politan BC (1983) . . . 405, 422, 554
People v Cook (1985) 30
People v Lashmett (1979) 30
People v St Amour (1980) 30
People v Sneed (1973) 30
People v Superior Court (1974) . . . 30
Pepita and Donkas, Re (1979) 965
Perera v Vandiyar (1953) 958
Perez-Adamson v Perez-Rivas (1987) . 111
Perl (P) (Exporters) Ltd v Camden LBC
(1984) 912
Perpetual Executors and Trustees Associ-
ation of Australia Ltd v Hosken
(1912) 148
Perri v Coolangatta Investments Pty Ltd
(1982) 214
Perrin v Lyon (1807) 76
Perry v Clissold (1907) 753
Perry v Davis (1858) 505
Perry v Sharon Development Co Ltd
(1937) 903

PAGE

Perry v Sidney Phillips & Son (1982) . 205
Perry v Woodfarm Homes Ltd (1975) . 742,
743, 751, 752
Persey v Bazley (1984) 363
Pertsoulis and Pertsoulis' Marriage, Re
(1980) 325, 326
Peterson v San Francisco Community
College District (1984) 952
Peterson's Estate, Re (1935) 297
Petrol Filling Station, Vauxhall Bridge
Road, London, Re (1969) . . . 586, 587
Pettey v Parsons (1914) 662, 663
Pettitt v Pettitt (1970) . . . 10, 233, 234,
235, 241, 242, 245, 246,
247, 249, 259, 260, 261,
263, 265, 267, 268, 272,
273, 278, 360, 397, 563,
725, 793, 794, 798, 808,
809, 812, 817
Pettiward Estates v Shepherd (1986) . 523
Pettkus v Becker (1981) . . . 245, 419, 814
Peyton v London Corpn (1829) . . . 642
Phillips v Barnett (1922) 1004
Phillips v Lamdin (1949) 24
Phillips v LB of Newham (1982) . . . 929
Phillips v Phillips (1861) 426
Phillips v Silvester (1872) 219
Phipps v Pears (1965) 655
Pickering v Rudd (1815) 28, 29
Pico v Columbet 308
Pieper v Edwards (1982) 686
Pilcher v Rawlins (1872) 48, 87, 92
Pinemain Ltd v Welbeck International
Ltd (1984) 521
Pines v Perssion (1961) 905
Pinewood Estate, Farnborough, Re
(1958) 713
Pink v Lawrence (1978) 241, 242
Pinnington v Galland (1853) 668
Piquet v Tyler (1978) 548
Pirie v Registrar-General (1963) . . 702, 707
Piromalli v Di Masi (1980) 681
Pitcher v Lockett (1966) 637
Pitcher v Tovey (1692) 443
Pitman v Nickerson (1891) 659
Pittortou (A Bankrupt), Re (1985): 883, 884
Platt v Ong (1972) 493, 503
Plaza Equities Ltd v Bank of Nova Scotia
(1978) 21
Plimmer v Mayor of Wellington (1884): 391,
393, 399, 413, 422
Pocock v Steel (1985) 1025
Poland v Earl Cadogan (1980) . . 728, 729
Polkinghorn v Wright (1845) 507
Pollicchio v Phoenix Assurance Co of
Canada (1978) 481
Pollock v Kumar (1977) 1015
Pollway Nominees Ltd v Croydon LBC
(1986) 927, 930
Port v Griffith (1938) 477

PAGE

Port Franks Properties Ltd v The Queen
(1980) 32
Posner v Scott-Lewis (1986) 475
Poster v Slough Estates Ltd (1968):   25, 141,
143, 426
Potter, Re (1970) 804
Potter v Duffield (1874) 210
Pountney v Clayton (1883) 17
Powell v Cleland (1948) 88, 1005
Powell v Ely (1980) 224
Powell v Linney (1983) 663
Powell v McFarlane (1977) . . . 744, 745,
747, 748, 749, 750
Power, Re (1947) 353
Power v Brighton (1984) . . . 250, 820
Power v Grace (1932) 317
Powers v Fowler (1855) 210
Pozzi, Re (1982) 327, 328
Practice Direction (Service of Notice to
Quit) (1965) 485
Practice Direction [1983] 1 WLR 4 . . 757
Practice Direction [1983] 1 WLR 150 . 150
Prah v Maretti (1982) 663
Pratt v McLeod (1982) 815
Precious v Reed (1924) 485
Predeth v Castle Phillips Finance Co Ltd
(1986) 621, 622
Premier Finance Co v Gravesande
(1985) 596
Preston v Greene (1909) 264
Preston Borough Council v Fairclough
(1982) 488
Price v Gould (1930) 1065
Price v Hilditch (1930) 664
Prior's Case (1368) 691, 693, 694
Pritchard v Briggs (1980) 137
Proctor v Kidman (1985) 153
Propert v Parker (1832) 477
Property & Bloodstock Ltd v Emerton
(1968) 617
Property & Reversionary Investment
Corpn Ltd v Secretary of State for the
Environment (1975) 147
Property Holding Co Ltd v Clark
(1948) 1000
Prosser (A) & Sons Ltd v Levy (1955) . 911
Proudfoot v Hart (1890) 923
Prudential Assurance Co Ltd v Newman
Industries Ltd (No 2) (1981) 421
Pryce v McGuinness (1966) 669
Public Trustee v Evans (1985) . . 332, 334
Public Trustee v Grivas (1974) . . 326, 327,
328, 336
Public Trustee v Hermann (1968) . . 642
Public Trustee of Manitoba and Le Clerc,
Re (1982) 334
Pugh v Pidgen (1987) 636
Pugh v Savage (1970) 650, 680, 681
Pulleng v Curran (1982) . . 480, 974, 982
Pupkowski, Re (1957) 333

PAGE

Purchase v Lichfield Brewery Co
(1915) 531, 533
Pure Oil Co v Byrnes (1944) 306
Purton's Estate and Guardianship, Re
(1968) 307
Putnam v Colvin (1984) 637
Putnam Organisation Ltd v Macdonald
(1979) 643
Pwllbach Colliery Co v Woodman
(1915) 671, 686
Pyer v Carter (1857) 674

Q

Quadramain Pty Ltd v Sevastapol In-
vestments Pty Ltd (1975-76) 588
Queen (The) v Smith (1981) . 397, 400, 418
Queen (The) v Tener (1985) . . . 633, 687
Queen (The) and Peters, Re (1983) . . 317
Queen (The) in Right of Manitoba and
Air Canada, Re (1978) 17, 27
Queen's Club Gardens Estates Ltd v
Bignell (1924) 437, 485, 486
Quennell v Maltby (1979) 611
Quick v Taff Ely BC (1986) . . 918, 921,
922, 923
Quilter v Mapleson (1882) 503

R

R v Abrol (1972) 956
R v Ahmad (1986) 956
R v Barnet London Borough Council,
ex p Nilish Shah (1983) 185
R v Bath County Council, ex p Sanger-
mano (1984) 767
R v Battersea, etc, Rent Tribunal, ex p
Parikh (1957) 985
R v Blankley (1979) 955
R v Bloomsbury and Marylebone County
Court, ex p Blackburne (1985) . 993, 1003
R v Bokhari (1974) 955
R v Brennan and Brennan (1979) . . . 955
R v Brentford Justices, ex p Catlin
(1975) 222
R v Bristol CC, ex p Browne (1979) . . 776
R v Camberwell Green Magistrates, ex
p Healey (1984) 934
R v Camden LBC, ex p Wait (1987) . . 775,
777
R v Camden LB Rent Officer, ex p Ebiri
(1981) 1032
R v Canterbury CC, ex p Gillespie
(1986) 1050
R v Cardiff City Council, ex p Cross
(1983) 916, 918, 919, 923, 930
R v Chief Rent Officer for Royal Borough
of Kensington and Chelsea, ex p
Moberley (1986) 1033
R v Clark (No 2) (1964) 639
R v Croydon London Borough Council,
ex p Toth (1986) 762
R v Dowsey (1903) 23

PAGE

R v Ealing London Borough Council,
ex p McBain (1985)   .   762, 770, 772, 776
R v Ealing London Borough Council,
ex p Sidhu (1982) 763, 766
R v East Hertfordshire District Council,
ex p Bannon (1986)   770
R v East Hertfordshire DC, ex p Hunt
(1985)   775
R v Eastleigh Borough Council, ex p
Beattie (1983) 768, 771, 937
R v Eastleigh Borough Council, ex p
Beattie (1984)   770
R v Eastleigh Borough Council, ex p
Evans (1984) 763, 769
R v Evangelos Polycarpou (1978)   .   .   .   956
R v Exeter CC, ex p Gliddon (1985)   .   .   772
R v Fox (1985) 535, 539
R v Hackney LBC, ex p Thrasyvoulou
(1986)   938
R v Hillingdon Homeless Persons Panel,
ex p Islam (1981)   764
R v Hillingdon London Borough Coun-
cil, ex p Islam (1983)   .   768, 770, 771, 774
R v Hillingdon London Borough Coun-
cil, ex p Puhlhofer (1986)   .   761, 764, 771,
778, 928, 934
R v Hillingdon LBC, ex p Streeting
(1980)   774
R v Howson (1966)   507
R v Hussey (1924) 537, 756
R v Islington LBC, ex p Knight (1984):   487
R v Kerrier DC, ex p Guppys (Bridport)
Ltd (1976)   929
R v Lambeth LBC, ex p Clayhope
Properties Ltd (1987)   927
R v Landry (1982)   537
R v LB of Camden, ex p Rowton
(Camden Town) Ltd (1983)   938
R v LB of Ealing, ex p Richardson
(1982)   931
R v LB of Hammersmith & Fulham, ex p
Duro-Rama (1983)   771
R v LB of Southwark, ex p Lewis Levy
Ltd (1983)   938
R v London Rent Assessment Panel, ex p
Chelmsford Building Co Ltd (1986)   . 1035
R v Lord Yarborough (1824)   33
R v Maldon DC, ex p Fisher (1986)   .   .   929
R v Mole Valley DC, ex p Minnett
(1983)   772
R v North Devon District Council, ex
p Lewis (1981) 767, 768, 769
R v Penwith District Council, ex p
Trevena (1984)   770
R v Phekoo (1981) 956, 957
R v Plymouth CC, ex p Freeman
(1987):   1046
R v Portsmouth CC, ex p Knight
(1983)   771
R v Pratt (1855)   636

PAGE

R v Purbeck District Council, ex p Cad-
ney (1985)   763
R v Reigate & Banstead DC, ex p Paris
(1984)   774
R v Rent Officer for LB of Camden, ex p
Plant (1981) 984, 996
R v Rent Officer of Nottingham Regis-
tration Area, ex p Allen (1985)   .   .   .   972
R v Rushmoor Borough Council, ex p
Barrett (1987)   736
R v Salford County Council, ex p
Devenport (1984) 770, 915
R v Slough BC, ex p Ealing LBC (1981):   774
R v South Herefordshire District Council,
ex p Miles (1983)   764
R v South Middlesex Rent Tribunal, ex p
Beswick (1976)   457
R v South West London SBAT, ex p
Barnett (1973)   1067
R v Southampton City Council, ex p
Ward (1984) 770, 773
R v Surrey Heath BC, ex p Li (1984)   .   771
R v Swansea City Council, ex p John
(1982) 769, 915
R v Swansea City Council, ex p Thomas
(1983)   770
R v Thanet District Council, ex p Reeve
(1981) 768, 772
R v Thornley (1980) 536, 538
R v Thurrock Borough Council, ex p
Williams (1981) 767, 768
R v Vale of White Horse DC, ex p Smith
and Hay (1984)   774
R v Wandsworth County Court, ex p
Wandsworth London Borough Council
(1975)   758
R v Wandsworth LBC, ex p Lindsay
(1986)   776
R v Wandsworth London Borough
Council, ex p Rose (1983)   768
R v Waveney District Council, ex p
Bowers (1983) 763, 767
R v Welwyn Hatfield District Council,
ex p Brinkley (1982) 635, 637
R v West Dorset District Council, ex p
Phillips (1985)   770
R v Westminster County Council, ex p
Ali (1983) 768, 771
R v Westminster County Council, ex p
Chambers (1982)   .   .   .   770, 775, 776
R v Whitby Magistrates, ex p Marsh
(1984) 458, 955
R v Williams (1735)   339
R v Wimbourne District Council, ex p
Curtis (1985)   770
R v Wyre BC, ex p Joyce (1983)   .   .   773
R v Yuthiwattana (1984)   956
R A Sanson Investments Ltd v Sanson
(1982) 451, 995
R B Policies at Lloyd's v Butler (1950):   740
RPC Holdings Ltd v Rogers (1953)   .   .   662

PAGE

R & P Properties Ltd v Baldwin (1939): 976
Raab v Caranci (1980) 748
Radaich v Smith (1959) . . . 439, 440, 449,
457, 459
Radford v Bonham (1963) . . . 1009, 1010
Raffaele v F & G Raffaele (1962) . 389, 391
Railway Comrs for NSW, Ex p (1941): 327
Railways Comr v Valuer-General (1974): 17
Raineri v Miles (1981) 217
Rains v Buxton (1880) 750
Rajbenback v Mamon (1955) . . . 993
Ramsay v Cooke (1984) 680, 682
Ramsay v Morrissette (1969) 952
Ramsay and Heselmann, Re (1983) . . 454
Ramsbottom v Snelson (1948) 461
Ramsden v Dyson (1866) 290, 390,
392, 393, 397, 400, 408
Rance v Elvin (1985) 657
Randall's Estate, Re (1942) 308
Rasmanis v Jurewitsch (1970): 333, 334, 336
Rathwell v Rathwell (1978) . 244, 246, 247,
269, 813
Ravenseft Properties Ltd v Davstone
(Holdings) Ltd (1980) 922
Rawlings v Rawlings (1964) . . . 822, 825
Rawson v Inhabitants of School District
No 5 in Uxbridge (1863) 75
Ray v Fairway Motors (Barnstaple) Ltd
(1968) 642
Ray v Hazeldine (1904) 686
Rayleigh Weir Stadium, Re (1954) . . 365
Rayner v Preston (1881) 220
Rea v Sheward (1837) 507
Reading BC v Ilsley (1981) 1060
Red House Farms (Thorndon) Ltd v
Catchpole (1977) 748
Reddin v Jarman (1867) 213
Redditch Benefit Building Society v
Roberts (1940) 890
Redland Bricks Ltd v Morris (1969) . . 643
Redspring Ltd v Francis (1973) . . . 1018
Reeve v Lisle (1902) 583
Refuge Assurance Co Ltd v Pearlberg
(1938) 610, 627
Regalian Securities Ltd v Ramsden
(1981) 974, 976, 1006, 1010
Regalian Securities Ltd v Scheuer
(1982) 1012, 1013, 1014
Regan & Blackburn Ltd v Rogers
(1985) 939
Regent v Millett (1976) 213
Regent Oil Co Ltd v J A Gregory (Hatch
End) Ltd (1966) . . . 522, 564, 702, 703
Regional Properties Ltd v City of London
Real Property Co Ltd (1981) . . . 941
Regis Property Co Ltd v Redman
(1956) 657
Registered Securities Ltd v Cummins
(1983) 217
Registrar-General of New South Wales
v Wood (1926) 315

PAGE

Registrar of Titles (Vic) v Paterson
(1876) 145
Rehfuss v McAndrew (1947) . . . 306, 308
Reid v Bickerstaff (1909) . . 713, 716, 717
Reid v Reid (1978) 307, 309, 313
Reid v Reid (1979) 245
Reidy v Walker (1933) 1001
Reilly v Booth (1890) 658
Reliance Permanent Building Society v
Harwood-Stamper (1944) 620
Remon v City of London Real Property
Co Ltd (1921) 431, 894, 1006
Renals v Cowlishaw (1878); affd (1879) . 702,
708, 713, 717
Restormel BC v Buscombe (1982) . . . 1047
Reuss v Picksley (1866) 210
Reynolds v Ashby & Son (1904) . . . 20
Richards v Dove (1974) 258
Richards v Green (1983) . . . 1010, 1012
Richards v Richards (1984) 785
Richards v Rose (1853) 686
Richardson v Landecker (1950) . . . 444
Richardson v Langridge (1811) . . . 431
Richardson v Richardson (1845) . . . 338
Richardson v Sydenham (1703) . . . 524
Riches v Hogben (1986): 386, 387, 397, 404,
405, 416, 419, 420, 421
Richter v Wilson (1963) 1021
Rickett v Green (1910) 530
Ricketts v Enfield Churchwardens
(1909) 524
Rider v Kidder (1805) 261, 265
Riechmann v Riechmann (1972) . . . 307
Riggs, Re (1901) 496
Right d Compton v Compton (1808) . 338
Rignall Developments Ltd v Halil
(1987) 126
Riley v Penttila (1974) . 644, 651, 652, 687,
744, 747, 749
Rimmer v Liverpool City Council
(1985) 914, 925, 948
Rimmer v Rimmer (1953) 259
Rio Algam Ltd and Turcotte, Re
(1979) 1021
Rivett v Rivett (1966) . 377, 378, 822, 823
Roake v Chadha (1984) 710, 712
Robbins v Jones (1863) 902, 911
Roberts v Macilwraith-Christie (1986) . 1018
Roberts v O'Neill (1983) 217
Roberts v Roberts (1941) 308, 313
Roberts v Roberts (1978) 309
Roberts Petroleum Ltd v Bernard Kenny
Ltd (1982) 870, 872
Robertson, Re (1944) 296
Robertson v Cilia (1956) 891
Robertson v Fraser (1871) 338
Robertson v Norris (1858) 624
Robertson v Norris (1859) 609
Robertson and Saunders, Re (1977) . . 397
Robichaud v Watson (1983) 331
Robinson v Bailey (1948) 661

PAGE

Robinson v Kilvert (1889) 477
Robinson v Robinson (1977) 241
Robinson v Rosher (1841) 531
Robinson v Torbay Borough Council
  (1982) 768
Robson v Hallett (1967) . 536, 537, 538, 539
Robson v Headland (1948) 1011
Robson-Paul v Farrugia (1969) . . 536, 538
Rochdale Canal Co v Radcliffe (1852) . 683
Roche v Sheridan (1857) 330
Rochefoucauld v Boustead (1897) . . . 237,
                                    238, 239
Rochester Investments Pty Ltd v
  Couchman (1969) 19
Rock Permanent Benefit Building Society
  v Kettlewell (1956) 92, 786
Rodenhurst Estates Ltd v W H Barnes
  Ltd (1936) 533
Rodewald v Rodewald (1977) 1052
Rodgers v Moonta Town Corpn (1981) . 397,
                                        467
Rodrigue v Dufton (1977) 325, 330
Roe v Russell (1928) 1003, 1006
Roe d Bree v Lees 431
Roe d Brune v Prideaux (1808) . . . 467
Rogers v Eller (1986) . . 404, 793, 794, 795,
                            799, 800, 802
Rogers v Hosegood (1900) 647, 703,
                    706, 707, 708, 710, 713
Rogers v Humphreys (1835) 608
Rogers v Hyde (1951) 982, 991
Rogers v Rice (1892) 503
Rogers' Question, Re (1948) . . . 268, 365
Roland House Gardens Ltd v Cravitz
  (1975) 1009, 1010, 1011
Rommel v Schambacher (1887) . . . 952
Rookes v Bernard (1964) 959
Rosenberg v Northumberland Building
  Society (1889) 589
Rosen (LM) Realty Ltd v D'Amore
  (1982) 379
Rosenfeldt v Olson (1985) . . . 332, 334
Rosher, Re (1884) 75, 137
Rösler v Rottwinkel (1986) 983
Rosling v Pinnegar (1986) 661, 662
Rossiter v Conway (1893) 537
Ross v Collins (1964) 1065, 1069
Rossvale Ltd v Green (1979) 448
Rothera v Nottingham City Council
  (1980) 339
Rouse v Bardin (1790) 639
Rousou v Photi (1940) 916
Routhan v Arun District Council
  (1982) 185
Rowbotham v Wilson (1857) 653
Rowhook Mission Hall, Horsham, Re
  (1985) 72
Royal Bank of Canada v Beyak (1981): 21,
                                    22, 24
Royal Bank of Canada v Grobman
  (1978) 576

PAGE

Royal Bank of Canada v Nicholson
  (1980) 612, 855
Royal Bank of Canada v Poisson (1980) . 857
Royal Bank of Canada and Saskatchewan
  Telecommunications, Re (1985) . . 22
Royal Court Derby Porcelain Co v Ray-
  mond Russell (1949) 1021
Royal Fishery of The Banne (1610) . . 640
Royal Life Saving Society v Page
  (1978) 982
Royal Philanthropic Society v County .
  (1985) 431, 443, 450, 460, 461
Royal Trust Co of Canada v Markham
  (1975) 896
Royal Victoria Pavilion, Ramsgate, Re
  (1961) 704
Ruabon Steamship Co v London Assur-
  ance (1900) 397
Rudd v Lascelles (1900) 216
Rudge v Richens (1873) 613
Ruff v Strobel (1978) 252
Rugby School (Governors) v Tannahill
  (1934); affd (1935): 496, 497, 498, 499, 500
Rukat v Rukat (1975) 882
Rupar v Rupar (1964) 264
Rupp v Kahn (1966) 300
Ruptash and Lumsden v Zawick (1956): 165,
                            311, 313, 314
Rushton (A Bankrupt), (1972) . . 295, 324
Russel v Russel (1783) 576
Russell v Archdale (1964) . . . 709, 713
Russell v Booker (1982) 975, 983
Russell v Scott (1936) 261, 264
Rutherford, Re (1977) 137
Ryall v Kidwell & Son (1914) 918
Ryan v LB of Camden (1982) 947
Ryder and Steadman's Contract, Re
  (1927) 355
Rye v Purcell (1926) 530
Rye v Rye (1962) 323, 433
Ryeville Properties Ltd v Saint-John
  (1980) 984
Rylands v Fletcher (1868) 915
Rymer (Grace) Investments Ltd v Waite
  (1958) 181, 192, 475, 530

S

SEDAC Investments Ltd v Tanner
  (1982) 501, 502, 514
S L Dando Ltd v Hitchcock (1954): . . 1011,
                                      1014
Saint v Jenner (1973) 662, 663
St Catherine's College, Oxford v Dorling
  (1980) 977
St Clair Beach Estates Ltd v MacDonald
  (1975) 748
St Edmundsbury and Ipswich Diocesan
  Board of Finance v Clark (No 2)
  (1975) 661, 685
St Marylebone Property Co Ltd v
  Fairweather (1963) 743, 751, 752

PAGE

St Saviour's Southwark (Churchwardens) v Smith (1762) 527
Salford City Council v McNally (1976): 928, 933, 934, 936
Saliba v Saliba (1976) 137
Salter v Clark (1904) 742, 753
Salter v Lask (1925) 1070
Salvation Army Trustee Co Ltd v West Yorkshire Metropolitan County Council (1981) 208, 400, 401, 402, 408, 410, 425
Salvin's Indenture, Re (1938) . . 646, 650
Sammon, Re (1979) 223, 323, 331
Sampson v Hodson-Pressinger (1981) . 915
Samuel v District Land Registrar (1984) 317, 323, 433
Samuel v Jarrah Timber and Wood Paving Corpn Ltd (1904) . . . 571, 582, 583, 587
Samuel Allen & Sons Ltd, Re (1907) . . 25
Samuel Keller (Holdings) Ltd v Martins Bank Ltd (1971) 612
Sanders v McDonald and Pringle (1981): 330, 536, 538
Sanders v Pope (1806) 491, 493
Sandhu and Yzereff, Re (1983) 1025
Sandon v Jervis (1859) 537
Sandys v Florence (1878) 952
Santiago v Immigration and Naturalization Service (1975) 413
Santley v Wilde (1899) 563, 586
Sarat Chunder Dey v Gopal Chunder Laha (1892) 403
Sarson v Roberts (1895) 904
Saulsberry v Saulsberry (1941) . . . 304
Saunders v Vautier (1841) 53, 354
Savage v Dunningham (1974) 260
Savva v Costa and Harymode Investments Ltd (1981) . . . 279, 290, 397, 402, 415, 418, 419
Sayers v Pyland (1942) 304, 306
Scala House and District Property Co Ltd v Forbes (1974) . 497, 498, 499, 500, 503
Scarf v Jardine (1882) 504
Schär, Re (1951) 342
Schebsman, Re (1944) 236
Schlichenmayer v Luithle (1974) . . . 300
Schnytzer v Wielunski (1978) 342
Schobelt v Barber (1967) . . . 333, 334
Schon v Camden LBC (1986) 956
Schoole v Sall (1803) 613
Schwab & Co Ltd v McCarthy (1976): 158, 176, 178, 185, 193, 488
Schwartz v Zamrl (1968) 431
Scott v Goulding Properties Ltd (1973): . 664
Scott v Martin (1987) 661
Scott v Pauly (1917) 263, 264
Scott v Scott (1963) 246, 247
Scott v Watson (1976) 952
Scouton & Co (Builders) Ltd v Gilyott & Scott Ltd (1972) 668, 672, 674

PAGE

Scratton v Brown (1825) 33
Scrimgoeur v Waller (1981) . . 438, 441, 460, 973, 993
Scurlock v Secretary of State for Wales (1976) 972
Scythes & Co Ltd v Gibsons Ltd (1927): 904
Sea View Gardens, Re Claridge v Tingey (1967) 199
Seaforth Land Sales Pty Ltd's Land (No 2), Re (1977) 671
Seal v London Borough of Greenwich (1981) 941
Secretary of State for Social Services v Beavington (1982) 433
Seddon v Smith (1877) 748
Sedgwick Forbes Bland Payne Group Ltd v Regional Properties Ltd (1981) . . 655, 672, 943
Seesholts v Beers (1972) 308, 309
Segal v Derrick Golf & Winter Club (1977) 656
Segal Securities Ltd v Thoseby (1963) . 505
Seidler v Schallhofer (1982) 794
Seifeddine and Governors & Co of Hudson Bay, Re (1980) 717
Selangor United Rubber Estates Ltd v Cradock (No 3) (1968) . . 120, 268, 812
Seldon v Davidson (1968) 262
Selim Ltd v Bickenhall Engineering Ltd (1981) 501
Selous Street Properties Ltd v Oronel Fabrics Ltd (1984) 518, 519
Selwyn v Garfit (1888) 615
Selwyn's Conveyance, Re (1967) . . . 709
Semayne's Case (1604) 512, 537
Serff v Acton Local Board (1886) . . . 669
Sergie, Re (1954) 434
Seton v Slade (1802) 575
Shaddock & Associates Pty Ltd v Parramatta City Council (1981) 206
Shah v Givert (1983) 758
Shaida v Kindlane Ltd (1982) . . 398, 402, 404, 413, 417, 421
Shakel v Duke of Marlborough (1819) . 631
Shanahan v Fitzgerald (1982) 219
Shankie-Williams v Heavey (1986) . . 205
Shannon Ltd v Venner Ltd (1965) . . 667
Sharman v Sharman (1893) 213
Sharp v Coates (1949) 135
Sharp v McArthur (1986) 454
Sharpe (A Bankrupt), Re (1980) . . . 262, 289, 290, 386, 405, 418, 419, 421, 425, 426, 554, 796, 797, 812
Sharpe v Manchester City Council (1977) 911, 914
Sharpe v Nicholls (1945) 1021
Shaw v Applegate (1977) 394, 396
Shaw v Foster (1872) . . 218, 219, 576, 577
Shaw v Groom (1970) 479
Shea v Moore (1894) 577

PAGE

Sheffield CC v Blaskey and Salis Properties Ltd (1986) 956
Sheldon v West Bromwich Corpn (1973) 920
Shelfer v City of London Electric Lighting Co (1895) 719
Shell-Mex & BP Ltd v Manchester Garages Ltd (1971): 450, 452, 454, 461, 995
Shell UK Ltd v Lostock Garage Ltd (1976) 588
Shelton v Vance (1951) 322
Shepherd v Braley (1981) . . . 1019, 1020
Shephard v Cartwright (1955) . . 261, 263
Sheppard v Northern Ireland Housing Executive (1984) 912, 914, 915
Sherren v Pearson (1887) 747
Shillabeer v Diebel (1980) . . 213, 742, 745
Shiloh Spinners Ltd v Harding (1973) . 82, 141, 143, 226, 491, 493, 503, 504, 520, 529, 532, 697
Shively v Bowlby (1894) 641
Short Bros (Plant) Ltd v Edwards (1979) 488, 993
Shrewsbury's (Countess) Case (1600) . 430
Shrimpton v Rabbits (1924) 1015
Shropshire County Council v Edwards (1982) 700, 702, 710
Siddiqui v Rashid (1980) 1018
Sidebotham v Holland (1895) 485
Sidmouth v Sidmouth (1840) 263
Sidnell v Wilson (1966) 501
Sidney Trading Co Ltd v Finsbury BC (1952) 1000
Siew Soon Wah v Yong Tong Hong (1973) . Re 416
Sigsworth, Re (1935) 332
Sikorski and Sikorski, Re (1979) . . . 577
Simmons v Montague (1909) . . . 577
Simmons v Pizzey (1979) 938
Simonds v Simonds (1978) 812
Simpson v Clayton (1838) 524
Simpson v Godmanchester Corpn (1897) 655
Simpson v Hartopp (1744) 512
Simpson v Knowles (1974) . . 444, 535, 658
Simpson v Wells (1872) 644
Sinclair v Brougham (1914) 556
Sinclair-Hill v Sothcott (1973) 219
Sinclair (Ed) Construction & Supplies Ltd v Grunthaler (1980) 114
Siney v Corpn of Dublin (1980) . . . 902, 903, 913
Sinton v Dooley (1910) 613
Six Arlington Street Investments Ltd v Persons Unknown (1987) 757
Skinner v Geary (1931) 979, 1008, 1009, 1010, 1011
Skull v Glenister (1864) 660
Slade v Guscott (1981) 536
Slater v Hoskins (1982) 958

PAGE

Slingsby's Case (1587) 340
Sloane v Mahon (1838) 609
Smalley v Quarrier (1975) 1005
Smallwood v Sheppards (1895) . . 213, 434
Smedley v Chumley & Hawke Ltd (1982) 922
Smith, Re (1892) 222
Smith v Bradford Metropolitan Council (1982) 482, 924, 949
Smith v Bristol County Council (1981) . 770
Smith v City Petroleum Co Ltd (1940) . 21
Smith v Daly (1949) 25
Smith v Eric S Bush (1987) 205
Smith v Evangelization Society (Incorporated) Trust (1933) 664
Smith v Littlewoods Organisation Ltd (1987) 951
Smith v Marrable (1843): 515, 903, 912, 916
Smith v Metropolitan Properties Ltd (1986) 428, 508
Smith v Morton (1972) 327
Smith v Neale (1857) 210
Smith v New England Aircraft Co (1930) 27, 28
Smith v Nottinghamshire County Council (1981) 543
Smith v Scott (1973) . . . 913, 914, 915
Smith v Seghill Overseers (1875) . . . 460
Smith v Smith (1895) 660
Smith v United States (1946) 305
Smith and Snipes Hall Farm Ltd v River Douglas Catchment Board (1949) . . 691, 692, 693, 694, 711
Snell v Mitchell (1951) 461
Snook v London and West Riding Investments Ltd (1967) 995
Snook v Mannion (1982) . . 536, 537, 538
Soar v Foster (1858) 263, 265
Solomon (A Bankrupt), Re (1967) . . 876
Solomon v Orwell (1954) 1006
Solomon v Vintners' Co (1859) . . 652, 679
Somers v W (1979) 47, 842
Somma v Hazelhurst and Savelli (1978): 447, 936, 995, 996, 998, 999
Sopwith v Stutchbury (1983): 459, 919, 1016
Sorensen and Sorensen, Re (1979) . . 317, 323, 325, 330
Sorochan v Sorochan (1986) . . . 419, 814
South Eastern Rly Co v Cooper (1924) . 661
South Holland DC v Keyte (1985) . . 455
South Staffordshire Water Co v Sharman (1896) 35, 36
South Western General Property Co Ltd v Marton (1982) 205
South Yarra Project Pty Ltd v Gentsis (1985) 269, 277, 281
Southampton (Lord) v Brown (1827) . 691
Southern Centre of Theosophy Inc v State of South Australia (1982) . . 32, 33
Southgate BC v Watson (1944) 431

PAGE

Southwark London Borough Council v Williams (1971) 754

Southwestern Lumber Co v Evans (1925) 25

Sovmots Investments Ltd v Secretary of State for the Environment (1979) . . 676

Sowerby v Sowerby (1982) 111

Spark v Meers (1971) 753

Speakman's Application, Re (1983) . . 720

Spears and Levy, Re (1975) 399

Spectrum Investment Co Ltd v Holmes (1981) 156, 743

Spencer's Case (1583) 141, 526, 530

Spicer v Martin (1888) 717

Spike and Rocca Group Ltd, Re (1980): 715

Spiller v Mackereth (1976) . . . 305, 309

Spiro v Lintern (1973) 859

Sport Internationaal Bussum BV v Inter-Footwear Ltd (1984) 493, 543

Spyer v Phillipson (1931) 24

Squarey v Harris-Smith (1981) 210, 671, 672, 674, 676, 678

Squire v C Brewer & Sons Ltd (1983) . 480, 523, 524

Squire v Rogers (1979-80): 306, 312, 313, 314

Stack v T Eaton Co (1902) 21

Staden v Tarjanyi (1980) 29

Stafford v Pearson-Smith (1962) . 677, 678

Staffordshire and Worcestershire Canal Navigation v Bradley (1912) 634

Stamford and Warrington (Earl), Re (1925) 369

Stamp Duties Comr (Queensland) v Livingston (1965) 233, 556

Standard Chartered Bank Ltd v Walker (1982) 620, 621, 622, 626

Standard Pattern Co Ltd v Ivey (1962): 494

Standard Property Investment plc v British Plastics Federation (1985): 113, 129

Standing v Bowring (1885) 263

Stanhope v Haworth (1866) 495

Stannard v Issa (1987) 720

Stanton v Southwick (1920) 917

Staples v Maurice (1774) . . . 317, 323, 326

Starlite Variety Stores Ltd v Cloverlawn Investments Ltd (1979) 213

Starrokate Ltd v Burry (1982) 501

State v McCoy (1883) 305

State Electricity Commission of Victoria & Joshua's Contract, Re 657, 671

State ex rel Thornton v Hay (1969) . . 642

State of Montana, ex rel Region II Child and Family Services Inc v District Court (1980) 1072

State of New Jersey v Baker (1979) . .1071, 1072

Stedman v Smith (1857) 305

Steadman v Steadman (1976) . . 213, 214

Stephens, ex p (1877) 24

Stephens v Gulf Oil Canada Ltd (1976): 136, 137, 588

PAGE

Stephens v Junior Army and Navy Stores Ltd (1914) 504

Stephens v Snell (1939) 640

Sterme v Beck (1863) 593

Stevahn v Meidinger (1952) 304

Stevens v Copp (1868) 523

Stevens v Stevens (1907) 782

Stevenson v Nationwide Building Society (1984) 205

Stewart v Higgins (1951) 1065

Stewart v Murdoch (1969) 76

Stiff v Stiff (1969) 330

Stilwell v Blackman (1968) . . 703, 709, 713

Stilwell v Simpson (1983) . . . 394, 397, 399, 404, 408, 415

Stocker v Planet Building Society (1879) 440

Stockler v Fourways Estates Ltd (1984): 112

Stockley v Knowsley MBC (1985) . . 919

Stokes v Costain Property Investments Ltd (1983) 59

Stone and Saville's Contract, Re (1962): 224

Storey v Robinson (1795) 512

Storey v Windsor (1743) 88

Stott v Ratcliffe (1982) 823

Strand and Savoy Properties Ltd, Re (1960) 434

Strand Securities Ltd v Caswell (1965) . 148, 162, 163, 175, 178, 182, 188

Street v Mountford (1984); revsd (1985) 427, 431, 438, 439, 440, 441, 443, 444, 448, 449, 450, 451, 452, 454, 455, 456, 457, 458, 459, 460, 461, 936, 939, 961, 964, 996, 997, 998, 1000, 1030, 1052

Stringer v Halton Borough Council (1982) 765

Strode v Parker (1694) 593

Stromdale and Ball Ltd v Burden (1952) 222

Strood Estates Co Ltd v Gregory (1936): 916

Stroyan v Knowles (1861) 642

Stuart v Joy (1904) 520

Stuart v Kingston (1923) 164

Stubbs v Slough BC (1980) 774

Stukeley v Butler (1615) 25

Sturge v Hackett (1962) 439

Sturges v Bridgman (1879) . . . 656, 682

Sturolson & Co v Weniz (1984): 447, 448, 999

Sudbrook Trading Estate Ltd v Eggleton (1983) 136, 211, 443

Suffield v Brown (1864) 673

Summers v Salford Corpn (1943) . 916, 917

Sumnal v Statt (1984) 1010

Supreme Court Registrar to Alexander Dawson Inc, Re (1976) 583

Surplice v Farnsworth (1844) 918

Sutcliffe, Re (1982) 75

PAGE

Sutherland (Duke) v Heathcote (1892):   438
Sutherland v Sutherland (1955)   . . .   883
Suttill v Graham (1977) 310, 311
Sutton v Dorf (1932)   1005
Sutton v Moody (1697) 34, 35
Sutton v O'Kane (1973) 142, 164
Sutton v Sutton (1984)   213
Sutton v Temple (1843)   902
Swain v Ayres (1888)   472
Swales v Cox (1981)   537
Swallow Securities Ltd v Isenberg
   (1985) 398, 402, 403, 410
Swan v Sinclair (1924)   687
Swan v Swan (1820)   312
Swan's Case (1592)   34
Swanbrae Ltd v Elliott (1986)   . . .   1064
Swansborough v Coventry (1832)   . . .   672
Swarzbaugh v Sampson (1936):   301, 303, 307
Swayne v Howells (1927)   438
Sweet & Maxwell Ltd v Michael-
   Michaels Advertising (1965)   659
Swetland v Curtiss Airports Corpn
   (1932)   27
Swift d Neale v Roberts (1764)   299
Swindon Waterworks Co Ltd v Wilts and
   Berks Canal Navigation Co (1875)   .   643
Swiss Bank Corpn v Lloyds Bank Ltd
   (1982) 563, 576, 577
Switzer & Co Ltd v Rochford (1906)   .   81
Syed Hussain v A M Abdullah Sahib &
   Co (1985)   993
Szabo v Boros (1967) 329, 330
Szachno, Krasinska and Skwarczynski v
   Gough (1978)   989
Szuba v Szuba (1951)   309

T

T & E Homes Ltd v Robinson (1979)   .   442
Taddeo v Taddeo (1978)   . .   245, 247, 261,
                              265, 266, 276
Tait-Jamieson v GC Smith Metal Con-
   tractors Ltd (1984)   32
Taj Din v Wandsworth London Borough
   Council (1983)   . .   762, 763, 771, 772, 775
Talbot-Ponsonby's Estate, Re (1937). .   77
Tan Chew Hoe Neo v Chee Swee Cheng
   (1929)   320
Tandon v Trustees of Spurgeons Homes
   (1982) 727, 731, 972
Tanner v Tanner (1975)   . . .   386, 544, 545,
                              548, 799
Tarjomani v Panther Securities Ltd
   (1983)   993
Tate & Lyle Food and Distribution Ltd
   v GLC (1983)   21
Tattersfield v Tattersfield and the New
   Zealand Insurance Co Ltd (1980)   . .   246
Tayler v Waters (1816)   546
Taylor v Auto Trade Supply Ltd
   (1972)   643
Taylor v Beal (1591)   942

PAGE

Taylor v Brindley (1947)   306
Taylor v Caldwell (1863)   451
Taylor v Knowsley BC (1985)   919
Taylor v London and County Banking
   Co (1901)   87
Taylor v Stibbert (1794) 91, 175
Taylor v Taylor (1956) 405, 418
Taylor v Taylor (1968)   . . .   111, 114, 365,
                              831, 836
Taylor and Willigar, Re (1980)   . . .   747
Taylor d Atkyns v Horde (1757)   . . .   63
Taylors Fashions Ltd v Liverpool Vic-
   toria Trustees Co Ltd (1982)   . .   390, 391,
         394, 396, 400, 402, 403,
             404, 407, 421, 524
Teape v Douse (1905)   . . .   433, 528, 529
Teasdale v Sanderson (1864)   313
Tecbild Ltd v Chamberlain (1969):   748, 749,
                                       750
Tehidy Minerals Ltd v Norman (1971):   679,
                                       684, 687
Telex (Australasia) Pty Ltd v Thomas
   Cook & Son (Australasia) Pty Ltd
   (1970) 476, 477
Temma Realty Co Ltd v Ress Enterprises
   Ltd (1968)   681
Tenhet v Boswell (1976) 298, 317
Tennant v Trenchard (1869)   631
Tepper's Will Trusts, Re (1987)   . .   75, 76
Te Rama Engineering Ltd v Shortlands
   Properties Ltd (1982)   . . .   398, 420
Tester v Harris (1964)   156
Tetley v Chitty (1986)   915
Tetragon Ltd v Shidasb Construction Co
   Ltd and Darabi (1981) 984, 1002
Teutenberg v Schiller (1955)   330
Texaco Antilles Ltd v Kernochan
   (1973) 716, 717
Thames Guaranty Ltd v Campbell
   (1985) 149, 575, 576, 577, 877
Thames Manufacturing Co Ltd v Per-
   rotts (Nichol & Peyton) Ltd (1984)   .   517,
                                       518, 519
Thatcher v C H Pearce & Sons (Con-
   tractors) Ltd (1968)   495
Theis v Muir (1951)   976
Thomas v Hayward (1869)   522
Thomas v Johnson (1973)   323
Thomas v National Union of Mine-
   workers (South Wales Area) (1986)   .   636,
                                       638
Thomas v Packer (1857)   468
Thomas v Rose (1968) 135, 138
Thomas v Sorrell (1673)   . . .   535, 539
Thomas v Thomas (1855)   745
Thomas v Thomas (1956)   . .   387, 389, 415
Thompson v City of Glasgow DC
   (1986)   1048
Thompson v Flynn (1936)   . . .   307, 309
Thompson v Park (1944)   548
Thompson v Potter (1980)   . . .   702, 718

PAGE

Thompson v Thompson (1976) 1052
Thompson v Ward (1871) 455
Thompson v Ward (1953) 1011
Thompson-Schwab v Costaki (1956) . 914
Thomson Electrical Works Ltd v Mc-
Graw (1976) 638
Thorndike v Hunt (1859) 88
Thorne v Smith (1947) 1021
Thornton v Thompson (1930) . . 531, 533
Thorp and the Real Property Act, Re
(1963) 333, 334
Thorpe v Brumfitt (1873) 645, 647
Thrasher v City of Atlanta (1934) . . 28, 29
Thrift v Thrift (1976) 307
Thurley v Smith (1984) 764, 767
Thurrock UDC v Shina (1972) 956
Thursby v Plant (1669) 521
Thwaites v Ryan (1984) 186, 208,
212, 233, 239, 255,
274, 277, 278, 281,
285, 286, 287, 855
Thynne v Earl of Glengall (1848) . . . 213
Thynne v Petrie (1975) 643
Tichborne v Weir (1892) 751, 752
Tickner v Buzzacott (1965) . . . 509, 752
Tickner v Hearn (1960) 1010
Tickner v Mole Valley District Council
(1980) 771
Tilbury v Silva (1890) 32
Tilbury West Public School Board and
Hastie, Re (1966) 73
Tilling v Whiteman (1980): 1005, 1025, 1026
Tiltwood, Re (1978) 702
Timber Top Realty Pty Ltd v Mullens
(1974) 405, 411
Timmins v Moreland Street Property Co
Ltd (1958) 211
Timms v Timms (1973) 796, 800
Tinker v Tinker (1970) 266
Tipler v Fraser (1976) 671
Titchmarsh v Royston Water Co Ltd
(1899) 669, 686
Tithe Redemption Commission v Run-
corn UDC (1954) 72, 635
Tito v Waddell (No 2) (1977) . . 236, 697
Tiverton Estates Ltd v Wearwell Ltd
(1975) 207, 210, 211
Todrick v Western National Omnibus Co
Ltd (1934) 645, 650, 660
Tollemache & Cobbold Breweries Ltd v
Reynolds (1983) 655
Tolman's Estate, Re (1928) 307
Tomlin v Luce (1889) 620
Tompkins v Rowley (1949) 1010
Tompkins v Superior Court of City and
County of San Francisco (1963) . 304, 536
Toner v Toner (1972) 258
Toobman (A Bankrupt), Re (1982) . . 878
Toohey v Gunther (1928) 586, 587
Toome Eel Fishery (Northern Ireland)
Ltd v Cardwell (1966) 633, 640

PAGE

Tophams Ltd v Earl of Sefton (1967) . 701,
702, 711
Topliss Showers Ltd v Gessey & Son Ltd
(1982) 115
Torbett v Faulkner (1952) 431
Tori, ex p (1977) 584, 585
Tormes Property Co Ltd v Landau
(1971) 1034
Torridge DC v Jones (1985) 1056
Tottenham Hotspur Football & Athletic
Co Ltd v Princegrove Publishers Ltd
(1974) 470, 472
Town and Country Investments Ltd v
Marks (1984) 1009, 1014
Town of Cascade v Cascade Co (1925) . 52
Townsend v Clifford (1973) 487
Traders Group Ltd v Mason (1975) . . 624
Trayfoot v Lock (1957) 1063
Trella and Anko Investments Ltd, Re
(1982) 904
Treloar v Nute (1976) . . . 743, 745, 748
Treml v Ernest W Gibson v Partners
(1984) 205
Trenberth (John) Ltd v National West-
minster Bank Ltd (1979) 28
Trentacost v Brussel (1980) 953
Treweeke v 36 Wolseley Road Pty Ltd
(1972-1973) 687
Trifid Pty Ltd v Ratto (1985) 442
Trimleston (Lord) v Hamill (1810) . . 609
Trustee of Estate of Royal Inns Canada
Ltd v Bolus-Revelas-Bolus Ltd (1982): 513
Trustees, Executors and Agency Co Ltd
v Acting Federal Comr of Taxation
(1917) 423
Trustees of Henry Smith's Charity v
Hemmings (1983) 1037
Trustees of Henry Smith's Charity v
Willson (1983) 505, 1006, 1037
Trustees of the Alcoholic Recovery Pro-
ject v Farrell (1976) 458
Tse Kwong Lam v Wong Chit Sen
(1983) 622, 623, 624,
625, 626
Tuck's Settlement Trust, Re (1978) . . 76
Tulk v Moxhay (1848) 139, 528,
550, 557, 698, 699, 705
Tunley v James (1982) 745, 794
Tunstall v Tunstall (1953) 831
Turismo Industries Ltd v Kovacs
(1977) 23
Turkington, Re (1937) 556
Turley v Mackay (1944) 138
Turner (A Bankrupt), Re (1974) . . 377, 877
Turner v Burton (1985) . . . 458, 758, 972
Turner v Jatko (1979) 514
Turner v Melladew (1903) 213
Turton v Turton (1987) 241
Tutton v Drake (1860) 512
Twentieth Century Banking Corpn Ltd
v Wilkinson (1977) 627, 629

PAGE

Tyrringham's Case (1584) 687
Tyson v Tyson (1960) 326

U

Ubhi v Nothey (1983) 958, 959
Ulrich v Ulrich and Felton (1968) . 250, 251
Ulster Bank Ltd v Shanks (1982) . . . 401,
                     832, 837, 838, 859
Unimin Pty Ltd v Commonwealth of
   Australia (1973-4) 633
Union Bank of Canada v Boulter-Waugh
   Ltd (1919) 165
Union Lighterage Co v London Graving
   Dock Co (1902) 669, 681
United Scientific Holdings Ltd v Burnley
   Borough Council (1978) . . . 42, 441, 442
United States v Allen (1980) 30
United States v Causby (1946) . . . 17, 27
United States v Jacobs (1939): 297, 298, 315
United States Surgical Corpn v Hospital
   Products International Pty Ltd (1983): 120
United Trust Co v Dominion Stores Ltd
   (1977) 165, 166
Unity Joint Stock Mutual Banking As-
   sociation v King (1858) 418
University College, London v Newman
   (1986) 185
University of Essex v Djemal (1980) . . 758
University of Prince Edward Island v
   President of the Students' Union of the
   University of Prince Edward Island
   (1977) 454
University of Reading v Johnson-Hough-
   ton (1985) 450, 451, 452, 461
Upper Hutt Arcade Ltd v Burrell and
   Burrell Properties Ltd (1973) . . . 470
Uzun v Ramadan (1986) 429

V

VT Engineering Co Ltd v Richard
   Barland & Co Ltd (1968) . . . 658, 660
Vacuum Oil Co Ltd v Ellis (1914) . . 612
Valentini v Canali (1889) 432
Van den Berg v Giles (1979) 418
Van Den Bosch v Australian Provincial
   Assurance Association Ltd (1968) . . 582
Vancouver City Savings Credit Union v
   Chambers (1976) 593
Vandermolem v Toma (1981) 1022
Vandervell v IRC (1966) 233, 291
Vandervell's Trusts (No 2), Re (1974) . 263,
                     264, 397
Vane v Lord Bernard (1716) 60
Vanek and Bomza, Re (1977) . . 500, 504
Vaughan v Hampson (1875) 539
Vedejs v Public Trustee (1985): 246, 247, 286
Veltrusy Enterprises Ltd and Gallant
   (1980) 1039
Vernazza v Ferro (1985) 989
Vernon v Bethell (1762) 579

PAGE

Verrall   v   Great   Yarmouth   BC
   (1981) 548, 549
Victa Sales Pty Ltd v Tucker (1970): 430, 431
Vinden v Vinden (1982) . . 399, 405, 420
Viney v Sunderland BC (1983) 922
Viveash Ltd v Feilen (1980) . . 1016, 1018

W

W & W (1976) 544
Wade v Marsh (1625) 511
Wadman v Calcraft (1804) 494
Wagener (WE) Ltd v Photo Engravers
   Ltd (1984) 517, 518
Waimiha Sawmilling Co Ltd v Waione
   Timber Co Ltd (1923) . . 164, 165, 168
Waimiha Sawmilling Co Ltd v Waione
   Timber Co Ltd (1926) 124
Wainwright   v   Leeds   City   Council
   (1984) 917, 919, 922
Waite v Taylor (1985) 636, 637
Waitzman v McGoldrick (1953) . . . 1069
Wakeham v Mackenzie (1968) 213
Wakeham v Wood (1982) 719
Wakeman, Re (1945) 353
Walker v Bower (1975) 211, 213
Walker v Boyle (1982) 205
Walker v Hall (1984) 248
Walker v Hobbs & Co (1889) . . . 918
Walker v Ogilvy (1974) 1014
Walker v Russell (1966) 747
Walker v Walker (1984) 243, 244,
                     261, 419, 795
Walker and Carlill & Carbolic Smoke
   Ball Corpn, Re (1980) 1025
Walker's Case (1587) 518
Waller v Waller (1967) . . . 365, 381, 831
Walliker v Deveaux (1959) 441
Wallingford v Mutual Society (1880) . . 593
Wallis v Hands (1893) 487
Wallis & Simmonds (Builders) Ltd, Re
   (1974) 576
Wallis's Cayton Bay Holiday Camp Ltd
   v Shell-Mex and BP Ltd (1975) . . . 744,
                     745, 746
Walsh   v   Griffiths-Jones   and   Durant
   (1978) 999
Walsh v Lonsdale (1882) . . 220, 323, 471,
                     511, 1051
Walsingham's Case (1573) 61, 62
Walter v Rumbal (1695) 972
Walters and Walters, Re (1978) . 329, 331
Waltham Forrest v Mills (1980) . . . 637
Walton Harvey Ltd v Walker and Hom-
   frays Ltd (1931) 549
Walton Stores Ltd v Sydney City Council
   (1968) 541, 659
Wandsworth Board of Works v United
   Telephone Co (1884) 28
Wandsworth LBC v Fadayomi (1987) . 1056
Wandsworth LBC v Winder (1985) . . 1051
Wanner v Caruana (1974) 585, 593

PAGE

Ward v Cannock Chase DC (1986) . . 950
Ward v Day (1864) 506, 511
Ward v Gold (1969) 28, 402
Ward v Kirkland (1967) . . 387, 398, 399,
400, 402, 408, 658,
674, 675, 684
Ward v Ryan (1875) 430
Ward (Helston) Ltd v Kerrier DC
(1984) 684
Wardlow v Pozzi (1959) 326
Ware v Cann (1830) 75
Ware v Lord Egmont (1854) 89
Waring (Lord) v London and Man-
chester Assurance Co Ltd (1935): 615, 617
Warmington v Miller (1973) . . . 217
Warner v Jacob (1882) 618, 619
Warner v LB of Lambeth (1984) . . . 935
Warner v Sampson (1958); revsd (1959): 58,
489, 502
Warner v Warner (1984): 280, 287, 288, 811
Warner (HA) Pty Ltd v Williams
(1946) 461
Warnes v Hedley (1984) . . 400, 401, 409,
419, 539, 794
Warnford Investments Ltd v Duckworth
(1979) 518, 520
Warren v Austin (1947) 1016
Warren v Keen (1954) 430, 481
Warren v Yoell (1944) 680
Warwick Grove Pty Ltd v Wright &
Howson (1979) 469, 470, 471
Warwick University v De Graaf (1975) . 757
Waterhouse v Waterhouse (1905) . . . 782
Waters v Weigall (1795) 942
Watkin v Watson-Smith (1986) . . . 225
Watkins v Emslie (1982) 406
Watson v Gass (1881-82) 313
Watson v Goldsbrough (1986): 397, 399, 402
Watson v Lucas (1980) . . 1065, 1066, 1068
Watts v Story (1983) . . . 405, 410, 411,
412, 801, 802
Watts v Waller (1973) 787
Waveney District Council v Wholge-
mouth (1985) 648
Wear v De Putron (1984) 262
Webb v Frank Bevis Ltd (1940) . . . 24
Webb v Paternoster (1619) . . . 540, 546
Webb v Pollmount Ltd (1966) . . 136, 179,
181, 524
Webb v Russell (1789) 693
Webb's Lease, Re (1951) 686
Wedd v Porter (1916) 481
Weedair (NZ) Ltd v Walker (1961) . . 29
Weg Motors Ltd v Hales (1962) . . . 434,
523, 530, 564, 573
Weh v Weh (1960) 313
Weirdale Investments Ltd and Canadian
Imperial Bank of Commerce (1981) . 593
Welch v Birrane (1975) 505
Welch v Nagy (1950) 991
Welch v Swasey (1909) 27

PAGE

Weld v Scott (1855) 747
Welford v Beezely (1747) 210
Wellington City Corpn v Public Trustee
(1921) 164
Wells v Joyce (1905) 591
Wells (Sir Thomas Spencer), Re (1933): 572
Wellsted's Will Trusts, Re (1949) . . . 353
Werth v London & Westminster Loan
and Discount Co (1889) 512
West v Rogers (1888) 503
West Bank Estates Ltd v Arthur (1967): 747
West Derby Union v Metropolitan Life
Assurance Society (1897) 585
West Layton Ltd v Ford (1979) . . . 480
Western Bank Ltd v Schindler (1977) . 607,
609, 896, 897
Western Fish Products Ltd v Penwith
District Council (1981) . . 397, 398, 413
Western Heritable Investment Co Ltd v
Husband (1983) 1036
Westhoughton UDC v Wigan Coal and
Iron Co Ltd (1919) 694
Westminster (Duke) v Guild (1985) . . 657,
907, 909, 910, 911, 915
Westminster (Duke) v Oddy (1984) . . 728
Westminster Bank Ltd v Lee (1956): 785, 786
Westminster City Council v Haymarket
Publishing Ltd (1981) 574
Westminster City Council v Select
Management Ltd (1984) . . . 908, 925
Weston v Henshaw (1950) . . 603, 806, 832
Wetherby Apartments v Tootell (1981): 441
Wettern Electric Ltd v Welsh Develop-
ment Agency (1983) 543
Whaley, Re (1908) 22, 24
Whatman v Gibson (1838) 698
Wheat v E Lacon & Co Ltd (1966) . . 445
Wheaton v Maple & Co (1893) . . . 680
Wheeldon v Burrows (1879) . 672, 673, 685
Wheeler v Baldwin (1934) 753
Wheeler v Horne (1740) 307
Wheeler v Mercer (1957) . . . 430, 431
Whissel Enterprises Ltd and Eastcal
Developments Ltd (1981) 465
Whitcomb v Minchin (1820) 625
White, Re (1928) 324
White v Bijou Mansions Ltd (1937): 114, 692
White v Cabanas Pty Ltd (No 2) (1970): 236,
269, 271, 273, 274, 292
White v City of London Brewery Co
(1889) 610
White v Exeter County Council (1981): . 768
White v Grand Hotel, Eastbourne, Ltd
(1913); affd (1915) 661
White v Lauder Developments Ltd
(1976) 700
White v Metcalf (1903) 628
White v Smyth (1948) 308
White v Williams (1922) 676
White Rose Cottage, Re (1965) . 161, 630
Whitehead, Re (1948) 418

PAGE

Whitehead v Clifford (1814) 487
Whiteley and Whiteley, Re (1975): 250, 254
Whitfield v Flaherty (1964) 333
Whitham v Kershaw (1886) 514
Whittingham v Whittingham (1979) . . 111,
                                164, 784, 851
Whitty v Scott-Russell (1950) 972
Wicks v Bennett (1921) . . . 163, 164, 165
Wigg v Wigg (1739) 87
Wight v IRC (1982) 303, 823
Wiles v Banks (1985) 685, 692
Wilford's Estate, Re (1879) 330
Wilkes v Goodwin (1923) 985
Wilkes v Larkcroft Properties Ltd
   (1983) 730
Wilkes v Spooner (1911) . . . 92, 127, 705
Wilkinson v Downton (1897) 959
Wilkinson v Haygarth (1847) 305
Wilkinson v Rogers (1864) 522
Wilks, Re (1891) 321, 325, 329
Williams, Re (1897) 555
Williams v Bosanquet (1819) 527
Williams v Coleman (1984) 401
Williams v Cynon Valley Council
   (1980) 773
Williams v Earle (1868) 522
Williams v Hensman (1861) . . . 320, 326,
                                329, 331
Williams v James (1867) 660, 662
Williams v Khan (1980) 1035
Williams v Mate (1983) 990
Williams v Morgan (1906) 629
Williams v Staite (1979) . . . 413, 414, 415,
                                416, 425
Williams v Unit Construction Co Ltd
   (1955) 694, 711
Williams v Usherwood (1983) . . 18, 668, 687
Williams v Walsh (1983) 730
Williams v Williams (1899-1900) . 313, 314
Williams v Williams (1970) 1063
Williams v Williams (1976) . . 825, 826, 878
Williams & Glyn's Bank Ltd v Barnes
   (1980) 595, 849, 857
Williams & Glyn's Bank Ltd v Boland
   (1979); affd (1981): 10, 65, 91, 105, 145, 147,
                163, 170, 171, 179, 181,
                187, 188, 191, 247, 249,
                350, 364, 366, 372, 373,
                375, 383, 385, 559, 601,
                603, 621, 783, 790, 832,
                833, 837, 841, 842, 843,
                844, 846, 847, 848, 849,
                850, 851, 853, 858, 859,
                861, 862, 865, 866, 896
Williams & Glyn's Bank Ltd v Brown
   (1979); affd (1981) 843
Williams Bros Direct Supply Ltd v
   Raftery (1958) 744, 748
Williams-Ellis v Cobb (1935) 635
Williamson v Pallant (1924) 1016
Williamson v Thompson (1979) . . . 1005

PAGE

Williamson Ltd v Lukey and Mulholland
   (1931) 213
Williamson's Estate v Williamson (1964): 297
Willis v Earl Howe (1893) 742, 753
Willis (J) & Sons v Willis (1986) . . . 415
Willits v Willits Estate (1982) 815
Willmott v Barber (1880) 393, 398,
                402, 403, 405, 407, 408,
                                     410
Wills v Wood (1984) 591, 594, 595
Wills' Trustees v Cairngorm Canoeing
   and Sailing School Ltd (1976) . 639, 640
Wilsher v Foster (1981) 486
Wilson v Bell (1843) . . 323, 326, 327, 329
Wilson v Bloomfield (1979) 205
Wilson v Brett (1843) 89
Wilson v Finch Hatton (1877) 904
Wilson v Pringle (1986) 959
Wilson v Rosenthal (1906) 480
Wilson v Rush (1980) 669
Wilson v Tavener (1901) 439
Wilson v Wilson (1969) . . . 242, 248, 362
Wilson's Settlements, Re (1972) . . . 692
Wiltshire County Council v Frazer
   (1984) . . . 72, 635, 637, 757, 758
Wimbledon and Putney Commons Con-
   servators v Dixon (1875) 668
Wimbush v Cibulia (1949) . . . 980, 1013
Wimbush v Levinski (1949) 981
Wimpey (George) & Co Ltd v Sohn
   (1967) 748, 749
Windsor Hotel (Newquay) Ltd v Allan: 701
Winkworth v Edward Baron Develop-
   ment Co Ltd (1986) . . . 181, 189, 190,
                245, 249, 255, 261,
                262, 277, 278, 279,
                280, 287, 288, 835,
                                850, 859
Winn v Bull (1877) 206
Winnipeg Condominium Corpn No 1
   and Stechley, Re (1979) 75
Wint v Monk (1981) 1018
Winter v Lord Anson (1827) 219
Winter Garden Theatre (London) Ltd v
   Millennium Productions Ltd (1948): 541,
                547, 548, 549, 553
Wirral BC v Smith and Cooper (1982): 485
Wirth v Wirth (1956) . . 244, 262, 263, 265
Wisbech St Mary Parish Council v Lilley
   (1956) 489
Wiscot's Case (1599) 337
Wolfe v Hogan (1949) 975, 1012
Wolff v Vanderzee (1869) 620
Wong v Beaumont Property Trust Ltd
   (1965) 671
Wong (Edward) Finance Co Ltd v John-
   son, Stokes & Master (1984) 206
Wood v Abrey (1818) 225
Wood v Carwardine (1923) 986
Wood v Leadbitter (1845) . . 538, 539, 540,
                                545, 548, 665

PAGE

Wood v Manley (1839) 540, 546
Wood v Nova Scotia (1981) 626
Wood v Wood (1982) 277, 811
Woodall v Clifton (1905) 524
Woodhouse v Walker (1880) 60
Woodhouse and Co Ltd v Kirkland
  (Derby) Ltd (1970) 645, 662
Woods v Donnelly (1982) 540, 546
Woodspring DC v Taylor (1982) . . . 1056
Woodstead Finance Ltd v Petrou
  (1986) 596, 598
Woodstock (A Bankrupt), Re (1979) . . 884
Woodward v Docherty (1974) 987
Woollahra Municipal Council v Local
  Government Appeals Tribunal (1975): 20
Woollerton and Wilson Ltd v Richard
  Costain Ltd (1970) 28
Woolley, Re (1903) 339
Wooton v Wooton (1984) 764, 767
Worth's Application, Re (1984) . . 718, 719
Wratten v Hunter (1978) . . 237, 239, 272
Wright v Bloom (1961) 298
Wright v Dean (1948) 114
Wright v Gibbons (1948-49) . . . 295, 297,
                        321, 322, 323, 326
Wright v Howell (1947) 980
Wright v Macadam (1949) . . . 659, 677
Wright v Stavert (1860) 439, 440
Wright v Wright (1981) 815
Wroth v Tyler (1974) 783, 786, 787,
                        788, 790, 819
Wrotham Park Estate Co Ltd v Parkside
  Homes Ltd (1974) 704, 705, 708,
                        709, 719

PAGE

Wycombe AHA v Barnett (1984) . 481, 919
Wykeham Terrace, Brighton, Sussex, ex
  p Territorial Auxiliary and Volunteer
  Reserve Association for the South East
  (1971) 757
Wyld v Clode (1983) 450, 1001
Wyld v Silver (1963) 644

Y

Yateley Common, Re (1977) 675
Yates v Bridgewater Estates Ltd (1982): 730
Yellowly v Gower (1855) 481
Yewbright Properties Ltd & Stone
  (1980) 1017
Yianni v Edwin Evans & Sons (1982) . 205
Yoland v Reddington (1982) 1018
York Bros (Trading) Pty Ltd v Commr
  of Main Roads (1983) 656
Young v Hichens (1844) 34
Young v McKittrick 311
Young v Van Beneen (1953) 442
Young v Young (1959) 263
Young v Young (1977) 311
Young v Young (1983) . . . 248, 252, 362

Z

Zamet v Hyman (1961) 857
Zanzonico v Zanzonico (1938) 306
Zapletal v Wright (1957) 72, 74, 77
Zaslow v Kroenert (1946) 305
Zeiss Stiftung (Carl) v Herbert Smith &
  Co (No 2) (1969) 281
Zetland (Marquess) v Driver (1939): 703, 708
Zimmerman v Burton (1980) 1069

Abbreviations

Bl Comm	W. Blackstone, *Commentaries on the Laws of England* (1st edn London 1765–1769)
Challis	*Law of Real Property* (3rd edn London 1911)
Co Litt	E. Coke, *The First Part of the Institutes of the Laws of England* or *A Commentary upon Littleton* (11th edn London 1719)
Emmet on Title	18th edn by J.T. Farrand, London 1983
Jiro	Journal of the Institute of Rent Officers
Litt	Littleton's Tenures (ed E. Wambaugh, Washington DC 1903)
Sheppard's Touchstone	W. Sheppard, *The Touchstone of Common Assurances* (London 1651)

THE GENERAL PART

A. Concepts

CHAPTER 1

Property

Property is necessarily a central element in any system of rules which is concerned with the governance of human activity. It is difficult to envisage a society which recognises no concept of property, for this concept is used by almost every social group in order to express certain relationships between individuals and the environment in which they live. Some philosophers have indeed perceived in the institution of property the vital prerequisite of civilised co-existence. David Hume was able to say, for instance, that

No one can doubt that the convention for the distinction of property, and for the stability of possession, is of all circumstances the most necessary to the establishment of human society, and that after the agreement for the fixing and observing of this rule, there remains little or nothing to be done towards settling a perfect harmony and concord.[1]

However, not all would share this view. For some social theorists the initial demarcation of property rights of any kind is a cause of profound regret.[2] For others it is a stimulus to radical change of the social order.[3] It is nevertheless undeniable that the concept of property plays an indispensable role in the organisation of our social and economic life. We can no more contemplate a society without some conception of property than we can imagine a society which has not yet discovered the device of contract. Indeed, it was John Locke who argued that the 'great and chief end...of men's uniting into common-wealths, and putting themselves under government, is the preservation of their property.'[4]

1. THE FUNCTION OF THE LAW OF PROPERTY

The law of property is not particularly concerned with 'things'; it is concerned much more deeply with the relationships which arise between persons in respect of 'things'. The law of property contains a crystallised expression of certain values, obligations and ideologies, all cast in sharp relief against the universe of 'things'. To embark on a study of property law unaware of this broader

---

1 *A Treatise of Human Nature* (Everyman's Library edn, London 1911), Vol II, p 196f (Book III, Part II).

2 'The first man who, having enclosed a piece of ground, bethought himself of saying "This is mine", and found people simple enough to believe him, was the real founder of civil society. From how many crimes, wars, murders, from how many horrors and misfortunes might not anyone have saved mankind, by pulling up the stakes, or filling up the ditch, and crying to his fellows: "Beware of listening to this impostor, you are undone if you once forget that the fruits of the earth belong to us all, and the earth itself to nobody"' (see J.-J. Rousseau, *Discourse on the Origin of Inequality* in *The Social Contract and Discourses* (Everyman's Library edn, London 1913), p 76).

3 This view is epitomised in Proudhon's often quoted remark that 'property is theft'. See *Qu'est-ce que la Propriété? Premier Mémoir* (Paris 1840), p 131.

4 *The Second Treatise of Civil Government* (ed J.W. Gough, Oxford 1946), para 124.

perspective would be to ignore the organic human dimension which makes the concept of property a central legal institution. It would also condemn the student to the misconception that the law of property is an arid and unexciting subject and would rob him of any clear vision of the important interface between property and everyday life. The student must of course begin by mastering the technical structures and concepts of property law. But to confine property law merely to its mechanical aspects is to force the law into an unrealistic moral and social vacuum. It is the wider social and economic dimension which gives the law both substance and direction.

(1) A social view of land law

This book contains an account of the basic elements of the English law of land. However, it also aims to present certain social and critical perspectives on the law of property, for it is in these extended perspectives that the technical rules of property law are most revealingly explained. As Alice Tay once said,[5] the 'concept of property, the way in which it is legally defined and the extent to which it is legally, socially and politically protected raise immediately the most fundamental problems of political philosophy and social life—the relationship between the individual and his social environment, between the citizen and the State and—in modern society—between the personal and the commercial.'

This book therefore sets out to explore some of the broader connotations of 'property' within the context of English land law. It examines the way in which the land lawyer uses and manipulates technical concepts in order to describe the accumulation of wealth and security. It discusses the way in which the underlying ideology of property law interacts with key issues of priority and efficiency. Above all, it depicts 'property' as a relation between individuals, and property law as a body of rules which ultimately governs the distribution of utility in socially valued resources.

(a) Distinctive features of land as a property form

Land law is that part of the general law which regulates the allocation of rights and obligations in relation to 'real' or 'immovable' property.[6] In separating off land as a subject of especial legal concern, English law merely follows the practice of most developed systems of law in regarding land as having enhanced qualities of utility and indestructibility which justify its distinction from other more perishable forms of property.[7] Since land provides the physical substratum for all social and economic interaction, the law of land is inevitably an expression of social status and an instrument of social engineering. All of us—even the truly homeless—live somewhere, and each therefore stands in some relation to land as owner-occupier, tenant, licensee or squatter. In this way land law impinges upon a vast area of social orderings and expectations, exerting a fundamental

5 'Property and Law in the Society of Mass Production, Mass Consumption and Mass Allocation', p 19, in *A Revolution in our Age: The Transformation of Law, Justice and Morals* (Canberra Seminars in the History of Ideas 1975).

6 The term 'real property' or 'realty' is often used in relation to rights in land precisely because early law gave the dispossessed landowner not a mere right of money compensation in respect of his loss, but a right instead to recover his land by 'real action', ie a right to require that the land be returned physically into his possession.

7 See *National Carriers Ltd v Panalpina (Northern) Ltd* [1981] AC 675 at 691A-B per Lord Hailsham of St Marylebone, 700B-E per Lord Russell of Killowen.

influence on the lifestyles of ordinary people. Quite apart from the residential dimension, when it is borne in mind that land has an enormous economic significance in terms of investment, business and agriculture, the importance of land as a property form becomes almost incalculable.

(b) Political dimension of property

It was Karl Renner who recognised that the institution of property leads automatically to an organisation similar to that of the state: 'Power over matter begets personal power'.[8] It follows from this view that property is ultimately a political relationship between persons. It is undeniable, moreover, that the law of property incorporates a series of critical value judgments. These value judgments reflect the body of cultural norms, the social ethics and the political economy prevalent in any given community. It is inevitable that property law should in this way serve as a vehicle for ideology, for 'property' has commonly been the epithet used to identify that which people most greatly value.

(2) Property, dependence and personality

Not only does 'property' identify resources of value. The label 'property' commonly points more subtly to relationships of dependence, in that dependence is the inescapable outcome of an unequal distribution of that which is valued. The terms 'property' and 'dependence' are thus positive and negative ways respectively of describing existing distributions of socially valued resources. It is clear, for instance, that an obvious kind of 'dependence' affects the status of the infant or minor and, significantly, English law declares that a legal estate in land cannot be owned by any person below the age of 18 years.[9] Starting from the premise of the infant's physical and mental immaturity, a technical legal rule has evolved which in turn confirms and reinforces a more general cultural image of the child's incompleteness as a legal and social personality. More pernicious is the way in which for centuries a similar process of reasoning resulted in the imposition of legal and social disadvantage on married women.[10] Only relatively recently has the law moved on from the position described by Blackstone, according to whom 'the very being or legal existence of the woman is suspended during the marriage'.[11]

---

8 *The Institutions of Private Law and Their Social Functions* (ed O. Kahn-Freund, London and Boston 1949), p 107.

9 Law of Property Act 1925, s 1(6) (post, p 71). The age of majority was lowered to 18 by Family Law Reform Act 1969, s 1(1).

10 Starting from a similar premise—the temporary physiological and economic incapacity imposed by motherhood—the law effectively denied the married woman sufficient legal personality to hold property in her own name. Almost all her property vested in her husband on marriage. Only with the enactment of the Married Women's Property Acts of 1870 and 1882 did the married woman regain the capacity to own property in her own right, and full recognition of her legal personality did not come until the passing of the Law Reform (Married Women and Tortfeasors) Act 1935. See generally Lee Holcombe, *Wives and Property* (Oxford 1983).

11 *Bl Comm*, Vol I, p 430. Blackstone was of course able to argue that the merger of the wife's personality with that of her husband was a most benevolent form of indulgence. '[W]e may observe that even the disabilities which the wife lies under are for the most part intended for her protection and benefit. So great a favourite is the female sex of the laws of England.' For a more sanguine account of the emancipation of the married woman, see O. Kahn-Freund, (1970) 33 MLR 601, (1971) 4 Human Rights Journal 493.

The abrogation or diminution of legal personality in terms of property law is usually made the more unacceptable by the pervasive association between a person's material substance and his or her sense of integrity as an individual.[12] The concept of property is inherently linked with some notion of an area of personal inviolability which is rooted deeply in the common law. This idea reflects itself in the origins of the action of trespass (both to person and to land) as the earliest and most important action at common law, and derives in turn from an even older Anglo-Saxon and Norse concept of 'seisin' which some claim lies behind the development of the specifically European ideal of social democracy.[13] In the analysis of Professor Tay,

Property is that which a man has a right to use and enjoy without interference; it is what makes him as a person and guarantees his independence and security. It includes his person, his name, his reputation, his chattels, the land that he owns and works, the house he builds and lives in and so on. These things are seen as his property in early law because they are seen as the reification of his will, as the tangible, physical manifestation of his work and his personality.[113]

2. THE MEANING OF PROPERTY

It is important at the outset to dispel one common lay notion concerning 'property'. Non-lawyers (and sometimes even lawyers) speak loosely of property as the *thing* which is owned. While this usage is harmless enough in day-to-day speech, it has the effect of obscuring certain salient features of property as a legal phenomenon, for semantically 'property' is the condition of being 'proper' to (or belonging to) a particular person.[15]

(1) Property is not a 'thing' but a 'relationship'

It was the philosopher, Jeremy Bentham, who had to remind lawyers that property is not a thing but a relationship. Bentham pointed out that 'in common speech in the phrase *the object of a man's property*, the words *the object of* are commonly left out; and by an ellipsis, which, violent as it is, is now become more

---

12 This association is, of course, a commonplace in literature. See, for instance, John Galsworthy, *The Forsyte Saga, Vol 1: The Man Of Property* (London 1906), p 44f: 'In his great chair with the book-rest sat old Jolyon, the figurehead of his family and class and creed, with his white head and dome-like forehead, the representative of moderation, and order, and love of property.' See also M.J. Radin, *Property and Personhood*, 34 Stanford LR 957 (1981-82); G. Trasler, 'The Psychology of Ownership and Possession', in P. Hollowell (ed), *Property and Social Relations* (London 1982), p 32.

13 It was Charles Reich who said that 'the institution called property guards the troubled boundary between individual man and the state. It is not the only guardian; many other institutions, laws, and practices serve as well. But in a society that chiefly values material well-being, the power to control a particular portion of that well-being is the very foundation of individuality' (*The New Property*, 73 Yale LJ 733 (1964)).

14 'Law, the citizen and the state', in E. Kamenka, R. Brown and A.E.-S. Tay (ed), *Law and Society* (London 1978), p 10. See also Alice Tay's interesting account of the significance of the concept of 'seisin' in 'Property and Law in the Society of Mass Production, Mass Consumption and Mass Allocation' (supra, note 5), p 7ff.

15 'The condition of being owned by or belonging to some person or persons' (*Oxford English Dictionary*, Vol. VIII, p 1471). The sense conveyed here is similar to that in which reference to a 'proper thing' meant, in archaic usage, 'one's own thing'. The *Oxford English Dictionary* gives the instance, under the heading 'proper', of Tindale who wrote in 1538 that 'Some call themselues poore, wythout hauyng ony thynge proper'. Similarly, an even earlier reference (dating from 1400) records that 'With his own propre Swerd he was slayn.'

familiar than the phrase at length, they have made that part of it which consists of the words *a man's property* perform the office of the whole.'[16] More recently Professor Macpherson has drawn attention to the way in which, in the transition from the pre-capitalist world to the world of the exchange economy, the distinction between a right to a thing (ie the legal relation) and the thing itself, became blurred. 'The thing itself became, in common parlance, the property'.[17]

(a) Potential multiplicity of competing users

At one level of analysis, then, 'property' is a relation between the owner and the thing (ie between a 'subject' and an 'object'). However, as has already been suggested, it is unreal to think simply in terms of 'the' owner of any particular thing. It is possible for conflicting claims to be brought by two or more 'subjects' in respect of the same 'object', and therefore the property lawyer is almost always concerned with the relative merits of different claims. In order to establish what belongs to, or is 'proper' to, any particular 'subject', he must first analyse the legal relations between a number of competing subjects vis à vis the same object. A further level of complexity arises because any particular 'object' of property may itself be capable of sustaining a wide variety of different (but not necessarily conflicting) claims. This is demonstrated most clearly in the case of land. Land may, for instance, be the object of a multiplicity of claims made simultaneously by an owner-occupier, a tenant, a building society, a neighbour who enjoys a right of way or restrictive covenant, or even by a spouse who has certain rights not to be evicted from the property.

(b) A network of 'property' relationships

In the ultimate analysis the law of property is concerned with entire networks of legal relationship existing between individuals in respect of things. 'Property' is thus the name given to the bundles of mutual rights and obligations which prevail between 'subjects' in respect of certain 'objects', and the study of property law accordingly becomes an inquiry into a variety of socially defined relationships and morally conditioned obligations. This relational view highlights certain characteristics of property which are essential to any real understanding of land law.

Professor Bruce Ackerman has spoken of the need to disabuse law students of their primitive lay notions regarding ownership.[18] In the words of Ackerman, 'only the ignorant think it meaningful to talk about owning things free and clear of further obligation.' Instead of defining the relationship between a person and 'his' things, property law considers the 'way rights to use things may be parcelled

---

16 *An Introduction to the Principles of Morals and Legislation* (ed by W. Harrison, Oxford 1948), p 337, note 1 (Chapter XVI, section 26).

17 'Capitalism and the Changing Concept of Property' in E. Kamenka and R.S. Neale (ed), *Feudalism, Capitalism and Beyond* (Canberra 1975), p 111. See also C.R. Noyes, *The Institution of Property* (New York and Toronto 1936), p 357 ('The term "property" may be defined to be the interest which can be acquired in external objects or things. The things themselves are not, in a true sense, property, but they constitute its foundation and material, and the idea of property springs out of the connection, or control, or interest which, according to law, may be acquired in them, or over them').

18 *Private Property and the Constitution* (New Haven and London 1977), p 26f.

out amongst a host of competing resource users'. Ackerman points out that each resource user is conceived as holding 'a bundle of rights vis à vis other potential users' and that the ways in which user rights may be legally packaged and distributed are 'wondrously diverse.' Ackerman concludes that

it is probably never true that the law assigns to any single person the right to use any thing in absolutely *any* way he pleases. Hence, it risks serious confusion to identify any single individual as *the* owner of any particular thing. At best, this locution may sometimes serve as identifying the holder of that bundle of rights which contains a range of entitlements more numerous or more valuable than the bundle held by any other person with respect to the thing in question. Yet, like all shorthands, talk about 'the' property owner invites the fallacy of misplaced concreteness, of reification. Once one begins to think sloppily, it is all too easy to start thinking that 'the' property owner, by virtue of being 'the' property owner, must *necessarily* own a particular bundle of rights over a thing. And this is to commit the error that separates layman from lawyer. For the fact (or is it the law?) of the matter is that property is not a thing, but a set of legal relations between persons governing the use of things.

(2) Property is a dynamic relationship

If property is a relationship, it is a dynamic relationship; the content of the relationship is liable to change. The 'subjects' of property may differ from one social era to another. The 'objects' of property are likewise liable to fluctuate with the passage of time and the emergence of new economic conditions. Above all, the ideology of property is profoundly influenced by changing factors of social, political and economic philosophy.

(a) The changing 'subjects' of property

An element of social control is exercised over the property relation in every society, in that each social group to a greater or lesser extent determines for itself the categories of person who may be recognised as the potential 'subjects' of property. In some societies of the past various classes of labourer or serf (eg slaves) were excluded from legal competence as potential 'subjects' of property. Even until relatively recently in England, the married woman was deprived of capacity to hold a legal title in her own name.[19] However, the present century has seen the 'emergence of a property-owning, particularly a real-property-mortgaged-to-a-building-society-owning, democracy.'[20] The years of greater affluence following the World Wars brought about, in the words of Lord Wilberforce,[1] 'the extension, beyond the paterfamilias, of rights of ownership, itself following from the diffusion of property and earning capacity.' Less obviously this diffusion of ownership rights has accentuated the demand that other kinds of right should be recognised as 'proprietary' rights on behalf of less advantaged social groups.[2] Those, for instance, who are not owners of the homes in which they live may wish to assert that their occupation rights (eg as tenants) represent a proprietary status equivalent to that of the owner-occupier.

---

19 Ante, p 7.
20 *Pettitt v Pettitt* [1970] AC 777 at 824B-C per Lord Diplock.
1   *Williams & Glyn's Bank Ltd v Boland* [1981] AC 487 at 508G.
2   Post, p 966.

(b) The changing 'objects' of property

If the 'objects' of property are those resources to which social or economic value is generally attached, it is inevitable that over time variations of social interest and concern should alter the emphasis of the property relationship. There was, for instance, an age in which both wives and slaves were regarded as appropriate 'objects' of property. In medieval England the husband was viewed as enjoying proprietary rights in relation to his wife, her domestic services and her productive capacity.[3] Much of the concern which generated this assessment of the spousal relationship was itself brought about by the supposed paramountcy of the need to ensure the devolution of property within a dynastic line of legitimate issue. However, the 'objects' of property are continually redefined by the prevalent social ethic, and today it is no longer acceptable that either wives or certain classes of labourer should be regarded as the 'objects' of a proprietary relation.

(i) *Transformation of material wealth*   The 'objects' of property can, however, change in more subtle degrees. For centuries the most highly prized 'object' of property in the common law world was land. In the 19th century and early 20th century the phenomenon of the company share came close to dislodging land as the pre-eminent 'object' of commercial value, at a time when the bulk of ordinary men and women owned little of value other than perhaps the clothes which they wore. In the modern post-industrial society, however, with the diffusion of ownership amongst classes never before entitled, the traditional concept of a man's wealth has undergone yet another transformation. Nowadays a person's material substance is no longer related particularly to the ownership of tangible assets designed for enjoyment and consumption; it is more readily expressed in terms of intangible, non-assignable, and often non-survivable, claims of a largely personal nature. The things which today are of real value to the man in the street are assets like his job, his pension, and the right to undisturbed possession of his home.[4] On the fringes of these new categories of property lie certain less well defined rights such as the right to education, the right to health and the right to a wholesome environment.[5]

(ii) *The 'new property'*   The changing concept of wealth in the modern world was classically described by Professor Charles Reich in a seminal law review article in 1964.[6] Reich drew attention to the dramatic changes taking place in the nature and forms of wealth in industrial democratic societies. In particular, he pointed to the way in which government has begun to operate today as a major distributor of wealth in the form of welfare payments, salaries for those in public service, pensions for those who have retired from employment, and many other forms of licence, franchise, subsidy and fiscal benefit. As Reich indicated, 'today's distribution of largesse is on a vast, imperial scale.' Reich went on to argue that the principal forms of wealth for most people in our society are

3 See Kevin Gray, *Reallocation of Property on Divorce* (Abingdon 1977), p 280ff.
4 See N.E. Simmonds, *The changing face of private law: doctrinal categories and the regulatory state*, (1982) 2 Legal Studies 257 at 267. See also P. Hollowell, 'Career: The Claim to Job Property', in P. Hollowell (ed), *Property and Social Relations* (London 1982), p 183.
5 See eg J.E. Cribbet, *Concepts in Transition: The Search for a New Definition of Property*, (1986) U of Illinois LR 1 at 24ff; R.P. Malloy, *Equating Human Rights and Property Rights*, 47 Ohio State LJ 163 (1986).
6 *The New Property*, 73 Yale LJ 733 (1964).

comprised in their employment or profession (and in various work-related benefits such as pensions) or in their dependency claims upon government (in the guise of social security payments).[7] These forms of wealth, which for Reich were concerned essentially with income security, have become in fact the 'new property', and Reich's major thesis was that this 'new property' should be accorded the same standard of legal protection as had been accorded in the past to more traditional entitlements of private property. In his view, the goal of future development in this area must be to 'try to build an economic basis for liberty today — a Homestead Act for rootless twentieth century man. We must create a new property.'[8]

The call for legal recognition of and protection for the 'new property' has intensified during the two decades since the publication of Reich's major article. In 1970, in its fundamentally significant decision in *Goldberg v Kelly*,[9] the Supreme Court of the United States acknowledged the 'new property' to be deserving of constitutional protection. In the years following this decision, the prominence of the 'new property' has been accentuated by developments in other fields of law.

(iii)   The changing balance of family, work and government   The emergence of the 'new property' can also be placed in the historical context of a more general shift in the relative importance of family, work and government as determinants of social status and as sources of economic security. Today, in an age of liberal divorce and increasingly attenuated family ties, the primary source of economic security for the individual is no longer the family but rather the individual's employment or his dependency relationship with government.

Professor Mary Ann Glendon has pointed to an interesting correlation between developments in the areas of family law and employment law during the past century.[10] Whereas a hundred years ago marriage and family life were subject to onerous legal regulation (particularly with respect to the legal termination of the marriage relationship), the employment relationship was dominated by the relatively unrestrained power of the master to engage and dismiss his servants. Since then legal developments in these cognate fields have led today to an almost total reversal of the respective conceptual starting-points of the law of work and family. While marriage is nowadays terminable more or less at will, the employment relationship is not normally terminable by the employer save on exceptionally clear and convincing grounds. As Glendon notes, the 'relationships that, unlike marriage and contract, are relatively hard to enter and leave today are the preferred sorts of new property — good jobs with good fringe benefits.'[11] These changes in the legal bonding of the individual, his family and his work have inevitably accorded a heightened significance to the 'new property' rights and 'security claims' which nowadays underpin the tripartite relationship between the individual, his employer and the government.

7 See S.F. Williams, *Liberty and Property: The Problem of Government Benefits*, 12 J of Legal Studies 3 (1983).
8 73 Yale LJ 733 at 787 (1964).
9 397 US 254 at 260ff, 25 L Ed 2d 287 at 295ff (1970).
10 See M.A. Glendon, *The New Family and the New Property*, 53 Tulane LR 697 (1979).
11 53 Tulane LR 697 at 708 (1979). See also M.A. Glendon and E.R. Lev, *Changes in the Bonding of the Employment Relationship: An Essay on the New Property*, 20 Boston College LR 457 (1979).

(iv) Residential security The jurisprudence of the 'new property' has emerged largely in the context of the individual's rights in the fields of employment and social security. However, an object which lies more immediately within the ambit of a 'Homestead Act for rootless twentieth century man' is the general provision of security in the enjoyment of residential accommodation.

The contemporary emphasis upon residential security is intensified by the peculiar forms of insecurity which result from economic recession, housing shortage and family breakdown. There is nowadays a very real sense in which the right to live in a house or flat free from the threat of arbitrary eviction, perhaps insulated from the full impact of market forces, has itself become a new form of proprietary right. It may not matter much whether the residential occupier has a legal title to the property which he occupies. His position is secure so long as the courts are prepared to recognise that he enjoys a 'status of irremovability'. Protected de facto possession of residential property has effectively become an informal version of title, entitlement to the 'use value' of property often being more important than entitlement to the 'exchange value' on the freehold market. Although residential property of course still has an important investment potential—a feature heightened in England by recent extensions of the tenant's 'right to buy'[12]—the significance of the 'use value', entirely divorced from title, should never be underestimated.

This book discusses many of the ways in which English land law has come to recognise claims to residential protection. There is—at least in theory—a general acceptance that residential security and decent housing provide essential preconditions for a life of reasonable dignity and purpose. The recognition that the residential occupier may have a certain 'status of irremovability' emerged first in the context of the law of landlord and tenant. However, a notion equivalent to 'security of tenure' has also emerged in other areas of land law where, particularly in the family context, extended forms of residential protection have been confirmed by law. Slowly but surely the law is moving towards a realisation of the idea that residential security is itself an integral component of the 'new property', and that the increased protection of housing rights may contribute significantly to a wider social distribution of the 'goods of life'. It is never easy, of course, to classify 'new property' claims in conventional property terms, but it may well be that the concept of property itself is currently undergoing a process of reformulation and redefinition.

(c) The contemporary redefinition of 'property'

During the present century claims of social welfare have been increasingly recognised through interventionist legislation in the fields of social security, housing and employment protection. By according legal force to various kinds of 'security claim', this legislation has already gone some distance towards ensuring a more equitable distribution of the 'goods of life'. The security claims recognised in these areas broadly cover the kinds of interest which are comprised within the 'new property'. Thus the claim to security in employment is recognised, at least to some extent, by legislation which protects the individual employee from 'unfair dismissal'; the claim to residential security, by the Rent and Housing Acts and other statutory means; the claim to income security, by the vast range of legislation which underpins the social security system. Inherent

12 See Chapter 19 (post, p 725).

in all these measures is a significant return to the idea of a 'status'. The individual receives the benefits of protective legislation, not because he has in any sense contracted or bargained to received them, but because he enjoys a defined 'status' which entitles him to some appropriate form of 'security'.[13]

All these developments tend to suggest that, by operating effectively as an agent of distributive justice, the 'new property' has initiated a redefinition of the ideology of property. In the conventional analysis, the concept of property is essentially negative and exclusory: the traditional concept of a property right comprises the right to exclude all others from the use or enjoyment of some thing.[14] The 'new property' comprises by contrast various kinds of claim *not* to be excluded from the use or enjoyment of some thing. Indeed it has been said that the idea of property is gradually being broadened to include a 'right to a kind of society or set of power relations which will enable the individual to live a fully human life.'[15] At least in some incipient form, this perspective may indicate an intellectual shift away from the idea that property is a private right to exclude from personally owned resources, and may point instead towards a reappraisal of property as a public right of access to socially valued resources.

It is this continual reshaping of the property concept which makes the law of property exciting and ensures a fertile response to constantly changing human needs and aspirations. This process is not new. Lawyers over the centuries have adapted the subjects and objects of property in order to meet altered social circumstances. For the equity lawyer, indelibly marked by his training in a jurisdiction of conscience, the ultimate value was the faithful discharge of moral obligation. Accordingly, with the development of the trust,[16] the medieval Chancellors of England converted the benefit of a moral obligation into a recognisable proprietary right. For the modern lawyer concerned with the 'new property', the paramount interest is the achievement of 'social justice' in a much more secular context. In a not dissimilar way, the law of the 'new property' acknowledges variant forms of a 'status of irremovability', thereby converting the benefit of a social obligation into a recognisable quasi-proprietary interest.

It may even be that the property law of the future will incorporate some new version of the trust device. It was the outstanding contribution of the old equity lawyers that they were able to fasten a trust upon the conscience of the legal owner of private property in order to give effect to the moral obligations owed to the cestui que trust.[17] In just the same way the 'new property' of the modern era may be seen as fastening a public trust upon the 'social property' comprised in the 'goods of life'. The recognition of such a trust makes the individual citizen a beneficiary of certain socialised obligations, thereby enabling him to enjoy a more equitable distribution of critically important welfare resources.

13 See *Johnson v Moreton* [1980] AC 37 at 67B per Lord Simon of Glaisdale.
14 See C.B. Macpherson, in E. Kamenka and R.S. Neale (ed), op cit, p 116ff.
15 Ibid, p 120. There are perfectly good historical antecedents for the claims presented by the 'new property', and indeed for the view that these claims may be the 'object' of 'property'. One need look no further than the 17th century to find political philosophers who entertained a similarly broad concept of property. In speaking unrestrainedly of 'things held in propriety', Thomas Hobbes observed that 'those that are dearest to a man are his own life, and limbs; and in the next degree, in most men, those that concern conjugal affection; and after them, riches and means of living' (*Leviathan* (Collins/Fontana edn, London 1978), p 300). The same latitude was demonstrated by John Locke, who propounded the idea that 'property' comprises a man's 'life, liberty and estate' and includes 'that property which men have in their persons as well as their goods' (*The Second Treatise of Civil Government* (ed by J.W. Gough, Oxford 1946), paras 87, 173).
16 Post, p 39.
17 Post, p 41.

Underlying the jurisprudence of the 'new property' is ultimately the theory that various forms of social and economic advantage are held in trust by nominees (eg by landlords, employers, investment institutions, fiscal authorities and so on). Under the regime of 'new property' it can be argued that a 'social trust' is imposed upon such nominee-owners by the conferment of status- related rights of enjoyment vested in deserving beneficiaries.[18] In this way the 'new property' can be made to give effect to a socialised version of the modern remedial constructive trust.[19]

18 For an interesting discussion of the general concepts of stewardship and public trust, see R.F. Babcock and D.A. Feurer, *Land as a Commodity 'affected with a Public Interest'*, 52 Wash LR 289 (1976-77); V.J. Yannacone, *Property and Stewardship—Private Property plus Social Interest equals Social Property*, 23 S Dak LR 71 (1978).
19 Post, p 811.

CHAPTER 2

Land

The great lawyers of a previous age were supremely conscious of the significance of land in human affairs. They were aware of the paradox of the integrity of man and his utter dependence upon his physical environment; of land as dignified by the habitation of man, yet alone providing the means for his survival; of land as a base for human striving and as an inspiration towards fleeting comprehension of something more.[1] The contemporary legal definition of 'land'—albeit broad in some respects—is but a pale shadow of these elevated perceptions.

1. THE LEGAL DEFINITION OF 'LAND'

For the modern property lawyer the word 'land' bears an extended meaning. According to section 205(1)(ix) of the Law of Property Act 1925, 'land' includes

land of any tenure, and mines and minerals, whether or not held apart from the surface, buildings or part of buildings (whether the division is horizontal, vertical or made in any other way) and other corporeal hereditaments; also a manor, an advowson, and a rent and other incorporeal hereditaments, and an easement, right, privilege, or benefit in, over, or derived from land.

As Blackstone said,[2] 'land' is 'a word of a very extensive signification'. For the purpose of the Law of Property Act 1925, it includes both 'corporeal hereditaments' and 'incorporeal hereditaments'. In broad terms 'corporeal hereditaments' refer to the physical and tangible characteristics of land, while 'incorporeal hereditaments' refer to certain intangible rights which may be enjoyed over or in respect of land.

2. CORPOREAL HEREDITAMENTS

Corporeal hereditaments comprise those 'substantial and permanent objects' which 'affect the senses',[3] the only objects which are truly 'permanent' being those constituted by or connected with immovable property. In the extended sense in which the term is used in English law, 'corporeal hereditaments' include not merely the physical clods of earth which make up the surface layer of land, but also all physical things which are attached to or are inherent in the ground. Thus the term 'corporeal hereditaments' comprehends such things as buildings, trees and subjacent minerals.[4]

(1) Cuius est solum eius est usque ad coelum et ad inferos

The extended significance of the term 'land' is sometimes more eloquently than accurately expressed in the Latin maxim, *cuius est solum eius est usque ad coelum et ad*

1 See, eg *Co Litt*, p 4a.
2 *Bl Comm*, Vol II, p 16.
3 *Bl Comm*, Vol II, p 17.
4 *Mitchell v Mosley* [1914] 1 Ch 438 at 450 (post, p 26).

inferos: he who owns the land owns everything reaching up to the very heavens and down to the depths of the earth. Whether accurate or not, this maxim articulates a notion of the sacrosanct nature of property rights in the common law,[5] and has tended to be invoked wherever necessary for the purpose of investing the landowner with all the rights required for reasonable enjoyment of his property.

Curiously enough, the maxim *cuius est solum...* cannot be traced back to Roman law,[6] and seems to be a brocard of medieval origin.[7] It contains a certain measure of truth as far as English law is concerned, for there is doubtless a general sense in which common lawyers have conceptualised 'land' as having an infinitely extended three-dimensional quality. However, the original Latin maxim is now subject to so many qualifications that it is virtually worthless as a statement of contemporary law.[8] In no sense can it be understood to mean that 'land' in English law comprehends the whole of the space from the centre of the earth to the heavens, not least since 'so sweeping, unscientific and unpractical a doctrine is unlikely to appeal to the common law mind.'[9] At most the maxim serves nowadays only as an approximate statement of the prima facie extent of the rights pertaining to owners of land[10] and of the extent of that ownership which is transferred by conveyance.[11]

(2) Buildings and other constructions

Another Latin maxim frequently invoked in the present context is the general

---

5 See eg *Lewvest Ltd v Scotia Towers Ltd* (1982) 126 DLR (3d) 239 at 240.
6 See Lord McNair, *The Law of the Air* (3rd edn, London 1964), p 393; J.C. Cooper, *Roman Law and the Maxim 'Cuius est Solum' in International Air Law*, (1952) 1 McGill LJ 23 at 26ff. It is unlikely that the maxim contains any residual trace of a belief in a flat earth. Contrary to popular conception, the medievals were not 'flat-earthers' (see C.S. Lewis, *The Discarded Image* (Cambridge 1964), p 142), but had fully adopted the traditional Aristotelian cosmology. The last educated man to espouse a flat earth theory seems to have been the sixth century Cosmas Indicopleustes, who believed the earth to be a flat parallelogram (see W.E.H. Lecky, *The Rise and Influence of Rationalism in Europe* (2nd edn London 1882), Vol I, p 269).
7 Its first recognised appearance seems to be in the 13th Century *Glossa Ordinaria* on the *Corpus Iuris* (*Digest*, VIII.2.1) by Accursius of Bologna (see H. Guibé, *Essai sur la navigation aérienne en droit interne et en droit international* (Paris 1912), p 35ff). It has been suggested that the maxim may have derived from even earlier Jewish origins (see (1931) 47 LQR 14; *Deuteronomy*, xxx: 11-14, *Isaiah*, vii: 11), but see D.E. Smith, *The Origins of Trespass to Airspace and the Maxim 'Cujus est solum ejus est usque ad coelum'*, (1982) 6 Trent Law Journal 33 at 38. For the earliest English reference, see the terminal note in *Bury v Pope* (1586) Cro Eliz 118, 78 ER 375, where the maxim is said to have been known from the time of Edward I (1239-1307). (It has been pointed out that Franciscus, the son of Accursius, appears to have travelled to England in 1274 at the invitation of Edward I (see McNair, *op cit*, p 397)). The maxim was later incorporated in *Co Litt*, p 4a; *Bl Comm*, Vol II, p 18.
8 In *Bernstein of Leigh (Baron) v Skyviews & General Ltd* [1978] QB 479 at 485C, Griffiths J dismissed the maxim as merely 'a colourful phrase'. The formula has been said to be 'imprecise' and 'mainly serviceable as dispensing with analysis' (*Commissioner for Railways et al v Valuer-General* [1974] AC 328 at 351G), and to have 'no place in the modern world' (*United States v Causby*, 328 US 256 at 261, 90 L.ed 1206 at 1210 (1946)). See also *Re The Queen in Right of Manitoba and Air Canada* (1978) 86 DLR (3d) 631 at 635, 637.
9 *Commissioner for Railways et al v Valuer-General* [1974] AC 328 at 351H-352A per Lord Wilberforce.
10 See eg *Pountney v Clayton* (1883) 11 QBD 820 at 838 per Bowen LJ.
11 See eg *National Carriers Ltd v Panalpina (Northern) Ltd* [1981] AC 675 at 708C, where Lord Russell of Killowen noted that a grant of a freehold estate in fee simple passes the land 'as to its surface and below its surface, and the airspace above, subject to exclusions'.

rule *superficies solo cedit* (a building becomes part of the ground).[12] Thus buildings constructed on foundations placed in the soil become themselves part of the 'land'.[13] Even the top floor of a high-rise block of flats comprises 'land'. A garage or garden shed or wall[14] likewise qualifies as 'land', provided that in each case it is firmly attached to the ground.

The rule *superficies solo cedit* is confirmed in section 62(1) of the Law of Property Act 1925, which provides that any conveyance of land is deemed to include by implication all buildings, erections, and fixtures attached to the land. Likewise, section 62(2) provides that any conveyance of land with houses or other buildings on it is deemed to include by implication 'all outhouses, erections, fixtures, cellars, areas, courts, courtyards, cisterns, sewers, gutters, drains, ways, passages, lights, [and] watercourses' appertaining to the land.[15]

(3) Strata titles

Section 205(1)(ix) of the Law of Property Act 1925 establishes beyond doubt that 'land' is capable of horizontal as well as vertical division, and that a land title can therefore relate to a slice of defined area or cubic space which is not grounded on the surface layer of the earth. A modern example of such an area is an upper-storey flat.

That there can be a horizontal stratification of rights in land is not a new idea. The possibility of horizontal division of land follows almost necessarily from the maxim *cuius est solum eius est usque ad coelum et ad inferos*. However attenuated the force of this maxim today, it is recognised that the landowner is at least to some limited extent competent to convey away separate estates in horizontal strata of his 'land'.[16] These strata may be subterranean. It is quite feasible, for instance, that one person should own the freehold estate in the surface layer of the ground while another person owns the freehold in a subjacent cavern,[17] or layer of minerals,[18] or underground cellar.[19]

(a) The 'flying freehold'

More controversial is the idea that separate freehold titles can be created above ground level. However, the idea is by no means novel. Coke allowed that 'a man may have an inheritance in an upper chamber though the lower buildings and soil be in another, and seeing it is an inheritance corporeal it shall pass by

---

12 This rule originates in Roman law (*Gaius*, 2.73; *Inst.* 2.1.29). See also S.S. Ball, *The Jural Nature of Land*, (1928-29) 23 Illinois LR 45 at 48.

13 *Mitchell v Mosley* [1914] 1 Ch 438 at 450.

14 *Moody v Steggles* (1879) 12 Ch D 261 at 267.

15 Post, p 674. Section 62 can be excluded by contrary intention expressed in the conveyance (see section 62(4)).

16 The strata need not even be horizontal. There is in principle nothing impossible about the conveyance of an estate in a sloping subterranean area (eg a cave or mineral bed) or in a sloping 'flying freehold' (eg an enclosed walkway across a street between different levels of adjacent buildings).

17 *Cox v Colossal Cavern Co*, 276 SW 540 at 542f (1925).

18 *Williams v Usherwood* (1981) 45 P & CR 235 at 253.

19 The possibility that there can, in this sense, be such a thing as a 'subterranean flying freehold' was conceded in *Grigsby v Melville* [1974] 1 WLR 80 at 83D-E. See also *Metropolitan Railway Co v Fowler* [1893] AC 416 at 420, 422.

livery.'[20] Although the horizontal stratification of estates in land has more often been achieved through the creation of leasehold rather than freehold estates, there seems to be nothing wrong in principle with the idea that a landowner may carve out of his own estate a 'flying freehold' which is not contiguous with ground level.[1] Although somewhat unusual in England, such titles do exist in certain parts of London, most notably in parts of Lincoln's Inn.

The principal objection to the 'flying freehold' is not conceptual but practical.[2] Planning considerations apart,[3] a freeholder has an inherent right to destroy his property or allow it to fall into disrepair. Thus a flying freehold is extremely vulnerable to the possibility that a subjacent freeholder may damage or prejudice the subjacent structure on which the 'flying freehold' physically rests. Of course the answer to this dilemma lies in fastening upon the subjacent owner the required positive duties of physical support and repair in relation to superior freeholders. This solution is, however, fraught with further difficulty since, in the current state of English law,[4] it is impossible to cause the burden of such positive covenants to run with the land so as to affect successors in title. The Law Commission has proposed that the law of covenants should be amended to make the burden of positive covenants transmissible as between freeholders,[5] and it seems likely that this change will occur in the fairly near future.

(b) The Australian model

Such a change in the law will almost certainly be accompanied by a movement towards increased use of the freehold estate in the conveyancing of flats.[6] This development would merely mirror the concept of 'strata titles' which was successfully pioneered in New South Wales in 1961[7] and which is now widespread in Australia.[8] Strata titles legislation of the Australian model has proved to be extremely flexible, even to the extent that it is possible to convey lots within a 'strata plan' which comprise cubic spaces of thin air,[9] or which include

20 *Co Litt*, p 48b. Challis adds that it seems 'clear on principle that if the house is burnt down or otherwise destroyed, the rights of the owner of the upper chamber cease, but the point does not appear to have been decided' (see *Challis*, p 54). The Law Commission expressed a contrary view on this point in 1984, observing that conveyances of freehold flats are drafted on the assumption that the freehold estate conferred is capable of lasting beyond the life of the building itself, ie is capable of surviving the destruction of the building. The Law Commission noted the preponderant view that 'an estate can exist in what has become mere airspace' (Law Commission, *Transfer of Land: The Law of Positive and Restrictive Covenants* (Law Com No 127, 26 January 1984), para 4.6). Moreover, it is generally assumed that the leasehold estate granted to a tenant does not end automatically with the destruction of a flat.

1 See S.M. Tolson, *'Land' without earth: Freehold Flats in English Law*, (1950) 14 Conv (NS) 350.
2 See *Bursill Enterprises Pty Ltd v Berger Bros Trading Co Pty Ltd* (1970-1971) 124 CLR 73 at 92 per Windeyer J.
3 Post, p 720.
4 Law Com No 127, para 4.6.
5 Post, p 721.
6 The Building Societies Association has advocated a switch from leasehold to freehold conveyancing of flats (see (1984) 128 SJ 538), a proposal which may be given added force by the recently exposed vulnerability of the mortgagee of leasehold titles (see *Abbey National Building Society v Maybeech Ltd* [1985] Ch 190, post, p 508).
7 See Conveyancing (Strata) Titles Act 1961 (NSW), now replaced by Strata Titles Act 1973.
8 See R. Sackville and M.A. Neave, *Property Law: Cases and Materials* (3rd edn 1981), p 358; [1986] Conv 222.
9 See Strata Titles Act 1973 (NSW), s 8(1)(f)(iii), resolving the point left open in *Rochester Investments Pty Ltd v Couchman* (1969) 90 WN (NSW) (Pt 1) 371 at 376G. See also *Burgchard v Holroyd Municipal Council* [1984] 2 NSWLR 164 at 169F.

not merely a dwelling but also a share of a communal garage, shed and swimming pool.[10]

(c) The 'commonhold' estate

In view of the steady disenchantment with the leasehold estate as the legal medium of flat ownership, it also seems likely that English law will eventually move towards the introduction of a new 'commonhold' estate in land. The Law Commission is currently investigating the possible adoption of a modified form of strata title or 'condominium title'[11] as the most appropriate form of ownership in respect of multi-occupied residential units which involve aspects of both private and communal user.[12]

If introduced, the new 'commonhold' estate in land will take its place beside the two historic estates known to English law, the freehold and the leasehold. In terms of the commonhold scheme the commonholder would have rights of individual ownership (similar to those of a freeholder) in respect of his own flat, while enjoying certain rights of co-ownership by way of membership of a company set up specifically to own and manage the communal parts of the building and grounds. It remains to be seen whether some version of the commonhold formula can command legislative approval.

(4) Fixtures

As indicated in section 62 of the Law of Property Act 1925, the statutory definition of 'land' includes 'fixtures' attached to the land. English law has effectively adopted the maxim *quicquid plantatur solo, solo cedit* (whatever is attached to the ground becomes a part of it),[13] but in so doing has had to fashion a slightly uneasy distinction between 'fixtures' and 'chattels'.

(a) The distinction between fixtures and chattels

'Fixtures' comprise that category of material objects which, when attached physically to the land, are regarded as becoming annexed to the realty.[14] Irrespective of their previous ownership, title to such objects thenceforth vests automatically and exclusively in the owner of the realty.[15] As fixtures, they are regarded as having merged with the 'land' by reason of some curious legal

---

10 *Woollahra Municipal Council v Local Government Appeals Tribunal* [1975] 2 NSWLR 594 at 603E.
11 Post, p 303. See [1985] Conv 305.
12 See B. Denyer-Green, *Commonhold and unitisation*, (1986) 16 CSW 140.
13 *Lancaster v Eve* (1859) 5 CB (NS) 717 at 727, 141 ER 288 at 293 per Williams J.
14 See *New Zealand Government Property Corpn v H. M. & S. Ltd* [1982] QB 1145 at 1160H-1161A. Fixtures become 'incorporated with the soil' (*Lancaster v Eve* (1859) 5 CB (NS) 717 at 728, 141 ER 288 at 293) or '*partes soli*' (*Bain v Brand* (1876) 1 App Cas 762 at 769). However, physical connection is not always necessary in order to constitute a particular physical thing an integral part of a freehold. 'Everybody knows that a key, although in its nature a chattel, belongs to the house, and passes with the freehold' (*Moody v Steggles* (1879) 12 Ch D 261 at 267 per Fry J).
15 The title of the former owner of a chattel is simply extinguished when the chattel is attached to realty, even if the attachment is carried out by someone else (*Reynolds v Ashby & Son* [1904] AC 466 at 472f, 475). The former owner has clearly lost any title to the now non-existent chattel, but may have a remedy for the tort of conversion. See also the related discussion of proprietary estoppel (post, p 386).

metamorphosis, and thus pass with all subsequent conveyances of the realty unless and until lawfully severed from the land.[16]

By contrast, the category of 'chattels' consists of physical objects which never lose their character as mere personalty, but which retain their 'chattel' status even though placed in some close relation with realty. Not being included within the realty, chattels do not automatically pass with conveyances of the 'land'.

The distinction between 'fixtures' and 'chattels' is not entirely straightforward. The distinction seems largely to turn on two separate but related tests as to the intention of the original owner of the object in question. As Blackburn J said in *Holland v Hodgson*,[17] these two tests relate to the degree of annexation present in the given circumstances and to the general purpose of the annexation. The intention of the annexor is material only in so far as it can be presumed from the degree and purpose of the annexation.[18]

(i) Degree of annexation The older of the two tests takes the more primitive form of an enquiry into the degree of the physical attachment between the object and the pre-existing realty. The more firmly or irreversibly the object is affixed to the earth or to a building thereon, the more likely is the object to be classified as a 'fixture'. However, as Blackburn J observed in *Holland v Hodgson*,[19] when 'the article in question is no further attached to the land than by its own weight it is generally considered to be a mere chattel'.[20]

On this basis the courts have been able to assign the status of 'fixture' to spinning looms bolted to the floor of a mill,[1] an automatic car wash machine bolted to the ground,[2] petrol pumps on a station forecourt,[3] and a bridge fixed on either side of a river.[4] Gas mains and service pipes embedded in the soil likewise lose their chattel character.[5] Consistently with principle, however, the courts have regarded as mere 'chattels' those objects which rest by their own weight, such as printing machinery,[6] a 'Dutch barn',[7] a mobile home,[8] and movable greenhouses.[9] Even if an object is attached to the realty only slightly and can be fairly easily removed, its character is prima facie that of a fixture.[10] Fixtures can thus include anything attached to 'land' by bolts, screws or nails. Somewhat to the surprise of the lay person, even such objects as a bathroom cabinet, overhead

---

16 *North Shore Gas Co Ltd v Commissioner of Stamp Duties (NSW)* (1939-40) 63 CLR 52 at 68.
17 (1872) LR 7 CP 328 at 334.
18 *Hobson v Gorringe* [1897] 1 Ch 182 at 193; *Stack v T. Eaton Co* (1902) 4 OLR 335 at 338; *Royal Bank of Canada v Beyak* (1981) 119 DLR (3d) 505 at 509.
19 (1872) LR 7 CP 328 at 335.
20 For a modern example, see *Deen v Andrews* [1986] 1 EGLR 262 at 264G. See also *Stack v T. Eaton Co* (1902) 4 OLR 335 at 338; *Plaza Equities Ltd v Bank of Nova Scotia* (1978) 84 DLR (3d) 609 at 631.
1 *Holland v Hodgson* (1872) LR 7 CP 328 at 340.
2 *Lombard and Ulster Banking Ltd v Kennedy* [1974] NI 20 at 23.
3 *Smith v City Petroleum Co Ltd* [1940] 1 All ER 260 at 261G-H; *Costa Investments Pty Ltd v Mobil Oil Australia Ltd* [1979] 1 SR (WA) 137 at 148.
4 *Montague v Long* (1972) 24 P & CR 240 at 246. Compare *Tate & Lyle Food and Distribution Ltd v GLC* [1983] 2 AC 509 at 534F (jetty).
5 *North Shore Gas Co Ltd v Commissioner of Stamp Duties (NSW)* (1939-1940) 63 CLR 52 at 67f, 70.
6 *Hulme v Brigham* [1943] KB 152 at 157. See also *Northern Press & Engineering Co v Shepherd* (1908) 52 SJ 715 (connection to motor or power supply irrelevant).
7 *Culling v Tufnal* (1694) Bull NP 34.
8 *Royal Bank of Canada v Beyak* (1981) 119 DLR (3d) 505 at 508f.
9 *H.E. Dibble Ltd v Moore* [1970] 2 QB 181 at 189A.
10 *Holland v Hodgson* (1872) LR 7 CP 328 at 335; *Stack v T. Eaton Co* (1902) 4 OLR 335 at 338.

heater or extractor fan, if attached to a wall, become prima facie part of the 'land'.

(ii) Purpose of annexation The degree of annexation is not in itself a conclusive test of the status of an object as a fixture or chattel. At most it provides a prima facie characterisation, which may be reversed by evidence of a contrary purpose as to the positioning of a given object in relation to the realty.[11] The more recent caselaw suggests that the relative significance of the degree of annexation has declined and that considerations of purpose are 'now of first importance'.[12] Generally the tests of degree and purpose coincide in result,[13] but this is not always or necessarily true.

It is clear, for instance, that certain objects which rest on the ground by their own weight may nevertheless be regarded as fixtures if the circumstances are such as to show that they were intended to become part of the land.[14] Thus, 'fixtures' can include heavy marble statues of lions,[15] and substantial 'garden ornaments',[16] if the presence of these items was integral to a permanent architectural design or if they were part of a general scheme for the improvement of the realty.[17]

Likewise, items which are firmly fixed to the realty may yet remain chattels if the purpose of the annexation was merely to facilitate enjoyment of them as chattels and if the degree of annexation was no more than was necessary for the achieving of that purpose.[18] The chattel character of such items survives if there was clearly no intention that they should attach *gratis* to the realty.[19] The category of affixed objects which thus persist as chattels includes such items as tapestries[20] and display cases of stuffed birds.[1]

An important element in the 'purpose test' appears to relate to whether the purpose of attachment was more heavily weighted towards promoting increased enjoyment of the object itself or towards maximising the use which could be made of the land.[2] The 'degree of annexation' test is thus dwarfed in importance

11 However, in the absence of a contrary intention, the prima facie inference to be drawn from the mode and degree of annexation will not be displaced (see *Berkley v Poulett* (1976) *Times*, 4 November).

12 *Hamp v Bygrave* (1983) 266 Estates Gazette 720 at 724. See also *Leigh v Taylor* [1902] AC 157 at 162 per Lord Macnaghten ('...its relative importance is probably not what it was in ruder or simpler times'); *In re Hulse* [1905] 1 Ch 406 at 411; *Commonwealth of Australia v New South Wales* (1920-1923) 33 CLR 1 at 34.

13 See eg *Royal Bank of Canada v Beyak* (1981) 119 DLR (3d) 505 at 509f.

14 The onus of proof that the items were intended to annex to the realty lies on those who assert that they have ceased to be chattels (see *Holland v Hodgson* (1872) LR 7 CP 328 at 335; *Haggert v Town of Brampton* (1897) 28 SCR 174 at 180f).

15 *D'Eyncourt v Gregory* (1866) LR 3 Eq 382 at 397. Compare, however, *Berkley v Poulett* (1976) *Times*, 4 November.

16 *Hamp v Bygrave* (1983) 266 Estates Gazette 720 at 726 (not garden gnomes but a number of large urns, a statue and a lead trough!)

17 See *D'Eyncourt v Gregory* (1866) LR 3 Eq 382 at 396. It is on this basis, for instance, that a dry stone wall, although resting only by its own weight, is regarded as part of the realty (*Holland v Hodgson* (1872) LR 7 CP 328 at 335).

18 *Hamp v Bygrave* (1983) 266 Estates Gazette 720 at 724; *Re Royal Bank of Canada and Saskatchewan Telecommunications* (1985) 20 DLR (4th) 415 at 417f.

19 *Leigh v Taylor* [1902] AC 157 at 159.

20 *Leigh v Taylor* [1902] AC 157 at 161. Compare, however, *In re Whaley* [1908] 1 Ch 615 at 619f, where a fixture classification was accorded to a picture and tapestry displayed in a house which had been rebuilt as a 'complete specimen of an Elizabethan dwelling-house'.

 1 *Viscount Hill v Bullock* [1897] 2 Ch 482 at 483ff.

 2 *Hellawell v Eastwood* (1851) 6 Ex 295 at 312, 155 ER 554 at 561 per Parke B.

by the question whether the purpose of the annexation was to improve the realty or to enhance the chattel.[3] If the purpose of affixing a chattel was to improve the freehold, then the object—even if only somewhat tenuously affixed—is more readily regarded as a fixture.[4] On this basis wall-to-wall carpeting affixed to the floors of a hotel has been considered a fixture since its attachment was intended for the better use of the building as a hotel rather than for the better use of the carpeting.[5] Likewise, the fact that an object is attached to the land in order to increase its commercial value for mortgage purposes may point irresistibly towards a fixture characterisation.[6] By contrast, a mobile home ranks as a mere chattel, since its attachment to the ground is intended to enhance only the enjoyment of the chattel rather than the enjoyment of the land.[7] Likewise, the installation of a television cable and equipment does not so much improve a building as make it possible for its occupiers to receive cable television.[8]

(b) Legal relevance of the distinction between fixtures and chattels

The distinction between fixtures and chattels—although sometimes elusive—is important for several legal purposes. Fixtures but not chattels pass with a conveyance of an estate in the land.[9] Fixtures can be the subject of theft only if severed from the land.[10] Writing is required in order to create an equitable charge over fixtures since they constitute an interest in land.[11] But perhaps the most significant distinction between fixtures and chattels relates to the circumstances in which they can be removed from the land.

(c) Rights of removal

A chattel may be removed from the land at any time by the owner of the chattel, subject to any contractual commitment (eg a television hire or hire-purchase agreement) which may regulate the location and use of the chattel. The right to remove fixtures is more complex.

(i) Removal by the freehold owner

The freehold owner who attaches fixtures to his own land may, of course, remove those fixtures at any time before he contracts to sell his estate to a stranger. The removal of his own fixtures is simply part and

---

3 Even this is not an easy test to apply. 'In a sense every chattel affixed to a building could be said to improve the building or else it would not be affixed' (*Credit Valley Cable TV/FM Ltd v Peel Condominium Corp No 95* (1980) 107 DLR (3d) 266 at 275). See also *Holland v Hodgson* (1872) LR 7 CP 328 at 339f.

4 *Holland v Hodgson* (1872) LR 7 CP 328 at 339; *Re Davis* [1954] OWN 187 at 190 per Spence J.

5 *La Salle Recreations Ltd v Canadian Camdex Investments Ltd* (1969) 4 DLR (3d) 549 at 556. Compare, however, *Holland v Hodgson* (1872) LR 7 CP 328 at 335.

6 *Haggert v Town of Brampton* (1897) 28 SCR 174 at 182; *Bank of Nova Scotia v Mitz* (1980) 106 DLR (3d) 534 at 539f.

7 *Lichty v Voigt* (1978) 80 DLR (3d) 757 at 761f. See also *Turismo Industries Ltd v Kovacs* (1977) 72 DLR (3d) 710 at 715.

8 *Credit Valley Cable TV/FM Ltd v Peel Condominium Corp No 95* (1980) 107 DLR (3d) 266 at 275. See also *Re Davis* [1954] OWN 187 at 190 (installation of bowling alley not for better use of building but for more efficient bowling).

9 Ante, p 18.

10 Theft Act 1968, s 4(2)(b), (c). See also *R v Dowsey* (1903) 29 VLR 453 at 456.

11 *Jarvis v Jarvis* (1893) 9 TLR 631 at 632; *North Shore Gas Co Ltd v Commissioner of Stamp Duties (NSW)* (1939-1940) 63 CLR 52 at 68.

parcel of his rights of ownership.[12] However, if the freehold owner contracts to sell his estate to another, the conveyance operates to pass to the purchaser all fixtures which were attached to the land at the date of the contract of sale,[13] unless both vendor and purchaser agreed to the contrary.[14]

(ii) Removal by a tenant for years All fixtures attached by a tenant or lessee accede prima facie to the realty, thus representing an uncompensated benefit for the landlord at the expense of the tenant.[15] In order to mitigate the harshness of this rule,[16] the law has conceded certain exceptions from the strict effect of annexation to the realty. Although a tenant is normally under no obligation to remove fixtures,[17] he has a right to remove any fixtures which he has attached for trade,[18] ornamental and domestic,[19] or certain agricultural[20] purposes. However, such fixtures remain the property of the landlord unless and until the tenant severs them from the realty,[1] which he must do (if at all) during his tenancy or within a reasonable time after its expiry.[2]

There is a certain judicial ambivalence as to whether the treatment of 'tenant's fixtures' truly represents an exception to a general rule of accession to the realty. It can be argued quite cogently that the caselaw concerning 'tenant's fixtures' merely comprises instances where the courts, by engaging in a more benevolent interpretation of the purpose of the annexation, have been more difficult to convince that the object attached to the land has lost its chattel character.[3]

12 *In re Whaley* [1908] 1 Ch 615 at 620. In certain circumstances removal of a fixture even by the freehold owner may require planning permission or listed building consent.
13 Law of Property Act 1925, s 62(1), (2); *Phillips v Lamdin* [1949] 2 KB 33 at 41f; *Hamp v Bygrave* (1983) 266 Estates Gazette 720 at 726. Between contract and conveyance the vendor is, in some sense, a trustee for the purchaser (post, p 217).
14 See J.E. Adams, (1986) 136 NLJ 652. It is even possible that the doctrine of proprietary estoppel may confer upon the purchaser the right to claim any chattels which were advertised in an estate agent's particulars of sale as being included in the sale of a house (post, p 399).
15 *North Shore Gas Co Ltd v Commissioner of Stamp Duties (NSW)* (1939-1940) 63 CLR 52 at 68.
16 See *Lombard and Ulster Banking Ltd v Kennedy* [1974] NI 20 at 23f; *Mancetter Developments Ltd v Garmanson Ltd* [1986] 2 WLR 871 at 876H-877A.
17 See *Never-Stop Railway (Wembley) Ltd v British Empire Exhibition (1924) Incorporated* [1926] Ch 877 at 886f (licensee's fixtures, but the same principle seems applicable to a lessee).
18 *Climie v Wood* (1869) LR 4 Exch 328 at 329f; *New Zealand Government Property Corpn v H. M. & S. Ltd* [1982] QB 1145 at 1157A-B, 1161E-F. The tenant's right to remove trade fixtures may be excluded by sufficiently clear terms in the lease (see *In re British Red Ash Collieries Ltd* [1920] 1 Ch 326 at 333; *Lombard and Ulster Banking Ltd v Kennedy* [1974] NI 20 at 26f). An action may lie for the tort of waste in respect of failure to make good any damage done by the removal of the tenant's fixtures, at least where the building is left no longer weather-proof (see *Mancetter Developments Ltd v Garmanson Ltd* [1986] 2 WLR 871 at 877D-878A, 882D-E).
19 *Spyer v Phillipson* [1931] 2 Ch 183 at 199ff, 208ff (ornamental panelling and fireplaces removable provided no substantial or irreparable damage was done).
20 Agricultural Holdings Act 1986, s 10.
1 See *Holland v Hodgson* (1872) LR 7 CP 328 at 336f; *Hobson v Gorringe* [1897] 1 Ch 182 at 191f; *Crossley Brothers Ltd v Lee* [1908] 1 KB 86 at 90; *North Shore Gas Co Ltd v Commissioner of Stamp Duties (NSW)* (1939-1940) 63 CLR 52 at 70. Compare, however, *In re Hulse* [1905] 1 Ch 406 at 411.
2 *Ex parte Stephens* (1877) 7 Ch D 127 at 130. When a lease expires or is surrendered, to be followed immediately by the grant of another term to the same tenant in possession, the tenant does not lose his right to remove fixtures installed during the first term. His right of removal is preserved to the end of the new term (*New Zealand Government Property Corpn v H. M. & S. Ltd* [1982] QB 1145 at 1160A). See (1982) 132 NLJ 786 (H.W. Wilkinson); (1982) 98 LQR 342.
3 For the suggestion that more exacting standards of annexation are applied as between landlord and tenant (thereby favouring the tenant), see *Fisher v Dixon* (1845) 12 Cl & Fin 312 at 328, 8 ER 1426 at 1433; *Webb v Frank Bevis Ltd* [1940] 1 All ER 247 at 251G-H; *Doran v Willard* (1873) 14 NBR 358 at 360; *Bank of Nova Scotia v Mitz* (1980) 106 DLR (3d) 534 at 538; *Royal Bank of Canada v Beyak* (1981) 119 DLR (3d) 505 at 506f.

(iii) Removal by a tenant for life Any fixtures attached by a tenant for life under a strict settlement likewise become part of the realty.[4] As such they must be left for the person next entitled (ie the remainderman), with the exception of trade and ornamental and domestic fixtures, which the tenant for life is entitled to remove if he wishes.[5]

(iv) Contractual rights to remove fixtures Certain categories of person may be given a contractual right to remove chattels which have been affixed to realty and which have therefore assumed the character of fixtures. For instance, equipment or machinery may be the subject of a contract for hire or hire-purchase. If that equipment or machinery has been attached to the land of the hirer, it becomes annexed to his realty, and the former chattel owner loses his title.[6] However, the latter may well reserve for himself a contractual right to remove the equipment or machinery in the event of default in the payment of the relevant hire charges or hire-purchase instalments. Such a contractual right of removal confers on the former chattel owner an equitable interest in the land known as a 'right of entry',[7] and this interest may be binding on third parties to whom the land is later conveyed.[8]

(5) Trees, plants and flowers

'Land' includes for legal purposes all trees, shrubs, hedges, plants and flowers growing thereon, whether cultivated or wild. Such forms of growth attach to the realty and are thus part of the estate owned by the landowner.[9] However, realty is capable of horizontal division and it is, in this sense, feasible to own and to convey a fee simple estate in a tree which is separate from the fee simple estate in the subjacent soil, provided that the tree has not yet been severed from the realty.[10]

Although ownership of living vegetable matter thus vests prima facie in the owner of the soil, it is now clear that no theft is committed by a stranger who, for non-commercial purposes, picks wild mushrooms, or flowers, fruit or foliage

---

4 On the role of the tenant for life under a strict settlement, see Chapter 23 (post, p 805).
5 *Lawton v Lawton* (1743) 3 Atk 13 at 15f, 26 ER 811 at 812; *In re Hulse* [1905] 1 Ch 406 at 410f.
6 Ante, p 20. See also *Lombard and Ulster Banking Ltd v Kennedy* [1974] NI 20 at 27f.
7 See *In re Morrison, Jones & Taylor Ltd* [1914] 1 Ch 50 at 58.
8 In unregistered land this right to remove hired fixtures is enforceable against all third parties other than a bona fide purchaser of a legal estate for value without notice (see *Poster v Slough Estates Ltd*[1968] 1 WLR 1515 at 1520G–1521C, post, p 141), and therefore binds a subsequent equitable mortgagee of the land (*In re Samuel Allen & Sons Ltd*[1907] 1 Ch 575 at 582). In registered land the right to remove hired fixtures is neither a minor interest nor an overriding interest, and cannot apparently be made to bind a purchaser at all—a result which has been described as 'unfortunate' (*Poster v Slough Estates Ltd supra* at 1521F per Cross J). See generally A.G. Guest and J. Lever, *Hire-Purchase, Equipment Leases and Fixtures*, (1963) 27 Conv (NS) 30.
9 *Bl Comm*, Vol II, p 18. See *Stukeley v Butler* (1615) Hob 168 at 317.
10 See *Liford's Case* (1614) 11 Co Rep 46b at 49a, 77 ER 1206 at 1211; *Stukeley v Butler* (1615) Hob 168 at 173, 80 ER 316 at 320; *John Austin & Sons Ltd v Smith* (1982) 132 DLR (3d) 311 at 319). The largest estate which can exist in a growing tree is presumably a fee simple conditional upon the life of the tree (see *Smith v Daly*[1949] 4 DLR 45 at 48). The characterisation of a forest as realty means that the fee simple in the trees may be owned by one person while the fee simple in the surface soil may be owned by someone else (see eg *Herlakenden's Case* (1589) 4 Co Rep 62a at 63b, 76 ER 1025 at 1029f; *Eastern Construction Co Ltd v National Trust Co Ltd*[1914] AC 197 at 208; *Southwestern Lumber Co v Evans*, 275 SW 1078 at 1082 (1925)). See also *Commonwealth of Australia v New South Wales* (1920-1923) 33 CLR 1 at 34.

from a plant growing wild upon the land.[11] Such actions do not constitute criminal damage either,[12] even if the motive is commercial, but may however comprise the torts of trespass and conversion.[13]

(6) Minerals and other inorganic substances

Minerals and other inorganic substances present in the ground comprise part of the realty and, unless reserved from the original grant to the landowner or severed from the realty by him, are annexed to the estate of the landowner.[14] Thus substances ranging from stone and mineral ores to gravel, sand and china clay comprise 'land' for legal purposes. To this principle there exist certain exceptions relating to hydrocarbons. Most notably, the ownership of all coal[15] and of all oil and natural gas[16] is vested exclusively in the state, and the landowner has no right to extract such commodities except by licence from the appropriate state agency.[17] The crown also has a prerogative right to mines of gold and silver.[18]

(7) Airspace

The Latin maxim, *cuius est solum eius est usque ad coelum et ad inferos*, has a qualified application to airspace contained within the vertical planes which mark the territorial boundaries of an estate in land.[19] There is no doubt that the rights of the owner extend to limited portions of airspace both above and below the ground level within those physical geographical boundaries. Thus a conveyance of an estate in the land (whether freehold or leasehold) is effective to convey the void space contained within an immediately subjacent cellar,[20] the void space contained between a false ceiling and an original ceiling,[1] and even the vacant underground spaces from which minerals have been worked out.[2] Likewise, a trespass is committed where an adjoining landowner uses a means of access situated on his own land for the purpose of gaining entry to a cave located partly beneath the surface of his neighbour's land.[3]

It is in connection with superjacent airspace that the principal difficulties arise. Some jurists go so far as to deny that such airspace is capable of ownership

---

11　Theft Act 1968, s 4(3). However, theft is committed if the entire plant is uprooted (see Theft Act 1968, s 4(1)). See also Wildlife and Countryside Act 1981, ss 13(1), 21(3).

12　Criminal Damage Act 1971, s 10(1)(b).

13　*Mills v Brooker* [1919] 1 KB 555 at 558 (post, p 28).

14　*Bl Comm*, Vol II, p 18. The subterranean limits of the landowner's rights may in some cases be curtailed by legislation. See *Goldblatt v Town of Hempstead*, 369 US 590 at 595f, 8 L Ed 2d 130 at 135 (1962) (Supreme Court of the United States upheld constitutional validity of town ordinance prohibiting, for safety reasons, excavation below the water table).

15　Coal Act 1938, s 3.

16　Petroleum (Production) Act 1934, s 1(1). See, however, *Earl of Lonsdale v Attorney-General* [1982] 1 WLR 887 at 947E.

17　See Petroleum (Production) Act 1934, s 2(1).

18　*Case of Mines* (1568) 1 Plowd 310 at 336, 75 ER 472 at 510.

19　See *Grigsby v Melville* [1974] 1 WLR 80 at 83F-G, 85G.

20　*Grigsby v Melville* [1974] 1 WLR 80 at 84F-G, 86G-H.

 1　*Graystone Property Investments Ltd v Margulies* (1984) 269 Estates Gazette 538 at 543. (It was sought to use this space for the construction of a mezzanine floor). See [1984] Conv 171.

 2　See *Mitchell v Mosley* [1914] 1 Ch 438 at 450.

 3　*Edwards v Sims*, 24 SW.2d 619 at 629 (1930); *Edwards v Lee's Administrator*, 96 SW.2d 1028 at 1029 (1936) (the 'Great Onyx Cave' in Kentucky).

at all.[4] However, irrespective of viewpoint on this issue, all seem to be agreed that some pragmatic distinction must be drawn between two different strata of airspace.

(a) The lower stratum

The lower stratum of airspace comprises that portion of the immediately superjacent airspace whose effective control is necessary for the landowner's reasonable enjoyment of his land at ground level.[5] There is no doubt that the landowner's rights extend to this stratum, whether his rights be analysed in terms of ownership or mere possession. As Douglas J once said in the Supreme Court of the United States, the landowner must have 'exclusive control of the immediate reaches of the enveloping atmosphere' since otherwise 'buildings could not be erected, trees could not be planted, and even fences could not be run.'[6]

(i) Vertical extent   Courts are notoriously unwilling to quantify the extent of the airspace which thus falls within the dominion of the landowner, but it seems unlikely in most cases to reach beyond an altitude of much more than 200 metres above roof level.[7] Even within this lower stratum the landowner may not enjoy unqualified dominion. He is subject to such restrictions as may be imposed by a local authority or state agency by way of planning or zoning regulation.[8]

(ii) Invasion   It would seem to follow that any lateral invasion of airspace at this low altitude is prima facie actionable in trespass.[9] It is well known that where the branches of a neighbour's tree overhang the land of an adjoining owner, the latter is entitled, without giving prior notice,[10] to lop off the branches which

---

4 See eg *Re The Queen in Right of Manitoba and Air Canada* (1978) 86 DLR (3d) 631 at 635 per Monnin JA ('...air and airspace are not the subject of ownership by anyone, either State or individual, but fall into the category of *res omnium communis*'). This ruling had a devastating impact on the attempt by Manitoba to impose a sales tax in respect of transactions on board aircraft flying over the province: the sales did not take place 'within the province'!

5 See *Swetland v Curtiss Airports Corporation*, 55 F.2d 201 at 203 (1932).

6 *United States v Causby*, 328 US 256 at 264, 90 L.ed 1206 at 1212 (1946). See, however, *Cheyenne Airport Board and City of Cheyenne v Rogers*, 707 P.2d 717 at 727ff (1985), where the Supreme Court of Wyoming upheld as constitutional a local zoning ordinance restricting the height of trees in properties situated in the approach zone to an airport. It was held that the ordinance could validly require the landowners to cut back a large cottonwood tree from 48 feet to the permissible height limit of 26 feet.

7 In *Smith v New England Aircraft Co*, 170 NE 385 at 393 (1930), the Supreme Court of Massachussetts regarded as trespass the overflight of an aircraft at a height of 100 feet. In Britain no aircraft may ever fly 'closer than 500 feet to any person, vessel, vehicle or structure' (Civil Aviation: The Rules of the Air and Air Traffic Control Regulations 1985 (SI 1985/1714), reg 5(1)(e)). An exception is made for aircraft 'while landing or taking off' (reg 5(2)(d)(i)) and for gliders 'while hill-soaring' (reg 5(2)(d)(ii)).

8 Post, p 720. The United States Supreme Court has upheld the constitutional validity of various kinds of restriction imposed for aesthetic or practical reasons on the 'air rights' of the landowner. See eg *Welch v Swasey*, 214 US 91 at 107, 53 L ed 923 at 930 (1909) (local restriction on height of buildings); *Penn Central Transport Company v City of New York*, 438 US 104 at 130f, 57 L Ed 2d 631 at 652f (1978) (rejection, as contrary to Landmarks Preservation Law, of proposal to cantilever a 55-storey building above facade of Grand Central Terminal held not to constitute a 'taking' of private property without just compensation).

9 There may also be an actionable nuisance (post, p 28).

10 *Lemmon v Webb* [1895] AC 1 at 6, 8.

intrude into his airspace, so long as he does not enter upon his neighbour's land for the purpose of so doing.[11] Likewise, either trespass or nuisance is committed through the projection of overhanging eaves,[12] advertising signs,[13] overhead cables and wires,[14] and the jibs of sky cranes.[15] Illicit invasion of airspace is caused even by the poking of a horse's head across a dividing fence,[16] and certainly by the intrusion of low-flying aircraft.[17] All trespasses are actionable *per se*,[18] and an injunction may be granted irrespective of whether damage has resulted.[19] However, the courts have tended to deny that trespass has occurred at all if the intrusion is purely trivial.[20]

(b) The higher stratum

Whatever its application to the lower stratum of airspace, it is now clear that the maxim *cuius est solum...* has no relevance at all to the higher stratum of airspace which lies beyond any reasonable possibility of purposeful use by the landowner

11 *Lemmon v Webb* [1895] AC 1 at 4; [1894] 3 Ch 1 at 14f, 17f, 24. (This right is probably better founded in the law of nuisance than in trespass: see *Lemmon v Webb* [1894] 3 Ch 1 at 24; *Bernstein of Leigh (Baron) v Skyviews & General Ltd* [1978] QB 479 at 485E). Because of the ever changing nature of the tree, neither the statute of limitations nor the law of prescription can validate the trespass (*Lemmon v Webb* [1895] AC 1 at 6). However, the adjoining owner commits a conversion if he appropriates either the branches or any fruit thereon (see *Mills v Brooker* [1919] 1 KB 555 at 558). Severance of fruit from the branch does not alter the ownership of the fruit. This remains after severance, as before, in the owner of the tree—even if the severance is caused by the action of the wind or the ripeness of the fruit (see *Mills v Brooker, supra* at 558 per Lush J).

12 *Baten's Case* (1610) 9 Co Rep 53b at 54a/b, 77 ER 810 at 811f; *Fay v Prentice* (1845) 1 CB 828 at 838, 840, 135 ER 769 at 773f; *Ward v Gold* (1969) 211 Estates Gazette 155 at 159. See also *Corbett v Hill* (1869-70) LR 9 Eq 671 at 673f.

13 *Gifford v Dent* [1926] WN 336; *Kelsen v Imperial Tobacco Co (of Great Britain and Ireland) Ltd* [1957] 2 QB 334 at 345.

14 *Barker v Corporation of the City of Adelaide* [1900] SALR 29 at 33f; *Graves v Interstate Power Co*, 178 NW 376 at 377 (1920). See also *Wandsworth Board of Works v United Telephone Co* (1884) 13 QBD 904 at 927 per Fry LJ.

15 *Graham v K.D. Morris & Sons Pty Ltd* [1974] Qd R 1 at 4D; *Lewvest Ltd v Scotia Towers Ltd* (1982) 126 DLR (3d) 239 at 240f (where it appeared that by trespassing the defendant building contractor was saving approximately $500,000, but Goodridge J ruled that if 'a third party can gain economic advantage by using the property of another, then it must negotiate with that other to acquire user rights. The Court cannot give it to him'). See also *John Trenberth Ltd v National Westminster Bank Ltd* (1979) 39 P & CR 104 at 106f; *Anchor Brewhouse Developments Ltd v Berkley House (Docklands) Development Ltd* (1987) *Times*, 3 April.

16 *Ellis v Loftus Iron Company* (1874) LR 10 CP 10 at 12ff ('That may be a very small trespass, but it is a trespass in law'). Compare *Gifford v Dent* [1926] WN 336, where Romer J thought that an occupier must have a right to 'put his head out of the window' even if his head therefore protruded into someone else's airspace. (The different perceptions here may turn on the presence or absence of actual damage—however irrelevant this variable is to the strict definition of trespass).

17 See *Smith v New England Aircraft Co*, 170 NE 385 at 393 (1930); *Thrasher v City of Atlanta*, 173 SE 817 at 826 (1934).

18 See eg *Woollerton and Wilson Ltd v Richard Costain Ltd* [1970] 1 WLR 411 at 413E.

19 See eg *Lewvest Ltd v Scotia Towers Ltd* (1982) 126 DLR (3d) 239 at 241. In *Woollerton and Wilson Ltd v Richard Costain Ltd* [1970] 1 WLR 411 at 416C, the operation of the injunction was suspended largely because the offending party had at all times offered a substantial sum as compensation for the trespass. Compare, however, *John Trenberth Ltd v National Westminster Bank Ltd* (1979) 39 P & CR 104 at 108.

20 See eg *Pickering v Rudd* (1815) 4 Camp 219 at 220, 171 ER 70 at 71, where Lord Ellenborough CJ thought no trespass was occasioned by 'firing [a gun] across a field *in vacuo*, no part of the contents touching it'. Compare, however, *Clifton v Viscount Bury* (1887) 4 TLR 8 at 9 (bullet fragments fell on land). See also *Lemmon v Webb* [1894] 3 Ch 1 at 11, 24 (no trespass by spreading tree roots but possible remedy in nuisance if damage caused).

below.[1] The borderline between the strata is inevitably somewhat imprecise, but the landowner's rights in superjacent airspace seem to be restricted to 'such height as is necessary for the ordinary use and enjoyment of his land and the structures upon it.'[2] Above this height the landowner 'has no greater rights in the air space than any other member of the public.'[3] Any other view would lead to 'the absurdity of a trespass at common law being committed by a satellite every time it passes over a suburban garden.'[4]

(i) Civil immunity of overflying aircraft It follows therefore that overflying aircraft commit no trespass when flying at a height of hundreds or thousands of feet,[5] since the mere intrusion of such aircraft into superjacent airspace causes no interference with any reasonable use to which the landowner may wish to put his land.[6] Section 76(1) of the Civil Aviation Act 1982 provides accordingly that no action shall lie in trespass or nuisance in respect of the flight of an aircraft over any property 'at a height above the ground, which, having regard to wind, weather and all the circumstances of the case is reasonable', provided that the aircraft complies with all relevant regulatory legislation.[7]

This statutory immunity does not necessarily cover all forms of overflight. It seems to be agreed that the 1982 Act confers only a right of 'innocent passage',[8] and that it would not, for instance, give tort immunity in respect of an aerobatic display in airspace above private property.[9] Slightly more difficult is the use of overflight for the purpose of aerial photography. Such overflight has been held to constitute neither trespass nor nuisance so long as the aircraft does not interfere

1 See the distinction indicated by Griffiths J in *Bernstein of Leigh (Baron) v Skyviews & General Ltd* [1978] QB 479 at 486D, 487F. See also S.S. Ball, *The Vertical Extent of Ownership in Land*, 76 U of Penn LR 631 (1928).

2 *Bernstein of Leigh (Baron) v Skyviews & General Ltd* [1978] QB 479 at 488A. See also *Staden v Tarjanyi* (1980) 78 LGR 614 at 621f; *Griggs v Allegheny County*, 369 US 84 at 88f, 7 L Ed 2d 585 at 588 (1962); *Laird v Nelms*, 406 US 797 at 799f, 32 L Ed 2d 499 at 503 (1972).

3 *Bernstein of Leigh (Baron) v Skyviews & General Ltd* [1978] QB 479 at 488B. See, for instance, the descriptions of the upper stratum of airspace as that which 'belongs to the world' (*Hinman v Pacific Air Transport*, 84 F.2d 755 at 758 (1936), affd 300 US 655, 81 L.ed 865 (1936)) and as 'free territory...a sort of "no-man's land"' (*Thrasher v City of Atlanta*, 173 SE 817 at 826 (1934)). The Air Commerce Act of 1926 (49 USC, s 171) declared a 'public right of freedom of interstate and foreign air navigation' in the navigable air space of the United States (see now 49 USC, s 1304 (Supp 1984)).

4 *Bernstein of Leigh (Baron) v Skyviews & General Ltd* [1978] QB 479 at 487G. At a level closer to earth, it is clear that a local authority byelaw cannot validly prohibit hang-gliding at *any* height above prescribed areas. The byelaw must specify a level below which the hang-glider is not allowed to fly (*Staden v Tarjanyi* (1980) 78 LGR 614 at 623). See also Civil Aviation: The Rules of the Air and Air Traffic Control Regulations 1985 (SI 1985/1714), reg 5(2)(d)(ii).

5 This was first recognised in relation to overflight in hot air balloons (see eg *Pickering v Rudd* (1815) 4 Camp 219 at 220f, 171 ER 70 at 71), but is now more generally acknowledged in relation to harmless air traffic in navigable airspace.

6 Excessive noise resulting from the overflight may be actionable in negligence (but see *Nova Mink Ltd v Trans-Canada Airlines* [1951] 2 DLR 241 at 244, 246, 266) or in nuisance.

7 See *Bernstein of Leigh (Baron) v Skyviews & General Ltd* [1978] QB 479 at 489H. The current regulations stipulate that, except 'while landing or taking off in accordance with normal aviation practice', no aircraft shall fly at less than 1,500 feet above the highest fixed object within 2,000 feet of the aircraft (Civil Aviation: The Rules of the Air and Air Traffic Control Regulations 1985 (SI 1985/1714), regs 5(1)(a)(ii), 5(1)(e)). The Civil Aviation Act 1982, s 76(2) imposes on the owner of the aircraft a strict liability for any material damage or loss caused by the aircraft in flight. See *Weedair (NZ) Ltd v Walker* [1961] NZLR 153 at 157.

8 Shawcross and Beaumont, *Air Law* (3rd edn 1966), p 561.

9 See J.E. Richardson, *Private Property Rights in the Air Space at Common Law*, (1953) 31 Can Bar Rev 117 at 120.

with the owner's use of his land (eg through the 'harassment of constant surveillance of his house from the air, accompanied by the photographing of his every activity').[10]

(ii) Aerial surveillance   More controversial is the use of aerial surveillance as a regular means of law enforcement. Overflight by police helicopters is regularly used not only for the purpose of traffic control, but also for the detection of crime and for the searching of areas which would otherwise be inaccessible in the absence of a properly obtained warrant. There is here a dangerous potential for invasion of the individual's right to privacy, the problem being intensified by the lack of any effective practice of accountability for policing activity.

There appears to be no English decision on the proper balance which requires to be maintained in this context between the individual's legitimate interest in his own freedom and privacy and the general public interest in the detection and due prosecution of crime. In the United States warrantless aerial searches have until recently been upheld as constitutionally valid,[11] at least so long as such searches are 'routine'.[12] However, there are now some indications that the courts may be starting to assert more control over the issue of 'backyard surveillance'. In *People v Cook*[13] the Supreme Court of California held by a majority that a warrantless aerial search conducted by police frustrated the individual's 'reasonable expectation of privacy from purposeful police surveillance of his backyard from the air'.[14] The Court firmly rejected the contention that 'the air lanes are modern highways' and that aerial surveillance by the police is 'but a form of routine "street patrol" to which the modern public must be deemed to be resigned.'[15]

In the view adopted by the majority in the Supreme Court, purposeful surveillance from the air 'simply lays open everything and everyone below— whether marijuana plants, nude sunbathers, or family members relaxing in their lawn chairs—to minute inspection.'[16] While conceding that 'one may have to put up with the occasional downward glance of a passing pilot or passenger',[17]

---

10 *Bernstein of Leigh (Baron) v Skyviews & General Ltd* [1978] QB 479 at 489G. See (1977) 93 LQR 491 (R. Wacks). (It did not help that the television company of which the plaintiff was chairman had recently made a series of films involving substantial aerial photography over wide areas of private property!) See also *E. I. du Pont de Nemours & Co v Christopher*, 431 F.2d 1012 at 1015 (1970), affd 400 US 1024, 27 L Ed 2d 637 (1971) (aerial photography an unlawful means of obtaining a trade secret).

11 See eg *Dean v Superior Court for County of Nevada*, 110 Cal Rptr 585 at 589f (1973) (observation of marijuana field); *People v Superior Court*, 112 Cal Rptr 764 at 765 (1974); *Burkholder v Superior Court*, 158 Cal Rptr 86 at 88f (1979); *People v Lashmett*, 389 NE.2d 888 at 890 (1979); *United States v Allen*, 633 F.2d 1282 at 1290 (1980); *People v St Amour*, 163 Cal Rptr 187 at 192 (1980). Compare, however, *People v Sneed*, 108 Cal Rptr 146 at 151 (1973) (helicopter search from position 20-25 feet above ground was 'unreasonable governmental intrusion into the serenity and privacy of [defendant's] backyard').

12 For an incisive criticism of American practice, see S.A. Higgins, *Aerial Surveillance: Overlooking the Fourth Amendment*, (1981-82) 50 Fordham LR 271 at 279.

13 221 Cal Rptr 499 (1985).

14 Post, p 636ff. In *Oliver v United States*, 80 L Ed 2d 214 at 224 (1984), the Supreme Court of the United States seemed to say that both 'the public and police lawfully may survey lands from the air', but this was not read in *People v Cook* as expressing approval of 'intense aerial scrutiny of an enclosed backyard'.

15 221 Cal Rptr 499 at 504.

16 221 Cal Rptr 499 at 505 per Grodin J.

17 221 Cal Rptr 499 at 501.

the majority refused to accept that the police should be allowed arbitrarily to violate the individual's reasonable expectation that his home and private yard would not 'be spied upon from the air by police officers scrutinising the property for evidence of crime.'[18] Accordingly, the Court denounced 'the Orwellian notion that precious liberties derived from the Framers [of the Constitution] simply shrink as the government acquires new means of infringing them.'[19] The Court observed that 'a society where individuals are required to erect opaque cocoons within which to carry on any affairs they wish to conduct in private, and the concomitant chill such a requirement would place on lawful outdoor activity, would be inimical to the vision of legitimate privacy which underlies [the] state Constitution.'[20] The defendant's conviction for the offence of unlawfully cultivating marijuana was therefore overturned.[1]

It seems unlikely that English courts will spring with similar vigilance to the defence of the privacy claims of the landowner.[2]

(8) Water

Although English law can contemplate with equanimity the conveyance of an estate in thin air, it has substantially more difficulty in relation to a conveyance of water. Inland water (whether a river or lake) is considered to be merely 'a species of land',[3] in that lawyers regard such areas of water as simply areas of 'land covered with water'.[4]

(a) Conveyancing implications

A conveyance of an estate in the land carries with it certain rights over the superjacent water,[5] whereas a grant of the water itself without reference to the land would pass merely a right of fishing.[6] A conveyance of riparian land bounded by a non-tidal river carries with it the soil *ad medium filum* (or to the

18 221 Cal Rptr 499 at 504. The police surveillance in this case occurred from a height of 1,600 feet, with the aid of photography using a 200 mm telephoto lens.
19 221 Cal Rptr 499 at 505.
20 221 Cal Rptr 499 at 501. The Supreme Court of the United States has since held by a five-to-four majority in *California v Ciraolo*, 90 L Ed 2d 210 at 217f (1986), that the Fourth Amendment protection of privacy is not violated by 'warrantless naked-eye observation' from an altitude of 1000 feet. See also *Dow Chemical Co v United States*, 90 L Ed 2d 226 at 238 (1986).
1 Lucas J entered a vigorous dissent, arguing that the '*only* privacy interest significantly infringed by such overflights is the interest of the marijuana grower in concealing his illegal crop . . . we are not concerned here with the privacy interests of nude sunbathers, religious cultists, political activists, or *anyone* except marijuana growers. The majority pays lip service to the self-evident principle that no one has a reasonable expectation of privacy in the conduct of his *criminal* affairs . . . but ultimately the majority fails to apply that sound principle here' (221 Cal Rptr 499 at 508).
2 Post, p 537. In particular it is noteworthy that the prohibition on aircraft flying within 500 feet of any person or structure (ante, p 27) has no application to an aircraft in the service of a police authority (Civil Aviation: The Rules of the Air and Air Traffic Control Regulations 1985 (SI 1985/1714), reg 5(2)(b)).
3 *Bl Comm*, Vol II, p 18.
4 *Ibid*, p 18. 'The solum of a river bed is a property differing in no essential characteristic from other lands' (*Attorney-General for British Columbia v Attorney-General for Canada* [1914] AC 153 at 167 per Viscount Haldane LC).
5 *Bl Comm*, Vol II, p 18.
6 *Bl Comm*, Vol II, p 19.

middle point of the river), whether the conveyance be of a freehold or leasehold estate.[7]

(b) Limits of the landowner's rights

The mere fact that rights over water are attributed to the owner of the underlying land does not necessarily confer upon that owner an absolute title to the water itself. It is clear that the landowner does not have any property as such in water which flows through his land in a defined channel (eg a river)[8] or in water which percolates through his land.[9] His right to abstract water is, for instance, strictly controlled by the requirement that he should obtain a licence to do so from the relevant water authority.[10] However, the landowner does have an exclusive right to fish in any non-tidal river which runs through his land.[11] If he owns only one of the banks of the river, he owns the subjacent land out to the *medium filum*,[12] and each riparian owner may fish as far across the river as he can reach by normal casting or spinning. So long as he stands on his own bank or wades out no further than the *medium filum*, each riparian owner may cast beyond the *medium filum*.[13]

(9) Avulsion and accretion

Titles to land are, in relatively rare cases, affected by the processes of avulsion and accretion. The common law recognises as a matter both of fairness and of convenience that where land is bounded by water the forces of nature are likely to cause changes in the boundary between the land and the water. Where these changes are gradual and imperceptible,[14] the law considers the title to the land as applicable to the land as it may be changed from time to time.[15]

---

7   *Tilbury v Silva* (1890) 45 Ch D 98 at 108f; *City of London Land Tax Commissioners v Central London Railway Co* [1913] AC 364 at 371, 379; *Southern Centre of Theosophy Inc v State of South Australia* [1982] AC 706 at 715G ; *Tait-Jamieson v G C Smith Metal Contractors Ltd* [1984] 2 NZLR 513 at 514.
8   *Mason v Hill* (1833) 5 B & Ad 1 at 24f, 110 ER 692 at 701.
9   *Ballard v Tomlinson* (1885) 29 Ch D 115 at 120f, 126.
10   Water Resources Act 1963, s 23(1), as amended by Water Act 1973, s 9. No licence is required if the water is abstracted merely for the domestic purposes of the occupier's household or for agricultural purposes other than spray irrigation (Water Resources Act 1963, s 24(2)(b)).
11   'The general principle is that fisheries are in their nature mere profits of the soil over which the water flows, and that the title to a fishery arises from the right to the solum' (*Attorney-General for British Columbia v Attorney-General for Canada* [1914] AC 153 at 167). See also *Ecroyd v Coulthard* [1898] 2 Ch 358 at 366, 374; *Jones v Llanrwst UDC* [1911] 1 Ch 393 at 401. If the right to fish is severed from the solum, it becomes a 'profit à prendre' (post, p 633). The public has no general right of fishing except in the open sea and in tidal waters (see *Blundell v Catterall* (1821) 5 B & Ald 267 at 294, 106 ER 1190 at 1199f).
12   *Micklethwait v Newlay Bridge Co* (1886) 33 Ch D 133 at 145, 152, 155; *Tait-Jamieson v G C Smith Metal Contractors Ltd* [1984] 2 NZLR 513 at 515f.
13   *Fothringham v Kerr* (1984) 48 P & CR 173 at 186f (House of Lords). See (1984) 134 NLJ 567.
14   The requirement that the relevant change be gradual and imperceptible is widely accepted. See Bl Comm, Vol II, p 262; *Attorney-General v McCarthy* [1911] 2 IR 260 at 277ff; *Southern Centre of Theosophy Inc v State of South Australia* [1982] AC 706 at 716C; *Clarke v City of Edmonton* [1929] 4 DLR 1010 at 1015; *Port Franks Properties Ltd v The Queen* (1980) 99 DLR (3d) 28 at 36.
15   Any change caused by the deliberate action of the claimant falls outside the doctrine of accretion (*Brighton and Hove General Gas Co v Hove Bungalows Ltd* [1924] 1 Ch 372 at 390; *Southern Centre of Theosophy Inc v State of South Australia* [1982] AC 706 at 720A).

(a) Effects on title

If part of a landowner's land is removed by erosion or 'diluvion' caused by an advance of the water, the landowner is treated as losing a portion of his land.[16] If, however, an addition is made to the land by wind-blown or water-borne deposit,[17] the landowner's land is regarded *pro tanto* as extending into the area which was previously water.[18] This doctrine of accretion does not apply to substantial and recognisable changes in boundary which take place suddenly. However, the mere fact that the leading-edge of a sand dune may move forward two or three feet in a perceptible jump over a 24 hour period in conditions of strong winds does not disqualify such an advance as an allowable accretion to the land, if in the long term the movement is imperceptible.[19] The title extended by accretion also confers a right to any minerals situated below the newly claimed land.[20] Land is accordingly conveyed prima facie subject to and with the benefit of such subtractions and additions as may take place over the course of time.[1]

(b) Mobile estates in land

It is even possible that land, the ultimate immovable, may in fact 'move', even though this can bring about the improbable result that someone holds title to a constantly mobile piece of land. For instance, it is quite feasible that the pattern of tide levels on a coastline may vary over time, with the result that the foreshore extending between the high- and low-tide marks shifts position. The foreshore is normally vested in the crown,[2] but if a portion of the foreshore has been conveyed to an individual (or more usually a local authority), the title conveyed may well, in the absence of a contrary intention, relate to a moving strip of foreshore.[3]

---

16 *Southern Centre of Theosophy Inc v State of South Australia* [1982] AC 706 at 716D. See also *Fellowes v Rother DC* [1983] 1 All ER 513 at 515a.

17 The distinction between these forms of deposit, even if possible, is irrelevant (*Southern Centre of Theosophy Inc v State of South Australia* [1982] AC 706 at 719H-720A, 720D).

18 *R v Lord Yarborough* (1824) 3 B & C 91 at 105, 107 ER 668 at 673; *Gifford v Lord Yarborough* (1828) 5 Bing 163, 130 ER 1023; *Dunstan v Hell's Gate Enterprises Ltd* (1986) 22 DLR (4th) 568 at 584. The doctrine of accretion applies equally to lakes and rivers (*Southern Centre of Theosophy Inc v State of South Australia, supra* at 715F). See H.W. Wilkinson, *Accretion, Avulsion and Diluvion*, (1982) 132 NLJ 1164; (1983) 99 LQR 412 (P. Jackson); W. Howarth, [1986] Conv 247.

19 *Southern Centre of Theosophy Inc v State of South Australia* [1982] AC 706 at 722F, 723B.

20 *Re Eliason and Registrar, Northern Alberta Land Registration District* (1981) 115 DLR (3d) 360 at 364.

1 This rule can be excluded by clear evidence of a contrary intention, but the mere fact that the grant of land was accompanied by a map delineating the boundary is not conclusive against the operation of the rule (see *Southern Centre of Theosophy Inc v State of South Australia* [1982] AC 706 at 716F-G; *Attorney-General v McCarthy* [1911] 2 IR 260 at 284).

2 See *Blundell v Caterall* (1821) 5 B & Ald 267 at 293, 304, 106 ER 1190 at 1199, 1203.

3 See *Baxendale v Instow Parish Council* [1982] Ch 14 at 23B-C (contrary intention shown). See also *Re Monashee Enterprises Ltd and Minister of Recreation and Conservation for British Columbia* (1979) 90 DLR (3d) 521 at 531. A movable fee simple seems not to be a fee simple absolute in possession, and can therefore take effect only under the Settled Land Act 1925 (see R.E. Annand, *'Movable Fees'*, [1982] Conv 208 at 211). See also *Scratton v Brown* (1825) 4 B & C 485 at 498, 107 ER 1140 at 1145.

(10) Wild animals

It is clearly established that wild animals[4] cannot, while alive, be the subject of absolute ownership in English law.[5] However, the landowner whose land they inhabit has a 'qualified property'[6] which arises *ratione soli*[7]: he has a right to hunt and catch such animals, thereby reducing them into his possession.[8] This 'qualified property' of the landowner in wild animals persists only so long as he 'can keep them in sight' and has 'power to pursue them'.[9] When the animals escape to the land of a neighbour, it is the latter who takes over the 'qualified property' in them.[10]

As soon as wild animals are killed, they become personalty and therefore proper objects of absolute ownership by the owner of the soil.[11] Thus if A kills a wild animal found on his own land, it belongs to him absolutely.[12] Likewise, if A trespasses on the land of B and there kills a wild animal, the absolute property

---

4 There is no definition of a 'wild animal' for this purpose, but in its common law usage the phrase is sufficiently narrow to exclude fish and sufficiently broad to encompass birds, insects and reptiles. The criterion of 'wildness' seems to require that an animal should not by habit or training live with or in association with or in the service of man (see *McQuaker v Goddard* [1940] 1 KB 687 at 696). The distinction between domesticated and undomesticated species is highly unsatisfactory. A homing pigeon is 'wild' (*Hamps v Darby* [1948] 2 KB 311 at 320f), as is a circus elephant (*Filburn v People's Palace and Aquarium Co Ltd* (1890) 25 QBD 258 at 260f; *Behrens v Bertram Mills Circus Ltd* [1957] 2 QB 1 at 15), whereas a camel is always 'tame' (*McQuaker v Goddard* [1940] 1 KB 687 at 694f).

5 *Case of Swans* (1592) 7 Co Rep 15b at 17b, 77 ER 435 at 438; *Blades v Higgs* (1865) 11 HLCas 621 at 638, 11 ER 1474 at 1481 per Lord Chelmsford; *Bl Comm*, Vol II, p 391.

6 *Bl Comm*, Vol II, p 391.

7 That is, 'in consideration of the property of the soil whereon they are found' (*Bl Comm*, Vol II, p 393). See also *Blades v Higgs* (1865) 11 HLCas 621 at 634, 11 ER 1474 at 1480 per Lord Westbury LC ('....ownership of the game is considered as incident to the property in the land'); *Kearry v Pattinson* [1939] 1 KB 471 at 479.

8 *Blades v Higgs* (1865) 11 HLCas 621 at 631, 11 ER 1474 at 1478f. This common law right is nowadays curtailed by conservationist legislation aimed at the protection of rare or endangered species, although such legislation still grants substantial immunity to the landowner or occupier (see eg Wildlife and Countryside Act 1981, ss 2(2), 4(3), 10(4), 27(1)). There are also anomalous exceptions to the landowner's rights which include the little known, but much flouted, provision contained in section 3 of the Game Act 1831 which prohibits hunting for game on Sundays and Christmas Day!

9 *Bl Comm*, Vol II, p 393 (swarm of bees). However, 'power to pursue' was construed in *Kearry v Pattinson* [1939] 1 KB 471 at 479 to mean 'lawful power' to pursue without committing trespass. However, provided the pursuit was lawful, Goddard LJ went so far as to suggest (at 481) that no stranger was entitled to frustrate the pursuit by intercepting the animal and capturing it himself (but compare *Young v Hichens* (1844) 6 QB 606 at 611, 115 ER 228 at 230). See also (1939) 17 Can Bar Rev 130; G.W. Paton, *Bees and the Law*, (1939-41) 2 Res Judicata 22. It is possible that interception of an animal which is in the course of being reduced into possession may now be theft (see Theft Act 1968, s 4(4)).

10 *Sutton v Moody* (1697) 1 Ld Raym 250 at 251, 91 ER 1063 at 1064; *Kearry v Pattinson* [1939] 1 KB 471 at 480f (swarm of bees). It has been suggested that certain distinctive or exotic animals (eg a tiger which has escaped from a zoo) must represent an exception to this rule (see T. Beven, *The Responsibility at Common Law for the Keeping of Animals*, 22 Harvard LR 465 at 481f (1908-09)). There may be an ancient doctrine of 'hot pursuit' which gives a landowner immunity from trespass when pursuing vermin from his own land on to a neighbour's land if the purpose of the incursion is merely the destruction of the vermin (see *Earl of Essex v Capel*, Hertford Assizes 1809, cited in *Locke on the Game Laws of England and Wales* (5th edn, London 1866), p 45), but even this immunity is somewhat dubious (see *Paul v Summerhayes* (1878) 4 QBD 9 at 11).

11 *Blades v Higgs* (1865) 11 HLCas 621 at 631, 11 ER 1474 at 1478f.

12 *Blades v Higgs* (1865) 11 HLCas 621 at 638, 11 ER 1474 at 1481 per Lord Chelmsford.

vests in **B**, both *ratione soli*[13] and because the trespasser may not profit by his wrong.[14] Anomalously, however, if A starts the chase on the land of B and hunts the animal into the land of C, where he eventually kills it, it seems that the absolute property in the animal vests inexplicably in A,[15] although A may well be liable in trespass to both B and C.[16]

(11) Fish

A landowner who by reason of the ownership of land owns also a right to fish in superajacent water[17] is regarded as having a 'qualified property' in fish found within the limits of his 'fishery'.[18] The fish become his absolute property only when he catches and kills them. If those fish are caught by some unauthorised person, the absolute property in the fish vests—on the analogy of wild animals— not in the trespasser but in the owner of the fishing rights.[19]

(12) Lost and hidden objects

In certain circumstances a landowner may have a right to lost or hidden things found in or on his land where the true owner's identity is unknown. In this context a primary distinction appears to be drawn between those things which are hidden *under* the surface of the land and those which are found merely resting *on* the land surface.

(a) Objects found within the ground

It is presumed that the owner in fee simple has possession of, and is therefore entitled to, all things concealed within the ground itself, even though before the date of discovery he was wholly unaware of the presence of the object and even though he is not the actual finder.[20] This rule has been supported by reference to the maxim *cuius est solum eius est usque ad coelum et ad inferos.*[1] A trespasser can assert

---

13 *Sutton v Moody* (1697) 1 Ld Raym 250 at 251, 91 ER 1063 at 1064, 5 Mod 375 at 376, 87 ER 715; *Earl of Lonsdale v Rigg* (1856) 11 Exch 654 at 675, 679, 682, 156 ER 992 at 1002ff, 1 Hurl & N 923 at 937, 156 ER 1475 at 1481; *Blades v Higgs* (1865) 11 HLC as 621 at 634, 11 ER 1474 at 1480.
14 *Blades v Higgs* (1865) 11 HLCas 621 at 632f, 11 ER 1474 at 1479.
15 *Sutton v Moody* (1697) 1 Ld Raym 250 at 251, 91 ER 1063 at 1064; *Churchward v Studdy* (1811) 14 East 249 at 251, 104 ER 596 at 597; *Blades v Higgs* (1865) 11 HLCas 621 at 633, 11 ER 1474 at 1479, but see the doubts expressed by Lord Chelmsford at 639f, 1482. In any event, A's ownership in this example holds good only so long as B's original entitlement arose merely *ratione soli*. If B were the owner of some special franchise, his rights would persist even if the animal were killed in the land of C (*Blades v Higgs* (1865) 11 HLCas 621 at 632f, 11 ER 1474 at 1479).
16 *Sutton v Moody* (1697) 1 Ld Raym 250 at 251, 91 ER 1063 at 1064.
17 Ante, p 31.
18 *Nicholls v Ely Beet Sugar Factory Ltd* [1936] Ch 343 at 347.
19 *Nicholls v Ely Beet Sugar Factory Ltd* [1936] Ch 343 at 347. The unlawful taking of the fish is not theft as such but may constitute an offence under Theft Act 1968, s 32(1), Sch 1, para 2(1).
20 *Elwes v Brigg Gas Company* (1886) 33 Ch D 562 at 568f (prehistoric longboat); *Attorney-General of the Duchy of Lancaster v G.E. Overton (Farms) Ltd* [1981] Ch 333 at 338C. *South Staffordshire Water Co v Sharman* [1896] 2 QB 44 is supportable on the ground that the rings found in this case were embedded in mud at the bottom of a pool of water (see *Parker v British Airways Board* [1982] QB 1004 at 1010E, 1013A).
1 *Elwes v Brigg Gas Company* (1886) 33 Ch D 562 at 568. See also *Parker v British Airways Board* [1982] QB 1004 at 1010C ('the chattel is to be treated as an integral part of the realty as against all but the true owner').

no lawful title to things found by him within the ground,[2] and may even be liable to prosecution if his find was facilitated by the use of a metal detector in a 'protected place' of archaeological importance.[3]

(b) Chattels found on the ground

At least until fairly recently the law relating to the finding of chattels has been somewhat unclear.[4] However, it now seems that an 'occupier' of a building has rights superior to those of a finder in respect of chattels found upon or in that building 'if, but only if, before the chattel is found, he has manifested an intention to exercise control over the building and the things which may be upon it or in it.'[5] This intention may be manifested either expressly or impliedly,[6] and the title to the discovered chattel depends on the individual facts of each case. Thus a valuable chattel found by a stranger on the floor of a bank vault belongs to the bank,[7] whereas the same chattel found in a public park belongs prima facie to the finder, there being in the latter instance no manifest intention on the part of the landowner or occupier to exercise the required degree of control.[8]

(i) 'Finders keepers'   The caselaw tends to suggest that there may be unsuspected legal force in the lay person's maxim 'finders keepers', and that the courts will not be easily convinced that the landowner or occupier has formulated the intention to control which is needed to rebut the popular aphorism. In *Parker v British Airways Board*[9] a gold bracelet found by a passenger on the floor of an executive lounge at Heathrow Airport was held to belong to that passenger when attempts to locate the true owner ultimately proved fruitless.[10] In *Bridges v Hawkesworth*[11] money found by a customer on the floor of a shop was held to belong to the finder rather than the shopkeeper. The finder's claim will normally prevail except in special circumstances involving, for instance, premises with extremely restricted access (eg a private house or bank vault), where the control exerted by the owner or occupier clearly indicates an overwhelming *animus possidendi* (or intention to possess).[12]

(ii) Trespassing finders   The rights of a trespassing finder are 'frail' but not wholly non-existent.[13] Although he cannot resist the claim of the occupier of the land on which the property was found, the common law gives him 'very limited

---

2 *Elwes v Brigg Gas Company* (1886) 33 Ch D 562 at 568. In the case of treasure trove, however, he may receive an ex gratia payment of the full value of the find notwithstanding his status as a trespasser (post, p 38).

3 Ancient Monuments and Archaeological Areas Act 1979, s 42(1).

4 *Parker v British Airways Board* [1982] QB 1004 at 1008B.

5 *Parker v British Airways Board* [1982] QB 1004 at 1018A. See also *South Staffordshire Water Co v Sharman* [1896] 2 QB 44 at 47.

6 *Parker v British Airways Board* [1982] QB 1004 at 1018B-C.

7 *Parker v British Airways Board* [1982] QB 1004 at 1019B, 1020C.

8 *Parker v British Airways Board* [1982] QB 1004 at 1019B-C.

9 *Parker v British Airways Board* [1982] QB 1004 at 1019D, 1020G-H, 1021E. See [1982] CLJ 242 (A. Tettenborn); (1982) 45 MLR 683 (S. Roberts).

10 The decision was supported by the argument that if 'finders had no prospect of any reward, they would be tempted to pass by without taking any action or to become concealed keepers of articles which they found' ([1982] QB 1004 at 1017B).

11 (1851) 21 LJQB 75 at 78.

12 *Parker v British Airways Board* [1982] QB 1004 at 1020B-C.

13 *Parker v British Airways Board* [1982] QB 1004 at 1009D.

rights' to retain the chattel—if only in order to prevent a 'free-for-all situation...in that anyone could take the article from the trespassing finder.'[14]

(13) Treasure trove

At common law the specific kind of find known as 'treasure trove' vests automatically in the crown, irrespective of whose land concealed the treasure.[15]

(a) Scope

The scope of 'treasure trove' is, however, fairly narrowly defined. In *Attorney-General of the Duchy of Lancaster v G.E. Overton (Farms) Ltd*[16] the Court of Appeal held that only objects of gold and silver are capable of constituting 'treasure trove'.[17] Moreover, for the term 'treasure trove' to apply properly to a coin (which is almost necessarily an alloy of some kind), the Court ruled that the coin must contain a 'substantial' amount of gold or silver.[18] 'Treasure trove' must be found concealed '*in* the earth, or other private place', and the owner of the treasure must be unknown.[19] A claim of 'treasure trove' can succeed only if it is inferable that the original owner hid the property with the intention of later recovery. The crown's claim to the treasure will fail if there is evidence that the original owner simply lost or abandoned it, although a heavy onus rests on the landowner to prove that the goods were lost or abandoned rather than merely temporarily hidden.[20]

The rationale underlying the law of treasure trove thus seems to be that if the original owner hides his treasure in a secret place, intending to reclaim it later, but then dies, his secret 'also dies with him', in which case the property vests in the crown. If, however, the original owner deliberately abandons or casually loses the treasure, he is presumed to have 'returned it into the common stock', in which case it 'belongs, as in a state of nature, to the first occupant, or finder'.[1]

---

14 *Parker v British Airways Board* [1982] QB 1004 at 1009D-E.
15 *Co Inst*, Part III, p 132. The only exception to crown ownership occurs where the landowner can prove that a crown franchise to receive treasure trove had been granted to one of his predecessors in title (see *Attorney-General v Trustees of the British Museum* [1903] 2 Ch 598 at 608). The ownership of goods which fall short of the definition of 'treasure trove' vests in the relevant landowner (see *Attorney-General of the Duchy of Lancaster v G.E. Overton (Farms) Ltd* [1981] Ch 333 at 338C).
16 [1982] Ch 277 at 291E, 293E. See [1981] Conv 385 (A.A. Preece); (1981) 125 SJ 92 (W.A. Greene).
17 This limitation excludes a vast range of other antiquarian finds from the scope of the royal prerogative in respect of treasure trove (see N.E. Palmer, *Treasure Trove and the Protection of Antiquities*, (1981) 44 MLR 178 at 180f). See also *Attorney-General of the Duchy of Lancaster v G.E. Overton (Farms) Ltd* [1982] Ch 277 at 293B-D.
18 [1982] Ch 277 at 291H, 294A; [1981] Ch 333 at 343B. The Court offered no arithmetic definition of 'substantial' beyond suggesting that the coins would require to be at least 50 per cent gold or silver (compare *Palser v Grinling* [1948] AC 291 at 317, post, p 987). In the present case the highest proportion of silver was only 18 per cent.
19 *Bl Comm*, Vol I, p 285. Goods are not treasure trove if found 'in the sea, or *upon* the earth' (*ibid*). It seems to be enough to establish the character of treasure trove that articles of gold or silver are concealed *in* a building or secreted in some private place (eg hidden in a thatched roof or inside furniture). See *Co Inst*, II, 576, III, 132; N.E. Palmer, (1981) 44 MLR 178 at 183.
20 See *Attorney-General v Trustees of the British Museum* [1903] 2 Ch 598 at 609f.
1 *Bl Comm*, Vol I, p 285f. The unfortunate nature (see [1980] CLJ 281 (D.E.C. Yale)) of this long accepted distinction is perhaps most clearly apparent in the fact that the Sutton Hoo burial find of 1939 did not qualify as 'treasure trove' because it consisted of abandoned goods. (The landowner in fact donated the hoard to the nation: see N.E. Palmer, (1981) 44 MLR 178 at 182). See also *Attorney-General v Trustees of the British Museum* [1903] 2 Ch 598 at 608f.

(b) Compensation for finders

It is the practice of the crown to make an ex gratia payment of the full value of the 'treasure trove' to a finder who immediately reports his discovery to the police or relevant local authority.[2] Such payments are intended to provide an incentive to finders to reveal their recovery of objects of archaeological interest and, for this reason, are paid even to those who were trespassers at the time of making the find.[3]

3.   INCORPOREAL HEREDITAMENTS

The concept of 'land' also includes 'incorporeal hereditaments'.[4] In contradistinction to 'corporeal hereditaments', which are tangible, 'incorporeal hereditaments' are not 'the object of sensation, can neither be seen nor handled, are creatures of the mind, and exist only in contemplation.'[5] An important modern example of this category of intangible rights is the right of way which one landowner, A, may have over the land of another, B. There are, however, other kinds of incorporeal hereditament known to English law, and they provide the subject matter of discussion elsewhere in this book.[6]

It is a curious feature of the English land lawyer's mode of thought that the benefit of the intangible rights which A enjoys over the land of B is conceptualised as becoming just as much part of A's 'land' as the very soil on which A's house is built. Thus, for example, the benefit of the right of way which A may have over the land of B is 'reified' and regarded as an integral piece of A's land. It follows that any future conveyance of A's 'land' to C will effectively transfer to C not only A's corporeal hereditaments but also the benefit of A's right of way over B's land.[7]

---

2 The payment is made to the finder rather than the landowner or occupier, but see, however, N.E. Palmer, (1981) 44 MLR 178 at 184. If no museum wishes to receive the find, it is returned without payment to the finder.
3 See Tim Bonyhady, *The Individual and the Environment: The Rights of Members of the Public in the English Countryside* (PhD dissertation, University of Cambridge 1985), p 459.
4 Ante, p 16.
5 *Bl Comm*, Vol II, p 17.
6 Post, pp. 81, 689.
7 See Law of Property Act 1925, s 62(1) (post, p 646f).

CHAPTER 3

Trust

The great codes of continental law follow Roman law in defining 'property' as the right to enjoy a thing and to dispose of it in the most absolute manner, ie, as the right to deal with that thing as one pleases and to exclude strangers from interference.[1] Property or ownership thus expresses itself as an absolute jural relationship between a person and a thing. The *dominium* of Roman law comprises both the legal title and the right of actual beneficial enjoyment. In other words, *dominium* treated as conceptually inseparable the owner's right to use, dispose of, and exclude others from, his property. The idea that *dominium* might be fragmented between a number of owners, each with a separate proprietary right to some aspect of *dominium*, was and still is unacceptable to civilian legal thought. *Dominium* is an indivisible unity.

This rather stolid conception of property and ownership has made it difficult for continental systems of law to accommodate the fragmentation of rights of title, use and enjoyment which is integral to the economic reality of property in a complex modern world. However, these problems have been largely resolved in English law and in most legal systems derived from the common law tradition. English law has been able to develop a more flexible concept of property simply because deeply grounded in the English lawyer's tradition is the institution of the 'trust'. Otto Kahn-Freund observed sagely that, in creating the trust, 'in some ways its most original contribution to jurisprudence', the English legal mind has made it 'unnecessary and impossible for itself to search for a definition of property in the continental sense.'[2] Maitland was able to say

Of all the exploits of Equity the largest and the most important is the invention and development of the Trust. It is an 'institute' of great elasticity and generality; as elastic, as general as contract. This perhaps forms the most distinctive achievement of English lawyers. It seems to us almost essential to civilisation, and yet there is nothing quite like it in foreign law.[3]

1. DEFINING THE 'TRUST'

Many attempts have been made to define the notion of a 'trust'.[4] The essence of a 'trust' is the idea that the trustee is the nominal owner of property but that the real or beneficial owner of that property is the 'beneficiary' or 'cestui que trust'. The central feature of a trust lies in the fact that the formal or 'titular' interest in

---

1 See *Code civil*, art 544; *Bürgerliches Gesetzbuch*, para 903; Swiss Civil Code, art 641.
2 *Introduction* to K. Renner, *The Institutions of Private Law and Their Social Functions* (London and Boston 1949), p 23.
3 *Equity* (2nd edn, London 1936), p 23. See also A. Nussbaum, *Sociological and Comparative Aspects of the Trust*, 38 Columbia LR 408 (1938); V. Bolgár, *Why No Trusts in the Civil Law?*, (1953) 2 AJCL 204.
4 See eg W.G. Hart, *What is a Trust?*, (1899) 15 LQR 294.

property vests in a nominee (or 'trustee') whose duty it is to deflect the beneficial enjoyment of the property to those who hold the 'equitable interests' under the trust.

(1) The function of a trust

In its classical form the trust is a device created expressly for a specific purpose. It is in effect an obligation arising out of a confidence reposed in one who holds property or who has had property conveyed to him. The obligation binds this person to apply the property faithfully in accordance with the confidence placed in him, ie, in accordance with the wishes of the creator of the trust and the expectations engendered in the beneficiaries. The most usual kind of trust may be represented diagrammatically as follows, where A, the owner of a legal estate in property, conveys that property to T as trustee, in order that T should hold 'on trust for' B, a named beneficiary:[5]

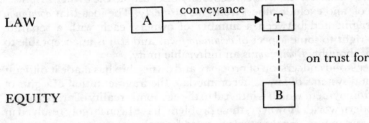

Fig. 1

(2) The functions of a trustee

Once such a trust has been created, its author, A, has no further part to play. The legal title in the trust property is held thereafter by T, who as title-holder is invested with administrative powers of 'management and disposition'. In other words, T is charged with the fiduciary responsibility of managing the trust property in such a way as to render it productive of income or other use value, subject always to the duty to divert the benefit (whether in the form of income or actual enjoyment) to the beneficiary, B.[6] It is a cardinal principle of trust law that T must never profit himself by reason of his office of trust.[7] His task is simply one of decision-making in the performance of the administrative duties connected with the trust. He manages the trust property and ultimately exercises powers of disposition in relation to that property. However, even the latter function is purely administrative. A disposition of the trust property simply converts that property into cash, which is still governed by the terms of the trust and which therefore requires to be reinvested in another form for the benefit of the person or persons entitled in equity.

5 It is not impossible that A may declare himself to be a trustee of his own legal title on behalf of B; or even that A himself owns only an equitable interest and can therefore, in effect, create only a subtrust of that equitable interest for B. However, these are more sophisticated examples of trust than the primary example discussed in *Fig.* 1.

6 The principles outlined here are exactly the same whether there is one trustee alone or several persons acting together as trustees, and whether the beneficiary is one person or many persons collectively.

7 See eg *Keech v Sandford* (1726) 2 Eq Cas Abr 741, 22 ER 629, Sel Cas T King 61 at 62, 25 ER 223 (post, p 269).

2. RELATIONSHIP BETWEEN LAW AND EQUITY

It is easily seen that the fundamental feature of a trust is that it makes possible a separation of the functions of administration and enjoyment. Although the trustee is invested with a formal title in the property, his ownership is purely nominal. If the trustee holds a legal title, that title is only a 'paper title'; the trustee, a mere 'paper owner'. The substance of beneficial enjoyment is reserved at all times for the beneficiary.

(1) Distinction between form and substance

Another important feature of the trust consists in the idea that the legal title is a mere matter of *form*, whereas the rights of beneficiaries represent *substance*. From its earliest days the common law of England was concerned only with form.[8] If asked to determine the ownership of a disputed piece of land, a court of common law would simply declare that full rights of ownership were vested in the person indicated by the paper title, ie, the person whose name appeared as transferee on the most recent deed of conveyance. The common law steadfastly declined to take cognisance of the moral obligation which the author of a trust had, by agreement, fastened on the conscience of the transferee of the paper title. The courts of common law regarded the formal title as exclusive of any rights in the supposed beneficiaries and as conclusive of any question relating to use, benefit or enjoyment.

(2) Development of the jurisdiction of equity

It was left to a jurisdiction founded upon conscience to remedy the defects of the common law. It was in the court of the Chancellor, and only in his court, that the moral obligations imposed on, and accepted by, the trustee were capable of enforcement. The court of the Chancellor, or the Court of Chancery as it came to be called, developed a body of rules which supplemented the rules of common law in the interest of achieving a greater equity in the dealings of men. This body of rules became known as 'equity', and it was by virtue of the 'equity' recognised by the Chancellor that the beneficiary of a trust could secure the enforcement of the trust reposed in his trustee. From the 14th century the Chancellors, although never denying that the trustee was the legal owner of the trust property, nevertheless began to give the beneficiary a remedy denied him by the courts of common law. The Court of Chancery insisted that the terms of the trust be observed and that the trust property be dealt with for the benefit of those persons named as beneficiaries or, as it came to be said, for the benefit of those persons 'entitled in equity'.

(3) Conflict between the jurisdictions of common law and equity

The courts of common law and equity thus diverged fundamentally in their approach to trust property. The courts of common law afforded a remedy only to the trustee; the court of equitable jurisdiction gave a remedy to the beneficiary. Not unnaturally conflict arose between these courts. The supremacy of the Court of Chancery became settled by the 17th century, but the mutual

8 See A.E.-S. Tay, 'The sense of justice in the Common Law', in E. Kamenka and A.E.-S. Tay (ed), *Justice* (London 1979), p 79.

antagonism of the courts of common law and equity was not resolved until late in the 19th century. The Supreme Court of Judicature Acts of 1873-1875 finally established that the rules of law and equity should be administered by all the courts of the land, so that the remedy obtained should no longer depend upon the precise court in which the plaintiff brought his action. Furthermore, in cases of conflict between law and equity, it was enacted that the rules of equity should prevail.[9]

In the orthodox analysis the changes of the late 19th century brought about a fusion merely of administration in respect of law and equity. 'The two streams of jurisdiction, though they run in the same channel, run side by side and do not mingle their waters.'[10] Although all courts may now grant legal and equitable remedies, the principles on which those remedies are granted remain distinct.

(4) Differences between legal and equitable remedies

There is one further procedural difference between law and equity which is of particular importance in land law. The characteristic remedy of the common law is the remedy of damages. The range of equitable remedies extends much more widely, embracing forms of relief which act *in personam* (eg decrees of specific performance, injunctions and orders for rectification). However, whereas the common law remedy of damages is available as of right once the plaintiff's case has been proved,[11] equitable remedies are always discretionary. Even if the plaintiff has proved his case, he may be denied equitable relief on the ground, for instance, that he has not come to court 'with clean hands'. That is, he may be precluded from relief simply because he has forfeited any claim to the assistance of equity by reason of his own inequitable or unconscionable conduct.[12]

3. THE ORIGIN AND TYPES OF TRUST

The modern concept of 'trust' developed from the more ancient institution of the 'use'.[13] Maitland attributed the derivation of the term 'use' not to the Latin *usus* but to the Latin *opus*.[14] In the vulgar or barbarous Latin of the 7th and 8th centuries, the phrase *ad opus* had already acquired a meaning of 'on behalf of'. Thus, if Coemgenus held land *ad opus Johannis*, he was under an obligation to hold land on behalf of Johannes. *Ad opus* became in time *ad oeps* or *ad eops*, emerging later in the form of the law-French *a son oes* and finally as the English 'to the use of'. Thus A might hold lands 'to the use of' B.

(1) The medieval 'use'

It was also Maitland who explained why, in the medieval context, it might be that A should hold lands 'to the use of' B. The device of the use arose in the 13th

---

9 Supreme Court of Judicature Act 1873, s 25(11) (post, p 471). See now Supreme Court Act 1981, s 49.
10 *Ashburner's Principles of Equity* (2nd edn by D. Browne, London 1933), p 18. Compare, however, *United Scientific Holdings Ltd v Burnley Borough Council* [1978] AC 904 at 925A-B per Lord Diplock.
11 The quantum of damages awarded remains, of course, a matter to be decided at the discretion of the court.
12 Post, p 469.
13 See generally A.W.B. Simpson, *A History of The Land Law* (2nd edn, Oxford 1986), p 173ff.
14 *Equity*, p 24.

and 14th centuries because of the restraints imposed by feudal law on the owner of land. The owner of land could not leave his land by will, for every germ of testamentary power in respect of land had been ruthlessly stamped out in the 12th century. Yet the claims of family endowment and the need for spiritual solace were strong. As Maitland pointed out,[15]

the Englishman would like to leave his land by will. He would like to provide for the weal of his sinful soul, and he would like to provide for his daughters and younger sons. That is the root of the matter...the law is hard upon him at the hour of death, more especially if he is one of the great.

For want of a testamentary alternative, recourse was had to the institution of the 'use'. The landowner typically conveyed his land inter vivos to friends, who were instructed to hold it to his 'use'. They could be directed to allow him enjoyment of the land during his lifetime, and could be given further instructions as to what they should do with the land on his death. They might well be directed in such an event to hold the land 'to the use of' other members of the deceased's family or 'to the use of' the Church. The latter form of use had the two-fold consequence of evading the Statutes of Mortmain, which prohibited the conveyance of lands to the Church, and of securing eternal rest for the soul of the 'feoffor to uses'.

The 'feoffment to uses' thus became a most flexible device.[16] A conveyance (or 'feoffment') of land might be made on terms which would prove highly beneficial to the 'feoffor'. Provided the 'feoffees' survived the 'feoffor', they could hold land to the uses indicated by the 'feoffor'. The utility of this scheme was so extensive, and the scheme itself became so commonplace, that in time it became standard practice to enfeoff a purely fictitious 'feoffee', so that a man of straw was caused to hold land 'to the use of' each beneficiary (or 'cestui que use').[17]

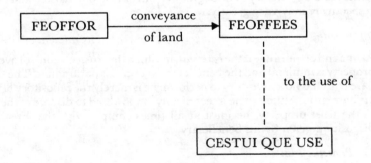

Fig. 2

(2) Development of the trust

Although the courts of common law looked only to the feoffee as the owner of the land, it was the Chancellor who by the 14th century had begun to enforce the use.

15 *The Collected Papers of Frederic William Maitland* (ed H.A.L. Fisher, Cambridge 1911), Vol III, p 335.
16 See W.F. Fratcher, *Uses of Uses*, 34 Missouri LR 39 (1969).
17 C.R. Noyes, *The Institution of Property* (New York, Toronto and London 1936), p 320.

It was natural of course that restrictions should later be imposed on the use, and in 1535 the Statute of Uses effectively abolished the power to create a use by will. However, within the next two centuries the foundations had been laid for an alternative device which was to perform most of the functions earlier discharged by the use. This device was the trust. From the late 17th century onwards the Court of Chancery began to fashion the principles which were to harden into the bleak and inflexible body of rules known as 'equity'—rules which were primarily (but not exclusively) concerned with the internal administration and external consequences of trusts of both real and personal property.

(3) **Historical significance of the trust**

In historical terms the major achievement of the trust was without doubt the final dismantling of the feudal system and its replacement by a new and much more flexible mechanism for the distribution of family wealth. In more recent times the trust has also developed a role as an extremely potent instrumentality of capitalism. One commentator has described the trust as 'a device of an individualistic character, conforming to the Anglo-Saxon system of economic liberalism'.[18] As a jural device, the trust is as essential to modern English law as is the institution of contract.

(4) **Types of trust**

The trust appears in a multiplicity of forms and may be directed towards a variety of purposes. In all its many forms the trust provides a medium by which the administrative and enjoyment functions pertaining to property may be separated and vested in different persons. The possible variations of the trust form depend on the precise way in which these functions are allocated between trustee and beneficiary. The degree of control vested in trustee and beneficiary respectively may vary greatly.

(a) *Bare trust*

At one end of the range is the *bare trust*, in which the trustee's control over the trust property is minimal and the beneficiary's control is paramount. The trustee of a bare trust has no active duty to perform: he is merely the repository of the naked or 'bare' title. Although he is technically empowered to dispose of the legal title in the trust property, he must at all times comply with the directions as to disposition given by his beneficiary.

(b) *Protective trust*

At the other end of the range of possible trusts is the *spendthrift* or *protective trust*, under which the beneficiary has no alienable interest and therefore no control over the trust property. Such trusts are frequently used to confer upon a beneficiary an interest which is terminable automatically on his insolvency, with the result that the trust estate is protected from the claims of the beneficiary's creditors.

(c) *Active trust*

At some intermediate point in the range of possible trusts is the *active* or *special*

18 Nussbaum, 38 Columbia LR 408 at 412 (1938).

trust—perhaps the most common of all types of trust. This is a trust in which the trustee is charged with the performance of active and substantial duties in respect of the control, management and disposition of the trust property, subject always to the fiduciary duty to deflect the benefit derived from that property towards the nominated beneficiaries.

(d) Other trusts

There also exist many other kinds of trust, such as the *trust for sale*, the *resulting trust*, and the *constructive trust*, but these are best explained later in the context in which they appear.[19]

4. EFFECT OF THE TRUST ON THIRD PARTIES

A trust is a fiduciary relationship with respect to property. The trustee holds typically the legal title to the trust property and exercises the appropriate powers of management and disposition. The beneficiary or 'cestui que trust' has an essentially personal right against his trustee to ensure that the latter carries out the terms of his trust. As Maitland pointed out,[20] the liability of the trustee is almost certainly of contractual origin. He is bound by the terms of the trust because he has bound himself: he has agreed with the author of the trust that he will faithfully observe the conditions on which the trust property was transferred to himself. The right of the cestui que trust is the benefit of an obligation—a right which is enforceable nowadays by appeal to the equitable jurisdiction of the courts. The cestui may apply for a court order directing his trustee to act conformably with the terms of his trust, or he may recover damages in respect of any breach of trust which has already occurred.

When stated in this way, it is apparent that the fiduciary relationship created by the trust should in principle affect the rights and obligations of only the trustee and the cestui. Third parties should not be subjected to the onerous liability undertaken voluntarily by the trustee. However, a proper understanding of the rights enjoyed by the cestui que trust begins with the realisation that equity, being a jurisdiction of conscience, gradually extended the ramifications of the private trust, thereby causing the trust to affect many categories of person other than the original trustee and cestui. This diffusion of trust liability occurred in the context of transfers of the trust property in favour of various kinds of third party (see *Fig. 3*).

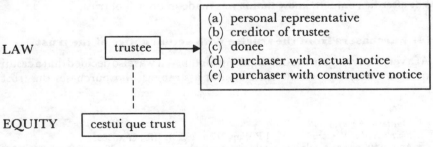

LAW | trustee →
(a) personal representative
(b) creditor of trustee
(c) donee
(d) purchaser with actual notice
(e) purchaser with constructive notice

EQUITY | cestui que trust

Fig. 3

19 Post, pp. 344, 244, 268.
20 *Equity*, p 110f.

(1) Persons who succeed to the rights of the trustee

The cestui que trust may enforce the trust against his original trustee. It was but a short step for equity to declare that the cestui que trust may also enforce the terms of the trust against all persons who by succession on the death of the trustee fill the place of that trustee. He may therefore enforce the trust against such persons as the trustee's personal representatives (ie, his executors in the case where the trustee dies testate, and his administrators in the case of death intestate). These persons are regarded as 'sustaining wholly or partially the *persona* of the original trustee and being bound by his obligations as regards the proprietary rights to which they have succeeded.'[1]

(2) Creditors of the trustee

The next step is to allow the cestui que trust to enforce the trust against the trustee's creditors.[2] The creditors may not claim the trust property in satisfaction of personal debts owed by the trustee, for the trust property is that to which the trustee is only nominally entitled as a paper owner. The benefit derived from the trust property belongs to the cestui que trust.[3]

(3) Donees of the trustee

Grave difficulties occur if the trustee, acting in breach of his trust, transfers the trust property to an innocent third party without receiving valuable consideration. There arises here a question of social, ethical and economic priority. Both the donee and the cestui que trust are entirely blameless, yet only one can prevail. It cannot be said that the donee is under any form of contractual liability towards the cestui, since the donee contracted with nobody. He is *ex hypothesi* utterly unaware of the existence of the trust. Yet, from a very early time, it has been accepted as a clear rule of equity that the donee should be compelled to observe the terms of the trust. It cannot be doubted that title has been validly transferred by the gift, but the cestui is allowed to enforce the trust against the donee (or 'volunteer'). 'Equity will not assist a volunteer'. A donee takes the gifted property subject to any equitable claims subsisting in relation to that property. Equity operates upon conscience, and it is sufficient to affect the conscience of the donee for this purpose that he has received something to which he was not entitled.[4] It would be 'against conscience' that he should retain the gift after he comes to know that it was made in breach of trust.

(4) Purchasers from the trustee with actual notice of the trust

At a very early stage in the development of equity, it was also decided that a cestui que trust may enforce the trust against a stranger who purchases the trust

---

1 Maitland, *Equity*, p 112.
2 *Finch v Earl of Winchelsea* (1715) 1 P Wms 277 at 282, 24 ER 387 at 389.
3 Ante, p 40. This principle is currently preserved in Insolvency Act 1986, ss 283(1)(a), (3)(a), 306 (post, p 876).
4 See eg *Burgess v Wheate* (1759) 1 Eden 177 at 195, 28 ER 652 at 659; *Re Diplock* [1948] Ch 465 at 503. The liability of the donee may rest on a theory of unjust enrichment (see Ames, *Lectures on Legal History*, p 255).

property with actual knowledge of the existence of the trust. The ground of liability in the third party is something akin to fraud. It is unconscientious— 'against conscience'—to buy what one knows to be held on trust for another. The purchaser is liable *ex delicto vel quasi*.[5] The basis for this conclusion is to be found in the simple but poignant law-French of 1471:

Si mon feoffee de trust etc enfeoffe un autre, que conust bien que le feoffor rien ad forsque a mon use, subpoena girra vers ambideux: scil auxibien vers le feoffee come vers le feoffor...pur ceo que en conscience il purchase ma terre.[6]

Thus the claims of equity operated upon the guilty conscience. If a stranger knowingly bought land held on trust, he did what was unconscientious and must now be regarded as holding on trust for me, for *en conscience il purchase ma terre*.

(5) Purchasers from the trustee with constructive notice of the trust

If equity had stopped there and gone no further, it would have been possible that purchasers would take good care to ensure that their consciences were not affected by actual notice of any trust which might exist. They would simply have 'shut their eyes' to the possible existence of a trust, and would have relied on the absence of actual notice as their ground of immunity from the obligation of the trust.

Equity accordingly developed the further rule that, in order to take the property free of the trust, the purchaser must not only be honest; he must also be diligent. He must have made all such investigation of the vendor's title and land as a prudent purchaser would have made, and he is affected with 'constructive notice' of all equitable rights of which he would have acquired actual notice had he made the proper enquiries. The trust may be enforced against any purchaser who would have known of the trust had he behaved as prudent purchasers behave in the conduct of their affairs.[7] Thus a standard of diligence has been elaborated by the courts in order to fasten upon the conscience of the unreasonable or disingenuous purchaser. If not actually guilty of *dolus*, such a purchaser is at least 'guilty of that sort of negligence which is equivalent to *dolus*. He had shut his eyes in order that he might not see.'[8]

At this point the long arm of equity stopped. Equity recognised that if the

5 Maitland, *Equity*, p 113. A.W. Scott attributed the liability of the purchaser with actual notice to the fact that he was 'colluding with the trustee in a breach of trust' (see *The Nature of the Rights of the Cestui Que Trust*, 17 Columbia LR 269 at 281 (1917)).

6 YB 11 Edw IV, fol 8: 'If my trustee conveys the land to a third person who knows well that the trustee holds for my use, I shall have a remedy in the Chancery against both of them: as well against the buyer as against the trustee: for in conscience he buys my land' (see Maitland, *Collected Papers*, Vol III, p 345).

7 'In the course of time it came to be held in the Court of Chancery that it would be unconscionable for the purchaser to take his stand on the facts that had come to his notice to the exclusion of those which ordinary prudence or circumspection or skill should have called to his attention. When the facts at his command beckoned him to look and inquire further, and he refrained from doing so, equity fixed him with constructive notice of what he would have ascertained if he had pursued the further investigation which a person of reasonable care and skill would have felt proper to make in the circumstances. He would not be allowed to say "I acted in good faith, in ignorance of those facts, of which I learned only after I took the conveyance", if those facts were such as a reasonable man in the circumstances would have brought within his knowledge' (*Somers v W* [1979] IR 94 at 108 per Henchy J).

8 Maitland, *Collected Papers*, Vol III, p 346.

purchaser who acquired ownership from the trustee was excusably ignorant of the rights of the cestui que trust, then he must be left to enjoy the ownership thus obtained. Since his conscience was unaffected, the Chancellor's equity had no hold upon him.[9] In *Pilcher v Rawlins*[10] James LJ regarded it as 'established law' that the purchaser's plea of 'a purchase for valuable consideration without notice is an absolute, unqualified, unanswerable defence, and an unanswerable plea to the jurisdiction of this Court.' James LJ accepted that the purchaser may be 'interrogated and tested to any extent' as to whether he gave valuable consideration or acted mala fide or had notice. But once a purchaser 'has gone through that ordeal', and has successfully maintained his unanswerable defence, then

this Court has no jurisdiction whatever to do anything more than to let him depart in possession of that legal estate, that legal right, that legal advantage which he has obtained. In such a case the purchaser is entitled to hold that which, without breach of duty, he has had conveyed to him.

In these circumstances there is no ground in equity for taking away that to which the purchaser is entitled at law. The purchaser has not himself undertaken any express obligation; he does not participate in the *persona* of the trustee; he has done no wrong; he has acted honestly and with due diligence. As Maitland said, 'Equity cannot touch him, because...his conscience is unaffected by the trust.'[11] Maitland added that this result could be formulated in either of two ways:

Formulation A

The cestui que trust may enforce his rights against
  (i) the trustee, *and*
 (ii) all who claim through the trustee as volunteers (personal representatives, devisees, donees), *and*
(iii) all those who acquire the trust property with actual or constructive notice of the trust.

Formulation B

The cestui que trust may enforce his rights against all persons *except* a bona fide purchaser of a legal title for valuable consideration without notice of the trust (whether actual or constructive).

Formulation B is now the more common means of stating the relevant proposition, and as such constitutes what is generally known as the *equitable doctrine of notice*. However, it is a statement of a negative kind, and it is not without interest that Maitland himself preferred *Formulation A* 'because it puts us at what is historically the right point of view—the benefit of an obligation has been so treated that it has come to look rather like a true proprietary right.'[12]

---

9 *Burgess v Wheate* (1759) 1 Eden 177 at 195, 28 ER 652 at 659 ('A conveyance with consideration without notice bars a trust').
10 (1872) 7 Ch App 259 at 268f.
11 *Equity*, p 115.
12 *Equity*, p 115.

5. THE INTEREST OF THE CESTUI QUE TRUST

The nature of the rights of the cestui que trust has traditionally been discussed in terms of the distinction between rights *in rem* and rights *in personam*.

(1) Rights *in personam*

A right *in personam* is a right to enforce the performance of an obligation undertaken by or imposed upon a specific person.[13] Such an obligation arises typically by reason of the law of contract, the law of torts, the law of trusts or indeed the law of property. The contractual promisee has rights *in personam* against his promisor. The victim of a tort has rights *in personam* against the tortfeasor. The cestui que trust has rights *in personam* against his trustee. It is possible to have rights *in personam* in respect of a thing. In each case, however, the rights concerned are rights enforceable only against the particular individual who has incurred liability by virtue of some transaction in law (whether contract, tort, trust, or licence). The identity or *persona* of the individual against whom enforcement proceedings are brought is highly relevant to the success of those proceedings, because there is no point in A's attempting to enforce against C a contract which A has concluded with B.[14] There is no point in A's attempting to recover damages from E in respect of a tort committed by D.[15]

(2) Rights *in rem*

A right *in rem* is, by contrast, a right which is enforceable not against merely one person but against the entire world.[16] The assertion of a right *in rem* is ultimately the assertion of some kind of ownership of a thing.[17] A right *in rem* is a right enforceable 'against the world' in respect of that thing; in some sense it represents the summation of all possible rights *in personam*.[18] If, in respect of the thing concerned, A is entitled to assert a right *in personam* against each and every individual in the world, the enforceability of his right is in no way dependent upon the precise identity of the individual against whom enforcement is sought (whether B, C, D, E, F...). A's right *in personam* is equally enforceable against all, and the *persona* of the individual enforced against ceases to be a determinant of A's ability to vindicate his rights. The *persona* no longer represents a relevant variable in the equation which leads to enforcement of what were originally

---

13 See J.L. Austin, *Lectures On Jurisprudence* (5th edn London 1885), Vol 1, p 370.

14 This is, of course, the doctrine of 'privity of contract'.

15 An exception to this proposition arises where E is D's employer and is therefore vicariously liable in respect of torts committed by D.

16 'The phrase *in rem* denotes the *compass*, and not the *subject* of the right' (J.L. Austin, op cit, p 369). 'A right *in rem* is usually defined to be a right available against the world at large, corresponding to a duty imposed upon the world at large; and by the world at large is meant indeterminate persons, an indefinite number of persons, not necessarily every one in the world; and it is to be distinguished from a right *in personam*, or obligation, which is a right available against determinate persons, corresponding to a duty imposed upon determinate persons' (A.W. Scott, 17 Columbia LR 269 at 273f (1917)).

17 For an argument to the effect that it is ultimately futile to search for 'the' owner of any particular thing, see Chapter 1 (ante, p 9).

18 It has been said that a 'right *in rem* is a name for a large number of rights *in personam*, actual or potential. A violation of a right *in rem* is always a violation of a definite one of these rights *in personam*' (W.W. Cook, *The Powers of Courts of Equity*, 15 Columbia LR 37 at 53 (1915)).

rights *in personam*. A's rights may just as comprehensively be described as rights against the thing itself, that is, as rights *in rem*.[19]

(3) Delineation of the boundaries of 'property'

The difference between rights *in rem* and rights *in personam* may seem academic. If rights are enforceable in any given situation, it matters not whether they are described as rights *in rem* or rights *in personam*. However, the distinction between rights *in rem* and rights *in personam* has a conventional significance in the law of land, because the borderline between these two categories of rights marks the boundaries of the 'proprietary right'. Only rights *in rem* are traditionally regarded as truly proprietary rights. Rights *in personam* are seen as purely personal rights which remain outside the realm of property law. According to Lord Wilberforce in *National Provincial Bank Ltd v Ainsworth*,[20] 'before a right or interest can be admitted into the category of property, or of a right affecting property, it must be definable, identifiable by third parties, capable in its nature of assumption by third parties, and have some degree of permanence or stability.'

The borderline between rights *in rem* and rights *in personam* is therefore crucial, for it expresses an important social judgment. The designation of a right as 'proprietary' is a kind of social accolade which signifies that a certain importance is attached to the entitlement in question. The interest concerned is sufficiently significant to merit public protection not merely vis à vis the participants in the private transaction which generated the interest, but vis à vis the entire world. It has been said that the 'basic badge of a proprietary right—that is, of an interest in property—is that unlike a personal right it is enforceable against the relevant property in the hands of third parties.'[1]

(4) Fluctuating boundary between rights *in rem* and rights *in personam*

The frontier between rights *in rem* and rights *in personam* has not yet been definitively settled. It is not impossible that a purely personal right may undergo a slow juristic metamorphosis, qualifying eventually for full recognition as a proprietary interest. Such an evolution is not unknown in the law of land, a prime example being the development which affected the law of restrictive covenants in the middle of the 19th century.[2] There are indications that a similar development is currently taking place in the law of contractual licences.[3]

(5) Cause and effect in the definition of 'proprietary status'

One of the most intriguing questions in this general context is whether a given right is enforced against third parties because it is a proprietary right, or whether

---

19 There is another, and rather different, sense in which the phrase 'right *in rem*' is sometimes used to describe a right in property which may be vindicated by the physical recovery of the physical property or *res* from the person into whose hands that property has come (as distinct from a mere action for money damages). However, this usage of 'right *in rem*' is less common than the meaning which has been attributed here (see W.W. Cook, 15 Columbia LR 37 at 43 (1915)).

20 [1965] AC 1175 at 1247G-1248A.

1 F.R. Crane, *Estoppel Interests in Land*, (1967) 31 Conv (NS) 332.

2 Post, p 698f.

3 Post, p 557f.

a given right acquires proprietary status precisely because it is enforced against such parties. Is curial enforcement the cause or the effect of proprietary character? This question is deeply bound up with the way in which the courts conceptualise the underlying issues in the context of property. It may even be that the balance of cause and effect is undergoing a noticeable reversal in some areas of property law today, as increasingly the courts fashion proprietary rights in order to give effect to what are thought to be the 'legitimate' moral expectations of litigants or the demands of conscionable conduct in their dealings.[4]

(6) Is the interest of the cestui que trust a right *in rem* or a right *in personam*?

The debate concerning the precise nature of the interest of the cestui que trust has traditionally centred on whether the cestui has a right *in rem* or merely a right *in personam*.[5] It is tempting, on first analysis of the trust concept, to say that two different forms of ownership are recognised in relation to the property which forms the subject matter of the trust. At law the owner is the trustee; in equity the owner is the cestui que trust. However, this view has not been accepted unqualifiedly in the orthodox teaching on the nature of the cestui's rights, for it seems to assert that the cestui has a right *in rem*, ie, that he is the 'equitable owner' of the trust property. Conventional doctrine tends towards the view that the cestui's rights are essentially and ultimately mere rights *in personam*.

(a) The orthodox view

The more generally accepted view of the nature of beneficial rights is that once expressed by Professor J.B. Ames, who observed that

A *cestui que trust* is frequently spoken of as an equitable owner of the land. This, though a convenient form of expression, is clearly inaccurate. The trustee is the owner of the land, and, of course, two persons with adverse interests cannot be owners of the same thing. What the *cestui que trust* really owns is the obligation of the trustee; for an obligation is as truly the subject-matter of property as any physical *res*.[6]

Maitland went further in his efforts to maintain that equitable estates and interests are not rights *in rem*. According to Maitland, the trustee 'is the owner, the full owner of the thing, while the cestui que trust has no rights in the thing.'[7] In Maitland's view, it was simply not true to say that 'whereas the common law said that the trustee was the owner of the land, equity said that the cestui que trust was the owner.' For Maitland there was an absurdity in the statement that before 1875 there were two courts of co-ordinate jurisdiction, one of which maintained that A was the owner, the other that B was the owner, of Blackacre:

That means civil war and utter anarchy...Equity did not say that the *cestui que trust* was the owner of the land, it said that the trustee was the owner of the land, but added that he was bound to hold the land for the benefit of the *cestui que trust*. There was no conflict here.[8]

---

4 Post, pp. 558f, 800.
5 See eg A.W. Scott, *The Nature of the Rights of the Cestui Que Trust*, 17 Columbia LR 269 (1917).
6 *Purchase for Value without Notice*, 1 Harvard LR 1 at 9 (1887-88).
7 *Equity*, p 47.
8 *Equity*, p 17. In this sense equity was true to its maxim: 'equity follows the law' (post, p 339). For a view contrary to that of Maitland, compare A.W. Scott, 17 Columbia LR 269 at 276 (1917).

In this way Equity fulfilled its historical purpose. 'Equity had not come to destroy the law, but to fulfil it. Every jot and every tittle of the law was to be obeyed, but when all this had been done something might yet be needful, something that equity would require.' But at every point equity presupposed the existence of common law. In Maitland's famous words,

It's of no use for Equity to say that A is a trustee of Blackacre for B, unless there can be some court that can say that A is the owner of Blackacre. Equity without common law would have been a castle in the air, an impossibility.[9]

The Supreme Court of Judicature Acts 1873-1875 declared, of course, that in any case of variance the rules of equity should prevail over the rules of law, but as Maitland shrewdly pointed out this only served to show that there had not been any conflict before 1875 as to the identity of the 'owner' of land held on trust. Had there been a conflict, the legislation would have had the effect of abolishing the entire law of trusts by its confirmation of the supremacy of equitable rules. B would have been recognised, in a situation of conflict, as the only owner of Blackacre. Such a conclusion is, however, patently untenable: the institution of the trust remains alive and well to this day.

Thus, in the conventional view of the matter, the interest of the cestui que trust comprises merely the benefit of an obligation—the obligation binding the trustee to observe and perform the duties of his trust. The right of a cestui is ultimately a right *in personam* against his trustee and against all persons claiming through him to the extent that the trust is fastened upon their conscience.[10]

(b)   The wider view

To other jurists it has seemed plausible to maintain that the rights of the cestui que trust comprise more than mere rights *in personam*. This wider view attributes greater significance to substance than to form. It recognises that the legal estate of the trustee is in most cases a mere 'shadow' following the equitable estate 'which is the substance'.[11] Support for this view may be found in the range of third parties against whom the cestui can enforce his rights. With the sole exception of the bona fide purchaser without notice, all third parties are bound by the trust, and in this sense the cestui is able to assert an 'equitable ownership' of the trust property against almost all the world.[12] Thus for Salmond

If we have regard to the essence of the matter rather than to the form of it, a trustee is not an owner at all, but a mere agent, upon whom the law has conferred the power and imposed the duty of administering the property of another person. In legal theory, however, he is

---

9   *Equity*, p 19.

10   It was essentially for this reason that Maitland preferred 'an enumeration of the persons against whom the equitable rights are good to a general statement that they are good against all, followed by an exception of persons who obtain legal rights *bona fide*, for value and without notice' (*Equity*, p 115).

11   See *Town of Cascade v Cascade Co*, 75 Mont 304 at 311 (1925). This wider view was the view typically espoused by Lord Mansfield CJ, who stated quite clearly in *Burgess v Wheate* (1759) 1 Eden 177 at 217, 28 ER 652 at 668, that 'trusts are considered as real estates, as the real ownership of the land.'

12   The immunity conferred on the bona fide purchaser is, of course, an undeniable qualification on the 'ownership' of the beneficiary. It was Langdell who pointed out that 'if equitable rights were rights *in rem*, they would follow the *res* into the hands of a purchaser for value and without notice' (*A Brief Survey of Equity Jurisdiction*, 1 Harvard LR 55 at 60 (1887-88)). See, however, A.W. Scott, 17 Columbia LR 269 at 278f.

not a mere agent but an owner. He is a person to whom the property of some one else is fictitiously attributed by the law, to the extent that the rights and powers thus vested in a nominal owner shall be used by him on behalf of the real owner. As between trustee and beneficiary, the law recognises the truth of the matter; as between these two, the property belongs to the latter and not to the former. But as between the trustee and third persons, the fiction prevails. The trustee is clothed with the rights of his beneficiary, and is so enabled to personate or represent him in dealings with the world at large.[13]

It is this perception of the cestui's true rights which ultimately underlies the rule in *Saunders v Vautier*[14] under which the beneficiary or beneficiaries of a trust may, if *sui iuris* (of full age and sound mind), terminate the trust and direct the trustee or trustees as to the disposition of the trust property.

Even Maitland was prepared to concede that the cestui has 'rights which in many ways are treated as analogous to true proprietary rights, to *iura in rem*.'[15] In his *Lectures on Equity*, he expressed the view that

The best answer may be that in history, and probably in ultimate analysis, it is *ius in personam*; but that it is so treated (and this for many important purposes) that it is very like *ius in rem*. A right primarily good against *certa persona*, viz the trustee, but so treated as to be almost equivalent to a right good against all—a *dominium*, ownership, which however exists only in equity. And this is so from a remote time.[16]

In his later writings it seems that Maitland mellowed even further towards a recognition that the cestui has rights which may be treated as ownership, or 'as some of those modalities of [*Eigenthum*] in which our medieval land law is so rich.'[17] In considering the question whether the rights of the 'destinatory' (or cestui) are rights *in rem* (*dinglich*) or mere rights *in personam* (*obligatorisch*), Maitland made reference to the wide categories of third party whose conscience is bound by the trust, and concluded:

Thus we come by the idea of an 'equitable ownership' or 'ownership in equity'. Supposing that a man is in equity the owner ('tenant in fee simple') of a piece of land, it makes very little difference to him that he is not also 'owner at law' and that, as we say, 'the legal ownership is outstanding in trustees.' The only serious danger that he is incurring is that this 'legal ownership' may come to a person who acquires it *bona fide*, for value, and without actual or constructive notice of his rights. And that is an uncommon event...I believe that for the ordinary thought of Englishmen 'equitable ownership' is just ownership pure and simple, though it is subject to a peculiar, technical and not very intelligible rule in favour of *bona fide* purchasers. A professor of law will tell his pupils that they must not think, or at any rate must not begin by thinking, in this manner. He may tell them that the destinatory's rights are in history and in ultimate analysis not *dinglich* but *obligatorisch*: that they are valid only against those who for some special reason are bound

---

13 *Jurisprudence* (12th edn by P.J. Fitzgerald, London 1966), p 256f. See also the statement of Isaacs J in *Hoystead v Federal Commissioner of Taxation* (1920) 27 CLR 400 at 422 that equity 'regards the cestui que trust of property as the true owner of the property itself.'
14 (1841) 4 Beav 115 at 116, 49 ER 282, Cr & Ph 240 at 249, 41 ER 482 at 485 (post, p 354).
15 *Equity*, p 110.
16 *Equity*, p 23.
17 *Collected Papers*, Vol III, p 343. In Maitland's day juristic debate in the area of property law was conducted largely in German—a factor which influenced much of Maitland's writing. Maitland clearly envied the greater expressive capacity of the German language: see for instance his remark that 'we have to envy our neighbours such a word as *Dinglichkeit*', a term which Maitland himself could render in English only in the rather ungainly form of 'thinglikeness' (see Pollock and Maitland, *The History of English Law* (2nd edn, London 1968), Vol 2, p 125).

to respect them. But let the Herr Professor say what he likes, so many people are bound to respect these rights that practically they are almost as valuable as if they were *dominium*.[18]

Ultimately the question whether a cestui que trust has rights *in rem* or rights *in personam* may simply be a matter of emphasis and perspective. From the earliest times there has been a willingness to concede that the cestui holds at the very least the benefit of an obligation and that this benefit may well, in some sense, comprise a *form* of 'equitable ownership'. This view receives support from an altogether more modern and more radical conception which sees the very *enforceability* of a claim to be the essence of a property right.[19]

18 *Collected Papers*, Vol III, p 349f.
19 Post, p 556.

CHAPTER 4

Tenures and estates

It is not easy to imagine, *tabula rasa*, how best to construct a coherent and systematic body of rules governing rights in and over land. During the course of eight centuries, English law has developed a framework of rules which functions today with admirable success, but it is far from obvious that, if the task of construction were begun again, the end result would necessarily resemble the law of real property in its present form. The conceptual points of departure which lie at the back of the law of real property contain little, if anything, of a particularly compelling or *a priori* nature. There is indeed nothing inevitable about the eventual shape of modern land law, but it remains true that the law of today is still heavily impressed with the form of ancient legal and intellectual constructs.

The present chapter is concerned with the conceptual starting points of English land law. From its earliest origins land law has comprised a highly artificial field of concepts, defined with meticulous precision, with the result that the inter-relation of these concepts is not unlike a form of mathematical calculus. The intellectual constructs of land law move, as Professor Lawson once said, 'in a world of pure ideas from which everything physical or material is entirely excluded.'[1] The law of land is logical and highly ordered, consisting almost wholly of systematic abstractions which 'seem to move among themselves according to the rules of a game which exists for its own purposes.' It is from this interplay of naked concepts that the creature of modern land law ultimately derives.

English law cannot be properly understood except in the light of its history,[2] and it is in the doctrines relating to tenures and estates that the historical roots of English land law are to be found. The present chapter is devoted to an examination of the way in which these doctrines provided the conceptual underpinnings for the modern law of land.

1. THE DOCTRINE OF TENURES

The origin of the medieval theory of English land law was the Norman invasion of England in 1066. From this point onwards the King considered himself to be the owner of all land in England. Since the Normans brought with them no written law of land, they initiated in their newly conquered territory what was effectively a system of landholding in return for the performance of services. According to this feudal theory, all land was owned by the Crown and was granted to subjects of the Crown only upon the continued fulfilment of certain

---

1 *The Rational Strength of the English Law* (London 1951), p 79.
2 See generally A.W.B. Simpson, *A History of The Land Law* (2nd edn, Oxford 1986); S.F.C. Milsom, *Historical Foundations of the Common Law* (2nd edn, London 1981); J.H. Baker, *An Introduction to English Legal History* (2nd edn, London 1979).

conditions. Land was never granted by way of an actual transfer of ownership, and the notion of absolute ownership other than in the Crown was therefore inconceivable. Pollock and Maitland were later to explain quite simply that all land in England 'must be held of the king of England, otherwise he would not be the king of all England.'[3] In their view, to have wished in medieval times for an ownership of land which was not subject to royal rights was 'to wish for the state of nature'.

It was a direct consequence of this theory that all occupiers of land were at best regarded as 'tenants', ie as holders of the land who in return for their respective grants rendered services of some specified kind either to the King himself or to some immediate overlord who, in his turn, owed services ultimately to the Crown. In this way there emerged a feudal pyramid, with the King at its apex, and it was the *doctrine of tenures* which defined the terms of the grant on which each tenant enjoyed his occupation of 'his' land.

(1) Classification of tenures

The feudal services rendered by 'tenants' were an integral part of early English land law, and in time became standardised and identifiable by the type of service exacted and performed. The different methods of landholding (differentiated according to the form of service required) were known as 'tenures', each tenure indicating the precise terms on which the land was held. The tenures were themselves subdivided into those tenures which were 'free' (and therefore formed part of the strict feudal framework) and those tenures which were 'unfree' (and appertained to tenants of lowly status who were *adscripti glebae*—effectively little better than slaves).

(a) Unfree tenures

The common labourer or 'villein tenant' originally had no place on the feudal ladder at all. He merely occupied land on behalf of his lord, and it was the latter who was deemed by the common law to have 'seisin'[4] of the land thus occupied. Villeinage (later called 'copyhold tenure'), although of an unfree nature, came in practice to enjoy increasing protection. This form of tenure retained its existence in law until the enactment of the property legislation of 1922–1925.

(b) Free tenures

The kinds of service provided by those who enjoyed free tenure included, for instance, the provision of armed horsemen for battle (the tenure of 'knight's service') or the performance of some personal service such as the bearing of high office at the King's court (the tenure of 'grand sergeanty'). These tenures were known as 'tenures in chivalry', and were distinct from the 'spiritual tenures' of 'frankalmoign' and 'divine service' (by which ecclesiastical lands were held in return for the performance of some sacred office) and the somewhat humbler 'tenures in socage' (which obliged the tenant to render agricultural service to his lord). With the passage of time, the military and socage tenures were

3 *The History of English Law* (2nd edn, London 1968), Vol 2, p 3.
4 Post, p 63.

commuted for money payments, but all tenures carried with them 'incidents' (or privileges enjoyed by the lord) which were often more valuable than the services themselves.

(2) The feudal pyramid

The consequence of medieval theory was the emergence of a kind of feudal pyramid of free tenants, with the actual occupiers of the land (the 'tenants in demesne') forming the base, their overlords ('mesne lords') standing in the middle—both receiving services and rendering services in their turn—and with the King at the apex receiving services from his immediate tenants ('tenants in chief').

(a) Subinfeudation

Pollock and Maitland described the system of tenures in terms of a series of 'feudal ladders', noting that 'theoretically there is no limit to the possible number of rungs, and . . . men have enjoyed a large power, not merely of adding new rungs to the bottom of the ladder, but of inserting new rungs in the middle of it.'[5] This process of potentially infinite extension of the feudal ladder was known as *subinfeudation*. However, subinfeudation carried the disadvantage that it tended to make the feudal ladder long and cumbersome, and in time the process of alienating land by *substitution* became more common. Under the latter device the alienee of land simply assumed the rung on the feudal ladder previously occupied by the alienor, and the creation of a new and inferior rung was no longer necessary.

(b) The Statute Quia Emptores

By the end of the 13th century a more modern concept of land as freely alienable property was beginning to displace the restrictive feudal order, and this evolution culminated in the enactment of Quia Emptores in 1290. The Statute Quia Emptores constituted a pre-eminent expression of a new preference for freedom of alienability as a principle of public policy. The major innovation contained in the Statute was the prohibition for the future of alienation by subinfeudation.[6] Following the enactment of 1290 only the Crown could grant new tenures, and the existing network of tenures could only contract with the passage of time. Every conveyance of land henceforth had the

---

5 Op cit, Vol 1, p 233. In one of the authentic examples provided by Pollock and Maitland, it could be said that '[i]n Edward I's day Roger of St German holds land at Paxton in Huntingdonshire of Robert of Bedford, who holds of Richard of Ilchester, who holds of Alan of Chartres, who holds of William le Boteler, who holds of Gilbert Neville, who holds of Devorguil Balliol, who holds of the king of Scotland, who holds of the king of England'. See also F.H. Lawson, *Introduction to the Law of Property* (London 1958), p 62 ('Tenure is a relation which looks both ways, towards a parcel of land and towards a lord').

6 The participants in the 17th and 18th century plantations of Ulster were commonly dispensed from the impact of the Statute Quia Emptores 1290, and thus had power to subinfeudate by way of 'fee farm grants' (post, p 73). The surviving effects of the subinfeudation which then took place are still obvious today in the extreme complexity of the 'pyramid titles' which create particularly acute difficulties in the conveyancing of urban land (see *Report of the Committee on Registration of Title to Land in Northern Ireland* (Cmd 512, 1967), para 116ff).

effect of substituting the grantee in the tenurial position formerly occupied by his grantor: no new relationship of lord and tenant was created by the transfer.

It is the Statute Quia Emptores which—quite unnoticed—still regulates every conveyance of land in fee simple today. Every such conveyance is merely a process of substitution of the purchaser in the shoes of the vendor, and the effect of the Statute during the last seven centuries has tended towards a gradual levelling of the feudal pyramid so that all tenants in fee simple today are presumed (in the absence of contrary evidence) to hold directly of the Crown as 'tenants in chief'.

(3) Virtual disappearance of the concept of tenure

The dismantling of the old feudal order was later accelerated by more direct measures aimed at a reduction of the forms of tenure. Under the Tenures Abolition Act 1660, almost all free tenures were converted into 'free and common socage' or 'freehold tenure'. By 1925 the only remaining tenures which enjoyed any importance were socage tenure and copyhold tenure. The Law of Property Act 1922 (which came into force on 1 January 1926) enfranchised all copyhold tenure, converting it automatically into freehold (ie socage) tenure.

There is therefore only one surviving form of tenure today—freehold tenure in socage—but the conceptual vestiges of the doctrine of tenures live on. It is still true that every parcel of land in England and Wales is held of some lord—almost invariably the Crown. It is still technically the case that no one owns land except the Crown, and that all occupiers of land are merely—in the feudal sense—'tenants'. However, for all practical purposes the doctrine of tenures is now obsolete.[7] Tenure of land for an estate in fee simple is now tantamount to absolute ownership of the land—or as close to total control of land as is nowadays possible. The doctrine of tenures has long been overtaken in importance by that other doctrine which explains much of English land law—the 'doctrine of estates'.

2.   THE DOCTRINE OF ESTATES

Whereas the doctrine of tenures served within the framework of medieval theory to indicate the conditions on which a grant of land was held, the *doctrine of estates* defined the effective duration of that grant. The doctrine still plays a fundamental role today in the classification of interests in land law.

(1) The concept of the 'estate'

Since it was intrinsic to the structure of medieval land law that the only owner of land was the King, it followed that his subjects—be they ever so great—were merely 'tenants', occupying the land on the terms of some grant derived ultimately from the largesse of the Crown. It was not initially clear what (if anything at all) the individual tenant could say he 'owned'.

---

7 Only in the context of the landlord-tenant relationship does the notion of tenure have much contemporary meaning (see Chapter 14, post, p 427). See also *Warner v Sampson* [1959] 1 QB 297 at 312f; (1959) 75 LQR 310 (P.V. Baker).

(a) The interposed abstraction

The answer to the conundrum was provided by the 'doctrine of estates'. As Professor F.H. Lawson pointed out, the solution arrived at in English law was 'to create an abstract entity called the estate in land and to interpose it between the tenant and the land.'[8] The object of the ownership enjoyed by each 'tenant' was not the land itself but a conceptual 'estate' in the land, each 'estate' differing from the others in temporal extent.

Thus, by resorting to an ingenious compromise, English law resolved at a stroke the apparent contradiction of theory and reality in the ownership of land. Although at one level the 'estate' in the land merely demarcated the temporal extent of the grant to the 'tenant', in practice it provided a functional (and theoretically acceptable) substitute form of ownership in respect of land. The doctrine of estates survives to the present day. Like the medieval 'tenant', the modern proprietor of land owns in some strict sense not the land, but rather an 'estate' in the land which confers specific rights and powers according to the nature of the 'estate'.[9]

(b) The dimension of time

The terminology of 'estates' introduced a fourth dimension of *time* into the description of the terms of grant enjoyed by the 'tenant'. Each 'estate' recognised by the common law simply represented a temporal 'slice' of the bundle of rights and powers exercisable in respect of land, and in the doctrine of estates there was developed a coherent set of rules classifying the diverse ways in which rights in land might be carved up in this dimension of time.[10]

It was the concentration on the rights and powers appurtenant to differing kinds of 'estate' which so sharply distinguished the common law view of real property from the continental emphasis on full ownership in the abstract sense (*dominium*).[11] An 'estate' denoted the *duration* of a grant of land from a superior owner within the vertical power structure which emanated from the Crown; and no man could grant another any greater 'estate' than that which he himself owned (*nemo dat quod non habet*).

(c) Successive estates in land

Through the doctrine of estates the common law was able to organise the allocation of certain powers of management, enjoyment and disposition over land in respect of particular periods or 'slices' of time. Moreover, as the law of real property became distanced from the physical reality of land and entered a world of almost mathematical abstraction, it was possible to accord an

---

8 Op cit, p 66f.
9 See *Minister of State for the Army v Dalziel* (1943-1944) 68 CLR 261 at 277 per Latham CJ ('In English law no subject can own lands allodially—he can own only an estate in land'). See also *Stokes v Costain Property Investments Ltd* [1983] 1 WLR 907 at 909E-F.
10 See R. Maudsley, *Escaping the Tyranny of the Common Law Estates*, 42 Missouri LR 355 (1977).
11 Ante, p 39. It was Otto Kahn-Freund who pointed out that '[o]wing to its habit of looking at the powers and rights arising from ownership rather than at ownership in the abstract, English law has been able to introduce the time element into the property concept. The continental notion of property, like the dominium of Roman law, contains, as a matter of principle, the element of eternity' (*Introduction* to Karl Renner, *The Institutions of Private Law and Their Social Functions* (London and Boston 1949), p 23).

immediate conceptual reality to each 'slice' of time represented by an 'estate'. In other words, any particular 'slice' of entitlement in the land could be viewed as having a present existence, notwithstanding that its owner was not entitled to possession of the land until some future date. In a world of concepts it was quite easy to conceive of rights to successive holdings of the land as 'present estates coexisting at the same time'.[12] It was ultimately this feature of the time-related aspect of the 'estate' in land which made it possible for the common lawyer to comprehend the notional reality of immediate dispositions of, and dealings with, future interests in land.

(d)   The doctrine of 'waste'

Precisely because the doctrine of estates recognised the feasibility of successive estates in the same land, rules were developed both at common law and in equity in order to restrain the current estate owner from prejudicing the value of the land in the hands of any successor (or 'remainderman'). These rules took the form of a doctrine relating to 'waste', 'waste' being defined as any action or inaction on the part of the estate owner which altered the physical character of the land.

Waste can be committed in several ways, although not all forms of waste lead to any legal remedy. The courts have been unwilling, for instance, to restrain the commission by a tenant for life of *ameliorating waste*, which merely has the effect of improving the land and of enhancing its value.[13] Only if the terms of his grant so stipulate can a tenant for life may be made liable for *permissive waste*, which comprises defaults of maintenance and repair leading to the delapidation of buildings situated on the land.[14] More serious is *voluntary waste*, which includes any positive diminution of the value of the land (for instance, by quarrying or by the cutting of timber). A tenant for life is liable for such waste unless the terms of his grant give him specific exemption by declaring him 'unimpeachable for waste'.[15] Even if a tenant for life is at common law unimpeachable for waste, in equity he can be restrained from the commission of *equitable waste* in the form of wanton destruction of the land to the prejudice of any remainderman.[16]

(2)   The freehold estates

The three freehold 'estates' known to the common law were the fee simple, the fee tail and the life estate, and each must now be examined in turn. Only one of these estates (the fee simple) is created with any frequency nowadays, the entailed interest and the life interest requiring to be created effectively behind some form of trust.

The key to the distinctions between them lies in the notion of time. The essence of the doctrine of estates has never been more elegantly captured than

---

12 F.H. Lawson, op cit, p 67.
13 See eg *Doherty v Allman* (1878) 3 App Cas 709 at 722f (conversion of dilapidated premises into dwelling-houses).
14 See eg *In re Cartwright* (1889) 41 Ch D 532 at 535f.
15 *Woodhouse v Walker* (1880) 5 QBD 404 at 406f.
16 See eg *Vane v Lord Bernard* (1716) 2 Vern 738 at 739, 23 ER 1082.

in the argument presented before the Court of Exchequer in the 16th century in *Walsingham's Case*.[17] Here it was said that

the land itself is one thing, and the estate in the land is another thing, for an estate in the land is a time in the land, or land for a time, and there are diversities of estates, which are no more than diversities of time.

(a) The estate in fee simple

The estate in fee simple has always been the primary estate in land.[18] It represents the amplest 'estate' which a 'tenant' can have in or over land.[19] As was said in *Walsingham's Case*,[20] 'he who has a fee-simple in land has a time in the land without end, or the land for time without end'. In so far as real property represents a 'bundle of rights' exercisable with respect to the land, 'the tenant of an unencumbered estate in fee simple has the largest possible bundle.'[1]

(i) Infinite transferability of the fee simple estate Although in theory each tenant in fee simple is still merely a tenant in chief of the Crown, the estate in fee simple is nowadays tantamount to absolute ownership of land. In terms of the feudal fiction, an estate in fee simple denotes a grant of land from the Crown in perpetuity—a right of tenure which endures for ever and which is capable, more or less indefinitely, of transfer inter vivos or of devolution on death. The owners of the fee simple estate may come and go but the estate remains, since it is of infinite duration. Each new owner steps into the shoes of his predecessor as a tenant in chief of the Crown—the modern effect of the Statute Quia Emptores of 1290.

(ii) Policy of unrestricted alienability The owner of an estate in fee simple is sometimes called a 'freeholder'—the owner of a freehold estate. Although modern legislation often curtails the fee simple owner's rights of use and enjoyment (for environmental and planning purposes[2]), there are relatively few limitations on his power to dispose of an estate in the land whether by will or by alienation inter vivos.[3] There is an important public policy which requires that land should be freely alienable in fee simple, since the unrestricted transferability of land is a vital precondition of a healthy and vibrant economy. Thus any grant or conveyance of an estate in fee simple subject to a condition which completely prohibits alienation by the grantee is in conflict with public policy. The offending condition is liable to be declared void at common law,[4] in which case the conveyance takes effect unconditionally.[5]

17 (1573) 2 Plowd 547 at 555, 75 ER 805 at 816f.
18 See J.L. Barton, (1976) 92 LQR 108.
19 'A fee simple is the most extensive in quantum, and the most absolute in respect to the rights which it confers, of all the estates known to the law' (*Challis*, p 218, cited with approval by Isaacs J in *Commonwealth of Australia v State of New South Wales* (1920- 1923) 33 CLR 1 at 42).
20 (1573) 2 Plowd 547 at 555, 75 ER 805 at 816f.
1 *Minister of State for the Army v Dalziel* (1943-1944) 68 CLR 261 at 285 per Rich J.
2 Post, p 720.
3 See, however, Inheritance (Provision for Family and Dependants) Act 1975; Race Relations Act 1976, s 21f.
4 *Co Litt*, p 223a.
5 Post, p 75.

(b) The entailed interest

A 'fee tail' or 'entailed interest' is an estate in land which endures so long as the original grantee (the 'tenant in tail') or any of his lineal descendants is alive.[6] Historically the entail provided a form of landholding designed to retain land within the family.[7] However, from the 16th century onwards, this purpose was commonly frustrated by the 'barring' of the entail by the tenant in possession—which usually had the effect of converting the entail into some form of fee simple.[8] The grantor's expressed intention is of course subverted by the barring of an entail,[9] but few tears are shed on this account nowadays, partly because it is widely accepted that the 'dead hand' of the grantor should not prevail for ever, and partly because an entailed interest generates an especially onerous liability to taxation.[10]

(c) The life interest

A life interest is plainly coextensive and coterminous with the life of the grantee.[11] Since 1925 it has been possible to create a life interest only behind a trust for sale[12] or under a strict settlement of land (in which case the owner of the life interest becomes the 'tenant for life').[13] If a life interest is conveyed to a stranger, it ranks merely as an interest *pur autre vie*, in that it still endures only for the lifetime of the original grantee. Unlike an entailed interest, a life interest cannot be unilaterally transformed into an interest of greater duration.

(3) Words of limitation

In accordance with the rules as to words of limitation now contained in section

6 As was said arguendo in *Walsingham's Case* (1573) 2 Plowd 547 at 555, 75 ER 805 at 817, 'he who has land in tail has a time in the land or the land for time as long as he has issues of his body'. An entailed interest in land can take effect nowadays only under a strict settlement governed by the complex machinery of the Settled Land Act (see Settled Land Act 1925, ss 1(1)(ii)(a), 20(1)(i)).

7 The fee tail frequently provided an instrument for giving effect to intricate patterns of landholding within an aristocratic dynastic family setting (see A.W.B. Simpson, *Introduction* to W. Blackstone, *Commentaries on the Laws of England* (Facsimile edn, Chicago and London, 1979), Vol 2, pp x-xi). Entails, said Samuel Johnson, 'are good, because it is good to preserve in a country, series of men, whom the people are accustomed to look up to as their leaders' (see A.W.B. Simpson, (1979) 24 Jur Rev (NS) 1).

8 The 'barring' of an entail may now be achieved quite easily either by will (see Law of Property Act 1925, s 176) or by means of a 'disentailing assurance', which comprises simply a declaration by deed executed by the tenant in tail that he henceforth holds a fee simple rather than an entailed interest.

9 Entails may occasionally be rendered unbarrable by statute. Examples are the entails conferred for public services upon the first Duke of Marlborough and the Duke of Wellington (see 6 Anne, c 6 (1706) , s 5; 6 Anne c 7 (1706), s 4; 54 Geo 3, c 161 (1814), s 28).

10 The enlargement of the interest of the tenant in tail immediately takes the land outside the clutches of the Settled Land Act 1925 (see *In re Alefounder's Will Trusts* [1927] 1 Ch 360 at 364) and operates to simplify the title to the land by sweeping all limited interests off the land. There has never been much sympathy for any sense of grievance which may be felt by the remainderman who, but for the barring of the entail, would have taken the fee simple in possession. No great injustice is worked against the latter if a right which was initially almost worthless (in view of the possibility of the barring of the entail) is in fact rendered completely worthless (when that possibility materialises).

11 '[H]e who has an estate in land for life has no time in it longer than for his own life' (see *Walsingham's Case* (1573) 2 Plowd 547 at 555, 75 ER 805 at 817).

12 Post, p 345.

13 Settled Land Act 1925, ss 1(1)(i), 19(1) (post, p 805).

60 of the Law of Property Act 1925, a conveyance of freehold land to any person 'without words of limitation, or any equivalent expression' is effective to pass to the grantee 'the fee simple or other the whole interest which the grantor had power to convey in such land, unless a contrary intention appears in the conveyance.'[14]

Thus a conveyance of freehold land without further reference to the estate or interest intended to be granted (eg Blackacre 'to X') is normally effective to invest the grantee with an estate in fee simple in the land. If the grantor wishes to dispose of some lesser estate in the land, he must actually employ 'words of limitation' in his grant (eg Blackacre 'to X in tail' or 'to X for life').[15]

(4) The concept of 'seisin'

The concept of 'seisin' is an early idea which lies at the root of the historical development of English land law. The notion of 'seisin' is part of the common law tradition that proprietary rights in land are based on physical possession rather than on abstract title. In its original form, seisin consisted essentially of the actual or de facto possession of land—quite irrespective of right. Such possession, even if wrongful, was accorded a certain protection by the common law 'in the interests of peace'.[16] Seisin was fact not right, although the right might flow from the fact and be reinforced by the passage of time.[17] As Pollock and Maitland wrote, a man is in 'seisin' of land 'when he is enjoying it or in a position to enjoy it.'[18]

(a) Seisin as intrinsic to estate ownership

Seisin thus expressed the organic element in the relationship between man and land and as such provided presumptive evidence of ownership within the medieval framework of rights in land. Furthermore only the person 'seised of' land could avail himself of an estate owner's rights in respect of that land. Since seisin was a matter of fact, even the thief could enjoy seisin and it is significant that he could be dispossessed only if the rightful estate owner brought against him the action of novel disseisin. In other words, it was the recovery of seisin which provided the first step towards recovery of the full rights of estate ownership.

(b) Feoffments with 'livery of seisin'

From the 15th century onwards, as Lord Mansfield was later to state,[19] seisin was the technical term used to 'denote the completion of that investiture, by which the tenant was admitted into the tenure; and without which, no freehold

---

14 Law of Property Act 1925, s 60(1).
15 Law of Property Act 1925, s 60(4).
16 See *Minister of State for the Army v Dalziel* (1943-1944) 68 CLR 261 at 276 per Latham CJ. Such was the force of the concept of seisin that the wrongful possessor was regarded as having a tortious fee simple which he could alienate and devise.
17 See A.E.-S. Tay, 'Property and Law in the Society of Mass Production, Mass Consumption and Mass Allocation', in *A Revolution in Our Age: The Transformation of Law, Justice and Morals* (Canberra Seminars in the History of Ideas, August 1975).
18 Op cit, Vol 2, p 34. See also F. W. Maitland, (1886) 2 LQR 481; (1888) 4 LQR 24, 286.
19 *Taylor d Atkyns v Horde* (1757) 1 Burr 60 at 107, 97 ER 190 at 216.

could be constituted or pass.' Indeed only the person seised could effect a 'feoffment' (or conveyance of freehold land) with 'livery of seisin' in the symbolic sense required by the common law. 'Livery of seisin' took the form of a solemn ceremony. The grantor and grantee entered upon the land conveyed and the feoffor, in the presence of witnesses, delivered the seisin to the feoffee either by some symbolic act, such as handing him a twig or sod of earth, or by expressing appropriate words of alienation and leaving him in possession of the land.[20]

The quaint ritual of feoffment with livery of seisin is no longer effective under English law to transfer an estate in land.[1] All interests in land now 'lie in grant' and may be conveyed 'without actual entry'.[2]

(c) The modern importance of seisin

Although seisin in its technical sense is no longer of much importance today, the emphasis which it placed on factual possession rather than abstract title continues to influence several areas of contemporary law.

(i) Relativity of title   The pragmatic process of modern conveyancing rests to some degree on the assumption that proof of continued de facto enjoyment of land by the vendor and his predecessors provides a good root of title for the purchaser.[3] The law of adverse possession likewise relies upon the significance of unhindered possession of land, in so far as uninterrupted enjoyment of land over a period of time stipulated by law effectively generates title to the land concerned.[4]

Moreover, the pre-eminent position accorded to de facto possession in English law ensures that there is no such thing as 'absolute title' to land.[5] All title is ultimately relative:[6] the title of the present possessor will customarily be upheld unless and until a better claim is advanced on behalf of somebody else. As Cockburn CJ observed in *Asher v Whitlock,*[7]

possession is good against all the world except the person who can shew a good title: and it would be mischievous to change this established doctrine . . . All the old law on the doctrine of disseisin was founded on the principle that the disseisor's title was good against all but the disseisee.

(ii) The common law concept of 'property'   It has also been said that the concept of seisin has laid an indelible mark upon the way in which the common lawyer

---

20   '"What's taking seizin?" said Dan, cautiously. "It's an old custom the people had when they bought and sold land. They used to cut out a clod and hand it over to the buyer, and you weren't lawfully seized of your land—it didn't really belong to you—till the other fellow had actually given you a piece of it—like this." He held out the turves' (Rudyard Kipling, *Puck of Pook's Hill* (London 1906), p 12). See also *Manton v Parabolic Pty Ltd* [1985] 2 NSWLR 361 at 367A-368C (post, p 223).

  1   That a title in land may be transferred by livery of seisin seems still to be a live possibility in the Canadian province of Ontario (see eg *Re Bouris and Button* (1976) 60 DLR (3d) 233 at 238).

  2   Law of Property Act 1925, s 51(1).

  3   Post, p 95. See *Minister of State for the Army v Dalziel* (1943-1944) 68 CLR 261 at 277.

  4   Post, p 740.

  5   Even the artificial concept of 'absolute title' as recorded in the Land Register is something of a misnomer (post, p 193).

  6   See B. Rudden, (1964) 80 LQR 63.

  7   (1865) LR 1 QB 1 at 5.

thinks of land. It was to the concept of seisin that Professor Alice Tay attributed 'the Englishman's concept of freedom—of his home as his castle'.[8] In her words, the common law has long maintained

a bias in favour of the factual situation—the citizen's actual behaviour and powers *against* the claims of privilege and authority as such . . . The role of the underlying seisin- possession concept in the common law is to recognise and protect those still important areas in which men live, work and plan as user-owners, to set out their rights and obligations, to give them an area of privacy in which they have a right to be free of state and community interference, to repel the unattractive neighbour, the busybody, the officious policeman, and to ensure that they allow their neighbours the same possibility of undisturbed enjoyment. Only in societies that do not have such protection do men realise how important this concept of personal security and inviolability is . . . It is also the base and shaper of the social sentiment that shrinks with distaste from the forcible eviction.

(iii) Protection of residential security   It is not without significance that the primarily physical or factual dimension bound up in the medieval notion of seisin finds a modern counterpart in the importance which is increasingly attached nowadays to the 'utility-based' aspects of land ownership and particularly to the protection of residential security. One of the themes of any account of modern English land law is the emergence of a contemporary emphasis on the use value of land as distinct from its exchange value.

A significant index of this development was provided, for instance, by the decision in *Williams & Glyn's Bank Ltd v Boland*.[9] In the Court of Appeal in this case Lord Denning MR construed the concept of the 'overriding interest' in registered land in language which was highly reminiscent of the concept of seisin.[10] He noted that, for the purpose of protection under the Land Registration Act 1925, 'actual occupation is matter of fact, not matter of law . . . It does not depend on title. A squatter is often in actual occupation.'[11] Thus, just as in the context of seisin the fact was instrumental in establishing the right, similarly in *Boland*'s case it was the fact of physical possession which ultimately conferred overriding status on a legal entitlement. The protection accorded in *Boland* to the rights of a spouse in the matrimonial home has since been extended, with reference to exactly the same concept of 'actual occupation', to other categories of dweller in the family home.[12]

8 'Law, the citizen and the state', in E. Kamenka, R. Brown and A.E.-S. Tay (ed), *Law and Society: The Crisis in Legal Ideals* (London 1978), p 11f.
9 [1981] AC 487 (House of Lords), [1979] Ch 312 (Court of Appeal) (post, p 843).
10 See Land Registration Act 1925, s 70(1)(g) (post, p 175).
11 [1979] Ch 312 at 332E. Lord Wilberforce ruled similarly in the House of Lords that the statutory phrase 'actual occupation' emphasises 'that what is required is physical presence, not some entitlement in law' ([1981] AC 487 at 505B).
12 Post, pp 171, 851.

B Structures

CHAPTER 5

Legal and equitable rights

The historical development of the English law of real property has been based
on a fundamental—albeit arbitrarily drawn—distinction between those
property rights in land which are designated as 'legal' rights and those which
are designated as merely 'equitable'. It is true to say that the distinction
between legal and equitable rights no longer retains the importance which it
once had, and that it may well fade into relative insignificance with the
comprehensive coverage of registered title.[1] Nevertheless any systematic
review of English land law must start from a rigorous analysis of the difference
between legal and equitable rights.

1. THE DISTINCTION BETWEEN 'LEGAL' AND 'EQUITABLE' RIGHTS

It might reasonably be expected that something fairly basic about land law
should appear in section 1 of the Law of Property Act 1925—and indeed it
does. In its terms section 1 surveys the entire field of proprietary rights in land,[2]
and outlines the way in which either 'legal' or 'equitable' quality can be
attached to those rights. The significance of this ascription of 'legal' or
'equitable' character derives, of course, from the days when 'legal' rights were
those rights which were recognised exclusively by the courts of common law,
while 'equitable' rights were enforced only by the courts of equity.[3] The
jurisdictions of law and equity have now been fused for more than a century,[4]
and legal and equitable rights are currently recognised and enforced in all
courts alike. However, the distinction between these two kinds of right is still
highly relevant—even decisive—in certain circumstances. This is particularly
true in the case of unregistered land, where the attribution of legal or equitable
character may fundamentally determine the effect of rights upon third parties
who purchase the land to which they relate.

It is for precisely this reason that section 1 of the Law of Property Act 1925
takes great pains to demarcate legal from equitable rights in land.

---

1 Post, p 144.
2 For the distinction between 'proprietary' and 'personal' rights in land see Chapter 3 (ante, p
49). It is important to note that section 1 of the Law of Property Act 1925 says nothing about
those categories of rights affecting land which are not truly proprietary rights as such but are
merely personal rights in land. The difference between 'proprietary' and 'personal' rights in
land rests ultimately on some intuitive perception that the former confer on the grantee some
kind of 'stake' in the land itself, whereas the latter confer merely a personal and usually
transient permission to live on or do something on the land in question. 'Personal' rights affect
only the immediate grantor and grantee: they are not normally regarded as capable of binding
third parties (post, p 180).
3 See A.W.B. Simpson, *A History of The Land Law* (2nd edn Oxford 1986), p 192ff.
4 See Supreme Court of Judicature Acts 1873-1875.

(1) The statutory criterion

Section 1 of the Law of Property Act 1925 draws a fairly sharp distinction between certain rights which are 'capable of subsisting or of being conveyed or created at law' and those rights which are capable of existence only in equity.

1.—(1) The only estates in land which are capable of subsisting or of being conveyed or created at law are —
(a) An estate in fee simple absolute in possession;
(b) A term of years absolute.

(2) The only interests or charges in or over land which are capable of subsisting or of being conveyed or created at law are —
(a) An easement, right, or privilege in or over land for an interest equivalent to an estate in fee simple absolute in possession or a term of years absolute;
(b) A rent charge in possession issuing out of or charged on land being either perpetual or for a term of years absolute;
(c) A charge by way of legal mortgage;
(d) . . . and any other similar charge on land which is not created by an instrument;
(e) Rights of entry exercisable over or in respect of a legal term of years absolute, or annexed, for any purpose, to a legal rentcharge.

(3) All other estates, interests, and charges in or over land take effect as equitable interests.

Section 1 thus distinguishes between
(a) two legal *estates* (section 1(1)) and five legal *interests* or *charges* (section 1(2)),[5] and
(b) all other proprietary rights in land—which must necessarily by reason of their exclusion from the first two subsections be equitable only (section 1(3)).

(2) The proper classification of rights in land

The distinction between 'legal' and 'equitable' rights in land is therefore both artificial and crude; but it is nonetheless clear. Whether an estate, interest or charge can ever be 'legal' depends quite simply on whether reference to it can be found in one or other of the categories contained in section 1(1) or (2). If the right in question is to be found there (eg a term of years absolute or a mortgage), then it is indeed capable of existing at law.[6] If it is not referred to within section

---

5 The rights referred to in section 1(1) and (2) are alike in that they are all potentially *legal* in character. The difference between estates, interests and charges consists in the fact that an 'estate' is a right in land owned or occupied by oneself, while an 'interest' or 'charge' tends to be a right acquired in or over somebody else's land. However, this formal distinction should not obscure the fact that the estates, interests and charges referred to in section 1(1) and (2) are all potentially legal rather than equitable. In the legislation consolidated in the 1925 enactments, all three kinds of legal right were thrown together in *one* subsection rather than the *two* subsections which appear as section 1(1) and (2) of the Law of Property Act 1925 (see Law of Property Act 1922, s 1(1)).

6 Section 1 of the Law of Property Act 1925 indicates merely whether a given property right is 'capable' of existing at law. Whether, within a particular context, that right *actually* constitutes a legal right depends usually on whether certain formalities (eg the use of a sealed document or deed) were observed in the granting of that right (post, p 221).

1(1) or (2)—as would be the case, for instance, with a restrictive covenant[7]—
then the right can only be equitable.[8]

2. LEGAL ESTATES

Section 1(1) marks out two possible *legal estates* in land—the 'freehold' and
'leasehold' estates respectively. Neither of these estates can be held by a minor,
ie, by a person who has not attained the age of 18 years.[9] These estates will now
be analysed in some detail.

3. THE FEE SIMPLE ABSOLUTE IN POSSESSION

The estate in fee simple absolute in possession is known as the 'freehold estate'
in English law. It is important to recognise the full significance of each element
in the name of this estate.[10]

(1) The meaning of 'absolute'

The term 'absolute' qualifies the character of a fee simple estate in such a way
as to distinguish it from various forms of modified fee such as the 'determinable'
and the 'conditional' fee simple. The fee simple absolute is nowadays much
more common than any of the modified fees, but the internal distinctions
between these fees may be quite difficult to draw.

(a) The determinable fee simple

A determinable fee simple is an estate of potentially perpetual duration which
is, however, liable to be cut short by the occurrence of some specified but
unpredictable event. An example would occur in a grant of Blackacre to A in
fee simple until A qualifies as a barrister. Here it is uncertain at the date of the
grant whether the determining event will ever happen.[11] The grant confers on
A a determinable fee simple which, because it is not 'absolute' in the terms of
section 1(1)(a) of the Law of Property Act 1925, can only be equitable.[12] As
such it must take effect behind some kind of trust arrangement.[13] Throughout
A's ownership of the determinable fee simple, the original grantor retains a
'possibility of reverter' in that A's estate will automatically terminate in favour

---

7 Post, p 700.
8 Moreover, the right is equitable in such a case irrespective of its mode of creation (eg even if
created by deed).
9 Law of Property Act 1925, s 1(6).
10 For the definition of the 'fee simple', see Chapter 4 (ante, p 61).
11 It is of the essence of a determinable fee that there is a possibility that the determining event
may *never* happen (see *Challis*, p 251). If, however, the specified determining event is bound to
occur sooner or later, no determinable fee simple can arise. For instance, a grant in fee simple to
A 'until the death of B' confers on A not a determinable fee simple, but an estate *pur autre vie*
(*Challis*, p 252) (ante, p 62).
12 Law of Property Act 1925, s 1(3). See *In re Ladypool Road Old National School, Birmingham* [1985]
Ch 62, [1984] 3 All ER 179.
13 Post, p 803.

of the revertee if the specified determining event occurs.[14] In this case the grantor's 'possibility of reverter' matures into a right to resume the fee simple absolute.

(i) Examples ancient and modern   No special language need be used to create a determinable fee simple so long as it is made plain that the durability of the fee simple estate is dependent on the continuance of some specified state of affairs or the non-occurrence of some specified future event.[15] The caselaw abounds with such curious examples as the grant of a fee simple 'during the time that such a tree shall grow',[16] or 'as long as the Church of St Paul shall stand',[17] or until X pay £100 to Y.[18] Nowadays determinable fees simple tend to be the product of statutory creation. In England and Wales, for instance, the relevant county highway authority is, in relation to the underlying soil of its public roads, statutorily invested with a fee simple estate determinable on those roads ceasing to be public highways.[19]

(ii) Subsequent impossibility   If the determining event indicated in the grant of a determinable fee simple later becomes impossible, the grantee's estate becomes a fee simple absolute and the grantor's possibility of reverter simply falls away.[20] If, in the example above of a grant to A in fee simple until he qualifies as a barrister, A dies without having thus qualified, his determinable fee becomes absolute and passes with his estate.

(iii) Invalidity on grounds of public policy   If, although it is somewhat rare, the limiting element in a determinable fee simple is vitiated by considerations of public policy, the determinable fee is rendered void in its entirety.[1] Since the limiting words are bound into the determinable fee simple as an integral component of the estate granted, any invalidity affecting those limiting words inevitably makes the entire grant defective.

(b) The conditional fee simple

A conditional fee simple is again an estate of potentially perpetual duration which is defeasible on the satisfaction of a 'condition subsequent'. An example would occur where Blackacre is granted to A 'on condition that he shall not qualify as a barrister'. The fee simple estate vested in A is liable to forfeiture if A qualifies as a barrister and thus fulfils the condition subsequent. As is the case with the determinable fee simple, the grant of a conditional fee provides, at least in theory, a potent means by which the owner of capital in the form of land

---

14 The determinable fee comes to an end without any entry or claim requiring to be made by the revertee (*Challis*, p 252). Possibilities of reverter are subject to the rule against perpetuities (Perpetuities and Accumulations Act 1964, s 12(1)(a)).
15 *Challis*, p 252.
16 *Ayres v Falkland* (1697) 1 Ld Raym 325 at 326, 91 ER 1112 at 1113.
17 2 Plowd 557, 75 ER 820.
18 For other examples of a determinable fee, see *Challis*, p 255ff. For a more recent example of a determinable fee simple, see *In re Rowhook Mission Hall, Horsham* [1985] Ch 62.
19 See Highways Act 1980, s 263; *Foley's Charity Trustees v Dudley Corporation* [1910] 1 KB 317 at 322, 324; *Tithe Redemption Commission v Runcorn UDC* [1954] Ch 383 at 403; *Wiltshire CC v Frazer* (1984) 47 P & CR 69 at 70, 72f.
20 *Challis*, p 254. See *In re Leach* [1912] 2 Ch 422 at 429.
 1 *Bl Comm*, Vol II, p 157. See *In re Moore* (1888) 39 Ch D 116 at 130, 132; *Zapletal v Wright* [1957] Tas SR 211 at 218.

may—however capriciously—impose on the grantees of his largesse an idiosyncratic preference as to beliefs, morals or lifestyle.[2]

(i) Ancillary 'rights of entry' It is normal to include in the grant of a conditional fee an express right of entry which entitles the grantor to forfeit the estate in the event of the fulfilment or breach of the specified condition.[3] Such rights of entry have sometimes been attached to a grant in fee simple in order to enforce payment of a rentcharge undertaken by the grantee of the land.[4] In certain parts of England[5] and Northern Ireland,[6] for instance, it has been a common conveyancing practice for land to be sold not for a capital sum but in consideration of a continuing income in the form of a perpetual rentcharge known as a 'fee farm rent'. Although such conveyances are no longer possible in England and Wales,[7] those fee farm grants which still subsist invest the grantee with merely a conditional fee simple, the estate conveyed being defeasible for non-payment of the required periodic sum.

(ii) Distinction between conditional and determinable fees It is notoriously difficult to maintain a strict distinction between the conditional and determinable forms of the fee simple.[8] At its root the distinction rests on the fact that in a determinable fee the limiting circumstance is integral to the formulation of the duration of the estate,[9] whereas in the conditional fee the limiting proviso operates to cut short the estate before it reaches out to its normal span.[10] The distinction is elusive in the extreme and is ultimately a matter of construction of the words used in the grant.[11] Any rationalisation of the distinction on purely

2 See eg *Jenner v Turner* (1880-81) 16 Ch D 188 at 196f per Bacon V-C: 'It is not competent to the court to inquire into the motives which may have induced the restriction. If it could be properly said they had been prompted by spite or malevolence the condition would nevertheless be valid; for the law does not prohibit testators from indulging such bad feelings, provided that no principle of public policy is thereby contravened.'

3 Post, p 82. It is now possible for the grantor in his conveyance to specify that the right of entry may be exercised by and on behalf of some person other than himself (Law of Property Act 1925, s 4(3)).

4 Rentcharges are discussed elsewhere (post, p 81).

5 Particularly in Manchester and East Lancashire, and around Bath and Bristol (see Law Commission, *Transfer of Land: Rentcharges* (Published Working Paper No 24, 1969), paras 10-14).

6 Much of the 17th and 18th Century plantation of Ulster was carried out effectively through the device of fee farm grants which still appear in chains of title to the present day (ante, p 57).

7 See Rentcharges Act 1977, s 2(1) (post, p 81).

8 The distinction has been described as 'little short of disgraceful to our jurisprudence' (*In re King's Trusts* (1892) 29 LR Ir 401 at 410 per Porter MR).

9 The determinable fee 'marks the bounds or compass of the estate, and the time of its continuance' (*Preston on Estates*, Vol 1, p 49). See also *Bl Comm*, Vol II, p 155; *Challis*, p 260f; *Re Tilbury West Public School Board and Hastie* (1966) 55 DLR (2d) 407 at 410.

10 The conditional fee 'has its operation in defeating the estate before it attains the boundary or has completed the space of time described by the limitation' (*Preston on Estates*, Vol 1, p 49). See also *Bl Comm*, Vol II, p 155; *Challis*, p 261. In the words of Laskin JA in *Re North Gower Township Public School Board and Todd* (1968) 65 DLR (2d) 421 at 424, a conditional fee involves a 'superadded condition upon a grant of a fee simple rather than an integral part of the very limitation of the estate created . . .' See also *Re Essex County Roman Catholic Separate School Board and Antaya* (1978) 80 DLR (3d) 405 at 409.

11 Certain words and phrases have come to be *indicia* of a fee simple upon condition subsequent (eg 'on condition that', 'provided that') and of a fee simple determinable (eg 'while', 'until', 'as long as'), but these rules of thumb are not necessarily conclusive (see *Hopper v Liverpool Corporation* (1943) 88 SJ 213 at 214; *Re North Gower Township Public School Board and Todd* (1968) 65 DLR (2d) 421 at 424).

semantic grounds is apt to be mocked by the almost indistinguishable duration of the estates created by the different forms of fee. An estate granted to A 'until he qualifies as a barrister' seems likely to last just as long as an estate granted 'on condition that he shall not qualify as a barrister.'

(iii) The legal quality of the conditional fee simple   The distinction between conditional and determinable fees would be almost entirely academic but for one vital substantive difference in their characterisation as property rights. By a sort of legislative accident, the conditional fee simple ranks as a *legal* estate in land, whereas the determinable fee is clearly equitable only. In strict logic, the absence of an 'absolute' quality should have the effect of relegating all conditional fees to merely equitable status in the terms of section 1(1)(a) of the Law of Property Act 1925. However, it was considered inconvenient that fee farm grants, which were all but grants in fee simple absolute, should not enjoy legal status.[12] Accordingly, section 7(1) of the Law of Property Act 1925 was amended in 1926 to provide that such grants should henceforth be treated for the purpose of the Act as grants of a fee simple absolute estate.[13] Whether or not intentionally, the amending provision appears to be sufficiently widely drafted to apply not merely to fee farm grants subject to a rentcharge, but to all forms of conditional fee simple which are subject to a right of entry.

(iv) Differences in the operation of conditional and determinable fees   There are also certain technical differences of operation and effect between conditional and determinable fees. *First*, whereas a determinable fee terminates automatically in favour of the revertee when the limiting event occurs, the conditional fee does not so terminate. The conditional fee continues to exist unless and until the grantor exercises his right of entry.[14] *Second*, the courts have tended to be somewhat more vigilant in applying rules of public policy to strike down undesirable conditions subsequent than has traditionally been the case with equivalent clauses contained in a determinable fee simple.[15] *Third*, if a condition subsequent is vitiated as contrary to public policy, the offending condition is merely struck out, leaving the grant as a fee simple absolute,[16] whereas in a determinable fee the grant is destroyed in its entirety.

(c) Judicial control over conditions and limitations

As indicated above, the courts have asserted a general jurisdiction to strike down certain kinds of condition or limitation attached to a grant in fee simple where the constraints concerned have been regarded as either impossible[17] or

---

12   There was a danger that such grants would have come within the cumbersome provisions of the Settled Land Act 1925 (post, p 803).

13   See Law of Property (Amendment) Act 1926, Schedule.

14   *Litt*, s 347; *Bl Comm*, Vol II, p 155; *Challis*, p 219. See *Matthew Manning's Case* (1609) 8 Co Rep 94b at 95b, 77 ER 618 at 620. The right of entry is subject to the rule against perpetuities (Perpetuities and Accumulations Act 1964, s 12(1)).

15   Post, p 75f.

16   *Bl Comm*, Vol II, p 156f. A void condition subsequent is simply 'treated as non scriptum' (*Gower v Public Trustee* [1924] NZLR 1233 at 1257 per Salmond J). See also *Morley v Rennoldson* (1843) 2 Hare 570 at 579f, 67 ER 235 at 239; *Zapletal v Wright* [1957] Tas SR 211 at 218.

17   Blackstone held conditions to be void 'if they be impossible at the time of their creation, or afterwards become impossible by the act of God or the act of the feoffor himself' (*Bl Comm*, Vol II, p 156). See also *Sheppard's Touchstone*, p 129; *Gower v Public Trustee* [1924] NZLR 1233 at 1255 (grant to X 'on condition that he shall not become a Roman Catholic', where X is already a Roman Catholic at the date of the grant).

illegal[18] or as inimical to public policy on moral, social or economic grounds. The judicial discretion to override the expressed wishes of grantors in such circumstances represents a significant diminution of the right of 'the owner' of property under English law to dispose of 'his' property in any way he will. There is in particular a disinclination to allow dispositions by which a testator seeks to direct the lives of his children from the grave.[19] The courts tend both to construe strictly any clause which purports to operate a forfeiture[20] and to exercise the equitable jurisdiction to relieve the defaulting party against the effect of forfeiture.[1]

(i) Restrictions on alienation In practice the courts guard jealously against restraints of an absolute or virtually absolute nature imposed upon the grantee of a fee simple, but have been remarkably tolerant of restraints which are merely partial or particular. In view of the public policy favouring the free alienability of land,[2] the courts have struck down conditions subsequent which wholly prohibit any form of alienation of the estate by the grantee,[3] or which allow alienation only to a named person.[4] However, the courts have been prepared to uphold clauses which prohibit alienation to a specific named person[5] or which permit alienation only to a member or members of an identifiable class or group of persons.[6] Some sort of compromise is thus struck

18 Blackstone gives the example of a grant to a man which is expressed to be defeasible 'unless he kills another' (*Bl Comm*, Vol II, p 157). The preclusion of illegality also implies that a condition subsequent cannot be allowed to frustrate the legally prescribed devolution of property. For instance, a condition subsequent cannot validly make a fee simple estate defeasible in the event of the grantee's intestacy (*In re Dixon* [1903] 2 Ch 458 at 460) or insolvency (*In re Machu* (1882) 21 Ch D 838 at 842). It is ironic that there is no objection if the offending clause appears in the form of a determinable interest (see eg *Graves v Dolphin* (1826) 1 Sim 66 at 67, 57 ER 503 at 504).

19 See *Clayton v Ramsden* [1943] AC 320 at 325 per Lord Atkin; *Re Sutcliffe* [1982] 2 NZLR 330 at 337. See also *Blathwayt v Baron Cawley* [1976] AC 397 at 427C-D; *In re Tepper's Will Trusts* [1987] 2 WLR 729 at 739A.

20 See *Rawson v Inhabitants of School District No 5 in Uxbridge* (1863) 89 Mass 125 at 127; *Pearson v Adams* (1912) 7 DLR 139 at 144f. The courts seem to require a greater degree of certainty in advance as to the scope of a condition subsequent than is needed when the condition is precedent (*Blathwayt v Baron Cawley* [1976] AC 397 at 424H-425A). It may be, as suggested by Lord Wright in *Clayton v Ramsden* [1943] AC 320 at 329, that the 'modern idea, perhaps, is that the beneficiary should be in a position to know beyond a peradventure what he is to do or not to do if he is to avoid a forfeiture. That must be ascertainable by him.' See *Clavering v Ellison* (1856) 3 Drew 451 at 470, 61 ER 975 at 982, (1859) 7 HLC 707 at 715f, 11 ER 282 at 285.

1 Post, p 493.

2 The power of alienation is seen as intrinsic to rights of ownership and an absolute restriction on alienation is therefore, in the words of Littleton, 'against reason' (*Litt*, s 360), in that it is repugnant to the essence of ownership in fee simple (*Co Litt*, p 223a; *Bl Comm*, Vol II, p 156). See *In re Rosher* (1884) 26 Ch D 801 at 812; *In re Elliot* [1896] 2 Ch 353 at 356; *Re Winnipeg Condominium Corp No 1 and Stechley* (1979) 90 DLR (3d) 703 at 706.

3 See also *Hood v Oglander* (1865) 34 Beav 513 at 522, 55 ER 733 at 737; *Byrne v Byrne* (1953) 87 ILTR 183 at 185f. 'Alienation' for this purpose includes a mortgage (*Ware v Cann* (1830) 10 B & C 433 at 438, 109 ER 511 at 513) and a testamentary disposition (*In re Jones* [1898] 1 Ch 438 at 443).

4 *Muschamp v Bluet*, Bridgman J 132 at 137, 123 ER 1253 at 1256; *Re Cockerill* [1929] 2 Ch 131 at 134f.

5 *Litt*, s 361; *Co Litt*, p 223a/b. See, however, *In re Rosher* (1884) 26 Ch D 801 at 813f.

6 *Doe d Gill v Pearson* (1805) 6 East 173 at 180, 102 ER 1253 at 1256; *In re Macleay* (1875) LR 20 Eq 186 at 189 (alienation permitted within 'the family'). Compare, however, *Crofts v Beamish* [1905] 2 IR 349 at 356f, 360; *In re Browne* [1954] Ch 39 at 50 (condition void where alienation restricted to small and diminishing group of 'brothers'). Where the class to which alienation is permitted is defined with reference to racial or sexual characteristics, the limiting clause seems not to be unlawful by reason of statute (see Race Relations Act 1976, s 21(1); Sex Discrimination Act 1975, s 30(1)). See J.F. Garner, *Racial Restrictive Covenants in England and the United States*, (1972) 35 MLR 478; J.D.A. Brooke-Taylor, [1978] Conv 24. However, this kind of clause would seem an entirely appropriate target for invalidation under general rules of public policy.

between the policy concern to render land easily commerciable and the countervailing impulse in favour of allowing personal control over the terms on which a private owner may dispose of his own property.

(ii)   Restrictions on marriage   In a similar way the state of marriage is regarded as a socially approved institution and the courts have been reluctant to uphold conditions subsequent which militate against the institution in its entirety.[7] Conditions subsequent have thus been invalidated which altogether preclude marriage[8] (as distinct from remarriage[9]) on the part of the grantee, but the courts have held good partial restraints on marriage which merely prohibit the grantee's marriage with a named person[10] or with any of an ascertainable class of persons.[11]

(iii)   Restrictions on religious belief   The courts have not been particularly astute to restrain attempts to perpetuate religious preference—bigoted or otherwise—in the grant of a fee simple, at least where there is no vitiating degree of uncertainty attaching to the faith prescribed or proscribed by the grantor.[12] In *Blathwayt v Baron Cawley*,[13] the House of Lords upheld a condition

---

7   'Conditions in restraint of marriage are odious' (*Long v Dennis* (1767) 4 Burr 2052 at 2055, 98 ER 69 at 72 per Lord Mansfield). The disfavour shown towards such conditions was justified in former times on grounds both of moral paternalism and of public policy. An absolute restraint upon marriage was liable to be condemned as hindering 'a great moral and social good...it tends to evil and the promoting of licentiousness; it tends to depopulation, the greatest of all political sins...' (*Low v Peers* (1770) Wilm 364 at 372, 97 ER 138 at 141). See also *Maddox v Maddox's Administrator*, 11 Grat (52 Va) 804 at 806 (1854); O.L. Browder, *Conditions and Limitations in Restraint of Marriage*, 39 Michigan LR 1288 (1940–41).

8   See eg *Morley v Rennoldson* (1843) 2 Hare 570 at 579f, 583, 67 ER 235 at 239f; *Jenner v Turner* (1880-81) 16 Ch D 188 at 197; *Duddy v Gresham* (1878) 2 LR Ir 442 at 464f. The courts may exceptionally uphold a condition prohibiting marriage where there was a clear and genuine intention in the grantor to provide for the grantee while he or she remained unmarried (see *Morley v Rennoldson*, supra at 580, 239; *Low v Peers* (1770) Wilm 364 at 377, 97 ER 138 at 143; *Jones v Jones* (1875-76) 1 QBD 279 at 283; *In re Elliott* [1918] 1 IR 41 at 43f). Compare the greater willingness to tolerate the use of marriage as a limiting circumstance in a determinable fee simple (*In re King's Trusts* (1892) 29 LR Ir 401 at 410; *Oliver v Menton* [1945] IR 6 at 11f; *Stewart v Murdoch* [1969] NI 78 at 82; *In re Dolan* [1970] IR 94 at 101).

9   Grants *durante viduitate* (for the duration of widowhood) have not been struck down as offensive to any consideration of public policy (see eg *Jordan v Holkham* (1753) Amb 209, 27 ER 139). Compare, however, the more enlightened approach evident in *Duddy v Gresham* (1878) 2 LR Ir 442, where a testator had left property to his widow on condition that she should not remarry, but should 'retire immediately after my death into a convent of her own choice'!

10   *Jarvis v Duke* (1681) 1 Vern 19 at 20, 23 ER 274 ('. . . such an example of presumptuous disobedience highly meriting such a punishment; she being only prohibited to marry with one man by name, and nothing in the whole fair garden of Eden would serve her turn but this forbidden fruit'). See also *Jenner v Turner* (1880-81) 16 Ch D 188 at 196; *In re Bathe* [1925] Ch 377 at 382; *In re Hanlon* [1933] Ch 254 at 260.

11   *Duggan v Kelly* (1847) 10 Ir Eq R 295 at 301f ('a Papist'); *Perrin v Lyon* (1807) 9 East 170 at 183f, 103 ER 538 at 543 ('a Scotchman'); *Jenner v Turner* (1880-81) 16 Ch D 188 at 197 ('a domestic servant').

12   See *Clayton v Ramsden* [1943] AC 320, where the House of Lords struck down as uncertain a prohibition of marriage with a person 'not of Jewish parentage and of the Jewish faith'. Compare, however, *Higgins v Bank of Ireland* [1947] IR 277 at 285f; *McCausland v Young* [1948] NI 72 at 94, [1949] NI 49 at 60; *Blathwayt v Baron Cawley* [1976] AC 397 at 425D-E, G, 429E-F; *In re Tuck's ST* [1978] Ch 49 at 62F, 65F, 66C; *In re Tepper's Will Trusts* [1987] 2 WLR 729 at 737A-C, 744G-745E.

13   [1976] AC 397. See generally J.D.A. Brooke-Taylor, [1978] Conv 24.

subsequent which had the effect of forfeiting the grantee's interest if he should 'be or become a Roman Catholic.'[14]

(iv) Other forms of discrimination There has been no significant inclination to import into this context supra-national guarantees against discrimination,[15] the view being expressed that discrimination 'is not the same thing as choice' and that 'neither by express provision nor by implication has private selection yet become a matter of public policy.'[16] The deference accorded the private prejudice of the propertied class is still substantial,[17] personal caprice becoming offensive to public policy only where it imposes a comprehensive fetter upon the operation of the free market in either private property[18] or the supporting institution of bourgeois marriage.[19]

(2) The meaning of 'in possession'

An estate in fee simple absolute in possession confers upon its owner an immediate right to occupation and enjoyment of the land from the effective date of the grant to him.[20] The term 'in possession',[1] when thus used in relation to the sole freehold estate at law, distinguishes this form of fee simple from those estates in fee simple which are merely 'in remainder' or 'in reversion'.

(a) Estates 'in remainder'

An interest 'in remainder' confers a present right to future enjoyment, in the sense that the 'remainderman' is excluded from immediate enjoyment only by

---

14 The actual grant in this case included an entailed interest, but the entail was duly barred by the tenant in tail (ante, p 62), who thereupon claimed that his fee simple was absolute and not conditional.

15 See eg The European Convention on Human Rights (1950), art 8 (right to respect for 'private and family life'), art 9 (right to freedom of religion).

16 *Blathwayt v Baron Cawley* [1976] AC 397 at 426B-C per Lord Wilberforce. See also Lord Cross of Chelsea at 429G-430A, Lord Edmund-Davies at 441D-E.

17 See eg *Re Talbot-Ponsonby's Estate* [1937] 4 All ER 309 at 313A (condition that grantee should not allow a named person to 'set foot upon' the property held valid). The private prejudices endorsed by the courts may, of course, be anti-establishment in character. See *Blathwayt v Baron Cawley* [1976] AC 397 at 442G, where Lord Fraser of Tullybelton thought that the courts would not regard as contrary to public policy a grant conditioned upon the grantee not sending his children to a fee-paying public school.

18 See the interesting statement of Lord Wilberforce in *Blathwayt v Baron Cawley* [1976] AC 397 at 426G that he found himself 'unpersuaded that, in relation to landed estates in which family attitudes and traditions may be strong and valued by testators, and moreover which may often involve close association with one or another Church, public policy requires that testators may not prefer one branch of the family to another upon religious grounds.'

19 The courts regard as void a condition which militates against the continued cohabitation of spouses (see *In re Johnson's WT* [1967] Ch 387 at 395B-C, 396C, F-G). See also *Zapletal v Wright* [1957] Tas SR 211 at 218, where a verbal condition subsequent requiring the continued cohabitation of de facto spouses was disregarded on the ground that it operated merely *in terrorem*. Compare *Andrews v Parker* [1973] Qd R 93 at 107B-D.

20 See *Pearson v IRC* [1981] AC 753 at 772A-D, where Viscount Dilhorne accepted the time-honoured proposition that an 'estate in possession' is one which gives 'a present right of present enjoyment'.

1 'Possession' is statutorily defined as including 'receipt of rents and profits or the right to receive the same' (Law of Property Act 1925, s 205(1)(xix)). Thus a fee simple absolute does not cease to be an estate 'in possession' merely because the owner grants a lease to a tenant. In the context of a legal lease both the landlord and the tenant have an estate 'in possession'.

reason of the presence of a prior interest or prior interests vested in somebody else.[2]

An example of a fee simple absolute in remainder would occur where X grants Blackacre to A for life, with remainder to B in fee simple. Here it is A who is entitled 'in possession' as from the date of the grant; B has merely a fee simple absolute in remainder. However, it is important to realise that B, although not immediately entitled 'in possession', does indeed receive a proprietary interest *at the date of the grant*. He receives a present right to future enjoyment, since his remainder will 'fall into possession' on the termination of A's prior interest (ie when A dies). This incidentally brings about the important consequence that if B predeceases A, B's present right to future enjoyment (ie his interest 'in remainder') will pass to B's estate to be claimed 'in possession' by the persons entitled thereunder when A eventually dies.

Attention must be drawn to one other implication attached to a fee simple absolute in remainder. It follows with remorseless logic from section 1(1)(a) of the Law of Property Act 1925 that such an estate, not being 'in possession', cannot be a legal estate. Regardless of the manner of its creation, it can only be an *equitable* fee simple absolute[3] and must therefore take effect behind some form of trust.[4]

(b) Estates 'in reversion'

An estate 'in reversion' is the sum total of the rights retained throughout by a grantor who fails to exhaust the entire interest in the land in the terms of his conveyance to a stranger.[5] In other words, if a grantor fails to dispose of the fee simple absolute in his land, he himself retains a fee simple 'in reversion' from the moment of his non-exhaustive grant, and this fee simple estate will fall back into possession on the expiration of the limited interests which he has granted away.

An example of a fee simple absolute in reversion arises where X grants Blackacre to A for life. A clearly takes a life interest 'in possession', but X, since he has not granted away the absolute interest in the land, takes the fee simple absolute 'in reversion' himself.[6] It should be noticed that, once again, this form of fee simple can only be equitable: it falls outside the terms of section 1(1)(a) of the Law of Property Act 1925.

4.   THE TERM OF YEARS ABSOLUTE

According to section 1(1)(b) of the Law of Property Act 1925, the only other estate in land which is capable of subsisting or of being conveyed or created *at law* is the 'term of years absolute'.[7] A term of years is the estate which a landlord

2 *Bl Comm*, Vol II, p 164; *Challis*, p 78f. A fee simple in remainder must be carefully distinguished from a 'contingent' fee simple, the vesting of which is subject to a 'condition precedent' (*Bl Comm*, Vol II, p 165).

3 Law of Property Act 1925, s 1(3).

4 Post, p 805.

5 '. . . if he, who was before possessed of the whole, carves out of it any smaller estate, and grants it away, whatever is not so granted remains in him' (*Bl Comm*, Vol II, p 175). See also *Challis*, p 78.

6 The 'reversion' which arises here by operation of law should be sharply distinguished from other forms of right which appear similar but which result from the conduct of the grantees themselves (eg the 'possibility of reverter' which rests with the grantor of a determinable fee simple and the 'right of entry' vested in the grantor of a fee simple which has been made the subject of a condition subsequent).

7 Ante, p 70; post, pp 427, 997.

confers upon his tenant, the qualifier 'absolute' appearing in this context to have no special significance.[8] A term of years is commonly known as a 'leasehold estate' and its owner as a leaseholder as distinct from a freeholder. A term of years is also often called simply a lease or tenancy.

(1) Distinguishing characteristic of the term of years

The distinguishing characteristic of a term of years is that it confers a right to occupy and enjoy land for a period of fixed maximum duration. It matters not whether that period is fixed and therefore self-determining or periodic and therefore renewable. The period may be one week or three thousand years: a term of years can exist in either case.[9] Being an estate in land, a term of years provides a flexible base for other transactions with the land. The term may itself become the subject matter of an 'assignment' (ie sale) or of a sublease.

(2) Social and economic functions of the lease

Leases of land are exceedingly important in both social and commercial terms. The device of the term of years plays a vital role in the provision of business premises for commercial enterprise, in the regulation of land use for agricultural purposes, and in the supply of residential housing.[10] Each of these spheres of operation was originally left to the free play of market forces, but nowadays the conduct of relations between landlord and tenant is controlled in a greater or lesser degree by regulatory legislation.[11] Perhaps the most conspicuous aspect of this legislation is that dealing with private residential tenancies. Historically the landlord, operating from a superior bargaining position, was frequently able to impose oppressive rents and conditions upon his tenants. However, the Rent Act legislation of the last seventy years has done much to redress the balance of power in the residential context, by affording substantial security of tenure and by establishing effective rent controls. Less extensive forms of protection for the tenant are provided by the statutory codes which govern other leasehold areas, ie, in respect of public sector residential tenancies, business tenancies and agricultural tenancies.

5. FORMAL CREATION OF ESTATES

With certain exceptions[12] no conveyance of land is effective to confer a legal

---

8 As defined in Law of Property Act 1925, s 205(1)(xxvii), a 'term of years absolute' retains its absolute character notwithstanding that it is determinable by notice given by either the landlord or the tenant or is determinable by reason of the landlord's exercise of a right of re-entry in the event of breach of covenant by the tenant.

9 A 'term of years absolute' is specifically defined as including 'a term for less than a year' (Law of Property Act 1925, s 205(1)(xxvii)). The longest lease on record seems to be one of 10 million years, granted on 3 December 1868 in respect of a plot for a sewage tank adjoining Columb Barracks, Mullinger, County Meath, Ireland (see N.D. McWhirter (ed), *Guinness Book of Records 1987* (London 1986), p 198).

10 In Great Britain approximately 33 per cent of the available housing stock is occupied by leaseholders under a term of years of some sort. See *General Household Survey 1985* (OPCS Monitor, Reference 86/1, 18 September 1986) p 6 (Table 7); Sir George Young, (1984) 15 Jiro (No 2), 6 at 7.

11 Post, pp 961, 1045.

12 These exceptions are spelt out in Law of Property Act 1925, s 52(2), the most important relating to assents by a personal representative (s 52(2)(a)) and certain kinds of lease not exceeding a term of three years (s 52(2)(d) in conjunction with s 54(2)) (post, pp 221, 464).

estate on the grantee unless the conveyance is made by deed.[13] The use of an unsealed form of writing for the grant of a fee simple absolute or a term of years results in the creation of only an equitable interest for the grantee.[14]

6.   LEGAL INTERESTS AND CHARGES

Section 1(2) of the Law of Property Act 1925 defines five categories of 'interest' or 'charge' capable of existence 'at law'.

(1)   Easements, rights and privileges (section 1(2)(a))

An easement is effectively a right to utilise somebody else's land in some limited way, the best example being a right of way over land belonging to a stranger.[15] If A, the owner of an estate in fee simple, grants his neighbour, B, a right of way over A's land, B is regarded in English law as having a proprietary right—of some kind—in or over A's land.

(a)   Requirements for legal character

Whether an easement is legal or equitable is determined largely by the terms of section 1(2)(a) of the Law of Property Act 1925, which includes within the rights 'capable' of existence at law any 'easement, right, or privilege in or over land for an interest equivalent to an estate in fee simple absolute in possession or a term of years absolute'. Whether an easement of the kind referred to here is *actually* legal in any given circumstances will depend on its creation by deed, statute or prescription.[16] However, section 1(2)(a) enables a distinction to be made between legal and equitable easements. It is a necessary, but not sufficient, condition of legal quality that an easement must conform to the characteristics as to duration which are laid down in section 1(2)(a).

(b)   Examples

If A by deed grants B an easement without limit of time, B's easement is legal, since its duration corresponds, in the terms of section 1(2)(a), to that of 'an estate in fee simple absolute in possession'. Likewise, if A by deed grants B an easement for a fixed period of time—whether long or short—B's easement is legal, since its duration is framed on the analogy of 'a term of years absolute', as referred to in the statute. However, if A grants B an easement for any period other than the two kinds of time-scale stipulated in section 1(2)(a), B's right can only be equitable. Section 1(2)(a) does not cover any easement granted for an indeterminate period other than in perpetuity, and therefore an easement granted, eg for B's life, or until such time as an alternative access is constructed, can only take effect in equity—even if granted by deed.[17]

---

13 Law of Property Act 1925, s 52(1). For further details of the rules regarding formalities, see Chapter 9 (post, p 221).

14 This demonstrates, incidentally, that it is quite possible to hold an *equitable* fee simple absolute in possession or an *equitable* term of years absolute. Section 1(1) of the Law of Property Act 1925 merely provides that it is these estates alone which have even the potentiality of *legal* existence.

15 Post, p 632.

16 Post, p 665.

17 Law of Property Act 1925, s 1(3).

(2) Rentcharges (section 1(2)(b))

A rentcharge is a right to a periodic payment of money charged on or issuing out of land other than under a lease or mortgage.[18] A rentcharge arises for instance where A has charged his own land with a payment of £100 per annum in favour of B. In such circumstances B is regarded as having a proprietary interest in A's land, and the characterisation of B's interest as legal or equitable turns on section 1(2)(b) of the Law of Property Act 1925. B's rentcharge can be legal only if it is 'either perpetual or for a term of years absolute', being equitable in all other cases.

Rentcharges are today fairly uncommon and are, in any case, in the process of being phased out of existence under the terms of the Rentcharges Act 1977.[19] This legislation recognises the anomalous nature of rentcharges in the modern context and provides that no new rentcharge may be created after 22 August 1977 'whether at law or in equity'.[20] Any instrument which purports to create a new rentcharge is declared void,[1] and all existing rentcharges are liable to be extinguished at the expiry of a period of sixty years beginning with the commencement of the 1977 Act or with the date on which the rentcharge in question first became payable, whichever is the later.[2]

(3) Mortgages (section 1(2)(c))

A mortgage is a form of security in real property taken by one who has advanced money on loan to the owner of land.[3] Although not of course confined to residential property, mortgage transactions have become the primary means of financing home ownership in fee simple or on long lease, the prospective home-owner often raising the bulk of the required purchase price by means of a loan from an institutional mortgagee such as a bank or building society or from a local authority.[4] The purchaser then acquires the fee simple or a long lease in the property purchased, granting a charge by way of legal mortgage as security for the loan.[5] The purchaser retains ownership of the estate throughout the loan term, although he is under a contractual obligation to repay both the capital sum advanced and any interest which it bears. The

---

18 Rentcharges Act 1977, s 1.
19 See Law Commission, *Report on Rentcharges* (Law Com No 68, August 1975).
20 Rentcharges Act 1977, s 2(1). However, this provision does not prohibit the creation of a rentcharge which has the effect of making the land on which the rent is charged settled land by virtue of Settled Land Act 1925, s 1(1)(v) (see Rentcharges Act 1977, s 2(3)(a)). The exempted class of rentcharge thus includes 'estate rentcharges' which arise where land is charged 'whether voluntarily or in consideration of marriage' with the payment of a periodic sum for the life of any person or for any lesser period. The embargo on new rentcharges covers only those created in a commercial context for money or money's worth.
1 Rentcharges Act 1977, s 2(2).
2 Rentcharges Act 1977, s 3(1). The owner of land subject to a rentcharge which is liable to extinguishment under section 3(1) may redeem the rentcharge by paying a redemption price calculated according to an algebraic formula contained in s 10(1). This right to redeem is not subject to the rule against perpetuities (see *Switzer & Co Ltd v Rochford* [1906] 1 IR 399 at 405f).
3 Mortgages are dealt with in detail in Chapters 16, 26 (post, pp 563, 887).
4 The role of the local authority as a mortgagee has been greatly increased by the 'right to buy' provisions introduced by Part I of the Housing Act 1980 (post, p 733).
5 This is nowadays a much more common means of creating a legal mortgage than the other mortgage device which is still permitted today, which involves the conferment on the mortgagee of a long lease in the property offered as security (Law of Property Act 1925, ss 85(1), 86(1)) (post, p 573).

home-owner—the mortgagor—is thereby enabled to acquire both a family base and a major capital asset by way of instalment purchase over a lengthy period (usually 20 or 25 years). Meanwhile the creditor—the mortgagee—is protected since the charge taken as security can always be enforced by taking possession of the property if the mortgagor becomes unable to discharge his obligations under the terms of the loan.

A charge granted 'by way of legal mortgage' is defined in section 1(2)(c) of the Law of Property Act 1925 as being capable of creation at law. If contained in a deed, such a charge is in fact *legal*.

(4) Miscellaneous charges (section 1(2)(d))

Section 1(2)(d) of the Law of Property Act 1925 refers to a group of legal charges on land not created by the voluntary transactions of individuals but imposed by statute. The categories of charge included here have been gravely diminished by repealing legislation,[6] and are now of little consequence.

(5) Rights of entry (section 1(2)(e))

A 'right of entry' has nothing to do with a right of way or any other easement.[7] A right of entry may be attached to a lease or rentcharge and, if so attached, is penal[8] rather than facultative. It consists essentially of the right to enforce forfeiture of the estate which is the subject matter of the lease or rentcharge. The right of entry becomes exercisable only in the event of default by, respectively, the tenant or the rentchargor, and its exercise results in a vesting or revesting of the delinquent's estate in the party exercising the right.[9] Far from comprising a 'right to use or draw profit from another man's land', the right of entry provides a means 'to take his land altogether away'.[10]

It is an intrinsic feature of a right of entry that it constitutes a proprietary right in the subject land which is somehow distinct from the proprietary right comprised in the lease or rentcharge to which it is appended. Thus A, the owner of an estate in fee simple, may have an extra proprietary right against his tenant, B, in the form of a right of entry expressly conferred on A by the terms of the lease. As a proprietary right in B's land, A's right of entry must be either legal or equitable. Section 1(2)(e) of the Law of Property Act 1925 specifically provides that a right of entry is legal if it is 'exercisable over or in respect of a legal term of years absolute'. Likewise, if A has annexed a right of entry to a rentcharge undertaken in his favour by B, that right of entry is legal if the rentcharge itself is legal. In all other cases the right of entry must be equitable only.[11]

---

6 Tithe rentcharge was abolished by the Tithe Act 1936, s 1, and land tax by the Finance Act 1963, Part V, Sch 14.
7 'To include a right of entry in the description of "equitable easement" offends a sense both of elegance and accuracy' (*Shiloh Spinners Ltd v Harding* [1973] AC 691 at 720B per Lord Wilberforce).
8 *Shiloh Spinners Ltd v Harding* [1973] AC 691 at 719E.
9 The exercise of the right of entry is subject to the court's jurisdiction to afford the defaulting party relief against forfeiture (post, p 493).
10 *Shiloh Spinners Ltd v Harding* [1973] AC 691 at 720C per Lord Wilberforce.
11 Law of Property Act 1925, s 1(3). See eg *Shiloh Spinners Ltd v Harding* [1973] AC 691 at 719B.

7. EQUITABLE INTERESTS

In the scheme of the Law of Property Act 1925 equitable interests in or over land are defined essentially by exclusion. Those proprietary rights in or over land which fail to qualify as 'legal' rights under the criteria of section 1(1), (2) take effect merely as 'equitable interests'.[12] These equitable interests and the conveyancing difficulties which they generate provide the subject matter of much of the remainder of this book.

8. SIGNIFICANCE OF THE DISTINCTION BETWEEN LEGAL AND EQUITABLE RIGHTS

A question must inevitably arise as to the reasons which underlie the strenuous efforts made in the Law of Property Act 1925 to distinguish *legal* from *equitable* rights. The sharpness of the distinction drawn by statute results from the fact that the borderline between legal and equitable rights has traditionally provided the starting point for the resolution of the central question of land law. This central issue relates to whether certain rights in land survive a transfer of that land to a purchaser, thereby remaining valid and enforceable against him. Given the pre-eminent importance of the transferability of land in an exchange economy, this question ranks as one of considerable social and commercial significance. Land law in practice means conveyancing—the quotidian business of effecting dispositions of property—and the scope of the problem becomes even larger once it is recognised that a 'conveyance' is defined broadly as including not merely the outright sale of property, but also a mortgage, charge, lease and assent relating to property.[13]

The fate of legal and equitable rights in the context of a conveyance is, of course, a matter of importance for both the purchaser and the owner of the rights in question. People tend to make the largest investment of their lifetime savings in one or other form of real property. It is a matter of more than marginal concern that the rights which they purchase should not be taken away, superseded or destroyed in any later transaction without proper compensation. Likewise the purchaser of land has a legitimate interest in knowing precisely which rights will be binding upon him in the aftermath of a purchase. Any uncertainty as to the effect of land transactions on various types of real property right has the effect of inhibiting purchasers and of stultifying dealings in land. No purchaser wants to risk his money if there is any real danger that the land purchased may be subject to adverse rights vested in others which render his title effectively or substantially worthless.

The social and economic implications involved here become even more acute if the 'purchaser' concerned is a mortgagee. In most instances mortgagees are large lending institutions which exist to finance the acquisition of realty for a wide range of commercial or residential purposes. Any inhibition placed on the availability of mortgage funds has immediately a potential impact on business life and the living patterns of millions. It was no mere casual

---

12 Law of Property Act 1925, s 1(3), (8).
13 Law of Property Act 1925, s 205(1)(ii). A 'purchaser' is likewise defined as including 'a lessee, mortgagee or other person who for valuable consideration acquires an interest in property . . .' (section 205(1)(xxi)).

afterthought which provoked the statement of Lord Upjohn in *National Provincial Bank Ltd v Ainsworth*[14] that

It has been the policy of the law for over a hundred years to simplify and facilitate transactions in real property. It is of great importance that persons should be able freely and easily to raise money on the security of their property.

Given these policy motivations, it is clear that the operation of an efficient conveyancing system depends heavily upon the achievement of a high degree of clarity in determining the fate of proprietary rights in the event of transactions with title. At least in historical terms, the answer to the central question of land law has turned ultimately on the characterisation of those rights as either *legal* or *equitable*. Although the importance of this distinction is being steadily eroded by the extension of the system of title registration,[15] it is this watershed between various sorts of right in land which still provides a vital key to resolving disputed issues of priority.

This can best be seen in the operation of two axioms which lie deeply embedded in the sedimentary layers of English land law. At some points today these two axioms still remain exposed to view, and provide an indispensable basis for the construction of solutions to land law problems. At other points they have been overlaid by different strata deposited by the later action of legislative change, although even here the erosive activity of judge-made law has occasionally stripped back the more recent strata to reveal the bed-rock of original principle.

The two most basic axioms of English land law are the following:

(i) legal rights bind the world;

(ii) equitable rights bind all persons except a bona fide purchaser of a legal estate for value without notice of those equitable rights.

(1) **Legal rights bind the world**

The force of the first axiom is simply explained. If B owns a *legal* right in or over land belonging to A (see *Fig.* 4), and C later acquires any interest in that land, B's right is binding on and effective against C. This result follows irrespective of whether C previously knew of B's right. The outcome rarely works injustice since almost all legal rights in or over land are evident on the face of the

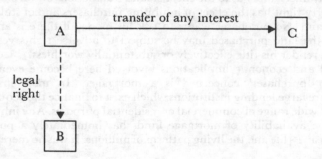

Fig. 4

14 [1965] AC 1175 at 1233G-1234A.
15 Post, p 144.

documents relating to title, and are therefore open to perusal by an intending purchaser.

Legal rights thus effectively take care of themselves. When land (or an interest in land) is transferred to *any* third party, legal rights previously attached to the land remain attached and are therefore binding on that third party. The axiomatic nature of this result works for both efficiency and clarity. The owner of legal rights knows that his position is secure notwithstanding the transfer of the land; likewise the purchaser is in general wholly aware that he takes his disposition subject to any legal rights which belong to others.

The simple logic of land law can be demonstrated in the following way. Suppose that A, the owner of a legal fee simple estate in Blackacre, grants a term of years (or lease) to B, and then transfers his fee simple (or 'freehold reversion'[16]) to C. If the term of years granted to B is a *legal* estate (as defined by the Law of Property Act 1925[17]), then it follows inexorably that C is bound by it.[18] The same result occurs *a fortiori* if C takes some lesser interest than a legal fee simple (eg if C is a mortgagee, or if C's interest is equitable rather than legal), for the binding effect of B's interest is not conditional on the precise nature of the interest taken by C. C is bound by B's legal right even if C is not a purchaser but is an adverse possessor (or 'squatter').[19] It is simply axiomatic that legal rights bind the world, and moreover that they bind the world irrespective of notice. It is entirely irrelevant whether C had any prior knowledge of the existence of B's rights.

The same reasoning is applicable to any other kind of legal interest owned by B. For example, if A, the owner of a legal fee simple estate in Blackacre, grants B a right of way over Blackacre, the effect of this easement on C (a subsequent purchaser from A) depends fundamentally on whether B's easement is characterised as legal or equitable. C is automatically bound by B's easement if the easement is properly classified as *legal* according to the canons contained in section 1(2)(a) of the Law of Property Act 1925 (eg if it was granted in perpetuity or for a fixed period of time).[20] Similarly, a mortgage granted by A to B is binding on C if it constitutes a legal mortgage within the terms of section 1(2)(c) of the Law of Property Act 1925 (eg if created by deed).[1] A right of entry, if legal within the terms of section 1(2)(e), is also binding on the world.[2] In all these cases it matters not what precise interest is taken by C. It is likewise irrelevant that C was at the date of purchase unaware of the rights of B, since the doctrine of notice has no application at all to legal rights.

(2) Equitable rights are governed by the doctrine of notice

According to the second axiom of English land law, equitable rights in or over land are binding on all persons *other than* a bona fide purchaser of a legal estate

16 Post, p 463.
17 Ante, p 70.
18 If B's term of years is not legal but equitable (eg if not created by deed in circumstances where a deed was required (see Law of Property Act 1925, ss 52(2)(d), 54(2))), its effect on C depends on different principles (post, pp 135, 159).
19 *In re Nisbet and Potts' Contract* [1906] 1 Ch 386 at 401.
20 Ante, p 80. If, however, the easement was granted for an indefinite period other than perpetuity or was granted otherwise than by deed, the easement can only be equitable and its impact on C turns on different principles (post, pp 141, 159).
1 Ante, p 70, post, p 573.
2 Post, p 82.

for value without notice of those equitable rights.[3] This basic proposition incorporates what is known as the *equitable doctrine of notice*,[4] and provides the historical method of determining whether an equitable interest granted to B in respect of A's land remains binding on a stranger, C, who later receives some interest in that land.

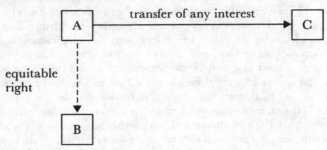

Fig. 5

It must be emphasised that this doctrine of notice, although forming a fundamental stratum of English land law, is nowadays heavily overlaid by various systems of registration of land interests.[5] It has also been superseded by certain statutory mechanisms for 'overreaching' prior equitable rights.[6] To this extent the doctrine is no longer the *comprehensive* arbiter of the binding effect of equitable interests.[7] It tends to play only a residual role in determining questions of priority when other methods have failed or are inapplicable.[8] Nevertheless the doctrine of notice holds a vital key even today to an understanding of the structure and function of the law of real property, and for this reason must be subjected to minute examination.

In terms of the doctrine of notice, equitable rights granted to B in respect of A's land are liable to be defeated by a third party purchaser who at the date of purchase had no notice or knowledge of their existence. In *Midland Bank Trust Co Ltd v Green*[9] Lord Wilberforce explained this doctrine as an instance of equity's tendency to fasten upon conscience, observing that the 'composite expression' of the doctrine was 'used to epitomise the circumstances in which equity would or rather would not do so.'[10]

The full implications of this 'composite expression' must now be investigated. Before the equitable doctrine of notice may operate in his favour and release him from pre-existing equitable rights, the purchaser must discharge a heavy onus. He must establish that he is a bona fide (good faith) purchaser of a legal estate for value without notice. The onus of proof rests clearly on him.[11] A purchaser who demonstrates that he is possessed of all these

3 *London and South Western Railway Co v Gomm* (1881-82) 20 Ch D 562 at 583; *In re Nisbet and Potts' Contract* [1906] 1 Ch 386 at 403, 405.
4 Ante, p 48.
5 Post, pp 110, 144.
6 Post, p 100.
7 Post, p 102.
8 Post, pp 102, 107.
9 [1981] AC 513 at 528D.
10 Ante, p 46.
11 *Attorney-General v Biphosphated Guano Co* (1879) 11 Ch D 327 at 337; *In re Nisbet and Potts' Contract* [1906] 1 Ch 386 at 403f; *Heneghan v Davitt* [1933] IR 375 at 377, 379; *Northern Bank Ltd v Henry* [1981] IR 1 at 19.

attributes is sometimes known simply as 'Equity's Darling'—one to whom the favour of equity has been extended.

(a) Bona fides

It is generally assumed that the requirement of bona fides or good faith on the part of the purchaser relates primarily to the element of notice. In order that the purchaser may claim immunity from equitable interests, he must show not only that he had no notice of those interests but also that his absence of notice was 'genuine and honest'.[12] Part of this idea is now incorporated in the concept of 'constructive notice',[13] but it may be that the requirement of good faith imports something more than a mere absence of notice. There are indications that even if the purchaser shows an absence of notice, the courts may still enquire into his honesty.[14] In other words, the requirement of good faith is neither obsolete nor descriptive merely of an absence of actual or constructive notice.[15] However, it seems in reality that nowadays this requirement is readily deemed to be satisfied, and little ever turns upon it.

(b) Purchase of a legal estate

In order to defeat pre-existing equitable rights, the purchaser must take a legal estate in the land concerned.[16] He must therefore purchase either a legal fee simple absolute in possession or a legal term of years.[17] Thus the freedom from prior equitable interests conferred by the doctrine of notice may be acquired by a purchaser of either a freehold or a leasehold. Moreover, by a special statutory fiction a third party lender who takes a charge 'by way of legal mortgage' is also regarded for some purposes as having purchased a legal estate.[18] He is deemed to have 'the same protection...as if' some form of term of years had been created in his favour by the mortgagor (ie, the borrower).[19]

If the purchaser takes only an equitable interest in the land, he is, in

---

12 *Midland Bank Trust Co Ltd v Green* [1981] AC 513 at 528E per Lord Wilberforce.
13 Ante, p 47, post, p 89.
14 See *Pilcher v Rawlins* (1872) 7 Ch App 259 at 269; *Oliver v Hinton* [1899] 2 Ch 264 at 273; *Taylor v London and County Banking Co* [1901] 2 Ch 231 at 256; *Midland Bank Trust Co Ltd v Green* [1981] AC 513 at 528F-G.
15 It is significant that the term 'purchaser', which appears in the statutory formulation of the notice doctrine contained in the Law of Property Act 1925, s 199(1)(ii) (post, p 89), is itself defined as incorporating an element of good faith (see Law of Property Act 1925, s 205(1)(xxi)).
16 Even a purchaser who has paid the purchase money in full is not safe if notice of the adverse equitable interest reaches him before the formal conveyance to him of the legal estate (*Wigg v Wigg* (1739) 1 Atk 382 at 384, 26 ER 244 at 245). However, this is true only in respect of those adverse equitable rights which existed prior to the contract to purchase. Any adverse equitable interest which arises between the date of contract and the date of the conveyance of the legal estate must concede priority to the purchaser, since the purchaser himself acquires an equitable interest at the date of contract (post, p 217). The latter situation is governed by the rule that where the equities are equal, the first in time prevails.
17 Law of Property Act 1925, s 1(1)(a), (b). Even a lessee at a rack rent constitutes a purchaser of a legal estate (*Goodright d Humphreys v Moses* (1775) 2 Wm Bl 1019 at 1022, 96 ER 599 at 600).
18 Law of Property Act 1925, s 87(1).
19 The grant of a long lease to the mortgagee is another method of creating a legal mortgage (post, p 573). See *Cave v Cave* (1880) 15 Ch D 639 at 646.

principle, subject to all prior equitable interests irrespective of notice.[20] The general rule is that where the equities are equal, the first in time prevails.[1]

(c) Purchase for value

The equitable doctrine of notice operates in favour only of a purchaser for value. The concept of a 'purchaser for value' may appear pleonastic, but it should be borne in mind that in the strictest common law sense[2] a 'purchaser' is one who takes property by reason of the act of another (as distinct from one whose title arises by operation of law). On this basis, even a donee (or 'volunteer') ranks technically as a 'purchaser', since his interest derives from an act of gift; whereas a squatter can never rank as a 'purchaser' *stricto sensu*, since his title derives from the legal effect of the mere effluxion of time.

In terms of the doctrine of notice it is therefore clear that one who seeks immunity from prior equitable interests must show not merely that he is a 'purchaser' in the technical sense, but also that he gave valuable consideration.[3] The status of 'Equity's Darling' can never be achieved by either a donee[4] or a squatter.[5] However, if the purchaser gave value, it is irrelevant whether the consideration given was adequate.[6]

(d) Absence of notice

The crux of the equitable doctrine of notice is, of course, the idea that immunity from prior equitable interests should be conferred only on those purchasers who, at the date of their purchase, had no knowledge or notice of the existence of such interests. Only in the absence of notice can it truly be said that the conscience of the purchaser is unaffected by adverse pre-existing rights.[7]

For this purpose 'notice' is given an extended meaning in the English law of real property. 'Notice' embraces not only 'actual' notice, but also 'constructive' and 'imputed' notice.

(i) Actual notice   Actual notice refers to matters of which the purchaser was consciously aware at the date of his purchase or which, in the statutory formulation of the doctrine of notice,[8] were 'within his own knowledge'.

---

20 *London and South Western Railway Co v Gomm* (1881-82) 20 Ch D 562 at 583. See eg *Cave v Cave* (1880) 15 Ch D 639 at 648f (one of purchasers was equitable mortgagee).
1 Post, p 604.
2 See *Powell v Cleland* [1948] 1 KB 262 at 272 for a recognition that, in its old common law significance, 'purchase' covers all means of acquisition otherwise than by descent or escheat. See also Inheritance Act 1833, s 1.
3 'Value' includes money, money's worth, marriage consideration, and even the satisfaction of an existing debt (*Thorndike v Hunt* (1859) 3 De G & J 563 at 569, 44 ER 1386 at 1388). If the transfer to the purchaser is for a money consideration, the purchaser does not rank as a 'purchaser for value' until he has paid the money over. He cannot plead the doctrine of notice in his own favour merely because a legal estate has been conveyed to him in advance of payment (*Story v Windsor* (1743) 2 Atk 630 at 631, 26 ER 776).
4 *Burgess v Wheate* (1759) 1 Eden 177 at 195, 28 ER 652 at 659.
5 *In re Nisbet and Potts' Contract* [1906] 1 Ch 386 at 406, 408, 410 (It is inconceivable that by his trespass a squatter should put himself in a more favourable position than if he had entered upon the land by right).
6 *Bassett v Nosworthy* (1673) Cas temp Finch 102 at 104, 23 ER 55 at 56.
7 Ante, p 48.
8 Law of Property Act 1925, s 199(1)(ii)(a).

Clearly no purchaser can be allowed to take priority over equitable interests whose existence was fully known to him, since otherwise the purchaser would be guilty of a form of equitable fraud.[9]

The source of the purchaser's knowledge is in most cases entirely irrelevant. If the purchaser has actual knowledge of an adverse equitable interest, it seems to matter not that this knowledge is derived from some person other than the vendor or that the purchaser came by the information fortuitously. However, it is probable that knowledge derived from casual conversations does not constitute actual notice except where the mind of the purchaser 'has in some way been brought to an intelligent apprehension of the nature of the incumbrance . . . so that a reasonable man, or an ordinary man of business, would act upon the information and would regulate his conduct by it . . .'[10]

By reason of a statutory fiction the formal registration of an equitable interest may sometimes constitute actual notice to the purchaser of the land affected by the registration.[11]

(ii) Constructive notice   Constructive notice relates to matters of which the purchaser would have been consciously aware if he had taken reasonable care to inspect both land and title.[12] It used to be thought that constructive notice arose only in circumstances of 'gross negligence' on the part of the purchaser,[13] but it seems at least since the Conveyancing Act 1882 that the standard of care required of the purchaser is perhaps somewhat higher.[14] Although phrased in a negative or restrictive form, section 199(1)(ii)(a) of the Law of Property Act 1925 indicates that the purchaser is prejudicially affected by notice of those matters which 'would have come to his knowledge if such inquiries and inspections had been made as ought reasonably to have been made by him . . .'

The classic description of the proper subject matter of the purchaser's inquiries is found in *Jones v Smith*.[15] Here, in a celebrated judgment, Wigram V-C reduced the categories of constructive notice to two classes of circumstances. The first comprises cases in which the purchaser has actual

9 See *Ware v Lord Egmont* (1854) 4 De GM & G 460 at 473, 43 ER 586 at 592 per Lord Cranworth: 'Where a person has actual notice of any matter of fact, there can be no danger of doing injustice if he is held to be bound by all the consequences of that which he knows to exist.'

10 *Lloyd v Banks* (1868) 3 Ch App 488 at 490f per Lord Cairns LC. See also *Barnhart v Greenshields* (1853) 9 Moo PCC 18 at 36, 14 ER 204 at 211 ('A purchaser is not bound to attend to vague rumours').

11 See eg Law of Property Act 1925, s 198(1) (post, p 114).

12 Ante, p 47.

13 See eg *Ware v Lord Egmont* (1854) 4 De GM & G 460 at 473, 43 ER 586 at 592 per Lord Cranworth. In *Jones v Smith* (1841) 1 Hare 43 at 56, 66 ER 943 at 949, Wigram V-C thought that a 'mere want of caution, as distinguished from fraudulent and wilful blindness' was not enough.

14 See Conveyancing Act 1882, s 3(1)(i) (now Law of Property Act 1925, s 199(1)(ii)(a)). It is a source of some perplexity (see *Northern Bank Ltd v Henry* [1981] IR 1 at 16) that section 3(3) of the 1882 Act (now section 199(3) of the 1925 Act) appears to provide that the purchaser is not to be affected by notice in any case in which he would not have been regarded as having constructive notice before the enactment of the statutory formula. Some comfort may perhaps be found in the observation of Lindley LJ in *Bailey v Barnes* [1894] 1 Ch 25 at 35 that the 1882 Act 'really does no more than state the law as it was before, but its negative form shews that a restriction rather than an extension of the doctrine of notice was intended by the Legislature.' The truth may be simply that 19th century judges were prone to stigmatise all actionable negligence as 'gross' or 'culpable' (see eg the statement of Rolfe B in *Wilson v Brett* (1843) 11 M & W 113 at 115, 152 ER 737 at 739, that negligence and gross negligence were 'the same thing, with the addition of a vituperative epithet').

15 (1841) 1 Hare 43 at 55, 66 ER 943 at 948.

notice of some defect or incumbrance in relation to the property, enquiry into which would disclose others: the purchaser is fixed with constructive notice of such matters as this further enquiry would have revealed.[16] The second category comprises cases in which the purchaser has 'designedly abstained from inquiry for the very purpose of avoiding notice.'

To these two categories there must now be added a third—perhaps today the most important. The purchaser is fixed with constructive notice of all those matters which a reasonable or prudent purchaser, acting with skilled legal advice,[17] would have investigated. He is judged objectively with reference to that which any ordinary purchaser, advised by a competent lawyer, would reasonably have inquired about or inspected for the purpose of obtaining a good title. A reasonable purchaser is one who 'not only consults his own needs or preferences but also has regard to whether the purchase may affect, prejudicially and unfairly, the rights of third parties in the property.'[18] Thus a reasonable purchaser can legally be expected to 'make such inquiries and inspections as would normally disclose whether the purchase will trench, fraudulently or unconscionably, on the rights of such third parties in the property.'[19] As Henchy J explained in *Northern Bank Ltd v Henry*,[20] 'the reasonable man, in the eyes of the law, will be expected to look beyond the impact of his decisions on his own affairs, and to consider whether they may unfairly and prejudicially affect his "neighbour", in the sense in which that word has been given juristic currency by Lord Atkin in *Donoghue v Stevenson*.'

Because the imposition of this standard of care represents a significant restraint on the ability of the purchaser to take free of adverse equitable interests,[1] the courts have been reluctant to extend the ambit of constructive notice to any large degree. A persuasive element of policy exerts an opposing tendency towards maximising the protection given to the purchaser of land.[2] The classic observation in this context is that of Farwell J, who stated in *Hunt v Luck*[3] that the 'doctrine of constructive notice, imputing as it does, knowledge which the person affected does not actually possess, is one which the Courts of late years have been unwilling to extend.'[4]

In consequence the duty of care expected of a purchaser covers only two major areas, concerning respectively an inspection of land and an inspection of title. An inspection of land may reveal facts which are inconsistent with the title

16 See eg *Birch v Ellames* (1794) 2 Anst 427 at 431f, 145 ER 924 at 926, where a mortgagee who lent money in the full knowledge that the borrower's title deeds were deposited with a third party was held to take subject to a prior mortgage which was secured by that deposit.

17 See *Northern Bank Ltd v Henry* [1981] IR 1 at 18 for the assertion by Kenny J that no prudent purchaser 'who was without legal qualifications would undertake the investigation of title to land.'

18 *Northern Bank Ltd v Henry* [1981] IR 1 at 9 per Henchy J. It is for this reason that the doctrine of notice is not tied to the standards observed by the prudent man of business. The latter is, almost by definition, no altruist and consequently sees no further than his own interests. As Henchy J said ([1981] IR 1 at 12), the 'test for constructive notice is legal reasonableness, not business prudence.'

19 [1981] IR 1 at 11.

20 [1981] IR 1 at 12.

1 See eg the discussion of protection for equitable rights under a trust for sale (post, p 836).

2 Post, p 96.

3 [1901] 1 Ch 45 at 48, affd [1902] 1 Ch 428 at 434f (post, p 837).

4 For evidence of the continued potency of this approach, see *Caunce v Caunce* [1969] 1 WLR 286 at 291H–292F (post, p 835).

offered by the vendor.[5] An inspection of the land may disclose the presence of persons other than the vendor, in which case the purchaser may be fixed with constructive notice of such rights as these persons may have in the property.[6] For instance, the presence of a tenant provides constructive notice of his leasehold interest[7] and of the terms of his lease,[8] but not necessarily of the rights of any person to whom the tenant may be paying rent.[9] It is now also quite likely that the purchaser is bound by the equitable rights of members of the vendor's family (and perhaps even of others) who are in joint occupation of the property with the vendor.[10]

An inspection of title comes within the scope of constructive notice in that the purchaser is fixed with constructive notice of all rights or interests affecting the land which would have been disclosed if he had investigated the vendor's title for the period allowed by statute.[11] The purchaser takes the land subject to any adverse equitable rights arising within that period, even where he has contracted for a shorter period of investigation than he is entitled by statute to require.[12] However, unless he positively chooses to investigate title for a longer period, the purchaser is not bound by equitable interests created before the beginning of the statutory period of title investigation.[13]

(iii) Imputed notice Imputed notice is notice which is attributed to a purchaser in virtue of knowledge possessed actually or constructively by some agent of his. The purchaser is deemed, for instance, to have notice of those matters of which his own solicitor was actually aware or should reasonably have been aware. This extension of the doctrine of notice is clearly necessitated by the widespread practice of employing legal advisers and other agents in the conduct of land transactions.

Imputed notice is now governed by section 199(1)(ii)(b) of the Law of Property Act 1925, which provides that this form of notice arises in respect of knowledge possessed actually or constructively by the purchaser's 'counsel, . . . solicitor or other agent'. However, imputed notice is subject to certain restrictions. The knowledge of a solicitor or other agent is imputed to

5 In extreme circumstances the scope of constructive notice may go even further. In *Hervey v Smith* (1856) 22 Beav 299 at 302, 52 ER 1123 at 1124, for instance, a purchaser of a house with fourteen chimney pots but only twelve flues was held to have received constructive notice of his neighbour's equitable easement to use the other two flues. See, however, *Allen v Seckham* (1879) 11 Ch D 790 at 794; R.A. Pearce, *Joint Occupation and the Doctrine of Notice*, (1980) 15 Ir Jur (NS) 211 at 213.

6 This possibility has been indirectly accentuated by the decision of the House of Lords in *Williams & Glyn's Bank Ltd v Boland* [1981] AC 487 (post, p 843). In *City of London Building Society v Flegg* [1987] 2 WLR 1266 at 1278G, Lord Oliver of Aylmerton observed that this formulation of the constructive notice doctrine is also reflected in the protection accorded by Law of Property Act 1925, s 14, to the interests of persons 'in possession or in actual occupation of land' (post, p 119).

7 *Hunt v Luck* [1902] 1 Ch 428 at 432.

8 *Taylor v Stibbert* (1794) 2 Ves 437 at 440f, 30 ER 713 at 714f.

9 *Hunt v Luck* [1901] 1 Ch 45 at 51, affd [1902] 1 Ch 428 at 434f (ante, p 90). The question of constructive notice becomes controversial here only if the vendor is not the person to whom the tenant is paying his rent.

10 Post, pp 842, 851.

11 The period of investigation of title fixed by statute now covers at least the 15 years preceding the current transaction. See Law of Property Act 1969, s 23 (post, p 221).

12 *In re Cox and Neve's Contract* [1891] 2 Ch 109 at 118; *In re Nisbet and Potts' Contract* [1906] 1 Ch 386 at 408.

13 Law of Property Act 1925, s 44(8).

the purchaser only if it arises within the current transaction of purchase, and only if the solicitor or other agent acquired his knowledge while acting in his capacity 'as such'.[14] Notice derived from any other transaction or circumstance is irrelevant and cannot be fastened upon the purchaser.[15]

(e) The destructive effect of purchase for value without notice

If the purchaser succeeds in establishing all the foregoing elements of the 'composite expression' which epitomises the doctrine of notice, he has an 'absolute, unqualified, unanswerable defence'[16] against adverse equitable claims. This defence is so complete that the mere fact of purchase for value without notice has the effect of *destroying* the equitable rights involved. The advent of a good faith purchaser of a legal estate is sufficient to obliterate those rights once and for all. They cannot thereafter revive even against a subsequent purchaser who *does* have notice of the fact that equitable rights once existed. This operation of the doctrine of notice was exemplified in *Wilkes v Spooner*[17] (see *Fig.* 6).

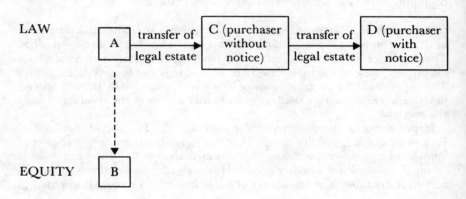

Fig. 6

On the facts presented in *Wilkes v Spooner*, C takes the legal estate free of B's equitable interest, since C is a bona fide purchaser of A's legal estate for value without notice. D likewise takes the legal estate free of B's equitable interest, albeit that he has notice of it, since B's interest has already been destroyed by

---

14 Law of Property Act 1925, s 199(1)(ii)(b).
15 See eg *Rock Permanent Benefit Building Society v Kettlewell* (1956) 168 Estates Gazette 397. (Although mortgagee's solicitor was mortgagor's brother and was therefore aware of mortgagor's matrimonial difficulties, such knowledge was not to be imputed to mortgagee under section 199(1)(ii)(b)).
16 *Pilcher v Rawlins* (1872) 7 Ch App 259 at 269.
17 [1911] 2 KB 473 at 487f. See also *Lowther v Carlton* (1741) 2 Atk 242, 26 ER 549 at 550 per Lord Hardwicke: 'It is certainly the rule of this court, that a man who is a purchaser with notice himself from a person who bought without notice, may shelter himself under the first purchaser, or otherwise it would very much clog the sale of estates.' See likewise *Nottingham Patent Brick and Tile Co v Butler* (1886) 16 QBD 778 at 788.

the earlier transfer to a good faith purchaser who had no notice of its existence.[18] B therefore has no rights *in rem*. Such rights as he retains are rights only *in personam*, ie, against A alone deriving from the transaction which gave B his rights in the first place.

18 This result does not apply, however, if A and D are the same person. A cannot destroy the equitable interest to which he is subject by selling the land to C and then purchasing that land from C (see eg *Barrow's Case* (1880) 14 Ch D 432 at 445).

CHAPTER 6

Outline of the 1925 legislation

The borderline between legal and equitable property rights in land was examined in Chapter 5.[1] The time has now come to outline the way in which both kinds of right are accommodated within the structure of the English law of real property (see generally *Fig.* 10[2]).

1. THE DISTINCTION BETWEEN REGISTERED AND UNREGISTERED LAND

The primary classification which requires to be drawn in modern English land law is the distinction between *registered* and *unregistered* land. More accurately, the relevant distinction is that which exists between land in respect of which title is registered and land where title remains unregistered. This major dichotomy heavily colours both the systematic organisation of land interests and the way in which these interests are protected in the context of a transfer of title.

(1) **The geographical distinction**

All land in England and Wales is held by way of either registered or unregistered title. No area of land can simultaneously comprise both registered and unregistered title, and the two regimes do not overlap except in anomalous and highly transitional situations. Certain geographical areas—mainly the large urban centres—have now been designated as areas of compulsory registration of title. The remainder of the country is still covered by the old system of unregistered title or, as it is sometimes called, 'old system title'[3].

(2) **The practical distinction**

The distinction between registered and unregistered title is best seen in practical conveyancing terms.

(a) *Registered title*

The essence of registered title is the idea that virtually all the pertinent details of ownership relating to a plot of land falling within an area of compulsory registration of title should be recorded definitively on a central register

---

1 Ante, p 69.
2 Post, p 109
3 The term 'old system' is a borrowing from the Australian jurisdictions, where 'old system' or 'general' land law is distinguished from the nowadays more common system of registration of title under Torrens legislation (post, p 146).

maintained by the Land Registry.[4] This Register is kept permanently updated and the theory of registered conveyancing is that a prospective purchaser need only consult the Land Register in order to discover all the relevant legal information about the land which he proposes to buy.

The law regulating registered titles is contained in the Land Registration Act 1925 and in the Land Registration Rules made pursuant to that Act.

(b) Unregistered title

In relation to that land where title is *not* registered, none of the details of ownership appears on any central record or register (with isolated exceptions such as those in respect of 'land charges', which are centrally recorded on the Land Charges Register[5]). In unregistered land, therefore, the purchaser must investigate title by means of perusal of the historical documents of title in the hope of eliciting the legal information which he requires before he decides to purchase.[6] In order to take a good title, the purchaser must be able to find a chain of ownership which stretches over a period of at least 15 years and leads to his proposed vendor. Only if the title asserted by his vendor is verified in this way can the purchaser of unregistered land safely pay over his purchase money and complete the transaction.[7]

The law pertaining to unregistered titles is found partly in the common law and partly in provisions scattered throughout the property legislation enacted in 1925.

(3) The relationship between registered and unregistered title

Compulsory registration of title in its present form was introduced only in 1926, and it was intended that it should gradually extend to cover all of England and Wales, thereby displacing the older system of unregistered conveyancing. So far the expansion of registered title has proceeded much more slowly than was anticipated,[8] and there remain substantial areas where title is still dealt with under the 'old system' rules.[9] It may seem strange that there are two systems of conveyancing operating side by side in this way. To add to the confusion, it happens not infrequently that identical factual problems arising in the different contexts of registered and unregistered conveyancing throw up diametrically opposed solutions.

The major emphasis in this book is placed upon the system of registered conveyancing. In other words, the system of registered title is viewed as the primary regime of land law in England and Wales, but so often the starting point for an understanding of registered land is provided by 'old system' conveyancing. It must not be forgotten in any event that a substantial minority of land transactions still concern unregistered title, and the law relating to this area is not yet ready to be discarded.

4 Post, p 147.
5 Post, p 113.
6 The process of unregistered conveyancing is described in detail in Chapters 7 and 9 (post, pp 125, 204).
7 Post, p 220.
8 It was initially expected that registration of title would cover the entire country within ten years of the enactment of the Land Registration Act 1925 (post, p 144).
9 Post, p 204.

2.   ALIENABILITY OF LAND AND FRAGMENTATION OF BENEFIT

The organisation of property rights in English land law is profoundly influenced by the perceived need to reconcile the potentially conflicting objectives of alienability of land and fragmentation of benefit. This need is just as acute in relation to registered as unregistered land.

(1) **The problem**

The pervasive (and almost intractable) problem of land law revolves around the extreme difficulty involved in satisfying the twin objectives of alienability and fragmentation.

(a) *Importance of alienability*

On the one hand it is quite clear that land must be allowed to be freely alienable or commerciable. Transactions in respect of legal estates in land (whether in the form of sale, lease or mortgage) must not be unduly restricted or hampered by law, for the uninhibited alienability of land is essential to the effective functioning of an exchange economy. Land is a highly marketable resource and it is vital that the market in land should not stagnate. As Lord Upjohn said in *National Provincial Bank Ltd v Ainsworth*,[10] it has been 'the policy of the law for over a hundred years to simplify and facilitate transactions in real property.'

(b) *Importance of fragmented benefits*

On the other hand there is a significant social interest in enabling land to be used as a means both of sharing out wealth and of allocating other kinds of benefit or utility which are incidental to land. It is highly desirable that the owner of a legal estate in land should be able to fragment, and thereby distribute, the benefits which are derived from land. These benefits may take various forms.

(i) Family interests   It is important, for instance, that land should provide a convenient and flexible medium of family endowment. The owner of a legal estate may well wish to grant various kinds of 'family' interest in land to his children, or he may simply wish to share the equitable ownership of the family home with a spouse or partner. The desideratum of endowment is recognised in any society which acknowledges both private ownership and the bonds of familial relationship, for endowment is integral to the intergenerational transfer of private wealth.

(ii) Commercial interests   Alternatively the owner of a legal estate in land may wish to fragment the benefit derived from the land not through the creation of 'family' equitable interests but rather through the granting away of 'commercial' equitable interests in or over the land.[11] Such rights may be of

10 [1965] AC 1175 at 1233G (post, p 840).
11 Ante, p 80.

considerable commercial or practical utility. The owner may, for example, decide to grant a stranger a right of way or the benefit of a restrictive covenant over his own land, thereby conferring on the stranger a portion of the utility which otherwise he himself would have retained in the land.

(c) Apparent contradiction of objectives

The twin objectives of alienability of title and fragmentation of benefit are, in the first analysis, set against each other in irreconcilable opposition. If the legal title in land is to be freely alienable, how can rights to various forms of fragmented benefit in that land be other than transient and defeasible rights which perish when the legal title passes into the hands of a purchaser? The interest of the alienee in taking title utterly free of conflicting rights militates directly against the objective of fragmentation of benefit. The free transferability of title seems to be in conflict with the durable creation— whether for family or commercial reasons—of lesser rights in the land which are capable of surviving subsequent dealings with the legal title.

(2) The solution

Perhaps the most distinctive achievement of modern English land law lies in the way in which it has largely resolved the inherent tension between the concerns of alienation and fragmentation. The accommodation of these divergent objectives of the law is made possible by a series of legislative provisions, confirmed in 1925, which simplify dealings with the legal estate in land. These provisions also ensure that fragments of benefit (which in the artificial schema of the Law of Property Act 1925 are almost always equitable interests[12]) are secured in such a way as to survive the alienation of the legal estate to a third party purchaser of the land. The outstanding success of the 1925 legislation consists in the way in which, in the context of land transfer, the law simultaneously facilitates the protection both of purchasers and of those who own various fragments of benefit[13].

3. PROTECTION OF PURCHASERS OF A LEGAL TITLE

The protection given to purchasers by the 1925 legislation rests upon two principal bases. *First*, the purchaser is favoured by a series of provisions which promote the free alienability of land titles. *Second*, the law now stipulates fairly narrowly the circumstances under which pre-existing rights in the land may remain binding on the purchaser after he takes his transfer.

(1) Free alienability of land titles

Two factors, above all others, have operated since 1925 to ensure the free alienability of land titles under English law. These factors operate indiscriminately in respect of both registered and unregistered land.

---

12 Ante, p 70.
13 See *City of London Building Society v Flegg* [1987] 2 WLR 1266 at 1272C–E per Lord Templeman.

(a) Restriction of the number of legal estates

The present line of demarcation between legal and equitable estates, interests and charges was finalised only in the Law of Property Act 1925. Before the commencement of this legislation many kinds of limited interest in land (eg a life interest and a fee tail) constituted legal estates in land. In order that a purchaser should take a good legal title, he had to require that the conveyance to him be executed by all persons holding any legal interest in the property. In other words he had to take his conveyance not merely from the owner of the fee simple absolute but possibly also from an assortment of limited owners. The purchaser's task in investigating all the component parts of a legal title might thus be rendered a quite horrifyingly complex and protracted affair.

The difficulty caused by the multifarious nature of legal estates in land has now been removed. Section 1(1) of the Law of Property Act 1925 deliberately restricts the number of possible legal estates in land to two—the fee simple absolute in possession and the term of years absolute.[14] All other interests in land take effect only behind one or other of these legal estates. Thus since 1 January 1926 (the commencement date of the 1925 legislation) all purchasers have known that the only person whose conveyance is necessary to transfer a freehold estate at law is the owner of an estate in fee simple absolute in possession. A conveyance of a mere limited interest is ineffective to pass the freehold title. It is correspondingly clear that since 1 January 1926 the only vendor competent to 'assign' (or convey) a leasehold legal estate is one who owns (or claims through the owner of) a term of years absolute.

(b) Restriction of the number of owners of a legal estate

Before the enactment of the property legislation of 1925, it was possible for even an absolute legal estate (eg a fee simple estate) to be held by, and therefore fragmented between, an almost limitless number of persons, each holding a specific share or proportion of that estate. In order to take a good legal title, the purchaser had to ensure not merely that his conveyance was signed by all the legal co-owners, but also that the individual title held by each was duly investigated[15]. Such a process was cumbersome, costly and time-consuming.

This disadvantageous feature of the law was removed, or at least substantially alleviated, by the 1925 legislation. The maximum number of persons who may hold a legal estate is now limited by statute to four.[16] The number of persons from whom the conveyance of a legal title must be taken is therefore at most four, and these four are regarded as owners of one and the same legal estate, with the result that the purchaser need investigate only *one* composite title.[17] In this way a much greater degree of simplicity and convenience is introduced into the process of title transfer.

(2) Limited liability of the purchaser to pre-existing interests

A further factor which ensures substantial protection for the purchaser of a legal title is the way in which the property legislation of 1925 circumscribes

---

14 Ante, p 70.
15 See *City of London Building Society v Flegg* [1987] 2 WLR 1266 at 1275G per Lord Oliver of Aylmerton.
16 Law of Property Act 1925, s 34(2), (3); Trustee Act 1925, s 34(2) (post, p 339).
17 Post, p 301.

fairly narrowly the conditions under which pre-existing rights in the land remain binding on him after he takes his transfer. This limited vulnerability on the part of the purchaser in respect of prior adverse interests has also the related effect of promoting the free alienability of land titles.

In analysing the relative immunity of the purchaser a distinction must be drawn between registered and unregistered land. In either case the practical problem under scrutiny is whether a right acquired by B in A's land remains binding on C, a subsequent owner of A's estate.

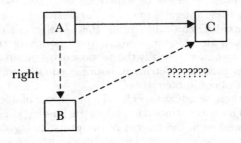

Fig. 7

(a) Legal rights in unregistered land

It is principally in relation to unregistered land or 'old system' conveyancing that the two basic axioms of English land law still retain some validity.[18] It remains almost entirely true that legal rights bind the world; with somewhat less accuracy it can be maintained that the impact of equitable rights on purchasers depends on some version of the equitable doctrine of notice.

In unregistered land legal rights, as defined with reference to section 1 of the Law of Property Act 1925, are automatically binding on and effective against all persons irrespective of notice.[19] In this sense, one of the earliest sedimentary layers of English land law is still thoroughly exposed to view in the law of unregistered title.

This means, of course, that the immunity given to purchasers of an unregistered title does not extend to immunity from pre-existing *legal* rights. The purchaser takes his title subject to these—and does so regardless of notice.[20] However, although he is bound by all legal interests affecting the land, the existence of such interests is usually obvious on physical inspection of the land or is readily apparent from the face of the documentary title investigated by him before completion of the purchase. It is unlikely in practice that the purchaser of a legal fee simple will be caught unawares by an existing legal lease or other legal interests or charges affecting the land.

---

18 Ante, p 84.
19 For special reasons (post, p 605), one particular legal interest relating to unregistered land—the 'puisne mortgage'—is taken outside the scope of this general rule of binding effect. The enforceability of a puisne mortgage against third parties depends on the registration of a Class C(i) land charge under Land Charges Act 1972, s 2(4).
20 Ante, p 85.

(b) Equitable rights in unregistered land

The other major axiom of land law dictates that equitable rights bind all persons other than a bona fide purchaser of a legal estate for value without notice.[1] The purchaser thus takes free of any equitable interests affecting the land of which he had no notice at the date of purchase.

Although this doctrine of notice operates substantially in favour of the purchaser of unregistered land, it is not entirely satisfactory even so far as he is concerned. In the strict terms of the doctrine, the purchaser takes his title subject to any equitable interests of which he *does* have notice, however inconvenient to him these interests may be. Furthermore, even if he has no actual notice of pre-existing equitable rights, there is always a possibility that he may be fixed by a deemed or 'constructive' notice of such rights—a consequence which can entirely stultify the purpose of his purchase. (The point will be taken up later that the doctrine of notice is equally prejudicial to the security of the owner of equitable rights.[2])

Notwithstanding these disadvantages for the purchaser of a legal estate, the equitable doctrine of notice continued to govern the binding effect of almost all equitable rights in land until the advent of the property legislation of 1925. However, the Law of Property Act 1925 sought in a rather fundamental way to modify the effect of the traditional doctrine of notice and this was done through the legislative confirmation of the device of 'overreaching'.

(i) The concept of 'overreaching'   'Overreaching' is a pivotal concept in the law of land. The term is used to describe the process by which a purchaser of a legal estate in land may be given an extended immunity from various forms of pre-existing equitable right—an immunity which goes beyond and largely supersedes the protection afforded the purchaser by the equitable doctrine of notice. To this extent the traditional doctrine of notice has now been displaced by an alternative means of guaranteeing the purchaser immunity from adverse rights.

(ii) Categories of overreaching transaction   Section 2(1) of the Law of Property Act 1925 allows the purchaser of a legal estate to 'overreach' (or defeat) many kinds of pre-existing equitable right affecting the land, 'whether or not he has notice' of those rights. This consequence is achieved through the declaration in section 2(1) that certain kinds of transaction with a legal title have a potentially 'overreaching' effect.[3] These transactions include a conveyance made under the powers conferred by the Settled Land Act 1925,[4] a conveyance made by 'trustees for sale',[5] a conveyance made by a mortgagee or personal representative,[6] and a conveyance made under court order.[7] By force of statute,

---

1 Ante, p 84.
2 Post, p 105.
3 Whether overreaching actually occurs in a given case depends on whether there has been compliance with the statutory preconditions of overreaching. These preconditions often require that the purchase moneys be paid to at least two trustees (post, p 356).
4 Law of Property Act 1925, s 2(1)(i) (post, p 806).
5 Law of Property Act 1925, s 2(1)(ii) (post, p 356).
6 Law of Property Act 1925, s 2(1)(iii) (post, p 616).
7 Law of Property Act 1925, s 2(1)(iv) (post, p 377).

the effect of such conveyances of a legal estate is normally to invest the purchaser with an absolute legal title free of any pre-existing equitable rights or powers.

(iii) Consequences of overreaching The device of overreaching radically extends the freedom from liability enjoyed by the purchaser of a legal estate. Provided that a potentially overreaching conveyance is conducted in the required manner,[8] the purchaser takes his title free of adverse equitable rights regardless of whether or not he had notice of such rights. However, the terms of section 2(1) of the Law of Property Act 1925 make it clear that 'overreaching' applies only to an equitable interest which is 'capable of being overreached' by the conveyance of a legal estate in the land. Not all kinds of equitable interest are thus capable.

In effect overreaching operates in relation to 'family' equitable interests, ie, those equitable interests which exist behind a trust for sale or under a strict settlement of land.[9] It is a matter of extreme importance that the purchaser of a legal estate in land should take his title free of such interests. It is often coincidentally true that those who own 'family' equitable interests have no real desire to retain their interests in the land after a legal estate in that land has been conveyed to a third party purchaser; they may be just as happy that their 'family' equitable interests should thereafter attach to the money proceeds of the conveyance or that such proceeds be reinvested in the purchase of new realty.

(iv) Operation of overreaching The operation of overreaching can be illustrated in the following way. Suppose that T^1 and T^2 hold a legal estate in fee simple as 'trustees for sale' on behalf of A and B, who each hold beneficial one-half shares in the property.[10] (This form of legal and equitable ownership probably covers

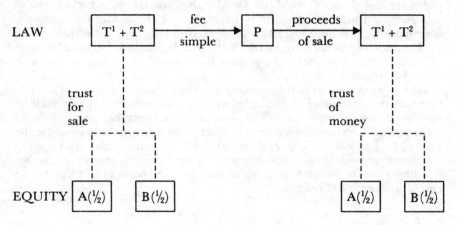

Fig. 8

8 Post, p 355.
9 Ante, p 96.
10 It will be seen later that it is quite possible that T^1 and T^2 may be the same people as A and B (post, p 347).

most matrimonial homes in England and Wales.) The equitable interests held by A and B behind this trust for sale are, in the contemplation of the Law of Property Act 1925, interests 'capable of being overreached'. If, as may well happen in the normal course of events, T^1 and T^2 sell and convey their legal estate to a purchaser, P, the overreaching mechanism normally comes into operation (see *Fig.* 8).

In accordance with section 2(1) of the Law of Property Act 1925, the conveyance to P overreaches (and therefore enables P to take free of) the equitable rights of A and B behind the trust. This result follows whether or not P had notice actual or constructive of the rights of A and B. However, although the equitable rights of A and B are, by this means, swept off the land conveyed to P, their rights are not in fact destroyed. As against P they are, of course, no longer effective—this is the whole purpose of the overreaching device. But the equitable rights of A and B remain binding on and enforceable against the trustees, T^1 and T^2, who now stand possessed not of land but of the capital proceeds of sale of land. In other words, the equitable rights of A and B are automatically translated by the overreaching conveyance into exactly equivalent interests in the money proceeds achieved by the sale. Each is the beneficial owner of half of these proceeds, and T^1 and T^2 are now effectively trustees of a sum of money. This conclusion is highly advantageous for all parties concerned. P takes a clean and unfettered title to the land, while the equitable rights of A and B are preserved after the conveyance by being diverted into money.

(v) Diminished role of the traditional doctrine of notice It can easily be seen that the device of overreaching has revolutionised the treatment of equitable interests in land during the period since 1925. In contrast to the earlier position, when all such rights were subject to the equitable doctrine of notice, many equitable rights are now simply swept off the land by an overreaching conveyance of an unregistered title. The role left to be played by the doctrine of notice is correspondingly diminished. As will be seen later,[11] the role of notice was further displaced by the introduction in the 1925 legislation of a limited scheme of land charge registration in respect of some of the non-overreachable equitable interests.

One important effect of the reorganisation of English land law in 1925 was therefore the subdivision of the field of equitable interests in unregistered land into three categories (see *Fig.* 10[12]). These categories comprise respectively (1) those equitable interests which are overreached on conveyance pursuant to the Law of Property Act 1925, (2) those equitable interests whose effect upon a purchaser depends on the registration of a land charge, and (3) those few remaining equitable interests whose impact on third parties still turns on the equitable doctrine of notice.

(c) Registered land

It is in relation to registered land that the twin axioms of land law have been most radically modified, to the point where the traditional starting points of the English law of real property are now scarcely recognisable.

11 *Post*, p 106.
12 *Post*, p 109.

Exactly the same legal and equitable interests exist in registered land. The line of demarcation between these interests is no different in relation to registered titles, the criteria of legal (as distinct from equitable) quality being laid down in section 1 of the Law of Property Act 1925.[13] However, it is from this point onwards that the law of registered land takes a different direction, for in it the rules of unregistered land are heavily overlaid by the principle of registration. The theory of registered title requires in effect that *all* land interests, whether legal or equitable, whether 'family' or 'commercial', be entered in the Land Register.[14] The Land Register is then regularly updated in order that it should at all times reflect the totality of property interests affecting any given plot of land falling within an area of compulsory registration of title.

(i) 'Major interests' and 'minor interests' The essential details of this registration scheme are very simple.[15] Certain legal estates in land (ie, the fee simple absolute in possession and terms of at least 21 years) are substantively registered under their own respective title numbers in the Land Register.[16] These registered interests (which might well be called 'major interests') then provide a focusing point for the registration of all other kinds of subsidiary interest affecting the land in question. In other words, the other subsidiary interests (many of them called 'minor interests') are entered on the Register against the 'major interest' to which they pertain. Provided that this process of registration is accurately and comprehensively carried out, the Register offers at all times a faithful record of all the interests relevant to any piece of land within an area of compulsory registration.

Of course the operation of the Land Register is more complicated in practice than is indicated by this introductory glimpse of its structure. Of particular difficulty is the existence of certain statutorily defined 'overriding interests' which exist outside the registration scheme but which nevertheless bind the land.[17] However, enough will have been gathered of the working of the

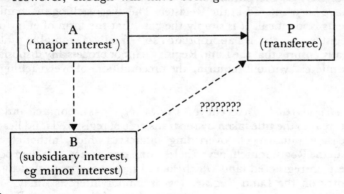

Fig. 9

13 Ante, p 70.
14 Registration of title must be sharply distinguished from registration of land charges under the Land Charges Acts 1925 and 1972. The latter form of registration represents an isolated form of registration available—rather confusingly—in respect of certain kinds of interest in *unregistered* land!
15 The operation of the Land Register is more fully described in Chapter 8 (post, p 144).
16 Post, p 151.
17 Post, p 170.

registration scheme to make it possible to understand the way in which purchasers (or 'transferees') of a registered title are given protection in the context of a transfer of the registered title (see *Fig.* 9).

(ii) Immunity of the transferee　In the law of registered land the distinction between legal and equitable rights is almost insignificant—except perhaps for the purpose of defining the 'major interests' against which all other registrations require to be effected. The essence of the scheme is that all land interests—whether legal or equitable—should be recorded on the Land Register, with the now controversial exception of 'overriding interests'.

The result of a transfer of a registered freehold 'major interest' (eg by A to P in *Fig.* 9) is spelt out by statute. According to section 20(1) of the Land Registration Act 1925, a 'disposition' of A's legal estate for valuable consideration confers that estate on P subject to 'the incumbrances and other entries, if any, appearing on the register' and subject to any 'overriding interests' which affect the estate transferred.[18] However, with the exception of these two kinds of interest the estate conferred on the transferee is declared to be 'free from all other estates and interests whatsoever'. Moreover, section 59(6) of the Land Registration Act 1925 provides that a purchaser of registered land takes free of any right unprotected by entry on the Register (other than 'overriding interests') 'whether he has or has not notice thereof, express, implied, or constructive'. The equitable doctrine of notice thus has no place at all within the regime of registered title.[19]

In theory therefore a very substantial degree of immunity from adverse rights is accorded to the purchaser of registered land. Apart from 'overriding interests' he is subject only to those interests positively recorded on the face of the Land Register at the date of his purchase. Moreover, it will be seen shortly that the transferee of a registered title can overreach 'family' equitable rights just as effectively as the purchaser of unregistered land, even where such interests have been entered in the Register. The overreaching mechanism in both contexts is identical. It is simply the case that the form of entry on the Land Register which is appropriate to 'family' equitable interests automatically ensures that the Land Registry cannot process any disposition of the 'major interest' without requiring the preconditions of overreaching to be fulfilled.[20]

(iii) 'Overriding interests'　In recent years, however, it has become clear that the principal threat to the title taken by the transferee of registered land lies in the ever increasing number of 'overriding interests' which, although never contained in the Register itself, nevertheless bind transferees. It is even possible that interests in registered land which should have been protected by some form of entry on the Land Register (eg as 'minor interests') may—in the absence of such protection—rank nonetheless as overriding interests. The over-protection of such interests has become a highly controversial feature of the registration scheme and produces the absurd consequence that protective entry on the Register is unnecessary and in many instances perhaps best avoided. The most dangerous development of all has been the judicial

18　Post, p 162.
19　Post, p 163.
20　Post, p 159.

confirmation that some of these 'overriding interests' are effective against the transferee even though the interests in question are potentially overreachable.[1]

4. PROTECTION FOR OWNERS OF FRAGMENTS OF BENEFIT

The major thrust of the English property legislation of 1925 is directed, in both registered and unregistered land, towards increased protection for the purchaser of a legal title. Yet one aspect of the remarkable achievement of this legislation is the fact that, although it confers heightened security on the purchaser, it simultaneously ensures a substantial degree of protection for those who own fragments of benefit in the land transferred. In this way the legislation facilitates both the free alienability of land titles and the durable creation of lesser entitlements in that land which are not destroyed by the act of transfer.

(1) Unregistered land

(a) Legal rights

The primary rule of unregistered land law is that legal rights bind the world. Legal rights thus require no artificial protection against third parties; their integrity is inviolable.[2] The equitable doctrine of notice has no relevance. If B, for instance, has been granted a legal term of years out of a fee simple estate owned by A in unregistered land, B's lease is wholly secure when A 'assigns the freehold reversion' (ie, conveys his legal title) to a purchaser, P. Likewise if B has a legal right of way over A's land, this easement is equally binding on P, a purchaser of A's legal title.

(b) Equitable rights

The degree of security enjoyed before 1926 by the owner of equitable interests in land was by no means so extensive as that accorded to the owner of a legal interest. Indeed, under the doctrine of notice, equitable rights are exceedingly insecure against purchasers of a legal estate, since they are liable to be destroyed if the purchaser has no notice of their existence. Equitable rights are commonly not referred to at all in the formal documents of title, and there is therefore a strong probability that a third party purchaser will not be fixed with notice and will take free of the rights in question. It may in many cases be highly inconvenient and wrong that equitable rights should be defeated in such a capricious way, especially where—as in the case of 'commercial' equitable interests—the rights have been created for valuable consideration. No equitable owner can sleep easily at night for fear that he may be confronted at any time by a purchaser of a legal estate for value who has no notice of his equitable rights. And of course once 'Equity's Darling' appears on the scene, equitable rights are destroyed for ever without any form of compensation.[3]

---

1 See eg *Williams & Glyn's Bank Ltd v Boland* [1981] AC 487 (post, pp 372, 843).
2 Ante, p 84.
3 Ante, p 92.

It was inevitable by 1925 that such uncertainty could no longer be allowed to attach to equitable rights, not least because this degree of vulnerability represents the antithesis of a rational law of property. It was for this reason that from 1 January 1926 legislative changes were introduced in order to protect equitable rights in unregistered land from the eminent possibility of wanton destruction by operation of the equitable doctrine of notice. The effect of these changes was to mitigate or modify much of the force of that doctrine.

The property legislation of 1925 introduced two major means of eliminating the insecurity of equitable interests vis à vis the bona fide purchaser of a legal estate for value without notice. *First,* it provided for a limited process of statutory 'overreaching' of equitable interests. *Second,* it established a system of formal 'land charge' registration in respect of certain equitable interests in unregistered land.

(i) Overreaching   It has already been seen that section 2(1) of the Law of Property Act 1925 confirmed a statutory facility of 'overreaching' in respect of 'family' equitable interests.[4] This device covers, for instance, equitable interests which arise under a strict settlement or behind a 'trust for sale', and ensures that, by complying with the statutory preconditions, the purchaser of a legal title may be guaranteed immunity from all pre-existing 'family' equitable rights. However, the beneficiaries under a settlement or trust are also protected by the overreaching process. They can, in theory at least, regard the conveyance of the legal estate with substantial indifference, since their equitable interests attach thereafter to the proceeds of the sale or other transaction. In effect, all that has happened is that the nature of the investment on their behalf—the character of the trust property—has undergone a transformation. With the disposition of the legal title to a third party, the beneficiaries' rights are swept off the land and on to the resulting capital proceeds. The third party takes the unregistered title free of their rights 'whether or not he has notice'. In this way security for the equitable interests is imaginatively coupled with facility for the purchaser.

(ii) Registration of land charges   The second innovation of the 1925 legislation was the introduction of a limited scheme of registration of equitable interests even within the domain of 'unregistered' land. Thus, in respect of 'commercial' equitable interests in unregistered land the Land Charges Act 1925 initiated a facility by which the owners of such interests can now register those interests as 'land charges' against the name of the owner of the legal estate in the land.[5]

Lest this introduction of a registration device in 'unregistered' land be thought unduly confusing, it must be borne in mind that the scheme of land charge registration seizes upon only one fairly small and isolated group of equitable interests in unregistered land, making these interests alone subject to a rule of registration. The limited scope of this form of registration in the Land Charges Register contrasts markedly with the theory of comprehensive registration of all interests (whether legal or equitable) in the rather different Land Register which controls matters of 'registered title'.[6]

4 Ante, p 100.
5 Post, p 113.
6 Ante, p 145.

The Land Charges Act 1925 has now been replaced by the Land Charges Act 1972. The operation of both Acts is similar and fairly straightforward. Whereas the effect of the device of 'overreaching' is to render notice on the part of a purchaser entirely irrelevant, land charge registration renders such notice altogether inescapable. The Land Charges Act modifies the traditional doctrine of notice by providing that the formal registration of certain kinds of equitable interest in the Land Charges Register 'shall be deemed to constitute actual notice . . . to all persons and for all purposes' of the existence of the right in question.[7]

In respect of 'commercial' equitable rights therefore, registration in the Land Charges Register has now become the only relevant or acceptable form of notice so far as third parties are concerned. By registering his interest as a land charge against the estate owner, the equitable owner effectively utilises the element of publicity inherent in formal registration, immediately fixing the world with statutory notice of his interest. He thus forecloses the possibility that any subsequent purchaser can ever claim to have bought a legal estate in the encumbered land *without* notice of his equitable interest. Once registered this equitable interest remains binding on the land into whosesoever hands the legal estate may later pass.

The scheme of land charge registration clearly removes many kinds of equitable interest in unregistered land from the scope of the conventional doctrine of notice, thereby diminishing yet further the role left to be played by this doctrine in modern land law. The principle underlying the registration scheme represents an ingenious means of combining security for various kinds of equitable owner with increased facility for third parties who deal with the legal estate.

Although several severe flaws will be seen later as emerging within this registration scheme,[8] its superficial advantages extend to both purchaser and equitable owner alike. By the simple act of registering his 'commercial' equitable interest, the incumbrancer effectively disables any subsequent purchaser from denying notice of his rights. At the same time the prospective purchaser is enabled, by a simple search of the Land Charges Register, to discover all the commercial equitable rights which affect his land. He is further protected by the rule that a registrable but unregistered interest is statutorily declared to be void as against him,[9] with the result that he takes his legal title subject only to those interests which have in fact been protected by entry on the Register. The purchaser is put in the position of knowing exactly what he is buying; while the rights of the equitable owner are made absolutely binding on all later purchasers through the artificial but inexorable medium of notice as provided by the Register.

(iii) Equitable rights still dependent on the traditional doctrine of notice The enactment in the 1925 Acts of the devices of overreaching and land charge registration was initially thought to have rendered almost redundant the orthodox doctrine of notice in its pre-1926 form. In their combined effect it was generally considered that these devices had made notice of equitable rights

7 Law of Property Act 1925, s 198(1) (post, p 114).
8 Post, p 130.
9 Land Charges Act 1972, s 4 (post, p 115).

either irrelevant or inescapable. However, during the period since 1925 it has become painfully obvious that the devices of overreaching and land charge registration have not exhausted the field of equitable interests in unregistered land. One of the most difficult problems to be found in modern unregistered conveyancing is the continued existence of a small, but consistently awkward, category of anomalous equitable rights which for one reason or another fall outside both major classifications of overreachable and registrable rights. To these interests the classical doctrine of notice is still applicable.[10]

(2) **Registered land**

The law of registered title offers, if anything, even greater protection to owners of fragments of benefit than is the case in the law of unregistered land. In registered land the significance of the distinction between legal and equitable rights is minimal. Almost all rights in registered land—of whatever kind—should be entered on the Land Register against the appropriate 'major interest'.[11] For example, 'commercial' and 'family' equitable interests are protectible as 'minor interests' by various forms of entry in the Register, and if so entered are binding upon later transferees of the registered title.[12] In particular, 'family' equitable interests are protectible primarily by the entry of a 'restriction' on the Register, which effectively ensures that any subsequent dealing with the registered title can be conducted only in such manner as will inevitably overreach the relevant equitable interests, thereby translating them into the equivalent interests in the capital proceeds received by the trustees.[13]

Thus, once again, the law of registered land strives towards a compromise between facility for the transferee and security for owners of lesser interests subordinate to the 'major' registered interest. The transferee may see the relevant details of title exposed on the face of the Land Register; the owners of such lesser interests may safeguard their rights by simple protective entry. However, as has been seen already,[14] one of the rogue developments in the modern law of registered title has been the extension of the category of 'overriding interests' which, although existing off the Register, become binding on transferees of the registered title. The over-large protection afforded such interests is currently under review. The present concern arises not least because the category of 'overriding interests' is sufficiently capacious to ensure that transferees often take title subject to rights which clearly should have been a matter of entry on the Register but which, for reasons of sheer negligence or otherwise, have not been so protected.

10 Post, pp 228, 836.
11 Ante, p 103; post, p 146.
12 Ante, p 103; post, p 159.
13 Ante, p 104; post, p 160.
14 Ante, p 103.

SYNOPSIS

The following diagram summarises the principal classifications and subdivisions introduced in this chapter.

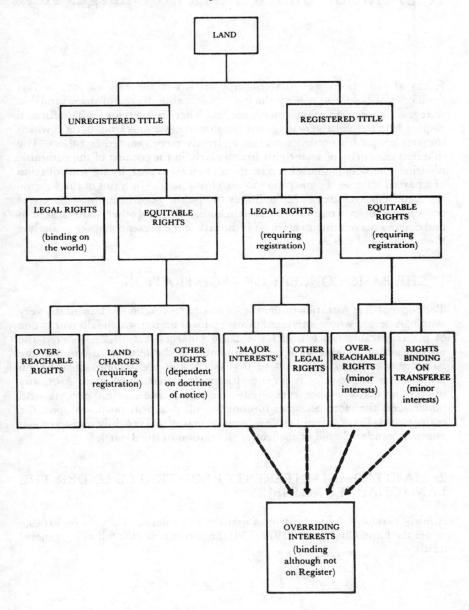

Fig. 10

CHAPTER 7

Registration under the Land Charges Act

It has already been seen that the application of the raw axioms or first principles of land law can produce a considerable degree of uncertainty in unregistered or 'old system' conveyancing.[1] There is room for both doubt and dispute as to the effectiveness against purchasers of various kinds of right which the vendor (or his predecessors) may already have granted to others. The inherent insecurity of such rights (particularly in the context of the equitable doctrine of notice) has now been removed, at least in part, by the introduction of a partial scheme of registration in *unregistered* land.[2] In terms of this scheme the Land Charges Act 1972 facilitates the public registration not merely of certain categories of equitable interest in land, but also of other matters, actions and documents relating to land.[3] It is the task of the present chapter to analyse the operation of this Act.

1. THE BASIC CONCEPT OF REGISTRATION

The concept of registration under the Land Charges Act is fundamentally very simple. A person who is interested in any claim or matter which falls within one of the registrable heads under the Land Charges Act 1972 is offered the opportunity of making an appropriate entry in the relevant division of the Register maintained pursuant to that Act.[4] The registration scheme then proceeds on the basis of two general and somewhat blunt rules. *First*, any interest or matter—once registered—is deemed to affect all persons with notice, and therefore becomes binding for all practical purposes upon the entire world. *Second*, a registrable interest or matter—if not duly registered—is normally rendered void or ineffective in relation to third parties.

2. MATTERS AND INTERESTS REGISTRABLE UNDER THE LAND CHARGES ACT 1972

A fairly carefully defined range of matters and interests is made registrable under the Land Charges Act 1972. This range comprises the following general heads.

---

1 Ante, p 105.
2 Ante, p 95.
3 Post, p 111.
4 The Register is maintained in Plymouth by the Land Charges Department of the Land Registry.

(1) Pending actions

The existence of certain kinds of litigation or disputed claim affecting a title to land may be the subject of a special entry in the register of pending actions which is maintained under the Land Charges Act 1972.

(a) Matters registrable as a pending action

The register of pending actions may be used for the registration of bankruptcy petitions filed on or after 1 January 1926 and for the entry of 'pending land actions'.[5] A 'pending land action' (or *lis pendens*) must comprise an action or proceeding pending in court 'relating to land or any interest in or charge on land'.[6] The definition of the matters registrable under this head thus covers most claims affecting the title to land or asserting some (even inchoate) proprietary interest in land. A pending land action may therefore include such disparate matters as a spouse's claim to a property adjustment order on divorce[7] and a claim of entitlement to an easement.[8] However, a pending land action cannot be registered in respect of a merely *monetary* claim in respect of land, with the result that registration cannot at present be used in order to protect such interests as a beneficiary's share in the proceeds of sale under a trust for sale.[9] It is possible, however, that the registration of a pending land action may provide a means of protecting the *occupation rights* not merely of beneficiaries under a trust for sale,[10] but also of persons who assert rights based on proprietary estoppel.[11]

(b) Effects of registration and non-registration

An entry in the register of pending actions has effect for an initial period of five years but is thereafter renewable for further periods of five years.[12] The inevitable consequence of such an entry is that any prospective purchaser of the land concerned is affected by a deemed 'actual notice' of potentially contentious issues relating to the title which he proposes to purchase.[13] However, a failure to register renders a pending land action ineffective against any purchaser 'without express notice of it'.[14] Likewise an unregistered petition in bankruptcy has no binding effect on 'a purchaser of a legal estate in good faith, for money or money's worth, without notice of an available act of bankruptcy'.[15]

---

5   Land Charges Act 1972, s 5(1). See (1986) 136 NLJ 157 (H.W. Wilkinson).
6   Land Charges Act 1972, s 17(1).
7   See *Whittingham v Whittingham* [1979] Fam 9 at 13E, but compare *Sowerby v Sowerby* (1982) 44 P & CR 192 at 195ff. See now *Perez-Adamson v Perez-Rivas* (1987) *Times*, 31 March, where the Court of Appeal held that even a general claim for property adjustment in respect of unidentified land, if registered as a lis pendens against specific property, could take priority over a mortgage charge subsequently executed by the other spouse.
8   See *Greenhi Builders Ltd v Allen* [1979] 1 WLR 156 at 159G.
9   *Taylor v Taylor* [1968] 1 WLR 378 at 384C, 385B-C.
10 Post, p 374.
11 See *Haslemere Estates Ltd v Baker* [1982] 1 WLR 1109 at 1119H-1120A; [1983] Conv 69 at 70 (post, p 425).
12 Land Charges Act 1972, s 8.
13 Law of Property Act 1925, s 198(1) (ante, p 107).
14 Land Charges Act 1972, s 5(7).
15 Land Charges Act 1972, s 5(8).

(2) **Writs and orders affecting land**

Certain kinds of writ or order issued in the enforcement of a court order or judgment may be registered in the register of writs and orders affecting land.[16] Included within this category are charging orders,[17] orders appointing a receiver or sequestrator of land,[18] and receiving orders in bankruptcy.[19] If duly registered, the writ or order is binding on all persons,[20] but if not so registered is generally ineffective against a 'purchaser of the land'.[1]

(3) **Annuities**

Certain annuities created between 1855 and 1926 were capable of entry in a register of annuities which was closed in 1925.[2] This register contains only anomalous annuities which by now must be almost extinct. Most modern annuities are registrable as Class C(iii) or Class E land charges under the Land Charges Act 1972.[3]

(4) **Deeds of arrangement**

Certain deeds of arrangement entered into by a bankrupt debtor for the benefit of his creditors may be recorded in the register of deeds of arrangement affecting land.[4] If so registered, they remain valid and effective against third parties for a renewable period of five years,[5] but if unregistered are void against any purchaser of the land concerned.[6]

(5) **Land charges**

By far the most important form of registration under the Land Charges Act 1972 relates to the 'land charge' properly so called.[7] The process of registration of such charges (and the legal consequences of registration) provide the subject matter of the remainder of this chapter.

---

16   As with pending actions, the registration is for a renewable period of five years (Land Charges Act 1972, s 8).
17   Land Charges Act 1972, s 6(1)(a). Charging orders are described in more detail in Chapter 26 (post, p 870). A *Mareva* injunction is not registrable under section 6(1)(a) (see *Stockler v Fourways Estates Ltd* [1984] 1 WLR 25 at 27B).
18   Land Charges Act 1972, s 6(1)(b).
19   Land Charges Act 1972, s 6(1)(c).
20   Law of Property Act 1925, s 198(1) (ante, p 107).
1   Land Charges Act 1972, s 6(4).
2   Land Charges Act 1925, s 4.
3   Post, pp 134, 143.
4   Land Charges Act 1972, s 7(1).
5   Land Charges Act 1972, s 8.
6   Land Charges Act 1972, s 7(2).
7   Registration of 'land charges' must be carefully distinguished from registration of 'local land charges' (see eg J.E. Adams, (1976) 40 Conv (NS) 106). A register of local land charges (which usually relate to such public matters as planning permissions or local government activities affecting property) is maintained by the relevant local authority in respect of both registered and unregistered land situated within its area.

3. REGISTRATION OF LAND CHARGES

Certain categories of statutorily defined charge are capable of registration in the Land Charges Register which is maintained pursuant to the Land Charges Act 1972. The initial paradox of this scheme for registration of 'land charges' is that it rather confusingly facilitates the registration of interests in *unregistered* land. This apparent difficulty disappears as soon as it is realised that the scheme embraces only one fairly small group of equitable rights in unregistered land and imposes on this isolated category a systematic regime of registration.[8]

(1) Mode of entry in the register

An interest registered in the Land Charges Register must be 'registered in the name of the estate owner whose estate is intended to be affected.'[9] This requirement causes a number of difficulties.

(a) Registration by a sub-purchaser

Not the least of the difficulties generated by a name-based register is that caused to the incumbrancer who is unaware that he is dealing with a sub-vendor. Such a difficulty occurs, for example, where A (the owner of a legal estate in fee simple in unregistered land) contracts to sell that estate to B. Before the appropriate conveyance is executed, B may well contract by way of sub-sale to convey the same legal estate to C. In this situation there are *two* land charges which qualify for registration under the terms of the Land Charges Act 1972. The first charge arises from the 'estate contract' entered into by A and B,[10] and is registrable by B against the name of the current 'estate owner', ie, A. The second charge arises from a further 'estate contract', ie, the contract of sub-sale between B and C.[11] Pending A's conveyance of his freehold title to B, this charge is likewise registrable against the name of A, who remains at all material times the 'estate owner'. If C, unaware that he is caught up in a sub-sale,

---

8 Precisely the same kinds of interest, if occurring in an area of registered title, are protected by entry on the Land Register. In this context, however, such interests are recorded as 'minor interests' (post, p 159), and entry usually takes the form of either a 'notice' or a 'caution' (post, p 160).

9 Land Charges Act 1972, s 3(1). As Walton J observed in *Standard Property Investment plc v British Plastics Federation* (1985) 53 P & CR 25 at 28ff, it is important that the land charges system should operate on the footing of 'some fixed point of reference, equally available to both parties which is . . . conclusive as to the name to be used.' Accordingly Walton J concluded that the name against which search should subsequently be made, is the name of the estate owner 'as disclosed by the conveyance to him or her' (post, p 129). It is possible that in rare circumstances the owner of a land charge may be required to register that charge against himself. Such a case arises for instance where a purchaser of land agrees to lease back the premises to the vendor on completion of the purchase. Here the vendor has a registrable estate contract pending completion which should be registered against himself as the current estate owner (see [1980] Conv 170).

10 A registrable 'estate contract' is statutorily defined as including 'a contract by an estate owner...to convey...a legal estate...' (Land Charges Act 1972, s 2(4)) (post, p 135).

11 The definition of an 'estate contract' is sufficiently wide to catch 'a contract...by a person entitled at the date of the contract to have a legal estate conveyed to him to convey...a legal estate...' (Land Charges Act 1972, s 2(4)) (post, p 135).

registers *his* estate contract against B, this registration is a nullity and is liable to be vacated.[12]

(b) 'Spite' registrations

The function of the Registrar in registering land charges is purely ministerial.[13] No inquiry is made at the date of registration into the validity of the charge registered, and there is no requirement that the estate owner be informed of the application for registration.[14] It is therefore possible that land charge registration may be used for tactical reasons in order to impose an apparent (but fictitious) blot on an owner's title. Such a registration may well delay or frustrate future transactions with the property affected, requiring the estate owner to take positive action to secure a vacation of the entry on the register.[15]

(2) Effect of registration

Once a proper registration has been effected against the name of the appropriate estate owner, that registration is, in the terms of section 198(1) of the Law of Property Act 1925, 'deemed to constitute actual notice...of the fact of such registration, to all persons and for all purposes connected with the land affected...'

This provision has great force.[16] It has even been held, for instance, that it overrides the protection apparently afforded a lessee by section 44(5) of the Law of Property Act 1925.[17] In *White v Bijou Mansions Ltd*[18] Simonds J took the view that, by virtue of section 198(1), a land charge registered by a stranger against the superior title of a lessor is binding on even a lessee or sublessee regardless of the fact that the latter have no right to investigate the lessor's title. By reason of the statutory fiction, the due registration of any land charge is deemed (in the widest terms possible) to constitute *actual notice* of the interest so registered.

12   Thus, if in such a case A duly conveys the legal estate to B, and B in breach of contract conveys that estate not to C but to X, C's only remedy lies in damages against B in respect of breach of contract (see *Barrett v Hilton Developments Ltd* [1975] Ch 237 at 244A, F; (1975) 39 Conv (NS) 65 (F.R. Crane)). In other words, C's land charge cannot bind X, for C's rights are *in personam* and not *in rem* (ante, p 49). There is, of course, no strict legal duty to register a land charge, and it therefore follows that any damages recovered by C in connection with B's breach of contract will not be reduced in view of C's improper registration (see *Wright v Dean* [1948] Ch 686 at 696).

13   See S.M. Cretney, (1969) 32 MLR 477 at 486f.

14   See eg *Taylor v Taylor* [1968] 1 WLR 378 at 383A–B.

15   See eg *Heywood v B.D.C. Properties Ltd* (No 2) [1963] 1 WLR 975 at 979ff; *Georgiades v Edward Wolfe & Co Ltd* [1965] Ch 487 at 503E, 506D–E; *Alpenstow Ltd v Regalian Properties Plc* [1985] 1 WLR 721 at 727B–G, 728B–C. See also S.M. Cretney, (1968) 118 NLJ 1167; *Barnett v Hassett* [1981] 1 WLR 1385 at 1389C. In some jurisdictions compensation may be claimed by the aggrieved estate owner in respect of loss flowing from improper registrations (see eg *Ed Sinclair Construction & Supplies Ltd v Grunthaler* (1980) 105 DLR (3d) 296 at 304; *Bedford Properties Pty Ltd v Surgo Pty Ltd* [1981] 1 NSWLR 106 at 107A).

16   See H.W.R. Wade, [1954] CLJ 89.

17   Under section 44 of the Law of Property Act 1925, an intending lessee or assignee is not entitled to examine the title to the freehold or to a leasehold reversion connected with the interest which he proposes to purchase. However, section 44(5), overturning the rule in *Patman v Harland* (1881) 17 Ch D 353, provides that such a lessee or assignee 'shall not...be deemed to be affected with notice of any matter or thing of which, if he had contracted that such title should be furnished, he might have had notice.'

18   [1937] Ch 610 at 619.

(3) **Effect of non-registration**

Just as the effect of registration is phrased in absolute terms in section 198(1) of the Law of Property Act 1925, so the consequence of failure to register a registrable interest is specified in similarly draconian language. The precise effect of non-registration depends on the category of land charge concerned, but the general result of failure to register is that the registrable interest is rendered void against certain kinds of purchaser.

(a) *Classes A, B, C(i), (ii) and (iii), and F*

A land charge of Class A, Class B, Class C(i), (ii) and (iii), or Class F is made 'void' for want of registration 'as against a purchaser of the land charged with it, or of any interest in such land...'[19] A 'purchaser' is defined as connoting any person (including a mortgagee or lessee) who gives 'valuable consideration'.[20]

(b) *Classes C(iv) and D*

An unregistered land charge of Class C(iv) or Class D is rendered 'void' against a somewhat narrower category of purchaser. Non-registration makes a charge within these Classes void merely 'as against a purchaser for money or money's worth of a legal estate in the land charged...'[1] An important statutory immunity is thus conferred on the purchaser, although in rare circumstances this immunity may be lost if the purchaser either fails to plead his statutory defence,[2] or is precluded from doing so by some argument based upon constructive trust[3] or estoppel.[4]

(c) *Differential effects of non-registration*

The different consequences attached to non-registration may have important practical results. Thus, for instance, non-registration by an incumbrancer causes a 'general equitable charge' (which belongs to Class C(iii)[5]) to become void as against a purchaser of *any* estate or interest—legal or equitable—in the land. However, a similar failure to register an 'estate contract' (which belongs to Class C(iv)[6]) makes the relevant charge void only as against a purchaser of a legal estate for money or money's worth. Unregistered land charges remain binding upon third party donees of the land affected, that is, upon those

---

19   Land Charges Act 1972, s 4(2), (5), (8). For reference to the Classes defined in the Land Charges Act, see post, p 133.

20   Land Charges Act 1972, s 17(1).

1   Land Charges Act 1972, s 4(6).

2   See eg *Balchin v Buckle* (1982) 126 SJ 412, (1982) *Times*, 1 June.

3   Post, p 268.

4   In *Old & Campbell Ltd v Liverpool Victoria Friendly Society* [1982] QB 133 (Note) at 159A, for instance, Oliver J held that the defendants, having represented to a tenant in two documents that his unregistered estate contract was still valid and subsisting, were estopped from pleading non-registration when the tenant later incurred substantial expenditure on the faith of that representation (post, p 386). Compare, however, the unwillingness in *Topliss Showers Ltd v Gessey & Son Ltd* [1982] ICR 501 at 518D-F, to allow estoppel to avert the consequences of non-registration where 'registration is a statutory requirement imposed as a matter of public policy'.

5   Post, p 134.

6   Post, p 135.

persons who have not given any valuable consideration in respect of the transaction of transfer (eg the recipient of land under a will or on intestacy).

(4) Irrelevance of the traditional doctrine of notice

The statutory consequences of non-registration are therefore spelt out clearly in the Land Charges Act 1972. Furthermore, where an unregistered charge is statutorily declared 'void' as against a purchaser, it is entirely irrelevant that at the date of the conveyance to him that purchaser had actual express knowledge—from another source—of the existence of the registrable but unregistered interest. Once 'void' by virtue of statute, the charge cannot be revitalised by any residual application of the traditional doctrine of notice. Towards this end the courts have rigorously maintained the integrity of the rules surrounding the registration of land charges.

(a) Preference for certainty over justice

It has always been a characteristic feature of the English property lawyer's thinking that he should prefer certainty over justice in the ascertainment of proprietary rights. The property legislation of 1925 was heavily influenced by this policy preference—not least in the approach adopted in respect of land charge registration. The major objective of the 1925 legislation was the simplification of conveyancing, and this objective is more effectively ensured in the context of land charges if the consequences of registration and non-registration are absolutely clear-cut and conclusive.

(i) Modification of the doctrine of notice It is for this reason that the traditional doctrine of notice is displaced or, more accurately, is drastically adapted by the land charges scheme. Under the Law of Property Act 1925 and the Land Charges Act 1925 the orthodox concept of notice suffered modification to the extent that registration of a land charge has now become the *only* recognised form of notice to third parties in respect of wide categories of commercial equitable interest. The law in this area thus follows the general tendency of English property law in ensuring certainty as to rights rather than in striving for justice as between parties. An interest which falls within the registrable heads under the Land Charges Act is *either* duly registered as a land charge and therefore rendered binding *or* is not so registered and is accordingly void against most purchasers.

(ii) Statutory incorporation of an amoral rule The overall efficiency of the system of land charge registration is thus promoted by the rule that the purchaser is not bound by notice of any registrable interest where such notice is obtained by him outside the register of land charges. According to section 199(1)(i) of the Law of Property Act 1925, a purchaser 'shall not be prejudicially affected by notice of...any instrument or matter capable of registration under the Land Charges Act [1972] . . . which is void or not enforceable as against him under that Act...by reason of the non-registration thereof.' By allowing the equitable doctrine of notice to be partially displaced by a 'mechanical principle of registration', the 1925 legislation thus gave effect to a 'shift from a moral to an amoral basis' in the protection of equitable interests in land.[7]

7   See H.W.R. Wade, [1956] CLJ 216 at 227.

A dramatic illustration of this ethical shift is found in *Hollington Bros Ltd v Rhodes*.[8] Here L contracted to grant a lease to T. This contract was in fact an 'estate contract' registrable as a land charge of Class C(iv),[9] but T neglected to register the charge against L. L then conveyed his legal estate in the property to P, expressly 'subject to and with the benefit of such tenancies as may affect the premises' (see *Fig.* 11).

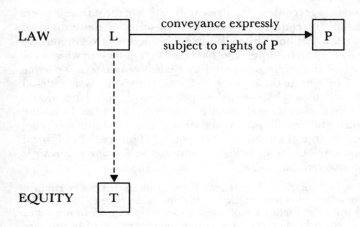

Fig. 11

Notwithstanding that P thus had actual express knowledge of the rights of T, P subsequently gave T notice to quit the premises, thereby effectively forcing T to negotiate a new lease. In proceedings brought by T, Harman J held that T's estate contract was void as against P by reason of its non-registration and ruled moreover that it was quite irrelevant that P had actual knowledge from another source of the existence of tenancies affecting the premises.[10] P was thus entitled to take his interest free of the adverse claims of an existing tenant—a result which was in ethical terms most unsatisfactory. The price paid by P had been calculated with reference to the existence of subsisting tenancies, but he was enabled to repudiate the existing incumbrances and coerce a re-negotiation at a new and higher rent level.[11]

(iii) Tension between certainty and justice Outcomes such as that demonstrated in *Hollington Bros Ltd v Rhodes* have, of course, been criticised as attaching a disproportionate penalty to the 'venial fault of non- registration'.[12] There is

8   [1951] 2 TLR 691.
9   Post, p 135.
10   'I do not see how that which is void and which is not to prejudice the purchaser can be validated by some equitable doctrine' ([1951] 2 TLR 691 at 696 per Harman J). See also *Coventry Permanent Economic Building Society v Jones* [1951] 1 All ER 901 at 904B-C per Harman J; *Beesly v Hallwood Estates Ltd* [1960] 1 WLR 549 at 558; *Buckley v SRL Investments Ltd and Cator and Robinson* (1971) 22 P & CR 756 at 764, 768.
11   There is nowadays a possibility that P's taking of title expressly 'subject to' the rights of T would raise a constructive trust in P to give effect to those rights (post, p 284).
12   H.W.R. Wade, [1956] CLJ 216 at 217.

indeed a certain 'defiance of ethics' where a purchaser with actual notice is allowed to trample over a third party's rights. Nevertheless even this result has one outstanding merit from the point of view of the traditionally minded property lawyer: it at least makes the position clear-cut. As Mahon J observed in *Carly v Farrelly*,[13] '[n]o stable system of jurisprudence could permit a litigant's claim to justice to be consigned to the formless void of individual moral opinion.'[14]

Thus, in the land charges context, the strict application of the statute renders unnecessary any difficult enquiry into the state of mind of the individual purchaser in each transaction. Either the incumbrancer has registered his interest and thereby made it binding, or he has failed to register—in which case his interest almost inevitably becomes void as against purchasers. To some extent efficiency is bought at the expense of fairness, and this is a trade-off which commends itself to most hard-nosed property lawyers. The latter would argue in any event that certainty and justice are not independent and absolute but interactive and highly conditional. When viewed in the dimension of time, certainty may well emerge as an intrinsic component of justice. The classical position of the property lawyer was clearly expressed in *Cowcher v Cowcher*,[15] where Bagnall J remarked that

in determining rights, particularly property rights, the only justice that can be attained by mortals, who are fallible and not omniscient, is justice according to the law; the justice which flows from the application of sure and settled principles to proved or admitted facts. So in the field of equity the length of the Chancellor's foot has been measured or is capable of measurement. This does not mean that equity is past childbearing; simply that its progeny must be legitimate—by precedent out of principle. It is well that this should be so; otherwise no lawyer could safely advise on his client's title and every quarrel would lead to a law suit.[16]

(b) Attempts to reintroduce a moral criterion

In its concern for long-term certainty rather than short-term justice, the law of property (and especially the law relating to land charges) is therefore largely indifferent to the relative moral claims of litigants. Nevertheless it is difficult to remain entirely insensitive to the ethical aspects of the relationship between purchaser and equitable incumbrancer, and several means have been suggested by which some sort of moral criterion can be restored to this area of the law of land charges.

(i) Protection for actual occupation It has been suggested that non-registration of a land charge should not have the effect of rendering void a registrable incumbrance belonging to a person who is *in actual occupation of the land*. Persons in actual possession of land may well have equitable interests of a fairly short-term nature in relation to which it is unrealistic to expect the vigilance of registration. The elderly widow who occupies property under an agreement for a lease has, in technical terms, a registrable estate contract. However, it seems unreasonable that the protection of her interest against third parties should rest

---

13   [1975] 1 NZLR 356 at 367.
14   See the equivalent discussion in relation to non-registration of rights under the Land Registration Act 1925 (post, p 162).
15   [1972] 1 WLR 425 at 430A-C.
16   See [1982] Conv 396.

exclusively on her registration of a Class C(iv) land charge—a registration which, in such circumstances and in the absence of legal advice, the lay person is highly unlikely to effect. It may seem much more reasonable that such a person should be able to rely for her protection upon her actual occupation of the land.[17] The fact of physical possession indicates to a purchaser just as effectively as the fact of registration that there is a possibility that the occupier has a proprietary interest of some kind in the land.

In the present state of the law, however, even the fact of actual occupation provides no protection for an incumbrancer who fails—albeit quite excusably—to register a land charge in respect of his interest. This conclusion seems not to be disturbed by section 14 of the Law of Property Act 1925, which provides that

This Part of this Act shall not prejudicially affect the interest of any person in possession or in actual occupation of land to which he may be entitled in right of such possession or occupation.

It was once thought that this provision enabled an incumbrancer in actual occupation to escape the consequences of non-registration.[18] However, it is now generally agreed that, in spite of the prominence afforded section 14 in recent cases,[19] the section is so limited in scope as to provide no assistance in the present problem.[20] The application of section 14 is expressly restricted to Part I of the Law of Property Act 1925. The consequences of non-registration of land charges are spelt out in a separate statute—the Land Charges Act[1]—and these consequences cannot therefore be muted by the saving provision contained in section 14 for the benefit of persons in possession.[2]

(ii) Relevance of actual but not constructive notice Another possible means of making the operation of the land charges system more 'just' lies in a compromise proposal that a purchaser should be prejudicially affected by actual notice (as

---

17 This idea is recognised, in the context of registered title, in section 70(1)(g) of the Land Registration Act 1925 (post, p 175).
18 See eg *Bendall v McWhirter* [1952] 2 QB 466 at 483.
19 See eg *City of London Building Society v Flegg* [1986] Ch 605 at 618F-620E (Court of Appeal), but compare now [1987] 2 WLR 1266 at 1278D-G (House of Lords).
20 See also *Coventry Permanent Economic Building Society v Jones* [1951] 1 All ER 901 at 904A-B; R.E. Megarry, (1952) 68 LQR 379 at 385.
1   There is here an ironic accident of legislative history. The Law of Property Act 1922 was, of course, the authentic source of the provisions which appear in a consolidated form in the 1925 legislation. Section 14 of the Law of Property Act 1925 was precisely foreshadowed by section 33 of the 1922 Act. However, when section 33 provided that nothing in Part I of the 1922 Act should 'prejudicially affect' the rights of actual occupiers, this saving provision clearly applied to the consequences of non-registration of land charges as then laid down in section 3(5) of Part I of the 1922 Act. When the 1922 Act was later consolidated, the land charges provisions (including section 3(5)) were diverted into a separate statute—the Land Charges Act. This formal restructuring of the 1922 legislation thus brought about the almost certainly unintended result that owners of land charges were (and still are) deprived of such protection as would otherwise be afforded by section 14 of the Law of Property Act 1925. See C. Harpum, (1977) 41 Conv (NS) 415 at 419 (n 31); M. Friend and J. Newton, [1982] Conv 213 at 215ff.
2   The general effect of this inevitably restricted construction of section 14 is to generate a blatant anomaly in the treatment of land charges as compared with the treatment of the rights of persons in 'actual occupation' of registered land (see Land Registration Act 1925, s 70(1)(g), post, p 175).

distinct from merely constructive notice) of an unregistered incumbrance.[3] On this footing, constructive notice would be relevant only where the incumbrancer is also in actual occupation of the land concerned.[4] In all other circumstances the definitive nature of the register would hold good unless, at the date of the transaction in question, the purchaser had actual knowledge of an unregistered land charge. In such a case—it is argued—the purchaser would be acting inconsistently with the requirements of conscience and would become a fair target for a limited application of the traditional doctrine of notice.

In spite of its attractions, however, this approach was firmly rejected by the House of Lords in *Midland Bank Trust Co Ltd v Green*.[5] This decision must now be examined in greater detail.

(5) Integrity of the system of land charge registration

The operation of the Land Charges Register is now largely overshadowed by the significant decision reached by the House of Lords in *Midland Bank Trust Co Ltd v Green*.[6] Here W, an owner of land in fee simple, granted his son, G, an option to purchase the land at a specified price which amounted to £22,500.[7] G failed to register this option as an estate contract under Class C(iv) of the Land Charges Act.[8] Six years later, in consequence of some family discord, W sought to revoke the option which he had earlier granted to G. Upon discovering that the option had never been registered by G, W quietly and speedily conveyed the land (which was by now worth £40,000) to his own wife, E, for a consideration of £500, with the clear intention of thereby defeating the unregistered option (see *Fig*. 12). G, who had at all material times been a tenant in occupation of the land, then purported to exercise his option. His mother declined to sell him the land in accordance with the option. G began proceedings against his father and the executors of his mother's estate—his mother having meanwhile died—claiming both a declaration that the option was binding on his mother's estate and an order of specific performance of the option. G then died and his executors, the plaintiff bank, continued the action with, of course, the benefit of a large sympathy factor weighing on behalf of G's bereaved widow and children.

---

3   This suggestion has been made particularly vigorously in the context of registered title, and is therefore considered in further depth in Chapter 8 (post, p 167). There are parallels in other registration areas for according relevance to actual but not constructive notice (see eg Land Charges Act 1972, s 5(7) (ante, p 111); Patents Act 1977, s 33(1)).

4   See eg H.W.R. Wade, [1956] CLJ 216 at 227.

5   [1981] AC 513. It is worth noting that the attempt to distinguish between actual and constructive notice in other areas of the law has not been without difficulty. Such a distinction provides a clear incentive for a purchaser to maintain a Nelsonian stance of wilful blindness in the face of the obvious. This possibility in its turn necessitates further (and more subtle) calibrations of the states of mind required to make a purchaser liable to adverse claims. See, for instance, the difficult gradations of knowledge which bear upon the imposition of constructive trusteeship on the ground of participation in a fraud perpetrated by a fiduciary (*Barnes v Addy* (1874) LR 9 Ch App 244 at 252ff; *Selangor United Rubber Estates Ltd v Cradock* (No 3) [1968] 1 WLR 1555 at 1580ff; *Nelson v Larholt* [1948] 1 KB 339 at 344; *Karak Rubber Co Ltd v Burden* (No 2) [1972] 1 WLR 602 at 633ff; *Belmont Finance Corpn Ltd v Williams Furniture Ltd* [1979] Ch 250 at 267G-268A; *United States Surgical Corpn v Hospital Products International Pty Ltd* [1983] 2 NSWLR 157 at 253D-254D.

6   [1981] AC 513, on appeal from [1980] Ch 590. See [1981] CLJ 213 (C. Harpum); [1981] Conv 361 (H.E. Johnson); (1981) 97 LQR 518 (B. Green); (1980) 96 LQR 8 (R.J. Smith).

7   G bought the option from his father for the sum of £1.

8   Post, p 136.

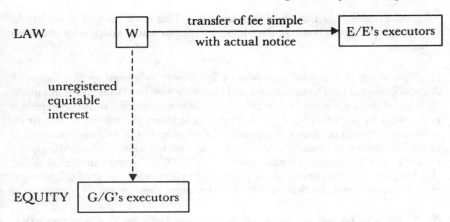

LAW   W   transfer of fee simple with actual notice   E/E's executors

unregistered equitable interest

EQUITY   G/G's executors

Fig. 12

By the time the action reached the courts, the value of the disputed land had inflated to over £400,000. It was plain that a decision against E's executors would effectively enable G's widow and children to buy the land for £22,500 in accordance with the option. A decision in favour of E's executors would result in a sale of the land and the division of the proceeds of sale between the five children of W and E, G's widow and children receiving in effect only 20 per cent of the value of the land.

The decision required in *Midland Bank Trust Co Ltd v Green* was essentially one relating to statutory construction. E's executors pleaded in their defence that the conveyance to E had been a bona fide sale and that E had been a 'purchaser for money or money's worth of a legal estate' for the purpose of what is now section 4(6) of the Land Charges Act 1972.[9] At first instance Oliver J upheld this defence and ruled that the unregistered option was not binding on E's estate.[10] This ruling was reversed by a majority decision in the Court of Appeal, only to be reinstated by the unanimous decision of the House of Lords. An analysis of the critical features emerging from this series of decisions highlights certain differences of judicial philosophy in relation to the law of property.

(a) Was there a purchase 'for money or money's worth'?

E's estate could take free of the unregistered option only if it could show that E had been a 'purchaser...for money or money's worth' within the meaning of the

---

9   Ante, p 115. The crucial provision in the *Green* litigation was of course the similarly worded predecessor provision found in Land Charges Act 1925, s 13(2). In order to aid the exposition of the provision currently in force, the courts' references in *Green* to section 13(2) are, in the following pages, rendered as references to section 4(6).

10   Oliver J confessed that he reached this conclusion 'with regret', since it seemed that G's clear rights had been 'deliberately frustrated by his parents in breach of the contract created by the option.' However, Oliver J took the view that, 'with the best will in the world', he could not allow his 'subjective moral judgment to stand in the way of...the clear meaning of the statutory provisions' ([1980] Ch 590 at 614D).

relevant provision of the Land Charges Act. This issue evoked a variety of responses at different levels in the hierarchy of courts concerned with the *Green* litigation.

(i) Requirement of 'adequate' consideration In giving judgment in the Court of Appeal in favour of G's executors, Lord Denning MR held that E had not given 'money or money's worth' within the terms of the immunity now conferred on purchasers by section 4(6). Lord Denning ruled that the statutory immunity from unregistered options presupposed the payment of 'a fair and reasonable value in money or money's worth: not an undervalue.'[11] Accordingly he regarded E's 'grotesquely small' payment of £500 as 'a gross undervalue' for this purpose and, furthermore, as providing evidence of a degree of collusion which 'would open the door to fraud of the worst description'.[12]

(ii) Rejection of the requirement of 'adequacy' Lord Denning's requirement that consideration be 'adequate' for the purpose of section 4(6) was conclusively rejected by the House of Lords. In delivering the only substantial speech in the House, Lord Wilberforce ruled that the purchaser need only show that she had provided 'valuable consideration'.[13] It was his view, moreover, that 'valuable consideration' is capable of including 'nominal consideration',[14] and that, had the decision been necessary, he would have had 'great difficulty' in any event in holding that £500 was merely a 'nominal sum of money'.[15] The House of Lords thus disposed of one of the principal bases for the decision of the majority in the Court of Appeal.

(b) Is there any requirement of good faith in section 4(6)?

The definition of 'purchaser' in the Land Charges Act does not impose any express requirement of good faith on the purchaser who claims the statutory

---

11 [1980] Ch 590 at 624E.
12 [1980] Ch 590 at 624D. Eveleigh LJ ([1980] Ch 590 at 628B-C) likewise thought that the true analysis of the transaction between W and E was that of 'a gift coupled with a token of £500 sought to be included to meet the requirements of [section 4] of the Land Charges Act...' Accordingly Eveleigh LJ held that the disputed conveyance had not been made 'for' money or money's worth within the meaning of section 4(6), the reference to payment having been inserted merely to add credibility to the claim of statutory immunity. Compare the dissenting judgment of Sir Stanley Rees ([1980] Ch 590 at 632A).
13 A 'purchaser' within the Land Charges Act 1972 is defined in terms of one who gives 'valuable consideration' (see Land Charges Act 1972, s 17(1)). In Lord Wilberforce's view, this statutory phrase is 'a term of art which precludes any enquiry as to adequacy' ([1981] AC 513 at 531E). Indeed, the only respect in which 'valuable consideration' is wider than the phrase 'money or money's worth' is that marriage consideration is included in the former concept but excluded from the latter ([1981] AC 513 at 531E).
14 'Purchaser' is defined in Law of Property Act 1925, s 205(1)(xxi) in terms of one who gives 'valuable consideration', a concept which is in turn defined as excluding 'a nominal consideration in money'. In the Court of Appeal Eveleigh LJ ([1980] Ch 590 at 629A) had thought that this definition was made relevant to the present case by the reference to 'purchaser' in Law of Property Act 1925, s 199(1)(i) (ante, p 116). He thus held that E could not invoke the parallel immunity conferred by section 199(1)(i), since, in his view, a purchase price of £500 constituted a merely nominal consideration. In the House of Lords, however, Lord Wilberforce not only disputed the meaning of 'nominal consideration' but also declined to accept that the definition of 'purchaser' contained in the Law of Property Act could be impliedly incorporated into the Land Charges Act ([1981] AC 513 at 531G-532B).
15 [1981] AC 513 at 532B.

immunity from unregistered land charges.[16] Yet the facts of *Midland Bank Trust Co Ltd v Green* offered every incentive for the infiltration of old equitable doctrines of good faith purchase into the construction of the Land Charges Act.[17] It was clearly possible to question whether E had acted in good faith in taking title from W with the deliberate object of defeating the unregistered option claimed by G. Here again divergent views were expressed by the courts.

(i) 'Fraud unravels everything' In the Court of Appeal both Lord Denning MR and Eveleigh LJ denied E's estate the protection of section 4(6) on the ground that E had not purchased in good faith. In Lord Denning's view, the statutory immunity could never avail a purchaser 'when the sale to him is done in fraud of the holder of the estate contract'.[18] In support of this conclusion Lord Denning invoked the general principle that 'fraud unravels everything', and that no court in the land 'will allow a person to keep an advantage which he has obtained by fraud'.[19] This concept of 'fraud' covered 'any dishonest dealing done so as to deprive unwary innocents of their rightful dues', and the hallmarks of such fraud included 'transactions done stealthily and speedily in secret for no sufficient consideration.'[20]

The majority in the Court of Appeal regarded the facts in *Midland Bank Trust Co Ltd v Green* as disclosing all the characteristics of 'fraud' thus defined, in that W and E had 'hatched a plot...[of which] the predominant purpose was to damage [G]'.[1] An absurdly low price (one eightieth of the current market value) had been paid over in connection with a secretly and swiftly executed transaction whose clear object had been to deprive G of his unregistered option. It would, said Lord Denning, be 'most unfair to [G], his widow and children', if the fraud perpetrated by W and E were allowed to succeed.[2] This view did not commend itself, however, to the House of Lords.

(ii) Rejection of any requirement of good faith In the House of Lords Lord Wilberforce expressed the firm conviction that the omission of any requirement of 'good faith' from the land charges legislation is entirely deliberate. To read into section 4(6) a requirement of good faith purchase would introduce 'the necessity of enquiring into the purchaser's motives and state of mind'[3]—a re-emergence of the very doctrine of notice which the 1925 legislation had sought to avoid.[4] In any event, as Lord Wilberforce observed, the notion of 'good faith' is inevitably so complex that the purchaser in the instant case could not necessarily be stigmatised as having acted unequivocally in bad faith.[5]

16 See Land Charges Act 1972, s 17(1) (formerly Land Charges Act 1925, s 20(8)).
17 See eg *Le Neve v Le Neve* (1748) 3 Atk 646 at 652, 26 ER 1172 at 1175ff, in relation to the operation of the Middlesex Registry Act 1708.
18 [1980] Ch 590 at 624F. Eveleigh LJ ([1980] Ch 590 at 627B-C) likewise imported a requirement of good faith by way of the definition of 'purchaser' in Law of Property Act 1925, s 205(1)(xxi). Compare, however, Lord Wilberforce ([1981] AC 513 at 529C-H).
19 *Lazarus Estates Ltd v Beasley* [1956] 1 QB 702 at 712.
20 [1980] Ch 590 at 625B.
1   [1980] Ch 590 at 622G, 625D. Compare, however, the dissenting judgment of Sir Stanley Rees ([1980] Ch 590 at 632F-633B).
2   [1980] Ch 590 at 622D.
3   [1981] AC 513 at 530A.
4   Ante, p 106.
5   'Suppose—and this may not be far from the truth—that the purchaser's motives were in part to take the farm from [G], and in part to distribute it between [G] and his brothers and sisters, but not at all to obtain any benefit for herself, is that acting in "good faith" or not?' ([1981] AC 513 at 530C-D per Lord Wilberforce).

It is significant that, in reaching this conclusion, the House of Lords expressed no dissent from Lord Denning's broad principle that 'fraud unravels everything'. In itself this proposition commands universal support: a party guilty of 'fraud' can never hope to win. It is, however, the definition and practical identification of 'fraud' which elude consensus. A majority of the Court of Appeal in *Midland Bank Trust Co Ltd v Green* found 'fraud' to be present in circumstances where the House of Lords was equally clear that 'fraud' was not in issue.[6]

(iii) Differing views of the function of property law The key to these discrepant interpretations of primary fact lies in a fundamental divergence of perspective on the proper function of the law of property. The majority in the Court of Appeal effectively viewed property law as a tool of distributive justice—in this instance as between family members competing for the largesse of their now deceased parents.[7] However, the dominant ideology of modern property law places an overwhelming emphasis upon the simple mechanics of contract and conveyance, leaving the morality of exchange almost wholly unquestioned. According to this view, the principal purpose of the law of property is to provide clarity and procedural efficiency in the combined operation of bargain and exchange. Moreover, the law of property implicitly assumes a world of bourgeois individualism in which all are presumed to be equal, self-determining and competent to transact freely for the purpose of private gain. Thus to the conventional property lawyer the transaction concluded has no significant moral dimension, since the law of property so clearly expresses a preference for certainty and efficiency over the claims of fairness or moral entitlement.

(iv) It is 'not fraud to take advantage of legal rights' The decision of the House of Lords in *Midland Bank Trust Co Ltd v Green* was entirely consistent with—indeed was ultimately inevitable in the context of—the amoral approach to economic relations which infuses the capitalist concept of property. While Lord Denning had asserted that 'fraud unravels everything', Lord Wilberforce preferred to invoke the well known principle that 'it is not fraud to take advantage of legal rights, the existence of which may be taken to be known to both parties'.[8] He pointed out that it had been perfectly open to G to protect his option by resorting to the simple mechanism of registration: this he had failed to do. In the words of Lord Wilberforce,

If the position was simply that the purchaser had notice of the option, and decided nevertheless to buy the land, relying on the absence of notification, nobody could contend that she would be lacking in good faith. She would merely be taking advantage of a situation, which the law has provided, and the addition of a profit motive could not create an absence of good faith.[9]

6   Compare *Waimiha Sawmilling Co Ltd v Waione Timber Co Ltd* [1926] AC 101 at 106 per Lord Buckmaster ('If the designed object of a transfer be to cheat a man of a known existing right, that is fraudulent...').
7   It appeared in *Midland Bank Trust Co Ltd v Green* that W had treated other members of the family more generously than G, a point which did not escape the notice of Lord Denning MR.
8   *In re Monolithic Building Co* [1915] 1 Ch 643 at 663 per Lord Cozens-Hardy MR.
9   [1981] AC 513 at 530A-B.

In other words, the House of Lords re-asserted the crude but efficient rule that the only form of notice relevant in the land charges context is the notice constituted by due entry in the Register. While conceding the existence of an exceptional category of vitiating 'fraud', the House found no such fraud to be present on the facts of the instant case, and declined to import any general moral criterion of good faith into the operation of what is now section 4(6) of the Land Charges Act 1972. As Lord Wilberforce said,

The case is plain: the Act is clear and definite. Intended as it was to provide a simple and understandable system for the protection of title to land, it should not be read down or glossed: to do so would destroy the usefulness of the Act. Any attempt to remould the Act to meet the facts of the present case, on the supposition that it is a hard one and that justice requires it, is...removed by the consideration that the Act itself provides a simple and effective protection for persons in [G's] position—viz—by registration.[10]

There are no easy solutions to the moral dilemmas which pervade many areas of property law. The law of property is not, and in a practical world never can be, a branch of moral philosophy.[11] The decision of the House of Lords in *Midland Bank Trust Co Ltd v Green* epitomises the traditional view of the busy property lawyer that there is much to be said in favour of trading off a little justice in return for enhanced security and certainty in commercial transactions.[12] However, this pragmatic approach will never satisfy all of the people all of the time. It may well be that, in the eyes of the law, it is not fraud to take advantage of the folly of another, but it remains an uncomfortable fact of life that most fraud consists in doing precisely that.

4. SEARCH OF THE LAND CHARGES REGISTER

Search of the Land Charges Register is governed by fairly complex rules both of statute and of judge-made law.

(1) Timing of search

It will at first sight seem somewhat strange that in unregistered or 'old system' conveyancing a prospective purchaser's investigation of title begins in earnest only after he has already entered into a contract to purchase.[13] It is, of course, only at this stage that the vendor becomes subject to any legal duty to show title to the land over the requisite period of time. During the interim between contract and conveyance, the purchaser must satisfy himself that the title offered is good. This he does by examining the deeds or documents of title relating to dispositions of the land during at least the preceding 15 years.[14]

---

10   [1981] AC 513 at 528A-B.
11   In *Midland Bank Trust Co Ltd v Green* the House of Lords effectively relegated G's estate to such non-proprietary remedies as might be available. The 'unfairness' of the result achieved by the House of Lords was somewhat mitigated by the fact the G's estate was held, in different proceedings before Oliver J, to be entitled to recover damages in respect of the negligence of G's solicitor in failing to register G's Class C(iv) land charge (see *Midland Bank Trust Co Ltd v Hett, Stubbs and Kemp (A Firm)* [1979] Ch 384 at 433B-D). G's estate was also successful in recovering damages against the estate of W for the tort of conspiracy (see *Midland Bank Trust Co Ltd v Green* (No 3) [1982] Ch 529 at 539H-540B, 541H-542A).
12   See *Holt, Renfrew & Co Ltd v Henry Singer Ltd* (1982) 135 DLR (3d) 391 at 399, for reference to the 'necessity of this business consideration predominating over the moral aspect'.
13   Post, p 209.
14   Law of Property Act 1969, s 23 (ante, p 95).

From the purchaser's point of view, this investigation must uncover a 'good root of title', ie, a valid document of title which is at least 15 years old.[15] It is, however, only *after* the exchange of contracts that the purchaser enjoys any contractual right of access to the historical documents of title which alone disclose the names of previous estate owners against whom land charges may have been registered.[16] The purchaser's right of access extends to all title deeds within the scope of the statutory 15 year period (or other agreed period), but does not extend back beyond the root of title.

(2) Process of search

Shortly before the projected date of completion it is usual for the purchaser to search the Land Charges Register against the names of estate owners comprised within the relevant title. If the first conveyance relating to the property which is at least 15 years old was executed in 1930, then the relevant title commences in 1930.

Search may be personal,[17] but most purchasers take advantage of the alternative 'official search' of the Register which is available upon application and the payment of a small fee. An 'official search' takes the form of a computer-aided check of the Land Charges Register for subsisting entries against the names of the estate owners included in the purchaser's requisition for search.[18]

(3) Effect of an official search

The principal advantage of an official search of the Land Charges Register consists in the fact that the result of the search is set out in a certificate issued to the intending purchaser.[19] The issue of this certificate has important implications.

(a) Conclusive nature of the certificate of official search

According to section 10(4) of the Land Charges Act 1972, '[i]n favour of a purchaser or an intending purchaser...the certificate, according to its tenor, shall be conclusive, affirmatively or negatively, as the case may be.'[20] Thus, even if the Registry mistakenly issues a clear or 'nil' certificate of official search in respect of a particular estate owner named in the relevant title, the certificate

15   Post, p 131. A 'good root of title' is, in effect, any instrument which unambiguously deals with or shows title to the whole legal and equitable interest in the correctly identified property. However, it is generally considered that instruments of mortgage, leases, and wills are insufficient for this purpose.

16   It is of course possible for the vendor to speed up or otherwise facilitate a transaction by affording access to the relevant documents before exchange of contracts, but this is still unusual in practice. See *Rignall Developments Ltd v Halil* [1987] 3 WLR 394 at 402E-F.

17   Land Charges Act 1972, s 9(1).

18   Land Charges Act 1972, s 10(1), (2).

19   A further advantage attracted by official search is that the purchaser is not bound by any entry made on the Register after the issue of the certificate (other than an entry made under a 'priority notice' pursuant to Land Charges Act 1972, s 11(1)-(3)), provided that completion of the purchaser's conveyance takes place within 15 working days of the date of issue of the certificate (Land Charges Act 1972, s 11(5), (6)).

20   See Land Charges Act 1925, s 17(3).

is *conclusive* according to its tenor. A land charge, albeit duly registered against such an estate owner, becomes utterly void.[1]

(b) Remedies in tort for any damage caused by negligent misstatement

The irrebuttable presumption contained in section 10(4) of the Land Charges Act 1972 effectively coerces the facts to accord with the fiction contained on the face of an inaccurate nil certificate. The purchaser can safely take the land free of the unnotified land charge, and the owner of the now destroyed charge is thrown back upon a remedy in damages against the Land Registry for the tort of negligence. Such an action is founded on the negligent misrepresentation which has been made by the Registry to the applicant for an official search and which has caused loss to a third party, the owner of the previously subsisting land charge.[2]

(c) Policy preference in favour of official search

It is clear that the underlying policy reflected in the Land Charges Act tends to ensure both certainty and facility in land transactions and, incidentally, to discourage personal searches of the Register. The latter point was borne out in *Oak Co-operative Building Society v Blackburn*,[3] where the Court of Appeal was concerned with the effect of a registration against an incorrect version of the name of the estate owner.[4] Russell LJ acknowledged that a personal searcher against the full correct name would not have encountered the registration in the present case and, not having the benefit of an official certificate of search, would have been affected by a 'deemed actual notice' under section 198(1) of the Law of Property Act 1925.[5] However, Russell LJ regarded the apparent unfairness of this outcome as largely countered by the consideration that 'anyone who nowadays is foolish enough to search personally deserves what he gets'.[6] In Russell LJ's acerbic view, if the aim of the Land Charges Act is 'to arrive at a sensible working system', that aim was more effectively furthered by

1   The effect of a clear certificate issued in error must be to extinguish (and not merely to suspend) the registered charge. Otherwise, the recipient of a clear certificate would be compelled to sell the land in his turn subject to the incumbrance, having bought the land free from the incumbrance on the strength of the clear certificate. Such a result would impose a palpable financial loss on the recipient of the certificate and would not therefore constitute an outcome 'in favour of [the] purchaser' as required by section 10(4) of the Land Charges Act 1972. In other words, the purchaser armed with an erroneously issued clear certificate of official search is a kind of statutory analogue of 'Equity's Darling'. His advent, like that of 'Equity's Darling', destroys existing incumbrances so that they cannot affect a later purchaser even though he has actual notice (see *Wilkes v Spooner* [1911] 2 KB 473 at 488, ante, p 92).

2   See *Ministry of Housing and Local Government v Sharp* [1970] 2 QB 223 (dealing with the equivalent problem in the analogous context of local land charges). An ambivalent provision in section 10(6) of the Land Charges Act 1972 purports to protect officers and employees of the Registry from personal liability for any loss arising, except where that loss is caused by an act of fraud. The clear intention is that persons aggrieved by the negligence of an officer or employee of the Registry should be able to recover damages on the basis of the vicarious liability of the Registry.

3   [1968] Ch 730.
4   Post, p 129.
5   [1968] Ch 730 at 743F-G.
6   [1968] Ch 730 at 744A-B.

upholding a slightly inaccurate registration than by 'protecting a personal searcher from his folly'.[7]

(4) Consequence of discovering a registered charge

The absolute nature of a land charge registration used to cause extreme difficulty if a purchaser discovered, shortly before completion, that the Land Charges Register did in fact contain some entry prejudicial to his intended use or enjoyment of the land. In the nature of things such a discovery would usually be made only after vendor and purchaser had exchanged contracts for the purchase of the land.

(a) Literal application of Law of Property Act 1925, s 198(1)

Such is the unqualified force of section 198(1) of the Law of Property Act 1925 that it was once thought that the purchaser in such a case must be deemed to have had 'actual notice' at the date of the contract of any subsisting registration disclosed later on search of the Register. This being so, the purchaser was then obliged to complete the contract and take a conveyance of the land notwithstanding that the sale was expressed to be 'free from encumbrances' and even though the land might well be valueless to him.[8]

(b) Curative effect of amending legislation

This 'indefensible' and quite inequitable rule[9] has been displaced in relation to contracts entered into since 1969. Where search reveals the existence of a registered land charge unknown to the purchaser at the date of the contract, the purchaser is now entitled to plead his ignorance as a ground for declining to complete the contract. According to section 24(1) of the Law of Property Act 1969, the issue is no longer to be determined with reference to the fictitious 'actual notice' imposed by section 198(1) of the Law of Property Act 1925. Instead the question whether, at the time of entering into the estate contract, the purchaser had knowledge of a registered land charge 'shall be determined by reference to his actual knowledge and without regard to the provisions of section 198...'

(5) Defective registration and defective search

To err is human. It is possible that mistakes (usually as to name[10]) may be made either in the process of registration of a land charge or in the process of search or—in rare concatenations of error—in both registration and search. The possibility of error arises from the fact that the Register of Land Charges is a register against names rather than title numbers or plots of land—a point which will be taken up later.[11]

---

7   [1968] Ch 730 at 744A. In practical terms it would be extremely difficult in any event for the personal searcher to provide convincing proof ex post facto that he had conducted his unsupervised search against the correct name of the estate owner.
8   See eg *In re Forsey and Hollebone's Contract* [1927] 2 Ch 379 at 392f.
9   See the criticisms advanced by H.W.R. Wade, [1956] CLJ 216 at 228ff.
10   For an ambiguity arising in relation to the precise plot of land concerned in an application for official search against a specific name, see *Du Sautoy v Symes* [1967] Ch 1146.
11   Post, p 130.

(a) Defective registration

The correct name against which a registration should be entered on the Land Charges Register is deemed to be the full name of the 'estate owner' as recorded on his deeds of title.[12] If the incumbrancer registers against any other name, such registration will not bind a third party who subsequently requisitions an official search against the full correct name.

In *Diligent Finance Co Ltd v Alleyne*[13] the first defendant, Erskine Owen Alleyne, was the estate owner of a matrimonial home. He deserted his wife, who later registered her statutory 'rights of occupation'[14] in the matrimonial home as a Class F land charge against the name of 'Erskine Alleyne'. Two months after the registration the first defendant negotiated an increased mortgage loan from the plaintiff moneylender, which duly requisitioned an official search of the Land Charges Register before taking a new legal charge on the property and releasing the loan moneys. The plaintiff company requisitioned its search against the name of the first defendant as recorded on his title deeds, 'Erskine Owen Alleyne'. The official search certificate made no reference to the Class F charge registered by the first defendant's wife. On receiving the increased advance the first defendant left the country and the plaintiff company eventually brought possession proceedings against the wife as second defendant.[15] Foster J held that in these circumstances the Class F registration against an incomplete version of the estate owner's name could not rank ahead of the plaintiff's legal charge where the plaintiff had obtained an official search certificate against the complete and correct version of that name.[16]

(b) Defective search

It is quite clear that a purchaser who requisitions an official search against an incorrect name must inevitably lose priority to an incumbrancer who has registered a land charge against the correct name of the estate owner as it appears on the title deeds.[17] By virtue of section 198(1) of the Law of Property Act 1925 such a purchaser is inescapably affected by a deemed 'actual notice' of the correct entry.

Somewhat more difficult is the issue of priority which arises where an incumbrancer has registered incorrectly, but the purchaser has likewise requisitioned an official search against the wrong name. This unlikely coincidence of error occurred in *Oak Co-operative Building Society v Blackburn.*[18]

---

12 *Standard Property Investment plc v British Plastics Federation* (1985) 53 P & CR 25 at 32.
13 (1971) 23 P & CR 346.
14 On statutory 'rights of occupation', see Chapter 22 (post, p 782).
15 Foster J acknowledged that it was 'unfortunate...that the Class F registration was not made against the proper name Erskine Owen Alleyne but only against Erskine Alleyne, but that is a mistake which I for my part cannot unfortunately rectify' ((1971) 23 P & CR 346 at 350). The debt owed to the plaintiff company amounted to only £700.
16 (1971) 23 P & CR 346 at 349f. See also *Standard Property Investment plc v British Plastics Federation* (1985) 53 P & CR 25 at 33.
17 This conclusion follows even if the search is requisitioned not against the name of the estate owner as disclosed by his title deeds, but against some more complete version of his name (eg the full names contained in his birth certificate). See *Standard Property Investment plc v British Plastics Federation* (1985) 53 P & CR 25 at 30ff. On the effect of other mistakes in a requisition of official search, see *Du Sautoy v Symes* [1967] Ch 1146.
18 [1968] Ch 730, on appeal from [1967] Ch 1169.

Here D^1 was an estate agent whose full name was 'Francis David Blackburn'. D^1 owned a dwelling-house in fee simple and he entered into an agreement to sell this property to D^3. D^3 was not legally represented; she agreed to pay a deposit of £100 and to pay the balance of the purchase price (£1,900) over a period of 15 years. D^3 subsequently registered this estate contract as a Class C(iv) land charge against the name of 'Frank David Blackburn', 'Frank' being the name by which D^1 was generally known in the locality. Several years later D^1 obtained a mortgage advance of £1,300 from P on the security of the property. Before accepting a legal charge on the property, P instructed their solicitor to requisition an official search of the Land Charges Register. The solicitor mistakenly applied for an official search against the name 'Francis Davis Blackburn'.[19] The search certificate made no reference to the subsisting entry against 'Frank David Blackburn'. D^1 was subsequently adjudicated bankrupt and some time later, in the words of Russell LJ, P 'roused themselves from torpor' and brought possession proceedings against D^3.

Under these circumstances the Court of Appeal was called upon to decide an issue which turned ultimately on the relative gravity of two errors—an error in the initial registration and an error in the requisition of official search. Reversing the judgment of Ungoed-Thomas J, the Court of Appeal took the 'broader view that so far as possible the system should be made to work in favour of those who seek to make use of it in a sensible and practical way.'[20] The Court thus concluded that D^3's registration should not be regarded as a nullity merely because D^1's formal name was 'Francis' and not 'Frank'. According to Russell LJ, a registration in 'what may be fairly described as a version of the full names of the vendor' is not rendered a nullity as against 'someone who does not search at all, or who (as here) searches in the wrong name', but would be a nullity as against someone who requisitioned an official search against the full correct name as disclosed by the deeds of title.[1]

5. THE BASIC FLAW OF THE LAND CHARGES SYSTEM

Any analysis of the caselaw under the Land Charges Act makes it increasingly apparent that the present land charges scheme suffers from a rather fundamental flaw.

(1) The problem

The basic problem underlying the registration of land charges lies in the fact that registration is effected against the *name* of the estate owner whose estate is

---

19   One of the hilarious features of this case is the fact that the solicitor who requisitioned the official search was himself called 'Davis' and appears, by error, to have transposed his own name into the search application!

20   [1968] Ch 730 at 743C.

1   [1968] Ch 730 at 743E-F. See (1968) 32 Conv (NS) 284 (F.R. Crane). It is clear that the Court of Appeal had little patience with the Oak Co-operative Building Society. The Building Society was even informed by the Registry of earlier charges on the property against the name of 'Francis David Blackburn', but had not been moved to inquire further. Russell LJ denied that the Court 'need shed any tears for the plaintiffs, who could easily have protected themselves by a proper search but which owing to the error of their solicitor they never made...[T]hey could without great trouble have caused somebody to visit the property in question, when they would have found the third defendant living there' ([1968] Ch 730 at 744B).

intended to be affected.[2] Names belong to people and, since people are mere mortals, their names are evanescent. As time passes, these names likewise disappear into the mists of history. The same is not true of land, which is immovable.[3]

(a) A practical example

The difficulty which unfolds itself is this. Suppose the following series of conveyances of a fee simple estate in a plot of land, Blackacre:

> A conveys to B in 1930
> B conveys to C in 1960
> C conveys to D in 1968
> D conveys to E in 1979
> E conveys to F in 1987

Suppose further that in 1936 B's neighbour, N, duly registered a restrictive covenant as a Class D(ii) land charge against the name of the current estate owner, B. It is almost certain that when F searched the Land Charges Register prior to completing his purchase in 1987, he did not discover the existence of N's incumbrance. In the normal case F's investigation of the title to Blackacre will have commenced with the conveyance by C to D in 1968—that is, with the first conveyance which by 1987 was at least 15 years old.[4] F will have had no contractual right of access to the earlier deeds of conveyance and therefore may never have heard of B (or A). Yet, according to the draconian terms of section 198(1) of the Law of Property Act 1925, N's registration against B constitutes 'actual notice' of N's equitable interest 'to all persons and for all purposes'. F is thus fixed with actual notice of N's restrictive covenant. The fact that F received a clear certificate of official search against the names of C, D and E is quite irrelevant. Through no real fault of his own F did not obtain a certificate of search against the name of B—and that is all that matters here. F is inescapably bound by a land charge which was duly registered, albeit behind a good root of title.

(b) The 'Frankenstein's monster'

The problem disclosed here is endemic in any system of name-registration which operates on the pragmatic assumption that those investigating title can entirely ignore events anterior to an artificial and arbitrarily defined 'root of title'. The difficulty was already sufficiently apparent to the Lord Chancellor's Committee on Land Charges which reported in 1956, when the statutory period of investigation of title was still 30 years.[5] In its report this Committee (which sat under the chairmanship of Roxburgh J) confessed itself unable to suggest any remedy for the grave defect which had been exposed in the

---

2   Land Charges Act 1972, s 3(1) (ante, p 113). It has been pointed out that name- registration is a perfectly suitable method of protecting land charges which have a limited expectation of life (eg estate contracts). However, other kinds of land charge (eg restrictive covenants) are commonly imposed in order to control the use of land over an indefinitely long period (see H.W.R. Wade, [1956] CLJ 216 at 222f).
3   Compare the basis of registration of title under the Land Registration Act 1925 (post, p 148).
4   Law of Property Act 1969, s 23 (ante, p 125).
5   Law of Property Act 1925, s 44(1) (post, p 221).

operation of the land charges scheme. The Committee conjectured that the inherently flawed name-register had been instituted in 1925 in the belief that all land in England and Wales would be covered by a system of compulsory registration of title within the following 30 years. This goal remained woefully unrealised in 1956, and the Roxburgh Committee could only recommend that the extension of compulsory registration of title should proceed apace.[6] As was said at the time, the draftsmen of the 1925 legislation 'appear to have succeeded in creating the conveyancing equivalent of a Frankenstein's monster, which with the passing years would become not only more dangerous but also more difficult to kill'.[7]

The problem of the hidden registration would still not have occasioned widespread difficulty if the minimum statutory period of investigation of title had remained as 30 years. In the example discussed above, this period would have embraced the conveyance from B to C in 1960, thus revealing to F the name of B as an earlier estate owner of Blackacre. However, in 1970 the statutory period of investigation of title was reduced to a mere 15 years,[8] and the problem was made instantly more acute. It became much more likely that purchasers would be trapped by registrations concealed behind a good root of title of whose existence they had no conceivable means of discovery. A partial remedy was therefore enacted in the Law of Property Act 1969.[9]

(2) A partial remedy

Section 25(1) of the Law of Property Act 1969 confers a right to compensation from public moneys on any purchaser of an estate or interest in land who suffers loss by reason of a registered land charge hidden behind a root of title. Thus, in relation to the dilemma of the concealed charge considered in the example above, the preferred legislative solution is that N's charge should remain binding on F in accordance with section 198(1) of the Law of Property Act 1925, but that any consequential loss falling on F should be assuaged by the award of money.

(a) Preconditions of statutory compensation

The availability of compensation (which is paid by the Chief Land Registrar[10]) is always subject to three statutory conditions. *First*, the completion of the transaction which occasions the loss must occur after the commencement date of the Law of Property Act 1969.[11] The compensation provision thus applies only to conveyances effected on or after 1 January 1970. *Second*, the purchaser must have no 'actual knowledge' of the charge at the date of completion of his

---

6   Cmd 9825 (July 1956), para 22.
7   See H.W.R. Wade, [1956] CLJ 216 at 220, who pointed out that it was quite impracticable even in 1956 to convert the Land Charges Register from a name-based register into a title- or land-based register. The 'herculean labour' required to effect the transition of millions of charges already registered now makes the task utterly impossible.
8   Law of Property Act 1969, s 23 (ante, p 125).
9   See Law Commission, *Report on Land Charges affecting Unregistered Land* (Law Com No 18, 1969), para 27.
10   Law of Property Act 1969, s 25(4).
11   Law of Property Act 1969, s 25(1)(a).

purchase.[12] *Third*, the charge in question must have been registered 'against the name of an owner of an estate in the land who was not as owner of any such estate a party to any transaction, or concerned in any event, comprised in the relevant title.'[13] In other words, the registration in respect of which compensation is sought must be truly concealed behind the root of title.

(b) Other practical precautions

The theoretical problem of concealed registrations has been largely avoided in practice because most registered land charges tend to be referred to in later title deeds so long as there remains any possibility that these charges remain relevant.[14] It is therefore a rare purchaser who can plead complete ignorance of a charge registered behind the root of title, but it is predictable that the day is fast approaching when the compensation provisions of the Law of Property Act 1969 will assume a more vital significance.

6. CATEGORIES OF REGISTRABLE LAND CHARGE

The categories of registrable land charge are defined in section 2 of the Land Charges Act 1972. There are six classes of land charge registrable in unregistered land, of which the most important are Classes C, D, and F.

(1) Class A

Class A charges comprise various kinds of land charge which derive ultimately from statute and which arise only on the making of some statutory application.[15]

(2) Class B

Class B charges likewise arise by virtue of statute, and include such charges as the Law Society's charge on land recovered or preserved for a legally assisted client under the Legal Aid Act 1974 in respect of unpaid contributions to the legal aid fund.[16] Class B charges differ from Class A charges in that they originate directly in the statute concerned and do not arise merely on the chargee's application.

---

12 Law of Property Act 1969, s 25(1)(b). For this purpose, 'actual knowledge' is to be determined without regard to the provisions of section 198(1) of the Law of Property Act 1925 (see Law of Property Act 1969, s 25(2)).
13 Law of Property Act 1969, s 25(1)(c).
14 The mere handing on of a series of official search certificates obtained on the occasion of purchase by each successive owner may not be enough in itself to compile an accurate or comprehensive record of all the charges affecting the land. There is, for instance, no necessary assurance that in each case the official search was requisitioned against the correct full names of former estate owners.
15 An example is the landlord's right to compensation under Agricultural Holdings Act 1986, s 86.
16 Legal Aid Act 1974, s 9(6) (post, p 324).

(3) Class C

Class C charges fall under four heads:

(a) Class C(i)

This class comprises the 'puisne mortgage', ie, a legal mortgage which is not protected by a deposit of documents relating to the legal estate affected. A puisne mortgage is therefore a second mortgage granted by a mortgagor who has already deposited his title deeds with the first mortgagee.[17] The second mortgagee, being unable to enjoy the security provided by retention of the title deeds, is offered the alternative security of being able to register his mortgage as a land charge notwithstanding that it is *legal*. Class C(i) thus provides a rare example of a legal interest which is registrable under the Land Charges Act: land charges are almost always *equitable* rights in or over land. The puisne mortgage is, however, included amongst the registrable categories simply for reasons of convenience and because of the additional security which registration confers on a second mortgagee.

(b) Class C(ii)

Class C(ii) comprises the 'limited owner's charge'. Such a charge arises where, for instance, a tenant for life of settled land[18] discharges out of his own pocket a liability to taxation attracted by the settled estate as a whole. The limited owner's charge is therefore an equitable charge which, if registered, secures the right of the limited owner (ie, the tenant for life) to reimbursement of the money paid by him to the Revenue.

(c) Class C(iii)

This class comprises the 'general equitable charge' and includes many kinds of equitable charge which are not otherwise registrable. Amongst the incumbrances registrable under Class C(iii) are a rentcharge granted for life (or 'equitable annuity'),[19] an equitable mortgage of a legal estate,[20] and an unpaid vendor's equitable lien on property sold. Class C(iii) does not, however, include any charge which is secured by a deposit of documents relating to the legal title affected.[1] Informal mortgages by deposit of title deeds are for this reason excluded from the registrable category.[2] Nor does Class C(iii) include any equitable charge which arises or affects an interest arising under a trust for sale or settlement of land.[3] Such charges are in any event governed by the normal process of overreaching on sale,[4] with the result that there is no reason for

---

17 Post, p 605.
18 Post, p 805.
19 Ante, pp 70, 81. 'Equitable annuities outside trusts for sale and settlements must be extremely rare, even if only because most kinds of annuity charged upon land make it settled land' (H.W.R. Wade, [1956] CLJ 216 at 224).
20 Post, p 576. Equitable mortgages of an equitable interest under a trust for sale or strict settlement of land are normally overreached on a conveyance of that land to a third party, and are thereafter satisfied out of the proceeds of sale (see Law of Property Act 1925, s 2(1)(i), (ii); Settled Land Act 1925, s 72(2)).
1 Land Charges Act 1972, s 2(4).
2 Post, p 576.
3 Land Charges Act 1972, s 2(4).
4 Ante, pp 100, 106.

enforcement against a later purchaser. Furthermore, Class C(iii) does not include either an agreement to share the proceeds of sale of land[5] or an estate agent's charge on those proceeds for the purpose of securing his commission.[6] The interest of the chargee in such cases is effectively an interest in money rather than an interest in land, and Class C(iii) is appropriate only in respect of interests in land.[7]

(d) Class C(iv)

Class C(iv) comprises the 'estate contract', which is statutorily defined as

a contract by an estate owner or by a person entitled at the date of the contract to have a legal estate conveyed to him to convey or create a legal estate, including a contract conferring either expressly or by statutory implication a valid option to purchase, a right of pre-emption or any other like right.[8]

(i) Conveyancing function of the estate contract It is integral to the conveyancing process that, from the very moment of exchange of contracts, the purchaser of a legal estate in land acquires not merely a *contractual* right but also a *proprietary* right. It is for precisely this reason that the Class C(iv) land charge is designed to protect the purchaser's estate contract, ie, the purchaser's right to require conveyance of the legal estate in accordance with the contract.[9] The purchaser's interest requires protection during the interim between contract and conveyance because there is always a possibility that the vendor may in breach of contract convey the legal estate to a third party who has no notice of the equitable rights created by the estate contract. Moreover, estate contracts by their very nature create merely short-term interests in land and are therefore peculiarly appropriate for protection under a system of name-registration such as the land charges scheme.[10] Ironically, however, it seems that estate contracts are in practice seldom registered by solicitors, being entered in the Land Charges Register only in cases of suspicion or delayed completion.[11]

(ii) Accepted forms of estate contract Estate contracts include not merely contracts for the sale of an estate in fee simple; they also include contracts for a lease[12] and contracts to create a mortgage of a legal estate. It matters not that the legal estate to be conveyed under the contract is greater than the estate currently vested in the estate owner,[13] although there is some doubt as to whether Class C(iv) can include an oral contract which is enforceable only on the basis of acts of part performance.[14]

5 *Thomas v Rose* [1968] 1 WLR 1797 at 1808G-H.
6 *Georgiades v Edward Wolfe & Co Ltd* [1965] Ch 487 at 501F, 504G, 508C.
7 In 1956 the Roxburgh Committee favoured the abolition of Class C(iii) with the exception of the category of mortgages (see *Report of the Committee on Land Charges*, para 13).
8 Land Charges Act 1972, s 2(4).
9 The legal estate in question may of course be either a freehold or a leasehold.
10 H.W.R. Wade, [1956] CLJ 216 at 222.
11 'Why it should be [the] collective practice [of conveyancing solicitors] to run this risk is a mystery, but the Land Registry must be grateful...for the volume of entries would be enormous, and "dead wood" would accumulate in the registry as fast as contracts were completed' (H.W.R. Wade, [1956] CLJ 216 at 223).
12 Post, p 468.
13 *Sharp v Coates* [1949] 1 KB 285 at 293.
14 See eg *Mens v Wilson* (1973) 231 Estates Gazette 843.

(iii) Options It is also clear that the category of registrable estate contract includes certain kinds of *option*.[15] The essence of an option for purchase is that the option holder is entitled to demand the conveyance of the relevant estate at any time of his choosing,[16] provided that he has first satisfied any conditions to which the option was made subject.[17] From the moment of its grant an option to purchase confers upon the grantee an equitable interest in the land concerned,[18] and the option can be revoked or varied only in accordance with the terms of the option itself.

An option to purchase a legal estate is registrable as a Class C(iv) charge,[19] as is also a tenant's option for renewal of his term under a lease.[20] Likewise a tenant may, under Class C(iv), register a notice served by him in respect of his right under the Leasehold Reform Act 1967 to purchase the freehold reversion or to acquire an enlarged lease.[1] A Class C(iv) charge may also be registered by a landlord in respect of any right which he may have to require his tenant to surrender (rather than assign) his leasehold term.[2]

(iv) Rights of pre-emption A fundamental distinction must be drawn between an option to purchase and a 'right of pre-emption'. Under an option the optionor grants to the optionee a right which is 'solely within the optionee's control to compel a conveyance of the optionor's land at a future date.'[3] By contrast, a 'right of pre-emption' confers upon its grantee merely a right of first refusal: the decision whether to sell at all lies always within the discretion of the grantor of

---

15   See generally D. Barnsley, *Land Options* (London 1978).

16   See *Canadian Long Island Petroleums Ltd v Irving Industries Ltd* (1975) 50 DLR (3d) 265 at 277 per Martland J. Under an option the right to purchase 'becomes crystallised immediately upon the option being granted and...exclusive control over whether a concluded contract for sale will come into existence resides in the optionee...The only act required to be done..is an act of the optionee signifying his intention to exercise the option' (*Kopec v Pyret* (1983) 146 DLR (3d) 242 at 248).

17   It is irrelevant that the purchase price is not stipulated in the terms of the option, so long as the option provides machinery by which the price can later be objectively ascertained without the necessity of any further agreement as to price between the parties (see *Kopec v Pyret* (1983) 146 DLR (3d) 242 at 248). In *Sudbrook Trading Estate Ltd v Eggleton* [1983] 1 AC 444, for instance, the House of Lords upheld the enforceability of an option where the price was to be settled by valuers nominated by the parties or, in default, by an umpire appointed by both parties. See [1981] Conv 448 (K. Hodkinson); [1982] CLJ 233 (C. Harpum and D. Lloyd Jones); (1982) 132 NLJ 818 (H.W. Wilkinson); (1982) 98 LQR 539 (J. Murdoch); (1983) 46 MLR 493 (P. Robertshaw). See also *Re Nishi Industries Ltd* (1979) 91 DLR (3d) 321 at 323f; *Lonergan v McCartney* [1983] 3 NIJB.

18   See *London and South Western Railway Co v Gomm* (1882) 20 Ch D 562 at 580f; *Webb v Pollmount Ltd* [1966] Ch 584 at 596D; *Frobisher Ltd v Canadian Pipelines & Petroleums Ltd* (1960) 21 DLR (2d) 497 at 532; *Stephens v Gulf Oil Canada Ltd* (1976) 65 DLR (3d) 193 at 215.

19   See eg *Midland Bank Trust Co Ltd v Green* [1981] AC 513 (ante, p 120).

20   *Beesly v Hallwood Estates Ltd* [1960] 1 WLR 549 at 558 (post, pp 395, 524). The Roxburgh Committee suggested that such options should cease to be registrable (*Report of the Committee on Land Charges*, para 15).

1   Leasehold Reform Act 1967, s 5(5) (post, p 730). The mere service of a statutory notice by the tenant under the 1967 Act confers no priority over a transferee from the landlord: the notice must also be registered (see *Buckley v S.R.L. Investments Ltd and Cator and Robinson* (1971) 22 P & CR 756 at 764).

2   *Greene v Church Commissioners for England* [1974] Ch 467 at 477B.

3   *Stephens v Gulf Oil Canada Ltd* (1976) 65 DLR (3d) 193 at 218. 'This feature of exclusive control by the optionee whereby he can, by his own unilateral act, compel the vendor to part with his interest in the subject-matter, does not permit the same indeterminacy of terms which characterises a right of first refusal at its inception' (*Kopec v Pyret* (1983) 146 DLR (3d) 242 at 248).

the right of pre-emption.[4] The essential characteristic of such a right of pre-emption thus consists in an intention on the part of the covenantor to give to the covenantee a preference over other potential buyers in the event that the covenantor should decide to sell.[5] Until that point, however, the grantee of the right of pre-emption has 'a mere spes which the grantor...may either frustrate by choosing not to fulfil the necessary conditions or may convert into an option and thus into an equitable interest by fulfilling the conditions.'[6]

Although the definition of a right of pre-emption usually causes little difficulty,[7] it is far from clear to what extent this kind of right is registrable under Class C(iv). Notwithstanding that the statutory definition of the Class C(iv) charge plainly includes a reference to a 'right of pre-emption',[8] the Court of Appeal held in *Pritchard v Briggs*[9] that such a right takes effect as an interest in land only when it becomes exercisable.[10] In other words, a right of pre-emption is registrable under Class C(iv) only if and when the vendor ultimately decides to sell the estate in question.[11] This conclusion has been heavily challenged, not least because it seems to contradict the pellucid wording of the statutory definition,[12] and the point remains shrouded in some confusion.[13]

(v) Contracts of agency It is also uncertain to what extent Class C(iv) applies to contracts of agency: there are conflicting views as to whether the class of

4 See *Brown v Gould* [1972] Ch 53 at 58F; *Stephens v Gulf Oil Canada Ltd* (1976) 65 DLR (3d) 193 at 217f. A right of first refusal operates in effect as a 'negative covenant on the part of the vendor not to part with his interest in the land until the first opportunity to purchase is accorded to the covenantee' (see *Canadian Long Island Petroleums Ltd v Irving Industries Ltd* (1975) 50 DLR (3d) 265 at 279f; *Kopec v Pyret* (1983) 146 DLR (3d) 242 at 247).

5 See *Kopec v Pyret* (1983) 146 DLR (3d) 242 at 247. If the original grant of the right of pre-emption stipulated a fixed purchase price which has since been rendered 'grossly inadequate' by the subsequent inflation of land values, there is a possibility that the agreement to grant the right will be struck down as void on grounds of public policy: the fixed price may be regarded as an invalid restriction upon alienation (ante, p 75). See *In re Rosher* (1884) 26 Ch D 801 at 811ff; *Hall v Busst* (1960) 104 CLR 206 at 216ff; *Saliba v Saliba* [1976] Qd R 205 at 207D-E.

6 *Pritchard v Briggs* [1980] Ch 338 at 418C-D per Templeman LJ.

7 In identifying whether a grant is one of option or of first refusal, the label applied by the parties themselves is not conclusive. The court may scrutinise the substance rather than the form of the transaction and need not 'adhere slavishly' to a label which misdescribes the relationship (see *Kopec v Pyret* (1983) 146 DLR (3d) 242 at 247).

8 Land Charges Act 1972, s 2(4) (ante, p 135).

9 [1980] Ch 338.

10 In *Kling v Keston Properties Ltd* (1983) 49 P & CR 212 at 217, Vinelott J pointed out that a vendor 'can hardly evince a desire to sell land more clearly than by contracting to sell it.' He therefore ruled that in that case the relevant right of pre-emption became an option and created an equitable interest in the land 'not later than the moment when the agreement for the grant of a lease was executed.' For a similar ruling, see *Kopec v Pyret* (1983) 146 DLR (3d) 242 at 252, where Scheibel J held that 'where the vendor has signified his intention to sell upon certain terms and holds himself ready to sell in the event those terms are met, the position of the preferential purchaser is transformed into that of a virtual optionholder.'

11 [1980] Ch 338 at 419F-G, 423A-B. There is authority in other jurisdictions for the proposition that, before it becomes exercisable, a right of pre-emption confers merely a personal right rather than a proprietary right (see *Stephens v Gulf Oil Canada Ltd* (1976) 65 DLR (3d) 193 at 217f) and cannot therefore constitute a registrable or caveatable interest in land (see *Re Rutherford* [1977] 1 NZLR 504 at 510). See also *Kopec v Pyret* (1983) 146 DLR (3d) 242 at 247.

12 Goff LJ went so far as to say that the legislation 'proceeded on a mistaken basis as to what the law was' ([1980] Ch 338 at 398A-399E).

13 For criticism of the decision in *Pritchard v Briggs*, see [1980] CLJ 35 (C. Harpum); (1980) 96 LQR 488 (H.W.R. Wade). See also A.R. Everton, [1982] Conv 177 at 180.

registrable estate contracts can include a *contract to create a contract* in relation to land. In *Turley v Mackay*,[14] for instance, Uthwatt J thought that Class C(iv) covered a contract 'under which one person is bound to a second person to create a legal estate in such a third person as the second person may direct.'[15] On this footing a contract by A to sell to any nominee put forward by B would itself qualify as an estate contract.

A more restrictive approach was applied in *Thomas v Rose*.[16] Here Megarry J agreed that Class C(iv) is sufficiently wide to cover a contract by A and B whereby A agrees to grant a legal estate (eg a lease) to X.[17] He was also prepared to concede that Class C(iv) includes a contract by A and B to convey or create a legal estate in favour of such persons as B shall direct.[18] In Megarry J's view, however, Class C(iv) is properly applicable only to those contracts 'which themselves bind the estate owner (or other person entitled) to convey or create a legal estate.'[19] No registration may be validly effected in respect of any contract which fails to impose on the estate owner a clear legal obligation to sell his estate to somebody.[20] In terms of this analysis Class C(iv) has no relevance to a contract 'at one remove' which merely provides 'machinery whereby such an obligation may be created by some other transaction'.[1] A contract between A and B conferring on B the power to accept 'any offer for the sale' of A's land is not a registrable estate contract: it is at most an authority to do some further act which may or may not bring an estate contract into being. In *Thomas v Rose*[2] Megarry J regarded such an agreement as constituting in essence a mere agency agreement regulating the disposal of land and providing for payment of the agent out of the proceeds of sale.

(4) Class D

Class D falls under three heads:

(a) Class D(i)

This class comprises an Inland Revenue charge for tax payable on death.

(b) Class D(ii)

This class comprises the 'restrictive covenant',[3] which for this purpose is defined as 'a covenant or agreement (other than a covenant or agreement

---

14 [1944] Ch 37 at 40.
15 This view was justified on the ground that the object of Class C(iv) is to 'secure that obligations affecting land may be registered by persons who have a commercial interest in seeing that those obligations shall be carried out' ([1944] Ch 37 at 41).
16 [1968] 1 WLR 1797 at 1804G, where Megarry J thought that *Turley v Mackay* was not a case which ought to be extended in its ambit. 'The agent's real claim in that case was for damages, and it is possible to wonder whether his contractual rights fell within the spirit of class C(iv).'
17 '[I]t matters not that the contract is a contract to create a legal estate in favour of someone other than a contracting party' ([1968] 1 WLR 1797 at 1804A-B).
18 It is irrelevant that the contract is not a firm contract in favour of a named person or that B never in fact gives any direction ([1968] 1 WLR 1797 at 1804B).
19 [1968] 1 WLR 1797 at 1805B-C.
20 [1968] 1 WLR 1797 at 1805C.
1   [1968] 1 WLR 1797 at 1805C.
2   [1968] 1 WLR 1797 at 1805F-G.
3   On restrictive covenants generally, see Chapter 18 (post, p 689).

between a lessor and a lessee) restrictive of the user of land and entered into on or after 1 January 1926'.[4]

(i) Function of the restrictive covenant A typical restrictive covenant may be taken to be an agreement between two neighbouring freeholders, A and B, to the effect that A shall not use his land, nor permit it to be used, for the purpose of any trade or business. This kind of restrictive covenant is almost invariably found in any residential context which involves multiple habitation in conditions of close proximity, the primary function of such a covenant being to preserve the essential preconditions of civilised domestic coexistence.

In all probability B will have obtained A's agreement to the restrictive covenant by the payment of money or by the offer of other valuable consideration (such as a reciprocal covenant by B himself).[5] A's undertaking clearly has contractual force and, by curtailing the potential scope of A's activities on his own property, has the general effect of promoting the amenity enjoyed by B in respect of his own property. A's covenant precludes him from using his premises as a rag merchant, bookmaker or indeed music teacher, and B plainly has a *contractual* interest in the due performance of A's promise.

(ii) Proprietary status of the restrictive covenant If the legal analysis of the relationship between A and B stopped at this point, the agreement framed between A and B would have no enduring impact upon third parties. Only the contracting parties may claim the benefit or be called upon to suffer the burden of contractual terms. No third party purchasing either A's land or B's land would be affected by a contract to which he was not privy. However, in the law of land B's interest in the performance of A's promise is not regarded as a purely contractual interest. Ever since the decision in *Tulk v Moxhay*,[6] the covenantee of a restrictive covenant has been viewed as having in some sense a *proprietary* interest in the covenantor's land to the extent that he enjoys a contractual right to control activities conducted on that land. Thus, as with the estate contract,[7] the contractual right tends to enlarge into, and to arrogate to itself the character of, a proprietary interest.

(iii) Relevance of the equitable doctrine of notice Since 1 January 1926 the proprietary interest acquired by the restrictive covenantee can take effect only as an equitable interest. It is clearly not included amongst the legal estates, interests and charges enumerated in section 1(1), (2) of the Law of Property Act 1925.[8] As such the proprietary right—the 'restrictive covenant'—is in principle fully subject to the equitable doctrine of notice. The burden of the restrictive covenant—the burden initially assumed by A—will bind all third parties who purchase A's land other than a bona fide purchaser for value of a legal estate without notice of the restrictive covenant.

(iv) Introduction of a rule of registration The equitable doctrine of notice is still relevant today in determining the binding effect of restrictive covenants which

---

4   Land Charges Act 1972, s 2(5). See generally R.G. Rowley, (1956) 20 Conv (NS) 370.
5   The restrictive covenant will normally be contractually enforceable even in the absence of valuable consideration. Most restrictive covenants are contained in a document under seal, and the presence of the seal imports consideration.
6   (1848) 2 Ph 774 at 777ff, 41 ER 1143 at 1144f (post, p 698).
7   Ante, p 135.
8   Ante, p 70.

were entered into by freeholders *before 1926*. However, in relation to restrictive covenants created by freeholders *after 1925*, the traditional doctrine of notice has been modified to the extent that the only recognised form of notice of the covenantee's equitable interest is now the notice which is ensured by registration of a Class D(ii) land charge.

(v) Enforcement of restrictive covenants Let us continue to suppose that A is the covenantor and B the covenantee in relation to a restrictive covenant which precludes trade or business user on A's land. A then sells and conveys his legal estate in fee simple to C, and B sells and conveys his legal estate in fee simple to D. May D now enforce the restrictive covenant against C?

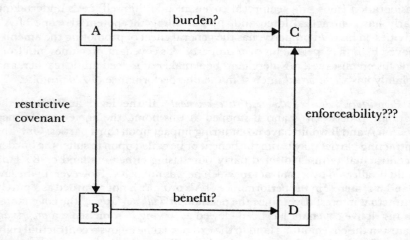

Fig. 13

The enforceability of the restrictive covenant as between C and D will turn on whether an affirmative answer can be given to two quite distinct questions.

—Has the burden of A's restrictive covenant been passed to C?
If the covenant was made after 1925 the only way in which the burden may 'run' with A's land is in consequence of the registration of a Class D(ii) land charge by B against the name of A. If such a registration was effected before A's conveyance to C, C cannot now deny that he received 'actual notice' of the restrictive covenant.[9] If B failed to register the land charge, the restrictive covenant becomes void as against C.[10]

—Has the benefit of the restrictive covenant been passed to D?
Unless the benefit of the restrictive covenant has indeed been passed to D, it will be entirely irrelevant that the land charge was duly registered against A. The benefit must have been conferred on D in one or other of the methods of transmission which are discussed later in Chapter 18.[11] For the moment it is sufficient to recognise simply that the restrictive covenant in question will be

9   Law of Property Act 1925, s 198(1) (ante, p 114).
10   Land Charges Act 1972, s 4(6) (ante, p 115).
11   Post, p 706.

enforceable against C at the behest of D only if *both* benefit *and* burden have been duly transmitted to the appropriate persons.

(vi) Exclusions from Class D(ii) Class D(ii) is so drawn as to exclude from its ambit not merely those restrictive covenants entered into before 1926 but also any restrictive covenant contained in a lease. In so far as leasehold restrictive covenants relate (or 'have reference'[12]) to the land leased, their enforcement against third parties is governed by a special framework of rules stemming from *Spencer's Case*.[13] However, it is possible that in certain circumstances a restrictive covenant between lessor and lessee may relate not to the user of the land demised but to the user of other land of the lessor. In such a case the enforcement of the restrictive covenant against third parties in unregistered land depends on the operation of the equitable doctrine of notice.[14] It is quite clear that no question of registration of a Class D(ii) charge can arise.

(c) Class D(iii)

This class comprises the 'equitable easement',[15] which is statutorily defined as 'an easement, right or privilege over or affecting land created or arising on or after 1 January 1926, and being merely an equitable interest.'[16] An equitable easement generally arises where a right in the nature of an easement has been created otherwise than by deed (eg by mere contract, unsealed writing or verbal grant) or has been created otherwise than for an interest equivalent to an estate in fee simple absolute in possession or a term of years absolute.[17]

(i) Uncertain coverage of Class D(iii) The Class D(iii) land charge has been the cause of much difficulty in practice. The very persons in whose favour such a charge may commonly arise are precisely those persons who will tend to be unaware of the need to secure protection by registration. Moreover the category of Class D(iii) charges is obscure and ill-defined.[18] It is far from certain which rights are registrable under this head. It has been held that Class D(iii) has no application to a tenant's right to remove fixtures at the end of a lease,[19] or to an equitable right of entry for breach of a leasehold covenant.[20] Such are the difficulties connected with the registration of equitable easements that the Roxburgh Committee suggested that Class D(iii) might be abolished altogether.[1]

(ii) Estoppel-based easements Many of the problems caused by Class D(iii) were exemplified in their most pressing form in *E.R. Ives Investment Ltd v High*.[2] Here

12 Law of Property Act 1925, ss 141(1), 142(1) (post, pp 521, 523).
13 (1583) 5 Co Rep 16a, 77 ER 72 (post, p 526).
14 *Dartstone v Cleveland Petroleum Co Ltd* [1969] 1 WLR 1807 at 1812A.
15 Easements are discussed more fully in Chapter 17 (post, p 632). The distinction between legal and equitable easements was outlined in Chapter 5 (ante, p 80).
16 Land Charges Act 1972, s 2(5).
17 Ante, p 80.
18 See H.W.R. Wade, [1956] CLJ 216 at 225f.
19 *Poster v Slough Estates Ltd* [1968] 1 WLR 1515 at 1521B-C.
20 *Shiloh Spinners Ltd v Harding* [1973] AC 691 at 721G. See [1973] CLJ 218 (Paul Fairest). The enforceability of such a right of entry against a later purchaser of the land therefore turns on the equitable doctrine of notice (post, pp 226, 532).
1 *Report of the Committee on Land Charges*, para 16.
2 [1967] 2 QB 379. See (1967) 31 Conv (NS) 338 (F.R. Crane).

the defendant, D, and X were neighbours. X began to construct on his property a block of flats the foundations of which marginally encroached upon D's land. D agreed to ignore the unintentional incursion on condition that he was granted a right of way for his car across X's yard. This right of way was not granted by deed and therefore constituted a merely equitable easement. As such it was never registered by D as a Class D(iii) land charge against the name of X. X later conveyed the fee simple estate in his property to Y, who knew of the earlier agreement. Y also knew that D had more recently built a garage on his own land which was accessible only across X's yard.[3] Moreover D contributed part of the cost of resurfacing this yard. Y in his turn sold and conveyed the legal estate to the plaintiff, P, expressly subject to the right of way enjoyed by D across the yard. P subsequently brought an action against D for trespass to the yard, claiming that D's equitable easement should have been registered against X as a Class D(iii) land charge. Since it had not been so registered, P contended, the charge now became void notwithstanding the actual knowledge which P had received.[4]

On the facts the merits of the case pointed clearly in favour of D. As an honest but uninformed layman it had never occurred to him that the agreement informally reached with X—largely as an act of grace on D's part—required formal protection vis à vis third parties. In contrast P was an investment company which had bought with full knowledge of the agreement and was quite prepared to plead the statute in order to further its own unconscionable dealing. It was not surprising that under these circumstances the Court of Appeal strained to uphold the county court judgment at first instance in favour of D.[5]

Danckwerts and Winn LJJ agreed that D's equitable right of way was rendered statutorily void against P for non-registration notwithstanding that P had purchased with actual notice of D's rights.[6] However, both judges held that P was 'estopped' (or precluded) from pleading non-registration by D in view of the past history of acquiescence in D's expenditure on the building of a garage in a particular position and on the resurfacing of the yard which now belonged to P.[7] This acquiescence, together with the doctrine of 'mutual benefit and burden',[8] created an 'equity' in favour of D which bound all subsequent purchasers who took the land with actual notice.[9] The 'equity' thus

---

3   Compare *Sutton v O'Kane* [1973] 2 NZLR 304 at 333.
4   Ante, p 116.
5   'Could anything be more monstrous and inequitable afterwards to deprive [D] of the benefit of what he has done?' ([1967] 2 QB 379 at 399F per Danckwerts LJ).
6   [1967] 2 QB 379 at 399B-C, 403E-F.
7   For a fuller treatment of estoppel, see Chapter 13 (post, p 386). Compare *Sutton v O'Kane* [1973] 2 NZLR 304 at 334.
8   This doctrine prescribes that when adjoining owners of land make an agreement to secure continuing rights and benefits for each of them in or over the land of the other, neither of them can take the benefit of the agreement and throw over the burden of it. This applies not only to the original parties but also to their successors. The successor who takes the continuing benefit must take it subject to the continuing burden. This principle has been applied, for instance, to neighbours who send their water into a common drainage system (*Hopgood v Brown* [1955] 1 WLR 213 at 226) and to purchasers of houses on a building estate who have the benefit of using the roads on that estate and are therefore subject to the burden of contributing to their upkeep (*Halsall v Brizell* [1957] Ch 169 at 182f). See also *Montague v Long* (1972) 24 P & CR 240 at 247f.
9   Post, p 425.

raised, unlike the equitable right of way, was not liable to registration under the Land Charges Act and was therefore unaffected by D's failure to register his easement.[10]

The third member of the Court of Appeal, Lord Denning MR, went even further. He held not merely that the estoppel prevented P from asserting a legally valid answer based on want of registration, but that D's equitable easement had not even been registrable in the first place. Lord Denning took the view that Class D(iii) embraces only those equitable easements which prior to the 1925 legislation ranked as legal interests in land but which were by virtue of that legislation relegated to merely equitable status. D's rights, however, arose directly from equitable doctrines based on acquiescence and the mutuality of benefit and burden and would, even before 1925, have ranked as rights subsisting only in equity.[11] Not being caught by the registration provisions of the Land Charges Act, they were governed simply by the traditional doctrine of notice.[12]

As Lord Denning observed,[13] the decision in *E.R. Ives Investment Ltd v High* illustrates the willingness of the courts to cut back the scope of the interests registrable under Class D(iii).[14] However, Lord Denning found this restrictive tendency 'not disturbing'[15] and moreover to be wholly in keeping with the Roxburgh Committee's proposal that Class D(iii) charges should be abandoned altogether. The Court of Appeal judgments in *E.R. Ives Investment Ltd v High* underscore the vagueness of the category of charges falling within Class D(iii). It seems clear that at least some equitable easements may also be analysed in terms of non-registrable estoppel-based rights which turn on the orthodox application of the concept of notice.[16]

(5) Class E

Class E land charges comprise annuities arising before 1926 but not registered until after the Land Charges Act 1925 came into force.

(6) Class F

Class F land charges comprise charges in respect of spousal rights of occupation which arise pursuant to the Matrimonial Homes Acts 1967 and 1983. The Class F charge plays so important a role in domestic conveyancing that it forms the subject of extensive consideration in Chapter 22.[17]

10   See also *Classic Communications Ltd v Lascar* (1985) 21 DLR (4th) 579 at 589f (post, p 387).
11   [1967] 2 QB 379 at 395E-396B. See C.V. Davidge, (1937) 53 LQR 259 at 260.
12   See also P.V. Baker, (1972) 88 LQR 336; D. Yates, (1974) 37 MLR 87. For reasoning similar to that of Lord Denning MR, see *Montague v Long* (1972) 24 P & CR 240 at 247f.
13   [1967] 2 QB 379 at 396C.
14   See also *Poster v Slough Estates Ltd* [1968] 1 WLR 1515 at 1521B (ante, p 25); *Shiloh Spinners Ltd v Harding* [1973] AC 691 at 721G (ante, p 141).
15   [1967] 2 QB 379 at 396C.
16   This has in turn provoked the criticism that estoppel interests fall outside the 'necessarily tidy world of the conveyancer', in that they tend to 'diminish both certainty of title and the availability of land on the market' (see F.R. Crane, (1967) 31 Conv (NS) 332 at 341f). The Law Commission has since recommended that in registered land the kind of 'equity' raised in *E.R. Ives Investment Ltd v High* should be protectible by entry on the register of the title affected (see Law Commission, Published Working Paper No 67: *Land Registration (Fourth Paper)* (April 1976), para 64ff).
17   Post, p 786.

CHAPTER 8

Registration of title

The present system of registration of title in England and Wales dates from the enactment of the Land Registration Act 1925. The registration scheme is administered by the Land Registry in accordance with the terms of the 1925 Act and in conformity with the Land Registration Rules prescribed pursuant to that legislation.[1]

Whether a particular property falls to be dealt with under the provisions of the Land Registration Act 1925 depends on whether that property is situated within an area currently designated as an area of compulsory registration of title.[2] The areas now so designated include most large urban centres, and it has been estimated that by 1987 the Land Registration Act covered areas containing 85 per cent of the population of England and Wales.[3] It was anticipated at first that unregistered land conveyancing would soon be superseded by registration of title,[4] but it now appears that this objective is still some distance from realisation.[5]

1. THE DISTINCTION BETWEEN REGISTERED AND UNREGISTERED CONVEYANCING

It is clear that registration of title now provides the primary regime of land law in England and Wales. The basic difference between registered and unregistered conveyancing consists in the fact that in unregistered conveyancing the purchaser must, on each occasion of purchase, undertake a fresh investigation of the title to be purchased. He must satisfy himself as to the validity of the title offered by examining the documents of title (ie, the 'title deeds') covering at least the last 15 years.[6] The basis of this practice is the pragmatic assumption that such investigation will reveal all the pertinent

---

1 See Land Registration Rules 1925 (SR & O 1925/1093).
2 See Land Registration: The Registration of Title Order 1984 (SI 1984/1693); Land Registration: The Registration of Title Order 1985 (SI 1985/1999).
3 See Law Commission, *Property Law: Third Report on Land Registration: A. Overriding Interests, B. Rectification and Indemnity, C. Minor Interests* (Law Com No 158, 31 March 1987), paras 1.2 (n8), 2.12 (n54).
4 Ante, p 132.
5 The Chief Land Registrar, in giving evidence to the Royal Commission on Legal Services, expressed the hope that the whole of England and Wales would be subject to compulsory registration 'by about 1985' (see *Report of the Royal Commission on Legal Services* (Cmnd 7648, October 1979), Vol 1, para 21.6. Present government policy involves an expectation that computerisation of the register will allow the programme of compulsory registration to be completed by 1994 (see *Parliamentary Debates, House of Commons, Official Report*, Vol 54 (Session 1983-1984), Cols 347f (Written Answer by the Solicitor-General, 17 February 1984)).
6 The process of unregistered conveyancing is described more fully in Chapters 6 and 7 (ante pp 94, 110).

details relating to the land which he proposes to buy. On the whole this
assumption is quite correct, but the principal defect of unregistered
conveyancing is precisely the fact that this cumbersome investigation of title
must be carried out on every occasion of purchase, irrespective of the length of
time which has elapsed since the last transfer and investigation of title. The
process of land transfer is thus self-perpetuating, repetitive, protracted and
costly.[7]

By contrast the objective which underlies the registration scheme contained
in the Land Registration Act 1925 is that the title to land should be investigated
only once—by the Chief Land Registrar.[8] All the details pertinent to the
ownership and enjoyment of that land (other than matters which are easily
discoverable on physical inspection of the land) are then recorded on a central
register—the Land Register. These details go far beyond the one isolated
category of interest—the 'commercial' equitable interest—which can be made
the subject of registration in the context of unregistered land.[9] Registration of
title involves the registration of almost every kind of interest in the land in
question—whether legal or equitable, 'family' or 'commercial'.

The aim of the registered land scheme is that the Land Register should
accurately reflect the totality of estates and interests created with reference to
any land falling within an area of compulsory registration. The register is then
kept accurate by regular up-dating of the information contained in it: there is a
requirement that all subsequent transactions affecting the registered land be
recorded on the register as a condition precedent to their effectiveness. The
intended result is that, at any given time, a prospective purchaser of registered
land should be able to verify, by a simple examination of the register, the exact
nature of all interests existing in or over the land which he proposes to buy.[10]
The historic searching of title which is characteristic of unregistered
conveyancing is thus rendered redundant, since the definitive record of the
register has eliminated all need for retrospective investigation.

2. THE BASIC FEATURES OF REGISTRATION OF TITLE

The scheme of title registration outlined above represented for many years an
aspiration of law reformers. In 1857 the Royal Commission on Land Transfer
and Registration defined the problem as one of finding a means of enabling

---

7   In *Williams & Glyn's Bank Ltd v Boland* [1981] AC 487 at 511D, Lord Scarman referred to
    unregistered conveyancing as the 'wearisome and intricate task of examining title...' For an
    excoriating account of the 'ritual dance' of conveyancers, see M. Joseph, *The Conveyancing
    Fraud* (London 1976), p 30ff.
8   There is some dispute as to the care and accuracy with which title is examined by the Land
    Registry before registration. Compare T.B.F. Ruoff and C. West, *Concise Land Registration
    Practice* (3rd edn London, 1982), 56ff, with [1983] Conv 329.
9   It is necessary to distinguish clearly between registration of *title* in the Land Register and
    registration of *land charges* in the Land Charges Register. The latter form of registration
    relates, somewhat confusingly, to unregistered land (ante, p 113). Of course, the interests
    which are registrable in the Land Charges Register are also protectible when they arise in the
    context of *registered land*, but in the latter case they are protected as 'minor interests', and are
    recorded in a quite different register, the Land Register, as an integral part of a much more
    general process of registration.
10 See eg *Registrar of Titles (Vic) v Paterson* (1876) 2 App Cas 110 at 116f.

owners 'to deal with land in as simple and easy a manner, as far as the title is concerned, and the difference in the nature of the subject matter may allow, as they can now deal with moveable chattels or stock.'[11] It has long been clear that the law of conveyancing can serve the interests of the community only if it provides a secure, efficient and inexpensive mode of land transfer—an objective of ever greater importance in a mobile and industrialised society.

(1) The three central principles

The archetypal scheme of title registration was introduced during the last century in the form of the 'Torrens Title' legislation enacted in Australia and New Zealand.[12] This legislation provided in many respects a model for the English enactments which culminated in the Land Registration Act 1925.

It has been said that the fundamental features of any scheme for registration of title, whether in the form of Torrens legislation or in the form of the Land Registration Act 1925, are three in number.[13] *First*, the register of title is intended to operate as a 'mirror', reflecting accurately and incontrovertibly the totality of estates and interests which at any time affect the registered land (the 'mirror principle'). *Second*, trusts relating to the registered land are kept off the title, with the result that third parties may transact with the registered proprietor safe in the assurance that the interests behind any trust will be overreached (the 'curtain principle'). *Third*, the state itself guarantees the accuracy of the registered title, in that an indemnity is payable from public funds if a registered proprietor is deprived of his title or is otherwise prejudiced by the operation of the registration scheme (the 'insurance principle').[14]

Notwithstanding the enunciation of these clear and high-sounding principles, it will emerge in the course of this chapter that title registration under the Land Registration Act 1925 has not eliminated all problems in the transfer of land. Difficulties remain, not least in relation to the extent to which the principles governing registered land truly diverge from those governing unregistered land. Both the structure and the detailed operation of the title registration scheme have recently been the subject of extensive deliberation by the Law Commission.[15] The Commission's proposals for reform, which are considered at various points throughout this chapter, are broadly aimed at bringing English law into closer accord with the three central principles referred to above.

---

11 *Report of the Commissioners on the Registration of Title with reference to the Sale and Transfer of Land* (CP 2215, 1857 - Session 2), para XL.
12 The Torrens scheme was first adopted in the Real Property Act 1858 (South Australia). There is some controversy as to whether Sir Robert Torrens was the true author of the scheme that bears his name. Torrens was accused by even his contemporaries of some degree of plagiarism (see R. Sackville and M. Neave, *Property Law* (3rd edn 1981), para 7.33). There is evidence to suggest that the fundamental concept of the 'Torrens' scheme was formulated by Dr Ulrich Hübbe, a German lawyer living in South Australia in the 1850s, and was modelled largely on the Hanseatic system of title registration (see Robinson, *Transfer of Land in Victoria* (1979), p 11ff).
13 See T.B.F. Ruoff, *An Englishman Looks at the Torrens System* (Sydney, Melbourne and Brisbane 1957), p 8.
14 See R. Stein, (1983-84) 9 Adelaide LR 267.
15 See eg Law Com No 158 (1987), post, p 201.

(2) A distinctively different system of land law

For many purposes it is true to say that the system of registered title contained in the Land Registration Act 1925 utilises existing concepts of unregistered land conveyancing and simply provides more streamlined conveyancing machinery.[16] There is, however, an important sense in which it is beginning to be realised that registration of title may achieve more than merely procedural changes in the law relating to land.

It is possible that the law of registered title will come in time to be recognised as a body of rules and concepts which is *substantively* quite different from the principles which regulate unregistered land.[17] It may well be that the classic concepts of unregistered land (eg the distinction between legal and equitable rights and the equitable doctrine of notice) will be rendered redundant by the steadily expanding scheme of registered title.[18] Under a system of registered title the only relevant distinction is that between 'major' and 'minor' interests; that is, between those rights which are roughly equivalent to absolute ownership of land and all other kinds of interest which diminish or qualify that ownership.[19] Interests of the latter variety are registered merely 'adjectivally', by subsidiary 'entry' on the register of the substantively registered title.

3. THE REGISTER

The Land Register is controlled by the Chief Land Registrar.[20] The Register is maintained both centrally at the Land Registry in London and regionally at thirteen district land registries.[1]

16 It has been suggested, somewhat mordantly, that the Land Registration Act 1925 'seems to be an example of the British genius for compromise...instead of a *completely efficient* Land Registry, which would make solicitors superfluous, a *semi-efficient* Land Registry [was] set up, which would cut out *half* the solicitor's work, while still allowing them to do the other half, but at substantially reduced costs...The only effect of setting up the Land Registry has been to make the solicitors' job easier' (see M. Joseph, *The Conveyancing Fraud* (London 1976), p 137f). There seems, incidentally, to be little foundation for the hope that registered land transactions can be carried out more easily or cheaply than those in unregistered land. In *Property & Reversionary Investment Corporation Ltd v Secretary of State for the Environment* [1975] 1 WLR 1504 at 1507D, Donaldson J recognised it as 'common ground that nowadays, when in unregistered land short title can be made, there is little, if any, saving in time or effort in dealing with a registered title.' It may be for this reason that the abolition in 1973 of solicitors' scale fees for conveyancing did not result in the intended downward levelling of unregistered conveyancing charges with the traditionally lower charges for registered conveyancing.
17 A significant step in this direction was taken by the decision of the House of Lords in *Williams & Glyn's Bank Ltd v Boland* [1981] AC 487 (post, pp 372, 843). In its most recent report the Law Commission accepted that 'there are substantive differences between registered and unregistered land' (Law Com No 158, para 2.5). The Commission saw 'little justification in trying at all costs to keep the two systems in step', and, in proposing changes in the registered land scheme, felt unconstrained 'by the fact that we might be creating or perpetuating distinctions from unregistered land. Registered conveyancing is after all to be the way forward, the new improving on the old.'
18 There are, however, sporadic attempts to re-introduce in the law of registered land something akin to the traditional doctrine of notice (see eg *Peffer v Rigg* [1977] 1 WLR 285 (post, p 166); *Lyus v Prowsa Developments Ltd* [1982] 1 WLR 1044 (post, p 284)).
19 Ante, p 103.
20 Land Registration Act 1925, s 126.
 1 See The Land Registration (District Registries) Order 1987 (SI 1987/360), Schedule.

(1) **The function of the Registrar and his staff**

The Chief Land Registrar is statutorily required to keep a Register of Title to all freehold and leasehold land within areas of England and Wales currently designated for compulsory registration.[2] It is accordingly the function of the Registrar and his staff to record in the Land Register all details pertinent to each individual title maintained at the Registry.[3] Each title is identified by the title number assigned to the plot of land concerned,[4] thus reinforcing the point that the Land Registration Act 1925 directs that registration be effected against an area of land identified numerically rather than against the name of the current estate owner (as is the case in relation to registration in the Land Charges Register[5]).

The Registrar is invested with a limited quasi-judicial capacity to determine questions and difficulties arising in the day-to-day operation of the register.[6] Alternatively the Registrar may obtain from the High Court a definitive ruling on any difficult question relating to the operation of the register.[7] The Registrar may also be required to give effect to any court order touching upon a registered title. On being served with a copy of a relevant court order, it is his function to make appropriate amendments of any register of title affected.

The Registrar and any staff acting under his authority are indemnified against any legal liability in respect of 'any act or matter done or omitted to be done in good faith in the exercise or supposed exercise' of their powers under the Land Registration Act 1925.[8]

(2) **The divisions of the Register**

The register of any individual title kept at the Land Registry is subdivided into three sections or 'parts',[9] each known itself as some sort of 'register'.

(a) *The 'Property Register'*

The Property Register under a particular title number records the advantageous features of the land in question. It contains a verbal description

---

2   Land Registration Act 1925, s 1(1). The register need not be kept in documentary form (see Land Registration Act 1925, s 1(2), as substituted by Administration of Justice Act 1982, s 66(1)). This proviso clearly heralds the advent of a fully computerised register, and the inspection and copying of such a register are envisaged by Land Registration Act 1925, s 113A as inserted by Administration of Justice Act 1982, s 66(2).

3   Land Registration Act 1925, ss 126, 127. Compare *Perpetual Executors and Trustees Association of Australia Ltd v Hosken* (1912) 14 CLR 286 at 295 per Isaacs J ('...the Registrar is not an automaton; he has a high and responsible public duty to discharge and he has an obligation to see that the purpose of the Act is neither destroyed nor prejudicially affected').

4   Land Registration Rules 1925, r 2.

5   Ante, p 113.

6   Land Registration Rules 1925, r 298(1). There is a right of appeal to the Chancery Division of the High Court (Land Registration Rules 1925, r 299). Accepted day-to-day practice in the Land Registry effectively creates the law which governs much of the business of the Registry, but Lord Denning MR warned in *Strand Securities Ltd v Caswell* [1965] Ch 958 at 977E that the Registrar is not allowed 'by his practice to make bad law'. See, however, [1981] Conv 395.

7   See eg *In re Boyle's Claim* [1961] 1 WLR 339 (post, p 175).

8   Land Registration Act 1925, s 131.

9   Land Registration Rules 1925, r 2.

of the land and a description by reference to a filed map, and notes such matters as easements, rights, privileges and covenants over other land which enure to the benefit of the land comprised within the title number.[10] If the title is leasehold, brief details of the lease are included.[11]

(b) The 'Proprietorship Register'

The Proprietorship Register indicates the name and address of the current registered proprietor of the estate represented by a particular title number.[12] This part of the Register also indicates whether the title enjoyed by the proprietor is 'absolute', 'good leasehold', 'qualified' or 'possessory'.[13] The Proprietorship Register similarly records any restrictions, cautions or inhibitions which affect or diminish the right of the registered proprietor to dispose of the land.[14]

(c) The 'Charges Register'

The Charges Register records all the disadvantageous or negative features of the legal ownership of the estate in question. Here are entered particulars (but not the amount) of mortgages and financial charges, together with liens and notices of leases. Also included are details of other incumbrances which adversely affect the land such as restrictive covenants, easements and rights of occupation under the Matrimonial Homes Act 1983.[15]

(3) The land certificate

The three subdivisions of the Land Register are correlated on one index card, a copy of which is issued to the current registered proprietor and is known as the 'land certificate'.[16] This certificate provides each registered proprietor with his immediate evidence of title, and is treated in the law of registered land as the rough equivalent of the title deeds provided by unregistered conveyancing.[17] The land certificate must normally be produced to the Registrar for appropriate amendment on any occasion of entry on the register of a 'restriction' or 'notice' against the relevant registered title.[18]

---

10 Land Registration Rules 1925, r 3.
11 Land Registration Rules 1925, r 5.
12 Land Registration Rules 1925, r 6. The price paid by the registered proprietor is entered only if the proprietor has so requested (Land Registration Rules 1925, r 247, as amended by Land Registration Rules 1976 (SI 1976/1332), rr 2, 3).
13 Post, p 154.
14 Land Registration Rules 1925, r 6.
15 Land Registration Rules 1925, r 7.
16 Land Registration Act 1925, s 63(1). The certificate is, however, retained in the Land Registry if and so long as the property concerned is subject to a registered charge by way of mortgage (see Land Registration Act 1925, s 65, post, p 605).
17 See eg *Thames Guaranty Ltd v Campbell* [1985] QB 210 at 233C-D; Land Registration Act 1925, s 66 (post, p 576).
18 Land Registration Act 1925, s 64(1), (2) (post, p 159). See, however, Land Registration Act 1925, s 64(5); Housing Act 1985, Sch 9A, para 5(3), as supplied by Housing and Planning Act 1986, s 8(2), Sch 2.

(4) Public access to the Land Register

One of the strange and controversial features of the Land Register is the fact that it is not at present open to public inspection[19]—a point which is not without political significance since the preclusion of access to the register ultimately frustrates any attempt to compile an accurate record of the allocation of land ownership in this country. As the law now stands, the register is open to inspection only by persons who possess the requisite authority. This authority may be given by the registered proprietor himself[20] or may be granted by court order.[1] In addition the Registrar has power to grant a special right of access to the police in connection with criminal investigations[2] or to an official receiver, liquidator or trustee in bankruptcy in connection with the insolvency of a registered proprietor.[3] A chargee or mortgagee is also given certain rights to requisition a search of the register in order to ascertain whether 'rights of occupation' under the Matrimonial Homes Act 1983 have been registered in respect of a relevant title.[4] Similarly, a residential tenant has a statutory right of access to the register of title relating to the premises occupied by him, although this right may be invoked only for the purpose of enabling him to ascertain the name and address of his immediate landlord.[5]

The denial of any more general right of public access to the Land Register is almost without parallel in other jurisdictions,[6] and has been criticised as symptomatic of 'the obsession with unnecessary secrecy which pervades British society'.[7] It was in direct response to objections of this kind that the Law Commission recently examined the closed nature of the Land Register, finally recommending in 1985 that the Register should be made available for general public scrutiny.[8] In the Commission's view, the abandonment of the rule of secrecy would not constitute any real invasion of the citizen's privacy, but would confer significant benefits particularly for the simplification of conveyancing.[9] It seems likely that the Commission's recommendation will soon be realised in statutory form.

---

19   Land Registration Act 1925, s 112(1).
20   Land Registration Act 1925, s 112(1)(i), as substituted by Administration of Justice Act 1982, s 67(1), Sch 5. An intending purchaser will usually be brought within this category of persons allowed access: authority to inspect the register may be conferred by a term in the contract of sale.
 1   Land Registration Act 1925, s 112(2), (3). A judgment creditor may now apply pursuant to Land Registration Act 1925, s 112(2) to be allowed to inspect the title of his judgment debtor. Such an application may be made ex parte and without the authority of the debtor (see *Practice Direction (Land Register: Inspection)* [1983] 1 WLR 150).
 2   Land Registration Act 1925, s 112A.
 3   Land Registration Act 1925, s 112AA(1), as introduced by Insolvency Act 1985, s 215.
 4   Land Registration Act 1925, s 112B.
 5   Land Registration Act 1925, s 112C, as inserted by Landlord and Tenant Act 1987, s 41(2), post, p 478.
 6   See Law Commission, *Property Law: Second Report on Land Registration: Inspection of the Register* (Law Com No 148, 25 July 1985), para 18(i).
 7   Comment of the National Consumer Council, as quoted in Law Com No 148, para 17(iii).
 8   Law Com No 148, para 21.
 9   Law Com No 148, para 20. The Commission thought that an open register would be entirely consistent with the principle that 'in an open society there should be freedom of information and publication'.

4. THE CLASSIFICATION OF INTERESTS IN REGISTERED LAND

The interests in land which require to be dealt with in terms of the Land Registration Act 1925 comprise largely the same kinds of interest which arise in the context of unregistered land: the only difference is one of terminology.[10] The range of possible interests in registered land includes 'registrable interests', 'minor interests',[11] 'overriding interests',[12] and 'registered charges'.[13]

5. REGISTRABLE INTERESTS

Registrable interests are those interests which are indicated in the Land Registration Act 1925 as being capable of substantive registration, ie, capable of registration in their own right under an individual title number. Under section 2(1) of the Act the only interests which may be substantively registered in this manner are those estates in land which are 'capable of subsisting as legal estates'.[14] Although the term is never used in the Act, such estates provide (with slight qualifications) the 'major interests' ancillary to which all other forms of entry in the Land Register (eg 'minor interests') are effected.[15]

A distinction must be drawn here between the registration provisions which relate to 'first registration' (ie, the initial inclusion of a registrable interest in the Land Register) and those provisions which govern subsequent transfers of a registered estate which has already been recorded in the Register.

(1) First registration of registrable interests

The initial entry of a registrable interest in the Land Register occurs either in pursuance of some rule of compulsion or (more rarely) in consequence of voluntary registration.

(a) Compulsory registration

First registration of a 'registrable interest' or 'major interest' is not effected automatically by reason of the designation of a geographical district as an area of compulsory registration of title. The requirement of entry in the Land Register begins to operate only with the first 'conveyance on sale of freehold land'[16] or grant of a lease which occurs *after* the date of such designation.[17] The

---

10 See generally D. Jackson, (1972) 88 LQR 93.
11 Post, p 159.
12 Post, p 170.
13 Post, p 193.
14 For this purpose the phrase 'legal estates' is defined by Land Registration Act 1925, s 3(xi) in terms which are sufficiently broad to catch all those 'estates', 'interests' and 'charges' referred to in Law of Property Act 1925, s 1(1), (2) (ante, p 70).
15 Ante, p 103.
16 A 'conveyance on sale' clearly excludes from first registration any transfer by way of gift or assent by personal representatives. The term 'sale' seems to require an exchange of property for a money consideration, and therefore almost certainly excludes an exchange of land for other land (see eg *In re National Westminster Group plc* [1985] 1 WLR 681 at 683C-D).
17 Land Registration Act 1925, s 123(1). It is of course true that it may be many years after an area has been designated as an area of compulsory registration before the first transaction occurs in respect of any given piece of land falling within that area.

estates which require substantive registration in such an event are spelt out in the Land Registration Act 1925.

(i) Freehold estates   It is clear that the interests which qualify for 'first registration' under the Land Registration Act 1925 include the legal fee simple absolute in possession. The first freehold purchaser following the effective date of compulsory registration may apply to have himself entered as the registered proprietor of the title purchased, in which case he is registered with either absolute or possessory title.[18] The registered freehold estate is thus the primary 'major interest' around which all other entries on the register are gathered.

(ii) Leasehold estates   A term of years absolute may likewise be the subject of substantive registration, subject to qualifications imposed by the Land Registration Act 1925 as amended. Not every lease can constitute a registrable title.[19] It is plain, for instance, that only a legal leasehold can qualify as a 'major interest'.[20] Moreover, in areas of compulsory registration the registration requirement affects only leases of a certain specified duration.[1] Leases granted for more than 21 years out of an unregistered title are compulsorily registrable on grant, and existing leases with more than 21 years unexpired at the date of assignment are likewise compulsorily registrable on assignment.[2] It is now clear that a leasehold estate is registrable notwithstanding that it may contain an absolute prohibition on alienation or assignment.[3]

The rules in respect of registration of leaseholds demonstrate that the landlord-tenant relationship may well produce *two* (if not more) registered estates, both of which require substantive registration under different title numbers and both of which are evidenced in separate land certificates. The tenant is required to register his term of years absolute quite independently of the substantive registration effected by his landlord.[4]

---

18   Land Registration Act 1925, s 4(a). The application for registration may be made by 'any estate owner holding an estate in fee simple', including a tenant for life (post, p 805), statutory owner, personal representative or trustee for sale. However, no application may be made by a mortgagee where there is a subsisting right of redemption or by a 'person who has merely contracted to buy land' (Land Registration Act 1925, s 4(b)).

19   See Land Registration Act 1925, s 8(1)(a). No registration may be effected in respect of a term of years which has been created as security for a mortgage loan (post, p 573), since other means exist in the scheme of registered title for protection of such interests (post, p 193).

20   Land Registration Act 1925, s 2(1).

1   Periodic tenancies, for instance, are never transferred in practice and their registration would serve no useful purpose in facilitating dealings in registered land (see Law Commission, *Property Law: Land Registration* (Law Com No 125, 26 October 1983), para 4.26(a)).

2   Land Registration Act 1925, s 123(1), as amended by Land Registration Act 1986, s 2(1). Land Registration Act 1925, s 8(1A), as supplied by Land Registration Act 1986, s 2(2), makes it clear than an application for registration can still be made if at the date of application for first registration a lease has 21 years or less to run (see Law Com No 125, paras 4.26ff). However, the amendments provided by the Land Registration Act 1986 apply only in relation to grants or assignments of leases after 1 January 1987 (see Land Registration Act 1986, s 2(5); The Land Registration Act 1986 (Commencement) Order 1986 (SI 1986/2117), para 2).

3   Land Registration Act 1925, s 8(2), as substituted by Land Registration Act 1986, s 3(1). See Law Com No 125, para 4.30.

4   The existence of the inferior interest must, however, be noted on the Charges Register of the superior title (see Land Registration Rules 1925, rr 7, 46).

(iii)   Easements   The existence of a legal easement benefiting land which is the subject of substantive registration may be entered in the Property Register of the relevant registered estate.[5]

(iv) Compulsory registration in non-compulsory areas   The requirement of first registration applies primarily in relation to 'registrable interests' in those areas of land which have been designated as areas of compulsory registration. However, a requirement of first registration is sometimes imposed in respect of 'registrable interests' arising *outside* those areas. The most notable examples occur in the context of sales and leases effected in pursuance of the 'right to buy' provisions now contained in the Housing Act 1985.[6] Thus first registration is mandatory—even outside compulsory areas—when a public sector tenant exercises his statutory right to demand a conveyance of a freehold or long leasehold estate in the property which he occupies.[7] The requirement of first registration also applies to the conveyance of a freehold estate to a tenant who has successfully fulfilled the terms of a shared ownership lease[8] and has therefore acquired a 100 per cent interest in the relevant property.[9] Mandatory first registration will likewise apply, outside compulsory areas, where unregistered land belonging to a public sector landlord is disposed of in favour of a private sector landlord who remains subject to the tenant's 'preserved right to buy'.[10]

(v) Consequences of failure to effect a first registration   In unregistered conveyancing the transfer of a legal estate (whether freehold or leasehold) is completed by the deed of transfer (ie, the conveyance from vendor to purchaser). The same is not true of registered conveyancing. Although the same process of contract and conveyance occurs in a dealing with a registered title, the transfer of any legal estate to the purchaser is effectual and complete only when the transferee is entered on the Land Register as the new registered proprietor of the estate concerned.

This general principle is given an apparently draconian effect in the context of the requirement of first registration. In areas of compulsory registration this requirement is, of course, triggered off by a conveyance or grant of some estate in land which has never yet been the subject of any entry on the register. The Land Registration Act 1925 provides accordingly that the legal title supposedly transferred by such a conveyance or grant is defeasible unless the transferee applies for a first registration of his registrable interest within two months from the date of execution of that conveyance or grant.[11] A failure by

5   Land Registration Rules 1925, rr 3(2)(c), 257.
6   Housing Act 1985, ss 118ff.
7   Housing Act 1985, s 154(1)(a). This registration requirement does not apply, however, to any freehold or leasehold estate granted by a public authority outside the terms of the Housing Act 1985.
8   Post, p 738.
9   Housing Act 1985, s 154(1)(b).
10   Housing Act 1985, Sch 9A, para 2(1), as supplied by Housing and Planning Act 1986, s 8(2), Sch 2.
11   Land Registration Act 1925, s 123(1). See *Buckley v S.R.L. Investments Ltd and Cator and Robinson* (1971) 22 P & CR 756 at 767. It has been made clear that section 123(1) does not apply to an omission of land from the scope of a first registration merely by reason of a defective description of the land to be registered. Section 123(1) is properly applicable only to cases which involve a 'total failure to register the conveyance on sale' (see *Proctor v Kidman* (1985) 51 P & CR 67 at 72 per Croom-Johnson LJ).

the transferee to apply for first registration renders the relevant transfer statutorily 'void so far as regards the grant or conveyance of the legal estate in the...land'.[12]

(b) Voluntary registration

It used to be the case before 1967 that first registrations could be made on a voluntary basis in respect of titles not included within areas designated for compulsory registration. This general facility of voluntary registration was finally withdrawn in 1967, not least because of the disproportionate demands which it imposed on the resources of the Land Registry.[13] Voluntary registration is now permitted only in exceptional circumstances specified by the Chief Land Registrar.[14] These circumstances include the case where title deeds have been lost or destroyed by reason of natural disaster (eg flooding), fire, theft, or other misfortune. Also included are certain cases of building estates which comprise at least 20 houses and sales by local authorities and development corporations in respect of residential properties or of land scheduled for residential development.[15]

(2) Possible grades of title

When the Land Registry receives an application for substantive registration of an estate in registered land, the quality of title to be accorded to the first registered proprietor must be graded within four possible classes. The class of title awarded is then indicated in the relevant Proprietorship Register.

(a) Absolute title

The highest class of title which may be granted on first registration is 'absolute title'. This form of title can be awarded in respect of both freehold and leasehold applicants.

(i) Applicant with freehold estate   Where the registered land is a freehold estate, a first registration with *absolute title*[16] statutorily invests the applicant with the full legal fee simple absolute in possession in the land[17] (together with all

---

12   Land Registration Act 1925, s 123(1). In spite of the apparent ferocity of the statutory language, it seems that in practice the registrar is almost always willing to extend the period allowed for first registration, provided that 'some accident or sufficient cause' can be shown justifying the exercise of a benevolent discretion (see Land Registration Act 1925, s 123(1), proviso). Compare T.B.F. Ruoff and R.B. Roper, *The Law and Practice of Registered Conveyancing* (5th edn London 1986), p 206f, and [1983] Conv 175.
13   Land Registration Act 1966, s 1(2).
14   Land Registration Act 1966, s 1(2).
15   H.M. Land Registry Press Notice (see [1983] Conv 172).
16   Absolute title cannot be awarded without the approval of the Registrar (Land Registration Act 1925, s 4). However, the Registrar has a discretion to approve a title as absolute notwithstanding that it is still open to objection on some score, provided that he has reason to believe that the holding under that title will not be disturbed (Land Registration Act 1925, s 13(c)).
17   Land Registration Act 1925, s 5. It has been held that section 5 invests the first registered proprietor with only the legal (and not the equitable) title (see *Epps v Esso Petroleum Co Ltd* [1973] 1 WLR 1071 at 1077E-G). This conclusion seems dubious (see *Barnsley's Conveyancing Law and Practice* (2nd edn by D.G. Barnsley and P.W. Smith, London 1982), p 27).

appurtenant rights), subject only to overriding interests, those minor interests which are entered on the register[18] and certain other interests of which he has notice.[19] Absolute title is granted in the case of almost all freehold applications for first registration.

The statutory effect of first registration with absolute title is, within the limits stated above, comprehensive and far-reaching. An absolute title, once awarded to the applicant, is conclusive to override or cure any defects in the applicant's title as it existed prior to first registration. In *In re 139 High Street Deptford, ex parte British Transport Commission*,[20] for instance, it was held that a first registration with absolute title was effective to invest the successful applicant with an estate in land which was not in fact owned by the vendor and which he therefore had no power to sell.[1]

(ii) Applicant with leasehold estate Absolute title is less frequently awarded to the applicant for first registration of a leasehold estate. Here absolute title can be conferred only if the Registrar is in a position to approve not only the applicant's title but also that relating to any superior freehold or leasehold estate.[2] This means that the applicant must deduce title to the Registrar's satisfaction not only in relation to his own leasehold but also in relation to all superior titles, unless the freehold is already registered.[3] This many lessees are unable to do, precisely because a lessee is not normally entitled to call for and investigate superior titles.[4]

If, however, absolute title is awarded to a leasehold applicant, the award operates effectively as a guarantee that the lease in question was validly granted. First registration of such a lease with absolute title is statutorily deemed to invest the successful applicant with possession of the leasehold interest together with all implied or expressed appurtenant rights and privileges.[5] The registration is subject to all the qualifications which affect a first registration of a freehold estate with absolute title,[6] with the further proviso that the applicant's new title is also subject to 'all implied and express covenants, obligations, and liabilities incident to the registered land'.[7]

(b) Good leasehold title

Even if absolute title cannot be awarded, a leasehold application for first

---

18 Mere entry on the register cannot, however, revitalise an interest which by the date of first registration has already ceased to be enforceable (eg on the ground of non-registration as a land charge). See *Kitney v MEPC Ltd* [1977] 1 WLR 981 at 992B-C, 994H-995B. See (1977) 41 Conv (NS) 356 (F.R. Crane); [1978] CLJ 13 (D.J. Hayton).
19 Land Registration Act 1925, s 5. The vulnerability to interests of which the applicant has notice applies only where the applicant is not entitled to the land for his own benefit (eg where he holds the land on trust for another).
20 [1951] Ch 884.
 1 The register was, however, rectified in favour of the former owner under Land Registration Act 1925, s 82(3)(a) ([1951] Ch 884 at 891f).
 2 Land Registration Act 1925, s 8(1), proviso (i).
 3 A registration with absolute title is not, however, impossible where, as is increasingly frequently the case, a dispositionary lease is granted by a lessor who is himself registered with absolute title.
 4 Law of Property Act 1925, s 44 (ante, p 114).
 5 Land Registration Act 1925, s 9.
 6 Land Registration Act 1925, s 5.
 7 Land Registration Act 1925, s 9(a).

registration will almost certainly result in the award of a *good leasehold title*. Such a title is, for all practical purposes, just as marketable as a leasehold which is registered with absolute title. The registered proprietor with good leasehold title is in exactly the same position as the recipient of an absolute title, except to the extent that a good leasehold title is held subject to any 'estate, right or interest affecting or in derogation of the title of the lessor to grant the lease'.[8] In other words, the Registrar, in awarding a good leasehold title, certifies his approval of the lease, but cannot guarantee that it was validly granted by the lessor.[9]

(c) Possessory title

It is open to the Registrar to grant a mere *possessory title* to any applicant for first registration who cannot produce sufficient documentary evidence of title and who therefore relies on a period of adverse possession of the land concerned. This possessory title is, however, subject to all adverse interests affecting the land which may later be shown to have existed at the date of first registration.[10]

Where freehold land is first registered with possessory title the Registrar may, and on application by the proprietor must, convert the title into an absolute title if he is 'satisfied as to the title' or if the land has been registered with possessory title for at least twelve years and he is satisfied that the proprietor is in possession.[11] A possessory title registered in respect of a leasehold may similarly be upgraded to a good leasehold title if the same conditions are fulfilled.[12]

(d) Qualified title

In extremely rare cases the Registrar may, with the applicant's consent, grant only a *qualified title* on first registration. Such cases arise where the applicant can establish title only in respect of a limited period or where there are other fundamental doubts as to the subject matter of the registration. A qualified title is highly precarious, being subject to any adverse interests which later emerge as having been in existence at the date of registration.[13]

8   Land Registration Act 1925, s 10.
9   The Registrar always retains a discretion to convert a good leasehold title into an absolute title if he is satisfied as to the title to the freehold and the title to any intermediate leasehold (Land Registration Act 1925, s 77(1), as amended by Land Registration Act 1986, s 1(1)).
10   Land Registration Act 1925, ss 6, 11. A possessory title may be subsequently rectified against the registered proprietor (without indemnity) for the purpose of giving effect to a superior title or if the possessory title was insufficiently grounded in a claim of adverse possession. See *Tester v Harris* (1964) 189 Estates Gazette 337 at 339, but compare *Spectrum Investment Co Ltd v Holmes* [1981] 1 WLR 221 at 230E-H.
11   Land Registration Act 1925, s 77(2), as amended by Land Registration Act 1986, s 1(1). If the relevant possessory title was registered before the commencement of the Land Registration Act 1986 on 1 January 1987, the required period of twelve years must occur *after* this commencement date, but nothing precludes the proprietor in such a case from reliance on the fifteen and ten year periods originally prescribed in Land Registration Act 1925, s 77(3)(b) (see Land Registration Act 1986, s 1(2)).
12   Land Registration Act 1925, s 77(2), as amended by Land Registration Act 1986, s 1(1).
13   Land Registration Act 1925, ss 7, 12. A qualified title may later be converted into absolute title (in the case of freehold land) or good leasehold title (in the case of leasehold land) if the Registrar is 'satisfied as to the title' (Land Registration Act 1925, s 77(3), as amended by Land Registration Act 1986, s 1(1)).

(e) A new statutory estate?

Under the Land Registration Act 1925 the legal estates in registered land have now become so heavily regulated by statutory incidents that it is sometimes suggested, in the field of registered land, that the common law estates have been replaced by some new and artificial kind of statutory registered estate.[14] This view has aroused much controversy[15] and, if correct, lends some credence to the theory that the principles of registered land are evolving into a significantly different law of property which recognises only the distinction between 'major' interests (ie, substantively registered titles) and 'minor' interests (ie, everything else).[16]

(3) Subsequent transfers of the registered estate

The foregoing rules circumscribe the initial entry or 'first registration' of a 'registrable interest' in the Land Register. Thereafter all transfers or assignments of the registered estate require to be recorded in the register as a condition precedent to their effectiveness at law.[17]

(a) The requirement of registration

The transfer of a registered estate (whether freehold or leasehold) is declared by statute to be 'completed' only when the registrar has entered on the register the name of the transferee as the proprietor of the estate transferred.[18] The accuracy of the register is thus maintained by imposing on each successive transferee of a registered estate an obligation to perfect his legal title by applying to be registered as the new proprietor.

(b) Consequences of non-registration of later transfers

Until the transferee of a registered estate has applied to be registered as the new proprietor, the transferor of that estate is deemed to remain proprietor.[19] The legal estate does not therefore pass until and unless such an application is made, but is not otherwise affected by the failure to secure registration of the transaction.[20]

In the absence of an application to register the transfer, the transferee retains

---

14 See *Chowood Ltd v Lyall* (No 2) [1930] 2 Ch 156 at 163 per Lord Hanworth MR; H. Potter, (1942) 58 LQR 356. Compare, however, *I.A.C. (Finance) Pty Ltd v Courtenay* (1963) 110 CLR 550 at 572 per Kitto J.
15 See R.C. Connell, (1947) 11 Conv (NS) 184, 232; (1949) 12 MLR 139 at 205 (H. Potter), 477 (A.D. Hargreaves).
16 Ante, p 147.
17 In other words, the requirement of registration of all such subsequent transactions applies whether or not the transaction involves a 'conveyance on sale'. All later transfers of the registered estate—even those by way of gift or devise—thus require to be recorded in the register.
18 Land Registration Act 1925, ss 19(1), 22(1). Likewise the express grant of any legal easement or other legal interest in registered land (apart from a registered estate) must be 'completed by registration' (Land Registration Act 1925, ss 19(2), 22(2)).
19 Land Registration Act 1925, ss 19(1), 22(1).
20 There is, in the context of later transactions with a registered estate, no equivalent of the rule in Land Registration Act 1925, s 123(1), which imposes a penalty of voidness for failure to apply for 'first registration' within two months (ante, p 153).

merely an equitable interest in the estate conveyed.[1] However, pending the registration of his transfer the transferee has a right to receive mesne profits accruing from the date of his unregistered conveyance.[2] Moreover, if the transferee actually receives such profits or if he himself goes into actual occupation of the land pending registration of the transfer, his equitable interest in the land constitutes an overriding interest which will bind any future purchaser who attempts to register a later transfer adverse to his interests.[3]

(c) Effect of registration of later transfers

In the Australian High Court in *Breskvar v Wall*,[4] Barwick CJ pointed out that schemes of land registration provide 'not a system of registration of title but a system of title by registration.' In other words, the title certified by the register is not ultimately historical or derivative, but 'is the title which registration itself has vested in the proprietor.'[5] Thus, provided that the transfer of a registered estate is duly recorded in the Land Register, the title enjoyed by the transferee depends on the force of statute rather than on any intrinsic validity in the transfer itself.

This truth is borne out in section 69(1) of the Land Registration Act 1925, which provides that the proprietor of land 'shall be deemed to have vested in him without any conveyance, where the registered land is freehold, the legal estate in fee simple in possession, and where the registered land is leasehold, the legal term created by the registered lease'.[6] It has been held that the formula contained in section 69(1) operates a 'statutory magic' which is sufficiently potent to invest the current registered proprietor with a full legal title even though the registered transfer to him may, for instance, have been a complete forgery.[7]

---

1   See *E.S. Schwab & Co Ltd v McCarthy* (1976) 31 P & CR 196 at 201 per Oliver J.
2   *Choudhury v Meah* (Unreported, Court of Appeal, 21 September 1981) per Lawton LJ.
3   Land Registration Act 1925, s 70(1)(g) (post, p 175). It is, of course, bizarre that the transferee can thus fail, with relative impunity, to apply for registration of his transfer. The Law Commission recommended as long ago as 1971 that section 70(1)(g) should be amended to ensure that no interest which is capable of substantive registration can ever constitute an overriding interest in default of due registration (see Law Commission, Published Working Paper No 37: *Land Registration (Second Paper)* (July 1971), para 14). In a more recent report, however, the Commission declared itself to be unconvinced of any current need to discourage 'off the register' conveyancing. The Commission preferred not to withdraw the protection at present afforded in this context to transferees in actual occupation, regarding the advantages and priorities secured by registration as a generally sufficient incentive towards the due registration of the new proprietor's title (see Law Com No 158, para 2.67).
4   (1971) 126 CLR 376 at 385.
5   (1971) 126 CLR 376 at 386.
6   This far-reaching vesting effect is expressly subject to 'overriding interests, if any, including any mortgage term or charge by way of legal mortgage...which has priority to the registered estate.'
7   *Argyle Building Society v Hammond* (1985) 49 P & CR 148 at 153, 155 per Slade LJ, quoting T.B.F. Ruoff and R.B. Roper, op cit, p 70. See also *Frazer v Walker* [1967] 1 AC 569 at 580F-581A, 585A-C. The vesting of a full legal title in the registering transferee does not, of course, preclude the possibility that the register may subsequently be rectified against him (post, p 194). In such cases, however, an indemnity may well be payable by way of compensation for the loss caused by rectification (post, p 199).

6. MINOR INTERESTS

A second category of interests in registered land is the category of minor interests. This category comprises a residual class of interests and includes those interests which do not otherwise rank as registrable or overriding interests or as registered charges.[8] Minor interests thus include those matters which in unregistered land are capable of protection under the Land Charges Act 1972; the rights of beneficiaries under a trust for sale or strict settlement; other equitable rights under the general law which relate to land and are not included in the foregoing categories; the rights, until registration, of those entitled to be registered in respect of a disposition to them; and leases granted prior to 1 January 1987 which contain an absolute prohibition on assignment and subletting or which were granted in consideration of a premium for a term of 21 years or less.

(1) Protection of minor interests

Minor interests qualify for protection not by means of substantive registration but by the subsidiary means of 'entry' on the register. This entry may take various forms, depending to some extent on the nature of the minor interest in question. Entry may be effected by way of 'restriction', 'notice', 'caution' or 'inhibition'.

(a) Restriction

The proprietor of any registered estate or registered charge is entitled to apply to the Registrar for the entry of a 'restriction' in the relevant Proprietorship Register.[9] A restriction cannot normally be entered unless the registered proprietor's land certificate is lodged for this purpose with the Registrar.[10] If the application is granted, the entry of the restriction has the effect of indicating that no disposition of, or transaction in relation to, the registered title can thenceforth be effected except in the manner expressly specified by the particular restriction. The protection provided by the entry of a restriction is peculiarly appropriate in the case of equitable interests which arise under a trust for sale or strict settlement.[11] In the case of such interests the restriction effectively stipulates that no further transaction with the title shall be registered

---

8 Land Registration Act 1925, s 3(xv).
9 Land Registration Act 1925, s 58(1). The Registrar has power of his own motion to enter a restriction (Land Registration Act 1925, s 58(3); Land Registration Rules 1925, r 39). A restriction may be entered at the behest of persons other than the registered proprietor (see Land Registration Act 1925, s 58(5); Land Registration Rules 1925, r 236). See also Housing Act 1985, Sch 9A, para 5(3) (as supplied by Housing and Planning Act 1986, s 8(2), Sch 2, post, p 739).
10 Land Registration Act 1925, s 64(1)(c). The Law Commission has now recommended that this requirement be discontinued in all cases where a beneficiary under a trust or settlement wishes to protect his equitable rights by entry of a restriction. On this basis a beneficiary would be able to apply for the entry of a restriction without the co-operation of the registered proprietor, although the Commission has proposed that the Registry be compelled to serve notice of the application on the proprietor (Law Com No 158, paras 4.53ff).
11 The Law Commission has recommended that the restriction should henceforth become the *only* permissible form of protection for such interests (Law Com No 158, para 4.52). At present the alternative protection of a notice or caution is also available.

by the Registrar unless all relevant capital moneys are paid to at least two trustees or to a trust corporation.[12] In this way it is ensured that the only transactions which can ever take place are those which inevitably have the effect of overreaching the beneficial interests in protection of which the restriction was entered. Enforcement of the terms of the restriction translates such interests into equivalent rights in the capital proceeds arising on the transaction.[13]

A desire to enforce compliance with the conditions of statutory overreaching is not necessarily the only reason for the entry of a restriction. Other kinds of restriction may be entered, as, for example, where it is wished to make the consent of a named person or body a prerequisite to any disposition of land.[14]

(b) Notice

Certain minor interests are protectible by the entry of a 'notice' on the Charges Register of the appropriate title,[15] although once again the registered proprietor's land certificate must normally be produced before the Registrar for this purpose.[16] The protection of a notice is available in respect of almost all those categories of rights which in unregistered land constitute registrable land charges.[17] Entry by notice is likewise appropriate for a range of other rights including legal easements and legal rentcharges. A notice may also be entered in order to protect the recipient of a charging order made against the registered proprietor pursuant to the Charging Orders Act 1979.[18] The entry of a notice (generally called a 'creditors' notice'[19]) is similarly appropriate for the purpose of protecting the interests of creditors pending the appointment of a trustee in bankruptcy in respect of the registered proprietor.[20] The effect of any notice, once entered, is that all subsequent transferees of the registered title to which it relates take that title subject to the rights protected by the notice.[1]

(c) Caution

Almost all forms of minor interest may be protected by the entry of a 'caution'

---

12   Land Registration Act 1925, s 58(2).
13   Ante, pp 100, 108.
14   For another example, see Housing Act 1985, Sch 9A, para 5(2)(b) (as supplied by Housing and Planning Act 1986, s 8(2), Sch 2).
15   Land Registration Act 1925, s 49(1).
16   Land Registration Act 1925, s 64(1)(c). See, however, the exceptions made in the case of entry of spousal rights of occupation under the Matrimonial Homes Act 1983 (Land Registration Act 1925, s 64(5), post, p 787) and the secure tenant's 'preserved right to buy' (Housing Act 1985, Sch 9A, para 5(3), as supplied by Housing and Planning Act 1986, s 8(2), Sch 2, post, p 183).
17   See Land Charges Act 1972, s 2 (ante, p 133). However, a second legal mortgage (which in unregistered land would rank as a puisne mortgage) is capable of substantive registration as a 'registered charge' in registered land (post, p 193), provided that the relevant land certificate is available to the Land Registry (see T.B.F. Ruoff and R.B. Roper, op cit, p 787).
18   Land Registration Act 1925, s 49(1)(g). See Chapter 26 (post, p 870). The Law Commission has recently recommended, however, that a charging order which takes effect exclusively against the equitable interest of the debtor as a beneficiary under a trust of registered land should be capable of protection by means of restriction only (see Law Com No 158, para 4.43).
19   Land Registration Act 1925, s 61(1).
20   Land Registration Act 1925, s 49(1)(f).

in the relevant Proprietorship Register.[2] There is no requirement that the registered proprietor should co-operate by making his land certificate available to the Registrar for this purpose. Although this facility for unilateral entry marks an important distinction between the caution and the notice, the caution is generally intended to achieve only a limited or temporary form of protection for some contentious matter.[3] The caution may take the form of either a 'caution against first registration'[4] or a 'caution against dealings'.[5] The effect of lodging a caution in either case is that no registration or dealing can be effected by the Registrar until a notice has been served on the cautioner giving him an opportunity to object.[6] If the cautioner's objection is successful, the Registrar has a broad discretion to take such action as he thinks appropriate, and this may involve the entry of a notice on the register in respect of the interest which was previously protected only by caution. If, however, the cautioner fails to substantiate his claim within 14 days, he is deemed to have been 'warned off' the register. In practice most cautions perform the role of a holding device which is aimed at the temporary suspension of dealings in the registered land until some superior form of protection becomes available.

(d) Inhibition

On the application of any interested person, both the court and the Registrar have power to enter an 'inhibition' on the register of title. This form of entry is made only rarely, but has the effect of precluding any dealing with the title either until the occurrence of some specified event or until further order.[7] The sorts of circumstance in which an inhibition may be appropriate include the case where the registered proprietor discovers that his land certificate has been lost or stolen, or where a bankruptcy order has been made in respect of the proprietor and there is a need to freeze possible dealings with title.[8]

(2) Search of the register

It is open to the intending purchaser of registered land to requisition an official search of the Land Register for the purpose of discovering the existence of

1 Land Registration Act 1925, ss 20(1)(a), 23(1)(b), 52.
2 See, however, Matrimonial Homes Act 1983, s 2(9) (post, p 787). The Registrar has no power to enter a caution of his own motion.
3 The means of protection for minor interests are not mutually exclusive: minor interests may often be protectible by any of several kinds of entry on the register (see *In re White Rose Cottage* [1965] Ch 940 at 949F–950B). The Law Commission has long advocated a rationalisation in this area which would draw a clear distinction between entries on the register which are contentious and those which are not. The Commission has expressed the view that an interest which is not disputed by the registered proprietor should always be protected by notice or (where appropriate) by restriction, whereas a disputed interest should always be protected by caution. See Law Commission, *Property Law: Land Registration (Fourth Paper)* (Published Working Paper No 67, April 1976), para 57f; Law Com No 158, para 4.38.
4 Land Registration Act 1925, s 53(1).
5 Land Registration Act 1925, s 54(1).
6 Land Registration Act 1925, s 55(1). See also Land Registration Rules 1925, r 220.
7 Land Registration Act 1925, s 57(1). The Law Commission has suggested that the facility of the inhibition should be extended to cover Mareva (and other) injunctions which relate to land (see Law Com No 158, paras 4.58ff).
8 Land Registration Act 1925, s 61(3), as amended by Insolvency Act 1985, Sch 8, para 5(3)(a).

minor interests entered against the title with which he is concerned.[9] The recipient of the official search certificate then acquires a 30 day priority period during which he may apply for the registration of his transfer,[10] safe in the knowledge that his title, when registered, will prevail over any supervening adverse entry made during the priority period.[11] If, however, the official search fails (because of some error in the Registry) to reveal a third party interest which has been duly protected, the transferee—albeit that he is entirely blameless—takes his title subject to the prior interest,[12] but is entitled to a statutory indemnity in respect of any loss suffered.[13]

(3) Competing minor interests

In those rare circumstances where two or more competing minor interests have been duly protected by entry against the same registered title, the issue of priority between them is not dictated by the respective dates of entry, but is generally governed by the respective dates of creation. Since minor interests take effect merely as equitable interests, the problem of priority inter se is resolved in favour of the minor interest which was created first, even though it may not have been entered in the register until after the date of entry of a competing minor interest of later creation. The priority accorded earlier creation gives way only where the owner of the first minor interest has behaved fraudulently or negligently or is estopped from asserting priority by reason of conduct which induced the second owner to act to his detriment in acquiring the later minor interest.[14]

(4) Effect of failure to protect a minor interest by entry on the register

One of the fundamental objectives of a system of registered title must be to ensure that the register remains an accurate record of the interests affecting registered titles. It is 'the cardinal principle' of title registration that 'the register is everything',[15] and it is therefore important that there should be a strong incentive towards protection of minor interests by means of the appropriate entry on the register.

The Land Registration Act 1925 accordingly contains provisions which are aimed at depriving unprotected minor interests of effect in the event of a transfer of the registered title to a third party. Under section 20(1), a disposition

---

9   The Land Registration (Official Searches) Rules 1986 (SI 1986/1536), r 3(1). Search applications are normally made in prescribed forms, but in some circumstances an up-dating search may be made by telephone or telex (r 7(1)).

10   The Land Registration (Official Searches) Rules 1986, r 2(1).

11   The Land Registration (Official Searches) Rules 1986, r 5.

12   *Parkash v Irani Finance Ltd* [1970] Ch 101 at 110H-111A. Compare the effect in unregistered land of Land Charges Act 1972, s 10(4) (ante, p 126), a provision which has no registered land equivalent.

13   Post, p 199.

14   See *Abigail v Lapin* [1934] AC 491 at 500ff; *Barclays Bank Ltd v Taylor* [1974] Ch 137 at 147E; *Strand Securities Ltd v Caswell* [1965] Ch 958 at 991B. The Law Commission has recently recommended that the existing rules as to the priority of minor interests should be reversed so that the priority of such interests inter se would normally be governed by their order of protection on the register (see Law Com No 158, para 4.98).

15   See *Fels v Knowles* (1906) 26 NZLR 604 at 620; *Bunt v Hallinan* [1985] 1 NZLR 450 at 458.

for valuable consideration of a legal estate in registered land (whether freehold or leasehold) has the effect of conferring that estate upon the transferee or grantee subject only 'to the incumbrances and other entries, if any, appearing on the register...and...to the overriding interests, if any, affecting the estate transferred or created'. The title of the new proprietor is statutorily declared to be 'free from all other estates and interests whatsoever'.[16] The same policy appears even more plainly in section 59(6), which declares that, with several exceptions,

a purchaser acquiring title under a registered disposition shall not be concerned with any...document, matter, or claim (not being an overriding interest...) which is not protected by a caution, or other entry on the register, whether he has or has not notice thereof, express, implied, or constructive.

(a) The orthodox rule

Sections 20(1) and 59(6) of the Land Registration Act 1925 seem to envisage that failure to protect a minor interest in registered land produces roughly the same consequence of voidness as that which results from a failure to register a land charge in respect of unregistered land.[17]

(i) The general irrelevance of notice Accordingly, in the context of registered land, an unprotected minor interest binds neither a 'transferee' within section 20(1) nor a 'purchaser' within section 59(6), irrespective of the state of mind of such persons.[18] As Cross J pointed out in *Strand Securities Ltd v Caswell*,[19] it is 'vital to the working of the land registration system that notice of something which is not on the register should not affect a transferee unless it is an overriding interest.'[20]

(ii) The rationale behind the rule This general denial of effect to unprotected minor interests is of course the cornerstone of any system of title registration.[1] The provision of statutory immunity from unprotected interests 'is designed to facilitate dealings with land; and it seems to mean that a man may purchase land safely from the registered proprietor, closing his mind to the mere fact of any unregistered interest.'[2] Once again it is the plain intention of the legislation that certainty and efficiency in the process of land transfer should prevail over

16   The proprietor's title is not of course free of other burdens arising by statute or under the common law which do not as such comprise an 'estate' or 'interest' in the land (eg liability to pay rates, the consequences of planning laws, and statutorily protected tenancies). See Law Com No 158, para 2.1.
17   In the context of unregistered land an unprotected land charge is usually void even as against a purchaser who has actual knowledge of the existence of the unregistered interest. See *Midland Bank Trust Co Ltd v Green* [1981] AC 513 (ante, p 120).
18   See *Miles v Bull (No 2)* [1969] 3 All ER 1585 at 1590D-H; *De Lusignan v Johnson* (1973) 230 Estates Gazette 499.
19   [1965] Ch 373 at 390A-B.
20   Overriding interests are discussed elsewhere (post, p 170).
1   See *Williams & Glyn's Bank Ltd v Boland* [1981] AC 487 at 503G-H, where in relation to title registration Lord Wilberforce emphasised that '[a]bove all, the system is designed to free the purchaser from the hazards of notice—real or constructive—which, in the case of unregistered land, involved him in enquiries, often quite elaborate, failing which he might be bound by equities'. See also *Parkash v Irani Finance Ltd* [1970] Ch 101 at 108A.
2   *Wicks v Bennett* (1921) 30 CLR 80 at 95.

short-term justice in matters of conflict between purchasers and owners of equitable interests.[3] Sections 20(1) and 59(6) of the Land Registration Act 1925 provide yet another illustration of 'the necessity of this business consideration predominating over the moral aspect'.[4] Concern for the integrity of the register ranks far ahead of any concern for the integrity of the purchaser.

(b) The exception for fraud

Notwithstanding the general irrelevance of notice under the Land Registration Act 1925, it has always been clear that cases of fraud or bad faith constitute an exception to the integrity of the register.[5] The statutory immunity from unprotected minor interests does not extend to a purchaser who seeks *fraudulently* to take advantage of a failure to enter such interests appropriately on the register.

As an exception to the integrity of the register, the concept of 'fraud' has no clear definition,[6] and its identification depends on the particular circumstances of each case.[7] In the present context 'fraud' seems to require more than a mere showing of 'equitable' or 'constructive' fraud.[8] The purchaser must be guilty of 'something in the nature of personal dishonesty or moral turpitude'.[9] Dishonesty of this kind involves 'some notion of taking from someone else, literally or metaphorically, that which is his due or due to him.'[10] Such a mental state is not easy to establish in a purchaser of a registered title, but may arise where the purchaser asserts a 'claim to hold the land for an unencumbered estate in wilful disregard of the rights to which it is known to be subject.'[11] Likewise, a fraudulent disregard of unprotected rights may be ascribed to the purchaser if 'his suspicions were aroused, and...he abstained from making inquiries for fear of learning the truth'.[12]

---

3   Ante, p 118.
4   See *Holt, Renfrew & Co Ltd v Henry Singer Ltd* (1982) 135 DLR (3d) 391 at 399.
5   See *De Lusignan v Johnson* (1973) 230 Estates Gazette 499 per Brightman J. See generally M.P. Thompson, *Registration, Fraud and Notice*, [1985] CLJ 280.
6   'No definition of fraud can be attempted, so various are its forms and methods' (*Stuart v Kingston* (1923) 32 CLR 309 at 359). See also *Moore v Moore* (1971) 16 DLR (3d) 174 at 185.
7   See *Bunt v Hallinan* [1985] 1 NZLR 450 at 461.
8   There must be 'actual fraud' (see *Assets Co Ltd v Mere Roihi* [1905] AC 176 at 210; *Bunt v Hallinan* [1985] 1 NZLR 450 at 458).
9   *Butler v Fairclough* (1917) 23 CLR 78 at 90; *Wicks v Bennett* (1921) 30 CLR 80 at 91; *Stuart v Kingston* (1923) 32 CLR 309 at 329 per Knox CJ. See also *Assets Co Ltd v Mere Roihi* [1905] AC 176 at 210; *Frazer v Walker* [1967] 1 AC 569 at 584C; *Whittingham v Whittingham* [1979] Fam 9 at 12F; *Bunt v Hallinan* [1985] 1 NZLR 450 at 458, 463.
10 *Sutton v O'Kane* [1973] 2 NZLR 304 at 322. Compare *Midland Bank Trust Co Ltd v Green* [1980] Ch 590 at 625B per Lord Denning MR (ante, p 123). See *Waimiha Sawmilling Co Ltd v Waione Timber Co Ltd* [1923] NZLR 1137 at 1175, where Salmond J indicated that 'the true test of fraud is not whether the purchaser actually knew for a certainty of the existence of the adverse right, but whether he knew enough to make it his duty as an honest man to hold his hand, and either to make further inquiries before purchasing, or to abstain from the purchase, or to purchase subject to the claimant's rights rather than in defiance of them.'
11 *Wellington City Corpn v Public Trustee* [1921] NZLR 423 at 433. In the words of Salmond J in *Waimiha Sawmilling Co Ltd v Waione Timber Co Ltd* [1923] NZLR 1137 at 1173, dishonesty connotes here 'a wilful and conscious disregard and violation of the right of other persons'.
12 *Assets Co Ltd v Mere Roihi* [1905] AC 176 at 210. There can be no 'fraud', however, if the purchaser acted on the advice of his lawyer that he was free to ignore rights which someone else claimed to have under an unregistered instrument (see *Bunt v Hallinan* [1985] 1 NZLR 450 at 462f). See also *Babcock v Carr* (1982) 127 DLR (3d) 77 at 84ff.

(c) Mere knowledge of the existence of unprotected rights is not fraud

It has always been vital in the present context that there should be a clear dissociation between fraud and notice: the traditional doctrine of notice must not be allowed to intrude upon the operation of the register.

(i) The historic dissociation of fraud and notice In surveying the registration schemes which were the forerunners of the Land Registration Act 1925, the Real Property Royal Commissioners of 1830 started from the premise that it is 'greatly for the public good, that civil rights should be capable of being ascertained without difficulty'. The Commissioners pointed out that a 'registered title possesses the advantages of certainty and security in a high degree, but they will be impaired, if preference be given to an unregistered over a registered deed, on the ground of notice.'[13] The Commissioners thus inveighed against the 'mischiefs' of letting in notice actual or constructive, and concluded that effect should always be denied to unregistered rights except 'in case of actual fraud'.[14]

These historic perceptions are now deeply embedded in the operation of most schemes of title registration throughout the common law world.[15] There is a general consensus that mere knowledge of the existence of unregistered rights does not connote a relevant degree of 'fraud' on the part of the purchaser.[16] As the High Court of Australia observed in *Wicks v Bennett*,[17] fraud in this area requires 'something more than mere disregard of rights of which the person sought to be affected had notice.' Title registration is intended to mark a 'complete break'[18] from the equitable rules which formerly governed land law priorities. In consequence there has been a general rejection, no less so in England than elsewhere, of any temptation to qualify the system of title registration by the importing of an equitable doctrine alien to its current purpose.

(ii) The occasional re-emergence of the doctrine of notice Given the dogmatic exclusion of mere knowledge from the concept of 'fraud', it is perhaps

---

13   *Report*, p 37. Compare *Agra Bank Ltd v Barry* (1874) LR 7 HL 135 at 149 per Lord Cairns ('It appears to me that the object of such a statute...is to give a premium to diligence in registration').

14   *Report*, p 39. The same disregard for notice except in cases of fraud was endorsed by a further Royal Commission in 1857 (see *Report of the Commissioners on the Registration of Title with reference to the Sale and Transfer of Land* (CP 2215, 1857 - Session 2), para LXXIII).

15   In some jurisdictions there is specific statutory confirmation that mere knowledge on the part of a purchaser that a trust or unregistered interest is in existence 'shall not of itself be imputed as fraud' (see eg New Zealand's Land Transfer Act 1952, s 182; Alberta's Land Titles Act (RSA 1980, c L-5), s 195). See generally D.J. Whalan, *The Meaning of Fraud under the Torrens System*, (1974-75) 6 NZULR 207; P. Butt, *Notice and Fraud in the Torrens System: A Comparative Analysis*, (1977-78) 13 Univ of Western Australia LR 354.

16   See eg *Union Bank of Canada v Boulter-Waugh Ltd* (1919) 46 DLR 41 at 48; *Waimiha Sawmilling Co Ltd v Waione Timber Co Ltd* [1926] AC 101 at 106ff; *Ruptash and Lumsden v Zawick* (1956) 2 DLR (2d) 145 at 159f; *Holt, Renfrew & Co Ltd v Henry Singer Ltd* (1982) 135 DLR (3d) 391 at 397, 408, 421f; *Re Pacific Cassiar Ltd and Esso Canada Resources Ltd* (1986) 28 DLR (4th) 104 at 117.

17   (1921) 30 CLR 80 at 91.

18   See *United Trust Co v Dominion Stores Ltd* (1977) 71 DLR (3d) 72 at 75 per Laskin CJC (dissenting).

inevitable that from time to time the caselaw should disclose instances where the courts have not been prepared to accept that the doctrine of actual notice has been fully extinguished.[19]

In England the clarity of the law relating to minor interests was thrown into some confusion by the decision in *Peffer v Rigg*.[20] Here B and X had married two sisters—one each—and therefore shared a common relative in the form of their mother-in-law, M. Partly in order to accommodate M during her old age, B and X joined together to buy a house. They contributed equally towards the purchase price of a property with registered title, although the property was transferred into the sole name of X. On these facts there arose an implied trust for sale, X holding the legal title as registered proprietor on behalf of himself and B as equitable tenants in common (see *Fig.* 14). The circumstances of this purchase were fully known to the entire family of M. Indeed the implied trust was subsequently confirmed expressly in a formal deed of trust drawn up by B and X, although B never took steps to protect his beneficial half-share by the entry of a minor interest on the register of X's title. Some time later X's marriage to A broke down and ended in divorce. As part of the divorce settlement X transferred the legal estate in the house to A, M having died by this stage. X purported to transfer the 'whole' of the property 'as beneficial owner', in consideration of the payment of £1 by A.

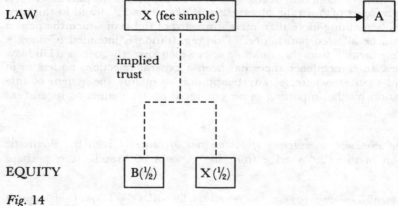

LAW   X (fee simple) ———————▶ A

implied trust

EQUITY   B(½)   X(½)

Fig. 14

A subsequently contended that the transfer invested her, as the new registered proprietor, with the legal estate in fee simple free of B's minor interest as a beneficiary behind the trust for sale. A argued that B's beneficial interest had become ineffective against her by reason of sections 20(1) and 59(6) of the Land Registration Act 1925. It was of course plain that A had at all times been perfectly well aware of the existence of B's interest in the property, since the entire family had been involved in resolving the accommodation needs posed by M. Nevertheless A was able to invoke considerable support for the

19   See eg *United Trust Co v Dominion Stores Ltd* (1977) 71 DLR (3d) 72 at 98, where Spence J voiced the opinion of the majority of the Supreme Court of Canada in holding that 'such a cardinal principle of property law cannot be considered to have been abrogated unless the legislative enactment is in the clearest and most unequivocal of terms'.

20   [1977] 1 WLR 285 (post, p 000). See (1977) 41 Conv (NS) 207 (F.R. Crane); (1977) 93 LQR 341 (R.J. Smith); [1977] CLJ 227 (D.J. Hayton); [1978] Conv 52 (J. Martin).

proposition that, irrespective of notice, an unprotected minor interest is unenforceable against a subsequent transferee or purchaser.[1]

Notwithstanding the clear provisions of sections 20(1) and 59(6), Graham J concluded that A held the newly transferred title on trust for herself and B as equitable tenants in common.[2] He took the view, first, that A was excluded from claiming any immunity from unprotected minor interests under section 20(1), since the transfer had been described by the parties themselves as involving only a 'nominal' consideration.[3] Section 20(1) requires that there be a transfer for 'valuable consideration', a phrase which for the purposes of the Act 'does not include a nominal consideration in money'.[4] Graham J then reinforced his decision by referring to the equitable doctrine which governs the 'knowing reception' of trust property transferred in breach of trust.[5] Since A 'knew...that the property was trust property when the transfer was made to her', Graham J held that she took the title 'on a constructive trust in accordance with general equitable principles'.[6]

The factor which, however, made the decision in *Peffer v Rigg* truly startling was the way in which Graham J cited the statutory definition of 'purchaser'[7] in support of his view that unprotected minor interests are rendered ineffective under section 59(6) only as against a purchaser 'in good faith'. A could not claim to be such a purchaser because she 'knew quite well' that X had held the property on trust.[8] Graham J thus ruled that a purchaser 'cannot...be in good faith if he has in fact notice of something which affects his title as in the present case.'[9]

This construction of the statute is quite remarkable in that, if applied broadly, it would drive a juggernaut through the provisions of the Land Registration Act 1925. Graham J's ruling appeared to produce the result that an unprotected minor interest remains binding on a purchaser with express actual notice, notwithstanding the clear wording of section 59(6) and the weight of the existing caselaw. It is certain that such a revitalisation of the

1 There was incidentally no question that P could claim the protection of an overriding interest by reason of 'actual occupation' (post, p 175), not least because he had never lived in the house in question.

2 [1977] 1 WLR 285 at 295E.

3 [1977] 1 WLR 285 at 293F. This ground for the decision was highly dubious. It was clear on the facts that A had also taken over a mortgage commitment in respect of the property under the terms of the divorce settlement, and her assumption of this liability must surely have constituted 'valuable consideration'.

4 Land Registration Act 1925, s 3(xxxi). Under section 20(4) unprotected minor interests remain binding on the transferee where a disposition is made 'without valuable consideration'.

5 Post, p 292.

6 [1977] 1 WLR 285 at 294E-F. Graham J emphasised that this constructive trust was 'a new trust imposed by equity and is distinct from the trust which bound [X].' Compare *Buck v Dickinson* (1978) 79 DLR (3d) 759 at 763.

7 For the purpose of the Land Registration Act 1925, 'purchaser' is defined as a 'purchaser in good faith for valuable consideration and includes a lessee, mortgagee, or other person who for valuable consideration acquires any interest in land or in any charge on land' (Land Registration Act 1925, s 3(xxi)). The word 'transferee' is left undefined by the Land Registration Act 1925, and it is therefore unclear whether this term incorporates any requirement of good faith.

8 [1977] 1 WLR 285 at 294E.

9 [1977] 1 WLR 285 at 294C. See *Marsden v Campbell* (1897) 18 LR (NSW) (Eq) 33 at 38, where a requirement of bona fides was interpreted to mean that the purchaser must take without notice of the rights of any occupant.

doctrine of notice in the context of registered land is contrary to principle, and highly likely that a moralistic view of the facts in *Peffer v Rigg* was allowed to coerce a legally unsupportable conclusion. It is not usually thought to be 'bad faith' for a purchaser to take advantage of the folly of those who fail to effect the appropriate registration in protection of their interests.[10] In *De Lusignan v Johnson*,[11] for instance, Brightman J expressly indicated that to allege 'bad faith' in this situation 'would be stretching the language'. He accordingly drew a sharp distinction between 'fraud' and mere 'notice of the existence or possible existence' of unprotected rights, taking the view that only the former provides a relevant ground of complaint against a purchaser of registered land. In *Peffer v Rigg* the primary motive underlying the disputed transfer of title from X to A was not to defraud B but rather to provide A with a home in the aftermath of divorce, and the case should not have been stigmatised as one involving 'bad faith' in the purchaser.[12]

(d) Recognised cases of 'fraud'

In cases of manifestly dishonest transfer of the registered title, it is clear that the court may exercise an *in personam* jurisdiction to prevent the Land Registration Act being used as an instrument of fraud.[13] In such instances the transferee is deemed to take the title subject to the unprotected minor interests which he has sought to disregard. The following circumstances, which are not mutually exclusive, provide examples of the kinds of conduct which have been classified as 'fraud' for this purpose.

(i) Deliberate ploy to defeat unprotected rights

The term 'fraud' is applicable to a transfer of a registered title which was intended quite blatantly to defeat an incumbrancer's rights while they remained unprotected. As Lord Buckmaster said in *Waimiha Sawmilling Co Ltd v Waione Timber Co Ltd*,[14] '[i]f the designed object of a transfer be to cheat a man of a known existing right, that is fraudulent'. Such a conveyance of title truly epitomises the *machinatio ad circumveniendum* which was condemned, perhaps overly broadly, by Lord Hardwicke LC in *Le Neve v Le Neve*.[15]

A label of 'fraud' is therefore liable to attach to a swiftly conducted transfer of a registered title to a friend for the deliberate purpose of defeating the equitable (and unprotected) rights of the transferor's wife.[16] Likewise a similarly motivated transfer to a company which is in reality the alter ego of the transferor is apt to be stigmatised as 'fraud'.[17] In *Jones v Lipman*,[18] for instance, Russell J held that an unprotected estate contract remained binding upon, and

---

10 See eg *In re Monolithic Building Co* [1915] 1 Ch 643 at 663; *Midland Bank Trust Co Ltd v Green* [1981] AC 513 at 530A-B (ante, p 124).
11 (1973) 230 Estates Gazette 499.
12 The authority of *De Lusignan v Johnson* was preferred in *Burr v Copp* [1983] CLY 2057.
13 Ante, p 123.
14 [1926] AC 101 at 106 (ante, p 124).
15 (1748) Amb 436 at 447, 27 ER 291 at 295.
16 *Efstratiou, Glantschnig and Petrovic v Glantschnig* [1972] NZLR 594 at 598f.
17 *Moore v Moore* (1971) 16 DLR (3d) 174 at 183, where the British Columbia Court of Appeal pointed out that 'incorporation of the company and the transfer by the husband to it was a device intended to defeat the rightful claims of the wife.'
18 [1962] 1 WLR 832.

specifically enforceable against, the transferee of a registered title. Here the transferee was a limited company which, on closer inspection, turned out to be merely the alter ego of the transferor who had earlier granted the estate contract to the present plaintiff. In Russell J's view, the defendant company was 'the creature of the first defendant [the transferor], a device and a sham, a mask which he holds before his face in an attempt to avoid recognition by the eye of equity'.[19]

(ii) Transfer expressly 'subject to' unprotected rights If a transfer of title is expressly stipulated to be 'subject to' unprotected minor interests, it is likely that the court will impose a constructive trust upon a transferee who later reneges upon the stipulation by claiming an unencumbered legal title.[20] 'Fraud' is clearly established by the transferee's deliberate disregard of the express terms on which the bargain between transferor and transferee was allowed to take effect.[1]

(iii) Collateral representation 'Fraud' is likewise present where the transfer of a registered title has been induced by a collateral representation made by the transferee that he will respect the unprotected rights of a third party. 'Fraud' may thus be found where a transferee initially indicated to the transferor either verbally or in writing that he would not disturb the rights of the unprotected incumbrancer.[2] If such a representation in fact induces in the vendor 'a false sense of security as to the purchaser's intention',[3] it may be fraudulent for the purchaser later to act inconsistently with its terms.[4]

(iv) Acquiescence in the exercise of unprotected rights If a transferee not merely knows of the existence of unprotected rights in the land transferred, but positively acquiesces in their continued exercise after the date of transfer, it may constitute a species of 'fraud' if the transferee subsequently claims to have taken title free of those rights.[5]

(e) Proposals for reform

The Law Commission has recently reviewed the current uncertainty surrounding the consequences of failure to protect a minor interest by appropriate entry on the register.[6] The Commission has recommended the introduction of a clear statutory requirement that all transferees and other

19 [1962] 1 WLR 832 at 836.
20 *Lyus v Prowsa Developments Ltd* [1982] 1 WLR 1044 at 1053F-G (post, p 285).
1 *Lyus v Prowsa Developments Ltd* [1982] 1 WLR 1044 at 1054G-H (post, p 284).
2 *Loke Yew v Port Swettenham Rubber Co Ltd* [1913] AC 491 at 502ff.
3 *Holt, Renfrew & Co Ltd v Henry Singer Ltd* (1982) 135 DLR (3d) 391 at 408.
4 Such a finding of 'fraud' is closely allied to the doctrine of estoppel by representation (post, p 400), and rests on clear proof of a causal link between the representation and the transfer (see eg *Holt, Renfrew & Co Ltd v Henry Singer Ltd* (1982) 135 DLR (3d) 391 at 410, 421f).
5 See eg *Maurice Demers Transport Ltd v Fountain Tire Distributors (Edmonton) Ltd* (1974) 42 DLR (3d) 412 at 420ff; *Gough v Kiddeys Korner Ltd* [1976] BCL 62.
6 Law Com No 158, paras 4.14ff.

purchasers who wish to take free from unprotected minor interests must take 'in good faith and for valuable consideration'.[7]

This proposal plainly clarifies the importance of valuable consideration in the present context, but it still leaves somewhat ambiguous the relevance of the third party's state of mind. The Commission envisaged, for instance, that its recommendation in this respect would cause the law of minor interests to diverge from that governing the registration of land charges in unregistered land.[8] The Commission nevertheless expressed its firm disapproval of the decision in *Peffer v Rigg*,[9] and suggested that statute law should make it clear that a transferee or purchaser is not to be 'deemed dishonest merely because he had actual knowledge of the unprotected minor interest in question.'[10] The Commission's deliberations thus seem to draw a crucial legal distinction between the purchaser who is aware of, and merely indifferent to, the unprotected status of a minor interest and the purchaser who positively and quite consciously manipulates that unprotected status for the overriding purpose of achieving some further advantage which is inconsistent with 'good faith'.

7. OVERRIDING INTERESTS

Overriding interests comprise a third important category of interests in registered land, being defined as including 'all the incumbrances, interests, rights, and powers not entered on the register but subject to which registered dispositions are by the Act to take effect.'[11] Most of the interests which fall within this 'intermediate, or hybrid, class'[12] are enumerated in section 70(1) of the Land Registration Act 1925,[13] and together represent a highly problematic area within the law of registered title.

(1) The function of the overriding interest

Overriding interests, as defined in the Land Registration Act 1925, are interests which bind the transferee of registered land notwithstanding that they are not recorded on the face of the register and notwithstanding that the transferee may have no actual knowledge of their existence. They are quite literally 'overriding'. Cumulatively they represent a group of interests in

---

7   Law Com No 158, para 4.15. In the Commission's view, the burden of showing an absence of good faith should be on the owner of the minor interest (Law Com No 158, para 4.17). If the purchaser were not a single individual but two or more persons, then an absence of good faith on the part of even one should be sufficient to enable the unprotected minor interest to prevail (ibid, para 4.16).

8   The Commission thought that the outcome in *Midland Bank Trust Co Ltd v Green* [1981] AC 513 (ante, p 120) did not represent an 'acceptable' resolution of the equivalent problem in registered land (see Law Com No 158, para 4.15).

9   [1977] 1 WLR 285 (ante, p 166).

10   Law Com No 158, para 4.15. The Commission thought it otherwise undesirable to fetter the courts in their application of the concept of 'good faith' to the facts of each individual case.

11   Land Registration Act 1925, s 3(xvi).

12   *Williams & Glyn's Bank Ltd v Boland* [1981] AC 487 at 503B per Lord Wilberforce.

13   See also Land Registration Rules 1925, r 258; Coal Act 1938, s 41; Coal Industry Nationalisation Act 1946, s 5; see Law Com No 158, Appendix B.

registered land which have been singled out either as having such distinct social importance or as involving such technical conveyancing difficulty as to merit a protection which derives not from the force of the register but from the force of statute.

(a) The conveyancing background of overriding interests

It is of the essence of the 'overriding interest' that certain kinds of right are made automatically binding on the transferee of registered land, even though they relate to matters which in unregistered conveyancing would not normally be included in title deeds or disclosed in abstracts of title. Since such matters would not therefore become apparent on an inspection of the documentary title (whether carried out by an intending purchaser or by the Land Registrar), they are matters in relation to which it is not possible to compile a trustworthy record on the register of title. As to these interests, the onus rests on persons dealing with registered land to seek information *outside* the register in the same manner and from the same sources as would persons dealing with an unregistered title. The purchaser of registered land must therefore obtain information about the possible presence of overriding interests by means of physical inspection of the land itself and by enquiries made of persons in occupation there. Overriding interests are supposed, in the main, to be rights which would become obvious to any purchaser who bothered to go and look at the property which he proposed to buy.

(b) The problematic nature of overriding interests

The principal difficulty posed by overriding interests is that their existence fundamentally distorts the mirror image of the register: the register can no longer be relied upon as a comprehensive record of the totality of interests in and affecting registered land. Another factor which exacerbates this difficulty is the circumstance that, in spite of the original (and vaguely comforting) theory that overriding interests will always be apparent upon physical inspection of the land, it is now quite clear that several categories of overriding interest may well remain undiscovered even by a purchaser who carefully inspects both land and title.[14] Recent decisions have tended, moreover, to increase rather than diminish the number of rights which may claim protected status as overriding interests.[15] The ultimate irony is that the transferee who is innocently ensnared by a virtually undiscoverable overriding interest does not qualify for any form of statutory compensation if the register is rectified to his prejudice in recognition of that overriding interest.[16]

It is hardly surprising, given these substantial drawbacks, that the Law Commission has given serious consideration to the proposal to 'close the cavernous crack in the mirror principle' by drastic amendment of the operation of overriding interests.[17] Although the Commission appeared

---

14   For explicit recognition of this point, see *Kling v Keston Properties Ltd* (1983) 49 P & CR 212 at 222 per Vinelott J; [1985] Conv 406 (J.E.M.).
15   See eg *Williams & Glyn's Bank Ltd v Boland* [1981] AC 487 (post, p 181).
16   Post, p 200.
17   Law Commission, *Property Law: Second Report on Land Registration (Provisional)* (November 1984), para 9.

initially to favour the virtual abolition of the entire category of overriding interests, it now seems more likely that the disadvantages created by such rights will soon be remedied in large measure by an extension of the indemnity provisions of the Land Registration Act 1925.[18]

(c) Loss of status as an overriding interest

It will quickly become apparent that the present state of registered land law permits some interests to enjoy a dual form of protection under the Land Registration Act 1925. In effect certain rights may be protected either by reason of their inclusion as minor interests on the register or by virtue of their status as overriding interests off the register.[19] It is quite clear, however, that an overriding interest is, by definition, an interest 'not entered on the register'.[20] If an overriding interest is at any stage the subject of some entry in the register, it ceases ipso facto to be an overriding interest and ranks thereafter as a minor interest.

It is also open to the Registrar, on receiving satisfactory proof of an overriding interest, to enter it in the register,[1] whereupon it ranks merely as a minor interest. Likewise the Registrar has discretion in appropriate cases to enter in the register a notice indicating that the land is free from overriding interests.[2] However, the powers thus vested in the Registrar only partially mitigate the problems inherent in the existence of those overriding interests which never reach the state of being recorded in the register.[3]

(2) The categories of overriding interest

Most of the categories of overriding interest in registered land are laid down in section 70(1) of the Land Registration Act 1925.[4] By far the most controversial of these categories is that referred to in section 70(1)(g),[5] but other significant kinds of overriding interest include the following.

(a) Section 70(1)(a)

Section 70(1)(a) confers the protection of an overriding interest in relation to a number of incorporeal hereditaments including rights of common, public rights, profits *à prendre*, rights of way, and 'other easements not being equitable easements required to be protected by notice on the register'. This provision is

---

18 Post, p 202. See Law Commission, *Property Law: Third Report on Land Registration: A. Overriding Interests, B. Rectification and Indemnity, C. Minor Interests* (Law Com No 158, 31 March 1987), para 2.7.
19 Post, p 191.
20 Land Registration Act 1925, s 3(xvi).
1   Land Registration Act 1925, s 70(3).
2   Land Registration Rules 1925, r 197.
3   So grave is the danger that a transferee of registered land may be trapped unwittingly by an overriding interest that many conveyancing solicitors attempt to divert responsibility for the discovery of overriding interests to the client-purchaser himself. Illusory indeed may be the protection which the lay person imagines he buys when he employs the services of a solicitor in a purchase of registered land.
4   See also Land Registration Rules 1925, r 258.
5   Post, p 175.

clearly apt to give overriding protection in registered land to such rights as legal easements and profits *à prendre* (whether legal or equitable),[6] but it is not nearly so plain that the provision covers equitable easements. It was indeed assumed by many that the somewhat ambiguous wording of section 70(1)(a) had the effect of excluding all equitable easements from the category of overriding interests, but this belief was shown to be unfounded in *Celsteel Ltd v Alton House Holdings Ltd.*[7] Here Scott J held that, although section 70(1)(a) does not give overriding protection to all equitable easements, it does (in conjunction with Land Registration Rules 1925, r 258[8]) confer such protection on equitable easements which are 'openly exercised and enjoyed' over the land which is the subject of the relevant transfer of title.[9]

(b) Section 70(1)(c)

Section 70(1)(c) provides that a liability to repair the chancel of a church may comprise a head of overriding interest. Liabilities of this kind have the effect of imposing on certain landowners a burden, of distinctly medieval origin, to bear the costs of repairing the chancels of probably one third of all parish churches in England and Wales.[10] The land affected by liability for chancel repairs has been estimated to cover nearly four million acres. The obligation involved is slightly quaint, but the transfer of the burdened land has in recent times exposed the transferee to an onerous and often wholly unexpected form of liability.[11] The Law Commission has now proposed that all chancel repair liability arising from the ownership of land should be phased out without compensation over a period of ten years,[12] and that failing a prompt abolition of this archaic form of liability all chancel repair obligations should become registrable local land charges.[13]

---

6 In this respect section 70(1)(a) seems to render otiose other statutory provisions which envisage that the grant of an easement or profit must be 'completed by registration' (see Land Registration Act 1925, ss 19(2), 22(2), ante, p 157). The Law Commission has recommended that the category of overriding interests should include only those easements and profits which arise by implied grant or reservation or by prescription (Law Com No 158, paras 2.26ff). This proposal, if implemented, would confer the status of a mere minor interest on expressly granted legal easements and profits which remain uncompleted by registration (ibid, para 2.26). Likewise, the Commission's recommendation would have the effect of reversing the decision in *Celsteel Ltd v Alton House Holdings Ltd* [1985] 1 WLR 204, thereby making all equitable easements protectible as minor interests only (ibid, para 2.33).
7 [1985] 1 WLR 204. See [1986] Conv 31 (M.P. Thompson).
8 Land Registration Rules 1925, r 258 provides that '[r]ights, privileges, and appurtenances appertaining or reputed to appertain to land or...enjoyed therewith or reputed or known as part or parcel of or appurtenant thereto, which adversely affect registered land, are overriding interests within section 70 of the Act...'
9 [1985] 1 WLR 204 at 220H-221D. The Court of Appeal subsequently confirmed the decision of Scott J without substantive comment on this point ([1986] 1 WLR 512). See Chapter 17 (post, p 648). See also *Payne v Adnams* [1971] CLY 6486.
10 See *Property Law: Liability for Chancel Repairs* (Law Com No 152, 20 November 1985), para 1.2.
11 See eg *Chivers & Sons Ltd v Air Ministry* [1955] Ch 585 at 594ff (land sold by Queens' College Cambridge).
12 Law Com No 152, para 4.18.
13 Law Com No 152, para 5.9f. The Law Commission has recommended that, pending implementation of Law Com No 152, chancel repair liability should no longer constitute a species of overriding interest, but should subsist as a form of 'general burden' (post, p 202) on the land affected. See Law Com No 158, para 2.81.

(c) Section 70(1)(f)

Pursuant to section 70(1)(f) and subject to other provisions of the Land Registration Act 1925, overriding interests also include 'rights acquired or in course of being acquired under the Limitation Acts'.[14] The operation of section 70(1)(f) was illustrated in *Bridges v Mees*.[15] Here P contracted to purchase from V the fee simple estate in an area of registered land. He paid the full purchase price and entered into occupation, but never obtained from V a transfer of the registered title and never protected his estate contract by entering a minor interest on the register. When nearly 20 years later V transferred the fee simple not to P but to D instead, P was able to argue successfully before Harman J that his contractual rights were protected under section 70(1)(f)—and also for that matter under section 70(1)(g)—by reason of his adverse possession.[16] D, although registered as the new proprietor, was therefore bound by P's overriding interest.

(d) Section 70(1)(k)

The protection of an overriding interest is likewise conferred by section 70(1)(k) on leases which are granted for a term not exceeding 21 years.[17] Although this provision no longer excludes leases which are obtained on payment of a fine or premium (ie, a capital sum as distinct from a periodic rent),[18] it is clear that the overriding interest protected under this head is confined to legal leases only and cannot apply to an equitable term of years.[19] However, equitable leases may, if

---

14 On the operation of the Limitation Act 1980, see Chapter 20 (post, p 740). The Law Commission has recommended that rights already acquired by adverse possession under the general law should continue to rank as overriding interests (Law Com No 158, para 2.36), but that rights which are still in the process of acquisition by adverse possession should retain their current degree of protection under some more direct provision outside and separate from the categories of overriding interest (ibid, para 2.37).

15 [1957] Ch 475.

16 [1957] Ch 475 at 484ff.

17 There has for a long time been a powerful argument to the effect that a lease which is not noted on the register ought not to be an overriding interest unless the tenant is in actual occupation and his existence is therefore discoverable on physical inspection of the property. This argument was, however, rejected by the Law Commission in one of its early Working Papers. The Commission expressed the view in 1971 that '[m]any short tenancies are informal and where they relate to dwelling-houses and flats are often granted without the tenant being legally represented. We cannot think that it would be desirable that a monthly tenant or even a tenant of a flat for, say, three years, who has not yet moved in, would have to register notice of this tenancy against the reversionary title at the Land Registry to protect himself against a purchaser of the reversion...Where there is a conflict we think that the law should incline in favour of the tenant. By not requiring occupation, the existing paragraph (k) does this and we agree with it' (Law Commission, *Property Law: Land Registration (Second Paper)* (Published Working Paper No 37, July 1971), para 89). See also Law Com No 158, paras 2.50ff.

18 See Land Registration Act 1925, s 70(1)(k), as amended by Land Registration Act 1986, s 4(1), (4).

19 *City Permanent Building Society v Miller* [1952] Ch 840 at 853. The Law Commission has recommended that section 70(1)(k) should expressly exclude discontinuous legal leases from the category of overriding interests (Law Com No 158, para 2.46). It is clear in any event that, even if a short lease constitutes an overriding interest under section 70(1)(k), the binding effect of the covenants contained in it is still governed by the ordinary rules (post, p 516) relating to the running of the benefit and burden of leasehold covenants (see Law Com No 158, para 2.49).

coupled with actual occupation by the tenant or the receipt of rents and profits from a subtenant, constitute an overriding interest under section 70(1)(g).[20]

(3) Operation of section 70(1)(g)

There is no doubt that the most dramatic species of overriding interest is that referred to in section 70(1)(g) of the Land Registration Act 1925. This category comprises

the rights of every person in actual occupation of the land or in receipt of the rents and profits thereof, save where enquiry is made of such person and the rights are not disclosed.[1]

(a) Purpose of section 70(1)(g)

The object of section 70(1)(g) was described by Lord Denning MR in *Strand Securities Ltd v Caswell*[2] as being to 'protect a person in actual occupation of the land from having his rights lost in the welter of registration.' Such a person may simply 'stay there and do nothing', but will nevertheless be protected since '[n]o one can buy the land over his head and thereby take away or diminish his rights'. In other words, an onus of enquiry is placed upon the purchaser and is ignored by him at his own peril.

Section 70(1)(g) was thus intended to benefit lay persons who own interests in registered land (perhaps of limited scope or duration) to whom it might not occur that protective entry in the register is required in the event of a transaction involving the registered title. In such cases it was considered that it might well be unfair to demand positive protective action in circumstances where the fact of actual occupation would signal to all prudent purchasers both the possible existence of undocumented interests affecting the land and the necessity of further enquiry.[3]

(b) Date on which the overriding interest takes effect

The date on which an overriding interest crystallises by reason of 'actual occupation' is the date on which the transferee of the registered title is entered on the register as the new proprietor of the estate in question.[4] Likewise, where a mortgage has been granted in respect of a registered title, the vital date is that on which the lender is entered on the register as proprietor of a registered

---

20 Post, p 181.
1 The concept of 'actual possession' appears first in this context in the judgment of Lord Loughborough LC in *Taylor v Stibbert* (1794) 2 Ves 437 at 440, 30 ER 713 at 714. For the first use of the phrase 'actual occupation', see *Barnhart v Greenshields* (1853) 9 Moo PCC 18 at 34, 14 ER 204 at 210. The idea of 'actual occupation' first appears in statutory form in the list of 'overriding interests' contained in Law of Property Act 1922, Sch 16, Part I, para 5(3)(i), amending Land Transfer Act 1875, s 18. Statutory equivalents of Land Registration Act 1925, s 70(1)(g), are found in Northern Ireland's Land Registration Act 1970, Sch 5, Part I, para 15, and in the Republic of Ireland's Registration of Title Act 1964, s 72(1)(j).
2 [1965] Ch 958 at 979G.
3 See Law Com No 158, para 2.6. It may even be that the inclusion of section 70(1)(g) in the Land Registration Act 1925 was altogether less remarkable against the background of the conveyancing practice of former times, when it was relatively unusual that completion should take place anywhere other than at the premises which were the subject of the instant transaction.
4 *In re Boyle's Claim* [1961] 1 WLR 339 at 344f.

charge.[5] In order to avoid any uncertainty over the date on which the application for registration is actually processed in the registry, the date of registration is deemed[6] in either case to be the date on which the application was lodged at the registry.[7] The 'rights'—whatever they may be—of any person in 'actual occupation' of the land on this crucial day become overriding.

(i) Dangers of the 'registration gap'   Although this outcome may be convenient in terms of registry practice, it is fraught with difficulty for the transferee or chargee of registered land. The vital date of registration occurs *after* completion of the contract of purchase,[8] and there is a danger that persons with adverse rights may enter into occupation of the property during the (sometimes lengthy) period which elapses between completion and the deemed date of registration.[9] This danger is particularly acute in the context of a purchase assisted by a contemporaneous mortgage. The registered chargee is rendered vulnerable to occupiers' rights which are set up in the period between completion and registration even though it was wholly impossible for him to discover their existence before advancing the loan moneys.[10]

(ii) Advantages of the 'registration gap'   The difficulties brought about by the 'registration gap' have caused the Law Commission to suggest that, in any future reform of overriding interests, the rights of occupiers should have significance as against transferees of registered land only if the claimants of these rights were in occupation at the date of completion.[11] The 'registration gap' has recently been shown, however, to confer one distinct and previously unsuspected advantage in the conveyancing process. In *City of London Building Society v Flegg*[12] a dwelling-house had been mortgaged by two trustees for sale without either the knowledge or the consent of other beneficiaries under the trust who were at all material times in actual occupation of the property. These beneficiaries later claimed that, by reason of actual occupation at the registration date of the mortgagee's charge, their equitable rights under the trust for sale (or at least the occupation rights incidental thereto[13]) would acquire the status of overriding interests. The House of Lords held, however, that section 70(1)(g) gives effect only to such 'rights' subsisting in reference to

---

5   Post, p 834.
6   See Land Registration Rules 1925, r 83(2), as substituted by Land Registration Rules 1978, r 8.
7   See also *E.S. Schwab & Co Ltd v McCarthy* (1976) 31 P & CR 196 at 204; *Kling v Keston Properties Ltd* (1983) 49 P & CR 212 at 218. Compare, however, *Paddington Building Society v Mendelsohn* (1985) 50 P & CR 244 at 247, where the county court judge had ruled that section 70(1)(g) requires actual occupation at the date of completion. The Court of Appeal disposed on the case on other grounds, but Browne-Wilkinson LJ declared himself to be 'far from saying that the judge's decision on that point was wrong'. On the unsatisfactory nature of the present uncertainty in this area, see Law Com No 158, para 2.76.
8   See Law Com No 158, para 2.57.
9   See also J. Russell, (1981) 32 NILQ 3 at 16.
10   Post, p 850.
11   See Law Com No 158, para 2.77. Compare the more cautious approach adopted in Law Commission, *Property Law: The Implications of Williams & Glyn's Bank Ltd v Boland* (Law Com No 115, August 1982), paras 18(ii), 34, and Appendix 2, para 12.
12   [1987] 2 WLR 1266 (post, pp 384, 601).
13   Post, p 374.

the land as are currently held by the persons in actual occupation at the registration date. Here the 'rights' of the beneficiaries had been overreached some time earlier on the execution of the mortgage charge and payment of the mortgage moneys to two trustees. It therefore inescapably followed that when the mortgagee came to register its charge, there would no longer exist any 'rights' in the beneficiaries which, by association with their undoubted actual occupation, could found a claim of overriding interest against the mortgagee.[14]

(c) Continuing enforceability of the overriding interest

Once an overriding interest has crystallised on the date of registration, this interest remains enforceable against the registering transferee or chargee, notwithstanding that the owner of the overriding interest ceases thereafter to occupy the land.[15] In other words, once the overriding interest materialises by virtue of actual occupation on the relevant date, its subsequent effectiveness against the transferee does not depend on continued actual occupation. Of course the conditions of section 70(1)(g) must be satisfied de novo in the event of any further transfer of the registered title.

(d) Protection of derivative interests

A derivative interest (eg a lease) which is subsequently carved out of an overriding interest enjoys the shelter of that overriding interest against any adverse claim brought by the transferee of the registered title. In *Marks v Attallah*,[16] for instance, E, as registered proprietor, held an estate in fee simple

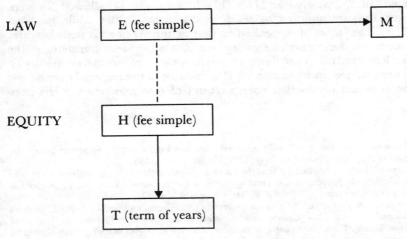

Fig. 15

14 'If, then, one asks what were the subsisting rights of the respondents referable to their occupation, the answer must be...that they were rights which, vis à vis the appellants, were, eo instante with the creation of the charge, overreached and therefore subsisted only in relation to the equity of redemption' ([1987] 2 WLR 1266 at 1287H–1288A per Lord Oliver of Aylmerton).
15 *London and Cheshire Insurance Co Ltd v Laplagrene Property Co Ltd* [1971] Ch 499 at 505A-B, 509E-F.
16 (1966) 198 Estates Gazette 685; (1966) 110 SJ 709.

on a bare trust for H. On the assumption[17] that H had an overriding interest vis à vis M (a transferee of the freehold from E), Ungoed-Thomas J was prepared to hold that M was also bound by the lease which H had granted to T after the effective date of registration of M's transfer (see *Fig.* 15). Although T himself could claim no overriding interest as such, he was entitled to rely on the overriding interest of H.[18]

(e) Protection for persons in receipt of rents and profits

In its terms section 70(1)(g) also affords the protection of an overriding interest to the rights of any person who, at the relevant date, is 'in receipt of the rents and profits' derived from the land, even though that person is not himself 'in actual occupation of the land'.[19]

(i) Protection for the commercial landlord

Section 70(1)(g) thus protects the rights of a non-resident landlord as well as those of his resident tenant: the landlord is protected by virtue of his receipt of rents and profits, and the tenant by virtue of actual occupation. It seems, however, that if section 70(1)(g) is to have this effect, the landlord must be in actual receipt of those rents and profits, and not merely have an unenforced right to receive the same.[20]

(ii) No rewards for generosity

Section 70(1)(g) does not apply, however, if the non-resident owner of an interest in land grants away mere rights of rent-free occupation. In such circumstances neither the licensor nor the licensee is protected. In *Strand Securities Ltd v Caswell*[1] a tenant, D, allowed his step-daughter and her children to reside rent-free in his flat while he lived elsewhere. The Court of Appeal ruled that neither D nor his step-daughter could assert an overriding interest against P, a subsequent transferee of the superior leasehold title, even though P was fully aware of the interest held by D. D was unprotected under section 70(1)(g) because at the material date he was neither in actual occupation nor in receipt of rent and profits.[2] His step-

---

17   This assumption was tested and confirmed when the issue was later presented before the Court of Appeal as *Hodgson v Marks* [1971] Ch 892 (post, p 185).

18   Ungoed-Thomas J pointed out that the Land Registration Act 1925 expressly provides that transfers should be 'subject to overriding interests, and not subject to overriding interests in any particular person' ((1966) 198 Estates Gazette 685 at 687).

19   The privilege thus accorded persons 'in receipt of the rents and profits' of land has been criticised by the Law Commission as inimical to the simplification of registered conveyancing. The Commission has recommended that the rights of such persons should no longer be made overriding by section 70(1)(g). See Law Com No 158, para 2.70.

20   See *E.S. Schwab & Co Ltd v McCarthy* (1976) 31 P & CR 196 at 205, 213. (Compare the more liberal definition of 'possession' in Land Registration Act 1925, s 3(xviii) and Law of Property Act 1925, s 205(1)(xix)). Even the retention of a deposit by way of security for rent appears to be inadequate to satisfy section 70(1)(g), not least since the effect of such a deposit as a deemed equivalent of rent will tend to become exhausted with the passage of time (see *E.S. Schwab & Co Ltd v McCarthy*, supra at 214 per Buckley LJ).

1   [1965] Ch 958.

2   The Court of Appeal acknowledged that the result would have been quite different if D's step-daughter had made a 'token' payment of rent—even 'a penny a week for the privilege of remaining there' ([1965] Ch 958 at 981A-B, 983D-E).

daughter, although in actual occupation, was likewise unprotected since her rights, being those of a bare licensee, did not even enter the threshold of section 70(1)(g).[3]

(4) Nature of the 'rights' protected by section 70(1)(g)

A strict analysis of section 70(1)(g) discloses the almost mathematical equation[4] that

$$\boxed{\text{'Rights'}} \;\; + \;\; \boxed{\begin{array}{c}\text{'actual occupation' or}\\ \text{receipt of rents and profits}\end{array}} \;\; = \;\; \boxed{\text{Overriding interest}}$$

In technical terms, the 'rights' do not themselves constitute the 'overriding interest' under section 70(1)(g),[5] but those 'rights', once found in conjunction with the factual element of 'actual occupation' or receipt of rents and profits, comprise in association an 'overriding interest'.[6] The 'overriding interest' is thus an amalgam of law and fact: pre-existing rights in statutory consort with one or other of the prescribed elements of physical occupation or receipt of money.

It is clear from this analysis that what becomes binding under section 70(1)(g) is not necessarily any occupancy on the part of the person who claims 'rights' under cover of that provision but rather the 'rights' which he claims. In other words, occupation of the land is not per se one of the 'rights' referred to in section 70(1)(g).[7] It is merely the trigger which activates the statutory protection of *any rights* belonging to the actual occupier—whatever those rights may be. Indeed, it may well be in a given case that the particular 'rights' protected under section 70(1)(g) are entirely unrelated to occupation of the land.[8]

Extensive though the sweep of section 70(1)(g) may thus appear to be, there are nevertheless certain implicit limitations on the range of interests which may come within its scope.

(a) The 'rights' must subsist in reference to land

Although section 70(1)(g) in broad terms attaches an overriding quality to the 'rights' of any person in actual occupation or in receipt of rents and profits, other provisions of the Land Registration Act 1925 impose implicit qualifications on the nature of the 'rights' concerned. For example, section

---

3 Post, p 182.
4 Speaking in the immediate context of *City of London Building Society v Flegg* [1987] 2 WLR 1266 at 1272H, Lord Templeman emphasised that there must be 'a combination of an interest which justifies continuing occupation plus actual occupation to constitute an overriding interest'.
5 See *Blacklocks v J.B. Developments (Godalming) Ltd* [1982] Ch 183 at 196E-F.
6 '[T]here is no logical difficulty in the association of a minor interest with another factor (ie actual occupation) being, qua association, an overriding interest' (*Williams & Glyn's Bank Ltd v Boland* [1981] AC 487 at 512A per Lord Scarman).
7 'Actual occupation is not an interest in itself' (*City of London Building Society v Flegg* [1987] 2 WLR 1266 at 1272H per Lord Templeman).
8 See eg *Webb v Pollmount Ltd* [1966] Ch 584 at 603C-D (specifically enforceable option to purchase land); *Kling v Keston Properties Ltd* (1983) 49 P & CR 212 at 215ff (right of pre-emption).

20(1) refers to overriding interests as interests 'affecting the estate transferred or created'. Likewise section 70(1) itself speaks of overriding interests as interests 'subsisting in reference' to 'registered land'. On the basis of these provisions, it is commonly maintained that section 70(1)(g) relates only to proprietary rights in land as already defined under the general law. In other words, section 70(1)(g) cannot apply to purely personal rights in or over land, which in terms of the general law of property remain mere rights *in personam* and never have any potential for binding third parties.[9]

This restriction was adverted to in *National Provincial Bank Ltd v Hastings Car Mart Ltd*[10] by Russell LJ, who was of opinion that section 70(1)(g) deals throughout only with 'rights in reference to land which have the quality of being capable of enduring through different ownerships of the land, according to normal conceptions of title to real property.' This view was confirmed by the House of Lords in the same case,[11] Lord Wilberforce emphasising that the 'whole frame of section 70...shows that it is made against a background of interests or rights whose nature and whose transmissible character is known , or ascertainable, aliunde, ie, under other statutes or under the common law.'[12] Lord Wilberforce thus concluded that, in order to ascertain what 'rights' come within the ambit of section 70(1)(g),

one must look outside the Land Registration Act and see what rights affect purchasers under the general law. To suppose that the subsection makes any right, of howsoever a personal character, which a person in occupation may have, an overriding interest by which a purchaser is bound, would involve two consequences: first that this Act is, in this respect, bringing about a substantive change in real property law by making personal rights bind purchasers; second, that there is a difference *as to the nature of the rights by which a purchaser may be bound* between registered and unregistered land; for purely personal rights cannot affect purchasers of unregistered land even with notice. One may have to accept that there is a difference between unregistered and registered land as regards what kind of notice binds a purchaser, or what kind of inquiries a purchaser has to make. But there is no warrant in the terms of this paragraph or elsewhere in the Act for supposing that the nature of the rights which are to bind a purchaser is to be different, excluding personal rights in one case, including them in another.[13]

---

9   This view of the status of personal rights in registered land is, of course, wholly consistent with the orthodox doctrine which holds that such rights have no effect on a purchaser in the corresponding context of unregistered land.

10   [1964] Ch 665 at 696.

11   *National Provincial Bank Ltd v Ainsworth* [1965] AC 1175.

12   [1965] AC 1175 at 1261F. This statement involves a somewhat circular definition of proprietary status as being rooted in the quality of transmissibility (post, p 557). See, however, *Guckian v Brennan* [1981] IR 478 at 486, where Gannon J pointed out that the Irish equivalent of section 70 'does not create burdens: it merely classifies burdens which are created aliunde.' See also *City of London Building Society v Flegg* [1987] 2 WLR 1266 at 1285G–H per Lord Oliver of Aylmerton.

13   [1965] AC 1175 at 1261B-E. A difference in the kind of notice which binds purchasers of unregistered and registered land respectively arises automatically from the fact that section 70(1)(g) creates an 'overriding interest' out of the rights of any person 'in receipt of the rents and profits' of registered land. It is quite clear that a purchaser of unregistered land occupied by a tenant is *not* thereby fixed with constructive notice of the landlord's rights (see *Hunt v Luck* [1901] 1 Ch 45 at 49, affd [1902] 1 Ch 428 at 432). Compare, however, Law Com No 158, para 2.70 (ante, p 178).

(b) 'Rights' accepted within the ambit of section 70(1)(g)

The orthodox reading of section 70(1)(g) is therefore that this provision refers only to 'rights' which have a recognisably proprietary character. The 'rights' capable of generating an overriding interest thus include such interests as an option to purchase a legal estate,[14] an equitable lease or tenancy,[15] the equitable interest of a beneficiary under a bare trust[16] or trust for sale,[17] the right to an unpaid vendor's lien,[18] the Rent Act entitlements of protected and statutory tenants,[19] the equitable proprietary rights of an estoppel licensee,[20] the right of a tenant to deduct from future rent the cost of repairs which his landlord has wrongfully failed to effect,[1] and the right to have a conveyance rectified in equity on the ground of mistake.[2] All such rights conform sufficiently to the traditional characteristics of a proprietary interest in land to be capable of 'subsisting in reference' to registered land for the present purpose.

(c) Rights excluded from the scope of section 70(1)(g)

Correspondingly it is quite consistent that section 70(1)(g) should exclude from its ambit those rights which, although related to land in some broad sense, are classified either by statute or by the general law of property as mere rights *in personam*. Section 70(1)(g) does not therefore include rights which are in essence purely personal or contractual.

(i) Personal rights to occupy the matrimonial home   The demarcation of the 'rights' falling within section 70(1)(g) arose most starkly when the courts were required to rule on the effect of the 'deserted wife's equity'.[3] In *National Provincial Bank Ltd v Ainsworth*,[4] the House of Lords finally, but conclusively, rejected the idea that this 'equity' could be anything more than a merely personal right effective

---

14   *Webb v Pollmount Ltd* [1966] Ch 584 at 603C-D; *Kling v Keston Properties Ltd* (1983) 49 P & CR 212 at 217ff; [1985] Conv 406 (J.E.M.).

15   *Grace Rymer Investments Ltd v Waite* [1958] Ch 831 at 849ff; *Greaves Organisation Ltd v Stanhope Gate Property Co Ltd* (1973) 228 Estates Gazette 725 at 729.

16   *Hodgson v Marks* [1971] Ch 892 at 934F-G (post, p 185).

17   *Williams & Glyn's Bank Ltd v Boland* [1981] AC 487 at 508A-B. See also *Winkworth v Edward Baron Development Co Ltd* (1986) 52 P & CR 67 at 78.

18   *London and Cheshire Insurance Co Ltd v Laplagrene Property Co Ltd* [1971] Ch 499 at 502H.

19   *National Provincial Bank Ltd v Hastings Car Mart Ltd* [1964] Ch 665 at 689 per Lord Denning MR. On the nature of a statutory tenancy, see Chapter 29 (post, p 1002). The Law Commission has pointed, however, to the difficulty that the degree of residential occupation sufficient to sustain a statutory tenancy under the Rent Act (post, p 1007) may not always amount to the 'actual occupation' required for the purpose of section 70(1)(g) (see Law Com No 158, para 2.15 (n 71)).

20   *National Provincial Bank Ltd v Hastings Car Mart Ltd* [1964] Ch 665 at 689 per Lord Denning MR.

 1   *Lee-Parker v Izzett* [1971] 1 WLR 1688 at 1693F-G (post, p 942).

 2   *Blacklocks v J.B. Developments (Godalming) Ltd* [1982] Ch 183 at 196D-E (post, p 197).

 3   During the 1950s and 1960s the Court of Appeal had developed a doctrine to the effect that a wife, in the event of desertion by her husband, acquired at the date of his departure an 'equity' in the matrimonial home which she could then successfully oppose against any purchaser from her husband. Such a purchaser would be bound (in the case of unregistered land) if he had notice of the 'equity' and (in the case of registered land) if the wife remained at all material times in 'actual occupation' within the terms of section 70(1)(g). See Chapter 22 (post, p 785).

 4   [1965] AC 1175 (post, p 786).

only against the other spouse.[5] In view of its nature and origin, the wife's 'equity' could not rank under the general law as a right *in rem* and, since it therefore lacked an essential proprietary character, it fell outside the scope of section 70(1)(g).[6]

This conclusion as to the non-proprietary status of matrimonial rights of occupation was then expressly preserved in the legislation which was swiftly introduced in order to replace the ill-fated doctrine of the 'deserted wife's equity'. This legislation, now consolidated in the Matrimonial Homes Act 1983, confers statutory 'rights of occupation' on specified categories of spouse,[7] but provides quite explicitly that a spouse's 'rights of occupation' can never constitute an overriding interest even though that spouse is in 'actual occupation' of the matrimonial home.[8]

(ii) Contractual licence   The precise status of the contractual occupation licence is currently a matter of some debate.[9] Such a licence, if accorded a proprietary status in the general law of land, is clearly capable of ranking as an overriding interest under section 70(1)(g). In *National Provincial Bank Ltd v Hastings Car Mart Ltd*[10] Lord Denning MR seemed prepared to include the contractual occupation licence as one of the 'rights' covered by section 70(1)(g). However, this approach conflicts somewhat with the conventional understanding of the status of the contractual licence under the general law,[11] and may be a more accurate reflection of the future development of the law than of its current state. For the time being it is highly doubtful whether such rights as the contractual licence can properly be described as 'rights' which come within the threshold of section 70(1)(g).[12]

(iii) Collateral contractual rights   It seems clear that collateral contractual rights cannot rank as overriding interests under section 70(1)(g) even on behalf of a person in actual occupation of the land. This result inevitably follows even

---

5   Post, p 786.
6   It should come as no great surprise to learn that in the Court of Appeal in *National Provincial Bank Ltd v Hastings Car Mart Ltd* [1964] Ch 665 at 689, Lord Denning MR had expressed a quite contrary view.
7   See Chapter 22 (post, p 782).
8   Matrimonial Homes Act 1983, s 2(8)(b) (post, p 789). (See Matrimonial Homes Act 1967, s 2(7)). Spousal 'rights of occupation' should of course be protected by the entry of a notice on the appropriate register of title (post, p 787).
9   Post, p 549.
10   [1964] Ch 665 at 688f.
11   Post, p 549. The orthodox rule is that the rights of a contractual licensee bind only the licensor, and that purchasers are never affected by a contractual licence even though they purchase with express notice of the licensee's rights (see *Clore v Theatrical Properties Ltd and Westby & Co Ltd* [1936] 3 All ER 483 at 490ff). However, Lord Denning's liberal view of section 70(1)(g) was in clear accord with his diligent efforts over many years to elevate the status of the contractual licence so that it should receive the same protection under the general law as that accorded to equitable proprietary rights (see eg *Errington v Errington and Woods* [1952] 1 KB 290 at 298ff; *Binions v Evans* [1972] Ch 359 at 367E-369C).
12   See, for instance, the extreme caution expressed on this point in *National Provincial Bank Ltd v Ainsworth* [1965] AC 1175 at 1239B-1240A per Lord Upjohn, 1251D-1252A per Lord Wilberforce. A non-contractual (or 'bare') licence is clearly excluded from the scope of section 70(1)(g). See *Strand Securities Ltd v Caswell* [1965] Ch 958 at 980C-D (ante, p 178); Law Com No 158, para 2.56.

though such rights may be collateral to other rights of a proprietary nature which undoubtedly do come within the compass of section 70(1)(g). In *Eden Estates Ltd v Longman*,[13] for instance, a tenant had agreed, on taking his tenancy, to pay the landlord a substantial deposit as security against non-payment of rent or breach of other covenants in the lease. The Court of Appeal declined to hold that this collateral agreement (which appeared to be entirely verbal in origin) was binding on a subsequent assignee of the landlord's interest. The tenant's contractual right to recover his deposit could not generate an overriding interest under section 70(1)(g) even though the tenant had remained at all times in 'actual occupation'.[14]

(d) Other statutory restrictions on the range of section 70(1)(g)

The operation of section 70(1)(g) is further limited by several express statutory restrictions on the 'rights' which are capable of protection under cover of an overriding interest.

(i) Equitable rights of settled land beneficiaries There is an explicit statutory prohibition against the inclusion within the field of overriding interests of any equitable rights arising under the Settled Land Act 1925. This prohibition takes the form of a clear directive that the equitable interests of beneficiaries under a strict settlement of land[15] may 'take effect as minor interests and not otherwise'.[16] There is therefore no possibility that such interests—even if coupled with actual occupation—can ever claim dual status as overriding interests under section 70(1)(g).[17]

(ii) Notice under the Leasehold Reform Act 1967 A further statutory exclusion arises under the Leasehold Reform Act 1967.[18] No overriding interest may ever be claimed in respect of any notice served by a qualifying tenant in support of his right to purchase a freehold or long leasehold title in property currently occupied by him.[19]

(iii) 'Preserved right to buy' On the fulfilment of certain conditions a 'secure tenant' in the public rented sector has a statutory right to purchase a freehold or a long leasehold estate in the property occupied by him.[20] Following the commencement of the Housing and Planning Act 1986, in the event of any disposal of that property to a private sector landlord the tenant's 'preserved right to buy' may be protected by the entry of a minor interest against the

---

13 Unreported, 19 May 1980 ([1982] Conv 239 (P.H. Kenny)). See also *Hua Chaio Commercial Bank Ltd v Chiaphua Industries Ltd* [1987] 1 AC 99 at 112D-113C (post, p 524).
14 See also *N.L.S. Pty Ltd v Hughes* (1966) 120 CLR 583 at 588ff.
15 Post, p 803.
16 Land Registration Act 1925, s 86(2).
17 The Law Commission has recently expressed the view that the exclusion of settled land beneficial interests from section 70(1)(g) is unjustifiable, not least because a strict settlement may sometimes be created informally and quite unintentionally in the context of 'family arrangements' (post, p 803). See Law Com No 158, para 2.69.
18 Post, p 725.
19 Leasehold Reform Act 1967, s 5(5).
20 Post, p 733.

register of the existing landlord's title.[1] However, if the 'preserved right to buy' is not duly protected in this way, it becomes ineffective against the new private sector landlord and is statutorily excluded from the category of overriding interests 'notwithstanding that the qualifying person is in actual occupation of the land'.[2]

(e) The 'rights' must have been enforceable at the date of transfer

Recent caselaw has also emphasised another implicit—but fairly obvious—limitation on the kinds of claim which may give rise to an overriding interest under section 70(1)(g). The operation of this paragraph necessarily presupposes some kind of transfer or dealing with a registered title, for its general effect is to render the pre-existing 'rights' of occupiers just as enforceable after the transfer as they were before. The use of the word 'rights' in this context requires not only that the relevant interest must have been in existence before the dealing, but also that it must, immediately before the dealing, have been enforceable as against the particular purchaser concerned, since otherwise it could not, quoad this purchaser, be meaningfully described as a 'right' at all for the purpose of section 70(1)(g).

Thus section 70(1)(g) cannot protect an occupier's interest against a subsequent transferee or chargee if the priority otherwise accorded the occupier's interest has been waived or diminished in advance of the relevant dealing with the registered title. In *Paddington Building Society v Mendelsohn,*[3] for instance, a registered title was purchased in the name of S, the purchase moneys being provided partly by S's mother, M, and partly through a mortgage loan advanced by P. M was clearly a beneficial tenant in common behind an implied trust of the registered title (see *Fig.* 16), and she moved into joint occupation of the property with S and his girl friend during the interim between the conveyance and P's registration of its charge over the property.

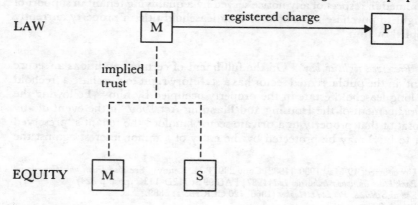

Fig. 16

---

1 Housing Act 1985, Sch 9A, para 5(2), as supplied by Housing and Planning Act 1986, s 8(2), Sch 2.

2 Housing Act 1985, Sch 9A, para 6(1(b), as supplied by Housing and Planning Act 1986, s 8(2), Sch 2.

3 (1985) 50 P & CR 244.

M later claimed that she had thereby acquired an overriding interest under section 70(1)(g) which was binding on P. The Court of Appeal held, however, that since M had both known and intended at the date of purchase that there was to be a charge in favour of P, the 'only possible intention to impute to the parties' was an intention that M's rights were to be 'subject to the rights' of P.[4] It then followed that M, having impliedly conceded priority to P, no longer retained at the date of P's registration of its charge any 'rights' as against P which were capable of protection under section 70(1)(g).[5] As Browne-Wilkinson LJ observed, '[i]f the rights of the person in actual occupation are not under the general law such as to give any priority over the holder of the registered estate, there is nothing in section 70 which changes such rights into different and bigger rights'.[6]

(5) Nature of 'actual occupation' for the purpose of section 70(1)(g)

Section 70(1)(g) affords protection to the rights of every person in 'actual occupation' of the land transferred or charged. The meaning of 'actual occupation' for this purpose must be sought in the caselaw, and raises difficulties similar to those found in connection with any statutory requirement of occupation or residence.[7]

(a) A primarily factual criterion

The definition of 'actual occupation' arose significantly for the first time in *Hodgson v Marks*.[8] Here H had been the owner of her house in fee simple. After the death of her second husband, she took in E as her lodger and soon came to regard him as a man of substance. She entrusted him with the management of her affairs, and at his suggestion executed a voluntary transfer of her registered title in his favour. E was duly registered as proprietor, the parties having

---

4   (1985) 50 P & CR 244 at 247. M had not signed the charge in favour of P, but as Mary Welstead has pointed out, '[i]nstead of the onus falling on the *purchaser* to investigate potential equitable claims, the onus seems to have shifted to the equitable owner to declare his rights to any purchaser of whom *he* has notice. If he does not so declare them he is deemed to have conceded priority to the purchaser...' (see [1985] CLJ 354 at 355). For evidence of the same approach in unregistered land, see *Bristol and West Building Society v Henning* [1985] 1 WLR 778 at 781G–782G (post, p 860).

5   For criticism of this application of the concept of estoppel, see Chapter 25 (post, p 860).

6   (1985) 50 P & CR 244 at 248. See also *E.S. Schwab & Co Ltd v McCarthy* (1976) 31 P & CR 196 at 205; *City of London Building Society v Flegg* [1987] 2 WLR 1266 at 1285E–F per Lord Oliver of Aylmerton.

7   Similar problems arise, for instance, in determining whether someone is in rateable occupation of property (see *Routhan v Arun DC* [1982] QB 502; *Locker v Stockport MBC* (1984) 83 LGR 652), or is 'resident' at Greenham Common for the purpose of inclusion on the electoral register (see *Hipperson v Newbury District Electoral Registration Officer* [1985] QB 1060). The law of landlord and tenant is bedevilled by requirements of continued residence (post, pp 990, 1008, 1064). Whether a person has been 'ordinarily resident' for the purpose of eligibility for a student grant has likewise provided a focus for controversy (see *R v Barnet LBC, ex parte Nilish Shah* [1983] 2 AC 309). In *University College, London v Newman* (1986) *The Times*, 8 January, the Court of Appeal held that a New Zealander who had spent most of three years 'bumming around' Europe had satisfactorily established that he had been 'ordinarily resident' in the European Community throughout this period.

8   [1971] Ch 892. See (1971) 35 Conv (NS) 225 (I. Leeming); (1972) 88 LQR 14 (J.L. Barton); (1973) 36 MLR 25 (R.H. Maudsley).

reached a verbal understanding that the transfer was simply nominal and that H should remain the real owner of the property. H and E continued to live together in the house after the transfer. However, E later dishonestly sold and transferred the legal estate to M without the knowledge or concurrence of H (see *Fig.* 17). E then died, and the present litigation concerned H's claim that her rights were protected against M by virtue of section 70(1)(g).

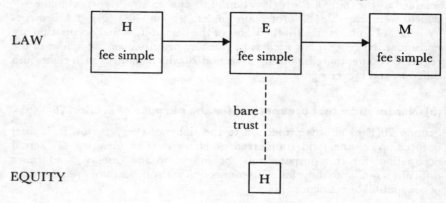

Fig. 17

It was accepted both by Ungoed-Thomas J and by the Court of Appeal that before the transfer to M, E had held the registered title on trust for H.[9] The major question now in dispute was whether H could assert her equitable rights as a trust beneficiary against the new registered proprietor, M. At the date when M presented his transfer document for registration,[10] H was of course still residing in the property.

(i) A test of 'actual and apparent occupation'   At first instance Ungoed-Thomas J held that H had not been in 'actual occupation' within the meaning of section 70(1)(g). He construed 'actual occupation' in the present context as connoting 'actual and apparent occupation...occupation by act recognisable as such', having taken the view that any other construction, by subjecting a purchaser to the rights of occupiers irrespective of notice, would mean that section 70(1)(g) had become 'not a form of notice at all, but its negation'.[11]

On the present facts it was clear that M had known of the existence of H when he contracted to purchase the property from E; he had seen H coming up the garden path on one occasion when he visited the property prior to the transfer. He had assumed that H was E's wife and that as such she had no

---

9   It was found that H had intended to retain the beneficial interest in the property, and that the original transfer had therefore brought about a resulting trust of the legal estate in favour of H ([1971] Ch 892 at 906D, 933C, G). H was not precluded from asserting the existence of such a trust vis à vis E, since resulting trusts are exempted from the requirements of formality normally imposed by Law of Property Act 1925, s 53(1) (post, p 243). Compare, however, *Thwaites v Ryan* [1984] VR 65 at 93.

10   Ante, p 176.

11   [1971] Ch 892 at 915C. Ungoed-Thomas J had proceeded on the premise that section 70(1)(g) was deliberately enacted as the statutory equivalent in registered land of the equitable doctrine of notice in unregistered land ([1971] Ch 892 at 915C-G).

beneficial interest in the property.[12] There was even some evidence to suggest that E had dishonestly attempted to implant such an impression in M's mind. Nevertheless Ungoed-Thomas J held that H had not been in 'actual occupation' for the purpose of section 70(1)(g), in that it would not have been apparent to a purchaser from the mere fact of her presence on the property that she was beneficially entitled.[13]

(ii) A test of physical fact　The ruling at first instance in *Hodgson v Marks* was reversed on appeal, the Court of Appeal holding that H's beneficial interest ranked as an overriding interest.[14] Russell LJ, while declining to 'lay down a code or catalogue of situations in which a person other than the vendor should be held to be…in actual occupation of registered land for the purposes of section 70(1)(g)',[15] had no doubt that on the present facts H had indeed been in 'actual occupation' of the property. The Court of Appeal construed this vital phrase quite literally, as connoting a mere physical presence on the part of persons other than the vendor.

In support of this conclusion, Russell LJ pointed to the general principle of common law and statute 'that a person in occupation is protected in his rights by that occupation'. In his view, a purchaser 'must pay heed to anyone in occupation if he is to be sure of getting a good title'. In thus placing the onus of enquiry firmly on the purchaser, Russell LJ declined to accept any sweeping proposition of law to the effect that the rights of any person who is in occupation will be overridden whenever the vendor is, or appears to be, also in occupation. It must, he said, 'depend on the circumstances, and a wise purchaser or lender will take no risks. Indeed, however wise he may be, he may have no ready opportunity of finding out; but nevertheless the law will protect the occupier.'[16]

It seems therefore in the aftermath of *Hodgson v Marks* that 'actual occupation' in the sense of section 70(1)(g) is to be construed largely as a matter of sheer physical fact. As Lord Denning MR observed in *Williams & Glyn's Bank Ltd v Boland*,[17] '"actual occupation" is matter of fact, not matter of law'. This approach was upheld by the House of Lords in the same case, Lord Scarman noting that, in section 70(1)(g), 'the statute has substituted a plain factual situation for the uncertainties of notice, actual or constructive, as the determinant of an overriding interest.'[18]

(b) Notional or symbolic 'actual occupation'

In spite of the apparently definitive ruling in *Williams & Glyn's Bank Ltd v Boland*, the concept of 'actual occupation' is still beset by certain difficulties which may make it almost impossible to determine whether title is being transferred subject to the adverse claims of persons in occupation.[19] The

---

12　This assumption was still current at the time of *Hodgson v Marks* but is no longer a safe one. See *Williams & Glyn's Bank Ltd v Boland* [1981] AC 487 (post, p 843).
13　Compare *Caunce v Caunce* [1969] 1 WLR 286 at 293G-294A (post, p 835).
14　[1971] Ch 892 at 934G-935A.
15　[1971] Ch 892 at 932C-D.
16　[1971] Ch 892 at 932D.
17　[1979] Ch 312 at 332E.
18　[1981] AC 487 at 511E-F.
19　For discussion of some of these difficulties, see Chapter 25 (post, p 829).

concept of 'actual occupation' cannot, for example, sensibly require uninterrupted personal presence on the land concerned. It is clear that some kinds of temporary absence will not detract from the 'actual occupation' which may be asserted by a person who is normally in residence. In this context the courts have applied something akin to the notions of *corpus possessionis* and *animus revertendi* which have become familiar in the law of landlord and tenant.[20] In effect, 'actual occupation' is regarded as subsisting so long as the temporarily absent occupier can point to some physical evidence or symbol of continued residence coupled with an intention to return to the property.[1]

(i) The family home   In *Chhokar v Chhokar*,[2] H held the registered legal title in the matrimonial home on a statutory trust for sale for himself and his wife, W, in equal shares. H agreed secretly to transfer that title at an undervalue to an acquaintance, P, H's intention being to rid himself of his wife while extracting for himself as much as he could of the outstanding equity in the matrimonial home.[3] H and P deliberately arranged that completion of the transfer should occur while W was in hospital having a baby. Immediately after the transfer of title, H disappeared with the balance of the proceeds of the sale and P advertised the property for sale at its full market value. When W emerged from hospital clutching her new-born child, she found that the locks had been changed and that she was denied access to her own home.[4]

Notwithstanding that W had clearly been absent from the property when P's new title was registered, Ewbank J regarded the continuing presence of W's furniture in the house as a notional or token occupation which was quite sufficient to constitute 'actual occupation' for the purpose of section 70(1)(g).[5] In view of W's consistent intention to resume residence, Ewbank J held without hesitation that she had an overriding interest binding on P.[6] It was somewhat

20   Post, pp 729, 1008.
1   See *Hoggett v Hoggett* (1980) 39 P & CR 121 at 130, where 'occupation' was not regarded as necessarily interrupted merely by the fact that the occupier might have gone into hospital for a few days, or gone on a weekend visit to a friend, or gone out shopping for a few hours (post, p 1010). In *Strand Securities Ltd v Caswell* [1965] Ch 958 at 981B, Lord Denning MR thought that section 70(1)(g) would be satisfied by vicarious occupation established through 'a servant or caretaker'. Compare, however, Russell LJ (at 985A-B), and see Law Com No 158, para 2.57.
2   [1984] FLR 313.
3   In the words of Ewbank J, the transaction between H and P was similar to that which might have taken place 'in relation to property...asserted to have fallen off the back of a lorry' ([1984] FLR 313 at 318A-B). P was fully aware of H's fraudulent intent.
4   She later did secure a re-entry into the premises but was then violently evicted by 'heavies' employed by P.
5   The *Chhokar* ruling represents a sharp contrast with the position of a wife in the family home before the decision of the House of Lords in *Williams & Glyn's Bank Ltd v Boland* [1981] AC 487. In *Bird v Syme-Thomson* [1979] 1 WLR 440 at 444A, D-E, Templeman J held that a wife who was physically resident in her home was not in 'actual occupation' of it since she was 'only there as a shadow of occupation of the owner'. The decision in *Chhokar* demonstrates that within a space of five years the courts' readiness to disregard a wife's occupation of the home as being merely vicarious had been replaced by a willingness to treat her occupation as 'actual' even though in most other legal contexts it would have been described as 'constructive' only.
6   [1984] FLR 313 at 317F. (This conclusion was not challenged in the subsequent appeal). Compare *Strand Securities Ltd v Caswell* [1965] Ch 958 at 985A-B, where Russell LJ was not prepared to accept that a valid claim of 'actual occupation' could be founded either on the presence of furniture or relatives or on the retention of a key by an absent occupier.

ironic that, before the litigation commenced, W had managed to return into residence in the home with her two children. Her husband then reappeared and was reconciled, and the family thereafter lived together happily much to the discomfiture of P, who ended up owning a house which he could neither occupy[7] nor sell[8] and from which he could derive no rental income.[9]

(ii) Other forms of property   It is quite feasible that an extended concept of 'actual occupation' may likewise affect other forms of property. In *Kling v Keston Properties Ltd,*[10] P was granted an option to purchase a garage which was later let on a long lease to D. In the dispute which followed, D parked her car across the entrance to this garage. This malicious action had the effect of trapping inside the garage a car belonging to P's wife which D plainly regarded as being wrongfully there. This being the impasse reached at the date of registration of D's lease, Vinelott J held that the enforced presence of the car in the garage constituted a form of 'actual occupation' of that garage on behalf of P, thus rendering his option an overriding interest binding on D.[11]

Broadly though the concept of 'actual occupation' may be construed, there are some factual circumstances to which it cannot apply. Mere user of a right of way cannot, for instance, constitute 'actual occupation' of the land over which that right of way is exercised.[12] A claim of easement necessarily implies some limited form of user,[13] and the intermittent exercise of a right of way simply lacks the intensity of user which even the minimal factual requirements of section 70(1)(g) seem to demand.

(6) Enquiry under section 70(1)(g)

Pursuant to section 70(1)(g) the rights of every person in actual occupation constitute an overriding interest 'save where enquiry is made of such person and the rights are not disclosed.' Clearly it was not the intendment of the legislature that this provision should preserve rights whose existence has been dishonestly concealed from a transferee or chargee of the land concerned. It is equally plain, however, that section 70(1)(g) imposes on the purchaser a responsibility to ensure that any person in actual occupation is asked 'what rights he or she has in the land'.[14]

---

7   Post, p 303.
8   Post, p 821.
9   Post, p 309.
10   (1983) 49 P & CR 212. See [1985] Conv 406 (J.E.M.).
11   (1983) 49 P & CR 212 at 218f. Vinelott J thought that the result would have been the same even if the car had not been trapped inside the garage. Even an intermittent user of the garage 'in the ordinary way' would have been sufficient to establish 'actual occupation'. Compare, however, *Epps v Esso Petroleum Co Ltd* [1973] 1 WLR 1071 at 1080A (regular parking of car on strip of land held not to be 'actual occupation').
12   *Celsteel Ltd v Alton House Holdings Ltd* [1985] 1 WLR 204 at 219E. See also Law Com No 158, para 2.57.
13   Post, p 657.
14   *Winkworth v Edward Baron Development Co Ltd* (1986) 52 P & CR 67 at 77 per Nourse LJ, who added that it was not sufficient for the purpose of section 70(1)(g) merely to ask all occupiers to confirm in writing that they held 'as bare licensees and not by virtue of any tenancy or lease'. The Court of Appeal's ruling in *Winkworth* was later reversed by the House of Lords on a different point which made section 70(1)(g) irrelevant ([1986] 1 WLR 1512). See Chapter 10 (post, p 288).

(a) Who must make the enquiry?

Section 70(1)(g) does not demand that the relevant enquiry necessarily be made by the purchaser of the registered title.[15] It seems that the relevant enquiry may be made by an agent. The terms of section 70(1)(g) are indeed disturbingly vague: there is no indication as to precisely when enquiry and disclosure ought to occur.[16]

(b) Of whom must the enquiry be made?

It is important to read the proviso to section 70(1)(g) with some care. In order to take the land free of overriding interests, a purchaser must make enquiry of the person whose rights would otherwise comprise an overriding interest.[17] In *Hodgson v Marks*[18] M may have made some enquiry as to the precise status or entitlement of H, but since he directed his enquiry only towards E, his enquiry was utterly irrelevant for the purpose of complying with section 70(1)(g). In order to guarantee immunity from the overriding interest, M would have had to make enquiry of H herself—and this he did not do. In the words of Russell LJ, 'reliance on the untrue ipse dixit of the vendor will not suffice'.[19] A heavy onus is often placed on the purchaser since he must make enquiry of persons whose occupation may not be at all apparent.[20] However, as Russell LJ stressed, the law will protect the occupier of registered land irrespective of the difficulty facing the purchaser.[1]

(7) The dual status of minor and overriding interests

Most schemes for the registration of land interests operate ultimately on the basis of two simple rules. *First,* if a registrable interest has in fact been duly entered on the register, it is binding on all purchasers regardless of whether they inspect the register. *Second,* a registrable right becomes void and unenforceable against purchasers if it is not entered on the register. In the latter

---

15   See [1980] Conv 161.
16   Much criticism has been directed at the fact that the scope of the enquiry enjoined by section 70(1)(g) is not even limited to any concept of 'reasonable' enquiry. The Law Commission has now endorsed the view that the statutory proviso concerning enquiry 'is in practice worthless...[and] performs no useful function' (Law Com No 158, para 2.59). Accordingly the Commission has recommended that this proviso be discontinued and that all categories of overriding interest (whether or not arising under section 70(1)(g)) be made explicitly subject to 'the jurisdiction of the courts to postpone them as against subsequent purchasers and lenders on the general grounds of fraud or estoppel' (ibid, para 2.75).
17   In *Winkworth v Edward Baron Development Co Ltd* (1986) 52 P & CR 67 at 77, Nourse LJ was prepared to accept that in most cases enquiry may properly be made of a solicitor acting for the person in actual occupation.
18   [1971] Ch 892 (ante, p 185).
19   [1971] Ch 892 at 932D. It is not enough to make enquiry of the hall porter in a block of flats as to the potential rights of occupiers of those flats. Such a porter is the agent of the landlord rather than any of the tenants, and has no authority to make (or withhold) any relevant reply under section 70(1)(g) (see *Kling v Keston Properties Ltd* (1983) 49 P & CR 212 at 220).
20   The onus placed on the transferee or chargee becomes even greater in cases of multiple occupation in the family context. See Chapter 25 (post, p 852).
 1   Ante, p 187. A purchaser of registered land is well advised to have written proof of enquiry (see [1980] Conv 361 (J. Martin)).

case it matters not that the purchaser has actual knowledge of the unprotected interest from another source.

These straightforward principles apply in the context both of registration of land charges[2] and registration of title.[3] The underlying motive is readily understandable—the rules are clear-cut and easily applicable. The medium of the public register serves as an effective form of notice. Moreover, the statutory sanction of voidness in the case of non-protection ensures that the register—whether it be the Land Charges Register or the Land Register—contains an accurate, current and comprehensive record of the interests affecting the land concerned.

(a) The existence of an overlap

It is against this background of principle that it appears particularly strange that the Land Registration Act 1925 should permit an area of overlap between minor and overriding interests in registered land. As the law of registered land currently stands, it is possible for the owners of certain kinds of equitable interest to claim a dual protected status in respect of their rights. Such equitable owners may assert priority over purchasers of the registered title *either* on the ground that they have duly protected their rights by the entry of minor interests on the register *or* on the quite different ground that their rights, taken in conjunction with 'actual occupation' under section 70(1)(g), qualify as overriding interests under that provision.[4]

The existence of this potential overlap was finally confirmed by the House of Lords in *Williams & Glyn's Bank Ltd v Boland*.[5] Here Lord Wilberforce, although impressed at first by the 'formidable' argument that the categories of minor interest and overriding interest are mutually exclusive, was finally convinced that there is no 'firm dividing line, or...unbridgeable gulf, between minor interests and overriding interests'.[6] He pointed to previous decisions in which potentially minor interests had found protection as overriding interests,[7] and regarded these decisions as confirming that 'the fact of occupation enables protection of the latter to extend to what without it would be the former.'[8]

(b) The undesirability of an overlap

It is therefore quite possible that a failure to protect a minor interest by entry on the register—far from incurring the penalty of voidness—may indeed have the paradoxical result of reinforcing that interest as an overriding interest.[9] It may

---

2 Ante, p 110.
3 Ante, p 163.
4 Ante, p 172.
5 [1981] AC 487 (post, pp 372, 843).
6 [1981] AC 487 at 508A.
7 See *Bridges v Mees* [1957] Ch 475 (ante, p 174) and *Hodgson v Marks* [1971] Ch 892 (ante, p 185).
8 [1981] AC 487 at 508A. Lord Scarman (at 512A) agreed that 'overriding interests and minor interests are, as categories, exclusive of each other', but found 'no logical difficulty in the association of a minor interest with another factor (ie actual occupation) being, qua association, an overriding interest.'
9 An overriding interest is, by definition, one which does not appear as a minor interest on the face of the register (ante, p 170).

appear strange that a scheme of registration can so operate that rights which are left unprotected qua minor interest are, in default of such protection, preserved as overriding interests.[10] It simply seems to be elementary good sense that any scheme directed towards securing the registration of interests should firmly attach disadvantage to a negligent failure to register. The inappropriateness of the overlap between minor and overriding interests is intensified when comparison is made between registered and unregistered land: it is quite often the case that exactly similar problems of land law priority result in diametrically different outcomes.[11]

(c) Future reform of section 70(1)(g)

The implications of the overlap between minor and overriding interests have inevitably attracted the attention of the Law Commission. Some consideration was given initially to the possibility that the categories of overriding interest might be abrogated in their entirety,[12] but the Commission has now concluded in favour of a much more limited reform of this area of the law.

Although intensely aware of the difficulties caused by the dual protection of interests within the registered land scheme, the Commission in its most recent proposals has attempted to strike some kind of social balance between the integrity of the register and the legitimate claims of actual occupiers of registered land.[13] Motivated by the benevolent view that 'it is not always reasonable to expect or sensible to require protection by registration',[14] the Commission has recommended the substantial retention of overriding interest protection for the rights of occupiers. It is true that by way of partial compromise the Commission simultaneously proposed that the range of potentially overriding interests be cut back by the exclusion of the rights of persons in receipt of the rents and profits of registered land.[15] However, the ultimate resolution of the tension between owners and occupiers of registered land was felt by the Commission to lie in a much more generous extension of statutory indemnity to those registered proprietors who are bound by overriding interests.[16]

---

10 See eg *Kling v Keston Properties Ltd* (1983) 49 P & CR 212 at 222 per Vinelott J ('It is disquieting that the system of land registration...should be so framed that a person acquiring an interest in registered land may find his interest subject to an option or right of pre-emption which has not been registered and notwithstanding that there is no person other than the vendor in apparent occupation of the property and that careful inspection and enquiry has failed to reveal anything which might give the purchaser any reason to suspect that someone other than the vendor had any interests in or rights over the property').

11 Compare eg *Hollington Brothers Ltd v Rhodes* [1951] 2 TLR 691 (ante, p 117) with *Grace Rymer Investments Ltd v Waite* [1958] Ch 831 (ante, p 181). In the former case an unregistered equitable lease in unregistered land was held to be void against a purchaser of the superior title, even though the purchaser had the clearest of express notice of the tenant's rights. In the latter case, the equivalent but unprotected estate contract was held to be an overriding interest. See generally Law Com No 158, para 2.5.

12 Ante, p 171.

13 Post, p 201.

14 Law Com No 158, para 2.64 (post, p 201).

15 Ante, p 178. Although minded to restrict the categories of overriding interest wherever possible, the Commission felt compelled in one respect to increase the overlap between minor and overriding interests. The Commission recommended that overriding interest protection be extended to settled land beneficial interests (ante, p 183).

16 Post, p 202.

8. REGISTERED CHARGES

A further category of right which may be created under the Land Registration Act 1925 is the 'registered charge'. Subject to any entry to the contrary on the register, the proprietor of registered land is statutorily empowered to mortgage that land by deed or otherwise in any manner which would have been permissible if the land had been unregistered.[17] It is the 'registered charge' which provides the standard method of mortgaging registered land. Such a charge, unless made by lease or sublease, takes effect as a 'charge by way of legal mortgage'.[18] A registered charge is therefore a legal interest which is capable of creation and disposition by means only of a 'registered disposition'.[19] As such, the registered charge can never qualify as a registrable interest, minor interest or overriding interest, and becomes fully effective only when the chargee is entered as the 'proprietor' of the charge on the relevant register of title.[20] Unless and until the charge is registered as a disposition, the chargee has an equitable interest only.[1]

Upon registration the chargee is issued with a charge certificate and, while the charge remains in effect, the chargor's land certificate is deposited in the Land Registry as security against further dealings by the estate owner.[2] Subject to any contrary indication on the register, registered charges on the same land rank as between themselves according to the order in which they are entered on the register, and not according to the order in which they are created.[3]

9. RECTIFICATION AND INDEMNITY

In spite of the much vaunted claim that an 'absolute title' is the ultimately secure form of title, it is an inherent feature of the Land Registration Act 1925 that no title registered under its provisions is ever quite absolute. Even a proprietor with supposedly 'absolute title' is liable to have the register of title rectified to his prejudice in certain circumstances. A power of rectification may be exercised by the court in eight specified instances, in six of which a like power of rectification is vested in the Registrar himself.[4]

There is nowadays increasing recognition of the close link which exists

---

17 Land Registration Act 1925, s 106(1).
18 Land Registration Act 1925, s 27(1).
19 Land Registration Act 1925, ss 3(xxii), 18(4), 21(4).
20 Land Registration Act 1925, s 26(1). It is a prerequisite to registration of the charge that the land certificate be produced to the Land Registry (T.B.F. Ruoff and R.B. Roper, op cit, p 794).
1   Land Registration Act 1925, s 106(2); *E.S. Schwab & Co Ltd v McCarthy* (1976) 31 P & CR 196 at 201, 212. Until completed by registration, the unregistered charge is a minor interest and is protectible by the entry of a notice or caution (Land Registration Act 1925, s 106(3)). A mortgage of an equitable interest (eg that of an equitable co-owner under a trust for sale) can never constitute a registered charge, but is capable of protection by entry of a caution (see *Elias v Mitchell* [1972] Ch 652 at 664B–D, post, p 371).
2   Land Registration Act 1925, s 65.
3   Land Registration Act 1925, s 29.
4   The Law Commission has suggested that the law be amended so that the Registrar and the court have identical jurisdiction in the matter of rectification (see Law Com No 158, para 3.19).

between rectification and the statutory categories of overriding interest. Rectification and overriding interests share the feature that they each provide a means of asserting an unregistered interest against the proprietor of registered land.[5] Together they merely represent different ways in which reliance on the register may ultimately prove to be misplaced.[6] The most important distinctions between these two large inroads into the principle of indefeasibility rest on the fact that overriding interests bind automatically whereas rectification is an essentially discretionary remedy. Moreover, rectification can affect any aspect of a registered title whilst overriding interests arise in relation only to a somewhat restricted list of rights.[7] However, even these differences do not obscure the reality that the future development of the law of registered land is likely to call for a greater harmonisation of the overriding interest provisions of the 1925 Act with the law relating to rectification and indemnity.[8]

(1) Grounds of rectification

The circumstances in which rectification may be obtained are enumerated largely in section 82(1) of the Land Registration Act 1925.[9] As soon as any one or more of the statutorily specified circumstances is shown to exist, there arises 'at least theoretical discretion to rectify any part of the register'.[10] The relevant circumstances include the following cases.

(a) Subsisting overriding interest

The court alone has jurisdiction to rectify the register of title where it has been held that some person is entitled to an interest or charge which is not currently on the register.[11] The most obvious example of this ground of rectification occurs where rectification is required in order to enter a subsisting overriding interest upon the register.[12]

(b) Interest wrongly omitted or included in the register

The court again has an exclusive discretion, exercisable on the application of any aggrieved person, to order rectification either for the purpose of entering on the register an interest which has been wrongly omitted by the Registrar on first registration,[13] or for the purpose of excluding from the register an interest which was wrongly included.

---

5   See Law Com No 158, para 1.4.
6   'In this respect, rectification is also a crack in the mirror principle' (Law Com No 158, para 2.10).
7   See Law Com No 158, para 1.4.
8   See Law Com No 158, para 2.10.
9   See also Land Registration Rules 1925, rr 13 (clerical errors), 14. It seems that the power to rectify under rule 14 is exercisable only by the Registrar and not by the court (see Law Com No 158, para 3.3).
10 *Argyle Building Society v Hammond* (1985) 49 P & CR 148 at 162 per Slade LJ, who also pointed out (at 157) that the jurisdiction to rectify 'plainly extends' to all the parts of register of title, ie, to the Property Register, the Proprietorship Register and the Charges Register alike.
11 Land Registration Act 1925, s 82(1)(a).
12 See eg *Chowood Ltd v Lyall (No 2)* [1930] 2 Ch 156 at 166.
13 See eg *Calgary and Edmonton Land Co Ltd v Discount Bank (Overseas) Ltd* [1971] 1 WLR 81 at 85A-C.

(c) Consent

The court or the Registrar may rectify the register in any case and at any time with the consent of all persons interested.[14]

(d) Entry obtained by fraud

Rectification may also be ordered where either the court or the Registrar is satisfied that an existing entry in the register has been 'obtained by fraud'.[15] In *Re Leighton's Conveyance*,[16] for instance, a daughter had fraudulently procured and registered a disposition of land from her mother, who had been unaware of the significance of the transaction. In these circumstances Luxmoore J was prepared to rectify the register by reinstating the mother as registered proprietor, although he declined to grant any rectification in respect of registered charges which the daughter had created while she was registered as proprietor.[17]

(e) Double registrations

The court and the registrar both have power to rectify the register where two or more persons have, by mistake, been registered as proprietors of the same registered estate or charge.[18]

(f) Wrongful registration of mortgagee

So long as a right of redemption currently subsists in the mortgagor, either the court or the registrar may order rectification where a mortgagee has been registered as proprietor of the land itself rather than merely as proprietor of a charge affecting the land.[19]

(g) Default of title

Rectification may be ordered by either the court or the Registrar where a legal estate has been registered in the name of a person who, if the land had not been registered, would not have been the estate owner.[20] This ground of rectification is frequently relevant in cases of adverse possession of registered land. In *Chowood Ltd v Lyall (No 2)*,[1] for example, title to an area of land had been registered in the name of a transferee, although the land in question had been adversely possessed by a third party for a sufficient period to extinguish the

---

14 Land Registration Act 1925, s 82(1)(c).
15 Land Registration Act 1925, s 82(1)(d).
16 [1936] 1 All ER 667.
17 [1936] 1 All ER 667 at 673. See also *Argyle Building Society v Hammond* (1985) 49 P & CR 148 at 158ff. In *Peffer v Rigg* [1977] 1 WLR 285 at 294G (ante, p 166), Graham J granted rectification of D^2's title under section 82(1), although he did not specify under which particular head he did so. It is possible that the circumstances present in this case may have constituted the case of an entry 'obtained by fraud'. See [1977] CLJ 227 at 231 (D.J. Hayton).
18 Land Registration Act 1925, s 82(1)(e).
19 Land Registration Act 1925, s 82(1)(f).
20 Land Registration Act 1925, s 82(1)(g).
 1 [1930] 2 Ch 156.

transferor's original title. Rectification was ordered in favour of a squatter who had acquired a good common law title by adverse possession.[2]

(h) Residual ground of rectification

Either the court or the Registrar may rectify the register where 'by reason of any error or omission in the register, or by reason of any entry made under a mistake, it may be deemed just to rectify the register'.[3] It is this provision which ultimately confirms that the jurisdiction to rectify the register is available on an extremely broad discretionary basis.[4]

Recent years have seen the emergence of an increasingly liberal approach to the exercise of the discretion to rectify. In *Orakpo v Manson Investments Ltd,*[5] for instance, P had executed a number of legal charges over his properties in favour of D as security for loans made to him by D. In each case D registered these charges against P's title, but it was held subsequently that the charges were unenforceable under section 6 of the Moneylenders Act 1927 and were not therefore proper entries on the register. D argued successfully that it was entitled, by subrogation, to unpaid vendor's liens in respect of the disputed transactions. Although the case was ultimately decided on other grounds by the House of Lords,[6] it was significant that the Court of Appeal expressed the court's discretion to rectify the register in wider terms than had hitherto been usual. Buckley LJ stated bluntly that 'if the present entries on the register do not reflect the true position, the register is open to rectification'.[7] He pointed out that the legal charges executed by P pursuant to the loan agreements required cancellation (which in itself would necessitate rectification), but saw no reason to preclude D from seeking entry on the register, by way of rectification, of suitable notices, cautions or restrictions to protect its subrogated rights. Buckley LJ considered that section 82(1)(a) and (h) might be applicable to the circumstances of the present case, indicating with particular reference to the latter ground of rectification that 'if there is an omission in the register of some entry which ought to be there for the protection' of D, then it was open to D simply to apply for rectification of the register to effect the necessary entry.[8]

This broad view of the basis for rectification has since been endorsed by the Law Commission. The Commission has recommended that rectification should be available wherever the register (whether through error or omission) 'does not reflect...the title to the land according to the rules of land law which

2   [1930] 2 Ch 156 at 168f.
3   Land Registration Act 1925, s 82(1)(h). See eg *Chowood Ltd v Lyall (No 2)* [1930] 2 Ch 156 at 165ff.
4   See *Argyle Building Society v Hammond* (1985) 49 P & CR 148 at 158ff. 'On the face of it, the paragraph appears wide enough to render all the other specific paragraphs largely superfluous' (Law Com No 158, para 3.7).
5   [1977] 1 WLR 347. See (1977) 41 Conv (NS) 210 (F.R. Crane).
6   [1978] AC 95. See (1977) 41 Conv (NS) 354 (F.R. Crane).
7   [1977] 1 WLR 347 at 360E.
8   [1977] 1 WLR 347 at 361A. Goff LJ was likewise of the opinion that D would be 'clearly entitled to have the register rectified under section 82 of the 1925 Act', but did not state any specific head under section 82(1) as being applicable ([1977] 1 WLR 347 at 370B-C).

prevail apart from registration of title'.[9] In the Commission's view, the only precondition is that such rectification must be 'just in all the circumstances', particularly where it is shown that there was fraud in obtaining an entry in the register, or if the transferee or grantee 'lacked good faith or did not give value'.[10]

(2) Effect of rectification

When the register is rectified by the removal of the name of the existing proprietor and the substitution of another person's name, the consequence is to vest the legal title in the new registered proprietor.[11] The former proprietor is thereafter divested of title, although it may be open to him to seek an indemnity in respect of any loss suffered by him by reason of the rectification.

Section 82(2) of the Land Registration Act 1925 provides that the register 'may be rectified...notwithstanding that the rectification may affect any estates, rights, charges, or interests acquired or protected by registration, or by any entry on the register, or otherwise.' This provision appears, in its express terms, to authorise orders for rectification which are not merely effective to rectify the title in question, but which also operate adversely upon the interests of innocent third parties whose rights are already duly protected by entry on the register or are supposedly overriding. However, the case law has not consistently accorded this extensive interpretation to section 82(2) and the exact scope of the provision remains unclear.

In *Freer v Unwins Ltd*,[12] for instance, a register of title was rectified by order of the Chief Land Registrar, by entering on the register notice of restrictive covenants affecting the land which had been wrongly omitted from it at the date of first registration. D was the assignee of a lease in the relevant land which had been granted prior to the rectification of the title, his lease being itself an overriding interest in the land. D had knowledge of the existence of the restrictive covenants but knew also that these covenants had not been protected by entry on the register. When P brought proceedings to enforce the restrictive covenants against D, Walton J held that D was not bound by them. According to Walton J, D's lease must, in accordance with section 19(2) of the Land Registration Act 1925, be deemed to have taken effect as if it were a registered disposition immediately on its being granted. Under section 20(1), therefore, it took effect subject to any entries appearing on the register at that date and subject to overriding interests (if any), but free from all other estates and interests.[13] The lease assigned to D was accordingly unaffected by the subsequent entry on the register of the restrictive covenant relating to the

---

9   Law Com No 158, para 3.34(1).
10   Law Com No 158, para 3.6.
11   Land Registration Act 1925, s 69(1). The right to rectification may itself constitute an overriding interest pursuant to Land Registration Act 1925, s 70(1)(g) (ante, p 181), provided that it is enjoyed in association with actual occupation. See *Blacklocks v J.B. Developments (Godalming) Ltd* [1982] Ch 183 at 196E-F ; [1983] Conv 169, 257.
12   [1976] Ch 288. See [1976] CLJ 211 (D.J. Hayton); (1976) 39 MLR 582 (J.M. Masson); (1976) 92 LQR 338 (R.J. Smith).
13   Ante, p 162. It seems that section 82(2) was not cited to the court (see Law Com No 158, para 3.8).

freehold title.[14] This decision thus provides a surprising instance of rectification in derogation of the rights of a freeholder but without prejudice to the rights of a leaseholder in the same land.[15]

A better example of the more likely intendment of section 82(2) is to be found in *Argyle Building Society v Hammond*.[16] In this case a former proprietor of a registered title alleged that during his absence abroad his title had been fraudulently transferred to his sister and her husband (the present defendants) by a forged instrument of which he knew nothing. The defendants had then charged the land to a building society in consideration of loan moneys which it advanced to them. The Court of Appeal was clear that, by reason of the 'statutory magic' of entry in the register,[17] the transfer (albeit forged) had been effective to vest the registered title in the defendants.[18] The Court ruled, however, that the original proprietor was entitled to rectification not only of the register of the defendants' fraudulently acquired title but also of the Charges Register containing the duly protected charge taken in all good faith by the mortgagee.[19] In the light of section 82(2), Slade LJ disregarded the objection that such a rectification of the Charges Register would deprive the innocent third party of its security.[20] The chargee, on suffering prejudice by reason of the rectification, would be entitled to an indemnity in respect of its loss.[1]

(3) Restrictions on rectification

Certain restrictions are imposed on the right to obtain rectification, largely because it is generally recognised that the unlimited availability of such a

14   [1976] Ch 288 at 298G. If D had been held bound by the restrictive covenants in question, it would have received a statutory indemnity in respect of its loss, and this might have been thought to provide a good ground for holding that D took subject to the unprotected covenants. However, this pragmatic approach was not adopted and the actual decision in *Freer v Unwins Ltd* merely leaves the even more puzzling question as to why title in this case was rectified in the first place. Walton J clearly considered the Registrar's decision in favour of rectification 'a very great surprise' ([1976] Ch 288 at 295B), presumably because the general scheme of the Land Registration Act 1925 is that a transferee (such as the original lessee) takes his interest in registered land free from all third party rights other than overriding interests and those interests which are duly protected by entry (Land Registration Act 1925, s 20(1)). See also [1980] CLJ 380f (D.J. Hayton).

15   The Law Commission has since declined to accept that the power of rectification is as limited as the decision in *Freer v Unwins Ltd* would tend to suggest. In the Commission's view, the court and the Registrar must have 'as full and ample a power of rectification as is needed to achieve justice' (Law Com No 158, para 3.8). The Commission has accordingly recommended that statute should make it absolutely clear that rectification 'may affect estates and interests already registered or protected or any existing overriding interests (ibid, para 3.34(3)).

16   (1985) 49 P & CR 148. See [1985] Conv 135 (A. Sydenham).

17   Ante, p 158.

18   (1985) 49 P & CR 148 at 155 (ante, p 158).

19   (1985) 49 P & CR 148 at 158ff.

20   Slade LJ distinguished *Re Leighton's Conveyance* [1936] 1 All ER 667 (ante, p 195) on the ground that it had not involved an altogether forged disposition of title (as in *Argyle Building Society v Hammond*) but merely a disposition executed by the proprietor herself, 'albeit under a mistake induced by fraud or other sharp practice' ((1985) 49 P & CR 148 at 161ff).

1   Land Registration Act 1925, s 83(4) provides that a 'proprietor of any registered land or charge claiming in good faith under a forged disposition shall, where the register is rectified, be deemed to have suffered loss by reason of such rectification and shall be entitled to be indemnified'.

remedy would be 'productive of future uncertainty and contrary to the raison d'être of registration of title.'[2] It is indeed entirely correct that sympathetic consideration should be given to the reasonable expectations of transferees of registered land who have paid the full purchase price, taken possession and become proprietors in reliance on the register of title. The motivation towards indefeasibility of the registered title is accordingly recognised in section 82(3) of the Land Registration Act 1925,[3] which provides that the register 'shall not be rectified, except for the purpose of giving effect to an overriding interest or an order of the court, so as to affect the title of the proprietor who is in possession...'.[4] Apart from the exceptional cases of the overriding interest and the court order, there are two further exceptions to the general rule that the register may not be rectified to the prejudice of the proprietor 'in possession'. These additional exceptions arise where the proprietor 'has caused or substantially contributed by fraud or lack of proper care' to the error or omission in respect of which rectification is sought,[5] and where 'for any other reason, in any particular case, it is considered that it would be unjust not to rectify the register against him'.[6]

(4) Indemnity

Subject to any contrary statutory provision, 'any person suffering loss by reason of any rectification of the register...shall be entitled to be indemnified.'[7] In addition, where an 'error or omission' has occurred in the register but the register is not rectified, any person suffering loss by reason of that error or omission is likewise entitled to be indemnified.[8] These provisions provide the

---

2   Law Com No 158, para 3.5. As Lord Elwyn-Jones LC declared in Parliament, it is 'important that the entry of a person on the Land Register as the registered proprietor of a piece of land should, so far as possible, be conclusive as to his title' (*Parliamentary Debates, Official Report, House of Lords*, Vol 386 (Session 1976–77), Col 871 (26 July 1977)).

3   In the words of the Law Commission, section 82(3) 'still embodies the best attempt at indefeasibility' (Law Com No 158, para 3.12).

4   The meaning of 'possession' in this context is not wholly clear (see Land Registration Act 1925, s 3(xviii)). It is likely, however, that the term applies only where there is physical possession by the registered proprietor and does not cover the case where the proprietor is merely in receipt of rents and profits derived from the land (see Law Com No 158, para 3.12). The Law Commission has suggested that it would conduce to 'greater consistency with the general and statutory principles of property law and conveyancing' if the apparent protection against rectification conferred by section 82(3) were redrafted 'so as to benefit registered proprietors who were prudent purchasers for value in good faith in actual occupation of the land' (Law Com No 158, para 3.15).

5   Land Registration Act 1925, s 82(3)(a), as substituted by Administration of Justice Act 1977, s 24(b). See *In re 139 High Street Deptford, ex parte British Transport Commission* [1951] Ch 884 at 890ff; *In re Sea View Gardens, Claridge v Tingey* [1967] 1 WLR 134 at 140H-141A.

6   Land Registration Act 1925, s 82(3)(c). See *Epps v Esso Petroleum Co Ltd* [1973] 1 WLR 1071 at 1080F-1083B; [1974] CLJ 60 (S.N. Palk); *Peffer v Rigg* [1977] 1 WLR 285 at 294G. The Law Commission has criticised this exception to the principle of indefeasibility as introducing 'too great an element of uncertainty into the registration system' (Law Com No 158, para 3.16). In the Commission's view, the register should be rectified against a bona fide purchaser for value in actual occupation only in order to give effect to an overriding interest or in favour of a trustee in bankruptcy (ibid, paras 3.13, 3.16, 3.18).

7   Land Registration Act 1925, s 83(1).

8   Land Registration Act 1925, s 83(2). See *Argyle Building Society v Hammond* (1985) 49 P & CR 148 at 158.

basis for the assertion that the scheme of registered title operates on the premise of a state-guaranteed title which is backed by automatic compensation in the event of any failure in the guarantee.[9]

(a) Restrictions on indemnity

The right to receive an indemnity in cases of prejudice is not as unqualified as might at first appear. Where a registered title is rectified to give effect to a subsisting overriding interest, the proprietor is ineligible for compensation. The oddly logical rationale for this exclusion is founded in the legal (though not social or commercial) reality that in such cases the proprietor has not technically suffered any loss. The title which he purchased was at all material times subject to the overriding interest in question; the only new feature in the factual situation is that now, for the first time, the proprietor knows about the qualification on his title. Thus, according to the unsympathetic argument, there can be no compensation where there has been no loss: the rectification has merely regularised a pre-existing position.[10] The right to indemnity is also withheld in other circumstances specified in the Land Registration Act 1925, such as the case where an applicant for the statutory indemnity 'has caused or substantially contributed by fraud or lack of proper care' to the loss in respect of which he claims compensation.[11]

(b) Incidence of indemnity claims

Where a right of indemnity is recognised, the indemnity is paid by the Chief Land Registrar out of moneys provided by Parliament. It appears that few indemnity claims are ever made. During the last decade the number of claims relating to first registration has averaged about 19 per year (with an average payment in each case of approximately £2,000).[12] These figures compare well with the average annual rate of 255,000 first registrations. It is, however, somewhat more alarming to note that, although the Land Registry collects fees from each applicant for registration, the indemnity moneys actually paid out amount to only 0.18 per cent of that fee income. This imbalance has given rise to the observation that the indemnity scheme provided under the Land Registration Act 1925 'must be the most expensive form of insurance ever devised', making the inefficiencies of insurance for tort claims look 'positively benign'.[13]

---

9   Land Registration Act 1925, s 83(11) creates a six year limitation period for most claims of indemnity, the period running from the date when the claimant knew (or ought to have known) of the existence of his claim. The Law Commission has recommended that the liability to pay indemnity should rank for limitation purposes as a simple contract debt and that the period of limitation should begin to run only from the date of rectification (Law Com No 158, paras 3.31f).

10   *In Re Chowood's Registered Land* [1933] Ch 574 at 581f. The Law Commission has since acknowledged the unfairness of this logic and has proposed that an indemnity be payable even where rectification is awarded on the basis of a subsisting overriding interest (post, p 202).

11   Land Registration Act 1925, s 83(5)(a), as substituted by Land Registration and Land Charges Act 1971, s 3(1).

12   R.J. Smith, (1986) 39 CLP 111 at 117. See also Law Com No 158, para 3.24, Appendix D.

13   R.J. Smith, (1986) 39 CLP 111 at 116.

10. FUTURE REFORM OF REGISTRATION OF TITLE

In its Third Report on Land Registration,[14] the Law Commission issued a series of highly significant proposals for the future development of the law of registered titles in England and Wales. In this Report the Commission addressed itself squarely to the difficulty of reconciling the security of property interests with the marketability of registered land. While accepting the theoretical validity of the 'ideal of a complete register of title', the Commission was not insensitive to the argument that it 'may be unjust to require that a particular interest be protected by registration on pain of deprivation.'[15] The Commission felt that the rights in question might often be readily discoverable on inspection of the land (in which case compulsory entry on the register would be unnecessary) or extremely informal or transient (in which case compulsory entry would be impracticable or undesirable).

(1) Two new guiding principles

In the light of these considerations the Commission enunciated two major principles as relevant to any reform of the law of registered land, the first principle necessarily conceding priority to the second.[16] *First*, the Commission endorsed the view that 'in the interests of certainty and of simplifying conveyancing, the class of right which may bind a purchaser otherwise than as the result of an entry in the register should be as narrow as possible.' *Second*, the Commission stipulated that 'interests should be overriding where protection against purchasers is needed, yet it is either not reasonable to expect or not sensible to require any entry on the register'. However, where the operation of the second principle might threaten loss to 'honest and careful purchasers', the Commission proposed that the ordinary indemnity provisions (and the vast surplus income derived from Land Registry fees) be made available for the purpose of compensating proprietors trapped unwittingly by overriding interests.

(2) Restriction of overriding interests

In order to implement the first principle the Commission recommended that the statutory categories of overriding interest be both rationalised and simplified.[17] Towards this end the Commission proposed that the present classes of overriding interest should be reformulated so as to cover only (i) legal easements and profits *à prendre* which arise (in either case) by operation of law[18]; (ii) rights acquired by adverse possession[19]; (iii) leases for 21 years or less[20]; (iv)

---

14 Law Commission, *Property Law: Third Report on Land Registration: A. Overriding Interests, B. Rectification and Indemnity, C. Minor Interests* (Law Com No 158, 31 March 1987).
15 Law Com No 158, para 2.6.
16 See Law Com No 158, para 2.6.
17 Law Com No 158, para 2.105.
18 On this basis overriding interests would thus exclude not only expressly granted legal easements and profits but also equitable easements (ante, p 173). The Commission also thought that many rights are at present quite superfluously referred to in the express terms of Land Registration Act 1925, s 70(1) (see Law Com No 158, paras 2.19ff).
19 Ante, p 174.
20 Ante, p 174.

rights of persons in actual occupation of land[1]; and (v) customary rights.[2] Other rights currently recognised as overriding interests would either be reclassified under a new category as 'general burdens' on registered land[3] or be relegated simply to the status of minor interest and protectible as such by appropriate entry in the register.[4]

(3) More equitable compensation for loss

The formulation of the Law Commission's second principle was underpinned by a novel and imaginative approach to the provision of compensation for those who suffer loss through the emergence of overriding interests. At present, as the Commission noted, the indemnity provisions of the Land Registration Act 1925 have no application to the case of overriding interests,[5] with the inevitable result that 'one (normally) innocent party must lose without compensation.'[6] The 'all or nothing' nature of this kind of outcome seems both unattractive and discriminatory,[7] not least since the considerable surplus funds accumulated by way of the Land Registry's fee income are more than sufficient to enable all loss to be adequately compensated.[8]

The Commission therefore proposed that, insofar as it felt unable to recommend the discontinuation of all statutory protection for overriding interests, an enhanced scheme of indemnity would represent a 'second best to the complete protection of purchasers'.[9] In the view of the Commission, 'the machinery of registered conveyancing ought to be oiled by means of a "state guarantee" of title', with the consequence that a right to indemnity should arise even where an overriding interest is asserted against a registered proprietor.[10] Thus, although 'as a matter of machinery' a registered proprietor would automatically take subject to all overriding interests, he would nevertheless be eligible for compensation from public funds in respect of his

---

1 The rights of persons in receipt of the rents and profits of land would thus cease to constitute an overriding interest (ante, p 178).

2 Post, p 643.

3 Law Com No 158, para 2.15. Such 'general burdens' would include such matters as statutory tenancies under the Rent Act (ibid, para 2.53), public rights (ibid, paras 2.79f), chancel repairs liability (ibid, para 2.81), and local land charges (ibid, para 2.94). The Commission envisaged that the Registrar would be invested with discretion to enter a note of 'general burdens' on the relevant register of title, but that, in spite of their superficial resemblance to overriding interests, 'general burdens' should never be subject to the provisions relating to rectification and indemnity (ibid, paras 2.15, 3.13).

4 Law Com No 158, para 2.108.

5 Ante, p 171.

6 Law Com No 158, para 2.10.

7 See Law Com No 158, paras 2.3, 2.10.

8 See Law Com No 158, paras 3.24ff.

9 Law Com No 158, para 2.12.

10 'An entirely innocent and properly careful purchaser for value of an "absolute" title, compelled and encouraged to rely upon the register, who finds his land subjected to an overriding interest might legitimately consider the system *not* to be "so far as is humanly possible, complete and perfect". He might equally legitimately look for compensation essentially because limitations of the system were accepted which still left him at some risk' (Law Com No 158, para 2.3).

loss.[11] The availability of such an indemnity, the Commission believed, would 'go some way to enabling an acceptable balance to be achieved between competing innocent interests'.[12] In this way rectification and indemnity could be made truly complementary remedies and, if the overriding interests in question were duly entered on the register in conjunction with the award of an indemnity,[13] the general effect would ultimately be the creation of a more complete register of title.

It remains to be seen whether the Law Commission's admirable proposals will be duly implemented in statutory form.

11 Law Com No 158, para 3.29. The Commission envisaged, however, that any indemnity paid under its proposals should be liable to be 'reduced where the applicant lacked proper care (ie was at fault or negligent) to such an extent as is thought just and equitable having regard to the applicant's share in the responsibility for the loss' (ibid, para 3.27).
12 Law Com No 158, para 2.12.
13 The Commission recommended that, as a precondition of indemnity, the Registrar should have discretion to rectify the register in order to give effect to the overriding interest (Law Com No 158, para 3.29).

CHAPTER 9

The conveyancing dimension

In England and Wales the process of land transfer is essentially a two-stage process: first contract, then conveyance (or 'completion' of the contract). In other words, when the preliminary negotiations between the prospective vendor and purchaser have taken place, the parties enter into a formal contract to execute in favour of the purchaser a conveyance of the legal estate in the land to be sold. The legal estate in question may be either an estate in fee simple (if the transaction related to a freehold) or a term of years (if the transaction related to a leasehold), and the transfer or assignment usually follows within four weeks of the exchange of contracts. In unregistered land the conveyance of a legal estate is effective forthwith to vest that legal estate in the purchaser. The process of transferring a title in registered land is essentially similar, with the qualification that a registered title may be alienated by mere document of transfer rather than deed of conveyance and the transfer of title is not final and complete until it is recorded in the Land Register.[1]

It is the concern of this chapter to trace some of the legal implications of the conveyancing process from the initiation of negotiations between vendor and purchaser to its conclusion in a completed transfer of title.

1. DEALINGS BEFORE EXCHANGE OF CONTRACTS

During the period before the exchange of contracts the purchaser and vendor negotiate agreement on such matters as the purchase price to be paid for the property and the precise extent of the property to be transferred. It is, for instance, possible for the parties to agree that certain fixtures and fittings should or should not pass as part of the realty.[2] The interval before the exchange of contracts also provides the purchaser with an opportunity to arrange the mortgage finance which he usually requires to enable him to buy the property.[3] Other matters which fall to be dealt with in advance of any exchange of contracts include the following.

(1) Preliminary enquiries

Before the parties reach the stage of exchanging contracts, it is customary for the purchaser to address 'preliminary enquiries' to his vendor. These enquiries, usually made in standard form, attempt to elicit information about existing disputes relating to the property, the ownership of boundary walls, hedges and fences, the existence of mains services to the property, rights of way, planning matters, compulsory purchase orders and the ownership and maintenance of

1   Ante, p 157.
2   Ante, p 24.
3   Post, p 563.

roads serving the property.[4] Although the responses to preliminary enquiries are by tradition unhelpfully vapid, the vendor bears a duty of care in relation to the accuracy of his replies.[5] An incorrect answer to a preliminary enquiry may found a liability in negligence.[6]

(2) Surveys

In advance of any exchange of formal contracts, the purchaser may also wish to commission a structural survey of the property which he proposes to buy. Moreover, any lending institution which helps to finance his purchase will certainly insist that some kind of survey is conducted on its own behalf (but at the purchaser's expense) in order that the security offered be shown to be reasonably sound.

Such surveys, if conducted negligently, provide a fertile source of legal liability. A surveyor who is careless in carrying out a survey commissioned privately by a potential purchaser before exchange of contracts is liable in negligence for the difference between the contracted purchase price and the true market value of the property at the date of purchase.[7] The damages awarded to the purchaser may also include interest on this difference in property values, together with damages for vexation and inconvenience.[8] It is also clear that a surveyor who values property for a building society owes a duty of care not only to the building society[9] but also to the mortgage applicant who proposes to purchase the property.[10] Furthermore, the building society may itself be vicariously liable to the mortgage applicant in respect of any loss caused by the negligence of the surveyor commissioned by the building society to report on the property in relation to which the mortgage loan is sought.[11]

4　See I.S. Wickenden and S.B. Edell, (1961) 25 Conv (NS) 336.

5　Carelessness cannot be cured by an attempted exclusion of liability in the eventual terms of the contract drawn up between vendor and purchaser (Misrepresentation Act 1967, s 3, as amended by Unfair Contract Terms Act 1977, s 8(1)). See *Walker v Boyle* [1982] 1 WLR 495 at 507A-E; [1982] CLJ 231 (S. Tromans); [1982] Conv 236 (K. Hodkinson); (1983) 80 Law Soc Gaz 326 (P.H. Kenny). See also *South Western General Property Co Ltd v Marton* (1982) 263 Estates Gazette 1090 at 1092; [1983] Conv 8.

6　See eg *Wilson v Bloomfield* (1979) 123 SJ 860; [1980] Conv 401.

7　*Perry v Sidney Phillips & Son* [1982] 1 WLR 1297 at 1302D-E, 1303F-H, 1304G, 1306C-D; [1984] Conv 60 (K. Hodkinson). The surveyor's duty of care is limited, however, to the potential purchaser who commissioned his survey. His negligence gives no cause of action in tort to potential purchasers of adjacent properties, even though their properties, when purchased, are discovered to contain the same defect (eg dry rot) which he failed to reveal in the commissioned survey (see *Shankie-Williams v Heavey* (1986) *The Times*, 12 May).

8　[1982] 1 WLR 1297 at 1302G-1303D, 1305F, 1307A-E. See also *Fisher v Knowles* (1982) 262 Estates Gazette 1083 at 1084; *Fryer v Bunney* (1982) 263 Estates Gazette 158 at 162ff; *Bolton v Puley* (1983) 267 Estates Gazette 1160 at 1163ff; *Treml v Ernest W. Gibson & Partners* (1984) 272 Estates Gazette 68 at 71ff; *Barrett v Dalgety New Zealand Ltd* [1979] BCL 341.

9　*London and South of England Building Society v Stone* [1983] 1 WLR 1242 at 1249H-1250A.

10　*Yianni v Edwin Evans & Sons* [1982] QB 438 at 456B-C; [1981] Conv 435 (M. Brazier and G. Pople); (1981) 131 NLJ 1181 (H.W. Wilkinson). See also *Smith v Eric S. Bush* (1987) *The Times*, 18 March, where the Court of Appeal held that it was not fair and reasonable, for the purposes of the Unfair Contract Terms Act 1977, that the surveyor should be able to rely on general disclaimers of negligence liability contained in the survey report and mortgage application.

11　See *Stevenson v Nationwide Building Society* (1984) 272 Estates Gazette 663 at 670. In this case, however, the building society was able to rely on a disclaimer clause contained in the prospective mortgagor's loan application, although it has since been questioned whether such a clause was truly effective in the light of the Unfair Contract Terms Act 1977 (see (1984) 272 Estates Gazette 333).

(3) Local authority searches

It is also common practice for the purchaser to use the period before exchange of contracts to requisition a search in respect of local land charges from his local authority.[12] The authority may be liable to the purchaser in negligence in respect of any misleading replies which cause him loss.[13]

(4) Agreement 'subject to contract'

It is usual that, while pre-contractual negotiations and enquiries are being pursued, the prospective vendor and purchaser will wish to express some kind of consensus ad idem in the matter of sale. It is invariable practice for vendor and purchaser at this stage to reach an agreement for sale 'subject to contract'. However, it is generally accepted that such an agreement, albeit in written form, is not contractually binding unless and until its terms are incorporated in a formal contract of sale signed and exchanged by the parties.[14]

It is, of course, the lack of legal consequence attaching to agreements 'subject to contract' which fosters the practice of 'gazumping' at times when the property market becomes unstable and volatile.[15] With total impunity the intending vendor can choose to disregard an existing agreement for sale 'subject to contract' if it emerges that a more favourable price can be extracted from another potential purchaser.[16] In a rising property market the total absence of legal obligation until the exchange of formal contracts can lead to highly inequitable results, not least because it creates the setting for that most unseemly form of competition between would-be purchasers—the 'contract race'.[17] There is much to be said in favour of the practice in Scots law which ensures that even informal agreements for the sale of land are contractually binding. Too often the 'gentleman's agreement' expressed in an agreement 'subject to contract' turns out to be merely, as Sachs J once said, 'a transaction in which each side hopes the other will act like a gentleman and neither intends so to act if it is against his material interests'.[18]

(a) Attempts to limit the 'subject to contract' proviso

In view of the inherent danger of inequity, judicial attempts were made, particularly during the early 1970s, to dislodge the well-entrenched suspensive

12   Ante, p 112.
13   See *L. Shaddock & Associates Pty Ltd v Parramatta City Council* (1981) 55 ALJR 713 at 715ff (High Court of Australia).
14   *Winn v Bull* (1877) 7 Ch D 29 at 32 per Jessel MR; *Coupe v Ridout* [1921] 1 Ch 291 at 297f; *Chillingworth v Esche* [1924] 1 Ch 97 at 104f; *Locket v Norman-Wright* [1925] Ch 56 at 62; *Keppel v Wheeler* [1927] 1 KB 577 at 592f; *Eccles v Bryant and Pollock* [1948] Ch 93 at 100f; *D'Silva v Lister House Development Ltd* [1971] Ch 17 at 28F.
15   'Gazumping' has been described as 'a practice as unattractive as its name' (see *Mulhall v Haren* [1981] IR 364 at 378 per Keane J).
16   It has even been pointed out that the duty of trustees to sell only at the best price reasonably obtainable may impose a duty to 'gazump'. See *Buttle v Saunders* [1950] WN 255 at 256; [1979] Conv 451.
17   The Law Society has attempted to control the practice of the 'contract race' by imposing a duty on the vendor's solicitor to disclose the existence of a 'contract race' to the solicitors acting for each prospective purchaser. See (1977) 74 Law Soc Gaz 834.
18   See *Goding v Frazer* [1967] 1 WLR 286 at 293B. See also *Edward Wong Finance Co Ltd v Johnson Stokes & Master* [1984] AC 296 at 307E, where Lord Brightman observed that 'the conception of courtesy as between vendor and purchaser would be a nonsense.'

effects of the 'subject to contract' rule. Where there was anything which remotely resembled a written memorandum of the contract of sale, considerable ingenuity was 'expended upon bringing about the downfall of the "gazumper"'.[19]

In *Griffiths v Young*,[20] for instance, the Court of Appeal was ready to hold that an agreement 'subject to contract' had been superseded by a subsequent unconditional offer and acceptance made by the same parties and communicated by telephone. Likewise, in *Law v Jones*[1] the Court of Appeal decided by a majority that the unilateral use of the phrase 'subject to contract' in correspondence between vendor and purchaser could not derogate from an oral contract for sale which had already been concluded between the parties. Moreover, the Court seemed to hold that such 'subject to contract' correspondence could itself provide the written memorandum which is required under section 40(1) of the Law of Property Act 1925[2] in order to ensure the enforceability of the earlier oral contract.

These decisions caused much consternation in the world of conveyancers. As Lord Denning MR observed in *Tiverton Estates Ltd v Wearwell Ltd*,[3] the decision in *Law v Jones* in particular falsified the belief of most practising solicitors that they could, on a sale of land, protect their clients by writing their letters 'subject to contract'. To the minds of solicitors, said Lord Denning, the decision 'virtually repealed the Statute of Frauds'. In his view, *Law v Jones* had 'sounded an alarm bell in the offices of every solicitor in the land', in that the ruling in this case seemed to expose the client to 'the full blast of "frauds and perjuries" attendant on oral testimony. Even without fraud or perjury, he is exposed to honest difference of recollections leading to law suits, from which it was the very object of the statute to save him.'[4]

It is now fairly clear that there has been a strong reaction against the decision in *Law v Jones*. In *Tiverton Estates Ltd v Wearwell Ltd*,[5] a differently constituted Court of Appeal decided that the insertion of the magical phrase 'subject to contract' effectively prevented correspondence from satisfying the requirement of a written memorandum under section 40(1) of the Law of Property Act 1925.[6] The authority of the decision in *Law v Jones* has been further weakened by subsequent cases which have tended to reinforce the traditional understanding of the 'subject to contract' proviso as used in normal conveyancing practice.[7] The use of the words 'subject to contract' is nowadays

19   See *Mulhall v Haren* [1981] IR 364 at 378.
20   [1970] Ch 675 at 685H–686D, 687A–E. See (1971) 35 Conv (NS) 55 (F.R. Crane).
1   [1974] Ch 112. See [1973] CLJ 214 (C.T. Emery); (1973) 37 Conv (NS) 282 (F.R. Crane).
2   Post, p 210.
3   [1975] Ch 146. See (1974) 38 Conv (NS) 127 (F.R. Crane); [1974] CLJ 42 (C.T. Emery);
     (1974) 37 MLR 695 (J.W. Tinnion); (1974) 90 LQR 1; (1974) 25 NILQ 333 (H. Wallace).
4   [1975] Ch 146 at 154A, 159G–160B. See also 1973) 117 SJ 293; *Mulhall v Haren* [1981] IR 364
     at 382.
5   [1975] Ch 146 at 160F–G, 161D, 171E.
6   It was significant that the Council of the Law Society expressed its view that the traditional
     status of 'subject to contract' correspondence had been vindicated by the approach adopted
     in *Tiverton Estates Ltd v Wearwell Ltd* (see (1973) 70 Law Soc Gaz 2637).
7   See *Daulia Ltd v Four Millbank Nominees Ltd* [1978] Ch 231 at 249B–250D; [1978] Conv 375
     (F.R. Crane); [1979] CLJ 31 (C. Harpum and D.L. Jones); (1979) 95 LQR 7 (H.W.
     Wilkinson); *Munton v GLC* [1976] 1 WLR 649 at 655D ; *Cohen v Nessdale Ltd* [1982] 2 All ER 97
     at 105a–j; [1982] Conv 71 (M.P. Thompson); *Alpenstow Ltd v Regalian Properties PLC* [1985] 1
     WLR 721 at 730A–B; [1985] CLJ 356 (C. Harpum); *Devlin v Northern Ireland Housing Executive*
     [1982] 17 NIJB, Transcript p 13ff; *Mulhall v Haren* [1981] IR 364 at 386. See generally R.W.
     Clark, [1984] Conv 173, 251.

agreed to be inconsistent with the existence of a concluded agreement 'save in the most exceptional cases'.[8]

(b) Applicability of the estoppel doctrine

It is not beyond the bounds of possibility that the more inequitable effects of the 'subject to contract' proviso may be challengeable by reference to the doctrine of proprietary estoppel.[9] It is quite common for an intending purchaser to incur expenditure or other detriment in advance of a formal contract for the purchase of land. In exceptional circumstances a valid claim of estoppel may arise if the would-be purchaser has detrimentally relied on some supposed contractual commitment between the vendor and himself.[10] In *Attorney-General of Hong Kong v Humphreys Estate (Queen's Gardens) Ltd,*[11] for instance, Lord Templeman conceded that it was 'possible but unlikely that in circumstances at present unforeseeable a party to negotiations set out in a document expressed to be "subject to contract" would be able to satisfy the court that...some form of estoppel had arisen to prevent both parties from refusing to proceed with the transactions envisaged by the document.'

In an ordinary transaction of purchase, however, it is highly unlikely that a purchaser will be held to have acquired some proprietary right by estoppel prior to contract.[12] For a claim of estoppel to succeed in such a case, it must be shown that the vendor created or encouraged an expectation in the purchaser that the vendor would not withdraw from a transaction which had been agreed in principle between the parties. There must also be strict proof that the purchaser relied on this expectation. The claim of estoppel failed in *Attorney-General of Hong Kong v Humphreys Estate (Queen's Gardens) Ltd*[13] precisely because it was clear that the purchaser had at all times known that the vendor retained the right to resile from the agreement which had been informally reached between them. As Lord Templeman pointed out, no estoppel could be founded on the mere fact that the purchaser had acted 'in the confident and not unreasonable hope that the agreement in principle would come into effect.'[14]

(c) Proposed reforms

The uncertain status of agreements which are 'subject to contract' has been kept under constant review by the Law Commission. In 1975 the Commission accepted that the 'subject to contract' proviso 'has drawbacks and is capable of being abused in certain circumstances'.[15] The Commission nevertheless

---

8   *Mulhall v Haren* [1981] IR 364 at 386. See *Alpenstow Ltd v Regalian Properties PLC* [1985] 1 WLR 721 at 730A-B, where Nourse J accepted that only in 'a very strong and exceptional context' will the words 'subject to contract' not be given their clear prima facie meaning.
9   See Chapter 13 (post, p 386).
10   See eg *Salvation Army Trustee Co Ltd v West Yorkshire MCC* (1981) 41 P & CR 179 (post, p 400); [1983] Conv 85.
11   [1987] 2 WLR 343 at 352H.
12   *Clark v Follett* [1973] STC 240 at 263f. See also *Thwaites v Ryan* [1984] VR 65 at 96. In *Salvation Army Trustee Co Ltd v West Yorkshire MCC* (1981) 41 P & CR 179 at 199, Woolf J was careful to emphasise that his upholding of a claim of estoppel on the unusual facts of that case was not intended to 'interfere with the normal conduct of negotiations "subject to contract"'.
13   [1987] 2 WLR 343 at 350A-B, 352H.
14   [1987] 2 WLR 343 at 349H.
15   Law Commission, *Report on 'Subject to Contract' Agreements* (Law Com No 65, January 1975), para 4.

expressed itself averse to any change which would give legal effect to agreements 'subject to contract' or impose any liability (civil or criminal) on a person who withdraws from such an agreement.[16] It was the belief of the Commission that the non-legal status of 'subject to contract' agreements was 'based on a sound concept, namely that the buyer should be free from binding commitment until he has had the opportunity of obtaining legal and other advice, arranging his finance and making the necessary inspection, searches and enquiries'.

Continuing abuse of the 'subject to contract' procedure during the years since 1975 has more recently led the Law Commission to make an important and extremely sensible proposal in relation to pre-contractual dealings with land. The Commission has not advocated that legally binding effect should be given to agreements which are entered into 'subject to contract'. Instead the Commission has formulated the recommendation that the prospective vendor and purchaser should put down a 'pre-contract deposit' as soon as an offer of purchase has been made and accepted 'subject to contract'.[17] These deposits would each comprise $\frac{1}{2}$ per cent of the purchase price of the property, and the parties would simultaneously enter into a written agreement to exchange formal contracts within four weeks. The pre-contract deposit would then be forfeited by any party who, otherwise than for good cause, withdrew or refused to exchange contracts within this period.[18]

The proposed 'pre-contract deposit' scheme provides an imaginative, albeit necessarily limited, form of protection against the evils of 'gazumping'.[19] The implementation of the scheme would, if nothing else, afford some compensation for the victim of 'gazumping' in respect of his wasted expenditure on professional fees connected with the abortive transaction.

2. THE EXCHANGE OF CONTRACTS

There are few rules relating to the required form or contents of a binding contract for the sale of land. Such a contract may be made quite validly in either oral or written form, although its enforceability depends on compliance with certain minimal evidential requirements imposed by statute. A contract of sale may be 'open', ie, may provide expressly for nothing beyond the identity of the parties, the definition of the subject matter and the price to be paid. The rights and duties of vendor and purchaser under an 'open' contract are then determined with reference to the general law of property. More common than 'open' contracts for the sale of land are 'closed' contracts which incorporate a number of standardised conditions relevant to the generality of land transactions. The most commonly used standard terms are those contained in the National Conditions of Sale,[20] the Law Society's Conditions of Sale,[1] and

16 Law Com No 65, para 4.
17 Law Commission, *Pre-Contract Deposits: A Practice Recommendation by the Conveyancing Standing Committee* (1987), para 5.
18 Ibid, para 7. The Law Commission envisaged the grounds of exception as including the case where a search or survey subsequently revealed 'nasty surprises' for the purchaser (para 8(a)).
19 The Standing Committee acknowledged, for instance, that the penalty of forfeiting the pre-contract deposit would have no deterrent effect at all in relation to a party who, by unjustified withdrawal from the 'subject to contract' agreement, stood to gain more than $\frac{1}{2}$ per cent of the purchase price of the relevant property (para 11).
20 20th Edn.
1 1984 Revision.

the Conveyancing Lawyers' Conditions of Sale.[2] The use of standard term conditions of sale substantially aids the process of land transfer.[3] The vendor, whose duty it is in any event to draw up the contract of sale, may adopt one or other set of standard conditions with such modifications as may appear appropriate to the circumstances of his particular sale.

(1) Requirement of a written memorandum

According to section 40(1) of the Law of Property Act 1925, no action may be brought upon any contract for the sale or other disposition of land or any interest in land 'unless the agreement upon which such action is brought, or some memorandum or note thereof, is in writing, and signed by the party to be charged or by some other person thereunto by him lawfully authorised.' This provision derives from the Statute of Frauds 1677 and is designed to prevent dispute over oral dealings in land.[4] Section 40(1) does not render void a purely oral contract for the sale of land: it merely provides that such a contract shall be unenforceable unless evidenced in some written memorandum. In practice, however, there is little confusion as to whether section 40(1) has been satisfied by the provision of a written memorandum or note, since most contracts for the sale of land are not only evidenced in writing but are actually contained in written form.

(a) *Form and contents of the memorandum*

There are few limitations on the form or contents of the memorandum which is required for the purposes of section 40. It is not necessary that the parties should have had present to their minds any intention to comply with the requirement of section 40.[5] It is enough simply that some note of all the material terms of the contract are recorded in documentary form,[6] and it is even possible that a written offer prior to contract may serve as the required memorandum of the terms of the agreement.[7]

(i) *Material terms*   The material terms to be recorded in the memorandum must describe the parties sufficiently clearly that their identity cannot be disputed.[8] The terms must also render ascertainable both the physical subject

---

2   See [1981] Conv 38.
3   It is, however, a salutary fact that the small print in such standard form contracts has binding effect even in relation to 'conditions which it is probable that nobody ever read' (see *Squarey v Harris-Smith* (1981) 42 P & CR 118 at 128ff).
4   The requirement of a written memorandum has no application, however, to any contract between A and B that A should purchase land from C (*Lees v Fleming* [1980] Qd R 162 at 167E-F).
5   *Welford v Beezely* (1747) 1 Ves Sen 6 at 7f, 27 ER 855 at 856; *In re Hoyle* [1893] 1 Ch 84 at 99; *Daniels v Trefusis* [1914] 1 Ch 788 at 798f.
6   *Hawkins v Price* [1947] Ch 645 at 659f; *Tiverton Estates Ltd v Wearwell Ltd* [1975] Ch 146 at 161G; *Mulhall v Haren* [1981] IR 364 at 394.
7   *Powers v Fowler* (1855) 4 El & Bl 511 at 517ff, 119 ER 187 at 189f; *Benecke v Chadwicke* (1856) 4 WR 687 at 688; *Smith v Neale* (1857) 2 CB (NS) 67 at 88, 140 ER 337 at 345; *Reuss v Picksley* (1866) LR 1 Ex 342 at 351. See also *In re New Eberhardt Co* (1889) 43 Ch D 118 at 129.
8   *Potter v Duffield* (1874) LR 18 Eq 4 at 7f; *Davies v Sweet* [1962] 2 QB 300 at 307f.

matter of the contract[9] and the price to be paid,[10] must specify a date for the handing over of possession to the purchaser,[11] and must afford evidence of other expressly agreed terms.[12]

(ii) Nature of the document Many differing kinds of document have been accepted as complying with section 40. The sorts of document which have been held to constitute a memorandum include a letter,[13] a clause in a will,[14] a receipt,[15] a telegram,[16] and even an entry in a diary,[17] provided in each case that the record of the contractual terms has been signed either by the party to be charged or by his 'lawfully authorised' agent.[18] Moreover, the section 40 requirement may be met by a joinder of documents, in that the courts have allowed plaintiffs to adduce parol evidence in order to link a number of separate and intrinsically incomplete documents until a complete memorandum is collected.[19] However, if two or more documents are to be joined in this way, one of the documents must be signed and must contain 'some reference, express or implied, to some other document or transaction'.[20]

(b) Recognition of an existing contract

It seems virtually certain that the decision of the Court of Appeal in *Law v Jones*,[1] which would have rendered oral contracts enforceable, no longer represents good law.[2] In *Law v Jones*, the Court of Appeal appeared to hold that subsequent 'subject to contract' correspondence might itself constitute the written memorandum required by section 40(1) of the Law of Property Act 1925. Buckley LJ was of the view that the note or memorandum required by section 40(1) need not itself acknowledge the existence of a contract, since it was 'not the fact of agreement but the terms agreed upon that must be found recorded in writing.'[3] However, in *Tiverton Estates Ltd v Wearwell Ltd*[4] a differently constituted Court of Appeal declined to follow *Law v Jones*, holding

9   *Davies v Sweet* [1962] 2 QB 300 at 306.
10 See *Sudbrook Trading Estate Ltd v Eggleton* [1983] 1 AC 444 (ante, p 136).
11 *Mulhall v Haren* [1981] IR 364 at 394. See also *Walker v Bower* [1975] NZ Recent Law 138 at 139.
12 *Hawkins v Price* [1947] Ch 645 at 654.
13 *Moore v Hart* (1682) 1 Vern 110 at 114, 23 ER 352 at 353; 1 Vern 201 at 202, 23 ER 412 at 413; *Longfellow v Williams* (1804) Peake Add Cas 225 at 226, 170 ER 252 at 253.
14 *In re Hoyle* [1893] 1 Ch 84 at 98ff; *Johnson v Nova Scotia Trust Co* (1974) 43 DLR (3d) 222 at 234.
15 *Evans v Prothero* (1852) 1 De GM & G 572 at 575, 42 ER 674 at 676; *Auerbach v Nelson* [1919] 2 Ch 383 at 386ff; *Newton-King v Wilkinson* [1976] 2 NZLR 321 at 325f. See also *Grime v Bartholomew* [1972] 2 NSWLR 827 at 836B (cheque coupled with receipt sufficient memorandum).
16 *McBlain v Cross* (1871) 25 LT 804 at 806.
17 *In re Hoyle* [1893] 1 Ch 84 at 96, 100.
18 The signature need be no more elaborate than a placing of initials or a printed name, provided that the intention was to authenticate the document (see *Hill v Hill* [1947] Ch 231 at 240; *Leeman v Stocks* [1951] Ch 941 at 947).
19 See *Long v Millar* (1879) 4 CPD 450 at 454ff.
20 *Timmins v Moreland Street Property Co Ltd* [1958] Ch 110 at 130 per Jenkins LJ. See also *Elias v George Sahely & Co (Barbados) Ltd* [1983] 1 AC 646 at 655A-656A; [1983] Conv 78 (M.P. Thompson).
1   [1974] Ch 112 (ante, p 207).
2   Ante, p 208.
3   [1974] Ch 112 at 124H.
4   [1975] Ch 146 at 160F-G, 171C-D.

instead that for the purpose of section 40(1) a memorandum or note must not only state the terms of the contract concerned, but must also contain an acknowledgement or recognition by the signatory to the document that a contract has been entered into. This view is now more generally accepted.[5]

(c) Future reform

In 1985 the Law Commission issued a working paper dealing with possible reforms of the law relating to contracts for the sale of land.[6] The Commission advocated the general principle that no future reform in this area should increase the likelihood of contracts for sale becoming binding before the parties have been able to obtain legal advice.[7] The Commission likewise saw, as general guidelines for the direction of any future changes, the need both to reduce the risk of injustice and to simplify the process of conveyancing.[8] Accordingly the Commission offered for public consultation a number of possible reforms of the law, ranging from a requirement that all contracts be in writing[9] to the suggestion that there be a 'cooling off' period after contract during which either party can withdraw.[10] The Commission expressed, extremely tentatively, its own preference for the introduction of a statutorily prescribed written form for all contractual dealings with land.[11] It saw such a prescribed format as having the advantages of establishing with greater clarity both the existence of a binding contract and the nature of the terms of that contract.[12] It is quite clear that a proposal of this kind, if implemented, would have highly beneficial effects for the conveyancing process as a whole and would also displace what is often felt to be the increasingly unsatisfactory operation of the doctrine of part performance in this area.[13]

(2) The doctrine of part performance

Irrespective of non-compliance with the provisions of section 40(1) of the Law of Property Act 1925, a contract for the sale of land may be actionable, even in the absence of writing, if there has been 'part performance'.[14] For this purpose part performance generally requires that the party seeking to enforce the contract has, in reliance upon that contract, undertaken some action to his own detriment or prejudice. The doctrine of part performance is thus closely related both to the doctrine of proprietary estoppel[15] and to the long-standing disinclination of the courts to allow a statute to be used as an instrument of fraud.[16]

---

5   See eg *Kelly v Park Hall School Ltd* [1979] IR 340 at 352; *Mulhall v Haren* [1981] IR 364 at 391.
6   Law Commission, *Transfer of Land: Formalities for Contracts for Sale etc of Land* (Working Paper No 92, July 1985).
7   Working Paper No 92, para 5.2(i).
8   Working Paper No 92, para 5.2(ii), (iii).
9   Working Paper No 92, para 5.12ff.
10   Working Paper No 92, para 5.30ff.
11   Working Paper No 92, para 5.17ff.
12   Working Paper No 92, para 5.17(i), (iii).
13   See Working Paper No 92, para 5.14.
14   Law of Property Act 1925, s 40(2).
15   See Chapter 13 (post, p 386).
16   Post, p 237. See *Maddison v Alderson* (1883) 8 App Cas 467 at 474 per Earl of Selborne LC; *Last v Rosenfeld* [1972] 2 NSWLR 923 at 927E-F; *Thwaites v Ryan* [1984] VR 65 at 91.

(a) Conditions of part performance

The doctrine of part performance renders a contract enforceable, even in the absence of a written memorandum, where the plaintiff has done acts which, on a balance of probability, are referable to and explicable only in terms of the existence of the contract alleged by the plaintiff. Although the acts need not be such as would demonstrate the precise terms of the contract,[17] the operation of the doctrine of part performance is premised on the current existence of an actual contract. Acts of reliance are irrelevant if performed on the footing of mere negotiations which may or may not ripen later into contract.[18] The doctrine is relevant, moreover, only if the plaintiff can establish a case for specific performance.[19] Since part performance is an equitable remedy, it is available only where the party seeking to rely on part performance has been guilty of no inequitable or unconscionable behaviour[20] and does not have access to any equally effective common law remedy.[1]

(b) Acts sufficient to constitute part performance

The requirements of part performance have been substantially relaxed in recent years. In *Steadman v Steadman*,[2] the House of Lords departed significantly from the classic requirements of the doctrine as laid down in *Maddison v Alderson*.[3] A claim of part performance may now be founded on any acts which can be shown to have been done in reliance on a contract, where it would in effect constitute a fraud if the defendant were to take advantage of the fact that the contract was not evidenced in writing. Relevant acts may include the payment of money either to the other contracting party[4] or to some third party,[5] the entry into possession of land with the vendor's consent,[6] or the making of substantial improvements or alterations to the land.[7] In *Sutton v Sutton*[8] it was held that part performance of an oral agreement for transfer of a

---

17 *Steadman v Steadman* [1976] AC 536 at 546F per Lord Morris of Borth-y-Gest.
18 *Thynne v Earl of Glengall* (1848) 2 HLC 131 at 158, 9 ER 1042 at 1052; *Re Foster, Ex parte Foster* (1883) 22 Ch D 797 at 811; *Biss v Hygate* [1918] 2 KB 314 at 317; *J.C. Williamson Ltd v Lukey and Mulholland* (1931) 45 CLR 282 at 300; *O'Rourke v Hoeven* [1974] 1 NSWLR 622 at 625E-F.
19 *McManus v Cooke* (1887) 35 Ch D 681 at 697; *Elliott v Roberts* (1912) 28 TLR 436 at 437f.
20 See *Coatsworth v Johnson* (1886) 55 LJQB 220 at 222f (post, p 470).
1   *Turner v Melladew* (1903) 19 TLR 273 at 274.
2   [1976] AC 536. See (1974) 90 LQR 433 (H.W.R. Wade); (1974) 38 Conv (NS) 354 (F.R. Crane); [1974] CLJ 205 (C.T. Emery).
3   (1883) 8 App Cas 467.
4   *Steadman v Steadman* [1976] AC 536 at 541B per Lord Reid, 565B per Lord Simon of Glaisdale, 570F-G per Lord Salmon. See also *In re Gonin, Decd* [1979] Ch 16 at 30G-H. Even the payment of a deposit which is retained pending the drawing up of a formal contract can constitute an act of part performance (see *Walker v Bower* [1975] NZ Recent Law 138 at 139).
5   See *Shillabeer v Diebel* (1980) 100 DLR (3d) 279 at 282.
6   *Smallwood v Sheppards* [1895] 2 QB 627 at 630; *Sharman v Sharman* (1893) 67 LT 834 at 836f; *Kingswood Estate Co Ltd v Anderson* [1963] 2 QB 169 at 181, 189, 193. See also *Wakeham v Mackenzie* [1968] 1 WLR 1175 at 1181D; *In re Gonin, Decd* [1979] Ch 16 at 31D-E; *Regent v Millett* (1976) 133 CLR 679 at 682f, affirming *Millett v Regent* [1975] 1 NSWLR 62.
7   *Lester v Foxcroft* (1701) Coll PC 108; *Reddin v Jarman* (1867) 16 LT 449 at 450; *Broughton v Snook* [1938] Ch 505 at 514ff; *Starlite Variety Stores Ltd v Cloverlawn Investments Ltd* (1979) 92 DLR (3d) 270 at 276.
8   [1984] Ch 184 at 193A-D. See [1984] Conv 152 (M.P. Thompson).

former matrimonial home could comprise the giving of consent to divorce on agreed financial terms. In *Steadman v Steadman*[9] it even appeared to be the majority view of the House of Lords that a sufficient act of part performance can arise where a purchaser instructs solicitors to prepare and submit a draft conveyance or transfer. Although the law lords were not agreed as to whether the acts relied upon must point to a contract in respect of *land*,[10] the view has subsequently been taken that a claim of part performance must indeed indicate the existence of a contract in relation to land.[11]

(3) Conditional contracts

It is possible for a binding contract for the sale of land to be made in conditional terms.[12] The courts have tended towards a generous view of the kinds of condition which may still be compatible with the existence of a binding contract for the sale and purchase of land. Effect may thus be given, for instance, to a contract which is expressed to be 'subject to survey,'[13] since this condition can be construed as imposing on the purchaser an obligation to act reasonably in obtaining a surveyor's report on the property and then in deciding whether to adopt its recommendations. Similarly, a binding contract may quite validly be conditioned upon the obtaining of a planning permission[14] or upon the purchaser's sale of his own property.[15]

Some conditions are, however, so vague or so general as to deprive an agreement of any genuine contractual force. Thus, for instance, a binding contract cannot be created by an acceptance of offered terms 'subject to the approval of' a named third party, although such an acceptance may constitute a counter-offer.[16] Likewise, a contract which is conditional on the availability of satisfactory mortgage finance for the purchaser is generally considered to be void for uncertainty,[17] although there are indications that the law on this point may be changing.[18]

(4) Manner of exchange of contracts

Until fairly recently the most common method of exchanging contracts for the sale of land, thereby rendering the contract in question legally binding, has

---

9   [1976] AC 536 at 540C per Lord Reid, 553H-554B per Viscount Dilhorne, 563A-B per Lord Simon of Glaisdale, 573D per Lord Salmon.
10 For the view that the contract need not refer to land, see [1976] AC 536 at 541C-D per Lord Reid, 554C-D per Viscount Dilhorne.
11 *In re Gonin, Decd* [1979] Ch 16 at 31B-D. See [1979] Conv 402 (M.P. Thompson).
12 See A.J. Oakley, (1982) 35 CLP 151. An option to purchase land is generally viewed, not as a conditional contract of sale, but as an offer which remains open and may be accepted at any time allowed by its terms (ante, p 136).
13 *Ee v Kakar* (1980) 255 Estates Gazette 879 at 881ff. See [1980] Conv 446 (J.E.A.); [1981] CLJ 23 (A.J. Oakley).
14 *McKillop v McMullan* [1979] NI 85.
15 *Perri v Coolangatta Investments Pty Ltd* (1982) 56 ALJR 445 at 448ff.
16 See *Framton v McCully* [1976] 1 NZLR 270 at 276. See also H.W. Wilkinson, [1985] Conv 90.
17 *Lee-Parker v Izzet (No 2)* [1972] 1 WLR 775 at 779F-G, 780A-B; (1976) 40 Conv (NS) 37; *Grime v Bartholomew* [1972] 2 NSWLR 827 at 837G.
18 See eg *Meehan v Jones* (1982) 42 ALR 463 at 470, 475ff (High Court of Australia). See also J. Phillips, (1975) 3 The Queensland Lawyer 113; B.H. Davis, (1977) 8 Cambrian LR 45.

consisted of a postal exchange of the two parts signed by vendor and purchaser respectively.

(a) Postal exchange

The general rule in the law of contract is that a postal acceptance of a contractual offer is complete when the offeree actually posts his acceptance to the offeror.[19] There has always been some doubt whether this postal rule applies to the exchange of contracts for sale of land, since the security sought by both parties in a land transaction seems to require that acceptance be complete only at the point of actual delivery of the acceptance to the offeror.[20] The legal conundrum involved here is now commonly obviated by the fact that most standardised sets of contractual conditions of sale provide that where the exchange of contracts is effected by post, the contract is made when the last part is actually posted.[1]

(b) Telephonic exchange

Just as the postal exchange of contracts has largely superseded any form of ceremonial exchange of contracts, so the postal mode of exchange is itself being gradually overtaken by telephonic exchange. The practical realities of modern 'chain transactions' increasingly require that solicitors should be able to use the medium of the telephone for the purpose of exchange. Accordingly in *Domb v Isoz*[2] the Court of Appeal recognised that the synchronised transactions which are required by such dealings often cannot be secured effectively by either physical or postal exchange. The Court therefore ruled that telephonic exchange may be used, under strictly regulated conditions,[3] where it appears both effectual and appropriate.[4] The Court took the view that an exchange of a written contract for sale is effected as soon as each part of the contract, duly signed by the appropriate party, is in the actual or constructive possession of the other party or of his solicitor. For this purpose constructive possession can arise by way of telephonic exchange, but only in circumstances where a contract signed by a client is 'in the physical possession of his own solicitor or in the possession of the solicitor on the other side who has agreed to hold that part to the order of the despatching solicitor.'[5] Used carefully, the practice of telephonic exchange can thus serve substantially to reduce the danger that any client may lose a bargain or be left without a home.

19 *Household Fire and Carriage Accident Insurance Co v Grant* (1879) 4 Ex D 216 at 219f.
20 *Eccles v Bryant and Pollock* [1948] Ch 93 at 99f per Lord Greene MR.
1 See eg National Conditions of Sale (20th edn), Condition 1(7)(ii); Law Society's Conditions of Sale (1984 Revision), Condition 10(1).
2 [1980] Ch 548. See [1980] Conv 227 (H.W. Wilkinson); (1980) 96 LQR 323.
3 '[A]s a matter of professional practice, exchange by telephone should only be carried out by a partner or proprietor of a firm of solicitors... [I]f two solicitors exchange by telephone, they should then and there agree and record identical attendance notes' ([1980] Ch 548 at 564E per Templeman LJ).
4 'A party's solicitor employed to act in respect of such a contract has, subject to express instructions, implied authority to effect exchange of contracts and so to make the bargain binding upon his client. This he can, in my judgment, do by any method which is effectual to constitute exchange' ([1980] Ch 548 at 557G per Buckley LJ). On exchange by telex, see [1982] Conv 245. See also [1980] Conv 87ff, 227.
5 [1980] Ch 548 at 564D per Templeman LJ.

(5) Deposits

It is customary for a deposit of 10 per cent of the purchase price to become payable by the purchaser on the exchange of contracts.[6] The requirement that such a deposit be paid is not a condition precedent to the existence of a binding contract, but is a fundamental contractual term which, if breached, entitles the injured party to sue for damages including the unpaid deposit.[7] The deposit operates effectively both as a part-payment of the contractually agreed purchase price and as a guarantee that the purchaser will complete the transaction. If the purchaser breaches the contract in such a way as to relieve the vendor from any further obligation under the terms of that contract, the vendor may retain any deposit already paid by the purchaser.[8] If, however, the contract goes off by reason of the vendor's default, the purchaser is of course entitled to recover his deposit money.

(6) Remedies for breach of contract

A contract for the sale of land, if breached by either party, may lead to a range of contractual remedies.

(a) Specific performance

A contract for the sale of a legal estate in land is one in respect of which equity will generally grant specific performance. In other words, if the vendor fails to convey the legal estate according to the terms of the relevant contract, the remedy available to the frustrated purchaser will normally consist not of compensatory damages, but of a court decree that the vendor do that which he promised to do, ie, execute the conveyance and thus transfer the legal estate to the contractual promisee. The rationale underlying this particular form of remedy is the recognition that, since the subject matter of a sale of land is unique, breach of a contract for the sale of land cannot usually be compensated adequately by a mere award of money.[9]

Since specific performance is an intrinsically equitable remedy, it is available not of right but only at the discretion of the court. The exercise of this discretion is normally, in its turn, dependent on a showing that there was a transaction for value evidenced in writing.[10] Equity will not usually assist a volunteer and a contract without writing will, in the absence of part performance, fail to comply with the terms of section 40 of the Law of Property Act 1925.[11] However, if the preconditions exacted by the equitable jurisdiction

---

6   See Law Society's Conditions of Sale (1984 Revision), Conditions 1(f), 9(1); National Conditions of Sale (20th edn), Condition 2. Except where he is expressly instructed so to do, it may constitute negligence on the part of a purchaser's solicitor to fail to make express provision for payment of a deposit under an open contract (see *Morris v Duke-Cohan & Co* (1975) 119 SJ 826). See also H.W. Wilkinson, *Deposits: Who Needs Them?*, (1984) 81 Law Soc Gaz 347; [1985] Conv 237.

7   *Millichamp v Jones* [1982] 1 WLR 1422 at 1430G-H. See also *Alarm Facilities Pty Ltd v Jackson Constructions Pty Ltd* [1975] 2 NSWLR 22 at 28F-29A.

8   The courts have an equitable jurisdiction to grant relief against forfeiture (see C. Harpum, [1984] CLJ 134). See also *Legione v Hateley* (1983) 46 ALR 1 at 12ff.

9   See *Hall v Warren* (1804) 9 Ves 605 at 608, 32 ER 738 at 739; *Hexter v Pearce* [1900] 1 Ch 341 at 346; *Rudd v Lascelles* [1900] 1 Ch 815 at 817.

10   See *Brunker v Perpetual Trustee Co* (1937) 57 CLR 555 at 599 per Dixon J.

11   Ante, p 210.

are satisfied, the remedy of specific performance is granted almost as a matter of course,[12] unless the purchaser has forfeited such help by reason of some unconscionable act or default[13] or if specific performance would prejudice the rights of third parties[14] or would cause a 'hardship amounting to injustice'.[15]

(b) Remedies in damages

In the case of failure to complete the contract, it is open to the aggrieved contracting party to rescind the contract and seek monetary compensation instead of specific performance of the contract. A failure to complete on the contractual date is remediable in damages for breach of contract or in damages in lieu of a decree for specific performance under the Supreme Court Act 1981.[16] However, no right to rescind arises until time becomes 'of the essence' by virtue of a notice to complete served by the party seeking completion or by virtue of unreasonable delay.[17] Where an aggrieved contracting party has treated another's repudiation or breach of contract as discharging the contract, or where an order for specific performance is not complied with, damages may be recovered not only for restitution and indemnity in respect of sums paid and expenses incurred, but also for loss of bargain.[18]

(7) The vendor as trustee

The ultimate effect of the rules relating to specific performance is that once a contract for the sale of a legal estate in land has been concluded, the eventual conveyance of that estate is virtually inevitable. Either the vendor will duly convey according to his contract or the purchaser will enlist the aid of equity towards this end by means of a decree of specific performance. The general inexorability of a due transfer of the legal estate then activates the equitable maxim that 'Equity looks on that as done which ought to be done'. Since the contract for sale ought (by one means or another) to lead to a conveyance of an estate in the land governed by the contract, equity regards the estate as having passed with the contract—provided that the contract was one in relation to which equity would have granted the remedy of specific performance. Thus the contract is effective to transfer the equitable ownership of the estate to the prospective purchaser, whether that estate be a fee simple or a term of years absolute.

---

12   *Patel v Ali* [1984] Ch 283 at 286G.
13   See *Coatsworth v Johnson* (1886) 55 LJQB 220 at 222f (post, p 470); *Harrigan v Brown* [1967] 1 NSWR 342 at 345ff.
14   *Warmington v Miller* [1973] QB 877 at 886F-G. There can, for instance, be no order for specific performance where the land in question has already been conveyed to a third party (see eg *Babcock v Carr* (1982) 127 DLR (3d) 77 at 85f).
15   *Patel v Ali* [1984] Ch 283 at 288D-E per Goulding J. See (1984) 100 LQR 337; (1984) 134 NLJ 685 (H.W. Wilkinson). See also *Roberts v O'Neill* (1983) 1 ILTR (NS) 14 at 15; *Registered Securities Ltd v Cummins* [1983] NZ Recent Law 246 at 247.
16   Supreme Court Act 1981, s 50.
17   See *Raineri v Miles* [1981] AC 1050; [1980] CLJ 21 (D.J. Hayton); [1980] Conv 77 (A. Sydenham).
18   *Johnson v Agnew* [1980] AC 367. See also A.J. Oakley, [1980] CLJ 58; M. Hetherington, (1980) 96 LQR 403; (1979) 42 MLR 696 (G. Woodman); [1979] Conv 293 (F.R. Crane).

It follows therefore that the vendor under a specifically enforceable contract of sale can be described as some form of trustee.[19] If a vendor (V) and a purchaser (P) go through the process of a contract and conveyance relating to a legal estate in Blackacre, their transaction takes the course indicated in *Fig.* 18.

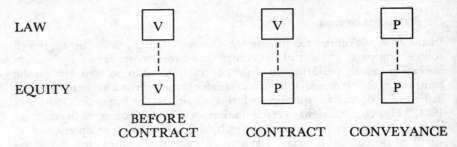

Fig. 18

Clearly the entire interest in Blackacre—both legal and equitable—is vested initially in V. However, from the moment when a specifically enforceable contract for sale is entered into with P, the equitable interest is treated in equity as belonging to P,[20] subject to a lien for the purchase money in favour of V.[1] When subsequently the conveyance of the legal estate is executed or the registered title transferred, the legal estate is effectively re-united with the equitable interest which passed with the contract.[2] It is plain, however, that between contract and conveyance the availability of the contractual remedy of specific performance has at least temporarily engrafted some sort of trust relationship upon the participants in the transaction.[3]

(a) Limitations on the vendor's trusteeship

Notwithstanding that a trust of some kind arises between contract and conveyance, it is plainly impossible to transpose into the law of vendor and purchaser the general law governing the rights and duties of trustees. Where there are rights outstanding on both sides, it may be that 'the description of the vendor as a trustee tends to conceal the essentially contractual relationship which, rather than the relationship of trustee and beneficiary, governs the rights and duties of the respective parties'.[4]

19 *Daire v Beversham* (1661) Nels 76 at 77, 21 ER 793 at 794; *Green v Smith* (1738) 1 Atk 572 at 573, 26 ER 360; *Paine v Meller* (1801) 6 Ves Jun 349 at 352f, 31 ER 1088 at 1089f; *Broome v Monck* (1805) 10 Ves 597 at 606, 32 ER 976 at 979; *Shaw v Foster* (1872) LR 5 HL 321 at 333, 338; *Lysaght v Edwards* (1876) 2 Ch D 499 at 507.
20 *Avondale Printers & Stationers Ltd v Haggie* [1979] 2 NZLR 124 at 141.
1 See *Howard v Miller* [1915] AC 318 at 326.
2 See V.G. Wellings, *The Vendor as Trustee*, (1959) 23 Conv (NS) 173; D. Waters, *Constructive Trust—Vendor and Purchaser*, (1961) 14 CLP 76.
3 See *Central Trust and Safe Deposit Co v Snider* [1916] 1 AC 266 at 272 per Lord Parker of Waddington; *Hoystead v Federal Commissioner of Taxation* (1920) 27 CLR 400 at 423 per Isaacs J. There remains some doubt as to the precise nature of the trust which arises in the vendor and even as to the point in time at which it arises (see *Chang v Registrar of Titles* (1975-76) 8 ALR 285 at 291; *Avondale Printers & Stationers Ltd v Haggie* [1979] 2 NZLR 124 at 141f). See also M.P. Thompson, [1984] Conv 43 at 44.
4 *Chang v Registrar of Titles* (1975-76) 8 ALR 285 at 295 per Jacobs J (High Court of Australia).

It is therefore only in a somewhat qualified sense that a vendor may properly be described as a trustee for his purchaser pending completion of a specifically enforceable contract. The vendor still enjoys a 'paramount right...to protect his own interest as vendor of the property'.[5] He still enjoys certain valuable rights in relation to the property. He has a right to remain in possession of the land until completion of the contract and payment of the purchase moneys,[6] and is entitled to the rents and profits which accrue before the date of completion.[7] Moreover, from the point of entering into a specifically enforceable contract of sale, the vendor retains an 'unpaid vendor's lien' over the property until the purchase moneys are paid in full.[8] However, once the vendor has received those purchase moneys in full, he becomes (until the date of completion) a 'bare trustee' for the purchaser.[9]

(b) Implications of the vendor's limited trusteeship

Certain consequences none the less flow from the equitable impact of a specifically enforceable contract for the sale of a legal estate in land. The purchaser, being now the beneficial owner of the land, henceforth has certain rights and responsibilities in relation to it.

(i) Vendor's duty of care The vendor is, by virtue of his limited trusteeship, burdened by fiduciary responsibilities towards his purchaser in respect of the management and preservation of the trust property during the period between contract and conveyance. The vendor may thus be liable to the purchaser if, by reason of his negligence, the subject matter of the contract of sale is damaged during this interim by trespassers[10] or by the elements,[11] or if the property is damaged by the vendor himself[12] or is prejudiced by unfavourable transactions entered into by the vendor.[13] Moreover, if the vendor in breach of contract sells the land instead to a third party, he stands in relation to the proceeds of that sale as a trustee on behalf of the contractual purchaser.[14]

5 *Shaw v Foster* (1872) LR 5 HL 321 at 338 per Lord Cairns LC.
6 *Gedye v Montrose* (1858) 26 Beav 45 at 49f, 53 ER 813 at 814f; *Phillips v Silvester* (1872) LR 8 Ch App 173 at 176f.
7 *Cuddon v Tite* (1858) 1 Giff 395 at 399, 65 ER 971 at 973. This differs from the 'inflexible rule' of equity that a trustee or fiduciary may never under any circumstances derive profit from his position of trust. See *Parker v McKenna* (1874) LR 10 Ch App 96 at 124 per James LJ; G.H. Jones, (1968) 84 LQR 472.
8 *Winter v Lord Anson* (1827) 3 Russ 488 at 492, 38 ER 658 at 660; *Nives v Nives* (1880) 15 Ch D 649 at 650; *Bridges v Mees* [1957] Ch 475 at 484; *In re Birmingham, Decd* [1959] Ch 523 at 528f; *London and Cheshire Insurance Co Ltd v Laplagrene Property Co Ltd* [1971] Ch 499 at 514C-D. An unpaid lender may later be subrogated to the vendor's lien after completion (see *Boodle Hatfield & Co v British Films Ltd* [1986] NLJ Rep 117 (post, p 575); *Bank of Ireland Finance Ltd v D.J. Daly Ltd* [1978] IR 79 at 82).
9 See eg *Bridges v Mees* [1957] Ch 475 at 484; *Chang v Registrar of Titles* (1975-76) 8 ALR 285 at 291; *Shanahan v Fitzgerald* [1982] 2 NSWLR 513 at 514G-515A.
10 *Clarke v Ramuz* [1891] 2 QB 456 at 460ff.
11 *Lucie-Smith v Gorman* [1981] CLY 2866.
12 *Lysaght v Edwards* (1876) 2 Ch D 499 at 507; *Cumberland Consolidated Holdings Ltd v Ireland* [1946] KB 264 at 269.
13 See *Abdulla v Shah* [1959] AC 124 at 132f (grant of unfavourable tenancies); *Sinclair-Hill v Sothcott* (1973) 226 Estates Gazette 1399 at 1401 (withdrawal of application for planning permission).
14 *Lake v Bayliss* [1974] 1 WLR 1073 at 1076D-E.

(ii) Insurable risk The trust relationship between vendor and purchaser has the further implication—of immediate practical concern to the latter—that the insurable risk in the subject matter of the contract passes concurrently with the equitable interest in the land. It is advisable therefore that the purchaser should buy insurance cover effective from the date of the contract, since it is generally accepted that the risk of destruction of the property passes to him as beneficial owner behind the trust of the legal estate.[15] On this basis, if a building on the land is destroyed by fire between contract and conveyance, the purchaser is still contractually bound to take the conveyance of the land and the charred remains at the full contracted purchase price.[16]

(iii) Role of the estate contract From the moment of the exchange of contracts the purchaser of land acquires not merely a contractual right but also a proprietary right. In the case of a freehold transaction, he acquires an equitable fee simple absolute in the property. This indirectly explains why one of the most significant categories of registrable land charge or minor interest—the 'estate contract'—is designed precisely to protect the right of the purchaser to require conveyance according to contract.[17] By virtue of the anticipatory effect of the equitable doctrine, the contractual right of the purchaser is recognised as a right in real property and (like any other commercial equitable interest) requires protection against third parties.

The same doctrine of equity has application to a contract to convey a lease or term of years. The contract itself is effective (under the doctrine in *Walsh v Lonsdale*[18]) to invest the tenant with an equitable interest in the land, ie, an equitable term of years. Furthermore, an imperfect conveyance of a leasehold interest (eg in writing instead of by deed) has a similar effect. Of course, in both cases the tenant can usually obtain specific performance of the lease by means of a court order that the landlord execute a lease in the proper form. However, the tenant often has no desire to seek specific performance since in equity he is already regarded as holding a term of years on conditions identical to those contained in the original contract or imperfect lease.[19] Thus, in many instances, a contract for a lease may never eventuate in a valid conveyance of the leasehold.

3. COMPLETION

By virtue of the exchange of contracts, vendor and purchaser are legally committed to complete the transaction. However, as Lord Erskine LC observed in *Hiern v Mill*,[20] 'no man in his senses would take an offer of a purchase from a man, merely because he stood upon the ground.' Mere possession by the vendor is not sufficient; the vendor must satisfy the purchaser that he has a good title to the property and that it is subject only to the adverse

---

15 *Lysaght v Edwards* (1876) 2 Ch D 499 at 507 per Jessel MR.
16 See eg *Lysaght v Edwards* (1876) 2 Ch D 499 at 507; *Rayner v Preston* (1881) 18 Ch D 1 at 6; *Budhia v Wellington City Corpn* [1976] 1 NZLR 766 at 768. For a strong counter-argument, see M.P. Thompson, *Must a Purchaser buy a Charred Ruin?*, [1984] Conv 43. See also Law of Property Act 1925, s 47.
17 Ante, pp 135, 159.
18 (1882) 21 Ch D 9 (post, p 471).
19 Post, p 472.
20 (1806) 13 Ves 114 at 122, 33 ER 237 at 240.

interests specified in the contract. If the title is unregistered, the vendor must supply an abstract of the title of the property which discloses dealings affecting the land during at least the past 15 years.[1] In the case of a registered title, the purchaser is given authority to inspect the Land Register for entries in respect of the vendor's title.[2] If either the abstract of title or the Land Register discloses apparent defects in the title offered, the purchaser may make 'requisitions' in order to clarify matters as to which doubt exists.

When satisfied that the title is in order, the purchaser sends to the vendor a draft conveyance, or, in the case of registered land, a draft form of transfer, for approval. When this draft is approved, the purchaser makes a final search of the Land Charges Register or Land Register, as is appropriate,[3] in order to ensure that the property remains free of undisclosed adverse interests. On the date fixed for completion (which is usually four weeks after the exchange of contracts), the purchaser pays over the balance of the purchase moneys and the vendor hands over the appropriate title deeds or documents. The transaction is now complete, except that in the case of registered land the document of transfer must be lodged at the Land Registry in order that the purchaser may be entered in the Register as the new proprietor.[4]

The foregoing is a brief description of the process by which a title is transferred from vendor to purchaser. Certain aspects of the transaction require greater emphasis.

(1) Formalities

By contrast with the relative informality with which a contract for the sale of land may be concluded, certain stringent requirements of form must be satisfied in the transfer of a legal estate in land. According to section 52(1) of the Law of Property Act 1925, '[a]ll conveyances of land or of any interest therein are void for the purpose of conveying or creating a legal estate unless made by deed.'[5] There are a number of exceptions to this rule, the most important of which relate to assents by personal representatives,[6] leases which are expressly exempted by statute from the requirement of formality,[7] and surrenders and conveyances which take effect by operation of law.[8]

(a) A deed must be signed, sealed and delivered

The substantial requirement of the deed is that it should be 'intended by the

1　Law of Property Act 1969, s 23. The maximum period in respect of which (in the absence of contrary contractual stipulation) the purchaser could insist on investigating title was originally fixed by the common law as 60 years (see *Barnwell v Harris* (1809) 1 Taunt 430 at 432, 127 ER 901). This period was progressively reduced to 40 years (Vendor and Purchaser Act 1874, s 1), 30 years (Law of Property Act 1925, s 44(1)), and now 15 years.
2　Ante, p 150.
3　Ante, pp 125, 161.
4　Ante, p 157.
5　Except as specified in the exceptions to the general principle in Law of Property Act 1925, s 52, an oral conveyance of a legal estate confers no interest in the land (see *Palfrey v Palfrey* (1974) 229 Estates Gazette 1593 at 1595). A parol grant has merely the force and effect of an interest at will (Law of Property Act 1925, s 54(1)). On interests at will, see Chapter 14 (post, p 430).
6　Law of Property Act 1925, s 52(2)(a).
7　Law of Property Act 1925, s 52(2)(d) (post, p 464).
8　Law of Property Act 1925, s 52(2)(c), (g).

party who does it to be the most solemn indication to the community that he really means to do what he is doing.'[9] In English law the validity of a deed has rested traditionally on compliance with the historic requirement that the deed must be signed, sealed and delivered. The force of these ancient conditions is today somewhat diminished.

(i) Signature   Where an individual executes a deed, he must either sign or place his mark upon the deed: sealing is no longer deemed sufficient.[10] Attestation of the signature is not a requirement,[11] although it is an exceedingly common practice for the signature to be witnessed. The signature need not, however, be in writing. It is sufficient—although not particularly desirable[12]— that the signature should take the form of an imprint by a rubber stamp with a facsimile signature or anything similar which clearly indicates an intention to authenticate the deed.[13] A corporation is deemed to have executed a deed if its seal is affixed to the document in the presence of, and is attested by, its clerk or secretary and a member of the board of directors or other governing body.[14]

(ii) Sealing   It used to be the case that 'no writing without a seal can be a deed',[15] but this rule was more appropriate to an age in which the general illiteracy of the population meant that a personal seal provided the only reliable means of authenticating a legal document. Nowadays the grantor's signature has acquired far greater practical significance than the seal in establishing the authenticity of the document concerned.[16] Section 73 of the Law of Property Act 1925 provides that where an individual executes a deed, he shall either sign or place his mark upon the same, and 'sealing alone shall not be deemed sufficient.' In any event, a seal tends today to be merely a mass-produced red adhesive paper disc which is attached to the bottom of the document concerned: the ceremony of sealing with the aid of sealing wax has almost entirely disappeared. Such is the diminishing mystique of the seal that in *First National Securities Ltd v Jones*[17] the Court of Appeal held that the requirement of a deed was satisfied by a signed document on which was printed a circle containing the letters 'LS'—representing *locus sigilli* (the place of a seal).[18]

(iii) Delivery   Although the idea of 'delivery' of a deed had its origin in some manual transfer of the relevant document, it has been clear since at least the

---

9   *Manton v Parabolic Pty Ltd* [1985] 2 NSWLR 361 at 367F-G.
10   Law of Property Act 1925, s 73(1).
11   See Law of Property Act 1925, s 75(1).
12   See eg *Goodman v J. Eban Ltd* [1954] 1 QB 550 at 561f.
13   *Bennett v Brumfitt* (1867) LR 3 CP 28 at 30f; *LCC v Agricultural Food Products Ltd* [1955] 2 QB 218 at 223ff; *R v Brentford Justices, ex parte Catlin* [1975] QB 455 at 462E-F.
14   Law of Property Act 1925, s 74(1).
15   *Sheppard's Touchstone of Common Assurances* (8th edn by E.G. Atherley, London 1826), p 56.
16   See *Stromdale and Ball Ltd v Burden* [1952] Ch 223 at 230, where Danckwerts J pointed out that 'with the spread of education, the signature became of importance for the authentication of documents'.
17   [1978] Ch 109 at 118E-F, 119H, 121A-B. Compare, however, *Re Smith* (1892) 67 LT 64 at 66.
18   See D.C. Hoath, *The Sealing of Documents—Fact or Fiction?*, (1980) 43 MLR 415.

17th century that a deed may be 'delivered by words without any act of delivery'.[19] Delivery of the signed and sealed document is nowadays taken to comprise any unilateral act or statement by the grantor which signifies that he adopts the deed irrevocably as his own.[20] The essential element of the deed is that it thus comprises 'the most solemn act that a person can perform with respect to a particular piece of property or other right'.[1]

(b) Reform of the existing requirements for a deed

It is curious to reflect on the importance attached historically to the requirement that a deed be signed, sealed and delivered by the grantor. Conveyancing, magic and sorcery have never been wholly unconnected phenomena, as is made clear by the medieval ritual and symbolism which attended the 'feoffment with livery of seisin'.[2] It is an interesting feature of the social anthropology of land law that the talismanic effect of a little red wafer is such as to confer upon certain transactions a legal efficacy which they would not otherwise possess. The use of a deed is more than a mere sine qua non of actionability.[3] It is a condition precedent to the validity of the conveyance or transfer which it contains. The significance of the seal is, however, much in decline in the present day. As long ago as 1937 Goddard J observed that 'a seal nowadays is very much in the nature of a legal fiction'.[4] In 1971 Lord Wilberforce, speaking extra-judicially in the House of Lords, castigated 'this medieval doctrine of the seal' and expressed the hope that 'we might have got rid of that mumbo-jumbo and aligned ourselves with most civilised countries'.[5]

In response to these long-standing criticisms of the formalities required in the execution of a deed, the Law Commission published a working paper in 1985 which proposed a vast simplification of the law relating to deeds.[6] The Commission provisionally recommended that the requirement of sealing should be abolished.[7] In its view, the seal is today 'a redundant formality without substantive purpose and easily overlooked.'[8] The Commission likewise proposed that the law would be simplified if the concept of delivery were abolished.[9] The Commission concluded, however, that the requirement of signature should remain,[10] adding that attestation should be made obligatory in unregistered conveyancing, as indeed it is already in registered conveyancing.[11] The Commission similarly envisaged that the formalities of a

19 *Co Litt*, p 36a.
20 See *Re Sammon* (1979) 94 DLR (3d) 594 at 597ff. See also D.E.C. Yale, *The Delivery of a Deed*, [1970] CLJ 52.
1 *Manton v Parabolic Pty Ltd* [1985] 2 NSWLR 361 at 369B-C.
2 ·Ante, p 64. For an historical account of the ritual solemnity attendant on transfers of land, see *Manton v Parabolic Pty Ltd* [1985] 2 NSWLR 361 at 367A-368C.
3 Compare Law of Property Act 1925, s 40(1).
4 Sixth Interim Report of the Law Revision Committee on *Statute of Frauds and the Doctrine of Consideration* (Cmd 5449, 1937), p 35.
5 *Parliamentary Debates, House of Lords, Official Report* (1970-71), Vol 315, Col 1213 (25 February 1971).
6 Law Commission, *Transfer of Land: Formalities for Deeds and Escrows* (Working Paper No 93, July 1985).
7 Working Paper No 93, para 8(2)(ii).
8 Working Paper No 93, para 8(2)(ii).
9 Working Paper No 93, para 8(2)(iv).
10 Working Paper No 93, para 8.2(iii).
11 Working Paper No 93, para 8.3(i). See Land Registration Rules 1925, r 98 and Schedule (Form 19).

deed should include a requirement of 'writing on some permanent substance...though perhaps extended to cover substances other than paper or parchment.'[12] This last proposal marked a recognition of the possibility that in days to come much material which is currently retained in written form may be preserved on a computer disk or in some other electronic form.

(2) Conveyancing practice

The conveyancing process has normally been conducted to date by solicitors acting for the vendor and purchaser respectively. In their hands the process is slow and costly,[13] and there has inevitably been large public concern as to whether the consumer of these legal services receives anything like value for money. The pattern of supply and demand has been further distorted by the fact that solicitors have long been the beneficiaries of a crude and quite remarkable monopolistic privilege in conveyancing matters. The Solicitors Act 1974 imposes criminal liability on any 'unqualified person' who receives any 'fee, gain or reward' for the purpose of drawing or preparing any instrument of transfer or charge or any other instrument relating to real or personal estate.[14] In this context, an 'unqualified person' is a person who is not qualified to act as a solicitor under section 1 of the 1974 Act.[15] The 1974 Act imposes no restriction on a lay person who merely wishes to do his own conveyancing; the prohibition strikes only at 'unqualified persons' who undertake conveyancing for a fee.

Over the years the solicitors' monopolistic control of conveyancing has tended to serve substantial vested interests and has accordingly been defended with the zeal which becomes strangely apparent when vested interests are threatened. The Royal Commission on Legal Services, which reported in 1979, vigorously resisted the introduction of a 'free-for-all' in which any person might offer conveyancing services without restriction.[16] The Commission took the view that it was only by virtue of the 'positive control' currently exercised by the responsible professional body that high standards of competence and ethical conduct could be maintained.[17] The Commission therefore not only endorsed the existing statutory monopoly enjoyed by solicitors but recommended that the monopoly should be extended to cover *contracts* for the sale of land.[18]

The Royal Commission's Report was seen by many as indicating an unnecessarily supine acceptance of the self-serving submissions made by a

---

12   Working Paper No 93, para 8.2(i).

13   See *In re Stone and Saville's Contract* [1962] 1 WLR 460 at 465, where Buckley J referred to the 'stately saraband which takes place between vendor and purchaser on a purchase of land'.

14   Solicitors Act 1974, s 22(1). In *Powell v Ely* (1980) *Times*, 22 May, this provision was even used—most oppressively—in the prosecution of an unqualified person who drafted divorce petitions in return for free accommodation and a weekly wage of £5 to £8.

15   Solicitors Act 1974, s 87(1).

16   *Final Report of the Royal Commission on Legal Services* (Cmnd 7648, October 1979), Vol 1, para 21.60(e).

17   Ibid, para 21.60(f).

18   Ibid, para 21.61. See now Solicitors Act 1974, s 22(3), as amended by Administration of Justice Act 1985, s 6(4). Indeed, the Commission was so anxious to give its enthusiastic support to the conveyancing monopoly of solicitors that it fell deep into the trap of the misplaced negative. In para 21.4 of its Report the Commission, by way of glorious misprint, went on record as advocating the imposition of criminal liability under Solicitors Act 1974, s 22, on all *qualified* persons who undertake conveyancing for a fee!

profession which was desperately anxious to preserve its entrenched monopoly. However, changes in this area have since been made irresistible both because of increasing public disquiet about the quality of legal services and because of the modern distaste for self-interested protectionism in professional life. The Administration of Justice Act 1985 accordingly makes provision for 'licensed conveyancing' to be carried out by persons who are not qualified solicitors.[19] With effect from May 1987 the 1985 Act legalises the delivery of conveyancing services by 'licensed conveyancers',[20] who are to be subject to professional controls administered by a Council for Licensed Conveyancers.[1] Past experience of the operation of market forces tends to suggest that this relaxation of the solicitors' conveyancing monopoly should conduce towards greater efficiency and economy in conveyancing services generally, without any consequent diminution in the standard of services or security at present offered to the consumer.

(3) Equitable jurisdiction to set aside unconscionable bargains

The law of real property is not a branch of moral philosophy; it is generally concerned only with the attainment of procedural efficiency in the transfer of land and not with the achievement of justice in the distribution of goods. Once the derivation of the vendor's title is clarified beyond technical dispute, the law of conveyancing raises no question either as to the substantive fairness of the fact that the vendor has land to convey or even as to the fact that the purchaser is possessed of the money consideration required for the transfer of title. This ethical neutrality is a pervasive characteristic of a capitalist system of property which is dominated both by the solid tug of money and by the inevitable advantage enjoyed by the wealthy and privileged over the poor and weak. It could not be pretended that the law of property in its traditional common law manifestation sets out either to direct or to endorse any redistribution of goods between the rich and the poor.

In only one area does the law of property make any concession to a conception of fairness as a criterion of legality in the transfer of property. There has always been an equitable jurisdiction to set aside a transaction at a considerable undervalue which has been entered into by a 'poor and ignorant' vendor acting without independent advice.[2] The persons who nowadays fall within the purview of this classical equitable formulation are those who, in contemporary idiom, comprise members of 'the lower income group' and who may be said to 'less highly educated'.[3] The court will exercise its equitable jurisdiction to relieve such vendors of the consequences of their dealings unless the purchaser discharges an onus of proof that the transaction in question was fair, just and reasonable.[4] This merciful jurisdiction is not, however, of wide

19 Administration of Justice Act 1985, s 11ff.
20 Administration of Justice Act 1985, s 11(4).
1   Administration of Justice Act 1985, s 12.
2   *How v Weldon and Edwards* (1754) 2 Ves Sen 516 at 518ff, 28 ER 330 at 331f; *Fry v Lane* (1888) 40 Ch D 312 at 322. See Lord Goff of Chieveley and Gareth Jones, *The Law of Restitution* (3rd edn, London 1986), p 257ff. See also M. Cope, (1983) 57 ALJ 279; *Chrispen v Topham* (1986) 28 DLR (4th) 754 at 758f.
3   *Cresswell v Potter* (1968) [1978] 1 WLR 255 (Note) at 257F-H per Megarry J. See also *Watkin v Watson-Smith* (1986) *Times*, 3 July.
4   *Wood v Abrey* (1818) 3 Madd 417 at 423f, 56 ER 558 at 560f; *Fry v Lane* (1888) 40 Ch D 312 at 322; *Hart v O'Connor* [1985] AC 1000 at 1024B-C; *Commercial Bank of Australia Ltd v Amadio* (1982-83) 46 ALR 402.

application. It cannot be invoked merely because the vendor has entered into an improvident transaction.[5] The discretion to set aside unconscionable bargains is exercised only in exceptional circumstances. In *Hart v O'Connor*,[6] for instance, Lord Brightman distinguished between transactions which are marked by 'procedural unfairness' (as, for instance, where there is an element of undue influence) and those which are adversely affected by 'contractual imbalance'. In his view, equity cannot set aside a transaction as an unconscionable bargain where 'there was no victimisation, no taking advantage of another's weakness, and the sole allegation was contractual imbalance with no undertones of constructive fraud'.[7]

4. PRIORITY OF INTERESTS AFTER THE CONVEYANCE OF A LEGAL ESTATE

One of the central questions of land law relates to the effect which the transfer of a legal estate has upon pre-existing equitable rights in the land conveyed. This issue is addressed in detail at several points in this book, but it may be helpful to summarise here some of the relevant principles.

(1) Equitable interests in unregistered land

The outline of the 1925 legislation which was contained in Chapter 6 should have made it clear that for conveyancing purposes the field of equitable interests in unregistered or 'old system' land subdivides into three distinct categories.[8] Some of these equitable interests are 'commercial' interests which are registrable in the Land Charges Register. Others comprise 'family' interests which are statutorily overreachable on a conveyance of the land and which take effect thereafter in proceeds of sale. In a twilight zone beyond these major categories of registrable and overreachable interests there lies a third (and ultimately residual) category of equitable rights in unregistered land. Since such rights are neither registrable nor statutorily overreached, their effect on a purchaser of land falls to be determined by the equitable doctrine of notice in its traditional formulation.[9]

The interests which fall into this third category are relatively few in number, but, being anomalous, they present problems in unregistered conveyancing disproportional to their prevalence. They provide the epicentre of many a minor earthquake amidst some of the more difficult terrain of land law.[10] Collectively they constitute the nightmare of the conveyancer in that they comprise unregistrable, non-overreachable and sometimes virtually undiscoverable equitable interests which may yet bind the purchaser on a basis of constructive notice. However, the threefold division of the field of equitable interests makes it possible to adopt a schematic approach to the resolution of

---

5   See *Mountford v Scott* [1975] Ch 258 at 264E.
6   [1985] AC 1000 at 1017H–1018C.
7   [1985] AC 1000 at 1024D.
8   Ante, p 102.
9   See eg *Shiloh Spinners Ltd v Harding* [1973] AC 691 at 721D, where Lord Wilberforce declared himself prepared to accept that 'there may well be rights, of an equitable character, outside the provisions as to registration and which are incapable of being overreached.'
10 See eg *E.R. Ives Investment Ltd v High* [1967] 2 QB 379 (ante, p 141).

problems of priority wherever the owner of an equitable interest in unregistered land is confronted by a purchaser of a legal estate in that land. Such questions of priority can always be answered by asking the following questions.

(a) Could the owner of the equitable interest have protected himself against the purchaser by means of a land charge registration?

If the owner of the equitable interest had rights which were capable of registration as a land charge, then
(i) if these rights were duly registered they now bind the purchaser[11];
(ii) if these rights were not duly registered they become, for want of registration, void against most categories of purchaser—even though the purchaser may have had actual knowledge of the rights at the date of his purchase.[12]

If, however, the equitable interest in question was not registrable and does not therefore become void for non-registration, then a second question must be raised:

(b) Was the equitable interest statutorily overreached by the purchase?

The transactions in land which attract the consequence of a statutory overreaching are detailed in section 2(1) of the Law of Property Act 1925. Such transactions comprise any 'conveyance'[13] to a purchaser of a legal estate in land which is effected (i) under the powers conferred by the Settled Land Act 1925, (ii) by trustees for sale, (iii) by a mortgagee or personal representative in the exercise of his paramount powers, or (iv) under an order of the court. It is clear that certain kinds of disposition of a legal estate in land (eg a conveyance by a bare trustee[14]) inherently lack any statutory overreaching capacity, for the purely artificial reason that they are not included within the statutory list of transactions which are detailed as having overreaching power. If, however, a particular equitable interest is in principle overreachable within the terms of section 2(1) of the Law of Property Act 1925, then

(i) if there was a compliance with the statutory preconditions for overreaching,[15] the equitable interest is overreached by force of statute and is henceforth satisfied out of the proceeds of the disposition;
(ii) if there was no compliance with the statutory preconditions for overreaching,[15] the purchaser cannot properly claim that he has overreached (or taken title free of) the equitable interest.

If for any reason the equitable interest is not overreached—either because it is inherently non-overreachable or because the statutory conditions were not

---

11   Law of Property Act 1925, s 198(1) (ante, p 114).
12   Land Charges Act 1972, s 4 (ante, p 115). See *Midland Bank Trust Co Ltd v Green* [1981] AC 513. Of course unprotected land charges are not universally void for reasons of non-registration. An unregistered estate contract remains valid, for instance, against a purchaser of an *equitable* interest in the land (see Land Charges Act 1972, s 4(6); *McCarthy and Stone Ltd v Hodge & Co Ltd* [1971] 1 WLR 1547 at 1555D-E).
13   A 'conveyance' is defined for the purpose of the Law of Property Act 1925 as including a mortgage, charge and lease of property (see Law of Property Act 1925, s 205(1)(ii)).
14   Ante, p 44. See eg *Hodgson v Marks* [1971] Ch 892 (post, p 185).
15   See eg Law of Property Act 1925, s 27(2) (ante, p 100; post, p 356).

fulfilled, the issue of priority must turn on the answer given to the final question.

(c) Was the purchaser a bona fide purchaser of a legal estate for value without notice?

The question of priority is ultimately determined by an application of the traditional doctrine of notice:

(i)   if the purchaser ranks as 'Equity's Darling', he takes the legal estate free of the equitable interest;

(ii)   if the purchaser was not a bona fide purchaser of a legal estate for value without notice, he is bound by the equitable interest.

Before 1926 this application of the equitable doctrine of notice would have provided the complete answer to any question of priority arising between the owner of an equitable interest and the purchaser of a legal estate in unregistered land. But since 1925 the doctrine of notice has been overlaid by the two devices of land charge registration and statutory overreaching, thus necessitating questions (a) and (b) in advance of question (c). In effect the registration of land charges renders notice inescapable; the process of statutory overreaching renders notice irrelevant. Taken in conjunction questions (a), (b) and (c) must inevitably disclose the fate of any equitable interest in unregistered land where a legal estate is purchased by a third party. The entire field of equitable interests may thus be divided into three major categories which simply serve to exhaust all the logical possibilities affecting the issue of priority between equitable owner and purchaser. The set of *equitable interests in unregistered land* can therefore be represented in terms of three sub-sets, to each of which one of the interrogatories (a) to (c) is appropriate.

SUB-SET 1	SUB-SET 2	SUB-SET 3
'COMMERCIAL' EQUITABLE INTERESTS	'FAMILY' EQUITABLE INTERESTS	UNREGISTRABLE NON-OVERREACHABLE INTERESTS
(protected by land charge registration)	(protected by effects of overreaching)	(protected by doctrine of notice)

QUESTION (a)   QUESTION (b)   QUESTION (c)

Fig. 19

(2) Equitable interests in registered land

In relation to registered land it is possible, in the current state of the law, to adopt a two-fold formula in the resolution of the equivalent issues of priority raised between the owners of equitable interests and a transferee of the legal title. The problem of priority can be determined by asking just two questions:

(a) Did the owner of the equitable interest have any interest capable of entry on the register as a minor interest?

If the answer to this question is in the affirmative and the right in question was duly entered as a minor interest, this entry of course prevails against the transferee.[16] If the right has not been so protected, there is some—albeit dubious—authority for the view that an unprotected minor interest is binding on a transferee who has actual knowledge of the existence of the right.[17] However, the better view is that (apart from cases of fraud) the transferee is unaffected by an unprotected minor interest 'whether he has or has not notice thereof, express, implied or constructive'.[18] If, on this view, a minor interest thus becomes ineffective as a minor interest, a further question must be posed.

(b) Can the owner of the equitable interest nevertheless claim any kind of overriding interest?

If the answer to this second question is in the affirmative, then even an unprotected minor interest may be saved as an overriding interest and may therefore be binding on the transferee of the registered title. The statutory protection afforded overriding interests may be available, for instance, on the ground that the owner of the equitable interest was at the effective date of transfer 'in actual occupation' of the land or 'in receipt of the rents and profits' thereof.[19]

The result is that the owner of an equitable interest in registered land may effectively have 'two bites at the cherry' in his claim for priority over the transferee of the registered title. He may, in some circumstances, be able to argue either that he has duly protected his interest by register entry or, in default of securing such protection, that his interest gave rise to an overriding interest which is binding on the transferee. This duplication of protection has in recent years raised profound difficulties in the conveyancing of registered titles,[20] but will become less extensive if legislative effect is given to the reform proposals made by the Law Commission.[1]

16   Land Registration Act 1925, s 20(1).
17   *Peffer v Rigg* [1977] 1 WLR 285 (ante, p 166).
18   Land Registration Act 1925, s 59(6).
19   Land Registration Act 1925, s 70(1)(g).
20   Ante, p 191; post, p 850.
1   Ante, p 201.

C. Holdings

CHAPTER 10

Trusts

Any claim to a beneficial interest[1] in real property necessarily presupposes the existence of some kind of trust.[2] As Lord Diplock indicated in *Gissing v Gissing*,[3] it must be shown 'that the person in whom the legal estate is vested holds it as a trustee upon trust to give effect to the beneficial interest of the claimant as cestui que trust.'[4] The present chapter is therefore devoted to an account of the origin of the various kinds of trust which have a role to play in the law of land.

1. ASCERTAINMENT OF BENEFICIAL OWNERSHIP

Fundamental to the ascertainment of the beneficial ownership of land is the proposition that a transfer of the legal title carries with it, prima facie, the absolute beneficial interest in the property conveyed.[5] Thus a conveyance to A of a legal title in land vests in A the whole of the beneficial interest unless some other person, B, is able to 'establish a basis upon which equity would intervene on [his or] her behalf.'[6] Equity will intervene on behalf of B only if such action is necessary in order to give effect to one or other of its doctrines.[7] Accordingly, equity's historic concern with conscience has manifested itself pre- eminently in a willingness in appropriate circumstances to call into existence some form of 'equitable' interest or ownership on behalf of B in opposition to the 'legal' title of A.[8] The recognition of such an entitlement amounts to the assertion of a trust relationship between A and B, under which A is conventionally described as holding his legal title on trust for B.

It is the purpose of the following pages to outline the circumstances under which such a trust will come into being. Three forms of trust are relevant in this context: (1) the express trust, (2) the resulting trust, and (3) the constructive trust. Sadly, however, the terminology used by courts and lawyers to refer to these different kinds of trust is somewhat lacking in uniformity and consistency.[9]

---

1 For an explanation of equitable or 'beneficial' ownership, see Chapter 3 (ante, p 51).
2 *Gissing v Gissing* [1971] AC 886 at 900B; *Burns v Burns* [1984] Ch 317 at 326F, 330H- 331A; *Allen v Snyder* [1977] 2 NSWLR 685 at 689F; *Thwaites v Ryan* [1984] VR 65 at 69.
3 [1971] AC 886 at 904G-H.
4 The onus is on the claimant to demonstrate that the beneficial entitlement does not coincide with the legal title (*Crisp v Mullings* (1976) 239 Estates Gazette 119 per Russell LJ). In *Bernard v Josephs* [1982] Ch 391 at 404H-405B, 407D-E the Court of Appeal held that, notwithstanding the arguments put forward by the defendant, everything in the surrounding circumstances of the case confirmed that the equitable ownership followed the legal title. See (1982) 98 LQR 518; [1982] Conv 444 (J. Warburton); [1983] CLJ 30.
5 *Pettitt v Pettitt* [1970] AC 777 at 813H-814A. See also *Vandervell v IRC* [1966] Ch 261 at 287G; *Gissing v Gissing* [1971] AC 886 at 902A; *Bernard v Josephs* [1982] Ch 391 at 402D; *Burns v Burns* [1984] Ch 317 at 330H, 336D.
6 *Allen v Snyder* [1977] 2 NSWLR 685 at 701E per Mahoney J.
7 *Commissioner of Stamp Duties (Queensland) v Livingston* [1965] AC 694 at 712E per Viscount Radcliffe; *Muschinski v Dodds* (1985) 62 ALR 429 at 452 per Deane J.
8 Ante, p 41.
9 See eg *Burns v Burns* [1984] Ch 317 at 336D-F, where May LJ described as a resulting trust what would more usually be termed a constructive trust. See also *Allen v Snyder* [1977] 2 NSWLR 685 at 691D; *Muschinski v Dodds* (1985) 62 ALR 429 at 437.

(1) **Classification of trusts**

Classification is arid, but confusion is worse. It may be appropriate at this point to indicate that the major classificatory distinction in the law of trusts is that between express and implied trusts. Implied trusts may be further subdivided into resulting and constructive trusts (*Fig.* 20).

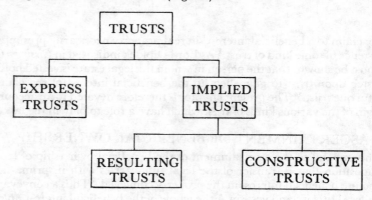

Fig. 20

It befits a jurisdiction which is less impressed by form than by substance that equity's recognition of the trust should ultimately be concerned with matters of intention. In the High Court of Australia in *Hepworth v Hepworth*,[10] Windeyer J observed that an 'intention, proved or presumed, that a trust should exist is at the base of every trust'. This proposition is borne out in the three cases of trust which are the focus of this chapter. The express trust is the very embodiment of an intention formulated by a legal owner as to the beneficial ownership of his property; the resulting trust gives effect to an intention presumed to have been formulated by the legal owner at the date of his acquisition of title; and the constructive trust arises in circumstances where it would be unconscionable not to give effect to a common intention which has provided the basis of the parties' mutual expectations and dealings.

(2) **Search for intentions as to beneficial ownership**

Ownership of the legal title in land is scarcely ever in doubt, since the identity of the current legal owner is usually firmly established by the last deed of conveyance (in the case of unregistered land) or by the relevant proprietorship register (in the case of registered land). In almost every case, therefore, the location of legal ownership is definitively ascertained by reference to a documentary source,[11] and indeed the primary purpose of the transfer documents which are used in conveyancing is to indicate with precision the name of the next legal owner or owners. These transfer documents may, of course, go on to clarify not merely matters of legal title but also details of beneficial ownership, and such a declaration of beneficial entitlement, if included in the conveyance, is generally conclusive.[12]

10   (1963) 110 CLR 309 at 317.
11   Compare, however, the case of acquisition through adverse possession (post, p 740).
12   *Pettitt v Pettitt* [1970] AC 777 at 813E per Lord Upjohn.

(a) Unexpressed beneficial ownership

It is possible, however, that the documentary title may remain completely silent as to the beneficial ownership of the land, in which case it is much more difficult to ascertain the nature and quantum of the equitable interests in that land. The details of beneficial ownership following transfer are frequently not contained in any formal document or other writing, and may come into question only at some much later stage when a dispute arises.[13] When this happens it becomes necessary to render explicit that which was previously left unexpressed.

(b) Extrinsic aids to the discovery of intention

The method by which beneficial ownership is determined under such circumstances was explained in classic terms by the House of Lords in *Pettitt v Pettitt*.[14] Here Lord Upjohn pointed to the extrinsic aids which may be called into play when the documentary title performs only its minimal function of dealing with the legal ownership. Certain residual evidential devices exist to enable the court to discover the parties' intentions in respect of beneficial ownership, and the court has recourse to these devices in the following order. *First*, the court may have regard to parol evidence as to the beneficial interests intended by the parties at the date of acquisition of the legal title.[15] *Second*, if such parol evidence is lacking or inadmissible or simply inconclusive, the court may draw inferences as to intention from the conduct of the parties both before and after the conveyance of the legal estate. *Third*, if even this fails to illuminate the relevant intentions of the parties, the court may apply the equitable presumptions as to intention. These presumptions represent merely the informed speculation of lawyers over the centuries as to the type of beneficial ownership most likely to have been intended by the parties in certain stylised situations.[16] The presumptions of equity are decisive of beneficial title only in the last resort and they prevail only in the absence of other more compelling evidence of actual intention.[17]

2. EXPRESS TRUSTS

The clearest example of a trust arises where A, the owner of a legal title in land, expressly declares himself to be a trustee of that title for B. Certain rules govern the creation and enforceability of such a trust.

---

13 Disputes as to beneficial ownership may arise in many contexts. The issue of ownership may be precipitated by a bankruptcy or death, or in connection with tax liability, or even in unusual contexts such as arose in *Heron v Sandwell MBC* (1980) 255 Estates Gazette 65, where the question affected the payment of an owner-occupier's supplement after compulsory purchase.

14 [1970] AC 777 at 813F-G.

15 Parol evidence may be given not only by the parties to a transaction of purchase, but also by others who are in a position to testify to their intentions at that time, eg relatives, solicitors etc (see *Hodgson v Marks* [1971] Ch 892 at 905C-E).

16 See *Pettitt v Pettitt* [1970] AC 777 at 823H per Lord Diplock (post, p 260); *Muschinski v Dodds* (1985) 62 ALR 429 at 450.

17 Post, p 261.

(1) Language creative of a trust

An express trust need not be couched in formal words; any words which plainly evince an intention to create a trust will be sufficient.[18] It is even possible that 'by the use...of unguarded language, a person may create a trust, as Monsieur Jourdain talked prose, without knowing it',[19] but unless an intention to create a trust is clearly to be collected from the language used and from the circumstances of the case, the courts will not be astute to discover indications of such an intention.[20]

(2) Subject matter of the trust

An express declaration of trust may extend to the entire equitable interest in the land (as where A constitutes himself a trustee for B absolutely). Alternatively, the declaration may extend merely to some limited interest in the land (as where A holds henceforth on trust to give effect to a life interest or a fractional share in B) or even to some functional equivalent of a limited interest (as where A undertakes to allow B rent-free occupation for life).[1]

No valid declaration of an express trust can be made in respect of property which does not yet exist or in which the declarant has no interest at the date of his purported declaration.[2] Nor, obviously, can the declarant create a trust of any larger estate than he himself owns.[3] However, with these qualifications an express trust can be declared at any time—whether on or after the declarant's acquisition of title—and in respect of any property in which the declarant is beneficially entitled.

(3) Requirement of formality

An express trust may thus take a wide variety of forms. The declaration of trust may nominate more than one beneficiary; it may allocate various kinds or sizes of equitable entitlement to numerous beneficiaries. However, irrespective of the content of the express trust, one overriding rule prevails in English law: a declaration of trust relating to land is enforceable only if evidenced in writing. Section 53(1)(b) of the Law of Property Act 1925 (which derives from the

18   *Cowcher v Cowcher* [1972] 1 WLR 425 at 430E; *Bloch v Bloch* (1981) 37 ALR 55 at 59.
19   *In re Schebsman, decd* [1944] Ch 83 at 104 per Du Parcq LJ. See also *Tito v Waddell (No 2)* [1977] Ch 106 at 211F.
20   Trusts affecting certain kinds of person (ie, the Crown and its governmental agencies) tend not to be justiciable in the courts. See *Tito v Waddell (No 2)* [1977] Ch 106 at 222F-G; *Guerin v The Queen* (1983) 143 DLR (3d) 416 at 469; *Aboriginal Development Commission v Treka Aboriginal Arts & Crafts Ltd* [1984] 3 NSWLR 502 at 518C, 519D. There are also certain kinds of property in relation to the acquisition of which the courts seem anxious not to apply trust principles (eg barristers' chambers). See *Appleby v Cowley* (1982) *Times*, 14 April.
1   Post, p 274.
2   *Dye v Dye* (1884) 13 QBD 147 at 157; *White v Cabanas Pty Ltd (No 2)* [1970] Qd R 395 at 407E. It is possible, however, that a constructive trust may attach to property which was not owned by the declarant at the date of his declaration of trust (see *Le Compte v Public Trustee* [1983] 2 NSWLR 109 at 111A, post, p 272).
3   *Dye v Dye* (1884) 13 QBD 147 at 157. A declaration of trust affecting the whole beneficial interest in co-owned land can be made only with the concurrence of all the co-owners (*Kronheim v Johnson* (1877) 7 Ch D 60 at 66).

Statute of Frauds 1677) contains a provision that

a declaration of any trust respecting any land or any interest therein must be manifested and proved by some writing signed by some person who is able to declare such trust or by his will.[4]

The date of the writing is irrelevant,[5] but without written evidence a declaration of trust relating to land is valid[6] but unenforceable.[7]

(4) Exemptions from the requirement of formality

The stern rule contained in section 53(1)(b) is subject to certain important exceptions, some of which go so far as to constitute 'a drastic judicial modification' of the statutory requirement of written evidence.[8]

If A , the owner of a legal title in land, attempts to deny the existence of a trust which he has already declared orally in B's favour, the only evidence of that trust is *ex hypothesi* oral or parol evidence. A's most obvious defence against B's claim is therefore that section 53(1)(b) excludes the very parol evidence which would substantiate the allegation of trust. However, there are some circumstances in which A is not entitled to shut out parol evidence of the trust in this way.

(a) Resulting, implied or constructive trusts

Certain kinds of trust are exempted from formal requirements of writing by the Law of Property Act itself. Section 53(2) provides that the requirement of formality does not affect the 'creation or operation of resulting, implied or constructive trusts'. Thus the parol nature of the evidence has no detrimental effect on B's claim against A if the same facts which underlie the express trust also give rise to a resulting or constructive trust. It is clear that the existence of an unenforceable express trust is not necessarily inconsistent with a claim alleging some other form of trust which is immune from the documentary requirements of section 53(1).[9] In this way an originally unenforceable oral declaration of trust for B may sometimes become enforceable not as an express trust, but as a resulting or constructive trust.

(b) Use of the statute as an instrument of fraud

The fundamental purpose of requiring certain formalities to be observed in the creation and operation of express trusts is the prevention of fraud which might otherwise operate against the trustee. However, this insistence on formality is

4   This provision is the modern emanation of section 7 of the Statute of Frauds 1677 (29 Car 2, c 3). For an account of the legislative motivations underlying this famous enactment, see Tim Youdan, *Formalities for Trusts of Land, and the Doctrine in Rochefoucauld v Boustead*, [1984] CLJ 306 at 307ff.
5   *Forster v Hale* (1798) 3 Ves 696 at 711, 30 ER 1226 at 1233; *Rochefoucauld v Boustead* [1897] 1 Ch 196 at 206.
6   *Gardner v Rowe* (1828) 5 Russ 258 at 262, 38 ER 1024 at 1025.
7   *Gissing v Gissing* [1969] 2 Ch 85 at 99A-B; [1971] AC 886 at 910E-F; *Cowcher v Cowcher* [1972] 1 WLR 425 at 430H-431A; *Midland Bank PLC v Dobson* [1986] 1 FLR 171 at 175C-D; *Wratten v Hunter* [1978] 2 NSWLR 367 at 371B.
8   T. Youdan, [1984] CLJ 306 at 325.
9   Post, pp 260, 270.

not pursued to the insensate degree that reliance upon an absence of writing is allowed to facilitate the commission of fraud by the trustee himself. There is a clear doctrine to the effect that equity will never permit a statute to be used as an instrument of fraud.[10] This doctrine affects the present context in two different ways.

(i) Part performance　The doctrine of part performance is a primary manifestation of the rule that equity will not allow a statute to be pleaded in defence of a fraud. Under this doctrine a relationship of contract or trust will be regarded as specifically enforceable, notwithstanding a non-compliance with statutory requirements of written evidence, if instead there is supporting evidence of acts of part performance which are clearly referable to the existence of the alleged contract or trust.[11] However, it is a condition of specific performance that the claimant should have provided consideration, for equity will not normally assist a volunteer.[12]

The doctrine of part performance may occasionally save an otherwise unenforceable oral trust declared by A in favour of B.[13] As Bagnall J observed in *Cowcher v Cowcher*,[14] the necessity for compliance with section 53(1)(b) is obviated if the declaration is contained in an agreement for consideration[15] of which equity would order specific performance. Part performance of the agreement by B would be sufficient to circumvent the formal requirement of written evidence. It could be argued, however, that the trust which thus becomes enforceable here is not so much the original orally declared trust but rather a new constructive trust based on detrimental reliance.[16]

(ii) The rule in Rochefoucauld v Boustead　A further instance of equity's abhorrence of fraud is found in the rule in *Rochefoucauld v Boustead*.[17] Here Lindley LJ, giving the judgment of the Court of Appeal, acknowledged the existence of a body of caselaw affirming the principle that 'the Statute of Frauds does not prevent proof of a fraud.'[18] Lindley LJ continued to say that

it is a fraud on the part of a person to whom land is conveyed as a trustee, and who knows it was so conveyed, to deny the trust and claim the land himself. Consequently, notwithstanding the statute, it is competent for a person claiming land conveyed to another to prove by parol evidence that it was so conveyed upon trust for the claimant,

---

10　*Hutchins v Lee* (1737) 1 Atk 447 at 448, 26 ER 284 at 285; *Forster v Hale* (1798) 3 Ves 696 at 713, 30 ER 1226 at 1234; *Lincoln v Wright* (1859) 4 De G & J 16 at 22, 45 ER 6 at 9; *McCormick v Grogan* (1869) LR 4 HL 82 at 97; *Booth v Turle* (1873) LR 16 Eq 182 at 187; *Rochefoucauld v Boustead* [1897] 1 Ch 196 at 206; *Organ v Sandwell* [1921] VLR 622 at 630; *Last v Rosenfeld* [1972] 2 NSWLR 923 at 927E.
11　Ante, p 212.
12　Ante, p 216. See *Midland Bank PLC v Dobson* [1986] 1 FLR 171 at 175E.
13　The operation of the law relating to part performance is expressly preserved in the context of section 53 of the Law of Property Act 1925 (see Law of Property Act 1925, s 55(d)).
14　[1972] 1 WLR 425 at 430H-431A, 431D, 435H, 436C, H.
15　The consideration may include marriage consideration (*Cowcher v Cowcher* [1972] 1 WLR 425 at 431A).
16　Post, p 268.
17　[1897] 1 Ch 196.
18　Ante, p 212.

and that the grantee, knowing the facts, is denying the trust and relying upon the form of the conveyance and the statute, in order to keep the land himself.[19]

The rule in *Rochefoucauld v Boustead* has a quite remarkable impact, but operates only within a fairly narrow range of circumstances. The rule cannot validate an express trust which is declared by A, with supposedly immediate effect, *before* the date of his acquisition of the legal title. Such a trust fails on the ground that the relevant trust property does not yet exist.[20] Nor can the rule render enforceable an oral declaration of trust made *after* the date of acquisition by which A purports to constitute himself a trustee of property which he already owns. Such a declaration is unenforceable since otherwise there would be no circumstances at all which came within the reach of section 53(1)(b).[1]

The rule in *Rochefoucauld v Boustead* therefore has a somewhat limited application, operating only where A acquires a title on terms of an oral undertaking that he will, from the moment of acquisition, hold on trust for B. However, within this context it seems not to matter whether A acquires his legal title by conveyance from B himself[2] or by conveyance from a complete stranger, X.[3] More surprising is the fact that it seems to be irrelevant whether B has provided any consideration for A's undertaking.[4] From the date of acquisition onwards, A is affected by a fiduciary obligation towards B, and it would be fraud in equity if A were to rely on the absence of written evidence as a ground for disavowing the trust on the terms of which he acquired title.

As Samuels JA pointed out in *Allen v Snyder*,[5] there is a certain ambiguity as to whether the trust which is enforced under the rule in *Rochefoucauld v Boustead* is more accurately characterised as the original express trust or as an entirely new constructive trust which is statutorily exempt from the requirement of written evidence.[6] On the one hand, it could be said, in view of equity's utter detestation of fraud, that the rule gives effect to the original express trust directly in the teeth of the statute.[7] Thus, without any attempt to surmount section 53(1)(b) by finding a resulting or constructive trust, 'equity simply enforce[s] the actual original trust upon which the person accepted the property in the first place'.[8] Such an approach epitomises the blunt view that it

19 [1897] 1 Ch 196 at 206.
20 Ante, p 236.
1   See *Wratten v Hunter* [1978] 2 NSWLR 367 at 371B.
2   *David v Szoke* (1974) 39 DLR (3d) 707 at 717.
3   See *Chattock v Muller* (1878) 8 Ch D 177 at 181; *Pallant v Morgan* [1953] Ch 43 at 48; *Devine v Fields* (1920) 54 ILTR 101 at 103f; *Organ v Sandwell* [1921] VLR 622 at 630; *McGillicuddy v Joy* [1959] IR 189 at 212ff; *Gilmurray v Corr* [1978] NI 99 at 104E-G.
4   See T. Youdan, [1984] CLJ 306 at 331f.
5   [1977] 2 NSWLR 685 at 699D-E.
6   See T. Youdan, [1984] CLJ 306 at 330ff.
7   It is significant that in *Rochefoucauld v Boustead* [1897] 1 Ch 196 at 208, the Court of Appeal specifically referred to the trust which it enforced as an 'express trust' and emphasised that the intention to create a trust had 'existed from the first'. Later, in *Hodgson v Marks* [1971] Ch 892 at 909B, Ungoed-Thomas J noted that the circumstances in *Rochefoucauld v Boustead* had been treated as 'falling exclusively within the section corresponding to section 53(1)(b) of the Law of Property Act 1925, and the defendants did not attempt to rely on any of the other provisions of section 53 to escape the operation of the principle.' See also *Organ v Sandwell* [1921] VLR 622 at 630; *David v Szoke* (1974) 39 DLR (3d) 707 at 717; *Allen v Snyder* [1977] 2 NSWLR 685 at 689F-G, 693A-B.
8   *Thwaites v Ryan* [1984] VR 65 at 91 per Fullagar J. As Fullagar J pointed out (at 93), it would be difficult to describe the trust enforced as 'implied or constructive' because it 'may often be actual and meticulously expressed'.

is preferable that the plain words of a statute should be ignored than that a fraud be permitted to succeed.[9] The alternative view is that the trust which is given effect is a new constructive trust which arises as soon as A asserts his legal title in derogation of the rights to which he has agreed to take subject.[10] This analysis does less violence to section 53(1)(b), since constructive trusts are clearly a case of statutory exception under section 53(2).

For most purposes, however, it matters not whether the trust enforced by the court is characterised as an express trust or as a constructive trust: both analyses result in the same conclusion. Historically, the express trust analysis seems more authentic, but the distinction remains otherwise a fairly arid issue except perhaps in one respect. In so far as the rule in *Rochefoucauld v Boustead* seems to be applicable even where B has provided no consideration at all for the benefit orally conferred by A,[11] the trust to which the rule gives effect must be express rather than constructive. It has long been accepted that no constructive trust can be claimed in the absence of a showing of 'detriment' or 'sacrifice' on the part of B.[12] Thus where B has given no consideration—or indeed where the consideration has moved from some third party instead—it seems preferable to say that B is enforcing an orally declared express trust which, but for the rule in *Rochefoucauld v Boustead*, would have been entirely unenforceable. However, such is the vacillating character of the trust given effect by the rule that the courts have sometimes—and almost certainly incorrectly—described the trust enforced on behalf of B in these circumstances as a constructive trust.[13]

(5) Conclusive effect of a declaration of trust

It is nowadays common, but not universal, conveyancing practice to include an express declaration of trust in a transfer of a legal estate to co-owners.[14] Being included in the document of conveyance, this declaration of course satisfies the statutory requirement of written evidence.

(a) The general principle

It is now clearly established in the caselaw that a declaration of trust

---

9   This approach, if correct, has been described as representing 'no less than the exercise by equity of a suspending or dispensing power denied the executive branch of government since the Bill of Rights 1689' (R.P. Meagher, W.M.C. Gummow and J.R.F. Lehane, *Equity: Doctrines and Remedies* (2nd edn 1984), para 1224. See, however, *Devine v Fields* (1920) 54 ILTR 101 at 103 per O'Connor MR: 'It is the duty of a court of equity to overcome all technicalities in order to defeat a fraud.'

10 Post, p 271. As Samuels JA said in *Allen v Snyder* [1977] 2 NSWLR 685 at 699E, the ambiguity is demonstrated most clearly in *Bannister v Bannister* [1948] 2 All ER 133.

11 Ante, p 239.

12 Post, p 276.

13 See eg *Neale v Willis* (1968) 19 P & CR 836 at 839 (post, p 276).

14 See the strenuous advice given to conveyancing solicitors by Bagnall J in *Cowcher v Cowcher* [1972] 1 WLR 425 at 442C, pointing out the wisdom of making an express declaration of the beneficial interests in property at the date of its acquisition. Ten years later, in *Bernard v Josephs* [1982] Ch 391 at 403E-F, Griffiths LJ expressed the wish that 'more heed had been paid' to this advice, not least because if a dispute as to beneficial ownership is later waged with the help of legal aid (as it often is), both parties may well 'see a large part of their share of the equity disappear in costs into the maw of the legal aid fund...' (post, p 359). See also *Goodman v Gallant* [1986] Fam 106 at 118F- G.

'necessarily concludes the question of title...for all time',[15] at least so long as the declaration is executed by the transferees as well as by the transferor.[16] This rule may have surprising implications.

(i) Declaration of beneficial joint tenancy If a legal title is conveyed into the joint names of A and B, subject to an expressly declared trust for themselves as beneficial joint tenants, the equitable rights of A and B are clarified definitively as those of joint tenants.[17] In other words, either A or B could at any time exercise the unilateral right of severance enjoyed by a beneficial joint tenant.[18] Both parties would then become beneficial tenants in common in equal shares, irrespective of the original proportions in which they contributed to the purchase price of the co-owned property and irrespective of the reasons which caused one party to desire a severance.[19] This result follows inexorably from the binding nature of what is effectively a signed settlement by the transferees regulating the beneficial terms on which they agreed to hold the legal estate: the transferees committed themselves at the outset to an equitable joint tenancy.

(ii) Declaration of other forms of beneficial ownership An express declaration of trust is commonly used to stipulate for beneficial joint tenancy in the family home.[20] However, a declaration of trust may take many forms, and is conclusive in its terms regardless of which precise form of beneficial ownership it provides.[1] Thus if a legal title is vested in A, B and C on trust for themselves as tenants in common in equal shares, it is entirely irrelevant that A, B and C may have contributed the purchase moneys in unequal proportions.[2] It would be

15 *Pettitt v Pettitt* [1970] AC 777 at 813E. See also *Gissing v Gissing* [1971] AC 886 at 905A. An express declaration of the beneficial interests also excludes any discretionary jurisdiction of the court to value the parties' equitable shares as of the date on which they ceased to live together. The proper date for the valuation of shares in such a case is the date of realisation of the property (*Turton v Turton* (1987) *Times*, 29 April).

16 *Robinson v Robinson* (1977) 241 Estates Gazette 153 at 155. In *Pink v Lawrence* (1978) 36 P & CR 98 at 101, Buckley LJ seemed to think it sufficient that the declaration of trust was inserted into the transfer document 'at the behest of the purchasers or their solicitors' and that the purchasers then took a vesting of the legal estate on the trust thus declared. See [1979] Conv 6.

17 *Pettitt v Pettitt* [1970] AC 777 at 813E per Lord Upjohn. See also *Mayes v Mayes* (1969) 210 Estates Gazette 935 at 937; *In re Johns' Assignment Trusts* [1970] 1 WLR 955 at 959C; *Boydell v Gillespie* (1970) 216 Estates Gazette 1505 at 1507; *Pink v Lawrence* (1978) 36 P & CR 98 at 101; *Brykiert v Jones* (1981) 2 FLR 373 at 376A-B; *Goodman v Gallant* [1986] Fam 106 at 110H-111A; [1986] CLJ 206 (S. Juss).

18 See the discussion of severance in Chapter 11 (post, p 317).

19 *Bedson v Bedson* [1965] 2 QB 666 at 689C-D; *Pettitt v Pettitt* [1970] AC 777 at 813E; *In re Johns' Assignment Trusts* [1970] 1 WLR 955 at 959C; *Bernard v Josephs* [1982] Ch 391 at 397F; *Goodman v Gallant* [1986] Fam 106 at 108D, 119D.

20 For reference to the modern popularity of this form of ownership in relation to the family home, see Chapter 11 (post, p 300).

1 Likewise, conclusive effect must be accorded a declaration which expressly negatives the existence of a trust in favour of persons who have undoubtedly made a financial contribution towards the purchase of the property (see *Godwin v Bedwell* (1982) *Times*, 10 March (Court of Appeal)). It is also possible to provide, by way of express declaration, that joint tenancy should prevail in equity until and unless severance occurs, and that in the event of severance the parties' respective interests should be unequal (see *Goodman v Gallant* [1986] Fam 106 at 119C).

2 *Brown v Staniek* (1969) 211 Estates Gazette 283. See also *Bedson v Bedson* [1965] 2 QB 666 at 689D-E.

equally irrelevant that part or all of the purchase moneys came from sources other than A, B and C.[3] It is clearly a matter of some importance that conveyancers should be able to rely on the face value of documents which purport to define in express terms both the legal and beneficial ownership of land.[4]

(b) Exceptions

Only extremely limited exceptions are permitted from the rule that an express declaration of trust has conclusive effect.

(i) Rescission for fraud or mistake   It is always open to a party to go behind the express terms of a trust where there has been 'fraud or mistake at the time of the transaction' by which the legal title is vested.[5] This ground of exception, if proved, may lead to rescission of the declaration, but the ground is difficult to establish. Mistake, for instance, is not constituted merely by a failure on the part of a lay person to understand the precise technical significance of the declaration of trust.[6] Indeed, in *Pink v Lawrence*,[7] the appalling result was brought about that the parties were held bound by a declaration of equitable joint tenancy which they had neither read nor signed, and which (it was conceded) they probably would not have understood anyway.

(ii) Rectification   Apart from cases of fraud or mistake, it is possible that a court may grant rectification of a declaration of trust in order to give effect to intentions which the parties clearly had at the date of the transaction, but which were expressed only imperfectly or not at all in the declared trust. In rare cases the court may, for instance, reinstate an original common intention that the parties should be equitable tenants in common rather than joint tenants,[8] or that one party rather than two should be beneficially entitled,[9] or even that two parties instead of one should be grantees of the legal title under the deed of conveyance.[10]

3. IMPLIED TRUSTS

Given that a conveyance of the legal title into the name of A carries prima facie the entire equitable interest too, substantial difficulties lie in the path of B, a

---

3   Compare, however, *City of London Building Society v Flegg* [1987] 2 WLR 1266 at 1269A–C, where the House of Lords seemed to envisage that the express trusts set out in a conveyance could be displaced by the fact that persons other than the designated beneficiaries had contributed financially towards the relevant purchase.

4   See [1979] Conv 6.

5   *Pettitt v Pettitt* [1970] AC 777 at 813E per Lord Upjohn. See also *Goodman v Gallant* [1986] Fam 106 at 116B.

6   *Mayes v Mayes* (1969) 210 Estates Gazette 935 at 937; *In re Johns' Assignment Trusts* [1970] 1 WLR 955 at 958G–H.

7   (1978) 36 P & CR 98 at 99.

8   See *In re Colebrook's Conveyances* [1972] 1 WLR 1397 at 1398H, but compare *Goodman v Gallant* [1986] Fam 106 at 116H–117C.

9   *Wilson v Wilson* [1969] 3 All ER 945 at 949A–B. Where the conveyance does not accurately represent the agreement of the parties, it may be possible for the court to give relief without actually employing the machinery of rectification (*Pink v Lawrence* (1978) 38 P & CR 98 at 101). See also *Gross v French* (1975) 238 Estates Gazette 39.

10   *Armstrong v Armstrong* (1979) 93 DLR (3d) 128 at 135.

claimant of an equitable interest, if he cannot base his claim on the express terms of a declaration of trust duly evidenced in writing. B's only remaining hope of making good his claim now rests largely on the contention that there exists in his favour, not an express trust, but an implied trust of some variety.

(1) Classification of implied trusts

Implied trusts are of essentially two kinds, the resulting trust and the constructive trust.[11] Whereas express trusts are founded directly on the expressly declared intentions of the parties, implied trusts arise by operation of law, albeit against the background of the parties' actual or presumed intentions.[12] Moreover, section 53(2) of the Law of Property Act 1925 makes it absolutely clear that the documentary requirements imposed in respect of trusts by section 53(1) have no application to the 'creation or operation of resulting, implied or constructive trusts.'

Although similar in the sense that they are implied rather than express and are alike freed from statutory requirements of formal writing, the resulting trust and the constructive trust have quite distinct spheres of operation. They are, however, easily confused one with another. Recent years have witnessed what an Australian judge has termed, with derogatory implication, an 'apparent amalgamation of resulting and constructive trusts into one congruent class.'[13] This compression of concepts has led to some uncertainty of doctrine. It may therefore be useful to attempt to separate out the notions involved in these classifications.

(2) Origin of implied trusts

Some of the ambiguity affecting this area of trust law may be traced to *Gissing v Gissing*.[14] Here, in what has become a classic point of reference in the law of trusts, Lord Diplock provided an incisive definition of the origin of implied trusts. He declared that

A resulting, implied or constructive trust—and it is unnecessary for present purposes to distinguish between these three classes of trust—is created by a transaction between the trustee and the cestui que trust in connection with the acquisition by the trustee of a legal estate in the land, whenever the trustee has so conducted himself that it would be inequitable to allow him to deny to the cestui que trust a beneficial interest in the land acquired. And he will be held so to have conducted himself if by his words or conduct he has induced the cestui que trust to act to his own detriment in the reasonable belief that by so acting he was acquiring a beneficial interest in the land.

This dictum has been frequently applied and sometimes misapplied, but it probably represents the best attempt yet to indicate the common elements

11 See *Cowcher v Cowcher* [1972] 1 WLR 425 at 431A.
12 *Avondale Printers & Stationers Ltd v Haggie* [1979] 2 NZLR 124 at 145.
13 *Allen v Snyder* [1977] 2 NSWLR 685 at 698D per Samuels JA. The English Court of Appeal has more recently confirmed that resulting and constructive trusts are not merely 'interchangeable' terms. In *Walker v Walker* (Unreported 12 April 1984), Browne-Wilkinson LJ emphasised that 'in many contexts there are crucial distinctions as to the circumstances which give rise to the existence of such trusts.' See also *Avondale Printers & Stationers Ltd v Haggie* [1979] 2 NZLR 124 at 145; *Muschinski v Dodds* (1985) 62 ALR 429 at 437.
14 [1971] AC 886 at 905B-C.

which underlie both the resulting and constructive trust. Such differences as exist between these two types of trust are best explained in the following way.[15] The effect of the resulting trust is designed to correspond with the intention, express or inferred, which controlled the relevant transaction between trustee and cestui que trust. The constructive trust, on the other hand, arises in circumstances where it would be a fraud for the trustee to assert an exclusive beneficial ownership.

4. RESULTING TRUSTS

A resulting trust comes into existence in certain stereotyped situations in English law, where a nominal purchaser of property (A) is deemed to hold on a trust which 'results' back to the person who has financed his purchase (B).[16] Under the resulting trust A takes merely the legal or paper title in the property and the equitable interest is presumed to belong to B, the 'real purchaser'.[17]

(1) Presumption of resulting trust

The origin of the resulting trust lies in a presumption as to the intended beneficial ownership of the property purchased.[18] This presumption gives way only if (and to the extent that) a contrary intention can be proved to have manifested itself in an enforceable form at the date of the purchase, or if the presumed resulting trust is itself displaced by a counter-presumption of equity.[19] In all other circumstances a resulting trust is presumed to come into existence wherever an interest in property[20] is purchased in the name of A, A having provided none or only part of the purchase price.[1] By operation of law,[2] a resulting trust arises in favour of B if (and to the extent that) B has provided money for that purchase. In the classic terms of Eyre CB in *Dyer v Dyer*,[3] a 'trust

---

15   See *Avondale Printers & Stationers Ltd v Haggie* [1979] 2 NZLR 124 at 145.
16   The word 'result' in this context is not used in any sense of causation and consequence, but rather in its root sense of 'leaping back' (Latin, *resultare*). A trust of the property springs back in favour of the real purchaser. See *Rathwell v Rathwell* (1978) 83 DLR (3d) 289 at 302 per Dickson J.
17   *Muschinski v Dodds* (1985) 62 ALR 429 at 432 per Gibbs CJ. See *Walker v Walker* (Unreported, Court of Appeal, 12 April 1984), where Browne-Wilkinson LJ held that 'a resulting trust arises where the facts alleged and proved consist of the payment of money by B to or for the benefit of A (otherwise than for the sole benefit of A) without a declaration of express trusts which fully exhaust the beneficial interest: in such a case the beneficial interest results to B to the extent that it is not exhausted by the express trust.'
18   *Gissing v Gissing* [1971] AC 886 at 902B.
19   *Calverley v Green* (1984) 56 ALR 483 at 488, 494; *Muschinski v Dodds* (1985) 62 ALR 429 at 432f, 449.
20   The property subject to a resulting trust may have a limited lifespan. It has been said, for instance, that there is 'no reason in principle' why a resulting trust cannot attach to a one-year tenancy, at least where—although it must happen rarely—such an estate is purchased for a premium (*Savage v Dunningham* [1974] Ch 181 at 184G).
1   *Pettitt v Pettitt* [1970] AC 777 at 814A; *Cowcher v Cowcher* [1972] 1 WLR 425 at 431B; *Wirth v Wirth* (1956) 98 CLR 228 at 235; *Goodfriend v Goodfriend* (1972) 22 DLR (3d) 699 at 702; *Allen v Snyder* [1977] 2 NSWLR 685 at 689G-690A; *Blackburn v Y V Properties Pty Ltd* [1980] VR 290 at 295, 301f; *Dullow v Dullow* [1985] 3 NSWLR 531 at 534E-F.
2   *Blackburn v Y V Properties Pty Ltd* [1980] VR 290 at 293; *Re Levy* (1982) 131 DLR (3d) 15 at 23.
3   (1788) 2 Cox Eq Cas 92 at 93, 30 ER 42 at 43.

of a legal estate...results to the man who advances the purchase-money.'[4] Thus, if B provides all the purchase money for a vesting of legal title in A, A is presumed (in the absence of evidence of contrary intention) to hold the legal title on a resulting trust for B absolutely (*Fig.* 21).[5]

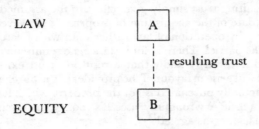

Fig. 21

The recognition that a trust relationship exists between A and B in these circumstances is a direct response to the supposed inequity of allowing A to retain property purchased in his own name without acknowledging the material assistance given in its purchase by B. It would generally be unconscionable to allow A to assert an absolute legal and beneficial title if B has paid moneys 'in the character of a purchaser'.[6] The doctrine of resulting trust accordingly recognises an 'equity' as inhering in B—an 'equity' which is founded on a perceived consensus that B will normally have been induced to finance A's purchase only by some expectation or belief that he would receive a tangible return for his contribution.[7]

(a) Ideology of the resulting trust

The resulting trust generated by the provision of purchase moneys is outstanding evidence of what Woodhouse J once termed 'the solid tug of money'.[8] In drawing a sharp distinction between the nominal and the real purchaser, equity has emphasised the pre-eminence of the cash nexus between man and his fellow man. Equity, it has been said, 'assumes bargains, and not gifts'.[9] In crude terms, people who pay money normally expect to get something for it. Today when B purchases property in the name of A there is, in

---

4   This dictum has been frequently cited with approval (see eg *Pettitt v Pettitt* [1970] AC 777 at 814B-E; *Gissing v Gissing* [1971] AC 886 at 902D).

5   *Calverley v Green* (1984) 56 ALR 483 at 485, 500. Money advanced by B to A on trust will, if invested by A in the acquisition of realty, produce a resulting trust for B (*McTaggart v Boffo* (1976) 64 DLR (3d) 441 at 457).

6   Post, p 248. See *Winkworth v Edward Baron Development Co Ltd* [1986] 1 WLR 1512 at 1516C-D per Lord Templeman.

7   See *Taddeo v Taddeo* (1978) 19 SASR 347 at 368, where Walters J attributed the operation of the resulting trust to equity's assumption that 'independently of any fraud...the purchaser...intended to act, and...was acting, in pursuance of his fiduciary duty.' See also *Gissing v Gissing* [1971] AC 886 at 902B; *Pettkus v Becker* (1981) 117 DLR (3d) 257 at 263.

8   *Hofman v Hofman* [1965] NZLR 795 at 800. See also *Reid v Reid* [1979] 1 NZLR 572 at 582 per Woodhouse J.

9   *Goodfriend v Goodfriend* (1972) 22 DLR (3d) 699 at 703 per Spence J (Supreme Court of Canada), quoting D. Waters, *The Doctrine of Resulting Trusts in Common Law Canada*, (1970) 16 McGill LJ 187 at 199. See also *Gorog v Kiss* (1977) 78 DLR (3d) 690 at 694.

the absence of a clear intention to donate or to lend, a presumption of resulting trust in favour of B; in our money-conscious world it is scarcely conceivable that B would have intended to confer a gratuitous benefit on A.[10]

The presumption of resulting trust thus reflects a socially perceived inference as to the likely intentions of A and B regarding attributions of ownership.[11] The doctrine of resulting trust simply gives effect to the assumed intentions of the parties at the date of the acquisition of property.[12] However, resulting trusts arise ultimately by operation of law rather than with reference to the actual intentions of the parties. There is, for instance, no requirement that a resulting trustee should necessarily know that a resulting trust exists.[13] Moreover, a resulting trust will arise in favour of the provider of the purchase moneys even if the property actually purchased is not the property which he intended should be purchased (eg if A wrongfully uses B's money in purchasing Whiteacre rather than Blackacre as agreed[14]).

(b) Time-frame of the relevant intentions

Intrinsic to the resulting trust is the idea that this form of trust is based on actual or presumed intentions existing at the date of acquisition of the property concerned. The time at which the beneficial interest 'crystallises' under the resulting trust is the date of acquisition,[15] and the only intentions relevant are those which were contemporaneous with that acquisition.[16] In strict terms a resulting trust cannot be raised by virtue of intentions which come into existence only at some later stage,[17] although the conduct of the parties subsequent to the acquisition date may be used as a basis for retrospective inference as to their actual intentions on that date.[18]

It is the timing of the relevant intentions which ultimately distinguishes the resulting trust from the constructive trust. The latter form of trust can be raised by intentions as to beneficial ownership which did not exist at the acquisition date and which were formulated or expressed only some time later.[19]

(c) Mode of acquisition of title

It matters not for the purpose of raising a resulting trust whether B purchases

10   For an alternative view that the presumption of resulting trust is 'completely anachronistic', see *Dullow v Dullow* [1985] 3 NSWLR 531 at 535A.
11   See *Pettitt v Pettitt* [1970] AC 777 at 823H-824A (ante, p 235). The presumption of resulting trust is sometimes explained as 'the fact of contribution evidencing an agreement'. It has also been described as a form of 'constructive agreement'. (see *Rathwell v Rathwell* (1978) 83 DLR (3d) 289 at 304 per Dickson J).
12   'Resulting trusts are as firmly grounded in the settlor's intent as are express trusts, but with this difference—that the intent is inferred, or is presumed as a matter of law from the circumstances of the case' (*Rathwell v Rathwell* (1978) 83 DLR (3d) 289 at 303).
13   *Tattersfield v Tattersfield and the New Zealand Insurance Co Ltd* [1980] BCL 1110.
14   *Scott v Scott* (1963) 109 CLR 649 at 663f (High Court of Australia).
15   *Bernard v Josephs* [1982] Ch 391 at 404F.
16   *Pettitt v Pettitt* [1970] AC 777 at 800F-G, 813D; *Gissing v Gissing* [1971] AC 886 at 897C, 900B-D, 905D; *Bernard v Josephs* [1982] Ch 391 at 404C; *Burns v Burns* [1984] Ch 317 at 327A; *Hohol v Hohol* [1981] VR 221 at 225f; *Baumgartner v Baumgartner* [1985] 2 NSWLR 406 at 417F.
17   See *Jeffries v Stevens* [1982] STC 639 at 651g.
18   *Gissing v Gissing* [1971] AC 886 at 906E; *Bernard v Josephs* [1982] Ch 391 at 404F-G; *Allen v Snyder* [1977] 2 NSWLR 685 at 707E-F; *Baumgartner v Baumgartner* [1985] 2 NSWLR 406 at 417E; *Vedejs v Public Trustee* [1985] VR 569 at 573.
19   Post, p 272.

property with his own funds, and directs that the legal title should be conveyed by the vendor into the name of A,[20] or whether A, using funds provided by B, purchases property in his own name.[1] In either case, if the moneys have been laid out by B 'in the character of a purchaser', there will be a presumption of resulting trust.[2] Nor does it matter whether the title is put in the name of A or in the joint names of A and B. If, in the latter case, B has provided all of the purchase moneys, A is presumed to take no beneficial interest and he holds the legal title merely as a trustee on a resulting trust for B.[3]

All these examples are, however, to be distinguished from a rather different case which under English law is dealt with quite separately. So far we have assumed a purchase in the name of A of property previously owned by V, a vendor. No resulting trust is presumed where B is the current owner of a legal title, which he then voluntarily transfers into the name of A.[4] Under these circumstances A takes both the legal and equitable title absolutely in the absence of any evidence of contrary intention.[5]

(d) Effect of joint contributions of money

If A and B both contribute towards a purchase of a legal title in A's name, there is a presumed resulting trust for A and B.[6] If A and B contribute unequally, they are presumed to hold beneficially as tenants in common in proportion to their respective contributions (*Fig.* 22).[7] If they contribute equally, their entitlement under the resulting trust is as joint tenants (*Fig.* 23),[8] each having the right to convert the beneficial joint tenancy into a tenancy in common in equal shares.[9]

---

20   *Pettitt v Pettitt* [1970] AC 777 at 814A; *Noack v Noack* [1959] VR 137 at 139; *Rathwell v Rathwell* (1978) 83 DLR (3d) 289 at 302.

1   *Bateman Television Ltd v Bateman and Thomas* [1971] NZLR 453 at 462.

2   See *Bateman Television Ltd v Bateman and Thomas* [1971] NZLR 453 at 462 per Turner J.

3   *Benger v Drew* (1721) 1 P Wms 781, 24 ER 613; *Noack v Noack* [1959] VR 137 at 139; *Calverley v Green* (1984) 56 ALR 483 at 492, 500.

4   Law of Property Act 1925, s 60(3). In *Hodgson v Marks* [1971] Ch 892 at 933D, Russell LJ still thought it a 'debatable question' whether a resulting trust arises on 'a voluntary transfer by A to stranger B'. It could be argued that in such circumstances the beneficial interest never leaves the transferor at all, but the preferable view nowadays seems to be that section 60(3) means what it says.

5   In jurisdictions where there is no statutory equivalent of the Law of Property Act 1925, s 60(3), a gratuitous transfer of title from A to B will produce a resulting trust in favour of B (see eg *Napier v Public Trustee (Western Australia)* (1980) 32 ALR 153 at 158).

6   *Calverley v Green* (1984) 56 ALR 483 at 485.

7   *Lake v Gibson* (1729) 1 Eq Ca Abr 290 at 291, 21 ER 1052 at 1053; *Aveling v Knipe* (1815) 19 Ves 441 at 444f, 34 ER 580 at 582; *Bull v Bull* [1955] 1 QB 234 at 236; *Brown v Robertson* (1962) 182 Estates Gazette 157; *Pettitt v Pettitt* [1970] AC 777 at 814B; *Gissing v Gissing* [1971] AC 886 at 907C; *Cowcher v Cowcher* [1972] 1 WLR 425 at 431B-C; *Williams & Glyn's Bank Ltd v Boland* [1981] AC 487 at 502F-G; *Goodman v Gallant* [1986] Fam 106 at 110F-H; *Scott v Scott* (1963) 109 CLR 649 at 663; *Taddeo v Taddeo* (1978) 19 SASR 347 at 365, 368; *Bloch v Bloch* (1981) 37 ALR 56 at 60, 62; *Calverley v Green* (1984) 56 ALR 483 at 500.

8   *Lake v Gibson* (1729) 1 Eq Ca Abr 290, 21 ER 1052; *O'Connell v Harrison* [1927] IR 330 at 336; *Efstratiou, Glantschnig and Petrovic v Glantschnig* [1972] NZLR 594 at 598; *Taddeo v Taddeo* (1978) 19 SASR 347 at 365. See also *Vedejs v Public Trustee* [1985] VR 569 at 575.

9   The law relating to 'severance' of beneficial joint tenancy is dealt with elsewhere (post, p 317).

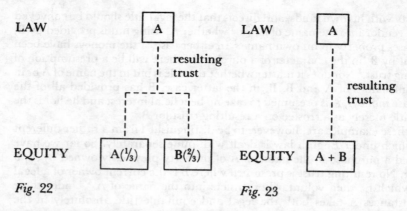

Fig. 22   *Fig. 23*

Since the ownership of the legal title is only a matter of nominal or paper title, exactly the same beneficial results would follow in either of these cases if the moneys of A and B were used to purchase a legal title in the names of A and B themselves[10] or—for that matter—in the joint names of A and X,[11] or of X, Y and Z. In such circumstances, the prima facie inference that equitable ownership follows the legal title is overborne by the more precise information concerning the source of the purchase money. In the absence of any contrary intention, a presumption of resulting trust would be raised in favour of A and B as providers of that money. Likewise, if a legal title were purchased in the joint names of A and B, using only the moneys of B, a resulting trust would presumed in favour of B (*Fig. 24*).[12]

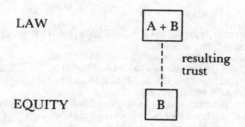

Fig. 24

(2) Definition of 'purchase money'

The presumption of resulting trust depends on a finding that B has acted 'in the character of a purchaser' by providing money for a purchase in the name of A.[13] Difficult questions are sometimes raised as to whether various forms of

10   *Crisp v Mullings* (1976) 239 Estates Gazette 119 at 121; *Walker v Hall* (1984) 14 Fam Law 21; *Re Hogg* (Unreported, Chancery Division, 1982 H No 2830, 11 July 1983); *Muschinski v Dodds* (1985) 62 ALR 429 at 432; *Calverley v Green* (1984) 56 ALR 483 at 485, 494.
11   *Hoare v Hoare* (1982) *Times*, 9 November.
12   *Wilson v Wilson* [1969] 3 All ER 945 at 949E-F; *Mellowes v Collymore* (Unreported, Court of Appeal, 27 November 1981); *Young v Young* [1983] Court of Appeal Bound Transcript 466; *Allied Irish Banks Ltd v McWilliams* [1982] NI 156 at 161C-D.
13   *Calverley v Green* (1984) 56 ALR 483 at 485.

financial contribution or liability constitute such a provision of 'purchase money' as to raise the presumption. Not every kind of contribution or assumption of liability can be attributed to an actual or presumed intention at the date of acquisition that beneficial ownership should result. In applying the doctrine of resulting trusts, the courts attach significance only to those money contributions made by B which can fairly be said to be 'referable to' the acquisition of title by A.[14]

Among the candidates for consideration as relevant forms of 'purchase money' are the following:

(a) Direct contribution to cash price

The clearest and easiest case concerns direct contributions to the cash price at which property is purchased. Regardless of the name or names in which the legal title is purchased, those who make direct contributions of cash at the date of acquisition are presumed, in the absence of all other evidence, to have intended to take beneficial interests commensurate with their respective contributions.[15] In other words, a direct cash payment is regarded as being sufficiently 'referable to' the acquisition of title to raise a resulting trust.[16] Thus, if a legal estate is conveyed to A for £60,000, A providing £20,000 out of his own free available moneys and B £40,000 out of his own free cash resources, a resulting trust is presumed under which A takes a one-third interest and B a two-thirds interest.[17] A and B are presumed, in effect, to have formulated a 'money consensus' that their respective beneficial interests should accord with the relative proportions of their contributions.[18] This 'money consensus' is contemporaneous with, and constitutive of, the resulting trust, and therefore requires no documentary formality under section 53(1)(b) of the Law of Property Act 1925.[19]

(b) Contribution of borrowed moneys

It is, however, somewhat rare for purchasers of land to finance their purchase entirely from their own freely available cash reserves.[20] It is much more common that part (or all) of the purchase price should consist of moneys borrowed from a third party such as a bank or building society.[1] If, in the situation just discussed above, the purchase price is raised by combining a direct cash contribution of £20,000 from A with a contribution of £40,000 which B has borrowed from X, a resulting trust is presumed on behalf of A and

---

14 *Burns v Burns* [1984] Ch 317 at 328H-329B. It may be difficult to establish the 'referable' character of a payment which was made some time *after* the acquisition of a particular property and full payment of its purchase price (see eg *Winkworth v Edward Baron Development Co Ltd* [1986] 1 WLR 1512 at 1515E-1516B, post, p 288).
15 *Pettitt v Pettitt* [1970] AC 777 at 794A-B; *Gissing v Gissing* [1971] AC 886 at 897A-B; *Cowcher v Cowcher* [1972] 1 WLR 425 at 431B-C; *Williams & Glyn's Bank Ltd v Boland* [1981] AC 487 at 502F-G; *Bernard v Josephs* [1982] Ch 391 at 403G.
16 *Burns v Burns* [1984] Ch 317 at 329B.
17 See *Cowcher v Cowcher* [1972] 1 WLR 425 at 431E-F (example (i)). See also *Gissing v Gissing* [1971] AC 886 at 907A-B.
18 *Cowcher v Cowcher* [1972] 1 WLR 425 at 436A-B.
19 *Cowcher v Cowcher* [1972] 1 WLR 425 at 436C-D.
20 *Bernard v Josephs* [1982] Ch 391 at 403G; *Burns v Burns* [1984] Ch 317 at 344D-E.
1 For an account of borrowing patterns, see Chapter 16 (post, p 563).

B in precisely the same proportions of one-third and two-thirds.[2] In other words, money borrowed in the sole name of B is regarded as the exact equivalent of money contributed from B's free available cash resources, which, as soon as X has lent the money to B, in a very real sense it is.[3]

(c) Assumption of liability to repay a loan of money

The example considered above suggests that an assumption of liability to repay borrowed money is always treated as having the same value in beneficial terms as a direct contribution of free cash. This is quite correct so long as a careful distinction is maintained between, on the one hand, the personal liability of B in relation to the lender X, and, on the other hand, the liability of A and B *inter se*, in respect of the loan money. It is the latter form of liability which is definitive of the presumed trust which results from B's contribution of borrowed moneys. There are two kinds of situation here which require attention.

(i) Assumption of loan liability by another beneficiary

The mere fact that B contributes money which has been borrowed from X on the strength of B's sole personal covenant to repay does not exclude the possibility that, as between themselves, A and B have nevertheless agreed to discharge the loan or mortgage liability by some combination of their joint financial efforts. If, for instance, A contributes £20,000 of his own free cash and also undertakes privately to B that he, A, will be responsible for half of the loan liability of £40,000 incurred under B's personal covenant with X, the proportions of beneficial ownership under the presumed resulting trust are immediately reversed. Under these changed circumstances A is presumed to be a beneficial tenant in common of a two-thirds share and B of only a one-third share. The altered balance flows from the fact that A's free cash, combined with his undertaking to share the loan liability, has now provided the source of £40,000 of the total purchase price of the property.[4] The proportions of resulting beneficial ownership will clearly vary in accordance with the proportion of B's loan liability which A privately agrees with B that he shall share.[5]

Whether any agreement has been reached by A and B as to the loan liability *inter se* is ultimately a question of fact, but any agreement found on the facts is again immune from the requirements of section 53(1)(b) provided that it existed at the date of acquisition. In *Power v Brighton*,[6] for instance, a legal estate was conveyed into the name of A, the purchase price being raised by means of a

2   *Cowcher v Cowcher* [1972] 1 WLR 425 at 431E-F (example (ii)).
3   For a strong argument to the effect that mortgage-generated contributions of cash should not be regarded as the direct equivalent of free cash, see *Ulrich v Ulrich and Felton* [1968] 1 WLR 180 at 186E per Lord Denning MR, who maintained that in the mortgage context the asset to which the beneficial shares attach is merely 'the equity of redemption in the property' (post, p 574). Diplock LJ (at 189F-G) likewise thought that to treat a mortgage liability as the direct equivalent of cash 'ignores the economic realities of modern mortgages of owner-occupied dwelling houses.' See also J. Levin, *The Matrimonial Home—Another Round*, (1972) 35 MLR 547 at 551; *Re Whiteley and Whiteley* (1975) 48 DLR (3d) 161 at 170f. It seems, however, that this approach no longer stands as good law (see *Cowcher v Cowcher* [1972] 1 WLR 425 at 433B).
4   *Cowcher v Cowcher* [1972] 1 WLR 425 at 431G-H.
5   *Cowcher v Cowcher* [1972] 1 WLR 425 at 431H-432A.
6   Unreported, Court of Appeal, 14 November 1984.

cash contribution from A, a cash contribution from B and a contribution of money advanced to A by X under a mortgage loan which A personally covenanted to repay to X. There was without doubt some kind of resulting trust, but dispute arose as to whether A's beneficial share thereunder should be calculated with reference not merely to her cash contribution but also to the loan money. It was found that, as is nowadays quite common, A and B had agreed throughout that the payment of the mortgage instalments should be fed by income derived from lettings of the trust property.[7] A majority in the Court of Appeal nevertheless held that, in the absence of convincing evidence of an explicit agreement *inter se* to share the mortgage liability,[8] the loan money for which A had assumed sole liability should be reckoned as the full equivalent of a cash contribution originating from her.

Dillon LJ dissented on this point, taking the view in the present circumstances that the loan money was irrelevant to the proportions of beneficial ownership. According to Dillon LJ, '[e]ssentially what is held on a resulting trust is the equity of redemption in the property subject to the mortgage.'[9] The fact that A had undertaken a sole personal liability in respect of the loan did not entitle her to claim this commitment as representing an enlarged financial contribution by her towards the purchase. If A were ever made liable on her personal covenant with X, she would, in Dillon LJ's view, have the ordinary right of any trustee to reimbursement by way of indemnity out of the trust property. The mere risk implicit in undertaking a personal liability in connection with the trust property did not therefore connote an extra element of consideration moving from her.

Thus there continues to be some doubt as to precisely how the assumption of loan liability should be taken into account in determining the proportions of beneficial ownership. However, the better view is that if there was an agreement between A and B at the date of acquisition as to how the loan liability should be apportioned informally as between themselves, then this agreement sets a marker for the quantification of the respective beneficial shares of A and B under a resulting trust. If such an agreement was reached at the date of acquisition but either A or B subsequently failed to discharge his allotted burden of the agreed loan liability, then the beneficial shares defined by the initial agreement are subject to variation in accordance with the money payments *actually* made by A and B respectively. Such an alteration of the original shareholding is almost certainly sanctioned—free of any requirement of written disposition of equitable interests—by the doctrine of constructive trust.[10]

It will normally be fairly rare that there is agreement between A and B at the acquisition date as to the precise shares in which they shall discharge a loan liability which was undertaken by A alone. In the absence of such an agreement, the *de facto* pattern of subsequent mortgage payments as between A

---

7   See eg *Annen v Rattee* (1985) 273 Estates Gazette 503 (post, p 256).

8   It is difficult to see why such an agreement could not have been found in the understanding between A and B that the mortgage repayments should be met out of the rents derived from the trust property. See also *Bernard v Josephs* [1982] Ch 391 at 405A.

9   See *Ulrich v Ulrich and Felton* [1968] 1 WLR 180 at 186E (ante, p 250); *Calverley v Green* (1984) 56 ALR 483 at 497.

10   Post, p 292. There is also the possibility that the final outcome as between A and B may be based upon the equitable principles governing the winding up of a joint venture (see eg *Muschinski v Dodds* (1985) 62 ALR 429 at 454f).

and B may provide cogent evidence of a common intention as of the date of acquisition that the beneficial ownership should be shared by both.[11] If this is the case, the quantum of their respective entitlements can only be assessed retrospectively in the light of the actual money payments made by both in discharge of the loan liability. In dealing with precisely this context in *Power v Brighton*, Dillon LJ may well have been absolutely correct to allocate no beneficial value to the merely potential exposure to liability which is involved in the personal covenant to repay the lender of moneys.[12]

(ii) Assumption of loan liability by another legal owner A related question sometimes arises as to whether the assumption of a joint loan liability by another legal owner in itself brings about a resulting trust of the co-owned legal estate.

The practical problem arises in the following way. A, although he wished to purchase a legal estate in his own name, may have found that he has had to include B's name on the title for any of a number of reasons. It may be, for instance, that B's name has been included on the title precisely in order to harness an enhanced borrowing power for the purpose of the purchase proposed by A.[13] However, the mere fact that B participates in the conveyance merely in order to maximise the borrowing power of A does not necessarily mean that B can be disregarded as a mere nominee or that there will be a resulting trust of the entire beneficial interest for A alone.[14] A and B will both take beneficial shares behind a resulting trust in proportions commensurate with their actual financial contributions to the total cash deposit and mortgage repayments.[15] A resulting trust will arise for A alone only if B makes no money payments of any kind whatsoever, and stands merely in the position of one who has lent at best a superficial borrowing power or credit status for the purpose of A's transaction.[16]

Alternatively, B may have been included within the legal title and joint mortgage liability simply because the lender of the mortgage moneys has refused to proceed without the additional security of knowing that B had expressly joined in the mortgage. Such a precaution is sometimes taken where B is discovered to be in joint occupation of the property to be mortgaged,[17] even though there is no intention on anyone's part that B should ever make any

11   Post, p 255.
12   See also *Allied Irish Banks Ltd v McWilliams* [1982] NI 156 at 161C-D.
13   The mortgage advance available will generally have been increased if B joins A on the legal title as a joint mortgagor, since the maximum advance available is usually calculated as a function of the joint income capacities of the mortgagors (post, p 565).
14   *Crisp v Mullings* (1976) 239 Estates Gazette 119; *Young v Young* [1983] Court of Appeal Bound Transcript 466; *Calverley v Green* (1984) 56 ALR 483 at 493.
15   *Bernard v Josephs* [1982] Ch 391 at 398A-B. However, an express declaration of trust for A and B as beneficial joint tenants is conclusive irrespective of the relative proportions of financial contribution: see *Mayes v Mayes* (1969) 210 Estates Gazette 935 at 937 (ante, p 241).
16   See eg *Hoare v Hoare* (1982) *Times*, 9 November; *Young v Young* [1983] Court of Appeal Bound Transcript 466. In *Allied Irish Banks Ltd v McWilliams* [1982] NI 156 at 161C-D, Murray J declined to attach any beneficial value to the mere assumption of personal liability by B in this situation, noting that any loss suffered by a trustee could be recouped by way of reimbursement from the trust property. See also *Clooney v Clooney*, 394 A.2d 313 at 316 (1978), but compare *Ingram v Ingram* [1941] VLR 95 at 98; *Ruff v Strobel* (1978) 86 DLR (3d) 284 at 295.
17   Post, p 860.

practical contribution towards the discharge of the mortgage liability.[18] It is probable that under these circumstances no beneficial interest is taken by B, even though technically, by joining in a personal covenant to repay the loan, he has exposed himself to a potential contractual liability to the lender.[19]

(d) Contribution of qualifying status or eligibility

A difficult question is posed where a legal title has been acquired partly by reason of money put up by B and partly by reason of a qualifying status or eligibility supplied by A. Such a case arose, for instance, in *Binmatt v Ali*,[20] where a local council sold a council house at a reduced price to the sitting tenant, A, the purchase money being provided by the tenant's son-in-law, B.[1] It was argued that the opportunity to purchase the property on advantageous terms was directly attributable to the previous occupation of the sitting tenant,[2] and that this contribution of status or eligibility was sufficient to raise a beneficial entitlement in her favour by way of resulting trust. The Court of Appeal left open the question whether the lending of A's name in this manner could create for A some beneficial share to be held in common with the undoubted beneficial interest of the money contributor, B.[3] On balance, it seems unlikely that a resulting trust would be regarded as applicable here, unless the courts were to adopt the not unattractive argument that A has made a contribution of money's worth measurable in terms of the reduction in price generated by A's status as a sitting or qualifying tenant.[4]

(e) Contribution to initial deposit or legal expenses

It is now clearly accepted that a money contribution by B to the initial deposit or legal expenses payable on the acquisition of a legal title will raise, in the absence of evidence of contrary intention, a resulting trust in favour of B.[5] Such a contribution casts B 'in the character of a purchaser', and provides presumptive evidence that both parties intended from the very outset that B should have some beneficial share in the property acquired.[6] The extent of the beneficial interest earned by B's contribution is not necessarily proportional to

---

18 See eg *Mellowes v Collymore* (Unreported, Court of Appeal, 27 November 1981) (mother-in-law in residence in family home).

19 The point was left open in *Mellowes v Collymore, supra,* but this conclusion seems to accord with the view so cogently expressed by Dillon LJ in *Power v Brighton, supra.*

20 Unreported, Court of Appeal, 6 October 1981.

1 The occurrence of this kind of issue is now increased by virtue of the 'right to buy' provision introduced by the Housing Act 1980 (post, p 736), and the problem could equally well arise as between a private landlord and tenant.

2 The Corporation would clearly not have countenanced such a sale to B, who had never occupied the property.

3 The issue was resolved here by granting A the right to reside in the property for the remainder of her life (although the precise basis on which this right was accorded is difficult to ascertain).

4 This rationalisation, while preserving the contribution-oriented basis of the doctrine of resulting trust, would nevertheless be difficult to apply where the shortfall in price was debatable or unquantifiable.

5 *Gissing v Gissing* [1971] AC 886 at 907E; *Davis v Vale* [1971] 1 WLR 1022 at 1026H; *Efstratiou, Glantschnig and Petrovic v Glantschnig* [1972] NZLR 594 at 598.

6 *Burns v Burns* [1984] Ch 317 at 344G.

the size of the contribution.[7] In particular, the fact that B has contributed towards the initial deposit or legal expenses may establish a framework of assumed intention in favour of beneficial co-ownership which makes it more feasible to regard subsequent payments by B as being 'referable to' the acquisition of the property.[8]

(f) Contribution of mortgage instalments

In some circumstances, as discussed above, there may well have been an express agreement between A and B as to the proportions in which each should assume liability for the discharge of a mortgage commitment incurred nominally by A in connection with his acquisition of a legal title.[9] Where such an agreement was reached, it provides prima facie evidence of the proportions in which A and B intended to be entitled beneficially under a resulting trust. However, even if no agreement was reached in express terms, it remains possible for the court to infer such an agreement from the factual pattern of the subsequent contributions made by A and B to the discharge of the mortgage commitment.

(i) Timing of the relevant intention

It is a strict rule that, for the purpose of establishing a resulting trust, the only relevant intention or agreement is that which was formulated at the date of acquisition in respect of the beneficial interests to be taken in the property acquired.[10] However, it is also clear that evidence of this contemporaneous intention may be found in the subsequent conduct of the parties concerned. Inferences drawn from post-acquisition conduct may reflect back upon, and thereby illuminate, the intentions which must have subsisted at the date of acquisition.[11]

(ii) Economic reality of the instalment mortgage

The context in which this process of inference is most highly relevant is that of the acquisition of a matrimonial home with the assistance of mortgage finance. As Lord Diplock conceded in *Gissing v Gissing*,[12] it would be 'unreasonably legalistic' to treat the relevant transaction involved in the acquisition of a matrimonial home as restricted to the actual conveyance of the fee simple into the name of one or other spouse. As Lord Diplock pointed out, the common intention of the spouses is 'more likely to have been concerned with the economic realities of the transaction than with the unfamiliar technicalities of the English law of legal and equitable interests

---

7   See *Efstratiou, Glantschnig and Petrovic v Glantschnig* [1972] NZLR 594 at 598, where payment of half of the deposit was held to generate a half-share in the entire beneficial interest under a resulting trust. See also *Pearson v Pearson* [1961] VR 693 at 699; *Re Whiteley and Whiteley* (1975) 48 DLR (3d) 161 at 170.

8   *Gissing v Gissing* [1971] AC 886 at 907F-H; *Burns v Burns* [1984] Ch 317 at 344G-H.

9   Ante, p 250.

10   *Bernard v Josephs* [1982] Ch 391 at 404C; *Burns v Burns* [1984] Ch 317 at 327A (ante, p 246).

11   In *Gissing v Gissing* [1971] AC 886 at 906E, Lord Diplock indicated that the conduct of parties subsequent to the acquisition of title is 'relevant if it is explicable only upon the basis of their having manifested to one another at the time of the acquisition some particular common intention as to how the beneficial interests should be held.' See also *Burns v Burns* [1984] Ch 317 at 327D; *Allen v Snyder* [1977] 2 NSWLR 685 at 707E-F; *Baumgartner v Baumgartner* [1985] 2 NSWLR 406 at 418B-D.

12   [1971] AC 886 at 906F-H.

in land.' In his view, the 'economic reality' underlying a mortgage-assisted acquisition is 'that the freeholder is purchasing the matrimonial home upon credit and that the purchase price is represented by the instalments by which the mortgage is repaid in addition to the initial deposit in cash.'[13] Thus the conduct of the spouses in relation to the payment of the mortgage instalments 'may be no less relevant to their common intention as to the beneficial interests in a matrimonial home acquired in this way than their conduct in relation to the payment of the cash deposit.'[14]

(iii) Quantification of beneficial interests   It is therefore clearly established that the financial contributions made at the actual date of acquisition do not necessarily provide a final or exclusive measure of the quantum of the beneficial interests taken by the contributors under a resulting trust of the legal estate acquired. Later payments of money can also rank as a contribution of 'purchase money' for the purpose of the same resulting trust. There are, for instance, certain circumstances in which a consistent pattern of contribution by B towards mortgage payments incurred by reason of A's acquisition of title may provide evidence from which it can be inferred that there was a common intention *ab initio* that beneficial ownership should be shared by both A and B.[15]

Such an inference will be even more readily made if there is evidence of 'regular and substantial direct contribution to the mortgage instalments'[16] or if the evidence of subsequent mortgage payments is reinforced by evidence of contribution to the initial cash deposit or legal expenses.[17] The quantum of beneficial ownership thus created by way of resulting trust can only be assessed in the light of the sum total of the financial contributions made by A and B both at acquisition and thereafter.[18] As Lord Diplock said in the context of a family home in *Gissing v Gissing*,[19] there is 'nothing improbable' in the spouses acting on 'the understanding that the wife should be entitled to a share which was not to be quantified immediately upon the acquisition of the home but should be left to be determined when the mortgage was repaid or the property disposed of, on the basis of what would be fair having regard to the total contributions, direct or indirect, which each spouse had made by that date.'[20] This approach was later confirmed in *Bernard v Josephs*,[1] where Kerr LJ, while agreeing that

13   See *Thwaites v Ryan* [1984] VR 65 at 93, for reference to the way in which 'modern phenomena affecting the acquisition of homes by most people may prolong the period of "acquisition"'.
14   See also *Bloch v Bloch* (1981) 37 ALR 55 at 64. Compare *Calverley v Green* (1984) 56 ALR 483 at 497.
15   *Gissing v Gissing* [1971] AC 886 at 900G; *Burns v Burns* [1984] Ch 317 at 345A; *McFarlane v McFarlane* [1972] NI 59 at 74; *Allen v Snyder* [1977] 2 NSWLR 685 at 707F-G.
16   *Gissing v Gissing* [1971] AC 886 at 908B-C. See also *Burns v Burns* [1984] Ch 317 at 329B, 344H-345A.
17   *Gissing v Gissing* [1971] AC 886 at 907F-G; *Burns v Burns* [1984] Ch 317 at 344G; *C v C* [1976] IR 254 at 258.
18   See *Bernard v Josephs* [1982] Ch 391 at 398B; *Burns v Burns* [1984] Ch 317 at 327B.
19   [1971] AC 886 at 909C-D.
20   See also *Winkworth v Edward Baron Development Co Ltd* [1986] 1 WLR 1512 at 1516C-D; *Burns v Burns* [1984] Ch 317 at 327A-B, 344E; *Baumgartner v Baumgartner* [1985] 2 NSWLR 406 at 418C-D.
 1   [1982] Ch 391 at 407G-H.

the parties' money contributions on acquisition 'necessarily provide the starting point for the declaration as to what their respective shares should be', conceded that the court should 'consider the ultimate position concerning the parties' rights' by reference to the totality of money contributions made before 'the common purpose of the implied trust...comes to an end'.

(iv) Requirement of 'referability'   The post-acquisition payment of mortgage instalments is therefore quite capable of ranking alongside other forms of financial contribution as a provision of 'purchase money' relevant for the purpose of raising a presumption of resulting trust. However, there is one all-important qualification upon the court's willingness to presume such a trust under these circumstances. The payments must be indicative of or 'referable to' a conscious or subjective belief on the part of the contributor that he or she was thereby acquiring a beneficial interest in the property concerned.[2] This requirement of referability seems to be more readily satisfied if the payments effectively facilitated the acquisition of the property,[3] or if the nominal owner of the legal title would not have been able to finance the purchase without their help,[4] or simply if the contributions were 'substantial'.[5]

In the absence of such a belief, the payment of mortgage instalments is utterly ineffective to generate a resulting trust. In *Annen v Rattee*,[6] for instance, B was a lodger in a flat owned by A^1 and A^2. In the absence of A^1 and A^2, B had over a long period enjoyed virtually exclusive occupation of the flat, in return for which he paid a large part of the mortgage instalments and other outgoings to which A^1 and A^2 were committed. However, the Court of Appeal took the view that B's contributions were quite reasonable payments made in respect merely of 'use and occupation' of the flat and as such could not provide the basis for any inference of a common intention that B should acquire a beneficial interest in the flat.[7] As Lord Diplock stressed in *Gissing v Gissing*,[8] each case 'must depend upon its own facts.'

(g) Contribution to general household expenses

The application of resulting trust doctrine to more general contributions to household expenses is somewhat less satisfactory. A legal title vested in the name of A alone may have been so acquired with the provision of A's own money together with a mortgage advance for which A is solely responsible. The prima facie inference disclosed by such circumstances is that A was intended to be the sole beneficial owner.[9] However, the question arises whether a resulting trust can be presumed in favour of B on the ground that B has contributed financially to the general expenses incurred by A's household, thereby freeing

2   *Burns v Burns* [1984] Ch 317 at 328H.
3   *Gissing v Gissing* [1971] AC 886 at 911A.
4   *Gissing v Gissing* [1971] AC 886 at 910H-911A.
5   *Gissing v Gissing* [1971] AC 886 at 902G; *Hazell v Hazell* [1972] 1 WLR 301 at 304G-H; *Hargrave v Newton* [1971] 1 WLR 1611 at 1613C; *Carley v Smith* (Court of Appeal, P No 7701392, 23 June 1980).
6   (1985) 273 Estates Gazette 503. See [1985] Conv 218, 371.
7   (1985) 273 Estates Gazette 503 at 504.
8   [1971] AC 886 at 907A.
9   *Bernard v Josephs* [1982] Ch 391 at 403G-H.

A *pro tanto* to discharge his mortgage commitment. This problem arises with particular acuteness in the context of a matrimonial or quasi-matrimonial home in which A and B have lived together. It is quite typical, for example, that A may have used his income to meet the mortgage payments on the property, while B has used his or her income in the payment of household bills or in the purchase of domestic consumables such as food and clothing.

(i) Response of the traditional property lawyer   There would seem to be a strong argument of fairness to the effect that B's financial contributions should generate for B an equitable share in the property which A has thus been freed to acquire. However, the doctrinaire approach of the property lawyer is as simple and logical as it is also unrealistic and unsubtle. If B spends money in the purchase of item X, he will generally acquire rights in item X; but he will not normally acquire rights in item Y, which has been bought by A, even if the fact that B has purchased item X indirectly enabled A to purchase item Y. Thus, in the hardened view of the property lawyer, the housewife who pays the household food or electricity bills with her own money thereby acquires lots of rights in the aforementioned food and electricity; but she does not magically acquire any rights in the house which meanwhile her husband has managed to purchase with his own money.[10] Her financial contributions towards the welfare of the family are not generally regarded as sufficiently enjoying the character of 'purchase money' to raise a resulting trust in her favour in respect of property bought by her husband.[11] The mere sharing of family living expenses does not in itself connote a joint contribution towards the acquisition of family property.[12] English law does not yet acknowledge the fact that families live in a factual community of goods and that the economic activity of spouses is characterised by constructive co-operation, by partnership endeavour and often by a certain division of labour.[13]

(ii) Requirement of 'referability'   Only in very special circumstances may financial contributions by B to A's general household expenditure be properly accounted as indirect contributions by B towards the purchase of A's property, thereby conferring a beneficial interest on B by way of resulting trust. These circumstances occur where it can be inferred from the conduct of A and B that there was a common intention on their part that B's payments in respect of other items should generate for B a beneficial share in A's acquired property.[14] As Lord MacDermott LCJ said in *McFarlane v McFarlane*,[15] A and B must have 'agreed to some quid pro quo in the nature of a proprietary benefit.' Where such an agreement can be proved, B's indirect contribution becomes 'as much the basis of a resulting trust as a direct contribution in money to the cost of acquiring a particular property.'[16]

10   *Burns v Burns* [1984] Ch 317 at 329C; *Allen v Snyder* [1977] 2 NSWLR 685 at 691C.
11   *Gissing v Gissing* [1971] AC 886 at 901B-C, 910G-H.
12   *Gissing v Gissing* [1971] AC 886 at 909G-H; *McGill v S* [1979] IR 283 at 289; *Niederberger v Memnook* (1982) 130 DLR (3d) 353 at 360.
13   Post, p 811.
14   *Gissing v Gissing* [1971] AC 886 at 909E-G; *McFarlane v McFarlane* [1972] NI 59 at 69, 71, 75; *Allen v Snyder* [1977] 2 NSWLR 685 at 707F-G; *Boccalatte v Bushelle* [1980] Qd R 180 at 184B.
15   [1972] NI 59 at 72.
16   [1972] NI 59 at 70.

This criterion has been expressed in the form that B's payments must be 'referable to the acquisition' of the property nominally vested in A.[17] A resulting trust emerges in this context only if there was some conscious agreement or bargain between A and B that their allocation of the burden of the family's financial commitments should eventuate in beneficial ownership for both.[18] The court has no authority to impute a common intention to this effect 'as a legal fiction for the purpose of achieving a result thought by the court to be just'.[19] There must have been a real and mutual understanding that B's assumption of responsibility for more general aspects of household expenditure was part of a deliberate design to free A to discharge the acquisition cost of the home itself.[20] It is somewhat easier to infer this kind of common intention where B has already made some direct financial contribution, for instance, to the initial deposit paid on or before acquiring the property.[1]

(iii) Judicial treatment of 'common intention'   It should not come as any great surprise that a common intention is rarely proved to the satisfaction of the court.[2] In *Gissing v Gissing*[3] the claimant wife alleged that she had made indirect contributions towards the purchase of the family home through her use of her own moneys on various forms of household and other family-related expenditure. The legal title in the home had been purchased in the name of the husband and he was solely responsible for repayment of the mortgage loan secured on the realty. In the absence of any express agreement between the spouses as to how the beneficial interest should be held,[4] the House of Lords declined to infer that her expenditure had been 'referable to' any bargain directed at beneficial co-ownership or could now be seen as reflecting a common intention that the wife should acquire any equitable share in the family home.[5]

Thus in the normal case, where the parties have given no consideration at the date of acquisition to the question of beneficial ownership, a trust claim

17   *Burns v Burns* [1984] Ch 317 at 328G-H; *Toner v Toner* (1972) 23 NILQ 208; *Allen v Snyder* [1977] 2 NSWLR 685 at 691B. It follows that if B's payments occurred after the process of acquisition was complete and any mortgage liability fully discharged, those payments are 'unrelated to the acquisition' and cannot found any equitable interest (see *McGill v S* [1979] IR 283 at 291f).

18   Proof of a 'substantial contribution...to family expenses' has been said to be a ground on which the court can properly infer that such payment is 'referable to the acquisition of the house since, in one way or another, it enables the family to pay the mortgage instalments' (*Burns v Burns* [1984] Ch 317 at 329A-B). See, however, the unsuccessful outcome of the claims pursued not merely in *Burns* itself, but also in *Richards v Dove* [1974] 1 All ER 888 at 894h-895c; *McFarlane v McFarlane* [1972] NI 59 at 73; *McKeown v McKeown* [1975] NI 135 at 142C-D; *Nemeth v Nemeth* (1977-78) 17 ALR 500 at 510; *In Re Barnes (A Bankrupt)* [1979] 4 NIJB, p 6.

19   *McFarlane v McFarlane* [1972] NI 59 at 76. See also *Gissing v Gissing* [1971] AC 886 at 900E-F, 904E-F; *In Re Barnes (A Bankrupt)* [1979] 4 NIJB, p 7; *Grant v Edwards* [1986] Ch 638 at 652F; *Baumgartner v Baumgartner* [1985] 2 NSWLR 406 at 412F-G.

20   *Gissing v Gissing* [1971] AC 886 at 903B-C; *Burns v Burns* [1984] Ch 317 at 329B-C, 330C-D; *Toner v Toner* (1972) 23 NILQ 208; *Nemeth v Nemeth* (1977-78) 17 ALR 500 at 510; *Boccalatte v Bushelle* [1980] Qd R 180 at 185E; *Northern Bank Ltd v Beattie* [1982] 18 NIJB, p 16f.

1   *Gissing v Gissing* [1971] AC 886 at 907G-908B; *Burns v Burns* [1984] Ch 317 at 344G-H.

2   Post, p 811.

3   [1971] AC 886.

4   [1971] AC 886 at 910E.

5   [1971] AC 886 at 911B-C.

premised on the existence of a common intention as of that date is inevitably doomed to failure.[6] Even if the relevant kind of common intention can be proved to have been present, the resulting trust is by no means one under which the contributors necessarily take equal shares,[7] unless the finances of the parties are so inextricably intermixed that 'an equitable knife must be used to sever the Gordian Knot.'[8] The recognition of disparate proportions of beneficial ownership may be much more common.[9]

It is interesting in this context to observe that a more realistic approach to resulting trusts is beginning to emerge in Australia. There is evidence that the Australian courts seem to be moving away from the orthodox strictures of the trust analysis as laid down by the New South Wales Court of Appeal in *Allen v Snyder*.[10] In *Baumgartner v Baumgartner*,[11] Kirby P led a majority in the same Court of Appeal in recognising a proportional beneficial entitlement on behalf of a de facto wife who had made merely indirect contributions towards the family home. In the view taken by Kirby P, the claimant, by pooling her income with that of her partner, had 'week by week evinced her intention in respect of the property. Week by week, in accepting it, [he] similarly evinced his intention'.[12] Kirby P thus concluded that, '[i]n combination with the undisputed evidence that the parties were living together at this time, planning and subsequently conceiving a child, inspecting and choosing the property together, the inference is inescapable that they intended this to be their home for the indefinite future and for their new family...Accordingly, they intended...that a trust should be created in favour of [the claimant] in proportion to the contribution each made to the purchase price.'[13] This benevolent interpretation of the intentions of cohabiting parties may well be the prelude to an overturning of *Allen v Snyder* when the appeal in *Baumgartner* finally reaches the High Court of Australia.

(h) Payment of periodic rent

In order to be relevant under the doctrine of resulting trusts, money payments must be made in connection with the acquisition rather than the use of a capital asset. This has a significance, for instance, in relation to flat-sharing arrangements, where it is common for a tenancy to be taken in the name of one of the flat-sharers, the others holding technically as contractual licensees from him. No resulting trust is presumed on the basis of money payments made by

6   *Gissing v Gissing* [1971] AC 886 at 900D-E.
7   *Gissing v Gissing* [1971] AC 886 at 897B, 903A-B; *McFarlane v McFarlane* [1972] NI 59 at 67.
8   *National Provincial Bank Ltd v Ainsworth* [1965] AC 1175 at 1236B. See also *Rimmer v Rimmer* [1953] 1 QB 63 at 73; *Pettitt v Pettitt* [1970] AC 777 at 803H-804A; *Gissing v Gissing* [1971] AC 886 at 908G; *Burns v Burns* [1984] Ch 317 at 345A; *McFarlane v McFarlane* [1972] NI 59 at 67.
9   See *Gissing v Gissing* [1971] AC 886 at 909C; *Bernard v Josephs* [1982] Ch 391 at 398C; *Falconer v Falconer* [1970] 1 WLR 1333 at 1336E-F. A one-third share was awarded in *Latter v McDonald* (Unreported, Court of Appeal, 26 February 1985); a one-fourth share in *Eves v Eves* [1975] 1 WLR 1338 at 1342H, 1343E, 1346A; and a one-fifth share in *Hall v Hall* (1982) 3 FLR 379 at 381H, 385C.
10 [1977] 2 NSWLR 685.
11 [1985] 2 NSWLR 406.
12 [1985] 2 NSWLR 406 at 418B-C.
13 [1985] 2 NSWLR 406 at 418C-D. Compare, however, the dissent of Mahoney JA (at 426E-427B).

flat-sharers who contribute proportionately to the rent charged to the nominal tenant.[14] The latter stands in no fiduciary relationship to the others, and it therefore follows that if he subsequently acquires a long lease in the flat on his own behalf, this valuable asset is not held on trust for the other erstwhile flat-sharers.[15] As Plowman J pointed out in *Savage v Dunningham*,[16] serious problems would result if flat-sharing were treated not as an entirely informal arrangement but as potentially generative of a trust. Each flat-sharer would, for instance, have a beneficial interest which would require written disposition within section 53(1)(c) of the Law of Property Act 1925 when he moved out.

(i) Contribution of domestic endeavour

It is clearly established that a contribution of domestic labour, even though performed over many years, does not constitute the equivalent of 'purchase money' for the purpose of raising a resulting trust.[17] The English law of real property notoriously refuses to attach any money value to the intangible (though not unquantifiable) contribution which the homemaker makes to the welfare of the family through services of domestic management and child care.[18] The courts take the view that 'the mere fact that parties live together and do the ordinary domestic tasks is...no indication at all that they thereby intended to alter the existing property rights of either of them.'[19]

(3) **Relationship between express and resulting trusts**

The mere existence of an unenforceable express trust of land does not foreclose the possibility that the same set of facts may also give rise to a valid resulting trust.[20] It might be thought that the explicitly declared intention contained in the express trust leaves no room for the implication of intention on which a resulting trust is supposedly based. However, this objection has not been sustained. Russell LJ observed in *Hodgson v Marks*[1] that 'if an attempted express trust fails, that seems...just the occasion for implication of a resulting trust, whether the failure be due to uncertainty, or perpetuity, or lack of form.'[2]

(4) **Displacement of the presumption of resulting trust**

As Lord Diplock noted in *Pettitt v Pettitt*,[3] the equitable presumptions as to intention are 'no more than a consensus of judicial opinion disclosed by

14   *Savage v Dunningham* [1974] Ch 181 at 184H-185A. See also *Annen v Rattee* (1985) 273 Estates Gazette 503.
15   *Savage v Dunningham* [1974] Ch 181 at 185G. The position might be different if the flat-sharers had jointly contributed a cash premium towards the purchase of the tenancy in the name of one of their number. See also *Malayan Credit Ltd v Jack Chia-M.P.H. Ltd* [1986] AC 549 at 561D-E.
16   [1974] Ch 181 at 185D-F.
17   See eg *Burns v Burns* [1984] Ch 317 at 342G.
18   Post, pp 811, 814.
19   *Burns v Burns* [1984] Ch 317 at 331A. See also *Button v Button* [1968] 1 WLR 457 at 462C (post, p 277).
20   *Hodgson v Marks* [1971] Ch 892 at 933B (ante, p 185).
1   [1971] Ch 892 at 933C.
2   See also *Dalton v Christofis* [1978] WAR 42.
3   [1970] AC 777 at 823H.

reported cases as to the most likely inference of fact to be drawn in the absence of any evidence to the contrary.' Presumptions shift the burden of adducing evidence, in that the onus of persuasion is thrown upon the party against whom the force of the presumption operates.[4] A presumption merely allocates the 'risk of non-persuasion'.[5] However, as an American judge once said,[6] 'presumptions may be looked on as the bats of the law, flitting in the twilight but disappearing in the sunshine of actual facts.' It follows that presumptions of intention ultimately prevail only where there is no convincing evidence of the actual intentions of the parties.

The presumption of resulting trust may be rebutted by any evidence[7] (including parol evidence) which unambiguously demonstrates that B, although providing all or part of the finance for a purchase in the name of A, did not actually intend to take a beneficial interest in the property.[8] Where one person has contributed all of the purchase money, it is his or her intention alone which is relevant; where two persons contributed, the intentions of both are material.[9] It seems, moreover, that the presumption of resulting trust may be rebutted either in whole or in part.[10] In *Napier v Public Trustee (Western Australia),*[11] for instance, the High Court of Australia held that the presumption had been rebutted as to the grant of a life interest in disputed property, but still operated in respect of the interest in remainder.[12]

Evidence which rebuts the presumption of resulting trust may take any of a number of forms.

(a) Gift

There may be evidence, for instance, that B intended to confer an entirely gratuitous benefit upon A in the form of the whole or part of the equitable ownership of the disputed property.[13] Evidence of a donative intention excludes any possibility of a resulting trust in favour of B.[14]

(b) Loan

Likewise, the presumption of resulting trust is displaced by proof that B

4   See *Russell v Scott* (1936) 55 CLR 440 at 451 per Dixon and Evatt JJ. See also *Calverley v Green* (1984) 56 ALR 483 at 499; *Muschinski v Dodds* (1985) 62 ALR 429 at 449.
5   *Carkeek v Tate-Jones* [1971] VR 691 at 695.
6   *Mackowik v Kansas City,* 94 SW 256 at 264 (1906) per Lamm J.
7   In determining whether the presumption of resulting trust has been rebutted, the acts and declarations of the parties forming part of the transaction are admissible as evidence either for or against the party who did the act or made the declaration. However, subsequent declarations are admissible as evidence only against the party who made them (see *Shephard v Cartwright* [1955] AC 431 at 445; *Cowcher v Cowcher* [1972] 1 WLR 425 at 436D-E; *Hepworth v Hepworth* (1963) 110 CLR 309 at 319; *Calverley v Green* (1984) 56 ALR 483 at 496; *Muschinski v Dodds* (1985) 62 ALR 429 at 433).
8   *Pettitt v Pettitt* [1970] AC 777 at 814F-G; *Allen v Snyder* [1977] 2 NSWLR 685 at 698F.
9   *Calverley v Green* (1984) 56 ALR 483 at 488f; *Muschinski v Dodds* (1985) 62 ALR 429 at 433.
10   *In re Kerrigan; Ex parte Jones* (1947) 47 SR (NSW) 76 at 82.
11   (1980) 32 ALR 153 at 155, 158.
12   See also *Rider v Kidder* (1805) 10 Ves Jun 360 at 368, 32 ER 884 at 887; *Dullow v Dullow* [1985] 3 NSWLR 531 at 540F-541D.
13   *Cowcher v Cowcher* [1972] 1 WLR 425 at 431C.
14   *Winkworth v Edward Baron Development Co Ltd* [1986] 1 WLR 1512 at 1516D; *Walker v Walker* (Unreported, Court of Appeal, 12 April 1984); *Taddeo v Taddeo* (1978) 19 SASR 347 at 366f (post, p 266). See also *Julian v Furby* (Unreported, Court of Appeal, No 79 15962, 24 November 1981)(gift of cost of B's labour on renovations).

provided the purchase moneys by way of loan.[15] A lender does not advance money 'in the character of a purchaser' and therefore takes no beneficial interest.[16] Were it otherwise, a lender could recover his money twice over,[17] and banks and building societies would moreover acquire a myriad of beneficial interests in the millions of homes bought on the strength of mortgage advances.

(c) Legally ineffective relationships

Similarly, no resulting trust can be claimed by an occupier of property who makes payments of money to the legal owner under circumstances where those payments are more in the nature of contributions to current living expenses and outgoings.[18] In such cases, where the payments are not attributable to any reasonable belief that a beneficial interest is being acquired, the contributor cannot be said to have advanced the money 'in the character of a purchaser'. There is often, particularly in the domestic or familial context, no intention that such payments should create any binding legal relationship at all.[19] The son who gives his mother part of his weekly wage packet while living at home does not thereby acquire a beneficial interest in realty.

Whether the presumption of resulting trust is rebutted in any of these ways is ultimately a matter of credibility and probability, determined with reference to the facts of each individual case.[20] It is in general unlikely that there will not be some living person who can, by his evidence, either confirm or rebut the resulting trust presumed from the payment of moneys. However, if all the available evidence is neutral as to the purpose of the money payment by B to A, the 'prima facie inference' will be that it was the common intention of A and B that there should be a resulting trust in proportion to the moneys contributed.[1]

(5) Presumption of advancement

In normal circumstances the onus of proving the donative intent of B falls, not unnaturally, upon A.[2] However, there is one rather distinct group of circumstances in which a different presumption of law comes into operation, thus effectively reversing the onus of proof. In these situations the presumption of resulting trust is displaced by a countervailing 'presumption of advancement' which, in a number of stereotyped situations, supports an inference of gift by supplying an all-important donative intent on the part of B.

---

15   *Winkworth v Edward Baron Development Co Ltd* [1986] 1 WLR 1512 at 1516D. See *Hussey v Palmer* [1972] 1 WLR 1286 at 1292E; *In re Sharpe (A Bankrupt)* [1980] 1 WLR 219 at 222E-F, 223A-B; *Hoare v Hoare* (1982) *Times*, 9 November; *Wear v DePutron* (Unreported, Court of Appeal, 6 March 1984); *Avondale Printers & Stationers Ltd v Haggie* [1979] 2 NZLR 124 at 145.
16   *In Re Cooke* (1857) 6 Ir Ch R 430 at 438; *Bateman Television Ltd v Bateman and Thomas* [1971] NZLR 453 at 459, 462.
17   *In Re Sharpe (A Bankrupt)* [1980] 1 WLR 219 at 223B.
18   See eg *Hannaford v Selby* (1976) 239 Estates Gazette 811 at 813 (post, p 278); *Baumgartner v Baumgartner* [1985] 2 NSWLR 406 at 419C.
19   Post, p 794.
20   For reference to the multiplicity of circumstances which may explain the payment of moneys in a domestic context, see Chapter 23 (post, p 808).
1   *Gissing v Gissing* [1971] AC 886 at 907C. See also *Seldon v Davidson* [1968] 1 WLR 1083 at 1090F; *Crane v Davis* (Unreported, Chancery Division, 8 May 1981).
2   *Wirth v Wirth* (1956) 98 CLR 228 at 235 per Dixon CJ.

The effect of the presumption of advancement is to establish that the disputed property belongs to A both at law and in equity,[3] the onus now shifting to B to rebut the inference that he intended to 'advance' A.[4]

(a) Relationships which raise a presumption of advancement

A presumption of advancement arises where property is nominally transferred to a person whose welfare the real purchaser of the property would naturally have wished to promote or 'advance'.[5] Accordingly, a special donative intent is presumed in favour of certain persons who come within the bonds of deemed familial affection[6] and for whom the real purchaser has some 'obligation in conscience to provide'.[7] By circumscribing the field of recognised 'advancement', the presumption casts an incidental and quite interesting light on socially perceived boundaries of personal and familial responsibility. Thus, in the absence of clear evidence of contrary intention at the time of purchase,[8] the presumption of advancement infers a donative intent where a father provides the consideration for a transfer into the name of his child[9] or where a person (male or female) purchases property in the name of someone in relation to whom he currently stands *in loco parentis*.[10] The presumption does not,

3 On the application of the presumption of advancement, 'the prima facie position remains that the equitable interest is presumed to follow the legal estate and to be at home with the legal title' (see *Calverley v Green* (1984) 56 ALR 483 at 500 per Deane J).

4 *Murless v Franklin* (1818) 1 Swan 13 at 18, 36 ER 278 at 280. See also *Sidmouth v Sidmouth* (1840) 2 Beav 447 at 454, 48 ER 1254 at 1257; *Pearson v Pearson* [1961] VR 693 at 698; *Martin v Martin* (1959) 110 CLR 297 at 303; *Pettitt v Pettitt* [1970] AC 777 at 814G per Lord Upjohn.

5 'The presumption is based on the concept that where a property is transferred to a person whom the transferor has an obligation to support, it is presumed to be an advance of the interest the dependant might reasonably expect to receive on the death of the transferor' (*Re Levy* (1982) 131 DLR (3d) 15 at 25). See also *Murless v Franklin* (1818) 1 Swan 13 at 17, 36 ER 278 at 280; *Dullow v Dullow* [1985] 3 NSWLR 531 at 535F-536A.

6 In *Wirth v Wirth* (1956) 98 CLR 228 at 237, Dixon CJ thought that 'the presumption of advancement doubtless in its inception was concerned with relationships affording "good" consideration'.

7 *Scott v Pauly* (1917) 24 CLR 274 at 281 per Isaacs J. In the words of Jessel MR in *Bennet v Bennet* (1879) 10 Ch D 474 at 477, 'the presumption of gift arises from the moral obligation to give'. See, however, *Calverley v Green* (1984) 56 ALR 483 at 486f.

8 Subsequent acts and declarations of the child (but not of the parent) may operate to rebut the presumed advancement (*Sidmouth v Sidmouth* (1840) 2 Beav 447 at 455, 48 ER 1254 at 1257). See also *Cowcher v Cowcher* [1972] 1 WLR 425 at 436D; *Charles Marshall Pty Ltd v Grimsley* (1956) 95 CLR 353 at 366; *Blackburn v Y V Properties Pty Ltd* [1980] VR 290 at 293.

9 *Dyer v Dyer* (1788) 2 Cox Eq Cas 92 at 93f, 30 ER 42 at 43; *Sidmouth v Sidmouth* (1840) 2 Beav 447 at 454, 48 ER 1254 at 1257; *Shephard v Cartwright* [1955] AC 431 at 445; *In re Vandervell's Trusts (No 2)* [1974] Ch 269 at 289A; *Charles Marshall Pty Ltd v Grimsley* (1956) 95 CLR 353 at 364; *Goodfriend v Goodfriend* (1972) 22 DLR (3d) 699 at 703; *Napier v Public Trustee (Western Australia)* (1980) 32 ALR 153 at 158; *Calverley v Green* (1984) 56 ALR 483 at 486, 501. The presumption also applies to an illegitimate child (*Soar v Foster* (1858) 4 K & J 152 at 160, 70 ER 64 at 67) and to an adopted child (*Standing v Bowring* (1885) 31 Ch D 282 at 287). A child is, of course, competent to hold a legal estate in land only if he has attained the age of 18 (Law of Property Act 1925, s 1(6)).

10 *Shephard v Cartwright* [1955] AC 431 at 445; *In re Vandervell's Trusts (No 2)* [1974] Ch 269 at 289A; *Charles Marshall Pty Ltd v Grimsley* (1956) 95 CLR 353 at 364; *Young v Young* (1959) 15 DLR (2d) 138 at 139; *Napier v Public Trustee (Western Australia)* (1980) 32 ALR 153 at 158; *Calverley v Green* (1984) 56 ALR 483 at 486, 501. The presumption of advancement thus applies to gifts to an illegitimate child (*Beckford v Beckford* (1774) Lofft 490 at 492, 98 ER 763 at 764), a stepson (*In re Paradise Motor Co Ltd* [1968] 1 WLR 1125 at 1140A), and a grandchild whose father is dead (*Edbrand v Dancer* (1680) 2 Ch Cas 26, 22 ER 829; *Soar v Foster* (1858) 4 K & J 152 at 160, 70 ER 64 at 67).

however, apply to a purchase in the name of a sister,[11] a son-in-law[12] or a nephew.[13] Nor does it rebut the presumption of resulting trust where property is purchased in the name of a parent or parent-in-law.[14]

(b) Applicability to mothers

It seems, moreover, still to be generally accepted that the presumption of advancement does not apply, even 'in these days of sex equality',[15] to a provision of money or transfer of other benefits by a mother to her own son or daughter.[16] This distinction between the cases of a father and a mother was once rationalised on the basis that the father was supposedly 'the head of the family' and therefore 'under the primary moral obligation to provide for the children of the marriage'.[17] However, the distinction comports very uneasily with modern notions of equality,[18] and is particularly difficult to justify in relation to benefits conferred on her children by a mother who is widowed, divorced or single.[19] In such cases it must surely require little evidence to establish a donative intent.[20]

(c) Applicability to spouses

Perhaps the most controversial issue of all is whether the presumption of advancement still applies as between husband and wife.[1] It is clear that such a presumption did once operate not only in favour of a married woman,[2] but also

---

11   *Noack v Noack* [1959] VR 137 at 140; *Gorog v Kiss* (1977) 78 DLR (3d) 690 at 694. It cannot be claimed that a brother stands *in loco parentis* to his sister (*O'Brien v Bean and Bean* (1957) 7 DLR (2d) 332 at 333).

12   *Knight v Biss* [1954] NZLR 55 at 57.

13   *Drury v Drury* (1675) 73 SS 205; *Russell v Scott* (1936) 55 CLR 440 at 451.

14   *Binmatt v Ali* (Unreported, Court of Appeal, 6 October 1981); *Groves v Christiansen* (1978) 86 DLR (3d) 296 at 301).

15   *Gross v French* (1975) 238 Estates Gazette 39 per Scarman LJ.

16   *Bennet v Bennet* (1879) 10 Ch D 474 at 478; *In re Vandervell's Trusts (No 2)* [1974] Ch 269 at 289A; *Preston v Greene* [1909] 1 IR 172 at 177f; *Lattimer v Lattimer* (1978) 82 DLR (3d) 587 at 590. Compare, however, *Bull v Bull* [1955] 1 QB 234 at 236, and *Rupar v Rupar* (1964) 49 WWR 226 at 234, where it seems to have been thought that the presumption of advancement could, in the absence of contrary intention, apply to a mother.

17   *Scott v Pauly* (1917) 24 CLR 274 at 282 per Isaacs J. It may be, however, that the onus on the child to prove a donative intent on the part of his mother will be fairly easily satisfied (see *Bennet v Bennet* (1879) 10 Ch D 474 at 479f per Jessel MR; *Main v Main* [1939] 1 DLR 723 at 725).

18   The starkly unjustifiable nature of the distinction appears in two cases concerning the ownership of lottery moneys won on a ticket purchased in the name of a child (compare *B v B* (1976) 65 DLR (3d) 460 at 466, with *Kiddle v Afoa and Afoa* (1984) NZ Recent Law 47).

19   In *Scott v Pauly* (1917) 24 CLR 274 at 282, Isaacs J thought that the presumption of advancement might apply to a widow. It may not require very strong evidence to show that a mother is *in loco parentis* (*Re Orme* (1883) 50 LT (NS) 51 at 53). The recent Australian caselaw discloses a marked willingness to extend the presumption to a mother (see *Dullow v Dullow* [1985] 3 NSWLR 531 at 536C, 541D-E).

20   *Edwards v Bradley* (1957) 9 DLR (2d) 673 at 678 (Supreme Court of Canada); *Lattimer v Lattimer* (1978) 82 DLR (3d) 587 at 590; *Dullow v Dullow* [1985] 3 NSWLR 531 at 534G.

1   It appears from *In Re Figgis* [1969] 1 Ch 123 at 144C that the presumption of advancement may still apply in respect of a joint bank account held by husband and wife (compare, however, *Re Berry (A Bankrupt)* [1978] 2 NZLR 373 at 378).

2   *Christ's Hospital v Budgin* (1712) 2 Vern 683 at 684, 23 ER 1043 at 1044; *Martin v Martin* (1959) 110 CLR 297 at 303; *Hepworth v Hepworth* (1963) 110 CLR 309 at 317.

in favour of a woman to whom property was transferred in express contemplation of a marriage which subsequently took place with the donor.[3] However, the presumption of advancement has never applied as between merely cohabiting parties.[4] Nor has it ever had any application in favour of a husband.[5] The relevance in modern conditions of the sex-discriminatory concept of 'advancement' is now highly questionable.[6] In its application in the marital context, the presumption was all too plainly an index of a former social climate in which wives enjoyed a far inferior status relative to that which they now occupy.[7] The archaic nature of the presumption was recognised by the House of Lords in *Pettitt v Pettitt*,[8] where Lord Diplock thought that it would be 'an abuse of legal technique...to apply to transactions between the post-war generation of married couples "presumptions" which are based upon inferences of fact which an earlier generation of judges drew as to the most likely intentions of earlier generations of spouses belonging to the propertied classes of a different social era.'[9]

The contemporary disfavour for the social philosophy of advancement has led to an almost irresistible movement away from the presumption, at least in the context of spousal transactions concerning land. It would seem that the presumption of advancement can now play only an extremely marginal role in determining between living spouses questions of equitable ownership.[10] In few cases will recourse to the presumption be necessary or conclusive, for it will be a rare case in which evidence of actual intention is completely absent. Where, however, the presumption is applicable, its strength may well require to be assessed relative to the date of the disputed purchase and to the age and social

3 *Moate v Moate* [1948] 2 All ER 486 at 487G-H; *Wirth v Wirth* (1956) 98 CLR 228 at 237f. See also *Ibbotson v Kushner* (1978) 84 DLR (3d) 417 at 419.
4 *Rider v Kidder* (1805) 10 Ves 360 at 367, 32 ER 884 at 887; *Soar v Foster* (1858) 4 K & J 152 at 162, 70 ER 64 at 68; *Collins v Sanders* (1956) 3 DLR (2d) 607 at 615; *David v Szoke* (1974) 39 DLR (3d) 707 at 716; *Allen v Snyder* [1977] 2 NSWLR 685 at 690B; *Calverley v Green* (1984) 56 ALR 483 at 495, 501f. See, however, *Napier v Public Trustee (Western Australia)* (1980) 32 ALR 153 at 154 per Gibbs ACJ; but compare now *Muschinski v Dodds* (1985) 62 ALR 429 at 432 per Gibbs CJ. It is always possible, of course, that there may be sufficient evidence of an actual donative intention to support the equitable entitlement of a cohabiting transferee (see *Murdock v Aherne* (1878) 4 VLR (E) 244 at 249; *Carkeek v Tate-Jones* [1971] VR 691 at 697ff).
5 *Pettitt v Pettitt* [1970] AC 777 at 815E-F; *Northern Bank Ltd v Henry* [1981] IR 1 at 18; *Allied Irish Banks Ltd v McWilliams* [1982] NI 156 at 161D; *Doohan v Nelson* [1973] 2 NSWLR 320 at 327D; *Brophy v Brophy* (1974) 3 ACTR 57 at 60; *Taddeo v Taddeo* (1978) 19 SASR 347 at 365, 367; *Muschinski v Dodds* (1985) 62 ALR 429 at 432.
6 It seems that the presumption of advancement still obtains in the Republic of Ireland (see *Heavey v Heavey* [1977] 111 ILTR 1 at 3; *M v M* [1980] 114 ILTR 46 at 49) and in Australia (see *Doohan v Nelson* [1973] 2 NSWLR 320 at 325E; *Napier v Public Trustee (Western Australia)* (1980) 32 ALR 153 at 158).
7 The presumption of advancement 'found its place in Victorian days when a wife was utterly subordinate to her husband. It has no place, or, at any rate, very little place, in our law today' (*Falconer v Falconer* [1970] 1 WLR 1333 at 1335H-1336A per Lord Denning MR).
8 [1970] AC 777 at 824C. See also Lord Reid (at 793E-F).
9 It is notable in any event that in *Pettitt* Lord Upjohn remained unrepentant about the role of the equitable presumptions. He acknowledged that they had been 'criticised as being out of touch with the realities of today', but maintained that 'when properly understood and properly applied to the circumstances of today...they remain as useful as ever in solving questions of title' ([1970] AC 777 at 813G-H). See also *Calverley v Green* (1984) 56 ALR 483 at 499 per Deane J.
10 *Pettitt v Pettitt* [1970] AC 777 at 811G; *Gissing v Gissing* [1971] AC 886 at 907C-D; *Re Berry (A Bankrupt)* [1978] 2 NZLR 373 at 378; *Napier v Public Trustee (Western Australia)* (1980) 32 ALR 153 at 154.

outlook of the particular spouses.[11] In *Re Hogg (Deceased)*,[12] for example, the presumption was held to be more readily applicable to spouses born at the end of the last century who married in 1930 with the benefit of a marriage settlement and who each possessed substantial capital assets of his or her own. Cultural factors may also influence the court, as in *Taddeo v Taddeo*,[13] where Bray CJ declined to apply a presumption of resulting trust in favour of an Italian wife, on the ground that there was evidence that she, 'as would be normal for a wife in Italy', had trusted her Italian husband 'to perform his moral obligation to use his money as well as hers for the benefit of the family without expecting any proprietary interest for herself'.

What little force the presumption retains can of course be rebutted by evidence of a contrary intention on the part of the spouses.[14] Only where this contrary intention involves some element of fraud or illegality will the courts decline to admit evidence tending to rebut the presumption of advancement.[15] Thus an advancement may still be presumed in favour of a married woman if the husband's motive in placing or purchasing property in her name was to defeat the potential claims of his own creditors. Such a transaction is vitiated by illegal purpose if it amounts to an agreement by the spouses to vest a title in the wife 'so that they might both pretend to anyone who became a creditor that she was the beneficial owner, but with a secret agreement that she would reconvey the interest to him when he wanted it'.[16] A husband cannot be heard to maintain as against his creditors that his family home belongs to his wife, while maintaining as against his wife that the house still belongs in equity to himself.[17] Likewise, a conveyance into a wife's name for tax reasons takes effect as a gift to her in equity too,[18] at least so long as the transaction was not merely an attempt to minimise the incidence of taxation, but involved a further element of criminal non-disclosure penalised by the relevant tax code.[19]

The combined operation of the presumptions of resulting trust and advancement in the spousal context is best explained in a number of examples.

(i) H's funds used for a purchase in the name of W   Where a husband purchases a legal title in his wife's name, it may be that in the absence of all other evidence

---

11   See *Doohan v Nelson* [1973] 2 NSWLR 320 at 326A.
12   Unreported, Chancery Division, 1982 H No 2830, 11 July 1983.
13   (1978) 19 SASR 347 at 366f.
14   *Organ v Sandwell* [1921] VLR 622 at 626, 629; *Allen v Snyder* [1977] 2 NSWLR 685 at 690A. In *Doohan v Nelson* [1973] 2 NSWLR 320 at 329C, significance was attached to the fact that the husband still used the wife's house as security for borrowings for his own purposes.
15   This application of the 'clean hands' doctrine was explained in terms of Lord Eldon LC's statement in *Muckleston v Brown* (1801) 6 Ves 52 at 69, 31 ER 934 at 942, that the plaintiff 'coming to equity to be relieved against his own act, and the defence being dishonest, between the two species of dishonesty the Court would not act; but would say, "Let the estate lie where it falls".' See also *Goodfriend v Goodfriend* (1972) 22 DLR (3d) 699 at 703, but compare *Moody v Cox & Hatt* [1917] 2 Ch 71 at 87f.
16   *David v Szoke* (1974) 39 DLR (3d) 707 at 719. See also *Gascoigne v Gascoigne* [1918] 1 KB 223 at 226f, but compare *Goodfriend v Goodfriend* (1972) 22 DLR (3d) 699 at 707.
17   See eg *Tinker v Tinker* [1970] P 136 at 141G-H; *Cantor v Cox* (1976) 239 Estates Gazette 121 at 123; *Maysels v Maysels* (1974) 45 DLR (3d) 337 at 345f, affd (1976) 64 DLR (3d) 765 (Supreme Court of Canada). See G. Kodilinye, *Restitution of Fraudulently Conveyed Property in England and Canada*, (1980) 9 Anglo-Am LR 28.
18   *Miller v Miller* (1983) 39 OR (2d) 74 at 81. See also *Martin v Martin* (1959) 110 CLR 297 at 305f.
19   *In re Emery's Investment Trusts* [1959] Ch 410 at 422.

he is presumed to have intended that she should take both the legal and equitable ownership.[20] However, it is questionable whether today the presumption of advancement retains even this degree of residual strength. Its severely diminished role under modern conditions was recently indicated by the Privy Council in *Neo Tai Kim v Foo Stie Wah*.[1] Here Lord Brightman declared that the presumption of advancement is 'not an immutable rule to be applied blindly where there is no direct evidence as to the common intention of the spouses. It is rather a guideline to be followed by the court in an appropriate case where it searches for the intention which ought, in the absence of evidence, to be imputed to the parties.'

(ii) H's funds used for a purchase in joint names   If a husband purchases a legal title in the joint names of himself and his wife, then in the total absence of all other evidence the spouses would seem to be joint tenants in equity also.[2] To this extent, again, the presumption of advancement has a residual function, but the position is more likely to be confirmed by evidence of an actual intention expressed by the spouses in favour of joint equitable ownership.[3]

(iii) W's funds used for a purchase in the name of H   If a wife purchases a legal title in her husband's name, he probably holds on a resulting trust for her,[4] 'but in practice there will in almost every case be some explanation (however slight) of this (today) rather unusual course.'[5]

(iv) W's funds used for a purchase in joint names   If a wife purchases a legal title in the joint names of herself and her husband, in the absence of any other evidence the inference may be that the spouses were intended to be joint owners in equity also. As Lord Upjohn once said, there seems to be 'no other reason for it.'[6] However, if this form of vesting is explicable on another footing (eg because the wife believed that she would not obtain a mortgage loan unless her husband was on the legal title), there may be a resulting trust for the wife absolutely as the sole provider of the moneys.[7]

20   *Pettitt v Pettitt* [1970] AC 777 at 815E per Lord Upjohn; *Pearson v Pearson* [1961] VR 693 at 698.
1   Unreported, Privy Council No 30 of 1982, 4 March 1985. See also *McFarlane v McFarlane* [1972] NI 59 at 75.
2   *Pettitt v Pettitt* [1970] AC 777 at 815E; *Re Hogg (Deceased)* (Unreported, Chancery Division, 1982 H No 2830, 11 July 1983); *Calverley v Green* (1984) 56 ALR 483 at 492. Compare, however, *Pearson v Pearson* [1961] VR 693 at 698, where the Full Court of the Supreme Court of Victoria thought that, in the absence of an actual donative intent, there would be a resulting trust for the provider of the purchase moneys.
3   There is a statutory presumption in some jurisdictions that a vesting of legal title in the joint names of husband and wife is prima facie proof that each spouse is intended on severance (post, p 317) to have a one-half beneficial interest in the property (see eg Ontario's Family Law Reform Act 1978 (RSO 1980, c 152), s 11(1)(a); Nova Scotia's Matrimonial Property Act 1980, s 21(1)(a)).
4   See eg *Northern Bank Ltd v Henry* [1981] IR 1 at 8, 18.
5   *Pettitt v Pettitt* [1970] AC 777 at 815E-F. See also *Pearson v Pearson* [1961] VR 693 at 698.
6   *Pettitt v Pettitt* [1970] AC 777 at 815F. Compare, however, *Pearson v Pearson* [1961] VR 693 at 698, where once again the Full Court thought that, absent an actual donative intent, there would be a resulting trust for the provider of the purchase moneys.
7   *Allied Irish Banks Ltd v McWilliams* [1982] NI 156 at 160D, 161D.

(v) Joint funds used for acquisition of a legal title If both spouses contribute to the purchase of a legal title, there is high authority for the view that they are to be taken, in the absence of all other evidence, as having intended to be beneficial owners in the proportions contributed.[8] For this purpose, it seems to be irrelevant whether the legal title is purchased in the name of the husband or of the wife or, indeed, in the names of both.[9] Even the fact that such a purchase is put in the name of the wife appears to be insufficient to found any claim to an advancement in her favour,[10] unless perhaps the husband's financial contribution is 'very small'.[11]

It has sometimes been suggested that if, in any of these situations, the husband makes a larger financial contribution than the wife, the excess of a moiety should be treated as an advancement of the wife, thereby bringing about a beneficial joint tenancy.[12] However, it seems far preferable to abandon even this residual notion of advancement in favour of saying simply that there is a presumed resulting trust for the spouses as beneficial tenants in common in arithmetic proportion to their respective contributions.[13]

5. CONSTRUCTIVE TRUSTS

The constructive trust is the most controversial and far-reaching of the devices used by equity in vindication of its own doctrines. In the words of Cardozo J, the constructive trust is

the formula through which the conscience of equity finds expression. When property has been acquired in such circumstances that the holder of the legal title may not in good conscience retain the beneficial interest, equity converts him into a trustee.[14]

Whether analysed as a 'right' or as a 'remedy',[15] the constructive trust involves a judicial finding that a person should be 'made liable in equity as trustee by the imposition or construction of the court of equity.'[16] Accordingly, the court may well acknowledge that A is the owner of the legal title in 'his' property, but still require that for reasons of consonance with equitable doctrine he should hold that title, in the character of a fiduciary, on an implied trust for B.[17] In its more dramatic manifestations, the imposition of a constructive trust on A amounts effectively to a decree of confiscation, awarding to B property which A had previously thought belonged to himself both at law and in equity. A court-ordered constructive trust which confers an

8 *Pettitt v Pettitt* [1970] AC 777 at 815F-G per Lord Upjohn; *McFarlane v McFarlane* [1972] NI 59 at 67 per Lord MacDermott LCJ. See eg *Re Rogers' Question* [1948] 1 All ER 328 at 330A.
9 *Pettitt v Pettitt* [1970] AC 777 at 815G.
10 See *McFarlane v McFarlane* [1972] NI 59 at 75 per Lowry J.
11 *Pettitt v Pettitt* [1970] AC 777 at 815G; *Calverley v Green* (1984) 56 ALR 483 at 494.
12 *Re Hogg (Deceased)* (Unreported, Chancery Division, 1982 H No 2830, 11 July 1983).
13 See *Hine v Hine* [1962] 1 WLR 1124 at 1132; *Bernard v Josephs* [1982] Ch 391 at 398A-C. See also *Pearson v Pearson* [1961] VR 693 at 698; *McFarlane v McFarlane* [1972] NI 59 at 74f; *Crisp v Mullings* (1976) 239 Estates Gazette 119 at 121.
14 *Beatty v Guggenheim Exploration Co*, 225 NY 380 at 386 (1919), quoted in *Binions v Evans* [1972] Ch 359 at 368C per Lord Denning MR.
15 See *Chase Manhattan Bank NA v Israel-British Bank (London) Ltd* [1981] Ch 105 at 124F-G per Goulding J; *Allen v Snyder* [1977] 2 NSWLR 685 at 703C.
16 *Selangor United Rubber Estates Ltd v Cradock (No 3)* [1968] 1 WLR 1555 at 1582A-B.
17 See *Muschinski v Dodds* (1985) 62 ALR 429 at 453 (High Court of Australia).

absolute interest on B has the double effect of confirming both the sole equitable title of B and the absence of any beneficial ownership in A.[18]

(1) Role of intention in the creation of the constructive trust

The liability of A as a constructive trustee does not depend directly on any intention on the part of A that he should hold property on trust for B.[19] The truth is usually quite the reverse, for the imposition of trust liability is normally the last result desired or contemplated by A.[20] Indeed, in most cases, A is made a constructive trustee by intervention of the court precisely because he has sought to *avoid* liability as a fiduciary. The imposition of constructive trusteeship rests primarily not upon intention, but upon the fact that A has, by some prior agreement or bargain, taken upon himself a fiduciary role which he cannot now be heard to disavow. As Dixon J said in *Cohen v Cohen*,[1] the constructive trust represents an instance 'where the equity is fastened upon the trustee not because he intended to become the fiduciary of property but because of the character of his dealings and in spite of his intention to take the property for himself.'[2] However, although not the direct product of intention, the constructive trust operates against the background of—and indeed is ultimately rooted in—some bargain or common intention which now makes the assertion of absolute beneficial entitlement unconscionable.[3]

(2) General principle underlying the constructive trust

It is an inveterate doctrine of equity that no person who holds property in a fiduciary capacity may ever be permitted to set up an inconsistent personal claim in respect of that property.[4] The rigour of this rule is preserved with great diligence. As long ago as *Keech v Sandford*[5] it was conceded that it 'may seem hard, that the trustee is the only person of all mankind' who is debarred from deriving personal advantage from the property which he holds on trust, but, as King LC said, 'it is very proper that rule should be strictly pursued, and not in the least relaxed.' This vigilance on the part of equity provides the basis of the constructive trust. A constructive trust will be imposed by the court in any case where a fiduciary seeks to deny that his title to property is qualified by his own status as a fiduciary.[6]

18 Not every constructive trust confers an absolute equitable interest on B. It is equally feasible, in certain circumstances, that a constructive trust may be imposed on A, directing him to hold on trust for some lesser equitable entitlement on the part of B (see eg *Bannister v Bannister* [1948] 2 All ER 133, post, p 282).
19 *Muschinski v Dodds* (1985) 62 ALR 429 at 450f.
20 See *Rathwell v Rathwell* (1978) 83 DLR (3d) 289 at 305.
 1 (1929) 42 CLR 91 at 100.
 2 See also *White v Cabanas Pty Ltd* (No 2) [1970] Qd R 395 at 408A; *Allen v Snyder* [1977] 2 NSWLR 685 at 690B; *McMahon v McMahon* [1979] VR 239 at 244; *South Yarra Project Pty Ltd v Gentsis* [1985] VR 29 at 37.
 3 See *Allen v Snyder* [1977] 2 NSWLR 685 at 693A-B; *Baumgartner v Baumgartner* [1985] 2 NSWLR 406 at 435A-B.
 4 *Parker v McKenna* (1874) 10 Ch App 96 at 124; *Meinhard v Salmon*, 164 NE 545 at 546 (1928); *Malsbury v Malsbury* [1982] 1 NSWLR 226 at 231C.
 5 (1726) 2 Eq Ca Abr 741, 22 ER 629, Sel Cas T King 61 at 62, 25 ER 223.
 6 'Strictly, constructive trusts arise where one who is already a trustee or otherwise clothed with fiduciary character seeks to retain an advantage from his trust' (*Cowcher v Cowcher* [1972] 1 WLR 425 at 431A).

(a) Role of bargain

It may well be asked how, for present purposes, a fiduciary status comes to impinge at all upon the ownership of a legal title in land. This question was addressed directly by the House of Lords in *Gissing v Gissing*.[7] Here Lord Diplock observed that the preceding caselaw on constructive trusts had largely passed over the first—and critical—stage in the analysis of this form of trust, ie, 'the role of...agreement...in the creation of an equitable estate in real property.'[8] The equitable interest to which the constructive trust gives effect results invariably from some anterior bargain or agreement relating to the property, by which an owner of a legal title has undertaken to give effect to an equitable entitlement in someone else.

(b) Role of conscience

It has already been seen that an express agreement by A, conferring on B a beneficial interest in A's land, is potentially creative of an express trust in respect of that land.[9] Such a declaration of trust is enforceable by B provided that it is evidenced in writing in accordance with section 53(1)(b) of the Law of Property Act 1925.[10] But if it is not evidenced by a duly signed document, the declaration of trust remains purely oral and therefore unenforceable as an express trust.[11]

This, however, is not the end of the story: the legal effect of the purely oral agreement is not yet spent. As Lord Diplock pointed out in *Gissing v Gissing*,[12] the court may still give effect to the agreement as to beneficial ownership, notwithstanding the absence of written evidence of the trust thereby declared. Equity's willingness to enforce a trust in this context is attributable quite simply to the fact that A, the legal owner, may have 'so conducted himself that it would be inequitable to allow him to deny to [B] a beneficial interest'. Such circumstances will arise, characteristically, if A 'by his words or conduct has induced [B] to act to his own detriment in the reasonable belief that by so acting he was acquiring a beneficial interest in the land.'[13] If by no other means, equity will frustrate the unconscionable behaviour of A through the imposition of a constructive trust in favour of B.[14] Unlike the antecedent oral declaration of trust, this constructive trust is fully enforceable by B, precisely because constructive trusts are, by section 53(2) of the Law of Property Act 1925, exempted from any requirement of formal writing.

(3) Component elements of the constructive trust

Given this account of the general principle underlying the constructive trust, it becomes possible to say that the imposition of a constructive trust requires

7   [1971] AC 886 (ante, p 258; post, p 810).
8   [1971] AC 886 at 904G. For reference in this context to the terminology of 'bargain', see *Grant v Edwards* [1986] Ch 638 at 651G-652B, 653D per Mustill LJ.
9   Ante, p 235.
10   If the trust is declared in proper form, the doctrine of constructive trust cannot be invoked to contradict it (see *Goodman v Gallant* [1986] Fam 106 at 116F-G).
11   Ante, p 236.
12   [1971] AC 886 at 905D-E.
13   [1971] AC 886 at 905B-C (ante, p 243).
14   See *Grant v Edwards* [1986] Ch 638 at 646H-647A per Nourse LJ.

proof of three elements. The facts must disclose (a) a common intention, (b) a change of position, and (c) equitable fraud.[15] These three elements are, however, almost inextricably inter-related. For the purpose of establishing a constructive trust, a common intention is recognised as relevant only if comprised within some form of 'bargain' under which one party changes his position. A change of position occurs in the relevant sense only if it is truly referable to a common intention that rights of beneficial ownership should be acknowledged by the legal owner. Equitable fraud is present only if the legal owner then tries to escape from the 'bargain' by asserting the absolute and exclusive nature of his own rights.

Thus stated, the constituent elements of the constructive trust bear a remarkable similarity to the features of proprietary estoppel.[16] It is not uncommon to find that in many cases arguments based on constructive trust and proprietary estoppel are pleaded in the alternative.[17] The elements of the constructive trust must now be examined more closely.

(4) Common intention

In strict theory every constructive trust derives ultimately from some bargain which affects the conscience of the party who is eventually made liable as constructive trustee.[18] For instance, if A, the owner of a legal title, has made some agreement to recognise the existence of equitable rights in B, it is unconscionable for A later to disown this common intention if, in the meantime, the agreement has induced a change of position by the other party to the agreement. Likewise, if A has purchased from X land which, to the knowledge of A, is already the subject of some bargain between B and X, then A will be made to hold that land on a constructive trust for B.

(a) Parties to the agreement or common intention

It follows that no crucial importance is attached to the precise origin of the agreement or common intention which underlies constructive trust liability. It is sufficient merely that there is some anterior 'bargain' relating to equitable rights in B which affects the property in such a way as to impinge on the conscience of A, the current legal owner. It matters not whether this 'bargain' was incorporated (as it more usually is) in an agreement between A and B directly[19] or whether it took the form of an undertaking given by A to a stranger, X.[20] It is even possible that the 'bargain' may not have been made by A at all, but may have been concluded between B and X in circumstances of which A has actual or deemed knowledge.[1] In all of these examples it may well

---

15   See *Ogilvie v Ryan* [1976] 2 NSWLR 504 at 516G–517A; *Hohol v Hohol* [1981] VR 221 at 225; *Butler v Craine* [1986] VR 274 at 283.
16   Post, p 387. See *Grant v Edwards* [1986] Ch 638 at 656H per Browne-Wilkinson V-C ('The two principles have been developed separately without cross-fertilisation between them: but they rest on the same foundation and have on all other matters reached the same conclusions').
17   Post, pp 419, 817.
18   See *Nemeth v Nemeth* (1977–78) 17 ALR 500 at 503.
19   See eg *Bannister v Bannister* [1948] 2 All ER 133 (post, p 282).
20   See eg *Binions v Evans* [1972] Ch 359 (post, p 551); *Lyus v Prowsa Developments Ltd* [1982] 1 WLR 1044 (post, p 284).
1   See eg *Peffer v Rigg* [1977] 1 WLR 285 (post, p 292); *White v Cabanas Pty Ltd* (No 2) [1970] Qd R 395 at 408B.

be that A's conscience is bound by the bargain in a way which makes him guilty of equitable fraud should he ever attempt to defeat the agreement.

(b) Time-frame of the agreement

Whereas a resulting trust can arise only in respect of an intention which is presumed to have been present at the date of acquisition of the trust property,[2] the precise timing of the agreement or 'bargain' which underlies the constructive trust appears to be altogether irrelevant. It matters not whether the agreement guaranteeing equitable rights for B precedes[3] or is contemporaneous with[4] the acquisition of the legal estate in the name of A. In either case A can be said to have taken his title subject to a fiduciary obligation towards B which, if breached by him, may lead to the imposition of a constructive trust.

The constructive trust is, however, capable of a somewhat wider application. It may be imposed in order to give effect to a 'bargain' or common intention to recognise beneficial rights in B, even though the relevant agreement between A and B occurred only some time *after* A's acquisition of title.[5] In this respect, the constructive trust is rather more flexible than the express trust. It is true that an express trust for B may be declared by A after the date on which he acquires his title to land, but the enforceability of this kind of post-acquisition trust is dependent upon compliance with the statutory requirement of written evidence.[6] However, a constructive trust arising in the same context is enforceable even though the agreement or common intention on which it is based was never statutorily evidenced.

(c) Form of the agreement or common intention

It is irrelevant whether A's agreement was overtly expressed in a form of words[7] or was merely a matter of clear inference from the conduct and mutual dealings of the parties.[8] In *Gissing v Gissing*[9] Lord Diplock indicated that, in so far as the

2   Ante, p 246.
3   This is so at least if the property concerned is specific and identifiable and was, at the time of the agreement, within the contemplation of both A and B (see *Le Compte v Public Trustee* [1983] 2 NSWLR 109 at 111A).
4   *Pettitt v Pettitt* [1970] AC 777 at 813D per Lord Upjohn.
5   See *Gissing v Gissing* [1971] AC 886 at 901D, 906E-F; *Bernard v Josephs* [1982] Ch 391 at 404D-E; *Burns v Burns* [1984] Ch 317 at 327D; *Layton v Martin* [1986] 2 FLR 227 at 236E-F; *Gough v Fraser* [1977] 1 NZLR 279 at 283; *Allen v Snyder* [1977] 2 NSWLR 685 at 691C; *McMahon v McMahon* [1979] VR 239 at 244; *Butler v Craine* [1986] VR 274 at 285ff.
6   *Wratten v Hunter* [1978] 2 NSWLR 367 at 371B (ante, p 239).
7   See *Grant v Edwards* [1986] Ch 638 at 647C, 654F. In the absence of written evidence, of course, a mere form of words constitutes an unenforceable declaration of trust (ante, p 237). However, what is unenforceable as an express trust may be effective as a constructive trust. In *Grant v Edwards*, supra at 655F-G, Browne-Wilkinson V-C emphasised that express verbal declarations of intended co-ownership—if present on the facts—make it unnecessary for the court to have recourse to inferences based on other forms of conduct.
8   That a common intention can be inferred from conduct has been widely accepted. See, eg *Gissing v Gissing* [1971] AC 886 at 900G, 902G, 908E-G; *Burns v Burns* [1984] Ch 317 at 336E-F, 344H-345A; *Grant v Edwards* [1986] Ch 638 at 648A-C; *Allen v Snyder* [1977] 2 NSWLR 685 at 691D; *McMahon v McMahon* [1979] VR 239 at 244; *Boccalatte v Bushelle* [1980] Qd R 180 at 185F; *Hohol v Hohol* [1981] VR 221 at 226; *Hayward v Giordani* [1983] NZLR 140 at 151; *Butler v Craine* [1986] VR 274 at 285. Proof of common intention is perhaps most frequently provided by evidence of expenditure 'referable to the acquisition' of the disputed property (see *Grant v Edwards*, supra at 647A-B).
9   [1971] AC 886 at 906B-C.

law of constructive trusts rests upon a common intention, 'the relevant intention of each party is the intention which was reasonably understood by the other party to be manifested by that party's words or conduct notwithstanding that he did not consciously formulate that intention in his own mind or even acted with some different intention which he did not communicate to the other party.'[10] In other words, the matter of intention is judged objectively rather than subjectively.[11] Effect is given to 'the inferences as to the intentions of parties to a transaction which a reasonable man would draw from their words or conduct and not to any subjective intention or absence of intention which was not made manifest at the time of the transaction itself.'[12]

In all cases, however, there must be evidence of an authentic agreement or common intention reached between A and B.[13] The court may 'infer' a common intention which is plainly evidenced by the conduct of A and B, but may not impute to them an intention which they never actually had.[14] At least according to the orthodox view, the court has no jurisdiction to impute to the parties a fictitious common intention that B should be beneficially entitled, even if it is highly probable that such an agreement would have been reached by the parties in any event had they only considered the issue[15] or would have been fair in all the circumstances.[16]

(d) Subject matter of the agreement

It is clear that a constructive trust may be raised in respect of any agreement or common intention entered into by A that a recognisable equitable right of property should be acknowledged as belonging to B. It is not necessary that 'the bargain...should include any express stipulation that [A] is in so many words to hold as trustee.'[17] It is enough that 'the bargain should have included a

---

10   See *Calverley v Green* (1984) 56 ALR 483 at 496; *Baumgartner v Baumgartner* [1985] 2 NSWLR 406 at 412F-G.

11   *Burns v Burns* [1984] Ch 317 at 336F. See also *Pearson v Pearson* [1961] VR 693 at 698.

12   [1971] AC 886 at 906C-D. See also *Eves v Eves* [1975] 1 WLR 1338 at 1342E.

13   *Allen v Snyder* [1977] 2 NSWLR 685 at 694A; *Baumgartner v Baumgartner* [1985] 2 NSWLR 406 at 435B. Statements can be found to the effect that the court may impute to the parties an artificial common intention which they never in fact had (see Lord Reid in *Pettitt v Pettitt* [1970] AC 777 at 795C-F; *Gissing v Gissing* [1971] AC 886 at 897F). However, this proposition has not commanded general support (see *Allen v Snyder*, *supra*, at 694B; *Muschinski v Dodds* (1985) 62 ALR 429 at 436f).

14   See *Butler v Craine* [1986] VR 274 at 285. For recognition of 'the uncertain boundaries between inference and conjecture', see *Doohan v Nelson* [1973] 2 NSWLR 320 at 329E. For a case on the borderline, see *Eves v Eves* [1975] 1 WLR 1338 at 1345D-F (post, p 815).

15   *Pettitt v Pettitt* [1970] AC 777 at 804H-805A, 810F, 816D; *Gissing v Gissing* [1971] AC 886 at 898C, 900E-F, 904E-F; *In re Densham (A Bankrupt)* [1975] 1 WLR 1519 at 1524E-F; *Burns v Burns* [1984] Ch 317 at 326D, 335G; *McFarlane v McFarlane* [1972] NI 59 at 71; *Allen v Snyder* [1977] 2 NSWLR 685 at 690F, 694A-B, 696F-G; *Avondale Printers & Stationers Ltd v Haggie* [1979] 2 NZLR 124 at 146; *McMahon v McMahon* [1979] VR 239 at 244; *Malsbury v Malsbury* [1982] 1 NSWLR 226 at 230B.

16   *Pettitt v Pettitt* [1970] AC 777 at 805A, 808B-C; *Gissing v Gissing* [1971] AC 886 at 900F; *Cowcher v Cowcher* [1972] 1 WLR 425 at 429H; *Burns v Burns* [1984] Ch 317 at 334B-C; *McFarlane v McFarlane* [1972] NI 59 at 77; *Allen v Snyder* [1977] 2 NSWLR 685 at 690D, F; *Avondale Printers & Stationers Ltd v Haggie* [1979] 2 NZLR 124 at 145f; *Baumgartner v Baumgartner* [1985] 2 NSWLR 406 at 412F-G.

17   *Bannister v Bannister* [1948] 2 All ER 133 at 136D. See also *White v Cabanas Pty Ltd (No 2)* [1970] Qd R 395 at 397F; *Baumgartner v Baumgartner* [1985] 2 NSWLR 406 at 444C.

stipulation under which some sufficiently defined beneficial interest in the property was to be taken by another.'[18]

(i) Origin of the rights enforced   It seems to be immaterial that the equitable rights which A undertakes to respect are pre-existing rights conferred by a separate agreement between, say, B and X; or that B would have had a contractual right in any event to recover damages from X for breach of that separate agreement.[19] A constructive trust can arise simply by reason of A's agreement to be bound by X's agreement, at least so long as X's agreement conferred some kind of equitable proprietary right on B.

It seems also to be irrelevant that the equitable entitlement which A's 'bargain' supposedly conferred on B is later confirmed by a purported testamentary disposition by A in B's favour.[20] Such a disposition is not necessarily inconsistent with, and therefore does not negative, the reality of the preceding common intention, particularly where the parties are lay persons who lack a 'sound understanding of the nature of equitable interests'.[1]

(ii) Recognised rights   Many different kinds of proprietary interest have been recognised as providing appropriate subject matter for a constructive trust. It has been held sufficient to ground constructive trust liability that A has undertaken either that B should have the entire equitable fee simple interest in A's property,[2] or merely that B should have some lesser equitable right such as a life interest,[3] an equitable share as a tenant in common,[4] an estate contract[5] (including an option to purchase[6]) or even a right to the conditional re-transfer of an interest already transferred by B to A.[7] However, the interest conferred or conceded by A—whatever its nature or quantum—must relate to a specific asset or to specific assets.[8]

(iii) Unconventional rights   Slightly more controversial is the suggestion made by Lord Denning MR in *Binions v Evans*[9] that a constructive trust may give

---

18   *Bannister v Bannister* [1948] 2 All ER 133 at 136D. In *Grant v Edwards* [1986] Ch 638 at 655G-H, Browne-Wilkinson V-C thought that the required assurance of beneficial entitlement would be sufficiently constituted by a legal owner's consistent verbal references to the property as 'our house' or to his life with the claimant as being based on the 'principle of sharing everything'. See also *Eves v Eves* [1975] 1 WLR 1338 at 1345B-C.

19   *Binions v Evans* [1972] Ch 359 (post, p 551); *Lyus v Prowsa Developments Ltd* [1982] 1 WLR 1044 at 1051E (post, p 284); *White v Cabanas Pty Ltd* (No 2) [1970] Qd R 395 at 399B-C. Indeed, the imposition of a constructive trust on A in *Binions v Evans* has since been explained as having been necessary to save X from an unmerited, but otherwise unavoidable, liability in damages to B (see *Lyus v Prowsa Developments Ltd*, supra, at 1051F-G).

20   *Hayward v Giordani* [1983] NZLR 140 at 144, 152. Compare, however, *Thwaites v Ryan* [1984] VR 65 at 82.

1   *Napier v Public Trustee (Western Australia)* (1980) 32 ALR 153 at 160.

2   *White v Cabanas Pty Ltd* (No 2) [1970] Qd R 395 at 399B-C, 406B; *Doohan v Nelson* [1973] 2 NSWLR 320 at 329E.

3   *Bannister v Bannister* [1948] 2 All ER 133 at 137B.

4   *Malsbury v Malsbury* [1982] 1 NSWLR 226 at 231E; *Hayward v Giordani* [1983] NZLR 140 at 145.

5   See eg *Lyus v Prowsa Developments Ltd* [1982] 1 WLR 1044.

6   *Avondale Printers & Stationers Ltd v Haggie* [1979] 2 NZLR 124 at 162, 164.

7   *Last v Rosenfeld* [1972] 2 NSWLR 923 at 937B. See also *Cadd v Cadd* (1909) 9 CLR 171 at 187.

8   *Layton v Martin* [1986] 2 FLR 227 at 237A-B, 238B.

9   [1972] Ch 359 (post, p 552).

effect to an undertaking by A that B should have a right which is not conventionally acknowledged as an equitable proprietary interest. The interest recognised by way of constructive trust in this case was, in Lord Denning's view, a contractual licence,[10] even though it is generally thought improbable that such a licence can ever constitute a property right in land.[11]

Lord Denning's approach may perhaps be rationalised, as it was by Dillon J in *Lyus v Prowsa Developments Ltd*,[12] on the footing that 'even if the beneficial interest of the claimant in the property concerned has not yet been fully defined, the court may yet intervene to raise a constructive trust on appropriate terms if to leave the defendant retaining the property free from all interest of the claimant would be tantamount to sanctioning a fraud on the part of the defendant.'[13] However, the limits of this broader approach are quickly reached if the subject matter of the 'bargain' between the parties is so ill-defined as not even faintly to resemble a recognised proprietary right. In *Layton v Martin*,[14] A had written a letter to B suggesting that B should come to live with him, in return for which A offered 'financial security during my life and financial security on my death.' This offer was held to be too vague to found any claim based on constructive trust (or indeed proprietary estoppel).[15]

(5) Change of position

In order that a constructive trust should arise, it is not sufficient merely that a common intention should have been expressed or a 'bargain' made that B should have some beneficial entitlement in A's land. If the assurance of beneficial entitlement remains purely oral, further elements are required. One of these is that there must be a 'change of position' by the party who relies upon the 'bargain' or agreement as to beneficial ownership.[16] As Lord Diplock stated in *Gissing v Gissing*,[17] if an express verbal agreement provides that the beneficial interest in A's land should be shared between A and B but fails to 'provide for anything to be done' by B, the agreement is 'a merely voluntary declaration of trust and unenforceable for want of writing.'[18] Traditionally equity will not assist a volunteer.[19]

It seems that the required 'change of position' itself involves two features, which in broad terms relate respectively to fact and motive:

10   [1972] Ch 359 at 367C, 369D.
11   Post, p 549. See also J.D. Davies, *Informal Arrangements Affecting Land*, (1979) 8 Sydney LR 578 at 579.
12   [1982] 1 WLR 1044 at 1053A.
13   See also *Eves v Eves* [1975] 1 WLR 1338 at 1342E-F, 1345B.
14   [1986] 2 FLR 227.
15   [1986] 2 FLR 227 at 238B. For a slightly more liberal approach in Australia, see *Malsbury v Malsbury* [1982] 1 NSWLR 226 at 230C-D; *Le Compte v Public Trustee* [1983] 2 NSWLR 109 at 111C, F.
16   For reference to the terminology of 'change of position', see *Burns v Burns* [1984] Ch 317 at 327G-H per Fox LJ.
17   [1971] AC 886 at 905E.
18   *Eves v Eves* [1975] 1 WLR 1338 at 1345B-C per Brightman J. See also *Grant v Edwards* [1986] Ch 638 at 656A; *Layton v Martin* [1986] 2 FLR 227 at 236H-237A (where Scott J pointed to the need for some 'quid pro quo moving from the claimant').
19   See *Midland Bank PLC v Dobson* [1986] 1 FLR 171 at 175E; *McFarlane v McFarlane* [1972] NI 59 at 73.

(a) There must be 'detriment' or 'sacrifice'

In order that an unenforceable oral trust declared by A should become enforceable by B, there must have been a change of position by B.[20] In the terms used by Lord Diplock in *Gissing v Gissing*,[1] B must have been induced by A to 'act to his own detriment'.[2] B must show that he has suffered some 'detriment' in reliance on A's undertaking as to the beneficial position,[3] or that he has otherwise made some 'material sacrifice' connected with the property.[4] The requirement of some form of 'contribution'[5] or 'consideration'[6] moving from B seems to be a strict precondition of the imposition of a constructive trust.[7] In this sense, the need to establish a change of position creates clear analogies between the constructive trust doctrine and both the doctrine of part performance[8] and the equitable willingness to grant specific performance of agreements for consideration.[9]

(i) Recognised forms The forms of 'detriment' or 'sacrifice' which denote a relevant change of position are manifold. The most obvious kind of 'detriment' or 'sacrifice' undertaken by claimants under a constructive trust is of a financial nature. Constructive trusts have been raised in cases where B has used his or her own moneys in paying (either in whole or in part) costs connected with the acquisition of property owned at law by A.[10] Normally payments made by B contemporaneously with A's acquisition generate a resulting trust for B in proportion to the moneys provided, since such a trust mirrors the presumed intentions of A and B as of that date. However, B's financial contributions may raise a constructive trust rather than a resulting trust *either* where A and B agree at the outset that the beneficial ownership should be in different proportions from those in which they actually contribute the purchase money,[11] *or* where B makes some subsequent financial contribution (eg towards

---

20 *Grant v Edwards* [1986] Ch 638 at 648D; *Ogilvie v Ryan* [1976] 2 NSWLR 504 at 517A.
1   [1971] AC 886 at 905C.
2   The claimant must be 'seen to act to her detriment on the faith of the common intention.' It is not enough, for instance, that in response to the legal owner's assurance of some entitlement the claimant has moved into his house. The law is 'not so cynical as to infer that a woman will only go to live with a man to whom she is not married if she understands that she is to have an interest in their home.' There must have been some 'conduct on which the [claimant] could not reasonably have been expected to embark unless she was to have an interest in the house' (*Grant v Edwards* [1986] Ch 638 at 648G). See also *Hohol v Hohol* [1981] VR 221 at 225.
3   *Christian v Christian* (1981) 131 NLJ 43 (post, p 277).
4   *Gissing v Gissing* [1971] AC 886 at 905F per Lord Diplock.
5   *Allen v Snyder* [1977] 2 NSWLR 685 at 691A per Glass JA. See also *Boccalatte v Bushelle* [1980] Qd R 180 at 185E.
6   *Taddeo v Taddeo* (1978) 19 SASR 347 at 365.
7   In *Neale v Willis* (1968) 19 P & CR 836 at 839, the Court of Appeal imposed a 'constructive trust' on A in favour of B, even though the consideration for A's oral undertaking to confer beneficial rights on B seems to have been provided not by B but by B's mother. However, the decision is far better analysed not as a case of constructive trust, but as involving an express declaration of trust which was made enforceable only by reason of the rule in *Rochefoucauld v Boustead*—of which principle it is indeed a textbook illustration (ante, p 240).
8   See *Taddeo v Taddeo* (1978) 19 SASR 347 at 365.
9   See *Cowcher v Cowcher* [1972] 1 WLR 425 at 431A.
10 For a further account of the operation of the constructive trust in the context of the family home, see Chapter 23 (post, p 811).
11 Post, p 285.

paying off a large part of the mortgage debt) in circumstances not foreseen at the date of A's acquisition.[12]

Relevant forms of 'detriment' have also included the making of payments for the improvement[13] or extension[14] of A's property. The courts have even been prepared to account as cognisable 'detriment' or 'sacrifice' the devotion of B's personal labour and energy towards the improvement of realty belonging to A.[15] In short, the claimant under a constructive trust 'must expend some money or do some other act, or omission, on the faith of his belief',[16] and 'detriment' can be simply defined as 'so acting on the faith of an expectation or belief that, if the expectation or belief be disappointed, the actor would suffer so substantially as to make it unconscionable for the other party to disappoint him'.[17]

(ii) Limits of 'detriment' and 'sacrifice' It remains the case, however, that the relevant forms of 'detriment' or 'sacrifice' are somewhat strictly circumscribed. For instance, no constructive trust is generated even by many years of faithful domestic endeavour on the part of a wife, mother and homemaker.[18] The contribution required of B must be in some sense property-related.[19] In *Christian v Christian*,[20] the claimant argued *inter alia* that she had suffered 'detriment' in the form of the social embarrassment caused by living with her de facto husband in a house situated in close proximity to the current home of the defendant's legal wife. Brightman LJ rejected this alleged 'detriment', observing that equity is 'concerned with the protection of property and proprietary interests, not with the protection of people's feelings.'[1] In his view, 'the only contributions, detriments and sacrifices, that move the court in this field are those of a monetary or proprietary nature.'[2] Likewise, in *Thwaites v*

---

12 See *Burns v Burns* [1984] Ch 317 at 327D, 329B; *Winkworth v Edward Baron Development Co Ltd* (1986) 52 P & CR 67 at 75, 79f.

13 *South Yarra Project Pty Ltd v Gentsis* [1985] VR 29 at 39.

14 *Hussey v Palmer* [1972] 1 WLR 1286 at 1289H, 1290E.

15 *Cooke v Head* [1972] 1 WLR 518 at 519G-H, 520F-G; *Eves v Eves* [1975] 1 WLR 1338 at 1340D-E, 1342F-G, 1344C-D, 1345C (post, p 815); *Hayward v Giordani* [1983] NZLR 140 at 142, 150, 152.

16 *Thwaites v Ryan* [1984] VR 65 at 90 per Fullagar J.

17 *Thwaites v Ryan* [1984] VR 65 at 95.

18 *Button v Button* [1968] 1 WLR 457 at 462A-C; *Gissing v Gissing* [1969] 2 Ch 85 at 98E-F; *Burns v Burns* [1984] Ch 317 at 327H, 331A-B, 345B-C; *Layton v Martin* [1986] 2 FLR 227 at 235H-236A, 238C-D; *C v C* [1976] IR 254 at 257. Compare *Hall v Hall* (1982) 3 FLR 379 at 381E-F per Lord Denning MR, but see now *Burns v Burns* [1984] Ch 317 at 331C-F, 342G (post, p 811).

19 However, it does not seem to be required that the detriment or 'sacrifice' incurred by B should necessarily relate to the precise land in respect of which the claim of constructive trust is made (see *Christian v Christian* (1981) 131 NLJ 43).

20 (1981) 131 NLJ 43 (post, p 406).

1 See the statement of Lawton LJ in *Wood v Wood* (Unreported, 1979 W No 1393, 7 July 1982), that the determination of property interests 'cannot be dealt with on the basis of sentiment...' This thought was echoed in *Winkworth v Edward Baron Development Co Ltd* [1986] 1 WLR 1512 at 1516C, where Lord Templeman observed that 'Equity is not a computer. Equity operates on conscience but is not influenced by sentimentality.'

2 '[T]he court is only entitled to look at the financial contributions or their real or substantial equivalent, to the acquisition of the house; that the husband may spend his weekends redecorating or laying a patio is neither here nor there, nor is the fact that the woman has spent so much of her time looking after the house, doing the cooking and bringing up the family' (*Burns v Burns* [1984] Ch 317 at 344E-F per May LJ).

Ryan,[3] the Supreme Court of Victoria declined to accept that the plaintiff had acted to his detriment in 'leaving his moribund marriage and moribund tenancy and going to live rent free in the pleasant home of his old friend.'

(iii) The net concept of 'detriment' or 'sacrifice'   The courts seem moreover to analyse even recognised forms of 'detriment' or 'sacrifice' in net terms. Thus a 'change of position', understood in the broadest sense, is seen as comprising the required degree of 'detriment' or 'sacrifice' only if it results in a net disadvantage to the individual concerned. In *Hannaford v Selby*,[4] for instance, the claimant's work in cultivating vegetables in his son-in-law's garden was not accounted to be 'detriment' in the relevant sense, since he was regarded as merely indulging his 'one absorbing hobby'. Likewise, in *Layton v Martin*[5] the claimant's housekeeping and other services had already been compensated at least in part by the award of a regular salary.[6]

(b) The change of position must be 'referable to' the 'bargain'

Detriment or sacrifice *per se* is insufficient to support a claim of constructive trust.[7] It must be shown that the claimant's change of position was 'referable to' the earlier 'bargain' or common intention that the legal owner should acknowledge some beneficial entitlement in the claimant. There must be some entirely conscious causal nexus between A's agreement and B's active willingness to undergo detriment or sacrifice.[8]

(i) Nature of the causal nexus   The notion of causation was stressed in Lord Diplock's classic exposition of the constructive trust in *Gissing v Gissing*.[9] Here Lord Diplock indicated that a constructive trust will arise only if the legal owner has 'induced' the claimant to act to his own detriment 'in the reasonable belief that by so acting he was acquiring a beneficial interest in the land.' This formulation seems to require a certain mental element or motivation on the part both of A, the legal owner, and of B, the claimant of an equitable interest. To raise a constructive trust, it must be shown not only that A's conduct 'was intended to induce [B] to act to his or her detriment upon the faith of the promise of a specified beneficial interest in the land', but also that B 'so acted with the intention of acquiring that beneficial interest.'[10]

---

3   [1984] VR 65 at 89.
4   (1976) 239 Estates Gazette 811 at 813.
5   [1986] 2 FLR 227 at 231F–G
6   See also *Heyland v Heyland* (1972) *The Times*, 25 January; *McPhee v McPhee* (1980) NZ Recent Law 42.
7   *Pettitt v Pettitt* [1970] AC 777 at 805E; *Gissing v Gissing* [1971] AC 886 at 900H, 901B–C, 909G–H, 910G–H; *Bernard v Josephs* [1982] Ch 391 at 404E–F; *Grant v Edwards* [1986] Ch 638 at 651F; *Allen v Snyder* [1977] 2 NSWLR 685 at 691C; *McGill v S* [1979] IR 283 at 289.
8   This is the traditional view outlined in the caselaw, but there are already indications of a changing emphasis in this area. In *Grant v Edwards* [1986] Ch 638 at 658B–D, Browne-Wilkinson V-C declined to express 'any concluded view' on the need for 'positive evidence' of 'conscious reliance' on the common intention (post, p 280). See also *Winkworth v Edward Baron Development Co Ltd* [1986] 1 WLR 1512 at 1515F, where the House of Lords looked (in vain) merely for some 'connection between the acquisition...and the payment'.
9   [1971] AC 886 at 905C.
10   [1971] AC 886 at 905G-H. This means, ironically, that if the claimant is 'almost wholly unmercenary', her claim of constructive trust will fail (see *Layton v Martin* [1986] 2 FLR 227 at 235B, 239H-240A).

Generally these requirements will occasion no difficulty where A and B have reached an express agreement as to the beneficial ownership of land vested at law in the name of A. The explicit nature of the agreement as to the respective beneficial interests of A and B obviates the need to demonstrate a positive causal connection between the verbal assurance of A and the detrimental reliance of B.[11] But in other cases where the relevant common intention as to beneficial title has not been communicated between A and B in express words, but is instead left to be inferred from their mutual conduct,[12] the acts or omissions alleged as 'detriment' by B must, according to Lord Diplock, be 'referable to the acquisition' of A's property.[13] Only if this test of 'referability' is satisfied can B rebut the normal legal inference that the sole title taken by A invests him also with the sole equitable interest.[14]

(ii) Failure of the Gissing claim   It was the application of this strict test of 'referability' which caused the failure of the wife's claim in *Gissing v Gissing*.[15] Here the House of Lords accepted that, in appropriate circumstances, either a resulting trust *ab initio* or a supervening constructive trust could be brought into existence by various forms of contribution made by B towards the cost of the acquisition or improvement of property vested at law in A. However, the mere fact that the wife in *Gissing* had made indirect financial contributions towards general household expenditure did not raise either form of trust in her favour in the absence of a showing that these contributions were made in conscious response to a 'bargain' with the legal owner directed towards bringing about beneficial co-ownership in the family home.[16] The wife failed because she was unable to provide credible evidence of an anterior common intention as between herself and her husband that her indirect financial contributions should be rewarded with a beneficial share in the home.[17]

(iii) Criticism of the 'referability' criterion   The fairness of the 'referability' criterion laid down in *Gissing v Gissing* has long been the subject of criticism.[18] In particular, it is clear that the application of this criterion penalises those lay persons who, in the confused circumstances of domestic life and financial pressure, fail to advert at a sufficiently conscious mental level to the

---

11   [1971] AC 886 at 905G-H. See eg *Le Compte v Public Trustee* [1983] 2 NSWLR 109 at 111C, E-F.
12   Ante, p 272. See eg *Winkworth v Edward Baron Development Co Ltd* (1986) 52 P & CR 67 at 75, 79.
13   [1971] AC 886 at 909G.
14   [1971] AC 886 at 909H-910A.
15   [1971] AC 886.
16   Ante, p 258; post, p 810.
17   In the absence of any 'discussion of the quid pro quo' to be provided by the claimant, the courts have attached significance to representations by the legal owner that the claimant should have the functional equivalent of some interest in his land (see *Grant v Edwards* [1986] Ch 638 at 653E-F). Such an approach verges upon the application of a doctrine of proprietary estoppel (post, p 406).
18   See eg *Hargrave v Newton* [1971] 1 WLR 1611 at 1613A-B; *Hazell v Hazell* [1972] 1 WLR 301 at 304C-D. However, Lord Denning MR's suggestion in *Falconer v Falconer* [1970] 1 WLR 1333 at 1336D-E that mere expenditure without the requisite intention can raise a trust has since been rejected as inconsistent with *Gissing v Gissing* (see *Savva v Costa and Harymode Investments Ltd* (1981) 131 NLJ 1114 per Ormrod LJ).

motivations and implications of their day-to-day actions.[19] Correspondingly, an unfair advantage in legal terms is conferred on those who are either more calculating in the advancement of their own self-interest or more sophisticated in their ability to provide (or fabricate) evidence *ex post facto* which bears out the claim that the detriment incurred by them was 'referable to' some agreement with the legal owner.[20]

(iv) Continuing force of the 'referability' criterion Notwithstanding these objections, the 'referability' criterion is still in common use.[1] In *Midland Bank PLC v Dobson*,[2] for instance, the claimant wife had clearly incurred detriment in the form of household expenditure on behalf of the family and renovation work done on the home which was vested at law in the name of her husband. The Court of Appeal ruled that, even after a marriage of 34 years, her husband did not hold the legal title on any trust for her. She had not demonstrated that she had been 'induced to act to her detriment upon the basis of a common intention of ownership of the house or that there was otherwise any nexus between the acquisition of the property and something provided or foregone by [her]'.[3]

It may be that the more recent decision of the Court of Appeal in *Grant v Edwards*[4] marks the beginning of a more liberal application of the requirement of 'referability'. This case concerned the effect of contributions to household expenses made by a de facto wife whose partner had undertaken sole responsibility for the repayment of the mortgage on the family home. Browne-Wilkinson V-C was not prepared to hold definitively that the claimant under a constructive trust must show 'positive evidence' of a 'conscious reliance' on a 'common intention'. It was enough that, without the woman's contributions, the man's means would have been 'insufficient to keep up the mortgage payments', and that her indirect contributions were therefore 'essentially linked to the payment of the mortgage instalments'.[5] The mere use of the claimant's money 'whether directly or indirectly' in the discharge of mortgage instalments provided, in Browne-Wilkinson V-C's view, 'a sufficient link between the detriment suffered by the claimant and the common intention'. The court can 'infer that she would not have made such payments were it not for her belief that she had an interest in the house.'[6] The de facto wife in this case was accordingly recognised as having acquired a one-half interest in the beneficial ownership.

19   See eg *McKeown v McKeown* [1975] NI 139 at 142C-D.
20   The force of these criticisms was indeed recognised by Lord Reid in *Gissing v Gissing* [1971] AC 886 at 897C-E. See also *Grant v Edwards* [1986] Ch 638 at 656B-D.
1   See eg *Grant v Sanderson* [1983] Court of Appeal Unbound Transcript 862; *Burns v Burns* [1984] Ch 317 at 327G-H, 328H-329B; *Warner v Warner* (Unreported, Court of Appeal, 11 July 1984); *Grant v Edwards* [1986] Ch 638 at 651G-H; *Winkworth v Edward Baron Development Co Ltd* [1986] 1 WLR 1512 at 1515F-G (post, p 288).
2   [1986] 1 FLR 171.
3   [1986] 1 FLR 171 at 177E. See also *Philip Lowe (Chinese Restaurant) Ltd v Sau Man Lee* (Unreported, Court of Appeal, 9 July 1985), where May LJ indicated that a showing of referability was 'at the very least a sine qua non of the existence of any such equity' as was claimed by the de facto wife. She was not awarded any beneficial interest because it was found that she had incurred detriment, not in any belief that she was thereby acquiring an equitable interest, but 'because she was part of the family' (post, p 404).
4   [1986] Ch 638. See [1986] Conv 291 (J. Warburton); [1986] CLJ 394 (D.J. Hayton); (1986) 130 SJ 347 (P.M. Rank).
5   [1986] Ch 638 at 656D-E.
6   *Grant v Edwards* [1986] Ch 638 at 656E-F.

(6) Equitable fraud

Before a constructive trust can be imposed, a third element must be established in addition to a mere 'change of position' premised on some 'bargain' between the relevant parties. This element is variously described in the caselaw, but in effect amounts to a requirement that 'equitable fraud'[7] be shown to exist on the part of the legal owner of the land.[8] 'Equitable fraud' has been said to provide the 'common denominator' or 'connecting link' which runs through the many categories of circumstance where constructive trusts have been imposed.[9]

(a) Unconscientious use of the legal title

The essence of 'equitable fraud' lies in what has been called the 'unconscientious use of the legal title'.[10] As Lord Diplock insisted, in a much misapplied passage of his speech in *Gissing v Gissing*,[11] a constructive trust will arise only where the legal owner, A, 'has so conducted himself that it would be inequitable to allow him to deny to [B] a beneficial interest in the land.'[12] However, the required inequity is plainly established by any 'disclaimer by the legal owner of the obligations of conscience based upon an express agreement, or common intention of the parties.'[13] Such a disclaimer would, in the words of Viscount Dilhorne in *Gissing v Gissing*,[14] amount to a 'breach of faith'.[15] Were A's disclaimer to remain unchecked, the 'suffering which would otherwise occur' on the part of B 'makes it "a fraud on B" for A to assert his rights, that is to say, makes it unconscionable of A to assert his rights.'[16]

(b) Attempted derogation from agreed entitlements

The constructive trust comes into play primarily in order to frustrate fraudulent designs.[17] It is clear that the fraud required to activate the constructive trust need not have been present in the original agreement or

---

7 See *Nocton v Ashburton* [1914] AC 932 at 953f per Viscount Haldane LC: 'In Chancery the term "fraud" thus came to be used to describe what fell short of deceit, but imported breach of a duty to which equity had attached its sanction...What it really means...is, not moral fraud in the ordinary sense, but breach of the sort of obligation which is enforced by a Court that from the beginning regarded itself as a Court of conscience.' For an early reference to 'equitable fraud', see *Lincoln v Wright* (1859) 4 De G & J 16 at 23, 45 ER 6 at 9. See also *Le Compte v Public Trustee* [1983] 2 NSWLR 109 at 111B, where Rath J thought that 'the words "the demands of justice and good conscience" should be read as exegetical of "fraud".'

8 See *Muschinski v Dodds* (1985) 62 ALR 429 at 435 per Gibbs CJ. See also the statement in *Carl Zeiss Stiftung v Herbert Smith & Co (No 2)* [1969] 2 Ch 276 at 301C-D per Edmund Davies LJ that 'want of probity' must always be proved in order to establish liability under a constructive trust. Compare, however, A.J. Oakley, (1973) 26 CLP 17 at 19f.

9 *Avondale Printers & Stationers Ltd v Haggie* [1979] 2 NZLR 124 at 159. See also *South Yarra Project Pty Ltd v Gentsis* [1985] VR 29 at 37.

10 *Ogilvie v Ryan* [1976] 2 NSWLR 504 at 518E per Holland J. See also *Baumgartner v Baumgartner* [1985] 2 NSWLR 406 at 412A-B.

11 [1971] AC 886 at 905C (post, p 810).

12 This dictum has sometimes been over-emphasised to the exclusion of the remainder of Lord Diplock's judgment (post, p 816).

13 *Allen v Snyder* [1977] 2 NSWLR 685 at 694E; *Baumgartner v Baumgartner* [1985] 2 NSWLR 406 at 435A-B.

14 [1971] AC 886 at 900B-C.

15 See also *Boccalatte v Bushelle* [1980] Qd R 180 at 186A.

16 *Thwaites v Ryan* [1984] VR 65 at 90.

17 *Avondale Printers & Stationers Ltd v Haggie* [1979] 2 NZLR 124 at 160.

'bargain' which guaranteed some kind of beneficial interest for B.[18] But a degree of 'equitable fraud' is present 'as soon as the absolute character of the conveyance is set up for the purpose of defeating the beneficial interest'.[19] Accordingly, a constructive trust will be imposed on A if he behaves inequitably by attempting to derogate from the beneficial rights conferred on B by the earlier 'bargain'. Moreover, A cannot escape from that 'bargain' by pleading its unenforceability through want of written evidence. There is a clear doctrine of equity to the effect that any 'reliance by the trustee on the statute requiring writing would be equitable fraud' itself.[20] Equity will never allow a statute to be used as an instrument of fraud.[1]

(7) Sphere of operation of constructive trusts

The following examples merely illustrate some of the general kinds of circumstance in which the constructive trust may be invoked in the law of land.

(a) Agreement that B should retain a beneficial interest in land purchased from B by A

One of the classic illustrations of the constructive trust doctrine occurs where B, a vendor, conveys the legal title in his land to A, a purchaser, on the strength of some oral undertaking by A that B shall retain a beneficial entitlement in the land even after the transfer. In such circumstances conscience demands that A be held to his agreement that the beneficial title should not belong solely to himself. The imposition of a constructive trust upon A can be quite easily rationalised here on the basis that B would never have parted with the property in the absence of such an oral undertaking from A.[2]

(i) The Bannister principle

In *Bannister v Bannister*[3] B, the sister-in-law of A, had conveyed her freehold interest in two cottages to A at a gross undervalue, upon A's oral undertaking that she would be allowed to live in one of the cottages rent-free for the remainder of her life. The conveyance made no reference to this oral promise. When A later sought to evict B on the ground that she was a mere tenant at will,[4] the Court of Appeal upheld the refusal of the county court to order possession against her.

In the view of the Court of Appeal, A, although the current legal owner by virtue of the conveyance, was bound by a constructive trust in favour of B. Scott LJ held that such a trust is 'raised against a person who insists on the absolute character of a conveyance to himself for the purpose of defeating a beneficial interest, which, according to the true bargain, was to belong to another.'[5] Here there had been a 'bargain', in the sense that B had been induced to convey the cottages to A partly in consideration of money payment and partly on the

---

18   *Bannister v Bannister* [1948] 2 All ER 133 at 136C, F-G; *Last v Rosenfeld* [1972] 2 NSWLR 923 at 934F.
19   *Bannister v Bannister* [1948] 2 All ER 133 at 136C-D. See also *Last v Rosenfeld* [1972] 2 NSWLR 923 at 934F; *Baumgartner v Baumgartner* [1985] 2 NSWLR 406 at 412A-B.
20   *Allen v Snyder* [1977] 2 NSWLR 685 at 692E; *Baumgartner v Baumgartner* [1985] 2 NSWLR 406 at 435A-B.
1   Ante, p 238.
2   See *Avondale Printers & Stationers Ltd v Haggie* [1979] 2 NZLR 124 at 163.
3   [1948] 2 All ER 133.
4   For a description of 'tenancy at will', see Chapter 14 (post, p 430).
5   [1948] 2 All ER 133 at 136C.

strength of his oral undertaking that B should enjoy a life interest in one cottage. Thus, even though the initial conveyance had not been fraudulent,[6] a fatal element of fraud was introduced as soon as A attempted to set up an absolute entitlement in himself in derogation of the beneficial rights which he had already agreed should be retained by B. Equitable fraud of this kind could not be covered up by the plea that 'no written evidence of the real bargain is available'.[7]

(ii) Extensions of the Bannister principle This application of the constructive trust is firmly established in other cases where there has been an unwritten agreement between A and B that B should retain either an absolute[8] or a limited[9] beneficial interest in land which he conveys to A. The precise nature or quantum of that interest is immaterial,[10] and it is generally accepted that the statutory requirement of writing can never be employed to 'smother proof of an oral arrangement creating a trust.'[11] For this purpose, moreover, it appears to be entirely irrelevant whether the purchase price paid by A is the full market value,[12] or is reduced in the light of the oral arrangement,[13] or is indeed non-existent.[14] The key question is simply 'whether the transferor would have parted with his property but for the oral undertaking of the transferee.'[15] If that question is answered in the negative, then A's renunciation of his promise or disavowal of the common intention formulated between A and B will 'operate in equity as a fraud' on B.[16]

(b) Agreement that B should retain a beneficial interest in land purchased by A from X

Another illustration of the constructive trust in operation arises where A purchases X's legal estate in land, having first agreed with the vendor that B

6   There was an express finding by the county court judge that no fraud was present in the conveyance ([1948] 2 All ER 133 at 135C).
7   [1948] 2 All ER 133 at 136D.
8   *Hutchins v Lee* (1737) 1 Atk 447 at 448, 26 ER 284 at 285; *Childers v Childers* (1857) 1 De G & J 482 at 492, 44 ER 810 at 814; *In re Duke of Marlborough* [1894] 2 Ch 133 at 146.
9   *Booth v Turle* (1873) LR 16 Eq 182 at 183, 188; *Bannister v Bannister* [1948] 2 All ER 133 at 136E-F; *Last v Rosenfeld* [1972] 2 NSWLR 923 at 936E.
10   *Bannister v Bannister* [1948] 2 All ER 133 at 136E-F; *Last v Rosenfeld* [1972] 2 NSWLR 923 at 936E; *Avondale Printers & Stationers Ltd v Haggie* [1979] 2 NZLR 124 at 163.
11   *Dalton v Christofis* [1978] WAR 42 at 46 per Smith J. See also *Organ v Sandwell* [1921] VLR 622 at 630.
12   *Last v Rosenfeld* [1972] 2 NSWLR 923 at 930B, 936B. It is arguable, however, that if A pays B the full market value there is then no element of 'detriment' or 'sacrifice' on the part of B sufficient to raise a constructive trust in his favour. Strictly speaking, this may well be true, in which case this situation is better analysed as involving an oral declaration of an express trust which, but for the rule in *Rochefoucauld v Boustead*, would have been unenforceable (ante, p 238). There is as always a lingering doubt as to the proper characterisation of the trust enforced by virtue of this rule, but it seems in accordance with principle to restrict the operation of the constructive trust to cases in which there has been a true 'change of position' by B in the shape of some 'detriment' or 'sacrifice'.
13   *Booth v Turle* (1873) LR 16 Eq 182 at 183, 188; *Bannister v Bannister* [1948] 2 All ER 133 at 134F.
14   *Hutchins v Lee* (1737) 1 Atk 447 at 448, 26 ER 284 at 285; *Childers v Childers* (1857) 1 De G & J 482 at 492, 44 ER 810 at 814; *In re Duke of Marlborough* [1894] 2 Ch 133 at 146. In some cases the transfer to the alleged trustee was expressed to be for valuable consideration, but the consideration was never in fact paid (see eg *Davies v Otty* (No 2) (1865) 35 Beav 208 at 213, 55 ER 875 at 877; *Haigh v Kaye* (1872) 7 Ch App 469 at 473f).
15   *Avondale Printers & Stationers Ltd v Haggie* [1979] 2 NZLR 124 at 163.
16   *Ibid.*

should retain a beneficial interest in that land even after the transfer to A.

Precisely these circumstances arose in *Lyus v Prowsa Developments Ltd.*[17] Here a development company, X, was the owner of an area of land on which it proposed to build a number of residential properties. The development was financed by a loan of money from a bank, Y, secured by way of a legal charge over X's land. Some time after the creation of this charge, X contracted with B to build a house on one plot within the development area and sell that plot to B. B paid a contractual deposit and waited for the house to be built. Before either the house or the transaction of purchase could be completed, X became insolvent and Y, in exercise of its statutory powers of sale as mortgagee, sold the property to A¹, another development company (*Fig.* 25). Although the transfer of the legal title to A¹ made no reference to B or his rights, the contract preceding the transfer made it quite clear that the transfer was expressly 'subject to' B's contractual rights under the estate contract between B and X. A¹ later transferred the same legal title to A², the contract for sale again stipulating that A² should take 'subject to' B's equitable rights under the original estate contract.

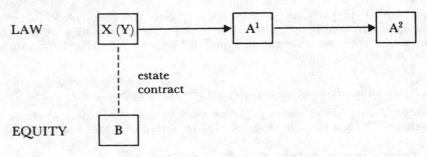

Fig. 25

B sued *inter alia* for a declaration that the estate contract was binding on A¹ and A².[18] Dillon J concluded that it had been 'a stipulation of the bargain' between Y and A¹ that A¹ would give effect to B's equitable rights under the original estate contract with X,[19] and that a similar stipulation had been made as between A¹ and A². Accordingly, Dillon J applied *Bannister v Bannister*[20] and held that both A¹ and A² had taken the legal estate on a constructive trust for B.[1] The 'fraud' present in this case lay very largely in A¹ 'reneging on a positive

17   [1982] 1 WLR 1044. See [1983] CLJ 54 (C. Harpum); [1983] Conv 64 (P. Jackson); (1983) 46 MLR 96 (P.H. Kenny); (1984) 47 MLR 476 (P. Bennett).
18   The estate contract had been duly protected by entry of a caution against X's registered title. However, this protection could not avail B as against Y, the bank-mortgagee, which derived overriding rights from a mortgage charge which was clearly prior to any rights which B had acquired under the later estate contract (see also Land Registration Act 1925, s 34(4)). In effect the issue of priority between B and A¹ and A² respectively was decided as if the caution had never been entered.
19   [1982] 1 WLR 1044 at 1053E.
20   [1948] 2 All ER 133 (ante, p 282).
1   [1982] 1 WLR 1044 at 1053F-G. See D.J. Hayton, (1983) 133 NLJ 188; C.T. Emery and B. Smythe, (1983) 133 NLJ 798.

stipulation in favour of [B] in the bargain under which [A¹] acquired the land.'[2] Specific performance was ordered against A² on the terms of the original estate contract.

(c) Agreement that B should acquire a beneficial interest in land purchased by A from X

It is possible that resort may be had to the constructive trust doctrine in order to give effect to an otherwise unenforceable agreement that B should acquire a beneficial interest in land purchased by A from X.

(i) Deviation from the shares generated by money contributions No recourse to the constructive trust doctrine will, of course, be needed if the agreed or presumed beneficial ownership follows the precise proportions in which A and B contributed moneys towards a purchase in the name of A. In such cases, where 'there is a correspondence between the proportions contributed and the beneficial interests intended', the agreement is enforceable—without any requirement of formal writing—as a resulting trust.[3]

If, however, the beneficial ownership, as agreed between A and B, is unrelated to their actual contributions, there arises in favour of B an 'express trust which lacks writing'.[4] It is in this context that the constructive trust may play a valuable role. To the extent that the agreed beneficial shares deviate from the ratio of actual money contributions—even if B claims a beneficial share unsupported by any actual money contribution[5]—the arrangement may still be enforceable as a constructive trust.[6]

(ii) Fiduciary consequences of an anterior bargain Underlying the imposition of a constructive trust in this situation is the notion it would be 'equitable fraud' for A to rely on the statutory requirement of writing in order to defeat the agreement reached between himself and B.[7] The existence of an anterior 'bargain' implies that A's conscience was bound—even at the date of acquisition—by an obligation to recognise equitable rights in B. It is the fact of agreement or common intention which supplies the vital link in the argument, for the obligation created by the 'bargain' casts A in the role of a fiduciary *ab initio*. As Fullagar J said in *Thwaites v Ryan*,[8] 'the trust existed *as the trustee took the property*. To set up the statute would be to steal what was in equity never his...[A] person who *accepts* property in a fiduciary capacity cannot set up in himself...the legal estate free of the trust.' It also follows that A's character as a

---

2   [1982] 1 WLR 1044 at 1054G-H. For another application of the same principle, see eg *Binions v Evans* [1972] Ch 359 at 368B, 370D-G (post, p 551).

3   *Allen v Snyder* [1977] 2 NSWLR 685 at 692A per Glass JA. See also *Bloch v Bloch* (1981) 37 ALR 55 at 64.

4   *Allen v Snyder* [1977] 2 NSWLR 685 at 692C-D per Glass JA, who pointed out that such an agreement, far from giving rise to a resulting trust, operates 'as a pro tanto rebuttal of the trusts resulting presumptively from the actual contributions.' See also *Cowcher v Cowcher* [1972] 1 WLR 425 at 431C, 433H.

5   In such a case, however, B's claim must be supported by evidence of some other form of 'detriment' or 'sacrifice'.

6   See *Calverley v Green* (1984) 56 ALR 483 at 497.

7   *Allen v Snyder* [1977] 2 NSWLR 685 at 692E.

8   [1984] VR 65 at 92f.

fiduciary at the very moment of acquisition will give rise to an allegation of 'equitable fraud' should he ever subsequently attempt to derogate from the rights in B to which he has agreed to take subject. Again in the words of Fullagar J,[9]

If A accepts property upon trust for B absolutely and then seeks to steal B's property by invoking the statute, equity is liable to say that A has received a benefit which binds his conscience and he cannot be allowed to assert against B the existence in A of something that A never had, namely the legal estate unencumbered by the trust. By invoking the statute A would be using it to steal from B property which, so far as A is concerned, was always the property of B.[10]

The well known decision of the Supreme Court of New South Wales in *Ogilvie v Ryan*[11] provides an example of the operation of the constructive trust in circumstances of purchase by A from X. Here B, a woman aged 62, had left her existing home in order to live with A in a house which he purchased in his own name for this purpose. Before moving into this property, A and B agreed orally that if B kept house and cared for A until he died—he was then aged 82—B would be entitled to live in the house rent-free for the remainder of her life. A and B then lived together on these terms for a further two years until A died. At this point, X, the executor of A's will, took proceedings for possession against B. Holland J held that X was bound by a constructive trust to give effect to the undertaking made by his predecessor in title, on the ground that it would be 'an unconscientious use of the legal title' if X were now to assert it in derogation of an interest conferred by A.[12] Even though B had made no contribution (financial or otherwise) towards the acquisition of legal title by A, an oral declaration of trust could have been enforced, in view of B's faithful performance of her side of the 'bargain', against A (and therefore against his personal representative). A had effectively acquired the property on terms that he should hold as a trustee for B.[13] As Holland J observed,[14]

an appropriate constructive trust will be declared in Equity to defeat a species of fraud, namely, that in which a defendant seeks to make an unconscionable use of his legal title by asserting it to defeat a beneficial interest in the property which he...has agreed to or promised; or which it was the common intention of the parties that the plaintiff should have, in return for benefits to be provided by, and in fact obtained from, the plaintiff in connection with their joint use or occupation of the property.[15]

(d)   Agreement that B should acquire a beneficial interest in land already owned by A

A significantly different question arises where A agrees with B that B should acquire some beneficial interest in land which is already owned by A at law. A

9   [1984] VR 65 at 91.
10   See also *Vedejs v Public Trustee* [1985] VR 569 at 572f.
11   [1976] 2 NSWLR 504. See M.A. Neave, *The Constructive Trust as a Remedial Device*, (1977- 78) 11 Melbourne ULR 343; I. Hardingham, *The Non-marital Partner as Contractual Licensee*, (1979- 80) 12 Melbourne ULR 356.
12   [1976] 2 NSWLR 504 at 518E.
13   See *Last v Rosenfeld* [1972] 2 NSWLR 923 at 928B-C; *Thwaites v Ryan* [1984] VR 65 at 94.
14   [1976] 2 NSWLR 504 at 518D-E.
15   It has been suggested that justice could have been done in this case (and in similar cases) through an application of the doctrine of estoppel rather than through the invocation of a constructive trust. See eg R.H. Maudsley, *Constructive Trusts*, (1977) 28 NILQ 123 at 133, 136ff; J.D. Davies, *Informal Arrangements Affecting Land*, (1979) 8 Sydney LR 578 at 583.

declaration of trust in B's favour made subsequently to A's acquisition of title is fully enforceable if evidenced in writing.[16] Difficulties arise, however, if some time *after* taking title A constitutes himself a trustee for B by means of purely oral declaration or agreement. In seeking to enforce his beneficial claim under these circumstances, B cannot invoke either the doctrine of resulting trust or the rule in *Rochefoucauld v Boustead*, since both of these are activated by intentions (actual or presumed) existing contemporaneously with A's acquisition of title.[17]

The same kind of objection would also be fatal to any claim based by B on constructive trust were the latter form of trust exclusively premised upon a fiduciary *acquisition* of legal title. In the circumstances now under discussion, B cannot of course argue that A acquired his legal estate as a fiduciary, since the trust alleged by B can only have come into existence, if at all, at some date subsequent to A's acquisition of the title concerned.

(i) Deferred assumption of fiduciary status It is clear, however, that the constructive trust doctrine is not dependent on a showing that A was a fiduciary at the date of his acquisition of title.[18] It is widely accepted that A's fiduciary character may arise at some much later date and that a constructive trust may be imposed in order to frustrate any attempt by A to deny that he has constituted himself a trustee for B by some act or agreement occurring subsequent to the acquisition date.[19] In such a case the constructive trust is imposed, not on the basis of any theory concerning the fiduciary acquisition of title, but on the basis of the argument that a later 'change of position' by B has conferred an advantage upon A, the beneficial effect of which he cannot now conscionably claim to retain.[20]

(ii) Reluctant recognition of post-acquisition constructive trusts The foregoing rationale closely resembles the concept of 'unjust enrichment' which provides the central feature of a much wider doctrine of the remedial constructive trust as applied, for instance, in the USA.[1] It is precisely the more open-ended nature of this application of constructive trust theory which makes the English courts fairly reluctant to admit constructive trust claims based on events occurring after the date of acquisition. However, such claims have been allowed, although usually only on strict proof that the supervening element of 'detriment' or 'sacrifice' on the part of B was truly 'referable to' some 'bargain'

16   Ante, p 236.
17   Ante, pp 239, 246.
18   See, however, *Thwaites v Ryan* [1984] VR 65 at 71, 93, where the excessively restrictive view was taken that the doctrine of constructive trust is inherently based upon acquisition in a fiduciary capacity and that a constructive trust cannot therefore arise by reason of events occurring after the date of acquisition. Compare, however, *Butler v Craine* [1986] VR 274 at 284f and see also *Gissing v Gissing* [1971] AC 886 at 905B-C (ante, p 243).
19   See eg *Gissing v Gissing* [1971] AC 886 at 901D, 906E, 908B-C; *Christian v Christian* (1981) 131 NLJ 43; *Mellowes v Collymore* (Unreported, Court of Appeal, 27 November 1981); *Burns v Burns* [1984] Ch 317 at 327D; *Warner v Warner* (Unreported, Court of Appeal, 11 July 1984); *Winkworth v Edward Baron Development Co Ltd* (1986) 52 P & CR 67 at 79f; *Grant v Edwards* [1986] Ch 638 at 651H-652A; *Butler v Craine* [1986] VR 274 at 287.
20   See *Nemeth v Nemeth* (1977-78) 17 ALR 500 at 506.
1   Post, p 812.

or common intention that a beneficial interest would be generated thereby.[2]

In *Bernard v Josephs*,[3] for example, Griffiths LJ conceded that it might 'in exceptional circumstances' be inferred that the parties had agreed to alter their beneficial interests subsequent to the acquisition of a quasi-matrimonial home. He instanced the hypothetical case in which 'the man bought the house in the first place and the woman years later used a legacy to build an extra floor to make more room for the children.' In such circumstances, 'the obvious inference' would be that the parties had agreed that the woman would acquire a share in 'the greatly increased value of the house produced by her money.' However, Griffiths LJ added ominously, 'this depends upon the court being able to infer an intention to alter the share in which the beneficial interest was previously held'. The 'mere fact' that one party 'has spent time and money on improving the property' would not normally be sufficient ground to justify such an inference.

(iii) Ambivalent judicial response   An illustration of the ambivalence with which the English courts approach constructive trust claims of this kind is provided by *Winkworth v Edward Baron Development Co Ltd*.[4] Here a matrimonial home was purchased in the name of a limited company owned and controlled by H and W. All of the purchase money was provided by the company, with the result that immediately following the purchase the entire beneficial interest in the property vested in the company alone. Some time after the acquisition W paid £8,600 of her own money to the company's bank, thereby reducing the company's overdraft on its current account with that bank. A majority in the Court of Appeal decided that this supervening payment raised a constructive trust in favour of W. Nourse LJ applied the principles stated in *Gissing v Gissing*, and held that W's payment had been 'referable to the acquisition' of the property.[5] In his view, it could reasonably be inferred that W and the company had formed a common intention that a beneficial interest in the property should be conferred on W.[6] Kerr LJ dissented, however, precisely on the ground that W's payment could not be attributed to any intention that it was to be referable to or on account of the purchase price which the company had paid for the property.[7]

When *Winkworth* was appealed, the House of Lords unanimously endorsed the dissenting judgment of Kerr LJ and reversed the ruling of the Court of Appeal. While not denying that a trust may arise *after* the date of acquisition, Lord Templeman pointed out that there had been 'no connection between the acquisition of [the property] and the payment of £8,600'.[8] The supervening payment made by W could not be said to be 'referable' to the acquisition of the

2   See the way in which constructive trust claims foundered for want of a proven common intention in *Grant v Sanderson* [1983] Court of Appeal Unbound Transcript 862; *Warner v Warner* (Unreported, Court of Appeal, 11 July 1984).
3   [1982] Ch 391 at 404D-F.
4   [1986] 1 WLR 1512 (House of Lords); (1986) 52 P & CR 67 (Court of Appeal).
5   (1986) 52 P & CR 67 at 74f.
6   (1986) 52 P & CR 67 at 73, 75. Once the requisite common intention was found, the court would 'not allow the [legal owner] to deny that interest and will construct a trust to give effect to it.'
7   (1986) 52 P & CR 67 at 83ff.
8   [1986] 1 WLR 1512 at 1515F.

house, not least because the property 'had already been bought and paid for in full'.[9] In the stern view adopted by the House of Lords, the payment into the company's bank account had not manifested 'an intention on the part of [W] to offer to buy a part interest' in the house.[10] Nor, by submitting to a reduction in its overdraft, had the company manifested 'an intention to sell to [W] a bizarre proportion of [the property] at a price which had never been negotiated and could never have been justified.'[11]

A somewhat controversial example of the way in which the constructive trust may cover post-acquisition agreements or arrangements is found in the decision of the Court of Appeal in *Hussey v Palmer*.[12] Here B, an elderly widow, had been invited to live in a house the legal title in which was already owned by her son-in-law, A. An extra bedroom was built for her as an extension to the existing house, and the cost of this construction was paid by B. Although the purpose of the arrangement had been to provide accommodation for B during her old age, the residence of B was brought to a premature end by domestic discord and B sought a return of her capital outlay.

It was typical of this kind of informal family arrangement that the parties had never spelt out clearly the legal implications of their relationship. The Court of Appeal nevertheless decided, by a majority, that a constructive trust existed in favour of B. Lord Denning MR stated the philosophy of the constructive trust in broad terms, holding it to be

a trust imposed by law whenever justice and good conscience require it. It is a liberal process, founded upon large principles of equity, to be applied in cases where the legal owner cannot conscientiously keep the property for himself alone, but ought to allow another to have the property or the benefit of it or a share in it. The trust may arise at the outset when the property is acquired, or later on, as the circumstances require. It is an equitable remedy by which the court can enable an aggrieved party to obtain restitution.[13]

Lord Denning thus ruled that it would be 'entirely against conscience that [A] should retain the whole house and not allow [B] any interest in it, or any charge upon it.'[14] The Court decided that A therefore held his legal title subject to an equitable interest in B proportionate to the value of her cash investment in the extension.

As is indicated by the fact that there was a dissent in *Hussey v Palmer*,[15] the applicability of a constructive trust in such circumstances is not entirely free of doubt. Although there was clearly a recognisable 'change of position' on the part of B, it is difficult to identify the relevant 'bargain' or common intention,[16]

9   [1986] 1 WLR 1512 at 1515E-F.
10   [1986] 1 WLR 1512 at 1516A.
11   [1986] 1 WLR 1512 at 1516B.
12   [1972] 1 WLR 1286. See (1973) 37 Conv (NS) 65 (D.J. Hayton); (1973) 89 LQR 2; (1973) 36 MLR 436 (T.C. Ridley).
13   [1972] 1 WLR 1286 at 1290A.
14   [1972] 1 WLR 1286 at 1291B.
15   [1972] 1 WLR 1286 at 1292C-D per Cairns LJ, who pointed out that B had herself testified in court to having merely 'lent' the money to A. In the view of Cairns LJ, 'it is going a very long way to say that...there was some misunderstanding by her of the legal position and that she was describing as a loan something which was not a loan at all.' Where there is documentary evidence which confirms the status of a transaction as a loan, this is enough to displace the possibility that a contribution of money may have generated a trust (see eg *In re Sharpe (A Bankrupt)* [1980] 1 WLR 219 at 222G-H).
16   See *Avondale Printers & Stationers Ltd v Haggie* [1979] 2 NZLR 124 at 145; M. Neave, (1978) 11 Melbourne ULR 343 at 361.

and even more difficult to pinpoint the precise kind of interest which A, even by inference, was supposed to have agreed to confer upon B.[17] The pivotal feature of the case was probably the inequitable nature of the conduct of A, who had behaved most oppressively and unfairly towards B,[18] and it may be that the majority decision was influenced more by such factors than by the technical requirements of constructive trust theory.[19]

(e) Agreement that B should acquire an enlarged beneficial interest in land owned by A

Further difficulties arise where a legal title in land is already vested in A, subject to an existing trust under which B has some beneficial entitlement. These difficulties occur if B later claims to have acquired an enlarged beneficial share over and above the quantum of beneficial entitlement already enjoyed by him under the original terms of the trust. It is one of the formal proprieties of a valid trust that the beneficial interests should crystallise in the intended proportions at the commencement of the trust,[20] and should not thereafter fluctuate arbitrarily or be otherwise varied except in accordance with the statutory requirements of writing.

(i) Strict application of trust principles   The present problem may easily arise if B makes supervening contributions of money towards the acquisition cost of A's property. In *Cowcher v Cowcher*,[1] for instance, the legal title in a matrimonial home was purchased in the name of A. However, the purchase price of £12,000 was raised effectively by means of a cash contribution of some £4,000 from B and a mortgage loan of £8,000 for repayment of which A undertook sole responsibility. These money contributions constituted what Bagnall J called a 'money consensus',[2] under which a presumed resulting trust arose for A and B in the precise proportions of their respective contributions.[3] The trust generated by this 'money consensus' was clearly immune from all requirements of writing or other formality.[4] When A's business later ran into difficulties, B used her own moneys to discharge in part A's mortgage responsibility. B claimed that, by reason of these supervening financial contributions, her

---

17 The interest recognised by Lord Denning MR as having been acquired by B under the court-imposed constructive trust seemed to hover ambivalently between a proportionate share in the beneficial ownership of the property and a mere lien for the money advanced by her ([1972] 1 WLR 1286 at 1291B-D). See *In re Sharpe (A Bankrupt)* [1980] 1 WLR 219 at 222H-223A. It is perhaps significant that a similar claim of constructive trust in favour of a mother-in-law was quickly brushed aside in *Broughall v Hunt* (Unreported, Chancery Division, 1 February 1983) in preference for a contractual licence solution (post, p 545). See also *Savva v Costa and Harymode Investments Ltd* (1981) 131 NLJ 1114.

18 There was evidence ([1972] 1 WLR 1286 at 1288D-E) that A had refused even to reply to a somewhat plaintive request made by B after her departure from the home for an allowance of £1 per week to help her out!

19 For a critical view of *Hussey v Palmer*, see *In re Sharpe (A Bankrupt)* [1980] 1 WLR 219 at 223A; *Avondale Printers & Stationers Ltd v Haggie* [1979] 2 NZLR 124 at 145; *Malsbury v Malsbury* [1982] 1 NSWLR 226 at 231B-C. It may be that, as was suggested in *Holiday Inns Inc v Broadhead* (1974) 232 Estates Gazette 951 at 1087 and *Savva v Costa and Harymode Investments Ltd* (1981) 131 NLJ 1114, the decision in *Hussey v Palmer* is better analysed as an illustration of the principle in *Ramsden v Dyson* (1866) LR 1 HL 129 (post, p 390). See the application of the law of proprietary estoppel in analogous circumstances in *Clayton v Green* (1979) NZ Recent Law 139 at 140.

20 *Bernard v Josephs* [1982] Ch 391 at 404F.

1 [1972] 1 WLR 425. See (1972) 35 MLR 547 (J. Levin).

2 Ante, p 249.

3 [1972] 1 WLR 425 at 431B-C.

4 [1972] 1 WLR 425 at 431C-D.

beneficial share under the trust of the matrimonial home had been increased from one-third to one-half.

B's claim, although apparently justified in terms of fairness, was rejected by Bagnall J. In his view, the beneficial interests under the trust had crystallised at the point of creation of the trust as shares of two-thirds and one-third for A and B respectively. These proportions fixed by the initial 'money consensus' were capable of subsequent variation only in strict compliance with section 53(1)(c) of the Law of Property Act 1925. This provision requires that 'a disposition of an equitable interest or trust subsisting at the time of the disposition must be in writing and signed by the person disposing of the same...'[5] In Bagnall J's analysis, any attempt to vary the beneficial shares achieved by the original 'money consensus' must be regarded as the consequence of some 'interest consensus' reached by the parties which, unlike the original 'money consensus', was not immune from the statutory requirement of writing. B's assertion of an extra beneficial entitlement necessarily involved a subsequent disposition of a one-sixth share in her favour. Bagnall J decided that her claim must fail for want of writing in compliance with section 53(1)(c).[6] B's beneficial entitlement was held to remain as a one-third share.[7]

The judgment of Bagnall J in *Cowcher v Cowcher* thus contains a stern ruling that the subsequent variation of the original beneficial shares fixed under a trust can operate only as an express disposition requiring writing.[8] This approach leads to obvious difficulties and the possibility of substantial injustice in those circumstances where parties make supervening contributions of money in a loose and informal manner, without having ever contemplated the necessity of compliance with a statutory requirement of writing. Moreover, it would seem exceedingly strange if a supervening contribution could generate a beneficial share where none existed before,[9] but could not augment a beneficial share already in existence.

5   Section 53(1)(c) derives ultimately from section 9 of the Statute of Frauds 1677. The object of both provisions is 'to prevent hidden oral transactions in equitable interests in fraud of those truly entitled, and making it difficult, if not impossible, for the trustees to ascertain who are in fact [their] beneficiaries' (*Vandervell v IRC* [1967] 2 AC 291 at 311B-C per Lord Upjohn). It is clear that section 53(1)(c) applies not merely to the disposition of equitable interests arising under an express trust, but also to the disposition of interests arising under a resulting trust (see *Cowcher v Cowcher* [1972] 1 WLR 425 at 432E) and also under a constructive trust (see *Oughtred v IRC* [1960] AC 206 at 230, 233; *Appleby v Cowley* (1982) *Times*, 14 April).

6   Bagnall J conceded ([1972] 1 WLR 425 at 432E-F) that, notwithstanding section 53(1)(c), 'a parole agreement for valuable consideration to vary the trusts, of which equity would grant specific performance' would have been 'as valid as an assignment in writing; for it would operate as an agreement for sale of an equitable interest upon which the vendor would become a trustee for the purchaser subject only to the payment of the consideration.' However, Bagnall J added that such an agreement could be implied from conduct 'only in the most exceptional circumstances' and that the mere payment by one beneficial owner of a mortgage instalment properly payable by the other could not normally imply an agreement to alter the beneficial interests. See also *Avondale Printers & Stationers Ltd v Haggie* [1979] 2 NZLR 124 at 142.

7   B was allowed to recover the amount of her supervening contributions (approximately £1,500) in addition to the value of her one-third equitable share (ante, p 249). However, the value of the extra one-sixth share which she unsuccessfully claimed would, by virtue of the considerable inflation of the land values involved, have been in the region of £7,000.

8   See also *Jeffries v Stevens* [1982] STC 639 at 651g for disapproval of the possibility of 'a wavering equity in...property'. By the same token, however, an initial beneficial entitlement cannot be forfeited merely by reason of the effluxion of time: it can normally be got out of its owner only by means of written disposition (see *Brykiert v Jones* (1981) 2 FLR 373 at 375G).

9   Ante, p 287.

(ii) Liberalising effects of the constructive trust   It now seems to be agreed that the dilemma exposed in *Cowcher* is best resolved through the application of a constructive trust. In *In re Densham (A Bankrupt)*[10] Goff J expressed some disapproval of the excessively rigid view adopted by Bagnall J as to the role of section 53(1)(c). Goff J was of the opinion that the original shares of beneficial ownership as fixed by actual money contribution at the date of purchase could indeed be varied by a subsequent 'interest consensus' without the necessity of compliance with section 53(1)(c). Thus if a legal title were purchased in the name of A, and A expressly agreed that B should receive a larger beneficial share under a trust than was strictly justified by B's money contribution towards that purchase, B could justifiably claim that larger share on the footing of a constructive trust. To hold the agreement in B's favour unenforceable for want of writing would, in Goff J's terms, be 'contrary to equitable principles' since it would be 'unconscionable for a party to set up the statute and repudiate the agreement.' A would become a 'constructive trustee of the property so far as necessary to give effect to the agreement.'[11] However, the major difficulty lying in B's path is the requirement that he prove the existence of an agreement or bargain for enhanced beneficial ownership and that his financial contribution was 'referable' to it.[12]

(f) Knowing reception by A of a title already held on trust for B

In all the examples considered so far, a constructive trust has been imposed on A because he has himself agreed to recognise the existence of beneficial rights in B or because he has agreed to give effect to somebody else's agreement to recognise such rights in B. There is, however, one instance in which A can be made a constructive trustee without having agreed to give effect to any rights held by B. This case arises where land already held by X on trust for B is conveyed to A. If, at the date of the conveyance, A had either actual or deemed knowledge of the trust, he cannot now be heard in all conscience to disavow his own fiduciary status. In effect he is made liable, as a constructive trustee, to give effect to a trust-generating intention previously existing between X and B.[13]

A controversial example of these circumstances occurred in *Peffer v Rigg*.[14] Here a legal title in a house had previously been vested in X as trustee for himself and B in equal shares. X then purported to transfer the 'whole' of the property 'as beneficial owner' to his ex-wife, A, who was at all material times fully aware of the existence of the trust. When A later contended that B's beneficial interest was ineffective against her, Graham J held that she had taken the legal title on a constructive trust for B, 'in accordance with general equitable principles'.[15] The judge was careful to emphasise that this constructive trust was 'a new trust imposed by equity and [was] distinct from the trust which bound [X]'.[16]

10   [1975] 1 WLR 1519. See (1976) 92 LQR 489 (F. Webb).
11   [1975] 1 WLR 1519 at 1525D-E. See, however, Insolvency Act 1986, s 339(3)(c) (post, p 886).
12   See Lord Diplock's reference in *Gissing v Gissing* [1971] AC 886 at 906E to the necessity for 'some subsequent fresh agreement, acted upon by the parties, to vary the original beneficial interests created when the matrimonial home was acquired'.
13   Ante, p 271.
14   [1977] 1 WLR 285 (ante, p 166).
15   [1977] 1 WLR 285 at 294F.
16   For other applications of the same principle, see *White v Cabanas Pty Ltd (No 2)* [1970] Qd R 395 at 400A-B, 406D; *Boccalatte v Bushelle* [1980] Qd R 180 at 186A.

CHAPTER 11

Co-ownership

Co-ownership is the term used to describe the form of ownership in which two or more persons are simultaneously entitled in possession to an interest or interests in the same property. Co-ownership thus connotes some form of concurrent (as distinct from successive) holding in respect of property, and is governed in English law by rules markedly different from those which regulate land which is the subject of a strict settlement under the Settled Land Act 1925.[1]

1. THE SOCIAL CONTEXT OF CO-OWNERSHIP

In social terms concurrent ownership of an estate or interest in land has nowadays become infinitely more common than the limited forms of successive ownership which are dealt with under the Settled Land Act 1925.

(1) The strict settlement

The device of the settlement evolved as a form of landholding designed primarily to satisfy the property-related aspirations of a distinctive social class living in a bygone era.[2] The purposes achieved by the settlement of land were gradually refined over the centuries,[3] but its broad aim was the intergenerational transfer of wealth within the family in an age when wealth was synonymous with land. Land was retained within the family essentially by conferring limited kinds of interest on key family members and (usually) by subjecting the property to resettlement every generation. In this way 'no single individual ever acquired an unfettered power to appropriate the family capital for his individual purposes'.[4]

Marriage settlements thus provided a medium of landholding which gave effect initially to the living arrangements ordained by a patriarchal figure—a paterfamilias. Furthermore, the interests created under the strict settlement were heavily determined by status and gender.[5] Status was determinative in the sense that the settled land interests were graded according to status within the family structure. Gender was relevant inasmuch as the male of the species

---

1 Post, p 803.
2 Ante, p 62.
3 See eg Lloyd Bonfield, *Marriage, Property and the 'Affective Family'*, (1983) 1 Law and History Review 297 at 298ff.
4 See A.W.B. Simpson, *Introduction* to W. Blackstone, *Commentaries on the Laws of England* (Facsimile edn, Chicago and London 1979), Vol 2, p xi.
5 For an account of the complex calibrations distinguishing the various forms of provision which could be made by a marriage settlement, see Lloyd Bonfield, *Marriage Settlements 1601 - 1740: The Adoption of the Strict Settlement* (Cambridge 1983).

was infinitely to be advanced in preference to the female. The archetypal settlement might well confer a mere life interest on a testator's widow while giving some form of entail in remainder to the testator's eldest son.

(2) A movement from status to contract

The modern demise of the strict settlement in favour of concurrent ownership is, in many ways, symptomatic of certain fundamental changes in social norms which have occurred during the last two centuries. Our own society has ceased to be regulated to the same degree by status and gender.[6] There is little doubt, for instance, that status has been displaced by contract as the conceptual basis of family relationships.[7] In a former age the relation of husband and wife was strictly defined in terms of the incidents of a lifelong status. Nowadays the continuance and quality of the spousal relationship are overshadowed by the reality of liberal divorce laws which recognise that marriage has become a form of permissive cohabitation, terminable at the will of either or both of the parties.[8] These changed social facts reflect themselves in our most important living arrangements—those which relate to the family home—with obvious implications for the law of real property.

(3) A new egalitarian ideal

Coupled with this movement from status-dependent relationships to voluntary co-operative relationships has been the wide acknowledgement of a new egalitarian ideal. This has been particularly evident in respect of the relationship between male and female, between husband and wife. Thus we no longer accept the sex-based lines of demarcation which, in real property terms, classed married women along with infants, idiots, traitors, felons and aliens, under the general heading of 'disabilities'. The modern emphasis in domestic living arrangements is placed very much more on the sharing of property by persons situated in a relation of equality—a relationship not constrained by the incidents of status but which springs from mutual consent and retains vitality only so long as that consent endures.

The social pattern described here is far removed from that of a former age which saw the grant of patriarchal largesse epitomised in the marriage settlement. Concurrent ownership of an absolute interest in land—rather than the successive entitlement to limited interests conferred by a settlement—has become the appropriate medium for the tangible expression of this newer social pattern. The vertical power structure embodied in settled land arrangements of the past has been largely displaced by the horizontal power relationships preferred in the more democratic, egalitarian, industrial and urban society of the 20th century.

---

6 See eg M.A. Glendon, *Power and Authority in the Family: New Legal Patterns as Reflections of Changing Ideologies,* (1975) 23 AJCL 1.
7 Post, p 793.
8 The literature is legion, but see particularly O.R. McGregor, *Equality, sexual values and permissive legislation: the English experience,* (1972) 1 Jnl Soc Pol 44; M.A. Glendon, *The New Family and the New Property* (Toronto 1981), p 11ff.

2. TYPES OF CO-OWNERSHIP

English law has known four types of co-ownership. They are respectively (i) joint tenancy, (ii) tenancy in common, (iii) tenancy by entireties, and (iv) coparcenary. The last two forms of co-ownership are for all practical purposes archaic.

3. JOINT TENANCY

The essence of joint tenancy consists in the theory that each joint tenant is 'wholly entitled to the whole' of the estate or interest which is the subject of co-ownership.[9] No joint tenant holds any specific share in the property himself, but each is (together with the other joint tenant or tenants) invested with the total interest in the land.[10] The whole is not so much the sum of the parts, for each and every part is itself co-extensive with the whole.[11] In Bracton's expressive language, each joint tenant *totum tenet et nihil tenet*[12]; each holds everything and yet holds nothing.[13]

(1) An undifferentiated form of co-ownership

Joint tenancy is thus an undifferentiated kind of co-ownership in which an entire estate or interest in property—rather than any defined proportion or aliquot share—is vested simultaneously in all the co-owners. The co-owned property is a single estate held by joint owners who are bound together in a 'thorough and intimate union of interest and possession'[14] and who together comprise but one composite person in the eyes of the law.[15]

(2) Absence of shareholding

Any reference to ownership in specific 'shares' (eg A owns a one-quarter interest and B a three-quarters interest) is normally sufficient to establish that A

---

9 In this context, the term 'tenant' has nothing necessarily to do with the landlord-tenant relationship: it merely signifies 'owner'. However, there arises here a possibility of ambiguity in that the total interest which is subject to 'joint tenancy' may well be either an estate in fee simple, or a life interest, or even a term of years (ie, a 'tenancy' in the landlord-tenant sense).

10 See *Wright v Gibbons* (1948-1949) 78 CLR 313 at 329 per Dixon J; *In re Rushton (A Bankrupt)* [1972] Ch 197 at 203A per Goff J.

11 'Joint tenancy is based on the theory that together the joint tenants have but one estate, not a number of estates equal to the number of joint tenants' (*In Re Estate of King*, 572 SW.2d 200 at 211 (1978)).

12 '*Quilibet totum tenet, et nihil tenet; scilicet, totum in communi, et nihil separatim per se*' (*Bracton*, fo 430 (Woodbine's edn), Vol 4, 336). See also *Co Litt*, p 186a.

13 See *Challis*, p 367.

14 *Bl Comm*, Vol II, p 182. So intimate is the union that, so far as vesting of title is concerned, it is irrelevant whether a joint tenant has made an equal (or indeed any) contribution to the purchase price of the co-owned property (see *Paluszek v Wohlrab*, 115 NE.2d 764 at 766 (1953); *Brockway's Estate v CIR*, 219 F.2d 400 at 403 (1954)).

15 'A gift of lands to two or more persons in joint tenancy is such a gift as imparts to them, with respect to all other persons than themselves, the properties of a single owner' (see Joshua Williams, *Principles of the Law of Real Property* (23rd edn by T.C. Williams, London 1920), p 143). See also *Duncan v Suhy*, 37 NE.2d 826 at 828 (1941); *In Re Lorch's Estate*, 33 NYS.2d 157 at 166 (1941); *Osterloh's Estate v Carpenter*, 337 SW.2d 942 at 946 (1960).

and B co-own not as joint tenants, but rather as tenants in common.[16] Even to say that A and B hold half-shares in property is, in strict terms, to indicate that A and B are tenants in common.[17]

Such ambivalence as may attach to the nature of co-ownership in equal shares or half- shares is almost certainly attributable to the fact that a joint tenancy is fairly easily convertible by 'severance'[18] into a tenancy in common in equal shares. In consequence, every joint tenancy is also potentially a tenancy in common in equal shares,[19] and every joint tenant is proleptically a co-owner in equal shares and thus entitled to dispose of his aliquot share or to grant a lease or life interest out of that share.[20] There is therefore an inevitable tendency on the part of lawyers to refer sometimes to joint tenants as being already entitled to equal shares,[1] but this merely reflects the extremely marginal nature of the legal distinction between the actual and the inchoate rights of the joint tenant.

(3) Distinguishing characteristics of joint tenancy

The distinguishing characteristics of joint tenancy are two in number. First, joint tenants enjoy as between themselves a 'right of survivorship'. Second, the existence of joint tenancy always presupposes the presence of the 'four unities'.

(a) Right of survivorship (ius accrescendi)

It has been said that the right of survivorship or *ius accrescendi* is the 'grand and distinguishing' incident of joint tenancy.[2] On the death of one of two joint tenants, the surviving joint tenant becomes the sole owner by right of survivorship. This doctrine was elegantly described by Blackstone:

When two or more persons are seised of a joint estate...the entire tenancy upon the decease of any of them remains to the survivors, and at length to the last survivor...The interest of two joint-tenants is not only equal or similar, but also is one and the same. One has not originally a distinct moiety from the other...but...each...has a concurrent

---

16 *Cowcher v Cowcher* [1972] 1 WLR 425 at 430H; *Paluszek v Wohlrab*, 115 NE.2d 764 at 766 (1953).

17 It may well be that Blackstone misled generations of lawyers when, in expounding Littleton's law-French (*Litt*, s 288), he taught that joint tenants are 'seised *per my et per tout*, by the half or moiety, and by all...' (*Bl Comm*, Vol II, p 182). See, for instance, *Doe d Aslin v Summersett* (1830) 1 B & Ad 135 at 140, 109 ER 738 at 739 per Lord Tenterden CJ. The word '*my*' is now generally agreed to have been the *mie* which in old French served as a negative expletive particle, rather than *mi* or 'half' as Blackstone seems to have believed. (So much should have been obvious in any event from the reflection that there may be more than two joint tenants; but see *Nielson-Jones v Fedden* [1975] Ch 222 at 228C). In effect, Littleton's phrase '*per my et per tout*' is merely a reiteration of Bracton's '*totum tenet et nihil tenet*'. On the 'singular infelicity' of Blackstone's translation, see Serjeant Manning's notes to *Daniel v Camplin* (1845) 7 Man & G 167 at 172, 135 ER 73 at 75 (note (c)). See also *Murray v Hall* (1849) 7 CB 441 at 455, 137 ER 175 at 180 (note (a)).

18 Post, p 317.

19 It was with this possibility in mind that Coke, while conceding that joint tenants are wholly seised of the whole, was nevertheless careful to point out that 'yet to divers purposes each of them hath but a right to a moiety, as to enfeoff, give, or demise, or to forfeit or lose by default in a *praecipe*' (*Co Litt*, p 186a).

20 See *Challis*, p 367. Such forms of alienation automatically bring about either a total or partial severance of the joint tenancy (post, p 321).

1 See eg *Bl Comm*, Vol II, p 182.

2 *De Witt v San Francisco*, 2 Cal 289 at 297 (1852). See also *In re Robertson* (1944) 44 SR (NSW) 103 at 105; *Matter of Estate of Oney*, 641 P.2d 725 at 727 (1982).

interest in the whole; and therefore, on the death of his companion, the sole interest in the whole remains to the survivor.[3]

(i) Operation of the survivorship principle The operation of the *ius accrescendi* may be illustrated in the following way. Suppose that a fee simple estate in Blackacre was vested originally in three joint tenants, A, B and C. If C now dies, the estate remains vested in A and B as the surviving joint tenants,[4] and C's entitlement is simply extinguished.[5] Regardless of whether C dies testate or intestate, no 'share' in Blackacre can devolve with his estate[6] because as a joint tenant C had no 'share' as such in the land.[7] He had no fraction of ownership which was capable of transmission on his death, since together with A and B he was wholly entitled to the whole. By virtue of the same argument, when C dies A and B are already fully entitled as joint tenants to the entire fee simple estate in Blackacre, and no further vesting in them as survivors is required.[8] No 'interest' passes to either of them on C's death[9]; the entire interest in the land merely 'survives' to them as the remaining joint tenants.

Similarly, if B predeceases A, the right of survivorship operates once more: B drops out of the picture, leaving A as the sole owner of the fee simple estate in Blackacre. At least in strict theory, A's ownership has been enlarged throughout the entire process only to the extent that he is no longer subject to the hazard of survivorship.[10] In reality, of course, there has been a 'distinct

3 *Bl Comm*, Vol II, p 183f. The *ius accrescendi* was described in *Wharton's Law Lexicon* (11th edn 1711), p 471, as 'a general concentration of property from more to fewer, by the accession of the part of him or them that die to the survivors or survivor, till it passes to a single hand, and the joint tenancy ceases'.

4 *Litt*, s 280; *Co Litt*, p 181a.

5 *Wright v Gibbons* (1948-1949) 78 CLR 313 at 323 per Latham CJ. See also *Green v Skinner*, 197 P 60 at 62 (1921); *Fleming v Fleming*, 174 NW 946 at 953 (1921).

6 The operation of survivorship is frustrated only rarely. An example arises where an application is made under the Inheritance (Provision for Family and Dependants) Act 1975 for provision out of the estate of a decedent. The 'severable share' of a deceased beneficial joint tenant may be treated as part of his net estate 'to such extent as appears to the court to be just in all the circumstances of the case' (Inheritance (Provision for Family and Dependants) Act 1975, s 9(1)).

7 Administration of Estates Act 1925, s 3(4); *Challis*, p 366, citing *Litt*, s 280; *Eastgate v Equity Trustees Executors And Agency Co Ltd* (1963-1964) 110 CLR 275 at 289f; *Dando v Dando*, 99 P.2d 561 at 562 (1940).

8 'Technically, joint tenants are originally entitled to all which they ever have' (*Fadden v Deputy Federal Commissioner of Taxation* (1943) 68 CLR 76 at 84). See also *In Re Peterson's Estate*, 45 P.2d 45 at 48f (1935); *Kleemann v Sheridan*, 256 P.2d 553 at 555 (1953); *Williamson's Estate v Williamson*, 380 SW.2d 333 at 338 (1964).

9 Except in the voracious view of the taxman, who, in defiance of the strict technicalities of land law, insists that a 'notional estate' (in the form of the appropriate aliquot share) has passed to the surviving joint tenant or tenants and is therefore chargeable to inheritance tax. See *Eastgate v Equity Trustees Executors And Agency Co Ltd* (1963- 1964) 110 CLR 275 at 284 per Kitto J, 290 per Menzies J; *United States v Jacobs*, 306 US 363 at 371, 83 L.ed 763 at 769 (1939); but compare *In Re Gerling's Estate*, 303 SW.2d 915 at 919 (1957). In England it seems that, for the purpose of inheritance tax, the value of a notional half-share under a joint tenancy is generally regarded by the Inland Revenue as being 45 per cent of the whole, the discount reflecting the fact that the co-owner did not enjoy complete control over the asset and that any realisation of the relevant value would have involved a transaction-cost for the vendor (see A.R. Mellows, *The Law of Succession* (4th edn, London 1983), p 196).

10 See *Eastgate v Equity Trustees Executors And Agency Co Ltd* (1963-1964) 110 CLR 275 at 283; *Craig v Federal Commissioner of Taxation* (1945) 70 CLR 441 at 452; *In Re Peterson's Estate*, 45 P.2d 45 at 48f (1935); *In Re Foster's Estate*, 320 P.2d 855 at 859 (1958).

shifting of economic interest, a decided change for the survivor's benefit'.[11] Moreover, it is irrelevant to the vesting of title in the survivor that he made little or no contribution towards the initial purchase of the property.[12]

Any doubt as to the identity of the surviving joint tenant is resolved in England by the rule governing *commorientes*. Under this rule where two or more persons have died in circumstances rendering it uncertain which survived the other or others, the deaths are presumed to have occurred in order of seniority, and the younger shall be deemed to have survived the elder.[13] The *commorientes* rule is not entirely satisfactory, and it is arguable that in the case of contemporaneous death the solution provided by the Uniform Simultaneous Death Act is much to be preferred.[14] Under this Act, which has been adopted for instance in California, the death of two or more joint tenants simultaneously is treated as a severance and an equal share of the property devolves with the estate of each decedent.[15]

(ii) Advantages of the survivorship principle   Joint tenancy, with its inherent right of survivorship, may at first sight appear somewhat capricious,[16] but the undifferentiated co-ownership of joint tenancy is ideal for some purposes. Ever since 1925 co-ownership of a legal estate in land (ie, of the fee simple absolute in possession or of a term of years absolute) has necessarily taken the form of joint tenancy.[17] The co-owners of a legal estate are automatically joint tenants and hold that estate as trustees. This fact has great importance both for the internal administration of the trust and for the conduct of transactions with strangers in respect of the trust property.

(iii) Avoidance of probate difficulties   It would be highly inconvenient if there had to be a new vesting of the trust property on every occasion of death within the trusteeship. It is however of the essence of joint tenancy that, on the death of

---

11 *United States v Jacobs*, 306 US 363 at 371, 83 L.ed 763 at 769 (1939) per Black J.

12 *Wright v Bloom*, 359 P.2d 1080 at 1083 (1961).

13 Law of Property Act 1925, s 184. This rule is, however, subject to any order of the court (see *In Re Lindop* [1942] Ch 377 at 382; *Hickman v Peacey* [1945] AC 304 at 316). See also Administration of Estates Act 1925, s 46(3), as added by Intestates' Estates Act 1952, s 1(4).

14 See *Hickman v Peacey* [1945] AC 304 at 314, 317, where Viscount Simon LC, while conceding that time is infinitely divisible, opined that section 184 of the Law of Property Act 1925 has no application if the relevant deaths are 'absolutely simultaneous'.

15 See Cal Prob Code, s 296.2; *In re Estate of Meade*, 39 Cal Rptr 278 at 282 (1964).

16 The Supreme Court of California has pointed out that 'a joint tenant's right of survivorship is an expectancy that is not irrevocably fixed upon the creation of the estate; it arises only upon success in the ultimate gamble—survival—and then only if the unity of the estate has not theretofore been destroyed...' (*Tenhet v Boswell*, 133 Cal Rptr 10 at 14 (1976) per Mosk J). Another American court has observed that, while the joint tenants of a fee simple estate are alive, 'each has a specialised form of life estate, with what amounts to a contingent remainder in the fee, the contingency being dependent upon which joint tenant survives' (*Green v Skinner*, 197 P 60 at 62 (1921)).

17 Post, p 339. Joint tenancy can exist even though one of the co-owners has the potential of perpetual existence. A corporate body, being an artificial person in the eyes of the law, enjoys in theory a kind of immortality. However, it is now legally feasible for a corporate body to become a joint tenant (see Bodies Corporate (Joint Tenancy) Act 1899, s1(1)). Moreover, survivorship operates in the sense that the jointly owned property devolves on the other joint tenant or tenants if the company is ever dissolved (see Bodies Corporate (Joint Tenancy) Act 1899, s1(2)).

a trustee, the surviving trustees are *already* invested with the entire interest in the property and no further vesting in their names is required.[18]

(iv) Facility of dealings with title Similarly, it has already been seen[19] that a purchaser from joint tenants need investigate only one title—the title held by each and all of the joint tenants—with the result that co-ownership by way of joint tenancy not only facilitates the internal management of the trust, but also promotes the free alienation of land. Thus joint tenancy serves admirably the needs which arise in connection with the administration and disposition of the legal title to property. Since the legal title is only a 'paper title', authorising its owners merely to exercise fiduciary powers of management and disposition, the caprice of survivorship is usually rendered quite harmless in reality, since it in no way affects the equitable (ie, beneficial) ownership of property. It is, of course, beneficial ownership which determines entitlements to the prospective proceeds of sale of the co-owned land.[20]

(v) Indestructibility of survivorship A unique and intimate union exists between joint tenants.[1] This identity of interest is so complete that the principal feature of their relationship—the right of survivorship—takes precedence over any testamentary disposition made by a joint tenant.[2] A disposition contained in the will of a joint tenant is entirely ineffective in respect of any land to which his joint tenancy relates, simply because a joint tenant has no specific share or interest which he can pass on his death.[3] Moreover, by the time the will takes effect survivorship has already operated.[4] The same point is expressed in the proposition that severance of a joint tenancy cannot normally be effected by

18 Moreover the appointment of new trustees may be made by the surviving trustee or trustees (Trustee Act 1925, s 36(1)) or by the court (Trustee Act 1925, s 41(1)). See also Trustee Act 1925, ss 36(7), 43. Where the appointment has been made by deed, a vesting of the land in the new trustees may be achieved by simple reliance on the vesting provisions contained in the Trustee Act 1925, s 40. There is normally no necessity for a re-conveyance of the trust property. See, however, Land Registration Act 1925, s 47(1) in relation to registered land.

19 Ante, p 98.

20 Ante, p 102.

1 There is much evidence to suggest that joint tenancy is almost exclusively a form of matrimonial or quasi-matrimonial tenure. It has been surmised that the sharp rise in the incidence of joint tenancies from the 1940s onwards may have been stimulated both by increasing social recognition of the emancipation of married women and by the ever-present reality of death under war-time conditions (see N.W. Hines, *Real Property Joint Tenancies: Law, Fact, and Fancy*, 51 Iowa LR 582 at 590, 623 (1965-66)).

2 It has been postulated that there is a 'deep-rooted need for survivorship—the people want it' (N. Sterling, *Joint Tenancy and Community Property in California*, 14 Pacific LJ 927 at 929 (1982-83).

3 'The event of death does not sever the joint tenancy because the right of the survivor of the joint tenants to have the entire interest is the essence of a joint tenancy; the event which triggers this legal effect cannot at the same time be the event which would destroy it' (*Re Levy* (1982) 131 DLR (3d) 15 at 25). See also *Swift d Neale v Roberts* (1764) 3 Burr 1488 at 1496f, 97 ER 941 at 946; *In Re Fritz' Estate*, 20 P.2d 361 at 363 (1933); *In Re Estate of Moy*, 31 Cal Rptr 374 at 377 (1963).

4 According to Coke, 'yet in consideration of Law there is a Priority of Time in an Instant, as here the Survivor is preferred before the Devise: for Littleton saith, that the Cause is that no Devise can take Effect till after the Death of the Devisor, and by his Death all the Land presently cometh by the Law to his Companion' (*Co Litt*, p 185b). See also *Bl Comm*, Vol II, p 186.

will.[5] Unless a severance of the joint tenancy has occurred inter vivos, the right of survivorship is indestructible.

(vi) Utility as an estate planning device   Not only does the right of survivorship override testamentary dispositions; it often has the effect of rendering testamentary gifts quite unnecessary. Where, for instance, the joint tenants are husband and wife, the operation of survivorship assumes most clearly its modern function as a simple and cost-effective estate planning device.[6] The *ius accrescendi* permits the co-owned estate to vest automatically in the survivor of the couple on the death of his or her partner—an outcome which seems in general to be desired by married couples.[7] In common with all other rules of intestate succession, survivorship is a speedy and inexpensive testamentary substitute designed to benefit a surviving partner while necessitating only minor administrative adjustments to the formerly joint title.[8]

(vii) Safety from unsecured creditors   A further, and rather more dubious, benefit of the survivorship principle is that its operation renders the surviving joint tenant or tenants immune from unsecured debts incurred independently by the deceased joint tenant during his lifetime.[9] On the death of the debtor the entire co-owned property vests by operation of law in the survivor or survivors free of any claims which may be advanced by the decedent's creditors.[10] Consistently with the theory of joint tenancy,[11] the decedent's estate has no interest in the co-owned property from which outstanding unsecured claims can be satisfied.[12] Unsecured creditors are therefore unable to reach into the joint tenancy after the debtor's death unless that debtor severed the joint tenancy before he died.[13]

---

5 The law of severance is dealt with elsewhere (post, p 317), but compare the effect of mutual wills (post, p 330).

6 Survivorship may even be coupled with added taxation advantages for the survivor, as is for instance the case under New Zealand's Joint Family Homes Act 1964, s 22(1) (post, p 882). For the motivation behind this conferment of tax exemption, see Vol 292, *New Zealand Parliamentary Debates*, 3692ff; Vol 340, *New Zealand Parliamentary Debates*, 2995ff.

7 In Britain joint tenancy has become the predominant form of freehold ownership for young married couples: see J.E. Todd and L.M. Jones, *Matrimonial Property* (London 1972), p 80; A.J. Manners and I. Rauta, *Family Property in Scotland* (1981), p 5.

8 Speaking of joint tenancy, one American commentator has pointed out that 'the people want it...because in most instances they want the survivor to get all the property in the event of death. It is the poor man's will; it is faster and, in "no tax" cases, it is cheaper. It works well in practice for people of modest means' (see Y.B. Griffith, *Community Property in Joint Tenancy Form*, 14 Stanford LR 87 at 108 (1961-62)). For the criticism that survivorship is nevertheless somewhat inflexible as a quasi-testamentary device, see N.W. Hines, 51 Iowa LR 582 at 598.

9 The unilateral creation of a *secured* charge over jointly owned property would normally have had the effect of severance (post, p 602).

10 *Irvine v Helvering*, 99 F.2d 265 at 269 (1938); *King v King*, 236 P.2d 912 at 913 (1951); *Frederick v Shorman*, 147 NW.2d 478 at 484 (1966); *Schlichenmayer v Luithle*, 221 NW.2d 77 at 83 (1974). The corollary is, of course, that if the *debtor* is the survivor, the creditors have access to the entire property formerly held under joint tenancy (see eg *Rupp v Kahn*, 55 Cal Rptr 108 at 112f (1966)).

11 Ante, p 295.

12 Unless a creditor can prove that the decedent deliberately put his property in joint tenancy form in order to defraud his creditors (post, p 884).

13 The effects of insolvency are examined more generally elsewhere (post, p 875).

Criticism has been directed at this rule which renders unsecured creditors extremely vulnerable when dealing with a debtor who contrives to tie up his property in joint tenancy form.[14]

(b) The 'four unities'

It is axiomatic that the 'four unities' must be present before a joint tenancy can be said to exist. These unities are the unities of possession, interest, title and time.[15] Only unity of possession is required as a precondition of tenancy in common.[16]

(i) Unity of possession Unity of possession means that each joint tenant is as much entitled to possession of every part of the co-owned land as the other joint tenant or tenants.[17] He may not physically delineate any part of the land as being 'his' land rather than that of any of his brethren,[18] nor prevent them from taking their appropriate share of the rents and profits derived from the land.[19] This unity of possession is only occasionally displaced by statutory intervention. Perhaps the best example of such intervention is provided by the Domestic Violence and Matrimonial Proceedings Act 1976, which empowers the court to oust even a joint tenant from the family home in cases of domestic violence.[20]

(ii) Unity of interest Unity of interest follows from the proposition that each joint tenant is 'wholly entitled to the whole'. The interest held by each joint tenant is therefore the same in extent, nature and duration. Joint tenancy cannot exist between persons holding interests of different natures or duration, eg between a freeholder and a leaseholder, an owner in possession and an owner in remainder, an owner of a fee simple interest and an owner of a life interest.[1]

The unity of interest enjoyed by joint tenants means that a purchaser from joint tenants need investigate only one title. It also brings about the

---

14 The California Law Reform Commission, for instance, has castigated this aspect of joint tenancy law as 'anachronistic' and has pointed out that 'the existing rule gives the surviving joint tenant an unjustified windfall at the expense of the creditors of the deceased joint tenant'. The Commission recommended that unsecured creditors of a deceased joint tenant be allowed to reach into the severable share of the debtor to the extent that his estate is insufficient to meet their claims (*Recommendation Relating To Non-Probate Transfers*, 15 Cal Law Revision Commission Reports (1980), 1620f). This is the rule currently incorporated in the Uniform Probate Code, s 6-107.

15 'This analysis has perhaps attracted attention rather by reason of its captivating appearance of symmetry and exactness, than by reason of its practical utility' (*Challis*, p 367). The requirement of the 'four unities' has not been literally adhered to in other jurisdictions: see eg *Estate of Grigsby*, 184 Cal Rptr 886 at 889 (1982).

16 Post, p 303.

17 The implications of unity of possession for joint tenants are the same as those for tenants in common (post, p 303).

18 *Swartzbaugh v Sampson*, 54 P.2d 73 at 75 (1936).

19 Post, p 304.

20 See Domestic Violence and Matrimonial Proceedings Act 1976, ss 1(1), (2), 4(1); *Davis v Johnson* [1979] AC 264, 317.

1 *Bl Comm*, Vol II, p 181.

consequence that the full legal estate in jointly owned property cannot be conveyed to a third party without the active participation of all the joint tenants, all of whom must put their signature to the transfer document.[2] A purchaser of a legal estate owned by joint tenants cannot take an unimpaired title if he receives a conveyance from only one of the joint tenants, since the purchaser can readily see on the face of the vendor's title document an explicit reference to the existence of a joint tenancy. It is indeed the mandatory participation of all the joint tenants in effecting dispositions of the joint property which has led in recent years to the proposal that all matrimonial homes should automatically be held by way of joint tenancy between husband and wife.[3] Only in this way can the law ultimately remove the insecurity which affects the position of one spouse if his or her partner should attempt to deal with title unilaterally or become insolvent.

(iii) Unity of title   Unity of title entails that each joint tenant must derive his title to the land from the same act or document.[4] Joint tenants, it was always said, 'are in under the same feudal contract or investiture'.[5]

(iv) Unity of time   Unity of time expresses the idea that the interest of each joint tenant must normally vest at the same time.[6]

4. TENANCY IN COMMON

Tenancy in common is firmly to be distinguished from joint tenancy. It is frequently said that, unlike joint tenants, tenants in common hold land in 'undivided shares'. The phrase 'undivided shares' may seem confusing at first, since it appears to conjure up a picture of the amorphous undifferentiated co-ownership which characterises joint tenancy. However, the key to the distinction between joint tenancy and tenancy in common lies in the reference to the word 'shares'.[7] It is only in the tenancy in common that the co-owners hold distinct shares at all. It is only of tenants in common that it can be meaningful to say, for instance, that A has a one-quarter interest and B a three-quarters interest, or even that A and B are each entitled to a one-half share. The allocation of shares or proportions is not possible as between joint tenants, who are of course wholly entitled to the whole.[8] Tenants in common are however owners of distinct shares, albeit in property which has not yet been divided up physically. It is not possible to point to one parcel or area of the co-owned land

2   See, however, P.W. Smith, [1980] Conv 191.
3   Post, p 862.
4   *Bl Comm*, Vol II, p 181.
5   See R. Preston, *Essay on Abstracts of Title* (1824), Vol 2, p 62.
6   *Bl Comm*, Vol II, p 181.
7   See eg *Re Davies* [1950] 1 All ER 120 at 123.
8   'A joint interest in equal shares is a contradiction in terms; the words of severance create a tenancy in common' (*Cowcher v Cowcher* [1972] 1 WLR 425 at 430H per Bagnall J). See also *Malayan Credit Ltd v Jack Chia- M.P.H. Ltd* [1986] AC 549 at 559E-G; *Bl Comm*, Vol II, p 193 (...'joint tenants do not take by distinct halves or moieties..').

rather than any other as belonging to a particular tenant in common:[9] tenants in common own specific, but undivided, shares in the land.[10]

The principal characteristics of tenancy in common are two in number: (i) there is no right of survivorship as between tenants in common, and (ii) only unity of possession is required.

(1) There is no right of survivorship

No right of survivorship obtains between tenants in common. The size of each tenant in common's share is a fixed quantum which cannot be altered by reason of the death of any other tenant in common. In the absence of a right of survivorship, the share of each passes on his death either in accordance with the terms of his will (if he died testate) or according to the rules of intestate succession.

(2) Only unity of possession is required

Of the four unities required in joint tenancy only unity of possession is an essential constitutive element of tenancy in common.[11] Unity of interest is not required; it is for precisely this reason that it is possible for one tenant in common to own, say, a one-third share in the co-owned property while another tenant in common owns a two-thirds share. Nor is unity of title or unity of time essential; as has just been seen, it is possible for the share of a tenant in common to be transmitted by will or on an intestacy to some third party. However, unity of possession is an indispensable component of tenancy in common, for without it there would exist no co-ownership at all.[12] There would merely be separate ownership of physically distinct areas of land.

As is true in respect of joint tenants,[13] the unity of possession enjoyed by tenants in common entails that each tenant in common is as much entitled to possession of the co-owned land as is any other tenant in common.[14] No tenant in common may physically demarcate any part of that land as his to the exclusion of his brethren.[15] Instead, each tenant in common has 'a right to

9   Coke described the tenancy in common enjoyed by two co-owners as applying to property which is 'common to them both...and neither of them knoweth his Part in several' (*Co Litt*, p 189a). This was later amplified in Blackstone's statement that 'because none knoweth his own severalty...they all occupy promiscuously' (*Bl Comm*, Vol II, p 191).

10 The tenancy in common has become a pivotal concept in the legal structuring of condominium ownership. Under this (largely transatlantic) form of co-ownership it is usual for each condominium dweller to own a specific unit in fee simple, but to be a tenant in common with the other condominium dwellers in respect of shared areas and accessways. See J.E. Cribbet, *Condominium–Home Ownership For Megalopolis?*, 61 Mich LR 1207 at 1215 (1962-63).

11 *Bl Comm*, Vol II, p 191f.

12 *Bl Comm*, Vol II, p 192.

13 Ante, p 301.

14 *Wight v IRC* (1982) 264 Estates Gazette 935 at 936f; *Swartzbaugh v Sampson*, 54 P.2d 73 at 75 (1936); *Dimmick v Dimmick*, 24 Cal Rptr 856 at 858 (1962). Compare, however, *Chhokar v Chhokar* [1984] FLR 313 at 332D-F, where Cumming-Bruce LJ refused to allow a tenant in common to assert any right to occupy a house which was already occupied by a married woman and her family (post, p 821).

15 Perhaps the most bizarre circumstances in which this principle has been applied arose in *Galasso v Del Guercio*, 276 A.2d 186 at 189f (1971). Here the Superior Court of New Jersey was called upon to resolve a dispute between co-owners as to which family member should be laid to rest in precisely which location in the family mausoleum.

exercise acts of ownership over the whole property',[16] subject to the qualification that in so doing he must not interfere with the like right of any other co- owner.[17] It follows that no tenant in common has any right to demand compensation in respect of the simultaneous enjoyment of the land by a fellow tenant in common except where the latter has received 'more than comes to his just share or proportion'.[18] However, this notion of a 'just share or proportion' has been construed so widely that in practice there is now relatively little left of the original rule that unity of possession precludes compensation claims between co-owners. The implications of unity of possession must now be explored in greater detail.

(a) Occupation and use

At common law each tenant in common had 'a perfect right'[19] to possession of the entire property and to the 'use and enjoyment of it in a proper manner'.[20] This right, which existed irrespective of the quantum of the tenant in common's undivided share, was influential in fixing the degree of mutual tolerance which the law still requires of co-owners in their dealings inter se.[1]

(i) Trespass and ouster It is now settled law, for instance, that no action will lie in trespass against a tenant in common merely because he exclusively occupies and exploits one part rather than another of the co-owned property.[2] He is not thereby taking 'more than comes to his just share or proportion'. Thus in *Jacobs v Seward*,[3] for instance, the House of Lords rejected a claim in trespass based partly upon the allegation that one tenant in common had cut a crop of grass on the co-owned land. Lord Hatherley LC declared that it was 'idle to talk of

---

16 *Griffies v Griffies* (1863) 8 LT (NS) 758 per Kindersley V-C. See also *Flynn v United States*, 205 F.2d 756 at 760 (1953).
17 *Saulsberry v Saulsberry*, 121 F.2d 318 at 321 (1941); *Sayers v Pyland*, 161 SW.2d 769 at 773 (1942); *Stevahn v Meidinger*, 57 NW.2d 1 at 7 (1952); *Tompkins v Superior Court of City and County of San Francisco*, 27 Cal Rptr 889 at 892 (1963); *Nasti v Verderosa*, 342 NYS.2d 40 at 41 (1973); *Jemzura v Jemzura*, 330 NE.2d 414 at 419 (1975).
18 This formula was first used in a statute of 1705 (4 Anne, c16, s 27) which gave both the joint tenant and the tenant in common an action of account in respect of profits derived from undue exploitation of the co-owned land by another cotenant. This statute has now been repealed (see Law of Property (Amendment) Act 1924, Sch 10), but the idea persists that co-owners are accountable to each other if one of them should take 'more than his proper share' (*Bull v Bull* [1955] 1 QB 234 at 237 per Denning LJ). Even before the repeal, this notion was construed as referring not merely to the 'receipt of issues and profits' but more widely to any 'receiving' in excess of one's 'just share' (see *Henderson v Eason* (1851) 17 QB 701 at 719, 117 ER 1451 at 1457).
19 *Henderson v Eason* (1851) 17 QB 701 at 720, 117 ER 1451 at 1458 per Parke B.
20 *Bull v Bull* [1955] 1 QB 234 at 237 per Denning LJ. The insistence upon use 'in a proper manner' is an echo of Lord Hatherley LC's statement in *Jacobs v Seward* (1872) LR 5 HL 464 at 474, that no action will lie against a tenant in common if he uses the co-owned property 'in an ordinary and legitimate way' or for 'a perfectly legitimate purpose'. It is less clear, however, whether Denning LJ was correct in thinking that the old authorities concerning tenancy in common at law are equally applicable after 1925 to tenancy in common in equity (post, p 374).
1 Post, p 308.
2 *Co Litt*, p 199b; *Bl Comm*, Vol II, pp 183, 194.
3 (1872) LR 5 HL 464 at 473.

trespass as a consequence of a man making hay upon his own field—for it is his own—or a moiety of it at least, and no definite portion of it is mapped out as his moiety.'[4]

A remedy for trespass is available against a tenant in common only in cases of 'ouster',[5] it being likewise settled law that no tenant in common may go so far as to turn another cotenant out of the property.[6] Moreover, the term 'ouster' is wide enough to cover not merely cases in which one tenant evicts or excludes another from the land,[7] but also those cases where he otherwise interferes with the common enjoyment of that land.[8] For the purpose of establishing trespass, however, this interference must be such as to tend towards the destruction of the co-owned property in its original form.[9] As Lord Hatherley LC pointed out in *Jacobs v Seward*,[10] 'where the act done by the tenant in common is right in itself, and nothing is done which destroys the benefit of the other tenant in common in the property, there no action will lie, because he can follow that property as long as it is in existence and not destroyed.'

(ii) Other forms of liability   It is possible that two other forms of claim may arise from an illegitimate user exercised by a tenant in common on the co-owned land. There appears to be no reason why the tort of nuisance cannot be alleged

4   However, as Lord Hatherley (at 474) and Lord Westbury (at 478) both conceded, there may have been a legitimate case for an accounting in respect of the profit made from the harvesting of the hay (post, p 307). See also *Harper v O'Neal*, 363 So.2d 930 at 932 (1978). It is clear beyond doubt that the harvesting co-owner cannot be guilty of theft (see *State v McCoy* (1883) NC 466; Annot, 17 ALR.3d 1394 at 1396).
5   *Co Litt*, p 199b; *Bl Comm*, Vol II, p 194; *Jacobs v Seward* (1872) LR 5 HL 464 at 472, 478. See also *Stedman v Smith* (1857) 8 E & B 1 at 6, 120 ER 1 at 3. Although the early cases often speak only of 'actual' ouster, it is probable that an action in trespass will lie even where the ouster is 'constructive', as for instance where an innocent tenant in common is just as surely caused— albeit by indirect means—to leave the co-owned property (see *Dennis v McDonald* [1982] Fam 63 at 70C, 71D). However, it seems that a statement by one tenant to the effect that the other tenant could leave if she did not like his behaviour does not constitute constructive ouster (*Diotallevi v Diotallevi* (1982) 134 DLR (3d) 477 at 479). See also *Spiller v Mackereth*, 334 So.2d 859 at 862 (1976).
6   *Bull v Bull* [1955] 1 QB 234 at 237 per Denning LJ. See also *Smith v United States*, 153 F.2d 655 at 661 (1946); *Zaslow v Kroenert*, 176 P.2d 1 at 5 (1946).
7   See *Bull v Bull* [1955] 1 QB 234 at 237. In *Jacobs v Seward* (1872) LR 5 HL 464 at 473, 477f, the House of Lords held that the mere putting of a lock upon a gate by one tenant in common could not constitute 'ouster', unless there was direct evidence that by this means another tenant in common had been intentionally denied entry. See also *Spiller v Mackereth*, 334 So.2d 859 at 862 (1976), but compare *Zaslow v Kroenert*, 176 P.2d 1 at 5f (1946), where there was manifest evidence of an intention to exclude the other cotenant, not least in the form of a change of locks and the prominent display of 'no trespassing' notices. For the suggestion that 'ouster' can occur where one co-owner unilaterally leases the property to a stranger, see *Oates v Oates* [1949] SASR 37 at 40.
8   See eg *Stedman v Smith* (1857) 8 E & B 1 at 7, 120 ER 1 at 3. Here D rested part of the roof of his wash-house on the top of a dividing wall which he co-owned with P. P was held to have been 'excluded from the top of the wall: he might have wished to train fruit trees there, or to amuse himself [sic] by running along the top of the wall'). See also *De La Cuesta v Bazzi*, 118 P.2d 909 at 915 (1941).
9   *Cubitt v Porter* (1828) 8 B & C 257 at 268, 108 ER 1039 at 1043.
10   (1872) LR 5 HL 464 at 475. The required degree of 'ouster' was not found either in *Cubitt v Porter* (destruction of old wall and building of new and better wall) or in *Ferguson v Miller* [1978] 1 NZLR 819 at 825. For an example of 'ouster' by destruction of the common property, see *Wilkinson v Haygarth* (1847) 12 QB 837 at 845, 116 ER 1085 at 1088 (removal of turf).

by one tenant in common against another,[11] although it may sometimes be difficult to prove that the alleged interference with the plaintiff's beneficial use of the land is sufficiently severe to meet the criterion of 'unreasonableness' which is constitutive of the tort.[12] It is also possible that one co-owner may be guilty of 'voluntary waste' by reason of his activity on the co-owned land,[13] but again it is both necessary and difficult to demonstrate that the activity in question has tended to the destruction of the property.[14] However, where waste is proved, the remedy for the other co-owner may take the form of either an action of account[15] or an injunction[16] or both.

(b) Rents and profits received from a stranger

If a tenant in common is not himself in occupation of the land, he is entitled to share in any rents and profits derived from the land (eg by way of a lucrative letting to a stranger). His rights in this respect are measured in strict proportion to the quantum of his individual share as a tenant in common,[17] so that, for instance, a tenant in common of a one- third interest is entitled to receive one third of the net rents and profits derived from the co-owned property.[18]

Tenants in common are liable to account inter se in respect of any income received by one tenant from a stranger in excess of his own 'just share or proportion'.[19] However, this liability to account applies only to actual (rather than constructive) receipts of income drawn from the property. Tenants in common are not fiduciaries one for another;[20] nor is their relationship one of

11   It is no longer thought to be essential to a successful claim of nuisance that the user complained of should have emanated from land other than that of the plaintiff (see eg *Hargrave v Goldman* (1963) 110 CLR 40 at 60; *Clearlite Holdings Ltd v Auckland City Corporation* [1976] 2 NZLR 729 at 736).

12   See eg *Ferguson v Miller* [1978] 1 NZLR 819 at 828, where McMullin J declined to apply the term 'nuisance' to a property developer's proposal to widen a carriageway on a co-owned access strip and resurface the accessway in permanent materials.

13   *Co Litt*, p 200b.

14   In *Ferguson v Miller* [1978] 1 NZLR 819 at 826, McMullin J considered the proposed development to be 'an act of repair rather than an act of waste.' See also *Jacobs v Seward* (1872) LR 5 HL 464, where the allegation of waste seems not even to have been raised.

15   *Sayers v Pyland*, 161 SW.2d 769 at 771f (1942).

16   See *The Durham and Sunderland Railway Co v Wawn* (1841) 3 Beav 119 at 123, 49 ER 47 at 48; *Foshee v Foshee*, 143 So.2d 301 at 303f (1962), 177 So.2d 99 at 101 (1965).

17   *Henderson v Eason* (1851) 17 QB 701 at 719, 117 ER 1451 at 1458.

18   However, the rents and profits shared in this way must be carefully confined to 'those receipts which can properly be regarded as rents and revenue of the common property itself as distinct from profits which the defendant [who ran a caravan park] may have made by his use and occupation of the common property (eg fees for services and for use of items of equipment)' (*Squire v Rogers* (1979-80) 27 ALR 330 at 345).

19   *Henderson v Eason* (1851) 17 QB 701 at 719, 117 ER 1451 at 1457f; *Kennedy v De Trafford* [1897] AC 180 at 187; *Bernard v Josephs* [1982] Ch 391 at 401C, 410B; *Chhokar v Chhokar* [1984] FLR 313 at 332G. See also *Zanzonico v Zanzonico*, 2 A.2d 597 at 598 (1938); *Rehfuss v McAndrew*, 33 So.2d 16 at 17 (1947); *American Oil Service v Hope Oil Co*, 15 Cal Rptr 209 at 214 (1961); *Jeffress v Piatt*, 370 SW.2d 383 at 386 (1963); *Squire v Rogers* (1979-80) 27 ALR 330 at 345. A co-owner's right to recover a share of rents and profits does not generate for him a lien for that sum upon the co-owned land (see *Brickwood v Young* (1905) 2 CLR 387 at 398; 86 CJS 417f).

20   *Kennedy v De Trafford* [1897] AC 180 at 189. See also *Pure Oil Co v Byrnes*, 57 NE.2d 356 at 361 (1944); *Taylor v Brindley*, 164 F.2d 235 at 240 (1947); *Britton v Green*, 325 F.2d 377 at 383 (1963). In spite of this basic statement of principle, it has sometimes been argued that the legal control of co-ownership relations has developed to the point where cotenants stand in a position tantamount to a fiduciary nexus (see D. Weible, *Accountability of Cotenants*, 29 Iowa LR 558 at 590 (1943-44); 86 CJS 377).

partnership or agency.[1] Even if one tenant in common is left to manage the property, he is under no duty to extract the maximum (or indeed any) rental value from the property.[2] There is therefore no liability to account for such rents or profits as might have been (but were not in fact) derived from prudent letting of the land to an outsider.[3]

(c) Profit derived from industry of one tenant in common

A different problem arises where one tenant in common enjoys sole occupation of the co- owned land and derives a profit or income from that land by reason of his own exertions.

(i) Legitimate profit

In *Henderson v Eason*,[4] Parke B thought that in many such instances it would be 'impossible' to say that the occupying co-owner 'has received more than comes to his just share.' He held that there is no liability to account for profits where a co-owner 'employs his capital and industry in cultivating the whole of a piece of land...in a mode in which the money and labour expended greatly exceed the value of the rent or compensation for the mere occupation of the land.'[5] In a 'hazardous venture' undertaken under such circumstances,[6] the risk of which is entirely his own,[7] the co-owner is entitled to retain all the produce of the venture.[8] In a spirited endorsement of free

1 *Leigh v Dickeson* (1884-85) 15 QBD 60 at 65. Of course, if there exists between the co- owners an agreement akin to partnership, under which one co-owner undertakes to manage the property for the common benefit, then there may arise a liability for 'wilful default' (see *Henderson v Eason* (1851) 17 QB 701 at 718f, 117 ER 1451 at 1457).

2 Nor, in the absence of agreement, may a co-owner demand any fee for his personal services in managing the property (see *Kahnovsky v Kahnovsky*, 21 A.2d 569 at 573 (1941); *Curl v Neilson*, 167 P.2d 320 at 322f (1946); *Combs v Ritter*, 223 P.2d 505 at 506 (1950); *Lewis v Latham*, 79 So.2d 811 at 814 (1955); *In Re Estate and Guardianship of Purton*, 441 P.2d 561 at 570 (1968); *Neal v Neal*, 470 SW.2d 383 at 386f (1971)).

3 *Wheeler v Horne* (1740) Willes 208 at 210, 125 ER 1135 at 1136; *Henderson v Eason* (1851) 17 QB 701 at 718f, 117 ER 1451 at 1457. In *Chhokar v Chhokar* [1984] FLR 313 at 332F, the wife was not required to account for any notional rent which she should have derived from her husband whom she allowed to live with her in the co-owned property. (Presumably the husband could have claimed that he was merely exercising his statutory rights of occupation under what is now the Matrimonial Homes Act 1983 (post, p 782)). See also *Boulter v Boulter* (1898) 19 LR (NSW) Eq 135 at 138f; *In Re Tolman's Estate* (1928) 23 Tas LR 29 at 31; *Thompson v Flynn*, 58 P.2d 769 at 771 (1936); *Mastbaum v Mastbaum*, 9 A.2d 51 at 54 (1939); *Riechmann v Riechmann*, 283 NE.2d 734 at 736 (1972); *Thrift v Thrift* (1976) 10 ALR 332 at 339.

4 (1851) 17 QB 701 at 720, 117 ER 1451 at 1458.

5 (1851) 17 QB 701 at 720f, 117 ER 1451 at 1458.

6 Parke B gave the example of cultivating hops. Compare, however, *Jacobs v Seward* (1872) LR 5 HL 464 at 474, 478. Here the cultivation of hay was considered not to be sufficiently hazardous, nor the investment of personal energy so excessive, as to exclude a liability to account, although Lord Hatherley LC conceded (at 476) that any expense incurred in making the hay would have to be allowed for in the accounting.

7 Parke B pointed out that 'if the speculation had been a losing one altogether, he could not have called for a moiety of the losses, as he would have been enabled to do had [the land] been cultivated by the mutual agreement of the cotenants' ((1851) 17 QB 701 at 721, 117 ER 1451 at 1458). For further reference to the profit-sharing implications of a risk- sharing agreement between co-owners, see *Anon* (1684) Skin 230, 90 ER 106.

8 This approach, correlating profit with risk, has been applied fairly widely to farming operations conducted by one co-owner (see eg *Swartzbaugh v Sampson*, 54 P.2d 73 at 75 (1936); *Black v Black*, 204 P.2d 950 at 953 (1949); *Reid v Reid* (1978) 87 DLR (3d) 370 at 372).

enterprise capitalism, Parke B concluded that the co-owner, in taking all the 'fructus industriales', receives in truth merely 'the return for his own capital and labour, to which his cotenant has no right.'[9] This statement almost certainly still represents good law, at least so long as the co-owner's activities have caused no long-term destruction of the revenue potential or capital value of the land.

(ii) Liability to account　In *Henderson v Eason* there is a clear implication that there may be some cases in which a co-owner will indeed have received more than his 'just share or proportion', even though his profit derives from engaging his own personal efforts in productive use of the co-owned land.[10] For instance, a co-owner may, by his industrious exploitation of the common land, have exhausted or diminished the capital value of the property through activities such as mining, quarrying or oil drilling.[11] Here, even though the co-owner has invested his own energy and risk-capital, he cannot retain the entire profit himself but must submit to a fair accounting with his cotenants.[12] His liability to account is not affected by the fact that he did not in any way exclude his cotenants from similar exploitation of the resource or even that he did not extract any more than his proportionate share of that resource.[13]

(d) Rent obligations as between tenants in common

It is often said that in the absence of agreement[14] no rent obligation can normally arise as between co-owners by reason merely of the fact that one tenant in common may happen to enjoy sole occupation of the entire co-owned property.[15]

(i) The general principle　Since tenants in common (and, for that matter, joint tenants) enjoy unity of possession, each is equally entitled with his brethren to

---

9　See also *Pico v Columbet*, 12 Cal 414 at 421. For a modern (and very similar) defence of the same approach, see L. Berger, *An Analysis of the Economic Relations between Cotenants*, 21 Arizona LR 1015 (1979).
10　See eg *Jacobs v Seward* (1872) LR 5 HL 464.
11　Such activities may technically constitute waste (see 86 CJS 420). In Britain the ownership of petroleum reserves is vested by statute in the Crown (ante, p 26).
12　*Payne v Callahan*, 99 P.2d 1050 at 1057 (1940). Such accounting relates only to the net profit derived from the operation. It allows the entrepreneur-cotenant reimbursement of the reasonable and necessary expenses incurred in extraction and marketing (see *Cox v Davison*, 397 SW.2d 200 at 203 (1965); *P & N Investment Corp v Florida Ranchettes Inc*, 220 So.2d 451 at 454 (1968)) and recognises his right to 'reasonable compensation' for his personal services (see *White v Smyth*, 214 SW.2d 967 at 975 (1948)).
13　*White v Smyth*, 214 SW.2d 967 at 975 (1948) (Supreme Court of Texas).
14　*M'Mahon v Burchell* (1846) 2 Ph 127 at 135f, 41 ER 889 at 893; 1 Coop T Cott 457 at 475, 47 ER 944 at 951; *Henderson v Eason* (1851) 17 QB 701 at 720, 117 ER 1451 at 1458; *Roberts v Roberts*, 150 SW.2d 236 at 237 (1941).
15　*M'Mahon v Burchell* (1846) 2 Ph 127 at 135, 41 ER 889 at 893; 1 Coop T Cott 457 at 475, 47 ER 944 at 951; *Kennedy v De Trafford* [1897] AC 180 at 190f; *Jones (A.E.) v Jones (F.W.)* [1977] 1 WLR 438 at 443B. See (1978) 41 MLR 208 at 209 (J. Alder). See also *In Re Randall's Estate*, 132 P.2d 763 at 766 (1942); *Rehfuss v McAndrew*, 33 So.2d 16 at 17 (1947); *Goforth v Ellis*, 300 SW.2d 379 at 383 (1957); *Baird v Moore*, 141 A.2d 324 at 329 (1958); *Parceluk v Knudtson*, 139 NW.2d 864 at 873 (1966); *Hunter v Schultz*, 49 Cal Rptr 315 at 319f (1966); *Seesholts v Beers*, 270 So.2d 434 at 436 (1972).

physical possession of the property.[16] The traditional view is that no tenant in common should be charged a rent for the sole enjoyment of that which is his 'perfect right' and which the other tenant or tenants in common are likewise free to enjoy.[17] The unilateral decision of one co-owner to vacate the land should not 'change his status into that of a landlord over the remaining cotenant in possession.'[18]

(ii) The proliferation of exceptions There have always been several exceptions to the basic principle of rent-immunity between co-owners. These categories of exception overlap to some extent, but all involve some trauma in the personal or family relationship of the co-owners. An occupation rent is payable, for instance, by a tenant in common whose sole occupation is achieved by the ouster or violent exclusion of another tenant in common.[19] A rent obligation may also be imposed by a court on or pending the granting of a divorce.[20] Alternatively, a rent liability may arise on the termination of a personal relationship in circumstances where it has become 'unreasonable' to expect continued joint occupation.[1] These circumstances of exception have so proliferated that in *Chhokar v Chhokar*[2] the Court of Appeal simply took the view that nowadays the proper test in determining the applicability of an occupation rent is whether the imposition of such an obligation upon a co-owner would be 'fair'.[3]

The exceptions to the principle of rent-immunity between co-owners have now become so numerous that the prima facie position today may well be that rent should be paid. In *Dennis v McDonald*,[4] for instance, Purchas J, in summarising the caselaw, pointed out that '[o]nly in cases where the tenants in common not in occupation were in a position to enjoy their right to occupy but chose not to do so voluntarily, and were not excluded by any relevant factor, would the tenant in common in occupation be entitled to do so free of liability to pay an occupation rent.' It appears, moreover, that the courts have

16   *Jacobs v Seward* (1872) LR 5 HL 464 at 473; *Bull v Bull* [1955] 1 QB 234 at 237.
17   *Henderson v Eason* (1851) 17 QB 701 at 720, 117 ER 1451 at 1458 per Parke B. See also *Griffies v Griffies* (1863) 8 LT (NS) 758; *McCormick v McCormick* [1921] NZLR 384 at 385; *Thompson v Flynn*, 58 P.2d 769 at 771 (1936); *Reid v Reid* (1978) 87 DLR (3d) 370 at 372.
18   *Seesholts v Beers*, 270 So.2d 434 at 437 (1972) per Walden J.
19   *Jones(A.E.) v Jones (F.W.)* [1977] 1 WLR 438 at 442B; *Dennis v McDonald* [1982] Fam 63 at 71D, 80A; *Bernard v Josephs* [1982] Ch 391 at 401B, 409B. See also *Mastron v Cotton* [1926] 1 DLR 767 at 768; *Luke v Luke* (1936) 36 SR (NSW) 310 at 314; *Szuba v Szuba* [1951] OWN 61 at 63; *Brunscher v Reagh*, 330 P.2d 396 at 398 (1958); *Lawrence v Lawrence*, 329 SW.2d 416 at 419f (1959); *Heyse v Heyse*, 176 NW.2d 316 at 320 (1970); *Palmer v Protrka*, 476 P.2d 185 at 190 (1970); *Spiller v Mackereth*, 334 So.2d 859 at 862 (1976); *Roberts v Roberts*, 584 P.2d 378 at 380 (1978).
20   See eg *Bedson v Bedson* [1965] 2 QB 666 at 682F; *Harvey v Harvey* [1982] Fam 83 at 89B; [1982] CLJ 228 at 230; *Brown v Brown* (1981) *Times*, 11 December.
1   *Cousins v Dzosens* (1981) *Times*, 12 December. See also *Bernard v Josephs* [1982] Ch 391 at 405F.
2   [1984] FLR 313 at 332E per Cumming-Bruce LJ.
3   The criterion of 'simple fairness' as the determinant of rent obligations between co-owners had already been propounded in New Zealand (see *Mayo v Mayo* [1966] NZLR 849 at 851). In *Chhokar* the Court considered it unfair to burden a wife with a rent obligation in favour of another tenant in common who had acted with 'moral turpitude' in conspiring with her husband to evict her from the matrimonial home (post, p 821).
4   [1982] Fam 63 at 71A-B.

frequently imposed a rent obligation on a sole occupier effectively as a condition of postponing a sale to which another co-owner would otherwise be entitled.[5] Likewise a co-owner who claims credit for improvements, repairs or other outgoings paid on the co-owned property may have to give credit for a notional rent to be assessed in respect of any sole occupation which he has enjoyed.[6]

(iii) Quantification of rent liability   There is a tendency in all cases to calculate the rent payable either on the analogy of a 'fair rent' for Rent Act purposes[7] or on the basis of a rough equation that any payment of mortgage interest by the sole occupier approximates to the appropriate rent.[8] It is perhaps worth pausing to reflect that the introduction of a periodic money liability between co-owners may compulsorily create between them a relationship of landlord and tenant,[9] with consequences under the Rent Act 1977 and the Supplementary Benefits Act 1976 which can only be described as interesting.[10]

The precise rationale for the payment of rent, particularly in cases of ouster, is increasingly unclear, although this uncertainty may have an impact upon the calculation of the amount payable. In *Dennis v McDonald*,[11] Purchas J envisaged the payment of rent as compensation to the non-occupying co-owner in respect of the *advantage* derived by the other co-owner from his sole occupation. However, the Court of Appeal in the same case[12] preferred to see the payment of rent more in terms of compensation for the *detriment* suffered by the ousted co-owner in consequence of the occupying co-owner's failure to discharge 'in due order' the trust behind which the co-ownership existed.[13] The distinction may appear insignificant, but the theory that rent is compensation payable by a trustee to a beneficiary was regarded by the Court of Appeal as rendering irrelevant the purpose to which the trustee then puts the property.[14] In particular, it meant that no deduction from the rent payable should be

5   The potential to do so was pointed out in *Dennis v McDonald* [1982] Fam 63 at 74A, and *Bernard v Josephs* [1982] Ch 391 at 411C, and appears to have been realised in practice in *Bedson v Bedson* [1965] 2 QB 666 at 682F, 683C; *Eves v Eves* [1975] 1 WLR 1338 at 1343A; *Cousins v Dzosens* (1981) *Times*, 12 December. See J.E. Martin, [1982] Conv 305 at 309.
6   Post, p 313.
7   *Dennis v McDonald* [1982] Fam 63 at 75E per Purchas J, 82A per Sir John Arnold P.
8   See eg *Leake v Bruzzi* [1974] 1 WLR 1528 at 1533B, H; *Suttill v Graham* [1977] 1 WLR 819 at 822C, 823H; *Bernard v Josephs* [1982] Ch 391 at 401B, 405G. In *Dennis v McDonald* [1982] Fam 63 at 75C, Purchas J rejected the suggestion that the occupation rent should be a rack rent, assessed in relation to half of the value of the capital asset, because 'this was not the concept behind an occupation rent.'
9   Post, p 431. For a denial that there is 'in reality' a tenancy here, see *Dennis v McDonald* [1982] Fam 63 at 81C per Sir John Arnold P.
10 It is perhaps for this reason that the courts have often been at pains to stress that the payments ordered do not strictly constitute an occupation 'rent' (see *Dennis v McDonald* [1982] Fam 63 at 81A; *Harvey v Harvey* [1982] Fam 83 at 89B). In *Dennis v McDonald* [1982] Fam 63 at 75E, Purchas J analysed the position of the rent-paying sole occupier as comprising a 'right to occupy the property akin to the sort of protection given to a protected tenant.'
11 [1982] Fam 63 at 70ff.
12 [1982] Fam 63 at 80G, 81F.
13 There is discussion in Chapter 12 (post, p 358) of the way in which the 1925 legislation generally superimposed a trust for sale upon the phenomenon of co-ownership.
14 [1982] Fam 63 at 81A. The 'breach of trust' approach may also create difficulties if the non-occupying co-owner was the sole trustee of the legal estate. See R. Schuz, (1982) 12 Family Law 108 at 114.

allowed merely on the ground that the payer was providing a home for the children of both co-owners.[15] Such a deduction would have been more appropriate on the former view, which fastens on the net advantage derived by the occupying co-owner in the totality of the circumstances.[16]

(e) Liability for repairs and improvements

The question sometimes arises whether any liability exists between co-owners in respect of moneys voluntarily expended by one co-owner on the repair or permanent improvement of the co- owned property.[17] The problems raised by such expenditure are complex, particularly in the case of tenancy in common, which is 'a tenure of an inconvenient nature, and...is unfit for persons who cannot agree amongst themselves.'[18]

(i) The general principle   The general principle applicable in this context was stated in *Leigh v Dickeson*.[19] Here the Court of Appeal held that no co-owner has the right to demand a contribution from his cotenants towards expenses which he has properly but voluntarily incurred in respect of repairs or improvements to the co-owned property.[20] However, this immunity from arbitrary calls for contribution does not avail the other co-owners if the repairs or improvements were effected by agreement with them[1] or at their express or implied request.[2] Nor does any immunity apply if the work was done pursuant to an existing obligation to a third party binding all the co-owners to maintain or repair their

---

15   [1982] Fam 63 at 80B-C.
16   For approval of the approach of Purchas J in preference to that of the Court of Appeal, see R. Schuz, *loc cit*, at 114; R. Cocks, *Co-ownership, Rights of Occupation and Obscurity*, [1984] Conv 198 at 205.
17   The payment of other forms of outgoings on the property (eg instalments payments under a mortgage) may raise similar questions as to the allowance of credits between co-owners (see *Leake v Bruzzi* [1974] 1 WLR 1528 at 1533B, H; *Suttill v Graham* [1977] 1 WLR 819 at 822C, 823H). Improvements made by spouses are singled out for special statutory treatment (see Matrimonial Proceedings and Property Act 1970, s 37, post, p 809).
18   *Leigh v Dickeson* (1884-85) 15 QBD 60 at 69 per Lindley LJ.
19   (1884-85) 15 QBD 60. This decision was in its turn confirmed and applied by the Australian High Court in *Brickwood v Young* (1905) 2 CLR 387 at 394f, 400. See also *Miller v Prater*, 100 SW.2d 842 at 844 (1937); *Lewis v Latham*, 79 So.2d 811 at 814 (1955); *Cox v Davison*, 397 SW.2d 200 at 201 (1965); *Cummings v Anderson*, 614 P.2d 1283 at 1287 (1980).
20   'If the law were otherwise, a part-owner might be compelled to incur expense against his will: a house might be situate in a decaying borough, and it might be thought by one co- owner that it would be better not to repair it' (*Leigh v Dickeson* (1884-85) 15 QBD 60 at 65 per Brett MR). Compare the law in many jurisdictions in the United States, where there is power to demand contributions from cotenants in respect of repairs which are absolutely necessary, although there is no similar liability in respect of permanent improvements (see 48A CJS 364, 86 CJS 445, 449f).
 1   *Anon* (1684) Skin 230, 90 ER 106; *Leigh v Dickeson* (1884-85) 15 QBD 60 at 64. See also *In re Holyman* (1935) 30 Tas LR 15 at 26, 29f; *Collier v Collier*, 242 P.2d 537 at 542 (1952); *Ruptash and Lumsden v Zawick* [1956] 2 DLR (2d) 145 at 158; *Young v Young*, 376 A.2d 1151 at 1157 (1977). However, a covenant by one co-owner to share the cost of repairs or improvements, being a positive covenant, does not run with the land to affect the covenantor's successors in title (post, p 695). See *Ruptash and Lumsden v Zawick* [1956] 2 DLR (2d) 145 at 160 (Supreme Court of Canada).
 2   *Leigh v Dickeson* (1884-85) 15 QBD 60 at 64, 66. It seems that a request or agreement will not be implied merely from the making of improvements or from their necessity or utility (*Young v McKittrick*, 267 Ill App 267).

property.[3] In such cases there is, of course, an immediate contractual liability to contribute towards the costs incurred.

Moreover, although it is impossible for a co-owner to assert an immediate and active entitlement to reimbursement as an independent head of claim against his cotenants,[4] a claim for contribution towards necessary expenditure gives rise to an 'equity' which may be vindicated defensively[5] by that co-owner when the value of the property is eventually realised or distributed between the cotenants.[6] In other words, a proportionate part of the money laid out by one co-owner on repair or improvement may be recovered later, usually from the proceeds of sale of the property, thus effectively sharing between all the co-owners the cost of any repair or improvement which has resulted in an enhanced sale price.[7] The rationale underlying this rule of reimbursement seems to be the prevention of unjust enrichment of other co-owners,[8] but this principle has no application where there was a clear intention to make a gift to the other co-owners of the value of the repair or improvement.[9]

It seems that this passive or dormant equity is available not only to a tenant in common but also to a joint tenant.[10] Thus any co-owner who is out of pocket may subsequently assert a lien upon the property (or the fund representing it) for the value of his repairs or improvements.[11] The equity of reimbursement which arises here does not immediately constitute a lien on the property, but comprises simply a right to have a lien decreed in respect of a co-owner's interest when the value of that property is ultimately realised or distributed

3   *Leigh v Dickeson* (1884-85) 15 QBD 60 at 66 per Cotton LJ. There is an indirect liability to contribute if the work was done by a co-owner who was also a trustee acting in the proper discharge of his duties (see *Gross v French* (1975) 238 Estates Gazette 39 at 41). The old writ *de reparatione facienda* (*Co Litt*, p 200b) seems to have been available only in the context of an existing obligation to third parties (see *Leigh v Dickeson* (1884-85) 15 QBD 60 at 67, 68f).

4   *Leigh v Dickeson* (1884-85) 15 QBD 60 at 65, 66; *Brickwood v Young* (1905) 2 CLR 387 at 395; *Squire v Rogers* (1979-80) 27 ALR 330 at 346.

5   For the original reference to a 'defensive' equity, see *Brickwood v Young* (1905) 2 CLR 387 at 395, 397.

6   *Leigh v Dickeson* (1884-85) 15 QBD 60 at 65, 67, 69; *In re Jones* [1893] 2 Ch 461 at 476; *In re Cook's Mortgage* [1896] 1 Ch 923 at 925; *Mayes v Mayes* (1969) 210 Estates Gazette 935 at 938; *Gross v French* (1976) 238 Estates Gazette 39 at 41; *Brickwood v Young* (1905) 2 CLR 387 at 395, 399; *Noack v Noack* [1959] VR 137 at 142f, 146.

7   '[O]ne party cannot take the increase in value, without making an allowance for what has been expended in order to obtain that increased value; in fact, the execution of the repairs and improvements is adopted and sanctioned by accepting the increased value' (*Leigh v Dickeson* (1884-85) 15 QBD 60 at 67).

8   See *Swan v Swan* (1820) 8 Price 518 at 519, 146 ER 1281; *Boulter v Boulter* (1898) 19 LR (NSW) Eq 135 at 137; *Re Byrne* (1906) 6 SR (NSW) 532 at 536; *Cummings v Anderson*, 614 P.2d 1283 at 1287f (1980).

9   *Noack v Noack* [1959] VR 137 at 146 (Full Court): 'No principle of equity can be invoked to recall a gift once made'.

10 *Re Byrne* (1906) 6 SR (NSW) 532 at 536. See also *Noack v Noack* [1959] VR 137 at 143, 146. Profound difficulties will, however, attach to any attempt to claim this equity on behalf of a deceased joint tenant, since it would involve 'a claim against an estate in which the joint tenant's interest had entirely ceased' (*Re Byrne* (1906) 6 SR (NSW) 532 at 536f). See D. Mendes da Costa, (1961-62) 3 Melbourne ULR 137 at 146, but compare *Isaryk v Isaryk* [1955] OWN 487 at 489, where the extinction of a joint tenant's interest on death was not thought to preclude his estate from recovering from a cotenant an excess over the latter's just share of rents and profits arising from the land, provided that action for such recovery was brought within the appropriate limitation period.

11 *Brickwood v Young* (1905) 2 CLR 387 at 397.

amongst all the co-owners.[12] The better view is that the measure of compensation in such cases should be related to the actual increment in value conferred on the property by the work done, rather than to the cost of doing the work.[13] On any footing, it is probably the case that minor refurbishments are to be completely disregarded on the ground that they are merely 'in the nature of ordinary maintenance' and thus do not constitute a permanent improvement of the realty.[14]

(ii) Equitable counterclaims There is an important limitation on the right of a co-owner to assert an 'equity' based on expenditure on repairs or improvements effected by him. Such a claim is normally allowable only if he submits to payment of an occupation rent in respect of any sole occupation enjoyed by him[15] or if he accounts for any rents and profits which he may have derived from lettings of the land.[16] The relevant principle here seems to be that he who comes to equity must himself do equity.[17] Thus, when the value of the co-owned land is finally distributed amongst the co-owners, there must be a counter-balancing of various types of income and expenditure connected with that land. Only in this way can it be ensured that each co-owner receives no

---

12 See *Mayes v Mayes* (1969) 210 Estates Gazette 935 at 938; *Gross v French* (1975) 238 Estates Gazette 39 at 41; *Dietsch v Long*, 43 NE.2d 906 at 916f (1942); *Ruptash and Lumsden v Zawick* [1956] 2 DLR (2d) 145 at 159 (SCC); *Canada Life Assurance Co v Kennedy* (1978) 89 DLR (3d) 397 at 401.

13 *Parker v Trigg* (1884) WN 27 at 28; *Watson v Gass* (1881-82) 45 LT (NS) 582 at 585; *Williams v Williams* (1899-1900) 81 LT (NS) 163; *Gross v French* (1975) 238 Estates Gazette 39 at 41; *Brickwood v Young* (1905) 2 CLR 387 at 398; *Mastin v Mastin's Administrator*, 50 SW.2d 77 at 79 (1932); *Noack v Noack* [1959] VR 137 at 146. Compare, however, the more restrictive view that compensation should be limited to the amount of the actual expenditure or the extent of the increment in value generated by that expenditure, whichever is the lesser figure (*In re Jones* [1893] 2 Ch 461 at 479; *In re Cook's Mortgage* [1896] 1 Ch 923 at 925; *Boulter v Boulter* (1898) 19 LR (NSW) Eq 135 at 137; *McMahon v The Public Curator of Queensland* [1952] St R Qd 197 at 202f (although here the court was prepared to allow the 'present day equivalent in value of the sums of money actually expended...in making the improvements')).

14 *McMahon v The Public Curator of Queensland* [1952] St R Qd 197 at 204 (painting of house).

15 Ante, p 310. See *Pascoe v Swan* (1859) 27 Beav 508 at 509, 54 ER 201 at 202; *Teasdale v Sanderson* (1864) 33 Beav 534, 55 ER 476; *Williams v Williams* (1899-1900) 81 LT (NS) 163; *McCormick v McCormick* [1921] NZLR 384 at 387f per Salmond J; *Roberts v Roberts*, 150 SW.2d 236 at 238 (1941); *Carkeek v Tate-Jones* [1971] VR 691 at 702f; *Reid v Reid* (1978) 87 DLR (3d) 370 at 372.

16 *Attorney-General v Magdalen College, Oxford* (1854) 18 Beav 223 at 255, 52 ER 88 at 100; *Pascoe v Swan* (1859) 27 Beav 508 at 509, 54 ER 201 at 202; *In Re Jones* [1893] 2 Ch 461 at 478; *Williams v Williams* (1899-1900) 81 LT (NS) 163; *Brickwood v Young* (1905) 2 CLR 387 at 398, 401; *Mastin v Mastin's Administrator*, 50 SW.2d 77 at 79 (1932). The offsetting of improvement costs in an accounting in respect of rents and profits provides an example of the case referred to by Brett MR in *Leigh v Dickeson* (1884-85) 15 QBD 60 at 64f: 'Sometimes money has been expended for the benefit of another person under such circumstances that an option is allowed to him to adopt or decline the benefit: in this case, if he exercises his option to adopt the benefit, he will be liable to repay the money expended...' (see *Squire v Rogers* (1979-80) 27 ALR 330 at 348). Yet because the taking of reciprocal accounts falls so clearly within the jurisdiction of equity, the approach of the courts is flexible and is heavily determined by notions of simple fairness (see eg *Baird v Moore*, 141 A.2d 324 at 330ff (1958); *Weh v Weh*, 164 A.2d 508 at 513 (1960)).

17 '[W]hile at common law...a tenant in common who occupies joint property without complaint from his cotenants is not required to account for the value of the use thereof, yet when he resorts to equity and seeks contribution from his cotenants for funds expended in the betterment of the common estate, it would seem that he should be required to do equity and allow as an offset the value of the use of the premises' (*Roberts v Roberts*, 150 SW.2d 236 at 238 (1941) (Supreme Court of Texas)).

more and no less than his proportionate share of the net rental value derived from the land during the period of co-ownership, together with his proper share of the net increase in the capital value of the land accruing over that period. This may require relatively refined calculation particularly where, for instance, the rents and profits drawn from the land have been ploughed back into the land in the form of permanent improvements.[18]

(iii) Impact of the equity on third parties   It is clear that the 'defensive' equity of a co-owner to receive compensation from his cotenants is a right which is not merely personal to the individual tenant who effects the improvements or repairs. The expenditure incurred by such a co-owner raises in his favour an equity attaching to the land, analogous to an equitable charge created by the owners for the time being, although enforceable only in the event of a later partition or distribution of the value of the land amongst the co-owners.[19] This 'equity' is fully capable of running with the land. Thus it may enure to the benefit of the successor in title of the original owner of the 'equity',[20] and may also bind the successor in title to the share of any other co-owner, except where that successor has purchased for value without notice.[1] It is by no means certain that such an 'equity' is capable of effective registration in a register of title.[2]

5. TENANCY BY ENTIRETIES

Before 1 January 1926 there existed in England a type of co-ownership known as the 'tenancy by entireties'. This type of co-ownership was restricted to husband and wife, and constituted the 'most intimate union of ownership known to the law.'[3] The tenancy by entireties was in effect a species of joint tenancy,[4] and was distinguished from joint tenancy only by its characteristic incident: it was unseverable.[5] In other words, the tenancy by entireties did not differ in its essential nature from a joint tenancy except in so far as neither tenant had the capacity to reduce the co-ownership to co-ownership in distinct

18   See eg *Squire v Rogers* (1979-80) 27 ALR 330 at 347.
19   *Brickwood v Young* (1905) 2 CLR 387 at 396; *Noack v Noack* [1959] VR 137 at 146.
20   *Brickwood v Young* (1905) 2 CLR 387 at 396. See also *Williams v Williams* (1899-1900) 81 LT (NS) 163, 68 LJ Ch 528 at 529; *In Re Jones* [1893] 2 Ch 461 at 476ff.
1   *Dietsch v Long*, 43 NE.2d 906 at 916f (1942); *Ruptash and Lumsden v Zawick* [1956] 2 DLR (2d) 145 at 159; *Squire v Rogers* (1979-80) 27 ALR 330 at 346. In this context the decision of the majority in the Ontario Court of Appeal in *Canada Life Assurance Co v Kennedy* (1978) 89 DLR (3d) 397 must be wrong. It was ruled that a contractual lien conferred on one tenant in common in connection with improvements effected by her took priority over a bona fide mortgagee of the share of the other tenant in common, even though the mortgagee was wholly unaware of the agreement between the two co-owners. See the strong dissent entered by Wilson JA ((1978) 89 DLR (3d) 397 at 410f).
2   See eg *Ruptash and Lumsden v Zawick* [1956] 2 DLR (2d) 145 at 159, where the Supreme Court of Canada held that even the entry of a caveat on the register of title of the co-owned property did not give notice to a purchaser of the existence of a co-owner's claim for a proportionate share of the cost of repairs effected before the sale of that property.
3   *Challis*, p 377.
4   *Ante*, p 295.
5   *Post*, p 317.

shares.[6] Instead tenants by entireties were for the duration of marriage rendered co-owners of the whole rather than of 'undivided shares'.[7] In this way the tenancy by entireties reflected the medieval theory of the indivisible unity of husband and wife. In terms of this theory the wife had no independent existence at law; her legal personality simply merged with that of her husband.[8] The effect of the tenancy by entireties was that any conveyance to husband and wife before 1883 rendered them compulsorily subject to this form of unseverable co-ownership.

(1) Conversion into joint tenancy

Of course the 'deeply rooted fiction' of conjugal unity could not survive the advent of more liberal views of the relationship of the sexes.[9] The creation of new tenancies by entireties was prohibited in 1882,[10] and all remaining tenancies by entireties were on 1 January 1926 converted automatically into joint tenancies.[11]

(2) Abortive revival of the tenancy by entireties

The tenancy by entireties is therefore now a mere curiosity of legal history, although more recently there has been an indirect attempt to resurrect the concept of an unseverable form of co-ownership in relation to property owned jointly by husband and wife.[12] In *Bedson v Bedson*,[13] Lord Denning MR seemed to hold that, where spouses own as joint tenants, neither can sever the joint tenancy and sell his own interest separately. In Lord Denning's view, if either spouse could sell his or her severable share, 'it would mean that the purchaser could insist on going into possession himself—with the other spouse there— which is absurd'.[14] However, this approach did not commend itself to all the members of the Court of Appeal in *Bedson*, Russell LJ considering the prohibition on unilateral severance to be 'without the slightest foundation in law or in equity'.[15] It is now clear that Lord Denning's revival of the defunct

---

6 *Registrar-General of New South Wales v Wood* (1926) 39 CLR 46 at 54. See *Challis*, p 376 (note); *United States v Jacobs*, 306 US 363 at 370, 83 L.ed 763 at 768 (1939); *In Re Estate of King*, 572 SW.2d 200 at 211 (1978).
7 Ante, p 302.
8 Ante, p 7.
9 In *Registrar-General of New South Wales v Wood* (1926) 39 CLR 46 at 53, Isaacs J observed that 'for the purposes of daily life' this fiction is 'so opposed to fact and experience and to present-day habits of thought that outside the solemn precincts of a Court no one in his senses would venture to affirm it.' See also *United States v Jacobs*, 306 US 363 at 369, 83 L.ed 763 at 768 (1939).
10 Married Women's Property Act 1882, ss 1, 5. See *Challis*, p 378.
11 Law of Property Act 1925, Sch 1, Part VI.
12 A more direct attempt to revive the tenancy by entireties is to be found in New Zealand's Joint Family Homes Act 1964, s 9(2)(c)(proviso), which states that neither spouse may sever the statutory joint tenancy under which a registered joint family home is held (post, p 882).
13 [1965] 2 QB 666 at 678B.
14 In coming to this conclusion, Lord Denning purported to rely on the Law of Property Act 1925, s 36(1), (3), although, as Plowman J later pointed out in *In re Draper's Conveyance* [1969] 1 Ch 486 at 493B, these provisions appear irrelevant to the proposition put forward.
15 [1965] 2 QB 666 at 690E.

tenancy by entireties is widely regarded as heretical.[16] Marital status alone does not inhibit unilateral severance of the equitable interest in a matrimonial home. As Russell LJ said in *Bedson v Bedson*,[17] it is 'inherent in the nature of the beneficial interest created that either joint tenant may sever at any time inter vivos.'

6. COPARCENARY

Coparcenary is a form of co-ownership which is now virtually extinct.[18] It arose before 1926 where a person died intestate leaving two or more persons as his 'heir', and in most instances coparcenary embodied the pernicious theory that it took two or more females to equal one male. Normally, under the pre-1926 rule of primogeniture, the eldest son of the intestate decedent constituted the 'heir'. However, if the decedent left not sons but daughters, those daughters inherited together as 'coparceners'.[19] Coparcenary was a hybrid form of co-ownership, bearing attributes of both joint tenancy and tenancy in common: coparceners held in undivided shares without any right of survivorship,[20] even though in most cases the 'four unities' were present.[1]

In the Administration of Estates Act 1925,[2] English law abandoned the general concept of descent to the 'heir', with the consequence that no new coparcenary can now occur save in those few exceptional cases where realty still descends to an 'heir'.[3] Coparcenary can therefore still emerge in two special cases, where two or more females (or their issue) are entitled on an intestacy. The first case occurs where the intestate was a 'lunatic or defective' of full age at the end of 1925 who never recovered his testamentary capacity.[4] The second case arises where the intestate was a tenant in tail who died without barring his entail.[5] In both situations the land is now held on trust for sale for the coparceners.[6]

---

16 See eg *In re Draper's Conveyance* [1969] 1 Ch 486 at 494A; *Cowcher v Cowcher* [1972] 1 WLR 425 at 430G-H; *Fleming v Hargreaves* [1976] 1 NZLR 123 at 127; *Harris v Goddard* [1983] 1 WLR 1203 at 1208G; (1966) 82 LQR 29 (REM). However, Lord Denning's dictum in *Bedson* has the dubious merit of being consistent with other recent indications that a beneficiary in possession of land has a *right* of occupation or at least has a right not to have that occupation prejudiced by the intervention of any third party (post, p 374). See also I.A. Saunders and A. McGregor, (1973) 37 Conv (NS) 270 at 272.
17 [1965] 2 QB 666 at 689C.
18 See *Bl Comm*, Vol II, p 187ff; *Challis*, p 373ff.
19 See also *Bl Comm*, Vol II, p 187; *Challis*, p 373f.
20 *Bl Comm*, Vol II, p 188. However, at common law each parcener was entitled as against his coparceners to a compulsory partition of the property (*Litt*, s 241).
1 See *Bl Comm*, Vol II, p 188; *Challis*, p 374f.
2 Administration of Estates Act 1925, s 45(1).
3 All land in which coparcenary still existed at the end of 1925 was automatically subjected to a statutory trust for sale behind which the coparceners took equitable interests as tenants in common (Law of Property Act 1925, Sch 1, Part IV).
4 Administration of Estates Act 1925, s 51(2).
5 Law of Property Act 1925, s 130(4); Administration of Estates Act 1925, ss 45(2), 51(4).
6 Where the intestate was a lunatic or defective, the trust for sale arises under the Administration of Estates Act 1925, s 33(1). Where he was a tenant in tail, the trust for sale is imposed by the Law of Property Act 1925, s 36(1), (2).

7. SEVERANCE

Certain acts or events cause the undifferentiated co-ownership of joint tenancy to crystallise into co-ownership in distinct and undivided shares.[7] The process by which joint tenancy may thus be converted into tenancy in common is known as severance,[8] and it is ultimately a 'mere matter of evidence' whether severance has occurred.[9]

(1) Facility of severance

Historically the common law has been willing to mitigate the hazards of survivorship by allowing severance to occur relatively easily.[10] Any act or event which is incompatible with the characteristic features of joint tenancy is apt to precipitate such a severance. Thus any dealing by a joint tenant which excludes the future operation of survivorship will result in severance. Joint tenancy depends, moreover, upon the continued existence of the three unities of possession, interest and title,[11] and the destruction of either unity of interest or unity of title will automatically bring about a severance.[12] For the purpose of severance under the common law rules the consent of the other joint tenant or joint tenants is not necessarily required,[13] and severance may in this sense be quite unilateral.[14] The major restriction upon the availability of severance is,

7 See A.J. McClean, (1979) 57 Can Bar Rev 1; P. Butt, (1979-82) 9 Sydney LR 568.
8 See *Harris v Goddard* [1983] 1 WLR 1203 at 1210E per Dillon LJ: 'Severance is...the process of separating off the share of a joint tenant, so that the concurrent ownership will continue but the right of survivorship will no longer apply. The parties will hold separate shares as tenants in common.'
9 *Crooke v De Vandes* (1805) 11 Ves 330 at 333, 32 ER 1115 at 1116. The onus of proof that severance has occurred rests upon the party seeking to establish severance (see *Flynn v Flynn* [1930] IR 337 at 343; *Re Denny* (1947) 116 LJR 1029 at 1031; *Greenfield v Greenfield* (1979) 38 P & CR 570 at 578; *Re Sorensen and Sorensen* (1979) 90 DLR (3d) 26 at 33; *Barton v Morris* [1985] 1 WLR 1257 at 1260G).
10 Ante, p 296. See *Cray v Willis* (1729) 2 P Wms 529, 24 ER 847 ('...the duration of all lives being uncertain, if either party has an ill opinion of his own life, he may sever the jointenancy...so that survivorship can be no hardship, where either side may at pleasure prevent it').
11 'The unity of time of vesting only applies to the original creation of the joint tenancy and cannot, therefore, be affected by any subsequent act' (*Re Murdoch and Barry* (1976) 64 DLR (3d) 222 at 225). See also *Nielson-Jones v Fedden* [1975] Ch 222 at 228F.
12 *Bl Comm*, Vol II, p 192. See eg *Power v Grace* [1932] 2 DLR 793 at 795; *Tenhet v Boswell*, 133 Cal Rptr 10 at 14 (1976); *In Re Estate of Estelle*, 593 P.2d 663 at 665 (1979); *First National Bank of Southglenn v Energy Fuels Corp*, 618 P.2d 1115 at 1118 (1980); *Minouk State Bank v Grassman*, 432 NE.2d 386 at 389 (1982); *Samuel v District Land Registrar* [1984] 2 NZLR 697 at 702. Destruction of unity of possession would, of course, terminate co-ownership altogether by means of 'partition' (post, p 341).
13 *Burke v Stevens*, 70 Cal Rptr 87 at 91 (1968). A form of unseverable joint tenancy (the 'tenancy by entireties') was available to husband and wife in England before 1926 (ante, p 314). In some jurisdictions joint tenancy has been made unseverable without the consent of all the joint tenants, with the express purpose of guaranteeing to each joint tenant the indestructibility of his right of survivorship (see eg Land Titles Act (Saskatchewan)(RSS 1978, c L-5), s 240; *Re The Queen And Peters* (1983) 141 DLR (3d) 508 at 516).
14 See *Staples v Maurice* (1774) 4 Bro Parl Cas 580 at 585, 2 ER 395 at 399. The joint tenants may of course bind themselves by agreement inter se not to do any act which will result in the severance of the joint tenancy (see *Re Debney* (1960) 60 SR (NSW) 471 at 473). However, even if such a contractual undertaking is broken (eg if one joint tenant sells his severable share to a stranger), it can sound only in damages against the errant co-owner: the illicit severance cannot prejudice the rights of the stranger (see *Fitts v Stone*, 166 SW.2d 897 at 899 (1942)). It seems also that an injunction may be available to restrain an impending dealing which threatens to sever the joint tenancy. See D. Mendes da Costa, (1961-62) 3 Melbourne ULR 137, 306, 433 at 440.

however, the rule that severance can be effected only inter vivos: there can be no unilateral severance by will.[15]

(2) Consequence of severance

In the absence of any contrary court order[16] or agreement between the co-owners[17], the aliquot shares which result from severance are always equal in size, irrespective of the proportions in which the joint tenants may have contributed initially towards the purchase price of the co-owned property.[18] The fact of severance, when it occurs, should be noted in a memorandum of severance signed by at least one of the joint tenants and endorsed on or annexed to the conveyance which created the joint tenancy.[19]

(3) Abolition of severance at law

Since the commencement of the Law of Property Act 1925, joint tenancy has been capable of severance only in respect of equitable interests in land: there can be no severance of a joint tenancy in a legal estate.[20] Section 36(2) of the Law of Property Act 1925 provides two major means of effecting severance in equity, and other circumstances of severance exist under more general doctrines of law. These methods of severance must be examined in turn.

8. SEVERANCE BY WRITTEN NOTICE

Section 36(2) of the Law of Property Act 1925 enables a joint tenant to effect a severance by giving to the other joint tenants a 'notice in writing' of his 'desire' to sever the joint tenancy. Although doubt has been expressed on the point,[1] it has been said that this provision radically altered the law of severance by introducing an entirely new method of severance as regards land.[2]

---

15   Ante, p 299. However, the execution of mutual wills by joint tenants may bring about a severance (post, p 330).

16   The court may, for instance, authorise an unequal division of proceeds of sale under the Matrimonial Causes Act 1973, ss 24(1), 24A, an order which would arguably have severing effect even before being duly performed (post, p 326).

17   An agreement deviating from equality of shares after severance may be present in rare cases of a partnership arrangement involving joint tenants (see eg *Barton v Morris* [1985] 1 WLR 1257 at 1262D-H), or may be incorporated in a declaration of trust (see *Goodman v Gallant* [1986] Fam 106 at 119C).

18   '[U]pon a severance the person severing will take 1/nth of the property beneficially, where "n" is the original number of the joint tenants' (*Nielson-Jones v Fedden* [1975] Ch 222 at 228E per Walton J). See also *Bedson v Bedson* [1965] 2 QB 666 at 689C; *Goodman v Gallant* [1986] Fam 106 at 119D.

19   Post, p 343. In registered land a 'restriction' (ante, p 159) should be entered on the register of title (see A. Kenny and P. Kenny, (1980) 80 Law Soc Gaz 1473 at 1475).

20   Law of Property Act 1925, s 36(2), ante, p 298, post, p 339. Thus severance by a co-owner who is a joint tenant both at law and in equity cannot affect his trusteeship of the legal estate. Although after severance he becomes a tenant in common in equity, he remains as a joint tenant of the legal estate until such time as he (i) retires from the trust, or (ii) 'releases' his legal estate to the other joint tenants (post, p 342), or (iii) dies.

1   See note 13. In *Burgess v Rawnsley* [1975] Ch 429 at 440B, Lord Denning MR thought section 36(2) merely declaratory of the pre-1926 law as to severance. See also *Hawkesley v May* [1956] 1 QB 304 at 313, as commented upon in *Davies v Davies* [1983] WAR 305 at 308 per Burt CJ.

2   See *Burgess v Rawnsley* [1975] Ch 429 at 444G per Browne LJ, 447E per Sir John Pennycuick; *Harris v Goddard* [1983] 1 WLR 1203 at 1208H per Lawton LJ.

(1) **Advantages**

The statutory method of severance by written notice is doubtless convenient.[3] It may be quite unilateral: no consent is required to be forthcoming from other joint tenants.[4] The severance is effective if there is evidence that the notice was duly posted to the other joint tenants[5]: it is not necessary that the notice should have been received by them.[6] The 'notice in writing' need not be signed[7] and may even take the form of a writ or originating summons by which proceedings are commenced for a judicial determination of the rights of the joint tenants inter se.[8] In *In re Draper's Conveyance*[9] a wife applied by summons under the Married Women's Property Act 1882[10] for an order directing a sale of the jointly owned matrimonial home and equal distribution of the proceeds of sale. The husband died shortly after the court had made the order requested, and Plowman J held that severance had occurred and that the wife now held the legal estate (as sole surviving trustee) on trust for herself and her husband's estate in equal shares.[11]

(2) **Limitations**

Severance by written notice is, however, subject to certain limitations. It has no reference to settled land,[12] and may well be inapplicable to cases in which the names on the legal title are not identical to the beneficiaries behind the trust (eg where A, B and C hold the legal estate on trust for sale for A, B, C and D, or where T^1 and T^2 hold the legal estate on trust for sale for X, Y and Z).[13] Likewise it seems that the written notice method of severance is not available if the co-owned land has already been sold: the land is no longer 'vested in joint

---

3   The written notice method of severance has the great advantage of speed and simplicity in circumstances where much can turn on the precise sequence of rapidly occurring events (see eg *First National Securities Ltd v Hegerty* [1985] QB 850 at 865B-E). For an appropriate form of words, see *Goodman v Gallant* [1986] Fam 106 at 109B.
4   *Harris v Goddard* [1983] 1 WLR 1203 at 1209B per Lawton LJ.
5   See Law of Property Act 1925, s 196.
6   *Re 88 Berkeley Road, NW 9* [1971] Ch 648 at 655C.
7   *In re Draper's Conveyance* [1969] 1 Ch 486 at 492A.
8   This seems to be the case at least so long as the writ or summons is coupled with a supporting affidavit, in circumstances where the two documents taken in conjunction clearly indicate a desire to sever (see *In re Draper's Conveyance* [1969] 1 Ch 486 at 492C). In *Burgess v Rawnsley* [1975] Ch 429 at 447F, Sir John Pennycuick thought that the 'notice in writing' could comprise either the writ or the summons or the affidavit.
9   [1969] 1 Ch 486. See (1968) 84 LQR 462 (P.V. Baker).
10   Compare the effect of an application under the Matrimonial Causes Act 1973 (post, p 320).
11   Plowman J based his decision both on the written notice provision in section 36(2) and on the old common law of severance (see [1969] 1 Ch 486 at 492B). It has been said that *In re Draper's Conveyance* can be treated as involving an act of a joint tenant 'operating upon' her own share (post, p 325).
12   Law of Property Act 1925, s 36(2).
13   It is possible that such a construction is compelled by the strict wording of section 36(2), '...where a legal estate...is vested in joint tenants beneficially...' However, there is much to commend a more liberal and more sensible construction which would enable all equitable joint tenants to take advantage of the facility of severance by written notice. See, in favour of this wider view, *Burgess v Rawnsley* [1975] Ch 429 at 439G per Lord Denning MR, 444F per Browne LJ, 447G per Sir John Pennycuick). See, *contra*, [1976] CLJ 20 at 24 (D.J. Hayton). It may, however, be 'unwise' to rely on the courts to apply the liberal approach here (*Emmet on Title*, p 325).

tenants beneficially', as seems to be required by section 36(2).[14] In such cases it may be that severance can be effected only by other means.

Perhaps the most important limitation on the scope of the written notice method of severance is that 'a desire to sever must evince an intention to bring about the wanted result immediately'.[15] Thus it is not enough that the written notice should express a desire to sever at some time in the future. It was on this ground that the Court of Appeal in *Harris v Goddard*[16] refused to find that severance had occurred where a spouse had merely included in her divorce petition a prayer that the divorce court might make such order respecting the matrimonial property 'as may be just.'[17]

9. THE *WILLIAMS v HENSMAN* METHODS OF SEVERANCE

Section 36(2) of the Law of Property Act 1925 makes it clear that severance can be effected in equity if a joint tenant does 'such other acts or things as would, in the case of personal estate, have been effectual to sever the tenancy in equity' before 1926. The classic authority on the pre-1926 forms of severance in personalty was provided in *Williams v Hensman*[18] by Page Wood V-C, who laid down three categories of circumstance which result in severance.[19]

These categories are now examined in turn. In general terms, in the context of a dealing between a joint tenant and a stranger the issue of severance tends to focus on whether the transaction in question has destroyed an essential unity of joint tenancy. Where, however, the context is that of a dealing of the joint tenants *inter se*, the more useful question seems to be whether any of the co-owners have evinced an intention which is clearly inconsistent with the future operation of the *ius accrescendi*.[20]

---

14   See *Nielson-Jones v Fedden* [1975] Ch 222 at 229E. See, *contra, Burgess v Rawnsley* [1975] Ch 429 at 440A per Lord Denning MR.

15   *Harris v Goddard* [1983] 1 WLR 1203 at 1209B per Lawton LJ. See also *Lyons v Lyons* [1967] VR 169 at 172.

16   [1983] 1 WLR 1203. See (1984) 100 LQR 161; [1984] Conv 148 (S. Coneys); (1984) 134 NLJ 63 (H.W. Wilkinson).

17   Both Lawton LJ (at 1209D) and Dillon LJ (at 1210H) also pointed out that the general prayer in the wife's petition could have been satisfied by relief which did not involve 'severance' at all. In the exercise of its discretion under the Matrimonial Causes Act 1973, the divorce court could have made an order extinguishing the interest of one or other spouse in the property or directing a resettlement on the spouses successively and not as concurrent owners. Compare *In re Draper's Conveyance* [1969] 1 Ch 486 (ante, p 319), where the claim plainly involved a severance of the beneficial joint tenancy.

18   (1861) 1 John & H 546 at 557, 70 ER 862 at 867, approved by the Privy Council in *Tan Chew Hoe Neo v Chee Swee Cheng* (1929) LR 56 Ind App 112 at 115. It was confirmed by Lawton LJ in *Harris v Goddard* [1983] 1 WLR 1203 at 1208H that the reference in section 36(2) to '...such other acts or things...' merely 'put into statutory language the other ways of effecting severance to which Page Wood V-C referred in *Williams v Hensman*.'

19   *Williams v Hensman* related to personalty, but the principles enunciated there have been applied indifferently to property real and personal. See *Burgess v Rawnsley* [1975] Ch 429; *Re Murdoch and Barry* (1976) 64 DLR (3d) 222 at 224; *McNab v Earle* [1981] 2 NSWLR 673 at 675G; *Abela v Public Trustee* [1983] 1 NSWLR 308 at 316E.

20   See *Bradley v Mann*, 525 P.2d 492 at 493 (1974), affd 535 P.2d 213 at 214 (1975); *Mangus v Miller*, 532 P.2d 368 at 369 (1975).

(1) Act of a joint tenant 'operating upon his own share'

According to Page Wood V-C, 'an act of any one of the persons interested operating upon his own share may create a severance as to that share.'[1] This mode of severance may be quite unilateral.[2] However, in order to amount to severance the 'act' of the joint tenant must be 'such as to preclude him from claiming by survivorship any interest in the subject-matter of the joint tenancy.'[3] In other words, the 'act' which operates upon the joint tenant's share must have a final or irrevocable character which effectively estops any future claim that longevity has conferred the benefits of survivorship on that co-owner.[4]

(a) Alienation inter vivos

A sufficient 'act' for the purpose of the rule in *Williams v Hensman* typically takes the form of a total or partial alienation of a joint tenant's share.[5] That this should be so is, in one sense, entirely consistent with the theory of joint tenancy. A joint tenancy is severed if one of the 'four unities' ceases to be present, as for instance would be the case if one joint tenant were to alienate his proprietary interest in the joint tenancy to a third party.[6] In such an event the stranger, as alienee, would not enjoy unity of title with the remaining joint tenants.[7]

There is, however, a logical difficulty at this point. In terms of the definition of joint tenancy, a joint tenant does not own an interest or 'share' which is sufficiently distinct to provide the subject matter of a disposition. The only way in which the alienor can validly dispose of an 'interest' is on the assumption that severance has already occurred. The act of alienation is thus, paradoxically, both the source and the vehicle of the interest conveyed. In some curious dislocation of time and causation, the completed act of transfer brings into being the very 'interest' which purported to be the subject matter of the transfer in the first place. It is small wonder that Dixon J observed in *Wright v Gibbons*[8] that joint tenancy is 'a form of ownership bearing many traces of the scholasticism of the times in which its principles were developed.'

1   (1861) 1 John & H 546 at 557, 70 ER 862 at 867.
2   *Harris v Goddard* [1983] 1 WLR 1203 at 1209B; *Clark v Carter*, 70 Cal Rptr 923 at 925 (1968); *Gonzales v Gonzales*, 73 Cal Rptr 83 at 87 (1968). The 'act' may even be dishonestly concealed from the other joint tenant or tenants (see eg *First National Securities Ltd v Hegerty* [1985] QB 850 (post, p 602); *Burke v Stevens*, 70 Cal Rptr 87 at 91 (1968)). See also *In Re Estate of Casella*, 64 Cal Rptr 259 at 265 (1967).
3   *In Re Wilks* [1891] 3 Ch 59 at 61 per Stirling J.
4   For express reference to the terminology of estoppel in this context, see *Re Murdoch and Barry* (1976) 64 DLR (3d) 222 at 229. Compare, however, A.J. McClean, (1979) 57 Can Bar Rev 1 at 29f.
5   If the relevant transfer requires registration in a register of title, such a transfer, if not for consideration, cannot constitute a severing 'act' unless and until it is duly registered (see *Golding v Hands, Golding and Boldt* [1969] WAR 121 at 126; *Re Murdoch and Barry* (1976) 64 DLR (3d) 222 at 228). The act of alienation may include a mortgage (see *First National Securities Ltd v Hegerty* [1985] QB 850 at 862G-H).
6   *Litt*, s 292; *Co Litt*, p 189a. See also *Partriche v Powlet* (1740) 2 Atk 54 at 55, 26 ER 430 at 431 per Lord Hardwicke LC: '*Alienatio rei praefertur iuri accrescendi*'. This proposition is yet another expression of one of the historic premises of English property law, ie, that the highest consummation of a thing lies in its alienation (ante, p 96).
7   *Bl Comm*, Vol II, p 185. See also *Re Murdoch and Barry* (1976) 64 DLR (3d) 222 at 225f.
8   (1948-1949) 78 CLR 313 at 330. Dixon J sought to reconcile the 'not altogether compatible aspects of joint tenancy' by resorting to Coke's proposition that 'to divers purposes' (eg alienation) each joint tenant is conceived as being entitled to an aliquot share (ante, p 296).

(i) Dealings with strangers The effect of this form of severance may be seen in the following examples. Suppose that A, B and C are joint tenants at law and in equity (see *Fig.* 26).

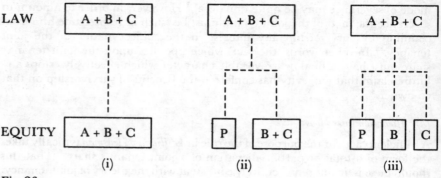

Fig. 26

If A transfers to P his 'share' or 'interest' in the joint tenancy, A thereby destroys the pre-existing unity of title and thus severs the joint tenancy.[9] This severance affects only the equitable ownership, since there can be no tenancy in common of a legal estate.[10] The result (as reflected in situation (ii) above) is that A, B and C will remain as trustees, holding the legal estate on trust for P (as a tenant in common owning a one-third share in equity) and B and C (as joint tenants inter se of the remaining two-thirds).[11]

Viewed objectively, this situation can still be described as disclosing a form of tenancy in common as between P, B and C. In strict analytical terms P is a tenant in common of a one-third share and the collective entity of (B + C) becomes a tenant in common of a two-thirds share. As between themselves, however, B and C are 'wholly entitled to the whole' of their two-thirds interest as joint tenants.[12] The right of survivorship will continue to operate between them with respect to this two-thirds interest unless and until either severs. In the event of such a severance A, B and C will still hold the legal estate as joint tenants, but will now hold it on trust for P, B and C as tenants in common each owning a one-third share in equity (ie, situation (iii) above).[13] The contradictions which appear in this context are more apparent than real, and merely mark the distinction between the external and the internal view of the property relations of P, B and C.

(ii) Dealings by joint tenants inter se Exactly the same kind of result will apply

9   This result follows even if A's 'share' is transferred to P by means of an instrument executed by P under a power of attorney and without the knowledge of the other joint tenants (see *Re Mills and Andrewes* (1983) 142 DLR (3d) 294).
10   Law of Property Act 1925, ss 1(6), 36(2), post, p 339.
11   *Litt*, s 294; *Co Litt*, p 189a; *Wright v Gibbons* (1948-1949) 78 CLR 313 at 323 per Latham CJ; *Bedson v Bedson* [1965] 2 QB 666 at 689D per Russell LJ.
12   See *Denne d Bowyer v Judge* (1809) 11 East 288 at 289, 103 ER 1014 at 1015; *Shelton v Vance*, 234 P.2d 1012 at 1014 (1951); *First National Bank of Denver v Groussman*, 483 P.2d 398 at 401, affd 491 P.2d 1382 (1971); *First National Bank of Southglenn v Energy Fuels Corp*, 618 P.2d 1115 at 1118 (1980).
13   It is entirely irrelevant to this outcome that P later transfers his share back to A (see *Palmer v Palmer*, 121 P.2d 822 at 825 (1942); *Alden v Alden*, 393 P.2d 5 at 6 (1964)).

where A, instead of transferring his interest to P, transfers it to B.[14] In such an event B acquires a dual status: he will become a tenant in common of a one-third interest in his own right and will be a joint tenant with C of the remaining two-thirds interest.[15] More difficult questions arise, however, if A and B as joint tenants *exchange* their 'interests' under the joint tenancy. Clearly, if A transfers his 'interest' to B one day before B transfers his 'interest' to A, two distinct severances will occur in close succession and A, B and C will all become tenants in common each as to a one- third share.[16] In *Wright v Gibbons*[17] precisely such transfers were made, but they were contained in one and the same instrument of transfer executed simultaneously by A and B. The High Court of Australia ruled that this mutual assurance or transposition of interests likewise had the effect of rendering A, B and C tenants in common each as to a one-third interest.[18]

(b) Alienation in equity

It would make no difference to the steps outlined above if, instead of transferring his 'interest' to P outright, A merely concludes a specifically enforceable contract to transfer to P.[19] Once again, equity looks on as done that which ought to be done, and the contract will operate in equity to transfer A's equitable interest to P under the doctrine in *Walsh v Lonsdale*.[20] The effect will be identical to that of an actual transfer.[1]

14   *Hammond v McArthur*, 183 P.2d 1 at 3 (1947). It has even been held that A may sever by transferring his 'share' to himself (infra), at least where such a transfer is made irrevocable, eg through registration or delivery of the deed of transfer (see *Re Murdoch and Barry* (1976) 64 DLR (3d) 222 at 228; *Re Sammon* (1979) 94 DLR (3d) 594 at 597; *McNab v Earle* [1981] 2 NSWLR 673 at 677A; *Re Lamanna and Lamanna* (1983) 145 DLR (3d) 117 at 119; but compare *Freed v Taffel* [1984] 2 NSWLR 322 at 324F, 325E). It is unlikely, however, that English courts will accept a self-dealing transfer as sufficient for severance (see *Rye v Rye* [1962] AC 496 at 514), in the absence of amending legislation such as that found in New Zealand's Property Law Act 1952, s 66A (see *Samuel v District Land Registrar* [1984] 2 NZLR 697 at 702).

15   See *Wright v Gibbons* (1948-1949) 78 CLR 313 at 324, 332; *In re Galletto's Estate*, 171 P.2d 152 at 156 (1946). B's two separate holdings will be distinguished by their different incidents: his joint tenancy of the two-thirds interest will still be subject to the right of survivorship.

16   *Wright v Gibbons* (1948-1949) 78 CLR 313 at 324f per Latham CJ.

17   (1948-1949) 78 CLR 313.

18   Dixon J thought that an exactly similar result would follow if A and B as joint tenants were to grant their two aliquot shares to X effectively as a trustee for A and B as tenants in common in equal shares ((1948-1949) 78 CLR 313 at 332).

19   *Brown v Raindle* (1796) 3 Ves 256 at 257, 30 ER 998 at 999; *Gould v Kemp* (1834) 2 My & K 304 at 309, 39 ER 959 at 961; *Wilson v Bell* (1843) 5 Ir Eq R 501 at 507; *Kingsford v Ball* (1852) 2 Giff (App) i at iii, 66 ER 294 at 295; *Caldwell v Fellowes* (1870) LR 9 Eq 410 at 418; *Re Hewett* [1894] 1 Ch 362 at 367. The elements of a specifically enforceable contract are discussed elsewhere (ante, p 216).

20   (1882) 21 Ch D 9 (post, p 471). Severance will not be defeated by the mere fact that the contracting joint tenant dies prior to the performance of his contract to transfer (see *Thomas v Johnson*, 297 NE.2d 712 at 714f (1973)).

1   See *Burgess v Rawnsley* [1975] Ch 429 at 443G; *Freed v Taffel* [1984] 2 NSWLR 322 at 325C. Severance will similarly occur if A declares himself a trustee of his own 'interest' on behalf of X (*Re Mee* (1971) 23 DLR (3d) 491 at 497; *Re Sorensen and Sorensen* (1979) 90 DLR (3d) 26 at 37; *Earl v Earl* [1979] 6 WWR 600 at 611); or if A transfers his 'interest' to T in order that T should hold on trust for A (*Staples v Maurice* (1774) 4 Bro Parl Cas 580 at 585, 2 ER 395 at 399; *Clark v Carter*, 70 Cal Rptr 923 at 925f (1968); *Re Murdoch and Barry* (1976) 64 DLR (3d) 222 at 226; *In the Marriage of Badcock and Badcock* (1979) FLC 90-723 at p 78,896). However, it seems that no severance will occur if A and B merely release their legal ownership in favour of C in order that C should hold on trust for A, B and C (*Groves v Christiansen* (1978) 86 DLR (3d) 296 at 306); or if A grants P an irrevocable but as yet unexercised option to purchase A's 'interest' (*Re McKee and National Trust Co Ltd* (1975) 56 DLR (3d) 190 at 196).

(c) Alienation by will

The alienation of a joint tenant's 'share' by will does not normally constitute an 'act...operating upon his own share' for the purpose of severance.[2] Neither death nor the execution of a testamentary document before death[3] is a severing event. The *ius accrescendi* prevails over the testamentary disposition,[4] and the gift is ineffective[5] except where all the joint tenants have made mutual wills.[6]

(d) Involuntary alienation

The severing event which operates upon a joint tenant's 'share' need not be voluntary. In a weak sense, the relevant act of alienation may be coerced by external circumstances which deprive the joint tenant of any true consent to the transfer of his share.[7] In a stronger sense, a bankruptcy affecting one of the joint tenants causes an immediate and involuntary assignment of the bankrupt's aliquot 'share' in favour of his trustee in bankruptcy[8] and thereby automatically severs the joint tenancy.[9] In such cases severance occurs without the consent of any of the joint tenants[10] and may ultimately lead to a sale of the co-owned property against their wishes.[11] It seems that severance is similarly produced by the making of a charging order under the Charging Orders Act 1979[12] in respect of a debtor joint tenant's beneficial interest in land,[13] or even by the imposition of a statutory charge in favour of the Law Society upon any interest 'recovered or preserved' for a joint tenant in legally aided litigation.[14]

---

2   Ante, p 299.
3   The execution of a will disposing of a joint tenant's share, although expressive of a severing intention, remains a revocable act until the testator's death and therefore lacks the definitive quality required by the first limb of the rule in *Williams v Hensman*. For an argument favouring severance by will, see N. Sterling, (1982-83) 14 Pacific LJ 927 at 952f.
4   '*Ius accrescendi praefertur ultimae voluntati* ' (*Co Litt*, p 185b). See *Moyse v Gyles* (1700) 2 Vern 385 at 386, 23 ER 846 at 847.
5   *Litt*, s 287; *Co Litt*, p 185b (ante, p 299).
6   Post, p 330.
7   See eg *Fleming v Hargreaves* [1976] 1 NZLR 123 at 126.
8   Post, p 876. See eg *In re Holliday (A Bankrupt)* [1981] Ch 405 at 411D, 421D (post, p 878).
9   *Morgan v Marquis* (1853) 9 Exch 145 at 147f, 156 ER 62 at 63; *Re White* [1928] 1 DLR 846 at 848; *Bedson v Bedson* [1965] 2 QB 666 at 690B; *In re Rushton (A Bankrupt)* [1972] Ch 197 at 203A; *In Re Blodgett*, 115 F.Supp 33 at 35 (1953); *Flynn v O'Dell*, 281 F.2d 810 at 817 (1960); *Canada Life Assurance Co v Kennedy* (1978) 87 DLR (3d) 397 at 400. In *Paten v Cribb* (1862) 1 QSCR 40 at 41, Lutwyche J observed that, for the purpose of severance, 'it makes no difference...whether one joint tenant has conveyed away his own share in his lifetime, or whether the law has done it for him.'
10 In jurisdictions where some form of homestead legislation is in force (post, p 881), this involuntary assignment is not usually regarded as falling within the control of the legislation. Being more in the nature of a vesting by operation of law, it does not constitute a disposition in respect of which the bankrupt's spouse has any power of veto. See eg *Containercare (Ireland) Ltd v Wycherley* [1982] IR 143 at 150.
11 Post, p 879.
12 Post, p 870.
13 The effect of a charging order absolute is to place the creditor in the same position as an equitable chargee (Charging Orders Act 1979, s 3(4)). Compare the severing effect brought about in the Republic of Ireland by the registration of a judgment mortgage against a joint tenant under the Judgment Mortgage (Ireland) Act 1850 (see *Containercare (Ireland) Ltd v Wycherley* [1982] IR 143 at 151).
14 *Bedson v Bedson* [1965] 2 QB 666 at 690G per Russell LJ (ante, p 315).

(e) Declaration of intention

Despite isolated statements to the contrary,[15] it seems fairly clear that a mere declaration of intention to sever is ineffective towards that end. Unless incorporated in a written notice[16] or contained in a specifically enforceable agreement to alienate the 'share' concerned,[17] it is difficult to see how a unilateral declaration by a joint tenant can truly be said to 'operate upon' his own share.[18] It is perhaps arguable, however, that severing significance should be attached to a declaration of intention which is evidenced in an irrevocable form akin to the conclusive effect achieved by the delivery of a deed[19] or the registration of a document.[20]

(f) Commencement of litigation

There is judicial support for the proposition that the formal commencement of litigation concerning a joint tenancy may constitute an 'act' operating upon the 'share' of the litigant joint tenant.[1] The objection has sometimes been raised that the mere commencement of legal proceedings is not a sufficiently conclusive 'act' upon which to found a severance since such proceedings can always be abandoned or discontinued.[2] However, the English courts have tended to regard the possibility of a discontinuance of the proceedings either as negligible[3] or as entirely irrelevant.[4]

---

15 See *Hawkesley v May* [1956] 1 QB 304 at 313 per Havers J; *In re Draper's Conveyance* [1969] 1 Ch 486 at 491G. Compare, however, (1976) 50 ALJ 246 at 249 (PB). Havers J's statement in *Hawkesley v May* was *obiter*, and has not been followed in other jurisdictions: see *Golding v Hands, Golding and Boldt* [1969] WAR 121 at 125f; *Re Murdoch and Barry* (1976) 64 DLR (3d) 222 at 228; *Re Sorensen and Sorensen* (1979) 90 DLR (3d) 26 at 39; *In the Marriage of Pertsoulis and Pertsoulis* (1980) FLC 90-832 at p 75,270f; *Davies v Davies* [1983] WAR 305 at 308; *Abela v Public Trustee* [1983] 1 NSWLR 308 at 314G; *Freed v Taffel* [1984] 2 NSWLR 322 at 324E.
16 Law of Property Act 1925, s 36(2).
17 *Partriche v Powlet* (1740) 2 Atk 54 at 55, 26 ER 430 at 431 per Lord Hardwicke LC. See also *Moyse v Gyles* (1700) 2 Vern 385 at 386, 23 ER 846 at 847; *Nielson-Jones v Fedden* [1975] Ch 222 at 231A.
18 *Davies v Davies* [1983] WAR 305 at 307 per Burt CJ.
19 Ante, p 222.
20 See *Re Murdoch and Barry* (1976) 64 DLR (3d) 222 at 228. A slightly wider view may have been expressed in *First National Securities Ltd v Hegerty* [1985] QB 850 at 862G-H, where Sir Denys Buckley thought that an application by one joint tenant for a loan secured on co-owned property might be a 'sufficient act of alienation' for the purpose of severance (post, p 602).
1   See *In re Draper's Conveyance* [1969] 1 Ch 486 at 492C (ante, p 319). See also *Harris v Goddard* [1983] 1 WLR 1203 at 1209H, where Lawton LJ thought that the service of the summons and the filing of the affidavit in *In re Draper's Conveyance* could have been 'acts effectual to sever' within *Williams v Hensman*.
2   See eg *In re Wilks* [1891] 3 Ch 59 at 61; *Nielson-Jones v Fedden* [1975] Ch 222 at 236C; *Munroe v Carlson* (1976) 59 DLR (3d) 763 at 765; *Rodrigue v Dufton* (1977) 72 DLR (3d) 16 at 19; *In the Marriage of Badcock and Badcock* (1979) FLC 90-723 at p 78,897; *In the Marriage of Pertsoulis and Pertsoulis* (1980) FLC 90-832 at p 75,272.
3   *In re Draper's Conveyance* [1969] 1 Ch 486 as interpreted in *Harris v Goddard* [1983] 1 WLR 1203 at 1210B. See in any event (1968) 84 LQR 463 (P.V.B.).
4   *Burgess v Rawnsley* [1975] Ch 429 at 440C, 447G. If *Burgess v Rawnsley* is correct in upholding the severing effect of an agreement which was later cancelled, it is difficult to see why severance is not irreversibly achieved by the mere commencement of litigation irrespective of the subsequent conduct of the parties.

(g) Court order

It has been suggested that severance is implicit in any court order resulting from litigation aimed at determining the rights of one joint tenant as against another. On this view, the order of the court itself effects a severance even before the order is duly carried through to performance. Support for this view in England has, however, been less than clear,[5] not least because the court order would not in any event constitute an 'act' of one of the joint tenants except in the strained sense that the proceedings were rooted in an action brought by at least one co-owner. Severance by mere court order has been justified elsewhere on the ground that an otherwise binding order (eg for sale and distribution of proceeds) would be rendered entirely abortive by the continued operation of the *ius accrescendi*: an untimely death before the court order is perfected should not have this capricious effect.[6] The solution in England may well be that severance is inherent in even an unperfected court order where the court's jurisdiction stems from legislation which empowers an alteration[7] (rather than merely a declaration[8]) of the rights of the joint tenants.

(2) Mutual agreement

The second method of severance referred to by Page Wood V-C in *Williams v Hensman*[9] was severance by 'mutual agreement' on the part of all the co-owners who currently enjoy the status of joint tenant. Although it may sometimes be difficult to distinguish this form of severance from the third method outlined by Page Wood V-C ('mutual conduct'),[10] it is clear that joint tenants by acting together may effectively agree *inter se* to sever their joint tenancy.[11] In the

5   In *Davies v Davies* [1983] WAR 305 at 306f, Burt CJ opined that the decision of Plowman J in *In re Draper's Conveyance* could have been reached on the footing that the court order in *In re Draper's Conveyance* itself effected the severance. However, Plowman J was careful to emphasise ([1969] 1 Ch 486 at 494D) that severance had been brought about by the summons and the affidavit and 'not by any order that was made'.

6   See *Re Johnstone* [1973] Qd R 347 at 351E; *Public Trustee v Grivas* [1974] 2 NSWLR 316 at 321E; *Gillette v Cotton* [1979] 4 WWR 515 at 525f; *In the Marriage of Pertsoulis and Pertsoulis* (1980) FLC 90-832 at p 75,272.

7   The legislation involved in the Australian cases cited in note 6 empowered a substantive alteration of rights and these decisions may thus provide better guidance as to the effect of a court order for sale and distribution of proceeds under the similarly broad provisions of the English Matrimonial Causes Act 1973, ss 24, 24A.

8   See *In re Draper's Conveyance* [1969] 1 Ch 486 at 494D, where Plowman J accepted that the court's power under section 17 of the Married Women's Property Act 1882 is merely declaratory of the existing rights of the parties and cannot authorise a conversion of these rights into a tenancy in common. It may be that the decisive factor in this context is the scope of the judicial discretion conferred by the relevant legislation. See also *Nielson-Jones v Fedden* [1975] Ch 222 at 236E.

9   (1861) 1 John & H 546 at 557, 70 ER 862 at 867 (ante, p 320).

10   Post, p 329. The possibility of confusion between 'mutual agreement' and 'mutual conduct' is intensified by judicial statements that the court will 'infer an agreement' to sever 'if the acts and dealings of the parties in respect to the joint property *indicate an intention* to treat it as property held in common and not jointly' (*Wilson v Bell* (1843) 5 Ir Eq R 501 at 507). See also *Mann v Bradley*, 535 P.2d 213 at 214 (1975). For an argument which fundamentally questions the validity of the distinction between 'mutual agreement' and 'mutual conduct', see A.J. McClean, (1979) 57 Can Bar Rev 1 at 16. See also *Lyons v Lyons* [1967] VR 169 at 171.

11   *Staples v Maurice* (1774) 4 Bro Parl Cas 580 at 585f, 2 ER 395 at 399; *Wardlow v Pozzi*, 338 P.2d 564 at 565 (1959). It seems that there must be mutuality between all the joint tenants existing at the date of the relevant agreement. There is no authority for severance where only some of those joint tenants are party to the agreement (see *Wright v Gibbons* (1948-1949) 78 CLR 313 at 322; *Tyson v Tyson* [1960] NSWR 177 at 180). Compare, however, A.J. McClean, (1979) 57 Can Bar Rev 1 at 2.

absence of contrary intention or arrangement, such a severance will result in a tenancy in common in equal shares.[12]

(a) Form of the agreement

Mutual agreement provides a flexible and informal mode of severance. The agreement need not take the form of a specifically enforceable contract[13]: it need not be evidenced in writing[14] and no valuable consideration need pass between the severing joint tenants.[15] Moreover, it is sufficient that the agreement is revocable and may never be carried through to performance: subsequent repudiation of the agreement will not detract from its severing quality.[16]

(b) Content of the agreement

The agreement may either contemplate severance in express terms or comprise merely an agreement that the joint tenants should deal with the property in a manner which necessarily involves severance.[17] Severing effect has thus been attributed, for instance, to an agreement between two joint tenants that on the death of either co-owner the interest of the decedent should be passed to their daughter.[18]

(i) Illustrations Severance will not normally result simply from an agreement by co-owners to join in a sale[19] or lease[20] of the jointly owned property to a third party.[1] Such action alone does not exclude the possibility of future survivorship

---

12 *Paterson v Paterson* (1980) 108 DLR (3d) 234 at 236.
13 Compare the case of severance under the first rule in *Williams v Hensman* (ante, p 323), where an agreement by A to transfer his 'share' to P constitutes an 'act...operating upon his own share' only if the agreement is specifically enforceable (see *Burgess v Rawnsley* [1975] Ch 429 at 446C per Sir John Pennycuick).
14 *Wilson v Bell* (1843) 5 Ir Eq R 501 at 507; *Lagar v Erickson*, 56 P.2d 1287 at 1288 (1936). Of course severance follows *a fortiori* where the agreement is in written form (see *Smith v Morton*, 106 Cal Rptr 52 at 55 (1972)). For the strong contention that, for the purpose of severance by 'mutual agreement', writing is indeed required under the old Statute of Frauds (now Law of Property Act 1925, s 40, ante, p 210), see A.J. McClean, (1979) 57 Can Bar Rev 1 at 16f; *Lyons v Lyons* [1967] VR 169 at 171.
15 'The significance of an agreement is not that it binds the parties; but that it serves as an indication of a common intention to sever...' (*Burgess v Rawnsley* [1975] Ch 429 at 446C per Sir John Pennycuick). See also *Frewen v Relfe* (1787) 2 Bro CC 220 at 224, 29 ER 123 at 125; *Gebhardt v Dempster* [1914] SALR 287 at 309; *Abela v Public Trustee* [1983] 1 NSWLR 308 at 315F.
16 *Burgess v Rawnsley* [1975] Ch 429 at 444D per Browne LJ; *Abela v Public Trustee* [1983] 1 NSWLR 308 at 314C, 315F.
17 *Burgess v Rawnsley* [1975] Ch 429 at 444A per Browne LJ, 446C per Sir John Pennycuick. See also *Wilson v Bell* (1843) 5 Ir Eq R 501 at 507; *Re Pozzi* [1982] Qd R 499 at 501C.
18 *McDonald v Morley*, 101 P.2d 690 at 692 (1940).
19 *Re Hayes' Estate* [1920] 1 IR 207 at 211; *Re Allingham* [1932] VLR 469 at 472; *County of Fresno v Kahn*, 24 Cal Rptr 394 at 397 (1962); *Lyons v Lyons* [1967] VR 169 at 172; *Public Trustee v Grivas* [1974] 2 NSWLR 316 at 320C; *Abela v Public Trustee* [1983] 1 NSWLR 308 at 314B. No severance is brought about by the compulsory acquisition of jointly owned land (see *Ex Parte Railway Commissioners for NSW* (1941) 41 SR (NSW) 92 at 95).
20 *Palmer v Rich* [1897] 1 Ch 134 at 143; *Lyons v Lyons* [1967] VR 169 at 170.
1 Nor will severance be brought about by a mere agreement between the joint tenants for a splitting of the rental income derived from a joint letting (see *Flannigan v Wotherspoon* [1953] 1 DLR 768 at 775f). Such an agreement does not exclude the possibility of survivorship in respect of the freehold reversion. For the same reason an agreement allowing one joint tenant sole residence of the property does not connote a severance by 'mutual agreement' (see *Gillette v Nicolls*, 262 P.2d 856 at 859 (1953); *Cole v Cole*, 294 P.2d 494 at 496 (1956); *Lyons v Lyons* [1967] VR 169 at 170; *Compton v Compton*, 624 P.2d 345 at 346 (1981)).

in respect of the capital proceeds of the transaction. However, an agreement that the proceeds of sale should be divided equally (or even unequally) between the co-owners does effect a severance, for the precise reason that further survivorship is now excluded.[2] Thus, where the joint tenants are spouses, severance may be brought about by a separation agreement which envisages a sale and distribution of the entire proceeds of sale in specific proportions,[3] or by a consent order made by a court to the same effect.[4] In *Nielson-Jones v Fedden*,[5] however, Walton J declined to find that severance had occurred by 'mutual agreement' where two spouses had signed a memorandum authorising the husband to organise a sale of the co-owned property and to employ some part of the proceeds in the purchase of a small dwelling-house for himself. This agreement was regarded as regulating only the 'use' and not the 'ownership' of the money proceeds of the sale.[6]

(ii) An extreme example   An extreme example of severance by 'mutual agreement' was provided by the controversial decision of the Court of Appeal in *Burgess v Rawnsley*.[7] Here two parties, H and R[8], joined in the purchase of a dwelling-house. The legal title was taken in joint names on trust for sale for themselves as beneficial joint tenants, each providing half of the purchase price. On the subsequent breakdown of the relationship, H negotiated with R to buy her out, and a county court judge found as a fact that R had orally agreed to sell her share in the house to H for a specified price. R subsequently revoked that agreement and demanded a higher price, but H died before negotiations could proceed further. The Court of Appeal held that H had indeed severed the beneficial joint tenancy before his death and that his estate was therefore entitled to a half-share in any proceeds of sale of the property. Both Browne LJ and Sir John Pennycuick reluctantly based this conclusion on the ground that severance had been effected by the agreement which the county court judge had found on the somewhat unsatisfactory evidence before him.[9]

2   *Crooke v De Vandes* (1805) 11 Ves Jun 330 at 333, 32 ER 1115 at 1116; *Flannigan v Wotherspoon* [1953] 1 DLR 768 at 776.

3   *Re McKee and National Trust Co Ltd* (1975) 56 DLR (3d) 190 at 196; *Re Pozzi* [1982] Qd R 499 at 502E. It seems that severance may be implied from the fact that joint tenants have agreed to divide between themselves the deposit paid over by the purchaser at the point of contract (see *Crooke v De Vandes* (1805) 11 Ves Jun 330 at 333, 32 ER 1115 at 1116; *Flannigan v Wotherspoon* [1953] 1 DLR 768 at 776), provided that this agreement apportions the whole and not merely part of the deposit (see *Nielson-Jones v Fedden* [1975] Ch 222 at 230D).

4   *Public Trustee v Grivas* [1974] 2 NSWLR 316 at 322C; *In Re Estate of Estelle*, 593 P.2d 663 at 666 (1979). A consent order may still have severing effect even though it fails to define precisely the respective shares of the parties in the proceeds of the court-ordered sale (see *Abela v Public Trustee* [1983] 1 NSWLR 308 at 316B).

5   [1975] Ch 222 at 229G.

6   See the criticism of this decision in *Burgess v Rawnsley* [1975] Ch 429 at 440B, 448B (post, p 331), but compare *Bank of British Columbia v Nelson* (1979) 17 BCLR 223.

7   [1975] Ch 429. See [1976] CLJ 20 (D.J. Hayton); (1975) 39 Conv (NS) 433 (F.R. Crane); (1976) 50 ALJ 246 (PB); (1976) 40 Conv (NS) 77 (J.F. Garner); (1977) 41 Conv (NS) 243 (S.M. Bandali).

8   The judgment of Lord Denning MR ([1975] Ch 429 at 435F-H) contains an account of a love story—as poignant as any to be found in the bleak pages of the law reports—which began at a scripture rally in Trafalgar Square.

9   'The evidence upon which that finding was based appears to be rather weak...' ([1975] Ch 429 at 445H per Sir John Pennycuick). See also [1975] Ch 429 at 442G, 443G per Browne LJ. It has been suggested that a doctrine of temporary severance may be appropriate in cases of short-lived agreement, with a reversion to joint tenancy when the agreement is terminated or revoked (see P. Butt, (1979-82) 9 Sydney LR 568 at 576f).

(3) Mutual conduct

The third method of severance adverted to by Page Wood V-C in *Williams v Hensman* has been termed severance by the 'mutual conduct' of the existing joint tenants. In the words of Page Wood V-C, severance may be effected 'by any course of dealing sufficient to intimate that the interests of all were mutually treated as constituting a tenancy in common.'[10] In spite of the close conceptual similarity, the balance of judicial opinion is now to the effect that this third category of severing circumstance is not 'a mere sub-heading of rule 2' of Page Wood V-C's categories.[11]

(a) General nature of 'mutual conduct'

'Mutual conduct' has been taken to comprise any conduct of the joint tenants which falls short of evidencing an express or implied agreement to sever but which nevertheless indicates a common intention that the joint tenancy should be severed.[12] Severance by 'mutual conduct' requires neither an express act of severance, nor a contract, nor a declaration of trust. It requires merely a consensus between the joint tenants, arising in the course of dealing with the co-owned property, which effectively excludes the future operation of a right of survivorship.[13]

(b) Examples of 'mutual conduct'

Examples of the 'course of dealing' required to establish severance are manifold and depend on the individual facts of each case. The following issues have featured near the centre of judicial concern.

(i) Long-term assumptions about ownership   It is clear that severance by 'mutual conduct' occurs where co-owners, although originally joint tenants, have acted over a long period of time on the assumption that each owns a severed share as a tenant in common.[14] However, the mere fact that joint property is for tax reasons included among the assets of a partnership with separate capital accounts for the co-owners does not necessarily constitute a severing 'course of dealing'.[15]

---

10   (1861) 1 John & H 546 at 557, 70 ER 862 at 867 (ante, p 320).
11   *Burgess v Rawnsley* [1975] Ch 429 at 447D per Sir John Pennycuick. See also [1975] Ch 429 at 439B per Lord Denning MR, 444F per Browne LJ; *Greenfield v Greenfield* (1979) 38 P & CR 570 at 577; *Abela v Public Trustee* [1983] 1 NSWLR 308 at 315A; contra, *In re Wilks* [1891] 3 Ch 59 at 61f; *Flynn v Flynn* [1930] IR 337 at 343; *Lyons v Lyons* [1967] VR 169 at 170f; *Nielson-Jones v Fedden* [1975] Ch 222 at 231B.
12   See *Abela v Public Trustee* [1983] 1 NSWLR 308 at 315G. A common intention to sever may be more readily inferred from a course of conduct where the joint tenants are married to each other (see *Harris v Goddard* [1983] 1 WLR 1203 at 1208F; *Estate of Gebert*, 157 Cal Rptr 46 at 51 (1979)) or where the personal relationship of the joint tenants has broken down (see *In the Marriage of Badcock and Badcock* (1979) FLC 90-723 at p 78,898; *Abela v Public Trustee* [1983] 1 NSWLR 308 at 315E). See also *Re Walters and Walters* (1978) 79 DLR (3d) 122 at 127.
13   See *Szabo v Boros* (1967) 64 DLR (2d) 48 at 49 per Davey CJBC.
14   See eg *Wilson v Bell* (1843) 5 Ir Eq R 501 at 507ff; *Re Denny* (1947) 116 LJR 1029 at 1037.
15   *Barton v Morris* [1985] 1 WLR 1257 at 1262D-H. See also *Brown v Oakshot* (1857) 24 Beav 254 at 258, 53 ER 355 at 357, but compare *Bedson v Bedson* [1965] 2 QB 666 at 690F per Russell LJ.

(ii) Mutual wills   The consensus required for 'mutual conduct' can be provided by the concurrent execution of mutual wills by two joint tenants, as for instance in the case of mutual wills which leave the respective share of each joint tenant to the survivor for life with remainder to some designated third party.[16]

(iii) Physical conversion of co-owned property   'Mutual conduct' is not necessarily constituted by a mere physical division of the co-owned property without partition or sale, where for reasons of convenience the joint tenants are left in sole and separate occupation of self-contained portions of the converted property.[17] A territorial realignment of this kind is not incompatible with continuing joint tenancy.[18]

(iv) Commencement of litigation   It seems that severance by 'mutual conduct' is not brought about simply by reason of the fact that the joint tenants have initiated court proceedings for partition[19] of the co-owned property or for a sale and distribution of proceeds.[20] However, it may well be that the formal commencement of such litigation between joint tenants effects a severance on other grounds.[1]

(v) Negotiations between joint tenants   Perhaps the most difficult issue in this area is whether a process of inconclusive negotiation between joint tenants in relation to their respective 'shares' can amount to 'mutual conduct'. Severance by 'mutual conduct' provided the ground on which Lord Denning MR preferred to rest his judgment in *Burgess v Rawnsley*.[2] In his view, this head of severance includes any 'course of dealing in which one party makes clear to the other that he desires that their shares should no longer be held jointly but be held in common.'[3]

This finding of 'mutual conduct' in the context of abortive negotiations for purchase did not, however, receive support from the other members of the Court of Appeal. Both Browne LJ[4] and Sir John Pennycuick[5] doubted whether a 'course of dealing' was sufficiently clearly established here to bring into play Page Wood V-C's third category of severing circumstance. Sir John

---

16   *In re Wilford's Estate* (1879) 11 Ch D 267 at 269; *In the Estate of Heys* [1914] P 192 at 195; *Szabo v Boros* (1967) 64 DLR (2d) 48 at 52. In *Re Bryan and Heath* (1980) 108 DLR (3d) 245 at 250, mutual wills distributing the respective shares of the co-owners among the surviving co-owner and the children of the family were held to constitute severance both by 'mutual agreement' and by 'mutual conduct'. See also *Re Sorensen and Sorensen* (1979) 90 DLR (3d) 26 at 38.

17   *Greenfield v Greenfield* (1979) 38 P & CR 570 at 578; *Sanders v McDonald and Pringle* [1981] CLY 1534; *Haughabaugh v Honald*, 5 Am D 548 at 550 (1812); *Stiff v Stiff*, 168 NW.2d 273 at 274 (1969).

18   Cp *Roche v Sheridan* (1857) 9 Ir Jur 409.

19   Post, p 341.

20   *Dando v Dando*, 99 P.2d 561 at 562 (1940); *Teutenberg v Schiller*, 291 P.2d 53 at 56 (1955); *Munroe v Carlson* (1976) 59 DLR (3d) 763; *Rodrigue v Dufton* (1977) 72 DLR (3d) 16.

1   Ante, p 325.

2   [1975] Ch 429 (ante, p 328).

3   [1975] Ch 429 at 439C.

4   [1975] Ch 429 at 444E.

5   [1975] Ch 429 at 447B.

Pennycuick admitted that 'where one tenant negotiates with another for some rearrangement of interest, it may be possible to infer from the particular facts a common intention to sever even though the negotiations break down.'[6] However, he thought such an inference to be entirely dependent on the individual facts of any given case.[7] In his view, the negotiations in *Burgess v Rawnsley*, 'if they can be properly described as negotiations at all', fell far short of warranting an inference of severance: 'one could not ascribe to joint tenants an intention to sever merely because one offers to buy out the other for £X and the other makes a counter-offer of £Y.'[8]

In other jurisdictions the courts have been more prepared to uphold severance as resulting from abortive or inconclusive negotiations between the joint tenants with respect to their individual 'shares'. This is particularly so where the negotiations have been incorporated in correspondence between the parties[9] or have been mediated through their respective legal advisers,[10] and where the parties have plainly begun to conceptualise their entitlements in terms of individualised shareholding.

(c) Limitations on 'mutual conduct'

Most of the limitations imposed on the concept of 'mutual conduct' stem from the judicial disinclination to accept that severance may be achieved by a merely unilateral and unwritten declaration of intention expressed by one of the joint tenants.[11] In this context the largely unspoken fear is that the facility of informal declaration, once admitted as a head of severance, would enable an unscrupulous joint tenant to hedge his bets in the gamble surrounding longevity. If the declarant subsequently failed to outlive his fellow co-owners, he would have ensured that a severed share devolved upon his own estate; if, however, he did survive them, he would be able simply to deny that he had ever made a severing declaration.[12] It was for this reason that in *Williams v Hensman*[13] Page Wood V-C emphasised explicitly that, in the absence of an express act of severance, 'it will not suffice to rely on an intention, with respect to the particular share, declared only behind the backs of the other persons interested.' Instead, ruled Page Wood V-C, it is imperative to 'find in this class of cases a course of dealing by which the shares of all the parties to the contest have been effected...'[14]

6   [1975] Ch 429 at 447A.
7   See also *Robichaud v Watson* (1983) 147 DLR (3d) 626 at 633.
8   [1975] Ch 429 at 447B. For a significant adoption of the observations of Sir John Pennycuick in preference to those of Lord Denning MR, see *Harris v Goddard* [1983] 1 WLR 1203 at 1211B per Dillon LJ.
9   *Ginn v Armstrong* (1969) 3 DLR (3d) 285 at 288. Compare *Nielson-Jones v Fedden* [1975] Ch 222 at 230C, 231A (ante, p 328); but see *Burgess v Rawnsley* [1975] Ch 429 at 440B per Lord Denning MR, who considered that *Nielson-Jones v Fedden* had been wrongly decided and that severance could instead have been upheld there on the basis of 'mutual conduct'.
10 *Re Walters and Walters* (1978) 79 DLR (3d) 122 at 127, affd (1978) 84 DLR (3d) 416n; *Robichaud v Watson* (1983) 147 DLR (3d) 626 at 636. See, however, A.J. McClean, (1979) 57 Can Bar Rev 1 at 23.
11 Ante, p 325.
12 In this context the formality of an irrevocable delivery or registration may be an all-important indication of a joint tenant's intention to exclude himself from the possibility of future survivorship (ante, pp 222, 325). See *Re Sammon* (1979) 94 DLR (3d) 594 at 600f.
13 (1861) 1 John & H 546 at 558, 70 ER 862 at 867.
14 The word 'effected' in this quotation must have the meaning of 'affected'. The latter word is used in the Law Journal report (see (1861) 30 LJ 878 at 880).

Thus while in *Burgess v Rawnsley* Sir John Pennycuick was quite ready to concede that the 'policy of the law as it stands today...is to facilitate severance at the instance of either party',[15] neither he nor any other member of the Court of Appeal was prepared to hold that severance could be effected either by an uncommunicated declaration by one joint tenant[16] or indeed by a mere verbal notice by one joint tenant to the other joint tenant or tenants.[17] It follows, *a fortiori*, that a declaration made by a joint tenant to a third party outside the joint tenancy is likewise incapable of bringing about a severance.[18]

10. SEVERANCE IN CONSEQUENCE OF UNLAWFUL KILLING

Severance of a joint tenancy may occur on a footing quite different from any so far considered. It is possible that severance may result, not from any lawful act of a joint tenant, but rather in consequence of the unlawful killing of one joint tenant by another.[19]

(1) The general rationale

In *Cleaver v Mutual Reserve Fund Life Association*,[20] Fry LJ gave classic expression to the view that 'no system of jurisprudence can with reason include amongst the rights which it enforces rights directly resulting to the person asserting them from the crime of that person.'[1] A forfeiture rule[2] is thus applied by the courts as a rule of public policy in order to ensure that no wrongdoer shall profit from his crime and, in particular, to ensure that 'a man shall not slay his benefactor and thereby take his bounty.'[3] This principle has a special application to joint tenants who, in fact if not in strict legal theory, derive benefit from the earlier decease of one of their number.[4]

15   [1975] Ch 429 at 448A, ante, p 317.
16   [1975] Ch 429 at 439C per Lord Denning MR, 444G per Browne LJ, 448A per Sir John Pennycuick.
17   [1975] Ch 429 at 439E per Lord Denning MR, 448A per Sir John Pennycuick.
18   *Greenfield v Greenfield* (1979) 38 P & CR 570 at 578 (communication to wife of other joint tenant held ineffective).
19   See generally Ames, *Can a Murderer Acquire Title by his Crime and Keep it?*, in *Lectures on Legal History* (1913), 310; J.W. Wade, 49 Harvard LR 715 (1935-36); Tim Youdan, *Acquisition of Property by Killing*, (1973) 89 LQR 235.
20   [1892] 1 QB 147.
 1   [1892] 1 QB 147 at 156, quoted with approval in *Beresford v Royal Insurance Co Ltd* [1938] AC 586 at 596 per Lord Atkin, and in *Helton v Allen* (1940) 63 CLR 691 at 709 (High Court of Australia). See also *Rosenfeldt v Olson* (1985) 16 DLR (4th) 103 at 120ff, (1986) 25 DLR (4th) 472 at 475.
 2   The term 'forfeiture rule' now has legislative status, being defined for the purpose of the Forfeiture Act 1982 as comprising 'the rule of public policy which in certain circumstances precludes a person who has unlawfully killed another from acquiring a benefit in consequence of the killing' (Forfeiture Act 1982, s 1(1)).
 3   *In the Estate of Hall* [1914] P 1 at 7 per Hamilton LJ. See also *Re Sigsworth* [1935] Ch 89 at 92; *In Re Giles* [1972] Ch 544 at 552B; *Re Nordstrom* (1962) 31 DLR (2d) 255 at 263. The courts in other jurisdictions are beginning to question whether the forfeiture rule is in every circumstance an inflexible rule of public policy. See eg the refusal to apply the rule in *Public Trustee v Evans* [1985] 2 NSWLR 188 at 193B-F (where one joint tenant killed her husband while attempting to avert lethal violence directed against herself and her children).
 4   Ante, p 297.

(2) The operation of the forfeiture rule

The operation of the forfeiture rule differs according to the number of joint tenants involved.

(a) Two joint tenants

The forfeiture rule operates easily in the case where the joint tenancy is limited to two persons who are joint tenants both of the legal estate and the equitable interest in the co- owned property. If, for instance, X and Y are joint tenants, and X unlawfully kills Y, it seems that X will remain invested with the legal estate by survivorship, but will hold it on trust for himself and Y's estate as tenants in common in equal shares,[5] subject only to the proviso that X may not take as a beneficiary under Y's estate.[6] In other words, the right of survivorship does not operate in an unqualified form: the killer cannot claim the benefit of the *ius accrescendi* in relation to the equitable interest. As Cardozo said,[7] 'the social interest served by refusing to permit the criminal to profit by his crime is greater than that served by the preservation and enforcement of legal rights of ownership.'

(i) Homicide as a severing event Although this conclusion has been accepted as correct in most jurisdictions, it is much less easy to articulate the precise legal reasoning which underlies the outcome stated above. Differing explanations have been put forward. It has sometimes been suggested that the act of killing constitutes so clear a violation of the intimate union of joint tenancy that the inherent feature of this co-ownership form—the right of survivorship—can no longer operate.[8] The rule of survivorship has, in effect, been displaced by reason of the unlawful attempt by one joint tenant to predetermine in his own favour the gamble on longevity.[9] A more widely accepted explanation is quite simply that homicide is itself a severing event.[10] However, this explanation has

---

5   *Re Thorp and the Real Property Act* (1963) 80 WN (NSW) 61 at 65; *Schobelt v Barber* (1967) 60 DLR (2d) 519 at 524; *Re Pechar (Deceased)* [1969] NZLR 574 at 587; *Rasmanis v Jurewitsch* (1970) 70 SR (NSW) 407 at 411; *Re Gore* (1972) 23 DLR (3d) 534 at 536. Where, as so frequently happens, the murder of Y is followed by the suicide of X, X's estate will hold the joint property at law on trust for X's estate and Y's estate as tenants in common in equal shares (see *Re Dreger* (1976) 69 DLR (3d) 47 at 49, 60). The beneficiary under both estates may well be the same person (see eg *Whitfield v Flaherty*, 39 Cal Rptr 857 (1964)). There is much to be said in favour of treating the murder-suicide phenomenon, not in terms of rules which aim to frustrate cupidinous slaying, but rather in terms analogous to the Californian rule relating to simultaneous death (ante, p 298). See *Johansen v Pelton*, 87 Cal Rptr 784 at 789 (1970).

6   *In re K* [1985] Ch 85 at 100G; *Johansen v Pelton*, 87 Cal Rptr 784 at 786, 788 (1970). This proviso is incorporated in California's Probate Code, s 258. See also *Re Pechar* [1969] NZLR 574 at 587.

7   See B.N. Cardozo, *The Nature of the Judicial Process* (New Haven and London 1969), p 43.

8   'This form of ownership implies mutual rights. Its subsistence depends upon a tacit understanding or consent to accept the risks and chances of the natural expectancy of life, but the risk that one joint tenant should feloniously slay the other is a risk which is not contemplated. This act is a repudiation of the terms on which they hold' (*In Re Barrowcliff* [1927] SASR 147 at 151 per Napier J). See also *Kemp v The Public Curator of Queensland* [1969] Qd R 145 at 149; *Bradley v Fox*, 129 NE.2d 699 at 705f (1955).

9   See *Re Pupkowski* (1957) 6 DLR (2d) 427 at 430. See (1957) 35 Can Bar Rev 966 (R. St J. Macdonald). In *In re K* [1985] Ch 85 at 100H, Vinelott J seemed prepared to accept that the operation of the forfeiture rule simply severs the joint tenancy.

10 *In re Barrowcliff* [1927] SASR 147 at 151; *Bradley v Fox*, 129 NE.2d 699 at 706 (1955); *Kemp v The Public Curator of Queensland* [1969] Qd R 145 at 149; *Johansen v Pelton*, 87 Cal Rptr 784 at 786, 788 (1970).

been criticised by some courts on the ground that it controverts the long-established principle that severance can be effected only before death.[11] Moreover, the proposition has been considered undesirable in so far as it seems to countenance the addition of homicide as an approved method of terminating joint tenancy![12]

(ii) Application of constructive trust principles   Increasingly the view is taken that the forfeiture imposed on the killer is best justified in terms of the application of an equitable doctrine of constructive trust based on unjust enrichment.[13] In other words, the killer is recognised as taking the entirety by survivorship but is, by reason of his misconduct, subjected to the full rigour of equitable control. He is made to hold the legal estate on a constructive trust for himself and the victim's estate in equal shares.[14]

(iii) Unjust enrichment   The constructive trust approach has major merits. The legal devolution of title is left untouched, while the principle of public policy is enforced through the medium of trust.[15] The imposition of a constructive trust efficiently prevents unjust enrichment:[16] the killer is stripped of any profit arising from his crime, but is not otherwise subjected to penalty or forfeiture in respect of his own inchoate interest under the joint tenancy.[17] Moreover, although the devolution of title is allowed to take its normal course, the relative culpability of the killer's conduct can be made relevant at this secondary stage in determining whether, and if so to what extent, a constructive trust should be imposed on the title-holder.[18] The constructive trust approach thus allows a flexible grading of response by the court to the relative wrongfulness of the co-owners.[19] Where a constructive trust is imposed, this trust is capable of binding a third party to whom the killer has transferred the property.[20]

11   See *Re Thorp and the Real Property Act* (1963) 80 WN (NSW) 61 at 63; *Rasmanis v Jurewitsch* (1970) 70 SR (NSW) 407 at 411C; *Public Trustee v Evans* [1985] 2 NSWLR 188 at 193A-B.

12   See *In Re King's Estate*, 52 NW.2d 885 at 889 (1952); *Abbey v Lord*, 336 P.2d 226 at 233 (1955); *Rasmanis v Jurewitsch* (1970) 70 SR (NSW) 407 at 412A.

13   See B.N. Cardozo, *The Nature of the Judicial Process*, p 42; *Scott on Trusts*, para 493.2 (p 3516f, 3520); *Abbey v Lord*, 336 P.2d 226 at 230, 231; *Re Pechar* [1969] NZLR 574 at 587f; Tim Youdan, (1973) 89 LQR 235 at 253f. See also the exposition of constructive trust doctrine in the context of unjust enrichment in *Rosenfeldt v Olson* (1985) 16 DLR (4th) 103 at 121ff, but see (1986) 25 DLR (4th) 472 at 476f.

14   *Bradley v Fox*, 129 NE.2d 699 at 706 (1955). In *In Re K* [1985] Ch 85 at 100F-H, Vinelott J noted this approach, but thought that English law already provided an easier solution.

15   See *Re Thorp and the Real Property Act* (1963) 80 WN (NSW) 61 at 65.

16   *Scott on Trusts*, para 492 (p 3495f), para 493 (p 3517); *Johansen v Pelton*, 87 Cal Rptr 784 at 787 (1970).

17   *Schobelt v Barber* (1967) 60 DLR (2d) 519 at 523f; *Re Gore* (1972) 23 DLR (3d) 534 at 536, 538; *Re Dreger* (1976) 69 DLR (3d) 47 at 60. There is a marked disinclination in the civil law area against the imposition of a double penalty where the killer has already been subjected to the censure of the criminal law. See *Schobelt v Barber, supra* at 523f; 41 Minnesota LR 639 at 654 (1956-57).

18   See *Abbey v Lord*, 336 P.2d 226 at 230 (1959); *Re Thorp and the Real Property Act* (1963) 80 WN (NSW) 61 at 63.

19   See *Re Public Trustee of Manitoba and LeClerc* (1982) 123 DLR (3d) 650 at 651, where the right of survivorship was allowed to operate freely in favour of a killer who had been found not guilty of manslaughter by reason of insanity. In strict terms the case involved no unlawful or wrongful act which could attract the imposition of a constructive trust by way of forfeiture. See also *In re Giles, decd* [1972] Ch 544 at 552A.

20   *Bradley v Fox*, 129 NE.2d 699 at 706 (killer transferred property to defence attorney as security for legal fees). However, the bona fide purchaser without notice should be protected (see Tim Youdan, (1973) 89 LQR 235 at 255f, commenting on *In re Cash (Deceased)* (1911) 30 NZLR 577 at 580f).

(iv) Form of the constructive trust remedy The precise form of the constructive trust required by public policy is open to question. Since the principal concern is that the killer should not be allowed to retain any benefit flowing to him from the slaying of his cotenant,[1] any benefit coming to him must be held on trust for someone other than himself.[2] In the two-man joint tenancy, this leads fairly clearly to the designation of the victim's estate as the appropriate recipient of that which the killer may not properly retain. Few courts have gone so far as to maintain that there should be a constructive trust for the victim's estate of the entire interest in the co-owned property.[3] The balance of authority favours a solution under which the killer holds the legal title in the co-owned property on constructive trust for himself and the victim's estate in equal shares.

Even this solution has been challenged on the ground that it indirectly confers upon the killer the benefit of retaining behind the constructive trust a severed one-half share which is henceforth free from the uncertainty of survivorship.[4] Had events taken their normal course, the survivor might well have lost the gamble of longevity anyway.[5] For this reason some courts and commentators have inclined towards a more sophisticated form of constructive trust which allows the killer only a life interest in one half of the co-owned property, the entirety being otherwise held on constructive trust for the victim's estate.[6] However, even this variant of the constructive trust approach is vulnerable to criticism,[7] and the preferable view seems to be the simpler conclusion that the co-owned property is held on constructive trust for the killer and his victim's estate equally.

(v) Forfeiture Act 1982 Although the conclusion stated above almost certainly represents the current law in England, the courts have recently been given a

---

1   In strict theory the killer has not acquired by his wrongful act any larger interest in the property than he had formerly, since joint tenants are each invested with the entire estate from the very inception of the joint tenancy (ante, p 297). However, the courts have had little hesitation in ruling that this 'common law fiction' should not be allowed to blind the eyes of equity to the fact that a wrongdoer has in reality benefited by his own wrongful conduct (see *Bradley v Fox*, 129 NE.2d 699 at 705 (1955); *National City Bank of Evansville v Bledsoe*, 144 NE.2d 710 at 714 (1957)).

2   'Where two persons have an interest in property and the interest of one of them is enlarged by his murder of the other, to the extent to which it is enlarged he holds it upon a constructive trust for the estate of the other' (*Restatement of the Law of Restitution* (St Paul 1937), s 188 (p 773)).

3   See *Colton v Wade*, 80 A.2d 923 at 926 (1951); *Neiman v Hurff*, 93 A.2d 345 at 347 (1952).

4   *Scott on Trusts*, para 493.2 (p 3520f).

5   It ought for this purpose to be immaterial that because of their respective ages or states of health it is probable that the killer would have been the survivor in any event (see *Restatement of the Law of Restitution*, s 188, comment a (p 773)).

6   This is the view favoured in the *Restatement of the Law of Restitution*, s 188 (p. 773f) and by Robert Goff and Gareth Jones, *The Law of Restitution* (2nd edn London 1978), p 489. (No preference is expressed in the 3rd edn 1986, p 630). See also *Colton v Wade*, 80 A.2d 923 at 925 (1951).

7   The restriction of the killer to a mere life interest in half of the joint property has been criticised as concentrating undue attention on what the victim has lost in derogation of what the killer has always had at least in inchoate form (see *Johansen v Pelton*, 87 Cal Rptr 784 at 791 (1970)). The 'life interest' approach may even comprise an unconstitutional deprivation of the killer's property interest (see *In Re Estate of Hart*, 135 Cal Rptr 544 at 547 (1982)). The 'life interest' approach has no application to the phenomenon of double killing (ie, murder followed by suicide) where, in any event, the public policy concern to prevent unjust enrichment of the killer is abundantly falsified by the killer's patent lack of interest in the fruits of his crime (see *Johansen v Pelton*, 87 Cal Rptr 784 at 789 (1970); *Re Gore* (1972) 23 DLR (3d) 534 at 537).

limited discretion to override the draconian effect of this forfeiture rule in cases other than those involving murder.[8] Section 2 of the Forfeiture Act 1982 empowers the court to modify the operation of the rule if, having regard to the conduct of the offender and of the deceased and other material circumstances, 'the justice of the case requires the effect of the rule to be so modified'.[9] The evidence available so far suggests that this discretion may not be liberally exercised.[10]

(b) More than two joint tenants

Where unlawful killing occurs between two joint tenants, the legal conclusion examined above is the same irrespective of whether the reasoning employed is that based on a supposed severance by reason of homicide or on an imposition of constructive trust.[11] However, the mode of legal reasoning adopted may well make a difference where the original joint tenancy comprises more than two co-owners.

Where A, B and C are joint tenants and A kills B unlawfully (C being entirely blameless), the resulting legal title is clearly vested in A and C as survivors. On the assumption that homicide effects a severance, a tenancy in common of the equitable interest would now arise between A as to one third, B's estate as to one third, and C as to one third. However, in *Rasmanis v Jurewitsch*,[12] the Court of Appeal of New South Wales preferred the constructive trust approach in ruling that any benefit flowing to the killer from his crime must be held on trust for some person other than himself. That person, decided the Court, was C. In other words, the equitable interests behind the constructive trust belong to C as a tenant in common of one-third, and to A and C as joint tenants of the remaining two-thirds. In this way any profit arising from A's wrong passes to C rather than A, and A retains merely a chance of survivorship in relation to a two-thirds interest. The justice achieved by this result may be questioned. It would be more consistent with the consensus attained in the case of two joint tenants that B's estate should take a one-third share, A and C remaining joint tenants of a two-thirds interest. While admittedly A must not be allowed to derive benefit from his crime, there is no convincing reason why C should benefit either.

11. SEVERANCE BY EQUITABLE INTERVENTION

There has been a tentative suggestion that a constructive trust may be imposed more broadly to bring about severance even in circumstances which do not involve the wrongful killing of one joint tenant by another. In *Public Trustee v Grivas*,[13] Bowen CJ in Eq did not exclude the possibility that equity might impose a constructive trust on a surviving joint tenant in a case where it would be unconscionable that such a survivor should take the entire benefit of the joint property by survivorship. Such an approach would render the survivor a

---

8　Forfeiture Act 1982, s 5.
9　Forfeiture Act 1982, s 2(2).
10　See eg *In Re K* [1985] 1 WLR 234 at 242ff, affirming [1985] Ch 85 at 100H-102A.
11　See *Rasmanis v Jurewitsch* (1970) 70 SR (NSW) 407 at 411F.
12　(1970) 70 SR (NSW) 407 at 412B-G.
13　[1974] 2 NSWLR 316 at 322D.

trustee on behalf of himself and the estate of the deceased joint tenant in equal shares, and would thus in effect result in severance.[14] This wider basis for severance awaits a more general acceptance by the courts.

12. SEVERANCE BY MERGER OF INTERESTS

Severance may also be brought about where the four unities which are characteristic of joint tenancy are destroyed by a 'merger' of interests. Such a merger occurs, for instance, where A, B and C are joint tenants for life, with remainder to D in fee simple, and A later acquires D's remainder. Such a transaction destroys unity of interest between A, B and C, in that A's life interest is seen as merging with the fee simple interest, and A's entitlement as becoming thereby distinguishable from that of B and C. Under these circumstances severance would occur in respect of the life interest, A becoming a tenant in common while B and C remain joint tenants for life. A similar result follows if A, B and C begin as joint tenants for life with remainder to A in fee simple. Oddly enough, the dual nature of A's initial entitlements seems not to connote any merger of interests which would precipitate a severance.[15] However, if C subsequently acquires A's fee simple in remainder, C's joint life interest is immediately severed.[16]

13. CONCURRENT INTERESTS IN THE PROPERTY LEGISLATION OF 1925

Integral to any understanding of concurrent interests in modern land law is the maintenance of a rigid distinction between ownership *at law* and ownership *in equity*. If this distinction is preserved, it becomes possible to view with equanimity the apparent contradiction that, for instance, the same persons may be simultaneously joint tenants at law and tenants in common in equity.

(1) Legal and equitable ownership

It is important to remember that the legal title to land, while of course it binds the whole world, is otherwise relatively unimportant. It comprises merely a 'paper title', indicating those persons who are entrusted with nominal ownership and the appropriate powers of management and disposition. In other words, the legal title is concerned with internal administration and formal transfer. The legal title in co-owned land invests the legal owner with fiduciary (and largely administrative) duties. Equitable ownership, by contrast, is concerned with actual beneficial enjoyment—enjoyment either of the residential utility conferred by occupation of the land or of the rents and profits derived from letting the land, and ultimately of course enjoyment of the proceeds resulting from any sale of the land.

14 The situation before the court in *Grivas* involved the death of a joint tenant occurring after a court order for sale of the joint property but before that order could be implemented (ante, pp 318, 326). See also *Gray v Gray*, 412 A.2d 1208 at 1211 (1980).
15 *Bl Comm*, Vol II, pp 181, 186. It has been doubted whether a modern court would adhere to the logic (or illogic) of this ancient rule: see D. Mendes da Costa, (1961-62) 3 Melbourne ULR 137, 306, 433 at 444.
16 *Morgan's Case* (t Eliz 1) 2 And 202, 123 ER 620; *Wiscot's Case* (1599) 2 Co Rep 60b, 76 ER 555 at 556f.

Thus, if A and B hold as joint tenants *at law* (ie, are joint tenants of a legal estate), all that is meant is that A and B are jointly invested with the paper title and are jointly charged with the managerial and dispositive functions connected with it. Since they are joint tenants, the right of survivorship operates between them. *In equity* A and B may also hold as joint tenants, but equally well—depending on the relevant circumstances—they may be tenants in common. There is nothing inherently inconsistent or incompatible in the proposition that A and B, although joint tenants at law, are tenants in common in equity. All that is now being said is that each has a distinct share in the fruits of beneficial enjoyment, that is, a distinct share in ultimately the money value of the co-owned property. Most importantly, when A and B (as legal joint tenants) convey their legal estate to a purchaser in execution of their trust, it is in their respective capacities as beneficial tenants in common that they may each claim a share in the capital proceeds of sale.

(2) Co-ownership at law

Historically the common law always preferred joint tenancy to tenancy in common as the medium of co-ownership, largely because the operation of survivorship tended to restrict the numbers of persons from whom feudal obligations might be due.[17] Later joint tenancy came to be preferred simply because conveyancers could more easily investigate the single title held by joint tenants than if the legal title were fragmented between tenants in common, each of whom could in turn dispose separately of his share. In short, the common law favoured the sweeping together of interests by means of survivorship and leaned away from tenancy in common. The law, said Holt CJ in 1700, 'loves not fractions of estates, nor to divide and multiply tenures'.[18]

(a) The common law presumption

The presumption at law was therefore in favour of joint tenancy, and wherever co-ownership existed in relation to a legal estate in land the co-owners were presumed to be joint tenants of that estate *except* where either one of the 'four unities' was absent or 'words of severance' had been employed in the terms of the grant to the co-owners. Words of severance could be either express or implied, and comprised any language which denoted that the grantees were intended to take distinct and identifiable shares in the land granted, thereby negating the presumption of joint tenancy.[19]

17   *Bl Comm*, Vol II, p 193. These feudal services and their incidents, which were owed by an occupier of land to his immediate superior in the tenurial relationship (ante, p 56), were of course more effectively secured if due from persons whose number was liable to decrease with the passage of time.
18   *Fisher v Wigg* (1700) 1 Salk 391 at 392, 91 ER 339 at 340.
19   See *Robertson v Fraser* (1871) 6 Ch App 696 at 699 per Lord Hatherley LC ('anything which in the slightest degree indicates an intention to divide the property must be held to abrogate the idea of a joint tenancy, and to create tenancy in common'. Examples of express words of severance include the terms 'equally' (see *Lewen v Dodd* (1595) Cro Eliz 443 at 444f, 78 ER 684 at 685; *Lewen v Cox* (1595) Cro Eliz 695 at 696, 78 ER 931 at 932; *Right d Compton v Compton* (1808) 9 East 267 at 276, 103 ER 575 at 579), to 'be divided between two' (see *Peat v Chapman* (1750) 1 Ves Sen 542, 27 ER 1193; *Re Crow* (1985) 12 DLR (4th) 415 at 422), and 'among' (*Richardson v Richardson* (1845) 14 Sim 526 at 528, 60 ER 462). Words of severance would be implicit in, for instance, a direction that the co-owners should pay an annuity to a third party 'in equal shares'.

(b) The presumption becomes irrebuttable

There has already been some discussion of the way in which the property legislation of 1925 sought to resolve the tension which existed before 1925 between the conflicting objectives of alienability of land and security of endowment.[20] The aim of alienability was promoted by a series of important provisions contained in the Law of Property Act 1925. Prior to this enactment it had been possible for a legal estate to be held in undivided shares, although the presumption of the law was clearly in favour of joint tenancy. The 1925 Act extended the presumption of the law to its logical conclusion by providing that co-ownership at law must now take only the form of joint tenancy and may never take the form of tenancy in common. Section 1(6) of the Law of Property Act 1925 provides unequivocally that a legal estate 'is not capable of subsisting or of being created in an undivided share in land'.

Tenancies in common can therefore no longer exist at law, and the effect of the 1925 Act is to sweep all co-ownership in undivided shares into equity.[1] The corollary of the mandatory nature of joint tenancy at law is the provision in section 36(2) of the Law of Property Act 1925 that 'no severance of a joint tenancy of a legal estate, so as to create a tenancy in common in land, shall be permissible'. The cumulative effect of the 1925 Act is to facilitate the purchaser of the legal estate, who no longer faces the risk of investigating title to a fragmented legal estate.[2] His task is further eased by the fact that the maximum number of persons who may be joint tenants of any legal estate held on trust for sale is now restricted to four.[3]

(3) Co-ownership in equity

Equity, in contrast to the common law, traditionally preferred tenancy in common to joint tenancy as the medium of co-ownership. Tenancy in common represents certainty and fairness in the property relations of co-owners. Each tenant in common holds a fixed beneficial interest immune from the caprice of survivorship.[4] Each share constitutes a tangible quantum of wealth which can serve as the subject of family endowment. Thus, whereas the law leaned in favour of joint tenancy largely for reasons of convenience, equity has always leaned towards tenancy in common for reasons of fairness.

(a) Equity follows the law

In consequence even prior to 1925 equity, as always following the law, was accustomed to treat co-owners as tenants in common in all cases in which they were accounted to be tenants in common in the eyes of the law. In other words, equity regarded co-owners as tenants in common in all cases where the 'four unities' were not present or where words of severance were expressed or

---

20 Ante, p 96.
1 Law of Property Act 1925, s 34(1). See also *Rothera v Nottingham City Council* (1980) 39 P & CR 613 at 617.
2 Ante, p 98; post, p 354.
3 See Trustee Act 1925, s 34(2); Law of Property Act 1925, s 34(2), (3).
4 Survivorship 'is looked upon as odious in equity' (*R v Williams* (1735) Bunb 342 at 343, 145 ER 694). See also *In Re Woolley* [1903] 2 Ch 206 at 211.

implied.[5] However, equity went further and in a number of special cases has always been prepared to presume—quite irrespective of the position at law—that in the absence of contrary agreement the co-owners hold as equitable tenants in common. These special cases involve circumstances in which equity is anxious to avoid the caprice of survivorship, and thus leans heavily in favour of tenancy in common even though the co-owners are joint tenants at law (see Fig. 27).

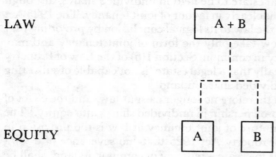

Fig. 27

(b) Special cases

It is now clear that the cases in which joint tenants at law are presumed to hold as tenants in common in equity are not rigidly circumscribed by the courts.[6] The circumstances in which equity may infer an intention to create a beneficial tenancy in common include the following.

(i) Partners   Where commercial partners acquire title to land for the purpose of their joint business enterprise, equity has always presumed that they hold the equitable interest in the land as tenants in common. The rationale for this equitable preference lies in the belief that the incidents of joint tenancy are inimical to commerce.[7] In particular the hazards of survivorship are alien to the essence of commercial partnership.

(ii) Mortgagees   Where two or more persons lend money on the security of property, equity presumes that the mortgagees are tenants in common as between themselves, even though as against the mortgagor they may have

---

5   Difficulty is, of course, occasioned by an ambivalent grant to 'A and B jointly and severally'. The rule has been clear since *Slingsby's Case* (1587) 5 Co Rep 18b at 19a, 77 ER 77 at 78, that this form of grant confers a joint tenancy if contained in a deed inter vivos, but creates a tenancy in common if contained in a will. The assumption here is presumably that, in the latter case, the final utterance of the moribund testator was the utterance which he intended to be definitive (see, however, *Bl Comm*, Vol II, p 193). A similar dilemma of construction arose more recently in *Joyce v Barker Bros (Builders) Ltd* (1980) *Times*, 26 February. Here land had been conveyed to a husband and wife 'in fee simple as beneficial joint tenants in common in equal shares'. Vinelott J held that this habendum clause created a joint tenancy in equity rather than a tenancy in common (see [1980] Conv 171 (J.E. Adams)).

6   See *Malayan Credit Ltd v Jack Chia-MPH Ltd* [1986] AC 549 at 560E per Lord Brightman.

7   See *Jeffereys v Small*, (1683) 1 Vern 217, 23 ER 424; *Lake v Craddock* (1732) 3 P Wms 158 at 159, 24 ER 1011 at 1012. See *Co Litt*, p 182a ('Ius accrescendi inter mercatores locum non habet').

taken their mortgage as joint tenants. The basis of this presumption is the belief that each mortgagee, irrespective of his posture towards the outside world, intended as against his co-mortgagee to 'lend his own and take back his own'.[8]

(iii) Purchasers who contribute money in unequal proportions By far the most important case in which equity prefers tenancy in common to joint tenancy arises where two or more persons contribute money in *unequal* proportions towards the purchase of property. Equity has consistently presumed that, as between persons who contribute differing amounts of money 'in the character of a purchaser', the resulting beneficial ownership ought to reflect the disparity of contribution.[9] The rights acquired by the contributors should not be regulated by the crude rule of survivorship.[10]

(iv) Business tenants In *Malayan Credit Ltd v Jack Chia-MPH Ltd*[11] Lord Brightman confirmed that the three cases cited above do not represent a definitive or exhaustive list of the special circumstances in which equity leans towards tenancy in common. There exist other cases in which equity may properly infer that, even though a legal title is held by way of joint tenancy, it was nevertheless intended that the parties should be tenants in common in equity. An example of such circumstances arose in *Malayan Credit Ltd v Jack Chia-MPH Ltd*, where the Privy Council upheld a beneficial tenancy in common where the grantees of a lease held the premises 'for their several individual business purposes'.[12]

14. TERMINATION OF CO-OWNERSHIP

Severance has the effect of converting co-ownership by joint tenancy into co-ownership by tenancy in common, but co-ownership may be altogether terminated or extinguished in any of the following ways.

(1) Partition

The unity of possession which is essential to both joint tenancy and tenancy in common is destroyed if the co-owned land is physically divided up or partitioned amongst the individual co-owners. Under section 28(3) of the Law of Property Act 1925, trustees for sale are now given power to effect a partition with the consent of their beneficiaries and to convey to each his separate portion of the realty. If the trustees or any of the beneficiaries refuse to consent to a partition, it is open to any person interested to apply to the court under section 30 of the Law of Property Act 1925, in which case the court may make

---

8   *Morley v Bird* (1798) 3 Ves 628 at 631, 30 ER 1192 at 1193. See also *In re Jackson* (1887) 34 Ch D 732 at 737, and compare now Law of Property Act 1925, s 111.
9   Where the contributions are equal in amount there is prima facie a joint tenancy between the contributors (ante, p 247).
10 For an account of the presumption of resulting trust, see Chapter 10 (ante, p 244).
11 [1986] AC 549 at 560E-F.
12 [1986] AC 549 at 560F.

'such order as it thinks fit'.[13] After partition there can be no co-ownership; there is merely separate ownership of the individual parcels of land which once comprised the co-owned realty.

(2) Union of the property in one joint tenant

Co-ownership clearly ends if a co-owned estate comes into the sole ownership of one joint tenant. In the context of a joint tenancy originally affecting both the legal and equitable interest in land, this may happen in two different ways.

(a) Release inter vivos

In strict terms a joint tenant has no interest with which he can deal unilaterally at law.[14] However, the Law of Property Act 1925 permits a joint tenant to 'release' his interest to the other joint tenant or tenants[15] and even makes provision for him to 'convey' his interest to another joint tenant.[16] It is clearly possible that the process of release may cause the entire co-owned interest to be held by only one of the original joint tenants, in which case all forms of co-ownership have been extinguished by the union in the single tenant.

(b) Operation of survivorship

The same effect may be brought about by the operation of survivorship.[17] If one of two remaining joint tenants dies without having effected a severance in equity, the entire interest both at law and in equity survives to the remaining tenant. Any trust for sale which previously gave effect to the co-ownership terminates with the demise of the joint tenancy.[18]

(i) The problem with subsequent dealings   It is expressly provided by section 36(2) of the Law of Property Act 1925 that nothing affects 'the right of a survivor of joint tenants, who is solely and beneficially interested, to deal with his legal estate as if it were not held on trust for sale.' There is, however, a practical difficulty here. The survivor is faced with the problem that if he should ever try to sell the property, his purchaser will require clear proof that none of the now deceased joint tenants brought about a severance of his equitable share prior to his death. In unregistered land the original joint tenancy will, of course, be

---

13   Post, p 377. Partition is rare in England, but is more common in other jurisdictions. On the criteria relevant to the court's discretion see eg *Schnytzer v Wielunski* [1978] VR 418 at 423ff (Property Law Act 1958 (Victoria), s 223); *Hayward v Skinner* [1981] 1 NSWLR 590 at 593F-595A (Conveyancing Act 1919 (New South Wales), s 66G(1), (4)). Partition may not be sanctioned by the court if its purpose is to evade planning controls or zoning regulations which prohibit subdivision of the land (see eg *Cochrane v Cochrane* (1980) 108 DLR (3d) 395 at 397f).

14   Ante, p 295.

15   Law of Property Act 1925, s 36(2). See *Harris v Goddard* [1983] 1 WLR 1203 at 1210F. Although it is open to a joint tenant to release his joint tenancy at any time subsequent to the creation of this form of co-ownership, it seems that he may disclaim his interest ab initio only if the other joint tenants are parties to his disclaimer (see *In Re Schär* [1951] Ch 280 at 285).

16   Law of Property Act 1925, s 72(4).

17   Ante, p 296.

18   See *In Re Cook* [1948] Ch 212 at 215f.

obvious from the face of the vendor's title deeds, and the vendor is consequently put on proof of a negative. If severance had occurred prior to the death of a deceased joint tenant, the purchaser would stand in clear danger of receiving only part of the beneficial interest in the land since the deceased's share would have devolved with his estate.

(ii) The statutory solution The survivor can always circumvent the present difficulty by appointing another trustee to act with him in giving what is conventionally regarded as an overreaching conveyance to the purchaser. However, legislation has now intervened in order to spare the surviving joint tenant both the inconvenience of such a manoeuvre and the impossibility of proving that no severance has ever taken place. Under section 1(1) of the Law of Property (Joint Tenants) Act 1964, the surviving joint tenant is deemed to be solely and beneficially entitled if he conveys as 'beneficial owner' or if the conveyance contains a statement that he is so interested. The 1964 Act has no application to registered land,[19] and is moreover ineffective in relation to unregistered land if a memorandum of severance has been attached to the title deeds[20] or if a receiving order (or a petition for one) has been registered under the Land Charges Act.[1] In all other cases, however, it is safe for a purchaser to rely on the presumption contained in the Act, and the purchaser thus takes priority over any owner of a severed share which was not the subject of a memorandum of severance.[2]

(3) Conveyance to a single third party

Co-ownership of land plainly terminates if the co-owners convey their land to a single third party. The purchaser takes the land free of all trusts if he pays the purchase moneys to at least two trustees. Of course, a conveyance of the land to more than one purchaser will create a new co-ownership in the land, as will a conveyance to a single purchaser in circumstances where two or more persons have contributed to the purchase moneys.[3]

---

19 Law of Property (Joint Tenants) Act 1964, s 3.
20 Law of Property (Joint Tenants) Act 1964, s 1(1)(a). On the 1964 Act, see (1964) 28 Conv (NS) 329; (1966) 30 Conv (NS) 27 (P. Jackson).
1   Law of Property (Joint Tenants) Act 1964, s 1(1)(b).
2   Even in the absence of a memorandum of severance, it is doubtful, however, that a purchaser with express notice of a severance can rely on the 1964 Act (see (1984) 100 LQR 149 (P. Jackson)).
3   Post, p 363.

CHAPTER 12

Trusts for sale

The device of the 'trust for sale' has nowadays become an integral feature of the law of co-ownership of land. There are few situations in English law in which co-ownership in possession does not bring into existence either expressly or impliedly some form of trust for sale, and it is for this reason that the operation of the trust for sale provides the subject matter of this chapter.

1. ORIGINS OF THE TRUST FOR SALE

During the 20th century the English law relating to co-ownership has adopted and modified for its own artificial purposes a form of trust holding whose origin was markedly different from its present function.

(1) Historical development

In its archetypal 19th century form the 'trust for sale' provided a means by which a testator could direct trusted friends (ie, his 'executors') to sell his property after his death and distribute the money proceeds to a number of specified beneficiaries. The duty of these 'trustees' was therefore unequivocal and immediate: they became immediately subject to a duty to convert (ie, to sell) the trust property, normally within a period of one year from the date of the testator's death (the so-called 'executor's year').

(2) Changing functions

As a legal device the trust for sale was initially more concerned with the exchange value of land than with its use value. The overriding emphasis was on property as capital rather than property as a means of utility. It was largely this conception of the trust for sale which was adopted in the property legislation of 1925 for the purpose of fulfilling a much broader function in regulating co-ownership of land. It is somewhat ironic that the modified version of the trust for sale which appeared so attractive in 1925 has now become—not least in the residential context—a somewhat inappropriate medium for the legal expression of co-ownership.[1]

(3) Static features

In spite of the initially somewhat strange nomenclature, it is important to remember that a 'trust for sale' of land does in fact exhibit the classic features of the trust concept.[2] As with any trust, the 'trust for sale' separates the functions of administration and enjoyment of property. Administration is vested in the

1   Post, p 367.
2   Ante, p 41.

trustees for sale as owners of the legal estate in the land. It is they who exercise the appropriate powers of management and disposition in relation to that estate. Enjoyment is, however, conferred upon the beneficiaries behind the trust for sale, ie, upon those who hold the equitable interests and on whose behalf the trustees are invested with the legal estate. Even so, the trust for sale is more than simply a *trust* of property: it is a trust *for sale*. Certain essential features have been superimposed on the basic trust device by the 1925 legislation, with the object of ensuring that the property held on 'trust' is ultimately converted and its money value distributed in the manner specified either by the settlor or by law.

(4) Successive and concurrent interests

It is possible to incorporate two quite different modes of beneficial entitlement within the framework of the trust for sale. A trust for sale can provide either for a succession of beneficial interests to be held in the land or for the equitable ownership of the land to be held by several persons absolutely and concurrently.

(a) The 'successive interest trust for sale'

Under a 'successive interest trust for sale' it is possible to provide for a succession of beneficial interests to be held in the land, as for instance where Blackacre is conveyed to trustees for sale on behalf of 'A for life, remainder to B for life, remainder to C in fee simple' (see *Fig.* 28).

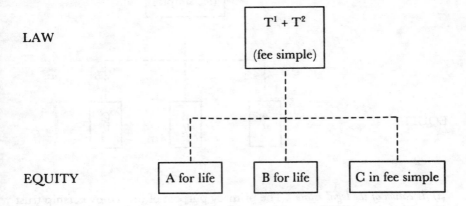

LAW $T^1 + T^2$ (fee simple)

EQUITY   A for life   B for life   C in fee simple

Fig. 28

(i) Location of the legal estate   This use of the trust for sale produces an effect which is remarkably similar to that achieved by a strict settlement created pursuant to the Settled Land Act 1925.[3] Under a trust for sale, however, the legal estate in the land and the attendant decision-making powers are not

3   Post, p 803.

vested, as is the case under a strict settlement,[4] in the beneficiary who is currently in possession (ie, A). The essence of the trust for sale is that the legal estate in the land is placed in the hands of separate trustees (T^1 and T^2),[5] who thereafter exercise all the decision-making powers with regard to the administration of the land and its eventual disposition.[6]

(ii) Operation of the trust   Under the trust for sale the trustees manage the property pending sale, allowing the beneficiary in possession at any given time either to reside on the land or to receive the rents and profits derived from the land. The trustees also exercise discretion as to the precise timing of sale, in which event the beneficial interests of A, B and C will normally be overreached and translated into the resulting proceeds.[7] In the absence of sale, the legal estate remains vested in the trustees and continues to be so vested regardless of death amongst the beneficiaries. If no sale occurs before C's beneficial interest falls into possession, C (if of full age) may call upon the trustees to vest the legal estate in himself, whereupon the trust for sale has terminated and C stands as absolute owner both at law and in equity.

(b) The 'co-ownership trust for sale'

A trust for sale more usually takes the form of a 'co-ownership trust for sale'. Such a trust provides for simultaneous entitlement in possession on the part of the beneficiaries, as where Blackacre is conveyed to trustees for sale on behalf of 'A, B and C in equal shares' (see *Fig.* 29).

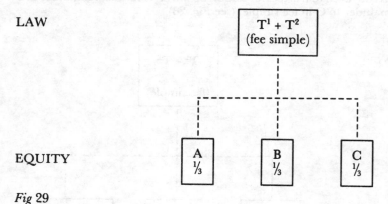

Fig 29

(i) Location of the legal estate   The primary purpose of the 'co-ownership trust for sale' is to provide for concurrent beneficial ownership of land rather than successive entitlements in equity. However, just as in the 'successive interest

---

4   Settled Land Act 1925, ss 19(1), 20(1), 38ff.
5   There is nothing, however, to preclude a beneficiary from also being a trustee (post, p 347).
6   A trust for sale in this form may be preferred to a strict settlement under the Settled Land Act 1925 precisely because it is, for some reason, thought desirable that the legal initiative in respect of management and disposition should be entrusted to persons other than the beneficiary in possession.
7   Ante, p 102, post, p 356.

trust for sale' (*Fig.* 28), the legal estate is vested in 'trustees for sale', and it is they who are charged with the exercise of powers of interim management and eventual disposition on behalf of the beneficiaries.

(ii) Operation of the trust In the 'co-ownership trust for sale' the interests of the beneficiaries are held simultaneously in possession, whether in specific proportions or otherwise. Whereas in the trust for sale outlined in *Fig.* 28 the beneficial interests (other than that of the final remainderman C) are limited and consecutive, the interests enjoyed by beneficiaries behind a 'co-ownership trust for sale' are absolute and concurrent. The beneficiaries have proportional rights in the income drawn from the land before sale, and usually enjoy specific shares of the capital proceeds of sale if and when sale takes place (see *Fig.* 29).

(iii) Division of functions The co-ownership trust for sale is nowadays very much more common than the successive interest trust for sale. But whether a trust for sale gives effect to successive or concurrent beneficial entitlements, at the heart of its structure lies the firm distinction between ownership of the legal estate (which is essentially a 'paper title') and ownership of the equitable interests (which carry beneficial enjoyment). The legal title is concerned with powers of management and disposition; the beneficial interests are concerned with money and actual occupation.

There is nothing, of course, to prevent trustees and beneficiaries from being the same people. T^1 and T^2 may hold a legal estate on trust for sale for *themselves* as beneficiaries. But even here there remains a vital division of function: T^1 and T^2 wear different hats at different times—those of trustee and beneficiary respectively. In the capacity of trustee for sale, each is the owner of the legal estate. In the capacity of beneficiary, each owns an equitable interest. Their various headgear must never be confused:

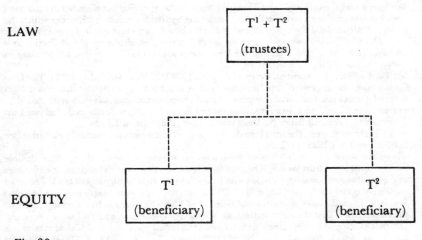

Fig. 30

(5) Express and implied trusts for sale

Trusts for sale arise either expressly or by implication. An express trust for sale arises where land is specifically vested in persons as trustees to hold 'on trust for sale' on behalf of certain beneficiaries. An implied trust for sale is normally the creation of some statutory provision, with the result that the terms 'implied trust for sale' and 'statutory trust for sale' may be used interchangeably. In the absence of an express trust for sale, an implied trust for sale arises by force of statute in almost every situation in which land is owned concurrently in possession by two or more persons.[8] A statutory trust for sale also occurs automatically on a death intestate.[9]

(a) 'Successive interest' trusts for sale

A 'successive interest trust for sale' can be created only *expressly*. In *Fig.* 28,[10] it is precisely the explicit nature of the direction that T^1 and T^2 should hold 'on trust for sale' which indeed brings about a trust for sale rather than a strict settlement.[11] Thus, where successive equitable interests in land are granted to designated beneficiaries, the grant inevitably takes the form of a strict settlement under the Settled Land Act 1925 unless the accompanying legal title is expressly directed to be held 'on trust for sale'.[12]

Trusts for sale are nowadays much more common than strict settlements.[13] The latter are rarely created deliberately,[14] and usually come into being only where a settlor has unwisely attempted to confer a life interest by informal means.[15] Here, in default of some explicit reference to a trust 'for sale', the ill-defined arrangement of the settlor initiates an imperfect settlement with all the disadvantages which ensue under the Settled Land Act 1925.[16]

---

8 An exceptional case is that of joint tenancy for life, which comprises a form of co-ownership in possession arising under a strict settlement (see Settled Land Act 1925, s 19(2)).

9 Administration of Estates Act 1925, s 33.

10 Ante, p 345.

11 To convey a legal estate to T^1 and T^2 merely 'on trust for' specified beneficiaries in succession would in fact produce a strict settlement under the Settled Land Act 1925, under which the person entitled to hold the legal estate would be the beneficiary currently in possession (rather than T^1 and T^2). Any conveyance to the latter 'on trust' would be simply ineffective as a conveyance of the legal estate, and the legal title would remain in the grantor pending its transfer to the appropriate tenant for life.

12 See *Peach v Peach* (Unreported, Court of Appeal, 1979 P 2745, 3 November 1981). The Law Commission has suggested that the priority thus accorded to the Settled Land Act 1925 should be terminated and that any grant of land which creates successive interests should be presumed to be held on a trust for sale unless this possibility is specifically excluded (see Law Commission, Working Paper No 94: *Trusts of Land* (1985), paras 3.3, 14.1).

13 As landholding devices, the trust for sale and the strict settlement are mutually exclusive (see Settled Land Act 1925, s 1(7)).

14 There are several powerful reasons nowadays for opting in favour of the more flexible arrangement of the trust for sale. The trust for sale substantially avoids the probate difficulties and quite disastrous tax implications which attach to the strict settlement of land. The strict settlement under the Settled Land Act 1925 has accordingly become extremely cumbersome and is little used under modern conditions. The Law Commission has already stated its provisional view that the strict settlement is 'excessively complex and no longer necessary' and that existing settlements should therefore be converted into some kind of trust of land (see Law Commission, Working Paper No 94 (1985), para 17.1). See also G.A. Grove, (1961) 24 MLR 123 at 127.

15 See Chapter 23 (post, p 803).

16 Post, p 805.

(b) 'Co-ownership' trusts for sale

A 'co-ownership trust for sale' may arise *either* expressly *or* by implication of statute. An express trust of this kind is created, for instance, by a conveyance of a legal estate 'to T^1 and T^2 on trust for sale for themselves in equity'. An implied trust for sale of the co-ownership variety arises, for example, where the legal estate is conveyed simply 'to A and B'. In the latter case statute intervenes to supply the existence of a trust for sale, more or less as a conveyancing device, with the result that the legal estate in the land is then held by A and B as trustees for sale presumptively for themselves in equity.[17]

2. STATUTORY DEFINITION OF THE 'TRUST FOR SALE'

The Law of Property Act 1925 adopted the familiar device of the 'trust for sale' and gave to it a central role in the restructuring of property law which took effect on 1 January 1926. A 'trust for sale' within the meaning of the Act is, however, accorded a somewhat specific definition which confines the statutory reference to 'an immediate binding trust for sale, whether or not exercisable at the request or with the consent of any person, and with or without a power at discretion to postpone the sale'.[18]

(1) Imposition of a duty

It is clear from the statutory definition that a 'trust for sale' necessarily imposes a 'trust' or duty upon the trustees. The essence of this trust is the *duty to sell* which is imposed on all trustees for sale by the very nature of their trust. If a mere *power of sale* has been conferred, then there can be no 'trust for sale'.[19] The distinction is ultimately one of construction of the words used in any express grant. However, a direction which somewhat ambiguously imposes a 'trust either to retain or to sell the land' is now properly construed as a trust to sell the land combined with a power to postpone the sale.[20]

(2) Immediacy of the trust

In terms of the statutory definition, a 'trust for sale' must be an 'immediate' trust for sale. This requirement of immediacy attaches, however, not to the sale but to the trust.

(a) Implied power to postpone sale

The existence of a 'trust for sale' does not necessitate an instant sale of the land. Indeed, section 25(1) of the Law of Property Act 1925 provides significantly that 'a power to postpone sale shall, in the case of every trust for sale of land, be

---

17   Post, p 360.
18   Law of Property Act 1925, s 205(1)(xxix).
19   The granting of a mere power of sale connotes the existence of a strict settlement of land, in which case that power of sale belongs properly, not to the trustees in the first instance, but to the tenant for life (post, p 805).
20   Law of Property Act 1925, s 25(4). See also Law of Property Act 1925, s 32(1), and *In re Hanson* [1928] Ch 96 at 99.

implied unless a contrary intention appears'.[1] However, the statutory definition produces the consequence that no trust for sale arises unless and until the land is impressed by a duty of sale in the trustees. If the 'trust' to sell arises only with effect from some future date, there is meanwhile no 'immediate' trust for sale. Any attempt to postpone the coming into effect of a trust for sale brings the relevant trust within the scope (at least initially) of the Settled Land Act 1925.[2]

(b) The 'trust for sale' as a device for retaining land

In effect a 'trust for sale' is in most cases a device of landholding directed not towards a *sale* but rather towards the *retention* of the land concerned—at least for the foreseeable future.[3] In imposing the (at first confusing) terminology of 'trust for sale' upon various forms of landholding, the Law of Property Act 1925 merely aims at a simplification of conveyancing. The use of a 'trust for sale' ensures that when, at some distant date, the land comes to be sold (ie, when the trust to sell is eventually 'executed'), the conveyancing machinery is already at hand to guarantee facility for the purchaser and security for those who own equitable interests. The device of overreaching enables the purchaser to take an unencumbered title, while beneficial interests relating to the land purchased are thenceforth satisfied out of the proceeds of the sale.[4] However, this outcome should not disguise the fact that, in most cases, unless and until a sale takes place the presence of a 'trust for sale' is nothing other than a convenient 'legal fiction'.[5]

(3) Binding nature of the trust

A 'trust for sale' must also be 'binding' in a highly specialised, but nowadays seldom crucial, sense. 'Trustees for sale' must be able, in dealing with a purchaser, to give a comprehensively overreaching conveyance of the legal estate, since otherwise the purchaser cannot acquire a clean title. A trust cannot constitute a 'binding trust for sale' where, for instance, the land subject to the trust is also the subject of legal or equitable entitlements arising *prior* to the trust which the trustees have no competence to overreach.[6] The caselaw on

---

1   For an instance of contrary intention, see *In re Atkins' Will Trusts* [1974] 1 WLR 761 at 767C-D. The Law Reform Committee observed that '[i]n many ways the reality is that a trust for sale is a power of sale' (see Law Reform Committee, *The powers and duties of trustees* (23rd Report, Cmnd 8733, October 1982), para 3.61).
2   Thus a grant of land to A for life, with remainder to B and C on trust for sale, creates a strict settlement during the lifetime of A. The trust becomes an 'immediate trust for sale' only on A's death. Compare, however, *Re Jacobson* [1970] VR 180 at 189 ('immediate binding trust for sale' consistent with conferment on widow of rent-free occupation pending sale).
3   See *In re Evers' Trust* [1980] 1 WLR 1327 at 1330G per Ormrod LJ ('[T]he trust for sale has become a very convenient and much used conveyancing technique. Combined with the statutory power in the trustees to postpone the sale, it can be used to meet a variety of situations, in some of which an actual sale is far from the intentions of the parties at the time when the trust for sale comes into existence').
4   Post, p 355.
5   *Williams & Glyn's Bank Ltd v Boland* [1979] Ch 312 at 336F-G per Ormrod LJ.
6   Additional overreaching powers appropriate to such a case are available only if the trust is converted into an *ad hoc* trust for sale under Law of Property Act 1925, s 2(2). The essence of an *ad hoc* trust for sale is that the trustees are either a trust corporation or persons appointed or approved by the court.

the meaning of the term 'binding' is confused,[7] but happily this aspect of the definition of a 'trust for sale' rarely causes problems in modern practice. The interpretation of the word 'binding' has an importance in demarcating the point in time at which a grant of land originally in the form of a strict settlement gives way to a trust for sale.[8] But, since strict settlements are now seldom created, the problem of construction is very much less pressing.

(4) Imposition of named consents

A trust for sale may be 'immediate' and 'binding' for the purpose of the Law of Property Act 1925 even though exercisable only at the request or with the consent of a named person or named persons. Thus, if a grantor of land wishes to render that land effectively unsaleable in the hands of his grantee, all he need do is to convey the land to trustees on trust for sale, specifying that sale is subject to the consent of some person who is extremely unlikely ever to agree to any sale.[9]

(a) Effect of an imposed consent

The technique of imposing a named consent in relation to the execution of a trust for sale may well be used for the purpose of ensuring, for instance, that a specific beneficiary under the trust is guaranteed rent-free use or occupation of the trust property for so long as he wishes.[10] Where this is done, the property can be disposed of only if and when sale accords with the needs and wishes of the named beneficiary.

(b) Legality of an imposed consent

The possibility that the exercise of a trust for sale may thus be controlled by requisite (and perhaps unobtainable) consents has brought about the rather strange consequence that land held supposedly on 'trust for sale' can, in some circumstances, be effectively incapable of sale. It is debatable whether the imposition of an unobtainable consent to the execution of a trust for sale is in truth compatible with the trustees' duty to sell,[11] but no challenge on this point

---

7   See eg *In re Leigh's Settled Estates* [1926] Ch 852; *In re Parker's Settled Estates* [1928] Ch 247; *In re Norton* [1929] 1 Ch 84. See also M.M. Lewis, (1938) 54 LQR 576.

8   This issue is, of course, vital in determining whether a purchaser of the land should look to the tenant for life or to the trustees for sale for a good conveyance of the legal title.

9   See *In re Inns* [1947] Ch 576 at 582.

10 See *In re Herklots' Will Trusts* [1964] 2 All ER 66 at 69I, 71C-D; *Ayer v Benton* (1967) 204 Estates Gazette 359 at 360.

11 There is, in relation to the trust for sale, no express equivalent of section 106 of the Settled Land Act 1925, which makes void any attempt to inhibit or restrict the exercise of a tenant for life's powers of disposition over settled land. The analogy provided by section 106 in a parallel field has of course stimulated the suggestion that, apart from the strictures necessarily imposed by a requisite named consent or the exercise of the trustees' power to postpone sale, the competence of a trustee for sale must be likewise irreducible. It might even be argued that section 106 is impliedly incorporated in the trust for sale provisions of the Law of Property Act 1925 by means of the reference in section 28(1) of that Act (post, p 352). However, sinuously attractive though these suggestions may be, the real truth is almost certainly that the respective policies of the trust for sale and the strict settlement are simply in conflict (see Law Commission, Working Paper No 94 (1985), para 8.5).

has yet been made in the courts. In theory the courts have jurisdiction under section 30 of the Law of Property Act 1925[12] to dispense with a requisite consent which is not forthcoming, but this jurisdiction has not yet been exercised in any reported decision.

3. THE RESPECTIVE ROLES OF TRUSTEE AND BENEFICIARY

The essence of most forms of the trust concept is the idea that the trustees hold the legal title to the trust property and are invested with powers of management and disposition. The beneficiaries merely benefit. Even if the trustees and the beneficiaries are the same persons, their functions are quite distinct.

(1) Powers of the trustees for sale

The powers exercisable by trustees for sale are defined by statute on an express analogy with the powers enjoyed by the tenant for life and settlement trustees under the Settled Land Act 1925.[13]

(a) Powers of management and disposition

The referential incorporation of Settled Land Act powers means that trustees for sale are invested with all the powers of management and disposition which would be enjoyed by a tenant for life and settlement trustees under a strict settlement.[14] Trustees for sale are therefore possessed of certain powers to grant leases[15] and mortgages[16] in respect of the land which they hold, and of course their ultimate power—that of sale[17]—is also a *duty*.

A trust for sale thus confers upon the trustees a mixture of powers and duties. The trust for sale itself imports a duty to sell coupled with a power at discretion to postpone sale. A power is by nature merely permissive; it is of the essence of a duty that its execution is mandatory. It may sometimes occur, of course, that trustees for sale cannot reach unanimity either in the discharge of their duty to sell the land or in the exercise of their power to postpone sale. In such a case the duty to sell overrides the power to postpone sale and is normally determinative

---

12   Post, pp 377, 382.

13   Law of Property Act 1925, s 28(1). See *In re Conquest* [1929] 2 Ch 353 at 358. These powers include the powers conferred during a minority by Settled Land Act 1925, s 102, even though no minority in fact exists in the context of the relevant trust for sale (see *In re Gray* [1927] 1 Ch 242 at 248).

14   These powers may be enlarged by express provision in the trust instrument (Settled Land Act 1925, s 109(1)). See *City of London Building Society v Flegg* [1986] Ch 605 at 612H- 613A).

15   In the absence of an expressly conferred extension of their power, the trustees are generally limited to granting leases for terms not exceeding 50 years (see Settled Land Act 1925, s 41). It has been recommended that the maximum term generally permissible could usefully be increased to 100 years, thereby enabling the grant of a 99 year term of years (see Law Reform Committee, *The powers and duties of trustees* (23rd Report, Cmnd 8733, October 1982), para 8.6).

16   See the limited mortgaging powers conferred on the tenant for life by Settled Land Act 1925, s 71.

17   See Settled Land Act 1925, s 38.

of the controversy. A trust 'for sale' must prevail (ie, the land must be sold) unless *all* the trustees agree to exercise the power to postpone sale.[18] Given the primacy of this duty to sell, if a recalcitrant trustee refuses to join his co-trustees in selling land held by them on trust for sale, an application may be made to the court in the last resort and the court may make 'such order as it thinks fit'.[19]

(b) Power to re-invest in land

Upon execution of their trust to sell, the trustees are responsible either for the proper investment of the proceeds of sale or (at the request of the beneficiaries) for the due distribution of those proceeds amongst the beneficiaries. In the absence of distribution the trustees have power[20] to re-invest the proceeds of sale in the purchase of other land which is then likewise held by them on trust for sale.[1] This useful power of reinvestment is, however, liable to one possible restriction. It is arguable that the trustees' power to re-invest in land is lost if at any point the trustees do not retain at least some land on trust for sale. By selling *all* the land originally held on trust for sale, the trustees may lose their status as 'trustees for sale',[2] in which case they become ordinary trustees of mere personalty and have as such no power to invest in realty.[3] For this reason it is sometimes said to be prudent for trustees for sale always to retain a small portion of land on trust for sale simply in order to preserve their character as 'trustees for sale'.

(2) Delegation of certain powers

It is open to trustees for sale to delegate certain of their statutory powers to any person of full age (other than a mere annuitant) who is currently entitled in possession to the net rents and profits of the land.[4] The powers which may be so delegated comprise the trustees' powers of management of the land and their

---

18   See *In re Mayo* [1943] Ch 302 at 304. There is a more detailed discussion elsewhere of the effect of disagreement between trustees for sale (post, p 819).
19   Law of Property Act 1925, s 30.
20   This power is derived from Settled Land Act 1925, s 73(1)(xi), as impliedly incorporated by Law of Property Act 1925, s 28(1).
1   Law of Property Act 1925, s 32(1).
2   By ceasing to hold *land*, it is arguable that the trustees lose their character as 'trustees for sale', as defined by Law of Property Act 1925, s 205(1)(xxix), and thereby fall outside the ambit of section 28(1). See *In re Wakeman* [1945] Ch 177 at 181f per Uthwatt J, but compare *In re Wellsted's Will Trusts* [1949] Ch 296 at 319.
3   Trustees of mere personalty have no power to invest any of their trust fund in land unless expressly authorised to do so by their trust instrument. Even where there is power to invest in land, the term 'investment' has been restrictively construed so as not to comprise the purchase of a house for the occupation of a beneficiary (see *In re Power* [1947] Ch 572 at 575). However, land is nowadays generally regarded as an extremely sound form of investment, and it has been recommended that the investment powers of ordinary trustees should be extended to cover the purchase of freeholds and certain leaseholds (see Law Reform Committee, *The powers and duties of trustees* (23rd Report, Cmnd 8733, October 1982), paras 3.2ff).
4   Law of Property Act 1925, s 29(1). A refusal by the trustees to delegate their powers in accordance with section 29 may become the subject of an application to the court under Law of Property Act 1925, s 30, which empowers the court to 'make such order as it thinks fit'.

powers of and incidental to leasing and accepting surrenders of leases.[5] The delegation must be made in writing signed by the trustees and is revocable by further signed writing.[6] If a delegation is made, the trustees cease to be liable for the acts or defaults of the delegate, since the delegate himself is thereafter deemed to have assumed the duties and liabilities of a trustee in relation to the exercise of the delegated powers.[7]

4. PROTECTION FOR A PURCHASER FROM TRUSTEES FOR SALE

One of the major achievements of the property legislation of 1925 was to make land generally marketable without simultaneously destroying its utility as a medium of family endowment. It is consistent with this policy that the trust for sale, as a conveyancing device, should enable a purchaser of any land held on trust for sale to acquire a good title free of the equitable interests of the beneficiaries. The legal title (whether it relates to registered or unregistered land) must be rendered freely alienable while fragments of beneficial ownership in the land are jealously safeguarded.

These twin objectives of facility for the purchaser and security for the beneficial owners are, in the context of the trust for sale, realised through the technical device of 'overreaching'.[8] This device effectively allows certain kinds of subsisting equitable interest to be swept off the land and on to the proceeds of sale, thereby affording the purchaser an absolute defence against any future claim founded on the equitable rights of trust for sale beneficiaries.

(1) Documentation in a trust for sale

Where land is held on an *express* trust for sale, the details of ownership (both legal and equitable) are often—although not necessarily—contained in two separate documents. One of these documents is a vesting document or conveyance which records the vesting of the legal title in the trustees for sale. The other document, if there is one, is a 'trust instrument' which records the equitable rights behind the trust. Normally a purchaser of the land need concern himself only with the first of these documents, since he knows that any equitable interests outlined in the trust instrument will be overreached on sale provided that he complies with the relevant statutory requirements. The primary protection for the purchaser therefore lies in his statutory claim to have overreached all subsisting beneficial interests, and it is a highly attractive incidental effect of the overreaching mechanism that these equitable rights are thereafter preserved as equivalent interests in the proceeds of sale.

---

5   Law of Property Act 1925, s 29(1). A trust for sale beneficiary, even though entitled to receive rents and profits, has no power to grant tenancies in the absence of a proper delegation under section 29, and any tenancy purportedly granted by him is not binding. In *Napier v Light* (1975) 119 SJ 166 at 167, the Court of Appeal held that two trust for sale beneficiaries, although together absolutely entitled and sui iuris, could not create a valid tenancy without the appropriate delegation. The rule in *Saunders v Vautier* ((1841) 4 Beav 115 at 116, 49 ER 282, Cr & Ph 240 at 249, 41 ER 482 at 485 (ante, p 53) gives beneficiaries authority merely to terminate the trust, not to commit their trustees to arbitrarily created tenancies.

6   Law of Property Act 1925, s 29(1).

7   Law of Property Act 1925, s 29(3).

8   The operation of 'overreaching' was explained in Chapter 6 (ante, p 100).

(2) The statutory conditions for 'overreaching'

Before a purchaser of land held on trust for sale can properly claim to have overreached, or taken title free of, the interests of beneficiaries under that trust, he must show that certain statutory conditions for overreaching have been satisfied. Section 2(1)(ii) of the Law of Property Act 1925 provides that

A conveyance to a purchaser of a legal estate in land shall overreach any equitable interest or power affecting that estate, whether or not he has notice thereof, if...the conveyance is made by trustees for sale and the equitable interest or power is at the date of the conveyance capable of being overreached by such trustees...and the statutory requirements respecting the payment of capital money arising under a disposition upon trust for sale are complied with...

The conditions laid down in this provision bear detailed examination.

(a) The conveyance must be 'made by trustees for sale'

No overreaching may occur in respect of a trust for sale except in the context of a 'conveyance'[9] made by 'trustees for sale'. 'Trustees for sale' are themselves defined in terms of 'persons...holding land on trust for sale',[10] and a 'trust for sale' is further defined as an 'immediate binding trust for sale'.[11] If, in the event of a disposition of the land, the purchaser fails to receive a conveyance made by 'trustees for sale', the overreaching mechanism described in section 2(1) of the Law of Property Act 1925 cannot operate in his favour.

(b) The equitable interests must be 'capable of being overreached '

The equitable interests which are 'capable of being overreached' by a purchaser are, in general, the equitable proprietary interests of trust for sale beneficiaries as joint tenants or tenants in common behind the trust. A conveyance of land held on trust for sale cannot entitle the purchaser to overreach 'commercial' equitable interests (such as estate contracts and restrictive covenants).[12] Interests of the latter kind continue to bind the land after the conveyance if—but only if—they have been protected by the appropriate form of registration or entry.[13]

Apart, however, from duly protected 'commercial' equitable rights, the only type of equitable interest which cannot be overreached on an ordinary conveyance by trustees for sale is an equity created *prior* to the trust for sale itself.[14] Such equitable interests rarely arise nowadays, and can be overreached by the purchaser only if recourse is had to the special machinery of an *ad hoc* trust for sale.[15]

---

9   A 'conveyance' within the Law of Property Act 1925 is defined as including, unless the context otherwise requires, 'a mortgage, charge, lease, assent, vesting declaration, vesting instrument, disclaimer, release and every other assurance of property or of an interest therein by any instrument, except a will...' (Law of Property Act 1925, s 205(1)(ii)).
10   Law of Property Act 1925, s 205(1)(xxix).
11   Ante, p 349.
12   Ante, p 96.
13   Ante, pp 113, 159. It must, of course, be remembered that in registered land certain rights remain binding on the transferee notwithstanding a failure to enter them on the register of title (see Land Registration Act 1925, s 70(1), ante, p 170).
14   There is, in the context of the trust for sale, no equivalent of Settled Land Act 1925, s 72(3). See *In re Ryder and Steadman's Contract* [1927] 2 Ch 62 at 82f.
15   Ante, p 350.

(c) Capital money must be paid over in the prescribed manner

It is a vital condition for overreaching under section 2(1)(ii) of the Law of Property Act 1925 that the purchaser must comply with 'the statutory requirements respecting the payment of capital money arising under a disposition upon trust for sale'. These statutory requirements are found in the provision that 'the proceeds of sale or other capital money shall not be paid to or applied by the direction of fewer than two persons as trustees for sale'.[16]

The requirement of payment to at least two trustees for sale is mandatory, overriding any contrary provision in the instrument (if any) which created the trust for sale.[17] Payment to fewer than two trustees precludes the purchaser from claiming that he has statutorily overreached the equitable interests under the trust for sale.[18] This is a rigid principle and admits of scarcely any exceptions. The two exceptions permitted by statute allow the purchaser to make payment to a trust corporation or to a sole personal representative.[19]

(3) The effects of overreaching

If the three statutory conditions for overreaching are satisfied, the purchaser of land held on trust for sale 'overreaches' the beneficial interests behind the trust.

(a) Purchaser can henceforth ignore all trusts

There is a clear provision in section 27(1) of the Law of Property Act 1925 that the purchaser who complies with the conditions of overreaching 'shall not be concerned with the trusts affecting the proceeds of sale of land subject to a trust for sale...or affecting the rents and profits of land until sale, whether or not those trusts are declared by the same instrument by which the trust for sale is created.'[20] In other words, the equitable interests behind the trust now take effect conclusively in the capital money arising from the disposition. The purchaser takes a good legal title free from all beneficial claims.[1]

---

16   Law of Property Act 1925, s 27(2), as substituted by Law of Property (Amendment) Act 1926, Schedule.
17   Law of Property Act 1925, s 27(2).
18   In such circumstances, these equitable interests remain binding on a purchaser of unregistered land unless he can show that he purchased without notice of them (post, p 836). In the case of registered land, the equitable interests may constitute overriding interests pursuant to Land Registration Act 1925, s 70(1)(g) (post, p 844).
19   Law of Property Act 1925, s 27(2). There is no provision for the payment of purchase money into court.
20   According to Lord Oliver of Aylmerton, it is 'tolerably clear that the scheme of the Act is to enable a purchaser or mortgagee, so long as he pays the proceeds of sale or other capital moneys to not less than two trustees or to a trust corporation, to accept a conveyance or mortgage without reference at all to the beneficial interests of co-owners interested only in the proceeds of sale and rents and profits until sale, which are kept behind the curtain and do not require to be investigated' (*City of London Building Society v Flegg* [1987] 2 WLR 1266 at 1277A-B).
1   Recent caselaw threatened to enter one extremely grave qualification upon the generality of this proposition. In *City of London Building Society v Flegg* [1986] Ch 605 (post, p 384), the Court of Appeal held that a purchaser of registered land did not necessarily obtain immunity from all beneficial interests merely by reason of payment to two trustees for sale. This ruling was, however, overturned on appeal to the House of Lords. See [1987] 2 WLR 1266 (ante, p 176; post, p 602).

(b) Purchaser is not answerable for the application of the proceeds

A receipt in writing in respect of the purchase money operates as a 'sufficient discharge' to the purchaser of land formerly held on trust for sale, and effectively exonerates him from seeing to the application of the proceeds of sale by the trustees or from being 'answerable for any loss or misapplication thereof.'[2] The combined effect of statute[3] is therefore that the purchaser who fulfils the three conditions for overreaching takes a legal title free both of the beneficial interests and of the terms of the trust.

(4) Other forms of protection for the purchaser

Although the protection offered the purchaser from trustees for sale lies primarily in overreaching, there are several additional forms of protection which operate in his favour.

(a) Consents

Where the execution of a trust for sale is made the subject of requisite consents to be obtained from two or more persons,[4] the consent of any two of such persons is deemed sufficient in favour of the purchaser.[5]

(b) Consultation

The purchaser is 'not concerned to see' that the trustees for sale have properly discharged any duty which they may have to consult their beneficiaries in accordance with the provisions of section 26(3) of the Law of Property Act 1925.[6]

(c) Postponement of sale

The purchaser is 'not concerned in any case with any directions respecting the postponement of a sale' contained in any instrument creative of the trust for sale.[7]

(d) Currency of the trust for sale

In order to activate all the statutory protections conferred on a purchaser from trustees for sale, the trust for sale is 'deemed to be subsisting until the land has been conveyed to or under the direction of the persons interested in the proceeds of sale'.[8]

---

2   Trustee Act 1925, s 14(1). A valid receipt cannot be given by a sole trustee other than a trust corporation (Trustee Act 1925, s 14(2)(a)).
3   See also Law of Property Act 1925, ss 2(1)(ii), 27(2).
4   Ante, p 351.
5   Law of Property Act 1925, s 26(1).
6   Law of Property Act 1925, s 26(3) (post, p 381).
7   Law of Property Act 1925, s 25(2) (ante, p 349).
8   Law of Property Act 1925, s 23.

5. THE IMPOSITION OF A TRUST FOR SALE IN ALL CASES OF CO-OWNERSHIP

It has been seen that the objectives of the property legislation of 1925 were essentially twofold: the achievement of facility for the purchaser of real property coupled with a guarantee of security for the owners of equitable interests in that property.[9] In the context of the co-ownership of land, the first objective was furthered by the prohibition of tenancies in common of the legal estate; both objectives were promoted by the policy, introduced in 1925, according to which a trust for sale was imposed upon all cases of co-ownership.

(1) The trust for sale as a conveyancing device

Under the scheme of the 1925 legislation a sale of land held on 'trust for sale' is rendered a specially efficacious method of disposing of realty. Section 2(1)(ii) of the Law of Property Act 1925 declares, as a matter of first principle, that a conveyance of the legal estate shall overreach all equitable interests affecting that estate provided that the conveyance is made by 'trustees for sale'. Accordingly it became vital in 1925 that, for purposes of conveyancing simplicity, all situations of co-ownership should be enabled to attract the peculiarly advantageous overreaching consequences which the statute attaches to a sale of land held on 'trust for sale.'[10] The only way in which the 1925 legislation could secure this result was by ensuring—even artificially— that henceforth all cases of co-ownership should necessarily be brought under the umbrella of a 'trust for sale'.

(a) Comprehensive coverage of the trust for sale

In terms of the intention which lay behind the 1925 Act, it mattered not whether the co-ownership related to the legal estate in land or to the equitable interest or indeed to both. In any case of co-ownership where a trust for sale was not already provided by the express terms of the relevant conveyance, the 1925 Act aimed to supply a trust for sale by statutory implication. By and large the Law of Property Act 1925 succeeds in ensuring that all cases of co-ownership in possession are comprehensively covered by a trust for sale. In several cases where the legislation fails to provide a trust for sale, the courts—by fair means or foul—have filled in the gaps.[11]

(b) Advantages of the trust for sale

The imposition of a trust for sale in all cases of co-ownership is, of course, only a conveyancing device. The trust for sale has no effect whatever on the nature or extent of the respective beneficial rights of the several persons interested.[12] The use of a trust for sale in this context brings into operation the conveyancing machinery which has already been examined,[13] thereby facilitating the process

---

9   Ante, p 97.
10   Ante, p 355.
11   Post, p 364.
12   *Goodman v Gallant* [1986] Fam 106 at 110E.
13   Ante, p 356.

of land transfer. The existence of a trust for sale ensures that a purchaser of co-owned land need be concerned only with the legal title. He need not concern himself with the equitable interests of the co-owners (whether as joint tenants or as tenants in common), because he knows that these beneficial interests are hidden behind the trust and will be overreached upon sale.

Similarly the beneficiaries behind the trust for sale are guaranteed certain forms of protection. The inclusion of equitable co-owners within the ambit of a 'trust for sale' gives them access to those protective provisions of the Law of Property Act 1925 which relate expressly to the 'trust for sale'.[14] The statutory activation of a trust for sale ensures that upon sale of the land the equitable interests of the beneficial co-owners are translated into equivalent interests in the proceeds of sale. Moreover, the beneficiaries are more generally protected throughout by the fact that the owners of the legal estate in the land are bound by strict duties of trusteeship.

The trust for sale represents the foremost legislative attempt to accommodate in the field of co-ownership the potentially conflicting interests of purchaser and co-owner. It will soon become apparent that, in view of the increased importance of residential utility during the years since 1925, the money-oriented concepts of the 1925 legislation are sometimes less than satisfactory.[15] However, the present concern is to examine the means by which a trust for sale emerges in various cases of co-ownership.

(2) Express trusts for sale

Little difficulty is occasioned by a transfer which expressly stipulates that the legal estate in the land conveyed shall be held 'on trust for sale'. A typical example arises where a transfer document is executed in favour of A and B to hold 'on trust for sale for themselves as beneficial joint tenants'.[16] Such a declaration of trust is conclusive of the nature and quantum of beneficial entitlement, at least if the transfer was executed by the purchasers themselves.[17] The existence of a trust for sale is clearly expressed on the face of the purchase deed, and the statutory provisions relevant to trusts for sale are plainly applicable.

(3) Implied trusts for sale

Slightly more controversial are the cases in which the paper title makes no express provision for a trust for sale in the context of co-ownership. However, in almost every case of co-ownership in possession, a trust for sale is supplied by implication of statute.[18] The following are some of the more obvious instances.

14 Post, p 380.
15 In *In re Evers' Trust* [1980] 1 WLR 1327 at 1330G, Ormrod LJ pointed out that the trust for sale 'has become a very convenient and much used conveyancing technique. Combined with the statutory power in the trustees to postpone the sale, it can be used to meet a variety of situations, in some of which an actual sale is far from the intentions of the parties when the trust for sale comes into existence' (ante, p 350).
16 As a matter of conveyancing practice it is nowadays usual, but not invariable, practice to include an express trust for sale in cases of co-ownership. See A. Kenny and P. Kenny, (1983) 80 Law Soc Gaz 1473 at 1474.
17 Ante, p 241.
18 The precise terms of the statutory trusts are recited in Law of Property Act 1925, s 35.

(a) Conveyance to joint tenants

A conveyance to joint tenants may take several forms, as is illustrated in the following examples.

(i) Conveyance to 'A and B'   Suppose that A and B purchase a legal estate in land and that the conveyance or transfer is simply executed in favour of 'A and B'.[19] The transfer document has performed its minimal purpose in identifying the new owners at law and there is no express stipulation as to beneficial ownership.[20] Suppose further that there is no available evidence relating to the intentions of A and B as to beneficial interest or as to the way in which the purchase money is contributed.[1]

In this situation the conveyance contains no express wording creative of a 'trust for sale'. A and B are clearly joint tenants of the legal estate,[2] and, in the absence of all other evidence, equitable ownership is left to be governed by the maxim that 'equity follows the law.'[3] A and B are therefore joint tenants in equity just as they are joint tenants at law (see *Fig.* 31).[4] The onus of proving otherwise rests on any person who would dispute that the beneficial entitlement coincides with the legal entitlement.[5]

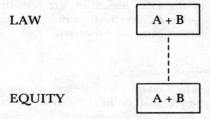

LAW   A + B

EQUITY   A + B

Fig. 31

Although there is no express trust for sale here, such a trust is supplied by implication of statute, and A and B are said to hold the legal estate in the land on trust for sale for themselves as beneficial joint tenants.[6]

---

19   In this case and in the following examples, it matters not whether the legal estate is a fee simple or a term of years absolute (eg a long lease).

20   The courts have delivered frequent exhortations about the desirability of including in the conveyance an express declaration of the beneficial interests in property at the date of purchase (*Cowcher v Cowcher* [1972] 1 WLR 425 at 442C; *Bernard v Josephs* [1982] Ch 391 at 403E).

1   The relevance of such matters in determining beneficial ownership is discussed elsewhere (ante, pp 235, 244).

2   Ante, p 339.

3   However, a conveyance into joint names at law does not necessarily mean joint tenancy or equality of shares in equity. If there is no express declaration of trust which is conclusive of beneficial entitlement, but there is evidence of disparate contributions towards the purchase, there will be beneficial tenancy in common (*Goodman v Gallant* [1986] Fam 106 at 118D).

4   *Pettitt v Pettitt* [1970] AC 777 at 814A; *Cowcher v Cowcher* [1972] 1 WLR 425 at 430E; *Bernard v Josephs* [1982] Ch 391 at 402B-C.

5   *Crisp v Mullings* (1975) 239 Estates Gazette 119 per Russell LJ.

6   Law of Property Act 1925, s 36(1). This provision is sufficiently wide to generate an implied trust for sale wherever there is a joint tenancy in equity (except where the land is settled land). A trust for sale thus arises by implication of statute where (i) A and B are joint tenants of the legal estate and B and C are joint tenants of the equitable interest (see *Hoare v Hoare* (1982) *The Times*, 9 November); (ii) A and B are joint tenants of the legal estate and A, B, C and D are joint tenants of the equitable interest (see *Mulley v Mulley*, Court of Appeal Unbound Transcript 1100, 28 November 1983); and—presumably—(iii) where A is sole owner of the legal estate, but A and B are joint tenants of the equitable interest (ante, p 247).

(ii) Conveyance to 'A and B' after purchase with unequal contributions   Suppose that A and B purchase a legal estate in land and that the conveyance is executed as before in favour of 'A and B'. As before, the conveyance makes reference neither to equitable ownership nor to the existence of a trust for sale, but let us suppose that there is clear evidence that A and B have contributed the purchase price in unequal proportions.

Once again A and B are necessarily joint tenants of the legal estate. In equity, however, they are tenants in common since the situation of unequal contribution is one in which equity—regardless of the position at law—leans in favour of undivided shares.[7] This kind of co-ownership is one of those cases not clearly caught by the terms of the Law of Property Act 1925, and there is thus no unequivocal statutory authority for the imposition of a trust for sale.[8] However, the courts have glossed the wording of the Act[9] in order to imply the existence of a statutory trust for sale.[10] A and B therefore hold the legal estate as joint tenants on trust for sale for themselves as beneficial tenants in common in shares proportionate to their respective contributions of money (see *Fig.* 32).

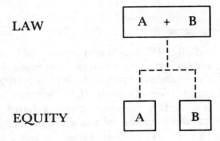

Fig. 32

(iii) Co-ownership of only the legal estate   Another and somewhat unusual case of co-ownership occurs where a trust for sale, if not express, is implied by virtue of statute. This case arises where a legal estate is vested in A and B as joint tenants in circumstances where the entire equitable interest is clearly vested in A alone (see *Fig.* 33).

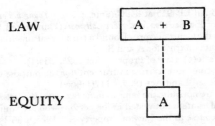

Fig. 33

7   Ante, p 341.
8   See *Concurrent interests in land*, (1944) 9 Conv (NS) 37 at 45.
9   Law of Property Act 1925, s 36(1).
10   *Re Buchanan-Wollaston's Conveyance* [1939] Ch 738 at 744; *Goodman v Gallant* [1986] Fam 106 at 110C-D. For a broad assertion that 'land held in undivided shares in possession must be held by trustees for sale', see *In re Hind* [1933] Ch 208 at 221 per Maugham J. See also (1944) 9 Conv (NS) 37 at 45.

Again, it has been accepted that this situation is covered by an implied trust for sale, although there seems to be no convincing statutory authority for the proposition.[11]

(iv) Conveyance to A and B on trust for C and D in equal shares   Another difficult case arises where a legal estate is conveyed to 'A and B on trust for C and D in equal shares'. This conveyance is plainly intended to create undivided shares for C and D, but the 1925 legislation prohibits such creation except under the provisions of either the Settled Land Act 1925 or the Law of Property Act 1925.[12] However, not a single provision in these statutes appears either to sanction the conferment of undivided shares on C and D in this way[13] or to imply the existence of a trust for sale under these circumstances.[14] There is nevertheless general agreement that, for reasons of conveyancing simplicity, the shares of C and D as equitable tenants in common must subsist behind a statutory trust for sale, although it is unsatisfactory to be unable to demonstrate the derivation of such a trust.[15]

(b) Conveyance to tenants in common

Special problems are raised after 1925 by a conveyance of land to persons as tenants in common. Clearly no legal estate can be held in undivided shares,[16] and this unusual form of conveyance is now given effect only in equity behind a trust for sale supplied by implication of statute. If, for instance, a legal estate is conveyed to A, B and C as tenants in common in equal shares, then provided that all are of full age the transfer is construed as a grant of the legal estate to A, B and C as joint tenants, to hold on an implied trust for sale for themselves as equitable tenants in common (see *Fig.* 34).[17] A similar result follows if a legal estate is conveyed to more than four persons as tenants in common (eg to A, B, C, D, E and F in equal shares). The first four persons named in the grant become necessarily joint tenants of the legal estate,[18] thereafter holding on an

---

11 *Wilson v Wilson* [1969] 3 All ER 945 at 949C (ante, p 242); *Young v Young* [1983] Court of Appeal Bound Transcript 466. See also *Mellowes v Collymore* (Unreported, Court of Appeal, 27 November 1981), where the Court of Appeal found a trust for sale in circumstances where A, B and C held a legal estate on trust for A and B.
12 Settled Land Act 1925, s 36(4); Law of Property Act 1925, s 34(1).
13 The conveyance cannot constitute a 'trust instrument' for the purpose of the Settled Land Act 1925, s 36(4): see Settled Land Act 1925, s 117(1)(xxxi).
14 The circumstances here are not quite the same as in *Re Buchanan-Wollaston's Conveyance* [1939] Ch 738 (p 379): the legal estate is not vested in the persons who are equitably entitled. The already questionable recourse to the Law of Property Act 1925, s 36(1) becomes even less tenable in the present case.
15 See (1944) 9 Conv (NS) 37 at 44. Essentially the same problem arose in *City of London Building Society v Flegg* [1986] Ch 605, [1987] 2 WLR 1266 (post, p 384), where A and B held a legal estate on an implied trust for A, B, C and D as equitable tenants in common. Both the Court of Appeal and the House of Lords proceeded on the premise that C and D were beneficiaries behind the trust for sale.
16 Ante, p 339.
17 Law of Property Act 1925, s 34(2).
18 The number of trustees permitted to hold a legal estate in land is restricted to four (ante, p 98).

implied trust for sale for all the grantees as tenants in common of the equitable interest (see *Fig.* 35).[19] In other words, the tenancy in common specified in the conveyance is given effect only in relation to the equitable interest in the property.[20]

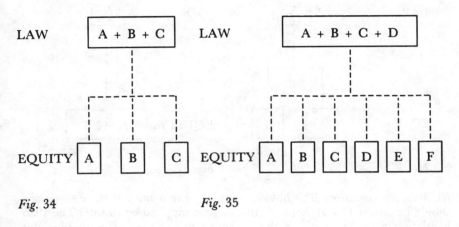

Fig. 34   *Fig. 35*

(c) Conveyance to a single co-owner

Perhaps the most problematic case of all is that which arises on a conveyance of a legal estate to a person who is recognised in equity as being either a joint tenant or a tenant in common. Suppose that A and B co-operate in the purchase of a legal estate in land, each contributing part of the purchase money, but that the legal title is taken solely in the name of A. If they contribute unequally, it is clear that, in the absence of any contrary intention, they are regarded as tenants in common of the equitable interest in the land in proportions fixed by their respective contributions (see *Fig.* 36).[1] If they contribute equally, they seem to be regarded as joint tenants of that equitable interest (see *Fig.* 37).[2] Difficulties emerge, however, if in either case the legal estate is conveyed not to A and B jointly but to A alone without any express declaration of trust for A and B as equitable co-owners. The co-ownership generated by these circumstances is undisclosed on the title: on the face of the purchase deed A appears to be solely entitled both at law and in equity. Moreover, these cases of co-ownership are plainly not covered by an express trust for sale. However, they are not uncommon and, if excluded from the aegis

---

19 Law of Property Act 1925, s 34(2). See eg *Persey and Another v Bazley* (1984) 47 P & CR 37 at 39; [1985] Conv 292 (J. Martin). 'The fact that the other owners of undivided shares are thereby excluded from any real control of the land has had to be sacrificed to the simplicity of conveyancing' (see (1944) 9 Conv (NS) 37 at 38).

20 If, in either of the cases considered here, the grant were made not by a deed inter vivos but by testamentary disposition, the legal estate would be held on an exactly similar trust for sale implied by statute, the only difference being that the legal estate would vest in the trustees of the will for the purpose of the Settled Land Act 1925 or (failing such trustees) would vest in the testator's personal representatives (Law of Property Act 1925, s 34(3)).

1   Ante, p 247.

2   Ante, p 247. See *Knightly v Sun Life Assurance Society Ltd* (1981) *The Times*, 23 July.

of a trust for sale, would provide a particularly significant breach in the general policy of the 1925 legislation that all cases of co-ownership in possession should be governed by a trust for sale.[3]

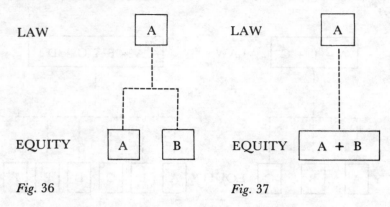

Fig. 36   *Fig. 37*

(i) A statutory omission   The obvious solution is that both of these situations should be covered by an implied trust for sale supplied by statute. The 1925 legislation arguably achieves this objective in the case of equitable joint tenancy (*Fig. 37*).[4] However, the legislation altogether fails to advert to the phenomenon of equitable tenancy in common where the legal title is held by one person alone (*Fig. 36*)—an omission which has been attributed to simple legislative oversight.[5] Nowhere does the legislation provide the much needed statutory authority for the implication of a trust for sale in this context. Nevertheless the problem has not remained unresolved.

(ii) A judicial solution   In *Bull v Bull*,[6] a mother and her adult son contributed unequal proportions of the purchase price of a dwelling-house which was duly conveyed into the sole name of the son. It was expressly found that the mother had not intended to make a gift of her contribution to the son.[7] They lived together in the house for some time, but in circumstances of discord following the son's marriage, the son brought proceedings for possession against his mother, arguing that she was merely a licensee and could therefore be evicted at will.

It seemed that the only way in which the courts could save the ageing mother from being thrown out of her home by her ungrateful offspring was by finding an implied trust for sale in her favour.[8] By this means the mother would be able

---

3   It is not without interest that the Law of Property Act 1922 contained a much clearer indication that all cases of equitable co-ownership were intended to be covered by at least an implied trust for sale. Section 10 of that Act (which was not duplicated in any of the 1925 legislation) was expressly directed at 'removing the difficulties incidental to land being held in undivided shares' and at 'preventing the creation of undivided shares in land, except under a settlement and behind a trust for sale...'

4   Law of Property Act 1925, s 36(1), ante, p 360.

5   See *Williams & Glyn's Bank Ltd v Boland* [1979] Ch 312 at 330C per Lord Denning MR.

6   [1955] 1 QB 234. See [1955] CLJ 155 at 156 (H.W.R. Wade); (1955) 18 MLR 303 (V. Latham), 408 (H.R. Gray); (1956) 19 MLR 312 (E.A. Forrest).

7   [1955] 1 QB 234 at 236.

8   Ironically it may well be that the desired objective could have been achieved by means other than the imposition of a 'trust for sale' (post, p 366).

to enjoy access to the statutory protection given to beneficial co-owners.[9] Despite the lacuna in the 1925 legislation,[10] Denning LJ in the Court of Appeal glossed the wording of section 36(4) of the Settled Land Act 1925 to produce the desired result that an equitable tenancy in common 'shall...only take effect behind a trust for sale' and that such a trust—if not express—is therefore implied by statute.[11]

(iii) Hidden consequences Although based on an extremely bold statutory construction,[12] *Bull v Bull* provides clear authority for the proposition that where a legal estate is purchased in the name of one, using the moneys of two or more, there arises an implied (or statutory) trust for sale of the legal estate on behalf of the contributors. In the context of the practical problem highlighted in the facts of *Bull v Bull*, this result represents a highly convenient solution.[13] However, for other purposes the implication of a trust for sale may prove to have less desirable consequences. The over-ready implication of a statutory trust for sale brings about the result that vast numbers of property owners are elevated to the status of trustee—a fiduciary status which will not only surprise the unwitting property owner but may also introduce unsuspected complications for third parties with whom he deals.[14]

9   Post, p 380.
10   It was thought at one time that the implication of a statutory trust for sale under analogous circumstances would involve 'straining the construction of too many of the provisions of the Property Legislation to be acceptable' ((1944) 9 Conv (NS) 37 at 46). See also M. Friend and J. Newton, *Undivided Shares and Trusts for Sale–A Draftsman's Error?*, [1982] Conv 213.
11   The Court's decision had the effect of making the mother a beneficiary behind a trust for sale. Thus she could not be arbitrarily evicted from the home which she had helped to buy, and the only way in which the son could effectively move her from the house was either by arranging a sale of the property (in which case the mother's interest would be translated into a share in the proceeds of sale) or by buying out her interest with cash (post, p 381).
12   Denning LJ's construction of this apparently irrelevant statutory provision does indeed seem rather strained. Section 36(4) provides that '[a]n undivided share in land shall not be capable of being created except under a trust instrument or under the Law of Property Act 1925, and shall then only take effect behind a trust for sale.' The circumstances present in *Bull v Bull* involved no trust instrument; nor were they covered by any provision in the Law of Property Act 1925 (hence the resort to the Settled Land Act 1925). However, Denning LJ read s 36(4) as if it contained no reference to such matters, thus reaching the convenient (if technically unwarranted) conclusion that a trust for sale must exist in every case of equitable tenancy in common. For a discussion of this flawed reasoning, see B. Rudden, (1963) 27 Conv (NS) 51.
13   It could be said that in *Bull v Bull* the Court of Appeal simply used common sense and a little ingenuity in filling one of the lacunae left in the 1925 legislation (see F.R. Crane, (1955) 19 Conv (NS) 146). The result reached in *Bull v Bull* had already been applied—although without reference to section 36(4) of the Settled Land Act 1925—in *Re Rogers' Question* [1948] 1 All ER 328 at 329A, and in *Re Rayleigh Weir Stadium* [1954] 1 WLR 786 at 790. Later cases have somewhat blandly assumed the existence of a statutory trust for sale in all situations of equitable tenancy in common where the legal estate is vested in one name only. See *Brown v Robertson* (1962) 182 Estates Gazette 157; *Kent v Regan* (1964) 192 Estates Gazette 545 at 547; *Waller v Waller* [1967] 1 WLR 451 at 453B, (1967) 31 Conv (NS) 140 (F.R. Crane); *Taylor v Taylor* (1968) [1968] 1 All ER 843 at 846I. See also W.J. Swadling, [1986] Conv 379.
14   Where, as in *Bull v Bull*, a trust for sale arises by implication of statute, there will be no reference to the trust on the face of the conveyance of the legal estate to the trustee. When the trustee later comes to sell the legal estate, he will appear to be offering a good title 'as beneficial owner' (post, p 830).

(iv) A 'straight trust' approach   There is, moreover, a slightly awkward surmise that the practical problem revealed on the facts in *Bull v Bull* could have been resolved without the necessity of invoking a trust for sale by somewhat dubious implication of statute. It has been suggested that precisely the same result could have been achieved by analysing the parties' rights as simply those of beneficiaries behind a 'straight trust' of land rather than the specialised 'trust for sale' enshrined in the legislation.[15]

(v) The accepted analysis   Notwithstanding the possibility of a 'straight trust' approach, the implication of a trust for sale in the circumstances of *Bull v Bull* has now been endorsed by the House of Lords. In *Williams & Glyn's Bank Ltd v Boland*,[16] Lord Wilberforce, in delivering the major speech, somewhat uncritically accepted the orthodox 'trust for sale' analysis as applied in this situation.[17] It thus appears fairly settled that, irrespective of the questionable nature of the original statutory construction, a trust for sale is implied by statute wherever a legal estate in land is vested in one owner following a joint purchase using the moneys of more than one contributor.

(d) Conveyance to co-owners one of whom is a minor

Further problems are raised by a conveyance of a legal estate to persons who include among their number one who is a minor. Land may be conveyed, for instance, to A, B and C, under circumstances where C is not yet aged 18. If the conveyance purports to transfer a legal estate to A, B and C as joint tenants, a clear statutory solution is provided. A and B take the legal estate, holding on an implied trust for sale for A, B and C as equitable joint tenants (*Fig. 38*).[18] If, however, the conveyance transfers the legal estate to A, B and C on trust for themselves as tenants in common, it seems that once again only A and B can

---

15   See eg (1970) 34 Conv (NS) 420 at 421 (F.R. Crane). Under the 'straight trust' analysis, there would be simply a trust of land of a character not essentially different from a trust of money or shares or other forms of property, but the trust would not be subject to the special statutory regime imposed on the artificially created 'trust for sale'. The main judicial support for the 'straight trust' analysis appears in the Court of Appeal in *Williams & Glyn's Bank Ltd v Boland* [1979] Ch 312 at 330C, 331A. Here Lord Denning MR resolved the difficulty of accommodating equitable co-ownership within the structure of the 1925 legislation by seeming to deny that the trust for sale has any application at all in the present context (see also R.J. Smith, (1979) 95 LQR 501; W.J. Swadling, [1986] Conv 379). However, his brethren in the Court of Appeal preferred to adopt the classic *Bull v Bull* trust for sale analysis (see [1979] Ch 312 at 333G per Ormrod LJ, 340A per Browne LJ). 'Straight trusts' of land may become more commonly accepted if and when effect is given to the recommendation that ordinary trustees be given a statutory power to invest in the purchase of land for one or more of the beneficiaries under a trust (see *The powers and duties of trustees*, Law Reform Committee Report No 23, Cmnd 8733 (October 1982), paras 3.5, 3.11).
16   [1981] AC 487 at 503D (post, pp 372, 843).
17   For a similar endorsement of the 'trust for sale' approach, see [1981] AC 487 at 510G per Lord Scarman.
18   Law of Property Act 1925, s 19(2).

take the legal estate, this time holding on an implied trust for sale for A, B and C as equitable tenants in common (*Fig. 39*).[19]

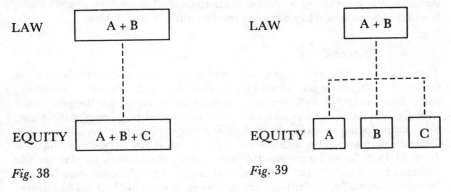

LAW   A + B

EQUITY   A + B + C

Fig. 38

LAW   A + B

EQUITY   A   B   C

Fig. 39

(4) The future of the trust for sale

It is clear that the concept of the trust for sale was adopted and manipulated by the framers of the 1925 legislation specifically in order to serve perceived conveyancing objectives. In this respect the terminology of 'trust for sale' was an appropriate reminder that the primary responsibility of the trustees lay in the performance of their duty to sell the co-owned property and to convert the land into a money form available either for re-investment or for distribution amongst the beneficiaries. During the years since 1925, however, it has become increasingly obvious that the language of 'trust for sale' provides a somewhat misleading description of the reality which underlies most circumstances of co-ownership of land. The conversion-oriented theory of the 1925 legislation compels co-owners of land to hold their legal title on some supposed trust 'for sale', although it is quite apparent that in practice this form of trust is more often aimed at the retention of land than at its alienation.[20] For this reason several proposals have been made in recent years for the replacement of the trust for sale by more realistically named devices which perform essentially the same function of modulating the rights and responsibilities inherent in co-ownership of land.

(a) A 'matrimonial home trust'

It has commonly been said that the terminology of 'trust for sale' is particularly inappropriate in relation to co-ownership of the matrimonial home. Most spouses have little interest in any immediate sale of their home but are rather more concerned—at least for the foreseeable future—to retain a secure base for themselves and their children. Accordingly in 1971 the Law Commission tentatively suggested that in the family context the device of the trust for sale should be replaced by a 'matrimonial home trust', on the ground that 'this is a far more appropriate term than "trust for sale" which to the layman seems to imply that the property must be sold.'[1] This in turn led to the Law

---

19   Law of Property Act 1925, s 19(5).
20   *Ante*, p 350.
1   *Family Law: Family Property Law* (Law Commission Published Working Paper No 42 (1971), para 1.115. See also I.A. Saunders and A. McGregor, (1973) 37 Conv (NS) 270 at 279.

Commission's later proposal that all matrimonial homes should be co-owned by spouses either in consequence of an express trust for sale or by virtue of a new statutory regime of co-ownership in the matrimonial home.[2] This worthwhile, but complex, proposal has not been implemented by legislation.[3]

(b) A new trust of land

The Law Commission has more recently mooted the question whether the device of the 'trust for sale' should not be abandoned altogether. In a working paper issued in 1985,[4] the Commission noted that the automatic imposition of a trust for sale on co-owners who may have purchased property for their own occupation 'is highly artificial and difficult to explain to a lay client.' The Commission inclined towards the view that the structure of co-ownership laid down in 1925 'is no longer suitable for modern conditions'. In place of the outmoded trust for sale, the Commission floated the possibility of introducing a 'new trust of land'.[5] Under this trust co-owned land would be held by trustees who enjoyed powers of sale and retention.[6] The Commission envisaged that under the new scheme, as under the present trust for sale, a purchaser would be able to take title from the trustees and, on condition of payment to at least two trustees, would overreach the interests of beneficiaries.[7]

The Law Commission's proposals for a 'new trust of land' have been the subject of wide public consultation. It remains to be seen whether the general reaction favours a retention of the inaccurately labelled but perfectly workable mechanism of the trust for sale or whether there is sympathy for the introduction of a device which is cosmetically more attractive.

6. RIGHTS OF OCCUPATION UNDER A TRUST FOR SALE

One of the most vexed questions of recent years has concerned whether the beneficiary under a trust for sale has, qua beneficiary, any *right of occupation* of the land held on trust.[8] This question has an importance not merely as between the beneficiary and his trustees, but also as against third parties who take a conveyance of the land from the trustees for sale. If a beneficial interest under a trust for sale does indeed carry with it an implicit right of occupation, the beneficiary may be able to assert this right either in opposition to any moves towards sale taken by the trustees or in derogation of the rights enjoyed by any eventual purchaser.

The law in this area has undergone significant development during the last 30 years, largely in response to changing perceptions of the function of property.

---

2   Post, p 862.
3   Post, p 865.
4   *Trusts of Land* (Law Commission Working Paper No 94, September 1985), para 6.4.
5   Working Paper No 94, para 6.1.
6   Working Paper No 94, paras 6.1, 7.5.
7   Working Paper No 94, para 9.1.
8   It is true, but for this purpose entirely irrelevant, that a trust for sale beneficiary may have rights of occupation derived otherwise than from his status as a beneficiary. He may well have statutory 'rights of occupation' pursuant to the Matrimonial Homes Act 1983 (post, p 782), but such rights are a quite separate phenomenon.

(1) The traditional view

There is considerable authority in the older cases for the proposition that a trust for sale beneficiary has no *right* as such to physical occupation of the land vested at law in the trustees for sale.[9] The beneficiary had, to be sure, a right to receive his due share of any rents and profits derived from the land, but could not insist on going into possession himself.[10] Possession was an attribute of the legal title. Thus, in the traditional view, occupation by a beneficiary was not a right but a privilege to be accorded or withheld by the trustees in the fiduciary exercise of their powers of management of the land.

This analysis survived the re-structuring of property law which culminated in the enactments of 1925.[11] In almost all cases of co-ownership the legal title was confirmed in 'trustees for sale'[12] who under their 'statutory trusts' had no express power to allow a beneficiary into occupation pending sale.[13] The orthodox view thus seemed clear that the trust for sale beneficiary had, in his capacity as beneficiary, no right to occupy the land. This position appeared, if anything, to be reinforced by an equitable doctrine which came to play an important part in the law of trusts for sale—the 'doctrine of conversion'.

(2) The doctrine of conversion

To the present day the trust for sale has been coloured, in a somewhat uncertain and fairly inconsistent manner, by the theory that the equitable interests of trust for sale beneficiaries comprise rights in personalty rather than rights in land. This is the theory known as the 'doctrine of conversion'.

(a) The spectral doctrine

It seems quite reasonable to suppose, a priori, that the equitable interests of beneficiaries under a trust for sale constitute rights of some sort in the *land* which is held on trust for sale. The net income drawn from the land is, after all, payable to any beneficiaries who are currently entitled in possession, and there has always been a possibility that the beneficiaries may be permitted to occupy the land itself. Notwithstanding these powerful indications, the historical development of the law of trusts for sale has been overshadowed by a doctrine which apparently insists that the equitable interest of the trust for sale beneficiary is at all times merely an interest in the prospective proceeds of sale of the land. In terms of this 'doctrine of conversion', the beneficiary holds no

---

9 Even before 1926 beneficiaries with equitable interests behind trusts of land were not entitled to physical possession as of right but only at the discretion of their trustees, duly controlled by the court. See *In re Bagot's Settlement* [1894] 1 Ch 177 at 180f; *In re Earl of Stamford and Warrington* [1925] Ch 162 at 171; (1955) 19 Conv (NS) 146 at 147 (F.R. Crane).

10 See eg *Hoysted v Federal Commissioner of Taxation* (1920) 27 CLR 400 at 410 per Knox CJ and Starke J (High Court of Australia).

11 See *In re Landi (Deceased)* [1939] Ch 828 at 835. The decision in *In re Landi* 'cannot...be reconciled with the proposition that equitable tenants in common can still claim possession as of right' ((1955) 19 Conv (NS) 146 at 147 (F.R. Crane)).

12 Ante, p 360ff.

13 Law of Property Act 1925, s 35. Doubtless if all the beneficiaries entitled under a trust for sale (being sui iuris) were to acquiesce in the allocation of possession to one or more of their number, there could be no question of breach of trust.

interest in land, but merely an interest in the money which the land represents. Quite how consistent has been the application of this theory is open to debate,[14] but there is little doubt that the doctrine of conversion has been perceived, rightly or wrongly, as having some role to play in the judicial implementation of the trust for sale.

(i) Rationale of 'conversion'   The rationale behind the spectral doctrine of conversion fastens upon the primacy of the trustees' duty to sell land held on trust for sale. Since 'equity looks on that as done which ought to be done',[15] equity anticipated the factual result brought about by the discharge of the trustees' duty to sell and converted the beneficiaries' interests into personalty from the very inception of an 'immediate, binding trust for sale'. Thus, even before sale took place—even if sale never took place—the doctrine of conversion supposedly insisted that the beneficiaries' rights be analysed proleptically as rights in *money* rather than rights in *land*.

(ii) Utility of 'conversion'   It is clear that the proper function of the doctrine of conversion has been to ensure clarity and certainty in the devolution of the beneficial interests subsisting behind an express trust for sale.[16] The great advantage conferred by the doctrine is that the devolution of such interests is not determined by largely fortuitous factors such as the precise timing of sale by the trustees.[17] It would be manifestly unsatisfactory that the character of a beneficiary's interest should hover arbitrarily between realty and personalty, and it is precisely this uncertainty which the original doctrine of conversion was designed to prevent. Under the doctrine all beneficial interests behind a trust for sale of land fall to be considered—both before and after sale—as interests in the prospective money proceeds only and therefore as 'personalty'.

(b) Misapplication of the theory of conversion

It is clear in retrospect that the true historical emphasis of the doctrine of conversion was the protection of the interests of beneficiaries within the framework of the trust for sale rather than any concern with the needs of parties outside the trust. That the doctrine should have the effect of conferring any benefit on strangers to the trust was entirely fortuitous, since the authentic purpose of the doctrine was simply to ensure the orderly and convenient

14   See eg S. Anderson, *The Proper, Narrow Scope of the Doctrine of Conversion*, (1984) 100 LQR 86.
15   Post, p 470.
16   See *Chandler v Pocock* (1880) 15 Ch D 491 at 496 per Jessel MR, who pointed out that the doctrine of conversion was not a rule which 'turns sovereigns into acres, or *vice versa*', but rather was a rule which 'works a conversion for the purpose of devolution.'
17   Were it not for the doctrine of conversion, the destination of a trust for sale interest left by will could well depend on whether the trustees for sale had sold the land before or after the date of the death of the testator/beneficiary. If the land had been sold the day before the testator/ beneficiary died, his beneficial interest under the trust for sale would rank as 'personalty' and pass to any designated recipient of his 'personal property'. If, on the other hand, the land had been sold by the trustees the day after his death, his beneficial interest would be characterised as 'real property' and would accordingly pass to the devisee of his 'realty'. The doctrine of conversion avoided these problems but, in characterising all equitable interests behind a trust for sale as personalty, was apt to create further difficulties (see eg *In re Kempthorne* [1930] 1 Ch 268 at 286, 290ff).

characterisation of interests on the death of a beneficial owner. Yet in recent times the doctrine has commonly been applied—or misapplied—in such a way as to facilitate the protection of third parties who purchase land from trustees for sale.

(i) The nexus with overreaching So great was the concentration on securing the protection of purchasers within the statutory scheme of 1925 that the original emphasis of the doctrine of conversion has since become obscured. The process of distortion was further accentuated by the tendency—pervasive in the enactments of 1925—to confine the significance of property to its value in immediate exchangeable cash terms. The concern for the interests of purchasers and the inclination to monetise all value operated in close conjunction. Both motivations caused the legislation to focus closely upon the need to ensure unrestricted alienability of title within an efficient property market. This in turn created a need for a mechanism which would enable the purchaser of land to take title free from fragments of benefit already vested in others which might prejudice or conflict with his own interest in the land.

Just such a mechanism was offered by the statutory device for the 'overreaching' of equitable interests behind a trust for sale. Moreover, the old theory of 'conversion' now seemed to offer an additional rationale for such overreaching. It became tempting to suggest that a purchaser from trustees for sale need never be concerned with the rights of beneficiaries since such rights had always been detached from the land and were at all times rights merely in prospective proceeds of sale. In *Irani Finance Ltd v Singh*,[18] for example, Cross LJ went so far as to assert that the 'whole purpose of the trust for sale' is to ensure, 'by shifting the equitable interests away from the land and into the proceeds of sale, that a purchaser of the land takes free from the equitable interests.' Cross LJ thought that to recognise the beneficiaries as having rights in the land itself—even 'for a limited period' pending sale of the land—would be 'inconsistent with the trust for sale being an "immediate" trust working an immediate conversion, which is what the Law of Property Act 1925 envisages'.[19]

(ii) Supposed exceptions from the scope of 'conversion' The full rigour of this 'conversion' theory could not always be maintained without offence to statutory intention. The courts allowed supposedly haphazard exceptions from the scope of an otherwise uncompromising doctrine. In *Cooper v Critchley*,[20] for instance, the Court of Appeal was of the opinion that a trust for sale beneficiary has an interest in 'land' for the purpose of section 40 of the Law of Property Act 1925.[1] Similarly, in *Elias v Mitchell*,[2] it was held that a beneficiary ranks as a 'person interested...in...land' for the purpose of protecting his beneficial interest as a minor interest by entry of a caution against a registered title.

18 [1971] Ch 59 at 80A (post, p 871).
19 [1971] Ch 59 at 80A-B.
20 [1955] Ch 431 at 439. See (1955) 19 Conv (NS) 148 (F.R. Crane); (1955) 71 LQR 177 (R.E.M.); [1955] CLJ 155 (H.W.R. Wade).
1   According to this provision, a contract for sale of 'any interest in land' is usually actionable only if evidenced in a written memorandum (ante, p 210).
2   [1972] Ch 652 at 664B-D. See (1972) 36 Conv (NS) 206 (D.J. Hayton).

(3) Retreat from a general theory of conversion

Although the so-called 'exceptions' to the doctrine of conversion were initially regarded as mere isolated deviations from an otherwise general doctrine, recent years have seen a remarkable retreat by the courts from the theory of conversion. Even on the historically dubious assumption that equity required an automatic conversion of trust for sale interests, it has increasingly been recognised that it is often quite unrealistic to relegate the rights of beneficiaries to a mere monetary interest. Such an analysis cannot be maintained with any conviction where the immediate and primary motivation underlying the trust for sale is not sale but rather retention of land.[3]

(a) Increasing importance of 'security claims'

The retreat from the general doctrine of conversion has coincided, not insignificantly, with an accumulation of emphasis during recent years on the importance of residential security. This changing emphasis is itself mirrored in a heightened awareness of 'security claims' in other fields of modern legislation such as those providing for employment security, social security and pension security. 'Security claims' of these kinds acquire a greatly increased importance in times of housing shortage, general economic recession, uncertain employment prospects and ever more frequent family breakdown. Consistent with the dominant need of the present age, the factor which unifies all such claims is the general quest not for dispositive power over 'things', but rather for enhanced security in the enjoyment of 'utility'.

(b) Changing perceptions of social status

There is nowadays also a more general acknowledgement that a married woman enjoys as of right a more elevated social status than was accorded to her in former times when the law was content to regard marriage as a form of 'disability'. This recognition is important in the present context since many trusts for sale relate to the family home and the categories of trust for sale beneficiary clearly include vast numbers of wives who have contributed financially to the acquisition of their homes.[4] It was inevitable that the opprobrium of sex-based discrimination should seem to attach to a doctrine which deprived a primary category of beneficiaries of any beneficial entitlement in the very property which was held on trust for sale for them and which they so visibly occupied.

(c) Reaction in the context of the family home

It came therefore as no surprise that the foremost challenge to the doctrine of conversion occurred in the context of the family home. It was clearly in this context that the doctrine failed most markedly to accord with social reality.[4]

The reaction against the doctrine of conversion emerged most dramatically in *Williams & Glyn's Bank Ltd v Boland*,[6] where the courts were indirectly

3   Ante, p 350.
4   Ante, p 254.
5   See, for instance, the closely related proposals to replace the trust for sale of family property by some kind of 'matrimonial home trust' or new form of land trust (ante, p 367).
6   [1981] AC 487 (House of Lords); [1979] Ch 312 (Court of Appeal). For a more detailed account of this litigation, see Chapter 25 (post, p 843).

required to determine the status of the equitable interest of a spouse-beneficiary behind a statutory trust for sale of the matrimonial home.[7] The Court of Appeal declined to apply the received doctrine of conversion, Ormrod LJ noting that in cases involving the family home 'the object of the trust was to provide a joint home and the last thing the parties contemplated was that the house should be sold and the cash divided between them.'[8] Ormrod LJ went on to acknowledge that the imposition of a trust for sale may have been 'an inescapable consequence' of a general legislative scheme directed towards the simplification of conveyancing, but was unwilling to press 'this legal fiction to its logical conclusion'.[9] He clearly felt that, in relation to a trust for sale of the family home, the rights of a beneficiary in possession were 'not accurately described as an interest in a sum of money, simpliciter',[10] and that these rights should not therefore be 'dismissed as a mere interest in the proceeds of sale except where it is essential to the working of the scheme to do so.'[11]

This disavowal of any universal formulation of conversion enabled the Court of Appeal to hold that a spouse-beneficiary behind a trust for sale has a right of occupation inherent in her beneficial entitlement which ranks as an overriding interest in registered land and enjoys priority over a chargee of the registered title.[12] On appeal this conclusion was upheld by the House of Lords, Lord Wilberforce observing that 'to describe the interests of spouses in a house jointly bought to be lived in as a matrimonial home as merely an interest in proceeds of sale, or rents and profits until sale, is just a little unreal'.[13]

(d) Present status of conversion

The present status of the equitable doctrine of conversion is nowadays a matter of some uncertainty. It seems to be generally, but not universally,[14] acknowledged that the doctrine has little (if any) relevance in the characterisation of the rights of a beneficiary behind a trust for sale of the family home. It is uncertain whether this liberated view of the doctrine extends to other forms of property (eg business or partnership property) which may equally well be held on trust for sale. It does, however, appear fairly clear that the much overworked doctrine of conversion is now tending towards its demise.[15] It has at last been realised that the notion of conversion is by no means

---

7 The point at issue was whether an equitable interest under a trust for sale could be properly described as 'subsisting in reference to' land for the purpose of section 70(1)(g) of the Land Registration Act 1925 (ante, p 179). Such an interest, if dismissed merely as an interest in prospective proceeds of sale, would be manifestly incapable of ranking as an overriding interest binding upon the chargee of the registered title.
8 [1979] Ch 312 at 336E-F. Lord Denning MR (at 329F) observed likewise that when 'a married man and his wife buy a house, they do it so as to live in it—so that it should be a home for them both and their children—for the foreseeable future. They do not intend to sell it—at any rate not for many years hence.'
9 [1979] Ch 312 at 336G. See [1979] CLJ 254 (M.J. Prichard).
10 [1979] Ch 312 at 336D.
11 [1979] Ch 312 at 336G-H.
12 Post, p 845.
13 [1981] AC 487 at 507F. See [1980] CLJ 243 (M.J. Prichard).
14 See eg *Harman v Glencross* [1985] Fam 49 at 54A-B, 55G-56C per Ewbank J, for an uninhibited reference to the continuing force of the conversion doctrine in the context of the family home. See also J. Warburton, *The Doctrine of Conversion–Fact or Fiction?*, [1986] Conv 415.
15 See [1979] CLJ 23 (M.J. Prichard).

crucial to the operation of overreaching under the Law of Property Act 1925, and that its supposed reinforcement of the process of overreaching is neither necessary nor helpful.[16] What is perhaps clearest of all is that the doctrine discloses no insuperable barrier in the way of asserting—at least in the context of residential property—that the trust for sale beneficiary has qua beneficiary a right of occupation.

(4) Recognition of the beneficiary's right to occupy

It was perhaps inevitable that the courts should eventually endorse the idea that the trust for sale beneficiary has an intrinsic right of occupation, at least where the property held on trust comprises some form of residential utility.[17] Such a conclusion is entirely consistent with the courts' increasing deference in recent years to the use value of property as distinct from its exchange or capital value. During the last 30 years or so the courts have begun to recognise that entitlement to unhindered enjoyment of residential property is usually more significant than entitlement to a mere cash value on sale. In this sense, the right to secure accommodation in a house or flat, free from the interventions of strangers, has itself become a species of property right.[18]

(a) Emergence of a right of occupation

The crucial development in the caselaw seems to have been the decision of the Court of Appeal in *Bull v Bull*.[19] Here Denning LJ was able, by somewhat devious means, to attribute a right of occupation to an equitable tenant in common who held beneficially behind an implied trust for sale of residential property. Starting from the quite accurate premise that legal tenants in common before 1926 had enjoyed concurrent rights of occupation,[20] Denning LJ considered that these rights of occupation were wholly unaffected by the fact that since 1925 a tenancy in common can exist only in equity. He concluded therefore that today all equitable tenants in common 'have the same right to enjoy the land as legal tenants used to have', and that pending sale each tenant in common is 'concurrently entitled with the other to the possession of the land and to the use and enjoyment of it in a proper manner'.[1]

(b) Confirmation of a right of occupation

The only difficulty with the analysis proffered by Denning LJ in *Bull v Bull* was that it ran directly counter to the orthodox view of the trust for sale beneficiary's position as represented, for instance, in the decision of the Court

---

16 See [1979] CLJ 251 (M.J. Prichard).
17 It is important to distinguish the beneficiary's intrinsic right of occupation from the artificial statutory 'rights of occupation' conferred on spouse-beneficiaries (and indeed on other categories of spouse) by the Matrimonial Homes Act 1983 (post, p 782).
18 This right of residential protection comprises a right to a 'security of tenure' not dissimilar to the 'status of irremovability' which is enjoyed by protected and statutory tenants under the Rent Act (post, p 1003), and as such is not easily assimilated within the canon of existing proprietary interests in land.
19 [1955] 1 QB 234 (ante, p 364).
20 Ante, p 304.
1 [1955] 1 QB 234 at 238.

of Appeal in *In re Landi (Deceased)*.[2] Nevertheless, in *Williams & Glyn's Bank Ltd v Boland*,[3] Lord Denning MR went even further. Relying in part on the authority of *Bull v Bull*, he declared forthrightly that, pending any sale of the family home, a spouse-beneficiary behind a trust for sale has 'an equitable interest in land'.[4] The relevant component of this interest for present purposes was the beneficiary's right of occupation, and it was this right which was eventually rendered 'overriding' against the chargee of the family home.[5]

The House of Lords was content in *Boland* to regard the equitable rights of tenants in common as merely 'subsisting in reference' to land,[6] but was otherwise prepared to confirm that the trust for sale beneficiary has a right of occupation in the property held on trust. Lord Wilberforce, although observing that the beneficiary's rights in respect of occupation were 'obscure', was ultimately happy to endorse the reasoning adumbrated in *Bull v Bull*.[7] Lord Scarman declared more boldly that an equitable tenant in common 'enjoys, by reason of her interest, a present right of occupation as well as a right to a share in the proceeds of sale, if and when the house is sold'.[8] This view was later to receive ample confirmation in the ruling of the House of Lords in *City of London Building Society v Flegg*.[9] Here Lord Oliver of Aylmerton accepted quite readily that a right of occupation 'derives from and is . . . fathered by the interest under the trust for sale.'[10] In the light of this high authority, it now seems that—however confused its historical antecedents—the trust for sale beneficiary's right of occupation has finally acquired an unchallengeable status in the law of co-ownership.

7. THE DECISION TO DEAL WITH CO-OWNED LAND

Peculiar problems surround the decision whether co-owned land should be sold, leased or mortgaged. The significance of any potential conflict of interest between co-owners is intensified by the fact that land is a uniquely flexible form of property. By its nature land provides not merely a medium of long-term capital accumulation, investment and exchange; it also has an importance as an asset for intermediate-term use and enjoyment. The question whether land should be disposed of at any given time often highlights an underlying tension between the 'exchange value' of land (ie, its potential for lucrative commercial exploitation) and its 'use value' (ie, its potential for continued beneficial occupation). It is true that some forms of dealing with land may reflect this tension in only an attenuated form. By means of a mortgage, for instance, owners of land may not be forced into an immediate or irrevocable choice between the realisation of the 'exchange value' and the 'use value' of their

---

2   [1939] Ch 828 (ante, p 369).
3   [1979] Ch 312.
4   [1979] Ch 312 at 331A, C.
5   [1979] Ch 312 at 333C (post, p 844).
6   Ante, p 179.
7   [1981] AC 487 at 507B-D.
8   [1981] AC 487 at 510G.
9   [1987] 2 WLR 1266.
10 [1987] 2 WLR 1266 at 1281E. Lord Oliver rationalised the beneficiary's possession or occupation as 'no more than a method of enjoying in specie the rents and profits pending sale in which he is entitled to share'.

land.[11] However, in all cases the question whether to deal with the co-owned land presents some kind of dilemma as to whether the land should be exploited as a means of raising cash or retained for beneficial enjoyment. Sooner or later these objectives become mutually incompatible, and difficulties arise when co-owners fail to agree as to what should be done.

Almost all forms of co-ownership in possession involve the existence of a trust for sale under the Law of Property Act 1925,[12] and it is of the essence of a trust for sale that the trustees are the persons invested with the decision-making powers of management and disposition. In this area there are two potential areas of difficulty. The first problem arises where the trustees cannot reach agreement *as between themselves* whether or not to sell (or otherwise dispose of) the co-owned land to which they hold legal title. The second problem occurs where, even though the trustees are unanimous in wishing to dispose of the co-owned land, some beneficiary under the trust for sale is anxious that the land should instead be retained for his or her own occupation.

(1) Dispute between the trustees themselves as to a proposed disposition

A fairly complex system of judge-made rules has developed to resolve disputes which arise between the trustees themselves as to whether a proposed disposition of the co-owned land should take place.

(a) The primary rule

The orthodox approach to trusts for sale of land holds that the prime object of a trust for sale is the conversion of the co-owned land into a monetary form in which all the beneficiaries may have equal enjoyment of their respective rights. Thus, in strict theory, a trust for sale is regarded as importing a mandatory duty to sell unless the trustees unanimously exercise their power to postpone sale.[13] In practice the trustees' duty to sell is frequently displaced by a unanimous exercise of the power to postpone sale, with the result that trustees for sale can be said to be invested with enormous discretion as to whether sale ever takes place.[14]

The duty to sell land held on trust for sale is suspended, however, only by the unanimous decision of the trustees.[15] If even one of the trustees positively wishes to execute the trust to sell, the other trustees may be compelled to join with him in giving a conveyance of the property. In *In re Mayo*[16] Simonds J held that any disagreement between the trustees as to the desirability of sale should normally be resolved in favour of discharging the primary purpose of the trust for sale. In

---

11   The mortgage transaction is commonly a device for allowing the mortgagor to enjoy both kinds of value simultaneously (post, p 563).

12   Ante, p 358.

13   An implied power to postpone sale is supplied by statute (see Law of Property Act 1925, s 25(1), ante, p 349).

14   See *In re Evers' Trust* [1980] 1 WLR 1327 at 1330G (ante, p 350).

15   A proposal to introduce a rule of decision by majority vote was rejected by the Law Reform Committee in 1982 (see Law Reform Committee, *The Powers and Duties of Trustees* (23rd Report, Cmnd 8733, October 1982), paras 3.60ff).

16   [1943] Ch 302 at 304.

the event of dispute the trust to sell will thus be held to prevail in the absence of proven mala fides in the trustee who presses for sale.[17]

The rule laid down in *In re Mayo* provides a prima facie (and usually conclusive) resolution of any disagreement between trustees as to sale of the co-owned property. In rare cases, however, it may happen that, although the fiduciary duty to sell is primary and even though a majority of the beneficiaries wishes that sale should occur, one of the trustees still adamantly refuses to join in effecting a conveyance of the co-owned estate to a third party. The conveyance cannot then proceed since the signature of all the trustees is required.[18] In these circumstances, those who press for sale may apply to the court under section 30 of the Law of Property Act 1925 for an order directing the recalcitrant trustee to co-operate in giving a conveyance of the land. Application may be made under section 30 '[i]f the trustees for sale refuse to sell...',[19] whereupon the court has a broad discretion to 'make such order as it thinks fit.'

(b) Exercise of discretion under Law of Property Act 1925, s 30

Although section 30 is aimed at assisting a party who wishes to compel the execution of a trust for sale, the express terms of section 30 reserve for the court a discretionary power to withhold enforcement of the trust for sale. The proper approach to this discretion was spelt out in *In re Buchanan-Wollaston's Conveyance*.[20] Here Sir Wilfred Greene MR indicated that the court of equity, when asked to enforce a trust for sale, 'must look into all the circumstances of the case and consider whether or not, at the particular moment and in the particular circumstances when the application is made to it, it is right and proper that such an order shall be made.' Above all the court must ask itself the question 'whether or not the person applying for execution of the trust for sale is a person whose voice should be allowed to prevail.'[1]

It is clear that the test to be applied under section 30 is not 'what is reasonable'.[2] As Devlin LJ pointed out in *Jones v Challenger*,[3] it is often entirely reasonable, for instance, that one trustee (if beneficially entitled) should wish to realise his equitable share in cash while another trustee who is likewise entitled should wish to continue to enjoy the use value of the property. The exercise of discretion pursuant to section 30 must therefore be governed by criteria other than some supposed standard of 'reasonableness'. It is against this background that the courts have developed a doctrine of 'secondary or collateral objects' underlying a trust for sale which may, in some circumstances, displace the primacy of the trustees' duty of sale.

17 See *In re Buchanan-Wollaston's Conveyance* [1939] Ch 738 at 748, where reference was made to the argument of the plaintiff trustee to the effect that the trustees had indeed determined the question of sale by vote, in that this vote had consisted of 'a vote at a meeting which he and he alone had attended, although the [other trustees] were invited to come'.
18 Ante, p 302.
19 Any 'person interested' may likewise invoke section 30 where the trustees refuse to exercise any of their powers under sections 28 and 29 (eg powers to grant leases and mortgages (ante, p 353)) or where any 'requisite consent' cannot be obtained.
20 [1939] Ch 738 at 747.
1 See eg *Chhokar v Chhokar* [1984] FLR 313 at 329f.
2 See *Jones v Challenger* [1961] 1 QB 176 at 180, 184; *Rivett v Rivett* (1966) 200 Estates Gazette 858; *Mayes v Mayes* (1969) 210 Estates Gazette 935 at 937; *In re Turner (A Bankrupt)* [1974] 1 WLR 1556 at 1558B-C.
3 [1961] 1 QB 176 at 184.

(c) Circumstances displacing the primacy of the duty to sell

Although the rule in *In re Mayo* emphasises the primacy of the trustees' duty to sell, Devlin LJ indicated in *Jones v Challenger*[4] that 'this simple principle' cannot prevail 'where the trust itself or the circumstances in which it was made show that there was a secondary or collateral object besides that of sale.'[5] Acknowledging that the conveyancing device of the trust for sale may nowadays serve a multiplicity of secondary purposes, Devlin LJ stated that, even in the absence of mala fides, it is 'wrong and inequitable for one of the parties to the trust to invoke the letter of the trust in order to defeat one of its purposes, whether that purpose be written or unwritten'.[6] In his view, there is 'something akin to mala fides if one trustee tries to defeat a collateral object in the trust by arbitrarily insisting on the duty of sale'.[7]

Accordingly the courts have consistently held that certain kinds of collateral object or underlying purpose in a trust for sale may have the effect of displacing the prime object of sale. If such a collateral purpose is still capable of fulfilment, the courts, in exercising their broad discretion under section 30, generally decline to grant an order for sale.[8] In such cases the courts will not permit the enforcement of the trust for sale unless, in all the circumstances, 'it is right and proper to order the sale'.[9] If, however, it appears that the collateral purpose of a trust for sale is no longer capable of fulfilment, the courts regard their discretion under section 30 as being 'of a much more limited character'[10] and tend therefore to sanction the proposed sale unless it is clearly inequitable to do so.

In practice the question whether the original trust purpose has wholly failed is apt to merge with the inquiry as to whose voice should in equity be allowed to prevail. In *Cousins v Dzosens*[11] the two forms of interrogatory were said to be 'really one and the same question', in that if 'there is still some outstanding equity to be satisfied, it must necessarily follow that the trust purposes cannot yet have been wholly exhausted; and if the entire purpose of the trust has not yet been accomplished, then there must be scope for equity to determine whether or not a sale should proceed.'

There are several broad kinds of circumstance in which the courts generally decline to accede to the argument that the initial or underlying purpose of the trust for sale has been frustrated and in which therefore the courts have exercised discretion against ordering a sale.

(i) Covenant not to sell without the consent of all the trustees   There is authority for the view that the court, in exercising jurisdiction under section 30, may not think it 'right and proper' to order sale where the trustees have already covenanted inter se not to dispose of the co-owned land without the concurrence of all the trustees.

---

4   [1961] 1 QB 176 at 181.
5   Devlin LJ stressed that *In re Mayo* had itself been 'a simple uncomplicated case of a trust for sale of freehold property, where the beneficiaries were brother and sister, and where there was no suggestion that either of them were intended to or even wished to occupy the property.'
6   [1961] 1 QB 176 at 181.
7   [1961] 1 QB 176 at 183.
8   *Rivett v Rivett* (1966) 200 Estates Gazette 858.
9   *Jones v Challenger* [1961] 1 QB 176 at 183.
10 *Rivett v Rivett* (1966) 200 Estates Gazette 858.
11 (1981) *The Times*, 9 December (John Waite QC).

In *In re Buchanan-Wollaston's Conveyance*[12] four individuals, who each owned separate but neighbouring properties overlooking the sea, combined to purchase a piece of land which they desired to keep as an open space in order to preserve their common sea view. The land was conveyed to them as joint tenants, and they therefore held the legal estate as trustees on trust for sale for themselves in the proportions of their respective financial contributions towards the purchase.[13] The parties then entered into a deed of covenant by which they mutually undertook not to part or deal with the co-owned land except with the unanimous consent of all parties or by majority vote. One of the trustees subsequently sold his own property and thus wished, notwithstanding the opposition of the other trustees, to withdraw his investment from the jointly held open land. He brought proceedings under section 30 for a court order directing his fellow trustees to join with him in selling that property and realising the proceeds. Farwell J refused at first instance to order such a sale, taking the view that the applicant for sale 'was putting forward a claim to equitable assistance merely to enable him thereby to escape from his contractual obligations'. To facilitate this course of action 'would be to disregard the well established rule of equity that he who seeks equity must do equity.'[4] Farwell J's decision was upheld by the Court of Appeal, Sir Wilfred Greene MR agreeing that the plaintiff 'could not...ask the Court to act in a way inconsistent with his own contractual obligations'.[15]

Thus, if trustees for sale have contractually displaced the primacy of the duty to sell, the court will not so exercise discretion under section 30 as to facilitate a breach of that contract.[16] Sale will not be ordered while the underlying contractual purpose subsists.[17]

(ii) Estoppel operating to make sale inequitable The court may likewise lean against sale in circumstances of estoppel, where it would be inequitable to order a sale of the co-owned property.[18] In *Jones (A.E.) v Jones (F.W.)*,[19] for instance, a father had induced his son to give up his employment and to contribute money towards the purchase of the father's house on the basis of a reasonable expectation, encouraged by the father, that the son could live in that house for the rest of his life. The Court of Appeal held that the father's widow (who had succeeded to the father's interests under the relevant trust for sale) was estopped from obtaining an order for sale under section 30. The Court took the view that section 30 should not be invoked so as to defeat the purpose originally contemplated by the father and son, which was to provide long-term housing for the latter.[20]

12 [1939] Ch 217, 738.
13 Ante, p 361.
14 [1939] Ch 217 at 223f.
15 [1939] Ch 738 at 745.
16 See also *L.M. Rosen Realty Ltd v D'Amore* (1982) 132 DLR (3d) 648 at 661 (damages for breach of contract).
17 In *In re Buchanan-Wollaston's Conveyance* [1939] Ch 738 at 747f, the Court of Appeal added that sale might be ordered if circumstances were to change, in that if 'all the parties died, and all their houses were sold, ...the Court, if asked to enforce a statutory trust for sale, would not be disposed to listen to arguments against such a sale adduced by people who had no real interest in keeping this land unsold.'
18 Estoppel is discussed more generally in Chapter 13 (post, p 386).
19 [1977] 1 WLR 438.
20 [1977] 1 WLR 438 at 442D-G, 443D-E.

(iii) Provision of a family home   The principles outlined in *In re Buchanan-Wollaston's Conveyance* have also been applied where the express or implied purpose underlying a trust for sale has been the provision of a family home in some form of co-ownership. In such cases, even if the orthodox view is accepted that the 'prime object' of the trust is sale, the trust clearly has a secondary or collateral purpose of providing a home for joint residential occupation by the members of a family. In exercising discretion under section 30, the courts have tended to order a sale of the family home where the collateral residential purpose has clearly been exhausted or frustrated, but have otherwise proved unwilling to allow the trust for sale to be executed while the initial purpose is still capable of fulfilment. This important body of caselaw is examined in greater detail elsewhere in the general context of residential security in the family home.[1]

(2) Rights of the beneficiary to affect the decisions of trustees for sale

So long as the rights of a trust for sale beneficiary were characterised as mere notional rights in the moneys of some future sale, it was quite consistent that decisions as to the proper management or disposition of the trust property should remain wholly within the control of the trustees for sale.[2] But as soon as the trust for sale beneficiary began to be seen as having an interest 'in' land and a correlative right to occupy that land,[3] it was inescapable that the courts should also recognise some right in the beneficiary to influence the decisions taken by the trustees for sale. In this context, the focal issue is the question whether, at any given stage, the land should be sold. It may well be that in a given case the trustees for sale are agreed as between themselves that sale should take place, only to find that one of their beneficiaries (not being a trustee) is resolutely opposed to such a prospect.

In a series of important developments during the last 30 years the courts have in many instances enabled the trust for sale beneficiary to intercept the decision-making processes of his trustees in order to ensure that his own preferences are not entirely ignored. These developments have conferred on the trust for sale beneficiary some measure of control over dealings by his trustees which threaten to prejudice his own enjoyment of the co-owned land. In such circumstances the beneficiary, although having no vote qua trustee in the matter of sale, is effectively given an opportunity to throw 'spanners into the works', by means of several tactical manoeuvres which may delay or frustrate a proposed sale which he wishes to prevent. There must be some closer examination of the devices which may be employed to protect the occupation interests of the beneficiary.

(a) Appointment of a second trustee

Where a single trustee for sale (as in *Bull v Bull*[4]) proposes to sell the land held on trust, it is open to any beneficiary to apply to the court for an injunction

---

1   Post, p 819.
2   Ante, p 369.
3   Ante, p 375.
4   [1955] 1 QB 234 (ante, p 364, post, p 381).

restraining sale until at least one other trustee has been appointed.[5] Of course the technical possibility of obtaining an injunction of this kind is of little use to a beneficiary who is unaware of an impending sale. Moreover, even an injunction will delay sale only temporarily since the single trustee is free to appoint one of his cronies as co-trustee to join with him in giving a good conveyance of the legal estate.[6]

(b) Duty of consultation

The Law of Property Act 1925 contains a special provision for consultation in relation to trusts for sale which arise by implication of statute.[7] Section 26(3) provides that the statutory trustees 'shall so far as practicable consult the persons of full age for the time being beneficially interested in possession...and shall, so far as consistent with the general interest of the trust, give effect to the wishes of such persons, or in the case of dispute, of the majority (according to the value of their combined interests) of such persons'.[8]

If the trustees attempt to sell the land without first discharging this duty of consultation, they may be restrained by injunction from completing the transaction.[9] However, the statutory duty of consultation is hedged about by qualifications, and ultimately comprises only a duty to listen coupled with a privilege to say 'no'. There is no duty in the trustees to *comply* with the wishes of the beneficiaries, except where these wishes are those of the majority shareholder(s) in equity and are also 'consistent with the general interest of the trust'. In *Bull v Bull*,[10] Denning LJ accepted that the son could have forced a sale of the property against the wishes of his mother if he so desired: all he needed to do was to appoint a second trustee for sale to act with him. In Denning LJ's view, the two trustees would 'no doubt have to consider the mother's wishes, but as the son appears to have made the greater contribution, he could in theory override her wishes about a sale'.[11]

(c) Implied consent of the beneficiary in possession

In *Bull v Bull*[12] Denning LJ pointed to a further 'practical difficulty' which a trust for sale beneficiary might lay in the way of trustees for sale who had

5   See *Waller v Waller* [1967] 1 WLR 451 at 453E-F, 454C; (1967) 31 Conv (NS) 140 (F.R. Crane). On the appointment of further trustees, see Trustee Act 1925, ss 36(1), 40(1) (ante, p 299).

6   See the Law Commission's proposal of 'trusteeship rights' in the matrimonial home (post, p 861).

7   Section 26(3) has no application to express trusts for sale, thereby providing support for Stephen Cretney's argument that in the Law of Property Act 1925 Parliament itself recognised 'the need to distinguish between cases where the trust for sale should be regarded as machinery, on the one hand, and those where it has been expressly chosen, when its logical consequences eg the conversion of the equitable interests may be implemented' ((1971) 34 MLR 441 at 442).

8   If a trust for sale beneficiary is bankrupt, the consultation pursuant to section 26(3) must not be with him, but with his trustee in bankruptcy. See *Fryer v Brooks* (Unreported, Court of Appeal, 19 July 1984).

9   See *Waller v Waller* [1967] 1 WLR 451 at 453D.

10   [1955] 1 QB 234 (ante, p 364).

11   [1955] 1 QB 234 at 238. See [1956] CLJ 157, where Professor H.W.R. Wade asked: 'What is the effect, one may wonder, of a provision of an Act of Parliament which operates only "in theory"?'

conformed with the minimal requirement of consultation stipulated by the Law of Property Act 1925. If such trustees still pressed for a sale, they would be confronted with the problem that 'so long as the [mother/beneficiary] is there, they could not sell with vacant possession.' Denning LJ proceeded to spell out for the beneficiary in possession under a trust for sale something akin to a 'status of irremovability'.[13] He held that by virtue of her *right* of occupation as an equitable tenant in common 'she could not be turned out by the trustees except with her consent.'[14]

(i) Dealing with an unavailable consent   In other words, Denning LJ appeared to suggest in *Bull v Bull* that a beneficiary in possession behind a trust for sale enjoys an implied right of consent to any disposition of the land proposed by the trustees for sale. If, as was the case in *Bull v Bull* itself, such a beneficiary adamantly refused to give her consent to a sale with vacant possession, she would effectively stultify the transaction proposed by the trustees.[15] The only recourse then available to the trustees would be an application to the court under section 30 of the Law of Property Act 1925 to dispense with the consent thus withheld.[16] Denning LJ anticipated that the court would make such an order only if 'satisfied that it was right and proper to do so and on such terms as to alternative accommodation as it thought fit to impose.'[17]

(ii) Limitations on the beneficiary's power of veto   The decision of the Court of Appeal in *Bull v Bull* has been criticised on the ground that it 'elevates the wishes of a beneficiary to the status of a "requisite consent"'.[18] In doing so the decision seems to confer upon the beneficiary in possession a fairly general power of veto over dealings by the trustees for sale. It may be that in this respect a distinction must be drawn between express and implied trusts for sale.

The relevant difficulty in this context arose in *Barclay v Barclay*,[19] where a testator had left his bungalow to be held on trust for sale, the proceeds of sale to be divided after his death between five members of his family. After his death the majority of the beneficiaries clearly wished the property to be sold in order that each might obtain his aliquot share of the wealth comprised in the bungalow. However, one of the beneficiaries, a son of the testator, had during his father's lifetime been allowed to occupy the bungalow following the break-up of his own marriage. After his father's death he continued to live in the property, greatly preferring to retain on his own behalf the utility which he enjoyed in the property rather than receive the one-fifth share in the capital which would be released by a sale. He therefore resisted sale, alleging that as a beneficiary in possession behind a trust for sale he had by implication a requisite consent which he declined to give.

12   [1955] 1 QB 234 at 238.
13   Post, p 968.
14   [1955] 1 QB 234 at 238.
15   'Why it should be in the power of a beneficiary with a minor interest to impede the execution of a trust for sale is something of a mystery' (H.W.R. Wade, [1955] CLJ 157). See also (1955) 18 MLR 303 (V. Latham).
16   Ante, p 352.
17   [1955] 1 QB 234 at 239. See also *City of London Building Society v Flegg* [1986] Ch 605 at 620A-B.
18   [1971] CLJ 44 at 45 (M.J. Prichard).
19   [1970] 2 QB 677. See (1970) 86 LQR 443 (P.V. Baker); [1971] CLJ 44 (M.J. Prichard).

It was plainly inequitable on the facts in *Barclay* that a marginal tenant in common should be able to frustrate the capital distribution desired by the other beneficiaries. Although confronted by the uncomfortable precedent of *Bull v Bull*, the Court of Appeal distinguished the earlier decision on the ground that there the 'prime object of the trust' had been that the son and mother 'should occupy the house together'.[20] In *Barclay*, however, Lord Denning MR considered the facts to be 'very different' since here the 'prime object of the trust was that the bungalow should be sold'.[1] The Court of Appeal without hesitation ordered in favour of sale.

(d) Overriding right of occupation

The ruling in *Barclay v Barclay* came 'perilously close'[2] to drawing a line between express trusts for sale (where the 'prime object' may well be sale) and statutory trusts for sale (where the 'prime object' may in fact be continued residence).[3] However, the terms of debate in this area were fundamentally altered—and in a sense made somewhat irrelevant—in the light of the more recent decisions of the courts.

It may well be true that a trust for sale beneficiary can temporarily delay a proposed dealing by his trustees by insisting on his statutory right to be consulted or by claiming some kind of consent requisite to sale. It is now clear, however, that there is one further—and very much more important—respect in which a beneficiary's wishes in the matter of disposition may impinge upon his trustees' dealings with the legal title in co-owned land. The caselaw of the last decade has revealed that the courts are willing to recognise that certain trust for sale beneficiaries may have an intrinsic right of occupation which is binding on third parties who deal with the land.

(i) Disposition by a single trustee for sale

Where land is held by a single trustee on a statutory trust for sale for beneficial co-owners, it seems that the right of occupation which each co-owner has qua beneficiary may be preserved notwithstanding an adverse dealing with the legal title by the trustee.[4] Thus, even though the single trustee may sell or mortgage the legal title, the occupation rights attached to the equitable interests may remain enforceable against the purchaser.

In registered land, this result will follow in relation to any trust for sale beneficiary who was in 'actual occupation' of the land at the date of the dealing.[5] In *Williams & Glyn's Bank Ltd v Boland*,[6] the House of Lords declared that 'the critically important right' of the spouse-beneficiary in that case was her 'right of occupation of the land'. It was this right which gave rise to an

---

20 [1970] 2 QB 677 at 684A. See also Edmund Davies LJ (at 684G) and Megaw LJ (at 685G-H).
1   [1970] 2 QB 677 at 684B.
2   [1971] CLJ 44 at 46 (M.J. Prichard).
3   For heavy criticism of the validity of such a distinction, see *Irani Finance Ltd v Singh* [1971] Ch 59 at 80 per Cross LJ.
4   See generally Chapter 25 (post, p 829). In strict terms the only single trustee for sale who can clearly give an overreaching conveyance is, of course, a trust corporation.
5   See Land Registration Act 1925, s 70(1)(g) (ante, p 175).
6   [1981] AC 487 at 511H per Lord Scarman.

overriding interest binding upon the chargee of the matrimonial home. The chargee was therefore unable to recover possession of the home for the purpose of exercising the mortgagee's statutory power of sale.[7]

In unregistered land the same outcome may well be achieved through the application of the traditional doctrine of notice.[8] The purchaser who deals with a single statutory trustee for sale is liable to be bound by the equitable interests (and correlative occupation rights) of the beneficial co-owners unless he can avail himself of the defence of the bona fide purchaser without actual or constructive notice.[9] It is clear in this context that a beneficial co-owner's residential occupation of the property may fix the purchaser with constructive notice of his or her rights.[10]

(ii) Disposition by two trustees for sale   It has always been thought that the interests of beneficial co-owners behind a trust for sale can have no effect on a purchaser who deals with at least two trustees for sale or with a trust corporation. For a long time it was confidently assumed that the mechanism of statutory overreaching operates in favour of such a purchaser, irrespective of whether the actual occupation enjoyed by the trust for sale beneficiaries would otherwise have founded an overriding interest in registered land or provided constructive notice in unregistered land.[11]

It was against this background that in *City of London Building Society v Flegg*[12] the Court of Appeal dropped a bombshell for all conveyancers. In this case, a registered title in a family home had been purchased in the name of A and B, much of the purchase money having been provided by X and Y, the parents of B. The conveyance to A and B contained an express trust for sale and explicitly declared that the trustees for sale, A and B, were possessed of the mortgaging powers of an absolute owner. Although the conveyance made no reference to X and Y, it was perfectly clear that they were beneficiaries behind the trust for sale of the registered title and indeed X and Y moved into joint occupation of the property with A and B.[13] Some time later, and without the knowledge or consent of either X or Y, A and B charged their legal title to a building society. A and B were subsequently made bankrupt and the building society sought to recover possession of the property, plainly imagining that the mortgage transaction executed by two trustees for sale had an unchallengeable overreaching effect on such equitable interests as might exist. This expectation was somewhat surprisingly falsified by the Court of Appeal, which held that X and Y, as beneficiaries in 'actual occupation', had interests in the property which were overriding in relation to the building society.

---

7   Ante, p 373; post, p 614. It is likely, however, that if the chargee had then proceeded to make the legal owner of the family home bankrupt, his trustee in bankruptcy would have been successful in pressing for a court order for sale under Law of Property Act 1925, s 30 (post, p 876). In such an eventuality the 'overriding interest' of the spouse-beneficiary would have the effect of entitling her not to resist sale, but merely to receive out of the proceeds of sale the value of her equitable share in priority to the claim of the chargee (post, p 862).

8   Post, p 841.

9   See *Caunce v Caunce* [1969] 1 WLR 286 at 289F-G (post, p 835).

10   *Kingsnorth Finance Co Ltd v Tizard* [1986] 1 WLR 783 at 792H-793A, 795B-C (post, p 842).

11   See eg J. Martin, [1980] Conv 361 at 362, [1981] Conv 219. Contra, C. Sydenham, [1980] Conv 427.

12   [1986] Ch 605 (post, p 601). See W.J. Swadling, [1986] Conv 379.

13   [1986] Ch 605 at 614E-F.

In support of this conclusion, the Court of Appeal relied on *Williams & Glyn's Bank Ltd v Boland*,[14] where (according to Dillon LJ) the reasoning of Lord Wilberforce did 'not depend at all...on the fact that in *Boland* there was only one registered proprietor of the land and therefore only one trustee for sale.'[15] In the view adopted by Dillon LJ, the protection of overriding interests under section 70(1)(g) of the Land Registration Act 1925 could be founded on a simple association existing between the equitable interest of a trust for sale beneficiary and the fact of 'actual occupation' of the property held on trust.[16] Thus, in the event of a dealing effected even by two registered proprietors, 'what would otherwise have been a minor interest capable of being overridden under the Law of Property Act 1925 by two trustees for sale, is, if protected by the fact of actual occupation of the land, elevated to the status of an overriding interest.'[17] Since no enquiry had been made of X and Y before the charge was executed, the Court held that the building society must take its mortgage subject to their overriding interests.[18]

This ruling immediately threatened a number of extraordinary consequences. *First*, a disposition by two trustees for sale would no longer automatically overreach otherwise overriding interests in registered land and probably would not overreach the equivalent equitable interests in unregistered land either. *Second*, the Court of Appeal's decision had the effect of ripping apart the 'curtain' behind which trust for sale equities had supposedly been concealed from the purchaser who deals with two trustees. *Third*, an onus was placed on the purchaser to identify all beneficiaries in possession (in either registered or unregistered land) and ensure that each gave consent to the transaction in hand. *Fourth*, if relevant consents were withheld, the only course available would be an application to court under section 30 of the Law of Property Act.[19]

The decision of the Court of Appeal in *Flegg* was the subject of much vigorous criticism on the ground that it undermined much of the structure of the property legislation of 1925.[20] Much to the relief of conveyancers, the ruling of the Court of Appeal has since been unanimously reversed by the House of Lords,[1] which firmly reinstated the orthodox understanding of the effects of a disposition made by two trustees for sale. It is once again clear beyond any doubt that the payment of purchase or other capital moneys to at least two trustees for sale conclusively overreaches the equitable claims of all beneficiaries under the trust.[2]

---

14   [1981] AC 487 (ante, p 383).
15   [1986] Ch 605 at 616H-617D.
16   [1986] Ch 605 at 617B-C.
17   [1986] Ch 605 at 617C.
18   Dillon LJ reinforced this ruling by reference ([1986] Ch 605 at 618D-620E) to Law of Property Act 1925, s 14, which, in his view, made it clear that the operation of overreaching under section 2(1)(ii) could not 'prejudicially affect the interest of any person in possession or in actual occupation of land to which he may be entitled in right of such possession or occupation'. See (1986) 136 NLJ 83 (H. Lewis).
19   Ante, p 382.
20   See [1986] CLJ 202 (C. Harpum); (1986) 136 NLJ 208 (D.J. Hayton); (1986) 49 MLR 519 (R.J. Smith); (1986) 102 LQR 349.
1   [1987] 2 WLR 1266.
2   See [1987] 2 WLR 1266 at 1275E-1277B per Lord Oliver of Aylmerton.

CHAPTER 13

Proprietary estoppel

One of the most significant movements occurring in the contemporary law of real property is the emergence of a new 'equity' based on the concept of 'estoppel'. As Browne-Wilkinson LJ observed in *Walker v Walker*,[1] the juristic basis of this new 'equity' and the circumstances in which it may arise are as yet 'ill defined', but the movement 'can only be regarded as a development of the doctrine of proprietary estoppel.' It is this 'equity', and the doctrine of proprietary estoppel by which it is raised, which together form the subject matter of the present chapter. It is increasingly clear that the doctrine of estoppel, although first adumbrated by the courts over a century ago, is beginning to play a substantial role in the ordering of rights in property. By identifying the circumstances in which certain claims may or may not be asserted in relation to titles in land, the doctrine has itself helped to reformulate the concept of a 'property right'—a consequence which of course has generated its own difficulties.

1. THE CENTRAL CONCERN OF PROPRIETARY ESTOPPEL

The central concern of the doctrine of proprietary estoppel is the notion of conscionable dealing in relation to land. The doctrine has been explained as having its root in 'the first principle upon which all courts of equity proceed', that is, 'to prevent a person from insisting on his strict legal rights—whether arising under a contract, or on his title deeds, or by statute—when it would be inequitable for him to do so having regard to the dealings which have taken place between the parties.'[2] The doctrine of proprietary estoppel thus shares a common origin with its contractual analogue of promissory estoppel,[3] but differs from it in certain important respects. First, proprietary estoppel can obviously arise even outside the scope of a contractual relationship,[4] although in practice proprietary estoppel and contractual relations often overlap.[5]

---

1   Unreported, Court of Appeal, 12 April 1984. See also *In re Sharpe (A Bankrupt)* [1980] 1 WLR 219 at 223D.
2   *Crabb v Arun DC* [1976] Ch 179 at 187H-188A per Lord Denning MR, citing *Hughes v Metropolitan Railway Co* (1877) 2 App Cas 439 at 448 per Lord Cairns LC.
3   See G.H.Treitel, *The Law of Contract* (6th edn London 1983), p 83ff.
4   *Holiday Inns Inc v Broadhead* (1974) 232 Estates Gazette 951 at 1087; *Riches v Hogben* [1986] 1 Qd R 315 at 339.
5   See eg *Tanner v Tanner* [1975] 1 WLR 1346 at 1350E (post, p 544), where Lord Denning MR described as a contractual licence something which might be more easily recognised in terms of proprietary estoppel. For conflicting views as to whether contractual licences and estoppels can logically overlap, see A. Briggs, [1981] Conv 212, [1983] Conv 285; M.P. Thompson, [1983] Conv 50. See also John Dewar, *Licences and Land Law: An Alternative View*, (1986) 49 MLR 741.

Second, proprietary estoppel may be relied on as a sword and not merely as a shield, thereby conferring a right of action where none would otherwise exist.[6] Third, the equity arising in connection with proprietary estoppel can bind third parties and, in this sense, appears to constitute a substantive equitable proprietary right.[7] The intrinsic elements of proprietary estoppel must now be examined closely.

2. THE GENERAL THEORY OF PROPRIETARY ESTOPPEL

The doctrine of proprietary estoppel has never been defined in one clear analytical formula, but has instead been expounded at different times by different judges in slightly divergent terms.[8] These varying formulae, although alike directed against unconscionable dealings with land, have not made for either certainty or consistency in the implementation of the basal premise of proprietary estoppel. Indeed, the common origin of these various formulations has rather tended to impose a spurious uniformity on the doctrine, concealing the fact that the courts were often trying to apply a supposedly homogeneous doctrine to significantly different fact-situations. However, there are now indications that the many conceptual strands which composed the core ideas of proprietary estoppel are in the process of being woven into one composite formula of equitable relief.

(1) Essential elements of proprietary estoppel

The raw essentials of the doctrine of proprietary estoppel are threefold. In some form or other, a proprietary estoppel comprises (i) an assurance, (ii) a reliance, and (iii) a detriment. If the owner of a title in land has expressly or impliedly given some assurance respecting present or future rights in his land, he cannot conscionably withdraw that assurance if the person to whom it was given has meanwhile relied upon it to his own detriment.[9] Thus stated, the elements of assurance, reliance and detriment are inter-dependent and therefore capable of definition only in terms of each other. An 'assurance' is present only if the person who gives it intends it to be relied upon. 'Reliance' occurs only if the person to whom the assurance is given then takes action detrimental to his own interests. In some ultimate sense, 'detriment' results only if the assurance, once relied upon, is withdrawn.

(2) Doctrinal roots of proprietary estoppel

The concatenation of ideas underlying proprietary estoppel emerges from three broad, and not entirely distinct, categories of case. These categories

6 *Crabb v Arun DC* [1976] Ch 179 at 187E; *Amalgamated Investment & Property Co Ltd v Texas Commerce International Bank Ltd* [1982] QB 84 at 105D-E; *Thomas v Thomas* [1956] NZLR 785 at 793; *Classic Communications Ltd v Lascar* (1985) 21 DLR (4th) 579 at 587. 'Purists may regret the use of the word "estoppel" as the name of a sword but it seems now too late to challenge the usage' (*Jackson v Crosby* (No 2) (1979) 21 SASR 280 at 287 per Bright J).
7 Post, p 425f.
8 For judicial reference to the wide variations in the formulation of the doctrine of proprietary estoppel, see *Ward v Kirkland* [1967] Ch 194 at 235D; *Cameron v Murdoch* [1983] WAR 321 at 350; *Riches v Hogben* [1986] 1 Qd R 315 at 327.
9 *In re Basham, decd* [1986] 1 WLR 1498 at 1503H. See also *Brinnand v Ewens* (1987) *Times*, 4 June.

comprise (1) the 'imperfect gift' cases, (2) the 'common expectation' cases, and (3) the 'unilateral mistake' cases. Irrespective of their classification, these cases all present the essential characteristics which embody the notion of proprietary estoppel, but each category of case in its turn gives a heightened emphasis to one or other of the constituent elements of assurance, reliance and detriment. As will appear later, the tendency in the modern caselaw is to synthesise the jurisprudence of proprietary estoppel so that it begins to compose a more unified doctrine based on a concept of 'detrimental reliance'. However, this threefold categorisation may still retain a residual importance, in that even today the response of the courts to estoppel claims seems in some respects to be graded with reference to criteria which differentiate slightly between these broad categories of circumstance.

3. CATEGORIES IN THE CASELAW

As indicated above the caselaw discloses that three somewhat overlapping categories of circumstance provide the doctrinal origins of proprietary estoppel.

(1) The 'imperfect gift' cases

The 'imperfect gift' cases relate typically to circumstances in which the courts, in applying the basic estoppel notion, have attached overwhelming significance to the element of 'assurance'. An assurance by X to Y that Y shall have rights in X's land is most clearly epitomised in a gift of that land by X to Y. However, a gift of an estate or interest in land must be effected in the appropriate form (eg by means of formal conveyance).[10] In default of such a formality, the gift remains incomplete and it is trite law that equity will not perfect an imperfect gift.[11] Equity will not normally enforce any claim by the putative donee based on the informal gift, no matter how sincere or convincing the assurance of the would-be donor that he wished to make a gift of the land.

(a) Exceptional assistance in the perfection of a gift

There are, however, some circumstances in which equity is prepared to depart from the normal rule in order to assist the vesting of a voluntary gift of realty. These circumstances are illustrated in classic form in *Dillwyn v Llewelyn*.[12] Here a father placed his son in possession of land belonging to the father, both parties signing an informal memorandum which evidenced an intention that the land should be given to the son for the purpose of providing him with a dwelling-house. The son immediately proceeded at vast expense to build a residence for himself on that land. Lord Westbury LC recognised the imperfect (and therefore abortive) nature of the purported gift of realty, but held that 'the subsequent acts of the donor may give the donee that right or ground of claim which he did not acquire from the original gift.'[13] On the present facts, a

10 Ante, p 221.
11 See *Milroy v Lord* (1862) 4 De G F & J 264 at 274, 45 ER 1185 at 1189 per Turner LJ.
12 (1862) 4 De G F & J 517, 45 ER 1285.
13 (1862) 4 De G F & J 517 at 521, 45 ER 1285 at 1286.

promise of gift had been made, and 'on the strength of that promise, with the knowledge of [the father]', the son had incurred substantial expenditure on the land. Accordingly, the son was held to have acquired 'a right from the subsequent transaction to call on the donor to perform that contract and complete the imperfect donation which was made.' Lord Westbury concluded that, since 'the subsequent expenditure by the son, with the approbation of the father, supplied a valuable consideration originally wanting', the memorandum signed by both must be regarded as 'an agreement for the soil extending to the fee-simple of the land'.[14] The Court decreed that the intention to give the fee simple estate must now be performed, even though title to the land had by this stage passed to the executors of the father's estate. In other words, an unambiguous (albeit informal) assurance of entitlement must be honoured in the light of the subsequent reliance upon it.

Although the issue in *Dillwyn v Llewelyn* was considered substantially on the analogy of the contractual doctrine of part-performance, Lord Westbury LC made an important reference to the idea that the donee had an 'equity' which entitled him to claim the estate purportedly given to him by the original and informal promise.[15] The attendant circumstances left no doubt but that the original intention had been to vest a fee simple in the donee.[16] The decision thus provides authority for the proposition that where a gratuitous assurance is given that an estate or interest in land will be transferred, there arises an 'equity' in favour of the promisee based upon proprietary estoppel, provided that the promisee suffers detriment in reliance on the assurance. Under these circumstances the doctrine of proprietary estoppel not only protects the informal promisee against adverse claims to possession; it affords the promisee a ground on which he may claim the assistance of the courts towards the perfection of the intended gift. This approach to imperfect gifts of realty has been followed in other cases, the courts regarding it as irrelevant whether the original assurance of rights is contained in writing or is merely oral.[17]

(b) Far-reaching consequences

The recognition of an 'equity' raised by an informal donee's detrimental reliance can, however, produce somewhat dramatic results. In *Pascoe v Turner*,[18] for instance, it emerged that P and D had lived in a de facto relationship in a house owned by P. When P moved out in order to live with another woman elsewhere, he informed D orally that she had nothing to worry about as the house and its contents were thenceforth entirely hers. D continued to live in the house and she later effected repairs and improvements to the house costing about £230, a figure which amounted to approximately one quarter of

14 (1862) 4 De G F & J 517 at 522, 45 ER 1285 at 1287.
15 (1862) 4 De G F & J 517 at 522, 45 ER 1285 at 1286f. *Dillwyn v Llewelyn* has subsequently been treated as involving a case of 'equitable estoppel by acquiescence' (see *Thomas v Thomas* [1956] NZLR 785 at 793).
16 Lord Westbury declared that the 'estate was given as the site of a dwelling-house to be erected by the son...No one builds a house for his own life only, and it is absurd to suppose that it was intended by either party that the house, at the death of the son, should become the property of the father.'
17 See *Thomas v Thomas* [1956] NZLR 785 at 793f; *Raffaele v F & G Raffaele* [1962] WAR 29 at 31 (but compare *Jackson v Crosby (No 2)* (1979) 21 SASR 280 at 289).
18 [1979] 1 WLR 431. See (1979) 129 NLJ 1193 (R.D. Oughton); [1979] Conv 379.

her available capital. When P later brought possession proceedings on the basis that D had a mere revocable licence to occupy, the Court of Appeal ruled that the fee simple in the house should be conveyed by P to D. Cumming-Bruce LJ applied *Dillwyn v Llewelyn*, holding that the circumstances raised in favour of D an 'equity', founded on proprietary estoppel, which could be satisfied only by ordering P to perfect his imperfect gift of the realty.[19]

(2) The 'common expectation' cases

Whereas the central feature of the 'imperfect gift' cases is a pellucid assurance of entitlement contained in an abortive gift of land, the element which comes to the fore in the 'common expectation' cases is the notion of 'reliance'. These cases concern not so much the situation where X has attempted to make a gift of land to Y, but rather the situation where X and Y have consistently dealt with each other in such a way as reasonably to cause Y to rely on a shared supposition that he would acquire rights of some kind in X's land. This is not to imply that the other key characteristics of proprietary estoppel are not present in such circumstances, but merely that the 'common expectation' cases particularly highlight the element of 'reliance'.

(a) Lord Kingsdown's speech in Ramsden v Dyson

The classic exposition of the 'common expectation' formulation of the doctrine of proprietary estoppel occurs in the dissenting speech of Lord Kingsdown in *Ramsden v Dyson*.[20] Here Lord Kingsdown stated that

If a man, under a verbal agreement with a landlord for a certain interest in land, or, what amounts to the same thing, under an expectation, created or encouraged by the landlord, that he shall have a certain interest, takes possession of such land, with the consent of the landlord, and upon the faith of such promise or expectation, with the knowledge of the landlord, and without objection by him, lays out money upon the land, a Court of equity will compel the landlord to give effect to such promise or expectation.[1]

Although, for the purpose of the instant decision, Lord Kingsdown couched his observations in terms of the landlord-tenant relationship, his remarks have been accepted as having a more general role in identifying the factors which can generate a proprietary estoppel.[2] In *Taylors Fashions Ltd v Liverpool Victoria Trustees Co Ltd*,[3] Oliver J pointed out that the circumstances postulated in Lord

---

19 The outcome in *Pascoe v Turner* is remarkable in that the equitable jurisdiction of the court was invoked effectively to bring about a redistribution of assets on the breakdown of a de facto marriage relationship. The manner and extent of the redistribution lay entirely within the discretion of the court, and the defendant was thereby enabled to circumvent the rule that a de facto spouse cannot claim property adjustment or financial provision from her partner on the demise of their relationship. See B. Sufrin, (1979) 42 MLR 574, and compare *McGill v S* [1979] IR 283 at 293 where Gannon J in the Irish High Court declined to follow *Pascoe v Turner*. See also *Gissing v Gissing* [1971] AC 886 at 910E-F.

20 (1866) LR 1 HL 129 at 170.

 1 See also *Gregory v Mighell* (1811) 18 Ves Jun 328 at 333, 34 ER 341 at 343. The doctrine of acquiescence has been traced back into the 15th Century (see Lord Goff of Chieveley and Gareth Jones, *The Law of Restitution* (3rd edn, London 1986), p 141).

 2 See *Crabb v Arun DC* [1976] Ch 179 at 194D per Scarman LJ.

 3 [1982] QB 133 (Note) at 147G.

Kingsdown's example of proprietary estoppel 'presuppose...the fostering of an expectation in the minds of *both* parties at the time but from which, once it has been acted upon, it would be unconscionable to permit the landlord to depart.' This formulation of the doctrine of proprietary estoppel is sometimes known as 'estoppel by encouragement' or 'estoppel by acquiescence'.[4]

(b) Classic illustrations of 'common expectation'

A good example of this form of proprietary estoppel is found in *Plimmer v Mayor etc of Wellington.*[5] Here a licensee of land had, at the request of the owner of that land, expended considerable sums of money on the extension of a jetty and the construction of a warehouse. The Judicial Committee of the Privy Council upheld a claim on behalf of appellants claiming through the licensee that the licence, although originally revocable, had been rendered irrevocable by reason of the expenditure. Sir Arthur Hobhouse declared that the parties could not 'go on dealing with one another in the way stated in this case for a series of years, except with a sense in the minds of both that the occupant has something more than a merely precarious tenure.'[6] The Privy Council decided that the circumstances fell 'within the principle stated by Lord Kingsdown as to expectations created or encouraged by the landlord', and that the appellants therefore had an 'equity arising from expenditure on land'.[7] Accordingly they had acquired 'an indefinite, that is practically a perpetual, right' to the jetty for the purposes of the original licence.

It has been accepted in numerous cases since *Plimmer* that a common expectation engendered by encouragement from the owner of land can give rise to an 'equity' based on proprietary estoppel. The classic features of this form of estoppel were demonstrated in *Inwards v Baker.*[8] Here a father had allowed his son to build a bungalow at his own cost on the father's land, the son thereafter going into occupation of the bungalow in the belief, encouraged by his father, that he would be allowed to live there during his lifetime. The father died without making any binding contract or other arrangements to this effect. The Court of Appeal nevertheless refused to permit the trustees under the father's will to obtain possession against the son, holding that the son had acquired by reason of his expenditure on the land an 'equity' which bound not only the father (while he was alive) but also his successors in title with notice.[9] In giving equitable relief, the Court took the view that the 'equity' could be satisfied only by holding that the son 'can remain there as long as he desires to [use it] as his home.'[10]

A similar application of the estoppel doctrine occurred in *E.R. Ives Investment Ltd v High.*[11] Here the defendant had incurred expenditure in reliance on an

---

4 The precise name given to the *Ramsden v Dyson* principle is 'really immaterial' (*Taylors Fashions Ltd v Liverpool Victoria Trustees Co Ltd* [1982] QB 133 (Note) at 151H per Oliver J).
5 (1884) 9 App Cas 699.
6 (1884) 9 App Cas 699 at 712.
7 (1884) 9 App Cas 699 at 713.
8 [1965] 2 QB 29. See (1965) 81 LQR 183 (R.H. Maudsley).
9 It has been pointed out that this decision, in conferring on the son a possessory licence for life, produced the undesirable result both of rendering the land pro tempore unsaleable and of discouraging the son from moving (see F.R. Crane, (1967) 31 Conv (NS) 332 at 342). For further criticism, see *Dodsworth v Dodsworth* (1973) 228 Estates Gazette 1115 (post, p 807).
10 [1965] 2 QB 29 at 37G. See also *Raffaele v F & G Raffaele* [1962] WAR 29 at 31.
11 [1967] 2 QB 379 (ante, p 141). See F.R. Crane, *Estoppel Interests in Land*, (1967) 31 Conv (NS) 332.

agreement reached with the plaintiff's predecessor in title, under which the defendant had undertaken to raise no objection to a trespass committed upon his land by reason of the encroachment of foundations into his land, provided that the defendant could enjoy a right of way across the predecessor in title's neighbouring property. The Court of Appeal held this agreement to be binding on the plaintiff. By reason of his detrimental reliance, the defendant had acquired an 'equity' founded on the fact that the plaintiff's predecessor had 'created in [the defendant's] mind a reasonable expectation that his access over the yard would not be disturbed.'[12] A similar approach was applied by the Court of Appeal in *Crabb v Arun DC*,[13] where one party had allowed himself to become landlocked in reliance on an 'agreement in principle' that he should have a right of access and egress over land belonging to an adjacent owner.

(3) The 'unilateral mistake' cases

A significant distinction can be drawn in the jurisprudence of proprietary estoppel between the 'common expectation' cases and the 'unilateral mistake' cases. Unlike the former category, which gives pre-eminence to the shared nature of the parties' assumptions as to their mutual rights, the 'unilateral mistake' cases apply the doctrine of proprietary estoppel to circumstances in which only one party has made any error about his rights. In the 'unilateral mistake' cases, primary importance is attached to the 'detriment' which is suffered by a party who innocently relies on his mistaken supposition that he has rights in land.[14] This branch of the doctrine of proprietary estoppel regards it as unconscionable that the owner of the land should wilfully stand by and allow such a person to incur 'detriment' by relying on his own uncorrected misapprehension of the true legal position.

(a) Lord Cranworth LC's speech in Ramsden v Dyson

The foremost statement of the 'unilateral mistake' approach is found in the speech of Lord Cranworth LC in *Ramsden v Dyson*.[15] Here the Lord Chancellor gave the following instance:

> If a stranger begins to build on my land supposing it to be his own, and I, perceiving his mistake, abstain from setting him right, and leave him to persevere in his error, a Court of equity will not allow me afterwards to assert my title to the land on which he had expended money on the supposition that the land was his own. It considers that, when I saw the mistake into which he had fallen, it was my duty to be active and to state my adverse title; and that it would be dishonest in me to remain wilfully passive on such an occasion, in order afterwards to profit by the mistake which I might have prevented.

The 'unilateral mistake' cases are remarkable in that they exemplify some of the very few instances in English law where the courts have recognised a right to payment or other compensation for services rendered gratuitously.[16] True

---

12   [1967] 2 QB 379 at 394G.
13   [1976] Ch 179 at 189E, 192A, 198G. See (1976) 40 Conv (NS) 156 (F.R. Crane); (1976) 126 NLJ 772 (M. Vitoria); (1976) 92 LQR 174 (P.S. Atiyah), 342 (P.J. Millett).
14   The 'detriment' will often flow directly from the fact that any physical improvements effected on the land in reliance on a mistaken belief accede to the realty (ante, p 20). Such improvements normally confer no rights upon the improver (post, p 397).
15   (1866) LR 1 HL 129 at 140f.
16   See Goff and Jones, *op cit*, p 137.

'unilateral mistake' cases are fairly rare,[17] and the facts which require to be proved in support of this kind of estoppel claim are narrowly prescribed.

(b) The Willmott v Barber probanda

It was over a century ago, in *Willmott v Barber*,[18] that Fry J, without making any explicit reference to any existing caselaw,[19] formulated his own definition of the notion of estoppel. In his view, a man is not to be deprived of his strict legal rights 'unless he has acted in such a way as would make it fraudulent for him to set up those rights.' Fraud of this kind depended on proof of five necessary elements. *First*, the claimant of an equity based on estoppel must have made a mistake as to his legal rights. *Second*, the claimant must have 'expended some money or must have done some act...on the faith of his mistaken belief'. *Third*, the owner of the land must know of the existence of his own right which is inconsistent with the right claimed by the claimant. *Fourth*, the owner must know of the claimant's mistaken belief of his rights. *Fifth*, the owner must have encouraged the claimant in his expenditure of money or in the other acts which he has done, either directly or by abstaining from asserting his legal right.

The five *probanda* laid down by Fry J related quite clearly and exclusively to unilateral mistake. The very essence of the 'fraud' which is required to activate the estoppel lies in the wilful and self-interested silence of one who knows his rights and who realises that he may profit by reason of the detriment suffered by one who, not knowing his rights, acts under a mistake. Such facts were not present in *Willmott v Barber*: here both plaintiff and defendant were alike mistaken as to their true legal rights.[20] The circumstances of the instant case could not properly be categorised as a genuine example of 'unilateral mistake', and the claim of estoppel was therefore rejected.

(c) Long-term effects of Willmott v Barber

The observations of Fry J were, however, destined to have a much more enduring impact, for they had the perhaps unintended effect of imposing a strait-jacket on the development of proprietary estoppel during the following hundred years. Unfortunately the five *probanda*, because they were not explicitly limited to the category of 'unilateral mistake', were for a long time regarded as applying to all claims of proprietary estoppel irrespective of the category into which they fell.[1]

---

17 See, however, *Hamilton v Geraghty* (1901) 1 NSWSR (Eq) 81.

18 (1880) 15 Ch D 96 at 105f.

19 *Ramsden v Dyson* (1866) LR 1 HL 129 had been cited during argument before Fry J.

20 Neither the plaintiff assignee of a lease nor his lessor had realised that the lease prohibited assignment of the lease without the lessor's consent. In Fry J's view, the lessor could not, by acquiescing in the plaintiff's expenditure, be estopped from asserting his right to refuse consent to the assignment since at the date of the supposed acquiescence he had not realised that he had a right of veto over assignments anyway.

1 It is noteworthy that this extensive view was not taken in the early days of the development of the estoppel doctrine. Only four years after *Willmott v Barber*, the Privy Council in *Plimmer v Mayor etc of Wellington* (1884) 9 App Cas 699 at 712, was careful to distinguish clearly between the categories of 'unilateral mistake' and 'common expectation', observing that in the instant case 'the equity is not claimed because the landowner has stood by in silence while his tenant has spent money on his land.'

The inevitable result was that the courts often attempted to force given fact-situations within Fry J's five *probanda*, even where the terminology of *Willmott v Barber* was ludicrously irrelevant or inapplicable to the circumstances in issue.[2] Likewise the courts were prone to dismiss claims based on proprietary estoppel where the *probanda* were not amply satisfied. In particular, the requirement that the estoppel claimant should have made a positive mistake as to his existing rights was apt to operate with some harshness in circumstances where the claimant was in no doubt as to the absence of any strict entitlement on his part, but had been led to expect that he would somehow and at some time acquire rights by relying upon the assurance given by the owner. The insistence on the five *probanda* thus caused special difficulty in the context of informal 'family arrangements',[3] where full awareness of the absence of any existing entitlement in strict law is not incompatible with a vague and ill-defined expectation of future entitlement.[4]

(d) Diminishing force of Willmott v Barber

In effect the rigid application of the *Willmott v Barber* criteria tended to attach supreme importance to the 'unilateral mistake' theory of estoppel as expounded by Lord Cranworth LC in *Ramsden v Dyson* and to divert attention away from the alternative 'common expectation' rationale found in Lord Kingsdown's judgment. Gradually it came to be recognised that the five *probanda* of Fry J did not constitute a comprehensive formula,[5] and the way was prepared for a broader restatement of the principle of estoppel. This restatement has largely reversed the balance of emphasis so that the modern law of proprietary estoppel more closely approximates to the approach adumbrated by Lord Kingsdown.

(4) The modern synthesis: 'detrimental reliance'

It fell to Oliver J in *Taylors Fashions Ltd v Liverpool Victoria Trustees Co Ltd*[6] to confirm a broader direction in the law of proprietary estoppel. The plaintiffs here were the assignees of a leasehold term granted by the predecessors in title of the defendants. Under the terms of the lease the lessee had been given an option to renew the lease at the expiration of the current term. At the commencement date of the lease, such an option was generally considered to run with the land and not to require protection by registration. A few months later the original lessor conveyed the freehold reversion to the defendants. In the firm belief that the option was still valid, the plaintiffs then incurred substantial expenditure on renovations and improvements of the demised premises. Only some years later—and somewhat to the surprise of conveyancers—did the courts make it clear that an option to renew a lease

---

2 See even *Crabb v Arun DC* [1976] Ch 179 at 195F-H.
3 Post, p 792.
4 For examples of 'hard cases' both in the family arrangement context and elsewhere, see *E & L Berg Homes Ltd v Grey* (1980) 253 Estates Gazette 473; *Stilwell v Simpson* (1983) 133 NLJ 894; *Coombes v Smith* [1986] 1 WLR 808.
5 See *Electrolux Ltd v Electrix Ltd* (1953) 71 RPC 23 at 33 per Evershed MR; *Shaw v Applegate* [1977] 1 WLR 970 at 978C-D, 980B-C.
6 [1982] QB 133 (Note). See (1981) 97 LQR 513; [1982] Conv 450 (P. Jackson).

constitutes a registrable land charge.[7] The ineluctible result here was that the plaintiffs' option was rendered void for non-registration.[8] When the defendants subsequently declined to renew the lease, the plaintiffs argued that the defendants, by acquiescing in the expenditure, had been estopped from pleading the voidness of the option. Oliver J rejected this claim of proprietary estoppel and held the defendants entitled to refuse to renew the lease.

(a) Restricted relevance of the Willmott v Barber probanda

It was clear on the facts of *Taylors Fashions* that the plaintiffs could not establish all of the *Willmott v Barber* criteria, not least because the defendants had at all material times been unaware of their own strict rights in the matter.[9] However, Oliver J declined to succumb to a slavish application of the *Willmott v Barber probanda*, basing his dismissal of the plaintiffs' estoppel claim on different, and much wider, grounds.[10] He pointed out that Fry J's *probanda*, while arguably relevant to certain claims of estoppel, made no sense at all in other cases. He drew a broad distinction between the 'common expectation' cases and the 'unilateral mistake' cases, observing that the strict *Willmott v Barber probanda* are more properly relevant (if at all) to the latter category of case 'where all that has happened is that the party alleged to be estopped has stood by without protest while his rights have been infringed.'[11] Oliver J found it 'readily intelligible' in cases of 'pure acquiescence' or 'mere passivity' that 'there must be shown a duty to speak, protest or interfere which cannot normally arise in the absence of knowledge or at least a suspicion of the true position.'[12] However, in the 'common expectation' cases exemplified in Lord Kingsdown's dictum in *Ramsden v Dyson*, 'there is no room for the literal application of the *probanda*, for the circumstances there postulated do not presuppose a "mistake" on anybody's part, but merely the fostering of an expectation in the minds of *both* parties at the time but from which, once it has been acted upon, it would be unconscionable to permit the landlord to depart.'[13]

(b) A more general basis for proprietary estoppel

Having rejected the universal applicability of the *Willmott v Barber probanda*, Oliver J proceeded to find support in the caselaw for 'a much wider equitable jurisdiction to interfere in cases where the assertion of strict legal rights is found

7 See *Beesly v Hallwood Estates Ltd* [1960] 1 WLR 549 (ante, p 136; post, p 524), affirmed by the Court of Appeal on different grounds ([1961] Ch 105).
8 Oliver J did not pretend that the defendants' case was 'overburdened with merit', but took the view that 'it is no part of a judge's function to seek to impose upon a party to litigation his own idiosyncratic code of commercial morality' ([1982] QB 133 (Note) at 135E-F). The option was of course still binding upon the original lessor ([1982] QB 133 (Note) at 143G).
9 They had not known that the plaintiffs were mistaken in believing that their option was still enforceable.
10 In Oliver J's view, the role of the court was not to inquire 'whether the circumstances can be fitted within the confines of some preconceived formula serving as a universal yardstick for every form of unconscionable behaviour' ([1982] QB 133 (Note) at 152A). See also *Andrews v Colonial Mutual Life Assurance Society Ltd* [1982] 2 NZLR 556 at 568.
11 [1982] QB 133 (Note) at 147B. Significantly, Oliver J thought that the strict relevance of the *probanda* even in 'unilateral mistake' cases 'must now be considered open to doubt.'
12 [1982] QB 133 (Note) at 146C, 147C.
13 [1982] QB 133 (Note) at 147G.

by the courts to be unconscionable.'[14] While the *Willmott v Barber* criteria may provide 'a valuable guide'[15] in determining the applicability of proprietary estoppel, the primary inquiry for the court is 'whether, in particular individual circumstances, it would be unconscionable for a party to be permitted to deny that which, knowingly or unknowingly, he has allowed or encouraged another to assume to his detriment'.[16] A circumstance such as the state of mind of the party alleged to be estopped thus becomes 'merely one of the relevant factors...in the overall inquiry.'[17]

The judgment of Oliver J in *Taylors Fashions* appears to have been a watershed in the law of proprietary estoppel. In the aftermath of *Taylors Fashions* it seems now to be accepted that 'the real question comes down simply to whether or not the assertion of strict legal rights would be unconscionable, without any detailed conditions or criteria being specified'.[18] Some categorisation of the cases will still be appropriate,[19] since, as emerges later, the requirements of estoppel continue to differentiate slightly between circumstances of 'common expectation' and 'unilateral mistake'.[20] But, in general terms, the strictures of the old *Willmott v Barber* approach have been very substantially relaxed.[1]

4. OPERATION OF PROPRIETARY ESTOPPEL

Attention must now be turned to the way in which the modern concept of proprietary estoppel operates in the caselaw. A successful claim of estoppel involves a showing of three elements: (1) an assurance, (2) a reliance, and (3) a detriment.

(1) Assurance

In order to found a claim of proprietary estoppel, it is vital that there should have been some assurance of entitlement given by the person whom it is sought to estop. There is in English law no doctrine akin to the Roman law concept of

---

14   [1982] QB 133 (Note) at 147B. The existence of this more extensive jurisdiction had already been suggested in *Shaw v Applegate* [1977] 1 WLR 970 at 980B-C per Goff LJ. (Compare, however, the cautionary remarks of Megarry V-C in *Haslemere Estates Ltd v Baker* [1982] 1 WLR 1109 at 1119G, and see the reminder in *Legione v Hateley* (1982-83) 46 ALR 1 at 18 that the estoppel doctrine provides no 'charter for idiosyncratic concepts of justice and fairness').
15   [1982] QB 133 (Note) at 153E, quoting *Crabb v Arun DC* [1976] Ch 179 at 194E per Scarman LJ.
16   [1982] QB 133 (Note) at 151H-152A.
17   [1982] QB 133 (Note) at 152A.
18   *Appleby v Cowley* (1982) *The Times*, 14 April, per Megarry V-C. See also *Amalgamated Investment & Property Co Ltd v Texas Commerce International Bank Ltd* [1982] QB 84 at 104D-E. A claim of proprietary estoppel succeeded in *In re Basham, decd* [1986] 1 WLR 1498, even though it was conceded (at 1508F-G) that the *Willmott v Barber* criteria had not been satisfied.
19   In *Taylors Fashions* [1982] QB 133 (Note) at 145ff, Oliver J undertook a meticulous analysis of the preceding caselaw which vindicated the view that slightly different considerations apply to the divergent categories of 'common expectation' and 'unilateral mistake'.
20   Post, p 408.
1   See, however, *Coombes v Smith* [1986] 1 WLR 808 at 817G-818B, where *Taylors Fashions Ltd v Liverpool Victoria Trustees Co Ltd* was not cited and the *Willmott v Barber* criteria were applied with full rigour.

negotiorum gestio,[2] which gave the provider of a voluntary service the right to claim remuneration or reimbursement.[3] One who voluntarily improves another's land without encouragement or promise of reward does so, in English law, 'entirely at his own risk.'[4] To confer benefit gratuitously and then expect reward is, to use the blunt terms of Lord Cranworth LC, a 'folly'.[5] Thus Oliver LJ was standing on solid ground when, in *Savva v Costa and Harymode Investments Ltd*,[6] he declared himself unable to accept the proposition that 'there is some category of proprietary estoppel outside the *Ramsden v Dyson* principle, resting simply on expenditure with consent.' In order to raise an equity there must have been a 'representation or expectation created by the landowner.'[7] The only exceptions to this principle tend to be of statutory origin[8] and are few in number.

(a) Source of the assurance

If a proprietary estoppel is effectively to restrain the exercise of rights normally incidental to a fee simple estate, the assurance on which the estoppel is based must have been given by the owner of the fee simple himself[9] or by his

---

2 See W.W. Buckland and A.D. McNair, *Roman Law and Common Law* (2nd edn, London 1952), p 344.
3 See W.W. Buckland, *A Text-book of Roman Law* (3rd edn by P. Stein, Cambridge 1963), p 537ff.
4 *Stilwell v Simpson* (1983) 133 NLJ 894. 'The general principle is, beyond all question, that work and labour done or money expended by one man to preserve or benefit the property of another do not according to English law create any lien upon the property saved or benefited, nor, if standing alone, create any obligation to repay the expenditure. Liabilities are not to be forced upon people behind their backs any more than you can confer a benefit upon a man against his will' (*Falcke v Scottish Imperial Insurance Co* (1886) 34 Ch D 234 at 248 per Bowen LJ). See also *Ruabon Steamship Co v London Assurance* [1900] AC 6 at 10, 15; *Pettitt v Pettitt* [1970] AC 777 at 818B; *In re Vandervell's Trusts* (No 2) [1974] Ch 269 at 299F, H; *Avondale Printers & Stationers Ltd v Haggie* [1979] 2 NZLR 124 at 155.
5 *Ramsden v Dyson* (1866) LR 1 HL 129 at 141. In England compensation for improvements cannot be claimed under any doctrine of unjust enrichment (see *Pettitt v Pettitt* [1970] AC 777 at 795G-H per Lord Reid).
6 (1981) 131 NLJ 1114.
7 *Ibid.* See also *Easterbrook v The King* [1931] 1 DLR 628 at 636; *Rodgers v Moonta Town Corporation* (1981) 37 ALR 49 at 53 per Gibbs CJ (High Court of Australia).
8 See eg Matrimonial Proceedings and Property Act 1970, s 37 (ante, p 311; post, p 809). Other jurisdictions provide more general statutory relief in respect of improvements effected under mistake of title. See eg Queensland's Property Law Act 1974-82, ss 196, 197 (*Newman v Powter* [1978] Qd R 383; *Ex parte Goodlet & Smith* [1983] 2 Qd R 792); Manitoba's Law of Property Act (RSM 1970, c L90), s 27 (*Re Robertson and Saunders* (1977) 75 DLR (3d) 507); Ontario's Conveyancing and Law of Property Act (RSO 1980, c 90), s 37 (*Geldhof v Bakai* (1983) 139 DLR (3d) 527). In some jurisdictions the statutory relief available does not even require proof of mistake (see British Columbia's Property Law Act (RSBC 1979, c 340), s 32: *Re Ferguson and Lepine* (1983) 141 DLR (3d) 187).
9 The assurance must come from some party qua owner of the land concerned (*Western Fish Products Ltd v Penwith DC* [1981] 2 All ER 204 at 218a-b). The relevant assurance may even come from the ultimate owner of land, ie, the Crown (see *Attorney-General to the Prince of Wales v Collom* [1916] 2 KB 193 at 204; *The Queen v Smith* (1981) 113 DLR (3d) 522 at 582). There is, however, no requirement that the promisor should already own the land in relation to which the assurance is made. The assurance may come, for instance, from a licensee who later acquires the legal estate (see *Watson v Goldsbrough* [1986] 1 EGLR 265 at 267F, where Browne-Wilkinson V-C held that an estoppel established against two licensees was 'fed' when they subsequently acquired a fee simple estate). See also *Riches v Hogben* [1986] 1 Qd R 315 at 321, 327, 342, where an estoppel claim was successfully based on a promise by a mother that she would purchase a house and put it in her son's name if he were prepared to emigrate to Australia to live near her.

employees or agents.[10] It is not sufficient to raise the equity that the assurance was given by a tenant of the freehold owner.[11] The party giving the assurance need not be human. A company acting through its employees and agents can give a relevant assurance,[12] but such an assurance is not meaningful if given to a related company which is controlled by identical shareholders and management.[13]

(b) Subject matter of the assurance

The assurance required to raise an 'equity' in the party to whom it is given must confirm in the latter an expectation that he will be the recipient of some interest or entitlement in the land which he would not otherwise have.[14]

(i) General nature of the rights promised The rights promised must be rights in or over land[15] and must be such as fall within the capacity of the owner to grant.[16] It is not sufficient that the owner should rather vaguely promise the claimant 'financial security' both before and after his death, without reference to any specific asset or assets.[17] An estoppel claim is not, however, precluded merely because the claimant's expectation did not relate to some clearly identified piece of property: a valid claim may arise from an expectation that the claimant would inherit the owner's residuary estate.[18]

The quality of the promised benefits as 'rights' may also depend rather crucially on the precise timing of their acquisition. Proprietary estoppel cannot operate if the rights promised have already passed to the claimant of the 'equity' before he incurs his expenditure or otherwise acts on the assurance given to him.[19] Doubt has been expressed whether a representation 'as to what will happen upon the representor's death or what will be in the representor's will' can be construed as an assurance that there should be a 'present

10 That an employee or agent can give a relevant assurance was confirmed by the Court of Appeal in *Ivory v Palmer* (1976) 237 Estates Gazette 411.
11 *Ward v Kirkland* [1967] Ch 194 at 241D; *Swallow Securities Ltd v Isenberg* (1985) 274 Estates Gazette 1028 at 1030. The point appears to have been implicit in *Willmott v Barber* (1880) 15 Ch D 96.
12 In *Swallow Securities Ltd v Isenberg, supra*, the Court of Appeal was prepared, *obiter*, to hold a landlord company estopped if the relevant assurance had been mediated through its resident porter in a block of flats.
13 *Te Rama Engineering Ltd v Shortlands Properties Ltd* [1982] BCL 692 (High Court of New Zealand). Casey J thought that the identical management would act as a 'barrier to concepts of inducement, encouragement, or acquiescence'.
14 In *Shaida v Kindlane Ltd* (Unreported, Chancery Division, 1976 S No 8501, 22 June 1982), Judge Baker QC upheld an estoppel claim based on an assurance that the defendants would transfer a freehold estate to the plaintiff's wife. In reliance on this assurance the plaintiff had effected improvements to the property. See also *Davies v Messner* (1975) 12 SASR 333 at 341.
15 Estoppel cannot be founded on a representation that planning permission will be available for a development on the claimant's land (*Western Fish Products Ltd v Penwith DC* [1981] 2 All ER 204 at 218h).
16 *Ezekiel v Orakpo and Scott* (Unreported, Court of Appeal, 1976 E No 1773, 20 February 1980) per Brightman LJ.
17 *Layton v Martin* [1986] 2 FLR 227 at 238G-239A. See also *Baumgartner v Baumgartner* [1985] 2 NSWLR 406 at 415C-D.
18 *In re Basham, decd* [1986] 1 WLR 1498 at 1510C-E. See [1987] CLJ 215 (D.J. Hayton).
19 *Avondale Printers & Stationers Ltd v Haggie* [1979] 2 NZLR 124 at 144. (This situation becomes problematic of course only if, as in this case, there is a subsequent re-transfer of the disputed rights to the party who gave the original assurance).

acquisition of that future right by the representee.'[20] It is clear, for instance, that a mere expression of opinion as to likely future entitlement cannot rank as an assurance for the purpose of estoppel.[1] However, in *In re Basham, decd*[2] an estoppel claim was successfully founded on acts undertaken not in reliance on a belief that the claimant had any existing rights, but on the faith of an undertaking that she would be granted rights in the future. The claimant and her husband had for many years looked after the claimant's elderly step-father, having been encouraged by him to believe that his entire residuary estate would become theirs on his death. It was held to be irrelevant that the claimant's expectations were not related to any existing entitlement,[3] and that she had never enjoyed even some lesser form of right in the property promised.[4]

(ii) Non-contractual acquisition of rights   Within the limits indicated above, the potential subject matter of the rights promised may take almost any form.[5] The courts have shown themselves willing in principle, and often in practice, to invoke the doctrine of proprietary estoppel to give effect to expectations of entitlement which vary from a fee simple interest in the land[6] to a right of pre-emption,[7] a lease,[8] a licence,[9] and even an easement.[10] Moreover, it is not essential that the precise nature of the promised entitlement should have been spelt out in terms of recognisable property rights. There is high authority for the view that 'the equity arising from expenditure on land need not fail merely on the ground that the interest to be secured has not been expressly indicated.'[11] The expectation engendered by the assurance may simply involve a fairly inarticulate understanding that the claimant of the 'equity' will acquire some rights of some kind.[12]

20   *Philip Lowe (Chinese Restaurant) Ltd v Sau Man Lee* (Unreported, Court of Appeal, 9 July 1985) per May LJ. See also *Layton v Martin* [1986] 2 FLR 227 at 238G-239D. *A fortiori*, if the estoppel claimant has actual knowledge that the representor has already made a will leaving the relevant property to somebody else (*Stilwell v Simpson* (1983) 133 NLJ 984). Compare, however, *Inwards v Baker* [1965] 2 QB 29 (ante, p 391), and see the way in which a Canadian court has imposed a constructive trust on the basis of the marriage vow 'With all my worldly goods I thee endow' (*Re Spears and Levy* (1975) 52 DLR (3d) 146 at 152, 154).
1   *E & L Berg Homes Ltd v Grey* (1980) 253 Estates Gazette 473 at 477 per Sir David Cairns.
2   [1986] 1 WLR 1498.
3   [1986] 1 WLR 1498 at 1509B.
4   [1986] 1 WLR 1498 at 1510B-C.
5   Even the inclusion of chattels within an estate agent's printed particulars of sale may constitute a representation that those items will pass with the conveyance of the realty, with the result that the vendor can be estopped from denying that they are within the scope of the sale (see *Hamp v Bygrave* (1983) 266 Estates Gazette 720 at 726).
6   *Pascoe v Turner* [1979] 1 WLR 431 (ante, p 389).
7   *Stilwell v Simpson* (1983) 133 NLJ 894.
8   *Watson v Goldsbrough* [1986] 1 EGLR 265 at 266F-H.
9   *Inwards v Baker* [1965] 2 QB 29 (ante, p 391); *Greasley v Cooke* [1980] 1 WLR 1306 (post, p 800).
10   *Ward v Kirkland* [1967] Ch 194; *Crabb v Arun DC* [1976] Ch 179; *Dewhirst v Edwards* [1983] 1 NSWLR 34 (post, p 684).
11   *Plimmer v Mayor etc of Wellington* (1884) 9 App Cas 699 at 713 per Sir Arthur Hobhouse. See also *Inwards v Baker* [1965] 2 QB 29 at 37B; *Denny v Jensen* [1977] 1 NZLR 635 at 638; *Vinden v Vinden* [1982] 1 NSWLR 618 at 624E; *Cameron v Murdoch* [1983] WAR 321 at 351 (affd (1985-86) 63 ALR 575 at 595). Compare, however, *Coombes v Smith* [1986] 1 WLR 808 at 818C-H.
12   See, for instance, *Baumgartner v Baumgartner* [1985] 2 NSWLR 406 at 414D, 419D-E, where Kirby P held that a valid estoppel claim could be founded on oral statements made by a de facto husband. He had constantly assured his partner that the family home would be 'a security for her' and had encouraged her to continue saving for 'our house'. Such assurances gave her an 'expectation of an indefinite right of residence'. It may not be sufficient, however, that the owner merely provides a written assurance, in general terms, of emotional and financial security (see *Layton v Martin* [1986] 2 FLR 227 at 238H-239D).

(iii) Non-contractual disposal of rights In extreme circumstances an 'equity' can arise, not on the basis of any assurance that the claimant would acquire new rights in any land, but on the basis of a representation that it would be safe for him to dispose of his existing rights in land. In *Salvation Army Trustee Co Ltd v West Yorkshire MCC*,[13] the defendant local authority was held to be estopped from declining to proceed with a purchase of the plaintiff's land after assurances had been given which led the plaintiff to purchase a substitute site for its activities. This result was remarkable, not least because the parties had never concluded any contract of sale,[14] but the circumstances present here were exceptional. It is unlikely that the doctrine of proprietary estoppel will be applied widely to enforce transactions of sale and purchase of land in advance of a formal contract.[15] Only rarely will an 'equity' be raised to support the non-contractual disposal of rights in land as distinct from facilitating the non-contractual acquisition of rights in land.

(c) The manner of the assurance

The assurance which generates the 'equity' may be express or implied; it may be 'active or passive'.[16] A proprietary estoppel will arise in either case if the present claimant of the 'equity' was led to believe that he would acquire rights over the land in question.

(i) Relevant forms of representation Relevant assurances may fall anywhere within the broad spectrum which ranges from a direct and positive request to incur expenditure, through encouragement and 'incitement', to mere silent abstention from the assertion of one's rights.[17] In determining the applicability of a proprietary estoppel, the courts look for evidence of 'anything done or left undone' which may have induced the detrimental reliance of the claimant.[18] It is clear that the assurance need not be made, and commonly is not made, in any manner which gives rise to contractual liability.[19]

(ii) Representation by silence It is in relation to the role of silence that the most controversial questions arise. It is clear that an estoppel can indeed be founded on conscious silence.[20] As Lord Wensleydale said in *Ramsden v Dyson*,[1] if a stranger 'builds on my land, supposing it to be his own, and I, knowing it to be mine, do not interfere, but leave him to go on, equity considers it to be

---

13 (1981) 41 P & CR 179. See [1983] Conv 85.
14 Ante, p 208.
15 Woolf J laid emphasis on the special circumstance that in the present case 'the arrangement for sale was part of a wider arrangement that involved the acquisition of an interest in other land and the sale and the acquisition were irretrievably interwoven...the acquisition and sale really amounted to the exchange of one site for another' ((1981) 41 P & CR 179 at 199).
16 *Warnes v Hedley* (Unreported, Court of Appeal, 31 January 1984) per May LJ.
17 *Ward v Kirkland* [1967] Ch 194 at 239B-C. See also *Taylors Fashions Ltd v Liverpool Victoria Trustees Co Ltd* [1982] QB 133 (Note) at 148E-F.
18 *E & L Berg Homes Ltd v Grey* (1980) 253 Estates Gazette 473 at 477 per Sir David Cairns.
19 There was, for instance, no contractual duty resting on the son in *Inwards v Baker* [1965] 2 QB 29 (ante, p 391) to take up his father's offer of land on which to build his bungalow.
20 See *The Queen v Smith* (1981) 113 DLR (3d) 522 at 583 (Federal Court of Appeal of Canada).
1 (1866) LR 1 HL 129 at 168.

dishonest in me to remain passive and afterwards to interfere and take the profit.'[2]

The courts are reluctant, however, to attach significance to mere silence on the part of a landowner unless it is quite clear that he deliberately intended that his silence should be construed as endorsing the supposed entitlement of the estoppel claimant.[3] In *Williams v Coleman*,[4] for instance, the Court of Appeal declined to uphold a claim of proprietary estoppel against a physically disabled lady confined to a wheelchair. Fox LJ thought that her silence in the face of adverse occupation could be explained simply on the basis that she 'wanted to avoid trouble' and therefore 'made no fuss'. It has likewise been held that inaction by a landlord in respect of past breaches of covenant by a tenant cannot constitute any assurance that the lease will not be forfeited by reason of future breaches.[5] Nor can mere inaction by a liquidator over a prolonged period during which a bankrupt improves his property be taken to connote the degree of encouragement or acquiescence required to generate a proprietary estoppel.[6] But if the owner of an interest in or over land remains wilfully silent about his interest in the knowledge that a mortgagee would otherwise be inhibited from accepting the land as security for a loan, this degree of non-disclosure may estop a future assertion of priority over the rights taken by the mortgagee.[7]

(d) The state of mind of the owner of the land

Certain difficulties in the application of the doctrine of proprietary estoppel relate to the state of mind which must be shown on the part of the owner of the land which is the subject of an estoppel claim.

(i) Must the owner know of the reliance by the claimant?
In order that a proprietary estoppel be raised, it is essential that a certain state of knowledge should have been present in the party whose strict rights it is sought to restrain. It must be shown that that party gave the relevant assurance, whether actively or passively, with the intention that it should be relied on to another's detriment.[8] Where the assurance is repeated over a period of time, during which reliance

---

2 In *Warnes v Hedley* (Unreported, Court of Appeal, 31 January 1984), Slade LJ readily accepted that 'in some circumstances passive conduct, even if unaccompanied by any words, may suffice to constitute the relevant encouragement, if the facts are such that it is reasonable for the other party so to construe it.' See also *Denny v Jensen* [1977] 1 NZLR 635 at 638.
3 See *Salvation Army Trustee Co Ltd v West Yorkshire MCC* (1981) 41 P & CR 179 at 196 per Woolf J.
4 Unreported, Court of Appeal, 27 June 1984.
5 *Boxbusher Properties Ltd v Graham* (1976) 240 Estates Gazette 463 at 465.
6 *Pennell v Nunn* (Unreported, Chancery Division, 1979 P No 105, 2 April 1982).
7 *Midland Bank Ltd v Farmpride Hatcheries Ltd* (1981) 260 Estates Gazette 493 at 497ff; *Ulster Bank Ltd v Shanks* [1982] NI 143 at 150A; *Bristol and West Building Society v Henning* [1985] 1 WLR 778 at 782G, 783C (post, p 860). An often quoted dictum is that of Lord Tomlin in *Greenwood v Martins Bank Ltd* [1933] AC 51 at 57: 'Mere silence cannot amount to a representation, but when there is a duty to disclose deliberate silence may become significant and amount to a representation' (see *Canadian Superior Oil Ltd v Paddon-Hughes Development Co Ltd* (1969) 3 DLR (3d) 10 at 16, (1970) 12 DLR (3d) 247 at 253; *Maurice Demers Transport Ltd v Fountain Tire Distributors (Edmonton) Ltd* (1974) 42 DLR (3d) 412 at 421).
8 Mere expressions of opinion cannot amount to assurances for the purpose of proprietary estoppel (see *E & L Berg Homes Ltd v Grey* (1980) 253 Estates Gazette 473 at 477 per Sir David Cairns, ante, p 399).

supervenes, it must be clear that there was knowledge that the assurance was being relied upon by the eventual claimant of the 'equity'.[9] It must be proved that the party giving the assurance knew[10] or ought to have known[11] that the claimant was acting in the belief that he was acquiring some entitlement on the strength of the assurance.

Usually there will be knowledge of such facts as that the claimant is engaging in expenditure on the improvement of land.[12] However, it is not necessary that the knowledge of the party sought to be estopped should extend to the precise nature of the disadvantage incurred by the claimant. In *Crabb v Arun DC*,[13] for instance, the Court of Appeal upheld an estoppel claim even though the defendant was unaware at the material time that the plaintiff was selling part of his land without reserving an appropriate right of way. Scarman LJ admitted that the Court was thus applying the estoppel doctrine where the defendant knew merely of the 'intention' of the plaintiff to rely on the assurance given, as distinct from having knowledge of 'the realisation of that intention'.[14] Scarman LJ nevertheless thought that a mere absence of notice of the precise prejudice incurred did not destroy the plaintiff's 'equity'. It was sufficient that the defendant had knowingly undertaken the risk that the plaintiff might act in reliance on the common expectation engendered by their mutual dealings.[15]

(ii) Must the owner know his own strict rights?   It used to be the accepted view that no claim of estoppel could be established unless the person who gave the original assurance was consciously aware at the time of his own strict proprietary rights.[16] As Fry J said in *Willmott v Barber*,[17] such a person 'must know of the existence of his own right which is inconsistent with the right claimed by the plaintiff.' Without such knowledge, he is 'in the same position as the plaintiff, and the doctrine of acquiescence is founded upon conduct with a knowledge of your legal rights.' However, this requirement of knowledge is nowadays confined to cases of 'pure acquiescence', where the only assurance given has taken the form of sheer silence or, at best, passive encouragement.[18]

---

9   *Griffiths v Williams* (1977) 248 Estates Gazette 947 at 949 per Goff LJ.
10   *Ward v Gold* (1969) 211 Estates Gazette 155 at 161; *Gross v French* (1975) 238 Estates Gazette 39 at 41; *Savva v Costa and Harymode Investments Ltd* (1981) 131 NLJ 1114; *Appleby v Cowley* (1982) *Times*, 14 April. In *Shaida v Kindlane Ltd* (Unreported, Chancery Division, 1976 S No 8501, 22 June 1982), Judge Baker QC described this requirement of knowledge as 'important, though not crucial'. See also *Denny v Jensen* [1977] 1 NZLR 635 at 639.
11   *Salvation Army Trustee Co Ltd v West Yorkshire MCC* (1981) 41 P & CR 179 at 194, 196; *Swallow Securities Ltd v Isenberg* (1985) 274 Estates Gazette 1028 at 1030 per Cumming-Bruce LJ; *Watson v Goldsbrough* [1986] 1 EGLR 265 at 266M, 267E.
12   Such knowledge may be actual or a matter of irresistible inference (see *E & L Berg Homes Ltd v Grey* (1980) 253 Estates Gazette 473 at 476, 479).
13   [1976] Ch 179 at 189D, 197H (ante, p 392).
14   [1976] Ch 179 at 197H-198A. However, where there is no knowledge even of an intention to rely on the assurance, the claim of proprietary estoppel must fail (see *Costagliola v English* (1969) 210 Estates Gazette 1425 at 1431). *A fortiori*, if there was a requirement (eg as a condition of grant aid) that the landowner be informed in advance of the intention to begin making improvements on the land (*Devlin v Northern Ireland Housing Executive* [1982] 17 NIJB, p 20 per Lord Lowry LCJ).
15   See however, *Coombes v Smith* [1986] 1 WLR 808 at 819H.
16   See eg *Ward v Kirkland* [1967] Ch 194 at 240B.
17   (1880) 15 Ch D 96 at 105.
18   *Taylors Fashions Ltd v Liverpool Victoria Trustee Co Ltd* [1982] QB 133 (Note) at 152A, 157B-C (ante, p 395).

Accordingly the owner's ignorance of his strict rights will provide no impediment to a claim of proprietary estoppel if the relevant assurance has taken a more forceful or active form.[19] Estoppel may apply if one party, although unaware of his precise rights, has by his words or conduct positively induced another party to rely on the strength of a common expectation generated by their dealings or negotiations.[20]

(iii) Must the owner know that the claimant is acting under a mistake? Again it used to be thought that, in order to establish a proprietary estoppel, a claimant must show that the owner knew that the claimant's belief in his own supposed rights was erroneous or mistaken.[1] However, after *Taylors Fashions Ltd v Liverpool Victoria Trustees Co Ltd*[2] this requirement seems to have been displaced at least in relation to cases of the 'common expectation' variety,[3] although it may have a greater relevance to cases of 'unilateral mistake'. As Oliver J pointed out, 'knowledge of the true position by the party alleged to be estopped becomes merely one of the relevant factors—it may even be a determining factor in certain cases—in the overall inquiry'.[4]

(2) Reliance

In order to raise an 'equity' based on proprietary estoppel, the claimant must show that he has acted in reliance upon the assurance given by the owner of the land.

(a) The causal link between assurance and detriment

It is the element of reliance which renders it unconscionable that an assurance, once given, should be subsequently withdrawn or denied. Reliance thus provides vital evidence of the causal link between the assurance given by one party and the detriment suffered by the other.

The courts have often stressed that the assurance must be an *effective* cause of detriment.[5] It must be proved that the assurance has 'induced'[6] the

---

19 It even seems to be irrelevant in such a case that the rights which the owner now seeks to enforce were not strictly pre-existing rights, but were instead rights which came into existence only upon the change of position induced by his assurance (see *Bank Negara Indonesia v Hoalim* [1973] 2 MLJ 3 at 5A-B per Lord Wilberforce).

20 That estoppel may be raised against a party who is innocently unaware of his own rights was confirmed, *obiter*, in *Canadian Superior Oil Ltd v Paddon-Hughes Development Co Ltd* (1969) 3 DLR (3d) 10 at 16f, (1970) 12 DLR (3d) 247 at 253. See also *Sarat Chunder Dey v Gopal Chunder Laha* (1892) 19 LR Ind App 203 at 215ff (Privy Council); *Cameron v Murdoch* [1983] WAR 321 at 351.

1 *Willmott v Barber* (1880) 15 Ch D 96 at 105.

2 [1982] QB 133 (Note) (ante, p 394).

3 [1982] QB 133 (Note) at 147B.

4 [1982] QB 133 (Note) at 152A.

5 In *Greasley v Cooke* [1980] 1 WLR 1306 at 1311C-E, Lord Denning MR seemed to suggest that there is a presumption of reliance once it is shown that 'a representation was calculated to influence the judgment of a reasonable man' (see also *Brikom Investments Ltd v Carr* [1979] QB 467 at 483A). Although followed in *Hamp v Bygrave* (1983) 266 Estates Gazette 720 at 726, this view has been criticised as inconsistent with authority and principle (see (1981) 125 SJ 539 at 540 (M.P. Thompson).

6 See *Dodsworth v Dodsworth* (1973) 228 Estates Gazette 1115 at 1117. In *Swallow Securities Ltd v Isenberg* (1985) 274 Estates Gazette 1028 at 1030, Cumming-Bruce LJ found it 'helpful to use the term "inducing an expectation" rather than the nearly synonymous verb "encouraging"...'

expectations of the party to whom it was given or has at least 'influenced'[7] his conduct. Accordingly, claims based on proprietary estoppel have been rejected by the courts on the ground that there was no evidence that the assurance was one of the operative causal factors bringing about the change of position in respect of which the 'equity' is claimed.[8] This has sometimes led to slightly surprising—and even harsh—decisions. The courts have on occasion declined to uphold estoppel claims in respect of improvements made to living conditions in the family home which, in the courts' view, the claimant would have effected in any case simply for reasons of domestic comfort or convenience.[9] Likewise the courts have refused to apply the doctrine of proprietary estoppel where it was felt that the claimant contributed money and labour, not in the belief that she was acquiring either an interest in the family home or a right to live there, but merely because 'she was part of the family'.[10]

(b) Change of position

The fundamental catalyst in the generation of rights by way of proprietary estoppel is the fact that there has been a change of position by the party to whom the assurance was given.[11] There must be palpable evidence that the claimant of the 'equity' has acted on the faith of the assurance given to him. This requirement has often been described in the caselaw as predicating that the claimant has suffered some form of 'detriment',[12] a usage which is perfectly acceptable so long as it is understood as referring to a factual disadvantage which demonstrates the reality of the reliance. As will be seen later,[13] the ultimate 'detriment' required to found a proprietary estoppel is the legal detriment which occurs only if the assurance initially given is unconscionably withdrawn. It may be altogether easier and less confusing to refer to the present requirement of factual detriment in terms of a 'change of position'.

(i) Improvement of realty It is sometimes said that the improvement of land constitutes the 'classic way'[14] in which the claimant of an 'equity' can establish

---

7 *Amalgamated Investment & Property Co Ltd v Texas Commerce International Bank Ltd* [1982] QB 84 at 105A per Goff J. See also *Coombes v Smith* [1986] 1 WLR 808 at 820A; *Layton v Martin* [1986] 2 FLR 227 at 235G.

8 See eg *Taylors Fashions Ltd v Liverpool Victoria Trustees Co Ltd* [1982] QB 133 (Note) at 156C per Oliver J, who distinguished between action undertaken 'on the faith of' a belief that the plaintiffs had a valid right of option (ante, p 394) and action undertaken merely 'in' that belief. See also *Avondale Printers & Stationers Ltd v Haggie* [1979] 2 NZLR 124 at 144; *Brinnand v Ewens* (1987) *Times*, 4 June.

9 See *E & L Berg Homes Ltd v Grey* (1980) 253 Estates Gazette 473 at 479 per Sir David Cairns; *Rogers v Eller* (Unreported, Court of Appeal, 20 May 1986). In *Stilwell v Simpson* (1983) 133 NLJ 894, it was considered that the claimant had effected the disputed improvements, not in response to the assurance given to him, but because it was 'natural to him to make the best of his home'.

10 *Philip Lowe (Chinese Restaurant) Ltd v Sau Man Lee* (Unreported, Court of Appeal, 9 July 1985) per May LJ. See also *Coombes v Smith* [1986] 1 WLR 808 at 820F-G; *Layton v Martin* [1986] 2 FLR 227 at 235H-236A.

11 'In cases of proprietary estoppel the factor which gives rise to the equitable obligation is A's alteration of his position on the faith of [an] understanding' (*In re Basham, decd* [1986] 1 WLR 1498 at 1504D).

12 See eg *Greasley v Cooke* [1980] 1 WLR 1306 at 1314A; *Riches v Hogben* [1986] 1 Qd R 315 at 341f.

13 Post, p 409.

14 *Shaida v Kindlane Ltd* (Unreported, Chancery Division, 1976 S No 8501, 22 June 1982) per Judge Baker QC.

that he has undergone a factual detriment or change of position in reliance on an assurance. It is certainly true that reliance is most clearly and tangibly expressed in the form of expenditure on improvements to realty, provided at least that these improvements are relatively 'permanent'[15] or 'substantial'.[16] Thus proprietary estoppels have been recognised where the claimant has built a dwelling-house on another's land,[17] or has financed an addition or extension to some existing construction.[18]

(ii) Disadvantage unrelated to land   It is clear, however, that 'the categories of detriment are not closed'.[19] There is no strict requirement that the change of position pleaded in support of an estoppel claim should necessarily involve any qualitative 'improvement' of land[20] or comprise expenditure on land belonging to the giver of the assurance[1] or, for that matter, comprise any form of expenditure related to land at all.[2] The disadvantage incurred by the relier may include such factors as a failure to reserve appropriate rights of way on the sale of his land.[3]

(iii) Personal effort and personal disadvantage   The estoppel claimant's change of position may be measurable in money terms,[4] but there is ample authority that the change of position required need not involve the payment of money.[5] It may instead take the form of a contribution of labour and services in the family home,[6] the working of a farm property,[7] the abandonment of an existing job and home in order to live near the person who provides the relevant assurance,[8]

---

15 *Griffiths v Williams* (1977) 248 Estates Gazette 947; *Taylor v Taylor* [1956] NZLR 99 at 103. In *Appleby v Cowley* (1982) *The Times*, 14 April, it was argued that a proprietary estoppel could be founded on an electrical re-wiring, redecoration and damp-repair of premises. However, Megarry V-C declined to say that such expenditure should be 'ignored', but thought it carried 'little weight' in that it did 'not represent much more than keeping the building in a usable state while it was being occupied.'
16 *Pascoe v Turner* [1979] 1 WLR 431 at 436B.
17 *Inwards v Baker* [1965] 2 QB 29 (ante, p 391).
18 *Hussey v Palmer* [1972] 1 WLR 1286 (post, p 797).
19 *Watts v Story* (Unreported, Court of Appeal, 14 July 1983) per Dunn LJ.
20 It is difficult, for instance, to imagine that the expenditure described in *Pennine Raceway Ltd v Kirklees MBC* [1983] QB 382 at 386B actually enhanced the utility of the land for any purpose other than that of using it for motor racing.
 1 *Willmott v Barber* (1880) 15 Ch D 96 at 105; *Dewhirst v Edwards* [1983] 1 NSWLR 34 at 49F. In *Cook v Minion* (1979) 37 P & CR 58 at 65, for instance, a claim of proprietary estoppel was upheld on behalf of an owner who had installed water closets on his own land in reliance on permission received from his neighbour for ancillary rights of drainage.
 2 *Holiday Inns Inc v Broadhead* (1974) 232 Estates Gazette 951 at 1087; *In re Basham, decd* [1986] 1 WLR 1498 at 1509D; *Riches v Hogben* [1986] 1 Qd R 315 at 342.
 3 *Crabb v Arun DC* [1976] Ch 179 at 197G (ante, p 402). See also *Vinden v Vinden* [1982] 1 NSWLR 618 at 624F.
 4 In *Timber Top Realty Pty Ltd v Mullens* [1974] VR 312 at 318, the Supreme Court of Victoria held that reliance on an assurance was sufficiently demonstrated where the claimant of the 'equity' sold land for an inadequate consideration to the person who gave the assurance. See also *Baumgartner v Baumgartner* [1985] 2 NSWLR 406 at 419C.
 5 *In re Sharpe (A Bankrupt)* [1980] 1 WLR 219 at 223E; *Greasley v Cooke* [1980] 1 WLR 1306 at 1311G, 1314A; *Watts v Story* (Unreported, Court of Appeal, 14 July 1983).
 6 *Greasley v Cooke* [1980] 1 WLR 1306 (post, p 800). See also *Hink v Lhenen* (1975) 52 DLR (3d) 301 at 315f, where what is essentially an estoppel claim is dealt with in terms of *quantum meruit*.
 7 *Beech v Beech* [1982] BCL 231 (High Court of New Zealand).
 8 *Jones (AE) v Jones (FW)* [1977] 1 WLR 438 at 442D. See also *Riches v Hogben* [1986] 1 Qd R 315 at 321 (where a son sold up at a loss and emigrated to Australia in order to live near his aged mother).

or indeed, perhaps, the undergoing of any sacrifice which is not of exclusively emotional significance.[9] The disadvantage incurred may comprise a foregoing of opportunities for a career outside the home,[10] a failure to purchase other land for use as a home,[11] and even a deliberate refraining from serving a statutory notice of application for a new lease.[12]

It has been said, however, that it is not sufficient merely to pay money towards the household expenses (such as food) or running costs (such as household bills), since this is more readily seen as a contribution to the current living expenses of the family.[13] Nor is an alteration of personal lifestyle necessarily a relevant change of position in the law of proprietary estoppel. In *Coombes v Smith*,[14] for instance, the claimant rested her allegation of change of position on the fact that she had left her husband to move in with the defendant, had allowed herself to become pregnant by him, and had generally looked after the child, the defendant and their shared home. It was held that none of these actions was sufficient to found a claim of proprietary estoppel, but simply represented the kind of conduct to be expected of the claimant 'as occupier of the property, as the defendant's mistress, and as [the child's] mother, in the context of a continuing relationship with the defendant'.[15] Moreover, it could not be demonstrated in any realistic way that the claimant's conduct had been induced by 'reliance on some mistaken belief as to her legal rights'.[16]

It may be, however, that the more recent decision of the Court of Appeal in *Grant v Edwards*[17] foreshadows a wider recognition of intangible personal sacrifice as being relevant to the foundation of an estoppel claim. Here Browne-Wilkinson V-C seemed prepared to accept that, if there was a common intention that the claimant should have an interest in the disputed property, 'any act done by her to her detriment relating to the joint lives of the parties is...sufficient detriment to qualify.'[18] In his view, the acts done need not be 'inherently referable to the house'.[19] They could indeed include such conduct as '[s]etting up house together, having a baby, [and] making payments to general housekeeping expenses', even though all such activity might be more accurately referable to 'the mutual love and affection of the parties and not specifically referable to the claimant's belief that she has an interest in the

---

9   See *Christian v Christian* (1981) 131 NLJ 43 (ante, p 277). See also *In re Basham, decd* [1986] 1 WLR 1498 at 1505G-H, where the claimant and her husband had 'subordinated their own interests to the wishes of the deceased'.

10   *Greasley v Cooke* [1980] 1 WLR 1306 at 1312A. Compare, however, *Coombes v Smith* [1986] 1 WLR 808 at 820H-821A.

11   *Cameron v Murdoch* [1983] WAR 321 at 360 (affirmed without comment by the Privy Council, (1985-86) 63 ALR 575 at 595). See also *In re Basham, decd* [1986] 1 WLR 1498 at 1505F, where the claimant and her husband had refrained from moving home in order that they could continue living near the claimant's step-father.

12   *Watkins v Emslie* (1982) 261 Estates Gazette 1192 at 1194, where the Court of Appeal rejected a claim of proprietary estoppel, not because inaction could not found the claim, but because the inaction had not been shown to have been induced by 'any assurances being given'.

13   *Hannaford v Selby* (1976) 239 Estates Gazette 811 at 813; *Griffiths v Williams* (1977) 248 Estates Gazette 947. See also *Baumgartner v Baumgartner* [1985] 2 NSWLR 406 at 415D.

14   [1986] 1 WLR 808. See [1986] CLJ 394 (D.J. Hayton).

15   [1986] 1 WLR 808 at 820F-G.

16   [1986] 1 WLR 808 at 820B.

17   [1986] Ch 638. See [1986] CLJ 394 (D.J. Hayton); [1986] Conv 291 (J. Warburton).

18   [1986] Ch 638 at 657B.

19   [1986] Ch 638 at 657B.

house.'[20] It remains to be seen whether this broader approach marks the path of future developments in the law of estoppel.

(iv) Shift in terminology The courts' definition of the element of reliance has become so broad that it is possible nowadays to see a subtle shift away from reference to 'detriment' to the terminology of 'change of position'.[1] In *Bhimji v Salih*,[2] for instance, Brightman LJ expressed the view that the doctrine of proprietary estoppel can apply only where 'the promisee has in fact acted to his detriment in the sense that...the promisee has altered his position in a way which would be to his disadvantage if the strict legal position remained unqualified.'[3] Likewise in *Greasley v Cooke*[4] Lord Denning MR considered it sufficient 'if the party, to whom the assurance is given, acts on the faith of it—in such circumstances that it would be unjust and inequitable for the party making the assurance to go back on it'. This movement towards a doctrine of 'acting' on the faith of an assurance is symptomatic of the more general contemporary tendency to re-state the several elements of proprietary estoppel in terms of a composite formula of unconscionability.[5]

(c) The state of mind of the estoppel claimant

In order that the doctrine of proprietary estoppel should operate, it is clear that there must have been some kind of misapprehension by the estoppel claimant as to the extent of his own entitlement.

(i) 'Unilateral mistake' cases The requirement of misapprehension was, of course, classically expressed in the form of the first *probandum* in *Willmott v Barber*,[6] where Fry J said that the claimant 'must have made a mistake as to his legal rights.' However, this requirement of 'mistake' has led to ambiguity, and the first *probandum* of *Willmott v Barber* probably applies in strict terms only to estoppel claims which truly fall within the category of 'unilateral mistake'. It is here that the requirement of 'mistake' makes perfect and literal sense. Lord Cranworth LC's exposition in *Ramsden v Dyson*[7] bases the operation of estoppel on the premise that the person who builds upon land in reliance upon the silent acquiescence of another wrongly 'supposes himself to be building on his own land'. The 'equity' in his favour arises directly from the dishonesty implicit in the true owner's failure to correct his misapprehension. An estoppel can arise in such a case only if the claimant acted under a positive mistake as to the nature

20 [1986] Ch 638 at 657A-B.
1 For an early reference to 'change of position' as an element of proprietary estoppel, see *E.R. Ives Investment Ltd v High* [1967] 2 QB 379 at 405F per Winn LJ. See also *In re Basham, decd* [1986] 1 WLR 1498 at 1504D. The terminology of 'change of position' is more commonly used in this context on the other side of the Atlantic (see eg *Maurice Demers Transport Ltd v Fountain Tire Distributors (Edmonton) Ltd* (1974) 42 DLR (3d) 412 at 423; *Mahony v Danis*, 469 A.2d 31 at 36 (1983) (Supreme Court of New Jersey)).
2 Unreported, Court of Appeal, 1978 B No 1099, 4 February 1981.
3 It was significant that Brightman LJ related this proposition directly to *Gissing v Gissing* [1971] AC 886 (ante, p 243).
4 [1980] 1 WLR 1306 at 1311G.
5 See *Taylors Fashions Ltd v Liverpool Victoria Trustees Co Ltd* [1982] QB 133 (Note) at 155C per Oliver J (ante, p 394); *Cameron v Murdoch* [1983] WAR 321 at 351.
6 (1880) 15 Ch D 96 at 105 (ante, p 393).
7 (1866) LR 1 HL 129 at 141 (ante, p 392).

or quantum of his existing rights.[8] As Lord Cranworth said, 'if a stranger builds on my land knowing it to be mine, there is no principle of equity which would prevent my claiming the land with the benefit of all the expenditure made on it. There would be nothing in my conduct, active or passive, making it inequitable in me to assert my legal rights.'[9]

(ii) 'Common expectation' cases   The requirement of mistake applies much less readily in the category of 'common expectation' cases.[10] Here the essence of the estoppel lies in the fact, not that a unilateral mistake about present entitlement has been made by someone, but that both parties have dealt with each other on the basis of a shared assumption as to their future rights. It is this important distinction between categories of estoppel claim which explains why in some cases the courts have demanded strict proof of 'mistake' on the part of the claimant,[11] while in other cases denying the necessity for proof of 'mistake' at all.[12] 'Mistake' in the *Willmott v Barber* sense is not required in the 'common expectation' category of case, except to the extent that the claimant has been induced to believe that he would receive some entitlement in the land which he would not otherwise have, and on the basis of that assurance exposed himself to recognisable legal prejudice.[13] In these circumstances it may well be that both parties originally believed and intended that the change of position should generate new rights as between themselves; the offence against conscience which attracts the operation of the estoppel is precisely the fact that subsequently one party unilaterally withdraws from that understanding.

(iii) Differentiation between mental states   Many of the 'hard cases' of the past[14] can be accounted for in retrospect as exemplifying a failure to acknowledge that slightly differing mental states are required for the purpose of estoppel claims in the apparently similar categories of 'common expectation' and 'unilateral mistake'. In estoppel claims based on 'common expectation', it

8   It seems that a 'unilateral mistake' can generate an estoppel even where the stranger has constructive notice of the fact that the land on which he builds is not his own. The relevant question is 'simply whether a mistake has been made, not whether the plaintiff ought to have made it' (see *Willmott v Barber* (1880) 15 Ch D 96 at 101 per Fry J). The knowledge required to bar a claim of estoppel based on 'unilateral mistake' is 'real knowledge which would involve a wilful act on the part of the party who has done the building' (*McMahon v Kerry County Council* [1981] ILRM 419 at 421).

9   See *Ezekiel v Orakpo and Scott* (Unreported, Court of Appeal, 1976 E No 1773, 20 February 1980), where Brightman LJ pointed out that the tenant, on whom had been conferred an option to purchase the freehold, had 'spent his money on that basis with his eyes open...His plans went awry, not because he was under any mistake or was misled by [the landlord], but because he ran out of money...Simply put, he was a speculator and his speculation did not pay off.'

10   As was pointed out in *Griffiths v Williams* (1977) 248 Estates Gazette 947 at 949, it is in any event difficult to pinpoint motivations in the 'common expectation' cases. Is the person who pays for improvements in her mother's home 'thinking predominantly of her own inheritance rather than the care and comfort of her mother'?

11   *Cullen v Cullen* [1962] IR 268 at 192; *Ezekiel v Orakpo and Scott* (Unreported, Court of Appeal, 1976 E No 1773, 20 February 1980) per Brightman LJ; *Salvation Army Trustee Co Ltd v West Yorkshire MCC* (1981) 41 P & CR 179 at 196; *Stilwell v Simpson* (1983) 133 NLJ 894.

12   *Ward v Kirkland* [1967] Ch 194 at 238B; *Holiday Inns Inc v Broadhead* (1974) 232 Estates Gazette 951 at 1087; *Griffiths v Williams* (1977) 248 Estates Gazette 947 at 949.

13   See eg *Griffiths v Williams* (1977) 248 Estates Gazette 947 at 949 per Goff LJ. Compare, however, *Coombes v Smith* [1986] 1 WLR 808 at 818B-H.

14   Ante, p 394. The 'hard cases' are not entirely a thing of the past: see *Coombes v Smith* [1986] 1 WLR 808.

seems to be required merely that the owner of land has induced in the claimant a belief that he 'would receive a sufficient interest in the land to justify the expenditure' or other disadvantage undertaken by the claimant.[15] The precise nature or quantum of the interest to be received need not have been specified at this point. It is sufficient simply that there is an expectation of some future entitlement of some recognisable kind,[16] and that the disadvantage incurred by the claimant is 'referable' to his belief that he would acquire some interest in or over the land.[17] It may be over-technical in the context of informal family arrangements to expect the lay person to formulate this expectation of entitlement in other than fairly vague and non-legal terms.[18] In the 'unilateral mistake' claims, however, there seems to be required in the claimant a state of mind much more akin to total misunderstanding of his existing entitlements.[19]

(3) Detriment

The doctrine of proprietary estoppel is firmly premised on a concept of detrimental reliance and, as Dixon J observed in *Grundt v Great Boulder Pty Gold Mines Ltd*,[20] the idea of estoppel is often simply expressed in terms that 'the party asserting the estoppel must have been induced to act to his detriment.' However, Dixon J pointed out that this proposition, although substantially correct, fails to bring out clearly the 'basal purpose of the doctrine', which is 'to avoid or prevent a detriment to the party asserting the estoppel by compelling the opposite party to adhere to the assumption on which the former acted or abstained from acting.' A moment's thought will confirm that no 'detriment' in the relevant sense ever truly arises unless and until the assurance which evoked the reliance is revoked or withdrawn. As Dixon J went on to say

the real detriment or harm from which the law seeks to give protection is that which would flow from the change of position if the assumption were deserted that led to it. So long as the assumption is adhered to, the party who altered his situation upon the faith of it cannot complain. His complaint is that when afterwards the other party makes a different state of affairs the basis of an assertion of right against him then, if it is allowed, his own original change of position will operate as a detriment.[1]

---

15 *Holiday Inns Inc v Broadhead* (1974) 232 Estates Gazette 951 at 1089. However, the estoppel claim will fail if the claimant cannot show credible evidence of some 'belief or expectation that she was being offered an interest in the house of the nature which she now claims' (*Warnes v Hedley* (Unreported, Court of Appeal, 31 January 1984) per Slade LJ). Likewise in *Clayton v Singh* (Unreported, Court of Appeal, 12 April 1984), the Court of Appeal dismissed an estoppel claim for want of evidence that the expenditure pleaded by the claimant had been referable to a genuine belief in his own entitlement.

16 It need not have been clear in the mind of the claimant how precisely the entitlement would arise; it is sufficient merely that he believed that he would become entitled 'in due course of time...in some way' (see *Cameron v Murdoch* [1983] WAR 321 at 354, 360). See also *Hardwick v Johnson* [1978] 1 WLR 683 at 687G.

17 The terminology of 'referability', reminiscent of *Gissing v Gissing* [1971] AC 886 at 909F-G (ante, p 278), seems to have been introduced in this context by May LJ: see *Warnes v Hedley* (Unreported, Court of Appeal, 31 January 1984); *Philip Lowe (Chinese Restaurant) Ltd v Sau Man Lee* (Unreported, Court of Appeal, 9 July 1985).

18 See the reference to 'hard cases' (ante, p 394).

19 For confirmation of this approach, see *Hastings Minor Hockey Association v Pacific National Exhibition* (1982) 129 DLR (3d) 721 at 728 (British Columbia Court of Appeal).

20 (1937) 59 CLR 641 at 674 (High Court of Australia).

1 See (1981) 44 MLR 461 at 463 (G. Woodman).

As Dixon J indicated, the element of 'detriment' which is integral to a claim of estoppel can thus be defined in terms of whether the claimant's original act or failure to act would, in view of the changed assumption, constitute for him a 'source of prejudice'.[2] The notion of 'prejudice' itself implies some distinction between acceptable and unacceptable outcomes, and is therefore capable of definition only in terms of whether it would be 'unfair or unjust' if the party who induced the expectation or assumed state of affairs 'were left free to ignore it.'[3]

(a) Legal detriment and the criterion of unconscionability

This reductionist interpretation of the element of 'detriment' finds significant echoes as the English caselaw moves closer towards a more composite criterion of unconscionability as the basis of proprietary estoppel. In *Watts v Story*,[4] for instance, Slade LJ thought it neither possible nor desirable to define the required 'detriment' except in terms of such 'prejudice...that it would be inequitable to allow the party who made the relevant representation to go back on it.' Likewise, in *Amalgamated Investment and Property Co Ltd v Texas Commerce International Bank Ltd*[5] Lord Denning MR expressed the view that all forms of estoppel can now be seen to 'merge into one general principle shorn of limitations.' This principle requires that when the parties to a transaction 'proceed on the basis of an underlying assumption—either of fact or of law— whether due to misrepresentation or mistake makes no difference—on which they have conducted the dealings between them—neither of them will be allowed to go back on that assumption when it would be unfair or unjust to allow him to do so.'[6]

(b) The test of unconscionability in practice

It used to be said that this test of estoppel, depending as it does on fairness or conscience, requires a degree of 'fraud' on the part of the person sought to be estopped.[7] However, the modern tendency is to commute this stringent epithet into a requirement that the plaintiff should 'establish as a fact that the defendant, by setting up his right, is taking advantage of him in a way which is unconscionable, inequitable or unjust.'[8] This formula frequently demands a complex and sophisticated evaluation of all the circumstances of a given case in

---

2   (1937) 59 CLR 641 at 675.
3   (1937) 59 CLR 641 at 675.
4   Unreported, Court of Appeal, 14 July 1983.
5   [1982] QB 84 at 122C.
6   See also *Dewhirst v Edwards* [1983] 1 NSWLR 34 at 49E; *Cameron v Murdoch* [1983] WAR 321 at 351.
7   *Willmott v Barber* (1880) 15 Ch D 96 at 105 (ante, p 393).
8   *Crabb v Arun DC* [1976] Ch 179 at 195B-C per Scarman LJ, who observed that 'fraud' was a word 'often in the mouths of those robust judges who adorned the bench in the 19th century', but is 'less often in the mouths of the more wary judicial spirits today who sit upon the bench'. See also *Swallow Securities Ltd v Isenberg* (1985) 274 Estates Gazette 1028 at 1030, where Cumming-Bruce LJ described the concept of 'taking an advantage of the defendant' as 'an essential ingredient of the equity'. It is clear, however, that a finding of 'unconscionable conduct' does not necessarily imply that the party estopped has 'acted reprehensibly' (*Salvation Army Trustee Co Ltd v West Yorkshire MCC* (1981) 41 P & CR 179 at 198).

order to establish whether it would be 'inequitable to permit [X] to resile from the assurances given to [Y].'⁹

(i) Restrictive approach of the courts In spite of the modern acceptance of a broadly based test of unconscionable dealing, the approach of the courts when faced with claims of proprietary estoppel tends to be restrictive. The courts treat such claims 'with a degree of caution',[10] mindful of the fact that the doctrine of proprietary estoppel may have the 'drastic effect of conferring on one person a permanent, irrevocable interest in the land of another, even though he has given no consideration for such acquisition, by way of contractual arrangement, and no legally effective gift of it has been made in his favour.'[11] There are slight indications that the courts may be even more restrictive when dealing with estoppel claims based on other forms of reliance than the expenditure of money on the land of the party whom it is sought to estop.[12] Above all there seems to be a judicial anxiety lest the courts should curtail the human impulse of generosity[13] by creating 'the impression that people are liable to be penalised for not enforcing their strict legal rights.'[14]

(ii) The measure of conscience Numerous factors affect the question whether the strict enforcement of rights is unconscionable. It is often patently obvious from the circumstances that it would be 'grossly inequitable' to leave one party without a remedy for a disadvantage which he has incurred in reliance on the basis of some legitimate expectation.[15] The courts are sometimes powerfully moved by the excessive or opulent nature of the unjust enrichment which would otherwise be conferred upon the maker of the original assurance.[16] However, each case is a matter of 'fact or degree',[17] and in evaluating the totality of the circumstances the courts have been particularly sensitive to the presence of counter-balancing advantages enjoyed by the relier which may partially or completely offset the disadvantage which he has suffered. Of especial importance in this context may be the fact that the claimant of an 'equity' through improvements has meanwhile enjoyed rent-free occupation,[18] or that the party sought to be estopped has in the past shown some forbearance towards the claimant[19] or made generous gifts of money in respect of the

9   *Watts v Story* (Unreported, Court of Appeal, 14 July 1983) per Slade LJ.
10   *Ibid*, per Slade LJ.
11   *Ibid*, per Slade LJ.
12   *Ibid*, per Slade LJ.
13   See *Marcroft Wagons Ltd v Smith* [1951] 2 KB 496 at 501 per Evershed MR (post, p 458).
14   *E & L Berg Homes Ltd v Grey* (1980) 253 Estates Gazette 473 at 479 per Ormrod LJ.
15   See eg *Timber Top Realty Pty Ltd v Mullens* [1974] VR 312 at 319.
16   See *Clayton v Green* (1979) NZ Recent Law 139 at 140, where it appeared that the plaintiff's contributions of cash had indirectly enabled her son-in-law (the present defendant) to instal in his home such 'luxury items' as a swimming pool and a carpeted bar!
17   *Watts v Story* (Unreported, Court of Appeal, 14 July 1983) per Dunn LJ.
18   *E & L Berg Homes Ltd v Grey* (1980) 253 Estates Gazette 473 at 477 per Brandon LJ, 479 per Sir David Cairns and Ormrod LJJ; *Watts v Story* (Unreported, Court of Appeal, 14 July 1983) per Slade LJ; *Hink v Lhenen* (1975) 52 DLR (3d) 301 at 316.
19   *Appleby v Cowley* (1982) *The Times*, 14 April 1982. Here Megarry V-C considered that, in view of a prolonged rent forbearance, the plaintiffs had received 'sufficient satisfaction' for their expenditure.

claimant's other commitments,[20] or that the claimant has received more by way of profits drawn from a business than she ever invested in that business in the first place.[1] The courts may therefore deny an estoppel claim if of the opinion that no net disadvantage would be suffered by the claimant if the assurance originally given were allowed to be withdrawn.[2]

(c) Bars to a claim of unconscionable behaviour

Several factors may operate as a bar in any given case to the claim that considerations of conscience require a holding of proprietary estoppel. Where, for instance, the parties have already agreed a contractually binding formula for compensating extra expenditure incurred by one, 'no intervention of equity is needed' in order to bring about a fair result.[3]

(i) Infringement of statute   More difficult questions arise if the expenditure on which the claim to an 'equity' is based was undertaken in breach of some statutory provision or regulation—a problem which is particularly live if the supposed 'equity' was grounded on some improvement to realty which required planning permission.[4] In *Chalmers v Pardoe*,[5] the Privy Council decided that the aid of equity could not be lent in support of an estoppel claim based on a land transaction which contravened regulatory legislation. In this respect, an estoppel claim may be barred for want of 'clean hands'.[6] However, the courts, although recognising the force of the argument of illegality, have sought almost any refuge to avoid having to sanction the unmerited retention of an unjustly received benefit by way of improvement.[7]

A lack of 'clean hands' will likewise defeat a claim to an 'equity' if the original assurance pleaded in aid by the estoppel claimant was procured by reason of his own false representations. In such a case 'it does not...lie in the mouth of the claimant to set up any form of estoppel.'[8]

---

20   *Jackson v Crosby* (No 2) (1979) 21 SASR 280 at 298, 302 per Zelling J (estoppel claim abated to the extent that defendant had helped to discharge previous mortgage created by plaintiff). See also *In re Basham, decd* [1986] 1 WLR 1498 at 1505E, where it was indicated that the claim of estoppel would not have succeeded if the claimant's labour on behalf of her step-father had received any 'commensurate reward...during his lifetime'.

1   *Cullen v Cullen* [1962] IR 268 at 282.

2   In *Watts v Story* (Unreported, Court of Appeal, 14 July 1983), Slade LJ agreed that the claimant of the 'equity' had failed to show 'that, when the benefits derived by him from his rent-free occupation of Apple House are set against any detriments suffered by him as a result of making the move from his flat in Leeds, he has on balance suffered any detriment in financial or material terms.'

3   *Appleby v Cowley* (1982) *The Times*, 14 April, per Megarry V-C.

4   Post, p 720.

5   [1963] 1 WLR 677 at 685.

6   See *Dewhirst v Edwards* [1983] 1 NSWLR 34 at 51B; *Jackson v Crosby* (No 2) (1979) 21 SASR 280 at 291 (Bright J).

7   In *Jackson v Crosby* (No 2) (1979) 21 SASR 280 at 301, the Supreme Court of South Australia ruled that the claimant of the 'equity' did not strictly come within the terms of a licensing requirement imposed on those carrying out building work 'for fee or reward', since what he did had been done for love not money. In *Lepel v Huthnance* (1979) NZ Recent Law 269, Speight J distinguished *Chalmers v Pardoe* on the grounds that in the instant case the breach of planning control had not been 'flagrant', that the local authority had taken no action in respect of the breach, and that in any event the duty to obtain the requisite planning permit had attached technically to the defendant as owner and occupier rather than to the plaintiff as claimant of the 'equity'.

8   *Ildebrando de Franco v Stengold Ltd* (Unreported, Court of Appeal, 14 May 1985) per Parker LJ.

(ii) Integrity of statutory duties and discretions   It is clear that no public body or agency can be estopped from performing a duty imposed on it by statute or from exercising a discretion conferred on it by legislation.[9]

5. THE EXTENT OF THE ESTOPPEL REMEDY

Once an 'equity' of estoppel has been established, the court must determine the proper scope of the remedy to be granted in the particular case.

(1) The general principle

The general principle of relief relevant to proprietary estoppel was stated over a century ago in *Plimmer v Mayor etc of Wellington*.[10] Here the Judicial Committee of the Privy Council held that when an 'equity' has been raised, 'the Court must look at the circumstances in each case to decide in what way the equity can be satisfied.'[11] The court may take into account all supervening circumstances occurring before the date of the hearing.[12] The court has an extremely wide discretion and formulates the remedy in terms of the 'minimum equity' required to do justice to the claimant.[13] The remedy awarded may involve the grant of a recognised proprietary interest in land, but may sometimes take the form of an occupation licence or a money remedy or lien for expenditure. In general terms, the court seeks to frame the remedy in accordance with the representation on which the claimant relied, so that the outcome of the litigation is that the claimant is given no more and no less than was promised in the original assurance.[14]

(2) Relevant criteria

The degree of discretion enjoyed by the court in fashioning the appropriate remedy is indeed substantial. As Lord Denning MR observed in *Crabb v Arun DC*,[15] here 'equity is displayed at its most flexible.'[16] It is clear that the remedy

---

9   *Western Fish Products Ltd v Penwith DC* [1981] 2 All ER 204 at 219c. See [1982] Conv 450 (P. Jackson); A. Bradley, [1981] 34 CLP 1 at 12ff. Compare *Santiago v Immigration and Naturalization Service*, 526 F.2d 488 at 494 (1975) per Choy J (dissenting).

10   (1884) 9 App Cas 699 at 714 (ante, p 391).

11   See also *Chalmers v Pardoe* [1963] 1 WLR 677 at 682; *Inwards v Baker* [1965] 2 QB 29 at 37B; *E R Ives Investment Ltd v High* [1967] 2 QB 379 at 395A; *Amalgamated Investment & Property Co Ltd v Texas Commerce International Bank Ltd* [1982] QB 84 at 122D.

12   *Williams v Staite* [1979] Ch 291 at 298F.

13   *Crabb v Arun DC* [1976] Ch 179 at 198G per Scarman LJ. See also *Cameron v Murdoch* [1983] WAR 321 at 360, where Brinsden J declared it to be his 'duty...to do equity and no more than equity and to give relief and no more relief than is necessary to satisfy the equity created by the representation.'

14   *Shaida v Kindlane Ltd* (Unreported, Chancery Division, 1976 S No 8501, 22 June 1982) per Judge Baker QC. For development of the argument that the doctrine of proprietary estoppel is merely a procedural mechanism which sanctions the informal creation of property rights in land, see S. Moriarty, (1984) 100 LQR 376. The argument, while interesting and challenging, may not explain the entirety of the caselaw (see eg *Griffiths v Williams* (1977) 248 Estates Gazette 947, ante, p 408), unless one simply accepts that 'perfect equity is seldom possible.' See also a convincing counter-argument by John Dewar, *Licences and Land Law: An Alternative View*, (1986) 49 MLR 741.

15   [1976] Ch 179 at 189F.

required in order to satisfy the 'equity' generated by proprietary estoppel is capable of fluctuation over the course of time. Developments subsequent to the date on which the 'equity' is initially raised may cause the court either to withhold relief from the claimant or to grant him relief in terms other than those which it would have been inclined to order at an earlier stage.[17]

(a) Misconduct

In some circumstances subsequent misconduct may be relevant to the court's response to a plea of proprietary estoppel.

(i) Effect on the inchoate 'equity'   It seems to be accepted that an inchoate 'equity' of estoppel may be offset by misconduct on the part of the claimant which occurs after the date on which that 'equity' originates. In *Williams v Staite*,[18] Cumming-Bruce LJ did not believe that 'the rights in equity of the [claimants] necessarily crystallise forever at the time when the equitable rights come into existence.' Instead the true analysis entailed that when the owner of land sought to enforce his strict legal rights against the claimant, all the relevant maxims of equity must be brought into play 'so that the court is entitled then on the facts to look at all the circumstances and decide what order should be made, if any, to satisfy the equity.' In such a case an estoppel claimant guilty of misconduct in relation to the owner of the land might well be considered to have come to the court without 'clean hands', with the result that he would be 'left with no right at all' and the legal owner would be at liberty to exercise his strict legal rights.[19]

In *Brynowen Estates Ltd v Bourne*,[20] for instance, there was clear evidence that the estoppel claimant had behaved in a 'quite extraordinarily disturbing and objectionable way', not least by swearing and making obscene gestures at visitors to the caravan park in respect of part of which she claimed an 'equity'.[1] The Court of Appeal had no hesitation in holding that any inchoate 'equity' of estoppel which might have been generated by the circumstances of the case had been amply negatived by the claimant's misconduct.

(ii) Effect on any court-ordered remedy   The court is less willing to have regard to subsequent misconduct where the claimant's 'equity' of estoppel has already

---

16   See the approving remarks of J.D. Davies, (1979) 8 Sydney LR 578 at 583ff, and (1980-81) 7 Adelaide LR 200 at 219.

17   In *Crabb v Arun DC* [1976] Ch 179 at 189G-190A, 192E, 199C-F, the Court of Appeal satisfied the 'equity' claimed by ordering the grant of an easement without compensation, even though had the same 'equity' been asserted earlier, it would have ordered the claimant to make some payment in respect of the right of access sought. However, during the intervening period the party denying the 'equity' had acted with 'high-handedness' and had moreover sterilised the user of an industrial estate by the denial of access, and for this the Court was prepared to impose a penalty. Another case of relevant change of circumstance arose in *Dodsworth v Dodsworth* (1973) 228 Estates Gazette 1115, where the Court of Appeal had regard to the fact that the legal owner had died subsequent to the date on which the 'equity' was first raised by an assurance of accommodation.

18   [1979] Ch 291 at 300G-H. See H. Bowie, (1981) 11 VUWLR 63.

19   [1979] Ch 291 at 299D per Goff LJ.

20   (1981) 131 NLJ 1212.

1   The claimant had also driven round the caravan park at speed late at night, continuously sounding her horn.

crystallised in the form of a remedy granted by the court.[2] In *Williams v Staite*[3] an 'equity' of estoppel had earlier resulted in the award to the claimants of a right of occupation for life. In relation to the remedy thus granted already, the Court of Appeal considered that 'subsequent excessive user or bad behaviour towards the legal owner cannot bring the equity to an end or forfeit it'.[4] Lord Denning MR had thought that there might be extreme circumstances under which even a court-ordered licence might be revoked on the ground of subsequent misconduct by the successful estoppel claimant,[4] but this reservation has not been adopted in the subsequent caselaw.[6]

(b) Use of estoppel as a 'sword' or as a 'shield'

It is now a commonplace that the doctrine of proprietary estoppel can be used as a sword and not merely as a shield.[7] However, there are some indications that when the 'equity' of estoppel is finally asserted before the court, the willingness of the court to grant a concrete remedy may be vitally affected by whether the estoppel argument is being used as a shield or a sword.

(i) Restraint upon positive or aggressive claims In *Stilwell v Simpson*,[8] for instance, the court refused to uphold a positive claim that the plaintiff was entitled to some interest or compensation in respect of improvements effected upon the defendant's property. The court noted that the plaintiff was a protected tenant of the defendant and therefore had in any event 'a life interest by statute'. However, the court added significantly that if there had not been a protected tenancy and the defendant (or a purchaser) had 'sought to eject the plaintiff', that would have been a different matter.[9] Likewise, in *Savva v Costa and Harymode Investments Ltd*,[10] the Court of Appeal indicated that it would have regarded much more favourably the plaintiff's plea of proprietary estoppel if the litigation had been precipitated by a threat from the defendant to dispossess the plaintiff and her children from the defendant's property.[11] As it was, the

---

2   See *J. Willis & Son v Willis* (1986) 277 Estates Gazette 1133, where Parker LJ compared the effect of misconduct on an inchoate 'equity', and concluded that there was 'a difference between the two situations'. See [1986] Conv 406 (M.P. Thompson).
3   [1979] Ch 291.
4   [1979] Ch 291 at 300B per Goff LJ. The Court of Appeal did, however, leave open the possibility that misconduct might give rise to an action in damages for trespass or nuisance or to an injunction restraining the misbehaviour. It appears in this case that the defendants, having already been granted an equitable licence by the county court on the ground of proprietary estoppel, informed the next purchaser of the disputed land that he was in for 'bloody trouble', which true to their word they proceeded to provide!
5   [1979] Ch 291 at 298B.
6   See eg *J. Willis & Son v Willis* (1986) 277 Estates Gazette 1133 per Parker LJ. See also the criticism in *McGill v S* [1979] IR 283 at 293 of the 'concept of a wavering licence terminable...upon the possibility of changeable circumstances affecting the licensee'. It would certainly be undesirable were the position of a purchaser from the licensor to depend on the relative iniquity or unpleasantness of the licensee's conduct at any particular point in time!
7   See *Crabb v Arun DC* [1976] Ch 179 at 187E; *Thomas v Thomas* [1956] NZLR 785 at 793; *Dewhirst v Edwards* [1983] 1 NSWLR 34 at 49E.
8   (1983) 133 NLJ 894.
9   *Ibid* per Sir Douglas Frank QC.
10 (1981) 131 NLJ 1114.
11 (1981) 131 NLJ 1114, where Oliver LJ pointed out that in such circumstances the plaintiff might well have been able to claim 'an irrevocable or indefinite licence of some sort to occupy'.

plaintiff was seeking an order directing either a transfer of the property to herself or a reimbursement in respect of improvements effected by her. Although dismissing this claim, the Court of Appeal referred to the 'prospective potential rights' which would accrue to the plaintiff if there ever were to be any threat to deny her 'the advantage of residing' in the home in which she had sought to 'provide a proper degree of amenity for the accommodation of the children'.[12]

(ii) Greater tolerance of defensive claims   Decisions like those just cited seem to show that proprietary estoppel may still be more readily accepted by the courts as a shield rather than as a sword. In other words, proprietary estoppel is sparingly used and the courts tend to apply the estoppel doctrine only where its use is quite essential in order to prevent gross injustice or where there is some immediate threat to the residential security of the claimant.

(3) Range of possible remedies

The court has virtually unlimited discretion in the matter of remedy, and the range of possible remedies includes the following.

(a) Grant of an unqualified estate or interest in land

It is possible that the court may determine that the 'equity' of estoppel can be satisfied only by an order directing the transfer of the fee simple estate to the estoppel claimant.[13] Such an order is rare, but has been made in circumstances such as those which occurred in *Pascoe v Turner*.[14] Here the Court of Appeal recognised that only the freehold title could protect the claimant from the 'ruthless' behaviour of her former lover and provide her with an interest which she might charge in order to raise finance for future repairs and improvements to the property.[15] In other cases the courts have seen fit to satisfy the 'equity' by granting or confirming a leasehold estate in land.[16] In appropriate circumstances the courts have granted rights akin to an easement,[17] or have allowed the claimant to purchase the disputed land at a discount.[18] Limitations or conditions may be attached to any interest granted by the court.[19]

12   (1981) 131 NLJ 1114 per Shaw LJ.
13   See eg *Dillwyn v Llewelyn* (1862) 4 De G F & J 517 at 523, 45 ER 1285 at 1287 (ante, p 388).
14   [1979] 1 WLR 431 at 439B (ante, p 389; post, p 818).
15   In *Riches v Hogben* [1986] 1 Qd R 315 at 321f, 327, 343 (ante, p 405), the Full Court of the Queensland Supreme Court ordered a transfer of the legal title to the estoppel claimant, subject to an equitable life interest for the maker of the relevant assurance, thereby enabling the latter to reside in a 'granny flat' associated with the property.
16   *Siew Soon Wah v Yong Tong Hong* [1973] AC 836 at 846B (Privy Council); *Andrews v Colonial Mutual Life Assurance Society Ltd* [1982] 2 NZLR 556 at 570. Compensation may be awarded if it is no longer possible or practicable to enforce a lease (see *Brownlee v Duggan* (1976) 27 NILQ 291).
17   *E R Ives Investment Ltd v High* [1967] 2 QB 379 at 396E, 406B (ante, p 391); *Crabb v Arun DC* [1976] Ch 179 at 190A, 192D, 199F (ante, p 392).
18   *Cameron v Murdoch* [1983] WAR 321 at 360 (affirmed by the Judicial Committee of the Privy Council, (1985-86) 63 ALR 575 at 595).
19   See eg *E R Ives Investment Ltd v High* [1967] 2 QB 379 at 395A (right of way so long as neighbour's foundations encroached); *Bank Negara Indonesia v Hoalim* [1973] 2 MLJ 3 at 5C (licence so long as claimant continued to practise his profession). It was accepted by Goff LJ in *Williams v Staite* [1979] Ch 291 at 300B-C, that any right granted by the court to an estoppel claimant might be limited in point of time or determinable on express conditions, in which case a court might later have to rule on whether the interest had expired or the determining event had occurred. See also *Riches v Hogben* [1986] 1 Qd R 315 at 321.

(b) Grant of a right to occupy

A more commonly granted remedy is a recognition by the court that the estoppel claimant has an irrevocable licence to occupy property rent-free either for life[20] or for some shorter period.[1] This form of order was made in *Inwards v Baker*[2] and *Greasley v Cooke*,[3] and often seems to mirror the ill-defined but nevertheless very real expectations of parties under informal family arrangements.[4]

The award of a right of occupation for life is, however, fraught with technical problems. There is a strong argument that the interest thereby conferred constitutes a 'life interest' which brings into play the cumbersome and improbable machinery of the Settled Land Act 1925.[5] In many cases it seems awkward and unlikely that the estoppel claimant should be invested with the over-large statutory powers of the 'tenant for life' under the Settled Land Act 1925.[6] In particular it is usually undesirable that the claimant should be able to call for a vesting in himself of the legal estate, and should then moreover have the legal capacity to sell, lease or mortgage that estate.[7] In order to avoid the complications of a strict settlement, the courts have tended to resolve the difficulty by making alternative kinds of order which involve either an award of monetary compensation for improvements effected by the claimant[8] or the compulsory grant of a long lease for life at a nominal rent and subject to an absolute covenant against assignment.[9]

(c) Grant of monetary compensation

There are some circumstances in which it is inappropriate to grant a remedy which involves any form of occupation right. It may, for instance, be impossible in practical terms to enforce a sharing arrangement between parties whose personal relationship has broken down.[10] Alternatively, the estoppel claimant may not have sought an occupation right in the first place[11] or may already have given up possession voluntarily.[12] It is, of course, perfectly possible in some

---

20 See *Pearce v Pearce* [1977] 1 NSWLR 170 at 177F. Compare *Binions v Evans* [1972] Ch 359 (ante, p 285). If it is no longer practicable to enforce such an occupation licence, money compensation may awarded in lieu (*Broughall v Hunt* (Unreported, Chancery Division, 1 February 1983)). See also (1983) 80 LSG 2198 (G. Gypps).

1 Post, p 798.
2 [1965] 2 QB 29 at 37G (ante, p 391).
3 [1980] 1 WLR 1306 at 1312B (ante, p 406; post, p 800).
4 Post, p 793.
5 See *Dodsworth v Dodsworth* (1973) 228 Estates Gazette 1115.
6 Post, p 805.
7 Settled Land Act 1925, s 19(1). See *Dodsworth v Dodsworth* (1973) 228 Estates Gazette 1115; *Griffiths v Williams* (1977) 248 Estates Gazette 947 at 949.
8 This was the solution adopted in *Dodsworth v Dodsworth* (1973) 228 Estates Gazette 1115.
9 See *Griffiths v Williams* (1977) 248 Estates Gazette 947 at 950, where Goff LJ proposed such an arrangement as a means of guaranteeing the estoppel claimant a lifelong right of occupation outside the ambit of both the Settled Land Act 1925 and the Rent Act 1977 (see F.R. Crane, (1967) 31 Conv (NS) 332 at 342). Goff LJ conceded that the nominal rent 'would be an obligation not contemplated when the representations were made to [the claimant]', but comforted himself with the thought that 'perfect equity is seldom possible'.
10 *Shaida v Kindlane Ltd* (Unreported, Chancery Division, 1976 S No 8501, 22 June 1982) per Judge Baker QC, giving the example of *Dodsworth v Dodsworth* (1973) 228 Estates Gazette 1115.
11 *Hamilton v Geraghty* (1901) 1 NSWSR (Eq) 81 at 88 per Darley CJ.
12 *Cushley v Seale* (Unreported, Court of Appeal, 28 October 1986).

cases for the court to satisfy the 'equity' through the award of money
compensation. This remedy appears particularly appropriate where the
'equity' is founded on expenditure for improvements which are not
substantial.[13] The court's discretion extends even to the basis adopted for
assessment of the compensation. In some cases compensation has been fixed
with reference to the enhanced value of the realty;[14] sometimes compensation
has been based on the actual cost of the improvements themselves, either with[15]
or without[16] payment of interest, or with some adjustment designed to counter-
balance the falling value of money over time.[17] In some cases the court has
ordered compensation on the basis of an intermediate figure representing a
compromise between the 'enhanced value' basis and the 'actual cost' basis.[18]

(d) Grant of a right of occupation coupled with monetary compensation

A further, and rather hybrid, form of remedy lies in an award which combines
an element of occupation with the grant of monetary compensation. Such a
remedy may involve the recognition that the estoppel claimant has a lien or
charge on the disputed property to the appropriate value of the improvements
effected[19] or of any money which has been given or loaned.[20] This lien on the
property may well be coupled with a right to occupy the property until such
time as the money is paid or repaid.[1]

(e) Inhibitory effect of estoppel remedies

At root all estoppel remedies involve the imposition of judicial restraint on the
exercise of what would otherwise be a strict legal entitlement. This means in
many cases that the owner of land is effectively restrained by injunction from
obtaining the arbitrary eviction of the estoppel claimant or from otherwise
causing him prejudice.[2] The common feature of all successful estoppel claims is
that the estoppel remedy inhibits the unconscionable assertion of strict legal

---

13   *Dodsworth v Dodsworth* (1973) 228 Estates Gazette 1115 at 1117; *Cushley v Seale* (Unreported,
      Court of Appeal, 28 October 1986).
14   *Montreuil v Ontario Asphalt Co* (1922) 69 DLR 313 at 334f; *Jackson v Crosby* (No 2) (1979) 21
      SASR 280 at 294f, 310; *Van den Berg v Giles* [1979] 2 NZLR 111 at 123; *The Queen v Smith* (1981)
      113 DLR (3d) 522 at 583. In *Lepel v Huthnance* (1979) NZ Recent Law 269 at 270, Speight J
      assessed compensation in terms of the added value of the property, rather than on the basis of
      the cost of the improvements, not least because the plaintiff's labour had been misdirected
      and the end result was not up to workmanlike standards.
15   *Morris v Morris* [1982] 1 NSWLR 61 at 64F.
16   *In re Whitehead* [1948] NZLR 1066 at 1071; *J.N. Elliot & Co (Farms) Ltd v Murgatroyd*
      (Unreported, Court of Appeal of New Zealand, CA 52/82, 12 September 1984).
17   *Cameron v Murdoch* [1983] WAR 321 at 351 (affirmed by the Judicial Committee of the Privy
      Council, (1985-86) 63 ALR 575 at 595).
18   *Clayton v Green* (1979) NZ Recent Law 139 at 140.
19   *Unity Joint Stock Mutual Banking Association v King* (1858) 25 Beav 72 at 78, 53 ER 563 at 565
      (although foreclosure decreed against both owner and holders of lien); *Hamilton v Geraghty*
      (1901) 1 NSWSR (Eq) 81 at 91; *Taylor v Taylor* [1956] NZLR 99 at 103f.
20   *Hussey v Palmer* [1972] 1 WLR 1286 at 1291A-C, as explained in *In re Sharpe (A Bankrupt)* [1980]
      1 WLR 219 at 222H-223A and *Savva v Costa and Harymode Investments Ltd* (1981) 131 NLJ 1114.
1   *Dodsworth v Dodsworth* (1973) 228 Estates Gazette 1115 at 1117; *In re Sharpe (A Bankrupt)* [1980]
      1 WLR 219 at 224B.
2   Strange results may flow from a finding of estoppel. In *Cullen v Cullen* [1962] IR 268 at 292,
      Kenny J deliberately intended that the upholding of an estoppel claim, while not conferring
      any immediate right upon the estoppel claimant, would enable him to be registered as the
      proprietor of the land at the end of the relevant limitation period.

rights against the estoppel claimant, sometimes indefinitely and sometimes merely until a compensatory award or interest has been granted in satisfaction of the 'equity' raised.

6. THE NATURE OF A PROPRIETARY ESTOPPEL

A number of difficulties are raised in analysing the nature of the 'equity' which is protected by the doctrine of proprietary estoppel.

(1) Relationship with constructive trust

There is without doubt a close relationship between the operation of proprietary estoppel and the device of the constructive trust.[3] It is clear that the doctrine of proprietary estoppel involves 'the same general principle as that invoked in *Gissing v Gissing*...namely, that courts applying equitable principles will prevent a person from insisting on his strict legal rights when it would be inequitable for him to do so having regard to the dealings which have taken place between the parties.'[4] The estoppel doctrine likewise gives effect to an 'equity of expectation' generated by past dealings,[5] and for this reason claims based on estoppel tend to go hand in hand with allegations of constructive trust.[6] Further confusion flows from the fact that the court, in concretising the 'equity' of estoppel in the grant of some interest in land, may award that interest behind a court-imposed 'constructive trust'.[7]

(a) Balance of emphasis

If there is a distinction between the doctrine of proprietary estoppel and the constructive trust as a substantive institution,[8] it may well be that 'estoppel puts weight on inducement, constructive trusts on undertakings.'[9] Expressed in another way, the constructive trust is ultimately based upon some concept of frustrated 'bargain'.[10] The 'equity' of estoppel is more clearly founded upon a concept of frustrated 'expectation', in circumstances where some 'holding out

---

3   For discussion of the constructive trust, see Chapter 10 (ante, p 268). It may be that a somewhat sharper distinction may be drawn between the notion of proprietary estoppel and the operation of the resulting trust (see *Walker v Walker* (Unreported, Court of Appeal, 12 April 1984) per Browne-Wilkinson LJ).

4   *Christian v Christian* (1981) 131 NLJ 43 per Brightman LJ. See also *Savva v Costa and Harymode Investments Ltd* (1981) 131 NLJ 1114 per Oliver LJ; *In re Basham, decd* [1986] 1 WLR 1498 at 1503H-1504F. Dickson J effectively used the language of estoppel in upholding a constructive trust in *Pettkus v Becker* (1981) 117 DLR (3d) 257 at 274 (post, p 814); *Sorochan v Sorochan* (1986) 29 DLR (4th) 1 at 7, 12f. See also *Hayward v Giordani* [1983] NZLR 140 at 147.

5   *Riches v Hogben* [1986] 1 Qd R 315 at 327, 339.

6   See eg *Christian v Christian* (1981) 131 NLJ 43; *Warnes v Hedley* (Unreported, Court of Appeal, 31 January 1984); *Walker v Walker* (Unreported, Court of Appeal, 12 April 1984); *Bristol & West Building Society v Henning* [1985] 1 WLR 778; *Philip Lowe (Chinese Restaurant) Ltd v Sau Man Lee* (Unreported, Court of Appeal, 9 July 1985).

7   See eg *In re Sharpe (A Bankrupt)* [1980] 1 WLR 219 at 225C-D (post, p 796); *In re Basham, decd* [1986] 1 WLR 1498 at 1504A-F.

8   On the constructive trust as a substantive institution, see Chapter 10 (ante, p 268). Compare the transatlantic use of the constructive trust as a remedial device (post, p 812).

9   J.D. Davies, (1980-81) 7 Adelaide LR 200 at 221.

10   Ante, p 270.

to the claimant that she had a beneficial interest' has comprised 'part of the inducement to her to do the acts relied on.'[11] Indeed the estoppel doctrine may be somewhat wider than the theory of constructive trust in that an estoppel claim can succeed where the claimant was promised not an equitable interest in land but the full legal interest.[12]

(b)   Range of recognised contributions

There are limits upon the kinds of contributory activity which are recognised as relevant forms of 'detriment' or 'sacrifice' within even the more liberal formulations of the substantive doctrine of constructive trust.[13] It seems, however, that the estoppel doctrine rests on 'wider equitable principles'[14] which provide relief in some cases where the strict application of constructive trust theory denies a remedy.[15] As was suggested by Browne-Wilkinson V-C in *Grant v Edwards*,[16] it is highly probable that the estoppel doctrine attaches significance to a somewhat broader range of contribution inclusive of the more intangible elements of domestic commitment and endeavour.[17]

(c)   Onus of proof

It is also possible that the party setting up an estoppel need not have formulated in his own mind so clear a concept of his own precise entitlement as appears to be currently required in order to establish a constructive trust.[18] The onus of proof in an estoppel claim may be easier in one further respect. Where, following assurances made by the owner, an estoppel claimant has adopted a course of conduct which is prejudicial or otherwise detrimental to himself, there is a rebuttable presumption that he adopted that course of action in reliance on the assurances.[19]

(d)   Extent of available remedies

It is sometimes suggested that the 'equity' comprised in a claim of proprietary estoppel is less effective than the 'equity' which is recognised when a court imposes a constructive trust on the owner of an estate in land.[20] However, this generalisation is misleading since there are respects in which the claim of proprietary estoppel is both narrower and wider than the orthodox application of constructive trust theory.

It is true that the estoppel remedy may lead in many cases to the judicial recognition of a 'lesser property right'[1] in the claimant than would normally be

11   *Grant v Edwards* [1986] Ch 638 at 657C per Browne-Wilkinson V-C.
12   *Riches v Hogben* [1985] 2 Qd R 292 at 299f, upheld on appeal [1986] 1 Qd R 315.
13   Ante, p 277.
14   *Morris v Morris* [1982] 1 NSWLR 61 at 63F-G.
15   However, for circumstances in which a claim based on constructive trust succeeded and an estoppel claim failed, see *Te Rama Engineering Ltd v Shortlands Properties Ltd* [1982] BCL 692 (ante, p 398).
16   [1986] Ch 638 at 657A-C (ante, p 406).
17   See eg *Greasley v Cooke* [1980] 1 WLR 1306 at 1312A (ante, p 406, post, p 800).
18   See *Bristol & West Building Society v Henning* [1985] 1 WLR 778 at 781F; *Vinden v Vinden* [1982] 1 NSWLR 618 at 623F, 625B.
19   *Coombes v Smith* [1986] 1 WLR 808 at 821E. See also *Grant v Edwards* [1986] Ch 638 at 657C; *In re Basham, decd* [1986] 1 WLR 1498 at 1507F-G.
20   *Pearce v Pearce* [1977] 1 NSWLR 170 at 177G.
1   *Bristol & West Building Society v Henning* [1985] 1 WLR 778 at 782B.

conferred by a constructive trust. The imposition of a constructive trust often involves, in essence, the allocation to one or other of the litigants of an aliquot share in the equitable ownership of property.[2] By contrast the recognition of a proprietary estoppel may found only 'the lesser property right of an irrevocable licence',[3] and in this sense may appear to provide an inferior or second-class form of remedy.

On the other hand, the estoppel remedy is sufficiently far-reaching that it sometimes rivals or even surpasses the relief that is commonly provided by the imposition of a constructive trust. As some of the estoppel cases demonstrate, the doctrine of proprietary estoppel is fully capable of leading to the conclusion that the claimant should be awarded not a mere partial interest in the disputed property but rather the fee simple interest itself.[4] Accordingly it is beginning to be recognised that a claim of proprietary estoppel 'may go a little further' than the kind of claim normally recognised under the head of constructive trust.[5]

(2) When does the 'equity' arise?

The 'equity' raised by proprietary estoppel is, of course, given a peculiarly concrete form when it is asserted and vindicated during the course of litigation. It is at this stage that the court, in determining the remedy required to satisfy the 'equity', recognises the claimant to be entitled to some appropriate right or interest in relation to the disputed land. However, as Browne-Wilkinson J observed in *In re Sharpe (A Bankrupt)*,[6] 'it cannot be that the interest in property arises for the first time when the court declares it to exist.' The claimant must already have a right before the court can grant a remedy in respect of its breach. Thus the 'equity' itself 'predates any order of the court', having arisen at an earlier point in the dealings of the parties.

(a) The inchoate 'equity'

It would appear that the 'equity' of estoppel arises as soon as the conscience of the landowner is affected by the transactions of the parties. It is to be noted that there need not be anything fraudulent or unjust in the initial negotiations of the parties. As Scarman LJ said in *Crabb v Arun DC*,[7] the 'fraud, if it be such, arises after the event, when the defendant seeks by relying on his right to defeat the expectation which he by his conduct encouraged the plaintiff to have.'[8] It is when the landowner unconscionably sets up his undoubted rights adversely to the legitimate demands of the claimant that the 'equity' comes into existence.

---

2 Ante, p 268.
3 *Bristol & West Building Society v Henning* [1985] 1 WLR 778 at 782D per Browne-Wilkinson LJ.
4 See eg *Pascoe v Turner* [1979] 1 WLR 431 at 439B (ante, p 416); *Riches v Hogben* [1986] 1 Qd R 315 at 321f, 327, 343 (ante, p 416).
5 *Shaida v Kindlane Ltd* (Unreported, Chancery Division, 1976 S No 8501, 22 June 1982) per Judge Baker QC.
6 [1980] 1 WLR 219 at 225H, citing in support *DHN Food Distributors Ltd v Tower Hamlets LBC* [1976] 1 WLR 852.
7 [1976] Ch 179 at 195C-D.
8 See *Taylors Fashions Ltd v Liverpool Victoria Trustees Co Ltd* [1982] QB 133 (Note) at 147H; *Olsson v Dyson* (1968-1969) 120 CLR 365 at 379. This approach bears certain similarities to the way in which the courts have applied the company law doctrine of 'fraud on the minority' (see *Prudential Assurance Co Ltd v Newman Industries Ltd* (No 2) [1981] Ch 257 at 307D per Vinelott J).

From this point onwards the claimant has some kind of inchoate right—or 'equity'—to bend the ear of the court of conscience to listen sympathetically to his tale.

(b) The concretised remedy

The mere fact that a claimant has acquired an inchoate 'equity' does not mean that he already has a right to be awarded any particular interest by way of remedy: the 'equity' crystallises only when concretised in the form of a specific property interest allocated by the court. But the importance of the 'equity' lies in the fact that it opens up to the claimant the jurisdiction of the court to consider his allegation against the good conscience of the landowner and, having listened, to allocate to him a particular form of proprietary interest by way of remedy.

(3) Does the 'equity' comprise a 'property interest' or 'interest in land'?

It is uncontroversial that the inchoate 'equity' generated by a claim of proprietary estoppel should be regarded as comprising an 'interest in land' for isolated purposes such as the award of compensation under the Town and Country Planning legislation.[9] However, it is usual to find such concessions closely coupled with a firm denial that the inchoate 'equity' can itself constitute a 'property interest' or 'interest in land' in the strict conveyancing sense.[10] It is distinctly unorthodox to assert the proprietary status of this kind of 'equity',[11] not least because of the extreme difficulty of placing it within the existing canon of rights and interests recognised in the Law of Property Act 1925. There is instead a rather half-hearted consensus that the estoppel claimant receives no property right in the strict sense unless and until a court finally awards him one or other of the recognised property rights in satisfaction of his 'equity'.

(a) An unorthodox view

Contrary to this traditional view of the status of the estoppel-based 'equity', it can be argued, however, that it is indeed proper and legitimate to regard the inchoate 'equity' of the estoppel claimant as a present right of property.[12] According to this alternative view, 'property' is not a thing but a relationship; and the essence of a 'property right' lies in the fact that it comprises a claim habitually recognised and enforced by the courts.[13]

---

9   *Pennine Raceway Ltd v Kirklees MBC* [1983] QB 382 at 389F, 391D-E. See [1983] Conv 317 (JEM). See also *Plimmer v Mayor etc of Wellington* (1884) 9 App Cas 699 at 714 (ante, p 391).

10   See eg *Pennine Raceway Ltd v Kirklees MBC* [1983] QB 382 at 391A.

11   The conventional view stems largely from the decision of the House of Lords in *National Provincial Bank Ltd v Ainsworth* [1965] AC 1175 (ante, p 50). See, however, the different view expressed by the High Court of Australia in *Latec Investments Ltd v Hotel Terrigal Pty Ltd* (1964-1965) 113 CLR 265 (post, p 572).

12   For an interesting argument that a licence coupled with an 'equity' may fall into some intermediate category of 'quasi-property' mid-way between rights *in rem* and rights *in personam*, see A.R. Everton, *Towards A Concept Of "Quasi-Property"?*, [1982] Conv 118 at 131f. See also S.M. Bandali, (1973) 37 Conv (NS) 402 at 409.

13   Ante, p 51.

In terms of this analysis, the 'equity' raised by a valid claim of proprietary estoppel can readily be seen as an equitable 'property right', in that it denotes a call upon conscience to which the courts will respond with the granting of a remedy. It is true that the particular remedy is selected at the discretion of the court, but the 'equity' of the estoppel claimant is otherwise not qualitatively different from the 'equity' of the cestui que trust to have property dealt with as the trust requires. As Isaacs J was accustomed to point out, the latter right 'is regarded for the purposes of equity as equivalent to a right in the property itself',[14] for equitable ownership is 'always commensurate with the right to relief in a Court of Equity.'[15] The 'equity' founded on proprietary estoppel is also susceptible to a 'property' characterisation. It was no mere accident that in *Hoystead v Federal Commissioner of Taxation*[16] Isaacs J viewed Lord Kingsdown's judgment in *Ramsden v Dyson* as being similarly 'based on the principle that equitable property is commensurate with equitable relief.'[17]

(b) A realist perspective

In realist terms the 'property right' *is* the recognition of the claim, and the enforceability of the claim is in fact all that is meant by the so-called 'property right'. It would be self-deception to regard the 'property interest' awarded by a court in satisfaction of the 'equity' of estoppel as being somehow invested with a larger 'property' significance than that which is being attributed here to the initial and inchoate 'equity' generated by the estoppel. In the last resort all that is denoted by either usage (whether the reference be to an 'equity' or to some comfortingly familiar 'property right') is that the courts will habitually enforce the claims thus respectively described in legal shorthand.

(c) The meaning of a 'property right'

It may, of course, be correctly concluded that it is not ultimately helpful to refer to anything as a 'property right', since at best this usage operates merely as an abbreviated reference to certain secondary characteristics which flow from the primary fact of enforcement through legitimated state power. When the arrogant nonsense of the 'property right' is finally stripped away, all that remains visible to the naked eye is the brute fact of enforcement.[18] The only relevant question, in a congeries of situations involving a variety of parties, concerns who will win. True it may be that the answer is conventionally rationalised in terms of justice or conscience. But whether the 'equity' generated by proprietary estoppel is or is not a 'property right' is not in itself a particularly interesting question.

---

14   *Glenn v Federal Commissioner of Land Tax* (1915) 20 CLR 490 at 503.
15   *Trustees, Executors and Agency Co Ltd v Acting Federal Commissioner of Taxation* (1917) 23 CLR 576 at 583.
16   (1920) 27 CLR 400 at 423.
17   Ante, p 390. It is consistent with this approach that in *Cameron v Murdoch* [1983] WAR 321 at 360, Brinsden J saw the plaintiffs' interest under their 'equity' as an 'equitable interest in specific assets'.
18   The notion of a 'property right' is, in this sense, a 'category of illusory reference' (see J. Stone, *Legal System and Lawyers' Reasonings* (London 1964), p 241ff).

(4) Can the benefit of the 'equity' pass to a third party?

It is important to know whether an 'equity' raised by proprietary estoppel may be asserted not by the party who originally relied on the relevant assurance but by his successor in title. To ask whether the inchoate 'equity' is or is not a 'property right' does not genuinely assist in the determination of this question, since a 'property' characterisation merely states the conclusion in advance without addressing the subtlety of the central issue.[19]

There seems to be some doubt as to whether an inchoate 'equity' can be asserted by successors in title. In *Fryer v Brook*,[20] for instance, Oliver LJ declined to decide the issue in definitive terms, but opined that the 'equity' was merely a 'personal interest' vested in the original estoppel claimant himself, and was 'rather akin to the personal right of occupation created by a statutory tenancy.'[1] As such it was not then capable of vesting in the claimant's trustee in bankruptcy.[2]

In *E.R. Ives Investment Ltd v High*,[3] however, an 'equity' based on proprietary estoppel was described by Lord Denning MR as being available also to successors in title.[4] It is possible that this statement meant only that successors in title could take advantage of the right of access which was awarded to the estoppel claimant in satisfaction of his 'equity', rather than that they could have asserted the inchoate 'equity' for the first time themselves. Only in the Australian caselaw is there a clear ruling that a successor in title can base an original claim to an inchoate 'equity' on the ground of an earlier assurance made to, and relied on by, his predecessor.[5] The balance of opinion in the English cases seems to incline against the transmissibility of the benefit of estoppel-based 'equities', but it may be that the Australian approach is a sign of future developments.[6]

(5) Can the burden of the 'equity' pass to a third party?

It may also be critically important to determine whether the 'equity' created by a proprietary estoppel is binding on third parties. The focus of concern here is the 'third-party impact' of the 'equity' as a mere inchoate right before it has

---

19   Post, p 555.
20   Unreported, Court of Appeal, 19 July 1984.
1   On the nature of the statutory tenancy, see Chapter 29 (post, p 1003). In *Jones (A E) v Jones (F W)* [1977] 1 WLR 438 at 443D, Lord Denning MR held that the defendant had an 'equity...of a possessory nature entitling [him] to remain in this house, but it would not...extend to the defendant's wife.'
2   In any event Oliver LJ found an alternative ground for his decision in section 22(3) of the Bankruptcy Act 1914.
3   [1967] 2 QB 379 at 395A. Winn LJ (at [1967] 2 QB 379 at 403A) declined to decide the 'subsidiary but important question whether Mr High's claim, if valid, is only a personal right'.
4   See however, F.R. Crane, (1967) 31 Conv (NS) 332 at 341.
5   *Hamilton v Geraghty* (1901) 1 NSWSR (Eq) 81 at 89; *Cameron v Murdoch* [1983] WAR 321 at 360 (affirmed (1985-86) 63 ALR 575 at 595). See M. Neave and M. Weinberg, *The Nature and Function of Equities*, (1978-80) 6 Tas ULR 24 at 30. It may be that the result of the tortuous litigation in *Neesom v Clarkson* (1842) 2 Hare 163, 67 ER 68, (1845) 4 Hare 97, 67 ER 576, can be seen as providing support for the same idea.
6   See the similar approach now adopted in relation to promissory estoppel in *Brikom Investments Ltd v Carr* [1979] QB 467 at 484G-485A per Lord Denning MR, citing in support the statement in *Co Litt*, p 352a,b that 'every estoppel ought to be reciprocal...privies in estate, as the feoffee, lessee & c...shall be bound and take the advantage of estoppels...'

crystallised in the form of some remedy granted by the courts.[7] It is, of course, clear that once the 'equity' has crystallised in a concrete judicial remedy, the interest thereby recognised in the claimant can more easily be made binding on third parties.[8]

(a) Unregistered land

It seems to be agreed that the 'equity' raised by proprietary estoppel does not constitute a land charge in the context of unregistered land.[9] It follows therefore that no facility of registration can be used in order to make such an 'equity' binding upon a purchaser of the land.[10] Equally plainly an inchoate 'equity' of estoppel does not rank as an equitable interest which is capable of being overreached under section 2(1) of the Law of Property Act 1925.

It is nevertheless clear that an 'equity' generated by proprietary estoppel can, under certain circumstances, run with the land,[11] so as to affect purchasers other than for value. An 'equity' of this kind, albeit not yet concretised in any court-ordered remedy, binds not merely the owner of the land, but also his trustee in bankruptcy,[12] his personal representatives,[13] an associated company,[14] and a successor local authority.[15]

(i) Application of the doctrine of notice The impact of the inchoate 'equity' on other third parties seems to turn on some version of the equitable doctrine of notice. It seems clear that an 'equity' raised by an assurance given by one owner of land is enforceable against a purchaser of a legal estate in that land who has actual notice of the circumstances which gave rise to the 'equity'.[16] It is less clear whether the 'equity' is binding on a purchaser of a legal estate with merely constructive notice.[17] If an estoppel-based 'equity' is treated as being

7 The maintenance of a distinction between the inchoate 'equity' and the eventual remedy may go some distance towards providing a solution to the problems raised by T. Bailey, [1983] Conv 99. It is all too easy to confuse the proprietary status of the inchoate 'equity' (ante, p 421) with the various kinds of property right which the courts may award in satisfaction of the 'equity'.
8 This appears to be true even where the estoppel is satisfied through the recognition that the claimant has an irrevocable licence (*In re Sharpe (A Bankrupt)* [1980] 1 WLR 219 at 224G). See *Williams v Staite* [1979] Ch 291, where the point seems to have been assumed without explicit argument.
9 *E.R. Ives Investment Ltd v High* [1967] 2 QB 379 at 395G, 400B, 405G; *Pascoe v Turner* [1979] 1 WLR 431 at 439A; *Bristol & West Building Society v Henning* [1985] 1 WLR 778 at 781F.
10 See [1982] Conv 80 (JEM). It has been suggested, on the basis of dicta in *Haslemere Estates Ltd v Baker* [1982] 1 WLR 1109 at 1119H-1120A per Megarry V-C, that an estoppel claim may be properly registrable under the Land Charges Act 1972 as a *lis pendens* (see [1983] Conv 69 at 70 (JEM)). This may be true, but would in any event require (i) that litigation should already have commenced and (ii) that the estoppel claim should assert an interest in land (see Land Charges Act 1972, s 17(1), ante, p 111).
11 The 'equity' can be traced into the proceeds of sale of the land and into further investments bought out of those proceeds (*Lepel v Huthnance* (1979) NZ Recent Law 269 at 270).
12 *In re Sharpe (A Bankrupt)* [1980] 1 WLR 219 at 224F.
13 *Inwards v Baker* [1965] 2 QB 29 at 37F; *Jones (A E) v Jones (F W)* [1977] 1 WLR 438 at 442F.
14 *E & L Berg Homes Ltd v Grey* (1980) 253 Estates Gazette 473 at 475.
15 *Salvation Army Trustee Co Ltd v West Yorkshire MCC* (1981) 41 P & CR 179 at 193.
16 *E.R. Ives Investment Ltd v High* [1967] 2 QB 379 at 393G, 400A,E, 405B. *A fortiori*, if the purchaser takes only an equitable interest in the land.
17 That a purchaser of a legal estate may be bound by mere constructive notice seems to emerge from *The Duke of Beaufort v Patrick* (1853) 17 Beav 60 at 78, 51 ER 954 at 961; *Bristol & West Building Society v Henning* [1985] 1 WLR 778 at 781G. See F.R. Crane, (1967) 31 Conv (NS) 332 at 339.

more or less equivalent to a conventional 'equitable interest in land', there would appear to be no reason in principle why a purchaser should not be bound if he has constructive notice. However, in *In re Sharpe (A Bankrupt)*[18] Browne-Wilkinson J did remark somewhat pointedly that the 'equity' raised in the case before him might be defeated by a purchaser from a trustee in bankruptcy, provided that such purchaser did not have 'express notice'.[19] On the other hand, if the 'equity' founded on proprietary estoppel is treated on the same footing as other 'equities',[20] it would follow that an estoppel-based 'equity' could be defeated by a purchaser for value of even an equitable interest in the land, provided that he has no notice actual or constructive.[1] The law in these respects awaits clarification.

(ii) Range of remedy open to successors in title It should be stressed that the precise nature of the remedy granted by the court against a successor in title may not be quite the same or as far-reaching as the remedy which the court might have granted had the 'equity' been asserted against the party who gave the initial assurance.[2]

(b) Registered land

There is less authority concerning the impact of inchoate estoppel claims on transferees of a title in registered land. However, it may be that the 'equity' raised by proprietary estoppel constitutes an overriding interest under section 70(1)(g) of the Land Registration Act 1925 if coupled with actual occupation on the part of the claimant.[3] Moreover, there is a possibility that the 'equity' is protectible as a minor interest by the entry of a caution[4] (or even a notice[5]) in the land register, although it is predictable that few such cautions will be entered in practice. However, the Law Commission has expressed the view that a requirement of registration in this context may 'add a further complication to the law'.[6] The most appropriate protection for estoppel claimants may ultimately lie in a general extension of existing powers of rectification under the Land Registration Act 1925.[7]

---

18 [1980] 1 WLR 219 at 226G.
19 For an argument in favour of limiting the category of purchasers affected by an 'equity' to those with actual or express notice, see M.P. Thompson, [1983] Conv 50 at 56. Professor R.H. Maudsley proposed a resolution of the present problem which turned on whether the estoppel claimant has exclusive possession of the land. He suggested that estoppel claimants who do not enjoy exclusive possession should be protected against (i) purchasers with actual notice, and (ii) volunteers. However, estoppel claimants who have exclusive possession should be protected against *every* person coming to the land except a purchaser for value without notice, actual or constructive (see (1956) 20 Conv (NS) 281 at 291ff).
20 Post, p 785.
1 See *Phillips v Phillips* (1861) 4 De G F & J 208 at 218, 45 ER 1164 at 1167.
2 Ante, p 416.
3 See *National Provincial Bank Ltd v Hastings Car Mart Ltd* [1964] Ch 665 at 689 per Lord Denning MR (ante, p 181). Compare, however, *Poster v Slough Estates Ltd* [1969] 1 Ch 495 at 507G per Cross J.
4 See T. Bailey, [1983] Conv 99 at 103.
5 See Law Commission, *Property Law: Land Registration (Fourth Paper)* (Published Working Paper No 67, April 1976), para 50. See also para 65f.
6 Law Commission, *Property Law: Second Report on Land Registration (Provisional)* (1984), para 57.
7 Ante, p 202.

CHAPTER 14

Leases

A 'term of years absolute' constitutes one of the two legal estates in land recognised today in English law.[1] In general terms a 'term of years' is created by some 'lease', 'demise' or 'tenancy' granted expressly or impliedly by a 'lessor' (or 'landlord'). This grant creates in the 'lessee' (or 'tenant') an interest in the land for a fixed period of certain maximum duration. Nevertheless, the grant of a lease differs from a conveyance of the other legal estate known to English law, the fee simple absolute, in that the conveyance of a leasehold interest does not represent a fully executed contract. Even after grant the lease is 'partly executory: rights and obligations remain outstanding on both sides throughout its currency'.[2]

Because the leasehold relationship formed no part of the feudal structure, the interest conferred by a lease or tenancy was originally regarded as lying outside the law of real property. The right to occupy another's land for a defined period of time was initially considered to be a mere right *in personam* which subsisted—at most—only in contract. Such an interest was not recognised as a right *in rem*.[3] It was only with the development of the action of ejectment in the 15th century that occupation rights of this kind—albeit conferred by contract—were acknowledged as constituting a new category of *property* right.[4] Thus, although the lease is today recognised as a potential legal estate in land,[5] it has always had a somewhat hybrid character, partaking of the nature of both realty and personalty. For this reason the term of years is sometimes called a 'chattel real'.[6]

1. ESSENTIAL ELEMENTS IN A 'LEASE' OR 'TENANCY'

In *Street v Mountford*[7] Lord Templeman pointed out that it is 'consistent with the elevation of a tenancy into an estate in land' that any grant of 'exclusive possession for a term at a rent' should result in the creation of a 'lease' or 'tenancy'. It is, however, readily apparent that this formula does not eliminate all difficulties in the definition of the leasehold estate.[8]

---

1 Ante, p 71.
2 *National Carriers Ltd v Panalpina (Northern) Ltd* [1981] AC 675 at 705G per Lord Simon of Glaisdale.
3 *Street v Mountford* [1985] AC 809 at 814E per Lord Templeman. See generally A.W.B. Simpson, *A History of The Land Law* (2nd edn Oxford 1986), p 71ff; F. Pollock and F.W. Maitland, *The History of English Law* (London 1968), Vol II, p 106ff.
4 See T. Plucknett, *A Concise History of the Common Law* (5th edn London 1956), p 574.
5 Law of Property Act 1925, s 1(1)(b) (ante, p 78).
6 See *National Carriers Ltd v Panalpina (Northern) Ltd* [1981] AC 675 at 708B-C per Lord Russell of Killowen.
7 [1985] AC 809 at 816B.
8 There is a definition of 'term of years absolute' in Law of Property Act 1925, s 205(1)(xxvii), but, being circular in nature, the statutory definition provides little assistance.

(1) Types of lease or tenancy

It has been said quite correctly that a lease is 'chameleonic in both character and function'.[9] In the legal systems of the common law world the leasehold device has been adapted and manipulated for an extremely broad range of purposes. It currently provides a legal vehicle for many forms of residential, commercial and agricultural user. The lease or tenancy has come to play a vital (and not particularly comfortable) role in mediating a host of contractual, consumer and conveyancing relationships. Essentially the same legal concept has had to do service for arrangements which, in their context and purpose, can differ as widely as the short-term letting for residential occupation and a leasehold term of 3,000 years used as mortgage security.[10] The multiplicity of uses to which the uniform concept of tenancy has been put only barely conceals the difficulties which are inherent in the indifferent application of the same legal rules to the periodic tenant who pays £50 per week for his bed-sit, the home-owner who has just paid £50,000 for a 99 year lease of a new flat, and the large commercial concern which rents a warehouse for £5,000 per year.

The types of tenancy known to English law include the following.

(a) Fixed term lease

The concept of the lease or tenancy may apply to the grant of exclusive possession for any fixed period of time. The period may be long or short, although the longer the term the greater is the tendency to use the terminology of 'lease' rather than 'tenancy'.

(i) Purchase of a long lease   A long lease may well comprise the grant of a term of 99 years, in which case the purchase of such an estate begins to resemble the purchase of an estate in fee simple. The grantee under a 99 year lease of a house or flat normally purchases his estate in the land on payment of an initial cash sum or 'premium' which is not dissimilar from the purchase price of a freehold estate in equivalent realty. Like the freeholder, the leaseholder may use the estate purchased as security for a loan covering all or part of the purchase price.[11] After acquisition the leaseholder's only remaining financial liabilities to his grantor relate to the continuing payment of what is usually a fairly nominal ground rent, together with payment of such periodic service or management charges as may be stipulated for in the covenants of the lease.

(ii) Leasehold as a marketable capital asset   The proprietor of the long leasehold stands possessed of an asset which, although necessarily of a wasting nature, will still for many years command an inflating market value on alienation (or 'assignment'). In other words, it is open to the leaseholder at any time to assign the unexpired portion of his term for such price as the current market will sustain,[12] and this price will continue for some time to run ahead of the initial

---

9   *219 Broadway Corp v Alexander's, Inc*, 387 NE.2d 1205 at 1207 (1979).

10   Post, p 573.

11   See, however, the problem raised by the recent decision in *Smith v Metropolitan Properties Ltd* (1986) 277 Estates Gazette 753 at 754 (post, p 508).

12   It is not uncommon, however, for a lease to contain a covenant prohibiting assignment except with the consent of the landlord (post, p 480).

purchase price of the lease at the commencement of the term. The leaseholder may alternatively deal with his estate by way of sublease.[13]

(iii) Termination A fixed term lease automatically comes to an end on the expiration of the period stipulated. At this point the reversion to the landlord 'falls in' and the land is no longer encumbered by the lease. The superior owner is once again free to resume physical possession and to deal with the property as he wishes.[14]

(b) Periodic tenancy

A 'term of years' may also take the form of a periodic tenancy which runs from week to week, or from month to month, or from quarter to quarter, or from year to year.[15] Such tenancies may be created either expressly or impliedly. A periodic tenancy continues indefinitely until determined by the giving of the appropriate notice.[16]

(i) The common law presumption There used to be a strong common law presumption that a periodic tenancy was impliedly created by the payment and acceptance of a periodic sum in the nature of rent.[17] Such circumstances were apt to generate a weekly, monthly, quarterly or yearly tenancy, depending on the period with reference to which the payment was calculated.[18] However, the reservation of rent and its payment on some periodic basis are not wholly incompatible with the existence of a mere tenancy at will.[19] In cases of dispute the court must ultimately examine the 'intentions of the parties in all the circumstances',[20] in order to determine whether it is 'right and proper to infer...that the parties had reached an agreement' for a periodic tenancy.[1] In many cases the preferred solution is still that of implied periodic tenancy but this is not always so.

(ii) Relevance of statutory protection of the tenant It has been said that in days of increased statutory control over the landlord's right of possession, the old common law presumption of periodic tenancy is 'unsound and no longer holds'.[2] In determining whether the mere fact of payment and acceptance of rent generates an implied periodic tenancy, the courts tend nowadays to draw inferences as to the parties' likely intentions in the light of the potential effects of

---

13   Post, p 463.
14   The generality of this proposition is qualified by the possibility that the tenant may enjoy some kind of security of tenure on the expiry of his lease (eg under the Rent Act). See Chapter 29 (post, p 961).
15   Law of Property Act 1925, s 205(1)(xxvii).
16   Post, p 485.
17   *Doe d Lord v Crago* (1848) 6 CB 90 at 98f, 136 ER 1185 at 1188f. This presumption 'dies very hard' (see *Longrigg, Burrough & Trounson v Smith* (1979) 251 Estates Gazette 847 at 849 per Ormrod LJ).
18   See *Cole v Kelly* [1920] 2 KB 106 at 132. For further discussion of the implied periodic tenancy, see p 466, post.
19   *Doe d Bastow v Cox* (1847) 11 QB 122 at 123, 116 ER 421 at 422; *Hagee (London) Ltd v A.B. Erikson and Larson* [1976] QB 209 at 214F-G.
20   *Cardiothoracic Institute v Shrewdcrest Ltd* [1986] 1 WLR 368 at 378C. See also *Doe d Cheny v Batten* (1775) 1 Cowp 243 at 245, 98 ER 1066 at 1067 per Lord Mansfield.
1   *Longrigg, Burrough & Trounson v Smith* (1979) 251 Estates Gazette 847 at 849. See also *Uzun v Ramadan* [1986] 2 EGLR 255 at 257 E-H.
2   *Longrigg, Burrough & Trounson v Smith* (1979) 251 Estates Gazette 847 at 849.

modern protective legislation.[3] However, the common law presumption still retains its force where, for instance, a tenancy unaffected by statutory prolongation has come to an end and the parties have not yet expressly agreed on the creation of a new tenancy. Under these circumstances the continuing payment and acceptance of a periodic rent may well generate a periodic tenancy 'on the footing that that is what the parties must have intended or be taken to have intended.'[4]

(c) Tenancy at will

A 'tenancy at will' arises where a person enjoys occupation of land with the consent of the owner in circumstances where either party may terminate the arrangement at will, ie, on demand.[5] A tenancy at will is something of a hybrid and its status in law is in many respects unclear. A tenancy at will is said to comprise a 'personal relation between the landlord and his tenant',[6] and a tenant at will, having no estate in the land, cannot assign his tenancy to a stranger.[7]

This being so, the tenant at will resembles the licensee, who likewise has no estate in the land and who avoids being classified as a trespasser only because the landowner consents to his occupancy.[8] However, the status of the tenant at will differs vitally from that of the mere licensee in that, even if he has no 'estate' as such, the tenant at will is accounted to be in 'possession' of the land.[9] It follows that the tenant at will can, unlike the licensee, maintain an action in trespass against a stranger[10] (although not against the owner himself[11]), and it has been held that he comes within the protection of the Rent Act.[12]

3 *Cardiothoracic Institute v Shrewdcrest Ltd* [1986] 1 WLR 368 at 379F-G. In this case, the potential impact of the protective scheme provided for business tenants by Part II of the Landlord and Tenant Act 1954 made the court unwilling to believe that the parties had intended, by mere payment and acceptance of rent, to create a periodic tenancy. See [1987] Conv 55 (J.E.M.).
4 *Cardiothoracic Institute v Shrewdcrest Ltd* [1986] 1 WLR 368 at 378B-C.
5 *Errington v Errington and Woods* [1952] 1 KB 290 at 296. No notice to quit is required in order to determine a tenancy at will (*Crane v Morris* [1965] 1 WLR 1104 at 1108B-C; *Cliffe v Cooper* (Unreported, Court of Appeal, 20 May 1985)), and it seems (sed quaere) that a tenancy at will may validly indicate a future date beyond which the tenancy shall not continue (*GLC v Minchin* (Unreported, Court of Appeal, 1979 G No 2837, 25 February 1981)). A tenancy at will is also terminated if the tenant commits acts of voluntary waste (see *Countess of Shrewsbury's Case* (1600) 5 Co Rep 13b, 77 ER 68 at 69; *Warren v Keen* [1954] 1 QB 15 at 21; *Nichols v R.A. Gill Ltd* (1975) 51 DLR (3d) 493 at 498). See also *Kater v Kater* (1960) 104 CLR 497 at 503.
6 *Wheeler v Mercer* [1957] AC 416 at 427 per Viscount Simonds. A tenancy at will is enjoyed by a person who is permitted to enjoy premises as a tenant rent free for an indefinite period (see *Doe d Groves v Groves* (1847) 10 QB 486 at 491f, 116 ER 185 at 187f; *Buck v Howarth* [1947] 1 All ER 342 at 343G).
7 See *Murphy v Ford* (1855) 5 ICLR 19 at 23; *Anderson v Tooheys Ltd* (1937) 54 WN (NSW) 21 at 23; *Victa Sales Pty Ltd v Tucker* [1970] 1 NSWR 737 at 739. Compare, however, *Ward v Ryan* (1875) IR 10 CL 17 at 19.
8 Post, p 535.
9 *Lynes v Snaith* [1899] 1 QB 486 at 488f. On the concept of 'possession', see post, pp 439, 446.
10 *Heslop v Burns* [1974] 1 WLR 1241 at 1253C; *Victa Sales Pty Ltd v Tucker* [1970] 1 NSWR 737 at 739.
11 Non-consensual entry by the owner amounts to a termination of the tenancy at will (see *Co Litt*, p 55b; *Doe d Bennett v Turner* (1840) 7 M & W 226 at 232f, 151 ER 749 at 751; *Landale v Menzies* (1909) 9 CLR 89 at 133).
12 *Francis Jackson Developments Ltd v Stemp* [1943] 2 All ER 601 at 603H-604A. It seems, however, that a tenant at will does not come within Part II of the Landlord and Tenant Act 1954 (see *Wheeler v Mercer* [1957] AC 416 at 426f, 428, 435; *Hagee (London) Ltd v A.B. Erikson and Larson* [1976] QB 209 at 215C, 216F; *Cardiothoracic Institute v Shrewdcrest Ltd* [1986] 1 WLR 368 at 376E-F).

It is of the essence of a tenancy at will that it continues indefinitely until terminated on demand by either party or brought to an end by the death of either.[13] However, a tenancy at will is nowadays unusual and slightly anomalous. It may be that such a tenancy 'can now serve only one legal purpose, and that is to protect the interests of an occupier during a period of transition.'[14] A tenancy at will normally confers only some form of intermediate status, and is readily converted into an estate in the land by way of implied periodic tenancy as soon as the tenant offers and the owner accepts some payment of rent which is referable to a year or aliquot part of a year.[15]

(d) Tenancy at sufferance

A tenancy at sufferance arises where a tenant who has enjoyed a perfectly valid terms of years holds over at the end of his term without the consent of the landlord.[16] It is the absence of the landlord's consent which distinguishes a tenancy at sufferance from a tenancy at will.[17] A tenant at sufferance has no 'tenancy' in any true sense and is not entitled to maintain any action in trespass.[18]

(2) The parties to a lease must be legally competent

Certain requirements of legal competence must be satisfied by the parties to a properly constituted term of years.

(a) Competent lessor

In order to grant a valid lease, the grantor must have legal competence to create a term of years in the subject land. In a very elementary sense it is clear that no lease is validly created unless the grantor himself has an estate in the land.[19] For instance, a company cannot effectively grant a term of years if title to the land in question is vested not in the company itself but in the name of the person who formed the company.[20] In any event, a corporate entity has no capacity to grant leases over its land unless a power to do so has been duly included in its memorandum of association.

(b) Competent lessee

The grantee of a lease must likewise have the legal competence required for the purpose of owning a term of years. The lessee must be a legal person such as an

---

13 *James v Dean* (1805) 11 Ves Jun 383 at 391, 32 ER 1135 at 1138; *Wheeler v Mercer* [1957] AC 416 at 427.

14 *Heslop v Burns* [1974] 1 WLR 1241 at 1253A per Scarman LJ.

15 Post, p 466. See *Roe d Bree v Lees*, 2 Wm Bl 1171 at 1173, 96 ER 691 at 692; *Richardson v Langridge* (1811) 4 Taunt 128 at 132, 128 ER 277 at 278; *Doe d Hull v Wood* (1845) 14 M & W 682 at 687, 153 ER 649 at 651; *Landale v Menzies* (1909) 9 CLR 89 at 129f.

16 See *Co Litt*, p 57b; *Remon v City of London Real Property Co Ltd* [1921] 1 KB 49 at 58.

17 *Wheeler v Mercer* [1957] AC 416 at 426.

18 *Schwartz v Zamrl* [1968] 2 NSWR 51 at 53; *Victa Sales Pty Ltd v Tucker* [1970] 1 NSWR 737 at 738f. He may, however, be eligible for protection under the Rent Act (post, p 971). See *Remon v City of London Real Property Co Ltd* [1921] 1 KB 49 at 58.

19 See *Southgate BC v Watson* [1944] KB 541 at 544; *Lewisham BC v Roberts* [1949] 2 KB 608 at 622; *Street v Mountford* [1985] AC 809 at 821B; *Royal Philanthropic Society v County* (1985) 276 Estates Gazette 1068 at 1071.

20 *Torbett v Faulkner* [1952] 2 TLR 659 at 660, 662.

individual or a corporate body.[1] Moreover, a corporate grantee must be duly empowered by the company constitution to be the recipient of leases.

Problems arise only rarely as to the legal competence of the lessee. However, two of the more common issues relate to the competence of (i) a grant to a minor and (ii) a grant to the lessor himself.

(i) Lease to a minor It is clear that a minor (ie, a person under the age of 18) is not competent to hold a legal estate in land,[2] and this necessarily means that a minor lacks capacity to hold any leasehold interest which ranks as a legal estate. This limitation on the competence of the lessee is seldom discussed but seems to be an inescapable conclusion of law. In strict terms a conveyance of a legal estate to a minor operates instead in the manner provided by the Settled Land Act 1925,[3] which means that the conveyance operates only as an agreement for valuable consideration to execute a settlement in favour of the minor.[4] The intending lessor meanwhile holds the estate on trust for the minor.[5]

Terms of years are not often conferred upon minors, but embarrassing consequences are introduced in those few areas where such leases are not unknown. A local authority which grants a council tenancy to a 17 year-old single mother has almost certainly no intention to activate the more obscure provisions of the Settled Land Act 1925.[6] It is extremely dubious whether such a grant constitutes a 'conveyance' within the meaning of that Act,[7] but if it does it seems that the landlord authority must hold on trust for the minor. In view of these difficulties, a tenancy agreement with a minor is much better analysed as creating an equitable[8] rather than a legal leasehold interest. Such a tenancy takes effect as a contract for a lease[9] and, since it relates to the supply of a 'necessary',[10] falls within one of the categories of contracts with minors which remain fully enforceable in law.[11]

---

1   A grant to a body which lacks legal personality is invalid as a lease. See eg *Congregational Christian Church v Iosefa Tauga* (1982) 8 Comm Law Bull 129 (grant to church invalid because church was an unincorporated association).
2   Law of Property Act 1925, s 1(6) (ante, p 71).
3   Law of Property Act 1925, s 19(1).
4   Settled Land Act 1925, s 27(1).
5   Ibid.
6   Post, p 803. The possibility that such a grant may occur has been greatly increased by the ruling of the House of Lords in *Eastleigh BC v Walsh* [1985] 1 WLR 525 that a tenancy (rather than a mere licence) may be conferred by the offer of temporary housing pending a decision as to eligibility as a homeless person for the purpose of what is now Housing Act 1985, s 58 (post, p 455).
7   The Settled Land Act 1925 does not define 'conveyance', but in the Law of Property Act 1925 the term is used only in relation to an assurance of a property interest 'by any instrument' (Law of Property Act 1925, s 205(1)(ii)).
8   Section 1(6) of the Law of Property Act 1925 does not, of course, prohibit the holding of an *equitable* interest by a minor.
9   Post, p 468.
10 See *Lowe v Griffith* (1835) 4 LJCP 94 at 96.
11 This view was endorsed by the Law Commission in 1984. The Commission sought to allay the concern expressed by some public landlord authorities, by pointing out that a minor is liable to pay the rent accruing during the currency of his contractual tenancy up to the date of any repudiation (*Law of Contract: Minors' Contracts* (Law Com No 134, 28 June 1984), para 5.15). See *Valentini v Canali* (1889) 24 QBD 166 at 167; *Davies v Beynon-Harris* (1931) 47 TLR 424. Compare *Can an under-18-year old be a contractual tenant?*, (1983) 147 Loc Gov Rev 259. See now Minors' Contracts Act 1987, s 1.

(ii) Lease to the lessor himself It has been clear since 1925 that, notwithstanding the terms of section 72(3) of the Law of Property Act 1925,[12] a person cannot grant a lease to himself of land of which he is the owner.[13] The major obstacle appears to consist in the absurdity of enforcing leasehold covenants against oneself.[14]

(3) A lease must have a fixed maximum duration

A term of years represents pre-eminently 'a time in the land' or 'land for a time'.[15] The grant of a lease or tenancy thus confers a right of exclusive possession of land for a quantum of time fixed in advance of the commencement date. From this proposition flow several implications.

(a) The lessor must retain a reversionary interest

A lease or tenancy always comprises the grant of a lesser estate out of a larger estate in land. It is therefore an integral feature of every term of years that the landlord is left with some kind of reversionary interest in the land.[16] In other words, there must always be a reversionary interest, retained throughout by the landlord, which 'falls in' at the end of the quantum of time represented by the lease. The presence of this reversionary interest in the landlord carries the important implication that he is regarded as holding an estate 'in possession' in the land even during the currency of the lease, 'possession' being defined broadly in the Law of Property Act 1925 as including 'receipt of rents and profits or the right to receive the same'.[17] The landlord's reversion is recognised as giving him an estate in the land sufficient, for instance, to provide him with a 'dominant tenement' for the purpose of enforcing restrictive covenants against a subtenant.[18]

(b) The lease must commence at a 'time certain'

The lease must commence at a 'time certain' which is either expressly fixed by the parties or is readily ascertainable before the start of the term.[19] In other

---

12 Section 72(3) provides that 'a person may convey land to or vest land in himself', but this has been construed as meaning merely that a sole executor may properly convey land to himself as devisee, or that a beneficial owner may convey land to himself as a trustee for charitable purposes (see *Rye v Rye* [1962] AC 496 at 514).
13 *Rye v Rye* [1962] AC 496 at 505 per Viscount Simonds, 514 per Lord Denning.
14 Compare eg Property Law Act 1952 (New Zealand), ss 49, 66A; *Harding v Commissioner of Inland Revenue* [1977] 1 NZLR 337 at 341; *Samuel v District Land Registrar* [1984] 2 NZLR 697 at 701f.
15 Ante, p 61.
16 *Re British American Oil Co Ltd and DePass* (1960) 21 DLR (2d) 110 at 115.
17 Law of Property Act 1925, s 205(1)(xix). There are always therefore at least two estates concurrently in possession in the landlord-tenant relationship, since both landlord and tenant enjoy 'possession' in the extended statutory sense.
18 *Hall v Ewin* (1888) 37 Ch D 74 at 79; *Teape v Douse* (1905) 92 LT 319 at 320; *Northern Ireland Carriers Ltd v Larne Harbour Ltd* [1981] 5 NIJB, Transcript, p 10 per Murray J.
19 *Bl Comm*, Vol II, p 143. There cannot in law be an agreement for a lease to commence at some unspecified future date. If a 'contract for a lease' (post, p 468) does not stipulate at least an ascertainable commencement date, there is no concluded contract (*Harvey v Pratt* [1965] 1 WLR 1025 at 1026D-E, 1027C). The commencement date cannot simply be taken to be the date of the contract (*Marshall v Berridge* (1881) 19 Ch D 233 at 239). See also *Lace v Chantler* [1944] KB 368 at 370; *Brown v Gould* [1972] Ch 53 at 61B; *Secretary of State for Social Services v Beavington* (1982) 262 Estates Gazette 551 at 554; *Kerns v Manning* [1935] IR 869 at 880; *McQuaid v Lynam* [1965] IR 564 at 574; *Omsac Developments Ltd v Colebourne* (1980) 110 DLR (3d) 766 at 768.

words, the lease must have a definite *terminus a quo*. If the commencement date is not specified, it may in some circumstances be inferred that the term begins immediately on the taking of possession, provided that there is no doubt as to the precise date on which this occurs.[20]

The commencement date of the lease may of course be postponed to a date considerably later than that of the instrument which creates the leasehold term, in which case the lease is known as a 'reversionary' lease.[1] However, a statutory penalty of voidness now attaches to any reversionary term granted at a rent or in consideration of a fine which is limited to take effect more than 21 years after the date of the instrument purporting to create it.[2]

(c) The term may be of any length

Subject to the requirement that its maximum duration be ascertainable, a term of years may relate to any length of time. The term may itself comprise merely a fraction of a year,[3] and could in theory be extremely short.[4] The term may equally well extend to vast expanses of time which begin to resemble a grant in fee simple.[5] A term of 99 years is commonly granted in respect of leasehold flats, and local authorities are statutorily empowered to grant terms of 125 years in respect of dwelling-houses covered by the 'right to buy' provisions of the Housing Act 1985.[6]

It is not even essential that the quantum of time in respect of which possession is granted under a lease should comprise one single continuous period. The advent of the phenomenon of 'holiday time-sharing'[7] has confirmed the idea that a lease may comprise an aggregate of discontinuous periods of time.[8] In

20 *James v Lock* (1977) 246 Estates Gazette 395 at 397.
1   Conversely the duration of a lease may be expressed with reference to a date which has already passed. It is, for instance, quite common in a 99 year lease that the 99 year period should be stipulated as running from a date prior to the granting of the lease (eg from the preceding quarter day).
2   Law of Property Act 1925, s 149(3). However, this provision does not affect the validity of a *contract* to create a lease at some future time which, when created by instrument, will then take effect either immediately or within 21 years of the date of that instrument (Perpetuities and Accumulations Act 1964, s 9(2)). See *In Re Strand and Savoy Properties Ltd* [1960] Ch 582 at 591; (1960) 76 LQR 352 (R.E.M.); *Weg Motors Ltd v Hales* [1962] Ch 49 at 68, 78.
3   Law of Property Act 1925, s 205(1)(xxvii) (ante, p 429).
4   It is probably true, however, that the shorter the supposed term, the greater the likelihood that the grant will be construed as conferring not a leasehold interest but a licence: see eg the 'coronation cases' (post, p 541). Nevertheless even short-term occupation may still give rise to a leasehold interest. In *National Carriers Ltd v Panalpina (Northern) Ltd* [1981] AC 675 at 714D, Lord Roskill agreed that a holiday-maker may well have a legal estate in a cottage let to him for a short period as a holiday home, although 'the estate in land which he acquires has little or no meaning for him.'
5   See *National Carriers Ltd v Panalpina (Northern) Ltd* [1981] AC 675 at 714B. The longest lease on record is an Irish lease comprising a grant for 10 million years (ante, p 79). Leases of 3,000 years are usual for the purpose of creating certain kinds of mortgage (post, p 573). For some reason the Irish tend to specialise in the granting of extremely long terms. Part of the Dublin cattle market was leased by John Jameson to the Dublin City Corporation on 21 January 1863 for a term of 100,000 years (see N. McWhirter (ed), *Guinness Book of Records* (27th edn Enfield, Middx, 1980), p 190). See also *In re Sergie* [1954] NI 1 (mortgage demise for 10,000 years).
6   Housing Act 1985, s 139(1), Sch 6, Part III, para 12(1).
7   See J. Edmonds, *International Timesharing* (2nd edn, London 1984), p 9ff.
8   As early as *Smallwood v Sheppards* [1895] 2 QB 627 at 630, it was recognised that a lease granting a right of occupation for three successive bank holidays could constitute a single letting.

Cottage Holiday Associates Ltd v Customs and Excise Commissioners,[9] Woolf J accepted as a lease a document which granted the lessee, in consideration of an initial premium, a right to occupy a holiday cottage for one week in each year for a term of 80 years.[10]

(d) The maximum duration of the lease must be ascertainable

Irrespective of the length of the term granted, it is an essential characteristic of a lease that it should confer an estate in land of certain maximum duration.[11] From the very outset a finite point (or *terminus ad quem*) must be either expressed or implicit or must be capable of being rendered certain. Thus, in *Lace v Chantler*,[12] no lease was held to exist where a right of occupation had been conferred 'for the duration of the war'.[13] Likewise a letting of premises 'for so long as the lessee shall use them' cannot create a valid leasehold term.[14]

This common law requirement of a pre-fixed maximum duration raises grave difficulties in the leasehold area. Many of these difficulties would remain unresolved but for several statutory interventions which ensure that at least some of the problematic cases are forced artificially, but nevertheless effectively, within the procrustean dimensions of the rule.

(i) Lease for life

Longevity being an unpredictable quality, a lease for life offends against the prescription that leases must be of fixed maximum duration.[15] A 'term of years' as defined in the Law of Property Act 1925 cannot therefore include a lease for life or a lease which is determinable on the death of some named person.[16] However, statute intervenes to reconcile the lease for life with the common law requirement. A lease for life, if granted at a rent or in consideration of a fine,[17] is automatically converted into a 90 year term.[18] The

---

9 [1983] QB 735 at 739D. However, Woolf J held that the length of the 'term' granted by such a lease was 80 weeks rather than 80 years ([1983] QB 735 at 739H-740F). Woolf J ([1983] QB 735 at 738A) expressly left open the effect of Law of Property Act 1925, s 149(3) (see D. Green, (1983) 80 Law Soc Gaz 2500 at 2501).

10 It may also be quite common nowadays that lessees of office buildings are not entitled to occupy the demised premises at certain times, eg at weekends (see *Cottage Holiday Associates Ltd v Customs and Excise Commissioners* [1983] QB 735 at 739G-H). See also [1983] Conv 319.

11 It does not follow that a lease must stipulate a *minimum* duration. It is the outer limit of the term which must be fixed or capable of being rendered certain. Provided that the maximum duration is certain, it is irrelevant that the term is capable of an earlier determination (eg through surrender or the operation of some limiting condition or through the lessor's exercise of a right of entry). See *Co Litt*, p 45; *Bl Comm*, Vol II, p 143.

12 [1944] KB 368 at 370f. See also *Eton College v Bard* [1983] Ch 321 at 332A.

13 See also *M.W. Investments Ltd v Kilburn Envoy Ltd* [1947] Ch 370 at 376. In view of the large number of supposed lettings affected, the ruling in *Lace v Chantler* had to be reversed by retroactive legislation (see Validation of War-time Leases Act 1944, s 1(1)). Compare, however, *Mrs Levin, Ltd v Wellington Co-operative Book Society* [1947] NZLR 83 at 86 (upholding lease determinable automatically three months after the cessation of active hostilities in war).

14 *Congregational Christian Church v Iosefa Tauga* (1982) 8 Comm Law Bull 129.

15 *Co Litt*, p 45; *Bl Comm*, Vol II, p 143.

16 Law of Property Act 1925, s 205(1)(xxvii).

17 A tenancy for life under which no rent or premium is payable may, somewhat inconveniently, fall within the Settled Land Act 1925. See *Binions v Evans* [1972] Ch 359 at 370D, 372E-G (post, p 807).

18 Law of Property Act 1925, s 149(6).

fixed term thus created is determinable after the death of the original lessee (or the dropping of any other specified life) by the giving of at least one month's written notice.[19]

(ii) Lease until marriage   Likewise a lease terminable upon the marriage of the lessee is converted into a 90 year term, determinable after the marriage of the original lessee by the giving of at least one month's written notice.[20]

(iii) Perpetually renewable lease   A perpetually renewable lease again fails, for want of a clear finite point, to qualify as a valid leasehold term. In theory such a grant could endure for ever, but is now converted automatically by statute into a term of 2,000 years[1] determinable only by the lessee.[2] There is nowadays a tendency for the courts to lean against construing a lease as a perpetually renewable lease in the absence of an unequivocal covenant to this effect.[3]

(iv) Time-share lease   It is clear that a 'time-share lease' can easily be drafted in such manner as to satisfy the requirement of certain maximum duration. In *Cottage Holiday Associates Ltd v Customs and Excise Commissioners*,[4] Woolf J recognised that there is a distinction between the lease which created the time-share interest and the interest itself. The lease might continue for 80 years, but the time-share interest conferred by it comprised a term of only 80 holiday periods of one week each. On any construction, no difficulty could arise here in respect of fixed maximum duration, not least because the rule against perpetuities ensures the imposition of a strict outer limit on all interests granted by the time-sharing arrangement.[5]

(v) Periodic tenancy   It may be more difficult to sustain the argument that a periodic tenancy satisfies the requirement of certain maximum duration. It is clear that a periodic tenancy (eg a weekly or monthly tenancy) commonly takes effect as a number of periods or units which confer on the tenant an estate in the land.[6] It is equally clear that a periodic tenancy continues indefinitely until

---

19   The statutory conversion also operates in relation to a *contract* to create a lease determinable by death or marriage (Law of Property Act 1925, s 149(6)).
20   Law of Property Act 1925, s 149(6). See, however, *Bass Holdings Ltd v Lewis* [1986] 2 EGLR 40.
1   Law of Property Act 1922, s 145, Sch 15, para 1. See *Parkus v Greenwood* [1950] Ch 644 at 648; *Caerphilly Concrete Products Ltd v Owen* [1972] 1 WLR 372 at 375F, 378C.
2   Law of Property Act 1922, Sch 15, para 10(1).
3   In order to qualify for statutory modification, the lease must contain an express covenant or obligation for perpetual renewal on identical terms. It is not enough, for instance, that a seven-year lease should contain a clause providing that if the tenant was desirous of taking a new lease and gave notice, the landlord would grant 'a new lease' for a further term of seven years 'at a rent to be agreed', and that 'such new lease' should contain a like covenant for renewal for a further seven years (see *Marjorie Burnett Ltd v Barclay* (1981) 258 Estates Gazette 642 at 644).
4   [1983] QB 735 at 740E-F.
5   See eg Perpetuities and Accumulations Act 1964, s 1(1).
6   *Commonwealth Life (Amalgamated) Assurance Ltd v Anderson* (1946) 46 SR (NSW) 47 at 49, 51; *Fink v McIntosh* [1946] VLR 290 at 292.

determined by the appropriate notice.[7] It constitutes 'an open-ended term with a series of possible termination dates which will only become effective if a valid notice to quit is served'.[8]

. In view of its open-ended nature the periodic tenancy is not viewed in English law as an aggregated series of distinct terms. Instead the units of time which constitute the periodic tenancy are seen as comprising one unbroken term which, unless and until duly determined, perpetually elongates itself by the superaddition of a fresh unit or period.[9] The term simply grows period by period 'as a single term springing from the original grant.'[10] There cannot be said to be a termination of one tenancy at the end of each period, followed by the commencement of a new letting or 'renewal' of the old letting.[11]

This being so, it is uncertain at the outset of a periodic tenancy what will be the maximum duration of the term created. As Russell LJ pointed out in *In re Midland Railway Co's Agreement*,[12] it 'cannot be predicated that in no circumstances will it exceed, for instance, 50 years'. In other words, the periodic tenancy has a certain *terminus a quo* but no certain *terminus ad quem*. In spite of this difficulty there is no serious doubt as to the leasehold quality of the periodic tenancy. The doctrinal embarrassment has been averted in several ways. It can be argued that the periodic tenancy passes the test of certain maximum duration in the sense that each occupational unit of time, as it is added to the preceding unit of time, is itself of strictly defined duration.[13] If, however, the common law requires that the maximum duration of a term be certainly known *in advance of its taking effect*, it may simply have to be conceded, as it was by Russell LJ in *In re Midland Railway Co's Agreement*,[14] that this

---

7 Post, p 485. By its very nature, a periodic tenancy does not expire by reason of the effluxion of time (*Queen's Club Gardens Estates Ltd v Bignell* [1924] 1 KB 117 at 130; *Mitchell v Wieriks, ex parte Wieriks* [1975] Qd R 100 at 102D).

8 Frank Webb, *Notices to quit by one joint tenant*, [1983] Conv 194 at 209.

9 *Legg v Strudwick* (1709) 2 Salk 414, 91 ER 359; *Jones v Mills* (1861) 10 CB NS 788 at 798, 142 ER 664 at 667; *Gandy v Jubber* (1865) 9 B & S 15 at 18, 122 ER 914 at 916; *Bowen v Anderson* [1894] 1 QB 164 at 167; *Queen's Club Gardens Estates Ltd v Bignell* [1924] 1 KB 117 at 130. It is for this reason that it is quite possible that a weekly tenancy may 'continue from week to week quite as long as a yearly tenancy from year to year' (*Jones v Chappell* (1875) LR 20 Eq 539 at 544).

10 *In re Midland Railway Co's Agreement* [1971] Ch 725 at 732F. For further recognition of the integrity of the original letting, see *Oxley v James* (1844) 13 M & W 209 at 214, 153 ER 87 at 89; *Bowen v Anderson* [1894] 1 QB 164 at 167; *Amad v Grant, Grosglik v Grant* (1947) 74 CLR 327 at 336; *In re Belajev* (1979) 22 SASR 1 at 4.

11 See *Jones v Chappell* (1875) LR 20 Eq 539 at 544. Compare, however, the careless remarks of Somervell LJ in *Leek & Moorlands Building Society v Clark* [1952] 2 QB 788 at 793. For the distinction between a periodic yearly tenancy and a perpetually renewable one-year tenancy, see *Gray v Spyer* [1922] 2 Ch 22 at 38f. It is significant (post, p 438) that the continuation of a periodic tenancy does not depend on the exercise after each unit of time of some kind of option to renew the letting. The tenancy continues as an integral term until duly determined by notice, and it has been pointed out that the true analogy for a notice to quit is with a break notice (see F. Webb, [1983] Conv 194 at 208).

12 [1971] Ch 725 at 732F. See [1971] CLJ 198 (D. MacIntyre). Compare, however, *Centaploy Ltd v Matlodge Ltd* [1974] Ch 1 at 11C; (1973) 89 LQR 457.

13 'Whether the tenancy be from year to year, quarter to quarter, month to month, or week to week, it is a tenancy for a definite term of a year, a quarter, a month, or a week, as the case may be, with the superadded provision that it is to continue for another definite term of the same period, unless, by proper notice to quit, it is terminated...' (*Commonwealth Life (Amalgamated) Assurance Ltd v Anderson* (1946) 46 SR (NSW) 47 at 50f).

14 [1971] Ch 725 at 732F-G.

requirement 'cannot...have direct reference to periodic tenancies.' In *Street v Mountford*[15] the House of Lords sidestepped the problem, taking the view that a tenancy arose from the grant of exclusive possession 'for a term at a rent'. That 'term' could be either a 'fixed or periodic term certain'.[16]

(vi) Service tenancy   In so far as a service occupancy is simply expressed as being co-terminous with the occupier's employment by the owner of property, there may be doubt as to whether the occupancy can constitute a tenancy. If the employee's employment, and therefore his occupancy of service accommodation, are of uncertain maximum duration, it may be that the common law requirement necessary for a leasehold estate is absent.[17] However, it is much more likely that where a periodic rent is paid for a service occupancy, there will arise an irresistible inference that there exists a periodic tenancy terminable by the appropriate notice in the event that the employment comes to an end.[18]

(4) The demised premises must be identified with certainty

All lands and all interests in land 'lie in grant',[19] and may therefore be made the subject matter of a lease or tenancy.[20] This carries the corollary that a lease may convey to the grantee not merely a corporeal hereditament but also various kinds of incorporeal hereditament. It is therefore quite possible to create a leasehold interest in a profit *à prendre* (such as shooting or fishing rights).[1]

(a) Conventions of leasehold conveyancing

Irrespective of the precise nature of the letting, it is a clear rule that the subject matter of a term of years must be described and identified with certainty.[2] This requirement is usually satisfied without excessive difficulty, particularly since the boundaries of the demised properties are often regarded as fixed, in the absence of contrary intention, by reference to certain conventions of leasehold conveyancing which have become rules of law. Thus, for instance, the external

15   [1985] AC 809 at 818C, 826G.
16   [1985] AC 809 at 818E. See also Lord Templeman's reference (at 826E) to a 'periodical term'.
17   See eg *Ball v Crawford* [1981] BCL 627 (New Zealand High Court). However, English courts seem not to have been particularly sensitive to the existence of this problem (see eg *Scrimgeour v Waller* (1981) 257 Estates Gazette 61).
18   This approach simply reduces the issue to the problem already dealt with in relation to periodic tenancies. The rationalisation seems attractive, but is not supported, for instance, by *Lace v Chantler* [1944] KB 368 at 370f (ante, p 435) where, in analogous circumstances, the payment of a weekly rent for an uncertain period did not save the arrangement from being void as a lease.
19   Law of Property Act 1925, s 51(1).
20   For a definition of 'land', see Chapter 2 (ante, p 16).
1   However, a lease of an incorporeal hereditament (eg where the grantee of a profit *à prendre* carves out a lesser interest in the profit for a stranger) cannot confer 'exclusive possession' in the sense of a right to exclude the owner of the title to the land (*Duke of Sutherland v Heathcote* [1892] 1 Ch 475 at 484). The lessee has at most a right to 'possession of his property, namely the incorporeal hereditament and its products' (*Hindmarsh v Quinn* (1914) 17 CLR 622 at 636). As lessee of the profit, however, he may defend his 'exclusive possession' of the profit by action in trespass (see *Swayne v Howells* [1927] 1 KB 385 at 393; *Mason v Clarke* [1955] AC 778 at 794).
2   *Goldsworthy Mining Ltd v Federal Commissioner of Taxation* (1972-1973) 128 CLR 199 at 211.

wall enclosing the demised premises is normally regarded as part of those premises.[3] A conveyance of a lease also passes void spaces above false ceilings in a flat.[4]

(b) Fluctuating boundaries

It is in any event sufficient that the description of the subject matter of a lease or tenancy is such as to enable the boundaries of the property to be ascertained or identified at any given time. Where, for example, the area of demised land fluctuates with changes in a littoral boundary caused by accretion,[5] the requirement of certainty is adequately met. The territorial limit of the lease is readily ascertainable, since it can simply be measured with reference to the surface as it exists from time to time.[6]

(5) A lease must confer a right of exclusive possession

It is an essential characteristic of any lease or tenancy that the grantee should be given a right to 'exclusive possession' of the demised premises,[7] and there can be no tenancy as such unless the occupier enjoys exclusive possession.[8] A grantee on whom has been conferred any lesser right cannot under any circumstances be a tenant,[9] for the right to exclusive possession is a *sine qua non* of the landlord-tenant relationship.

(a) Exclusive possession as territorial control

As Windeyer J declared in *Radaich v Smith*,[10] the legal right to exclusive possession is 'the proper touchstone' of the lease or tenancy.[11] In particular, it is usually this element alone which confers the degree of territorial control necessary to enable the tenant effectively to carry out the purpose (whether commercial or residential) for which he took the letting.[12] The common law requirement of 'exclusive possession' is a constant reminder of the fact that

3　*Sturge v Hackett* [1962] 1 WLR 1257 at 1265. A lease of a flat prima facie conveys an estate in the external walls of that flat, but not in the external walls of other flats in the same building (*Campden Hill Towers Ltd v Gardner* [1977] QB 823 at 834F-G).

4　*Graystone Property Investments Ltd v Margulies* (1983) 269 Estates Gazette 538 at 541f (ante, p 26).

5　Ante, p 32.

6　*Goldsworthy Mining Ltd v Federal Commissioner of Taxation* (1972-1973) 128 CLR 199 at 211f.

7　See *Wright v Stavert* (1860) 2 E & E 721 at 727, 121 ER 270 at 273; *Radaich v Smith* (1959) 101 CLR 209 at 214 ('The true test of a supposed lease is whether exclusive possession is conferred upon the putative lessee'); *Hull v Parsons* [1962] NZLR 465 at 468.

8　*Street v Mountford* [1985] AC 809 at 818E per Lord Templeman. Thus, for example, the right to park a car in a large garage can take the form of a lease only if the right relates to an identified parking bay rather than to the entire parking area in general (see *Harley Queen v Forsyte Kerman* [1983] CLY 2077).

9　See *Street v Mountford* [1985] AC 809 at 816C. Such a grantee will be in most cases a mere licensee (see eg *Wilson v Tavener* [1901] 1 Ch 578 at 581; *Peakin v Peakin* [1895] 2 IR 359 at 362; *Daalman v Oosterdijk* [1973] 1 NZLR 717 at 720).

10　(1959) 101 CLR 209 at 223.

11　See also *Armstrong v Armstrong* [1970] 1 NSWR 133 at 135; *Goldsworthy Mining Ltd v Federal Commissioner of Taxation* (1972-1973) 128 CLR 199 at 212.

12　See *Radaich v Smith* (1959) 101 CLR 209 at 215, 217.

privacy is seen as an intrinsic component of ownership of an 'estate' within the capitalist concept of property.[13]

The authority of the Australian High Court in *Radaich v Smith* was enthusiastically endorsed by the House of Lords in *Street v Mountford*,[14] which pointed out that the hallmark of exclusive possession is entirely consistent with the 'elevation of a tenancy into an estate in land.'[15] Lord Templeman acknowledged that the tenant with exclusive possession 'is able to exercise the rights of an owner of land, which is in the real sense his land albeit temporarily and subject to certain restrictions.'[16] One of the most dramatic indicia of his ownership of an estate in land is the ability of the tenant to 'keep out strangers and keep out the landlord unless the landlord is exercising limited rights reserved to him by the tenancy agreement to enter and view and repair.'[17] It is thus a fundamental characteristic of a term of years—whether the term is long or short—that the tenant's right of exclusive possession gives him a degree of physical control over the demised premises which enables him to vindicate his ownership by way of an action in trespass even as against his own landlord.[18] Conversely an arrangement under which an owner has genuinely reserved a contractual right to exclude an occupier from the premises for a specific portion of each day may be destructive of any claim to exclusive possession and therefore of any claim to a tenancy.[19]

(b) 'Exclusive possession' distinguished from 'exclusive occupation'

The key element of 'overall control' later becomes vital in distinguishing between the 'exclusive possession' which is indicative of a true tenancy and the 'exclusive occupation' which often characterises many licences.[20] 'Exclusive occupation' is not synonymous with the right of 'exclusive possession' which is the attribute of a tenancy. It is often the case that persons who are allowed to enjoy sole occupation in fact are not necessarily to be taken as having been given a right of 'exclusive possession' in law.[1] Many contractual licensees and lodgers (eg students in university halls of residence, residents in a hotel, and persons living in an old people's home) undoubtedly enjoy sole occupation in this sense, but equally clearly have no tenancy.[2]

---

13   Ante, p 14.

14   [1985] AC 809 (post, p 449).

15   [1985] AC 809 at 814E-F, 816B. See Law of Property Act 1925, s 1(1)(b) (ante, p 78).

16   It has always been clearly recognised that the tenant's right to exclusive possession is not inconsistent with the imposition of restrictions as to the uses to which he may put the land (see *Glenwood Lumber Co Ltd v Phillips* [1904] AC 405 at 408; *Re British American Oil Co Ltd and DePass* (1960) 21 DLR (2d) 110 at 117ff).

17   [1985] AC 809 at 816B-C. See also *Lewis v Bell* [1985] 1 NSWLR 731 at 734F-G. It is widely accepted that a reservation to the landlord, either by contract or statute, of a limited right of entry for the purpose of viewing or repairing the premises, is not inconsistent with a tenant's right of exclusive possession (see eg *Radaich v Smith* (1959) 101 CLR 209 at 222). For a statutory right of entry, see Landlord and Tenant Act 1985, ss 8(2) (post, p 917), 11(6).

18   See *Wright v Stavert* (1860) 2 E & E 721 at 728f, 121 ER 270 at 273; *Stocker v Planet Building Society* [1879] 27 WR 877 at 878.

19   See eg *Markou v Da Silvaesa* (1986) 52 P & CR 204 at 222 (post, p 456), where throughout an agreement for 26 weeks' occupation, the owner had effectively reserved a contractual right to exclude the occupiers from their residence every day between 10.30 a.m. and 12.00 midday.

20   Post, p 446.

1   *Radaich v Smith* (1959) 101 CLR 209 at 223.

2   Post, p 455.

(c) Circumstances negating exclusive possession

Any attempt to confer a right of 'exclusive possession' on two or more persons simultaneously otherwise than as joint tenants or tenants in common[3] must inevitably be self-contradictory and meaningless.[4] It follows, *a fortiori*, that if premises are shared in joint occupation with the supposed landlord, so that exclusive possession cannot be claimed by either, there is no question of tenancy.[5] An occupier's mere possession of a key to the premises constitutes proof neither of 'exclusive possession' nor of 'exclusive occupation'.[6]

(6) Rent or other consideration

An obligation on the part of the tenant to pay rent or, more properly, to perform 'rent-service', has been traditionally considered to be an integral aspect of the tenurial relationship of landlord and tenant. Correspondingly, the landlord's right to receive rent or 'rent-service' has tended to be regarded as a normal incident annexed to his reversion in the land. In recent years, however, there has been a distinct movement away from this tenurial view towards a more contractual analysis of the concept of rent. The courts have begun to characterise rent as not so much the incident of a kind of tenure, but rather the contractual consideration paid in return for the tenant's right of exclusive possession.[7]

(a) Necessity for rent or other money payment

When seen from the viewpoint of the landlord, the lease or tenancy is nowadays primarily an instrument for the commercial exploitation of land. Most leases and tenancies are therefore granted expressly in consideration of money or money's worth, in which case the leasehold character of the arrangement is quite clear. In order to create a leasehold interest, however, it is not in strict terms essential that a rent should be reserved,[8] although in the absence of an express covenant for rent the common law is fairly ready to imply a promise to

---

3 Ante, p 295.
4 *Wetherby Apartments v Tootell* (Unreported, Court of Appeal, 27 October 1981); *Hindmarsh v Quinn* (1914) 17 CLR 622 at 630.
5 *Pearch v Gycha* (1953) 73 WN (NSW) 122; *Walliker v Deveaux* (1959) 78 WN (NSW) 409 at 410; *Armstrong v Armstrong* [1970] 1 NSWR 133 at 135.
6 *Michel v Volpe* (1967) 202 Estates Gazette 213. Moreover, the possibility of tenancy may well be negatived if the owner retains a key and uses it for occasional access (see *Garland v Johnson* (Unreported, Court of Appeal, 24 February 1982); *Markou v Da Silvaesa* (1986) 52 P & CR 204 at 211, 222).
7 See eg *C.H. Bailey Ltd v Memorial Enterprises Ltd* [1974] 1 WLR 728 at 732B-D, 735B-C; *United Scientific Holdings Ltd v Burnley BC* [1978] AC 904 at 935A.
8 See *Knight's Case* (1588) 5 Co Rep 54b at 55a, 77 ER 137 at 138; *Re British American Oil Co Ltd and DePass* (1960) 21 DLR (2d) 110 at 115. The presence or absence of a rent seems to be irrelevant to the definition of a 'term of years' in Law of Property Act 1925, s 205(1)(xxvii), although the absence of a money rent may have the effect of precluding a tenancy from some special forms of statutory protection (see eg Rent Act 1977, s 5(1), post, p 983). It may be significant, as the contractual rather than tenurial view of the leasehold relationship nowadays gains predominance, that the courts are beginning to suggest that the payment of rent is a sine qua non of a tenancy (see eg *Street v Mountford* [1985] AC 809 at 818C, 821B, 826E per Lord Templeman; *Scrimgeour v Waller* (1981) 257 Estates Gazette 61 at 63 per Sir David Cairns).

pay reasonable compensation for the loss of land use caused to the landlord by reason of the occupation of the tenant.[9]

(b) Certainty of rent obligation

Where a rent[10] is reserved in the terms of a lease or tenancy, that rent must be either certain or capable of being calculated with certainty at the due date for payment.[11] The historic rationale for the requirement of a 'rent certain' is that the landlord's remedy of distress for unpaid rent (ie, the right to remove goods to the value of the default[12]) can operate only where the rent obligation is clearly defined.[13]

(i) Variable rent Under this qualified requirement of certainty, it is quite possible that the rent due from the tenant may fluctuate over time,[14] even if the fluctuation is wholly the result of unilateral decision by the landlord. The variability of the rent obligation is irrelevant so long as the rent payable is ascertainable with certainty at the due date for payment. Thus a leasehold provision that a council tenant's rent is 'liable to be increased or decreased on notice being given' is not void for uncertainty, even though such a clause admittedly renders the rent level 'dependent...on the whim of the landlords.'[15]

(ii) Indeterminate rent Although the courts are disinclined to strike down purposeful transactions as void on the ground of uncertainty,[16] there are some circumstances in which a tenancy is inevitably invalidated by uncertainty as to the rent obligation. Thus a tenancy 'at a rent to be agreed' is vitiated by uncertainty,[17] at least where the tenancy contains no formula for quantifying

9   See *Dean and Chapter of Rochester v Pierce* (1808) 1 Camp 466 at 467, 170 ER 1023. However, it may not necessarily follow that a tenancy always arises wherever the landowner demands compensation for use and occupation. See *Northern Ireland Housing Executive v McCann* [1979] NI 39 at 43E (regular payments demanded from squatters in initially unlawful occupation).

10 For the rules of certainty in relation to the capital purchase price of options to renew a lease or to purchase a reversion, see Chapter 7 (ante, p 136).

11 *Greater London Council v Connolly* [1970] 2 QB 100 at 109A. If the rent, although quantifiable at the due date, has not yet been ascertained, it cannot be demanded retrospectively for periods preceding the date when it finally is quantified (*Re Essoldo (Bingo) Ltd's Underlease* (1971) 23 P & CR 1 at 4f).

12 Post, p 510.

13 See *In re Knight, ex parte Voisey* (1882) 21 Ch D 442 at 457; *Greater London Council v Connolly* [1970] 2 QB 100 at 112D; *United Scientific Holdings Ltd v Burnley BC* [1978] AC 904 at 935B-C. For evidence of the diminishing impact in this area of the conceptual restrictions imposed by the largely archaic law of distress, see *T & E Homes Ltd v Robinson* [1979] 1 WLR 452 at 456H-457A.

14 Coke gave the example of a rent-service comprising the shearing of 'all the sheep pasturing within the lord's manor' (*Co Litt*, p 96a). See also *Kendall v Baker* (1852) 11 CB 842 at 850, 138 ER 706 at 710 (rent riding on the price of wheat).

15 *Greater London Council v Connolly* [1970] 2 QB 100 at 109D, 111H. A rent may be validly tied to some index of inflation (see eg *Blumenthal v Gallery Five Ltd* (1971) 220 Estates Gazette 31 at 33; *Re Collins Cartage & Storage Co Ltd and McDonald* (1981) 116 DLR (3d) 570 at 571f; *Trifid Pty Ltd v Ratto* [1985] WAR 19 at 29).

16 *Greater London Council v Connolly* [1970] 2 QB 100 at 108F; *Brown v Gould* [1972] Ch 53 at 56F.

17 *King's Motors (Oxford) Ltd v Lax* [1970] 1 WLR 426 at 429A; *King v King* (1980) *The Times*, 26 June; *Young v Van Beneen* [1953] 3 DLR 702 at 704f.

the rent.[18] However, a tenancy is not regarded as being void for uncertainty merely because the rent is to be fixed 'having regard to the market value of the premises'[19] or is to be quantified as the current 'market rental'.[20] The concept of 'market rental' has a well known meaning in the context of landlord-tenant negotiations, and the courts will, if necessary, provide machinery for assessing the value of such a rental in any given case.[1]

(iii) Rent in kind Although it is usual for rent to be expressly reserved in money terms, there is no objection in principle to a rent which is fixed in some other way,[2] eg in the form of services in kind,[3] bottles of wine,[4] or other chattels.[5] Where a rent is fixed in money terms, nothing turns on the adequacy of the consideration.[6]

2. THE DISTINCTION BETWEEN 'LEASE' AND 'LICENCE'

A lease (or tenancy) confers upon the occupier a proprietary estate to which is annexed a right of exclusive possession enforceable against all persons including the landlord.[7] By contrast, a licence confers upon the occupier not an estate in the land but merely a personal permission to occupy.[8] When described in abstract terms, the lease appears wholly different in nature from the licence. However, the distinction has proved in practice to be much more problematical,[9] not least because the factual and physical evidence of a lease 'on the ground' often seems to differ in no substantial respect from that of a contractual licence. Both cases may well involve the payment of a rent in return for the right to some form of exclusive occupancy for a pre-fixed period of time.

---

18 *Brown v Gould* [1972] Ch 53 at 58C. In *Beer v Bowden (Note)* [1981] 1 WLR 522, the Court of Appeal upheld a lease for 10 years which fixed an annual rent for the first five years, but provided that thereafter the rent should be such rent 'as shall...be agreed'. Geoffrey Lane LJ indicated (at [1981] 1 WLR 522 at 527G-H) that the lease was saved from voidness only by reason of the tenant's 'subsisting estate in land' and the concession by the tenant that 'some rent must be paid in respect of these premises'. The Court implied an obligation to pay a 'fair rent'.

19 *Brown v Gould* [1972] Ch 53 at 61F, 62C.

20 *Andrews v Colonial Mutual Life Assurance Society Ltd* [1982] 2 NZLR 556 at 565.

1   *Andrews v Colonial Mutual Life Assurance Society Ltd* [1982] 2 NZLR 556 at 565. See also *Sudbrook Trading Estate Ltd v Eggleton* [1983] 1 AC 444 at 484A per Lord Fraser of Tullybelton (ante, p 136).

2   *Co Litt*, p 142a. However, it does not necessarily follow that non-monetary forms of consideration will necessarily constitute 'rent' for all legal purposes. See eg Rent Act 1977, s 5(1) (post, p 973).

3   *Co Litt*, p 96a (ante, p 442); *Doe d Tucker v Morse* (1830) 1 B & Ad 365 at 369, 109 ER 822 at 824; *Duke of Marlborough v Osborn* (1864) 5 B & S 67 at 74, 122 ER 758 at 761; *Barnes v Barratt* [1970] 2 QB 657 at 666D, 670F-G.

4   *Pitcher v Tovey* (1692) 4 Mod 71 at 75f, 87 ER 268 at 271.

5   *Co Litt*, p 142a. It is not impossible that the rent should be the annual rendering of one peppercorn.

6   *Royal Philanthropic Society v County* (1985) 276 Estates Gazette 1068 at 1072.

7   Ante, p 440.

8   See *Street v Mountford* [1985] AC 809 at 816C. Licences are discussed in Chapter 15 (post, p 535).

9   See A. Waite, *Distinguishing between Tenancies and Licences*, (1980) 130 NLJ 939, 959.

(1) **Significance of the distinction**

The blurred nature of the distinction between the lease and the licence has been responsible for much of the confusion which was until recently endemic in the law of landlord and tenant.[10] Yet the distinction—however elusive—is a vital determinant of a host of legal issues.

(a) *The common law of landlord and tenant*

In the common law of landlord and tenant the lease-licence distinction derives an immediate relevance from the fact that a proprietary estate in land is conferred by a lease but never by a licence. Only a tenant, for instance, has an estate in the land which is capable of assignment to a stranger.[11] Furthermore, it is orthodox teaching that leases—but not most kinds of licence—are capable of binding a transferee of land.[12] Only a tenant[13]—and not a licensee[14]—is entitled to sue a third party for nuisance or trespass. Only a tenant—and not a licensee—may properly be subject to the remedy of distress for arrears of rent.[15] A licensee—but not normally a tenant—is subject to the 'short-cut' summary procedure for the recovery of possession under RSC, Ord 113.[16]

(b) *The ambit of protective legislation*

The distinction between lease and licence is also vital in defining the coverage of various schemes of protective legislation. Perhaps the most controversial function of this conceptual divide has been to delineate the scope of full protection under the Rent Act 1977.[17] The ample benefits conferred by this Act apply only to the tenant and not to the licensee.[18] Similarly the distinction between lease and licence serves to fix the boundaries of the statutory code regulating business tenancies.[19] The definitional knife-edge separating lease

---

10 See *National Carriers Ltd v Panalpina (Northern) Ltd* [1981] AC 675 at 714A per Lord Roskill.
11 Post, p 463. See *Richardson v Landecker* (1950) 50 SR (NSW) 250 at 255; *Lewis v Bell* [1985] 1 NSWLR 731 at 735G.
12 Ante, p 85.
13 *Harper v Charlesworth*(1825) 4 B & C 574 at 585, 107 ER 1174 at 1178; *Street v Mountford* [1985] AC 809 at 816B-C (ante, p 440). It seems that, in order to maintain an action in trespass, the tenant must be in possession (see *Simpson v Knowles* [1974] VR 190 at 195).
14 A licensee has no right to sue a third person in respect of a disturbance of his rights (*Hill v Tupper* (1863) 2 H & C 121 at 127, 159 ER 51 at 53 (post, p 648)). See also *Hull v Parsons* [1962] NZLR 465 at 467f (nuisance and trespass); *Malone v Laskey* [1907] 2 KB 141 at 151 (nuisance); *Nunn v Parkes & Co* (1924) 158 LT Jo 431 (nuisance); *Simpson v Knowles* [1974] VR 190 at 195 (trespass); *Oldham v Lawson (No 1)* [1976] VR 654 at 657 (nuisance); *Moore v MacMillan* [1977] 2 NZLR 81 at 89 (trespass); *Lewisham BC v Roberts* [1949] 2 KB 608 at 622.
15 The assertion by the owner of a right to distrain upon the goods of the occupier may operate virtually as an estoppel, precluding the owner from any future claim that the occupier had merely a licence (see eg *Carden v Choudhury* (Unreported, Court of Appeal, 29 February 1984)).
16 *Markou v Da Silvaesa* (1986) 52 P & CR 204 at 226.
17 Post, p 961.
18 Rent Act 1977, s 1 (post, p 971). A contractual licence may, however, qualify for the limited protection given to 'restricted contracts' (post, p 1040).
19 Landlord and Tenant Act 1954, s 23(1). The distinction between tenancy and licence is now no longer vital to the operation of the protective codes regulating either secure tenancies (see Housing Act 1985, s 79(3)) or agricultural tenancies (see Agricultural Holdings Act 1986, s 2(2)(b)).

from licence may also affect even wider categories of problems, ranging from the level of compensation payable to a householder on compulsory purchase[20] to the quantification of entitlement to supplementary benefits[1] and the allocation of legal liability for defective premises.[2]

(c) Rare instances of superior protection for the licensee

Although it is generally true that a tenancy confers on the occupier a greater degree of legal protection than does a licence in equivalent circumstances, this is not always the case. A licensee may sue the licensor in negligence for failure to exercise reasonable care in safeguarding the licensee's belongings from burglary.[3] A similar claim on behalf of a tenant founders on the fact that the tenant is the owner of an 'estate' in the land and is himself responsible for the defence of his right to exclusive possession of that land. It is also significant that various forms of licence in land—notably the 'irrevocable licence' or licence based on proprietary estoppel—have been accorded a degree of security of tenure which may well exceed that conferred by a tenancy.[4]

(2) Competing criteria of exclusive possession and expressed intention

The recent history of the law of landlord and tenant has been heavily influenced by the constant opposition of two factors, both of which have claimed primacy as the determinants of whether a given occupancy ranks in law as a tenancy or as a licence. These two factors are, respectively, the elements of exclusive possession and the expressed intention of the parties. It is clear in retrospect that these apparently disparate elements interact in large measure and some degree of confusion, in terms of both substantive law and legal terminology, was perhaps inescapable. As always in the law of landlord and tenant, this confusion has been more readily apparent in the law of residential tenancies than in respect of commercial lettings.

(a) Historical primacy of exclusive possession

It used formerly to be quite clear that a tenancy rather than a licence was the inevitable product of any agreement which conferred a right of 'exclusive possession' at a rent for a defined period.[5] This moderately sharp boundary between the lease and the licence had existed from medieval times,[6] and tended to minimise dispute as to the character of various kinds of occupancy.

The overriding significance of 'exclusive possession' prevailed in the caselaw

---

20 See *David v LB of Lewisham* (1977) 34 P & CR 112 at 115f; *McHugh v LB of Islington* (1984) 270 Estates Gazette 1095 at 1096 (post, p 460).
1   See (1984) 59 Welfare Rights Bulletin 2.
2   Defective Premises Act 1972, s 4(1) (post, p 800). See *Wheat v E. Lacon & Co Ltd* [1966] AC 552 at 579A-B, 579F-580A; *McDonagh v Kent AHA* (Unreported, Court of Appeal, 7 October 1985).
3   *Appah v Parncliffe Investments Ltd* [1964] 1 WLR 1064 at 1067.
4   See eg *Hardwick v Johnson* [1978] 1 WLR 683 at 689H (post, p 800).
5   See eg *Marcroft Wagons Ltd v Smith* [1951] 2 KB 496 at 501; *Landale v Menzies* (1909) 9 CLR 89 at 100f.
6   See [1985] CLJ 351 at 352.

relating to residential accommodation until the mid-1970s.[7] This caselaw demonstrates fairly clearly that the factual enjoyment of exclusive occupation was effectively taken to be a conclusive indication of tenancy except in those relatively rare instances where the 'possession' apparently pertaining to an actual occupier could more properly be attributed instead to some other person as the relevant 'estate' owner. In such cases the occupier had no legal right of 'exclusive possession' but merely a de facto privilege of 'exclusive occupation',[8] a fine distinction which turns not on the quality of 'exclusiveness' but rather on the definition of 'possession'.[9]

(i) 'Exclusive possession' distinguished from 'exclusive occupation' The exceptional cases in which exclusive occupancy still gave rise to a licence comprised those circumstances where in reality overall territorial control of the premises was exercised not by the actual occupier but by the landowner himself. The landowner thus retained 'possession' in its strict legal sense, and the actual occupier was left with a mere *factum* of 'exclusive occupation'. In such circumstances the occupier's status was at best that of a contractual licensee, even though his occupation might be for a fixed period and in consideration of the payment of 'rent'. If it could not even be shown that the parties had intended to enter into a legally binding relationship, the occupier's status was simply that of a bare licensee.

(ii) The 'Facchini v Bryson categories' The approach outlined above found perhaps its foremost expression in *Facchini v Bryson*.[10] Here, after reviewing the contemporary caselaw, Denning LJ indicated that exclusive occupation for a fixed period at a rent pointed invariably towards the existence of a tenancy except in those cases where 'there has been something in the circumstances, such as a family arrangement, an act of friendship or generosity, or such like, to negative any intention to create a tenancy.'[11] Where accommodation was provided in such circumstances, the occupier might well enjoy exclusive occupation. Nevertheless there was present in each of Denning LJ's examples some limiting factor which effectively denied the occupier that degree of overall control which is intrinsic to the legal right to 'exclusive possession'. The occupier could not with credibility claim either that he had a 'stake' in the

---

7   It is sometimes thought that the turning-point occurred earlier in *Cobb v Lane* [1952] 1 All ER 1199. However, the effect of this decision was simply to mark the abandonment of the old doctrine that a 'tenancy at will' (ante, p 430) arose once a person had been in exclusive occupation of another's land for an *indefinite* period (see eg *Doe d Tomes v Chamberlaine* (1839) 5 M & W 14 at 16, 151 ER 7; *Lynes v Snaith* [1899] 1 QB 486 at 488). Notwithstanding this movement away from the 'tenancy at will' (see *Heslop v Burns* [1974] 1 WLR 1241 at 1252A-G), the caselaw until the mid-1970s can still be rationalised on the basis that exclusive occupation at a rent for a term always gave rise to a tenancy in the true sense except in the circumstances referred to in the '*Facchini v Bryson* categories'.

8   This distinction was explained earlier (ante, p 440), and was well understood in the last century. In *Bradley v Baylis* (1881) 8 QBD 195 at 216, Jessel MR spoke (albeit in slightly different terminology) of the 'guest at an inn, or a visitor at a country house, who may have the exclusive use of a room, and yet not be in occupation of it, in a legal sense.'

9   Ante, p 439.

10   [1952] 1 TLR 1386 at 1389.

11   The '*Facchini v Bryson* categories' are examined in greater detail later in this chapter (post, p 457).

property or that he was entitled to invoke the law of trespass in defence of an 'estate' in the land.

The general effect of the *Facchini v Bryson* approach was that until the mid-1970s an exclusive occupancy of residential premises was regarded as giving rise to a licence only if that occupancy involved some domestic or quasi-familial element, or if the motivation behind the provision of accommodation was charitable or therapeutic, or was in some other way entirely personal to the particular occupier. In view of the cyclical movement of the law during the last ten years, it may well be true that most of the *Facchini v Bryson* categories still represent good law today.[12]

(b) Intrusion of paramount intention

For some 25 years the '*Facchini v Bryson* categories' operated to ensure a heavy bias towards a tenancy characterisation in most cases of exclusive occupancy. During the mid-1970s, however, the controlling influence of these categories came to be questioned. An important catalyst in the process was the steady proliferation of the occupation licence as a prominent mode of land-holding in the rented housing sector.[13] The emergence of the accommodation licence can be attributed very largely to the desire of property owners to escape the significant extension of Rent Act control from 1965 onwards.[14] It became increasingly attractive to avoid the effect of this legislation through the granting to residential occupiers of a contractual licence rather than a tenancy. However, this method of circumventing the Rent Acts remained suspect so long as the '*Facchini v Bryson* categories' imposed severe limits on the classes of case in which 'exclusive occupation' could be enjoyed outside the landlord-tenant relationship.

(i) Rejection of the 'Facchini v Bryson categories'   It was against this background that the stranglehold of the '*Facchini v Bryson* categories' was successfully challenged in 1978 in *Somma v Hazelhurst and Savelli*.[15] Here, in circumstances which were physically indistinguishable from those of most joint tenancies, a property owner purported to grant a young cohabiting couple two separate residential occupation 'licences' in respect of their shared double room.[16] The case clearly failed to qualify under any of the *Facchini v Bryson* criteria, being a straightforward instance of a commercial transaction concluded between persons dealing at arm's length. Nevertheless the Court of Appeal not only declined to overturn the superficial label of licence. It rejected the relevance of the '*Facchini v Bryson* categories' altogether, elevating in their place a test based on the expressed intentions of the parties. Cumming-Bruce LJ saw 'no reason why an ordinary landlord not in any of these special categories should not be able to grant a licence to occupy an ordinary house.'[17] If both parties intended

---

12   Post, p 457.
13   See *Heslop v Burns* [1974] 1 WLR 1241 at 1252C-D per Scarman LJ.
14   Post, p 994.
15   [1978] 1 WLR 1014. See [1979] CLJ 38.
16   The licences were supposedly for 'non-exclusive occupation', but this qualification appears to have been included merely as a sham device to preclude the occupiers from claiming the 'exclusive possession' which is the *sine qua non* of a tenancy (post, p 998).
17   [1978] 1 WLR 1014 at 1024H-1025A. See also *Sturolson & Co v Weniz* (1984) 272 Estates Gazette 326 at 329f.

to create a licence and could 'frame any written agreement in such a way as to demonstrate that it is not really an agreement for a lease masquerading as a licence', the Court could detect no 'reason in law or justice why they should be prevented from achieving that object.'

From this point onwards, the expressed intention of the parties became the governing test of the distinction between a tenancy and a licence.[18] In effect the legal status of an occupancy could be dictated by the expressly imposed intention of the stronger bargaining party, who, in the residential sector at least, was almost inevitably the landlord.[19] The only constraint on this process stemmed from the courts' reservation of a residual power to renounce a 'sham' transaction. This power was exercised in only the rarest of cases.[20]

(ii) High point of the relevance of expressed intention   The primacy accorded to expressed intention as the arbiter of the tenancy-licence distinction reached its zenith in 1984 in the decision of the Court of Appeal in *Street v Mountford.*[1] Here, in an ordinary commercial setting in the residential sector, the occupier was given a right of exclusive occupancy of a self-contained flat on payment of a weekly 'licence fee'. The agreement signed by the occupier was expressly described as a 'licence agreement', and the occupier specifically and in writing disavowed any intention to take a tenancy.[2]

The Court of Appeal held that, while the 'fact of exclusive occupation' was 'a most important pointer' as to the intentions of the parties, 'their true intentions are the decisive consideration in determining whether an agreement creates a tenancy...or a licence.'[3] Here the unequivocal written acknowledgement by the occupier that no tenancy was intended was conclusive in favour of a licence characterisation.[4] The Court of Appeal disregarded the fact that, judged in subjective terms, the occupier almost certainly had not shared the owner's desire to create merely a licence. In Slade LJ's view, the issue was one of objective intention, in that the true question was 'not what the defendant wanted to get but what [she] actually got.'[5] The Court supported its finding of licence by detailed reference to the clauses of the written agreement, which it described as bearing almost exclusively 'the hallmarks of a licence rather than a tenancy'.[6]

This decision, reached—it is fair to say—with some considerable misgiving,[7]

---

18   This approach was applied not merely in the residential sector but also in relation to business tenancies (see *Rossvale Ltd v Green* (1979) 250 Estates Gazette 1183; *Matchams Park (Holdings) Ltd v Dommett* (1984) 272 Estates Gazette 549 at 555).

19   See eg *Aldrington Garages Ltd v Fielder* (1978) 37 P & CR 461 at 468; *Sturolson & Co v Weniz* (1984) 272 Estates Gazette 326 at 329f.

20   Post, p 996.

1   (1984) 49 P & CR 324, (1984) 271 Estates Gazette 1261. See (1984) 81 Law Soc Gaz 2355 (P.H. Kenny); [1984] JSWL 292 (M.A. Jones).

2   The owner of the flat—a local solicitor—has since said that this form of agreement was explicitly framed with reference to the decisions emerging from the Court of Appeal during the period 1977-1979. He claimed to have 'decided to take the Court of Appeal at its word and drafted a document, using the simplest possible terms, expressed to be a personal non-assignable licence' (see R. Street, *Coach and Horses Trip Cancelled?*, [1985] Conv 328 at 329).

3   (1984) 49 P & CR 324 at 330 per Slade LJ.

4   (1984) 49 P & CR 324 at 331f.

5   (1984) 49 P & CR 324 at 333, quoting *Aldrington Garages Ltd v Fielder* (1979) 37 P & CR 461 at 476 per Stephenson LJ.

6   (1984) 49 P & CR 324 at 329.

7   Post, p 998.

was to precipitate a quite dramatic reversal of judicial policy when the case reached the House of Lords.

(c) Reinstatement of the primacy of exclusive possession

The House of Lords in *Street v Mountford*[8] overturned the conclusion of the Court of Appeal and decided that the facts of the case disclosed the existence of a tenancy rather than a licence. In so doing, the House of Lords overruled *Somma v Hazelhurst and Savelli* and reinstated the old test of 'exclusive possession' as the primary determinant of the presence of a leasehold estate in land.

In the view adopted by the House of Lords, where the 'only circumstances are that residential accommodation is offered and accepted with exclusive possession for a term at a rent, the result is a tenancy,'[9] and the parties 'cannot turn a tenancy into a licence merely by calling it one.'[10] Lord Templeman, who delivered the only substantial speech in the House, was powerfully moved by the consideration that if exclusive possession at a rent for a term does not constitute a tenancy, then 'the distinction between a contractual tenancy and a contractual licence of land becomes wholly unidentifiable.'[11] Unless these three hallmarks are 'decisive', the task of differentiation becomes 'impossible...save by reference to the professed intention of the parties or by the judge awarding marks for drafting.'[12]

The net result of this decision is that the 'professed intention of the parties' is no longer the determinant of the precise legal status of the occupancy agreed by them.[13] *Street v Mountford* produced a conclusion which, on first impression, seems both improbable and somewhat bizarre. Although the occupier had signed a written acknowledgement that she had no tenancy, this was indeed precisely the interest which the House of Lords decided had been conferred upon her by the disputed agreement.

(3) Identification of the 'nature and quality' of an occupancy

It is quite correct that the ruling of the House of Lords in *Street v Mountford* should be seen as a remarkable turning point in the law of landlord and tenant, but it certainly does not eliminate every difficulty attaching to the elusive distinction between tenancy and licence.

The effect of the decision in *Street v Mountford* is clearly to displace the element of expressed intention as the decisive variable in the identification of a

---

8   [1985] AC 809. For the losing landlord's view, see R. Street, [1985] Conv 328. See also [1985] CLJ 351 (S. Tromans); (1985) LAG Bulletin 77; [1986] JSWL 46 (D. Hoath).
9   [1985] AC 809 at 827A-B.
10 [1985] AC 809 at 821C. See *Errington v Errington and Woods* [1952] 1 KB 290 at 298.
11 [1985] AC 809 at 825C.
12 [1985] AC 809 at 826E. Lord Templeman observed that the same realisation had already occurred, a quarter of a century before, in the High Court of Australia. In *Radaich v Smith* (1959) 101 CLR 209 at 222, Windeyer J had emphasised the 'self-contradictory and meaningless' quality of any assertion that a person legally entitled to exclusive possession for a term is a mere licensee. In his view, '[t]o say that a man who has, by agreement with a landlord, a right of exclusive possession for a term is not a tenant is simply to contradict the first proposition by the second.' See also *Goldsworthy Mining Ltd v Federal Commissioner of Taxation* (1972-1973) 128 CLR 199 at 212; *Lapham v Orange City Council* [1968] 2 NSWR 667 at 670f; *Lewis v Bell* [1985] 1 NSWLR 731 at 734E-F.
13 [1985] AC 809 at 819G-H.

tenancy. From now on, as Lord Templeman stated, 'the only intention which is relevant is the intention demonstrated by the agreement to grant exclusive possession for a term at a rent.'[14] However, as Lord Templeman himself conceded, it may sometimes be difficult to know whether an agreement, on its true construction, confers in strict terms a right of 'exclusive possession' which is referable to the existence of a tenancy. The court must therefore scrutinise the 'nature and quality'[15] of any disputed occupancy in order to determine whether the occupier has been granted the right to 'exclusive possession' in the relevant sense.[16] This task may be just as elusive as was the original distinction between tenancy and licence.

(a) Irrelevant or ambivalent factors

The determination whether a given occupancy constitutes a lease or a licence is ultimately 'a question of law...to be decided upon the basis of the primary facts'.[17] The difficulty facing the court is that, even after the House of Lords' ruling in *Street v Mountford*, many of the 'primary facts' remain neutral or ambivalent as between tenancy and licence.

(i) Exclusiveness of occupation Factual exclusiveness of occupation does not indicate unambiguously the existence of a tenancy. 'Exclusive occupation', not being the same thing as the right to 'exclusive possession',[18] points indifferently towards both tenancy and licence. The mere fact that an occupier enjoys 'exclusive occupation' is not necessarily inconsistent with a right of 'exclusive possession' vested in someone else, and it is only the right to 'exclusive possession' in the full legal sense which can provide the unequivocal indicium of a tenancy.[19]

(ii) Descriptive labels The House of Lords' decision in *Street v Mountford* emphatically confirms the long-standing doctrine that the superficial label attached to a transaction is not necessarily definitive of its legal status.[20] The descriptive labels (eg 'lease', 'tenancy' or 'licence') applied by the parties themselves have only a persuasive and not a conclusive quality,[1] and the court

---

14   [1985] AC 809 at 826G. See also *Royal Philanthropic Society v County* (1985) 276 Estates Gazette 1068 at 1072; *Lewis v Bell* [1985] 1 NSWLR 731 at 736D-737C.
15   *Marchant v Charters* [1977] 1 WLR 1181 at 1185G.
16   *Street v Mountford* [1985] AC 809 at 825B-C.
17   *Carden v Choudhury* (Unreported, Court of Appeal, 29 February 1984) per Arnold P. The issue is decided on a balance of probabilities (see *University of Reading v Johnson-Houghton* (1985) 276 Estates Gazette 1353 at 1356).
18   Ante, p 440.
19   Clarity in this area is not assisted by the fact that the courts have often used the terms 'exclusive possession' and 'exclusive occupation' as if they were interchangeable. Something of this confusion is present even in the speech of Lord Templeman in *Street v Mountford* [1985] AC 809. There is a strong argument for regarding the element of 'exclusive possession' as being truly present only in a lease or tenancy (see eg [1986] JSWL 46 at 49 (D. Hoath)).
20   *Shell-Mex & BP Ltd v Manchester Garages Ltd* [1971] 1 WLR 612 at 615D, 618D-E; *Euston Centre Properties Ltd v H & J Wilson Ltd* (1982) 262 Estates Gazette 1079 at 1082; *University of Reading v Johnson-Houghton* (1985) 276 Estates Gazette 1353 at 1355; *Irish Shell and BP Ltd v John Costello Ltd* [1981] ILRM 66 at 70.
1   *Wyld v Clode* (Unreported, Court of Appeal, 7 December 1983) per Arnold P; *Guppys (Bridport) Ltd v Brookling* (1984) 269 Estates Gazette 846 at 850.

retains an undoubted jurisdiction to override any appellation or 'false label' if it does not correspond with the inner reality of the transaction in hand.[2] It is open to the court in appropriate circumstances to regard a supposed 'licence' as constituting in substance a lease,[3] and a supposed 'lease' or 'tenancy' as comprising in truth a mere licence.[4]

(iii) Subjective intentions As Purchas LJ stressed in *Markou v Da Silvaesa*,[5] no decisive significance is to be attached to the 'actual subjective intention of the parties, even if they are ad idem, ...unless they do not intend to enter into the agreement at all'.[6] This point was made even more graphically in *Street v Mountford* itself, where Lord Templeman stated that

If the agreement satisfied all the requirements of a tenancy, then the agreement produced a tenancy and the parties cannot alter the effect of the agreement by insisting that they only created a licence. The manufacture of a five-pronged implement for manual digging results in a fork even if the manufacturer, unfamiliar with the English language, insists that he intended to make and has made a spade.[7]

(iv) Duration of the occupancy It is strictly irrelevant to an occupier's legal classification whether his occupancy is permanent or merely temporary.[8] The mere effluxion of time cannot convert a licensee into a tenant.[9]

(v) References to 'rent' It is of no significance that the parties refer to the money consideration for the occupancy as 'rent', and even make use of a 'rent book'. Such terminology provides no more than a 'convenient means of verbal reference to the payments.'[10]

(vi) Provision of furniture It is not decisive of the legal character of an occupancy whether the premises concerned are furnished or unfurnished.[11]

---

2   *Greenstreet v Moorchat Ltd* (Unreported, Court of Appeal, 1981 G No 3845, 12 November 1982) concerned a 'management contract' under which the occupier agreed to pay £416,000 per annum ('payable weekly') in return for the privilege of being 'manager' of an all-night cinema in Soho. The Court of Appeal construed this as a lease. See also *Baron Hamilton v Edgar* (1953) 162 Estates Gazette 568.
3   See eg *Addiscombe Garden Estate Ltd v Crabbe* [1958] 1 QB 513 at 525; *Demuren v Seal Estates Ltd* (1978) 249 Estates Gazette 440 at 444; *O'Malley v Seymour* (1978) 250 Estates Gazette 1083 at 1088; *University of Reading v Johnson-Houghton* (1985) 276 Estates Gazette 1353 at 1356; *McDonagh v Kent AHA* (Unreported, Court of Appeal, 7 October 1985); *Irish Shell and BP Ltd v John Costello Ltd* [1981] ILRM 66 at 71. See (1982) 17 Ir Jur (NS) 121 (T.A.M. Cooney).
4   See eg *Taylor v Caldwell* (1863) 3 B & S 826 at 832, 122 ER 309 at 312; *Clore v Theatrical Properties Ltd and Westby & Co Ltd* [1936] 3 All ER 483 at 490, 491; *R.A. Sanson Investments Ltd v Sanson* (Unreported, Court of Appeal, 11 March 1982).
5   (1986) 52 P&CR 204 at 230.
6   On the absence of an intention to create any legal relationship, see p 457 post.
7   [1985] AC 809 at 819E-F.
8   *Marchant v Charters* [1977] 1 WLR 1181 at 1185F.
9   *Markou v Da Silvaesa* (1986) 52 P & CR 204 at 212.
10   *Street v Mountford* (1985) 49 P & CR 324 at 328 per Slade LJ. See also *Lewis v Bell* [1985] 1 NSWLR 731 at 738G.
11   *Marchant v Charters* [1977] 1 WLR 1181 at 1185F.

(vii) Potential application of the Rent Act   The potential application of the Rent Act is entirely irrelevant to the problem of determining the legal effect of the rights granted by an agreement for residential occupation.[12] As Geoffrey Lane LJ said in *Aldrington Garages Ltd v Fielder*,[13] if the parties stipulate expressly for a licence rather than a tenancy 'they should not be prevented from that course by the courts bending over backwards to ensure that landlords do not manage to avoid the provisions of the Rent Acts.' In his view, the mere fact that such agreements 'may result in enhanced profits for the owners does not necessarily mean that the agreements should be construed as tenancies rather than as licences.'[14]

(viii) Non-performance of contracted obligations   The exercise or failure to exercise rights provided for in the parties' agreement is 'not of decisive importance' in determining the legal character of the occupancy.[15] Thus, even though there has in fact been no performance of a contractual obligation to provide the occupier with 'attendance', the mere fact that such services were stipulated for in the parties' agreement may be effective to classify their status in terms of licence rather than tenancy.[16]

(b) Consideration of documents and circumstances

It is well established that, in seeking to assess whether the 'nature and quality' of an occupancy discloses a grant of 'exclusive possession' in the strict sense, the court will look to the substance of the disputed transaction and not merely to its external form.[17] In determining whether the grantee was entitled to 'exclusive possession' or merely to the use of land 'for limited purposes', the court must consider 'the purpose of the grant, the terms of the grant and the surrounding circumstances'.[18]

(i) Written agreements   It may be somewhat easier to determine whether rights of occupancy reflect the 'exclusive possession' postulated of a tenant where those rights are conferred by some written document. As Purchas LJ stated in *Markou v Da Silvaesa*,[19] the court must 'construe the document as a whole in order to determine the nature and quality of the occupancy under the terms of the agreement reached between the parties...Subject to the agreement on its face appearing to be a sham, the effect in law of the agreement must depend

---

12   *Street v Mountford* [1985] AC 809 at 819G-H; *Markou v Da Silvaesa* (1986) 52 P & CR 204 at 214f, 230.
13   (1978) 37 P & CR 461 at 468.
14   The decision in *Aldrington Garages Ltd v Fielder* was disapproved in *Street v Mountford* [1985] AC 809 at 826A, but there was no criticism of this particular dictum.
15   *Markou v Da Silvaesa* (1986) 52 P & CR 204 at 230.
16   *Markou v Da Silvaesa* (1986) 52 P & CR 204 at 222.
17   *Shell-Mex & BP Ltd v Manchester Garages Ltd* [1971] 1 WLR 612 at 618D-E; *Demuren v Seal Estates Ltd* (1978) 249 Estates Gazette 440 at 444; *University of Reading v Johnson-Houghton* (1985) 276 Estates Gazette 1353 at 1355; *Gatien Motor Co Ltd v Continental Oil Co of Ireland Ltd* [1979] IR 406 at 414, 420.
18   *Street v Mountford* [1985] AC 809 at 817G-H.
19   (1986) 52 P & CR 204 at 229.

upon its construction in accordance with the normal rules in the context of its factual matrix and genesis.'[20]

The courts are reluctant to 'award marks for drafting' or to 'draw up a "shopping list" of clauses' in any given agreement which respectively argue in favour of either tenancy or licence.[1] However, a careful construction of the written agreement will usually indicate whether a right to 'exclusive possession' has been genuinely conferred upon or genuinely denied to the occupier concerned. In this process of construction the courts are entitled to disregard 'sham' terms as being entirely ineffective and therefore severable from the agreement.[2] The issue is one of substance. If the agreement confers and imposes on the grantee in substance the rights and obligations of a tenant, and on the grantor in substance the rights and obligations of a landlord, then this finding is indeed conclusive in favour of tenancy.[3] If this is not the case, the grantee must then be a licensee.

The presence or absence of a right to 'exclusive possession' may be inferable from some of the written terms of an occupancy agreement. In *Lewis v Bell*,[4] for instance, the Court of Appeal of New South Wales pointed out the special significance of any terms bearing upon the transferability of the occupier's rights. A leasehold estate is inherently assignable to third parties,[5] and a term which affirms the occupier's right to transfer his entitlement to a third party carries the clear implication that the occupier has an 'exclusive possession' sufficient to sustain such a transfer. Somewhat paradoxically, a term which expressly prohibits the assignment of the occupier's rights likewise reinforces the occupier's claim to 'exclusive possession', since the specific restraint on transfer impliedly concedes that the occupier would otherwise have been competent to alienate his rights.[6] However, a term which stipulates merely that the occupier's rights are personal to him and are for that reason non-transferable has the effect of negativing any implication of 'exclusive possession'.[7] Likewise a term which entitles the owner at his convenience to move the occupier from one room to another within the same house fairly clearly negatives any claim of 'exclusive possession' which the occupier might otherwise have in respect of the room originally allocated to him.[8]

(ii) Unwritten agreements Where the written terms of an occupancy agreement are either lacking or inconclusive, the proper classification of the occupancy must rest on more elusive factors such as the surrounding circumstances of the case.[9] In such an instance the distinction between the tenant and the lodger

---

20 Purchas LJ added that he found 'difficulty in excluding the respective positions of the parties from an analysis of the genesis and factual matrix of the agreement' ((1986) 52 P & CR 204 at 230).
1   *Markou v Da Silvaesa* (1986) 52 P & CR 204 at 230.
2   *Markou v Da Silvaesa* (1986) 52 P & CR 204 at 215.
3   *Addiscombe Garden Estates Ltd v Crabbe* [1958] 1 QB 513 at 522 per Jenkins LJ.
4   [1985] 1 NSWLR 731 at 735G-736A.
5   Post, p 463.
6   References to subletting may not connote quite so clearly the existence of a tenancy (see *Lewis v Bell* [1985] 1 NSWLR 731 at 738G).
7   *Lewis v Bell* [1985] 1 NSWLR 731 at 735G.
8   *Markou v Da Silvaesa* (1986) 52 P & CR 204 at 222.'
9   See *Lewis v Bell* [1985] 1 NSWLR 731 at 735C-E.

rests ultimately on some intuitive perception as to whether the occupier has a 'stake' in the premises which would sustain an action in trespass even against the owner or which would provide the occupier with an 'estate' capable of assignment to a stranger.[10] As Lord Denning MR indicated in *Marchant v Charters*,[11] the legal characterisation of the occupancy depends ultimately on 'the nature and quality of the occupancy.' The crucial question is:

Was it intended that the occupier should have a stake in the room or did he have only permission for himself personally to occupy the room, whether under a contract or not, in which case he is a licensee?[12]

This question itself demonstrates the ultimately inescapable interaction between elements of intention and the conferment of 'exclusive possession'.

(4) Implied exclusions from the concept of 'tenancy'

At the heart of the House of Lords' ruling in *Street v Mountford* lies the legal formula that the grant of 'exclusive possession at a rent for a term' is constitutive of a tenancy. It is unusual for a court to formulate definitional criteria in quite so positive a manner, but the House of Lords' approach was carefully drawn so as impliedly to exclude a number of situations from the definition of tenancy.

(a) 'Exclusive possession' referable to some other category of legal relationship

The qualification that the grant must be 'at a rent for a term' is important since, as Lord Templeman pointed out in *Street v Mountford*,[13] it is quite possible to enjoy exclusive possession outside the landlord-tenant relationship. The owner in fee simple, the trespasser,[14] the mortgagee in possession[15] and the purchaser allowed into possession before completion[16] all illustrate in their respective ways the possibility that the conferment of the right to exclusive possession is 'referable to a legal relationship other than a tenancy.'[17]

Since the ruling in *Street v Mountford*, the Court of Appeal has added one further (and surely questionable) example to this list. It seems that exclusive possession outside the landlord-tenant relationship may be enjoyed by an occupier whose provision of accommodation is referable to the fulfilment by a local authority of its statutory duty under the homeless persons legislation.[18]

---

10   See *Barnes v Barratt* [1970] 2 QB 657 at 669G-H; *Shell-Mex and BP Ltd v Manchester Garages Ltd* [1971] 1 WLR 612 at 617H-618A. The student who lives in a bed-sitting room provided in a hostel or hall of residence has, for instance, no 'estate' which he can meaningfully transfer to a stranger. See, however, *University of Prince Edward Island v President of the Students' Union of the University of Prince Edward Island* (1977) 70 DLR (3d) 756 at 760.
11   [1977] 1 WLR 1181 at 1185G.
12   See also *Maxwell v Brown* (1982) 35 OR (2d) 770 at 772; *Re Ramsay and Heselmann* (1983) 148 DLR (3d) 764 at 766.
13   [1985] AC 809 at 818E.
14   Post, p 744.
15   Post, p 605.
16   However, if an occupier enters into possession with the ultimate intention of negotiating a purchase of the property, and that purchase never materialises, the occupancy will still rank as a tenancy if the facts otherwise satisfy the *Street v Mountford* criteria of 'exclusive possession at a rent for a term' (see *Bretherton v Paton* [1986] 1 EGLR 172 at 174H). Compare *Sharp v McArthur* (Unreported, Court of Appeal, 9 June 1986).
17   [1985] AC 809 at 826H-827A.
18   See Housing (Homeless Persons) Act 1977, s 3(4), now Housing Act 1985, s 63(1).

Although granted 'exclusive possession' of council accommodation pending the outcome of a 'homelessness inquiry', such a person will have merely a licence,[19] unless the local authority has quite explicitly offered him a 'tenancy'.[20]

(b) Occupancy of the 'lodger'

Even if a residential occupier enjoys rights 'at a rent for a term', he may still be excluded from the status of tenant if he does not also have a right to 'exclusive possession'. In *Street v Mountford*, the House of Lords sought on this basis to delineate a distinct legal classification of 'lodger' as representing a category of occupier who is impliedly excluded from the status of tenant. Indeed Lord Templeman went so far as to say that 'save in exceptional circumstances' the only live question in the determination of the status of a residential occupancy is henceforth the inquiry 'whether...the occupier is a lodger or a tenant'.[1]

(i) Distinction between the 'lodger' and the 'tenant' The House of Lords thus drew a primary distinction between the 'tenant' and the 'lodger'. Either can enjoy residential accommodation at a rent for a term, but the crucial distinction between these two classes of occupier rests in the location of overall control in respect of the premises. A lodger is entitled to live in the premises 'but cannot call the place his own.'[2] In particular, stated Lord Templeman, an occupier is a 'lodger' if the landlord provides attendance or services 'which require the landlord or his servants to exercise unrestricted access to and use of the premises.'[3] If, however, the landlord does not contract to provide the occupier with either attendance or services, the grant is one of tenancy.[4] In such circumstances the express reservation of limited rights for the landlord to enter and view the state of the premises or to repair and maintain 'only serves to emphasise the fact that the grantee is entitled to exclusive possession and is a tenant.'[5]

---

19   *South Holland DC v Keyte* (1985) 19 HLR 97 at 101ff (post, p 774).
20   See *Eastleigh BC v Walsh* [1985] 1 WLR 525 at 530F-H; [1985] Conv 217.
1   [1985] AC 809 at 827E-F.
2   [1985] AC 809 at 818A. See *Allan v Liverpool Overseers* (1874) LR 9 QB 180 at 191f. Central to early legal definitions of the term 'lodger' was the idea that lodgers 'submit themselves to [the owner's] control' (*Ancketill v Baylis* (1882) 10 QBD 577 at 586) and that the owner 'retains his character of master of the house, and...retains the general control and dominion over the whole house' (*Thompson v Ward* (1871) LR 6 CP 327 at 361). In *Bradley v Baylis* (1881) 8 QBD 195 at 219, Jessel MR saw the owner of lodgings as one who 'gives to the "inmates"...merely a right of ingress and egress, and retains to himself the general control, with...a right to interfere, a right to turn out trespassers, and so on...' See also N. Madge, (1985) LAG Bulletin 77 at 78.
3   [1985] AC 809 at 818A. It is not the provision of services or attendance as such which negatives the possibility of tenancy (see eg Rent Act 1977, s 7, post, p 985). The decisive factor is the absence of any right to resist intrusion.
4   [1985] AC 809 at 818C. It was conceded in *Street v Mountford* [1985] AC 809 at 818D, 826B-C, that there had been no provision of attendance or services. In *Markou v Da Silvaesa* (1986) 52 P & CR 204 at 218, Ralph Gibson LJ regarded it as still an open question whether a licence could exist even though the landlord provided no attendance or services. This possibility was subsequently confirmed by the ruling of the Court of Appeal in *Brooker Settled Estates Ltd v Ayers* (1987) *The Times*, 13 February, although it is not easy to reconcile the result with Lord Templeman's approach ([1985] AC 809 at 818C).
5   [1985] AC 809 at 818C-D.

The 'lodger' classification endorsed in *Street v Mountford* simply confirms existing authority relating to the status of serviced accommodation. Only a licence arises in such cases, since the occupancy conferred is so clearly personal to the occupier and the supervision of his activities so intrusive as to exclude any possibility that he has an 'estate' in the land. Traditional examples within this category include the long-term hotel resident,[6] the lodger in a furnished room,[7] and the resident in an old people's home,[8] all of whom can be said to enjoy a mere 'exclusive occupation' as distinct from a right of 'exclusive possession'.[9]

(ii) Provision of attendance or services   In view of the emphasis placed in *Street v Mountford* on the relevance of attendance or services, it seems likely that such provision will become a critical area of dispute in the future. Already it is clear that the foisting of unwanted attendance or services upon the occupier bids fair to replace the express disavowal of tenancy as a standard means of establishing the licensee status of the occupier.[10]

In *Markou v Da Silvaesa*,[11] for instance, an occupancy agreement referred explicitly and at some length to promised attendance which included the provision of a housekeeper, cleaning and lighting of common parts, window cleaning, provision of a telephone, the collection of rubbish and the laundering of bed linen. The Court of Appeal took the view, however, that a mere contractual undertaking to provide attendance is not in itself conclusive in favour of a licence classification. Such a result follows within the *Street v Mountford* guidelines only if the attendance or services provided actually 'require' the exercise of unrestricted access by the owner or his servants to the premises concerned.[12] The occupier may still be able to claim a tenancy if in practice the contracted attendance is provided without the necessity of actual entry into the occupier's premises.[13] However, the mere fact that contractually stipulated attendance is declined by the occupier or is never actually provided by the owner does not convert a licence into a tenancy.[14]

6   *Appah v Parncliffe Investments Ltd* [1964] 1 WLR 1064 at 1071; *Luganda v Service Hotels Ltd* [1969] 2 Ch 209 at 217D. See also *Re Canadian Pacific Hotels Ltd and Hodges* (1979) 96 DLR (3d) 313 at 318 (hotel retained 'a general, over-all control of the property').

7   *Marchant v Charters* [1977] 1 WLR 1181 at 1185G-H ('attractive bachelor service apartments', ie, bed-sits each with its own gas-ring). This decision was approved in *Street v Mountford* [1985] AC 809 at 824G-825C. See also *Maxwell v Brown* (1982) 35 OR (2d) 770 at 772, where the rules and restrictions imposed by the owner of a rooming house as to cooking privileges and the number of occupants were held sufficient to deny the occupier a 'stake in the room'. Compare, however, *Guppys (Bridport) Ltd v Brookling* (1984) 269 Estates Gazette 846 at 850, where the character of the occupancy depended largely on whether the owner's 'janitor' had exercised effective control over the admission of visitors—particularly of the opposite sex.

8   *Abbeyfield (Harpenden) Society Ltd v Woods* [1968] 1 WLR 374 at 376F-H, as approved in *Street v Mountford* [1985] AC 809 at 824B.

9   It is well established that the 'exclusiveness' of the occupation enjoyed by such persons is not prejudiced or diminished by reason merely of the fact that staff may enter the room daily to make the bed and clean the room or that a landlady has a right of access at all times (see *Luganda v Service Hotels Ltd* [1969] 2 Ch 209 at 219D-F).

10   See the discussion in Chapter 29 (post, p 997) of devices aimed at evasion of the Rent Act.

11   (1986) 52 P & CR 204; (1986) 278 EG 618 (post, p 997).

12   (1986) 52 P & CR 204 at 211. However, it is sufficient for this purpose that the right of 'unrestricted access' is exercised merely with reasonable frequency.

13   (1986) 52 P & CR 204 at 216f.

14   (1986) 52 P & CR 204 at 212, 230.

(5) Express exclusions from the concept of 'tenancy'

In addition to formulating a positive statement of the criteria of tenancy, the House of Lords also adverted in *Street v Mountford* to certain kinds of occupancy which, although exclusive, would not necessarily constitute a tenancy. Amongst these exempted categories Lord Templeman numbered the occupier who is 'an object of charity or a service occupier'.[15] He expressly excluded the possibility of tenancy in such cases either on the ground that the occupier's apparent possession should be treated in law as the 'possession' of someone else,[16] or on the ground that the circumstances negatived the intention to enter into any legal contractual relationship at all.[17]

(a) Re-emergence of the 'Facchini v Bryson categories'

Lord Templeman's approach seems in large measure to revive the old '*Facchini v Bryson* categories' as instances in which the factual enjoyment of exclusive occupation at a rent for a term does not necessarily generate a relation of landlord and tenant. The '*Facchini v Bryson* categories' comprised cases where there was 'something in the circumstances, such as a family arrangement, an act of friendship or generosity, or such like, to negative any intention to create a tenancy.' As Windeyer J was to observe later in *Radaich v Smith*,[18] these exceptional instances are probably best regarded as cases where a factual exclusiveness of occupation fell significantly short of the right to 'exclusive possession' in the true legal sense.

(b) Modern relevance of the 'Facchini v Bryson categories'

In view of the cyclical movement of the law which culminated in *Street v Mountford*, most of the '*Facchini v Bryson* categories' probably represent good law today.[19] The old caselaw based on these categories provides useful (and still supportable) illustrations of the forms of occupancy expressly excluded by the House of Lords from the ambit of the modern landlord-tenant relationship.

(i) Accommodation based on 'charity'

In *Street v Mountford*[20] Lord Templeman indicated that the occupier who is 'an object of charity' will normally be excluded from the status of tenant. Although no definition of 'charity' was given, this proviso seems to be a contemporary evocation of the old *Facchini v Bryson* principle that residential arrangements underpinned by altruism generate only a licence, even though the occupier enjoys exclusive occupation. Even before the decision in *Street v Mountford*, the courts consistently denied the character of a tenancy to arrangements which smacked of a charitable or therapeutic nature. Findings of licence rather than tenancy were accordingly upheld in the cases of long-term residents of a YWCA hostel,[1] an old people's

---

15 [1985] AC 809 at 818E.
16 [1985] AC 809 at 818F-G.
17 [1985] AC 809 at 819C, 820D.
18 (1959) 101 CLR 209 at 223 (ante, p 439).
19 Ante, p 446.
20 [1985] AC 809 at 818E.
1   *R v South Middlesex Rent Tribunal, ex parte Beswick* (1976) 32 P & CR 67 at 69.

home,[2] and a rehabilitative hostel for former alcoholics.[3] No tenancy can be claimed by a person who enjoys temporary shelter provided by a religious order.[4] Consistently with the ruling in *Street v Mountford*, such cases are now apt to be classified as involving accommodation provided to 'lodgers'.[5]

More recently, in *Brent People's Housing Association Ltd v Winsmore*,[6] Lord Templeman's exception for charity-based accommodation was invoked in order to establish the licensee status of an occupier who lived in a house managed by a 'single homeless project group' sponsored by a registered (and necessarily charitable) housing association. The absence of any right of 'exclusive possession' vested in the occupier was underscored by the fact that all the residents in the house lived under the close supervision of local authority social workers who were employed full-time at the house to provide support, advice and general assistance. The denial of tenant status probably extends to many other kinds of sheltered or 'special needs' accommodation.[7]

(ii) Accommodation based on friendship or generosity   It is uncertain whether Lord Templeman's reference to 'charity' is sufficiently wide to incorporate the old 'friendship or generosity' cases which, under the *Facchini v Bryson* guidelines, were held normally to comprise instances of mere licence.

In the law of landlord and tenant generosity was never left to be its own dubious reward. In the classic case of *Marcroft Wagons Ltd v Smith*,[8] a landlord, acting in response to 'the ordinary decencies of human life',[9] had allowed the daughter of his now deceased tenants to remain in occupation in the immediate aftermath of her double bereavement, paying the same rent as had obtained under those tenancies. The Court of Appeal was unwilling to penalise the landlord's compassionate 'indulgence' by imposing on him the strictures of Rent Act control,[10] and the Court therefore rejected the daughter's contention that she had acquired a new tenancy.[11] In *Street v Mountford*,[12] the House of Lords approved this decision as one in which the parties evidenced no intention to contract at all. However, it seems altogether preferable to rationalise

2   *Abbeyfield (Harpenden) Society Ltd v Woods* [1968] 1 WLR 374 at 376F-H.
3   *Trustees of the Alcoholic Recovery Project v Farrell* (1976) LAG Bulletin 259.
4   *R v Whitby Magistrates, ex parte Marsh* (Unreported, Queen's Bench Divisional Court, 26 November 1984) (Priory of the Order of the Holy Paraclete).
5   See eg [1985] AC 809 at 824B.
6   Unreported, County Court, 20 November 1985. See *Rent Acts: Selected Case Law Guide* (Institute of Rent Officers Educational Trust), Vol 1, p 347; (1986) 17 Jiro (Ed Supp) No 1, p ii.
7   By contrast the absence of any particularly charitable or therapeutic motive underlying the provision by local authorities of 'short life accommodation' may now convert such residential arrangements into a tenancy (see N. Madge, (1986) Legal Action 97). It has become quite common for a local authority to create 'licences' in favour of 'short life user groups' (SLUGs) in relation to empty properties awaiting repair or demolition. The SLUGs then confer further 'licences' on individual occupiers. One of the immediate effects of *Street v Mountford* may have been to destroy the validity of this 'licence' classification and, by making local authority recovery potentially more difficult, to jeopardise the future of such short life accommodation schemes.
8   [1951] 2 KB 496.
9   [1951] 2 KB 496 at 502.
10   Evershed MR was particularly anxious that the courts should do nothing which might inhibit or stultify the already rare human impulse towards altruism (see [1951] 2 KB 496 at 501).
11   In *Turner v Burton* (Unreported, Court of Appeal, 12 March 1985), a mere revocable licence was found where the occupier had initially asked for accommodation for 'one or two weeks at most' and was then allowed to stay on for a few more weeks because he had lost his job.
12   [1985] AC 809 at 820D.

Marcroft Wagons Ltd v Smith on the footing that the occupation there did not amount to 'exclusive possession' in the true legal sense.[13]

The decision in *Marcroft Wagons Ltd v Smith* set the pattern for a number of cases in which occupancy motivated by altruism was held to give rise to a mere licence.[14] On closer analysis these rulings now seem of dubious merit. It is not especially easy to understand why the fact that a particular transaction has been induced by friendship or generosity should necessarily bring the transaction within an exceptional category. Indeed, it can be observed that until the effect of the transaction has been determined, it is impossible to appreciate the extent of the grantor's generosity or to know quite how far the ties of friendship have carried him.[15]

(iii) Accommodation provided under a 'gentleman's agreement' A rather more convincing exception from the scope of the tenancy is that category of cases in which the non-profit-making nature of an occupancy ensures that the courts characterise the arrangement merely as a licence. In *Garland v Johnson*,[16] for instance, a flat-owner who had recently been the victim of a burglary reached a 'gentleman's agreement' with a casual acquaintance, under which the latter was given a temporary right to occupy the former's flat during his absence abroad. The Court of Appeal upheld the existence of a mere licence here, partly on the ground that the occupancy was a personal occupancy 'in the role of a caretaker or a friend looking after the place',[17] and partly because the agreed payments to be made by the occupier were so minimal as to fall far short of an economic rent. In truth, the occupier had no 'stake in the land', but had merely been permitted, on part-payment of 'expenses', to occupy the flat 'as a precaution against burglars'.[18] The owner had not sought commercial gain but merely an occupier whom he could trust.[19]

Whether, after *Street v Mountford*, the occupation typified in *Garland v Johnson* is rationalised as pertaining to a 'lodger' or 'an object of charity', or simply as disclosing no intention to enter into contractual relations, it seems clear that the same circumstances today would still be seen as generating only a licence to occupy.

(iv) Occupancy of a domestic or quasi-familial character In *Street v Mountford*[20] the House of Lords thought it quite possible that 'surrounding circumstances' may demonstrate a plain absence of any 'intention to create legal relationships'.[1] In

---

13   See R. Street, [1985] Conv 328 at 331; D.N. Clarke, [1986] Conv 39 at 43.
14   See J.W. Harris, *Licences and Tenancies—The Generosity Factor*, (1969) 32 MLR 92. It should not be assumed that an occupancy coloured by circumstances of friendship or generosity always gave rise to a licence. See eg *Sopwith v Stutchbury* (1983) 17 HLR 50 at 55 (express grant of tenancy to friend in aftermath of broken marriage).
15   See *Radaich v Smith* (1959) 101 CLR 209 at 220 per Taylor J.
16   Unreported, Court of Appeal, 24 February 1982.
17   Per Eveleigh LJ. 'Caretaker's agreements' of this kind seem to have been long accepted in Ireland as giving rise only to a licence (see *Davies v Hilliard* (1967) 101 ILTR 50 at 56; *Gatien Motor Co Ltd v Continental Oil Co of Ireland Ltd* [1979] IR 406 at 421).
18   Per Eveleigh LJ.
19   Once again, the element of overall control seems to have been a decisive factor. Eveleigh LJ noted that the parties had 'treated the place,...in their mutual contemplation, not as the [occupier's] flat but as the [owner's] home.'
20   [1985] AC 809 at 826H.
1   In *Markou v Da Silvaesa* (1986) 52 P & CR 204 at 226f, Purchas LJ thought that the issue of intention to create legal relations raised 'philosophical questions of social policy which...lie within the especial province of the legislature'.

support of this proposition, Lord Templeman referred to the caselaw which exemplified the old '*Facchini v Bryson* categories'.

Under the *Facchini v Bryson* guidelines, loose informal arrangements for occupancy within a familial or quasi-familial context were apt to be analysed as disclosing no intention to create any legal relationship at all, and therefore as creative merely of a revocable licence.[2] In *Barnes v Barratt*,[3] for instance, the Court of Appeal declined to attach the label of 'tenancy' to an arrangement under which a couple were provided with exclusive occupation of three rooms in a house in return for their performance of cooking and other domestic services and their payment of certain household bills. There existed here merely a 'personal licence to occupy', not least, as Sachs LJ emphasised, because the situation 'was closely akin to those produced by family arrangements to share a house.'[4] Similarly, a mere licence was found in *Heslop v Burns*,[5] where the relationship between the owner and the occupiers was not only 'very akin to a family arrangement'[6] but also marked by an extreme degree of generosity on the part of the former towards the latter.[7]

In *Street v Mountford*[8] the House of Lords considered these cases to be supportable as examples of a hiatus of contractual intent, but once again it may be better to view them as cases in which the occupier was not truly invested with 'exclusive possession'. It is probable, however, that on one or other of these bases most family arrangements will still rank as mere licences today.

(v) Service occupancy   In *Street v Mountford*[9] the House of Lords expressly indicated service occupancy as a form of occupancy entirely personal to the occupier and therefore incompatible with the relationship of landlord and tenant. As Lord Templeman observed, 'the possession and occupation of the servant is treated as the possession and occupation of the master and the relationship of landlord and tenant is not created.'[10] This exception from the scope of tenancy is entirely consistent with the *Facchini v Bryson* guidelines, under which it was accepted that rights of occupancy granted to an employee resulted in a licence rather than a tenancy provided that the occupancy was 'strictly ancillary to the performance of the duties which the occupier has to perform' within the employment relationship.[11]

Street v Mountford thus confirms that if an employee is required to occupy his employer's premises for the better performance of his duties, the employee then

---

2   See eg *Booker v Palmer* [1942] 2 All ER 674 at 677C (evacuees); *Cobb v Lane* [1952] 1 All ER 1199 at 1201A (brother). See also *Errington v Errington and Woods* [1952] 1 KB 290 at 298; *Peakin v Peakin* [1895] 2 IR 359 at 361f (occupation allowed to owner's sisters was 'not an independent possession by them').

3   [1970] 2 QB 657.

4   [1970] 2 QB 657 at 670A. Sharing between family members is apt to create merely a licence (see *David v LB of Lewisham* (1977) 34 P & CR 112 at 115f; *Armstrong v Armstrong* [1970] 1 NSWR 133 at 135).

5   [1974] 1 WLR 1241.

6   [1974] 1 WLR 1241 at 1252G ('second home' of owner).

7   There seems to have been some ground for believing that the owner had formed a romantic attraction for one of the occupiers (see [1974] 1 WLR 1241 at 1244C).

8   [1985] AC 809 at 824E-F.

9   [1985] AC 809 at 818E, 827A.

10   [1985] AC 809 at 818F-G. Service occupancy is discussed further in Chapter 29 (post, p 992).

11   *Smith v Seghill Overseers* (1875) LR 10 QB 422 at 428. See also *Dobson v Jones* (1844) 5 Man & G 112 at 120, 134 ER 502 at 506; *Scrimgeour v Waller* (1981) 257 Estates Gazette 61 at 64; *Royal Philanthropic Society v County* (1985) 276 Estates Gazette 1068 at 1072. See [1986] Conv 215 (P.F. Smith).

ranks as a mere licensee.[12] In such circumstances the occupancy permitted to the employee—however exclusive in its nature—is entirely personal to him and is wholly dependent upon the specific relationship created by his employment.[13] The position may be different if the accommodation provided by an employer is not aimed at facilitating the better or more convenient performance of the employee's contract of service. Where the employee's occupancy is coincidental to rather than contingent upon his employment—and especially if the accommodation might just as readily have been allocated to a non-employee—the courts seem much more willing to identify the status of the accommodation in terms of tenancy.[14] Whether this distinction is either logical or fair is highly questionable.[15]

(6) Application of *Street v Mountford* in relation to business occupancy

The decision in *Street v Mountford* is clearly of primary application in the residential context. However, precisely the same task of distinguishing between tenancy and licence arises in relation to commercial or business occupancy.

Although the distinction in the non-residential sector cannot, of course, rest upon the borderline between 'tenant' and 'lodger', largely the same indicia of tenancy prevail in the commercial context as in the residential sphere. If anything, the courts have tended rather more consistently in the business context to invoke the criterion of 'overall control' as the determining factor in the identification of a tenancy. In *Shell-Mex and BP Ltd v Manchester Garages Ltd*,[16] the Court of Appeal construed an agreement relating to a petrol filling station as a merely personal licence. Lord Denning MR attached particular significance to a stipulation contained in the agreement that the owners should be allowed unimpeded access to the premises, observing that this clause seemed to connote that the owners 'remain in possession themselves'.[17]

This approach has now simply been intensified by the emphatic re-assertion in *Street v Mountford* of the decisive influence of the legal right to exclusive possession. In *University of Reading v Johnson-Houghton*,[18] for instance, a grant of rights to train and exercise racehorses was scrutinised most carefully in order to discover whether the grantee had acquired such a right. The status of the agreement as a tenancy was confirmed when it appeared that the grantee had a

---

12 *Glasgow Corporation v Johnstone* [1965] AC 609 at 626E-G; *Street v Mountford* [1985] AC 809 at 818G; *H.A. Warner Pty Ltd v Williams* (1946) 73 CLR 421 at 429 per Dixon J. See now *Gibson v Death* (Unreported, Court of Appeal, 17 June 1986).

13 See eg *Ramsbottom v Snelson* [1948] 1 KB 473 at 477 (chauffeur or gardener); *Macann v Annett* [1948] NZLR 116 at 120; *Snell v Mitchell* [1951] NZLR 1 at 3 ('live-in' housekeepers).

14 'Where the purpose of placing the employee in occupation of the premises is to give him the benefit of a dwelling place whether as a concession or as part of his recompense for his services or in consideration of a deduction from his wages, he is regarded as having an independent occupation of the premises and the relation is construed as landlord and tenant' (*H.A. Warner Pty Ltd v Williams* (1946) 73 CLR 421 at 429 per Dixon J). See also *Hughes v Overseers of Chatham* (1843) 5 Man & G 54 at 78, 134 ER 479 at 488; *Dover v Prosser* [1904] 1 KB 84 at 85f; *Facchini v Bryson* [1952] 1 TLR 1386 at 1389; *Royal Philanthropic Society v County* (1985) 276 Estates Gazette 1068 at 1072.

15 Post, p 998.

16 [1971] 1 WLR 612.

17 [1971] 1 WLR 612 at 616B-C, approved in *Street v Mountford* [1985] AC 809 at 824D-E.

18 (1985) 276 Estates Gazette 1353. See [1986] Conv 275 (C.P. Rodgers).

right to exclude even the owner from the area concerned. Clearly in this context—even more so than in the residential sector—everything turns on 'the nature of the transaction itself' as disclosed by the written terms of the occupancy and the surrounding circumstances.[19]

3. FLEXIBILITY OF LEASEHOLD ARRANGEMENTS

The potential flexibility of leasehold arrangements may be demonstrated with reference to the following diagram:

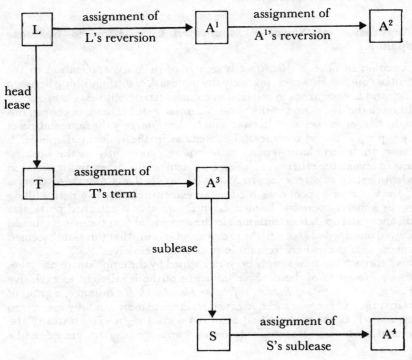

Fig. 40

In *Fig.* 40 L, the owner of an estate in fee simple absolute, has granted a lease to T. This grant had the effect of investing T with an estate in the land (a 'term of years absolute'), thereby precluding L from resuming occupation of the land until the termination of the lease. The sum total of the rights meanwhile retained by L is known as a 'reversion', ie, the residue of the rights reversionary upon the lease. The essence of a legal lease is that both lessor and lessee are invested with a legal estate in possession.[20] Each has an estate in the land with which—at least in theory—he may deal quite independently.

---

19 See also *London & Associated Investment Trust PLC v Calow* [1986] 2 EGLR 80 at 84D; [1987] Conv 137 (S. Bridge).
20 Ante, p 433.

(1) Subsequent dealings by L

It is open to L subsequently to assign his 'reversion' to an assignee, A^1, by conveying to him a fee simple estate in the land which is subject to the lease. A^1 may thereafter execute a further assignment of the 'reversion' to A^2, the 'reversion' steadily increasing in value as the lease approaches its expiry.

(2) Subsequent dealings by T

Meanwhile T has been invested with an estate in the land with which he can deal either by way of assignment or by way of sublease. In *Fig.* 00, T assigns the unexpired portion of his term of years to A^3,[1] who in his turn creates a sublease in favour of S. S in due course assigns the unexpired portion of his sublease to A^4. A^2 now holds the legal fee simple in possession, and both A^3 and A^4 hold terms of years absolute in possession. At this stage the relationship of landlord and tenant exists *first*, between A^2 and A^3 and *second*, between A^3 and A^4. In this way the relationship of landlord and tenant can be duplicated many times over within the leasehold context, with an infinite number of terms of years being carved out of the initial grant by L to T. In this process the distinction between assignment and sublease is subtle but important.

(a) Assignment

The distinguishing feature of an assignment is that it comprises a disposition to the assignee of the assignor's entire interest in the land,[2] thereby putting the assignee into the shoes of the assignor as henceforth the tenant under the lease. The assignor thereafter retains no interest, estate or reversion in the land, although, as will be seen later,[3] this does not mean that his obligations under the lease are necessarily terminated at this point.

(b) Sublease

By contrast the essence of a sublease consists in the fact that the lessee retains an immediate reversion in the land, the sublease bringing into existence a new tenurial relationship between sublessor and sublessee. A sublease can thus be granted only for some lesser period of time than the term enjoyed by the sublessor. Effectively the sublessor merely carves a subsidiary estate out of his own interest in the land, meanwhile retaining a reversion on the sublease thereby created which will take effect (even if only fleetingly) at the termination of the sublease.[4] Whether a particular dealing has produced a

---

1 Even if T's assignment is in breach of a covenant in the lease prohibiting assignment, the assignment to A^3 is valid, although the wrongful assignment may provide a ground for forfeiting the lease against A^3 (see *Old Grovebury Manor Farm Ltd v W. Seymour Plant Sales and Hire Ltd (No 2)* [1979] 1 WLR 1397 at 1398G; *Governors of the Peabody Donation Fund v Higgins* [1983] 1 WLR 1091 at 1095E-G, 1097C-D; *Massart v Blight* (1951) 82 CLR 423 at 440).
2 See *Milmo v Carreras* [1946] KB 306 at 310.
3 Post, p 517.
4 '[W]hen the grant is for the residue of the term of the grantor, there must be an exception of the last day or the last hour, or of some other period of the term' (*Jameson v London and Canadian Loan Agency Co* (1897) 27 SCR 435 at 442 per Strong CJ).

sublease or an assignment is ultimately judged as a matter of substance and not of form, and the court accordingly has power to override any label falsely attached to the transaction.[5]

4. FORMALITIES OF LEASES AND TENANCIES

The creation and assignment of most kinds of lease are subject to certain statutory requirements of formality. A leasehold interest in land comprises at least potentially a legal estate, and therefore the creation and assignment of such an interest are subject to fairly stringent rules relating to formality.

(1) **Creation**

The statutory requirements of formality in respect of the initial grant or creation of leasehold interests are contained in an uncoordinated series of provisions in the Law of Property Act 1925.[6] The starting point is the proposition that 'all conveyances of land or of any interest therein are void for the purpose of conveying or creating a legal estate unless made by deed'.[7] An exception is then made in relation to 'leases or tenancies...not required by law to be made in writing'.[8] Further investigation of the statute reveals that no writing of any kind is required for the creation of 'leases taking effect in possession for a term not exceeding three years...at the best rent which can be reasonably obtained without taking a fine'.[9] All other interests in land, if not created in writing, have the 'force and effect of interests at will only'.[10] The net effect of these provisions is that a legal lease or tenancy for a period not exceeding three years can be created in writing or even orally.[11]

Special problems arise in relation to three kinds of lease or tenancy.

(a) *Periodic tenancies*

It follows from the provisions of the Law of Property Act 1925 that a legal periodic tenancy may be created without any kind of formality,[12] even though it is possible that the tenancy may continue indefinitely for much more than three years.[13] Such a tenancy may be created simply by verbal grant.[14]

---

5   *Milmo v Carreras* [1946] KB 306 at 310; *Gaumont v Luz* (1980) 111 DLR (3d) 609 at 614f.
6   These provisions stem from the Statute of Frauds 1677, ss 1, 2, and the Real Property Act 1845, s 3.
7   Law of Property Act 1925, s 52(1). Section 52(2) details certain exceptions to this basic principle, one of the exceptional cases relating to 'conveyances taking effect by operation of law' (s 52(2)(g)).
8   Law of Property Act 1925, s 52(2)(d).
9   Law of Property Act 1925, s 54(2). A 'fine' (or 'premium') is a lump sum payment which is sometimes demanded as part of the consideration for the grant of a term of years.
10 Law of Property Act 1925, s 54(1).
11 *Kushner v Law Society* [1952] 1 KB 264 at 272.
12 *In re Knight, ex parte Voisey* (1882) 21 Ch D 442 at 456, 458; *Hammond v Farrow* [1904] 2 KB 332 at 335.
13 It seems to be determinative that, at the commencement of the periodic tenancy, it is entirely uncertain that the tenancy will continue for more than three years and eminently possible that it may come to a conclusion sooner (see *In re Knight, ex parte Voisey* (1882) 21 Ch D 442 at 456; *Duncan v Paki* [1976] 2 NZLR 563 at 565).
14 *Kushner v Law Society* [1952] 1 KB 264 at 274.

Moreover, a periodic tenancy may be created either expressly or impliedly. An express periodic tenancy is one which is granted, for instance, 'from week to week' or 'from month to month'. An implied periodic tenancy arises where a property owner accepts rent paid on a periodic basis by a 'tenant at will'[15] (ie, one who occupies land with the consent of the owner) or by a tenant under a formally invalid lease.[16] In these cases the precise nature of the tenancy is determined prima facie by the period with reference to which the rent payable is calculated, not by the frequency with which that rent is actually paid.[17] Where a landlord accepts rent paid on a periodic basis by a 'tenant at sufferance'[18] (ie, one who holds over at the end of a valid tenancy), that payment may well be construed as giving rise to a weekly tenancy notwithstanding that the original tenancy comprised a fixed term of one year.[19]

(b) Renewable leases

The fact that a lease for a period not exceeding three years contains an option for renewal does not convert that lease into a term exceeding three years, even though the total period of possession enjoyed by the tenant may ultimately extend beyond three years.[20] The option for renewal, if exercised by the tenant, merely has the effect of creating a fresh lease for a new term.[1] No formality is required in respect of either the first term or the second term, provided that the second term does not itself exceed three years.

(c) Determinable leases

The requirement of formal creation by deed applies to a lease which is granted for a definite term in excess of three years, notwithstanding that the lease may be determinable by the tenant within the first three years.[2] The determinable 90 year term into which most leases for life are converted by statute[3] is, however, immune from the requirement of formal creation since the term of 90 years takes effect by operation of law.[4]

---

15 Ante, p 430.
16 Post, p 466.
17 Thus in the absence of some express description of the precise nature of the tenancy, a tenant whose rent obligation amounts to '£520 per annum payable weekly' is presumed to hold a yearly tenancy, whereas a tenant whose rent obligation amounts to '£10 per week' is presumed to hold a weekly tenancy (see *Ladies' Hosiery & Underwear Ltd v Parker* [1930] 1 Ch 304 at 328f). See also *E.O.N. Motors Ltd v Secretary of State for the Environment* (1981) 258 Estates Gazette 1300, where there was an agreement that rent should be paid every quarter 'on the basis of £20 per week'. This agreement was held to give rise to a weekly tenancy notwithstanding that the rent was paid in quarterly instalments. Although the tenant had been in possession for four years, Sir Douglas Frank QC, sitting as a deputy High Court judge, observed that the tenancy 'continues to be a tenancy for one week, however long it may last.'
18 Ante, p 431.
19 See *Adler v Blackman* [1952] 2 All ER 41 at 44A-B, affd [1953] 1 QB 146 at 150ff.
20 *Hand v Hall* (1877) 2 Ex D 355 at 358.
 1 *Lewis v Stephenson* (1898) 67 LJQB 296 at 300; *Gerraty v McGavin* (1914) 18 CLR 152 at 163f; *Minister v New South Wales Aerated Water and Confectionery Co Ltd* (1916) 22 CLR 56 at 78; *195 Crown Street Pty Ltd v Hoare* [1969] 1 NSWR 193 at 199. See also *Re Whissel Enterprises Ltd and Eastcal Developments Ltd* (1981) 116 DLR (3d) 174 at 176f.
 2 *Kushner v Law Society* [1952] 1 KB 264 at 274.
 3 Ante, p 435.
 4 Law of Property Act 1925, s 52(2)(g) (ante, p 464).

(2) **Assignment**

The exemption from formality accorded to certain kinds of lease or tenancy applies only to the *creation* of such terms of years. It is clear that the *assignment* of any legal leasehold interest must—irrespective of its duration—be effected formally by deed. Thus a yearly tenancy, although perfectly capable of oral creation, must be assigned by deed if it is to invest the assignee with a legal estate in the land.[5]

(3) **Informal and equitable leases**

At law it has always been clear that no lease or tenancy can be validly created or conferred by any document which fails to satisfy the strict requirements of formality which may be appropriate to the execution or assignment of a term of years.[6] Any purported conveyance of a leasehold interest otherwise than in the requisite formal manner is statutorily declared to be 'void for the purpose of conveying or creating a legal estate.'[7] However, it is equally clear in English law that such a transaction is not necessarily to be regarded as wholly ineffectual. It is possible that an informal lease, although void as a conveyance of a legal estate in land, may nevertheless enjoy some other form of validity either at law or in equity.

This is best explained in terms of a series of fairly logical steps which the courts have taken in seeking to give some kind of effect to a formally defective lease. Let us assume for this purpose that L, an owner of a legal estate in fee simple, has attempted to convey a seven year lease to T, but that the grant of this term is contained merely in an informal written document not under seal. In other words, L has not created the lease by deed as required by the Law of Property Act 1925, s 52(1). L's document cannot therefore convey to T a *legal* lease for a term of seven years, but may nevertheless bring about the following consequences.

(a) *Tenancy at will*

A 'tenancy at will'[8] arises by implication where the tenant under a formally invalid lease enters into possession of the land with the consent of the landlord.[9] Thus T, if allowed into occupation of the 'demised' premises, immediately acquires the status of a tenant at will.[10]

(b) *Implied periodic tenancy*

As soon as a periodic rent is offered by a tenant at will in virtue of his occupation of land, and that payment is accepted by the landowner, the tenancy at will is

---

5   *Botting v Martin* (1808) 1 Camp 317 at 319, 170 ER 970 at 971.
6   Ante, p 464.
7   Law of Property Act 1925, s 52(1) (ante, p 464).
8   Ante, p 430.
9   *Braythwayte v Hitchcock* (1842) 10 M & W 494 at 497, 152 ER 565 at 567.
10   Ante, p 465.

automatically converted by implication of law into a periodic tenancy.[11] Thus, in the present example, T becomes entitled, from the first payment of rent, to a 'term of years' in the full sense.[12]

(i) Duration of the term The precise duration of this periodic tenancy is governed prima facie by the period with reference to which the rent is payable.[13] However, it takes little to raise a presumption that the implied periodic tenancy generated by the tenant's payments is a yearly tenancy.[14] The fact that rent is paid 'by reference to a year, or aliquot part of a year, affords evidence of a tenancy from year to year.'[15] Thus the payment of a quarterly rent raises a presumption of a periodic tenancy from year to year,[16] although this presumption can be rebutted.[17] In principle even the payment of a weekly rent will normally result in an implied term from year to year,[18] although there is some suggestion in the caselaw that a yearly tenancy comes about only if the tenant continues to pay a periodic rent for at least a whole year,[19] or if there is some other evidence that the rent was paid 'with reference to a yearly holding'.[20]

(ii) Terms of the implied periodic tenancy The terms on which T holds his implied periodic tenancy are governed by the rule confirmed in *Martin v Smith.*[1] T's

11   *Hamerton v Stead* (1824) 3 B & C 478 at 483, 107 ER 811 at 813; *Anderson v Midland Railway Co* (1861) 3 E & E 614 at 622, 121 ER 573 at 576.

12   *Moore v Dimond* (1929) 43 CLR 105 at 112. However, the periodic tenancy thereby created continues only for the term originally contemplated in the ineffective legal demise (ie, in the present example seven years). The implied periodic tenancy thus expires at the end of that term by the effluxion of time without notice to quit (see *Doe d Davenish v Moffatt* (1850) 15 QB 257 at 265, 117 ER 455 at 458; *Moore v Dimond*, supra at 113). It is of course liable in the meantime to an earlier determination by notice to quit (see *Doe d Davenish v Moffatt*, supra; *Rodgers v Moonta Town Corporation* (1981) 37 ALR 49 at 54).

13   *Martin v Smith* (1874) LR 9 Ex 50 at 52; *Adams v Cairns* (1901) 85 LT 10 at 11.

14   Since the 18th century a consistently strong presumption has existed in favour of this form of tenure (see *Doe d Martin and Jones v Watts* (1797) 7 TR 83 at 85f, 101 ER 866 at 868; *Lowe v Adams* [1901] 2 Ch 598 at 601; *Moore v Dimond* (1929) CLR 105 at 116). See generally *Bl Comm*, Vol II, p 147; W.S. Holdsworth, *History of English Law* (2nd edn, London 1937), Vol VII, p 244f.

15   *Moore v Dimond* (1929) 43 CLR 105 at 114. See *Braythwayte v Hitchcock* (1842) 10 M & W 494 at 497, 152 ER 565 at 567; *Landale v Menzies* (1909) 9 CLR 89 at 129f.

16   See eg *Lee v Smith* (1854) 9 Ex 662 at 665, 156 ER 284 at 285; *Croft v William F. Blay Ltd* [1919] 2 Ch 343 at 349, 357. The original, but abortive, lease may well have specified a rent of £X per annum payable quarterly. In such circumstances, a quarterly payment by a tenant at will 'implies a yearly tenancy because it is part of the compensation for a year's holding' (*Moore v Dimond* (1929) 43 CLR 105 at 117).

17   A provision that the tenant only (and not the landlord) should be entitled to give notice to quit would, for instance, be repugnant to the concept of a periodic tenancy (*Doe d Warner v Browne* (1807) 8 East 165 at 166, 103 ER 305 at 306). See also *Roe d Brune v Prideaux* (1808) 10 East 158 at 187, 103 ER 735 at 746.

18   *Moore v Dimond* (1929) 43 CLR 105 at 116f.

19   *Moore v Dimond* (1929) 43 CLR 105 at 122f per Isaacs J. See also *Knight v Benett* (1826) 3 Bing 361 at 364, 130 ER 552 at 553; *Arden v Sullivan* (1850) 14 QB 832 at 839, 117 ER 320 at 323; *Hunt v Allgood* (1861) 10 CB (NS) 253 at 257, 142 ER 448 at 450.

20   However, such evidence is not generally difficult to find. In *Moore v Dimond* (1929) 43 CLR 105 at 123, Isaacs J was prepared to accept evidence of 'relevant conduct' including 'entry upon or retention of possession upon the faith of an agreement'. Such an agreement is readily established by the abortive grant of a legal lease.

1   (1874) LR 9 Ex 50 at 52.

tenancy is deemed to incorporate by implication all the terms of the original, but abortive, legal lease in so far as those terms are compatible with and transferable to T's periodic tenancy.[2] Thus T's periodic tenancy will be taken prima facie to include any covenant in the invalid letting which related, for instance, to restrictions on the use of the premises or to a right of entry reserved for the landlord.[3] However, a leasehold term requiring T to redecorate the premises at the end of the seventh year is inconsistent with a periodic tenancy which by its nature is, at most, a tenancy from year to year.[4]

(iii) Legal quality of the implied periodic tenancy   No special formality of creation is required of the periodic tenancy which arises by implication from T's entry into possession and payment of rent. Being at most a yearly tenancy, it need not be created by deed or other writing.[5] T's term of years arises by sheer implication from conduct, and takes effect as a legal estate in the land. As such it remains binding on L (and, indeed, on any assignee of L's reversion) until either the appropriate notice to quit is given or the originally contemplated period of seven years expires.

(c) Contract to create a lease

In terms of the foregoing analysis, T's formally invalid lease for seven years is partially saved as a yearly tenancy at law and thus enjoys a certain limited effect as a legal transaction. However, there is another quite different way in which T's abortive seven-year term may still be given some force both at law and in equity.

There is for lawyers a general reluctance to concede that a transaction which has been voluntarily and deliberately entered into by persons of full age and sound mind should be prejudiced by a failure to comply with a simple requirement of formal execution. It is therefore quite frequently the case that where a conveyance of a legal estate is deprived of effect for some technical reason, the transaction is nevertheless regarded both at law and in equity as a *contract* for valuable consideration to convey the relevant legal estate at some later stage when the impediment has been removed or rectified.[6] In other words, a transaction which was intended to operate by way of conveyance is given a limited effect in contract; that which should have acted *in rem* acts in this instance merely *in personam*.

This approach, when translated into terms of the present problem, brings about the result that an invalid attempt to create a legal lease is treated both at law and in equity as a binding contract to execute such a lease. Thus, by means of a now well established fiction, the ineffective conveyance of a legal estate to T is deemed to constitute an *agreement* to convey that legal estate to him.[7] On this basis, L is regarded as contractually obligated to convey a seven-year lease to T by deed. This deemed contract is subject to several controls.

2   *Doe d Rigge v Bell* (1793) 5 TR 471 at 472, 101 ER 265 at 266; *Arden v Sullivan* (1850) 14 QB 832 at 839, 117 ER 320 at 323; *Croft v William F. Blay Ltd* [1919] 2 Ch 343 at 349.
3   See eg *Thomas v Packer* (1857) 1 H & N 669 at 672f, 156 ER 1370 at 1371f.
4   *Martin v Smith* (1874) LR 9 Ex 50 at 52. However, such a covenant would be enforceable if in fact T continued to occupy, as a yearly tenant, for the originally anticipated term of seven years (*Martin v Smith*, supra at 52f).
5   Law of Property Act 1925, ss 52(2)(d), 54(2) (ante, p 464).
6   Compare eg Settled Land Act 1925, ss 13, 27(1).
7   *Parker v Taswell* (1858) 2 De G & J 559 at 570f, 44 ER 1106 at 1111.

(i) Formalities The contractual relationship between L and T is governed by the usual requirement of formality affecting contracts for the sale or other disposition of land or of any interest in land. In accordance with section 40 of the Law of Property Act 1925, neither L nor T may bring any action to enforce their contract for a lease unless the contract is sufficiently evidenced in writing or is supported by part performance.[8] However, given that section 40 is satisfied, and provided that valuable consideration moves from T to L, the contract for a seven-year lease between L and T is enforceable both at law and in equity.

(ii) Protection against third parties By virtue of the agreement to create a legal estate in his favour, T has acquired an 'estate contract' which is protectible against third parties who may deal with L's reversionary title. T may register this estate contract as a Class C(iv) land charge in the case of unregistered land,[9] and may enter a minor interest on L's title in the case of registered land.[10]

(iii) Remedies for breach Given that a contract is deemed to exist between L and T, the common law remedy for any failure by L to convey the intended legal estate to T consists in the award of money damages to T as compensation for breach of contract. However, the ineffective legal transaction is also regarded in equity as a contract for a lease, and the remedy offered by equity in respect of breach of contracts relating to land goes much further than the traditional common law remedy of compensatory damages. A contract for the transfer of an interest in land is a contract of which equity will usually grant specific performance.[11] Since the subject matter of the contract for a lease is unique and irreplaceable, equity takes the view that the loss suffered by non-performance of the contract is not normally compensable in money terms. The only adequate remedy for breach of that contract is therefore an order that L do that which he is taken to have promised to do, ie, convey a legal lease to T by deed.

Being an equitable remedy, the decree of specific performance is not available as of right: its award lies within the discretion of the court. However, the court will normally grant specific performance provided certain conditions are fulfilled. *First*, there must of course be compliance with section 40 of the Law of Property Act 1925. *Second*, the claimant of specific performance must have given value: 'equity will not assist a volunteer'. *Third*, that claimant must not have forfeited his claim to equitable assistance through unconscionable or inequitable conduct: 'he who comes into equity must come with clean hands'.

In the immediate context, this last condition means that the court has a discretion to withhold specific performance from either party[12] if there is conduct which alienates the sympathy of equity. Such conduct may, for instance, include a failure to fulfil obligations fixed by the original and abortive

8   Ante, p 210.
9   Ante, p 135.
10   Ante, p 159.
11   Ante, p 216.
12   Even the landlord may be precluded from obtaining specific performance if, by his conduct, he has forfeited the assistance of the equitable jurisdiction (*Warwick Grove Pty Ltd v Wright & Howson* [1979] 1 SR (WA) 69 at 73). In such a case the court will simply decline to compel the tenant to execute the legal lease.

legal lease.[13] However, the court will not usually refuse its aid unless the breaches alleged are 'gross and wilful'.[14] The court has discretion, for instance, to grant specific performance on behalf of a tenant notwithstanding his breach of a term for rent payment, where the relevant arrears have since been paid to the landlord and accepted by him.[15] Nor is a landlord guilty of 'unclean hands' merely because he has tendered to the tenant a lease containing more onerous terms than those in the original (but invalid) lease (eg by including a clause demanding 20 per cent of the consideration moving on each subsequent assignment).[16]

Provided the conditions of equitable relief are satisfied, T has a right to compel the specific performance of his agreement for a lease. It is inevitable, therefore, that T's agreement for a lease will now eventuate in the conveyance of the original leasehold estate to him—either by reason of L's voluntary fulfilment of the contract or in pursuance of a decree of specific performance. The legal inevitability of performance of the contract at the instance of either L or T now secures the last link in the long chain of the present argument.

(d) Anticipatory effect of equity

Since the availability of specific performance of T's contract for a lease makes the execution of a formal seven-year lease at law virtually inevitable, equity anticipates the due performance of the contractual obligation. In the words of the maxim, 'equity looks on that as done which ought to be done'. Equity is therefore prepared to adjudge the rights and obligations of L and T on the fictitious basis that the undertaking contained in the as yet unexecuted contract has already been performed, ie, that a seven-year term has already been conferred by L on T. The respective rights and duties of L and T are thus fixed in equity as though L had already conveyed a seven-year term to T.

This fiction cannot of course extend to the point of holding that T is actually invested with a *legal lease* for seven years, for there has been no formal conveyance of such an estate. However, it does enable T to maintain that he has an *equitable lease* for seven years.[17] As Lord Chelmsford LC observed in *Parker v Taswell*,[18] 'the intention of the parties having been that there should be

---

13 *Coatsworth v Johnson* (1886) 55 LJQB 220 at 222f (breach of covenant in agreement to cultivate land in 'a good and husbandlike manner'). See also *Australian Hardwoods Pty Ltd v Commissioner for Railways* [1961] 1 WLR 425 at 432. The doctrine can also apply to unfulfilled conditions precedent where there is no waiver by the landlord (see *Cornish v Brook Green Laundry Ltd* [1959] 1 QB 394 at 407; *Euston Centre Properties Ltd v H & J Wilson Ltd* (1982) 262 Estates Gazette 1079 at 1082).

14 *Parker v Taswell* (1858) 2 De G & J 559 at 573, 44 ER 1106 at 1112. See also *Upper Hutt Arcade Ltd v Burrell and Burrell Properties Ltd* [1973] 2 NZLR 699 at 703.

15 *Baxton v Kara* [1982] 1 NSWLR 604 at 610D-E. The courts tend not to refuse equitable assistance where, under a legal lease, relief against forfeiture (post, p 493) would have been granted (see *Parker v Taswell* (1858) 2 De G & J 559 at 573, 44 ER 1106 at 1112). A mere delay by the tenant in seeking specific performance of the contract for a lease does not fetter the equitable jurisdiction to award such relief (see *Tottenham Hotspur Football & Athletic Co Ltd v Princegrove Publishers Ltd* [1974] 1 WLR 113 at 122B-C; *Baxton v Kara*, supra at 611E).

16 *Warwick Grove Pty Ltd v Wright & Howson* [1979] 1 SR (WA) 69 at 73. (The tenant is not bound to execute a formal lease in such terms, but specific performance of a more conventional lease may be ordered).

17 This conclusion is valid, however, only so long as T's contract for a lease is specifically enforceable (see *Euston Centre Properties Ltd v H & J Wilson Ltd* (1982) 262 Estates Gazette 1079 at 1082).

18 (1858) 2 De G & J 559 at 570, 44 ER 1106 at 1111.

a lease...the aid of equity [is] only invoked to carry that intention into effect.' T is therefore regarded in equity as holding on terms identical to those originally contained in the abortive conveyance of a legal seven-year term.[19]

(4) Resolution of the conflict between law and equity

The conclusion reached in the foregoing argument is that a formally defective lease in writing is not wholly without effect, even though the term purportedly conveyed is in excess of three years. If the tenant enters into possession and begins to pay rent to the landlord, he is regarded thenceforth as holding on a legal periodic (usually yearly) tenancy. Moreover, if the transaction between landlord and tenant is specifically enforceable as a contract for a lease, the tenant will be treated as holding on an equitable tenancy on precisely the terms contained in the original formally defective lease.

A major difficulty occurs, however, if a conflict arises in any particular case between the leasehold obligations created by the implied legal periodic tenancy and those recognised under the equitable lease which comes into being under the doctrine in *Parker v Taswell*. Which obligations are to prevail?

This problem posed itself, apparently for the first time, in *Walsh v Lonsdale*.[20] Here D granted P a seven-year lease in writing, one of the terms of the tenancy being that P should pay each year's rent in advance. No lease under seal was executed, but P entered into possession and proceeded for some time to pay rent in arrear, thereby seeming to become a yearly periodic tenant at law. D then demanded a year's rent in advance and, on P's refusal to pay rent in advance, distrained for it (by seizing P's goods). P brought an action seeking both damages for trespass and a decree of specific performance of the informal lease. These facts disclosed a clear conflict between P's yearly tenancy (under which as a matter of law rent was payable in arrear) and the seven-year equitable lease which arose in accordance with *Parker v Taswell* (in terms of which rent was expressly payable in advance). The liability of D in trespass obviously turned on the question whether the legal periodic tenancy or the equitable seven-year lease was conclusive of the rights and duties of the parties.

In an historic judgment the Court of Appeal decided that, in consequence of the Judicature Acts 1873-1875, any conflict between the rules of law and equity should be resolved by an application of the rules of equity.[1] D's act in distraining upon the goods of P had therefore been perfectly lawful since D's rights were to be measured in terms of the equitable seven-year lease which had expressly stipulated that rent was due in advance.

With admirable clarity the Court disposed of the problem of apparently co-existing yet incompatible estates in the land. Jessel MR declared that

there are not two estates as there were formerly, one estate at common law by reason of the payment of rent from year to year, and an estate in equity under the agreement.

---

19 In *Parker v Taswell* (1858) 2 De G & J 559 at 573, 44 ER 1106 at 1112, Lord Chelmsford LC construed the parties' obligations as if the stipulations of their original informal agreement had been 'converted into a covenant according to the intention of the parties'. See also *Warwick Grove Pty Ltd v Wright & Howson* [1979] 1 SR (WA) 69 at 73. The doctrine stemming from *Parker v Taswell* is often, and with some historical inaccuracy, referred to in terms of a tenant's entitlement to a '*Walsh v Lonsdale* equity' (see eg *Cornish v Brook Green Laundry Ltd* [1959] 1 QB 394 at 406f).

20 (1882) 21 Ch D 9.

1 Supreme Court of Judicature Act 1873, s 25(11); see now Supreme Court Act 1981, s 49(1) (ante, p 42).

There is only one Court, and the equity rules prevail in it. The tenant holds under an agreement for a lease. He holds, therefore, under the same terms in equity as if a lease had been granted, it being a case in which both parties admit that relief is capable of being given by specific performance. That being so, he cannot complain of the exercise by the landlord of the same rights as the landlord would have had if a lease had been granted.[2]

It is thus perfectly plain that a tenant who enters into possession under a specifically enforceable contract for a lease[3] holds not a legal periodic tenancy from year to year, but rather an equitable tenancy on the same terms as those contained in the abortive informal grant.[4] However, if the conditions of specific enforceability are not met,[5] the obligations of the parties are governed by the terms appropriate to the legal periodic tenancy which is implied from the tenant's entry into possession and payment of rent.[6] An equitable tenancy cannot co-exist with a legal periodic tenancy, and the doctrine founded on the equitable jurisdiction to order specific performance effectively ensures that the terms of the equitable tenancy prevail where (and only where) the remedy of specific performance is available.

The doctrine of *Walsh v Lonsdale* has come to apply to a wide range of purportedly legal transactions which are vitiated by non-compliance with some legal formality. The doctrine establishes a principle of general application to such transactions as the granting of easements, profits and mortgages, and brings about the effect that informal grants in any of these cases are construed as contracts which, if capable of specific performance, are regarded as grants of equitable interests of the relevant kind.[7]

(5) Is a contract for a lease as good as a lease itself?

The effect of the doctrine of *Walsh v Lonsdale* is, in most cases, to convert a formally defective lease or a mere contract for a lease into a perfectly valid

---

2   (1882) 21 Ch D 9 at 14f. However, as Jessel MR pointed out, the tenant could not, on this premise, be turned out on six months' notice as would have been the case had he been merely a tenant from year to year. Under the equitable lease, the tenant had the right to insist that the landlord could re-enter only for breach of covenant.

3   The principle of *Walsh v Lonsdale* applies even where the agreement is embodied in a consent order of the court confirming a compromise between the parties (see *Tottenham Hotspur Football & Athletic Co Ltd v Princegrove Publishers Ltd* [1974] 1 WLR 113 at 122A).

4   See *Swain v Ayres* (1888) 21 QBD 289 at 293; *Goldstein v Sanders* [1915] 1 Ch 549 at 556; *Tottenham Hotspur Football & Athletic Co Ltd v Princegrove Publishers Ltd* [1974] 1 WLR 113 at 121G-H; *Industrial Properties (Barton Hill) Ltd v Associated Electrical Industries Ltd* [1977] QB 580 at 598B-C, 610C.

5   The doctrine in *Walsh v Lonsdale* is applicable 'only in those cases where specific performance can be obtained between the same parties in the same court, and at the same time as the subsequent legal question falls to be determined' (*Manchester Brewery Co v Coombs* [1901] 2 Ch 608 at 617 per Farwell J). This may mean that the full effect of *Walsh v Lonsdale* may not apply as between one of the original parties and an assignee of the other (see R.J. Smith, *The Running of Covenants in Equitable Leases and Equitable Assignments of Legal Leases*, [1978] CLJ 98 at 102).

6   *Coatsworth v Johnson* (1886) 55 LJQB 220 at 222f. Although technically more potent than an equitable interest in that it binds the world, a legal periodic tenancy suffers from the grave defect that it may be determined at any time by the appropriate notice to quit. The protection given a legal yearly tenancy (ie, determinable on six months' notice) falls very far short of that available under an equitable lease (which must be allowed to run its full course except where a right of re-entry arises for breach of covenant).

7   Post, pp 540, 576.

equitable lease on exactly the same terms. In view of this result, it is often said that an agreement for a lease is as good as a lease itself.[8] For this reason the parties to a contract for a lease may well not seek specific performance at all and may be quite content to allow their obligations to be governed by a contract which never eventuates in the conveyance of a legal estate to the tenant. For most purposes the mere contract is as efficacious as the legal lease itself. Yet the substantial truth of this proposition tends to conceal certain significant respects in which a contract for a lease falls vitally short of the conveyance of a leasehold estate.[9]

(a) Parties are dependent on the availability of specific performance

The doctrine in *Walsh v Lonsdale* is entirely dependent on the availability of the discretionary remedy of specific performance. It is for the party who seeks to rely on the doctrine to establish that he is entitled to specific performance of the contract for a lease. Thus the status of a tenant as an equitable tenant under *Walsh v Lonsdale* is dependent on the theoretical willingness of the court to grant the discretionary remedy of specific performance of his contract for a lease. If this contract is one in respect of which equity cannot or will not grant specific performance, the tenant's position is then very different from that which would have obtained if a formal legal lease had been granted in the first place. In such a case the tenant's only remedy in respect of default by his landlord will be a mere action in damages for breach of contract, and in the meantime his rights will simply be those (much less secure) rights which exist by virtue of the periodic tenancy implied at law.[10]

(b) There is no 'privity of estate' under a contract for a lease

Certain leasehold covenants are binding on assignees of the original lessor and lessee respectively where there exists 'privity of estate'.[11] However, it is generally considered that 'privity of estate' arises only where a leasehold term is validly granted as a legal estate in the land and all subsequent assignments by either lessor or lessee are formally executed by deed. In the conventional view, no 'privity of estate' can obtain in relation to a contract for a lease quite simply because there exists no 'estate' to which anyone can be 'privy'. The net result is that leasehold covenants entered into by the original lessee under a contract for a lease may not be enforceable against his assignees—an illustration of the general rule that the benefit but not the burden of a contract is assignable. This is one important respect in which, at least from the point of view of the lessor, a contract for a lease is certainly not as good as a lease.

8 See eg *In Re Maughan, Ex parte Monkhouse* (1885) 14 QBD 956 at 958; *Lowther v Heaver* (1889) 41 Ch D 248 at 264 per Cotton LJ. Indeed, there are even certain respects in which a contract for a lease offers more liberal remedies than does the equivalent legal lease. Under a contract for a lease, for instance, the landlord enjoys the benefit of an *implied* right of entry in the event of breach by the tenant (post, p 482).

9 'Although it has been suggested that the decision in *Walsh v Lonsdale* takes away all differences between the legal and equitable estate, it, of course, does nothing of the sort, and the limits of its applicability are really somewhat narrow' (*Manchester Brewery Co v Coombs* [1901] 2 Ch 608 at 617 per Farwell J).

10 Ante, p 466.

11 Post, p 526.

(c) Equitable tenant cannot claim the benefit of Law of Property Act 1925, s 62

The 'general words' provision of section 62 of the Law of Property Act 1925 is activated only by a deed of 'conveyance' of a legal estate.[12] Section 62 cannot therefore be invoked by a tenant under a contract for a lease,[13] with the result that no easements can be implied in favour of such a tenant on the basis of the 'general words'.[14]

(d) Equitable tenant cannot plead purchase of a legal estate without notice

In the law relating to unregistered land, it is quite impossible for an equitable tenant to claim immunity from prior unregistrable, non-overreachable equitable interests. The binding effect of such interests is still governed by the equitable doctrine of notice,[15] and in advance of acquiring a legal term of years the contractual tenant cannot claim to be a bona fide purchaser of a legal estate for value without notice.[16]

(e) Equitable tenant is insecure against third parties

Perhaps the most important deficiency of a contract for a lease consists in the fact that the tenant is insecure against a third party who purchases his landlord's title (see *Fig. 41*).

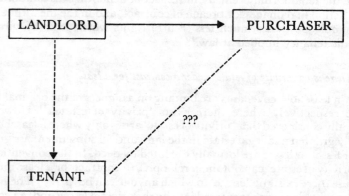

Fig. 41

(i) Unregistered land If the contract is specifically enforceable, the tenant is regarded as holding an equitable lease. Such an interest, if held in unregistered land, ought to be registered as a Class C(iv) land charge against the name of the landlord.[17] If not so registered, the equitable tenant's lease becomes void against any purchaser of a legal estate for money or money's worth, irrespective of the purchaser's state of mind.[18]

---

12   'Conveyance' is defined in Law of Property Act 1925, s 205(1)(ii).
13   *Borman v Griffith* [1930] 1 Ch 493 at 497f.
14   Post, p 676.
15   Ante, p 107.
16   Ante, p 87.
17   Ante, p 135.
18   Land Charges Act 1972, s 4(6). See *Midland Bank Trust Co Ltd v Green* [1981] AC 513 at 527H-528A (ante, p 115).

If for some reason the contract for a lease is not specifically enforceable, the tenant has at best a legal periodic tenancy which, although binding on the purchaser, may be determined by the appropriate notice to quit at the end of the relevant period.

(ii) Registered land If a specifically enforceable contract for a lease relates to registered land, the tenant has an equitable interest which should be protected as a minor interest.[19] Such an interest, if not duly protected, is ineffective against a transferee of the landlord's registered title, subject only to the possibility that the tenant's interest may, in some circumstances, become binding as an 'overriding interest'.[20]

If, conversely, the tenant's contract for a lease is not capable of specific performance, his position is that of a legal periodic tenant whose rights are binding on the transferee of the landlord's title,[1] but which may nevertheless be terminated at any time by the appropriate notice to quit.

5. LEASEHOLD COVENANTS

Under English law a lease usually contains certain express and implied obligations incumbent upon landlord and tenant respectively, giving rise to correlative rights in the other party to the leasehold relationship.

(1) Express obligations of the landlord

Most formal leases contain a wide range of express covenants entered into by the landlord stipulating responsibility in respect of such matters as repair, insurance, rights of access, options for renewal and the like. The precise content of these covenants is left to be determined largely by the parties themselves, although the normal balance of bargaining power as between landlord and tenant ensures that the express burdens of the leasehold relationship are usually allocated more heavily to the tenant than the landlord. Where, however, a landlord has undertaken an express obligation, the courts tend to construe the relevant covenant strictly according to its terms.[2]

(2) Implied obligations of the landlord

In the absence of express contrary agreement, a lease impliedly imposes certain traditionally defined obligations on the landlord. These obligations vary slightly depending on the legal or equitable nature of the lease.

---

19 Ante, p 159.
20 Land Registration Act 1925, s 70(1)(g). See *Grace Rymer Investments Ltd v Waite* [1958] Ch 831 at 849, 851.
1   Land Registration Act 1925, s 70(1)(k) as amended by Land Registration Act 1986, s 4(1) (ante, p 174).
2   See eg *Posner v Scott-Lewis* [1986] 3 WLR 531 at 537H-538A (covenant to employ resident porter in block of flats).

(a) Legal lease

The implied obligations of the landlord under a legal lease include the following.

(i) Covenant for quiet enjoyment   The leasehold covenants include an implied covenant by the landlord to permit the tenant 'quiet enjoyment' of the premises let.[3] The covenant has nothing to do with noise-free enjoyment of the demised premises, but impliedly guarantees that the tenant shall be immune from the exercise of adverse rights over the land.[4] The landlord thus has a duty to ensure that the tenant remains free of any physical interference with or interruption of his enjoyment of the demised premises during the currency of the lease.

Although the landlord's obligation is not absolute, it covers not merely his own conduct (whether rightful or wrongful) but also the rightful acts[5] of any person claiming 'under' him. In *Celsteel Ltd v Alton House Holdings Ltd (No 2)*,[6] however, the Court of Appeal found no breach of the landlord's covenant for quiet enjoyment where a tenant complained that his occupation had been disturbed by the lawful exercise of rights by persons who had earlier been granted tenancies of adjacent property by a former owner of the present landlord's reversion. Such persons did not claim their adverse rights 'under' the present landlord but rather 'under' his predecessor in title. Their rights had been created by virtue of a title which was prior to that of the current landlord and which was therefore superior to it, and the exercise of those rights could not cause the present reversioner to be in breach of his covenant to afford quiet enjoyment.

There is further discussion of the implied covenant for quiet enjoyment in Chapter 28.[7]

(ii) Covenant against derogation from grant   A landlord has an implied obligation not to 'derogate from his grant'.[8] This obligation has been described as 'a principle which merely embodies in a legal maxim a rule of common honesty'.[9] The landlord may not grant land to the tenant on terms which effectively or substantially negative the utility of the grant.[10] Neither the landlord nor any

---

3   *Budd-Scott v Daniell* [1902] 2 KB 351 at 356f; *Markham v Paget* [1908] 1 Ch 697 at 715f; *Kenny v Preen* [1963] 1 QB 499 at 511.
4   See *Hudson v Cripps* [1896] 1 Ch 265 at 268. The covenant for quiet enjoyment has been described as being 'an ordinary incident of a tenancy…it is of the very essence of the tenancy' (*Kanizaj v Brace* [1954] NZLR 283 at 284).
5   In *Malzy v Eichholz* [1916] 2 KB 308 at 315f, for example, a landlord was held not to have breached the covenant for quiet enjoyment where one tenant complained of acts of nuisance committed, without the landlord's authority or concurrence, by other tenants.
6   [1987] 1 WLR 291 at 294B-D.
7   Post, p 957.
8   See generally D.W. Elliott, (1964) 80 LQR 244; M.A. Peel, (1965) 81 LQR 28.
9   *Harmer v Jumbil (Nigeria) Tin Areas Ltd* [1921] 1 Ch 200 at 225 per Younger LJ.
10 A grantor 'having given a thing with one hand is not to take away the means of enjoying it with the other' (*Birmingham, Dudley and District Banking Co v Ross* (1888) 38 Ch D 295 at 313 per Bowen LJ). Actual physical interference with the tenant's activities need not be shown in order to prove that a derogation has occurred (see *Telex (Australasia) Pty Ltd v Thomas Cook & Son (Australasia) Pty Ltd* [1970] 2 NSWR 257 at 266).

person claiming under him[11] may engage in conduct which is inconsistent with the purpose for which the lease was granted.[12] In *Harmer v Jumbil (Nigeria) Tin Areas Ltd*,[13] for instance, the Court of Appeal held that the obligation not to derogate from grant had been breached where a landlord, having leased land for the express purpose of storing explosives, allowed adjoining land to be used for mining operations which endangered the furtherance of the tenant's enterprise.[14] The implied covenant against derogation from grant is likewise breached where a landlord carries out noisy renovations in the same building which render the demised premises unfit for the specialised purposes envisaged by the tenant.[15] Most conduct which breaches the landlord's duty to afford quiet enjoyment represents also a derogation from the leasehold grant,[16] but this is not always or necessarily so.[17]

(iii) Covenants in respect of state of repair There is in general no implied guarantee by the landlord as to the state of repair or fitness of the subject matter of any letting. The broad rule is *caveat emptor*. However, this degree of legal abstention is now qualified by a number of exceptions (arising both at common law and by statute) which impose on the landlord various kinds of duty in relation to the physical condition of the premises leased. Most of these duties relate to standards of repair and fitness required in residential accommodation, and the law governing this area is examined in some detail in Chapters 27 and 28.[18]

(b) Equitable lease

Under an equitable lease (or contract for a lease)[19] there is an implied term, which may be displaced by contrary agreement, that the formal lease when executed should contain 'the usual covenants'.[20] These covenants include the traditional qualified covenant by the landlord to permit quiet enjoyment to the contractual tenant.[1]

(3) Other statutory obligations of the landlord

Apart from their statutory responsibilities in respect of repair and fitness of premises, landlords (or their agents) are subject to other important obligations imposed by statute. These obligations include the following.

---

11 *Aldin v Latimer Clark, Muirhead & Co* [1894] 2 Ch 437 at 447; *Molton Builders Ltd v City of Westminster LBC* (1975) 30 P & CR 182 at 186.
12 The benefit of the landlord's obligation not to derogate from grant may also be claimed by those who take under the tenant (see *Molton Builders Ltd v City of Westminster LBC* (1975) 30 P & CR 182 at 186).
13 [1921] 1 Ch 200 at 225.
14 See also *Mount Cook National Park Board v Mount Cook Motels Ltd* [1972] NZLR 481 at 496. Compare *Port v Griffith* [1938] 1 All ER 295 at 299E-300G.
15 *Telex (Australasia) Pty Ltd v Thomas Cook & Son (Australasia) Pty Ltd* [1970] 2 NSWR 257 at 266 (where the tenant traded in hearing aids and audiometric equipment). See also *Aldin v Latimer Clark, Muirhead & Co* [1894] 2 Ch 437 at 444.
16 See *Robinson v Kilvert* (1889) 41 Ch D 88 at 95ff; *Malzy v Eichholz* [1916] 2 KB 308 at 314.
17 See eg *Grosvenor Hotel Co v Hamilton* [1894] 2 QB 836 at 840.
18 Post, pp 901, 946.
19 Ante, p 468.
20 *Propert v Parker* (1832) 3 My & K 280 at 281, 40 ER 107.
 1 *Hampshire v Wickens* (1878) 7 Ch D 555 at 561.

(a) Disclosure of certain information

The landlord of premises occupied as a dwelling is now statutorily obliged to supply his tenant with certain kinds of information which may prove vital for the effective enforcement of the tenant's rights.

(i) Identity of the landlord   If the tenant of 'premises occupied as a dwelling' makes a written request for the landlord's name and address *either* to any person who demands or last received rent payable under the tenancy *or* to any agent of the landlord in relation to the tenancy, that person must within 21 days supply the tenant with a written statement of the information requested.[2] In the case of a corporate landlord, the tenant may make a further written request that he be informed of the name and address of every director and of the secretary of the landlord company.[3]

(ii) Assignment by the landlord   In the event of any assignment of the landlord's reversion on a tenancy of premises which consist of or include a dwelling, the new landlord is statutorily obliged to give the tenant written notice of the assignment and of the landlord's name and address within at most two months of the date of the assignment.[4]

(b) Provision of rent book

Where a tenant has a right to occupy premises as a residence in consideration of a rent which is payable weekly, the landlord must provide a 'rent book or other similar document for use in respect of the premises'.[5] Any rent book provided in pursuance of this duty must contain such details as the name and address of the landlord,[6] and certain statutorily prescribed information relating to rent and

---

2   Landlord and Tenant Act 1985, s 1(1). The period of 21 days begins with the date of receipt of the request. Non-compliance is a criminal offence (section 1(2)), but only the identity of the immediate landlord need be disclosed (section 1(3)). Any written demand (eg for rent) which is made to a residential tenant must contain the name and address of the landlord (Landlord and Tenant Act 1987, s 47(1)). The landlord of every residential tenant must furthermore furnish his tenants with written advice of an address in England and Wales at which notices (eg notices of proceedings) may be served (Landlord and Tenant Act 1987, s 48(1)). Until such an address is notified to the tenant, no rent or service charge otherwise due from the tenant can be treated as due (Landlord and Tenant Act 1987, s 48(2)). See also Land Registration Act 1925, s 112C (ante, p 150).
3   Landlord and Tenant Act 1985, s 2(1). The obligations of disclosure imposed by Landlord and Tenant Act 1985, ss 1, 2, have no reference to business tenancies governed by Part II of the Landlord and Tenant Act 1954 (see Landlord and Tenant Act 1985, s 32(1)), but do apply in the case of statutory tenancies under the Rent Act (see Landlord and Tenant Act 1985, s 1(3)).
4   Landlord and Tenant Act 1985, s 3(1). This provision catches statutory tenancies, and is activated by 'any conveyance other than a mortgage or charge' of the landlord's interest (Landlord and Tenant Act 1985, s 3(4)). In default of such a notice, the former landlord remains liable to the tenant on the covenants of the lease (Landlord and Tenant Act 1985, s 3A, as added by Landlord and Tenant Act 1987, s 50).
5   Landlord and Tenant Act 1985, s 4(1). This requirement does not apply, however, if the rent includes a payment in respect of board and the value of that board to the tenant forms 'a substantial proportion of the whole rent' (Landlord and Tenant Act 1985, s 4(2)).
6   Landlord and Tenant Act 1985, s 5(1).

other particulars of the tenancy.[7] Failure to comply with any of these requirements constitutes a criminal offence,[8] but such failure does not invalidate the tenancy or render the rent thereunder irrecoverable.[9] The statutory rules relating to rent books are often ignored by landlords, and there is a strong argument for more vigorous enforcement of this branch of the law on behalf of residential tenants.[10]

(c) Restrictions in respect of service charges

The Landlord and Tenant Act 1985 imposes certain duties on the landlord in respect of 'service charges'[11] which are payable by the tenant in a block of flats. Where a service charge is payable in advance of any expenditure, the landlord may demand only such amount as is 'reasonable' and must make any necessary adjustment by way of rebate after the relevant costs have been incurred.[12] The landlord can recover the costs of relevant services or works in respect of a given period only to the extent that those costs (eg the costs of repairs) were 'reasonably incurred' and the services provided or works carried out were 'of a reasonable standard'.[13]

In any case in which the costs of proposed works exceed a statutorily prescribed amount,[14] the landlord must obtain at least two estimates for the works[15] and must supply these together with a written notice for the tenant's observations.[16] A tenant may in writing require the landlord to supply him with a written summary of costs incurred in connection with service charges,[17] and the tenant also has rights to inspect accounts, receipts and other documents supporting this summary.[18]

---

7   Landlord and Tenant Act 1985, s 5(1)(a), (b). See The Rent Book (Forms of Notice) Regulations 1982 (SI 1982/1474), Schedule. The prescribed information must include details of the tenant's right not to be harassed or unlawfully evicted and of his right (where necessary) to receive help with payment of his rent. See (1984) 134 NLJ 4 (M. Haley).
8   Landlord and Tenant Act 1985, s 7(1).
9   *Shaw v Groom* [1970] 2 QB 504 at 516E-F, 526B-D; *Lambeth LBC v Udechuku* (1981) 41 P & CR 200 at 208. A tenant is not guilty of participating in any fraud upon the Inland Revenue merely because he suspects that his landlord's refusal to supply a rent book is related to an unwillingness to leave a permanent trace of the rent payments made (see *Chukwu v Iqbal* (Unreported, Court of Appeal, 30 January 1985) per Fox LJ).
10   See D.C. Hoath, [1978-79] JSWL 3.
11   A 'service charge' is defined as an amount which is payable by a tenant of a flat, as part of or in addition to rent, in respect of 'services, repairs, maintenance, or insurance or the landlord's costs of management' and which varies in whole or part according to the relevant costs (Landlord and Tenant Act 1985, s 18(1)).
12   Landlord and Tenant Act 1985, s 19(2).
13   Landlord and Tenant Act 1985, s 19(1).
14   The prescribed limit is whichever is the greater of £25 multiplied by the number of flats in the building or £500 (Landlord and Tenant Act 1985, s 20(2)).
15   Landlord and Tenant Act 1985, s 20(3)(a). At least one estimate must be provided by 'a person wholly unconnected with the landlord'.
16   Landlord and Tenant Act 1985, s 20(3)(b), (c).
17   Landlord and Tenant Act 1985, s 21(1). If there are more than four flats in the building, the summary must be certified as 'fair' by a qualified accountant (Landlord and Tenant Act 1985, s 21(6)).
18   Landlord and Tenant Act 1985, s 22(2).

(4) Express obligations of the tenant

The express terms of leases both formal and informal tend to impose extensive liabilities and disabilities on the tenant. These may range from such matters as the imposition of an express liability to pay a stipulated rent to an absolute undertaking by the tenant not to assign or sublet the premises.[19] If the tenant expressly covenants in a more qualified form not to assign or sublet the premises without the landlord's consent, there is a statutory implication that such consent shall not be unreasonably withheld.[20] If the tenant expressly covenants not to make improvements or alterations to the demised premises without the landlord's consent, it is again implied by statute that such consent shall not be unreasonably withheld.[1] A covenant by the tenant not to use the premises except for a specified purpose does not constitute a positive undertaking to use the premises for that purpose.[2] No liability attaches to the tenant if under such circumstances he makes no use of the land at all.[3]

(5) Implied obligations of the tenant

In the absence of contrary stipulation in the lease, certain obligations are imposed on the tenant by implication of law. These include a covenant to pay rent[4] and rates.[5] The tenant's implied duties are, however, limited in content and nature. The courts will, for instance, be slow to imply additional covenants such as a covenant that the tenant should not use the premises for immoral purposes.[6]

(a) Obligation not to commit waste

There is an implied duty in the tenant not to commit waste. The extent of this duty depends on the character of the tenancy concerned.

(i) Fixed term of years　A tenant holding under a fixed term of years is, in the absence of contrary agreement, liable for both voluntary and permissive

---

19　An absolute prohibition may be waived by the landlord, but he cannot be compelled to permit a proposed assignment or sublease even if he is acting wholly unreasonably. A covenant against assignment or subletting of 'any part of' the demised premises is breached by an assignment or subletting of the whole of the premises (*Field v Barkworth* [1986] 1 WLR 137 at 139F-G, 140E-F), but a covenant which simply relates to the whole is not broken by a transaction in respect of only a part (*Wilson v Rosenthal* (1906) 22 TLR 233).

20　Landlord and Tenant Act 1927, s 19(1). See *Bickel v Duke of Westminster* [1977] QB 517 at 524C-G; *Bocardo SA v S & M Hotels Ltd* [1980] 1 WLR 17 at 23F-24G; *Bromley Park Garden Estates Ltd v Moss* [1982] 1 WLR 1019; [1983] Conv 140 (L. Crabb). Consent may reasonably be withheld on the ground that an assignee may claim protection under the Leasehold Reform Act 1967 (see *Norfolk Capital Group Ltd v Kitway Ltd* [1977] QB 506 at 514D, 516A, F-G), but not necessarily on the ground that the Rent Act will come into operation (see *West Layton Ltd v Ford* [1979] QB 593 at 605A-C). See also *Leeward Securities Ltd v Lilyheath Properties Ltd* (1983) 17 HLR 35 at 47ff; P.F. Smith, *Covenant against assignments and sublettings: A review of recent developments*, [1986] 6 RRLR 240.

1　Landlord and Tenant Act 1927, s 19(2).

2　*Marquis of Bute v Guest* (1846) 15 M & W 160 at 165, 153 ER 804 at 807; *Lacon v Laceby* [1897] WN 39.

3　See *Pulleng v Curran* (1982) 44 P & CR 58 at 68; *Australian Safeway Stores Pty Ltd v Toorak Village Development Pty Ltd* [1974] VR 268 at 273.

4　Ante, p 441.

5　*Squire v C. Brewer & Sons Ltd* (Unreported, Court of Appeal, 15 July 1983).

6　*Burfort Financial Investments Ltd v Chotard* (1976) 239 Estates Gazette 891 at 893.

waste.[7] On this basis a tenant for years is liable for any repair for which his landlord is not expressly or impliedly responsible.[8]

(ii) Yearly tenancy The liability of a yearly tenant is probably somewhat different from that of other periodic tenants. A yearly tenant is liable for voluntary waste,[9] but is liable for permissive waste only if he fails to weatherproof the premises.[10] He is not liable for 'fair wear and tear'.[11]

(iii) Other periodic tenancies It is of course clear that the tenant must not damage the premises wilfully or negligently,[12] but it seems that, in the absence of express contract, periodic tenants other than the yearly tenant have no general duty to put and keep the premises in repair.[13] The only duty of the periodic tenant is to use the premises in a 'husbandlike' or 'tenantlike' manner.[14] As Denning LJ explained in *Warren v Keen*,[15] this means merely that the tenant 'must do the little jobs about the place which a reasonable tenant would do'. He must mend the electric light when it fuses; he must unstop the sink when it is blocked by his waste. If he goes away for any length of time during winter, he must turn off the water and empty the boiler.[16] However, the weekly or monthly tenant bears no liability for disrepair which is caused by 'fair wear and tear or lapse of time'.[17]

(b) 'Usual covenants' in an equitable lease

Under an equitable lease or contract for a lease, the obligations impliedly undertaken by the tenant are taken, in the absence of express agreement, to include 'the usual covenants'.[18] These covenants comprise[19] undertakings by

7   *Yellowly v Gower* (1855) 11 Exch 274 at 293f, 156 ER 833 at 841f. On the meaning of 'waste', see Chapter 4 (ante, p 60).
8   Compare, however, *Warren v Keen* [1954] 1 QB 15 at 20, where Denning LJ seemed to say that even a tenant for years has no general duty to carry out repairs.
9   *Marsden v Edward Heyes Ltd* [1927] 2 KB 1 at 6ff.
10 *Wedd v Porter* [1916] 2 KB 91 at 100; but see *Warren v Keen* [1954] 1 QB 15 at 20.
11 *Warren v Keen* [1954] 1 QB 15 at 20.
12 *Warren v Keen* [1954] 1 QB 15 at 20.
13 *Warren v Keen* [1954] 1 QB 15 at 20.
14 *Warren v Keen* [1954] 1 QB 15 at 20; *Firstcross Ltd v Teasdale* (1984) 47 P & CR 228 at 233. See also *Bickman v Smith Motors Ltd* [1955] 5 DLR 256 at 257; *Gallo v St Cyr* (1983) 144 DLR (3d) 146 at 148f, 153.
15 [1954] 1 QB 15 at 20.
16 *Warren v Keen* [1954] 1 QB 15 at 20. See also *Pollicchio v Phoenix Assurance Co of Canada* (1978) 79 DLR (3d) 453 at 461. Compare, however, *Wycombe AHA v Barnett* (1984) 264 Estates Gazette 619 at 621 (post, p 919).
17 *Warren v Keen* [1954] 1 QB 15 at 20.
18 It was held in *Flexman v Corbett* [1930] 1 Ch 672 at 678 that the list of 'usual covenants' is neither fixed nor closed.
19 These, together with the landlord's implied covenant for quiet enjoyment (ante, p 476), are the 'usual covenants' as classically expounded by Jessel MR in *Hampshire v Wickens* (1878) 7 Ch D 555 at 561 (see *Chester v Buckingham Travel Ltd* [1981] 1 WLR 96 at 99G). It is clear, however, that other covenants may also be 'usual' in particular contexts. The content of the 'usual covenants' turns on the circumstances of each case and is influenced both by the practice of conveyancers in the relevant district (*Flexman v Corbett* [1930] 1 Ch 672 at 678) and by the character of the property concerned. See eg *Chester v Buckingham Travel Ltd* [1981] 1 WLR 96 at 101D-E.

the tenant to pay rent, to pay tenant's rates and taxes, to keep and deliver up the premises in repair at the end of the term, and to permit the landlord to enter and inspect the premises where the landlord is responsible for any repair. In addition, and in sharp contrast with the law of forfeiture under a legal lease, the landlord under an equitable lease has an *implied* right of re-entry at least in respect of non-payment of rent[20] and possibly also nowadays in respect of any breach of covenant.[1]

(6) Statutory obligations of the tenant

Statute provides the source for many of the obligations which are imposed on certain categories of tenant. Most of the responsibilities of the 'secure tenant' of local authority housing are, for instance, laid down in the Housing Act 1985.[2] More generally a tenant may be subject to important rights of entry reserved by statute on behalf of his landlord. In a tenancy governed by section 8 or section 11 of the Landlord and Tenant Act 1985,[3] the landlord, on giving the tenant 24 hours' notice in writing, has a right of entry 'at reasonable times of the day' for the purpose of viewing the condition and state of repair of the demised premises.[4]

(7) Unlawful leasehold practices

Under English law there are few general restrictions on the kinds of clause or covenant which may be inserted in a tenancy agreement or lease. It is, for instance, open to the landlord, if he so chooses, to require that the demised premises should be occupied only as a private residence for one family, or that no children should live in the property, or that the tenant should not keep a domestic pet on the premises.

(a) Discrimination on grounds of race or sex

Statute only rarely interferes with the content of leasehold undertakings or with letting practices in general. It is, however, unlawful for a landlord to discriminate on grounds of race or sex either in the 'terms on which he offers...premises'[5] or in refusing altogether an application for a tenancy.[6]

---

20 *Hodgkinson v Crowe* (1875) 10 Ch App 622 at 626.
1   See *Chester v Buckingham Travel Ltd* [1981] 1 WLR 96 at 105E–F; (1981) 97 LQR 385 (G. Woodman); (1981) 131 NLJ 545 (H.W. Wilkinson).
2   Post, p 1050.
3   Post, pp 916, 918.
4   Landlord and Tenant Act 1985, ss 8(2), 11(6). It has also been suggested that under a local authority tenancy the council always has an implied right to enter demised premises for the purpose of repair (see *Smith v Bradford Metropolitan Council* (1982) 4 HLR 86 at 91f, post, p 924).
5   Race Relations Act 1976, s 21(1)(a); Sex Discrimination Act 1975, s 30(1)(a). These provisions do not apply, however, to an owner-occupier of the premises unless he uses the services of an estate agent or otherwise advertises the vacant accommodation (see Race Relations Act 1976, s 21(3); Sex Discrimination Act 1975, s 30(3)).
6   Race Relations Act 1976, s 21(1)(b); Sex Discrimination Act 1975, s 30(1)(b). Likewise these provisions have no application to an owner-occupier of the premises unless he uses the services of an estate agent or otherwise advertises the vacant accommodation (see Race Relations Act 1976, s 21(3); Sex Discrimination Act 1975, s 30(3)).

Likewise grounds of race or sex may not be used by a landlord in order to justify the differential provision of access to any benefits or facilities in relation to the premises,[7] or to justify the eviction or detrimental treatment of the tenant.[8] However, none of these prohibitions has any application to 'small premises'[9] where the landlord would otherwise be compelled to share accommodation (such as a bathroom or kitchen) with other occupiers.[10]

Where the licence or consent of the landlord (or any other person) is required for any assignment or subletting by the tenant, it is likewise unlawful for such licence or consent to be withheld on discriminatory grounds of race or sex.[11] Once again 'small premises' are exempted from the operation of this statutory restraint.[12]

(b) The American comparison

The English experience in this area lags somewhat behind that of many American jurisdictions, where suspect classifications have been recognised as extending well beyond race and sex. On constitutional and other grounds the courts have struck down leasehold terms which discriminate against tenants who have children,[13] or who are unmarried cohabitees,[14] or are single parents, or which discriminate according to other suspect criteria.

In *Marina Point Ltd v Wolfson*,[15] for instance, the printed form of lease signed by the tenants, a married couple, contained a clause prohibiting residence in the landlord's apartment complex by children under the age of 18. On the subsequent birth of the tenants' child, the landlord company refused to renew the lease and eventually took eviction proceedings. The Supreme Court of California held that the landlord's exclusion of children violated California's Unruh Act which guarantees equal treatment for all citizens 'in all business establishments of every kind whatsoever'.[16] Tobriner J ruled that the Act did not permit a business enterprise to enforce a 'blanket exclusion' of families with minor children, even if children 'as a class' are 'noisier, rowdier, more mischievous and more boisterous than adults'.[17] The Act did not sanction the

---

7   Race Relations Act 1976, s 21(2)(a); Sex Discrimination Act 1975, s 30(2)(a).
8   Race Relations Act 1976, s 21(2)(b); Sex Discrimination Act 1975, s 30(2)(b).
9   'Small premises' have a statutory definition (see Race Relations Act 1976, s 22(2); Sex Discrimination Act 1975, s 32(2)).
10 Race Relations Act 1976, s 22(1); Sex Discrimination Act 1975, s 32(1).
11 Race Relations Act 1976, s 24(1); Sex Discrimination Act 1975, s 31(1).
12 Race Relations Act 1976, s 24(2); Sex Discrimination Act 1975, s 31(2).
13 See L.D. Barnett, *Child Exclusion Policies in Housing*, 67 Ky LJ 967 (1978-79); G.M. Travalio, *Suffer the Little Children—But Not in My Neighborhood*, (1979) 40 Ohio St LJ 295; A.W. Beck, *Apartment for rent: Adults only; no children allowed*, 15 Cal W LR 219 (1979-80); J.D. Segal, *The Enforceability of Age Restrictive Covenants in Condominium Developments*, 54 So Cal LR 1397 (1980-81); *Why Johnny can't rent any more—An Examination of laws prohibiting discrimination against families in rental housing*, 94 Harv LR 1829 (1981); S. Schovanec, *Landlord and Tenant: Is Discrimination Against Children Permissible in Oklahoma?*, 36 Okla LR 361 (1983). See also S.V. MacCallum and A.J. Bradbrook, (1977-78) 6 Adelaide LR 439.
14 See M.G. Connolly, *The Rights of Unmarried Cohabiting Couples to Housing in New York*, 11 Fordham Urban LJ 381 (1982-83).
15 640 P.2d 115 (1982).
16 California Civil Code, s 51. In *Halet v Wend Investment Co*, 672 F.2d 1305 at 1308f (1982), an adults-only letting policy was also challenged as racially discriminatory, in that it operated with 'greater impact...on blacks and Hispanics because more of those households included minor children'.
17 640 P.2d 115 at 124.

exclusion of an entire class of individuals from access to facilities 'on the basis of a generalised prediction that the class "as a whole" is more likely to commit misconduct than some other class of the public.'[18] Accordingly the Supreme Court, by a majority,[19] declined to allow the landlord company to recover possession, Tobriner J observing that a society which 'sanctions wholesale discrimination against its children in obtaining housing engages in suspect activity.'[20]

6. TERMINATION OF LEASES AND TENANCIES

There are many possible ways in which a lease or tenancy may come to an end in English law. These ways include the following.

(1) Effluxion of time

A lease or tenancy for a fixed term automatically terminates on the expiry of the stipulated period without any requirement that the tenant should be given any form of notice to quit. In some contexts, however, the expiry of a contractually agreed fixed term does not terminate all the tenant's rights. Under Part II of the Landlord and Tenant Act 1954, for instance, many categories of business tenant are given a statutory right to request the grant of a new lease.[1] Under the Rent Act 1977 many kinds of residential tenant are deemed to be 'statutory' tenants on the expiry of a fixed term.[2] Moreover, a lease which is expressly limited to continue only so long as the tenant abstains from breaching any covenant takes effect as a lease which is determinable by a proviso for re-entry on such breach.[3]

(2) Notice to quit

A lease or tenancy may be determinable by notice to quit. The availability of this method of termination depends to some extent on the quality of the tenancy concerned.

(a) Fixed term tenancies

In the case of a fixed term of years a notice to quit is effective only if the parties have expressly agreed that this should be so, since otherwise such a lease simply continues until the expiry of the term. A long lease sometimes contains

---

18   640 P.2d 115 at 125. The Supreme Court did, however, concede that in a different context an age-limited admission policy would be perfectly permissible under the Unruh Act in relation to retirement communities or housing complexes reserved for the elderly (640 P.2d 115 at 128). However, the Court distinguished sharply between the conditions required for meeting such specialised housing needs and the 'wholesale exclusion of children from an apartment complex otherwise open to the general public'.
19   See the interesting dissent of Richardson J (640 P.2d 115 at 129ff).
20   640 P.2d 115 at 129.
1   See generally D. Yates and A.J. Hawkins, *Landlord And Tenant Law* (2nd edn London 1986), p 637ff.
2   Post, p 1002.
3   Law of Property Act 1925, s 146(7).

provision for a 'break notice' which allows the tenant to determine the lease by notice at any of a number of stipulated intervals before the expiry of the term granted.

(b) Periodic tenancies

It is intrinsic to the concept of a periodic tenancy that it should be determinable by a notice to quit given by either the landlord or the tenant.[4] A notice to quit given by only one of two or more joint landlords is effective to terminate a periodic tenancy.[5] Likewise a periodic tenancy may be determined by a notice given by only one of a number of joint tenants.[6] Where a tenant has died intestate in mid-term, the landlord's notice to quit should be served upon the President of the Family Division of the High Court.[7]

In the absence of express agreement between landlord and tenant, the length of the notice required in order to terminate a periodic tenancy is governed in the first instance by the common law and depends on the nature of the tenancy concerned.

(i) Common law rules A yearly tenancy may be determined by not less than half a year's notice expiring at the end of a year of the tenancy.[8] In the case of all other periodic tenancies, the notice required at common law comprises at least one full period (eg one month's notice in the case of a monthly tenancy,[9] and one week's notice in the case of a weekly tenancy[10]). In each case the notice must (in the absence of contrary agreement) expire on the last day of a completed period of the tenancy.[11] Thus a notice to quit in relation to a weekly

---

4 See *Centaploy Ltd v Matlodge Ltd* [1974] Ch 1 at 15A-B, where the Court of Appeal regarded as repugnant and void a term which made a weekly tenancy determinable only by the tenant. Compare, however, *In re Midland Railway Co's Agreement* [1971] Ch 725 at 733F-734A, where the Court of Appeal upheld a proviso which imposed a precondition rather than a prohibition on determination by the landlord.

5 *Doe d Aslin v Summersett* (1830) 1 B & Ad 135 at 140ff, 109 ER 738 at 739f; *Parsons v Parsons* [1983] 1 WLR 1390 at 1399A; [1984] Conv 166 (J.T.F.). See generally F. Webb, [1983] Conv 194.

6 *Leek and Moorlands Building Society v Clark* [1952] 2 QB 788 at 793; *Greenwich LBC v McGrady* (1983) 46 P & CR 223 at 224.

7 *Practice Direction (Service of Notice to Quit)* [1965] 1 WLR 1237. The death of the tenant does not in itself terminate a tenancy, and if the tenant dies intestate the residue of his tenancy vests in the President of the Family Division (Administration of Estates Act 1925, s 9, as amended by Administration of Justice Act 1970, s 1, Sch 2). See *Wirral BC v Smith and Cooper* (1982) 4 HLR 81 at 84; (1983) 80 Law Soc Gaz 883 (M. Lee).

8 *Sidebotham v Holland* [1895] 1 QB 378 at 383. The notice need not be (but usually is) in writing (see *Doe d Lord Macartney v Crick* (1805) 5 Esp 196 at 197, 170 ER 784).

9 A month for this purpose is a calendar month (see Law of Property Act 1925, s 61(a)). Thus a month's notice should expire on the corresponding day of the next month (ie, a notice to quit given on 14 May should expire on 14 June). Where there is no 'corresponding day' (eg in relation to a month's notice given on 31 May), the notice should be made to expire on 30 June). See *Dodds v Walker* [1981] 1 WLR 1027 at 1030E-F.

10 *Queen's Club Gardens Estates Ltd v Bignell* [1924] 1 KB 117 at 124.

11 See *Kemp v Derrett* (1814) 3 Camp 510 at 511, 170 ER 1463 at 1464; *Precious v Reedie* [1924] 2 KB 149 at 151f. The courts in England and elsewhere have refused to split hairs over the question whether a notice to quit on the anniversary date of a periodic tenancy is as effective as a notice to quit on the last day of the relevant period. In *Sidebotham v Holland* [1895] 1 QB 378 at 383, Lindley LJ observed that 'a notice to quit at the first moment of the anniversary ought to be just as good as a notice to quit on the last moment of the day before.' See also *Crate v Miller* [1947] KB 946 at 948f; *Municipality of Metropolitan Toronto v Atkinson* (1977) 78 DLR (3d) 142 at 147f per Laskin CJC.

tenancy cannot be made to expire during the currency of a week.[12] The same approach is applicable mutatis mutandis to monthly and quarterly periodic tenancies.[13]

(ii) Statutory intervention The common law rules relating to notice must now be read subject to the overriding provision contained in the Protection from Eviction Act 1977 that in the case of residential premises no notice to quit has any validity if it is given less than four weeks before the date on which it is to take effect.[14] This requirement applies irrespective of whether the notice is given by the landlord or by the tenant. In either case the notice must be in writing.[15]

Where the landlord gives the tenant notice to quit, the written notice must include certain statutorily prescribed information[16] which assures the tenant that even after the notice has expired the landlord must take proceedings in court before the tenant can be lawfully evicted. The tenant must also be informed that he may be able to obtain free legal advice relating to his rights.[17] In effect every effort must be made to ensure that the notice to quit does not have an intimidating impact on the occupier or inhibit his exercise of such legal rights as he may have. A notice which fails to include the prescribed information is invalid and ineffective to determine the tenancy.[18]

(3) Forfeiture

In the event of a breach of covenant by the tenant, a lease may become determinable according to the rules of forfeiture. The law in relation to forfeiture is discussed in detail in the general context of remedies available to the landlord.[19]

(4) Surrender

A lease or tenancy may be determined by a surrender of the tenant's interest to his immediate landlord. If the landlord accepts the surrender, the tenant's term of years merges forthwith in the landlord's reversion and is extinguished. A

---

12   *Queen's Club Gardens Estates Ltd v Bignell* [1924] 1 KB 117 at 124ff; *Lynch v Dolan* [1973] IR 319 at 328.
13   *Ex parte Maddocks; Re Brown* [1968] 3 NSWR 651 at 652.
14   Protection from Eviction Act 1977, s 5(1)(b). Section 5 of the 1977 Act is equally applicable to restricted contracts (post, p 1040). See *Lambeth LBC v Udechuku* (1981) 41 P & CR 200 at 208. A notice which is too short may be cured by an agreement on the part of the recipient to waive his strict rights (see *Elsden v Pick* [1980] 1 WLR 898 at 906A-B, 907H-908A, 909B).
15   Protection from Eviction Act 1977, s 5(1)(a).
16   Protection from Eviction Act 1977, s 5(1)(a). See The Notices to Quit (Prescribed Information) Regulations 1980 (SI 1980/1624), Schedule. The landlord need not use the precise form of wording set out in these regulations, provided he transmits in substance the information required (see *Beckerman v Durling* (1981) 6 HLR 87 at 90; *Wilsher v Foster* [1981] CLY 1546).
17   The currently prescribed information is less extensive (and subtly less protective) than was the case under the regulations formerly in force. See The Notices to Quit (Prescribed Information)(Protected Tenancies and Part VI Contracts) Regulations 1975 (SI 1975/2196).
18   A notice to quit is not invalidated by reason of the fact that it contains more information than is required by the Protection from Eviction Act 1977 (see *Meretune Investments v Martin* [1984] CLY 1917).
19   Post, p 490.

surrender offered by only one of two or more joint tenants is ineffective.[2] A surrender of the tenant's term may be made either expressly or impliedly by operation of law.[1]

(a) Express surrender

Since the surrender of a tenant's term is effectively a disposition of an estate in the land,[3] an express surrender must be contained in a deed in order to be effective at law.[4] It is also likely that equity would be prepared to give effect to an express surrender made by mere writing.[4] However, surrender is not achieved by a document which merely manifests an intention on the part of the tenant to give up possession at some future stage.[5] Surrender must be accompanied by some (even notional) delivery up of possession and cannot operate in futuro.[6]

(b) Surrender by operation of law

Surrender occurs by operation of law where, with the landlord's concurrence, the tenant consciously does some act which is inconsistent with the continuance of the tenancy.[7] This form of surrender is ultimately founded on the doctrine of estoppel.[8] Implied surrender effectively requires 'a change of possession, or something that is equivalent to a change of possession',[9] in circumstances where it would subsequently be unconscionable for the tenant to plead the absence of a formal deed of surrender.

(i) Actual delivery up of possession Where an implied surrender is premised on some claim of actual delivery up of possession by the tenant, it must be shown that the tenant has intentionally and unequivocally removed all evidence of his possession under the former tenancy. The return of the tenant's key,

---

20 *Leek and Moorlands Building Society v Clark* [1952] 2 QB 788 at 795; *Greenwich LBC v McGrady* (1983) 46 P & CR 223 at 224.

1 *Foster v Robinson* [1951] 1 KB 149 at 155.

2 It has nevertheless been held, somewhat surprisingly, that the landlord to whom a surrender is made is not an 'acquiring authority' within the Land Compensation Act 1973. Thus a tenant who surrenders a local authority tenancy on the assurance that alternative council accommodation will be provided has no entitlement to a 'disturbance payment' (see *R v Islington LBC, ex parte Knight* [1984] 1 WLR 205 at 210E-G).

3 Law of Property Act 1925, s 52(1). See *Hoggett v Hoggett* (1980) 39 P & CR 121 at 126. This requirement applies even to the surrender of an orally granted tenancy.

4 See *Hoggett v Hoggett* (1980) 39 P & CR 121 at 126. It is possible that an oral surrender, evidenced by writing or acts of part performance, would be sufficient in equity. See, however, *Townsend v Clifford* (1973) 228 Estates Gazette 135 at 139, 141.

5 *Re Humphrey and Ontario Housing Corporation* (1979) 96 DLR (3d) 567 at 569.

6 *Whitehead v Clifford* (1814) 5 Taunt 518 at 519, 128 ER 791 at 792.

7 *Fredco Estates Ltd v Bryant* [1961] 1 All ER 34 at 46G; *Mavromatis v Mavromatis* [1968] 1 NSWR 647 at 649. No formality is required in respect of a surrender by operation of law (Law of Property Act 1925, s 52(2)(c)), but it is not sufficient that the parties enter into a mere parol agreement to surrender which is unsupported by any confirmatory act of delivery of possession (see *195 Crown Street Pty Ltd v Hoare* [1969] 1 NSWR 193 at 199).

8 *Foster v Robinson* [1951] 1 KB 149 at 155 per Evershed MR. See also *Wallis v Hands* [1893] 2 Ch 75 at 82.

9 *Hoggett v Hoggett* (1980) 39 P & CR 121 at 126. See also *Oastler v Henderson* (1877) 2 QBD 575 at 578.

accompanied by the tenant's going out of occupation, represents a classic instance of surrender by operation of law.[10] However, it must be clear that the tenant's actions were intended to mark the surrender of his term[11] and were accepted by the landlord as doing so. The mere vacation of the rented property does not necessarily connote a surrender by the tenant, even if he discontinues his payment of rent.[12] In such a case it is always open to the landlord to regard the tenancy as subsisting and to sue for the arrears of rent. The courts may, however, be more ready to find a surrender by operation of law where a departing tenant has left behind him sizeable arrears of rent and remains absent for a substantial period of time.[13]

In determining whether surrender has occurred, the courts have tended to apply the Rent Act concepts of 'corpus possessionis' and 'animus revertendi'.[14] There is no surrender by operation of law while there remains any physical or symbolic evidence (or 'corpus') of the tenant's occupation or so long as the tenant has any intention (or 'animus') to return to the property. Thus the tenant's 'corpus' of possession can be preserved intact where the tenant has departed but his wife,[15] his furniture,[16] or his dog[17] remain at the premises. Moreover, a continuing 'corpus' of possession can be maintained vicariously where the tenant's wife, even though physically absent during the relevant period, intends to return to the property.[18]

(ii) Constructive delivery up of possession   There may even be a constructive delivery up of possession, as for instance where a tenant does not relinquish his possession but accepts some new residential status inconsistent with that enjoyed under the former tenancy.[19] It seems, however, that where one kind of letting arrangement is supposedly replaced by another the court will not accept

10   See *E.S. Schwab & Co Ltd v McCarthy* (1976) 31 P & CR 196 at 205, although Oliver J (at 206ff) doubted whether, in the case of registered land, such a surrender could in the absence of a registered disposition be effective to vest in the landlord anything more than a mere equitable interest in the tenant's lease. See also *Palfrey v Palfrey* (1974) 229 Estates Gazette 1593 at 1595.
11   See *Heath Estates Ltd v Burchell* (1979) 251 Estates Gazette 1173 at 1174.
12   *Addy v Donnelly* [1983] Court of Appeal Bound Transcript 506. The surrender of a statutory tenancy under the Rent Act 'is no easy matter' (*Hulme v Langford* (1985) 50 P & CR 199 at 202 per Stephenson LJ), not least because the courts are disinclined to allow the protection conferred by a special statutory regime to be contracted, or still less, given away (post, p 991). See also *Mavromatis v Mavromatis* [1968] 1 NSWR 647 at 651.
13   *Preston BC v Fairclough* (1982) 8 HLR 70 at 73.
14   Post, p 1008.
15   *Old Gate Estates Ltd v Alexander* [1950] 1 KB 311 at 318ff. The tenant can be said to retain a 'corpus' of possession even where, against his will, his wife insists upon exercising either her common law right to reside in the matrimonial home (see *Middleton v Baldock* [1950] 1 KB 657 at 662ff) or her statutory 'rights of occupation' under the Matrimonial Homes Act 1983 (see *Hoggett v Hoggett* (1980) 39 P & CR 121 at 126ff). See generally Chapter 22 (post, p 781).
16   *Old Gate Estates Ltd v Alexander* [1950] 1 KB 311 at 317.
17   *Hoggett v Hoggett* (1980) 39 P & CR 121 at 126f.
18   *Hoggett v Hoggett* (1980) 39 P & CR 121 at 127f (wife in hospital for operation).
19   See *Foster v Robinson* [1951] 1 KB 149 at 159 (post, p 992), where the tenant accepted a rent-free licence for life and Evershed MR thought it irrelevant for the purpose of this surrender that the key had not been 'handed over and then been handed back the next minute' to mark the superseding of the old relationship by a new and different one. See also *Palfrey v Palfrey* (1974) 229 Estates Gazette 1593 at 1595; *Short Bros (Plant) Ltd v Edwards* (1979) 249 Estates Gazette 539 at 542.

that there has been a valid surrender of the earlier tenancy unless there is clear evidence of the grant of a new tenancy or licence.[20]

(5) Disclaimer

A lease or tenancy may be terminated by various kinds of disclaimer. One such form of disclaimer occurs where the tenant denies or repudiates his landlord's title. In such a case the tenant's lease becomes automatically liable to forfeiture on the basis that repudiation of the superior title is incompatible with the tenant's fundamental obligation to do nothing to prejudice the interests of his landlord.[1]

Another kind of disclaimer may arise on the bankruptcy of the tenant. It is open to the tenant's trustee in bankruptcy to disclaim a subsisting lease owned by the bankrupt if that lease comprises property which is 'unsaleable or not readily saleable' or is likely to give rise to a 'liability to pay money or perform any onerous act'.[2] Such a disclaimer has the effect of terminating the lease and releasing both the bankrupt and his estate from all further liability in connection with it.[3]

(6) Merger

A lease may be determined by merger where the tenant acquires the landlord's reversion and holds both interests in the same name and in exercise of the same legal capacity.[4] Under these circumstances—at least so long as there is no contrary intention—the lease merges with the reversionary title and is extinguished.[5]

(7) Frustration

It has been recognised for a long time that the individual covenants contained in a lease may be suspended or discharged in so far as supervening impossibility of performance affects continuing or future obligations.[6] Only fairly recently, however, has it been accepted that the contractual doctrine of frustration may sometimes apply to the existence of the lease as a whole.[7] In *National Carriers Ltd v Panalpina (Northern) Ltd*,[8] the House of Lords ruled by a majority that a lease

20 *Hulme v Langford* (1985) 50 P & CR 199 at 203ff. Here the tenant had requested that the landlord should transfer a tenancy out of his name into that of his wife. However, the Court of Appeal held that, in order to be effective, such a surrender would necessarily have involved a 'tripartite agreement' between the tenant, the landlord and the wife.

1 *Doe d Ellerbrock v Flynn* (1834) 1 CM & R 137 at 141, 149 ER 1026 at 1028; *Wisbech St Mary Parish Council v Lilley* [1956] 1 WLR 121 at 125; *Warner v Sampson* [1959] 1 QB 297 at 312f.

2 Insolvency Act 1986, s 315(1), (2)(b). The disclaimer may require the approval of the court (Insolvency Act 1986, s 317).

3 Insolvency Act 1986, s 315(3)(a).

4 It is not sufficient, for instance, that the tenant should have acquired the reversion merely qua personal representative (*Chambers v Kingham* (1878) 10 Ch D 743 at 746).

5 See Law of Property Act 1925, s 185.

6 *Cricklewood Property and Investment Trust Ltd v Leighton's Investment Trust Ltd* [1945] AC 221 at 240.

7 For the older law, see *Cricklewood Property and Investment Trust Ltd v Leighton's Investment Trust Ltd* [1945] AC 221 at 228ff.

8 [1981] AC 675. See [1981] Conv 227 (K. Hodkinson); (1981) 32 NILQ 162 (B. Dickson); [1981] CLJ 217 (S. Tromans); (1982) 60 Can Bar Rev 619 (J.T. Robertson).

can be affected by frustration, although the cases in which the doctrine will be applicable are likely to be 'exceedingly rare'.[9] It must be shown that a 'supervening event' has brought about such a 'fundamental change of circumstances as to enable the court to say—"this was not the bargain which these parties made and their bargain must be treated as at an end".'[10] In the *National Carriers* case itself the only access road leading to the demised premises had been closed by the local authority for a period of 18 months during a ten-year lease. The House of Lords declined to accept that this interruption of access had been of sufficient gravity to frustrate the entire lease.[11]

(8) Enlargement

There exists a little used facility pursuant to section 153 of the Law of Property Act 1925 for the enlargement of certain long leases into a fee simple estate.[12] It is open to the tenant to execute a deed of enlargement in respect of a lease which was granted for a term in excess of 300 years, of which at least 200 years remain unexpired.[13] Qualifying leases must not be liable to be determined by re-entry for condition broken,[14] nor must any rent of money value be payable.[15] After enlargement the tenant takes the fee simple subject to all the same covenants and provisions which governed the now extinguished lease.[16]

7. LANDLORD'S REMEDIES FOR BREACH OF COVENANT BY THE TENANT

The landlord has a number of remedies in respect of the tenant's breach of the covenants contained (either expressly or impliedly) in a lease. These remedies include the following.

(1) Forfeiture of the lease

The right to 're-enter' the demised premises and forfeit the lease or tenancy is the most draconian weapon in the armoury of the landlord whose tenant has committed a breach of covenant. Almost all well drafted leases contain a stringent forfeiture clause which provides that in the event of any breach by the tenant 'it shall be lawful for the landlord to re-enter upon the demised premises and peaceably to hold and enjoy the demised premises thenceforth as if this lease had not been made and the term hereby granted shall absolutely determine...'

9   [1981] AC 675 at 692B-D, 697A.
10 [1981] AC 675 at 717D per Lord Roskill.
11 [1981] AC 675 at 697G-698A, 707B-F, 718A. It is quite possible, however, that the answer would have been different in the case of a more lengthy interruption of access.
12 See also the operation of the Leasehold Reform Act 1967 (post, p 725).
13 Law of Property Act 1925, s 153(1). A sublease can be enlarged only if it was created out of a superior term which is itself capable of enlargement under the Law of Property Act 1925 (see Law of Property Act 1925, s 153(2)(ii)).
14 Law of Property Act 1925, s 153(2)(i).
15 Law of Property Act 1925, s 153(1)(b).
16 Law of Property Act 1925, s 153(8).

As will appear later, the exercise of the landlord's right of re-entry is qualified by the court's discretion to grant equitable relief against forfeiture. It is clear, however, that this discretion to relieve against forfeiture cannot be evaded by the mere insertion in a tenancy agreement of a provision which enables the landlord to terminate the tenancy in the event of breach by the tenant by giving a shorter period of notice than would otherwise be required. Such a clause is regarded as the functional equivalent of a forfeiture clause,[17] although the same view is not taken in relation to a clause which permits the landlord to terminate the tenancy in the event of breach by giving the same period of notice as would have been applicable in the absence of such breach.[18]

(a) Purpose of the right of re-entry

The clear purpose of the landlord's right of re-entry is to provide the landlord with a realistic form of security in the event of the tenant's failure to discharge his obligations under the lease.[19] In other words, the landlord is not relegated to a mere monetary claim in respect of the tenant's breach,[20] but may use the threat of recovery of possession as a lever to enforce compliance with the covenants. Sometimes, however, the landlord's only substantial concern when faced with a defaulting tenant is to ensure the termination of the tenancy and the eviction of the tenant from the premises.

(b) Right of re-entry as a proprietary right in land

A landlord's right of re-entry constitutes a species of proprietary interest in the land demised to the tenant.[1] If exercisable 'over or in respect of a legal term of years absolute', the right of re-entry is itself a legal right.[2] Such a right of re-entry is enforceable against the entire world—even against persons who are not in strict terms bound by the covenants to which the right of re-entry relates.[3] If annexed to an equitable term of years, the right of re-entry is equitable only[4] and may be binding on some third parties.[5] Whether legal or equitable in quality, the right of re-entry need not be exercised immediately at the point when it arises.[6] Except in circumstances of release, abandonment or waiver,[7] the right of re-entry may be exercised at any time within the period fixed by the Statutes of Limitation.[8]

(c) General conditions for exercise of a right of re-entry

Under a legal term of years the landlord's right to re-enter and forfeit the lease arises only if the lease itself contains an express proviso for re-entry or if the lease

---

17　*Richard Clarke & Co Ltd v Widnall* [1976] 1 WLR 845 at 850F-G.
18　*Clays Lane Housing Co-operative Ltd v Patrick* (1985) 49 P & CR 72 at 78f.
19　See *Howard v Fanshawe* [1895] 2 Ch 581 at 588; *Di Palma v Victoria Square Property Co Ltd* [1984] Ch 346 at 360D; *Direct Food Supplies (Victoria) Pty Ltd v D.L.V. Pty Ltd* [1975] VR 358 at 359.
20　As Lord Erskine LC pointed out in *Sanders v Pope* (1806) 12 Ves 282 at 289, 33 ER 108 at 110, the landlord may come 'from time to time against an insolvent estate'.
1　Ante, p 82.
2　Law of Property Act 1925, s 1(2)(e).
3　*Shiloh Spinners Ltd v Harding* [1973] AC 691 at 717C, G.
4　Law of Property Act 1925, s 1(3).
5　For the effect of an equitable right of re-entry on third parties, see p 531, post.
6　*Owendale Pty Ltd v Anthony* (1966-1967) 117 CLR 539 at 557.
7　Post, p 740.
8　*Matthews v Smallwood* [1910] 1 Ch 777 at 786.

is phrased in such a way that the performance of the tenant's obligations is rendered a 'condition' on which the future subsistence of the lease depends.[9] A right of re-entry cannot otherwise be implied in a legal lease. It seems, however, that a right of re-entry is impliedly contained in every equitable lease not merely in respect of non-payment of rent[10] but also in relation to other breaches of covenant by the tenant.[11]

(d) Restrictions upon exercise of the right of re-entry

In view of the potentially far-reaching nature of the landlord's right of re-entry, its exercise is subject to certain important restrictions. In the famous words of Coke, 'the law leans against forfeitures'.[12]

(i) Residential leases   It is, for instance, unlawful to enforce a right of re-entry under a residential lease 'other than by proceedings in court while any person is lawfully residing in the premises'.[13] No matter how heinous the breach committed by the tenant, any re-entry against a residential tenant without a court order for possession will give rise to serious criminal liability.[14] In such circumstances it is quite dangerous for the landlord to take at face value the wording of the forfeiture clause in his lease.

(ii) Non-residential leases   Although the requirement of legal process has no strict application to the exercise of a right of re-entry in non-residential leases, it is comparatively rare for a landlord under a business lease to re-enter without first obtaining a court order for possession. However, peaceable re-entry remains an option in relation to a business lease,[15] subject only to the possibility that in certain circumstances the exercise of the landlord's right of re-entry may give rise to criminal liability. It is an offence under the Criminal Law Act 1977 for any person without lawful authority to use or to threaten violence for the purpose of securing entry into any premises where, to his knowledge, there is someone present who is opposed to the entry.[16] Thus peaceable re-entry

---

9   *Doe d Henniker v Watt* (1828) 8 B & C 308 at 315f, 108 ER 1057 at 1060.
10   A proviso for re-entry in the case of non-payment of rent constitutes one of the 'usual covenants' (ante, p 481) which will be implied into a contract for a lease (*Hodgkinson v Crowe* (1875) 10 Ch App 622 at 626).
11   *Chester v Buckingham Travel Ltd* [1981] 1 WLR 96 at 105E-G.
12   *Co Litt*, pp 201b, 202a; *Duppa v Mayho* (1669) 1 Wms Saund 282 at 287, 85 ER 366 at 375 (Note).
13   Protection from Eviction Act 1977, s 2. In respect of residential tenancies which are protected under the Rent Act 1977, the landlord must obtain not only a court order sanctioning forfeiture but also an order granting him possession under Rent Act 1977, s 98(1) (post, p 1015).
14   Post, p 954.
15   It has been pointed out that peaceable re-entry may be particularly attractive to the landlord under a business tenancy on the ground that it avoids the delay which usually attends a county court or High Court possession hearing (see M. Green, (1983) 80 Law Soc Gaz 328). It is not, however, open to a landlord to effect a peaceable re-entry against a tenant by means of an agreement with a subtenant under which the latter consents to have the locks changed but otherwise to remain in occupation as a direct tenant of the landlord (see *Ashton v Sobelman* [1987] 1 WLR 177 at 187A-C).
16   Criminal Law Act 1977, s 6(1) (post, p 756).

becomes a realistic option for the business landlord only where the demised premises are, at least temporarily, unoccupied by the tenant.[17]

(iii) Tenant's right to relief against forfeiture The most important general limitation on the successful exercise of a landlord's right of re-entry lies in the possibility that the tenant may be able in appropriate circumstances to obtain relief against forfeiture.

It is clear that from the earliest times courts of equity have asserted the right to relieve against the forfeiture of property on the ground that such a penalty is disproportionate to the breach upon which the forfeiture is premised.[18] Equity still 'expects men to carry out their bargains and will not let them buy their way out by uncovenanted payment'. However, as Lord Wilberforce emphasised in *Shiloh Spinners Ltd v Harding*,[19] the courts which today exercise equitable jurisdiction retain the right 'in appropriate and limited cases' to relieve against forfeiture for breach of covenant or condition 'where the primary object of the bargain is to secure a stated result which can effectively be attained when the matter comes before the court, and where the forfeiture provision is added by way of security for the production of that result.'

Thus, despite the aggressive tone of most leasehold forfeiture clauses, it is somewhat rare for a lease ultimately to be forfeited to the landlord if the tenant's breach is capable of remedy and the purpose of the landlord-tenant relationship is still capable of fulfilment.[20] It is also clear that the right to seek relief against forfeiture passes to assignees of the original tenant, even though the assignment is itself wrongful because made in breach of covenant.[1]

(e) Forfeiture for non-payment of rent

The precise operation of forfeiture for non-payment of rent[2] depends on whether recourse is had to the jurisdiction of the county court or of the High Court.[3] In either case the landlord's right to re-enter must be preceded by a

---

17 See M. Green, (1983) 80 Law Soc Gaz 328.

18 'Where a penalty or forfeiture is designed merely as a security to enforce the principal obligation, it is as much against conscience to allow any party to pervert it to a different and oppressive purpose, as it would be to allow him to substitute another for the principal obligation' (J. Story, *Commentaries on Equity Jurisprudence* (12th edn 1877), Vol II, p 561). See also *Sanders v Pope* (1806) 12 Ves 282 at 289, 33 ER 108 at 110.

19 [1973] AC 691 at 723G-H. See also *Sport Internationaal Bussum B.V. v Inter-Footwear Ltd* [1984] 1 WLR 776 at 783H, 785G.

20 'When the landlord can be made whole by the payment of the money, there will rarely be reason to refuse the tenant relief from re-entry or forfeiture' (*Badley v Badley* (1983) 138 DLR (3d) 493 at 502). See also *Platt v Ong* [1972] VR 197 at 198.

1 *Old Grovebury Manor Farm Ltd v W. Seymour Plant Sales & Hire Ltd (No 2)* [1979] 1 WLR 263; *Re Hurontario Management Services Ltd and Menechella Brothers Ltd* (1983) 146 DLR (3d) 110 at 112. The original tenant loses any right after assignment to apply for relief against forfeiture (see *Re Francini and Canuck Properties Ltd* (1982) 132 DLR (3d) 468 at 471, post, p 525).

2 The practical operation of forfeiture for non-payment of rent may be extended by reason of the common practice under which the payment of a maintenance or service charge under a lease is expressly covenanted as a form of additional rent (see eg *Di Palma v Victoria Square Property Co Ltd* [1986] Ch 150 at 158C).

3 The county court has jurisdiction in relation to premises whose rateable value does not exceed £2,000. A landlord who unnecessarily issues proceedings in the High Court may find that he is penalised in the matter of costs (*Lircata Properties Ltd v Jones* [1967] 1 WLR 1257 at 1261F).

formal demand for rent[4] unless the requirement of formal demand is obviated either by the express terms of the lease[5] or by statute. Section 210 of the Common Law Procedure Act 1852 provides that there is no requirement of formal demand if at least half a year's rent is in arrear and the goods present on the premises and available for distress are insufficient to cover the arrears due. These conditions are fairly easily met since goods are deemed unavailable for distress if contained in premises which are locked.[6]

(i) Tenant's right to have possession proceedings stayed   Notwithstanding the existence of a right in the landlord to re-enter for non-payment of rent, the courts have traditionally restrained the exercise of this right. Since the purpose of the proviso for re-entry is merely to secure the payment of rent,[7] it follows that 'when the rent is paid, the end is obtained; and therefore the landlord shall not be permitted to take advantage of the forfeiture'.[8]

In possession proceedings brought in the High Court for non-payment of rent, the tenant is therefore entitled to have the proceedings stayed if he pays all rent arrears and costs before the date of trial.[9] Somewhat anomalously this right arises only if at least six months' rent is in arrear.[10] If the tenant does not satisfy the conditions which automatically entitle him to have the possession action stayed, he is relegated to seeking the exercise in his favour of the courts' general equitable discretion to grant relief against forfeiture.

(ii) The court's general discretion to grant relief against forfeiture   The High Court has a general discretion, rooted in its ancient equitable jurisdiction, to grant relief against forfeiture. In the leasehold context this discretion is exercisable in cases where less than six months' rent is in arrear and the tenant tenders full payment before the trial date. It is similarly exercisable where the tenant tenders payment of all arrears and costs subsequent to the granting of a possession order,[11] provided in general that application for relief is made within

---

4   The archaic process of 'formal demand' must be made either at an appointed place or on the demised premises and should require that the exact rent owed should be paid before sunset on the last date for due payment (see *Duppa v Mayho* (1669) 1 Wms Saund 282 at 287, 85 ER 366 at 374f (Note)).

5   Almost all professionally drafted leases today stipulate that the landlord should be exempted from making 'formal demand' for the rent.

6   *Doe d Chippendale v Dyson* (1827) M & M 77 at 78, 173 ER 1087; *Hammond v Mather* (1862) 3 F & F 151, 176 ER 68. See also County Courts Act 1984, s 139(1).

7   Ante, p 491.

8   *Wadman v Calcraft* (1804) 10 Ves Jun 67 at 69, 32 ER 768 at 769. See also *Baxton v Kara* [1982] 1 NSWLR 604 at 609G-610C; *Badley v Badley* (1983) 138 DLR (3d) 493 at 502.

9   Common Law Procedure Act 1852, s 212. It seems that payment by a third party is not sufficient (*Matthews v Dobbins* [1963] 1 WLR 227 at 229ff). The tenant has a similar right to terminate county court proceedings on the payment of all rent arrears and costs not less than five days before the trial date (County Courts Act 1984, s 138(2)).

10   *Standard Pattern Co Ltd v Ivey* [1962] Ch 432 at 438, but compare (1962) 78 LQR 168 (R.E.M.). See also *Di Palma v Victoria Square Property Co Ltd* [1984] Ch 346 at 366A-B.

11   Supreme Court Act 1981, s 38(1). This jurisdiction to grant relief can be invoked by the tenant even where the landlord exercises a right of lawful and peaceable re-entry without the interposition of the legal process (*Howard v Fanshawe* [1895] 2 Ch 581 at 588). See also *Lovelock v Margo* [1963] 2 QB 786 at 788; *Abbey National Building Society v Maybeech Ltd* [1985] Ch 190 at 201F-G.

six months of the execution of the judgment for possession.[12] The High Court's discretion may be exercised notwithstanding physical re-entry by the landlord,[13] in which case the tenant simply continues to hold under the old lease.[14] However, no discretion can be exercised in favour of the tenant if the landlord has already re-let the premises to a stranger.[15]

The jurisdiction to relieve against forfeiture is exercised with what often appears at first sight to be an over-indulgent forbearance towards the tenant.[16] It is generally possible for a tenant to stave off the effects of forfeiture by paying up arrears of rent at the last possible moment, a past record of continuous arrears being regarded as irrelevant to the question whether discretion should be exercised in his favour.[17] Thus in *Bhimji v Salih*,[18] for instance, the Court of Appeal admitted that the defendant had an 'appalling record as a tenant', having run up a total of almost £3,000 in rent arrears. Throughout the lease he had been consistently in arrear with his rent, had been 'a deplorable tenant', had breached other covenants of the lease, and in the view of Brightman LJ was guilty of 'thoroughly unmeritorious behaviour'. The Court nevertheless granted him relief against forfeiture since he had lodged the arrears with his solicitors by the date of the appeal from the judgment for possession. Brightman LJ pointed out that there was 'nothing that the landlord can currently complain of; he can only complain of the past.'[19]

Similarly the tenant may avert forfeiture in county court proceedings if he pays up all arrears and costs within four weeks of the court possession order or within such further period as the court may think fit to allow.[20] However, if the tenant fails to do this, he is liable to have the possession order enforced against him and he is thereafter barred from all further relief.[1] In the case of tenancies protected under the Rent Act 1977 or the Housing Act 1985, further

---

12 Common Law Procedure Act 1852, s 210. In strict terms this time limit applies only where the circumstances are such that the landlord is exempted from making a formal demand for rent, but it is highly probable that this limitation applies more generally by analogy to all but truly exceptional cases (see *Di Palma v Victoria Square Property Co Ltd* [1984] Ch 346 at 366C; *Thatcher v C.H. Pearce & Sons (Contractors) Ltd* [1968] 1 WLR 748 at 755G-756A).

13 *Howard v Fanshawe* [1895] 2 Ch 581 at 586ff; *Belgravia Insurance Co Ltd v Meah* [1964] 1 QB 436 at 444.

14 *Supreme Court Act* 1981, s 38(2).

15 *Stanhope v Haworth* (1866) 3 TLR 34.

16 See *Ladup Ltd v Williams & Glyn's Bank PLC* [1985] 1 WLR 851 at 860E-F per Warner J.

17 See *Gill v Lewis* [1956] 2 QB 1 at 14; *Newbolt v Bingham* (1895) 72 LT 852 at 854. In *Bhimji v Salih* (Unreported, Court of Appeal, 1978 B No 1099, 4 February 1981), Brightman LJ expressed the tentative opinion that such liberal views are 'probably directed to a case where all that was due for rent and costs had actually been paid when the equitable jurisdiction of the court was invoked'.

18 Unreported, Court of Appeal, 1978 B No 1099, 4 February 1981.

19 Brightman LJ did emphasise, however, that in view of the circumstances of the case the tenant could never again expect to be granted relief against forfeiture.

20 County Courts Act 1984, s 138(3), (4), (5), as amended by Administration of Justice Act 1985, s 55(2). The calamitous outcome achieved in *Di Palma v Victoria Square Property Co Ltd* [1986] Ch 150 is thus less likely to recur. The county court has discretion to relieve against forfeiture after a re-entry (whether preceded by court action or merely peaceable), provided that application is made within six months of such re-entry (County Courts Act 1984, ss 138(9A) (as supplied by Administration of Justice Act 1985, s 55(4)), 139(2).

1   The tenant is thereby excluded from obtaining relief even in the High Court, as was demonstrated with disastrous consequences in *Di Palma v Victoria Square Property Co Ltd* [1986] Ch 150.

restrictions are imposed on the landlord's recovery of possession on the ground of non-payment of rent.[2]

(f) Forfeiture for breach of other covenants

Forfeiture for breach of covenants other than the covenant to pay rent is now governed strictly by statute. Section 146 of the Law of Property Act 1925 lays down a special notice procedure in respect of such covenants which differs markedly from the rules relating to forfeiture for non-payment of rent.[3] Apart from several exceptional instances withdrawn from its scope,[4] section 146 is mandatory and cannot even be excluded by contrary contractual provision.[5]

(i) Contents of a 'section 146 notice'   Under section 146(1) the landlord cannot enforce any right of re-entry or forfeiture, either by court action or by peaceable re-entry, unless he has first served a valid statutory notice on the tenant[6] and the tenant has failed within a reasonable time to comply with the terms of that notice. The 'section 146 notice' must specify the particular breach of which complaint is made.[7] It must require that the tenant remedy the breach 'if the breach is capable of remedy',[8] and it must normally require that the tenant make compensation in money for the breach.[9] In addition, if the notice relates to a breach of the tenant's repairing covenants, it must make visible reference to various rights to protection enjoyed by the tenant under the Leasehold Property (Repairs) Act 1938.[10] Any notice which fails to comply with section 146 is rendered invalid[11] and any purported forfeiture based upon an invalid notice is void.[12]

(ii) Purpose of the notice procedure As Slade LJ pointed out in *Expert Clothing Service & Sales Ltd v Hillgate House Ltd*,[13] it is 'an important purpose' of the section 146 procedure 'to give even tenants who have hitherto lacked the will or the means

2   Post, pp 1022, 1056.
3   Section 146 has no application to breaches of the covenant to pay rent (Law of Property Act 1925, s 146(11)).
4   See Law of Property Act 1925, s 146(8), (9).
5   Law of Property Act 1925, s 146(12).
6   As to the meaning of service, see Law of Property Act 1925, s 196. If there is more than one tenant, the notice must be served on all (*Blewett v Blewett* [1936] 2 All ER 188 at 190).
7   Law of Property Act 1925, s 146(1)(a). The notice must be sufficiently specific to enable the tenant to provide an effective remedy (*Fletcher v Nokes* [1897] 1 Ch 271 at 273f). In the case of disrepair by the tenant it is usual to append to the notice a schedule of delapidations prepared by a builder or surveyor.
8   Law of Property Act 1925, s 146(1)(b).
9   Law of Property Act 1925, s 146(1)(c). It is clear, however, that the landlord need not demand monetary compensation if he does not want it (*Lock v Pearce* [1893] 2 Ch 271 at 276, 279f). In *Rugby School (Governors) v Tannahill* [1935] 1 KB 87 at 91, for instance, Rugby School was not required to demand that it share by way of compensation in income derived through prostitution!
10   Leasehold Property (Repairs) Act 1938, s 1(4) (post, p 500).
11   For instance, a section 146 notice is invalid if it omits to require that the tenant remedy a breach of covenant which is 'capable of remedy' in the statutory sense (see eg *Glass v Kencakes Ltd* [1966] 1 QB 611 at 622; *Expert Clothing Service & Sales Ltd v Hillgate House Ltd* [1986] Ch 340 at 362A, 365B.
12   *In re Riggs* [1901] 2 KB 16 at 20.
13   [1986] Ch 340 at 358A.

to comply with their obligations one last chance to summon up that will or find the necessary means before the landlord re-enters'.

The precise way in which this inducement operates is itself dependent on whether the breach in question is 'capable of remedy' within the meaning of section 146(1). Where a breach is 'capable of remedy', the real object of the section 146 notice procedure is to afford the tenant two opportunities before the landlord proceeds to enforce his right of re-entry.[14] *First,* the notice gives the tenant the opportunity to remedy his breach 'within a reasonable time' after the service of the notice.[15] *Second,* the notice procedure further allows the tenant to apply to the court for relief from forfeiture. However, where the tenant's breach is not 'capable of remedy', there is clearly no point in providing him with the first of these opportunities,[16] and the object of the notice procedure is simply to enable the tenant to throw himself upon the court's equitable jurisdiction to grant relief.[17]

(iii) Remediable breaches of covenant In the case of a remediable breach of covenant, the section 146 notice must give the tenant a reasonable period of time within which to comply with its terms.[18] The reasonableness of the time allowed is intricately linked with the remediability of the breach,[19] but it is generally thought that a period of three months is sufficient. If remedial action is taken and reasonable compensation is paid by the tenant within that time, the landlord is then unable to show that the statutory condition precedent to his ability to enforce the forfeiture has been fulfilled.[20] If, however, compliance with the notice is not forthcoming within that time, the landlord may proceed to enforce the forfeiture either in person or by action,[1] subject only to the tenant's rights to obtain relief against forfeiture at any time before actual re-entry.[2]

(iv) Irremediable breaches of covenant It is clear that some breaches of covenant by a tenant are, in effect, irremediable.[3] In such cases the section 146 notice need not require that the tenant make any remedy of the breach.[4] It is sufficient merely that the landlord serves a section 146 notice which specifies that the breach has occurred and which demands that money compensation be paid by

---

14 *Expert Clothing Service & Sales Ltd v Hillgate House Ltd* [1986] Ch 340 at 351B.
15 Law of Property Act 1925, s 146(1).
16 *Expert Clothing Service & Sales Ltd v Hillgate House Ltd* [1986] Ch 340 at 351C.
17 The court always has jurisdiction to grant relief, but it has been described as 'a bold course' to grant relief against forfeiture in the case of a breach which is 'incapable of remedy' (*Dunraven Securities Ltd v Holloway* (1982) 264 Estates Gazette 709 at 711).
18 A 'reasonable time' depends ultimately on the facts of the individual case (see *Hick v Raymond & Reid* [1893] AC 22 at 29).
19 See, for example, the conceptual connection made in *Expert Clothing Service & Sales Ltd v Hillgate House Ltd* [1986] Ch 340 at 357B-C.
20 *Scala House and District Property Co Ltd v Forbes* [1974] QB 575 at 585B.
1   *Expert Clothing Service & Sales Ltd v Hillgate House Ltd* [1986] Ch 340 at 362D-E.
2   Post, p 502.
3   This is expressly envisaged in the terms of Law of Property Act 1925, s 146(1). See *Expert Clothing Service & Sales Ltd v Hillgate House Ltd* [1986] Ch 340 at 362E.
4   Such a requirement would be 'pointless' where remedy within a reasonable time is impossible (*Expert Clothing Service & Sales Ltd v Hillgate House Ltd* [1986] Ch 340 at 357A). See also *Rugby School (Governors) v Tannahill* [1935] 1 KB 87 at 91, 94; *Dunraven Securities Ltd v Holloway* (1982) 264 Estates Gazette 709.

the tenant.[5] After a reasonable interval[6] the landlord is then free to enforce the forfeiture, subject only to the tenant's possible rights to claim relief against that forfeiture.[7]

(v) Concept of capability of remedy In view of the 'limited guidance' to be derived from the authorities,[8] it is not necessarily easy to determine whether a particular breach of covenant is of such a character as to be incapable of remedy. There is, of course, a sense in which no breach of covenant can ever truly be remedied. The breach, once committed, cannot be undone or expunged from the record,[9] and the caselaw of the past has certainly applied this blunt construction at least in relation to the breach of negative user covenants.[10] However, since section 146(1) clearly contemplates that some breaches are 'capable of remedy', this extreme approach cannot provide a conclusive or definitive interpretation.[11]

It is now beginning to be accepted that the 'concept of capability of remedy' turns on 'whether the harm that has been done to the landlord by the relevant breach is for practicable purposes capable of being retrieved.'[12] Thus, by a subtle semantic shift, the test of the remediability of a *breach* has become a test of the remediability of the *damage* caused by that breach. As Slade LJ indicated in *Expert Clothing Service & Sales Ltd v Hillgate House Ltd*,[13] the 'ultimate question' is whether the 'harm' suffered by the landlord would be 'effectively remedied' if the tenant were to comply within a reasonable time with a section 146 notice demanding both remedy and compensation. Only if the answer to this question is in the negative may a section 146 notice validly omit to require that the tenant remedy his breach.

In this way the sharp point of the 'remediability issue' has moved away from judicial assessments of the intrinsic quality of the tenant's act or default towards a consideration of the consequential effect of the tenant's breach as measured in terms of irretrievable long-range damage to the landlord's interests.[14] A breach is 'capable of remedy' within the meaning of the statute if, but only if, the landlord can be restored within a reasonable time to the position he would have been in if no breach had occurred.[15] In this sense, therefore, 'a breach which has been remedied has been demonstrated to have been a breach which was ab initio capable of being remedied.'[16] If, however, the effects of the tenant's default cannot be cured either within a reasonable time or at all, then his breach is not 'capable of remedy' in the relevant statutory sense.[17]

5   It may nevertheless be prudent for the landlord to proceed cautiously by demanding that the tenant's breach be remedied if, in the statutory terminology, it is 'capable of remedy'.
6   Two days are not enough for this purpose (see *Horsey Estate Ltd v Steiger* [1899] 2 QB 79 at 91f), but fourteen days are sufficient (*Civil Service Co-operative Society Ltd v McGrigor's Trustee* [1923] 2 Ch 347 at 356; *Scala House and District Property Co Ltd v Forbes* [1974] QB 575 at 589B-D).
7   Post, p 502.
8   *Expert Clothing Service & Sales Ltd v Hillgate House Ltd* [1986] Ch 340 at 351C.
9   *Expert Clothing Service & Sales Ltd v Hillgate House Ltd* [1986] Ch 340 at 362E-F.
10 See eg *Rugby School (Governors) v Tannahill* [1934] 1 KB 695 at 701f.
11 *Hoffman v Fineberg* [1949] Ch 245 at 253.
12 *Expert Clothing Service & Sales Ltd v Hillgate House Ltd* [1986] Ch 340 at 355B-C.
13 [1986] Ch 340 at 358C-D.
14 The 'remediability issue', thus stated, must be examined at the date of issue of the section 146 notice (*Expert Clothing Service & Sales Ltd v Hillgate House Ltd* [1986] Ch 340 at 362E).
15 *Expert Clothing Service & Sales Ltd v Hillgate House Ltd* [1986] Ch 340 at 362 E-F.
16 *Expert Clothing Service & Sales Ltd v Hillgate House Ltd* [1986] Ch 340 at 364E-F.
17 *Expert Clothing Service & Sales Ltd v Hillgate House Ltd* [1986] Ch 340 at 362F.

(vi) Remediability of positive covenants This pragmatic approach enables some approximate predictions to be made as to the status of certain kinds of breach under section 146(1). A breach of a positive covenant (whether it be a continuing breach or a 'once and for all' breach) will normally be capable of remedy,[18] since such a breach can usually be cured by belated performance of the covenanted action.[19] Thus in *Expert Clothing Service & Sales Ltd v Hillgate House Ltd*[20] the Court of Appeal held that the tenant's breach of a covenant to reconstruct premises within a specified time was 'capable of remedy' by performance out of time, since the landlord would not suffer irretrievable prejudice if the tenant tendered late performance of his covenant and made adequate money compensation for his breach.[1] An effective remedy can be provided for a 'once and for all' breach of covenant if that which ought to have been done can be done within a reasonable time during the subsistence of the term.[2]

It may not ultimately be possible to maintain that the breach of a positive covenant is always 'capable of remedy',[3] but it is certainly difficult to think of examples of such breaches which are not.[4]

(vii) Remediability of negative covenants The 'remediability issue' in relation to negative covenants may produce somewhat different results. The decision of the Court of Appeal in *Scala House and District Property Co Ltd v Forbes*[5] provides binding authority that there cannot be any remedy in respect of a 'once and for all' breach of a negative covenant such as a covenant prohibiting the assignment or subletting of the demised premises.[6] It used to be thought that no breach of any negative covenant could ever be remedied by the tenant, even if the prohibited user ceased before the service of the section 146 notice.[7] However, the better view now appears to be that remedy is possible in relation to negative covenants where the breach is of a *continuing* nature.[8] In such cases

---

18 *Expert Clothing Service & Sales Ltd v Hillgate House Ltd* [1986] Ch 340 at 355B.
19 *Rugby School (Governors) v Tannahill* [1934] 1 KB 695 at 701; *Expert Clothing Service & Sales Ltd v Hillgate House Ltd* [1986] Ch 340 at 355C. See also *Bass Holdings Ltd v Morton Music Ltd* (1987) *Times*, 6 April.
20 [1986] Ch 340.
1 The most substantial damage imposed on the landlord by the tenant's breach flowed from the fact that the reconstructed premises would have commanded a higher rental value. However, as the Court of Appeal indicated (at 356A), this kind of loss was amply compensable in money. The Court further pointed out (at 358A-B) that the landlord would have been entitled to include in the section 146 notice a 'tight timetable' for the fulfilment of the tenant's obligation to reconstruct.
2 *Expert Clothing Service & Sales Ltd v Hillgate House Ltd* [1986] Ch 340 at 362H-363A.
3 See *Expert Clothing Service & Sales Ltd v Hillgate House Ltd* [1986] Ch 340 at 354H-355A, 358F, where Slade LJ hypothesised that irremediability might attach, for instance, to the breach of a covenant to insure the demised property if the premises had already been burnt down without insurance cover having been obtained.
4 *Expert Clothing Service & Sales Ltd v Hillgate House Ltd* [1986] Ch 340 at 362H-363A. There seems to be no decided English case in which the breach of a positive covenant has been held incapable of remedy (see *Expert Clothing Service & Sales Ltd v Hillgate House Ltd*, supra at 358F).
5 *Scala House and District Property Co Ltd v Forbes* [1974] QB 575 at 588D. See (1973) 89 LQR 460; [1974] CLJ 54 (D.J. Hayton).
6 See also *Expert Clothing Service & Sales Ltd v Hillgate House Ltd* [1986] Ch 340 at 354G, 363A.
7 See *Rugby School (Governors) v Tannahill* [1934] 1 KB 695 at 701; *Scala House and District Property Co Ltd v Forbes* [1974] QB 575 at 588A-B. Compare, however, *Rugby School (Governors) v Tannahill* [1935] 1 KB 87 at 90.
8 It is well established that a breach of a covenant as to user of premises constitutes a continuing breach (see *Cooper v Henderson* (1982) 263 Estates Gazette 592 at 593).

the vital determinant is whether the harm caused to the landlord by the tenant's breach can be retrieved by the cesser of the prohibited activity.

It is clear that in some instances the mere cesser by the tenant of the offending user cannot constitute an adequate remedy simply because even a complete cesser does not remove the 'stigma' which the tenant's wrongful activities have caused to attach to the premises.[9] Thus the use of the demised premises in breach of covenant as a brothel cannot be remedied by mere cesser of the immoral user (even if accompanied by the payment of compensation).[10] As O'Connor LJ observed in *Expert Clothing Service & Sales Ltd v Hillgate House Ltd*,[11] 'the taint lingers on and will not dissipate within a reasonable time.' Likewise the involvement of the tenant in any serious criminal activity in relation to the demised premises may constitute a breach incapable of remedy.[12] In *Dunraven Securities Ltd v Holloway*[13] the Court of Appeal regarded as irremediable the conduct of a tenant who had taken a lease of shop premises in Soho supposedly for the sale of old and modern prints, books and objets d'art, but who had instead used the premises as a sex shop.[14]

Equally clearly there are some continuing breaches of a negative covenant where cesser of the prohibited user accompanied by reasonable compensation can constitute a sufficient remedy.[15] If such cesser provides an adequate remedy, then if the cesser occurs before the service of the section 146 notice, that notice need not demand that remedy be made. The only issue outstanding at this stage will be the payment of compensation for the tenant's breach,[16] and the tenant can avert forfeiture simply by paying the required compensation. If cesser has not yet occurred, the section 146 notice must not only demand compensation but must also require that cesser occur within such time as is reasonable.

(viii) Forfeiture for breach of the tenant's repairing covenant Forfeiture for breach of a tenant's covenant to repair merits special attention since further limits on the enforceability of such a covenant are contained in the Leasehold Property

9 *Expert Clothing Service & Sales Ltd v Hillgate House Ltd* [1986] Ch 340 at 357D-E.
10 *Rugby School (Governors) v Tannahill* [1935] 1 KB 87 at 90f, 93f; *Egerton v Esplanade Hotels, London, Ltd* [1947] 2 All ER 88 at 92A. However, it is possible that such a breach is remediable by a tenant who takes immediate action directed at forfeiture in order to terminate an immoral or illegal user by his subtenant of which he was previously unaware (see eg *Glass v Kencakes Ltd* [1966] 1 QB 611 at 629; *Re Vanek and Bomza* (1977) 74 DLR (3d) 175 at 180; but compare the doubts expressed on this point in *Scala House and District Property Co Ltd v Forbes* [1974] QB 575 at 587B-C). See also *British Petroleum Pension Trust Ltd v Behrendt* (1985) 276 Estates Gazette 199 at 202, where Purchas LJ declined to regard a breach of a covenant against immoral user as remediable, particularly since the tenant had effectively shut his eyes to the conduct of his subtenant.
11 [1986] Ch 340 at 362G.
12 See *Hoffman v Fineberg* [1949] Ch 245 at 257 (illicit gaming club); *Ali v Booth* (1966) 110 SJ 708 at 709 (conviction of restaurateur under food hygiene regulations); *Kelly v Purvis* (1983) 80 Law Soc Gaz 410 (illegal use of licensed massage parlour as brothel).
13 (1982) 264 Estates Gazette 709 at 711. See (1983) 133 NLJ 485 (H.W. Wilkinson); (1983) 127 SJ 232 (D.W. Williams).
14 Although the tenant had not been prosecuted under the Obscene Publications Act 1959, magistrates had made a forfeiture order in respect of books, magazines and films found on the premises.
15 Examples would appear to be provided by the breach of such covenants as not to place window boxes in the windows of a residential flat (see *Expert Clothing Service & Sales Ltd v Hillgate House Ltd* [1986] Ch 340 at 362G) or not to use the demised premises for residential purposes (see *Cooper v Henderson* (1982) 263 Estates Gazette 592 at 594).
16 *Expert Clothing Service & Sales Ltd v Hillgate House Ltd* [1986] Ch 340 at 362H.

(Repairs) Act 1938. This Act was introduced in order to counteract a prevalent mischief which enabled an unscrupulous landlord to purchase the reversion on a long lease and then harass the tenant with exaggerated lists of dilapidations, not for the purpose of protecting the landlord's reversion but rather in order to coerce an early surrender of the term.[17]

The Leasehold Property (Repairs) Act 1938 provides some degree of protection for the tenant by imposing special restrictions on the availability of certain kinds of remedy for breaches of a tenant's covenant to repair.[18] The Act applies only to leases for a term of seven years or more,[19] of which at the relevant time at least three years remain unexpired.[20] The Act requires in effect that the landlord obtain the sanction of the court before pursuing remedies of forfeiture or damages. The Act does not, however, restrict the availability to the landlord of any remedy either by way of mandatory injunction[1] or by way of action for a debt due under the lease.[2]

Where the landlord seeks either forfeiture of the lease or damages on the basis of a tenant's breach of his covenant or agreement to keep or put the demised premises in repair,[3] the landlord must first serve on the tenant a notice as specified in section 146 of the Law of Property Act 1925.[4] The tenant then has a statutory right within 28 days of the service of this notice to serve on the landlord a counter-notice claiming the benefit of the 1938 Act.[5] Where a counter-notice is duly served, no proceedings (by action or otherwise) may be taken by the landlord for the purpose of re-entry or recovery of damages unless the court gives its leave.[6] The court's leave is available only on the grounds specified in the Act,[7] of which the most important is that the present actuality

17 On the intendment of the legislation, see *Sidnell v Wilson* [1966] 2 QB 67 at 76; *Hamilton v Martell Securities Ltd* [1984] Ch 266 at 278E-F. See generally P.F. Smith, [1986] Conv 85.

18 For even more specific restrictions on the landlord's remedies for the tenant's default in respect of internal decorative repairs, see Law of Property Act 1925, s 147.

19 Leasehold Property (Repairs) Act 1938, s 7(1). A lease of an agricultural holding is excluded.

20 Leasehold Property (Repairs) Act 1938, s 1(1).

 1 There is venerable authority against the granting of a mandatory injunction for the specific enforcement of a tenant's repairing obligation (post, p 514), but compare *S.E.D.A.C. Investments Ltd v Tanner* [1982] 1 WLR 1342 at 1349F, where it was suggested that such a remedy is open to the landlord (see [1983] Conv 71).

 2 The 1938 Act certainly does not preclude the landlord from suing for a debt due under the lease such as legal costs and surveyor's fees incurred in the preparation of a section 146 notice (*Middlegate Properties Ltd v Gidlow-Jackson* (1977) 34 P & CR 4 at 9).

 3 The 1938 Act has no application to such covenants as to take out and maintain insurance on the demised premises (*Farimani v Gates* (1984) 271 Estates Gazette 887 at 888f) or to clean toilets on the demised premises (*Starrokate Ltd v Burry* (1982) 265 Estates Gazette 871 at 872).

 4 Leasehold Property (Repairs) Act 1938, s 1(1), (2). The landlord's notice directed towards forfeiture is invalid unless it indicates 'in characters not less conspicuous than those in any other part of the notice' the tenant's right to serve a counter-notice (Leasehold Property (Repairs) Act 1938, s 1(4)). A section 146 notice relating to the recovery of damages for breach of covenant must be served at least one month before the commencement of the action (Leasehold Property (Repairs) Act 1938, s 1(2)).

 5 Leasehold Property (Repairs) Act 1938, s 1(1), (2).

 6 Leasehold Property (Repairs) Act 1938, s 1(3). A landlord's application for the court's leave under section 1(3) is a pending land action within Land Charges Act 1972, s 17(1) and is therefore protectible by the entry of a caution in registered land (*Selim Ltd v Bickenhall Engineering Ltd* [1981] 1 WLR 1318 at 1323H-1324A).

 7 However, in order to obtain leave the landlord need only make out a prima facie case or a bona fide arguable case that at least one of the grounds is satisfied. The standards of proof are 'lowly' (*Land Securities PLC v Receiver for the Metropolitan Police District* [1983] 1 WLR 439 at 444D-E, 445A; [1983] Conv 323 (P.F. Smith)).

or imminent likelihood of substantial diminution of the value of the landlord's reversion makes immediate remedy of the breach imperative.[8] The court may also grant leave where 'special circumstances...render it just and equitable that leave should be given'.[9]

There may be one potentially serious trap for the landlord under the terms of the 1938 Act. It seems that the entire scheme of the Act contemplates that the landlord's service of a section 146 notice should precede any actual remedy of the tenant's breach of his repairing covenant.[10] Accordingly it was held in *S.E.D.A.C. Investments Ltd v Tanner*[11] that the court had no jurisdiction to grant a landlord leave to pursue a claim in damages against the tenant if, in the interests of procuring an immediate remedy,[12] the landlord had already effected the necessary repairs before purporting to serve a section 146 notice on the tenant.[13] If this decision is correct, the landlord may be unable to recover his expenditure on urgently conducted repairs.[14]

(g) Relief against forfeiture for breaches other than non-payment of rent

Irrespective of whether the covenant breached by the tenant is or is not 'capable of remedy' within section 146 of the Law of Property Act 1925, there is always a possibility that the court may grant the tenant relief against forfeiture. As Lord Erskine LC remarked in *Davis v West*,[15] where 'there is no fraud, and the party is capable of giving complete compensation, it is the province of a Court of Equity to interfere, and give relief against the forfeiture for breach of other covenants, as well as that for payment of rent.' This jurisdiction is now confirmed by statute. Section 146(2) of the Law of Property Act provides that where the landlord is proceeding, by action or otherwise, to enforce his right of re-entry, the tenant may apply for relief against forfeiture, and the court has a discretion to grant or withhold relief as it thinks fit.[16] If the court decides to grant relief, it may do so on such terms as to costs, expenses, damages,

---

8　Leasehold Property (Repairs) Act 1938, s 1(5)(a).
9　Leasehold Property (Repairs) Act 1938, s 1(5)(e).
10　See *S.E.D.A.C. Investments Ltd v Tanner* [1982] 1 WLR 1342 at 1347G-H.
11　[1982] 1 WLR 1342 at 1348G-H. See [1983] Conv 72 (P.F. Smith);
12　There was evidence that the landlord feared that the premises, unless repaired as a matter of urgency, might present a danger of injury to passing pedestrians. He therefore intervened swiftly in order to protect himself from liability ([1982] 1 WLR 1342 at 1344A).
13　In effect the section 146 notice was invalid because it required a remedy for a breach which had already been remedied by the landlord's anxious and precipitate action ([1982] 1 WLR 1342 at 1348F-G).
14　The courts have since sought to curtail the highly inconvenient result produced by the *S.E.D.A.C. Investments* decision. See eg *Hamilton v Martell Securities Ltd* [1984] Ch 266 at 281B-C, where a similar claim by a landlord to recover the cost of urgently conducted repairs was held to be a claim in debt for a liquidated sum rather than a claim for unliquidated damages. On this view the landlord's claim required no judicial sanction under the 1938 Act, a decision since supported in *Colchester Estates (Cardiff) v Carlton Industries PLC* (1984) 271 Estates Gazette 778 at 779. See (1984) 100 LQR 338; [1984] Conv 231 (J.E.M.); (1984) 270 Estates Gazette 908 (S. Bickford-Smith). See also *Elite Investments Ltd v T.I. Bainbridge Silencers Ltd* [1986] 2 EGLR 43 at 49H; [1986] Conv 140 (P.F. Smith).
15　(1806) 12 Ves 475 at 476, 33 ER 180.
16　However, since section 146(1) is restricted in its terms to forfeiture 'under any proviso or stipulation in a lease', there is no jurisdiction to grant relief where the landlord forfeits the lease at common law on the ground of the tenant's denial of the landlord's title (*Warner v Sampson* [1958] 1 QB 404 at 424).

compensation or injunctions to restrain future breach or otherwise[17] as it thinks appropriate in the circumstances.[18]

Relief may be sought by a tenant even after an order for possession has been made but before actual re-entry occurs.[19] However, re-entry by the landlord terminates the tenant's opportunity to apply for relief.[20] By way of sharp contrast with the rules concerning forfeiture for non-payment of rent, in the present context the court has no jurisdiction to grant relief against forfeiture even within the limited period of the six months immediately following actual re-entry.[1]

(i) Guidelines for the exercise of discretion Certain guidelines have emerged in the exercise of the court's discretion to grant relief against forfeiture under section 146(2) of the Law of Property Act 1925. The court must have regard to the conduct of the applicant for relief, and must consider in particular the wilfulness of his default, the gravity of the breach and the disparity between the value of the property of which forfeiture is claimed and the extent of the damage caused by the breach.[2]

(ii) Irremediable breaches Relief is usually (but not always[3]) granted where the tenant's breach has been remedied.[4] Conversely, it is clear that the court will rarely grant relief where the tenant's breach is not 'capable of remedy' in terms of section 146.[5] Although the court is certainly possessed of power to grant relief even in relation to an irremediable breach,[6] the very circumstances which made the breach incapable of remedy may also provide good grounds for refusing relief against forfeiture.[7] Save in exceptional cases,[8] it is the 'established practice' of the court not to grant relief where the breach involves immoral user.[9]

---

17 See eg *McIvor v Donald* [1984] 2 NZLR 487 at 493, where in relation to a similar statutory provision the New Zealand Court of Appeal held that relief could be granted on terms that the tenant submit to a programme designed to have him remedy his defaults.

18 Law of Property Act 1925, s 146(2). See, in relation to virtually identical provisions, *Platt v Ong* [1972] VR 197 at 201f; *Dickeson v Lipschitz* [1972] 106 ILTR 1 at 3.

19 *West v Rogers* (1888) 4 TLR 229; *Egerton v Jones* [1939] 2 KB 702 at 707ff.

20 *Quilter v Mapleson* (1882) 9 QBD 672 at 675ff; *Pakwood Transport Ltd v 15 Beauchamp Place* (1978) 36 P & CR 112 at 117, 119.

1 *Rogers v Rice* [1892] 2 Ch 170 at 172; *Abbey National Building Society v Maybeech Ltd* [1985] Ch 190 at 198E-G.

2 *Shiloh Spinners Ltd v Harding* [1973] AC 691 at 723H-724A. The court is statutorily directed to have regard to the conduct of the parties and 'all the other circumstances' of the case (Law of Property Act 1925, s 146(2)).

3 See eg *Clifford v Johnson's Personal Representatives* (1979) 251 Estates Gazette 571 at 573, where the Court of Appeal approved a holding that 'a single man...unemployed for two years [with] no prospect of work in his field in the area...does not come within any reasonable ground for relief from forfeiture.' It was also a relevant factor that the granting of relief would have meant that the landlord was saddled with a protected tenant in respect of part of the premises.

4 *Earl Bathurst v Fine* [1974] 1 WLR 905 at 908A.

5 See eg *Dunraven Securities Ltd v Holloway* (1982) 264 Estates Gazette 709 at 711 (ante, p 500).

6 *Scala House and District Property Co Ltd v Forbes* [1974] QB 575 at 589D; *McIvor v Donald* [1984] 2 NZLR 487 at 491.

7 See *Ali v Booth* (1966) 110 SJ 708 at 709.

8 See eg *Central Estates (Belgravia) Ltd v Woolgar (No 2)* [1972] 1 WLR 1048 at 1053D-1054B.

9 *G.M.S. Syndicate Ltd v Gary Elliott Ltd* [1982] Ch 1 at 10D-E.

(iii) Trivial breaches The tenor of the caselaw suggests that, whereas the wilful transgressor must accept the penalty of his wrongdoing,[10] the transgressor whose breach is unintentional and relatively minor may confidently expect relief against forfeiture.[11] Thus, for instance, relief may be granted where in violation of his covenant the tenant has kept a pet on the demised premises, so long as the animal has not interfered with the reasonable enjoyment of other tenants or unduly frustrated the expectations of those other tenants.[12] It would be 'absurd' if a landlord could terminate a tenancy if the tenant's breach comprises some purely trivial conduct such as the keeping of a single goldfish in a bowl or the feeding of a few crumbs of bread to one sparrow or the shaking of a duster out of the window or the placing of paper in a corridor.[13]

(h) Waiver of breach

The landlord's exercise of a right of re-entry for breach of the tenant's covenants is subject to the operation of the doctrine of waiver.

(i) Principle of waiver Even if a lease provides that the tenant's term of years shall be void in the event of a breach of covenant, it is clear that the lease does not ipso facto become void. The tenant is not permitted to take advantage of his own wrong[14] and the landlord has a right to elect whether to treat the lease as forfeited or as remaining in force.[15] This election need not be made immediately,[16] but once made it cannot be retracted.[17]

It is against this background that waiver of forfeiture operates. A landlord is precluded from seeking re-entry (though not in general from recovering damages or arrears[18]) if with knowledge[19] of the tenant's default he does some act which unequivocally indicates his intention to regard the lease as

---

10 'Established and...sound principle requires that wilful breaches should not, or at least should only in exceptional cases, be relieved against, if only for the reason that the [injured party] should not be compelled to remain in a relation of neighbourhood with a person in deliberate breach of his obligations' (*Shiloh Spinners Ltd v Harding* [1973] AC 691 at 725E-F per Lord Wilberforce).

11 *Re Vanek and Bomza* (1977) 74 DLR (3d) 175 at 180.

12 *Re London Housing Authority and Coulson* (1978) 82 DLR (3d) 754 at 756ff (two cats); *Re Kay and Parkway Forest Developments* (1982) 133 DLR (3d) 389 at 392f (dog).

13 *Re Miller and Zuchek* (1982) 132 DLR (3d) 142 at 149. Such actions would constitute a breach of the covenants commonly found in residential leases of even as long as 99 years in duration.

14 *Owendale Pty Ltd v Anthony* (1966-1967) 117 CLR 539 at 589.

15 *Expert Clothing Service & Sales Ltd v Hillgate House Ltd* [1986] Ch 340 at 359C.

16 *Owendale Pty Ltd v Anthony* (1966-1967) 117 CLR 539 at 557f.

17 *Scarf v Jardine* (1882) 7 App Cas 345 at 360; *Expert Clothing Service & Sales Ltd v Hillgate House Ltd* [1986] Ch 340 at 359C.

18 *Stephens v Junior Army and Navy Stores Ltd* [1914] 2 Ch 516 at 523.

19 The knowledge required for the purpose of implied waiver is sufficiently present where the landlord or any of his agents or employees is aware of the tenant's breach of covenant. See eg *Metropolitan Properties Co Ltd v Cordery* (1980) 39 P & CR 10 at 16f, where the knowledge acquired by the landlord's porters in a block of flats was attributed to the landlord. Compare *Official Custodian of Charities v Parway Estates Developments Ltd* (1984) 270 Estates Gazette 1077 at 1080, where disclosure of the tenant's breach in the *London Gazette* was held not to fix the landlord with deemed knowledge of that breach.

subsisting.[20] Both knowledge and active recognition of the subsistence of the lease are necessary. One without the other is ineffective to constitute a waiver of the landlord's right to forfeit.[1] Waiver, where it does occur, may be either express or implied.

(ii) Implied waiver of forfeiture Although an implied waiver of forfeiture can arise in many kinds of circumstance, it seems that conduct in relation to rent may 'fall into a special category'.[2] An implication of waiver is almost inevitable where a landlord, with actual or constructive knowledge that a breach has occurred, continues unambiguously to demand[3] or to accept[4] any rent which falls due after the breach.[5] The mere fact that rent is accepted 'without prejudice' to the right to forfeit[6] or is accepted by reason of clerical error[7] cannot prevent the acceptance from operating as a waiver. Moreover, the act of distraining for rent waives any right to forfeit the lease on the ground of rent arrears accruing before the date of the distress.[8]

Waiver may also occur, although somewhat less automatically, in other categories of case. In matters not connected directly with the payment of rent,

---

20 The legal effect of an act relied on as constituting waiver must be considered objectively, without regard to the motive or intention of the landlord or the actual understanding or belief of the tenant (*Central Estates (Belgravia) Ltd v Woolgar (No 2)* [1972] 1 WLR 1048 at 1054D). As was pointed out by Slade LJ in *Expert Clothing Service & Sales Ltd v Hillgate House Ltd* [1986] Ch 340 at 360D, this means that the doctrine of waiver is 'quite capable in some instances of operating harshly, most particularly where there has been an acceptance of rent by the landlord.'

1 *Perry v Davis* (1858) 3 CB (NS) 769 at 777, 140 ER 945 at 948.

2 *Expert Clothing Service & Sales Ltd v Hillgate House Ltd* [1986] Ch 340 at 360D-E.

3 *Segal Securities Ltd v Thoseby* [1963] 1 QB 887 at 899; *David Blackstone Ltd v Burnetts (West End) Ltd* [1973] 1 WLR 1487 at 1498E-F; *Welch v Birrane* (1975) 29 P & CR 102 at 112; *Expert Clothing Service & Sales Ltd v Hillgate House Ltd* [1986] Ch 340 at 359C-F. In order to amount to waiver, the demand for rent must be effectively communicated to the tenant. It is not enough, for instance, that it is addressed to the tenant's wife (*Trustees of Henry Smith's Charity v Willson* [1983] QB 316 at 332F-333A).

4 *Croft v Lumley* (1858) 6 HLCas 672 at 713, 10 ER 1459 at 1475; *Davenport v R* (1877) 3 App Cas 115 at 131f; *Oak Property Co Ltd v Chapman* [1947] KB 886 at 898; *Expert Clothing Service & Sales Ltd v Hillgate House Ltd* [1986] Ch 340 at 359C-D; *Larking v Great Western (Nepean) Gravel Ltd* (1940) 64 CLR 221 at 240; *Owendale Pty Ltd v Anthony* (1966-1967) 117 CLR 539 at 557f, 588; *Baxton v Kara* [1982] 1 NSWLR 604 at 608. In *Foxell v Mendis* (Unreported, Court of Appeal, 19 May 1982), however, Stephenson LJ pointed out that it is 'not an easy thing to waive the forfeiture of a statutory tenancy by the acceptance of rent'. For the proposition that there may be a distinction between rent accepted from a statutory tenant and that accepted from a contractual tenant, see *Oak Property Co Ltd v Chapman*, supra at 898f; *Trustees of Henry Smith's Charity v Willson* [1983] QB 316 at 331C-G; [1983] Conv 248 (J. Martin).

5 There is, however, no waiver of forfeiture if money is 'received in respect of the tenant's use of the land but not in its quality as rent' (*Larking v Great Western (Nepean) Gravel Ltd* (1940) 64 CLR 221 at 240). There is therefore no waiver by the landlord if he receives payments from the tenant in the form of 'mesne profits'.

6 *Segal Securities Ltd v Thoseby* [1963] 1 QB 887 at 897f; *Central Estates (Belgravia) Ltd v Woolgar (No 2)* [1972] 1 WLR 1048 at 1054E; *Expert Clothing Service & Sales Ltd v Hillgate House Ltd* [1986] Ch 340 at 359D-E.

7 *Central Estates (Belgravia) Ltd v Woolgar (No 2)* [1972] 1 WLR 1048 at 1052F-G, 1055D-F.

8 *Doe d Flower v Peck* (1830) 1 B & Ad 428 at 437, 109 ER 847 at 850; *Kirkland v Briancourt* (1890) 6 TLR 441. A request by a landlord that the Department of Health and Social Security should deduct rent arrears (or even current payments for use and occupation) from statutory benefit payments made to the occupier has been held not to operate as a waiver of a demand for possession (*Northern Ireland Housing Executive v Duffin* [1985] 8 NIJB 62 at 71f). Compare, however, *Northern Ireland Housing Executive v McGinn* (Unreported).

the courts seem to be more 'free to look at *all* the circumstances of the case'[9] in considering whether a landlord's actions are consistent with his avoiding the lease. Waiver may well arise where the landlord, with knowledge of a breach giving him a right of re-entry, engages in action so unequivocal as to be consistent only with the continued existence of the landlord-tenant relationship. Such conduct includes, for instance, an agreement by the landlord to grant the tenant a new lease commencing on the normal determination of existing letting,[10] or, in some circumstances, the proffering of a mere negotiating document which contemplates continued contractual relations.[11]

(iii) Temporal scope of the waiver   In the case of a 'once and for all breach',[12] any proven waiver of forfeiture precludes any claim by the landlord to forfeit the lease on the ground of the particular breach which has occurred,[13] but does not operate as a general waiver in relation to similar breaches in the future.[14] However, waiver in respect of a continuing breach of covenant can be withdrawn at any time subsequently by the landlord, whereupon his right to claim forfeiture of the lease is revitalised.[15] In the absence of some plea based upon estoppel, the tenant is not entitled to argue that one prolonged period of waiver gives him any right or expectation that the waiver of a continuing breach should continue indefinitely.[16]

(j) Effect of forfeiture

The exercise of the landlord's right of re-entry has a number of important consequences (both actual and potential) for the tenant and for other persons.

(i) Effect on tenant   The mere fact that a lease or tenancy has been determined does not entitle the landlord to claim trespass against the tenant if the latter remains in occupation. The landlord's right to immediate possession is not enough for this purpose. It is necessary that he should convert his right to possession into actual possession by means of re-entry on the premises.[17]

---

9   *Expert Clothing Service & Sales Ltd v Hillgate House Ltd* [1986] Ch 340 at 360E-F. In *Chrisdell v Tickner* (1987) *Times*, 11 May, the Court of Appeal held that a landlord's failure to take any action in relation to a suspected breach of the tenancy agreement did not amount to a waiver of the breach where the landlord had not been sufficiently confident that a judge would disbelieve the tenant's denial of the alleged breach.

10 See eg *Ward v Day* (1864) 5 B & S 359 at 363, 122 ER 865 at 866.

11 *Expert Clothing Service & Sales Ltd v Hillgate House Ltd* [1986] Ch 340 at 360F-G.

12 For the distinction between a 'once and for all' breach and a breach of a continuing nature, see p 499, ante. It seems that breach of a covenant to insure premises is not a continuing breach (see *Farimani v Gates* (1984) 271 Estates Gazette 887 at 889; but compare *Larking v Great Western (Nepean) Gravel Ltd* (1940) 64 CLR 221 at 236 per Dixon J). See also *Church Commissioners for England v Nodjoumi* (1985) 135 NLJ 1185; (1986) 136 NLJ 255 (H.W. Wilkinson).

13 *Farimani v Gates* (1984) 271 Estates Gazette 887 at 889.

14 Law of Property Act 1925, s 148(1).

15 *Doe d Ambler v Woodbridge* (1829) 9 B & C 376 at 377f, 109 ER 140. There is no need to serve a further section 146 notice (*Farimani v Gates* (1984) 271 Estates Gazette 887 at 888).

16 *Cooper v Henderson* (1982) 263 Estates Gazette 592 at 594.

17 *Butcher v Butcher* (1827) 7 B & C 399 at 402, 108 ER 772 at 773; *Jones v Chapman* (1849) 2 Exch 803 at 821, 154 ER 717 at 724; *Lows v Telford* (1876) 1 App Cas 414 at 426; *Hegan v Carolan* [1916] 2 IR 27 at 30f; *Haniotis v Dimitriou* [1983] 1 VR 498 at 500.

However, once re-entry occurs the tenant becomes a trespasser. The landlord may now use such force as is reasonably necessary to expel his former tenant, provided that the latter has been requested to leave and has been given a reasonable opportunity of doing so.[18]

It seems unclear whether on re-entering the landlord must give notice requiring the removal within a reasonable time of any goods left on the premises by the former tenant.[19] However, if such notice is given and ignored the landlord may remove the goods from the premises without incurring any liability in trespass. This is so at least if the goods are carried 'to a convenient distance' and deposited 'in a proper and convenient place for the use of the plaintiff',[20] and if the landlord does no unnecessary damage.[1] A right of distress damage feasant may be asserted by the landlord where the presence of the tenant's belongings on the premises causes actual damage, although it is possible that the costs of removal may amount to actual damage for this purpose.[2] This latter right is, however, subject to the normal limitation that the remedy of distress may not be claimed in respect of things in actual use by their owner.[3]

(ii) Effect on subtenant It is trite law that the forfeiture of a head lease necessarily and automatically destroys any sublease created out of that head lease.[4] However, it is also clear that a subtenant has an independent right under section 146(4) of the Law of Property Act 1925 to seek relief against forfeiture.[5] The court has a broad discretion to grant relief on such terms as it thinks fit.[6] In particular the court may invest the subtenant with an entirely new estate[7] in the demised premises on such terms as are deemed appropriate,[8]

---

18 *Polkinghorn v Wright* (1845) 8 QB 197 at 206f, 115 ER 849 at 853; *Haniotis v Dimitriou* [1983] 1 VR 498 at 500.

19 *Haniotis v Dimitriou* [1983] 1 VR 498 at 501f.

20 *Houghton v Butler* (1791) 4 TR 364 at 365f, 100 ER 1066 at 1067. See also *Rea v Sheward* (1837) 2 M & W 424 at 426, 150 ER 823 at 824.

1 *Neville v Cooper* (1834) 2 C & M 329 at 331, 149 ER 786 at 787. In *Haniotis v Dimitriou* [1983] 1 VR 498 at 502, Brooking J left for future litigation the hypothetical case 'of the Stradivarius put out on to the footpath', suggesting that relevant arguments at that stage would include the contention that such a small object was not 'encumbering' the landlord's premises, or 'doing damage' to him, or that the law will not permit the remedy of self-help where the resulting loss to the tenant is wholly disproportionate to the injury averted by the landlord.

2 *Jamieson's Tow & Salvage Ltd v Murray* [1984] 2 NZLR 144 at 149, but compare *R v Howson* (1966) 55 DLR (2d) 582 at 597.

3 *Jamieson's Tow & Salvage Ltd v Murray* [1984] 2 NZLR 144 at 150 (illegally parked car towed away with driver still sitting resolutely at steering wheel).

4 *Great Western Railway Co v Smith* (1876) 2 Ch D 235 at 253; *G.M.S. Syndicate Ltd v Gary Elliott Ltd* [1982] Ch 1 at 8C. See generally Stephen Tromans, [1986] Conv 187.

5 Section 146(4) relates to forfeiture for breach of *any* covenant (whether or not for non-payment of rent). See (1984) 134 NLJ 717 (H.W. Wilkinson).

6 In *Chatham Empire Theatre (1955) Ltd v Ultrans* [1961] 1 WLR 817 at 820, for instance, relief was granted on condition that the subtenant paid up that proportion of the total arrears of rent which corresponded with his part of the premises comprised within the head lease.

7 The new lease is 'a quite distinct piece of property from the old' (*Cadogan v Dimovic* [1984] 1 WLR 609 at 613H). See also *Official Custodian for Charities v Mackey* [1985] Ch 168 at 183E. In effect the head lessor may be forced into privity of contract with the former sublessee, but the coercion of such a legal relationship may itself be inequitable if it is unreasonable to saddle the head lessor with a lessee whom he would never willingly have contracted to accept (see *O'Connor v J.G. Mooney & Co Ltd* [1982] ILRM 373 at 383).

8 Law of Property Act 1925, s 146(4).

subject to the proviso that the subtenant may not require a lease to be granted to him for any longer term than he had under his original sublease.[9] Moreover, the court has discretion to grant relief in respect of part only of the premises comprised in the head lease. Thus, in the absence of any express restriction of the landlord's right to re-enter on part only of those premises, the court may grant relief to a tenant in respect of one portion of the premises while refusing relief to a subtenant who has been in possession of another part of the premises,[10] or vice versa.

(iii) Effect on mortgagee   Forfeiture has a potentially devastating effect on any security enjoyed by a third party who has taken a mortgage over the leasehold estate of the tenant. The termination of the tenant's estate in the land destroys the mortgage. However, a legal mortgagee has a right to seek relief against forfeiture under section 146(4) of the Law of Property Act 1925.[11] Moreover, it is possible that the ancient and inherent equitable jurisdiction of the courts to grant relief against forfeiture may be available in favour of either a legal mortgagee who has failed to claim relief before re-entry by the landlord,[12] or an equitable mortgagee or equitable chargee of a leasehold interest.[13] It has been suggested that this residual equitable jurisdiction may be exercised even after forfeiture has been completed by judgment and execution,[14] and that the court will generally grant relief on the payment of appropriate compensation.[15]

The applicability of the court's inherent jurisdiction in this context is not wholly clear of doubt.[16] In *Smith v Metropolitan City Properties Ltd*,[17] for instance, Walton J thought it 'quite fantastic' that, by enacting Law of Property Act 1925, s 146, Parliament could be regarded as having intended to leave the inherent equitable jurisdiction untrammelled. If correct, this conclusion means that a lease containing a forfeiture clause can no longer be viewed as an acceptable security for a mortgagee where there is any possibility that the landlord may succeed in concealing forfeiture proceedings from the mortgagee until it is too late for the latter to seek relief. On this basis the mortgaging of leasehold flats would be severely jeopardised.[18]

---

9   The term of the original sublease is taken to include any extension imposed pursuant to any relevant statutory code (eg Part II of the Landlord and Tenant Act 1954). See *Cadogan v Dimovic* [1984] 1 WLR 609 at 614D-E.

10   *G.M.S. Syndicate Ltd v Gary Elliott Ltd* [1982] Ch 1 at 12E-F, following *Dumpor's Case* (1603) 4 Co Rep 119b, 76 ER 1110. See [1981] Conv 381 (R. Griffith).

11   See *Official Custodian for Charities v Mackey* [1985] Ch 168 at 183B-C; [1985] Conv 50. The mortgagee's right to claim relief under section 146(4) may arise on the ground that the mortgagee took the security of a long sublease (post, p 573) and therefore now has standing as a subtenant. Alternatively, if the mortgage was under a charge expressed to be by way of legal mortgage, the chargee has (by virtue of Law of Property Act 1925, s 87(1)) the same right to apply for relief as if he were possessed of a sub-term less by one day than the term of the charged lease (see *Abbey National Building Society v Maybeech Ltd* [1985] Ch 190 at 198C-D).

12   *Abbey National Building Society v Maybeech Ltd* [1985] Ch 190 at 204C. See [1985] Conv 50.

13   *Ladup Ltd v Williams & Glyn's Bank PLC* [1985] 1 WLR 851 at 860H-861A. See [1985] Conv 407.

14   *Hare v Elms* [1893] 1 QB 604 at 607f.

15   *Ladup Ltd v Williams & Glyn's Bank PLC* [1985] 1 WLR 851 at 860E-F. See generally Stephen Tromans, [1986] Conv 187.

16   See (1986) 136 NLJ 339 (P.F. Smith).

17   (1986) 277 Estates Gazette 753 at 754.

18   See (1986) 136 NLJ 254.

(iv) Effect on squatter A squatter who has acquired a title by adverse possession against a leaseholder has no sufficient interest in the lease to enable him to apply for relief against its forfeiture.[19]

(k) Proposals for reform

In 1985 the Law Commission completed an exhaustive review of the current law relating to the forfeiture of leases and tenancies.[20] The Commission formed the view that the existing law of forfeiture is 'unnecessarily complicated, is no longer coherent and may give rise to injustice.'[1] In particular the Commission pointed to the anomalous way in which the law at present incorporates two almost entirely separate regimes, one relating to forfeiture for non-payment of rent and the other relating to all other cases.[2] The Commission accordingly recommended the abolition of the existing law of forfeiture and its replacement by a new system.[3] The key feature underlying the Commission's recommendation was the recognition that re-entry by the landlord almost invariably occurs nowadays in the constructive form of commencement of legal proceedings, actual re-entry being unlawful in many cases.[4] The Commission thus proposed to rationalise the present procedure by acknowledging that the landlord's proceedings, which at present have to be framed as proceedings for possession, are in reality proceedings designed to terminate the tenancy.[5]

The Commission therefore proposed the introduction by legislation of a new 'termination order scheme'.[6] Under this scheme there would be no distinction between termination for non-payment of rent and termination for other reasons, and every tenancy would remain in full force until the court made a 'termination order' determining the date on which the tenancy should end.[7] The landlord would be able to base his application for a termination order on any of a number of 'termination order events', which would broadly cover all breaches of express or implied leasehold covenant and the bankruptcy of the tenant.[8] Termination on any of these grounds would no longer depend on the inclusion of an express forfeiture clause in the covenants of a lease,[9] and would still remain available even where the consequences of a termination order event had been remedied.[10]

The court, on hearing an application for termination, would have a discretionary power to make either an 'absolute order' for termination[11] or a 'remedial order' which would end the tenancy 'if, but only if, the tenant failed to take specified remedial action within a specified time'.[12] An absolute order

---

19 *Tickner v Buzzacott* [1965] Ch 426 at 434.
20 *Codification of the Law of Landlord and Tenant: Forfeiture of Tenancies* (Law Com No 142, 21 March 1985). See [1986] Conv 165 (P.F. Smith).
1   Law Com No 142, para 1.3.
2   Law Com No 142, para 3.11.
3   Law Com No 142, para 1.3.
4   Law Com No 142, para 3.4.
5   Law Com No 142, para 3.5.
6   Law Com No 142, paras 3.7, 3.26ff.
7   Law Com No 142, para 4.1.
8   Law Com No 142, paras 5.1ff.
9   Law Com No 142, paras 5.3ff.
10 Law Com No 142, para 7.13.
11 Law Com No 142, paras 9.15ff.
12 Law Com No 142, paras 9.21ff.

would in general be appropriate only where a termination order event was either of such serious character that the tenant 'ought not in all the circumstances to remain tenant of the property',[13] or comprised a wrongful assignment or an insolvency event under circumstances in which the court was satisfied that no remedial action would be adequate and satisfactory to the landlord.[14]

The Law Commission's proposals represent a most useful reformulation of the law of forfeiture. It remains to be seen whether the Commission's recommendations provide a spur to legislative action.

(2) Distress

Distress is an ancient common law remedy which entitles the landlord, in appropriate circumstances, summarily to seize goods found on the demised premises, sell them up and recoup from the proceeds of sale any arrears of rent owed by the tenant.[15] Although sometimes described as an obsolete remedy,[16] distress is not infrequently used, especially by local authority landlords, as a means of recovering arrears of rent from a defaulting tenant.[17]

As a remedy founded in self-help, distress is anomalous and somewhat controversial. Except in the case of protected and statutory tenancies,[18] there is no requirement that any due process of law be interposed before the landlord distrains upon his tenant's goods.[19] Precisely because it is a potentially traumatic remedy, the exercise of distress is subject to a number of restrictions, some of which are rooted in statutory provisions of some antiquity.

(a) General restrictions on the right to distrain

Distress may be levied only in respect of arrears of rent.[20] No other breach of

---

13 Law Com No 142, paras 9.33ff. This guideline was intended by the Law Commission to 'militate against the doctrine of "stigma"' (para 9.39).

14 Law Com No 142, paras 9.43ff.

15 One of the best modern accounts of the law of distress is contained in *Distress for Rent* (Law Commission Working Paper No 97, May 1986), Chapter 2.

16 *Abingdon RDC v O'Gorman* [1968] 2 QB 811 at 819E. See the reference to distress as a 'relic of feudalism' in Law Commission, *Landlord and Tenant: Interim Report on Distress for Rent* (Law Com No 5, 1966), para 5.

17 See (1978) LAG Bulletin 57 (A. Arden); Law Commission Working Paper No 97 (May 1986), para 3.3. Distress has also been advocated as an attractive alternative to other remedies for commercial arrears (see *Distress for Rent: Best Remedy for Commercial Arrears*, (1980) 1 PLB 33). The argument is that distress provides a faster and less cumbersome form of remedy than re-entry, which may rebound on the landlord, leaving him with empty premises and no rent. An alternative to distress exists in the form of execution against the goods of the tenant either through the issue of a warrant of execution (CCR (1981), Ord 26, r 1) or on application to the High Court for a writ of *fieri facias*. Both forms of process tend to be more heavily encumbered by technical difficulty than even the remedy of distress. See [1983] Conv 444 (A. Hill-Smith); (1986) 136 NLJ 546 (M. Haley).

18 Rent Act 1977, s 147(1) (post, p 1039). The Law Commission has recommended that the leave of the county court be a prerequisite of distress in relation to any kind of residential tenancy (Law Com No 5, para 26).

19 Distress has been abolished in many jurisdictions (see eg Judgments (Enforcement) Act (Northern Ireland) 1969, s 122), and is of doubtful constitutional validity in other jurisdictions (see eg Constitution of the Republic of Ireland, art 43). In 1968 the Payne Committee recommended the abolition in England of distress for rent (see *Report of Committee on the Enforcement of Judgment Debts* (Cmnd 3909, February 1969), para 924).

20 The right to levy distress is limited to six years of rent arrear (Limitation Act 1980, s 19). There is no right to distrain for mesne profits (*Bridges v Smyth* (1829) 5 Bing 410 at 413, 130 ER 1119 at 1120; *Alford v Vickery* (1842) Car & M 280 at 283, 174 ER 507 at 508).

covenant entitles the landlord to distrain upon the goods of his tenant. Moreover, distress is intrinsically a landlord's remedy, and is therefore available only where there is a tenancy[1] and never where there is merely a licence.[2] The landlord must, at the date of the distress, be possessed of the immediate reversion on the tenancy in relation to which he seeks to distrain. This means, in effect, that distress cannot generally be levied against a subtenant,[3] and a subtenant's goods are in any event exempted by statute from any distress levied by a head lessor against a head lessee.[4]

The landlord's right to distrain arises as soon as any rent is in arrear during the subsistence of the tenancy,[5] and the right continues for six months after the termination of the tenancy if the former tenant is still in occupation of the same premises.[6] However, the remedies of distress and forfeiture are mutually exclusive.[7] Distress is premised on an affirmation of the landlord-tenant relationship, while forfeiture marks an unequivocal election by the landlord to terminate that relationship.[8] It follows therefore that distress cannot lawfully be levied where the landlord has already exercised his right to re-enter the demised premises.[9] Recourse to common law distress is likewise excluded if the landlord has already obtained a court judgment for the arrears of rent.[10]

(b) Time and manner of lawful distress

The time and manner of lawful distress are regulated by rather archaic and not

---

1 The corollary is that an owner who distrains on the goods of one who occupies his premises is estopped from alleging that the occupier is merely a licensee, at least if the other requirements of a lease (ante, p 429) are also present. See *Ward v Day* (1863) 4 B & S 337 at 357, 122 ER 486 at 493; *Carden v Choudhury* (Unreported, Court of Appeal, 29 February 1984) (ante, p 444).

2 *Hancock v Austin* (1863) 14 CB (NS) 634 at 639f, 143 ER 593 at 596; *Ward v Day* (1863) 4 B & S 337 at 356ff, 122 ER 486 at 493.

3 See *Wade v Marsh* (1625) Lat 211, 82 ER 350.

4 Law of Distress Amendment Act 1908, s 1.

5 This is so even if rent is payable in advance (see *Walsh v Lonsdale* (1882) 21 Ch D 9 at 14f, ante, p 471). There is no requirement at common law that the landlord should make any further demand for rent before distraining (*Kerby v Harding* (1851) 6 Exch 234 at 240f, 155 ER 527 at 530).

6 Landlord and Tenant Act 1709, ss 6, 7. Thus the right to distrain is lost if a local authority rehouses elsewhere former tenants who have been evicted for rent arrears.

7 *Bank of Montreal v Woodtown Developments Ltd* (1980) 99 DLR 739 at 743; *Country Kitchen Ltd v Wabush Enterprises Ltd* (1981) 120 DLR (3d) 358 at 361.

8 'It could be said that [the landlord], by its actions, attempted "to have its cake and eat it too", ie, to enjoy the fruits of both forfeiture and distraint at the same time or at least whichever one suited its purpose...this [the landlord] was not entitled to do' (*Country Kitchen Ltd v Wabush Enterprises Ltd* (1981) 120 DLR (3d) 358 at 362). It seems the mutually exclusive nature of the remedies cannot be reversed even by express contractual provision (*Re Coopers & Lybrand Ltd and Royal Bank of Canada* (1982) 137 DLR (3d) 356 at 360f).

9 *Kirkland v Briancourt* (1890) 6 TLR 441. Forfeiture will be established by any 'act so inconsistent with the continuance of the [tenant's] term that [the landlords] were estopped from denying that it was at an end' (*Oastler v Henderson* (1877) 2 QBD 575 at 577). Thus the landlord's right to distrain is lost if he changes the locks on the doors of the demised premises and denies the tenant entry (*Country Kitchen Ltd v Wabush Enterprises Ltd* (1981) 120 DLR (3d) 358 at 363; *Re Coopers & Lybrand Ltd and Royal Bank of Canada* (1982) 137 DLR (3d) 356 at 359), but not if he merely sends a letter demanding payment of existing arrears of rent (*Cameron v Eldorado Properties Ltd* (1981) 113 DLR (3d) 141 at 145).

10 *Chancellor v Webster* (1893) 9 TLR 568 at 569 (even though the judgment debt remains unsatisfied).

always rational rules. Distress cannot be levied between sunset and sunrise[11] nor on a Sunday.[12] Entry to the premises must not be made by breaking an outer door,[13] but inner doors may be broken down once entry has been achieved.[14] Entry through an open window is permissible,[15] but not through a window which, although unlocked, is closed.[16]

The landlord may distrain in person, but it is more normal to employ the services of a bailiff.[17] Not only must a bailiff have the authority of the landlord (usually in the written form of a warrant of distress); he must also hold a written certificate issued by the county court which entitles him to act in this capacity.[18]

(c) Exemption for privileged goods

The process of distraint involves in principle the seizure of any goods found on the demised premises,[19] subject only to certain common law[20] and statutory exceptions in respect of privileged goods. Among the categories of goods immune from seizure are clothes and bedding (to a total value of £100) and tools of trade (to a total value of £150)[1]; perishable foods,[2] tenant's fixtures,[3] the property of lodgers,[4] and things in actual use. Things 'in actual use' include articles which are immune from seizure simply on the ground that a breach of the peace would otherwise almost necessarily occur.[5] It is not certain how far the last exemption extends, but it seems that a tenant can effectively resist attempts at distress simply by switching on any kind of electrical apparatus in his home before the landlord or bailiff arrives to carry out the distress (eg television set, radio, refrigerator, washing machine, cooker).[6] Distress can be

11   *Aldenburgh v Peaple* (1834) 6 C & P 212 at 213, 172 ER 1212; *Tutton v Darke* (1860) 5 H & N 647 at 650, 157 ER 1338 at 1340.
12   *Werth v London & Westminster Loan and Discount Co* (1889) 5 TLR 521 at 522.
13   *Semayne's Case* (1604) 5 Co Rep 91a at 92b, 77 ER 194 at 198; *Hancock v Austin* (1863) 14 CB (NS) 634 at 640, 143 ER 593 at 596; *Gordon v Phelan* (1881) 15 ILTR 70 at 72; *Cassidy v Foley* [1904] 2 IR 427 at 428.
14   *Browning v Dann* (1735) Bull NP 81.
15   *Long v Clarke* [1894] 1 QB 119 at 121.
16   *Nash v Lucas* (1867) LR 2 QB 590 at 594f.
17   County Courts display the names of certificated bailiffs (who are often solicitors), and there is a Certificated Bailiffs' Association.
18   See Law of Distress (Amendment) Act 1888, s 7. The Distress for Rent Rules 1983 (SI 1983/1917) now provide for general certificates valid for a year and thereafter renewable.
19   It is, however, unlawful for the landlord to assert any lien over goods of the tenant which already happen to be in the possession of the landlord as bailee (*Finlayson v Taylor* (1983) *Times*, 14 April).
20   At common law coins were always immune from distress unless contained in a closed purse or bag (*East India Co v Skinner* (1695) 1 Botts P L 259; Law Commission Working Paper No 97 (May 1986), para 2.40). Compare, however, the unusual form of purported distress used in *Bank of Montreal v Woodtown Developments Ltd* (1980) 99 DLR 739 (landlord placed his own representatives in charge of cash register in tenant's shop).
1   Law of Distress (Amendment) Act 1888, s 4; County Courts Act 1984, s 89(1); The Protection from Execution (Prescribed Value) Order 1980 (SI 1980/26), art 2.
2   *Morley v Pincombe* (1848) 2 Exch 101 at 102, 154 ER 423.
3   *Simpson v Hartopp* (1744) Willes 512 at 514f, 125 ER 1295 at 1296f; *Darby v Harris* (1841) 1 QB 895 at 898f, 113 ER 1374 at 1376; *Crossley Bros Ltd v Lee* [1908] 1 KB 86 at 90f.
4   See Law of Distress Amendment Act 1908, s 1.
5   *Simpson v Hartopp* (1744) Willes 512 at 516, 125 ER 1295 at 1297; *Storey v Robinson* (1795) 6 TR 138 at 139, 101 ER 476 at 477; *Field v Adames* (1840) 12 Ad & El 649 at 652, 113 ER 960 at 962.
6   See (1978) LAG Bulletin 57 (A. Arden).

levied on the goods of innocent strangers which are present on the premises,[7] subject to a right in the true owner to reclaim his property by serving a statutory declaration on the landlord or bailiff.[8]

(d) Sale

The landlord or bailiff who levies distress with the intention of selling up the goods seized must give the tenant, or leave at the demised premises, a notice which states the cause for the distress and stipulates the place of sale.[9] No sooner than five days later[10] the goods may be sold—usually by auction—and the landlord may recoup the arrears of rent from the proceeds, returning the balance (if any) minus expenses to the tenant. The landlord is not permitted to purchase the goods himself, and there is a duty to obtain the best price possible.[11] It is generally thought that the sale of goods which have been the subject of an illegal distress does not pass a good title to the purchaser.[12]

(e) Proposed abolition of distress

In a recent examination of the law of distress, the Law Commission found this area of the law to be 'riddled with inconsistencies, uncertainties, anomalies and archaisms' and the Commission accordingly adopted the view that reform was 'long overdue'.[13] In the opinion of the Commission, the defects in the present law of distress are 'so fundamental and widespread that very little purpose would be served by collecting up the existing principles from the statutes and common law and restating them in modern terms in a codifying statute.'[14] The Commission has provisionally concluded that the remedy of distress for rent 'is a relic from the ancient laws of England which has no place in modern society',[15] and has thus proposed that this form of distress should be abolished.[16]

(3) Damages for breach of covenant

Damages may be awarded by the court where a landlord proves breach by the tenant of any covenant other than a covenant respecting payment of rent. Except where the breach is of a repairing covenant, damages are assessed on the usual contractual basis.[17] Their purpose is to place the landlord in the

---

7   *Juson v Dixon* (1813) 1 M & S 601 at 606ff, 105 ER 225 at 227.
8   Law of Distress Amendment Act 1908, s 1. The owner of the goods may obtain an ex parte interlocutory injunction to restrain sale, even though the required declaration is made through the agency of his solicitor (see *Lawrence Chemical Co Ltd v Rubinstein* [1982] 1 WLR 284 at 291C-E, 292F-H).
9   Distress for Rent Act 1689, s 1; Distress for Rent Act 1737, s 9.
10   Distress for Rent Act 1689, s 1.
11   There is a duty, akin to that of a mortgagee exercising his power of sale (post, p 620), to use reasonable care in conducting the sale. An independent appraisal of the goods is mandatory only if requested in writing by the tenant (Law of Distress (Amendment) Act 1888, s 5). Compare, however, *Cameron v Eldorado Properties Ltd* (1981) 113 DLR (3d) 141 at 147ff.
12   See the application of the principle *nemo dat quod non habet* in comparable circumstances in *Trustee of Estate of Royal Inns Canada Ltd v Bolus-Revelas-Bolus Ltd* (1982) 136 DLR (3d) 272 at 279.
13   *Distress for Rent* (Law Commission Working Paper No 97, May 1986), para 5.1(1).
14   Working Paper No 97, para 5.1(2).
15   Working Paper No 97, para 5.1(5).
16   Working Paper No 97, paras 4.66, 5.1(5).
17   See *Anson's Law of Contract* (26th edn by A.G. Guest, Oxford, 1984), p 491ff.

position—in so far as this can be done by means of a monetary award—in which he would have been if there had been no breach by the tenant. Damages for breach of a tenant's covenant to keep or put premises in repair cannot exceed the amount by which the value of the reversion has been diminished through the breach.[18]

(4) Action for arrears of rent

The effect of the Limitation Act is that a maximum of six years' arrears of rent may be recovered in an action brought by the landlord in respect of a tenant's non-payment of rent.[19] There is therefore no prescriptive right to freedom from the obligation to pay rent.

(5) Injunction

It is possible in appropriate circumstances for the landlord to seek the discretionary remedy of the injunction for the purpose of restraining breaches of certain covenants in the lease.[20] However, no mandatory injunction is available to enable the landlord to compel the tenant's performance of a covenant to repair the demised premises.[1]

(6) Damages for waste

The landlord may, in appropriate cases, recover damages for the tort of waste committed by the tenant. The measure of damages is represented by the diminution in the value of the reversion less a discount which allows for the fact that payment is being made some time before the reversion falls into possession.[2]

8. TENANT'S REMEDIES FOR BREACH OF COVENANT BY THE LANDLORD

The tenant has access to a wide range of remedies in respect of breach of covenant by the landlord.

(1) Remedies for disrepair

The most usual breach by the landlord relates to covenants to put or keep the demised premises in repair. The tenant's remedies in respect of disrepair or poor conditions of housing are discussed in greater detail in Chapter 27.[3]

---

18 Landlord and Tenant Act 1927, s 18(1). The landlord is not entitled to damages for mental distress caused by the tenant's breach of his covenant to repair (see eg *Turner v Jatko* (1979) 93 DLR (3d) 314 at 316f). For restrictions on the landlord's recovery of damages, see Leasehold Property (Repairs) Act 1938, s 1(2) (ante, p 501).
19 Limitation Act 1980, s 19.
20 Post, p 528.
1 *Hill v Barclay* (1810) 16 Ves 402 at 405f, 33 ER 1037 at 1038. Compare, however, *S.E.D.A.C. Investments Ltd v Tanner* [1982] 1 WLR 1342 at 1349F (ante, p 502), where it was suggested that the remedy of mandatory injunction may be open to the landlord.
2 *Whitham v Kershaw* (1886) 16 QBD 613 at 617.
3 Post, p 939.

(2) **Independence of the covenants of landlord and tenant**

Although the tenant has access to a wide range of remedy for breach of his landlord's covenants, English law still adheres to the principle that there is in general no interdependence between the proper performance of the covenants of landlord and tenant respectively.[4] A breach of the landlord's responsibilities under a lease (eg by denial of quiet possession or by failure to repair) does not usually relieve the tenant of the burden of his own obligations.[5] The tenant has, for instance, no right to take part in a 'rent strike' in order to bring pressure to bear upon the defaulting landlord.[6] He must instead avail himself of some existing remedy by way of damages or injunction or specific performance. If the tenant withholds rent, he is liable to be sued for arrears by the landlord and may find that his non-payment of rent affords the landlord a ground for forfeiting the lease and recovering possession.

This weakness in the tenant's position has been countered in other jurisdictions by the introduction of legislation which reverses the traditional independence of covenanted obligations in the leasehold context. In Ontario, for instance, it has been enacted that 'the common law rules respecting the effect of the breach of a material covenant by one party to a contract on the obligation to perform by another party apply to tenancy agreements.'[7] Likewise the Uniform Residential Landlord and Tenant Act adopted in several American jurisdictions specifically allows the tenant to raise a breach of covenant by the landlord as a defence in any action for possession for non-payment of rent.[8]

(3) **Proposals for reform**

In England the Law Commission has recently proposed that the tenant should have a new right to seek termination of a tenancy on the ground of breach of covenant by his landlord.[9] This proposal, if implemented, would conclude a rather inglorious chapter of English law in which 'not even the worst possible conduct by a landlord...gives the tenant the right to end the tenancy'.[10] The Law Commission's recommendation envisages that the tenant would have the right to apply to court for a termination order based on any of a number of 'termination order events',[11] the court retaining discretion either to grant the

---

4　This principle is itself in marked contrast with the historic principle of English contract law that breach of a material covenant by one contracting party relieves the other contracting party of his obligations under the contract (see *Kingston v Preston* (1773) 2 Doug 689, 99 ER 437 per Lord Mansfield). See generally W.M. McGovern, *Dependent Promises in the History of Leases and Other Contracts*, 52 Tulane LR 659 at 666ff (1977-78); J.A. Humbach, *The Common-Law Conception of Leasing: Mitigation, Habitability, and Dependence of Covenants*, 60 Wash Univ LQ 1213 (1982-83).

5　For partial exceptions to this rule, see *Smith v Marrable* (1843) 11 M & W 5, 152 ER 693 (post, p 903); *Lee-Parker v Izzet* [1971] 1 WLR 1688 (post, p 942).

6　See eg *Bishop v Moy* [1963] NSWR 468 at 469f.

7　Landlord and Tenant Act (RSO 1980, c 232), s 89. Compare, however, *Re Burke and Arab* (1980) 130 DLR (3d) 38 at 51, affd (1983) 141 DLR (3d) 766. See generally *Poverty and the Residential Landlord-Tenant Relationship* (Report by A.J. Bradbrook, Canberra 1975), p 16.

8　Uniform Residential Landlord and Tenant Act, s 4.105. See also Mich Comp Laws Ann (Supp 1972), s 600.5741. See generally M.A. Glendon, *The Transformation of American Landlord-Tenant Law*, 23 Boston College LR 503 at 532f (1982).

9　*Codification of the Law of Landlord and Tenant: Forfeiture of Tenancies* (Law Com No 142, 21 March 1985), paras 17.10ff.

10　Law Com No 142, para 17.2.

11　Law Com No 142, paras 18.4ff.

termination requested (together with compensation for the tenant[12]) or to make a 'remedial order' requiring the landlord to take specified remedial action within a specified time.[13]

8. ENFORCEABILITY OF LEASEHOLD COVENANTS IN A LEGAL LEASE

The device of the leasehold estate offers great potential flexibility in terms of assignment and the creation of subleases.[14] The enforceability of leasehold covenants presents little problem as between the original lessor and lessee, but becomes more difficult as successive assignees and subtenants become increasingly remote from the initial contractual relationship. It is nevertheless important that the law should provide a framework of liability and consequent enforcement which ensures the effective 'policing' of the original covenants of the lease in the more distant leasehold relationships which exist beyond the nexus of lessor and lessee. English law provides this framework by a combination of common law and statutory rules.[15]

The precise ambit of these rules depends on whether the lease in question is legal or equitable in nature.[16] Attention in the following pages is directed first to relationships of liability under a legal lease. *Fig.* 42 contains a representation of a typical network of leasehold relationships, flowing from a legal head lease, which may readily serve as a model for the present discussion. It is assumed in the following discussion not only that the head or superior lease is legal[17], but that all subsequent assignments are effected by deed and are likewise legal. Thus, in terms of *Fig.* 42, L creates a lease in favour of T and then assigns his own reversion to A^1. T later assigns his term of years to A^2, who in turn assigns to A^3, who finally sublets to S.

(1) Liability as between L and T

The relationship of L and T is quite simply contractual. Privity of contract exists between L and T, and each is therefore liable to the other on all the covenants of the lease, irrespective of whether those covenants 'touch and concern' the demised land.[18] Moreover, the contractual nexus involves in

---

12   Law Com No 142, para 19.15.
13   Law Com No 142, paras 19.16ff.
14   Ante, p 462.
15   See generally D. Gordon, [1987] Conv 103. The Law Commission, in recommending a general reformulation of the law of positive and restrictive covenants (post, p 721), has made it clear that its proposals are not intended to affect the traditional rules relating to the enforceability of covenants between landlord and tenant. See *Transfer of Land: The Law of Positive and Restrictive Covenants* (Law Com No 127, 26 January 1984), paras 3.9, 24.11.
16   The distinction between legal and equitable leases is discussed elsewhere (ante, p 464).
17   It matters not for the purposes of exposition whether the lease between L and T is the head lease. Exactly the same principles, transposed as it were one octave down, would apply if L were not himself the freeholder but were instead a leaseholder holding on the covenants of a legal lease.
18   Reference is made elsewhere to covenants which 'touch and concern' (post, p 521).

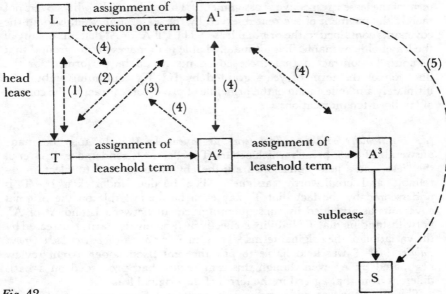

Fig. 42

principle a continuing liability on both sides throughout the entire term in the absence of some contractually agreed release.[19]

(a) T's liability survives assignment of the term

The durability of the contractual nexus is such that even the assignment of T's term to A^2 (and later to A^3) cannot relieve T of responsibility for the due performance of his leasehold obligations.[20] It also follows, however, that L continues to be liable to T in respect of breaches of covenant committed by L while T was in possession, notwithstanding that T has since assigned his term to A^2.[1]

(i) T's liability on the original covenants of the lease

It is trite law that, in the absence of contrary agreement with L, T remains liable throughout the entire

19 The liability of any surety of T also extends to the whole of the term of the lease (see *Thames Manufacturing Co Ltd v Perrotts (Nichol & Peyton) Ltd* (1984) 271 Estates Gazette 284 at 287). However, L has no right to recover from receivers appointed by T's mortgagees any moneys paid by sublessees during the period before T's lease is declared forfeit by the court (*Official Custodian for Charities v Mackey (No 2)* [1985] 1 WLR 1308 at 1313H-1314A).

20 'When the lessee assigns, the privity of estate between him and the lessor is destroyed; the privity of contract remains' (*W.E. Wagener Ltd v Photo Engravers Ltd* [1984] 1 NZLR 412 at 424). It is of course open to L and T to agree contractually that T's liability should not survive assignment of his term. However, the limitation of T's liability in this way is unusual—a fact which the Law Commission has ascribed to 'the unequal bargaining power of landlords and tenants' (see *Landlord and Tenant: Privity of Contract and Estate; Duration of Liability of Parties to Leases* (Law Commission Working Paper No 95, March 1986), para 7.1(c)). An exception to the general rule of T's continuing liability arises under a perpetually renewable lease (ante, p 436). The lessee under such a lease is not liable after assignment of his term (Law of Property Act 1922, Sch 15, para 11).

1 *City and Metropolitan Properties Ltd v Greycroft Ltd* (1987) *The Times*, 29 January.

term of the lease irrespective of assignment.[2] This enduring liability covers not merely the payment of the rent reserved by the lease,[3] but extends to all the covenants contained in the original lease.[4] Thus, if A^2 or A^3 defaults on any of the leasehold covenants, T is ultimately liable in damages on the ground that he initially contracted that those covenants would be performed for the duration of the term of years granted by L.[5] T's continuing liability is ultimately a manifestation of the principle of privity of contract in the context of landlord-tenant relations.

(ii) T's liability on the original terms as varied In that he may be made answerable for *any* breach which occurs, T is effectively rendered an insurer of the lease, and a heavy onus of care is thereby imposed on T to select only a reliable and creditworthy assignee.[6] The burden undertaken by T is underscored by the fact that T may even be made liable on the original covenants as amended by subsequent agreement between L and A^2 or A^3, notwithstanding that T's liability is effectively (and involuntarily) increased by the variation of the original terms.[7] Thus, in *Selous Street Properties Ltd v Oronel Fabrics Ltd*[8] T was held liable to pay the rent fixed under a rent review negotiated by A^2 even though this rent review had proceeded on a basis different from that agreed in the terms of the original lease.[9]

This approach was evidenced in an even more extreme form in *Centrovincial*

2 *Walker's Case* (1587) 3 Co Rep 22a at 23a, 76 ER 676 at 680; *Baynton v Morgan* (1888) 22 QBD 74 at 82 per Lopes LJ; *Arlesford Trading Co Ltd v Servansingh* [1971] 1 WLR 1080 at 1082G. See also *195 Crown Street Pty Ltd v Hoare* [1969] 1 NSWR 193 at 195; *Francini v Canuck Properties Ltd* (1982) 35 OR (2d) 321 at 323a; *W.E. Wagener Ltd v Photo Engravers Ltd* [1984] 1 NZLR 412 at 417.

3 *Warnford Investments Ltd v Duckworth* [1979] Ch 127 at 138G–139A, 141H–142A. It is now a chilling fact of life for the original lessee that he may even have to pay statutory interest (under Supreme Court Act 1981, s 35A) on rent unpaid by his assignee. See eg *Allied London Investments Ltd v Hambro Life Assurance Ltd* (1984) 269 Estates Gazette 41 at 42ff, 270 Estates Gazette 948 at 950 ('Of course the expectation, commercially speaking, is that the assignee will pay, but the assignor does not by assignment get rid of one jot or tittle of his original liability').

4 *Thames Manufacturing Co Ltd v Perrotts (Nichol & Peyton) Ltd* (1984) 271 Estates Gazette 284 at 286f (T liable in damages for A^2's breach of repairing and decorating covenant and breach of covenant to surrender and yield up possession).

5 *Warnford Investments Ltd v Duckworth* [1979] Ch 127 at 138H. Since T is no longer in possession, there is no purpose in any attempt by L to seek injunctive relief or forfeiture against him.

6 In most cases L will already have made assurance doubly sure by including in the lease a covenant prohibiting any assignment or subletting without his prior consent. However, the mere fact that L has consented to T's assignment to A^2 does not impliedly release T from his original liability or discharge him from responsibility for breaches occurring after the date of assignment (*Thames Manufacturing Co Ltd v Perrotts (Nichol & Peyton) Ltd* (1984) 271 Estates Gazette 284 at 286).

7 T's liability may, however, be reduced to nil by one particular subsequent event. If it appears that there has been 'some operation conducted upon the lease' (eg surrender of the whole), T's liability to pay rent is terminated (*Allied London Investments Ltd v Hambro Life Assurance Ltd* (1984) 269 Estates Gazette 41 at 46). See also *195 Crown Street Pty Ltd v Hoare* [1969] 1 NSWR 193 at 196f, 200.

8 (1984) 270 Estates Gazette 643 at 650.

9 For a critical view of the vulnerability of the original lessee who is exposed to liability on any terms which a subsequent (and possibly hard-pressed) assignee may be forced to accept, see (1984) 81 Law Soc Gaz 2214 at 2215 (K. Reynolds).

Estates PLC v Bulk Storage Ltd.[10] Here T was held liable to pay a much higher revised rent agreed between L and A[2] even though the rent review had occurred without T's knowledge or consent. In Harman J's view, this result proceeded not on any footing of agency, but simply on the basis that 'each assignee is the owner of the whole estate and can deal with it so as to alter it or its terms. The estate as so altered then binds the original tenant, because the assignee has been put into the shoes of the original tenant and can do all such acts as the original tenant could have done'.[11] As Harman J pointed out, there is machinery ready to hand by which the original tenant can ensure that no rent review ever takes place without his knowledge or consent. All he need do is grant not an assignment of the whole of his unexpired term, but rather a sublease on identical terms for the same period minus two or three days.[12]

(iii) Increasing recourse to the enforcement of secondary liability In realistic commercial terms the primary target for enforcement in the event of breaches occurring after assignment is usually the defaulting assignee himself. However, the original lessee's secondary liability is by no means theoretical or unimportant.[13] In an era of frequent corporate insolvency, it is now increasingly common for lessors to have recourse to what—for the original lessee at least—is an unanticipated form of liability, and the courts have enforced the secondary liability of the original lessee in a surprisingly wide range of circumstances. It seems that the original lessee's inability after assignment to ensure compliance with his covenants is entirely irrelevant to his continuing liability.[14]

(iv) T's rights to indemnity If T is made to answer in damages for the defaults of subsequent assignees, T has in theory a right to be indemnified in respect of any liability which he has had to discharge personally. This right to indemnity (if not express) arises both by way of quasi-contract[15] and under statute,[16] but is

---

10 (1983) 46 P & CR 393 at 396ff.

11 (1983) 46 P & CR 393 at 396.

12 (1983) 46 P & CR 393 at 398.

13 The original lessor cannot, of course, recover twice over for the same breach of covenant by an assignee. He may choose whether to enforce the primary liability of the defaulting assignee or the secondary liability of the original lessee, but the remedies are alternative not cumulative (*Brett v Cumberland* (1619) Cro Jac 521 at 523, 79 ER 446 at 447). For the lessee who is sued the extent of liability may not be minimal or of academic interest only. In *Allied London Investments Ltd v Hambro Life Assurance Ltd* (1984) 269 Estates Gazette 41, the original tenant was sued for over £48,000, and in *Selous Street Properties Ltd v Oronel Fabrics Ltd* (1984) 270 Estates Gazette 643, the original tenant was held liable for arrears amounting to £110,000.

14 It is immaterial, for instance, that after his assignment to A[2] T is powerless to compel A[2] to carry out covenanted repairs or other obligations imposed on T by the original lease (*Thames Manufacturing Co Ltd v Perrotts (Nichol & Peyton) Ltd* (1984) 271 Estates Gazette 284 at 286).

15 *Moule v Garrett* (1872) LR 7 Exch 101 at 104; *Selous Street Properties Ltd v Oronel Fabrics Ltd* (1984) 270 Estates Gazette 643 at 747f. See Lord Goff of Chieveley and Gareth Jones, *The Law of Restitution* (3rd edn London 1986), pp 310, 312ff. If T is made liable for the default not of A[2] but of A[3], T's right of indemnity is available against A[3] directly (see *Baynton v Morgan* (1888) 22 QBD 74 at 82).

16 Law of Property Act 1925, s 77; Land Registration Act 1925, s 24(1)(b).

apt to prove ineffective simply because the defaulting assignee is usually insolvent.[17]

(v) Proposals for reform   The enforcement of a continuing liability against the original lessee has been so widely criticised in recent years that in 1985 the Law Commission was moved to examine the operation of the privity of contract principle in the leasehold relationship.[18] The Commission has now largely acknowledged the intrinsic unfairness of continuing liability, and has recognised that landlords are often given excessive protection at the expense of tenants who have long since ceased to have any interest in the leasehold property.[19]

The Commission has therefore provisionally concluded that the imposition of liability on the original lessee unjustifiably duplicates the liability which arises against the tenant's assignees by reason of 'privity of estate'.[20] Accordingly the Commission has proposed the total abrogation of the privity of contract principle as between landlord and tenant, at least to the extent that it relates to leasehold covenants which bind successors in title.[1] In the view of the Commission, leasehold covenants should bind the parties only 'while they continue to own their respective interests in the property'. The Commission has also suggested the enactment of legislation which would declare void any contract which sought to preserve a continuing liability after assignment except in cases where it could be demonstrated that such liability was 'fair and reasonable'.[2]

(b) L's liability survives assignment of the reversion

It follows from the contractual nature of the initial leasehold commitment that L's liability on the covenants of the lease likewise survives the assignment of his reversion to A[2] (or later to A[3]),[3] unless the covenants in question clearly impose liability only on the person who for the time being owns the reversionary estate.[4]

---

17   Insolvency on the part of the defaulting assignee is almost certainly the reason why L is suing T rather than the actual wrongdoer (see eg *Warnford Investments Ltd v Duckworth* [1979] Ch 127). T's right to indemnity usually provides only illusory comfort since T can recover no more from a man of straw than L could recover in respect of the primary liability for breach of covenant. It may therefore be prudent for the otherwise defenceless assignor, if possessed of sufficient bargaining power (but see (1983) 127 SJ 832 (G.L. Leigh)), expressly to reserve a right of re-entry against his assignee in the event of any breach by the latter for which the assignor is made liable. See eg *Shiloh Spinners Ltd v Harding* [1973] AC 691 (ante, pp 82, 141, 226).

18   *Landlord and Tenant: Privity of Contract and Estate; Duration of Liability of Parties to Leases* (Law Commission Working Paper No 95, March 1986).

19   Working Paper No 95, paras 3.1ff.

20   Working Paper No 95, paras 3.17ff.

1   Working Paper No 95, para 6.2.

2   Working Paper No 95, para 6.16(d).

3   *Stuart v Joy* [1904] 1 KB 362 at 367f. L's vulnerability to an action based on his original covenants not only survives the assignment of his reversion to A[1], but can provide the basis for action against him even by an assignee of T's term of years, eg by A[2] or A[3] (see *Celsteel Ltd v Alton House Holdings Ltd* (No 2) [1987] 1 WLR 291 at 296D-E; [1986] 1 WLR 666 at 672G-H. See also Law of Property Act 1925, s 142(2).

4   *Bath v Bowles* (1905) 93 LT 801 at 805.

(2) Liability of T to A[1]

The liability of T towards A[1] rests upon a statutory basis. Under section 141(1) of the Law of Property Act 1925,[5] the assignment of L's reversionary estate to A[1] passes to A[1] the benefit of all the covenants and conditions originally entered into by T in so far as those obligations have 'reference to the subject-matter' of the lease.[6]

(a) Covenants which 'touch and concern' the demised land

The reference in section 141(1) to covenants which have 'reference to the subject-matter' of the lease means effectively that A[1] receives the benefit of only those covenants which, in the older terminology, 'touch and concern' the demised premises.[7]

(b) Purpose of the 'touch and concern' requirement

The concept of 'touching and concerning' covenants has no application to the original lessor and lessee, but is aimed at restricting the binding effect of leasehold covenants in relation to other participants in a leasehold arrangement.[8] In other words, not every covenant contained in a lease is enforceable outside the immediate contractual nexus of lessor and lessee.[9] Such extensive impact is accorded only to those covenants which intrinsically affect the lessor in his capacity as lessor and the lessee in his capacity as lessee. The 'touch and concern' requirement thus excludes covenants which are of exclusively personal or private significance for the parties to the lease. The 'touch and concern' requirement is fulfilled only where 'the parties, as laymen and not as lawyers, would naturally regard the covenant as intimately bound up with the land, aiding the promisee as landowner or hampering the promisor in a similar capacity'.[10]

---

5   This provision originates in the Grantees of Reversions Act 1540 (32 Hen VIII, c 34). See *Thursby v Plant* (1669) 1 Saund 237 at 240, 85 ER 268 at 270, for the statement that this statute 'transferred the privity of contract'. See also *Bickford v Parson* (1848) 5 CB 920 at 930, 136 ER 1141 at 1145, where Wilde CJ held that the 1540 Act 'annexes, or rather creates, a privity of contract between those who have privity of estate'.

6   Section 141(1) clearly has no reference to undertakings entered into by any third party. For instance, A[1] cannot receive the benefit of a third party's surety covenant on behalf of T either under section 141(1) or—for that matter—under sections 62(1), 56(1) or 78(1) of the Law of Property Act 1925 (*Pinemain Ltd v Welbeck International Ltd* (1984) 272 Estates Gazette 1166 at 1169ff; [1986] Conv 50 (S. Murdoch)). Compare, however, *Coastplace Ltd v Hartley* [1987] 2 WLR 1289 at 1295A-1299C; *Kumar v Dunning* (1987) *Times*, 16 April.

7   It has been accepted that the two sets of terminology are merely differing formulations of the same idea (see *Hua Chaio Commercial Bank Ltd v Chiaphua Industries Ltd* [1987] 2 WLR 179 at 182B-C per Lord Oliver of Aylmerton; *Davis v Town Properties Investment Corporation Ltd* [1903] 1 Ch 797 at 805; *Breams Property Investment Co Ltd v Stroulger* [1948] 2 KB 1 at 7).

8   'The line of cleavage between covenants which do and do not touch or concern the land has always been somewhat artificial, but it expresses the principle that not every contractual provision can be turned into an interest in land, since interests in land must be of finite and familiar character' ([1957] CLJ 148 at 149 (H.W.R. Wade)).

9   See *Thursby v Plant* (1669) 1 Saund 237 at 239f, 85 ER 268 at 269. The 'touch and concern' requirement is found in many, but not all, common law jurisdictions. Compare, for instance, the disparaging remarks made by Gibson J in the Irish Court of Appeal in *Lyle v Smith* [1909] 2 IR 58 at 76.

10   *Abbott v Bob's U-Drive*, 352 P.2d 598 at 604 (1960) (Supreme Court of Oregon).

(c) Application of the 'touch and concern' requirement

The 'touch and concern' criterion is elusive and perhaps ultimately intuitive.[11] The requirement operates largely to limit the enforcement of leasehold covenants to those promises in whose due performance the respective estate owners under a lease have a peculiar economic interest *qua estate owner*.[12] A 'touching and concerning' covenant is thus demarcated from those other covenants, albeit contained in the same lease, in whose due performance the promisee has no higher or more distinctive economic interest than any other person who is not party to the lease.

(i) 'Touching and concerning' covenants undertaken by T   Although the conceptual distinction between those covenants which 'touch and concern' and those which do not remains highly artificial, in practice most leasehold covenants do 'touch and concern' the demised premises. Amongst the category of covenants which have been accepted as having this quality are positive covenants such as the covenant by the lessee to pay rent,[13] or to repair the premises,[14] or to cultivate land in a particular manner.[15] Likewise certain negative covenants by the lessee 'touch and concern'.[16] Amongst these are a lessee's undertaking to use property for domestic purposes only,[17] or to retail only the lessor's brand of product on the premises,[18] or not to assign the lease without the lessor's consent,[19] or not to permit a named person to be involved in the conduct of business on the premises.[20]

11   It is notoriously difficult to propose a definition of 'touching and concerning' covenants which is not flawed by circularity. This vitiating factor ultimately afflicts the famous test in *Congleton Corpn v Pattison* (1808) 10 East 130 at 135, 103 ER 725 at 727, which defined a 'touching and concerning' covenant as one which 'affected the nature, quality, or value of the thing demised, independently of collateral circumstances; or if it affected the mode of enjoying it.' See also *Hua Chaio Commercial Bank Ltd v Chiaphua Industries Ltd* [1987] 2 WLR 179 at 187E, where Lord Oliver of Aylmerton observed that to ask whether a particular covenant 'affects the landlord qua landlord or the tenant qua tenant is an exercise which begs the question. It does so only if it runs with the reversion or with the land respectively.'

12   'The touch and concern requirement...pertains to what the normal expectations of society would be as to whether this particular benefit or burden so relates to the owner in his capacity as owner that the average person would assume that the law would decree that such benefit or burden would accompany the ownership' (L. Berger, *A Policy Analysis of Promises Respecting the Use of Land*, 55 Minnesota LR 167 at 219f (1970-71)).

13   *Parker v Webb* (1693) 3 Salk 5, 91 ER 656. However, a covenant to pay an annual sum to a third person does not 'touch and concern' (*Mayho v Buckhurst* (1617) Cro Jac 438 at 439, 79 ER 374 at 375).

14   *Matures v Westwood* (1598) Cro Eliz 599 at 600, 78 ER 842; *Williams v Earle* (1868) LR 3 QB 739 at 751f.

15   *Chapman v Smith* [1907] 2 Ch 97 at 103.

16   The operation of Law of Property Act 1925, s 141(1) thus neatly circumvents the difficulties which until relatively recently have plagued the transmission of the benefit of restrictive covenants between freeholders (post, p 709). See eg *Re Memvale Securities Ltd's Application* (1975) 233 Estates Gazette 689 at 693.

17   *Wilkinson v Rogers* (1864) 2 De GJ & S 62 at 67ff, 46 ER 298 at 300f.

18   *Clegg v Hands* (1890) 44 Ch D 503 at 518, 522f (beer); *Regent Oil Co Ltd v J.A. Gregory (Hatch End) Ltd* [1966] Ch 402 at 431E-F, 432F (petrol). By contrast, a lessor's covenant not to compete with the lessee's business does not 'touch and concern' (*Thomas v Hayward* (1869) LR 4 Ex 311 at 312).

19   *Williams v Earle* (1868) LR 3 QB 739 at 749f; *Goldstein v Sanders* [1915] 1 Ch 549 at 556; *Cohen v Popular Restaurants Ltd* [1917] 1 KB 480 at 482.

20   *Lewin v American & Colonial Distributors Ltd* [1945] Ch 225 at 235.

(ii) Purely personal or collateral covenants In effect only covenants by the lessee which are of a purely personal or collateral nature fall outside the ambit of 'touching and concerning' covenants. Examples of such covenants would include a covenant to perform some personal service for the lessor and a covenant for forfeiture of the lease on the criminal conviction of the lessee or any occupier of the land.[1]

(d) L's remedies after assignment of the reversion

When L assigns his reversion to A^1, A^1 acquires an exclusive right to sue in respect of breaches of covenant whensoever committed.[2] L henceforth loses the right of action, and A^1 is entitled to any appropriate remedy even in respect of breaches committed prior to the date of assignment,[3] unless those breaches were waived by L.[4] L is still liable, however, on all the lessor's covenants contained in the original lease, and may even be sued by later assignees of T on such of those covenants as 'touch and concern' the land.[5]

(3) Liability of A^1 to T

The liability of A^1 to T also rests on a statutory base. Under section 142(1) of the Law of Property Act 1925, the assignment of L's reversionary estate to A^1 passes to A^1 the burden of all the covenants and conditions originally entered into by L^6 in so far as the obligations contained therein 'have reference to the subject-matter of the lease'.[7]

(a) Application of the 'touch and concern' requirement

Once again the obligations undertaken by L which 'have reference to the subject-matter of the lease' are those which, in the older formulation, 'touch and concern' the demised premises. 'Touching and concerning' covenants include covenants by L to repair or to insure the demised premises, to supply water to those premises,[8] to give T quiet possession of the premises,[9] and not to

---

1   *Stevens v Copp* (1868) LR 4 Ex 20 at 24ff.
2   It is irrelevant for this purpose that T assigned his term of years to A^2 before L's assignment of the reversion in favour of A^1 and that 'privity of estate' (post, p 526) never existed between A^1 and T (see *Arlesford Trading Co Ltd v Servansingh* [1971] 1 WLR 1080 at 1082F-G).
3   *In Re King* [1963] Ch 459 at 488f, 497 (damages for L's breach of covenant to rebuild); *London & County (A. & D.) Ltd v Wilfred Sportsman Ltd* [1971] Ch 764 at 784D (right of re-entry in respect of rent arrears); *Arlesford Trading Co Ltd v Servansingh* [1971] 1 WLR 1080 at 1082E-F (right to sue for arrears of rent).
4   *London & County (A. & D.) Ltd v Wilfred Sportsman Ltd* [1971] Ch 764 at 783B.
5   *Celsteel Ltd v Alton House Holdings Ltd* (No 2) [1986] 1 WLR 666 at 672H.
6   A 'covenant' within section 142(1) need not be a covenant under seal and may even arise outside the document which constitutes the lease (see *Weg Motors Ltd v Hales* [1962] Ch 49 at 73, 76f; but compare *Eden Park Estates Ltd v Longman* (Unreported, Court of Appeal, 19 May 1980)). However, a covenant comes within section 142(1) only if it was actually 'entered into by a lessor'. It is not enough that it would have been inserted into the lease if the lessee had chosen to claim an equity of rectification in his favour (see *Squire v C. Brewer & Sons Ltd* (Unreported, Court of Appeal, 15 July 1983) per Slade LJ).
7   A^1 cannot be made liable, however, in respect of breaches committed by L prior to the assignment of the reversion (*Pettiward Estates v Shephard* [1986] 6 CL 173). See also D. Gordon, [1987] Conv 103 at 105.
8   *Jourdain v Wilson* (1821) 4 B & Ald 266 at 267, 106 ER 935.
9   *Celsteel Ltd v Alton House Holdings Ltd (No 2)* [1986] 1 WLR 666 at 672H.

develop adjoining land.[10] L's covenant that the rent paid by T should be inclusive of rates likewise 'touches and concerns'.[11] The burden of all such covenants runs automatically with the land so as to bind the reversionary estate in the hands of A^1. Somewhat anomalously, A^1 is not bound to return to T any deposit paid by T to L at the commencement of the lease in respect of future payments of rent.[12] Such a deposit is regarded—rather unfairly—as paid under an agreement which is merely 'collateral' to the lease and which therefore creates only rights *in personam* between T and L.

(b) Options conferred by L on T

The 'touching and concerning' category has also been held to include a lessor's covenant to renew the lease,[13] but not—strangely—a right of pre-emption conferred on the lessee,[14] or an option under which the lessor covenants to sell his reversion to the lessee at a pre-fixed price.[15] Here the relevant distinction seems to rest on the basis that whereas an option for renewal of the lease is a matter of peculiar interest to the lessee qua lessee, a right of pre-emption and an option to purchase the reversion confer no greater benefit on the lessee than on any third party. Indeed such rights affect the parties not *qua* lessor and lessee but *qua* vendor and purchaser, and are therefore truly 'collateral to the relationship of landlord and tenant'.[16] Nowadays, however, it is generally considered that even the lessor's covenant for renewal of the lease is a dubious case for inclusion within the category of 'touching and concerning' covenants, and the courts have accordingly limited the practical effect of its inclusion.

It was at first thought, with the enactment of section 142(1) of the Law of Property Act 1925, that the burden of L's covenant to renew T's lease would run with the land so as automatically to bind A^1, the assignee of L's reversion.[17] This may still be true in respect of registered land, since T (if in actual occupation of the land or in receipt of the rents and profits thereof) can usually claim that his option for renewal constitutes an overriding interest.[18] However, in *Beesly v Hallwood Estates Ltd*[19] Buckley J held—to the suprise of many[20]—that

10   *Ricketts v Enfield Churchwardens* [1909] 1 Ch 544 at 555.
11   *Squire v C. Brewer & Sons Ltd* (Unreported, Court of Appeal, 15 July 1983) per Fox LJ.
12   *Hua Chaio Commercial Bank Ltd v Chiaphua Industries Ltd* [1987] 2 WLR 179 at 187F-188B per Lord Oliver of Aylmerton; *Eden Park Estates Ltd v Longman* (Unreported, Court of Appeal, 19 May 1980) (ante, p 183). See also *Re Dollar Land Corporation Ltd v Solomon* (1963) 39 DLR (2d) 221 at 226.
13   *Richardson v Sydenham* (1703) 2 Vern 447, 23 ER 885; *Simpson v Clayton* (1838) 4 Bing (NC) 758 at 780, 132 ER 981 at 989. These rulings have been regarded by some as anomalous (see eg *Muller v Trafford* [1901] 1 Ch 54 at 60), but compare (1981) 125 SJ 816 at 817 (M.P. Thompson).
14   *Charles Frodsham & Co Ltd v Morris* (1974) 229 Estates Gazette 961 at 962.
15   *Woodall v Clifton* [1905] 2 Ch 257 at 279.
16   See *Davenport Central Service Station Ltd v O'Connell* [1975] 1 NZLR 755 at 757.
17   See eg *Wolstenholme & Cherry's Conveyancing Statutes* (12th edn, London 1932), p 246.
18   Land Registration Act 1925, s 70(1)(g) (ante, p 175). Compare *Webb v Pollmount Ltd* [1966] Ch 584 at 603C-D (option to purchase freehold) (ante, p 181).
19   [1960] 1 WLR 549 at 557 (ante, p 136). See also *Taylors Fashions Ltd v Liverpool Victoria Trustees Co Ltd* [1982] QB 133 (Note) at 142G-143G.
20   See eg *Taylors Fashions Ltd v Liverpool Victoria Trustees Co Ltd* [1982] QB 133 (Note) at 138B (ante, p 394). Compare the strongly critical view expressed in (1981) 125 SJ 816 at 817f (M.P. Thompson).

a lessee's option to renew his lease constitutes an estate contract.[1] In unregistered land such a contract requires to be registered against the lessor prior to the assignment of the reversion,[2] and if not so registered becomes statutorily void against a purchaser of a legal estate for money or money's worth.[3] Thus the mere fact that T's option for renewal 'touches and concerns' is almost entirely irrelevant in unregistered land to the question of its impact on A[1], since A[1] will be bound by an unregistered option only if he is someone other than a purchaser for money or money's worth (ie, a donee).

(c) T's remedies after assignment of the term

Section 142(1) of the Law of Property Act 1925 affords T an important statutory basis for enforcement of leasehold covenants against A[1]. However, T is in the difficult position of having virtually no access to legal remedy (other than by way of indemnity) after assigning his term to A[2]. After the assignment T holds no estate in the land and therefore has no standing either to apply for relief against forfeiture of the lease[4] or to sue in respect of breaches of covenant committed by L (or by any subsequent assignee of the reversion). In effect the assignment of T's term has transferred with it the right to seek legal remedies appertaining to the estate assigned, while leaving T entirely vulnerable to action brought against him on his original leasehold covenants.

(4) Other forms of liability based on 'privity of estate'

For over four centuries it has been clear in English law that liability on the covenants of a legal lease may extend beyond merely those parties who are affected by privity of contract or by its statutory extension to assignees of the reversion. The covenants of the lease may reach far outside the immediate contractual nexus of L and T, and are regarded as enforceable as between all formal assignees of either L or T.

There are merely two constraints placed on the enforceability of leasehold covenants. *First*, only those leasehold covenants which 'touch and concern' the

---

1   The option for renewal is thus put effectively on a par with a lessee's option to purchase the lessor's reversion and a lessee's right of pre-emption, in that all such rights may now constitute estate contracts registrable by the lessee. However, the fact that a covenant for renewal 'touches and concerns' the demised land ensures that the benefit of the option passes with assignments of the lessee's term.

2   Ante, p 135. Even in registered land the option for renewal should be protected by the entry of a minor interest in the register of the lessor's title (ante, p 159). However, an unprotected option, although ineffective as a minor interest (Land Registration Act 1925, s 59(6), ante, pp 163, 190), is often valid as an overriding interest.

3   Land Charges Act 1972, s 4(6). In *Beesly v Hallwood Estates Ltd* [1960] 1 WLR 549 at 557f, Buckley J rejected the argument that a lessee's option to renew is indelibly annexed to the land by Law of Property Act 1925, s 142(1), so that the burden runs with the reversion without the requirement of registration. Section 142(1) applies in its terms only 'if and so far as the lessor has power to bind' the reversioner, and Buckley J took the view that this section does not empower a lessor to bind a reversioner 'in respect of any obligation which the legislature has said shall not be enforceable against such reversioner.' An example of such an obligation, in Buckley J's view, is an unregistered estate contract, and the effect of the Land Charges Act is therefore 'to take such an obligation out of the scope of section 142 upon a purchase of the reversion for money or money's worth taking place while the obligation is unregistered.'

4   *Re Francini and Canuck Properties Ltd* (1982) 132 DLR (3d) 468 at 471.

demised premises are capable of enforcement. *Second*, no covenant can be enforced unless there exists a 'privity of estate' between plaintiff and defendant.

(a) The 'touch and concern' requirement

This requirement has already been discussed.[5] It draws a line of distinction, uncertain in theory but usually fairly clear in practice, between those covenants which are integral to the relationship of landlord and tenant and those covenants which are merely collateral to that relationship.

(b) 'Privity of estate'

'Privity of estate' is a wider concept than that comprised in the notion of 'privity of contract', being the term used to describe a legal relationship based on successive interests in the same leasehold estate. 'Privity of estate' embraces all persons within the framework of a leasehold relationship who currently stand vis à vis each other in the position of landlord and tenant.

(i) Inclusion within 'privity of estate'

In *Fig.* 42,[6] 'privity of estate' thus includes all those who can trace their leasehold status directly to the 'estate' comprised within the head lease, ie, A^1, A^2 and A^3. Each of these persons, during the currency of his tenure, can trace his position to one or other side of the notional feudal divide (or 'estate') which separates landlord from tenant and places them in a relationship of tenure. Each stands in the shoes of either the original lessor or the original lessee. Each is therefore 'privy' to the 'estate' of the head lease.

(ii) Exclusion from 'privity of estate'

The one person in *Fig.* 42 who is not 'privy' to the estate of the head lease is S, the sublessee. S is 'privy' not to the estate of the head lease but to the estate comprised within a different lease of which he is more immediately a party. He is, of course, 'privy' to the estate of the sublease granted him by A^3.[7]

(iii) Binding impact of 'privity of estate'

It was in the historic ruling of the Court of King's Bench in *Spencer's Case*[8] that the consequence of 'privity of estate' was first clearly spelt out. The Court held that leasehold covenants 'run with the land' so as to affect assignees of the term who are 'privy' to the relevant estate. Thus both the benefit and the burden of the original lessee's covenants pass to assignees of the term, provided only that the covenants in question 'touch and concern' the demised land.

In *Spencer's Case* the Court was able to draw upon the analogy of the Grantees of Reversions Act 1540,[9] which, in a similar way, transmitted to assignees of the

---

5   Ante, p 521.
6   Ante, p 517.
7   In diagrammatic terms, the test of 'privity of estate' turns on whether the party concerned can trace his position back horizontally to the original landlord-tenant relationship to which it is claimed he is 'privy'. S cannot do this in relation to the estate of the head lease between L and T.
8   (1583) 5 Co Rep 16a at 17b, 77 ER 72 at 75.
9   Ante, p 521.

reversion both the benefit and the burden of 'touching and concerning' covenants entered into by the original lessee. The 1540 Act (and its modern equivalent[10]) represent simultaneously a statutory extension of 'privity of contract' in favour of the assignee of the reversion and an application of the idea of 'privity of estate'.

Spencer's Case provides even today the linchpin of leasehold enforceability. It is ultimately by virtue of this decision that the original covenants of every legal lease are made potentially binding on all subsequent assignees of either the term[11] or the reversion.[12] These results follow irrespective of the nature or duration of the leasehold estate granted, and subject only to the proviso that *Spencer's Case* applies only to covenants which 'touch and concern' the land.

(iv) Temporary nature of 'privity of estate' Since 'privity of estate' denotes the relationship which exists between those who stand *pro tempore* in the shoes of the original lessor and lessee, the liability imposed by *Spencer's Case* is necessarily dependent on the duration of a given tenure. Unlike the liability of the original lessee, which is unassignable and therefore coextensive with the lease, the liability of each successive assignee of the term relates only to breaches committed while in possession of the land. Thus, in *Fig.* 42,[13] A^2 is not liable under *Spencer's Case* in respect of breaches of covenant committed prior to the assignment to himself.[14] Nor is A^2 liable in respect of breaches committed by A^3 after the assignment of the term to the latter,[15] unless on taking the assignment A^2 expressly covenanted to become liable for the residue of the term.[16] However, for all breaches whensoever occurring T bears an enduring liability throughout the leasehold term.[17]

The overall result of the ruling in *Spencer's Case* is that all 'touching and concerning' covenants undertaken by T in the original lease with L are enforceable against A^2 and A^3 in respect of breaches committed during their respective periods of possession. The proper plaintiff in either case is L (before he assigns the reversion to A^1) and A^1 thereafter (even in respect of breaches committed before the assignment to him[18]).

10   Law of Property Act 1925, ss 141(1), 142(1).
11   See eg *Williams v Bosanquet* (1819) 1 Brod & B 238 at 262f, 129 ER 714 at 723.
12   See eg *Celsteel Ltd v Alton House Holdings Ltd (No 2)* [1986] 1 WLR 666 at 673A. (Here the application of *Spencer's Case* is simply confirmed by section 142(1) of the Law of Property Act 1925).
13   Ante, p 517.
14   *Grescot v Green* (1700) 1 Salk 199, 91 ER 179; *St Saviour's Southwark (Churchwardens) v Smith* (1762) 3 Burr 1271 at 1272f, 97 ER 827. This result follows even though A^2 pays a lower price for the assignment deliberately in view of the prior breach (*Hawkins v Sherman* (1828) 3 C & P 459 at 461, 172 ER 500 at 502). Liability for rent unpaid by T and A^2 is therefore subject to apportionment between the two with reference to the date of assignment of the term (see *Glass v Patterson* [1902] 2 IR 660 at 676ff).
15   *Onslow v Corrie* (1817) 2 Madd 330 at 340f, 56 ER 357 at 360; *Paul v Nurse* (1828) 8 B & C 486 at 488f, 108 ER 1123 at 1124. A^2 is, however, liable even after the assignment to A^3 in respect of breaches committed while he was himself in possession of the land (*Harley v King* (1835) 2 Cr M & R 18 at 22f, 150 ER 8 at 10.
16   *J. Lyons & Co Ltd v Knowles* [1943] 1 KB 366 at 368ff.
17   Ante, p 517.
18   Ante, p 523.

(5) Liability of S to L or A[1]

The liability of a sublessee on the covenants of a head lease presents different kinds of problem in English law.

(a) Absence of 'privity of estate'

In *Fig.* 42[19] it is clear that S is not 'privy' to the same estate in the land as are both L and A[1].[20] S's relationship of 'privity' is not with the head lease between L and T at all, but with the sublease between A[3] and himself. In principle, therefore, even those covenants of the head lease which 'touch and concern' the land are unenforceable against S either by L or, after assignment of the reversion, by A[1]. The vital element of 'privity of estate' is not present. Neither L nor A[1] may recover a money remedy from S (eg arrears of rent or damages for breach of covenant),[1] precisely because the proper remedy in either case lies in an action against S's immediate superior, A[3], who does stand in a relationship of 'privity of estate' to the head lease.

(b) Other remedies against S

Notwithstanding the fact that the want of 'privity of estate' renders S immune from monetary recovery on the covenants of the head lease, there are other forms of remedy which enable either L or A[1] (as the case may be) to enforce leasehold covenants either directly or indirectly against S. The legal insulation of S from L and A[1] is far from complete.

(i) Enforcement of restrictive covenants　It is clear that L (or, after assignment of the reversion, A[1]) may be able to obtain an injunction restraining S from further breach of a restrictive covenant contained in the head lease, even though S is not 'privy' to that head lease.

This possibility finds its roots in the decision of Lord Cottenham LC in *Tulk v Moxhay*,[2] which effectively converted restrictive covenants into a species of proprietary interest capable of running with land and binding any purchaser other than a purchaser of a legal estate for value without notice.[3] This doctrine, when applied in the leasehold context, ensures that a restrictive covenant contained in the head lease between L and T is enforceable by way of injunction,[4] outside the area demarcated by privity of estate, against *any* occupier who takes possession of the demised premises with notice of the

19　Ante, p 517.
20　*Garry Denning Ltd v Vickers* [1985] 1 NZLR 567 at 570.
1　For the criticism that the immunity thus granted to the sublessee reinforces an unsupportable distinction between the respective positions of assignee of the term and sublessee, see W.B. Jaccard, *The Scope of Liability between Landlord and Subtenant*, (1980-81) 16 Col Jnl of Law and Soc Prob 364.
2　(1848) 2 Ph 774 at 778f, 41 ER 1143 at 1144f.
3　Post, p 699.
4　See the quintessentially Victorian melodrama of *Hall v Ewin* (1887) 37 Ch D 74 at 78ff (where a sub-under-lessee breached a head lease covenant prohibiting 'noisome or offensive trade, business or employment' by holding an exhibition of wild beasts in his back garden). See also *Teape v Douse* (1905) 92 LT 319 at 320; *Northern Ireland Carriers Ltd v Larne Harbour Ltd* [1981] 5 NIJB, Transcript, p 10. The restrictive covenant binds even a licensee who occupies the premises (*Mander v Falcke* [1891] 2 Ch 554 at 557f).

existence of that covenant.[5] The equitable doctrine thus represents an important limitation on the immunity of S in respect of the covenants agreed between L and T.[6]

(ii) Remedy of forfeiture There exists a further—albeit indirect—means of enforcement against S in respect of conduct in breach of covenants contained in the head lease between L and T. In the event of such conduct by S,[7] any right of re-entry which was expressly reserved by L in the head lease becomes exercisable against A[3]. Re-entry brings about a forfeiture of not only A[3]'s lease but S's sublease also,[8] subject only to any rights to relief against forfeiture which may be claimed by either A[3] or S.[9]

10. ENFORCEABILITY OF LEASEHOLD COVENANTS IN AN EQUITABLE LEASE

The rules governing the enforceability of covenants under an equitable (or informal) lease[10] differ in certain respects from those which obtain in relation to a legal lease. These rules will be discussed still with reference to the framework of leasehold relationships depicted in *Fig.* 42.[11]

(1) Liability as between L and T

Here the result is not different if the transaction concluded by L and T is not a legal lease but merely a specifically enforceable contract for a lease. L and T are still bound, now perhaps even more obviously, by a nexus of contract which endures throughout the entire term. All the leasehold obligations which form part of that contract are enforceable between them, without regard to whether these obligations 'touch and concern' the demised land.

(2) Liability of T to A[1]

In this context the existence of a mere contract for a lease produces no difference in the liability of T to A[1]. Section 141(1) of the Law of Property Act

---

5   S invariably has notice of restrictive covenants contained in the head lease. Such covenants will almost certainly have been recited in identical terms in the covenants of the sublease. In any event S had the right, before taking his sublease, to call for the head lease (see *Gosling v Woolf* [1893] 1 QB 39 at 40, (1893) 68 LT 89 at 90) and is therefore affected by constructive notice of its contents (*Teape v Douse* (1905) 92 LT 319 at 320).
6   In unregistered land the equitable doctrine of notice still governs the effect on a sublessee of restrictive covenants contained in a head lease. Restrictive covenants between lessor and lessee are never registrable as a Class D(ii) land charge (Land Charges Act 1972, s 2(5), ante, p 141). In registered land such covenants are not capable of protection by the entry of a notice on the register (Land Registration Act 1925, s 50(1)), but are automatically binding on a transferee or underlessee by virtue of Land Registration Act 1925, s 23(1)(a), (2).
7   It is irrelevant that, for want of 'privity of estate', S was not technically bound by the covenant in question (*Shiloh Spinners Ltd v Harding* [1973] AC 691 at 717G).
8   Ante, p 507.
9   Ante, p 502.
10 Ante, p 466.
11 Ante, p 517.

1925[12] applies equally to an equitable lease,[13] thereby ensuring that A[1] can sue T in respect of those covenants which have 'reference to the subject-matter' of the lease.[14]

(3) Liability of A[1] to T

The liability of A[1] to T under an equitable lease is likewise governed by section 142(1) of the Law of Property Act 1925,[15] which applies indiscriminately to legal and equitable terms of years.[16] A[1] is liable to T on all undertakings in the original informal lease which 'have reference to the subject-matter of the lease', subject only to one complicating factor which is primarily of importance in unregistered land.

An equitable lease constitutes an estate contract and, in the case of unregistered land, there arises a prudential requirement of registration. Therefore unless T registers the equitable lease as a Class C(iv) land charge against L, the informal term is rendered statutorily void—notwithstanding section 142(1)—against any assignee who purchases the legal reversionary estate for money or money's worth.[17] If T neglects to register his estate contract in unregistered land, his informal lease is effectively binding on A[1] only if A[1] is someone other than a purchaser of a legal estate for money or money's worth (eg a donee or a purchaser of an equitable interest in the land). Ironically none of these issues is relevant in relation to the same problem in registered land, since here it is clearly established that an unprotected informal lease gives rise to an overriding interest on behalf of an equitable lessee who is in actual occupation of the land or in receipt of its rents and profits.[18]

(4) Liability of assignees

It is well established that the benefit of an equitable lessee's covenants, so far as they 'touch and concern' the demised premises, can run with the assignment of the reversion. Thus, if *Fig.* 42[19] were taken as representing a series of transactions with an equitable head lease, A[1] would be entitled to enforce 'touching and concerning' covenants against T.[20]

The major distinction between the enforceability of legal and equitable leases probably emerges in relation to the liability of assignees of the equitable lease.

(a) The traditional doctrine

Orthodox doctrine holds that *Spencer's Case*[1] does not apply to an equitable lease and that therefore the burden of an equitable lessee's leasehold

---

12   Ante, p 521.
13   *Rickett v Green* [1910] 1 KB 253 at 259; *Rye v Purcell* [1926] 1 KB 446 at 451ff.
14   Ante, p 521.
15   Ante, p 523.
16   *Weg Motors Ltd v Hales* [1962] Ch 49 at 73.
17   Land Charges Act 1972, s 4(6). See eg *Hollington Bros Ltd v Rhodes* [1951] 2 TLR 691 at 696 (ante, p 117). Compare the reasoning in *Beesly v Hallwood Estates Ltd* [1960] 1 WLR 549 at 557f (ante, p 525).
18   Land Registration Act 1925, s 70(1)(g). See *Grace Rymer Investments Ltd v Waite* [1958] Ch 831 at 849, 851 (ante, pp 181, 192).
19   Ante, p 517.
20   *Manchester Brewery Co v Coombs* [1901] 2 Ch 608 at 617ff.
1   (1583) 5 Co Rep 16a, 77 ER 72 (ante, p 526).

obligations does not pass with the assignment of his term to a third party.[2] On this view, it is impossible in *Fig.* 42 for either L or A^1 (as the case may be) to recover arrears of rent or any other money remedy for breach of covenant from A^2 or A^3.[3] This strange result emerges most clearly from the decision of the Divisional Court in *Purchase v Lichfield Brewery Co.*[4]

The traditional view goes even further and regards the introduction of any equitable link in an otherwise legal chain of leasehold relationships as similarly having the effect that the burden of the lessee's covenants does not pass.[5] Thus, for instance, an equitable assignment[6] to A^2 of a legal lease granted by L to T does not effectively fasten the burden of T's leasehold obligations upon A^2.[7]

(i) Rationale of the traditional view   It is generally assumed that the refusal to apply *Spencer's Case* in the context of an equitable lease is premised upon the absence of 'privity of estate' stemming from the lease between L and T. In other words, since the head lease between L and T takes the form merely of an equitable term, there exists no 'estate' in the legal sense to which anyone can be 'privy'. Thus, on this reasoning, one of the essential preconditions for enforcement against an assignee of the term is absent, and the issue of liability is now determined by the elementary rule that the benefit but not the burden of a contract is assignable.

(ii) Accepted qualifications of the traditional view   Even if the conventional wisdom of *Purchase v Lichfield Brewery Co* is accepted, it must be remembered that this limitation on the liability of assignees excludes only the recovery of money remedies. In appropriate circumstances it remains open for either L or A^1 (as the case may be) to invoke two other kinds of remedy against a defaulting assignee under an equitable lease. *First*, the owner of the reversionary estate is entitled to seek an injunction against any further breach by A^2 or A^3 of a restrictive covenant contained in the equitable head lease.[8] *Second*, the reversioner is likewise entitled to re-enter against a defaulting assignee of the equitable term, thereby forfeiting the lease.[9]

In the case of an equitable lease of unregistered land, the availability of both of these remedies against assignees can be explained on the basis of first principle. In such a context the restrictive covenant and the right of re-entry both constitute equitable proprietary rights which are neither overreachable

---

2   See generally R.J. Smith, *The Running of Covenants in Equitable Leases and Equitable Assignments of Legal Leases*, [1978] CLJ 98 at 113ff.

3   Money recovery can always be made from T on the basis of his original and durable contractual liability (ante, p 517). See *Camden v Batterbury* (1860) 7 CB (NS) 864 at 878ff, 141 ER 1055 at 1061.

4   [1915] 1 KB 184 at 187ff.

5   See R.J. Smith, [1978] CLJ 98 at 113ff.

6   Ante, p 466.

7   *Moores v Choat* (1839) 8 Sim 508 at 523, 59 ER 202 at 208; *Robinson v Rosher* (1841) 1 Y & C CC 7 at 11, 62 ER 767 at 768; *Moore v Greg* (1848) 2 Ph 717 at 722ff, 41 ER 1120 at 1122f; *Cox v Bishop* (1857) 8 De GM & G 815 at 822ff, 44 ER 604 at 607f; *Thornton v Thompson* [1930] SASR 310 at 313; *Chronopoulos v Caltex Oil (Australia) Pty Ltd* (1982-83) 45 ALR 481 at 489.

8   Ante, p 528.

9   L may well have reserved an express right of re-entry for breach, but in any event it seems that a right of re-entry is implied on behalf of L in most, if not all, equitable leases (ante, p 482).

nor registrable as land charges,[10] thus remaining binding on all persons other than a purchaser of a legal estate for value without notice.[11] In view of the equitable nature of the lease out of which they take their assignments, neither A^2 nor A^3—irrespective of the issue of notice—can claim to have purchased a legal estate. In the case of an equitable lease of registered land, it is arguable that the restrictive covenant and the right of re-entry constitute, as against A^2 and A^3, overriding interests on behalf of the reversioner as a person who is 'in receipt of the rents and profits' of land.[12]

(b) Alternative approaches

It is widely accepted that the result generally attributed to *Purchase v Lichfield Brewery Co* is anomalous, and for this reason various alternative approaches have been proposed as a means of ensuring the enforceability of the covenants in an equitable lease against assignees. However, it is not at all clear that any of these approaches will be readily accepted in England, and the matter awaits a more comprehensive statutory resolution.

(i) Abrogation of the distinction between law and equity   By far the most radical assault yet mounted on the orthodox doctrine concerning the liability of assignees occurred in *Boyer v Warbey*.[13] Here Denning LJ appeared to suggest that the difference between legal and equitable leases was eliminated by the fusion of law and equity in the Judicature Act 1873. Thus, in Denning LJ's view, there is 'no valid reason nowadays why the doctrine of covenants running with the land—or with the reversion—should not apply equally to agreements under hand as to covenants under seal.' To this the purist is bound to object that the 1873 Act fused at most the administration of law and equity,[14] and *Boyer v Warbey* has tended to be seen as representing a somewhat maverick view of the issue. However, it has been suggested in other jurisdictions that 'privity of estate' is not necessarily confined to legal relationships, but may exist even under an equitable lease.[15] If this view were adopted, the authority of *Spencer's Case* would simply transmit the burden of the equitable lessee's covenants to assignees of the term, at least in so far as these covenants 'touched and concerned' the land.

(ii) Implied contract   It has been suggested that another avenue of escape from the inconvenient result of *Purchase v Lichfield Brewery Co* lies in the argument that it may be possible to imply that a fresh contract (and therefore a new privity of contract) arises if the assignee from the original equitable lessee goes into

---

10   The restrictive covenant is not protectible by entry on any register (see Land Charges Act 1972, s 2(5); Land Registration Act 1925, s 50(1)). Likewise, in *Shiloh Spinners Ltd v Harding* [1973] AC 691 at 721D, G (ante, p 141), the House of Lords decided that an equitable right of re-entry in a lease is not registrable within any category of land charge.
11   Ante, p 107.
12   Land Registration Act 1925, s 70(1)(g) (ante, p 178). See also Land Registration Act 1925, s 23(1)(a), (2).
13   [1953] 1 QB 234 at 245f.
14   Ante, p 42.
15   See eg *Dufaur v Kenealy* (1908) 28 NZLR 269 at 295; *De Luxe Confectionery Ltd v Waddington* [1958] NZLR 272 at 278, 283f.

possession, pays rent, and is accepted by the reversioner as the current tenant.[16] This possibility was left open in *Purchase v Lichfield Brewery Co* itself, where Lush J appeared rather pointedly to attribute the absence of privity of contract to the fact that the assignees 'never went into possession or were recognised by the landlord'.[17] This argument, although not entirely free of difficulty,[18] holds the most hopeful key to the resolution of the present dilemma.

(iii) New periodic tenancy A further, and more debatable, approach seeks to fasten liability upon the assignee of the equitable lease on the basis that an implied legal periodic tenancy arises as soon as the assignee enters into possession and pays a periodic rent to the current reversioner.[19] The traditional objection to such an analysis rests on the argument that *Walsh v Lonsdale* excludes the possibility that a legal periodic tenancy may coexist with a specifically enforceable contract for a lease.[20] However, this difficulty presents no obstacle if—as some suggest—this aspect of the ruling in *Walsh v Lonsdale* is applicable only in the 'two-party situation' as between the original lessor and lessee.[1]

(iv) Other equitable techniques It is also sometimes suggested that monetary liability can be fixed upon assignees of an equitable lease by invocation of the principle of 'mutual benefit and burden'[2] or estoppel.[3] However, there is as yet little support in the caselaw for these techniques of imposing liability.

(5) Liability of S to L or A[1]

The liability of S under an equitable lease is much the same as under a legal lease. There seems to be no possibility that the owner of the reversion can obtain a money remedy against a sublessee, but he may be able to enforce a

16 See R.J. Smith, [1978] CLJ 98 at 105f. If novation is to be pleaded successfully as a ground of action against the assignee, it may be prudent to secure a new privity of contract by arranging a tripartite agreement between reversioner, lessee and assignee, which extinguishes all liability on the part of the lessee. See *De Luxe Confectionery Ltd v Waddington* [1958] NZLR 272 at 284; R.T. Fenton, *The Assignment of Informal Leases*, (1976-77) 7 NZULR 342 at 347, 352.

17 [1915] 1 KB 184 at 188f. In *Purchase v Lichfield Brewery Co* the assignees of the equitable lease had received their assignment by way of mortgage security and were not therefore in the same position as their assignor for the purpose of the availability of specific performance of the lease. It may be that other kinds of assignee—in relation to whom specific performance is available—are more readily subject to the doctrine of *Walsh v Lonsdale* (ante, p 472). See eg *De Luxe Confectionery Ltd v Waddington* [1958] NZLR 272 at 277. This surmise may itself be questioned (see eg p 530, ante), but if correct makes it arguable that the doctrine of *Walsh v Lonsdale* simply renders the monetary liability of such assignees equivalent to the liability which would have existed if a decree of specific performance had been granted and a legal lease had come into effect.

18 There is a substantial body of caselaw which denies that novation is possible through a mere entry into possession and payment of rent by the assignee (see *Camden v Batterbury* (1860) 7 CB (NS) 864 at 878ff, 141 ER 1055 at 1061; *Cox v Bishop* (1857) 8 De GM & G 815 at 822ff, 44 ER 604 at 607f; *Thornton v Thompson* [1930] SASR 310 at 313f; *Rodenhurst Estates Ltd v W.H. Barnes Ltd* [1936] 2 All ER 3 at 6). For other difficulties, see R.J. Smith, [1978] CLJ 98 at 106ff.

19 Ante, p 466.

20 See *Manchester Brewery Co v Coombs* [1901] 2 Ch 608 at 617f.

1 R.J. Smith, [1978] CLJ 98 at 108f. See, in support, *Chronopoulos v Caltex Oil (Australia) Pty Ltd* (1982-83) 45 ALR 481 at 489.

2 R.J. Smith, [1978] CLJ 98 at 110.

3 See *Rodenhurst Estates Ltd v W.H. Barnes Ltd* [1936] 2 All ER 3 at 12ff, but compare *Chronopoulos v Caltex Oil (Australia) Pty Ltd* (1982-83) 45 ALR 481 at 488f.

restrictive covenant by injunction.[4] Moreover, any forfeiture which takes effect against an assignee of the equitable lease automatically terminates S's sublease,[5] subject only to statutory controls such as the provision of certain rights to relief against forfeiture.[6]

4   Ante, p 528.
5   Ante, p 507.
6   Ante, p 502.

CHAPTER 15

Licences

Reference has already been made in Chapter 14[1] to the distinction between the licence and the lease. The essential difference between these two concepts lies in the fact that a lease creates an estate or proprietary interest in land, whereas, at least in the conventional understanding, a licence creates only a personal permission to be present on land. The permission conferred by the licence merely legitimates what would otherwise be the tort of trespass. In the time-honoured words of Vaughan CJ in *Thomas v Sorrell*,[2] a licence 'properly passeth no interest nor alters or transfers property in any thing, but only makes an action lawful, which without it had been unlawful.' A licensee does not have 'possession' of the land in even the way that a tenant at will enjoys 'possession',[3] and in consequence the licensee is unable to sue in either trespass or nuisance.[4] In general the licensee has no right to take action against any third party in respect of a disturbance of his rights.[5] His remedy (if any) lies only as against his licensor.

Although licences may assume various forms and perform a multiplicity of purposes, the law has in the past recognised four slightly overlapping categories: the bare licence, the licence coupled with the grant of an interest, the contractual licence and the licence based on proprietary estoppel.

1. BARE LICENCES

A 'bare licence' is a mere personal permission to enter upon land. It comprises a permission granted otherwise than for consideration, and performs the minimal function of equipping the lawful occupier or visitor with a defence against any claim of trespass on the land.[6] If the licensee strays beyond the geographical or temporal scope of the permission granted to him, his status becomes automatically that of trespasser.[7]

---

1 Ante, p 443.
2 (1673) Vaugh 330 at 351, 124 ER 1098 at 1109.
3 Ante, p 430.
4 *Malone v Laskey* [1907] 2 KB 141 at 151 (nuisance); *Nunn v Parkes & Co* (1924) 158 LT Jo 431 (nuisance); *Hull v Parsons* [1962] NZLR 465 at 467f (nuisance and trespass); *Simpson v Knowles* [1974] VR 190 at 195 (trespass); *Oldham v Lawson* (No 1) [1976] VR 654 at 657 (nuisance); *Moore v MacMillan* [1977] 2 NZLR 81 at 89 (trespass).
5 *Hill v Tupper* (1863) 2 H & C 121 at 127, 159 ER 51 at 53 (post, p 648).
6 'No man can set his foot upon my ground without my licence' (*Entick v Carrington* (1765) 19 State Trials 1029 at 1066 per Lord Camden CJ). See also *Morris v Beardmore* [1981] AC 446 at 464C-D per Lord Scarman. Entry upon land without this licence renders the intruder a trespasser (see eg *R v Fox* [1985] 1 WLR 1126 at 1129G-H).
7 *O'Keeffe v Irish Motor Inns Ltd* [1978] IR 85 at 94, 100.

(1) Creation

A bare licence may be created either expressly or impliedly. A common example of express conferment is the dinner or party invitation. A bare licence need not, however, be written or even oral: it can arise by implication from either circumstances or conduct.[8] It seems probable (but not beyond all dispute) that a valid licence can be granted unilaterally by one of two co-owners of land.[9] A doubt remains in this context since, as was said by Traynor J in *Tompkins v Superior Court of City and County of San Francisco*,[10] one joint owner's right of privacy should not be left 'completely at the mercy of another with whom he shares legal possession.'[11]

(a) Implied licence

One of the pervasive difficulties with the implied licence is that it can arise in an extremely wide variety of situations. It seems, for instance, that the residential status of a child in the family home rests upon a bare licence both before and after his attainment of the age of majority.[12] A bare licence is often present in many other kinds of informal arrangement for family living.[13]

In a slightly different context it is now settled law that, in the absence of a locked gate or some other notice, the occupier of a dwelling-house gives an implied licence to any member of the public to come through his garden gate (if he has one) and up to his front door in order to inquire whether he may be admitted to the house or perform some other act on the land.[14] An implied licence of this kind extends to such persons as the postman, the milkman,[15] an election canvasser[16] and a police officer,[17] provided in each case that the person concerned has a genuine and legitimate reason to be present[18] or proposes to conduct 'lawful business'.[19]

8   *Faulkner v Willetts* [1982] RTR 159 at 164H. See also Occupiers' Liability Act 1957, s 2(6).
9   See eg *Robson-Paul v Farrugia* (1969) 20 P & CR 820 at 825; *Slade v Guscott* [1981] CLY 719. Compare, however, *Sanders v McDonald and Pringle* [1981] CLY 1534. See also *Jolliffe v Willmett & Co* [1971] 1 All ER 478 at 483g-484f.
10   27 Cal Rptr 889 at 892 (1963).
11   In *Tompkins* the Supreme Court of California held that a police officer could not rely on a permission to enter co-owned premises which had been given by only one of the co-owners, at least where there was no emergency and the officer did not explain to the co-owner in residence that he had the consent of an absent co-owner. See also *R v Thornley* (1980) 72 Cr App R 302 at 305.
12   Post, p 782.
13   Post, p 794.
14   *Robson v Hallett* [1967] 2 QB 939 at 951F, 953G-954A. See also *Snook v Mannion* [1982] RTR 321 at 326C-D; *Nevill v Halliday* [1983] 2 VR 553 at 556; *Halliday v Nevill* (1984) 155 CLR 1 at 7. The implied licence of the general public has been held equally applicable to an occupier's back door (see *Pamplin v Fraser* [1981] RTR 494 at 500H; *Snook v Mannion* [1982] RTR 321 at 327A-B). The implied licence to approach business premises may be more limited. See *Great Central Railway Co v Bates* [1921] 3 KB 578 at 581f; *Mackay v Abrahams* [1916] VLR 681 at 684f; but compare *Davis v Lisle* [1936] 2 KB 434 at 438ff.
15   *Holden v White* [1982] QB 679 at 687D-E; [1983] CLJ 48 (J.R. Spencer).
16   *Evans v Forsyth* (1979) 90 DLR (3d) 155 at 156.
17   *Robson v Hallett* [1967] 2 QB 939 at 952A-B, 953F-954A. See also *Dobie v Pinker* [1983] WAR 48 at 51, 68.
18   *Nevill v Halliday* [1983] 2 VR 553 at 556.
19   *Robson v Hallett* [1967] 2 QB 939 at 954A. In *Lambert v Roberts* [1981] 2 All ER 15 at 19d, Donaldson LJ was prepared to extend this implied licence to knock on the door to all citizens (including police officers) who 'reasonably think that they have' legitimate business on the premises. The 'business' need not be with the occupier of the house (see *Brunner v Williams* [1975] Crim LR 250).

It seems, moreover, that the implied licence which arises in this context is not ordinarily restricted to presence on the open driveway or path for the purpose of going to the entrance of the house. As the High Court of Australia pointed out in *Halliday v Nevill*,[20] a passer-by is not rendered a trespasser 'if, on passing an open driveway with no indication that entry is forbidden or unauthorised, he or she steps upon it either unintentionally or to avoid an obstruction such as a vehicle parked across the footpath.' Nor is there any trespass if the passer-by goes upon the driveway or path 'to recover some item of his or her property which has fallen or blown upon it or to lead away an errant child.' The law is 'not such an ass' that the implied or tacit licence in such a case is restricted to stepping over the item of property or around the child for the purpose of going to the entrance and asking the householder whether the item of property can be reclaimed or the child led away.[1]

(b) 'An Englishman's home is his castle'

In its operation within the domestic curtilage, the law of implied licences trenches peculiarly upon the general principle that 'an Englishman's home is his castle'.[2] This brocard has 'immense importance in the history of this country, and it still has immense importance.'[3] The implied licence exercised by an investigating police officer extends only to the area outside the dwelling-house.[4] Further entry may be made only with the clear licence of the occupier (or of some person acting on his behalf[5]) or in pursuance of some common law[6] or statutory police power.[7] The question whether a bare licence to *enter* premises has been granted to a police officer is ultimately one of fact, but the courts tend to assume that the owner or occupier of premises has granted such a licence unless he has in some way manifested an intention to exclude.[8]

20 (1984) 155 CLR 1 at 7.
1   (1984) 155 CLR 1 at 7. See also *Lincoln Hunt Australia Pty Ltd v Willesee* [1986] 4 NSWLR 457 at 460C-E.
2   It was affirmed as early as 1604 that '[t]he house of every one is to him as his castle and fortress' (see *Semayne's Case* (1604) 5 Co Rep 91a at 91b, 77 ER 194 at 195). The rule is of course subject to exceptions, but it is for the police to justify a forcible entry (*McLorie v Oxford* [1982] QB 1290 at 1296B per Donaldson LJ). For an extensive review of the maxim that 'an Englishman's home is his castle', see *Nevill v Halliday* [1983] 2 VR 553 at 561ff. It has been held that a householder may use all necessary force (including potentially lethal force) against a trespasser who invades his home (see *R v Hussey* (1924) 18 Cr App R 160 at 161). Nowadays, however, it will be rare that this principle can properly be invoked in defence of homicide.
3   *Swales v Cox* [1981] QB 849 at 855A-B per Donaldson LJ. See M.J. Speziale, *Is a House a Castle?*, 9 Conn LR 110 (1976-77).
4   *Robson v Hallett* [1967] 2 QB 939 at 951F; *Snook v Mannion* [1982] RTR 321 at 327E.
5   *Robson v Hallett* [1967] 2 QB 939 at 954C. That a licence may be effectively granted by some person acting on the occupier's authority is clear from *Rossiter v Conway* (1893) 58 JP 350 at 351; *Jones v Lloyd* [1981] Crim LR 340 at 341; *Nevill v Halliday* [1983] 2 VR 553 at 557.
6   *Sandon v Jervis* (1859) El Bl & El 935 at 940f, 120 ER 758 at 760. See eg *Hart v Chief Constable of Kent* [1983] RTR 484 at 491E-F (right of 'hot pursuit').
7   See eg Police and Criminal Evidence Act 1984, ss 8(1), 17(1), 18(1). This does not, however, mean that evidence obtained by trespassing police officers is necessarily inadmissible in subsequent criminal proceedings (see *R v Fox* [1985] 1 WLR 1126 at 1131H, 1132D-E).
8   *Nevill v Halliday* [1983] 2 VR 553 at 556. See eg *Faulkner v Willetts* [1982] RTR 159 at 164C-D, where the Divisional Court found an implied licence where a woman opened her front door to a police officer and walked back into the house, giving the officer the impression that he had an implied invitation to follow her into the house. Compare *R v Landry* (1982) 34 OR (2d) 697 at 704, where the Ontario Court of Appeal held by a majority that a police officer who entered a home through an open door did not do so in pursuance of any implied licence and was therefore a trespasser.

(2) **Revocation**

It is generally said that a bare licence is revocable at will by the licensor,[9] without any necessity of prior notice[10] and without any requirement that there be compliance with rules of natural justice.[11] In particular it is clear that the ordinary householder may arbitrarily exclude from his land any person who lacks an entitlement, whether legal or equitable, whether by way of common law or under statute, to maintain a presence there.[12] Quite apart from the practicalities of the matter, there is no way in which the bare licensee, being a mere volunteer, can have his exclusion from the land restrained by the equitable remedy of injunction.

(a) *Mode of revocation*

A bare licence is effectively revoked by any words or conduct which sufficiently indicate that a permission to be present on land has been withdrawn. The crucial (and primarily factual) issue is whether the language or conduct used is such as to intimate a request to leave the property.[13] It seems that a bare licence can be validly revoked by one of two or more joint owners acting unilaterally[14] or by some person acting on behalf of the true owner or occupier.[15] A bare licence is revoked automatically by the death of the licensor or the assignment of his land.[16]

(b) *Effect of revocation*

Following upon the revocation of a bare licence, it becomes the duty of the

9   *Wood v Leadbitter* (1845) 13 M & W 838 at 844f, 153 ER 351 at 354 (even where the licence was granted under seal). See also *Mayfield Holdings Ltd v Moana Reef Ltd* [1973] 1 NZLR 309 at 315.
10   *Lambert v Roberts* [1981] 2 All ER 15 at 19d.
11   A private landowner may exclude any person from his land without assigning any reason. The principles of natural justice do not apply to the exercise of private rights in respect of property (*Heatley v Tasmanian Racing and Gaming Commission* (1977) 14 ALR 519 at 538). However, it may be that the power to exclude a licensee from a public facility (eg a public racecourse) should be treated as a public power subject to requirements of due process (see *Forbes v New South Wales Trotting Club Ltd* (1979) 25 ALR 1 at 28). For further development of the idea that the owner of quasi-public premises (eg a shopping plaza) cannot exclude members of the public on a mere whim, see *Harrison v Carswell* (1976) 62 DLR (3d) 68 at 73f per Laskin CJC (dissenting).
12   *Forbes v New South Wales Trotting Club Ltd* (1979) 25 ALR 1 at 28.
13   In *Gilham v Breidenbach* [1982] RTR 328 at 331E-F, a Divisional Court declined to interfere with a decision by magistrates who had decided, after hearing extracts from the *Oxford English Dictionary*, that the phrase 'fuck off' was to be interpreted as 'coarse abuse rather than a request to leave'. Donaldson LJ thought that the 'precise meaning of that observation was supremely a matter for the justices with their knowledge of the local vernacular'. See also *Snook v Mannion* [1982] RTR 321, but compare *Halliday v Nevill* (1984) 155 CLR 1 at 19, where Brennan J declared himself 'unable to adopt the reasoning in these cases. To imply that a police officer who is pursuing a fugitive on to his home ground has the fugitive's permission to enter and remain there until the police officer's work is done is...contrary to the inference ordinarily to be drawn from those facts.'
14   *Robson-Paul v Farrugia* (1969) 20 P & CR 820 at 825; *Sanders v McDonald and Pringle* [1981] CLY 1534; *Annen v Rattee* (1985) 273 Estates Gazette 503 at 507. See, however, *R v Thornley* (1980) 72 Cr App R 302 at 305f.
15   *Robson v Hallett* [1967] 2 QB 939 at 954B.
16   Revocation in these circumstances is the inevitable consequence of the highly personal nature of the bare licence.

licensee to leave the property 'with all reasonable speed'.[17] The licensee has a 'reasonable' time within which to vacate the licensor's premises,[18] but he becomes a trespasser unless he acts with 'reasonable expedition'.[19] It is clear, for instance, that a police officer whose implied licence has been withdrawn has a 'reasonable time to leave the premises by the most appropriate route'.[20] In relation to a bare licence enjoyed in the longer-term context of a 'family arrangement',[1] a 'reasonable' period of time for the vacation of property is determined largely by the practicalities of finding alternative accommodation. In such cases the period may perhaps be as long as twelve months.[2]

2. LICENCES COUPLED WITH THE GRANT OF AN INTEREST

Another form of licence long recognised by the common law is the 'licence coupled with the grant of an interest'. Such a licence usually comprises a permission to enter upon another's land for the specific purpose of abstracting something from that land (eg timber, minerals, fish, crops, or game).[3] In effect this form of licence combines the grant of an interest (such as a profit *à prendre*[4]) with an ancillary permission to enter the land in order to realise or exploit that interest.[5]

(1) Types of 'interest'

It seems that no authoritative definition has yet been given by the courts of the categories of 'interest' within the present context to which a licence may be attached.[6] The types of 'interest' so far accepted for this purpose have included not merely interests in land and chattels but also—more dubiously—the 'interest' which a licensee may have in attending a creditors' meeting[7] or in seeing a cinema performance[8] or in continuing work on a building site.[9] As Megarry J pointed out in *Hounslow LBC v Twickenham Garden Developments Ltd*,[10]

17   *Lambert v Roberts* [1981] 2 All ER 15 at 19c.
18   *Robson v Hallett* [1967] 2 QB 939 at 952G-953A. The licensor is bound to allow the licensee a reasonable time to remove himself, and the withdrawal of the licence becomes effective only after that period has expired (*Minister of Health v Bellotti* [1944] KB 298 at 309). The expiry of this period marks the inception of a state of trespass (see *Warnes v Hedley* (Unreported, Court of Appeal, 31 January 1984)). The period allowed for removal is sometimes called 'packing up time' (see *Hounslow LBC v Twickenham Garden Developments Ltd* [1971] Ch 233 at 242B, 244E).
19   *Robson v Hallett* [1967] 2 QB 939 at 954D.
20   *Robson v Hallett* [1967] 2 QB 939 at 954D.
 1   Post, p 794.
 2   See eg *E. & L. Berg Homes Ltd v Grey* (1980) 253 Estates Gazette 473 at 477. See also *Hannaford v Selby* (1976) 239 Estates Gazette 811 at 813 (six months allowed).
 3   *Muskett v Hill* (1839) 5 Bing (NC) 694 at 707f, 132 ER 1267 at 1272f; *Wood v Leadbitter* (1845) 13 M & W 838 at 844f, 153 ER 351 at 354f; *Hounslow LBC v Twickenham Garden Developments Ltd* [1971] Ch 233 at 243D.
 4   Post, p 633.
 5   See eg *Thomas v Sorrell* (1673) Vaugh 330 at 351, 124 ER 1098 at 1109; *Wood v Leadbitter* (1845) 13 M & W 838 at 844f, 153 ER 351 at 354f.
 6   *Hounslow LBC v Twickenham Garden Developments Ltd* [1971] Ch 233 at 243G per Megarry J.
 7   *Vaughan v Hampson* (1875) 33 LT 15 at 16.
 8   *Hurst v Picture Theatres Ltd* [1915] 1 KB 1 at 7ff.
 9   *Hounslow LBC v Twickenham Garden Developments Ltd* [1971] Ch 233 at 244G, 248F.
10   [1971] Ch 233 at 244D, H.

such cases involve 'no shred of proprietary interest in the...land or any chattels on it', yet, if correctly decided, make it difficult 'to see any fair stopping place in what amounts to an interest, short of any legitimate reason for being on the land.' It may therefore be best to regard the licence coupled with a grant as restricted to proprietary interests only.[11]

(2) Creation

In so far as the permission to enter on land is here the adjunct of some recognised proprietary interest, it is necessary that this proprietary interest should itself have been the subject of valid creation. In the case of a profit *à prendre*, the interest concerned must have been formally granted by deed[12] or duly acquired by prescription.[13] The same formality of grant is not required where the licence is linked to a proprietary interest of a chattel character, as for instance in the case of a licence to enter on land and remove a crop of already harvested hay or cut timber.[14]

(3) Revocation

It has always been a general common law principle that a licence coupled with the grant of a proprietary interest is irrevocable during the subsistence of the proprietary interest to which it pertains.[15] So long as the proprietary interest in question was validly created,[16] the licence is co-extensive with it and enjoys the same legal character.[17] In so far as legal rights bind the world, such a licence enjoys the perpetually binding effect attributed to the proprietary interest to which it is annexed. The licence coupled with an interest is therefore not only binding on the licensor and all his successors in title,[18] but is itself capable of assignment to third parties.[19]

11   See eg *Mayfield Holdings Ltd v Moana Reef Ltd* [1973] 1 NZLR 309 at 315 per Mahon J.
12   On the *Walsh v Lonsdale* principle (ante, p 472), equity is normally prepared to regard a profit which has been granted for value by informal writing as a specifically enforceable agreement to grant an interest (post, p 665). See *James Jones & Sons Ltd v Earl of Tankerville* [1909] 2 Ch 440 at 443. Equity is therefore willing to give effect by way of injunction to a licence coupled with such an interest (*Frogley v Earl of Lovelace* (1859) John 333 at 339f, 70 ER 450 at 453; *Chandler v Kerley* [1978] 1 WLR 693 at 697D- E; *Woods v Donnelly* [1982] NI 257 at 263G).
13   Post, pp 678, 684.
14   See eg *James Jones & Sons Ltd v Earl of Tankerville* [1909] 2 Ch 440 at 442; *Wood v Manley* (1839) 11 A & E 34 at 37, 113 ER 325 at 326.
15   *Doe d Hanley v Wood* (1819) 2 B & Ald 724 at 738ff, 106 ER 529 at 534ff; *Wood v Manley* (1839) 11 A & E 34 at 37, 113 ER 325 at 326; *Wood v Leadbitter* (1845) 13 M & W 838 at 845, 153 ER 351 at 354; *Hounslow LBC v Twickenham Garden Developments Ltd* [1971] Ch 233 at 243D; *Mayfield Holdings Ltd v Moana Reef Ltd* [1973] 1 NZLR 309 at 314; *Woods v Donnelly* [1982] NI 257 at 263A-C. The licence is irrevocable even if coupled with an informal grant of a proprietary interest effective only in equity (see *James Jones & Sons Ltd v Earl of Tankerville* [1909] 2 Ch 440 at 442f).
16   *Wood v Leadbitter* (1845) 13 M & W 838 at 845, 153 ER 351 at 354f.
17   See *Woods v Donnelly* [1982] NI 257 at 263C, where Hutton J held that a licence granted for life to draw sand and gravel could not be terminated without consent during the grantee's life. A 'licence coupled with an interest' is irrevocable 'so long as the term of the grant of the ancillary interest continues' (*Patel v Patel* [1983] Court of Appeal Unbound Transcript 930 per Slade LJ).
18   *Webb v Paternoster* (1619) Palm 71 at 72f, 81 ER 983 at 984; 2 Rolle 143, 81 ER 713; Popham 151, 79 ER 1250.
19   *Muskett v Hill* (1839) 5 Bing (NC) 694 at 707f, 132 ER 1267 at 1273f. The assignability of the licence may be restricted by an expression of contrary intention (see *Woods v Donnelly* [1982] NI 257 at 263C).

3. CONTRACTUAL LICENCES

A 'contractual licence' comprises a permission to be present on land which derives its force from some contract express or implied. It differs from the bare licence in that it is not granted gratuitously but is founded upon valuable consideration moving from the licensee.[20]

The precise legal status of the contractual licence is today a matter of some controversy. The essential dilemma revolves around the question whether the contractual licence should be regarded as conferring merely rights in contract or as also having a proprietary dimension. It may well be that the law in relation to contractual licences is currently undergoing the same process of evolution which in the 19th century led to the recognition of the restrictive covenant as a proprietary interest of an equitable character.[1] Although it is nowadays quite clear in which direction legal developments are headed, it is certainly not yet settled law that the contractual licence has acquired proprietary status.

(1) The disparate functions of the contractual licence

The ambivalence which surrounds the contractual licence is accounted for in part by the fact that it is above all a chameleonic device which has been adapted at different times and in wildly divergent contexts in order to fill various sorts of legal hiatus.

(a) Short-term functions

At one end of the spectrum the contractual licence provides the legal medium for relationships of an extremely short-term and intensely purposive character. The contractual licence frequently supplies a personal permission to be present on another's land for the purpose of business or entertainment. It is the contractual licence which underlies the right of the cinema fan to sit in the auditorium or that of the football spectator to cheer from the terraces.[2] It was the contractual licence which provided the legal basis of the classic 'coronation cases' of 1903 where would-be spectators had hired rooms in order to watch a coronation procession which was in fact postponed by reason of the illness of King Edward VII.[3] Temporary parking in a commercial car park usually takes effect behind a contractual licence.[4]

---

20 *Horrocks v Forray* [1976] 1 WLR 230 at 236C-E per Megaw LJ.
1   Post, pp 557, 698.
2   *Winter Garden Theatre (London) Ltd v Millennium Productions Ltd* [1948] AC 173 at 189; *Hurst v Picture Theatres Ltd* [1915] 1 KB 1 at 7. In *Hurst* the Court of Appeal rationalised the licence as one coupled with the grant of an interest (ante, p 539), but it is better analysed simply as a contractual licence. For criticism of the reasoning in *Hurst*, see *Cowell v Rosehill Racecourse Co Ltd* (1937) 56 CLR 605 at 621ff, 652; *Mayfield Holdings Ltd v Moana Reef Ltd* [1973] 1 NZLR 309 at 315. Compare, however, *Hounslow LBC v Twickenham Garden Developments Ltd* [1971] Ch 233 at 244G-245A, 248F.
3   *Krell v Henry* [1903] 2 KB 740 at 750.
4   *Ashby v Tolhurst* [1937] 2 KB 242 at 249. Compare, however, the bailment analysis applied in *Davis v Pearce Parking Station Pty Ltd* (1954) 91 CLR 642 at 647; *Walton Stores Ltd v Sydney City Council* [1968] 2 NSWR 109 at 112ff. The bailment analysis may, of course, result in the imposition of a different standard of care.

(b) Medium-term functions

The contractual licence is also quite capable of serving a number of medium-term objectives. The building contractor who works on a construction site enjoys a contractual licence to be present on another's land.[5] 'Front of the house rights' in a theatre are commonly enjoyed by way of contractual licence.[6] On payment of his annual subscription the member of a golf club acquires a contractual licence to play on the course and to enjoy a package of benefits, privileges and club facilities.[7]

(c) Long-term functions

At the other end of the spectrum the contractual licence has come, during the last 40 years, to play a rather different role from any mentioned so far. The contractual licence has emerged as a common residential device peculiarly appropriate to modern social conditions. The contractual licence has acquired a wholly unaccustomed prominence as a 'possible mode of land-holding—a mode which had certainly not been developed into anything like its current maturity in the 19th century.'[8] The contractual licence thus provides the legal explanation for the social reality of occupancy enjoyed by lodgers[9] and by a wide range of family members living in informal and loosely organised 'family arrangements'.[10]

(d) Disjunctions of time and concept

The difficulties evident in the contemporary law of contractual licences are those which inevitably arise where one phrase, itself of somewhat ill-defined scope, has to do service for a range of purposes which differ broadly in context and time-scale. The formative concepts relevant to the law of contractual licences were hammered out during the 19th and early 20th centuries some time before the residential dimension of the contractual licence began properly to emerge.[11] Rules which were quite appropriate for short- or medium-term dealings have now come to appear entirely inapposite to the expectations of parties caught up in long-term residential arrangements. Conversely, ideas which would seem bizarre in the context of the 'cinema ticket' cases acquire a certain plausibility—and indeed a certain legal necessity—in the context of other kinds of arrangement which fall within the compass of the contractual licence.

---

5   *Hounslow LBC v Twickenham Garden Developments Ltd* [1971] Ch 233 at 246C, 247B-D; *Mayfield Holdings Ltd v Moana Reef Ltd* [1973] 1 NZLR 309 at 316.
6   *Clore v Theatrical Properties Ltd and Westby & Co Ltd* [1936] 3 All ER 483 at 490.
7   *The Banstead Downs Golf Club v The Commissioners* (1974) VATTR 219 at 227.
8   *Heslop v Burns* [1974] 1 WLR 1241 at 1252C-D per Scarman LJ.
9   In the residential context there seems to be a presumption in favour of contractual licence rather than bare licence. The onus is on the licensor to prove that only a bare licence was present and that no monies were paid (see *Patel v Patel* [1983] Court of Appeal Unbound Transcript 930 per Slade LJ).
10   'Family arrangements' are discussed further in Chapter 23 (post, p 792).
11   Even in the 1930s the Rent Acts were as yet in their infancy, and the possibility that this legislation might be circumvented through the grant of a contractual occupation licence had not been fully realised. This process of circumvention has now of course come full circle with the ruling of the House of Lords in *Street v Mountford* [1985] AC 809 (ante, p 449; post, p 1000).

(2) Terms of the contractual licence

A contractual licence may be created either expressly or impliedly and its terms are left to be ascertained by normal contractual principles. Some terms may be stipulated explicitly by the parties, but it is quite possible that other terms may be supplied by implication from the conduct and expectations of the parties.

(a) Implied term for quiet enjoyment

It is possible that some kinds of contractual licence will be held to contain an implied undertaking by the licensor to afford quiet enjoyment to the licensee.[12] In *Smith v Nottinghamshire County Council*,[13] for instance, a number of students living in a hall of residence complained that their preparation for an examination had been prejudicially affected by noisy repairs which their polytechnic had insisted on carrying out during term time. The Court of Appeal held that there had indeed been a breach of a contractual term that the polytechnic, as a contractual licensor, should do nothing without just cause to disturb the students from getting on with their studies with reasonable quietude in their own rooms.

(b) Implied term relating to fitness for purpose

As is demonstrated by *Smith v Nottinghamshire County Council*, the judicial implication of terms has done much to make the contractual licence resemble the functional equivalent of a tenancy.[14] In one respect, however, the courts have gone even further and have been willing to imply in the contractual licence a term which has never been implied in any lease. In *Wettern Electric Ltd v Welsh Development Agency*,[15] Judge John Newey QC was prepared to imply into a contractual occupation licence a term that the premises hired should be fit for the purposes envisaged by the licensee.[16] Here the plaintiffs had been unable to carry on their business in the licensed premises because, shortly after moving in, they discovered foundations defects which made the property dangerous and unusable. The defendants were found to be in breach of an implied term of fitness and were therefore liable in damages.[17] The willingness of the courts to imply such terms on the basis of 'business efficacy'[18] may well counterbalance the perceived attraction—judged from the landowner's viewpoint—which the contractual licence has seemed to enjoy over the lease.

---

12   On the covenant for quiet enjoyment implied in a lease, see Chapter 14 (ante, p 476).
13   (1981) *Times*, 13 November.
14   However, although the contractual licensee may invoke the contractual doctrine of frustration (see *Krell v Henry* [1903] 2 KB 740 at 751ff; *National Carriers Ltd v Panalpina (Northern) Ltd* [1981] AC 675 at 690H-691A, 694A-B), he enjoys no special rights in respect of fixtures (*C & P Haulage v Middleton* [1983] 1 WLR 1461 at 1468B-C) and cannot invoke on his own behalf the equitable doctrine of relief against forfeiture (*Sport Internationaal Bussum BV v Inter-Footwear Ltd* [1984] 1 WLR 776 at 794C-G).
15   [1983] QB 796. See (1983) 34 NILQ 349 (Norma Dawson); (1983) 80 Law Soc Gaz 2195 (H.W. Wilkinson); [1983] Conv 319 (J.E.M.).
16   For a discussion of the courts' reluctance to imply an equivalent term in the context of a lease, see Chapter 27 (post, p 904).
17   [1983] QB 796 at 809A-E.
18   See *The Moorcock* (1889) 14 PD 64 at 68, cited in *Wettern Electric Ltd v Welsh Development Agency* [1983] QB 796 at 809A-B.

(c) Implied terms as to residential security

In the relatively recent past the practice of contractual implication in relation to licences has been carried to controversial extremes.

(i) The Tanner v Tanner licence In *Tanner v Tanner*,[19] for example, a young mother of twins gave up a Rent Act protected tenancy in order to move into a house bought by the father of her children. When he later evicted her from that house, the Court of Appeal awarded the woman compensation for the loss of a 'contractual licence'. According to Lord Denning MR, the house had obviously been 'provided for her as a house for herself and the twins for the foreseeable future'.[20] Having suffered the detriment of giving up her protected tenancy, she had acquired a contractual licence to 'have accommodation in the house for herself and the children so long as they were of school age and the accommodation was reasonably required for her and the children'.[1] The Court thus regarded the expectations of the parties as having given rise to a form of residential security which, although terminable in changed circumstances,[2] was none the less compensable by damages where the licence had already been wrongfully terminated.[3]

(ii) Retreat from the Tanner v Tanner licence Although in the years following *Tanner v Tanner* the courts have occasionally implied the existence of a contractual licence from circumstances of family cohabitation,[4] the reasoning applied in that case has been subjected to severe criticism.[5] It is unlikely that the courts would nowadays be quite so ready to give implied contractual status to supposed undertakings whose scope and time-scale can scarcely have been present to the minds of the parties.[6] In *Chandler v Kerley*,[7] for instance, the defendant and her ex-husband conveyed their former matrimonial home to the plaintiff who was at this time the defendant's lover. It was intended that the defendant and the two children of the broken marriage should continue to live there, and the plaintiff paid a purchase price which was some £5,000 below the

---

19   [1975] 1 WLR 1346. See (1976) 92 LQR 168 (J.L. Barton).
20   [1975] 1 WLR 1346 at 1350B.
1   [1975] 1 WLR 1346 at 1350E.
2   [1975] 1 WLR 1346 at 1350F. For criticism of the 'concept of a wavering licence', see *McGill v S* [1979] IR 283 at 293 (ante, p 415).
3   See I.J. Hardingham, *The Non-Marital Partner as Contractual Licensee*, (1979-80) 12 Melbourne ULR 356.
4   See eg *Broughall v Hunt* (Unreported, Chancery Division, 1 February 1983). See (1983) 80 Law Soc Gaz 2198 (G. Gypps). The courts have even gone so far as to attribute a notional cash value to a *Tanner v Tanner* licence in the reallocation of resources between husband and wife on divorce (see *W v W* (Financial Provision: Lump Sum) [1976] Fam 107 at 113A-B).
5   See eg *McGill v S* [1979] IR 283 at 292. The factual situation present in *Tanner* could have been much better analysed in terms of proprietary estoppel (ante, p 386). It is perhaps significant that, as the contractual shortcomings of *Tanner* became increasingly evident, Lord Denning proceeded to address essentially the same problems in terms not of contractual licence but of the estoppel doctrine (see eg *Greasley v Cooke* [1980] 1 WLR 1306 (post, p 800)).
6   Compare eg the reluctance of a differently constituted Court of Appeal to find a contractual licence in *Horrocks v Forray* [1976] 1 WLR 230 at 238H-239C, 239E. Even in *Tanner v Tanner* [1975] 1 WLR 1346 at 1350E-F, Lord Denning MR had been forced to concede that there was 'no express contract...but the circumstances are such that the court should imply a contract by the plaintiff—or, if need be, impose the equivalent of a contract by him...' See also the hesitation expressed by Browne LJ (at 1351E).
7   [1978] 1 WLR 693. See [1979] Conv 184 (J.M. Masson).

probable market value of the property. Within six weeks of the purchase, the plaintiff terminated his relationship with the defendant and brought an action for possession. The Court of Appeal held that the defendant enjoyed a contractual licence terminable on reasonable notice which, in the circumstances, was fixed as a period of 12 calendar months. Significantly the Court declined to imply a contractual term that the defendant should have an occupation licence for life. Lord Scarman thought it 'wrong...to infer, in the absence of an express promise, that the plaintiff was assuming the burden of housing another man's wife and children indefinitely, and long after his relationship with them had ended.'[8]

(3) Revocation

From the middle of the 19th century onwards it was settled law that a contractual licence could be effectively revoked by the licensor at any time, notwithstanding that the revocation constituted a gross breach of contract. Of course the revocation gave the licensee a right to sue for contractual damages,[9] and the measure of those damages was determined by ordinary contractual principles.[10] It was, however, accepted as clear doctrine in *Wood v Leadbitter*[11] that the breach of a contractual licence could not give rise to any further liability (whether in tort or otherwise) if, following the revocation, the licensee were forcibly ejected or barred from the land.[12]

While contractual damages still remain available as a remedy for breach of a contractual licence,[13] developments during the present century have made it clear that damages no longer represent the only (or even the most important) remedy available to the contractual licensee. More recent developments are deeply rooted in a new found willingness of the courts to imply a negative contractual term in restraint of revocation. The movement of the law in this area has had the indirect effect not only of altering the rules as to the revocability of contractual licences but also of transforming the status of the contractual licence within the broader field of property concepts. As always the jural character of a right is heavily determined by the nature and extent of the remedies which the courts are prepared to award for its violation.

8   [1978] 1 WLR 693 at 698G-H. See A.A.S. Zuckerman, (1980) 96 LQR 248 at 257.
9   In *Hounslow LBC v Twickenham Garden Developments Ltd* [1971] Ch 233 at 249B-C, Megarry J referred to the 'old distinction' between the licensor's power to revoke the licence effectively and his right or liberty to do it lawfully. 'He had the power: he did it: if he did it wrongfully he may have to pay damages: but still he did it.'
10   The court should not, for example, place the aggrieved party in a better financial position than if the contract had been duly performed (*C & P Haulage v Middleton* [1983] 1 WLR 1461 at 1467H-1468A). It used to be thought that the contractual damages appropriate in the 'cinema ticket' cases amounted simply to the price of the ticket, but it may be that, following *Jackson v Horizon Holidays Ltd* [1975] 1 WLR 1468 at 1472B-C, the damages will now include an element of compensation for lost enjoyment and disappointment.
11   (1845) 13 M & W 838 at 855, 153 ER 351 at 359.
12   See also *Hounslow LBC v Twickenham Garden Developments Ltd* [1971] Ch 233 at 243D-E; *Heatley v Tasmanian Racing and Gaming Commission* (1977) 14 ALR 519 at 534.
13   See eg *Tanner v Tanner* [1975] 1 WLR 1346 at 1351C, where the Court of Appeal awarded compensation of £2,000 in respect of the wrongful termination of a contractual licence. See also the award of £1,500 in *Broughall v Hunt* (Unreported, Chancery Division, 1 February 1983), where in similar circumstances Judge Michael Wheeler QC admitted that he was 'frankly placed in a position of having to pluck a figure off a wall'. Compare the rather less generous quantification adopted in *Ivory v Palmer* (1976) 237 Estates Gazette 411 at 413.

(a) The 'implied contract' theory

It has come to be accepted that in a contractual licence the element of licence is not a separate entity but is merely one of the manifestations of the contract in which it is contained.[14] Thus, where a contract contains a permission to occupy land for a specific purpose or period of time, it is often possible to spell out in the contract an implied negative obligation on the part of the licensor, ie, an obligation not to revoke the licence before the completion of that purpose or period. Such a term may be implied, for instance, in contractual licences which confer on the licensee a right to watch a theatre performance[15] or to carry out a building operation.[16] This development has facilitated an even more important step in the evolution of the law.

(b) The 'licence coupled with an equity'

The implication of a negative term in restraint of revocation has revolutionised the power of the courts to govern the rights conferred by a contractual licence, not merely as between the contracting parties themselves but also as against third parties. The crucial development in this context has come through the increased willingness of the courts to exercise their equitable jurisdiction in respect of the 'licence coupled with an equity'.

In the Court of Appeal in *National Provincial Bank Ltd v Hastings Car Mart Ltd*,[17] Lord Denning MR adverted to a long line of cases which establish the legal implications of the phenomenon known as the 'licence coupled with an equity'. Lord Denning drew an analogy between such a licence and the 'licence coupled with an interest', which has long been recognised as conferring on the licensee an irrevocable right binding on third parties.[18] He explained the 'licence coupled with an equity' as arising if

> the owner of land grants a licence to another to go upon land and occupy it for a specific period or a prescribed purpose, and on the faith of that authority the licensee enters into occupation and does work, or in some other way alters his position to his detriment, then the owner cannot revoke the licence at his will. He cannot revoke the licence so as to defeat the period or purpose for which it was granted. A court of equity will restrain him from so doing. Not only will it restrain him, but it will restrain any successor in title who takes the land with knowledge of the arrangement that has been made.[19]

Lord Denning then gave two further examples of the application of this rule: the doctrine of 'proprietary estoppel'[20] and the equitable approach to contractual licences.

---

14   See *Millennium Productions Ltd v Winter Garden Theatre (London) Ltd* [1946] 1 All ER 678 at 680E-H; *Hounslow LBC v Twickenham Garden Developments Ltd* [1971] Ch 233 at 246C.
15   *Hurst v Picture Theatres Ltd* [1915] 1 KB 1 at 10.
16   *Hounslow LBC v Twickenham Garden Developments Ltd* [1971] Ch 233 at 247B-C.
17   [1964] Ch 665 at 684ff.
18   Ante, p 540.
19   [1964] Ch 665 at 686. For expositions of the doctrine that a licence, once acted upon, is irrevocable, see *Webb v Paternoster* (1619) 2 Rolle 143, 81 ER 713; Palm 71 at 72f, 81 ER 983 at 984; Popham 151, 79 ER 1250; *Tayler v Waters* (1816) 7 Taunt 374 at 384, 129 ER 150 at 153; *Wood v Manley* (1839) 11 A & E 34 at 37f, 113 ER 325 at 326; *Hounslow LBC v Twickenham Garden Developments Ltd* [1971] Ch 233 at 255A-F; *Woods v Donnelly* [1982] NI 257 at 266D-F.
20   The estoppel dimension of the 'licence coupled with an equity' is the subject of Chapter 13 (ante, p 386).

(c) The equitable approach to contractual licences

The major modern development in the law relating to contractual licences finds its origin in the same basic idea of conscience which is embodied in the doctrine of proprietary estoppel.[1] Where a contractual licence contains, either expressly or by implication, a negative obligation binding the licensor not to revoke the licence during the currency of the contract, the courts have increasingly recognised the existence of an equitable jurisdiction to restrain the licensor by injunction from wrongful eviction of the licensee before the termination of the contract.[2] As the Court of Appeal explained in *Winter Garden Theatre (London) Ltd v Millennium Productions Ltd*,[3] the court will not assist the licensor to act in breach of his contractual undertaking.[4]

(i) The Errington decision   One of the first significant demonstrations of the new equitable approach occurred in the decision of the Court of Appeal in *Errington v Errington and Woods*.[5] Here a father, wishing to provide a home for his son who had recently married, purchased a house in his own name on mortgage loan. He promised that if his son and daughter-in-law continued in occupation of the house and paid all the instalments of the mortgage loan, he would then transfer the property to them absolutely. The son and his wife entered into occupation and began to make repayments of the loan to the building society. The father later died, leaving all his property (including the house) to his widow, the present plaintiff. Shortly after the father's death, the son left his wife and went to live with his widowed mother. The daughter-in-law, the defendant in the present proceedings, continued to occupy the house and to make the appropriate repayments to the building society. The plaintiff then brought an action for possession, alleging that the defendant had a mere revocable licence to occupy the house.

The Court of Appeal unanimously rejected the claim for possession and declined to eject the daughter-in-law. Denning LJ found that the father's promise was 'a unilateral contract—a promise of the house in return for their act of paying the instalments. It could not be revoked by him once the couple

---

1   The precise differences between the contractual licence and the licence associated with proprietary estoppel have been the subject of lively debate. See A. Briggs, [1981] Conv 212, [1983] Conv 285; M.P. Thompson, [1983] Conv 50. See also A.R. Everton, [1982] Conv 119, 177.

2   See *Chandler v Kerley* [1978] 1 WLR 693 at 697C per Lord Scarman ('Where the parties have contracted for a licence, equity will today provide an equitable remedy to protect the legal right...'). See also *Mayfield Holdings Ltd v Moana Reef Ltd* [1973] 1 NZLR 309 at 316. Of course, injunctive relief can be granted only where the relevant negative obligation is express or can be implied from the dealings between the parties. Where no such undertaking is present, the contractual licence is determinable on the giving of reasonable notice (see *Patel v Patel* [1983] Court of Appeal Unbound Transcript 930). If the licence is terminated in breach of contract, the licensee's remedy lies in a mere action for damages (see *Ivory v Palmer* (1976) 237 Estates Gazette 411 at 413ff).

3   [1946] 1 All ER 678 at 685 per Lord Greene MR (reversed by the House of Lords on different grounds, [1948] AC 173). See also Sir R. Evershed, (1954) 70 LQR 326 at 331ff.

4   See *Hounslow LBC v Twickenham Garden Developments Ltd* [1971] Ch 233 at 248C-E. Compare the quite different approach adopted in Australia, where the courts have preferred not to allow injunctive relief to sanction a continuing trespass. See eg *Graham H. Roberts Pty Ltd v Maurbeth Investments Pty Ltd* [1974] 1 NSWLR 93 at 102D-F, 105F-106B, 108D-G; Sir Anthony Mason, (1980) 11 U Qd LJ 121 at 129.

5   [1952] 1 KB 290. See generally H.W.R. Wade, (1948) 64 LQR 57; R.H. Maudsley, (1956) 20 Conv (NS) 281.

entered on performance of the act.'[6] This being so, the couple were licensees who enjoyed 'a permissive occupation short of a tenancy', but who also had 'a contractual right, or at any rate, an equitable right to remain so long as they paid the instalments, which would grow into a good equitable title to the house as soon as the mortgage was paid.'[7] The couple thus had a 'licence coupled with an equity', the 'equity' consisting precisely in the fact that the courts would grant equitable relief to prevent their ejection in breach of contract.[8]

(ii) The availability of injunctive relief The effect of *Errington*, if correctly decided, is to reverse the rule in *Wood v Leadbitter* that contractual licences are always de facto revocable. The position nowadays appears to be that, practicalities of time and circumstance permitting, an injunction may be available in the discretion of equity to restrain a threatened breach of a contractual licence.[9] Where injunctive relief is available the court may also be prepared to grant the further remedy of specific performance in order to ensure that the terms of a contractual licence are indeed duly carried out.[10] The remedy of injunction now seems to be available in most cases in which the licensee manages to raise his complaint before a threatened revocation takes effect.[11] If, however, no application for an injunction can be made before the revocation becomes effective, the licensee is relegated to a mere action in damages for breach of contract.[12]

There may of course be certain circumstances in which equity is either unwilling or unable to grant the discretionary remedy of injunction, notwithstanding that a threatened revocation is in clear breach of contract. In *Thompson v Park*,[13] for instance, the Court of Appeal held that a highly personal sharing arrangement was not enforceable by way of injunction.[14] Equity cannot enforce 'an agreement for two people to live peaceably under the same roof.'[15] The Court thus held that under these circumstances the revocation of a

6   [1952] 1 KB 290 at 295.
7   [1952] 1 KB 290 at 296. See *Hardwick v Johnson* [1978] 1 WLR 683 at 689H (post, p 800). Compare *Millett v Regent* [1975] 1 NSWLR 62 at 68A-B, 72F-73A, 74D, where similar circumstances were treated as constituting acts of part performance sufficient to exclude the statutory requirement that contracts relating to land should be evidenced in writing (ante, p 212).
8   Denning LJ fully recognised that at law they had no right to remain, 'but only in equity, and equitable rights now prevail' ([1952] 1 KB 290 at 298). The case is 'a classic illustration of equity supplementing a contractual right so as to give effect to the intention of the parties to the arrangement' (*Chandler v Kerley* [1978] 1 WLR 693 at 697H- 698A per Lord Scarman).
9   *Winter Garden Theatre (London) Ltd v Millennium Productions Ltd* [1946] 1 All ER 678 at 684; *Foster v Robinson* [1951] 1 KB 149 at 156 (as cited in *Binions v Evans* [1972] Ch 359 at 367D); *Hounslow LBC v Twickenham Garden Developments Ltd* [1971] Ch 233 at 247B- C, 248F; *Piquet v Tyler* [1978] CLY Unreported Court of Appeal Case No 119. Compare, however, *Mayfield Holdings Ltd v Moana Reef Ltd* [1973] 1 NZLR 309 at 318ff.
10 See eg *Verrall v Great Yarmouth BC* [1981] QB 202 at 216A-F, 218B, 220D-F (specific performance granted to enforce booking of public hall for National Front meeting).
11 Compare *Tanner v Tanner* [1975] 1 WLR 1346 at 1352D.
12 *Tanner v Tanner* [1975] 1 WLR 1346 at 1351A-C; *Broughall v Hunt* (Unreported, Chancery Division, 1 February 1983). It is also possible that a licensee who has been wrongfully ejected from the land in breach of his contractual licence may successfully seek damages for assault and battery (see eg *Hurst v Picture Theatres Ltd* [1915] 1 KB 1 at 11, 15).
13 [1944] KB 408.
14 Here the owners of two schools had agreed to share occupation of premises which were owned by one of them.
15 [1944] KB 408 at 409.

contractual licence, although wrongful, was nevertheless effective, with the consequence that when the ejected licensee forcibly re-entered the premises he was guilty of trespass.[16] Although the point remains somewhat unclear, it is possible that the observations made later by the House of Lords in *Winter Garden Theatre (London) Ltd v Millennium Productions Ltd*[17] have at least the effect of relieving the contractual licensee of liability for trespass in this kind of case.

(4) Effect of the contractual licence on third parties

Another element in the modern transformation of the contractual licence concerns the effect which a contractual licence exerts on third parties who deal with land affected by such a licence.

(a) The traditional rule

The received doctrine of contractual licences holds that a contractual licence confers on the licensee no proprietary interest in the land.[18] This orthodox view is founded on a firm belief that the rights of contractual licensees are at all times rights in contract, not rights in property. From this it inevitably follows that the rights generated by a contractual licence bind only the licensor and licensee, and cannot bind a purchaser of the land even though he may have actual notice of the licence. For these propositions there is extremely strong authority in the decisions of the House of Lords in *King v David Allen and Sons, Billposting, Ltd*[19] and of the Court of Appeal in *Clore v Theatrical Properties Ltd and Westby & Co Ltd.*[20]

(b) The gradual transformation

The orthodox view of the contractual licence of course represents sound commonsense in relation to those licences which have only a short lifespan and which are directed towards intensely purposive activity. It would be absurd, for instance, to suggest that the holder of a cinema ticket has a proprietary interest in the cinema. The Chief Justice of Australia tersely remarked on one occasion that '[f]ifty thousand people who pay to see a football match do not obtain fifty thousand interests in the football ground.'[1]

One of the pervasive problems in the law of contractual licences is, however, that the field of contractual licences also includes rights which take effect over a

---

16 [1944] KB 408 at 411f. In *Hounslow LBC v Twickenham Garden Developments Ltd* [1971] Ch 233 at 249F-G, Megarry J confessed to 'feeling great difficulty' about the grounds given for this decision. He suggested that the case was decided 'quasi in furore' by way of heated response to the licensee's 'high-handed and riotous behaviour'.

17 [1948] AC 173. See *Verrall v Great Yarmouth BC* [1981] QB 202 at 216C-G, 219C-E.

18 A very typical observation is that of Slade LJ in *Patel v Patel* [1983] Court of Appeal Unbound Transcript 930, to the effect that 'it would be a heresy to suggest that the mere fact that a licence to occupy land has been given for consideration renders it irrevocable or confers any interest in the land on the licensee.'

19 [1916] 2 AC 54 at 59, 61f. See also the firm rulings of the Australian High Court in *Minister of State for the Army v Dalziel* (1943-1944) 68 CLR 261 at 300; *Howie v New South Wales Lawn Tennis Ground Ltd* (1955-1956) 95 CLR 132 at 156f.

20 [1936] 3 All ER 483 at 490ff. See also *Walton Harvey Ltd v Walker and Homfrays Ltd* [1931] 1 Ch 274 at 277.

1 *Cowell v Rosehill Racecourse Co Ltd* (1937) 56 CLR 605 at 616 per Latham CJ.

much longer time-scale. In relation to such licences the attribution of proprietary character is not nearly so bizarre, and it is not therefore surprising that in recent years attempts have been made to modify the traditional analysis of the contractual licence. Once again these developments are closely connected with the liberal intervention of equity.

(c) The impact of the 'licence coupled with an equity'

The emergence of an equitable jurisdiction to restrain the revocation of contractual licences has indirectly made it possible to suggest that at least some kinds of contractual licence have an extended impact upon third parties. In *Errington v Errington and Woods*,[2] Denning LJ pointed out that the fusion of law and equity, taken in conjunction with the new approach adumbrated in the *Winter Garden* case,[3] had brought about the result that

a licensor will not be permitted to eject a licensee in breach of a contract to allow him to remain...This infusion of equity means that contractual licences now have a force and validity of their own and cannot be revoked in breach of contract. Neither the licensor nor anyone who claims through him can disregard the contract except a purchaser for value without notice.

In other words Denning LJ regarded the equitable approach to licences as having transformed a purely personal right into what he described in later cases as a 'licence coupled with an equity' and, finally, as an 'equitable licence'.[4] The protective vigour of the courts in satisfying the 'equity' effectively converted contractual licences into rights of property.[5] The approach adopted in *Errington* subsequently provided the basis for an extension of the law relating to family and other living arrangements. In each case the courts, where appropriate, applied the concept of the 'licence coupled with an equity'—whether that 'equity' be founded on estoppel or on contract—in order to 'give effect to the expectations of the parties when making their arrangement'.[6] The 'equity' thus recognised was then jealously protected against all third parties except a purchaser without notice.

(d) The high-point of the Denning doctrine

Throughout his judicial career Lord Denning tried to elevate the contractual licence to the status of an equitable interest in land. Notwithstanding the

---

2   [1952] 1 KB 290 at 298f.
3   [1948] AC 173, [1946] 1 All ER 678 (ante, p 547).
4   See *Hardwick v Johnson* [1978] 1 WLR 683 at 688H.
5   This approach did not, however, go unchallenged. Can it really be so easy, asked Professor H.W.R. Wade, 'to cross the chasm which lies between contract and property?' (see (1952) 68 LQR 337 at 348). That chasm had of course been crossed before—for example in the case of the restrictive covenant (post, p 699)—but the courts have strictly defined the qualities which must be possessed by restrictive covenants before they cross the threshold of the law of property. A restrictive covenant qualifies as a proprietary interest only if it clearly restricts the user of one defined area of land (the 'servient tenement') for the 'benefit' of another defined area of land (the 'dominant tenement'). This imposition of constraints on the doctrine proceeding from *Tulk v Moxhay* (1848) 2 Ph 774, 41 ER 1143, represented, as Professor Wade pointed out, a 'decisive repudiation of the notion that the mere fact that an equitable remedy was available was enough to turn a contract into an interest in land binding purchasers with notice'.
6   *Chandler v Kerley* [1978] 1 WLR 693 at 698F per Lord Scarman.

suggestion that such a development could properly be achieved only by statutory intervention,[7] Lord Denning consistently maintained that in unregistered land the contractual licence was governed by the equitable doctrine of notice,[8] and that in registered land the contractual licence, although unregistrable, could generate an overriding interest.[9] Thus, at least in the context of those long-term arrangements where equity was prepared to protect the licensee from wrongful revocation, a contractual licence had the capacity to affect third parties who purchased the land.

The high-point of the Denning doctrine came in *Binions v Evans*.[10] Here the defendant, D, had been allowed by X, the trustees of the estate for which her late husband had worked, to reside rent-free in a cottage on that estate for the remainder of her life. This permission was granted in a written agreement which, inter alia, imposed on D an obligation to maintain the interior of the cottage and to keep the garden in good condition. It was provided that D could terminate the arrangement on giving four weeks' notice. D continued to live in the cottage (which had already been her home for some 50 years). X then conveyed the property to the present plaintiffs, P, expressly subject to the rights enjoyed by D. Notwithstanding that P had secured the purchase at a reduced price in view of D's occupation, P brought possession proceedings against D, who was by this stage 79 years of age.

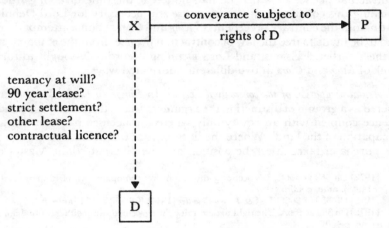

Fig. 43

7 See eg *National Provincial Bank Ltd v Hastings Car Mart Ltd* [1964] Ch 665 at 699 per Russell LJ. On appeal the House of Lords, although cautious as to the current status of the contractual licence, was less definite about the need for legislation and was not wholly unsympathetic to the idea of further judicial development (see *National Provincial Bank Ltd v Ainsworth* [1965] AC 1175 at 1239E per Lord Upjohn, 1251E per Lord Wilberforce).
8 It is clear that a contractual licence cannot be registered as any kind of land charge.
9 See *National Provincial Bank Ltd v Hastings Car Mart Ltd* [1964] Ch 665 at 688f. Compare, however, Russell LJ (at 699). It seems likely that a contractual licence cannot support a caveat under Torrens title legislation. See *Re P. T. Stevens Earthmoving Pty Ltd's Caveat* [1975] Qd R 69 at 70D, but compare *Pearce v Pearce* [1977] 1 NSWLR 170 at 179G-180A.
10 [1972] Ch 359. See R.J. Smith, [1973] CLJ 123; (1972) 36 Conv (NS) 266 (J.E. Martin), 277 (D.J. Hayton); (1972) 88 LQR 336 (P.V. Baker); (1972) 35 MLR 551 (A.J. Oakley); (1973) 117 Sol Jo 23 (B.W. Harvey).

The success of P's possession action clearly depended on the status of the rights held by D. In the Court of Appeal Lord Denning MR took the view that the original written agreement could not have conferred on D either a determinable 90 year lease[11] or indeed any other kind of lease.[12] Moreover, it could not be said that D was either a tenant at will[13] or a tenant for life under any kind of strict settlement.[14] Instead, Lord Denning ruled that D had been granted a contractual licence to reside in the cottage for the remainder of her life.[15] In accordance with authority he then held that the courts of equity would not allow the occupier under such a contract to be evicted in disregard of the contract.[16] Since P had bought the property expressly 'subject to' the contractual rights of D, they were bound by a 'constructive trust to permit the defendant to reside there during her life, or so long as she might desire.'[17] The constructive trust arose here 'for the simple reason that it would be utterly inequitable for the plaintiffs to turn the defendant out contrary to the stipulation subject to which they took the premises'.[18]

(e) The doctrinal difficulties

The result achieved by Lord Denning in *Binions v Evans* was controversial in that it ensured that a purchaser of unregistered land was bound by a contractual licence of which he had notice at the time of taking title.[19] In reaching this conclusion, it was of course still necessary for Lord Denning to distinguish the contrary precedents of *King* and *Clore*.[20] Some attempt therefore had to be made to free the law of contractual licences from the embarrassment of these earlier decisions, and Lord Denning accordingly sought to turn the flank of *King* and *Clore* in two different but related ways.

(i) Actual occupation of the contractual licensee

In *Binions v Evans*[1] Lord Denning offered as a ground of distinction the argument that a third party is bound by a licence coupled with an equity only where the licensee has been 'in actual occupation of the land'. Where the licensee is not in actual occupation when the purchaser takes title, 'the position may be different.'[2] The Master of the

---

11   [1972] Ch 359 at 366C. D's occupation was rent-free (compare Law of Property Act 1925, s 149(6), ante, p 435).

12   [1972] Ch 359 at 366G-H. See *Lace v Chantler* [1944] KB 368 at 371 (ante, p 435).

13   [1972] Ch 359 at 366A. The right to determine the agreement was neither mutual nor at will (ante, p 430).

14   [1972] Ch 359 at 366E-G (post, p 807).

15   The other two judges in the Court of Appeal (Megaw and Stephenson LJJ) preferred, although not with any great conviction, to analyse D's rights in terms of the Settled Land Act 1925 (post, p 807).

16   'In my opinion the defendant, by virtue of the agreement, had an equitable interest in the cottage which the court would protect by granting an injunction against the landlords restraining them from turning her out' ([1972] Ch 359 at 369C-D).

17   [1972] Ch 359 at 369D.

18   [1972] Ch 359 at 368B. See also *Errington v Errington and Woods* [1952] 1 KB 290 at 299. For further description of the operation of the constructive trust, see Chapter 10 (ante, p 268).

19   See eg *DHN Food Distributors Ltd v LB of Tower Hamlets* [1976] 1 WLR 852 at 859H; [1977] CLJ 12 (D.J. Hayton).

20   Ante, p 549.

1   [1972] Ch 359 at 369A-B.

2   *National Provincial Bank Ltd v Hastings Car Mart Ltd* [1964] Ch 665 at 688. This distinction has at least the merit that it accords with the special significance accorded in registered land to the rights of those in 'actual occupation' (see Land Registration Act 1925, s 70(1)(g), ante, p 175).

Rolls was thus able to reconcile the divergent results achieved in *King* and *Errington*, but was forced to assert—surely erroneously[3]—that in *Clore* the licence to exercise 'front of the house' rights in a theatre could 'not properly be said to be actual occupation'.[4]

This rationalisation of *Clore* is fraught with difficulty. In *National Westminster Bank Ltd v Hastings Car Mart Ltd*,[5] for instance, Russell LJ declared himself simply unable to accept that *King* 'depends for its validity on the fact that the licence had not yet been acted upon'.[6] At the end of the day, as Russell LJ indicated, the inexorable truth of the matter is that the real basis for the decisions in *King* and *Clore* was the court's refusal in both cases to accept that a contractual licence is anything other than a private agreement binding only the immediate parties. It creates no proprietary interest in land. In coming to this conclusion, Russell LJ was unmoved by the impact of equitable intervention following *Winter Garden Theatre (London) Ltd v Millennium Productions Ltd*.[7] He confessed that he found it

not easy to see, on authority, how that which has a purely contractual basis between A and B is, though on all hands it is agreed that it is not to be regarded as conferring any estate or interest in property on B, nevertheless to be treated as producing the equivalent result against a purchaser C, simply because an injunction would be granted to restrain A from breaking his contract while he is still in a position to carry it out.[8]

(ii) Conveyance 'subject to' the rights of the contractual licensee In *Binions v Evans* Lord Denning sought an alternative (and somewhat more powerful) ground for distinguishing the contrary precedents of *King* and *Clore*. He pointed out that in neither of those cases had there been any 'trace of a stipulation, express or implied, that the purchaser should take the property subject to the right of the contractual licensee.'[9] In *Binions v Evans*, however, the purchasers had not only taken title with actual express knowledge of the adverse rights of D; they had expressly agreed, in their contract of purchase, to take 'subject to' her rights.[10]

The imposition of a constructive trust under these circumstances is much more consonant with equitable principle. It is entirely consistent with the standard principles of constructive trust theory that the use of a 'subject to' formula should activate the judicial imposition of a constructive trust.[11] In this respect the judgment of Lord Denning in *Binions v Evans* is eminently supportable, but it still provides no solid authority for the proposition that a

---

3 See eg *National Provincial Bank Ltd v Hastings Car Mart Ltd* [1964] Ch 665 at 698 per Russell LJ.
4 *National Provincial Bank Ltd v Hastings Car Mart Ltd* [1964] Ch 665 at 688.
5 [1964] Ch 665 at 697.
6 There is profound difficulty with any line of distinction drawn with reference to actual occupation by a contractual licensee. See eg R.H. Maudsley, (1956) 20 Conv (NS) 281 at 295, for confirmation that the difference between an executory and an executed licence was not relied on in *King*'s case and indeed had been regarded as irrelevant for 100 years before that.
7 [1948] AC 173 (ante, p 547).
8 [1964] Ch 665 at 698.
9 [1972] Ch 359 at 368G.
10 P were in fact supplied with a copy of the earlier agreement which conferred those rights on D.
11 Ante, p 283.

contractual licence has any capacity to bind third parties in the absence of a taking of title 'subject to' the rights of the licensee.[12]

(f) The present position

The present position in relation to the third-party impact of the contractual licence is one of considerable confusion. The question of third-party impact is, of course, fairly irrelevant where a contractual licence comprises merely a short-term permission to be present on land (eg the 'cinema ticket' case). But where a contractual licence represents a longer-term arrangement, the issue assumes a much more fundamental significance for property lawyers. For the academic there is the nice point as to the precise location of the borderline between property and contract.[13] For the conveyancer the question is one of some practical importance, for the ever-present fear of the conveyancer is that the purchaser of land may be trapped, and his title rendered less valuable, by an unregistrable, non-overreachable and effectively undiscoverable equitable interest.

During the years following *Binions v Evans* it was beginning to seem that the effluxion of time, if nothing else, would give a quietus to Lord Denning's unconventional view of the effects of the contractual licence on third parties. But just when the old orthodoxy appeared to be regaining its control over the conveyancing dimension, a further decision of the Court of Appeal threw the law once again into some turmoil. In *Midland Bank Ltd v Farmpride Hatcheries Ltd*[14] a differently constituted Court of Appeal accepted without question that a contractual licence was fully capable of binding a purchaser of the land affected. On the facts of this case (which concerned unregistered land), the only remaining question then concerned whether the purchaser had constructive notice of the rights of the contractual licensee. As it happened the purchaser was held not to be fixed with such notice, but the significant feature of the decision was the Court's willingness to envisage that in unregistered land a contractual licence ranks alongside all other unregistrable, non-overreachable equitable rights and is ultimately governed by the doctrine of notice.

The confusion in this area was compounded by a later decision by yet a different Court of Appeal in *Patel v Patel*.[15] Here Slade LJ, in dealing with a residential licence, reaffirmed 'the general rule...that a mere licence to occupy land, albeit of a contractual nature, as opposed to a lease, does not confer any interest on the licensee in the land.' Indeed Slade LJ went so far as to declare it to be a 'heresy' to suggest that 'the mere fact that a licence to occupy land has been given for consideration renders it irrevocable'.

---

12   See, for instance, the insistence of Browne-Wilkinson J in *In re Sharpe (A Bankrupt)* [1980] 1 WLR 219 at 225G-H, that an irrevocable licence can create an 'interest in land' only in association with some kind of constructive trust.

13   See eg A. Briggs, [1981] Conv 212, [1983] Conv 285; M.P. Thompson, [1983] Conv 50. For an incisive examination of the implications of the licence debate, see John Dewar, *Licences and Land Law: An Alternative View*, (1986) 49 MLR 741.

14   (1981) 260 Estates Gazette 493 (Buckley, Shaw and Oliver LJJ). See [1982] Conv 67 (R.E. Annand); (1982) 132 NLJ 68 (H.W. Wilkinson). See also *Pennine Raceway Ltd v Kirklees Metropolitan BC* [1983] QB 382 at 389F (contractual licensee recognised, in a less than 'strict conveyancing sense', as 'a person interested in land' for the purpose of statutory compensation in the event of a withdrawal of planning permission). See [1983] Conv 317 (J.E.M.).

15   [1983] Court of Appeal Unbound Transcript 930 (Dunn and Slade LJJ).

Perhaps the only point which now remains clear is the need for a definitive ruling from the House of Lords on the proprietary status of the contractual licence. Such a ruling would, however, involve a significant consideration of the boundaries of the property concept, and this itself raises a question as to the meaning of 'property' and, in particular, of 'equitable rights of property'. There are certain movements in the contemporary jurisprudence of property which make it not at all impossible that the contractual licence will one day be recognised as a species of property interest.

(5) The meaning of 'property' and 'equitable rights of property'

Throughout this book reference has been made to 'property' as connoting not a thing but a relationship.[16] In effect 'property' is accurately characterised not in the form of any reification of wealth, but rather in terms of socially defined relationships and morally conditioned obligations. This point is especially true of 'equitable rights of property', and has an important implication for the issue whether a contractual licence can ever bind a purchaser of land. In *National Provincial Bank Ltd v Hastings Car Mart Ltd*,[17] Russell LJ was of the opinion that a contractual licence cannot bind third parties since, in his analysis, a contractual licence created not a right of 'property' but merely a personal right affecting the land. It followed from this premise that, since only proprietary rights have the quality of binding third parties, a contractual licence cannot affect even a third party who takes the land with actual notice.

(a) Cause and effect in the characterisation of 'property'

It can, however, be argued that to approach problems of this kind in terms of a 'property' analysis is to turn the process on its head and to begin with a conclusion. Where an equitable interest is protected against third parties, the reality of the matter is not that it is protected in this way because it is 'property', but rather that it is 'property' precisely because—ultimately through the equitable intervention of the courts—it is indeed protected.[18] To address the question in terms of a 'property' analysis is to argue at one remove from the legal reality that underlies the debate, and often invites obfuscation of the issue.

(b) The priority of obligation

To say that a person is a beneficiary or has an equitable interest in property is not to say that he owns a 'thing' but to indicate that someone owes him an obligation.[19] This idea becomes a little clearer if for the unhelpful term 'beneficiary' is substituted the less modern but more literally expressive term 'cestui que trust'. Trusts, said Lindley LJ, 'are equitable obligations to deal with property in a particular way'.[20] As Isaacs J once observed, 'the right of the

16 Ante, p 8.
17 [1964] Ch 665 at 697ff.
18 Compare C.B. Macpherson, 'The Meaning of Property', in C.B. Macpherson (ed), *Property: Mainstream and Critical Positions* (Oxford 1978), p 3: 'Property is not thought to be a right because it is an enforceable claim: it is an enforceable claim only because and in so far as the prevailing ethical theory holds that it is a necessary human right'.
19 Ante, p 51.
20 *In re Williams* [1897] 2 Ch 12 at 18.

cestui que trust to have the property dealt with as the trust requires is regarded for the purpose of equity as equivalent to a right in the property itself, but only commensurate with his particular right *in personam*.'[1]

(c) Rights to relief emerge as a species of 'property'

An 'equitable right of property' is therefore simply a right to equitable relief in the face of the assertion by another of legal rights in the same 'thing'.[2] This right to relief is premised upon a perceived obligation binding the legal owner to deal with the property honestly and in good faith. An effective claim to such relief metamorphoses imperceptibly into the kind of right which, in legal shorthand, is termed a 'right of property'. As was once said in the context of the equitable rules of tracing, equitable intervention, although starting 'from a personal equity...ended, as was so often the case, in creating what were in effect rights of property, though not recognised as such by the common law'.[3]

(d) The necessity of equitable relationship

Thus, in the creation of an 'equitable right of property', the existence of a moral duty is logically anterior to the recognition of a proprietary right. In the beginning was not a right but a relationship—a relationship which was enforced through the granting of a remedy. This is clear from the fact that where there is no relationship there can be no equitable right, as for instance where property is owned by one person absolutely. In *Comr of Stamp Duties (Queensland) v Livingston*,[4] Viscount Radcliffe spoke of the 'fallacy' contained in the assumption that for all purposes and at every moment of time the law requires the separate existence of two different kinds of estate or interest in property, the legal and the equitable. In his view such an assumption was quite unnecessary since when 'the whole right of property is in a person...there is no need to distinguish between the legal and equitable interest in that property...Equity in fact calls into existence and protects equitable rights and interests in property only where their recognition has been found to be required in order to give effect to its doctrines.'[5]

(e) The analogy of intellectual property

Whole areas of equitable jurisdiction can be understood only on the basis that an equitable right of property is protected not because it has first been

---

1   *Glenn v Federal Comr of Taxation* (1915) 20 CLR 490 at 503 (ante, p 423).
2   For the emergence of this idea in the law of estoppel, see Chapter 13 (ante, p 422). See also *Chase Manhattan Bank NA v Israel-British Bank (London) Ltd* [1981] Ch 105 at 124F-G per Goulding J: 'Within the municipal confines of a single legal system, right and remedy are indissolubly connected and correlated, each contributing in historical dialogue to the development of the other, and save in very special circumstances it is as idle to ask whether the court vindicates the suitor's substantive right or gives the suitor a procedural remedy as to ask whether thought is a mental or a cerebral process. In fact the court does both things by one and the same act.'
3   *Sinclair v Brougham* [1914] AC 398 at 441f per Lord Parker of Waddington.
4   [1965] AC 694 at 712C-E.
5   Thus a man cannot be a trustee for himself alone (*Re Heberley* [1971] NZLR 325 at 333, 346). See also *Re Turkington* [1937] 4 All ER 501 at 504F.

characterised as 'property', but because equitable intervention is imperative in order to satisfy the demands of ethical dealing within a given social or commercial relationship. This is particularly true, for example, of the law which protects the integrity of trade marks and regulates the use of confidential information. Holmes J once remarked that 'the word "property" as applied to trademarks and trade secrets is an unanalysed expression of certain secondary consequences of the primary fact that the law makes some rudimentary requirements of good faith'.[6]

(f) The analogy of the restrictive covenant

The same approach can be found at the root of the law relating to restrictive covenants. It is striking that the decision which is generally accepted as marking the conferment of proprietary character on restrictive covenants is not actually phrased in these terms at all. In *Tulk v Moxhay*,[7] Lord Cottenham LC did not hold the restrictive covenant to be binding on the third party purchaser on the ground that it was in some sense 'property', or because (as he would have expressed the same idea) it 'ran with the land'. Instead, he agreed that 'the question is not whether the covenant runs with the land, but whether a party shall be permitted to use the land in a manner inconsistent with the contract entered into by his vendor, and with notice of which he purchased.' He concluded that the restrictive covenant should be enforced against the purchaser on the morally-laden ground that 'nothing could be more inequitable than that the original purchaser should be able to sell the property the next day for a greater price, in consideration of the assignee being allowed to escape from the liability which he had himself undertaken.'[8]

(g) The hallmarks of a 'property right'

The distinction between proprietary and personal rights was expounded in conventional terms by the House of Lords in *National Provincial Bank Ltd v Ainsworth*.[9] Here Lord Wilberforce declared that before a right or interest can be admitted into the 'category of property, or of a right affecting property', it must be 'definable, identifiable by third parties, capable in its nature of assumption by third parties, and have some degree of permanence or stability.'[10]

According to the traditional view a contractual licence does not sufficiently demonstrate these indicia of 'property', although it might be observed that, in so far as Lord Wilberforce's criterion of proprietary character rests upon a requirement of 'permanence or stability', the courts' definition of 'property' is self-fulfilling. There are other respects in which the exclusion of the contractual licence from the realm of 'property' may be subjected to challenge.

---

6   *E.I. Du Pont de Nemours Powder Co v Masland*, 244 US 100 at 102 (1917). See also *Jones v Bouffier* (1911) 12 CLR 579 at 613 per Isaacs J.
7   (1848) 2 Ph 774, 41 ER 1143 (post, p 698).
8   (1848) 2 Ph 774 at 777f, 41 ER 1143 at 1144.
9   [1965] AC 1175 at 1247G-1248A.
10 See also *National Provincial Bank Ltd v Hastings Car Mart Ltd* [1964] Ch 665 at 696 per Russell LJ.

(i) Transferability It seems strange to exclude the contractual licence from the category of property rights on the ground that the interest of the licensee fails to comply with some supposed criterion of transmissibility, when the only really difficult problem posed by the admission of such licences usually relates only to the effect of a transfer of the interest of the *licensor*. It is the assignment of the latter's interest which is controversial. Contractual licences—particularly in the context of family arrangements—are rarely if ever assigned, largely because the security conferred by the licence is normally envisaged from the outset as a purely personal and non-transmissible benefit.

(ii) Changing perceptions of 'property' The dogma which requires that a property interest be both identifiable by, and capable of transmission to, third parties may well represent an increasingly obsolete conception of 'property' in the context of the modern world. As a dogma it is pervaded by an image of property as something commerciable—as something belonging essentially in the world of exchange relationships. This view is not particularly apposite to many of the kinds of property which enjoy social significance today.

The substance of the modern citizen is no longer intrinsically related to the 'ownership' of tangible and freely alienable assets, but is nowadays more readily expressed in terms of intangible, non-assignable, often non-survivable claims of an essentially personal nature. The social desire which underlies all such claims—whether in the field of employment, pensions or income maintenance—is the general quest not for dispositive power over 'things', but rather for security in the enjoyment of 'utility'.[11] The unifying factor here is the claim to a new dimension of security in respect of the legal bonding of home, work and family. The so-called 'new property'[12] is, of course, as profoundly related to the emerging importance of residential security as it is to employment security, pension security and social security. The definition of 'property' is constantly on the move, and in the light of current developments it may be wrong arbitrarily to exclude contractual licences from the field of 'property'.

(iii) Injunctive relief and rights of 'property' In other contexts it has become readily apparent that 'as a practical matter' the granting of injunctive relief, when 'unlimited in point of time', can be equivalent to a transfer of property order.[13] The 'status of irremovability' enjoyed, for example, by the Rent Act protected tenant is recognised as 'one of the most significant rights of property' which an individual may hold.[14] Beyond a certain point procedural relief and substantive rights begin to meld, creating a protected status which is difficult to classify in traditional property law terms.

(iv) Property rights and personal rights The courts are only slowly starting to recognise that, at least in the area of residential security, property rights and personal rights are not distinct but interactive.[15] During the last two decades the judicial development of the law of licences has occurred against the

---

11   Ante, p 372.
12   Ante, p 11.
13   See *Cantliff v Jenkins* [1978] Fam 47 (Note) at 51F-G per Stamp LJ.
14   *Mafo v Adams* [1970] 1 QB 548 at 557G-H per Widgery LJ (post, p 1003).
15   See Sir R. Evershed, (1954) 70 LQR 326 at 331, 341.

backdrop of the ill-fated doctrine of the 'deserted wife's equity'.[16] Reference has since been made to the fact that in *National Provincial Bank Ltd v Ainsworth* 'the personal rights of the deserted wife were not allowed to override the property rights of the husband'.[17] In *Davis v Johnson*[18] Lord Denning MR ventured to suggest that such a concept of 'rights of property' was now 'quite out-of-date'. He declared that

It is true that in the 19th century the law paid quite high regard to rights of property. But this gave rise to such misgivings that in modern times the law has changed course. Social justice requires that personal rights should, in a proper case, be given priority over rights of property.[19]

The immediate context of this observation was, of course, the legislative intervention contained in the Domestic Violence and Matrimonial Proceedings Act 1976.[20] It may be that the elevation of the contractual licence to proprietary status in lawyers' terms will similarly require statutory intervention.[1]

16   See Chapter 22 (post, p 785) for a description of the way in which in *National Provincial Bank Ltd v Ainsworth* [1965] AC 1175 the House of Lords finally and conclusively determined that the 'deserted wife's equity' had no capacity to affect a purchaser.
17   *Davis v Johnson* [1979] AC 264 at 274E.
18   [1979] AC 264 at 274F.
19   See also *Williams & Glyn's Bank Ltd v Boland* [1979] Ch 312 at 333A.
20   Ante, p 301.
 1   See *National Provincial Bank Ltd v Ainsworth* [1965] AC 1175 at 1239E per Lord Upjohn, 1251E per Lord Wilberforce.

D. Incumbrances

CHAPTER 16

Mortgages

In cold legal terms the device of the mortgage (and the closely related device of the 'charge') are designed to provide creditors with a valuable form of security for loan moneys advanced by them. When analysed in social and human terms, mortgage finance can be said to play a vital part in the realisation of the life chances and aspirations of a large section of the population. The unprecedented availability of mortgage funds has, more than any other single factor, promoted the ideology of home ownership in Britain. As Lord Diplock once observed,[1] the last 40 years have witnessed 'the emergence of a property-owning, particularly a real-property-mortgaged-to-a-building-society-owning, democracy.' By 1985 the proportion of owner-occupation in Great Britain had risen to 62 per cent of all households,[2] 37 per cent of all households being subject to some current mortgage liability.[3] Accordingly it can be estimated that there are almost six million mortgages on residential properties in Britain.[4]

1. DEFINITIONS

In the law of mortgage there exists a technical distinction between a 'mortgage' and a 'charge'.

(1) Mortgage

In strict terms a 'mortgage' is a disposition of some interest in land or other property[5] 'as a security for the payment of a debt or the discharge of some other obligation for which it is given.'[6] The 'mortgagee' (ie, the lender of money) is thereby placed in the privileged position of being a secured creditor of the 'mortgagor' (ie, the borrower of money), with the consequence that he enjoys priority over the latter's unsecured creditors if the latter becomes insolvent. For the purpose of recovering the amount of his loan, the mortgagee enjoys not merely a personal right based on his contract of loan with the borrower, but also a proprietary right, potentially enforceable against third parties, to realise

---

1 *Pettitt v Pettitt* [1970] AC 777 at 824C.
2 Central Statistical Office, *Social Trends No 17* (1987 edn London), p 137.
3 *General Household Survey 1985* (OPCS Monitor, Reference 86/1, 18 September 1986), p 6 (Table 7).
4 Of these mortgage loans 79 per cent are provided by building societies, 8 per cent by local authorities, 5 per cent by insurance companies and pension funds, and 10 per cent by banks (Central Statistical Office, *Social Trends No. 17* (1987 edn London), p 148 (Table 8.24)).
5 Most kinds of property—even a mortgage itself—may be the subject of a mortgage.
6 *Santley v Wilde* [1899] 2 Ch 474 per Lindley LJ. See also *Swiss Bank Corpn v Lloyds Bank Ltd* [1982] AC 584 at 595C-D per Buckley LJ.

the value of the mortgaged property. Mortgage transactions today represent one of the safest ways of lending money since ultimately the property offered as security can be sold by the mortgagee and the proceeds of sale applied in the repayment of the loan.

(2) Charge

Again in strict terms a 'mortgage' should be distinguished from a 'charge' over property. Whereas a mortgage actually invests the mortgagee with an interest in the secured property, a charge confers no such interest but merely gives the 'chargee' certain rights (eg in respect of possession and sale) over the property charged as security for the loan.[7] Nevertheless the practical distinction between mortgages and charges is relatively unimportant and nowadays the charge may be regarded as virtually a species of mortgage.[8] The rules discussed in this chapter apply generally to both mortgages and charges.

2. THE SOCIAL SIGNIFICANCE OF MORTGAGE FINANCE

The institution of the mortgage exerts a profound effect upon ordinary people in a variety of ways. From the viewpoint of the private individual, his mortgage commitment becomes a central concern in his life. By mortgaging or charging realty he is enabled to obtain a loan of substantial capital which he may then apply for a number of purposes including—most significantly—the purchase of realty. The capital money is normally repayable over a long term (eg 25 years). His repayment of this loan may take the form of periodic payments of both capital and interest (as in the ordinary 'repayment' or 'instalment' mortgage).[9] Alternatively, the entire capital sum borrowed may be left outstanding during the mortgage term, the mortgagor meanwhile servicing the loan by paying periodic interest (as in the 'endowment' mortgage).[10]

The mortgage transaction will almost certainly represent the largest single form of financial indebtedness incurred by the ordinary individual during his lifetime. For him the availability of mortgage finance has a multi-faceted significance.

(1) The dream of home ownership

The major impact of mortgage finance has been to make the dream of home

7   An equitable charge 'does not pass either an absolute or special property to the creditor or any right of possession, but only a right of realisation by judicial process in case of non-payment of the debt' (*London County and Westminster Bank Ltd v Tompkins* [1918] 1 KB 515 at 528). See also *Weg Motors Ltd v Hales* [1962] Ch 49 at 77.

8   The distinction is finally blurred by the reference in the 1925 legislation to a 'charge by way of legal mortgage' (Law of Property Act 1925, ss 1(2)(c), 85(1)). See *Grand Junction Co Ltd v Bates* [1954] 2 QB 160 at 168f; *Regent Oil Co Ltd v J.A. Gregory (Hatch End) Ltd* [1966] Ch 402 at 431B-E.

9   During the early years of the mortgage term, most of each periodic payment will comprise interest rather than capital, the relative proportions of capital and interest altering during the course of the term.

10   Under an endowment mortgage the borrower provides additional security for the loan by assigning to the mortgagee a policy of life assurance taken out on the borrower's life. The life assurance is so calculated as to yield a capital sum equivalent to the mortgage debt on the date of its maturing or in the event of the earlier death of the mortgagor.

ownership a reality for ordinary people. Mortgage finance offers the borrower an opportunity to become an owner-occupier of his dwelling-house in circumstances where he would not otherwise be able to afford to purchase such a property. Many institutional mortgagees (such as building societies, banks, local authorities and insurance companies) are prepared to advance funds on the security of a mortgage in order to facilitate home ownership for the private citizen. The individual is thereby enabled simultaneously to buy a house or flat with the borrowed money[11] and to offer the home thus purchased as security for the loan advanced to him.[12] The borrower retains the freehold or leasehold estate in the property throughout the mortgage term, and is enabled to acquire both a family base and a major capital asset essentially by means of instalment purchase spread over half a lifetime.

(2) The effect on life styles

The availability of mortgage finance has a significant impact on the life chances of the individual borrower. The nature of his tenure as a home-owner will be an important status determinant during his life. It may affect his personal life and marriage prospects. It will certainly affect his creditworthiness for many purposes: the possession of a permanent home base is generally considered to be a good indicator of financial reliability. The nature of his tenure may also control the timing of both his marriage and the arrival of his children, and may well determine the ultimate size of his family.

(3) The effect on family finance

It may well be that the availability of mortgage finance has done more than any form of taxation to redistribute private wealth in this country during the present century.[13] Its significance can be seen in the following ways.

(a) Capital accumulation

Home ownership (even with the aid of borrowed money) has provided for most people a hitherto unparalleled means of access to capital accumulation. Given the steady increase in land values and the general effects of inflation, it is highly probable that the ownership of realty over even a short period of time will generate a capital gain for the owner which can safely be measured in five figures. This capital may not be immediately realisable, but it nevertheless provides an asset against which further money may be borrowed. An increase in the amount of the borrower's mortgage loan may enable him to effect improvements or extensions to his home, ranging in social purpose from the construction of a new sun patio to the provision of a self-contained annexe for ageing parents.

---

11 Mortgagees will normally advance loans totalling 2.5 or 3 times the borrower's gross annual income plus half of his spouse's gross annual income, but few mortgagees will lend 100 per cent of the purchase price of property.
12 Building societies are specifically empowered by Building Societies Act 1986, s 10(5) to advance money for the purchase of registered land 'notwithstanding that the advance is made before the borrower is registered as proprietor of the estate'.
13 For a description of the way in which the extension of home ownership has brought millions of citizens within the 'propertied classes', see Chapter 19 (post, p 725).

(b) Upward mobility and commercial expansion

Capital increments, whether or not ploughed back into the realty, provide in their turn a springboard for the upwardly mobile, in that steady capital gains coupled with the borrower's increasing mortgage capacity facilitate his moving home to a bigger house in a better area. Alternatively, if the borrower is a businessman, he may use the family home as security for a bank loan earmarked for the creation or extension of his commercial operations. (This possibility of course raises the difficult question whether a home-owner should be any more free to offer his family base as a security for entrepreneurial purposes than a landlord to own another's home for the purpose of deriving personal profit.[14])

(c) The redistribution of income over the family life-cycle

Another major, but more subtle, effect of the availability of mortgage finance is to redistribute the application of income over the average family life-cycle. Since the burden of the domestic mortgage commitment shifts housing costs from the later to the earlier stages of the family life-cycle, it has been said that the relatively new phenomenon of home ownership acts 'as an indirect subsidy paid by the young to the old, or, more precisely, forces individual households to subsidise their own old age in their late teens and twenties.'[15] This in turn means that elderly home-owners are better able to survive on minimal pension benefits than are elderly tenants, thereby diminishing (at least on the part of those who favour increased home ownership) any real political incentive to care effectively for the elderly. These disparities in the distribution of wealth and social welfare are then intensified by the fact that the more affluent middle-aged, who have by and large completed the payments on their homes, are in a position to use their surplus income in further personal investment or consumption or in helping their own children to realise the same ambition of home ownership.

(4) The political dimension of mortgages

Mortgage finance enjoys a certain public importance not least because the ideology of home ownership has a clear political dimension.

(a) The tendency towards preservation of the status quo

Home ownership, particularly if achieved with the aid of mortgage finance, breeds political conservatism.[16] The enlightened self-interest of the owner-

---

14 Post, p 970.
15 J. Kemeny, *The Myth of Home Ownership* (London 1981), p 59.
16 It was Harold Bellman, one of the leading figures in the early building society movement, who in 1927 saw clearly that the 'working man who is merely a tenant has no real anchorage, no permanent abiding place, and in certain circumstances is fair prey for breeders of faction and revolutionaries of every sort and condition. Home-ownership is a civic and national asset. The sense of citizenship is more keenly felt and appreciated, and personal independence opens up many an avenue of wide responsibility and usefulness. The benefits of home-ownership are not merely material, but ethical and moral as well. The man who has something to protect and improve—a stake of some sort in the country—naturally turns his thoughts in the direction of sane, ordered, and perforce economical government. The thrifty man is seldom or never an extremist agitator. To him revolution is anathema; and as in the earliest days Building Societies acted as a stabilising force, so today they stand...as a "bulwark against Bolshevism and all that Bolshevism stands for".' See H. Bellman, *The Building Society Movement* (London 1927), p 53f.

occupier represents a form of political capital for those who are inclined towards the preservation of the status quo. It is also the case that the ready provision of mortgage funds effectively endorses approved patterns of life style and political demeanour. In that mortgage finance may serve either domestic or entrepreneurial purposes, the very institution of the mortgage bespeaks a flexibility of choice and self-determination which is rooted in the political philosophy of the right rather than the left. It is, of course, the former influence which has moulded the English law of real property, and it should thus come as no surprise to note that in *National Provincial Bank Ltd v Ainsworth*[17] Lord Upjohn declared that

It has been the policy of the law for over a hundred years to simplify and facilitate transactions in real property. It is of great importance that persons should be able freely and easily to raise money on the security of their property.

(b) The public sector tenant's 'right to buy'

In recent times the most notable political initiative in favour of home ownership has been the controversial introduction of the council tenant's 'right to buy'.[18] The provisions of the Conservative-inspired Housing Act 1980[19] conferred on qualifying council tenants a right to purchase their own homes with the help of mortgage finance provided from public funds controlled by the Housing Corporation. The then Secretary of State for the Environment commended the scheme to Parliament as fostering 'a deeply ingrained desire for home ownership' and as stimulating 'the attitudes of independence and self-reliance that are the bedrock of a free society.'[20] In his view the 'right to buy' scheme was destined to 'transform the personal prospects of millions of our citizens, offering to turn them at their wish from tenants to owners. It will establish their rights as individuals above the bureaucracies of the State. It will come to be seen among the finest traditions and philosophies of the Conservative Party.'[1]

(5) Comparison of the positions of the mortgagor and the periodic tenant

In superficial terms it often seems that the owner-occupier who purchases his home with the aid of mortgage finance is in a wholly different position from the periodic tenant who rents his home. It is indeed true, of course, that the owner-occupier owns a substantial proprietary estate in the land, and is eligible to receive income tax relief based on mortgage interest paid by him.[2] He is entitled to sell the land and to retain any capital gain made by reason of the

---

17 [1965] AC 1175 at 1233G-1234A.
18 Post, p 733.
19 These provisions are now contained in Housing Act 1985, Part V.
20 Mr M. Heseltine, *Parliamentary Debates, House of Commons, Official Report*, Vol 976 (Session 1979-1980), Col 1445 (15 January 1980).
 1 Ibid, Col 1460. Given this rousing attribution to the Tory credo, it is scarcely surprising that the scheme for the sale of council housing was so bitterly opposed by the Labour Party.
 2 A taxpayer may claim income tax relief to the extent of the interest which is payable on any loan not exceeding £30,000 which is used for the purchase or improvement of land (Finance Act 1972, s 75, as amended by Finance Act 1974, s 19, Sch 1, and Finance Act 1986, s 20).

sale.[3] Likewise he may dispose of the property by will, and by means of certain exemptions in respect of inheritance tax[4] he will be able to pass on to another generation the substance of the wealth which is tied up in the property. The owner-occupier enjoys ultimate security of tenure because his estate in the land is unlimited. He generally pays no rent to any other person. He fully participates in the 'home-owning democracy' with all the attendant psychological benefits of prestige and irremovability. At first sight the tenant who merely rents his home enjoys nothing comparable with these social and economic advantages. However, it is important to scrutinise with some care the alleged disparity between the mortgagor and the renter.

(a) Political manipulation of relative status

Much political vigour has been invested in the assertion of a basic commitment to home ownership as a superior form of tenure when measured against tenure in the rented sector. The 'almost mystical reverence for home-ownership'[5] finds expression in sincere speeches about the 'deeply ingrained'[6] or 'natural'[7] desire for owner-occupation. Accordingly the policy of encouraging home ownership has effectively stigmatised rented housing as the preserve of the second-class citizen, and the renter, instead of enjoying the status of part-owner of housing stock,[8] is made the subject of invidious comparisons between the 'owner' and the 'tenant'. The very fact that the public sector tenant is now given a statutory right to improve his lot by buying (ie, borrowing) and therefore 'owning' his own home[9] further underlines the negative discrimination which has been practised against the renter in Britain and which has conduced to the general running-down of the rented sector.

(b) Are the utilities and obligations of mortgagor and tenant dissimilar?

Ironically the rights and duties of the mortgagor and the tenant may not be essentially dissimilar. From the point of view of the occupier there may often be little practical difference between money paid periodically by way of rent and money paid periodically as interest and capital repayment on a mortgage loan. Mortgage interest tax relief may, in some cases, be counterbalanced by the tenant's receipt of a rent or rate rebate or housing benefit.[10]

The apparently unlimited rights of use and enjoyment which pertain to an owner-occupier are nowadays severely curbed by planning law, building consent regulations and other forms of public and private control of land use. The owner-occupier's title to the incremental capital value of his property in the event of sale may turn out to be a somewhat illusory benefit, since his rights

---

3   A capital gain made on the disposal of a dwelling-house is not chargeable to capital gains tax if the house was the individual's 'only or main residence' throughout the period of ownership (Capital Gains Tax Act 1979, s 101(1)).

4   Capital Transfer Tax Act 1984, Sch 1, as amended by Finance Act 1986, Sch 19, para 36.

5   J. Kemeny, *The Myth of Home Ownership* (London 1981), p 11.

6   *Parliamentary Debates, House of Commons, Official Report*, Vol 976 (Session 1979-1980), Col 1445 (15 January 1980) (Mr M. Heseltine).

7   *Fair Deal for Housing* (Cmnd 4728, London 1971), p 4.

8   Post, p 966.

9   See Housing Act 1985, s 118(1) (post, p 733).

10   Post, p 1051.

are significantly eroded by the fact that the proceeds of that sale often require to be ploughed back into the purchase of a new property in an inflated housing market. Even the freedom of testamentary disposition supposedly enjoyed by the owner-occupier is substantially modified by legislation which permits claims to be brought against his estate by certain classes of statutory dependant for whom he has not made reasonable provision.[11]

(c) Does the renter really have less security of tenure?

The significance of the owner-occupier's participation in the 'property-owning democracy' must be assessed, moreover, in the context of the gradual shift in ideology which has occurred in the rented sector during the last 10 or 20 years. The extension of security of tenure in both the private and the public rented sectors has gone a long way towards establishing for the residential tenant a more solid base of 'homestead rights' not dissimilar to the housing security enjoyed by the freeholder.[12] This tendency is accentuated as residential housing stock comes increasingly to be regarded not as an essentially commerciable commodity of exchange but primarily as a social resource whose 'allocation' should be governed by considerations of social justice and equity. In terms of this collectivist perspective, what is nowadays regarded as important and valuable is not ownership of the right to dispose, but rather ownership of the right to use and enjoy under living conditions of reasonable security and dignity. It is significant, for instance, that much of the legislation of the last two decades in the parallel areas of residential tenancies and residential mortgages has been directed towards protection of the occupier's right not to be evicted from his home arbitrarily or without just cause.[13]

(d) Does the mortgagor really enjoy greater mobility?

It is sometimes said that home ownership founded on mortgage finance provides the individual with a greater mobility than is enjoyed by the occupier who merely rents his home. It must indeed be true that the owner-occupier is more mobile, at least in the geographical sense, than the individual who rents in, say, the public sector. However, this claim should not be pitched too high. There are important respects in which the apparent mobility of the owner-occupier has turned out to be illusory.

(i) The 'new feudalism' Once installed as a home-owner on the strength of a mortgage advance, the borrower becomes subtly tied to his current employment. The legal bonding of employer and employee is no less dictated by the economic necessities of the employee's mortgage commitment than by the advent of modern employment protection legislation. The dream of home ownership made possible by funds borrowed on mortgage has introduced a new feudal age in which the residential occupier is once again *adscriptus glebae*: he is no longer in a position to afford excessive labour mobility. He himself

11 Inheritance (Provision for Family and Dependants) Act 1975, ss 1–3.
12 See the reference to the Rent Act legislation bringing abo ut a situation in which we have 'all but reverted to copyhold tenure' in the rented sector (J.S. Colyer, (1965) 29 Conv (NS) 429 at 463).
13 Post, p 891.

acquires a vested financial interest in his mortgage, since the capital value of his property is inflating year by year, and he relies increasingly heavily on his payment of mortgage interest as a means of reducing the marginal rate of taxation to which his income is liable.

(ii) 'Shared ownership' schemes Potential access to institutional mortgage funds may confer a mobility not enjoyed by a renter who remains at the mercy of waiting lists for council housing. However, the apparent advantage of mobility is nowadays frequently negatived by the huge discrepancy in house prices across the nation. The exorbitant realty values currently prevailing in London and the South East have conduced to the result that an income base which is quite sufficient to finance a certain standard of home ownership elsewhere in England and Wales is simply inadequate to command the mortgage resources required to obtain a similar standard of accommodation in the prosperous South East. This pattern of shortfall has made a hollow mockery of many an attempt to move from an area of industrial recession to a location of new and flourishing industry. It is often the case that people with mortgageable incomes cannot afford to make the move without inflicting on their families a disastrous drop in their standard of living.

One of the more intriguing by-products of this 'mobility trap' is the encouragement recently given to the novel concept of 'shared ownership'.[14] The essential feature of a 'shared ownership' scheme is that the aspiring homeowner is enabled (with the aid of mortgage finance) to purchase a defined quantum of ownership in his house, leaving the balance of the ownership to be purchased later when he can better afford to do so. The mortgagor meanwhile pays a periodic rent in proportion to that quantum of ownership which he has not yet purchased. It remains to be seen whether this unprecedented fusion of different sorts of estate ownership survives to become a popular means of home acquisition.

(e) Perceptions of social status, self-esteem and solidarity

In the light of the considerations outlined above, the functional differences between the positions of the mortgagor and the periodic tenant may well be more apparent than real. Differences there certainly are, but it was Otto Kahn-Freund who so cogently pointed out that 'the social function of the building society mortgage is very closely akin to that of the urban lease. The "ownership" of a house bought with a building society mortgage (and collateral security) has the economic function of a tenancy combined with the ideological function of property.'[15]

The differences which remain between the mortgagor and the renter are measured more realistically in terms of their respective perceptions of social status, self-esteem and community solidarity. The prospective renter in Britain undergoes a process of 'selection' by his landlord which can be intrusive, humiliating and sometimes discriminatory. Moreover, the power-relationship inherent in landlordism extends well beyond the initial selection of 'suitable' or 'deserving' tenants, and exerts an impact upon the general freedom of life style

14 Post, p 737.
15 'Introduction', in K. Renner, *The Institutions of Private Law and Their Social Functions* (London and Boston 1949), p 35f.

enjoyed by the occupier. It has been said, with some insight, that the 'wider ideological importance of tenure derives mainly from the effect of different forms of tenure on the degree to which life styles and interests become privatised.'[16] These differences of degree are apparent in even the most trivial of ways. The owner-occupier, but not the council tenant, can choose the colour of his own front door! The private sector tenant, but not the home-owner, is subject to a stranger's control over the hours during which he may listen to his stereo. Yet a community of renters generally enjoys a common interest and solidarity unknown—except perhaps when the closure threatens the local primary school—by the atomised denizens of the average middle-class home-owning neighbourhood.

3. THE CREATION OF LEGAL MORTGAGES

In the historical pattern of the English law of mortgage, security interests in land have been created by means of the manipulation of existing estates and interests in the land of the borrower of money. This practice has brought about the consequence that the law of mortgage is heavily marked by fiction. As Maitland said,[17] the mortgage transaction is 'one long suppressio veri and suggestio falsi'.[18] Lord Macnaghten declared in *Samuel v Jarrah Timber and Wood Paving Corpn Ltd*[19] that 'no one...by the light of nature ever understood an English mortgage of real estate.'

(1) Pre-1926 modes of creation

In order to understand the modern law of mortgage it is necessary to bear in mind the means by which prior to 1926 a legal mortgage of land could be created. Before the commencement of the 1925 legislation, a legal mortgage of freehold land was effected by the conveyance of a fee simple estate to the mortgagee, subject to a covenant for re-conveyance on redemption of the mortgage (ie, on repayment of the loan).[20] A legal mortgage of leasehold land took the form of an assignment to the mortgagee of the residue of the mortgagor's term of years in the land, subject to a proviso for re-assignment by the mortgagee on the repayment of the loan. The creditor's security for the loan was thus, in either case, the debtor's legal title in the land mortgaged. If the mortgagor failed to redeem the mortgage by the date stipulated for repayment of the capital sum, the mortgagee was entitled at common law to retain his security unencumbered by any further interest vested in the mortgagor.

(2) The mortgagor's equity of redemption

From the seventeenth century onwards, however, equity intervened in a

---

16 J. Kemeny, op cit, p 64. 'In practice home ownership both encourages the work force to participate more closely in the mode of production and ideologically reflects the generalised atomisation and egoism in bourgeois society' (P. Beirne, *Fair Rent and Legal Fiction* (London 1977), p 107).
17 *Equity* (London 1936), p 182.
18 See P. Jackson, *The Need to Reform the English Law of Mortgages*, (1978) 94 LQR 571.
19 [1904] AC 323 at 326.
20 See A.W.B. Simpson, *A History of The Land Law* (2nd edn Oxford 1986), p 242f.

manner which was to make the traditional method of mortgage more than slightly fictitious. Although the mortgagee was entitled to enjoy physical possession of the land, equity compelled him to account to the mortgagor in respect of any profit derived from that land in excess of the interest due under the contract of loan. Thus there ceased to be any material advantage for the mortgagee in exercising his right to possess the land and the mortgagor was commonly left in possession himself even though he no longer retained the legal title.

Furthermore, although the common law attached drastic consequences to a failure by the mortgagor to repay the capital debt by the date fixed, equity regarded the mortgagor as entitled to redeem the mortgage at any time, even by tendering repayment of the loan *after* that date had passed. The mortgagor could therefore effectively ignore the date on which the debt fell due, in the knowledge that equity would assist him in compelling a re-conveyance or re-assignment even if repayment were delayed until long after that date.[1] Only if the Court of Chancery in the exercise of its equitable jurisdiction considered it reasonable to grant a decree of 'foreclosure' would the mortgagor's equitable rights be terminated and the mortgagee permitted to take a free title to the land. Unless and until such a decree was granted, the sum total of the mortgagor's equitable rights in respect of the mortgaged realty was termed his *equity of redemption*. This 'equity of redemption' simply marked the view of equity that, irrespective of the strict legal and contractual position, the mortgagor remained in substance the owner of the mortgaged land—albeit subject to the mortgage created in favour of his creditor. The inviolability in equity of the borrower's right to redeem the mortgage thus inverted the legal relationship of the parties to the mortgage transaction, and the mortgagor's 'equity' came to be seen as constituting a proprietary interest in the land which could itself be bought, sold and mortgaged.[2]

(3) Post-1925 modes of creation

The developments brought about by the intervention of equity were finally rationalised in the Law of Property Act 1925, it being wholly irrelevant for present purposes whether the land concerned is registered or unregistered.[3]

---

1   Equity was willing to allow this forbearance in favour of the borrower since the value of the lender's security (ie, the land) might greatly exceed the sum lent and it therefore seemed inequitable that the mortgagor should forfeit the entire security for failure to repay on the date fixed in the contract of loan. When it became clear that, in view of the stance adopted by equity, the contractual date of redemption was rendered academic, it became customary to fix this date a mere six months after the entry into the contract of loan. It may also be that the fixing of an early (and therefore effectively fictitious) date for repayment under the strict terms of the loan was influenced by the fact that whereas a certain spiritual opprobrium attached to the charging of interest before the loan was due for repayment, the exaction of interest thereafter was regarded by Church doctrine as constituting a wholly legitimate form of 'compensation' (*interesse*) for failure to restore the principal by the date promised. See R.H. Tawney, *Religion and the Rise of Capitalism* (Harmondsworth 1938), p 54.

2   See *Casborne v Scarfe* (1738) 1 Atk 603 at 605f, 26 ER 377 at 379, (1738) 2 Jac & W 194, 37 ER 600; *Latec Investments Ltd v Hotel Terrigal Pty Ltd (In Liquidation)* (1964-1965) 113 CLR 265 at 277. See also A.W.B. Simpson, op cit, p 245. The proprietary status of the 'equity of redemption' is so clearly established that it may even be claimed by the crown as bona vacantia (see *Re Sir Thomas Spencer Wells* [1933] Ch 29 at 48, 55, 63).

3   Law of Property Act 1925, ss 85(3), 86(3).

(a) Legal mortgages of freehold land

Since the commencement of the Law of Property Act 1925 it has been impossible to mortgage land by the process of conveyance and re-conveyance of the fee simple estate.[4] Instead, section 85(1) of that Act provides that a legal mortgage of freehold land may be effected 'either by a demise for a term of years absolute, subject to a provision for cesser on redemption, or by a charge by deed expressed to be by way of legal mortgage.'

(i) Legal mortgage by long demise Under the first of the methods of legal mortgage envisaged by section 85(1), the security granted to the lender takes the form of a long lease in the borrower's land (usually in practice a term of 3,000 years).[5] The mortgagee is thus invested with a legal estate—a term of years absolute— in the borrower's land, and is in theory entitled to enjoy possession of that land as a long leaseholder. Once again, a mortgage has been created by the manipulation of the existing estates which lie dormant in the land, but this method of freehold mortgage is not nowadays so commonly used as the other form introduced by section 85(1).

(ii) Legal mortgage by charge Section 85(1) also permits the freehold land to be mortgaged by means of a 'charge by deed expressed to be by way of legal mortgage'. This charge, although not conferring on the chargee any legal term as such[6] or indeed any proprietary interest in the land at all, is statutorily deemed to invest the chargee with 'the same protection, powers and remedies (including the right to take proceedings to obtain possession...)' as if a leasehold term of 3,000 years had been created in his favour.[7]

(b) Legal mortgages of leasehold land

It has likewise been impossible since 1925 to mortgage a leasehold estate by means of assignment and re-assignment of the borrower's term of years.[8] Instead, section 86(1) of the Law of Property Act 1925 provides that a legal mortgage of leasehold land may be effected either by a subdemise for a term of years absolute, subject to a provision for cesser on redemption, or by a charge by deed expressed to be by way of legal mortgage.

(i) Legal mortgage by long subdemise The method of subdemise requires that the borrower carve a sublease for the lender out of his own leasehold estate, the sublease being 'less by one day at least than the term vested in the mortgagor'.[9]

4   Any attempt after 1925 to mortgage a freehold by conveyance of a fee simple estate necessarily operates as a demise of the land to the mortgagee for a term of 3,000 years (Law of Property Act 1925, s 85(2)(a)).

5   The real value of the mortgagor's interest in the land is, of course, not so much the (fairly sterile) freehold reversion on a 3,000 year term, but rather the equity of redemption which he also still retains (ie, the right to repay the loan and secure the termination of the mortgagee's technical leasehold interest).

6   *Weg Motors Ltd v Hales* [1962] Ch 49 at 74, 77.

7   Law of Property Act 1925, s 87(1).

8   Law of Property Act 1925, s 86(1). Any such assignment by way of mortgage now operates necessarily as a subdemise to the mortgagee for a term of years ten days less than the term supposedly assigned (Law of Property Act 1925, s 86(2)(a)).

9   There is a statutory proviso that where the subdemise requires the licence of the lessor, this licence shall not be unreasonably refused (Law of Property Act 1925, s 86(1)).

Once again this rather cumbersome mode of mortgaging is nowadays less often used than the straightforward method of charge by way of legal mortgage.

(ii) Legal mortgage by charge Even a leasehold estate may be mortgaged by means of a 'charge by deed expressed to be by way of legal mortgage',[10] and such a charge assures the lender equivalent protection to that which would have been conferred by a mortgage subdemise.[11]

(4) The overall effect of the 1925 legislation on mortgages

The changes introduced by the 1925 legislation have had the effect of injecting a much greater realism into the law and practice of mortgages.

(a) Legal title remains in the borrower

The mortgagor's continuing occupation of the land during the mortgage term is now openly acknowledged by the fact that he is permitted to retain his full legal title throughout.[12] This retention of formal title nowadays provides an important key to capital accumulation for the upwardly mobile private citizen. The mortgagor is automatically entitled to the steadily inflating value of the mortgaged property even though initially he may have purchased the property entirely with borrowed funds. The mortgagee, in closer accord with the reality of the situation, takes merely a security interest (by way of charge or lease) over the land, and is entitled only to the return of his capital together with appropriate interest thereon.

(b) The 'equity of redemption'

The mortgagor still retains his equity of redemption, and the effective value of this right is the difference at any given point in time between the market value of the land and the sum of the mortgage debt currently outstanding.[13] Such is the significance of the mortgagor's equity of redemption that the contractual date for repayment of the mortgage loan is rendered entirely academic. For this reason most modern mortgage deeds contain a clause—which strikes terror into the heart of only the uninformed lay person—apparently requiring repayment of the entire capital sum within a very short period (eg three or six months) of the granting of the loan.

(c) The inescapability of statutory control

The net effect of the provisions contained in the Law of Property Act 1925 is

---

10   Law of Property Act 1925, s 86(1).
11   Law of Property Act 1925, s 87(1)(b).
12   That the 'owner' of the land is the mortgagor (rather than the mortgagee) is apparent from the fact that it is the former who is bound by statutory (eg rating) obligations imposed on the 'owner' (see *Westminster City Council v Haymarket Publishing Ltd* [1981] 1 WLR 677 at 680C).
13   Thus, if a property has a market value of £100,000 and is currently subject to a mortgage debt of £60,000, the value of the mortgagor's equity of redemption is £40,000. The value of this equity will tend to increase both in consequence of the steady inflation of land values and by reason of the gradual discharge of the mortgage debt.

that all transactions which in substance secure a loan of money upon the borrower's real property must inevitably operate by way of mortgage under the terms of the Act. The courts have jurisdiction to determine whether any credit transaction (no matter in what guise presented or obscured) is in reality a mortgage transaction. In *Grangeside Properties Ltd v Collingwoods Securities Ltd*[14] Harman LJ referred to

the ancient law, which had always been that Chancery would treat as a mortgage that which was intended to be a conveyance by way of security between A and B. Once a mortgage, always a mortgage and nothing but a mortgage, has been a principle for centuries...It could not be that [the 1925 Act] is intended to sweep away the view of the law which had always been that if you proved the thing was a mortgage, equity would allow you to have your equity of redemption to redeem on payment of the mortgage money, interest and costs.[15]

Thus, in a manner not unlike the way in which the courts test transactions in the rented sector,[16] the courts examine the inner substance rather than the external form of credit transactions, in order to ensure that those who borrow money on the security of land actually receive the legal protection promised by statute to mortgagors.[17]

4. THE CREATION OF EQUITABLE MORTGAGES

The possibility of an equitable mortgage or charge in respect of realty is implicit in section 1(2)(c) of the Law of Property Act 1925.[18] An equitable mortgage or charge may arise in several ways.

(1) Mortgage of an equitable interest

A mortgage may remain equitable precisely because it is created in respect of merely an equitable interest in the mortgagor's land. The owner of an equitable interest in or subsisting in reference to land[19] may effect a mortgage of his interest by assigning that interest to the lender of money. The assignment is subject to a proviso for re-assignment on repayment of the loan.[20] Such a mortgage is necessarily equitable, and unless made by will must be in writing as required by section 53(1)(c) of the Law of Property Act 1925.[1]

---

14 [1964] 1 WLR 139 at 142f.
15 'Once a mortgage always a mortgage' has been described as 'merely an expression of the general principle as to fraud in its application to mortgages' (*Last v Rosenfeld* [1972] 2 NSWLR 923 at 931E). See also *Seton v Slade* (1802) 7 Ves 265 at 273, 32 ER 108 at 111.
16 Ante, p 450; post, p 995.
17 It is also the case that the *lender* of money is deprived of substantial protection unless his advance is secured by way of mortgage. An unsecured creditor finds himself in dire straits if the loan goes sour, although in rare circumstances such a lender may possibly rely on the equitable doctrine of subrogation. See the remarkable rescue operation successfully mounted in *Boodle Hatfield & Co v British Films Ltd* [1986] NLJ Rep 117, where a firm of solicitors had made an unsecured advance to its client in order to facilitate the completion of a purchase. See [1986] Conv 149; (1986) 136 NLJ 83, 117.
18 Ante, p 81.
19 Ante, p 373.
20 See *Thames Guaranty Ltd v Campbell* [1985] QB 210 at 234F-G.
1 Ante, p 291.

(2) Informal mortgage of a legal interest

An equitable mortgage may also arise where the owner of a legal estate in land effects an informal mortgage of his estate by failing to use either of the modes of legal mortgage indicated as appropriate in the Law of Property Act 1925. An example occurs where a landowner mortgages his legal estate otherwise than by deed. The consequence of such a transaction is that 'equity looks on that as done which ought to have been done'. The informal mortgage (ie, the mortgage created by imperfect means) is regarded, under the doctrine in *Walsh v Lonsdale*,[2] as having the same effect as a contract to create a legal mortgage of realty. If the imperfect mortgage would have been specifically enforceable as an agreement to create a legal mortgage, it is then treated as giving rise to an equitable mortgage.[3] The preconditions of specific enforceability require, however, that there should have been compliance with section 40 of the Law of Property Act 1925.[4] It must therefore be shown that the agreement was evidenced in writing or that it was supported by a sufficient act of part performance.[5]

(3) Equitable mortgage by deposit of documents of title

It has long been accepted, under a doctrine stemming from *Russel v Russel*,[6] that an equitable mortgage of land may be effected by a deposit of the title deeds relating to that land[7] coupled with an intention on the part of the owner that the depositee should hold the title deeds as his security for a loan of money.[8] Such a deposit is effectively construed as a sufficient act of part performance to amount to evidence of a contract to create a mortgage.[9]

Although this method of mortgage somewhat controversially ignores the historic concern for writing expressed in the Statute of Frauds 1677,[10] no further formality is required to make such an equitable mortgage effective.[11] It

---

2   Ante, p 471.
3   See eg *In re Beetham; Ex parte Broderick* (1887) 18 QBD 766 at 768; *Swiss Bank Corpn v Lloyds Bank Ltd* [1982] AC 584 at 594H-595A, D-E; *Hoofstetter v Rooker* (1895) 22 OAR 175 at 179; *Re Collens* (1983) 140 DLR (3d) 755 at 757f.
4   *Swiss Bank Corpn v Lloyds Bank Ltd* [1982] AC 584 at 595D-E.
5   Ante, p 210ff.
6   (1783) 1 Bro CC 269 at 270, 28 ER 1121 at 1122. See J.H.G. Sunnucks, (1970) 33 MLR 131.
7   In relation to registered land the deposit of the land certificate has precisely the same effect (Land Registration Act 1925, s 66).
8   If this intention is present, it is probably unnecessary to deposit all of the title deeds relating to a plot of unregistered land, provided that the documents actually deposited constitute material evidence of title (see *Royal Bank of Canada v Grobman* (1978) 83 DLR (3d) 415 at 428).
9   See *Swiss Bank Corpn v Lloyds Bank Ltd* [1982] AC 584 at 594H-595A; *Thames Guaranty Ltd v Campbell* [1985] QB 210 at 218F; *Bank of Ireland Finance Ltd v D.J. Daly Ltd* [1978] IR 79 at 82. The mere delivery of documents will be effective without any express written or verbal agreement to mortgage, since the court will readily infer an intention to provide security as between debtor and creditor (see *Shaw v Foster* (1872) LR 5 HL 321 at 339f; *In re Wallis & Simmonds (Builders) Ltd* [1974] 1 WLR 391 at 395A-E).
10 It is indeed somewhat extraordinary that an equitable mortgage can be made without any writing at all. See, for instance, the regret with which Maitland was forced to accept the existence and continued force of the doctrine stemming from *Russel v Russel* (*Equity*, p 199). See also *Edge v Worthington* (1786) 1 Cox 211 at 212, 29 ER 1133.
11 'The right created by the deposit is not limited to keeping the deeds until the money has been paid but gives an equitable estate in the lands' (*Allied Irish Banks Ltd v Glynn* [1973] IR 188 at 192).

is sufficient that there is a mere act of deposit,[12] coupled with the intention of thereby providing real security.[13] In practice, however, most mortgages by deposit are nowadays accompanied by some form of written memorandum (often under seal) confirming the intentions of the parties.[14] An insistence upon the deposit of title documents has become an increasingly powerful weapon in the hands of banks, this means being frequently used to obtain some form of security for the bank in the event that a customer's overdraft should reach a dangerously high level.

(4) Equitable charge

Although a charge differs slightly in nature from a mortgage,[15] an equitable charge may arise where land is charged in equity with some obligation such as the repayment of a debt.[16] Thus, in *Matthews v Goodday*,[17] it was accepted that a written contract by B charging his real estate to A in the sum of £500 would not constitute an 'agreement to give a legal mortgage', but would amount to 'a security by which he equitably charged his land with the payment of a sum of money.'[18] Thus, even though there is no deposit of any title document, a mere informal written agreement under which property is to be security for a debt creates an equitable charge.[19] There must, however, be a common intention to make the land a form of security as such. A mere agreement that a lender should share in the proceeds of sale in priority to the debtor is not enough to create an equitable charge over the property.[20]

5. REFORM OF THE LAW OF MORTGAGES

Such is the complexity of the present modes of mortgage creation that the Law Commission is currently investigating a comprehensive reform of the law of mortgage. In order to simplify and rationalise the law the Commission has tentatively proposed that all existing methods of mortgaging land should be

---

12 A joint owner of a freehold estate cannot validly create an equitable mortgage on that estate by means of a merely unilateral deposit of the documentary title without the consent of the other joint tenant or tenants (see *Thames Guaranty Ltd v Campbell* [1985] QB 210 at 233C-D).

13 There must be a genuine intention that the deposit of the documentary title should operate as security for the advance. It is not sufficient that, after an agreement has been made to provide security, the documentary title happens to come into the hands of the creditor for some other purpose (*In re Beetham; Ex parte Broderick* (1887) 18 QBD 380 at 383f, 766 at 769f; *Bank of Ireland Finance Ltd v D.J. Daly Ltd* [1978] IR 79 at 82).

14 If, however, a deposit of documents is accompanied by an actual written charge, it is the express terms of this charge which are definitive (see *Shaw v Foster* (1872) LR 5 HL 321 at 339f; *Thames Guaranty Ltd v Campbell* [1985] QB 210 at 241D-E).

15 See eg *Shea v Moore* [1894] 1 IR 158 at 168.

16 'An equitable charge which is not an equitable mortgage is said to be created when property is expressly or constructively made liable, or specially appropriated, to the discharge of a debt or some other obligation, and confers on the chargee a right of realisation by judicial process, that is to say, by the appointment of a receiver or an order for sale' (*Swiss Bank Corpn v Lloyds Bank Ltd* [1982] AC 584 at 595A-B per Buckley LJ).

17 (1861) 31 LJ Ch 282 at 283.

18 See also *Freeway Mutual Pty Ltd v Taylor* (1978-79) 22 ALR 281 at 285.

19 *Simmons v Montague* [1909] 1 IR 87 at 95f; *Bank of Ireland Finance Ltd v D.J. Daly Ltd* [1978] IR 79 at 82.

20 *Re Sikorski and Sikorski* (1979) 89 DLR (3d) 411 at 415f.

abolished and that a new 'Formal Land Mortgage' should be created for use over any interest in land.[1] The new standardised mortgage would be created by deed,[2] and is envisaged as having attributes defined de novo by statute.[3] Under the Formal Land Mortgage the mortgagor would still retain title to the mortgaged property, and the mortgagee would acquire a 'sui generis proprietary interest' consisting of such rights in the mortgaged property as are thought necessary for the protection and enforcement of the security.[4] The Law Commission has likewise proposed the introduction of a standardised 'Informal Land Mortgage',[5] which would comprise the informal (but written) grant of a security in land under which the principal right of the Informal Mortgagee would be to have the mortgage perfected.[6]

The Law Commission has tendered a number of aspects of the proposed reform for wide public consultation and it remains to be seen whether a consensus emerges in favour of the changes preferred by the Commission.

6. THE DISCHARGE OF MORTGAGES

Mortgages may be discharged, and the mortgagor's equity of redemption extinguished, in a number of ways. These methods of discharge include the sale of the mortgaged property under the mortgagee's power of sale,[7] foreclosure,[8] and the operation of the Limitation Act 1980.[9] However, the simplest means of discharge arises on the repayment of all mortgage moneys owed to the mortgagee. A receipt for the outstanding moneys which is written on or annexed to the mortgage deed in the form required by statute is effective to discharge a mortgage of unregistered land.[10] A registered charge affecting registered land is normally discharged on the making of the prescribed form of application to the Land Registry under the Land Registration Rules.[11] Discharge by repayment occurs most commonly when the mortgagor sells his property and makes the repayment of his mortgage debt a first call on the proceeds of sale received on the transaction.[12]

---

1   *Land Mortgages* (Law Commission Working Paper No 99, August 1986), para 4.1 (Proposal I).
2   Ibid, para 5.3.
3   Ibid, para 5.2.
4   Ibid, para 5.2. See also paras 5.21 - 5.28.
5   Ibid, para 5.4.
6   Ibid, para 5.5
7   Post, p 614.
8   Post, p 628.
9   Neither the mortgagor nor any person claiming through him may assert any right to redeem the mortgage where the mortgagee has been in possession in his capacity as mortgagee for a period of at least twelve years (Limitation Act 1980, s 16). See also *Park v Brady* [1976] 2 NSWLR 329 at 336B.
10 Law of Property Act 1925, s 115(1). The discharge of building society mortgages is expressly governed by Building Societies Act 1986, Sch 4, para 2.
11 Land Registration Rules 1925, r 151 (Form 53).
12 It has been a common conveyancing practice for completion to occur before the vendor's outstanding mortgage is actually discharged. The purchaser completes effectively on the basis of a mere undertaking by the vendor's solicitor that the mortgage debt will be discharged out of the proceeds of sale and the deed of discharge forwarded subsequently to the new owner. It seems that this practice (the so-called 'Hong Kong style of completion') is no longer safe and may indeed expose the purchaser's solicitor to liability in negligence (see *Edward Wong Finance Co Ltd v Johnson Stokes & Master* [1984] AC 296 at 308G).

7. PROTECTION FOR THE MORTGAGOR

Two truisms about human experience have influenced the historical development of the law of mortgage. First, those who lend money commercially are more powerfully motivated by the wish to acquire personal profit than by any desire to render useful service to their community. Second, borrowers of money tend to be pictured (at least in the frozen frame of the historic stereotype) as necessitous persons who lack bargaining power and who are therefore especially vulnerable to harsh or unconscionable dealing. As Lord Henley LC declared in *Vernon v Bethell*,[13] 'necessitous men are not, truly speaking, free men, but, to answer a present exigency, will submit to any terms that the crafty may impose upon them.'

(1) Relaxation of the rules prohibiting usury

The truisms outlined above both found expression in the medieval canon law's abhorrence of usury and the sin of avarice.[14] The initially inflexible rule of the Church prescribed that no man might lawfully charge money for a loan. To do so was not only contrary to Scripture.[15] It was, in the famous words of R.H. Tawney,[16] 'contrary to nature, for it is to live without labour; it is to sell time, which belongs to God, for the advantage of wicked men; it is to rob those who use the money lent, and to whom, since they make it profitable, the profits should belong...' As Tawney perhaps somewhat mischievously pointed out, 'the true descendant of the doctrines of Aquinas is the labour theory of value. The last of the Schoolmen was Karl Marx.'[17]

The practice of usury touched on another very sensitive nerve within the medieval scheme of economic ethics. This scheme regarded all commercial intercourse as subordinate in importance to the salvation of the soul, and saw all business life as but one aspect of personal conduct and therefore subject to overriding rules of personal morality. The medieval commercial ethic thus insisted on equity in bargaining, and correspondingly condemned all abuse of superior status or superior bargaining power. Usury was prohibited not least because it was often the most conspicuous kind of extortion practised against the poor and the needy.

The intellectual and doctrinal assumptions which underlay the proscription of usury were, of course, radically affected by the Protestant Reformation, the arrival of a new age of capitalism and the Calvinist acceptance of the rightness and the inevitability of commercial enterprise. But while Luther condemned even the minor fictions by which the canonists had tried to evade the laws against usury, Calvin was later to declare that the charging of interest was not intrinsically unlawful.[18] Indeed, to charge money as the price of a loan was simply to require the debtor to concede some small part of his profit to the

---

13 (1762) 2 Eden 110 at 113, 28 ER 838 at 839.
14 See J.T. Noonan, *The Scholastic Analysis of Usury* (Cambridge Mass, 1957), p 11ff; B.N. Nelson, *The Idea of Usury* (2nd edn Princeton 1969), p 3ff; S. Homer, *A History of Interest Rates* (2nd edn, New Brunswick, NJ 1977), p 69ff.
15 Exodus xxii.25; Luke vi.35.
16 *Religion and the Rise of Capitalism* (Harmondsworth 1938), p 55.
17 Op cit, p 48.
18 J.T. Noonan, op cit, p 365ff.

creditor with whose capital assistance the gain had been achieved. The Calvinist doctrine held the exaction of interest to be legitimate, provided that the rate of interest did not exceed certain stated limits, provided that the creditor did not require an excessive security, and provided always that loans were extended gratis to the poor. The Protestant ethic of thrift, industry and sanctification through one's calling replaced the medieval detestation of usury, first by a qualified tolerance of certain forms of money-lending and finally by the elevation of a new ethic of investment. The lender entered into a community of risk with the borrower, and therefore rightly took his 'fair share of the profits, according to the degree in which God has blessed him by whom the money is used.'[19]

(2) **The historic role of equity**

Over the last three centuries the English law of mortgage has practised a cautious regulation of credit transactions related to land, and in this respect the jurisdiction of equity has played a role of pivotal importance.[106] At every stage in the evolution of the law of mortgage since the 17th century, equity has been prepared to intervene on grounds of conscience in the relationship of mortgagor and mortgagee, with the object of preventing any exploitation of the former by the latter. Equity has been particularly conscious of the possibility that the lender of money may abuse his superior bargaining strength and economic capacity by imposing on the borrower oppressive or unconscionable terms of dealing. The balance of legal protection in the mortgage transaction has therefore tended in favour of the mortgagor rather than the mortgagee.

(3) **The modern mortgage transaction**

Although equity's protective emphasis is still a potent influence in the modern law of mortgage, it could hardly be claimed that the typical mortgage of today—the granting of a legal charge over the family home—falls neatly within such historical stereotypes of the mortgage transaction as the merchant's means of raising trading credit or as the last resort of the poor in time of need. The social function of the modern mortgage has more to do with family consumption than with the needs of trade or production or even with the requirements of a rudimentary and brutal form of social security. The typical mortgage transaction of today is a means of providing residential security for much of the population. Thus, while the law still strikes down inequitable or unconscionable dealing in the area of credit transactions,[1] the impact of legislation on the law of mortgage has in recent years been more concerned with the protection of the residential utility enjoyed by the mortgagor and his family.

---

19   W. Ames, *De Conscientia et eius iure vel Casibus, Libri Quinque* (Amsterdam 1630), Book V, p 289 (Chapter XLIV, xiv, R.1), *De Contracto Usurario.*

20   Equity was, in effect, beginning to take over the jurisdiction covered by the law against usury, although the usury legislation was not finally abolished until 1854 (see Usury Laws Repeal Act 1854).

1   See eg Consumer Credit Act 1974, ss 137ff (post, p 594).

(4) The rule against 'collateral advantages'

The focus of equitable concern for the mortgagor rested traditionally on the perceived need to protect the mortgagor's 'equity of redemption', since this 'equity' represents in effect the summation of the borrower's rights in the property which has been offered as security. Towards this end equity developed a loose and not always consistent amalgam of rules prohibiting a mortgagee from stipulating for any 'collateral advantage' in a mortgage transaction which might be deemed unfair or unconscionable. In particular equity propounded the 'quaintly labelled'[2] doctrine which insisted that no 'clogs or fetters' should be imposed on the exercise of the mortgagor's equity of redemption.[3] The doctrine was almost a temporal expression of some notion that the debtor should always be free, by the mere act of full repayment, to be restored completely to the state of grace and perfect liberty from which he fell with the advent of the mortgage debt. As Walker LJ declared in *Browne v Ryan*,[4]

When a transaction appears, or has been declared to be a mortgage, Courts of Equity regard the instrument only as a security for the repayment of the principal, interest, and costs named and secured, and the mortgagor is entitled to get back his property as free as he gave it, on payment of principal, interest, and costs, and provisions inconsistent with that right cannot be enforced. The equitable rules, 'once a mortgage always a mortgage,' and that the mortgagee cannot impose any 'clog or fetter on the equity of redemption', are merely concise statements of the same rule.

(a) High-point of the 'clogs and fetters' doctrine

In its most extreme form, the prohibition against 'clogs and fetters' invalidated any condition in a mortgage transaction which tended either to inhibit the realistic possibility of redemption of the mortgage or to prevent the debtor from regaining in full his unencumbered status by mere repayment of all moneys owed. Offending terms were liable simply to be struck down as null and void. Of course, the avoidance of formally agreed contractual terms represented a remarkable denial of the principle of sanctity of contract, and the history of the 'clogs and fetters' doctrine provides a fascinating account of the confrontation between the irresistible force of equity and the immovable object of traditional contract doctrine. The fluctuating fortunes of the 'clogs and fetters' prohibition epitomise the resolute opposition of the requirements of conscience and the commercial ethic of late 19th century capitalism.

(b) Retreat from the 'clogs and fetters' doctrine

Nowadays the caselaw on the 'clogs and fetters' doctrine seems to have a certain fin-de-siècle quality and the authorities are not wholly reconcilable. It is quite clear that modern courts have had less occasion (and probably less desire) to apply the same censure to mortgage terms which would have attracted the displeasure of judges of an earlier generation.[5] Even by 1914 it

2 *Bannerman Brydone Foster & Co v Murray* [1972] NZLR 411 at 429 per Woodhouse J.
3 See B. Wyman, 21 Harvard LR 459 (1907-08); G.L. Williams, (1944) 60 LQR 190.
4 [1901] 2 IR 653 at 676.
5 See the reference by Lord Mersey in *G. & C. Kreglinger v New Patagonia Meat and Cold Storage Co Ltd* [1914] AC 25 at 46 to the doctrine of 'clogs and fetters' as being 'like an unruly dog, which, if not securely chained to its own kennel, is prone to wander into places where it ought not to be.'

was being declared by Lord Parker of Waddington in *G. & C. Kreglinger v New Patagonia Meat and Cold Storage Co Ltd*[6] that

> there is now no rule in equity which precludes a mortgagee...from stipulating for any collateral advantage, provided such collateral advantage is not either (1) unfair and unconscionable, or (2) in the nature of a penalty clogging the equity of redemption, or (3) inconsistent with or repugnant to the contractual and equitable right to redeem.

It is likely that the courts' scrutiny of mortgage terms is nowadays governed, as is suggested by the *Kreglinger* case, by a somewhat more narrow and more flexible test of fairness. Accordingly, the older caselaw requires to be interpreted carefully in the light of the *Kreglinger* criteria, which more clearly delineate the circumstances in which the courts will intervene in the context of mortgage transactions. Nevertheless the disfavour of oppressive terms and 'clogs' retains a residual strength in the contemporary law and now also finds expression in modern statute law. The protection afforded the mortgagor is evident primarily in the following areas.

(5) Attempted exclusion of the right to redeem

It is traditional for equity to direct its sharpest gaze upon any provision which has the effect of negating the mortgagor's 'equity of redemption'. The clearest and most conclusive form in which such a provision may appear comprises a mortgage term which potentially removes from the mortgagor the possibility of ever redeeming his mortgage.[7] What is relevant in this context is not the degree of risk that the mortgagor's equity of redemption may be excluded, but rather the fact that there exists any risk at all.

(a) The rule

In *Samuel v Jarrah Timber and Wood Paving Corpn Ltd*[8] the mortgagee of a quantity of debenture stock was by the terms of the mortgage given an option to purchase the stock outright within twelve months of the date of the loan secured by the mortgage. When the mortgagee purported to exercise this option, the mortgagor sought a declaration that the option was illegal and void in that it excluded the mortgagor's equity of redemption. The House of Lords granted the declaration, somewhat reluctantly in view of the fact that in this case a 'perfectly fair bargain' had been concluded between two parties 'each of whom was quite sensible of what they were doing'.[9] However, the option was invalidated simply because 'at the same time a mortgage arrangement was made between them.' Such is the vigilance of equity to ensure that 'a mortgagee can never provide at the time of making the loan for any event or condition on which the equity of redemption shall be discharged...'[10]

---

6   [1914] AC 25 at 61.
7   It is a cardinal principle of the law of mortgage that the mortgagor has a *legal* right to redeem the mortgage on the redemption date fixed by the mortgage deed. Once that date has passed, the mortgagor thereafter enjoys for the indefinite future an *equitable* right to redeem until such time as his equity of redemption is finally extinguished by foreclosure or sale (post, p 616). See *Van Den Bosch v Australian Provincial Assurance Association Ltd* [1968] 2 NSWR 550 at 552.
8   [1904] AC 323.
9   [1904] AC 323 at 325.
10   [1904] AC 323 at 327.

(b) The rationale

The courts' disfavour of options for purchase which are incorporated within a mortgage transaction[11] is grounded upon the argument that such options change 'the nature of the transaction from a transfer by way of security to what is essentially a potential transfer on sale, at the option of the mortgagee.'[12] There is always a danger that this transmutation may have been the result of unfair bargaining by an unscrupulous mortgagee. However, the protective concern of equity was stretched to the limit in *Samuel v Jarrah Timber and Wood Paving Corpn Ltd*, where the House of Lords was clearly reluctant to allow the vigilance of equity to be used as 'a means of evading a fair bargain come to between persons dealing at arms' length and negotiating on equal terms.' As Lord Macnaghten pointed out,[13] the directors of a trading company in search of financial assistance 'are certainly in a very different position from that of an impecunious landowner in the toils of a crafty money-lender.'

(c) Restrictive application of the rule

The countervailing principle of freedom of contract not only underlies the House of Lords' diffidence as to the result achieved in the *Jarrah Timber* case but also explains the willingness of the House to reach a different result on the barely distinguishable facts of *Reeve v Lisle*.[14] Here an option for purchase of part of the secured property was granted to a mortgagee ten days *after* the date of execution of the mortgage transaction. The House of Lords upheld the option as valid since it derived from a transaction which was separate from and independent of the original mortgage transaction.

The rationale underlying the distinction between *Jarrah Timber* and *Reeve v Lisle* is thus supposedly the idea that the mortgagor, once he has obtained the loan which he seeks, is no longer vulnerable to unconscionable dealing by his mortgagee in respect of a later and quite separate transaction.[15] However, the ultimate test turns on whether there has been, in the view of equity, unconscionable dealing between mortgagor and mortgagee. The mere fact that a mortgage and an option are contained in separate documents executed on different days does not necessarily exclude the possibility of a vitiating clog on the equity of redemption.[16] The essential issue before the court is whether the two documents represent 'in substance a single and undivided contract or two distinct contracts.'[17]

---

11 See also *Harper v Joblin* [1916] NZLR 895 at 915f; *Baker v Biddle* (1923) 33 CLR 188 at 194, 196f; *Laurin v Iron Ore Co of Canada* (1978) 82 DLR (3d) 634 at 645. The grant to the mortgagee of a mere right of pre-emption is less likely to attract equitable censure since such a grant confers on the mortgagee no right to demand the sale of the property (see *Orby v Trigg* (1722) 9 Mod 2, 88 ER 276).
12 P.B. Fairest, *Mortgages* (2nd edn London 1980), p 26.
13 [1904] AC 323 at 327.
14 [1902] AC 461.
15 For criticism of the logic of the distinction, see P.B. Fairest, op cit, p 27f. Compare, however, *Lewis v Frank Love Ltd* [1961] 1 WLR 261 at 271; (1961) 77 LQR 163 (P.V. Baker).
16 *Re Supreme Court Registrar to Alexander Dawson Inc* [1976] 1 NZLR 615 at 627.
17 *G. & C. Kreglinger v New Patagonia Meat and Cold Storage Co Ltd* [1914] AC 25 at 39 per Viscount Haldane LC. In *Bay of Islands Electric Power Board v Buckland* (Unreported, A No 48/1976, 10 July 1978), the Supreme Court of New Zealand upheld an option which had been granted to the mortgagee in advance of the mortgage and which was proved to be a quite separate transaction.

(6) Postponement of the date of redemption

It is not impossible that a mortgage, instead of excluding altogether the mortgagor's right to redeem, should merely include a contractual term which *postpones* the earliest permissible date of redemption. It is, of course, customary for a formal redemption date to be set at a relatively short distance (eg six months) from the date of the mortgage transaction, since the mortgagor retains an equity to redeem the mortgage long after this date has passed.[18] However, the contractual terms of a mortgage may sometimes postpone the earliest date at which redemption may occur,[19] since the effect of such a term is to guarantee for the mortgagee a secure investment over a long period at a favourable rate of interest. In certain circumstances this type of provision may operate so unilaterally in favour of the mortgagee that the courts will hold it to be invalid and unenforceable.[20] The test is ultimately one of degree as to whether the postponement effectively renders the equity of redemption illusory or valueless, in which case it would be unconscionable to uphold the postponement clause in its literal terms.

(a) Exceptional intervention of equity

In *Fairclough v Swan Brewery Co Ltd*[1] the mortgagor was contractually precluded from exercising his right of redemption during most of the period of the leasehold term which provided the subject matter of the mortgage. The mortgagor's leasehold estate was for a term of 17 $\frac{1}{2}$ years, and according to the terms of the mortgage his right to redeem arose at the earliest only six weeks before the expiry of that lease. The Judicial Committee of the Privy Council upheld a claim by the mortgagor to redeem at an earlier date, ruling that 'equity will not permit any device or contrivance being part of the mortgage transaction or contemporaneous with it to prevent or impede redemption.'[2] In this case the mortgage had been rendered 'for all practical purposes...irredeemable', since on redemption the effective value to the mortgagor of an almost expired lease would have been minimal.

(b) The more general approach

The facts of *Fairclough* are of course exceptional, and later cases have not adopted so wide a view of the inequity of postponed redemption. As Mason J of the Australian High Court ruled in *Hyde Management Services Pty Ltd v F.A.I. Insurances Ltd*,[3] 'at common law and in equity...the borrower has no right to repay principal before the day named for repayment in the loan agreement,

---

18   Ante, p 572.
19   Of course, in the absence of any stipulation that the mortgagor may not pay off before a specified date, there is nothing to prevent him from tendering full payment at any time and requiring that the mortgage be discharged (see *G.A. Investments Pty Ltd v Standard Insurance Co Ltd* [1964] WAR 264 at 267; *Ex parte Tori* [1977] Qd R 256 at 260D-E).
20   See E.H. Bodkin, (1941) 5 Conv (NS) 178.
1   [1912] AC 565.
2   [1912] AC 565 at 570.
3   (1979) 53 ALJR 502 at 503.

unless the agreement itself gives him such a right.'[4] It seems therefore that repayment may normally be postponed quite validly until such date as may be fixed by the parties in the instrument of mortgage. The court will not endorse any claim by the mortgagor to redeem in advance of that date unless it turns out that the mortgagee was not equally precluded from prematurely calling in the loan[5] or that the postponement term is in all the circumstances unconscionable or oppressive.[6]

This general approach to contractually retarded redemption dates was amply demonstrated in *Knightsbridge Estates Trust Ltd v Byrne*,[7] where the Court of Appeal was confronted with a mortgage term which stipulated that the loan advanced should not be repaid before the expiry of 40 years from the granting of the mortgage. The loan had been obtained at an interest rate of $6\frac{1}{2}$ per cent per annum, and when later the mortgagor wished to avail himself of a general fall in interest rates by borrowing money elsewhere, he claimed to be entitled to redeem the mortgage before the expiration of the stipulated period. The Court of Appeal held, however, that the validity of the original loan terms was not prejudiced by the contractual postponement of the date for redemption. Sir Wilfred Greene MR made it clear that 'equity does not reform mortgage transactions because they are unreasonable.' Equity is concerned, he said, 'to see two things—one that the essential requirements of a mortgage transaction are observed, and the other that oppressive or unconscionable terms are not enforced.'[8] Thus, in the present case, the postponement of the date of redemption could not be challenged on the ground that postponement was permissible only for a 'reasonable' period. The true ground of equitable intervention arose where the contractual right of redemption was rendered 'illusory' by postponement of the right to redeem, as had occurred in *Fairclough v Swan Brewery Co Ltd*.

The Court thus declined to intervene in the *Knightsbridge Estates* case, where from the start the mortgagor had bargained at arm's length for a long-term loan of a substantial sum (£310,000) on the most advantageous terms available at the time. The resulting agreement was 'a commercial agreement between two important corporations experienced in such matters' and had 'none of the features of an oppressive bargain where the borrower is at the mercy of an unscrupulous lender.'[9] The Court of Appeal was not prepared to view the agreement made 'as anything but a proper business transaction'. Any other result would have placed 'an unfortunate restriction on the liberty of contract of competent parties who are at arm's length'.[10] Moreover, it would have led to the 'highly inequitable' consequence that whereas the mortgagor would from

4   See *Burrough v Cranston* (1840) 2 Ir Eq R 203 at 205; *Brown v Cole* (1845) 14 Sim 427, 60 ER 424; *West Derby Union v Metropolitan Life Assurance Society* [1897] AC 647 at 649ff. It is significant that some jurisdictions confer a statutory right on the mortgagor to pay off the principal at any time during the agreed mortgage term, but only on condition that he also pays interest for the entirety of the originally agreed term. See eg Conveyancing Act 1919 (New South Wales), s 93(1); *Wanner v Caruana* [1974] 2 NSWLR 301 at 306C-D.
5   See *Bovill v Endle* [1896] 1 Ch 648 at 650f; *Ex parte Tori* [1977] Qd R 256 at 257D.
6   See *Morgan v Jeffreys* [1910] 1 Ch 620 at 629; *G.A. Investments Pty Ltd v Standard Insurance Co Ltd* [1964] WAR 264 at 266; *Ex parte Tori* [1977] Qd R 256 at 260D.
7   [1939] Ch 441.
8   [1939] Ch 441 at 457.
9   [1939] Ch 441 at 455.
10 [1939] Ch 441 at 455.

the outset have had the right to redeem at any time (thereby subjecting the lender to the inconvenience of profitable re-investment[11]), the mortgagee would have had no right to require repayment of the loan otherwise than by the specified contractual instalments.[12]

(7) Solus agreements

It is not uncommon, where the mortgagor and mortgagee conduct a common trading concern, for the terms of the mortgage to require that the mortgagor refrain from any commercial competition prejudicial to the mortgagee's own business operation. These restrictions appear most frequently in the form of a 'solus tie' by which a mortgagee such as a petrol company or a brewery imposes on the mortgagor a condition that the latter shall deal only in the products manufactured or distributed by the mortgagee.

The possibility that a mortgage transaction may thus confer a collateral advantage on the mortgagee has activated the watchful concern of equity, initially because the securing of collateral benefits for the mortgagee was in the past a common means of circumventing the laws against usury.[13] More recently the vigilance of equity has been reinforced if not supplanted by another ground of concern—this time expressed by the common lawyers—that solus clauses in a mortgage agreement may offend the contractual doctrine against unreasonable restraints of trade.

(a) The equitable distaste for superadded obligations

Even after the repeal of the usury laws equity viewed the solus tie with suspicion, partly because it gave scope for coercive bargaining or commercial exploitation on the part of the mortgagee, and also because the 'advance of money with a superadded obligation' seemed so over-protective of the mortgagee as to offend against 'the settled principles of equity'.[14]

(i) The old rule of thumb   The caselaw in this area is not wholly consistent,[15] but it seems that the courts were usually prepared to strike down as void any collateral benefit for a mortgagee which purported to remain in force *after* the redemption of the mortgage.[16] A solus tie not limited to the actual (as distinct from potential) duration of a mortgage was liable to be regarded as invalid,

11   See *Hyde Management Services Pty Ltd v F.A.I. Insurances Ltd* (1979) 53 ALJR 502 at 505.
12   The decision of the Court of Appeal was affirmed by the House of Lords, but on the different ground that the mortgage in question constituted a debenture within the Companies Act 1929, ss 74, 380, and was not invalidated on the ground of postponement of the redemption date (see [1940] AC 613). However, the House of Lords threw no doubt on the reasoning applied by the Court of Appeal.
13   'A man shall not have interest for his money, and a collateral advantage besides for the loan of it, or clog the equity of redemption with any by-agreement' (*Jennings v Ward* (1705) 2 Vern 520 at 521, 23 ER 935). In view of the development of the law since 1705 (post, p 587), this statement cannot now stand unqualified (see *Biggs v Hoddinott* [1898] 2 Ch 307 at 321; *G. & C. Kreglinger v New Patagonia Meat and Cold Storage Co Ltd* [1914] AC 25 at 38; *Re Petrol Filling Station, Vauxhall Bridge Road, London* (1969) 20 P & CR 1 at 7).
14   *Noakes & Co Ltd v Rice* [1902] AC 24 at 31; *Toohey v Gunther* (1928) 41 CLR 181 at 192.
15   The difficult case is generally taken to be *Santley v Wilde* [1899] 2 Ch 474, but this decision was heavily criticised by the House of Lords in *Noakes & Co Ltd v Rice* [1902] AC 24 at 31f, 34.
16   See eg *Noakes & Co Ltd v Rice* [1902] AC 24 at 29, 33; *Bradley v Carritt* [1903] AC 253 at 266.

since such a tie—if allowed to remain in force after redemption—could be seen as repugnant to the mortgagor's equity to redeem.[17] The mortgagor would be in a distinctly less favourable position after redemption than he occupied before the grant of the mortgage. Full repayment of all moneys owed would not have the effect of restoring the status quo ante, since the restrictive trading condition would still remain in operation. Conversely the courts generally upheld solus clauses whose force was in terms limited to the actual continuance of the mortgage security,[18] since in such cases there was no danger that redemption of the mortgage would leave the borrower still encumbered by some obligation towards the lender.

(ii) The qualification imposed by the Kreglinger case The distinctions outlined in the older decisions probably remain good law today, with an important qualification imposed by the decision of the House of Lords in *G. & C. Kreglinger v New Patagonia Meat and Cold Storage Co Ltd.*[19] Here Viscount Haldane LC indicated that although equity would continue to control any bargain so framed that 'the right to redeem was cut down',[20] the parties to a mortgage are entirely free to 'stipulate for a collateral undertaking, outside and clear of the mortgage'.[1] No objection can be raised against such a collateral advantage, provided that it does not comprise 'remuneration for the use of the money'[2] or constitute any 'part of the consideration given for the mortgage'.[3] If the collateral advantage is thus neither a 'part of the mortgage transaction' nor 'one of the terms of the loan',[4] but is instead 'part of another kind of transaction',[5] it falls completely outside the ambit of the equitable objection to clogs on the equity of redemption.[6] A collateral advantage included in a wholly independent transaction may therefore endure even beyond the redemption of the mortgage, provided that the advantage is not otherwise unconscionable.[7]

Thus it was that in the *Kreglinger* case itself the House of Lords upheld the validity, even after redemption of the mortgage, of an agreement that the mortgagor would not sell a specified product to any person other than the lender so long as the lender was willing to purchase at not less than the best price offered by any third party. This agreement was regarded as part of a wholly different transaction from that of the mortgage, even though it was contained in the same document and even though it may have been 'in the nature of a collateral bargain the entering into which was a preliminary and separable condition of the loan'.[8]

---

17   See *Toohey v Gunther* (1928) 41 CLR 181 at 192.
18   *Biggs v Hoddinott* [1898] 2 Ch 307 at 313ff, 321ff.
19   [1914] AC 25.
20   See *Re Petrol Filling Station, Vauxhall Bridge Road, London* (1969) 20 P & CR 1 at 7: 'The purpose of the [equitable] jurisdiction is to ensure that the transaction, whose "real nature and substance" was "one of mortgage simply," should be limited to a mortgage, that is, to a mortgage being "a mere security for money".'
1   [1914] AC 25 at 39.
2   *Noakes & Co Ltd v Rice* [1902] AC 24 at 34 per Lord Davey.
3   *De Beers Consolidated Mines Ltd v British South Africa Co* [1912] AC 52 at 67. See *Re Petrol Filling Station, Vauxhall Bridge Road, London* (1969) 20 P & CR 1 at 6.
4   *Samuel v Jarrah Timber and Wood Paving Corpn Ltd* [1904] AC 323 at 329 per Lord Lindley.
5   *Re Petrol Filling Station, Vauxhall Bridge Road, London* (1969) 20 P & CR 1 at 9.
6   *Re Petrol Filling Station, Vauxhall Bridge Road, London* (1969) 20 P & CR 1 at 8.
7   *Re Petrol Filling Station, Vauxhall Bridge Road, London* (1969) 20 P & CR 1 at 7.
8   [1914] AC 25 at 39.

It is not easy, however, to draw a firm distinction between, on the one hand, a collateral benefit which although apparently a sine qua non of the mortgage advance is conferred 'outside the security...[and] in substance independent of it',[9] and, on the other hand, a collateral agreement which is 'part of the consideration given for the mortgage'[10] and which is therefore vulnerable to the censure of equity. It may be for this reason that the more recent legal challenge to solus agreements has tended to be based on a rather different objection stemming from the law of contract.

(b) Invalid restraints of trade

There is a general doctrine in the law of contract that agreements which operate unreasonably in restraint of trade are void on the ground of public policy.[11] In the more recent past solus agreements by mortgagors have been subjected, with varying degrees of success,[12] to challenge on this basis.[13] In general it seems that the courts are prepared to uphold solus agreements which are limited in their stipulated duration to relatively short periods (eg five years), but would not be willing to countenance a tie which extended over a period of 21 years unless such a prolonged tie is grounded in a clear case of economic necessity.[14]

(8) Judicial control of 'oppressive and unconscionable' terms

The courts have always claimed an overriding equitable jurisdiction to strike down any term in a mortgage transaction which tends to operate in an 'oppressive or unconscionable' manner.[15] The courts' inherent supervisory function is significant, but should not be overstated since its effects are demonstrated only in exceptional cases. The areas in which judicial intervention has been most clearly evident concern the rates of interest levied on mortgage loans.

(a) Legality of variable interest rates

The modern domestic mortgage is a quite remarkable form of transaction. Most mortgages of residential property are concluded between an owner-occupier and a building society. Such mortgages are, of course, covered by the general law relating to mortgages, but they differ slightly from the ordinary

---

9   [1914] AC 25 at 41.
10   *De Beers Consolidated Mines Ltd v British South Africa Co* [1912] AC 52 at 67.
11   G.H. Treitel, *The Law of Contract* (6th edn London 1983), p 341ff.
12   See eg *Shell UK Ltd v Lostock Garage Ltd* [1976] 1 WLR 1187 at 1199C; *Alec Lobb (Garages) Ltd v Total Oil (Great Britain) Ltd* [1985] 1 WLR 173 at 180D; *Irish Shell & BP Ltd v Ryan* [1966] IR 75 at 99; *Continental Oil Co of Ireland Ltd v Moynihan* (1977) 111 ILTR 5 at 9f.
13   The doctrine against restraint of trade has been held to have no application to restrictive covenants undertaken by persons purchasing or leasing land where those persons had no previous right to trade at all on the land in question. The doctrine applies only where a pre-existing freedom is given up (*Esso Petroleum Co Ltd v Harper's Garage (Stourport) Ltd* [1968] AC 269 at 298B-C, 309A-F, 316F-317A, 325B-F). See also *Quadramain Pty Ltd v Sevastapol Investments Pty Ltd* (1975-1976) 133 CLR 390 at 401; *Stephens v Gulf Oil Canada Ltd* (1976) 65 DLR (3d) 193 at 203f.
14   *Esso Petroleum Co Ltd v Harper's Garage (Stourport) Ltd* [1968] AC 269 at 303E-304B, 320F-321E, 330B, 340C-E. See the reference to a 'rule of thumb' in *Alec Lobb (Garages) Ltd v Total Oil (Great Britain) Ltd* [1985] 1 WLR 173 at 178H-179A; [1985] Conv 141 (P. Todd).
15   See *Knightsbridge Estates Trust Ltd v Byrne* [1939] Ch 441 at 457.

mortgage of realty in that they are affected by certain rules which apply specifically to transactions entered into by building societies.[16] Under the building society mortgage the mortgagor is required to become a member of the building society which advances him money on loan,[17] and the rules of the society are impliedly incorporated into the mortgage transaction itself.[18] All building societies reserve the right, on serving notice on their borrowers, to alter the rate of interest payable on mortgage loans. In other words, the rate of interest payable by the mortgagor is not fixed throughout the period of the loan, but fluctuates in accordance with the rate stipulated from time to time by the society itself.[19]

The open-ended contract thus concluded between the mortgagor and mortgagee is little short of astonishing. The mortgagor agrees to pay *any* rate of interest demanded by the lender of the money. There is some question as to whether either party is competent to contract on this basis, or indeed as to whether the terms of such a contract of loan are sufficiently certain to support a binding legal relationship.[20] It has been observed that this unilateral power to vary the interest rate payable, if 'reserved to an individual mortgagee in an ordinary mortgage, would savour of being harsh and unconscionable' and would therefore be liable to be struck down as invalid and unenforceable.[1] However, it seems that no legal challenge has ever been raised as to the right of building societies to adjust interest rates at their discretion, partly because it is recognised that building societies constitute a special case. It is clear that a building society which tethered itself to a rigid rate of interest in a long-term transaction would be 'hopelessly exposed to the risk of having to pay more to its investors than it was currently receiving from its borrower.'[2] Moreover, building society interest rates are subject in any event to a large element of quasi-public control in that the variation of interest rates is indirectly related to the general economic strategy of the government of the day.[3]

(b) Control of harsh interest rates

While the protection of most borrowers rests largely on the responsible exercise of power by the large institutional lenders[4] and the underlying element of

---

16 The principal enactment regulating the operation of building societies is the Building Societies Act 1986.
17 Building Societies Act 1986, s 10(1).
18 *Rosenberg v Northumberland Building Society* (1889) 22 QBD 373 at 380.
19 The absence of a fixed interest rate is also a feature of mortgage loans made by other institutional lenders such as banks and local authorities.
20 The argument based on uncertainty has, however, been dismissed in the context of unilaterally variable interest rates in a debenture (see *ANZ Banking Group (NZ) Ltd v Gibson* [1981] 1 NZLR 513 at 525).
1 Wurtzburg and Mills, *Building Society Law* (14th edn, London 1976), p 166.
2 Ibid, p 165.
3 In view of the potential legal objection to the unilateral nature of mortgage interest rate adjustments, it is nevertheless significant that most building societies, when raising the interest rate, are prepared to offer their borrowers such alternative facilities as repayment over a longer period of time. Such conciliatory gestures are probably wise, since it has been considered to be 'open to doubt if an unlimited power simply to vary the interest rate at discretion would be legally valid' (Wurtzburg and Mills, op cit, p 166).
4 The Payne Committee on the Enforcement of Judgment Debts reported in 1969 that it had received no evidence 'to establish or to suggest that the Building Societies impose harsh or unconscionable obligations on their borrowers' (*Report of the Committee on the Enforcement of Judgment Debts* (Cmnd 3909, 1969), para 1354).

governmental regulation, no such protection is available for the individual who borrows on mortgage from another individual or from a credit company or other fringe financial institution. The protection of such borrowers depends ultimately on the important residual power of the courts to declare void any mortgage term which is 'oppressive' or 'unconscionable'.[5]

A dramatic illustration of the courts' powers in this context occurred in *Cityland and Property (Holdings) Ltd v Dabrah*.[6] Here the plaintiff company had sold a residential property to the defendant, who was the existing occupier. The balance of the purchase price was raised by a loan from the plaintiff secured upon the property in question. The mortgage granted to the plaintiff made no provision for the payment of interest as such, but required that the defendant pay by monthly instalments a sum which exceeded the loan moneys by a figure which was described by the plaintiff as a 'premium'. The plaintiff reserved the right to recover on demand the full outstanding balance of the sum payable by the defendant in the event of any default at any time. On the facts it was calculable that the premium payable by the mortgagor represented, over a three year period, an interest rate of 19 per cent per annum. Moreover, since the entire capital debt was recoverable immediately in the case of default, the 'premium' (taken as a proportion of the capital sum lent) effectively constituted a capitalised interest rate of 57 per cent. Goff J held that the imposition of this rate of interest was in the circumstances 'unfair and unconscionable', and that the mortgagee was entitled to require only a 'reasonable' rate of interest, which he fixed at 7 per cent per annum.[7] The 'premium' agreed between the parties was unenforceable since it conferred an unconscionable collateral advantage in favour of the mortgagee.[8]

Cityland and Property (Holdings) Ltd v Dabrah remains the only well known instance in recent years in which the court has exercised its inherent equitable power to rewrite a mortgage bargain concluded by the parties themselves. It is clear, however, that the conscionableness of a specific rate of interest will vary in accordance with the relative bargaining positions of mortgagor and mortgagee. In *Cityland and Property (Holdings) Ltd v Dabrah* there was a plain disparity of bargaining power as between mortgagor and mortgagee, and there was also a strong suspicion that the mortgagor had agreed to disadvantageous terms only because, as the sitting tenant in the property, he had been threatened with eviction on the expiry of his lease.

The decision in *Cityland and Property (Holdings) Ltd v Dabrah* is not, however, without parallel. The courts have long exercised a similar jurisdiction under the Moneylenders Acts 1900-1927 to set aside 'harsh and unconscionable'

---

5   An early attempt to restrict mortgage interest rates by statute was contained in the Increase of Rent and Mortgage Interest (War Restrictions) Act 1915 (post, p 961).

6   [1968] Ch 166.

7   [1968] Ch 166 at 180D.

8   The plaintiff was nevertheless granted an order for possession against the defendant. At first sight the approach adopted by Goff J seems to conflict with the insistence of the Court of Appeal in *Knightsbridge Estates Trust Ltd v Byrne* [1939] Ch 441 at 457 (ante, p 585) that the relevant test is not one of 'reasonableness' but rather one of 'conscionableness'. It is perhaps noteworthy that the *Knightsbridge Estates* case was not cited before Goff J. As Browne-Wilkinson J observed in *Multiservice Bookbinding Ltd v Marden* [1979] Ch 84 at 110D-E, Goff J appears to have treated the words 'unreasonable' and 'unconscionable' as being interchangeable. However, as Browne-Wilkinson J went on to say, it 'was unnecessary for [Goff J] to distinguish between the two concepts, since on either test the premium was unenforceable.'

transactions,[9] and disparity of bargaining strength has played an important part in determining the exercise of this discretion.[10] In *Carringtons Ltd v Smith*,[11] for instance, a borrower who was 'intelligent and a man of business' was held to be unable to upset an interest rate of 50 per cent on a transaction of loan. In *Wells v Joyce*,[12] however, the court was prepared to re-open an unfavourable loan which had been pressed on a Connemara farmer 'of rustic mind'.

(c) Index-linked interest rates

It is not unnatural, particularly in an age of inflation, that the lender of money should wish to ensure that he is compensated for any fall in the value of money occurring during the term of the loan. Unless he receives such compensation, the principal sum when finally returned to him is bound to be less valuable in real terms than the loan which was made at the beginning of the transaction. The obvious means by which a mortgagee may seek to counteract the deleterious effects of inflation lies in some index-linking of the capital and interest repayments due under a mortgage. However, the legality of this protective technique was until relatively recently a matter of considerable doubt.[13]

(i) Challenge based on grounds of public policy It used to be asserted that index-linked loans were invalidated on grounds of public policy. The force of this argument was convincingly removed by the decision in *Multiservice Bookbinding Ltd v Marden*.[14] Here the terms of a mortgage of commercial premises provided that the loan could not be called in by the mortgagee, nor the mortgage redeemed by the mortgagor, within ten years of the date of the grant of the mortgage, and that interest should be payable at 2 per cent above Minimum Lending Rate on the entire capital sum throughout the duration of the loan. Furthermore, the mortgage included a provision which stipulated that any repayment of interest or capital should increase or decrease in accordance with alterations in the rate of exchange between the pound sterling and the Swiss franc subsequent to the commencement of the loan.

The clear object of these provisions was to ensure that the lender was protected against both domestic inflation and any fall in the value of the pound sterling on the international money market. Ten years after the commencement of the loan period, the mortgagor sought to redeem the mortgage on terms to be declared by the court. The mortgagor claimed that

9   The Court of Appeal declined in *Wills v Wood* [1984] CCLR 7 at 11, 17, to apply the Moneylenders Acts (and the statutory requirement of a licence) to a private individual who from time to time invested his savings in the making of mortgage loans at normal interest rates to a limited number of borrowers selected by his own solicitor. However, for a more stringent view of deeply disturbing aspects of this case, see (1983) LAG Bulletin (September) 9ff; (1984) Legal Action (April), p 7. See also (1986) 136 NLJ 980.
10 See H.W. Wilkinson, (1980) 130 NLJ 749; Lord Goff of Chieveley and Gareth Jones, *The Law of Restitution* (3rd edn London 1986), p 260f.
11 [1906] 1 KB 79 at 92ff.
12 [1905] 2 IR 134 at 142ff. See also *Kevans v Joyce* [1896] 1 IR 442 at 462ff, 485ff.
13 See eg Wurtzburg and Mills, op cit, p 167f; *Nationwide Building Society v Registry of Friendly Societies* [1983] 1 WLR 1226 at 1228B-C.
14 [1979] Ch 84. See [1978] CLJ 211 (A.J. Oakley); (1978) 128 NLJ 1251 (H.W. Wilkinson); (1979) 42 MLR 338 (W.D. Bishop and B.V. Hindley); [1978] Conv 318 (F.R. Crane). See generally H.W. Wilkinson, *Index-Linked Mortgages*, [1978] Conv 346.

the payment clause contained in the mortgage was void and unenforceable on grounds of public policy. During the intervening period the value of the pound sterling had depreciated relative to the Swiss franc to such an extent that at the date of redemption the mortgagee would, in return for the original loan of £36,000, have received almost £133,000 by way of payments of capital and interest.

Browne-Wilkinson J gave judgment in favour of the mortgagee, holding that an index-linked money obligation could not be said to be contrary to public policy. He treated the 'Swiss franc uplift' provision as a form of index-linking, and was clearly moved by the consideration that 'unless lenders can ensure that they are repaid the real value of the money they advanced, and not merely a sum of the same nominal amount but in devalued currency, the availability of loan capital will be much diminished.' This, in Browne-Wilkinson J's view, 'would surely not be in the public interest.'[15]

(ii) Challenge based on equitable objections The mortgagor's challenge on grounds of public policy therefore failed, but the mortgagor went on to claim that the mortgage terms were in any event unenforceable on the ground that they were 'unconscionable' or 'unreasonable'. Browne-Wilkinson J took the view that such a challenge can succeed only if the mortgagor can show 'that the bargain, or some of its terms, was unfair and unconscionable: it is not enough to show that, in the eyes of the court, it was unreasonable.'[16] Moreover, a bargain is not 'unfair and unconscionable' unless one of the parties to it 'has imposed the objectionable terms in a morally reprehensible manner...in a way which affects his conscience.'[18][1] Although he declined to limit the categories of unconscionable bargain, Browne-Wilkinson J gave as the classic example of such a bargain the case 'where advantage has been taken of a young, inexperienced or ignorant person to introduce such a term which no sensible well-advised person or party would have accepted.'

In the present case, however, Browne-Wilkinson J was not prepared to stigmatise the terms of the mortgage transaction as 'unconscionable' or 'oppressive', although he did concede that these terms had been 'unreasonable'.[18] The terms had not been 'imposed...in a morally reprehensible manner', in that there had been no great inequality of bargaining power between the parties. The parties had, moreover, received the benefit of independent legal advice, and the loan related to commercial premises which had trebled in value during the loan period. Above all, the mortgagee was not 'a professional moneylender' and there was no evidence of 'any sharp practice of any kind' by him. Browne-Wilkinson J refused to regard the 'Swiss franc uplift' element as representing in any sense a 'premium or collateral advantage'.[19] In ensuring that he is repaid the real value of his

15   [1979] Ch 84 at 104G-H.
16   [1979] Ch 84 at 110E.
17   [1979] Ch 84 at 110F.
18   'In particular I consider that it was unreasonable both for the debt to be inflation proofed by reference to the Swiss franc and at the same time to provide for a rate of interest two per cent above bank rate—a rate which reflects at least in part the unstable state of the pound sterling. On top of this interest on the whole sum was to be paid throughout the term. The defendant made a hard bargain. But the test is not reasonableness.'([1979] Ch 84 at 112B-C).
19   [1979] Ch 84 at 111C.

original advance, the lender 'is not stipulating for anything beyond the repayment of principal.'[20]

(iii) Potential impact of index-linking The *Multiservice Bookbinding* case thus established that there is no objection in principle to the index-linking of mortgage commitments, and the practice of index-linking has been further stimulated by the government's increasing use of this technique in borrowing money by way of issue of treasury stock.[1] This general disposition in favour of upholding the legality of index-linked mortgage payments has now been taken to the extent that even building societies, which enjoy a bargaining strength quite disproportionate to that of the individual borrower, have been allowed to take advantage of this facility for reversing the effects of the falling purchasing power of money.[2] However, the practice of index-linking building society repayments, if widely adopted, would dramatically erode the value of realty as a means of fairly rapid capital accumulation for the private citizen, who would find himself required to share with his building society a large portion of the inflated equity which he acquires during his period of ownership.[3]

(d) Penal interest rates

The courts also have power to invalidate rates of mortgage interest which are imposed for penal purposes without any consideration of whether they comprise a genuine pre-estimate of the damage suffered by the mortgagee in the event of the mortgagor's default. In an area which is curiously bereft of modern English authority, it seems that the courts have tended to strike down clauses which, on default by the mortgagor, increase the interest rate beyond the primary rate normally payable.[4] Somewhat illogically the courts have declined to interfere if the mortgage agreement merely allows the mortgagor a reduction or discount from the normal or primary rate if he makes punctual payment.[5] There is, however, authority for regarding as void a provision that, upon default by the mortgagor, a flat rate of interest becomes payable for the balance of the mortgage term on the entirety of the outstanding debt.[6] Such a clause bears all the hallmarks of an in terrorem stipulation designed to force mortgagors to adhere to their bargains and contains none of the ingredients of a genuine pre-estimate of loss.

---

20 [1979] Ch 84 at 111C.
1 See *Nationwide Building Society v Registry of Friendly Societies* [1983] 1 WLR 1226 at 1228C.
2 See *Nationwide Building Society v Registry of Friendly Societies* [1983] 1 WLR 1226 at 1231D-E.
3 See H. Cohen, (1984) 134 NLJ 437 at 439.
4 *Holles v Wyse* (1693) 2 Vern 289 at 290, 23 ER 787; *Strode v Parker* (1694) 2 Vern 316 at 317, 23 ER 804 at 805. It is possible that a provision for increased interest in the case of default on an instalment mortgage would not be regarded as penal or repugnant (see eg *C. J. Belmore Pty Ltd v A.G.C. (General Finance) Ltd* [1976] 1 NSWLR 507 at 509E). Some jurisdictions statutorily prohibit the imposition of a higher interest rate on arrears than on principal not in arrears. See eg Canada's Interest Act (RSC 1970, c I-18), s 8(1); *Vancouver City Savings Credit Union v Chambers* (1976) 59 DLR (3d) 753 at 758; *Re Weirdale Investments Ltd and Canadian Imperial Bank of Commerce* (1981) 32 OR (2d) 183 at 190; *Beauchamp v Timberland Investments Ltd* (1984) 4 DLR (4th) 485 at 487ff.
5 *Sterne v Beck* (1863) 32 LJ Ch 682 at 684f; *Wallingford v Mutual Society* (1880) 5 App Cas 685 at 702; *Re Jones's Estate* [1914] 1 IR 188 at 192ff.
6 *Wanner v Caruana* [1974] 2 NSWLR 301 at 306F.

(9) **Extortionate credit bargains under the Consumer Credit Act 1974**

Further protection against unconscionable dealing is now provided for mortgagors by the Consumer Credit Act 1974, which empowers the court to reopen 'extortionate' credit bargains.[7] The 1974 Act has no application to loans made by a building society or local authority,[8] but does govern loans advanced by banks and finance companies. In its application to mortgages, the legislation tends to direct its focus not upon first mortgages of residential property but upon second mortgages and short-term transactions entered into within the 'fringe area' dominated by non-institutional lenders. Borrowers in this 'fringe area' stand in need of considerable legal protection, being almost by definition the 'poorer risk' borrowers who cannot obtain loan facilities from one of the institutional lenders.

(a) *The court's powers to reopen 'extortionate' credit bargains*

A court which finds a credit bargain 'extortionate' is authorised by section 137(1) of the Consumer Credit Act 1974 to 'reopen the credit agreement so as to do justice between the parties.' Once the Act is invoked by a debtor, the onus is on the creditor to prove that the credit bargain is not 'extortionate'.[9] Unless he can do this, the court may set aside in whole or part any obligation imposed by that bargain on the debtor or may otherwise alter the terms of the agreement.[10]

(b) *Meaning of 'extortionate' bargain*

In terms of section 138(1) of the Act, a credit bargain is 'extortionate if it...requires the debtor or a relative of his to make payments...which are grossly exorbitant, or...otherwise grossly contravenes ordinary principles of fair dealing.'[11] This statutory language has been the subject of some judicial amplification.

(i) *Underlying reality of 'extortionate' bargaining* It has been suggested that although the statutory jurisdiction seems to 'contemplate at least a substantial imbalance in bargaining power of which one party has taken advantage',[12] the word 'extortionate' may not necessarily cover precisely the same conduct as is envisaged under the traditional rubric of 'harsh and unconscionable' dealing.[13] The term 'extortionate' is comprehensively defined in section 138

---

7   The court's power in this respect is not restricted, as is usual under the Consumer Credit Act 1974, to loans of less than £15,000 (see Consumer Credit Act 1974, ss 8(2), 16(7)). See The Consumer Credit (Increase of Monetary Limits) Order 1983 (SI 1983/1878).

8   Consumer Credit Act 1974, s 16(1).

9   Consumer Credit Act 1974, s 171(7).

10   Consumer Credit Act 1974, s 139. A debtor's trustee in bankruptcy may apply for the setting aside or variation of any 'extortionate' credit transaction which the debtor entered into within the three years preceding the commencement of his bankruptcy (Insolvency Act 1986, s 343(2)).

11   See *Davies v Directloans Ltd* [1986] 1 WLR 823 at 836G-837A.

12   *Wills v Wood* [1984] CCLR 7 at 15. Compare the reference to abuse of a 'dominant position' in Article 86 of the Treaty of Rome, and see *Matthew v Bobbins* (1981) 41 P & CR 1 at 7 (post, p 993).

13   See, however, *Castle Phillips Finance Co Ltd v Khan* [1980] CCLR 1 at 3.

itself, and the old authorities on the meaning of 'harsh and unconscionable' conduct may not provide authoritative guidance in this statutory context.[14] At any rate it has been pointed out that the controlling notion in section 138(1) is that of 'extortionate' rather than merely 'unwise' transactions.[15] The borrower certainly cannot be heard to complain in retrospect that he should have been protected from undertaking an imprudent debt.[16]

(ii) Statutory criteria In determining whether a credit bargain is 'extortionate', the court must have regard to such evidence as is adduced concerning 'interest rates prevailing at the time it was made'[17] and to 'any other relevant considerations'.[18] In particular, the court is directed,[19] in relation to the debtor, to have regard to his age, experience, business capacity,[20] state of health, and the degree to which, at the time of making the credit bargain, he was under financial pressure.[1] In relation to the creditor, the court is directed[2] to take account of the degree of risk accepted by him (having regard to the value of any security provided), his relationship with the debtor, and whether or not a colourable cash price was quoted for any goods or services included in the credit bargain.

(c) Judicial treatment of interest rates

Notwithstanding the legislative concern to suppress unfair or oppressive dealing in the area of consumer credit, it is difficult to find any case in which the court has regarded an interest rate as being sufficiently excessive to render a credit bargain 'extortionate' within the meaning of the Act.[3]

---

14 See *Davies v Directloans Ltd* [1986] 1 WLR 823 at 831C-E.
15 *Wills v Wood* [1984] CCLR 7 at 15.
16 *Wills v Wood* [1984] CCLR 7 at 17; *Davies v Directloans Ltd* [1986] 1 WLR 823 at 837H. See also *Williams & Glyn's Bank Ltd v Barnes* (Unreported, Gibson J, 26 March 1980)(post, p 849).
17 Consumer Credit Act 1974, s 138(2)(a). It was finally recognised in *Davies v Directloans Ltd* [1986] 1 WLR 823 at 835D that only the annual percentage rate of interest (APR), calculable from the HMSO's Consumer Credit Tables, gives any indication of the true rate of interest charged, and that this should be the relevant figure for the purpose of section 138(2)(a). An APR of 35 per cent could well be expected in a first mortgage granted by a 'fringe' lender to a borrower unable to raise funds from a bank or building society (see *Davies v Directloans Ltd* [1986] 1 WLR 823 at 836E).
18 Consumer Credit Act 1974, s 138(2)(c).
19 Consumer Credit Act 1974, s 138(3).
20 The fact that both debtor and creditor are experienced and successful businessmen tends to rebut any allegation that their bargain was 'extortionate' (see *Arrowfield Finance v Kosmider* [1984] CCLR 38 at 49).
 1 'Nearly every purchaser who borrows money in order to complete his purchase is under some degree of financial pressure. It is only if the lender takes advantage of the pressure that this factor is...relevant in considering whether the loan is extortionate' (*Davies v Directloans Ltd* [1986] 1 WLR 823 at 832G).
 2 Consumer Credit Act 1974, s 138(4).
 3 For a rare instance, see *Barcabe Ltd v Edwards* [1983] CCLR 11 at 12, where a county court judge thought it '*prima facie* exorbitant' to lend money at a flat rate of 100 per cent, when other similar lenders charged approximately 20 per cent. The APR for the loan in this case was actually 319 per cent, and the court substituted a flat interest rate of 40 per cent (ie, an APR of 92 per cent). Compare the approach adopted in Canada, where an interest rate double that normally obtainable is regarded as prima facie harsh and unconscionable (see *Krocker v Midtown Mortgage & Loans Ltd* (1975) 52 DLR (3d) 286 at 290ff).

(i) Practical application of the statute A. *Ketley Ltd v Scott*[4] provided the first opportunity for the High Court to apply the terms of sections 137-140 of the Consumer Credit Act 1974. In a decision which was to become an important point of reference in this area, Foster J declined to hold that an annual rate of interest of 48 per cent was 'extortionate' in the statutory sense.[5] The defendants had sought a loan from the plaintiff company at very short notice for the purpose of completing a purchase of the flat in which they lived. They signed a number of documents in great haste, including a legal charge for a loan for three months at 12 per cent interest. One of the defendants had already charged the property to secure a bank overdraft, but this fact was not disclosed to the plaintiff in the present transaction. In refusing to grant relief, Foster J had regard not only to this element of deceit[6] but also to the fact that the extraordinary nature and urgency of the transaction justified the imposition of a higher rate of interest than that normally charged by banks and building societies. The defendants had known exactly what they were doing, and had not been subject to real financial pressure. Although already entitled to a protected tenancy in the property, they simply wished to purchase that property at what was a temporary bargain price.[7]

(ii) The judicial dilemma Although no great merit attaches to the conduct of the defendants in A. *Ketley Ltd v Scott*, the facts of the case are typical of the sorts of circumstance which feature in section 137 applications. The borrower is often a person of limited means who by reason of mismanagement or misfortune has rendered himself the victim of his own overweening material ambitions. Typically, such a borrower has already exhausted the patience of institutional lenders in connection with existing loans, and is on the verge of either bankruptcy or repossession of his home. His only remaining hope of averting disaster lies in a further loan or re-mortgaging arrangement with the most shady of lenders.

These circumstances almost inevitably predetermine the conclusion that the borrower represents an exceedingly poor risk, which in turn justifies the exaction of a high rate of interest. Moreover, since the borrower would be uniformly adjudged a poor risk by the few lenders still prepared to deal with him, even a monstrous rate of interest is not discordant with the 'interest rates prevailing' generally at the bottom end of the credit market in relation to borrowers within this risk category. In *Woodstead Finance Ltd v Petrou*,[8] for instance, the defendant had charged her home in order to stave off her

---

4   [1980] CCLR 37. See (1980) 130 NLJ 749 (H.W. Wilkinson).
5   It was later claimed that this decision had laid down a general rule that an interest rate can never be 'extortionate' if it does not exceed 48 per cent. This suggestion was, however, vigorously denied by Dillon LJ in *Castle Phillips Finance Co Ltd v Williams* (Unreported, Court of Appeal, 25 March 1986). The borrower in this case had agreed a bridging loan at 4 per cent per month (ie, at an APR of 67.7), which the Court of Appeal considered quite excessive. Although it did not reopen the transaction, the Court ordered that the conduct of the plaintiff finance company, which Dillon LJ described as 'dishonest', be referred for further action to the Director General of Fair Trading.
6   Deceit or non-disclosure of all relevant facts tends to be fatal to applications for a reopening of a credit bargain (see eg *First National Securities Ltd v Bertrand* [1980] CCLR 5 at 22; *Premier Finance Co v Gravesande* [1985] CCLR 1 at 7).
7   [1980] CCLR 37 at 43f.
8   (1986) *Times*, 23 January.

husband's bankruptcy. Although Browne-Wilkinson V-C confessed that to his 'untutored eye' the interest rate of 42 per cent per annum appeared 'very harsh', it could not be stigmatised as 'extortionate'. In view of the husband's 'appalling record in relation to payments' and given the 'parlous financial condition' of the couple, the loan arrangement and the rate of interest were 'normal for a risk of this kind'. Thus, somewhat ironically, the more desperate and vulnerable the borrower, the more justified is the imposition of a high interest rate, and the less able are the courts to intervene in terms of supposedly protectionist legislation.

(10) The doctrine of undue influence

A limited form of protection is available to mortgagors under the general equitable doctrine that the court may set aside, or decline to enforce, any bargain reached by means of undue influence. It was once thought that the relationship between banker and borrower was apt to raise a presumption of undue influence sufficient to vitiate loan transactions wherever it was clear that the borrower had received no independent advice as to the effect of the transaction on his rights.[9] This broad approach, which flourished during the mid-1970s, placed a heavy reliance on the fashionably continental concept of 'abuse of a dominant position' in the context of an 'inequality of bargaining power' between the parties.[10]

(a) Rejection of the liberal approach

The liberal application of the notion of undue influence was finally rejected in definitive terms by the House of Lords in *National Westminster Bank Plc v Morgan*.[11] Here a husband and wife, as joint owners of their matrimonial home, had signed a charge over that property in favour of the bank in order to secure a short-term loan to tide the husband over a period of financial difficulty. The wife subsequently alleged that the bank manager had exercised undue influence in obtaining her signature during a somewhat 'tense' visit by him to their home. It was clear that both spouses had been desperately anxious not to lose their home, but the House of Lords declined to accept that these circumstances disclosed a true case of undue influence.

In coming to this conclusion, Lord Scarman rooted the concept of undue influence in a 'victimisation of one party by the other.'[12] In order that a plea of undue influence should succeed, he held, the 'wrongfulness' of the transaction must be shown: there must be shown to be a dealing 'in which an unfair advantage has been taken of another.'[13] In Lord Scarman's view, however, the mere relationship of banker and customer is in itself insufficient to introduce any vitiating element of undue influence in the absence of evidence that the transaction concluded by them 'constituted a manifest disadvantage to the

9   This view is often, but somewhat inaccurately, traced back to the judgment delivered by Lord Denning MR in *Lloyds Bank Ltd v Bundy* [1975] QB 326.
10   Ante, p 225. See also *Morrison v Coast Finance Ltd* (1966) 55 DLR (2d) 710 at 713.
11   [1985] AC 686.
12   [1985] AC 686 at 705A, citing *Allcard v Skinner* (1887) 36 Ch D 145 at 182f.
13   [1985] AC 686 at 707B.

party seeking to avoid it, explicable only on the basis that undue influence has been used to procure it.'[14]

On the present facts the claim of undue influence was countered by two circumstances. First, the transaction had not been unfair to the wife.[15] In the context of 'an ordinary banking transaction'—albeit one directed at saving the family home from the hands of creditors—the bank had no duty to ensure that independent legal advice was received by the wife.[16] Second, as the judge at first instance had found, the transaction had not been 'manifestly disadvantageous' to the wife, in that it had 'provided what to her was desperately important, namely the rescue of the house'.[17]

The ruling of the House of Lords in *National Westminster Bank Plc v Morgan* has severely cut back the scope of the doctrine of undue influence, in that the absence of independent advice for the borrower (or indeed for any guarantor) is no longer automatically fatal to the lender's claim to enforce his rights. However, as Oliver LJ added in *Coldunell Ltd v Gallon*,[18] once it is shown that the party in a dominant position has achieved a bargain in itself unconscionable, then that party is 'saddled with the burden of establishing affirmatively that no domination was practised to bring the transaction about—as for instance by demonstrating not merely the availability but the fact of separate and independent advice.'

(b) Restrictive impact of the 'manifest disadvantage' requirement

Subsequent cases have extended *Morgan* to loans advanced by finance companies and other lenders. However, the restrictive impact of the requirement of 'manifest disadvantage' is clearly demonstrated in *Woodstead Finance Ltd v Petrou*.[19] Here Browne-Wilkinson V-C held that the issue of 'manifest disadvantage' must be analysed with reference to the position prevailing at the date of the loan transaction which it was sought to set aside. On this basis he was wholly unable to accede to any plea of undue influence, precisely because the couple's finances at that stage were so overwhelmingly parlous that almost any means of warding off financial disaster would then have seemed preferable to the bankruptcy which for them lay only days away. Far from the loan representing a 'manifest disadvantage' to the borrower, it provided the only remaining straw at which she and her husband could clutch.[20]

(c) Exceptional relief for mortgagors

There exist at least two exceptional kinds of situation where, notwithstanding

14   *Coldunell Ltd v Gallon* [1986] 2 WLR 466 at 474G per Oliver LJ, providing a slightly more elegant version of what was said by Lord Scarman at [1985] AC 686 at 704G-H. See also *Goldsworthy v Brickell* [1987] 2 WLR 133 at 154C.
15   [1985] AC 686 at 709D.
16   [1985] AC 686 at 709D.
17   [1985] AC 686 at 702A.
18   [1986] 2 WLR 466 at 474H. It is clear, however, that the *Morgan* ruling provides no authority for the view that the presumption of undue influence applies only where one party to a transaction has assumed a role of dominating influence over the other (see *Goldsworthy v Brickell* [1987] 2 WLR 133 at 155B-C, 163D-E, 164F-G, 165D-E).
19   (1986) *Times*, 23 January (ante, p 596).
20   Compare *Midland Bank Plc v Phillips* (1986) *The Times*, 28 March.

the ruling in *National Westminster Bank Plc v Morgan*, a mortgagor (or guarantor of a loan) may be granted some form of relief from the strict terms of a loan transaction.

(i) The 'agency' exception It is clear that the courts may refuse to enforce a mortgage transaction where some person who 'could reasonably be expected to have influence over' a prospective mortgagor has acted effectively as an agent for the mortgagee in procuring the due execution of the relevant documents.[1]

In *Kings North Trust Ltd v Bell*[2] the sole legal owner of a matrimonial home had fraudulently misrepresented to his wife the scope and purpose of a secured loan in order to obtain her consent to the mortgage demanded by the lender. The Court of Appeal accepted that at all material times the wife had owned a beneficial interest in the property,[3] and refused to enforce the security against her. The Court held that the mortgagee had failed to ensure that she received independent advice and had simply left it to her husband to extract the required signature from her by any means he chose. Although there is in English law no presumption of undue influence as between husband and wife,[4] Dillon LJ took the view that, in the absence of independent advice, a consent obtained by means of actual undue influence on the husband's part could not be upheld. A principal (however innocent) who instructs an agent to achieve a particular end (eg the signing of a document by a mortgagor-spouse) is liable for any fraudulent misrepresentation made by the agent in achieving that end.[5]

Likewise in *Avon Finance Co Ltd v Bridger*[6] a son dishonestly persuaded his ageing parents to charge their home in order (although they were unaware of the fact) to secure a loan advanced to himself. There is no presumption of undue influence as between a son and his parents,[7] but here the son had been expressly authorised by the mortgagee to procure the execution of the mortgage. Brandon LJ considered the relationship 'between a son in the prime of life and parents in the evening of life' to be clearly 'a relationship in which it should be appreciated that the possibility of influence exists.'[8] In such circumstances the mortgagee was subject to an overriding duty to ensure that the mortgagors received independent legal advice. In default of such advice the Court of Appeal held the security to be unenforceable against the mortgagors where—as was manifestly the case here—their signatures had been induced by the son's undue influence and deception.[9]

1 See *Chaplin & Co Ltd v Brammall* [1908] 1 KB 233 at 237; *Kings North Trust Ltd v Bell* [1986] 1 WLR 119 at 124C, 125A-B.
2 [1986] 1 WLR 119. See [1986] Conv 213 (J.E.M.); (1986) 102 LQR 351.
3 [1986] 1 WLR 119 at 120G.
4 *Bank of Montreal v Stuart* [1911] AC 120 at 137; *Kings North Trust Ltd v Bell* [1986] 1 WLR 119 at 123D-E.
5 [1986] 1 WLR 119 at 124A.
6 [1985] 2 All ER 281.
7 *Coldunell Ltd v Gallon* [1986] 2 WLR 466 at 475A. See (1986) 102 LQR 351.
8 [1985] 2 All ER 281 at 288a.
9 [1985] 2 All ER 281 at 286g. If, however, the unfair pressure emanates from a person to whom the mortgagee has given no such authority, the signatures obtained cannot be set aside on the ground of undue influence. In the absence of any effective agency relationship between the mortgagee and the person who actually procures the execution of the mortgage, the transaction cannot be undone even though it has been induced by thoroughly reprehensible conduct on the part of a self-interested, but wholly unauthorised, intermeddler (see eg *Coldunell Ltd v Gallon* [1986] 2 WLR 466 at 480H-481C; [1986] Conv 213 (J.E.M.); (1986) 102 LQR 351). See also *Midland Bank plc v Perry* (1987) *Times*, 28 May.

(ii) The banker's self-imposed duty of care In *National Westminster Bank Plc v Morgan*[10] Lord Scarman placed particular emphasis on the fact that the bank manager never 'crossed the line' between a normal banking transaction and one in which he 'goes further and advises on more general matters germane to the wisdom of the transaction'. It is probable that a bank has no general duty to explain to a mortgagor or guarantor the effect of a relevant transaction,[11] but this broad proposition is likely to be true only in respect of a bank's dealings with strangers rather than with its existing customers.[12] Thus if, in the *Morgan* situation, a wife is an existing customer and the bank takes it upon itself to explain the legal implications of a mortgage or guarantee which she is required to sign, the bank may become liable to her in damages if it negligently misrepresents the scope or effect of her agreement. In *Cornish v Midland Bank plc*,[13] for instance, the Court of Appeal held a bank liable in negligence where it had failed to inform a wife of the vital fact that, in signing a legal charge in favour of the bank, she was signing an 'all monies' term which covered all future—and potentially unlimited—borrowings by her husband.

8. PROTECTION FOR THE MORTGAGEE

Important policy considerations underlie the legal protection given to mortgagees. In order that the flow of mortgage finance should be sustained, particularly for the purpose of facilitating home purchase, it is essential that certain safeguards and remedies be maintained on behalf of those who lend money on the security of real property.[14] The forms of protection or facility afforded the mortgagee include the following.

(1) Investigation of title by the mortgagee

It is customary for the lender to investigate the title offered by a borrower before taking a mortgage as security for the loan to be advanced.[15] Where a building society lends on an 'acquisition mortgage', it often instructs the purchaser's solicitor to investigate title not merely on behalf of the purchaser but also on behalf of the building society itself.[16]

Although investigation of the borrower's title normally ensures that the mortgagee takes a sound and reliable security, it is clear that lenders will do well to proceed with an abundance of caution. Among the hidden dangers lying in wait for the mortgagee are the following kinds of interest, any of which may diminish or destroy the effective value of the mortgagee's security.

10 [1985] AC 686 at 708G, 709C.
11 See *O'Hara v Allied Irish Banks Ltd* [1985] BCLC 52 at 53.
12 *Cornish v Midland Bank plc* [1985] 3 All ER 513 at 522a.
13 [1985] 3 All ER 513 at 520f-g, 521j.
14 See eg the deference to public policy expressed by Browne-Wilkinson J in *Multiservice Bookbinding Ltd v Marden* [1979] Ch 84 at 104G-H (ante, p 592).
15 On the precise scope of the mortgagee's duty of enquiry, see Chapter 25 (post, p 829).
16 The investigation of title carried out on behalf of the building society is, of course, at the expense of the applicant for the building society loan. The purchaser/mortgagor thus pays the same solicitor twice for doing the same job, once on his own behalf and again on behalf of the building society. It is usual practice for the solicitor to charge a lower fee in respect of the work done for the building society, with the net result that the purchaser/mortgagor pays roughly one-and-one-half times the cost of the job.

(a) Equitable interests of beneficiaries behind a trust for sale

In relation to a mortgage of land which is subject to an implied trust for sale,[17] recent caselaw has introduced a degree of hazard for the mortgagee which was not previously thought to be present. The Law of Property Act 1925 does not provide any authority for the overreaching of equitable interests behind such a trust unless the mortgage funds are duly paid to at least two trustees for sale.[18] Several potential problems arise in this context.

(i) Loan moneys advanced to a sole trustee for sale It is quite possible that land which is vested in the name of one person only may be held on a statutory trust for sale for a number of beneficiaries whose existence is not of course apparent on the face of the legal title. A mortgagee who is unaware that the land offered to him as security is governed by such a statutory trust will be equally unaware of the need to pay two trustees.[19] Being unable to claim the benefit of the statutory provision for overreaching, such a mortgagee stands in danger of losing priority to the equitable interests of beneficiaries behind the trust. This means that in registered land the mortgagee becomes vulnerable to the adverse claims of beneficiaries who at the material time were 'in actual occupation' of the land.[20] In unregistered land the mortgagee may likewise find that he takes his security subject to the rights of beneficiaries of whom he is deemed to have had constructive notice.[1]

The danger that the mortgagee may be bound by prior equitable entitlements becomes particularly acute in the context of the family home. As was said by Lord Denning MR in *Williams & Glyn's Bank Ltd v Boland*,[2] '[a]nyone who lends money on the security of a matrimonial home nowadays ought to realise that the wife may have a share in it.' The only practical solution for the mortgagee in cases of doubt is to ensure that the mortgage is executed by all the co-owners of the land (either legal or equitable) or that he receives a formal disclaimer of priority from all persons in actual occupation of the land (whether the land be held by way of registered or unregistered title).[3]

(ii) Loan moneys advanced to two trustees for sale Of course, if a mortgagee is aware of the existence of a trust for sale, he will clearly insist that the mortgage be executed jointly by the trustees for sale and that they duly give him a receipt in respect of the loan moneys paid over to them. It was long assumed that this procedure would unfailingly entitle the mortgagee to overreach all beneficial interests behind the trust. This expectation was recently challenged in *City of London Building Society v Flegg*,[4] where the Court of Appeal ruled that a mortgage charge granted by two trustees did not necessarily enable the mortgagee to take

---

17 Ante, p 348.
18 Law of Property Act 1925, ss 2(1)(ii), 27(2).
19 See Chapter 12 (ante, p 363) for a description of the way in which an implied (or statutory) trust for sale could easily come into being without anyone being aware of its existence.
20 Land Registration Act 1925, s 70(1)(g). See eg *Williams & Glyn's Bank Ltd v Boland* [1981] AC 487 (post, p 843).
1   See eg *Kingsnorth Finance Co Ltd v Tizard* [1986] 1 WLR 783 at 792H-793A (post, p 842).
2   [1979] Ch 312 at 332G (post, p 849).
3   Even these safeguards may not necessarily guarantee that the mortgagee's priority is altogether beyond challenge (post, p 856).
4   [1986] Ch 605 at 617C-D, 619H-620A (ante, p 384; post, p 861).

free of all adverse claims by beneficiaries. In *Flegg*'s case the Court of Appeal held, somewhat controversially, that a mortgage executed by legal co-owners did not effectively overreach the interests of other beneficiaries who were in actual occupation of the secured property. This decision, which seriously undermined much of the legal protection afforded to mortgagees, was, however, overruled conclusively when the further appeal in *Flegg* came before the House of Lords.[5] The ruling of the House of Lords vindicates the orthodox understanding of the overreaching mechanism in this context, with the result that it is now clear that a dealing by two trustees for sale entitles the mortgagee to take free of the equitable interests of other beneficiaries.

(iii) Loan moneys advanced to a fraudulent trustee for sale A further hazard for the mortgagee of land held on trust for sale lies in the possibility of a wholly fraudulent transaction with regard to a jointly held legal title. Recent developments have demonstrated, however, that the degree of risk for the mortgagee is not now so great as was once feared.

In *First National Securities Ltd v Hegerty*[6] a husband and wife ('H' and 'W' respectively) were joint owners of the legal and equitable interest in a dwelling-house which was held on a statutory trust for sale. H dishonestly obtained a mortgage advance on the security of this property by forging W's signature on an instrument which purported to charge the jointly owned legal estate in favour of the lender. H then left the country with the loan money and, when he defaulted on the mortgage repayments, the mortgagee brought proceedings for payment and applied ex parte for a charging order under the Charging Orders Act 1979.[7]

In these circumstances it was clear that the fraudulently executed charge could have no operation upon the jointly owned legal title in the property, precisely because W had not in fact executed the instrument of charge.[8] Nor could the mortgagee claim to have statutorily overreached the equitable interests belonging to H and W, since there had been no true dealing with two trustees for sale. The forged charge could not affect W's equitable interest behind the trust for sale because she was wholly uninvolved in H's dishonest transaction.[9] However, the abortive legal charge had of course severed any joint tenancy which existed in equity,[10] and the only question remaining was whether that charge could now be seen as enjoying a residual effect against H's severed equitable share.

When roughly the same circumstances had arisen some years previously in *Cedar Holdings Ltd v Green*,[11] the Court of Appeal had decided that the fraudulently executed legal mortgage was not effectual to charge even H's beneficial interest in the property. This ruling was based at least in part on a reluctant application of the equitable doctrine of conversion.[12] Under section

5   [1987] 2 WLR 1266 at 1270A per Lord Templeman, 1276E-1277B per Lord Oliver of Aylmerton. A mortgagee who in good faith advances money to two trustees is statutorily exonerated of any further concern with the propriety or purpose of the mortgage or with the application of the mortgage moneys (Trustee Act 1925, s 17; Law of Property Act 1925, s 27(1)).
6   [1985] QB 850.
7   Post, p 870.
8   [1985] QB 850 at 863A (ante, p 301f).
9   [1985] QB 850 at 863A.
10   [1985] QB 850 at 854B, 862G-H.
11   [1981] Ch 129.
12   Ante, p 369.

63(1) of the Law of Property Act 1925, every conveyance is declared to be 'effectual to pass all the estate, right, title, interest, claim, and demand which the conveying parties respectively have, in, to, or on the property conveyed, or expressed or intended so to be...' In *Cedar Holdings*, the Court of Appeal held that H's interest under the trust for sale of the co-owned property was an interest in proceeds of sale and not in 'the property' purportedly conveyed by the charge, and therefore could not be affected by section 63(1).[13]

This dogmatic approach was not followed in *First National Securities Ltd v Hegerty*. Here Bingham J pointed out that the application of the doctrine of conversion in *Cedar Holdings* had since been explicitly rejected by the House of Lords in *Williams & Glyn's Bank Ltd v Boland*.[14] Bingham J was thus in no doubt that the abortive legal charge was still effective to create a valid equitable charge in favour of the lender in relation to H's beneficial interest in the property.[15] This view was upheld by the Court of Appeal,[16] with the result that the lender was then able to apply successfully for a charging order which conferred locus standi to apply for a sale of the property pursuant to section 30 of the Law of Property Act 1925.[17] A sale, if ordered under this provision, would in effect enable a recovery of the loan money from the cash value of H's share of the proceeds.

(b) Other beneficial interests under trusts and settlements

The problems of the mortgagee are not confined to equitable rights concealed behind an implied trust for sale. Similar difficulties may afflict a lender who advances money on the security of land which is held on a bare trust not disclosed by the paper title.[18] Moreover, if the mortgagee is unaware that the land over which he takes his security is settled under the Settled Land Act 1925, the mortgage may itself be null and void.[19]

(c) Tenancies by estoppel

The mortgagee is also vulnerable to tenancy agreements granted by the mortgagor before he acquired the legal title which has been offered as security. In *Church of England Building Society v Piskor*,[20] the mortgagor had obtained possession of land in advance of the completion of his purchase. During the interim before completion he purported to grant periodic tenancies to two tenants who moved in before the date of the conveyance to the mortgagor. When the mortgagee later sought possession of the property on the ground of

---

13   [1981] Ch 129 at 141E-F, 146C.
14   [1981] AC 487 at 507F-G per Lord Wilberforce.
15   [1985] QB 850 at 854B-C.
16   [1985] QB 850 at 862H-863A.
17   Post, p 876.
18   See eg *Hodgson v Marks* [1971] Ch 892 at 934G (ante, p 185). Here the real loser was the second defendant, the Cheltenham and Gloucester Building Society, which had advanced the purchase moneys to the first defendant, the purchaser. The Court of Appeal was not overly sympathetic towards the building society. Russell LJ observed that 'it is plain that it made no inquiries on the spot save as to repairs; it relied on [the first defendant], who lied to it; and I waste no tears on it' ([1971] Ch 892 at 932B).
19   See eg *Weston v Henshaw* [1950] Ch 510 at 520. Compare, however, *In Re Morgan's Lease* [1972] Ch 1 at 9A-B.
20   [1954] Ch 553.

default by the mortgagor, the Court of Appeal held that the rights of the tenants took priority over the mortgage. The tenancies had been mere 'leases by estoppel' during the period before completion, since the lessor had not yet acquired the legal estate out of which they might be created. However, as soon as the legal estate passed to the mortgagor/lessor on completion, these tenancies automatically became legal tenancies. This metamorphosis occurred during the *scintilla temporis* which in theory intervenes between the passing of the legal estate to the mortgagor and the disposition of mortgage in favour of the lender of the purchase moneys.[1] The rights of the tenants thus crystallised as legal rights in the instant when the 'estoppel was fed' by the conveyance of the legal estate.[2]

(d) Unregistered contractual rights

A mortgagee who takes merely an equitable security over the mortgagor's property faces special difficulties. Whereas a legal mortgagee may ignore contractual rights which should have been protected by registration in the Land Charges Register or in the Land Register but which were not so protected, an equitable mortgagee is much more vulnerable. Thus an equitable mortgagee of unregistered land may be bound by a prior land charge (even if unregistered), on the basis that 'where the equities are equal, the first in time prevails'.

In *McCarthy & Stone Ltd v Julian S. Hodge & Co Ltd*[3] it was held that an unregistered estate contract should take priority over a later equitable mortgagee of the encumbered property, since the latter could not claim the immunity conferred by statute upon a 'purchaser for money or money's worth...of a legal estate in the land'.[4] The effect of the unregistered estate contract therefore turned on an application of the traditional doctrine that where the equities are equal, the first in time prevails. The result would not have been different if the land in question had been held by registered title, since the unprotected contractual right would have acquired protection as an overriding interest provided that the owner of the estate contract was 'in actual occupation' at the date of the equitable mortgage.[5]

(2) Deposit of title documents

Various rules requiring the deposit of title documents afford the legal mortgagee a substantial safeguard against any prejudicial dealings with the legal title by the mortgagor. Section 85(1) of the Law of Property Act 1925 provides that a first mortgagee has a legal right throughout the mortgage term to retain the title deeds pertaining to the mortgaged property. This safeguard is

---

1 Post, p 834.
2 [1954] Ch 553 at 561, 564f. A similar result would have followed if title had been registered, since the tenants would have been protected by Land Registration Act 1925, s 70(1)(g), (k) (ante, pp 175, 174). If, however, the tenants had had a mere contract for a tenancy, their rights in unregistered land would have depended on the registration of a Class C(iv) land charge, and, in registered land, on the existence of 'actual occupation' for the purpose of Land Registration Act 1925, s 70(1)(g).
3 [1971] 1 WLR 1547 at 1555D. See [1972A] CLJ 34 (P.B. Fairest).
4 See Land Charges Act 1972, s 4(6) (ante, p 115).
5 Ante, p 181.

available, of course, only to a mortgagee of unregistered land. However, much the same effect is achieved in the context of registered land by section 65 of the Land Registration Act 1925, which requires that the mortgagor's land certificate be deposited in the Land Registry until redemption of the mortgage.[6]

A second mortgagee of unregistered land obviously cannot enjoy the same security of deposit of the title deeds. However, in unregistered land a second mortgage may be protected as a Class C(i) land charge (if the mortgage is legal),[7] and as a Class C(iii) land charge (if the mortgage takes the form of an equitable charge).[8] In registered land the problem of protecting the second chargee is alleviated by the fact that the relevant land certificate is retained by the Land Registry while any charge remains registered against the title.[9]

Apart from restraining prejudicial dealings by the mortgagor, the practice of depositing title documents with the mortgagee of unregistered land facilitates any later exercise of the mortgagee's power of sale. Should that power ever become exercisable,[10] he is already equipped with the necessary documents of title for the purpose of dealing with third parties.

9. THE MORTGAGEE'S RIGHT TO POSSESSION

The English law of mortgage arms the mortgagee with a number of important rights and remedies by way of safeguard against the possibility of default by his mortgagor. Crucial in this context is the right of the mortgagee to enter into possession of the mortgaged land. This right has been the subject of some controversy, since it impinges perhaps more directly than any other right of the mortgagee upon the security of tenure enjoyed by the mortgagor, whether he be the owner of residential or commercial property.

(1) Origin of the legal mortgagee's right to possession

A legal mortgage confers on the mortgagee a legal estate in the mortgaged property,[11] and a legal charge is statutorily deemed to have an equivalent effect.[12] It is established doctrine in the English law of mortgage that, as an incident of this estate in the land, the mortgagee has 'an unqualified right to possession of the mortgaged property.'[13] This right to possession arises as soon as the mortgage is made and is not dependent on any default by the mortgagor.

---

6   Ante, p 193. The mortgagor has a statutory right to inspect and make copies (at his own expense) of the title documents in the custody or power of the mortgagee (Law of Property Act 1925, s 96(1)). This right cannot be excluded by contract. On redemption of a mortgage, the mortgagee must hand the title deeds over either to the mortgagor or to the next mortgagee (see Law of Property Act 1925, s 96(2)).
7   Ante, p 134.
8   Ante, p 134.
9   Land Registration Act 1925, s 65.
10   Post, p 614.
11   Law of Property Act 1925, ss 85(1), 86(1) (ante, p 573).
12   Law of Property Act 1925, s 87(1) (ante, p 573).
13   *Mobil Oil Co Ltd v Rawlinson* (1982) 43 P & CR 221 at 223 per Nourse J. See [1982] Conv 453 (P. Jackson); (1983) 133 NLJ 247 (H.W. Wilkinson).

As Harman J graphically pointed out in *Four-Maids Ltd v Dudley Marshall (Properties) Ltd*,[14] the mortgagee 'may go into possession before the ink is dry on the mortgage unless there is something in the contract, express or by implication, whereby he has contracted himself out of that right.'[15] Moreover, a mortgagor who resists his mortgagee's demand for possession automatically becomes a trespasser,[16] and, in the absence of any relevant statutory restriction, the mortgagee is then entitled to make a peaceable entry without the necessity of first obtaining a court possession order.[17]

(2) Exclusion of the mortgagee's right to possession

The mortgagee's inherent right to enter into possession may be negatived either by statutory restrictions[18] or by mortgage terms which expressly or impliedly reserve the right of possession to the mortgagor instead.[19]

(a) Express exclusion

It is not uncommon, for instance, that a building society mortgage should expressly grant the mortgagor a right of possession until default. It has been held that such a mortgage term constitutes an implied exclusion of the mortgagee's right to possession before default occurs.[20]

(b) Implied exclusion

It is also possible that the mortgagee's right to possession may be excluded by implication from the terms and attendant circumstances of the mortgage transaction.

(i) Instalment mortgages In *Esso Petroleum Co Ltd v Alstonbridge Properties Ltd*[1] Walton J accepted that the court will be particularly ready to find an implied term in an instalment mortgage that the mortgagor is to be entitled to remain in possession against the mortgagee unless he makes some default in payment of

---

14   [1957] Ch 317 at 320. See (1957) 73 LQR 300 (R.E.M.).
15   See also *Alliance Perpetual Building Society v Belrum Investments Ltd* [1957] 1 WLR 720 at 723.
16   *Birch v Wright* (1786) 1 TR 378 at 383, 99 ER 1148 at 1152; *Jolly v Arbuthnot* (1859) 4 De G & J 224 at 236, 45 ER 87 at 92.
17   See *McPhail v Persons (Names Unknown)* [1973] Ch 447 at 456D-457B (post, p 756). In strict terms there is no general requirement of legal process prior to the exercise of peaceable entry by a mortgagee who wishes to assert his paramount right to possession. However, there is always a danger that such entry may generate criminal liability under the Protection from Eviction Act 1977, s 1 (post, p 955) or the Criminal Law Act 1977, s 6(1) (post, p 756), and in practice it is highly unusual for a mortgagee to resort to peaceable entry without the benefit of a court possession order. There is also some question whether section 36 of the Administration of Justice Act 1970 has impliedly inserted a requirement of due legal process in relation to residential mortgages (post, p 893).
18   Post, p 892.
19   *Doe d Roylance v Lightfoot* (1841) 8 M & W 553 at 564f, 151 ER 1158 at 1163. Where the mortgagee's right to possession has been excluded by contract, an injunction may be granted to restrain the mortgagee from going into possession in breach of his contract (*Doe d Parsley v Day* (1842) 2 QB 147 at 156, 114 ER 58 at 62).
20   *Birmingham Citizens Permanent Building Society v Caunt* [1962] Ch 883 at 890.
1   [1975] 1 WLR 1474.

one of the instalments. Walton J added, however, that 'there must be something upon which to hang such a conclusion in the mortgage other than the mere fact that it is an instalment mortgage.'[2]

(ii) Other mortgages The tenor of Walton J's cautionary remark is borne out in other cases in which the courts have proved somewhat slow to find that the right to possession has been impliedly reserved to the mortgagor rather than the mortgagee.[3] In *Western Bank Ltd v Schindler*[4] the defendant mortgagor had borrowed £32,000 from the plaintiff mortgagee on the terms of an endowment mortgage which provided that no payment of capital or interest was contractually due until ten years after the date of execution of the mortgage. Notwithstanding the absence of any financial default by the mortgagor, the mortgagee subsequently claimed a right to possession *within* the ten year period, in order to preserve the value of the security. The Court of Appeal unanimously upheld the mortgagee's claim to possession in these circumstances.[5]

The Court was unwilling to accept the argument that a contractual term excluding this right should normally be implied 'if and for so long as the terms of the mortgage preclude the mortgagee from making immediate demand for payment or otherwise immediately enforcing his security.' Buckley LJ agreed that the fact that a mortgage was an instalment mortgage might make it easier for a court to find such an implied term, but held that even this fact would not be conclusive.[6] In the present case the mortgagee's right to possession was not lightly to be held to have been excluded by implication, since only this right could effectively protect the mortgagee's legitimate interest in ensuring that at the redemption date the property would still represent a good security for a substantial debt of capital and interest. As Scarman LJ pointed out, the only way in which the mortgagee could ultimately guarantee that the mortgaged property was properly managed and maintained, and the value of the security preserved throughout the loan term, was if the court upheld the mortgagee's claim to possession in the absence of a clear contractual exclusion of that right.[7]

(c) Attornment clauses

The *attornment clause* provides a nowadays somewhat unusual means of excluding the mortgagee's right to possession. It used to be common practice to insert in deeds of mortgage an attornment clause which had the result of creating a purely nominal landlord-tenant relationship between the parties to the mortgage.[8] Under an attornment clause the mortgagor holds effectively as a tenant of the mortgagee, and the object of the clause is to make available to

---

2   [1975] 1 WLR 1474 at 1484B.
3   See R.J. Smith, [1979] Conv 266 at 268ff.
4   [1977] Ch 1. See (1977) 40 MLR 356 (C. Harpum).
5   [1977] Ch 1 at 16A, 19G, 26F.
6   [1977] Ch 1 at 10C-D.
7   'So far from implying a term excluding the common law right, I would expect, as a matter of business efficacy, that the mortgagee would in these circumstances require its retention' ([1977] Ch 1 at 17F).
8   The rent payable under the tenancy was often a purely nominal rent such as the 2½p stipulated for in *Peckham Mutual Building Society v Registe* (1981) 42 P & CR 186 at 188.

the mortgagee the additional possessory remedies open to the landlord.[9] There is, however, one respect in which the inclusion of an attornment clause significantly qualifies the mortgagee's right to enter into possession. Precisely because a notional tenancy is created between mortgagor and mortgagee, the latter is required to terminate the tenancy by serving a notice to quit as a necessary preliminary to any exercise of the right to possession.[10]

The attornment clause does not, however, confer on a residential mortgagor any of the other forms of protection afforded tenants under the Rent Act legislation.[11] The mortgagor is not, for instance, entitled to the minimum period of four weeks' notice to quit which is generally applicable in the area of residential lettings.[12] In *Alliance Building Society v Pinwill*[13] Vaisey J held that the statutory requirement of a minimum period of notice protects only 'a real tenant against a real landlord under a real "residential letting"'.[14] The insertion of an attornment clause in a mortgage is now somewhat rare.[15]

(3) Exercise of the mortgagee's right to possession

It is now widely accepted that a legal mortgagee is entitled to go into possession of the mortgaged property even in the absence of default by the mortgagor and even though the date fixed for redemption has not yet passed. Entry into physical occupation is impossible only where the land is subject to a lease which is binding on the mortgagee either because it was created prior to the mortgage[16] or because it was created thereafter with the mortgagee's consent.[17] However, in such cases the mortgagee may assume 'possession' in the sense of the right to receive the rents and profits due under the relevant lease.[18]

It is nevertheless extremely rare in practice for a mortgagee to exercise his right to go into possession during the currency of a mortgage. There is in general a 'tacit agreement' between mortgagor and mortgagee that possession should be exercised de facto by the mortgagor in all cases except those of actual

---

9   'Notwithstanding the *contra proferentem* principle of construction, I cannot believe that it was intended by the draftsman that the attornment clause should in any way benefit the mortgagor' (*City Mutual Life Assurance Society Ltd v Lance Creek Meat Works Pty Ltd* [1976] VR 1 at 11).

10   *Hinckley and Country Building Society v Henny* [1953] 1 WLR 352 at 355.

11   Post, p 961.

12   See *Peckham Mutual Building Society v Registe* (1981) 42 P & CR 186 at 188f.

13   [1958] Ch 788 at 792.

14   Compare, however, P.B. Fairest, op cit, p 89, who points out that the landlord-tenant relationship created by the attornment clause has a 'quite surprising reality' in other contexts.

15   See Wurtzburg and Mills, *Building Society Law* (14th edn, London 1976), p 184f.

16   A prior legal lease would thus be binding (ante, p 85).

17   See *Rogers v Humphreys* (1835) 4 Ad & E 299 at 313, 111 ER 799 at 804; *In re Ind Coope & Co Ltd* [1911] 2 Ch 223 at 231. However, the mortgagee is not bound by leases granted by the mortgagor after the execution of the mortgage which were not authorised by statute or by the mortgagee himself (*Rogers v Humphreys* (1835) 4 Ad & E 299 at 313, 111 ER 799 at 804; *Dudley and District Benefit Building Society v Emerson* [1949] Ch 707 at 714). The mortgagee himself may grant new leases (see *Chapman v Smith* [1907] 2 Ch 97 at 102), although such lessees are of course subject to the mortgagor's equity of redemption. See also Law of Property Act 1925, s 99(2).

18   *Moss v Gallimore* (1779) 1 Doug 279 at 283, 99 ER 182 at 184. See Law of Property Act 1925, s 205(1)(xix) (ante, p 433). The tenant may be directed to pay his rent henceforth to the mortgagee rather than to the mortgagor (*Horlock v Smith* (1842) 6 Jur 478).

default.[19] While this tacit consent continues to operate, the mortgagor's possessory status has been described as effectively that of a tenant at sufferance.[20] However, he is under no duty to account for any rents and profits derived from the land,[1] and is liable for waste only if the land ceases by reason of his waste to constitute an adequate security for the mortgage debt.[2]

(a) Factors inhibiting actual exercise of the mortgagee's right

The principal object of most mortgages is that the mortgagor should remain in occupation of the land which forms the subject matter of the security.[3] Indeed, it is not going too far to say that, apart perhaps from the exceptional circumstances typified in *Western Bank Ltd v Schindler*,[4] a mortgagee will never nowadays seek possession unless a default has already occurred. Several factors have conduced to this result.

(i) Statutory control over residential property In the residential context the exercise of the mortgagee's right to possession has become subject to an important measure of statutory control. The court now has a discretion under section 36 of the Administration of Justice Act 1970 to regulate the recovery of possession by the mortgagee where there appears to be a realistic possibility that the mortgagor may remedy his default within a reasonable period of time.[5]

(ii) Mortgagee's strict liability to account A mortgagee who goes into possession of the mortgaged property becomes subject to the particularly stringent control of equity in his dealings with the property.[6] If, while in possession, he intercepts the rents and profits drawn from the land in order to ensure the payments due to him under the mortgage, he is liable to account strictly to the mortgagor for any income which he thus receives.[7] Furthermore, the mortgagee may not derive any profit other than the return of the principal and interest stipulated for in the terms of the mortgage.[8]

The mortgagee's duties are rendered even more onerous by the fact that he is liable on the footing of 'wilful default'.[9] In consequence he must account to the

---

19 See *Moss v Gallimore* (1779) 1 Doug 279 at 283, 99 ER 182 at 184; *Christophers v Sparke* (1820) 2 Jac & W 223 at 235, 37 ER 612 at 617. See also B. Rudden, (1961) 25 Conv (NS) 278.
20 See *Green v Burns* (1879) 6 LR Ir 173 at 176 per Palles CB; *Fairclough v Marshall* (1878) 4 Ex D 37 at 48.
1 *Ex parte Calwell* (1828) 1 Mol 259; *Campion v Palmer* [1896] 2 IR 445 at 455ff.
2 *King v Smith* (1843) 2 Hare 239 at 243f, 67 ER 99 at 101f; *Harper v Aplin* (1886) 54 LT 383 at 384.
3 See eg *Four-Maids Ltd v Dudley Marshall (Properties) Ltd* [1957] Ch 317 at 321, where Harman J made the point that building societies 'are not desirous of going into possession, nor would they do business if they were able to go into possession whenever they liked. The whole object of building societies is to maintain the householder in possession of his house so long as he pays the instalments to the society...'
4 [1977] Ch 1 (ante, p 607).
5 Post, p 891. See also Housing Act 1985, Sch 17, para 1(2), (3).
6 *Robertson v Norris* (1859) 1 Giff 428 at 436, 65 ER 986 at 989.
7 *Lord Trimleston v Hamill* (1810) 1 Ball & B 377 at 385. See H.E. Markson, (1979) 129 NLJ 334.
8 For instance, a mortgagee in possession may not (even by an express mortgage term) impose any charge for his management of the land, since this would be to usurp the function of a receiver (*Comyns v Comyns* (1871) 5 IR Eq 583 at 587f).
9 *Lord Trimleston v Hamill* (1810) 1 Ball & B 377 at 385; *Sloane v Mahon* (1838) 1 Dr & Wal 189 at 192, 195; *Mobil Oil Co Ltd v Rawlinson* (1982) 43 P & CR 221 at 224.

mortgagor not only in respect of any rents and profits actually received, but also in respect of that income which he would have received if he had managed the property with 'due diligence'.[10] Thus in *White v City of London Brewery Co*[11] a mortgagee who entered into possession and let the mortgaged property as a 'tied' public house (for the benefit of his own brewery business) was held liable to account for the greater rents which he would have received had he let the property as a 'free' house.[12] If the mortgagee himself goes into personal occupation of the property, he is chargeable with the best occupation rent obtainable on the open rental market in respect of those premises.[13]

The net result of these stringent rules is that if the mortgagee's primary concern is with the income derived from the mortgaged land, his objectives are in general much better served through the exercise of his statutory power to appoint a receiver[14] than by entry into possession subject to the strict control of equity in the matter of accounting. The handling of rents and profits by a receiver is not subject to the same rigorous surveillance of equity.[15]

(b) Does the mortgagee have a right or merely access to a remedy?

In practice the mortgagee who nowadays exercises his right to possession is not concerned to attach the income drawn from the land, but rather to obtain vacant possession of the property in order that he may sell on the open market and thereby recoup the outstanding loan moneys. Thus possession is almost invariably sought as a preliminary to the mortgagee's exercise of his statutory power of sale.[16]

It follows that in practice a mortgagee hardly ever seeks to go into possession unless and until there is some default by the mortgagor, because it is only at this point that the mortgagee's statutory power of sale becomes exercisable.[17] Since the taking of possession has now become effectively 'an adjunct of the power of sale',[18] it has been questioned whether the mortgagee's right to possession would not be described more accurately in terms of access to a remedy rather than in terms of an absolute and inherent right. As a right which technically subsists from the date of the mortgage, it is in most cases a profoundly misleading fiction. It can be argued that the terminology of remedy is distinctly more appropriate, since in reality the mortgagee's inherent right to possession lies dormant in all situations except those in which the mortgagee's security is threatened by an actual default on the part of his mortgagor.

---

10   See *Chaplin v Young* (No 1) (1864) 33 Beav 330 at 337f, 55 ER 395 at 398.
11   (1889) 42 Ch D 237 at 249.
12   Similarly, a mortgagee in possession is liable to account for the notional rent of property which he has allowed to remain unoccupied and for due rent which he has failed without good cause to recover from his tenants (*Noyes v Pollock* (1886) 32 Ch D 53 at 61).
13   *Metcalf v Campion* (1828) 1 Mol 238 at 239; *Marriott v Anchor Reversionary Co* (1861) 3 De GF & J 177 at 193, 45 ER 846 at 852. If, however, there is no realistic evidence that the property could have been let out profitably, this rental value may be nil, in which case the mortgagee is not guilty of wilful default (see eg *Fyfe v Smith* [1975] 2 NSWLR 408 at 413F-414A).
14   Law of Property Act 1925, s 101(1)(iii) (post, p 627).
15   *Refuge Assurance Co Ltd v Pearlberg* [1938] Ch 687 at 691f.
16   See *Mobil Oil Co Ltd v Rawlinson* (1982) 43 P & CR 221 at 224.
17   Post, p 614.
18   See R.J. Smith, [1979] Conv 266.

(i) Brief emergence of the remedial perspective The remedial perspective received reinforcement from the decision of the Court of Appeal in *Quennell v Maltby.*[19] Here the owner of a house in fee simple mortgaged the property to a bank by way of security for his bank overdraft. Although the mortgage contained a prohibition against any lettings of the property without the bank's consent,[20] the owner made an unauthorised letting of the house to two university students. On the expiry of the contractual period of the letting, the owner wished to sell the property with vacant possession on the open market, but the tenants claimed to be statutory tenants and refused to leave. The owner then unsuccessfully requested the bank to assert possession of the property *qua mortgagee.* He managed, however, to persuade his own wife to pay off the moneys owing to the bank, and in consequence the bank transferred its mortgage over the property to the wife. It was she who brought the present action for possession against the two students, claiming that as mortgagee she had an absolute right to take possession.

The entire course of dealings involved here smacked heavily of collusion, and not surprisingly perhaps the Court of Appeal declined to allow the protective effect of the Rent Act to be frustrated by an evasive device. It was plain that the owner would not have been entitled to evict the tenants had he sought possession under the Rent Act. Lord Denning MR pointed out that to allow the owner's wife to achieve in the present proceedings an objective which he could not have achieved in Rent Act proceedings would open the way to widespread evasion of the Rent Acts.[1]

Lord Denning noted that the wife's action for possession was not motivated by any desire to enforce the security or to obtain repayment of the loan moneys. She had brought the present action 'simply for an ulterior purpose of getting possession of the house, contrary to the intention of Parliament, as expressed in the Rent Acts.'[2] Lord Denning therefore suggested that 'in modern times equity can step in so as to prevent a mortgagee, or a transferee from him, from getting possession of a house contrary to the justice of the case.'[3] Thus a mortgagee would be restrained by the court from getting possession 'except where it is sought bona fide and reasonably for the purpose of enforcing the security and then only subject to such conditions as the court thinks fit to impose.'[4] In the present case the ulterior object of the transaction had been to enable the owner and his wife to obtain possession of their home 'in order to resell it at a profit.' In these circumstances the Court of Appeal held that the mortgagee's claim to possession should not be enforced.

(ii) Return to the right-based approach Although the result attained by the Court of Appeal in *Quennell v Maltby* did admirable justice on the facts of the case,[5] the excessively broad sweep of Lord Denning's judgment is at variance with the

---

19 [1979] 1 WLR 318. See [1979] CLJ 257 (R.A. Pearce).
20 A mortgagor normally has a statutory power of leasing (see Law of Property Act 1925, s 99).
 1 [1979] 1 WLR 318 at 322C-D.
 2 [1979] 1 WLR 318 at 323C. On the operation of the Rent Acts, see Chapter 29 (post, p 961).
 3 [1979] 1 WLR 318 at 322G-H.
 4 [1979] 1 WLR 318 at 322H.
 5 Bridge and Templeman LJJ favoured an alternative basis for reaching the same result, ie, that the wife was in substance suing as an agent of her husband (see [1979] 1 WLR 318 at 323E, 324F).

conventional understanding that, contractual agreement apart, a mortgagee has an absolute right to possession from the commencement of the mortgage term.[6] Lord Denning treated the mortgagee's right to possession effectively as a remedy dependent on the equity of the case rather than as an original and inherent right. It seems almost certain that this approach does not represent good law, not least because it renders otiose the protection afforded the mortgagor under section 36 of the Administration of Justice Act 1970.[7] Moreover, there has been a return in the recent caselaw to the orthodox view that the mortgagee has a right to possession ab initio,[8] regardless of any default[9] and regardless even of the existence of a counterclaim by the mortgagor for a sum which exceeds the mortgage debt.[10] The better view nowadays therefore seems to be that the mortgagee's right to possession is more appropriately conceptualised as a paramount right rather than as a discretionary remedy.[11]

(4) Does the equitable mortgagee have a right to possession?

Much more doubt surrounds the question whether an equitable mortgagee or equitable chargee has an inherent right to possession similar to that enjoyed by the legal mortgagee.[12] The latter's right to possession is, of course, an incident of the legal estate which is created by the mortgage itself or implied on his behalf by statute.[13] In consequence it seems unlikely that, in the absence of some express conferment by the terms of the mortgage, a right of possession can be claimed by a mere equitable mortgagee or chargee unless and until such a right has been granted by a court.[14]

It is sometimes suggested that the doctrine in *Walsh v Lonsdale*,[15] by drawing an analogy between legal and equitable rights, has the indirect effect of conferring a right of possession upon even the equitable mortgagee,[16] but the weight of judicial authority runs counter to this assertion.[17] It is clear, however,

6   'A Court of Equity never interferes to prevent the Mortgagee from assuming the possession' (*Marquis Cholmondeley v Lord Clinton* (1817) 2 Mer 171 at 359, 35 ER 905 at 976). See F.W. Maitland, *Equity* (2nd edn London 1936), p 186, where it is pointed out that equity would never interfere with a claim to possession at common law except on terms of payment off of the whole principal, interest and costs, an equity which Maitland described as a 'mock equity', since it required payment in full and implied the termination of the mortgagor-mortgagee relationship itself.
7   See R.J. Smith, [1979] Conv 266 at 268.
8   *Barclays Bank Plc v Tennet* (Unreported, Court of Appeal, 6 June 1984); *National Westminster Bank Plc v Jones* (Unreported, Court of Appeal, 3 December 1984).
9   *Mobil Oil Co Ltd v Rawlinson* (1982) 43 P & CR 221 at 223f.
10   See *Barclays Bank Plc v Tennet* (Unreported, Court of Appeal, 6 June 1984), following *Samuel Keller (Holdings) Ltd v Martins Bank Ltd* [1971] 1 WLR 43 at 47H-48B, 51C-D.
11   See *Park v Brady* [1976] 2 NSWLR 329 at 335E.
12   See H.W.R. Wade, (1955) 71 LQR 204.
13   Law of Property Act 1925, s 87(1) (ante, pp 573, 605).
14   See *Barclays Bank Ltd v Bird* [1954] Ch 274 at 280; *Royal Bank of Canada v Nicholson* (1980) 110 DLR (3d) 763 at 765f. The absence of a right to possession carries the further implication that the equitable mortgagee has no inherent right to receive the rents and profits derived from the land (*Finck v Tranter* [1905] 1 KB 427 at 429; *Vacuum Oil Co Ltd v Ellis* [1914] 1 KB 693 at 703, 708).
15   Ante, p 471.
16   See *Antrim County Land, Building, and Investment Co Ltd v Stewart* [1904] 2 IR 357 at 364 per Palles CB.
17   See eg *Ladup Ltd v Williams & Glyn's Bank Plc* [1985] 1 WLR 851 at 855B.

that even if the equitable mortgagee or chargee has no automatic right of possession, either may nevertheless apply to the court for an order putting him into possession.[18]

10. REMEDIES AVAILABLE TO THE LEGAL MORTGAGEE

In the event of default under a legal mortgage the mortgagee has available to him a number of remedies which operate directly against the mortgagor.[19] These remedies are in general concurrent and cumulative, and include the following.

(1) Action on the mortgagor's personal covenant to repay

Since the mortgage transaction is ultimately rooted in a contract of loan, it remains open to the mortgagee to sue the mortgagor on his personal covenant to repay the mortgage loan and interest.[20] The mortgagee cannot take action on the mortgagor's covenant before the legal redemption date stipulated by the mortgage,[1] but even a sale of the mortgaged property pursuant to his power of sale does not preclude the mortgagee from suing on the mortgagor's covenant in respect of any remaining financial loss.[2] The mortgagee is entitled only to simple interest upon any interest left in arrears, unless the mortgage contained an agreement (either expressly or by necessary implication) for the payment of compound interest.[3]

The recovery of arrears of interest is statute-barred six years after becoming due,[4] and the recovery of the mortgage principal is statute-barred after the expiration of twelve years from the date when the right to receive that money accrued.[5]

---

18   The court has power under section 90(1) of the Law of Property Act 1925 to vest a legal estate in the mortgagee sufficient to enable him to assume possession (see *Ladup Ltd v Williams & Glyn's Bank Plc* [1985] 1 WLR 851 at 855B-C). The court also has an inherent jurisdiction to put an equitable mortgagee in possession (see *Re O'Neill* [1967] NI 129 at 135).

19   He may also have remedies against third parties. If, for instance, the mortgagor of a leasehold term causes his lease to become forfeit by reason of his default, the mortgagee may have access to the inherent equitable jurisdiction of the court for relief against forfeiture (ante, p 508).

20   In practice most institutional lenders are reluctant to increase the (perhaps temporary) financial difficulties of hard-pressed borrowers by suing on the personal covenant for repayment. The remedy of sale is always available if these difficulties cannot be resolved within a reasonable period.

1   *Bolton v Buckenham* [1891] 1 QB 278 at 281f; *Sinton v Dooley* [1910] 2 IR 162 at 165.

2   *Rudge v Richens* (1873) LR 8 CP 358 at 361f; *Schoole v Sall* (1803) 1 Sch & Lef 176.

3   *Ex parte Bevan* (1803) 9 Ves 223 at 224, 32 ER 588; *Fergusson v Fyffe* (1841) 8 Cl & F 121 at 141, 8 ER 49 at 57; *Daniell v Sinclair* (1881) 6 App Cas 181 at 189f; *Deutsche Bank v Banque des Marchands de Moscou* (1931) 4 LDAB 293; *Domaschenz v Standfield Properties Pty Ltd* (1977) 17 SASR 56 at 61.

4   Limitation Act 1980, s 20(5). This limitation does not apply, however, if the mortgagor seeks to redeem the mortgage either in redemption proceedings (*Elvy v Norwood* (1852) 5 De G & Sm 240 at 243, 64 ER 1099 at 1100; *Holmes v Cowcher* [1970] 1 WLR 834 at 836G) or in foreclosure proceedings brought by the mortgagee (*Dingle v Coppen* [1899] 1 Ch 726 at 746). There is likewise no limitation on the arrears of interest which may be recouped from the proceeds of sale received by a mortgagee who exercises his statutory power to sell the mortgaged property (see *Holmes v Cowcher* [1970] 1 WLR 834 at 837G).

5   Limitation Act 1980, s 20(1).

(2) Exercise of the power of sale

The most usual remedy invoked by the mortgagee in the event of serious default by his mortgagor is the exercise of the mortgagee's power of sale. Since vacant possession is almost inevitably an essential condition of a good sale price, the exercise of this power of sale is normally preceded by the mortgagee's recovery of possession of the mortgaged property.

(a) When the power of sale arises

The mortgagee has no common law power of sale over mortgaged property. An express power of sale is sometimes conferred by the terms of the mortgage deed, but a similar power is now supplied in any event by the provisions of the Law of Property Act 1925.[6] Under section 101 the mortgagee's statutory power of sale *arises* if three conditions are satisfied. *First*, the mortgage in question must have been effected by deed.[7] *Second*, the mortgage money must have become due.[8] Thus the mortgagee's power of sale may arise if the legal date for redemption has passed or even if any instalment of the mortgage money has become due under an instalment mortgage.[9] *Third*, the mortgage must itself contain no expression of contrary intention which would have the effect of precluding a power of sale in the foregoing circumstances.[10]

Section 101 of the Law of Property Act 1925 operates as a filter to section 103. If the conditions of section 101 are met, the mortgagee may proceed to exercise his power of sale in terms of section 103.

(b) When the power of sale becomes exercisable

Whereas three cumulative conditions must be satisfied in order that the mortgagee's statutory power of sale should *arise*, that power becomes *exercisable* only if the mortgagee can show that any one of three conditions specified in section 103 of the Law of Property Act 1925 has been met.

(i) The three conditions In the absence of an express power of sale conferred by the mortgage instrument itself, the mortgagee may not exercise his statutory power of sale unless and until *either* the mortgagor has been in default for three months following the service upon him of a notice requiring payment of the mortgage money,[11] *or* some interest under the mortgage has remained unpaid for two months after becoming due,[12] *or* there has been a breach of some mortgage term 'other than and besides a covenant for the payment of mortgage money or interest thereon.'[13]

---

6 The scope of the mortgagee's power of sale and the circumstances of its exercise may, of course, be varied or extended by the express terms of the mortgage deed (Law of Property Act 1925, s 101(3)).
7 Law of Property Act 1925, s 101(1).
8 Law of Property Act 1925, s 101(1)(i).
9 *Payne v Cardiff RDC* [1932] 1 KB 241 at 251, 253.
10 Law of Property Act 1925, s 101(4).
11 Law of Property Act 1925, s 103(i).
12 Law of Property Act 1925, s 103(ii).
13 Law of Property Act 1925, s 103(iii).

If any one of these conditions is satisfied, the mortgagee has statutory authority to proceed with a sale of part or all of the mortgaged property.[14] Unlike the remedy of foreclosure,[15] the exercise of the mortgagee's power of sale does not require the sanction or leave of any court. Even though he is not personally invested with the mortgagor's estate, the mortgagee is statutorily clothed with full power to give a conveyance of this estate freed from all property rights over which the mortgage had priority, but subject of course to those rights which themselves rank prior to the mortgage.[16] The Law of Property Act 1925 in effect confers on the mortgagee a power of compulsory sale over a title which does not belong to him at law.[17]

(ii) Premature sale It is important to distinguish between the point in time at which the power of sale arises and that at which it becomes exercisable. The mortgagee has no power at all to sell until the statutory power arises. If he purports to sell the property in advance of this date, the premature transaction transfers to the purchaser merely those rights which the mortgagee enjoyed qua mortgagee, and is entirely ineffective to pass the mortgagor's legal estate.

More doubt surrounds the effect of a sale by a mortgagee in whose favour the statutory power of sale has arisen but has not yet become exercisable. The purchaser's title is statutorily declared to be unimpeachable,[18] although such a sale clearly exposes the selling mortgagee to an action in damages brought by the mortgagor.[19] It seems, however, that the purchaser cannot claim any immunity under statute if at the time of the sale he had actual notice that the power of sale was not exercisable or that there was some other impropriety in the sale.[20] Thus the purchaser may be prejudicially affected, for instance, by actual notice that at the date of the sale the mortgagor was not in fact in default of his interest payments under the mortgage. It is doubtful that the purchaser can be bound by merely constructive notice of irregularities in the matter of sale,[1] although in *Bailey v Barnes*[2] Stirling J warned that the purchaser must not 'wilfully shut his eyes and abstain from making inquiries which might have led to a knowledge of impropriety or irregularity'.

(c) Effect of sale by the mortgagee

Where a mortgagee sells under his statutory or express power of sale, his

---

14   Law of Property Act 1925, s 101(1)(i).
15   Post, p 628.
16   Law of Property Act 1925, s 104(1).
17   Law of Property Act 1925, ss 88(1), 89(1). The mortgagee's sale is not a transaction 'by which the mortgagor, through the medium of an agent, is disposing of his own property. It is one by which his property is being divested from him' (*Forsyth v Blundell* (1972-1973) 129 CLR 477 at 500).
18   Law of Property Act 1925, s 104(2).
19   Law of Property Act 1925, s 104(2).
20   *Lord Waring v London and Manchester Assurance Co Ltd* [1935] Ch 310 at 318. To uphold such a purchaser's title would be 'to convert the provisions of the statute into an instrument of fraud' (*Bailey v Barnes* [1894] 1 Ch 25 at 30). Likewise a good title may not be asserted by a purchaser who had actual knowledge of an irregularity in the mortgagee's exercise of an express (as distinct from statutory) power of sale (*Selwyn v Garfit* (1888) 38 Ch D 273 at 280).
1   Indeed section 104(2) of the Law of Property Act 1925 seems to release the purchaser from any concern 'to see or inquire' whether the mortgagee has properly exercised his power of sale. See, however, the critical view expressed by P.B. Fairest, op cit, 95f.
2   [1894] 1 Ch 25 at 30.

conveyance is effective to vest in the purchaser the mortgagor's full legal estate (whether freehold or leasehold), subject to any legal mortgage which has priority to that of the selling mortgagee.[3] The conveyance otherwise operates to confer on the purchaser a good legal title, enabling him to overreach all interests which are capable of being overreached (eg subsequent mortgages, the selling mortgagee's mortgage and the mortgagor's equity of redemption).[4]

In particular it seems that the purchaser, having once taken his conveyance from the selling mortgagee, is unaffected by any estate contract entered into by the mortgagor during the course of the mortgage term. In *Duke v Robson*[5] a mortgagor had contracted to sell his estate to P^1 for £25,000 and P^1 had quite properly registered this transaction as a Class C(iv) land charge.[6] Before this contract was completed, the relevant mortgagee purported to exercise its statutory power of sale by contracting to sell the mortgaged estate to a different purchaser, P^2, for £45,000 (see *Fig.* 44). The Court of Appeal refused to restrain the completion of the latter contract. The Court affirmed Plowman J's view at first instance that, while the mortgage remained unredeemed, all that the mortgagor could contract to sell was his equity of redemption.[7] This equity of redemption, together with P^1's interest in it by virtue of his registered estate contract, was clearly liable to be overreached by a conveyance in pursuance of the mortgagee's paramount power of sale.[8]

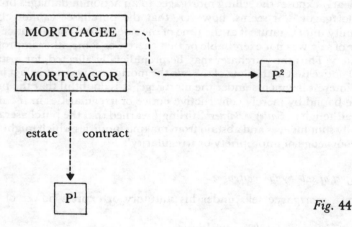

Fig. 44

This solution is now mirrored in the context of the identical problem in registered land. In *Lyus v Prowsa Developments Ltd*[9] Dillon J took the view that the purchaser from the mortgagee would take free of the mortgagor's contractual

---

3   Law of Property Act 1925, ss 88(1), 89(1).
4   Law of Property Act 1925, ss 2(1)(iii), 88(1)(b), 89(1)(b).
5   [1973] 1 WLR 267. See (1973) 37 Conv (NS) 210 (F.R. Crane).
6   Ante, p 135.
7   [1973] 1 WLR 267 at 271D-F.
8   [1973] 1 WLR 267 at 275B-C. Russell LJ (at 275F-H) left open the possibility that P^1, who had the prospect of re-selling the property for £60,000, would be able to formulate a claim in damages against the mortgagor on the ground of his inability to convey the property free from incumbrances for the contractual price of £25,000!
9   [1982] 1 WLR 1044 at 1047G-1048A (ante, p 284).

commitment to sell, even though this contract had been duly protected against the mortgagor as an estate contract and even though the mortgagee had actually consented at the time to the mortgagor's dealing with a stranger.[10] In the registered land context this result is dictated even more definitively by section 34(4) of the Land Registration Act 1925, which stipulates that, on the completion of the mortgagee's sale by registration, his charge 'and all incumbrances and entries inferior thereto shall be cancelled.'

Upon the exercise of the mortgagee's power of sale, the mortgagor's equity of redemption is extinguished,[11] and he can bring no complaint against the mortgagee except where it can be shown that the power of sale was exercised in an improper, harsh or oppressive manner.[12]

(d) Absence of any statutory standard of fair dealing

In recent years some controversy has surrounded the nature of the duties imposed by law on the mortgagee who acts in exercise of his power of sale. The Law of Property Act 1925 clearly envisages that some exercises of the power of sale may be improper or irregular.[13] However, it may perhaps reflect the latent capitalist emphasis of the 1925 legislation that, except in relation to the application of the proceeds of the sale, this statute does not expressly impose any specific ethical standard or code of conduct on the selling mortgagee.[14] It has been left to the courts to supply an implication that the mortgagee must fulfil certain expectations of equity in his exercise of the power of sale.[15]

(e) Mortgagee's duty in relation to the application of proceeds

On the exercise of his power of sale the mortgagee is statutorily rendered a trustee of the resulting proceeds of sale. The application of these proceeds is governed by section 105 of the Law of Property Act 1925, which directs that the proceeds should be held in trust by the mortgagee, to be applied *first*, in payment of all costs, charges and expenses properly incurred by him in connection with the sale; *second*, in discharge of the mortgage money and interest due under his mortgage; and *third*, in payment of the residue to the mortgagor.

---

10 The actual decision in this case turned on a quite different point involving the law of constructive trusts (ante, p 268).

11 In strict terms the statutory power is exercised as soon as the mortgagee contracts to sell the property. In the absence of some form of equitable fraud by the mortgagee (post, p 626), the mortgagor is from this point onwards disabled from redeeming the mortgage. He cannot frustrate the contracted sale by a belated payment of the moneys due under the mortgage (see *Lord Waring v London and Manchester Assurance Co Ltd* [1935] Ch 310 at 318; *Property & Bloodstock Ltd v Emerton* [1968] Ch 94 at 114F-115B; *Forsyth v Blundell* (1972-1973) 129 CLR 477 at 499).

12 The court has an inherent jurisdiction to restrain the improper or oppressive exercise of the mortgagee's power of sale (see *Clark v National Mutual Life Association of Australasia Ltd* [1966] NZLR 196 at 197).

13 See Law of Property Act 1925, s 104(2).

14 Compare eg Victoria's Transfer of Land Act 1958 (No 6399), s 77(1); Queensland's Property Law Act 1974, s 85(1).

15 See *Henry Roach (Petroleum) Pty Ltd v Credit House (Vic) Pty Ltd* [1976] VR 309 at 312.

(f) General duty of the selling mortgagee

Although a selling mortgagee thus becomes a trustee of the proceeds of sale, it is commonly said that he is not in strict terms a trustee of the power of sale itself.[16] This power is given to him, not for the benefit of another, but 'for his own benefit, to enable him the better to realise his debt.'[17] It is clear that the exercise of the power of sale is not a fiduciary exercise,[18] and the mortgagee has 'rights of his own which he is entitled to exercise adversely to the mortgagor.'[19] However, as Cross LJ pointed out in *Cuckmere Brick Co Ltd v Mutual Finance Ltd,*[20] the position of the selling mortgagee is at least 'ambiguous', since it is equally clear that he must 'pay some regard to the interests of the mortgagor when he comes to exercise the power.' The law of mortgage thus holds somewhat inscrutably that, in exercising his power of sale, the mortgagee is entitled to give first, but not exclusive, consideration to his own interests.[1]

There has been much difference of opinion as to the proper balance to be maintained between the respective interests of the mortgagor and mortgagee. Assessed purely in terms of immediate financial self-interest, the mortgagee's only concern in sale is to obtain with speed and efficiency a sufficient price to cover the amount of his outstanding loan. However, a sale which satisfied only this minimal purpose would almost always inflict grave prejudice on the mortgagor, since any sale at an undervalue erodes the effective value of his equity of redemption. A sale price which is adequate to meet only the costs of the sale and the outstanding mortgage moneys leaves no surplus at all for the mortgagor.

The ambiguity of the mortgagee's position was for a long time reflected in the divergent and sometimes inconsistent criteria applied by the courts in determining the propriety of a mortgagee's exercise of his power of sale.[2] It now seems clear, however, that the conduct of the selling mortgagee is to be judged with reference to two criteria, one subjective in nature and the other objective. The mortgagee must act in good faith; he must also discharge a duty of reasonable care towards his mortgagor. The mortgagor has a valid ground for complaint if either of these criteria has not been met.

(i) Subjective criterion of good faith   There is an elementary requirement of good faith in the exercise of the mortgagee's power of sale. This subjective criterion demands that the mortgagee should not deal 'wilfully and recklessly...with the property in such a manner that the interests of the mortgagor are sacrificed'.[3]

Equity's traditionally heavy emphasis on this requirement of good faith at first led the courts to deny that mere carelessness in the matter of sale could ever

---

16   *Cuckmere Brick Co Ltd v Mutual Finance Ltd* [1971] Ch 949 at 965F; *Frost Ltd v Ralph* (1981) 115 DLR (3d) 612 at 622; *Commercial and General Acceptance Ltd v Nixon* (1981-82) 38 ALR 225 at 226, 233, 243.
17   *Warner v Jacob* (1882) 20 Ch D 220 at 224 per Kay J.
18   See Paul Finn, *Fiduciary Obligations* (Sydney 1977), p 10.
19   *Farrar v Farrars Ltd* (1888) 40 Ch D 395 at 411.
20   [1971] Ch 949 at 969F.
1   See *Palmer v Barclays Bank Ltd* (1972) 23 P & CR 30 at 35; *Henry Roach (Petroleum) Pty Ltd v Credit House (Vic) Pty Ltd* [1976] VR 309 at 313.
2   *Cuckmere Brick Co Ltd v Mutual Finance Ltd* [1971] Ch 949 at 966B.
3   *Kennedy v De Trafford* [1897] AC 180 at 185 per Lord Herschell. See also *Barns v Queensland National Bank Ltd* (1906) 3 CLR 925 at 942f; *Pendlebury v Colonial Mutual Life Assurance Society Ltd* (1912) 13 CLR 676 at 680, 694, 700.

be a ground of liability for the mortgagee.[4] Thus it used to be thought that the mortgagee's only obligation to the mortgagor was simply 'not to cheat him'.[5] According to this earlier view, the court would not interfere 'even though the sale be very disadvantageous', unless the sale price was 'so low as in itself to be evidence of fraud' or there was evidence of 'corruption or collusion with the purchaser'.[6]

It is an interesting feature of the recent development of the law of mortgage throughout the common law world that there has been a general rejection of the idea that the subjective requirement of good faith stands alone as the exclusive criterion of the mortgagee's conduct. It now seems clear that his behaviour must also measure up to an objective standard of reasonableness.[7]

(ii) Objective criterion of reasonable behaviour There have always been isolated statements in the caselaw that the selling mortgagee should 'behave...as a reasonable man would behave in the realisation of his own property, so that the mortgagor may receive credit for the fair value of the property sold.'[8] These statements have gathered force in recent years, and it has come to be increasingly held that the mortgagee is indeed answerable for negligence in the conduct of the sale.[9] He cannot exercise his power of sale arbitrarily, but must 'act in a prudent and business-like manner, with a view to obtain as large a price as may fairly and reasonably, with due diligence and attention, be under the circumstances obtainable.'[10] The injection of this objective criterion of reasonableness has done much to elevate the standard of dealing required of the mortgagee.

(iii) Fusion of subjective and objective criteria The conduct nowadays expected of the selling mortgagee involves a fusion of subjective and objective elements, and requires that the mortgagee should practise not only good faith but also reasonable care. As Salmon LJ said in *Cuckmere Brick Co Ltd v Mutual Finance Ltd*,[11] the mortgagee 'owes both duties'.[12] These two duties may well interact one with another. In the Australian High Court in *Forsyth v Blundell*,[13] Menzies J likewise expressed the view that to 'take reasonable precautions to obtain a proper price is but part of the duty to act in good faith.'[14] This blending of concepts ensures that the legitimate primacy of the mortgagee's self-interest is not inconsistent with 'having regard to the interests of others or with taking reasonable care to protect the interests of others.'[15]

4   *Pendlebury v Colonial Mutual Life Assurance Society Ltd* (1912) 13 CLR 676 at 700; *British Columbia Land & Investment Agency v Ishitaka* (1911) 45 SCR 302 at 317.
5   *Cuckmere Brick Co Ltd v Mutual Finance Ltd* [1971] Ch 949 at 966B per Salmon LJ.
6   *Warner v Jacob* (1882) 20 Ch D 220 at 224.
7   See *Goldcell Nominees Pty Ltd v Network Finance Ltd* [1983] 2 VR 257 at 262.
8   *McHugh v Union Bank of Canada* [1913] AC 299 at 311.
9   *Holohan v Friends' Provident and Century Life Office* [1966] IR 1 at 21ff, 25.
10 See *Matthie v Edwards* (1846) 2 Coll 465 at 480, 63 ER 817 at 824.
11 [1971] Ch 949 at 966C.
12 It is significant that as long ago as *Farrar v Farrars Ltd* (1888) 40 Ch D 395 at 411, Lindley LJ had ruled that the mortgagor had no redress provided the mortgagee 'acts bona fide and takes reasonable precautions to obtain a proper price'.
13 (1972-1973) 129 CLR 477 at 481.
14 See eg *Frost Ltd v Ralph* (1981) 115 DLR (3d) 612 at 617, where the mortgagee's precipitate action, in selling at an undervalue one day after the mortgagor failed to redeem, constituted not only a lack of reasonable care on the mortgagee's part, but also strong evidence of mala fides.
15 *Henry Roach (Petroleum) Pty Ltd v Credit House (Vic) Pty Ltd* [1976] VR 309 at 313.

The twin concepts of good faith and reasonable care make their presence felt in the contemporary caselaw in differing ways and with differing results. The objective requirement of reasonable care has tended to generate a negligence liability in damages in respect of any financial loss caused by the careless exercise of a mortgagee's power of sale. The force of the subjective requirement of good faith has been demonstrated primarily in relation to conflicts of interest affecting the mortgagee and in the willingness of the courts to set aside sales transacted in the face of any such conflict. It may be easier here to deal first with the requirement of reasonable care.

(g) Mortgagee's duty of objectively reasonable care

The objective requirement of reasonable care has come to exert an impact on much of the mortgagee's conduct in the exercise of his power of sale, most noticeably in relation to the price achieved by the sale.

(i) Sale price Building society mortgagees have long been subject to a statutory duty to take 'reasonable care to ensure' that the price achieved on the exercise of their power of sale is 'the best price that can reasonably be obtained'.[16] Likewise a local authority mortgagee, on exercising its right to vest mortgaged property in itself,[17] must account to the mortgagor for the 'value of the house at the time of the vesting'.[18] This value is statutorily deemed to be the price which the interest vested in the authority would realise if the house, freed of the relevant incumbrance, were 'sold on the open market by a willing vendor'.[19]

It is also clear that other kinds of mortgagee nowadays owe some duty of care at common law in respect of the price at which the mortgaged property is ultimately realised.[20] This duty of care is owed not only to the mortgagor himself,[1] but also to any guarantor of the mortgage loan.[2] The mortgagee's duty is moreover non-delegable,[3] with the result that the mortgagee is not relieved from his responsibility merely because he entrusts the sale of the mortgaged property to an apparently competent or experienced agent.[4] In

16   See now Building Societies Act 1986, s 13(7), Sch 4, para 1(1)(a), (2). See also *Reliance Permanent Building Society v Harwood-Stamper* [1944] Ch 362 at 372ff.

17   Post, p 624.

18   Housing Act 1985, Sch 17, para 3(1)(a).

19   Housing Act 1985, Sch 17, para 3(2).

20   This duty of care is premised on the 'neighbour' principle adumbrated by Lord Atkin in *Donoghue v Stevenson* [1932] AC 562 at 580, and has been rationalised with reference to the 'proximity' existing between the mortgagee and the mortgagor (and his guarantor if any). See *Cuckmere Brick Co Ltd v Mutual Finance Ltd* [1971] Ch 949 at 966D; *Standard Chartered Bank Ltd v Walker* [1982] 1 WLR 1410 at 1415F-G.

1   See *Johnson v Ribbins* (1975) 235 Estates Gazette 757 at 759; *Standard Chartered Bank Ltd v Walker* [1982] 1 WLR 1410 at 1415E-G; *Clark v UDC Finance Ltd* [1985] 2 NZLR 636 at 638f.

2   *Standard Chartered Bank Ltd v Walker* [1982] 1 WLR 1410 at 1415E-G; *American Express International Banking Corpn Ltd v Hurley* [1985] 3 All ER 564 at 571f.

3   *Wolff v Vanderzee* (1869) 20 LT 353 at 354; *Tomlin v Luce* (1889) 41 Ch D 573 at 575f, (1889) 43 Ch D 191 at 194; *Cuckmere Brick Co Ltd v Mutual Finance Ltd* [1971] Ch 949 at 973A. See also *ANZ Banking Group Ltd v Bangadilly Pastoral Co Pty Ltd* (1978) 19 ALR 519 at 540.

4   See *Commercial and General Acceptance Ltd v Nixon* (1981-82) 38 ALR 225 at 227, 233, 237, 248. The non-delegable responsibility of the mortgagee is unaffected by the probability nowadays that the injured mortgagor has a valid claim in negligence directly against the mortgagee's agent (see *Cuckmere Brick Co Ltd v Mutual Finance Ltd* [1971] Ch 949 at 973C- E; *Commercial and General Acceptance Ltd v Nixon* (1981-82) 38 ALR 225 at 234f, 243).

Cuckmere Brick Co Ltd v Mutual Finance Ltd,[5] Salmon LJ described the duty of the selling mortgagee as comprising a responsibility to 'take reasonable precautions to obtain the true market value of the mortgaged property at the date on which he decides to sell it.'[6] The mortgagee is not entitled to adopt *any* arrangement or accept *any* price merely because it will see him paid out.[7] He has no right to sacrifice the interest of the mortgagor (or indeed of subsequent mortgagees) in the surplus of the proceeds of the sale.[8]

Whether a mortgagor has discharged his duty of care is a question of fact in each case.[9] In *Cuckmere Brick Co Ltd v Mutual Finance Ltd,*[10] for instance, a mortgagee realised the mortgaged property through sale by auction. Although informed expressly of a relevant (but fairly complex) planning permission relating to the property, the mortgagee failed to make adequate reference in the auction advertisements to the full extent of the permission. In consequence the land was sold at an undervalue, and the Court of Appeal held that the mortgagee was liable in damages to the mortgagor for breach of the duty of care which it owed to the latter.[11] There is, however, no necessary inference of negligence if, as in *Palmer v Barclays Bank Ltd,*[12] the mortgagee and his agent had never been informed by the mortgagor of the availability of any planning permission and were therefore wholly unaware of its existence.[13]

(ii) Timing of the sale It is orthodox law that once his power of sale has accrued, the mortgagee is entitled to exercise it for his own purposes whenever he chooses to do so.[14] In *Cuckmere Brick Co Ltd v Mutual Finance Ltd*[15] Salmon LJ

5   [1971] Ch 949 at 968H-969A.
6   Salmon LJ preferred not to refer to the concepts of 'proper price' (which was 'perhaps a little nebulous') or 'best price' (which 'might suggest an exceptionally high price'). See also *Standard Chartered Bank Ltd v Walker* [1982] 1 WLR 1410 at 1415E per Lord Denning MR; *Predeth v Castle Phillips Finance Co Ltd* (1986) 279 Estates Gazette 1355 at 1356.
7   *Henry Roach (Petroleum) Pty Ltd v Credit House (Vic) Pty Ltd* [1976] VR 309 at 313. See eg *Frost Ltd v Ralph* (1981) 115 DLR (3d) 612 at 617, 622; *Forsyth v Blundell* (1972- 1973) 129 CLR 477 at 510.
8   *Commercial and General Acceptance Ltd v Nixon* (1981-82) 38 ALR 225 at 226, 243. There is some suspicion that the decision of both the Court of Appeal and the House of Lords in *Williams & Glyn's Bank Ltd v Boland* [1981] AC 487, [1979] Ch 312 (ante, p 372, post, p 843) may have been influenced by the bank mortgagee's fairly ruthless sale for £1,500 of a part of the secured property which was probably worth in the region of £22,500 (see (1978) 36 P & CR 448 at 451).
9   The content of this duty of care does not vary in proportion to the degree of experience possessed by the mortgagee as vendor. In other words the same standard of care is demanded of the small investor as of the institutional lender (see *Commercial and General Acceptance Ltd v Nixon* (1981-82) 38 ALR 225 at 233).
10   [1971] Ch 949. See (1971) 87 LQR 303.
11   Compare *Bank of Cyprus (London) Ltd v Gill* [1980] 2 Lloyds Rep 51 at 54. See (1982) 132 NLJ 883 (H.W. Wilkinson). See also *Predeth v Castle Phillips Finance Co Ltd* (1986) 279 Estates Gazette 1355 at 1358f, where the Court of Appeal held that there had been a want of reasonable care where the mortgagee authorised a 'crash sale' of the mortgaged property (see [1986] Conv 442 (M.P. Thompson)).
12   (1972) 23 P & CR 30 at 36.
13   It could be argued, however, that the mortgagee's failure to advertise a relevant planning permission is largely negatived by the fact that any serious prospective purchaser would normally discover the existence of the planning permission on requisitioning a local authority search (see *Goldcell Nominees Pty Ltd v Network Finance Ltd* [1983] 2 VR 257 at 277f).
14   It is, of course, clear that a mortgagee who takes possession of a security with a view to selling it must account to the mortgagor for any loss occurring through his (or his agent's) negligence in dealing with the property between the date of his taking possession and the date of the sale (*Commercial and General Acceptance Ltd v Nixon* (1981-82) 38 ALR 225 at 242). See eg *Norwich General Trust v Grierson* [1984] CLY 2306.
15   [1971] Ch 949 at 965G.

thought that it 'matters not that the moment may be unpropitious and that by waiting a higher price may be obtained.'[16] It was his view that the mortgagee 'has a right to realise his security by turning it into money when he likes.'[17]

It seems likely, however, that the mortgagee's prerogative to determine the date of sale is now coloured by his overriding duty to exercise reasonable care in the matter of sale. In *Standard Chartered Bank Ltd v Walker*,[18] Lord Denning MR acknowledged the existence of dicta to the effect that a mortgagee may determine the timing of sale quite arbitrarily. He observed that these dicta did not necessarily imply that a mortgagee 'can sell at the worst possible time. It is at least arguable that, in choosing the time, he must exercise a reasonable degree of care.'[19]

(iii) Other preliminaries or modalities of the sale The mortgagee's duty to afford reasonable protection for the interests of his mortgagor imposes on him a duty of care in relation to other preliminaries or modalities of the sale. In organising the sale the mortgagee must act in the same way as would a 'prudent vendor' who wishes to sell property belonging to himself.[20] The mortgagee must, for example, take reasonable steps to ascertain the value of the property before sale.[1] He must also make a reasonable effort to bring the proposed sale to the attention of all persons likely to be interested.[2] There is, for instance, a want of due care where the mortgagee fails to follow up the possibility of a higher price, knowing that a prospective purchaser is prepared to pay more than an existing offer.[3] Where there are two or more interested potential purchasers, they must be brought into competition with each other so as to obtain the highest price sustainable by the available market.[4] Whether the sale is by public auction or private treaty, the mortgagee must bring to the notice of interested parties the 'potentiality of the property to be sold'.[5] The mortgagee is under no strict duty

---

16   See also *Davey v Durrant* (1857) 1 De G & J 535 at 553, 44 ER 830 at 838; *Farrar v Farrars Ltd* (1888) 40 Ch D 395 at 398, 411; *Barns v Queensland National Bank Ltd* (1906) 3 CLR 925 at 942; *Tse Kwong Lam v Wong Chit Sen* [1983] 1 WLR 1349 at 1355B, 1359F-G; *Predeth v Castle Phillips Finance Co Ltd* (1986) 279 Estates Gazette 1355 at 1356.

17   Nor has the mortgagor any valid complaint if the mortgagee, by threatening to exercise his statutory power of sale, pressurises the mortgagor into selling the mortgaged property at an unfavourable time (*Page v Barclays Bank Ltd* (Unreported, Court of Appeal, 1979 P 3253, 14 July 1980)).

18   [1982] 1 WLR 1410 at 1415G.

19   See the test of negligence applied in *Bank of Cyprus (London) Ltd v Gill* [1980] 2 Lloyds Rep 51 at 54, where the Court of Appeal approved a decision by Lloyd J that, although the mortgagee was not obliged to wait on a rising market or for a market to recover, he must nevertheless take proper steps to secure the best price available at the time in question.

20   *Tse Kwong Lam v Wong Chit Sen* [1983] 1 WLR 1349 at 1359G-H; *Commercial and General Acceptance Ltd v Nixon* (1981-82) 38 ALR 225 at 233. This criterion certainly represents a tightening up of standards when compared with earlier cases (see eg *British Columbia Land & Investment Agency v Ishitaka* (1911) 45 SCR 302 at 317 per Duff J).

1   *Pendlebury v Colonial Mutual Life Assurance Society Ltd* (1912) 13 CLR 676 at 683; *Henry Roach (Petroleum) Pty Ltd v Credit House (Vic) Pty Ltd* [1976] VR 309 at 313; *Frost Ltd v Ralph* (1981) 115 DLR (3d) 612 at 617; *Tse Kwong Lam v Wong Chit Sen* [1983] 1 WLR 1349 at 1357H-1358A.

2   *Henry Roach (Petroleum) Pty Ltd v Credit House (Vic) Pty Ltd* [1976] VR 309 at 313. In *Davey v Durrant* (1857) 1 De G & J 535 at 560, 44 ER 830 at 840, Knight Bruce LJ was not prepared to hold that a mortgagee can never accept a fair offer from a private buyer until he has advertised the property for sale.

3   *ANZ Banking Group Ltd v Bangadilly Pastoral Co Pty Ltd* (1978) 19 ALR 519 at 544f.

4   *Forsyth v Blundell* (1972-1973) 129 CLR 477 at 509.

5   *Henry Roach (Petroleum) Pty Ltd v Credit House (Vic) Pty Ltd* [1976] VR 309 at 313.

to consult either the mortgagor or other mortgagees as to a proposed sale, but a failure to do so may in some circumstances point to a lack of good faith on his part.[6]

(iv) Sales by auction Although the mortgagee may have a duty to seek expert advice as to the method of sale,[7] there is no legal obligation to hold a sale by auction.[8] Indeed sale by public auction rather than by private treaty does not in itself prove the validity of a transaction,[9] particularly since an auction which produces only one bid obviously provides no guarantee that a true market value has been achieved.[10] The mortgagee commits no breach of his duty of care merely because prior to auction he sells the property privately without first informing the mortgagor.[11] In some cases it may be entirely consistent with the discharge of his duty that he should accept a suitably high pre-emptive bid made by a private purchaser who wishes to 'kill' the sale and withdraw the property from auction.[12]

If, however, the mortgagee chooses to sell by public auction, he has a non-delegable duty[13] to ensure that the auction is preceded by appropriate advertisement.[14] The mortgagee may be exposed to a claim in damages for negligence if a relevant newspaper advertisement was carried only once,[15] or allowed only a minimal lead time before the auction date,[16] or was hidden 'in the middle of a mixed grill of auction advertisements' ranging from sales of china and bric-à-brac to old furniture and power tools.[17] The mortgagee may also be liable for negligence if he sells properties of widely differing types and attractions in one block.[18]

The mortgagee's duty of care also renders him vicariously liable for the actual conduct of the auction sale. The precise date chosen for the day of auction may reflect prejudicially upon the price achieved on sale.[19] A reserve

---

6   *Goldcell Nominees Pty Ltd v Network Finance Ltd* [1983] 2 VR 257 at 272, 278. See also *ANZ Banking Group Ltd v Bangadilly Pastoral Co Pty Ltd* (1978) 19 ALR 519 at 523, 546.

7   *Tse Kwong Lam v Wong Chit Sen* [1983] 1 WLR 1349 at 1357H, 1359G.

8   *Frost Ltd v Ralph* (1981) 115 DLR (3d) 612 at 624.

9   *Tse Kwong Lam v Wong Chit Sen* [1983] 1 WLR 1349 at 1355G.

10 *Tse Kwong Lam v Wong Chit Sen* [1983] 1 WLR 1349 at 1356H-1357A. See also *ANZ Banking Group Ltd v Bangadilly Pastoral Co Pty Ltd* (1978) 19 ALR 519 at 544, where 'there was in truth only one bidder' at the auction.

11 *Davey v Durrant* (1857) 1 De G & J 535 at 560, 44 ER 830 at 840; *Goldcell Nominees Pty Ltd v Network Finance Ltd* [1983] 2 VR 257 at 262. Such a sale may, however, indicate bad faith if the mortgagee had earlier undertaken to consult the mortgagor over any proposal to transact a private sale in advance of the auction (see *Goldcell Nominees Pty Ltd v Network Finance Ltd* [1983] 2 VR 257 at 278).

12 *Johnson v Ribbins* (1975) 235 Estates Gazette 757 at 761.

13 *Commercial and General Acceptance Ltd v Nixon* (1981-82) 38 ALR 225 (ante, p 620).

14 *Pendlebury v Colonial Mutual Life Assurance Society Ltd* (1912) 13 CLR 676 at 683ff; *Henry Roach (Petroleum) Pty Ltd v Credit House (Vic) Pty Ltd* [1976] VR 309 at 313; *Commercial and General Acceptance Ltd v Nixon* (1981-82) 38 ALR 225 at 231.

15 *Commercial and General Acceptance Ltd v Nixon* (1981-82) 38 ALR 225 at 226, 231. It was crucial here that the mortgagee failed to ensure that the advertisement appeared in the Wednesday edition of a daily newspaper which was the normal forum for each week's auction advertisements of real estate (see [1980] Qd R 153 at 156C).

16 *Commercial and General Acceptance Ltd v Nixon* (1981-82) 38 ALR 225 at 226, 231, [1980] Qd R 153 at 156B-C (two days). See also *ANZ Banking Group Ltd v Bangadilly Pastoral Co Pty Ltd* (1978) 19 ALR 519 at 523, 545.

17 *Nixon v Commercial and General Acceptance Ltd* [1980] Qd R 153 at 156C-D.

18 *Aldrich v Canada Permanent Loan & Savings Co* (1897) 24 OAR 193 at 194, 197f.

19 See eg *ANZ Banking Group Ltd v Bangadilly Pastoral Co Pty Ltd* (1978) 19 ALR 519 at 523, 545 (auction two days before Christmas).

price should be set with the benefit of expert advice,[20] and the auctioneer informed of that price well before the commencement of the auction.[1] It may well be a breach of the mortgagee's duty if details of the reserve price are disclosed to any individual prospective purchaser in advance of the auction,[2] or indeed are announced at the auction itself to all the potential bidders collectively.[3]

(h) Mortgagee's duty of subjective good faith

The impact of the mortgagee's duty of good faith is nowadays most obviously apparent in the courts' response to cases where there is a potential conflict between the interest of the mortgagee as vendor in obtaining the highest price and some collateral interest of the mortgagee in achieving a lower price for the purchaser. As Jacobs J observed in *ANZ Banking Group Ltd v Bangadilly Pastoral Co Pty Ltd*,[4] the requirement of bona fides in a mortgagor 'is concerned with a genuine primary desire to obtain for the mortgaged property the best price obtainable consistently with the right of a mortgagee to realise his security.' This goal is obviously jeopardised where the mortgagee either consciously or unconsciously grants preferment to a conflicting commercial interest on the part of the purchaser, and the closer the association between mortgagee and purchaser, the less likely is the court to allow the transaction of sale to stand. The 'legitimate purpose' of the mortgagee's power of sale is to secure repayment of the mortgage money, and if the mortgagee 'uses the power for another purpose...or to serve the purposes of other individuals...the Court considers that to be a fraud in the exercise of the power'.[5]

Conflicts of interest affecting the mortgagee tend to arise in two slightly different categories of circumstance.

(i) Sale to the mortgagee or to his representative The first category of case comprises circumstances in which any purported sale by the mortgagee is simply void and ineffective. It is quite clear, for instance, that the mortgagee cannot, in exercise of his power of sale, effect a valid sale of the mortgaged property either to himself alone or to himself and others.[6] A sale by a person to himself 'is no sale at all',[7] even though the sale price be the full value of the mortgaged property.[8]

20   *Tse Kwong Lam v Wong Chit Sen* [1983] 1 WLR 1349 at 1357H.
1   *Tse Kwong Lam v Wong Chit Sen* [1983] 1 WLR 1349 at 1358A, where Lord Templeman indicated that a want of due care may be present if the auctioneer is not instructed to do more than 'put the property under the hammer'. Such a procedure 'may be appropriate to the sale of second hand furniture but is not necessarily conducive to the attainment of the best price for freehold or leasehold property'.
2   *Goldcell Nominees Pty Ltd v Network Finance Ltd* [1983] 2 VR 257 at 263, 278. See also *Tse Kwong Lam v Wong Chit Sen* [1983] 1 WLR 1349 at 1358C.
3   *Industrial Enterprises Inc v Schelstraete* (1975) 54 DLR (3d) 260 at 274.
4   (1978) 19 ALR 519 at 522 (High Court of Australia).
5   *Robertson v Norris* (1858) 1 Giff 421 at 424f, 65 ER 983 at 984 per Stuart V-C.
6   *Martinson v Clowes* (1882) 21 Ch D 857 at 860; *ANZ Banking Group Ltd v Bangadilly Pastoral Co Pty Ltd* (1978) 19 ALR 519 at 542. Some jurisdictions confer on the mortgagee a specific statutory authority to buy in at auction (see eg New Brunswick's Property Act (RSNB 1952, c 177), s 42(1)(a); *Traders Group Ltd v Mason* (1975) 53 DLR (3d) 103 at 117).
7   *Farrar v Farrars Ltd* (1888) 40 Ch D 395 at 409 per Lindley LJ. An important exception to this principle is provided by Housing Act 1985, Sch 17, para 1(1), which allows a local authority mortgagee to vest in itself by deed any house in respect of which it is entitled to exercise a power of sale. This relaxation of the normal rule is subject both to the leave of the county court and to a statutory scheme of compensation and accounting to the mortgagor (ante, p 620).
8   *Farrar v Farrars Ltd* (1888) 40 Ch D 395 at 409.

Precisely the same fate awaits any attempt to sell the mortgaged property to a trustee for the mortgagee,[9] or to the mortgagee's solicitor[10] or other agent.[11]

(ii) Sale to an associated person A more flexible view is taken of a mortgagee's sale to a less closely associated person or entity such as a business acquaintance or a company in which the mortgagee is himself a shareholder. Such a transaction is not necessarily ineffective, but the normal onus of proof is reversed and a burden rests on the mortgagee to demonstrate positively that his 'desire to obtain the best price was given absolute preference over any desire that an associate should obtain a good bargain.'[12] It is simply the case that the court will scrutinise carefully the sale effected by the mortgagee once it appears that the circumstances surrounding that sale tend to impeach his bona fides.[13]

There is, for instance, no hard and fast rule that a mortgagee may not sell to a company in which he is interested.[14] As Lord Templeman ruled in *Tse Kwong Lam v Wong Chit Sen*,[15] the mortgagee and the company seeking to uphold the transaction 'must show that the sale was in good faith and that the mortgagee took reasonable precautions to obtain the best price reasonably obtainable at the time.' In *Tse Kwong Lam*, however, the exercise of the mortgagee's power of sale had taken the form of a public auction at which the only bidder was the mortgagee's wife, acting as the representative of the family company of which both were directors and shareholders.[16] There was no competitive bidding at the auction; the property was purchased at the reserve price which had been fixed by the mortgagee and which was, of course, clearly known to the purchaser; and the purchase was financed from funds provided by the mortgagee himself. In such circumstances the Privy Council had no doubt that the mortgagee had failed to show that 'in all respects he acted fairly to the borrower and used his best endeavours to obtain the best price reasonably obtainable for the mortgaged property.'[17]

The critical question in every case is whether there was an independent bargain between mortgagee and purchaser.[18] It is open to the court to find that no fair bargain has been proved where, for instance, the selling mortgagee appears to have been 'either consciously or unconsciously overborne' by the fact that the purchaser was a business client and acquaintance of some commercial substance in the local community.[19]

---

9   *Downes v Grazebrook* (1817) 3 Mer 200 at 209, 36 ER 77 at 80; *ANZ Banking Group Ltd v Bangadilly Pastoral Co Pty Ltd* (1978) 19 ALR 519 at 542.

10 *Martinson v Clowes* (1882) 21 Ch D 857 at 860.

11 *Downes v Grazebrook* (1817) 3 Mer 200 at 209, 36 ER 77 at 80; *Whitcomb v Minchin* (1820) 5 Madd 91, 56 ER 830; *Martinson v Clowes* (1882) 21 Ch D 857 at 860.

12 *ANZ Banking Group Ltd v Bangadilly Pastoral Co Pty Ltd* (1978) 19 ALR 519 at 522. See *Tse Kwong Lam v Wong Chit Sen* [1983] 1 WLR 1349 at 1356G-H.

13 *Goldcell Nominees Pty Ltd v Network Finance Ltd* [1983] 2 VR 257 at 263.

14 *Farrar v Farrars Ltd* (1888) 40 Ch D 395 at 409f; *Tse Kwong Lam v Wong Chit Sen* [1983] 1 WLR 1349 at 1355A; *ANZ Banking Group Ltd v Bangadilly Pastoral Co Pty Ltd* (1978) 19 ALR 519 at 543.

15 [1983] 1 WLR 1349. See [1984] Conv 143 (P. Jackson).

16 See also *ANZ Banking Group Ltd v Bangadilly Pastoral Co Pty Ltd* (1978) 19 ALR 519 (purchase at auction by an associate company controlled by the mortgagee).

17 [1983] 1 WLR 1349 at 1355F-G.

18 *ANZ Banking Group Ltd v Bangadilly Pastoral Co Pty Ltd* (1978) 19 ALR 519 at 544.

19 *Goldcell Nominees Pty Ltd v Network Finance Ltd* [1983] 2 VR 257 at 274.

(j) Remedies for the mortgagor

The mortgagor's remedies for the improper exercise of the mortgagee's power of sale seem to depend largely on whether the irregularity falls within the category of mere carelessness or is more accurately described in terms of bad faith.

(i) Damages for carelessness by the mortgagee Section 104(2) of the Law of Property Act 1925 provides a remedy in damages against the mortgagee in favour of the mortgagor who suffers loss by virtue of an improper exercise of the mortgagee's statutory power of sale. Consistently with this provision, it seems to be accepted that damages represent the appropriate remedy where the mortgagor's complaint is that the selling mortgagee failed to exercise reasonable care to obtain the true market value of the mortgaged property.[20]

(ii) Setting aside the sale because of 'fraud on the power' It seems, however, that more far-reaching remedies may be available where the particular exercise of a mortgagee's power of sale goes beyond a case of mere carelessness and is more akin to equitable fraud or a 'fraud on the power'.[1] In this more extreme category of case the mortgagee's sale is liable to be set aside completely, with the result that the mortgagor recovers the equity of redemption of which he has been unjustly deprived.[2] The circumstances which merit this more dramatic remedy do not necessarily involve any actual fraud (in the common law sense) or any collusion between the mortgagee and the purchaser, but comprise those cases where the bona fides of the mortgagee has been irreparably placed in question by evidence of his 'wilful or reckless disregard of the interests of the mortgagor',[3] or by his transacting in the face of a clear conflict of interests.[4]

In *Tse Kwong Lam v Wong Chit Sen*[5] the Privy Council held that rescission of the relevant sale would, 'as a general rule', have been the appropriate remedy for the aggrieved mortgagor. However, Lord Templeman imposed the rider that the complainant will be left to a mere remedy in damages if it is 'inequitable as between the borrower and the purchaser for the sale to be set aside.'[6] In *Tse Kwong Lam* the remedy of rescission was indeed rendered inequitable because of the mortgagor's 'inexcusable delay' in prosecuting his

---

20   It is significant that only a money remedy was sought (and awarded) in *Cuckmere Brick Co Ltd v Mutual Finance Ltd* [1971] Ch 949 at 958B. See *Brutan Investments Pty Ltd v Underwriting and Insurance Ltd* (1980) 58 FLR 289 at 294f; *Wood v Bank of Nova Scotia* (1981) 112 DLR (3d) 181 at 183. The mortgagor's remedy for a want of 'reasonable care' resulting in a mortgagee's sale at an undervalue is sometimes described in terms of an equitable 'allowance' or account (see *Standard Chartered Bank Ltd v Walker* [1982] 1 WLR 1410 at 1416B; *General Credits (Finance) Pty Ltd v Stoyakovich* [1975] Qd R 352 at 354B- C).

1   *Forsyth v Blundell* (1972-1973) 129 CLR 477 at 496 per Walsh J. For the suggestion that the mortgagee's sale may be impeached as a fraudulent conveyance, see J.C. McCoid, *Constructively Fraudulent Conveyances: Transfers for Inadequate Consideration*, 62 Texas LR 639 (1983). See also *Durrett v Washington National Insurance Co*, 621 F.2d 201 at 204 (1980); *Abramson v Lakewood Bank and Trust Co*, 647 F.2d 547 at 549 (1981).

2   *Tse Kwong Lam v Wong Chit Sen* [1983] 1 WLR 1349 at 1359H-1360A.

3   *Forsyth v Blundell* (1972-1973) 129 CLR 477 at 496. See *Brutan Investments Pty Ltd v Underwriting and Insurance Ltd* (1980) 58 FLR 289 at 295f.

4   See eg *Goldcell Nominees Pty Ltd v Network Finance Ltd* [1983] 2 VR 257 at 278f.

5   [1983] 1 WLR 1349 at 1359H.

6   [1983] 1 WLR 1349 at 1360A.

counterclaim. The mortgagor was thus relegated to damages, which were measured as the difference between the actual sale price and the best price reasonably obtainable at the date of sale.[7]

(3) Appointment of a receiver

The option of appointing a receiver provides the mortgagee with a further remedy for default by his mortgagor which is rather different from either the remedy of action on the mortgagor's personal covenant or the remedy of forced sale.

(a) Preconditions for appointment

The mortgagee has a statutory power to appoint in writing such person as he thinks fit to act as a receiver of the income of the mortgaged property.[8] This power becomes available in the same circumstances and on the same conditions as those which cause the statutory power of sale to arise and to become exercisable.[9]

(b) Functions of the receiver

The appointment of a receiver may be particularly useful if the mortgagee does not presently wish to realise his security or otherwise undertake the responsibility of going into possession of the mortgaged property.[10] The duty of the receiver is to collect all the income derived from the mortgaged land and to ensure that from that income there is payment of all sums due by way of rents, rates, taxes, his own commission, insurance premiums, repairs and, of course, interest owing under the mortgage.[11] Any surplus income is payable to the person, usually the mortgagor, who would otherwise have been entitled to the rents and profits of the property.[12]

(c) Liability for the receiver's actions

The receiver is deemed by statute to be the agent of the *mortgagor*.[13] It follows therefore that, unless the mortgage deed otherwise provides, the mortgagor

---

7   [1983] 1 WLR 1360H. The damages award of HK $ 950,000 can only have been a fraction of the hearing-date value of the land which the mortgagor had effectively hoped to recover through an award of rescission.
8   Law of Property Act 1925, ss 101(1)(iii), 109(1).
9   Law of Property Act 1925, s 109(1). Thus a receiver cannot be appointed while the mortgagor still has a legal right to redeem the mortgage, eg in advance of a legal redemption date which has been clearly stipulated in the mortgage (see *Twentieth Century Banking Corpn Ltd v Wilkinson* [1977] Ch 99 at 104D). However, the mere fact that a mortgagee has gone into possession does not preclude his appointment of a receiver (see *Refuge Assurance Co Ltd v Pearlberg* [1938] Ch 687 at 693), although in registered land the mortgagee must first be registered as the proprietor of a charge over the property (see *Lever Finance Ltd v L.N. & H.M. Needleman's Trustee* [1956] Ch 375 at 382).
10 A receiver is not governed by the strict liability for wilful default which attaches to a mortgagee who enters into possession (ante, p 609).
11 Law of Property Act 1925, s 109(8). See *Marshall v Cottingham* [1982] Ch 82.
12 Law of Property Act 1925, s 109(8).
13 Law of Property Act 1925, s 109(2).

becomes solely liable for any acts or defaults of the receiver even though he has had no hand in his appointment.[14] The mortgagee is not responsible for what the receiver does whilst he is the mortgagor's agent unless the mortgagee directs or interferes with the receiver's activities.[15]

(4) Foreclosure

Foreclosure is the most draconian remedy open to the mortgagee in the event of default by his mortgagor. An order for foreclosure effectively abrogates the mortgagor's equity of redemption and leaves the entire value of the mortgaged property in the hands of the mortgagee. Foreclosure is thus directed primarily at the recovery of the mortgagee's capital investment.

(a) Legal effects of foreclosure

Unlike the exercise of the statutory power of sale, the drastic remedy of foreclosure requires the interposition of some judicial control and is therefore available only on application to the court.[16] A court order for *foreclosure absolute* operates to vest the mortgagor's entire estate (whether freehold or leasehold) in the mortgagee, without compensation for the mortgagor and subject only to those legal mortgages which have priority to the mortgage in respect of which the foreclosure has been obtained.[17]

Notwithstanding that he has obtained foreclosure absolute, the mortgagee may still sue the mortgagor on his personal covenant to repay, provided the mortgagee retains the mortgaged property in his possession.[18] The mortgagee is, however, precluded from such action if, having foreclosed, he then sells the property to a third party.[19] In this event it is plainly inequitable that the mortgagee should be allowed to continue to pursue the mortgagor for any deficiency resulting from the sale. The mortgagee who sells following a foreclosure is not subject to the same duty of care which weighs upon the mortgagee who exercises a statutory power of sale.[20] It would therefore be grossly unfair to hold the foreclosing mortgagee to be unaccountable to the mortgagor in the matter of the price achieved by the sale yet able to recover from the latter any shortfall which supposedly remains.[1]

14   Law of Property Act 1925, s 109(2). See eg *White v Metcalf* [1903] 2 Ch 567 at 570ff.
15   *American Express International Banking Corp v Hurley* [1985] 3 All ER 564 at 571g.
16   *Ness v O'Neil* [1916] 1 KB 706 at 709. To the general rule there are statutory exceptions of very minor significance (see eg Small Dwellings Acquisition Act 1899, s 5(1)).
17   Law of Property Act 1925, ss 88(2), 89(2). (All subsequent mortgage terms or charges are statutorily extinguished by the foreclosure.) In registered land the order for foreclosure is completed by the cancellation of the registered charge and the registration of the former chargee as the sole proprietor of the land (Land Registration Act 1925, s 34(3)).
18   *Kinnaird v Trollope* (1888) 39 Ch D 636 at 642. However, such further action on the mortgagor's covenant gives the latter a new equity of redemption (see *Lockhart v Hardy* (1846) 9 Beav 349 at 356, 50 ER 378 at 380; *Palmer v Hendrie* (1859) 27 Beav 349 at 351, 54 ER 136 at 137). In some jurisdictions the mere fact of foreclosure extinguishes any further capacity to sue on the mortgagor's covenant to repay (see eg Manitoba's Mortgage Act (RSM 1970, c M200), s 16; *Manitoba Development Corp v Berkowits* (1980) 101 DLR (3d) 421 at 422ff).
19   *Kinnaird v Trollope* (1888) 39 Ch D 636 at 642; *Gordon Grant & Co Ltd v Boos* [1926] AC 781 at 784ff; *Lloyds and Scottish Trust Ltd v Britten* (1982) 44 P & CR 249 at 256f; *Burnham v Galt* (1869) 16 Gr 417 at 419.
20   Ante, p 620.
1   See *Bank of Nova Scotia v Dorval* (1980) 104 DLR (3d) 121 at 125.

(b) Preconditions of foreclosure

The mortgagee cannot resort to foreclosure as a remedy until, at the very least, the mortgagor has ceased to have any legal right to redeem the mortgage. Only then does the mortgagor acquire his 'equity' to redeem the mortgage, and it is the possible extinguishment of this equity which is in question in foreclosure proceedings.

Where a mortgage contains an express proviso for redemption, the mortgagor's legal right to redeem is lost only when he fails to comply with the terms of that proviso.[2] The mortgagor's legal right to redeem clearly ceases, for instance, if the date set at law for redemption has already passed.[3] Likewise, the mortgagor puts himself in breach of a proviso for redemption if his legal right to redeem was explicitly made conditional on the punctual payment of capital and interest and he has defaulted in this respect.[4] However, even if the mortgage contains no express proviso for redemption, the court can still order a foreclosure if the mortgagor's default is of such a nature as to bar him at law from recovering his property and to justify the court in extinguishing his equity of redemption.[5] In this respect a mortgagee may be able to obtain a foreclosure even though the circumstances fall short of those which entitle him to exercise his statutory power to sell or to appoint a receiver.[6]

(c) Procedure of foreclosure

Foreclosure proceedings are normally conducted in the High Court. If the court decides to grant an order for foreclosure, it first makes an order for *foreclosure nisi*. This order directs that accounts be taken and provides that unless the mortgagor repays the mortgage moneys due within a period stipulated by the court,[7] the mortgage will be foreclosed. If no such payment is forthcoming, the court makes an order for *foreclosure absolute*, which has the effect of transferring the mortgagor's estate to the mortgagee. However, during the interim between the order nisi and the order absolute, it is open to the mortgagor or the mortgagee to apply to the court for an order directing a sale of the property rather than foreclosure.[8] This alternative form of order may be granted in the discretion of the court, and has the consequence that at least part of the value of the mortgaged property may be salvaged for the mortgagor.

Even after the court has made an order for foreclosure absolute, it is possible for the mortgagor to request the court to 're-open' the order.[9] The court thus

---

2 *Twentieth Century Banking Corpn Ltd v Wilkinson* [1977] Ch 99 at 105A.
3 Ante, p 572.
4 See eg *Kidderminster Mutual Benefit Building Society v Haddock* [1936] WN 158. Compare the refusal to order foreclosure in *Williams v Morgan* [1906] 1 Ch 804 at 810, where the express proviso for redemption clearly preserved the mortgagor's right to redeem at law until a stipulated date irrespective of prior default.
5 *Twentieth Century Banking Corpn Ltd v Wilkinson* [1977] Ch 99 at 105A-C.
6 See *Twentieth Century Banking Corpn Ltd v Wilkinson* [1977] Ch 99 at 104E-F. Ironically, if the mortgagee can show himself entitled to foreclosure, the court has a discretion to direct a sale anyway (Law of Property Act 1925, s 91(2)).
7 This period is usually six months.
8 Law of Property Act 1925, s 91(2).
9 A mortgagor's application to re-open an order for foreclosure absolute may be registrable as a pending land action, thereby guarding against the possibility that the mortgagee may proceed with a sale of the foreclosed property (see *Re Pacific Savings & Mortgage Corp and Can-Corp Development Ltd* (1982) 135 DLR (3d) 623 at 640).

has even further discretion to prevent the final destruction of the mortgagor's equity of redemption.[10] The remedy of foreclosure becomes statute-barred twelve years after the date when the relevant mortgage moneys fell due.[11]

(d) Modern incidence of foreclosure

Foreclosure is rarely sought today, and even more rarely granted. It is usually much more convenient for the mortgagee to exercise his statutory power of sale. Moreover, the court's powers to stay possession proceedings under section 36 of the Administration of Justice Act 1970 have now been extended to actions for foreclosure.[12] The courts have been increasingly reluctant to grant orders for foreclosure, particularly in the context of a rapidly rising property market, because an order for foreclosure may have the effect of transferring to the mortgagee a much more valuable property than the property over which he initially took his security. In such circumstances foreclosure would confer an increasingly valuable asset on the mortgagee at what must inevitably be a substantial undervalue.

11. REMEDIES   AVAILABLE   TO   THE   EQUITABLE MORTGAGEE

The remedies available to an equitable mortgagee differ in some respects from those which are open to a legal mortgagee, largely because the equitable mortgagee takes no legal estate or interest in the land offered as security. The equitable nature of the security, although not affecting the mortgagee's ability to sue on the mortgagor's personal covenant to repay, nevertheless has the following repercussions.

(1) Exercise of the power of sale

The statutory power of sale conferred by section 101(1) of the Law of Property Act 1925 is available in respect of any mortgage which has been effected by deed.[13] Thus some equitable mortgagees may have access to the statutory power,[14] but most equitable mortgagees are excluded from exercising the statutory power on the ground that their mortgages were effected by purely informal means.[15] Such mortgagees have no automatic right to sell, but are entitled to apply to the court under section 91 of the Law of Property Act 1925,

---

10   See *Campbell v Holyland* (1877) 7 Ch D 166 at 172ff per Jessel MR.
11   Limitation Act 1980, s 15(1).
12   Administration of Justice Act 1970, s 36, as amended by Administration of Justice Act 1973, s 8(2) (post, p 891).
13   Ante, p 614. If the statutory power is available, it is possible that the equitable mortgagee is competent to convey the full *legal* estate of his mortgagor (see *In re White Rose Cottage* [1965] Ch 940 at 951C; but compare *In re Hodson and Howe's Contract* (1887) 35 Ch D 668 at 671, 673). The matter may be put beyond doubt by conferring on the mortgagee an irrevocable power of attorney to convey the mortgagor's legal estate.
14   Sale with vacant possession may, however, provide some problem since it is not entirely clear that an equitable mortgagee has the same right to possession as a legal mortgagee (ante, p 612).
15   This exclusion would not, of course, apply where the equitable mortgage was effected by a memorandum of deposit under seal (ante, p 577).

and the court may in its discretion direct either that the mortgaged property be sold[16] or that a legal term of years be vested in the mortgagee, thereby converting him into a legal mortgagee for the purpose of entitlement to exercise the statutory power of sale.[17] An equitable chargee likewise has no automatic power of sale, but may nevertheless request the court for an order for sale.[18]

(2) Appointment of a receiver

The statutory power to appoint a receiver is available only in respect of mortgages created by deed,[19] but in the absence of such creation the court may be asked to appoint a receiver.[20]

(3) Foreclosure

The court has power to order foreclosure of an equitable mortgage or to order a judicial sale in lieu of foreclosure.[1] In the case of an equitable mortgage, however, foreclosure takes the form of a court order that the mortgagor convey the legal title in the mortgaged property into the name of the mortgagee.

16   Law of Property Act 1925, s 91(2).
17   Law of Property Act 1925, s 91(7).
18   See *Matthews v Goodday* (1861) 31 LJ Ch 282 at 283; *London County and Westminster Bank Ltd v Tompkins* [1918] 1 KB 515 at 528. See also Law of Property Act 1925, s 90(1); *Ladup Ltd v Williams & Glyn's Bank Plc* [1985] 1 WLR 851 at 855B-C.
19   Law of Property Act 1925, s 101(1) (iii).
20   Supreme Court Act 1981, s 37(1), (2), formerly Supreme Court of Judicature (Consolidation) Act 1925, s 45. See *Shakel v Duke of Marlborough* (1819) 4 Madd 463, 56 ER 776.
 1   *James v James* (1873) LR 16 Eq 153 at 154. However, a mere equitable chargee cannot foreclose (see *Tennant v Trenchard* (1869) 4 Ch App 537 at 542; *Ladup Ltd v Williams & Glyn's Bank Plc* [1985] 1 WLR 851 at 855B), but can only seek a court order for sale in lieu of foreclosure.

CHAPTER 17

Easements and profits à *prendre*

Easements and profits à *prendre* comprise some of the most important rights which one landowner may acquire over the land of another. The law relating to profits is of fairly ancient origin,[1] but the law of easements has developed in more recent times as a means of enabling the private landowner to plan land use and to enhance the enjoyment or utility of his own land.

It was noted in Chapter 1 that the law of property is made more complex by the fact that it is possible for a number of people to acquire different, but compatible, rights in or over the same thing.[2] Thus A may own a fee simple estate in his land while his neighbour, B, simultaneously has a right to use part of A's land in a certain way or indeed a right to prevent a certain kind of use of A's land. The rights which may be created between A and B provide the subject matter of the law relating to easements, profits and also covenants.[3] These rights may well bind A and B as a matter of contract, but for the land lawyer the question inevitably arises whether the rights in question will bind third parties such as the successors in title of A and B respectively. In reality, of course, the rights created by private agreement are usually intended to be not merely contractual but also proprietary, in the sense that they should affect all who come to the land.

Since the concern here is with the borderline of the law of property, it should come as no surprise that the law has traditionally imposed certain stringent limitations both as to the kinds of right which may qualify as easements and profits and also as to their mode of creation or acquisition. The marketability of land would be gravely affected if these restrictive rules were not clear and rigorously applied. Land titles would otherwise become encumbered by useless and anti-social user-rights of dubious enforceability, vested in unspecified or unidentifiable third parties. The resulting chaos would be inimical to the large social interest which pervades the law of property—the interest that property should be readily alienable.

1. DEFINITIONS AND DISTINCTIONS

An easement is an incorporeal hereditament,[4] comprising in essence either a positive or a negative right of user over the land of another. In effect an easement is a right annexed to one piece of land (a 'dominant tenement') to utilise land of different ownership (a 'servient tenement') in a particular way

---

1 See A.W.B. Simpson, *A History of The Land Law* (2nd edn Oxford 1986), p 106ff.
2 Ante, p 9.
3 Covenants are dealt with in Chapter 18 (post, p 689).
4 Ante, p 38.

or, indeed, to prevent the owner of that other land from utilising his own land in a particular way.[5] An easement cannot extend a right of user to the point where it becomes a right to take the natural produce of another's land or any part of his soil: such a right is classified not as an easement but as a profit *à prendre*. An easement is ultimately a privilege without profit which the owner of one tenement has over another tenement, by which the servient owner permits (or refrains from) certain activities on his own land for the advantage of the dominant tenement.

The concept of the easement must be distinguished from a number of other rights which may exist over land. These include the following.

(1) Profits *à prendre*

A profit *à prendre* confers a right to take part of the soil, minerals or natural produce of the servient tenement.[6] A profit thus differs from an easement in that the latter right is essentially a privilege without profit. A profit may comprise a right to take either some part of the servient land itself (eg gravel or turf[7]) or something which grows on that land (eg grass or crops) or indeed fish[8] or wild animals[9] which are found on the servient owner's land or in his waters.[10] A profit may be granted in conjunction with a licence, in which case the licence is irrevocable during the term of the profit.[11] The fact that in given circumstances a profit is not exclusive in nature does not derogate from its proprietary character as a profit.[12]

(a) A profit may exist 'in gross'

A profit is further distinguishable from an easement in that a profit may exist 'in gross', ie, the owner of the profit need not be the owner of any adjoining or neighbouring land or indeed of any land at all.[13] There need not be a 'dominant tenement'. The rules relating to easements are quite different, and it is an essential condition of an easement that the easement be appurtenant to 'dominant' land.[14]

---

5   Thus described, a negative easement differs little if at all from a restrictive covenant (post, p 700).
6   *Alfred F. Beckett Ltd v Lyons* [1967] Ch 449 at 482B. See also *The Queen v Tener* (1985) 17 DLR (4th) 1 at 16f (Supreme Court of Canada).
7   See *Convey v Regan* [1952] IR 56 at 61; *In re Bohan* [1957] IR 49 at 54ff.
8   See *Kerry CC v O'Sullivan* [1927] IR 26 at 29f; *Toome Eel Fishery (Northern Ireland) Ltd v Cardwell* [1966] NI 1.
9   See *Finlay v Curteis* (1832) Hayes 496 at 499f.
10 The subject matter of a profit *à prendre* must be something which is capable of ownership. A right to take water itself cannot be a profit, since water is not capable of being owned (*Alfred F. Beckett Ltd v Lyons* [1967] Ch 449 at 481G–482A).
11 Ante, p 540.
12 *Unimin Pty Ltd v Commonwealth of Australia* (1973-4) 2 ACTR 71 at 78. It is the right of severance which results in the holder of the profit *à prendre* acquiring title to the thing severed. He does not own the subject matter of the profit while it remains in situ (see *The Queen v Tener* (1985) 17 DLR (4th) 1 at 17).
13 *Bl Comm*, Vol II, p 34. See *The Queen v Tener* (1985) 17 DLR (4th) 1 at 17.
14 Post, p 644.

(b) Scope of the profit

A profit in gross is said to be 'unstinted' in the sense that it may be exhaustive of the fruit or produce of the servient land.[15] By contrast, a 'profit appurtenant' (ie, a profit which is annexed to some nearby dominant tenement) may not be exhaustive, but is limited to the needs of the dominant tenement.[16]

(2) Licences

A licence grants a permission to do something on or affecting land which would otherwise constitute a trespass.[17] Licences are distinguishable from easements in the following respects.

(a) Types of permissible user

The categories of user which are capable of recognition as easements are both relatively limited and restrictively defined. By contrast a licence may be used to permit the conduct of almost any activity on the land of the licensor (ranging from the daily delivery of milk to the holding of an open-air pop festival). A licence may in some circumstances comprise an element of exclusive occupation of land, but any claim to exclusive rights of user is incompatible with the concept of easement.[18]

(b) Creation

The creation of easements often requires compliance with rules of formality,[19] but licences may be created without any formality at all. Furthermore, an easement cannot exist in gross,[20] but a licence need not be related to the ownership of any dominant tenement.

(c) Effect on third parties

An easement creates a proprietary interest which is capable of benefiting and binding third parties. At least in the conventional view, a licence does not generate any similar proprietary effect.[1]

(3) Restrictive covenants

Restrictive covenants are agreements restrictive of the user of land for the benefit of other land adjoining or in the vicinity. Restrictive covenants are closely related to easements both in terminology and in substance, so much so that it has been said that restrictive covenants are in essence negative

---

15   See eg *Staffordshire and Worcestershire Canal Navigation v Bradley* [1912] 1 Ch 91 at 103.
16   *Bailey v Stephens* (1862) 12 CB NS 91 at 108, 110, 142 ER 1077 at 1084; *Lord Chesterfield v Harris* [1908] 2 Ch 397 at 410; *Anderson v Bostock* [1976] Ch 312 at 315F-G, 318B, 318H-319A.
17   For an examination of the law of licences, see Chapter 15 (ante, p 535).
18   Post, p 657.
19   Post, p 665.
20   Post, p 644.
1   Ante, p 549.

easements.[2] Certain differences nevertheless exist between the easement and the restrictive covenant. Easements are enforceable both at law and in equity. Restrictive covenants are the creature of equity and are enforceable only in equity. Moreover, easements may be acquired by prescription (ie, long user),[3] while restrictive covenants may never be acquired in this way. Once again, while the permissible subject matter of an easement is relatively circumscribed, the possible content of a restrictive covenant is virtually unlimited.

(4) Public rights

Public rights are rights which are exercisable by anyone, whether he owns land or not, merely by virtue of his being a member of the public. Some public rights resemble profits *à prendre* (eg the public right of fishing). Other public rights are akin to easements (eg the public right in respect of the highway). However, all public rights are distinct from easements,[4] since they do not presuppose the existence of any dominant tenement and are never the subject of a specific grant to any individual.[5]

The more important public rights include the following.

(a) Rights of passage along the highway

Certain kinds of user of the public highway[6] are enjoyed as a matter of public right,[7] and every highway authority has a responsibility both at common law[8] and under statute[9] to assert and protect the rights of the public to the use and enjoyment of the highways within its area.

(i) Content of the citizen's rights

Every citizen has a right of passage and re-passage along any highway (including the pavement[10]) over which the public

---

2 Post, p 700. Easements were recognised much earlier in the common law. Restrictive covenants have been accorded proprietary effect only since the mid-19th century (post, p 698).

3 Post, p 678.

4 The public right of passage along the highway is sometimes—albeit inaccurately—referred to in somewhat loose terms as an 'easement' (see eg *Harrison v Duke of Rutland* [1893] 1 QB 142 at 154 per Lopes LJ).

5 For the best modern account of public rights, see T.J. Bonyhady, *The Individual and the Environment: The Rights of Members of the Public in the English Countryside* (PhD dissertation, University of Cambridge, 1985).

6 The 'highway' is defined as including not only the 'carriageway' over which there is a right of way for vehicular traffic but also the adjoining 'footway' on either side where there is merely a public right of way on foot (see Highways Act 1980, ss 328(1), 329(1)). See also *Hubbard v Pitt* [1976] QB 142 at 175D.

7 A public highway need not necessarily lead to any public place (see *Williams-Ellis v Cobb* [1935] 1 KB 310 at 320). If a highway is maintainable by the relevant statutory highway authority at public expense, that authority holds a determinable fee simple interest in the surface of the highway and in so much of the subjacent land and superjacent airspace as is required for the discharge of its statutory duties (see *Foley's Charity Trustees v Dudley Corpn* [1910] 1 KB 317 at 322; *Tithe Redemption Commission v Runcorn UDC* [1954] Ch 383 at 398; *Wiltshire County Council v Frazer* (1984) 47 P & CR 69 at 72; Highways Act 1980, s 263 (ante, p 72)).

8 *R v Welwyn Hatfield DC, ex parte Brinkley* (1982) 80 LGR 727 at 735.

9 Highways Act 1980, s 130(1).

10 *News Group Newspapers Ltd v SOGAT '82* [1986] IRLR 337 at 346.

has acquired a right of way either by statute[11] or by reason of dedication and acceptance at common law.[12] The public right of passage is of a somewhat limited nature. Citizens have a 'right to pass and repass at their pleasure for the purpose of legitimate travel'[13] and also for 'purposes incidental to passage'.[14] Any other form of user of the highway constitutes a trespass against the owner of the top-soil in the highway[15] and may well involve a criminal obstruction of the highway.[16]

(ii) Criminal obstruction of the highway The scope of the public right of passage and re-passage on the highway has tended to be defined, not so much by any positive explication given by the courts, as by the delimiting effects imposed by various forms of criminal liability derived from statute.

Of these heads of liability the most important is that created by the offence of wilful obstruction of 'free passage along a highway'.[17] In the absence of 'lawful

11 A public highway may be specifically designated as such by statute. There is a general (although rebuttable) statutory presumption that a way is deemed to have been dedicated as a public highway where the way has been 'actually enjoyed by the public as of right and without interruption for a full period of 20 years' (Highways Act 1980, s 31(1)). See *Gloucestershire CC v Farrow* [1985] 1 WLR 741 at 745H-746G.

12 Dedication and acceptance are generally inferred from the fact of long user (*Cubitt v Lady Caroline Maxse* (1873) LR 8 CP 704 at 715). The intention to dedicate a way to the public is commonly rebutted by an annual and symbolic closure of the route for one day for the purpose of denying public access as of right (see *British Museum Trustees v Finnis* (1833) 5 C & P 460 at 465, 172 ER 1053 at 1056).

13 *Harrison v Duke of Rutland* [1893] 1 QB 142 at 154. See also *Hickman v Maisey* [1900] 1 QB 752 at 757; *Waite v Taylor* (1985) 149 JP 551 at 553; *Thomas v National Union of Mineworkers (South Wales Area)* [1986] Ch 20 at 64A.

14 *Hubbard v Pitt* [1976] QB 142 at 149G-150A per Forbes J, who explained that '[a] tired pedestrian may sit down and rest himself. A motorist may attempt to repair a minor breakdown...[I]t is permissible to queue for tickets at a theatre or other public place of entertainment, or for a bus.' Even then such user is limited in duration to 'a reasonable while', and must be exercised 'reasonably and in such a way as not unduly to obstruct other users' ([1976] QB 142 at 150D). See also *Hadwell v Righton* [1907] 2 KB 345 at 348; *Iveagh v Martin* [1961] 1 QB 232 at 273; *Waite v Taylor* (1985) 149 JP 551 at 553; *Cooper v Metropolitan Police Commissioner* (1985) 82 Cr App R 238 at 242.

15 *Harrison v Duke of Rutland* [1893] 1 QB 142 at 154; *Hubbard v Pitt* [1976] QB 142 at 150C-F, 175C-D. See eg *R v Pratt* (1855) 4 El & Bl 860 at 865, 867f, 119 ER 319 at 321f (hunting on highway); *Hickman v Maisey* [1900] 1 QB 752 at 756ff (racing tout spying on horse trials). An injunction will issue to restrain an individual who 'persistently follow[s] another on a public highway, making rude gestures or remarks in order to annoy or vex' (*Thomas v National Union of Mineworkers (South Wales Area)* [1986] Ch 20 at 64D). There is, however, no trespass by the child who chases his ball into the roadway or runs across the roadway in play (see *Culkin v McFie and Sons Ltd* [1939] 3 All ER 613 at 620F-G). See, however, Highways Act 1980, s 161(3).

16 Highways Act 1980, s 137(1). For reference to potential liability for public and private nuisance, see *Hubbard v Pitt* [1976] QB 142 at 175A, E.

17 Highways Act 1980, s 137(1). 'Unless it is de minimis any stopping on the highway is prima facie an obstruction' (see *Hirst v Chief Constable of West Yorkshire* (1986) *Times*, 19 November). Under Highways Act 1980, s 137(2), a police constable has power to arrest without warrant any person 'whom he sees committing an offence under this section'.

18 See *Nagy v Weston* [1965] 1 WLR 280 at 284C-D. No defence can be raised on the basis that the defendant has operated a street stall in the same position for several years and has duly paid rates (*Pugh v Pidgen* (1987) *Times*, 2 April). In the absence of malpractice, oppression, caprice or opprobrious behaviour, it is lawful for the police to stop cars randomly on the highway for the purpose of detecting crime (including drunken driving). See *Beard v Wood* [1980] RTR 454 at 459E-H; *Chief Constable of Gwent v Dash* [1986] RTR 41 at 48G.

authority or excuse',[18] obstruction encompasses anything other than a passing and re-passing along the highway or activity ancillary to such passage.[19] Whether the use made of the highway by a member of the public is 'so unreasonable as to amount to obstruction' is a question of fact and degree in every case.[20] The offence of obstruction tends in practice to catch many 'relatively minor activities which some of the public might consider to be beneficial'.[1] The offence has also been applied—somewhat dangerously—to the conduct of activities on the footpath or sidewalk which are deemed to be unpleasant, socially undesirable or obtrusive in relation to passers by.[2]

A further form of criminal liability arises where 'without lawful authority or excuse' any person deposits 'any thing whatsoever on a highway to the interruption of any user of the highway'.[3] It is a specially designated criminal offence to deposit a builder's skip on the highway without the permission of the relevant highway authority.[4] Moreover, a local authority has power to require the removal of any 'structure' erected or set up on the highway without lawful authority.[5]

(iii) Protest and demonstration on the public highway The nature of the public right of user of the highway also performs a significant function in delimiting the citizen's right in relation to certain forms of protest and demonstration. In *Hubbard v Pitt*[6] a majority in the Court of Appeal upheld the granting of an interlocutory injunction restraining the picketing of an estate agent's premises carried out by a local tenants' organisation. The majority decision may, however, have been based more upon an allegation of private nuisance than upon any suggestion that the demonstration on the pavement outside the estate agent's premises had constituted either a trespass or a criminal obstruction.[7] In his dissenting judgment Lord Denning MR was prepared to discharge the injunction altogether, noting specifically that the presence of half a dozen people for three hours on a Saturday morning was 'not an unreasonable use of

---

19 See *Waite v Taylor* (1985) 149 JP 551 at 553, where May LJ pointed out that there is no obligation 'to keep moving all the time', so long as the 'stopping is part and parcel of passing and re-passing along the highway and is ancillary to it (such as a milkman stopping to leave a milk bottle on a doorstep).' Likewise, in *Cooper v Metropolitan Police Commissioner* (1985) 82 Cr App R 238 at 242, Tudor Evans J thought that there is clearly 'a right to look in a shop window or to talk to a passing friend without committing an offence'.

20 *Nagy v Weston* [1965] 1 WLR 280 at 284D-E.

1 *Waite v Taylor* (1985) 149 JP 551 at 553. Criminal liability has thus been imposed—with expressions of judicial regret—on hot dog vendors (*Nagy v Weston* [1965] 1 WLR 280 at 284F; *Pitcher v Lockett* (1966) 64 LGR 477 at 479), mobile snack bars (*Waltham Forrest v Mills* [1980] RTR 201 at 205G-H), and street buskers juggling with lit firesticks in a pedestrian precinct (*Waite v Taylor*, supra at 553f).

2 *Cooper v Metropolitan Police Commissioner* (1985) 82 Cr App R 238 at 242ff (club tout seeking to persuade passing pedestrians to enter Soho club).

3 Highways Act 1980, s 148(c). See *Putnam v Colvin* [1984] RTR 150 at 158B-E (placing of pots with shrubs in cul-de-sac to prevent unlawful parking itself unlawful).

4 Highways Act 1980, s 139(1), (3). The criminal offence also includes leaving a skip on the highway for longer than the permitted period (*Craddock v Green* (1983) 81 LGR 235 at 239f).

5 *R v Welwyn Hatfield DC, ex parte Brinkley* (1982) 80 LGR 727 at 734ff (gypsy caravans). Possession of the highway may also be recovered under RSC Ord 113 (post, p 757). See *Wiltshire County Council v Frazer* (1984) 47 P & CR 69 at 74ff.

6 [1976] QB 142.

7 [1976] QB 142 at 180C-D, 189C-D.

the highway'.[8] In the words of the Master of the Rolls, 'so long as good order is maintained, the right to demonstrate must be preserved.'[9]

The liberal tenor of Lord Denning's approach has been invoked more recently in *Hirst v Chief Constable of West Yorkshire*.[10] Here a number of 'animal rights' protesters had exhibited banners and distributed leaflets in a pedestrian precinct outside a shop which sold fur coats. Their convictions on charges of wilful obstruction of the highway were quashed by the Divisional Court of Queen's Bench, Otton J observing that the courts have long recognised the right of free speech and the right to peaceful protest on matters of public concern, subject to the need for peace and good order. However, the Court confirmed the stern warning given by Lord Denning MR in *Hubbard v Pitt*[11] that any violence 'should be firmly handled and severely punished'.

(iv) Industrial protest   A difficult balance requires to be maintained between the right of the citizen to use the highway as a forum for legitimate protest and the right of other citizens to enjoy uninterrupted user of the same highway for their own legitimate purposes. This issue has arisen with some force in connection with the crossing of picket lines during strikes. In *Thomas v National Union of Mineworkers (South Wales Area)*,[12] Scott J held that working miners were entitled under the general law to exercise their right to go to work 'without unreasonable harassment by others'. Since the working miners had a 'right to use the highway for the purpose of going to work',[13] they were entitled to an injunction protecting that right from 'unreasonable interference' by a group of 50 to 70 striking miners who on a daily basis hurled verbal abuse at them from the picket line.[14] In this rather special sense Scott J seemed to suggest that unreasonable collective interference with public rights of user of the highway constitutes 'a species of private nuisance'.[15]

The decision in *Thomas v National Union of Mineworkers (South Wales Area)* also indicates that the courts may be more prepared to allow the highway to be utilised as a means of protest by private or informal interest groups (such as 'animal rights' protesters) than by more highly organised representatives of unionised labour. Whether such an approach is right or wrong, the public right of user of the highway was jeopardised by the distinctly questionable ruling given in *Moss v McLachlan*.[16] Here, in a decision which bodes ill for civil liberties

8   [1976] QB 142 at 174H-175A ('They did not interfere with the free passage of people to and fro'). Lord Denning was of the opinion (at 175C-D) that neither the aggrieved estate agent nor the local highway authority had any right of action in trespass.
9   [1976] QB 142 at 179A.
10   (1986) *The Times*, 19 November.
11   [1976] QB 142 at 178H-179A.
12   [1986] Ch 20 at 64E-F. See [1985] CLJ 374 (K.D. Ewing).
13   [1986] Ch 20 at 64E.
14   [1986] Ch 20 at 65A-C. Regular picketing at the home of a working miner was held to be a common law nuisance, 'regardless of the number of people involved and regardless of the peaceful nature of their conduct' ([1986] Ch 20 at 65C-D).
15   [1986] Ch 20 at 64E. In *News Group Newspapers Ltd v SOGAT '82* [1986] IRLR 337 at 346, Stuart-Smith J held that the owner of land adjoining the highway has a 'right of access to the highway from any part of his premises.' An actionable private nuisance arises in the event of interference with this right, so long as the obstruction of access amounts to 'an unreasonable use of the highway'. In this case the daily presence of 50 to 200 dismissed print workers outside Rupert Murdoch's newspaper plant at Wapping was considered to be an 'unreasonable obstruction of the highway'. See also *Thomson Electrical Works Ltd v McGraw* (1976) 61 DLR (3d) 548 at 552f; F.P. Davidson, (1982) 33 NILQ 341.
16   (1985) 149 JP 167.

in days to come, a Divisional Court upheld a supposed right in the police to turn back convoys of 'flying pickets' from proceeding along the highway towards the scene of an organised labour demonstration. Skinner J held that police officers operating on a motorway were acting within the execution of their duty when they stopped cars carrying persons 'who appeared to be striking miners'.[17] The police had sought to justify their action on the basis that the continued progress of the vehicles gave rise to a reasonable expectation that a breach of the peace would ensue in the form of a mass demonstration at a colliery some miles distant.[18] In accepting this explanation, the Divisional Court endorsed the restriction of free movement along the highway on grounds of an apprehended (but as yet unproven) unlawfulness of the ultimate objective of the journey undertaken.[19]

This monstrous decision sets an extremely dangerous precedent for the censoring of lawful activities of entirely innocent persons on some ground of visual similarity to other persons who are deemed inimical to an officially defined social interest.[20] Even in relation to those who look like trouble, the ill-drawn law in respect of breach of the peace must be sparingly applied. The ruling in *Moss v McLachlan* has highly disturbing implications not merely for public rights in respect of the highway, but also for certain important freedoms of speech, association and assembly.

(v) Public nuisance Some forms of user of the highway may involve the criminal offence of public nuisance.[1] It is clear, however, that not every obstruction of the highway constitutes a public nuisance. There must in addition be some 'unreasonable use of the highway by the defendant'.[2] Thus a march or procession which is conducted in an orderly manner is not a public nuisance, even though it may involve obstruction of the highway.[3] In determining the reasonableness of any particular user, the court must 'balance the rights of those who wish to demonstrate with those who wish to exercise their rights of passage.'[4] A meeting or demonstration on the highway is not necessarily unlawful,[5] although it is 'more likely to be than a procession'.[6]

---

17   (1985) 149 JP 167 at 168.
18   (1985) 149 JP 167 at 170ff.
19   Compare *Wills' Trustees v Cairngorm Canoeing and Sailing School Ltd*, 1976 SLT 162 at 191 where, in dealing with the analogous right of passage on navigable waters, Lord Wilberforce expressed the view that 'once a public right of passage is established, there is no warrant for making any distinction, or even for making any enquiry, as to the purpose for which it is exercised. One cannot stop a canoe, any more than one can stop a pedestrian on a highway, and ask him what is the nature of his use.'
20   Compare the statement of Wilson J in *Rouse v Bardin* (1790) 1 H Bl 351 at 355, 126 ER 206 at 208, that members of the public have a right to use the public highway 'for all purposes and at all times'.
1   A public nuisance may arise in connection with an 'unlawful act which endangers lives, safety, health, property or comfort of the public or by which the public are obstructed in the exercise or enjoyment of any right common to all Her Majesty's subjects' (*News Group Newspapers Ltd v SOGAT '82* [1986] IRLR 337 at 346).
2   *Lowdens v Keaveney* [1903] 2 IR 82 at 87f; *R v Clark* (No 2) [1964] 2 QB 315 at 320f.
3   *News Group Newspapers Ltd v SOGAT '82* [1986] IRLR 337 at 346. See now the stringent controls imposed on public processions by Public Order Act 1986, s 11ff.
4   *News Group Newspapers Ltd v SOGAT '82* [1986] IRLR 337 at 346.
5   See *Burden v Rigler* [1911] 1 KB 337 at 339f.
6   *News Group Newspapers Ltd v SOGAT '82* [1986] IRLR 337 at 346.

Public nuisance is also actionable as a civil wrong if it 'materially affects the reasonable comfort and convenience of life of a class of Her Majesty's subjects' who come within the sphere or 'neighbourhood' of its operation.[7] The plaintiff must, moreover, show particular damage 'other than and beyond the general inconvenience suffered by the public.'[8] In *News Group Newspapers Ltd v SOGAT '82*,[9] Stuart-Smith J ruled that the holding of mass demonstrations outside Rupert Murdoch's print plant at Wapping constituted an actionable public nuisance. The demonstrations were directed by sacked print workers both against the plaintiffs' continuing employees and against lorry drivers who distributed the plaintiffs' newspapers. Stuart-Smith J held that the targets of these demonstrations comprised a sufficiently numerous 'class' for the purpose of rendering the mass show of force an actionable civil wrong.[10] The print firm had a right for its employees and visitors to pass on all roads (including pavements) approaching the plant, 'unobstructed by pickets or demonstrators acting in an abusive, insulting, threatening or violent manner.'[11] Injunctions were granted restricting the demonstrations at Wapping to a picket line consisting of no more than six workers whose function was confined to peaceful communication and persuasion.[12]

(b) Rights of passage in navigable waters

There is at common law a public right of navigation in non-tidal waters. This right is subject to statutory regulation,[13] and entitles the citizen to exercise only reasonable rights of user which are incidental to a right of passage and re-passage.[14] The reasonableness of any particular user is measured with reference to the 'capacity and quality of the river'.[15]

(c) Rights of fishing

From ancient times there has been a right, vested in members of the public, to fish in the sea[16] and in all tidal and salt waters.[17] There is, of course, no public right of fishing in non-tidal rivers,[18] and it is highly unlikely that any such right exists in relation to inland non-tidal lakes.[19]

---

7   *Attorney General v P.Y.A. Quarriers Ltd* [1957] 2 QB 169 at 184.
8   *News Group Newspapers Ltd v SOGAT '82* [1986] IRLR 337 at 346.
9   [1986] IRLR 337.
10   *News Group Newspapers Ltd v SOGAT '82* [1986] IRLR 337 at 346. Stuart-Smith J thought that the 'class' requirement probably does not apply at all to obstruction of the highway, since obstruction in this context can generally be presumed to affect the public at large.
11   *News Group Newspapers Ltd v SOGAT '82* [1986] IRLR 337 at 357. See now the wide formulation of the offences related to riot, violent disorder, affray, intimidation and harassment contained in Public Order Act 1986, ss 1-5.
12   *News Group Newspapers Ltd v SOGAT '82* [1986] IRLR 337 at 357.
13   See eg Water Resources Act 1963, s 79(3), (4); Countryside Act 1968, s 22(6).
14   Thus, for instance, the right of passage does not confer any entitlement to indulge in wildfowling on a river (see *Lord Fitzhardinge v Purcell* [1908] 2 Ch 139 at 166).
15   *Wills' Trustees v Cairngorm Canoeing and Sailing School Ltd*, 1976 SLT 162 at 191 per Lord Wilberforce.
16   '[E]very man may fish in the sea of common right' (1466) YB Mich 8 Edw IV, pl 30, quoted by T.J. Bonyhady, op cit, p 412.
17   *Stephens v Snell* [1939] 3 All ER 622H; *Case of the Royal Fishery of the Banne* (1610) Dav 55, 80 ER 540 at 541. Private fisheries can exist in such waters only if created prior to Magna Carta 1215 (see *Stephens v Snell*, supra at 622G).
18   Ante, p 32.
19   See *Johnston v O'Neill* [1911] AC 552 at 568, 577f, 592f. Compare, however, *Toome Eel Fishery (Northern Ireland) Ltd v Cardwell* [1966] NI 1 at 12 per Lord MacDermott CJ.

(d) Rights of recreational user

Under English law members of the public have only limited public rights of recreational user in respect of land and water. There is no general right to ramble over hills and open countryside.[20] There is no public right to swim at the shore or walk upon the foreshore.[1] Such activities represent at best some form of tolerated user in respect of which the landowner by long tradition—in the generality of cases—seeks no remedy in trespass. In *Attorney-General v Antrobus*,[2] for instance, Farwell J denied the existence of a public right of access to the megalithic monument at Stonehenge, and underlined the legal impossibility that any member of the public may acquire a *ius spatiandi*[3] (or right to wander at large) over open countryside.[4] There does, however, appear to be a public right to navigate at will over the surface of non-tidal inland waters.[5]

In respect of access to the recreational outdoors, English law contrasts unfavourably with the law of other jurisdictions. There is in England no general right of access to open or uncultivated countryside, although substantial de facto access is enjoyed in a somewhat ill-defined way. The need for a more satisfactory confirmation of a general right of access is now more pressing than ever. The threatened privatisation of water authorities is likely to frustrate the access previously enjoyed by walkers and climbers across large catchment areas in the hills. There is a very real fear that, as the price of agricultural land steadily declines, the owners of scenic open spaces will compensate either by increasing afforestation or even by imposing access charges upon those who merely wish to roam around or climb in wild and open country.[6]

The American courts are, by contrast, much more willing to infer the existence of an implied licence on the part of private landowners for public access to wide areas of open space.[7] American courts have also invoked doctrines of customary right and public trust (or *ius publicum*[8]) in order to

---

20 See *Earl of Coventry v Willes* (1863) 9 LT 384 at 385; *Hammerton v Honey* (1876) 24 WR 603 at 604. The National Parks and Access to the Countryside Act 1949, ss 60ff, brought into existence machinery for the creation of public rights of access to the countryside by means of access agreements and orders. However, these procedures have ensured that no more than 0.3 per cent of the total area of England and Wales is covered by access arrangements (see T.J. Bonyhady, op cit, p 251).

1 *Brinckman v Matley* [1904] 2 Ch 313 at 324; *Alfred F. Beckett Ltd v Lyons* [1967] Ch 449 at 482E-F. Such rights may be enjoyed only by way of licence.

2 [1905] 2 Ch 188 at 208.

3 Post, p 652.

4 See also *In re Ellenborough Park* [1956] Ch 131 at 184 per Evershed MR. See generally T.J. Bonyhady, op cit, p 200ff.

5 See eg *Marshall v Ulleswater Steam Navigation Co* (1871) LR 7 QB 166 at 172 (Ullswater); *Bloomfield v Johnston* (1868) IR 8 CL 68 at 87ff, 111f (Lough Erne); *Micklethwait v Vincent* (1892) 67 LT 225 at 230 (Norfolk Broads).

6 See P. Sedgwick, 'The access debate', in *High* (February 1987), p 24. Compare S. Tompkins, *The Theft of the Hills* (The Ramblers' Association London 1986).

7 See *McKee v Gratz*, 260 US 127 at 136, 67 L Ed 167 at 170 (1922) per Holmes J ('The strict rule of English common law as to entry upon a close must be taken to be mitigated by common understanding with regard to the large expanses of uninclosed and uncultivated land in many parts, at least, of this country. Over these it is customary to wander, shoot, and fish at will until the owner sees fit to prohibit it. A licence may be implied from the habits of the country').

8 See *Shively v Bowlby*, 152 US 1 at 11ff, 38 L Ed 331 at 336ff (1894).

rationalise the public acquisition, by implied dedication, of recreational easements over beaches.[9]

(5) Natural rights

Landowners have certain 'natural rights' which are protected by the law of torts.[10] Natural rights are distinguishable from easements in that they come into being automatically and are not the subject of any grant.

(a) Right to support for land

The most important 'natural right' is the landowner's right to support for his land.[11] Every landowner has a right to enjoy his own land in its natural state and is therefore entitled to have his land supported by that of his neighbour.[12]

(i) Extent of the right   In practical terms the landowner has a right that the lateral thrust exerted on his soil by his neighbour's land should not be removed (eg by mining or excavating operations on the neighbour's land which cause subsidence).[13] This natural right of support avails the land only in its original state unencumbered by buildings or other constructions.[14] It does not comprise any right to support for buildings on the land.[15] If the action of a neighbour in demolishing a contiguous and supporting building or wall causes a landowner's house to collapse, he has no remedy in the absence of a duly acquired easement of support.[16] If, however, the neighbour's activities on his land would have caused the subsidence of land in any event, irrespective of the presence of buildings thereon, the damages recoverable for the violation of the natural right of support for land may include damages in respect of any buildings which have been affected.[17]

(ii) Remedies   Action which prejudices the landowner's natural right to support gives rise to a liability in damages and may even be the subject of a

9   See eg *State ex rel Thornton v Hay*, 462 P.2d 671 at 673ff (1969); *Gion v City of Santa Cruz*, 465 P.2d 50 at 55ff (1970); *Department of Natural Resources v Ocean City*, 332 A.2d 630 at 633ff (1975); *County of Los Angeles v Berk*, 605 P.2d 381 at 389ff (1980). See M.L. Bryan, *Which Way to the Beach? Public Access to Beaches for Recreational Use*, 29 So Car LR 627 (1977-79).
10   Violation of a natural right is actionable in the law of nuisance (see *Clerk and Lindsell on Torts* (15th edn London 1982), para 23-56ff).
11   See generally J.F. Garner, (1948) 12 Conv (NS) 280.
12   *Backhouse v Bonomi* (1861) 9 HL Cas 503 at 512f, 11 ER 825 at 829; *Bognuda v Upton & Shearer Ltd* [1972] NZLR 741 at 760.
13   *Dalton v Angus & Co* (1881) 6 App Cas 740 at 808; *Byrne v Judd* (1908) 27 NZLR 1106 at 1118ff.
14   *Latimer v Official Co-operative Society* (1885) 16 LR Ir 305 at 308.
15   *Public Trustee v Hermann* [1968] 3 NSWR 94 at 108.
16   *Peyton v London Corpn* (1829) 9 B & C 725 at 735ff, 109 ER 269 at 273f; *Ray v Fairway Motors (Barnstaple) Ltd* (1968) 20 P & CR 261 at 264; *Green v Belfast Tramways Co* (1887) 20 LR Ir 35; *Gateley v H. & J. Martin Ltd* [1900] 2 IR 269 at 272f.
17   *Stroyan v Knowles* (1861) 6 H & N 454 at 465, 158 ER 186 at 191; *Hunt v Peake* (1860) 29 LJ Ch 785 at 787; *Ray v Fairway Motors (Barnstaple) Ltd* (1968) 20 P & CR 261 at 268; *Public Trustee v Hermann* [1968] 3 NSWR 94 at 108f. See generally E.H. Bodkin, (1962) 26 Conv (NS) 210.

mandatory injunction.[18] However, the natural right to support is not infringed if the land which has been excavated and the adjacent land from which lateral support has thereby been removed were both, at the date of excavation, within the common ownership of one person.[19] A subsequent purchaser of the portion of land from which lateral support has been removed cannot claim any violation of his 'natural right' in the event of a later collapse of his land, but may be able to sue in negligence.[20]

(b) Other natural rights

Other forms of natural right may exist. The landowner has, for instance, a natural right to water where it flows naturally in a defined channel through or past his land.[1] This natural right, being part of the fee simple estate in the land, passes without any express provision on the conveyance of that estate.[2] However, since natural rights cannot arise in respect of buildings, there is no such thing as a natural right to even 'a single ray of light'.[3] Rights to light can be created or acquired only as easements.[4]

(6) Local customary rights

Local customary rights differ from easements in that they are not necessarily appurtenant to any dominant tenement but are exercisable generally by the members of a particular local community such as a town[5] or a parish.[6] Customary rights have been held to extend to such activities as the use of an access path to the local church,[7] the playing of sports and pastimes on a piece of land,[8] the drying of fishing nets in a certain location,[9] and the holding of an

---

18   See *Redland Bricks Ltd v Morris* [1969] 2 All ER 576 at 579H-580F; *Economy Shipping Pty Ltd v A.D.C. Buildings Pty Ltd and Fischer Constructions Pty Ltd* [1969] 2 NSWR 97 at 106; *Grocott v Ayson* [1975] 2 NZLR 586 at 590. It seems that the withdrawal of support is not actionable in itself but only when actual damage ensues (*Taylor v Auto Trade Supply Ltd* [1972] NZLR 102 at 108; *Bognuda v Upton & Shearer Ltd* [1972] NZLR 741 at 760). Damages cannot be awarded in respect of prospective loss flowing from the infringement of a natural right, with the result that de minimis violations of the right, even if accompanied by trivial damage, are not properly the subject of any remedy (see *Hirst v Klomp* (1981) NZ Recent Law 359 at 360).

19   *Blewman v Wilkinson* [1979] 2 NZLR 208 at 211ff. See also *Jennings v Sylvania Waters Pty Ltd* [1972] 2 NSWLR 4 at 14C-D.

20   *Blewman v Wilkinson* [1979] 2 NZLR 208 at 212, 215, 217. See also *Bognuda v Upton & Shearer Ltd* [1972] NZLR 741 at 757ff. An action for loss of support may lie against the person withdrawing support even though he has since ceased to own the land adjoining that from which support was withdrawn (*Thynne v Petrie* [1975] Qd R 260 at 262F-G).

1   *Chasemore v Richards* (1859) 7 HL Cas 349 at 382, 11 ER 140 at 153; *Swindon Waterworks Co Ltd v Wilts and Berks Canal Navigation Co* (1875) LR 7 HL 697 at 704ff; *Jennings v Sylvania Waters Pty Ltd* [1972] 2 NSWLR 4 at 10E. There is no natural right to water which percolates underground in an undefined channel (see *Bradford Corpn v Pickles* [1895] AC 587 at 592, 595, 600). See also J.S. Fiennes, (1938) 2 Conv (NS) 203; P. Brett, (1950) 14 Conv (NS) 154.

2   *Jennings v Sylvania Waters Pty Ltd* [1972] 2 NSWLR 4 at 12B-D.

3   C.J. Gale, *Law of Easements* (12th edn, London 1950), p 6.

4   See *Earl Putnam Organisation Ltd v Macdonald* (1979) 91 DLR (3d) 714 at 717f.

5   *New Windsor Corporation v Mellor* [1975] Ch 380 at 391C-D.

6   *Brocklebank v Thompson* [1903] 2 Ch 344 at 354.

7   *Brocklebank v Thompson* [1903] 2 Ch 344 at 355.

8   *New Windsor Corporation v Mellor* [1975] Ch 380 at 392H.

9   *Mercer v Denne* [1905] 2 Ch 538 at 577ff.

annual 'fair or wake'.[10] Local customary rights can arise at common law only if
they are ancient,[11] certain, reasonable and continuous.[12]

2. ESSENTIAL CHARACTERISTICS OF AN EASEMENT

In *In re Ellenborough Park*[13] Danckwerts J defined the essential qualities of an
easement in the following terms:

(1) there must be a dominant and a servient tenement; (2) an easement must
accommodate the dominant tenement, that is, be connected with its enjoyment and for
its benefit; (3) the dominant and servient owners must be different persons; and (4) the
right claimed must be capable of forming the subject-matter of a grant.

There is a strong tendency to accord the status of an easement to any right
which satisfies these requirements,[14] irrespective of the precise label which the
right in question may have been given by the parties themselves.[15]

(1) There must be a dominant tenement and a servient tenement

An easement cannot exist 'in gross' but only as appurtenant to a defined area of
land.[16] An easement must in effect be linked with two parcels of land. There
must be a 'dominant tenement' in favour of which the easement is created or
acquired,[17] and there must be a 'servient tenement' over which the easement is
exercised or exercisable. It is irrelevant that the servient tenement may serve
more than one dominant tenement.[18]

(a) Requirement of two tenements

The requirement of a relationship of dominance and servience was laid down
clearly by Cresswell J in *Ackroyd v Smith*.[19] Here the plaintiff and the defendant
owned adjoining areas of land. The plaintiff's predecessor in title had granted
to an earlier owner of the adjoining land a right to use a road across his land.
When this right was subsequently claimed as an easement, Cresswell J held the

---

10   *Wyld v Silver* [1963] Ch 243 at 256, 266.
11   In theory 'ancient' rights must pre-date 1189, but in practice the requirement of ancient
     origin is satisfied by evidence of uninterrupted long user for 20 years (or perhaps within living
     memory), provided always that there is no proof that the user actually originated after 1189
     (see *Simpson v Wells* (1872) LR 7 QB 214 at 217; *Mercer v Denne* [1905] 2 Ch 538 at 577).
12   *Lockwood v Wood* (1844) 6 QB 50 at 64, 115 ER 19 at 24; *Daly v Cullen* (1958) 92 ILTR 127 at
     130.
13   [1956] Ch 131 at 140.
14   See J.F. Garner, (1983) 127 SJ 95, 115.
15   See eg *Riley v Penttila* [1974] VR 547 at 560 (a 'liberty' to use and enjoy an area of land
     construed as an easement).
16   *Commissioner of Main Roads v North Shore Gas Co Ltd* (1967) 120 CLR 118 at 134 per Windeyer J;
     Gas & Fuel Corpn of Victoria v Barba [1976] VR 755 at 763. See generally M.F. Sturley, (1980)
     96 LQR 557. Compare the law of New Zealand which has by statute dispensed with the
     general requirement of a dominant tenement (see Property Law Act 1952, s 122).
17   Thus, for instance, a member of a golf club cannot acquire any easement to play golf, since
     there exists no dominant tenement in the sense required (*Banstead Downs Golf Club v The
     Commissioners* (1974) VATTR 219 at 226).
18   See eg *In re Ellenborough Park* [1956] Ch 131 at 175 (post, p 651); *Harada v Registrar of Titles*
     [1981] VR 743 at 751.
19   (1850) 10 CB 164 at 187ff, 138 ER 68 at 77.

right to be a mere licence on the ground that a 'right unconnected with the enjoyment or occupation of the land cannot be annexed as an incident to it.' The right concerned in the present case had been granted 'for all purposes' to the 'owners and occupiers' of the adjoining land and to 'all persons having occasion to resort thereto'. This right was held to be too ample to qualify as an easement, on the principle that a right of way cannot be granted in gross, and 'no one can have such a way but he who has the land to which it is appendant'.[20] A right granted in gross was, in the view of Cresswell J, 'personal only, and cannot be assigned'.[1] Cresswell J rationalised this rule by reference to a sentiment which pervades the early law of easements and covenants.[2] He ruled that

It is not in the power of a vendor to create any rights not connected with the use or enjoyment of the land, and annex them to it: nor can the owner of land render it subject to a new species of burthen, so as to bind it in the hands of an assignee. 'Incidents of a novel kind cannot be devised, and attached to property, at the fancy or caprice of any owner'.

Within this statement is contained the implicit concern lest an easement in gross impose 'clogs upon the title' which may render the servient land unmarketable.[4] This rationale for the requirement of a dominant tenement is today somewhat open to challenge.[5] It may be that the abolition of the rule which forbids easements in gross would nowadays promote rather than impede the optimal utilisation of land. Sometimes, of course, this rule is effectively relaxed by statute in order to confer certain rights of use and inspection upon those bodies which operate vital public services and utilities (eg electricity, gas and water authorities).[6] In such cases the requirement of a dominant tenement

---

20 (1850) 10 CB 164 at 188, 138 ER 68 at 77. If, however, the formal grant of the easement had been limited to the person in possession of the dominant tenement, the right of way would also have been available to other persons who had express or implied authority from the dominant tenant. See eg the reference in *Baxendale v North Lambeth Liberal and Radical Club Ltd* [1902] 2 Ch 427 at 429 to 'members of [the grantee's] family, servants, visitors, guests and tradespeople'. See also *Woodhouse and Co Ltd v Kirkland (Derby) Ltd* [1970] 1 WLR 1185 at 1190F-H; *Hammond v Prentice Brothers Ltd* [1920] 1 Ch 201 at 216; *Grinskis v Lahood* [1971] NZLR 502 at 509.

1 (1850) 10 CB 164 at 188, 138 ER 68 at 77. This case has been said to be 'not easy to understand' (*Todrick v Western National Omnibus Co Ltd* [1934] Ch 561 at 572). It is probably best explained as a case in which the purposes for which the relevant right was granted 'were to a great extent unconnected with the use of the close to which that right was claimed as appurtenant' (*Thorpe v Brumfitt* (1873) 8 Ch App 650 at 657 per Mellish LJ).

2 Post, p 698.

3 (1850) 10 CB 164 at 188, 138 ER 68 at 77f, quoting *Keppell v Bailey* (1834) 2 My & K 517 at 535, 39 ER 1042 at 1049.

4 See M.F. Sturley, (1980) 96 LQR 557 at 562f.

5 It has been questioned, for instance, whether a company which runs a helicopter shuttle service should be obliged to make the slightly disingenuous claim that its West End office constitutes the 'dominant tenement' in respect of some distant landing pad over which it exercises rights (see M.F. Sturley, (1980) 96 LQR 557 at 565, 567).

6 'The gas company has...no true easement; for there is no true dominant tenement unless it be said to be the gas works' (*Commissioner of Main Roads v North Shore Gas Co Ltd* (1967) 120 CLR 118 at 133 per Windeyer J). However loose and inaccurate the use of the term 'easement' in this context (see C. Sweet, (1916) 32 LQR 70 at 79ff), such easements seem to comprise a category of 'statutory easements' which are appurtenant only to some enterprise rather than to any particularly convincing dominant tenement (see J.F. Garner, (1956) 20 Conv (NS) 208).

is abrogated in order to further certain public or community-related purposes.[7] However, it is arguable that the requirement should also be abrogated even in relation to easements which are directed at wholly private purposes.

(b) An easement may run with both tenements

An easement is a proprietary right in the sense that, once duly created and acquired, it annexes a burden to the servient tenement and an equivalent benefit to the dominant tenement in such manner as to affect the successors in title of either tenement. The precise effects of the easement on third parties depend to some extent on the legal or equitable quality of the easement[8] and on whether it relates to unregistered or registered land. The relevant problems arise where A has granted an easement to B (see *Fig.* 45). Are C and D affected by respectively the burden and benefit of that easement?

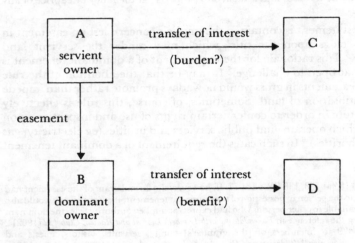

Fig. 45

(i) Unregistered land Where an easement is appurtenant to a dominant tenement, it becomes notionally affixed to that tenement in the same way that fixtures become annexed to realty.[9] In consequence the benefit of the easement

---

7 Alternatively it can perhaps be said that the dominant tenement relevant to such easements comprises both corporeal and incorporeal hereditaments (see *Re Salvin's Indenture* [1938] 2 All ER 498 at 506D-F), the latter being the similar rights of user which a public utility acquires in other adjoining lands. See *Gas & Fuel Corporation of Victoria v Barba* [1976] VR 755 at 763f. That a dominant tenement may consist of incorporeal property is clear from *Hanbury v Jenkins* [1901] 2 Ch 401 at 422f.

8 Ante, p 80.

9 Ante, p 20. In particular, there is a prima facie inference that the easement becomes appurtenant to each and every part of the dominant tenement (see *Callard v Beeney* [1930] 1 KB 353 at 360f; *Laurie v Winch* [1952] 4 DLR 449 at 456f; *Re Maiorana and the Conveyancing Act* [1970] 1 NSWR 627 at 634; *Re Gordon and Regan* (1985) 15 DLR (4th) 641 at 645). In consequence the law of easements has avoided the problems which once bedevilled the law of restrictive covenants in relation to subsequent fragmentation of the dominant tenement (post, p 709).

passes with any subsequent conveyance by deed of the land concerned.[10] Thus, in *Fig.* 45, the benefit of the easement granted by A to B can be invoked by D, regardless of whether the easement was legal or equitable.

The mere fact that the benefit of an easement remains an incident of the dominant tenement in the hands of B's successor does not, however, mean that the right is enforceable against A's successor, C. This result will follow only if the burden of the easement was effectively transmitted to C under the rules which govern the binding effect of land interests in English law. There is here, of course, a difficulty for the lay person who imagines in his innocence that there can be no 'benefit' for anyone unless someone else is simultaneously subject to a correlative 'burden'.[11] However, the land lawyer approaches the issue of enforceability in an artificial manner which at first seems semantically confusing. 'Benefit' and 'burden' are treated as separate and unconnected phenomena, the transmission of which is governed by divergent principles. The apparent illogic of this approach is less bizarre when considered in the forensic context. Any action to enforce an easement will succeed only if the plaintiff can be shown to have the 'benefit', and the defendant the 'burden', of the easement in question. Thus, for the land lawyer, the real questions are whether (in *Fig.* 45) the 'benefit' of the easement concerned has been got out of B into D, and the 'burden' out of A into C.

In unregistered land, the rules governing the transmission of the burden of easements are relatively straightforward. If the easement granted by A to B was legal, its burden will automatically affect the servient tenement in the hands of C since legal rights bind the world.[12] If the easement was equitable, its binding effect on C depends on whether B registered the easement as a Class D(iii) land charge against A.[13]

(ii) Registered land In registered land the benefit of B's easement is likewise a proprietary incident of the dominant tenement and passes with any transfer of B's estate.[14] The burden of the easement should normally be entered by B on the register of A's title,[15] and if protected in this way is clearly binding on C, the transferee of the servient tenement (see *Fig.* 45).[16]

A legal easement also constitutes an overriding interest,[17] and thus binds a successor in title of the servient tenement even where no attempt has been made to secure the entry of a minor interest on the register. Somewhat

---

10   *Godwin v Schweppes Ltd* [1902] 1 Ch 926 at 932. See also Law of Property Act 1925, ss 62(1), 187(1) (post, p 674); *Leech v Schweder* (1874) 9 Ch App 463 at 474f; *Graham v Philcox* [1984] QB 747 at 757E-F, 764F-G. The benefit of the easement may therefore be enjoyed by the occupier for the time being of the dominant land even if he is a mere lessee of that land (see *Thorpe v Brumfitt* (1873) 8 Ch App 650 at 655f).

11   See, however, *Rogers v Hosegood* [1900] 2 Ch 388 at 395 per Farwell J.

12   Ante, p 85.

13   Ante, p 141. There is some possibility in this context that an unregistered land charge may still be enforceable against C on grounds of estoppel if C had knowledge of its existence at the time of the transfer to him (see *E.R. Ives Investment Ltd v High* [1967] 2 QB 379, ante, p 141).

14   Reference to a legal easement may be entered on the property register of the relevant dominant tenement (Land Registration Rules 1925, rr 3(2)(c), 252, 254, 257 (ante, p 149)).

15   Land Registration Rules 1925, r 41. See *Celsteel Ltd v Alton House Holdings Ltd* [1985] 1 WLR 204 at 220E-F.

16   Land Registration Act 1925, ss 20(1)(a), 23(1)(b).

17   Land Registration Act 1925, s 70(1)(a); Land Registration Rules 1925, r 258 (ante, p 173).

controversially,[18] however, it appears that the protection of an overriding interest may also be available in respect of at least some categories of equitable easement.[19] An equitable easement may occasionally occur in association with actual occupation by the person entitled to the benefit of the easement, in which case the easement is protected under the Land Registration Act 1925, s 70(1)(g).[20] In *Celsteel Ltd v Alton House Holdings Ltd*,[1] moreover, Scott J held that an equitable right of way could also be protected as an overriding interest pursuant to the Land Registration Act 1925, s 70(1)(a), where such an easement was 'openly exercised and enjoyed' as appurtenant to the dominant tenement at the date of the relevant transfer of the servient tenement.[2] In view of the confused state of the law in this area, there is a strong argument for the elimination of overriding status for any unprotected equitable easement.[3]

(2) The easement must 'accommodate' the dominant tenement

No right may qualify as an easement unless it can be shown that the right confers benefit on the dominant tenement as distinct from some merely personal advantage on the dominant owner.[4] The criterion of benefit rests ultimately on whether the dominant tenement is accommodated and its use made more beneficial by the right in question.

(a) Exclusion of purely personal or commercial advantages

The classic example of a purely personal advantage which could not be claimed as an easement is the right which was alleged by the plaintiff in *Hill v Tupper*.[5] Here the owner of a canal leased land on the canal bank to the plaintiff and purported to grant him a 'sole and exclusive' right to put pleasure boats on the canal. The plaintiff subsequently contended that he had acquired an

18 See eg Law Commission, *Property Law: Third Report on Land Registration: A. Overriding Interests, B. Rectification and Indemnity, C. Minor Interests* (Law Com, No 158, 31 March 1987), paras 2.31ff.

19 It had been assumed by many commentators that this possibility was excluded by the fact that Land Registration Act 1925, s 70(1)(a) expressly covers only easements other than 'equitable easements required to be protected by notice on the register' (see M.P. Thompson, [1986] Conv 31). However, this provision is ambivalent since there is no strict requirement that a person entitled to an equitable easement should necessarily protect it by entry on the register.

20 *Celsteel Ltd v Alton House Holdings Ltd* [1985] 1 WLR 204 at 220G. If, however, the easement in question is a right of way, it is unlikely that there will be actual occupation of the servient tenement (see *Celsteel Ltd v Alton House Holdings Ltd*, supra at 219E (ante, p 189)). Indeed such occupation may well be incompatible with the essentially non-exclusive character of an easement (see M.P. Thompson, [1986] Conv 31 at 36).

1   [1985] 1 WLR 204 at 220H-221D. The Court of Appeal did not subsequently interfere with this ruling ([1986] 1 WLR 512).

2   Land Registration Rules 1925, r 258 provides that rights, privileges and appurtenances 'appertaining or reputed to appertain to land...which adversely affect registered land' constitute overriding interests within Land Registration Act 1925, s 70.

3   See M.P. Thompson, [1986] Conv 31 at 37. See Chapter 8 (ante, p 173).

4   *Dukart v District of Surrey* (1978) 86 DLR (3d) 609 at 616 (Supreme Court of Canada). There must be dominant land, but not necessarily a dominant building (see *Commonwealth v Registrar of Titles (Victoria)* (1918) 24 CLR 348 at 353, 355). See also *Waveney DC v Wholgemouth* (1985) *The Times*, 11 July.

5   (1863) 2 H & C 121, 159 ER 51.

easement in respect of the canal which was enforceable against the defendant, the landlord of a nearby inn, who unlawfully interfered with the plaintiff's trade by putting rival boats on the same canal. This claim to an easement was not upheld by the court, which took the view that the plaintiff had acquired merely a licence which was, of course, unenforceable except against the licensor.

The ground for the decision in *Hill v Tupper* is somewhat unclear. Pollock CB observed that a 'new species of incorporeal hereditament cannot be created at the will and pleasure of the owner of property.'[6] Martin B held that to admit the right claimed by the plaintiff 'would lead to the creation of an infinite variety of interests in land, and an indefinite increase of possible estates.'[7] Such statements appear to be yet further expressions of the policy against imposing 'clogs' which might tend to make a title uncommerciable or inalienable. However, perhaps the most potent factor in the minds of the judges in this case was their clear apprehension that the right claimed by the plaintiff was not appurtenant to any dominant tenement. Pollock CB cited *Ackroyd v Smith*[8] in support of the proposition that it is impossible to create easements in respect of 'rights unconnected with the use and enjoyment of land.' In the present case it was scarcely realistic to argue that the plaintiff's contractual rights over the canal were such as to make his occupation of the land on the canal bank more convenient. The area in question included a landing stage, and it was clearly the case that this landing stage facilitated the plaintiff's use of the canal rather than vice versa.[9]

It may also be that in *Hill v Tupper* the court felt disinclined to allow a purely commercial advantage to be claimed as an easement. The plaintiff was seeking in effect to assert a commercial monopoly in respect of the business of putting pleasure boats on the canal in question. There was no sense in which the plaintiff's occupation of the alleged dominant tenement was enhanced by the easement, because his use of that land was entirely incidental to his entrepreneurial exploitation of the waterway.[10] It is also possible that the judgments in *Hill v Tupper* concealed a distaste for rights which are over-broad. It is characteristic of the easement that it should not smack of exclusiveness of possession or control.

(b) Requirement of propinquity

In order to support the claim that a given right 'accommodates' the alleged dominant tenement, there is some requirement of propinquity in relation to the

---

6   (1863) 2 H & C 121 at 127, 159 ER 51 at 53.
7   (1863) 2 H & C 121 at 128, 159 ER 51 at 53.
8   (1850) 10 CB 164, 138 ER 68 (ante, p 644).
9   See *In re Ellenborough Park* [1956] Ch 131 at 175. It is possible that the right claimed would have been upheld as an easement if it had provided an effective means of access and egress from the plaintiff's land and the defendant's boats had interfered with that access.
10 See *In re Ellenborough Park* [1956] Ch 131 at 175, where Evershed MR said, with reference to *Hill v Tupper*, that 'it is clear that what the plaintiff was trying to do was to set up, under the guise of an easement, a monopoly which had no normal connexion with the ordinary use of his land, but which was merely an independent business enterprise. So far from the right claimed sub-serving or accommodating the land, the land was but a convenient incident to the exercise of the right.' See, however, [1956] CLJ 24 at 25 (R.N. Gooderson).

servient and dominant tenements. There is no rule that the dominant and servient land must be contiguous,[11] but the servient land must at least be sufficiently closely situated to confer a practical benefit on the dominant land.[12] It is for this reason that the example is often given that there cannot be 'a right of way over land in Kent appurtenant to an estate in Northumberland'.[13]

(c) Nature of the accommodation or benefit conferred

It is an elusive task to define in positive terms the nature of the benefit which must be shown to have been conferred on the alleged dominant tenement. There is, of course, a crude sense in which in the law of easements all benefits are ultimately enjoyed by people rather than by land.[14] In *Dukart v District of Surrey*,[15] however, the Supreme Court of Canada spoke of the need to show that 'the dominant tenement is accommodated, serviced or supported by the servient tenement'. There must be between the dominant tenement and the servient tenement 'a connection of real benefit to the former...which is of such a character as would ordinarily be classified as a right or condition running with the land and not merely a contractual right enuring to the benefit only of persons who are parties thereto at its inception.'

(i) Enhancement of land value   The test whether a particular right increases the market value of the benefited land is relevant but not conclusive.[16] There are many kinds of right which may have this effect, but not all would qualify as easements. As the Court of Appeal indicated in *In re Ellenborough Park*,[17] there must be some 'sufficient nexus between the enjoyment of the right and the use of [the dominant property].' Thus a right granted to the purchaser of a particular house to use the Zoological Gardens free of charge or to attend Lord's Cricket Ground without payment, although undoubtedly increasing the value of the property conveyed, could not at law run with the property as an easement. Such rights would be 'wholly extraneous to, and independent of, the use of a house as a house, namely as a place in which the householder and his family live and make their home.'

(ii) Exclusiveness of benefit is not necessary   Such benefit as is conferred by an easement need not relate exclusively to the dominant owner. It is not fatal, for instance, to the status of an easement that it comprises a right of way which is capable of benefiting not merely the dominant tenement but also 'any passer-by, wholly unconnected with the dominant tenement, who chooses to use it as a short cut'.[18]

---

11   *Re Salvin's Indenture* [1938] 2 All ER 498 at 506G; *Harada v Registrar of Titles* [1981] VR 743 at 751f. See also *In re Ellenborough Park* [1956] Ch 131 at 175 (where the requirement of benefit was satisfied even in respect of those houses which did not front on to the park).

12   *Bailey v Stephens* (1862) 12 CB (NS) 91 at 115, 142 ER 1077 at 1086; *Todrick v Western National Omnibus Co Ltd* [1934] Ch 561 at 572ff, 580f, 589ff; (1934) 50 LQR 313; *Pugh v Savage* [1970] 2 QB 373 at 381C-D; *Dewhirst v Edwards* [1983] 1 NSWLR 34 at 51E-F.

13   See *Bailey v Stephens* (1862) 12 CB (NS) 91 at 115, 142 ER 1077 at 1086 per Byles J; *Todrick v Western National Omnibus Co Ltd* [1934] Ch 561 at 580.

14   Post, p 703.

15   (1978) 86 DLR (3d) 609 at 616.

16   *In re Ellenborough Park* [1956] Ch 131 at 173.

17   [1956] Ch 131 at 174. See [1956] CLJ 24 (R.N. Gooderson); (1956) 72 LQR 16 (R.E.M.).

18   *In re Ellenborough Park* [1956] Ch 131 at 172.

(iii) Benefit to trade conducted on the dominant tenement It seems to be a sufficient accommodation of the dominant tenement that the right claimed as an easement should facilitate or benefit some trade or business which is carried on in the dominant land. In *Moody v Steggles*,[19] for instance, Fry J held that the owner of a public house might claim an easement to hang a signboard on the adjoining house. A commercial benefit extracted from business conducted on the servient tenement is not, however, enough to validate the claim of easement.[20]

(iv) Integral aspects of commodious domestic living In the residential context it seems that the test of accommodation requires the making of ultimately social judgments as to the kinds of benefit or advantage which are integral to the domestic arrangements required for commodious living. In *In re Ellenborough Park*,[1] for example, a number of owners of residential properties had been given a right of common enjoyment of a park or pleasure ground which was enclosed by their houses and which was vested in trustees. Each adjoining owner paid a proportionate part of the cost required to maintain the pleasure ground as a well stocked and carefully ordered garden. The Court of Appeal held that the right granted each purchaser of 'full enjoyment...of the pleasure ground' was capable of forming the subject matter of an easement. Underlying this decision was an almost unspoken value judgment that 'the use of a garden undoubtedly enhances, and is connected with, the normal enjoyment of the house to which it belongs'.[2] In the present circumstances the park had become the 'communal garden for the benefit and enjoyment of those whose houses adjoined it or were in its close proximity'[3] and as such amply satisfied the 'requirement of connexion with the dominant tenements to which it is appurtenant.'[4]

As this case demonstrates, the definition of qualifying rights in the law of easements is heavily coloured by an element of value judgment. Such judgments relate not only to the sorts of activity claimed as amounting to an easement, but also to the relative degree of merit which is thought to attach to the party advancing the claim. In *In re Ellenborough Park* the Court of Appeal had little difficulty in applying the terminology of easements to the civilised user by civilised people of a communal garden situated in an excessively bourgeois location.

(v) A purely recreational user may not be an easement There is some authority in English law for the view that a mere right of 'recreation and amusement' can never qualify as an easement since such a right lacks any capacity to confer

---

19 (1879) 12 Ch D 261 at 266ff. See also *Ellis v Mayor of Bridgnorth* (1863) 15 CB (NS) 52 at 78, 143 ER 702 at 712; *Leon Asper Amusements Ltd v Northmain Carwash & Enterprises Ltd* (1966) 56 DLR (2d) 173 at 176.

20 See *Hill v Tupper* (1863) 2 H & C 121, 159 ER 51 (ante, p 648).

1 [1956] Ch 131.

2 [1956] Ch 131 at 174 per Evershed MR. See also *Riley v Penttila* [1974] VR 547 at 559f ('For gracious living it has been found for a very long time...necessary to have space in areas around a house for the purposes of a garden and recreation, and even of a park. Undoubtedly, it adds to the enjoyment of the occupation of such house property').

3 [1956] Ch 131 at 174.

4 [1956] Ch 131 at 175.

'utility and benefit' on land.[5] There can in short be no easement merely to have fun. Consistent with this limitation is the once widely accepted notion that the concept of an easement cannot encompass a *ius spatiandi*, ie, 'a privilege of wandering at will over all and every part of another's field or park'.[6]

It is clear, however, that neither of these restrictions on the scope of easements is absolute. In *In re Ellenborough Park*[7] the Court of Appeal agreed that a *ius spatiandi*, being an 'indefinite and unregulated privilege', would indeed lack the essential qualities of an easement. The Court nevertheless considered a *ius spatiandi* to be 'substantially different' from the grant in the present case, which comprised 'the provision for a limited number of houses in a uniform crescent of one single large but private garden'.[8] Moreover, although in the view of Evershed MR 'a garden is a pleasure—on high authority, it is the purest of pleasures',[9] the right claimed here was 'appurtenant to the surrounding houses as such', and constituted 'a beneficial attribute of residence in a house as ordinarily understood.'[10] The Court of Appeal thus concluded that the use of the communal garden 'for the purposes, not only of exercise and rest but also for such domestic purposes as...taking out small children in perambulators or otherwise...is not fairly to be described as one of mere recreation or amusement, and is clearly beneficial to the premises to which it is attached.'[11]

(3) The dominant and servient tenements must be owned or occupied by different persons

An easement is by definition a right over somebody else's land. It is therefore impossible that the same person should both own *and occupy* the dominant and servient tenements, since it is a nonsense that a man should have rights against himself.[12] It is, however, quite feasible that a tenant should acquire an easement over his landlord's land, since although in this situation there is common ownership of the dominant and servient tenements, there is no

---

5   *Solomon v Vintners' Company* (1859) 4 H & N 585 at 593, 157 ER 970 at 974; *Mounsey v Ismay* (1865) 3 H & C 486 at 498, 159 ER 621 at 625. See H.S. Theobald, *The Law of Land* (2nd edn, London 1929), p 263.

6   *In re Ellenborough Park* [1956] Ch 131 at 176 per Evershed MR. See *International Tea Stores Co v Hobbs* [1903] 2 Ch 165 at 172; *Attorney-General v Antrobus* [1905] 2 Ch 188 at 198ff.

7   [1956] Ch 131 at 176.

8   [1956] Ch 131 at 176. In *Dukart v District of Surrey* (1978) 86 DLR (3d) 609 at 616, the Supreme Court of Canada took the view that *In re Ellenborough Park* had established that some kinds of ius spatiandi are sufficiently determinate to deserve easement status. The Supreme Court pointed in particular to the fact that in *In re Ellenborough Park* Evershed MR had emphasised ([1956] Ch 131 at 179) that an easement may include a right of 'wandering at will round each and every part of the garden except of course, such parts as comprise flower beds, or are laid out for some other purpose, which renders walking impossible or unsuitable.' In *Dukart* the Supreme Court held, on similar grounds, that there can be a easement to wander at large over a beach beside a resort development. See also *Riley v Penttila* [1974] VR 547 at 559, where an easement was held to arise on the basis of a right of enjoyment of a defined area for recreation which had been given not to the public but to a limited number of lot holders.

9   [1956] Ch 131 at 179. The idea that a garden is a numinous place goes back as far as the first garden, where Adam communed with God in the cool of the evening.

10   [1956] Ch 131 at 179.

11   [1956] Ch 131 at 179.

12   *Morris v Edgington* (1810) 3 Taunt 24 at 30, 128 ER 10 at 13. See *B. & W. Investments Ltd v Ulster Scottish Friendly Society* (1969) 20 NILQ 325.

common occupation.[13] Likewise a landlord may equally well acquire an easement in respect of land which is the subject of a lease to his own tenant.[14]

(4) The easement must be capable of forming the subject matter of a grant

It is commonly said that all easements 'lie in grant'. That is, no right can successfully be claimed as an easement which could not have been granted by deed. This requirement imposes certain stringent conditions on the kinds of rights which can constitute an easement, as also on the circumstances in which a valid easement may be created.

(a) There must be a capable grantor and a capable grantee

It follows from the requirement of capacity for grant that the existence of any easement presupposes both a competent grantor and a competent grantee.

(i) Capable grantor No easement can be claimed if at the date of creation of the supposed easement the servient land was owned by someone who was legally incompetent to grant an easement (eg a statutory or other corporation which has no duly constituted authority to grant away easements over its land[15]). A less obvious case of incompetent grant arises where an easement (eg a right of way) has already been validly created as appurtenant to a particular dominant tenement. In such circumstances and in the absence of contrary agreement,[16] the dominant owner has no power to grant any share of that same easement to the owner of an adjoining tenement supposedly for the benefit of that adjoining tenement.[17]

It is possible (although not entirely clear) that an easement may be the subject of a valid unilateral grant by one of a number of joint owners of the servient tenement, provided that the encumbrance does not interfere with the rights of the other co-owners to possession and enjoyment of that land.[18] Conversely, where a person expressly grants an easement over land to which he currently has no title but to which he later acquires title, then in the period between the grant and the acquisition of the legal title the grantor is estopped as against the grantee from denying the grant.[19] The subsequent acquisition of the legal title feeds the estoppel so that thereafter, and perhaps also retrospectively, the grant operates as effectively as if the grantor had had title at the date of his grant.[20]

---

13 See *Borman v Griffith* [1930] 1 Ch 493 at 499 (post, p 676).
14 *Beddington v Atlee* (1887) 35 Ch D 317 at 332.
15 *Mulliner v Midland Railway Co* (1879) 11 Ch D 611 at 619ff.
16 *Clapman v Edwards* [1938] 2 All ER 507 at 512D-H.
17 *Bannister v Chiene* (1902) 22 NZLR 628 at 631. See also *Classic Communications Ltd v Lascar* (1985) 21 DLR (4th) 579 at 584.
18 *Hedley v Roberts* [1977] VR 282 at 288f. Compare, however, *Paine & Co Ltd v St Neots Gas & Coke Co* [1939] 3 All ER 812 at 824A-D.
19 *Rowbotham v Wilson* (1857) 8 El & Bl 123 at 145, 120 ER 45 at 54, (1860) 8 HLC 348 at 364, 11 ER 463 at 470.
20 *Hedley v Roberts* [1977] VR 282 at 285.

(ii) Capable grantee   Likewise no easement may be claimed if the alleged dominant owner was at the time legally incompetent to receive such a grant (eg a company without power to acquire easements,[1] or a fluctuating body of persons such as 'the inhabitants for the time being' of a named village[2]).

(b) The right must be sufficiently definite

In order to qualify as an easement, a right must be sufficiently definite. There is, for instance, no easement such as a right to a prospect or view.[3] Such a right may be acquired only by way of a restrictive covenant which precludes the owner of the neighbouring land from building on his land in such a way as to obstruct the view which it is desired to protect.[4] Likewise there is no such easement as a right to the uninterrupted access of light or air except through defined apertures in a building.[5] There is no easement of indefinite privacy.[6] Nor does English law recognise as an easement any claim to wander at will over land.[7]

(c) The right must be within the general nature of the rights traditionally recognised as easements

The law of easements has been generally constrained by the innately conservative principle that the categories of admissible easement must not dramatically overstep the boundaries of the kinds of easement already recognised.

(i) Novelty is not necessarily an objection   It is often said that the list of easements is not closed. As Lord St Leonards observed in *Dyce v Lady James Hay*,[8] 'the category of servitudes and easements must alter and expand with the changes that take place in the circumstances of mankind.'[9] The courts are nevertheless traditionally reluctant to admit new kinds of right to the status of easement,[10] and have not usually been prepared to recognise as easements rights which lie markedly outside the range of rights which have hitherto been acknowledged

1   *National Guaranteed Manure Co Ltd v Donald* (1859) 4 H & N 8 at 17f, 157 ER 737 at 741.
2   Such a body may, however, enjoy a local customary right as distinct from an easement (ante, p 643).
3   *William Aldred's Case* (1610) 9 Co Rep 57b at 58b, 77 ER 816 at 821; *Campbell v Paddington Corpn* [1911] 1 KB 869 at 875f.
4   See eg *Buckleigh v Brown* [1968] NZLR 647 at 651ff.
5   See *Levet v Gas Light & Coke Co* [1919] 1 Ch 24 at 27. The High Court of Australia has recognised the right to the uninterrupted access of light and air as an easement, even though not limited to access through defined apertures (see *Commonwealth v Registrar of Titles (Victoria)* (1918) 24 CLR 348 at 353ff). The English Court of Appeal has rationalised the easement of light enjoyed by the domestic greenhouse on the ground that a greenhouse is 'not to be regarded simply as a garden under glass, but as a building with apertures, namely, the glass roof and sides'. See *Allen v Greenwood* [1980] Ch 119 at 129C per Goff LJ; [1979] Conv 298 (F.R. Crane).
6   *Browne v Flower* [1911] 1 Ch 219 at 225 per Parker J.
7   *In re Ellenborough Park* [1956] Ch 131 at 176ff (ante, p 652).
8   (1852) 1 Macq 305 at 312.
9   Cited with approval in *Commonwealth v Registrar of Titles (Victoria)* (1918) 24 CLR 348 at 353 per Griffith CJ.
10   See eg *Hill v Tupper* (1863) 2 H & C 121, 159 ER 51 (ante, p 649).

as easements. A new category of right is occasionally admitted within the list of easements,[11] but in many other cases rights alleged to be easements have been rejected not least because the rights claimed were in the nature of negative easements and therefore more appropriately created and protected as restrictive covenants.

(ii) Reluctance to accept new negative easements There is some indication that the category of negative easements is nowadays virtually closed. In *Phipps v Pears*,[12] for instance, the plaintiff sought damages from the defendant on the ground that the latter had demolished his adjoining house thereby exposing the unpointed flank wall of the plaintiff's house to the rigours of the weather.[13] The plaintiff's action was based upon a supposed easement of protection from the weather, but the Court of Appeal denied that any such right could exist as an easement.[14] Lord Denning MR conceded that a right to support from an adjoining building had long been recognised as constituting a possible easement. However, such a right partakes of the nature of both positive and negative easements, in the sense that it comprises not merely a right that one's neighbour should not remove his building but also a right for the protected building to exert a sideways thrust or lean upon the adjoining building.[15] A supposed right to protection from the weather is 'entirely negative' and, in Lord Denning MR's view, is effectively 'a right to stop your neighbour pulling down his own house.' Such a right, being essentially negative, 'must be looked at with caution' since the law 'has been very chary of creating any new negative easements'.[16]

This reluctance to recognise new negative easements was justified in *Phipps v Pears* on the ground that any contrary view would tend towards an undue restriction of the rights of neighbouring owners to enjoyment of their own land. The Court of Appeal was thus disinclined to 'hamper legitimate development', since, given the appropriate planning permissions,[17] 'every man is entitled to

---

11 See eg *Simpson v Godmanchester Corpn* [1897] AC 696 at 701ff, where the House of Lords held that an easement could comprise the right to enter on to another's land in order to open and shut sluice gates on a canal. See also *Attorney-General of Southern Nigeria v John Holt & Co (Liverpool) Ltd* [1915] AC 599 at 617.

12 [1965] 1 QB 76. See [1964] CLJ 203 (K. Scott).

13 See now Building Act 1984, s 82(1)(b), under which a local authority may require the weatherproofing of surfaces exposed by demolition.

14 See also *Giltrap v Busby* (1970) 21 NILQ 342; *Marchant v Capital & Counties Property Co Ltd* (1982) 263 Estates Gazette 661; (1983) 80 Law Soc Gaz 84 (D.W. Williams).

15 It has since been noted that *Phipps v Pears* did not concern any claim to support to the gable wall, merely a claim to be protected from the weather (see *Bradburn v Lindsay* [1983] 2 All ER 408 at 414j). The courts have tended to be much more responsive where the plaintiff alleges interference with an easement of support for his building or with an easement to have a party wall kept weatherproof (see eg *Tollemache & Cobbold Breweries Ltd v Reynolds* (1983) 268 Estates Gazette 52 at 56; *Bradburn v Lindsay*, supra at 413e; *Brace v South East Regional Housing Association Ltd* (1984) 270 Estates Gazette 1286 at 1288). See [1984] Conv 54 (P. Jackson).

16 [1965] 1 QB 76 at 82G-83A. For a critical view of this rationale, see (1964) 80 LQR 318 (R.E.M.); M.A. Peel, (1964) 28 Conv (NS) 450 at 451ff. It has since been doubted whether Lord Denning's rejection of an easement of protection from the weather was intended to apply as between tenements which are separated horizontally rather than vertically (see *Sedgwick Forbes Bland Payne Group Ltd v Regional Properties Ltd* (1981) 257 Estates Gazette 64 at 70 per Oliver J).

17 Planning permission is required even for the demolition of property, if the demolition is part of a scheme of redevelopment of the site (see *London County Council v Marks & Spencer Ltd* [1953] AC 535 at 541f).

pull down his house if he likes.'[18] In Lord Denning's view the only way in which an owner may protect himself in such circumstances is by extracting from his neighbour a restrictive covenant that the neighbour will not take action which prejudices the owner's enjoyment of his property.[19]

(iii) Range of recognised easements   Notwithstanding the clear element of judicial caution in this context, the courts have over the years accepted many widely varying kinds of right as constitutive of an easement. An easement may thus comprise a right to do something on the servient tenement (eg to use a right of way,[20] to store goods,[1] or to advertise a business[2]). An easement may also comprise a right in the dominant owner to prevent the servient owner from doing certain acts on the servient land which he would otherwise be entitled to perform, subject of course to the danger that such a right may be considered to be both negative and novel and therefore not in the nature of an easement.[3]

An easement may even sanction the performance of acts affecting the servient land which would otherwise constitute a nuisance.[4] In *Sturges v Bridgman*[5] the defendant claimed to have acquired an easement by reason of long user to generate an excessive amount of noise and vibration in the course of his conduct of business as a confectioner. The Court of Appeal held that no easement had been acquired on the facts, but acknowledged that an easement to make noise could have been created by long user if during the period of user the noise had amounted to an actionable nuisance and the servient owner had not availed himself of the appropriate remedy in the law of tort.[6]

---

18   [1965] 1 QB 76 at 83A ('If it exposes your house to the weather, that is your misfortune. It is no wrong on his part. Likewise every man is entitled to cut down his trees if he likes, even if it leaves you without shelter from the wind or shade from the sun').
19   [1965] 1 QB 76 at 83E-F.
20   *Borman v Griffith* [1930] 1 Ch 493 at 499.
1   *Attorney-General of Southern Nigeria v John Holt & Co (Liverpool) Ltd* [1915] AC 599 at 617.
2   *Moody v Steggles* (1879) 12 Ch D 261 at 266ff; *Henry Ltd v McGlade* [1926] NI 144 at 151f.
3   Some negative rights have nevertheless been acknowledged as easements. In *Ough v King* [1967] 1 WLR 1547 at 1553A-C, for instance, the Court of Appeal upheld an easement of access to light flowing through a defined aperture. This right was effectively a right to prevent a neighbour from building on his land in such a way as to obstruct that right to light, and in the circumstances the Court of Appeal upheld an award of damages in favour of the aggrieved dominant owner (post, p 663).
4   For the potentially dangerous doctrine that an immunity from nuisance liability may also arise by necessary implication from a statute which regulates an environmentally hazardous activity, see *Allen v Gulf Oil Refining Ltd* [1981] AC 1001 at 1014A-C, 1016F, 1024A-B; [1981] CLJ 226 (J.A. Jolowicz); (1980) 43 MLR 219 (R.A. Buckley). See also *York Bros (Trading) Pty Ltd v Commr of Main Roads* [1983] 1 NSWLR 391 at 397D-398A; but compare *City of Campbellton v Gray's Velvet Ice Cream Ltd* (1982) 127 DLR (3d) 436 at 441ff.
5   (1879) 11 Ch D 852. See also *Miller v Jackson* [1977] QB 966 at 978G, where even Lord Denning MR held that there is 'no such easement known to the law as a right to hit cricket balls into your neighbour's land'. Compare, however, (1977) 93 LQR 481 (R.M. Goode); (1978) 41 MLR 334 (R.A. Buckley). The rights of the cricketers in *Miller v Jackson* were somewhat perversely upheld on other grounds, but other courts have been less inclined to allow the rights of neighbouring householders to be 'subordinated to the leisurely pursuits of sportsmen'. See *Kennaway v Thompson* [1981] QB 88 at 94E-95A (power boat racing), and compare the disobliging view taken of domestic bombardment by golf balls in *Lester-Travers v City of Frankston* [1970] VR 2 at 9f; *Segal v Derrick Golf & Winter Club* (1977) 76 DLR (3d) 746 at 749f.

(iv) An easement must not impose any positive burden on the servient owner It is generally considered intrinsic to the concept of an easement that the role of the servient owner should be essentially passive. A true easement requires of the servient owner nothing more than an act of sufferance, in that he must either allow the dominant owner to do something on the servient land or abstain from some action of his own on that land which would otherwise be entirely legitimate.[7] In the absence of contrary agreement, an easement must not normally involve the servient owner in any expenditure of money or in any positive or onerous action.[8] Thus, for instance, no claim of easement can be based on an undertaking to maintain a supply of hot water.[9] Likewise the mere existence of a right of way imposes on the servient owner no duty to carry out necessary repair or maintenance of the way.[10] A tenant's easement to use drains running through his landlord's premises imposes no duty on the landlord to keep those drains in repair.[11]

Only rarely has it been held that an easement may properly impose any positive duty on the servient owner. In *Jones v Price*,[12] however, the Court of Appeal held that a right to require a neighbour to maintain a boundary fence can be validly acquired as an easement. This fencing easement has nevertheless been described as being 'in the nature of a spurious easement',[13] and it is doubtful whether it can arise otherwise than by prescription.[14] It is also possible that a landowner whose property fronts on to the sea may be burdened by an easement to repair the sea wall.[15]

(v) An easement must not amount to exclusive occupation or joint user It is always said, consistently with the limited nature of rights of easement, that no claim can be

---

6   (1879) 11 Ch D 852 at 863ff. See also *In re The State Electricity Commission of Victoria & Joshua's Contract* [1940] VLR 121 at 125f; D. Wittman, (1980) 9 Jnl of Legal Studies 557.

7   See, however, A.J. Waite, [1985] CLJ 458, for the argument that this limitation on the scope of the easement is a relatively recent development in English law and that some easements of positive obligation may have survived intact to the present day.

8   See *Liverpool City Council v Irwin* [1977] AC 239 at 256D-E per Lord Wilberforce.

9   *Regis Property Co Ltd v Redman* [1956] 2 QB 612 at 627f. A distinction must be maintained between a right to the supply of water and a right to the uninterrupted passage of water over the land of another. The former right cannot exist as an easement because it imposes on the owner of the alleged servient tenement a positive obligation to secure the supply and probably to pay for that supply. By contrast, a mere right to the uninterrupted passage of water from the land of another can constitute an easement, since it imposes an essentially negative obligation (see *Rance v Elvin* (1985) 50 P & CR 9 at 15ff).

10 *Jones v Pritchard* [1908] 1 Ch 630 at 637f. The servient owner may be liable to his own visitors in respect of any injury which they sustain in using the right of way, but otherwise bears no liability either at common law or under the Occupiers' Liability Act 1957 to any other person who may use the right of way. See *Holden v White* [1982] QB 679 at 684A-B, 685D, 687E-F; (1982) 98 LQR 541 (K. Stanton); [1983] CLJ 48 (J.R. Spencer); [1983] Conv 58 (R. Griffith). Compare *Bartlett v Robinson* (1980) 25 SASR 552.

11 *Duke of Westminster v Guild* [1985] QB 688 at 702H-703C, 704A. Where the maintenance of an easement requires positive action, the dominant owner has an implied right to enter the servient land, eg for the purpose of executing repairs (see *Jones v Pritchard* [1908] 1 Ch 630 at 638).

12 [1965] 2 QB 618 at 633D-E, 639C.

13 *Lawrence v Jenkins* (1873) LR 8 QB 274 at 279.

14 Where this kind of easement exists, however, it is of some importance, for instance, in determining the respective rights and obligations of holders of grazing rights on open moorland. See *Crow v Wood* [1971] 1 QB 77 at 84E-G; *Egerton v Harding* [1975] QB 62 at 68B-F; [1975] CLJ 34 (C.F. Kolbert). See also A.J. Bradbrook, (1979) 53 ALJ 306.

15 *Keighley's Case* (1610) 10 Co Rep 139a at 139b, 77 ER 1136 at 1137.

recognised as an easement if it involves an element of exclusive possession or joint occupation of the supposedly servient land.[16] It is never very clear how strictly this negative characteristic of an easement is applied by the courts, and it is likely that the prohibition against exclusiveness represents an intuitive rather than a reasoned response to the validity of certain claims of easement.[17]

In *Copeland v Greenhalf*,[18] for instance, the defendant was a wheelwright who had for 50 years used a narrow strip of land belonging to the plaintiff for the purpose of storing vehicles awaiting and undergoing repair. Upjohn J held that the prescriptive right claimed by the defendant was too extensive to constitute an easement in law. In his view, the right claimed went 'wholly outside any normal idea of an easement' since it amounted to a 'claim to a joint user of the land by the defendant'.[19] Indeed the defendant was arrogating to himself 'the whole beneficial user' of one strip of the land in question. Such a claim could not be established as an easement since it was 'virtually a claim to possession of the servient tenement, if necessary to the exclusion of the owner.'[20] There was, said Upjohn J, no authority in support of the idea that 'a right of this wide and undefined nature can be the proper subject-matter of an easement.'[1]

The criterion of non-exclusive possession has been frequently applied in testing whether a particular right is capable of being an easement.[2] In *Ward v Kirkland*[3] the plaintiff claimed to have a right to enter an adjoining farmyard in order to maintain the wall of his cottage abutting on to that farmyard. Ungoed-Thomas J held that the right claimed was capable of existence as an easement, since the right involved no more than monthly visits to the servient land for the purposes of window-cleaning.[4] In *Grigsby v Melville*,[5] however, Brightman J doubted whether a right of storage in a cellar could constitute an easement in circumstances where the claim amounted to 'an exclusive right of user over the whole of the confined space representing the servient tenement'.[6]

---

16 See *Reilly v Booth* (1890) 44 Ch D 12 at 21f, 24f, 26f. A transfer of title or exclusive ownership of a building is inconsistent with the concept of easement (see *Bursill Enterprises Pty Ltd v Berger Bros Trading Co Pty Ltd* (1970-1971) 124 CLR 73 at 91 per Windeyer J).

17 One implication of the non-exclusive nature of an easement is the inability of its owner to maintain an action in trespass (see *Paine & Co Ltd v St Neots Gas & Coke Co* [1939] 3 All ER 812 at 823G-H; *Simpson v Knowles* [1974] VR 190 at 195).

18 [1952] Ch 488.

19 [1952] Ch 488 at 498. Compare *V. T. Engineering Co Ltd v Richard Barland & Co Ltd* (1968) 19 P & CR 890 at 895f.

20 [1952] Ch 488 at 498.

1 [1952] Ch 488 at 498. See also *Harada v Registrar of Titles* [1981] VR 743 at 753, where the right of a public electricity authority to position pylons on private land and to prohibit the landowner from building thereon was considered to be a claim of joint user and thus inconsistent with a claim of easement.

2 *Attorney-General of Southern Nigeria v John Holt & Co (Liverpool) Ltd* [1915] AC 599 at 617; *Capar v Wasylowski* (1983) 146 DLR (3d) 193 at 200f.

3 [1967] Ch 194.

4 The right could not be defeated on the ground that it comprised a user which 'would in effect exclude the defendant from the use of part of the farmyard next to the cottage, or interfere substantially with such use' ([1967] Ch 194 at 223C). The right contended for in no way resembled a claim of 'possession or joint possession of part of the defendant's property' ([1967] Ch 194 at 223E).

5 [1972] 1 WLR 1355 at 1364G.

6 Brightman J's decision was upheld by the Court of Appeal ([1974] 1 WLR 80), but without further consideration of the question of exclusive user or possession. The disinclination to uphold claims of easement in respect of confined spaces may account for the ruling in *Dikstein v Kanevsky* [1947] VLR 216 at 219, that there can be no easement to use an elevator.

Peculiar problems have been raised by the question whether there can be an easement to park a car. It seems likely that easements may be validly created for this purpose provided that the rights claimed do not amount to an arrogation of exclusive beneficial user of the entire servient tenement. The courts have tended to uphold as easements those parking rights which are strictly limited in point of time[7] or which relate only to a general area of land[8] rather than to a numbered or individualised parking bay.[9]

The criterion of non-exclusive possession does not appear to have been applied uniformly throughout the caselaw.[10] It seems obvious, for instance, that there can be no easement to build a house on another man's land.[11] In *Berger Bros Trading Co Pty Ltd v Bursill Enterprises Pty Ltd*,[12] however, it was held that an easement could comprise a right to demolish an existing building and rebuild on the site where the grant in question conferred no rights in respect of land beneath the surface.[13] There are other instances in which the courts have upheld as easements rights which clearly did constitute exclusive possession or user. The truth may simply be that the courts have employed the supposed requirement of non-exclusive user as a smokescreen for judicial discretion, invoking the requirement in order to strike down claims felt to be unmeritorious, while suppressing the requirement in cases where it has been thought that a remedy should be given. In *Wright v Macadam*,[14] for example, the Court of Appeal had no hesitation in recognising as an easement a right claimed by a hard-pressed tenant to store coal in a coal shed provided by her landlord. It may well be that in reality this right was one of exclusive user,[15] but it is also clear that the Court of Appeal did not look particularly kindly upon the fact that the landlord had asserted a right to make an extra charge for use of the coal shed and had pulled down the coal shed before the date of the hearing.

7   *Leon Asper Amusements Ltd v Northmain Carwash & Enterprises Ltd* (1966) 56 DLR (2d) 173 at 176ff (parking only after 6 pm each day).
8   *Sweet & Maxwell Ltd v Michael-Michaels Advertising* [1965] CLY 2192; *Newman v Jones* (Unreported, 22 March 1982, Megarry V-C).
9   See (1973) 37 Conv (NS) 60 (D.J. Hayton). A right to park in a strictly defined space may more plausibly connote the grant of a leasehold interest (see *Harley Queen v Forsyte Kerman* [1983] CLY 2077, ante, p 439). See also (1976) 40 Conv (NS) 317. Yet another possibility is that car parking is a form of bailment (see *Walton Stores Ltd v Sydney City Council* [1968] 2 NSWR 109 at 112f, ante, p 541), although this analysis may be applicable only where custody of the vehicle has actually been transferred (eg through a handing over of car keys). See *Fred Chappell Ltd v National Car Parks Ltd* (1987) *Times*, 22 May. A claim to use a right of way as a parking lot may be too extensive to support a valid claim of easement (*Keefer v Arillotta* (1977) 72 DLR (3d) 182 at 189).
10 It has even been suggested that *Copeland v Greenhalf* is a decision per incuriam (see [1973] CLJ 30 at 33 (J.R. Spencer)).
11 *Pitman v Nickerson* (1891) 40 NSR 20.
12 [1970] 1 NSWR 137 at 140.
13 On appeal the High Court of Australia avoided the issue by construing the grant not as an easement but as a conveyance of a stratum interest (see *Bursill Enterprises Pty Ltd v Berger Bros Trading Co Pty Ltd* (1970-1971) 124 CLR 73 at 76, 91f).
14 [1949] 2 KB 744 at 751ff. See (1959) 66 LQR 302 (R.E.M.).
15 In *Grigsby v Melville* [1972] 1 WLR 1355 at 1364F, Brightman J noted that the 'precise facts in *Wright v Macadam* in this respect are not wholly clear from the report and it is a little difficult to know whether the tenant had exclusive possession of the coal shed or of any defined portion of it. To some extent a problem of this sort may be one of degree.' See also *Miller v Emcer Products Ltd* [1956] Ch 304 at 316, where the Court of Appeal held that the right to use a lavatory on another's premises was capable of constituting an easement—although this must have involved some element of at least intermittently exclusive possession. See (1956) 72 LQR 172 (R.E.M.); *Hedley v Roberts* [1977] VR 282 at 289.

(5) Common easements

Amongst the most common easements are those which confer a right of way and those which relate to access to light. These easements deserve further consideration.

(a) Rights of way

A right of way is essentially a right to pass and re-pass along a way and to do things which are reasonably ancillary to such passage.[16]

(i) Content of the right of way   A right of way confers not merely a right to pass and re-pass, but also a right to halt on the way for a reasonable period of time for the purpose of loading and unloading a vehicle.[17] Although a right of way does not confer any right to leave vehicles unattended on the way or to station gantries, cranes, hoists or other loading equipment on the way,[18] it does give the grantee certain rights over the superjacent airspace. The grantee can thus insist that the way remain unobstructed, not necessarily *usque ad coelum*, but to such height as is 'reasonable in all the circumstances'.[19]

(ii) Relation to the dominant tenement   So long as a right of way is demonstrably beneficial to the occupation of the dominant tenement to which it is appurtenant, it is irrelevant that other land intervenes between the dominant and servient tenements.[20] However, a right of way which is supposedly appurtenant to a particular dominant tenement may not be used colourably for the real purpose of enjoying a further access across that dominant tenement to some other property.[1] The circumstances of such a case negative any claim that benefit is conferred upon the supposed dominant tenement.

(iii)   Construction of an express grant   Where a right of way is the subject of an express grant, its precise scope falls to be construed in the light of the

---

16   *V.T. Engineering Ltd v Richard Barland & Co Ltd* (1968) 19 P & CR 890 at 896. Compare the public right to pass along the highway (ante, p 635).
17   *Bulstrode v Lambert* [1953] 1 WLR 1064 at 1071; *McIlwraith v Grady* [1968] 1 QB 468 at 476E; *V.T. Engineering Ltd v Richard Barland & Co Ltd* (1968) 19 P & CR 890 at 894; *Grinskis v Lahood* [1971] NZLR 502 at 509; *Deanshaw and Deanshaw v Marshall* (1978) 20 SASR 146 at 150.
18   *V.T. Engineering Ltd v Richard Barland & Co Ltd* (1968) 19 P & CR 890 at 896.
19   *V.T. Engineering Ltd v Richard Barland & Co Ltd* (1968) 19 P & CR 890 at 895. Here the grantee was held to be entitled to a reasonable amount of 'vertical swing space' for a hoist, but Megarry J ruled that the right of way could not confer rights to a 'lateral swing space' since this would 'in effect sterilise a strip of land of indefinite depth on each side of the way'.
20   *Todrick v Western National Omnibus Co Ltd* [1934] Ch 561 at 572f.
1   *Allen v Gomme* (1840) 11 A & E 759 at 770, 113 ER 602 at 607; *Skull v Glenister* (1864) 16 CB (NS) 81 at 103, 143 ER 1055 at 1063; *Williams v James* (1867) LR 2 CP 577 at 580, 582; *Harris v Flower* (1904) 74 LJ Ch 127 at 132; *Bracewell v Appleby* [1975] Ch 408 at 417H-418A; *Smith v Smith* (1895) 14 NZLR 4 at 6; *Grinskis v Lahood* [1971] NZLR 502 at 509; *Re Gordon and Regan* (1985) 15 DLR (4th) 641 at 647f. An exception to this principle occurs where, at the date of the grant, the dominant tenement was itself used as a means of access to the other property (see *Nickerson v Barraclough* [1980] Ch 325 at 336D-E). See also *National Trust v White* [1987] 1 WLR 907 at 913C-D.

surrounding circumstances at the date of the grant.[2] Of these circumstances one of the most material is the 'nature of the locus in quo over which the right of way is granted'.[3] Thus the sheer physical characteristics of the way granted may indicate that rights which are otherwise unlimited in their terms of grant must by necessary implication be cut back to more restricted forms of user.[4]

Where an easement of way is not expressly subject to any restriction as to the form of user, the courts have been disinclined to hold that the permissible user is cut down by the past practice of the dominant owner[5] or is impliedly limited to certain kinds of person.[6] In particular an unlimited right of way may be exercised for any purpose related to the contemporary user of the dominant tenement, even though this user may differ from the original user at the date of the express grant. In the absence of express contrary stipulation in the grant, there is no doctrine that a right of way must be confined to purposes consistent with the user of the dominant tenement as of the date of grant.[7] A right of way granted for general purposes in respect of a house thus survives the conversion of that house into a hotel,[8] although there is always the possibility that any excessive user of the original easement will be actionable as nuisance.[9]

(iv) Fluctuations in user under an express grant While subsequent changes of user of the dominant tenement are in themselves immaterial, it is clear that objection may be raised if the changed user imposes an excessive burden on the servient tenement relative to the burden which existed at the date of grant. In *Jelbert v Davis*,[10] for instance, a dominant tenement had originally been used for agricultural purposes only. The dominant owner subsequently obtained planning permission to position up to 200 holiday caravans on the site. The Court of Appeal attached no significance to the change in the *form* of user of the dominant land, but upheld an objection that the *volume* of user of the access

2 *St Edmundsbury and Ipswich Diocesan Board of Finance v Clark* (No 2) [1975] 1 WLR 468 at 476G–477B; *Bridgwood v Keates* (Unreported, Court of Appeal, 1 November 1983). If the terms of a conveyance do not sufficiently describe the extent of a right of way, reference may be had for this purpose not only to the plan annexed to the conveyance but also to any planning permission which delimited the scope of the relevant access (*Scott v Martin* [1987] 1 WLR 841 at 849D–850A).

3 *Cannon v Villars* (1878) 8 Ch D 415 at 420 per Jessel MR.

4 A right granted in respect of a passageway which was only 2 ft 11 in wide is necessarily restricted to foot traffic (*Bridgwood v Keates* (Unreported, Court of Appeal, 1 November 1983)).

5 *Bridgwood v Keates* (Unreported, Court of Appeal, 1 November 1983).

6 See *Bridgwood v Keates* (Unreported, Court of Appeal, 1 November 1983), where Oliver LJ refused to hold that an access to a back door was restricted by implication to 'trade visitors', thereby precluding access by the dominant owner herself or her children. In this case the real substance of the grievance expressed by the dominant owner's neighbours was the fact that she was accustomed in effect to use her back door as the principal entrance to her house. The Court of Appeal refused to intervene, although noting that if this user became 'excessive' then it would be actionable as nuisance (post, p 662).

7 *South Eastern Railway Co v Cooper* [1924] 1 Ch 211 at 222f; *Grinskis v Lahood* [1971] NZLR 502 at 508. It may still be true that an easement of way granted as appurtenant to an open space cannot be invoked if that open space is subsequently built upon (see *Allen v Gomme* (1840) 11 A & E 759 at 772, 774, 113 ER 602 at 607f).

8 *White v Grand Hotel, Eastbourne, Ltd* [1913] 1 Ch 113 at 116f (affirmed by Court of Appeal, (1915) 84 LJ Ch 938); *Robinson v Bailey* [1948] 2 All ER 791 at 796B–G; *Jelbert v Davis* [1968] 1 WLR 589 at 594H–595B; *Grinskis v Lahood* [1971] NZLR 502 at 509.

9 See eg *Rosling v Pinnegar* (1986) *Times*, 16 December.

10 [1968] 1 WLR 589.

route to this site was liable to become excessive. In the view of Lord Denning MR, the proposed user was likely to be 'so extensive as to be outside the reasonable contemplation of the parties at the time the grant was made'.[11] An injunction was granted.[12]

The mere alteration of a dominant tenement to which a right of way has been appurtenant does not necessarily extinguish the right of way. In *Graham v Philcox*,[13] a subsequent enlargement of the original dominant tenement was held to have no effect on the existence of the easement, so long as the character and extent of the burden imposed on the servient tenement by the extended dominant tenement were not excessive.

(v) Scope of a prescriptively acquired right of way   Different rules govern a right of way which has been acquired by prescription.[14] Such a right is for ever limited to the kind of user which prevailed during the period which gave rise to the prescriptive claim.[15] However, a prescriptively acquired easement is not affected by a subsequent increase in user as distinct from a change in the fundamental character or purpose of the original user.[16]

(vi) Interference with rights of way   Any wrongful interference with a private right of way is potentially a nuisance in relation to which either damages or an injunction (or both) may be sought.[17] However, not every form of interference is actionable.[18] A right of way cannot, by definition, confer rights of exclusive user, and it necessarily follows that the threshold of actionable nuisance is reached only when there is 'substantial' interference with the way as granted,[19] in a form which is plainly obstructive of its reasonable use.[20] Each case raises an

---

11   [1968] 1 WLR 589 at 596A, F. See *Malden Farms Ltd v Nicholson* (1956) 3 DLR (2d) 236 at 239ff, where the dominant tenant, who had recently built a holiday beach resort, was restrained from allowing the general public (who came 'by the hundreds') to use a lake shore pathway which had originally been granted as a private right of way to an unspoilt piece of shoreline. See also *Grinskis v Lahood* [1971] NZLR 502 at 509f. Compare *National Trust v White* [1987] 1 WLR 907 at 913G-914G.

12   For further discussion of the remedy appropriate in cases of unreasonable or excessive user, see *Rosling v Pinnegar* (1986) *Times*, 16 December.

13   [1984] QB 747 at 756D-757A, 764D-765A (conversion of two flats into single dwelling-house, where one of the flats had earlier enjoyed a right of way over adjoining land). See [1985] CLJ 15 (S. Tromans); [1985] Conv 60 (P. Todd).

14   Post, p 678.

15   *Ballard v Dyson* (1808) 1 Taunt 279 at 286, 127 ER 841 at 844; *Williams v James* (1867) LR 2 CP 577 at 582; *Bradburn v Morris* (1876) 3 Ch D 812 at 823; *R.P.C. Holdings Ltd v Rogers* [1953] 1 All ER 1029 at 1032B-C. See also *Cargill v Gotts* [1981] 1 WLR 441 at 447H-448A.

16   *British Railways Board v Glass* [1965] Ch 538 at 562E-563A, 567G-568D (increase from 6 to 30 caravans on site); *Woodhouse & Co Ltd v Kirkland (Derby) Ltd* [1970] 1 WLR 1185 at 1190H-1191A. For the present purpose a prescriptive claim is not vitiated merely because the original easement involved user by horse-drawn vehicles, while the modern user is by way of motor car (*Lock v Abercester Ltd* [1939] Ch 861 at 863f), or because the original user has dwindled away to less onerous traffic on foot (*Davies v Stephens* (1836) 7 C & P 570 at 571, 173 ER 251 at 252). See also *Cargill v Gotts* [1981] 1 WLR 441 at 448H-449B.

17   *Saint v Jenner* [1973] Ch 275 at 280A-E; *McKellar v Guthrie* [1920] NZLR 729 at 731.

18   *Celsteel Ltd v Alton House Holdings Ltd* [1985] 1 WLR 204 at 216E.

19   *Hutton v Hamboro* (1860) 2 F & F 218 at 219, 175 ER 1031 at 1032; *Keefe v Amor* [1965] 1 QB 334 at 347D; *Pettey v Parsons* [1914] 2 Ch 653 at 662, 665.

20   *Keefe v Amor* [1965] 1 QB 334 at 346G; *Celsteel Ltd v Alton House Holdings Ltd* [1985] 1 WLR 204 at 217B.

issue of fact and degree. No actionable interference occurs, for example, where an adjacent building enroaches into a roadway by merely two feet,[1] but there may well be a remedy where the width of the way is more than halved.[2] The erection of a gate across the way constitutes no nuisance so long as the dominant owner is allowed free access at all times,[3] or so long as the gate is kept open at least during the dominant owner's business hours.[4] The installation of a large cattle grid may be a source of actionable nuisance,[5] but the courts have looked more kindly on the construction of speed ramps on a driveway.[6]

(b) Rights of light

In the absence of any natural right of access to light,[7] the preservation of access to sunlight must be sought by way of either a duly acquired easement of light or a restrictive covenant which precludes adverse building development. Rights of light are commonly acquired as a prescriptive easement and are often termed 'ancient lights'.[8] In English law at any rate, an easement of light can arise only in respect of light which comes through a defined aperture (such as a window[9]), and easements of light are therefore restricted to buildings.[10] The obstruction of part of the light reaching a building on the dominant tenement can constitute an actionable nuisance.

(i) Quantum of light The dominant owner is entitled to the uninterrupted access through his ancient windows of sufficient light to enable him to enjoy comfortable use of the building for the purposes of his occupancy,[11] whether that use is residential or business.[12] Judged against the criterion of 'ordinary

---

1 *Clifford v Hoare* (1874) LR 9 CP 362 at 370ff.
2 *Celsteel Ltd v Alton House Holdings Ltd* [1985] 1 WLR 204 at 218C-G. See also *Powell v Linney* (1983) 80 Law Soc Gaz 1982.
3 See *Flynn v Harte* [1913] 2 IR 322 at 326ff. The existence of a right of way is not inconsistent with a duty in the dominant owner to close the gate after use (see *Lister v Rickard* (1969) 113 SJ 981; *Gohl v Hender* [1930] SASR 158 at 163f).
4 *Pettey v Parsons* [1914] 2 Ch 653 at 662ff; *Lister v Rickard* (1969) 113 SJ 981.
5 *Powell v Linney* (1983) 80 Law Soc Gaz 1982.
6 *Saint v Jenner* [1973] Ch 275 at 279D.
7 Ante, p 643.
8 Post, p 684.
9 Ante, p 654. See *Levet v Gas Light & Coke Co* [1919] 1 Ch 24 at 27.
10 In other jurisdictions there has been much greater interest in the more general question of easements of solar access. See eg *Prah v Maretti* 321 NW.2d 182 at 187ff (1982); D.D. Goble, *Solar Rights: Guaranteeing a Place in the Sun*, 57 Oregon LR 94 (1978); P.D. Devlin, 17 Calif Western LR 123 (1980-81); A.J. Bradbrook, (1982) 5 Univ of New South Wales LJ 229; (1983) 15 U of W Australia LR 148; A.E. Blenkhorn, 32 Cleveland State LR 497 (1983-84).
11 *Colls v Home and Colonial Stores Ltd* [1904] AC 179 at 187, 198, 204; *Allen v Greenwood* [1980] Ch 119 at 130A-B, 135A-B. In *Carr-Saunders v Dick McNeil Associates Ltd* [1986] 1 WLR 922 at 928E-F, Millett J reiterated the 'well established' rule that no actionable wrong is committed if 'the amount of light remaining is sufficient for the comfortable enjoyment of his property by the dominant owner according to the ordinary notions of mankind.'
12 A photographic studio may be entitled to an unusually large quantity of light (see *Allen v Greenwood* [1980] Ch 119 at 133C-D, 136G-H), but a church, even if it has stained glass windows, cannot prescribe for more light than is needed in order to be 'comfortably used according to the ordinary requirements of people attending church' (see *Newham v Lawson* (1971) 22 P & CR 852 at 859f).

user',[13] the relevant issue in any alleged interference with light is not 'How much light has been taken away?' but rather 'How much light is left?'[14]

(ii) Fluctuations in user   The dominant owner is not entitled to impose an increased burden on the servient tenement merely by altering either the user of his building[257] or the position or size of his windows.[16] However, an easement of light acquired under the Prescription Act 1832 relates to the building as a whole and not to a particular room within it.[17] The extent of the dominant owner's right is neither increased nor diminished by the actual use to which the dominant tenement has been put in the past[18] or by any extraordinary use to which he now chooses to put the premises or any of the rooms in them.[19] The court must therefore take account not only of present use, but also of 'other potential uses to which the dominant owner may reasonably be expected to put the premises in the future'.[20] In *Carr-Saunders v Dick McNeil Associates Ltd*,[1] for instance, it was not fatal to the dominant owner's allegation of obstruction that he had, during the prescription period, altered his premises by subdividing one large room into a number of smaller rooms. The windows had remained unchanged, even though the rooms behind them had not, and the dominant owner was therefore entitled to damages in respect of the elevation of an adjacent building which had recently obstructed the access of reasonable light to the reconstructed rooms.

(iii) Actionable interference   The courts are nowadays disinclined to adopt inflexible methods of quantifying the degree of obstruction with light which gives rise to an actionable nuisance. There is no longer any '45 degrees rule',[2] and in *Carr-Saunders v Dick McNeil Associates Ltd*[3] Millett J resisted any rigid application of a '50-50 rule', under which an interference with light is actionable only where more than 50 per cent of the floor area of a room receives

---

13   The light required for 'ordinary user' depends also on the nature of the building concerned. A greenhouse may need much more light than a warehouse (see *Allen v Greenwood* [1980] Ch 119 at 131B, 135A-B). The standard of light enjoyed by way of easement may extend beyond that which would be justified by 'ordinary user' if the servient owner has, eg during the prescription period, been aware of a specially enhanced or heightened requirement of light for the particular purposes of the dominant owner (see *Allen v Greenwood*, supra at 132D-F, 136A-B).

14   *Higgins v Betts* [1905] 2 Ch 210 at 215 per Farwell J. See also *Carr-Saunders v Dick McNeil Associates Ltd* [1986] 1 WLR 922 at 928F.

15   *Colls v Home and Colonial Stores Ltd* [1904] AC 179 at 203.

16   *Smith v Evangelization Society (Incorporated) Trust* [1933] Ch 515 at 533ff; *Scott v Goulding Properties Ltd* [1973] IR 200 at 219ff.

17   *Colls v Home and Colonial Stores Ltd* [1904] AC 179 at 204; *Price v Hilditch* [1930] 1 Ch 500 at 508; *Carr-Saunders v Dick McNeil Associates Ltd* [1986] 1 WLR 922 at 928D.

18   *Price v Hilditch* [1930] 1 Ch 500 at 506ff; *Carr-Saunders v Dick McNeil Associates Ltd* [1986] 1 WLR 922 at 928F-G.

19   *Carr-Saunders v Dick McNeil Associates Ltd* [1986] 1 WLR 922 at 928G.

20   *Carr-Saunders v Dick McNeil Associates Ltd* [1986] 1 WLR 922 at 928H. See also *Moore v Hall* (1878) 3 QBD 178 at 182.

1   [1986] 1 WLR 922 at 929F-930F.

2   *Colls v Home and Colonial Stores Ltd* [1904] AC 179 at 210; *Fishenden v Higgs & Hill Ltd* (1935) 153 LT 128 at 131f, 136f, 143f. This rule operated against obstructions which rose above a line extended upwards from a room at a 45 degree angle out through the centre of a window.

3   [1986] 1 WLR 922 at 927B-C.

one lumen of light at table level. He took the view that the dominant owner is simply entitled to such access of light 'as will leave his premises adequately lit for all ordinary purposes for which they may reasonably be expected to be used.'[4]

3. CREATION OF EASEMENTS AND PROFITS

An easement or profit *à prendre* can exist *at law* only if certain conditions are fulfilled. *First*, the easement or profit must be held 'for an interest equivalent to an estate in fee simple absolute in possession or a term of years absolute'.[5] *Second*, the easement or profit must be created by statute, by deed or by prescription. In all other cases the easement or profit must be equitable. There is no exception even in the case of an easement or profit which is granted for a period of three years or less, since there is no analogy with the rules concerning the informal creation of legal leases.[6]

(1) Informal creation

In the absence of statutory or prescriptive creation, an easement or profit which is granted *informally* has only equitable status.[7] It is possible, however, that an equitable easement or profit may be created by a written document not under seal[8] or even by a mere oral agreement,[9] provided in either case that the transaction is a transaction for value or is supported by a sufficient act of part performance.

(2) Distinction between grant and reservation

Easements and profits may be created by means of either grant or reservation. The difference between grant and reservation turns on the identity of the party in whose favour the easement or profit is created. The following examples use a right of way as a working basis for discussion.

(a) Grant

Grant arises typically where a landowner (V) disposes of part of his land to a stranger (P) as in *Fig.* 46, on terms that P shall henceforth be entitled to the benefit of an easement over the land retained by V.[10] In this case the easement concerned is created in favour of P, the transferee of the land.

---

4   [1986] 1 WLR 922 at 928G-H.
5   Law of Property Act 1925, s 1(2)(a).
6   Ante, p 464.
7   See *Wood v Leadbitter* (1845) 13 M & W 838 at 843, 153 ER 351 at 354; *Mason v Clarke* [1954] 1 QB 460 at 468, 471.
8   *Frogley v Earl of Lovelace* (1859) Johns 333 at 339f, 70 ER 450 at 453; *May v Belleville* [1905] 2 Ch 605 at 613. This result is merely another application of the doctrine of *Walsh v Lonsdale* (ante, p 472).
9   *McManus v Cooke* (1887) 35 Ch D 681 at 697; *Bayley v Marquis Conyngham* (1863) 15 ICLR 406 at 410ff.
10   Grant need not, of course, occur only in the event of a severance or subdivision of an existing ownership, in that it is always open to a landowner to grant away easements or profits over his land. It is simply the case that grant tends to occur most frequently in cases of subdivision, where the minds of the parties are most clearly directed towards a consideration of their future needs in relation to their respective properties.

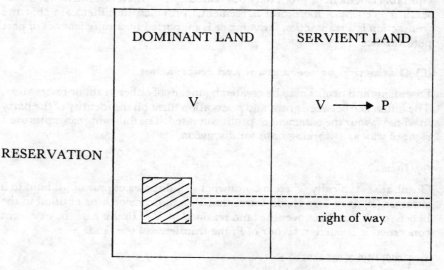

Fig. 46

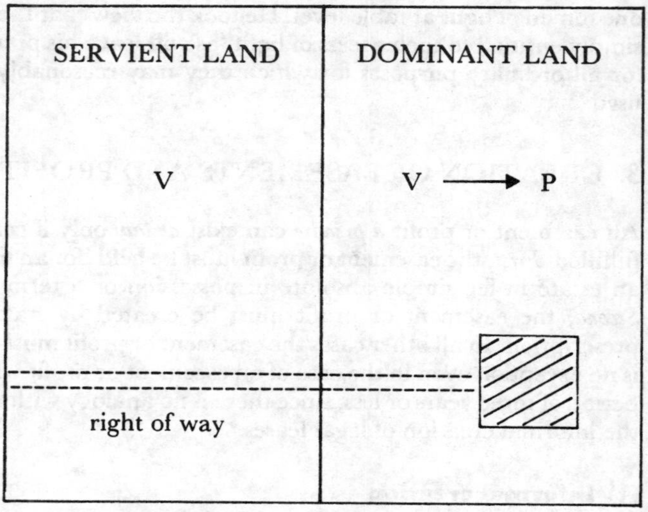

Fig. 47

(b) Reservation

Reservation arises where the original landowner (V) disposes of part of his land to P, as in *Fig. 47*, on terms that V shall nevertheless retain an easement over the land purchased by P. In this case the easement concerned is one created in favour of V, the transferor of the land.

The rules relating to the creation of easements and profits are made very much easier if the distinction between grant and reservation is borne in mind.

The essential difference between grant and reservation is whether the right in question is granted to the transferee of the land conveyed or is reserved by the transferor in favour of the land retained. In the case of grant, the servient tenement is in the hands of V; in the case of reservation, the servient tenement is that of P.

4. GRANT OF EASEMENTS AND PROFITS

Grant of an easement or profit *à prendre* may be brought about by express grant, implied grant, prescription or estoppel.

(1) Express grant

Express grant may in turn arise in two cases—by means of express words of grant and by means of statute.

(a) Express words of grant

This is the most common form of grant and, as such, presents relatively few complications.[11] Express words of grant are normally incorporated in the conveyance or transfer of a legal estate where it is intended that the purchaser should enjoy certain rights by way of easement over the land retained by the vendor. There is no legal requirement that the grant should make any explicit reference to the dominant tenement or in any other way identify the land benefited by the easement.[12]

After 1925 the grant of an easement or profit without words of limitation confers the most ample interest which the grantor of the easement is competent to confer, unless a contrary intention is apparent. Thus an easement granted expressly in a conveyance of the grantor's fee simple estate is effective to grant an easement for an interest equivalent to a fee simple. Moreover, in the absence of specifically restrictive terms in the original grant or any contrary intention expressed in the conveyance to the grantee, an easement which is granted in connection with the creation of a leasehold estate is not necessarily coterminous with that estate and therefore appertains to the land without limit of time.[13] An easement which is expressly granted for

---

11 Easements are, however, subject to the rule against perpetuities (see *Dunn v Blackdown Properties Ltd* [1961] Ch 433 at 438), and there is therefore always a possibility that a grant may be rendered void on the ground of perpetuity (see eg *Newham v Lawson* (1971) 22 P & CR 852 at 855f).

12 The court simply examines all the relevant circumstances in order to determine whether there was in fact a dominant tenement benefited by the supposed easement (see *Johnstone v Holdway* [1963] 1 QB 601 at 612; *Shannon Ltd v Venner Ltd* [1965] Ch 682 at 693G-694A; *Gas & Fuel Corpn of Victoria v Barba* [1976] VR 755 at 764). The rule on this point is different in other common law jurisdictions. In New South Wales (although not in Victoria), no easement is enforceable against a third party unless the instrument which creates the interest clearly indicates both the land to which the benefit is appurtenant and the land which is subject to the burden of the easement (Conveyancing Act 1919, s 88(1)). See *Maurice Toltz Pty Ltd v Macy's Emporium Pty Ltd* (1969) 91 WN (NSW) 591 at 599D-F; *Papadopoulos v Goodwin* [1982] 1 NSWLR 413 at 417B-418E.

13 *Graham v Philcox* [1984] QB 747 at 761A-D.

the term of a lease is an easement for an interest equivalent to a term of years absolute and may be likewise legal.[14]

(b) Statute

Easements and profits may be granted expressly by statute. Such grants are often made in favour of public utilities for the purpose of the better management or execution of the function with which they are charged. Thus statutorily created easements exist in favour of public utility undertakings which provide and maintain supplies of gas, electricity, water and sewerage.[15]

(2) Implied grant

There are certain cases in which the grant of an easement will be implied in favour of the purchaser of land. These cases of implied grant fall into roughly four categories.

(a) Necessity

In certain circumstances the courts are willing to imply the grant of an easement on the ground of necessity,[16] the classic case of necessity in this context being that of the 'landlocked close'.[17] If V sells land to P which has no means of access except across land retained by V, it is clear that the courts will imply on behalf of P an easement of access even though the conveyance or transfer to P makes no express reference to such a right.[18] It is for V to select the particular route of access,[19] but once nominated this route cannot later be varied without agreement.[20]

(i) Criterion of 'necessity'   For the present purpose a case of 'necessity' does not arises on a mere showing that a particular access would be convenient or even 'reasonably necessary' for the proper enjoyment of the alleged

14   Ante, p 80.
15   Ante, p 645.
16   See P. Jackson, (1981) 34 CLP 113; P.G. Glenn, 58 North Carolina LR 223 (1979-80).
17   See D.A. Stroud, (1940) 56 LQR 93; A.J. Bradbrook, (1983) 10 Sydney LR 39. It is possible that there may be other species of easement which are implied from necessity. For the suggestion that necessity may generate an obligation of support as between adjoining terraced or semi-detached houses, see *Williams v Usherwood* (1983) 45 P & CR 235 at 254. It is also likely that in these circumstances an implied obligation of support can be founded on the rule in *Wheeldon v Burrows* (post, p 672). See eg *Scouton & Co (Builders) Ltd v Gilyott & Scott Ltd* (1972) 221 Estates Gazette 1499.
18   *Pinnington v Galland* (1853) 9 Exch 1 at 12f, 156 ER 1 at 6; *Pearson v Spencer* (1861) 1 B & S 571 at 584, 121 ER 827 at 831; *B. & W. Investments Ltd v Ulster Scottish Friendly Society* (1969) 20 NILQ 325.
19   *Bolton v Bolton* (1879) 11 Ch D 968 at 972; *Deacon v South-Eastern Railway Co* (1889) 61 LT 377 at 379; *Brown v Alabaster* (1887) 37 Ch D 490 at 500; *Barba v Gas & Fuel Corpn of Victoria* (1976) 136 CLR 120 at 132. The route selected must, however, be convenient (see *Pearson v Spencer* (1861) 1 B & S 571 at 585, 121 ER 827 at 832). If the servient owner fails to point out the way, the grantee must take the nearest way possible (see *Wimbledon and Putney Commons Conservators v Dixon* (1875) 1 Ch D 362 at 369f).
20   *Deacon v South-Eastern Railway Co* (1889) 61 LT 377 at 379.

dominant tenement.[1] The claimant must establish that, without the provision of the desired access, his tenement cannot be used at all.[2] It is not fatal to the claim of necessity that some of the surrounding land belongs to third parties and not to the vendor,[3] or that there exist alternative ways open to the landlocked owner by way of precarious user.[4] It is, however, vital that the necessity pleaded by the purchaser or by his successor in title should have existed at the date of conveyance of the land and not be merely a form of necessity which arose after that date.[5]

(ii) Extent of the implied right   An implied way of necessity confers only a right to pass and re-pass along the route of access to the landlocked dominant tenement. It has been held that the dominant owner cannot plead a similar ground of necessity in support of such ancillary easements as those relating to drainage, sewerage and the supply of electricity.[6] It is just possible, however, that an implied grant of these auxiliary rights would be supportable on a principle of non-derogation from grant.[7]

(iii) An overriding rule of public policy?   It has been suggested that implied easements of necessity rest ultimately on some rule of public policy. In *Nickerson v Barraclough*,[8] for instance, it was argued that the terms of the conveyance of a landlocked close from V to P had expressly negatived any right of way in favour of P. When the existence of a possible easement of necessity became a matter of dispute between the successors in title of P and V, Megarry V-C made reference at first instance to a 'rule of public policy which requires that land should not be rendered unusable by being landlocked'.[9] An important aspect of this policy was, in his view, the idea that 'no transaction should, without good reason, be treated as being effectual to deprive any

1   Compare the position in New Zealand where there is a much more general power vested in the courts to make an order on behalf of a landlocked owner granting access through the land of neighbours (Property Law Act 1952, s 129B). Land is 'landlocked' if 'there is no reasonable access to it' as defined in Property Law Act 1952, s 129B(1)(c). See *Murray v Devonport BC* [1980] 2 NZLR 572 (Note); *Hutchison v Milne* [1980] 2 NZLR 568; *Wilson v Rush* [1980] 2 NZLR 577; *Mowat v Federated Farmers of New Zealand (Waikato Provincial District) Inc* [1980] 2 NZLR 585; *Mitchell v Rands* [1982] BCL 204; *Gardner v Howie* [1983] BCL 495; *Cooke v Ramsay* [1984] 2 NZLR 689.
2   See *Union Lighterage Co v London Graving Dock Co* [1902] 2 Ch 557 at 573.
3   *Serff v Acton Local Board* (1886) 31 Ch D 679 at 683f; *Barkshire v Grubb* (1881) 18 Ch D 616 at 620.
4   See *Barry v Hasseldine* [1952] Ch 835 at 839. The availability of an alternative route enjoyable as of right is, of course, destructive of any claim of necessity, even though that alternative is inconvenient (see *Titchmarsh v Royston Water Co Ltd* (1899) 81 LT 673 at 675).
5   *Holmes v Goring* (1824) 2 Bing 76 at 84, 130 ER 233 at 237; *Corpn of London v Riggs* (1880) 13 Ch D 798 at 806ff. See also *B.O.J. Properties Ltd v Allen's Mobile Home Park Ltd* (1980) 108 DLR (3d) 305 at 312ff.
6   See eg *Pryce v McGuinness* [1966] Qd R 591 at 607f (where the dominant owner successfully claimed a right of way, but was otherwise marooned in his landlocked close). See also *Union Lighterage Co v London Graving Dock Co* [1902] 2 Ch 557 at 573.
7   Ante, p 476; post, p 672.
8   [1980] Ch 325. See (1980) 96 LQR 187 (P. Jackson); (1980) 130 NLJ 204 (H.W. Wilkinson); [1980] Conv 95 (J.T.F.).
9   [1980] Ch 325 at 334D. See E.H. Bodkin, (1973) 89 LQR 87; T.A.M. Cooney, (1979) 14 Ir Jur (NS) 334.

land of a suitable means of access.'[10] On the facts of the present case Megarry V-C saw no good reason for depriving the land in question of any access to the highway.[11] He regarded his conclusion as being supported by the long-standing rule that a grantor may not 'derogate from his grant'.[12] In *Nickerson v Barraclough* the original vendor had sold building land as such and, according to Megarry V-C, to negative any means of access to that land in the terms of the conveyance would constitute 'a plain instance of derogation'.[13]

Megarry V-C's judgment was reversed by the Court of Appeal.[14] Here Brightman LJ ruled that 'the doctrine of way of necessity is not founded upon public policy at all but upon an implication from the circumstances.'[15] The Court held that a way of necessity can exist only in association with a grant of land and rests on the implication, drawn from the circumstances of the case, that unless some way is implied a parcel of land will be inaccessible. Considerations of public policy are relevant therefore only to the extent that the courts may *frustrate* a contract where the underlying intention is contrary to public policy.[16]

(iv) Access to neighbouring land for the purpose of repair   English law does not at present provide any general means by which a person who requires to have access to neighbouring land for the purpose of carrying out necessary works on his own land can lawfully enter his neighbour's land without that neighbour's permission. The problem raised here is most pressing, for instance, where a landowner requires to repair part of his property (eg a roof gutter) which immediately abuts on to adjoining land. In order to remedy the deleterious effects of an unreasonable (but at the moment unchallengeable) refusal of access by an unhelpful neighbour, the Law Commission has recently proposed that the law be amended to make a right to such access available on application to the county court.[17] This right of access would be limited to the purpose of carrying out 'preservation work' such as cleaning, decoration, care, maintenance and repair,[18] and would not cover optional improvements

---

10   [1980] Ch 325 at 334H-335A. Megarry V-C recognised, however, that a way of necessity will not be implied in the case of every landlocked close, since there are certain circumstances in which 'there may be good reason why the land should be deprived of all access'. He cited as examples the case where the land 'may contain large quantities of highly toxic substances with a long life' and the somewhat less disturbing case where it is 'desired to produce a bird sanctuary that will, as far as possible, be free from any disturbance' ([1980] Ch 325 at 334G).

11   The relevant conveyance was thus construed, not as negativing the implication of a way of necessity, but merely as freeing V from any obligation to make up proposed new roads ([1980] Ch 325 at 335H-336A).

12   Ante, p 476.

13   [1980] Ch 325 at 335B.

14   [1981] Ch 426. See (1982) 98 LQR 11 (P. Jackson); L. Crabb, [1981] Conv 442.

15   See eg *North Sydney Printing Pty Ltd v Sabemo Investment Corpn Pty Ltd* [1971] 2 NSWLR 150 at 160D-E, cited in *Nickerson v Barraclough* [1981] Ch 426 at 440G.

16   [1981] Ch 426 at 441A.

17   *Rights of Access to Neighbouring Land* (Law Com No 151, Cmnd 9692, December 1985), para 3.42.

18   Law Com No 151, paras 4.2, 4.7. The Commission envisaged that the county court would have power to order compensation to be paid to the neighbour for any loss, damage or injury suffered as a result of the access, but not for the nuisance or inconvenience of the access itself (paras 4.48ff).

and alterations.[19] The right of access granted by the court would not be a permanent right, but would merely be a 'one-off' right appropriate to a particular need.[20] No legislation embodying the Law Commission's proposal has yet appeared.[1]

(b) Common intention

Easements may be implied in favour of the grantee of property in order to give effect to a common intention of the grantor and grantee of that property. Such easements may not be essentially different from those implied from necessity, in that a common intention to grant a particular easement will normally be found only in cases of necessity.[2] In *Pwllbach Colliery Co Ltd v Woodman*,[3] Lord Parker of Waddington stated that the law will readily imply the grant of 'such easements as may be necessary to give effect to the common intention of the parties to a grant of real property, with reference to the manner or purposes in and for which the land granted...is to be used.'[4] Lord Parker added, however, that 'it is essential...that the parties should intend that the subject of the grant...should be used in some definite and particular manner'.[5]

The principle of implication from common intention was illustrated in *Wong v Beaumont Property Trust Ltd.*[6] Here the defendant's predecessor in title had leased the basement of premises to the plaintiff's predecessor in title for the express purpose of use as a restaurant. The plaintiff later bought the remainder of the lease, intending to use the premises as a Chinese restaurant. He covenanted to comply with public health regulations and to eliminate all noxious smells and odours. In fact, unknown to the parties at the date of the assignment of the lease, these obligations could be performed only by the installation of a new ventilation system leading through the upstairs premises retained by the defendant. The Court of Appeal held that the plaintiff was entitled to assert an easement of necessity in respect of the construction of the ventilation duct which would enable him to comply both with the terms of the lease and with public health regulations.[7]

---

19 Law Com No 151, para 4.8.
20 Law Com No 151, para 4.62f.
 1 The compulsory acquisition of easements is already available on a more extensive scale in other jurisdictions. Compare eg Queensland's Property Law Act 1974, s 180 (see *Tipler v Fraser* [1976] Qd R 272; *Ex parte Edward Street Properties Pty Ltd* [1977] Qd R 86; *Re Seaforth Land Sales Pty Ltd's Land* (No 2) [1977] Qd R 317; H. Tarlo, (1979) 53 ALJ 254); British Columbia's Property Law Act (RSBC 1979, c 340), s 32 (see *Re Ferguson and Lepine* (1982) 128 DLR (3d) 188).
 2 See eg *Nickerson v Barraclough* [1980] Ch 325 at 336D, where Megarry V-C expressed the view that a 'way of necessity' should be 'more accurately referred to as a way implied from the common intention of the parties, based on a necessity apparent from the deeds'. The affinity between the grounds of necessity and common intention is again evident in *B.O.J. Properties Ltd v Allen's Mobile Home Park Ltd* (1980) 108 DLR (3d) 305 at 315f.
 3 [1915] AC 634 at 646f.
 4 See also *Squarey v Harris-Smith* (1981) 42 P & CR 118 at 127 per Oliver LJ.
 5 [1915] AC 634 at 647 ('It is not enough that the subject of the grant...should be intended to be used in a manner which may or may not involve this definite and particular use').
 6 [1965] 1 QB 173. See (1964) 80 LQR 322 (R.E.M.).
 7 [1965] 1 QB 173 at 181E, 183E-F. See also *In re The State Electricity Commission of Victoria & Joshua's Contract* [1940] VLR 121 at 125f (implied grant of easement to transmit noise).

(c) Quasi-easements (the rule in Wheeldon v Burrows)

A third category of implied grant was confirmed by the rule in *Wheeldon v Burrows*.[8] This doctrine is but another illustration of the more general rule in English law that a grantor 'may not derogate from his grant'.[9] In other words, he must not grant land to another on terms which effectively negate the utility of the grant for the grantee.[10] This presumption against derogation from grant may of course be ousted by contrary agreement.[11]

(i) Operation of the rule   The rule in *Wheeldon v Burrows* operates in the event of a subdivision of land (see *Fig.* 48). The rule confers on P, the transferee of a part of V's land, the benefit of any user over the land retained by V, which V himself had earlier found it convenient to exercise on his own behalf during the period prior to the subdivision. However, since this user could not have been said to constitute an easement before the transfer to P—for the simple reason that both tenements were then under the common ownership and occupation of V[12]—the rights impliedly granted to P under *Wheeldon v Burrows* are usually referred to as *quasi-easements*.[13] In effect P receives as quasi-easements such rights over the tenement still retained by V which V had previously found to be necessary for the proper enjoyment and utilisation of the tenement now transferred to P.[14] Thus if V, while he lived in the quasi-dominant tenement prior to subdivision of his land, had been accustomed to pass and re-pass over land which he still retains after the subdivision, this user may now be claimed by P as of right in relation to what has become a quasi-servient tenement (see *Fig.* 48). The rule in *Wheeldon v Burrows* is capable, moreover, of extending far beyond rights of way. Where, for instance, V originally owned two adjoining houses, the rule may equally well operate to imply a right of support on behalf of P if he purchases one of these houses from V.[15]

---

8   (1879) 12 Ch D 31.

9   Ante, p 476. See eg *Bayley v Great Western Railway Co* (1884) 26 Ch D 434 at 453; *Nelson v Walker* (1910) 10 CLR 560 at 582.

10   See *Birmingham, Dudley and District Banking Co v Ross* (1888) 38 Ch D 295 at 313 per Bowen LJ (ante, p 476).

11   *Borman v Griffith* [1930] 1 Ch 493 at 499; *Squarey v Harris-Smith* (1981) 42 P & CR 118 at 123, 128f.

12   Ante, p 652.

13   See *Nelson v Walker* (1910) 10 CLR 560 at 582, where Isaacs J explained quasi-easements as 'such things enjoyed *de facto* during unity of possession as would, had that unity not existed, have been easements.'

14   See *Australian Hi-Fi Publications Pty Ltd v Gehl* [1979] 2 NSWLR 618 at 621B. If, instead of retaining some land after the subdivision, V were simultaneously to convey the subdivided tenements to P and Q respectively, each purchaser would obtain by way of implied grant the same rights over the land of the other as he would have received if that other land had been retained by V (see *Swansborough v Coventry* (1832) 9 Bing 305 at 309, 131 ER 629 at 631).

15   *Scouton & Co (Builders) Ltd v Gilyott & Scott Ltd* (1972) 221 Estates Gazette 1499. See also Law of Property Act 1925, s 38. It may even be that the rule in *Wheeldon v Burrows* provides a means for a landlord to enforce a repairing obligation undertaken by a tenant even though the landlord has failed to reserve the appropriate right of entry for this purpose in the express terms of the lease (see *Sedgwick Forbes Bland Payne Group Ltd v Regional Properties Ltd* (1981) 257 Estates Gazette 64 at 68).

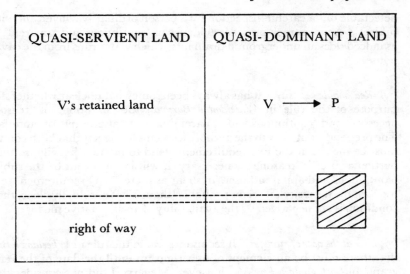

QUASI-SERVIENT LAND	QUASI- DOMINANT LAND
V's retained land	V ⟶ P
right of way	

Fig. 48

(ii) Conditions of operation There are certain limitations upon the kinds of right which may pass to a transferee of land under the rule in *Wheeldon v Burrows*. The rule has no reference to 'mere personal conveniences',[16] but applies only to those rights which are intrinsically capable of being easements. Furthermore, in *Wheeldon v Burrows*[17] Thesiger LJ indicated that

[O]n the grant by the owner of a tenement of part of that tenement as it is then used and enjoyed, there will pass to the grantee all those continuous and apparent easements (by which, of course, I mean *quasi* easements), or, in other words, all those easements which are necessary to the reasonable enjoyment of the property granted, and which have been and are at the time of the grant used by the owners of the entirety for the benefit of the part granted.[18]

These limiting conditions must be examined in more detail.

(iii) 'Continuous and apparent' user The requirement of 'continuous and apparent' user[19] does not appear to be applied by the courts with any great strictness. The requirement has been held to be satisfied by any user which is enjoyed over substantial periods of time[20] and which is discoverable or

16   *Nelson v Walker* (1910) 10 CLR 560 at 584 per Isaacs J.
17   (1879) 12 Ch D 31 at 49.
18   The *rule* in *Wheeldon v Burrows* is to be distinguished from the actual decision in that case, which concerned implied reservations (post, p 685). A 'helpful translation' of the rule in *Wheeldon v Burrows* is to be found in *Borman v Griffith* [1930] 1 Ch 493 at 499 (see *Horn v Hiscock* (1972) 223 Estates Gazette 1437 at 1441 per Goulding J).
19   It has been suggested that the criterion of 'continuous and apparent' user was borrowed in the 19th century from the analogous concepts of continuous and apparent servitudes in French law. See *Suffield v Brown* (1864) 4 De GJ & S 185 at 195, 46 ER 888 at 892; *Dalton v Angus & Co* (1881) 6 App Cas 740 at 821; A.W.B. Simpson, *The Rule in Wheeldon v Burrows and the Code Civile*, (1967) 83 LQR 240.
20   'Continuous user' is not necessarily incessant user, but refers to permanent rather than merely temporary user (see Gale, *Law of Easements* (1st edn London 1839), p 53).

detectable on 'a careful inspection by a person ordinarily conversant with the subject'.[1] A worn track provides evidence of 'continuous and apparent' user,[2] as indeed does an underground drain into which water runs from the eaves of a house.[3]

(iv) Reasonable necessity   It has always been somewhat unclear whether, for the purpose of the rule in *Wheeldon v Burrows*, the conditions of 'reasonable necessity' and 'continuous and apparent' user are alternative or cumulative.[4] The preponderant view in the authorities seems to suggest that both conditions must be met,[5] but the two requirements tend to interact heavily, so that if a particular user is 'reasonably necessary' it will in any event be the subject of 'continuous and apparent' user. In so far as there is any requirement to show 'reasonable necessity', it seems probable (though not absolutely clear) that this condition is not negatived by the availability of an alternative means of access.[6]

(v) User at the date of transfer   It seems integral to the rule in *Wheeldon v Burrows* that there must be an element of user right up until the date of the relevant grant. In *Costagliola v English*,[7] however, Megarry J did not consider that an 'established means of access' was deprived of status as a quasi-easement merely because it had not been 'actively enjoyed to any great extent' during the 10 or 11 months preceding the relevant conveyance.

(vi) Application to contracts   It has been clear since *Borman v Griffith*[8] that the rule in *Wheeldon v Burrows* applies not only to legal grants (eg on the conveyance of an estate in fee simple or a term of years), but also to grants which take effect only in equity (eg on a contract for a lease[9]).

(d) Law of Property Act 1925, s 62

Another form of implied grant is made possible by the operation of the 'word-saving provision' contained in section 62 of the Law of Property Act 1925.[10]

1   *Pyer v Carter* (1857) 1 H & N 916 at 922, 156 ER 1472 at 1475. See also *Scouton & Co (Builders) Ltd v Gilyott & Scott Ltd* (1972) 221 Estates Gazette 1499.
2   *Hansford v Jago* [1921] 1 Ch 322 at 337ff. See also *Horn v Hiscock* (1972) 223 Estates Gazette 1437 at 1441, where Goulding J looked for a 'plainly visible road' over the property 'for the apparent use' of the alleged quasi-dominant tenement.
3   *Pyer v Carter* (1857) 1 H & N 916 at 922, 156 ER 1472 at 1475.
4   The judgment of Thesiger LJ is itself ambiguous. See *Ward v Kirkland* [1967] Ch 194 at 224D-225A. The ambivalence on this issue is not diminished by the observations of Oliver LJ in *Squarey v Harris-Smith* (1981) 42 P & CR 118 at 124.
5   See eg *Bayley v Great Western Railway Co* (1884) 26 Ch D 434 at 452f; *Horn v Hiscock* (1972) 223 Estates Gazette 1437 at 1441; *Israel v Leith* (1890) 20 OR 361 at 367; *Floyd v Heska* (1975) 50 DLR (3d) 161 at 167. In *Costagliola v English* (1969) 210 Estates Gazette 1425 at 1431, Megarry J applied the requirement of 'reasonable necessity' in circumstances where there was some doubt as to the continuity of the disputed user.
6   See *Costagliola v English* (1969) 210 Estates Gazette 1425 at 1431; *Horn v Hiscock* (1972) 223 Estates Gazette 1437 at 1441.
7   (1969) 210 Estates Gazette 1425 at 1429.
8   [1930] 1 Ch 493 at 499. See (1930) 46 LQR 271 (H.P.); [1932] CLJ 219 (K.K.L.). See also *Horn v Hiscock* (1972) 223 Estates Gazette 1437 at 1441.
9   Ante, p 472.
10   See P. Jackson, (1966) 30 Conv (NS) 340.

Section 62 contains 'general words' which, unless excluded in express terms,[11] imply into any conveyance of a legal estate in land a number of rights thenceforth to be enjoyed by the grantee of that estate. Under section 62(1), every conveyance of land

shall be deemed to include and shall by virtue of this Act operate to convey, with the land, all buildings, erections, fixtures, commons, hedges, ditches, fences, ways, waters, watercourses, liberties, privileges, easements, rights, and advantages whatsoever, appertaining or reputed to appertain to the land or any part thereof, or, at the time of conveyance, demised, occupied, or enjoyed with, or reputed or known as part or parcel of or appurtenant to the land or any part thereof.

In very similar terms section 62(2) provides that every conveyance of land which has 'houses or other buildings thereon' is deemed to include all 'cisterns, sewers, gutters, drains, ways, passages, lights, watercourses, liberties, privileges, easements, rights, and advantages' appertaining or reputed to appertain to the land or buildings.

Section 62 is an exceedingly ample provision. It has the effect of passing to any grantee of land the benefit of existing easements, profits, privileges and rights which appertain to that land, or are reputed to appertain to it, or which are at the date of the conveyance enjoyed with that land.[12] However, the provision goes even further, and under certain circumstances creates entirely new easements and profits out of many kinds of quasi- easement, right and privilege subsisting at the date of the conveyance which activates section 62. It is therefore possible that rights which were not easements properly so called before the conveyance may be translated to the status of easement thereafter.

(i) Relation to the rule in Wheeldon v Burrows Section 62 of the Law of Property Act 1925 is in many respects of somewhat wider significance than the rule in *Wheeldon v Burrows*. Although section 62 is not competent to convert into easements rights which, by their very nature, are incapable of being easements,[13] there is no requirement that the rights to which section 62 has reference should be 'continuous and apparent' or 'necessary to the reasonable enjoyment of the land granted'[14] or even that there be proof of actual user at the date of the conveyance.[15] Moreover, section 62 seems to provide a mode of

---

11 Law of Property Act 1925, s 62(4).
12 The notion of enjoyment is not synonymous with user, and therefore section 62 does not require actual proof of user at the date of the conveyance (*In Re Yateley Common* [1977] 1 WLR 840 at 850H-851A). In *Re Broxhead Common, Whitehill, Hampshire* (1977) 33 P & CR 451 at 463f, however, Brightman J found it impossible to say that grazing rights which had not been exercised for some 21 or 22 years prior to the relevant conveyance were 'enjoyed' or reputed to be appurtenant to the land for the purpose of section 62(1). See also *Penn v Wilkins* (1974) 236 Estates Gazette 203.
13 See *Lewis v Meredith* [1913] 1 Ch 571 at 579 per Neville J; *Green v Ashco Horticulturist Ltd* [1966] 2 All ER 232 at 239C.
14 In *Goldberg v Edwards* [1950] Ch 247 at 256, for instance, the Court of Appeal held that section 62 could apply to a way of access through a landlord's house which was clearly not necessary for the tenant in view of the fact that he had a quite separate means of access to the premises which had been let to him. See (1950) 66 LQR 302 (R.E.M.). See also *Baron Hamilton v Edgar* (1953) 162 Estates Gazette 568 at 569; *Ward v Kirkland* [1967] Ch 194 at 229G.
15 *Re Broxhead Common, Whitehill, Hampshire* (1977) 33 P & CR 451 at 463.

implied grant relevant to profits,[16] which almost certainly are not covered by the rule in *Wheeldon v Burrows*.[17]

(ii) Section 62 operates only on a conveyance of a legal estate   There are several important restrictions on the operation of section 62. Of these the most obvious is that the provision is activated only by a deed of conveyance of a legal estate in land, although it is immaterial whether that legal estate be freehold or leasehold.[18] Section 62 can never be invoked by a tenant under a contract for a lease.[19]

(iii) Requirement of 'prior diversity of occupation'   An even more severe limitation on the scope of section 62 takes the form of a judge-made rule which drastically restricts the number of situations in which the provision is conceivably relevant. In *Sovmots Investments Ltd v Secretary of State for the Environment*,[20] Lord Edmund-Davies confirmed that section 62 operates only where there has been some 'diversity of ownership or occupation of the quasi-dominant and quasi-servient tenements prior to the conveyance'.[1] This gloss is undoubtedly correct since without at least some element of prior diversity of ownership or occupation it would be difficult to point to any 'rights' or 'liberties' or 'privileges' which might meaningfully have existed before the conveyance to which section 62 relates.[2] However, this requirement of 'prior diversity of occupation' means that section 62 is inapplicable in the very context where the rule in *Wheeldon v Burrows* finds its most frequent application, ie, where there is a subdivision of land which was formerly subject to common ownership and occupation.[3]

(iv) Application to the landlord-tenant relationship   The requirement of 'prior diversity of occupation' has the effect that the primary impact of section 62 on the implied grant of easements is in the landlord-tenant context, for it is in precisely such a case that the required diversity of occupation prior to conveyance can be found. A landlord (L) may own two adjacent plots of land in fee simple, living on one of them himself and leasing the other to a tenant (T). It is possible that during the currency of the lease L may permit T to use, for instance, a means of access running across the plot which is occupied by L. T's user of this access is 'precarious' in the sense that L could, if he so wished, revoke at any time the bare permission (or licence) thus granted for T to use this route. In other words, T's user arises initially by grace and favour of L, not as a matter of entitlement under the lease.

16   *White v Williams* [1922] 1 KB 727 at 737ff.
17   Ante, p 672.
18   'Conveyance' is defined in Law of Property Act 1925, s 205(1)(ii).
19   *Borman v Griffith* [1930] 1 Ch 493 at 497f.
20   [1979] AC 144 at 176C, following *Long v Gowlett* [1923] 2 Ch 177 at 200 per Sargant J. See (1977) 127 NLJ 695 (H.W. Wilkinson).
1   See C. Harpum, (1977) 41 Conv (NS) 415; [1979] Conv 113. Compare P. Smith, [1978] Conv 449; [1979] Conv 311.
2   See also *Squarey v Harris-Smith* (1981) 42 P & CR 118 at 129 per Oliver LJ.
3   Ante, p 672.

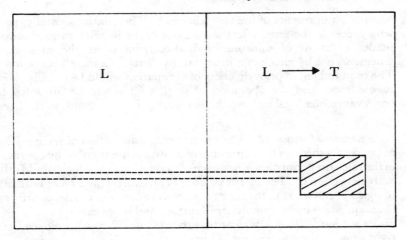

Fig. 49

Section 62 will operate against the background thus described if L subsequently by deed grants to T a legal estate in the land which T already occupies. This grant by deed might, for instance, take the form of a renewal of the term of years which T has enjoyed in the past, or it may comprise a conveyance to T of the freehold reversion in the premises previously rented by T (see *Fig.* 49). In either case the conveyance to T will activate section 62 and will have the effect of vesting in T the legal estate (whether freehold or leasehold) *coupled with a right by way of easement* to continue against L the user which had previously been merely precarious.[4] This result flows directly from the fact that section 62 of the Law of Property Act 1925 implies into the conveyance from L to T all such users as previously comprised 'privileges...appertaining...to the land'. What was merely a licence before the conveyance is now converted into an easement. Moreover, since T's new easement has been incorporated by implication within a deed of conveyance, it is clothed with legal character and binds any successor in title.

Section 62 thus provides a means whereby a purely precarious user may be elevated to the status of a legal easement upon the conveyance to a tenant, thereby giving him a right of indefinite enjoyment.[5] The operation of section 62 turns, however, on the fact that prior to the conveyance there was diversity of

4   *International Tea Stores Co v Hobbs* [1903] 2 Ch 165 at 170ff. Compare, however, *Green v Ashco Horticulturist Ltd* [1966] 2 All ER 232 at 239E-H, where on the facts Cross J held that the tenant's intermittent consensual privilege of access through his landlord's premises was not such a user as could have been the subject of a grant of a legal right, and for this reason section 62 was inapplicable. In this case there was evidence that the user was extremely precarious, in that the access in question had been permitted to the tenant only at times when the landlord did not find such user inconvenient. See also *Wright v Macadam* [1949] 2 KB 744 at 747ff, where the Court of Appeal applied section 62 on the renewal of a term of years.

5   See *Lewis v Meredith* [1913] 1 Ch 571 at 579; *Wright v Macadam* [1949] 2 KB 744 at 751; *Goldberg v Edwards* [1950] Ch 247 at 255f; *Stafford v Pearson-Smith* (1962) 182 Estates Gazette 539 at 541.

occupation in respect of the two tenements. There is, incidentally, no reason why precisely the same effect should not occur in relation to a conveyance made in favour of someone who already occupies the quasi-dominant tenement, not by virtue of a lease, but by virtue of a mere licence to occupy. The requirement of prior diversity of occupation would be equally satisfied in such a case, and the operation of section 62 would be attracted by any conveyance of a legal estate (whether freehold or leasehold) to the licensee.

(v) Avoidance of section 62   The far reaching implication of section 62 can be averted only through the expression of contrary intention[6] or by the revocation of the relevant permission in advance of the conveyance which would otherwise activate section 62. The mere existence of an express (and more limited) grant of rights of easement in the terms of a conveyance does not necessarily exclude the acquisition by the purchaser of further and more extensive implied rights under section 62(1), if it is clear that the vendor effectively enjoyed the larger right prior to the conveyance in question.[7]

(vi) Jurisdiction to rectify   The court retains an equitable jurisdiction to rectify any conveyance which mistakenly transfers to a grantee more rights than were intended in the relevant contract for sale. Thus, in *Clarke v Barnes*,[8] the court rectified a conveyance which had failed to exclude as against the purchaser the user of a right of way over other land retained by the vendor. The equitable jurisdiction was available to rectify the vendor's omission to exclude the effect of section 62, even though the purchaser maintained that he had contracted to purchase the land on the assumption that the right of way in question was included in the conveyance. However, the remedy of rectification will not be extended in order to assist any vendor who has acted otherwise than in good faith.

(3) Prescription

A third method of acquisition of easements and profits *à prendre* is provided by the law of prescription or long user. This area of law has become extremely complex over the years, and as long ago as 1966 the Law Reform Committee by a majority recommended the total abolition of the concept of prescriptive acquisition.[9] No reform has yet occurred, although the existing law is marked

---

6   Law of Property Act 1925, s 62(4). Section 62 is commonly excluded in standard form Conditions of Sale, although there has been some expression of judicial disquiet that this provision can be ousted by a clause buried in the small print of a contract of sale which the parties may never have read (see *Squarey v Harris-Smith* (1981) 42 P & CR 118 at 128, 130).

7   *Gregg v Richards* [1926] Ch 521 at 529ff. See also *Stafford v Pearson-Smith* (1962) 182 Estates Gazette 539 at 541.

8   [1929] 2 Ch 368 at 380ff.

9   *14th Report of the Law Reform Committee* (Cmnd 3100, 1966), para 32. A minority of the Committee recommended the retention of a prescription period of 12 years' user in respect of easements (see (1967) 30 MLR 189 (H.W. Wilkinson)). Among the main considerations leading to the majority proposal that prescriptive acquisition be abolished entirely was the argument that 'there is little, if any, moral justification for the acquisition of easements by prescription, a process which either involves an intention to get something for nothing or, where there is no intention to acquire any right, is purely accidental.'

by 'much unnecessary complication and confusion'.[10] Prescriptive acquisition is something of a hybrid, since it combines elements of fictitious express grant with implications from long-term user.

(a) Rationale of prescriptive acquisition

There is in English law generally a strong policy bias in favour of the legitimacy of a user which has been exercised de facto over long periods of time.[11] This consideration underlies the law of adverse possession,[12] and likewise affords the conceptual basis of prescriptive acquisition.[13] Prescription provides the ground on which the courts may uphold as lawful the long user of any right in the nature of an easement or profit à prendre. Although there may be no evidence of any actual grant, the law of prescription spells an often fictitious grant out of the fact of prolonged enjoyment of rights over the land of another. As Fry J said in *Moody v Steggles*,[14] it is 'the habit, and...the duty, of the court, so far as it lawfully can, to clothe the fact with right'. The process of prescription must, however, be distinguished from that of adverse possession under the Limitation Act. The latter process extinguishes old titles, whereas prescription has the effect of generating new rights. Limitation thus has a negative and extinctive effect, whereas prescription is positive and creative in its mode of operation.[15]

(b) General principles of prescriptive acquisition

The basis of prescriptive acquisition is not merely long user per se. In order that a claim of prescription should succeed, it is necessary that there be a history of continuous user in fee simple as of right. The nature of the required user has traditionally been described in terms borrowed from Roman law. It is commonly said that the user must be *nec vi, nec clam, nec precario*.[16] That is, the user must have been exercised without force, without secrecy and without permission. The onus of proof lies on the claimant.[17]

(i) Continuous user as of right The user which founds a prescriptive claim must be continuous user as of right, although the degree of continuity required is dependent on the nature of the right claimed. The mere fact that user is intermittent does not destroy a claim of continuous user,[18] but frequency of user

10   *Tehidy Minerals Ltd v Norman* [1971] 2 QB 528 at 543F per Buckley LJ. Compare, for instance, the almost total exclusion of the prescriptive principle from the operation of Torrens title legislation (see *Dewhirst v Edwards* [1983] 1 NSWLR 34 at 48A-D).
11   Ante, p 64.
12   Post, p 740.
13   See *Clippens Oil Co Ltd v Edinburgh and District Water Trustees* [1904] AC 64 at 69f per Earl of Halsbury LC.
14   (1879) 12 Ch D 261 at 265.
15   See M.J. Goodman, *Adverse Possession or Prescription? Problems of Conflict*, (1968) 32 Conv (NS) 270; S. Anderson, *Easement and Prescription–Changing Perspectives in Classification*, (1975) 38 MLR 641.
16   *Eaton v Swansea Waterworks Co* (1851) 17 QB 267 at 275, 117 ER 1282 at 1285; *Solomon v Vintners' Co* (1859) 4 H & N 585 at 602, 157 ER 970 at 977.
17   *Earl De La Warr v Miles* (1881) 17 Ch D 535 at 591; *Gardner v Hodgson's Kingston Brewery Co Ltd* [1903] AC 229 at 233.
18   *Axler v Chisholm* (1978) 79 DLR (3d) 97 at 101.

may well affect the validity of the claim. Thus, for instance, a prescriptive claim to a right of way may succeed where there has been user on six to ten occasions each year for 35 years,[19] but not where there have been merely three occasions of user, each separated by an interval of twelve years.[20]

Prescriptive user must, moreover, be based upon an assumption of right,[1] for it is only against a background of assumed entitlement that the courts can go so far as to imply the existence of the grant from which the lawful exercise of an easement or profit is deemed to have derived. It follows that no claim of right can be premised on activity which is itself unlawful in any sense other than that necessarily involved in the trespass which is eventually cured by prescriptive acquisition.[2] It appears, however, that it is no bar to the acquisition of rights by long user that the claimant suffered from a mistaken belief that he owned the disputed land anyway.[3] If anything, the claimant's misapprehension confirms rather than vitiates the claim of rightful user.[4]

(ii) User in fee simple   A further feature of the general law of prescription consists in the fact that prescription is traditionally based on user in fee simple. The user alleged must be user by or on behalf of a fee simple owner against a fee simple owner.[5] Thus at common law there can be no prescriptive acquisition of an easement or profit for life or for a term of years,[6] and any claim to prescriptive acquisition at common law must inevitably fail if the user began against an occupier of the servient land who was not entitled in fee simple (eg a tenant for life or a tenant for years).[7] In such circumstances it would almost certainly be unreasonable to hold the fee simple owner bound by a prescriptive

---

19   *Diment v N.H. Foot Ltd* [1974] 1 WLR 1427 at 1430G. Likewise, the continuity of user of a roadway leading to a summer home is not vitiated by the fact that the access is closed off during winter (*Estey v Withers* (1975) 48 DLR (3d) 121 at 127f). Nor is continuity of user interrupted by an agreement between the claimant and the landowner to alter the route of access (*Davis v Whitby* [1973] 1 WLR 629 at 631C-D).

20   *Hollins v Verney* (1884) 13 QBD 304 at 315. See also *Ramsay v Cooke* [1984] 2 NZLR 680 at 687, where continuous user as of right could not be pleaded on the basis of 'merely isolated occasions when the tenant of the land had given permission by way of licence for use for a specific limited and temporary purpose'.

1   See *Earl De La Warr v Miles* (1881) 17 Ch D 535 at 591 per Brett LJ; *Hanna v Pollock* [1900] 2 IR 664 at 671.

2   The court 'will not recognise an easement established by unlawful activity'. See *Cargill v Gotts* [1981] 1 WLR 441 at 446H, where the Court of Appeal held that the plaintiff could not rely, for the purpose of establishing prescriptive acquisition of an easement to draw water, on his abstraction of water from a mill pond without the appropriate licence under the Water Resources Act 1963. See (1980) 96 LQR 500, (1981) 97 LQR 382 (P. Jackson).

3   *Capar v Wasylowski* (1983) 146 DLR (3d) 193 at 200ff.

4   A mistaken belief that the claimant owns the alleged servient tenement vitiates the claim of easement only if, in reliance on his assumption, the claimant has exercised acts of ownership involving exclusive possession of that tenement. See *Attorney-General of Southern Nigeria v John Holt & Co (Liverpool) Ltd* [1915] AC 599 at 617f; *Warren v Yoell* [1944] 1 DLR 118 at 129f; *Capar v Wasylowski* (1983) 146 DLR (3d) 193 at 201.

5   *Davis v Whitby* [1973] 1 WLR 629 at 630E.

6   *Gayford v Moffatt* (1868) 4 Ch App 133 at 135; *Wheaton v Maple & Co* [1893] 3 Ch 48 at 63; *Kilgour v Gaddes* [1904] 1 KB 457 at 460.

7   *Pugh v Savage* [1970] 2 QB 373 at 383G-H. (Some of the problems connected with tenure by limited owners are eased by the Prescription Act 1832, ss 7, 8). See also A.K. Kiralfy, (1948) 13 Conv (NS) 104.

user of which he may not have been aware and which, in any event, he may have been utterly powerless to prevent.[8]

(iii) User nec vi It is clear that forcible user will vitiate any claim to entitlement as of right. For this purpose the notion of forcible user includes not merely a violent exercise of the user, but also any insistence upon a particular user in the face of continuing protest from the supposedly servient owner.[9]

(iv) User nec clam The user which founds a prescriptive claim must not be surreptitious or in any way concealed. In *Union Lighterage Co v London Graving Dock Co*,[10] for instance, the Court of Appeal declined to accept that a prescriptive claim had been established by a defendant who fixed the side of a dock to the soil of a wharf by means of underground rods which remained undetected for more than 20 years.[11] Romer LJ held that a prescriptive right to an easement over another's land could be acquired only 'when the enjoyment has been open—that is to say, of such a character that an ordinary owner of the land, diligent in the protection of his interests, would have, or must be taken to have, a reasonable opportunity of becoming aware of that enjoyment.'[12]

(v) User nec precario No prescriptive claim can be based on a user which is permissive, ie, precariously founded on a licence from the landowner.[13] User enjoyed under licence from the alleged servient owner cannot support any claim of prescription, since the element of permission inherent in such user is clearly destructive of any claim that the user was a matter of independent entitlement.[14] However, a user which originates in a permission granted by the landowner may later lose its permissive character and arrogate to itself a kind

---

8 See *Pugh v Savage* [1970] 2 QB 373 at 383G-H per Cross LJ. Here, however, the Court of Appeal took the view (at 383H-384A, 386F) that a user which commenced against a fee simple owner is not prejudiced if the land in question is subsequently occupied by a tenant at some intermediate stage during the prescription period. See also *Piromalli v Di Masi* [1980] WAR 173 at 176.

9 *Dalton v Angus & Co* (1881) 6 App Cas 740 at 786. See eg *Eaton v Swansea Waterworks Co* (1851) 17 QB 267 at 275, 117 ER 1282 at 1285.

10 [1902] 2 Ch 557.

11 See also *Liverpool Corpn v H. Coghill and Son Ltd* [1918] 1 Ch 307 at 314 (secret discharge of factory effluent into sewer generated no easement by long user).

12 [1902] 2 Ch 557 at 571. See eg *Capar v Wasylowski* (1983) 146 DLR (3d) 193 at 199. It may be that the burden of proof is upon a landowner to rebut the presumption that he had knowledge of long user of a way over his land (see *Diment v N.H. Foot Ltd* [1974] 1 WLR 1427 at 1434F-G). However, in cases involving other kinds of easement where the user is either less obvious or extremely intermittent, the onus may be on the prescriptive claimant to prove that the alleged servient owner knew, or had reasonable means of knowledge, of the acts of user (*Davies v Du Paver* [1952] 2 All ER 991 at 997F-G; *Temma Realty Co Ltd v Ress Enterprises Ltd* (1968) 69 DLR (2d) 195 at 198). At the very least any onus of rebuttal which rests on the landowner in these circumstances is easily satisfied (see *Axler v Chisholm* (1978) 79 DLR (3d) 97 at 101f).

13 *Henderson v Volk* (1982) 35 OR (2d) 379 at 383. It is fatal at common law to rest any prescriptive claim on an alleged contractual right in respect of the relevant user (see *Norton v Williams* [1939] NZLR 1051 at 1055).

14 Enjoyment merely at the will and pleasure of the owner is inconsistent with a claim of right (*Gardner v Hodgson's Kingston Brewery Co Ltd* [1903] AC 229 at 234ff). See eg *Goldsmith v Burrow Construction Co Ltd* (1987) *Times*, 31 July (locking of gate on path for substantial periods rendered user merely precarious).

of rightful quality if there is evidence that subsequent acts of user ceased to be reliant on the initial element of licence.[15]

Whereas user by way of permission or licence precludes any prescriptive claim, the entire law of prescription rests upon some notion of *acquiescence*,[16] ie, an acquiescence by the servient owner in the exercise by a dominant owner of rights which are acknowledged to be a matter of entitlement in favour of the latter. In *Dalton v Angus & Co*,[17] Fry J took the view that, in this sense, acquiescence necessarily presupposes on the part of the servient owner (1) a knowledge of the acts done[18]; (2) a power in him to stop the acts or to sue in respect of them; and (3) an abstinence on his part from the exercise of such a power.[19] Thus, in *Dalton v Angus & Co*, the House of Lords held that the plaintiff had acquired a right of support for his building by reason of 20 years' enjoyment, and could therefore sue the defendant in respect of the damage caused by the removal of the lateral support provided by the defendant's adjoining house.[20]

The courts are not over-ready to find that the required degree of acquiescence by the alleged servient owner has been established on the facts of any given case. A landowner's 'mere tolerance of a trespass' which continues over many years will not necessarily clothe that trespass with the character of a user as of right.[1] As the Ontario Court of Appeal held in *Henderson v Volk*,[2] 'neighbourly acquiescence' in the occasional use of a path 'during inclement weather or in times of emergency such as a last minute attempt to catch a bus' should not too readily be accepted as evidence of submission to the use. The courts tend to proceed with caution before upholding a prescriptive claim, since the essence of prescription is to 'subject a property owner to a burden without compensation.'[3] The over-eager finding of successful prescriptive user 'may discourage acts of kindness and good neighbourliness; it may punish the kind and thoughtful and reward the aggressor.'[4]

---

15 See *Gaved v Martyn* (1865) 19 CB NS 732 at 744f, 144 ER 974 at 979f. However, the making by the claimant of periodic payments to the landowner tends to indicate that a continuing user was acknowledged to be permissive only (*Gardner v Hodgson's Kingston Brewery Co Ltd* [1903] AC 229 at 231ff).

16 *Sturges v Bridgman* (1879) 11 Ch D 852 at 863 per Thesiger LJ.

17 (1881) 6 App Cas 740 at 773f.

18 Acquiescence is not, however, vitiated if the servient owner is unaware that he owns the land himself (*Capar v Wasylowski* (1983) 146 DLR (3d) 193 at 199).

19 This statement of the principle of acquiescence closely resembles the doctrine of proprietary estoppel, particularly where the prescriptive claimant undertakes expenditure in the belief that there has been acquiescence in his assumption of right (see eg *Annally Hotel Ltd v Bergin* (1970) 104 ILTR 65 at 66ff).

20 It is difficult to see how in practice such a prescriptive claim could have been frustrated by the adjoining owner otherwise than by demolishing his building within the prescription period of 20 years. At common law, however, a servient owner could always frustrate the prescriptive acquisition of a right of access to light by erecting a 'spite fence' to obstruct the light. Nowadays the servient owner can achieve the same objective under the Rights of Light Act 1959 by registering a notional 'spite fence' in the local land charges register (Rights of Light Act 1959, s 2).

1 *Ramsay v Cooke* [1984] 2 NZLR 680 at 685f. See later *Cooke v Ramsay* [1984] 2 NZLR 689.

2 (1982) 35 OR (2d) 379 at 384.

3 *Henderson v Volk* (1982) 35 OR (2d) 379 at 384.

4 *Henderson v Volk* (1982) 35 OR (2d) 379 at 384 per Cory JA. It is a constant refrain in the law of easements that 'between neighbours there must be give as well as take' (see *Costagliola v English* (1969) 210 Estates Gazette 1425 at 1431 per Megarry J).

(c) Grounds of prescriptive acquisition

At common law prescription depends on the idea that long user is evidence of past grant. In other words, the fact of long user is deemed to provide evidence that the easement or profit now claimed was once duly granted in proper form, and any easement or profit established by prescription is therefore necessarily legal. The theory of prescriptive acquisition is, however, deeply marked by fiction.

(i) Common law presumption from long user At common law it was presumed that a long user stemmed from a valid grant if that user had continued 'from time whereof the memory of men runneth not to the contrary',[5] a date which was somewhat arbitrarily fixed as 1189.[6] Any user which commenced before this date was apt to provide an unimpeachable basis for a claim of prescriptive acquisition. With the passage of time it came to be presumed by the courts of common law that if a user as of right for more than 20 years could be shown at any point, this user must have commenced before 1189.[7] However, this benevolent fiction was liable to be frustrated if it could be shown that a particular user could not possibly have been exercised or enjoyed at all times since 1189[8] or if there had been unity of possession between the dominant and servient tenements at any stage since 1189.[9]

(ii) Lost modern grant In order to remedy the deficiencies of the common law presumption from user, the courts later developed the doctrine of 'lost modern grant'.[10] This doctrine conceded that user dating back to 1189 could not be proved. It therefore allowed prescriptive claims to be made on the basis of a fiction that 20 years' user provided evidence of a 'modern grant' (ie, a grant by deed at some date after 1189) which had since been misplaced and lost.[11] The doctrine of 'lost modern grant' was upheld by the House of Lords in *Dalton v Angus & Co*,[12] the only conditions for its application being proof of 20 years' enjoyment as of right, coupled with an absence of any evidence that the putative grantor was legally incompetent.[13] Proof of continuous user as of right

5   *Co Litt*, p 114b.
6   Statute of Westminster I, 1275, c 39.
7   *Clancy v Whelan and Considine* (1958) 92 ILTR 39 at 43f. The required period was sometimes stated to involve continuous user within living memory (*Hanna v Pollock* [1900] 2 IR 664 at 700).
8   Thus an easement of access to light could not be claimed in respect of a building which had clearly been constructed only since 1189 (*Duke of Norfolk v Arbuthnot* (1880) 5 CPD 390 at 393, 402). See also *Hanna v Pollock* [1900] 2 IR 664 at 693, 700f. For similar reasons there can be no presumption of user since before 1189 in New Zealand (see *New Zealand Loan and Mercantile Agency Co Ltd v Wellington Corpn* (1890) 9 NZLR 10 at 18f).
9   Post, p 687.
10 See *Angus & Co v Dalton* (1877) 3 QBD 85 at 94, where Lush J made his classic reference to the 'revolting fiction of a lost grant'.
11 See *Bryant v Foot* (1867) LR 2 QB 161 at 181; *Dalton v Angus & Co* (1881) 6 App Cas 740 at 811ff; *Hanna v Pollock* [1900] 2 IR 664 at 694, 697f.
12 (1881) 6 App Cas 740.
13 The presumption of grant may be rebutted by evidence that the putative grantor suffered from mental incapacity or was a corporation which lacked the legal capacity to grant away rights of easement (see *Rochdale Canal Co v Radcliffe* (1852) 18 QB 287 at 314f, 118 ER 108 at 118). See also *Oakley v Boston* [1976] QB 270 at 280F-281A, 285C-E.

for a period of 20 years is therefore usually sufficient nowadays to found a claim of prescriptive acquisition.[14]

(iii) Prescription Act 1832   Some of the difficulties of the common law are dealt with in the Prescription Act 1832, but this statute has been justly described as 'one of the worst drafted Acts on the Statute Book'.[15] The Act is intended to supplement, rather than displace, the other grounds of prescription, but its provisions are available only where some litigation has arisen in relation to an alleged incumbrance.

In respect of easements other than easements of light, the 1832 Act provides that user as of right and without interruption for 20 years cannot be defeated by evidence that such user commenced after 1189.[16] An easement enjoyed for 40 years as of right and without interruption is deemed to be 'absolute and indefeasible' unless enjoyed by written consent or agreement.[17] The periods of time pleaded in support of a prescriptive claim under the statute must be the periods 'next before some suit or action' in which the claim is challenged.[18] There is a further provision to the effect that no act of obstruction is deemed to be an interruption until it has been submitted to or acquiesced in for one year after the party interrupted had notice both of the interruption and of the person making it.[19]

Slightly different rules apply to the prescriptive acquisition of easements of light. Under the Prescription Act 1832, the actual enjoyment of access to light for a period of 20 years without interruption renders that access 'absolute and indefeasible' unless it was enjoyed merely by reason of written consent or agreement.[20] The Prescription Act 1832 also provides that a profit *à prendre* which has been enjoyed as of right and without interruption for 30 years 'next before some suit or action' cannot be defeated by proof that the profit arose only after 1189.[1] Moreover, a period of 60 years' user on the same terms makes the prescriptive claim to the profit 'absolute and indefeasible'.[2]

(4) Estoppel

A further method of creation of easements and profits lies in the operation of the doctrine of proprietary estoppel.[3] This doctrine is the subject of an extended discussion in Chapter 13.[4]

14   See *Tehidy Minerals Ltd v Norman* [1971] 2 QB 528 at 546A, 552A-B. It may even be that the presumption of a lost modern grant cannot be rebutted by evidence that no grant was in fact ever made (see *Angus & Co v Dalton* (1878) 4 QBD 162 at 172f, 187; *Tehidy Minerals Ltd v Norman*, supra at 552B).

15   *14th Report of the Law Reform Committee* (Cmnd 3100, 1966), para 40.

16   Prescription Act 1832, s 2.

17   Prescription Act 1832, s 1. It is likely that, contrary to the position at common law (ante, p 681), an oral permission will bar a claim under the statute only if the relevant oral licence or consent was given or renewed during the statutory period of user (see *Gardner v Hodgson's Kingston Brewery Co Ltd* [1903] AC 229 at 236).

18   Prescription Act 1832, s 4.

19   Prescription Act 1832, s 4. However, the mere fact that the Prescription Act 1832 is excluded by an interruption lasting more than one year does not preclude the possibility of a valid claim on the basis of lost modern grant (see *Ward (Helston) Ltd v Kerrier DC* (1984) 24 RVR 18 at 19).

20   Prescription Act 1832, s 3. There is no requirement here that the user should have been as of right; it may be merely precarious (*Colls v Home and Colonial Stores Ltd* [1904] AC 179 at 205).

1   Prescription Act 1832, s 1.

2   Prescription Act 1832, s 1.

3   See eg *Ward v Kirkland* [1967] Ch 194; *Crabb v Arun DC* [1976] Ch 179; *Dewhirst v Edwards* [1983] 1 NSWLR 34 (ante, pp 399, 416).

4   Ante, p 386.

5. RESERVATION OF EASEMENTS AND PROFITS

Reservation is the converse of grant and occurs where a vendor reserves for himself easements or profits over a portion of the land which he conveys to a purchaser. The technique of reservation is nowadays much simpler than it used to be before the enactment of the property legislation of 1925. Once again the reservation may be either express or implied.

(1) Express reservation

If a vendor wishes to retain any right in the nature of an easement or profit *à prendre* in respect of land which he conveys to a purchaser, it is open to him to do so by means of express words contained in the document of transfer.[5] The precise extent of a reservation is ultimately a matter of construction of the words used in the light of the general principle that the terms of a grant are, in cases of doubt or ambivalence, to be construed *against* the grantor. In the past the courts were accustomed to regard the reservation of an easement or profit as constituting in law a 'regrant' of that right by the purchaser of the servient tenement, with the consequence that the *contra proferentem* rule of construction operated not in favour of the servient owner but in favour of the party who had in effect reserved the right for himself (ie, the dominant owner). After 1925 it was generally considered that the balance of advantage conferred by this rule of construction had been reversed by the provision in section 65(1) of the Law of Property Act 1925 that a reservation shall 'operate at law without...any regrant'. However, the more recent caselaw seems somewhat perversely to favour the proposition that an express reservation of an easement or profit is still to be construed against the servient owner and in favour of the dominant tenant.[6]

(2) Implied reservation

It is a rule of general application that if a vendor wishes to reserve any rights over land granted away, he must do so expressly in clear and unambiguous terms.[7] In *Wheeldon v Burrows*,[8] a vendor claimed a right of access to light as impliedly reserved in his conveyance to a purchaser. This claim was denied by the Court of Appeal on the ground that reservation can arise only by reason of express stipulation in the terms of the conveyance. To this rule there appear to be only two exceptions.[9]

5　It is even possible that a reservation in favour of C may be created by a conveyance of a legal estate by A to B which in its express terms purports to be subject to an easement (albeit not yet in existence at the date of the conveyance) for the owner or occupier of a specified dominant tenement (Law of Property Act 1925, s 65(2)). Such a conveyance creates an easement for C, to which C is entitled and which he may enforce even though he is not actually referred to by name in A's conveyance (see *Wiles v Banks* (1985) 50 P & CR 80 at 87ff).

6　See *Johnstone v Holdway* [1963] 1 QB 601 at 612f; (1963) 79 LQR 182 (R.E.M.); *St Edmundsbury and Ipswich Diocesan Board of Finance v Clark (No 2)* [1975] 1 WLR 468 at 478F-G. Compare *Cordell v Second Clanfield Properties Ltd* [1969] 2 Ch 9 at 15B-16B.

7　*Broomfield v Williams* [1897] 1 Ch 602 at 616; *Wiles v Banks* (1985) 50 P & CR 80 at 83f.

8　(1879) 12 Ch D 31.

9　The *rule* in *Wheeldon v Burrows* applies, of course, only as a ground of implied grant, not as a means of implied reservation (see *Barton v Raine* (1981) 114 DLR (3d) 702 at 706).

(a) Necessity

The implication of a reservation of necessity is rare. The only circumstances in which such an implied reservation will be accepted by the courts arise where a vendor conveys away all the land surrounding the land retained by himself, in circumstances in which the only possible access to the land retained lies across the land conveyed away. An easement of access will be implied in such a case, since without such a reservation the vendor's land would be rendered unusable.[10] It is not sufficient that the easement claimed should be necessary to the reasonable enjoyment of the land retained. It must be shown that, without the easement, the vendor's land would be completely sterilised. In *Ray v Hazeldine*,[11] Kekewich J held that no easement could be impliedly reserved where the vendor retained an adjoining property which permitted a means of access. In order that an easement of necessity should arise by implied reservation, it is vital that the vendor's land should have become completely landlocked.[12]

(b) Common intention

In rare circumstances an easement will be implied into a conveyance on behalf of the vendor in order to effectuate some common intention which was left unexpressed by that conveyance.[13] A heavy onus of proof rests on the vendor who wishes to show that a reservation was mutually intended.[14]

6. EXTINGUISHMENT OF EASEMENTS AND PROFITS

There is in English law no statutory provision for the discharge or modification of easements or profits which have become redundant or obstructive with the effluxion of time.[15] There are, however, several ways in which easements and profits may be extinguished at common law.

---

10   Ante, p 669. See *Titchmarsh v Royston Water Co Ltd* (1899) 81 LT 673 at 675; *Barry v Hasseldine* [1952] Ch 835 at 838f; *Maude v Thornton* [1929] IR 454 at 457.

11   [1904] 2 Ch 17 at 20f.

12   Thus no implied reservation of a right of way may be claimed where the vendor has available to him a legal entitlement (as distinct from a mere permission) to use an alternative access (*Barry v Hasseldine* [1952] Ch 835 at 839). There is some authority to the effect that a reservation of necessity is extinguished if the claimant subsequently acquires an alternative means of access (see *Holmes v Goring* (1824) 2 Bing 76 at 83ff, 130 ER 233 at 237). Compare, however, *Maude v Thornton* [1929] IR 454 at 458.

13   *Pwllbach Colliery Co v Woodman* [1915] AC 634 at 646f (ante, p 671).

14   See *In re Webb's Lease* [1951] Ch 808 at 820. Implied reservation has, however, been held to give a mutual right of support after the sale of one of two adjoining houses by their common owner (see *Richards v Rose* (1853) 9 Exch 218 at 221, 156 ER 93 at 94f). See also *Barton v Raine* (1981) 114 DLR (3d) 702 at 706ff.

15   Compare Law of Property Act 1925, s 84 (post, p 720). The New Zealand courts have power under Property Law Act 1952, s 127, to modify or extinguish an easement on the ground that its continued existence 'would impede the reasonable user of the land'. See *Masters v Snell* [1979] 1 NZLR 34 at 40ff. There is a similar power in New South Wales (Conveyancing Act 1919, s 89(1)). See *Manly Properties Pty Ltd v Castrisos* [1973] 2 NSWLR 420; *Pieper v Edwards* [1982] 1 NSWLR 336.

(1) Unity of possession and ownership

It follows from the characteristics attributed to easements and profits that any such rights are extinguished automatically if at any time the dominant and servient tenements pass into the ownership and possession of the same person.[16]

(2) Release

Release may be express or implied.

(a) Express release

The dominant owner may release his rights expressly. In the case of a legal easement or profit, such a release must be contained in a deed.[17] However, in relation to an equitable easement or profit, it is sufficient if the dominant owner releases his rights by means of an informal agreement which is supported by consideration given by the servient owner or which is attended by circumstances in which it would be inequitable to revive the rights thereby abrogated.[18]

(b) Implied release

An easement or profit may be released impliedly in cases of abandonment of the exercise of the right coupled with a clear intention to release the right in question.[19] However, mere non-user of a right of way does not necessarily constitute abandonment,[20] since 'it is one thing not to assert an intention to use a way, and another thing to assert an intention to abandon it.'[1] A long suspension of user may nevertheless render it necessary for the owner of the relevant right either to provide an explanation for the non-user[2] or to show that during the period of suspension some indication was given of his intention to preserve his entitlement.[3] Failing such evidence, it is often said that an

---

16   *Tyrringham's Case* (1584) 4 Co Rep 36b at 38a, 76 ER 973 at 980; *The Queen v Tener* (1985) 17 DLR (4th) 1 at 17 (Supreme Court of Canada). See also J.D.A. Brooke-Taylor, (1977) 41 Conv (NS) 107.

17   *Lovell v Smith* (1857) 3 CB (NS) 120 at 126f, 140 ER 685 at 687.

18   *Davies v Marshall* (1861) 10 CB (NS) 697 at 710f, 142 ER 627 at 633.

19   *Swan v Sinclair* [1924] 1 Ch 254 at 266; *Tehidy Minerals Ltd v Norman* [1971] 2 QB 528 at 553D-F. Alterations to, or demolition of, a structure situated on the dominant tenement (eg a mill which enjoys an easement of water) may provide the required evidence of an intention to abandon user (see *Liggins v Inge* (1831) 7 Bing 682 at 693, 131 ER 263 at 268). In *Costagliola v English* (1969) 210 Estates Gazette 1425 at 1431, Megarry J conceded the 'undoubted similarities' between the doctrines of abandonment and proprietary estoppel, but thought it wrong to 'equate' them.

20   *Crossley & Sons Ltd v Lightowler* (1867) 2 Ch App 478 at 482; *Swan v Sinclair* [1924] 1 Ch 254 at 266; *Treweeke v 36 Wolseley Road Pty Ltd* (1972-1973) 128 CLR 274 at 282ff, 302ff; *Riley v Penttila* [1974] VR 547 at 570; *Re Kileel and Kingswood Realty Ltd* (1980) 108 DLR (3d) 562 at 565; *Barton v Raine* (1981) 114 DLR (3d) 702 at 710; *McIntyre v Porter* [1983] 2 VR 439 at 444.

1   *James v Stevenson* [1893] AC 162 at 168 per Sir Edward Fry. Abandonment is 'not...to be lightly inferred' (*Gotobed v Pridmore* (Court of Appeal Transcript No 498A of 1970, p 12f); *Williams v Usherwood* (1983) 45 P & CR 235 at 256).

2   *Treweeke v 36 Wolseley Road Pty Ltd* (1972-1973) 128 CLR 274 at 288 per Walsh J; *Riley v Penttila* [1974] VR 547 at 570ff; *McIntyre v Porter* [1983] 2 VR 439 at 444.

3   *Moore v Rawson* (1824) 3 B & C 332 at 337f, 107 ER 756 at 759; *Crossley & Sons Ltd v Lightowler* (1867) 2 Ch App 478 at 482; *Riley v Penttila* [1974] VR 547 at 570.

intention to abandon may be presumed after a discontinuation of user for 20 years.[4]

4   *Moore v Rawson* (1824) 3 B & C 332 at 339, 107 ER 756 at 759. Compare, however, *Cook v Bath Corpn* (1868) LR 6 Eq 177 at 180. Where 20 years have not yet elapsed, it may be possible to found the extinguishment of an easement on the doctrine of proprietary estoppel (ante, p 386). However, there may be problems in proving the necessary elements of knowledge and reliance required in a claim of estoppel (see *Costagliola v English* (1969) 210 Estates Gazette 1425 at 1431).

CHAPTER 18

Covenants

The law of covenants provides an important means by which landowners may control the use of land. In the context of real property a 'covenant' is an agreement under seal in which one party (the 'covenantor') promises another party (the 'covenantee') that he will or will not engage in some specified activity in relation to a defined area of land. As between covenantor and covenantee the covenant is then fully enforceable as a form of contract.[1] It is the task of this chapter to examine the legal principles which give effect to *private* covenants in respect of *freehold land*.[2]

1. THE FUNCTION OF COVENANTS IN THE PLANNING OF LAND USE

It is nowadays clear that covenants enjoy a wider significance in land law than is explained merely by their contractual effect as between covenantor and covenantee. Although initially founded in contract, covenants have come to provide a means by which certain obligations relating to land use can be made to 'run with the land' so as to benefit and burden not only the original covenanting parties but also their successors in title. By extending their operation outside the realm of contract, covenants may effectively impose controls over land use which bind all parties into whose hands the land may come at any future time.

(1) Development of private control of land use

The basic principles governing the creation and enforcement of covenants respecting land were formulated during a period when government agencies played little part in planning the use and development of the community's land resources. It was accordingly both natural and inevitable that the law should seek to give long-term effect to the agreements by which landowners attempted to regulate land use through private treaty, and the law of covenants came in this way to provide a particularly important facility for the private planning of land use.

Although this function of the covenant device has more recently been given a socialised form in planning legislation, the law of private covenants still retains a broad significance. Increasingly complex schemes have been introduced in order to make private covenants widely enforceable between freeholders, not least because the existence of valid and enforceable covenants may make land

---

1 The agreement has legal efficacy because the seal imports consideration and averts the strict question of whether consideration was provided for the promise given by the covenantor.
2 Covenants relating to leasehold land were discussed in Chapter 14 (ante, p 516).

much more valuable on the open market. The existence of a comprehensive scheme of restrictive covenants binding all purchasers may greatly enhance the market attraction of a particular site or area of development, in that prospective purchasers are thereby assured that local amenities or the desirable characteristics of the neighbourhood will be preserved indefinitely in the future.

(2) Positive and negative covenants

Covenants may take the form of either *positive* covenants or *negative* covenants. A positive covenant is one which imposes on the covenantor an obligation to perform some specified act or activity in relation to a defined piece of land. A positive covenant may, for instance, stipulate that the covenantor shall maintain his neighbour's boundary fence in good repair. By contrast, a negative covenant restricts disadvantageous developments on other land in the vicinity of the covenantee's property. A negative (or 'restrictive') covenant may, for example, preclude the covenantor from using his own land for the purpose of conducting trade or business. Such a covenant clearly promotes the amenity enjoyed by the covenantee on his land, by curtailing the potential scope of the activities conducted on the covenantor's land. The negative covenant may enable the covenantee to live in pleasant surroundings untroubled by the presence of nearby factories belching smoke or by neighbours who insist upon using their homes as a base for private commercial enterprise.

(3) The boundary between contract and property

As a contractual obligation a covenant is of course enforceable only as between the original covenantor and covenantee. If the legal analysis of covenants were to stop at this point, the private agreements of covenantors and covenantees would have no enduring impact upon third parties, for the doctrine of privity of contract confines the benefit and burden of contractual terms to the contracting parties alone. It is, however, of great importance that the benefit and burden created by a private covenant should be capable of transmission to third parties, since otherwise all obligations would be destroyed on a transfer of land. It would, moreover, be open to any covenantor to free himself of his covenanted obligations by the simple expedient of a collusive sale and reconveyance. It is essential for ethical and commercial reasons that the benefit and burden of a covenant should run with the land to which they relate, no matter into whose hands that land may subsequently pass.

This objective of freely transmissible obligation is to some extent realised today by the law governing covenants in respect of freehold land. There is, however, a certain public interest that the law of covenants should be clear, and the law defines fairly rigidly the circumstances in which covenants may not merely have contractual force but may also impose benefits and burdens upon third parties. It is important that these rules should tend to be restrictive rather than over-broad. If covenants of *any* kind, however loose or ill-defined, were allowed to bind third parties, there is a strong possibility that the encumbered land would be rendered effectively unmarketable. No purchaser would wish to buy land under circumstances where its future use had already been fettered by trivial or obscure covenants governing the activities permissible on that land. It is for good reason therefore that the law of covenants has striven to maintain the frontier between contract and property.[3]

The transmission to third parties of covenanted benefits and burdens is simultaneously governed in English law by rules of respectively common law and equitable origin. These must be examined in turn.

2. COVENANTS AT LAW

The common law rules relating to the transmission of covenants are of ancient origin.[4] It has been clear from early times that at law a covenantor need not own any estate in land. The law will nevertheless enforce his covenant under certain circumstances, whether that covenant be positive or negative. These propositions were first established by *The Prior's Case*[5] in 1368, where it was held that a positive covenant to sing divine service in a chapel might be enforced at law even though the covenantor had no estate in land which could be burdened by the obligation. The approach adopted in *The Prior's Case* has been applied in more recent times, as in *Smith and Snipes Hall Farm Ltd v River Douglas Catchment Board*,[6] where the Court of Appeal enforced the defendant's positive covenant to repair and maintain the floodbanks of a river. There is, however, a requirement at common law that the *covenantee* must hold some estate in land to which the benefit of the covenant may accrue.[7]

(1) Effect of Law of Property Act 1925, s 56

Difficulties have arisen in recent years concerning the scope of the benefit conferred by covenants at law. It is clear that, on purely contractual principles, a covenant may confer an enforceable benefit upon any party who is expressly named as the covenantee in the deed of covenant.[8] At common law there was for many years a strict rule that no person could sue on a deed made inter partes[9] unless he was *named* in that deed as a party.[10] This rule was modified in the mid-19th century,[11] and the current position is elucidated in section 56(1) of the Law of Property Act 1925. According to this provision,

3 See H.W.R. Wade, (1952) 68 LQR 337 at 347f ('If there were no frontier, there would be no limit to the new incidents of property which could be invented. But rights which can bind third parties ought to be of a limited and familiar kind; for otherwise purchasers might have to investigate an infinite variety of incumbrances, and would often have no means of knowing the real effect of some fancy or imaginative transaction to which they were strangers. Therefore the law has striven to draw lines of demarcation round the special interests which, exceptionally, may be created by contract or covenant').

4 See A.W.B. Simpson, *A History of The Land Law* (2nd edn Oxford 1986), p 116ff.

5 (1368) YB 42 Edw III, pl 14, fol 3A.

6 [1949] 2 KB 500 at 506f, 514f. See (1949) 12 MLR 498 (A.K.R. Kiralfy).

7 If the covenantee parts with the land benefited by the covenant before any breach of the covenant occurs, he can recover only nominal damages in any action brought against the covenantor, since the real loss is likely to have fallen upon the person to whom he has conveyed the land.

8 Thus if C is *named* in the covenant as a covenantee, as for instance where A covenants expressly with B *and* C to confer benefit upon C, C is automatically entitled to sue in the event of breach, precisely because he is one of the contracting parties.

9 A deed made inter partes is to be distinguished from a *deed poll*, ie, a deed executed unilaterally by one party.

10 See *Lord Southampton v Brown* (1827) 6 B & C 718 at 719f, 108 ER 615 at 616.

11 Real Property Act 1845, s 5.

A person may take an immediate or other interest in land or other property, or the benefit of any condition, right of entry, covenant or agreement over or respecting land or other property, although he may not be named as a party to the conveyance or other instrument.

(a) The doctrine of contractual privity

Few statutory provisions have generated so much confusion as section 56(1), and its effects are still not entirely clear. It was at one time thought that this section had abrogated the entire doctrine of privity of contract,[12] but the rather ambivalent utterances of the House of Lords in *Beswick v Beswick*[13] indicate on balance that this is not so. Thus, if A covenants with B to confer a benefit upon C, C is still disabled from enforcing the covenant, since he is excluded from doing so by the rules of privity.[14]

(b) Generic descriptions

The better view appears to be that section 56(1) merely removes the old rule which restricted the enforceable benefit of a covenant to those parties who were expressly referred to *by name* in the original deed of covenant. After 1925 it is no longer a precondition of a successful claim to a covenanted benefit that the claimant-beneficiary should actually have been *named* in the covenant. It is sufficient that he is designated as a covenantee under some *generic* description.[15]

Thus, for instance, a covenantor may covenant with a named party (eg the vendor of land) and also with the 'owners for the time being' of identified adjoining plots of land. In such cases the benefit of the covenant may be enforced not only by the *named* covenanting party but also by those other owners who are included in the category of covenantees, albeit that their inclusion is merely by generic reference.[16] The only limitation on this application of section 56(1) is the requirement that those who are generically described as relevant covenantees may claim the covenanted benefit only if they are existing and identifiable individuals at the date of that covenant.[17]

---

12   See eg *Smith and Snipes Hall Farm Ltd v River Douglas Catchment Board* [1949] 2 KB 500 at 514ff per Denning LJ; *Beswick v Beswick* [1966] Ch 538 at 556G-557C per Lord Denning MR.
13   [1968] AC 58. See (1967) 30 MLR 687 (G.H. Treitel).
14   See *White v Bijou Mansions Ltd* [1937] Ch 610 at 624f, [1938] Ch 351 at 365.
15   It is possible that this restrictive construction of section 56(1) of the Law of Property Act 1925 has not entirely refuted the idea that a third party may sue for the benefit of a contract. In *Beswick v Beswick* [1968] AC 58 the House of Lords thought that section 56(1) could not facilitate the recovery of a contractual benefit by a non-party. However, a majority of the House formed this view on the assumption that section 56(1) is confined to real property and not because such a recovery is necessarily excluded by the contractual doctrine of privity. Only two judges in the House of Lords explicitly rejected Lord Denning's view of section 56(1) (see [1968] AC 58 at 94C-D per Lord Pearce, at 106A-E per Lord Upjohn).
16   See eg *Wiles v Banks* (1985) 50 P & CR 80 at 87ff (ante, p 685).
17   See *Kelsey v Dodd* (1881) 52 LJ Ch 34 at 39; *Forster v Elvet Colliery Co Ltd* [1908] 1 KB 629 at 636f; *Grant v Edmondson* [1931] 1 Ch 1 at 27; *Bohn v Miller Bros Pty Ltd* [1953] VLR 354 at 358; *In re Ecclesiastical Comrs for England's Conveyance* [1936] Ch 430 at 441f; *Re Wilsons' Settlements* [1972] NZLR 13 at 32. Thus section 56(1) does not enable a covenant to confer benefit directly upon *future* purchasers of plots of land. A covenant which purports to be made with a named owner of land 'and with his successors in title' does not bring the successors in title within the scope of section 56(1). In such a case, only the named individual can rank as a covenantee of the promise.

(2) **Transmission of the benefit of a covenant**

With the foregoing qualifications, a covenant is clearly enforceable in contract by the original covenantee,[18] but greater difficulty is posed by the question whether the benefit[19] of that covenant can be transmitted at law to a third party. The common law lays down fairly strict conditions as to the passing of the benefit.[20] In order that the benefit of a covenant should run with the covenantee's land at law, several conditions must be satisfied.

(a) *The covenant must 'touch and concern' the land*

It must be shown that the covenant was entered into for the benefit of the land owned by the covenantee and not merely for his personal benefit. The test of whether a covenant 'touches and concerns' the land[1] is essentially the same as that which is applied in the context of leasehold covenants,[2] with the obvious qualification that the land in question here is of course the land of the covenantee rather than any land of the covenantor.[3] It must, in effect, be shown that between the covenant and the covenantee's land there is some connection which approximates to that required by the equitable rules of annexation.[4] As Tucker LJ held in *Smith and Snipes Hall Farm Ltd v River Douglas Catchment Board,*[5] a covenant which 'touches and concerns' the covenantee's land 'must either affect the land as regards mode of occupation, or it must be such as per se, and not merely from collateral circumstances, affects the value of the land.'[6]

(b) *The covenantee must have a legal estate in the land benefited*

A covenant can run with the land at law only if made with a covenantee who has a legal estate in the land benefited.[7] No benefit can pass at law where the original covenantee has a merely equitable interest in his land.

(c) *The assignee of the land must have a legal estate in the land benefited*

There used to be a rule at common law that any third party who sought to claim at law the benefit of a covenant relating to land must show that he had the *same* legal estate in that land as the original covenantee. In other words, if

---

18 This is true except where the covenantee has already assigned the benefit of the covenant to some other party. For a similar principle in the context of leaseholds, see Chapter 14 (ante, p 523).

19 For an explanation of this use of the term 'benefit' and the corresponding term 'burden', see Chapter 17 (ante, p 647).

20 See E.H. Scamell (1954) 18 Conv (NS) 546.

1 For this purpose the covenantee's land is usually a corporeal hereditament, but may also include an incorporeal hereditament such as an easement (see *Gaw v Córas Iompair Éireann* [1953] IR 232 at 257f). See W.N. Harrison, (1957) 3 U of Qd LJ 165.

2 Ante, p 521.

3 It is in fact irrelevant whether the covenantor has any land to be burdened. See *The Prior's Case* (1368) YB 42 Edw III, pl 14, fol 3A.

4 Post, p 707.

5 [1949] 2 KB 500 at 506.

6 Tucker LJ also ruled that the required connection between the covenant and the land concerned need not appear expressly in the terms of the covenant but may be proved by extrinsic evidence: '*Id certum est quod certum reddi potest*' ([1949] 2 KB 500 at 508).

7 *Webb v Russell* (1789) 3 TR 393 at 402, 100 ER 639 at 644.

the original covenantee was an owner in fee simple, the benefit of the covenant could pass only to a third party who similarly owned the land in fee simple.[8] However, this requirement was not imposed in *The Prior's Case*[9] itself, and always constituted a somewhat doubtful feature of the common law rules on the passing of the benefit. In *Smith and Snipes Hall Farm Ltd v River Douglas Catchment Board*,[10] the Court of Appeal took the view that the common law requirement had finally been abrogated by section 78(1) of the Law of Property Act 1925.[11] In *Smith*'s case the original covenantee had later sold his dominant tenement to P^1, who in his turn leased the land to P^2. The Court allowed an action for damages for breach of covenant on the suit of both P^1 (the owner in fee simple) and P^2 (who held merely a term of years). It was held that section 78(1) rendered the covenant in question enforceable on behalf of not only the original covenantee but all successors in title and all persons deriving title from such successors.

(d) There must have been an intention that the benefit should run with the land owned by the covenantee at the date of the covenant

In *Smith and Snipes Hall Farm Ltd v River Douglas Catchment Board*,[12] Tucker LJ indicated that it must be shown that 'it was the intention of the parties that the benefit [of the covenant] should run with the land'. This element of intention provides perhaps the central and most important precondition for the running of a covenanted benefit at law.[13]

(e) Other means of transmitting covenanted benefits at law

If the foregoing conditions are satisfied, the benefit of a covenant (whether positive or negative) may pass at law to a third party who takes an estate in the benefited land. The legal rules for the transmission of benefit have, in the main, existed since the earliest days of the common law. Equity was later to formulate its own rules for the passing of the benefit of covenants, and did so on the assumption that it was following the rules laid down by the common law.[14] However, the common law rules continue to apply in cases which are not covered under the rules developed by equity, as for instance where the covenantor has no land upon which the burden of the covenant can be imposed.

---

8 See, eg *Westhoughton UDC v Wigan Coal and Iron Co Ltd* [1919] 1 Ch 159 at 171.
9 (1368) YB 42 Edw III, pl 14, fol 3A.
10 [1949] 2 KB 500.
11 Section 78(1) of the Law of Property Act 1925 provides that a covenant 'relating to any land of the covenantee shall be deemed to be made with the covenantee and his successors in title and the persons deriving title under him or them, and shall have effect as if such successors and other persons were expressed' (post, p 710).
12 [1949] 2 KB 500 at 506. See, however, D.W. Elliott (1956) 20 Conv (NS) 43 at 53. *Smith and Snipes Hall Farm Ltd v River Douglas Catchment Board* was followed in *Williams v Unit Construction Co Ltd* (1955) 19 Conv (NS) 262.
13 In *Smith and Snipes Hall Farm Ltd v River Douglas Catchment Board* [1949] 2 KB 500, the deed in question showed that the object of the covenant was 'to improve the drainage of land liable to flooding and prevent future flooding'.
14 Post, p 706.

(f) Statutory covenants for title

There is a special statutory provision in relation to the most important covenants relating to land, ie, covenants in respect of title. Various covenants for title are implied by section 76 of the Law of Property Act 1925. Section 76(6) provides that the benefit of these covenants is 'annexed and incident to, and shall go with, the estate or interest of the implied covenantee, and shall be capable of being enforced by every person in whom that estate or interest is, for the whole or any part thereof, from time to time vested'.

(g) Assignment of choses in action

There exist further statutory means which facilitate the transmission of covenanted benefits at common law. The benefit of a covenant which is not exclusively personal may, for instance, be assigned as a chose in action under section 136 of the Law of Property Act 1925. In order to be effective at law, this form of assignment requires to be in writing, and express written notice of the assignment must be served upon the covenantor.

(3) Transmission of the burden of a covenant

Whereas the benefit of a covenant can pass at law to third parties, it is a dogmatic principle of the common law that a covenanted burden cannot pass in such a way as to become directly enforceable against assigns or successors in title of the original covenantor.[15] In *Austerberry v Oldham Corpn*[16], the Court of Appeal confirmed as a clear rule of law that the burden of a covenant between freeholders cannot run with the land.[17] This rule is, of course, consonant with the general principle that the benefit, but never the burden, of a contract can be assigned to a third party. It was indeed this unwillingness to hold covenants enforceable at law against the covenantor's successors in title which ultimately made it necessary for equity to provide a means by which at least the burden of restrictive covenants could be made to run with the land.[18]

(a) Modern disadvantages of non-transmissible burdens

Although the principle of *Austerberry v Oldham Corpn* was clearly motivated by a policy that land should remain unfettered for future generations, the implications of that decision are nowadays a matter of considerable

---

15 It is one of the eternal mysteries of English land law that section 79(1) of the Law of Property Act 1925 seems never to have been invoked as a means of transmitting the burden of a positive covenant from one freeholder to another. This provision declares that a covenant relating to the covenantor's land 'is deemed to be made by the covenantor on behalf of himself his successors in title and the persons deriving title under him or them, and...shall have effect as if such successors or other persons were expressed'. The New Zealand equivalent of this provision (Property Law Act 1952, s 64) has been invoked in order to permit the transmission between freeholders of a positive duty to repair a right of way (see *S.J. Allen (South Island) Ltd v Crowe* (1980) NZ Recent Law 118). See also [1970] NZLJ 67 (F.M. Brookfield).

16 (1885) 29 Ch D 750 at 781. See also *Jones v Price* [1965] 2 QB 618 at 633E-F, 639G, 646D.

17 Lindley LJ thought that the burden of a positive covenant could run with the land only if the covenant amounted, upon the true construction, 'to either a grant of an easement, or a rent-charge, or some estate or interest in the land' ((1885) 29 Ch D 750 at 781).

18 Post, p 698.

disadvantage. It has been pointed out, for instance, that the principle 'impedes transactions in land which have become socially desirable.'[19] The anxiety of judges in the 19th century to limit the kinds of incumbrance which might be imposed upon the freehold estate is not particularly apposite under the vastly changed conditions of modern life where most people live in large cities. The property law of the 19th century was highly individualistic and made little provision for 'freeholders living like battery hens in urban developments' where much of the land area may consist of amenities which belong to none personally but which are socially necessary for all.[20] The non-transmissible character of positive burdens has, moreover, made it difficult to envisage the possibility of freehold conveyancing of flats.[1]

(b) Avoidance devices

The common law principle in respect of covenanted burdens is so profoundly inconvenient that various devices have been used to circumvent it and achieve by indirect means a result which is impossible by direct means.[2] These devices include the following:

(i) Chain of covenants Although the burden of a freehold covenant cannot be made to run with the covenantor's land, something like this result can be circuitously achieved by causing a chain of indemnity covenants to be undertaken by successive purchasers of the covenantor's land. The original covenantor still remains liable, of course, on the terms of his initial covenant but, in the event of a violation by a subsequent purchaser, the original covenantor is able to sue on the indemnity covenant in order to recover any damages which he may have been required to pay to the original covenantee (or his successors in title). The chain of indemnity covenants may extend indefinitely, each succeeding purchaser of the covenantor's land entering into a covenant to indemnify his predecessor in title in respect of any future breaches.

In practice, however, the utility of the chain of covenants is lessened or even destroyed by reason of the death or disappearance of the original covenantor or because the chain of indemnities is interrupted. A further disadvantage with the device of indemnity covenants is the fact that even if the chain of covenants remains intact, the only remedy available to the covenantor is an action in damages, whereas the remedy which he really wants is an injunction or order of specific performance.

---

19 See H.W.R. Wade, [1972B] CLJ 157.
20 See [1972B] CLJ 157 at 158, for the view that the rule in *Austerberry v Oldham Corpn* is inappropriate today in view of 'the tendency of an overcrowded population to live in "developments" where they are more and more dependent upon shared amenities such as roads, stairways and gardens, and where lapses by individual owners from the general standards of repair and maintenance will affect the amenity and value and even perhaps the physical stability of neighbouring homes. The law has failed to provide any mechanism by which the necessary obligations can be made to run satisfactorily with freehold land.' See also C.D. Bell, (1984) 128 SJ 323.
1 Ante, p 19.
2 See A. Prichard, (1973) 37 Conv (NS) 194.

(ii) Conversion of leasehold into freehold There are two statutory means by which a long lease may be converted into a freehold estate. Under section 153 of the Law of Property Act 1925, a long lease[3] may be enlarged into a freehold if certain conditions are fulfilled. If this occurs, the freehold becomes subject 'to all the same covenants...as the term would have been subject to if it had not been so enlarged'.[4] This device may be significant in the present context since the freehold is then governed by the principle which applies to leasehold covenants, ie, the principle that the burden of covenants may run with the estate.[5] A similar result is brought about by the enfranchisement of a long lease under the Leasehold Reform Act 1967.[6]

(iii) Doctrine of 'mutual benefit and burden' Once again, the burden of a freehold covenant may pass indirectly to a successor in title of the covenantor by virtue of the doctrine of 'mutual benefit and burden'.[7]

(iv) Reservation of a right of entry It is possible to reserve a right of entry in respect of land, on terms that the right of entry becomes exercisable on events which amount to a violation of a positive covenant.[8] Such a right of entry, if duly created, becomes a legal interest in the land[9] and thus runs with the burdened land so as to affect the successors in title of the covenantor.[10]

3. COVENANTS IN EQUITY

One of the most revolutionary contributions made by equity in the area of property comprises the development during the 19th century of special equitable rules governing covenants between freeholders. This body of rules was of great importance in regulating the urban and industrial development of England before the advent of planning legislation. The new equitable regime relating to covenants has come to supplement, and indeed very largely displace, the common law rules relating to the transmission of the benefit and burden of covenants.

3 A long lease is defined for this purpose as a lease which was originally created for at least 300 years of which not less than 200 years are unexpired, which involves the payment of no rent or money value, and which is not liable to be determined by re-entry for condition broken (see Law of Property Act 1925, s 153(1), (2)).

4 Law of Property Act 1925, s 153(8).

5 Ante, p 525. See T.P.D. Taylor, (1958) 22 Conv (NS) 101.

6 Leasehold Reform Act 1967, s 8(3) (post, p 725).

7 Ante, p 82. See *Halsall v Brizell* [1957] Ch 169 at 182f; (1957) 73 LQR 154 (R.E.M.); (1957) 21 Conv (NS) 160 (F.R. Crane); [1957] CLJ 35 (H.W.R. Wade); *E.R. Ives Investment Ltd v High* [1967] 2 QB 379 at 394B-E; *Tito v Waddell (No. 2)* [1977] Ch 106 at 289ff per Megarry V-C, who held (at 303E) that the doctrine covers not merely successors in title but also anybody 'whose connection with the transaction creating the benefit and burden is sufficient to show that he has some claim to the benefit whether or not he has a valid title to it.' See also (1977) 41 Conv (NS) 432 (F.R. Crane); E.P. Aughterson, [1985] Conv 12.

8 See *Shiloh Spinners Ltd v Harding* [1973] AC 691 at 717C, G-H (ante, p 141). It is, of course, possible that relief may be granted against forfeiture (ante, p 493).

9 Ante, p 82. Compare the use of essentially fictitious rentcharges as a means of enforcing positive covenants between freeholders. See *Clem Smith Nominees Pty Ltd v Farrelly* (1980) 20 SASR 227 at 253; *Davison Properties Ltd v Manukau City Council* (1980) NZ Recent Law 225; B. Hunter, (1963-66) 2 Adelaide LR 208.

10 The right is, however, subject to the rule against perpetuities (see S.M. Tolson (1950) 14 Conv (NS) 350 at 354ff).

(1) Developments in the caselaw

The mid-19th century was a period of significant expansion, when the tension was greatest between the desire to keep land unfettered by private covenants (and therefore profitable for industrial development) and the conflicting desire to curb the effects of commercial and urban growth (by preserving residential amenity for the private householder). These conflicting policies were reflected in the caselaw of the period. In *Keppell v Bailey*,[11] for instance, Lord Brougham refused to allow that 'incidents of a novel kind can be devised and attached to land at the fancy and caprice of any owner.' He thus declined to enforce the burden of a covenant against a successor in title of the original covenantor, taking the view that such a burden, if enforced, would fetter the use and development of the land in perpetuity.[12]

(a) The decision in Tulk v Moxhay

The emphasis had altered significantly by the time *Tulk v Moxhay*[13] came to be decided by the courts in 1847. The ruling of Lord Cottenham LC in this case is usually taken as marking the inception of a major development in the equitable rules concerning freehold covenants,[14] thus reversing the earlier disinclination of equity to allow land to be sterilised by the imposition of permanently binding freehold covenants.

In *Tulk v Moxhay*, the plaintiff had sold a vacant piece of land in Leicester Square to E, who covenanted on behalf of himself, his heirs and his assigns that he would keep and maintain that land 'in an open state, uncovered with any buildings, in neat and ornamental order.' The land subsequently passed by a further conveyance into the hands of the defendant. The defendant's conveyance had not contained any such covenant as that spelt out in the original conveyance from the plaintiff, but it was common ground that he had had notice of the restrictive covenant imposed in respect of the open land. When the defendant attempted to build on the open land in defiance of the covenant, the plaintiff sought an injunction to prevent him from doing so. Lord Cottenham LC upheld a decision at first instance granting the plaintiff the relief required.

Lord Cottenham took an entirely different view from that adopted earlier by Lord Brougham in *Keppell v Bailey*. In the present case, Lord Cottenham held that an injunction should be granted restraining the defendant from acting in violation of the restrictive covenant, not because the burden of such a covenant might run either at law or in equity, but rather because equity asserts a stern view on matters of conscience. The Lord Chancellor accepted the argument that the real question was

not whether the covenant runs with the land, but whether a party shall be permitted to use the land in a manner inconsistent with the contract entered into by his vendor, and with notice of which he purchased. Of course, the price would be affected by the

11   (1834) 2 My & K 517 at 535, 39 ER 1042 at 1049.
12   (1834) 2 My & K 517 at 536f, 39 ER 1042 at 1049f.
13   (1848) 2 Ph 774, 41 ER 1143.
14   It has been pointed out that the decision reached in *Tulk v Moxhay* had been anticipated in two poorly reported cases decided by Sir Lancelot Shadwell, *Whatman v Gibson* (1838) 9 Sim 196 at 207, 59 ER 333 at 338, and *Mann v Stephens* (1846) 15 Sim 377 at 378, 60 ER 665 at 666. See A.W.B. Simpson, *A History of The Land Law* (2nd edn Oxford 1986), p 257f.

covenant, and nothing could be more inequitable than that the original purchaser should be able to sell the property the next day for a greater price, in consideration of the assignee being allowed to escape from the liability which he had himself undertaken.[15]

In order to preclude such an unconscionable outcome, Lord Cottenham concluded that the court should enforce the relevant covenant against any party purchasing with notice of it, 'for if an equity is attached to the property by the owner, no one purchasing with notice of that equity can stand in a different situation from the party from whom he purchased.'[16]

(b) The reception of Tulk v Moxhay in the caselaw

The decision in *Tulk v Moxhay* was broadly based. Equity was prepared to intervene in restraint of any unconscionable conduct in respect of a contractual undertaking of which the wrongdoer—although not himself a contracting party—nevertheless had notice. The argument which had prevailed before Lord Cottenham LC was capable of wide application. Indeed, the view adopted in *Tulk v Moxhay*, far from leading to a sterilisation of land use, could even be seen as promoting the commerciability of land. As Lord Cottenham clearly recognised, unless restrictive covenants could be enforced against the covenantor's successors, 'it would be impossible for an owner of land to sell part of it without incurring the risk of rendering what he retains worthless.'[17] The ruling in *Tulk v Moxhay* was, accordingly, applied with enthusiasm during the years which followed that decision. The ruling was applied to both positive and negative covenants; it was applied on behalf of litigants who held no estate in the land benefited by the covenant; it was even applied outside the realm of real property.[18]

(c) The evolution of a new proprietary interest

The doctrine in *Tulk v Moxhay* had a dramatic effect upon both the law of contract and the law of property. The covenantee was widely regarded as having not merely a contractual interest in the performance of the covenant made with him, but also a *proprietary* interest in the land of the covenantor. Moreover, the covenantee's proprietary interest could run with the land of the covenantor, so as to bind all those into whose hands that land came, until eventually the covenantor's land was conveyed to a bona fide purchaser of a legal estate for value without notice of the covenant. The covenantee was thus given a contractual right to control activities on the land of the covenantor, and, by virtue of the equitable doctrine, that contractual right enlarged into— and arrogated to itself the status of—a proprietary right in land.[19]

(d) Gradual restriction of the scope of Tulk v Moxhay

It was inevitable that, with the passage of time, the broad doctrine of *Tulk v Moxhay* should be somewhat modified. Aware of the potential scope of the doctrine, the courts had begun even during the closing decades of the 19th

15   (1848) 2 Ph 774 at 777f, 41 ER 1143 at 1144.
16   (1848) 2 Ph 774 at 778, 41 ER 1143 at 1144.
17   (1848) 2 Ph 774 at 777, 41 ER 1143 at 1144.
18   See A.W.B. Simpson, op cit, p 259.
19   See S. Gardner, *The Proprietary Effect of Contractual Obligations under Tulk v Moxhay and De Mattos v Gibson*, (1982) 98 LQR 279 at 293ff.

century to limit its application by defining precise qualities which required to be possessed by covenants before they could rank as equitable interests in the land of the covenantor.[20] In *London and South Western Railway Co v Gomm*,[1] Jessel MR was already re-interpreting the doctrine in *Tulk v Moxhay* as 'either an extension in equity of the doctrine of *Spencer's Case* to another line of cases, or else an extension in equity of the doctrine of negative easements.'[2] Thus the new doctrine had its 'wings clipped'.[3] Covenants began to be enforced against third parties on the same conditions as attached to the enforcement of easements, with the result that equity imposed such extra requirements as that there be a servient and a dominant tenement.[4]

Attention must now be turned to the limitations which equity thus imposed on the category of covenants capable of enforcement against successors in title.

(2) Characteristics of enforceable covenants

As the doctrine in *Tulk v Moxhay* was slowly refined, it became clear that certain requirements must be fulfilled in respect of a covenant relating to land before that covenant can be enforced in equity otherwise than between the original parties.

(a) The covenant must be restrictive or negative

If the application of *Tulk v Moxhay* was to be limited by analogy with the doctrine of negative easements, the first limiting factor to emerge was the rule that equity would take cognisance of only those covenants which are truly negative or restrictive in nature.[5] In *Haywood v Brunswick Permanent Benefit Building Society*,[6] the Court of Appeal held that equity had no jurisdiction to enforce against an assignee from the covenantor a positive covenant to build and repair.[7] In the view of Brett LJ, equity would henceforth enforce only those covenants 'restricting the mode of using the land'.[8] Thus, from at least this point onwards, the burden of a positive covenant became unenforceable, either at law or in equity, against successors of the original covenantor. Furthermore, since the purview of equity was now confined to restrictive covenants, the

---

20   See H.W.R. Wade, (1952) 68 LQR 337 at 348.
1   (1882) 20 Ch D 562 at 583. See also *In re Nisbet and Potts' Contract* [1905] 1 Ch 391 at 397 per Farwell J.
2   This did not, and does not, necessarily mean that restrictive covenants in fact *are* easements (see *Norton v Kilduff* [1974] Qd R 47 at 53E-G per Hart J). See also *White v Lauder Developments Ltd* (1976) 60 DLR (3d) 419 at 427.
3   See *Challis*, p 185.
4   See eg *Newton Abbot Co-Operative Society Ltd v Williamson & Treadgold Ltd* [1952] Ch 286 at 293 per Upjohn J.
5   See C.D. Bell, *Tulk v Moxhay Revisited*, [1981] Conv 55. For the view that the doctrine in *Tulk v Moxhay*, as originally formulated, applied only to negative covenants, compare R. Griffith, *Tulk v Moxhay Reclarified*, [1983] Conv 29, but see also [1983] Conv 327 (C.D. Bell). The idea that the original doctrine related to both positive and negative covenants seems to be supported by *Morland v Cook* (1868) LR 6 Eq 252 at 265f; *Cooke v Chilcott* (1876) 3 Ch D 694 at 701f.
6   (1881) 8 QBD 403.
7   See *Shropshire CC v Edwards* (1983) 46 P & CR 270 at 274.
8   (1881) 8 QBD 403 at 408. In Brett LJ's view, 'if we enlarged the rule as it is now contended, we should be making a new equity, which we cannot do.'

remedy given by equity in respect of enforceable restrictive covenants became pre-eminently the remedy of injunction.

(i) Criterion of negative or restrictive quality   The question whether a covenant is *restrictive* always involves a test of substance. A covenant phrased in a positive manner may nevertheless constitute a restrictive covenant, as is the case, for instance, with a covenant 'to use the property for residential purposes only'.[9] Conversely, a covenant 'not to let the property fall into disrepair' is, on closer examination, a positive repairing covenant. A rule of thumb commonly used to test the nature of a covenant of dubious status is the question whether the covenant requires the expenditure of money for its performance. If the covenantor is required 'to put his hand into his pocket', the covenant cannot be negative in nature.[10]

(ii) Function of restrictive covenants   Restrictive covenants are widely used for the purpose of preserving the residential character of a district or neighbourhood. Restrictive covenants commonly require the covenantor to refrain from conducting any trade or business on his land[11] or to refrain from building within a certain distance from the frontage of his property or even to refrain from erecting certain kinds of construction on his land.[12] A covenant not to 'cause or permit' a certain specified form of user is not, however, breached merely because the covenantor later agrees to sell the land affected to a third party who, to his knowledge, intends to engage in one of the proscribed forms of user.[13]

(b) The covenant must accommodate a dominant tenement

In conformity with the theory that the equitable rules about restrictive covenants merely extend the rules relating to negative easements, it has come to be accepted that equity will take cognisance only of those covenants which create a relationship of benefit between two separate plots of land.

---

9   See *German v Chapman* (1877) 7 Ch D 271 at 277f, 280.

10   See *Haywood v Brunswick Permanent Benefit Building Society* (1881) 8 QBD 403 at 409 per Cotton LJ.

11   The enforcement of a restrictive covenant against business user may provide a solution for the vexed problem of the neighbour who keeps a huge lorry parked semi-permanently on the street outside his home (see *McDonagh v Cromie* [1982] 9 BNIL 72). See also *Balchin v Buckle* (1982) 126 SJ 412 (injunction and £250 damages).

12   See eg *Clothier v Snell* (1966) 198 Estates Gazette 27 at 28 (restrictive covenant against any building other than bungalow). A covenant prohibiting any building other than a private dwelling-house is infringed by the construction of flats (*Carmichael v Ripley Finance Co Ltd* [1974] 1 NZLR 557 at 559), but not by the erection of a covered swimming pool in the grounds of a private house (*Harlow v Hartog* (1978) 245 Estates Gazette 140). A covenant limiting construction on a site to one house is breached by a subsequent conversion of that one house into two dwelling units (*Lawton v S.H.E.V. Pty Ltd* [1969] 2 NSWR 238 at 241f). See also *Windsor Hotel (Newquay) Ltd v Allan* (1980) 77 Law Soc Gaz 733 (large barbeque held to be a 'building').

13   *Tophams Ltd v Earl of Sefton* [1967] 1 AC 50 at 64D, 68G, 75A-76A.

(i) Requirement of a dominant tenement   It is nowadays accepted as clear that a restrictive covenant can be enforced only if it relates to a defined servient tenement and is appurtenant to an ascertainable dominant tenement.[14] The covenantee must own an estate in the dominant tenement and the covenantor an estate in the servient tenement.[15] Furthermore, the party who seeks to enforce the restrictive covenant must show that his tenement—although not necessarily contiguous with—is at least reasonably proximate to the servient tenement, since otherwise the requirement of benefit is unlikely to be satisfied. As was indicated by Pollock MR in *Kelley v Barrett*[16], 'land at Clapham would be too remote and unable to carry a right to enforce...covenants in respect of...land at Hampstead.'[17]

The requirement of dominant ownership was affirmed most clearly in *London County Council v Allen*.[18] Here the Court of Appeal held that the plaintiff was unable to enforce a restrictive covenant against the covenantor's successor, on the ground that the plaintiff was not in possession of, or interested in, any land for the benefit of which the covenant had been taken.[19] The requirement that there be a dominant tenement carries the additional implication that if the covenantee parts with all the land for the benefit of which the restrictive covenant was taken, he ceases to be able to enforce the covenant except against the original covenantor.[20] Even as against the latter, his remedy is limited to the recovery of nominal damages.

There are, of course, certain exceptional cases in which the requirement of dominant ownership is modified or even entirely abrogated.[1] Following the decision in *Hall v Ewin*,[2] for instance, it has been clear that a lessor's reversion provides a sufficient dominant tenement for the enforcement of restrictive

---

14   The terminology of dominance and servience mirrors the language of easements (ante, p 644). In English law there is no strict requirement that the deed of covenant should positively and clearly identify the dominant and servient tenements. It is sufficient that the dominant land is ascertainable with reasonable certainty (see *Renals v Cowlishaw* (1879) 11 Ch D 866 at 868f; *Shropshire CC v Edwards* (1983) 46 P & CR 270 at 275). Compare the law of New South Wales on this point (Conveyancing Act 1919, s 88(1), ante, p 667). See *Re Louis and the Conveyancing Act* [1971] 1 NSWLR 164 at 178A; *Clem Smith Nominees Pty Ltd v Farrelly* (1978) 20 SASR 227 at 236f.

15   A restrictive covenant is extinguished by unity of possession of the dominant and servient tenements, unless revived by their common owner in a subsequent transfer of one of those tenements (see *In re Tiltwood* [1978] Ch 269 at 280F). See G.M. Bates, (1980) 54 ALJ 156.

16   [1924] 2 Ch 379 at 404.

17   See also *McGuigan Investments Pty Ltd v Dalwood Vineyards Pty Ltd* [1970] 1 NSWR 686 at 690f (covenant held incapable of benefiting land 17 miles distant from supposed dominant tenement); *Clem Smith Nominees Pty Ltd v Farrelly* (1978) 20 SASR 227 at 236 (covenant not enforced where tenements separated by 35 km).

18   [1914] 3 KB 642. See D.J. Hayton, (1971) 87 LQR 539 at 542f.

19   The result reached in this case has now been reversed by statute (Town and Country Planning Act 1971, s 52). See also *Tophams Ltd v Earl of Sefton* [1967] 1 AC 50 at 81A per Lord Wilberforce.

20   See *Chambers v Randall* [1923] 1 Ch 149 at 157f per Sargant J; *Formby v Barker* [1903] 2 Ch 539 at 550f; *Miles v Easter* [1933] Ch 611 at 630f; *Pirie v Registrar-General* (1963) 109 CLR 619 at 628. In *Thompson v Potter* [1980] BCL 764, for instance, the original covenantee was held to be unable for this reason to enforce against an assignee from the original covenantor.

1   In a somewhat different context, the requirement of dominant ownership is altogether dispensed with on the last sale under a scheme of development (post, p 716), the common vendor retaining at this point nothing which even remotely resembles a dominant tenement. See *Re Mack and the Conveyancing Act* [1975] 2 NSWLR 623 at 630E.

2   (1887) 37 Ch D 74 (ante, p 528). See also *Regent Oil Co Ltd v J.A. Gregory (Hatch End) Ltd* [1966] Ch 402 at 433A-B, F per Harman LJ.

covenants contained in a lease.[3] Nowadays, moreover, many public and quasi-public bodies are dispensed by statute from any requirement of dominant ownership. In consequence of the inconvenient ruling in *London County Council v Allen*,[4] numerous bodies have been given specific authority to enforce restrictive covenants in gross, ie, even though they are not possessed of any dominant land which might serve as a base for enforcement in the conventional sense.[5]

(ii) Criterion of benefit No restrictive covenant can be enforced in equity unless the covenant in question was made for the benefit and protection of dominant land retained by the covenantee.[6] In this context a 'benefit' must be 'something affecting either the value of the land or the method of its occupation or enjoyment'.[7] Thus, for example, a covenant which forbids a covenantor to compete with a business conducted on the covenantee's land can properly be held to 'touch and concern' or 'benefit' the land in the required sense.[8]

In the past certain difficulties have afflicted the question whether a particular restrictive covenant can be said to confer true benefit upon an alleged dominant tenement which is excessively large. In *In re Ballard's Conveyance*,[9] for instance, a restrictive covenant had been made in favour of a covenantee who retained approximately 1,700 acres of land. Clauson J held that the covenant was not enforceable at the behest of the covenantee's successor in title, since it could not reasonably be maintained that the covenant in question conferred benefit upon the entirety of such an extensive dominant tenement as that claimed by the successor.[10] The strictness of this approach has since been relaxed in the more recent caselaw. The courts tend nowadays to presume that a covenant confers benefit upon the alleged dominant tenement

3 Likewise a mortgagee's interest in mortgaged land is a sufficiently real interest to enable the mortgagee to enforce a restrictive covenant affecting the land (see *Regent Oil Co Ltd v J.A. Gregory (Hatch End) Ltd* [1966] Ch 402 at 433D-F (ante, p 564)).
4 [1914] 3 KB 642 (ante, p 702).
5 The dispensation extends, for instance, to local authorities (see Housing Act 1985, s 609), the National Trust (see National Trust Act 1937, s 8; *National Trust v Midlands Electricity Board* [1952] 1 All ER 298 at 302A), and the Nature Conservancy Council (Countryside Act 1968, s 15(4)).
6 See *Formby v Barker* [1903] 2 Ch 539 at 552 per Vaughan Williams LJ. It used to be said, in the hallowed terminology of the law of covenants, that the restrictive covenant must 'touch and concern' the land of the covenantee (see eg *Rogers v Hosegood* [1900] 2 Ch 388 at 395; *In Re Ballard's Conveyance* [1937] Ch 473 at 480; *Marquess of Zetland v Driver* [1939] 1 Ch 1 at 8). However, in more recent times the courts have tended to move away from the concept of covenants which 'touch and concern' the covenantee's land, in favour of a requirement that the restrictive covenant should 'benefit' the covenantee's land. See D.J. Hayton, (1971) 87 LQR 539 at 544.
7 *In re Gadd's Land Transfer* [1966] Ch 56 at 66B per Buckley J.
8 *Newton Abbot Co-operative Society Ltd v Williamson and Treadgold Ltd* [1952] Ch 286 at 293f. It remains a salutary thought that '[t]he protection of land, qua land, does not have any rational or, indeed, any human significance, apart from its enjoyment by human beings, and the protection of land is for its enjoyment by human beings' (*Stilwell v Blackman* [1968] Ch 508 at 524G-525A per Ungoed-Thomas J).
9 [1937] Ch 473. See G.R.Y. Radcliffe (1941) 57 LQR 203 at 210f.
10 While conceding that a breach of the covenant might well affect a portion of the successor's land in the vicinity of the covenantor's property, Clauson J was of opinion that 'far the largest part of this area of 1,700 acres could not possibly be affected by any breach of any of the stipulations'. Nor in his view did the court have jurisdiction to 'sever' the covenant and treat it as relevant to part only of the area. ([1937] Ch 473 at 480f).

unless it can be shown that such a view cannot reasonably be held.[11] In other words, it seems that the validity of a restrictive covenant will be upheld 'so long as an estate owner may reasonably take the view that the restriction remains of value to his estate.' The restriction will not be discarded 'merely because others may reasonably argue that the restriction is spent.'[12]

(c) The covenant must have been intended to run with the covenantor's land

A restrictive covenant may be phrased in such a way that it binds only the covenantor.[13] In all other cases, however, it is presumed that the burden of a restrictive covenant is intended to run with the land of the covenantor. This is the effect of section 79(1) of the Law of Property Act 1925, which provides that, unless a contrary intention is expressed, a covenant 'relating to any land of a covenantor or capable of being bound by him, shall be deemed to be made by the covenantor on behalf of himself his successors in title and the persons deriving title under him or them, and...shall have effect as if such successors and other persons were expressed'.[14]

(3) General principles of enforceability of restrictive covenants

In order that a restrictive covenant should be enforceable between parties other than the original covenantor and covenantee, it is necessary to show first that the covenant in question conforms to the characteristics which equity demands of any 'restrictive covenant'.[15] It is also essential that the party who seeks to enforce the restrictive covenant should be able to establish both that he is entitled to the *benefit* of the covenant and that the person against whom he seeks enforcement is subject to the *burden* of the covenant.[16] If he can prove only one of these requirements, his action must fail. Successful enforcement depends upon an appropriate transmission of both the benefit and the burden originally taken by covenantee and covenantor respectively (see *Fig.* 50). In other words, it is essential that the plaintiff should be able to show that

(i) the benefit of the restrictive covenant has been duly transmitted to him,
    and

(ii) the burden of the restrictive covenant has been duly transmitted to the defendant.

11 See eg *Wrotham Park Estate Co Ltd v Parkside Homes Ltd* [1974] 1 WLR 798 at 808D, where Brightman J stated that there 'can be obvious cases where a restrictive covenant clearly is, or clearly is not, of benefit to an estate. Between these two extremes there is inevitably an area where the benefit to the estate is a matter of personal opinion, where responsible and reasonable persons can have divergent views sincerely and reasonably held...[I]n such cases, it is not for the court to pronounce which is the correct view...the court can only decide whether a particular view is one which can reasonably be held.' See [1974] CLJ 214 (C.T. Emery); *Lord Northbourne v Johnston & Son* [1922] 2 Ch 309 at 318ff.
12 *Wrotham Park Estate Co Ltd v Parkside Homes Ltd* [1974] 1 WLR 798 at 808F. See G.H. Newsom, [1974] JPL 130 at 133.
13 See *In re Royal Victoria Pavilion, Ramsgate* [1961] Ch 581 at 589.
14 In this context, 'successors in title' are deemed to include the owners and occupiers for the time being of relevant land (Law of Property Act 1925, s 79(2)). Section 79 has reference only to restrictive covenants entered into on or after 1 January 1926 (Law of Property Act 1925, s 79(3)).
15 Ante, p 700.
16 Ante, p 140.

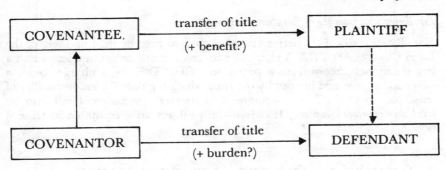

Fig. 50

(4) Transmission of the burden of a restrictive covenant

In consequence of the doctrine proceeding from *Tulk v Moxhay*,[17] the restrictive covenant has become an equitable interest in the covenantor's land. Prior to the enactment of the 1925 legislation, in common with other equitable interests in land, a restrictive covenant was binding on all persons except a bona fide purchaser for value of a legal estate without notice.[18] It was therefore unenforceable against any purchaser for value of a legal estate in the covenantor's land who had no notice of the covenant,[19] or indeed against *any* successor in title of such a person.[20] The transmission of the burden of a restrictive covenant was, in effect, governed quite simply by the equitable doctrine of notice.

(a) Introduction of a registration requirement

The property legislation of 1925 of course effected major alterations both in the law of restrictive covenants and, more generally, in the application of the doctrine of notice. Most kinds of restrictive covenant made after 1925 now constitute a land charge of Class D(ii).[1] The transmission of the burden of such a restrictive covenant depends upon whether (in the case of unregistered land) that covenant has been duly registered in the Land Charges Register[2] or (in the case of registered land) has been duly protected as a minor interest by entry of a notice or caution in the Land Register.[3]

Thus, in *Fig.* 50, the plaintiff will be able to enforce the restrictive covenant against the defendant as successor in title to the covenantor only if the covenantee had protected the incumbrance by the appropriate register entry prior to the transfer of title by the covenantor. If the restrictive covenant was duly protected, the defendant is now inescapably bound by it; if not, the defendant takes the freehold free of the burden of the covenant.[4]

---

17 (1848) 2 Ph 774, 41 ER 1143 (ante, p 698).
18 Ante, p 85.
19 A restrictive covenant does, however, bind an adverse occupier of the servient land, precisely because he is not a *purchaser* (see *In Re Nisbet and Potts' Contract* [1906] 1 Ch 386 at 401ff, 408f (ante, p 88)).
20 See *Wilkes v Spooner* [1911] 2 KB 473 at 487f (ante, p 92). See also *Nottingham Patent Brick and Tile Co v Butler* (1886) 16 QBD 778 at 788.
1 Ante, p 138.
2 Ante, p 140. See *Wrotham Park Estate Co Ltd v Parkside Homes Ltd* [1974] 1 WLR 798 at 809A.
3 Ante, p 159.
4 Ante, p 140.

(b) Exceptions from the registration requirement

Not all categories of restrictive covenant are governed by the provisions of the Land Charges Act 1972. A restrictive covenant made between a lessor and a lessee can never constitute a protectible Class D(ii) land charge. Such a covenant is governed instead by the rules which regulate the enforceability of leasehold covenants.[5] Furthermore, a restrictive covenant entered into by freeholders *before* 1 January 1926 is still fully subject to the equitable doctrine of notice.

(5) Transmission of the benefit of a restrictive covenant

In order that the benefit of a restrictive covenant should be transmitted in equity to a successor in title of the covenantee,[6] it is necessary not only that the covenant should 'touch and concern' or 'benefit' some dominant land, but also that the benefit be transmitted in one or more of the modes prescribed by equity. Historically, these modes of transmission have tended to be defined in fairly stringent terms. Nowadays, however, there is a strong contrary tendency on the part of the courts to relax the strict requirements of equity by allowing the appurtenant quality of a covenant to be determined with reference to the intentions of the covenanting parties rather than in accordance with stipulated requirements of form.[7] This gradual movement away from technicality and heavy formalism has certainly done much to simplify the law of restrictive covenants.[8]

If the benefit of a restrictive covenant is to be transmitted in equity to a successor in title of the covenantee, it must be shown that that benefit was effectively *annexed* to the covenantee's land, or was expressly *assigned* to the successor, or has become enforceable by reason of the presence of a *building scheme* or *scheme of development*. It is sometimes said that these equitable modes of transmission of benefit are merely an elucidation of the common law rules governing the passing of the benefit of covenants.[9] It is indeed possible that the benefit of a restrictive covenant may be held to pass *at law* if the common law conditions for transmission are fulfilled, even though successful enforcement of the covenant depends ultimately on the transmission of the burden in accordance with *equitable* principles.[10] There are, however, certain

---

5   Ante, p 516. If the restrictive covenant—albeit contained in a lease—related to land not comprised within that lease, the position is governed by the equitable doctrine of notice (see *Dartstone Ltd v Cleveland Petroleum Co Ltd* [1969] 3 All ER 668 at 672D-G (ante, p 141)).

6   See S.J. Bailey, [1938] CLJ 339.

7   It has been pointed out that the modern tendency is 'to assimilate the law of covenants to the law of easements, where no formalities are required for establishing the right as appurtenant to the dominant tenement' (see H.W.R. Wade, [1972B] CLJ 157 at 163).

8   The trend of recent developments in this area is, however, vulnerable to the inevitable conveyancer's objection that the law now 'detracts from the vital characteristics of all property interests viz. definability, ascertainability, and stability, and... the uncertainty thereby created casts doubt on many titles, thus inhibiting the marketability and the development of land' (see D.J. Hayton, (1971) 87 LQR 539).

9   *Rogers v Hosegood* [1900] 2 Ch 388 at 397.

10 See eg *Rogers v Hosegood* [1900] 2 Ch 388 at 395ff.

circumstances in which the benefit of a restrictive covenant can be claimed only by virtue of the equitable rules concerning transmission, and these cases are essentially situations in which the common law rules are not satisfied. There can be no passing of the benefit at law if, for instance, either the covenantee or his successor has merely an equitable interest in land,[11] or if the covenantee's successor takes title to part only of the original dominant tenement.[12] In such circumstances, the transmission of the benefit of a restrictive covenant rests entirely upon the operation of the equitable rules.

(6) Annexation

Annexation is the metaphorical 'nailing' of the benefit of a restrictive covenant to a clearly defined area of land belonging to the covenantee, in such a way that the benefit passes with any subsequent transfer of the covenantee's interest in that land. Annexation has traditionally comprised a formal recognition that both covenantor and covenantee intend that the benefit should run with the land so as to avail future owners of that land. Once that intention has been manifested in the express terms of the covenant, the benefit of that covenant is notionally fastened upon, or annexed to, the covenantee's land. The benefit thereafter passes automatically to all successive owners, tenants and occupiers of the land irrespective of knowledge or notice and without any specific assignment.[13] In recent years, however, the linguistic formalism required in annexation has tended to be relaxed by the courts, with the result that it is now possible to distinguish three different types of annexation.

(a) Express annexation

Express annexation is the oldest and least controversial form of annexation. Express annexation arises where the deed which contains the restrictive covenant includes some clear and formal expression of intention that the benefit of the covenant should run with the land to which the covenant is appurtenant. In other words, a formula of annexation is embedded in the very document which brings the restrictive covenant into being.

(i) Formulae of express annexation It is always a question of construction whether the benefit of any restrictive covenant is in fact intended to run with a defined piece of land. It is generally accepted that the benefit is effectively annexed to a particular piece of land if that land is sufficiently defined in the instrument containing the covenant *and* the covenant is expressed to be made 'for the benefit of the land' or 'for the benefit of the [owner] in his capacity of

---

11 See *Fairclough v Marshall* (1878) 4 Ex D 37 at 44ff.
12 See *Miles v Easter* [1933] Ch 611 at 630 per Romer LJ ('...at law the benefit could not be assigned in pieces. It would have to be assigned as a whole or not at all').
13 In the words of Collins LJ in *Rogers v Hosegood* [1900] 2 Ch 388 at 407, annexation is effective to make the benefit of a covenant run, 'not because the conscience of either party is affected, but because the purchaser has bought something which inhered in or was annexed to the land bought.' It is for this reason, of course, that 'the purchaser's ignorance of the existence of the covenant does not defeat the presumption [that the benefit passes on a sale of the land]' ([1900] 2 Ch 388 at 408). See also *Pirie v Registrar-General* (1963) 109 CLR 619 at 628.

owner of a particular property'.[14] The use of such formulae is clearly indicative of an intention that the benefit of the relevant covenant should not be personal to the covenantee, but should enure to the advantage of future owners of the covenantee's land.

Thus in *Rogers v Hosegood*,[15] for instance, the Court of Appeal was able to find an effective annexation in the parties' clearly expressed 'intent that the covenant may enure to the benefit of the vendors [ie, the covenantees] their successors and assigns and others claiming under them to all or any of their lands adjoining'.[16] In *Renals v Cowlishaw*,[17] however, a claim of annexation was rejected where a covenant had been made merely with the vendors, 'their heirs, executors, administrators, and assigns'. It was fatal in this case that no reference had been made to the land which was intended to receive the benefit. Annexation is essentially a conferment of benefit upon *land*, not upon *persons*, and it is therefore imperative that the covenant to be enforced should incorporate some reference to land.

(ii) Express annexation to a large dominant tenement   In the past there has been some difficulty as to whether there could be an effective annexation where a restrictive covenant purported to confer benefit upon the *whole* of an excessively large dominant tenement.[18] The court in *In re Ballard's Conveyance*[19] was plainly unwilling to sever a covenanted benefit and treat it as specific only to a portion of the alleged dominant tenement. However, it has long been clear that none of the problems raised by *In re Ballard's Conveyance* have any substance if the benefit of the relevant restrictive covenant has been annexed, not to the undifferentiated whole of a large dominant tenement, but to 'each and every part' of that tenement.[20] In the case of annexation to 'each and every part', the covenantee's successors are entitled to claim the benefit of the covenant in respect of *any* part of a large dominant tenement which is particularly adversely affected by any breach of the covenant, provided always that the successor has a proprietary interest in the portion of land in respect of which he claims the benefit.

(iii) Fragmentation of the dominant tenement   Most instances of express annexation effected since *Marquess of Zetland v Driver*[1] have made clear reference to 'each and every part' of the covenantee's land or have used words

---

14   *Osborne v Bradley* [1903] 2 Ch 446 at 450 per Farwell J. See also *Drake v Gray* [1936] Ch 451 at 466, where Greene LJ stated that there are 'two familiar methods of indicating in a covenant of this kind the land in respect of which the benefit is to enure. One is to describe the character in which the covenantee receives the covenant. That is the form which is adopted here, a covenant with so and so, owners or owner for the time being of whatever the land may be. Another method is to state by means of an appropriate declaration that the covenant is taken "for the benefit of" whatever the lands may be.'

15   [1900] 2 Ch 388 at 408.

16   It was of no great importance that this formula of annexation defined the benefited tenement in only general terms (ante, p 702).

17   (1878) 9 Ch D 125 at 130f (affd (1879) 11 Ch D 866). See *Rogers v Hosegood* [1900] 2 Ch 388 at 396, 408.

18   These difficulties are now substantially reduced in the light of the decision of Brightman J in *Wrotham Park Estate Co Ltd v Parkside Homes Ltd* [1974] 1 WLR 798 (ante, p 704).

19   [1937] Ch 473 (ante, p 703).

20   See *Marquess of Zetland v Driver* [1939] Ch 1 at 10. In this case the Marquess of Zetland succeeded in depriving the citizens of Redcar in Yorkshire of the facility of 'an eating-house for the consumption of fried fish and other food' ([1939] Ch 1 at 3).

1   [1939] Ch 1.

of similar import. The result of such annexation is that any subsequent purchaser from the covenantee may claim the benefit of the covenant as annexed to the subject matter of *his* purchase even though he may have purchased only a part of the original dominant tenement. Thus fragmentation of the dominant tenement does not prevent the covenant from being enforceable at the behest of successors in title of the original covenantee.

Until fairly recently, however, there was a real danger that, in the absence of an annexation to 'each and every part' of the covenantee's land, a subsequent purchaser of only a part of the dominant tenement would be unable to claim a benefit which had originally been annexed to the whole of that tenement.[2] For a period technical complexity seemed to threaten good sense and to elevate arid formalism in the law of restrictive covenants.[3] However, in *Federated Homes Ltd v Mill Lodge Properties Ltd*,[4] Brightman LJ finally declared that 'if the benefit of a covenant is, on a proper construction of a document, annexed to the land, prima facie it is annexed to every part thereof, unless the contrary clearly appear'.[5] This observation, although technically obiter dictum,[6] clearly reflected the general relaxation during recent years of the rules relating to restrictive covenants, although falling somewhat short of the simplification which has been achieved in other jurisdictions by the more direct means of statutory intervention.[7]

2   See *Russell v Archdale* [1964] Ch 38 at 47 per Buckley J; (1962) 78 LQR 334, 482 (R.E.M.). See also *Re Arcade Hotel Pty Ltd* [1962] VR 274 at 287ff (Full Court of the Supreme Court of Victoria). There was also a risk that a successor in title of the covenantee might himself be disabled from claiming a benefit originally annexed to the undifferentiated whole if he later sold a part of that whole to a third party, on the ground that in such circumstances the vendor no longer retained the entire dominant tenement to which that benefit had been annexed. See *Stilwell v Blackman* [1968] Ch 508 at 519D-F, where, as in *Russell v Archdale*, the point was obiter because there was on the facts a valid *assignment* of the benefit of the restrictive covenant in question. See P.V. Baker (1968) 84 LQR 22, and compare *In Re Selwyn's Conveyance* [1967] Ch 674 at 689A-B; (1968) 31 MLR 459 (J.W. Harris).

3   For reference to a 'somewhat muddy corner of legal history', see *Griffiths v Band* (1974) 29 P & CR 243 at 246 per Goulding J. It is noteworthy that the technical principles adumbrated in *Russell v Archdale* and *Stilwell v Blackman* have no counterpart in the law relating to assignment (post, p 712) or, for that matter, in the law of easements (ante, p 646).

4   [1980] 1 WLR 594 at 606G. Brightman LJ had already resolved some of the present problems in *Wrotham Park Estate Co Ltd v Parkside Homes Ltd* [1974] 1 WLR 798 at 806E, where he had held that a successor in title—albeit that he had sold away a part of the dominant tenement—might nevertheless claim the benefit if he could show that he retained 'in substance' the dominant tenement for the benefit of which the covenant was unqualifiedly taken.

5   Brightman LJ confessed to finding the 'idea of the annexation of a covenant to the whole of the land but not to a part of it a difficult conception fully to grasp' ([1980] 1 WLR 594 at 606F). See also Megaw LJ (at 608B-C). In *Re Arcade Hotel Pty Ltd* [1962] VR 274 at 291, Scholl J anticipated the Court of Appeal's construction by 18 years: 'Is there then some particular virtue in the addition of the words "or any part thereof" to the description of the benefited land?... why should the benefit of the covenant not be understood to be distributed over the benefited land, in the same way as the burden over the burdened land? I can see no logical reason why not; and as a mere matter of language I can see no such reason.'

6   The remarks of the Court of Appeal in this respect have been criticised as inconsistent with earlier authorities. Compare eg *Miles v Easter* [1933] Ch 611 at 628 per Romer LJ (see G.H. Newsom (1981) 97 LQR 32 at 48f).

7   See, for instance, s 79A of the Property Law Act 1958 (No 6344) of Victoria, as inserted by the Transfer of Land (Restrictive Covenants) Act 1964 (No 7130) in response to the ruling in *Re Arcade Hotel Pty Ltd* [1962] VR 274. Section 79A provides that when the benefit of any restrictive covenant 'purports to be annexed...to other land the benefit shall unless it is expressly provided to the contrary be deemed to be and always to have been annexed to the whole and to each and every part of such other land capable of benefiting from such restriction.' This reform vindicates the dissenting judgment of Sholl J in *Re Arcade Hotel Pty Ltd* [1962] VR 274 at 291. See also *Re Miscamble's Application* [1966] VR 596 at 598ff.

(b) Implied annexation

It is still uncertain whether annexation of a covenanted benefit may arise by implication from circumstances.[8] There is judicial support for the suggestion that annexation, although not expressed in the deed containing the restrictive covenant, may nevertheless have been so obviously intended by the covenanting parties that to ignore it would be 'not only an injustice but a departure from common sense'.[9] On this basis annexation of the benefit of a restrictive covenant may be implied from the circumstances surrounding a deed of covenant, where it is clear that the covenant had reference to a defined piece of land and that the parties themselves intended that the benefit should attach to the land rather than to the covenantee personally.[10]

(c) Statutory annexation

One of the more dramatic developments of recent years in the area of restrictive covenants is the way in which the courts have at last begun to have recourse to long dormant provisions of the Law of Property Act 1925.[11] Section 78(1) of this Act provides that

A covenant relating to any land of the covenantee shall be deemed to be made with the covenantee and his successors in title and the persons deriving title under him or them, and shall have effect as if such successors and other persons were expressed. For the purposes of this subsection in connexion with covenants restrictive of the user of land 'successors in title' shall be deemed to include the owners and occupiers for the time being of the land of the covenantee intended to be benefited.

At first sight, section 78(1) appears to provide, in statutory language, a formula of annexation no less efficacious than the classic formula which was upheld in *Rogers v Hosegood*.[12] Yet to the obvious puzzlement of many commentators,[13]

---

8 For the view that implied annexation is possible, see H.W.R. Wade, [1972B] CLJ 157 at 169f. The doctrine of implied annexation is, however, criticised by D.J. Hayton, (1971) 87 LQR 539; P.V. Baker (1968) 84 LQR 22 at 30. See also E.C. Ryder, (1972) 36 Conv (NS) 20.

9 *Marten v Flight Refuelling Ltd* [1962] Ch 115 at 133 per Wilberforce J. See (1962) 26 Conv (NS) 298 (J.F. Garner). Even in *Rogers v Hosegood* [1900] 2 Ch 388 at 408, Collins LJ, delivering the judgment of the Court of Appeal, held that annexation merely requires some 'indication in the original conveyance, or in the circumstances attending it, that the burden of the restrictive covenant is imposed for the benefit of the land reserved.'

10 See *Shropshire CC v Edwards* (1982) 46 P & CR 270 at 277f. It may well be that schemes of development are ultimately an instance of annexation by implication from surrounding circumstances (post, p 715).

11 For the suggestion that section 62 of the Law of Property Act 1925 may be sufficient to enable the benefit of a restrictive covenant to pass on a conveyance of the dominant land, see H.W.R. Wade, [1972B] CLJ 157 at 175; D.J. Hayton, (1971) 87 LQR 539 at 567, 570. This view was endorsed by Judge John Mills QC at first instance in *Federated Homes Ltd v Mill Lodge Properties Ltd* (see [1980] 1 WLR 594 at 601C-D). Compare, however, *Rogers v Hosegood* [1900] 2 Ch 388 at 398; *Shropshire CC v Edwards* (1982) 46 P & CR 270 at 278f; *Roake v Chadha* [1984] 1 WLR 40 at 47F-G.

12 Ante, p 708.

13 'Why the decided cases make no reference to this legislation is a mystery...why...should counsel never argue the point, judges never mention it, and textbooks not discuss it?' (H.W.R. Wade, [1972B] CLJ 157 at 171ff.) See also G.R.Y. Radcliffe, (1941) 57 LQR 203 at 205.

section 78(1) was until recently never regarded as supplying a general statutory implication of the necessary words of annexation.[14]

The spell was finally broken by the decision of the Court of Appeal in *Federated Homes Ltd v Mill Lodge Properties Ltd*.[15] The restrictive covenant involved here contained a reference to 'any adjoining or adjacent property retained by' the covenantee. One parcel of the covenantee's adjoining lands was subsequently transferred to the present plaintiff, and the question arose whether the benefit of the original restrictive covenant could be claimed by the plaintiff on the basis of a valid annexation.[16] The Court was of the opinion that it could be so claimed on the basis of section 78(1). Brightman LJ rejected any narrow interpretation of section 78(1) as 'merely a statutory shorthand for reducing the length of legal documents'.[17] He thought that in the present case 'the benefit of [the] covenant was annexed to the retained land, and...this is a consequence of section 78...'[18] In his view, the actual wording of the restrictive covenant had been sufficient to intimate that the covenant was one 'relating to...land of the covenantee' within the sense of section 78(1). The remainder of section 78(1) was therefore activated by this conclusion, with the result that the statute supplied the words necessary to complete the required formula of annexation,[19] thereby causing the benefit of the restrictive covenant in question 'to run with the...land and therefore to be annexed to it.'[20]

14   Section 78(1) could, arguably without offence to legislative intention, have been treated as implying a statutory formula of annexation in every deed containing a restrictive covenant which is clearly intended to confer a benefit upon a defined area of land. However, for many years the orthodox view of section 78(1) was that it provided merely 'word-saving' facility, operating only when a valid annexation had *already* been established without reliance on the subsection, but nevertheless making it unnecessary to name the covenantee's successors in title (see D.J. Hayton (1971) 87 LQR 539 at 554).

15   [1980] 1 WLR 594. See (1980) 43 MLR 445 (D.J. Hayton); [1980] JPL 371 (G.H. Newsom); (1980) 130 NLJ 531 (T. Bailey); [1980] Conv 216 (A. Sydenham).

16   The restrictive covenant in issue in this case was clearly enforceable by the covenantee's successor in title on the ground of a valid chain of express assignments, but the Court nevertheless dealt with the possibility that the covenant had also been the subject of an effective annexation.

17   Such an interpretation seemed to Brightman LJ 'to fly in the face of the wording of the section' ([1980] 1 WLR 594 at 604D). In *Tophams Ltd v Earl of Sefton* [1967] 1 AC 50 at 73A-C, Lord Upjohn had dismissed section 79, the companion section of section 78, as having purely 'word-saving significance'. In *Federated Homes*, however, Brightman LJ referred to section 79 as a provision which 'involves quite different considerations' and which provides no 'helpful analogy' ([1980] 1 WLR 594 at 606B).

18   [1980] 1 WLR 594 at 603H.

19   'If, as the language of setion 78 implies, a covenant relating to land which is restrictive of the user thereof is enforceable at the suit of (1) a successor in title of the covenantee, (2) a person deriving title under the covenantee or under his successors in title, and (3) the owner or occupier of the land intended to be benefited by the covenant, it must, in my view, follow that the covenant runs with the land, because ex hypothesi every successor in title to the land, every derivative proprietor of the land and every other owner and occupier has a right by statute to the covenant. In other words, if the condition precedent of section 78 is satisfied— that is to say, there exists a covenant which touches and concerns the land of the covenantee— that covenant runs with the land for the benefit of his successors in title, persons deriving title under him or them and other owners and occupiers' ([1980] 1 WLR 594 at 605A-C). Brightman LJ professed to find support for his view of the impact of section 78 in *Smith and Snipes Hall Farm Ltd v River Douglas Catchment Board* [1949] 2 KB 500, and *Williams v Unit Construction Co Ltd* (1955) 19 Conv (NS) 262. See, however, G.H. Newsom (1981) 97 LQR 32 at 44ff.

20   [1980] 1 WLR 594 at 607C. See also *S.J. Allen (South Island) Ltd v Crowe* (1980) NZ Recent Law 118. The liberal approach of *Federated Homes* has since been applied in *Bridges v Harrow LBC* (1981) 260 Estates Gazette 284 at 290; [1982] Conv 313 (F. Webb).

The views expressed by the Court of Appeal in *Federated Homes Ltd v Mill Lodge Properties Ltd* have proved to be highly controversial.[1] It has been pointed out that if section 78 of the Law of Property Act 1925 indeed imposes an automatic annexation effect, this may possibly render otiose the entire device of express assignment as an alternative means of transmitting the benefit of restrictive covenants.[2] The Court of Appeal has also been criticised on the ground that, in determining a question of annexation, which 'is not a question of words but of intention', it seemed to attach paramount significance to statutory words which are 'neutral as to intention'.[3] If the decision in *Federated Homes Ltd v Mill Lodge Properties Ltd* is correct, it would seem to follow that section 78(1) has the extraordinary effect of creating an automatic annexation quite irrespective of the intentions of covenantor and covenantee.[4] In *Roake v Chadha*,[5] however, the original covenanting parties had expressly stipulated that their covenant should 'not enure for the benefit of any owner or subsequent purchaser of any part of the...estate unless the benefit...shall be expressly assigned'. Judge Paul Baker QC held that section 78 could not be applied here so as to pass the benefit of a covenant which had so clearly excluded the consequence of annexation. When construed as a whole against the background of its explicit terms, the relevant covenant simply did not relate to, and was not annexed to, the land of the covenantee. Under these circumstances section 78 was left with no proper role to play. It remains to be seen whether subsequent decisions likewise limit the otherwise impressive span of the liberalising decision in *Federated Homes*.

(7) Assignment

A second method of transmitting the benefit of a restrictive covenant in equity is provided, in the conventional view, by the device of express assignment of that benefit.[6] Thus, even though a successor in title of the covenantee cannot claim to enforce the covenant on the basis of an effective annexation, he may be able to show that the benefit of the covenant has been expressly assigned to him.

(a) Relation between assignment and annexation

It may well be that the broad view of annexation adopted by the Court of Appeal in *Federated Homes Ltd v Mill Lodge Properties Ltd*[7] has removed much of the scope left for the law of assignment of covenanted benefits. Nevertheless the device of assignment, to the extent that it remains a means of transmitting benefit, differs from the device of annexation in the following respects.

---

1   For the view that *Federated Homes* may be confined to much narrower limits than is generally supposed, see P.N. Todd, *Annexation After Federated Homes*, [1985] Conv 177.

2   (1980) 43 MLR 445 at 447 (D.J. Hayton).

3   See G.H. Newsom (1981) 97 LQR 32 at 34. Unlike section 79(1) (ante, p 704), section 78(1) makes no allowance for the expression of 'a contrary intention' by the parties to the covenant.

4   It is such considerations as these which have caused the leading authority on the law of restrictive covenants to express the opinion that 'it really seems almost impossible that the view of Brightman LJ can be correct' (see G.H. Newsom (1981) 97 LQR 32 at 48). See also G.H. Newsom, (1982) 98 LQR 202.

5   [1984] 1 WLR 40 at 46B-H. See [1984] Conv 68 (P.N. Todd).

6   See L.H. Elphinstone, (1952) 68 LQR 353.

7   [1980] 1 WLR 594 (ante, p 711).

(i) Difference of focus Annexation and assignment are directed at quite different targets. Annexation involves the attachment of benefit to *land*; assignment involves the conferment of benefit upon a *person*.

(ii) Difference of timing Annexation and assignment occur (if at all) at different times. Annexation is effected at the date of the making of the restrictive covenant. Assignment is effected, perhaps many years later, on subsequent transfers of the covenantee's title to later purchasers of the dominant land.[8]

(iii) Difference of effect Annexation and assignment have quite different effects. Annexation has the effect of fastening the benefit of a restrictive covenant upon the dominant land for ever, with the result that the benefit passes automatically with that land on any subsequent transfer of title. Assignment is, at least according to one view, efficacious only in respect of the immediate assignee, with the result that the benefit of the restrictive covenant requires to be assigned afresh with every subsequent transfer of the dominant land.[9]

The law of assignment contrasts markedly with that of annexation, in that it was thought until relatively recently that a benefit unqualifiedly annexed to the whole of a dominant tenement could not be claimed by a successor in title of merely a portion of that land.[10] There has never been any corresponding limitation in respect of the assignment of covenanted benefits, notwithstanding that these benefits may originally have been annexed to the entirety of a dominant tenement.[11] Fragmentation of the dominant land has no prejudicial impact upon assignment since assignment is an essentially personal transaction which involves the transmission of a benefit from one individual to another.

(b) Preconditions of assignment

Assignment is usually effected by means of express words of assignment inserted into the document of transfer executed by the covenantee in favour of his successor in title or executed by that successor in favour of a later purchaser. Certain specific conditions must be fulfilled in order that assignment be effective, but in general terms the essential requirement is that assignor and assignee should express some agreement that the benefit shall pass to the latter.

(i) The covenant must have been taken for the protection or benefit of land owned by the covenantee at the date of the covenant The assignee of the benefit of a restrictive

---

8 It is not impossible that a successor in title of the covenantee may claim the benefit of a covenant on the basis of both assignment and annexation (ante, p 706). Assignment and annexation are not, in this sense, mutually exclusive.

9 See *In re Pinewood Estate, Farnborough* [1958] Ch 280 at 287. There is, however, weighty support for the alternative view that assignment effects a 'delayed annexation'. See *Renals v Cowlishaw* (1878) 9 Ch D 125 at 130f; *Rogers v Hosegood* [1900] 2 Ch 388 at 408; *Reid v Bickerstaff* [1909] 2 Ch 305 at 320; but compare *Stilwell v Blackman* [1968] Ch 508 at 526C-E. See also S.J. Bailey, [1938] CLJ 339 at 360f; [1957] CLJ 146 (H.W.R. Wade); P.V. Baker, (1968) 84 LQR 22 at 31f; H.W.R. Wade, [1972B] CLJ 157 at 166.

10 Ante, p 709.

11 See, for instance, the cases where assignment was held to be effective under circumstances in which supposedly annexation would not have passed the benefit to the plaintiff (*Russell v Archdale* [1964] Ch 38 at 47f; *Stilwell v Blackman* [1968] Ch 508 at 528G-529A (ante, p 709)).

covenant must be able to show that the covenant was originally taken for the benefit or protection of land owned by the covenantee at the date of the covenant.[12] If this were not so, the covenant would be a 'covenant in gross', and would be unenforceable except as between covenantor and covenantee. It is permissible to prove this requirement by showing that the circumstances surrounding the making of the covenant clearly establish that the covenant was intended to benefit the covenantee's land. In *Newton Abbott Co-operative Society Ltd v Williamson and Treadgold Ltd,*[13] for instance, Upjohn J was prepared to accept that the requirement of intended benefit was met by a covenant which precluded the covenantor from conducting trade in competition with the business carried on by the covenantee on his nearby premises. It was quite clear here that the covenant had been taken for the protection of the covenantee's land.

(ii)   The assignment must be contemporaneous with the transfer of the dominant land   If the assignee of the benefit of a restrictive covenant seeks to enforce that benefit against the original covenantor, he need prove only that the benefit has been duly assigned to him as a chose in action. However, if he seeks to enforce the covenant against a successor in title to the servient land, he must show that the benefit was assigned to him contemporaneously with the transfer of the title in the dominant land. In other words, he must establish that the assignment was part of the transaction of transfer.[14] If the benefit of a restrictive covenant becomes separated from the dominant land, it ceases to be operative.[15]

(iii)   The dominant tenement must be ascertainable   In *Miles v Easter*[16] the Court of Appeal held that the land benefited by the restrictive covenant which the assignee seeks to enforce must be 'ascertainable' or 'certain'. As Romer LJ indicated in this case, it is impossible to ascertain the existence and location of the dominant land for this purpose unless these are 'indicated in the conveyance or have been otherwise shown with reasonable certainty'. It is clear, however, that the dominant land will be regarded as sufficiently identified if it is ascertainable with reference to extrinsic evidence.[17]

---

12   *Miles v Easter* [1933] Ch 611 at 625 per Bennett J. See (1933) 49 LQR 483 (H.A. Hollond). This case is sometimes known as *In re Union of London and Smith's Bank Ltd's Conveyance.*

13   [1952] Ch 286 at 293f.

14   See *Miles v Easter* [1933] Ch 611 at 632; *Newton Abbot Co-operative Society Ltd v Williamson & Treadgold Ltd* [1952] Ch 286 at 294. See also L. Elphinstone, (1952) 68 LQR 353.

15   See *Miles v Easter* [1933] Ch 611 at 632, where Romer LJ explained the assignability of a covenant as being necessary to enable the covenantee to 'dispose of his property to advantage'. This protection is not, however, necessary if he has already managed to sell the dominant land to a third party without simultaneously assigning the benefit.

16   [1933] Ch 611 at 631.

17   See eg *Newton Abbot Co-operative Society Ltd v Williamson & Treadgold Ltd* [1952] Ch 286 at 297, where Upjohn J considered that he was entitled to 'look at the attendant circumstances to see if the land to be benefited is shown "otherwise" with reasonable certainty.' See also *Re Memvale Securities Ltd's Application* (1975) 233 Estates Gazette 689 at 691, for confirmation that 'it is permissible to identify the land benefited dehors the deed'. Compare, however, D.J. Hayton, (1971) 87 LQR 539 at 568ff.

(8) Scheme of development

A third method of transmitting the benefit of restrictive covenants in equity is provided by the 'scheme of development' or 'building scheme'.[18] It is not unusual for a property developer to subdivide a large area of land into plots with the intention of selling those plots seriatim to individual purchasers. In order to preserve the value of each plot and the residential amenity of the whole area, the vendor commonly extracts certain restrictive covenants from each purchaser in turn. The object of the exercise is plainly to institute a scheme of mutually enforceable restrictive covenants which will be valid not only for the initial purchasers vis à vis each other but also as between all successors in title of the original covenantors. This aim, if duly realised, has the effect of creating a 'local law' for maintaining the character of the neighbourhood for the indefinite future.

(a) The problem

The transmission of the burden of restrictive covenants undertaken by the original purchasers of the individual plots depends, of course, simply on the due registration against those purchasers of the relevant incumbrances created in favour of the developer of the site.[19] The transmission of the benefit received by the developer as covenantee is, however, a matter of somewhat greater difficulty. As the developer extracts restrictive covenants from each initial purchaser, the dominant tenement to which each covenant appertains is of course the area constituted by the plots of land as yet unsold by the developer, and this area inevitably shrinks with each successive sale. The dominant tenement in respect of any one covenant does not include the plots which have already been sold away, and neither annexation nor assignment can enable the covenantee to distribute the benefits of later covenants to earlier purchasers.[20] Given the irreversible chronology of the transfers on sale, the enforcement of the original restrictive covenants must fairly quickly break down in the absence of some other more general mechanism for transmitting the covenanted benefits to all purchasers and their successors in title.

(b) The solution

The solution to the problem outlined above lies in the distinctly equitable rules which have evolved for the governance of 'schemes of development'. If a 'scheme of development' is present in any given circumstances, equity takes the view that the restrictive covenants appurtenant to each and every plot of land comprised within the scheme can be enforced by all who currently own land covered by the scheme.[1] If a 'scheme of development' is shown to exist, it matters not whether the party seeking to enforce a relevant covenant is an

---

18 According to Megarry J in *Brunner v Greenslade* [1971] Ch 993 at 999F, '"scheme of development"...is the genus; "building scheme" a species.'
19 *Emmet on Title*, p 552f. See also (1928) 78 LJ 39 (J.M.L.).
20 See *Re Louis and the Conveyancing Act* [1971] 1 NSWLR 164 at 178F.
1   A 'scheme of development' need not necessarily relate to the subdivision of land in a horizontal plane. Such a scheme can arise in relation to units formed by other kinds of subdivision (see *Hudson v Cripps* [1896] 1 Ch 265 at 268ff (flats); *Re Spike and Rocca Group Ltd* (1980) 107 DLR (3d) 62 at 64f (tenanted units in shopping plaza)).

original covenantor or a successor in title.² Within a proven 'scheme of development', restrictive covenants are enforceable on a general basis, quite irrespective of the relative timing of the original covenants or of the date of purchase by either of the parties in any enforcement action.³ The chronology of covenant and purchase is utterly irrelevant, both conceding priority to the overwhelming force of an equitable principle of conscience.⁴ The 'scheme of development' thus has a special equitable character which makes it quite immune from the normal rules governing the enforceability of restrictive covenants.⁵

(c) Changing criteria

The equitable consequence of a finding that there exists a 'scheme of development' is, of course, a vast simplification of the difficulties which would otherwise bedevil the enforceability of the mutual covenants of the participants in such a scheme. In view of the potent effects of a 'scheme of development', the courts used to impose severely restrictive preconditions for establishing such a scheme.

(i) The original preconditions   The constituent elements of the 'scheme of development' were described in classic terms in *Elliston v Reacher*.⁶ Here Parker J laid down strict requirements in relation to any enforcement of the covenants comprised within such a scheme. It must be proved (1) that both the plaintiff and defendant derive title from one common vendor, (2) that the common vendor laid out the estate in defined plots in advance of the sales of the plots now owned by plaintiff and defendant respectively, (3) that the restrictions imposed by the common vendor were intended to be for the benefit of all of the plots within the scheme, and (4) that the plaintiff and defendant (or their predecessors in title) purchased their respective plots on the footing that the restrictions imposed were mutually enforceable by the owners of all the plots within the scheme. It was further stipulated by the Court of Appeal in *Reid v Bickerstaff*⁷ that the area to which the 'scheme of development' extends must be clearly defined.

(ii) Subsequent relaxation of the requirements   So ferocious were the conditions thus laid down for the existence of a 'scheme of development' that between 1908 and 1965 it seems that such a scheme was upheld in only two reported English cases.⁸ More recently, however, the courts have relaxed the

---

2   The scheme of development 'crystallises' on the disposition of the first plot sold within the scheme, and all land comprised within the scheme is automatically bound by the terms of the scheme (*Brunner v Greenslade* [1971] Ch 993 at 1003F-G).
3   Thus, under the equity of a 'scheme of development', even prior purchasers can take the benefit of covenants entered into by later purchasers (see *Re Louis and the Conveyancing Act* [1971] 1 NSWLR 164 at 183D-E).
4   It is even irrelevant that, on the final sale under a 'scheme of development', the covenantee (logically) retains no dominant tenement to which the last purchaser's covenant could be said to appertain. In this case the requirement of benefit to dominant land is simply dispensed with (see *Re Mack and the Conveyancing Act* [1975] 2 NSWLR 623 at 630D-F, ante, p 702).
5   A 'scheme of development' cannot be enforced if unity of seisin intervenes during the course of the scheme, but the scheme can revive if and when that unity once again disappears (see *Texaco Antilles Ltd v Kernochan* [1973] AC 609 at 625E-626D).
6   [1908] 2 Ch 374 at 384.
7   [1909] 2 Ch 305 at 319.
8   See *Newman v Real Estate Debenture Corpn Ltd and Flower Decorations Ltd* [1940] 1 All ER 131.

requirements demanded of an enforceable 'scheme of development', by having regard to the equitable principles which regulated 'schemes of development' prior to *Elliston v Reacher*.[9] In the 19th century, for instance, it was much more generally recognised that the authentic basis for the enforcement of 'schemes of development' was the idea of community of interest.[10] As Lord Macnaghten said in *Spicer v Martin*,[11] 'community of interest necessarily...requires and imports reciprocity of obligation'.[12] The intended mutuality of the covenants created within the 'scheme of development' was seen as generating a 'local law' for the area covered by the scheme.[13] This mutuality attracted the protection of a jurisdiction founded upon notions of conscience, for it gave rise to 'an equity which is created by circumstances and is independent of contractual obligation'.[14]

As Megarry J observed in *Brunner v Greenslade*,[15] when the broader perspective of equity is adopted '[t]he major theoretical difficulties based on the law of covenant seem...to disappear.' The courts have accordingly tended to return to the authentic root of equitable obligation which underlies the 'scheme of development'. In *In re Dolphin's Conveyance*,[16] for instance, the court was presented with a scheme which was defective in terms of the traditional requirements of a 'scheme of development' as laid down in *Elliston v Reacher*. The scheme lacked a single common vendor, and the vendors had not, prior to the relevant sales, laid out the estate or any defined portion of it in pre-determined lots. Stamp J nevertheless held that there was a valid 'scheme of development' in existence.[17] He noted that in the present case it had been intended 'as well by the vendors as the several purchasers...to lay down what has been referred to as a local law for the estate for the common benefit of all the several purchasers of it.'[18] There had been a clear intention that each purchaser should 'have, as against the other purchasers, in one way or another, the benefit of the restrictions to which he had made himself subject.'[19] Accordingly Stamp J found in favour of the existence of a 'scheme of development', not on the ground of any implication derived from the existence of the four points specified by Parker J in *Elliston v Reacher*, but rather on the basis of 'a wider principle'.[20] In Stamp J's view, there arose on the present facts an 'equity'

---

9   'I accordingly think that in this case I am fabricating no new equity, but merely emphasising an established equity' (see *Brunner v Greenslade* [1971] Ch 993 at 1005H per Megarry J).

10 See *Child v Douglas* (1854) Kay 560 at 572, 69 ER 237 at 242; *Renals v Cowlishaw* (1878) 9 Ch D 125 at 129 (affd (1879) 11 Ch D 866); *Nottingham Patent Brick and Tile Co v Butler* (1885) 15 QBD 261 at 268f (affd (1886) 16 QBD 778).

11 (1888) 14 App Cas 12 at 25.

12 See *Re Seifeddine and Governors & Co of Hudson Bay* (1980) 108 DLR (3d) 671 at 679.

13 See *Reid v Bickerstaff* [1909] 2 Ch 305 at 319 per Cozens-Hardy MR.

14 *Lawrence v South County Freeholds Ltd* [1939] Ch 656 at 682 per Simonds J. See also *Re Mack and the Conveyancing Act* [1975] 2 NSWLR 623 at 629F-630C.

15 [1971] Ch 993 at 1005G.

16 [1970] Ch 654. See (1970) 86 LQR 445 (P.V. Baker); (1970) 117 SJ 798 (G.H. Newsom).

17 See also *Baxter v Four Oaks Properties Ltd* [1965] Ch 816 at 828B-E, but compare the stubborn adherence to *Elliston v Reacher* in Canada (*Re Lakhani and Weinstein* (1981) 118 DLR (3d) 61 at 67f).

18 For other references to the implications of a 'local law' or 'common law' designed to govern a defined area, see *Baxter v Four Oaks Properties Ltd* [1965] Ch 816 at 826B per Cross J; *Texaco Antilles Ltd v Kernochan* [1973] AC 609 at 624E per Lord Cross of Chelsea.

19 [1970] Ch 654 at 662A.

20 See also *Re Mack and the Conveyancing Act* [1975] 2 NSWLR 623 at 634E-F.

which was ultimately founded on the 'common interest and the common intention actually expressed in the conveyances themselves.'[1]

(d) The modern requirements

By returning to its broad origins in obligations of reciprocity and conscience, the courts have been able to re-fashion the 'scheme of development' so that it once more becomes a useful and workable device in the enforcement of restrictive covenants.[2] It is now generally accepted that a 'scheme of development' is created where there is an intention that a well defined area of land should be sold off in units or plots and that, for the benefit of the common purchasers inter se, restrictive obligations should be imposed on the user of each portion sold.

It seems that ultimately there are but two requirements which are universally insisted upon, and if these two requirements are fulfilled, it matters not greatly that the other requirements elucidated by Parker J in *Elliston v Reacher* are not satisfied.

(i) There must be a 'scheme'

It is essential to a 'scheme of development' that there should be a *scheme*. If the evidence presented in favour of a scheme rests upon the terms of a series of conveyances, it may well be fatal to the existence of a supposed scheme that none of those conveyances show any defined area over which reciprocal obligations are to be enforceable.[3] Although there is no requirement that the area covered by the scheme should necessarily have been subdivided into plots of uniform or predetermined size,[4] the absence of lotting may make it much more difficult to prove that there was any coherent intention to create an effective 'local law'.[5]

(ii) There must be a mutually perceived common intention

The essence of a 'scheme of development' is reciprocity. It must be shown that each participant in the scheme alike purchased on the footing that all would be mutually bound by, and mutually entitled to enforce, a defined set of restrictions.[6] Evidence of such

1   [1970] Ch 654 at 664C-D, citing *Nottingham Patent Brick and Tile Co v Butler* (1885) 15 QBD 261 at 268 per Wills J.

2   For reference to the possibility that the vigilant enforcement of a 'scheme of development' may protect the character and amenity of a housing estate 'to a standard which planning control would lamentably have failed to achieve', see *Re Hornsby's Application* (1968) 20 P & CR 495 at 502. See also *Re Mack and the Conveyancing Act* [1975] 2 NSWLR 623 at 635A-B.

3   *Lund v Taylor* (1975) 31 P & CR 167 at 175. The absence of any 'scheme' accounted for the failure of the claims put forward in *Harlow v Hartog* (1977) 245 Estates Gazette 140; *In re Crest Homes Plc's Application* (Unreported, Lands Tribunal, LP/19/1982, 12 January 1984); *Thompson v Potter* [1980] BCL 764.

4   *Baxter v Four Oaks Properties Ltd* [1965] Ch 816 at 828C-E.

5   *Baxter v Four Oaks Properties Ltd* [1965] Ch 816 at 828C; *In re Crest Homes Plc's Application* (Unreported, Lands Tribunal, LP/19/1982, 12 January 1984); *Re Worth's Application* (Unreported, Lands Tribunal, 12 July 1984).

6   It has even been said that 'the equitable doctrine of the common building scheme...was concerned with notice of a vendor's intention and not with the existence of a covenant in actual fact. It is possible to envisage a case where there was never one covenant contained in a conveyance and yet there might be a common building scheme, because purchasers purchased on the basis that there would be such covenants' (*Re Louis and the Conveyancing Act* [1971] 1 NSWLR 164 at 178D-E per Jacobs JA).

a common intention may be found in the terms of the individual conveyances to the several purchasers,[7] but in the absence of such evidence, the court may seek out extrinsic evidence as to the circumstances of the original purchases. The existence of a 'scheme of development' may be negatived if it cannot be shown, for instance, that the estate plan was brought to the attention of any of the individual purchasers.[8] Similarly, no scheme is established where there is no evidence that the prospective purchasers were told that the vendor was proposing to exact similar covenants, or indeed any covenants, from the purchasers of other plots.[9] The existence of a 'scheme of development' is unlikely to be inferred from the mere entry of restrictive covenants in a charges register.[10]

(9) Remedies for breach of restrictive covenants

A range of remedies may be available to a plaintiff who successfully claims both that he is entitled to the benefit of a restrictive covenant and that the defendant is subject to its burden and in breach of its terms.[11] The court may award damages if the injury to the plaintiff's rights is small, if the damage can be estimated in money and would be adequately compensated by a small money payment, and if it would be oppressive to the defendant to grant a mandatory injunction.[12] In other cases, however, the court may be prepared to award a mandatory injunction. In *Wakeham v Wood*,[13] the defendant had acted in 'flagrant disregard of the plaintiff's rights' by constructing, in breach of covenant, a building which obstructed the plaintiff's view of the sea. The Court of Appeal was not inclined to enable the defendant to 'buy his way out of his wrong' and granted a mandatory order requiring the demolition of the obstruction.[14]

7   In determining the intentions of the original and subsequent purchasers, the court will have regard to as many of the relevant instruments of conveyance as possible (see C.H.S. Preston and G.H. Newsom, *Restrictive Covenants affecting Freehold Land* (7th edn, London 1982) p 61f). See, however, *Re Worth's Application* (Unreported, Lands Tribunal, 12 July 1984), where the relevant conveyances failed to disclose evidence of any scheme.
8   *Lund v Taylor* (1975) 31 P & CR 167 at 174; *Harlow v Hartog* (1978) 245 Estates Gazette 140. In the case of an estate sold by auction, however, it may be sufficient that the covenants to be entered into by each purchaser were set out in the auction particulars. See *Lund v Taylor*, supra at 174; *In re Crest Homes Plc's Application* (Unreported, Lands Tribunal, LP/19/1982, 12 January 1984). Compare, however, *Carmichael v Ripley Finance Co Ltd* [1974] 1 NZLR 557 at 560.
9   *Lund v Taylor* (1975) 31 P & CR 167 at 174. See also *Nottingham Patent Brick and Tile Co v Butler* (1885) 15 QBD 261 at 269. The existence of a coherent common intention may also be put in doubt by any subsequent waiver of breaches or inconsistent or irregular imposition of the restrictions on other purchasers (see *Re Lakhani and Weinstein* (1981) 118 DLR (3d) 61 at 67f).
10   *In re Crest Homes Plc's Application* (Unreported, Lands Tribunal, LP/19/1982, 12 January 1984).
11   It is always open to the defendant in proceedings brought for the enforcement of a restrictive covenant to request leave to apply to the Lands Tribunal for discharge or modification of the covenant (Law of Property Act 1925, s 84(9)).
12   *Shelfer v City of London Electric Lighting Co* [1895] 1 Ch 287 at 322. See also *Federated Homes Ltd v Mill Lodge Properties Ltd* [1980] 1 WLR 594 at 607E-F; *Arbutus Park Estates Ltd v Fuller* (1977) 74 DLR (3d) 257 at 261ff.
13   (1982) 43 P & CR 40 at 45.
14   (1982) 43 P & CR 40 at 45, 47. See also *Wrotham Park Estate Co Ltd v Parkside Homes Ltd* [1974] 1 WLR 798 at 809D-F, 811A-C; *Lund v A.J.A. Taylor & Co Ltd* (1974) 230 Estates Gazette 363 at 367. A mandatory injunction may be refused if the plaintiff stood by while the work progressed (see *Clothier v Snell* (1966) 198 Estates Gazette 27 at 28).

(10) Modification and discharge of restrictive covenants

The existence of a restrictive covenant affecting a particular piece of land clearly fetters to some extent the kinds of activity which may be conducted on that land. It is sometimes undesirable that this inhibition upon land use should continue indefinitely, and it may be in the interests of social utility that the restrictions imposed by the covenant should be abrogated or otherwise modified.

It is for this reason that section 84(1) of the Law of Property Act 1925 confers a discretionary power upon the Lands Tribunal to discharge or modify any restrictive covenant (with or without compensation) on a number of grounds.[15] The Lands Tribunal may exercise this power where, for instance, by reason of changes in the character of the property concerned or the neighbourhood or otherwise, the restriction is deemed 'obsolete',[16] or where the continued existence of the restriction 'would impede some reasonable user of the land for public or private purposes'.[17] In the latter case covenants may be discharged or modified where they no longer, in relation to the respective dominant owners, secure 'any practical benefits of substantial value or advantage to them'.[18] The Tribunal's power is also exercisable where the persons entitled to the benefit of the restriction have agreed expressly or by implication to its discharge or modification,[19] and where the proposed discharge or modification 'will not injure' the persons entitled to the benefit of the restriction.[20]

(11) Planning and compulsory purchase law

It has already been mentioned that much of the law relating to the control of land use has been brought within the public domain by modern legislation. The field of planning law and compulsory purchase is now governed by an extremely wide range of statute law and delegated legislation. This area of law is indeed vast and lies outside the scope of this book.[1]

(12) Reform of the law of covenants

It has for long been recognised that the law of covenants in England is in need of radical reform. As long ago as 1965 the Wilberforce Committee acknowledged

---

15   See generally E.H. Bodkin, (1943) 7 Conv (NS) 17; Norma Dawson, (1978) 29 NILQ 223. The court has jurisdiction under section 84(2) of the Law of Property Act 1925 to declare whether given land is affected by a restrictive covenant.
16   Law of Property Act 1925, s 84(1)(a). There is inevitably great difficulty in showing that a restrictive covenant entered into in recent years is obsolete (see *Balchin v Buckle* (1982) 126 SJ 412).
17   Law of Property Act 1925, s 84(1)(aa), as inserted by Law of Property Act 1969, s 28. See *Stannard v Issa* [1987] 2 WLR 188 at 194G-H.
18   Law of Property Act 1925, s 84(1A). The Tribunal will not, however, discharge or modify a covenant which secures a 'practical benefit' in the form of the preservation of a landscape view which is visible, not from the dominant land itself, but from land in its vicinity, and which is threatened by a proposed housing development. See *Gilbert v Spoor* [1983] Ch 27 at 33A-C, 35G-36B; [1982] Conv 452 (P.H. Kenny). See also *Re Speakman's Application* [1983] JPL 680 at 681; *Re Mercian Housing Society Ltd's Application* (1972) 23 P & CR 116 at 122ff.
19   Law of Property Act 1925, s 84(1)(b).
20   Law of Property Act 1925, s 84(1)(c).
1   See generally P. McAuslan, *Land, Law and Planning* (London 1975); *The Ideologies of Planning Law* (Oxford 1980); K. Davies, *Law of Compulsory Purchase and Compensation* (4th edn London 1984); D. Hughes, *Environmental Law* (London 1986).

that many positive covenants in respect of property in this country are quite unenforceable in practice because of the unsatisfactory nature of the rules relating to the burden of those covenants.[2] The Committee agreed that the time had come for statutory intervention 'to introduce legal order and consistency into the present (inevitably) haphazard techniques of multi-unit property development'.[3]

No legislation was ever introduced to implement the proposals of the Wilberforce Committee. In 1984, however, the Law Commission issued a renewed proposal for the comprehensive reformulation of the law of freehold covenants, both positive and negative, which rested heavily on the analogy of the law of easements.[4] The Commission envisaged the creation of a new interest in land (the 'land obligation'), by means of which it would be possible to impose both positive and negative obligations on one piece of land (the 'servient land') for the benefit of another piece of land (the 'dominant land').[5] 'Land obligations' are to comprise two types of obligation. It is proposed that they should include 'neighbour obligations' (which represent the equivalents of existing positive and negative covenants)[6] and 'development obligations' (which relate to the kinds of reciprocal obligation much needed for the regulation of multi-occupied areas such as blocks of flats).[7] The Law Commission has recommended that the 'land obligation' should always be made in writing. Moreover a legal land obligation must be contained in a deed and must be made for a term equivalent to a fee simple absolute in possession or for a term of years absolute.[8] Any other 'land obligation' has merely equitable status.[9]

The Law Commission's proposed scheme, if implemented, will have the highly beneficial consequence that the extremely technical rules relating to the transmission of the benefits and burdens of covenants will disappear.[10] It is envisaged that all land obligations (including legal obligations) must be protected by the registration of a new category of Class C land charge (in the case of unregistered land) and by entry on the register of the titles of both dominant and servient tenements (in the case of registered land).[11] The benefits and burdens created by the 'land obligation' will thereafter attach to the relevant tenements and will be enforceable only as between the current owners of the respective tenements.[12] In other words, the person burdened by a land obligation will cease to be liable under it when he ceases to be owner of the relevant servient land.[13]

Although the Law Commission attached to its report a draft Land Obligations Bill, no legislation has yet been introduced in Parliament to give effect to its provisions.

2   See *Report of the Committee on Positive Covenants Affecting Land* (Cmnd 2719, 1965).
3   Ibid, para 9.
4   *Transfer of Land: The Law of Positive and Restrictive Covenants* (Law Com No 127, 26 January 1984).
5   Law Com No 127, paras 4.21, 5.2.
6   Law Com No 127, paras 6.3ff.
7   Law Com No 127, paras 6.7ff.
8   Law Com No 127, paras 5.2, 8.8f.
9   Law Com No 127, paras 5.2, 8.8f.
10   Law Com No 127, para 4.22.
11   Law Com No 127, paras 9.4ff, 9.14ff.
12   Law Com No 127, paras 4.22, 10.2ff.
13   Law Com No 127, para 11.32.

SPECIAL PROBLEMS

E. A property-owning democracy?

CHAPTER 19

The tenant's 'right to buy'

In *Pettitt v Pettitt*[1] Lord Diplock observed that over the years a range of social, economic and demographic factors had conduced towards 'the emergence of a property-owning, particularly a real-property-mortgaged-to-a-building-society-owning, democracy.' At the beginning of the First World War there were only approximately 800,000 home owners in England, comprising some 10 per cent of all households.[2] By 1951 the owner-occupied sector accounted for 3,900,000 dwelling-houses or 31 per cent of the total housing stock.[3] The decade of the 1970s alone saw an expansion of the owner-occupied sector from 49 per cent to 55 per cent of all housing stock in the United Kingdom,[4] and by 1985 this proportion had increased to 62 per cent.[5] It can be estimated that there are today some 13 million home owners living in the United Kingdom.[6] This dramatic shift towards home ownership is, of course, the product of many contributory factors, but foremost amongst these has undoubtedly been the liberal extension of mortgage facilities to broad sections of the population,[7] coupled with the emergence of home ownership not only as a popular ideal but as the object of determined political striving.[8]

There is no doubt that during the present century home ownership has operated as an immensely powerful engine of wealth creation and wealth distribution. The phenomenon of home ownership has brought millions of citizens within the 'propertied classes'. The expansion of the so-called 'property-owning democracy' has been particularly promoted in recent years by two significant legislative devices—the right to leasehold enfranchisement or extension introduced by the Leasehold Reform Act 1967 and the 'right to buy' conferred on public sector tenants by the Housing Act 1980. This chapter examines the contribution which these statutory schemes have made to the general shift from leasehold to freehold tenure.

1. LEASEHOLD ENFRANCHISEMENT AND EXTENSION

A controversial means of leasehold enfranchisement is contained in the

1 [1970] AC 777 at 824C.
2 John Stanley MP, Minister for Housing and Construction, Department of the Environment, 'Government Policies on Home Ownership in the 1980s', in SHAC, *Home Ownership in the 1980s* (Policy Paper No 3, July 1980), p 6.
3 'Trends in Housing and Household Tenure', in Building Societies Association Bulletin No 44 (October 1985), p 20.
4 See Office of Population Censuses and Surveys, *General Household Survey 1978* (London 1980), p 31 (Table 3.1); Central Statistical Office, *Social Trends No 11* (1981 edn London), p 145 (Table 9.4).
5 Central Statistical Office, *Social Trends No 17* (1987 edn London), p 137.
6 See Central Statistical Office, *Social Trends No 16* (1986 edn London), p 133; *Social Trends No 17* (1987 edn London), p 137.
7 On the role of the mortgage, see Chapter 16 (ante, p 563).
8 See Chapter 21 (post, p 760).

Leasehold Reform Act 1967.[9] The principal object of this legislation is to confer on certain tenants holding long leases a right compulsorily to purchase either the freehold reversion or an extended term of years in the property which they occupy.

(1) The legislative motivation

In the residential context long leases almost invariably take one or other of two forms. They may comprise 'building leases', typically for 99 years, under which the original tenant agreed to pay a (usually fairly nominal) ground rent and to construct a house on the site to be delivered up in good repair at the end of the term. Alternatively the long lease may be a 'premium lease' for a similar period, acquired by the original tenant in consideration of a capital payment or premium and supplemented by continuing payments of a low periodic ground rent. The premium paid by the tenant—particularly in relation to a 99 year lease—often approaches the freehold price of similar property. In addition the tenant normally undertakes a contractual responsibility to carry out all running repairs to the property during the currency of the lease and to yield up the property in good repair at the end of the term.

On the expiry of a 'building lease' or 'premium lease' the demised premises (inclusive of any construction, improvements or repairs effected by the tenant) revert to the landlord without any compensation for the tenant. For over a hundred years there has been pressure for some legislative intervention to remedy the possible injustice suffered by the tenant in consequence of the relative imbalance in this form of landlord-tenant relationship. In 1966 the Labour Government of the day issued a White Paper which recognised that residential long leases have 'worked very unfairly against the occupying leaseholder'.[10] This Paper pointed to the fact that, although the freeholder had provided the land, it was the leaseholder who in the vast majority of cases had either built the house at his own expense or had borne the cost of improvements and maintenance during the currency of the term.[11] It was acknowledged to be 'quite indefensible, if justice is to be done as between freeholder and occupying leaseholder', that property which had been cherished and improved as the home of the leaseholder should revert without compensation to the landlord at the expiry of the term.[12]

The Government accordingly proposed a legislative reform of long leaseholds based on the fundamental principle that 'the freeholder owns the land and the occupying leaseholder is morally entitled to the ownership of the building which has been put on and maintained on that land.'[13] This recommendation provided the motive force for the Leasehold Reform Act

9   See N.D.M. Parry, (1983) 127 SJ 113, 129.
10   *Leasehold Reform in England and Wales* (Cmnd 2916, 1966), para 1. The White Paper referred in particular to the fact that, in the case of many of the leasehold estates built in the second half of the 19th century, landowners had used their monopoly power to prevent development taking place on other than leasehold terms. As these leases began to fall in, 'leaseholders are now experiencing the full harshness of the leasehold system' (ibid, para 3).
11   Cmnd 2916, para 1. The injustice to the leaseholder was especially acute where he had financed his purchase of the leasehold interest by means of a mortgage loan and, in view of the wasting nature of the leasehold asset, ended up with nothing to show for his investment.
12   Cmnd 2916, para 1.
13   Cmnd 2916, para 2.

1967, which was formulated precisely on the premise that 'the land belongs in equity to the landowner and the house belongs in equity to the occupying leaseholder.'[14] The 1967 Act seeks to give effect to this perception by conferring on the tenant a statutory right to acquire the freehold by buying out the landlord compulsorily.[15]

(2) Qualifying conditions

Under the Leasehold Reform Act 1967 the right to leasehold enfranchisement or extension is hedged about by important qualifications.

(a) Eligible property

The Leasehold Reform Act 1967 applies only to premises which consist of a 'house', which for this purpose is defined as including 'any building designed or adapted for living in and reasonably so called, notwithstanding that the building is not structurally detached, or was or is not solely designed or adapted for living in, or is divided horizontally into flats or maisonettes'.[16]

It is ultimately a question of law whether it is reasonable to call a building a 'house'.[17] The mere fact of a mixed residential and business user does not disqualify property from the terms of the 1967 Act. In *Tandon v Trustees of Spurgeons Homes*,[18] for instance, a majority in the House of Lords was prepared to accept that the Act was capable of application to leasehold premises which comprised a shop with living accommodation above.[19] As long as a building of mixed use can reasonably be called a house, it comes within the statutory definition 'even though it may also reasonably be called something else'.[20] With certain exceptions, the rateable value of 'houses' within the 1967 Act must not exceed £750 (or £1,500 in Greater London),[1] although these limits nowadays include most properties and exclude only those of an unusually large or luxurious nature.

(b) Eligible tenancy

In order to be eligible under the Leasehold Reform Act 1967, the tenant must demonstrate that his term fulfils certain statutory conditions.

14 Cmnd 2916, para 4.
15 Any attempt by contractual means to exclude or modify the tenant's rights under the Leasehold Reform Act 1967 is in principle void (see Leasehold Reform Act 1967, s 23(1)). See, however, *Buckley v S.R.L. Investments Ltd and Cator and Robinson* (1971) 22 P & CR 756 at 767.
16 Leasehold Reform Act 1967, s 2(1). Thus a 'house' can comprise terraced or semi-detached houses or an entire house divided up into flats or maisonettes. The statutory term cannot apply, however, to a tower block of flats, since this could not 'reasonably' be called a house (see *Lake v Bennett* [1970] 1 QB 663 at 671A). An individual flat or maisonette cannot be claimed to be a 'house' (Leasehold Reform Act 1967, s 2(1)(a)). See [1982] Conv 241.
17 *Tandon v Trustees of Spurgeons Homes* [1982] AC 755 at 767B-C per Lord Roskill.
18 [1982] AC 755 at 766F-H. See [1982] Conv 378. See also *Lake v Bennett* [1970] 1 QB 663 at 671C, 672D-E.
19 'Tenants who live over the shop are not to be denied the right conferred by the Act...merely because the building in which they work and live accommodates the two uses' ([1982] AC 755 at 766F-G per Lord Roskill).
20 [1982] AC 755 at 767B per Lord Roskill.
1 Leasehold Reform Act 1967, s 1(1)(a), as amended by Housing Act 1974, s 118. The rateable value of property may be reduced in accordance with Housing Act 1974, Sch 8, in order to take account of tenants' improvements (Housing Act 1980, s 141, Sch 21, para 2). See *Pearlman v Keepers and Governors of Harrow School* [1979] QB 56 at 67C.

(i) 'Long tenancy'   A qualifying tenant must show that he has a 'long tenancy' as defined by the Act. A 'long tenancy' is, in general, a term certain which when granted was in excess of 21 years,[2] notwithstanding that it may have been terminable before the end of that period by notice, re-entry, forfeiture or otherwise.[3]

(ii) 'Low rent'   Qualifying tenancies include only those tenancies which are 'at a low rent'.[4] A 'low rent' is for this purpose defined as any rent which, when measured at a yearly rate, is not equal to or more than two-thirds of the rateable value appropriate to the property,[5] or, in respect of certain tenancies, does not exceed two-thirds of the 'letting value' of the property.[6] In the latter case the 'letting value' of the property is calculated on a basis which includes the decapitalised value of any lawfully obtainable premiums on the letting,[7] with the result that the Act operates even more favourably to the tenant than would otherwise be the case.

It follows incidentally that the tenancies to which the 1967 Act applies are not generally covered by the Rent Act 1977, precisely because the annual rent payable under a protected or statutory tenancy must comprise at least two-thirds of the relevant rateable value.[8]

(iii) Residence qualification   In order to be eligible under the 1967 Act, the tenant must satisfy a residence qualification. He must be able to show either that he has occupied the relevant house[9] as his only or main residence for a period of at least three years prior to notifying his desire to exercise his statutory rights, or that he has so occupied the house for periods together totalling three years during the ten years prior to the service of his notice.[10]

In *Poland v Earl Cadogan*[11] the Court of Appeal regarded the issue of residence in this context as raising a question of mixed fact and law. The criterion of residence as a condition of eligibility under the Leasehold Reform Act seems to

2   Certain categories of lease are excluded either in whole or in part from the scope of the Leasehold Reform Act 1967. Such categories include leases of National Trust property (Leasehold Reform Act 1967, s 32), and shared ownership leases (Housing Act 1985, s 173(1)).
3   Leasehold Reform Act 1967, s 3(1). See *Eton College v Bard* [1983] Ch 321 at 330C, 332C- E; [1984] Conv 136 (R. Griffith). There are now restrictions on the application of the Leasehold Reform Act 1967 to leases which are terminable on the death of some person other than the tenant, eg a royal life (see Housing Act 1980, s 141, Sch 21, para 3). Where a term is granted for less than 21 years subject to a covenant for renewal without payment of any premium (but not for perpetual renewal), the Act will nevertheless apply to the renewed term (Leasehold Reform Act 1967, s 3(4)). It has been suggested, however, that this provision may be capable of being avoided through the simple expedient of a covenant to pay a fresh premium on renewal (see (1980) 1 PLB 11).
4   Leasehold Reform Act 1967, s 1(1)(a).
5   Leasehold Reform Act 1967, s 4(1).
6   Leasehold Reform Act 1967, s 4(1), proviso.
7   *Manson v Duke of Westminster* [1981] QB 323 at 333B-C, 335D-E. See also *Johnston v Duke of Westminster* [1986] AC 839 at 845E.
8   See Rent Act 1977, s 5(1) (post, p 983).
9   It is sufficient that he has occupied only part of the house (see *Harris v Swick Securities Ltd* [1969] 1 WLR 1604 at 1607E-F).
10   Leasehold Reform Act 1967, s 1(1)(b), as amended by Housing Act 1980, s 141, Sch 21, para 1(1). See *Harris v Plentex* (1980) 40 P & CR 483 at 485f. The occupation must be 'in right of the tenancy', and the Act thus takes no account of residence by a person who holds a tenancy as a bare trustee (see *Duke of Westminster v Oddy* (1984) 270 Estates Gazette 945 at 946).
11   [1980] 3 All ER 544 at 549e.

be construed more strictly than the requirement of continued residence for the purpose of a statutory tenancy under the Rent Act.[12] The Leasehold Reform Act plainly contemplates that the tenant's residence may be discontinuous,[13] but where the tenant is not physically in occupation 'the onus is firmly on him to show that the steps which he has taken to maintain occupation are clear.'[14] Absence on a 'short holiday' may be no bar to a claim of 'residence',[15] but the longer the period of absence the more difficult it may be to infer continued occupation.[16] Residence may be maintained through the vicarious physical occupation of the tenant's family (wife or children), but, except where the period of absence is short, it is distinctly less easy to claim residential occupation on the basis merely that the tenant has left furniture in the house or that there is a caretaker.[17] In *Poland v Earl Cadogan* itself, the tenant was held to have put himself outside the ambit of the Leasehold Reform Act in going abroad and leaving it to his daughter and Harrods to sublet his house.[18]

(3) The tenant's statutory rights

The Leasehold Reform Act confers on a qualifying tenant two substantive rights. *First*, the tenant has a right to require that his existing lease be replaced by a new tenancy for a term which expires 50 years after the expiry date of the existing tenancy.[19] *Second*, the tenant has an alternative right to the enfranchisement of his lease, in that he is entitled compulsorily to purchase the freehold in the demised premises.[20]

(a) Manner of exercise

The exercise of the tenant's rights to enfranchisement or extension of his lease may be set in motion by the service on the landlord of a written notice in the prescribed form which indicates his desire to avail himself of one or other of his statutory entitlements.[1] Where the tenant has served such a notice, the landlord may not, during the currency of the tenant's claim, bring any proceedings to terminate the tenancy without the leave of the court.[2] Such leave may be granted, however, if there is evidence that the tenant's claim to enfranchisement or extension of his lease was not made in good faith, as for instance where the tenant was seeking to purchase the freehold merely in order to escape a forfeiture based on his breach of the leasehold covenants.[3]

---

12 *Poland v Earl Cadogan* [1980] 3 All ER 544 at 549a-b per Waller LJ. Megaw LJ (at 551d) was more ready to find assistance in the Rent Act application of the notion of *animus possidendi*. On the Rent Act requirement, see Chapter 29 (post, p 1008).
13 *Poland v Earl Cadogan* [1980] 3 All ER 544 at 548j, 550e.
14 *Poland v Earl Cadogan* [1980] 3 All ER 544 at 549c-d per Waller LJ.
15 *Poland v Earl Cadogan* [1980] 3 All ER 544 at 549d.
16 *Poland v Earl Cadogan* [1980] 3 All ER 544 at 549d.
17 *Poland v Earl Cadogan* [1980] 3 All ER 544 at 549d.
18 [1980] 3 All ER 544 at 549f, 550j.
19 Leasehold Reform Act 1967, s 14(1).
20 Leasehold Reform Act 1967, s 8(1).
1 Leasehold Reform Act 1967, ss 8(1), 14(1), 22, Sch 3. Such notices may be served at any time during the original term of years, but a tenant's notice in respect of a proposed freehold acquisition cannot be served later than the term date of his lease (Leasehold Reform Act 1967, s 16(1)(a)). Once the notice is served, there is a limitation period of 12 years (see *Collin v Duke of Westminster* [1985] QB 581 at 603F).
2 Leasehold Reform Act 1967, Sch 3, para 4(1).
3 See eg *Central Estates (Belgravia) Ltd v Woolgar* [1972] 1 QB 48 at 55H-56A, 56G-57A.

The mere right to serve such a notice does not in itself constitute an interest in the land, and cannot therefore be regarded as having the character of a land option.[4] However, the rights which accrue to the tenant in consequence of serving a notice under the Leasehold Reform Act can be protected against any subsequent transferee of the landlord's interest through registration of a Class C(iv) land charge (in the case of unregistered land)[5] and by the entry of a minor interest in the register of title (in the case of registered land).[6]

(b) Price

The financial terms on which the tenant's rights to extension or enfranchisement may be exercised are stipulated in the Leasehold Reform Act.

(i) Leasehold extension   Where the tenant exercises his right to obtain a 50 year extension of his existing lease, no price or premium is payable other than the rent due under the lease. That rent is calculated initially as a ground rent which represents the letting value of the site at the commencement of the new tenancy (exclusive of the value of buildings on it).[7]

(ii) Leasehold enfranchisement   Where the tenant exercises his right to purchase the landlord's freehold reversion, the price payable to the landlord is determined in accordance with one or other of two methods of valuation, the so-called '1967 basis of valuation' and the '1974 basis of valuation'.

The '1967 basis of valuation' applies to less valuable properties with a rateable value not exceeding £500 (or £1,000 in Greater London). The relevant price is that which the house, if sold on the open market by a willing seller, might be expected to realise on the twin assumptions that the tenant has exercised his statutory right to obtain a 50 year extension of his lease and that the purchaser is someone other than the tenant himself.[8] The net effect of these assumptions is that the tenant pays approximately the site value of the property (ie, the value of the property excluding any buildings on the site).[9] The price payable on this basis may be remarkably minimal.[10]

4   Ante, p 136. The tenant who has not yet served a notice thus has no right to receive compensation for loss of his rights in the event of compulsory purchase of the property (*Johnson v Sheffield CC* (1982) 43 P & CR 272 at 277).

5   Ante, p 136. An unregistered notice is rendered void against a purchaser for money or money's worth, irrespective of his knowledge of the tenant's rights under the Leasehold Reform Act (see *Buckley v S.R.L. Investments Ltd and Cator and Robinson* (1971) 22 P & CR 756 at 763f, 768).

6   Ante, p 159. It is clear that the tenant's rights arising from service of his notice can never constitute an overriding interest pursuant to Land Registration Act 1925, s 70(1)(g) (Leasehold Reform Act 1967, s 5(5), ante, p 183).

7   Leasehold Reform Act 1967, s 15(2)(a). After the expiry of 25 years from the term date of the original lease a higher rent may become payable in accordance with Leasehold Reform Act 1967, s 15(2)(b).

8   Leasehold Reform Act 1967, s 9(1), as amended by Housing Act 1969, s 82.

9   The operative value can never exceed the present value of the right to take possession in 50 years' time. See *Jones v Wrotham Park Settled Estates* [1980] AC 74 at 108F-G.

10   See eg *Yates v Bridgewater Estates Ltd* (1982) 261 Estates Gazette 1001 at 1002, *Williams v Walsh* (1983) 268 Estates Gazette 915 at 920 (£10 for freehold of properties subject to leases of respectively 971 years and 950 years unexpired); *Divis v Middleton* (1983) 268 Estates Gazette 157 (£665 for freehold of property subject to unexpired term of 89 years); *Re London & Winchester Properties Ltd's Appeal* (1983) 267 Estates Gazette 685 at 686, *Wilkes v Larkcroft Properties Ltd* (1983) 268 Estates Gazette 903 at 906 (£560 and £420 respectively for freeholds of properties subject to unexpired terms of 17 years).

The '1974 basis of valuation' applies to properties with a rateable value between £500 and £750 (or between £1,000 and £1,500 in Greater London).[11] The price payable in such cases is calculated as the amount which the house, if sold on the open market by a willing seller, might be expected to realise on the assumption that at the end of the tenancy the tenant had a right to remain in possession as a statutory tenant under Part I of the Landlord and Tenant Act 1954.[12] This basis of valuation is more favourable to the landlord and is intended to provide a price which is approximately equivalent to the market value of the site and house as occupied by a sitting and statutorily protected tenant.

In default of agreement between landlord and tenant, the price payable is determined by a local Leasehold Valuation Tribunal, with a right of appeal to the Lands Tribunal.[13]

(4) The 'human rights' challenge

One of the underlying assumptions of the Leasehold Reform Act 1967 is that the true investment input in a qualifying lease derives essentially from the tenant, either in the form of the capital premium for which the leasehold term was initially purchased or by way of the tenant's construction and maintenance of a dwelling-house on the site. On this basis no great harm is done to the landlord by the compulsory enfranchisement or extension of the existing term. In the case of a building lease the landlord has contributed only a site value which is now almost certainly dwarfed by the tenant's investment of capital. In the case of a premium lease the landlord could be said to have extracted a fair capital value at the outset of the term. There is something to be said for the view that a tenant who holds a largely unexpired long lease should be recognised as effectively the absolute owner of the property, in which case the Leasehold Reform Act 1967 plays an valuable function in enabling the position to be regularised.

On the other hand, however, it can be argued that the Leasehold Reform Act 1967 'greatly favours the tenant'[14] and is in effect 'an expropriatory Act'.[15] Under its terms the landlord may be required to submit to the compulsory purchase by his tenant of a property which represents an increasingly valuable

---

11 Leasehold Reform Act 1967, s 9(1A), as amended by Housing Act 1974, s 118(4). See *Norfolk v Trinity College Cambridge* (1976) 32 P & CR 147 at 152ff. In *Effra Investments Ltd v Stergios* (1982) 264 Estates Gazette 449 at 453, for instance, a purchase price of £34,500 was determined in relation to a freehold property valued at £70,000 with vacant possession where the tenant had served his notice one month before the expiry of a 99 year lease.

12 In *Mosley v Hickman* (1986) 278 Estates Gazette 728 at 729, 732, the Court of Appeal held that where the tenant had already obtained a 50 year extension of his lease and subsequently, before expiry of the original term date of the tenancy, applied for the freehold, the price payable had to be calculated on the basis of the property as subject to the extended lease. The availability of this opportunity to manipulate valuations resulted in the landlord's receiving much less than market value by way of compensation. This loophole in the Leasehold Reform Act 1967 has now been removed by Housing and Planning Act 1986, s 23(1).

13 Housing Act 1980, s 142, Sch 22.

14 *Tandon v Trustees of Spurgeons Homes* [1982] AC 755 at 761A per Lord Wilberforce (dissenting).

15 *Manson v Duke of Westminster* [1981] QB 323 at 332C per Stephenson LJ. It may well be that recent cases have exposed fundamental divergences of judicial philosophy in relation to the proper role and scope of the Leasehold Reform Act 1967. See eg *Tandon v Trustees of Spurgeons Homes* [1982] AC 755; [1982] Conv 378 at 380f.

capital asset. Especially as a long leasehold term reaches towards its term date, it may seem unfair to deprive the landlord of his steadily appreciating asset at a price which often appears to be derisory. It is often painfully clear that the benefits of the 1967 Act are not confined to the relatively deprived or disadvantaged. Indeed, the position is quite the reverse since, in spite of its socialist origins, the Act is primarily of benefit to those who are already possessed of sufficient capital resources or borrowing power to acquire long leases in the first place. As with so much else in this life, to those to whom much has been given shall even more be given.

In 1984 growing dissatisfaction with the operation of the Leasehold Reform Act 1967 led to litigation before the European Court of Human Rights by trustees acting on behalf of the Duke of Westminster, the freehold owner of large areas of Belgravia.[16] The Westminster family trust complained that the Leasehold Reform Act 1967 contravened the requirement in the European Convention on Human Rights that '[n]o one shall be deprived of his possessions except in the public interest...'[17] Between 1979 and 1983 the Westminster family trust had been involved in 80 leasehold enfranchisements by its tenants, and it was estimated that the Westminster estate might ultimately be subject to between 500 and 800 enfranchisement applications by long leaseholders. Although the unencumbered freehold value of the properties so far enfranchised varied from £44,000 to £225,000, the prices paid by the tenants had ranged from £2,500 to £111,000. Many of the enfranchising tenants had since sold up their newly acquired freeholds, some at an instant profit of over £100,000. It was alleged that losses already totalling over £2,500,000 had been sustained by reason of these compulsory sales on other than open-market terms.[18]

Notwithstanding this evidence the European Court rejected the claim that the compulsory transfer of property under the Leasehold Reform Act 1967 constitutes a breach of the Convention on Human Rights. The Court was of the opinion that the compulsory transfer of property from one individual to another 'may, depending upon the circumstances, constitute a legitimate means for promoting the public interest'.[19] The Court upheld the Leasehold Reform Act 1967 on the ground that the 'taking of property in pursuance of a policy calculated to enhance social justice within the community can properly be described as being "in the public interest".'[20] The aim striven for by the 1967 Act was 'legitimate',[1] in that, although the applicants' complaint was not 'groundless',[2] the United Kingdom Parliament's belief in the existence of social injustice in 1967 'was not such as could be characterised as manifestly unreasonable' in view of the relative capital investments of landlord and

---

16   *Case of James* (Case No 3/1984/75/119, European Court of Human Rights, 21 February 1986).
17   Article 1 of Protocol No 1 to the European Convention on Human Rights.
18   *Case of James*, Court Judgment, para 29.
19   *Case of James*, Court Judgment, para 40. The Court cited in support the U.S. Supreme Court's endorsement of state legislation for the compulsory transfer of title from lessors to lessees in the interests of reducing the concentration of land ownership (see *Hawaii Housing Authority v Midkiff*, 467 US 229 at 241ff, 81 L Ed 2d 186 at 198ff (1984)).
20   *Case of James*, Court Judgment, para 41.
1   Ibid, para 47.
2   Ibid, para 49.

tenant.[3] The Court ultimately rejected the instant complaint on the ground that 'modern societies consider housing of the population to be a prime social need, the regulation of which cannot entirely be left to the play of market forces.' There must be legislative competence to secure 'greater social justice in the sphere of people's homes...even where such legislation interferes with existing contractual relations between private parties and confers no direct benefit on the State or the community at large.'[4]

2. THE PUBLIC SECTOR TENANT'S 'RIGHT TO BUY'

An increasingly significant aspect of the charter of rights conferred on the public sector tenant takes the form of his statutory 'right to buy' the home in which he lives. This right, introduced in the Housing Act 1980 and now contained in the Housing Act 1985, was intended to satisfy 'a deeply ingrained desire for home ownership'.[5] Promotion of the 'right to buy' has now become a central feature of Tory Party policy, promising in the unrestrained language of its government sponsors to 'transform the personal prospects of millions of our citizens, offering to turn them at their wish from tenants to owners'.[6] The ready provision of this 'right to buy' has immediate political leverage in so far as it supposedly 'ensures the wide spread of wealth through society, encourages a personal desire to improve and modernise one's own home, enables parents to accrue wealth for their children and stimulates the attitudes of independence and self-reliance that are the bed-rock of a free society'.[7]

There is little doubt that the introduction of the public sector 'right to buy' has significantly affected the nature and distribution of home-ownership in England and Wales. In spite of its controversial political origins, the 'right to buy' has now been exercised by almost one million council tenants,[8] thus bringing somewhat closer the apparent reality of a 'property-owning democracy'. However, the undeniable popular success of the 'right to buy', when assessed against a background of unprecedented and catastrophic housing shortage, only barely conceals the fact that much needed public housing stock has been sold off and withdrawn from circulation in order to gratify a desire for capital accumulation at the expense of those who in housing terms are most heavily disadvantaged. It is not at all clear that 'property-owning' and 'democracy' are ultimately compatible if the extension of home ownership can be achieved only at the cost of reinforcing existing inequalities in the housing market and intensifying the growing cleavage between one nation which consists of those who have and that other nation which comprises those who do not.

---

3 Ibid, para 49. The Court laid great emphasis on the fact that any 'windfall profits' gained through onward sales by the enfranchising tenants had been made, not at the expense of the applicants who had received the statutorily prescribed compensation, but at the expense of the predecessors in title of the enfranchising tenants (para 69).

4 Ibid, para 47. The Court's comments in this respect are as relevant to the social legitimacy of Rent Act legislation as to the function of the Leasehold Reform Act 1967. On the question of constitutional challenge to Rent Act legislation, see Chapter 29 (post, p 970).

5 Mr M. Heseltine (Secretary of State for the Environment), *Parliamentary Debates, House of Commons, Official Report*, Vol 976 (Session 1979-1980), Col 1445 (15 January 1980).

6 Ibid, Col 1460.

7 Ante, p 567.

8 See R.N.D. Hamilton, (1986) 130 SJ 906.

(1) Nature of the 'right to buy'

The Housing Act 1985 confers on certain qualifying categories of 'secure tenant'[9] the right, in statutorily defined circumstances, to purchase either the freehold or a long leasehold term in the property in which the secure tenant lives. The secure tenant is entitled to acquire the freehold if his dwelling-house is a 'house' and his landlord owns the freehold.[10] If his dwelling-house is not a 'house' but is a flat or if his landlord is not the owner of the freehold, the secure tenant has a right to be granted a long lease for a term of usually not less than 125 years at a rent which does not exceed £10 per annum.[11]

Where a qualifying secure tenancy is a joint tenancy, the 'right to buy' belongs to all the tenants jointly.[12] A secure tenant may also nominate not more than three 'members of his family'[13] to share the 'right to buy' with him, but may validly do so only if those members are not already joint tenants but occupy the dwelling-house as their 'only or principal home'.[14] Moreover, unless the landlord otherwise consents, any nominated family member must either be a spouse of the secure tenant or a person who has resided with the secure tenant for at least twelve months.[15] Where a qualifying tenant nominates other family members to share his 'right to buy', that right belongs to them all jointly.[16]

(2) Conditions of eligibility

The 'right to buy' is conferred by the Housing Act 1985 on any secure tenant who satisfies a complicated series of statutory conditions.

(a) Qualifying property

The 'right to buy' is capable of application to any dwelling-house within the definition of the 1985 Act. A dwelling-house is a 'house' if it is 'a structure reasonably so called',[17] and a dwelling-house which is not a house is a 'flat'.[18] Where a building is divided horizontally, the resulting residential units are 'flats' rather than 'houses',[19] but a vertical division of a building into semi-detached or terraced houses produces separate 'houses' within the meaning of the Act.[20]

The Housing Act 1985 excludes certain kinds of property from the scope of the 'right to buy'. Among the excluded categories are properties of which the landlord is a charitable housing trust or housing association,[1] or is a co-

---

9 A 'secure tenancy' is defined in Housing Act 1985, s 79ff. See Chapter 30 (post, p 1045).
10 Housing Act 1985, s 118(1)(a).
11 Housing Act 1985, s 118(1)(b), Sch 6, Part III, paras 11, 12(1).
12 Housing Act 1985, s 118(2).
13 Membership of the tenant's family is, for this purpose, defined in Housing Act 1985, s 186 in terms identical to those which govern the statutory devolution of a public sector tenancy (post, p 1060). Compare Housing Act 1985, s 113.
14 Housing Act 1985, s 123(1).
15 Housing Act 1985, s 123(2).
16 Housing Act 1985, s 123(3).
17 Housing Act 1985, s 183(2). Compare Leasehold Reform Act 1967, s 2(1) (ante, p 727).
18 Housing Act 1985, s 183(3).
19 Housing Act 1985, s 183(2)(a).
20 Housing Act 1985, s 183(2)(b).
1 Housing Act 1985, Sch 5, para 1.

operative housing association.[2] Also excluded from the statutory 'right to buy' are dwelling-houses which have features which are substantially different from those of ordinary dwelling-houses and which have been designed or converted to make them suitable for occupation by physically disabled persons.[3] Nor does the 'right to buy' arise if the dwelling-house in question is particularly suitable for occupation by persons of pensionable age and has been the subject of a letting either to a person of pensionable age or to a physically disabled person.[4]

(b) Qualifying tenants

A secure tenant qualifies for the 'right to buy' if he has been a secure tenant of a public sector landlord for a period of at least two years,[5] although neither the landlord nor the dwelling-house need have been the same during the whole of this period.[6] Where the secure tenancy is a joint tenancy, it is sufficient that this condition is satisfied by only one of the joint tenants.[7] Even though the claimant of the 'right to buy' has not himself resided for a period of two years, the requisite residence may comprise residence either by a spouse with whom he was living at the date on which he claimed the 'right to buy'[8] or by a spouse who died prior to his claiming the 'right to buy' but with whom he was living at the date of her death.[9]

The 'right to buy' is not available if any person to whom that right belongs is an undischarged bankrupt or has a bankruptcy petition pending against him or a receiving order in force against him.[10] Nor can the 'right to buy' be exercised if the tenant, at any stage before the completion of his purchase, becomes the subject of a possession order made against him on any of the grounds which permit the landlord to recover possession under the Housing Act 1985.[11] If the law were not so, as Slade LJ pointed out in *Enfield LBC v McKeon*,[12] a secure tenant would always be able to frustrate the enforcement of any possession order against him—no matter how good the ground on which it was made—by the simple device of claiming the 'right to buy'.

2 Housing Act 1985, Sch 5, para 2.
3 Housing Act 1985, Sch 5, paras 6-8. This exception is intended to relate to such features as the installation of ramps, specially widened doors, lifts and specially lowered cooking surfaces. It does not cover the mere installation of an additional downstairs lavatory which is wholly incapable of accommodating a wheelchair (see *Freeman v Wansbeck DC* (1983) 82 LGR 131 at 134ff).
4 Housing Act 1985, Sch 5, para 11, as substituted by Housing and Planning Act 1986, s 1.
5 Housing Act 1985, s 119(1). This qualifying period need not be a continuous period (Housing Act 1985, Sch 4, para 1), nor need it be a period immediately preceding the tenant's exercise of his 'right to buy' (see Housing Act 1980, s 27(3); Housing Act 1985, Sch 4, para 2(a)).
6 See Housing Act 1980, s 1(3)(a).
7 Housing Act 1985, s 119(2).
8 Housing Act 1985, Sch 4, para 2(a).
9 Housing Act 1985, Sch 4, para 2(b). A child of a secure tenant may be able to count towards the residence requirement certain periods during which he occupied his parent's dwelling-house as his only or principal home after the age of sixteen (Housing Act 1985, Sch 4, para 4).
10 Housing Act 1985, s 121(2).
11 Housing Act 1985, s 121(1). See *Enfield LBC v McKeon* [1986] 1 WLR 1007 at 1015G-H, where the Court of Appeal held that a tenant's attempt to exercise her 'right to buy' had been effectively pre-empted by the Council's recovery of possession on the ground that the accommodation afforded by the house was more extensive than was required by the tenant.
12 [1986] 1 WLR 1007 at 1015F-G.

(3) Terms of purchase

A secure tenant may claim to exercise his 'right to buy' by serving a written notice to that effect on the landlord.[13] Where the 'right to buy' has been validly claimed, the terms on which the tenant's purchase is to be concluded are specified in complex provisions of the Housing Act 1985, as amended by the Housing and Planning Act 1986.

(a) Discounted price

The qualifying tenant has a right to purchase either the freehold or a long leasehold term at the price which such an interest would achieve on the open market,[14] minus a discount which is variable in accordance with the duration of the pre-existing secure tenancy.[15] In the case of a house the appropriate discount ranges from 32 per cent to a maximum of 60 per cent after 30 years of qualifying residence.[16] In the case of a flat the relevant discount ranges from 44 per cent to a maximum of 70 per cent.[17]

There is, of course, a clear danger that the availability of purchase at a discounted price may facilitate private profiteering at public expense. In order to preclude this possibility, the Housing Act 1985 imposes in cases of 'early disposal' an obligation to repay in part or whole any discount which was made in favour of the tenant on the exercise of his 'right to buy'.[18] On purchase the tenant is required to covenant to repay a statutorily prescribed portion of that discount in the event of any onward sale of the fee simple or grant of a long lease[19] during the three years immediately following his purchase.[20]

---

13   Housing Act 1985, s 122(1). See The Housing (Right to Buy) (Prescribed Forms) Regulations 1986 (SI 1986/2194), effective 7 January 1987.
14   Housing Act 1985, ss 126(1)(a), 127(1)-(3).
15   Housing Act 1985, s 126(1)(b). The maximum discount allowable is currently fixed as £35,000. See Housing Act 1985, s 131(2); The Housing (Right to Buy) (Maximum Discount) Order 1986 (SI 1986/2193), effective 7 January 1987.
16   Housing Act 1985, s 129(2)(a), as substituted by Housing and Planning Act 1986, s 2. The discount is increased by one per cent for each complete year by which the qualifying period exceeds two years.
17   Housing Act 1985, s 129(2)(b), as substituted by Housing and Planning Act 1986, s 2. The discount is increased by two per cent for each complete year by which the qualifying period exceeds two years.
18   Any liability arising under this obligation to repay the discount constitutes a charge which may be protected under Land Registration Act 1925 by entry against the purchaser's registered title (Housing Act 1985, s 156(3)). Certain disposals are exempted from the liability to repay the discount (see Housing Act 1985, s 160(1)), eg a disposal on divorce in pursuance of a property transfer order made under Matrimonial Causes Act 1973, s 24. However, this exception relates only to a transfer or settlement which involves 'continued occupational enjoyment of the property by a spouse and/or children of the family...whereby no liquid cash advantage is gained' (*R v Rushmoor BC, ex parte Barrett* [1987] 1 All ER 353 at 357j-358a). The immunity does not therefore cover a sale ordered under Matrimonial Causes Act 1973, s 24A, where the net proceeds of sale are divided between the spouses.
19   Where the purchasing tenant subsequently grants a lease, the 'early disposal' provisions are relevant only where the lease comprises a term (other than a mortgage term) exceeding 21 years otherwise than at a rack rent (Housing Act 1985, s 159(1)(b)).
20   Housing Act 1985, s 155(1),(2), as amended by Housing and Planning Act 1986, s 2(3). The amount of discount repayable is reduced by one-third for each complete year which has elapsed after the acquisition and before the disposal.

(b) Right to mortgage finance

The qualifying tenant who exercises his 'right to buy' is entitled to leave the whole or part of the purchase price outstanding on the security of the dwelling-house or, if the landlord is a housing association, to have the whole or part of that amount advanced to him by the Housing Corporation by way of mortgage loan.[1] A secure tenant who purchases a long lease in a flat is entitled to require that the landlord should include in his notice of the purchase price an estimate of the service charges (including repair costs) which will be payable during the first five years following the tenant's exercise of his 'right to buy'.[2] This estimate is binding on the landlord,[3] and the tenant has a statutory right to loan facilities sufficient to cover service charges for repairs during the first ten years.[4]

(c) Terms and covenants affecting the new title

The completion of a purchase under the 'right to buy' terminates any secure tenancy previously enjoyed by the purchasing tenant.[5] Thereafter the position of the purchaser is governed largely by the terms and covenants which are attached by the Housing Act 1985 to the conveyance of his freehold or the grant of his lease.[6] In particular the conveyance or grant cannot exclude or restrict the general words implied under section 62 of the Law of Property Act 1925,[7] except where the purchasing tenant consents or the exclusion or restriction is made 'for the purpose of preserving or recognising an existing interest of the landlord in tenant's incumbrances or an existing right or interest of another person'.[8]

(4) Shared ownership leases

It is possible that the attempt by a secure tenant to claim his 'right to buy' under the Housing Act 1985 may result in the grant to him of a hybrid form of lease known as a 'shared ownership lease'. The right to be granted a 'shared ownership lease' arises where a secure tenant has established his 'right to buy' but is not entitled to a full mortgage for the purpose of completing his purchase.[9] In these circumstances the tenant is entitled to the grant of a lease which combines features of long leasehold ownership and periodic tenancy.

---

1 Housing Act 1985, s 132(1).
2 Housing Act 1985, ss 125(4)(a), 125A(1),(2), as substituted by Housing and Planning Act 1986, s 4(1),(2). The landlord must also provide an estimate of likely improvement contributions payable by the tenant over a similar period (Housing Act 1985, ss 125(4)(b), 125B(1),(2), as substituted by Housing and Planning Act 1986, s 4(1),(2)). See also The Housing (Right to Buy) (Service Charges) Order 1986 (SI 1986/2195), effective 7 January 1987.
3 Housing Act 1985, Sch 6, Part III, para 16C(1), as supplied by Housing and Planning Act 1986, s 4(4).
4 Housing Act 1985, s 450A(1), as supplied by Housing and Planning Act 1986, s 5.
5 Housing Act 1985, s 139(2).
6 Housing Act 1985, s 139(1). See generally Housing Act 1985, Sch 6.
7 Ante, p 674.
8 Housing Act 1985, Sch 6, para 1.
9 Housing Act 1985, s 143(1). The claimant must also have paid a deposit of £100 (Housing Act 1985, s 142(1)(c)).

(a) Principle of shared ownership

Under a 'shared ownership lease' the claimant tenant does not purchase either a freehold or a leasehold estate in the entire property outright, but instead purchases a notional proportion of the property on a long lease (normally of 125 years[10]) while remaining a periodic tenant in respect of the remainder. In effect, the occupier under the 'shared ownership lease' purchases an equity share in the property and pays a rent in respect of the remaining share, with the result that the traditional common law estates in the property are subjected to a complicated and subtle form of shared ownership between landlord and tenant.

The tenant may claim to exercise his right to be granted a 'shared ownership lease' by serving on the landlord a written notice which specifies the 'initial share' which he proposes to acquire.[11] This 'initial share' must comprise at least 50 per cent of the whole ownership of the property and may be any higher multiple of 12.5 per cent.[12] The intended effect of the 'shared ownership lease' is that the 'initial share' should correspond roughly to the amount in respect of which the tenant can reasonably expect to be able to discharge a mortgage liability while paying the normal periodic rent due in respect of the remaining percentage of ownership of the house.[13]

(b) Principle of progressive purchase

The 'shared ownership lease' when granted contains terms and covenants prescribed by statute.[14] The lease must confer on the tenant a right to acquire 'additional shares' in the dwelling-house (in multiples of 12.5 per cent),[15] and for this purpose the tenant is given a statutory right to increased mortgage facilities.[16] The tenant may thus increase the proportion of his capital share in the dwelling-house in accordance with later increases in his financial resources and general creditworthiness.[17] When the tenant has by progressive stages completed the acquisition of 100 per cent of his dwelling-house, he is entitled (if his landlord owns a fee simple estate) to require that the landlord should convey that freehold to him.[18] Where the landlord's interest is itself a leasehold estate, the tenant who acquires 100 per cent of the initially shared ownership is effectively entitled to the entire leasehold interest at a rent of £10 per annum.[19]

---

10   Housing Act 1985, Sch 6, para 12(1).
11   Housing Act 1985, s 144(1).
12   Housing Act 1985, s 145(2), (3). The claimant tenant is entitled to a discounted purchase price in accordance with the duration of the existing secure tenancy (Housing Act 1985, s 148(1)).
13   Shared ownership leases have now been withdrawn from the jurisdiction of the rent officer under the Rent Act 1977 (see Rent Act 1977, s 5A(1), as supplied by Housing and Planning Act 1986, s 18, Sch 4, para 1(2), post, p 983).
14   Housing Act 1985, s 151(1). See Housing Act 1985, Sch 8, Sch 6, Parts I and III.
15   Housing Act 1985, Sch 8, para 1(1).
16   Housing Act 1985, Sch 9, para 1(1). See The Housing (Right to a Shared Ownership Lease) (Further Advances Limit) Regulations 1985 (SI 1985/758).
17   On the purchase of an 'additional share', the rent payable by the tenant is correspondingly diminished (Housing Act 1985, Sch 8, para 4(1)).
18   Housing Act 1985, Sch 8, para 2(1).
19   Housing Act 1985, Sch 8, para 5.

(5) The 'preserved right to buy'

A new dimension of complexity has arrived to bedevil the operation of the secure tenant's 'right to buy' under the Housing Act 1985. The Housing and Planning Act 1986 contains measures designed to protect the tenant's 'right to buy' where the landlord's interest in his dwelling-house is 'privatised', ie, transferred from public ownership into ownership within the private sector. Where the secure tenant's dwelling-house is the subject of such a disposal to a private sector landlord, the tenant is given a 'preserved right to buy' which is effective against the new landlord in exactly the same terms as formerly against the original public sector landlord.[20] The bindingness of this 'preserved right to buy' on the new landlord depends, however, on the entry of the right against the appropriate register of title,[1] and if not duly registered in this way the 'preserved right to buy' will become entirely ineffective.[2]

---

20 Housing Act 1985, s 171B(1), as supplied by Housing and Planning Act 1986, s 8(1).
1   Housing Act 1985, Sch 9A, para 5(4), as supplied by Housing and Planning Act 1986, s 8(2), Sch 2 (ante, p 183). The existing public sector landlord must, and a qualifying tenant may, apply for the appropriate registration.
2   Housing Act 1985, Sch 9A, para 6(2).

CHAPTER 20

Adverse possession

The law of adverse possession presents one of the oldest, yet also most imprecise, aspects of the concept of property. Stemming ultimately from some idea of title by successful taking, acquisition through adverse possession seems at first not to have any affinity at all with the 'property-owning democracy'. However, the law of adverse possession, by pressing to its limit the essential relativity of title in English law, operates at the very margins of the property concept to extend rights in land to those who have no formal title.

The acquisition of rights by adverse possession operates in conjunction with the Limitation Act and differs markedly from any form of acquisition by conveyance or transfer. The essential feature of acquisition by adverse possession is the idea that if the owner of property fails within a certain period to secure the eviction of a squatter or trespasser from his land, his own title is extinguished and he is thereafter statutorily barred from recovering possession of the land. Title to land being ultimately relative, the intruder thus acquires—as an indirect effect of the Limitation Act—a title which enables him to remain in possession.

1. THE RATIONALE OF ACQUISITION BY ADVERSE POSSESSION

The law of adverse possession gives effect to the pragmatic expectation, born no doubt in the more physical climate of earlier times, that a property owner will rise with rugged fortitude to assert his title against unlawful intruders. The Limitation Act reflects a policy that 'those who go to sleep upon their claims should not be assisted by the courts in recovering their property'.[1] An equally potent element of policy underlying the Act is the idea that 'there shall be an end of litigation'. From the earliest origins of the 'seisin-possession' concept in the common law, there has been a large social interest in 'the quieting of possession'.[2] As Lord St Leonards observed as long ago as 1852,[3] all limitation statutes are intended to prevent the 'rearing up of claims at great distances of time when evidences are lost'.[4]

Thus it has come about that the modern Limitation Act (the Limitation Act 1980) is in part directed towards extinguishing titles which have not been vindicated within the period specified by statute. It seems likely that the law of

1 *R.B. Policies at Lloyd's v Butler* [1950] 1 KB 76 at 81.
2 *Dundee Harbour Trustees v Dougall* (1852) 1 Macq 317 at 321.
3 See *A'Court v Cross* (1825) 3 Bing 329 at 332f, 130 ER 540 at 541, where Best CJ pointed out that a Statute of Limitation is 'an act of peace. Long dormant claims have often more of cruelty than of justice in them'.
4 The first statute of limitation was the Limitation Act 1623. The current statute, the Limitation Act 1980, came into force on 1 May 1981.

adverse possession still has a valid role in the contemporary legal world,[5] in that it is generally accepted that 'certainty of title to land is a social need and occupation of land which has long been unchallenged should not be disturbed'.[6] Moreover, as the emphasis of the law turns increasingly to the protection of residential security, the law of adverse possession has the merit of ensuring that de facto possession does not diverge too markedly from de iure title.[7]

2. THE PERIOD OF LIMITATION

The broad principle underlying the law of adverse possession is the rule that no action may be brought for the recovery of land after the expiration of a statutorily prescribed period of time running from the date when the right of action first accrued.[8] The period prescribed differs according to the nature of the particular action, but at the termination of the appropriate period the action for recovery becomes statute-barred.

(1) The general rule

The Limitation Act 1980 lays down as a general rule that '[n]o action shall be brought by any person to recover any land after the expiration of twelve years from the date on which the right of action accrued to him'.[9]

(a) Accrual of the right of action

In order that a right of action should accrue, thereby causing the period of limitation to begin to run, the land concerned must be 'in the possession of some person in whose favour the period of limitation can run'.[10] The possession here referred to is commonly known as 'adverse possession'. Thus the limitation period begins to run from the date of the owner's dispossession by an adverse possessor[11] or from the date of the inception of adverse possession by a

---

5 See M. Dockray, *Why Do We Need Adverse Possession?*, [1985] Conv 272.
6 See Law Reform Committee, *Report on Acquisition of Easements and Profits by Prescription* (14th Report, Cmnd 3100, 1966), para 36.
7 See M. Goodman, (1970) 33 MLR 281 at 282f. It is a salutary fact that the law of adverse possession is often the consumer's ultimate remedy for the deficiencies of modern conveyancing techniques. For an even more bizarre application of adverse possession, see *DeRocco v Young* (1981) 120 DLR (3d) 169 at 173, where a convicted murderer was held to be capable (after his release from prison) of acquiring a title by long possession of his victim's land, even though he was barred by public policy from claiming any interest in the victim's land by way of the beneficial interest which had been left to him in her will (ante, p 332).
8 For reference to a 'tenuous if picturesque' form of adverse possession, see A.R. Everton, *Built in a Night...*, (1971) 35 Conv (NS) 249. See also (1972) 36 Conv (NS) 241, (1975) 39 Conv (NS) 427.
9 Limitation Act 1980, s 15(1). The limitation period is 30 years in respect of actions brought by the Crown and 60 years in respect of actions brought by the Crown to recover foreshore (Limitation Act 1980, Sch 1, paras 10, 11). Other provisions in the Limitation Act 1980 deal specifically with the accrual of rights of action in relation to future interests, settled land and land held on trust for sale (Limitation Act 1980, s 18, Sch 1, para 4).
10 Limitation Act 1980, Sch 1, para 8(1). Adverse possession cannot be claimed by any person who is not legally competent to hold title (eg an unincorporated association of persons (see *Afton Band of Indians v Attorney-General of Nova Scotia* (1978) 85 DLR (3d) 454 at 463ff)).
11 Limitation Act 1980, Sch 1, para 1.

third party following a 'discontinuance' of possession by the original owner.[12]

(b) Aggregation of periods of adverse possession

The limitation period prescribed by statute may be established by a series of adverse possessors of land. In other words, if X (the original 'paper owner') is dispossessed of his land by A who, in his turn, is dispossessed by B, B may claim the period of A's adverse possession as if it were his own in defence to any action for recovery brought by X, provided that the two periods together total at least 12 years.[13] B is, however, vulnerable to any action for recovery which is brought against him by A before B's independent period of adverse possession has prevailed for at least 12 years.

The adverse possession of successive trespassers can operate cumulatively to extinguish an existing title only if the periods of adverse possession are continuous. If A abandons his adverse possession within the limitation period and, after an interval, B begins adversely to possess, B cannot add to his possession the period of adverse possession earlier established by A.[14] The break in adverse possession will have restored the true owner's title to its pristine force, and the statutory limitation period starts afresh from the inception of B's possession.[15]

(2) Special rules in respect of tenancies

Special rules govern adverse claims in respect of land which is the subject of a term of years. No tenant can claim adverse possession against his landlord during the currency of his tenancy, not least because the tenant is estopped from denying his landlord's title.[16] The possession of a tenant cannot be considered adverse until the period covered by the last payment of rent has expired.[17]

(a) Dispossession of a tenant by a squatter

If the tenant is dispossessed by a third party during the currency of his lease, the intruder's adverse possession begins to be effective immediately as against the tenant,[18] but the statutory limitation period does not begin to run as against the landlord until the expiry date of the lease.[19] A tenancy from year to year or for any other period is normally treated as being determined for this purpose at the expiration of the first year or other period.[20] However, where any rent has

---

12   Limitation Act 1980, Sch 1, para 8(1).
13   Limitation Act 1980, s 15(1). See *Willis v Earl Howe* [1893] 2 Ch 545 at 553f; *Salter v Clark* (1904) 4 SR (NSW) 280 at 288; *Mulcahy v Curramore Pty Ltd* [1974] 2 NSWLR 464 at 476D-E.
14   Limitation Act 1980, Sch 1, para 8(2).
15   *Willis v Earl Howe* [1893] 2 Ch 545 at 554; *Mulcahy v Curramore Pty Ltd* [1974] 2 NSWLR 464 at 476E.
16   *Shillabeer v Diebel* (1980) 100 DLR (3d) 279 at 283.
17   See *Hayward v Chaloner* [1968] 1 QB 107 at 122C-D per Russell LJ.
18   *Perry v Woodfarm Homes Ltd* [1975] IR 104 at 130.
19   Limitation Act 1980, Sch 1, para 4. See also *Perry v Woodfarm Homes Ltd* [1975] IR 104 at 120; *Gioukouros v Cadillac Fairview Corp Ltd* (1984) 3 DLR (4th) 595 at 605.
20   Limitation Act 1980, Sch 1, para 5(1). See *Palfrey v Palfrey* (1974) 229 Estates Gazette 1593 at 1595.

subsequently been received in respect of the tenancy, the right of action is treated as having accrued on the date of the last receipt of rent.[1]

(b) Surrender of a dispossessed tenant's term

Some difficulty has arisen over the question whether a dispossessed tenant can effectively surrender to his landlord a leasehold term which, from the tenant's viewpoint, has already become statute-barred against the squatter. Such a manoeuvre may be attempted in the hope of accelerating the landlord's right to possession. On the assumption that the land concerned was unregistered, the House of Lords held by a majority in *St Marylebone Property Co Ltd v Fairweather*[2] that the landlord is entitled in these circumstances to recover possession from the squatter, on the ground that the latter's possession defeated only the rights of the tenant and not the superior title of the landlord. However, this reasoning is inherently vulnerable to the objection that a tenant who has lost all his title to a leasehold estate is in no position to deal effectively with that estate, having nothing which he can either surrender or assign.[3] The highly suspect analogy of *St Marylebone Property Co Ltd v Fairweather* has been resisted in the context of registered land, where it is clear that in equivalent circumstances the squatter is entitled, after 12 years' adverse possession, to be registered as proprietor of the land.[4] Thereafter any purported surrender by the tenant is entirely ineffective to merge any leasehold interest with the landlord's superior title.[5]

3. DISPOSSESSION AND DISCONTINUANCE OF POSSESSION

It is clear law that under the Limitation Act the person claiming land by possession must show either (i) a 'discontinuance by the paper owner followed by possession' or (ii) a 'dispossession' (or 'ouster') of the paper owner.[6] True cases of dispossession or ouster are nowadays somewhat rare, and most of the difficulties in the law of adverse possession have arisen in the context of 'discontinuance' of possession by the paper owner followed by the inception of 'possession' on the part of an intruding squatter.

(1) 'Discontinuance' of possession by the paper owner

Except in cases of ouster or physical dispossession, a claim of adverse possession can succeed only if it can be shown that there was a 'discontinuance' of possession by the paper owner.[7]

1　Limitation Act 1980, Sch 1, para 5(2).
2　[1963] AC 510 at 540ff, 548. See (1962) 78 LQR 541 (H.W.R. Wade).
3　See eg *Perry v Woodfarm Homes Ltd* [1975] IR 104 at 114, 119, 130f.
4　Land Registration Act 1925, s 75 (post, p 751).
5　*Spectrum Investment Co v Holmes* [1981] 1 WLR 221 at 230E-231C. See (1981) 32 NILQ 254 (H. Wallace); [1981] Conv 157 (C. Sydenham); [1982] Conv 201 (P.H. Kenny). The same result would follow in registered land even if the squatter did not apply to be registered as proprietor, since his possessory rights ought in any event to comprise an overriding interest pursuant to Land Registration Act 1925, s 70(1)(f) (ante, p 174).
6　*Treloar v Nute* [1976] 1 WLR 1295 at 1300E per Sir John Pennycuick.
7　For the inevitable consequence of failure to show a 'discontinuance', see *Maguire v Browne* (1913) 17 CLR 365 at 368f.

(a) Presumption in favour of the paper owner

Any claim based on an alleged 'discontinuance' of possession requires the rebuttal of a fairly heavy presumption that possession is retained prima facie either by the paper owner or by some person who claims through him.[8] In the absence of evidence to the contrary, the owner of the paper title is deemed to remain in possession. He is regarded as maintaining a constructive possession of the land even if he is not in actual possession of the whole of it.[9]

(b) Retention for future use

It is usually not difficult to determine whether there has been a 'discontinuance' of possession by the paper owner. However, the problematical case is that in which the paper owner allows his land to lie dormant for the time being, while intending to put the land to some specific use in the future.

There is strong authority for the view that the paper owner does not necessarily discontinue his possession of land merely because neither he nor any person claiming through him currently makes use of the land.[10] Nor does a 'discontinuance' of possession occur even if some other person meanwhile enjoys physical occupation of the land, provided that the paper owner intends throughout to retain the land for a specific use or purpose at some later date.[11] In such a case, as Lord Denning MR said in *Wallis's Cayton Bay Holiday Camp Ltd v Shell-Mex and BP Ltd*,[12] the true owner does not lose his title to the land 'simply because some other person enters on it and uses it for some temporary...or...seasonal purpose...even if this temporary or seasonal purpose continues year after year for 12 years, or more.'

(2) Inception of 'possession' by a third party

In cases of adverse possession arising otherwise than by 'ouster', it is essential to show not merely that there has been a 'discontinuance' of possession by the paper owner, but also that there has been an inception of 'possession' by an adverse occupier. Without the element of a new 'possession' asserted by an intruder there would of course be no right of action in the paper owner to be statute-barred through the effluxion of time. For present purposes, however, the concept of 'possession' is given a qualified meaning. 'Possession' can be attributed to the intruder only if he can show that he has both factual possession and the requisite 'intention to possess' (*animus possidendi*).[13]

---

8   *Powell v McFarlane* (1977) 38 P & CR 452 at 470. See also *Re Lundrigans Ltd and Prosper* (1982) 132 DLR (3d) 727 at 731.

9   See *Fletcher v Storoschuk* (1981) 128 DLR (3d) 59 at 62; *Masidon Investments Ltd v Ham* (1983) 39 OR (2d) 534 at 545d.

10   *Leigh v Jack* (1879) 5 Ex D 264 at 271 per Cockburn CJ. See also *Riley v Penttila* [1974] VR 547 at 562.

11   See *Leigh v Jack* (1879) 5 Ex D 264 at 271ff; *Williams Brothers Direct Supply Ltd v Raftery* [1958] 1 QB 159 at 170ff.

12   [1975] QB 94 at 103D. See (1975) 39 Conv (NS) 57 (F.R. Crane); [1975] CLJ 32 (D. Macintyre); (1975) 91 LQR 7 (J.L. Barton).

13   See *Powell v McFarlane* (1977) 38 P & CR 452 at 470 per Slade J.

(a) Factual possession

The factual possession required in the present context is of a special kind. The possession which causes time to run under the Limitation Act must be 'open, not secret; peaceful, not by force; and adverse, not by consent of the true owner'.[14]

(i) Possession must be exclusive to the claimant   No claim of adverse possession may be founded on possession which is not exclusive to the claimant.[15] A possession which is, for instance, exercised at different times by several members of one family cannot grow into a possessory title for one of those family members alone.[16] The claimant's possession must be a 'single and conclusive possession'.[17]

(ii) Possession must be 'adverse' to the paper owner   The possession which is relevant under the Limitation Act comprises only that which is truly 'adverse' to the paper owner. It follows therefore that any possession which is concurrent with that of the paper owner is insufficient as a foundation of possessory title.[18] Nor can 'adverse' possession be claimed on the basis of any occupation which is exercised with the consent or licence[19] of, or by way of lease[20] from, the paper owner. There is, moreover, a tendency to find that any possession exercised by one family member against another within the context of a loosely organised family arrangement is not in any real sense 'adverse', but is more realistically attributed to some form of implied licence.[1]

(iii) Doctrine of 'implied licence'   The courts used to apply a doctrine of 'implied licence' in determining whether a squatter could validly claim 'possession' of land which the paper owner, having no immediate use for the land, had left unoccupied.

Being reluctant to allow an encroacher or squatter to acquire a good title against the true owner, the courts traditionally gave an extremely narrow interpretation to the notion of 'possession' in this context.[2] In *Wallis's Cayton*

14   *Mulcahy v Curramore Pty Ltd* [1974] 2 NSWLR 464 at 475D per Bowen CJ.
15   *Clement v Jones* (1909) 8 CLR 133 at 139 per Griffith CJ.
16   *Morris v Pinches* (1969) 212 Estates Gazette 1141.
17   *Powell v McFarlane* (1977) 38 P & CR 452 at 470, although Slade J conceded that 'there can be a single possession exercised by or on behalf of several persons jointly'.
18   *Treloar v Nute* [1976] 1 WLR 1295 at 1300E per Sir John Pennycuick. Thus the paper owner and the intruder cannot both be in possession at the same time (see *Powell v McFarlane* (1977) 38 P & CR 452 at 470).
19   *Hughes v Griffin* [1969] 1 WLR 23 at 30A, 31G, 32F; *Palfrey v Palfrey* (1974) 229 Estates Gazette 1593 at 1595; *Wallis's Cayton Bay Holiday Camp Ltd v Shell-Mex and BP Ltd* [1975] QB 94 at 103F-G; *Murphy v Murphy* [1980] IR 183 at 195, 202; *Bellew v Bellew* [1982] IR 447 at 464. A merely verbal acknowledgement by an occupier that he holds possession with the permission of the paper owner is sufficient to prevent time from running under the Limitation Act (see *Blakeney v MacDonald* (1981) 116 DLR (3d) 402 at 413ff).
20   *Shillabeer v Diebel* (1980) 100 DLR (3d) 279 at 283. However, rights originally granted as rights of way may subsequently enlarge into a possessory title if the paper owner fails to challenge a more extensive user by the grantee which is no longer referable to any lawful right of easement but is wholly inconsistent with such a right (see *Thomas v Thomas* (1855) 2 K & J 79 at 83ff, 69 ER 701 at 703f; *Keefer v Arillotta* (1977) 72 DLR (3d) 182 at 188f).
1   *Murphy v Murphy* [1980] IR 183 at 195. See eg *Tunley v James* (Unreported, Court of Appeal, No 81 03701, 7 April 1982); *Fruin v Fruin* [1983] Court of Appeal Bound Transcript 448.
2   See *Wallis's Cayton Bay Holiday Camp Ltd v Shell-Mex and BP Ltd* [1975] QB 94 at 114C-D per Ormrod LJ.

Bay Holiday Camp Ltd v Shell-Mex and BP Ltd,[3] for instance, a majority in the Court of Appeal held that the occasional acts of user pleaded by the trespasser in this case were insufficient to constitute 'adverse possession'. For Lord Denning MR the line between 'acts of user' and 'acts of possession' was 'too fine for words', and the Master of the Rolls did not think that it lay in a trespasser's mouth 'to assert that he used the land of his own wrong as a trespasser.'[4] Instead the user exerted by the trespasser was, in his view, to be ascribed to a mere 'licence or permission of the true owner.'[5] The doctrine of implied licence was thus applied effectively as a matter of law so as to preclude the inception of any adverse possession by a stranger.

This highly restrictive aspect of the law of limitation was finally amended in 1980.[6] It is now clear that, in determining whether a person occupying land is in adverse possession of the land, it is no longer to be 'assumed by implication of law that his occupation is by permission of the person entitled to the land merely by virtue of the fact that his occupation is not inconsistent with the latter's present or future enjoyment of the land.'[7] It is still, however, open to the courts to apply the concept of the implied licence—just as before 1980—where a finding of implied permission is 'justified on the actual facts of the case.'[8]

(iv) Adverse possession need not be hostile The mere fact that possession must be 'adverse' does not mean that it must necessarily be hostile. It is quite possible that time may run under the Limitation Act even as against a paper owner who is entirely unaware that title to the land was conveyed to him long ago.[9] It is equally possible that adverse possession may occur without either the paper owner or the adverse possessor having any knowledge of it at all.[10] A title may be acquired through adverse possession even though the claimant, through ignorance or mistake, is unaware of the true ownership of the property.[11] It is sufficient simply that he has asserted a factual possession objectively comprising 'acts...which are inconsistent with [the paper owner's] enjoyment of the soil for the purposes for which he intended to use it'.[12]

---

3 [1975] QB 94.
4 [1975] QB 94 at 103F ('By using the land, knowing that it does not belong to him, he impliedly assumes that the owner will permit it: and the owner, by not turning him off, impliedly gives permission').
5 See also *Gray v Wykeham Martin* (Court of Appeal Transcript No 10A of 1977), where the Court of Appeal thought that 'any sensible and neighbourly person who exercised control over a piece of land and had not any particular use for it at the time would have given a licence to anybody who wanted to use it in the way the plaintiff did.' The plaintiff must have realised that she was 'being allowed as of grace to carry on as before during these times of food shortage.'
6 See Limitation Amendment Act 1980, s 4.
7 Limitation Act 1980, Sch 1, para 8(4). See Law Reform Committee 21st Report, *Final Report on Limitation of Actions* (Cmnd 6923, 1977), para 3.47ff; (1977) 244 Estates Gazette 291, 375 (D. Brahams).
8 Limitation Act 1980, Sch 1, para 8(4). See P. Jackson, (1980) 96 LQR 333 at 335f; [1986] Conv 434 (G. McCormack).
9 *Palfrey v Palfrey* (1974) 229 Estates Gazette 1593 at 1595.
10 *Murphy v Murphy* [1980] IR 183 at 202.
11 *McGugan and McNeill v Turner* [1948] 2 DLR 338 at 344ff; *Beaudoin v Aubin* (1981) 125 DLR (3d) 277 at 292; *Guild v Mallory* (1983) 144 DLR (3d) 603 at 619.
12 *Leigh v Jack* (1879) 5 Ex D 264 at 273 per Bramwell LJ.

(v) Possession must be open The possession which founds a claim of adverse possession must be open, notorious and unconcealed.[13] The requirement of visibility ensures that the paper owner is given every opportunity of challenging the possession before it can ripen into an unimpeachable title.[14]

(vi) Examples of factual possession The requirement of factual possession signifies the necessity that adverse possession should involve some appropriate degree of exclusive physical control over the land in question. The kinds of 'possession' required for the purpose of establishing this element of physical control must depend upon the circumstances of each case.[15] The acts relied upon as evidencing the 'possession' of the claimant need not have been uninterrupted,[16] but it must be shown that 'the alleged possessor has been dealing with the land in question as an occupying owner might have been expected to deal with it and that no-one else has done so.'[17] It is clear that acts of possession done on parts of the land to which a possessory title is sought may be 'evidence of possession of the whole'.[18]

In *Powell v McFarlane*,[19] for instance, Slade J indicated that the question of 'possession' must be determined with particular reference to 'the nature of the land and the manner in which land of that nature is commonly used or enjoyed.'[20] Thus, in Slade J's view, absolute physical control of open land is normally impracticable 'if only because it is generally impossible to secure every part of a boundary so as to prevent intrusion'.[1] The erection of fencing is, however, 'useful evidence of occupation to the exclusion of others',[2] and it has been said that only rarely will extensive fencing fail to demonstrate the adverse

---

13 *Lord Advocate v Lord Lovat* (1880) 5 App Cas 273 at 291, 296; *McConaghy v Denmark* (1880) 4 SCR 609 at 632f; *Sherren v Pearson* (1887) 14 SCR 581 at 585.

14 See eg *Re Lundrigans Ltd and Prosper* (1982) 132 DLR (3d) 727 at 729ff, where the Newfoundland Court of Appeal rejected a claim of adverse possession based on the presence in a wilderness area of two log cabins which were not visible either from the ground or from the air.

15 *Lord Advocate v Lord Lovat* (1880) 5 App Cas 273 at 288; *Bligh v Martin* [1968] 1 WLR 804 at 811F; *Murphy v Murphy* [1980] IR 183 at 193.

16 *Bligh v Martin* [1968] 1 WLR 804 at 811F-G; *Mulcahy v Curramore Pty Ltd* [1974] 2 NSWLR 464 at 475F. In *Re Taylor and Willigar* (1980) 99 DLR (3d) 118 at 125f, it was held sufficient that the disputed property was used only in summer months and not at other times 'when the snow and ice of winter preclude their use in any practicable sense'.

17 *Powell v McFarlane* (1977) 38 P & CR 452 at 471.

18 *Powell v McFarlane* (1977) 38 P & CR 452 at 471 ('Whether or not acts of possession done on parts of an area establish title to the whole area must, however, be a matter of degree'). See also *Halifax County Pulp Co Ltd v Rutledge* (1982) 131 DLR (3d) 199 at 206ff; *Walker v Russell* (1966) 53 DLR (2d) 509 at 524ff. Compare, however, *Weld v Scott* (1855) 12 UCQB 537 at 540, for the suggestion that the area which may be claimed by the adverse possessor is confined to that covered by his 'pedal possession'.

19 (1977) 38 P & CR 452 at 471.

20 See also *Kirby v Cowderoy* [1912] AC 599 at 603; *Bligh v Martin* [1968] 1 WLR 804 at 811F-H; *McDonell v Giblin* (1904) 23 NZLR 660 at 662; *Riley v Penttila* [1974] VR 547 at 561; *West Bank Estates Ltd v Arthur* [1967] 1 AC 665 at 678A-B per Lord Wilberforce.

1 (1977) 38 P & CR 452 at 471.

2 *Mulcahy v Curramore Pty Ltd* [1974] 2 NSWLR 464 at 475E. Compare, however, *Fruin v Fruin* [1983] Court of Appeal Bound Transcript 448, where the Court declined to accept as evidence of adverse possession a fence one of whose purposes had been to restrain a senile family member who was 'apt to wander'. See also *Riley v Penttila* [1974] VR 547 at 564ff, where the purpose of a fence and netting was primarily to facilitate the playing of tennis rather than to exclude the true owner.

possession required for a successful claim of possessory title.[3] Of course, the absence of fencing does not in itself prove a lack of possession.[4] Relevant 'possession' can be established by a variety of other uses of the land, as for instance where the claimant has used the land for shooting[5] or for grazing and storage purposes,[6] or even where the claimant has simply erected prominent 'no trespassing'[7] or 'no dumping'[8] signs on the land.

Trivial or equivocal acts by the adverse occupier will not be sufficient to prove 'possession'. In *Tecbild Ltd v Chamberlain*,[9] for instance, the Court of Appeal declined to attach significance to the fact that the claimant's children had been accustomed to play on the disputed plots of land as and when they wished and that the family ponies had been tethered and exercised there.[10] As the Court of Appeal confirmed, 'trivial acts of trespass' do not constitute adverse possession.[11] It must be demonstrated that the adverse occupier established a possession which was wholly inconsistent with and in denial of the rights of the paper owner as the legal owner of the land concerned.[12]

(b) Intention to possess (animus possidendi)

The *animus possidendi* which is required for the inception and retention of 'possession' by an adverse occupier was classically defined by Lindley MR in *Littledale v Liverpool College*[13] as comprising an 'intention of excluding the owner as well as other people'. This element of intention is not necessarily easy to establish. It is readily assumed, in the absence of clear contrary evidence, that the requisite intention is present in the paper owner or any other person with a right of possession of the land (eg an existing adverse possessor).[14] Thus, for instance, even the slightest acts done by or on behalf of a paper owner will be found in practice to negative any supposed 'discontinuance' of his own possession.[15]

(i) Restrictive application by the courts

The requirement of *animus possidendi* has

---

3   *George Wimpey & Co Ltd v Sohn* [1967] Ch 487 at 512A per Russell LJ. See eg *Seddon v Smith* (1877) 36 LT 168 at 169 per Cockburn CJ ('Enclosure is the strongest possible evidence of adverse possession').
4   *Mulcahy v Curramore Pty Ltd* [1974] 2 NSWLR 464 at 475E.
5   *Red House Farms (Thorndon) Ltd v Catchpole* (1977) 244 Estates Gazette 295 at 297ff.
6   *Treloar v Nute* [1976] 1 WLR 1295. See (1978) 41 MLR 204 (P.F. Smith).
7   *Powell v McFarlane* (1977) 38 P & CR 452 at 478.
8   *Hughes v Mulholland & McCann Ltd* [1982] 7 BNIL 72. See also *Raab v Caranci* (1980) 97 DLR (3d) 154 at 157ff, affd (1980) 104 DLR (3d) 160 (building of small wall).
9   (1969) 20 P & CR 633.
10 Compare *Powell v McFarlane* (1977) 38 P & CR 452 (ante, p 747).
11 (1969) 20 P & CR 633 at 644, 646. See eg *Attersley v Blakely* (1970) 13 DLR (3d) 39 at 47; *Re MacEachern and MacIsaac* (1978) 81 DLR (3d) 20 at 29.
12 See *Moses v Lovegrove* [1952] 2 QB 533 at 538.
13 [1900] 1 Ch 19 at 23. See more recently *Powell v McFarlane* (1977) 38 P & CR 452 at 471f, where Slade J indicated that *animus possidendi* involves 'the intention, in one's own name and on one's own behalf, to exclude the world at large, including the owner with the paper title if he be not himself the possessor, so far as is reasonably practicable and so far as the processes of the law will allow.'
14 Ante, p 744.
15 *Leigh v Jack* (1879) 5 Ex D 264 at 272; *Williams Brothers Direct Supply Ltd v Raftery* [1958] 1 QB 159 at 171. See *Re St Clair Beach Estates Ltd v MacDonald* (1975) 50 DLR (3d) 650 at 656; *Masidon Investments Ltd v Ham* (1983) 39 OR (2d) 534 at 553f.

been applied fairly restrictively by the courts.[16] The success of any claim by a trespasser to have acquired 'possession' rests on clear and affirmative evidence that the trespasser 'not only had the requisite intention to possess, but made such intention clear to the world.'[17] Although this intention is not necessarily incompatible with mistake or ignorance as to the true ownership of the land in question,[18] it must be shown that the claimant consciously acted in a manner which was objectively consistent with a claim to title on his own behalf. The conduct of the adverse possessor must have been such as to demonstrate an apparent intention to exclude the paper owner from such uses as he might have wished to make of his property.[19] It is not enough for this purpose that the particular manner or degree of the claimant's occupation deprived the paper owner of uses of his own property of which he never intended or desired to take advantage.[20] Nor is it sufficient if the claimant's conduct indicates not so much a settled intention to exclude the true owner as an intention to confer a particular benefit upon himself.[1]

(ii) Equivocal acts When the inception of 'possession' has to be inferred from equivocal acts, the intention with which these acts are performed becomes 'all-important'.[2] In *Powell v McFarlane*,[3] Slade J confirmed that 'compelling evidence' of *animus* is required where a trespasser's user of land does not by itself clearly betoken an intention on his part to claim the land as his own to the exclusion of the true owner.[4] In this case Slade J declined to find the necessary *animus* proved on behalf of a plaintiff who, at the age of 14, had begun to use land for the purpose of grazing his cow. In Slade J's view, the conduct of one so young was 'not necessarily referable' to any intention to dispossess the paper owner and to occupy the land 'wholly as his own property'.[5]

(iii) Proof of intention In the absence of concealed fraud,[6] it is generally

16 For cases in which the courts have rejected claims to possessory titles by trespassers for want of sufficient evidence of the requisite intent, see eg *Littledale v Liverpool College* [1900] 1 Ch 19 at 23ff; *George Wimpey & Co Ltd v Sohn* [1967] Ch 487 at 508F-G; *Tecbild Ltd v Chamberlain* (1969) 20 P & CR 633 at 643ff.
17 (1977) 38 P & CR 456 at 472 per Slade J. See generally M. Dockray, [1982] Conv 256, 345.
18 Ante, p 746.
19 *Keefer v Arillotta* (1977) 72 DLR (3d) 182 at 193.
20 *Keefer v Arillotta* (1977) 72 DLR (3d) 182 at 193. See also *Masidon Investments Ltd v Ham* (1983) 39 OR (2d) 534 at 550ff.
1   *Murnane v Findlay* [1926] VLR 80 at 88. See eg *Riley v Penttila* [1974] VR 547 at 562ff (where a tennis court had been built on the disputed ground). See also *Masidon Investments Ltd v Ham* (1983) 39 OR (2d) 534 at 550f.
2   *Littledale v Liverpool College* [1900] 1 Ch 19 at 23 per Lindley MR. See also *Clement v Jones* (1909) 8 CLR 133 at 140; *Riley v Penttila* [1974] VR 547 at 562.
3   (1977) 38 P & CR 452 at 476.
4   If the trespasser's acts are 'open to more than one interpretation and he has not made it perfectly plain to the world at large by his actions or words that he has intended to exclude the owner as best he can, the courts will treat him as not having had the requisite *animus possidendi* and consequently as not having dispossessed the owner' ((1977) 38 P & CR 452 at 472).
5   (1977) 38 P & CR 452 at 478. See also *Re MacEachern and MacIsaac* (1978) 81 DLR (3d) 20 at 28f.
6   Where the paper owner establishes that he was the victim of a fraud perpetrated by the adverse occupier or that any fact relevant to his right of action was deliberately concealed from him by the occupier, the period of limitation does not begin to run until the plaintiff could with reasonable diligence have discovered the fraud or concealment (Limitation Act 1980, s 32(1)). Protection is provided for innocent third parties who purchase property for valuable consideration (Limitation Act 1980, s 32(3)).

irrelevant in the law of adverse possession that the paper owner is ignorant of the fact that he has been dispossessed.[7] However, in view of the drastic results of a change of possession, a person who seeks to dispossess a paper owner must 'at least make his intentions sufficiently clear so that the owner, if present at the land, would clearly appreciate that the claimant is not merely a persistent trespasser, but is actually seeking to dispossess him'.[8] Courts will attach 'very little evidential value' to retrospective assertions of the required *animus*, because 'they are obviously easily capable of being merely self-serving, while at the same time they may be very difficult for the paper owner positively to refute'.[9] For the same reason even contemporary declarations by an adverse occupier to the effect that he is intending to assert a claim to the land provide but little support for a claim of 'possession' at the relevant time unless they are specifically brought to the attention of the true owner.[10] In general, as Sachs LJ said in *Tecbild Ltd v Chamberlain*,[11] 'intent has to be inferred from the acts themselves.'

(iv) Restrictive impact on squatters   It has been said that in *Powell v McFarlane* Slade J imposed such onerous restrictions upon the notion of *animus possidendi* that few squatters, if any, could satisfy it. Indeed, the heavy reliance upon a strict test of *animus* has allegedly emerged as 'yet another weapon in the armoury to be deployed against squatters'.[12] It is this interface with the law of squatting which has made the determination of *animus possidendi* so crucial and which has doubtless conduced to the restrictiveness of the courts' application of the concept of 'possession'.

It is trite law that the status of 'possession' confers on the possessor valuable privileges not only against the world at large, but also against the owner of the land concerned. It entitles even the trespasser to maintain an action in trespass against anyone who enters the land without his consent, with the sole exception of a person who has a better title to possession than himself.[13] The possessor has moreover one valuable element of protection against even the owner himself. Until 'possession' of land has actually passed to the trespasser, the owner may validly exercise the remedy of self-help against him.[14] However, once 'possession' has been taken over by the trespasser, this remedy is no longer available to the owner, and the intruder's position becomes correspondingly more secure. If he does not then leave the land voluntarily, the owner will find himself obliged to bring proceedings for possession and for this purpose to prove his title.[15]

7   *Rains v Buxton* (1880) 14 Ch D 537 at 540f.
8   *Powell v McFarlane* (1977) 38 P & CR 452 at 480.
9   *Powell v McFarlane* (1977) 38 P & CR 452 at 476.
10 *Powell v McFarlane* (1977) 38 P & CR 452 at 476.
11 (1969) 20 P & CR 633 at 643.
12 P. Jackson (1980) 96 LQR 333 at 334.
13 Ante, p 64; post, p 751.
14 Post, p 755.
15 See generally *Powell v McFarlane* (1977) 38 P & CR 452 at 476 per Slade J.

4. THE OPERATION OF THE LIMITATION ACT 1980

The operation of the Limitation Act 1980 is essentially negative in nature. The effluxion of the limitation period does not create a title in the adverse possessor, but has the effect of extinguishing the former title of the paper owner.[16] Under section 17 of the Limitation Act 1980, the paper owner's right of action to recover his land and the title on which that right is based are alike terminated on the expiry of the limitation period.

(1) Relativity of title

In English law title to land is always relative,[17] land titles being secure only if and to the extent that no other person can assert a better claim. This produces the consequence that if the paper owner whose title has been extinguished was himself a fee simple owner, the successful adverse possessor acquires a title in fee simple which is unimpeachable. Nobody can now claim a better title than the adverse possessor, since the only person who could have challenged him is now statute-barred from proceeding with any action for recovery of the land.

(a) Unregistered land

In unregistered land, although the adverse possessor is effectively entitled to a legal estate in fee simple absolute,[18] his long possession for 12 years does not in itself operate any *transfer* of title from the paper owner. The Limitation Act does not effect a parliamentary conveyance of the land concerned,[19] this possibility being ruled out precisely because the paper owner's title has been completely extinguished by the operation of the statute. However, when the extinguishing effect of the Limitation Act is placed in conjunction with the positive effect of adverse possession, the indirect consequence is that the adverse possessor is enabled to claim a new title of his own.

(b) Registered land

In the case of registered land, so long as the paper owner remains registered as the relevant proprietor in the Land Register, it cannot be quite true to say that his title has been extinguished by the operation of the Limitation Act. However, the Land Registration Act 1925 provides that where, if the land in question were not registered, the estate of the existing registered proprietor would have been extinguished, his estate in registered land shall be 'deemed to be held by the proprietor for the time being in trust for the person who, by virtue of the [Limitation] Acts, has acquired title against any proprietor'.[20]

---

16 The effect of the Limitation Act is to extinguish the true owner's title, rather than merely to render his right of re-entry unenforceable (see *Mulcahy v Curramore Pty Ltd* [1974] 2 NSWLR 464 at 476A).
17 Ante, p 64.
18 Post, p 752.
19 *Tichborne v Weir* (1892) 67 LT 735 at 736f. See also *St Marylebone Property Co Ltd v Fairweather* [1963] AC 510 at 535; *Perry v Woodfarm Homes Ltd* [1975] IR 104 at 122f.
20 Land Registration Act 1925, s 75(1).

Moreover, the adverse possessor of registered land may apply to be registered as proprietor of that land,[1] and in the meantime his rights are regarded as an 'overriding interest' with reference to that land.[2]

(2) Rights of third parties

Precisely because there has been no transfer or assignment of title by the paper owner to the adverse possessor, the latter is not affected by certain rules of land law which impinge upon a transferee or assignee. Thus, for instance, a squatter (even after 12 years of adverse possession) cannot claim to take title free of equitable interests binding the land, because he can never establish status as a bona fide *purchaser* without notice. He has not *purchased* the land, but has instead taken title by operation of law. In this case equitable interests such as restrictive covenants are binding upon him,[3] and this is so regardless of whether these interests have been duly registered or protected by the incumbrancer.[4]

Where the land occupied by an adverse possessor was the subject of a lease, the squatter cannot be sued directly for rent or damages by the landlord on the ground of a breach of leasehold covenants. The squatter is not an *assignee* of any term of years and is therefore not covered by the doctrine of 'privity of estate'.[5] However, even if he is not strictly liable to observe the covenants of the lease, the adverse occupier is still vulnerable to the landlord's exercise of a right of re-entry contained in that lease in the event of non-performance of the covenants. The squatter is thus liable to suffer forfeiture and is, moreover, entirely unable to claim any right to relief against such forfeiture.[6]

(3) Inchoate rights of the squatter

An important consequence of the principle of relativity of title is the fact that, even before his possessory title has been completed, the adverse possessor acquires certain inchoate rights in the land occupied by him.

(a) Nature of the squatter's rights

Even before the paper owner becomes statute-barred from recovery, the squatter acquires incipient rights in the land which are good against all the world except those persons who (like the paper owner) are meanwhile able to assert a better title.[7] From the inception of his 'possession' the squatter is

1 Land Registration Act 1925, s 75(2).
2 Land Registration Act 1925, s 70(1)(f) (ante, p 174).
3 *In re Nisbet and Potts' Contract* [1906] 1 Ch 386 at 402ff. See F.W. Maitland, *Equity* (2nd edn, London 1936), p 116.
4 Ante, p 88.
5 *Tichborne v Weir* (1892) 67 LT 735 at 737f (ante, p 526); *St Marylebone Property Co Ltd v Fairweather* [1963] AC 510 at 535; *Perry v Woodfarm Homes Ltd* [1975] IR 104 at 120. The ousted tenant continues to be contractually liable on his covenants (see *Perry v Woodfarm Homes Ltd*, supra at 130).
6 *Tickner v Buzzacott* [1965] Ch 426 at 434E-G (ante, p 509). The threat of forfeiture may indirectly force the squatter to perform the leasehold covenants (see *Perry v Woodfarm Homes Ltd* [1975] IR 104 at 120).
7 *Asher v Whitlock* (1865) LR 1 QB 1 at 5.

recognised as having an estate in fee simple, despite the fact that his possession of the land was initially tortious and notwithstanding that until the 12 year period of limitation has expired he may be turned out by legal process.[8]

(b) Transmissibility

Having acquired an estate in fee simple by his own wrong, the squatter—even within the limitation period—is fully competent to assign his rights *inter vivos* or to dispose of them by will.[9] If he dies intestate, his rights devolve upon his next of kin. An assignee from a squatter may count the squatter's period of possession towards the period of 12 years of adverse possession which are required to establish the completion of the limitation period in favour of the *assignee*.[10] Even without any transfer of the squatter's inchoate fee simple estate,[11] the period of his possession may be added to the possession of the next successive squatter on the land so as to enable the latter to claim a completed possessory title after an aggregate of 12 years.[12]

5. RECOVERY OF POSSESSION BY THE PAPER OWNER

Under the Limitation Act any action for the recovery of land from which the paper owner has been dispossessed must be brought *before* the expiration of the limitation period. After the expiration of that period, the right of recovery becomes statute-barred and the title of the paper owner is extinguished. It thus becomes extremely important that any steps taken by the paper owner for recovery of his land are initiated before the end of the limitation period.

(1) No defence of necessity

The recovery of land by a paper owner has been rendered somewhat more controversial in an era when 'squatting' has become a common means of coercing political action or expressing political or other protest. The 'sit-in' has emerged as a standard non-violent method of protest, whether the issue at stake be a proposed mass redundancy at the work-place, supposedly oppressive action taken by university authorities or the obscenity of empty property sitting idle at a time of severe homelessness. During recent years, however, the judicial reaction to 'squatting' and 'sit-ins' has taken the form of a stern reinforcement of the legal power of the paper owner of the land concerned. The courts have not been prepared to endorse any social or political justification for the

---

8   See *Wheeler v Baldwin* (1934) 52 CLR 609 at 632 per Dixon CJ; *Spark v Meers* [1971] 2 NSWLR 1 at 12A-C. The squatter is even entitled to claim compensation in the event of compulsory purchase of the land before his possessory title is confirmed under the Limitation Act (see *Perry v Clissold* [1907] AC 73 at 79f).

9   *Asher v Whitlock* (1865) LR 1 QB 1 at 6f; *Wheeler v Baldwin* (1934) 52 CLR 609 at 632f; *Allen v Roughley* (1955) 94 CLR 98 at 108, 130ff; *Mulcahy v Curramore Pty Ltd* [1974] 2 NSWLR 464 at 476C.

10 *Asher v Whitlock* (1865) LR 1 QB 1 at 6f; *Mulcahy v Curramore Pty Ltd* [1974] 2 NSWLR 464 at 476D.

11 *Willis v Earl Howe* [1893] 2 Ch 545 at 553; *Salter v Clarke* (1904) 4 SR (NSW) 280 at 288; *Mulcahy v Curramore Pty Ltd* [1974] 2 NSWLR 464 at 471A-B.

12 Ante, p 742.

dispossession of a paper owner from 'his' property. The idea that the existing distribution of land may itself express or conceal inequity is not a notion which the courts have been ready to explore.[13]

In *McPhail v Persons (Names Unknown)*[14] a group of homeless persons secured entry to residential premises which had been left unoccupied and locked by the owner. The owner brought proceedings for the recovery of possession. In the Court of Appeal, Lord Denning MR defined a 'squatter' as 'one who, without any colour of right, enters on an unoccupied house or land, intending to stay there as long as he can.'[15] Lord Denning held that the Court could not entertain, by way of defence, a plea by a squatter that 'he was homeless and that this house or land was standing empty, doing nothing.' No such excuse could be of any avail in law, since, as Lord Denning himself had said in *Southwark LBC v Williams*,[16] if homelessness were once admitted as a defence to trespass, 'no one's house could be safe'. The courts 'must, for the sake of law and order, take a firm stand. They must refuse to admit the plea of necessity to the hungry and the homeless: and trust that their distress will be relieved by the charitable and the good.'[17]

(2) Criminal liability

Far from being justifiable on grounds of a social or compassionate nature, the adverse occupation of residential premises is now in certain circumstances made a criminal offence by the Criminal Law Act 1977. Under this Act a criminal offence is committed by any person who, having entered premises as a trespasser, fails to leave those premises on being required to do so by or on behalf of either a 'displaced residential occupier'[18] or a 'protected intending occupier'[19] of those premises.[20]

Within the fairly recent past there has been a significant reinforcement of the power of the criminal law to deal with cases of trespass to private property. Public concern has been particularly aroused where a trespass takes the form of occupation by a mass motorised convoy of squatters who swarm locust-like from the land of one innocent owner to that of another or who invade ancient monuments (such as Stonehenge) at midsummer. Symptomatic of the modern tightening up of the law is the introduction of a new criminal offence by the Public Order Act 1986. This legislation confers a power upon a 'senior police officer' to direct persons to leave land if the officer 'reasonably believes' that

---

13   In the Republic of Ireland the Supreme Court has rejected the suggestion that the use of legal process against trespassers for the vindication of the landowner's possessory rights is an unconstitutional form of discrimination against the 'landless classes' (see *Dooley v Attorney General* [1977] IR 205 at 210).
14   [1973] Ch 447. See A.M. Prichard, (1976) 40 Conv (NS) 255; [1973] CLJ 220 (D. Macintyre).
15   [1973] Ch 447 at 456B.
16   [1971] Ch 734 at 744B-C.
17   [1971] Ch 734 at 744C-D. See also *Kensington and Chelsea LBC v Wells* (1974) 72 LGR 289 at 297ff per Roskill LJ; *Northern Ireland Housing Executive v Fox* [1981] 3 BNIL 62.
18   A 'displaced residential occupier' is defined in Criminal Law Act 1977, s 12(3) (post, p 756).
19   A 'protected intending occupier' is defined in Criminal Law Act 1977, s 7(2).
20   Criminal Law Act 1977, s 7(1). Criminal trespass is punishable summarily by six months' imprisonment and/or a fine not exceeding £1,000 (Criminal Law Act 1977, s 7(10)). See [1978] CLJ 11.

two or more such persons have entered land as trespassers and 'are present there with the common purpose of residing there for any period'.[1] In order properly to exercise this power, the senior police officer must also have reason to believe that 'reasonable steps' have been taken by or on behalf of the occupier to ask them to leave and that the trespassers have caused damage to property on the land or have used 'threatening, abusive or insulting words or behaviour' or that the trespassers 'have between them brought twelve or more vehicles on to the land'.[2] A criminal offence is committed by any person who, knowing that a direction to leave the land has been given by a senior police officer, fails to leave the land 'as soon as reasonably practicable' or who, having left, returns as a trespasser within the following three months.[3] The offence is, however, limited in scope in that the 'land' to which it applies does not include buildings (other than agricultural buildings or scheduled ancient monuments) and does not include land forming part of a highway.[4]

(3) Civil remedies

There are three possible civil remedies available for the purpose of assisting the paper owner to recover possession from trespassers who occupy his land.[5]

(a) Remedy of self-help

It is quite clear that where strangers have taken over occupation of land, the paper owner of that land may exercise the remedy of self-help at any stage *before* the occupying strangers acquire 'possession' of the property in the sense currently required by the law of adverse possession.

(i) Preconditions of self-help The availability of the remedy of self-help is terminated by the inception of 'possession' on the part of the trespasser, and it is for precisely this reason that the concept of 'possession' is defined so restrictively by the courts.[6] A householder who returns home from holiday to find his house occupied by squatters is entitled to throw the intruders out of his house without further ceremony. They were trespassers when they entered his house and they continued to be trespassers so long as they remained there

---

1 Public Order Act 1986, s 39(1).
2 Public Order Act 1986, s 39(1).
3 Public Order Act 1986, s 39(2). The offence is punishable by three months' imprisonment and/or a fine. A uniformed police constable has power to arrest without warrant any person whom he 'reasonably suspects' of committing an offence under this provision (Public Order Act 1986, s 39(3)).
4 Public Order Act 1986, s 39(5).
5 Damages may also be awarded in respect of trespass, in which case the damages may cover not only the diminution in the value of the land but also the cost of any works reasonably required in order to restore the owner's enjoyment of his land (see *Heath v Keys* (1984) *The Times*, 28 May). Where a group of trespassers join in a squat, all may be made liable in negligence on a 'joint venture' basis for damage which has been caused by one member only of the group (see *Bushell v Hamilton* (1981) 113 DLR (3d) 498 at 502). See also *Lamb v Camden LBC* [1981] QB 625. A landowner whose title is not in issue is prima facie entitled to an interlocutory injunction to restrain trespass on his land even though he has suffered no damage (see *Patel v W.H. Smith (Eziot) Ltd* [1987] 1 WLR 853 or 861C-E).
6 Ante, p 750.

awaiting the householder's return. The owner has not acquiesced in their presence in his house, and the vital consequence in law is that their occupation is not such as to enable them to allege that they ever gained 'possession' for the purpose of adverse possession.[7] In such a case, the owner is not obliged to go to the courts to obtain possession. He is entitled, if he so desires, to take the remedy into his own hands. As Lord Denning MR observed in *McPhail v Persons (Names Unknown)*[8] the owner 'can go in himself and turn them out without the aid of the courts of law.' However, although Lord Denning considered the legality of this particular remedy 'beyond question', he cautioned that self-help 'is not a course to be recommended because of the disturbance which might follow'.[9]

(ii) Limitations on self-help   If the owner himself uses force to secure the eviction of the trespassers, it is clear that he must use no more force than is reasonably necessary for the purpose.[10] The exercise of self-help is also subject to the important qualification imposed by the Criminal Law Act 1977. Under section 6(1) of this Act it is a criminal offence for any person without lawful authority to use or to threaten violence for the purpose of securing entry into any premises if, to his knowledge, there is someone present on those premises who is opposed to his entry.[11] This provision inevitably applies to some trespassers, but is not of course relevant to a squatter who enters premises by non-violent means. Simply by virtue of his de facto possession of the property, such a trespasser is entitled to resist trespass by others, although his claims must naturally give way in the face of any superior claim (eg by the real owner) to regain possession.

The Criminal Law Act 1977 provides a defence to any charge of violent entry for any person who is kept out of his own living accommodation by trespassers. Such a person has a defence to a charge under section 6 of the Act if he can prove that he was a 'displaced residential occupier' seeking to secure access to residential premises from which he had been excluded by the trespasser.[12] Apart from the case where the displaced occupier is himself a trespasser,[13] the status of 'displaced residential occupier' is defined as attaching to 'any person who was occupying any premises as a residence immediately before being excluded from occupation by anyone who entered those premises...as a trespasser'.[14] Such a person continues to rank as a 'displaced residential occupier' so long as he continues to be excluded from occupation of the premises by the original trespasser or by any subsequent trespasser.

The 'possession' of a lawful occupier (eg a tenant or licensee) may not be terminated by recourse to the remedy of self-help, even where the interest granted to the occupier has duly expired. Once 'possession' has been enjoyed by a tenant or licensee the occupier cannot be evicted except by due process of

---

7   See Sir F. Pollock, *Torts* (15th edn, London 1951), p 292.
8   [1973] Ch 447 at 456D-E.
9   [1973] Ch 447 at 456E.
10   See *Hemmings v Stoke Poges Golf Club Ltd* [1920] 1 KB 720 at 747. Compare *R v Hussey* (1924) 18 Cr App R 160 at 161 (ante, p 537).
11   This provision would apply, for instance, to a trespasser who breaks a door or window in order to secure entry, but not to one who merely manipulates a yale-type lock or window catch with a thin piece of metal (see Law Commission, *Report on Conspiracy and Criminal Law Reform* (Law Com No 76, 1976), para 2.61). See also (1985) LAG Bulletin (October), p 5.
12   Criminal Law Act 1977, s 6(3).
13   Criminal Law Act 1977, s 12(4).
14   Criminal Law Act 1977, s 12(3).

law. In such cases a criminal offence is committed by any person who seeks to secure the eviction of the occupier by any means other than that of court order for possession.[15]

(b) Remedy by action for possession

Although the law provides a displaced owner with the remedy of self-help in certain circumstances, this is not usually a course to be encouraged. As Lord Denning MR said in *McPhail v Persons (Names Unknown)*,[16] '[i]n a civilised society, the courts should themselves provide a remedy which is speedy and effective: and thus make self-help unnecessary.' In England the legal process by which a displaced owner can dislodge trespassers from his property has traditionally taken the form of the common law action for possession. By the late 1960s and early 1970s, however, it had become obvious that this remedy was subject to certain disadvantages. The procedure of the action for possession was particularly ineffective where the occupiers of premises were unidentifiable and could not therefore be named as defendants in proceedings taken against them.[17] There were also great difficulties in making a possession order where one squatter followed another in quick succession.

(c) Remedy by summons

Some relief from the technical defects of the common law action for possession came in 1970 when the Supreme Court Rules and County Court Rules were reformulated to provide a summary 'short-cut' procedure for the recovery of possession against trespassers. This procedure was intended to be used only in straightforward cases where there is no doubt that the occupiers of land are trespassers.

(i) The 'fast possession action'

The 'fast possession action' now provided by RSC Ord 113 (in the High Court) and by CCR Ord 24 (in the county court) lends substantial assistance to landowners who are dispossessed by trespassers or squatters. The landowner may invoke a speedy remedy by summons against any person who occupies his land without his consent. He may issue an originating summons claiming possession even though he cannot identify the squatters by name.[18] The court may make an order for possession five days after the service of the summons,[19] and even this period may be shortened in cases of urgency.[20] The court has no discretion to withhold or suspend the order for

---

15 Ante, p 65; post, p 955.

16 [1973] Ch 447 at 457B-C.

17 See *In Re Wykeham Terrace, Brighton, Sussex, ex Parte Territorial Auxiliary and Volunteer Reserve Association for the South East* [1971] Ch 204 at 209F.

18 See *McPhail v Persons (Names Unknown)* [1973] Ch 447 at 458E per Lord Denning MR ('A summons can be issued for possession against squatters even though they cannot be identified by name and even though, as one squatter goes, another comes in'). See also *Warwick University v De Graaf* [1975] 1 WLR 1126 at 1129H-1130B; *Wiltshire CC v Frazer* (1984) 47 P & CR 69 at 71.

19 *Practice Direction (Chancery: Procedure)* [1983] 1 WLR 4. Once the writ of possession is granted, it must be executed by the sheriff as soon as is reasonably practicable (*Six Arlington Street Investments Ltd v Persons Unknown* [1987] 1 WLR 188 at 192G-H).

20 See RSC Ord 113, r 6(1), as substituted by *The Rules of the Supreme Court (Amendment No 3) 1986* (SI 1986/2289), post, p 759.

possession once the case for possession has been established.[1] The 'short-cut' procedure is not appropriate, however, where there exists any serious triable issue, eg whether the occupier is a tenant or licensee,[2] or has a defence available to him,[3] or where there is a complicated claim as to title.[4]

(ii) Extended scope   The procedure by way of summons has proved to be an expeditious means of recovering possession of land from a wide variety of trespassers. It has been used successfully against such persons as students participating in a campus 'sit-in',[5] gypsies illegally camping on a roadside,[6] and residential licensees who refuse to vacate premises following the expiry of their licence.[7] Once a possession order has been granted, it can be enforced against any person who subsequently returns to the site or premises covered by the original order, provided that there is a 'plain and sufficient nexus between the original recovery of possession and the need to effect further recovery of the same land.'[8]

An order for possession under the procedure by way of summons may extend to a larger area of the owner's property than is adversely affected by the occupation in respect of which relief is initially sought. In *University of Essex v Djemal*,[9] for instance, a group of university students occupied the university's administrative offices as a protest. Faced with a summons under RSC Ord 113, they vacated the occupied premises but threatened to take further direct action if the university did not agree to their demands. The university continued with legal proceedings, and Walton J made an order for possession under RSC Ord 113, but limited the order to that part of the university premises which had been occupied.[10] The Court of Appeal took the view, however, that RSC Ord 113 confers 'a jurisdiction directed to protecting the right of the owner of property to the possession of the whole of his property, uninterfered with by unauthorised adverse possession'.[11] Because there was a threat that the students might occupy other parts of the university's premises, the Court of Appeal extended Walton J's possession order to cover the whole of the university's premises.

1   See *McPhail v Persons (Names Unknown)* [1973] Ch 447 at 458E-G per Lord Denning MR ('There is no provision for giving any time. The court cannot give any time. It must, at the behest of the owner, make an order for recovery of possession. It is then for the owner to give such time as he thinks right to the squatters. They must make their appeal to his goodwill and consideration, and not to the courts'). See also *Northern Ireland Housing Executive v McAuley* [1974] NI 233 at 235ff.
2   See *Henderson v Law* (1984) 17 HLR 237 at 241; *Markou v Da Silvaesa* (1986) 52 P & CR 204 at 217, 226, 230f.
3   *Shah v Givert* (1983) LAG Bulletin 54. See N. Madge, (1983) LAG Bulletin 53.
4   *Cudworth v Masefield* (1984) *Times*, 16 May.
5   *University of Essex v Djemal* [1980] 1 WLR 1301.
6   *Wiltshire CC v Frazer* (1984) 47 P & CR 69 at 75ff.
7   *GLC v Jenkins* [1975] 1 WLR 155 at 157A, 160B; *Turner v Burton* (Unreported, Court of Appeal, 12 March 1985). There was also a suggestion in 1980 that the summons procedure should be extended to the recovery of possession in respect of tenancies covered by the Rent Acts, but this proposal proved to be so controversial that it was eventually abandoned as politically unfeasible (see (1980) LAG Bulletin 201).
8   *Wiltshire CC v Frazer* [1986] 1 WLR 109 at 113D. See also *R v Wandsworth County Court, ex parte Wandsworth LBC* [1975] 1 WLR 1314 at 1318H-1319A.
9   [1980] 1 WLR 1301. See [1981] Conv 317 (A.A. Preece).
10   The part last occupied had been Level 6 of the Social and Comparative Studies building.
11   [1980] 1 WLR 1301 at 1304E per Buckley LJ.

(iii) Recent reform of RSC Ord 113 Within recent years even the 'fast possession action' has been open to criticism as a mechanism which operates too slowly and formally to provide an effective remedy when it is most needed. This criticism has been made particularly acutely in relation to much publicised cases where farmers have been unable to recover possession of their land from armies of participants in a 'hippie convoy' in time to prevent irremediable damage to growing crops or silage.

In response to this sort of concern the process of summary recovery of land has been further facilitated by adjustments made to RSC Ord 113 with effect from early 1987.[12] Summary proceedings under RSC Ord 113 may now be heard and determined by a master rather than a judge.[13] The process of serving the summons is made significantly easier. Service on unnamed defendants may be effected either by affixing a copy of the summons and the accompanying affidavit either to the main door or other conspicuous part of the premises occupied or by affixing a sealed transparent envelope containing the same to stakes which for this purpose are specially placed in the ground 'at conspicuous parts of the occupied land'.[14] The delay before the making of any final order for possession is also significantly reduced. Such an order may be made (in the case of residential premises) when five clear days have elapsed since the date of service and (in the case of other land) when two clear days have so elapsed.[15] These periods may be further reduced 'in case of emergency and by leave of the court'.[16] The net effect of the changes is significantly to strengthen the interests of private property against the adverse claims of intruders.

12 See *The Rules of the Supreme Court (Amendment No 3) 1986* (SI 1986/2289), which came into operation on 12 January 1987.
13 RSC Ord 113, r 1A, as introduced by SI 1986/2289. The Lord Chancellor's Department, in sponsoring the amendment of RSC Ord 113, did not accept the proposal that ex parte possession orders should be made possible under RSC Ord 113.
14 RSC Ord 113, r 4(2), as substituted by SI 1986/2289.
15 RSC Ord 113, r 6(1), as substituted by SI 1986/2289.
16 RSC Ord 113, r 6(1), as substituted by SI 1986/2289.

CHAPTER 21

Homelessness

Perhaps the most marked feature of the inequalities demonstrated in the contemporary housing market is the unprecedented degree of homelessness which has emerged during the last ten years. Official housing policy during this period has taken the form of a 'relentless drive into owner occupation'.[1] While the extension of the 'property-owning democracy' has been promoted politically as a desirable social objective, government finance for public sector housing investment has been subject to increasingly savage cut-back. The reinforcement of the public sector tenant's 'right to buy' has led to the disposal into private ownership of the more desirable council houses,[2] leaving the remaining public housing stock to diminish in supply and to deteriorate rapidly in quality.[3]

Government housing policy of recent years has inevitably exerted a considerable impact on an already strained housing market. Less affluent households have been encouraged to aspire to a home ownership which, particularly with increasing economic recession and job redundancy, has proved difficult to finance.[4] Unlucky families whose dreams of home ownership have been shattered by mortgage default join the swelling numbers on waiting lists for council houses which are not being built. Those who do not manage to obtain accommodation either with relatives or in the declining private rental market are then relegated to the ranks of the 'homeless'. Accordingly in Great Britain in 1985 a total of some 109,000 households were accepted by local authorities as 'homeless'.[5] This official figure excludes the single homeless and takes no account either of those who have no 'priority need' or of those who make no application to any local housing authority. The figure therefore seems to be a substantial under-estimate of the true level of homelessness prevalent today.[6]

1. GENERAL AIM OF THE HOMELESSNESS LEGISLATION

The enactment of the Housing (Homeless Persons) Act 1977 marked the introduction of a highly significant piece of social legislation. The basic aim of this Act, most of which is now consolidated in Part III of the Housing Act 1985,

1 A. Arden, *The Housing Act 1980* (London 1980), p x.
2 Ante, p 733.
3 Post, p 1049.
4 For evidence of an increase in the number of families made homeless by reason of mortgage default, see J. Ivatts, *Homelessness Legislation: A Study of the Housing (Homeless Persons) Act 1977* (London 1984), p 103.
5 Central Statistical Office, *Social Trends No 17* (1987 edn London), p 147 (Table 8.20). This figure compares with 97,000 households accepted as homeless in 1984 and 53,000 households in 1978 (see *Social Trends No 10* (1980 edn London 1979), p 206 (Table 9.21)).
6 See J. Ivatts, op cit, p 95.

was to impose on local housing authorities a clear statutory duty to house homeless families. The Act also sought to provide distinct guidelines for determining whether a homeless family falls within the responsibility of one local authority rather than another. It was hoped in this way to inject a certain administrative uniformity into strategies for dealing with the homeless and to end the social mischief which arose where homeless persons were endlessly passed from one local authority to another or from one department to another within the same local authority.[7]

Against the background of current housing policy, it is clear that the homeless persons legislation has visited a quite impossible task not only upon the housing authorities which are charged with its implementation but also upon the courts before which housing authority action may subsequently be challenged. So severe have these difficulties become that in *R v Hillingdon LBC, ex parte Puhlhofer*,[8] the House of Lords felt constrained to impose severe limitations on the scope of the homeless persons legislation. Lord Brightman ruled—somewhat in the teeth of the statute—that the Act was 'not an Act which imposes any duty upon a local authority to house the homeless.'[9] It is 'an Act to assist persons who are homeless, not an Act to provide them with homes.' In Lord Brightman's view, the statutory intendment was 'to provide for the homeless a lifeline of last resort; not to enable them to make inroads into the local authority's waiting list of applicants for housing.'[10] It is, however, highly dubious whether the social purpose of the legislation can be eviscerated in this way and the limiting effect of the *Puhlhofer* decision has since been tempered by amending legislation which indicates that the statute cannot properly be read down in so drastic a manner.[11]

2. CONDITIONS OF ELIGIBILITY

Part III of the Housing Act 1985 imposes on a local authority a duty to provide full and permanent rehousing for certain groups of homeless persons who come within its area of responsibility. This duty is, however, graded in accordance with a number of criteria, and in some circumstances the duty is of a lesser degree, consisting in reality only of an obligation to furnish a homeless person with 'advice and appropriate assistance' towards securing accommodation.

In order to qualify as a proper object of the local authority's ultimate legal obligation to provide permanent housing, an applicant must satisfy a number of conditions. He must be able to show (1) that he is 'homeless',[12] (2) that he has a 'priority need',[13] and (3) that he did not become homeless 'intentionally'.[14] The applicant must moreover have a 'local connection' with the area covered by the housing authority to which he makes application.[15] Each of these

---

7 For a critical examination of the legislation, see P.W. Robson and P. Watchman, [1981] JSWL 1, 65; P.Q. Watchman and P. Robson, *Homelessness and the Law* (Glasgow 1983); D. Hoath, *Homelessness* (London 1983).
8 [1986] AC 484. See [1986] JSWL 305 (D. Hoath).
9 [1986] AC 484 at 517B.
10 [1986] AC 484 at 517C.
11 See Housing Act 1985, s 58(2A), as supplied by Housing and Planning Act 1986, s 14(1), (2) (post, p 766).
12 Housing Act 1985, s 65(1).
13 Housing Act 1985, s 65(2).
14 Housing Act 1985, s 65(2).
15 Housing Act 1985, s 67(2).

conditions is based on criteria which are defined more closely in the statute and which are elaborated in the Code of Guidance issued in conjunction with the Housing Act 1985 and to which each housing authority is required to have regard.[16]

(1) Definition of homelessness

For the purpose of the Housing Act 1985 a person is regarded as 'homeless' if he has 'no accommodation in England, Wales or Scotland.'[17] Within these terms an applicant qualifies as 'homeless' if there is no accommodation which he is entitled to occupy by virtue of any property interest (eg a tenancy)[18] or by way of express or implied licence.[19] No applicant is 'homeless' if he enjoys a status of irremovability conferred on him either by statute (eg under the Rent Act 1977[20]) or by any rule of law.[1]

(a) Constructive homelessness

The statutory concept of homelessness is amplified by the direction that a person shall be regarded as 'homeless' within the meaning of the Housing Act 1985 even in certain circumstances where accommodation is at least nominally available for his occupation. These cases of constructive homelessness arise where the applicant has accommodation but cannot secure entry to it,[2] or can occupy it only at the risk of probable or realistically apprehended violence from some other person who resides in the accommodation.[3] A further instance of constructive homelessness arises where the applicant's accommodation consists of a 'movable structure, vehicle or vessel designed or adapted for human habitation' and there is no place where he is entitled or permitted both to place it and to reside in it.[4]

(b) Temporary or crisis accommodation

The Housing Act 1985 seems to stipulate that a claim of homelessness cannot be made by any person who enjoys rights in the nature of a licence, whether express or implied, which entitle him to occupy accommodation. It is clear, however, that an applicant may nonetheless rank as 'homeless' if, for instance, his residence with a relative is only temporary and the relative wants the applicant to leave.[5] In any event, as Lord Lowry pointed out in *Taj Din v Wandsworth LBC*,[6] it is 'still a matter for debate whether the terms

---

16   Housing Act 1985, s 71(1). See Code of Guidance (2nd edn), issued by the Department of the Environment, the Home Office and the Welsh Office. The Code is not a binding statute (see *De Falco v Crawley BC* [1980] QB 460 at 478A), but its terms are highly persuasive.
17   Housing Act 1985, s 58(1).
18   Housing Act 1985, s 58(2)(a). Homeless status is also precluded by the existence of a court order entitling the applicant to occupation of the relevant accommodation.
19   Housing Act 1985, s 58(2)(b).
20   Post, p 968.
1   Housing Act 1985, s 58(2)(c).
2   Housing Act 1985, s 58(3)(a).
3   Housing Act 1985, s 58(3)(b). Compare, however, *R v Croydon LBC, ex parte Toth* (1986) Legal Action 124.
4   Housing Act 1985, s 58(3)(c).
5   See eg *R v Ealing LBC, ex parte McBain* [1985] 1 WLR 1351 at 1353E.
6   [1983] 1 AC 657 at 678D. See [1982] JSWL 176 (P.Q. Watchman).

"occupation" and "occupy" are appropriate to describe the position of a person sharing a house as a guest without having any portion of the accommodation definitely allotted to him'.

It is also plain that much of the social purpose of the homelessness legislation would be destroyed if those who enjoy mere precarious rights of short-term shelter were ruled out of statutory protection. In *Taj Din v Wandsworth LBC*[7] Lord Lowry held that 'to be homeless and to have found some temporary accommodation are not mutually inconsistent concepts'. In his view, a person does not cease to be 'homeless' merely by 'having a roof over his head or a lodging, however precarious'.[8] Thus living in temporary crisis accommodation (such as a battered women's refuge) does not take the occupier outside the 'homeless' category.[9] A person may be 'homeless' even though he is accustomed, whenever space is available, to sleep in a night centre which provides shelter for the homeless.[10]

(c) Domestic violence

It has been a consistently controversial question whether the victim of domestic violence may properly leave home and present herself to her housing authority as a 'homeless' person.[11] The Housing Act 1985 at least superficially appears to treat as homelessness those circumstances in which a person can occupy accommodation only at the risk of violence.[12] However, the courts seem increasingly to take the view that, before claiming to be 'homeless', the person who fears violence must first exhaust all other remedies (such as the exclusion of the violent partner from the shared home).[13] An applicant who has failed to seek such remedies may well be held to have rendered herself 'homeless intentionally'.[14]

(i) Denial of 'homeless' status It is possible that the courts will deny that an applicant is 'homeless' at all if she has failed to apply for a court order under the Matrimonial Homes Act 1983 or the Domestic Violence and Matrimonial Proceedings Act 1976 for the purpose of excluding her erstwhile partner from the former family home.[15] In *McAlinden v Bearsden and Milngavie DC*[16] Lord McDonald held that 'homeless' status could not be claimed by an applicant who had left her existing home and simply 'elected to sit back and claim the preference afforded to a person who satisfied the definition of homelessness'. The courts have certainly not been over-ready to uphold a recourse to the public housing obligation on supposedly trivial evidence of possible violence or fear of domestic harassment.[17]

---

7   [1983] 1 AC 657 at 677F.
8   [1983] 1 AC 657 at 677F.
9   *R v Ealing LBC, ex parte Sidhu* (1982) 2 HLR 45 at 53f. See [1982] JSWL 237 (P.Q. Watchman).
10 *R v Waveney DC, ex parte Bowers* [1983] QB 238 at 243C.
11 See M. Bryan, [1984] JSWL 195.
12 Housing Act 1985, s 58(3)(b) (ante, p 762).
13 See *R v Eastleigh BC, ex parte Evans* (1984) 17 HLR 515 at 523ff.
14 Post, p 769.
15 Post, p 784. See generally David Pearl, 'Public Housing Allocation and Domestic Disputes', in M.D.A. Freeman (ed), *Essays in Family Law 1985* (London 1986), p 20.
16 1986 SLT (OH) 191 at 192D, G-H.
17 *R v Purbeck DC, ex parte Cadney* (1985) 17 HLR 534 at 537.

(ii) Availability of exclusion orders The extreme confusion of the law in this area is indicated moreover by the response which has been elicited by applications for exclusion orders. In *Wooton v Wooton*,[18] for instance, a de facto wife applied for an exclusion order against her partner, who had previously been violent and now threatened to burn the house down. The Court of Appeal declined to make an exclusion order on the ground that, if evicted, the male partner would not qualify for assistance under the homelessness legislation, whereas the female partner would be able to invoke that legislation in her favour if *she* were to vacate the shared home.[19] To refuse a battered woman an exclusion order on such grounds may well be thought to represent a condonation of the violence which led to the application.[20]

(d) Reasonableness of association

Any sensible determination of whether an applicant currently has access to 'accommodation' or is indeed truly 'homeless' can be made only in the context of the familial or other associations around which the applicant wishes to base his residential life. The Housing Act 1985 thus provides that an applicant is not to be treated as having 'accommodation' in the statutory sense unless his existing accommodation is available (as of right or by way of licence) not only for himself but also for 'any other person who normally resides with him as a member of his family or in circumstances in which it is reasonable for that person to reside with him'.[1] This provision clearly invests the local housing authority with a significant discretion as to the types of personal association which may legitimately afford a basis for any claim of collective homelessness.[2]

(e) Qualitative test as to existing 'accommodation'

It has been a deeply vexed question in recent years whether the availability of 'accommodation' for an applicant under the homelessness legislation is to be judged with reference to any qualitative assessment of his existing living conditions. Prior to 1986 it was generally assumed that in some circumstances the inherent quality of the applicant's current living conditions could be so defective or substandard that the applicant could quite properly allege that he had no 'accommodation' at all within the meaning of the legislation and that he was therefore 'homeless'.[3] This view was, however, severely shaken by the decision of the House of Lords in *R v Hillingdon LBC, ex parte Puhlhofer*.[4]

(i) The Puhlhofer ruling In *Puhlhofer* the applicants, a married couple, lived with two young children of the family (aged 3 and 1) in one room in a guest house. No cooking or laundry facilities were available at the premises and, apart from

18   [1984] FLR 871 at 874B-C per Dunn LJ.
19   Compare *Thurley v Smith* [1984] FLR 875 at 878E-H, where the Court of Appeal made an exclusion order against a male partner who was both alcoholic and violent.
20   See [1985] JSWL 372 at 374 (M. Bryan).
1   Housing Act 1985, s 58(2). A member of the applicant's de iure family need not show that it is 'reasonable' for him to reside with the applicant (*R v Hillingdon Homeless Persons Panel, ex parte Islam* (1981) *Times*, 10 February). See also Housing Act 1985, s 75.
2   See D. Hoath, *'Split Families' and Part III of the Housing Act 1985*, [1987] JSWL 15.
3   See eg *R v South Herefordshire DC, ex parte Miles* (1983) 17 HLR 82 at 92.
4   [1986] AC 484. See [1986] JSWL 305 (D. Hoath).

breakfast, the family had to eat outside the guest house. It was clear that there
was practically no room to move inside this accommodation, since most of the
floor space was taken up with two beds, a cradle, a pram and children's toys.[5]
When their second child was on its way the applicants claimed that they were
'homeless' in that their existing living space was overcrowded and wholly
inappropriate for the needs of their growing family. In particular the
applicants alleged that their personal relationship had been damaged by the
tension induced by their confined conditions. Following the birth of the second
child it was also clear that their children were likewise suffering emotional and
other traumas in consequence of the overcrowding. The local housing
authority nevertheless rejected the claim of homelessness, adopting the view
that the single room constituted 'accommodation' for the purpose of the Act.
This finding was challenged by way of proceedings for judicial review.

The House of Lords, although expressing 'deepest sympathy' for the plight
of the applicants,[6] held that their application for housing had been correctly
rejected. In delivering the only major speech, Lord Brightman pointed to the
fact that the homelessness legislation had not placed any qualifying adjective
before the word 'accommodation'.[7] There was accordingly no statutory
indication, either express or by way of necessary implication, that an
applicant's current living conditions must be 'appropriate' or 'reasonable'
before he could be excluded from the scope of the legislation.[8] Existing living
space was not disqualified as 'accommodation' merely because it was unfit for
human habitation[9] or statutorily 'overcrowded'.[10] The statutory definition of
'overcrowding' might occasionally be relevant in so far as 'accommodation
must, by definition, be capable of accommodating'. In the view of Lord
Brightman, however, the definition of 'accommodation' was ultimately a
'question of fact to be decided by the local authority' in accordance with the
'ordinary meaning of that word in the English language'.[11] Thus, while there
were clearly some living places which 'could not properly be regarded as
accommodation at all',[12] the applicants in the instant case could not claim that
they had no 'accommodation' for the purpose of the Act.

(ii) The reaction to Puhlhofer The *Puhlhofer* decision showed the courts to be
deeply sensitive—and indeed overly sensitive—to the problems faced by local
authorities in attempting 'in extremely difficult circumstances' to perform
their duties under the homeless persons legislation 'with due regard for all their
other housing problems'.[13] The living conditions suffered by the *Puhlhofer*
applicants and their young family were undoubtedly appalling, and the ruling
of the House of Lords generated a public outcry to the effect that the homeless

5   [1986] AC 484 at 488E-F.
6   [1986] AC 484 at 518C per Lord Brightman.
7   [1986] AC 484 at 517D.
8   [1986] AC 484 at 517E. See eg *Stringer v Halton BC* [1982] CLY 1464 (caravan in which
    woman and four-year-old son had to sleep in chairs or on floor nevertheless held to be
    'accommodation')
9   Post, p 917.
10 Post, p 936.
11 [1986] AC 484 at 517F-G.
12 [1986] AC 484 at 517F ('[I]t would be a misuse of language to describe Diogenes as having
    occupied accommodation within the meaning of the Act').
13 [1986] AC 484 at 518F.

persons legislation, if correctly construed in this way, required an immediate amendment of balance and direction.[14]

With uncharacteristic swiftness, the widespread criticism of the *Puhlhofer* decision led to the amendment in the Housing and Planning Act 1986 of the statutory concept of homelessness. As altered by the 1986 Act, the Housing Act 1985 now stipulates that a person shall not be treated as having 'accommodation' for the purpose of the homelessness legislation 'unless it is accommodation which it would be reasonable for him to continue to occupy'.[15] These words counteract the rigidity of the *Puhlhofer* construction and it seems likely that the courts will in future apply a more broadly qualitative test in determining whether an applicant currently has access to 'accommodation' of a standard which precludes any further claim under the Act.[16]

(2) Definition of 'priority need'

The obligations of housing authorities under Part III of the Housing Act 1985 are delimited by reference to the concept of 'priority need'.[17] The definition of 'priority need' effectively excludes from the scope of the homelessness provisions most categories of single person living alone. A 'priority need for accommodation' arises essentially where a homeless person has dependent children who reside (or might reasonably be expected to reside) with him or her.[18] Where the applicant actually has dependent children living with him at the date of the authority's determination, it is irrelevant whether or not they can reasonably be expected to live with him.[19]

A single homeless person presents a 'priority need' only where such a person is pregnant,[20] or is homeless or 'threatened with homelessness'[1] as a result of any emergency such as flood, fire or any other disaster,[2] is 'vulnerable' as a

14   See (1986) Legal Action (March) 1, 29.
15   Housing Act 1985, s 58(2A), as supplied by Housing and Planning Act 1986, s 14(1), (2). However, in determining whether continued occupation would be reasonable, it is proper to have regard to 'the general circumstances prevailing in relation to housing in the district of the local housing authority' to which the applicant has applied for help with his housing (see Housing Act 1985, s 58(2B)).
16   The Housing and Planning Act 1986 also contains a direction that a housing authority, in exercising its duties pursuant to Housing Act 1985, ss 65-68, shall for the purpose of determining whether accommodation is suitable have regard to Parts IX - XI of the Housing Act 1985, which relate respectively to slum clearance, overcrowding and houses in multiple occupation (see Housing Act 1985, s 69(1), as substituted by Housing and Planning Act 1986, s 14(1), (2)).
17   Housing Act 1985, s 65(2). Of 227,000 homelessness enquiries made in Great Britain in 1985, 99,000 were found to involve a case of 'priority need' (see Central Statistical Office, *Social Trends No 17* (1987 edn London), p 147 (Table 8.21)).
18   Housing Act 1985, s 59(1)(b). Households with dependent children made up 62 per cent of the cases of homelessness accepted by local authorities in 1985 (see Central Statistical Office, *Social Trends No 17* (1987 edn London), p 147 (Table 8.20)).
19   A 'priority need' is not dependent on a showing that the applicant has been awarded a full custody order in respect of the children in question (see *R v Ealing LBC, ex parte Sidhu* (1982) 2 HLR 45 at 56f).
20   Housing Act 1985, s 59(1)(a). A 'priority need' also arises where pregnancy affects a person with whom the homeless applicant resides or might reasonably be expected to reside.
1   A person is regarded as being 'threatened with homelessness' if it is 'likely that he will become homeless within 28 days' (Housing Act 1985, s 58(4)).
2   Housing Act 1985, s 59(1)(d). The making of a demolition order (under Housing Act 1985, s 265) does not qualify as a 'disaster' within the meaning of this provision (*Noble v South Herefordshire DC* (1983) 17 HLR 80 at 81).

result of old age,[3] mental illness or handicap,[4] physical disability or 'other special reason'.[5] In the present context the notion of vulnerability extends to any person who is 'less able to fend for [himself] so that injury or detriment will result when a less vulnerable man will be able to cope without harmful effects'.[6] Only certain kinds of vulnerability constitute cases of 'priority need'. The concept can be properly applied to an applicant who suffers both from alcoholism and a brain injury caused through accident, but not to an applicant who merely has a drink problem.[7] There is an indication in the Code of Guidance that the requirement of vulnerability can be satisfied in relation to a homeless young person who is 'at risk of sexual or financial exploitation',[8] even if such exploitation has not yet occurred.[9]

(3) Definition of intentional homelessness

A further limitation on the statutory obligations imposed by Part III of the Housing Act 1985 is provided by the novel concept of intentional homelessness. This concept was adopted originally in the Housing (Homeless Persons) Act 1977[10] and is now incorporated in the 1985 Act. The housing authority's duties become fully operative in relation to any given applicant only if the authority is 'not satisfied that he became homeless intentionally'.[11] For this purpose a person becomes 'homeless intentionally' if he 'deliberately does or fails to do anything in consequence of which he ceases to occupy accommodation which is available for his occupation and which it would have been reasonable for him to continue to occupy'.[12] These provisions have become a notorious source of difficulty.

(a) Nature of relevant conduct

Intentional homelessness may arise from any deliberate act or omission, but an act or omission 'in good faith on the part of a person who was unaware of any

3   The Code of Guidance suggests that a man above 65 years of age should be treated as 'vulnerable' (Code, para 2.12(c)(i)).
4   See *R v Bath CC, ex parte Sangermano* (1984) 17 HLR 94 at 101.
5   Housing Act 1985, s 59(1)(c). See, however, *Wooton v Wooton* [1984] FLR 871 at 874B, where the Court of Appeal thought that a male partner, who had a tendency to behave violently while suffering epileptic seizures, would not be able to claim any 'priority need' for rehousing if he were excluded from the family home. See [1985] JSWL 372 at 373 (M. Bryan).
6   *R v Waveney DC, ex parte Bowers* [1983] QB 238 at 244H-245A. See [1983] JSWL 252 (P.Q. Watchman).
7   *R v Waveney DC, ex parte Bowers* [1983] QB 238 at 246A-C. See also *Thurley v Smith* [1984] FLR 875 at 878E-H. There is, however, no requirement that the vulnerability be 'substantial' before it can give rise to a 'priority need' (see *R v Waveney DC, ex parte Bowers*, supra at 245G-H).
8   Code of Guidance, para 2.12(c)(iii).
9   *Kelly v Monklands DC* (Court of Session (OH), 12 July 1985).
10 Housing (Homeless Persons) Act 1977, s 17.
11 Housing Act 1985, s 65(2). The onus of proof rests on the housing authority; no onus rests on the applicant to satisfy the authority that he did not become 'homeless intentionally' (see *R v Thurrock BC, ex parte Williams* (1981) 1 HLR 128 at 134ff; *R v North Devon DC, ex parte Lewis* [1981] 1 WLR 328 at 332F).
12 Housing Act 1985, s 60(1). See eg *Lazare v Slough BC* (1981) LAG Bulletin 66, where a finding of intentional homelessness was upheld in circumstances in which the behaviour of the male applicant towards his mother-in-law had caused the latter to ask the applicants to leave her home.

relevant fact is not to be treated as deliberate'.[13] The leeway afforded by this proviso is, however, somewhat limited in that it applies only where the applicant was ignorant of a material fact and not simply unaware that his actions or omissions would have a certain result as a matter of law. Thus a finding of 'intentionality' may be based upon a rent or mortgage default which leads to the legal consequence of eviction, even though the applicant did not appreciate at the time that his non-payment would be the eventual cause of his homelessness.[14] The result may be different if the applicant suffered from a genuine misapprehension of fact, eg that his mortgage interest was being paid automatically by the Department of Health and Social Security.[15] Voluntary removal from existing secure accommodation may lead to intentional homelessness, but the applicant's decision to move is not 'deliberate' if he was unaware that his new accommodation was merely short-term and insecure.[16]

(i) Indirect causal nexus A finding of intentional homelessness must be based on some act or omission for which the applicant is directly or indirectly responsible. Such behaviour comprises not merely voluntary removal from existing accommodation, but also any conduct which becomes a proximate cause for the loss of accommodation. 'Intentionality' may be founded, for instance, on misconduct at or connected with the work place which the applicant must have known would lead to dismissal and the loss of tied accommodation.[17] 'Intentionality' may also derive from a voluntary resignation of employment which likewise causes the loss of tied accommodation,[18] but 'intentionality' is not necessarily present where the applicant is dismissed for mere incompetence[19] or is the victim of a constructive dismissal.[20]

(ii) Changes in family status or living arrangements Acts or omissions which have the effect of altering family living arrangements or familial status do not in general bring about a case of intentional homelessness. It is clear, for instance, that an applicant does not become 'homeless intentionally' merely because she becomes pregnant with the result that her existing accommodation is no longer suitable[1] or that she is no longer welcome there. The applicant's implementation of a desire to have his family reside with him does not raise a case of intentional homelessness where his existing accommodation, although adequate to house him on his own, is inadequate to house his family as well.[2] It

---

13 Housing Act 1985, s 60(3).
14 *Robinson v Torbay BC* [1982] 1 All ER 726 at 730g. See also *R v Eastleigh BC, ex parte Beattie* (1984) 17 HLR 168 at 173f. The Code of Guidance indicates that wilful and persistent refusal to pay rent should usually result in a finding of 'intentionality' (para 2.15).
15 *White v Exeter CC* (1981) LAG Bulletin 287.
16 *R v Wandsworth LBC, ex parte Rose* (1983) 11 HLR 105 at 114f.
17 *R v Thanet DC, ex parte Reeve* (1981) 6 HLR 31 at 35. See also *Goddard v Torridge DC* (1981) LAG Bulletin 287; *Jennings v Northavon DC* (1981) LAG Bulletin 287.
18 *R v North Devon DC, ex parte Lewis* [1981] 1 WLR 328 at 334C-E; *R v Thanet DC, ex parte Reeve* (1981) 6 HLR 31 at 34.
19 *R v Thurrock BC, ex parte Williams* (1981) 1 HLR 128 at 137f.
20 *R v Thurrock BC, ex parte Williams* (1981) 1 HLR 128 at 136.
1 *R v Eastleigh BC, ex parte Beattie* (1983) 10 HLR 134 at 141 (post, p 771).
2 *R v Hillingdon LBC, ex parte Islam* [1983] 1 AC 688 at 708F-G, 715E-F. See [1982] JSWL 101 (P.Q. Watchman); (1982) 45 MLR (D.C. Hoath). See also Housing Act 1985, s 75 (post, p 770), and *R v Westminster CC, ex parte Ali* (1983) 11 HLR 83 at 93.

is possible, however, that the failure of an evicted family member to exhaust remedies in domestic law in respect of exclusion from the home may constitute a case of 'intentionality',[3] although it would be improper for a housing authority, as a matter of inflexible policy, to make the exhaustion of such remedies a precondition of help.[4]

(b) Nature of responsibility

A successful application under Part III of the Housing Act 1985 may impose on a housing authority an obligation to secure accommodation not only for the applicant but also for any person who might reasonably be expected to reside with him. It therefore becomes an important, but difficult, question whether intentional homelessness which affects one member of a family group necessarily precludes a homelessness application by other members of the same residential unit.

(i) Presumption of collective liability In *R v North Devon DC, ex parte Lewis*,[5] the de facto husband of the applicant had become homeless by virtue of the fact that he had voluntarily given up the employment on which the family's tied accommodation depended. Woolf J held that the housing authority was not entitled to treat members of the same family unit as tainted automatically by the misconduct of one member of that unit.[6] The applicant in *Lewis* was not therefore precluded from making a separate application as a homeless person, even though her partner might indirectly benefit from her eligibility.[7] However, Woolf J took the view that the homelessness legislation 'requires consideration of the family unit as a whole' and that it can be presumed, in the absence of contrary evidence, that the conduct of one family member in becoming intentionally homeless is 'conduct to which the other members of the family were a party.'[8] It was found in *Lewis* that the woman had acquiesced in her cohabitee's decision to terminate his employment and Woolf J held accordingly that she too had rendered herself 'homeless intentionally'.[9]

(ii) Guilt by association The courts have since applied the *Lewis* ruling to a broad range of circumstances in which an applicant for housing is deemed—often somewhat harshly—to have been implicated in misconduct which has led to the forfeiture of secure accommodation and which has therefore conduced to the homelessness of the entire family unit. In *R v Swansea CC, ex parte John*,[10] a 67 year-old council tenant was evicted by the council on the ground of the

---

3   *R v Eastleigh BC, ex parte Evans* (1984) 17 HLR 515 at 523f. See, however, Code of Guidance, para 2.16 ('A battered woman who has fled the marital home should never be regarded as having become homeless intentionally because it would clearly not be reasonable for her to remain').
4   See *Eastleigh BC v Betts* [1983] 2 AC 613 at 627H-628A.
5   [1981] 1 WLR 328.
6   [1981] 1 WLR 328 at 333B-C.
7   [1981] 1 WLR 328 at 333E-F.
8   [1981] 1 WLR 328 at 333G-H.
9   [1981] 1 WLR 328 at 333H-334E. Woolf J thought that exactly the same result would follow if a wife were to acquiesce in her husband's spending the rent money on drink ([1981] 1 WLR 328 at 334A-B).
10   (1982) 9 HLR 56 at 62.

nuisance and annoyance caused by her uncontrollably alcoholic partner. She was held to have made herself intentionally homeless in that, by failing to sever her relationship with him, she had effectively acquiesced in his conduct.[11] Likewise a council tenant whose husband and children have terrorised the immediate neighbourhood can be held to have rendered herself 'homeless intentionally' if the family is evicted for causing nuisance and annoyance.[12] A finding of 'intentionality' is not, however, justified if there is evidence that the applicant, far from acquiescing in the misconduct which led to the homelessness, dissociated herself from it and remonstrated with the family member who was directly responsible for it.[13]

(c) The applicant must 'cease' to occupy accommodation

In order to attract a finding of intentional homelessness, the applicant must have ceased to occupy accommodation which was both available for his occupation and reasonable for him to *continue* to occupy.[14] It is clear that no such finding can be made in relation to accommodation in which the applicant has not yet lived. It follows that intentional homelessness cannot arise merely because the applicant unreasonably rejects an offer of accommodation made by the housing authority acting under Part III of the Housing Act 1985.[15] However, although the authority cannot reject the applicant as intentionally homeless, it can nevertheless claim, in the absence of any material change of circumstance, that it has already discharged its statutory obligation towards him in full.[16]

(d) The abandoned accommodation must have been 'available for...occupation'

There can be no finding of 'intentionality' unless the accommodation abandoned by the applicant was 'available for his occupation',[17] a phrase which is further defined as requiring that the accommodation be available 'for occupation both by him and by any other person who might reasonably be expected to reside with him'.[18] In *R v Wimbourne DC, ex parte Curtis*,[19] a wife had been granted under the terms of a separation agreement a right to occupy the

---

11 See also *R v Swansea CC, ex parte Thomas* (1983) 9 HLR 64 at 69f; [1983] JSWL 356 (P.Q. Watchman).
12 *R v Salford CC, ex parte Devenport* (1984) 82 LGR 89 at 96f, 99f. See also *Smith v Bristol CC* (1981) LAG Bulletin 287; *R v Southampton CC, ex parte Ward* (1984) 14 HLR 114 at 120, 136ff; *R v East Hertfordshire DC, ex parte Bannon* (1986) Legal Action 124.
13 See *R v West Dorset DC, ex parte Phillips* (1985) 17 HLR 336 at 340ff (where the applicant turned on her husband during the interview with the housing authority's homeless persons officer, blaming her husband for the loss of their tenancy). See also *R v Eastleigh BC, ex parte Beattie* (1984) 17 HLR 168 at 177f; *R v Penwith DC, ex parte Trevena* (1984) 17 HLR 526 at 532.
14 Housing Act 1985, s 60(1).
15 *R v Westminster CC, ex parte Chambers* (1982) 6 HLR 24 at 28; *R v Ealing LBC, ex parte McBain* [1985] 1 WLR 1351 at 1354G-H.
16 *R v Westminster CC, ex parte Chambers* (1982) 6 HLR 24 at 29f (post, p 776).
17 Housing Act 1985, s 60(3).
18 Housing Act 1985, s 75. See *R v Hillingdon LBC, ex parte Islam* [1983] 1 AC 688 at 708E- F, where Lord Wilberforce pointed out that 'rooms in two separate continents' could not be combined to make up 'available' accommodation for a family (ante, p 768).
19 (1985) 18 HLR 79.

former matrimonial home unless and until she remarried or cohabited with another man. When she later brought somebody else to live with her in the home, her occupancy rights were duly terminated by a sale of the property effected by her separated husband. Under the circumstances the Divisional Court declined to find the woman intentionally homeless. The Court held that the accommodation had not been 'available' for her in the first place, in that it had not been accommodation which was open—as might reasonably have been expected—to be shared with her new partner.[20]

(e) It must have been 'reasonable' for the applicant to continue to occupy the accommodation

An applicant cannot be held to be 'homeless intentionally' unless it would have been 'reasonable for him to continue to occupy' his existing accommodation. In determining this question of reasonableness, the housing authority may have regard to 'the general circumstances prevailing in relation to housing' within its area.[1] In effect the authority can turn down an application for housing on the ground that other residents in the same area were living in conditions which were even worse than those of the applicant.[2] There is also the potent consideration that applicants should not, by means of homelessness applications, be able to 'jump the queue' in relation to those who for years have been on waiting lists for council tenancies. It is quite legitimate that, by giving weight to this consideration, a housing authority should seek to prevent the homelessness legislation being used as a form of pre-emptive bid for public housing.[3]

Following the decision of the House of Lords in *R v Hillingdon LBC, ex parte Puhlhofer*,[4] it is nowadays less likely that continued occupation of existing accommodation will be considered unreasonable merely because that accommodation is inherently substandard. Nevertheless, as Lord Brightman stressed, accommodation 'must, by definition, be capable of accommodating',[5] and the courts may not think it 'reasonable' for an applicant and his family to continue to live in conditions which are grossly overcrowded.[6] Other factors which may make it no longer 'reasonable' for the applicant to have continued in his existing accommodation may include the availability of a job elsewhere,[7] or the fact that possession proceedings were pending against him on grounds which offered no reasonable possibility of successful defence.[8] It is not 'reasonable' to remain in occupation where eviction is either inevitable[9] or

20 (1985) 18 HLR 79 at 81f.
1 Housing Act 1985, s 60(4). This provision is not exhaustive as to the circumstances to which the court may have regard (see *R v LB of Hammersmith & Fulham, ex parte Duro-Rama* (1983) 9 HLR 71 at 77).
2 See Code of Guidance, para 2.16.
3 See *Tickner v Mole Valley DC* (1980) LAG Bulletin 187.
4 [1986] AC 484 (ante, p 764).
5 [1986] AC 484 at 517G-H.
6 See *Krishnan v LB of Hillingdon* (1981) LAG Bulletin 137; *R v Eastleigh BC, ex parte Beattie* (1983) 10 HLR 134 at 141; *R v Westminster CC, ex parte Ali* (1983) 11 HLR 83 at 93.
7 *R v Hillingdon LBC, ex parte Islam* [1983] 1 AC 688 at 717F per Lord Lowry.
8 *R v Surrey Heath BC, ex parte Li* (1984) 16 HLR 79 at 89; [1984] JSWL 370 (M.A.J.); *R v Portsmouth CC, ex parte Knight* (1983) 82 LGR 184 at 191. See also [1985] JSWL 368 at 370 (D. Hoath).
9 Occupants who move before a notice to quit takes effect are not necessarily to be regarded as intentionally homeless (see *Taj Din v Wandsworth LBC* [1983] 1 AC 657 at 668B per Lord Wilberforce).

imminent,[10] or where the accommodation was obtained in the first place by means of deception.[11]

(f)   There must be a causal link between the applicant's conduct and the cesser of occupation

In order that homelessness should be intentional, there must be some causal link between a cessation of occupation and the homelessness which is the source of the instant application. This issue raises essentially a problem of 'remoteness' in determining whether there is a chain of causation between a past abandonment of accommodation and the applicant's present dilemma.[12] In *Dyson v Kerrier DC*,[13] for instance, the applicant had deliberately surrendered the tenancy of a council flat and had thereafter taken a short-term tenancy of a house which was the subject of a winter letting only. When she was rendered homeless on the termination of this short-term letting, the Court of Appeal held that a finding of intentional homelessness could properly be based on the facts surrounding the voluntary termination of the earlier tenancy.[14] The applicant did not therefore come within the scope of the legislation, even though she was the mother of a young child and had moved to the short-term accommodation in order to live next door to her sister, with whom she had previously shared the council flat.

The *Dyson* decision indicates that the courts are ready to regard a single incident of intentional homelessness as thereafter tainting the status of the homeless on a fairly long-term basis.[15] The disqualification imposed by an initial element of 'intentionality' is not removed merely because the applicant would eventually have become involuntarily homeless even if he had continued to occupy the original accommodation.[16] However, as the House of Lords made clear in *Taj Din v Wandsworth LBC*,[17] the intentionally homeless person may be able to purge or expunge his original 'intentionality' by showing that he has since obtained intervening settled accommodation elsewhere. If this has occurred, he is then free to apply to his housing authority on the basis of any fresh incident of homelessness which affects his new accommodation, since the chain of causation leading from the first incident has been truncated. If, however, an intentionally homeless person simply continues in a state of homelessness without interruption, there is no new incident of homelessness on which he can rely.[18]

10   *R v Mole Valley DC, ex parte Minnett* (1983) 12 HLR 49 at 57.
11   *R v Exeter CC, ex parte Gliddon* [1985] 1 All ER 493 at 497e-f.
12   *R v Thanet DC, ex parte Reeve* (1981) 6 HLR 31 at 35.
13   [1980] 1 WLR 1205.
14   [1980] 1 WLR 1205 at 1215A-B. See the mixed reaction to this decision in *Taj Din v Wandsworth LBC* [1983] 1 AC 657 at 667H-668A per Lord Wilberforce, 678F per Lord Lowry.
15   This principle has been applied even to those who leave secure accommodation in other countries and who upon arrival in England enjoy only short-term and unsatisfactory accommodation before becoming homeless. See eg *De Falco v Crawley BC* [1980] QB 460 at 478G-H. See also *Lambert v Ealing LBC* [1982] 1 WLR 550 at 556D-E, 558F-G; [1982] JSWL 233 (P.Q. Watchman).
16   *Taj Din v Wandsworth LBC* [1983] 1 AC 657 at 668A per Lord Wilberforce, 671F-G per Lord Fraser of Tullybelton, 679F per Lord Lowry. Compare, however, Lord Russell of Killowen (at 673H-674A) and Lord Bridge of Harwich (at 682D-E, 685G-686A). See [1982] JSWL 176 (P.Q. Watchman).
17   [1983] 1 AC 657 at 668A, 686A.
18   See *R v Ealing LBC, ex parte McBain* [1985] 1 WLR 1351 at 1355D-E.

(4) Definition of 'local connection'

Responsibility as between local authorities in respect of particular homeless persons is allocated largely on the basis of a person's 'local connection' with one or other local authority area.[19] A person may claim a relevant 'local connection' on the ground that he is, or in the past was, normally resident in a particular district and that his residence there is or was a matter 'of his own choice'.[20] Likewise 'local connection' may be claimed on the ground of employment in,[1] or family associations with,[2] a particular district, or 'because of special circumstances'.[3] These matters are all merely grounds of 'local connection', and it is vital that the applicant should be able to show not only one of the grounds but also that the grounds afford evidence of a real 'local connection'.[4]

If an applicant has no relevant 'local connection', a housing authority may transfer to another authority the full housing duty under Part III of the Housing Act 1985,[5] but may not shuffle off any other lesser responsibility which the Act imposes (eg a duty to provide 'advice' and appropriate 'assistance').

3. DUTIES OF THE HOUSING AUTHORITY

The duties of the relevant housing authority take different forms at different stages in a homelessness application.

(1) Duty to make inquiries

If a local housing authority has reason to believe that an applicant is either homeless or threatened with homelessness, the authority has a duty to make such inquiries as are necessary to verify whether the applicant is indeed a victim of actual or threatened homelessness.[6] If so satisfied the authority must then make any further inquiries necessary in order to verify whether the

---

19   The 'local connection' requirement does not apply if the applicant has no 'local connection' anywhere in England, Wales or Scotland. See *R v Hillingdon LBC, ex parte Streeting* [1980] 1 WLR 1425 at 1433C, 1439B-D; [1981] JSWL 124; *R v Hillingdon LBC, ex parte Islam* [1983] 1 AC 688 at 717A-C.

20   Housing Act 1985, s 61(1)(a). See also Housing Act 1985, s 61(2)(b), (3).

1   Housing Act 1985, s 61(1)(b). See, however, *R v Vale of White Horse DC, ex parte Smith and Hay* (1984) 17 HLR 160 at 166ff; *Eastleigh BC v Betts* [1983] 2 AC 613 at 627F-628G (less than six months insufficient).

2   Housing Act 1985, s 61(1)(c).

3   Housing Act 1985, s 61(1)(d). Association with a particular church may not be a special circumstance (see *R v Vale of White Horse DC, ex parte Smith and Hay* (1984) 17 HLR 160 at 165).

4   *Eastleigh BC v Betts* [1983] 2 AC 613 at 627C-E; [1984] JSWL 365 (P.Q. Watchman).

5   Housing Act 1985, s 67. A housing authority which finds that an applicant is not intentionally homeless but has no 'local connection' can transfer housing responsibility to another authority with whom the applicant does have a 'local connection', even though that other authority has already determined the applicant to be intentionally homeless. See *R v Slough BC, ex parte Ealing LBC* [1981] QB 801 at 814C-D, 816F-H; (1981) LAG Bulletin 17 (A. Arden).

6   Housing Act 1985, s 62(1). The onus is not on the applicant to prove that he is homeless (see *R v Reigate & Banstead DC, ex parte Paris* (1984) 17 HLR 103 at 110f). Of 227,000 homelessness applications made to local housing authorities in 1985, 66,000 were rejected on the ground that the applicant was not found to be 'homeless'. See Central Statistical Office, *Social Trends No 17* (1987 edn London), p 147 (Table 8.21).

applicant has a 'priority need' or became 'homeless or threatened with homelessness intentionally', and may make further inquiries as to the applicant's 'local connection'.[7] The authority has a duty to secure that accommodation is made available for the applicant pending the outcome of these inquiries, if the authority has reason to believe that the applicant is homeless and has a 'priority need'.[8]

Uncertainty surrounds the extent of the investigation which must be carried out before a housing authority may properly conclude that an applicant has become homeless or threatened with homelessness 'intentionally'. The authority is under no 'positive duty to conduct detailed CID-type inquiries' in determining the reason for homelessness,[9] but may be in breach of its statutory obligation if it fails to consider all the relevant elements in each case.[10]

(2) Duty to give reasonable consideration

It seems that, in discharging its duty under the Housing Act 1985, the authority must at least to some extent observe the rules of natural justice, eg by allowing both sides of the case to be heard and considered.[11] In *R v Wyre BC, ex parte Joyce*,[12] for example, the Divisional Court of Queen's Bench granted judicial review of a council's decision to reject a homelessness application made by a former homeowner who had defaulted on her mortgage. Forbes J held that the authority had failed to make proper inquiries in that it had not given the applicant any opportunity to explain why she had been unable to keep up her payments. Similarly there may be a violation of the rules of natural justice if an authority fails to consider each case individually but for instance adopts a general policy of treating as 'intentionally' homeless all persons evicted for rent arrears.[13] However, in determining a homelessness application the authority is not required to act 'as if it were a court of law' but is merely required to act 'reasonably'.[14] The authority may have regard to hearsay evidence, and is not necessarily under any duty to confront the applicant with every aspect of the information uncovered by its inquiries.[15]

(3) Duty of notification

A housing authority has a statutory duty to inform an applicant in writing of its decision as to whether he is homeless or threatened with homelessness and has a priority need.[16] It must also notify him in writing of the reasons for any adverse decision which restricts its responsibility to him under Part III of the Housing Act 1985.[17]

7   Housing Act 1985, s 62(2).
8   Housing Act 1985, s 63(1). The standard of the accommodation provided in pursuance of this duty is not necessarily as high as that required in relation to accommodation which is offered in compliance with the authority's full housing duty under Housing Act 1985, s 65(2) (see *Hamilton DC v Brown* [1982] SCOLAG 185).
9   *Lally v Kensington and Chelsea Royal Borough* (1980) *Times*, 27 March.
10   See *Barry v LB of Newham* (1980) LAG Bulletin 142.
11   *Afan BC v Marchant* (1980) LAG Bulletin 15; *Stubbs v Slough BC* (1980) LAG Bulletin 16.
12   (1983) 11 HLR 73 at 79f.
13   *Williams v Cynon Valley Council* (1980) LAG Bulletin 16.
14   *R v Southampton CC, ex parte Ward* (1984) 14 HLR 119 at 136.
15   *R v Southampton CC, ex parte Ward* (1984) 14 HLR 119 at 136.
16   Housing Act 1985, s 64(1), (2), (5).
17   Housing Act 1985, s 64(3), (4), (5).

(4) Duties to assist the homeless

The precise content of the housing authority's duty towards the homeless is calibrated according to the degree to which any given applicant can show that he satisfies the statutory conditions.

(a) Duty to secure that accommodation becomes available for occupation

In relation to a person who is shown to be homeless, to have a priority need and not to have become homeless intentionally, the local housing authority is under a 'duty...to secure that accommodation becomes available for his occupation'.[18] This accommodation may be provided either by the authority itself or by some other person or body at the instance of the authority.[19] There is no requirement that permanent accommodation should be made available immediately, and the authority may discharge its duty 'in stages' which progress towards the provision of a secure permanent base.[20] However, an applicant who fulfils the statutory criteria is ultimately entitled to be provided with accommodation which is indefinite in duration. The housing authority cannot regard its duty to secure accommodation as discharged merely because it has provided accommodation for a longer period than would normally have been enjoyed in any event under the applicant's last tenancy or licence.[1]

(i) Suitability of accommodation A housing authority's statutory obligation is discharged only if the accommodation which it secures is 'appropriate' for the applicant.[2] The accommodation must be 'available for his occupation' in the sense that it must be available not only for the applicant but also for 'any other person who might reasonably be expected to reside with him'.[3] The accommodation must therefore be suitable in relation to the size of the applicant's family, the character of the local area and the prospects for local employment.[4] While the accommodation offered need not be situated in the area in which the applicant currently lives, the authority cannot discharge its duty by securing accommodation in a city 150 miles away with which the

---

18 Housing Act 1985, s 65(2).
19 See Housing Act 1985, s 69(1), as substituted by Housing and Planning Act 1986, s 14(1), (3). Homeless persons may be required to pay 'reasonable' charges in respect of the accommodation secured by the housing authority (Housing Act 1985, s 69(2)). See (1986) Legal Action 125.
20 *R v East Hertfordshire DC, ex parte Hunt* (1985) 18 HLR 51 at 55. See [1987] JSWL 67 (B. Walsh). In 1985, almost 15,500 households who had been officially accepted as homeless were given temporary accommodation. Of this number 4,500 were in bed and breakfast accommodation, 5,000 in hostels, and 6,000 in short-life dwellings. See Central Statistical Office, *Social Trends No 17* (1987 edn London), p 147. A Parliamentary written answer given on 3 July 1986 revealed that there were 2,960 households accommodated in bed and breakfast establishments in London alone (see *Parliamentary Debates, House of Commons, Official Report*, Vol 100 (Session 1985-86), Col 596w). A single hotel in Hounslow accommodates 850 homeless persons (see (1986) Legal Action 124).
1 *R v Camden LBC, ex parte Wait* [1987] 1 FLR 155 at 163A-B; [1987] JSWL 123 (M.A.J.). See also *Taj Din v Wandsworth LBC* [1983] 1 AC 657 at 678D; *Eastleigh BC v Walsh* [1985] 1 WLR 525 (ante, p 455).
2 *Parr v Wyre BC* (1982) 2 HLR 71 at 78; *R v Westminster CC, ex parte Chambers* (1982) 6 HLR 24 at 29.
3 Housing Act 1985, s 75.
4 *Parr v Wyre BC* (1982) 2 HLR 71 at 78. See [1982] JSWL 236 (P.Q. Watchman).

applicant has no prior connection.[5] It is also now clear that in determining the suitability of accommodation, the authority must have regard to the provisions of the Housing Act 1985 relating to slum clearance, overcrowding and houses in multiple occupation.[6]

(ii) Further offers of accommodation The full housing obligation imposed on a local authority by the Housing Act 1985 is discharged by the making of one offer of appropriate accommodation.[7] The authority is under no obligation to keep making offers to a homeless person who unreasonably refuses the accommodation which is available, even though the applicant's original state of unintentional homelessness subsists 'for a protracted period'.[8] As McCullough J held in *R v Westminster CC, ex parte Chambers*,[9] one offer suffices if, in reality, the applicant 'is experiencing one incidence of unintentional homelessness'. However, a second incidence of homelessness will impose on the housing authority a 'fresh duty', and such a 'second incidence' may arise through a material change in the applicant's circumstances which renders the first offer of accommodation now inappropriate even though it would have been entirely reasonable for him to accept the offer at the time when it was originally made. In *R v Ealing LBC, ex parte McBain*,[10] for instance, a female applicant, who then had only one child, declined accommodation which seemed entirely suitable for her. The Court of Appeal nevertheless held that the housing authority's obligation towards her revived when, on giving birth to a second child, the applicant could show that her circumstances had materially changed. The applicant did not forfeit the right to any further statutory assistance if her circumstances were subsequently so altered 'that the accommodation originally offered would, in the event, have been quite unsuitable.'[11]

(b) Duty to take reasonable steps to secure that accommodation does not cease to be available for occupation

In relation to a person who can show that he is unintentionally threatened with homelessness and has a 'priority need', the local housing authority is under a 'duty...to take reasonable steps to secure that accommodation does not cease to be available for his occupation'.[12]

(c) Duty to secure that accommodation becomes available for temporary occupation

Where a housing authority recognises that an applicant is homeless and has a

---

5   *Parr v Wyre BC* (1982) 2 HLR 71 at 78. Compare *R v Bristol CC, ex parte Browne* [1979] 1 WLR 1437 at 1443D-F.
6   Housing Act 1985, s 69(1), as substituted by Housing and Planning Act 1986, s 14(3). See, however, *R v Wandsworth LBC, ex parte Lindsay* (1986) Legal Action 124, where a housing authority was held not to have acted unreasonably in offering a ninth-floor maisonette with a dangerous balcony to a mother of two young children.
7   *R v Westminster CC, ex parte Chambers* (1982) 6 HLR 24 at 29; *R v Ealing LBC, ex parte McBain* [1985] 1 WLR 1351 at 1354F-1355B.
8   *R v Westminster CC, ex parte Chambers* (1982) 6 HLR 24 at 29.
9   (1982) 6 HLR 24 at 29f.
10 [1985] 1 WLR 1351. See [1987] JSWL 64 (B. Walsh).
11 [1985] 1 WLR 1351 at 1356C-D per Ackner LJ.
12 Housing Act 1985, s 66(2).

'priority need' but is also satisfied that he became homeless 'intentionally', the authority is statutorily obliged merely to 'secure that accommodation is made available for his occupation for such period as it considers will give him a reasonable opportunity of securing accommodation for his occupation'.[13] The authority must meanwhile furnish the applicant with 'advice' and such 'assistance' as it considers appropriate in the circumstances in any attempts which the applicant may make to find other accommodation.[14]

The period for which the housing authority may provide accommodation in pursuance of this aspect of its statutory duty may well extend to three or four months in those areas in which it is generally difficult to find accommodation at short notice.[15] In *Lally v Kensington and Chelsea Royal Borough*,[16] Browne-Wilkinson J struck down as 'unreasonable' the general policy implemented by the defendant council of allowing no more than 14 days for applicants to find other accommodation. It is clear that the standard of the temporary accommodation need not be as high as that required in relation to accommodation which is offered in compliance with the authority's full housing duty.[17]

(d) Duty to provide 'advice' and appropriate 'assistance'

In other cases, where the housing authority is not even satisfied that the applicant has demonstrated a 'priority need', the authority's duty is further down-graded, becoming a mere duty to render 'advice' and such 'assistance' as it considers 'appropriate' to the applicant's attempts to secure that accommodation becomes available for his occupation.[18] In many cases such 'advice' and 'assistance' simply take the form of pointing the applicant to bed-and- breakfast accommodation, which the applicant proceeds, typically at vast public expense, to occupy in the medium or long term.

4. REMEDIES

A powerful remedy is open to an aggrieved applicant in respect of the way in which a local housing authority has handled his application under Part III of the Housing Act 1985. Any challenge to the basic determination reached by the authority must be made by way of proceedings for judicial review,[19] in which case the onus lies on the applicant to show that the decision reached in

---

13 Housing Act 1985, s 65(3)(a). Where the applicant is 'threatened with homelessness intentionally', the authority's duty relates to the applicant's attempts to ensure that accommodation does not cease to be available for his occupation (Housing Act 1985, s 66(3)).

14 Housing Act 1985, s 65(3)(b).

15 *Lally v Kensington and Chelsea Royal Borough* (1980) *Times*, 27 March.

16 (1980) *Times*, 27 March.

17 See *Hamilton DC v Brown* [1982] SCOLAG 185; *R v Camden LBC, ex parte Wait* [1987] 1 FLR 155 at 162G-H.

18 Housing Act 1985, s 65(4). In 1985, 52,000 out of a total of 227,000 homelessness enquiries resulted in a giving of mere 'advice' and 'assistance'. See Central Statistical Office, *Social Trends No 17* (1987 edn London), p 147 (Table 8.21).

19 *Cocks v Thanet DC* [1983] 2 AC 286 at 294D-E. See [1983] JSWL 300 (P.Q. Watchman); (1983) 46 MLR 645 (M. Sunkin); (1983) 99 LQR 166 (H.W.R.W.).

his case is void on administrative law principles.[20] There has been a tendency in recent years for the remedy of judicial review to become an almost standard means of challenging every exercise of discretion by local housing authorities. In *R v Hillingdon LBC, ex parte Puhlhofer*[1] Lord Brightman expressed himself to be 'troubled' at the 'prolific use' of judicial review in this context. While accepting that the action or inaction of a local authority 'is clearly susceptible to judicial review where they have misconstrued the Act, or abused their powers or otherwise acted perversely', Lord Brightman nevertheless thought that 'great restraint' should be exercised in giving leave to proceed by judicial review.[2] In his view this form of remedy should not be used to monitor the actions of housing authorities under the homelessness legislation 'save in the exceptional case'.[3] In a clear indication of the future demeanour of the courts, Lord Brightman urged that decisions of fact should be left by the courts to the 'public body to whom Parliament has entrusted the decision-making power save in a case where it is obvious that the public body, consciously or unconsciously, are acting perversely'.[4]

This remarkable attempt to restrict access to appropriate legal remedy is, of course, a function of the quite desperate circumstances under which housing authorities are expected to administer the homelessness legislation. Where already overburdened housing resources are strained beyond their limit, it is inevitable that something should give way. In the absence of any realistic political will to remedy the particular social evil, the link which has broken apart is the integrity of the legal mechanism for relief. In the present context a wide gulf has opened up between the actual implementation of the homelessness legislation and the original social intendment of that legislation. The immediate damage is to the quality of life of the increasing numbers of homeless people. Perhaps more insidious is the damage cynically inflicted on constructive interpretations of the plain wording of well-intentioned social legislation.

20 *Cannock Chase DC v Kelly* [1978] 1 WLR 1 at 6D.
1   [1986] AC 484 at 518B.
2   [1986] AC 484 at 518B-C.
3   [1986] AC 484 at 518C.
4   [1986] AC 484 at 518D-E.

F. Residential security in the family home

CHAPTER 22

Rights of occupation

It is by now clearly established in English law that rights of occupation in land can derive from equitable entitlement under a trust for sale.[1] A beneficial co-owner behind such a trust of the family home has, qua beneficiary, an intrinsic right to occupy that property in common with any other similarly entitled beneficiaries.[2] The present chapter is, however, devoted to occupation rights which are independent of beneficial entitlement under any trust for sale. The individual members of a family may well have occupation rights in the family home which are derived from quite different sources rooted either in common law or in statute.

1. RIGHTS OF OCCUPATION ENFORCEABLE AGAINST OTHER FAMILY MEMBERS

Quite independently of title or beneficial ownership, certain rights of occupation in the family home are enforceable against other family members.

(1) The wife's common law right to occupy

It is clear that at common law a wife has a right of occupation in the matrimonial home.[3] Her entitlement in this respect is somewhat anomalous. If the home is owned by her husband, she resides there not as a trespasser nor even as a licensee,[4] but in virtue of her status as a wife. Her common law right of occupation is sui generis,[5] in that the right to be housed by her husband arises from the fact of marriage itself and is an integral component of the dependency-related notion of spousal maintenance.[6]

(a) Effect of the common law right

The wife's common law right of occupation is binding only on her husband and is not enforceable against third parties.[7] If, however, the right of occupation is

---

1 Ante, p 374.
2 There is a discussion in Chapter 25 (post, p 829) of the conditions under which a beneficial co-owner's right of occupation may be enforceable against purchasers of the family home.
3 This does not necessarily mean that the wife has any right at common law to insist on sharing residential accommodation in which her husband has set up a new home with a different partner (*Nanda v Nanda* [1968] P 351 at 354C, 357D-E).
4 *National Provincial Bank Ltd v Ainsworth* [1965] AC 1175 at 1232F.
5 *National Provincial Bank Ltd v Ainsworth* [1965] AC 1175 at 1232F per Lord Upjohn.
6 See *Gurasz v Gurasz* [1970] P 11 at 16B-C.
7 *National Provincial Bank Ltd v Ainsworth* [1965] AC 1175; *Gurasz v Gurasz* [1970] P 11 at 16C. The wife's common law right cannot be enforced if the home is owned jointly by the husband and a third party (*Chaudhry v Chaudhry* [1987] 1 FLR 347 at 350G-H).

threatened by an impending sale of the home by her husband, the wife may seek to have the sale restrained by court injunction.[8] Nowadays in an era of greater sex equality, it may even be that the spousal right to be housed has become a mutual right and may be claimed by either husband or wife.[9]

(b) Restricted scope of the common law right

The common law right to occupy the matrimonial home is available only to a de iure spouse. No similar rights exist at common law either in favour of a de facto spouse or in favour of a minor child (whether legitimate or not). A de facto spouse obviously cannot claim any right of occupation derived from the fact of marriage, and, although the point is not entirely clear, it seems that a minor child is likewise unable to claim any right of occupation based on status. Except in cases of beneficial entitlement or court order, such rights of residence as are enjoyed by a child of the family appear to rest on the concept of revocable licence both before and after his attainment of the age of majority.[10]

(2) Statutory 'rights of occupation'

The spouse's common law right of occupation in the matrimonial home is now reinforced by statute. The Matrimonial Homes Act 1967 conferred statutory 'rights of occupation' on certain categories of spouse, and these rights are now consolidated and extended by the Matrimonial Homes Act 1983. The rights created by this legislation are entirely sex-neutral, with the result that they may in appropriate cases be invoked by either husband or wife, but the statute confers no rights of occupation on family members other than a spouse.[11]

(a) Nature of the statutory 'rights of occupation'

The Matrimonial Homes Act 1983 confers on specified categories of qualifying spouse a bundle of rights known collectively as statutory 'rights of occupation'. In terms of section 1(1) of the Act a qualifying spouse, if in occupation of the matrimonial home, has a 'right not to be evicted or excluded from the dwelling house or any part thereof by the other spouse' except in pursuance of a court order.[12] Furthermore, if not in occupation of the matrimonial home, a qualifying spouse has a 'right with the leave of the court...to enter into and occupy the dwelling house'.[13]

---

8   *Lee v Lee* [1952] 2 QB 489 at 491f. Such an injunction is available unless the husband provides his wife with reasonable suitable alternative accommodation.

9   See eg *Harman v Glencross* [1985] Fam 49 at 58B-C per Ewbank J.

10   *Metropolitan Properties Co Ltd v Cronan* (1982) 44 P & CR 1 at 8. See also *Waterhouse v Waterhouse* (1905) 94 LT 133 at 134; *Stevens v Stevens* (1907) 24 TLR 20 at 21; *Egan v Egan* [1975] Ch 218 at 221D.

11   Compare the equivalent Scottish legislation, which does apply under certain circumstances to a 'cohabiting couple'. The Matrimonial Homes (Family Protection) (Scotland) Act 1981, s 18 empowers the court to grant 'occupancy rights' to a 'non-entitled partner' for a limited period where 'a man and a woman are living with each other as if they were man and wife'.

12   Matrimonial Homes Act 1983, s 1(1)(a). See generally O. Kahn-Freund, (1970) 33 MLR 601 at 610ff.

13   Matrimonial Homes Act 1983, s 1(1)(b). A spouse is regarded as still 'in occupation' of the matrimonial home even though absent temporarily in hospital (*Hoggett v Hoggett* (1980) 39 P & CR 121 at 128).

The statutory 'rights of occupation' are purely personal rights[14] and in themselves have no binding impact on purchasers of the matrimonial home unless registered in the appropriate manner.[15] The recipient of the statutory rights retains those rights for the duration of the marriage or until the other spouse himself ceases to have any beneficial, contractual or statutory right to occupy the home.[16] A spouse may at any time renounce his statutory rights in whole or part by means of a written release.[17]

(b) Categories of spouse covered by the statutory rights

The statutory 'rights of occupation' are available to any spouse who cannot claim a right of occupation by virtue of any beneficial interest or under any contract or statute, but whose spouse is entitled to occupy a dwelling house on one or other of these bases.[18] The range of the Matrimonial Homes Act 1983 is best illustrated by reference to the various patterns of ownership shown in *Fig.* 51.

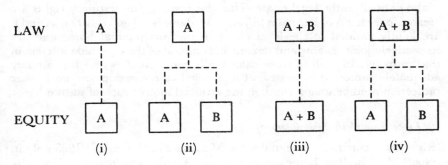

Fig. 51

(i) The non-entitled spouse In superficial terms the statutory rights are restricted to those spouses who have no right to occupy the family home other than the right of occupation derived at common law from the status of marriage. Indeed the scheme of the Matrimonial Homes Act was originally directed towards the protection of 'the bare wife'[19] who was wholly denuded of all proprietary rights

---

14 See *Wroth v Tyler* [1974] Ch 30 at 46F-G, where Megarry J described the rights as comprising 'a personal and non-assignable statutory right...the right may be said to be one which readily fits into any category known to conveyancers before 1967; the phrase sui generis seems apt, but of little help.'

15 Post, p 786. The enforcement of one spouse's statutory rights against the other spouse does not depend on any kind of registration (*Hoggett v Hoggett* (1980) 39 P & CR 121 at 127).

16 Matrimonial Homes Act 1983, s 1(10).

17 Matrimonial Homes Act 1983, s 6(1).

18 Matrimonial Homes Act 1983, s 1(1). It is not, for instance, necessary that the entitled spouse should own the legal title in the matrimonial home, since this may be held by a third party on trust to give effect to a beneficial interest in the entitled spouse (see Matrimonial Homes Act 1983, s 1(8)). For the purpose of determining whether one spouse has an existing right to occupy a dwelling house, any right to possession conferred on a mortgagee by virtue of his mortgage is to be disregarded (Matrimonial Homes Act 1983, s 8(1)).

19 This graphic phrase was frequently used by Lord Denning MR (see *Gurasz v Gurasz* [1970] P 11 at 17D; *Williams & Glyn's Bank Ltd v Boland* [1979] Ch 312 at 328C).

in the home (whether legal or equitable). Thus, if A and B are married, B will enjoy the statutory 'rights of occupation' in case (i) above (*Fig.* 51).

(ii) The beneficial co-owner The initial ambit of the Matrimonial Homes Act was extended in 1970[20] to confer the statutory 'rights of occupation' on a spouse who owns an equitable but not a legal interest in the home.[1] Such a spouse is brought within the framework of the parent statute through a fiction which effectively confers statutory rights by suspending existing rights. An equitable owner is, for present purposes, treated as if he or she were not entitled to occupy the dwelling house by virtue of his or her beneficial entitlement.[2] Thus denuded of any proprietary right of occupation, the equitable co-owner comes neatly within the terms of section 1(1) of the 1983 Act. Statutory 'rights of occupation' are, accordingly, enjoyed by B in case (ii) above (see *Fig.* 51).

(iii) The legal co-owner The only cases in which 'rights of occupation' are not granted by the Matrimonial Homes Act are those in which an equitable owner is also entitled to the legal estate. Thus, for instance, no statutory rights are created for either A or B in cases (iii) and (iv) above (see *Fig.* 51), where A and B are jointly entitled to the legal estate in the matrimonial home and are respectively joint tenants and tenants in common of the equitable interest in that property. In both of these cases the occupation of A and B is already adequately protected by reason of their legal co-ownership and no further protection need be sought through the artificial intervention of statute.[3]

(c) Property to which the statutory rights apply

'Rights of occupation' arise under the Matrimonial Homes Act 1983 only in respect of a 'dwelling house',[4] a term which is defined as including inter alia 'any building or part thereof which is occupied as a dwelling'.[5] The statutory rights cannot be claimed in respect of any property which has never served as a matrimonial home of the spouses in question.[6] If, however, these preconditions are fulfilled, it is irrelevant whether the matrimonial home to which the statutory rights attach is held by freehold or leasehold title, or whether, if the property is held on a tenancy, that tenancy is contractual or statutory.

(d) Judicial regulation of the statutory rights

Where one spouse has statutory 'rights of occupation' in the matrimonial home[7] and even where the spouses are joint tenants of the legal estate in that property,[8] it is open to either spouse to apply for a court order regulating the

---

20 Matrimonial Proceedings and Property Act 1970, s 38.
1   See Chapter 10 (ante, p 244) and Chapter 23 (post, p 808) for an examination of the circumstances which may generate beneficial ownership in the family home.
2   Matrimonial Homes Act 1983, s 1(11).
3   See *Harman v Glencross* [1986] Fam 81 at 90D, 94A.
4   Matrimonial Homes Act 1983, s 1(1).
5   Matrimonial Homes Act 1983, s 10(1). See the comparable definitional discussion necessitated by Rent Act 1977, s 1 (post, p 971).
6   Matrimonial Homes Act 1983, s 1(10). See *Whittingham v Whittingham* [1979] Fam 9 at 16B.
7   Matrimonial Homes Act 1983, s 1(2).
8   Matrimonial Homes Act 1983, s 9(1).

occupation of the home. The court may make such order as it thinks 'just and reasonable', having regard to 'the conduct of the spouses in relation to each other and otherwise, to their respective needs and financial resources, to the needs of any children and to all the circumstances of the case'.[9] The court may declare, enforce, restrict or terminate the statutory 'rights of occupation',[10] or prohibit, suspend or restrict the exercise by either spouse of the right to occupy the home.[11] The court's power to regulate 'rights of occupation' in these ways has become both important and controversial in the context of domestic violence.[12]

2. RIGHTS OF OCCUPATION ENFORCEABLE AGAINST PERSONS OUTSIDE THE FAMILY

Neither the common law rights of occupation enjoyed by spouses nor the 'rights of occupation' created by the Matrimonial Homes Act 1983 have any binding impact on persons outside the family. The purely personal nature of these rights is such that they have no effect on any third party to whom the matrimonial home may be transferred or mortgaged. This can raise a difficult problem where the legal owner of a matrimonial home disposes of either the legal title or some security interest in the property in favour of a stranger. It becomes very probable in such a case that the occupation rights enjoyed by the legal owner's spouse will be destroyed by the transaction.

(1) The 'deserted wife's equity'

It was precisely in order to protect occupation claims in the family home against the assertion of rights by third parties that during the 1950s the Court of Appeal developed the doctrine of the 'deserted wife's equity'.

(a) The doctrine

The doctrine of the 'deserted wife's equity' held that if a husband abandoned his wife, leaving her in occupation of the family home, the deserted wife acquired at the date of desertion an 'equity' which she could successfully oppose against any third party to whom her husband sold or mortgaged the home. In this way the common law rights of occupation enjoyed by a deserted wife were binding on any purchaser who took with notice of those rights.[13]

(b) Disadvantages

The doctrine of the 'deserted wife's equity', although motivated by strong family considerations,[14] proved eventually to be unacceptable in terms of

---

9 Matrimonial Homes Act 1983, s 1(3).
10 Matrimonial Homes Act 1983, s 1(2)(a).
11 Matrimonial Homes Act 1983, s 1(2)(b).
12 See *Richards v Richards* [1984] AC 174.
13 For the development of this doctrine, see *Bendall v McWhirter* [1952] 2 QB 466 at 475ff; *Ferris v Weaven* [1952] 2 All ER 233 at 236F-H; *Lee v Lee* [1952] 2 QB 489 at 492; *Jess B Woodcock & Sons Ltd v Hobbs* [1955] 1 WLR 152 at 154ff; *Westminster Bank Ltd v Lee* [1956] Ch 7 at 17ff. See also F.R. Crane, (1955) 19 Conv (NS) 343.
14 Ante, p 65.

conventional concepts of property law. The 'deserted wife's equity' became a nightmare for practising conveyancers since it represented an unregistrable, non-overreachable incumbrance which could bind purchasers on the basis of even constructive notice.[15] In effect the doctrine imposed an embarrassing onus of enquiry on any third party entering into any transaction (eg sale, lease or mortgage) with a man whose household included a resident adult female. In order to be safe from adverse claims to occupy, the purchaser had to inquire, first, whether this woman was the wife of the vendor/lessor/mortgagor and, second, whether the marriage (if there was one) was happy and stable.[16] The problem of enquiry was far-reaching. Where a husband's bank overdraft was secured on the matrimonial home, the bank might even be required to make enquiries as to his matrimonial behaviour before honouring his cheques.[17]

(c) Rejection

The doctrine of the 'deserted wife's equity' was finally destroyed in *National Provincial Bank Ltd v Ainsworth*.[18] Here the House of Lords conclusively rejected the idea that the deserted wife's rights of occupation in the matrimonial home were other than personal rights enforceable against the husband alone. Her common law rights of occupation have no impact on third parties.

(2) Registration of statutory 'rights of occupation'

The almost immediate consequence of the House of Lords' ruling in *National Provincial Bank Ltd v Ainsworth* was the enactment of the Matrimonial Homes Act 1967 (now consolidated as the Matrimonial Homes Act 1983), which was designed to fulfil some of the purposes previously served by the judge-made doctrine of the 'deserted wife's equity'. The Act conferred statutory 'rights of occupation' in the matrimonial home on certain categories of spouse, but these rights are, of course, rights *in personam* and effective only against the other spouse. However, the Matrimonial Homes Act provides a process of registration by which mere rights *in personam* may effectively be transformed into rights *in rem*.[19]

(a) Process of registration

Where one spouse enjoys statutory 'rights of occupation' under section 1(1) of

---

15   See *Rock Permanent Building Society v Kettlewell* (1956) 168 Estates Gazette 397 where Harman J described the 'equity' as 'a new terror in the surveyor's professional life' and as 'a sore subject between lawyers...a thorn in the flesh of the equitable branch of the law...'

16   See the trenchant criticisms expressed by property lawyers of the traditional mould in *Westminster Bank Ltd v Lee* [1956] Ch 7 at 22; *National Provincial Bank Ltd v Hastings Car Mart Ltd* [1964] Ch 665 at 699 per Russell LJ; *National Provincial Bank Ltd v Ainsworth* [1965] AC 1175 at 1234C-E per Lord Upjohn, 1249A-B per Lord Wilberforce. See also R.E. Megarry, (1952) 68 LQR 379 at 383.

17   See *Wroth v Tyler* [1974] Ch 30 at 42G.

18   [1965] AC 1175. See O.Kahn-Freund, (1970) 33 MLR 601 at 608ff; F.R. Crane, (1965) 29 Conv (NS) 254 at 464.

19   The Matrimonial Homes Act thus 'uses the machinery of publicity in order to transform the internal right of enjoyment into a modification of title' (O. Kahn-Freund, (1970) 33 MLR 601 at 610).

the Matrimonial Homes Act 1983, these rights constitute a registrable charge on any beneficial estate or interest held by the other spouse.[20]

(i) Entry in the register   In the case of unregistered land a Matrimonial Homes Act charge may be registered against the name of the relevant estate owner as a Class F land charge,[1] and in the case of registered land may be entered by notice as a minor interest affecting the appropriate registered title.[2] In either context the Matrimonial Homes Act charge may be entered in the relevant register notwithstanding that the registering spouse is not currently in occupation (eg because he or she has been expelled from the home or has indeed left the home voluntarily).[3] However, a spouse may never register a charge in respect of more than one dwelling-house at any one time.[4]

(ii) Registration for ulterior motives   A Matrimonial Homes Act registration can be effected quite unilaterally. It seems, somewhat controversially, to be the 'positive practice' of the Registry not to serve notice of the application for registration upon the owner of the legal estate.[5] The ease with which a charge can be registered, when combined with the potentially hostile impact of such a registration, has often provoked the criticism that the Matrimonial Homes Act facilitates 'spite' registrations. Megarry J observed in *Wroth v Tyler*[6] that the legislation has 'put into the hands of all spouses with statutory rights of occupation a weapon of great power and flexibility.' Particularly if registration occurs at an inconvenient moment in the process of contract and conveyance, the registering spouse is presented with a relatively simple, speedy and secret means of frustrating any proposed sale of the matrimonial home with which he

20   Matrimonial Homes Act 1983, s 2(1). 'Parliament has looked with particular favour upon a spouse's right to occupy the matrimonial home and has given it the status of an equitable interest...with consequential priority over subsequent equitable interests created by the other spouse...provided that the owner of the subsequent interest has notice, and notice is given by the registration of a Class F land charge or the equivalent notice on the title in the case of registered land' (*Harman v Glencross* [1986] Fam 81 at 94A-B).
1   Land Charges Act 1972, s 2(1), (7).
2   Matrimonial Homes Act 1983, s 2(8)(a). The statutory 'rights of occupation' may not be protected by the lodging of a caution (Matrimonial Homes Act 1983, s 2(9)), but the entry of a notice in the register of title does not (unlike most cases of entry of a notice) require the production of the land certificate of the registered proprietor (Land Registration Act 1925, s 64(5), as supplied by Matrimonial Homes and Property Act 1981, s 4(1)). A notice may thus be entered without the knowledge of the other spouse (post, p 788). The Law Commission has recommended that the statutory rights should henceforth be protected by notice only if the registered proprietor consents to the entry, and should in all other cases be protected by the entry of a caution (*Property Law: Third Report on Land Registration* (Law Com No 158, 31 March 1987), para 4.41).
3   *Watts v Waller* [1973] QB 153 at 175G. However, it is an improper use of the registration machinery to register a charge not for the purpose of protecting and preserving a spouse's right to 'enter into and occupy' the matrimonial home, but for some ulterior motive such as to freeze the proceeds of sale of the property (see *Barnett v Hassett* [1981] 1 WLR 1385 at 1388H, 1389C).
4   Matrimonial Homes Act 1983, s 3.
5   See *Wroth v Tyler* [1974] Ch 30 at 39B; T.B.F. Ruoff and R.B. Roper, *Law and Practice of Registered Conveyancing* (4th edn, London 1979), p 747. The practice of leaving the landowner unwarned of the registration has been severely criticised (see *Wroth v Tyler* [1974] Ch 30 at 39C), but compare Law Commission, *Family Law: Third Report on Family Property: The Matrimonial Home (Co-ownership and Occupation Rights) and Household Goods* (Law Com No 86, June 1978), para 2.85ff.
6   [1974] Ch 30 at 46B.

does not agree.[7] The stubborn or ruthless spouse is thus enabled to force on his partner a purely private and unshared desire for domestic inertia or, even worse, is enabled to require the other spouse to buy off the charge. Considerations such as these led Megarry J in *Wroth v Tyler*[8] to condemn the Matrimonial Homes Act charge as 'a companion in obloquy for what in *Keeves v Dean*...Scrutton LJ stigmatised as *monstrum horrendum informe ingens*.'[9]

(iii) Release of rights and cancellation of registration The Matrimonial Homes Act 'rights of occupation', even if registered, cease to have effect on the death of the spouse against whose estate they are registered[10] and normally come to an end on the termination of a marriage otherwise than by death.[11] There is provision for cancellation of any registration of the statutory rights in either of these events or if the court itself exercises its discretion to terminate one spouse's 'rights of occupation'.[12] A spouse may also 'release' his 'rights of occupation' in writing,[13] or may by writing agree that his 'rights of occupation' should be postponed behind some later charge on the same estate or interest.[14]

It is, moreover, an implied term of any contract for the sale of the home with vacant possession that the vendor will before completion procure the cancellation of any registration of subsisting 'rights of occupation'.[15] Considerable problems ensue if the vendor fails to secure the release of his spouse's 'rights of occupation' and the cancellation of any existing registration. In *Wroth v Tyler*,[16] for instance, a wife had secretly entered her rights on the register of her husband's title on the day following his exchange of contracts. Her action had the disastrous consequence of exposing him to liability towards his purchaser for breach of contract. The wife, who had not wanted to move house, obstinately declined to remove the entry. This refusal eventually brought about the bankruptcy of her husband (who was unable to pay the contractual damages), with the ironic result that her rights were defeated in any event by her husband's trustee in bankruptcy.[17]

7   See *Wroth v Tyler* [1974] Ch 30 (infra). Compare, however, *Barnett v Hassett* [1981] 1 WLR 1385 at 1388H, 1389C (ante, p 787).
8   [1974] Ch 30 at 64A-B.
9   Post, p 1007.
10   Matrimonial Homes Act 1983, s 2(4)(a).
11   Matrimonial Homes Act 1983, s 2(4)(b).
12   Matrimonial Homes Act 1983, s 5(1).
13   Matrimonial Homes Act 1983, s 6(1).
14   Matrimonial Homes Act 1983, s 6(3). A mortgagee who obtains priority in this way is entitled to exercise his power of sale free of any spousal 'rights of occupation', although difficulties may arise if the mortgagee failed to warn the spouse releasing the rights of the need for independent legal advice (ante, p 600).
15   Matrimonial Homes Act 1983, s 4(1). A solicitor may be liable in negligence for failing to ensure the appropriate cancellation of rights (see *Holmes v Kennard & Son* (1984) 49 P & CR 202 at 210f).
16   [1974] Ch 30.
17   Matrimonial Homes Act 1983, s 2(7), but see now Insolvency Act 1986, s 336(2)-(5) (post, p 881). As Megarry J observed ([1974] Ch 30 at 64F), 'there should be displayed in every conveyancer's office the minatory legend Cave uxorem'. The Law Commission has, however, defended the wife's exercise of her right to register her rights of occupation, arguing that such registration is 'not rendered an abuse merely because it may interfere with smooth conveyancing. It is an essential step in protecting her substantive rights and we think that to introduce restrictions on that exercise would be contrary to the policy of the Act' (see Law Commission, *Family Law: Third Report on Family Property: The Matrimonial Home (Co-ownership and Occupation Rights) and Household Goods* (Law Com No 86, June 1978), para 2.83). See also D.J. Hayton, *The Femme Fatale in Conveyancing Practice*, (1974) 38 Conv (NS) 110.

(b) Effect of registration

Once protected by entry in the appropriate register, a spouse's statutory 'rights of occupation' become binding on and enforceable against almost all third parties.[18] The one notable exception to this principle relates to the trustee in bankruptcy of the spouse against whom registration is effected. Spousal 'rights of occupation', even though duly registered, are at best effective for only a limited period against such a trustee in bankruptcy.[19] The mere registration of statutory rights cannot preclude indefinitely the possibility that the matrimonial home may have to be sold with vacant possession in order to meet the outstanding claims of the bankrupt spouse's creditors. The incidence of bankruptcy is, of course, considerably increased in circumstances of marital breakdown, not least because a husband's financial resources may be impossibly stretched by the strain of attempting to support two family units. Few men can afford successive polygamy. In the immediate context, as so often in land law, the commercial interest (as represented here by the husband's creditors) prevails over the family interest (as typically represented here by a deserted family's need of residential security).[20]

(c) Consequence of non-registration

It is a clear consequence of a spouse's failure to register the statutory 'rights of occupation' that these rights become ineffective against a purchaser for value of any interest in the land.[1] Moreover, in relation to registered land the Matrimonial Homes Act 1983[2] specifically excludes any possibility that the unprotected rights may be claimed as an overriding interest even on behalf of a spouse who remains 'in actual occupation' of the matrimonial home.[3]

3. THE FUTURE OF THE MATRIMONIAL HOMES ACT

From the very enactment of the Matrimonial Homes Act 1967 the scheme of statutory 'rights of occupation' has been fraught with difficulty.

(1) Mass invalidation of charges

The consequence of non-registration of the Matrimonial Homes Act 'rights of occupation' reveals one curious and significant feature of the benefits supposedly conferred by this legislation. In the case of most other registrable incumbrances in respect of land, the plain statutory expectation is that

---

18 Law of Property Act 1925, s 198(1) (ante, p 114); Land Registration Act 1925, s 20(1) (ante, p 162).
19 Insolvency Act 1986, s 336(2)-(5), displacing the effect of Matrimonial Homes Act 1983, s 2(7) (post, p 881).
20 Ante, pp 257, 279. There is here an irony of legislative history. The judge-made doctrine of the 'deserted wife's equity' held that the deserted wife's right of occupation was fully opposable against even her husband's trustee in bankruptcy (see *Bendall v McWhirter* [1952] 2 QB 466 at 478, but compare *National Provincial Bank Ltd v Ainsworth* [1965] AC 1175 at 1240B).
1 Land Charges Act 1972, s 4(8) (ante, p 115); Land Registration Act 1925, ss 20(1), 59(6) (ante, p 162).
2 Matrimonial Homes Act 1983, s 2(8)(b).
3 Land Registration Act 1925, s 70(1)(g) (ante, p 182).

registration will be effected in all situations where registration is appropriate, on pain of the dire penalty that rights left unregistered will become ineffective against third parties.[4] It can hardly have been the case, however, that the legislature contemplated that there would be mass registrations in respect of all matrimonial homes, regardless of the stability of the relevant marriage relationship. Such vigilance on the part of those who enjoy Matrimonial Homes Act 'rights of occupation' would have the disastrous effect of swamping the registries with literally millions of applications for registration. In *Wroth v Tyler*[5] Megarry J thought that 'it would not be surprising if in fact the Act in the main has been operating on a basis of the mass invalidation of the statutory charges for want of registration, with registration being effected only in cases of actual or impending disputes.'

(2) Lack of public awareness

It seems anomalous that the operation of a statute of such wide social significance should depend on the ignorance or apathy of the citizens whose protection it is designed to secure. A further irony consists in the fact that the registration of spousal rights of occupation is often abused for malicious purposes by those who need protection least, but is frequently not effected by those who stand most clearly in need of the protection which registration provides.[6] This raises at least some question as to the desirability of legislation which in practice requires that protection of occupation should depend not only on a high level of awareness of the legal need to register rights but also on a willingness to undertake an 'essentially hostile type of proceeding'.[7] As Ormrod LJ indicated in *Williams & Glyn's Bank Ltd v Boland*,[8] the remedy offered by the Matrimonial Homes Act is 'usually "too little and too late"'.

(3) Automatic co-ownership of the matrimonial home

The fundamental difficulty associated with the Matrimonial Homes Act is the fact that an inherently worthwhile measure of reform has been substantially vitiated by the attempt to engraft family-based rights on to an existing system of registration of incumbrances governed by the general law of property. The problems which have arisen under the Matrimonial Homes Act are almost entirely attributable to the fact that this statute is not rooted unequivocally in family considerations such as those which underpin the homestead legislation in force in other parts of the Commonwealth.

It is perhaps inevitable that the security of spouses will be assured only when the Matrimonial Homes Act 1983 finally gives way to a rule of automatic co-ownership of the legal estate in the matrimonial home during marriage—a

4   Ante, p 190.
5   [1974] Ch 30 at 46A-B.
6   See *Williams & Glyn's Bank Ltd v Boland* [1979] Ch 312 at 328E-F per Lord Denning MR, who pointed out that the Matrimonial Homes Act 'was of precious little use to [the wife], at any rate when she was living at home in peace with her husband. She would never have heard of a Class F charge: and she would not have understood it if she had.'
7   *Williams & Glyn's Bank Ltd v Boland* [1979] Ch 312 at 339F.
8   [1979] Ch 312 at 339G.

regime not brought about by the application of commercialist principles of property law but resulting instead from the status of marriage. The social purpose of the current matrimonial homes legislation would be more effectively achieved through the statutory imposition of such a scheme of co-ownership.[9] The adoption of this solution would mean that no disposition of the legal estate could ever occur without the active participation of both spouses. Both would have to sign any document of transfer, lease or mortgage. A spouse's occupation of the matrimonial home would thus be rendered absolutely secure against hidden transactions with the title and there would be no need for any hostile registration to be effected where existing marital tension already threatens domestic harmony. A principle of automatic co-ownership would cut clean through the difficulties which have been exposed in the operation of the Matrimonial Homes Act, but as yet no legislation incorporating this principle has been enacted in England.[10]

9　Post, p 862.
10　Compare the presumption of joint tenancy of the matrimonial home introduced by Marriage Act 1958 (Victoria), s 161(4)(b), as amended by Marriage (Property) Act 1962, s 3 (see eg *Hogben v Hogben* [1964] VR 468 at 472f). The Victorian legislation has now been superseded for almost all practical purposes by the federal jurisdiction exercised under the Family Law Act 1975. However, it has been proposed that the Victorian model could serve as a basis on which to construct a new and comprehensive matrimonial property regime in Australia both during and on the termination of marriage (see Parliament of the Commonwealth of Australia, *Family Law in Australia* (Report of the Joint Select Committee on the Family Law Act, July 1980), Vol 1, para 5.158 (Recommendation 37)). The Australian Law Reform Commission has left open the question of a statutory presumption of joint ownership of the matrimonial home (*Matrimonial Property Law* (Discussion Paper No 22, June 1985), paras 178ff).

CHAPTER 23

Family arrangements

Some of the most difficult problems of land law occur where the doctrinaire principles of property intersect with the realities of family living. Nowhere has this been more obvious than in the attempts made in English law during the last 20 years to regulate the area of 'family arrangements'.

1. INFORMAL ORIGINS OF FAMILY ARRANGEMENTS

It is an inherent characteristic of the property relations of family members that these relations are marked by a greater degree of informality and by a lesser degree of specificity than are usually present in the property relations of strangers. That this should be so is explained by a number of factors.

(1) Non-commercial nature of familial relations

Familial relations are in general non-commercial and do not often involve the prudential calculation of cash advantage which so heavily colours the relationships of strangers. It is normally the case that hard bargaining and the cold definition of legal rights are alien to the spirit in which family interaction is conducted. It is also generally true that younger members of family groups are subject to some measure of disability (both legal and economic), and are therefore more likely to be the beneficiaries of transactions motivated by a wholly non-commercial sense of generosity.

(2) Significance of long-term social credit

It is undeniable, of course, that there is also a more subtle sense in which the reciprocity which is so keenly sought in the hard-nosed bargaining of strangers is no less effectively secured in the family context. Since family living implies at least some continuity of relationship between family members, the expected reciprocity of family transactions may take many years to be fully realised. As William J. Goode once said,[1] the continuity of family relationships means that husband and wife, as well as children, 'enjoy a much longer line of social credit than they would have if they were engaged in random social interaction with strangers.' This in turn means that 'an individual can give more at one time to a family member, knowing that in the long run this will not be a loss, for the other person (or someone else) is likely to reciprocate at some point.' The net result is that members of family and kinship groups commonly participate in informally based living arrangements which are negotiated—if they are

---

1   'The Resistance of Family Forces to Industrialisation', in J.M. Eekelaar and S.N. Katz (ed), *Marriage and Cohabitation in Contemporary Societies* (Toronto 1980), p xiv.

discussed at all—not in clearly defined terms of legal entitlement, but rather in vaguely expressed terms of anticipated mutuality.

2. THE ANALYTICAL PROBLEMS RAISED BY FAMILY ARRANGEMENTS

It is the concern of the present chapter to examine some of the law relating to informal 'family arrangements'. The legal problems raised in this area are not inconsiderable. Family arrangements may take a diversity of forms, and are commonly characterised by obscure intentions, unexpressed terms, mixed motives and a high degree of mutual misunderstanding.[2] There is nevertheless a strong impulse to ensure that the law of property applies indifferently to all kinds of cohabitation, whether that cohabitation be heterosexual, homosexual, platonic, dual or multiple in nature. A further dimension of difficulty is introduced by the sharing of accommodation with elderly or incapacitated relatives—a phenomenon of increasing frequency as the proportion of old people in the community continues to rise and the present housing problem becomes ever more acute.[3]

(1) Problems of contractual classification

It is far from easy to analyse the effect of family arrangements by reference to traditional legal categories.[4] Indeed, by nature and form such arrangements are so unlegalistic that for many years the courts declined on principle to attribute to family members any intention at all to create legally actionable relationships. For many people, discussion of the legal implications of their living arrangements would, in any case, be inconsistent with the mutual trust on which their relationship is based.[5] It was Atkin LJ who observed in *Balfour v Balfour*[6] that family arrangements

are outside the realm of contracts altogether. The common law does not regulate the form of agreements between spouses. Their promises are not sealed with seals and sealing wax. The consideration that really obtains for them is that natural love and affection which counts for so little in these cold Courts...The parties themselves are advocates, judges, Courts, sheriff's officer and reporter. In respect of these promises each house is a domain into which the King's writ does not seek to run, and to which his officers do not seek to be admitted.[7]

It is clear, however, that this non-interventionist view no longer retains the force which it once had. As appears from much of the remainder of this chapter, the courts are increasingly willing to accept and to enforce some degree of contractual ordering of family relationships by the parties themselves.[8]

---

2   In view of their frequently chaotic and indeterminate nature, Croom-Johnson LJ has described such situations as 'family non-arrangements' (see *Rogers v Eller* (Unreported, Court of Appeal, 20 May 1986)).
3   Central Statistical Office, *Social Trends No 17* (1987 edn London), p 31 (Chart 1.5).
4   See J.D. Davies, (1979) 8 Sydney LR 578 at 580f.
5   See *Doohan v Nelson* [1973] 2 NSWLR 320 at 324G-325A.
6   [1919] 2 KB 571 at 579.
7   See also *Pettitt v Pettitt* [1970] AC 777 at 796A; *Burns v Burns* [1984] Ch 317 at 335C.
8   See *Hardwick v Johnson* [1978] 1 WLR 683 at 688A-E. See also G. Temple, *Freedom of Contract and Intimate Relationships*, 8 Harvard Jnl of Law and Public Policy 121 (1985).

(2) **Problems of property classification**

It is just as problematical to assimilate family arrangements within the law of property. The rights conferred by such arrangements almost invariably lack the clarity of definition which marks out a right of property[9] and are often vitiated by non-compliance with some requirement of written form. The technicalities of property law are 'terra incognita and rather frightening to many people',[10] and it is not surprising that the legal aspects of domestic life are often left ill-defined and vague.

(3) **Problems of public policy**

Where a family arrangement involves some kind of de facto relationship, the application of property law has tended in the past to be complicated by factors of public policy. A pervasive influence in this area has been the fear lest the conferment of property rights be confused with a rewarding of supposed immorality.[11] It is only in relatively recent years that the courts have regarded themselves as no longer bound to use the withholding of property or other rights as a means of evidencing an official social displeasure with unorthodox living arrangements.[12] This altered direction does not necessarily reflect a new judicial liberalism or even an incipient principle of moral neutrality in the courts. In many cases the new approach is more clearly the product of a judicial desire to deprive unmarried male cohabitees of any possible haven of effective legal immunity. Alongside this motivation there has been a strong impulse to ensure that unmarried partners should not be able to contract out of legal control by opting deliberately for some autonomous or supposedly free-thinking relationship above and beyond the law.[13]

In the absence of any systematic resolution of the problems posed by diffuse relationships of cohabitation, recent years have witnessed the emergence of a number of different approaches to the property difficulties caused by family arrangements. These approaches tend to merge into each other with distressing terminological imprecision, thus making clear exposition of the relevant principles an almost impossible task. The range of analytical solutions evidenced in the caselaw includes the following.

3. LEGALLY INEFFECTIVE RELATIONSHIPS

It is clear that some family arrangements have no significant long-term legal effect other than that created by a bare or contractual occupation licence.[14] In

---

9   'The conception of a normal married couple spending the long winter evenings hammering out agreements about their possessions seems grotesque...' (*Pettitt v Pettitt* [1970] AC 777 at 810E-F per Lord Hodson). See also *Gissing v Gissing* [1971] AC 886 at 896B-D per Lord Reid; *Burns v Burns* [1984] Ch 317 at 334H; *Doohan v Nelson* [1973] 2 NSWLR 320 at 323F; *C v C* [1976] IR 254 at 258; *McGill v S* [1979] IR 283 at 289.

10   *Gissing v Gissing* [1971] AC 886 at 896B per Lord Reid.

11   See *Holman v Johnson* (1775) 1 Cowp 341 at 343, 98 ER 1120 at 1121.

12   See eg *Seidler v Schallhofer* [1982] 2 NSWLR 80 at 89G-91A; *Niederberger v Memnook* (1982) 130 DLR (3d) 353 at 356f.

13   [1982] CLJ 30 at 34.

14   See eg *Tunley v James* (Unreported, Court of Appeal, No 81 03701, 7 April 1982); *Warnes v Hedley* (Unreported, Court of Appeal, 31 January 1984); *Rogers v Eller* (Unreported, Court of Appeal, 20 May 1986).

Hoskins v Hoskins,[15] for instance, three brothers owned a small chain of shops. When one of the brothers married, he was allowed, with his new wife and children, to move into rent-free accommodation above one of the shops owned by the partnership. The purpose of the arrangement was supposedly short-term and was intended to last only until a more permanent home could be found. Shortly thereafter the marriage broke down by reason of the desertion of the husband. The wife resisted the claim for possession which was eventually brought against her by her husband's brothers, but the Court of Appeal had no doubt that her status was merely that of a bare licensee under 'an ad hoc short-term licence free of charge'. In the circumstances it was quite impossible to impute to the parties any intention to create an indefinite or irrevocable accommodation licence.

Even where money changes hands under a family arrangement, the arrangement itself can rest so heavily upon the presence of a gift relationship between the parties that there is no question of loan-based contractual rights or equity shareholding behind any sort of resulting or constructive trust.[16] It is entirely feasible that payments of money may pass between members of the same family without any intention that a binding legal relationship of any kind should arise.[17] There is a ready presumption in the domestic context that payments of money merely represent contributions towards current living expenses and outgoings[18] rather than contributions which generate a beneficial or other entitlement in the family home for the contributor.[19] It can only rarely be the case, for instance, that a beneficial interest in the home is acquired by the son who lives at home with his parents and gives his mother part of his weekly wage packet.

Even a pattern of regular payments into a common pool may result in no more than the minimal protection afforded under an occupation licence. In *Hannaford v Selby*,[20] for example, a young couple bought a house in their own names with the aid of a mortgage loan. They moved into this property with their children and with the wife's elderly parents. Over a substantial period of time the parents paid £5 per week into the family purse, and the wife's father indulged his 'one absorbing hobby' by working hard in the garden. When friction developed between the three generations living in the house, the wife's parents claimed to have acquired a beneficial interest in the home on the ground that their financial contributions had generated some form of trust in their favour. This argument was rejected by Goulding J, who took the view that their weekly payments had not been made with any intention of acquiring an interest in the property, but represented simply 'a contribution to expenses

---

15 Unreported, Court of Appeal, 3 December 1981.
16 Evidence of a donative intention excludes any possibility of a resulting trust (ante, p 261).
17 See eg *Walker v Walker* (Unreported, Court of Appeal, 12 April 1984), where a father had announced at his son's wedding that he proposed to give the newly married couple money to set up a house. See also *Julian v Furby* (Unreported, Court of Appeal, No 79 15962, 24 November 1981), where a father-in-law was held to have made a gift of his labour in effecting improvements.
18 *Gross v French* (1975) 238 Estates Gazette 39 at 41; *Rogers v Eller* (Unreported, Court of Appeal, 20 May 1986). See also *Baumgartner v Baumgartner* [1985] 2 NSWLR 406 at 419C.
19 The contributor cannot usually be said to have advanced the money 'in the character of a purchaser' (ante, p 262).
20 (1976) 239 Estates Gazette 811.

in consideration of being allowed to live with the plaintiffs in the house.'[1] Accordingly the parents' occupation licence was revocable on reasonable notice.[2]

4. LOAN

Another possible analysis of legal relations within a family arrangement is that based on some express or (more usually) implied contract of loan. Any presumption of trust which might otherwise arise on the purchase of a family home may be displaced by evidence that the contributor of moneys intended merely to make a loan.[3] It is clear that a lender does not advance money 'in the character of a purchaser' and can take no aliquot beneficial interest in property acquired with his money.[4] In such a case his rights comprise essentially the right to recover the debt by way of action on the contract of loan.

(1) Occupation lien pending repayment

In recent years, however, the loan analysis has proved to have several important implications. It is quite common in the context of family arrangements that money should be lent towards the purchase of property on the understanding that the lender should have some form of residential privilege in the property pending the repayment of his loan. It is also frequently the case in such arrangements that no term date is fixed in relation to the loan and there may be only the haziest of intentions as to how or when the money is to be repaid. Particularly where the lender is an elderly person, the provision of loan moneys returnable at some unspecified future date tends to merge obscurely with an anticipated devolution of property by way of succession. In such circumstances the courts have often recognised the primarily contractual nature of the relationship, while awarding the lender some form of occupation lien pending repayment. This form of remedy is readily coupled, in somewhat imprecise association, with related notions of irrevocable licence, constructive trust and proprietary estoppel.

(2) The protection of the lender

Both the flexibility and the uncertainty of the law in this area were demonstrated in *In re Sharpe (A Bankrupt)*.[5] Here S had acquired a leasehold interest in a shop and maisonette, much of the purchase price of this property being contributed by S's 77 year-old aunt, J. In order to raise her contribution to the property, J had sold her existing home and had moved into the maisonette with S and his wife on the understanding that she would be able to

---

1   (1976) 239 Estates Gazette 811. Compare, however, *Timms v Timms* (1973) 226 Estates Gazette 1565, where the Court of Appeal preferred to find in favour of a tenancy rather than a family arrangement.
2   (1976) 239 Estates Gazette 811 at 813 (six months' notice given).
3   Ante, p 261.
4   *In re Cooke* (1857) 6 Ir Ch R 430 at 438.
5   [1980] 1 WLR 219. See [1980] Conv 207 (J. Martin); (1980) 96 LQR 336 (G. Woodman); A.R. Everton, [1982] Conv 119 at 125ff.

stay there for as long as she wished. S later became bankrupt and his trustee in bankruptcy contracted to sell the leasehold premises to P with vacant possession. When S's trustee in bankruptcy moved for vacant possession, J argued that she had an interest in the premises.

Browne-Wilkinson J declined to hold that J had an interest in the property by way of resulting trust, taking the view that the moneys paid by J had been paid by way of loan.[6] However, he was inclined to agree that J had acquired 'something less than an aliquot share of the equity in the premises, namely, the right to stay on in the premises until the money she provided indirectly to acquire them has been repaid.'[7] Browne-Wilkinson J accepted that such a right had a somewhat mixed derivation which drew support from analogous concepts of proprietary estoppel, constructive trust and irrevocable licence. In his view the right claimed by J was based upon 'the line of recent Court of Appeal decisions which has spelt out irrevocable licences from informal family arrangements, and in some cases characterised such licences as conferring some equity or equitable interest under a constructive trust.'[8]

Browne-Wilkinson J thought that the principles lying behind these decisions had not yet been 'fully explored' and pointed out that 'on occasion it seems that such rights are found to exist simply on the ground that to hold otherwise would be a hardship to the plaintiff.'[9] He was, however, of the opinion that recent authorities had established the proposition that

[I]f the parties have proceeded on a common assumption that the plaintiff is to enjoy a right to reside in a particular property and in reliance on that assumption the plaintiff has expended money or otherwise acted to his detriment, the defendant will not be allowed to go back on that common assumption and the court will imply an irrevocable licence or trust which will give effect to that common assumption.[10]

Accordingly Browne-Wilkinson J concluded that the circumstances in which J had lent her money to facilitate the purchase in the name of S plainly gave rise to 'some right' in J. It was relevant that J had 'only loaned the money as part of a wider scheme, an essential feature of which was that she was to make her home in the property to be acquired with the money loaned'.[11] Browne-Wilkinson J ruled that the right thus generated on J's behalf, 'whether it be called a contractual licence or an equitable licence or an interest under a constructive trust',[12] was binding not only upon S but also upon S's trustee in bankruptcy, who simply stepped into the shoes of the debtor. J had a right to

---

6 [1980] 1 WLR 219 at 222F. The loan analysis of the relationship was made inevitable by the fact that, after S became bankrupt, J (acting on her solicitor's advice) obtained from him a promissory note for £15,700. The parties thereby clearly indicated that the moneys paid by J to S were to be repayable.

7 [1980] 1 WLR 219 at 223B-C. For other attempts to resolve the 'granny flat' problem, see *Hussey v Palmer* [1972] 1 WLR 1286 (ante, p 289); *Broughall v Hunt* (Unreported, Chancery Division, 1 February 1983); *Clayton v Green* (1979) NZ Recent Law 139; *Lepel v Huthnance* (1979) NZ Recent Law 269.

8 [1980] 1 WLR 219 at 223C.

9 [1980] 1 WLR 219 at 223C-D.

10 [1980] 1 WLR 219 at 223E-F.

11 [1980] 1 WLR 219 at 223H.

12 [1980] 1 WLR 219 at 224A.

live in the property until her loan was repaid, and it followed that the trustee in bankruptcy took the property subject to that right.[13]

5. IRREVOCABLE LICENCE

There has been an increasing tendency in recent years for the courts to invoke the concept of the licence in order to resolve the property problems created by ill-defined living arrangements. Just as family arrangements lend themselves only with difficulty to conventional property classification, so it is no accident that the occupation licence—itself currently in some limbo in the law of property[14]—has emerged in this context as an appropriate explanatory device.

There is a distinct chronological pattern in the way in which the courts have drawn on the concept of licence in order to regulate those aspects of domestic living arrangements which are left untouched by other, more heavily property-oriented, concepts. In *Pettitt v Pettitt*[15] and *Gissing v Gissing*[16] the House of Lords effectively precluded the law of trusts from having much positive application to informal family arrangements. The required elements of conscious understanding or 'common intention' in which the House of Lords rooted the origins of trust were inevitably alien to the informal and chaotic nature of most kinds of family arrangement.[17] The device of the licence suddenly seemed to provide the flexibility of approach to family arrangements which the clumsy and doctrinaire concepts of trust law so conspicuously lacked.

Developments in this area over the past two decades have been closely linked with the emerging recognition of the phenomenon known as the 'licence coupled with an equity'.

(1) The 'licence coupled with an equity'

Already in *National Provincial Bank Ltd v Hastings Car Mart Ltd*,[18] Lord Denning MR had adumbrated his understanding of the 'licence coupled with an equity'.[19] This notion represented a constructive cross-fertilisation of the old common law concept of the 'licence coupled with a grant'[20] with the traditional equitable doctrine that an 'equity' may be raised by detrimental reliance on a freely given undertaking. Thus, in the *National Provincial Bank* case, Lord Denning had held that a 'licence coupled with an equity' arises where 'the owner of land grants a licence to another to go upon land and occupy it for a specific period or a prescribed purpose.' If 'on the faith of that

---

13   [1980] 1 WLR 219 at 224F-225D (ante, p 262). Although this was sufficient to dispose of the issue between J and S's trustee in bankruptcy, Browne-Wilkinson J observed that P, who was not a party to the present proceedings, would not necessarily be bound by such rights as J might have. In fact, Browne-Wilkinson J indicated that 'as a purchaser without express notice' P might well take priority over J in any action for specific performance of his contract ([1980] 1 WLR 219 at 226G). See Chapter 13 (ante, p 426).
14   See Chapter 15 (ante, p 549).
15   [1970] AC 777 (ante, p 246).
16   [1971] AC 886 (ante, p 258).
17   See Chapter 10 (ante, p 258).
18   [1964] Ch 665 at 686ff (ante, p 546).
19   This concept had long been a part of Lord Denning's jurisprudence. See *Errington v Errington and Woods* [1952] 1 KB 290 at 295ff (ante, p 547).
20   Ante, p 539.

authority' the licensee enters into occupation and does work 'or in some other way alters his position to his detriment', then the owner is precluded from revoking the licence at his will. The court, acting in exercise of its equitable jurisdiction, will restrain not only the original licensor, but also any 'successor in title who takes the land with knowledge of the arrangement that has been made.'

This articulation of the 'licence coupled with an equity', one of Lord Denning's most important and distinctive contributions to the law of property, was to stimulate several related developments in the field of both contractual licences and proprietary estoppel.[1]

(2) Contractual licence

Following the effective foreclosure of traditional trust remedies by the critical decisions in *Pettitt* and *Gissing*, the Court of Appeal evinced a clear tendency in the early 1970s to seek a resolution of the property dimension of family arrangements in some extended version of the contractual licence. Typical of this movement was the decision in *Tanner v Tanner*.[2] Here the Court of Appeal held that a young mother had been offered accommodation, by way of implied contractual licence, by the father of her two twin children. By giving up her former flat in order to move into a house provided by her lover, the woman had acquired a contractual right to accommodation so long as her children 'were of school age and the accommodation was reasonably required for her and the children'.[3] The woman was accordingly awarded £2,000 as compensation when she was later wrongfully evicted from the house.

The decision in *Tanner* was nevertheless to raise almost as many questions as it purported to resolve. Lord Denning MR had reached his unorthodox conclusion in this case by reference to an implied contractual undertaking which can only be described as somewhat artificial.[4] He had been prepared, 'if need be...[to] impose the equivalent of a contract by' the woman's lover.[5] He even seemed at one point in his judgment to invoke a doctrine of remedial constructive trust,[6] arguing that by his wrongful termination of the woman's licence the plaintiff had 'obtained an unjust benefit and should make restitution.'[7] It is not perhaps surprising that the more extreme aspects of this doctrine of implied contractual licence were disavowed in other 'family arrangement' cases.[8] As the *Tanner* approach seemed increasingly to lack credibility, the focal point of the 'family arrangement' decisions began instead to move away from strained implications of contract towards more overtly equitable devices of licence and proprietary estoppel.[9]

1　Ante, p 386.
2　[1975] 1 WLR 1346 (ante, p 544). See also I.J. Hardingham, (1979-80) 12 Melbourne ULR 356.
3　[1975] 1 WLR 1346 at 1350E.
4　Ante, p 544.
5　[1975] 1 WLR 1346 at 1350F.
6　Post, p 811.
7　[1975] 1 WLR 1346 at 1351B.
8　Ante, p 544. See eg *Horrocks v Forray* [1976] 1 WLR 230 at 238H-239E; *Chandler v Kerley* [1978] 1 WLR 693 at 698G-H; *Johnson v Johnson* (Unreported, Court of Appeal, 11 March 1986); *Rogers v Eller* (Unreported, Court of Appeal, 20 May 1986).
9　See E. Ellis, (1979) 95 LQR 11.

(3) Equitable licence

A slightly different form of the licence approach emerged temporarily with the decision of the Court of Appeal in *Hardwick v Johnson*.[10] Here the plaintiff was a mother who, in her own name, purchased a house for occupation by her son and daughter-in-law. It was arranged that the couple would pay the mother £7 per week, and it had been vaguely supposed by all concerned that these periodic payments would eventually counter-balance the purchase price. It was not clear, however, whether the payments were in respect of rent or represented instead a kind of instalment purchase of the house. Nor were any terms agreed as to an eventual conveyance of the property to the couple, although it was probably anticipated that the house would be inherited by them.

The arrangement broke down when the husband left his wife, and the mother purported to terminate the right of the wife to occupy the house. Lord Denning MR ruled that, in dealing with informal and ill-defined family arrangements of this kind, the court has to 'look at all the circumstances and spell out the legal relationship...and will find the terms of that relationship according to what reason and justice require.'[11] He considered that the present arrangement created a 'personal licence...in the nature of an equitable licence'. He therefore held that the licence was not revocable at the will of the mother, and that the court would not order possession in her favour at least so long as the daughter-in-law was ready to pay the £7 per week.[12]

Even this approach may have appeared to be an over-broad response to the messy and ill-defined complexities of family arrangements,[13] and it was not long before the courts had moved again in the direction of a revitalised version of the doctrine of proprietary estoppel.

(4) Proprietary estoppel

Towards the end of the 1970s it became increasingly clear that the jurisprudence of proprietary estoppel might afford a flexible means of enabling the courts to do justice in the light of the interaction and expectations of the litigants in 'family arrangement' cases.[14] The remedies available on a showing of proprietary estoppel ranged from the recognition of long-term occupation rights in the claimant to the award of money compensation for services rendered.[15]

(a) Occupation rights

A typical example of the way in which the courts could fashion discretionary relief in this area was provided by the decision of the Court of Appeal in *Greasley v Cooke*.[16] Here the defendant, C, cross-claimed for a declaration that she had a

---

10   [1978] 1 WLR 683.
11   [1978] 1 WLR 683 at 688D.
12   [1978] 1 WLR 683 at 689E-F. See also *Timms v Timms* (1973) 226 Estates Gazette 1565, where a payment of 'rent' by one sister-in-law to another was found to have created a tenancy.
13   For extremely limiting remarks about the scope of *Hardwick v Johnson*, see *Hoskins v Hoskins* (Unreported, Court of Appeal, 3 December 1981); *Rogers v Eller* (Unreported, Court of Appeal, 20 May 1986).
14   For a discussion of the doctrine of proprietary estoppel, see Chapter 13 (ante, p 386).
15   Ante, p 416.
16   [1980] 1 WLR 1306. See [1981] Conv 154 (R.E. Annand); (1981) 44 MLR 461 (G. Woodman).

right to occupy a house rent-free for the remainder of her life. She had entered the house at the age of 16 as a living-in maid to the then owner, a widower with four children. She had at first been paid a weekly wage, but after eight years of paid employment she had begun to cohabit in the house with one of the owner's sons, K. For almost the next 30 years C looked after members of the family, including a daughter who suffered from severe mental illness, but received during this period no financial reward for her services. C was later to allege that she had not asked for payment precisely because she had been encouraged by members of the family (including G, one of the present plaintiffs) to believe that she could regard the property as her home for the rest of her life.

When both the original owner and his son, K, had died, the remaining members of the family brought an action for possession against C. The county court judge declined to recognise that any proprietary estoppel had arisen in favour of C, holding that such a claim must fail because C had spent no money on the property. This decision was reversed by the Court of Appeal in a ruling which plainly met the justice of the case but which may well have strained the doctrine of proprietary estoppel beyond its proper bounds. Lord Denning MR emphasised that neither the expenditure of money nor strict proof of reliance was a necessary element in a claim of proprietary estoppel.[17] Here it was sufficient that C had 'stayed on in the house', looking after its needy occupants, 'when otherwise she might have left and got a job elsewhere.'[18] Lord Denning thus led the Court of Appeal in holding that an 'equity' had been raised in favour of C, in that she had acted on the faith of an assurance given to her 'in such circumstances that it would be unjust and inequitable for the party making the assurance to go back on it.'[19] C was accordingly given a right of residence in the house for the remainder of her life.

(b) Money compensation

Not every successful plea of proprietary estoppel in a family arrangement will result in the award of rights of occupancy. Where an estoppel is shown to exist, it is the long-established practice of the court to grant only such remedy as is required to satisfy the 'equity' raised in favour of the particular claimant.[20] In some cases it is eminently possible that the 'minimum equity' required for the purpose of doing justice to the claimant may amount to no more than an order for money compensation. In *Dodsworth v Dodsworth*,[1] for instance, the owner of a bungalow had allowed the present defendants (who were her younger brother and his wife) to live with her in that property. The defendants proceeded to spend some £700 on improvements to the bungalow in the expectation that they could live in the property during the indefinite future. It was not contested

17 [1980] 1 WLR 1306 at 1311G-1312A. In a phrase which has since been somewhat misunderstood, Lord Denning expressed the view that there was 'no need for her to prove that she acted to her detriment or to her prejudice'. Some have taken this statement to mark an abrogation of any requirement of detriment in estoppel cases, but this interpretation has since been expressly disavowed by Dunn LJ in *Watts v Story* (Unreported, Court of Appeal, 14 July 1983). See also *Greasley v Cooke* [1980] 1 WLR 1306 at 1313H-1314A per Dunn LJ.
18 [1980] 1 WLR 1306 at 1312A.
19 [1980] 1 WLR 1306 at 1311G-H.
20 Ante, p 413.
1 (1973) 228 Estates Gazette 1115 (ante, p 418).

that an equity of estoppel had arisen on these facts, but the Court of Appeal considered that the appropriate remedy in the circumstances comprised merely the return of the defendants' capital outlay together with some compensation for the labour invested in making the improvements.[2] The defendants' complaint had been essentially that it would be unfair to evict them in the light of their detrimental reliance on the assurances given to them, but in the Court's view this objection was easily deflected by a simple reimbursement of the money expended by them.[3]

(c) *Retreat from the wide application of estoppel*

Although the estoppel doctrine often appears to supply the adaptable framework required for dealing satisfactorily with the diffuse and uncertain circumstances of 'family arrangement' cases, it is by no means clear that subsequent courts have viewed liberal applications of the estoppel approach with any great favour.

There has been a tendency in recent years for the courts to emphasise more keenly the requirement that the estoppel claimant be shown to have incurred a 'detriment' which extends beyond mere emotional trauma or the inconvenience of a changed lifestyle.[4] In *Watts v Story*,[5] for instance, the Court of Appeal rejected a claim of estoppel in spite of substantial evidence of disadvantage suffered by the claimant. The claimant here had given up a Rent Act protected flat and had moved from a settled life in his home town in order to live with and look after his elderly grandmother. There was evidence that she had promised him that, in return for his services, her house would be his when she died. In rejecting the claim of estoppel, Slade LJ declared that it was right in such cases to approach estoppel claims 'with a degree of caution' not least because, if successful, the plea of estoppel 'may have the drastic effect of conferring on one person a permanent, irrevocable interest in the land of another, even though he has given no consideration for such acquisition, by way of contractual arrangement, and no legally effective gift of it has been made in his favour.'[6]

(d) *Doctrinal controversy*

In the current English caselaw on proprietary estoppel there appears to be a divergence of approach between the formalistic-conservative stance adopted by the hard-nosed property lawyers and the liberal-humane view favoured by more imaginative judicial souls. Epitomising the former approach, Judge Jonathan Parker QC ruled in *Coombes v Smith*[7] that no estoppel could be

---

2   (1973) 228 Estates Gazette 1115 at 1117. The defendants' occupation was secured pending their reimbursement. See also *Mayes v Mayes* (1969) 210 Estates Gazette 935 at 938.

3   Other complicating factors were the death of the owner during the hearing and the fear expressed by the Court of Appeal lest the remedy granted to the defendants should bring them within the scope of the Settled Land Act 1925 (post, p 803).

4   See eg *Christian v Christian* (1981) 131 NLJ 43; *Coombes v Smith* [1986] 1 WLR 808 (ante, p 406).

5   Unreported, Court of Appeal, 14 July 1983 (ante, p 412).

6   An estoppel will not be raised by reason of the mere fact that occupants have been permitted to stay in residence for an extremely long period of time without any express indication that they would ever be turned out. Something more is needed in the form of an assurance of entitlement to continue to reside (see *Rogers v Eller* (Unreported, Court of Appeal, 20 May 1986)).

7   [1986] 1 WLR 808 (ante, p 406).

founded on the action of a female claimant who had moved in with her lover, had borne his child and had assumed the general role of homemaker, wife and mother in the domestic base provided by him. In *Grant v Edwards*,[8] however, the Court of Appeal (and in particular Browne-Wilkinson V-C) displayed a quite contrary willingness to have regard, in similar circumstances, to ordinary acts of domestic endeavour as the foundation of a claim of proprietary estoppel. It is as yet too early to predict with any certainty in which direction this opposition of approach will be resolved. There are, however, increasing indications that the English courts are now somewhat embarrassed by the apparent inability of the law to provide satisfactory remedies for those who have devoted labours of love in the context of ultimately abortive family arrangements.

6. LIFE INTEREST

Over the years the law of family arrangements has been further complicated by the possibility that the ill-defined terms of an informal residential privilege may slip unnoticed within the clutches of the Settled Land Act 1925, thereby attracting consequences which are both inconvenient and almost certainly unintended by the relevant parties.

(1) Definition of a Settled Land Act 'settlement'

The Settled Land Act 1925 imposes a special regime of estate ownership on certain statutorily defined patterns of landholding. A 'settlement' within the meaning of the Settled Land Act 1925 (sometimes called a 'strict settlement' or 'Settled Land Act settlement') arises in two generalised kinds of situation: (1) where successive and limited equitable interests are carved out of ownership of a legal estate in land,[9] and (2) where an absolute (as distinct from a limited) interest in land is conferred on a grantee who is subject to some disability,[10] liability[11] or contingency[12] which detracts from his capacity or entitlement to hold such an interest.

Most of the circumstances caught within the terms of the Settled Land Act 1925 are now archaic and are only rarely found in practice. This is somewhat ironic since the 1925 Act contains in perfected form certain fairly sophisticated devices for the legal articulation of the strict settlement. Just as the strict settlement reached its zenith of refinement as a legal institution, other factors began to operate in such a way as to render the strict settlement an unsuitable (if not fiscally disastrous) form of landholding.[13] Today the strict settlement has been almost wholly displaced by the trust for sale,[14] and the ingenuity of lawyers is now more commonly devoted to avoiding rather than promoting the creation of strict settlements of land.

---

8 [1986] Ch 638 at 657A-B.
9 See eg Settled Land Act 1925, s 1(1)(ii)(a) (entailed interest).
10 See eg Settled Land Act 1925, s 1(1)(ii)(d) (legal estate granted to a minor).
11 See eg Settled Land Act 1925, ss 1(1)(ii)(c) (determinable fee), 1(1)(v) (family rentcharge).
12 See eg Settled Land Act 1925, s 1(1)(iii) ('springing' interest).
13 The tax consequences which flow from the creation of a strict settlement are onerous in the extreme, taxation falling on the full capital value of the estate on the termination of each successive interest (see A. R. Mellows, *The Law of Succession* (4th edn London 1983, p 304)).
14 See Chapter 12 (ante, p 348).

(2) Application to life interests

The relatively broad ambit of the statutory notion of 'settlement' nevertheless ensures that the Settled Land Act 1925 is sometimes applicable in circumstances where its operation would not normally be anticipated. One of these cases involves the informal family arrangement under which a landowner grants some kind of occupation right to another person for the lifetime of the latter. Under section 1(1)(i) of the Act a settlement is deemed to arise where 'any land...stands for the time being limited in trust for any persons by way of succession.' This formula seems apt to apply to the grant of a life interest, since such an interest is necessarily equitable in nature and necessarily involves some element of succession on its termination. It is possible that even a loosely worded conferment of such a right may be held to come within the 1925 Act.[15]

(a) The Bannister ruling

A crucial decision in the present context was the ruling of the Court of Appeal in *Bannister v Bannister*.[16] Here the defendant had conveyed her freehold interest in two cottages to her brother-in-law, the present plaintiff, on his oral undertaking that she could thereafter live in one of the cottages rent-free for the remainder of her life. The conveyance failed to incorporate this oral promise, but when the plaintiff later sought possession against the defendant, the Court of Appeal held that he was bound by a constructive trust to give effect to her interest. This interest, said Scott LJ, was an equitable life interest determinable on her ceasing to live in the cottage.[17] The imposition of the constructive trust had 'the effect of making the beneficiary a tenant for life within the meaning of the Settled Land Act'.[18]

(b) Doubts left by the Bannister ruling

The Court of Appeal had no need in *Bannister*'s case to pursue the implications of holding that the defendant came within the Settled Land Act. It has since been doubted, however, whether this aspect of the Court's ruling can have been correct.[19] The inter vivos creation of a strict settlement requires the execution of at least two deeds (a trust instrument and a vesting document),[20] and it seems wholly impossible that the defendant in *Bannister* could properly have become a tenant for life by way of merely oral grant.[1] Nevertheless the decision of the Court of Appeal in *Bannister* provides an uncomfortable precedent in support of the proposition that a purely oral grant may attract the operation of the Settled Land Act.

---

15 See eg *In re Gibbons* [1920] 1 Ch 372 at 377ff (option to occupy and enjoy use of a house); *Peach v Peach* (Unreported, Court of Appeal, 1979 P 1475, 3 November 1981) (right to receive rents and profits for life). Even a non-exclusive right to reside for life may raise a settlement (see *Re Potter* [1970] VR 352 at 354ff).

16 [1948] 2 All ER 133 (ante, p 282).

17 [1948] 2 All ER 133 at 136B.

18 [1948] 2 All ER 133 at 137B-C.

19 See A.J. Hawkins, (1966) 30 Conv (NS) 256; J.A. Hornby, (1977) 93 LQR 561.

20 Settled Land Act 1925, s 4(1).

1 It has been suggested that in such cases the court order itself may be the instrument which constitutes the settlement within Settled Land Act 1925, s 1(1) (*Griffiths v Williams* (1977) 248 Estates Gazette 947 at 950 per Goff LJ). See also [1978] Conv 250 at 251.

(3) **Conveyancing consequences**

Further doubts as to the correctness of *Bannister* are raised upon a closer examination of the conveyancing consequences which follow a finding that an informally granted life interest falls within the Settled Land Act 1925.

(a) *Vesting of the legal estate in the tenant for life*

Once the qualifying terms of the Act have been satisfied, the cumbersome machinery provided by the statute is liable to come into operation. The grantee of an ill-defined personal right of occupation, so long as he is a 'person of full age...for the time being beneficially entitled under a settlement to possession of settled land for his life',[2] qualifies as the statutory 'tenant for life'. As such he is entitled, under the scheme of the Settled Land Act,[3] to call for a vesting of the full legal estate in his name.[4] In *Bannister*'s case this would have involved the somewhat improbable result that the defendant, having conveyed the legal estate to her brother-in-law, would immediately have been entitled to insist that the legal estate should be reconveyed to her as tenant for life. However unattractive in the present context, this consequence merely reflects the fundamental design which lies at the root of the Settled Land Act—that the tenant for life should hold two distinct interests in the land. Thus, if X is the tenant for life, the position is as follows.

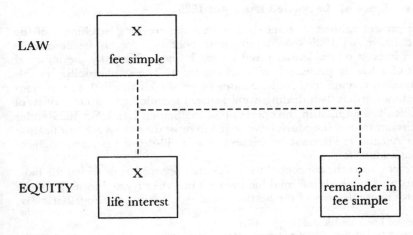

Fig. 52

Here X, the tenant for life under a strict settlement, holds the legal estate merely as a fiduciary. He effectively holds the legal estate on the trusts of the

---

2   Settled Land Act 1925, s 19(1).
3   It is central to the entire scheme of the Settled Land Act 1925 that, wherever possible, the full legal estate should be held by the person who for the time being is currently entitled to an equitable interest in possession (see eg Settled Land Act 1925, s 20(1)).
4   Settled Land Act 1925, s 9(2).

settlement[5] on behalf both of himself (as the owner of an equitable life interest) and of the person entitled thereafter in remainder or reversion.[6] He derives no benefit from his ownership of the legal estate, having in relation to it only statutory powers of management and disposition. As tenant for life he is invested with the Settled Land Act powers of sale,[7] lease[8] and mortgage[9] over the legal estate. The quantum of X's benefit under the terms of the strict settlement is, however, confined to the extent of his own equitable life interest. He is entitled to occupy and enjoy the land during his lifetime (or to receive the rents and profits drawn from the land during that time).

(b) Exercise of the tenant for life's dispositive powers

Even if X, in exercise of his statutory power of sale as tenant for life,[10] sells and conveys the legal estate to a stranger, he does not receive the proceeds of sale himself. Under the scheme of the 1925 Act there is a requirement that the capital proceeds should be paid over to specially appointed 'trustees of the settlement'.[11] If this occurs, the purchaser takes the legal estate entirely free of the trusts of the settlement.[12] The equitable interests of the settled land beneficiaries are overreached by the conveyance,[13] and take effect thereafter as equivalent interests in the capital moneys. X's equitable life interest in the land, when overreached, would take the form of a lifetime right to receive the income from the proceeds of sale as invested by the settlement trustees.

(4) Avoidance of the Settled Land Act 1925

In the present context it seems strange that the creaking machinery of the Settled Land Act 1925 should grind into operation merely because some limited interest or residential privilege has been conferred by the informal means of a loosely phrased family arrangement. The implausibility of this consequence is reinforced in those cases where the parties had no conscious understanding that their dealings would attract specific legal effects. In view of the difficulties implicit in the operation of the Settled Land Act 1925 under such circumstances, the courts have begun to resist the over-ready application of that Act to the informal conferment of some ill-defined personal right of occupation for life.

In recent years the concept of the residential licence has provided the most obvious way in which informal life interests may be diverted away from the dangerous complexities of the Settled Land Act.[14] It is not altogether clear,

---

5   Settled Land Act 1925, ss 16(1)(i), 107(1).
6   For an explanation of estates in remainder and in reversion, see Chapter 5 (ante, p 77).
7   Settled Land Act 1925, s 38.
8   Settled Land Act 1925, s 41ff.
9   Settled Land Act 1925, s 71(1).
10   Any attempt to inhibit or fetter the tenant for life's exercise of his statutory powers is void and ineffective (Settled Land Act 1925, s 106(1)).
11   This requirement is regarded as being of such importance to the security of the settled land beneficial interests that the Act declares void any purported conveyance of the legal estate which does not result in a payment of capital moneys to the settlement trustees or into court (Settled Land Act 1925, s 18(1)). See *Weston v Henshaw* [1950] Ch 510 at 519; but compare *In re Morgan's Lease* [1972] Ch 1 at 7E-9C. See also D.W. Elliott, (1971) 87 LQR 338; R.H. Maudsley, (1973) 36 MLR 25 at 28f; R. Warrington, [1985] Conv 377.
12   Settled Land Act 1925, s 72(2), (3).
13   Law of Property Act 1925, s 2(1)(i) (ante, p 100).
14   For a discussion of the law of licences, see Chapter 15 (ante, p 535).

however, that there is a judicial consensus that the licence construction can properly exclude the inconvenient and heavy-handed operation of the Settled Land Act. The ambivalence on this point was apparent in the decision of the Court of Appeal in *Binions v Evans*.[15] Here D had been granted a right of rent-free residence in a cottage for the remainder of her life. A majority in the Court of Appeal still felt constrained by grudging deference to *Bannister v Bannister* to hold that this grant was caught by the Settled Land Act 1925.[16] However, Lord Denning MR declined to apply *Bannister* precisely on the ground that it would have been 'entirely contrary to the true intent of the parties' that D should have acquired, by reason of the grant, a statutory power of sale or lease of the property under the Settled Land Act.[17]

Lord Denning accordingly found a ready escape route in *Binions v Evans* in the form of a severely restrictive construction of section 1(1)(i) of the Settled Land Act 1925, taking the view that the statutory reference to 'land...limited in trust' covers only the case where land is 'expressly limited' in trust and where there is a genuine 'succession of one beneficiary after another'.[18] In an informal arrangement of the kind present in *Binions v Evans*, there was no true 'limitation' of land and therefore no 'settlement'. Thus, although ultimately reaching the same result as his brethren in the majority, Lord Denning did so by way of a finding of contractual licence.[19] Subsequent decisions have echoed this disquiet with the *Bannister* ruling,[20] and there is now a divergent line of authority to the effect that there can be such a phenomenon as a licence for life which exists outside the clutches of the Settled Land Act 1925.[1] Licences for life have frequently been awarded in satisfaction of the 'equity' raised by proprietary estoppel.[2]

The approach adopted by Lord Denning in *Binions v Evans*, although heavily reinforced by common sense, is not however easily reconciled with the circumstances and the ruling in *Bannister*.[3] On the one hand it is the deliberate policy of the 1925 legislation that land should be rendered easily marketable,[4] and there is therefore a strong argument in favour of maximising the coverage of the Settled Land Act, thereby extending as widely as possible its

---

15   [1972] Ch 359. For the full facts of this case, see Chapter 15 (ante, p 551).

16   'I realise that the application of the Settled Land Act 1925 may produce some odd consequences' ([1972] Ch 359 at 370D-G per Megaw LJ). See also Stephenson LJ (at 372E-G). See, however, *Ivory v Palmer* (1976) 237 Estates Gazette 411 at 413, where Cairns LJ thought that the majority view in *Binions v Evans* had 'stretched to the very limit the application of the Settled Land Act'.

17   [1972] Ch 359 at 366D. For further reference to the over-large powers which would be made available under the Settled Land Act 1925, see also *Dodsworth v Dodsworth* (1973) 228 Estates Gazette 1115; *Griffiths v Williams* (1977) 248 Estates Gazette 947 at 949.

18   [1972] Ch 359 at 366E-F.

19   [1972] Ch 359 at 367C (ante, p 552).

20   Such is the embarrassment caused by *Bannister* that in *Ivory v Palmer* (1976) 237 Estates Gazette 411 at 416 Browne LJ was at pains to stress that 'the court did not in fact...base its decision on the Settled Land Act 1925, but on more general principles of the law of trusts.'

1   *Foster v Robinson* [1951] 1 KB 149 at 158ff (post, p 992); *Ivory v Palmer* (1976) 237 Estates Gazette 411 at 413 per Cairns LJ.

2   See eg *Inwards v Baker* [1965] 2 QB 29 at 37; *Greasley v Cooke* [1980] 1 WLR 1306 at 1312B.

3   See eg *Griffiths v Williams* (1977) 248 Estates Gazette 947 at 950, where Goff LJ questioned whether *Dodsworth v Dodsworth* (1973) 228 Estates Gazette 1115 might not have been decided per incuriam on the ground that the Court of Appeal in the latter case did not advert to section 1 of the Settled Land Act 1925.

4   Ante, p 96.

conveyancing and overreaching machinery.[5] On the other hand, there is the very real difficulty that this resolution introduces into the relationship of the parties a statutory mechanism which was never intended by them to be relevant and is usually most unwelcome to them. The law here remains in a state of some confusion, although there seems to be a preponderant tendency to avoid the complications of the Settled Land Act if at all possible.[6]

7. ALIQUOT SHARES BEHIND A TRUST

There was an extensive discussion in Chapter 10[7] of the circumstances in which various forms of payment or contribution may generate entitlement to an aliquot share behind a trust. There is, of course, nothing inherently implausible about the idea that a trust may be raised on the basis of the conduct of parties to a 'family arrangement'. However, a note of caution inevitably surrounds the application of trust law to transfers of value within a familial context. Such transfers are, in principle, equally explicable on the basis of gift or loan.[8] It is quite possible that payments made in connection with a family arrangement were intended—if indeed there was any relevant intention at all—to fall within one or other of these categories rather than attract the operation of the law of trusts.[9] The issue is likely to depend ultimately on the credibility of the available evidence.[10] Moreover, English law does not in strict terms recognise any law of matrimonial property or special regime of 'family assets'. The mere fact that persons are married to each other or are members of the same family has no automatic effect on their respective property entitlements. The property relations of family members are still governed in principle by the somewhat bleak and inflexible rules of the general law of property.

(1) The role of intention

The root problem in the contemporary English law of family property lies in the dogmatic requirement that some conscious intention as to beneficial title be demonstrated as the minimal condition for the creation of equitable co-ownership. In almost all family arrangements the search for such intentions is unreal.

(a) Improvements

In *Pettitt v Pettitt*[11] the House of Lords firmly rejected a husband's claim that he had acquired an equitable share in his wife's home on the ground of the many improvements he had carried out in the property. In the absence of evidence of

---

5   Ante, p 100.
6   In *Griffiths v Williams* (1977) 248 Estates Gazette 947 at 950, for instance, the Court of Appeal was so anxious to escape the possible implications of the Settled Land Act that it effectively resolved the residential problems of the parties by dictating, with only the barest consent of those parties, an alternative solution in terms of the grant of a long tenancy at a nominal rent.
7   Ante, p 233.
8   See *Hardwick v Johnson* [1978] 1 WLR 683 at 688D.
9   Ante, p 261.
10 See eg *Kent v Regan* (1964) 192 Estates Gazette 545 at 547.
11 [1970] AC 777.

agreement or common intention that his work should reflect itself in a changed beneficial ownership of that property, the House of Lords declined to hold that every minor improvement performed by the husband had some proportionate reflex effect upon the quantum of the spouses' respective entitlements in the equitable ownership of the house.[12]

Within a short time, however, the force of the decision in *Pettitt* was reversed by statute. Section 37 of the Matrimonial Proceedings and Property Act 1970 declares that where a husband or wife 'contributes in money or money's worth to the improvement' of property in which either spouse is beneficially entitled, the spouse 'so contributing shall, if the contribution is of a substantial nature...be treated as having then acquired...a share or an enlarged share' in the other's beneficial interest. The operation of this provision is 'subject to any agreement between them to the contrary express or implied', and seems in effect to create a rebuttable presumption of common intention as between husband and wife that certain kinds of improvements made by either to the property of the other shall generate a beneficial entitlement for the 'improving' spouse. The quantum of equitable entitlement created by reason of the improvement is, in the first instance, a matter to be agreed by the spouses.[13] In default of agreement, however, quantum is to be determined by the court in terms of what 'may seem in all the circumstances just'.[14]

Section 37 is a little used and not entirely happy provision. It drives a somewhat uncomfortable distinction between contributions made towards the 'improvement' of property and contributions made towards the acquisition or retention of property. It is clear, moreover, that the provision confers benefit only upon a husband or wife and not upon other members of family groups. There is no statutory definition of 'improvement', but section 37 has been applied to confer an enhanced equitable share even on the basis of such mundane contributions as the installation of central heating in the family home.[15]

(b) Contributions of money or effort towards acquisition or retention

Although the distinction between improvements and other forms of contribution is admittedly somewhat artificial,[16] the law of trusts operates quite differently in relation to contributions of money or effort which are directed towards the acquisition or retention of property. In the latter context there is no statutory presumption of intention equivalent to that contained in section 37 of the Matrimonial Proceedings and Property Act 1970.

(i) Requirement of 'referability' In *Gissing v Gissing*[17] the House of Lords stressed that the beneficial ownership of property is ultimately determined by the intentions of the parties to the relevant acquisition. These intentions may be expressed by the parties or inferred from their conduct, but cannot be imputed to them retrospectively when it is quite clear that they never consciously

---

12 'It is only in the bitterness engendered by the break-up of the marriage that so bizarre a notion would enter their heads' ([1970] AC 777 at 826B per Lord Diplock).
13 Matrimonial Proceedings and Property Act 1970, s 37.
14 Matrimonial Proceedings and Property Act 1970, s 37.
15 *In Re Nicholson* [1974] 1 WLR 476 at 482G-483C.
16 See eg *Pettitt v Pettitt* [1970] AC 777 at 794A-E per Lord Reid.
17 [1971] AC 886 (ante, p 258).

formulated *any* common intention with regard to the equitable ownership of the property in question.[18] The courts have no jurisdiction to subject disputed property to a trust merely on the ground that such a result 'would be fair in all the circumstances'[19] or indeed would have been agreed by the parties themselves at the time if they had only considered the matter.[20] Instead a trust of property can arise only where there is a valid declaration of trust or where the beneficial claimant has made contributions of money or effort which 'it can be inferred' are 'referable to the acquisition' of the family home.[1]

(ii) Lord Diplock's rationale of trust law   In *Gissing v Gissing*[2] Lord Diplock sought to explain the genesis of the trust in terms of one comprehensive formula. In a passage which has since become a locus classicus in the law of real property, he declared that a trust, whether resulting, implied or constructive,

is created by a transaction between the trustee and the cestui que trust in connection with the acquisition by the trustee of a legal estate in the land, whenever the trustee has so conducted himself that it would be inequitable to allow him to deny to the cestui que trust a beneficial interest in the land acquired.

Couched in these terms, Lord Diplock's articulation of trust doctrine instantly appears to endorse the idea that the court may award a trust interest ex aequo et bono whenever it would be 'inequitable' not to do so. However, Lord Diplock proceeded immediately to qualify his statement, observing that, in the situation to which he had just referred, the trustee

will be held so to have conducted himself if by his words or conduct he has induced the cestui que trust to act to his own detriment in the reasonable belief that by so acting he was acquiring a beneficial interest in the land.

So far from supporting any wide understanding of the trust remedy, Lord Diplock's dictum—when read as one conjoined formula—constitutes a plainly restrictive application of trust doctrine.[3] This conclusion is confirmed by the merest glance at the actual decision reached by the House of Lords in *Gissing*. In this case the claimant wife, during a marriage of some 25 years' duration, had made indirect financial contributions towards the purchase of the family home through the use of her own moneys on various forms of household and other family-related expenditure. The House of Lords nevertheless denied her any beneficial entitlement in the property, which was vested at law solely in the name of her husband.

(iii) The failure of the Gissing claim   The failure of the wife's claim in *Gissing* was not rooted in any argument that it was 'inequitable' to grant her a beneficial share in the matrimonial home. Her failure rested simply on the absence of any convincing evidence that the parties had ever consciously formulated a 'bargain' or 'quid pro quo' under which her contributions could be said to have been induced by a belief that she was thereby acquiring some beneficial entitlement. For want of any conscious agreement to share the beneficial title,

---

18   Ante, p 258.
19   [1971] AC 886 at 900F per Viscount Dilhorne.
20   [1971] AC 886 at 898C, 900E-F, 904E-F (ante, p 273).
1   [1971] AC 886 at 909F-G per Lord Diplock.
2   [1971] AC 886 at 905B-D (ante, p 243).
3   See eg *Allen v Snyder* [1977] 2 NSWLR 685 at 694B-695C.

the House of Lords declined to infer that the wife's expenditure had been 'referable to' the acquisition of the family home.[4]

(iv) Criticism of the Gissing ruling   The decision of the House of Lords in *Gissing* is open to severe criticism on grounds of social justice.[5] However, the approach applied in that case was inevitably constrained by the fact that behind the equitable presumption of resulting trust there lies the 'solid tug of money'.[6] The more solid the tug, the more ready will be the presumption of resulting trust. The indirect contribution made by the wife in *Gissing* was not sufficiently 'solid' to raise the required inference of intention and, given the primary importance of intention, the House of Lords was absolutely correct in so holding. The wife in that case (and indeed most wives) would have continued to make her appropriate contribution to the marriage partnership without regard to any anticipation of immediate reward or tangible pay-off—and this for at least two reasons. *First,* the wife never contemplated that her marriage would break down and thus require that the respective property rights of the parties be crystallised. *Second,* it is an intrinsic characteristic of family life that the constructive contributions of family members are motivated less by the mercenary incentives of an exchange economy than by higher principles of love and duty.

It is clear the requirement of 'referability' has operated as a sharp brake upon successful claims to beneficial entitlement on the part of family members. The insistence in *Gissing* that equitable co-ownership be premised on some demonstrable 'common intention' has thrown almost insuperable obstacles even in the way of those who have contributed substantially to the success of a joint venture and who stand most clearly in need of legal protection.[7] In *Burns v Burns,*[8] for example, the Court of Appeal sent away empty-handed a de facto wife who had lived with her partner for 17 years, had borne and reared two children by him, and had contributed both money and household services to the relationship.[9] In *Wood v Wood*[10] a similar result caused Lawton LJ to observe that the outcome should provide a 'cautionary tale for women who cohabit with men without having clear understandings with them about their property dealings one with the other.' In his view, 'questions of property rights as between cohabitees cannot be dealt with on the basis of sentiment, they have got to be dealt with in accordance with the law of property.'

(2) The 'new model' or remedial constructive trust

English law has traditionally regarded the constructive trust as a substantive

4   Ante, p 279.
5   Ante, p 279.
6   Ante, p 245.
7   See eg *Hannaford v Selby* (1976) 239 Estates Gazette 811; *Grant v Sanderson* [1983] Court of Appeal Unbound Transcript 862, 20 April 1983; *Warner v Warner* (Unreported, Court of Appeal, 11 July 1984).
8   [1984] Ch 317 (ante, p 258).
9   The property problems of spouses are now usually resolved with reference to the extended discretionary powers of the divorce court to grant property adjustment and other ancillary relief pursuant to the Matrimonial Causes Act 1973, ss 24(1), 25. These powers were introduced by the Matrimonial Proceedings and Property Act 1970 after the decisions in *Pettitt* and *Gissing,* and have effectively moved the focus of 'family arrangement' problems from de iure marriage to de facto marriage and other familial relationships.
10   Unreported, Court of Appeal, 1979 W No 1393, 7 July 1982.

institution analogous to the express trust.[11] A constructive trust arises where, in relation to defined property, some person has undertaken a fiduciary role which thereafter he cannot be heard to disavow.[12] In such circumstances, the person concerned is made liable *as though* he were a trustee. As Ungoed-Thomas J indicated in *Selangor United Rubber Estates Ltd v Cradock (No 3)*,[13] he is 'made liable in equity as trustee by the imposition or construction of the court of equity'.

In its adherence to a substantive doctrine of constructive trusts, English law now contrasts sharply with the application of constructive trust theory in certain other jurisdictions.

(a) The North American constructive trust

In the North American model, for instance, the constructive trust is an overtly remedial mechanism.[14] It provides a third head of civil obligation, ranking alongside but still rather distinct from, contract and tort, in which the court subjects a person holding title to property to an equitable duty to convey it to, or to hold it on trust for, another on the ground that the current title holder would be 'unjustly enriched' if he were permitted to retain the property beneficially.[15] The constructive trust in this sense is closely linked with the emergence of the law of restitution as a third major form of civil liability in the common law world.[16] This remedial perspective is not without respectable antecedents,[17] but its importance lies nowadays in the fact that it opens up a range of almost uncontrollably diverse applications.

(b) The English response to the 'unjust enrichment' principle

The remedial dimension of the constructive trust has not been accorded a rapturous reception in English jurisprudence. In *Pettitt v Pettitt*,[18] Lord Reid

11 *Avondale Printers & Stationers Ltd v Haggie* [1979] 2 NZLR 124 at 147.
12 Ante, p 269.
13 [1968] 1 WLR 1555 at 1582 A-B.
14 See *Chase Manhattan Bank NA v Israel-British Bank (London) Ltd* [1981] Ch 105 at 126G-127D; *Simonds v Simonds*, 408 NYS.2d 359 at 362ff (1978). See also J.L. Dewar, *The Development of the Remedial Constructive Trust*, (1982) 60 CBR 265.
15 The American *Restatement of Restitution* provides that 'a person who has been unjustly enriched at the expense of another is required to make restitution to that other' (para 1). Likewise, where 'a person holding title to property is subject to an equitable duty to convey it to another on the ground that he would be unjustly enriched if he were permitted to retain it, a constructive trust arises' (para 160). See also A.W. Scott, (1955) 71 LQR 39, *Law of Trusts* (3rd edn, Boston and Toronto 1967), Vol V, p 3413; D.W.M. Waters, *The Constructive Trust* (London 1964).
16 See Lord Goff of Chieveley and Gareth Jones, *The Law of Restitution* (3rd edn London 1986). See also *Beatty v Guggenheim Exploration Co*, 225 NY 380 at 386 (1919), where Cardozo J described the constructive trust as 'the formula through which the conscience of equity finds expression. When property has been acquired in such circumstances that the holder may not in good faith retain the beneficial interest, equity converts him into a trustee'.
17 See eg *Moses v Macferlan* (1760) 2 Burr 1005 at 1012, 97 ER 676 at 681, where Lord Mansfield pointed out that 'the gist of this kind of action is that the defendant, upon the circumstances of the case, is obliged by the ties of natural justice and equity to refund the money...'
18 [1970] AC 777 at 795G-H. See also *In re Sharpe (A Bankrupt)* [1980] 1 WLR 219 at 225G, where Browne-Wilkinson J declared the 'constructive trust as a remedy' to be 'a novel concept in English law'.

expressed the opinion that the doctrine of unjust enrichment, whilst applicable to money claims, is not necessarily appropriate in relation to real property.[19] The English courts have always seen the origin of the trust as founded in some common intention or conscious bargain directed towards the diffusion of equitable ownership. The inevitable result of this approach has been the frequent denial of equitable entitlement in the context of family arrangements, purely and simply on the ground that the relevant participants failed to advert in any precise or legalistic way to the property consequences of their relationship.[20] In this respect the decision of the House of Lords in *Gissing v Gissing*[1] has exerted a stranglehold on the development of any rational law of family property in England. The application of trust doctrine in *Gissing* was ultimately unsympathetic to the realities of family living, since the House of Lords effectively required that beneficial entitlement be proved on the basis of intentions which are rarely articulated or even contemplated in the daily round of domestic life.

(c) 'Unjust enrichment' and family property

It is clear, however, that the day is slowly coming when the courts will no longer feel bound to search for—or disingenuously to fashion—phantoms of common intention in order to resolve the property relations of disaffected participants in family arrangements.[2] In this context it cannot escape notice that the North American constructive trust is more highly sensitive to the realities of family life which are so grievously falsified by the English application of trust doctrine. The 'remedial' constructive trust arises quite independently of the vagaries of intentions which may or may not have been formulated by the parties.[3] It substitutes the broad principle of restitution of unjust enrichment for a sterile and ritualistic preoccupation with ultimately illusory figments of common intention.

(i) Canadian developments   The application of a liberal doctrine of constructive trust has revolutionised the law of family property in Canada.[4] In *Rathwell v Rathwell*[5] the Supreme Court of Canada invoked a wide concept of remedial constructive trust in order to confer a half-share in the matrimonial property on a wife who had made substantial domestic contributions to the marriage partnership. In the words of Dickson J, the application of the constructive trust

comprehends the imposition of trust machinery by the Court in order to achieve a result consonant with good conscience. As a matter of principle, the Court will not allow any man to appropriate to himself the value earned by the labours of another. That principle is not defeated by the existence of a matrimonial relationship between the parties; but, for the principle to succeed, the facts must display an enrichment, a

---

19   See also *Orakpo v Manson Investments Ltd* [1978] AC 95 at 104C per Lord Diplock.
20   *Ante*, p 279.
1   [1971] AC 886 (ante, pp 258, 279).
2   [1982] CLJ 30 at 33. See also *Hayward v Giordani* [1983] NZLR 140 at 145 per Cooke J.
3   See *Hayward v Giordani* [1983] NZLR 140 at 148, 149.
4   See generally Mary Welstead, *Domestic Contribution and Constructive Trusts: The Canadian Perspective*, (1987) 2 Denning LJ 151. See also J.D. McCamus and L. Taman, (1978) 16 Osgoode Hall LJ 741; A.J. McClean, (1982) 16 UBCLR 155.
5   (1978) 83 DLR (3d) 289.

corresponding deprivation, and the absence of any juristic reason—such as a contract or disposition of law—for the enrichment.[6]

This approach was taken one step further in *Pettkus v Becker*,[7] where the Supreme Court of Canada similarly applied the remedial constructive trust for the purpose of recognising the entitlement of a de facto wife to one-half of the family assets acquired through her joint efforts with her partner in his farm business.[8] In terms which closely resembled the language of proprietary estoppel, Dickson J noted that 'where one person in a relationship tantamount to spousal prejudices herself in the reasonable expectation of receiving an interest in property and the other person in the relationship freely accepts benefits conferred by the first person in circumstances where he knows or ought to have known of that reasonable expectation, it would be unjust to allow the recipient of the benefit to retain it.'[9]

This recognition was extended yet again in *Sorochan v Sorochan*,[10] where the Supreme Court invoked the principle of 'unjust enrichment' to confer a substantial share of quasi-matrimonial property on a homemaker and mother. Dickson CJC acknowledged that the claimant's unwaged domestic endeavour had clearly conferred a 'benefit' upon her partner, resulting in a corresponding 'deprivation' to herself.[11] There being no 'juristic reason' in the form of any obligation (contractual or otherwise) to perform such household services, the claimant was awarded a constructive trust of part of her de facto husband's land plus a money sum of $20,000.

(ii) Significance of the remedial constructive trust   The North American (and particularly the Canadian) articulation of constructive trust theory is interesting because it widens considerably the conditions which activate the imposition of a trust on the owner of a legal estate.[12] If the trigger for the traditional presumption of resulting trust is a contribution of money, it may well be that contributions of labour provide the trigger for the application of the constructive trust based on 'unjust enrichment'. Moreover, this development may be symptomatic of the contemporary emergence of the 'new property', one of the strongest features of which is the recognition that men and women have a 'property' in their own labour.[13] The remedial constructive trust also mirrors something of the advances which are being made in other jurisdictions through the development of the doctrine of proprietary estoppel. However, the 'unjust enrichment' constructive trust seems to incorporate a more positive and ultimately more realistic emphasis upon the element of

6   (1978) 83 DLR (3d) 289 at 306. For confirmation of the three constitutive elements of the constructive trust, see *Sorochan v Sorochan* (1986) 29 DLR (4th) 1 at 5 per Dickson CJC.
7   (1980) 117 DLR (3d) 257.
8   Tragically the successful plaintiff never received her award of $150,000. She committed suicide in November 1986 (see *Montreal Gazette*, 11 November 1986), driven to despair by a legal system which had allowed her former partner to frustrate in large measure all attempts made by her to enforce the court order in her favour. The only sums paid over by the defendant, amounting to $68,000, were in fact seized by the plaintiff's lawyer for legal fees. See Mary Welstead, (1987) 2 Denning LJ 151.
9   (1980) 117 DLR (3d) 257 at 274.
10   (1986) 29 DLR (4th) 1.
11   (1986) 29 DLR (4th) 1 at 6f.
12   There is, for instance, no need to relate specific contributions to particular assets (see *Nuti v Nuti* (1980) 108 DLR (3d) 587 at 603, (1982) 122 DLR (3d) 384).
13   Ante, p 11.

'benefit' conferred on the recipient of the relevant contribution of services or money. Estoppel theory is still largely dominated by the inquiry whether 'detriment' has been incurred by the contributor. It is often the case that an emphasis on the benefit conferred more accurately reveals the true value of the respective contributions made in the context of family arrangements.

(d) The 'new model' constructive trust

The remedial constructive trust has conferred a new freedom on the courts in other jurisdictions to do justice in the resolution of the property rights within family arrangements.[14] Some version of this liberated form of constructive trust doctrine flourished in England—at least briefly—during the 1970s.[15] The remedial constructive trust—marked as it is by its close association with the Protestant work ethic—found its foremost protagonist in the English courts in the predictable shape of Lord Denning MR. In *Cooke v Head*,[16] the former Master of the Rolls declared that the courts would 'impose or impute' a constructive trust 'whenever two parties by their joint efforts acquire property to be used for their joint benefit'.[17] *Cooke v Head* involved parties to a de facto relationship, but Lord Denning pointed out that the constructive trust doctrine was applicable to 'husband and wife, to engaged couples, and to man and mistress, and maybe to other relationships too.'[18]

Perhaps the most clear-cut application of the constructive trust for remedial purposes occurred in *Eves v Eves*.[19] Here a de facto wife claimed to have effected extensive improvements to a house vested at law in the sole name of her partner.[20] The Court of Appeal awarded her one quarter of the beneficial ownership in the property, Lord Denning MR basing his reasoning on a liberal theory of constructive trust.[1] He observed that 'a few years ago even equity would not have helped' a claimant in the position of the plaintiff, but noted that 'things have altered now. Equity is not past the age of child bearing. One of her latest progeny is a constructive trust of a new model. Lord Diplock brought it into the world and we have nourished it.'[2] Lord Denning proceeded to cite in his support the passage in *Gissing v Gissing* containing Lord Diplock's famous summary of the rationale of all trust doctrines.[3] It was noticeable,

14 See eg *McGrath v Hilding*, 394 NYS.2d 603 at 606f(1977); *Clooney v Clooney*, 394 A.2d 313 at 316 (1978); *Wright v Wright*, 311 NW.2d 484 at 485f (1981); *In re Estate of Eriksen*, 337 NW.2d 671 at 674 (1983); *Willits v Willits Estate* (1982) 14 Sask R 114 at 126f; *Pratt v MacLeod* (1982) 129 DLR (3d)·123 at 132ff; *Palachik v Kiss* (1983) 146 DLR (3d) 385 at 391ff; *Murray v Roty* (1983) 147 DLR (3d) 438 at 443ff; *O'Neill v Mehain* (1985) 57 BCLR 64 at 68.

15 See also Marcia Neave, *The Constructive Trust as a Remedial Device*, (1978) 11 Melbourne ULR 343.

16 [1972] 1 WLR 518 at 520F.

17 See, however, *Brown v Stokes* [1980] BCL 802.

18 [1972] 1 WLR 518 at 520G. Compare *Hankinson v Kyle* [1982] BCL 1014.

19 [1975] 1 WLR 1338. See (1976) 92 LQR 489 (F. Webb); R.H. Maudsley, (1977) 28 NILQ 123 at 132f.

20 Apart from redecorating the entire house and demolishing a garden shed single-handed, it had been the formidable achievement of the claimant to wield a 14 lb sledgehammer to break up an area of concrete at the front of the house, dump the rubble in a skip, and prepare the garden for turfing ([1975] 1 WLR 1338 at 1340D-E).

1 The other judges in the Court of Appeal, Browne LJ and Brightman J, were more cautious and preferred to find a more traditional basis for reaching the same conclusion (ante, p 277).

2 [1975] 1 WLR 1338 at 1341F-G.

3 Ante, pp 243, 810.

however, that in the remainder of his judgment Lord Denning appeared to concentrate on the first part of Lord Diplock's dictum to the virtual exclusion of the second (and severely limiting) passage.[4] In fact, Lord Diplock's speech when read closely in context provides no support for the proposition that a new head of inequitable conduct is disclosed whenever, in the absence of a contract or relevant common intention, the court considers that it would be fair to cause beneficial ownership to be shared by two or more parties who have acquired property by joint efforts.[5] In *Gissing* precisely this proposition was rejected,[6] and the applicant wife there lost her case.

(e) Property-based objections to the remedial constructive trust

Lord Denning's attempts to introduce a more liberal principle of constructive trust were evident in other cases of the 1970s.[7] However, the application of the remedial constructive trust proved to be excessively controversial in the English context,[8] and did not survive Lord Denning's retirement from the bench. The remedial constructive trust, together with its companion principle of 'unjust enrichment', had already been rejected in forthright terms by many other Commonwealth jurisdictions,[9] and there was at the beginning of the 1980s a general reinforcement of the orthodox jurisprudence of trust law.

(i) The 'formless void of individual moral opinion'   One reason for the submergence of the 'new model' constructive trust in England has lain in the powerful objection that the imposition of such a trust constitutes an argument of last resort. For the hard-nosed property lawyer, the 'finding' of a remedial constructive trust is an act of sheer intellectual bankruptcy, amounting effectively to a judicial confession that no convincing reason can be found in law for giving judgment in favour of a deserving plaintiff. The law of remedial constructive trusts has also been condemned as a law of 'palm-tree justice' under which past decisions are worthless as precedent and future decisions are entirely unpredictable. As Mahon J pointed out in *Carly v Farrelly*,[10] no 'stable

---

4   For criticism of this overly selective technique, see *Avondale Printers & Stationers Ltd v Haggie* [1979] 2 NZLR 124 at 146f per Mahon J.

5   Lord Denning MR consistently declined in other cases to adopt Lord Diplock's notion of 'referable' contributions (ante, p 279). See *Hargrave v Newton* [1971] 1 WLR 1611 at 1613B-D, where Lord Denning found the concept 'very difficult to apply', and thus preferred 'to take the simple test: did the wife make a substantial contribution, direct or indirect, to the acquisition of the house or the repayment of the mortgage or the loan?' See also *Hazell v Hazell* [1972] 1 WLR 301 at 304C-E.

6   Ante, p 273.

7   See eg *Heseltine v Heseltine* [1971] 1 WLR 342 at 346D-F; *Hussey v Palmer* [1972] 1 WLR 1286 at 1289H-1290D (ante, p 289).

8   See A.J. Oakley, (1973) 26 CLP 17.

9   See eg *Avondale Printers & Stationers Ltd v Haggie* [1979] 2 NZLR 124 at 144ff. In *Allen v Snyder* [1977] 2 NSWLR 685 at 700F-701A, Samuel JA observed in the New South Wales Court of Appeal that in *Eves v Eves* Lord Denning had 'proclaimed the legitimacy of equity's latest progeny, plucked by Lord Diplock from her capacious womb, and it was named "a constructive trust of a new model." But I would respectfully suggest that Lord Diplock's speech in *Gissing v Gissing* gives no warrant for identifying him as midwife; his Lordship, by exemplifying the trustee's inequitable conduct as the basis of the trust, is expressing no novelty...[T]he legitimacy of the new model is at least suspect; at best it is a mutant from which further breeding should be discouraged.'

10   [1975] 1 NZLR 356 at 367.

system of jurisprudence could permit a litigant's claim to justice to be consigned to the formless void of individual moral opinion'.

(ii) Unfair prejudice to third party interests A further objection comprises the weighty argument that the imposition of a remedial constructive trust unfairly prejudices interests which are jealously protected by the law of property—the interests of innocent third parties.[11] In the present context part of the problem is precisely the fact that any beneficial interest awarded by way of constructive trust gains an automatic priority over creditors of the constructive trustee in the event of any insolvency affecting the latter.[12] Furthermore, even if the constructive trustee remains perfectly solvent, there is always a danger that third parties who purchase the trust property from him may find themselves fixed with deemed notice of the constructive beneficiary's equitable interest.[13]

(f) Future developments

Although strong objections undoubtedly exist to the over-ready application of trust law to family arrangements, it is not impossible that future developments in England will see the emergence of a more liberal position. There is already an incipient revolt against the tyranny of the 'common intention' requirement. In *Bernard v Josephs*,[14] for instance, Griffiths LJ agreed that there is 'of course an air of unreality about the whole exercise' and that the court can only view 'broadly' the conduct of the parties in its search for their 'unexpressed and probably unconsidered intentions as to...beneficial ownership'. Fairly recently the Court of Appeal of New Zealand refused in *Hayward v Giordani*[15] to exclude the possibility that the court might properly impose a constructive trust, on the Canadian analogy, in response to an allegation of 'unjust enrichment'. Cooke J found the approach of the Canadian Supreme Court 'very helpful...in working out the property rights of common law spouses', and indicated that to him it seemed 'only a small step to eliminate the need to strain for proof of common intention'.[16]

It is likely that this movement towards a more sympathetic application of trust law will find an echo in England. Although it seems improbable that there will be a revival of the 'new model' constructive trust of the 1970s, there have already been signs that the Court of Appeal is prepared to relax the requirement of 'referability' in the creation of trusts of the family home.[17] Ultimately it may be that, in the interests of social justice, the courts will return to the approach adumbrated by Lord Reid in *Pettitt v Pettitt*[18] and *Gissing v Gissing*.[19] Here Lord Reid, albeit a lone voice in the House of Lords, urged that the courts be free to impute to family members a 'deemed intention' with respect to beneficial ownership based on the likely intentions of reasonable persons. Lord Reid made clear his sense of disquiet with any requirement of

---

11 See A.J. Oakley, *Constructive Trusts* (2nd edn London 1987), p 4ff.
12 Ante, p 46.
13 Ante, p 365; post, p 836.
14 [1982] Ch 391 at 404B. See [1983] CLJ 30.
15 [1983] NZLR 140.
16 [1983] NZLR 140 at 148.
17 See eg *Grant v Edwards* [1986] Ch 638 (ante, p 280). See also (1987) 50 MLR 94 (B. Sufrin).
18 [1970] AC 777 at 795C-G.
19 [1971] AC 886 at 897C-G.

actual or inferred common intention as the necessary foundation of beneficial entitlement, noting that, if such a requirement were held to be good law, he himself 'could not contemplate the future results of such a decision with equanimity.'[20] It would rather appear that time has proved Lord Reid correct.

8. PROPERTY TRANSFER ORDER

Except when granting ancillary relief between spouses on divorce,[1] English courts have no general statutory discretion to reallocate property by transfer order as between the participants in a family arrangement.[2] There is, however, one slightly surprising context in which such a power is effectively available to the courts. In *Pascoe v Turner*,[3] for instance, P and D had lived in a de facto relationship in a house owned by P. When P later moved out in order to live with another woman elsewhere, he informed D orally that she had nothing to worry about as the house and its contents were thenceforth entirely hers. D subsequently effected improvements to the house costing about £230, a figure which amounted to one quarter of her available capital. When P later brought possession proceedings on the basis that D had a mere revocable licence to occupy, the Court of Appeal ruled that the fee simple in the house should be transferred to D.

This rather startling result was reached on the ground of proprietary estoppel.[4] Here an estoppel was held to arise on the basis of D's (albeit modest) expenditure coupled with P's tacit acquiescence. In deciding the extent of the 'minimum equity' required in order to do justice to D, the Court thought that the only appropriate way in which D's 'equity' could be satisfied in the present circumstances was by perfecting the imperfect oral gift of realty made by P.[5] The Court was influenced towards this conclusion by the fact that P was a relatively rich man who had pursued his possession action against D 'with a ruthless disregard of the obligations binding on conscience'. The granting of a mere licence remedy was thought insufficient to protect D against future manifestations of this ruthlessness,[6] and the Court decided that the 'equity' in favour of D could be satisfied only by 'compelling the plaintiff to give effect to his promise and her expectations'.[7]

---

20   *Gissing v Gissing* [1971] AC 886 at 897G.
1   See Matrimonial Causes Act 1973, ss 24(1), 25(1)-(4), 25A.
2   For a proposal that such a jurisdiction be introduced by legislation, see C. Harpum, (1982) 2 Oxford Jnl of Legal Studies 277 at 287.
3   [1979] 1 WLR 431. See [1979] Conv 379; (1979) 42 MLR 574 (B. Sufrin); (1979) 129 NLJ 1193 (R.D. Oughton).
4   [1979] 1 WLR 431 at 436D.
5   [1979] 1 WLR 431 at 438A.
6   A further motive for awarding a remedy which went beyond the grant of a mere licence was the need to equip D with a mortgageable estate in the land for the purpose of raising finance for such further improvements to the realty as might prove to be required ([1979] 1 WLR 431 at 439A-B).
7   [1979] 1 WLR 431 at 439B.

CHAPTER 24

The decision to sell the family home

There has been some discussion in earlier chapters of the ways in which family members may be able to influence decisions as to the possible sale of the home in which they live. A spouse who has either a beneficial interest or no interest at all may be able to stultify any proposed sale of the family home by registering 'rights of occupation' under the Matrimonial Homes Act 1983.[1] Moreover, a beneficial co-owner (other than one who is also entitled at law) may have a quite independent right to occupy the family home.[2] The latter right is an incident of equitable entitlement under a trust for sale, and seems in effect to confer upon the beneficial co-owner a right of consent to any proposed transaction with the legal title in the property.[3]

The present chapter is concerned with the special problem which arises where sale of the family home is proposed by an owner of the *legal* estate, but is vehemently opposed either by another co-owner of that same legal estate or indeed by a beneficial co-owner. Such disagreements centre around the operation of trusts for sale, precisely because any co-ownership of the family home necessarily involves some form of trust for sale.[4]

1. SECTION 30 OF THE LAW OF PROPERTY ACT 1925

It is not unusual in the event of a breakdown in a family relationship that there should be disagreement as to whether the family home should be sold. Some members of the family may wish the property to be sold and the proceeds of sale distributed in the appropriate beneficial shares, while other members may simply wish to remain living in the home. If the issue arises on the granting of a divorce, the court has of course an extensive jurisdiction under the Matrimonial Causes Act 1973 to determine the pattern of the family's future living arrangements. There are, however, several other broad categories of circumstance which do not involve a dissolution of marriage, but in which the future of the family home may likewise become a matter of dispute.

If in such cases the family home has hitherto been held on trust for sale (either express or implied), contentious questions of sale can ultimately be resolved by means of an application to the court under section 30 of the Law of Property Act 1925. This provision confers on the court an apparently unfettered

---

1 See Chapter 22 (ante, p 786). See eg *Wroth v Tyler* [1974] Ch 30.
2 See Chapter 12 (ante, p 374).
3 Ante, p 381. Such consent, if withheld, may be the subject of an application to court under Law of Property Act 1925, s 30 (ante, p 377), in which case the court has discretion to dispense with the unobtainable consent and make an order directing sale. However, before any order for sale is granted, the court 'would be able to go into the merits of the proposed eviction of the person in occupation in all the circumstances of the case' (see *City of London Building Society v Flegg* [1986] Ch 605 at 620A-B per Dillon LJ).
4 See Chapter 12 (ante, p 358).

discretion to 'make such order as it thinks fit',[5] and may be invoked in a variety of situations 'by any person interested'.

(1) The factual context

The problem towards which section 30 of the Law of Property Act 1925 is directed appears in its most acute form where two spouses or de facto partners hold the legal estate in the family home on trust for sale for themselves.[6] If, as trustees for sale, the parties cannot agree whether or not to sell their home, either may invoke the court's jurisdiction under section 30. It is likewise open to a beneficial co-owner (other than a trustee) to have recourse to section 30 where the trustee or trustees for sale insist on selling the family home in defiance of the wishes of the beneficial co-owner.[7]

(2) The primary rule

In strict theory a trust for sale imports a mandatory duty to sell unless the trustees unanimously exercise their power to postpone sale.[8] In the context of the family home this approach automatically predicates that any dispute as to the desirability of sale should be determined conclusively in favour of sale, the only necessary preliminary being possibly the appointment of a second trustee for sale.[9] However, the resolution of a thoroughly human impasse by reference to mere dogma has little attraction in the family context. Not surprisingly the primacy of the duty to sell has been heavily modified by the courts in order to take into account the specific needs and vulnerabilities which are present in the diffuse and complex world of family relations.

2. THE COLLATERAL PURPOSE OF A TRUST FOR SALE OF THE FAMILY HOME

The courts have refined a more subtle and flexible approach in relation to applications under section 30 for sale of the erstwhile family home. Even though technically the prime object of a trust for sale may be sale itself, a trust for sale of a family home is in reality founded on the collateral purpose of providing a residential base for family occupation.[10] The courts have therefore tended to exercise their discretion under section 30 with reference to whether that original collateral purpose is still capable of fulfilment.[11]

---

5   Ante, p 377.
6   Ante, p 359.
7   Ante, p 382.
8   The significance of collateral or secondary purposes underpinning a trust for sale is discussed in Chapter 12 (ante, p 377).
9   Ante, p 376.
10 Ante, p 350.
11 This approach is applicable even outside the immediate family context. See eg *Power v Brighton* (Unreported, Court of Appeal, 14 November 1984), where the court declined to order a sale of property held on an implied trust for sale. The property had been purchased for the purpose of providing a home for the new legal owner, who had funded the acquisition with contributions of money from friends. When those contributors desired to withdraw their respective cash investments, the Court of Appeal held that the 'underlying purpose of the trust' was still in existence and therefore precluded sale.

(1) Survival of the collateral purpose

No sale of the family home will normally be ordered pursuant to section 30 where the collateral purpose underlying the trust for sale subsists and is capable of fulfilment. In *Jones v Challenger*,[12] for instance, Devlin LJ observed that where property is acquired by a husband and wife for the purpose of providing a matrimonial home, 'neither party has a right to demand the sale while that purpose still exists'. Thus sale of the matrimonial home cannot in general be compelled under section 30 while the spouses otherwise continue to live amicably as husband and wife.

This broad rule of thumb is capable of surprising extensions, since the courts seem prepared to adopt the same approach in certain classes of application for sale under section 30 made by third parties.[13] In *Chhokar v Chhokar*,[14] a husband (H) had held the registered title in the matrimonial home on an implied trust for sale for himself and his wife (W). In fraud of W, H then transferred the registered title to P (a casual acquaintance) and disappeared with the proceeds of sale, while P vandalised the house with the intention of preventing any re-entry by W and her children. The Court of Appeal had little difficulty in confirming that under these circumstances P had taken the registered title subject to the overriding interest of W as a beneficial co-owner,[15] thereafter holding that title on trust for sale for himself and W. W, being a woman of some determination, later re-entered her former home and rendered it once again capable of habitation. In defiance of all human expectation H later reappeared with contrite demeanour and, upon being reconciled with W, proceeded to live with her and their children in the original family home.

When P applied for a court order for sale under section 30, Ewbank J inclined in favour of sale on the ground that it was 'quite wrong' that P should provide H and W with a house of substantial value 'free of charge'.[16] This ruling was reversed by the Court of Appeal. Cumming-Bruce LJ referred to the now traditional distinction between the matrimonial or quasi-matrimonial cases, where the court will have regard to 'the underlying purpose of the trust', and the 'third party' cases, where for instance the court 'will usually pay great regard to the voice of a trustee in bankruptcy' who presses for sale on behalf of the 'innocent creditors'.[17] In the view of Cumming-Bruce LJ, the circumstances in *Chhokar* more properly belonged in the first category. Although the 'scoundrel' P had no 'matrimonial privity' with W, he had sought by his 'monstrous fraud' to 'intermeddle in the wife's interests in the matrimonial home' and was not therefore truly a 'stranger to the marriage'.[18]

On this analysis and in view of the reconciliation of H and W, the original trust for sale and its 'underlying objects' were still subsisting at the date of P's application for sale, and there appeared now to be no special reason for frustrating the initial intention of H and W to use the property as their matrimonial home. Indeed all the merits of the case pointed the other way, in

---

12　[1961] 1 QB 176 at 182.
13　See, however, Chapter 26 (post, p 876) for discussion of the usual outcome of section 30 applications made by the trustee in bankruptcy of either spouse.
14　[1984] FLR 313 (ante, pp 188, 303).
15　Ante, p 188.
16　[1984] FLR 313 at 322B-C.
17　[1984] FLR 313 at 327E-G.
18　[1984] FLR 313 at 328C-G.

that P's role in the transaction had been 'from first to last...stamped with immoral stigma.'[19] The proper conclusion was therefore that in equity the voice of W should be allowed to prevail and no sale should be ordered under section 30.[20]

(2) Destruction of the collateral purpose

If the underlying object of the family home trust is frustrated by later events and can no longer be achieved, it seems that 'some very special circumstances need to be shown to induce the court not to order a sale.'[1] However, the decision whether a sale should be ordered lies within the discretion of the court and the presence or absence of the original collateral purpose of the trust for sale is merely one, albeit highly persuasive, factor influencing the exercise of this discretion.[2]

(a) Supervening divorce

It has often been said that the purpose of a matrimonial home trust for sale has failed if the relationship of the trustees breaks down and there no longer exists a marriage in relation to which the property is required as a 'matrimonial home'. In such a case the primacy of the duty to sell is restored—at least according to the view expressed in the older cases. In the words of Devlin LJ in *Jones v Challenger*,[3] it is not 'inequitable' in this event for one of the spouses to want to realise his investment. Accordingly the courts have tended to order sale under section 30 where the initial purpose of a trust for sale of the matrimonial home has been frustrated by the divorce of the trustees.[4] If the 'prime object' of the trust is to have any weight, 'the preservation of the house as a home for one of them singly is not an object at all.'[5]

19   [1984] FLR 313 at 330E-F. Cumming-Bruce LJ declared it difficult 'to find language which, with becoming moderation, describes the moral turpitude of every step taken by [P] throughout this transaction' ([1984] FLR 313 at 330G).

20   The villain P ended up owning the registered title (and a beneficial half-share) in a house which he could neither occupy (ante, p 303) nor sell, and from which he could derive no rental income (ante, p 309). W, on the other hand retained her own beneficial half-share and was furthermore guaranteed rent- and mortgage-free accommodation for the indefinite future, together with the more dubious benefits of cohabitation with her reconciled husband. However, as Cumming-Bruce LJ observed ([1984] FLR 313 at 331H), there was no room here for the shedding of 'crocodile tears' on behalf of P merely because his unlawful enterprise had not succeeded. ('I can see no reason for giving him anything more than the court in an unreported case gave to the money-lender who had rights over a debtor. The proceedings are recorded in a play of Shakespeare'.)

1   *Re Holliday (A Bankrupt)* [1980] 3 All ER 385 at 391f per Goff LJ. See also *Rivett v Rivett* (1966) 200 Estates Gazette 858.

2   Any dogmatic assertion that the subsistence or destruction of the initial purpose of the trust is the only criterion is ultimately inconsistent with the discretionary nature of the jurisdiction conferred by section 30 (see *Luciv v Filinov* (Unreported, Court of Appeal, 15 May 1980) per Megaw LJ).

3   [1961] 1 QB 176 at 184.

4   *Jones v Challenger* [1961] 1 QB 176 at 183. The underlying purpose of the trust is likewise considered spent when, by reason of the separation of the legal owners, the marriage is dead in fact though not yet in law (see *Rawlings v Rawlings* [1964] P 398 at 416, 419, but compare the vigorous dissent by Willmer LJ (at 414). See also *Bedson v Bedson* [1965] 2 QB 666 at 680A.

5   *Jones v Challenger* [1961] 1 QB 176 at 184. Most decisions nowadays as to the future disposition of the matrimonial home on divorce are not made pursuant to Law of Property Act 1925, s 30, but under the different (and rather more specialised) jurisdiction of the divorce courts pursuant to Matrimonial Causes Act 1973, ss 23-25.

(b) Breakdown of co-operative relationships

A similar approach has been applied in other cases where a trust for sale indirectly serves the purpose of extended family living. In *Rivett v Rivett*,[6] for instance, the legal title in a family home was owned jointly by a widower and his son, the purpose of the arrangement being that both should occupy the home together. When the arrangement was disrupted by personal discord, Goff J ruled that the estrangement of father and son had terminated the original purpose of the trust, in that one of 'the two entities' for whom the home had been intended was no longer able to derive any realistic benefit.[7] A sale of the property was thus ordered, even though the home was still required as a residence by the son, his wife and their children.[8]

If, however, the original purpose of a trust for sale was to provide a home for two co-owners during their joint lifetimes and thereafter for the survivor, the court will not order sale at the behest of the personal representatives of the deceased tenant in common. Thus in *Stott v Ratcliffe*[9] the Court of Appeal declined to order sale where the explicit object of the acquisition of the co-owned property had been to secure a home for the survivor after the death of her partner.[10]

(3) **Opposition of approaches under section 30**

Even on the assumption that, in dealing with section 30 applications, the court should refer to the collateral purpose of the trust for sale, the caselaw on the family home discloses an underlying tension. This tension exists between, on the one hand, a predominantly commercialist view of the trust for sale as a device whose object is the protection of the monetary shares of beneficial co-owners and, on the other hand, a more utility-oriented view of the trust for sale as a machinery device whose prime object is the provision of a family home for medium- to long-term residential occupation. In relation to whether weight should be given to a defined collateral purpose, there seems to have been a relentless opposition between the 'property-oriented' and 'family-oriented' approaches.

(a) The property-oriented approach

The adoption of a property-oriented approach has inclined the court towards ordering a sale of co-owned property wherever there is any danger that a

---

6 (1966) 200 Estates Gazette 858.
7 It was not sufficient here that the son had offered to raise £2,000 in part payment of his father's share. It was clear that the balance of the father's share would have to remain indefinitely locked up in the house.
8 See also *Luciv v Filinov* (Unreported, Court of Appeal, 15 May 1980).
9 (1982) 126 SJ 310. See also *Jones (A.E.) v Jones (F.W.)* [1977] 1 WLR 438 at 442G, where the Court of Appeal led by Lord Denning MR declined to order sale of the disputed property at the behest of a trustee, on the ground that such an order would 'defeat the very purpose of the acquisition, namely that the [beneficiary currently in possession] would be able to be there for his life and remain in it as his home.' Since rent may not be chargeable from a resident co-owner by a non-resident co-owner (ante, p 309), it has been pointed out that the court's refusal to order sale is sometimes tantamount to the making of a maintenance order against the latter (see J. Martin, [1980] Conv 361 at 376).
10 See also *Wight v IRC* (1982) 264 Estates Gazette 935 at 936f.

refusal to order sale would either prejudice the monetary value of a beneficiary's equitable share or otherwise keep that share locked up in the property for an unduly lengthy or indefinite period.

(i) Wasting assets   Where the family home is held on a term of years there has been an inclination more readily to order sale under section 30, since a delayed sale may dramatically affect (if not destroy) the money value of the share of the beneficial co-owner who is pressing for sale.[11] If, however, the leasehold term concerned is relatively long, the urgency of sale is considerably abated not least because the asset which is subject to co-ownership is not a wasting asset but is liable to inflate in value.[12]

(ii) Size of the family home   Another factor particularly relevant to a property-oriented view of section 30 relates to the size of the family home and its suitability for the needs of the beneficial co-owner who resists sale. There is a leaning in favour of sale where a home, having once served as the base for a family, is excessively large for one person living there on his or her own.[13] In such circumstances it may well be just and equitable to release the cash shares of the beneficial co-owners.

(iii) Needs of minor children   Nowhere has the property-oriented view of section 30 been more evident than in relation to the position of minor children resident in the family home. In the past a commercialist view of the trust for sale has dissuaded the court from attaching much significance to the presence of children when deciding whether to order a sale of the family home. In *Burke v Burke*,[14] for instance, Buckley LJ thought that the interests of children are 'only incidentally to be taken into consideration...so far as they affect the equities in the matter as between the two persons entitled to the beneficial interests in the property.' To treat the children's father as being 'obliged to make provision for his children by agreeing to retain the property unsold' was, said Buckley LJ, to 'confuse with a problem relating to property considerations which are relevant to maintenance.'[15]

(b) The family-oriented approach

In recent years the property-oriented approach to the family home has been strongly challenged by a much more utilitarian view of trusts for sale in the family home. This family-oriented approach has increasingly moved the courts to exercise discretion under section 30 against ordering a sale of the home.

(i) Needs of minor children   Under the family-oriented approach to section 30, the presence of minor children of the family is seen as prolonging the collateral purpose of the trust for sale beyond the termination of the mutual relationship of the trustees or beneficiaries. In recent years it has come to be questioned whether the underlying purpose of a trust for sale is indeed truly spent when a marriage or family relationship breaks down, in that it often happens that the

11   See *Jones v Challenger* [1961] 1 QB 176 at 187 (lease with only six years to run).
12   See *Mayes v Mayes* (1969) 210 Estates Gazette 935 at 937.
13   See *Jackson v Jackson* [1971] 1 WLR 1539 at 1543G-H.
14   [1974] 1 WLR 1063 at 1067D. (*Burke v Burke* was not strictly a case involving a section 30 application, but arose on an application under Married Women's Property Act 1882 which required that the court decide whether to order the sale of the matrimonial home).
15   [1974] 1 WLR 1063 at 1067E.

home continues to be required as accommodation for the children of the family.[16]

An index of this new perspective was provided by *Williams v Williams*,[17] where a trustee for sale applied under section 30 for an order directing the sale of the jointly owned former matrimonial home. Although the two trustees for sale had been divorced, the plaintiff's ex-wife continued to live in the property with the children of the marriage. The plaintiff sought a sale and equal division of the proceeds in order that he could extract his capital investment from the house and apply it for other purposes. The Court of Appeal declined to order a sale which would have had the effect of evicting the plaintiff's ex-wife and children. Lord Denning MR drew a distinction between 'the old approach' (as applied in *Jones v Challenger* and *Burke v Burke*) and a 'modern view', which he proceeded to expound. Referring to Buckley LJ's approach in *Burke v Burke* as 'now out-dated', Lord Denning indicated that the exercise of discretion under section 30 had been cross-fertilised by the family code which now operates in the reallocation of property on divorce. He stressed that the courts 'nowadays have great regard to the fact that the house is bought as a home in which the family is to be brought up. It is not treated as property to be sold, nor as an investment to be realised for cash.'[18]

In *Williams v Williams* Lord Denning strongly emphasised the importance of the 'use value' rather than the 'capital value' of such property as the family home. The decision reflected the way in which the bleak and inflexible rules of property law have been increasingly coloured during recent years by considerations which are much more sympathetic to the realities of family life. In preferring the residential security of the ex-wife and children above the achievement of capital liquidity for the ex-husband,[19] the Court of Appeal's judgments marked a significant development in the courts' sensitivity to the balance which exists in this area between property considerations and family considerations.[20]

16   Thus, in *Rawlings v Rawlings* [1964] P 398 at 419, Salmon LJ opined that the court would not execute the trust where there were young children, since the original purpose of the trust 'would no doubt have been to provide a home for them'. See the much more startling (and surely inaccurate) statement of Lawton LJ in *Burke v Burke* [1974] 1 WLR 1063 at 1068D: 'If the circumstances are such that the parents buy a house in which to accommodate themselves and any children of the marriage, for my part I cannot see why the children should not be beneficiaries under any implied trust which may come into existence on the purchase of the home'.

17   [1976] Ch 278.

18   [1976] Ch 278 at 285E-F.

19   In *Browne v Pritchard* [1975] 1 WLR 1366 at 1371H, in the context of property adjustment under the Matrimonial Causes Act 1973, Ormrod LJ had dismissed an argument that a wife would be 'kept out of her money' if the court did not order an immediate sale of the former matrimonial home and division of the proceeds. He pointed out that the wife in that case was 'not being kept out of her money. If the marriage had not broken down...she would never have touched a penny of the value of the house, because investment in a home is the least liquid investment that one can possibly make. It cannot be converted into cash while the children are at home and often not until one spouse dies unless it is possible to move into much smaller and cheaper accommodation.'

20   The underlying tension in the caselaw has not, however, quite disappeared. In *Re Holliday (A Bankrupt)* [1980] 3 All ER 385 at 393a-b, Goff LJ reiterated the more commercialist view of section 30, preferring the approach taken by Buckley LJ in *Burke v Burke* to that expressed by Salmon LJ in *Rawlings v Rawlings*. In Goff LJ's view, the collateral purpose of a matrimonial home trust for sale ended on divorce or marital breakdown, but the existence of children remained 'a factor incidentally to be taken into account so far as they affect the equities in the matter as between the persons entitled to the beneficial interests in the property.' However, the preservation of the house as a home for the children could 'be no more an object than its preservation as a home for the spouse.'

(ii) Balance of respective needs   The family-oriented approach to section 30 has enabled the court to respond to a wide variety of competing needs presented by members of a family.[1] It is clear, for instance, that the court may, in its discretion, withhold a sale of the family home where a co-owner who wishes to retain the home is out of work.[2] The more recent caselaw seems to confirm that the family-oriented view has now acquired a controlling relevance in the determination of section 30 applications relating to the family home.

In *In re Evers' Trust*,[3] for instance, the Court of Appeal was faced with what was essentially a security claim following the breakdown of a de facto family relationship.[4] Here a couple had lived together as man and wife for several years, purchasing a home in joint names largely with the aid of a joint mortgage loan. When the parties later separated, the woman and three children (including two from an earlier union) remained in the house. The Court of Appeal refused the man's application for a court order for sale under section 30. Ormrod LJ observed that the approach revealed in the judgment of Lord Denning MR in *Williams v Williams*[5] had considerable advantages 'in these "family" cases', in that it enabled the court 'to deal with substance, that is, reality, rather than form, that is, convenience of conveyancing'.[6]

Thus, while the 'usual practice' of the courts in section 30 applications has been to order a sale and division of the proceeds, thereby 'giving effect to the express purpose of the trust', Ormrod LJ agreed that the court must in every case have regard to the 'underlying purpose' of the trust in question.[7] In the present case, the interests of children, both legitimate and illegitimate, were to be considered, and it was moreover clear that the underlying purpose of the trust for sale had been to provide a home for the couple and their three children 'for the indefinite future'. The Court of Appeal, in declining to order sale under section 30, took into account that the man now had a secure home with his own mother and had no present need to realise his investment,[8] while the woman was prepared to accept full responsibility for the outstanding mortgage liability and would have found it extremely difficult to rehouse herself if the property had been sold.[9] The Court therefore postponed any question of sale, but indicated that sale might become appropriate at some future stage if

1   Because of the family-oriented nature of these factors, it has been said that all section 30 applications relating to the home (whether matrimonial or quasi-matrimonial) should be dealt with by the Family Division rather than the Chancery Division (see *Bernard v Josephs* [1982] Ch 391 at 401F).
2   *Mayes v Mayes* (1969) 210 Estates Gazette 935 at 937.
3   [1980] 1 WLR 1327. See [1981] Conv 79 (A. Sydenham).
4   Pointing out that this was the first occasion on which the Court of Appeal had been faced with a section 30 application in respect of property jointly titled in an unmarried couple, Ormrod LJ said: 'This is a situation which is occurring much more frequently now than in the past, and is a social development of considerable importance with which the courts are now likely to have to deal from time to time ([1980] 1 WLR 1327 at 1330A).
5   [1976] Ch 278 (ante, p 825).
6   [1980] 1 WLR 1327 at 1332H-1333A. Ormrod LJ also pointed out that the family-oriented approach to section 30 'brings the exercise of discretion under this section, so far as possible, into line with the exercise of the discretion given by section 24 of the Matrimonial Causes Act 1973.'
7   [1980] 1 WLR 1327 at 1330G-H.
8   'It is an excellent one, combining complete security with considerable capital appreciation in money terms' ([1980] 1 WLR 1327 at 1334B per Ormrod LJ).
9   [1980] 1 WLR 1327 at 1334B-C.

circumstances changed, as for instance if the woman remarried or if it became financially possible for her to buy the man out.[10]

(iii) Relevance of public housing policy It is not wholly impossible that the property- and family-oriented approaches to disputed questions of sale of the matrimonial home may some day be coloured more overtly by the general issue of public housing policy. It may just be that increased pressure on public housing resources will at some future date provide a ground on which the courts will decline to order the sale of co-owned homes under section 30. In *Bernard v Josephs*[11] Kerr LJ observed that 'above all, in these times of housing shortage, a sale has the disadvantage that the property ceases to be available as a home for either of the parties.' This consideration—whether rightly or wrongly entertained—has become a dominant concern under the Matrimonial Causes Act 1973,[12] and certainly influenced the court in *Bernard v Josephs* to hold that the order for sale in that case should not be enforced if the defendant were willing and able to buy out the plaintiff's share for cash.

10   [1980] 1 WLR 1327 at 1334D-G.
11   [1982] Ch 391 at 410D. See [1983] CLJ 30 at 33f.
12   See eg *Harvey v Harvey* [1982] Fam 83 at 88E-F; [1982] CLJ 228 at 230f.

CHAPTER 25

Dealings with the family home

In the field of English land law one of the more pressing questions of recent years has concerned the degree to which a sale or mortgage of the family home adversely affects the residential security enjoyed by members of the family. The present chapter is therefore devoted to the issue whether the occupation rights of family members can be prejudiced by dealings with the legal title of which they are unaware and to which they do not consent.

1. THE FOCUS OF THE PROBLEM

In the context of third-party dealings with title, some aspects of the law relating to residential security are clear and moderately uncontroversial.

(1) The solely owned family home

Where a family home is not subject to any form of co-ownership at all (either legal or equitable), the only residential protection against purchasers[1] which is offered by English law arises through registration of such statutory 'rights of occupation' as are conferred by the Matrimonial Homes Act 1983.[2] This form of protection is, of course, available only to spouses, and the relevant 'rights of occupation' are binding upon a purchaser of the legal title in the family home only if there has been recourse to the essentially hostile process of entry in the register.[3]

(2) Co-ownership of the legal title

It is likewise the case that few difficulties arise where there is co-ownership of the legal estate in a family home. In such a case the presence of joint tenancy on the face of the documentary title inevitably signals to any purchaser the existence of a trust for sale in respect of the property. The immediate practical consequence is that the purchaser will insist on paying any relevant capital moneys to at least two trustees, whereupon all equitable interests under the trust for sale will be overreached, attaching thereafter to the proceeds of the transaction.[4]

---

1 The term 'purchaser' is used here in its extended statutory sense, which includes both a lessee and a mortgagee (see Law of Property Act 1925, s 205(1)(xxi); Land Registration Act 1925, s 3(xxi)). A chargee of a legal estate in land is statutorily declared to stand in the same position as if he had taken a legal estate (ie, a long leasehold) in the land charged by way of legal mortgage (see Law of Property Act 1925, s 87(1); Land Registration Act 1925, s 3(i), ante, p 573).

2 Ante, p 782.

3 Ante, p 786.

4 Ante, p 354, but see the doubts introduced briefly by the decision of the Court of Appeal in *City of London Building Society v Flegg* [1986] Ch 605 (ante, p 384; post, p 861).

(3) **Undisclosed equitable co-ownership**

It is where there is undisclosed co-ownership of the equitable interest in the family home that the real problem arises. An implied trust for sale may easily come into existence where a home is purchased in the name of A alone, in circumstances in which the purchase price has been raised by the financial contributions of A and B.[5] Intractable difficulties become apparent in this context if A, the legal owner and sole trustee for sale, then engages in some transaction of sale or mortgage with P (see *Fig.* 53).

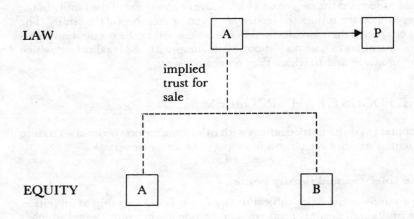

Fig. 53

(a) *The problem for the purchaser*

A trust for sale generated in these circumstances necessarily exists *dehors* the paper title offered to the purchaser, and it is quite possible that the latter will have no idea that his vendor is in fact a trustee for sale.[6] Quite reasonably the purchaser will believe that the vendor is dealing as 'beneficial owner' of the land, ie, as the sole owner of the entire legal and equitable interest in the land. Accordingly it will never occur to the purchaser to pay the capital moneys arising on the transaction to two trustees. However, in the absence of compliance with this formality the purchaser cannot claim that he has statutorily overreached all existing equitable interests.[7]

(b) *The problem for the equitable co-owner*

An equally awkward difficulty awaits the equitable co-owner whose rights are concealed behind a statutory trust for sale. What happens to a family member whose home has been sold or mortgaged without his or her participation,

---

5   Ante, p 363.
6   It is quite possible that the vendor will not be aware of this fact either (ante, p 365).
7   Ante, p 355.

knowledge or consent?[8] Is a wife or partner (perhaps together with minor children) to be evicted from the home in deference to a prior claim of the purchaser? The answer to these questions reflects in large measure the kind of residential security offered in English law to those who live in the family home. The legal response also illuminates the underlying tension which has long existed in English property law between policy considerations of residential security and conveyancing convenience.

2. THE LEGAL EFFECT OF THE SINGLE TRUSTEE'S DEALINGS

A preliminary question arises as to whether a dealing by a single trustee for sale with the legal title in the family home has any effect at all as a legal transaction.

(1) Unregistered land

The clear expectation of the property legislation of 1925 was that there should be no dealings with the legal title of any land held in co-ownership except where those dealings were conducted by at least two trustees for sale. Payment of capital moneys to at least two such trustees was intended to confer upon the purchaser a title which was statutorily declared free of pre-existing co-ownership interests,[9] whilst providing a safeguard for the financial interests of the equitable co-owners.[10]

(a) The rule

In view of the importance of ensuring an overreaching of equitable interests, it used to be thought that a single statutory trustee lacked the competence to deal unilaterally with his own legal title by way of either sale or mortgage.[11] If this

---

8   Of course few problems arise in practice if the disposition is effected with the knowledge or consent of all concerned. There must be thousands of conveyances completed each year by vendors who are sole trustees for sale although neither they nor their purchasers realise this fact. However, failure to comply with the conditions of statutory overreaching usually makes no difference to anyone, since the proceeds of the sale are generally re-invested in the purchase of another family home and the beneficial co-owners could, if necessary, claim to trace their equitable rights into the new property. The Law Commission has proposed, within the context of a new regime of statutory co-ownership of the matrimonial home, that each spouse should have rights to ensure that the other spouse's share of the proceeds of sale of a former home is used in the acquisition of a new one (see *Family Law: Third Report on Family Property: The Matrimonial Home (Co-ownership Rights) and Household Goods* (Law Com No 86, 13 June 1978), paras 1.365ff).

9   Law of Property Act 1925, ss 2(1)(ii), 27(1) (ante, p 356).

10   See *Taylor v Taylor* [1968] 1 WLR 378 at 382G per Danckwerts LJ; Law Com No 86, para 1.250.

11   See *Bull v Bull* [1955] 1 QB 234 at 238 per Denning LJ; *Waller v Waller* [1967] 1 WLR 451 at 453C. Compare, however, *Tunstall v Tunstall* [1953] 1 WLR 770 at 771. In favour of the 'two trustee' rule are the twin considerations that a sole trustee for sale acts in clear breach of his trust when he purports to deal with his legal title, and cannot in any event give a 'valid receipt' for any proceeds paid to him (see Trustee Act 1925, s 14(2). This provision could, at least in theory, make it difficult for a purchaser subsequently to prove that he was a 'purchaser for value'—a point which may be crucial later (post, p 836)).

were the case, any purported conveyance by such a trustee would be a mere nullity[12] and would simply have no effect at law.[13]

It is now clear, however, that a disposition of sale or mortgage effected by a de facto legal owner—albeit a sole trustee for sale—is in general terms quite unchallengeable as a valid transaction with the legal title.[14] Notwithstanding the force of the 'two trustee' rule, the dealing by the single trustee is currently regarded as being a good transaction at law, even though it is concluded wrongfully and in breach of trust.[15]

(b) The unspoken rationale

This generally accepted outcome reflects a cogent argument of public policy, in that a contrary holding (ie, that a single trustee's dealings are automatically void at law) would have placed purchasers in grave jeopardy. The purchaser who took a title from an apparently single vendor would have been subjected in every case to an intolerable burden of enquiry. In order to take a good legal title he would have had to satisfy himself of the non-existence of a trust for sale. How could a purchaser ever prove this negative in relation to a vendor with whom he had had no antecedent dealings and who might well in years past have been the recipient of money contributions creative of a trust for sale? The acceptance *sub silentio* that a sole trustee for sale can deal effectively in respect of a legal estate held on statutory trust for sale simply marks the intuitive premise of the property lawyer that the purchaser of land ought to be protected.[16]

(2) Registered land

In registered land the issue is even clearer. There is no doubt that a disposition or charge of a registered proprietor's legal estate is a valid transaction in relation to that estate, even though the proprietor is in truth a sole trustee for

---

12   It is significant that the penalty of voidness attaches to an irregular conveyance of a legal estate by a tenant for life of settled land who acts outside his statutory authority (see Settled Land Act 1925, s 18(1)(a); *Weston v Henshaw* [1950] Ch 510 at 519f). Since the powers of trustees for sale are modelled on the analogy of the Settled Land Act powers (ante, p 352), it can be argued that the settled land rule is effectively carried over into the context of the implied trust for sale (see S.M. Clayton, [1981] Conv 19). However, it seems improbable that Parliament would have preferred to achieve a comparable result in the case of the trust for sale by means of a mere tenuous inference from the Settled Land Act rather than an express provision in the Law of Property Act 1925 (see B. Rudden, (1963) 27 Conv (NS) 51 at 56).

13   There is even some indication that this result was intended by the legislature. See Law of Property Act 1925, s 27(2) (ante, p 356), which seems to leave open the inference that, where capital money does arise on a transaction by trustees for sale, it is indeed 'necessary to have more than one trustee' and that the absence of a second trustee invalidates the disposition at law.

14   See eg *Caunce v Caunce* [1969] 1 WLR 286 (post, p 835); *Kingsnorth Finance Co Ltd v Tizard* [1986] 1 WLR 783 at 785C; *Ulster Bank Ltd v Shanks* [1982] NI 143 at 144E per Murray J (although here no trust for sale as such was involved). For a query as to the mortgaging powers of trustees for sale, see however (1986) 49 MLR 519 at 523 (R.J. Smith).

15   See, however, [1979] CLJ 23 at 26 (M.J. Prichard). In *Northern Bank Ltd v Henry* [1981] IR 1 at 19, Kenny J expressly left open the question whether a disposition by a bare trustee, likewise acting wrongfully and in breach of trust, has any legal validity.

16   Ante, pp 90, 96. See also *Property Law: The Implications of Williams & Glyn's Bank Ltd v Boland* (Law Com No 115, Cmnd 8636, August 1982), para 10(i), footnote 26.

sale acting in breach of his trust.[17] The trustee has all the powers conferred by statute upon the 'proprietor' of the registered title,[18] and these powers may include a power to transfer the fee simple interest,[19] to grant a lease,[20] and to charge the registered land by way of mortgage.[1]

Unless the proprietor's competence is limited by the entry of a 'restriction' on the register of his title, his powers are freely exercisable if and so long as he remains registered as 'proprietor'.[2] If, however, a restriction is entered on behalf of an equitable co-owner, the Land Registry is effectively precluded from registering any further dealing with the title under which capital money arises, except where the disposition is effected by at least two trustees or by a trust corporation or by order of the Registrar.[3] Where no restriction or other appropriate entry is present on the register, a disposition by a sole trustee has full effect at law,[4] although quite different considerations may affect the enforceability of the equitable interest of the aggrieved co-owner.[5]

3. THE EQUITABLE EFFECT OF THE SINGLE TRUSTEE'S DEALINGS

Given that a sole trustee for sale is competent to deal validly and effectively with his legal title, the issue of protection for equitable co-ownership interests in the family home revolves around the question whether the purchaser takes his title free of such interests. If he does take free of the equitable rights of other co-owners, the residential protection enjoyed by equitable co-owners not represented on the title is gravely diminished. If conversely those equitable rights are binding on the purchaser, an important step has been taken towards guaranteeing the residential security of many kinds of family member.[6]

(1) Range of parties involved

It must be remembered that the 'purchaser' involved in the present context may well be a mortgagee or chargee of the family home.[7] As Murray J said in

17 The registration of the dealing operates by 'statutory magic' to confirm the legal effect of the dealing in favour of the transferee or chargee (Land Registration Act 1925, ss 20(1), 69(1)), despite any defect which may have attended the manner of disposition (see *Argyle Building Society v Hammond* (1985) 49 P & CR 148 at 155 (ante, p 158).
18 Ante, p 154. The term 'proprietor' is defined in the Land Registration Act 1925, s 3(xx) as 'the registered proprietor for the time being of an estate in land or of a charge'.
19 Land Registration Act 1925, s 18(1).
20 Land Registration Act 1925, ss 18(1)(e), 21(1).
1   Land Registration Act 1925, s 25(1) (ante, p 193).
2   Ante, p 157.
3   Ante, p 159.
4   No question was raised as to the validity as a legal transaction of the mortgage effected by a sole trustee for sale in *Williams & Glyn's Bank Ltd v Boland* [1981] AC 487 (post, p 843). In *Knightly v Sun Life Assurance Society Ltd* (1981) *The Times*, 23 July, Nourse J expressly rejected an argument that such a mortgage was legally ineffective. For a similar approach in relation to the transfer of an estate in fee simple, see also *Chhokar v Chhokar* [1984] FLR 313 (post, p 847). A disposition of the registered title by a bare trustee is likewise effective at law, even though the trustee is acting in breach of trust (see *Hodgson v Marks* [1971] Ch 892 at 899C).
5   Post, p 843.
6   If the purchaser is bound by the rights of equitable co-owners, he will merely have stepped into the shoes of the vendor as a sole trustee for sale, and must thereafter hold the legal estate on behalf of himself and any other beneficiary whose interest has not been overreached.
7   Ante, p 829.

Northern Bank Ltd v Beattie,[8] the phrase 'the eternal triangle' has nowadays taken on a new meaning for the judge in the Chancery Division. A typical dispute may involve 'a husband-mortgagor of his matrimonial home, a bank mortgagee of that home, and an estranged wife still living in the home', but essentially the same issues may arise in relation to a much wider range of members of the legal owner's family. The equitable co-owners of the family home may well include such persons as the legal owner's parents, or his de facto partner, his child, his spinster aunt, his homosexual lover, or many other persons who may have helped to finance his purchase of the home. The application of land law principles is indifferent to the precise nature of their relationship.

(2) Special significance of the mortgage transaction

The priority problem under discussion here arises even more frequently with a mortgage of the family home than in the case of a sale or lease of that property.[9] Where the legal owner tries to sell or lease the family residence, other members of his family are more likely to be aware of the impending disposition and are therefore in a position more readily to assert such equitable rights as they may have. However, a mortgage of land is usually a much less visible transaction and in any case the continued occupation of the home by other family members will not necessarily cause alarm to the mortgagee or precipitate disclosure of their co-ownership rights.

(a) Acquisition mortgage

In the case of an acquisition mortgage, the creation of the mortgage or charge is never quite contemporaneous with the mortgagor's acquisition of the legal title in the land which is offered as security.[10] In the theory of unregistered conveyancing a *scintilla temporis* is interposed between the arrival of the legal title in the home-buyer and the creation of the mortgage charge which secures the loan which enabled him to acquire that legal title.[11] In registered conveyancing there may well be an even longer delay before the mortgagee's security is complete.[12] In either circumstance there is the distinct possibility that equitable co-ownership rights may have intervened before the mortgagee receives his security, as for instance would be the case if part of the purchase price for the acquisition were contributed by other family members.[13] The vital question is whether these rights should enjoy priority over the mortgagee.

(b) Post-acquisition mortgage

The problem of priority is raised particularly acutely by a second mortgage or further advance which is granted perhaps many years after the original

8   [1982] 18 NIJB, p 1 (High Court of Northern Ireland).
9   For a problem arising on sale, see *Chhokar v Chhokar* [1984] FLR 313 (ante, p 188).
10 Ante, p 604.
11 See *Church of England Building Society v Piskor* [1954] Ch 553 at 564f (ante, p 603).
12 Ante, p 176; post, p 850.
13 See Law Com No 115, paras 33ff (post, p 866).

purchase of the property[14] and which may be concluded by a sole legal owner without the knowledge or participation of any of his family.[15] The transaction may even comprise a purely informal mortgage of the property by deposit of title documents for the purpose of obtaining a business loan or securing a bank overdraft.[16] In the case of a post-acquisition mortgage, beneficial co-ownership interests may already have been generated quite silently by a range of contributory activity on the part of family members during the period since the initial acquisition of the property.[17] The question inevitably arises whether the lender takes his security subject to these undisclosed equitable rights, or whether he indeed acquires priority over equitable co-owners and can therefore in the last resort recover his loan by forcing a sale of the family home.

The answer to these questions must be sought both in the law of unregistered land and in the law of registered title.

(3) Unregistered land

Typical of the kinds of circumstance which underlie the present enquiry were the facts which presented themselves in *Caunce v Caunce*.[18] Here a husband and wife (hereafter referred to as H and W respectively) purchased a house in unregistered land, contributing the purchase moneys unequally. The property was conveyed into the name of H alone. There thus arose on the facts an implied trust for sale of the fee simple, H holding as a sole trustee on behalf of himself and W as equitable tenants in common. Some time after the acquisition of this matrimonial home, H, acting without the knowledge or consent of W, charged the property by way of legal mortgage to Lloyds Bank in order to secure a loan of money advanced to himself (see *Fig. 54*).

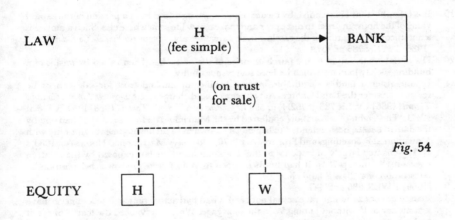

Fig. 54

---

14 Ante, p 565.
15 This possibility is given a strange twist where the legal title in the family home is vested in a company (see eg *Winkworth v Edward Baron Development Co Ltd* (1986) 52 P & CR 67, ante, p 288).
16 Ante, p 576.
17 Ante, p 808.
18 [1969] 1 WLR 286.

When later the bank did not receive the repayments due under the loan, it sought possession of the property against W, who by this stage was living there alone. At the date of the possession hearing, H was bankrupt and, in the euphemism of the judge, 'in default of appearance'.[19]

The contest in *Caunce v Caunce* clearly concerned two innocent parties, both duped by reason of the dishonesty of a third person. When the relevant facts came to light, the bank, which had made no enquiry of W, was doubtless aghast to discover that it had lent money on the security of a property which (unknown to it) was held on trust for sale. For her part, W was horrified to learn that the family home had been mortgaged to the hilt.[20] The legal question was whether the bank took priority over the equitable interest which belonged to W as a tenant in common behind the undisclosed statutory trust for sale.

Stamp J held that the bank did take priority and he therefore made an order for possession against W. The process of statutory overreaching which normally protects co-ownership interests had not occurred; nor did W have any kind of interest which could have been validly registered as a land charge against H.[1] In the result Stamp J took the view that the issue of priority turned on a residual application of the equitable doctrine of notice.[2] Given this premise, the only live question left in *Caunce* was whether the bank had had constructive notice of the equitable rights of W,[3] and here the answer was in the negative.

The decision in *Caunce v Caunce* certainly indicates that, in the context of an implied trust for sale of unregistered land,[4] the present issue of priority depends on the equitable doctrine of notice. In other words, the purchaser from a single statutory trustee for sale takes free of adverse equitable interests only if he ranks as a bona fide purchaser of a legal estate for value without notice (either actual

---

19   It is inferable that H intended, by means of this mortgage, to extract a portion of the capital value of the house in order to disappear and make a new life somewhere else. Such a motive is a not uncommon feature of the caselaw in this area (see also *Kingsnorth Finance Co Ltd v Tizard* [1986] 1 WLR 783 at 787A).

20   H's initial contribution to the purchase price of the house had been raised by means of a building society loan for which he bore sole responsibility.

1   In unregistered land an equitable interest behind an implied trust for sale cannot be registered under the Land Charges Act either as a land charge (see *Kingsnorth Finance Co Ltd v Tizard* [1986] 1 WLR 783 at 792H) or as a *lis pendens* (see *Taylor v Taylor* [1968] 1 WLR 378 at 384C). The 'rights of occupation' conferred by the Matrimonial Homes Act 1967 had not, by the date of *Caunce*, been extended to beneficial co-owners. This development came only with Matrimonial Proceedings and Property Act 1970, s 38—now Matrimonial Homes Act 1983, s 1(11)—enacted largely in response to the shortcomings in the law exposed by the result in *Caunce* itself (ante, p 784). It had not been open to W in *Caunce* to protect her position by registration of a Class F land charge.

2   [1969] 1 WLR 286 at 289G.

3   Plainly the bank did not have actual notice: if it had had actual notice, it would never have lent money to H without joining W in the mortgage. When it advanced the loan moneys, it had no idea that it was dealing with a trustee for sale.

4   The position is quite different in relation to an *express* trust for sale of the family home. Here, of course, it is quite impossible for the purchaser to disclaim notice of the trust affecting the property. If the legal title expressly reveals the existence of a trust for sale, the purchaser must deal with and pay his money to at least two trustees, even if this means that he must demand the appointment of a second trustee, since otherwise the transaction will not overreach the equities behind the trust. Furthermore, if the legal title is already vested in two or more joint tenants, any conveyance executed by only one such trustee will not even produce a good conveyance at law. An effective disposition of a jointly held legal title requires the active participation of all the joint tenants (ante, p 302).

or constructive).[5] However, this proposition marks not the conclusion but the beginning of an inquiry which is both complex and subtle.

(a) Nature of constructive notice

Most of the caselaw in this area is concerned primarily with the rather desperate attempts of beneficial co-owners to fix the relevant purchaser with constructive notice of their undisclosed equitable interests behind a trust for sale. It is not easy either to define the factual circumstances which fasten constructive notice on a purchaser or to determine whether the purchaser has indeed discharged his duty of careful enquiry.[6] It seems, however, to be settled law that a purchaser will be bound by adverse equities only if he has failed to make reasonable enquiries as to the possible existence of undisclosed co-ownership.

(b) Restrictive applications of constructive notice

The traditional approach of English courts disfavours any unnecessary extension of the concept of constructive notice.[7] Purchasers are not lightly to be held to have a duty of enquiry into otherwise undisclosed rights in the land which they seek to purchase. It has been said, moreover, that the 'commonness or otherwise of the right which may be disclosed by the enquiry cannot...affect the reasonableness or otherwise of making any enquiry.'[8] The issue depends not upon the nature of the right but upon the individual circumstances of the case.

A number of factors may be relied upon as fixing a purchaser with constructive notice of the undisclosed rights of equitable co-owners, but the relevant caselaw in this area reveals that until relatively recently there has been a severely restrictive application of the doctrine of notice.

(i) Origin of purchase moneys

In *Caunce v Caunce*,[9] W argued that the bank-mortgagee was fixed with constructive notice by reason of the fact that her own financial contribution towards the acquisition of the family home had originally been withdrawn from an account at the very same branch of the very same bank which some five years later advanced the disputed mortgage moneys to H. She contended that the bank should have realised that her substantial withdrawals of cash arose in connection with the purchase of the family home and that she therefore had some share in its equitable ownership as a tenant in common behind a trust.

---

5   See also *Williams & Glyn's Bank Ltd v Boland* [1979] Ch 312 at 330D, 334C; *Kingsnorth Finance Co Ltd v Tizard* [1986] 1 WLR 783 at 792H-793A; J.F. Garner, (1969) 33 Conv (NS) 240. The same result appears to follow even if the co-ownership is not analysed in terms of a trust for sale (see *Ulster Bank Ltd v Shanks* [1982] NI 143 at 150H; *Allied Irish Banks Ltd v McWilliams* [1982] NI 156 at 161F; *Northern Bank Ltd v Beattie* [1982] 18 NIJB, p 20).
6   There may be a difference between the question whether a party is fixed with constructive notice and whether 'it is reasonable in the circumstances to pursue enquiry' (see *Midland Bank Ltd v Farmpride Hatcheries Ltd* (1980) 260 Estates Gazette 493 at 497 per Shaw LJ).
7   See *Hunt v Luck* [1901] 1 Ch 45 at 48 (ante, p 90).
8   *Midland Bank Ltd v Farmpride Hatcheries Ltd* (1981) 260 Estates Gazette 493 at 498 per Oliver LJ.
9   [1969] 1 WLR 286 at 291C-F.

Stamp J rejected this argument on the ground that such a view would 'place on the bank an intolerable burden and would stretch the doctrine of constructive notice to a point beyond its proper limits.'[10] He was not attracted by the suggestion that a bank-mortgagee should be bound to conduct an enquiry into the financial relations between husband and wife before it could safely advance money on the security of property vested in the name of one.[11] Such a proposition, if once accepted, could not logically be confined to a duty of enquiry into the financial relations of merely the vendor/mortgagor and his spouse. As Stamp J pointed out, the bank would on the same principle be obliged to conduct research into not only the bank account of the vendor/mortgagor's spouse but perhaps also that of his father or other relatives[12]—a proposal of patent absurdity.

(ii) Manner of dealing   The circumstances of *Northern Bank Ltd v Henry*[13] were for all material purposes identical to those which arose in *Caunce v Caunce*.[14] Here McWilliam J ruled in the Irish High Court that a bank-mortgagee was not fixed with constructive notice of the equitable interest of the mortgagor's wife simply because the mortgagor had requested the mortgagee to direct all correspondence to him at his business address rather than at the family home.[15] Such a fact did not place upon the bank a duty to inquire whether the wife enjoyed some as yet undisclosed equitable right in the property.[16]

(iii) Joint occupation of the family home   In the present context it has often been crucial to determine whether a purchaser is fixed with constructive notice by virtue merely of the fact that, at the date of the disputed transaction, an equitable co-owner was in joint occupation of the property together with the vendor.

In *Caunce v Caunce*, W argued that her own occupation of the matrimonial home at the time of the mortgage transaction was sufficient to fix a duty of further enquiry upon the bank-mortgagee as to whether she had any interest in

10   [1969] 1 WLR 286 at 291G-H, citing in support *Hunt v Luck* [1901] 1 Ch 45 at 48. For a similar reluctance to extend the role of constructive notice in this area, see *Ulster Bank Ltd v Shanks* [1982] NI 143 at 150F.
11   Here is exposed the not always obvious tension between rights to protection and rights of privacy in the domestic context. Stamp J took the view that 'in this day and age husbands and wives ought to be able to bank at the same bank without having their accounts analysed by the bank in order to find out if one of them is deceiving the other. The exercise which, it is submitted, ought to have been conducted in the present case would—so it seems to me—have been more appropriate to a police inquiry or that of a detective agency than to a bank manager who often no doubt arranges finances daily in the ordinary course of business' ([1969] 1 WLR 286 at 292F).
12   [1969] 1 WLR 286 at 292G.
13   [1981] IR 1.
14   This case involved a bare trust of the family home, a husband holding on trust for his wife as sole beneficiary, but the reasoning expressed by the courts is equally applicable to the situation of the trust for sale.
15   [1981] IR 1 at 6. The point was not taken up by the Supreme Court on appeal.
16   However, both McWilliam J at first instance ([1981] IR 1 at 6) and Henchy J in the Supreme Court ([1981] IR 1 at 10) were prepared to hold the bank fixed with constructive notice by reason of its failure to enquire whether there was any litigation pending or threatened in respect of the property offered as security. These questions are normally a matter of formal enquiry between conveyancers (ante, p 204), and failure to make such enquiry was 'foolhardy'.

the property offered as security. However, Stamp J declined to accept that W's cohabitation with H had been other than 'wholly consistent with the sole title offered by the husband to the bank'.[17] W had not been 'in apparent occupation or possession' since her presence in the family home was 'ostensibly because she was the husband's wife...' The bank was therefore perfectly entitled to assume that W was in occupation simply because she was married to the apparent owner, H. It is not unusual, even in these days, that a wife should actually live with her husband, and in Stamp J's view the fact of joint residence was not in itself so remarkable as reasonably to cause the bank to suspect that W was in residence not merely qua dutiful wife but also qua beneficial co-owner.[18]

Certain wider implications are triggered off by the view that shared residential occupation can be explained merely by reference to a familial relationship. In *Caunce v Caunce*, for instance, Stamp J pointed out that there were many other persons whose presence in a family home would be similarly compatible with the sole title ostensibly vested in the vendor. Such persons would include, for instance, 'the vendor's father, his Uncle Harry or his Aunt Matilda, any of whom, be it observed, might have contributed money towards the purchase of the property.'[19] In Stamp J's view, the mere fact of joint residence in the family home by any of these persons could be 'wholly consistent with the title offered' by the vendor and would not be sufficiently noteworthy to put a purchaser on enquiry as to the possibility of an undisclosed beneficial entitlement.[20] Thus, even though such occupiers might in truth be equitable co-owners behind some implied trust for sale, a purchaser was not to be fixed with constructive notice of their rights merely by reason of a failure to make further enquiries on the premises. Any contrary holding would be adverse to the public interest in that bank-mortgagees would be rendered 'snoopers and busybodies in relation to wholly normal transactions of mortgages.'[1]

(c) The conveyancing perspective

This restrictive application of the doctrine of notice is, of course, entirely consistent with the hard-nosed conveyancer's view of land law priorities. The conveyancing perspective places a premium on the free commerciability of land, thereby elevating the 'exchange value' in preference to the 'use value' of

17 [1969] 1 WLR 286 at 293G.
18 In *Caunce* the mortgagor was still in residence in the family home at the time of the mortgage, although he left shortly thereafter with the loan money. Stamp J was careful to emphasise that the decision would have been quite different if the vendor were not in occupation 'and one finds another party whose presence demands an explanation and whose presence one ignores at one's peril' ([1969] 1 WLR 286 at 294A). In such a case the presence on the premises of an apparent stranger is clearly inconsistent with the sole title ostensibly offered by the legal owner, and any purchaser who continues to deal with the absent legal owner takes subject to all equitable interests (other than that of the vendor) which may exist behind any implied trust for sale.
19 [1969] 1 WLR 286 at 293H.
20 See, however, *Nelthorpe v Holgate* (1844) 1 Collyer 203 at 212, 215, 63 ER 384 at 388f, where it was said that the presence of the vendor's mother in the property sold 'may well' have fixed the purchaser with constructive notice of the mother's life interest in that property.
1 There is of course a duty in the purchaser to inspect the land as well as the title in respect of which he transacts (ante, p 90), but see *Northern Bank Ltd v Henry* [1981] IR 1 at 6 per McWilliam J (post, p 842).

land.[2] Transactions in realty are naturally facilitated by reducing the burden of enquiry imposed on purchasers and by protecting the latter from the claims of undetected beneficial co-owners.[3] The commercialist concern for smooth conveyancing practice can be promoted only by claiming priority over the social interest which favours residential protection for family members.[4]

(d)   The mortgage perspective

There is a further dimension to the generally persuasive policy that the burden of enquiry fastened upon purchasers should not be increased save for good cause. It is a cogent fact of economic life that banks and other institutional lenders would not be so ready to lend money on the security of realty if the law were to impose added risks for the bona fide mortgagee.[5] In the older caselaw it is significant that the money interest was consistently allowed to prevail over the residential interests of family members. The 'solid tug of money',[6] coupled with a pragmatic desire not to inhibit lenders from financing home ownership and entrepreneurial endeavour, has traditionally exerted an hypnotic influence over the determination of priorities in this area.

(e)   The modern approach to occupation rights

Recent years have witnessed a more general recognition of the importance of residential security in the family home.[7] It was inevitable that this shift in approach would eventually be reflected in a more sympathetic ordering of priorities in the present context. In consequence the rights of beneficial co-owners in the family home have been promoted significantly by developments both legislative and judge-made.

(i)   Class F land charge   The residential protection enjoyed by certain equitable co-owners has now been improved—at least in theory—by the extension of the

2   Ante, p 375. It is the traditional view of the property lawyer that 'where the equities are equal the purchaser should prevail, for the policy of the law is to favour alienability and clean titles' (H.W.R. Wade, [1956] CLJ 216 at 219). See also G. Woodman, (1980) 96 LQR 336 at 340.

3   In *Caunce v Caunce* [1969] 1 WLR 286 at 292H, Stamp J relied heavily on the famous dictum of Lord Upjohn in *National Provincial Bank Ltd v Ainsworth* [1965] AC 1175 at 1233G-1234A, that it 'has been the policy of the law for over a hundred years to simplify and facilitate transactions in real property. It is of great importance that persons should be able freely and easily to raise money on the security of their property' (ante, p 567).

4   The decision in *Caunce v Caunce* [1969] 1 WLR 286 epitomised the orthodox property lawyer's view that it is virtually conclusive of any issue of priority in land law to declare the matter to be essentially a problem of conveyancing or banking practice. It was consistent with this view that the law should tend towards minimising any possible duty of enquiry as to the equitable entitlements of wives and other family members concealed behind statutory trusts. Emphasising that 'the practice of conveyancers carries great weight', Stamp J pointed out 'how unworkable and undesirable it would be if the law required such an enquiry—an enquiry...which would be as embarrassing to the enquirer as it would be...intolerable to the wife and the husband' ([1969] 1 WLR 286 at 294C).

5   The bulk of housing finance in this country is provided by banks, building societies and local authorities (ante, p 563), and there seems little doubt that the availability of credit for the purpose of financing home-ownership would be adversely affected by the imposition of onerous legal liability on the lender. See *Multiservice Bookbinding Ltd v Marden* [1979] Ch 84 at 104H (ante, p 592).

6   *Hofman v Hofman* [1965] NZLR 795 at 800 per Woodhouse J.

7   Ante, p 65.

statutory scheme of 'rights of occupation' provided under the Matrimonial Homes Act.[8] The scope of the Matrimonial Homes Act was enlarged in 1970 precisely in order to cover spouses who own an equitable share in the matrimonial home but are not represented on the legal title.[9] In unregistered land a spouse who is beneficially entitled under a trust for sale of the matrimonial home may nowadays protect his or her statutory 'rights of occupation' by the simple act of registering a Class F land charge. Such registration renders the spousal 'rights of occupation' automatically binding on any purchaser of the family home.[10]

It is nevertheless one of the ironies of the legislative process that the extended coverage of the Matrimonial Homes Act has not in practice resulted in any greater residential protection for spouse-beneficiaries in the family home. It is highly likely that a spouse-beneficiary will never have heard of Class F land charges and in most instances the much vaunted 'rights of occupation' provided by Parliament are simply rendered void as against purchasers for want of registration.[11] It must nevertheless be clearly understood that the 'rights of occupation' conferred by the Matrimonial Homes Act are quite distinct from any equitable proprietary interest which a spouse may also have as a co-owner of the family home.[12] The latter entitlement may still of course be pleaded as a basis for priority over the purchaser, but this is merely to re-introduce the application of the equitable doctrine of notice.

(ii) Changing judicial outlook The traditional approach to problems of residential security tended heavily towards increased protection for purchasers from a single statutory trustee for sale at the expense of the beneficiaries behind the trust, even though the latter might be in actual occupation of the land. However, important developments in judicial outlook during recent years have now made this robust preference seem much less tenable.

A new stance with regard to residential security in the family home began to make itself apparent during the 1970s, not merely in the English courts but also in other jurisdictions. An initial indication of the shift towards a more liberal outlook came in the registered land case of *Hodgson v Marks*,[13] where a similar question arose as to the scope of enquiry incumbent upon a purchaser of land held on trust. Russell LJ declared himself unable to accept a 'general proposition' that enquiry need not be made of any person on the premises if the proposed vendor himself appears to be in occupation.[14] Russell LJ was not, however, prepared to formulate any 'code or catalogue of situations in which a person other than the vendor should be held to be in occupation of unregistered

---

8 Ante, p 782.
9 Matrimonial Proceedings and Property Act 1970, s 38, introducing Matrimonial Homes Act 1967, s 1(9), which is now Matrimonial Homes Act 1983, s 1(11) (ante, p 784). The motivation for the 1970 amendment is to be found in Law Commission, *Family Law: Report on Financial Provision in Matrimonial Proceedings* (Law Com No 25, July 1969), para 60.
10 Ante, p 789.
11 Land Charges Act 1972, s 4(8); see *Williams & Glyn's Bank Ltd v Boland* [1979] Ch 312 at 328F per Lord Denning MR (ante, p 790).
12 Ante, p 374.
13 [1971] Ch 892 (ante, p 185).
14 In so far as *Caunce v Caunce* might have seemed to lay down such a proposition, Russell LJ was unwilling to agree ([1971] Ch 892 at 935A).

land for the purpose of constructive notice of his rights'.[15] The matter must depend on the circumstances.[16]

The idea that purchasers might be fixed with a duty of enquiry as to the possible equitable entitlements of family members then received significant support in the Irish jurisdictions. In *Northern Bank Ltd v Henry*,[17] the Supreme Court held that a mortgagee had constructive notice of the rights of a wife-beneficiary under a trust of the matrimonial home. Parke J took the view that 'any person who was offered a title to a matrimonial home by one spouse should have been alerted to the possibility that the other spouse might have a claim...to at least a share in the beneficial interest in the property.'[18] This forthright approach almost immediately found a following in the High Court of Northern Ireland.[19]

In *Kingsnorth Finance Co Ltd v Tizard*[20] the English courts finally confirmed this steady movement towards a less restrictive application of constructive notice in the context of co-ownership.[1] Here the legal title in the disputed property was in fact held by a husband on an implied trust for sale for himself and his estranged wife. The home provided a residence for the husband and two children of the family. The wife slept in the house only in the husband's absence and otherwise lived in separate accommodation nearby, usually visiting the home twice a day in order to cook meals for the children. The husband, although merely a single statutory trustee, secretly charged the legal title to a finance company and then disappeared to America with one of the

15   [1971] Ch 892 at 932C-D.
16   Russell LJ added ominously that 'a wise purchaser or lender will take no risks' ([1971] Ch 892 at 932C-D). A similar cutting back of the scope of *Caunce* was evident again in the context of registered land in *Williams & Glyn's Bank Ltd v Boland* [1981] AC 487 where, although the House of Lords expressly declined to overrule *Caunce*, Lord Scarman indicated (at 511G) that he himself was 'by no means certain' that the case had been correctly decided. Lord Wilberforce expressed approval (at 505E) of the observations of Russell LJ in *Hodgson v Marks*, and in the Court of Appeal Ormrod LJ ([1979] Ch 312 at 335D) thought that *Caunce* might well be decided differently.
17   [1981] IR 1 (ante, p 90). See R.A. Pearce, *Joint Occupation and the Doctrine of Notice*, (1980) 15 Ir Jur (NS) 211. This conclusion seems to have been heavily influenced by the total failure of the bank-mortgagee to make any enquiry whatsoever as to whether persons other than the mortgagor were in occupation of the property. The mortgage had been granted rather hurriedly in response to the bank's insistence on the provision of some collateral security in respect of the mortgagor's rapidly increasing bank overdraft. In the words of Kenny J, quoting counsel, the bank was 'prepared to take whatever interest in the property the husband had "warts and all"' ([1981] IR 1 at 19).
18   [1981] IR 1 at 21. See also *Somers v W* [1979] IR 94 at 111, 114f, where the mere fact that a purchaser knew that she was dealing with a family home was held to be enough to fasten upon her a duty to enquire as to the possible beneficial entitlement of the vendor's wife. Failure to enquire fixed the purchaser with constructive notice and excluded her from the protection given to a purchaser 'in good faith' as defined in the Family Home Protection Act 1976, s 3(3)(a), (6).
19   See *Allied Irish Banks Ltd v McWilliams* [1982] NI 156 at 161H-162A; *Northern Bank Ltd v Beattie* [1982] 18 NIJB, p 20. In both cases Murray J dismissed a bank's application for possession of the family home, holding that the bank had made no enquiry at all as to the possible beneficial rights of the mortgagor's wife and was therefore bound by constructive notice of such rights as she turned out to have.
20   [1986] 1 WLR 783. See (1986) 136 NLJ 771 (P. Luxton); [1986] Conv 283 (M.P. Thompson).
1   In *Bristol and West Building Society v Henning* [1985] 1 WLR 778 at 781G, Browne-Wilkinson LJ had already accepted without demur the ruling at first instance that a woman's occupation of the family home could constitute constructive notice of her equitable rights. The case was, however, decided by the Court of Appeal on different grounds (post, p 860).

children, leaving the wife to defend the mortgagee's inevitable action for possession. Before any charge had been taken over the home, the mortgagee's agent had made a pre-arranged visit to the premises on a Sunday afternoon for the purpose of the usual mortgagee's inspection and valuation. It was clear in retrospect that the time of the visit had been fixed by the husband to coincide with the wife's absence from the home and that all signs of her occupation had been 'temporarily eliminated' by the husband.[2] The agent of course discovered evidence of occupation by two teenage children, but was told by the husband that their mother had left the home some time before and lived elsewhere.

On these facts the mortgagee's action for possession was rejected by the High Court. The husband had originally described himself in his loan application as being 'single', and Judge Finlay QC held that the agent's reference in his report to the presence of the children should have alerted the mortgagee to the need to make further enquiry as to the possible rights of a wife.[3] Here the wife had indeed been in 'occupation' of the property in that she had been present 'virtually every day for some part of the day'.[4] The failure to make further enquiry as to her possible entitlements, coupled with a form of inspection which Judge Finlay QC condemned as unsatisfactory,[5] led the court to the conclusion that the mortgagee was fixed with constructive notice of the wife's equitable interest under the trust for sale.[6]

Although it is somewhat early to judge, it seems likely that the decision in *Kingsnorth Finance Co Ltd v Tizard* is symptomatic of a more liberal judicial approach to the protection of the residential interests of equitable co-owners behind a statutory trust for sale of unregistered land. If this tentative conclusion is correct, the law of unregistered land will merely reflect the developments which had already occurred in the law of registered title.

(4) Registered land

Exactly the same problem of priority which has been discussed in unregistered land terms has posed itself in the law of registered title. The relevant issues reached the House of Lords in 1980 in the conjoined appeals in *Williams & Glyn's Bank Ltd v Boland* and *Williams & Glyn's Bank Ltd v Brown*.[7] Both cases concerned the question whether a wife-beneficiary under an implied trust for sale could claim priority over a bank to which her husband had charged the family home by way of legal mortgage as security for a business loan (see *Fig. 55*). In both cases it was alleged (and generally accepted) that the wife had acquired an equitable share in the home by reason of her past financial contributions towards its purchase. It was likewise common ground that in neither case had the bank made any enquiry of the wife before advancing the mortgage moneys to her husband; each wife claimed that she had had no contemporary knowledge of the creation of the mortgage charge.

2 [1986] 1 WLR 783 at 793C.
3 [1986] 1 WLR 783 at 792D.
4 [1986] 1 WLR 783 at 788E.
5 Judge Finlay QC was not satisfied that in the present circumstances a 'pre-arranged inspection on a Sunday afternoon fell within the category of "such inspections which ought reasonably to have been made," the words in section 199 of the Law of Property Act 1925...' ([1986] 1 WLR 783 at 795B).
6 [1986] 1 WLR 783 at 794E.
7 [1981] AC 487 (hereafter referred to collectively as *Boland*).

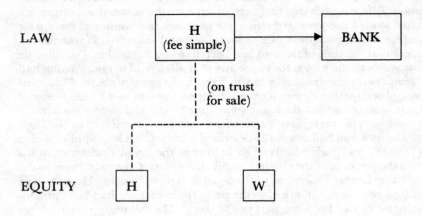

Fig. 55

The House of Lords reached the conclusion that an equitable co-owner concealed behind an implied trust for sale of the family home can have an 'overriding interest' which binds those who unwittingly deal with a sole trustee for sale. Since in *Boland* the right which thus became 'overriding' was the right of occupation carried by an equitable interest under a trust for sale,[8] the bank was held to be unable to exercise the mortgagee's normal right to recover possession of the property for the purpose of selling up and recouping the outstanding loan.[9] This decision has not only clarified the law of registered land but has had a profound collateral effect in coercing the law of unregistered land towards a parallel conclusion.

(a)   The legal issues raised in Boland's Case

Many questions of priority in registered land can be resolved simply by tackling two issues in turn.[10] Can the interest for which priority is sought be protected *either* as a minor interest *or* as an overriding interest within the scheme of the Land Registration Act 1925? The relevant principles of registered land law do not in general depend on whether the parties involved are married or related by family connection,[11] but once again the outcome provides some index of the residential security conferred by the law on family members.[12]

8   Ante, p 373.
9   In *Williams & Glyn's Bank Ltd v Boland* the plaintiff bank succeeded in its action for possession before Templeman J ((1978) 36 P & CR 448), only to lose in the subsequent appeals to the Court of Appeal ([1979] Ch 312) and the House of Lords ([1981] AC 487). On the Court of Appeal's ruling, see [1979] Conv 377 (F.R. Crane); (1979) 42 MLR 567 (W.T. Murphy); [1979] CLJ 254 (M.J. Prichard); (1979) 95 LQR 501 (R.J. Smith); (1979) 129 NLJ 700 (H.W. Wilkinson). On the House of Lords' decision, see (1980) 43 MLR 692 (S. Freeman); [1980] Conv 361 (J. Martin); [1980] CLJ 243 (M.J. Prichard); (1981) 97 LQR 12 (R.J. Smith).
10   See Chapter 9 (ante, p 228).
11   See *Williams & Glyn's Bank Ltd v Boland* [1981] AC 487 at 502F per Lord Wilberforce.
12   The registered land outcome is particularly significant because registration of title is most prevalent in urban areas, which in their turn are most likely to throw up problems related to co-ownership and cohabitation in family form (ante, p 294).

(i) Protection for minor interests In *Boland* there had clearly been several means of protection available to W as an equitable co-owner behind an implied trust for sale of the family home. W could have protected two kinds of interest by entry on the register of H's title. She could have entered her equitable proprietary interest as a minor interest;[13] she could similarly have protected her spousal 'rights of occupation' arising under the Matrimonial Homes Act.[14] She took neither course of action, with the result that both of these entitlements were rendered entirely ineffective against the bank-mortgagee unless they could provide the basis for an 'overriding interest' under section 70(1)(g) of the Land Registration Act 1925.[15]

(ii) Protection for overriding interests The crucial question in *Boland* therefore related to whether either of W's entitlements could rank as an overriding interest binding the bank as registered chargee. One half of the answer to this question was already clear beyond the shadow of a doubt. Spousal 'rights of occupation' under the Matrimonial Homes Act can never be an overriding interest: this possibility is unambiguously precluded by legislation.[16] The only question left was whether a co-owner's equitable proprietary interest could give rise to an overriding interest within section 70(1)(g) of the Land Registration Act 1925.[17] In the absence of any enquiry addressed to W by the bank-mortgagee, this question ultimately turned on whether W could be said to have been 'in actual occupation' of the land at the effective date of the bank's charge.[18] The House of Lords decided this issue in the affirmative, but in so doing left problems which will almost certainly require legislative attention.

(b) Actual occupation of the family home

The question whether joint occupation of the family home by a wife-

---

13 In the Court of Appeal Ormrod LJ seemed to suggest that W's equitable interest could not have constituted a minor interest, since it could not have been overreached by a conveyance from a single trustee for sale ([1979] Ch 312 at 337F). However, this assertion was expressly rejected in the House of Lords by Lord Roskill ([1981] AC 487 at 512F-G). It is nevertheless clear that the protection of an equitable proprietary interest as a minor interest normally requires the co-operation of the registered proprietor (ante, p 159)—and this may not always be forthcoming.

14 Matrimonial Homes Act 1967, s 2(7), now Matrimonial Homes Act 1983, s 2(8); Land Registration Act 1925, s 64(5) (ante, p 160).

15 Land Registration Act 1925, s 59(6). There is no doubt that the apparent negligence of W in failing to take appropriate protective action played some part in determining the course of the litigation (post, p 858).

16 Matrimonial Homes Act 1967, s 2(7), now Matrimonial Homes Act 1983, s 2(8)(b) (ante, p 182).

17 It has been seen elsewhere (ante, p 372), that one of the major obstacles in the way of an affirmative outcome was removed fairly early in the *Boland* litigation. It was accepted by all concerned that, despite the doctrine of conversion, an equitable interest behind a trust for sale is a right subsisting in reference to land in a sense sufficient to satisfy the definitional requirements of Land Registration Act 1925, s 70(1).

18 Lord Wilberforce pointed out ([1981] AC 487 at 504B) that the equitable doctrine of notice affecting purchasers of unregistered land 'has no application even by analogy to registered land.' Lord Scarman likewise stressed ([1981] AC 487 at 511E) that the Land Registration Act 1925 has 'substituted a plain factual situation for the uncertainties of notice, actual or constructive, as the determinant of an overriding interest.' The House of Lords even rejected ([1981] AC 487 at 508E) an attempt to import the equitable doctrine of notice into registered land via Land Registration Act 1925, s 74. See also [1979] Ch 312 at 343D per Browne LJ; [1979] CLJ 254 at 256 (M.J. Prichard).

beneficiary amounts to 'actual occupation' by her touches deeply upon perceptions of the relative social and economic status of husband and wife. It was significant that the caselaw prior to *Boland* had seemed to contain sex-biased perceptions of the significance of a married woman's presence and function in the family home. The older decisions consistently reinforced the idea that a wife's residence in the home was subordinated to, and submerged within, the occupation enjoyed by her husband.

(i) The 'shadow' theory   In *Bird v Syme Thomson*,[19] a case which concerned facts virtually identical to those of *Boland*, Templeman J had rejected a wife-beneficiary's claim that she had an overriding interest in respect of a leasehold flat. In his view, 'when a mortgagor is in actual occupation of the matrimonial home, it cannot be said that his wife also is in actual occupation.'[20] 'Actual occupation' in the statutory sense thus belonged exclusively to the owner of the registered title, the wife being present 'only...as a shadow of occupation of the owner.'[1] Templeman J reiterated this view in giving judgment for the bank-mortgagee at first instance in *Boland*.[2] He pointed to the 'wide and almost catastrophic' nature of the extensive burden of enquiry which would be forced on prospective purchasers by any other holding.[3]

Until 1980 this fear of opening up a 'Pandora's box' of insoluble complications had dissuaded the courts from any liberal construction of 'actual occupation' for the purpose of section 70(1)(g). The burden of enquiry imposed on the purchaser of registered land was deliberately restricted in order to facilitate the operations of conveyancers and bankers. The courts played safe and insisted that no equitable co-owner—not even a spouse—could ever claim to have any interest overriding a purchaser of the registered title. In particular, the courts consistently endorsed the view that those who lend money expect to be repaid in full even if that means that wives and families must be evicted from their homes—a view somewhat crudely expressed in the adage that 'an Englishman's home is his bank manager's castle!'

(ii) Rejection of gender-discrimination   One of the major drawbacks of the 'shadow' theory was that it seemed to compel the scarcely plausible conclusion that a woman who was physically resident in the home, who lived, cooked, washed clothes and reared children in the home, was not 'in actual occupation' of that home for the purpose of section 70(1)(g) of the Land Registration Act 1925. The 'shadow' theory of a wife's residence in the family home was

---

19 [1979] 1 WLR 440. See [1979] CLJ 23 (M.J. Prichard); [1979] Conv 72 (F.R. Crane).
20 [1979] 1 WLR 440 at 444A.
 1 [1979] 1 WLR 440 at 444E.
 2 (1978) 36 P & CR 448 at 454.
 3 It has been pointed out that Lord Templeman is a judge with lengthy experience of conveyancing practice at the Chancery Bar and was a member of the Royal Commission on Legal Services whose Report (Cmnd 7648, 1979) was very much concerned with the conveyancing process (see S. Freeman, (1980) 43 MLR 692 at 693). It is of interest to note that four years after giving judgment for the bank-mortgagee in *Boland*, Lord Templeman, speaking in a House of Lords' debate, saw 'no reason why the *Boland* decision which protects [a wife] should not stand' (*Parliamentary Debates, House of Lords, Official Report*, Vol 437 (Session 1982-1983), Col 649 (15 December 1982)).

therefore finally and convincingly refuted in *Boland*. Here both the Court of Appeal and the House of Lords firmly rejected any suggestion that the presence pleaded as 'actual occupation' should in some sense be adverse to that of the registered owner.[4]

The concept of vicarious occupation through a spouse was condemned by the Court of Appeal in *Boland* as 'unrealistic and anachronistic'[5] since it represented the law 'a hundred years ago when the law regarded husband and wife as one: and the husband as that one.'[6] It would be difficult, said Ormrod LJ, to 'imagine clearer examples of "actual occupation" in the ordinary sense' than the case of a wife living with her husband in the matrimonial home.[7] In the House of Lords, Lord Wilberforce noted that the 'shadow' theory is now 'heavily obsolete'[8] and that the statutory phrase 'actual occupation' is neutral between male and female, involving 'no question of matrimonial law, or of the rights of married women or of women as such.'[9] It was 'unacceptable' to suggest that the apparent occupation of the wife of a vendor/mortgagor could be 'satisfactorily accounted for by his',[10] and Lord Wilberforce had no difficulty in concluding that 'a spouse, living in a house, has an actual occupation capable of conferring protection, as an overriding interest, upon rights of that spouse.'[11]

(c) The significance of the Boland decision

The decision in *Williams & Glyn's Bank Ltd v Boland* has exerted a dramatic impact upon the law of co-ownership interests in both registered and unregistered land. The importance of the decision (and indeed its correctness) can be measured in several ways.

(i) Reversal of the traditional property perspective The *Boland* case was remarkable not least because it involved a stark confrontation between the need for streamlined conveyancing practice and the requirement of social justice for the family. The eventual ruling in *Boland* demanded in effect that the purchaser of registered land should at his own risk prove a negative—that is, satisfy himself

---

4 [1981] AC 487 at 505B per Lord Wilberforce, echoing the view of Ormrod LJ in the Court of Appeal ([1979] Ch 312 at 339A).
5 [1979] Ch 312 at 343B per Browne LJ.
6 [1979] Ch 312 at 332C per Lord Denning MR. Ormrod LJ voiced the objection that the notion of vicarious occupation through a wife 'resurrects the outmoded concept of the head of the family' ([1979] Ch 312 at 338H).
7 [1979] Ch 312 at 338F. 'Visit the home and you will find that [the wife] is in personal occupation of it just as much as [the husband] is. She eats there and sleeps there just as he does. She is in control of all that goes on there—just as much as he. In no respect whatever does the nature of her occupation differ from his...' ([1979] Ch 312 at 332D-E per Lord Denning MR).
8 [1981] AC 487 at 505G.
9 [1981] AC 487 at 502E. See also [1979] Ch 312 at 333D-E per Ormrod LJ.
10 [1981] AC 487 at 505G-H.
11 [1981] AC 487 at 506C. The pre-*Boland* view of the position of a wife in the family home has now been turned on its head. In *Bird v Syme-Thomson* [1979] 1 WLR 440 at 444E Templeman J held that a wife who was physically resident in her home was not in 'actual occupation'. In *Chhokar v Chhokar* [1984] FLR 313 at 317F, a wife was unhesitatingly declared to be in 'actual occupation' notwithstanding that she was clearly absent from the property at the relevant time—she had been physically excluded from the house (ante, p 188).

that no overriding interest impinges upon the interest which he takes. Reliance can no longer be placed on an apparently unencumbered legal title: the purchaser must take special steps to ascertain whether there are persons other than the vendor/mortgagor in actual occupation of the property. He must then make enquiry of all persons living in the property who might conceivably claim equitable co-ownership rights capable of protection by way of overriding interest. The imposition of such an onerous duty of enquiry militates heavily against the traditionally vigorous preference of English land law for protection of the purchaser.[12]

(ii) Allocation of risk The fundamental question underlying the *Boland* litigation related quite simply to the extent to which a lender of money should be required as a matter of policy to take the risk of a defect in the borrower's title in any property offered as security. In *Boland* the House of Lords ruled in favour of increasing the risk imposed on the lender, thereby leaving it to the latter to adopt means of self-protection. Lord Wilberforce saw this 'extension of the risk area' for purchasers as following necessarily from 'the extension, beyond the paterfamilias, of rights of ownership, itself following from the diffusion of property and earning capacity.'[13] This shift in the balance of risk was strongly supported by the law lords' use of the rhetoric of social justice. The House of Lords effectively traded off protection for the bank against a higher social interest—that of greater security for the family in its occupation of the matrimonial home.[14]

(iii) Triumph of 'social justice' The *Boland* ruling thus disclosed a concerted policy decision to uphold the integrity of the family home in preference to the convenience of conveyancers. Lord Denning MR declared in the Court of Appeal in *Boland* that the courts 'should not give monied might priority over social justice'.[15] In his view the bank was 'not entitled to throw these families out into the street—simply to get the last penny of the husband's debt.'[16] He did not see that this new approach would cause any difficulty to conveyancers[17] or

---

12   Ante, p 90.
13   [1981] AC 487 at 508G. For further discussion of the emergence of a 'property-owning democracy', see Chapters 19 - 21.
14   This approach is in keeping with a noticeable tendency over recent years for the House of Lords to infuse a new direction in particular areas of law 'if it be thought to be socially necessary'. See *Davis v Johnson* [1979] AC 264 at 348F; *Gillick v West Norfolk AHA* [1986] AC 112 at 171E, 183B.
15   [1979] Ch 312 at 333A.
16   [1979] Ch 312 at 333C. Lord Denning even went so far as to fasten an obligation of social morality upon institutional lenders: 'If a bank is to do its duty, in the society in which we live, it should recognise the integrity of the matrimonial home. It should not destroy it by disregarding the wife's interest in it—simply to ensure that it is paid the husband's debt in full—with the high interest rate now prevailing' ([1979] Ch 312 at 332H-333A). It is perhaps significant that in *Boland* the bank had sanctioned a sale of the mortgagor's property (valued at £22,500) for merely £1,500 ((1978) 36 P & CR 448 at 450f).
17   See the comparable remarks of Lord Denning MR in *Brikom Investments Ltd v Carr* [1979] QB 467 at 484F: 'I prefer to see that justice is done: and let the conveyancers look after themselves'.

impair the proper conduct of businesses,[18] since

> [a]nyone who lends money on the security of a matrimonial home nowadays ought to realise that the wife may have a share in it. He ought to make sure that the wife agrees to it, or to go to the house and make inquiries of her. It seems to me utterly wrong that a lender should turn a blind eye to the wife's interest or the possibility of it—and afterwards seek to turn her and the family out—on the plea that he did not know she was in actual occupation.[19]

The House of Lords unanimously confirmed this relegation of the commercial interest of the bank-mortgagee behind the claim to family security. Lord Wilberforce acknowledged that this outcome might 'add to the burdens of purchasers, and involve them in enquiries which in some cases may be troublesome.'[20] He was not, however, unhappy to see a 'departure from an easy-going practice of dispensing with enquiries as to occupation beyond that of the vendor and accepting the risks of doing so.'[1] The intensification of the duty of enquiry was simply the inevitable concomitant of 'the widespread development of shared interests of ownership.'

An even more robust unconcern for the protests of conveyancers emerged in the speech of Lord Scarman, who thought that the alleged difficulties in conveyancing and banking practice had been 'exaggerated'. In his view, 'bankers and solicitors exist to provide the service which the public needs. They can—as they have successfully done in the past—adjust their practice, if it be socially required.'[2] In Lord Scarman's view, the 'achievement of social justice' now required that the courts give a meaning to section 70(1)(g) which militated in favour of, and not against, the preservation of those rights of co-ownership in the family home which the courts have come to recognise over the past three decades as having been earned by various kinds of family member.[3]

(iv) Was justice done? Notwithstanding the powerful appeal to wider sentiments of social justice, the correctness of the *Boland* decision has since been

---

18   The husbands in *Boland* were both small businessmen who had gone bankrupt when Williams & Glyn's called in their respective loans. It was therefore particularly unfortunate that Williams & Glyn's chose 1979 to run a series of advertisements in the national press containing such announcements as 'Williams & Glyn's believes businesses should make their bank managers work harder for them...Call in and see your local Williams & Glyn's manager soon. You've nothing to lose...' (*Guardian*, 12 July 1979). A certain piquancy attached to the Bank's assurance (*Guardian*, 8 May 1979) that 'Williams & Glyn's believes small businesses deserve all the help a bank can give...we encourage managers to visit customers on their home ground...That's a higher degree of commitment than many banks undertake. But then Williams & Glyn's Bank is a rather different kind of bank...' The propensity of Williams & Glyn's Bank to call in business loans at short notice became the subject of considerable concern in 1979 (see *Economist*, 5 - 11 May 1979). However, in *Williams & Glyn's Bank Ltd v Barnes* (Unreported, 26 March 1980), Gibson J upheld the bank's claim that money lent on overdraft is prima facie repayable on demand.
19   [1979] Ch 312 at 332G. Ormrod LJ likewise minimised the conveyancing difficulties which had been so heavily stressed by the bank, observing that 'one cannot help noticing a tendency to express them in unusually strong language' ([1979] Ch 312 at 339B-C).
20   [1981] AC 487 at 508G.
1   [1981] AC 487 at 508H.
2   [1981] AC 487 at 510B-C.
3   Ante, p 249ff.

questioned in both moral and practical terms.[4] It is at least dubious whether a beneficial co-owner deserves protection if he or she has failed to take advantage of the freely available protection provided by registration.[5] Quite apart from the danger of collusive and fabricated claims of equitable co-ownership,[6] it remains exceedingly questionable whether the wives in *Boland* should have been allowed to enjoy the prospects of their husbands' business prosperity, while retaining an immunity from the shared misfortune of their adversity. Had success attended the commercial enterprises for which the secured loans were obtained, the wives would no doubt have participated indirectly in their spouses' good fortune. There is a powerful argument in support of the proposition that the risks inherent in the pursuit of a business enterprise are not fairly susceptible of a narrower allocation than its benefits.[7]

4. THE PROBLEMS LEFT IN THE MODERN LAW

Recent caselaw developments in both registered and unregistered land have had the effect of creating entirely new hazards for purchasers who unwittingly deal with a statutory trustee for sale. The decision in *Williams & Glyn's Bank Ltd v Boland* makes it extremely likely that the occupation rights implicit in the interests of undisclosed trust beneficiaries will become overriding interests in registered land. The ruling in *Kingsnorth Finance Co Ltd v Tizard*[8] dramatically increases the possibility that purchasers of unregistered land will be fixed with constructive notice of the rights of equitable co-owners in residence in the family home behind some implied and undetected trust for sale.

These parallel developments have left a number of grave difficulties for purchasers. The dilemma facing the purchaser is particularly acute in relation to registered land in that registered transactions (whether of sale or mortgage) are not finally complete until the deemed date of registration.[9] There is therefore a substantial possibility that persons with beneficiary status will have moved into occupation[10] of the family home during the period intervening

---

4   Even Lord Wilberforce was to confess, in an extra-judicial statement in 1985, that he had subsequently 'had some misgivings about whether or not we were right' in *Boland* (see *Parliamentary Debates, House of Lords, Official Report*, Vol 460 (Session 1984-85), Col 1271 (5 March 1985)). See also the bitter reproach delivered by Lord Templeman in *Winkworth v Edward Baron Development Co Ltd* [1986] 1 WLR 1512 at 1515C.

5   One of the bank's counsel, Robert Reid QC, was later to condemn the decision in *Boland* as 'one of the furthest extensions of what is sometimes called "The Nanny State"; that is the state in which people are presumed incapable of taking any coherent decision for themselves about any important matter' (see *Williams & Glyn's Bank Ltd v Boland: Report of a Conference on Problems of Conflict of Interest in the Matrimonial Home* (1981), p 26).

6   Post, p 858. The wives in *Boland* were not locked in mortal matrimonial combat with their respective husbands. Rather it was the case that each husband was seeking grimly to hang on to the family home by opposing against the bank his wife's alleged equitable interest under a statutory trust for sale. The Law Commission has pointed to the danger that 'occupiers' rights may often be invoked primarily to frustrate proceedings brought by a mortgagee against the legal owner, as in fact they were in *Boland* itself' (Law Com No 115, para 30).

7   See S. Freeman, (1980) 43 MLR 692 at 696.

8   [1986] 1 WLR 783 (ante, p 842).

9   Ante, p 834.

10   Post, p 852.

between the handing over of purchase or mortgage moneys and the true date of transfer of title or effective charge.[11]

Among the remaining difficulties for the purchaser (in either registered or unregistered land) are the following.

(1) Range of relevant co-owners

The modern caselaw now makes it somewhat uncertain which categories of person in joint occupation with a vendor are to be considered as being in relevant occupation for the purpose of either registered or unregistered land.

(a) Extension beyond the category of spouse

The class of beneficial co-owners eligible for protection in either registered or unregistered land is not necessarily confined to a spouse of the vendor.[12] In both contexts it is clear that a relevant degree of joint residential occupation in a domestic menage may be asserted by an extensive range of persons. The persons who fall within this category may have gained beneficiary status through contributions to the acquisition, extension or improvement of the property in which they live.[13] In relation to each of them there arises therefore a more or less onerous duty of further enquiry by the purchaser.

(i) De facto partners   Once it is accepted that joint residence by a spouse-beneficiary in the family home ranks as relevant occupation, it becomes difficult to exclude a de facto partner from the ambit of proper enquiry on the part of a purchaser.[14] Any other approach would in effect require that the intending purchaser should confront his vendor with an embarrassingly intrusive question as to the marital status of any adult resident of the opposite sex apparently living with the vendor.[15]

---

11   See Law Com No 115, paras 31, 34. The interim period may be as long as six or eight weeks (see Robert Reid QC in *Williams & Glyn's Bank Ltd v Boland: Report of a Conference on Problems of Conflict of Interest in the Matrimonial Home* (1981), p 30). Even if registration of the title or security is effected promptly within a matter of days, the danger of an interloper-beneficiary is still present (see [1981] Conv 84).

12   See eg *Williams & Glyn's Bank Ltd v Boland* [1981] AC 487 at 508F, where Lord Wilberforce pointed out that in registered land section 70(1)(g) of the Land Registration Act 1925 potentially protects the 'interests of spouses, and indeed, in theory, of other members of the family or even outside it.' In the Court of Appeal in *Boland* Ormrod LJ had pointed out that the appellant wives were 'relying not upon their position as married women, but upon their property rights as ordinary citizens.' It was purely 'incidental' that the wives were married to the persons in whom the legal estate was vested ([1979] Ch 312 at 333D-E).

13   For a discussion of the (sometimes unexpected) forms of contribution which may generate equitable co-ownership of the family home, see Chapter 23 (ante, p 808). A contribution towards the installation of central heating may be sufficient (see *In Re Nicholson*, [1974] 1 WLR 476 at 482H).

14   In *Williams & Glyn's Bank Ltd v Boland* [1979] Ch 312 at 333F, Ormrod LJ thought that exactly the same legal principles would apply even if the co-owners concerned 'were not married or were of the same sex as the legal proprietors.' In the House of Lords, Lord Wilberforce envisaged that overriding interests could easily arise in 'the case of a man living with a mistress, or of a man and a woman—or for that matter two persons of the same sex—living in a house in separate or partially shared rooms' ([1981] AC 487 at 506B).

15   It was precisely this kind of complication which helped to doom the 'deserted wife's equity' of the 1950s and 1960s (ante, p 786). For reference to the undesirability of such enquiries, see *National Provincial Bank Ltd v Hastings Car Mart Ltd* [1964] Ch 665 at 700 per Russell LJ, [1965] AC 1175 at 1234C-E per Lord Upjohn, at 1249B per Lord Wilberforce; *Hastings and Thanet Building Society v Goddard* [1970] 1 WLR 1544 at 1548E per Russell LJ; *Whittingham v Whittingham* [1979] Fam 9 at 17G-H per Balcombe J.

(ii) Other family members   If residence by a de facto spouse in the family home is a relevant factor, it then becomes artificial (and indeed impossible) to exclude from the scope of the purchaser's enquiries other members of a wider kinship group. Equitable co-ownership in a family home may well extend to the vendor's parents,[16] his 'Uncle Harry' and 'Aunt Matilda',[17] and other assorted relatives, perhaps even including children. Any of these persons could be a beneficiary behind an implied trust for sale. Any of them could be in joint occupation of the family home together with the owner of the legal estate. The equitable interest of each is now rendered potentially binding on purchasers merely by reason of their shared occupation of the family home.

(iii) Unorthodox domestic groupings   It seems, furthermore, that any duty of enquiry triggered off by de facto cohabitation must apply also in relation to the members of unusual or unorthodox domestic relationships (eg homosexual partners, two 'old cronies', platonic friends,[18] polygamous spouses or members of a *ménage à trois*.[19] To distinguish between such social groupings on the basis of lifestyle or sexual practice would inevitably be arbitrary and discriminatory.[20]

(b) Definition of occupation

The difficulties facing the purchaser are increased by the penumbra of uncertainty which surrounds the notion of 'occupation'.[1] It is clear, in both registered and unregistered land, that a beneficial co-owner's occupation of the family home may become enforceable against a purchaser of that property notwithstanding that the degree of residential occupation is partial and discontinuous,[2] or even subject to substantial interruption.[3] The recognition of even intermittent occupation concedes unexpected significance in the present context to the more unusual or unorthodox forms of informal cohabitation.

(2) Range of relevant enquiry

An onus is now placed on the purchaser (and particularly on a mortgagee) either to ascertain whether any occupier of the family home (other than the

---

16   The numbers of old people are expected to increase during the late 1980s and 1990s, and the phenomenon of multiple occupation of the family home may well acquire a new significance as the extended family re-groups in order to pool resources in the face of economic adversity, housing shortage and scarcity of fuel predicted for those years. See L.H. Elrod, *Housing Alternatives for the Elderly*, (1979-80) 18 J Fam L 723 at 745.

17   See *Caunce v Caunce* [1969] 1 WLR 286 at 293H (ante, p 839).

18   See eg *Carega Properties SA v Sharratt* [1979] 1 WLR 928 (post, p 1070).

19   That property problems arise within such groupings is well illustrated in *Philip Lowe (Chinese Restaurant) Ltd v Sau Man Lee* (Unreported, Court of Appeal, 9 July 1985) (ante, p 280).

20   For a similar problem in the law of tenancies, see Chapter 31 (post, p 1071).

1   For the classic analysis of possession in terms of *corpus* and *animus*, see Chapter 29 (post, p 1008).

2   See *Kingsnorth Finance Co Ltd v Tizard* [1986] 1 WLR 783 at 788D-E, where Judge Finlay QC considered that there is no requirement of 'continuous and uninterrupted presence; such a notion would be absurd'. In this case the relevant 'presence' of a wife-beneficiary was not 'negatived by regular and repeated absence' (ante, p 842).

3   See eg *Chhokar v Chhokar* [1984] FLR 313 (ante, p 188).

vendor) claims a proprietary interest or to adopt one or more of the rather desperate defensive measures to which reference will be made later in this chapter.[4]

(a) Manner and scope of enquiry

The enquiry made by a purchaser in the present context may ultimately extend to some kind of inspection of the property in order to discover how many people live there.[5] Questions may have to be raised as to the nature or quality of the relationship between the joint occupiers whose presence is disclosed by such an inspection.[6] These questions may not, however, elicit any clear response. How can enquiry be made meaningfully of an occupier with beneficiary status who is an infant,[7] or is senile, or is temporarily absent from the home?[8] How can enquiry be made fairly of an occupier who is unaware that he or she has rights in the first place?

(b) Onerous nature of enquiry

The burdensome nature of such enquiries has caused serious concern to bankers and conveyancers alike.[9] In *Williams & Glyn's Bank Ltd v Boland* counsel for the bank expressed the view that the banking world desired and needed 'a workable system' and that this goal would be made quite unattainable if lenders (and other purchasers) were required to make comprehensive, distasteful and intrusive enquiries in every case.[10] The reaction to *Boland* from

4 Post, p 855.
5 In *Boland* the law lords actively contemplated during argument that a duty might be placed on a purchaser to search through the bedrooms in a house in order to see who slept with whom, and to rummage through wardrobes in order to determine the gender of the occupiers! See *Kingsnorth Finance Co Ltd v Tizard* [1986] 1 WLR 783 at 791D-E.
6 It may, for instance, be vital for the purchaser to distinguish between the vendor's wife or mistress (who may have a beneficial interest in the premises) and his lodger or au pair (who almost certainly is not so entitled). Yet the difference in terms of external appearance may not be particularly great or obvious.
7 A child may well be a beneficiary under a trust for sale of the family home, as for instance where part of the purchase moneys originated in a fund held on trust for that child. In *Bird v Syme-Thomson* [1979] 1 WLR 440 at 444D, Templeman J implied that the minor children of a vendor would not be able to claim the benefit of section 70(1)(g) of the Land Registration Act 1925. However, there appears to be no authority in support of this view (see, incidentally, J. Martin, [1980] Conv 361 at 372). A child, if beneficially entitled and in actual occupation of registered land, would seem to have an overriding interest 'save where enquiry is made of such person and the rights are not disclosed' (ante, p 189). There is an absurdity in holding that proper enquiry can be made of a baby-beneficiary or that the latter's gurgling replies amount to a non-disclosure of his or her rights! There appears to be no easy solution to the problem of the infant beneficiary. To hold that enquiry must be made of the child's parent or guardian may be to play into the hands of the one person who has a vested interest in not disclosing the child's beneficial entitlement (ante, p 190).
8 Ante, p 188.
9 The Law Commission has quoted estimates supplied by the Building Societies Association which show that over 75 per cent of mortgages of matrimonial homes are now in joint names, but, as the Commission noted, this 'still leaves a considerable residue of existing and future purchases which have been or will be taken in the name of a sole legal owner' (see Law Com No 115, paras 29, 60).
10 [1981] AC 487 at 502C. Indeed, so anxious was the bank to obtain a declaratory ruling from the House of Lords in support of a 'workable system' that the bank undertook, in the event of a favourable judgment, not to pursue any order for possession against the respondent wives.

the banking and conveyancing world was predictably fierce.[11] It has been alleged that the additional enquiries necessitated by the *Boland* ruling have added millions of pounds to the cost of domestic conveyancing.[12]

(i) Is justice ultimately done to the purchaser? The dilemma posed for lawyers in the present context takes the form of the following choice between efficiency and justice. Should the law assuage the fear that increased burdens of enquiry may cripple a 'workable system' of conveyancing and impede the efficient handling of millions of transactions with title? Or should the law instead protect the residential security of family members who may be the luckless victims of financial misfortune or mismanagement on the part of the registered proprietor of the family home? Yet the argument of justice may not be entirely one-sided.

Even the Law Commission, which for 20 years has been the firmest advocate of family property rights,[13] has been moved to conclude that it is '*not* acceptable in principle that a purchaser should be at risk of being bound by an interest which, however extensive his enquiries, he is unable to discover.'[14] Nor did the Commission consider it 'satisfactory in principle that the present state of the law as declared in *Boland* should expose lenders, whether institutional or not, to additional financial risks.'[15] Inevitably the *Boland* ruling has merely rebounded on the countless businessmen who can no longer obtain bank overdraft facilities merely by proffering documents of title for the purpose of informal mortgage of the family home.[16] The Law Commission has therefore declared that *Boland*, while consistent with the 'current social policy which favours the protection of the wife in the matrimonial home', is inconsistent with 'the policy of property law which upholds the security of titles, the marketability of land and the simplification of conveyancing.'[17]

(ii) The social calculus The basic problem underlying the present issue is the fact that the courts have attempted to give effect to perceived goals of social

---

11 In a letter to *The Times*, 24 June 1980, Derek Wheatley, Legal Adviser, Lloyds Bank Head Office, condemned the *Boland* decision on the ground that '[i]nevitably the cost of house purchase will rise as will the difficulty of borrowing upon the security of house property.' Speaking extra-judicially, Lord Templeman has observed that 'no one has great sympathy for lenders or banks but the point is that at the end of the day it is the borrower who pays, unless there is some speedy and efficient method of conveyancing' (see *Parliamentary Debates, House of Lords, Official Report*, Vol 437 (Session 1982-1983), Col 650 (15 December 1982)).

12 The Law Society has estimated the extra cost in domestic conveyancing at 'around £7 million per year' (see Law Commission, *Property Law: Second Report on Land Registration (Provisional)* (November 1984), para 8). The Law Commission has pointed out that this expenditure 'cannot be regarded as in the nature of a premium for comprehensive insurance cover:...the precautions paid for do not necessarily eliminate the risks' (Law Com No 115, para 43).

13 For an account of the Law Commission's fine record in this area, see Chapters 22, 23 (ante, pp 781, 792).

14 Law Com No 115, para 62.

15 Law Com No 115, para 64. In the jocular pages of the *Conveyancer*, attention was rightly drawn to the property lawyer's new concern lest the fearsome 'Wagbol' creep up behind him and do something nasty! (see [1981] Conv 17).

16 See *Parliamentary Debates, House of Lords, Official Report*, Vol 437 (Session 1982-1983), Col 648 (Lord Templeman) (15 December 1982).

17 Law Com No 115, para 70.

policy by judicial manipulation of the conveyancing system.[18] When it is asked whose presence in jointly occupied property is sufficient to bind third parties, the real answer is that occupation will be protected in the case of those persons whose residential security is generally recognised as having a claim to social (and therefore legal) priority. It is ultimately a social calculus which decides the issue. Social arguments mould the law by defining the categories of persons whose residential protection has become a matter of overriding social concern. The decision of the House of Lords in *Boland* was, at its roots, a statement of social ethics about the importance of protecting the occupation of the married woman in the matrimonial home.[19] It can be expected that the courts will similarly endorse the claims to residential security presented by such joint occupiers as the de facto wife, Uncle Harry, Aunt Matilda, and the ageing parent—all of whom have acquired beneficiary status behind implied trusts by virtue of small contributions to the purchase, extension or improvement of the family home. It is less likely that there will be the same enthusiasm to accord protection to homosexual cohabitees[20] or to the participants in a freewheeling suburban commune.

(3) Methods of defeating undisclosed co-ownership interests

In view of the recent intensification of the risks undertaken by purchasers of a family home, considerable energy has been invested by conveyancers in seeking ways to minimise the hazards posed by undisclosed co-ownership interests in both registered and unregistered land. Amongst the methods commonly adopted for this purpose are the following.

(a) Enquiry of the vendor/mortgagor

In order to neutralise the adverse rights of occupiers in the family home, it is necessary first to ascertain whether any such occupiers exist.[1] The purchaser of property ostensibly owned both at law and in equity by one person only is well advised to enquire directly of that person as vendor/mortgagor whether any

---

18 It is noticeable that courts in other jurisdictions have not been prepared to strain conveyancing machinery in order to afford spouses protection against third parties who have the benefit of a mortgage charge from the legal owner of the family home (see eg *Royal Bank of Canada v Nicholson* (1981) 112 DLR (3d) 364 at 367; *Containercare (Ireland) Ltd v Wycherley* [1982] IR 143 at 153). An Australian commentator has said that 'it would be striking at the most basic tenets of the Torrens system' to apply in the *Boland* situation any of the statutory exceptions to the Torrens principle of indefeasibility of title (see P. Butt, *Conveyancing and the Rights of Persons in Occupation*, (1981) 55 ALJ 119 at 123).

19 See eg the extra-judicial statement by Lord Simon of Glaisdale that, although many of the issues were 'highly technical', running through the judgments in *Boland* was 'a strong sense of the social issues that were involved' (*Parliamentary Debates, House of Lords, Official Report*, Vol 437 (Session 1982-1983), Col 641 (15 December 1982)).

20 In the context of public sector tenancies, for instance, the courts have refused to uphold a claim to residential security on behalf of a lesbian (*Harrogate Borough Council v Simpson* (1984) 17 HLR 205 at 210, post, p 1060). See also *Thwaites v Ryan* [1984] VR 65 at 93.

1   Physical inspection of the premises prior to completion of the transaction, while advisable, is not necessarily conclusive in favour of the purchaser and may not be realistic in the context of 'chain' transactions of sale and purchase (see Law Com No 115, paras 39f). Such an inspection may not detect all the existing occupiers (ante, p 853) and, in any event, new occupiers may arrive during the period between the inspection and the effective date of the transaction (ante, p 850).

other persons are in actual occupation of the property.[2] Such an enquiry, if answered both honestly and accurately, will resolve the difficulties exposed by *Boland*, since the purchaser is thereby enabled to make separate approaches to each person named in order to extract a release of his or her rights.[3] However, the major disadvantage of this form of protection for a purchaser is that misleading or dishonest representations made by a vendor/mortgagor cannot operate to the prejudice of the rights of any equitable co-owner whose entitlement has not been disclosed.[4] Those rights will nonetheless continue to bind the purchaser, thus limiting the utility of this kind of enquiry.[5]

(b) Requirement of express consent from putative beneficiaries

If the purchaser is aware of the identity of other persons in actual occupation of the land in question, it is open to him to seek from these persons an express consent to the transaction in hand. In the case of a mortgage of the legal estate, this is most effectively achieved by requiring any putative beneficial co-owner to join with the sole legal owner in executing the mortgage charge. Such consent can be made a condition *sine qua non* of the transaction and will preclude any future claim that an occupier has a beneficial co-ownership interest which enjoys priority over the purchaser.[6]

(i) Undue influence   The obtaining of express consents is, however, fraught with latent danger for the mortgagee. There is a possibility that an occupier who supplies such a consent may subsequently claim that he or she was the victim of undue influence and that the consent is therefore vitiated.[7] It seems therefore that, in order to be unimpeachable, any consent signed by a putative co-owner

2   See R.J. Smith, (1979) 95 LQR 501 at 505. The vendor is now asked in the standard Preliminary Enquiries before contract to give the full names, and ages if under 18, of all persons, other than the vendor, in actual occupation of the property. It has even been suggested, somewhat lightheartedly, that the Land Registry should serve an 'official notice of inquiry' upon 'The Occupier(s)' at any given address and that failure to reply within fourteen days should be conclusive evidence of the non-existence of an overriding interest (see [1980] Conv 85, but compare [1980] Conv 311, 313). The Law Commission has firmly rejected the suggestion (see Law Com No 115, Appendix 2, para 15).

3   Although the validity of such a release of rights is open to question (infra), this procedure has been adopted by many institutional lenders, eg the Halifax Building Society, which requires all declared occupiers to sign a form of consent to the proposed mortgage (Form L26) or further advance (Form L27).

4   See the statement of Russell LJ in *Hodgson v Marks* [1971] Ch 892 at 932D, that 'reliance on the untrue ipse dixit of the vendor will not suffice' to protect the purchaser (ante, p 190). This observation, although made in the context of registered land, must also represent the position in relation to unregistered land. The Law Commission has dismissed the suggestion that a declaration by the vendor should be statutorily deemed conclusive as to the existence or non-existence of co-ownership rights (Law Com No 115, Appendix 2, paras 21ff).

5   The purchaser may have a remedy in either contract or tort in respect of a misrepresentation made by the vendor, but an award of damages will be of little avail to a mortgagee if the only asset from which such an award might be satisfied is the property subject to the mortgage. This property may well have been rendered unsaleable by reason of the adverse claim of the beneficial co-owner.

6   However, the release of rights operates only as against the purchaser; the rights remain intact as against the legal owner or against the proceeds of sale in his hands.

7   The law relating to the setting aside of unconscionable bargains is discussed elsewhere (ante, p 225). The Law Commission has pointed out that some occupiers may be legally incapable of giving a valid consent to a release of their rights, referring specifically to the cases of the mentally infirm and persons under the age of 18 (see Law Com No 115, para 42(i)(b)).

should stipulate expressly and unambiguously its legal effect on such rights as the signatory may have.[8] If this is done, it is unlikely that the consent can be set aside on the ground that a purchaser such as a bank-mortgagee has exerted undue influence over the signatory.[9]

(ii) No duty to ensure independent legal advice It is clear, moreover, that in the absence of some special relationship of confidence, a bank normally has no obligation to advise a borrower on the prudence of any lending which it makes to him.[10] Until relatively recently it has been less clear whether a bank has any similar duty in relation to the borrower's spouse.[11] However, in *National Westminster Bank Plc v Morgan*,[12] the House of Lords held that in the context of 'an ordinary banking transaction' a bank has no duty to ensure that independent legal advice is received by a wife who joins in a mortgage of the matrimonial home.[13]

While the *Morgan* ruling has plainly limited the responsibility imposed on a bank-mortgagee in the present context, it is possible that there remain more indirect sources of liability. There is in English law no presumption of undue influence as between husband and wife.[14] However, it may just be that a mortgagee has a special duty to insist that independent advice is obtained where the circumstances are such that husband-mortgagor himself 'could be expected to have influence over' the signatory of the consent.[15]

(c) Strict proof of beneficial entitlement

It is increasingly common for purchasers, when confronted by a party claiming rights as an equitable co-owner, to demand strict proof of the supposed

---

8   See *Zamet v Hyman* [1961] 1 WLR 1442 at 1446 per Lord Evershed MR. Forms L26 and L27 used by the Halifax Building Society (ante, p 856) merely require the 'Occupier' to confirm that 'the effect of this form of consent has been explained'.

9   In *National Westminster Bank Plc v Morgan* [1985] AC 686, the House of Lords disapproved the view expressed by Lord Denning MR in *Lloyds Bank Ltd v Bundy* [1975] QB 326 at 339C that a presumption of undue influence, arising from 'inequality of bargaining power', arises between banker and customer. See C.J. Barton and P.M. Rank, *Undue Influence–A Retreat?*, [1985] Conv 387.

10 See *Williams & Glyn's Bank Ltd v Barnes* (Unreported, Gibson J, 26 March 1980).

11 In a pre-*Morgan* case, *Midland Bank Ltd v Goodall* (CA Unbound Transcript 1064, 1 November 1983), the Court of Appeal held that such duty as a bank might have was fully satisfied by the inclusion in the letter of consent signed by the mortgagor's wife of a printed warning that the document 'should be signed only after consulting a Solicitor or other professional adviser'. Form L26 used by the Halifax Building Society (ante, p 856) requires the Occupier to confirm that he 'has been advised of the right to have independent legal advice on its effect'. Form L27—the form of consent to further advance—contains the advice 'Before signing this form please see your own solicitor if you are not sure of its effect'.

12 [1985] AC 686 at 709D per Lord Scarman. It is noteworthy that other jurisdictions have been generally unsympathetic to the suggestion that a bank has a duty to ensure that a wife should receive independent professional advice before guaranteeing her husband's mortgage debt (see eg *Royal Bank of Canada v Poisson* (1980) 103 DLR (3d) 735 at 738).

13 In *Morgan* the mortgagors were joint tenants of the legal title, but this does not make the approach of the law lords inapplicable to a co-owner who is entitled only in equity.

14 *Bank of Montreal v Stuart* [1911] AC 120 at 137; *Kings North Trust Ltd v Bell* [1986] 1 WLR 119 at 123D-E.

15 See *Kings North Trust Ltd v Bell* [1986] 1 WLR 119 at 124C, 125A-B (ante, p 599). See also the fairly strict requirement of legal advice imposed by the High Court of Australia in *Bank of New Zealand v Rogers* (1941) 65 CLR 42 at 87.

equitable entitlement. Priority can be obtained over the mortgagee only if there is in fact co-ownership of the family home in equity,[16] and it is entirely predictable that the purchaser's first line of attack should be a denial that any beneficial entitlement exists.[17]

It is often painfully true that the only evidence for the existence of a statutory trust for sale consists of vague, unsubstantiated, self-serving and possibly even collusive claims of financial contribution towards a purchase many years before. At first instance in *Williams & Glyn's Bank Ltd v Boland*,[18] for instance, there was clearly a fear in the mind of Templeman J that a fabrication of joint financial contribution might enable the bankrupt husband to save his matrimonial home from the hands of his creditors under cover of a fictitious beneficial interest claimed on behalf of his wife. It is significant that Templeman J was at every point careful to say merely that the wife 'claimed' to have made the cash contributions which supposedly generated a statutory trust of the husband's legal title. Moreover, the wife in *Boland* had failed to register her 'rights of occupation' under the Matrimonial Homes Act 1967 and Templeman J was acutely aware that it would 'really make that Act a nonsense' if the spouse of the legal owner 'could say or allege at any time that he or she had contributed to the purchase price', thereby laying the foundation for an overriding interest.

This caution was reiterated in *Midland Bank plc v Dobson*,[19] where Fox LJ observed that 'assertions made by a husband and wife as to a common intention formed 30 years ago regarding joint ownership, of which there is no contemporary evidence and which happens to accommodate their current need to defeat the claims of a creditor, must be received by the courts with caution.'[20] However, there are also innumerable cases in which past financial contributions are none the less real for being difficult to prove. Yet the law of property has proved remarkably resistant in recent years to claims of co-ownership of the family home.[1] In few other areas is the law quite so technical and unpredictable as in its treatment of the assertion that a particular kind of contributory activity has generated an equitable share for the contributor.[2]

(d) Application of estoppel doctrine

Perhaps the most controversial of the arguments increasingly used for the protection of purchasers rests on the judicial willingness to apply something akin to a doctrine of estoppel against beneficial co-owners of the family home.

---

16   *Williams & Glyn's Bank Ltd v Boland* itself concerned a preliminary point of law and it was therefore assumed for this purpose that W was entitled as an equitable co-owner behind a trust for sale.

17   This line of attack has been used successfully in relation to both unregistered land (see *Midland Bank plc v Dobson* [1986] 1 FLR 171 at 177G) and registered land (see *Anglia Building Society v Lewis* (Unreported, Court of Appeal, No 8008681, 29 January 1982); *Anand v Gill* [1983] CA Bound Transcript 302).

18   (1978) 36 P & CR 448 at 454.

19   [1986] 1 FLR 171 at 174D.

20   In *Knightly v Sun Life Assurance Society Ltd* (1981) *Times*, 23 July, a wife-mortgagor sought—unsuccessfully—to assert a beneficial entitlement on behalf of her husband who had no wish to be involved in the instant litigation and who maintained throughout that he had no equitable interest in the mortgaged property.

1   Ante, p 279.

2   See Law Com No 115, para 55.

The courts have shown themselves disinclined to allow a beneficial co-owner deliberately to remain silent about his or her equitable rights at the date of the relevant transaction, only to assert those rights later as having priority over the third party who dealt in good faith with the legal owner.[3] The force of this estoppel doctrine is merely intensified if the original silence as to equitable entitlement was calculated to induce the third party to enter into a transaction in which he would not otherwise have engaged.[4] Under such circumstances the owner of the undisclosed rights cannot be heard conscionably to raise those rights in derogation of an interest or security taken by the purchaser from a sole trustee for sale.[5]

(i) Requirement of participation in the transaction   In deciding whether to apply the doctrine of estoppel in the area of security transactions, the courts have drawn a necessary distinction between those cases in which a husband has negotiated a business mortgage without the knowledge of the wife-beneficiary and those cases in which the beneficial co-owner has been fully aware of the transaction and its importance for the family.[6] In the former category of case the courts have not penalised the undisclosed beneficiary for her silence.[7] However, in cases falling within the latter category, the courts have been all too ready to disallow any claim by family members to override the priority apparently conferred by a mortgage upon a third party.[8] The courts have taken the view that wilful non-disclosure of an interest capable of undermining the security offered 'would be conduct which would leave the owner of the equitable interest open to the charge of coming to the court with hands that were not clean.'[9] In circumstances of this kind, the equitable owner must be estopped from claiming priority: any other approach is 'unarguable' and 'would go near

3   See eg *Midland Bank Ltd v Farmpride Hatcheries Ltd* (1981) 260 Estates Gazette 493 at 497 per Shaw LJ, 498f per Oliver LJ.
4   On the role of representation by silence in the law of estoppel, see Chapter 13 (ante, p 400). It is certainly questionable whether an estoppel of this kind can be raised if the purchaser merely informs an occupier that it will be assumed, in the absence of reply within seven days, that the latter claims no adverse interest in the property (but see J. Russell, (1981) 32 NILQ 3 at 21).
5   It has been suggested that a wife of the legal owner might be estopped from asserting her rights against a purchaser if she appeared to acquiesce in the sale, for example by showing the purchaser around the house and encouraging him in expenditure (see [1980] Conv 361 at 368 (J. Martin); *Spiro v Lintern* [1973] 1 WLR 1002 at 1013B-D). Compare *Hodgson v Marks* [1971] Ch 892 at 934A (resulting trust).
6   For explicit reference to this distinction, see *Anglia Building Society v Lewis* (Unreported, Court of Appeal, No 8008681, 29 January 1982) per Dunn LJ; *Paddington Building Society v Mendelsohn* (1985) 50 P & CR 244 at 248f per Browne-Wilkinson LJ.
7   The foremost example within this category is *Williams & Glyn's Bank Ltd v Boland* [1981] AC 487. See also *Winkworth v Edward Baron Development Co Ltd* (1986) 52 P & CR 67 at 77 (reversed on other grounds [1986] 1 WLR 1512, ante, p 288).
8   See *Knightly v Sun Life Assurance Society Ltd* (1981) *Times*, 23 July; *Bristol and West Building Society v Henning* [1985] 1 WLR 778 at 782G, 783C. In *Ulster Bank Ltd v Shanks* [1982] NI 143 at 150A, it was considered highly relevant that the wife-beneficiary had been present during at least part of the negotiations between the husband-mortgagor and the bank manager.
9   *Ulster Bank Ltd v Shanks* [1982] NI 143 at 150D per Murray J. Likewise Browne-Wilkinson LJ declared in *Bristol and West Building Society v Henning* [1985] 1 WLR 778 at 782G that he 'would not impute to the parties an intention to mislead the society by purporting to offer the unencumbered fee simple of the property as security when in fact there was to be an equitable interest which would take priority to the society.' See (1986) 49 MLR 245 (M.P. Thompson).

to saying that our system of conveyancing permits a mortgagor to obtain money under a false pretence.'[10]

(ii) Limitations on the Boland ruling   The courts have taken this estoppel approach so far that it threatens seriously to cut back the scope of 'overriding interests' in the registered land context. In *Paddington Building Society v Mendelsohn*,[11] the Court of Appeal made it clear that section 70(1)(g) of the Land Registration Act 1925 provides protection only to those rights which, by their 'inherent quality', are enforceable rights at the date of the relevant transfer.[12] In this case an equitable owner was deemed, by non-disclosure of her rights to a mortgagee, to have conceded priority to the latter. Accordingly the Court held that her rights were no longer enforceable rights at the date of registration of the mortgage charge, even though she remained 'in actual occupation' of the family home. Her equitable rights never came within the threshold of section 70(1)(g).[13] It is questionable whether this erosion of the protection afforded family property rights is truly justifiable as an application of the essential idea of proprietary estoppel.[14]

(e)   Requirement of joint conveyance or mortgage

Until recently it has always been assumed that, as a last resort, a purchaser dealing with a family home may obtain an unimpeachable title simply by insisting on taking a joint conveyance or mortgage.[15] Thus, even though the vendor/mortgagor may appear to be solely entitled both at law and in equity, any fear that a latent co-ownership might exist in equity can be completely ignored if the vendor/mortgagor adds another name to the title, with the result that the property is now owned by two trustees for sale.

(i)   Overreaching advantages   The motivation which underpins this manoeuvre is clearly the idea that the purchaser, in dealing explicitly with two trustees, is automatically assured that any sale or mortgage under these circumstances will overreach any equitable interests otherwise asserted by putative co-owners hidden behind an implied trust for sale.[16]

10   *Knightly v Sun Life Assurance Society Ltd* (1981) *Times*, 23 July per Nourse J. Compare *Bristol and West Building Society v Henning* [1985] 1 WLR 778 at 781G-782A, where Browne-Wilkinson LJ observed that there was a 'risk that the common sense answer in this case may get lost in the many different technicalities which can arise. The basic fact is that the mortgage was granted to the society with the full knowledge and approval of Mrs Henning.' The judge noted that the 'logical result' of the wife's argument claiming priority was that she would be 'entitled to stay in possession indefinitely without making any payment. That would be a strange result which I would be reluctant to reach.'
11   (1985) 50 P & CR 244 at 248.
12   Ante, p 184.
13   (1985) 50 P & CR 244 at 248f.
14   See [1985] CLJ 354 (Mary Welstead).
15   This rather desperate expedient is not without precedent in the law of real property, since this solution was commonly applied to remove doubt about possible severances under a joint title before the enactment of the Law of Property (Joint Tenants) Act 1964 (ante, p 343). See [1980] Conv 458.
16   Overreaching effect will be achieved under the Law of Property Act 1925, s 2(1)(ii), even though a disposition made without due consultation (see Law of Property Act 1925, s 26(3)) will constitute a breach of trust giving rise at least in theory to a remedy in damages.

(ii) Possible flaws This mode of protection for the purchaser is not particularly apt to evoke enthusiastic participation from the vendor,[17] who is put to the inconvenience and expense of finding a second legal owner.[18] More seriously, however, recent developments threatened for a time to expose a flaw in this technique which would have negated much of its utility for the purpose of defeating the occupation rights of beneficial co-owners. In *City of London Building Society v Flegg*[19] the Court of Appeal held that even payment to two trustees for sale did not necessarily ensure that the undisclosed equitable interests were statutorily overreached, but this ruling has now been rejected conclusively by the House of Lords.[20] Accordingly it remains good law that a dealing by two trustees for sale enables a purchaser to take free of all adverse beneficial interests in the family home.

(f) Insurance

An alternative way of freeing purchasers from the hazard represented by adverse equitable rights in the family home lies in the device of insurance.[1] In the area of mortgage transactions some insurance companies now offer a scheme under which the insurer contracts to take over the security, together with a transfer of the lender's mortgage, if an equitable owner emerges to assert binding rights against the mortgagee.[2] However, liability insurance is not a panacea. It is predictable that any insurance scheme of this kind would make it a condition of cover that the purchaser had taken all reasonable care to limit the insured risk in the first place by making enquiry as to the possible existence of undisclosed co-ownership of the property—which is the very burden which the purchaser seeks to minimise.

(g) Bankruptcy

The ultimate recourse for a mortgagee who is trapped by undisclosed co-ownership interests may lie in forcing a bankruptcy. The mortgagor, if sued by the mortgagee on the repayment covenant contained in the mortgage, may be made bankrupt. The mortgagor's trustee in bankruptcy then has locus standi

---

17 The Law Commission has reported that there appears to be 'considerable reluctance to request a sole owner to arrange for a joint disposition: such a request, by bringing into question the beneficial ownership of the property, intrudes into affairs which are normally regarded as private to the owner's household' (Law Com No 115, para 42(ii)).

18 The Law Commission has proposed that a beneficial owner of the matrimonial home should have statutory 'trusteeship rights'. These rights would include a right to prevent other persons becoming trustees of the home without the consent of the spouse-beneficiary, and a right for the latter himself or herself to apply to the court for appointment as a trustee (see *Family Law: Third Report on Family Property: The Matrimonial Home (Co-Ownership and Occupation Rights) and Household Goods* (Law Com No 86, June 1978), paras 1.295ff).

19 [1986] Ch 605 (ante, pp 384, 601). See also C. Sydenham, [1980] Conv 427, but compare J. Martin, [1981] Conv 219; Law Com No 115, para 89).

20 [1987] 2 WLR 1266 (ante, p 385).

1 It is significant that in *Williams & Glyn's Bank Ltd v Boland* [1979] Ch 312 at 332H-333A, Lord Denning MR seemed to regard the 'high interest rate now prevailing' in respect of bank loans as providing the institutional lender with an informal mechanism of insurance against the risks of security transactions.

2 See J.E. Adams, *American Title Insurance in an English Context*, [1979] Conv 322; C. Sydenham, [1980] Conv 427 at 432. An insurance scheme of this sort is currently offered by the Sun Alliance Insurance Co.

to apply under section 30 of the Law of Property Act 1925 for a sale of the property concerned.[3] Under the provisions of the Insolvency Act 1986 it is extremely unlikely that the court will postpone sale for more than a limited period of perhaps one year.[4] At this point the property must be sold up, releasing the cash value of the mortgagor's equitable share in at least partial satisfaction of the mortgage debt.[5]

In these circumstances the mere fact that another beneficial owner has a binding or 'overriding' interest in the property does not preclude the possibility of sale at the behest of the trustee in bankruptcy. The binding or 'overriding' nature of such an interest means not that a sale can be resisted, but only that the owner of the binding or 'overriding' interest is entitled on sale to be paid the value of his or her interest *in priority to* all other claims including that of the mortgagee.[6]

5. PROPOSALS FOR REFORM

During the last ten years the special problem of adverse dealings with the family home has become inextricably associated with more general proposals for reform of the law of matrimonial property. Most of the discussion in this area has been heavily influenced by the proposed regime of statutory co-ownership of the matrimonial home which was contained in the Law Commission's *Third Report on Family Property* in 1978.[7]

(1) A statutory scheme of co-ownership

By 1978 the Law Commission had concluded that, except in cases involving death or divorce, the legal rights which spouses need in respect of their matrimonial home are essentially twofold.[8] *First*, each spouse needs a 'right of control' in order to ensure that the property is not sold, mortgaged or otherwise disposed of without his or her consent. *Second*, each spouse also needs a 'money right' in order to safeguard his or her due share of any money proceeds realised by such dealings as may take place. Both of these rights are already enjoyed by joint tenants of the legal title in the matrimonial home.[9] However, neither right

---

3   Ante, pp 377, 819.
4   Insolvency Act 1986, s 336(5) (post, p 881).
5   Post, p 884.
6   This was precisely the approach adopted by Murray J in the High Court of Northern Ireland in *Northern Bank Ltd v Beattie* [1982] 18 NIJB, Transcript, p 25. In technical terms such a solution probably represents the outcome which should have occurred in *Williams & Glyn's Bank Ltd v Boland* [1981] AC 487. It seems clear that if the bank in *Boland* had gone one step further and had issued a bankruptcy notice, it could then have forced a sale of the property notwithstanding the wife's overriding interest. This was later admitted expressly by Lord Hailsham LC speaking extra-judicially in the House of Lords (see *Parliamentary Debates, House of Lords, Official Report*, Vol 437 (Session 1982-1983), Col 663 (15 December 1982)). However, it is likely that the bank, having undertaken not to press for possession if it won the case (ante, p 853), felt that it could not honourably seek a bankruptcy sale in the immediate aftermath of losing the case.
7   *Family Law: Third Report on Family Property: The Matrimonial Home (Co-Ownership and Occupation Rights) and Household Goods* (Law Com No 86, June 1978).
8   Law Com No 86, paras 1.230f.
9   Ante, p 302.

is available in any effective form to a spouse who owns merely a beneficial interest in the home or to a spouse who owns no interest at all.[10]

(a) Automatic joint tenancy in equity

In the light of the needs thus identified, the Law Commission's *Third Report on Family Property* recommended the adoption of a statutory scheme of co-ownership of the matrimonial home.[11] This new regime was intended to apply to most dwelling-houses in which either spouse was entitled to an equitable interest in possession.[12] Irrespective of the state of the legal title, all spouses (other than existing legal co-owners[13]) would become joint tenants of the equitable interest in their matrimonial home.[14] The imposition of joint tenancy would apply even where both spouses were already equitable tenants in common behind an implied trust for sale.[15] In all cases the regime of mandatory co-ownership would take effect behind a statutory trust for sale.[16]

(b) Protection through registration

The Law Commission envisaged that the statutory regime in the matrimonial home should be based on the registration of co-ownership rights. Accordingly the Commission recommended that any equitable co-owner not represented on the legal title should be able to protect his or her new statutory equitable interest either by registering a Class G land charge (in the case of unregistered land)[17] or by entering a restriction in the register of title (in the case of registered land).[18] In either context registration would inevitably ensure that a purchaser was bound by the registering spouse's beneficial interest under the statutory co-ownership scheme.[19]

(c) Advantages of the scheme

The merits of the Law Commission's proposal were clear.[20] Registration would

---

10   Law Com No 86, paras 1.234ff.
11   Law Com No 86, para 1.1.
12   Law Com No 86, paras 1.18ff. The scheme of statutory co-ownership was subject to a number of exceptions covering homes acquired before marriage, property interests given to a third party, and exclusory agreements drawn up by the spouses themselves (see Law Com No 86, paras 1.104ff).
13   The Law Commission recognised that there would be no need for 'statutory co-ownership' in cases where the spouses had already imposed co-ownership on their home in express terms, eg by means of a conveyance to themselves expressly as joint tenants of the legal estate (Law Com No 86, para 1.3).
14   Law Com No 86, paras 1.18, 1.54ff.
15   'Both interests...should be thrown into the melting pot and should emerge in the form of statutory co-ownership' (Law Com No 86, para 1.28).
16   Law Com No 86, para 1.62.
17   Law Com No 86, para 1.318.
18   Law Com No 86, para 1.328. It has always been possible under the Land Registration Act 1925 to enter a restriction in respect of an equitable interest behind a trust for sale (ante, p 159). The Law Commission's recommendation would merely make such an entry even more imperative, since the protection of the overriding interest would simultaneously be withdrawn (post, p 865). In order to avoid the difficulty that the registered proprietor might refuse to co-operate in the entry of the restriction, the Law Commission proposed that the production of the land certificate should not be necessary in these circumstances (ibid, para 1.329) and that the registry should not give the registered proprietor notice of the restriction having been entered (ibid, para 1.330).
19   Law Com No 86, paras 1.320, 1.331.
20   See (1983) 46 MLR 330 (W.T. Murphy).

have the double consequence of making the consent of both spouses essential for dealings with the matrimonial home, and of safeguarding the rights of both in any capital moneys which might arise.

(i) The 'right of control'   In practical terms registration of co-ownership rights would prevent any dealing with the matrimonial home which did not involve the active co-operation of the registering spouse-beneficiary. In this way registration would effectively impose a 'consent requirement' in respect of all subsequent transactions with the legal title,[1] and the Law Commission believed that the introduction of this 'consent requirement' would achieve for the registering spouse the 'right of control' which the Commission had analysed as a primary legal need.[2]

(ii) The 'money right'   The Law Commission further envisaged that registration of co-ownership rights should constitute notice not only of the registering spouse's beneficial interest under the statutory trust but also of his or her 'consent requirement' in respect of the proposed transaction.[3] Once registration was effected, no third party dealing with the legal owner could ever disclaim knowledge of the trust.[4] A purchaser would be able to transact in safety only if he paid all capital money to two trustees, thereby acquiring the benefit of overreaching.[5] In the Law Commission's view, transactions in unregistered land which did not result in a payment to two trustees would not overreach the equitable interests of the statutory co-owners,[6] while in the case of registered land such transactions would simply not be processed by the Land Registry and would thus remain incomplete.[7] By this means the Law Commission clearly intended that the introduction of a 'registration requirement' would indirectly enforce compliance with the 'two trustee' rule,[8] while simultaneously ensuring that the registering spouse's beneficial interest was adequately safeguarded in the form of a share in the capital proceeds of the transaction.

(d) The 'registration requirement'

In order to promote certainty and clarity in the operation of the co-ownership scheme, the Law Commission proposed the introduction of a strict 'registration requirement' under which an equitable co-ownership interest would become enforceable against a purchaser or lender if, but only if, the interest were registered in the appropriate manner.[9] Thus any failure by an equitable co-

1   Law Com No 86, paras 1.320f.
2   Law Com No 86, para 1.231
3   Law Com No 86, paras 1.319, 1.328. See Land Registration Act 1925, s 58(1)(b), (3).
4   'The registration facility thus remedies, for relevant land, the unsatisfactory feature of the present law about the two trustee rule in relation to land that is unregistered: that there is no satisfactory way to ensure that a purchaser has notice of the circumstances which bring the rule into play' (Law Com No 86, para 1.320).
5   Law of Property Act 1925, ss 2(1)(ii), 27(2) (ante, p 355).
6   Law Com No 86, para 1.320.
7   Law Com No 86, para 1.331. The presence of a restriction on the register of title prevents the Land Registry from registering any transaction conducted otherwise than in accordance with terms of the restriction (ante, p 159).
8   Law Com No 86, para 1.321.
9   Law Com No 86, paras 1.317ff.

owner to take the necessary protective action would render the relevant interest entirely unenforceable against third parties.[10] An unregistered charge would be deemed to be void 'no matter whether the purchaser has notice of the trust, or of the beneficial interest, in other ways or from other sources'.[11]

In order to reinforce this 'registration requirement', the Commission urged that statute law should declare, for the avoidance of doubt, that an equitable interest under a trust for sale could never constitute an overriding interest in registered land.[12] The Commission was clearly of the view that it should not be possible for a statutory co-owner to derive protection from 'actual occupation' of the matrimonial home at the date of the disputed transaction.[13]

(e) Criticisms of the co-ownership scheme

The Law Commission's proposals in respect of matrimonial home rights were necessarily complex. Perhaps the most acute difficulty raised by the entire scheme of statutory co-ownership turned on the fact that protection was made to depend ultimately on some active step of land charge registration or formal entry in the Land Register. If a major problem with the existing Class F registration is precisely the fact that, for reasons of ignorance or sheer inertia, qualifying spouses neglect to register their rights,[14] it seemed scarcely likely that the same spouses would be any more ready to register their 'Class G' entitlements.

(2) The Boland ruling and its implications

The Law Commission's proposal for statutory co-ownership was introduced in the House of Lords as a Private Member's Bill during the 1979-1980 session, only to founder through lack of parliamentary time.[15] However, interest in the Law Commission's recommendations revived with the ruling of the House of Lords in *Williams & Glyn's Bank Ltd v Boland*. This decision amply falsified the Commission's preferred view, as expressed in its Report in 1978, that an interest under a trust for sale constitutes nothing more than a minor interest in the law of registered land.[16]

---

10 Law Com No 86, paras 1.322(a), 1.332. The Law Commission envisaged that an unprotected interest would, on the analogy of the Class F land charge (ante, p 115), be unenforceable against the purchaser of *any* interest in the land and not merely the purchaser of a legal estate. An unregistered interest would thus be void even as against an equitable mortgagee, thereby protecting banks which take informal (and therefore equitable) charges on domestic property.

11 Law Com No 86, para 1.322. ('This is consistent with the principles of the existing law about registration, and in particular with section 199(1) of the Law of Property Act 1925...[A]ny other solution would involve purchasers in making the enquiries which we are anxious to avoid').

12 In the view of the Commission, such an interest should never 'amount to an overriding interest, whether it belongs to a wife or to anyone else' (Law Com No 86, para 1.333). The Commission's Report was, of course, issued in advance of the ruling in *Williams & Glyn's Bank Ltd v Boland* [1981] AC 487.

13 Law Com No 86, paras 1.322(a)(i), 1.333.

14 Ante, p 790.

15 The sponsor of the Bill, Lord Simon of Glaisdale, later agreed that a Bill of this complexity had been beyond the capacity of a private Member (*Parliamentary Debates, House of Lords, Official Report*, Vol 437 (Session 1982-1983), Col 642 (15 December 1982)).

16 Law Com No 86, para 1.333.

(a) Acknowledged defects of Boland

The Law Commission reported in 1982 on the implications of the decision in *Boland*.[17] The Commission acknowledged that the *Boland* ruling had to some extent improved the position of co-owners and thus promoted the social policy of protecting the interests of wives in the matrimonial home.[18] However, the Commission felt that *Boland* was unduly detrimental to the interests of purchasers and lenders, in that the law had become uncertain and therefore prejudicial both to the security of titles and to the ready marketability of land.[19] Moreover, the increased cost and complexity of transactions in the aftermath of *Boland* were not counter-balanced by any corresponding security achieved on behalf of co-owners of the family home. In the Commission's view, therefore, even the *Boland* ruling provided inadequate protection for co-ownership interests.[20]

(b) The renewed initiative of the Law Commission

The Law Commission accordingly sought to resolve the difficulties exposed in *Boland* by re-issuing in substantially unamended form the proposal made in 1978 for a statutory scheme of automatic co-ownership in the matrimonial home.[1] This proposal cast a sharpened focus upon the need to enforce a requirement of registration. The Commission reiterated its conclusion that questions of priority under the new scheme should depend neither on the doctrine of notice (in the case of unregistered land) nor on the protection given to overriding interests (in the case of registered land).[2] Instead the security of equitable co-ownership interests in both contexts should turn on upon the presence or absence of a protective entry in a register.[3] The legal response would be clear-cut, but certainty would have been bought at the price of penalising those who fail to take protective action.[4]

The Commission gave further consideration to the objection that registration does not provide a particularly apt mechanism for the residential protection of ordinary lay persons who may not appreciate the need to take positive action in defence of their rights.[5] The Commission concluded,

---

17   *Property Law: The Implications of Williams & Glyn's Bank Ltd v Boland* (Law Com No 115, Cmnd 8636, August 1982). The Commission repeated its recommendation that an equitable interest behind a trust for sale should never be protectible as an overriding interest in registered land (para 24).

18   Law Com No 115, paras 45, 67.

19   Law Com No 115, paras 27ff, 57ff, 68f. The Law Commission referred to the risk imposed on purchasers in terms of the classic 'pig in a poke' (ibid, para 28).

20   Law Com No 115, para 46ff. The Law Commission stressed, for instance, that a co-owner's rights will not be 'overriding' in registered land terms unless he or she is in actual occupation at the relevant time (ibid, para 47).

1   Law Com No 115, para 115.

2   Law Com No 115, para 74(ii).

3   The Law Commission saw a particular advantage in the fact that a registration requirement would at last 'create consistency between the protection of statutory rights of occupation under the Matrimonial Homes Act...and the protection of rights of occupation derived from beneficial interests.' It would also reinforce consistency between registered and unregistered conveyancing by making the protection of beneficial trust interests by registration available in both contexts alike (Law Com No 115, para 74(iv)).

4   It is perhaps a nice question whether a solicitor acting for a sole legal owner would have any duty to advise that owner's spouse to register his or her rights under the co-ownership scheme.

5   The Law Commission had thought in 1978 that '[a]lmost the only situation in which registration is necessary is that in which marital disharmony gives rise to the fear that one spouse's interests may not be accorded their due weight' (Law Com No 86, para 1.336).

however, that the advantages of an imposed registration requirement considerably outweighed the disadvantages.[6] In fact, in its Report of 1978, the Commission had conceded the undesirable nature of the registration requirement in respect of only one area. The Commission felt that the registration mechanism would prove unwieldy where a sole legal owner offered the matrimonial home as security not for an 'acquisition mortgage' but for a 'further advance' perhaps many years after the acquisition of the property.[7]

(3) The Land Registration and Law of Property Bill 1985

Once again the Law Commission's endorsement of a general scheme of co-ownership failed to materialise in statutory form,[8] but wide recognition of the difficulties now present in relation to dealings with the matrimonial home led in 1985 to a further parliamentary initiative sponsored by the Lord Chancellor, Lord Hailsham. The Land Registration and Law of Property Bill 1985 aimed to reduce the scope of the enquiries forced upon a purchaser or mortgagee by decisions such as *Boland*. The Bill provided, in rather cumbersome terms,[9] that the protection of an overriding interest in registered land should, in the present context, be available only to the spouse of the vendor or mortgagor.[10] The protection of the *Boland* ruling was thus to be withdrawn from all other categories of beneficial co-owner whose existence lay concealed behind an implied trust for sale of a family home.[11] The Bill thus effected a compromise in registered land: the *Boland* ruling was preserved on behalf of spouses, but the protection of all other kinds of family member was to depend conclusively on registration.[12]

Not surprisingly the flawed provisions of the 1985 Bill met substantial opposition both within and without Parliament and were eventually quietly suppressed. It would without doubt have been difficult to justify the differential

6 A crucial factor in favour of a registration requirement was the consideration that 'whilst registration of his interest would eliminate the risk to the co-owner and failure to register would not affect the co-owner's rights against the legal owner, under the present law neither enquiries nor any other precaution can wholly eliminate the risk to the purchaser' (Law Com No 115, para 82).

7 If, for instance, the legal owner obtained overdraft facilities from his bank on the security of his home, the bank 'could not reasonably be required to make a search [of the register] every time a cheque was presented' (Law Com No 86, para 1.351). The Law Commission therefore suggested that in the case of a further advance the lender should be adversely affected by failure to obtain the consent of a spouse-beneficiary only if *either* that spouse's consent had been required for the original mortgage and had been duly obtained *or* that spouse served a notice in writing on the lender stating that his or her consent was required (Law Com No 86, para 1.352f).

8 The government made it clear that it gave a higher priority to the promotion of legislation in other areas (*Parliamentary Debates, House of Lords, Official Report*, Vol 437 (Session 1982-1983), Cols 659-662 (Lord Hailsham LC) (15 December 1982)). See [1983] Conv 87.

9 See the disobliging comments of Lords Mishcon and Wilberforce (*Parliamentary Debates, House of Lords, Official Report (Fifth Series)*, Vol 460 (Session 1984-85), Cols 1270ff).

10 Land Registration and Law of Property Bill 1985, clause 1(1).

11 The Bill likewise provided that a purchaser or mortgagee of unregistered land should not be affected by notice of the beneficial rights of any co-owner (other than a spouse) who shared occupation with the sole vendor or mortgagor (see Land Registration and Law of Property Bill 1985, clause 2).

12 The 1985 Bill effectively gave expression to an earlier statement by Lord Hailsham LC to the effect that, contrary to the predictions of conveyancers, 'the world has not come to an end as a result of the decision in *Boland*' (see *Parliamentary Debates, House of Lords, Official Report*, Vol 437 (Session 1982-1983), Col 662 (15 December 1982)).

treatment which the Bill sought to accord to the rather similar residential claims presented by spouses and other categories of family member, particularly when the current tendency in family law is directed towards the assimilation of the incidents of de iure and de facto marriage.[13]

(4) The Law Commission's proposed reform of overriding interests

After further consideration of the impact of the *Boland* ruling and the fate of earlier reform proposals, the Law Commission has now concluded in favour of a rather different kind of solution to the problems in this area. In its most recent report on land registration,[14] the Commission has suggested that the rights of those 'in actual occupation' should continue to give rise to an overriding interest as against transferees and chargees, but that all such third parties adversely affected by an overriding interest should be indemnified against loss by the payment of compensation from public moneys.[15] This proposal would give ample weight to the fact that 'society generally (which includes purchasers and mortgagees) should recognise and respect' equitable rights of ownership in the family home.[16] If incorporated in legislative form, the Commission's recommendations will provide — at least in registered land — an admirable resolution of a dilemma which has already existed far too long.

13   See *Parliamentary Debates, House of Lords, Official Report (Fifth Series)*, Vol 460 (Session 1984-85), Cols 1270ff.
14   *Property Law: Third Report on Land Registration: A. Overriding Interests, B. Rectification and Indemnity, C. Minor Interests* (Law Com No 158, 31 March 1987).
15   Ante, p 202.
16   Law Com No 158, para 2.63.

CHAPTER 26

Financial crisis and the owner-occupier

Since the late 1970s Britain has suffered an industrial and commercial recession of a character unknown since the 1930s. Redundancy followed by long-term unemployment has become for many a structural feature of life. What is perhaps novel about this period of economic depression is that it coincides for the first time with a public endorsement of the ethic of home ownership in fee simple.[1] It is of course inevitable that the more general economic climate should reflect itself in an increasing incidence of financial crisis in the owner-occupied family home. Some measure of the way in which family living has been hit by current economic difficulties is provided by the statistic that the number of repossessions of family homes by building society mortgagees rose from 3,000 in 1980 to 16,590 in 1985.[2] The number of bankruptcy adjudications made by the county courts likewise rose from 2,607 in 1980 to 5,560 in 1984.[3] Financial problems affecting the principal family breadwinner clearly have a direct impact upon residential security in the home.[4]

This chapter is concerned with the legal protection which is afforded owner-occupation of the family home during times of financial crisis. It will become obvious that the primary challenge placed before both courts and legislature in this area is the search for a proper balance between competing considerations of commercial utility and family security. It should come as no surprise that the historic pattern of English law has tended towards the protection of the commercial interests of the creditor in preference to the preservation of the less tangible and less articulate interests of the family as an organic and vulnerable social entity. The long-standing antagonism between 'money interests' and 'family interests' is, however, undergoing constant adjustment and recent developments have done something to reinforce the family's claim to greater protection against the particular impact of general economic adversity.

---

1 Ante, p 725.
2 Central Statistical Office, *Social Trends No 17* (1987 edn London), p 149 (Table 8.25); *Parliamentary Debates, House of Commons, Official Report,* Vol 99 (Session 1985-86), Col 130 (Written Answer, 10 June 1986). The fact that many of these repossessions involved a voluntary surrender by the mortgagor indicates that the default problem is seriously underestimated on a mere scrutiny of judicial statistics (see *Land Mortgages* (Law Commission Working Paper No 99, August 1986), para 1.3). The alarming reality is that in 1985 some 49,600 mortgagors in the United Kingdom were between six and twelve months in arrear with their payments (*Social Trends No 17*, p 149 (Table 8.25)). See also [1986] Conv 67 at 68.
3 See *Judicial Statistics* (Annual Report 1981, Cmnd 8770), p 39 (Table C.3(b)); *Judicial Statistics* (Annual Report 1985, Cmnd 9864), p 89 (Table 7.15).
4 In England in 1985, 10 per cent of all households accepted as homeless were rendered homeless in consequence of a court order for mortgage default (see *Parliamentary Debates, House of Commons, Official Report,* Vol 99 (Session 1985-86), Col 128ff (Written Answer, 10 June 1986)).

1. ENFORCEMENT OF CHARGING ORDERS

The device of the charging order now provides an increasingly important mechanism for the legal recovery of debts. In this context it has become clear that the charging order can exert a devastating impact upon the security of the family home.

(1) Origin and function of the charging order

Under the Charging Orders Act 1979 it is open to a creditor, on obtaining a High Court or county court judgment in respect of a debt, to apply to the court for a 'charging order' for the purpose of enforcing the judgment or order in his favour.[5] The court has a discretion to decide whether to make a charging order,[6] and if the creditor's application is successful the court first makes an order nisi and then an order absolute.[7]

(a) Effect of the charging order

If the creditor's application is granted by the court, the charging order has the effect of imposing on specified property of the debtor a 'charge for securing the payment of any money due...under the judgment or order'.[8] The charging order thus converts what was at most a contractual debt into an enforceable security with proprietary attributes. The judgment creditor may protect his charge against third parties by the expedient of a registration against the debtor's name under the Land Charges Act 1972 (in the case of unregistered land)[9] or by the entry of a notice in the register of the debtor's title (in the case of registered land).[10]

(b) Realisation of the charge

The principal advantage of a charging order is that the charge imposed by the court becomes enforceable 'in the same manner as an equitable charge created by the debtor by writing under his hand.'[11] Accordingly the judgment creditor has a right to invoke legal process in the realisation of his security,[12] and is entitled to apply to the court either for an order for sale of the property charged or for the appointment of a receiver.[13]

---

5   Charging Orders Act 1979, s 1(1). The creditor's application may be made ex parte (RSC Ord 50, r 1(2)).
6   Charging Orders Act 1979, s 1(5) (post, p 872).
7   Certainly where the matter arises only as between the creditor and the debtor, the burden of showing cause why a charging order nisi should not be made absolute is on the judgment debtor (see *Roberts Petroleum Ltd v Bernard Kenny Ltd* [1982] 1 WLR 301 at 307E; *Harman v Glencross* [1985] Fam 49 at 56H). However, the mere fact that a court may decline to make an order absolute does not of course discharge the debt owed to the creditor (see *Harman v Glencross* [1985] Fam 49 at 58D).
8   Charging Orders Act 1979, s 1(1).
9   Land Charges Act 1972, s 6(1)(a) (register of writs and orders affecting land).
10 Land Registration Act 1925, s 49(1)(g), as inserted by Charging Orders Act 1979, s 3(3).
11 Charging Orders Act 1979, s 3(4).
12 Ante, pp 564, 631.
13 See *Midland Bank Plc v Pike* (1986) *Financial Times*, 18 April.

(2) **Property on which the charge may be imposed**

A court, acting in exercise of its powers under the Charging Orders Act 1979, may impose a charge on a wide range of the debtor's assets including 'any interest held by the debtor beneficially' in land, specified securities or funds in court, or 'under any trust'.[14]

(a) *Application to beneficial interests behind a trust for sale*

The express language of the Charging Orders Act 1979 deliberately sets out to cure a defect which existed in the law prior to the enactment of the 1979 Act,[15] by clarifying beyond all doubt that a charging order may effectively operate upon the equitable interest of a beneficial co-owner behind a trust for sale.[16]

(b) *Operation of a charging order in relation to the family home*

The reformulated language of the Charging Orders Act 1979 now makes it quite feasible for a creditor to obtain a charging order in respect of an interest in a jointly owned family home.[17] In such cases the charge imposed by the court attaches of course only to the equitable share of the debtor.[18] This plainly entitles the chargee to realise the value of that share by applying to the court for an order for its sale, but in view of the limited market for merely equitable interests the sale of such a share holds little attraction for most creditors. It is, however, of very much greater significance that the chargee ranks as a 'person interested' for the purpose of proceedings under section 30 of the Law of Property Act 1925.[19] Armed with his charging order, the judgment creditor has locus standi to apply to the court for an order directing the sale of the entire co-owned land, his own charge being satisfied out of the proceeds attributable to the debtor's aliquot share.[20] Given the traditional preference in favour of creditors under section 30,[1] it becomes acutely apparent that the charging order carries a realistic and highly potent threat to residential security in the family home.[2]

---

14 Charging Orders Act 1979, s 2(1)(a).
15 The predecessor of the Charging Orders Act 1979, section 35(1) of the Administration of Justice Act 1956, applied somewhat more narrowly to the debtor's 'interest in land'. In *Irani Finance Ltd v Singh* [1971] Ch 59 at 79B-F, the Court of Appeal held that an equitable interest behind a trust for sale of land, being an interest merely in the proceeds of sale (ante, p 371), was not therefore available as an object of a charging order.
16 The limitations imposed by the equitable doctrine of conversion have now been removed by the express wording of the Charging Orders Act 1979 (see *National Westminster Bank Ltd v Stockman* [1981] 1 WLR 67 at 69C).
17 *Harman v Glencross* [1985] Fam 49 at 54B. If the judgment debtor was the sole owner of the family home, the charging order clearly operates upon the entire equitable interest. The resulting charge will enable the creditor to apply for sale unless, of course, the debtor's spouse has made sale impossible by her prior registration of 'rights of occupation' under the Matrimonial Homes Act 1983 (post, p 872).
18 The imposition of the charge effects a severance of any beneficial joint tenancy (ante, p 324).
19 Ante, p 377.
20 *Midland Bank Plc v Pike* (1986) *Financial Times*, 18 April.
1 Post, p 877.
2 As was noted somewhat wryly in *Midland Bank Plc v Pike* (1986) *Financial Times*, 18 April, the chargee appears to have a better prospect of obtaining an order for sale under section 30 than does a co-owner!

(3) The court's discretion whether to make a charging order

In view of its potentially drastic consequences, the making of a charging order is not mandatory on proof of a judgment debt.[3] A wide judicial discretion attaches both to the decision whether a charging order should be made at all[4] and to subsequent decisions whether a charging order, once made, should be discharged or varied.[5] In all such decisions[6] the court must consider 'all the circumstances of the case',[7] and in particular must have regard to evidence of the 'personal circumstances of the debtor'[8] and whether any other creditor would be 'unduly prejudiced' by the making of the order.[9]

(a) The necessity for discretion

In the general context of proceedings between debtor and creditor under the Charging Orders Act 1979, the creditor, although not entitled to a charging order as of right, is normally justified in expecting that a charging order will be made.[10] However, this proposition is far from absolute,[11] and in the rather special context of the family home it has been said that references to 'any presumption one way or the other' are unhelpful.[12] In dealing with the family home the court must seek to 'strike a balance between the normal expectation of the creditor and the hardship to the wife and children if an order is made.'[13]

(i) Considerations in favour of the creditor

On behalf of the creditor it is a significant consideration that the debtor's spouse may fairly be called on to share the debtor's adversity, just as doubtless she would have been willing in different circumstances to share in any prosperity which might have come his way.[14] In many instances the debtor's wife may also have had the opportunity, by registration of her statutory rights of occupation, to acquire priority over any charging order obtained against her husband.[15] Moreover, as Balcombe

---

3 See the recommendation of the Law Commission (*Report on Charging Orders* (Law Com No 74, Cmnd 6412, 1976), para 43).
4 Charging Orders Act 1979, s 1(5).
5 Charging Orders Act 1979, s 3(5). The jurisdiction to discharge or vary a charging order is open only to a 'person interested in any property to which the order relates', but this may include the debtor's spouse (*Harman v Glencross* [1985] Fam 49 at 56C-D, [1986] Fam 81 at 89H-90B, E-G).
6 The matters prescribed for consideration in section 1(5) are by necessary implication relevant also to decisions on discharge or variation (*Harman v Glencross* [1985] Fam 49 at 55C-D).
7 In the context of a jointly owned matrimonial home, the court has 'a duty at least to consider' whether the debtor's wife 'ought not to be given notice of the hearing so that she can be heard and...all the circumstances of the case can be considered' (*Harman v Glencross* [1985] Fam 49 at 54G-H, [1986] Fam 81 at 89D-E).
8 Charging Orders Act 1979, s 1(5)(a). See *Harman v Glencross* [1986] Fam 81 at 103D-E.
9 Charging Orders Act 1979, s 1(5)(b).
10 See *Roberts Petroleum Ltd v Bernard Kenny Ltd* [1982] 1 WLR 301 at 307A; *First National Securities Ltd v Hegerty* [1985] QB 850 at 366A-B.
11 The proposition is necessarily qualified where, for instance, the judgment creditor finds himself in competition with other creditors (see *Harman v Glencross* [1986] 2 WLR [1986] Fam 81 at 93A).
12 *Harman v Glencross* [1985] Fam 49 at 57B.
13 *Harman v Glencross* [1986] Fam 81 at 104A per Fox LJ.
14 *Harman v Glencross* [1985] Fam 49 at 59A-B.
15 *Harman v Glencross* [1986] Fam 81 at 94A-C.

LJ pointed out in *Harman v Glencross*,[16] not all judgment creditors are 'faceless corporations'. Some are private individuals for whom the denial or postponement of a charging order may entail just as much domestic hardship as for the debtor.[17]

(ii) Considerations in favour of the debtor and his family On behalf of the debtor and his family, however, it is often a relevant consideration, as in *Harman v Glencross*,[18] that the debtor's wife was not a party to the indebtedness incurred by her husband. Moreover, the creditor could easily have insisted on taking some security prior to advancing money or credit to the debtor but clearly failed to do so.[19] In some circumstances it may be conclusive in favour of the debtor's family that the operation of a charging order on the debtor's beneficial share will precipitate a sale of the family home and leave insufficient funds to rehouse the debtor's wife and children.[20] In *Harman v Glencross*[1] Ewbank J decided that the balance of these considerations pointed overwhelmingly against the making of a charging order, and the Court of Appeal declined to disturb his exercise of discretion.[2]

(b) Relationship with section 30 proceedings

It is, of course, a standard contention of judgment creditors that a charging order should be made fairly automatically in relation to the family home, leaving factors of discretion to be dealt with in any later application by the creditor for a court order for sale under section 30 of the Law of Property Act 1925.[3] In general, however, the courts have resisted such attempts to exclude the exercise of discretion under the Charging Orders Act 1979. In *Harman v Glencross*[4] Ewbank J took the brutally realistic view that to postpone the exercise of discretion until an application is heard under section 30 'is failing to do justice to a wife', since the 'only real question' with which the court is concerned in section 30 proceedings is 'how long is the wife to continue to have possession and not whether there should be a sale at all.'[5]

(c) Relationship with property adjustment on divorce

A complicating factor in the exercise of discretion under the Charging Orders Act 1979 is frequently the consideration that the making of a charging order in respect of the debtor's beneficial interest in his family home may prejudice any claim which his wife might otherwise have under the Matrimonial Causes Act 1973 for property adjustment in the event of divorce.[6] In an extreme, but not

---

16 [1986] Fam 81 at 93F.
17 [1986] Fam 81 at 93G-H.
18 [1986] Fam 81 at 98C.
19 [1986] Fam 81 at 98C.
20 *Harman v Glencross* [1985] Fam 49 at 59F.
 1 [1985] Fam 49 at 59F. See [1985] Conv 129 (P.F. Smith).
 2 [1986] Fam 81 at 98G, 105G. See [1986] Conv 218 (J. Warburton).
 3 Post, p 876.
 4 [1985] Fam 49 at 58A-B.
 5 This somewhat sanguine assessment was endorsed in the Court of Appeal by Balcombe LJ ([1986] Fam 81 at 96B), but compare now Insolvency Act 1986, s 336(3), (4), (5) (post, p 881).
 6 If a charging order is made, clearly any subsequent order for the transfer of property made in matrimonial proceedings (see Matrimonial Causes Act 1973, s 24(1)) will take effect subject to the charging order (see *Harman v Glencross* [1986] Fam 81 at 102B, 103G).

uncommon, case the imposition of a charge on the debtor's beneficial interest in the family home may leave no property at all in his name against which a property adjustment order in favour of his wife can operate. The value of the beneficial interest (if any) retained by the wife is unlikely to be adequate to purchase suitable alternative accommodation for herself and the children.[7] In such circumstances the exercise of discretion under the Charging Orders Act 1979, although superficially an issue arising merely as between debtor and creditor, represents in reality a conflict between the commercial law jurisdiction conferred by the 1979 Act and the matrimonial jurisdiction conferred by the Matrimonial Causes Act 1973.[8] Under the ground-rules enunciated by the Court of Appeal in *Harman v Glencross*,[9] the timing of the respective applications becomes a crucial consideration.

(i) Charging order made before debtor's wife applies for ancillary relief   If a charging order is made absolute *before* the debtor's wife applies for ancillary relief on divorce, then her appeal for a judicial consideration of her circumstances is most properly made under section 30 of the Law of Property Act 1925 in the context of a subsequent application by the creditor for an order directing the sale of the family home.[10]

(ii) Charging order made after debtor's wife applies for ancillary relief   If, however, the charging order is made *after* the wife applies for ancillary relief,[11] then the court has power to make the charging order absolute and unconditional, but may normally do so only if the balance of the proceeds of sale (after the judgment debt has been satisfied) are 'clearly sufficient to provide adequate alternative accommodation for the wife and children.'[12] If, as is more usual, the proceeds released by sale are unlikely to be sufficient for this purpose, the creditor's application for an order absolute should normally be transferred to the court's family jurisdiction and considered in conjunction with the wife's application for property adjustment. In this way one court (and one court only) is in a position to consider all the relevant circumstances of the case.[13]

The transfer of the charging order application to the matrimonial jurisdiction does not, however, detract from the essentially commercial character of the subsequent proceedings,[14] and the creditor has a justifiable expectation of recovering his debt.[15] Only in exceptional circumstances is the court ever justified in ordering an outright transfer of the debtor's share to his

---

7   *Harman v Glencross* [1986] Fam 81 at 97B-C, 104A-B.
8   *Harman v Glencross* [1986] Fam 81 at 103F.
9   [1986] Fam 81.
10   [1986] Fam 81 at 99A-B. See also *First National Securities v Hegerty* [1985] QB 850 at 868B.
11   It would not normally constitute a proper exercise of the court's discretion under Matrimonial Causes Act 1973, s 24, to order an immediate property transfer to the wife for the express purpose of frustrating a pending application for a charging order (*Harman v Glencross* [1986] Fam 81 at 103G-H).
12   [1986] Fam 81 at 99C-D. See eg *Llewellin v Llewellin* (Unreported, Court of Appeal, Transcript No 640 of 1985, 30 October 1985). In this context, the provision of 'adequate alternative accommodation' is not inconsistent with the wife and children being 'housed at a lower standard than they might reasonably have expected...' ([1986] Fam 81 at 99F).
13   [1986] Fam 81 at 99D-E, 105E-F.
14   [1986] Fam 81 at 103F, 105F.
15   [1986] Fam 81 at 99E-F.

wife, thereby leaving nothing on which the judgment creditor's charging order can ever bite.[16] The creditor's legitimate interest should be relegated only if and to the extent that it is 'necessary to protect the wife's right to occupy (with the children where appropriate) the matrimonial home.'[17] With this end in view, the Court of Appeal suggested in *Harman v Glencross* that a compromise solution may well lie in the equivalent of the *Mesher* order which at one time enjoyed currency under the Matrimonial Causes Act 1973.[18] A charging order based on the *Mesher* analogy imposes a charge on the debtor's share in the family home but effectively postpones its enforcement so long as the house is occupied by the wife and a child of the family who is under the age of 17 and in full time education.[19] Such an order thus guarantees the creditor a deferred recovery of his debt, while alleviating at least temporarily the hardship inevitably suffered by the debtor's family.[20]

(d) Relationship with bankruptcy proceedings

It is not at all unlikely that a creditor may seek a charging order in respect of a debtor who is on the verge of bankruptcy. In these circumstances, as Balcombe LJ indicated in *Harman v Glencross*,[1] there may be little point in denying the creditor his charging order since it is only a matter of time before the occupation rights of the debtor's wife are defeated by a creditor who chooses to make the debtor bankrupt.[2]

2. EFFECTS OF BANKRUPTCY

Bankruptcy is personal financial crisis in its most extreme form, leading as it does to a severe diminution of legal capacity for the individual who is the subject of a bankruptcy order.[3] Bankruptcy tends to occur in close association with such events as redundancy, business failure or marriage breakdown,[4] and in each case the advent of bankruptcy has a potentially devastating impact on family life.[5] This impact is intensified by the fact that frequently the only substantial capital asset available to meet the claims of creditors is the family home in which the bankrupt's wife and children (and often the bankrupt himself) are still living.[6]

---

16 [1986] Fam 81 at 100A.
17 [1986] Fam 81 at 99G per Balcombe LJ.
18 See *Mesher v Mesher* [1980] 1 All ER 126n.
19 Fox LJ pointed out ([1986] Fam 81 at 104F-G) that section 3(1) of the Charging Orders Act 1979 empowers the court to make a charging order subject to the condition that the creditor should not seek to enforce his charge by means of an order for sale during a specified period.
20 Fox LJ agreed ([1986] Fam 81 at 105A-B) that *Mesher* type orders were not in the long term particularly favourable from the wife's viewpoint, but thought that in a dispute between the wife and the husband's creditor 'the interests of the creditor cannot be disregarded.'
1 [1986] Fam 81 at 100B.
2 See now Insolvency Act 1986, ss 264ff (post, p 881).
3 See eg Insolvency Act 1986, s 284(1).
4 It is not impossible that a divorced husband may become bankrupt under the financial strain of attempting to support two families.
5 'Eviction from the family home...may be a disaster not only to the debtor himself...but also to those who are living there as his dependants who may not, and often do not, have any legal or beneficial rights in the property which they can enforce' (*Insolvency Law and Practice* (Report of the Review Committee chaired by Sir Kenneth Cork, Cmnd 8558, June 1982), para 1116).
6 See generally C. Palley, *Wives, Creditors and the Matrimonial Home* (1969) 20 NILQ 132; C. Hand, *Bankruptcy and the Family Home*, [1983] Conv 219.

(1) **Application for sale of the family home**

When bankruptcy affects a person who is a beneficial co-owner of the family home, section 30 of the Law of Property Act 1925 provides the primary forum for the resolution of those conflicts of interest which unavoidably arise between the creditors and the family of the bankrupt.[7] Even though only one member of the family has become bankrupt, it is virtually inevitable that the family home will be the subject of an application for a court order for sale under this section.[8]

(a) *Locus standi of the trustee in bankruptcy*

The application under section 30 is usually initiated not by the bankrupt or his spouse (either or both of whom may desperately wish to retain the home),[9] but by the bankrupt's trustee in bankruptcy. Any property owned beneficially by the bankrupt (ie, the bankrupt's 'estate') vests by operation of law in his trustee in bankruptcy,[10] who is then statutorily bound to 'get in, realise and distribute' that estate in satisfaction of the claims of creditors.[11] Where the bankrupt was beneficially entitled to a share in a jointly owned family home, it has been quite clear since *In Re Solomon (A Bankrupt)*[12] that the trustee in bankruptcy ranks as a 'person interested' within the meaning of section 30 and may therefore apply for an order for sale of the entire co-owned property. The court, in determining this application, has discretion to make 'such order as it thinks fit'.

(b) *Nature of the discretion exercised under section 30*

The section 30 jurisdiction highlights the recurring tension between the legitimate claims of commercial creditors and the competing claims of family members to residential security at a time of peculiar crisis. The resolution of this tension must now be sought both in the existing caselaw on the exercise of the section 30 discretion and in the terms of the Insolvency Act 1986.[13]

(i) *The orthodox view of the exercise of discretion*   Prior to the commencement of the Insolvency Act 1986, it was consistently maintained by the courts that, even

---

7   Ante, p 377. The Cork Committee noted quite rightly that where the family home is in the sole ownership of the debtor, section 30 of the Law of Property Act 1925 (which relates only to the execution of trusts for sale) confers no discretion upon the court to permit his family continued possession of that home for any length of time against the wishes of the trustee in bankruptcy. See *Insolvency Law and Practice* (Cmnd 8558, June 1982), para 1117.

8   Post, p 877.

9   Self-induced bankruptcy is, in rare cases, used in an attempt to defeat the first wife's claims for property adjustment on divorce (see eg *In Re Holliday (A Bankrupt)* [1981] Ch 405 at 412G, 414C-D; *In Re Lowrie (A Bankrupt)* [1981] 3 All ER 353 at 355j-356a).

10   Insolvency Act 1986, ss 283(1)(a), (3)(a), 306. The estate which thus vests in the trustee in bankruptcy cannot include a mere right on the part of a bankrupt spouse to apply for property adjustment on divorce. Such a right does not constitute 'property' in any sense recognisable in bankruptcy law (see eg *Deloitte, Haskins & Sells Ltd v Graham* (1983) 144 DLR (3d) 539 at 543).

11   Insolvency Act 1986, s 305(2).

12   [1967] Ch 573 at 586.

13   The relevant provisions of the Insolvency Act 1986 came into force on 29 December 1986, a micro-second after the coming into effect of the Insolvency Act 1985, whose provisions were consolidated in the 1986 Act. See The Insolvency Act 1985 (Commencement No 5) Order 1986 (SI 1986/1924).

though a section 30 application was initiated by a trustee in bankruptcy, the matter remained ultimately one of discretion for the court.[14] There could not be said to be any presumption (either rebuttable or irrebuttable) in favour of the trustee in bankruptcy.[15] According to the Court of Appeal in *Thames Guaranty Ltd v Campbell*,[16] the result of the contest between the family and the creditors is 'by no means a foregone conclusion.' The discretion of the court 'is a real one and in considering whether or not to order a sale, the court must weigh the conflicting legal and moral claims of the creditors on the one hand and those of the wife on the other, taking all relevant facts, including the existence of children, into account'.

(ii) The historic record   Notwithstanding the protestations of neutrality made by the courts, a review of the caselaw relating to section 30 reveals that in almost every instance the question of priority between commercial and family claims has been resolved conclusively in favour of the trustee in bankruptcy.[17] The courts have been consistently ready to exercise their discretion under section 30 in favour of fairly immediate sale, even though the family home might still be required for the bankrupt's wife and children.[18] Once again the 'solid tug of money' (as represented in the claims of creditors) has tended to prevail over the 'family interest' implicit in the housing needs of the wife and children.[19] Although the courts have steadily maintained that the relevant question is simply 'whose voice in equity ought to prevail',[20] it is impossible to find a single case in which the voice of the trustee in bankruptcy has not eventually prevailed.[1] The section 30 discretion has been exercised uniformly in favour of sale of the family home (usually within three months) in order that the bankrupt's share of the proceeds be released for the satisfaction of his debts.[2]

---

14   *In Re Turner (A Bankrupt)* [1974] 1 WLR 1556 at 1558A; *In Re Densham (A Bankrupt)* [1975] 1 WLR 1519 at 1531E; *In Re Holliday (A Bankrupt)* [1981] Ch 405 at 420C.

15   *In Re Turner (A Bankrupt)* [1974] 1 WLR 1556 at 1558B per Goff J.

16   [1985] QB 210 at 239A-B.

17   See eg *In Re Densham (A Bankrupt)* [1975] 1 WLR 1519 at 1532B; *Bird v Syme-Thomson* [1979] 1 WLR 440 at 445E-F; *In Re Lowrie (A Bankrupt)* [1981] 3 All ER 353 at 358h, 359h; *In Re Holliday (A Bankrupt)* [1981] Ch 405 at 425G.

18   See *Harman v Glencross* [1985] Fam 49 at 58A-B (ante, p 875) for a rare admission that under section 30 the 'only real question' is 'how long is the wife to continue to have possession and not whether there should be a sale at all.'

19   See eg the statement of Cumming-Bruce LJ in *Chhokar v Chhokar* [1984] FLR 313 at 327G that, because he represents 'innocent creditors', the court 'will usually pay great regard to the voice of a trustee in bankruptcy'.

20   *In Re Turner (A Bankrupt)* [1974] 1 WLR 1556 at 1558C. See also *Chhokar v Chhokar* [1984] FLR 313 at 329F-330H.

1   The caselaw has tended to have a self-fulfilling quality. See eg *In Re Bailey (A Bankrupt)* [1977] 1 WLR 278 at 283C, where Walton J attributed great significance to the fact that 'no case of the many referred to yet has thrown up the case where [the trustee in bankruptcy's] voice was not allowed to prevail.'

2   It seems to have been regarded as extremely relevant in the caselaw that the trustee in bankruptcy was statutorily *bound* (by Bankruptcy Act 1914, ss 48ff) to realise the debtor's assets (see eg *In Re Turner (A Bankrupt)* [1974] 1 WLR 1556 at 1558E; *In Re Densham (A Bankrupt)* [1975] 1 WLR 1519 at 1531G). It has been suggested that if section 30 is invoked not by a trustee in bankruptcy, but merely by a mortgagee, different considerations may be applicable. It may well be that sale would be less readily ordered at the behest of a mortgagee who, unlike a trustee in bankruptcy, has no statutory *duty* as such to realise the mortgagor's assets (see R.J. Smith, (1979) 95 LQR 501 at 506; J. Martin, [1980] Conv 361 at 376ff).

(iii) Hard cases   Typical of the commercialist bias of the court in section 30 applications is the decision in *In Re Bailey (A Bankrupt).*[3] Here the two trustees for sale of a former matrimonial home had been divorced and the ex-husband was declared bankrupt. His ex-wife was still living in the property with a 16 year old son of the marriage. In the course of the section 30 proceedings brought by the trustee in bankruptcy, she requested that sale of the matrimonial home be postponed for two years in order that the son might complete his studies at the local school and take his GCE 'A' level examinations.

Although the ex-wife had urged that the court should follow the family-oriented approach to section 30 demonstrated by the Court of Appeal in *Williams v Williams,*[4] Megarry V-C distinguished this decision on the ground that it 'was not a bankruptcy case, but a husband and wife case.'[5] In other words, Megarry V-C considered that the intervention of the trustee in bankruptcy materially altered the nature of the exercise under section 30. In his view, the 'husband and wife' cases were irrelevant for the present purpose since they 'were not cases in which matters of commercial obligation arose, as in the case of bankruptcy.' Moreover, he said, 'bankruptcy has, in relation to the matrimonial home, its own claim to protection.' In *Bailey,* therefore, the claims of the ex-wife and child were ultimately considered to be insufficiently weighty to counterbalance the third party concerns represented by the trustee in bankruptcy,[6] and the court refused to grant any postponement of the sale.

Walton J concurred in this decision, preferring to emphasise 'the purely property aspect of the matter.'[7] He pointed out that the maxim *pacta sunt servanda,* 'although somewhat out of fashion, must be borne in mind. A person must discharge his liabilities before there is any room for being generous. One's debts must be paid, and paid promptly...'[8] Walton J conceded that there might be special circumstances where the court 'would hesitate long before making an immediate order for sale',[9] but ruled that such circumstances were not present in this case.[10]

In only one reported decision prior to the Insolvency Act 1986 has there been any aberration from the solid preference expressed throughout the caselaw for the claims of creditors. In *In Re Holliday (A Bankrupt)*[11] an ex-wife was still living

3   [1977] 1 WLR 278.
4   [1976] Ch 278 (ante, p 825).
5   [1977] 1 WLR 278 at 281F-G.
6   Megarry V-C thought it improbable that the sale of the matrimonial home would affect the son's educational prospects other than very slightly ([1977] 1 WLR 278 at 282F-G).
7   [1977] 1 WLR 278 at 283E. Walton J observed that the present decision 'may be yet another case where the sins of the father have to be visited on the children, but that is the way in which the world is constructed, and one must be just before one is generous' ([1977] 1 WLR 278 at 284E).
8   [1977] 1 WLR 278 at 283A-B.
9   The circumstances postulated included the case where, for example, a house had been specially adapted to suit the needs of a handicapped child ([1977] 1 WLR 278 at 284B-C).
10   In *In Re Toobman (A Bankrupt)* (1982) *Times,* 3 March, Warner J ordered the sale of the family home in exercising a similar discretion under Bankruptcy Act 1914, s 108(1). Here the bankrupt's wife suffered from severe heart disease and anxious depression and her doctor certified that her condition was largely attributable to her husband's financial problems and the constant threat of losing their home. Warner J nevertheless thought that there was 'no definite period, short of Mrs Toobman's life' for which he could 'usefully postpone the sale'. Her state of health did not justify keeping the creditors out of their money during her lifetime, 'with only statutory interest at 4 per cent per annum to compensate them.'
11   [1981] Ch 405. See [1981] Conv 79 (A. Sydenham); (1981) 97 LQR 200 (C. Hand).

in the former matrimonial home with three young children. Her ex-husband had been adjudicated bankrupt on his own petition,[12] but the extent of his outstanding liabilities was fairly small (in the region of £6,000). The Court of Appeal considered that the ex-wife had 'strong and justifiable grounds' for arguing that an immediate sale would be 'unfair' to her. The Court had particular regard to the bankrupt's conduct in leaving his wife for another woman, and to the fact that his ex-wife was now 'saddled with the burden of providing a proper home for her children' without the resources necessary for this purpose.[13] In view of the extreme hardship in which the ex-wife found herself, the Court declined to order an immediate sale of the property (in which there was in any event an ample equity of some £27,000).[14] Instead the Court postponed sale for five years (by which time the two eldest children would be over 17 years of age), while reserving the power to enforce the trust for sale on the application of any interested party should circumstances change in the meantime.[15]

It is significant that subsequent courts have gone out of their way to disavow any suggestion that the temporary concession to hardship demonstrated in *In Re Holliday (A Bankrupt)* marked the beginning of a more general departure from the otherwise contrary pattern of the caselaw under section 30.[16]

(c) Changes introduced by the Insolvency Act 1986

Many of the shortcomings of the English law of insolvency were addressed by a Review Committee, chaired by Sir Kenneth Cork, which reported in 1982. This Committee concluded that it would be 'consonant with present social attitudes to alleviate the personal hardships of those who are dependent on the debtor but not responsible for his insolvency, if this can be achieved by delaying for an acceptable time the sale of the family home.'[17] The substance of this recommendation is now incorporated in the Insolvency Act 1986, although in a rather complex form which omits some of the more subtle refinements of the original proposal.

In the following ways the 1986 Act significantly adjusts the balance to be struck between family and commercial interests on bankruptcy.

(i) Limited security of tenure for the bankrupt himself

The 1986 Act confers on the bankrupt himself certain 'rights of occupation' as against the trustee in bankruptcy in respect of any dwelling-house in which the bankrupt was

---

12 On the general irrelevance of the motive underlying a self-induced bankruptcy, see *Ex parte Painter* [1895] 1 QB 85 at 91; *In Re Harry Dunn* [1949] Ch 640 at 647; *In Re A Debtor* [1967] Ch 590 at 596C; *Re Mottee* (1977) 29 FLR 406 at 415.
13 [1981] Ch 405 at 424A-B.
14 [1981] Ch 405 at 424D, 425D-E. It may be significant that Goff LJ died before the final judgments were delivered.
15 [1981] Ch 405 at 424E.
16 See the statement of Balcombe LJ in *Harman v Glencross* [1986] Fam 81 at 95F-H that the decision in *Holliday* was 'very much against the run of the recent authorities' and represented a 'high water-mark for the protection of the wife and children under section 30'. See also *In Re Lowrie (A Bankrupt)* [1981] 3 All ER 353 at 356a ('One can scarcely..imagine a more exceptional set of facts...'); [1982] Conv 74 (A. Sydenham).
17 *Insolvency Law and Practice* (Cmnd 8558, June 1982), para 1118.

beneficially entitled.[18] These rights, although framed on the analogy of 'rights of occupation' under the Matrimonial Homes Act 1983,[19] are quite independent of such rights as the bankrupt's spouse (if any) may have under the latter statute.[20] Moreover, the bankrupt's 'rights of occupation' are expressed to be conditional on his living with some persons under the age of 18 with whom he has at some previous time occupied the dwelling-house in question.[1]

The bankrupt's 'rights of occupation' are deemed to take effect under the Matrimonial Homes Act 1983,[2] and include a right not to be evicted or excluded from the dwelling-house except with the leave of the court.[3] Thus any attempt by the trustee in bankruptcy to realise the cash value of the bankrupt's home necessarily involves an application to court for the termination of the bankrupt's 'rights of occupation'. This application, although treated as an application under section 1 of the 1983 Act,[4] is determined by the bankruptcy court with reference to criteria laid down in the Insolvency Act 1986. Accordingly the court must make 'such order...as it thinks just and reasonable having regard to the interests of the creditors, to the bankrupt's financial resources, to the needs of the children and to all the circumstances of the case other than the needs of the bankrupt.'[5] The statutory criteria are unranked and somewhat general in their tenor, in strong contrast with the express recommendation of the Cork Committee that, in balancing familial and commercial interests, the court should 'give primary consideration to the welfare of dependant children, to the circumstances of the wife, and to the situation of dependant parents who are resident in the family dwelling.'[6]

The significance of these provisions of the Insolvency Act 1986 lies in the fact that important elements of due legal process and judicial discretion are now necessarily interposed before any sale of the bankrupt's home may take place. Moreover, this statutory protection is available irrespective of whether the bankrupt's ownership of his home was joint or sole,[7] the only relevant precondition being that he should be living at the material time with persons under the age of 18. The bankrupt's security of tenure is, however, severely curtailed by an overriding statutory direction which relates to any case in which more than one year has elapsed since the bankrupt's estate vested in his trustee. In determining any application made at this later stage for a termination of the bankrupt's 'rights of occupation', the court is directed to assume, 'unless the circumstances of the case are exceptional, that the interests

18 Insolvency Act 1986, ss 337(1), (2). The bankrupt cannot claim any right of occupation qua beneficial owner, since his own beneficial interest has of course vested in his trustee in bankruptcy (see Insolvency Act 1986, s 306(1)).

19 Ante, p 782.

20 Insolvency Act 1986, s 337(2).

1 Insolvency Act 1986, s 337(1)(b). This condition is somewhat more restrictive than the terms of the Cork Report, which recommended (para 1124f) that statutory protection should also be available where the home was currently occupied by the debtor's wife or cohabitee or by the debtor together with 'a dependant parent of the debtor or of his wife who has been living there as part of the family on the basis of a long term arrangement.'

2 Insolvency Act 1986, s 337(3)(a).

3 Insolvency Act 1986, s 337(2)(a)(i).

4 Ante, p 784.

5 Insolvency Act 1986, s 337(5).

6 *Insolvency Law and Practice* (Cmnd 8558, June 1982), para 1129.

7 See *Insolvency Law and Practice* (Cmnd 8558, June 1982), para 1117 (ante, p 876).

of the bankrupt's creditors outweigh all other considerations.'[8] This provision clearly signals that the bankrupt's home will rarely be immune from sale for more than a limited adjustment period of one year following his bankruptcy.

(ii) Limited security of tenure for the bankrupt's spouse The Insolvency Act 1986 also confirms a form of limited security of tenure arising by virtue of any 'rights of occupation' which the bankrupt's spouse may enjoy independently under the Matrimonial Homes Act 1983.[9] In the event of bankruptcy, such rights can now be terminated only on application to the bankruptcy court, which is statutorily directed to make 'such order...as it thinks just and reasonable'.[10] The court's discretion is once again structured by reference to a number of statutory criteria. These criteria, which are similar to those which govern applications to terminate the 'rights of occupation' of the bankrupt himself,[11] are again controlled by the injunction that the interests of the bankrupt's creditors shall normally be regarded as paramount in all applications made more than one year after the vesting of the bankrupt's estate in his trustee.[12]

(iii) Limited postponement of the execution of a trust for sale Where the bankrupt and his spouse (or former spouse) are trustees for sale of a dwelling-house, any application for sale made by the trustee in bankruptcy under section 30 of the Law of Property Act 1925 must now be addressed to the bankruptcy court.[13] This court is directed to determine the application with reference to precisely the same criteria which govern the discretionary termination of the 'rights of occupation' enjoyed by the bankrupt's spouse under the Matrimonial Homes Act 1983.[14] Once again the court's discretion is peremptorily limited, save in 'exceptional' circumstances, by the instruction that in any application made more than one year after the trustee in bankruptcy is invested with the bankrupt's estate the court must assume that 'the interests of the bankrupt's creditors outweigh all other considerations.'[15]

(iv) Comparison with homestead legislation It is the clear purpose of the Insolvency Act 1986 to induce a better and more compassionate balance in the consideration of competing interests in the family home on bankruptcy. In particular the new legislative compromise aims at establishing a legal mechanism which delays rather than cancels the rights of creditors.[16] The

---

8   Insolvency Act 1986, s 337(6).
9   The bankrupt's spouse is expressly precluded from acquiring statutory 'rights of occupation' (eg by reason of marriage) during the period which intervenes between the presentation of the petition for a bankruptcy order and the vesting of the bankrupt's estate in a trustee (Insolvency Act 1986, s 336(1)).
10   Insolvency Act 1986, s 336(4).
11   The criteria are adapted to include reference also to the conduct of the spouse 'so far as contributing to the bankruptcy' (s 336(4)(b)), the needs and financial resources of the spouse (s 336(4)(c)) and, of course, the needs of any children (s 336(4)(d)).
12   Insolvency Act 1986, s 336(5).
13   Insolvency Act 1986, s 336(3).
14   Insolvency Act 1986, s 336(4). A trustee for sale, even though a spouse, does not of course have 'rights of occupation' under the Matrimonial Homes Act 1983. Such rights are not conferred upon an owner of the legal estate (ante, p 784).
15   Insolvency Act 1986, s 336(5).
16   See *Insolvency Law and Practice* (Cmnd 8558, June 1982), para 1118.

heightened emphasis thus accorded to the residential expectations of family members is indeed a significant advance on the pattern of decision-making evident in the antecedent caselaw under section 30. However, even the innovative measures of the Insolvency Act 1986 fall short of the objectives of the 'homestead legislation' which is currently in force in New Zealand and in many of the common law jurisdictions of Canada and the United States. At the heart of each of these homestead schemes is a large presumption in favour of long-term security of tenure in the family home. By contrast, the balance of emphasis expressed in the Insolvency Act 1986 still heavily favours the recovery of creditors' claims, at most subject to a limited delay in the enforcement of those claims against family assets.

One of the oldest and most typical schemes of homestead rights is contained in New Zealand's Joint Family Homes Act 1964. Under this statute it is possible for spouses to register their home as a 'joint family home'.[17] Upon registration the spouses become legal and beneficial joint tenants,[18] and while the joint family home settlement remains registered the interests of the husband and wife are unaffected by bankruptcy or assignment for the benefit of creditors.[19] Creditors of either spouse may oppose the initial registration,[20] but may subsequently attack the joint family home settlement only on the limited grounds laid down in the Act.[1]

Under the Act the court retains a discretion to cancel any existing joint family home registration,[2] but it is clear that this discretion will not be exercised in favour of sale merely because one of the spouses has been declared bankrupt.[3] Cancellation followed by sale and distribution will be ordered only in fairly exceptional circumstances. Such circumstances may arise, however, where there has been unconscientious dealing by the debtor with his creditors,[4] or where *both* spouses have been adjudicated bankrupt and there remains a very substantial equity from which the creditors could be satisfied without undue hardship to the family.[5] Even if the court decides in a particular case that the joint family home must be sold up to meet the claims of creditors, the proceeds of that sale remain to a level specified by statute immune from third

17　Joint Family Homes Act 1964, s 5. Registration is entirely voluntary.
18　Joint Family Homes Act 1964, s 9(1)(b).
19　Joint Family Homes Act 1964, s 9(2)(d). See *Official Assignee v Lawford* [1984] 2 NZLR 257 at 263.
20　Joint Family Homes Act 1964, s 6(1).
1　Joint Family Homes Act 1964, ss 16-20.
2　Joint Family Homes Act 1964, s 16(1).
3　See eg *Official Assignee of Pannell v Pannell* [1966] NZLR 324 at 325, where Wilson J did not think the very considerable total of the bankrupt's debts or the large number of his creditors to be 'sufficient, without more, to warrant...an order for sale.'
4　See *Official Assignee of Pannell v Pannell* [1966] NZLR 324 at 326.
5　See eg *Official Assignee v Lawford* [1984] 2 NZLR 257 at 264ff, where even after satisfaction of the creditors' claims the equity amounted to over $70,000. The Court of Appeal considered that this surplus was sufficient to enable the bankrupts to purchase a quite adequate home and that 'on an objective view the present appellants and their family cannot possibly be said to be in a situation of hardship...True, their standard of living has fallen; the home will be more modest and they no longer own a yacht...' ([1984] 2 NZLR 257 at 265). Compare *Rukat v Rukat* [1975] Fam 63 at 73F ('The rich gourmet who because of financial stringency has to drink vin ordinaire with his grouse may well think that he is suffering a hardship; but sensible people would say he was not').

party claims,[6] with the result that the family salvages something from the calamity of insolvency.[7]

The priorities expressed in the Joint Family Homes Act 1964 are quite different from those which have prevailed hitherto in the English law of bankruptcy. The New Zealand legislation was enacted with the express object of promoting the stability and permanence of family life as a higher social end than that represented by commercial security for the creditor.[8] The 1964 Act indeed embodies a remarkable and imaginative attempt to strike a humane social balance between competing interests, and it is highly arguable that English law would be enriched by the enactment of similar legislation.

(d) The equity of exoneration

If and when a trustee in bankruptcy finally succeeds in obtaining a court order for the sale of jointly owned property, the division of the resulting proceeds of sale may be affected by the operation of the 'equity of exoneration'. This little known equity is founded on the general proposition that if two joint owners of property charge that property in order to secure the debts of only one of the joint owners, the other joint owner stands merely in the position of a surety and is entitled, as between the two joint owners, to have the secured indebtedness discharged so far as is possible out of the equitable interest of the debtor.[9] The equity of exoneration in effect allocates more fairly as between joint mortgagors the ultimate burden of an indebtedness which was incurred for the benefit of only one co-owner.

(i) Operation of the equitable principle of exoneration

(i) *Operation of the equitable principle of exoneration* The operation of this equitable doctrine can be demonstrated in a practical context where two co-owners of a family home have jointly charged that property as security for the debts of one co-owner who is subsequently adjudicated bankrupt. Such a charge may well arise, for instance, where a bank insists on the provision of some security in respect of the husband's bank overdraft. Were it not for the equity of exoneration, the burden of this indebtedness could quite properly be thrown in exactly equal proportions upon the funds which represent the beneficial half-shares of the co-owners in the net proceeds of an enforced bankruptcy sale. However, the equity of exoneration entitles the bankrupt's

---

6   In the event of cancellation of a joint family home registration on the ground of bankruptcy, $34,000 must be set aside for the beneficiaries of the joint family home settlement, notwithstanding that this pro tanto defeats the claims of creditors (see Joint Family Homes Act 1964, s 16(1)(a), as amended by Joint Family Homes (Specified Sum) Order 1985 (SR 1985/60)).

7   Similar schemes of limited immunity from the effects of bankruptcy are contained in Canadian provincial legislation. See eg Alberta's Exemptions Act (RSA 1980, c E-15), s 1(1)(k); Saskatchewan's Exemptions Act (RSS 1965, c 96), s 2(1), para 11.

8   See Vol 292, *New Zealand Parliamentary Debates*, 3493ff (Hon T.C. Webb, Attorney-General); Vol 340, *New Zealand Parliamentary Debates*, 2294 (Hon J.R. Hanan, Minister of Justice). In *Fairmaid v Otago District Land Registrar* [1952] NZLR 782 at 786, North J described the legislation as ensuring that 'husband and wife can live contentedly in their home in the knowledge that it is secured to them as a family home so long as they need it whatever the vicissitudes of life may bring.' See also *Sutherland v Sutherland* [1955] NZLR 689 at 691; *Official Assignee v Lawford* [1984] 2 NZLR 257 at 261.

9   See *In Re Pittortou (A Bankrupt)* [1985] 1 WLR 58 at 61B.

co-owner to insist that the burden of the creditors' claims should be diverted primarily on to the bankrupt's share in those proceeds. The result of this process is to enhance the proprietary interest of the bankrupt's co-owner and to augment that co-owner's eventual money recovery.[10]

(ii) Relevance of intention   The equity of exoneration depends upon the presumed intention of the parties.[11] The equity comes into play only if it can be inferred from the circumstances of the case that the joint mortgagors together intended that the burden of the secured indebtedness should fall primarily on the share of the actual debtor.

Thus the equity cannot operate if the indebtedness in question was incurred for the purpose of financing a higher standard of living for both co-owners and their family.[12] In other words, the equity cannot be invoked if in reality both joint mortgagors received and enjoyed the benefits of the indebtedness.[13] Thus, in *In Re Pittortou (A Bankrupt)*,[14] Scott J held that the equity of exoneration should be confined to payments other than those made for the 'joint benefit of the household'. On this basis the bankrupt's wife was not entitled to any exoneration in respect of debts arising in connection with the running of the joint family household. She was, however, entitled to require that debts incurred by her husband for purely business purposes and in supporting another woman should be treated as charged primarily on his own half-share in the mortgaged property.[15]

(2) Adjustment of prior transactions at an undervalue

Except in respect of debts incurred by the bankrupt jointly with some other person, the claims of the bankrupt's creditors can only be met out of that property in which the bankrupt is himself beneficially interested.[16] Although the realisation of the bankrupt's assets may necessitate the sale of property in which other persons also claim an interest, the only money value available for distribution amongst the bankrupt's creditors is that which corresponds to the aliquot share of the bankrupt himself. Other co-owners, although exposed to an involuntary sale, are nevertheless entitled to receive the money value of their own aliquot shares intact, since they are in principle under no obligation to contribute to the discharge of the bankrupt's debts.

(a) Reviewability of prejudicial transactions

In the present context the bankruptcy of one beneficial co-owner of a family home does not therefore make the beneficial share of any other co-owner vulnerable to an enforced distribution amongst the bankrupt's creditors. This

---

10   *In Re Pittortou (A Bankrupt)* [1985] 1 WLR 58 at 61F. See also *In Re A Debtor (No 24 of 1971)* [1976] 1 WLR 952 at 955.
11   *In Re Pittortou (A Bankrupt)* [1985] 1 WLR 58 at 62A.
12   See *Paget v Paget* [1898] 1 Ch 470 at 475ff; *In Re Pittortou (A Bankrupt)* [1985] 1 WLR 58 at 62G.
13   *In Re Woodstock (A Bankrupt)* (Unreported, Walton J, 19 November 1979).
14   [1985] 1 WLR 58 at 62H.
15   [1985] 1 WLR 58 at 62H-63A. See also *Re Berry* [1976] 2 NZLR 449 at 451f; *Farrugia v Official Receiver in Bankruptcy* (1982) 43 ALR 700 at 703.
16   Insolvency Act 1986, s 283(1)(a), (3)(a).

broad principle is, however, subject to one important qualification. There is clearly a danger that a debtor, with an eye to the possibility of a future bankruptcy, may think it advantageous to 'off-load' his assets (either in whole or in part) in favour of some close associate who will supposedly enjoy immunity from the bankruptcy process. For many years, therefore, the courts have been invested with a statutory jurisdiction to negative the effects of prejudicial transactions of this kind.[17]

This jurisdiction, which is now confirmed in substantially similar terms in the Insolvency Act 1986,[18] has a clear application to the family home. The net effect of the jurisdiction is to give the trustee in bankruptcy access to the money value of beneficial shares in the family home other than the share of merely the bankrupt himself. Moreover, although the jurisdiction is aimed primarily at transactions entered into in bad faith for the purpose of defrauding creditors, there is the chilling possibility that the trustee in bankruptcy may be able to recover the money value of beneficial interests which have been acquired quite innocently by other members of the bankrupt's family.

(b) Identification of transactions 'at an undervalue'

The trustee in bankruptcy may apply to the court for an order in relation to certain kinds of transaction which the bankrupt has entered into 'at an undervalue'.[19] If the transaction in question was entered into at a statutorily 'relevant time',[20] the court must 'make such order as it thinks fit for the purpose of restoring the position to what it would have been' had the transaction not taken place.[1] The court's powers include a power to order that any property transferred by the transaction (or the proceeds of its sale) be vested in the trustee in bankruptcy,[2] or that the other party in the transaction make money compensation to the bankrupt's estate in respect of any 'benefits received' under the transaction.[3]

A transaction is defined as being 'at an undervalue' if any of three independent conditions is fulfilled.

(i) Transactions by way of gift

Any transaction with a third party is considered to be 'at an undervalue' where the bankrupt 'makes a gift to that person' or otherwise agrees to receive no consideration for the transaction.[4] This provision has wide implications, for it instantly renders vulnerable any gift of a beneficial share in the family home which the bankrupt has made to a third party within the statutorily relevant period. For example, the wife who has been the

---

17 See Bankruptcy Act 1914, s 42; Law of Property Act 1925, s 172 (both provisions repealed by Insolvency Act 1985, Sch 10).
18 Insolvency Act 1986, ss 339ff.
19 Insolvency Act 1986, s 339(1). There are ancillary provisions (in section 340) which deal in similar terms with any 'preference' which the bankrupt has given to another person. The term 'preference' (as defined in section 340(3)) is, for instance, wide enough to cover any advantage or concession which carries a supposed priority in bankruptcy.
20 See Insolvency Act 1986, ss 339(1), 341(1)(a) (post, p 887).
1   Insolvency Act 1986, s 339(2).
2   Insolvency Act 1986, s 342(1)(a), (b).
3   Insolvency Act 1986, s 342(1)(d).
4   Insolvency Act 1986, s 339(3)(a).

recipient of a half-share in the matrimonial home by way of gift from her husband may suddenly find that her beneficial interest is subject to distribution amongst her husband's creditors in the event of a subsequent bankruptcy. Thus, far from salvaging at least some portion of the beneficial value of the family home in the disaster of insolvency, the bankrupt's spouse discovers to her horror that the entire proceeds of the enforced sale are clawed back into the bankrupt's distributable estate.

(ii) Transactions for marriage consideration   The transactions of the bankrupt are likewise deemed to be 'at an undervalue' if entered into 'in consideration of marriage'.[5] Thus any beneficial interest in the family home which was given to the bankrupt's wife on the occasion of marriage may be reviewable later at the instance of the trustee in bankruptcy. That which a man gives can be taken away again—by his trustee in bankruptcy.[6]

(iii) Transactions for significantly less than full consideration   The definition of 'undervalue' is also sufficiently extensive to catch any transaction with a third party which is entered into by the bankrupt 'for a consideration the value of which, in money or money's worth, is significantly less than the value, in money or money's worth, of the consideration provided by the [bankrupt].'[7] This cumbersome form of words is designed to encompass transactions which involve a net disposition of value by the bankrupt.

This broad understanding of prejudicial transactions can give rise to an even more subtle hazard for those who claim beneficial rights in the family home. In certain circumstances, for instance, it is clear that the doctrine of constructive trust can justify a claim to a quantum of beneficial entitlement which would not be supportable by way of a resulting trust based on the claimant's actual contributions of money or money's worth.[8] Such a case arose in *In Re Densham (A Bankrupt)*,[9] where Goff J agreed that a constructive trust could be invoked by a wife whose husband had agreed that she should enjoy joint beneficial ownership of the matrimonial home even though her own money contributions towards its purchase had been fairly minimal. A resulting trust based on her actual money contributions would have entitled her to a one-ninth share in equity, but the successful plea of constructive trust confirmed a joint ownership which, when severed by her husband's bankruptcy,[10] gave her a presumptive half-share in equity.

Goff J was compelled, however, to hold that the operation of the constructive trust had effected a net disposition of value in her favour which was now reclaimable by her husband's trustee in bankruptcy.[11] To the extent to which her half-share exceeded the equitable quantum to which a resulting trust

5   Insolvency Act 1986, s 339(3)(b).
6   The provisions of the Insolvency Act 1986 are, of course, sex-neutral in the sense that the gender of the bankrupt is irrelevant. However, as the Cork Committee noted, it is easier for the sake of simplicity to assume that the bankrupt is male (see *Insolvency Law and Practice* (Cmnd 8558, June 1982), para 1125).
7   Insolvency Act 1986, s 339(3)(c).
8   Ante, p 285.
9   [1975] 1 WLR 1519 (ante, p 292).
10   Ante, p 324.
11   [1975] 1 WLR 1519 at 1529C.

would have entitled her,[12] she had received a disposition of beneficial interest from her husband which was not supported by sufficient consideration 'in a commercial sense'.[13] Thus the increased interest which the court with one hand awarded by way of constructive trust, the court with its other hand took away again in administering the law of bankruptcy. The court ordered a sale under section 30 of the Law of Property Act 1925, and the wife was left with only the value of the one-ninth share to which she was originally entitled on the basis of resulting trust.[14]

Although the *Densham* ruling involved the application of the Bankruptcy Act 1914, it is likely that a similar approach would be adopted in the construction of the even more specific terms of the Insolvency Act 1986. The danger is thus intensified that those who claim shares in the family home by way of constructive rather than resulting trust may find that their shares are highly vulnerable to a divesting in favour of a bankrupt's estate.[15]

(c) Definition of the statutorily 'relevant time'

A bankrupt's prior dealings with third parties are liable to be reopened on bankruptcy only where those dealings occurred within the *five* years immediately preceding the presentation of the petition which resulted in his bankruptcy.[16] However, even transactions which fall within this prescribed period are immune from review if they were entered into more than *two* years before the presentation of the bankruptcy petition and the bankrupt can prove that he was not insolvent at the date of the transaction and did not become insolvent in consequence of it.[17] The rule of mandatory reviewability applies only in respect of those transactions which were entered into within the two years immediately before the presentation of the bankruptcy petition.[18]

3. RECOVERY OF POSSESSION BY A MORTGAGEE

Possession proceedings brought by a mortgagee represent another way in which financial crisis within the family may threaten security of tenure in the family home.[19] The enforcement of the mortgagee's right to possession is almost

---

12    $\frac{1}{2} - \frac{1}{9} = \frac{7}{18}$
13   [1975] 1 WLR 1519 at 1529C. See also *In Re Barnes (A Bankrupt)* [1979] 4 NIJB, p 5f, where Lowry LCJ went so far as to suggest that there must be 'a contractual obligation on the bankrupt' to concede to his wife the beneficial interest which she now opposes against his trustee in bankruptcy. Her 'mere' provision of household services was, in the absence of some agreement, insufficient consideration for the present purpose.
14   [1975] 1 WLR 1519 at 1531E-1532C.
15   Although Matrimonial Causes Act 1973, s 39 (as amended by Insolvency Act 1986, Sch 14) expressly provides that a court-ordered property adjustment on divorce may be reviewable under Insolvency Act 1986, ss 339, 340, the compromise of claims under the Matrimonial Causes Act 1973 may provide a sufficient form of consideration to guarantee the immunity of a bankrupt's spouse (see *In Re Abbott (A Bankrupt)* [1983] Ch 45 at 56E; [1983] Conv 240 (R. Griffith)).
16   Insolvency Act 1986, s 341(1)(a).
17   Insolvency Act 1986, s 341(2).
18   In this respect the Insolvency Act 1986 effectively preserves the rule contained in Bankruptcy Act 1914, s 42(1).
19   On the law of mortgage generally see Chapter 16 (ante, p 563).

always a precursor to the exercise of the mortgagee's power of sale and the necessarily traumatic dispossession of a family from its home.[20] In view of these far-reaching implications for the mortgagor and his family, both the courts and the legislature have developed several forms of relief which may enable the hard-pressed borrower to avert the threat of recovery of possession by the mortgagee and consequent sale of the family home. Among the lifelines thrown to the mortgagor and his family are the following.

(1) Payment of mortgage interest by way of supplementary benefit

A mortgagor who qualifies for supplementary benefits may be able to claim the interest payable on his mortgage loan as part of his entitlement to supplementary benefit.[1]

(a) Inclusion of mortgage interest within 'housing requirements'

The 'housing requirements' which are taken into account in calculating a claimant's entitlement to supplementary benefit include 'mortgage payments'.[2] These payments are in turn defined[3] as including amounts of 'interest' payable in respect of any 'loan. . . taken out to defray money applied for the purpose of acquiring an interest in the home'.[4] It is irrelevant whether the loan is a first or second mortgage loan, a bank loan or even a private or unsecured loan, but the loan must be connected with the acquisition of an interest in the home rather than with the mere improvement of the home.[5] The Department of Health and Social Security can provide a written guarantee of mortgage interest payments, which may help to persuade the mortgagee (and particularly the institutional mortgagee) to accept 'interest only' payments for the duration of the mortgagor's financial difficulties.[6]

The provision of mortgage interest by way of supplementary benefit provides invaluable assistance for an 'assessment unit' which finds itself in financial difficulty. However, the interest payments thereby discharged out of public funds are liable to restriction if they are 'excessive'.[7] For this purpose

---

20　Ante, p 610.
1　The supplementary benefits rules have been amended—somewhat controversially—so that during the first 16 weeks of any period of unemployment affecting the mortgagor only half of the mortgage interest due is payable as supplementary benefit. See Supplementary Benefit (Requirements) Regulations 1983 (SI 1983/1399), reg 15(1)(b)(ii), as amended by Supplementary Benefit (Housing Requirements and Resources) Amendment Regulations 1987 (SI 1987/17), reg 2(3) (effective from 26 January 1987).
2　Supplementary Benefit (Requirements) Regulations 1983 (SI 1983/1399), reg 14(1)(a).
3　Supplementary Benefit (Requirements) Regulations 1983, reg 15(3), as amended by Supplementary Benefit (Housing Requirements and Resources) Amendment Regulations 1987 (SI 1987/17), reg 2(3).
4　The housing requirement covers only the net outlay of the mortgagor on mortgage interest after deduction, where applicable, of income tax at the basic rate (Supplementary Benefit (Requirements) Regulations 1983, reg 15(4)(a)).
5　The allowable mortgage payments do not cover any extra interest on accrued mortgage arrears (see CSB 467/1983), or the life assurance premiums payable in connection with an endowment mortgage (see R(SB) 46/83), or any interest on a loan which was taken out in order to repay an earlier loan even if that earlier loan was granted for the purpose of acquiring an interest in the home (see R(SB) 21/85).
6　See generally J. Tunnard and C. Whately, *Rights Guide for Home Owners* (4th edn, London 1983), p 44ff.
7　Supplementary Benefit (Requirements) Regulations 1983, reg 21(1).

amounts are deemed to be 'excessive' if and to the extent that 'the home, excluding any part which is let or is normally occupied by boarders, is unnecessarily large for the assessment unit and any other non-dependants, or is located in an unnecessarily expensive area.'[8] This proviso is capable of operating oppressively against the interests and wishes of an already beleaguered family unit, but it is clear that benefit is not to be restricted if, 'having regard to the relevant facts, it is not reasonable to expect the assessment unit to seek alternative cheaper accommodation'.[9]

(b) Exclusion of capital repayments from 'housing requirements'

The relevant regulations give effect to the broad principle that supplementary benefit covers only payments of interest and not payments of capital. The official view underlying this principle seems to be the idea that, provided the claimant's accommodation is safeguarded, 'public funds ought not to be used to increase the capital assets' of those on welfare benefit.[10] It should be noted, however, that even the payment of mortgage interest will normally conduce to a degree of capital accumulation since the home-owner, if maintained in occupation, is thereby enabled to retain at least part of the inflationary increase in the capital value of his property.

(2) Right of the mortgagor's spouse to tender payment of mortgage monies

A spouse who enjoys 'rights of occupation' under the Matrimonial Homes Act 1983[11] is entitled to tender payment in her own name of any mortgage liability affecting her dwelling-house, and such payments by her are statutorily declared to be 'as good as if made...by the other spouse.'[12] Thus the mortgagor's spouse is armed with an important right to compel the mortgagee to accept payment by her in lieu of payments by the true mortgagor, thereby withdrawing from the mortgagee a potential ground for the exercise of his power of sale.[13]

Of course, the mere right to make vicarious payment on the mortgagor's behalf is of singularly little use to a spouse who lacks the required financial resources. It is nevertheless quite possible that the mortgagor's spouse may be entitled to supplementary benefit, as indeed will be the case if she is deserted by the mortgagor. It is then clear that, for the purpose of computing her claim to benefit, her 'housing requirements' will include the payment of mortgage interest if it can be shown that the mortgagor 'has left the home and either cannot or will not pay the interest' on the mortgage.[14]

---

8 Supplementary Benefit (Requirements) Regulations 1983, reg 21(2). See CSB 1016/1982.
9 Supplementary Benefit (Requirements) Regulations 1983, reg 21(3). Even if it is reasonable to expect the unit to move to cheaper accommodation, the restriction of benefit is postponed for six months if the claimant was able to meet the mortgage commitment when it was originally entered into, and may be postponed for a further six months 'if and so long as the claimant uses his best endeavours to obtain cheaper accommodation' (reg 21(4)).
10 See *Report of the Committee on One-Parent Families* (Cmnd 5629, July 1974), Vol 1, para 6.126.
11 Ante, p 782.
12 Matrimonial Homes Act 1983, s 1(5).
13 Ante, p 614.
14 Supplementary Benefit (Requirements) Regulations 1983, reg 15(7), as amended by Supplementary Benefit (Housing Requirements and Resources) Amendment Regulations 1987 (SI 1987/17), reg 2(3). It matters not for this purpose whether the claimant was married to the mortgagor or, indeed, whether the mortgage commitment was originally undertaken by them jointly.

(3) **The court's inherent jurisdiction to grant relief to the mortgagor**

If neither the mortgagor nor his spouse or partner is able to forestall a mortgagee's possession proceedings by any of the above means, it is possible that some temporary relief may be available either before or even after the making of a possession order in favour of the mortgagee. A limited access to such relief lies in the exercise of the inherent equitable jurisdiction of the High Court to grant relief to a mortgagor who has hit financial difficulties.

(a) Liberal exercise of a merciful discretion

The exercise of the inherent jurisdiction has in the past enabled the court to assert some control over the enforcement of the mortgagee's right to possession, largely through the adjournment of possession proceedings in order to give more time to the mortgagor. The jurisdiction is exercisable by the Masters of the Chancery Division, and provides a temporary form of relief which may allow hard-pressed mortgagors to resolve their financial difficulties and repay overdue mortgage moneys.[15] The court's exercise of discretion in this matter is based on the convention that 'the court has never allowed a mortgagee to enforce his rights under the mortgage in the face of a concrete offer by the mortgagor to redeem.'[16]

The court's discretion to temporise was at first exercised quite liberally, one famous Chancery Master describing his function as being akin to that of a 'social worker rather than a Judge'.[17] It was the task of the Master, if matters were not altogether hopeless, to encourage the borrower to re-organise his finances and to keep his home by paying off mortgage arrears in agreed instalments.[18] It has since been said that the generous approach adopted by Chancery Masters was 'no doubt assisted by the benevolent attitude which the Legislature had by then assumed towards tenants faced with eviction by their landlords.'[19] The analogy drawn—at least tacitly—between the respective positions of the home-owner and the renter was soon to constitute a recurring cross-reference in the law relating to the protection of residential mortgagors.[20]

(b) Modern restrictions on the inherent jurisdiction

In recent years the court's inherent jurisdiction to stay possession proceedings against mortgagors has been exercised much more sparingly.[1] In *Birmingham Citizens Permanent Building Society v Caunt*,[2] Russell J held that the inherent

---

15   In the celebrated words of Clauson LJ, 'the facts and the circumstances of the case were brought before the Court, and in proper cases the wind was tempered to the shorn lamb, time being given for payment and so forth...' (*Redditch Benefit Building Society v Roberts* [1940] Ch 415 at 420). This jurisdiction is exercisable both in proceedings commenced by writ and in proceedings commenced by originating summons (see RSC Ord 88, r 7).
16   *Mobil Oil Co Ltd v Rawlinson* (1982) 43 P & CR 221 at 225.
17   See Master Ball, *The Chancery Master*, (1961) 77 LQR 331 at 351.
18   The lengths to which Chancery Masters were prepared to go appears in Master Ball's frank admission that, if necessary, the Master was generally willing to use 'time and technicality as weapons against a too stony-hearted plaintiff' ((1961) 77 LQR 331 at 351).
19   *Mobil Oil Co Ltd v Rawlinson* (1982) 43 P & CR 221 at 224 per Nourse J.
20   Post, p 891.
1   For a description of the judicial reaction against what was seen as excessive indulgence shown towards borrowers, see *Mobil Oil Co Ltd v Rawlinson* (1982) 43 P & CR 221 at 224.
2   [1962] Ch 883 at 891. See (1962) 78 LQR 171 (R.E.M.).

jurisdiction merely empowers the court to adjourn a hearing 'for a short time' in order to 'afford the mortgagor a limited opportunity to find means to pay off the mortgagee or otherwise satisfy him if there was a reasonable prospect of either of those events occurring.'[3] As Russell J indicated, however, it is unlikely that even in these circumstances an adjournment will be granted for a period of more than 28 days.[4]

(4) The court's statutory power to delay the recovery of possession

The decision in *Birmingham Citizens Permanent Building Society v Caunt* did much to restore to the mortgagee the balance of power which some imagined had been removed by the steady development of the court's inherent jurisdiction.[5] However, the net effect of the tightening-up of the court's inherent jurisdiction was to accentuate the demand for a new statutory form of relief against possession actions relating to the family home. In 1969 the Payne Committee on the Enforcement of Judgment Debts recognised that a succession of governments had 'for some years encouraged the purchase, instead of the renting, of houses by persons of modest means.' The Committee therefore concluded that where a mortgagor, because of financial difficulties, falls into arrears with his mortgage instalments, the courts should be 'empowered, subject to proper safeguards, to extend to the mortgagor the same protection in relation to the continued occupation of the house as would be given to a tenant of a property of a similar rateable value.'[6] In effect the Committee accepted that the expansion of the 'property-owning democracy' had fixed on the government of the day a broad social responsibility to assimilate mortgagors within the same kind of protective legislation as that which benefits residential tenants.[7]

The statutory relief proposed by the Payne Committee was almost immediately introduced by section 36 of the Administration of Justice Act 1970. This important legislative initiative now enables the court in the context of possession proceedings to grant relief to residential mortgagors in much the same way in which relief is granted against forfeiture in the landlord-tenant relationship.[8]

---

3   See also *London Permanent Benefit Building Society v De Baer* [1969] 1 Ch 321 at 338B, F.
4   [1962] Ch 883 at 908. See, however, *Braithwaite v Winwood* [1960] 1 WLR 1257 at 1264ff.
5   'Equity was never and should never be in the hands of the judges a sword to attack any part of the security itself, and the right to possession was an important part of that security, more particularly in the association with the ability to give vacant possession on the exercise of the power of sale' (*Birmingham Citizens Permanent Building Society v Caunt* [1962] Ch 883 at 896). See also *Robertson v Cilia* [1956] 1 WLR 1502 at 1508; (1957) 73 LQR 18 (R.E.M.).
6   *Report of the Committee on Judgment Debts* (Cmnd 3909, February 1969), para 1386(d). The Committee accepted (para 1386(b)) that the 'responsible building societies have proved themselves to be tolerant and understanding with those of their borrowers who have fallen into arrears with their instalments through misfortune, and not infrequently they enter into reasonable and satisfactory arrangements for the discharge of arrears without initiating or pursuing a claim for possession'. However, as the Committee went on to note, 'unfortunately all mortgagees are not responsible building societies...' See also *Report of the Committee on One-Parent Families* (Cmnd 5629, July 1974), Vol 1, para 6.116ff.
7   For a similar comparison with the protection from eviction conferred on protected and statutory tenants under the Rent Act legislation, see *Hughes v Waite* [1957] 1 WLR 713 at 715 per Harman J.
8   Ante, p 569; post, p 1022.

(a) Preconditions for the exercise of the statutory discretion

Section 36 of the Administration of Justice Act 1970 confers on the court a wide power to adjourn possession actions brought by mortgagees or to postpone the giving of possession in respect of a 'dwelling-house'[9] for such period or periods 'as the court thinks reasonable'.[10] The court's discretion is exercisable in any claim for possession of residential property in which

it appears to the court that in the event of its exercising the power the mortgagor is likely to be able within a reasonable period to pay any sums due under the mortgage or to remedy a default consisting of a breach of any other obligation arising under or by virtue of the mortgage.[11]

(i) An initial defect of drafting   As it stands, the wording of section 36 contains a severe drafting imperfection which threatened initially to destroy the protective import of the provision. In *Halifax Building Society v Clark*[12] the plaintiff building society sought an order for possession against the deserted wife of the mortgagor and Pennycuick V-C ruled that it was impossible for her to satisfy the preconditions for the exercise of discretion under section 36. In the present case the mortgage instalments in arrear amounted to only £100, but on the husband's default the entire capital debt of over £1,400 became 'due' in accordance with the strict terms of the mortgage. Even if the mortgagor's wife exercised her right to tender vicarious payments,[13] it was quite obvious that there was no realistic prospect that she could raise this larger sum 'within a reasonable period'.[14] It was indeed highly unlikely that she could within a short period pay off a sum which it had been anticipated originally would take another 20 years to discharge.

This rather grave defect in the legislation was remedied by the enactment of section 8(1) of the Administration of Justice Act 1973, which redefines the phrase 'any sums due' in section 36(1) of the 1970 Act as referring only to such

9   The term 'dwelling-house' includes 'any building or part thereof which is used as a dwelling' (Administration of Justice Act 1970, s 39(1)), an extended meaning which may go too far. As Roger Smith has pointed out, section 36 thus seems capable of application to an entire office block which contains somewhere within it a caretaker's flat (see [1979].Conv 266 at 271). Moreover, it is irrelevant that part of the premises comprised in a 'dwelling-house' is used 'as a shop or office or for business, trade or professional purposes' (Administration of Justice Act 1970, s 39(2)).

10   Administration of Justice Act 1970, s 36(2). A similar power is vested in the county court in respect of any application by a local authority mortgagee for a re-vesting of a property which has been purchased by a sitting tenant with the assistance of local authority finance (Housing Act 1985, Sch 17, para 1(2), (3)). The county court may adjourn proceedings by the local authority mortgagee or postpone the date for execution of the authority's deed for 'such period as the court thinks reasonable' and on such terms with regard to mortgage payments as the court thinks fit.

11   Administration of Justice Act 1970, s 36(1). Section 89 of the Housing Act 1980 introduces certain severe restrictions on the court's exercise of discretion in making possession orders in respect of land (post, p 1024). In general the court may not postpone possession for more than 14 days from the making of a possession order, but this draconian rule does not apply in possession actions brought by mortgagees (see Housing Act 1980, s 89(2)(a)).

12   [1973] Ch 307. See (1973) 89 LQR 171 (P.V. Baker); (1973) 36 MLR 550 (P. Jackson); (1973) 37 Conv (NS) 213 (F.R. Crane).

13   See Matrimonial Homes Act 1983, s 1(5) (ante, p 889).

14   [1973] Ch 307 at 313G-H. See also *Governor and Company of the Bank of Scotland v Grimes* [1985] QB 1179 at 1190C-F.

amounts as the mortgagor would have expected to be required to pay if the mortgage had not contained a default clause rendering the entire mortgage monies payable in the event of any of the instalments falling into arrear.[15] Section 8(1) thus overturns the decision in *Halifax Building Society v Clark*, and effectively reinstates what was almost certainly the intention of the legislature in framing the 1970 Act.[16] The court may therefore adjourn possession proceedings or stay the execution of a possession order if there is a likelihood that during the interim the mortgagor will be able to find not only any mortgage instalments which have fallen into arrear but also any other instalments which may become due during the period of postponement.[17]

(ii) The broad coverage of section 36 As amended by the Administration of Justice Act 1973, the statutory discretion under section 36 provides valuable assistance for many mortgagors who run into temporary financial difficulties, whether by reason of unemployment, short-time working, redundancy or marital difficulties.[18] Although clearly not all judges agree on the point,[19] it has been said that the Administration of Justice Acts 1970 and 1973 together represent a form of 'social legislation' in which 'Parliament has attempted to give legislative shelter to a wide class of owner-occupiers'.[20] It is consistent with the nature of such legislation that the court's discretion to give relief to domestic mortgagors should be construed liberally, and indeed the courts have confirmed that the section 36 jurisdiction may be invoked not only in relation to instalment mortgages but also in relation to endowment mortgages.[1]

(b) Does section 36 now impose a requirement of due legal process?

It is a curious feature of section 36 of the Administration of Justice Act 1970 that the protective discretion of the court arises only where 'the mortgagee...brings an action in which he claims possession of the mortgaged property...'[2] The apparent corollary is that the benevolent effect of section 36 cannot be invoked by a residential mortgagor if his mortgagee simply asserts his paramount right

---

15   See Stephen Tromans, [1984] Conv 91.
16   Even before the enactment of section 8 of the Administration of Justice Act 1973, the problem addressed in *Halifax Building Society v Clark* had arisen in *First Middlesbrough Trading and Mortgage Co Ltd v Cunningham* (1974) 28 P & CR 69 at 74, and the Court of Appeal declined to adopt the construction applied in *Halifax Building Society v Clark*. For an argument that the ratio of *Cunningham*'s case may still be wider (and therefore more favourable to the mortgagor) than section 8 of the Administration of Justice Act 1973, see R.J. Smith, [1979] Conv 266 at 274f.
17   Administration of Justice Act 1973, s 8(2). See *Peckham Mutual Building Society v Registe* (1981) 42 P & CR 186 at 189.
18   For a consideration of the factors relevant to the exercise of the statutory discretion, see R.J. Smith, [1979] Conv 266 at 279f.
19   See [1983] Conv 80 (P.H. Kenny).
20   *Centrax Trustees Ltd v Ross* [1979] 2 All ER 952 at 955f per Goulding J.
1   *Governor and Company of the Bank of Scotland v Grimes* [1985] QB 1179 at 1188G, 1190G. See [1985] Conv 407 (J.E.M.), but compare *Lord Marples of Wallasey v Holmes* (1976) 31 P & CR 94 at 97. Section 36 has no application to the enforcement of charging orders (ante, p 870), but see Charging Orders Act 1979, s 1(5). See also the refusal in the Irish Republic to apply the comparable Family Home Protection Act 1976, s 7(1) to the enforcement of a judgment mortgage in *Containercare (Ireland) Ltd v Wycherley* [1982] IR 143 at 150.
2   Administration of Justice Act 1970, s 36(1).

to possession by peaceful re-entry without court action. There is, however, a patent absurdity in the idea that section 36 should solicitously protect the mortgagor in court proceedings for possession, while leaving him hopelessly vulnerable to an extra-curial recovery of possession. This result is sufficiently anomalous to have prompted the suggestion[3] that section 36 impliedly abrogates the mortgagee's inherent common law right to go into possession at any time of his choosing without first seeking a court order.[4] There is a powerful argument in favour of the conclusion that a mortgagee may nowadays assert his right to possession only after due legal process.

This suggestion, although not without attraction, has not yet gained judicial support of any kind. Indeed, recent dicta have if anything tended to confirm the conventional view that the mortgagee may re-enter arbitrarily if he chooses.[5] In the absence of strong authority it seems difficult to maintain that the orthodox understanding of the mortgagee's paramount right to possession at common law has been subverted by a mere implication from statute.[6] On balance it seems likely that the anomaly which appears to exist can be removed only by an express legislative provision, and that meanwhile the practical protection of residential mortgagors under section 36 is most unsatisfactorily preserved by the fact that, for one reason or another,[7] most mortgagees in reality enforce their security only after court proceedings for possession.

(c) Procedural rights for the mortgagor's spouse

Statutory intervention has conferred a number of procedural rights on the spouse of a mortgagor, for the purpose of enabling such a spouse more effectively to take advantage of the important discretion enjoyed by the court under section 36 of the Administration of Justice Act 1970. The motive behind these recent initiatives stems from the disadvantage which is inevitably suffered by a spouse who does not know that her partner's financial difficulties are beginning to jeopardise the security of the family home.

(i) No right to be informed of mortgage arrears   The statutory right[8] of a mortgagor's spouse to tender mortgage payments is not of much value to a spouse who is unaware that her husband's mortgage payments have fallen into arrear. In *Hastings and Thanet Building Society v Goddard*[9] the Court of Appeal held that there is no statutory justification for requiring that a building society should inform the mortgagor's wife of her husband's default in order that she should have an opportunity to tender payments herself. Russell LJ thought that any contrary view was 'impracticable because a building society can scarcely be expected to keep track of the matrimonial status of its mortgagors.'[10] Likewise the Court refused to accept that notice of a

3   See eg A. Clarke, [1983] Conv 293.
4   Ante, p 605.
5   Ante, p 612.
6   See, however, *Remon v City of London Real Property Co Ltd* [1921] 1 KB 49 at 59, in relation to a comparable problem under the early Rent Act legislation. See A. Clarke, [1983] Conv 293 at 296.
7   Ante, p 609 (note 3).
8   Ante, p 889.
9   [1970] 1 WLR 1544. See (1971) 35 Conv (NS) 48 (F.R. Crane).
10   [1970] 1 WLR 1544 at 1548E.

mortgagee's possession proceedings should be served on the mortgagor's spouse (where she was not a joint tenant of the property), since her statutory rights of occupation in the matrimonial home are in no way binding on the mortgagee.[11] The only right which the spouse may assert against the mortgagee is the right to pay any moneys still owing to him and thereby prevent him from exercising his right to take possession.

The decision in *Hastings and Thanet Building Society v Goddard*, although heavily criticised,[12] remains good at common law. The ruling leads in practice to the unfortunate result that a deserted wife who discovers too late that her husband has allowed substantial mortgage arrears to accrue, may then find herself precluded from any effective argument that the court's discretion should be extended in her favour under the Administration of Justice Act. A partial remedy for the shortcomings of the common law has now been provided in legislative form.[13]

(ii) Right to be joined as a party in possession proceedings The mortgagor's spouse, if entitled to tender vicarious mortgage payments, is now given a statutory right to apply to the court to be joined as a party in any possession proceedings brought by a mortgagee to enforce his security in respect of a dwelling-house.[14] The court must accede to her application if it sees no 'special reason' against it,[15] provided that it is satisfied that there is a realistic possibility that the spouse may be able to attract the benevolent operation of the court's discretion under section 36 of the Administration of Justice Act 1970.[16]

This statutory right at least gives the mortgagor's spouse locus standi in possession proceedings to present a case for consideration under section 36,[17] but still fails to tackle the difficulties faced by a spouse who is entirely unaware that possession proceedings are afoot against her mortgagor-husband. A compromise solution has been introduced by statute in order to meet these difficulties.

(iii) Right to be served with notice of possession proceedings It is now clear that any mortgagee who seeks to enforce his security in land which comprises a dwelling-house is statutorily obliged to serve notice of his possession action on any spouse who has protected her 'rights of occupation' in that property by

---

11 Compare *Harman v Glencross* [1985] Fam 49 at 54G-H (ante, p 873).
12 See D.A. Nevitt and J. Levin, *Social Policy and the Matrimonial Home*, (1973) 36 MLR 345 at 349f. The Finer Committee on One-Parent Families expressed the view that 'the courts have seemed to be more concerned with reducing the administrative burdens of building societies than with safeguarding families in their homes...' (*Report of the Committee on One-Parent Families* (Cmnd 5629, July 1974), Vol 1, para 6.120).
13 For the background to the legislation, see *Third Report on Family Property: The Matrimonial Home (Co-ownership and Occupation Rights) and Household Goods* (Law Com No 86, June 1978), para 2.25ff.
14 Matrimonial Homes Act 1983, s 8(2).
15 Matrimonial Homes Act 1983, s 8(2)(a).
16 Matrimonial Homes Act 1983, s 8(2)(b).
17 Dunn LJ recognised in *Anglia Building Society v Lewis* (Court of Appeal, No 8008681, 29 January 1982) that even if the mortgagor's spouse is unsuccessful in invoking section 36, the mere fact that the possession order is formally entered against her name also will tend to strengthen her claim to be provided with alternative accommodation by her local housing authority.

registration of a Class F land charge (in unregistered land) or entry of the appropriate notice (in registered land).[18] This provision affords a further incentive towards protection of the 'rights of occupation' conferred by the Matrimonial Homes Act 1983, by guaranteeing that a spouse who duly protects her rights cannot lose her home at least without having an opportunity to be joined and heard as a party in the mortgagee's possession action. The spouse's right to notice of possession proceedings clearly imposes a burden of search on any mortgagee who intends to initiate possession proceedings, but in days of increased emphasis on residential security this result may not seem entirely unreasonable.[19]

(d) Limits of the court's discretion

The court's discretion under section 36 of the Administration of Justice Act 1970 is subject to certain general limitations which severely cut back the protection potentially offered to the residential mortgagor.

(i) No discretion in the absence of a realistic ability to pay arrears   Before the court's discretion can properly be exercised in favour of a mortgagor, it must appear to the court that the mortgagor is 'likely to be able within a reasonable period to pay any sums due under the mortgage'. Even when the effect of amending legislation is taken into account,[20] there is no scope for the exercise of *any* discretion by the court if the mortgagor (or his spouse[1]) cannot provide realistic evidence of at least some ability to pay off arrears of mortgage money.[2] Simply to ask for time to pay is not enough to attract the exercise of the court's discretion.

(ii) No discretion to postpone proceedings indefinitely   Even if the court is able to exercise discretion in favour of the mortgagor, there are substantial restrictions upon the terms on which it may do so. In *Royal Trust Co of Canada v Markham*,[3] for instance, the Court of Appeal ruled that it had no jurisdiction to order suspension of possession proceedings *sine die*.[4] The court must define the period during which the proceedings may be adjourned or any possession order stayed. In any event relief may be granted to the mortgagor only in respect of such period of time as is 'reasonable'. The Payne Committee on the Enforcement of Judgment Debts considered that a period of six months would be sufficient in most cases,[5] but the period may well be longer or shorter depending on the circumstances.[6]

---

18   Matrimonial Homes Act 1983, s 8(3).
19   English law in this respect still does not go as far as, for instance, the law in Ontario, which requires that notice of mortgagees' possession actions be given to 'all persons in actual possession' in order to enable them to apply for relief (see Rules of Practice (Ont), Rule 567(2); *Canada Trustco Mortgage Co v McLean* (1983) 143 DLR (3d) 101 at 104).
20   Administration of Justice Act 1973, s 8 (ante, p 892).
1   See Matrimonial Homes Act 1983, s 8(2), (3) (ante, p 895).
2   See eg *Williams & Glyn's Bank Ltd v Boland* [1981] AC 487 at 509C-D; *Peckham Mutual Building Society v Registe* (1981) 42 P & CR 186 at 189. Compare *Centrax Trustees Ltd v Ross* [1979] 2 All ER 952 at 954h, 957f-g.
3   [1975] 1 WLR 1416 at 1423C, 1424A-B.
4   Compare, however, the suggestion in *Western Bank Ltd v Schindler* [1977] Ch 1 at 14E-G.
5   *Report* (Cmnd 3909, 1969), para 1388.
6   See R.J. Smith, [1979] Conv 266 at 278f; D. McConnell, *Defending Mortgage Possession Actions*, (1985) Legal Action 121; A. Brewer and S. Jarvis, *The Reasonable Period: Suspension of Mortgage Possession Hearings in the County Court*, (1986) Legal Action 96.

(iii) No discretion before moneys have become due There is some doubt as to whether section 36 of the Administration of Justice Act 1970 can have any application where no mortgage moneys of any kind have yet become due. In *Western Bank Ltd v Schindler,*[7] two members of the Court of Appeal thought that section 36 must be applicable irrespective of the absence of actual default, since otherwise a blameless mortgagor would be put in a less advantageous position than a defaulting mortgagor who can rely on section 36. Goff LJ was, however, of the view that, on strict construction, section 36 cannot apply where there is no money due or any other default present on the facts of the case.[8] This restrictive approach has since received some confirmation in *Habib Bank Ltd v Tailor.*[9] Here the Court of Appeal ruled that the Administration of Justice Acts had no application to a mortgage given as security for a bank overdraft, under which no money was due unless and until repayment was demanded by the bank.[10]

4. ASSERTION OF PRIORITY BY A BENEFICIAL OWNER

Even if none of the foregoing forms of assistance or relief is available to the mortgagor and his family, there remains one means by which it is possible that the occupiers of a family home may yet be able to defeat a mortgagee's claim to possession. Recent caselaw has demonstrated that it may be open to various kinds of family member to assert priority over a mortgagee on the ground that he took his security subject to their undisclosed rights as beneficial co-owners behind a statutory trust for sale. This area of law has nowadays become so important and so controversial as to merit extensive treatment in Chapter 25.[11]

7   [1977] Ch 1 at 13D-E per Buckley LJ, 19F per Scarman LJ.
8   [1977] Ch 1 at 26E. See (1977) 40 MLR 356 (C. Harpum).
9   [1982] 1 WLR 1218. See [1983] Conv 80 (P.H. Kenny); (1983) 133 NLJ 247 (H.W. Wilkinson).
10   [1982] 1 WLR 1218 at 1225F.
11   Ante, p 829.

G. A charter of rights for residential tenants

CHAPTER 27

The environmental quality of tenanted accommodation

It is clear that certain basic standards of amenity must be met by any form of residential housing which seeks to provide conditions conducive to a civilised, humane and purposive existence. The social function of the law of housing is therefore directed very largely towards guaranteeing residential tenure of reasonable decency and security, not least because the achievement of this aim is nowadays seen as significantly related to the promotion and protection of a happy personal and family life. It is difficult to inspire children to a sense of social responsibility if their housing conditions provide constant and irrefutable evidence of an irresponsible and uncaring society.

This chapter outlines the legal mechanisms which are aimed at the preservation and enhancement of the environmental quality of tenanted accommodation. The landlord-tenant relationship covers a broad spectrum of legal devices and social contexts. At one end of the spectrum the law of landlord and tenant must ensure that the periodic tenant has effective enjoyment of a 'social right' to decent housing, so far as possible free of the adverse physical conditions which are a function of poverty. However, the same law of landlord and tenant also regulates the housing conditions of a different social and economic group which can afford to purchase long leases in residential flats. It has become increasingly clear that the tenant who 'owns' a flat in a private residential block is just as helpless in the hands of his landlord's management company in the matter of repairs and maintenance as is the periodic tenant at the mercy of his landlord.[1]

The feature which unifies the law relating to the quality of tenanted accommodation is that the problems of poor housing are, at root, problems of economic deprivation. The primary housing problem in England today is not one of physically defective housing stock—although there is plenty of that around. It is instead a problem of inadequate income: poor housing survives only because there are poor people.[2] Since poverty at least in this country is an essentially relative phenomenon, the quality of residential housing becomes an area of legal concern in relation to a wide variety of social groups. There is currently a housing crisis of alarming proportions amongst the disadvantaged, the disabled and the unemployed. There is another—albeit less pressing—problem in relation to the housing conditions of the young urban professional such as the teacher or the nurse who can only just afford to pay the mortgage on his or her tiny flat in a crumbling tenement.

1   Concern in this area led to the setting up of the Nugee Committee, which reported in 1985. See *Report of the Committee of Inquiry on the Management of Privately Owned Blocks of Flats* (Chairman: E.G. Nugee QC, 1985), Vol 1. The Nugee Committee's Report was, in its turn, instrumental in the enactment of the Landlord and Tenant Act 1987.

2   This conclusion was confirmed in one of the most far-reaching surveys ever conducted into the subject of poverty. See *Poverty in Australia* (Australian Government Commission of Inquiry into Poverty, First Main Report, April 1975), Vol 1 (the 'Henderson Report'), p 176 ('we conclude that direct income support would be more effective than public housing').

1. THE PRINCIPLE OF CAVEAT EMPTOR

Until some point during the 19th century the primary rule governing the residential fitness of tenanted accommodation was the unsympathetic principle of *caveat emptor*. The leasehold device was conceptualised very much in terms of a conveyance of an estate in land which conferred upon the lessee a right to exclusive possession. So long as he was given exclusive possession at the commencement of the lease, the lessee's obligation to pay rent was absolute and unqualified.[3] The lessee had no right, after the commencement of the lease, to complain about the fitness of the land for his purpose. He was deemed to assume all risks attached to the condition of the land unless he had reached some contrary agreement with the lessor. In other words, the lessee hired at his peril, and the lessor gave no implied undertaking as to the physical condition of the land or (in the case of a building) as to its state of repair.

(1) Origin of the principle

The immunity thus conferred on the lessor was doubtless due in great measure to the fact that the subject matter of leases was more commonly agricultural land than residential dwellings.[4] The courts were greatly concerned to prevent the extension of lessors' duties in agrarian leases.[5] This approach inevitably coloured the courts' view of residential lettings, as evidenced by Erle CJ's famous observation that 'fraud apart, there is no law against letting a tumble-down house.'[6] The common law principle was clear: 'the lessee must make his objections to the condition of the premises before taking the lease.'[7] It went almost without saying that the lessor had no responsibility to maintain the land during the currency of the lease. The law simply epitomised the rule of laissez faire.[8]

(2) Retreat from the principle

The common law principle, even if appropriate in a rural and largely agrarian context, could not remain unaffected by the social and economic changes brought about by the creation of an urbanised proletariat during the early years of the 19th century. A myriad of houses 'suitable for...use...by members of

---

3   The tenant's rent obligation was held to survive a number of calamities. See *Paradine v Jane* (1647) Aleyn 26 at 27f, 82 ER 897 at 898 (dispossession during civil war); *Monk v Cooper,* (1727) 2 Stra 763, 93 ER 833 at 834; *Belfour v Weston* (1786) 1 TR 310 at 312, 99 ER 1112 at 1113 (destruction of premises by fire). Compare, however, *Graves v Berdan* 26 NY 498 (1863).

4   See the explanation offered in *Siney v Corporation of Dublin* [1980] IR 400 at 408 per O'Higgins CJ.

5   See eg *Sutton v Temple* (1843) 12 M & W 52 at 65, 152 ER 1108 at 1113 (cattle died of lead poisoning in field).

6   *Robbins v Jones* (1863) 15 CB (NS) 221 at 240, 143 ER 768 at 776. See *Anns v Merton LB* [1978] AC 728 at 768E per Lord Salmon ('The immunity of a landlord who sells or lets a house which is dangerous or unfit for habitation is deeply entrenched in our law'.) The exception made for fraud may be important. See eg *Gordon v Selico Co Ltd* [1986] 1 EGLR 71 at 77J, where a vendor of a long lease was held liable in damages for the tort of deceit where he had fraudulently concealed the existence of dry rot in a flat sold to the plaintiffs.

7   H. Tiffany, *Treatise on the Law of Landlord and Tenant* (1912), p 572f.

8   See J.I. Reynolds, *Statutory Covenants of Fitness and Repair: Social Legislation and the Judges,* (1974) 37 MLR 377 at 378ff.

the working classes'[9] quickly formed in orderly patterns of squalid misery around the factories, textile mills, coal-pits and iron-works of the industrial revolution.[10] This sudden aggregation of residential dwellers in large industrial conurbations[11] inevitably gave an unprecedented prominence to the legal issue of habitability in the residential sector.[12]

The response of bourgeois law to these developments was rather less substantial than the human and social problems to which they gave rise.[13] Even the modern law relating to the residential fitness of rented dwellings still comprises a piecemeal collection of provisions derived from the common law and sporadic statutory intervention.

2. THE LANDLORD'S LIABILITY AT COMMON LAW

The common law has made a partial contribution towards the development of a recognised standard of habitability in residential lettings. This contribution has come through the declaration of an implied condition in certain kinds of lease, together with the gradual extension of the law relating to nuisance and negligence.

(1) Implied condition of fitness for human habitation

A significant exception to the common law principle of *caveat emptor* in landlord-tenant relations was established in 1843 in *Smith v Marrable*.[14]

9   This terrible statutory phrase was to recur in legislation dating from the Housing of the Working Classes Act 1885 to the present day (see eg Rent Act 1977, s 101(2)). See also *Chorley BC v Barratt Developments (North West) Ltd* [1979] 3 All ER 634 at 639a–c; R.G. Lee, *The Demise of the Working Classes*, [1980] Conv 281.

10   Some of the early industrialists and landowners took care to provide decent housing conditions for the workers, but all too often the new housing took the form of the back-to-back terraces, cellar dwellings or courtyard dwellings which became the slums of the future (see A. Briggs, *Victorian Cities* (Harmondsworth, Middx 1968), p 226f; J. Burnett, *A Social History of Housing 1815–1970* (London 1978), pp 11, 54ff).

11   In 1801 approximately 80 per cent of the population of England and Wales was still 'rural' and only 20 per cent lived in towns of more than 5,000 inhabitants. By 1851 54 per cent of the population had become urban dwellers, and there were already ten urban centres of more than 100,000 inhabitants each, accounting in total for a quarter of the population of the entire country (see J. Burnett, op cit, p 6f).

12   The full horror of some of the housing supposedly suitable for use by members of the working classes is apparent in the *First Report of the Royal Commission on the Housing of the Working Classes* (PP 1884–85, XXX), p 11f. The Commissioners recorded that in Bristol 'privies actually exist in living rooms'; that in Liverpool they found 'walls...alive with vermin'; and that in Southwark some houses had 'large cracks and holes in the walls large enough for a man to enter'. The Commissioners also referred (at p 12) to the curiously modern complaint of 'jerry building'.

13   The nature of the interest which even a supposedly enlightened 19th century landlord had in the living conditions of his tenants is apparent in the earnest statement that 'sanitary improvements lead to higher rentals being obtained and to the tenants enjoying better health, and, consequently, being in a better position to pay the said rent'. (G.H. Larmuth, *A Practical Guide to the Law of Landlord and Tenant* (Manchester 1878), p 45).

14   (1843) 11 M & W 5 at 8f, 152 ER 693 at 694. The American parallel is *Ingalls v Hobbs*, 31 NE 286 at 287 (1892), citing *Smith v Marrable* in support. There has always been a special exception at common law governing the liability of a lessor who sells a leasehold estate in a house which is still in the process of construction. The vendor is impliedly taken to warrant the suitability of materials used, the quality of the workmanship and the fitness of the house for habitation (see *Perry v Sharon Development Co Ltd* [1937] 4 All ER 390 at 393A–B; *Siney v Corporation of Dublin* [1980] IR 400 at 408).

(a) Content of the implied condition of fitness

In *Smith v Marrable* the tenant, on taking possession, had discovered the premises to be infested with bugs. The Court of Exchequer held it to be an implied condition in the letting of any furnished house that the premises should be reasonably fit for habitation. The tenant was therefore entitled to quit the letting without notice.[15] According to Parke B, 'if the demised premises are incumbered with a nuisance of so serious a nature that no person can reasonably be expected to live in them, the tenant is at liberty to throw them up.'[16]

(b) Limitations of the implied condition of fitness

The ruling in *Smith v Marrable* is, however, subject to certain grave limitations. The implied condition of fitness for habitation relates only to the condition of the premises at the commencement of the letting; it does not cover defects arising thereafter.[17] The implied condition does not apply to ordinary disrepair which merely renders habitation unpleasant or inconvenient[18] as distinct from dangerous or impossible.[19] The implied condition applies only to a residential tenancy.[20] It has no relevance to unfurnished premises,[1] with the effect that nowadays almost all council tenancies and certainly all long (eg 99 year) leases of residential flats[2] are excluded from its scope. Even in relation to furnished premises, the implied condition does not extend to dangerous appliances or furnishings supplied by the landlord.[3] Because the landlord's liability arises *ex contractu*, no person other than the tenant can maintain an action for breach of the implied condition.[4]

The potentially fertile scope of *Smith v Marrable* has thus been disastrously curtailed, thereby frustrating an important opportunity for the construction of a comprehensive common law standard of habitability in residential lettings.

---

15 See also *Collins v Barrow* (1831) 1 M & Rob 112 at 114, 174 ER 38 at 39. The tenant is under no obligation to give the landlord an opportunity to remedy the defect (*Wilson v Finch Hatton* (1877) 2 Ex D 336 at 341).

16 The decision is itself something of an accident. Later in the same year (in *Hart v Windsor* (1843) 12 M & W 68 at 87, 152 ER 1114 at 1122) Parke B confessed that he believed his ruling in *Smith v Marrable* to have been founded on unsupportable authority, and he refused to extend that ruling to unfurnished lettings.

17 *Hart v Windsor* (1843) 12 M & W 68 at 85f, 152 ER 1114 at 1121; *Sarson v Roberts* [1895] 2 QB 395 at 397f.

18 See eg *Maclean v Currie* (1884) Cab & El 361 (cracked plaster).

19 See eg *Bird v Lord Greville* (1884) Cab & El 317; *Collins v Hopkins* [1923] 2 KB 617 at 628 (property vacated by person with infectious disease). See generally (1982) 79 Law Soc Gaz 1567 (D.W. Williams).

20 See *Bradford House Pty Ltd v Leroy Fashion Group Ltd* (1982-83) 46 ALR 305 at 313. Compare, however, G.G. Greenfield and M.Z. Margolies, *An Implied Warranty of Fitness in Nonresidential Leases*, 45 Albany LR 855 (1980-81); J.A. Marley, *Landlord-Tenant—Should a Warranty of Fitness be implied in Commercial Leases?*, 13 Rutgers LJ 91 (1981-82).

1 *Hart v Windsor* (1843) 12 M & W 68 at 87, 152 ER 1114 at 1122; *Lane v Cox* [1897] 1 QB 415 at 417. The landlord's immunity prevails even though he has brought about the defect himself and is aware of its existence (see *Bottomley v Bannister* [1932] 1 KB 458 at 468; *Cruse v Mount* [1933] Ch 278 at 282; *Davis v Foots* [1940] 1 KB 116 at 121; *Scythes & Co Ltd v Gibsons Ltd* [1927] 2 DLR 834 at 838; *Re Trella and Anko Investments Ltd* (1982) 122 DLR (3d) 713 at 716).

2 See eg *Gordon v Selico Co Ltd* [1986] 1 EGLR 71 (although the tenant under a long lease may sometimes have a damages remedy for the tort of deceit).

3 *Pampris v Thanos* [1968] 1 NSWR 56 at 58 (tenant's wife electrocuted on contact with faulty refrigerator).

4 *Cameron v Young* [1908] AC 176 at 180f; *Pampris v Thanos* [1968] 1 NSWR 56 at 58.

(c) Scope for a more general warranty of habitability?

Some idea of what might have been achieved by the common law becomes apparent in the development of housing law in the United States during the 1960s and 1970s. Over this period there occurred what some have described as a 'revolution' in the residential landlord-tenant relationship,[5] the central feature of which was the recognition of an 'implied warranty of habitability' in all residential lettings whether furnished or not.

The symbolic turning-point in this reorientation of American landlord-tenant law is traditionally seen as the judgment of Judge Skelly Wright in *Javins v First National Realty Corporation*[6] in 1970. However, the change of direction can be traced further back to cases like *Pines v Perssion*,[7] where it was declared that the 'need and desirability of adequate housing for people in this era of rapid population increases is too important to be rebuffed by that obnoxious legal cliché, *caveat emptor.*' It now seems clear that the introduction of the general warranty of habitability in residential tenancy relations was heavily influenced both by the more questioning climate induced by the Vietnam War and by a judicial response to the civil rights movement and the plight of the largely black population of slum-dwellers on the East and West coasts.[8]

In *Javins v First National Realty Corporation*[9] the tenants of an apartment block in Washington DC had declined to pay rent on the ground that their landlord was guilty of approximately 1,500 violations of the Housing Regulations of the District of Columbia. Judge Wright, sitting in the United States Court of Appeals, held that the tenants' obligation to pay rent was dependent on the landlord's performance of his obligations, which included an implied warranty to maintain the premises in habitable condition.[10]

The reasoning employed by Judge Wright in coming to this conclusion has become a classic exposition of the legal nature of the residential landlord-tenant relationship. Fundamental to Judge Wright's analysis was the conceptual transformation of the tenancy relationship from its doctrinal starting-point in a conveyance of a leasehold estate in (largely agrarian) land to its modern social function as a consumer contract. As Judge Wright indicated,[11]

When American city dwellers, both rich and poor, seek 'shelter' today, they seek a well known package of goods and services—a package which includes not merely walls and

---

5   See eg E.H. Rabin, *The Revolution in Residential Landlord-Tenant Law: Causes and Consequences*, 69 Cornell LR 517 (1983-84). See also M.A. Glendon, *The Transformation of American Landlord-Tenant Law*, 23 Boston College LR 503 (1982).

6   428 F.2d 1071 (1970).

7   111 NW.2d 409 at 413 (1961).

8   See E.H. Rabin, 69 Cornell LR 517 at 546ff. In a letter to Professor Rabin in 1982, Judge Skelly Wright recalls having been influenced by 'the fact that, during the nationwide racial turmoil of the sixties and the unrest caused by the injustice of racially selective service in Vietnam, most of the tenants in Washington, DC slums were poor and black and most of the landlords were rich and white' (69 Cornell LR at 549).

9   428 F.2d 1071 (1970).

10   Judge Wright was already a remarkable and somewhat controversial figure, having once been described (greatly to his credit) as 'the most hated man in New Orleans' (see J. Bass, *Unlikely Heroes* (1981), p 114). He ordered desegregation of educational institutions in Louisiana even before the Supreme Court's landmark decision in *Brown v Board of Education*, 347 US 483 (1954).

11   428 F.2d 1071 at 1074.

ceilings, but also adequate heat, light and ventilation, serviceable plumbing facilities, secure windows and doors, proper sanitation, and proper maintenance.[12]

This novel perception of the nature of the tenancy agreement entailed certain important consequences. The analogy with the provision of goods and services made instantly more feasible the implication of a warranty that those goods and services should be reasonably fit for their designed purpose. In the view of Judge Wright, the tenancy contract is a commercial transaction in which the tenant 'seeks to purchase from his landlord shelter for a specified period of time'.[13] In common with the average consumer of goods and services, the tenant is not generally capable of assessing the fitness of the product supplied, and therefore relies inevitably on 'the skill and bona fides of his landlord at least as much as a car buyer must rely upon the car manufacturer.'[14] Since the tenancy specifies 'a particular period of time during which the tenant has a right to use his apartment for shelter, he may legitimately expect that the apartment will be fit for habitation for the time period for which it is rented.'[15]

On the basis of these considerations Judge Wright ruled that the traditional *caveat emptor* rule, which effectively imposed all repair obligations during the tenancy on the tenant himself, 'was really never intended to apply to residential urban leaseholds'.[16] The contract principles established in other areas of the law 'provide a more rational framework for the apportionment of landlord-tenant responsibilities.'[17] In other words, the time had now come for the landlord-tenant relationship to take its rightful place as a branch of the law of consumer protection.

The initiative of *Javins* has left a lasting—although still controversial—mark on American landlord and tenant law.[18] It has reversed the negative effect of

---

12   'The value of the lease today...is that it gives the tenant a place to live, and he expects not just space but a dwelling that protects him from the elements of the environment without subjecting him to health hazards' (*Foisy v Wyman*, 515 P.2d 160 at 164 (1973)).

13   428 F.2d 1071 at 1079. Judge Wright was trained in the civil law of Louisiana, under which a lease (as in all civilian systems) belongs to the sphere of contract not property law.

14   428 F.2d 1071 at 1079. This consideration was intensified by the inequality of bargaining power present between landlord and tenant.

15   428 F.2d 1071 at 1079. See also *Green v Superior Court of City and County of San Francisco*, 517 P.2d 1168 at 1175 (1974), where in the Supreme Court of California Tobriner J observed that 'in most significant respects, the modern urban tenant is in the same position as any other normal consumer of goods...A tenant may reasonably expect that the product he is purchasing is fit for the purpose for which it is obtained, that is, a living unit'.

16   428 F.2d 1071 at 1080. Judge Wright had stressed (at 1078) that the modern tenant is usually possessed of 'a single, specialised skill unrelated to maintenance work; he is unable to make repairs like the "jack-of-all-trades" farmer who was the common law's model of the lessee. Further, unlike his agrarian predecessor who often remained on one piece of land for his entire life, urban tenants today are more mobile than ever before. A tenant's tenure in a specific apartment will often not be sufficient to justify efforts at repairs'.

17   428 F.2d 1071 at 1080.

18   For other applications of the *Javins* doctrine, see Chapter 28 (post, p 953). See eg *Foisy v Wyman*, 515 P.2d 160 at 164 (1973), where the Supreme Court of Washington applied a warranty of habitability even though the tenant's rent was specially reduced because of the defects in the premises ('We believe this type of bargaining by the landlord with the tenant is contrary to public policy and the purpose of the doctrine of implied warranty of habitability'). Some commentators have even gone so far as to support the warranty of habitability quite explicitly as a device aimed at 'a significant expropriation or redistribution away from people who are owners of low-income property'. See Duncan Kennedy, *In favor of the Warranty of Habitability, In Brief* (May 1987) p 8.

the rule in *Smith v Marrable* and has entrenched in the American law of landlord and tenant the more humane principle that the landlord is contractually liable to supply his tenants with decent housing conditions throughout the term of the tenancy.[19] By contrast, English common law remains tethered to the limitations of *Smith v Marrable*, and has therefore been forced to seek the same goal, somewhat imperfectly, through tortuous and fragmented initiatives of statute law. It remains a matter of curious surmise that in England the control of environmental quality in the residential tenancy relationship may implicitly have been traded off for the security of tenure and rent control which, ironically, is so conspicuously lacking in the United States.

(2) Implied contractual duty of care

The fact that the landlord-tenant relationship is normally, at its roots, a contractual relationship has facilitated a more positive move towards the achievement of better housing conditions for tenants under English law. The recent caselaw has demonstrated the courts' increasing willingness to imply on the part of the landlord certain contractual duties of care which have the indirect effect of promoting the residential utility enjoyed by tenants. Such duties of care may well arise where the landlord retains within his control common parts of a building over which the individual tenants enjoy rights in the nature of an easement. In such circumstances a duty of care is fixed upon the landlord to preserve the amenities enjoyed by the tenants.

(a) Content of the contractual duty of care

A most important contribution was made to the development of the landlord's duty of care by the decision of the House of Lords in *Liverpool City Council v Irwin*.[20] Here council tenants living in flats in the upper storeys of a high-rise block withheld rent on the ground that the lifts, staircases and rubbish chutes in their building were not maintained by the council in a safe or efficient condition. There was evidence that the lifts were almost continuously out of order and the stairways unlit largely because of the activity of vandals living on the estate. The House of Lords ruled that certain duties of care on the part of the landlord were to be implied into the contract of tenancy as a matter of 'necessity'.[1] In the absence of any express undertaking by the landlord authority, Lord Wilberforce held that the council was under a contractual duty to 'take reasonable care to keep in reasonable repair and usability' the

---

19 Similar motivations lay behind the recommendation in Ontario that the landlord should bear a statutory responsibility for providing and maintaining residential premises 'in a good state of repair and fit for habitation during the tenancy and for complying with health, safety and maintenance and occupancy standards required by law' (Ontario Law Reform Commission, *Report on Landlord and Tenant Law* (1976), p 133ff; Residential Tenancies Act (ORS 1980, c452), s 28(1)). See also *Fleischmann v Grossman Holdings Ltd* (1978) 79 DLR (3d) 142 at 146ff; *Gaul v King* (1980) 103 DLR (3d) 233 at 238.

20 [1977] AC 239.

1 [1977] AC 239 at 254F. See also Lord Salmon (at 263A). Both the 'business efficacy' test and the landlord's implied obligation not to derogate from his grant (ante, p 476) were invoked in somewhat similar circumstances in *Karaggianis v Malltown Pty Ltd* (1979) 21 SASR 381 at 390ff. See, however, the limitation imposed on the doctrine prohibiting derogation from grant in *Duke of Westminster v Guild* [1985] QB 688 at 703F.

common parts and facilities in the building.[2] The maintenance of such facilities as lifts, stairways and rubbish chutes could not simply be regarded as 'conveniences provided at discretion: they are essentials of the tenancy without which life in the dwellings, as a tenant, is not possible.'[3] As Lord Salmon asked with some force, '[c]an a pregnant woman accompanied by a young child be expected to walk up 15...storeys in the pitch dark to reach her home? Unless the law...imposes an obligation upon the council at least to use reasonable care to keep the lifts working properly and the staircase lit, the whole transaction becomes inefficacious, futile and absurd'.[4]

Having thus adopted a commendably enlightened approach to a vexingly common problem of housing management, the House of Lords then somewhat blunted its own initiative by holding that the council had not been shown to be in breach of its contractual obligation of care. It was clear that the council had made considerable efforts, despite the depredations committed by the local vandals, to maintain the efficiency of communal facilities in the flats.[5] The House stressed that the council's implied obligation to repair and maintain was not absolute. Such an obligation would itself have been 'unreasonable',[6] and the substance of the tenants' counter-claim for damages accordingly failed.[7]

Ironically, it seems that the tenants may have made a grave tactical error in alleging the existence of an *absolute* duty of care in the landlord. In the House of Lords Lord Salmon reached his conclusion 'with some reluctance and doubt', opining that the tenants' counter-claim might well have succeeded if they had pleaded that the landlord was subject to a duty merely to take 'reasonable care'.[8]

The ruling in *Liverpool City Council v Irwin* is a significant landmark in the law of landlord and tenant in that the implied contractual duty of care endorsed in this decision may enable tenants, in appropriate circumstances, to recover damages from the landlord for mere loss of amenity without the necessity of showing any physical injury or damage.[9]

2   [1977] AC 239 at 256G. See also *Karaggianis v Malltown Pty Ltd* (1979) 21 SASR 381 at 392 (mandatory injunction to restore lift and escalator service to the sixth floor).
3   [1977] AC 239 at 254F-G.
4   [1977] AC 239 at 262A-B.
5   In coming to their conclusion, some of the law lords were influenced (see [1977] AC 239 at 257C-D, 269D-E) by Lord Denning MR's judgment in the Court of Appeal ([1976] QB 319 at 332E-H). Here the Master of the Rolls had pointed out that the council 'did their best to cope with these troubles...They have been beaten by the vandals and hooligans.' Lord Denning then continued to express a quite astonishing degree of prejudice against council tenants, who pay 'very low rents' and are 'allowed, in practice, virtual security of tenure'. He alleged that in the present case the tenants were 'all, in a sense, responsible for the deplorable state of affairs...[C]ollectively the tenants could do much to improve the situation. They should do their part in disciplining these youngsters.'
6   [1977] AC 239 at 256G. See also Lord Cross of Chelsea (at 259F-G), Lord Edmund-Davies (at 269C-D).
7   It now seems that the aggrieved tenants could have taken steps leading to the service on the City Council of an improvement notice under section 21 of the Health and Safety at Work etc Act 1974 (see *Westminster City Council v Select Management Ltd* [1984] 1 WLR 1058 at 1061H, post, p 925). This would have had the effect of compelling the Council to restore the lifts and other common facilities to a functional state. The only difficulty is that the 'enforcing authority' for the 1974 Act would have been the City Council itself!
8   [1977] AC 239 at 263C-G. Lord Salmon agreed that the lifts had been 'out of action inordinately often and only a little more than half the time on account of vandalism.'
9   It is significant that Lord Wilberforce was not prepared in principle to leave tenants at the mercy of the council's response to 'administrative or political pressure' ([1977] AC 239 at 254G). See also Lord Salmon (at 261C).

(b) Limitations of the implied contractual duty

Important though the implied contractual duty of care may be, it has its limitations. As the House of Lords made clear in *Liverpool City Council v Irwin*,[10] the duty impliedly fixed upon the landlord may be excluded by the simple expedient of express contractual provision.[11] Moreover, it seems that the implication of a landlord's duty of care will be more readily made in relation to high-rise blocks designed for multiple occupation than in relation to other kinds of tenancy.[12]

(i) Limitation to circumstances of necessity The scope of the landlord's implied contractual obligation is significantly restricted by the courts' tendency to imply a contractual duty of care only in those circumstances where the absence of such a duty would render the contract of tenancy 'inefficacious, futile and absurd'.[13] Thus in *O'Leary v LB of Islington*[14] a landlord authority was held to be under no implied duty of care to enforce for the benefit of one of its tenants a nuisance clause contained in its tenancy agreement with another of its tenants.[15] The Court of Appeal adopted an exceptionally limited view of the management function of the housing authority, ruling in effect that the authority was under no obligation to 'police' the performance of the tenants' duties to respect the quality of residential life on a council housing estate. The landlord's intervention was considered unnecessary to give effect to the plaintiff's tenancy agreement, since the plaintiff himself had a perfectly good remedy in tort directly against his obnoxious neighbour.

Likewise, in *Collins v Northern Ireland Housing Executive*[16] Carswell J declined to hold that a tenancy agreement was rendered 'inefficacious, futile and absurd' merely because of frequent breakdowns in the district heating system which provided the source of space heating on the plaintiffs' housing estate. No contractual term could be implied that the landlord authority should maintain the system in proper repair or at a given state of efficiency, since defects in the system affected only 'the quality of enjoyment of the facilities supplied, not...the basic ability to use the accommodation.'[17] Carswell J held that, even

---

10 [1977] AC 239 at 259E, 260C.
11 See eg *Coughlan v The Mayor of the City of Limerick* (1977) 111 ILTR 141 at 142.
12 [1977] AC 239 at 254G, 256E-F, 270B-C. See *Duke of Westminster v Guild* [1985] QB 688 at 699B-C; *Gordon v Selico Co Ltd* [1986] 1 EGLR 71L.
13 See *Liverpool City Council v Irwin* [1977] AC 239 at 262A-B per Lord Salmon. The courts are therefore less ready to imply a contractual duty of care where the express terms of the lease were intended to 'provide a comprehensive code in regard to repair and maintenance of the block' (see *Gordon v Selico Co Ltd* [1986] 1 EGLR 71K-72A). Compare the more liberal approach applied in the United States in *Javins v First National Realty Corporation*, 428 F.2d 1071 (1970) (ante, p 905), and see D. Tiplady, *Recent Developments in the Law of Landlord and Tenant: the American Experience*, (1981) 44 MLR 129 at 141f.
14 (1983) 9 HLR 81 at 86, 89.
15 The local authority had tried its best, but failed, to get the nuisance-prone neighbour to change her ways (see (1983) 9 HLR 81 at 84).
16 [1984] 17 NIJB, Transcript p 21.
17 [1984] 17 NIJB, Transcript p 21. However, Carswell J was prepared (at p 25) to imply a contractual term that the pricing structure of the heating charges should be 'fair and reasonable'. In his view it would not be 'fair and reasonable' that the landlord authority should refuse to refund standing charges in respect of those periods when no heat at all was furnished to the tenant. The tenant could recover some proportion of his payments in quasi-contract or on the basis of unjust enrichment, but, according to Carswell J, could do so only in respect of continuous periods of deprivation of heat lasting more than one week. A week was 'the shortest period which can be regarded as...a divisible part of the contract' (p 26).

though the landlord authority was in sole control of the heating system and made standing charges for its use, the tenant could, if necessary, always 'resort to auxiliary methods of heating...and still continue to occupy the accommodation demised'.[18]

(ii) Limitation to contracting parties   Perhaps the most obvious limitation upon the scope of a landlord's implied contractual duty of care is quite simply the fact that the duty, if it exists at all, is owed only to the other contracting party, the tenant. The liability of the landlord to non-contracting parties (such as members of the tenant's family) can be established only with reference to other forms of common law or statutory responsibility.

(3) Implied covenant for quiet enjoyment

There is in every lease an implied covenant or contractual term[19] binding the landlord to give 'quiet possession' to the tenant.[20] The landlord's obligation is intended to ensure that the tenant enjoys freedom from any physical interference with the demised land by either the landlord or any person for whom the landlord is responsible. The liability founded on the implied covenant plays some part in protecting the tenant's right to certain standards of amenity in the land demised. As Lord Denning MR ruled in *McCall v Abelesz*,[1] the implied covenant extends to any conduct which 'interferes with the tenant's freedom of action in exercising his rights as tenant', and therefore covers 'any acts calculated to interfere with the peace or comfort of the tenant, or his family'.[2]

In the present context, there may be a breach of the implied covenant for quiet enjoyment where, for instance, a burst water pipe in premises retained by the landlord causes water to flow into, and cause damage to, the premises occupied by the tenant.[3] However, it is probable that no liability accrues to the landlord in the absence of some wilful or negligent omission or commission by him.[4] There is a clear breach of the implied covenant where the landlord maliciously cuts off the supply of gas or electricity to the tenant.[5]

18   [1984] 17 NIJB, Transcript p 22.
19   In strict terms a 'covenant' exists only in relation to a lease by deed, but there is an equivalent implied contractual term for quiet enjoyment in tenancies not granted by deed (see *Budd-Scott v Daniell* [1902] 2 KB 351 at 355f).
20   Ante, p 476. See also M.J. Russell, (1976) 40 Conv (NS) 426.
1   [1976] QB 585 at 594E.
2   See also *Kenny v Preen* [1963] 1 QB 499 at 513, 515.
3   *Anderson v Oppenheimer* (1880) 5 QBD 602 at 607. See also *Martins Camera Corner Pty Ltd v Hotel Mayfair Ltd* [1976] 2 NSWLR 15 at 24A-C. Likewise, where a landlord has covenanted with a tenant to maintain other parts of a block of flats, failure to keep the building waterproofed may amount to a breach of the covenant for quiet enjoyment (*Gordon v Selico Co Ltd* [1985] 2 EGLR 79 at 83D).
4   See *Anderson v Oppenheimer* (1880) 5 QBD 602 at 607f; *Booth v Thomas* [1926] Ch 397 at 403, 411. The covenant for quiet enjoyment cannot be invoked so as to impose on the landlord a positive obligation to perform repairs which otherwise would not be his responsibility (see *Duke of Westminster v Guild* [1985] QB 688 at 703F).
5   *McCall v Abelesz* [1976] QB 585 at 594D.

(4) The landlord's liability in negligence

The law of negligence provides an additional (and sometimes vital) form of protection for the residential amenity enjoyed by tenants.[6]

(a) Defects arising after the commencement of the tenancy

There is authority, stemming largely from the decision of the House of Lords in *Cavalier v Pope*,[7] to the effect that a landlord cannot be liable to a tenant in negligence by reason of the defective nature of the demised premises at the commencement of the tenancy.[8] It is clear, however, that liability in negligence can arise in respect of events occurring after the commencement date.[9]

(i) Damage emanating from premises retained by the landlord

It is well established, for instance, that a claim in negligence may lie against a landlord if, by some action or omission on premises retained within his exclusive possession and control, damage is caused to that part of the premises demised to the tenant.

A typical problem in this context arises where the landlord grants away tenancies of flats in a building, while retaining for himself exclusive possession over such parts of the building as the roof or the service ducts. Under such circumstances, the landlord owes a duty of care at common law (and not merely in consequence of an express covenant entered into by him[10]). He must take reasonable care to remedy defects in his own premises of which he has notice (eg an excessive accumulation of drainwater) which may cause damage to the premises of his tenants.[11] This form of negligence liability has been applied to give the tenant a remedy against his landlord for such damage to the demised premises as that caused by a failure to clear a blocked rain-water gutter[12] or a downpipe,[13] or to avoid the overflow of water from a basin and pipe,[14] or to prevent an invasion of cockroaches from the service ducts.[15] However, the tenant cannot claim negligence on the part of the landlord merely because some defect in a drain situated in the property retained by the landlord prevents the outflow of the tenant's own drainwater.[16]

6 There is always of course the possibility that one tenant may sue another tenant directly in respect of negligence which leads to loss of amenity (see *Elfassy v Sylben Investments Ltd* (1979) 91 DLR (3d) 96). However, the defendant in such an action may be able to plead successfully that he had no reason to suspect the existence of the problem which caused the damage of which the plaintiff now complains. In *Hawkins v Dhawan* (1987) *Times*, 11 February, the Court of Appeal held that just as every dog must be 'allowed its first bite', so a tenant's washbasin must be allowed its first flood, even though the overflow escapes to the premises of a neighbouring tenant.

7 [1906] AC 428 at 430ff. See *Bottomley v Bannister* [1932] 1 KB 458 at 477.

8 See *Robbins v Jones* (1863) 15 CB (NS) 221 at 240, 143 ER 768 at 776; *Bottomley v Bannister* [1932] 1 KB 458 at 477; *Otto v Bolton and Norris* [1936] 2 KB 46 at 54; *Davis v Foots* [1940] 1 KB 116 at 121, 124; *McGowan v Harrison* [1941] IR 331 at 337.

9 See *Clerk & Lindsell on Torts* (15th edn, London 1982), paras 10-27, 12-39.

10 *Martins Camera Corner Pty Ltd v Hotel Mayfair Ltd* [1976] 2 NSWLR 15 at 24E-F.

11 *Cockburn v Smith* [1924] 2 KB 119 at 129. See also *Duke of Westminster v Guild* [1985] QB 688 at 701C-E.

12 *Hargroves, Aronson & Co v Hartopp* [1905] 1 KB 472 at 477.

13 *Martins Camera Corner Pty Ltd v Hotel Mayfair Ltd* [1976] 2 NSWLR 15 at 26E.

14 *A. Prosser & Sons Ltd v Levy* [1955] 1 WLR 1224 at 1233.

15 *Sharpe v Manchester City Council* (1977) 5 HLR 71 at 76.

16 *Duke of Westminster v Guild* [1985] QB 688 at 702E-F. See [1985] Conv 66 (P. Jackson).

In the absence of personal injury or damage to property, however, the landlord owes no duty of care to avoid causing inconvenience or discomfort to his tenant. In *Collins v Northern Ireland Housing Executive*,[17] for example, Carswell J refused to hold a landlord authority guilty of actionable negligence in respect of the frequent malfunctioning in deepest winter of the heating system provided in its flats.

(ii) Damage caused by third parties   It is possible that a landlord may be liable in negligence even where the defect has been caused maliciously through vandalism committed by unknown third parties. In *Sheppard v Northern Ireland Housing Executive*,[18] the landlord authority, although aware of the problem, had failed to take effective action to prevent vandals from using access to air inlets on the roof of a block of flats as a means of obstructing soil pipes. Lord Lowry LCJ held the authority liable to a tenant for damage caused when her flat was flooded by sewage, expressly holding that the authority's tenants were 'neighbours in the *Donoghue v Stevenson* sense'.[19]

This liberal approach has not, however, been adopted by the English courts. In *King v Liverpool City Council*[20] the plaintiff was a tenant in a block of flats owned by the local authority. When the flat immediately above her flat became vacant, she requested the landlord authority to board it up so as to secure it against intruders. The landlord authority took no effective steps in this direction, with the result that on three occasions vandals broke into the vacant flat and damaged water pipes, thus allowing water to escape and cause damage in the plaintiff's flat. The Court of Appeal rejected the claim brought by the plaintiff in negligence. The Court confirmed that although there is no principle of law excluding negligence liability for damage caused by the deliberate wrongdoing of a third party, such liability can arise only where there is some special relationship between the defendant and the third party or where the injury to the plaintiff is the inevitable and foreseeable result of the defendant's act or omission.[1] In the instant case it had been found that, in view of the 'extensive area' of the local authority's responsibility and the 'regrettable, but established, social climate at present being experienced' in Liverpool,[2] it had not been 'possible for effective steps to be taken...which could defeat the activities of vandals.'[3] This finding operated, in the words of Purchas LJ, to 'restrict the ambit of the duty to take any positive steps to secure the property',[4] with the consequence that the landlord authority was not in breach of any duty owed to the plaintiff.[5]

17   [1984] 17 NIJB, Transcript, p 32f (ante, p 909).
18   [1984] 1 NIJB.
19   [1984] 1 NIJB, Transcript, p 4.
20   [1986] 1 WLR 890.
1   See *Home Office v Dorset Yacht Co Ltd* [1970] AC 1004 at 1030A-C, 1032D; *P. Perl (Exporters) Ltd v Camden LBC* [1984] QB 342 at 359C-E; *Paterson Zochonis Ltd v Merfarken Packaging Ltd* [1983] FSR 273 at 298ff per Robert Goff LJ.
2   [1986] 1 WLR 890 at 901B.
3   [1986] 1 WLR 890 at 901D. See *Smith v Littlewoods Organisation Ltd* [1987] 2 WLR 480 at 499F, where Lord Mackay of Clashfern accepted this argument as a complete vindication of the result in *King*. Lord Goff of Chieveley also regarded *King* as 'rightly decided' ([1987] 2 WLR 480 at 510C).
4   [1986] 1 WLR 890 at 901D-E.
5   [1986] 1 WLR 890 at 901E, 902B-E.

The decision in *King v Liverpool City Council* represents a substantial abrogation of a landlord's wider responsibility to protect the residential interests of his tenant. The judicial debate in this case, being conducted in almost metaphysical terms of autonomous action, control, and causation, served to obscure the simple point that the landlord authority—although fully apprised of the situation—had not even taken the relatively straightforward precaution of securing the adjacent vacant premises with effective plywood boarding or metal sheeting.[6] The outcome in *King* contrasts remarkably with a more enlightened philosophy which views the landlord-tenant relationship, particularly in the public sector, as involving the delivery of a 'package' of consumer utilities which include not least an element of security in the immediate neighbourhood of the tenanted property.

(iii) Damage caused by neighbours There is, however, no general duty of care which obliges a landlord to exercise diligence on behalf of one tenant in selecting only civilised tenants to live in neighbouring premises.[7] Nor, oddly enough, does the 'neighbour principle' of *Donoghue v Stevenson* require the landlord to enforce standards of good neighbourliness on behalf of one tenant as against other neighbouring tenants.[8]

(b) Defects existing at the commencement of the tenancy

A more controversial question relates to the increasingly strong impulse to impose negligence liability on a landlord in respect of defects present in the demised premises at the date of the letting. The argument in favour of fixing the landlord with such liability is forceful, particularly where the landlord has special knowledge of latent defects and concealed dangers of which the tenant, on taking the letting, could not have been expected to be aware.

In *Siney v Corporation of Dublin*,[9] the Irish Supreme Court acknowledged the traditional view against liability for initial defects, but held that the principle of *Donoghue v Stevenson* might apply where a landlord authority carelessly exercised statutory powers under a scheme of housing legislation which had been intended to confer benefit and protection on its tenants.[10] Thus the authority was liable in respect of an inherent ventilation defect which caused excessive condensation and the growth of fungus over the walls of the tenant's flat. *Siney*

---

6   [1986] 1 WLR 890 at 892C-G. Following the resulting flood in her flat the plaintiff tenant left to live with her sister until she was rehoused by the Council three months later. The Council then had the nerve to counterclaim for arrears of rent ([1986] 1 WLR 890 at 892G).
7   *Smith v Scott* [1973] Ch 314 at 322A-B, E-F; *O'Leary v LB of Islington* (1983) 9 HLR 81 at 87f.
8   *O'Leary v LB of Islington* (1983) 9 HLR 81 at 88.
9   [1980] IR 400 at 414f, 421f. See T. Kerr and R. Clark, (1980) 15 Ir Jur (NS) 32.
10   The approach of the Supreme Court was in large part a response to the increasing tendency of the English courts to afford a remedy in negligence in respect of physical injury and economic loss resulting from the carelessness of statutory bodies involved in controlling or certifying the quality of building operations (see eg *Dutton v Bognor Regis UDC* [1972] 1 QB 373 at 392B-D, 406H-407A; *Anns v Merton LB* [1978] AC 728 at 758D-F, 760G, 767A-B). It was, for instance, regarded as particularly relevant in *Siney v Corporation of Dublin* [1980] IR 400 at 414 that the landlord authority had exercised supervision over the design of the tenant's flat and had inspected it before granting the letting—supposedly to ensure that it was fit for human habitation.

has since been cited by the English Court of Appeal in *Rimmer v Liverpool City Council*,[11] in support of a more general movement away from the strictures of *Cavalier v Pope*.

(5) The landlord's liability for nuisance

There is no doubt that a tenant, being in possession or occupation of land, has locus standi to sue in respect of the tort of nuisance.[12] It has been less clear whether he may ever sue his landlord (as distinct from other tortfeasors). However, the courts now seem willing to entertain the possibility that the landlord has committed on premises retained or controlled by him a nuisance in respect of which his tenant may complain.[13]

(a) Acts of the landlord himself

It follows that an action in nuisance may lie where the acts of the landlord on his own land unduly interfere with the tenant's comfortable and convenient enjoyment of the demised premises.[14] Such acts would include the landlord's disconnection of water and electricity supplies and interference with washing and toilet facilities.[15] Likewise, a defect arising in that part of the premises still controlled by the landlord may constitute an actionable nuisance if damage is caused to the tenant's premises.[16]

(b) Acts of other tenants

It is well established that a landlord is not in general liable for a nuisance committed by his tenant, since the person to be sued in nuisance is the occupier of the property from which the nuisance emanates.[17] Thus a landlord bears no liability in nuisance simply because he grants a letting to a tenant whom he knows to be nuisance-prone.[18] Nor does any implied term in a tenancy make

---

11   [1985] QB 1 at 15A.
12   *Inchbald v Robinson* (1869) LR 4 Ch App 388 at 395ff; *Jones v Chappell* (1875) LR 20 Eq 539 at 543f.
13   *McCall v Abelesz* [1976] QB 585 at 599F; *Guppys (Bridport) Ltd v Brookling* (1984) 269 Estates Gazette 846 at 946. As indicated in the latter decision, the courts are even prepared to contemplate the award of exemplary damages for nuisance. See M.J. Russell, *Nuisance by Landlords*, (1977) 40 MLR 651.
14   See *Thompson-Schwab v Costaki* [1956] 1 WLR 335 at 338.
15   *Guppys (Bridport) Ltd v Brookling* (1984) 269 Estates Gazette 846.
16   See *Sharpe v Manchester City Council* (1977) 5 HLR 71 at 75f (invasion of cockroaches from service ducts); *Sheppard v Northern Ireland Housing Executive* [1984] 1 NIJB (blocked sewage pipe) (ante, p 912).
17   *Smith v Scott* [1973] Ch 314 at 321B. However, if the landlord either expressly or impliedly reserves a right to enter and repair the demised property, he retains a 'sufficient basis of control' to enable a nuisance liability to be fastened on him in respect of defects arising on the demised premises (see *Heap v Ind Coope and Allsopp Ltd* [1940] 2 KB 476 at 483; *Mint v Good* [1951] 1 KB 517 at 521, 527f; *Carter v Murray* [1981] 2 NSWLR 77 at 79F).
18   *Smith v Scott* [1973] Ch 314 at 321E-F. Here the landlord authority was held not liable in nuisance for the noise emerging from the home of one of its own tenants, not least because the latter's tenancy agreement expressly prohibited the committing of nuisance. However, the Court of Appeal has since pointed out that it could well have been argued that the landlord authority's non-enforcement of the tenant's contractual undertaking not to commit nuisance had resulted in the landlord's 'adopting his tortious behaviour' (see *Page Motors Ltd v Epsom and Ewell BC* (1982) 80 LGR 337 at 347f).

the landlord compellable to seek contractual remedies against another tenant who is nuisance-prone.[19]

A nuisance liability can arise in the landlord in respect of his tenants' activities only where he has either expressly or impliedly authorised a tenant to commit nuisance.[20] There is thus a possibility that a landlord's nuisance liability vis à vis one tenant may be founded on acts committed by other tenants in occupation of a different part of the landlord's property.[1] This may sometimes prove to be a potent mechanism of redress in disputes arising between neighbours in a crowded multiple residential context.[2] In *Sampson v Hodson-Pressinger*,[3] for instance, a tenant complained of the noise penetration caused by another tenant's quite normal use of an immediately superjacent, but defectively constructed, roof terrace. The Court of Appeal held the landlord liable in nuisance on the ground that, although he was not himself responsible for the construction of the terrace, he had nevertheless taken an assignment of the reversion in the knowledge that its faulty construction would cause disturbance to the plaintiff.[4]

(6) The landlord's liability under *Rylands v Fletcher*

The rule in *Rylands v Fletcher*[5] imposes a liability on the owner or controller of a dangerous 'thing' which escapes and does damage. There are obvious respects in which this form of tort liability may impinge on the standard of habitability of residential lettings. It is clear, for instance, that a landlord who allows water to overflow from his premises into those of his tenant is liable under the rule for damage caused by the escape.[6] There is in this sense a close nexus between the liability of a landlord under the rule in *Rylands v Fletcher* and his liability in negligence.[7] However, the courts have declined to accept that a tenant may invoke the rule in *Rylands v Fletcher* in order to make the landlord liable for the tortious acts of other tenants of his who live in the neighbourhood.[8] Noxious

---

19   *O'Leary v LB of Islington* (1983) 9 HLR 81 at 86.
20   *Harris v James* (1876) 35 LT 240 at 241; *Hilton v James Smith & Sons (Norwood) Ltd* (1979) 251 Estates Gazette 1063 at 1067f. It is sufficient that the nuisance is 'certain to result from the purposes for which thĕ property is let' (*Smith v Scott* [1973] Ch 314 at 321C). See also *Tetley v Chitty* [1986] 1 All ER 663 at 671e-f.
1   The landlord may even bear a liability in nuisance for acts committed by non-tenants. See eg *Sheppard v Northern Ireland Housing Executive* [1984] 1 NIJB (local vandals).
2   Another remedy for aggrieved tenants is to persuade their landlord to recover possession from the nuisance-prone tenant on the ground of misconduct. This may bring about the rather dire consequence that the evicted tenant is regarded as 'intentionally homeless' and does not therefore fall within the ambit of the local authority's statutory duty to house homeless persons. See eg *R v Salford City Council, ex parte Devenport* (1984) 82 LGR 89 at 97 (eviction by council on ground of failure to control violence and vandalism committed by children of problem family). See also *R v Swansea City Council, ex parte John* (1982) 9 HLR 56 at 61f (tenant 'acquiesced in' misconduct of alcoholic and violent cohabitee).
3   [1981] 3 All ER 710. See [1982] Conv 155; [1982] CLJ 38 (M. Owen).
4   [1981] 3 All ER 710 at 714j. The offending tenant upstairs was considered to be an entirely innocent party. Although she would have been strictly liable in damages for her nuisance, the Court was prepared to regard this as an appropriate case for complete indemnity from the landlord, who was made to pay £2,000 damages.
5   (1868) LR 3 HL 330.
6   See eg *Martins Camera Corner Pty Ltd v Hotel Mayfair Ltd* [1976] 2 NSWLR 15 at 27B.
7   Indeed in *Cockburn v Smith* [1924] 2 KB 119 at 133, Scrutton LJ based the landlord's negligence liability on a 'modified doctrine of *Rylands v Fletcher*'. See also *Duke of Westminster v Guild* [1985] QB 688 at 701F-H.
8   *Smith v Scott* [1973] Ch 314 at 321F-G.

neighbours (and the noise created by them) may escape and do damage, but they do not constitute dangerous 'things' likely to do mischief in the sense required by *Rylands v Fletcher*.

3. THE LANDLORD'S LIABILITY UNDER STATUTE

The limited innovation brought about at common law in *Smith v Marrable*[9] has been adopted and extended in certain statutory provisions relating to the residential fitness of tenancies. However, the extremely fragmented and piecemeal nature of these provisions has prompted the observation that the current legislation in respect of the environmental quality of housing is 'a dog's breakfast which badly needs to be overhauled and consolidated.'[10] In any event the restricted ambit of some of these provisions is often as remarkable as the tenor of their curial exposition.

(1) Implied terms as to fitness for human habitation

Section 8(1) of the Landlord and Tenant Act 1985,[11] which applies only to tenancies[12] at a low rent,[13] imposes two implied contractual terms in the letting of a dwelling-house.[14] These terms comprise a condition that the house is 'fit for human habitation at the commencement of the tenancy' and a further (and rather more significant) undertaking that the house 'will be kept by the landlord fit for human habitation during the tenancy'.[15]

(a) Purpose

In *Summers v Salford Corporation*[16] the House of Lords recognised the forerunner of section 8(1) as being aimed at 'social amelioration', and as having been 'designed for the purpose of compelling landlords of small dwellings such as are

9   (1843) 11 M & W 5, 152 ER 693 (ante, p 903).
10 J. Perry and M. Gibson, *Roof* (July/August 1981), p 23f. For an incisively critical view of the English strategy for housing renewal, see J.N. Hawke and G.A. Taylor, [1984] JSWL 129; D. Hughes, [1984] JSWL 137.
11 This provision originated in Housing of the Working Classes Act 1890, s 75, and subsequently appeared in an extended form in Housing, Town Planning etc Act 1909, s 15(1), Housing Act 1936, s 2(1) and Housing Act 1957, s 6(2). The section applies equally to a tenancy of part of a house (Landlord and Tenant Act 1985, s 8(6)(a)), and applies just as readily to a statutory tenancy as to a contractual tenancy (see Rent Act 1977, s 3(1), although compare *Strood Estates Co Ltd v Gregory* [1936] 2 KB 605 at 624f).
12 Local authority tenancies are included (*R v Cardiff City Council, ex parte Cross* (1983) 81 LGR 105 at 115f).
13 Landlord and Tenant Act 1985, s 8(4). This exclusion is designed to prevent the section from applying to long leases at a low ground rent. To the disadvantage of the tenant, the landlord may include rates and other outgoings for which he is responsible in determining whether the rent falls within the statutory limits (*Rousou v Photi* [1940] 2 KB 379 at 385). See J.I. Reynolds, (1974) 37 MLR 377 at 383.
14 See *O'Brien v Robinson* [1973] AC 912 at 927B-D.
15 Section 8(1) has no application to a tenancy for more than three years granted upon terms that the tenant puts the premises into a condition reasonably fit for human habitation (Landlord and Tenant Act 1985, s 8(5)).
16 [1943] AC 283 at 293, 297.

normally inhabited by the working classes to see that their tenants are properly and decently housed.'[17] The overtly protective nature of this social legislation is underscored by the fact that the implied terms cannot be excluded by express contractual provision.[18] The statutory terms are intended to 'protect working people by a compulsory provision, out of which they cannot contract, against accepting improper conditions.'[19]

(b) Relevant standard

For the purpose of section 8(1), a house is 'unfit for human habitation' only if it is 'not reasonably suitable for occupation' by reason of one or more of a number of stated defects, which include its condition of repair, stability, freedom from damp, internal arrangement, natural lighting, ventilation, water supply, and drainage, sanitation and cooking facilities.[20] As Lord Wright pointed out in *Summers v Salford Corporation*,[1] '[t]he words of the Act are meant to be wide and elastic, because they are to be applied to the needs and circumstances of poor people living in confined quarters.' The court, he added with revealing candour, 'has to condescend to realise what these are.' Thus, in the *Summers* case itself the landlord's statutory obligation was held to have been breached where a broken sash-cord had the effect of jamming a bedroom window, thereby impairing ventilation.[2] In *Stanton v Southwick*,[3] however, a house which had been overrun by rats was not considered unfit for human habitation. It was found that the rats did not live and breed in the house itself, but were merely accustomed to enter it from the sewer outside.[4]

(c) Limitations

Section 8(1) has other severe limitations. The landlord's obligation arises only when he is notified of the relevant defect.[5] Moreover, the section has no application if the property cannot be rendered fit for human habitation at reasonable expense.[6] The statutory rent limits now exclude from the section all

17 As Salter J observed in *Jones v Geen* [1925] 1 KB 659 at 668, 'the standard of repair required...is naturally...a humble standard'. Quite how humble appears in another judgment of Salter J in *Stanton v Southwick* [1920] 2 KB 642 at 646 (infra).

18 Landlord and Tenant Act 1985, s 8(1).

19 *Summers v Salford Corporation* [1943] AC 283 at 293.

20 Landlord and Tenant Act 1985, s 10.

1 [1943] AC 283 at 294.

2 [1943] AC 283 at 297f. See, however, *Wainwright v Leeds City Council* (1984) 270 Estates Gazette 1289 at 1290, where Dunn LJ observed that a house pervaded by damp was not 'unfit for human habitation'.

3 [1920] 2 KB 642 at 646.

4 Salter J thought that the statutory term would be breached only if the rats 'were regularly there and, as it were, formed part of the house.' Even by 1942 the House of Lords had doubts as to whether this decision was correct (see *Summers v Salford Corporation* [1943] AC 283 at 295).

5 *Morgan v Liverpool Corporation* [1927] 2 KB 131 at 141, 143, 150f, 153; *McCarrick v Liverpool Corporation* [1947] AC 219 at 229f. The notice requirement is not statutory in origin! It seems to be a superadded condition supplied by the courts on the ground of 'business efficacy' (see *McCarrick* at 224, 232), and is particularly difficult to justify in view of the express conferment on the landlord of a statutory right of entry for the purpose of inspection (Landlord and Tenant Act 1985, s 8(2)). See J.I. Reynolds, (1974) 37 MLR 377 at 387ff; *Gaul v King* (1980) 103 DLR (3d) 233 at 241f.

6 *Buswell v Goodwin* [1971] 1 WLR 92 at 97A. See J.I. Reynolds, (1974) 37 MLR 377 at 384, but compare M.J. Robinson, (1976) 39 MLR 43. On the issue of 'reasonable expense', compare Housing Act 1985, s 189(1) (post, p 928).

but the oldest and very poorest residential lettings,[7] in relation to which total demolition rather than repair almost inevitably represents the less expensive alternative.[8] So far as the tenant is concerned, the scope of section 8(1) is disastrously circumscribed, but where a breach does occur the tenant is entitled to withhold the payment of rent, and he (but not other members of his family[9]) may sue for damages for breach of the implied contractual term.[10]

In view of the virtually ineffective role of section 8(1), more attention has focused on another statutory provision designed to secure decent housing conditions for tenants.

(2) Implied covenant for repair and maintenance

Certain important obligations of repair and maintenance are imposed by section 11(1) of the Landlord and Tenant Act 1985.[11] These obligations take the form of an implied covenant[12] on the part of the landlord in a lease of a dwelling-house for a term of less than seven years.[13]

(a) Content of the implied covenant

Under section 11(1) the landlord impliedly undertakes to keep in repair[14] the 'structure and exterior' of the dwelling-house.[15] The 'structure' includes the walls of the demised premises and even a large plate-glass window.[16] The

7   In relation to tenancies granted on or after 6 July 1957, the annual rent limit is £80 in London and £52 elsewhere (Landlord and Tenant Act 1985, s 8(4)). This limit has—rather incredibly—remained unchanged for 20 years, even though, as Lawton LJ pointed out in *Quick v Taff Ely BC* [1986] QB 809 at 821D-E, the present day equivalents allowing for inflation would be at least six times greater. There is an overwhelming case for a new statutory definition of 'low rent' (*Quick v Taff Ely BC,* supra at 817B, 821E). See also *R v Cardiff City Council, ex parte Cross* (1983) 81 LGR 105 at 116.
8   Section 8(1) has no application to a dwelling which a local housing authority is using to provide short-term accommodation pending demolition, provided that accommodation is 'adequate for the time being' (Housing Act 1985, s 302(c)). On the housing standard envisaged by section 8, see generally (1977) LAG Bulletin 206 (D. Ormandy).
9   *Ryall v Kidwell & Son* [1914] 3 KB 135 at 140f, 143. See J.I. Reynolds, (1974) 37 MLR 377 at 381f.
10   *Walker v Hobbs & Co* (1889) 23 QBD 458 at 460.
11   This provision was previously contained in Housing Act 1961, ss 32, 33.
12   A 'covenant' differs from a 'condition' (cp Landlord and Tenant Act 1985, s 8(1)), in that breach of a 'condition' by the landlord (as distinct from a breach of 'covenant') entitles the tenant to terminate the tenancy forthwith, rather than simply to sue for damages or other remedy (see *Surplice v Farnsworth* (1844) 7 Man & G 576 at 584f, 135 ER 232 at 235f).
13   Landlord and Tenant Act 1985, s 13(1). Section 11(1) applies only to leases granted on or after 24 October 1961, and there is a further specific exclusion of tenancies within the Agricultural Holdings Act 1948 (Landlord and Tenant Act 1985, s 14(3)) and of certain business tenancies within Part II of the Landlord and Tenant Act 1954 (Landlord and Tenant Act 1985, s 32(2)).
14   The obligation to 'keep' in repair implies an obligation to restore the premises to a state of repair if they are in a state of disrepair at the date of grant of the tenancy (*Liverpool City Council v Irwin* [1977] AC 239 at 269F-G). If the landlord executes repairs pursuant to section 11(1), he must also make good consequential damage to the decorative order of the dwelling-house (*Bradley v Chorley BC* (1985) 17 HLR 305 at 308f).
15   Landlord and Tenant Act 1985, s 11(1)(a). This obligation extends expressly to drains, gutterings and external pipes.
16   *Boswell v Crucible Steel Co* [1925] 1 KB 119 at 122f. However most domestic windows will normally fall under the tenant's duty to repair (Landlord and Tenant Act 1985, s 11(2)(a)). For an argument that the landlord may be responsible under section 11(1) to replace windows damaged by vandals, see D. Hoath, *Damage caused by Vandalism: Responsibility as between Landlord and Tenant,* (1986) LAG Bulletin 22.

'exterior' includes steps and flagstones giving access to the house,[17] but not a patio in the back-yard.[18] The roof of a building, even though not strictly part of the demised premises, can in some circumstances constitute part of the 'structure' or 'exterior' in respect of a flat on the top floor (but not a lower floor) of a building or block of flats.[19]

The landlord also impliedly undertakes under section 11(1) to keep in repair and 'proper working order' installations for the supply of water, gas and electricity,[20] facilities for sanitation,[1] and installations for space heating and heating water.[2] A breach of this covenant is instantly committed by any landlord who cuts off the supply of gas or electricity as a means of harassment of the tenant.[3]

(b) Range of application

Although relevant only to short leases of less than seven years,[4] section 11(1) applies not merely to legal leases, but also to equitable leases,[5] local authority tenancies,[6] and leases which are determinable at the landlord's option before the expiration of seven years from the commencement of the term.[7] The landlord's implied covenant cannot normally be excluded by contrary contractual provision.[8] The repairing obligation may even arise outside the circumstances defined in the statute if the landlord, by demanding an enhanced rent on the basis that the Act applies, has thereby estopped himself from denying that a tenant is protected under section 11(1).[9]

17 *Brown v Liverpool Corporation* [1969] 3 All ER 1345 at 1346I.
18 *Hopwood v Cannock Chase DC* [1975] 1 WLR 373 at 377H-378A, 378C-D.
19 *Douglas-Scott v Scorgie* [1984] 1 WLR 716 at 721C-D; [1984] JSWL 228 (M.A. Jones)); [1984] Conv 229.
20 Landlord and Tenant Act 1985, s 11(1)(b). The obligation to repair and maintain water installations does not imply any covenant by the landlord to lag water pipes. See *Wycombe AHA v Barnett* (1982) 264 Estates Gazette 619 at 621, but compare *Stockley v Knowsley MBC* (1985) 17 HLR 376 at 378f. Curiously, the tenant's failure to lag the pipes himself does not seem to be a breach of his duty to act in a 'tenant-like manner' (see (1983) 127 SJ 627 (D.W. Williams)).
1 Landlord and Tenant Act 1985, s 11(1)(b). It is irrelevant that the facilities, whether or not by reason of inherent design defect, have never been in 'proper working order'. See *Liverpool City Council v Irwin* [1977] AC 239 at 257E, 264C-D, 270A, C-D (£5 damages for faulty lavatory cistern).
2 Landlord and Tenant Act 1985, s 11(1)(c). See *Taylor v Knowsley BC* (1985) *Times*, 26 March (£100 awarded for loss of hot water for five months).
3 *McCall v Abelesz* [1976] QB 585 at 594C-D.
4 The landlord's implied covenant thus has no application to a 99 year lease of a residential flat (see eg *Gordon v Selico Co Ltd* [1985] 2 EGLR 79 at 80H-J).
5 *Brikom Investments Ltd v Seaford* [1981] 1 WLR 863 at 867E. See [1981] Conv 397.
6 *Wycombe AHA v Barnett* (1982) 264 Estates Gazette 619 at 621. See *R v Cardiff City Council, ex parte Cross* (1983) 81 LGR 105 at 115; *Wainwright v Leeds City Council* (1984) 270 Estates Gazette 1289 at 1290; *Taylor v Knowsley BC* (1985) 17 HLR 376 at 378f (see (1986) 136 NLJ 78 (H.W. Wilkinson)). In the case of a 'secure tenancy' the landlord is now obliged to inform the tenant 'in simple terms' of the landlord's statutory repairing covenant (Housing Act 1985, s 104(1)(c)). It seems that if the landlord is the Crown (in the form of a government department), Housing Act 1985, s 11(1) has no application (see *Department of Transport v Egoroff* (1986) 278 Estates Gazette 1361).
7 Landlord and Tenant Act 1985, s 13(2)(b). See eg *Sopwith v Stutchbury* (1983) 17 HLR 50 at 61f. Section 13(2)(b) effectively brings periodic tenancies within section 11(1).
8 Landlord and Tenant Act 1985, ss 11(4), 12(1). See, however, section 12(2).
9 *Brikom Investments Ltd v Seaford* [1981] 1 WLR 863 at 869C-D. The estoppel doctrine is discussed in Chapter 13 (ante, p 386).

(c) Requirement of notice

As in the case of section 8(1) of the Landlord and Tenant Act 1985, no liability arises for the landlord under section 11(1) unless and until he is notified of the relevant defect.[10] Once again, this notice requirement seems to have no statutory origin.[11] Nevertheless it has been preserved in the caselaw even though, in the words of Sir John Donaldson MR in *McGreal v Wake*,[12] it 'penalises the conscientious landlord and rewards the absentee.' What the Master of the Rolls did not say was that the person most heavily penalised by the notice requirement is, of course, the tenant himself. Its effect is to preclude the tenant from relief under the implied statutory covenant where injury or loss has resulted suddenly from a latent and previously invisible defect.[13]

(d) Limitations on the scope of the duty

Once again, the statutory obligations imposed on the landlord have been accorded only a limited utility in promoting adequate housing conditions for tenants. The landlord's implied covenant does not extend to the common parts of tenanted property (eg stairways and lifts in blocks of flats),[14] or to external walls of the building which are not also walls of the tenant's own premises,[15] since such areas are not strictly the subject matter of any letting to the tenant.[16] Nor does the landlord's implied covenant cover any defect which the tenant himself should remedy by virtue of his duty to use the premises in a tenant-like manner.[17] The landlord is under no duty to rebuild or reinstate the premises in the case of destruction or damage by fire, tempest, flood or 'other inevitable accident'.[18]

---

10   *O'Brien v Robinson* [1973] AC 912 at 926A, 930B. The notice need not come directly from the tenant. In *McGreal v Wake* (1984) 269 Estates Gazette 1254 at 1256, the Court of Appeal held it to be sufficient that the tenant had complained to his local council, which then served on the landlord a 'repair notice' under what is now Part VI of the Housing Act 1985 (post, p 926). However, it has not yet been decided whether a landlord's knowledge arising entirely *aliunde* the tenant fixes the statutory obligation on the landlord (see *O'Brien v Robinson* [1973] AC 912 at 928G). Given the fragile status of the notice requirement in the first place, it is highly arguable that knowledge from any source should be sufficient (see Law Commission, *Report on Obligations of Landlords and Tenants* (Law Com No 67, 11 June 1975), para 122ff). It is clear that knowledge acquired by the landlord's employee is imputed to the landlord (*Sheldon v West Bromwich Corporation* (1973) 25 P & CR 360 at 363f). See also *Dinefwr BC v Jones* (1987) *Times*, 27 June.

11   See the critical view expressed by J.I. Reynolds, (1974) 37 MLR 377 at 386ff, but compare M.J. Robinson, (1976) 39 MLR 43 at 49ff.

12   *McGreal v Wake* (1984) 269 Estates Gazette 1254. See [1984] Conv 229.

13   See eg *O'Brien v Robinson* [1973] AC 912 at 915G–926A (collapsing ceiling). The imposition of a notice requirement has not been thought necessary in relation to parallel legislation in other jurisdictions (see eg *Gaul v King* (1980) 103 DLR (3d) 233 at 242).

14   *Liverpool City Council v Irwin* [1977] AC 239 at 257D–E, 270A.

15   *Campden Hill Towers v Gardner* [1977] QB 823 at 834F–G.

16   On this basis it has even been said that the landlord's statutory covenant does not apply, for instance, to the maintenance of a boiler in the basement of a block of flats which heats the water supplied to all the flats in the building (*Campden Hill Towers v Gardner* [1977] QB 823 at 835C, H). See (1979) 129 NLJ 691 (D.J. Hughes), and compare *Douglas-Scott v Scorgie* [1984] 1 WLR 716 at 721C–D.

17   Landlord and Tenant Act 1985, s 11(2)(a).

18   Landlord and Tenant Act 1985, s 11(2)(b).

(e) Limitations on the concept of 'repair'

It is elementary, in terms of the covenant implied by section 11(1), that the landlord is under no obligation to do anything at all 'until there exists a condition which calls for repair.'[19] The concept of 'repair' has caused enormous difficulty.

(i) Disrepair does not include loss of amenity In construing the concept of 'repair', the courts have imposed the unfortunate limitation that 'disrepair is related to the physical condition of whatever has to be repaired, and not to questions of lack of amenity or inefficiency.'[20]

Thus, in *Quick v Taff Ely BC*,[1] the Court of Appeal held the implied statutory covenant substantially inapplicable to a council house where 'very severe condensation' had rendered the living conditions of the tenant and his family 'appalling'.[2] The Court rejected the argument that disrepair comprised any state which is 'inherently inefficient for living in or ineffective to provide the conditions of ordinary habitation'.[3] The ample evidence of extensive condensation damage to bedding, clothing and furniture was, in the Court's view, irrelevant in the absence of any 'evidence at all of physical damage to the walls...or the windows'.[4] The landlord's statutory duty relates only to the 'structure and exterior' of the dwelling-house. Here there was no damage to the tenant's walls, merely lots of mould on them!

In *Quick v Taff Ely BC* the Court of Appeal insisted on construing the implied statutory covenant for 'repair' in precisely the same way as if it had been contained in an express covenant in a private lease.[5] In particular, the Court was firmly of the opinion that the level of the landlord's statutory duty to repair is in no way accentuated or increased by reason of the fact that the landlord 'is a local authority, which is discharging a social purpose in providing housing for people who cannot afford it'.[6] The Court declined, however, to attach significance to the fact that the plaintiff's condensation problem would have been alleviated if he had kept the central heating on more continuously and at higher temperatures. Dillon LJ observed that '[i]f there is disrepair which the council is by its implied covenant bound to make good, then it is no answer for the council to say that, if the tenant could have afforded to spend more on his central heating, there would have been no disrepair, or less disrepair.'[7]

---

19 *Quick v Taff Ely BC* [1986] QB 809 at 821F per Lawton LJ. ('As a matter of the ordinary usage of English that which requires repair is in a condition worse than it was at some earlier time').
20 *Quick v Taff Ely BC* [1986] QB 809 at 818C-D per Dillon LJ.
1   [1986] QB 809. See [1986] Conv 45.
2   [1986] QB 809 at 815A. There was evidence of extensive fungus or mould growth; bedding, clothes and other fabrics had become mildewed and rotten; the living room was scarcely ever used because of the smell. It might be wondered why, under such circumstances, the local authority landlord should contest the tenant's claim. The horrifying reality appeared to be that the cost of remedying this kind of complaint across the entire range of the defendant local authority's housing stock would have been in the region of £9 million ([1986] QB 809 at 816F-G). The tenant in *Quick* was subsequently rehoused by the local authority.
3   [1986] QB 809 at 817F.
4   [1986] QB 809 at 819G.
5   [1986] QB 809 at 817H-818A.
6   [1986] QB 809 at 817G-H.
7   [1986] QB 809 at 820G-H. (The tenant here had been unemployed for five years and lived on supplementary benefit).

(ii) Liability for original defects   If the unsympathetic and restrictive application of commercial criteria to social housing needs operates to the disadvantage of the local authority tenant in one context, the same approach must surely operate in his favour in another context. It has tended to be the traditional view that the landlord's implied statutory covenant relates merely to the repair and maintenance of existing installations and facilities, and confers on the tenant no right to insist on the *improvement* of the property beyond its condition at the date of grant of his tenancy. In other words, section 11(1) does not supply a covenant to give 'a different thing' from that which the landlord granted with the tenancy.[8] On this basis, it is said, the landlord's implied undertaking cannot therefore apply to an inherent design defect in the tenant's housing.

This narrow approach is typified in *Wainwright v Leeds City Council*.[9] Here the Court of Appeal held that a landlord was under no obligation to provide a damp-proof course, even though this was the only practical means of eradicating the problem of damp and condensation in the tenant's house. The landlord's duty did 'not go beyond repairing the thing which was the subject of the demise, namely in this case a house without a damp-proof course.'[10] To add insult to injury, the Court rationalised this restrictive construction in terms of freedom of contract. Dunn LJ endorsed counsel's argument that 'the tenant had a choice whether to take an old house, or whether or not to take a house without any method of waterproofing and, having chosen to take the house that he did, he cannot ask the landlord to improve the house so that it is a different house from the house which he originally took.'[11] However, freedom of contract is generally spurious in the residential landlord-tenant context and particularly so in this case, where the tenant was in his 50s, unemployed and educationally subnormal. The Court nevertheless ruled that when he looked to his local council for accommodation, he had no right under section 11(1) to be provided with a house free of damp.[12]

A quite different approach to 'repair' may be adopted, however, if the statutory repairing covenant is to be construed on the model of express repairing covenants contained in private leases. In this area there has been a recent but fairly general recognition, stemming from *Ravenseft Properties Ltd v Davstone (Holdings) Ltd*,[13] that an express covenant to 'repair' can extend to the remedying of an inherent design defect if the 'repair' can be 'done in a sensible way' only 'by getting rid of the design defect'.[14]

It is significant that this new judicial trend in dealing with express repairing covenants was not cited to the Court of Appeal in *Wainwright v Leeds City*

8   See the parallel case of *Lister v Lane & Nesham* [1893] 2 QB 212 at 216f, as applied in *Pembery v Lamdin* [1940] 2 All ER 434 at 437H-438A; *Liverpool City Council v Irwin* [1976] QB 319 at 329A per Lord Denning MR.
9   (1984) 270 Estates Gazette 1289.
10   (1984) 270 Estates Gazette 1289 at 1290. Compare *Viney v Sunderland BC* (1983) LAG Bulletin (September), p 13 (failure of existing damp-proof course).
11   (1984) 270 Estates Gazette 1289 at 1290.
12   It is fair to record that the council had attempted, without success, to eliminate the damp problem by means other than the insertion of a damp-course. The real difficulty lay in the fact that the property was a century-old back-to-back terraced house in a run-down area of Leeds.
13   [1980] QB 12 at 22D. See [1979] Conv 429 (P.F. Smith); (1979) 129 NLJ 839 (H.W. Wilkinson). See also *Smedley v Chumley & Hawke Ltd* (1982) 44 P & CR 50 at 55f; *Elmcroft Developments Ltd v Tankersley-Sawyer* (1984) 270 Estates Gazette 140 at 142.
14   *Quick v Taff Ely BC* [1986] QB 809 at 822B-C.

Council, and that in *Quick v Taff Ely BC*,[15] Lawton LJ expressed approval of the *Ravenseft* decision. While accepting for the purpose of the statutory repairing covenant that 'neither a landlord nor a tenant is bound to provide the other with a better house than there was to start with', he pointed out that 'almost all repair work requires some degree of renewal' and that therefore 'problems of degree arise as to whether after the repair there is a house which is different from that which was let.'[16] This may well mark the inception of a somewhat broader and enlightened approach to the concept of 'repair' under section 11(1) of the Landlord and Tenant Act 1985.

(f) Limitations on the standard of repair

The standard of any repair required by the landlord's implied repairing covenant is relative to the 'age, character and prospective life of the dwelling-house and the locality in which it is situated.'[17] This means in practice that the repairing obligation is not measured objectively. The statutory standard of repair may tend towards a minimal obligation where the dwelling-house is so severely sub-standard that its expected use is confined to the short-term only.[18] Virtually derelict property with an extremely limited life span may thus be let to the poor and otherwise homeless on terms which effectively lie outside the reach of the landlord's statutory covenant. Where the property belongs to a local authority, it is often the case that with the express approval of the courts[19] the admitted shortcomings of the accommodation are traded off against a low rent.[20]

(3) Liability under the Defective Premises Act 1972

Section 4 of the Defective Premises Act 1972 contains an innovation which extends the right of residential occupiers to enjoy proper housing conditions.[1] This provision, which confers benefits only on tenants and not on licensees,[2] imposes on the landlord a statutory duty to take reasonable care to prevent personal injury or property damage which might be caused by defects in the state of the demised premises.

(a) Conditions under which the landlord's duty of care arises

The landlord's duty of care under section 4(1) arises only where he is responsible, under the terms of the tenancy, for the 'maintenance or repair' of

15 [1986] QB 809 at 822D-E.
16 [1986] QB 809 at 821H.
17 Landlord and Tenant Act 1985, s 11(3). 'The standard of repair may depend on whether the house is in a South Wales valley or in Grosvenor Square' (*Quick v Taff Ely BC* [1986] QB 809 at 821F per Lawton LJ).
18 Compare *Payne v Haine* (1847) 16 M & W 541 at 545, 153 ER 1304 at 1306; *Proudfoot v Hart* (1890) 25 QBD 42 at 51; *LB of Newham v Patel* (1978) 13 HLR 77 at 83ff. See D. Hughes, [1984] JSWL 137 at 148.
19 See eg *LB of Newham v Patel* (1978) 13 HLR 77 at 83, 85.
20 It can be argued that it would be entirely irresponsible for the local authority to spend public money—already in short supply—on any substantial repair of property scheduled for redevelopment.
1 See the critical observations of J.R. Spencer, [1975] CLJ 48 at 75.
2 *McDonagh v Kent AHA* (Unreported, Court of Appeal, 7 October 1985) (ante, p 445). Section 4 does, however, apply to local authority tenants (see *R v Cardiff City Council, ex parte Cross* (1983) 81 LGR 105 at 115).

the premises.[3] However, the Act construes such responsibility in broad terms. Even if under the terms of the tenancy the landlord has not expressly undertaken any repairing obligation, he is still taken to owe a duty of care within section 4(1) if he has expressly or impliedly[4] reserved for himself 'the right to enter the premises to carry out any description of maintenance or repair'.[5] There is thus an inherent trap in the common practice of including in leases an express reservation to the landlord of the right, in the event of the tenant's failure to carry out repairs under a repairing covenant, to enter and carry out the repairs himself. The landlord comes under the statutory duty of care, thereby exposing himself to a potential liability to third parties without giving him any effective remedy against his tenant.[6]

The landlord's duty of care arises only if he actually knew or if he 'ought in all the circumstances to have known' of the relevant defect.[7] However, it is not a precondition of the landlord's liability that the tenant should first notify him of the defect,[8] and this provides a significant respect in which the liability imposed on the landlord under the Defective Premises Act 1972 is wider than that now imposed under section 11(1) of the Landlord and Tenant Act 1985.[9] Moreover, there is an even more stringent provision in the Defective Premises Act 1972 prohibiting any attempt in the contract of tenancy to restrict or exclude the landlord's liability.[10]

(b) Content of the duty

The landlord's duty is not absolute.[11] His statutory duty is owed not to the world at large, but only to 'persons who might reasonably be expected to be affected by defects in the state of the premises'.[12] In relation to such persons, the landlord is obliged to take only 'such care as is reasonable in all the circumstances to see that they are reasonably safe from personal injury or from damage to their property caused by a relevant defect'.[13] Thus, for instance, in *Issitt v LB of Tower Hamlets*[14] the landlord authority was held free of liability for

3   Defective Premises Act 1972, s 6(3). Such responsibility includes any duties of repair or maintenance impliedly undertaken by the landlord pursuant to Landlord and Tenant Act 1985, ss 8(1), 11(1) (ante, pp 916, 918). See Defective Premises Act 1972, s 4(5).
4   It has been opined that under a local authority tenancy, the council always has an implied right to repair any part of its property and to enter demised premises for that purpose (see *Smith v Bradford Metropolitan Council* (1982) 4 HLR 86 at 91f).
5   Defective Premises Act 1972, s 4(4). However, section 4(4) stipulates that the extended coverage of the Act does not apply in relation to any defect which has arisen from, or continued because of, the tenant's own failure to carry out an express contractual obligation of his own.
6   See *Hamilton v Martell Securities Ltd* [1984] Ch 266 at 271D-F.
7   Defective Premises Act 1972, s 4(2). Constructive knowledge of defects may attach to a local authority whose appointed officials fail to detect the relevant defects by inspection (*Clarke v Taff Ely BC* (1980) 10 HLR 44 at 52f).
8   Section 4(2) makes it quite clear that the landlord's knowledge may arise 'whether as the result of being notified by the tenant or otherwise'.
9   Ante, p 920.
10 Defective Premises Act 1972, s 6(3). Compare Landlord and Tenant Act 1985, ss 11(4), 12 (ante, p 919).
11 Cf *Gaul v King* (1980) 103 DLR (3d) 233 at 243 ('The object of the legislation is to provide reasonable standards for rental premises. This does not mean that the Legislature intended the lessors should be insurers.')
12 Defective Premises Act 1972, s 4(1).
13 Defective Premises Act 1972, s 4(1).
14 Unreported, Court of Appeal Unbound Transcript 1115, 6 December 1983.

an accident to a child caused by a defective window catch, since, in the view of Griffiths LJ, 'any responsible parent' would have put a screw in rather than waiting for the council workman to call round.

It matters not whether the 'relevant defect' was present at the commencement of the tenancy or materialised only later.[15] However, the defect must have originated in, or continued because of, an 'act or omission by the landlord' which was a breach of his obligation to repair or maintain or would have been such if he had had the requisite knowledge.[16] The landlord is not therefore liable in respect of inherent design defects, which by their very nature are not attributable to any failure by him to repair or maintain.[17]

(4) Liability under the Health and Safety at Work etc Act 1974

Although it is not entirely clear that this result was contemplated by the legislature, it seems that certain aspects of the residential tenant's right to adequate housing conditions are indirectly secured under the Health and Safety at Work etc Act 1974.

Section 4(2) of this Act imposes a duty to take reasonable care to ensure that all means of access to and egress from the relevant premises, together with any 'plant or substance...provided for use' on those premises, are 'safe and without risks to health'. The duty bears only upon a person who has control of the relevant premises 'in connection with the carrying on by him of a trade, business or other undertaking (whether for profit or not)'.[18] Moreover, the statutory duty relates only to 'non-domestic premises' and only in favour of non-employees.[19] In *Westminster City Council v Select Management Ltd*,[20] it was held that the statutory duty was fully applicable in respect of the lifts in a block of residential flats managed by the defendant company,[1] and that improvement notices served on the company under the 1974 Act had therefore been properly served.[2] Taylor J pointed out that a lift constituted 'plant' for the purpose of the Act and ruled that the common parts of a block of flats were not 'domestic premises' within the meaning of the statute.[3]

This somewhat surprising application of the Health and Safety at Work etc Act 1974 thus provides a useful remedy for the residential tenant who finds that the management company which controls the common parts of his block of flats persistently ignores its responsibility in respect of lifts, stairways, and

---

15 Defective Premises Act 1972, s 4(3).
16 Defective Premises Act 1972, s 4(3).
17 See eg *Rimmer v Liverpool City Council* [1985] QB 1 at 7D-E (post, p 948); *McDonagh v Kent AHA* (Unreported, Court of Appeal, 7 October 1985)(post, p 949).
18 Health and Safety at Work etc Act 1974, s 4(4).
19 Health and Safety at Work etc Act 1974, s 4(1).
20 [1984] 1 WLR 1058 at 1061E-G. See (1985) 48 MLR 589 (B. Barrett); [1986] Conv 45.
1 Taylor J thought that the statutory duty would be raised in favour of workmen who came to repair the lifts or electrical installations ([1984] 1 WLR 1058 at 1061D).
2 Health and Safety at Work etc Act 1974, s 21. Taylor J thought that in relation to visitors to the flats a lift would constitute, within the statutory terms, 'plant...provided for their use' ([1984] 1 WLR 1058 at 1061E-F). The same must be true in relation to residents of the flats themselves. Compare *Liverpool City Council v Irwin* [1977] AC 239 (ante, p 907).
3 [1984] 1 WLR 1058 at 1060H-1061B.

electrical installations in the common parts of the buildings.[4] The tenant may request the proper officer of his local authority to serve an improvement notice under section 21 of the Act for the purpose of compelling the discharge of the company's responsibility.[5]

(5) Control of noise pollution

The residential amenity enjoyed by tenants is also subject to some measure of local authority supervision pursuant to the Control of Pollution Act 1974. A local authority has power under section 58(1) of this Act to serve an 'abatement notice' in respect of any 'noise amounting to a nuisance'.[6] This notice is served on the 'person responsible for the nuisance',[7] and may require the abatement of the nuisance and the undertaking of any necessary repair directed towards this end. It is a criminal offence to contravene the requirements of a section 58 notice 'without reasonable excuse'.[8]

The importance of section 58 in landlord-tenant relations was demonstrated in *A. Lambert Flat Management Ltd v Lomas*.[9] Here two tenants in a block of flats complained to the local authority about the excessive noise caused by the operation of the lifts in their block. The company which managed the flats entirely ignored the abatement notice served on it by the local authority, and was held to have been correctly convicted of the criminal offence created under the section.

(6) Repair notice under the Housing Act 1985

A further, and likewise administratively based, control over the environmental quality of tenanted accommodation is provided by the power of the local housing authority to issue repair notices in respect of sub-standard housing.

4   The setting up of the Nugee Committee in 1984 marked the increasing concern to remedy the apparent impotence of many private flat-owners in the face of indifferent or wholly cynical management of privately owned blocks of flats. The Committee reported with proposals which have since been incorporated in the Landlord and Tenant Act 1987. When this Act comes into force, it will give certain important forms of protection to the tenants of residential blocks. This protection will include the conferment of rights of first refusal on disposals by the landlord (s 1ff), the right to apply to court for the appointment of a manager in respect of the block (s 21ff), certain rights of compulsory acquisition of the landlord's interest (s 25ff), and other kinds of protection in relation to service charges (s 41f). See also [1985] Conv 162; [1986] Conv 12 (A.J. Hawkins).

5   Failure to comply with this notice may lead to criminal liability under Health and Safety at Work etc Act 1974, s 33(1).

6   The only relevance of the tort of nuisance in section 58 proceedings is to establish the level of noise which exists (*A. Lambert Flat Management Ltd v Lomas* [1981] 1 WLR 898 at 905F, 906F).

7   Control of Pollution Act 1974, s 58(2). The 'person responsible for the nuisance' is defined in Control of Pollution Act 1974, s 73(1), and may include a management company employed to administer lettings in a block of flats (see eg *A. Lambert Flat Management Ltd v Lomas* [1981] 1 WLR 898). If the 'person responsible' cannot be found, the notice may be served on the owner of the premises even though he has no previous knowledge of the nuisance (*A. Lambert Flat Management Ltd v Lomas*, supra at 905C-D). The person served with the notice has a right of appeal to the magistrates' court (Control of Pollution Act 1974, s 58(3)).

8   Control of Pollution Act 1974, s 58(4). Reasonable excuse includes such factors as illness, non-receipt of the notice and absence abroad, but not an allegation that the original abatement notice was invalid (*A. Lambert Flat Management Ltd v Lomas* [1981] 1 WLR 898 at 904E-F, 907B-C).

9   [1981] 1 WLR 898.

(a) Premises in a 'state of disrepair' (s 190)

It is open to an 'occupying tenant' to make representations directly to his local housing authority about the quality of his accommodation. He may complain that his 'house',[10] although not unfit for human habitation, is in such a 'state of disrepair' that *either* 'substantial repairs are necessary to bring it up to a reasonable standard',[11] *or* 'its condition is such as to interfere materially with the personal comfort of the occupying tenant'.[12] If satisfied that this is so, the housing authority has a discretion to serve a 'repair notice' requiring the execution of appropriate repair works within a reasonable time.[13]

A highly relevant, but not conclusive, factor influencing the exercise of this discretion is the question whether the expenditure required under section 190 bears a reasonable relation to the increased open market value of the refurbished property with a sitting tenant.[14] However, the courts are well aware of the huge windfall which comes the way of the owner who is able to free even a delapidated property of its sitting tenant.[15] The courts have been accordingly astute to counter any temptation for owners to allow property to fall into chronic disrepair in order later to evict unwanted protected or statutory tenants on the plea that the property is 'unfit for human habitation'.

In *Kenny v Kingston upon Thames Royal LBC*,[16] for instance, the Court of Appeal upheld a repair notice where the cost of the repairs required were almost double the anticipated increase in capital value. In view of the fact that the owner had been content to allow the property to sink gradually into decay, the Court had regard to 'policy considerations' favouring the protection of tenants and to the fact that the 'ultimate value of the building' would greatly exceed the cost of the repairs when the existing tenancy eventually came to an end.

(b) Premises 'unfit for human habitation' (s 189)

An even more far-reaching power is vested in the local housing authority in relation to housing which is considered 'unfit for human habitation'. It is open to any tenant—as indeed to any other person—to request a local justice of the peace or local parish or community council to refer an allegation of substandard housing to the proper officer of the local housing authority. On receiving a written complaint from any of these persons,[17] the local authority's

---

10 The statutory definition of a 'house' in Housing Act 1985, s 207, is not particularly helpful, and it is far from clear, for instance, that the term can be construed to include a privately owned block of purpose-built flats (see *Pollway Nominees Ltd v Croydon LBC* [1986] 3 WLR 277 at 280F-H per Lord Bridge of Harwich, where the point was conceded by counsel). Compare, however, *R v Lambeth LBC, ex parte Clayhope Properties Ltd* (1987) *Times*, 17 June, where the Court of Appeal held that a flat in a block was a 'part of a building' but was not a 'house'. Thus, although a leaseholder could be required to carry out repairs in his particular flat, he could not be required to carry out repairs to the roof and common parts of the block.
11 Housing Act 1985, s 190(1)(a) (formerly Housing Act 1957, s 9(1A)).
12 Housing Act 1985, s 190(1)(b).
13 Housing Act 1985, s 190(2). The housing authority has no power to require 'works of internal decorative repair'.
14 Compare Housing Act 1985, s 189(1) (infra).
15 See *Hillbank Properties Ltd v Hackney LBC* [1978] QB 998 at 1006H, 1010H-1011C.
16 (1985) 274 Estates Gazette 395 at 397.
17 The local authority may act even in the absence of formal complaint (Housing Act 1985, s 606(3)).

environmental health officer is required to inspect the premises in order to determine whether they are 'unfit for human habitation'.[18]

(i) Implications of a finding of unfitness   The criteria of unfitness for human habitation are, for this purpose, identical to those applied with reference to section 8(1) of the Landlord and Tenant Act 1985.[19] However, the mere fact that a dwelling is 'unfit for human habitation' does not mean that the occupier is without 'accommodation'. Such an occupier is not a 'homeless' person within the meaning of Part III of the Housing Act 1985,[20] and is therefore not entitled to invoke the statutory duty of the local housing authority to provide him with housing.[1] Nor is he entitled to claim that a dwelling which is 'unfit for human habitation' is necessarily 'prejudicial to health' and therefore a 'statutory nuisance' within the Public Health Act 1936.[2] His remedy lies instead in the power vested in his housing authority to issue a 'repair notice'.

(ii) The 'repair notice'   If, on report from the environmental health officer, the housing authority is satisfied that the house is indeed 'unfit for human habitation', the authority must serve a repair notice,[3] unless satisfied that the house is not capable of being rendered fit for human habitation 'at reasonable expense'.[4]

The repairs which the housing authority thus has power to order are not confined to work merely on the existing shell of a house, but can extend to improvement of the house by way of extension. The housing authority can require not only such repairs as the treatment of rotten timbers,[5] but can also, for instance, direct the construction of an entirely new bathroom and inside toilet.[6]

(iii) Reasonableness of expenditure on repairs   In determining the reasonableness of the expense of any repair, regard must be had to the estimated cost of the works necessary to render the premises fit for human habitation and the value

---

18   Housing Act 1985, s 606(2) (formerly Housing Act 1957, s 157(2)). This procedure is often the most effective means of forcing a local housing authority to take action in cases of severely sub-standard housing. According to Tom Hadden, the section 606 route is frequently 'the best and quickest method of securing a closing order and rehousing for the occupants' (*Housing: Repairs and Improvements* (London 1979), p 67).

19   Compare Housing Act 1985, s 604(1) with Landlord and Tenant Act 1985, s 10 (ante, p 917).

20   Ante, p 765.

1   *R v Hillingdon LBC, ex parte Puhlhofer* [1986] AC 484 at 717E, although see now Housing Act 1985, s 58(2A), as supplied by Housing and Planning Act 1986, s 14(2) (ante, p 766).

2   See *Salford City Council v McNally* [1976] AC 379 at 389C-D, where Lord Wilberforce observed that 'while a house which is by its condition "prejudicial to health" is likely to be "unfit for human habitation", the converse is not necessarily the case.'

3   Housing Act 1985, s 189(1) (formerly Housing Act 1957, s 9).

4   Housing Act 1985, s 189(1).

5   *Kimsey v Barnet LBC* (1976) 3 HLR 45.

6   See *Harrington v Croydon Corporation* [1968] 1 QB 856 at 869A. This case concerned an 'improvement notice' (post, p 931) rather than a 'repair notice', but relevance can be found in Salmon LJ's comment that building a new bathroom on to the existing dwelling would not 'make it into a different dwelling'. The essence of 'repair' likewise turns on whether the dwelling after the execution of works is 'the same dwelling' as before those works were carried out (ante, p 922).

which it is estimated the premises will have when the works are completed.[7] This deceptively simple formula has been construed to mean that premises are not repairable at 'reasonable expense' if the cost of the necessary works[8] exceeds the difference between the value of the freehold in its unrepaired state[9] and its value after repair,[10] as diminished by the presence of a sitting tenant.[11] The means and financial position of the owner are, in general, irrelevant to the issue of reasonableness.[12]

If the house cannot be rendered fit for human habitation 'at reasonable expense',[13] the housing authority must[14] adopt other more stringent measures. It must serve a 'time-and-place' notice aimed at inducing the owner voluntarily to undertake the necessary repairs irrespective of the cost to himself.[15] If this fails to produce the desired result, the authority must then make either a demolition or a closing order[16] or take steps towards the compulsory purchase of the condemned housing for purpose of providing short-term accommodation pending demolition.[17]

(iv) Immunity for local authority tenancies There exists one extremely unfortunate exception from the scope of the environmental health officer's

---

7   Housing Act 1985, s 206. See generally D.J. Hughes, (1978) 29 NILQ 122; D. Morgan, [1979] Conv 414; J.N. Hawke and G.A. Taylor, [1984] JSWL 129 at 131.

8   The cost to the owner must take into account such factors as lost interest on money borrowed to finance the repairs (*Kimsey v Barnet LBC* (1976) 3 HLR 45 at 65), loss of rent during repairs (*Kimsey v Barnet LBC*, supra at 53) increased rental value after repair (*Ellis Copp & Co v LB of Richmond upon Thames* (1976) 3 HLR 55 at 64f), and available grant aid (*Harrington v Croydon Corporation* [1968] 1 QB 856 at 870A-B). A local authority repairs grant is automatically available to any person on whom a repair notice is served under Housing Act 1985, ss 189, 190 (see Housing Act 1985, s 494(1)).

9   The freehold value of the property in its unrepaired state may sometimes tend towards zero (see *Kimsey v Barnet LBC* (1976) 3 HLR 45 at 52).

10 This formula is most clearly enunciated in *Kimsey v Barnet LBC* (1976) 3 HLR 45 at 52. The relevant value is the value of the freehold on the open market after the repair has been effected (rather than its investment value). See *Inworth Property Co Ltd v Southwark LBC* (1977) 3 HLR 67 at 70f. For the argument that this formula offers 'considerable scope for profit' to the owner and that the relevant comparison should be between the current vacant possession value and the repaired tenanted value, see (1982) 3 PLB 27.

11 *Kimsey v Barnet LBC* (1976) 3 HLR 45 at 52. See, however, *Hillbank Properties Ltd v Hackney LBC* [1978] QB 998 at 1006F-1007B, but compare now *Phillips v LB of Newham* (1982) 43 P & CR 54 at 56.

12 *Leslie Maurice & Co Ltd v Willesden Corporation* (1953) 3 HLR 12 at 15. See also *Hillbank Properties Ltd v Hackney LBC* [1978] QB 998 at 1008B-C, where Lord Denning MR envisaged that the court might quash or modify a repair notice served on 'a poor widow who has only one house which she lets out to bring in some rent.'

13 The effect of Housing Act 1985, s 189(1) is to create a presumption in favour of repair rather than demolition, but it has been recognised that 'questions of housing policy' are material to the decision whether to issue a repair notice under section 189(1) or a 'time-and-place' notice under section 264(1). See *R v Maldon DC, ex parte Fisher* (1986) 18 HLR 197.

14 The duty is mandatory (see *R v Kerrier DC, ex parte Guppys (Bridport) Ltd* (1976) 32 P & CR 411 at 418). See, however, Tom Hadden, op cit, p 71, for the view that 'no local authority makes a serious attempt to apply the letter of the law in this context'.

15 Housing Act 1985, s 264(1).

16 Housing Act 1985, s 265(1).

17 Housing Act 1985, s 300(1). Compulsorily purchased property can be used by the local authority for providing accommodation so long as it is 'of a standard which is adequate for the time being'. Such property is frequently used to relieve the pressures imposed on the local authority's housing stock by the statutory duty to house homeless persons (post, p 777).

power to condemn housing as 'unfit for human habitation'. The environmental health officer has been held to have no jurisdiction in relation to houses owned and controlled by the local authority itself within its own area.[18] The immunity thus conferred on local authorities is supposedly justified by the absurdity implicit in a local authority having to serve a repair notice upon itself. However, this exemption produces the quite appalling anomaly that the council tenant is placed in a much less advantageous position than the private tenant in terms of capacity to control the residential fitness of his accommodation.[19]

(c) Administrative enforcement by the housing authority

A repair notice under the Housing Act 1985 is served on the 'person having control of the house',[20] who then has a right of appeal to the county court.[1] If a repair notice is not complied with, the local housing authority may decide in its discretion to execute the necessary repairs itself[2] and to recover the cost from the defaulter.[3]

It is clear that the residential security of the tenant is gravely affected by the service of a repair notice. For this reason, the housing authority may serve a copy of the repair notice on the tenant as well as on the 'person having control of the house'.[4] There seems—somewhat anomalously—to be no provision for a similar service on the tenant where the premises are not repairable at reasonable expense and are therefore made the subject of a demolition or closing order.[5] However, in recent years the courts have allowed the tenant to challenge the housing authority's determination by way of judicial review, in

18   *R v Cardiff City Council, ex parte Cross* (1983) 81 LGR 105 at 114.
19   The council tenant is relegated to a complaint in relation to a 'statutory nuisance' under Public Health Act 1936, s 99 (post, p 933).
20   Housing Act 1985, ss 189(1), 190(1). For the purpose of both sections, the 'person having control of the house' is the person who is in actual or constructive receipt of the rack rent of the premises, ie, a rent not less than two-thirds of the full net annual value of the premises (Housing Act 1985, s 207). In a letting by a freeholder to an occupying tenant under a long lease at a ground rent below the rack rent, the 'person having control' is the tenant rather than the freeholder (*Pollway Nominees Ltd v Croydon LBC* [1986] 3 WLR 277 at 282E per Lord Bridge of Harwich, 287D-E per Lord Goff of Chieveley). This construction, although probably entirely unforeseen by Parliament, may well compel the 'startling and impractical' result that the 'person having control of the house' is a collective entity consisting of 43 persons having interests in different parts of a mansion block (see *Pollway Nominees Ltd v Croydon LBC* [1986] 3 WLR 277 at 285C-D, 286B).
1   Housing Act 1985, s 191(1). An unfit house with vacant possession is generally of greater value to the landlord than a fit house subject to the rights of a sitting tenant (see *Hillbank Properties Ltd v Hackney LBC* [1978] QB 998 at 1006D, 1010H-1011C). There is a strong incentive for the landlord to contend that the property, while 'unfit for human habitation', is not repairable at reasonable cost. If this ground of appeal is upheld, a demolition or closing order may be made, which of course terminates the rights of existing tenants to Rent Act protection. In the case of a successful appeal against a repair notice under Housing Act 1985, s 189, the housing authority may purchase the property, if necessary by compulsory means (Housing Act 1985, s 192(1)).
2   Housing Act 1985, s 193(1). However, the authority must exercise a genuine discretion before executing works at the owner's expense, otherwise the cost cannot be recovered from that owner (*Elliott v Brighton BC* (1981) 258 Estates Gazette 441 at 445f).
3   Housing Act 1985, s 193(3), Sch 10. In some cases the 'person having control of the house' will himself be a tenant, in which case he may be able to recover from the landlord some portion of any cost met by him in complying with the repair notice (Housing Act 1985, s 199(1)).
4   Housing Act 1985, ss 189(3), 190(3).
5   Housing Act 1985, s 268(1).

order that the tenant should not be denied the opportunity to assert that his home *is* repairable at reasonable cost.[6]

(7) Improvement notice under the Housing Act 1985

The Housing Act 1985 contains another measure which is aimed at raising housing standards and enhancing the quality of life enjoyed both by tenants and by other residential occupiers. Part VII of the Act empowers the local housing authority to serve 'improvement notices' in relation to dwellings within its area.[7] This power differs from the statutory controls under Part VI of the Housing Act 1985[8] and under the Public Health Act 1936,[9] in that an improvement notice need not be premised on any finding that a dwelling is in a state of disrepair[10] or is unfit for human habitation.

(a) General conditions for the service of an improvement notice

There are three general conditions for the service of an improvement notice under Part VII of the Housing Act 1985.

(i) Lack of standard amenities The basic precondition for the service of an improvement notice is that a dwelling lacks 'one or more of the standard amenities'.[11] These 'standard amenities' are defined[12] as including a fixed bath or shower,[13] a wash-hand basin and a sink (all supplied by hot and cold water), together with a water closet.[14] A 'standard amenity' is present in a dwelling only if provided for the 'exclusive use' of the occupants of that dwelling. Thus, if the tenants of two dwellings share a bathroom or lavatory, both dwellings are deficient in a standard amenity.[15] The objection that to require a bathroom for every dwelling consisting of a single room would 'set an inconceivably high standard' has been dismissed by the courts. Any danger of setting too high a standard is mitigated by the fact that the burden imposed on the owner is expressly limited to 'reasonable expense'.[16]

---

6 *R v LB of Ealing, ex parte Richardson* (1982) 4 HLR 125 at 130.
7 Previously Housing Act 1974, s 85ff.
8 Ante, p 926.
9 Post, p 933.
10 Housing Act 1985, s 209(a).
11 Housing Act 1985, s 209(a).
12 Housing Act 1985, ss 237, 508(1).
13 If it is not reasonably practicable for the fixed bath or shower to be in a bathroom, such installations can be positioned in any other part of the dwelling except a bedroom (Housing Act 1985, s 508(1) (Note 2)). Even in 1984, 29 per cent of all tenants of private rented accommodation still lacked sole use of a bath or shower (see Central Statistical Office, *Social Trends No 16* (London 1986), p 135 (Table 8.6).
14 A water closet need not be in the dwelling itself, but should be reasonably accessible (Housing Act 1985, s 508(1) (Note 3)). Again the most recent available figures (for 1984) indicate that 29 per cent of all tenants of private rented accommodation still lack sole use of an inside toilet (see Central Statistical Office, *Social Trends No 16* (London 1986), p 135 (Table 8.6).
15 *F.F.F. Estates Ltd v LB of Hackney* [1981] QB 503 at 520B-C.
16 See *F.F.F. Estates Ltd v LB of Hackney* [1981] QB 503 at 518H-519A.

(ii) Improvement at reasonable expense   Under section 209(b) of the 1985 Act, the dwelling must be capable of improvement 'at reasonable expense' to either the 'full standard'[17] or, failing that, to the 'reduced standard'.[18] The criterion of 'reasonable expense', although not defined in Part VII, is interpreted in a manner broadly similar to the construction applied in relation to section 189 of the 1985 Act.[19] Thus the courts have tended to measure the cost of the relevant improvements in relation to the value of the improved dwelling 'as a saleable asset in the hands of the landlord'.[20] However, by calculating the latter value as a reduced figure in view of the continuing occupation of sitting tenants, it is often the case that the increased market value of the property is found not to justify the cost of improvements.[1] In such circumstances the residential occupiers are denied the benefits afforded by compulsory improvement, and the inevitable result is not the amelioration of housing standards but the gradual delapidation of the property to the point where it is 'unfit for human habitation'. The owner can then sell the property with vacant possession and recover a large capital profit.[2]

(iii) Age of the building   The third general condition for the service of an improvement notice is that the dwelling must have been provided, either by erection or by the conversion of a building already in existence, before 3 October 1961.[3]

(b) Procedure of service

An 'occupying tenant'[4] of a dwelling which is not in a general improvement area[5] or a housing action area[6] may make written representations to the local housing authority regarding the lack of standard amenities in his dwelling.[7] If satisfied that the general conditions for the service of an improvement notice are met, the authority must either serve a provisional improvement notice on the person having control of the building[8] or give the tenant written reasons for

---

17   The 'full standard' is attained where the dwelling is provided with all the standard amenities for the exclusive use of its occupants, is in 'reasonable repair', conforms with any relevant government requirement with respect to thermal insulation, is 'in all other respects fit for human habitation', and is likely to have a lifespan as a dwelling of at least 15 years (Housing Act 1985, s 234(1)).

18   The 'reduced standard' is attained where the local housing authority dispenses in respect of a specified property with any of the conditions required for the attainment of the 'full standard' (Housing Act 1985, s 234(2)). The requirement of 'standard amenities' cannot be dispensed with in the case of a 'house in multiple occupation' (post, p 938) (Housing Act 1985, s 234(3)).

19   Ante, p 928.

20   *F.F.F. Estates Ltd v LB of Hackney* [1981] QB 503 at 525E.

1   *F.F.F. Estates Ltd v LB of Hackney* [1981] QB 503 at 525F.

2   For criticism of this formula in the context of section 189 of the Housing Act 1985, see (1982) 3 PLB 27 (ante, p 929), and compare the more realistic approach applied under section 190 in *Kenny v Kingston upon Thames Royal LBC* (1985) 274 Estates Gazette 395 at 397 (ante, p 927).

3   Housing Act 1985, s 209(c).

4   The procedure is not therefore available to licensees. It is also clear that no improvement notice may be served in respect of property owned by a local authority or other public or quasi-public body (Housing Act 1985, s 232(2)).

5   See Housing Act 1985, s 253.

6   See Housing Act 1985, s 239.

7   Housing Act 1985, s 212(1).

8   If the dwelling is situated in a general improvement area or a housing action area, the local housing authority may itself take the initiative in serving a provisional improvement notice (Housing Act 1985, s 210(1)).

not doing so.[9] The provisional notice specifies required improvements and nominates a 'time and place' at which the authority's proposals may be discussed by all concerned.[10] If negotiations do not lead to a voluntary undertaking to effect the appropriate improvements within 12 months of the tenant's first written representations, the authority may serve a final improvement notice requiring specified works to be done within a further period of 12 months.[11]

The person who has control of the dwelling has a right of appeal to the county court against service of the final improvement notice.[12] If the appeal is not upheld (or if no appeal is made), the improvement notice becomes operative.[13] The local housing authority must make an intermediate grant for works required in providing a dwelling with the standard amenities,[14] and is statutorily obliged to offer a loan to meet that part of the expenses of compulsory improvement not covered by grant aid.[15] In the event of non-compliance with the improvement notice, the local housing authority may perform the works of improvement itself,[16] and may recover the costs of doing so from the defaulter.[17]

(8) Intervention in the case of 'statutory nuisance'

The concept of 'statutory nuisance' provides a further ground on which a local authority may intervene in cases of alleged housing disrepair.[18]

(a) Definition

A 'statutory nuisance' arises, within the meaning of section 92 of the Public Health Act 1936, where any premises are 'in such a state as to be prejudicial to health or a nuisance'.[19] The situations thus covered include such eventualities

---

9   Housing Act 1985, s 212(3).
10 Housing Act 1985, s 213(1).
11 Housing Act 1985, ss 215(1), (2), 216(1). Care must be taken to ensure that the improvement notice contains the statutorily required information (see eg *Canterbury City Council v Bern* (1981) 44 P & CR 178 at 187ff). A final improvement notice is registrable as a local land charge (ante, p 112) (Housing Act 1985, s 215(4)).
12 Housing Act 1985, s 217. The county court has power in certain circumstances to order that a contribution towards the cost of the improvements be made by some third party who will benefit from the execution of the works (Housing Act 1985, s 217(5)). However, such a levy cannot be made in relation to a protected or statutory tenant (see *Harrington v Croydon Corporation* [1968] 1 QB 856 at 873B-874B, 882C-D).
13 Various forms of criminal liability attach to persons who obstruct the execution of works required by an improvement notice (see Housing Act 1985, ss 221(2), 223(1)).
14 Housing Act 1985, s 474(1)(a).
15 Housing Act 1985, s 228(1).
16 Housing Act 1985, s 220(1). The person having control has the right to demand that the local housing authority should purchase his interest in the dwelling (Housing Act 1985, s 227(1)).
17 Housing Act 1985, s 220(6), Sch 10.
18 See D.J. Hughes, (1976) 27 NILQ 1, 131, 233. For an excellent account, see J. Luba, (1982) LAG Bulletin 85.
19 See also Public Health Act 1936, s 343(1) (definition of 'prejudicial to health'). A 'statutory nuisance' also includes 'any accumulation or deposit which is prejudicial to health or a nuisance' (Public Health Act 1936, s 92(1)(c)). For the proper approach to be applied by magistrates, see *Salford City Council v McNally* [1976] AC 379 at 389F-390A. It is clear that medical evidence is not a *sine qua non* of establishing that premises are 'prejudicial to health' (*McCorley v Chief Executive of Birmingham City Council* (Unreported, Queen's Bench Divisional Court, CO/464/83, 12 January 1984)). A local authority may also be liable in damages where injury is caused by its failure to discharge its duty under Public Health Act 1936, s 72(2) to collect house refuse (see *Dear v Newham LBC* (1987) *Times*, 10 April.

as structural defects in houses, crumbling plaster,[20] the presence of toxic blue asbestos,[1] and blocked drains and lavatories.

A particular source of complaint in this area is the problem of damp and mould caused by domestic condensation.[2] It is clear that disrepair caused by damp can lead to a finding of 'statutory nuisance'.[3] However, the courts have been reluctant to allow the Public Health Act to be used as a forum for complaints which are more closely related to design defects in housing than to 'public health' complaints arising from housing conditions.[4] In *Dover DC v Farrar*,[5] for instance, a Divisional Court refused to apply the term 'statutory nuisance' to damp and decay caused where the local authority-installed heating system had, for many tenants, proved to be too expensive to run as intended. The tenants had turned to alternative means of heating which were cheaper but less effective in combatting condensation. However, this decision was later distinguished by another Divisional Court in *GLC v LB of Tower Hamlets*.[6] Here Griffiths LJ declared that where a property is, by reason of the peculiar aspects of its construction, 'wholly exceptionally vulnerable to condensation', the landlord cannot escape any liability for danger to the health of those living there 'by asserting that the occupants should have used wholly abnormal quantities of fuel.'[7]

The mere fact that the landlord is not in breach of any of his obligations as landlord, whether in tort or in contract,[8] constitutes 'persuasive' but by no means 'conclusive' evidence that the landlord is freed of responsibility for a 'statutory nuisance'.[9] It is clear, however, that the presence of a 'statutory nuisance' does not entitle the occupier to present himself before his local housing authority as a 'homeless' claimant for housing,[10] except where it is no longer 'reasonable for him to continue to occupy' the accommodation in question.[11]

(b) Complaint made by local authority

A complaint relating to a statutory nuisance may be made by any tenant (or other occupier) to the local authority's environmental health officer, who has

20   *Coventry City Council v Quinn* [1981] 1 WLR 1325 at 1328E-F.
1   *R v Camberwell Green Magistrates, ex parte Healey* (Unreported, Queen's Bench Divisional Court, CO/305/84, 10 October 1984).
2   For reference to the standard attempt by local authorities to pass dampness off as merely condensation—as if this mattered—see (1979) LAG Bulletin 190 (D. Ormandy). See also D. Watkinson, (1986) Legal Action 49.
3   *Patel v Mehtab* (1980) 5 HLR 78 at 83; *Coventry City Council v Quinn* [1981] 1 WLR 1325 at 1329E; *McCorley v Chief Executive of Birmingham City Council* (Unreported, Queen's Bench Divisional Court, CO/464/83, 12 January 1984).
4   Interference with 'comfort' does not bring a case within the 'health' limb of the Public Health Act 1936 (*Salford City Council v McNally* [1976] AC 379 at 389E).
5   (1980) 2 HLR 35 at 38.
6   (1983) 15 HLR 54 at 61.
7   In this case the tenant's flat was built on a raised level and was therefore exposed to the elements not only on three sides but also underneath. A finding of 'statutory nuisance' was upheld.
8   See eg Landlord and Tenant Act 1985, s 11(1) (ante, p 918).
9   *Birmingham DC v Kelly* (1985) 17 HLR 572 at 579f per Woolf J. See also *Clayton v Sale UDC* [1926] 1 KB 415 at 426.
10   This seems to follow from the decision of the House of Lords in *R v Hillingdon LBC, ex parte Puhlhofer* [1986] AC 484 at 517D-G, (ante, p 764). The operation of the homelessness provisions of Part III of the Housing Act 1985 is discussed in Chapter 21 (ante, p 760).
11   See Housing Act 1985, s 58(2A), to be supplied by Housing and Planning Act 1986, s 14(2).

power to serve on the owner of the premises an 'abatement notice' requiring that the condition be remedied.[12] If no remedial action is taken in response to the abatement notice or if, in the opinion of the local authority, the nuisance is likely to recur on the same premises, the authority must initiate the issue of a summons in the magistrates' court.[13] This court, if it upholds the complaint of statutory nuisance, has power to make either a 'nuisance order' requiring the nuisance to be abated[14] or an order prohibiting further residential use of a building until it has been rendered fit for human habitation.[15]

(c) Complaint made by individual tenant

If the local authority fails to institute proceedings for the abatement of a statutory nuisance, it is open to the aggrieved private individual[16] to lay a complaint before the magistrates' court under section 99 of the Public Health Act 1936.[17] If the complaint is found proved,[18] the court may then order the nuisance to be abated and may require the local authority itself to take steps to remove the nuisance at the owner's expense.[19] The owner does not abate the nuisance merely by removing the existing occupiers and thus causing the relevant property to be kept vacant.[20] Abatement requires positive action to be effected on the premises, although it is possible that abatement may be held to occur where a house has been 'effectively rendered incapable of being occupied, eg having all services permanently cut off and being boarded up prior to eventual demolition'.[1]

An obvious difficulty arises where the landlord against whom the complaint of 'statutory nuisance' is raised is the local authority itself. It is clear, however, that a local authority landlord may be the subject of a magistrates' court order and that such an order may properly require the local authority to execute specific works of repair in relation to the property.[2] Nevertheless, the courts have emphasised that there is a need for the magistrates' court to exercise its

---

12   Public Health Act 1936, s 93.
13   Public Health Act 1936, s 94(1). A fine may also be imposed (Public Health Act 1936, s 94(2)). It is a valid defence for the defendant to show that his act or default is not responsible for the continuance of the nuisance. See eg *Warner v LB of Lambeth* (1984) 15 HLR 40 at 51f, where a local authority tenant announced that she could not tolerate the conditions existing while the authority tried to repair her council house. She insisted that she wanted to be rehoused rather than repaired, but then turned down a series of offers of alternative local authority accommodation!
14   Public Health Act 1936, s 94(2).
15   Public Health Act 1936, s 94(2).
16   The section 99 procedure is available even to a local authority tenant (see eg *Coventry City Council v Doyle* [1981] 1 WLR 1325).
17   As to the contents of the information to be laid before the magistrates, see *Warner v Lambeth LBC* (1984) 15 HLR 40 at 51.
18   The relevant date for determining the existence of a statutory nuisance is the date of the hearing in the magistrates' court (*Coventry City Council v Doyle* [1981] 1 WLR 1325 at 1338B-C).
19   Public Health Act 1936, s 99. Any expenses reasonably incurred by the local authority in abating a nuisance covered by a nuisance order may be recovered from the owner of the property (Public Health Act 1936, s 96(1)). The successful complainant is also entitled to recover expenses incurred in bringing the section 99 proceedings (*Coventry City Council v Doyle* [1981] 1 WLR 1325 at 1338E-F).
20   *Lambeth LBC v Stubbs* (1980) 78 LGR 650 at 656, 660.
1   See *Coventry City Council v Doyle* [1981] 1 WLR 1325 at 1339E-F.
2   *Birmingham DC v Kelly* (1985) 17 HLR 572 at 579f.

jurisdiction under the Public Health Act 1936 'with discretion and common sense'.[3] It has been said that the magistrates 'should bear in mind the fact that a local authority...has very heavy housing responsibilities and the procedure under Part III of the Act must not be used as a method of obtaining for particular tenants benefits which they were well aware did not exist when they took the tenancies in question and which if they were provided could put those tenants in a favoured position in relation to other tenants who are also being housed by the authority.'[4]

(9) Overcrowding

One element which figures more prominently than most in detracting from the residential quality of life enjoyed by tenants is quite simply the factor of overcrowding. Fitness for human habitation tends to be inversely proportional to the number of occupants of a defined space, and there is therefore a strong call for legal control to be asserted over the number of tenants permissible in multiple residential living units.

There are essentially two sources of such control in modern English housing law. Both are now contained in the Housing Act 1985 and both are in terms applicable to tenants and licensees alike. However, since the effect of the House of Lords' decision in *Street v Mountford*[5] is to alter the distribution of residential occupiers significantly in favour of a tenancy classification, the control of overcrowding is dealt with here in the primary context of tenanted accommodation.

(a) Prohibition of statutory 'overcrowding'

The primary control in respect of overcrowded accommodation is contained in Part X of the Housing Act 1985.

(i) Definition of 'overcrowding' in Part X of the Housing Act 1985   Part X of the Housing Act 1985 confirms a statutory definition of 'overcrowding'.[6] In terms of this definition,[7] a 'dwelling'[8] is 'overcrowded' when the number of persons 'sleeping'[9] in the dwelling is such as to contravene *either* a 'room standard' *or* a 'space standard'. The 'room standard' is violated when the number of rooms 'available as sleeping accommodation'[10] is such that 'two persons of opposite sexes who are not living together as husband and wife must sleep in the same room.'[11] A child under the age of ten is left out of account for the purpose of this

3   See *Salford City Council v McNally* [1976] AC 379 at 390A.
4   *Birmingham DC v Kelly* (1985) 17 HLR 572 at 581 per Woolf J.
5   [1985] AC 809 (ante, p 449).
6   See Housing Act 1957, s 77(1).
7   Housing Act 1985, s 324.
8   A 'dwelling' is unhelpfully defined as 'premises used or suitable for use as a separate dwelling' (Housing Act 1985, s 343).
9   The concept of 'overcrowding' is, for some reason, related exclusively to the activity of sleeping. There is no 'overcrowding' if an excessive number of persons merely 'use' rather than sleep in the relevant dwelling (see *Somma v Hazelhurst and Savelli* [1978] 1 WLR 1014 at 1029A) (ante, p 447, post, p 998).
10   A room is 'available as sleeping accommodation' if it is 'of a type normally used in the locality either as a bedroom or as a living room' (Housing Act 1985, s 325(2)(b)).
11   Housing Act 1985, s 325(1).

computation.[12] The 'space standard' is contravened when the number of persons[13] sleeping in a dwelling exceeds the 'permitted number'[14] appropriate to the number of rooms or floor area available as sleeping accommodation.[15]

(ii) Criminal liability The importance of the concept of 'overcrowding' lies in the fact that both the 'occupier'[16] and the landlord[17] may be guilty of a criminal offence by causing or permitting a dwelling to be overcrowded. The local housing authority has power to serve a notice on either the occupier or the landlord requiring that the 'overcrowding' be abated.[18] The landlord is criminally liable only if he or his letting agent had reasonable cause to believe that the dwelling would become overcrowded,[19] or failed to make inquiries of the proposed occupier as to the 'number, age and sex' of the persons who would be allowed to sleep in the dwelling,[20] or if he fails to comply with an abatement notice served by the local housing authority.[1]

(iii) Repossession of overcrowded property The local housing authority has power both to require information from the occupier as to the persons sleeping in the dwelling,[2] and to enter the premises on notice given for the purpose of verifying this information.[3] The housing authority may ultimately, in default of any response to a duly served abatement notice, apply to the county court for an order that vacant possession be given to the landlord.[4] Such an order will normally bring about the result that the occupiers become 'homeless' persons whom it is the duty of the local authority to rehouse.[5]

12 Housing Act 1985, s 325(2)(a).
13 No account is taken of a child under one year old, and a child aged between one and ten is reckoned as 'one-half of a unit' (Housing Act 1985, s 326(2)(a)).
14 The 'permitted number' is defined in Housing Act 1985, s 326(3). Where, for instance, two rooms are 'available', the permitted total of slumbering occupants is three; in the case of four rooms, $7\frac{1}{2}$ slumbering occupants (s 326(3), Table I). The floor area test (s 326(3), Table II) is more complicated, but permits, for example, two slumbering occupants in sleeping accommodation measuring 110 sq ft or more.
15 Housing Act 1985, s 326(1). The statutory limit is fixed by whichever formula produces a smaller number.
16 Housing Act 1985, s 327(1). There are certain exceptions to criminal liability, relating to visiting members of the occupier's family (s 329) and the case where the occupier has obtained a licence from the local housing authority (s 330).
17 Housing Act 1985, s 331(1). Any rent book supplied by the landlord must specify the permitted number of persons in relation to the dwelling (s 332(1)(b)), and the local housing authority has power to require the production of the rent book (s 336(1)).
18 Housing Act 1985, ss 331(2)(c), 338(1).
19 Housing Act 1985, s 331(2)(a).
20 Housing Act 1985, s 331(2)(b).
1 Housing Act 1985, s 331(2)(c).
2 Housing Act 1985, s 335(1).
3 Housing Act 1985, ss 337(1), 340(1).
4 Housing Act 1985, s 338(2).
5 The mere decision to have more children, thereby inducing a condition of statutory 'overcrowding', does not amount to 'intentional homelessness' which would disqualify the parents from assistance under Part VI of the Housing Act 1985. See *R v Eastleigh BC, ex parte Beattie* (1983) 10 HLR 134 at 141 per Woolf J. (It was later found that there was no 'overcrowding' on the facts (Unreported, Queen's Bench Division, CO/449/84, 18 September 1984)).

(b) Control of houses in 'multiple occupation'

Part XI of the Housing Act 1985 provides a further form of control in relation to houses in 'multiple occupation' (HMOs), which are often, but not always, privately owned and privately run bed-and-breakfast hostels offering last-resort accommodation to the poor and chronically disadvantaged and to migrant or casual workers.[6]

(i) The local authority's supervisory powers   Under the Housing Act 1985 the local housing authority is given significant powers to control the quality of residential life in an HMO. This control is not only relevant to overcrowding, but also gives the housing authority power to regulate and direct such aspects of life in an HMO as those concerning fitness for occupation,[7] repairs,[8] fire precautions,[9] and standards of management.[10] The local housing authority may ultimately make a 'control order' in respect of an HMO which effectively enables the authority to take over the HMO if such action is 'necessary...in order to protect the safety, welfare or health of persons living in the house'.[11]

(ii) Definition   A 'house in multiple occupation' within Part XI of the Housing Act 1985 is defined as a 'house which is occupied by persons who do not form a single household'.[12] There is for this purpose no statutory definition of a 'household', and in *Simmons v Pizzey*[13] the House of Lords held that the constitution of a 'household' is a 'question of fact and degree'. Thus a hostel which contains over a thousand bedrooms for single men constitutes a house in mutiple occupation, since its occupants cannot be said in any way to comprise 'a single household'.[14] Likewise, a refuge for battered wives, with a large population which fluctuated with fortuitous arrivals and departures, could not be described as 'a single household'.[15]

(iii) Overcrowding notice under Part XI of the Housing Act 1985   In relation to HMOs the local housing authority has power under the Housing Act 1985 both to limit the maximum number of individuals or households allowed to occupy the property in its current condition,[16] and to enforce these limits by means of

6   Those who have the stomach to read of the kinds of living conditions tolerated in the 1980s under a free enterprise economy might care to consult *R v LB of Southwark, ex parte Lewis Levy Ltd* (1983) 8 HLR 6 at 8f.
7   Housing Act 1985, s 352ff.
8   Housing Act 1985, ss 352(2), 372, 375ff.
9   Housing Act 1985, s 365ff.
10   Housing Act 1985, s 369ff. A criminal offence is committed by any person who knowingly contravenes or without reasonable excuse fails to comply with the management code issued by the Secretary of State under section 369 (Housing Act 1985, s 369(5)). It is not necessary in this context to prove that the defendant had knowledge of the defects in the premises managed by him (*City of Westminster v Mavroghenis* (1983) 11 HLR 56 at 60).
11   Housing Act 1985, s 379(1)).
12   Housing Act 1985, s 345. A hotel providing bed and breakfast accommodation is 'occupied' for this purpose where a local authority uses it as merely temporary accommodation for homeless persons (*R v Hackney LBC, ex parte Thrasyvoulou* (1986) 18 HLR 370).
13   [1979] AC 37 at 59F-G. See (1978) 41 MLR 195 (D.C. Hoath).
14   *R v LB of Camden, ex parte Rowton (Camden Town) Ltd* (1983) 10 HLR 28.
15   [1979] AC 37 at 56A, 60B-E (Erin Pizzey's refuge in Chiswick).
16   Housing Act 1985, s 354(1).

the service of an 'overcrowding notice'.[17] The local authority also has power to prosecute any person who knowingly fails to comply with such a notice.[18]

The occupants of HMOs are more likely to be licensees than tenants, but the potential application to tenants of Part XI of the Housing Act 1985 is illustrated in *LB of Hackney v Ezedinma*.[19] This case concerned the prosecution of an estate agent who managed lettings of a house to, in all, eight students. The local authority had restricted to three the maximum number of 'households' permitted to occupy the house in its existing condition, and the question arose whether the present lettings exceeded the permissible limit. The Divisional Court held that it would have been open to the magistrates to hold that each student constituted a separate 'household' for the purpose of the statute. However, the Court acquitted the defendant, on the ground that there was 'just sufficient' evidence that the students constituted in total no more than three 'households'.[20] There was some evidence that the single tenants had lived in groups, sharing between them a total of three kitchens.[1] The living conditions of the students thus fell marginally outside the purview of what is now Part XI of the Housing Act 1985, but, in view of *Street v Mountford*,[2] there are now bound to be many more tenants who come within the scope of local authority supervision of multiple occupation.

4. THE TENANT'S REMEDIES FOR BREACH OF LANDLORD'S REPAIRING COVENANTS

The tenant's rights in respect of the residential quality of his accommodation are vitally dependent upon his ability to secure an adequate and effective remedy for disrepair which has occurred in consequence of default by his landlord. In view of the general principle within the landlord-tenant relationship that the performance of the parties' respective obligations is not inter-dependent,[3] it is not wise (and may indeed be disastrous[4]) for the tenant to withhold payment of rent or service charges on the ground of his landlord's patent failure to discharge a duty to repair. The tenant must seek to vindicate his rights through the legitimate channels which the law affords him. The remedies open to the tenant include the following.

(1) Damages for breach of covenant

It is of course clear that the tenant may sue the landlord for damages for breach of any repairing covenant expressly or impliedly undertaken by the landlord in the lease.[5]

17 Housing Act 1985, s 358(1).
19 Housing Act 1985, s 355(2).
20 [1981] 3 All ER 438.
20 [1981] 3 All ER 438 at 442d.
1   [1981] 3 All ER 438 at 442c.
2   [1985] AC 809 (ante, p 449).
3   Ante, p 515.
4   See eg *Di Palma v Victoria Square Property Co Ltd* [1986] Ch 150 (ante, p 495).
5   See the substantial damages awarded for breach of Landlord and Tenant Act 1985, s 11 (ante, p 918) in *Downie v LB of Lambeth* (1986) Legal Action 95. An action for damages for breach of the landlord's repairing covenant, even if coupled with an application for a mandatory injunction, cannot be registered as a pending land action within Land Charges Act 1972, s 17(1). See *Regan & Blackburn Ltd v Rogers* [1985] 1 WLR 870 at 875D-E; [1985] Conv 406; (1986) 136 NLJ 157 (H.W. Wilkinson).

(a) The general principle

It was reiterated by the Court of Appeal in *Calabar Properties Ltd v Stitcher*[6] that in assessing the tenant's damages for breach of a landlord's repairing covenant, the court starts from 'the fundamental principle' that the purpose of such damages is 'so far as is possible by means of a monetary award, to place the plaintiff in the position which he would have occupied if he had not suffered the wrong complained of...' The object of the award is 'not to punish the landlord but...to restore the tenant to the position he would have been in had there been no breach.'[7]

(b) Measure of the tenant's loss

It follows from the general principle above that damages must be assessed as the difference between the value of the property to the tenant in its condition of disrepair and the value which the property would have had if the landlord had fulfilled his repairing obligation.[8] However, in *Calabar Properties Ltd v Stitcher*[9] Griffiths LJ indicated that the court cannot simply apply 'one set of rules to all cases regardless of the circumstances of the case. The facts of each case must be looked at carefully to see what damage the tenant has suffered and how he may be fairly compensated by a monetary award.'

Thus if a tenant has taken a letting with the intention (known to the landlord) of subletting the property, the 'difference in value to the tenant' may be measured by his loss of rent if he cannot let the property because of the landlord's breach.[10] If the tenant is driven out of occupation by the breach and forced, for instance, to sell a long leasehold by way of assignment of his term, then the 'difference in value to the tenant' may be represented by the discrepancy between the selling price and the price which he would have obtained if the landlord had observed the repairing covenant.[11]

The fall in the value of the demised property as a marketable asset provides no true guide to the tenant's loss in the more normal case where the tenant took the letting with the intention of living in the property himself and wishes to continue to live there after the necessary repairs have been carried out.[12] In such circumstances, the 'reality' of the tenant's loss is 'the temporary loss of the home' in which he would have lived permanently if the landlord had performed his covenant.[13] Thus, in *Calabar Properties Ltd v Stitcher*[14] the Court of Appeal considered that the damages awarded the tenant could properly have included the cost of redecoration and a sum to compensate for the discomfort

---

6   [1984] 1 WLR 287 at 295G-H.
7   [1984] 1 WLR 287 at 297F. See (1984) 81 Law Soc Gaz 1269 (D.W. Williams); [1984] Conv 230 (J.E.M.); (1984) LAG Bulletin 51 (N. Madge and D. Watkinson).
8   See *Calabar Properties Ltd v Stitcher* [1984] 1 WLR 287 at 296C.
9   [1984] 1 WLR 287 at 297F-G.
10   [1984] 1 WLR 287 at 299D. See *Hewitt v Rowlands* (1924) 93 LJKB 1080 at 1082.
11   [1984] 1 WLR 287 at 293E-F, 297H-298A, 299D-E.
12   [1984] 1 WLR 287 at 298A. Here, in the view of Griffiths LJ, it would be 'wholly artificial' to award damages on the basis of loss in market value (given in any event that the tenancy has a sufficiently long term to command a market value in the first place).
13   [1984] 1 WLR 287 at 293D.
14   [1984] 1 WLR 287 at 298B, 299F.

and loss of enjoyment and health involved in living in a damp and deteriorating flat.[15]

The Court of Appeal in *Calabar Properties* also took the opportunity to scotch the prevalent view that damages could never include the cost of reasonable alternative accommodation whilst repairs were being carried out.[16] It was the unanimous view of the Court that the landlord would be liable for any reasonable sum spent on providing alternative accommodation after the demised property became uninhabitable by reason of the landlord's disrepair.[17] However, the landlord's liability for the costs of alternative accommodation for the tenant arises only in respect of those costs which are incurred after the landlord has received notice of the want of repair and a reasonable time has elapsed in which the repair could have been carried out.[18] Thus, as Griffiths LJ pointed out, there would have been no breach of the landlord's repairing obligation (and therefore no liability in damages) if the landlord had sent workmen round to carry out the repairs promptly on receiving notice of the defect and the tenant for her own convenience had decided to move to a hotel while the repairs were conducted.[19]

The approach adopted by the Court of Appeal in *Calabar Properties* is reflected in the greater realism apparent in more recent assessments of the discomfort and distress inflicted on the tenant by a landlord's default in the matter of repair. Although in some cases the courts have simply refunded the tenant a proportion of the rent paid,[20] other cases have resulted in very substantial awards or settlements where disrepair has rendered the premises more or less uninhabitable.[1]

(2) Order for specific performance

Although the remedy of specific performance is not available for the enforcement of a tenant's repairing obligation,[2] it seems that the courts may be prepared in appropriate circumstances to order specific performance of a landlord's covenant to repair. In *Jeune v Queens Cross Properties Ltd*,[3] Pennycuick V-C held that although the jurisdiction to grant this remedy should be

---

15   The tenant was awarded £3,000 in respect of 'all the unpleasantness of living in the flat while it deteriorated' and £4,606 in respect of necessary redecoration and internal repairs. See also *Fryer v Bunney* (1981) 263 Estates Gazette 158 at 164 (£500 for having survived conditions which were 'rather nasty'); *Seal v London Borough of Greenwich* (1981) LAG Bulletin 237; *McGreal v Wake* (1984) 269 Estates Gazette 1254 at 1256 (ante, p 920). See generally (1982) LAG Bulletin 66 at 69 (J. Luba); (1984) 134 NLJ 357 (J. Luba); (1984) LAG Bulletin 53.
16   [1984] 1 WLR 287 at 297E-F. The Court agreed, however, that the tenant could not recover the running costs or outgoings on the property (eg rates, rent and service charges) during the period when the tenant's flat was uninhabitable ([1984] 1 WLR 287 at 291G-H). See *Green v Eales* (1841) 2 QB 225 at 238, 114 ER 88 at 93.
17   [1984] 1 WLR 287 at 291G-H, 298A-B, 299F.
18   Ante, p 920.
19   [1984] 1 WLR 287 at 298D-E.
20   See eg *Do Rosario v Dewing* (1982) LAG Bulletin 91 at 92 (two-thirds of a 'fair rent' returned by way of damages); *McCoy & Co v Clark* (Unreported, Court of Appeal, 19 March 1982).
1   See eg *Hubble v Lambeth LBC* (1986) Legal Action 50 (£4,000); *Fraser v Hopewood Properties* [1986] 1 CL 217 (£2,000); *Meah v LB of Tower Hamlets* (1986) Legal Action 135 (£3,284).
2   *Hill v Barclay* (1810) 16 Ves 402 at 405f, 33 ER 1037 at 1038; *Regional Properties Ltd v City of London Real Property Co Ltd* (1981) 257 Estates Gazette 64 at 66.
3   [1974] Ch 97 at 101C-D.

'carefully exercised', an order of specific performance might well be appropriate where there has been 'a plain breach of a covenant to repair and there is no doubt at all what is required to be done to remedy the breach.'[4] This discretion to award specific performance in favour of the tenant has now been expressly confirmed by statute.[5] In exceptional circumstances a mandatory injunction compelling repairs may even be made at an interlocutory stage if the effect of the disrepair is to expose tenants to 'a real risk of damage to health'.[6]

(3) Remedies of self-help

Further relief in the case of disrepair lies in the form of three similar, but distinct, remedies available to the tenant on a basis of self-help. These remedies comprise the old common law right to recoup the cost of necessary repairs from future rent payments and the equitable right to set off a damages claim in respect of disrepair against the landlord's claim for rent.[7] The 'secure tenant' also has access to a new statutory scheme of self-help provided by the Housing Act 1985.

(a) Common law right of recoupment from future rent

Recent caselaw has given new force to an ancient common law remedy enjoyed by the tenant in cases of breach by the landlord of any covenant (whether express or implied) to repair the demised premises.[8] In *Lee-Parker v Izzet*[9] Goff J confirmed the existence of a right in the tenant to execute the covenanted repairs himself and then deduct the cost of those repairs from future payments of rent.[10] The tenant who takes advantage of this right is *pro tanto* immune from any action by the landlord for arrears of rent and also has in the same degree an answer to any claim by the landlord to distrain upon his goods.[11]

(i) Preconditions of self-help   The form of self-help endorsed in *Lee-Parker v Izzet* provides a valuable remedy for the victim of disrepair by the landlord.

---

4   See also *Francis v Cowcliffe* (1977) 33 P & CR 368 at 374ff; *Peninsular Maritime Ltd v Padseal Ltd* (1981) 259 Estates Gazette 860 at 868; (1984) 81 Law Soc Gaz 1269 (D.W. Williams).

5   Housing Act 1974, s 125(1). See *Parker v Camden LBC* [1986] Ch 162 at 173G-H; (1982) LAG Bulletin 66 at 68 (J. Luba).

6   *Parker v Camden LBC* [1986] Ch 162 at 174C, where Donaldson MR pointed out that the failure of a local authority landlord to repair and restart boilers which supplied heating and hot water made both elderly and very young occupiers of housing on a council estate vulnerable to 'a far from fanciful risk of death'.

7   See *Melville v Grapelodge Developments Ltd* (1979) 39 P & CR 179 at 186.

8   The remedy can be traced back at least as far as *Taylor v Beal* (1591) Cro Eliz 222, 78 ER 478. See also *Waters v Weigall* (1795) 2 Anst 575 at 576, 145 ER 971. The legitimacy of broad formulations of the common law doctrine has been questioned (see P.M. Rank, *Repairs in lieu of Rent*, (1976) 40 Conv (NS) 196). However, the doctrine seems to have a good common law pedigree (see A. Waite, *Repairs and Deduction from Rent*, [1981] Conv 199).

9   [1971] 1 WLR 1688 at 1693F-G. See also *Melville v Grapelodge Developments Ltd* (1979) 39 P & CR 179 at 186.

10   This principle has been extended to allow the cost of necessary repairs to be recovered by the reduction of rent arrears already in existence (*Asco Developments Ltd v Gordon* (1978) 248 Estates Gazette 683). Thus, by withholding the payment of his rent, a tenant can save up the capital cost of necessary repairs which his landlord refuses to carry out (see (1973) LAG Bulletin 173 (S. Sedley)). See also *Knockholt Proprietary Ltd v Graff* [1975] Qd R 88 at 90G-91A.

11   *Lee-Parker v Izzet* [1971] 1 WLR 1688 at 1693A-B, 1695H. See (1982) LAG Bulletin 66 at 67 (J. Luba); A. Waite, *Set-off and Distress for Rent*, (1984) LAG Bulletin 66.

However, the availability of the remedy is dependent on certain strict conditions. It is clear that the tenant's right to recoup the costs of repairs out of rent owed to the landlord arises only if the landlord is in breach of his repairing covenant[12] and if the tenant has given notice to him of the need for repair.[13] Moreover, the right to make deductions from rents owed applies only in relation to such portion of the tenant's expenditure as is reasonable and proper in all the circumstances of the case.[14] The existence of a *Lee-Parker v Izzet* right in the tenant does not impliedly arm him with an easement to enter other parts of the landlord's property in order to carry out repairs which the landlord has covenanted (but failed) to execute.[15]

(ii) Proprietary status of the remedy The tenant's remedy of self-help under *Lee-Parker v Izzet* would be severely limited if it availed only against the landlord in possession at the date of the initial default in respect of covenanted repairs. It is therefore a matter of some importance that the tenant's right to make rent deductions on the ground of essential expenditure on repairs constitutes a proprietary right capable of binding a third party who purchases his landlord's reversion. In registered land the *Lee-Parker v Izzet* right ranks as an overriding interest on behalf of a tenant who remains 'in actual occupation' of the land,[16] and in unregistered land comprises a non-registrable, non-overreachable right which binds all except a purchaser for value without notice. Thus the tenant's rights under the *Lee-Parker v Izzet* doctrine are not lost merely by reason of a change of landlord.

(b) Equitable set-off

If instead of paying for necessary repairs which the landlord should have effected, the tenant cross-claims for damages for breach of the landlord's covenant, it seems that the tenant has an equitable right to set off his unliquidated claim for damages against a liquidated claim by the landlord in respect of any non-payment of rent.[17] The remedy of set-off may be even more valuable than the common law right to make deductions from rent. The equitable set-off can cover consequential damage flowing from the landlord's breach,[18] while the common law remedy enables the tenant to recoup merely the cost of reasonable repairs.[19]

12   There is no right to make a deduction in respect of repairs which fall outside the landlord's covenants (*Lee-Parker v Izzet* [1971] 1 WLR 1688 at 1693H).
13   *Lee-Parker v Izzet* [1971] 1 WLR 1688 at 1693H; *British Anzani (Felixstowe) Ltd v International Marine Management (UK) Ltd* [1979] 2 All ER 1063 at 1070b.
14   *Lee-Parker v Izzet* [1971] 1 WLR 1688 at 1693G, 1695H-1696A. See A. Waite, [1981] Conv 199 at 206f.
15   *Sedgwick Forbes Bland Payne Group Ltd v Regional Properties Ltd* (1981) 257 Estates Gazette 64 at 68.
16   *Lee-Parker v Izzet* [1971] 1 WLR 1688 at 1691G.
17   *British Anzani (Felixstowe) Ltd v International Marine Management (UK) Ltd* [1979] 2 All ER 1063 at 1068d-h, 1074c-d. The right to a set-off arises, however, only if it would be inequitable to allow the landlord to recover the rent in the face of the tenant's claim (see (1979) LAG Bulletin 210 at 211 (A. Arden)).
18   *British Anzani (Felixstowe) Ltd v International Marine Management (UK) Ltd* [1979] 2 All ER 1063 at 1070a-c, f-g, 1076h-j.
19   It has been suggested that the landlord cannot contractually exclude the tenant's equitable right to a set-off (see R.C.A. White, *Self-help — When to withhold payment*, (1981) LAG Bulletin 182 at 184).

(c) The statutory 'right to repair'

'Secure tenants', as defined by the Housing Act 1985,[20] are now given a statutory 'right to repair' in respect of certain kinds of defect in the condition of their accommodation. This 'right to repair' is currently outlined in a statutory instrument approved under the Housing Act 1985.[1] In relation to any 'qualifying repair',[2] the secure tenant may serve on his landlord a 'tenant's repair claim'.[3] The landlord authority may refuse to accept the claim on any of a number of specified grounds[4] (or may accept the tenant's claim with modifications[5]), but must otherwise consent to the relevant repairs being effected at the landlord's expense either by some person approved by the landlord[6] or by the tenant himself.[7] If the landlord authority fails either to accept the tenant's repair claim or to provide a satisfactory ground for refusing it, the tenant may ultimately carry out the necessary repairs and claim payment for them from the landlord authority.[8]

The 'right to repair' scheme is an important component of the emerging charter of rights for the 'secure tenant'. There is, however, provision within the scheme for setting off due payments from the landlord authority against rent arrears owed by the tenant,[9] and this may ironically mean that public sector landlords will be able to recoup vast arrears of rent owed by council tenants by way of general improvement of the public housing stock.[10]

(4) Appointment of receiver

A rather unusual remedy for the victim of disrepair was used for the first time in *Hart v Emelkirk Ltd*.[11] Here Goulding J, on the application of the tenants of a mansion block, appointed a nominated surveyor to act as receiver in respect of the demised premises.[12] The landlord company had for some time made no effort at all to discharge its obligation to repair and maintain the main

---

20 See Housing Act 1985, s 79ff (post, p 1045).
1   The Secure Tenancies (Right to Repair Scheme) Regulations 1985 (SI 1985/1493). See Housing Act 1985, s 96(1).
2   A 'qualifying repair' is any repair 'which the landlord of a secure tenant is obliged by a repairing covenant to carry out, other than a repair to the structure or exterior of a flat' (SI 1985/1493, reg 1(2)).
3   SI 1985/1493, reg 3(1).
4   SI 1985/1493, reg 5, Annex B, Parts 1 and 2. It is a mandatory ground of refusal that the landlord's costs in effecting the repair would be less than £20 (Ground 1), and a discretionary ground of refusal that the landlord's costs in effecting the repair would be more than £200 (Ground 4).
5   SI 1985/1493, reg 7(1)(b), 8(1)(iv).
6   SI 1985/1493, reg 7(2).
7   SI 1985/1493, reg 7(3)(i).
8   SI 1985/1493, reg 11.
9   SI 1985/1493, reg 23(1).
10 See (1986) 130 SJ 380 at 383.
11 [1983] 1 WLR 1289 at 1291H. See [1984] Conv 230; (1983) LAG Bulletin 55.
12 The High Court has power under section 37(1) of the Supreme Court Act 1981 to appoint a receiver wherever it 'appears...just and convenient to do so'.

structure of the block.[13] The tenants sued for a mandatory injunction to compel the due performance of the landlord's covenant. In view of the urgent need to prevent further structural deterioration in the flats, it was held that pending the trial of their action a receiver should be appointed to receive the rents from the tenants and to manage the entire property in accordance with the landlord's obligations.[14]

This remedy may provide much needed instant relief for the occupants of mismanaged tenanted property, but is subject to the restrictive qualification that the courts seem unwilling to appoint a receiver to act in respect of housing owned and managed by a local authority.[15] There is, moreover, the difficulty that even in relation to privately let premises the appointment of a receiver is likely to prove ineffective in practice if the income (inclusive of any service charge or other property or money which can be put under the control of the receiver) is patently inadequate to meet the cost of repairs.[16] It is therefore said that a receiver is well advised not to take office unless he is satisfied that the assets of which he is appointed a receiver are sufficient to meet his own remuneration or unless he has obtained an enforceable indemnity in this regard from one of the parties to the litigation. The receiver has no general right to be indemnified by either landlord or tenant in respect of expenditure incurred on repairs or of remuneration due to him. As Vinelott J observed in *Evans v Clayhope Properties Ltd*,[17] these unfortunate constraints serve as a reminder of the limitations inherent in the power to appoint a receiver and detract considerably from the potential utility of this form of remedy for the tenant.

13   For judicial recognition of the problem of the negligent landlord, see *Clayhope Properties Ltd v Evans* [1986] 1 WLR 1223 at 1231C-E. Concern at the apparent helplessness of the long leaseholder in a mansion block led the Nugee Committee in 1985 to propose increased safeguards for the tenant (see *Report of the Committee of Inquiry on the Management of Privately Owned Blocks of Flats* (Chairman: E.G. Nugee QC, 1985), Vol 1). These safeguards included the extension to the county courts of the High Court power to appoint a receiver (para 7.2.17), and the conferment on tenants of a collective right of first refusal to purchase the block when the landlord wishes to dispose of his interest (para 7.9.13ff). The proposals of the Nugee Report have now been largely incorporated in the Landlord and Tenant Act 1987 (ante, p 926). Ultimately the solution may lie in the introduction of some form of freehold or 'commonhold' ownership of flats (para 7.9.11) (ante, p 20).

14   See also *Daiches v Bluelake Investments Ltd* [1985] 2 EGLR 67 at 70A-D. Although the receivership order vests no interest in the land in either the receiver or the tenant, the order is registrable by the tenant under Land Charges Act 1972, s 6 (ante, p 112) and Land Registration Act 1925, s 54 (see *Clayhope Properties Ltd v Evans* [1986] 1 WLR 1223 at 1230F, 1231F). The tenant is thus given advance warning of any attempt by the landlord to 'offload' the freehold.

15   *Parker v Camden LBC* [1986] Ch 162 at 173B-D, 176E-F, 179A-D. See Housing Act 1985, s 21(1) (formerly Housing Act 1957, s 111(1)).

16   *Evans v Clayhope Properties Ltd* [1987] 1 WLR 225 at 231A-B.

17   [1987] 1 WLR 225 at 230G.

CHAPTER 28

Safety in and around the home

It is a notorious fact of life that the home is a potentially injurious, and sometimes lethal, environment: most accidents to children occur within the domestic curtilage. Such mishaps are usually the consequence of the negligence of the victim or of some member of his family, but some accidents may give rise to a liability in the landlord either at common law or pursuant to statute. The sources of legal liability for accidents in and around the home of the residential tenant closely mirror the forms of liability already explored in relation to the residential fitness of that dwelling.

1. THE LANDLORD'S LIABILITY AT COMMON LAW

The forms of common law liability fixed upon a landlord in respect of personal injuries in the home revolve around the contractual duties expressed or implied in the tenancy agreement and around the traditional heads of liability in tort. The most significant seem to be the following.

(1) Implied contractual duty of care

The decision of the House of Lords in *Liverpool City Council v Irwin*[1] demonstrates the willingness of the courts, at least in principle, to exact from the landlord the discharge of an implied contractual duty of care to ensure a reasonable level of safety in relation to areas over which the landlord retains control or possession. The tenants' complaint in this case concerned mere loss of residential amenity as distinct from physical injury or damage. However, it is clear that the implied contractual duty of care may afford a remedy in damages in respect of physical harm also, even though this head of liability is subject to all the same disadvantages which were recognised earlier as attaching to purely contractual remedies.[2]

The circumstances in which the landlord's implied contractual duty of care may be invoked by a tenant are illustrated in *Dunster v Hollis*.[3] Here the plaintiff tenant was injured by a fall on a delapidated external stairway leading from the street to the building containing his rented rooms. Lush J held the landlord to be in breach of his 'implied contractual obligation to keep the access in a reasonably safe condition', since otherwise the tenant 'cannot enjoy the use of the rooms which he has contracted to take.'[4] Lush J declined to hold the landlord subject to an absolute duty to guarantee the tenant's safety under all

1   [1977] AC 239 (ante, p 907).
2   Ante, p 910.
3   [1918] 2 KB 795.
4   [1918] 2 KB 795 at 802.

conditions. He ruled, however, that the landlord's obligation of care extends not merely to concealed dangers or traps, but also to defects which are entirely visible and obvious to the tenant.[5]

(2) Liability in negligence

Once again a distinction must still be maintained between defects and defaults which are present at the commencement of a tenancy and those which arise later.

(a) Defects and defaults arising after the commencement of the tenancy

It is quite clear that a landlord may be liable in damages for any foreseeable personal injury caused by his negligence in respect of defects or defaults arising after the commencement of the tenancy.[6] For any negligence liability to arise, there must of course be some breach of duty by the landlord. Prima facie evidence of such a breach may be provided by the landlord's failure to fulfil implied statutory duties of repair or maintenance.[7]

In that it extends potentially to others beyond the tenant, the landlord's negligence-based liability is wider than his liability under the implied contractual duty of care. However, the landlord's liability in negligence is not absolute; he is liable only to take reasonable care to ensure the safety of those persons who might reasonably be expected to be affected by his actions or defaults. If the landlord has breached no duty of care (either express or implied), there can be no liability in negligence.[8] In *Ryan v LB of Camden*,[9] for instance, the Court of Appeal declined to hold a local authority to be in breach of its duty of care towards a six-month old baby who had suffered severe contact burns after falling on an exposed and uninsulated central heating pipe in a bedroom of a council flat. In the view taken by the Court, the local authority had been under no duty to lag the hot water pipe. The authority was entitled to rely on the child's parents to protect it from the danger presented by the central heating system,[10] and was therefore not liable for a kind of harm which was not reasonably foreseeable by either the parents or the local authority.[11]

(b) Defects and defaults existing at the commencement of the tenancy

It is less clear, in view of the House of Lords' restrictive ruling in *Cavalier v Pope*,[12] that any negligence liability can be fixed on the landlord in respect of defects or defaults existing at the commencement date of a tenancy.[13] It is in

---

5   [1918] 2 KB 795 at 803. See also *Fanjoy v Gaston* (1982) 127 DLR (3d) 163 at 168f (landlord liable for accident caused largely because matting on the steps provided insufficient friction in wet weather, there was no handrail and the electric light at the entrance had burned out).
6   Ante, p 911.
7   See eg *Gaul v King* (1980) 103 DLR (3d) 233 at 244.
8   See eg *McAuliffe v Moloney* [1971] IR 200 at 203.
9   (1982) 8 HLR 75.
10   (1982) 8 HLR 75 at 84, 89f. 'The amenity of a well warmed house imposed an obligation upon parents to keep their children away from the pipes, and experience showed that they apparently succeeded' (per Cumming-Bruce LJ).
11   (1982) 8 HLR 75 at 78f, 87, 90. Contrast the approach of the Supreme Court of New Jersey in *Coleman v Steinberg*, 253 A.2d 167 at 170ff (1969).
12   [1906] AC 428.
13   See 62 Harvard LR 669 (1948-49).

this context that the recent English caselaw points towards a significant development.

In *Rimmer v Liverpool City Council*,[14] a local authority, with the help of its own architects and works department, designed and constructed a block of flats. The plaintiff tenant injured himself when he tripped and fell through a thin glass panel which formed part of an internal wall in his flat.[15] The Court of Appeal upheld a decision that the local authority was liable in negligence. The Court took the view that the authority owed not merely the tenant but also his wife and child 'a duty to take such care as was reasonable in all the circumstances to see that [each] was reasonably safe from personal injury caused by the glass panel.'[16] The authority was in breach of this duty, it being irrelevant that the tenant had previously complained of the dangerous nature of the panel[17] and that the expense of replacing all similar panels in council flats would be great.[18]

Stephenson LJ, delivering the judgment of the Court of Appeal, sidestepped the increasingly inconvenient authority of *Cavalier v Pope* by making reference to the more recently established liability imposed on a builder towards those injured by his negligence in building.[19] It was already accepted that the builder's liability is not in any relevant respect diminished merely by the fact that he is also the owner of the land.[20] Stephenson LJ therefore distinguished *Cavalier v Pope* as a case relating only to the liability of a 'bare landlord' as distinct from that of a 'builder owner'.[1] *Cavalier v Pope* in no way precluded a landlord of an unfurnished house from being liable to his tenant for defects rendering it dangerous if the landlord had constructed the premises himself.[2]

The decision of the Court of Appeal in *Rimmer v Liverpool City Council* clearly marks the beginning of the end for the rule in *Cavalier v Pope*, although, as suggested in *Rimmer*,[3] legislation may be required in order to achieve the final removal of this obdurate rule.[4]

14   [1985] QB 1.
15   There was evidence that the original specification for the glass had been reduced, as a cost-cutting device, from ¼inch wired glass to ⅛inch pattern glass.
16   [1985] QB 1 at 13G-H. For a recent American parallel, see the ruling of the Supreme Court of California in *Becker v IRM Corp*, 213 Cal Rptr 213 (1985); R. Deeb, 20 Loyola of Los Angeles LR 323 (1987).
17   [1985] QB 1 at 14A-B, E-F. The plaintiff's knowledge of the danger could not therefore preclude his action for negligence. The plaintiff had been informed by the council that the glass panel was a standard feature and that nothing could be done about it. The Court of Appeal doubted whether, as a tenant, he would have had any right (let alone a duty) to remove the panel.
18   [1985] QB 1 at 16B.
19   The turning point seems to have been the judgment of Lord MacDermott LCJ in *Gallagher v N. McDowell Ltd* [1961] NI 26 at 44, cited with approval in *Anns v Merton LBC* [1978] AC 728 at 758H-759A, 768A.
20   [1985] QB 1 at 12E.
1   [1985] QB 1 at 14G. Although declining to treat *Cavalier v Pope* as overruled, Stephenson LJ said pointedly (at 9H) that the decision 'must be kept in close confinement.' See also *Collins v Northern Ireland Housing Executive* [1984] 17 NIJB, Transcript, p 23.
2   [1985] QB 1 at 13E-F, following *Anns v Merton LBC* [1978] AC 728 at 768E-G per Lord Salmon.
3   [1985] QB 1 at 16B-C.
4   'This immunity long remained singularly stubborn to the civilized demand of the modern age for a general duty of care' (J.G. Fleming, *The Law of Torts* (6th edn, Sydney, Melbourne and Perth 1983), p 454). It is noticeable that courts in other jurisdictions have felt much more free to ignore the fetters of *Cavalier v Pope* (see eg *Basset Realty Ltd v Lindstrom* (1980) 103 DLR (3d) 654 at 670).

2. THE LANDLORD'S LIABILITY UNDER STATUTE

Statute has significantly extended the landlord's liability for accidents occurring in and around the home. The most significant innovations include the following.

(1) Implied terms of the tenancy

The terms relating to residential fitness which are implied by the Landlord and Tenant Act 1985[5] plainly provide the tenant with some form of redress in respect of domestic accidents. However, in view of the limitations inherent in these statutory terms,[6] a more fertile ground of recovery for the tenant lies in the Defective Premises Act 1972.

(2) Liability under the Defective Premises Act 1972

Section 4 of the Defective Premises Act 1972 imposes on the landlord, in defined circumstances, a duty to take reasonable care to prevent any personal injury which might be caused by the landlord's default in the discharge of his duties of repair and maintenance.[7]

This provision has acquired considerable significance in the law relating to domestic accidents, not least because the landlord's liability is not exclusively towards the tenant. The statutory liability extends in favour of 'all persons who might reasonably be expected to be affected by defects in the state of the premises'.[8] Thus, in *Clarke v Taff Ely BC*,[9] section 4 was held to found an action in damages in respect of the personal injuries suffered when a friend of the tenant stood on a table in order to help redecorate the ceiling. The floor under the table was rotten, and its collapse threw the enthusiastic helper to the ground.[10] Moreover, the landlord may be liable under section 4 even in respect of defects introduced into the premises by another tenant. In *Smith v Bradford MC*[11] the tenant suffered injury when falling from a paved area in his garden which had been constructed defectively by a previous tenant. The landlord authority was held liable in damages because it had reserved a right of entry for the purpose of maintenance and repair.[12]

Wide though the terms of liability may be under the Defective Premises Act 1972, there are limitations on the statutory duty of care owed thereunder by the landlord to his tenant. In *McDonagh v Kent AHA*,[13] for instance, a tenant suffered horrendous injuries in consequence of falling down a steep and narrow

---

5 Landlord and Tenant Act 1985, ss 8(1), 11(1) (ante, pp 916, 918).
6 Ante, pp 917, 920.
7 For the respects in which the Defective Premises Act 1972 is wider than other heads of liability, see p 924.
8 Defective Premises Act 1972, s 4(1) (ante, p 924).
9 (1980) 10 HLR 44 at 53.
10 The local authority had sent its employees on many previous occasions to execute specific works of repair on the pathway, windows, roof and sink unit in the house. The failure of any of these employees to make any attempt to test the floor for defects fixed the landlord authority with constructive notice of the defect within the meaning of section 4(2) (ante, p 924).
11 (1982) 4 HLR 86.
12 See Defective Premises Act 1972, s 4(4) (ante, p 924).
13 Unreported, Court of Appeal, 7 October 1985.

staircase which was only partially protected by a handrail.[14] The Court of Appeal held, however, that the landlord was not in breach of the statutory duty of care where the alleged defect was not due to disrepair or lack of maintenance as such,[15] but was inherent in the original design and construction of the tenant's house.[16]

3. THE LANDLORD'S LIABILITY IN RESPECT OF CRIME

It is of the essence of a lease or tenancy that the tenant is granted a right to exclusive possession of the rented premises. It follows as a general proposition that the responsibility falls thereafter on the tenant to protect the rented premises and their occupiers against criminal invasion by third parties. The landlord is, for instance, under no duty of care to safeguard the tenant's belongings from burglary.[17] The tenant is himself responsible for the defence of his own 'estate' in the land. There are, however, certain partial exceptions to the general immunity of the landlord for criminal activity adverse to his tenant.

(1) Liability for agents and employees

It is clear that a landlord may be vicariously liable in negligence for losses caused by criminal activity on the part of his agent or employee while acting within the scope of his authority.[18] In *Nahhas v Pier House (Cheyne Walk) Management Ltd*,[19] for example, a landlord was held liable for losses suffered by a tenant who, on going into hospital, had left the keys to her flat with the landlord's burglary-prone porter. The High Court considered that the landlord had been negligent in failing to discover the extensive criminal record of the employee.

(2) Local authority liability for vandalism

Another potential liability affecting the landlord arises where the landlord is a local authority. A landlord authority may become liable in negligence for the activities of vandals on unoccupied property belonging to the authority where those activities cause injury or damage to a local authority tenant in adjoining premises.[20] In *Ward v Cannock Chase DC*[1] a local authority which had failed to repair its own vacant property was liable to an adjacent freeholder in respect of

---

14   The victim was rendered tetraplegic by her fall. Had damages been awarded under the Defective Premises Act 1972, they would have been in the sum of £163,667.
15   O'Connor LJ was unwilling to recognise the absence of part of the handrail as a 'defect' within the meaning of the Defective Premises Act 1972, and was certainly not prepared to hold that the landlord authority was in breach of any duty to repair or maintain merely because it had failed to extend the handrail to cover the entire staircase.
16   The Court of Appeal regarded it as irrelevant that the staircase in question (constructed almost a century ago) would not have satisfied the requirements of the Building Regulations 1972.
17   *Appah v Parncliffe Investments Ltd* [1964] 1 WLR 1064 at 1067 (ante, p 445).
18   *Lloyd v Grace, Smith & Co* [1912] AC 716 at 731.
19   (1984) 270 Estates Gazette 328 at 333.
20   This problem becomes particularly common in a run-down area where some council tenants are still in residence. The local authority may gradually take over run-down houses or flats and keep them vacant pending demolition and redevelopment.
1   [1986] Ch 546 at 562G-H, 569F-571C.

damage indirectly caused to his house by the depredations of vandals in the neighbouring property. Precisely the same liability would have attached to the local authority if the neighbouring plaintiff had been one of its tenants rather than a freeholder,[2] but the ambit of the landlord authority's duty of care may be cut back if, as in *King v Liverpool City Council*,[3] there are no effective means available for eliminating the threat of vandalism. The heavy cost of preventive action against vandalism has led the courts in recent cases to evince a growing disinclination to impose any general principle of liability in this context. In *Smith v Littlewoods Organisation Ltd*,[4] for instance, Lord Goff of Chieveley thought it impossible to sustain the wide proposition that there is any 'general duty on owners or occupiers of property...to take reasonable care to see that it [is] proof against the kind of vandalism which was calculated to affect adjoining property'.

(3) A general duty to preserve the tenant from crime?

One of the most interesting developments in the law of landlord and tenant in the United States has been the increasing recognition of a duty in the landlord to provide security from criminal attack in respect of both the goods and the person of the residential tenant.[5]

(a) Extension of tort liability

This development came first through an extension of tort liability. In *Kline v 1500 Massachussetts Ave Apartment Corp*[6] a District Court of Appeals took the first move away from the traditional rule that the landlord-tenant relationship does not in itself impose on the landlord any duty to protect the tenant from the crime of a third party. The Court viewed this long-standing immunity as inapplicable to 'the landlord-tenant relationship in multiple dwelling houses.'[7] While conceding that the landlord 'is no insurer of his tenants' safety', the Court insisted that 'he certainly is no bystander'. Accordingly the Court held a landlord liable in damages for the injuries suffered by a tenant who was assaulted in the common hallway of her apartment house, under circumstances where the landlord had had notice of repeated criminal assaults on those premises.

Significance was attached by the Court in *Kline* to the fact that the landlord is usually the party best positioned to take precautionary measures to minimise the risk of crime to which his tenants are exposed.[8] Moreover, the Court

---

2 *O'Leary v LB of Islington* (1983) 9 HLR 81 at 88 per Ackner LJ ('If the principle of *Donoghue v Stevenson* is to be applied, who more readily comes within the category of a neighbour than the adjoining occupier?')

3 [1986] 1 WLR 890 at 901B-E (ante, p 912).

4 [1987] 2 WLR 480 at 510C-D.

5 See S.C. Kifer, *Security: A New Standard for Habitability*, (1980-81) 42 U Pitt LR 415; C.F. Van Benschoten, *The Landlord's Duty in New York to protect his Tenant against Criminal Intrusions*, (1980-81) 45 Albany LR 988; O.L. Browder, *The Taming of a Duty-the Tort Liability of Landlords*, (1982-83) 81 Mich LR 99; I.W. Merrill, *Landlord Liability for Crimes Committed by Third Parties against Tenants on the Premises*, 38 Vand LR 431 (1985).

6 439 F.2d 477 (1970).

7 439 F.2d 477 at 481.

8 439 F.2d 477 at 484.

pointed out that 'the most analogous relationship to that of the modern day urban apartment house dweller is not that of a landlord and tenant, but that of innkeeper and guest.'[9] The Court was thus able to rationalise the liability of the modern landlord on the analogy of the heightened obligation which the common law had always fastened upon the innkeeper to ensure the safety of his guests.[10] While not subject to an absolute duty to ensure the personal safety of his guests,[11] the common innkeeper is liable to take reasonable care that his guests should not suffer injury through his negligence.[12]

In line with the reasoning in *Kline*, the landlord's duty of care to protect the tenant from third party crime has been widely applied in the United States.[13] The landlord's liability is not absolute, but depends heavily on the facts of each case.[14] However, one of the more striking demonstrations of tort liability in this context has been the willingness of the courts to impose liability on colleges and universities where inadequate security has led to the rape of students in campus dormitories.[15] In recent decisions the responsibility of the landlord institution to ensure the safety of its students has verged on a rule of strict liability.[16]

(b) Implied warranty of habitability

The result reached in *Kline* has been confirmed by the more recent extension of the implied contractual warranty of habitability[17] to cover the landlord's

---

9   439 F.2d 477 at 485. The analogy stems from *Javins v First National Realty Corporation*, 428 F.2d 1071 at 1077 (1970), where it was pointed out that the medieval inns had been 'the only multiple dwelling houses known to the common law'. In strict property law terms, of course, the innkeeper's guest has (unlike the tenant) no estate in the realty (see *De Wolf v Ford*, 86 NE 527 at 529f (1908)), but, as the court declared in *Javins* at 1074, today's 'city dweller...on the third floor of a tenement has little interest in the land 30 or 40 feet below, or even in the bare right to possession within the four walls of his apartment.'

10 'For centuries it has been settled law in all jurisdictions where the common law prevails that the business of an innkeeper is of a quasi public character, invested with many privileges, and burdened with correspondingly great responsibilities' (*De Wolf v Ford*, 86 NE 527 at 529 (1908)).

11 *Calye's Case* (1584) 8 Co 32a, 77 ER 520. 'The innkeeper...is not an insurer of the safety, convenience, or comfort of the guest' (*De Wolf v Ford*, 86 NE 527 at 530 (1908)).

12 *Sandys v Florence* (1878) 47 LJQB 598 at 600. See also *Mastad v Swedish Brethren*, 85 NW 913 at 914 (1901); *Rommel v Schambacher*, 11 A 779 (1887); *Gurren v Casperson*, 265 P 472 at 473 (1928).

13 For other instances of landlord liability for breach of a duty of care, see *Ramsay v Morrissette*, 252 A.2d 509 at 512f (1969) (assault); *Johnston v Harris*, 198 NW.2d 409 at 411 (1972) (robbery); *Feld v Merriam*, 461 A.2d 225 at 231f (1983) (assault); *Scott v Watson*, 359 A.2d 548 at 553ff (1976) (murder); *Holley v Mt Zion Terrace Apartments, Inc*, 382 So.2d 98 at 101 (1980) (murder); *O'Hara v Western Seven Trees Corporation Intercoast Management*, 142 Cal Rptr 487 at 490f (1977) (rape).

14 The landlord is required only to take reasonable precautions, but these may include, for instance, the provision of adequate lighting in the common parts of the premises (*Kwaitkowski v Superior Trading Co*, 176 Cal Rptr 494 at 495, 500 (1981)).

15 *Mullins v Pine Manor College*, 449 NE.2d 331 at 338ff (1983); *Miller v State*, 467 NE.2d 493 at 497 (1984). See also *Peterson v San Francisco Community College District*, 205 Cal Rptr 842 at 846f (1984). It is, in English law, a moot question whether a student's occupation can constitute a tenancy (ante, p 454).

16 In *Mullins v Pine Manor College*, 449 NE.2d 331 at 339 (1983), the landlord institution was held liable notwithstanding that it had employed security guards and even though no rapes had ever before occurred on the premises. The court held that the landlord's precautions were inadequate precisely because they were unsuccessful in preventing the intrusion of the assailant.

17 Ante, p 905.

liability for third party crime. In *Trentacost v Brussel*[18] the tenant, a 61 year old widow, had been mugged and beaten in an attack on an internal stairway in her apartment block. The Supreme Court of New Jersey held the landlord liable to her in negligence, on the ground that muggings were a foreseeable result of the landlord's failure to secure the entrance to the common areas of an apartment building in a crime-ridden neighbourhood.[19]

A majority in the Supreme Court was prepared, however, to go somewhat further and hold the landlord liable on the implied contractual warranty of habitability recognised in *Javins v First National Realty Corporation*.[20] Pashman J argued that since 'crime is an inescapable fact of modern life', an apartment 'is clearly not habitable unless it provides a reasonable measure of security from the risk of criminal intrusion.'[1] He thus concluded that 'the landlord's implied warranty of habitability obliges him to furnish reasonable safeguards to protect tenants from foreseeable criminal activity on the premises.'[2] The landlord was in breach of this implied undertaking since he had neglected to instal even the simplest of locks on the entrance door to the block. He had done nothing at all to 'protect against the threat of crime which seriously impaired the quality of residential life in his building.'

Before joining in the general applause occasioned by the imposition of a form of social responsibility upon landlords, it is worth pondering the following. Given that low-income housing is the location of most residential crime, it can be argued that recognition of a warranty of habitability in this context merely passes the cost of security measures on to poor tenants via increased rents. In other words, the 'bill will be paid, not by the owner, but by the tenants. And if...the incidence of crime is greatest in the areas in which the poor must live, they, and they alone, will be singled out to pay for their own police protection'.[3] To this the hard-bitten cynic might well respond that, in this life, you only get what you pay for. Put more kindly, however, the crucial question is whether the tenants are to receive some protection or none at all. Two sure things emerge from the historical record—tenants lack both the resources and the collective organisation to buy their own protection; and landlords will not provide the protection voluntarily.

(c) Implied contractual promise to preserve security

The contractual approach was taken even further in *Flood v Wisconsin Real Estate Investment Trust*.[4] Here a tenant was awarded nearly $400,000 in damages against her landlord in respect of injuries suffered when she was assaulted and raped by burglars whom she surprised in her apartment. A District Court held

---

18   412 A.2d 436 (1980).
19   412 A.2d 436 at 441 (1980) ('a callous disregard for the residents' safety in violation of ordinary standards of care').
20   428 F.2d 1071 (1970) (ante, p 905).
 1   412 A.2d 436 at 443 (1980).
 2   412 A.2d 436 at 443 (1980). It was considered that to restrict the relevant 'premises' merely to the individual dwelling units, would render the common areas in an apartment block 'a "no man's land" for the purpose of assessing habitability.' Moreover, the landlord's implied undertaking was held to exist independently of his knowledge of any risks.
 3   *Goldberg v Housing Authority of Newark*, 186 A.2d 291 at 298 (1962).
 4   503 F.Supp 1157 (1980).

that her tenancy agreement contained an implied warranty that the landlord would maintain the same level of security as was present at the commencement of the tenancy.[5] The landlord was therefore liable in contract, since there was evidence that the security patrol provided by the landlord had become less frequent during the course of the tenancy.[6]

(d) Comparison with England

There is in the recent judicial development of the American law of landlord and tenant a degree of social awareness and innovative boldness which contrasts markedly with the reluctance of the English courts to impose on landlords a duty to protect their tenants against the high incidence of crime in the depressed housing estates of large inner cities. Such a duty is unlikely to satisfy the test of 'necessity' or 'business efficacy' laid down in *Liverpool City Council v Irwin*[7] as governing the implication of a contractual duty of care.

The extension of housing standards to incorporate some form of guarantee of security against third party crime may represent a development of the future in England. In the meantime the protection of tenants from criminal intrusion seems to remain within the province of the criminal rather than the civil law.[8]

4. PROTECTION AGAINST UNLAWFUL EVICTION

There is a timeless social sentiment which abhors the forcible eviction of a man and his family from their home. In English law the roots of this general distaste for violent eviction are buried in the 'seisin-possession' concept which has influenced the law of land from its earliest days.[9] Regardless of the merits of the case, eviction is not merely the forcible vacation of property; it is the destruction of someone's way of life.

Counter-balanced against this general social antipathy towards unlawful extrusion of residential occupiers is the sometimes urgent desire of the landlord to rid himself of a turbulent, or merely inconvenient, tenant. The implications of Rent Act and other statutory protection of tenants are frequently so far-reaching that the landlord, deprived of any lawful means of terminating the tenant's protected status, resorts to violent means directed towards the same end. The precipitating factor is often the substantial cash incentive of a sale with vacant possession on the open market.

The landlord's use of self-help in such a case is quite unlawful.[10] Section 2 of the Protection from Eviction Act 1977 provides that where any premises are let as a dwelling on a lease which is subject to a right of re-entry or forfeiture, it is unlawful to enforce that right 'other than by proceedings in court while any

---

5   503 F.Supp 1157 at 1160.
6   503 F.Supp 1157 at 1160.
7   [1977] AC 239 (ante, p 907).
8   See eg *Knox v Anderton* (1982) 147 JP 340 at 343f, where the Divisional Court upheld the conviction of a defendant for possession of an offensive weapon on an upper landing on a block of flats on a council housing estate. This location was held to constitute a 'public place' within the meaning of section 1 of the Prevention of Crime Act 1953.
9   Ante, p 8.
10   The lawful means of terminating a tenancy are described in Chapter 14 (ante, p 484).

person is lawfully residing in the premises'. Similar requirements of due process of law are interposed by the 1977 Act where a statutorily unprotected tenant continues to reside in premises after the end of his tenancy,[11] and where a licensee under a 'restricted contract'[12] likewise remains in residence after the expiry of his agreement.[13]

English law provides not merely criminal sanctions, but also civil and administrative remedies in respect of unlawful eviction of the tenant from his home.

(1) Criminal sanctions

The primary criminal sanctions applicable to the unlawful eviction of a tenant are contained in the Protection from Eviction Act 1977.[14] The relevant terms of the Act provide protection for the 'residential occupier'—a phrase which includes any 'person occupying...premises as a residence, whether under a contract or by virtue of any enactment or rule of law'.[15] Although clearly not referable to trespassers or casual (ie, non-contractual) lodgers,[16] the class of 'residential occupier' includes not only tenants—whether contractual or statutory—but also contractual licensees.[17]

The Protection from Eviction Act confirms the existence of two criminal offences,[18] conviction for either of which may render the wrongdoer liable to a maximum fine of £400 and imprisonment for·a maximum term of two years.[19] Where either offence has been committed by a company (eg the landlord's management company), criminal proceedings may be initiated against not only the corporate entity but also any director, manager, secretary or 'other similar officer', if it can be proved that the offence was committed 'with the

11 Protection from Eviction Act 1977, s 3(1). This provision includes a tenant who does not qualify as a 'protected' or 'statutory' tenant under Rent Act 1977, ss 1, 2, but who nevertheless has a 'restricted contract' (see Protection from Eviction Act 1977, s 3(2A)).
12 Post, p 1040.
13 Protection from Eviction Act 1977, s 3(2A). This provision applies only to licences entered into after 28 November 1980 (compare *R v Blankley* [1979] Crim LR 166). The Protection from Eviction Act 1977 also applies to an occupier under a 'rental purchase agreement' as defined by Housing Act 1980, s 88(4), post, p 1001 (see Housing Act 1980, Sch 25, para 61).
14 Further criminal liability may arise in connection with the offences of using and threatening violence to secure entry to premises under Criminal Law Act 1977, s 6(1) (ante, p 756). See A.J. Ashworth, [1979] JSWL 79f.
15 Protection from Eviction Act 1977, s 1(1). The 'premises' may include the composite unit of a caravan parked on the landowner's land (*Norton v Knowles* [1969] 1 QB 572 at 576F. It may even be that a landlord is himself a 'residential occupier' if he occupies part of the premises (see *Harassed landlords*, (1977) 121 SJ 361).
16 'Residential occupier' cannot therefore include someone who is provided with temporary shelter and solace by a religious order (*R v Whitby Magistrates, ex parte Marsh* (Unreported, Queen's Bench Divisional Court, CO/625/84, 26 November 1984) (ante, p 458).
17 Ante, p 541.
18 Formerly contained in Rent Act 1965, s 30(1), (2). See (1979) 123 SJ 629 (H.E. Markson); A.J. Ashworth, [1979] JSWL 76.
19 Protection from Eviction Act 1977, s 1(4). See the prison terms of two years upheld in *R v Bokhari* (1974) 59 Cr App R 303 at 305 (prolonged harassment of 84 year old lady); three months in *R v Brennan and Brennan* [1979] Crim LR 603 (landlord without previous convictions who used the services of a 'very large man and an alsatian dog' to evict a group of students from their rented premises: 'Loss of liberty should be the usual penalty where landlords used threats or force, in the absence of unusual mitigation'). See (1979) LAG Bulletin 52, 249. Local authorities, through the agency of their harassment officers, have power to prosecute (Protection from Eviction Act 1977, s 6), but are frequently unwilling to act (see eg *McCall v Abelesz* [1976] QB 585 at 598C; (1981) LAG Bulletin 75).

consent or connivance of', or was 'attributable to any neglect on the part of', such a person.[20]

(a) Unlawful eviction

A criminal offence is committed under section 1(2) of the Act if any person unlawfully deprives the residential occupier of his occupation, or attempts to do so, 'unless he proves that he believed, and had reasonable cause to believe, that the residential occupier had ceased to reside in the premises.'[1] In *R v Yuthiwattana*[2] the Court of Appeal emphasised that an unlawful deprivation of occupation for this purpose must have the character of an 'eviction'. Thus the offence outlined in section 1(2) is committed where the occupier is required to leave the premises, not necessarily permanently, but at least for 'months or weeks'.[3] However, a 'locking-out' case, in which the occupier is merely shut out of premises overnight or for a short period of time, cannot give rise to an offence under section 1(2). Such a case is more appropriately prosecuted under section 1(3).[4]

(b) Harassment

A related criminal offence is committed under section 1(3) of the 1977 Act by any person who does 'acts'[5] which are 'calculated to interfere with the peace or comfort of the residential occupier or members of his household, or persistently withdraws or withholds services reasonably required for the occupation of the premises as a residence'.[6] However, such is the 'serious stigma' and 'social obloquy' attached to this 'truly criminal offence',[7] that a specific intent is required in the wrongdoer. Criminal liability for harassment arises only if the wrongdoer can be shown to have acted 'with intent to cause the residential occupier...to give up the occupation of the premises...or to refrain from exercising any right or pursuing any remedy in respect of the premises.'[8]

The offence of harassment can vary greatly. At one end of the scale the relevant acts may comprise no more than the intermittent but persistent

20   Protection from Eviction Act 1977, s 1(6).
1   Section 1(2) may apply even where the premises comprise only one room (*Thurrock UDC v Shina* (1972) 23 P & CR 205 at 207). See the fines of £1,000 imposed in *Sheffield CC v Blaskey and Salis Properties Ltd* (1986) Legal Action 135.
2   (1984) 16 HLR 49 at 63.
3   (1984) 16 HLR 49 at 63.
4   (1984) 16 HLR 49 at 63 (landlady refused to replace tenant's missing key). See [1981] Conv 377 (M. Wasik).
5   The word 'acts' includes a single act (*R v Evangelos Polycarpou* (1978) 9 HLR 129 at 131), but may not include an omission to act. It has been held that no offence is committed under section 1(3) merely because the landlord fails to rectify damage caused by repair work which was itself lawfully undertaken (*R v Ahmad* (1986) 130 SJ 554 at 555). Compare, however, *R v Yuthiwattana* (1984) 16 HLR 49, where a failure to replace the tenant's key came within section 1(3). See also (1986) Legal Action 125.
6   On the importance of 'persistently', see *R v Abrol* (1972) 116 SJ 177.
7   *R v Phekoo* [1981] 1 WLR 1117 at 1126G.
8   Protection from Eviction Act 1977, s 1(3). Thus no offence is committed if the defendant landlord reasonably believed the object of his attentions to be a squatter or trespasser rather than a 'residential occupier' (*R v Phekoo* [1981] 1 WLR 1117 at 1127A-B, 1128D) or if the landlord was 'utterly indifferent to, and unconcerned for', the tenant (*McCall v Abelesz* [1976] QB 585 at 598A, G). An intention to cause purely temporary disruption of occupation while repair works are carried out does not amount to an 'intent to cause the residential occupier . . . to give up . . . occupation', but may nevertheless connote an intent to cause him to 'refrain from exercising' his rights or pursuing any appropriate remedy (see *Schon v Camden LBC* [1986] 2 EGLR 37 at 39 F-H).

withdrawal by the landlord of such services as the domestic supply of water, gas and electricity.[9] At the other end of the scale the acts may constitute 'more serious threats which are tantamount to the statutory crime of blackmail'.[10] It is clear, however, that section 1 of the Protection from Eviction Act 1977 is merely a penal provision and, in itself, creates no statutory cause of action for damages in the victim.[11] The victim of eviction or harassment must look for compensation to the relevant remedies provided under civil law.

(2) Civil remedies

It is expressly stated in section 1(5) of the Protection from Eviction Act 1977 that the imposition of criminal liability under section 1 in no way prejudices 'any liability or remedy...in civil proceedings' which may arise from the same acts of eviction or harassment.[12] In consequence the courts have proved increasingly willing in recent years to award substantial civil damages to tenants who have suffered wrongful eviction or harassment at the hands of their landlord.[13] The aggrieved tenants have commonly alleged a congeries of torts and breaches of contract,[14] the recognised causes of action including the following.

(a) Breach of the landlord's covenant for quiet enjoyment

Any attempt by the landlord directed towards harassment or unlawful eviction of the tenant will constitute a breach of the landlord's implied covenant for quiet enjoyment.[15] The landlord's conduct may thus give rise to an action in damages or to an injunction on behalf of the tenant,[16] but harassment as such does not entitle the tenant to terminate the tenancy.[17]

9 *R v Phekoo* [1981] 1 WLR 1117 at 1126G.
10 *R v Phekoo* [1981] 1 WLR 1117 at 1126H. The phenomenon of the landlord's snake neatly coiled up in the tenant's bath is not unknown to legal advisers who practise in this area.
11 *McCall v Abelesz* [1976] QB 585 at 594C, 597F. However, it is open to the aggrieved individual to lay an information on oath concerning his eviction before magistrates, which may lead to the issue of a warrant for the arrest of the offending landlord. The landlord may then be remanded on bail, one of the conditions of which can be set as the reinstatement in possession of the evicted tenant. The criminal procedure can thus provide by indirect means an immensely practical and potent form of injunction (see (1982) LAG Bulletin, December, p 14).
12 See *McCall v Abelesz* [1976] QB 585 at 594B-C.
13 See (1979) LAG Bulletin 114. In *Drane v Evangelou* [1978] 1 WLR 455 at 461E-F, Lawton LJ observed that '[t]o deprive a man of a roof over his head...is one of the worst torts which can be committed.'
14 'The cases...must be rare in which eviction...does not found claims both in contract and in tort' (*Millington v Duffy* (1984) 17 HLR 232 at 235).
15 Ante, p 476. See R.L. Archdale, (1986) 130 SJ 601.
16 See *McCall v Abelesz* [1976] QB 585 at 594G, but compare (1979) 42 MLR 223 at 227f. An imaginative use of the criminal process (and particularly of conditions for bail) may effectively give the dispossessed tenant all the benefits of a civil injunction (supra).
17 This causes no real disadvantage to the tenant who holds a short periodic tenancy, since he can simply give the appropriate notice to quit. It presents more difficulty for the tenant with a longer fixed term, who is unable to quit the letting and find alternative accommodation. He is not even entitled to withhold rent (*Amrani v Oniah* [1984] CLY 1974). His remedy lies exclusively in damages for breach of the landlord's covenant. For the unsatisfactory nature of the tenant's rights, see *Poverty and the Residential Landlord-Tenant Relationship* (Research Report by Adrian Bradbrook, Canberra 1975), p 49. It has been suggested that the courts should apply in favour of the tenant a doctrine of 'constructive eviction' which dates back to the New York case of *Dyett v Pendleton* (1826) 8 Con (NY) 727. See A.J. Bradbrook, *The Role of the Judiciary in Reforming Landlord and Tenant Law*, (1975-76) 10 Melbourne ULR 459 at 466.

Examples of a breach of the landlord's covenant for quiet possession include a changing of the locks,[18] the removal of doors and windows,[19] the removal of the tenant's belongings,[20] the truncation of mains services[1] or central heating[2] in the tenant's home, actual or threatened violence aimed at inducing the departure of the tenant,[3] and the physical replacement of one tenant by another.[4] Even the eviction of a statutory tenant following the issue of a court order for possession, but before its execution by officers of the court, amounts to a breach of the covenant for quiet enjoyment.[5]

The tenant's right to damages for breach of the covenant for quiet enjoyment is not prejudiced by the fact that he himself may be in breach of some of the terms of the letting.[6] It is well established that the tenant's due payment of rent or performance of other covenants cannot—even by express words—be made a condition precedent of the tenant's right to quiet enjoyment of the premises.[7] The court may award not only general damages for loss suffered, but also 'aggravated' damages for injury to feelings.[8] If the eviction of the tenant is permanent, it is not necessarily easy to assess the loss suffered in having to seek other accommodation, quantification of the tenant's loss being particularly difficult if the tenant had a statutory tenancy which was potentially life-long in duration.[9] Although the point is disputed, it seems possible that the court may

---

18   *Ubhi v Nothey* (1983) LAG Bulletin 105; *Amrani v Oniah* [1984] CLY 1974; *Barnett v Djordjevic* (1984) LAG Bulletin 124 (£750 for three days out of possession); *Chukwu v Iqbal* (Unreported, Court of Appeal, 30 January 1985).

19   *Lavender v Betts* [1942] 2 All ER 72 at 73H.

20   *Chrysostomou v Georgiou* (1982) LAG Bulletin 33.

1   *Perera v Vandiyar* [1953] 1 WLR 672 at 675f.

2   *Malloy and Lunt v Alexander* [1982] CLY 1747.

3   See *McMillan v Singh* (1985) 17 HLR 120 at 123, where the landlord threw the tenant's camp bed and suitcase out into the garden with the immortal words, 'If you come back in here again, I'll fucking kill you' (£500 damages).

4   *McMillan v Singh* (1985) 17 HLR 120 at 122.

5   *Kyriacou v Pandeli* [1980] CLY 1648.

6   It would be different if the entire contract of tenancy were tainted by illegality, since in this case neither party could enforce its terms. However, the courts are slow to find such illegality. In *Chukwu v Iqbal* (Unreported, 30 January 1985), the Court of Appeal awarded damages to a tenant notwithstanding the fact that the tenant had known that the landlord was not declaring the rent to the Inland Revenue.

7   *Dawson v Dyer* (1833) 5 B & Ad 584 at 588, 110 ER 906 at 907f; *Edge v Boileau* (1885) 16 QBD 117 at 120; *Slater v Hoskins* [1982] 2 NZLR 541 at 551. The equitable doctrine of 'clean hands' has no application to a common law claim for damages (*McMillan v Singh* (1985) 17 HLR 120 at 124).

8   *McMillan v Singh* (1985) 17 HLR 120 at 125 (£250 aggravated damages); *Ashgar v Armed* (1984) LAG Bulletin 124 (£500 aggravated damages). Damages for breach of contract may include an element of compensation for the 'mental upset and distress' caused by the landlord's conduct (*McCall v Abelesz* [1976] QB 585 at 594E). This may include damages for inconvenience and distress caused to members of the tenant's family (*McCall v Abelesz*, supra at 594F). See the award of £500 damages for distress and inconvenience in *Millington v Duffy* (1984) 17 HLR 232 at 236. The court may more readily award aggravated damages where the breach of the covenant for quiet enjoyment is accompanied by a tort (eg trespass). See *Muljee v Rezaul Haque* (Unreported, Court of Appeal, 25 October 1985).

9   Even in these cases damages awards tend to be ludicrously small. It has been pointed out that more realistic awards would reach towards five rather than three figures, and would then exceed the limits of county court jurisdiction (see R. Clayton and H. Tomlinson, *Damages for Loss of a Rent Act Tenancy*, (1986) LAG Bulletin 10). In *Muljee v Rezaul Haque* (Unreported, 25 October 1985), the Court of Appeal held that the protected nature of the tenancy lost by reason of eviction was 'an element capable of increasing the damages for breach of the covenant for quiet enjoyment' (£1,860 awarded).

also grant 'exemplary' or 'punitive' damages in order to 'teach the defendant that a ruthless and cynical disregard of the plaintiff's rights for his own profit is not an appropriate method of proceeding'.[10]

(b) Torts of assault and battery

The tenant who suffers violent and unlawful eviction may well have an action in damages for the torts of assault and battery.[11] Battery includes any form of intentional 'hostile' touching[12] of the tenant by the landlord (or his agents). It is even possible that the infliction of emotional distress or nervous trauma upon a tenant may give rise to liability under the little-used rule in *Wilkinson v Downton*.[13]

(c) Tort of trespass

The tenant may vindicate his inherent right to exclusive possession of the demised premises by means of a civil action for trespass to his land.[14] Such trespass is almost certainly involved in any attempt to secure his unlawful eviction from the property by physical means,[15] and the courts have indicated, moreover, that exemplary damages may be awarded 'whenever it is necessary to teach a wrongdoer that tort does not pay.'[16]

(d) Tort of nuisance

Some forms of harassment by a landlord may amount to an actionable nuisance. In *Guppys (Bridport) Ltd v Brookling*[17] the Court of Appeal awarded exemplary damages for nuisance to tenants whose residential comfort had been devastated by the landlord's attempts to re-build their premises around them and convert the property into self-contained flats for more affluent occupiers.

10   *McMillan v Singh* (1985) 17 HLR 120 at 125 per Arnold P (£250 exemplary damages awarded in order to negative the landlord's profit from a re-letting at a higher rent). Exemplary damages may be awarded even though the circumstances constitute harassment falling short of eviction (see *De Silva v Qureshi* (1984) LAG Bulletin 47 (£500 exemplary damages plus £500 general damages for removal of mains services)). Likewise, exemplary damages may be awarded even though the unlawful eviction involves only a single person rather than a family (see *Ubhi v Nothey* (1983) LAG Bulletin 105). No principle of 'double jeopardy' precludes the award of exemplary damages where the landlord has already been fined heavily under the Protection from Eviction Act 1977 (*Ashgar v Armed* (1984) LAG Bulletin 124).

11   See eg *Edwards v Marbyn* (1980) LAG Bulletin 17 (£150 for assault, together with £50 for inconvenience, £25 special damages, £475 aggravated damages and £300 exemplary damages, and fines and costs totalling £250); *Moran v Duffy* (1982) LAG Bulletin 34 (£1,000 for punch in face and injury to finger).

12   *Wilson v Pringle* [1986] 3 WLR 1 at 11A.

13   [1897] 2 QB 57. See eg *Newby v Alto Riviera Apartments*, 131 Cal Rptr 547 at 552ff (1976); D. Tiplady, *Recent Developments in the Law of Landlord and Tenant: the American Experience*, (1981) 44 MLR 129 at 147f.

14   Ante, p 755.

15   See eg *Drane v Evangelou* [1978] 1 WLR 455 at 457C-G ('monstrous behaviour'). See (1979) 42 MLR 223 (D. Morgan).

16   *Rookes v Bernard* [1964] AC 1129 at 1227 per Lord Devlin, applied to the case of unlawful eviction in *Drane v Evangelou* [1978] 1 WLR 455 at 459D, 462D-E; *Millington v Duffy* (1984) 17 HLR 232 at 235f; *Amrani v Oniah* [1984] CLY 1974.

17   (1984) 269 Estates Gazette 846 at 946 (£1,000 damages for each tenant).

(e) Tort of wrongful interference with goods

It is also open to a dispossessed tenant to sue for damages for the tort of wrongful interference with goods. This remedy may be particularly advantageous where the tenant had intended to give up possession in any event, whereupon the landlord violently accelerated the process of departure. In *Caruso v Owen*[18] the landlord removed the belongings of the tenant, a research student, while he was away from his rented house. The tenant recovered £3,000 damages for loss of his PhD notes, which the landlord had burned on a bonfire in the garden.[19]

(3) Administrative remedies

There is, at least in theory, an administrative remedy for evicted tenants under the terms of the Housing Act 1985. The local housing authority's duty to provide accommodation for the 'homeless'[20] extends to a person who 'has accommodation but...cannot secure entry to it'[1] or who is 'threatened with homelessness'.[2] In the latter case, the local housing authority may be under a duty to 'take reasonable steps to secure that accommodation does not cease to be available for his occupation.'[3] In practice this should mean that the local authority takes steps to invoke section 1(3) of the Protection from Eviction Act 1977 in order to protect the occupation of the tenant who is under threat of unlawful eviction.[4] There is, however, little evidence that local authorities are particularly diligent in this regard.[5]

---

18 (1983) LAG Bulletin 106 (Willesden County Court).
19 The damages were assessed with reference to the maintenance grant normally awarded for the period which the student estimated he would need to do his research again.
20 The duties of the local housing authority in respect of homeless persons are discussed more generally in Chapter 21 (ante, p 760).
1 Housing Act 1985, s 58(3)(a).
2 Housing Act 1985, s 58(4).
3 Housing Act 1985, s 66(2).
4 Ante, p 956.
5 Ante, p 763.

CHAPTER 29

Statutory protection in the private sector

For over 70 years successive Rent Acts have provided the mainstay of the statutory protection conferred on residential tenants in the private rented sector. First introduced in 1915, the Rent Act legislation has survived a number of amendments and consolidations, exerting a consistent and durable influence over the entire field of housing law. Just as portents of demise began to gather around the Rent Act, the House of Lords' decision in 1985 in *Street v Mountford*[1] demonstrated that the Act has an even more extensive impact than had generally been imagined. On any analysis, therefore, the Rent Acts represent a remarkable corpus of legislation, mirroring in their own way many of the social, economic and ideological changes which have occurred during the present century. The legislation has come to be one of the pre-eminent expressions of the idea that all citizens have a social right to residential living conditions of reasonable security and dignity.

1. HISTORY AND SOCIAL PHILOSOPHY OF THE RENT ACTS

That the Rent Act legislation should have acquired such long-lasting importance is one of the ironies of parliamentary intervention. The first Rent Act, the Increase of Rent and Mortgage Interest (War Restrictions) Act 1915, was conceived as an emergency solution to a supposedly short-term problem.

(1) The origins of the Rent Acts

The outbreak of the Great War in 1914 inevitably generated shortages of the resources, money-supply and labour-power required for the private construction of dwelling-houses for the working classes. In circumstances of accentuated demand for housing, landlords were enabled to demand (and obtain) increasingly higher rents, not least because wages in the munitions industry were relatively good.[2] Ordinary working-class families not employed in that industry were unable, however, to meet the new levels of rent demanded. The predictable result was the frequent eviction of such families and the rise of a new class of profiteering landlords who did not scruple to extort private advantage from the poor in the midst of war-time exigency. Evictions were accompanied by a growing working-class fury—most notably in Glasgow—which found expression in bitter and voluble protest and, more tangibly, in the prosecution of increasingly determined rent strikes.[3]

1 [1985] AC 809 (ante, pp 427, 449).
2 See P. Beirne, *Fair Rent and Legal Fiction* (London 1977), p 77.
3 See P.Q. Watchman, 'The Origin of the 1915 Rent Act', (1980) Law and State (No 5) 20 at 24f.

(a) The immediate background of the 1915 Act

In the face of widespread protest Asquith's government still refused to act until eventually its hand was forced by an extraordinary concatenation of events. In the autumn of 1915 Clydeside was close to a social convulsion which has been aptly described as a 'crisis of legality'.[4] The very munitions workers whose high wages had enabled the landlords to exploit housing shortages provided the focal point of a new but related form of civil unrest. The Munitions of War Act, introduced in July 1915, imposed a heavy-handed and almost military form of discipline upon the munitions industry in an attempt to coerce the work-force to contribute more efficiently to the war effort.[5] Within a couple of months not only had the munitions issue conduced to the emergence of 'a grass-roots organisation committed to class struggle',[6] but the munitions workers had joined in holy alliance with the protest against rent increases. The situation rapidly deteriorated in the direction of a widespread breakdown of the rule of law. Matters came to a head when, in November 1915, a local factor served eviction summonses on 18 of his tenants. In the face of street demonstrations, massive working-class protest and the threat of a general withdrawal of labour from the munitions factories and shipyards, the government gave way.[7] Within eight days the government had introduced legislation in Parliament directed at the restriction of rent levels, and within a month the government's reluctant proposals had become law.

Only truly exceptional circumstances could have brought about, so quickly and so decisively, the introduction of a measure which was plainly inimical to large vested interests in Parliament. The central issues raised by the Increase of Rent and Mortgage Interest (War Restrictions) Bill were never discussed by Parliament.[8] There seems to have been a general agreement that the Bill incorporated a necessary but purely temporary measure which could be justified only in the exigency of a war-time emergency.[9] However, while many inveighed in Parliament against the ruinous socialist tendencies promoted by the Bill,[10] few perceived that the legislation would prove to be far from

---

4   See P.Q. Watchman, (1980) Law and State (No 5) 20 at 23.

5   Under the Munitions of War Act 1915, strikes by munitions workers were forbidden by law and local munitions tribunals were instituted to try offenders against the new code of discipline.

6   P.Q. Watchman, (1980) Law and State (No 5) 20 at 30. See generally David Englander, *Landlord and Tenant in Urban Britain 1838-1918* (Oxford 1983), p 210ff.

7   *The Glasgow Herald* (30 October 1915) reported the words of Paddy Dollan, 'The law of eviction was the law of the propertied classes. [And] they of the working class would respect no law which sanctioned the eviction of a working class family'. See P.Q. Watchman, (1980) Law and State (No 5) 20 at 37.

8   A great deal of Parliament's attention was devoted to the effect of the Bill on levels of mortgage interest as distinct from levels of rent. See eg *Parliamentary Debates, House of Commons, Official Report (Fifth Series)*, Vol 76 (Session 1914-15), Cols 434-438, 454-456, 726, 732-736, 754-757, 792-794.

9   See *Parliamentary Debates, House of Commons, Official Report (Fifth Series)*, Vol 76 (Session 1914-15), Cols 429, 720, 733, 753, 765, 781, 798f. See especially the statement of Sir W. Essex (at Col 789) that the Bill was 'being supported on all the benches of this House because there is not a man hardly who dares get up in this House and say a word against it, whatever he may feel'.

10   See eg *Parliamentary Debates, House of Commons, Official Report (Fifth Series)*, Vol 76 (Session 1914-15), Col 435 (Sir F. Banbury).

temporary and would indeed go a long way to undermine the existing balance of property rights.[11]

(b) The Increase of Rent and Mortgage Interest (Restrictions) Act 1920

Although designed as a short-term measure, the 1915 legislation was subsequently consolidated and extended in the Increase of Rent and Mortgage Interest (Restrictions) Act 1920.[12] The Minister of Health, who moved the second reading of the 1920 Bill in the House of Commons, conceded that the legislation represented an 'interference with economic laws',[13] but it was already clear that the Rent Act had come to stay. Ironically the most important innovation of the 1920 Act—the introduction of a principle of statutory succession on the death of the tenant—went almost unnoticed by Parliament.[14] Yet the protective impact of the modern Rent Act rests largely on the association between fair rents and the security of tenure effectively brought about by the devolution of tenancies on death.

(c) Subsequent history of the Rent Act legislation

The Rent Act legislation has since arrogated to itself a life and substance never contemplated by its framers. For many decades now the statute has imposed some measure of social control in the private sector over the relationship between landlords and residential occupiers—a control which is aimed at preventing exploitation of the latter by the former. The maintenance of this control clearly restricts freedom of contract in the housing market and has had the broad effect of inhibiting the exercise by private owners of formerly sacrosanct rights of property.

(i) *Political influences* The history of the Rent Acts subsequent to 1920 has, of course, been marked by fluctuations of political and economic policy.[15] Extensions of the legislation have tended to occur during periods of Labour administration.[16] Restrictions of the legislation have in general been instituted

---

11 For a rare recognition that the legislation would be far from temporary in scope and indeed marked a 'breaking through the whole of the rules governing private property', see *Parliamentary Debates, House of Commons, Official Report (Fifth Series)*, Vol 76 (Session 1914-15), Col 788f (Sir W. Essex).

12 The continuation of the Rent Act legislation after the First World War has since been explained as having been intended to 'deal with the critical housing shortage which followed the demobilisation of immense numbers of the armed forces' (see *Harrison v Hammersmith and Fulham LBC* [1981] 1 WLR 650 at 661B).

13 *Parliamentary Debates, House of Commons, Official Report (Fifth Series)*, Vol 129 (Session 1920), Col 2236 (4 June 1920). There was recognition even in 1915 that the Rent Act would 'thrust a crowbar into the business relations of this country' (see *Parliamentary Debates, House of Commons, Official Report (Fifth Series)*, Vol 76 (Session 1914-15), Col 733 (Sir Thomas Whittaker)).

14 See however, *Parliamentary Debates, House of Commons, Official Report (Fifth Series)*, Vol 129 (Session 1920), Col 2261 (4 June 1920); Vol 130, Col 1929f (21 June 1920).

15 For a historical survey of the antagonism between two camps broadly labelled as 'controllers' and 'free marketeers', see Barry Pearce, 'Private Rental Housing: a problem of Political Schism', in D. Anderson and D. Marsland (ed), *Home Truths* (London 1983), p 24ff.

16 See eg the Rent Acts of 1965, 1968 and 1974. In *Homes for the Future* (1985) the National Executive Committee of the Labour Party announced its intention to strengthen the existing Rent Act legislation and to repeal the 'failed shorthold tenancies scheme'.

by Conservative administrations.[17] Yet neither of the political parties with government experience has done anything effective to halt the decline of the private rented sector in a period of increasingly horrendous housing shortage.

(ii) Decline in the private rected sector   One of the most important social statistics of the present century relates to the transformation in modes of tenure of the private home. Before the First World War 90 per cent of all dwellings were privately rented.[18] As late as 1951 the private rented sector still accounted for 50 per cent of the market.[19] Since then the incidence of private letting has declined dramatically.[20] The proportion of households living in privately rented accommodation decreased from 15 per cent in 1971 to 7 per cent in 1985.[1] For this decline there are many explanations, but the central dilemma seems to relate to the relative poverty of those occupiers who resort to the private rental market. Many tenants are simply unable, because of low income, to pay an economic rent, and the Environment Committee of the House of Commons concluded in 1982 that the imposition of higher rents would merely aggravate existing problems of overcrowding and homelessness.[2] In consequence the landlord's rates of return on Rent Act protected dwellings are not usually comparable with those available on other—much more easily managed—forms of investment. Depressed rates of financial return, coupled with the impact of security of tenure and the difficulties of repossession, have made private letting an increasingly unattractive option. It is clear that the private sector will never truly revitalise in the absence of some fundamental reorganisation of the system of housing finance designed to negative the competitive effects of the heavy forms of subsidy already available in respect of owner-occupied and publicly rented accommodation.[3]

(iii) The net balance of the Rent Act   The field of Rent Act jurisprudence is pervaded by the debate whether increased statutory control over private lettings is ultimately counterproductive. There is a strong argument to the effect that the net consequence of the Rent Act has been the constricted supply of dwellings available for private letting.[4] However, this argument has only limited attractions and did not, for instance, dissuade the House of Lords in *Street v Mountford*[5] from recognising the extensive application of the Rent Act in the context of many so-called 'licences'. In the light of this important decision the present coverage of the Rent Act is difficult to estimate, but it is probably

---

17   See eg the Housing Act 1980, which imposed many important qualifications on the rights enjoyed by private sector tenants under the Rent Act. See D.C. Hoath, *The Housing Act 1980: A New Rent Act*, [1981] JSWL 257, 335; *Making Money from the Housing Act 1980*, (1980) 1 PLB 25.

18   John Stanley MP (Minister for Housing and Construction), *Government Policies on Home Ownership in the 1980s*, in *Home Ownership in the 1980s* (SHAC Policy Paper 3, 1980), p 6.

19   Sir George Young, (1984) 15 Jiro (No 2), 6 at 7.

20   See generally *The Private Rented Housing Sector* (First Report from the House of Commons Environment Committee), Vol 1 (HC 40-1, 13 July 1982), Chapter 2.

1   *General Household Survey 1985* (OPCS Monitor, Reference GHS 86/1, 18 September 1986), p 6 (Table 7).

2   See *The Private Rented Housing Sector*, supra, para 86.

3   See B.J. Pearce, *Private Rental Housing: Prospects for a Political Consensus*, [1983] 32 Housing Review 117 at 118.

4   Post, p 996. See also Sir George Young, (1984) 15 Jiro (No 2) 6 at 8.

5   [1985] AC 809 (ante, p 449; post p 1000).

fair to say that something in excess of 1.4 million dwellings (or 9 per cent of the housing stock of England and Wales) still come within the ambit of the Act.[6]

(iv) Revival of judicial concern The ruling in *Street v Mountford* was the culmination of a new judicial concern with rented housing which emerged slowly but steadily during the 1970s and 1980s. The courts played their part in the dialectic between the political philosophies which favoured respectively the extension and the contraction of the Rent Act operation. It is significant that during the 1970s the Court of Appeal seemed prepared to let the 'decontrollers' have their way, in the hope that this might stimulate the overall supply of private rented accommodation.[7] Yet there were indications that many judges were becoming increasingly willing to endorse the protective policy found in the Rent Act.[8] In *Davis v Johnson*,[9] for instance, Lord Scarman declared that he found 'nothing illogical or surprising in Parliament legislating to over-ride a property right, if it be thought to be socially necessary...[T]he restriction or suspension for a time of property rights is a familiar aspect of much of our social legislation: the Rent Acts are a striking example.' The same judge pointed out in *Horford Investments Ltd v Lambert*[10] that the

policy of the Rent Acts was and is to protect the tenant in his home, whether the threat be to extort a premium for the grant or renewal of his tenancy, to increase his rent, or to evict him...The Rent Acts have throughout their history constituted an interference with contract and property rights for a specific purpose—the redress of the balance of advantage enjoyed in a world of housing shortage by the landlord over those who have to rent their homes.[11]

The future of the Rent Act lies, however, in the hands of politicians rather than judges. It remains to be seen whether the House of Lords' ruling in *Street v Mountford* marks the beginning of a new era of invigorated protectionist policy in the private rental sector. The cynic will be alert to the possibility that the recent revival of apparent concern for the interests of the residential tenant only barely conceals a much more pressing fiscal reality. It is quite clear that the 'fair rent' controls which were indirectly strengthened by *Street v Mountford* provide a mechanism for limiting public expenditure on housing needs. In so far as the housing needs of the poorer citizen are financed by housing benefit, the enforcement of statutory control over rents paid to private landlords effectively prevents the diversion of public funds into the hands of private entrepreneurs. The operation of a free rental market may have had to concede priority to restrictions on public spending, with the somewhat paradoxical

6   Central Statistical Office, *Social Trends No 16* (London 1986), p 133; *Report of the Inquiry into British Housing* (Chairman: HRH The Duke of Edinburgh, July 1985), p 23. As the Parliamentary Under Secretary of State for the Department of the Environment said in 1984, the private rented sector, although 'now small in terms of the total housing market...can still play a disproportionate part in meeting the needs of certain groups of people' (see Sir George Young, (1984) 15 Jiro (No 2), 6 at 7).

7   Post, p 996.

8   This approach contrasted strongly with the open antagonism with which the courts treated the early Rent Acts (see eg R.E. Megarry, *The Rent Acts* (10th edn, London 1967), p 9f).

9   [1979] AC 317 at 348E-G.

10 [1976] Ch 39 at 52D-E. In *Feyereisel v Turnidge* [1952] 2 QB 29 at 37, Denning LJ declared that 'the guiding light through the darkness of the Rent Acts is to remember that they confer personal security on a tenant in respect of his home.'

11 See also *Re Pepita and Donkas* (1979) 101 DLR (3d) 577 at 590.

result that the protectionist policy of the Rent Act has circuitously become an instrument of Tory policy.[12]

(2) The changing ideology of property

The law relating to residential tenancies is fundamentally concerned with human dignity and decency. Its primary application is in the provision of a secure domestic base for a wide range of family and other social interactions and a temporary base for the relatively large numbers of people on the move between jobs and marriages.

The modern Rent Act seeks to attain these objectives by assuring the private tenant both a certain 'status of irremovability' and a guarantee that only a 'fair rent' will be asked as the price of his security of tenure.[13] The overall effect is in many cases to confirm at fair rents the existence of residential tenancies which—irrespective of their contractually agreed duration—are not terminable within the lifetime of the original tenant or indeed during the lifetime of some of the members of his family. To this extent the social interest in residential security for the family has been allowed to override the claim of the property owner to dispose freely of his land in accordance with the nominal terms of the lease.[14] The corollary of this recognition is the gradual metamorphosis of the legal position of the protected residential tenant.

(a) Social rights of property

The Rent Act may initially appear to provide only for a temporary restriction or suspension of the property rights belonging to the landlord. In reality, however, the legislation confers on eligible residential tenants certain 'social rights of property' which prevail over strict legal entitlements as defined in the orthodox law of property or as fixed by private agreement between landlord and tenant.[15]

Under the Rent Act the tenant's mere right to enjoy possession for a limited period has now been extended—often indefinitely—by force of statute, with the consequence that it begins much more closely to resemble some qualified claim of ownership. While by force of statute the protected tenant has become almost the grantee of some kind of entailed interest, the landlord's rights are, in sharp contrast, stripped back to a bare reversion.[16] Rent Act legislation has the clear effect of 'preventing a landlord from obtaining in the foreseeable future

---

12   Post, p 1032.
13   Security of tenure and rent restriction constitute an indivisible form of protection for the tenant. The two measures are plainly interdependent, since one blade alone of the double-edged sword of the Rent Act would provide merely illusory protection for the tenant (see eg *Blake v Attorney General* [1982] IR 117 at 141 per O'Higgins CJ). In the absence of security of tenure a landlord, although restricted to charging a fair rent, could evict at any time; without 'fair rent' control the landlord could likewise rid himself of an unwanted tenant simply by raising the level of the rent.
14   An important catalyst in this process has been the universal consensus that 'a good and secure home is essential to successful family life'. See eg *Report of the Committee on One-Parent Families* (Cmnd 5629, July 1974), Vol 1, para 6.1.
15   See E.H. Rabin, *The Revolution in Residential Landlord-Tenant Law: Causes and Consequences*, 69 Cornell LR 517 (1984).
16   Post, p 970. See also M.A. Glendon, *The Transformation of American Landlord-Tenant Law*, 23 Boston College LR 503 at 544 (1982).

any benefit at all from his property',[17] and of causing 'an almost permanent alienation from the landlord of the right to get possession of the premises'.[18]

(b) False dichotomies

There is, of course, a source of potential confusion in any discussion of the respective rights of landlord and tenant. It was pointed out in Chapter 1[19] that there is a certain unreality in any search for 'the' owner of any particular 'thing'. The law of property is concerned not with things but with relationships. As Professor Bruce Ackerman has said,[20]

property law discusses the relationships that arise *between people* with respect to things. More precisely, the law of property considers the way rights to use things may be parcelled out amongst a host of competing resource users. Each resource user is conceived as holding a bundle of rights vis à vis other potential users...Hence it risks serious confusion to identify any single individual as *the* owner of any particular thing.

In examining the operation of the Rent Act it is therefore fundamentally important to eliminate the false dichotomy between the 'ownership' supposedly retained by the landlord and the 'mere' use or possession enjoyed by the residential tenant. The long history of the Rent Acts has comprised various kinds of inter-change between the bundles of user claims enjoyed by landlord and tenant respectively, the inter-change in every case being premised ultimately on some allegedly overriding principle of social justice.

(c) Distributive justice

The Rent Acts represent a response to the sad but timeless capacity of man to exploit the economic necessity of his fellow man when demand for a particular resource—here housing—is not met by an adequate supply. Ultimately the Rent Act is concerned with a problem of distributive justice—the allocation of one of the elementary 'goods' of life, ie, access to reasonable housing and living conditions. In superficial terms the legislation seeks to achieve its social objective through a partial displacement of the normal market forces which would otherwise dominate the allocation of the primary economic resource of housing stock. Nothing should, however, obscure the underlying reality, which is that, in common with so many innovations in the modern law of residential tenancies,[1] the Rent Act serves 'the moral principle of redistribution of wealth from landlord to tenant'.[2]

(d) A shift in the meaning of 'property'

The property implications of Rent Act legislation are consistent with certain contemporary trends in the jurisprudence of property. Attention was drawn in

---

17   *Blake v Attorney-General* [1982] IR 117 at 122 per McWilliam J.
18   *Blake v Attorney-General* [1982] IR 117 at 140 per O'Higgins CJ.
19   Ante, p 9.
20   B.A. Ackerman, *Private Property and the Constitution* (Yale UP 1977), 26f.
1   For a description of other innovations relating to the environmental quality of tenanted accommodation, see Chapter 27 (ante, p 901).
2   See C.J. Meyers, 27 Stanford LR 879 at 882 (1974-75).

Chapter 1 to the argument advanced by Professor C.B. Macpherson that whereas the concept of a property right has traditionally comprised a *right to exclude* all others from the use or enjoyment of something, the newly emerging idea of property consists essentially of a *right not to be excluded* from the use or enjoyment of something.[3] Thus the idea of property is constantly being 'broadened...to include...a right to a kind of society or set of power relations which will enable the individual to live a fully human life.'

This analysis is in sympathetic accord with Charles Reich's now classic plea for a recognition of 'the new property' as the basis for 'a Homestead Act for rootless twentieth century man'.[4] If correct, this analysis indicates an intellectual shift at the core of the property notion away from the idea of a private right to exclude from personally owned resources towards the idea of a public right of access to socially valued resources. Such a development is, of course, entirely consistent with the contemporary emergence of 'new property rights' which comprise essentially highly personal, intangible, non-commerciable claims relating to various kinds of personal security.[5] It may even be that these forms of 'new property' prefigure some idea of a public trust, under which socially valued assets (eg housing, pensions, and jobs) can be viewed as held by nominee owners on trust for defined categories of beneficiary.[6]

Coinciding with this shift is the advent of the welfare state—an institution which for many purposes has taken over the allocative function of the market in relation to the 'goods' of life. It is not difficult to locate the role of Rent Act legislation within this general pattern of development. Some writers, like Macpherson, see the entire evolutionary process in this area as securing the right of the citizen to 'that kind of society which is instrumental to a full and free life', and therefore to 'a set of power relations that permits a full life of enjoyment and development of one's human capacities.' Others have not viewed the current trend with such favour. Kamenka and Tay, for instance, have measured the 'decline in respect for private property' partly in terms of 'the demand for *access* as independent of ownership and as something that ought to be maintainable against it.'[7]

(e) A 'status of irremovability'

Irrespective of ideological standpoint there is little doubt that there is currently in progress something in the nature of a redefinition of the general concept of

---

3   See C.B. Macpherson, 'Capitalism and the Changing Concept of Property', in E. Kamenka and R.S. Neale (ed), *Feudalism, Capitalism and Beyond* (Canberra 1975), p 116ff.

4   C. Reich, *The New Property*, 73 Yale LJ 733 (1964).

5   Ante, pp 11, 372, 558.

6   For a reference to the way in which the development of rent and eviction control has caused the landlord to be 'treated more and more like a public utility and less and less like an ordinary business person', see L. Berger, *The New Residential Tenancy Law-Are Landlords Public Utilities?*, 60 Nebraska LR 707 at 715 (1981).

7   'Beyond Bourgeois Individualism: the Contemporary Crisis in Law and Legal Ideology', in E. Kamenka and R.S. Neale (ed), op cit, p 133. Alice Tay has pointed in particular to the dangers implicit in the contemporary movement towards 'a bureaucratic-administrative, regulatory and even confiscatory resources-allocation concern, in which the state stands above property owners as the representative of a general "socio-political" interest' (see 'Law, the citizen and the state', in E. Kamenka, R. Brown and A.E.-S. Tay (ed), *Law and Society* (London 1978), p 13).

property. This redefinition emerges in the Rent Act in the form of a legally protected 'status of irremovability'[8] vested in the residential tenant. This status of irremovability cannot be classified easily within the framework of existing proprietary rights in land. In some very real sense the right to live in a house or flat, free from the threat of arbitrary eviction, free from the exploitative and oppressive impact of normal market forces, has itself become a new form of property right.[9] Entitlement to the 'use value' of residential property has in this context become more significant than entitlement to its 'exchange' or 'capital value' as a disposable asset on the freehold property market.

(f) A return from contract to status

The idea of 'status' is indeed central to the entire scheme of the Rent Act. The whole point of the Act is that the rights of the tenant are defined in terms of a status rather than by contract—a feature which nowadays is not uncharacteristic of social legislation in an increasingly collectivist world.[10] This fact represents a partial reversal of Henry Sumner Maine's famous dictum of 1861 that 'the movement of the progressive societies has hitherto been a movement *from Status to Contract.*'[11]

Maine's dictum and its eventual rejection across large areas of social legislation were adverted to by the House of Lords in *Johnson v Moreton*.[12] Here Lord Simon of Glaisdale pointed to the way in which even within Maine's lifetime changing social and economic circumstances were beginning to cast a somewhat bleaker shadow upon the pre-eminent position ascribed by Maine to the contractual ordering of society. Even in the 19th century the law 'began to back-pedal' from the formerly sacrosanct principle of freedom of contract.[13] Above all, the prerequisites for the beneficent operation of the laissez-faire ideology were 'palpably lacking' in the area of landlord and tenant. The supply of land could not expand immediately and flexibly in response to demand and generally, as Lord Simon went on to observe,[14]

a man became a tenant rather than an owner-occupier because his circumstances compelled him to live hand-to-mouth; the landlord's purse was generally longer and his command of knowledge and counsel far greater than the tenant's. In short, it was held, the constriction of the market and inequality of bargaining power enabled the landlord to dictate contractual terms which did not necessarily operate to the general benefit of society. It was to counteract this descried constriction of the market and to redress this descried inequality of bargaining power that the law— specifically, in the shape of legislation—came to intervene repeatedly to modify freedom of contract between landlord and tenant. Since Maine the movement of many 'progressive' societies has been reversed. The holding of a statutory or protected tenancy is rather a status than a pure creature of contract.

(g) Unlawful expropriation?

The operation of the Rent Act is, of course, controversial simply because it

8   Post, p 1003.
9   See C. Hand, *The Statutory Tenancy: An Unrecognised Proprietary Interest,* [1980] Conv 351.
10 See eg Lesar, (1961) 9 U Kansas LR 369.
11 *Ancient Law* (Everyman's Library edn, London 1917), p 100.
12 [1980] AC 37. See N.D.M. Parry, [1980] Conv 117.
13 [1980] AC 37 at 66F.
14 [1980] AC 37 at 66H-67B.

seems to deprive 'the' property owner of much of the utility which he imagined he had by virtue of being 'the' property owner. The statute is doubly controversial because it intervenes within a primarily commercial relationship in order to impose standards of social morality. The Rent Act legislation subverts the basic rule in property law of caveat emptor and reflects a viewpoint which, when expressed in an extreme form, holds it to be immoral for one individual to own another's home for personal profit.

It is interesting to note that in 1981 the Rent Act legislation of the Republic of Ireland was subjected to a constitutional challenge of a kind which is, of course, quite impossible in England.[15] The argument of constitutional infirmity was raised in *Blake v Attorney General*,[16] on the ground that the operation of the Irish Rent Act was both arbitrary and discriminatory. McWilliam J held that the legislation concerned was repugnant to the constitutional protection afforded rights of property.[17] In his view, 'a group of citizens arbitrarily selected has been deprived of property for the benefit of another group of citizens without compensation, with no limitation on the period of deprivation, and with no indication of any occasion which necessitates their selection for this purpose from amongst the general body of citizens.'[18]

This judgment was later upheld by the Supreme Court, where O'Higgins CJ observed that the statutory scheme was 'arbitrary and unfair' in that 'tenants of controlled dwellings are singled out for specially favourable treatment, both as to rent and as to the right to retain possession, regardless of whether they have any social or financial need for such preferential treatment and regardless of whether the landlords have the ability to bear the burden of providing such preferential treatment.'[19] The eventual result of the successful constitutional challenge was the introduction of new legislation which now provides for the administrative assessment of such rents as may be deemed 'just and proper'.[20] By this means it is assumed, although it is not yet certain, that the legislation cannot be condemned as mounting an 'unjust attack' on the property rights of the private landlord.

2. DEFINITION OF A 'PROTECTED TENANCY'

So stringent are the implications of protected status under the Rent Act that the courts have traditionally interpreted the legislation somewhat restrictively

---

15 Ireland's Rent Restrictions Act 1960 was framed in terms broadly similar to the English Rent Acts.
16 [1982] IR 117.
17 Article 40, s 3(2) of the Irish Constitution protects 'from unjust attack' the 'property rights of every citizen'.
18 [1982] IR 117 at 126.
19 [1982] IR 117 at 140. This decision was immediately followed by the introduction of the Housing (Private Rented Dwellings) Bill 1981, which sought to phase out controlled rents over a period of five years. However, even this provision was declared by the Supreme Court to be an unconstitutional attack on the property rights of landlords (see *In the Matter of Article 26 of the Constitution and in the Matter of The Housing (Private Rented Dwellings) Bill, 1981* [1983] IR 181 at 191).
20 Housing (Private Rented Dwellings) Act 1982, s 13(2), as amended by Housing (Private Rented Dwellings) (Amendment) Act 1983.

and therefore adversely to the interests of the residential occupier. The gates of the Rent Act do not open wide to all comers. Those who seek the full protection of the statute must show that they qualify in terms of section 1 of the Rent Act 1977. This deceptively simple provision merits close scrutiny. The most difficult question under the Rent Act relates to definitional issues concerning eligibility for protection, and it is an altogether easier task to outline the provisions which apply once a tenancy is shown to fall within the dragnet of the legislation.

Section 1 of the Rent Act 1977 defines a 'protected tenancy' as 'a tenancy under which a dwelling-house (which may be a house or part of a house) is let as a separate dwelling'. This definition is subject to exceptions both express and implied, although categories of occupancy which are excluded from full protected status under the Rent Act may nevertheless qualify for the lesser degree of protection given by the Act to restricted contracts.[1]

A protected tenancy under section 1 must meet the following conditions.

(1) There must be a 'tenancy' and not a mere 'licence' or other arrangement

It is fundamental that full Rent Act protection applies only to those forms of occupancy which have the strict character of a 'tenancy'. Section 1 of the Rent Act 1977 has no relevance either to a mere licence to occupy or to any other residential arrangement which falls short of conferring a tenancy. The elusive distinction between the tenancy and the licence has been discussed extensively elsewhere,[2] and is not dealt with here in any detail except in so far as it relates to various evasive mechanisms which have been developed by landlords for the purpose of circumventing the intrusive reach of the Rent Act.[3]

Once a tenancy has been found to satisfy the qualifying conditions of section 1 of the 1977 Act, it is entirely irrelevant whether that tenancy is a periodic tenancy or a fixed term, a legal or an equitable tenancy, a tenancy by estoppel or a subtenancy.[4] Moreover, in relation to tenancies granted on or after 14 August 1974, it matters not whether the tenancy covers furnished or unfurnished premises.[5]

(2) The tenancy must relate to a 'dwelling-house'

It is clear from section 1 of the Rent Act 1977 that the subject of a 'protected tenancy' must be a 'dwelling-house'. However, there is no statutory definition of the term 'dwelling- house' other than the plain indication in section 1 that a dwelling-house for this purpose may comprise 'either a house or part of a house'. It is a notorious feature of English housing legislation that statutory

1 See Rent Act 1977, s 19(2) (post, p 1040).
2 Ante, p 443.
3 Post, p 997.
4 See Rent Act 1977, s 152(1).
5 The Rent Act exemption in respect of furnished tenancies was removed with effect from this date by Rent Act 1974, s 1(1). However, for the purpose of determining the applicability of the Rent Act to tenancies granted before 14 August 1974, it may still be necessary to inquire whether the amount of rent fairly attributable to the provision of furniture 'forms a substantial part of the whole rent' payable by the tenant (see eg *Mann v Cornella* (1980) 254 Estates Gazette 403 at 405f; [1981] Conv 9).

definitions of the pivotal term 'house' are either inadequate or non-existent,[6] and the courts have not been overly anxious to provide a judicial definition where the legislature has failed.[7] In consequence, it has generally been considered a mere question of fact in any given case whether a building or any part of a building thus qualifies as a 'dwelling-house'.[8]

In the flexible view thus taken by the courts,[9] almost any building which has been constructed or adapted for residential occupation constitutes a 'dwelling-house' for the purpose of the Rent Act.[10] The benefits conferred by a protected tenancy may therefore apply to many kinds of accommodation, whether in the form of an entire house, a self-contained flat, a single bed-sitting room, or even non-adjacent premises (perhaps within different buildings[11]). The limiting factor seems to be not the physical or structural nature of the premises claimed as a 'dwelling-house' but rather the *purpose* of the letting of which those premises are the subject.[12]

(3) The rent payable must be quantifiable in definite monetary terms

As has already been indicated,[13] it is at least questionable whether in English law the term 'tenancy' is capable of including an arrangement under which no

6   See, for instance, P.H. Halstead, 'To be or not to be (a house): that is the question', [1984] Conv 121. For a rare attempt to provide a workable definition of the word 'house', see Leasehold Reform Act 1967, s 2(1) (ante, p 727).

7   In *Gravesham Borough Council v Secretary of State for the Environment* (1982) *Times*, 10 November), McCullough J justified this reticence on the ground that 'fewer difficulties are caused by leaving undefined words of common usage found in statutes.' He was prepared to commit himself only to the proposition that a 'dwelling-house' comprises 'a building which provides facilities required for daily private domestic existence.'

8   See *Scurlock v Secretary of State for Wales* (1976) 238 Estates Gazette 47; *Horford Investments Ltd v Lambert* [1976] Ch 39 at 51H per Scarman LJ. Compare however, *Tandon v Trustees of Spurgeons Homes* [1982] AC 755 at 761E, 767C, where the House of Lords decided that a question of *law* arises where a court determines whether a building is a 'house' within the meaning of the definition contained in section 2(1) of the Leasehold Reform Act 1967 (ante, p 727).

9   This judicial flexibility is akin to the approach of the man in Professor Hart's famous example who says 'I can recognise an elephant when I see one but I cannot define it' (see H.L.A. Hart, *The Concept of Law* (Oxford 1961), p 13).

10   See eg *Horsford v Carnill* (1951) 157 Estates Gazette 243, 158 Estates Gazette 287, where it was argued that a cave might constitute a 'dwelling-house'. (The case was finally compromised). It seems that, on an analogy with *Makins v Elson* [1977] 1 WLR 221 at 223H, a 'dwelling-house' will also cover a 'mobile home' which has been immobilised, jacked up on a concrete base and connected to mains services. Jurisdiction is commonly accepted by the rent officer in such a case (see D. Baskerville, 'Caravans', (1984) 15 Jiro (No 2) 10), and the Court of Appeal has endorsed this approach (*Turner v Burton* (Unreported, 12 March 1985). Compare, however, *R v Rent Officer of Nottingham Registration Area, ex parte Allen* (1985) 52 P & CR 41 at 45; [1985] Conv 353.

11   See eg *Langford Property Co Ltd v Goldrich* [1949] 1 KB 511 at 518 (non-adjacent flats within the same block); *Whitty v Scott-Russell* [1950] 2 KB 32 at 42 (semi-detached house and cottage without internal intercommunication). Here the vital question seems to be whether the letting of two premises can be construed as a single letting of premises which in aggregate comprise a single 'dwelling-house' (see *Hampstead Way Investments Ltd v Lewis-Weare* [1985] 1 WLR 164 at 169G, post, p 1012) or merely as simultaneous lettings of separate premises, either tenancy being terminable without prejudice to the other. See 'More than One Dwelling', (1983) 14 Jiro (No 2) 14. That two sets of premises can form the subject matter of a single tenancy is clear from *Walter v Rumbal* (1695) 1 Ld Raym 53 at 55, 91 ER 931 at 933.

12   Post, p 974.

13   Ante, p 441.

rent or other consideration is payable to the landlord.[14] However, it is clear that, for the purpose of determining whether a dwelling-house has been 'let' within the meaning of section 1 of the Rent Act 1977, there must be a tenancy under which a rent is paid in terms which have a quantifiable money value. The machinery of the Rent Act for rent restriction and control[15] would be totally inoperable if the consideration for the tenant's occupation were not ultimately expressible in terms of money.[16]

(a) Performance of services

The requirement of a quantifiable money rent means that no protected tenancy can arise where the tenant's obligations to his landlord are expressed merely in terms of the performance of onerous services for the latter or in terms of some other payment or privilege in kind.[17] The Rent Act will apply only if a definite monetary value can be attributed to the discharge of the tenant's obligations or if the parties agree on some method for calculating a monetary equivalent.[18]

(b) Payments of money other than as 'rent'

Even if the tenant pays money to his landlord, such payment does not necessarily constitute 'rent' for the purpose of attracting Rent Act protection. The tenancy may fall outside the Rent Act if, for instance, the landlord demands payment in respect of merely the hire of furniture. Moreover, it is arguable that no protected tenancy is created by an arrangement under which the tenant, in what is otherwise rent-free accommodation, undertakes to discharge other—perhaps unrelated—liabilities incurred by the landlord (eg items of household expenditure such as rates, gas or electricity bills), or even to make donations to some third party nominated by the landlord.[19] Such diversionary tactics are often thought by landlords to guarantee immunity from the Rent Act, although it is likely—and indeed desirable—that the courts

---

14 Since the full protection of the Rent Act applies only to tenancies, it could of course be argued that no great wrong is done by excluding from protection an occupier who enjoys rent-free accommodation. However, even this point is highly debatable.

15 Post, p 1031.

16 See *Barnes v Barratt* [1970] 2 QB 657 at 667E per Sachs LJ.

17 See *Hornsby v Maynard* [1925] 1 KB 514 at 523ff (tenant agreed to give landlord rent-free accommodation of part of the demised premises); *Barnes v Barratt* [1970] 2 QB 657 at 668G-H (performance of domestic chores and payment of general household bills). It may be that the absence of any rent payment in *Heslop v Burns* [1974] 1 WLR 1241 contributed to the Court of Appeal's finding in that case in favour of a licence rather than a tenancy (ante, p 460).

18 In *Montague v Browning* [1954] 1 WLR 1039 at 1044f, a distinct money value was attributable to the tenant's occupation under a service tenancy in that his wages were subject to a regular fixed deduction in respect of that occupation (compare *Meier v Lucas* (Unreported, Court of Appeal, 4 March 1986)). It appears, however, that this kind of rationalisation is not open to the court if the agreement which authorises the deduction from the employee's wages also expressly stipulates that his occupation of his employer's property is to be 'rent-free' (see *Scrimgeour v Waller* (1981) 257 Estates Gazette 61 at 63).

19 See eg *Michel v Volpe* (1967) 202 Estates Gazette 213, where the occupier was contractually obliged to make 'donations' to a periodical called 'The Vanguard' produced by the person who provided her accommodation. The Court of Appeal held that this arrangement created a licence rather than a subtenancy, even though the occupier's 'donations book' was eventually replaced by 'a kind of rent book'.

should declare such a device to be merely an unconvincing disguise for what is in reality a protected tenancy.[20]

A strong argument in favour of recognising obligatory payments to third parties as a form of rent lies in the fact that such payments (if disclosed) are treated for tax purposes as the equivalent of rent received by the property owner. In *Jeffries v Stevens*[1] Walton J held that payments made direct by an occupier to a bank and insurance company in discharge of liabilities under the property owner's mortgage constituted 'receipts arising to a person from, or by virtue of, his ownership of an estate or interest in or right over...land'.[2] Such payments—whether or not they constituted 'rent' in strict terms—were therefore taxable under Schedule A, being made in respect of the occupation of the taxpayer's land.

(4) The dwelling-house must be let 'as a separate dwelling'

Statutory protection under section 1 of the Rent Act 1977 extends only to those dwelling-houses which are let 'as a separate dwelling'. These apparently innocuous words have been accorded a strict construction by the courts.[3] There are at least three elements in this phrase which require special consideration.

(a) Purpose of the letting

The word 'as' imports purpose, and it is a 'principle of cardinal importance' in Rent Act jurisprudence that the purpose of a letting (and therefore the question of statutory protection) depend 'upon the terms of the tenancy, not upon subsequent events.'[4] The decisive factor is the original purpose of the letting[5] rather than the actual user of the premises by the tenant.[6]

In some circumstances the intention to let premises 'as a separate dwelling' may simply be excluded by considerations of practical feasibility which necessarily limit the nature of potential use of those premises. In *Grosvenor*

---

20 Post, p 1000.
1 [1982] STC 639 at 651b.
2 Income and Corporation Taxes Act 1970, s 67.
3 See *Hampstead Way Investments Ltd v Lewis-Weare* (Unreported, Court of Appeal, 24 February 1984) per Eveleigh LJ: 'I can see good reason for a strict interpretation of "let as a separate dwelling", because a landlord ought not to find himself saddled with a statutory tenant when neither he nor the tenant when agreeing to the tenancy intended to be dealing with premises coming within the Act.'
4 *Horford Investments Ltd v Lambert* [1976] Ch 39 at 52B per Scarman LJ.
5 See eg *Regalian Securities Ltd v Ramsden* [1981] 1 WLR 611 at 616C, where the House of Lords accepted that at the date of the relevant tenancy and for many years thereafter a flat and maisonette had been occupied together 'as a single family home or...as "one unit of habitation".' It mattered not therefore that the tenant later granted a subletting of the flat while remaining in occupation of the maisonette.
6 De facto user of premises for residential purposes cannot alter the original character of a letting and bring it within the Rent Act, if the intention at the time of letting was to create a business tenancy under the Landlord and Tenant Act (see eg *Wolfe v Hogan* [1949] 2 KB 194 at 204ff). It has been pointed out that, if the position were otherwise, the 'tenant could stop, start, stop, start, as long as he liked, juggling between the two Acts of Parliament' (see *Pulleng v Curran* (1982) 44 P & CR 58 at 70). See also the famous, but often misquoted, dictum of Bankes LJ in *Epsom Grand Stand Association Ltd v Clarke* [1919] WN 170 at 171: 'If an agreement were to let premises as a barn, the tenant, even though he lived there, could not be heard to say that they were let as a dwelling-house'.

(Mayfair) Estates v Amberton,[7] for instance, the Court of Appeal declined to hold that two flats had been 'let as a separate dwelling' within the meaning of the Rent Act. It appeared that at the relevant date (ie, the date of the letting) a couple who had taken a letting of both flats together could not possibly have used the flats 'as a single dwelling'. One of the flats was still lawfully occupied by three existing licensees, and there was no evidence that the parties had intended at the date of the letting that there should be an early removal of these licensees in order to enable the tenants to use both flats as a single dwelling. It was irrelevant that there was a remote possibility that the licensees would vacate their flat at some unspecified future date.

In the present context the intentions of landlord and tenant are to be sought primarily in any express term of the letting which stipulates its purpose,[8] and, in the absence of such a term, are left to be inferred from the circumstances of the letting taken as a whole.[9] No merely unilateral change of user by the tenant can modify the original purpose of the letting thus ascertained, unless amounting to a consensual variation of the tenancy agreement.[10] Such a variation need not be express, but can be implied in circumstances where the original contemplation of the parties has been superseded by a change in user which is fully known to, and accepted by, the landlord.[11]

(b) The 'singular construction' of 'separate dwelling'

Recent judicial decisions have shown the indefinite article in the phrase 'let as a separate dwelling' to deserve a degree of respect quite disproportionate to its length. In order to attract protection under section 1 of the Rent Act 1977, it is essential that the tenancy granted should be intended to provide one (and only one) unit of habitation: only then can the house truly be said to be let as 'a' separate dwelling. Moreover, the relevant date for determining this question of intention is the date on which the tenancy was granted.[12]

(i) Unrestrictive aspects Curiously enough, there seems to be no requirement that the dwelling unit should necessarily be intended to become the separate

---

7   (1983) 265 Estates Gazette 693 at 694. See [1984] Conv 151.
8   In *Wolfe v Hogan* [1949] 2 KB 194 at 204, Denning LJ indicated that such a term would normally be conclusive. It is clear, however, that the mere presence of an express contractual undertaking, eg not to use property except as a 'strictly private residence' will not predetermine the test of residential purpose if the intentions of both parties at the date of letting were in reality different (see *Grosvenor (Mayfair) Estates v Amberton* (1983) 265 Estates Gazette 693 at 696).
9   See *Wolfe v Hogan* [1949] 2 KB 194 at 204f per Denning LJ: 'If the house is constructed for use as a dwelling-house, it is reasonable to infer the purpose was to let it as a dwelling. But if, on the other hand, it is constructed for the purpose of being used as a lock-up shop, the reasonable inference is that it was let for business purposes. If the position were neutral, then it would be proper to look at the actual user.' See also *Russell v Booker* (1982) 263 Estates Gazette 513 at 516 per Slade LJ.
10   See *Russell v Booker* (1982) 263 Estates Gazette 513 at 516 (change from agricultural to residential user unsuccessfully claimed as transferring tenancy from the protection of the Agricultural Holdings Act 1948 to that of the Rent Act 1977).
11   See *Wolfe v Hogan* [1949] 2 KB 194 at 205. The continued acceptance of rent by the landlord may well connote an affirmative consent to a variation of the original terms, but the court will be reluctant to spell such a variation out of merely an alleged constructive knowledge by the landlord of a change of user (see *Russell v Booker* (1982) 263 Estates Gazette 513 at 516).
12   *Grosvenor (Mayfair) Estates v Amberton* (1983) 265 Estates Gazette 693 at 694.

dwelling of the person to whom the tenancy is granted.[13] It is irrelevant, for instance, that the protected tenant never 'dwells' in the premises at any time but immediately sublets the entire unit to a single subtenant.[14] Alternatively, it is immaterial that the original tenant later sublets part of the dwelling-house to some other person while retaining possession of part of the premises himself.[15] In either of these circumstances it is still accurate to say that, for the purpose of the statute, there was initially a letting of the premises to the tenant as 'a' separate dwelling (though not necessarily as *his* separate dwelling or even permanently as 'a' separate dwelling). However, as Scarman LJ remarked in *Horford Investments Ltd v Lambert*,[16] the words in the statutory phrase 'mean what they literally say'.[17]

(ii) Capricious outcomes   Logical though this may seem, the strictly singular construction of the words 'let as a separate dwelling' leads to certain arguably capricious results. In the *Horford Investments* case a non-resident tenant, Lambert, sublet to others property which had already been adapted for multiple residential occupation at the date of the letting to himself (see *Fig. 56*).

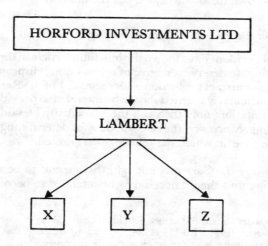

Fig. 56

<hr />

13   Compare, however, (i) the position under section 2(1)(a) of the Rent Act 1977, where the existence of a 'statutory tenancy' is expressly premised upon the continued residence of the statutory tenant (post, p 1007); (ii) the position under section 23(1) of the Landlord and Tenant Act 1954, where the existence of a protected business tenancy presupposes that premises are 'occupied' by the tenant (post, p 1038).

14   See *Feather Supplies Ltd v Ingham* [1971] 2 QB 348 at 353A; *Horford Investments Ltd v Lambert* [1976] Ch 39 at 51A. The subtenant may also have a protected tenancy under the Rent Act (see Rent Act 1977, s 152(1)).

15   See *Regalian Securities Ltd v Ramsden* [1981] 1 WLR 611 at 614H.

16   [1976] Ch 39 at 52F.

17   There is substantial support in the caselaw for a singular construction of the key phrase in section 1 of the Rent Act 1977. See eg *R & P Properties Ltd v Baldwin* [1939] 1 KB 461 at 470; *Theis v Muir* [1951] EGD 292; *Herbert v Byrne* [1964] 1 WLR 519 at 526.

Seeking to maximise his profit from the rental income derived from his subtenants, he later applied to have a fair rent registered in respect of his own superior tenancy.[18] The Court of Appeal held that his own tenancy could not be claimed as a protected tenancy within the Rent Act since it was obvious from the circumstances that the property had been let to him, not as 'a' separate dwelling, but rather as a *number* of separate dwellings or units of habitation.[19]

This is the inevitable construction of section 1 of the Rent Act 1977 where, at the commencement of a non-residential tenancy, a dwelling-house has already been converted into multiple residential accommodation (eg by subdivision into a number of self-contained flats or bedsits).[20] In the *Horford Investments* case, this construction was wholly consistent with the wider policy of the Rent Act which, as Scarman LJ pointed out,[1] was not concerned with 'the protection of an entrepreneur such as Lambert whose interest is exclusively commercial.' Yet it would seem that an entrepreneur in the position of Lambert can generally acquire protected status under the Rent Act by the simple expedient of ensuring that the conversion of his dwelling-house into multiple units of habitation does not occur until after the commencement of his own tenancy.[2]

(iii) Rebound effects on residential occupiers A further anomaly resulting from the 'singular construction' of section 1 of the Rent Act 1977 was exposed in *St Catherine's College, Oxford v Dorling*.[3] Here a landlord, Dorling, granted a letting of a house to a college on terms that the college would permit the house to be 'used as private residence only in occupation of one person per room...'(sic).[4]

18 It was likewise open to each of his subtenants to apply for the registration of a fair rent in respect of his own accommodation. However, the 'fair rent' in respect of the entire property comprised within the superior tenancy would almost certainly have been less than the sum of the 'fair rents' obtainable in respect of each of the relevant parts. Moreover, the risk that the rental income derived from the subtenants might be reduced from a market rent to a fair rent could well be minimised by reliance on the twin forces of ignorance and inertia, and might in any event be lessened by judicious manipulation of the duration and terms of the subtenancies themselves.

19 The Court of Appeal felt compelled to this conclusion in spite of the anomalies implied by it. In particular, Russell LJ observed ([1976] Ch 39 at 48A) that 'it seems somewhat anomalous to find that a letting of premises comprising a shop and one unit of habitation is within protection (see eg *British Land Co Ltd v Herbert Silver (Menswear) Ltd* [1958] 1 QB 530 in this court), while a letting of premises comprising two units of habitation is not.'

20 However, this construction is patently inapplicable to rented premises which are inherently incapable of multiple residential user (eg if consisting of one bedroom) or if such user would contravene legislation designed to prevent 'overcrowding' (ante, p 936) or to regulate houses in multiple occupation (ante, p 938).

1 [1976] Ch 39 at 52D.

2 See *Horford Investments Ltd v Lambert* [1976] Ch 39 at 48A per Russell LJ. As always, the determining factor is the original purpose of the letting as expressed in the terms of the tenancy or as inferred from the surrounding circumstances, rather than the subsequent user itself (ante, p 974). This being so, the entrepreneur will normally acquire Rent Act protection for himself in this situation unless both he and his landlord clearly contemplated at the beginning of the tenancy that there should be multiple residential user at some later date.

3 [1980] 1 WLR 66. See (1979) LAG Bulletin 211.

4 The motive underlying this transaction was the desire of the landlord to ensure that the actual occupiers would be excluded from statutory protection by the Rent Act 1977, s 8(1) (post, p 983).

The college proceeded to sublet individual rooms in the house as bedsits for five of its students, each sharing certain communal facilities and each paying a proportionate part of the rent payable by the college under the superior letting (see *Fig. 57*).

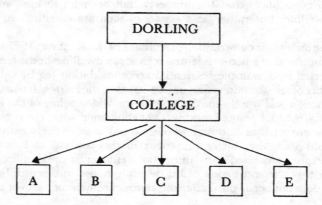

Fig. 57

Five days after entering into the superior letting, the college applied, much to the surprise of the landlord, for the registration of a fair rent in respect of that letting. Although the motive of the college seems to have been a genuine (and entirely laudable) desire to pass the likely reduction in rent on to its students, the Court of Appeal unanimously held that the college was not a protected tenant. The terms of the letting to the college expressly envisaged multiple residential occupation by students of the college, and it could not be said therefore that the house had been let to the college 'as a separate dwelling'.[5]

Not the least of the difficulties of the 'singular construction' of section 1 is therefore the fact that the courts are unable to distinguish between, on the one hand, the entrepreneur who wishes to use the Rent Act as an aid to profiteering in the private rental market and, on the other hand, the tenant who wishes to claim Rent Act protection precisely in order to confer a benefit upon his multiple subtenants.[6] Moreover, the *Dorling* decision illustrates rather neatly the moral crux of the Rent Act question: are the courts to permit a little wrong in order that a greater good ensue?[7] Although disclaiming it as a ground for the Court's decision, Megaw LJ drew attention to the likelihood that the operation of a benevolent scheme, aimed at increasing the supply of student

---

5   Moreover, as Eveleigh LJ pointed out ([1980] 1 WLR 66 at 72A), the 'existence of someone able to go of his own right to all the rooms of the premises is one of the hallmarks of a dwelling-house. That is completely absent on the findings in this case.'

6   Nor, it is fair to say, did the Court of Appeal in *Dorling* seem particularly anxious to draw such a distinction. The Court was frankly appalled by the action of the college in applying for a fair rent five days after signifying consent to the contractual rent level. See Megaw LJ at [1980] 1 WLR 66 at 72G, who somewhat wickedly hoisted the college on its own petard by observing that it might not now think it 'appropriate that the undergraduates should bear the consequences of the college having seen fit to agree a rent which it believed (if indeed it did so believe) was a rent higher than the fair rent.'

7   Post, p 996.

accommodation in a crowded university town, would be jeopardised rather than strengthened if colleges were able to subvert the parties' expectations by claiming Rent Act protection in respect of the head leases made available to them through the good offices of local property owners.[8]

(c) Nature of a 'separate dwelling'

Further difficulty is caused by the legal concept of a 'separate dwelling': it is by no means easy to identify the domestic activities which constitute the necessary and sufficient characteristics of such a dwelling. Once again the issue of statutory construction raises questions both as to the purpose of the tenancy and as to the wider purpose of the Rent Act. In *Skinner v Geary*[9] Scrutton LJ repeated his frequent assertion that the 'principal object' of the Rent Act legislation is to 'protect a person residing in a dwelling-house from being turned out of his home.'[10] The focus of the courts' attention has thus come to rest upon the question whether the premises for which protection is claimed can be described as a 'home', and this consideration in its own turn has been said to require the application of 'a certain amount of common sense'.[11]

(i) Capacity to sustain a separate domestic existence It is clear, for instance, that the mere fact that a letting comprises one room only does not prevent that room from being the 'separate dwelling' of the tenant, provided that the room in question is 'the only place where he moves and has his being.'[12] However, something turns on whether the premises claimed as a 'separate dwelling' are intrinsically capable of sustaining the separate domestic existence of the tenant. In *Metropolitan Properties Co (FGC) Ltd v Barder*[13] the Court of Appeal refused to apply the term 'separate dwelling' to the letting of a 'tiny room' across the corridor from a flat which the same tenant rented by virtue of an earlier agreement. The room contained a wash-basin but no lavatory facilities, and its size, furnishings and use as an au pair's bedroom merely went to confirm that its use was nothing more than as 'an annexe or overflow of the flat'.[14]

(ii) Fragmentation of domestic activity between different premises There are other even more difficult cases in which the quotidian activities of the tenant are distributed over several premises only one of which falls within the scope of the relevant letting. A tenant may, for instance, sleep in one room and carry on other domestic activities in other premises.[15] The courts have been reluctant to

8   [1980] 1 WLR 66 at 72E. Ironically, it now appears that a college or university authority, although excluded from the scope of a protected tenancy in the circumstances of *Dorling*'s case, may nevertheless be able to claim that it occupies the premises for the purpose of a 'business', thereby coming within the protection of Part II of the Landlord and Tenant Act 1954 (see *Groveside Properties Ltd v Westminster Medical School* (1983) 9 HLR 118 at 120).

9   [1931] 2 KB 546 at 560.

10   See also *Haskins v Lewis* [1931] 2 KB 1 at 14.

11   *Curl v Angelo* [1948] 2 All ER 189 at 190D per Lord Greene MR.

12   Ibid.

13   [1968] 1 WLR 286.

14   [1968] 1 WLR 286 at 294C per Edmund Davies LJ.

15   Similar (but not identical) questions as to the nature of a 'separate dwelling' arise in other contexts, eg in deciding whether a tenant occupies a dwelling-house 'as his residence' for the purpose of claiming a statutory tenancy under the Rent Act 1977, s 2(1)(a) (post, p 1012), or has 'the exclusive occupation of any accommodation' for the purpose of claiming a protected or statutory tenancy under the Rent Act 1977, s 22(1) (post, p 981).

describe the demised premises as a 'home' if 'the tenant carried on elsewhere activities which it was essential should have been carried on on those premises so as to be able to properly say that they were his "home".'[16]

The courts seem to have taken the view that the particular activity ('if it can be so called'[17]) of sleeping is peculiarly relevant to the essence of a 'separate dwelling'.[18] In *Wright v Howell*,[19] the Court of Appeal held that the word 'dwelling' included 'all the major activities of life, particularly sleeping, cooking and feeding'. Since, however, the tenant slept not in the rented premises, but in a flat in the same building belonging to his parents- in-law, the letting was denied the status of a 'separate dwelling'.[20] On the other hand, the mere fact that a tenant uses the demised premises for the purpose of sleeping will not necessarily cause the court to attribute the character of a 'dwelling' to those premises if the tenant is accustomed to carry on all his other activities in a different tenement altogether.[1] In other words, it appears to be generally recognised that user for the purpose of sleeping is a necessary but not sufficient element in the constitution of a 'separate dwelling'. However, each case depends ultimately upon its own facts,[2] and there are some cases in which it would seem harsh to hold that the status of a 'separate dwelling' is lost merely because the tenant does not sleep on the premises,[3] or because his domestic activities are distributed over more than one tenement.[4]

Less has been said judicially about the other activities which may be thought to comprise major components of domestic living. It seems to be accepted, for the purpose of establishing that there has been a letting of a 'separate dwelling', that there is no requirement that the tenant 'must always show that the premises were a complete home'.[5] In other words, the mere fact that such activities as cooking or eating take place elsewhere should not necessarily destroy the otherwise protected status of a letting.[6] The possibility also seems to

---

16 *Hampstead Way Investments Ltd v Lewis-Weare* (Unreported, Court of Appeal, 24 February 1984) per May LJ.
17 *Curl v Angelo* [1948] 2 All ER 189 at 190G per Lord Greene MR.
18 See R.E. Megarry, *The Rent Acts* (10th edn 1967), p 85.
19 (1947) 204 LT Jo 299 at 300.
20 See also *Wimbush v Cibulia* [1949] 2 KB 564 at 569 per Jenkins LJ.
1   See eg *Curl v Angelo* [1948] 2 All ER 189 at 190H-191A; *Hampstead Way Investments Ltd v Lewis-Weare* [1985] 1 WLR 164 at 171H per Lord Brandon of Oakwood. See also [1985] Conv 224 (P.F. Smith).
2   *Curl v Angelo* [1948] 2 All ER 189 at 192G per Lord Greene MR.
3   Compare, for instance, the more flexible approach adopted in New Zealand, where it was held in *McCarthy v Preston* [1951] NZLR 1091 at 1093 that the premises in which the tenant 'spends most of his waking hours, away from his work' could for statutory purposes constitute a 'place where he lives or dwells' even though he never slept there.
4   It seems inequitable, if essential aspects of living are split between two premises, that the tenant should render himself ineligible for Rent Act protection in respect of *either* of the premises. The unfairness is intensified if both premises are rented from the same landlord under different lettings. However, in the latter case, it may be possible to argue that the two lettings—although separated in point of time—should be construed as a combined single letting (see eg *Wimbush v Cibulia* [1949] 2 KB 564 at 570; *Hampstead Way Investments Ltd v Lewis-Weare* [1985] 1 WLR 164 at 169G, post, p 1012).
5   *Hampstead Way Investments Ltd v Lewis-Weare* (Unreported, Court of Appeal, 24 February 1984) per Eveleigh LJ.
6   In *Hampstead Way Investments Ltd v Lewis-Weare, supra,* Eveleigh LJ inclined towards the argument advanced by counsel that 'it would be unthinkable that a one-room flat occupied by an elderly person was not protected because he or she fed at other premises.'

be recognised that property originally let as a 'separate dwelling' may continue to be entitled to protection even though subsequently the tenant ceases to use the premises for some of the purposes for which a home is used.[7] As always, the purpose of the letting is to be judged as of the date on which the tenancy was granted and not on the basis of actual user as demonstrated by later events.[8]

(d) Implications of sharing arrangements

Further difficulties arise under the Rent Act in respect of sharing arrangements in a dwelling-house.[9] There can be no protected tenancy under the Act if the person who grants the tenancy also occupies a dwelling-house within the same building.[10] Thus the resident landlord is exempted from the full rigour of the statute.[11] Other sharing arrangements which require attention include the following.

(i) Multiple lettings If the landlord does not reside on the premises but merely lets to persons in multiple occupation, each living unit is regarded as having been 'let as a separate dwelling' for the purpose of the Rent Act, notwithstanding that the tenants enjoy the right to share certain accommodation such as a kitchen, bathroom or lavatory. Regardless of the fact that part of the accommodation is shared, each tenant qualifies for full protection under section 1 of the Rent Act 1977, provided that he retains exclusive possession of at least *some* accommodation (eg a private bed-sitting room in a shared house).[12] Section 1 cannot apply, however, if the sharing is so comprehensive as to preclude any claim to exclusive possession in respect of even part of the premises.[13]

(ii) Letting to joint tenants Exclusive possession of an entire house, flat or other living unit may be granted to a number of persons as joint tenants. Although the Rent Act surprisingly omits any reference to the phenomenon of joint tenancy,[14] it is clear that joint tenants are to be regarded as one person in law

---

7 See eg *Wimbush v Levinski* [1949] 2 KB 564, as interpreted by Eveleigh LJ in *Hampstead Way Investments Ltd v Lewis-Weare, supra.*
8 Ante, p 974. As Eveleigh LJ noted in *Hampstead Way Investments Ltd v Lewis-Weare, supra*, this approach has the merit that it 'coincides with common sense and humanity.' Unless this approach was adopted, Eveleigh LJ could foresee the case of 'a widower and widow, each with a family living in adjacent flats owned by the same landlord. They marry and use one flat for sleeping and the other for living during the day. It could be said that neither is now occupied as a complete home and consequently neither husband nor wife would be entitled to protection.'
9 See T.M. Aldridge, (1974) 118 SJ 3; J.E. Adams, (1976) 120 SJ 125.
10 Rent Act 1977, s 12.
11 Post, p 987.
12 Rent Act 1977, s 22(1).
13 See eg *Choudhury v Meah* (Unreported, Court of Appeal, 21 September 1981), where the overcrowding of premises in Soho was so gross as to destroy any possible claims of exclusive possession.
14 See *Howson v Buxton* (1929) 139 LT 504 at 506, where Scrutton LJ thought that there was 'a good deal to be said for the view that the legislature had not definitely present to its mind that there might be joint tenants, and that it has continually used the phrase "tenant" without any nice consideration of what would happen if there were more than one tenant.' See also J. Martin, [1978] Conv 436.

for the purpose of determining whether property has been let 'as a separate dwelling'. Thus in principle joint tenants are together eligible for full protected status under section 1 of the Rent Act 1977.[15]

(iii) Letting to a tenant who grants contractual licences It may sometimes occur that a tenancy of a dwelling-house is granted to an individual who in his turn grants contractual occupation licences to a number of persons, the result being that both the tenant and his licensees share some parts of the house. Although the licensees are clearly excluded from full Rent Act protection, the original tenant may still enjoy protected status. The dwelling-house has been let to him 'as a separate dwelling' within section 1 of the Rent Act 1977 notwithstanding that he shares some parts of the premises (eg a kitchen, bathroom or lavatory) with others.[16]

(e) Mixed user of premises

The Rent Act is in general concerned only with the occupation of residential premises; lettings of business premises are governed by Part II of the Landlord and Tenant Act 1954. Difficulties clearly arise under the Rent Act in respect of residential premises which are used in part for the purpose of a business conducted by the tenant.

The fact that part of a dwelling-house is used for a business purpose is enough to disqualify that letting from Rent Act protection, unless the tenant's business activities are merely incidental to the residential occupation and do not comprise a significant purpose of his occupation taken as a whole.[17] The relevant degree of commercial user of residential premises is always a question of fact in each individual case, but the protection of the Rent Act apparently extends to a tenant who takes in a few lodgers at minimal rents without reaping any substantial pecuniary advantage from such activity.[18]

3. EXPRESS EXCLUSION FROM THE SCOPE OF A PROTECTED TENANCY

Quite apart from the implied exclusions from the scope of the 'protected tenancy' under the Rent Act 1977, there are certain situations which are expressly exempted from full Rent Act coverage.

A tenancy cannot be a protected tenancy if the dwelling house in question either has or (at any relevant time) has had too high a rateable value.[19] The

---

15 Several other problems are posed under the Rent Act by joint tenancies (post, pp 999, 1005).
16 See *Baker v Turner* [1950] AC 401 at 417 per Lord Porter; *Rogers v Hyde* [1951] 2 KB 923 at 932 per Lord Asquith.
17 See Rent Act 1977, s 24(3); *Cheryl Investments Ltd v Saldanha, Royal Life Saving Society v Page* [1978] 1 WLR 1329 at 1333F-H, 1336D-E; *Pulleng v Curran* (1982) 44 P & CR 58 at 71. The Canadian courts have ruled that the residential character of premises is displaced only by a predominating business user (*Re Hahn and Kramer* (1980) 97 DLR (3d) 141 at 144).
18 *Lewis v Weldcrest Ltd* [1978] 1 WLR 1107 at 1118A-C, 1119G-H, 1122A-B. It would, however, be otherwise if the tenant let a large number of rooms in a spacious house for the purpose of obtaining considerable profit. Such a tenancy would fall not under the residential code of the Rent Act but under the business code contained in the Landlord and Tenant Act 1954 ([1978] 1 WLR 1107 at 1121H-1122A per Waller LJ).
19 Rent Act 1977, s 4(1).

intention behind this exclusion is to take luxury accommodation outside the ambit of the legislation, almost all other accommodation falling within the stipulated rateable value limits.[20] Likewise there can be no protected tenancy if the tenant pays no rent at all or pays an annual rent which is less than two-thirds of the relevant rateable value.[1]

No protected tenancy can arise where a dwelling-house is let together with (and for a purpose subsidiary to) other land.[2] Nor can a protected tenancy be created if the dwelling-house forms part of an agricultural holding,[3] comprises premises licensed for the sale of alcohol,[4] or is the subject of any letting by the Crown or by a government department.[5] Also excluded are the majority of shared ownership leases,[6] and lettings by a local authority,[7] the Commission for the New Towns,[8] a development corporation,[9] housing association,[10] or housing co-operative.[11] No protected tenancy can be claimed where a letting is made to a student by a specified educational institution.[12]

There remain three other important cases of express exclusion from full protected status under the Rent Act.

(1) The 'holiday lettings' exemption

The European Court of Justice pointed out in *Rösler v Rottwinkel*[13] that a letting of holiday accommodation does not share the same social purpose as a long-term lease of residential property, in that 'the rented property is not an essential part of the holidaymaker's livelihood.' The absence of any paramount claim to statutory protection is evident under the Rent Act 1977, which provides that a tenancy is not a 'protected tenancy' if its purpose is to confer on the tenant the right to occupy a dwelling-house 'for a holiday'.[14] It is now

---

20   The ineffectiveness for this purpose of the current rateable value limits is illustrated by the 'handsome period country house' complete with staff flat, outbuildings, stable and large garden in dispute in *Hill v Rochard* [1983] 1 WLR 478 at 480D-E. See P.F. Smith, [1983] Conv 320 at 323: 'Gone indeed are the days when the Acts were merely aimed at the oppressed'!
1   Rent Act 1977, s 5(1) (ante, p 973). It is this provision which alone excludes most long leases with a nominal ground rent from the provisions of the Rent Act. See also *Griffiths v Williams* (1977) 248 Estates Gazette 947 at 950; Landlord and Tenant Act 1954, Part I. There is a danger that unfit dwellings in relation to which a nil or nominal rent is fixed (ante, p 933) will fall outside the Rent Act (see [1981] Conv 325).
2   Rent Act 1977, ss 6, 26(1). See *Bradshaw v Smith* (1980) 255 Estates Gazette 699 at 701ff. There is for this purpose a definition of 'agricultural land' in General Rate Act 1967, s 26(3)(a) (see *Russell v Booker* (1982) 263 Estates Gazette 513 at 514f).
3   Rent Act 1977, s 10. See Agricultural Holdings Act 1986, s 1(1).
4   Rent Act 1977, s 11.
5   Rent Act 1977, s 13(1), as amended by Housing Act 1980, s 73(1). See *Crown Estate Commissioners v Wordsworth* (1982) 6 HLR 99.
6   Rent Act 1977, s 5A(1), as supplied by Housing and Planning Act 1986, s 18, Sch 4, para 1(2).
7   Rent Act 1977, s 14(a), (b), (c). However, most public or quasi-public tenancies now receive statutory protection as 'secure tenancies' under Housing Act 1985, ss 79ff (post, p 1045).
8   Rent Act 1977, s 14(d).
9   Rent Act 1977, s 14(e).
10   Rent Act 1977, s 15(1). See eg *Goodman v Dolphin Square Trust Ltd* (1979) 38 P & CR 257 at 266.
11   Rent Act 1977, s 16.
12   Rent Act 1977, s 8. See Protected Tenancies (Exceptions) Regulations 1986 (SI 1986/541).
13   (Case 241/83) [1986] QB 33 at 53B-D.
14   Rent Act 1977, s 9. The European Court of Justice has ruled that holiday lets abroad are governed by the national law of the situs (*Rösler v Rottwinkel* (Case 241/83) [1986] QB 33 at 59G-60A).

widely acknowledged that the holiday let has been extensively used by landlords as a means of circumventing Rent Act control.[15] The holiday lettings exemption has indeed generated a remarkable expansion of the tourist industry in the most surprising areas of large cities.[16]

(a) Definition of a 'holiday'

There is no statutory definition of 'holiday' for Rent Act purposes, and the question whether a letting is a holiday letting is always an issue of fact.[17] Left to their own devices, the courts have defined a 'holiday' as 'a temporary suspension of one's normal activity not necessarily implying a period of recreation.'[18] Thus, although the perfectly plain meaning of a 'holiday' would seem to involve a cessation of labour, it has been held that a 'holiday' letting may be validly granted to a tenant who is on a 'working holiday'.[19]

(b) The courts' jurisdiction to reject a 'sham'

The mere fact that a letting is expressly specified to be a 'holiday letting' does not preclude the court's jurisdiction to overturn the superficial label if it misrepresents the substance of a transaction. However, until fairly recently the courts have not seemed particularly responsive to the argument that improbable holiday lets should be stigmatised as a 'sham'.[20]

The onus is clearly on the tenant to prove that the label is a 'sham', rather than on the landlord to rebut any adverse inference.[1] The tenant's burden of proof is substantial. In *Buchmann v May*[2] the Court of Appeal ruled that a false label of holiday let could not be challenged on the ground of either an inequality of bargaining power or the tenant's failure to apprehend the legal significance of the express term. The prima facie evidence of the parties' intentions, as contained in the superficial description, was conclusive in the absence of any claim by the tenant that there was either a 'sham' or misrepresentation or any ground for rectification.[3] There are, however, incipient signs of a new realism in the courts' approach. In *R v Rent Officer for LB of Camden, ex parte Plant*,[4] for instance, Glidewell J refused to uphold the label of holiday letting in relation to a tenancy which had been granted for occupation of a flat by a number of student nurses. The landlord was perfectly aware that

---

15   See *Residential round-up—stop worrying about the Rent Act*, (1981) 2 PLB 22; (1979) 123 SJ 86.

16   It is almost certainly the case that, following the de-control of furnished tenancies in the Rent Act 1974, landlords have simply redefined formerly exempt furnished lettings as currently exempt holiday lets (see S. Weir, *Roof* (October 1975), p 11ff; N. Finnis, *Roof* (May 1978), p 74ff). See also *R v Rent Officer for LB of Camden, ex parte Plant* (1981) 257 Estates Gazette 713 at 718.

17   *Francke v Hakmi* [1984] CLY 1906.

18   See *Francke v Hakmi* [1984] CLY 1906, where the only qualification seemed to be that the 'holiday' must involve an intention 'to resume one's normal activity at its conclusion'.

19   See also *McHale v Daneham* (1979) 123 SJ 86. For critical comment, see (1984) 128 SJ 537.

20   See eg *Tetragon Ltd v Shidasb Construction Co Ltd and Darabi* (1981) 7 HLR 113 at 117f, where, somewhat surprisingly, the Court of Appeal was not unduly perturbed by a 'holiday letting' granted to a company!

1   *Ryeville Properties Ltd v Saint-John* [1980] CLY 1598.

2   [1978] 2 All ER 993 at 998h.

3   A lesser onus may rest on a tenant whose understanding of English is poor (see *Francke v Hakmi* [1984] CLY 1906).

4   (1981) 257 Estates Gazette 713. See (1981) LAG Bulletin 67.

the occupiers were not on holiday but were working instead as students, and the court held that there was 'clear evidence' that the purpose expressed in the tenancy agreement was not the 'true purpose' of that agreement.[5] The tenancy was therefore protected under the Rent Act 1977.[6]

Despite several proposals to confine the scope of the Rent Act exemption to genuine holiday arrangements, Parliament has not yet seen fit to circumscribe the definition of a 'holiday' letting.[7]

(2) The 'board or attendance' exemption

A tenancy is not a protected tenancy if under the tenancy a dwelling-house is 'bona fide let at a rent which includes payments in respect of board or attendance'.[8] The onus is on the landlord to establish that the tenancy comes within the scope of this immunity,[9] and it is clear that the allocation of rent to board or attendance must be genuine.[10] However, board or attendance is significant only if provided as a matter of strict contractual liability under the tenancy. It is entirely irrelevant that the landlord makes a charge for meals which he is not contractually obliged to supply or that the tenant does not in actual fact receive the board or attendance to which he is contractually entitled. The crucial feature in the 'board or attendance' exemption is not de facto provision, but de iure entitlement.[11]

(a) Definition of 'board'

The provision of *any* board is sufficient to displace the protected tenancy.[12] There is no statutory definition of 'board', and it is not entirely clear what the term covers. It seems that 'board' would not be constituted by 'an early morning cup of tea',[13] but would include a breakfast supplied by the landlord.[14] The concept of 'board' covers the provision of 'such food as...would ordinarily be consumed at daily meals and would be obtained and prepared by a tenant for himself, if it were not provided by somebody else.'[15] For this purpose a 'continental breakfast' is sufficient.[16]

5   (1981) 257 Estates Gazette 713 at 718.
6   For another case of 'misdescription', see *Foxell v Mendis* (Unreported, Court of Appeal, No 81 17755, 19 May 1982).
7   In 1980, for instance, Parliament rejected the proposal that the holiday letting exemption should be available only in respect of a dwelling-house approved by the local authority as a 'short-term dwelling' (*Parliamentary Debates, House of Commons, Official Report* (Standing Committee F), Vol IX (Session 1979–80), Col 2317ff (22 April 1980)).
8   Rent Act 1977, s 7(1).
9   *Palser v Grinling* [1946] KB 631 at 635.
10 *Palser v Grinling* [1948] AC 291 at 310.
11 *Michael v Phillips* [1924] 1 KB 16 at 26f; *Palser v Grinling* [1948] AC 291 at 311. However, the fact that food is provided in different or less accessible premises or only at times unsuitable for the tenant may disqualify the provision as board (see *Rita Dale v Adrahill Ltd and Ali Khan* [1982] CLY 1787, post, p 986).
12 In *Wilkes v Goodwin* [1923] 2 KB 86 at 93, Bankes LJ thought that a tenancy would be excluded from the Rent Act by any amount of board which 'is not ruled out of consideration by the application of the rule *de minimis non curat lex*.'
13 *Wilkes v Goodwin* [1923] 2 KB 86 at 110 per Younger LJ.
14 See *R v Battersea, etc, Rent Tribunal, ex parte Parikh* [1957] 1 WLR 410 at 412 (A mere sandwich will not take a tenancy outside the Rent Act).
15 *Wilkes v Goodwin* [1923] 2 KB 86 at 110.
16 *Holiday Flat Co v Kuczera*, 1978 SLT (Sh Ct) 47. This concession was felt to be an inevitable consequence of the British entry into the European Economic Community!

(i) Sham provision of board   The Rent Act does not in plain terms exclude the possibility that the 'board' may consist of merely the periodic provision of pre-packaged food or uncooked raw ingredients, and it is notorious that the 'board' exemption is frequently and disingenuously claimed by landlords who simply arrange for periodic deliveries of milk and packets of breakfast cereals and the like.[17] The relative ease with which this particular Rent Act immunity may be obtained represents one of the weakest features of the legislation.[18]

(ii) Recent restrictions   Increasing criticism of the widespread abuse of the 'board' exemption has led to a slightly more restrictive approach in the recent caselaw. It may not be a sufficient provision of 'board' if the landlord merely undertakes to supply meals in a different building 250 yards away, particularly if the landlord knows that his tenant has normally left to go to work at the time stipulated.[19] There is at least a heavy implication that the 'board' must be available at the premises let to the tenant.[20] For this reason a Scottish Sheriff's Court held in *Gavin v Lindsay*[1] that there was no true provision of 'board' where, at the landlord's expense, the tenant could opt either to obtain breakfast at a local café or to collect the raw ingredients from a local general store. The Sheriff decided that 'board' implied not merely 'substance' (ie, food) but also 'service' on the part of the landlord in the form of the preparation and setting out of food and the clearing up after the meal. The mere right to collect rations from a nearby shop could not constitute 'board'. This qualification may now place in some legal jeopardy the standard practice of delivering the mere ingredients of meals to the tenant's premises.[2]

(b) Definition of 'attendance'

There is likewise no statutory definition of 'attendance', but the term was understood by the House of Lords in *Palser v Grinling*[3] to comprise 'service personal to the tenant performed by an attendant provided by the landlord...for the benefit or convenience of the individual tenant in his use or enjoyment of the demised premises.'

(i) Illustrations   The personal attendance must be specifically directed towards the individual tenant's dwelling-house, typical examples including nowadays fairly archaic practices such as the carrying of coals[4] or delivery of letters or messages[5] to the tenant and the removal of refuse from his premises.[6]

---

17   See (1981) 2 PLB 22.
18   In 1980 Parliament rejected a proposal aimed at abolishing the 'board or attendance' exemption in respect of all new tenancies (*Parliamentary Debates, House of Commons, Official Report* (Standing Committee F), Vol IX (Session 1979–80), Col 2317ff (22 April 1980)).
19   *Rita Dale v Adrahill Ltd and Ali Khan* [1982] CLY 1787. See (1982) LAG Bulletin 39.
20   See, however, (1982) 3 PLB 4.
1   Glasgow and Strathkelvin Sheriff's Court (27 June 1985). See *Rent Acts: Selected Case Law Guide* (Institute of Rent Officers Educational Trust), Vol 1, p 338. See (1985) 16 Jiro Educational Supplement (No 3), p iii; (1985) Scolag 153; (1986) Legal Action 31.
2   See also *Leech Leisure Ltd v Hotel and Catering Industry Training Board* (1984) *Times*, 18 January. See F. Pearey, *Bed and Breakfast*, (1987) 17 Jiro (No 4), p 7, for an indication of a general tendency on the part of rent officers to view 'bed and breakfast' cases with grave suspicion.
3   [1948] AC 291 at 310f per Viscount Simon.
4   *Palser v Grinling* [1948] AC 291 at 318.
5   *Wood v Carwardine* [1923] 2 KB 185 at 191f.
6   *Palser v Grinling* [1948] AC 291 at 318.

The judge-made definition excludes any services provided for tenants communally, such as the provision of a lift service or a supply of hot water to all the tenants in a block of flats or the provision of cleaning services in the common parts of a building.[7] The installation of a resident porter in charge of a main entrance-door does not constitute 'attendance' in the required sense.[8]

(ii) Requirement of substantiality　Unlike 'board', where any amount suffices to exclude the Rent Act, 'attendance' rules out a protected tenancy only if 'the amount of the rent which is fairly attributable to attendance, having regard to the value of the attendance to the tenant, forms a substantial part of the whole rent.'[9] In *Palser v Grinling*,[10] the House of Lords ruled with some profundity that 'substantial' means 'considerable, solid or big'. On the facts of the case the House decided without much difficulty that an allocation of £4 to 'attendance' out of a total rent of £175 was not a 'substantial part', but declined to quantify the criterion of substantiality in any general percentage terms or by means of any mathematical formula.[11] Some guidance on the test of substantiality is, however, to be found in the caselaw on the former (and similarly phrased) 'furnished premises' exemption.[12] In this context it has been held that a furniture allocation valued at 14 per cent of the rent payable is 'substantial...though...very near the borderline',[13] while allocations valued at 7 per cent[14] and 9 per cent[15] have been regarded as falling below the borderline.[16]

(3) The 'resident landlord' exception

Perhaps the most important express exclusion from full protected status under the Rent Act concerns tenancies where the landlord resides on the premises.[17] The 'resident landlord' exception was introduced by the Rent Act 1974 in order to replace the immunity previously conferred on furnished tenancies,[18] and it applies only to tenancies granted on or after 14 August 1974.[19] Section 12 of the 1977 Act lays down certain restrictive conditions for the operation of the exemption.

7　*Palser v Grinling* [1948] AC 291 at 318.
8　*Palser v Grinling* [1948] AC 291 at 318.
9　Rent Act 1977, s 7(2).
10　[1948] AC 291 at 317.
11　[1948] AC 291 at 317.
12　See eg Rent Act 1968, s 2(3) (ante, p 971).
13　*Woodward v Docherty* [1974] 1 WLR 966 at 970G.
14　*Christophedis v Cuming* (1976) 239 Estates Gazette 275.
15　*Mann v Cornella* (1980) 254 Estates Gazette 403 at 407.
16　Compare, however, *Grant v Gresham* (1979) 252 Estates Gazette 55 at 57 (17 or 18 per cent not 'substantial' for the purpose of Landlord and Tenant Act 1954, s 43(1)(d)(i)).
17　In 1984 resident landlord lettings comprised 6 per cent of all current private residential lettings (Sir George Young, (1984) 15 Jiro (No 2) 6 at 7).
18　Ante, p 971. Most tenancies which are excluded from section 1 of the Rent Act 1977 by reason of the 'resident landlord' exception will constitute 'restricted contracts' (post, p 1040).
19　A tenancy granted before 14 August 1974 is not deprived of full protected status by reason of the presence of a resident landlord, but may well be excluded on the ground that the premises were furnished (see *Mann v Cornella* (1980) 254 Estates Gazette 403 at 405f).

(a) Property to which the tenancy relates

The 'resident landlord' exception applies where the tenant's dwelling-house forms 'part only of a building' in which the landlord also resides and the building in which both live is not a 'purpose-built block of flats'.[20]

(i) Definition of 'part only of a building'   It is not always easy to determine whether a tenant's dwelling-house forms 'part only' of the same building in which the landlord has his residence. This definitional problem is ultimately rooted in some peculiarly Anglo-Saxon perceptions of 'social space' within the crowded conditions of modern urban living.[1]

The primary purpose of the 'resident landlord' exemption is plainly to permit a property owner to grant lettings of rooms in his own home to strangers without thereby incurring the full rigour of the Rent Act.[2] The resident landlord is effectively allowed to trade off some of his domestic privacy in return for the statutory assurance of substantial immunity from any possible claim to protected status on the part of the intruding tenant. In *Bardrick v Haycock*[3] Scarman LJ observed that section 12 is aimed 'at the mischief of that sort of social embarrassment arising out of close proximity—close proximity which the landlord had accepted in the belief that he could bring it to an end at any time allowed by the contract of tenancy.'

The 'resident landlord' exception has thus been construed as relating only to those living units which are so inter-connected (structurally or otherwise) as to make it impossible for people to 'live separate lives without embarrassment'.[4] The exception applies most clearly where a landlord simply rents out a room in his own home. The exception has also been upheld where a landlord and his tenant live in adjoining premises which have been internally reconstructed by the demolition of dividing walls and the insertion of an inter-communicating door.[5] In such cases the possibility of socially compromising contact remains an ever-present reality. The 'resident landlord' immunity cannot be claimed, however, where the parties live in adjoining terraced houses without such internal connections.[6] Nor does the exemption apply where the landlord lives in an extension which is tied structurally to, but is not internally linked with, an adjoining block of flats.[7]

An important feature of the 'social proximity' test seems to be whether the two dwelling units have a separate external access.[8] The existence of separate front doors minimises to the point of insignificance the personal trauma of

---

20   Rent Act 1977, s 12(1)(b).
1   For an apt expression of these perceptions, see W.H. Auden's *Thanksgiving for a Habitat* (*Collected Poems* (ed by E. Mendelson, London, 1976), p 519): 'Some thirty inches from my nose, The frontier of my Person goes'.
2   See *Report of the Committee on the Rent Acts* (the Francis Committee) (Cmnd 4609, 1971), p 234 (Minority Report).
3   (1976) 31 P & CR 420 at 424 per Scarman LJ.
4   *Barnes v Gorsuch* (1982) 43 P & CR 294 at 298.
5   *Guppy v O'Donnell* (1979) 129 NLJ 930.
6   *Bardrick v Haycock* (1976) 31 P & CR 420 at 425. Semi-detached houses are near the borderline, but (although it is ultimately a question of fact) they are probably not to be regarded as being parts of the same building (see *Humphery v Young* [1903] 1 KB 44 at 46). Compare *Cook v Minion* (1979) 37 P & CR 58 at 63.
7   *Bardrick v Haycock* (1976) 31 P & CR 420 at 425.
8   *Bardrick v Haycock* (1976) 31 P & CR 420 at 425.

social proximity. The overall 'social space' apportioned between the two dwelling units is also significant: small adjoining properties tend to be more readily considered as constituting one single building.[9]

(ii) Joint residence in a 'purpose-built block of flats' The 'resident landlord' exception cannot normally be claimed where both the landlord and the tenant live in a building which is a 'purpose-built block of flats'.[10] Such flats are pre-eminently designed to minimise the adverse social and personal complications of multiple occupation.[11] The only case in which the landlord's exemption can apply within a purpose-built block arises where a resident within the block lets one or more of the rooms in his own flat to a subtenant.[12] In such a case the danger of embarrassing proximity revives notwithstanding the purpose-built nature of the premises, and it is therefore open to the landlord to avail himself of the section 12 exemption.

(b) Landlord's residence in another part of the same building

It is a strict condition of the availability of the 'resident landlord' exemption that the tenancy should have been granted by a person who, at the time of the grant, 'occupied as his residence another dwelling-house' in the same building.[13]

(i) Definition of 'landlord' It is of course possible that the 'landlord' may be a composite entity comprising several persons who are jointly entitled to the landlord's interest.[14] It is clear, however, that the 'resident landlord' exception may be claimed provided at least one of those persons was in residence at the grant of the tenancy and has remained in residence since that date.[15] In *Cooper v Tait*[16] Eveleigh LJ attributed this conclusion to a legislative preference to 'encourage people to divide up...accommodation...to create more than one dwelling-house without being afraid that they would be unable again to have their premises under their own sole control and occupation because of the presence of a protected tenant.'

---

9   *Griffiths v English* (1982) 261 Estates Gazette 257; [1983] Conv 147 (J.E.M.). See also *Cook v Minion* (1979) 37 P & CR 58 at 63.

10 A 'purpose-built block of flats' is defined in Rent Act 1977, Sch 2, para 4. The building must have been a 'purpose-built block of flats' when originally designed and constructed (*Vernazza v Ferro* (Unreported, Court of Appeal, 26 June 1985)). It is not enough that a large Victorian house has at some later stage been substantially reconstructed and converted into flats (*Barnes v Gorsuch* (1982) 43 P & CR 294 at 297; [1983] Conv 146).

11 *Bardrick v Haycock* (1976) 31 P & CR 420 at 424f. See, however, *Barnes v Gorsuch* (1982) 43 P & CR 294 at 298f.

12 Rent Act 1977, s 12(1)(a), as amended by Housing Act 1980, s 65(1).

13 Rent Act 1977, s 12(1)(b).

14 Other problems arising from joint tenancy of the landlord's interest or the tenant's interest are discussed elsewhere (ante, p 981; post, p 1005).

15 *Szachno, Krasinska and Skwarczynski v Gough* [1978] Conv 6; (1977) 41 Conv (NS) 225; *Cooper v Tait* (1984) 48 P & CR 460 at 462. It seems that section 12 is available even if the non-resident owners of the landlord's interest are unaware of the letting (*Chetwynd v Boughey* [1981] CLY Unreported Case 167 (Court of Appeal)). See also (1983) 80 Law Soc Gaz 87 (P.M.L. Glover).

16 (1984) 48 P & CR 460 at 462.

(ii) Definition of 'residence'   In order to qualify for the 'resident landlord' exemption, the landlord must be able to assert a continuous occupation of part of the premises 'as his residence'.[17] The concepts of occupation and residence are construed, for this purpose, on a direct analogy with the nature and quality of the continued residence which is required to sustain the existence of a statutory tenancy.[18] Thus the benefit of section 12 may not be available to a landlord who is unable to show substantial use of the property as a home, as for instance where he retains a merely nominal occupation of one small room in the demised premises.[19] Occasional or token residence is apt to be dismissed as a 'sham', but it is possible nevertheless that the landlord's residence can be maintained by proxy in the form of his wife or mother.[20] However, no 'residence' can be claimed by or on behalf of the landlord unless the premises reserved out of the letting for occupation by the landlord are intrinsically capable of constituting a realistic home. A mere potting-shed or basement sun-lounge, although reserved for the exclusive occupation of the landlord, cannot comprise 'another dwelling-house' within the same building for the purpose of establishing the landlord's exemption.[1]

(c) Requirement of continuous residence by landlord

The 'resident landlord' exemption is available only if the interest of the landlord has, throughout the period since the grant of the tenancy, belonged continuously to some person (not necessarily the original landlord) who has resided in another dwelling-house in the same building.[2] Certain minor intermissions in residence are permitted by express statutory provision.[3] Where the premises are vested in personal representatives on the death of the landlord, any intermission in residence not exceeding two years in duration has no effect on the continuity of residence required under the 'resident landlord' exemption.[4]

4. CONTRACTUAL DEVIATIONS FROM THE RENT ACT

The net effect of the Rent Act legislation is to confer upon the statutory tenant certain rights of a quasi-proprietary nature. These rights, not being property

---

17   Rent Act 1977, s 12(1)(b), (c). The 'resident landlord' exception is therefore not available to a landlord company.

18   Post, p 1008. See Rent Act 1977, Sch 2, para 5.

19   See *Cliffe v Standard* (1982) 132 NLJ 186, where the Court of Appeal withheld 'resident landlord' status from a landlord who retained a furnished room in the tenanted property but slept at a nearby house with his wife and children.

20   *Lyons v Caffery* (1983) 266 Estates Gazette 213 at 214. The presence of a resident housekeeper installed by the landlord cannot connote residence by the landlord himself (see *Markou v Da Silvaesa* (1986) 52 P & CR 204). However, any services or attendance provided by that housekeeper which require that she should have unrestricted access to the occupier's premises may well indicate that the occupier is not a tenant at all but a mere 'lodger' or licensee (ante, p 445).

1   *Lyons v Caffery* (1983) 266 Estates Gazette 213 at 214; [1983] Conv 147.

2   Rent Act 1977, s 12(1)(c).

3   Rent Act 1977, Sch 2, para 1

4   Rent Act 1977, Sch 2, para 2A. See *Williams v Mate* (1983) 263 Estates Gazette 883 at 885; [1983] JSWL 121 (M. Davey); *Caldwell v McAteer* (1984) 269 Estates Gazette 1039 at 1040; [1985] Conv 127.

rights in the conventional sense, are best defined in terms of status rather than contract: the Rent Act tenant has a 'status of irremovability'.[5] In effect Parliament has intervened between landlord and tenant in order to remedy a serious imbalance of economic power and to protect the party whose bargaining power is handicapped by his personal circumstances.

By attaching a framework of tenants' rights to a legislatively defined status, Parliament has gone some distance towards compensating for the aleatory distribution of economic power in an imperfect world. The Rent Act counteracts the contractual imbalance between landlord and tenant by securing for the latter the kind of rights for which he would have bargained had he been a free agent endowed with equal negotiating strength. However, difficult issues of policy are raised by the question whether landlord and tenant may legitimately employ the device of contract to diminish the protection which has been conferred as an incident of status. Is the tenant at liberty to bargain away his artificial immunity from normal market forces? Is he free not to be free?

(1) Contracting out of the Rent Act

It is a cardinal (albeit non-statutory) feature of Rent Act jurisprudence that a protected or statutory tenant has no competence in law to bargain away his protection under the Act.[6] Just as it is not open to a tenant to contract into the protection of the Rent Act,[7] equally the protected or statutory tenant who remains in possession cannot validly contract out of the rights afforded him by statute.[8] His rights are publicly conferred as incidents of a status defined by the Rent Act and cannot be diminished or destroyed by private agreement. It follows that no contractual provision,[9] no estoppel,[10] and a fortiori no 'mere statement of his wishes or intentions'[11] can abrogate his protection under the Act.[12] As Lord Greene MR declared in *Brown v Draper*,[13] the tenant can be deprived of his statutory protection only by voluntarily giving up possession to his landlord or by having a court order for the recovery of possession made against him. Until either of these events occurs, the tenant is 'under the shelter of the Act, whether or not he so desires.'[14]

---

5 Post, p 1003.
6 *Baxter v Eckersley* [1950] 1 KB 480 at 485.
7 An ineligible tenant cannot attract the operation of the Rent Act by mere contract with his landlord (see *Rogers v Hyde* [1951] 2 KB 923 at 931).
8 *Brown v Draper* [1944] KB 309 at 313.
9 See the analogous authority on agricultural tenancies (*Johnson v Moreton* [1980] AC 37; *Keen v Holland* [1984] 1 WLR 251 at 261C).
10 See *Welch v Nagy* [1950] 1 KB 455 at 460, 464; *Keen v Holland* [1984] 1 WLR 251 at 261D-F.
11 See *Brown v Draper* [1944] KB 309 at 313, where the Court of Appeal regarded as ineffective a tenant's declaration in open court—made largely to spite his estranged wife—that he had no further claim to the rented premises.
12 It is difficult to predict whether the courts will treat the term which invalidly purports to contract away the protection of the Act as rendering the entire transaction void (see eg *Amoco Australian Pty Ltd v Rocca Bros Motor Engineering Co Pty Ltd* [1975] AC 561 at 578B-G) or as merely severable (see eg *Ailion v Spiekermann* [1976] Ch 158 at 163A-B). The better view is probably that the courts will strive to enforce the transaction without the ineffective term (see *Carney v Herbert* [1985] AC 301 at 317A-B).
13 [1944] KB 309 at 313.
14 [1944] KB 309 at 313.

The grounds on which the court may order the recovery of possession in favour of a landlord are examined elsewhere.[15] There is, however, some considerable controversy as to the kind of circumstances in which a tenant can be said to have put himself outside the reach of the Rent Act by a voluntary giving up of possession.

(a) Contractual exchange of licence for tenancy

It has proved not at all easy to determine whether there has been a voluntary delivery up of possession by a tenant who agrees to exchange his protected status for mere rights of licence. In an area which is unusually characterised by appalling decisions, one case above all remains as a blot on English jurisprudence. In *Foster v Robinson*[16] a farm labourer had for many years occupied one of his employer's cottages by way of a protected tenancy at a half-yearly rent. When the tenant ceased work by reason of age and infirmity, his employer orally offered to replace the existing contractual tenancy by the grant of rent-free occupation of the cottage for the remainder of the labourer's life. This offer was duly accepted, but when the labourer died four years later and his daughter claimed a Rent Act tenancy by succession, the employer denied that the occupancy had remained within the protection of the statute.

The circumstances were of course open to the suspicion that the landlord had coerced an old and sick man to contract away his undoubted Rent Act status in return for a trivial rent forbearance during the last four years of his life.[17] There would indeed be something rather shabby about a transaction by which a landlord—at minimal cost—purchased his freedom from Rent Act constraints which might otherwise have endured for at least another generation. However, the county court judge found that there had been an 'effective genuine transaction' under which there was a 'delivery up of possession under the former tenancy and a resuming of possession under a new transaction immediately afterwards.'[18] When the case reached the Court of Appeal, Evershed MR conceded that he was 'by no means sure' that re integra he would have reached the same decision.[19] Nevertheless the Court of Appeal upheld the first instance court's conclusion that there had been an implied surrender of the contractual tenancy by operation of law. Evershed MR was clear that if, at the date of the disputed exchange of rights, 'the key had been handed over and then been handed back the next minute that would have symbolised the delivery up of possession'. He did not think that it 'vitally matters that that performance was not gone through.'[20]

The circumstances of *Foster v Robinson* illustrate the constant danger that unfair pressure may be brought to bear on a tenant—particularly where the landlord is also the tenant's employer—in order to coerce the tenant into

---

15   Post, p 1015.
16   [1951] 1 KB 149.
17   So conscious was Evershed MR of this possible construction of the events that he professed himself in the Court of Appeal to be 'very anxious to avoid any suggestion that a decision in the plaintiff landlord's favour would open the door to devices whereby a landlord could go to a sick tenant and get him to agree to some arrangement which was really to the advantage of the landlord and the grave disadvantage of the tenant.'
18   [1951] 1 KB 151 at 159.
19   [1951] 1 KB 151 at 158.
20   [1951] 1 KB 151 at 159.

exchanging substantial rights under the Rent Act in return for much less valuable rights.[1] There are, however, some tentative signs that the courts are nowadays somewhat less inclined to find that a tenant has validly consented to an implied surrender of his statutory rights in return for a mere contractual licence. The courts' reluctance is particularly marked if the agreement does not take effect immediately[2] or if the full legal impact of this exchange has not been spelt out in explicit terms for the benefit of the tenant.[3]

(b) Consent order

It is clear that an agreement by a statutory tenant to give up possession in return for payment is not illegal, unlawful or contrary to public policy.[4] However, such an agreement is not necessarily capable of specific performance through the making of a court order for possession.[5] The inhibition on contracting out of Rent Act protection applies even to a consent order for possession, in so far as it constitutes an attempted waiver by the tenant of an existing statutory entitlement.[6] The court has jurisdiction to make a consent order for possession only if the tenant's consent marks a recognition by him either that he has never been or has now ceased to be a statutory tenant or that a good ground of recovery of possession exists under Schedule 15 of the Rent Act 1977.[7]

(2) Evasion

In view of the severe strictures imposed by Rent Act control there is an inevitable temptation for landlords to grant lettings which are contractually structured so as to circumvent the provisions of the Act. Over the years much

---

1   In a similarly dreadful decision in *Matthew v Bobbins* (1981) 41 P & CR 1 at 8, the Court of Appeal ruled that the terms of a licence forced upon a Rent Act protected employee were 'fair...[or] at any rate not grossly unfair.' Waller LJ thought that in days when 'there is all the protection of the Employment Acts, and the opportunity of going to an industrial tribunal', no presumption of undue influence could be pleaded on behalf of the employee ((1981) 41 P & CR 1 at 9). See (1981) 131 NLJ 1022 (A. Waite); (1980) LAG Bulletin 189. See also *Scrimgeour v Waller* (1981) 257 Estates Gazette 61 at 63.

2   See *Short Bros (Plant) Ltd v Edwards* (1979) 249 Estates Gazette 539 at 542f.

3   See eg *Palfrey v Palfrey* (1974) 229 Estates Gazette 1593 at 1595; *Glastonbury Royal British Legion Club Ltd v Govier* (Unreported, Court of Appeal, No 80/00664, 9 September 1981); *Addy v Donnelly* [1983] CA Bound Transcript 506. See also *Tarjomani v Panther Securities Ltd* (1983) 46 P & CR 32 at 42.

4   *Rajbenback v Mamon* [1955] 1 QB 283 at 286; *R v Bloomsbury and Marylebone County Court, ex parte Blackburne* (1985) 275 Estates Gazette 1273 at 1274.

5   In *R v Bloomsbury and Marylebone County Court, ex parte Blackburne* (1985) 275 Estates Gazette 1273 at 1274, the Court of Appeal refused to allow a consent order to stand even though the tenant had already accepted payment of his costs and an offer of £11,000 for surrender of his statutory rights. Estoppel could not be invoked to confer jurisdiction where none existed, although the tenant of course was liable to repay the costs and clearly lost any claim to the quit money.

6   *Barton v Fincham* [1921] 2 KB 291 at 296ff; *Middleton v Baldock* [1950] 1 KB 657 at 669f.

7   *R v Bloomsbury and Marylebone County Court, ex parte Blackburne* (1985) 275 Estates Gazette 1273 at 1274. See also *Syed Hussain v A.M. Abdullah Sahib & Co* [1985] 1 WLR 1392 at 1397D-E per Lord Keith of Kinkel. (It is, however, of some interest that the Privy Council reserved its opinion as to the possible binding effect of an agreement given by a tenant in pursuance of a compromise involving the payment of money). See also A. Firth and L. Blake, (1984) **Legal Action** 98.

ingenuity has been devoted to the development of devices whose sole object is to enable landlords to evade the impact of the statutory protection conferred on residential tenants. By the early 1980s these devices had become sufficiently prevalent to cause commentators to question whether the Rent Act had in reality become irrelevant to landlord-tenant relations.[8] In 1982 the House of Commons Environment Committee expressed its concern at the number of lettings being granted supposedly outside the Rent Act, noting that 'in certain areas, especially in Inner London, such lettings form a significant proportion of available vacant accommodation.'[9] However, more recent developments indicate that the courts may now have closed many of the loopholes exploited by landlords, with the result that the protective effect of the Rent Act has been significantly reinforced.

(a) 'Avoidance' and 'evasion'

Deeply entrenched in the philosophy of the Rent Act is the maintenance of a strict distinction between the concepts of 'avoidance' and 'evasion'. 'Avoidance' is the entirely legitimate objective of arranging legal relations so that they do not attract the operation of regulatory legislation. 'Evasion' involves the use of essentially deceptive devices in order to avert the operation of regulatory legislation where it would otherwise clearly apply.[10] It is trite law that avoidance is lawful, but that evasion is illegal and will be rejected as such by the courts. However, the borderline between avoidance and evasion is somewhat blurred,[11] and in consequence the courts have generally struck down only those Rent Act evasions which can be characterised as a 'sham'. The practical distinction between avoidance and evasion has thus tended to focus on the identification of 'sham' transactions, not least because a 'sham' usually represents only a thinly disguised attempt to contract out of the provisions of the Rent Act.

(b) 'Genuine transactions' and 'shams'

The prohibition against contracting out of a statute would be both comprehensive and conclusive were it not for the proposition that parties to a

8   '...it seems as though with present arrangements landlords can, with a fair degree of impunity, often get around the constraints intended by the Rent Act' (J. Doling, *Have the Rent Acts become irrelevant?*, (1984) 270 Estates Gazette 1148). See also J. Doling, *How Much Protection Do The Rent Acts Provide?*, [1983] JPL 713; *Residential round-up—stop worrying about the Rent Act*, (1981) 2 PLB 22.

9   *The Private Rented Housing Sector* (First Report from the House of Commons Environment Committee), Vol 1 (HC 40-1, 13 July 1982), para 89. The Committee observed (ibid, para 90) that 'there is considerable evidence to suggest that many of the deliberate exclusions from Rent Act protection to deal with, for example, hostels, are no longer simply being used genuinely to provide specialised forms of short-term accommodation.'

10   'A property owner is entitled to arrange his affairs so as not to get his property enmeshed in the Rent Acts. What he is not entitled to do is to arrange his affairs in one way, which brings his property within the Rent Acts, and then to dress them up in another way so as to give the impression that it is outside the Rent Acts' (*O'Malley v Seymour* (1978) 250 Estates Gazette 1083 at 1088 per Lawton LJ). See also *Gatien Motor Co Ltd v Continental Oil Co of Ireland Ltd* [1979] IR 406 at 416.

11   In the analogous area of tax law the moral and legal distinctions between avoidance and evasion have become so uncertain that the mirky middle-ground between the concepts has been termed 'avoision' (see A. Seldon (ed), *Tax Avoision* (London 1979), p 4).

transaction are entirely free under English law so to order their affairs that they never come within the range of the statute in the first place.[12] There can be no question of contracting out of the Rent Act if the parties never originally crossed the threshold of the legislation.

For this reason the courts have developed an elusive distinction between 'genuine transactions' and 'shams'.[13] The 'contracting-out' problem simply does not arise in a 'genuine transaction', where the contract of the parties accurately records their bona fide intention to enter into a legal relationship to which the statute has no application anyway. A 'sham' occurs by contrast where the parties engage in actions or execute documents 'which are intended by them to give to third parties or to the court the appearance of creating...legal rights and obligations different from the actual legal rights and obligations (if any) which the parties intend to create.'[14] 'Sham' terms are intrinsically deceptive,[15] in that they are wilful misdescriptions of the parties' true relationship, but they are not in themselves illegal or contrary to public policy. They are simply ineffective and therefore to be disregarded by the court.[16]

(i) The courts' general approach to 'shams'   There is an important social concern that shams should be uncovered by the courts. As Denning LJ pointed out in *Facchini v Bryson*,[17] if the courts are not astute to denounce the sham transaction, 'we should make a hole in the Rent Acts through which could be driven—I will not in these days say a coach and four—but an articulated vehicle.' Until relatively recently, however, the courts have been slow to stigmatise transactions as sham. While constantly affirming that the court 'has to be especially wary and especially careful to see that the wool is not being pulled over its eyes',[18] the judges took the view that the parties' intentions should not be categorised as 'bogus or unreal or as sham' merely on the ground that the court 'disapproves of the bargain'.[19] In *Aldrington Garages Ltd v Fielder*[20]

---

12   This has been a conventional starting-point for the courts in the law of taxation (see *IRC v Duke of Westminster* [1936] AC 1 at 19 per Lord Tomlin; *Helvering v Gregory*, 69 F.2d 809 at 810 (1934) per Judge Learned Hand; but compare now *Furniss v Dawson* [1984] AC 474 at 526F-527E).

13   See generally A. Nicol, *Outflanking Protective Legislation-Shams and Beyond*, (1981) 44 MLR 21.

14   *Snook v London and West Riding Investments Ltd* [1967] 2 QB 786 at 802E per Diplock LJ, who added that 'for acts or documents to be a "sham"...all the parties thereto must have a common intention that the acts or documents are not to create the legal rights and obligations which they give the appearance of creating. No unexpressed intentions of the "shammer" affect the rights of a party whom he deceived.' See also *Hoggett v Hoggett* (1980) 39 P & CR 121 at 125.

15   The Court of Appeal has confirmed that the notion of a 'sham' applies with no less force in relation to business lettings than in relation to residential lettings (see *Greenstreet v Moorchat Ltd* (Unreported, 1981 G No 3845, 12 November 1982), ante, p 451). In the commercial context, moreover, there is also the ironical twist that 'sham' terms are sometimes used in order to dress up a gratuitous licence in the form of a lease (see eg *R.A. Sanson Investments Ltd v Sanson* (Unreported, Court of Appeal, 11 March 1982)).

16   *Markou v Da Silvaesa* (1986) 52 P & CR 204 at 215.

17   [1952] 1 TLR 1386 at 1390.

18   *Aldrington Garages Ltd v Fielder* (1978) 37 P & CR 461 at 469.

19   *Somma v Hazelhurst and Savelli* [1978] 1 WLR 1014 at 1025A-B. See also *Shell-Mex and BP Ltd v Manchester Garages Ltd* [1971] 1 WLR 612 at 619B-D; *Donald v Baldwyn* [1953] NZLR 313 at 321.

20   (1978) 37 P & CR 461 at 468 (ante, p 452).

Geoffrey Lane LJ argued forcefully against the courts 'bending over backwards to ensure that landlords do not manage to avoid the provisions of the Rent Acts.' The same judge entered a vigorous defence of the entrepreneurial impulse, taking the view that there is 'nothing wrong in trying to escape the provisions of [the Rent] Acts or, indeed, in trying to increase one's profits if one can legitimately do so.'[1]

In the result the courts, while expressing a superficial willingness to strike down a sham, rarely intervened in any case other than that of gross fraud on the Rent Act.[2] Indeed, it may well be that during the late 1970s and early 1980s the courts allowed the boundary between legitimate avoidance and illicit evasion of the Rent Act to shift around in response to some perceived need to stimulate rather than fetter the supply of rented accommodation in large urban centres.[3] There had always been an argument to the effect that the operation of the Rent Act is ultimately counterproductive. In terms of this argument, Rent Act control tends to strangulate the supply of residential lettings by inhibiting those who would otherwise be willing to release accommodation on to the rental market for short-term and easily recoverable occupation.[4]

By the early 1980s, however, it had become obvious that judicial pragmatism had not opened up an abundant supply of rented housing. Instead the courts' failure to challenge any but the most blatant of shams had effectively brought about a measure of de-control of rented lettings which simply enabled landlords more easily to recover possession from occupiers. Possession, once obtained, led typically to a swift sale on the freehold market and the consequent realisation by the landlord of the dramatic inflation in property values which had accrued during the 1970s.[5] In more recent years, therefore, it is significant that the courts have adopted a less tolerant stance in relation to Rent Act evasions. A new temper was evident, for instance, in *R v Rent Officer for LB of Camden, ex parte Plant*.[6] Here Glidewell J had little difficulty in concluding that an alleged holiday let was a sham, adding somewhat pointedly that he had 'managed to remain reasonably upright while achieving that result.' There are, of course, counter-examples which do not disclose the same degree of judicial activism, but the tenor of contemporary developments was aptly summed up in Lord Templeman's exhortation in *Street v Mountford*[7] that 'the court should...be astute to detect and frustrate sham devices and artificial transactions whose only object is to disguise the grant of a tenancy and to evade the Rent Acts.'

(ii) Identification of a 'sham'   In practical terms the real clue to the presence of a 'sham' seems to be the inclusion of written terms which are so inconsistent, incomprehensible or improbable as to raise a presumption that they cannot

1   (1978) 37 P & CR 461 at 471.
2   See, however, *Demuren v Seal Estates Ltd* (1978) 249 Estates Gazette 440; *O'Malley v Seymour* (1978) 250 Estates Gazette 1083.
3   This is probably the most charitable explanation for the decision of the Court of Appeal in *Somma v Hazelhurst and Savelli* [1978] 1 WLR 1014 (post, p 998).
4   The attraction of this argument was demonstrated by the introduction in the Housing Act 1980 of a new mandatory ground for possession in the case of 'protected shorthold tenancies' (post, p 1028).
5   See J. Kemeny, *The Myth of Home Ownership* (London 1981), p 28.
6   (1981) 257 Estates Gazette 713 at 718.
7   [1985] AC 809 at 825H.

possibly represent the true intentions of the parties. In *Demuren v Seal Estates Ltd*,[8] for instance, the grantee of a one-year 'licence' had been required to make immediate payment by a series of post-dated cheques of all the monthly instalments due. The dubious status of this 'licence' was intensified by the fact that, notwithstanding his acceptance of the cheques, the 'licensor' supposedly retained a unilateral right to terminate the 'licence' at any time by giving one week's notice. The Court of Appeal found these terms 'irreconcilable' and pointed out that there was 'something so badly wrong with this agreement that one is bound to look at it with the gravest suspicion.'[9] The agreement was declared to be a 'sham' designed to conceal the existence of a Rent Act protected tenancy.

The relevance of unrealistic or sloppily drafted clauses was again exemplified in *Markou v Da Silvaesa*.[10] Here a residential 'licence' purported to grant the occupiers 'merely a personal privilege to use' their furnished flat on each day during a 26-week period 'between the hours of midnight and 10.30 am and between noon and midnight but at no other times.' Moreover the 'licensor' expressly reserved a right to remove or substitute 'such articles of furniture from the flat as [he] may see fit.' Although neither of these clauses had ever been strictly enforced, the Court of Appeal noted that the terms of the agreement apparently authorised the 'licensor' to insist that the occupiers should remove themselves and all their belongings from the flat for one and a half hours each day. Moreover, the agreement seemed to give the 'licensor' the right at his whim to denude the flat of all furniture supplied for the purpose of occupation by the 'licensees'. The Court thought it unlikely that such 'astonishingly extreme'[11] terms could represent a true description of the nature of the possession intended to be enjoyed by the respective 'licensees'. Each clause was 'bizarre'[12] and 'so extraordinary...that it calls for an explanation.'[13] Nicholls LJ found that it strained his credulity 'too far' to suppose that such terms comprised a 'genuine record of the transaction' when 'the basic clause in [the] agreement is an artificial contrivance intended to mislead and thereby to create or strengthen a claim by the landlord that the agreement was outside the Rent Acts.'[14] Accordingly the Court ruled that it was at least arguable that the entire transaction was one of tenancy rather than mere licence.

(c) Particular evasive devices

Over the years a number of standard techniques of Rent Act evasion have been developed which now require especially strict scrutiny in view of the ruling of the House of Lords in *Street v Mountford*.[15] The success of such techniques has tended in the past to rest upon the fact that the nominal label attached to any evasive transaction is conclusive unless positively challenged by the occupier,

---

8 (1978) 249 Estates Gazette 440.
9 (1978) 249 Estates Gazette 440 at 443.
10 (1986) 52 P & CR 204; (1986) 278 Estates Gazette 618.
11 (1986) 52 P & CR 204 at 215 per Ralph Gibson LJ.
12 (1986) 52 P & CR 204 at 215 per Ralph Gibson LJ.
13 (1986) 52 P & CR 204 at 224 per Nicholls LJ.
14 (1986) 52 P & CR 204 at 226.
15 [1985] AC 809 (ante, p 449).

and many occupiers are deterred by one reason or another from undertaking such a challenge.[16] Among the evasive devices frequently encountered are the following.

(i) Licence   An obvious evasive technique involves the explicit acknowledgement by the occupier that no tenancy was intended to be created by his occupancy agreement. Indeed, it used to be a fairly common practice for an intending occupier to be required to sign a declaration, incorporated within the written agreement itself, which specifically denied that his rights were other than those of a licensee. Although superficial labels are never conclusive,[17] such language (particularly if accompanied by multiple references to the 'licensor' and 'licensee') was almost always persuasive in pointing towards the 'licence' character of the agreement in question.[18]

During the early 1980s, however, the courts began to feel increasingly uncomfortable about the ease with which a tenancy classification could be averted by landlords who exploited their superior bargaining power through the 'device of letting by licence rather than a tenancy.'[19] The natural conclusion of this judicial disquiet was the House of Lords' decision in *Street v Mountford*[20] that the grant of exclusive possession for a term at a rent almost inevitably generates a tenancy even in the face of the parties' express disavowal of any intention to produce that result. It follows that nowadays even the most explicit denial of the tenancy status of a letting will be ineffectual if the classic indicia of a tenancy are also present. The courts will be even more ready to disregard a 'false label' which amounts to a 'sham' or wilful misdescription of the parties' relationship.

The courts' new-found willingness to disregard 'sham' terms has proved particularly significant in the area of the 'non-exclusive occupation licence'. This kind of licence acquired such prominence during the late 1970s and early 1980s that it became difficult to find residential accommodation in the large cities except on the terms of such a licence. The non-exclusive occupation licence provided characteristically for multiple occupation of living accommodation in a manner not dissimilar to joint tenancy, but with the crucial difference that each occupier was artificially denied exclusive possession of the premises. Without exclusive possession there could be no tenancy, with the consequence that none of the occupiers was eligible for protection under the Rent Act.[1]

The primary recognition of the legal effect of the non-exclusive occupation licence occurred in the Court of Appeal's ruling in 1978 in *Somma v Hazelhurst*

---

16   An interesting role has been played in this respect by rent officers in the exercise of their jurisdiction to entertain applications for registration of a 'fair rent' (post, p 1032). One rent officer has made the candid but not atypical admission that his own approach to questionable letting devices has been to determine the arrangement to be a tenancy and invite the 'owner' to challenge this determination in the county court (see L.N. Biddulph, *Avoidances, Evasions-Licences, A Growing Problem*, (1983) 14 Jiro (No 1), 25 at 26).

17   Ante, p 450.

18   See eg *Somma v Hazelhurst and Savelli* [1978] 1 WLR 1014 at 1026D (ante, p 447).

19   *Street v Mountford* (1984) 49 P & CR 324 at 333 per Griffiths LJ. See also Slade LJ at 331.

20   [1985] AC 809 at 827A-B.

1   Nor did any of the occupiers qualify for the protection given to restricted contracts (post, p 1040), since the clear implication of Rent Act 1977, s 19(6) is that an occupier under such a contract must also enjoy exclusive occupation of at least some part of the premises.

and Savelli.[2] Here an unmarried man and woman had both signed 'licence agreements' in respect of a double bed-sitting room. Both agreements explicitly indicated that the 'licensor' was unwilling to grant either occupier exclusive possession of the room, and this unwillingness was reinforced by the express reservation on behalf of the 'licensor' of a right to 'use' the room in common with the occupiers[3] and even to nominate a replacement in the event that one of the occupiers should leave.[4] The clear intention of these terms was that neither occupier should be able to claim exclusive possession. The couple proceeded to pay rent separately to the 'licensor', the latter providing a single receipt for these payments. The Court of Appeal somewhat surprisingly declined to treat the couple as being the unit which they undoubtedly constituted, holding instead that each had a distinct and separate occupation licence.[5] In effect the very unity of possession which is an essential characteristic of joint tenancy was treated as rebutting the exclusiveness of possession which is integral to the concept of tenancy. In consequence neither occupier was eligible for any form of Rent Act protection.[6]

The decision in *Somma* was widely understood as providing landlords with a foolproof means of circumventing the Rent Act through the granting of fictitious 'licences' for non-exclusive multiple occupation. Indeed the ruling seemed to imply that the Rent Act was rendered wholly inapplicable if a landlord merely reserved himself a right (never in fact intended to be exercised) to use accommodation in common with even a single occupier.[7] Although followed in a number of subsequent decisions,[8] *Somma* was, however, overruled

2   [1978] 1 WLR 1014. See [1979] CLJ 38; (1979) 42 MLR 331 (M. Partington); (1979) LAG Bulletin 87 (A. Arden); [1980] Conv 27 (P. Robson and P. Watchman).
3   This implausible right of common user of one room was challenged by the occcupiers on the ground of illegality, in that (it was argued) the reservation expressed an intention to contravene the statutory prohibition of 'overcrowding' (ante, p 936). However, the Court of Appeal rejected this objection ([1978] 1 WLR 1014 at 1028H–1029A) on the ground that the 'overcrowding' legislation applies only where an excessive number of adults 'sleep' in, rather than merely 'use', the same room!
4   At first instance the county court judge had thought it a 'most revolting' idea that the 'licensor' should be technically entitled to introduce a substitute 'licensee' of a different sex to succeed to the vacancy. However, this objection cut little ice in the Court of Appeal, Cumming-Bruce LJ indicating ([1978] 1 WLR 1014 at 1028E–G) that moralistic argument on this point was somewhat irrelevant given the status of the current occupiers' relationship!
5   Compare, however, *Walsh v Griffiths-Jones and Durant* [1978] 2 All ER 1002 at 1010d–e; [1979] CLJ 38. Here a joint tenancy was upheld where, in virtually identical circumstances, two young (male) graduates of Trinity College, Cambridge had been granted non-exclusive occupation licences in respect of their shared flat. The discrepant results in *Somma* and *Walsh* give rise to the strong suspicion of the legal realist that the courts may have looked more kindly on a couple of Trinity graduates, bristling with sincerity at the threshold of their new careers in the metropolis, than upon a man and woman who merely preferred to live in sin! See also *McHugh v LB of Islington* (1984) 270 Estates Gazette 1095.
6   It appeared to weigh heavily with the Court ([1978] 1 WLR 1014 at 1025H–1026C) that the occupiers' rent obligations were calculated quite separately, although it was very clear that neither occupier would have entered into an agreement alone and that the couple had agreed to the terms offered only because they were in urgent need of accommodation. Joint tenants are, of course, jointly and severally liable for rent, although this consideration was not regarded as precluding a joint tenancy in *Walsh v Griffiths-Jones and Durant* [1978] 2 All ER 1002 at 1010a–b or *Demuren v Seal Estates Ltd* (1978) 249 Estates Gazette 440 at 443. See (1978) LAG Bulletin 265 (A. Arden).
7   See, however, *O'Malley v Seymour* (1978) 250 Estates Gazette 1083 at 1087f.
8   See *Aldrington Garages Ltd v Fielder* (1978) 37 P & CR 461 at 472; *Sturolson & Co v Weniz* (1984) 272 Estates Gazette 326 at 330.

finally in *Street v Mountford*.[9] Here the House of Lords stigmatised the grant of rights of non-exclusive user in *Somma* as plainly having a 'sham nature'. If the 'sham' terms were accordingly disregarded, it followed inescapably that the occupiers had been in reality joint tenants, since they had taken the room as residential accommodation with exclusive possession in order that they might 'live together in quasi-connubial bliss making weekly payments.'[10]

It is clear that the House of Lords' decision in *Street v Mountford* has effectively destroyed the potential of most forms of the non-exclusive occupation licence as an instrument for evasion of Rent Act control. In *Caplan v Marden*,[11] for instance, the Sheffield County Court had little difficulty in upholding a claim of joint tenancy where three students had been granted three identical agreements purporting to grant each non-exclusive rights of 'licence' over the upper part of a house.[12] It is, of course, still possible that a non-exclusive occupation licence may be validly granted outside the reach of the Rent Act if there is a genuine arrangement to share residential accommodation. In *Brooker Settled Estates Ltd v Ayer*[13] the Court of Appeal upheld such a licence in the context of a flat-sharing arrangement in which the owner of the flat had reserved a right to put another person into occupation of a bedroom and all the flat-sharers had a right of access to all parts of the flat. In general, however, non-exclusive occupation licences are nowadays likely to be scrutinised with grave suspicion, and the attention of those landlords minded to evade the Act has already turned to alternative devices directed towards achieving the same end.[14]

(ii) Rent-free tenancy coupled with extortionate hire of furniture   A further technique sometimes used for the purpose of evading Rent Act control is the grant of a 'rent-free' tenancy under which the tenant is obliged to hire furniture or other chattels at extortionate rates. Although the absence of any 'rent' *stricto sensu* is clearly aimed at excluding the operation of the Act,[15] it should not be difficult for the court to stigmatise such a blatant device as a 'sham'.[16]

(iii) Rent-free tenancy coupled with obligatory payment to a third party   A similar form of Rent Act evasion occurs where the grantee of a supposedly 'rent-free' tenancy is contractually obliged to make equivalent payments in discharge of the landlord's financial obligations to third parties.[17] It is probable that the court would declare such a contractual term to be a 'sham' and thus to be ineffective as a means of circumventing the Rent Act.[18]

9   [1985] AC 809 at 825H-826A.
10   [1985] AC 809 at 825G.
11   *Rent Acts: Selected Case Law Guide* (Institute of Rent Officers Educational Trust), Vol 1, p 348. See (1986) Legal Action 30; (1986) 136 NLJ 131.
12   See also *Felix v Karacritos and Jachni* (1986) Legal Action 30; *Felix v Rajar and Mahindra* (1986) Legal Action 30; *Felix v Lockwood* (1986) Legal Action 164.
13   (1987) *Times*, 13 February.
14   Ante, p 983; post, p 1001.
15   See Rent Act 1977, s 5(1) (ante, p 983, post, p 1001).
16   See eg *Irish Shell and BP Ltd v John Costello Ltd* [1981] ILRM 66 at 71. Compare, however, *Maclay v Dixon* [1944] 1 All ER 22 at 23D-H, where the Court of Appeal did not strike down a highly dubious manoeuvre involving furniture.
17   Ante, p 973.
18   See eg the insistence in *Sidney Trading Co Ltd v Finsbury BC* [1952] 1 All ER 460 at 462A per Lord Goddard CJ that if 'there is a sum of money which the tenant agrees to pay as a consideration for the tenancy, it is for this purpose a rent.' See also *Property Holding Co Ltd v Clark* [1948] 1 All ER 165 at 173H-174A.

(iv) Options to purchase and 'rental purchase' Evasion of the Rent Act is occasionally attempted either under cover of some 'contract' by the residential occupier to purchase a freehold or long lease in his accommodation or under cover of some scheme of 'deferred' or 'rental purchase' of the property.[19] The essential characteristic of such schemes is that the occupier is required to pay periodic sums supposedly in respect of occupation pending completion of a contract of sale or as instalments directed towards an eventual conveyance of the property if and when the entire purchase price has been paid to the owner.

In reality, of course, such arrangements scarcely ever result in any transfer of an estate in the land and are merely a thinly disguised form of letting at a periodic rent unaccompanied by any plausible intention on either side that there should be a conveyance. The courts have traditionally regarded the 'rental' or 'deferred' purchase with great suspicion, and have been ready to reject such agreements as a blatant 'sham' where the circumstances disclose no genuine intention to sell an estate in the property.[20] Likewise a contract for sale is apt to be disregarded as a 'sham' if the purchaser fails to buy the property within the relevant option period but is immediately granted a further 'option to purchase' while remaining in occupation at the same periodic rent.[1]

(v) The 'company let' In recent years much use has been made of the 'company let' as a means of circumventing the Rent Act.[2] The essence of a 'company let' is that the landlord agrees to grant a tenancy to a company rather than to any individual or group of individuals, even though the clear purpose of the letting is to facilitate residential occupation by individuals connected with the company. In strict legal form (although not in reality), the landlord grants a letting to the company as an artificial entity, whereupon the company grants a sublease or licence to each intended occupier. In the most blatant manifestation of the 'company let', the landlord causes the intending occupiers to purchase an 'off-the-peg' company precisely in order that the immediate grantee of the letting should be the corporate entity.

The utility of the 'company let' lies in the fact that a company cannot assert any personal or domestic residence in property,[3] and thus can never claim the security of tenure which is effectively afforded to a statutory tenant.[4] Although

---

19   See B.M. Hoggett, *Houses on the Never-Never: Some Legal Aspects of Rental Purchase*, (1972) 36 Conv (NS) 325.

20   See eg *Martin v Davies* (1952) 7 HLR 120 at 131ff, where a further dubious feature of the agreement was the fact that the contractual repayment period actually exceeded the unexpired term of the 'vendor's' leasehold interest in the property! See also Housing Act 1980, s 88(1), which introduced one welcome form of relief for occupiers under a 'rental purchase agreement' (as defined in Housing Act 1980, s 88(4)). Where court proceedings for possession are brought against such occupiers, the court may adjourn the proceedings, or stay or suspend the execution of any possession order, or postpone the date for possession (post, p 1022). See also H.A. Frazer and J.C.W. Wylie, *The Rent Restriction Law of Northern Ireland*, (1971) 22 NILQ 99 at 122f.

1   See eg *Aujla v Tuffin* [1981] CLY 1550.

2   Post, p 1008.

3   *Reidy v Walker* [1933] 2 KB 266 at 271f; *Hiller v United Dairies (London) Ltd* [1934] 1 KB 57 at 63.

4   See *Hiller v United Dairies (London) Ltd* [1934] 1 KB 57 at 63f. There is likewise no danger in a 'company let' that the tenancy may devolve upon family members by succession (*Wyld v Clode* (Unreported, Court of Appeal, 7 December 1983) per Arnold P). However, there is nothing to prevent a corporate tenant from applying for registration of a 'fair rent' during the term of a protected tenancy (*Carter v S.U. Carburetter Co* [1942] 2 KB 288 at 291).

such lettings now represent an increasingly common abuse of the Rent Act, the courts have been reluctant to castigate such lettings as a 'sham'.[5] It seems that the 'company let'—except perhaps in its most extreme and disingenuous guise—may currently be one of the most effective means of deflecting the long-term security of tenure otherwise acquired under the Rent Act by a residential occupier and members of his family.

(vi) Use of a business tenancy   It is not impossible that the grant of a spurious 'business tenancy' may be used in order to conceal a Rent Act protected letting of residential premises. It is not unknown for landlords to prefer potential exposure to the much less stringent terms of Part II of the Landlord and Tenant Act 1954,[6] rather than face the rigours of the Rent Act. However, the courts have not shown themselves overly astute to strike down a nominally 'business' letting even where the label is belied by the landlord's waiver of an express prohibition of residential user.[7]

(vii) Manipulations of express exceptions to the Rent Act   Other forms of Rent Act evasion involve the manipulation of express exceptions to Rent Act coverage. These exceptions are dealt with elsewhere,[8] and the kinds of manipulation exploited by landlords include the disingenuous use of 'holiday lets',[9] insubstantial claims to the 'board' or 'attendance' exemption,[10] and the spurious assertion of 'resident landlord' status.[11] The courts are increasingly prepared to strike down the cynical abuse of such exceptions to Rent Act protection.

5. THE STATUTORY TENANCY

Provided that a tenancy of a dwelling-house does not fall within any of the express or implied exceptions specified by the Rent Act 1977, it constitutes a 'protected tenancy' for the purpose of the Act so long as there is a continuing contractual relationship between landlord and tenant. The duration of that contractual relationship is fixed by the terms of the tenancy agreement. However, when the contractual period comes to an end (either by the effluxion of time or after the service of a notice to quit), it is integral to the Rent Act scheme that the tenancy continues to subsist, not as a 'protected tenancy' based on the parties' contract, but as a 'statutory tenancy' which derives its legal effect from the Rent Act itself.[12] In other words, it is possible that the expired protected tenancy may receive almost literally a new lease of life in the form of a

---

5   See eg *Firstcross Ltd v East West (Export/Import) Ltd* (1981) 41 P & CR 145 at 158; (1981) LAG Bulletin 40 (A. Arden); *Tetragon Ltd v Shidasb Construction Co Ltd and Darabi* (1981) 7 HLR 113 at 118. Compare the willingness of the Court of Appeal in *Evans v Engelson* (1980) 253 Estates Gazette 577 at 578 to pierce the corporate veil in favour of a landlord company which wished to claim the benefit of the Rent Act.
6   Post, p 1038.
7   See eg *Cooper v Henderson* (1982) 263 Estates Gazette 592 at 593f.
8   Ante, p 983.
9   Ante, p 984.
10   Ante, p 986.
11   Ante, p 990.
12   Rent Act 1977, s 2(1)(a).

'statutory tenancy' which enjoys substantially the same protection under the Rent Act as did the former contractual tenancy.[13] So valuable is this protection that the courts have recognised that often the possession of a statutory tenancy is 'one of the most significant rights of property' which an individual may hold.[14] Under the Rent Act protected tenancies and statutory tenancies are together known as 'regulated tenancies'.

(1) Nature of a statutory tenancy

The statutory tenancy created by the Rent Act is a highly anomalous jural phenomenon. A statutory tenancy is not the product of any conscious grant by the landlord. The truth is quite the reverse, for a statutory tenancy arises in effect where a former tenant holds over without his landlord's consent.[15] In strict terms the statutory tenancy is no tenancy at all[16]; it comprises merely a 'right or a bundle of rights' created by statute and 'does not fit easily into such classifications as movables and immovables, corporeal and incorporeal hereditaments or any of the other common law conceptions of property.'[17] However, as Evershed MR remarked in *Marcroft Wagons Ltd v Smith*,[18] the statutory tenancy illustrates 'one of the features of modern times', in that the rights of occupation created thereby are notable for 'having in most respects the attributes of a tenancy but lacking the estate in land which is a necessary incident of a tenancy.'

(a) The statutory tenant has a 'status of irremovability'

It is difficult to assimilate the statutory tenancy within the doctrine of estates,[19] for the statutory tenant has no estate or interest known to the common law.[20] All he has is a negatively expressed and largely personal right to be 'free from disturbance'[1] by his landlord unless and until some court of competent

---

13 A statutory tenant is subject to and entitled to the benefit of all the terms and conditions of the original contract of tenancy, so far as they are consistent with statute (Rent Act 1977, s 3(1)).

14 See *Mafo v Adams* [1970] 1 QB 548 at 557G-H. Even if measured in purely financial terms, the right to a statutory tenancy may be surprisingly valuable (see, for example, the agreement that the landlord pay a statutory tenant £11,000 as 'quit money' in *R v Bloomsbury & Marylebone County Court, ex parte Blackburne* (1985) 275 Estates Gazette 1273). See also *Brown v Ministry of Housing and Local Government* [1953] 2 All ER 1385 at 1392D-E.

15 *Keeves v Dean* [1924] 1 KB 685 at 694.

16 '[I]t is a pity that that expression was ever introduced. It is really a misnomer' (*Keeves v Dean* [1924] 1 KB 685 at 690). See also *Roe v Russell* [1928] 2 KB 117 at 131; *Drury v Johnston* [1928] NI 25 at 30; *McCullough v Ministry of Commerce for Northern Ireland* [1961] NI 75 at 81; *McKinty v Belfast Corporation* [1973] NI 1 at 11.

17 *McKinty v Belfast Corporation* [1973] NI 1 at 11. See also *Chelsea Investments Pty Ltd v Federal Commissioner of Taxation* (1966) 115 CLR 1 at 7.

18 [1951] 2 KB 496 at 500.

19 In some ways the statutory tenancy, with its capacity for devolution upon members of the tenant's family (post, p 1062), rather tantalisingly resembles a modern form of fee tail, but the analogy is partial and imperfect.

20 *Keeves v Dean* [1924] 1 KB 685 at 690, 697; *Dudley and District Benefit Building Society v Emerson* [1949] Ch 707 at 717; *Harrington v Croydon Corporation* [1968] 1 QB 856 at 873D, 882D; *McCullough v Ministry of Commerce for Northern Ireland* [1961] NI 75 at 81; *McKinty v Belfast Corporation* [1973] NI 1 at 11.

1 *Keeves v Dean* [1924] 1 KB 685 at 697. See also *Brown v Ministry of Housing and Local Government* [1953] 2 All ER 1385 at 1392E; *McCullough v Ministry of Commerce for Northern Ireland* [1961] NI 75 at 81.

jurisdiction makes an order for the recovery of possession on behalf of that landlord.[2] It is for this reason that the statutory tenant is often referred to as having a mere 'status of irremovability'.[3] This absence of a legal estate in the land can be demonstrated in several contexts.

(i) Destruction of the dwelling-house   If the statutory tenant's dwelling-house is completely demolished by fire, war damage or other cause, the statutory tenancy perishes with the house.[4] In equivalent circumstances, however, a contractual tenant may claim that his tenancy extends prima facie to any new house constructed on the same site.[5] A contractual tenant clearly has an estate in the land itself rather than merely a qualified statutory right not to be removed from a dwelling unit located on the land.

(ii) Non-transferability of the statutory tenant's rights   A further sharp contrast with the position of the contractual tenant is provided by the fact that the statutory tenant has no interest in the land which is capable of either unilateral assignment inter vivos[6] or testamentary disposition[7] to a third party. The statutory tenant thus lacks the uninhibited and independent capacity to transfer ownership which is conventionally regarded as the intrinsic incident of a property right.[8]

It also follows that, since a statutory tenancy lacks the quality of a proprietary estate, it cannot pass to the tenant's trustee in bankruptcy. A statutory tenant who becomes bankrupt is therefore protected from eviction.

---

2   Post, p 1015. The statutory tenancy appears to constitute a classic example of Hohfeldian 'immunity' (see W.N. Hohfeld, *Fundamental Legal Conceptions as Applied in Judicial Reasoning* (ed by W.W. Cook, New Haven, 1923), p 60ff).

3   The origin of the phrase seems to be a remark made by Lush J in *Keeves v Dean* [1924] 1 KB 685 at 686. See also *Marcroft Wagons Ltd v Smith* [1951] 2 KB 496 at 501; *Jessamine Investment Co Ltd v Schwartz* [1978] QB 264 at 272H-273A; *McKinty v Belfast Corporation* [1973] NI 1 at 11f.

4   *Ellis & Sons Amalgamated Properties Ltd v Sisman* [1948] 1 All ER 44 at 47A, F-G; *Phillips v Barnett* [1922] 1 KB 222 at 225.

5   See *McKinty v Belfast Corporation* [1973] NI 1 at 12.

6   *Keeves v Dean* [1924] 1 KB 685 at 695; *Atyeo v Fardoe* (1979) 37 P & CR 494 at 496; *Chelsea Investments Pty Ltd v Federal Commissioner of Taxation* (1966) 115 CLR 1 at 7; *Lifshitz v Forest Square Apartments Ltd* (1982) 36 OR (2d) 175 at 179. In England the only way in which the statutory tenant may effectively transfer his rights is through a written agreement to which his landlord is a party (Rent Act 1977, Sch 1, para 13(1), (2)). Compare, however, New York State Division of Housing and Community Renewal Regulations, s 2500.2, which permits a vacating tenant to pass his tenancy on to a remaining member of his immediate family. Since such a family member would have been protected in the event of the tenant's death (see New York City Rent and Eviction Regulations, s 56(d), post, p 1064), it has been declared 'inequitable and untenable to destroy such a right just because the [tenant] moved elsewhere rather than died' (*M. & L. Jacobs Inc v DelGrosso* 490 NYS.2d 963 at 968 (1985)). See also *Goodman v Ross*, 79 NYS.2d 791 at 792 (1948); *Herzog v Joy*, 428 NYS.2d 1 at 3 (1980).

7   *John Lovibond & Sons Ltd v Vincent* [1929] 1 KB 687 at 693ff; *Marcroft Wagons Ltd v Smith* [1951] 2 KB 496 at 501.

8   See eg *Doe d Mitchinson v Carter* (1798) 8 TR 57 at 60, 101 ER 1265 at 1266 per Lord Kenyon CJ; *Keeves v Dean* [1924] 1 KB 685 at 695. It is, however, open to the court on or after granting a decree of divorce to direct that one spouse shall cease to be the statutory tenant of a dwelling-house and that the other spouse shall be deemed to be so entitled (Matrimonial Homes Act 1983, Sch 1, Part II, para 3(1)). This power overrides any prohibition against assignment contained in the original tenancy agreement. See *Buckingham v Buckingham and London Brick Co Ltd* (Unreported, 12 May 1978); (1979) 129 NLJ 52 (N.E. Hickman); (1986) 136 NLJ 134 at 135 (S. Maidment).

His rights cannot be extinguished by any disclaimer of his tenancy on the part of his trustee in bankruptcy.[9] However, the date of bankruptcy is the vital determinant since if it occurs during the contractual term while a protected tenancy still subsists, the tenant's term vests in his trustee in bankruptcy, who is then free either to affirm or disclaim the contract.[10] A trustee in bankruptcy who takes over a protected tenancy cannot subsequently claim any form of statutory tenancy, since the trustee cannot claim residence for the purpose of Rent Act 1977, s 2(1).[11]

(iii) Irrelevance of strict property rules It is clearly accepted that the Rent Acts are not in pari materia with the Law of Property Act 1925.[12] Accordingly the courts have declined to adhere slavishly to the conventional rules of property law in elaborating the implications of the statutory tenancy. In *Lloyd v Sadler*,[13] for instance, the Court of Appeal allowed a unilateral claim to a statutory tenancy to be made by only one of the original contractual tenants,[14] even though the strict theory of joint tenancy[15] would normally have required that the conditions of eligibility for a statutory tenancy should be met by the composite entity consisting of all of the original joint tenants. However, Lawton LJ pointed out that the Rent Act 'gives protection to persons, not to legal concepts such as joint tenants'.[16] Since the security of tenure conferred by the Rent Act is 'a matter of personal and individual interest',[17] the Court refused to allow the doctrinal technicalities of joint tenancy to frustrate the status of irremovability claimed by the one tenant who had complied with the requirements for a statutory tenancy.[18]

(b) Quasi-proprietary aspects of a statutory tenancy

Notwithstanding that some of the traditional characteristics of a property right are lacking, the statutory tenancy is a hybrid concept and plainly exhibits some countervailing features which are much more closely analogous to the rights of proprietary entitlement enjoyed by the ordinary contractual tenant.[19]

(i) Right to sue in trespass Foremost amongst these quasi-proprietary incidents is the right which the statutory tenant enjoys as against all the world to remain

---

9   *Sutton v Dorf* [1932] 2 KB 304 at 308.
10 See *Smalley v Quarrier* [1975] 1 WLR 938 at 943E, 945D-E; *Fletcher v Davies* (1980) 257 Estates Gazette 1149.
11 Post, p 1007. See *Eyre v Hall* (1986) 280 Estates Gazette 193 at 195).
12 See *Powell v Cleland* [1948] 1 KB 262 at 273.
13 [1978] QB 774 (post, p 1007).
14 One of the original joint protected tenants had left during the contractual term in order to get married.
15 Ante, p 301.
16 [1978] QB 774 at 789A.
17 [1978] QB 774 at 791A. See [1978] Conv 436 (J. Martin).
18 As Shaw LJ said (at 790H), the 'identity of interest which subsists during the term of the grant is not bound to persist in a statutory appendage to it.' The decision in *Lloyd v Sadler* was later to create an uncomfortable backdrop to the issue which was presented to the courts in *Tilling v Whiteman* [1980] AC 1 (post, p 1025). See also *Williamson v Thompson* (1979) 251 Estates Gazette 955 at 959f.
19 See Catherine Hand, *The Statutory Tenancy: An Unrecognised Proprietary Interest?*, [1980] Conv 351.

in possession until duly dispossessed by order of the court. Until such an order is made and executed, the statutory tenant is competent to assert his right of exclusive possession by an action in trespass against any person (including the landlord) who enters the premises without his permission.[20] In other words, the statutory tenant enjoys that traditional and most characteristic right of the property owner in common law jurisprudence—the right to exclude others from enjoyment.

(ii) Right to grant sublettings Even if the statutory tenant has no estate at common law, he clearly has some statutorily created interest in the land which is sufficient not only to enable him to sublet at least part[1] (if not indeed the whole[2]) of the premises but also to entitle him to maintain an action of ejectment against the subtenant.[3]

(iii) Right to compensation for compulsory purchase The statutory tenant's interest is sufficiently substantial to make him eligible for compensation in the event of compulsory purchase of his premises.[4]

(iv) The statutory tenant's rights and duties are binding on third parties The quasi-proprietary nature of the statutory tenancy is underscored by the fact that it remains binding on successors in title of the landlord.[5] Moreover, the statutory tenant and his successors are in principle subject to the burdens[6] and entitled to the benefits[7] of the contractual tenancy which immediately preceded the statutory tenancy.

Thus, although not comprising a common law estate in the land, the statutory tenancy constitutes 'an interest in relation to the land'[8] which carries all the indicia of the 'new property' which is beginning to exert an impact on orthodox notions of property ownership.[9] The category of 'new property'

20 *Keeves v Dean* [1924] 1 KB 685 at 694. See *Cruise v Terrell* [1922] 1 KB 664 at 669f; *Remon v City of London Real Property Co Ltd* [1921] 1 KB 49 at 58f; *Chelsea Investments Pty Ltd v Federal Commissioner of Taxation* (1966) 115 CLR 1 at 7.
 1 *Roe v Russell* [1928] 2 KB 117 at 130f; *Regalian Securities Ltd v Ramsden* [1981] 1 WLR 611 at 614H. However, the statutory tenant cannot confer any estate or interest on the subtenant, since the statutory tenant 'cannot carve something out of nothing' (*Solomon v Orwell* [1954] 1 All ER 874 at 876), but the subtenant may now be protected under Rent Act 1977, s 137.
 2 See *Trustees of Henry Smith's Charity v Willson* [1983] QB 316 at 325D-E; [1983] Conv 248 (J. Martin).
 3 *Lask v Cohen* [1925] 1 KB 584 at 588. See *McCullough v Ministry of Commerce for Northern Ireland* [1961] NI 75 at 83.
 4 *Brown v Ministry of Housing and Local Government* [1953] 2 All ER 1385 at 1392A; *McCullough v Ministry of Commerce for Northern Ireland* [1961] NI 75 at 84f, 97f. Compare, however, *McKinty v Belfast Corporation* [1973] NI 1 at 14, where McVeigh LJ declined to hold that a statutory tenancy constituted property in respect of which malicious damage compensation could be paid pursuant to Criminal Injuries Act (Northern Ireland) 1956, s 4(4).
 5 See Land Registration Act 1925, s 70(1)(g) (ante, p 181). See also *Linden v Wigg* [1968] 2 NSWR 603 at 605.
 6 Rent Act 1977, s 3(2).
 7 *Hewitt v Rowlands* (1924) 93 LJKB 1080 at 1082f (landlord's duty to repair); *Lavender v Betts* [1942] 2 All ER 72 at 73D-E (landlord's covenant for quiet enjoyment).
 8 *Chelsea Investments Pty Ltd v Federal Commissioner of Taxation* (1966) 115 CLR 1 at 7 per Windeyer J. This recognition may be vital, for instance, for the purpose of establishing that the rights of a statutory tenant comprise rights 'subsisting in reference' to land pursuant to Land Registration Act 1925, s 70(1)(g) (ante, p 179). See also *Linden v Wigg* [1968] 2 NSWR 603 at 605.
 9 Ante, p 9.

comprises precisely those rights which are of an intangible, non-disposable, non-survivable and substantially personal nature. In view of its highly ambivalent nature, it is not surprising that in *Marcroft Wagons Ltd v Smith*[10] Evershed MR spoke of the perplexity which the concept of statutory tenancy is apt to provoke. Adopting Virgil's description of the Cyclops,[11] Evershed MR opined that with the advent of the statutory tenancy,

a new 'monstrum horrendum, informe, ingens', has come into our ken—the conception of a statutory tenancy—the conception that a person may have such a right of exclusive possession of property as will entitle him to bring an action for trespass against the owner of that property but which confers no interest whatever in the land.

These considerations led Evershed MR to agree that the statutory tenancy is most accurately represented in terms merely of a 'statutory right of irremovability'.

(2) The statutory tenant must first have been a protected tenant

A statutory tenancy arises only on the termination of a protected tenancy under section 1 of the Rent Act 1977.[12] The statutory tenant must be able to show that, 'immediately before that termination', he was entitled to a protected tenancy of the dwelling-house.[13] This means, in effect, that the privileges accorded to the statutory tenant are dependent on his having fulfilled all the requirements for recognition of a protected tenancy in relation to the preceding contractual tenancy. Amongst these was the requirement that the premises should, at the commencement of the protected tenancy, have been let 'as a separate dwelling'.[14]

(3) The statutory tenant must occupy the dwelling-house as his residence

Unlike the position under a protected or contractual tenancy,[15] a requirement of continued residence is imposed on the statutory tenant. In accordance with section 2(1)(a) of the Rent Act 1977, the statutory tenancy remains in force only 'if and so long as he occupies the dwelling-house as his residence'.[16] Thus, whereas a non-resident tenant may enjoy a protected tenancy during his contractual term, a statutory tenant forfeits his status as soon as he ceases to make residential use of the property.[17] It follows incidentally that if the tenant

---

10 [1951] 2 KB 496 at 501.

11 Virgil, *Aeneid*, III, 658.

12 Rent Act 1977, s 2(1)(a).

13 It is irrelevant that he was not the *only* person entitled to that protected tenancy. Where two persons take a protected tenancy as joint tenants and one dies or ceases to occupy the dwelling-house before the contractual term ends, the remaining joint tenant will become the statutory tenant if still in occupation at that point (*Lloyd v Sadler* [1978] QB 774 at 791C, ante, p 1005).

14 Ante, p 974.

15 Ante, p 976.

16 This phrase must be construed with reference to the body of caselaw which developed in this area between 1920 and 1968 (see Rent Act 1977, s 2(3)).

17 *Brown v Brash and Ambrose* [1948] 2 KB 247 at 254.

is an artificial person such as a company, any claim to a statutory tenancy is generally precluded by the inability of such a tenant to assert any personal residence in rented property.[18]

(a) Purpose of the requirement of continued residence

This requirement of continued residence is related to the broader objects of the Rent Act legislation. The Rent Acts have always regarded private housing as a social resource which requires careful allocation, and the legislation has consistently been concerned with the efficient management of housing stock. As Scrutton LJ explained in *Skinner v Geary*,[19] one object of the Acts has been 'to provide as many houses as possible at a moderate rent.' A non-resident tenant conflicts with the social (and to some extent redistributive) policy of the Rent Acts in that he is 'withdrawing from circulation that house which was intended for occupation by other people.' Likewise, in *Brown v Brash and Ambrose*,[20] Asquith LJ pointed out that the 'clear policy' of the Acts is 'to keep a roof over the tenant's or someone's head, not over an unoccupied shell, and to economise rather than sterilise housing accommodation.' Thus the phenomenon of the non-resident tenant is tolerated only in relation to a protected tenancy, being penalised in the case of the statutory tenancy by the immediate withdrawal of the tenant's 'status of irremovability'.

(b) The 'continuity' problem

Clearly it cannot be necessary for the preservation of his status of irremovability that a statutory tenant should be 'compelled to spend twenty-four hours in all weathers under his own roof for three hundred and sixty-five days in the year.'[1] Accordingly the courts have construed the requirement of continuity in a relatively liberal manner, drawing support for this purpose from the familiar Roman law notion that the concept of possession includes elements of both *corpus* and *animus*. Thus the statutory tenant is secure so long as he can demonstrate some physical evidence of continuing possession (a *factum* or *corpus possessionis*) coupled with a particular mental state (*animus possidendi* or *animus revertendi*),[2] the *corpus possessionis* representing merely 'some visible state of affairs in which the animus possidendi finds expression'.[3]

(i) Corpus possessionis The *corpus possessionis* does not necessarily take the form of personal occupation by the tenant, but may comprise any 'deliberate symbol of continued occupation'.[4] Thus a sufficient *corpus possessionis* is maintained where the statutory tenant instals in the premises some caretaker or

---

18   See *Firstcross Ltd v East West (Export/Import) Ltd* (1981) 41 P & CR 145 at 151ff (ante, p 1002). There is a (rarely exercised) jurisdiction vested in the court to declare a 'company let' to be a sham (ante, p 1001).
19   [1931] 2 KB 546 at 564.
20   [1948] 2 KB 247 at 254.
1   *Brown v Brash and Ambrose* [1948] 2 KB 247 at 254 per Asquith LJ.
2   *Brown v Brash and Ambrose* [1948] 2 KB 247 at 254f; *Hallwood Estates Ltd v Flack* (1950) 155 Estates Gazette 408.
3   *Brown v Brash and Ambrose* [1948] 2 KB 247 at 255.
4   *Brown v Brash and Ambrose* [1948] 2 KB 247 at 255.

representative whose function it is to preserve the premises for his ultimate return.[5] The retention of furniture in the property may likewise constitute a symbolic extension of residential occupation on behalf of the absent tenant.[6]

(ii) Animus possidendi and animus revertendi While he is in personal physical occupation of the premises the statutory tenant is assumed to have an *animus possidendi* sufficient to establish his continuing residential status for the purpose of the Rent Act. This *animus possidendi* survives through merely intermittent periods of absence which do not in themselves indicate a cesser of occupation.[7] However, a tenant's absence from the premises may become sufficiently prolonged or unintermittent to compel a prima facie inference that his occupation has ceased. In such cases an onus passes to the tenant to establish that he has a 'de facto intention to return after his absence'.[8] This *animus revertendi* must exist continuously throughout the tenant's absence, and even then its mere assertion may not be convincing unless the tenant 'couples and clothes his inward intention with some formal, outward, and visible sign of it'.[9] If, however, the tenant can support the alleged *animus* by demonstrating the existence of a continuing *corpus possessionis*, he will rebut the presumption that his statutory tenancy has ended.[10]

Whether the tenant can show the required combination of *corpus* and *animus* is always 'a question of fact and degree' in any given case.[11] If at any stage during his absence the tenant abandons his intention to return, his statutory tenancy terminates and cannot be revitalised by a later resumption of the original intention.[12] However, *animus revertendi* is not lost merely because a tenant's willingness to return is expressly subject to some reasonable condition. The intention would not, for instance, be destroyed where a tenant who has been violently treated by her husband refuses to return to the premises while he continues to live there.[13]

5 *Brown v Brash and Ambrose* [1948] 2 KB 247 at 254f; *Roland House Gardens Ltd v Cravitz* (1975) 29 P & CR 432 at 435; *Foley v Galvin* [1932] IR 339 at 362, 365f; *McCabe v McGonigle* [1956] IR 162 at 167f; *Fridberg v Doyle and Ryan* [1981] ILRM 370 at 371. Compare *Skinner v Geary* [1931] 2 KB 546 at 569f (where the persons installed in actual occupation 'were not there to preserve the house as a residence' for the tenant).

6 *Brown v Brash and Ambrose* [1948] 2 KB 247 at 255; *Bevington v Crawford* (1974) 232 Estates Gazette 191; *Gofor Investments Ltd v Roberts* (1975) 29 P & CR 366 at 372; *Roland House Gardens Ltd v Cravitz* (1975) 29 P & CR 432 at 438, 440; *Atyeo v Fardoe* (1979) 37 P & CR 494 at 497; *Hoggett v Hoggett* (1980) 39 P & CR 121 at 128; *Minishull v Donovan* (Unreported, Court of Appeal, P No 8000042, 3 July 1980).

7 *Brown v Brash and Ambrose* [1948] 2 KB 247 at 254.

8 *Brown v Brash and Ambrose* [1948] 2 KB 247 at 254 per Asquith LJ. See also *Roland House Gardens Ltd v Cravitz* (1975) 29 P & CR 432 at 437f; *Radford v Bonham* (Unreported, Court of Appeal, Unbound Transcript 939, 6 July 1983).

9 However, Asquith LJ warned in *Brown v Brash and Ambrose* [1948] 2 KB 247 at 254 against the supposition that the statutory tenant 'can absent himself for five or ten years or more and retain possession and his protected status simply by proving an inward intention to return after so protracted an absence'.

10 *Minishull v Donovan* (Unreported, Court of Appeal, P No 8000042, 3 July 1980).

11 *Brown v Brash and Ambrose* [1948] 2 KB 247 at 254; *Atyeo v Fardoe* (1979) 37 P & CR 494 at 499.

12 *Radford v Bonham* (Unreported, Court of Appeal, Unbound Transcript 939, 6 July 1983); *Town and Country Investments Ltd v Marks* (Unreported, Court of Appeal, 11 December 1984).

13 See *Hoggett v Hoggett* (1980) 39 P & CR 121 at 128.

(c) Temporary absence of the tenant

The 'principal object' of the Rent Acts has traditionally been to 'protect a person residing in a dwelling-house from being turned out of his home.'[14] Thus the legislation is not intended to give long-term protection to a tenant who sublets the entire dwelling-house or who cannot show substantial use of the property as a home.[15]

It does not inevitably follow that every temporary absence on the part of the tenant terminates his statutory tenancy.[16] Provided that there is an *animus revertendi*,[17] the tenant does not lose his statutory tenancy simply because of some deliberate absence from the property. His statutory privilege remains, for instance, even though he goes away on holiday,[18] or goes to look after a dying parent,[19] or leaves in order to escape a violent spouse,[20] or sublets part of the property,[1] or moves out of sub-standard accommodation for health reasons while renovations are carried out.[2] Nor is a statutory tenancy forfeited by certain kinds of involuntary absence such as confinement in a hospital.[3] Of course the mere retention of a *corpus possessionis* cannot preserve a statutory tenancy if the facts do not bear out the tenant's assertion of a realistic intention to return.[4] But where there is a 'real hope of return coupled with the practical possibility of its fulfilment within a reasonable time',[5] the tenant's absence may extend for quite lengthy periods of time.[6]

(d) Vicarious residence by members of the tenant's family

It is firmly established that a statutory tenant may preserve a continuing residential status by reason of occupation which is exercised vicariously through members of his own family. In other words, residence on the part of

---

14   *Haskins v Lewis* [1931] 2 KB 1 at 18; *Skinner v Geary* [1931] 2 KB 546 at 560.
15   *Haskins v Lewis* [1931] 2 KB 1 at 14.
16   *Roland House Gardens Ltd v Cravitz* (1975) 29 P & CR 432 at 436; *Al-Sabrya (Jersey) Ltd v Willis* [1983] CA Bound Transcript 445. See *Hoggett v Hoggett* (1980) 39 P & CR 121 at 127f, where, in the context of what was conceded to be an analogous problem, Sir David Cairns thought that occupation would not be given up either by going into hospital for a few days or by going on a weekend visit to a friend or by going out shopping for a few hours.
17   *Skinner v Geary* [1931] 2 KB 546 at 569.
18   *Roland House Gardens Ltd v Cravitz* (1975) 29 P & CR 432 at 438f.
19   *Richards v Green* (1983) 268 Estates Gazette 443; [1984] Conv 151.
20   See *Hoggett v Hoggett* (1980) 39 P & CR 121 at 128 (ante, p 188).
1   *Regalian Securities Ltd v Ramsden* [1981] 1 WLR 611 at 614H-615A.
2   *Atyeo v Fardoe* (1979) 37 P & CR 494 at 498.
3   *Tompkins v Rowley* (1949) EGD 314; *Tickner v Hearn* [1960] 1 WLR 1406 at 1411ff. Compare, however, *Brown v Brash and Ambrose* [1948] 2 KB 247 at 254, where the Court of Appeal was not prepared to allow a tenant to rely on his involuntary imprisonment as 'preventing him from taking steps to assert possession by visible action'. According to Asquith LJ, the tenant's non-occupation was not involuntary in that 'he committed intentionally the felonious act' which brought about his conviction! See also *Sumnal v Statt* (1984) 271 Estates Gazette 628 at 632f.
4   See eg *Radford v Bonham* (Unreported, Court of Appeal, Unbound Transcript 939, 6 July 1983), where the Court rejected a claim to a statutory tenancy where there was only a 'mere hope or chance of returning'. Likewise, in *Al-Sabrya (Jersey) Ltd v Willis* [1983] CA Bound Transcript 445, a 'future and indeterminate intention' was thought 'quite insufficient'. See also *Duke v Porter* (1986) 280 Estates Gazette 633 at 635.
5   *Tickner v Hearn* [1960] 1 WLR 1406 at 1410. See also *Dixon v Tommis* [1952] 1 All ER 725 at 726H, 727D (retirement home).
6   See eg *Gofor Investments Ltd v Roberts* (1975) 29 P & CR 366 at 372f (10 years).

relatives may itself constitute a *corpus possessionis* which, in combination with the appropriate *animus revertendi*, fulfils the requirement for continuation of the statutory tenancy.[7]

(i) Occupation by a spouse In one special instance the notion of vicarious residence has been formalised by statute, in that occupation on the part of the spouse of a statutory tenant is now acknowledged by legislation as sustaining the possession of that tenant during his absence from the premises.[8] This recognition is of primary assistance to a spouse who has been deserted by the statutory tenant, but cannot operate to prolong a statutory tenancy beyond the date of divorce.[9] The granting of a divorce patently terminates any *animus revertendi* which might have existed until that point.

(ii) Occupation by other family members The continuing presence of a de facto wife may also preserve a statutory tenancy on behalf of an absent partner,[10] but the statutory tenancy falls away as soon as the tenant formulates an intention to remain permanently away from the premises.[11] It is also clear that residence by the children of a statutory tenant may constitute a sufficient form of occupation on his behalf,[12] provided that there is a true *animus revertendi*.[13]

(e) The 'second home' problem

It has long been accepted that the Rent Act requirement of continued residential occupation by the statutory tenant may be satisfied notwithstanding that the rented premises are used as merely *one* of his homes.[14]

---

7   See *Skinner v Geary* [1931] 2 KB 546 at 562, where Scrutton LJ gave his famous example of the 'sea captain who may be away for months but who intends to return, and whose wife and family occupy the house during his absence.' See generally (1983) 133 NLJ 5 (P.F. Smith).
8   Matrimonial Homes Act 1983, s 1(6). This provision is a modern echo of the older caselaw under the Rent Acts under which the courts were affected 'consciously or unconsciously [by] the shadow of the old common law doctrine that husband and wife are one in law' (*S.L. Dando Ltd v Hitchcock* [1954] 2 QB 317 at 325). See, however, *Hulme v Langford* (1985) 50 P & CR 199 at 205f, for a suggestion that Matrimonial Homes Act 1983, s 1(6) may not affect statutory tenancies.
9   *Robson v Headland* (1948) 64 TLR 596 at 598f; *Heath Estates Ltd v Burchell* (1979) 251 Estates Gazette 1173 at 1174; *Metropolitan Properties Co Ltd v Cronan* (1982) 44 P & CR 1 at 4f; [1982] Conv 384. It is, of course, open to the divorced spouse of a statutory tenant to apply for a transfer of the statutory tenancy into her own name (Matrimonial Homes Act 1983, Sch 1, Part I, paras 1, 2 (ante, p 1004).
10 A de facto spouse cannot of course claim the benefit of Matrimonial Homes Act 1983, s 1(6), but it is still possible to regard her presence in the property as representing a *corpus* of possession on behalf of the absent tenant (see eg *Brown v Brash and Ambrose* [1948] 2 KB 247 at 255).
11 *Thompson v Ward* [1953] 2 QB 153 at 164f; *Colin Smith Music Ltd v Ridge* [1975] 1 WLR 463 at 466G.
12 *Roland House Gardens Ltd v Cravitz* (1975) 29 P & CR 432 at 438f; *Atyeo v Fardoe* (1979) 37 P & CR 494 at 498 (son).
13 See, however, *Metropolitan Properties Co Ltd v Cronan* (1982) 44 P & CR 1 at 7f. It is clearly not open to an absent statutory tenant to nominate a legal stranger (whether his divorced wife or indeed any other person) to occupy the premises in a representative capacity on his behalf, where he himself has no intention or wish to return into residence (see *Heath Estates Ltd v Burchell* (1979) 251 Estates Gazette 1173 at 1174).
14 *Kavanagh v Lyroudias* [1985] 1 All ER 560 at 562d-e; *Hampstead Way Investments Ltd v Lewis-Weare* [1985] 1 WLR 164 at 168D, 169F.

There is no theoretical objection to the possibility that a person may occupy more than one dwelling-house as his 'home',[15] even though this opens up the possibility that he is entitled to claim a statutory tenancy in relation to any or all of these properties.[16]

The phenomenon of the 'second home' nevertheless raises serious problems in practice.[17] Where a person owns one dwelling-house which he occupies as his home for most of the time, and is at the same time the tenant of another dwelling-house which he occupies only rarely or for limited purposes, it is a question of 'fact and degree' whether he truly occupies the latter dwelling-house 'as his second home'.[18] This question resolves itself into two related queries.[19]

(i) Is the second property a 'residence'?   A statutory tenancy continues under Rent Act 1977, s 2(1)(a) only so long as the tenant occupies the dwelling-house as his 'residence'.[20] The loaded meaning of the term 'residence' invests this condition with a difficulty similar to that which affects the definition of a 'separate dwelling' for the purpose of section 1.[1] The two tests differ in that the element of purpose referred to in section 1 is fixed almost irreversibly at the commencement of the tenancy,[2] whereas the critical element of purpose under section 2(1)(a) clearly varies with de facto changes of user by the tenant. It is therefore quite possible that even though the 'initial purpose' test of section 1 is satisfied, the tenant may fall outside the scope of a statutory tenancy if he later ceases to use the premises as a 'residence' in the specific sense required by section 2(1)(a).[3]

In *Hampstead Way Investments Ltd v Lewis-Weare*[4] the House of Lords indicated that the premises in relation to which a statutory tenancy is claimed must be occupied 'as a complete home in itself'. There was evidence in this case that the tenant, whose job required him to work unsocial hours, used a room in a rented flat only for the limited purpose of sleeping during the day-time. The House of Lords held that this marginal use could not ground any claim to a statutory tenancy, since the remainder of the tenant's social and domestic life was conducted in a house which he had bought for himself and his family half a mile away.[5] Although conceding that in certain rare instances two separate

---

15   There may, however, be some moral objection (see *Richards v Green* (1983) 268 Estates Gazette 443).

16   *Langford Property Co Ltd v Tureman* [1949] 1 KB 29 at 33f; *Regalian Securities Ltd v Scheuer* (1982) 5 HLR 48 at 56; *Hampstead Way Investments Ltd v Lewis-Weare* [1985] 1 WLR 164 at 169F.

17   See D.W. Williams, *The Two-Home Man and the Rent Acts*, (1983) 133 NLJ 677; J. Driscoll, (1985) LAG Bulletin 142.

18   *Hampstead Way Investments Ltd v Lewis-Weare* [1985] 1 WLR 164 at 169G-H. The question is a 'jury question to be determined by applying ordinary common sense' (*Beck v Scholz* [1953] 1 QB 570 at 575).

19   That the two queries are distinct was confirmed in *Kavanagh v Lyroudias* [1985] 1 All ER 560 at 562f-g.

20   The onus rests on the landlord to prove on a balance of probability a cesser of the tenant's occupation of the premises as his 'residence' (*Ali Reza Suleyman v Knapp* (Unreported, Court of Appeal, 9 March 1983) per Cumming-Bruce LJ).

1   Ante, p 979.

2   See *Wolfe v Hogan* [1949] 2 KB 194 at 204f (ante, p 975).

3   See *Hampstead Way Investments Ltd v Lewis-Weare* (Unreported, Court of Appeal, 24 February 1984) per May LJ).

4   [1985] 1 WLR 164 at 171B. See [1985] Conv 224 (P.F. Smith).

5   [1985] 1 WLR 164 at 171G-H. See also *Regalian Securities Ltd v Scheuer* (1982) 5 HLR 48 at 56ff.

properties could be regarded as 'a combined or composite home',[6] Lord Brandon thought that here the distance between the tenant's two properties excluded the possibility that they could be seen as 'constituting together a single unit of living accommodation'.[7]

This decision brings about the awkward consequence that if essential aspects of domestic living are split between two rented premises, no statutory tenancy can be claimed in respect of either property, since neither constitutes 'a complete home' in the required sense.[8] In *Kavanagh v Lyroudias*,[9] a tenant enjoyed separate lettings from the same landlord of two adjoining properties. Because of the cramped conditions in each house, he was accustomed to sleep and study in one property while carrying on all other aspects of his domestic life in the other property. The Court of Appeal held that he was not entitled to a statutory tenancy of the property containing his bedroom and study, in that his 'persistent partial user' of these premises did not extend to 'all those activities which are essential to enable them to exhibit the characteristics of a complete home.'[10]

(ii) Does the tenant 'occupy' the premises? Even if the relevant property constitutes 'a complete home in itself', the tenant must be able to show a frequency of user of the premises sufficient to support a claim that he 'occupies' them as his second home.[11] This requires at least that he should make use of the property 'on a reasonably substantial number of occasions'.[12] By contrast with the rather strict requirement in respect of the residential integrity of the 'second home', this test seems to be fairly easily satisfied.[13] It does not matter that the tenant's presence in his second home is only occasional or intermittent. A statutory tenancy may be maintained, for instance, by a person whose principal residence is situated in the country but who stays in a London flat on one or two days per week.[14] Likewise an urban dweller may claim a statutory tenancy in respect of a country retreat which he uses only for a couple of days each weekend.[15] Rent Act protection is also available in respect of sporadic

6   [1985] 1 WLR 164 at 171B-C. See eg *Wimbush v Cibulia* [1949] 2 KB 564 at 570 (ante, p 980).
7   [1985] 1 WLR 164 at 171F. It was conceded to be irrelevant that the statutory tenant's stepson used the premises as a 'complete home' for himself.
8   *Hampstead Way Investments Ltd v Lewis-Weare* [1985] 1 WLR 164 at 169F-G.
9   [1985] 1 All ER 560.
10 [1985] 1 All ER 560 at 562g. Although declining to rule on the correctness of this decision, Lord Brandon observed in *Hampstead Way Investments Ltd v Lewis-Weare* [1985] 1 WLR 164 at 171C-D that there the Court of Appeal had quite properly posed the question whether the relevant property was used 'as a complete home in itself', but had failed to ask the further (and in his view necessary) question as to whether two adjacent properties could nevertheless be viewed as 'a combined or composite home'.
11 One extremely revealing index of residence seems to be consumption of gas or electricity as evidenced in household bills (see eg *Ali Reza Suleyman v Knapp* (Unreported, Court of Appeal, 9 March 1983)).
12 *Al-Sabrya (Jersey) Ltd v Willis* [1983] CA Bound Transcript 445.
13 In *Hampstead Way Investments Ltd v Lewis-Weare* (Unreported, Court of Appeal, 24 February 1984), May LJ thought this discrepancy to be 'arguably unjust'.
14 *Bevington v Crawford* (1974) 232 Estates Gazette 191.
15 *Regalian Securities Ltd v Scheuer* (1982) 5 HLR 48 at 56.

occupation by a travelling businessman[16] or by a tenant who is absent abroad for all but two or three months of each year.[17]

The limits of the court's tolerance are reached only where the tenant uses the second premises 'not as a home but merely for occasional occupation as a matter of convenience.'[18] Thus a casual intermittent occupation of a holiday home[19] or a working studio[20] is not enough to 'imprint upon that user the characteristics of user as a home'.[1] It is inconsistent with the principle and purpose of the Rent Acts that statutory protection should attach to premises which the tenant uses only as a temporary resort of convenience or pleasure.[2]

(f) The nominal tenant

It is possible that the requirement of continued residence may be satisfied by the occupation of some person other than the nominal tenant where the landlord is aware that 'the real tenant is somebody else'.[3] However, this qualification upon the general rule applies somewhat rarely, and only in any event if the landlord grants the tenancy to a nominal tenant 'as a sham and for the purpose of being free of the burdens of the Rent Acts to which he would otherwise be subject in respect of the "real" tenant.'[4] Where, for instance, a landlord lets a dwelling-house to a father in the knowledge that the purpose of the letting is occupation by a child, it seems that the occupying child is not entitled to a statutory tenancy on the expiration of the contractual tenancy.[5]

6. SECURITY OF TENURE

The categories of tenancy which at present fall within the ambit of full Rent Act protection are the 'regulated' protected tenancy and the 'regulated' statutory tenancy.[6] Under a 'regulated' tenancy of either kind, the tenant acquires a certain security of tenure. If the tenant is not prepared to vacate his

---

16 *Bromley Securities Ltd v Matthews* (Unreported, Court of Appeal, 23 February 1984).
17 *Bevington v Crawford* (1974) 232 Estates Gazette 191 at 193. It appeared that the tenant in this case spent most of the year running a golf course which he owned in Cannes. Lord Denning MR pointed out, however, that the wealth of the tenant was entirely irrelevant to the applicability of the Rent Act.
18 *Al-Sabrya (Jersey) Ltd v Willis* [1983] CA Bound Transcript 445. See also a reference to a 'house of convenience' in *Town and Country Investments Ltd v Marks* (Unreported, Court of Appeal, 11 December 1984).
19 *Walker v Ogilvy* (1974) 28 P & CR 288 at 292f; *Regalian Securities Ltd v Scheuer* (1982) 5 HLR 48 at 56f.
20 *Regalian Securities Ltd v Scheuer* (1982) 5 HLR 48 at 58f; *Ali Reza Suleyman v Knapp* (Unreported, Court of Appeal, 9 March 1983).
 1 *Regalian Securities Ltd v Scheuer* (1982) 5 HLR 48 at 56 per Cumming-Bruce LJ.
 2 *Beck v Scholz* [1953] 1 QB 570 at 575. See also *Minishull v Donovan* (Unreported, Court of Appeal, P No 8000042, 3 July 1980).
 3 *Metropolitan Properties Co Ltd v Cronan* (1982) 44 P & CR 1 at 5. See also *Heath Estates Ltd v Burchell* (1979) 251 Estates Gazette 1173.
 4 *Metropolitan Properties Co Ltd v Cronan* (1982) 44 P & CR 1 at 5. See also *S.L. Dando Ltd v Hitchcock* [1954] 2 QB 317 at 322; *Cove v Flick* [1954] 2 QB 326 at 327f (Note).
 5 *Metropolitan Properties Co Ltd v Cronan* (1982) 44 P & CR 1 at 5.
 6 The older category of 'controlled' tenancy (which was essentially a tenancy granted prior to 6 July 1957) had become exceedingly rare by 1980. Almost all 'controlled' tenancies were automatically converted into 'regulated' tenancies by Housing Act 1980, s 64(1).

dwelling-house voluntarily, his landlord cannot obtain possession without (i) terminating his contractual tenancy (if such is still in force) and (ii) obtaining a court order for possession, thereby terminating the statutory tenancy which automatically arises at the end of the contractual tenancy.[7] A court will make an order for possession against a protected or statutory tenant only on the grounds specified in the Rent Act 1977.[8] Some of these grounds are discretionary grounds for the recovery of possession; others are mandatory.

(1) Discretionary grounds for possession

Pursuant to section 98(1) of the Rent Act 1977, no court order for possession can properly be made unless

(a) the court considers it 'reasonable to make such an order',
   AND
(b) EITHER the court is satisfied that 'suitable alternative accommodation is available for the tenant or will be available for him when the possession order takes effect,
   OR the circumstances are such as are specified in any of the Cases in Part I of Schedule 15 of the Rent Act 1977.

(a) Reasonableness of the possession order

It is a precondition of any possession order (other than one obtained on the mandatory grounds contained in Part II of Schedule 15) that the court should consider it 'reasonable to make such an order'.[9] This criterion of reasonableness confers a substantial discretion on the court.[10] The court must take into account 'all relevant circumstances as they exist at the date of the hearing'.[11] It is clear that the Court of Appeal will be slow to disturb the conclusions reached by a lower court on the question of reasonableness.[12] There is, moreover, no right of appeal on any question of *fact* arising in connection with Cases 1 to 6 and 9 of Schedule 15.[13]

(i) Nature of breach by the tenant If possession is sought against a tenant on the basis of some breach of covenant under his tenancy agreement, the precise nature of that breach may be highly relevant to the issue whether it is

---

7   Protection for residential occupiers who are not statutorily protected tenants is conferred by Protection from Eviction Act 1977, s 3, as amended by Housing Act 1980, s 69(1).
8   See A. Arden, (1976) LAG Bulletin 280, (1978) LAG Bulletin 10, 186, (1979) LAG Bulletin 11; A. Harvey, (1981) LAG Bulletin 279.
9   The question is not whether it is 'reasonable' for the landlord to want to recover possession, but whether it is 'reasonable' for the court to order possession in his favour. See *Shrimpton v Rabbits* (1924) 131 LT 478 at 479; *Foxell v Mendis* (Unreported, Court of Appeal, No 81 17755, 19 May 1982).
10 The court has an 'overriding discretion' (see *Cresswell v Hodgson* [1951] 2 KB 92 at 95).
11 *Cumming v Danson* [1942] 2 All ER 653 at 655E.
12 See *Cresswell v Hodgson* [1951] 2 KB 92 at 96; *Hill v Rochard* [1983] 1 WLR 478 at 485G; *Battlespring Ltd v Gates* (1983) 268 Estates Gazette 355; *Pazgate Ltd v McGrath* (1984) 17 HLR 127 at 134. A possession order, if successfully appealed against by the tenant, may lead either to the restoration of the tenant's possession or to an order for money compensation for the tenant (see *Pollock v Kumar* (1977) 242 Estates Gazette 371).
13 County Courts Act 1984, s 77(6)(d).

'reasonable' to make a possession order. It is not normally 'reasonable' to evict a tenant on the ground of some default which is both temporary and remediable and which is indeed remedied by the date of the hearing.[14] Likewise it is scarcely 'reasonable' to order possession where a tenant's rent default relates, for example, to only one missing instalment of the rent due.[15] The award of possession to the landlord must usually be premised on some serious, continuing[16] or irremediable[17] default by the tenant, or on the presence of substantial arrears of rent. It may, however, be 'reasonable' to allow the landlord to recover possession where substantial work is required to repair delapidations which have occurred during the tenant's occupation.[18]

(ii) Nature of the consequences of repossession   The likely consequences of a possession order may have an important bearing on whether it is 'reasonable' to make such an order. It is relevant to, but not conclusive of, the court's deliberations that the tenant is a single male who, if evicted, will not be eligible for rehousing by his local authority as a homeless person.[19] Conversely the availability of suitable alternative accommodation may make it not unreasonable to order possession against the tenant.[20]

The question whether it is 'reasonable' to evict often tends to merge with the issue of suitable alternative accommodation,[1] and it may not be reasonable to evict a tenant if the alternative accommodation offered is relatively disadvantageous to him. In *Warren v Austin*,[2] for instance, the Court of Appeal thought it unreasonable that a tenant should have to move to smaller accommodation where he could no longer derive a much needed supplement to his income from taking in lodgers. Similarly, in *Battlespring Ltd v Gates*,[3] the Court of Appeal declined to make a possession order in respect of a flat in which a widow had lived for 35 years and to which she was sentimentally attached, even though her new landlords had offered her superior accommodation in the immediate neighbourhood.

(b) Suitable alternative accommodation

A court may make a possession order against a tenant if it thinks it 'reasonable' to do so and if it is satisfied that 'suitable alternative accommodation' is available for the tenant or will be available for him when the possession order

---

14   *Foxell v Mendis* (Unreported, Court of Appeal, No 81 17755, 19 May 1982) per Stephenson LJ.
15   *Sopwith v Stutchbury* (1983) 17 HLR 50 at 68.
16   See eg *Foxell v Mendis* (Unreported, Court of Appeal, No 81 17755, 19 May 1982), where the Court of Appeal dismissed the appeal against a possession order precisely because the tenant's breach was a 'serious nuisance' which was continuing at the date of the county court hearing.
17   See eg *Pazgate Ltd v McGrath* (1984) 17 HLR 127 at 134, where an unlawful assignment in breach of covenant made it 'reasonable' to order possession against the assignee.
18   *Viveash Ltd v Feilen* (Unreported, Court of Appeal, 16 January 1980).
19   *Johnnie Johnson Housing Trust Ltd v Sandon* (Unreported, Court of Appeal, No 81 01105, 23 June 1982).
20   *Viveash Ltd v Feilen* (Unreported, Court of Appeal, 16 January 1980).
1   Post, p 1016.
2   [1947] 2 All ER 185 at 186H. See also *Williamson v Pallant* (1924) 131 LT 474 at 475; *Fisher v Macpherson*, 1954 SLT (Sh Ct) 28 at 29.
3   (1983) 268 Estates Gazette 355 at 356. See [1984] JSWL 53 (R.G. Lee); [1984] Conv 152 (R.G. Lee).

takes effect.[4] The meaning of 'suitable alternative accommodation' is further explained in Part IV of Schedule 15 of the Rent Act 1977.[5]

(i) Proximity to place of work Under Part IV of Schedule 15 the landlord may recover possession if the replacement accommodation is 'reasonably suitable to the needs of the tenant and his family as regards proximity to place of work'.[6] Proximity to the work-place is always a 'question of fact and degree',[7] and requires to be measured 'in a commonsense way'.[8] It may well be unreasonable to require a tenant to move to new accommodation which would necessitate two or three hours of travel each day using a combination of buses and trains.[9]

(ii) Suitability to the needs and means of the tenant Even if the circumstances satisfy the test of 'proximity to place of work', it must also be shown that the alternative accommodation is *either* 'similar as regards rental and extent' to the accommodation provided by the relevant local housing authority for persons with equivalent needs to those of the tenant and his family,[10] *or* 'reasonably suitable to the means of the tenant and to the needs of the tenant and his family as regards extent and character'.[11]

It is clear that alternative accommodation cannot be deemed 'suitable' unless it is similarly Rent Act protected,[12] but the courts have not proved to be generally sympathetic to complaints by tenants that the proposed accommodation is unsuitable.[13] Alternative accommodation can be held to be 'suitable' even though it does not provide 'equal facilities and advantages in

---

4   Rent Act 1977, s 98(1)(a). A certificate of the local housing authority that the authority will provide suitable alternative accommodation is conclusive of the availability of suitable alternative accommodation for the purpose of section 98(1)(a) (see Rent Act 1977, Sch 15, Part IV, para 3). A deferred order may be made in order to enable proposed alternative accommodation, although not immediately available, to be rendered 'suitable' (see *Yewbright Properties Ltd v Stone* (1980) 40 P & CR 402 at 410).
5   Rent Act 1977, s 98(4).
6   Rent Act 1977, Sch 15, Part IV, para 5(1). In some circumstances (eg where the tenant is a freelancer who travels widely to various locations) a 'place of work' may be an 'area' (see *Yewbright Properties Ltd v Stone* (1980) 40 P & CR 402 at 407).
7   *Yewbright Properties Ltd v Stone* (1980) 40 P & CR 402 at 407.
8   'Proximity' does not relate simply to 'distance as the crow flies'. The court must take into account 'not only what the distance is along such routes as are available but also the means of transport available to the tenant concerned and the amount of time and the degree of inconvenience involved in making the journey' (*Yewbright Properties Ltd v Stone* (1980) 40 P & CR 402 at 411).
9   *Yewbright Properties Ltd v Stone* (1980) 40 P & CR 402 at 411.
10   The reference here to the tenant's family may require a judicial determination as to the existence of a familial nexus (post, p 1064). See eg *Kavanagh v Lyroudias* [1985] 1 All ER 560 at 563d-f, where the Court of Appeal declined to accept that two male friends could constitute a 'family' for the purpose of Rent Act 1977, Sch 15, Part IV, para 5(1).
11   Rent Act 1977, Sch 15, Part IV, para 5(1). A certificate of the local housing authority that the accommodation proposed is suitable for a family of equivalent size to that of the tenant is conclusive as to the suitability of the accommodation for this purpose (see Rent Act 1977, Sch 15, Part IV, para 5(2)). Alternative accommodation cannot be deemed to be 'suitable' if its occupation by the tenant and his family would result in 'overcrowding' within the meaning of Part X of the Housing Act 1985 (ante, p 936). See Rent Act 1977, Sch 15, Part IV, para 6.
12   See eg *Leeward Securities Ltd v Lilyheath Properties Ltd* (1983) 17 HLR 35 at 48.
13   See eg *Gladyric Ltd v Collinson* (1983) 267 Estates Gazette 761 at 762; [1984] Conv 151 (J.E.M.); *Matthews v Bucknell* (Unreported, Court of Appeal, 13 February 1984).

every respect' to those of the existing accommodation.[14] The fact that the tenant may not be able to house all of his furniture in smaller premises does not in itself make those premises unsuitable.[15] Moreover, in *Siddiqui v Rashid*[16] the Court of Appeal accepted that the 'character' of the proposed accommodation may extend to environmental factors,[17] but that the tenant could not be heard to object that the new accommodation would make it more difficult for him to pursue his existing social, cultural and devotional interests and commitments.

The replacement accommodation need not be such that 'all the fads and fancies and preferences of the tenant shall be gratified to the full.'[18] In *Hill v Rochard*,[19] for instance, the tenants had lived for 16 years in a large and isolated country house with a paddock and outbuildings where they were able to keep lots of household animals. When the landlords offered to rehouse them in a spacious house on a housing estate in the nearby village, the tenants objected to the likely alteration of the lifestyle to which they had been accustomed. The Court of Appeal nevertheless upheld the suitability of the alternative accommodation, Dunn LJ observing that the reference to 'needs' in Part IV of Schedule 15 was a reference merely to 'needs for housing'.[20] The Court took the view that the Rent Act was not intended to protect 'incidental advantages'[1] relating to the tenants' 'peculiar wishes and desires, their own particular taste for amenities, which go again beyond their needs even for a person who is entitled to sustain a high standard of living.'[2] The alternative accommodation offered by the landlords was such as would enable the tenants to 'live

---

14 *Viveash Ltd v Feilen* (Unreported, Court of Appeal, 16 January 1980) per Templeman LJ. It is possible, for instance, that even a mere part of the tenant's existing accommodation can in some circumstances constitute 'suitable alternative accommodation' (see *Mykolyshyn v Noah* [1970] 1 WLR 1271 at 1277B-C; *Wint v Monk* (1981) 259 Estates Gazette 45; *Yoland v Reddington* (1982) 263 Estates Gazette 157).

15 *Mykolyshyn v Noah* [1970] 1 WLR 1271 at 1278A-B; *Festing v Costas* (Unreported, Court of Appeal, 10 December 1984).

16 [1980] 1 WLR 1018 at 1023E-F; [1980] Conv 443 (R.G. Lee).

17 See eg *Redspring Ltd v Francis* [1973] 1 WLR 134 at 138B-C, where Buckley LJ was not prepared to uphold the suitability of accommodation which was 'situated in an area which is offensive as the result of some industrial activity in the neighbourhood, which perhaps creates offensive smells or noises, or which is extremely noisy as a result of a great deal of traffic passing by, or in some other respect is much less well endowed with amenities than the accommodation which the tenant is required to vacate'. In *Redspring Ltd v Francis*, the Court of Appeal declined to evict the tenant from a flat in a quiet residential road in order that he should move to a flat in a busy traffic thoroughfare, which (unlike his existing flat) had no garden but did have a fish and chip shop next door. See also *Minchburn Ltd v Fernandez* [1986] 2 EGLR 103 at 104K-105B.

18 *Clark v Smith* (Unreported, 16 July 1920), cited in *Hill v Rochard* [1983] 1 WLR 478 at 483E.

19 [1983] 1 WLR 478; [1983] Conv 320 (P.F. Smith); (1983) 268 Estates Gazette 882 (D.W. Williams).

20 [1983] 1 WLR 478 at 484G. Eveleigh LJ likewise thought that the court was limited to considering the tenant's 'needs...for accommodation for the purpose of habitation...Proximity to entertainment, recreation or sport is not relevant on the test of suitability, and proximity to a paddock or stable is...also not relevant' ([1983] 1 WLR 478 at 486D-E). See also *Roberts v Macilwraith-Christie* (Unreported, 25 September 1986), where the Court of Appeal thought it irrelevant that the proposed alternative accommodation would give the tenant access merely to Shepherd's Bush Green rather than the more attractive public garden in Kensington Square to which she was accustomed.

1 [1983] 1 WLR 478 at 485D.

2 [1983] 1 WLR 478 at 486G. See, however, *De Markozoff v Craig* (1949) 93 SJ 693, where the Court of Appeal held premises to be unsuitable because of the absence of a garden in which the tenant's child could play.

reasonably comfortably...in a reasonably similar way' to the lifestyle led in the existing accommodation,[3] and the Court of Appeal therefore upheld the making of a possession order.

(c) The Cases in Part I of Schedule 15

Quite apart from any claim that suitable alternative accommodation is available for the tenant, the recovery of possession by a landlord may be based upon one or more of Cases 1 to 10 contained in Part I of Schedule 15 of the Rent Act 1977. These Cases provide grounds for repossession which relate in the main either to defaults by the tenant or to the necessary protection of the landlord's interests,[4] although it must still be shown in each instance that it is 'reasonable' to make a possession order. The most important Cases are the following.

(i) Case 1 Case 1 may be invoked where the tenant has failed to pay or tender any rent lawfully due or is in breach of any other lawful obligation of the tenancy (express or implied).[5]

(ii) Case 2 Case 2 arises where the tenant (or any person residing or lodging with him) has been guilty of conduct which is 'a nuisance or annoyance' to adjoining occupiers,[6] or has been convicted of using the dwelling-house or allowing the dwelling-house to be used for immoral or illegal purposes. A possession order can be made under Case 2 notwithstanding that the conduct complained of has since abated.[7]

In the context of Case 2, 'nuisance' is not construed in its strict common law sense.[8] Together with the term 'annoyance', it bears an ordinary non-technical meaning connoting such activities as would disturb a reasonable occupier of normal sensitivity.[9] Case 2 is therefore capable of application to almost any conduct which prejudices harmonious co-operative living in crowded urban conditions.[10] Case 2 embraces (but is not restricted to) acts of 'drunkenness,

3   [1983] 1 WLR 478 at 485E.
4   *Cobstone Investments Ltd v Maxim* [1985] QB 140 at 151C.
5   See A. McAllister and S. McGrath, (1986) Legal Action 21. Where the terms of a tenancy agreement prohibit user of the premises for any immoral purpose, there is no breach by reason merely of the fact that two persons live there in de facto cohabitation (*Heglibiston Establishment v Heyman* (1978) 36 P & CR 351 at 360ff).
6   'Adjoining occupiers' need not be immediate neighbours, in the sense of persons occupying premises which are physically contiguous or coterminous. For the purpose of Case 2 'adjoining occupiers' are those who are 'near enough to be affected by [the tenant's] conduct on the premises, and may therefore include flat-dwellers two or more floors distant (see *Cobstone Investments Ltd v Maxim* [1985] QB 140 at 147E, 151B; [1985] Conv 167 (T.J. Lyons)).
7   *Florent v Horez* (1983) 268 Estates Gazette 807 at 809.
8   *Shepherd v Braley* (Unreported, Court of Appeal, 26 February 1981) per Watkins LJ.
9   No intention is required to be shown on the part of the tenant under Case 2. The word 'guilty' means 'no more than what was done by way of creating a nuisance or annoyance was knowingly done by the person said to be responsible for it' (*Shepherd v Braley* (Unreported, Court of Appeal, 26 February 1981)).
10 Value judgments are inevitably called for in this context. See eg *Re Mastercraft Construction Co Ltd and Baldwin* (1978) 87 DLR (3d) 551 at 554, where a Canadian court was required to measure the freedom of a tenant to use CB radio in his own home against the social and other values represented in his neighbours' unimpaired reception of television transmissions. The court preferred to uphold television viewing, on the ground that television sets 'cannot be considered luxuries—but have come to be necessities in our Canadian society—which has developed its own built-in pressures and anxieties.'

abuse, noise, obstruction, or violence'.[11] Case 2 is satisfied, for instance, by evidence that one tenant carried out a 'vendetta' against another tenant, playing back at high volume tape recordings of music produced in the complainant's adjoining room.[12] The noise caused by a dozen dogs kept for breeding purposes has been said to constitute relevant 'nuisance' and 'annoyance'.[13] 'Annoyance' can comprise verbal abuse and the use of obscene language.[14] Case 2 can also include the use of residential premises as a base for organising a political pressure group, if such activity involves the constant coming and going of visiting strangers.[15]

On the other hand, Case 2 does not normally apply to mere isolated acts by a tenant which do not in themselves comprise 'matters of gravity', at least where the tenant has been in occupation for a lengthy period of time.[16] It is unlikely that de facto cohabitation by a tenant will nowadays be thought to constitute 'nuisance' or 'annoyance' within Case 2.[17] Moreover, it may well be that greater margins of tolerance are required in relation to certain classes of tenant whose lifestyle involves more than usual noise and disturbance.[18]

(iii) Case 3   Case 3 may be pleaded where the tenant (or any person residing or lodging with him) has been guilty of waste, neglect or default thereby causing the condition of the dwelling-house to deteriorate.[19]

(iv) Case 4   Case 4 may be relevant where the tenant's ill-treatment has caused the deterioration of furniture provided for use under the tenancy.

(v) Case 5   Case 5 applies where the tenant has given notice to quit, and the landlord has relied on that notice to his prejudice (eg by contracting to sell or let the property to a third party).

(vi) Case 6   Case 6 may be raised where the tenant has assigned or sublet the whole dwelling-house without consent. For the purpose of Case 6 it is clear that

11   *Cobstone Investments Ltd v Maxim* [1985] QB 140 at 151C-D. See, however, *O'Leary v LB of Islington* (1983) 9 HLR 81 (ante, p 915).
12   *Crowder v Mercer* (Unreported, Court of Appeal, 6 March 1981).
13   *Shepherd v Braley* (Unreported, Court of Appeal, 26 February 1981)).
14   *Cobstone Investments Ltd v Maxim* [1985] QB 140 at 143C; *Johnnie Johnson Housing Trust Ltd v Sandon* (Unreported, Court of Appeal, No 81 01105, 23 June 1982).
15   *Florent v Horez* (1983) 268 Estates Gazette 807 at 809.
16   See *Matthews v Ahmed* (Unreported, Court of Appeal, 29 January 1985), where both Hollings J and Cumming-Bruce LJ expressed awareness of the possibility that vague allegations of 'nuisance' or 'annoyance' were being used by the landlord as a pretext for getting rid of an unwanted tenant.
17   Compare eg *Heglibiston Establishment v Heyman* (1978) 36 P & CR 351 at 360ff, with *Benton v Chapman* [1953] CLY 3099. In *Legg v Coole and Sheaff* (1978) LAG Bulletin 189, the Court of Appeal held that there is no obligation on a prospective tenant to volunteer information to his future landlord that he is not married to the person with whom he proposes to occupy the premises. See also *Atkisson v Kern County Housing Authority*, 130 Cal Rptr 375 at 379ff(1976); C.S. Dalton, *Privacy Rights, Visitors Rules and Public Housing*, 62 Boston ULR 325 (1982).
18   See *Clarey v Principal and Council of The Women's College* (1953) 90 CLR 170 at 175, where the High Court of Australia held that a landlord who lets to university students 'can only reasonably expect that such students will keep late hours' and that such occupation will be marked by 'noises made by such acts as walking about, scraping chairs along the floor, having baths, talking and laughing, and preparing for bed.'
19   In *Holloway v Povey* (1984) 271 Estates Gazette 195, the Court of Appeal thought that a tenant's serious neglect of a garden could entitle the landlord to invoke Case 3. See also *Foxell v Mendis* (Unreported, Court of Appeal, No 81 177755, 19 May 1982), where the tenant's unusual ablutionary practices were held to be 'waste' within Case 3.

the term 'tenant' therefore includes a former tenant,[20] and Case 6 can be invoked even though the tenancy contains no prohibition against assignment or subletting.[1]

(vii) Case 8 Case 8 applies where the tenant was a service tenant of the landlord and, this employment having now ceased, the landlord reasonably requires the dwelling-house for occupation as a residence for some person engaged in his whole-time employment.[2] The tenant against whom this Case is raised must have been in the landlord's employment at the beginning of the tenancy, but need not have known that the tenancy was intended to be coterminous with his contract of employment.[3] It seems likely that Case 8 can operate even where the employer terminates the tenant's employment by unlawful dismissal, since the employee's redress in such a case lies in an action in respect of the wrongful dismissal.[4]

(viii) Case 9 Case 9 can be pleaded where a Rent Act protected dwelling-house is 'reasonably required' by the landlord[5] for residential occupation by himself or by any son or daughter of his over 18 years, or by his father or mother or father-in-law or mother-in-law. The Court of Appeal held in *Kidder v Birch*[6] that this accommodation requirement need not be immediate. Possession under Case 9 may quite properly be sought where the need for accommodation is 'in the ascertainable and not distant future', perhaps (although not necessarily) within the following twelve months.

The landlord who invokes Case 9 must normally be the legal and equitable owner of the property.[7] A landlord company cannot in general seek to avail itself of Case 9,[8] and if there are joint landlords the dwelling-house must be reasonably required by all of them.[9] Case 9 is never available to a landlord who

---

20   *Pazgate Ltd v McGrath* (1984).17 HLR 127 at 133, 272 Estates Gazette 1069; [1985] Conv 353 (J.E.M.).
1   *Leith Properties Ltd v Byrne* [1983] QB 433 at 439H, 443E-G; [1983] Conv 155 (J.E. Martin).
2   The potential availability of Case 8 somewhat dubiously led the Court of Appeal in *Matthew v Bobbins* (1981) 41 P & CR 1 at 7f to conclude that an employer was not guilty of any abuse of a 'dominant position' in causing his employee to accept a residential licence in exchange for a protected tenancy (ante, p 993).
3   *Braithwaite & Co Ltd v Elliot* [1947] KB 177 at 181, 183; *Royal Court Derby Porcelain Co v Raymond Russell* [1949] 2 KB 417 at 424f. See also *R.F. Fuggle Ltd v Gadsden* [1948] 2 KB 236 at 240ff.
4   See *Re Rio Algom Ltd and Turcotte* (1979) 88 DLR (3d) 759 at 761.
5   See *Richter v Wilson* [1963] 2 QB 426 at 430.
6   (1983) 46 P & CR 362 at 364; [1982] Conv 444 (J.E. Martin); (1983) 127 SJ 741 (D.W. Williams); [1986] Conv 274 (J.E.M.). If a landlord recovers possession under Case 9 by dishonest misrepresentation, the dislodged tenant is entitled to compensation (see *Thorne v Smith* [1947] KB 307 at 312ff (landlord proceeded to sell the property)).
7   Thus, for instance, a landlord who has no beneficial interest in the property (eg a personal representative) cannot normally invoke Case 9, not least because doing so would in most cases constitute a breach of trust (see *Sharpe v Nicholls* [1945] KB 382 at 386, 389). Compare, however, *Patel (Mahendrakumar) v Patel (Bharat)* [1981] 1 WLR 1342 at 1346G-1347A, where the Court of Appeal found exceptional circumstances which precluded any breach of trust by the personal representatives. See [1982] Conv 443 (J.E.M.). See also *Bostock v Tacher de la Pagerie* (1987) *Times*, 27 February.
8   See, however, *Evans v Engelson* (1979) 253 Estates Gazette 577 at 578, where the landlord company was the alter ego of the respondent and the Court of Appeal accordingly thought it 'commonsense to pierce the corporate veil' for the purpose of Case 9.
9   *Baker v Lewis* [1947] KB 186 at 190; *McIntyre v Hardcastle* [1948] 2 KB 82 at 90; *Mangaroo v Mangaroo* (Unreported, Court of Appeal, 15 January 1981). See also *Re Blok- Glowczynski and Stanga* (1979) 93 DLR (3d) 517 at 521f.

has 'become landlord by purchasing the dwelling-house' after a date stipulated by statute,[10] the object of this provision being to protect a sitting tenant against the possibility that a new owner may buy up the reversion in his home and then immediately invoke the ground for possession contained in Case 9.[11]

There is a special proviso to Case 9 in the form of a 'greater hardship' test under which the onus of proof rests on the tenant.[12] No possession order may be made under Case 9 if the court is satisfied that, 'having regard to all the circumstances, including the question whether other accommodation is available for the landlord or the tenant, greater hardship would be caused by granting the order than by refusing to grant it'.[13] In applying the 'greater hardship' criterion, the court must inquire inter alia into the finances of the parties and their respective capacities to raise and service a mortgage loan.[14] A tenant's ineligibility for council housing may balance the 'greater hardship' test in his favour.[15] The court is also entitled to take into account in the tenant's favour that alternative unfurnished Rent Act protected accommodation is often virtually unobtainable.[16] Yet there are some circumstances in which the accommodation needs presented by the landlord are so pressing as to demand the operation of Case 9.[17] Ill-health on the part of the landlord may be a decisive factor.[18]

(d) The court's residual discretion

Even if one or other of the discretionary grounds for possession has been established against a tenant, the court still retains under section 100 of the Rent Act 1977[19] a broad discretion to adjourn proceedings (or to suspend[20] or put

10   In most cases arising today, the statutorily relevant date is 24 May 1974.
11   Case 9 is available, however, to an owner who, after the statutorily relevant date, purchases property which is unoccupied or has already been vacated by the last tenant. In such circumstances the owner has not 'become landlord by purchasing' and therefore retains the right to invoke Case 9 in respect of a subsequent letting to a new tenant (*Arya v Leon* [1983] Court of Appeal Bound Transcript 501, 15 November 1983).
12   *Mangaroo v Mangaroo* (Unreported, Court of Appeal, 15 January 1981) per Ormrod LJ.
13   Rent Act 1977, Sch 15, Part III, para 1. See *Manaton v Edwards* (1985) 276 Estates Gazette 1256 at 1257f; *Alexander v Mohamadzadeh* [1985] 2 EGLR 161 at 163D-G; (1986) 136 NLJ 447 (H.W. Wilkinson); [1986] Conv 273 (J.E.M.). The 'greater hardship' test tends in practice to intermesh with the further questions whether the landlord can be said 'reasonably' to require the accommodation within the terms of Case 9 and whether it is 'reasonable' to make a possession order at all under Rent Act 1977, s 98(1). In *Lethbridge v Banin* (Unreported, Court of Appeal, P No 8003848, 16 January 1981), Oliver LJ described it as not being 'either right or practicable to separate [these] questions'.
14   See eg *Lethbridge v Banin* (Unreported, Court of Appeal, P No 8003848, 16 January 1981). See also *Bradshaw v Baldwin-Wiseman* (1985) 49 P & CR 382 at 384 (Case 9 not applicable on behalf of successful professional man against 73 year-old tenant 'of very modest means').
15   See *Fernandes v Parvardin* (1982) 264 Estates Gazette 49.
16   *Bassett v Fraser* (1981) 9 HLR 105 at 108f.
17   *Abiafo v Lord* [1984] CLY 1920 (landlord's son aged 18 and daughter aged 16 would otherwise have to share bedroom).
18   See eg *Mohan v Manning* [1981] CLY 1554.
19   As amended by Housing Act 1980, s 75.
20   More than one suspension may be granted, but an order for an indefinite suspension (although clearly within the power of the court) should be made only 'on extremely rare occasions and when very special circumstances exist' (*Vandermolen v Toma* (1981) 9 HLR 91 at 101). Otherwise the tenant would continually have hanging above his head a 'sword of Damocles' (at 104 per Templeman LJ).

back the date of possession under a possession order) for such period or on such terms as the court thinks fit.[1] In the context of Part I of Schedule 15 of the 1977 Act, the court will grant possession to the landlord only if it is 'reasonable' to do so.[2] Often the draconian effect of eviction renders it plainly unreasonable to order possession against the tenant even though the facts fall clearly within one of the statutory Cases. In many instances the immediate effect of a possession order is simply to impose another burden on the already hard-pressed resources of the local housing authority.[3]

If the court grants discretionary relief pursuant to section 100, it must impose conditions respecting the payment of any outstanding arrears of rent except in cases of 'exceptional hardship' or where such an order would otherwise be 'unreasonable'.[4] Where a tenant is already at least 13 weeks in arrears with his rent, it is open to the appropriate local authority to divert rent payments to a landlord from any entitlement which the tenant may have to housing benefit.[5] Moreover, a landlord may be able to obtain an ex parte order for direct payment to himself of the tenant's housing benefit where the tenant is still in occupation but is likely to continue to default in his payment of rent.[6]

(2) Mandatory grounds for possession

Part II of Schedule 15 of the Rent Act 1977 sets out certain grounds (Cases 11 to 20) which, if proved, lead automatically to the making of a possession order against the tenant.[7] These mandatory grounds for the recovery of possession alike require that the landlord should have given written notice to the tenant *before* the commencement of the tenancy that he might seek to repossess under a particular Case. The importance of this requirement of written notice was explained in *Bradshaw v Baldwin-Wiseman*,[8] where Griffiths LJ observed that it

---

1 The usual forum for possession proceedings under the Rent Act is the county court. The broad suspensory jurisdiction conferred by section 100 may be invoked by a spouse or former spouse of the tenant, even after the tenancy has been terminated on the ground of the tenant's non-payment of rent, so long as the spouse or former spouse is still in occupation of the dwelling-house. See Rent Act 1977, s 100(4A), (4B), as supplied by Housing Act 1980, s 75(3), reversing the effect of *Penn v Dunn* [1970] 2 QB 686. See also A. Arden, [1982] Conv 334 at 337ff.
2 Ante, p 1015.
3 This in turn may raise the question whether a tenant has jeopardised his eligibility as a 'homeless person' by making himself intentionally homeless (ante, p 767).
4 Rent Act 1977, s 100(3), as substituted by Housing Act 1980, s 75(2). The court's powers are not, however, subject to the constraints imposed by Housing Act 1980, s 89(1), post, p 1024 (see Housing Act 1980, s 89(2)(c)).
5 See The Housing Benefits Regulations 1985 (SI 1985/677), reg 44(2)(b). See also The Supplementary Benefit (Claims and Payments) Regulations 1981 (SI 1981/1525), reg 15B, 16.
6 *Berg v Markhill* (1985) 17 HLR 455 at 457. Such an order operates not against the authority paying the housing benefit but against the tenant himself.
7 Rent Act 1977, s 98(2). It is now possible to obtain possession under Cases 11 to 20 by way of originating application as distinct from ordinary action (see The Rent Act (County Court Proceedings for Possession) Rules 1981 (SI 1981/139)). Under this special procedure the landlord's action may be heard by a registrar and in chambers, and the period intervening between the service of the plaintiff's affidavit on the defendant and the hearing can be as little as seven days (see [1981] JSWL 159). The advantage of the special procedure is thus that the landlord is enabled to have his possession action heard earlier, although not necessarily at less length (see *Minay v Setongo* (1983) 45 P & CR 190 at 194f).
8 (1985) 49 P & CR 382 at 385.

'is of the utmost importance to a tenant that he should appreciate when he takes rented property whether or not he is obtaining a secure tenure. I can think of nothing likely to have a greater effect on the way people order their lives than the knowledge one way or the other whether or not they have a secure home.' There is a presumption that a notice which has been sent by the landlord has been received by the tenant. However, this presumption may be rebutted on the evidence, in which case a notice duly sent but never received cannot be said to have been 'given' for the purpose of the Rent Act.[9]

Cases 11 to 20 leave virtually no room for the exercise of discretion. In making an order for possession under Part II, the court may not postpone the giving up of possession to a date later than 14 days after the making of that order unless 'it appears to the court that exceptional hardship would be caused by requiring possession to be given up by that date'.[10] Even where 'exceptional hardship' is present, possession cannot be postponed to a date later than six weeks after the making of the court order.[11]

Some of the most important Cases within Part II operate by way of reference to stipulated conditions for the recovery of possession which are contained in para 2 of Part V of Schedule 15.[12] For the purpose of clarity these conditions are outlined here:

(a) the dwelling-house is required as a residence for the owner or any member of his family who resided with the owner when he last occupied the dwelling-house as a residence;

(b) the owner has retired from regular employment and requires the dwelling-house as a residence;

(c) the owner has died and the dwelling-house is required as a residence for a member of his family who was residing with him at the time of his death;

(d) the owner has died and the dwelling-house is required by a successor in title as his residence or for the purpose of disposing of it with vacant possession;

(e) the dwelling-house is subject to a mortgage, made by deed and granted before the tenancy, and the mortgagee —

(i) is entitled to exercise a power of sale conferred on him by the mortgage or by section 101 of the Law of Property Act 1925; and

(ii) requires the dwelling-house for the purpose of disposing of it with vacant possession in exercise of that power;

(f) the dwelling-house is not reasonably suitable to the needs of the owner, having regard to his place of work, and he requires it for the purpose of disposing of it with vacant possession and of using the proceeds of that disposal in acquiring, as his residence, a dwelling-house which is more suitable to those needs.

(a) Case 11

Case 11 arises where the landlord is an 'owner-occupier' who, having let his home temporarily to a tenant, seeks to recover possession from the tenant on

---

9   See *Minay v Setongo* (1983) 45 P & CR 190 at 193f.
10   Housing Act 1980, s 89(1).
11   Housing Act 1980, s 89(1).
12   Rent Act 1977, s 98(5). See Housing Act 1980, s 66(1), (3), and Sch 7.

the ground that one of the conditions set out in Schedule 15, Part V, para 2(a) and 2(c) - (f) is satisfied. Of these conditions the most important is that contained in para 2(a), ie, that 'the dwelling-house is required as a residence for the owner or any member of his family who resided with the owner when he last occupied the dwelling-house as a residence'.

(i) Comparison with Case 9 Case 11 is superficially similar to, but in substance rather different from, the ground of possession contained in Case 9.[13] Case 11 is mandatory in its operation whereas Case 9 is discretionary. Case 11 (unlike Case 9) requires that the landlord must himself have occupied the dwelling-house as his residence prior to the letting to the present tenant.[14] Under Case 11 the landlord must normally have served a written notice on the tenant at the commencement of the tenancy, informing him that possession was ultimately recoverable under Case 11. There is no 'greater hardship' test under Case 11.[15]

(ii) Meaning of 'required' For the purpose of recovering possession under Case 11 there is no necessity that the landlord should demonstrate that the dwelling-house is 'reasonably' required as a residence. In *Kennealy v Dunne*[16] the Court of Appeal held it to be sufficient that the dwelling-house is 'required'. The landlord need show nothing more than that the property is 'bona fide wanted and genuinely intended to be occupied as a residence at once, or at any rate within a reasonable time, but so wanted and intended whether reasonably or unreasonably'.[17] Stephenson LJ found force in the contention that the purpose of Case 11 is to enable an owner to give up his home temporarily in order to 'take up a post in another part of the country or abroad', secure in the knowledge that on his return he can 'resume life in his own home, without being confronted with all the difficulties' encountered by a landlord who seeks to recover possession under Case 9.[18]

It seems under Case 11 that the landlord need not require *all* of the dwelling-house as a residence for himself or a member of his family.[19] Moreover, if two or more persons are joint owners of the dwelling-house in question, Case 11 permits the recovery of possession even though the property is required as a residence for only one of the owners.[20]

(iii) Meaning of 'residence' Case 11 inevitably raises some question as to the nature and extent of the proposed occupancy needed in order to show that a

---

13 Ante, p 1021.
14 However, there is no longer any requirement that the landlord should have resided in the dwelling-house *immediately* prior to the letting currently in dispute. See Rent (Amendment) Act 1985, s 1(1), reversing the effect of *Pocock v Steel* [1985] 1 WLR 229. (The change is retrospective: see *Hewitt v Lewis* [1986] 1 WLR 444 at 448H-449A).
15 Ante, p 1022.
16 [1977] QB 837 at 850A-B, 851B-C; (1977) 41 Conv (NS) 287 (D. MacIntyre).
17 [1977] QB 837 at 849D-E. The Canadian courts have likewise adopted the view that, in the present context, there is no implication that the landlord must show that he 'needs' the premises (see *Re Walker And Carlill & Carbolic Smoke Ball Corporation* (1980) 99 DLR (3d) 498 at 502f; *Re Higgins and Mathot* (1984) 45 OR (2d) 377 at 379).
18 [1977] QB 837 at 849E-F.
19 See *Kelley v Goodwin* [1947] 1 All ER 810 at 812G (involving Case 9); *Re Sandhu and Yzereff* (1983) 140 DLR (3d) 761 at 763.
20 *Tilling v Whiteman* [1980] AC 1 at 19D, 21E-F; [1980] CLJ 27. Compare *Lloyd v Sadler* [1978] QB 774 (ante, p 1005).

dwelling-house is required 'as a residence' either for the owner or for some member of his family. In *Naish v Curzon*,[1] for instance, the landlord lived and worked in South Africa. He invoked Case 11 in order to recover possession of a house in England which he had let to a tenant. His visits to England had always been somewhat short and discontinuous, and it appeared that during the four years immediately preceding the relevant hearing he had spent only some seven weeks in the country. The tenant claimed that it could be extrapolated from the intermittent pattern of the landlord's presence in England that he was seeking possession of the property not for use as a future 'residence' but merely in order to facilitate his 'occasional holiday visits'. However, the Court of Appeal ordered possession under Case 11, Oliver LJ taking the view that Case 11 does not impose 'any sort of requirement of permanence or lack of intermittency in the residence which is required by the landlord.'[2]

The impression that the courts have not been overly sympathetic towards the tenant in the context of Case 11 was strengthened by a further decision of the Court of Appeal in *Najia Naim v Bemrose*.[3] Here the landlords, who were normally resident in Singapore, owned two properties in England and granted lettings in respect of both of them. The landlords invoked Case 11 against the tenant of one of these properties in immediate response to her application for the determination of a fair rent. The landlords admitted that their intention was to sell the property within a year or two, but the Court of Appeal found none of these facts inconsistent with a bona fide intention[4] on the part of the landlords to return into residence at least intermittently pending such a sale.[5] In awarding possession under Case 11, Arnold P attached importance to Lord Wilberforce's statement in *Tilling v Whiteman*[6] that the underlying policy of Case 11 is to 'induce occupiers of dwelling-houses...to make their premises available for letting to others, on the basis that on their return they would be able, without dispute, to regain possession.' Here, once again, is the moral crux of the Rent Act: should the Rent Act be construed in favour of landlords (and therefore adversely to tenants) precisely in order to stimulate a ready supply of rented accommodation for the needy consumer?[7]

(iv) Familial nexus   Case 11 provides a ground of recovery of possession where a dwelling-house is required as a residence either for the 'owner-occupier'

1   (1986) 51 P & CR 229.
2   (1986) 51 P & CR 229 at 241. The Court of Appeal expressly drew on the analogous requirement of continuous residence which is applicable to a statutory tenant (ante, p 1007). It is difficult, however, to avoid the strong suspicion that a less substantial degree of occupancy is needed for the purpose of making Case 11 available to a landlord than is required to enable a statutory tenant to maintain a second home within the protection of the Rent Act.
3   Unreported, 17 March 1986.
4   In some Canadian jurisdictions, the fact that the landlord returns into residence for at least a year following a successful repossession raises a rebuttable presumption as to his bona fides (see British Columbia's Residential Tenancy Act (RSBC 1980, c 48), s 13; *Re Holdom and Lucas* (1983) 143 DLR (3d) 133 at 135).
5   Cumming-Bruce LJ professed to see nothing in the case to suggest that the court was being 'taken for a ride' or had been 'misled by a cosmetic and artificial device'.
6   [1980] AC 1 at 18F.
7   In so far as Case 11 was grafted on to the Rent Act only in 1965 (see Rent Act 1965, s 14), there has always been some dispute as to whether it should be construed in such a way as to reinforce the existing protective policy of the Rent Act or whether it should be taken to reflect a retrenchment upon tenants' rights to be construed liberally in the landlord's favour (see [1980] CLJ 27 at 30f).

himself or for 'any member of his family' who satisfies the stipulated residence requirement. Case 11 thus involves (at least potentially) some consideration of familial nexus, and can be invoked on behalf of a somewhat wider range of persons than those who come within the ambit of Case 9.[8] The phrase used in Case 11, 'member of his family', is generally taken to include those de facto relationships which generate entitlement to a statutory tenancy by succession.[9]

(v) Dispensing with the requirement of written notice   Under Case 11 the court may in some circumstances dispense with the requirement that the landlord should have served a written notice at the commencement of the tenancy, warning the tenant that possession was ultimately recoverable under Case 11. The court has a statutory discretion to award possession to the landlord, notwithstanding that no such notice was served, if 'of opinion that...it is just and equitable to make an order for possession'. This discretion may be exercised in favour of a landlord who has sent a notice to his tenant which was never received by the latter,[10] or in favour of a landlord who has given his tenant merely oral notice of his intention to resort to Case 11.[11] It is, however, extremely doubtful that the court will grant the same indulgence to a landlord who never made any attempt at all to provide his tenant with the appropriate Case 11 notice.[12] In *Bradshaw v Baldwin-Wiseman*[13] the Court of Appeal declined to allow the discretionary exception to be used to circumvent an 'obvious and important' form of protection for the tenant under the Rent Act. It was not 'just and equitable' to dispense with the notice requirement in relation to a letting which had not initially been intended as a temporary letting under Case 11, but which had always been envisaged as carrying with it the security of the Rent Acts.[14]

(b) Case 12

Case 12 may be relevant where a landlord, with the intention of later occupying a dwelling-house as his residence on retirement from regular employment, meanwhile let that property on a regulated tenancy prior to his retirement.[15] Case 12 is established if the tenant was duly served with a written notice at the commencement of the tenancy that possession was recoverable under Case 12[16] and if one of the conditions set in Schedule 15, Part V, para 2(b)–(e) is now satisfied.[17] Case 12 is thus primarily relevant where the owner-landlord finally retires from regular employment and requires the dwelling-house as his home.

---

8   Ante, p 1021.
9   Post, p 1064.
10   *Minay v Setongo* (1983) 45 P & CR 190 at 193ff.
11   *Fernandes v Parvardin* (1982) 264 Estates Gazette 49 at 50.
12   *Minay v Setongo* (1983) 45 P & CR 190 at 195.
13   (1985) 49 P & CR 382 at 385. See [1985] Conv 354 (J.E.M.); [1985] JSWL 298 (M.A.J.).
14   (1985) 49 P & CR 382 at 388.
15   However, the landlord need not have *bought* the property with the intention of using it as his future retirement home. Such an intention was required by Case 12 in its original form in Schedule 15 of the Rent Act 1977, but is now made unnecessary by Housing Act 1980, s 66(4).
16   As under Case 11, the court has discretion under Case 12 to dispense with this requirement of written notice if 'of opinion that...it is just and equitable to make an order for possession'.
17   Ante, p 1024.

(c) Case 19

Case 19 was added by the Housing Act 1980 to the Cases contained in Part II of Schedule 15 of the Rent Act 1977.[18] It provides a mandatory ground for the recovery of possession of property let on a 'protected shorthold tenancy'. Although introduced at the end of a long list of Cases for repossession, Case 19 enjoys a significance which belies its deceptively innocuous position, for it strikes at the very basis of protected status under the Rent Act.[19]

(i) Definition of a 'protected shorthold tenancy'   A 'protected shorthold tenancy' is defined as a protected tenancy which is granted after the commencement of the Housing Act 1980 for 'a term certain of not less than one year nor more than five years', and which satisfies certain other stipulated conditions.[20] It must be a tenancy which cannot be terminated by the landlord before the expiry of the term except in pursuance of a provision for re-entry or forfeiture for non-payment of rent or breach of any other obligation of the tenancy.[1] There is a requirement that the landlord should, not later than the commencement of the tenancy, have given the tenant a valid notice stating that the tenancy is to be a protected shorthold tenancy.[2] There was originally a general requirement that a 'fair rent' registration be in force in relation to the dwelling-house at the commencement date or be applied for within 28 days of that date.[3] However, this requirement has now been discontinued,[4] thus destroying the initially intended trade-off between fair rent and security of tenure in respect of shorthold tenancies.

(ii) Recovery of possession   If a protected shorthold tenant does not give up possession voluntarily at the end of his period certain, the landlord may commence proceedings for possession not later than three months after the expiry of a further written notice indicating to the tenant that possession will be sought under Case 19.[5]

As is the case with all protected tenancies under the Rent Act, no shorthold tenant may be evicted except by order of the court. However, Case 19 provides that if the court is of opinion that it is 'just and equitable' to make an order for possession, the court 'may treat the tenancy under which the dwelling-house

---

18   Housing Act 1980, s 55(1). See P.F. Smith, [1982] Conv 29; V. Fisher, (1982) 132 NLJ 55.

19   See A. Arden, (1980) LAG Bulletin 33; (1980) LAG Bulletin 266f.

20   Housing Act 1980, s 52(1).

1   Housing Act 1980, s 52(1)(a). A protected shorthold tenancy is, however, terminable by the tenant on giving the landlord written notice of one month (if the term certain is two years or less) or three months (if the term certain is more than two years) (see Housing Act 1980, s 53(1)).

2   Housing Act 1980, s 52(1)(b).

3   Housing Act 1980, s 52(1)(c).

4   The Protected Shorthold Tenancies (Rent Registration) Order 1987 (SI 1987/265), para 2. See Housing Act 1980, s 52(4). The protection of compulsory 'fair rent' registration was withdrawn in respect of shorthold tenancies outside Greater London in 1981 (The Protected Shorthold Tenancies (Rent Registration) Order 1981 (SI 1981/1578), para 2), but, with effect from 4 May 1987, this denial of protection has now been extended even to the Greater London area.

5   This notice must itself be of at least three months in duration (Housing Act 1980, s 55(1)). See also The Protected Shorthold Tenancies (Notice to Tenant) Regulations 1987 (SI 1987/267).

was let as a protected shorthold tenancy', notwithstanding that no notice was given by the landlord at the commencement of the tenancy indicating the existence of a protected shorthold tenancy, and notwithstanding that no 'fair rent' registration has ever been obtained in respect of the property.[6] This provision, if construed liberally, would enable the court to deem many ordinary protected tenancies granted after 1980 to be 'protected shorthold tenancies', thus bringing such tenancies without warning within the scope of the automatic ground of possession contained in Case 19. There is, however, some reason for believing that the courts are reluctant to give Case 19 so unrestricted an application.[7]

Where a possession order is made under Case 19, the county court has only an extremely limited discretion to postpone the operation of the order. The maximum suspension of any order is for a period of 14 days, extendable in cases of 'exceptional hardship' for a period not exceeding six weeks from the date of the possession order.[8]

(iii) Policy of the protected shorthold The introduction of the 'protected shorthold tenancy' was a politically motivated device intended to turn the flank of the protective policy embodied in the Rent Act. At one level it was doubtless a genuine attempt to entice owners to release more residential property on to the private rental market by the promise of easily recoverable possession after short-term occupation.[9] However, the underlying motive behind the shorthold tenancy has been seen by some as comprising a more far-reaching concern to emasculate the social philosophy of Rent Act legislation, by altering the balance of bargaining power on the housing market in favour of the owner of private property.[10] The innovation of the shorthold tenancy is an implicit repudiation of the idea that residential tenants may acquire 'social rights of property' in their homes.

The concept of the shorthold tenancy is not itself entirely new, having been the subject of several private member's Bills introduced unsuccessfully in Parliament prior to 1980.[11] However, even these Bills contained important

---

6 Housing Act 1980, s 55(2). Compare Rent Act 1977, Sch 15, Part II, Cases 11 and 12 (ante, p 1027).

7 See eg *Bradshaw v Baldwin-Wiseman* (1985) 49 P & CR 382 at 388 (ante, p 1027).

8 Housing Act 1980, s 89(1).

9 It can, however, be argued that an earlier measure of statutory 'de-control' in the housing area, the Rent Act 1957, was followed not by an increase but by a marked decrease in the availability of private residential lettings. See *Social Trends No 16* (London 1986), p 133 (Chart 8.1); M. Partington, *Landlord and Tenant* (2nd edn London 1980), p 14f; J. Hillman, *The shrinking pool of private-rented housing*, (1980) 53 New Society 17. The statistical evidence seems to suggest that the removal of Rent Act protection is more closely associated with re-sale on the open freehold market (ante, p 996). See also Institute of Rent Officers, *A Response to the Report of the Inquiry into British Housing* (1986), paras 1.3.3ff, 6.2.6.

10 The Labour Party is pledged to an early repeal of the shorthold provisions in their present form. See *Parliamentary Debates, House of Commons, Official Report* (Standing Committee F), Vol IX (Session 1979-80), Col 1180 (Mr G Kaufman, Opposition Spokesman on Housing) (18 March 1980).

11 See eg the Housing (Shorthold Tenancies) Bill introduced on 19 May 1976 (*Parliamentary Debates, House of Commons, Official Report* (1975-76), Vol 911, Col 1445), and on 30 January 1979 (*Parliamentary Debates, House of Commons, Official Report* (1978-79), Vol 961, Col 1240).

forms of protection for the tenant which are not present in Case 19.[12] Although Case 19 can have no application to protected tenancies granted before the commencement of the Housing Act 1980, it is clear that few protected tenancies are now likely to be granted except on the terms of a shorthold tenancy (which may be for as short a period as one year).[13] This result, taken in conjunction with the right of public sector tenants to purchase their homes in fee simple,[14] has done much to tilt the balance on the private rental market in favour of the landlord. Those who cannot afford to buy their own home, who cannot command mortgage resources, who are ineligible for local authority housing, are thrown even more helplessly on the mercy of an increasingly constricted market in private residential lettings.

It is not difficult to see how the introduction of the shorthold tenancy strikes at the basis of Rent Act protection for residential tenants.[15] The major purpose of the Rent Act is to mitigate the disparity in bargaining power otherwise evident in a situation of free contracting on the private rental market. This legislative purpose has hitherto been achieved by substituting for the normal operation of market forces a protective scheme which guarantees for the residential tenant certain rights not grounded in contract but founded upon status.[16] This purpose is severely jeopardised by the innovation of the shorthold tenancy, which at least partially relegates the basis of the tenant's protection to the realm of contract.

The shorthold tenancy also offends the fundamental premise that the twin tenets of long-term security of tenure and restriction of rents together constitute an indivisible basis for the protected status of the tenant under the Rent Act.[17] Although a shortholder will enjoy security of tenure during his term, he is by definition deprived of long-term security. For the first time in decades there is now a separation between the two prongs of Rent Act protection, tenants under Case 19 having now lost in their entirety the benefits conferred by the statutory restriction of rents.[18]

12   Several safeguards were unsuccessfully proposed at the committee stage in the House of Commons' consideration of the Housing Bill 1980 (see *Parliamentary Debates, House of Commons, Official Report* (Standing Committee F), Vol IX (Session 1979–80), Cols 1125f (11, 13 March 1980)). These included amendments which would have ensured (1) that the relevant dwelling-house should be vacant for a continuous period of at least 6 months immediately preceding the commencement of the Housing Act 1980; (2) that the landlord be required to give a right of 'first refusal' to any sitting shortholder where the landlord wished to create a new shorthold on the termination of an expired shorthold; (3) that the Rent Officer be required to countersign a written shorthold lease, doing so only after satisfying himself that the parties were 'aware of their rights and obligations under shorthold tenure'.

13   The ruling of the House of Lords in *Street v Mountford* [1985] AC 809 (ante, p 1000) has now made it somewhat less feasible for landlords to circumvent the Rent Act by 'sham' devices.

14   Ante, p 733.

15   The existence of the shorthold also affects the freedom of other kinds of tenant. The possibility that property may now be exploited by way of shorthold letting without any prospect of long-term intrusion upon the landlord's reversion has been held to justify a head-lessor's refusal to consent to alternative (and more prejudicial) forms of residential letting proposed by the head-lessee (see *Leeward Securities Ltd v Lilyheath Properties Ltd* (1983) 17 HLR 35 at 48).

16   Ante, p 969.

17   Ante, p 966.

18   Ante, p 1028.

(d) Overcrowding

There is one other circumstance in which, irrespective of the nature of the tenancy involved, an order for possession will be made virtually automatically. This occurs where a dwelling-house is 'overcrowded' within the meaning of the Housing Act 1985 with the result that the occupier is rendered criminally liable.[19] In such a case the occupier's immediate landlord may obtain possession under section 101 of the Rent Act 1977, but this provision is restricted in its scope to a 'dwelling-house which consists of premises used as a separate dwelling by members of the working classes or of a type suitable for such use'.[20]

7. RESTRICTION OF RENTS

The second basic feature of the protection afforded the regulated tenant under the Rent Act 1977 lies in the measure of statutory control exercisable over the rent which may lawfully be charged by the landlord. Under the scheme of the Rent Act the tenant need pay nothing more than an administratively determined 'fair rent' as the price of his security of tenure. This restriction of the rent payable not only displaces the normal operation of market forces but also cuts through the principle of sanctity of contract between landlord and tenant. A determination of 'fair rent' plainly overrides the rent agreed contractually between the parties, even though in most cases a 'fair rent' in relation to a dwelling-house is considerably less than the rent obtainable on an open and uncontrolled market.[1]

(1) Application for a 'fair rent' determination

Both landlord and tenant have a statutory right to apply to the local rent officer for registration of a 'fair rent' in respect of any dwelling subject to a regulated tenancy.[2] The local authority has a similar right,[3] and local authorities nowadays make increasingly frequent applications for a 'fair rent'

---

19 Ante, p 937.
20 Rent Act 1977, s 101(2). It has been said in another context that the phrase 'houses intended to be used as dwellings for the working classes' is today 'anachronistic' and liable to be condemned as containing a hint of paternalism (see *Chorley BC v Barratt Developments (North West) Ltd* [1979] 3 All ER 634 at 637f, 639b; see also *H.E. Green and Sons v Minister of Health* (No 2) [1948] 1 KB 34 at 38). Yet it is surprising that such perceptions of social stratification have been preserved for so long even in modern legislation. See also R.G. Lee, *The Demise of the Working Classes*, [1980] Conv 281.
1   In *Blake v Attorney General* [1982] IR 117 at 139, the success of the constitutional challenge mounted against the validity of the Irish Rent Act legislation (ante, p 970) was founded in part on the argument that the rent chargeable under the statutory scheme was 'oppressively uneconomic'.
2   Rent Act 1977, s 67(1). It is the duty of the rent officer to prepare and keep up to date a register of all registered rents within his area of jurisdiction (Rent Act 1977, s 66(1)). The register is open to public inspection, and in practice provides a means of ensuring that rents applicable in the same locality are broadly comparable.
3   Rent Act 1977, s 68(1).

determination simply as a means of limiting the amount of public funds otherwise milked away by private landlords.[4]

(2) **Registration of a 'fair rent'**

The application for registration of a fair rent is determined in the first instance by the local rent officer.[5] The rent officer must first be 'satisfied' that his jurisdiction is properly founded in respect of any particular application,[6] and in cases where he is so satisfied must then proceed to fix a 'fair rent'.[7]

(a) *Effects of registration*

The 'fair rent' determined by the rent officer is effective from the date of registration,[8] and the maximum rent thereafter recoverable in respect of any contractual period is limited to this registered rent.[9] The 'fair rent' registered is exclusive of rates,[10] but it is open to the rent officer to register a variable 'fair rent' in order to take account of reasonable fluctuations in any service charges payable by the tenant as a component of his rent.[11]

If the tenant has already contracted to pay more than the registered 'fair

---

4   Ante, p 965. Where the tenant is in receipt of housing benefit, ie, his accommodation costs are covered by state-funded benefit, he has no direct incentive to challenge a rent which exceeds a 'fair rent'. During recent years it is quite clear that private landlords have in many cases charged exorbitant rents, confident in the knowledge that such rents would be automatically paid from public funds.

5   The Rent Officer Service was established in 1965, and operates from a number of 'shop front' premises in designated urban areas. Rent officers are officers of the Crown (as distinct from civil servants). They have formed a distinct professional body (the Institute of Rent Officers), which publishes the *Journal of the Institute of Rent Officers* (Jiro).

6   The rent officer's jurisdiction is 'like that of an arbitrator. It stems from...an assumption that there is a protected tenancy'. The rent officer has no jurisdiction to 'decide' that there *is* such a tenancy (see *R v Camden LB Rent Officer, ex parte Ebiri* [1981] 1 WLR 881 at 884D-F per Donaldson LJ). In practice many rent officers simply assume that there is jurisdiction except in the clearest of cases, and invite the landlord to challenge that assumption in the county court under Rent Act 1977, s 141 (see also N. Madge, (1981) LAG Bulletin 236).

7   In the event of dispute as to the precise status of an occupancy, the rent officer is obliged to determine and register a 'fair rent' as soon as he is 'satisfied' of the existence of a regulated tenancy, even though his assumption of jurisdiction remains open to challenge (*R v Camden LB Rent Officer, ex parte Ebiri* [1981] 1 WLR 881 at 881F).

8   Rent Act 1977, s 72, as amended by Housing Act 1980, s 61(1). Before the commencement of the Housing Act 1980, registrations were normally back-dated to the date of application, thus conferring a substantial advantage on the tenant. For discussion of the way in which the present law penalises the tenant, see (1981) LAG Bulletin 67, 236 (N. Madge).

9   Rent Act 1977, s 44(1). Moreover, the registration attaches to the dwelling-house as such, with the result that the benefit of a 'fair rent' achieved by one tenant can, in the absence of a variation, be claimed by any subsequent tenant. However, if after the registration date there is some 'material change...in the specification of the dwelling-house' (eg through the addition or subtraction of a room or rooms) or a 'material change in the particulars with regard to the tenancy' (eg through the provision of furniture in an initially unfurnished dwelling), then the registered rent no longer represents the maximum recoverable rent for the purpose of section 44(1). See *Metrobarn Ltd v Gehring* [1976] 1 WLR 776 at 780B-C; *Kent v Millmead Properties Ltd* (1982) 44 P & CR 353 at 357; [1983] Conv 147 (F. Webb).

10 Rent Act 1977, s 71(2). See also *Aristocrat Property Investments Ltd v Harounoff* (1982) 43 P & CR 284 at 292f.

11 *Firstcross Ltd v Teasdale* (1984) 47 P & CR 228 at 239. See [1983] Conv 90, but compare [1983] Conv 175 (J.T.F.).

rent', the excess is not recoverable by the landlord.[12] Indeed if the tenant has actually paid a rent in excess of the registered 'fair rent', he may recover that excess from the landlord either directly or by deducting it from any rent still due to the landlord.[13] When the contractual period of the tenancy comes to an end, the tenant need not pay more than the last contractual rent or the relevant registered rent, whichever is the lower.[14]

One of the more surprising statistics of Rent Act coverage is that 'fair rents' are currently registered in respect of only one third of the lettings which fall within the regulated sector.[15] It has, moreover, been estimated that 95 per cent of those rents which are registered relate to unfurnished premises.[16] It seems to be the case that most furnished tenants—for one reason or another—never get around to having a 'fair rent' registered in respect of their accommodation.

(b) Appeal and variation

If the rent officer's determination is not accepted by the parties, the matter can be referred to a rent assessment committee.[17] If the rent assessment committee declines to interfere with the rent determined by the rent officer, the rent so fixed cannot normally be varied for a period of two years.[18] Within this two-year period, however, it is open to the landlord and the tenant to make a joint application for cancellation or alteration of the registered 'fair rent',[19] and it is always possible for either to allege that by reason of a relevant change of circumstance the registered rent no longer represents a fair rent.[20] Any increase in rental which is allowed on this ground need not be limited, however, to the value of the alterations in the condition of the property which gave rise to the right to apply for variation.[1]

12 Rent Act 1977, s 44(2).
13 Rent Act 1977, s 57. No excess may be recovered more than two years after the date of payment (see Rent Act 1977, s 57(3)). Compare the six year limitation period imposed on the landlord's right to sue for arrears of rent (ante, p 514).
14 However, if the contractual rent at that point is lower than the rent which is registrable as a 'fair rent', the landlord may increase the rent to a fair rent by serving notices of increase in the prescribed form.
15 Sir George Young (Parliamentary Under Secretary, Department of the Environment), (1984) 15 Jiro (No 2), 6 at 7.
16 Central Statistical Office, *Social Trends No 16* (London 1986), p 133.
17 See The Rent Assessment Committees (England and Wales) Regulations 1971 (SI 1971/1065), as amended by The Rent Assessment Committees (England and Wales) (Amendment) Regulations 1981 (SI 1981/1783); [1982] JSWL 226; [1983] Conv 260.
18 Rent Act 1977, s 67(3), as amended by Housing Act 1980, s 60(1). It is open to the landlord to apply for cancellation of the registered rent within the two-year period if the tenant has quit possession (see Rent Act 1977, s 73(1A), as supplied by Housing Act 1980, s 62(2)). Before the commencement of the Housing Act 1980, registered rents were immune from alteration for three years. The changes effected in 1980 were symptomatic not only of the impact of inflation on the real value of rents but also of a new legislative sympathy for the entrepreneurial impulse as applied to the housing market.
19 Rent Act 1977, s 73(1)(c).
20 Rent Act 1977, s 67(3). It is not open to a tenant simply to apply for re-registration of an existing 'fair rent': there must be a fresh determination by the rent officer (see *R v Chief Rent Officer for Royal Borough of Kensington and Chelsea, ex parte Moberley* [1986] 1 EGLR 168 at 169J-M; [1986] Conv 274 (J.E.M.)).
1   *London Housing and Commercial Properties Ltd v Cowan* [1977] QB 148 at 152E-F. There is no longer provision for phasing in any permitted rent increase over a period of one year (The Rent (Relief from Phasing) Order 1987 (SI 1987/264)). See formerly Rent Act 1977, Sch 8, as amended by Housing Act 1980, s 60(3).

(3) Certificates of 'fair rent'

It is possible to apply for a 'certificate of fair rent' before any letting occurs, simply in order to discover what rent would be considered by the rent officer to represent a 'fair rent' if the premises were subsequently let.[2] The rent indicated in the certificate will determine the amount of any 'fair rent' registrable on an application made within two years of the date of issue of the certificate.[3]

(4) Assessment of a 'fair rent'

In determining the amount of a 'fair rent', the rent officer is statutorily directed to have regard to 'all the circumstances (other than personal circumstances)' of the case.[4]

(a) General approach

In *Mason v Skilling*[5] Lord Kilbrandon pointed out that the fixing of a fair rent 'calls for a skilled estimate of a hypothetical figure, namely, the rent which a landlord would demand and a tenant would be prepared to pay if the market were roughly in a state of equilibrium, without serious shortage or surplus of subjects available for letting.' The House of Lords ruled that it is open to a rent officer to adopt 'any method or methods' of ascertaining such a fair rent, provided that he does not use 'any method which is unlawful or unreasonable'.[6]

(i) Capital return or comparable value?   One of the most controversial questions in the context of 'fair rents' is whether the determination of a 'fair rent' should be reached by having regard to the registered rents of comparable dwellings or by making reference to a notional level of return on the landlord's capital investment.[7] Consideration of the latter factor is clearly germane in so far as there is any concern that 'a fair rent should be fair to the landlord as well as fair to the tenant'.[8]

It is clear, however, that it is open to either a rent officer or a rent assessment committee to have regard to the more 'obvious and direct'[9] method for assessing a 'fair rent', that is, by having regard to available evidence of the relevant 'comparables'.[10] In recent years the courts have tended to attach

---

2   Rent Act 1977, s 69(1). See *Guppys Properties Ltd v Knott* (1980) 253 Estates Gazette 907 at 909. After the commencement of the Housing and Planning Act 1986, a public sector landlord which proposes to sell dwellings on a council estate to a private landlord will likewise be able to apply to the rent officer for a certificate of fair rent (Rent Act 1977, s 69(1A), as supplied by Housing and Planning Act 1986, s 7(1)). This certificate will be declaratory of the rent deemed 'fair' after the privatisation of any given tenancy (post, p 1058).
3   Rent Act 1977, s 69(4), as amended by Housing Act 1980, Sch 25, para 40.
4   Rent Act 1977, s 70(1). See R.G. Lee, *Fair rents—legal sense from economic nonsense*, (1984) 4 Oxford Jnl of Legal Studies 287.
5   [1974] 1 WLR 1437 at 1443B-C.
6   [1974] 1 WLR 1437 at 1439G per Lord Reid.
7   See eg (1979) LAG Bulletin 128.
8   *Mason v Skilling* [1974] 1 WLR 1437 at 1440A-B per Lord Reid. See also S.J. Sheldon, *Rethinking Rent Control: An Analysis of 'Fair Return'*, 12 Rutgers LJ 617 (1980-81).
9   *Mason v Skilling* [1974] 1 WLR 1437 at 1439H.
10   See *Tormes Property Co Ltd v Landau* [1971] 1 QB 261 at 267A.

increasing importance to 'comparables' as a means of guiding the determination of 'fair rents'.[11] In *Ellis & Sons Fourth Amalgamated Properties Ltd v Southern Rent Assessment Panel*,[12] Mann J rejected the contention that the landlords had been entitled to a certain level of 'return on a capital sum achievable in an open and free market'. He observed that in the present context the court was 'not concerned with the world of open and free markets', and he could not 'see how the committee could have derived assistance from any consideration such as that the landlords would not let at that rent because they would get too low a rate of return on the capital asset which they would otherwise realise in a free market.'[13]

(ii) Relevance of inflation Where a rent has been registered on a property, the effects of subsequent inflation do not entitle the landlord to demand that the 'fair rent' should be proportionately up-rated on re-registration of the same dwelling-house. The impact of inflation is merely one of the factors which may be relevant to the exercise.[14]

(b) Relevant factors

Certain factors are statutorily declared to be relevant to the assessment of a 'fair rent'. These include the following.

(i) Condition of the dwelling-house In fixing a 'fair rent', the rent officer must have particular regard to the age, character, locality and state of repair of the dwelling-house.[15] Perhaps surprisingly the Court of Appeal held in *Williams v Khan*[16] that the existence of a closing order in relation to the dwelling-house[17] does not of itself provide conclusive evidence that the fair rent registrable in respect of the premises should be either nominal or nil.[18]

11　See eg *London Rent Assessment Committee v St George's Court Ltd* (1984) *Times*, 28 April, where the Court of Appeal held that 'weighty reasons' were necessary before it would be permissible for a rent assessment committee to depart substantially from recent fair rent assessments for comparable properties.

12　(1984) 270 Estates Gazette 39 at 40.

13　It is, of course, unrealistic to ignore the fact that the landlord, if a freeholder (and to a lesser degree if a leaseholder) is also steadily accumulating a capital profit in terms of the aggregating capital value of the property (see J. Kemeny, *The Myth of Home- Ownership* (London 1981), p 27f). It has been held that the increasing capital value of the property should not be taken into account in fixing a 'fair rent', in that capital appreciation does not have any impact on rent levels in the market (*Midanbury Properties (Southampton) Ltd v Houghton* (1981) 131 NLJ 803). See also *R v London Rent Assessment Panel, ex parte Chelmsford Building Co Ltd* [1986] 1 EGLR 175 at 176M-177B.

14　*Kovats v Corporation of Trinity House* (1981) 262 Estates Gazette 445 at 446. Compare the Rent (Northern Ireland) Order 1978, art 22(4), which provides for automatic periodic increases in registered rents in line with inflation.

15　Rent Act 1977, s 70(1)(a).

16　(1980) 43 P & CR 1 at 16f. Compare, however, *Black v Oliver* [1978] QB 870 at 880G, 884G-H; [1978] Conv 407. See also [1980] Conv 389.

17　Such an order may be made on the ground that the property is unfit for human habitation (ante, p 927).

18　For a 'fair rent' assessment on a house inhabited by a poltergeist, see *McGhee v LB of Hackney* (1969) 210 Estates Gazette 1431 at 1433 (The appropriate rent was, incidentally, 25p per week in 1969 values).

(ii) Condition of any furniture   In determining a 'fair rent', the rent officer must also have particular regard to the quantity, quality and condition of any furniture provided for use under the tenancy.[19] The 'fair rent' arrived at is neither raised nor lowered by reference to any improvement or deterioration caused by the tenant to such furniture.[20]

(iii) Lawful premiums   From the commencement date of the relevant provision in the Housing and Planning Act 1986, the assessment of a 'fair rent' must also take into account any premium or sum in the nature of a premium lawfully paid by the tenant in connection with the grant, renewal, continuance or assignment of his tenancy.[1]

(c) Irrelevant factors

Certain factors are statutorily declared to be irrelevant to the determination of a 'fair rent'.

(i) Personal circumstances   In fixing the level of a 'fair rent', the rent officer is directed to take no account of 'personal circumstances'.[2] This exclusion ensures that the financial means of both the particular landlord and the particular tenant are irrelevant to the assessment of a 'fair rent'. In *Mason v Skilling*,[3] moreover, the House of Lords was of the opinion that the regulated tenant's rights to security of tenure likewise represent a purely personal circumstance which must be excluded from consideration in so far as it might affect the assessment of a 'fair rent'.[4]

(ii) Scarcity value   The rent officer is directed to disregard any element of 'scarcity value' within a particular 'locality' when determining a 'fair rent'.[5] The motive underlying this direction is plainly that any inherent amenities or advantages possessed by the dwelling-house in question should be reflected in the rent assessed, but that no regard should be had to any increase in the market rent which would confer on the landlord a wholly unmeritorious increase in rent simply because of an excess of demand over supply in any 'locality'.[6]

---

19   Rent Act 1977, s 70(1)(b).
20   Rent Act 1977, s 70(3)(e).
1   Rent Act 1977, s 70(1)(c), as added by Housing and Planning Act 1986, s 17(2).
2   Rent Act 1977, s 70(1).
3   [1974] 1 WLR 1437 at 1440E-F.
4   Thus, in fixing a 'fair rent' on the basis of notional capital return, the value of the capital tied up in the dwelling-house should be assessed on the basis of vacant possession.
5   It is to be 'assumed that the number of persons seeking to become tenants of similar dwelling-houses in the locality on the terms (oth er than those relating to rent) of the regulated tenancy is not substantially greater than the number of such dwelling-houses in the locality which are available for letting on such terms' (Rent Act 1977, s 70(2)). See *Western Heritable Investment Co Ltd v Husband* [1983] 2 AC 849 at 854E-F per Lord Fraser of Tullybelton, 856C-D per Lord Keith of Kinkel. See also P.Q. Watchman, [1985] Conv 199.
6   The rent officer, in deciding whether there exists an overall scarcity to be discounted, must 'pick a really large area that gives [him] a fair appreciation of the trends of scarcity and their consequences' (*Metropolitan Property Holdings Ltd v Finegold* [1975] 1 WLR 349 at 354A-B). Thus the presence in the immediate vicinity of some amenity (eg a school, zoo, theatre or swimming pool) which has not been provided by the landlord cannot be a ground for raising a 'fair rent'.

(iii) Other disregards It is also clear that the assessment of a 'fair rent' is to be reached without making any reduction on account of any disrepair or defect for which the tenant is responsible.[7] Likewise the rent officer must have no regard to any improvements effected by the tenant himself,[8] unless such improvements were required of the tenant under the terms of the tenancy.[9]

(5) The direction of reform

In 1985 the Report of the Duke of Edinburgh's Inquiry into British Housing endorsed the proposal that there should be a new basis for setting rents in both the public and private sectors. The recommendations made in this Report indicate a possible direction of reform of the Rent Act. The Inquiry concluded that all residential sector rents should be related to the capital (vacant possession) value of the properties concerned, thereby reflecting their popularity in market terms.[10] The Inquiry envisaged that 'capital value rents' would not be unregulated open market rents, but would be set in such a way as to achieve for the landlord a reasonable annual return on his capital investment. The Inquiry based the thrust of its recommendations on the (supposedly informed) surmise that a real return of approximately 4 per cent on capital value would be adequate to attract investment from financial institutions.[11] By supporting the proposal that 'capital value rents' should aim at this level of return, the Inquiry hoped to provide the cash incentive required for substantial re-investment in the housing market and renovation of the housing stock contained within it.[12]

The Inquiry's recommendations have been accorded a somewhat guarded welcome by the Institute of Rent Officers.[13] While acknowledging the need for a much revitalised rental market, the Institute has pointed out that the decline of private renting in this country has not been a direct result of a 'low rent' policy. This decline is attributed instead to a combination of social and economic factors, not least of which are 'the different perceptions which the general public and politicians have of this form of housing'.[14] The Institute has expressed doubt as to whether a system of 'capital value rents' based on a standard national percentage of, say, 4 per cent of capital value, would yield an acceptable uniformity of return across a country in which house prices vary so greatly.[15] Accordingly the Institute has proposed that the 'fair rents' fixed under the Rent Act should be replaced by 'equitable rents', which, while based on the concept of rent assessment by reference to capital values, would also have regard to 'variable equity growth'.[16] Thus in localities experiencing

---

7 Rent Act 1977, s 70(3)(a).
8 'This is consistent with the broad policy behind the Act...to preclude the landlord from taking, in additional rent, the benefit of works carried out by his tenant at his own, that is to say, at the tenant's, expense' (*Trustees of Henry Smith's Charity v Hemmings* (1983) 45 P & CR 377 at 381).
9 Rent Act 1977, s 70(3)(b).
10 *Report of the Inquiry into British Housing* (1985), p 19.
11 Ibid, p 19.
12 Ibid, p 51.
13 Institute of Rent Officers, *A Response to the Report of the Inquiry into British Housing* (October 1986).
14 Ibid, p 1. See also paras 1.4.1ff.
15 Ibid, paras 3.4.2ff, 4.3.2ff.
16 Ibid, para 4.1.1ff.

higher than national average equity growth, the applied yield factor would be relatively lower than elsewhere, the respective differentials continuing in force until such time as local equity growth rates fell into line with the national average.

No action has yet been taken to introduce either 'capital value rents' or 'equitable rents', but it is possible that both broadly foreshadow the future operation of the Rent Act. Either basis for the computation of rents would mean a marked departure from the level of comparable 'fair rents' at present enforced under this legislation. Another (somewhat less attractive) direction for future reform lies in the proposal that all new private residential lettings should be governed not by the Rent Act, but by the regulatory code heretofore applied only to business lettings under Part II of the Landlord and Tenant Act 1954. Pursuant to this legislation the tenant has a right, on the termination of his contractual tenancy, to request that a new tenancy be granted to him on terms which are either agreed between the parties or (in default of agreement) fixed by the court. Although the landlord may oppose the grant of a new tenancy only on certain limited grounds provided by statute,[17] it has been rare for the duration of any new tenancy granted by court order under the 1954 Act to exceed the length of the original term.

8. PROHIBITION OF UNLAWFUL PAYMENTS BY A REGULATED TENANT

It would make a nonsense of the Rent Act scheme if the 'fair rent' restriction on the amounts recoverable by a landlord could be circumvented by the exaction of an initial money consideration for the grant, renewal or assignment of a regulated tenancy. For this reason the Rent Act seeks to illegalise various kinds of lucrative trading in relation to regulated tenancies.[18]

(1) Premiums on grant, renewal or continuance

It is a criminal offence for any person[19] to require or receive a premium or loan as a condition of, or in connection with, the grant, renewal or continuance of a protected tenancy,[20] and the court may accordingly order the repayment of any illicit premium (or 'key money'[1]) so paid.[2]

---

17   Landlord and Tenant Act 1954, s 30(1).
18   'In the context of housing accommodation the most obvious and facile way of operating a black market where rents are controlled is to demand a premium—ie, a capital payment in connection with the grant etc of a tenancy over and above the rent as held statutorily below its true market rate. The history of rent control is a history of attempts to control the black market in rented housing accommodation by penalising criminally and nullifying civilly the taking of premiums' (*Farrell v Alexander* [1977] AC 59 at 87H-88A per Lord Simon of Glaisdale).
19   The ambit of the criminal provision is extensive, for the term 'any person' is wide enough to include such persons as landlords, tenants, agents, middlemen and relatives. Criminal liability here does not require that the recipient of the premium should necessarily have been some person already in receipt of rent (*Farrell v Alexander* [1977] AC 59 at 71E-G, 77B-F, 96A-B; (1977) 40 MLR 216 (A.S. Owen)). See also *Adair v Murrell* (1981) 263 Estates Gazette 66 at 69f (illegal premium recoverable from tenant's trustee in bankruptcy).
20   Rent Act 1977, s 119(1). (The maximum penalty is a fine of £100).
1   See *Kiriri Cotton Co Ltd v Ranchhoddas Keshavji Dewani* [1960] AC 192 at 205 per Lord Denning.
2   Rent Act 1977, s 125(1). See *Kiriri Cotton Co Ltd v Ranchhoddas Keshavji Dewani* [1960] AC 192 at 205. See also Lord Goff of Chieveley and Gareth Jones, *The Law of Restitution* (3rd edn London 1986), pp 125f, 408; R.C.A. White, (1981) LAG Bulletin 182.

For the present purpose the term 'premium' includes any pecuniary consideration received in addition to rent,[3] and may be sufficiently wide to cover any payments required or received otherwise than as rent. It is possible, for instance, that an excessive security deposit charged on a letting may constitute an unlawful 'premium'.[4] For this purpose an excessive deposit comprises any deposit which exceeds one-sixth of the annual rent payable by the tenant and is not 'reasonable in relation to the potential liability in respect of which it is paid'.[5]

(2) Premiums on assignment

The Rent Act contains a similar prohibition against premiums and loans on the assignment of protected tenancies,[6] although a proper apportionment of outgoings or money spent on alterations and fixtures is permissible.[7] For the purpose of all these provisions, the charging of an excessive price for furniture which the tenant is required to purchase under the terms of his tenancy is regarded as a premium.[8]

(3) Advance payments of rent

It is a criminal offence for the landlord to require the payment of rent excessively in advance of the rental period to which the rent relates.[9] Such requirement of advance payment is void and unenforceable, and rent for any rental period to which a prohibited requirement relates is irrecoverable from the tenant and, if already paid, may be recovered from the landlord.

9. RESTRICTION OF THE RIGHT TO LEVY DISTRESS

Where a tenant holds under a regulated tenancy, the landlord's right to distrain upon his goods is subject to an important limitation under the Rent Act 1977.[10] No distress may be levied except by leave of a county court.[11]

---

3   See the definition of 'premium' in Rent Act 1977, s 128(1). In *Hampstead Way Investment v Mawdsley* [1980] CLY 1617, a landlord had agreed that if the divorced wife of a previous tenant paid off rent arrears owed by him, she could have a regulated tenancy of the premises. It was held that the amount of these arrears represented an unlawful premium which was recoverable by her (see (1980) LAG Bulletin 295 (A. Arden)).
4   Rent Act 1977, s 128(1)(c), as substituted by Housing Act 1980, s 79.
5   Housing Act 1980, s 79(c). Some Canadian jurisdictions restrict the deposit payable by the tenant to merely one month's rent (see Ontario's Residential Tenancies Act (RSO 1980, c 452), s 9(1); but compare *Re Veltrusy Enterprises Ltd and Gallant* (1980) 110 DLR (3d) 100 at 102f).
6   Rent Act 1977, s 120(1), (2). The fear was once expressed that these provisions might render unlawful the payment of a premium on the assignment of a long lease, where an escalating ground rent subsequently took the letting outside the general immunity conferred by Rent Act 1977, s 5 (ante, p 983). See A.M. Prichard, *Unsaleable Flats*, (1980) 130 NLJ 271; but compare [1982] Conv 169.
7   Rent Act 1977, s 120(3), (4).
8   Rent Act 1977, s 123(1). See, however, *Nock v Munk* (1982) 263 Estates Gazette 1085 at 1087f.
9   Rent Act 1977, s 126(1).
10 On distress generally, see Chapter 14 (ante, p 510). The Law Commission has tentatively proposed the abolition of the remedy of distress (see *Distress for Rent* (Law Commission Working Paper No 97, May 1986), para 5.1(5)).
11 Rent Act 1977, s 147(1).

Furthermore, on any application for leave to levy distress against a regulated tenant, the county court is possessed of all the same powers with respect to adjournment, stay, suspension, postponement and otherwise as are conferred by section 100 of the Rent Act 1977 in relation to proceedings for possession of such a dwelling house.[12]

10. RESTRICTED CONTRACTS

Full protection under the Rent Act 1977 is available only in respect of the 'regulated tenancy' in either its 'protected' or 'statutory' form. Other kinds of residential arrangement may nevertheless qualify for the protection which is afforded under the Rent Act to the 'restricted contract'.[13] The latter protection is in many respects similar to, but less sophisticated and much less effective than, the protection conferred upon the regulated tenancy.

(1) Definition

A 'restricted contract' is defined in the Rent Act 1977 as 'a contract...whereby one person grants to another person, in consideration of a rent which includes payment for the use of furniture or for services, the right to occupy a dwelling as a residence'.[14] A restricted contract may be either a tenancy or a licence, but there is a clear implication in the Rent Act that a restricted contract can never exist unless the occupier is entitled to 'exclusive occupation' of at least some accommodation within a dwelling-house.[15] But where the occupier has such a right, it is irrelevant that he is also entitled to 'the use in common with any other person of other rooms or accommodation in the house.'

(a) Express inclusions

Several other kinds of residential circumstance are expressly brought within the ambit of the 'restricted contract'. A tenancy which is precluded from being a protected tenancy by reason only of the 'resident landlord' exception[16] is declared to constitute a restricted contract 'notwithstanding that the rent may not include payment for the use of furniture or for services'.[17] Similarly the absence of a rent component in respect of furniture or services does not preclude the possibility of a restricted contract where a tenant has exclusive occupation of some accommodation but shares the use of other accommodation in common either with his landlord or with his landlord and other persons.[18]

---

12   Ante, p 1022.
13   See the statement of Sir David Cairns in *Baldock v Murray* (1981) 257 Estates Gazette 281 at 282, that the tenancies excluded from full protection by reason of Rent Act 1977, ss 8-12, 'are all capable of being restricted contracts.'
14   Rent Act 1977, s 19(2). Restricted contracts used to be known as 'Part VI contracts' in the terminology of Rent Act 1968.
15   See Rent Act 1977, s 19(6).
16   Rent Act 1977, s 12 (ante, p 987).
17   Rent Act 1977, s 20.
18   Rent Act 1977, s 21. This provision is applicable, however, only where the tenant would have had a protected tenancy but for the element of common user or the presence of a resident landlord (Rent Act 1977, s 21(c)). In other words, the occupation cannot give rise to a restricted contract if it is precluded from being a protected tenancy for some other reason, eg that the rateable value of the property lies outside the Rent Act limits.

The restricted contract thus defined applies to most contractual occupation licences. Such licences can never, of course, qualify as protected tenancies under the Rent Act simply by reason of the fact that they are 'licences' as distinct from 'tenancies'. To claim even a restricted contract, however, the contractual licensee must show that he is entitled to exclusive occupation of at least some part (eg a separate bed-sitting room) of the dwelling-house in question.[19]

(b) Express exclusions

Certain residential arrangements are expressly excluded from possible status as a restricted contract. No restricted contract can arise where the relevant dwelling-house has a rateable value in excess of specified statutory limits.[20] Nor can a contract constitute a restricted contract if it creates a regulated tenancy.[1] No restricted contract can exist in relation to a letting by the Crown or by a government department,[2] or to a tenancy granted by a housing association or housing trust or by the Housing Corporation.[3] Nor can a restricted contract comprise any contract 'for the letting of any premises at a rent which includes payment in respect of board if the value of the board to the lessee forms a substantial proportion of the whole rent'.[4]

(2) Security of tenure

Restricted contracts fall within the jurisdiction of the area rent tribunal, which has power to provide certain forms of indirect protection for occupiers holding under a restricted contract. The security of tenure conferred on a restricted contract differs according to whether the contract was granted before or after the commencement date of the Housing Act 1980.[5]

(a) Restricted contracts granted before the Housing Act 1980

Complicated provisions govern the security of tenure enjoyed under a restricted contract which was concluded before the commencement date of the Housing Act 1980. In general terms, the occupier under such a contract has in the first instance no security of tenure at all. The rent tribunal has power to order a postponement of any notice to quit which is served on the occupier, but this jurisdiction in matters of security of tenure is exercisable only in

---

19 Rent Act 1977, s 21(a).
20 Rent Act 1977, s 19(4). The designated limits are such as to rule out only luxury accommodation.
1   Rent Act 1977, s 19(5)(a). Thus the borderline between the restricted contract and the protected tenancy is strictly preserved. The wording of section 19(5)(a) is, however, somewhat ambiguous (see *Baldock v Murray* (1981) 257 Estates Gazette 281 at 282).
2   Rent Act 1977, s 19(5)(b), as amended by Housing Act 1980, s 73(2).
3   Rent Act 1977, s 19(5)(e). The Housing Corporation is a public body which is statutorily empowered to purchase and develop land for lease or sale, and to lend money to and control the operations of housing associations. Its powers were greatly expanded by the Housing Act 1974.
4   Rent Act 1977, s 19(5)(c).
5   The commencement date was 29 November 1980.

conjunction with an application to a rent tribunal for registration of a 'reasonable' rent.[6]

' *(i) Applications for registration of a 'reasonable' rent* If after a restricted contract has been referred to a rent tribunal for rent registration, the landlord serves on the occupier a notice to quit the premises, that notice cannot normally take effect before the expiry of a period of six months following the tribunal's determination of the reference.[7] If a notice to quit is served before the occupier has made any application for rent registration, the occupier may refer the restricted contract to a rent tribunal for rent registration at any time *before* the expiry of the notice to quit. In this event, the protective jurisdiction of the rent tribunal will be activated by the reference in respect of rent, with the result that it is open to the tribunal to order a postponement of the notice to quit for a period of up to six months.[8] Further postponements may be granted in the discretion of the tribunal, although the tribunal may in any case substitute a shorter period than six months.

(ii) Necessity for court proceedings Even where the rent tribunal's discretion to postpone possession has finally been exhausted, there exists one last protection for the occupier under a restricted contract. It is not lawful for the owner to enforce his right to possession except by proceedings in court.[9]

(iii) Special ground of repossession Even the limited security of tenure conferred on the pre-1980 restricted contract can be overridden by a special ground of recovery which is available in certain circumstances to the owner of property subject to a restricted contract. A ground of immediate recovery of possession is open to an owner-occupier who, by virtue of a restricted contract, has granted the right to occupy a dwelling to another person. Such an owner-occupier may recover possession on the expiry of a notice to quit if 'at the time the notice is to take effect, the dwelling is required as a residence for the owner-occupier or any member of his family who resided with him when he last occupied the dwelling as a residence'.[10]

This right of recovery is, however, constrained by certain conditions. *First*, the 'owner-occupier' must originally have occupied the dwelling in question 'as a residence'. *Second*, he must at or before the commencement of the restricted contract have given to the occupier a notice in writing 'that he is the owner-occupier within the meaning of [section 105].' *Third*, the owner-occupier must not occupy any part of the dwelling-house during the currency of the restricted contract.

6   Post, p 1043.
7   Rent Act 1977, s 103(1).
8   Rent Act 1977, s 104(1). However, even this limited security of tenure is lost if the occupier fails to apply to the tribunal within the period of the notice to quit (see Rent Act 1977, s 104(1)(c)). Moreover, the protective powers of the rent tribunal are in any event available only if a notice to quit is required in order to terminate the restricted contract in question. No notice to quit is necessary in the case of either a fixed term or an occupation licence: both come to an end automatically in accordance with their terms.
9   Protection from Eviction Act 1977, s 3(1).
10 Rent Act 1977, s 105. This provision is effectively the analogue of the mandatory ground for possession in respect of a regulated tenancy under Case 11 of the Rent Act 1977, Sch 15, Part II (ante, p 1024).

(b) Restricted contracts granted after the Housing Act 1980

The law relating to security of tenure is substantially different in relation to restricted contracts granted *after* the commencement of the Housing Act 1980. Sections 103 to 106 of the Rent Act 1977 have no application to such contracts.[11] Instead it is provided that a court may grant a postponement of no longer than three months in respect of any order for possession made in favour of the owner of the property.[12] It therefore becomes much easier for the owner to recover his property, but the limited security of tenure now enjoyed by the occupier under a post-1980 restricted contract is supplemented by the disappearance of the owner-occupier's ground of repossession under section 105 of the Rent Act 1977. Moreover, even if he is merely a licensee the occupier under a post-1980 restricted contract cannot ultimately be evicted except by court order.[13]

(3) Restriction of rents

In the case of a restricted contract either the owner or the occupier (or indeed the local authority) may refer the contract to a rent tribunal for the determination of a 'reasonable' rent.[14] The tribunal may then fix a 'reasonable' rent after making inquiries and hearing any representations made by either party.[15] The rent so fixed is entered in a register of rents maintained by the relevant local authority,[16] and may not be the subject of any reference to a rent tribunal during the following two years except where both owner and occupier apply jointly for a reconsideration of the rent or where, by reason of a change of circumstance, the registered rent is no longer a 'reasonable' rent.[17] It is illegal to require or receive any amount in excess of a registered rent,[18] and any excess paid is recoverable by the occupier.[19]

11 Housing Act 1980, s 69(3).
12 Rent Act 1977, s 106A(2), (3), as added by Housing Act 1980, s 69(2). In granting relief under Rent Act 1977, s 106A, the court must impose conditions as to payment of rent and arrears except in cases of 'exceptional hardship' or where such an order would otherwise be 'unreasonable' (see Rent Act 1977, s 106A(4), as added by Housing Act 1980, s 69(2)). However, the court's powers are not subject to the restrictions contained in Housing Act 1980, s 89 (ante, p 1024). Section 89 normally limits the court's power to postpone the date for the giving up of possession to a mere 14 days after the date of the court order, but see the exception made in the case of restricted contracts (Housing Act 1980, s 89(2)(d)).
13 Protection from Eviction Act 1977, s 3(2A), as added by Housing Act 1980, s 69(1). In the absence of any duly served notice to quit or court order for possession, an occupier under a restricted contract who is summarily evicted is not relegated to a mere claim in damages for breach of contract. He may regain possession by way of proceedings under CCR, Ord 24 (see eg *Borg v Rogers* (Unreported, Court of Appeal, 30 November 1981)). Where the occupier does not seek to be reinstated in possession, substantial exemplary damages may still be awarded for unlawful eviction (see eg *Chrysostomou v Georgiou* (1982) LAG Bulletin 33).
14 Rent Act 1977, s 77(1). In practice 'reasonable' rents are almost always higher than 'fair' rents in respect of the same premises, thus confirming, incidentally, the idea that 'fair' rents are by definition 'unreasonable' rents.
15 Rent Act 1977, s 78(2).
16 Rent Act 1977, s 79(1).
17 Rent Act 1977, s 80(2), as amended by Housing Act 1980, s 70(1).
18 Rent Act 1977, s 81(1).
19 Rent Act 1977, s 81(3).

(4) Prohibition of unlawful premiums

The provisions of the Rent Act which prohibit certain premiums[20] are extended to apply to similar payments which are required as a condition of the grant, renewal, continuance or assignment of rights conferred by a restricted contract, so long as the rent payable under that contract is registered.[1]

20   Ante, p 1038.
1   Rent Act 1977, s 122(1), (2).

CHAPTER 30

Statutory protection in the public sector

For more than 70 years the Rent Acts have provided some form of statutory protection for the residential tenant in the private sector. It was not until the enactment of the Housing Act 1980 that any equivalent regime was introduced for the residential tenants of various kinds of public and quasi-public landlord. Prior to 1980, as Brandon LJ observed in *Harrison v Hammersmith and Fulham LBC*,[1] there had been a broad assumption that it was 'safe and proper to give to local authority landlords a complete discretion with regard to the eviction of public sector tenants, and to rely on them to exercise such discretion fairly and wisely.' The Housing Act 1980 was not, however, a response to any immediate or urgent crisis in housing accommodation. Its purpose was instead 'the social one of giving to tenants in the public housing sector, so far as reasonably practicable, the same kind of protection from being evicted from their homes without good and sufficient cause as had been enjoyed by tenants in the private housing sector for many decades under the Rent Acts.'[2]

Accordingly Chapter II of Part I of the Housing Act 1980 was largely directed towards an assimilation of rights as between public and private sector tenants 'in the general interests of social equality and non-discrimination'.[3] The Act introduced a new legal status for the public sector tenant as a 'secure tenant', and in recognising this category of tenant the statute went a long way towards establishing a 'charter of rights' in the area of public housing. This 'charter of rights' has a huge coverage in terms of the national population, extending in 1984 to some 6,065,000 homes in Great Britain and thereby accounting for 27.9 per cent of all households.[4]

The protection conferred on public sector tenants by the Housing Act 1980 is now contained in Part IV of the Housing Act 1985. Although the 1985 Act extends to the public sector many of the protective devices which have been pioneered under successive Rent Acts, the new public sector regime differs from the current Rent Act in certain important respects. The present chapter is largely devoted to an exploration of these differences.

1. DEFINITION OF 'SECURE TENANCY'

The central concept in Part IV of the Housing Act 1985 is that of the 'secure tenancy'. This form of tenancy underpins the statutory code relating to the

---

1 [1981] 1 WLR 650 at 661D-E. See [1982] Conv 218 (P.F. Smith).
2 [1981] 1 WLR 650 at 661C.
3 [1981] 1 WLR 650 at 661D.
4 OPCS Monitor, *General Household Survey* (Reference GHS 86/1, 18 September 1986), p 5f. See also Building Societies Association Bulletin No 44 (October 1985), p 21 (Table 2). The proportion of households falling within the public housing sector has declined from 34 per cent in 1981, this trend being attributable to the exercise by council tenants of their statutory 'right to buy'.

public residential sector, affording in effect the analogue of the 'protected tenancy' in the private residential sector. The 'secure tenancy', as defined by the Housing Act 1985, carries with it a number of significant implied terms for the regulation of the landlord-tenant relationship. The 'secure tenant' is, moreover, 'secure' in the sense that he enjoys a relative permanence of tenure which can be terminated only by a court order based on one or other of the grounds stipulated in the 1985 Act. The 'secure tenant' enjoys in addition one special right—the 'right to buy'—which has little if any parallel in the private landlord-tenant relationship.[5]

(1) The two conditions

Before a tenancy can attain recognition as a 'secure tenancy', it must be shown that two statutorily prescribed conditions are fulfilled. A 'secure tenancy' exists for the purpose of the Housing Act 1985 only if the conditions described in the Housing Act 1985 as respectively 'the landlord condition' and 'the tenant condition' are simultaneously satisfied.[6] If either of these conditions ceases to be fulfilled in respect of any given tenancy, that tenancy automatically ceases to be a 'secure tenancy'.

(a) The landlord condition

The essence of 'the landlord condition' is that the dwelling-house must belong to one or other of a number of public or quasi-public bodies. These bodies include a local authority, a new town corporation, an urban development corporation, the Development Board for Rural Wales, the Housing Corporation, a charitable housing trust and specified housing associations and housing co-operatives.[7] However, the landlord condition is not satisfied where the landlord's interest is jointly owned and only one of the joint owners is a prescribed authority.[8] It may therefore be open to a local authority to use a joint letting device in order to frustrate the 'right to buy' which would otherwise be available to the tenant as a 'secure tenant'.

(b) The tenant condition

The essence of 'the tenant condition' is that the tenant must be an 'individual' and must occupy the relevant dwelling-house as his 'only or principal home'.[9]

(i) The tenant must be an 'individual' This element of 'the tenant condition' mirrors the way in which a statutory tenancy under the Rent Act is available only to a human tenant.[10] However, the Housing Act 1985 does depart from

---

5   On the 'right to buy', see Chapter 19 (ante, p 733). See also the limited 'rights of first refusal' now conferred on certain private residential tenants in connection with the sale of their landlord's reversion (Landlord and Tenant Act 1987, s 1 ante, p 926).
6   Housing Act 1985, s 79(1).
7   Housing Act 1985, s 80(1).
8   *R v Plymouth CC, ex parte Freeman* (1987) *Times*, 23 April.
9   Housing Act 1985, s 81.
10   Ante, p 1007.

the historic pattern of housing legislation in its explicit recognition of the possible existence of joint tenancy.[11] It is clear that a secure tenancy may be held by joint tenants, provided that each of the joint tenants is an 'individual' and at least one of them occupies the dwelling-house as his 'only or principal home'.[12]

(ii) The tenant must occupy the dwelling-house as his 'only or principal home' There is no statutory explication of the idea that the tenant must occupy the dwelling-house as his 'only or principal home'. It is likely that this phrase is to be construed on a par with the interpretation accorded similar terminology in the Leasehold Reform Act 1967.[13] It is thus feasible in theory that a public sector tenant may also own another house. However, it seems clear that the Housing Act 1985 will not be interpreted on the benevolent analogy of the Rent Act statutory tenancy so as to enable a tenant to occupy more than one dwelling-house as a secure tenant.[14]

(2) There may be either a tenancy or a licence

In a major departure from the pattern of the Rent Act, the definition of the 'secure tenancy' is specially extended to cover not merely a tenancy in the strict sense[15] but also a licence to occupy a dwelling-house,[16] provided that the licence otherwise fulfils the conditions required of a secure tenancy.[17] The precise coverage of the secure tenancy does not therefore depend on the controversial borderline between the concepts of tenancy and licence.[18] This statutory assimilation of tenancies and licences does not, however, extend to any licence which was granted as a 'temporary expedient' to a person who entered the relevant dwelling-house 'or any other land' as a trespasser.[19] Thus it is clear that no secure tenancy can be claimed by a person who, for instance, enters vacant local authority property initially as a squatter but who is later given some short-life occupation licence in respect of that property.[20]

(3) There must be a 'dwelling-house'

A secure tenancy can arise only in relation to a 'dwelling-house'.[1] Little guidance is given by the Housing Act 1985 as to the meaning of this term other

---

11 Ante, p 981.
12 Housing Act 1985, s 81.
13 See Leasehold Reform Act 1967, s 1(1)(b) (ante, p 728). See also *Frost v Feltham* [1981] 1 WLR 452 at 455D-G.
14 The secure tenancy may be either a periodic or a fixed term, although the latter form is somewhat rare.
15 Ante, p 429.
16 Housing Act 1985, s 79(3).
17 This proviso was formerly made explicit in Housing Act 1980, s 48(1), and had for instance the effect of excluding from the Housing Act such arrangements as the genuine non-exclusive occupation licence (see *Family Housing Association v Miah* (1982) 5 HLR 94 at 101). The precise wording of Housing Act 1980, s 48(1) does not appear in the 1985 Act, but the sense seems to be preserved in the requirement that a secure tenancy can arise only where a dwelling-house has been 'let as a separate dwelling'.
18 Ante, p 443.
19 Housing Act 1985, s 79(4).
20 See also *Restormel BC v Buscombe* (1982) 14 HLR 91 at 98ff.
1   Housing Act 1985, s 79(1).

than that it may comprise 'a house or part of a house'.[2] For want of any more substantial aid to construction, the interpretation of the term must follow the analogy of the Rent Act 1977.[3]

(4) The relevant dwelling-house must be 'let as a separate dwelling'

A secure tenancy can likewise exist only where the relevant dwelling-house is 'let as a separate dwelling'.[4] This unanalysed phrase, which occurs in the direct Rent Act analogy, contains a veritable jungle of complication, not least in respect of the 'singular construction' to be accorded to lettings falling within the Act.[5] The proper construction of the phrase must sadly incorporate all the foibles exposed in the equivalent Rent Act context.[6]

(5) Express exclusion from the scope of a secure tenancy

Certain lettings are expressly excluded from the scope of the 'secure tenancy'. These exceptions include long leases for a term exceeding 21 years[7] and tenancies granted in conjunction with a contract of employment where the employee is required to occupy a dwelling-house 'for the better performance of his duties'.[8] No secure tenancy can arise from a letting to a student who is given notification by his landlord of his insecure status under the Housing Act 1985.[9] A tenancy granted by a local authority to a homeless person in pursuance of Part III of the Housing Act 1985[10] does not normally become a secure tenancy until twelve months after the local authority has notified the applicant for accommodation that it regards him as 'homeless' within the meaning of the Act.[11] A tenancy may also be excluded from security for a period of one year if it was granted to a person who (not having been resident in the district immediately prior to the grant) required temporary accommodation in order to take up an offer of employment which was available to him within that district or surrounding area.[12]

2. LOCAL AUTHORITY ALLOCATION OF SECURE TENANCIES

The management of public sector housing is dominated nowadays by two factors, the excess of demand over supply and the steady deterioration of pubicly owned housing stock.

2 Housing Act 1985, s 112(1).
3 Ante, p 971.
4 Housing Act 1985, s 79(1).
5 Ante, p 975.
6 See eg *Thompson v City of Glasgow DC* 1986 SLT (Lands Tr) 6 at 10E–H, where it was held that a room had not been 'let as a separate dwelling' in that the essential living activities of the occupier were not confined to the premises let.
7 Housing Act 1985, s 115(1), Sch 1, para 1.
8 Housing Act 1985, Sch 1, para 2(1). This exception is extended to cover certain police officers and firemen (para 2(2), (3)).
9 Housing Act 1985, Sch 1, para 10(1)
10 Ante, p 775.
11 Housing Act 1985, Sch 1, para 4(1). See *Family Housing Association v Miah* (1982) 5 HLR 94 at 100; *Eastleigh BC v Walsh* [1985] 1 WLR 525 at 530F–H (ante, p 455).
12 Housing Act 1985, Sch 1, para 5(1).

(1) The current state of the public housing sector

Local housing authorities are statutorily charged with a responsibility to consider both 'housing conditions in their district' and 'the needs of the district with respect to the provision of further housing accommodation'.[13] Each housing authority is invested with a power (but is not subjected to any duty) to provide housing accommodation through the construction of new houses, conversion of existing buildings or acquisition of new properties.[14] It was nevertheless clear that by 1986-1987 net public expenditure on housing had fallen in cash terms by some 27 per cent as against the equivalent level of expenditure in 1980-1981.[15] Likewise the annual net gain in United Kingdom public sector housing stock, which had averaged 170,000 dwelling-houses during the 1960s and 139,000 dwelling-houses as recently as the period 1976-1980, dwindled by 1985 to 43,000 dwelling-houses.[16] As if this picture were not already bleak, local authorities in England and Wales reported that 321,000 of the dwellings owned by them in April 1985 were 'difficult to let'.[17] The defective condition of much public sector housing has in fact resulted in 120,000 local authority dwellings lying vacant.[18] Meanwhile there were in 1984 nearly 922,000 applicants on waiting lists for local authority accommodation, of whom a chilling 14 per cent had been waiting for nine years or more.[19]

(2) Selection of council tenants

The factors outlined above convert the allocation of council housing into an extremely complex exercise in distributive justice. Each local housing authority has virtually unlimited discretion in the way in which it allocates its available housing stock to those on waiting lists.[20] Most authorities apply some form of residence qualification and most inevitably use some version of a 'points system' in assessing the relative needs of applicants.[1] Virtually the only statutory direction governing a housing authority's selection of tenants is the injunction that 'a reasonable preference' should be given to persons occupying insanitary or overcrowded houses, to persons having large families, to persons living 'under unsatisfactory housing conditions', and to persons who have been found to be 'homeless' within the terms of Part III of the Housing Act 1985.[2]

The applicant for housing probably has, in the first instance, nothing more

---

13 Housing Act 1985, s 8(1).
14 Housing Act 1985, s 9(1).
15 Central Statistical Office, *Social Trends No 17* (1987 edn London), p 143 (Chart 8.13). These percentages are not adjusted for price inflation.
16 *Social Trends No 17*, p 143 (Table 8.12).
17 *Social Trends No 17*, p 144 (82 per cent of these dwellings being situated in metropolitan areas).
18 *Social Trends No 17*, p 144.
19 *Social Trends No 17*, p 144f (Table 8.15). In the case of those currently in privately rented accommodation, this proportion rose to 17 per cent.
20 Housing Act 1985, s 21(1). See, however, Sex Discrimination Act 1975, s 30(1); Race Relations Act 1976, s 21(1) (ante, p 483).
1 See (1973) LAG Bulletin 170. Each housing authority must publish a summary of its rules for determining priority as between applicants in the allocation of its housing accommodation (Housing Act 1985, s 106(1)(a)), and the rules must be made freely available for inspection at all reasonable hours in the council's principal office (Housing Act 1985, s 106(2)).
2 Housing Act 1985, s 22.

than a mere right to have his application considered fairly, but any failure by an authority to accord 'fair' consideration is challengeable by way of proceedings for judicial review. In *R v Canterbury CC, ex parte Gillespie*,[3] for instance, a housing applicant (who had two children) had left a council dwelling in another area which she had held as a joint tenant with her erstwhile cohabitee. The housing authority to whom she now applied refused to accept her on to its waiting list. It justified this refusal on the ground that it had a policy of declining (except in certain strictly defined circumstances which were clearly inapplicable here) to consider any application made by a person who had an interest in a local authority dwelling in any other area. The applicant then attempted in vain to surrender her existing joint tenancy, but was thereafter unwilling to take proceedings to oust her former cohabitee since to do so would have made him homeless. The housing authority to whom she had applied later decided to accept her on to its list, but to refuse to consider her for accommodation.

The applicant was subsequently successful in obtaining judicial review of the authority's exercise of its discretionary powers in the management and control of its housing stock.[4] Simon Brown J, while conceding that a local authority was perfectly entitled to formulate general guidelines for the exercise of discretion, held that the housing authority could not apply such guidelines blindly without a proper assessment of 'the individual considerations of the applicant's case'. The applicant's challenge was successful not because the authority's allocations policy was 'intrinsically irrational', but because it constituted a 'rule which requires to be followed slavishly rather than merely a stated general approach which is always subject to an exceptional case and which permits each application to be individually considered.'

3. TERMS OF THE SECURE TENANCY

The terms of a secure tenancy comprise, in part, terms derived from the common law of landlord and tenant and, in part, terms which are stipulated by statute. Every landlord authority which grants a secure tenancy must publish up-to-date information about its secure tenancies,[5] which explains 'in simple terms' the effect of the express terms of its secure tenancies, the provisions of Part IV of the Housing Act 1985 and the statutory 'right to buy',[6] and the extent of the landlord's repairing obligations under the Landlord and Tenant Act 1985.[7] The landlord under a secure tenancy must also supply every secure tenant with a copy of this information together with a written statement of the terms of the tenancy, 'so far as they are neither expressed in the lease or written tenancy agreement (if any) nor implied by law'.[8]

---

3   (1986) Legal Action 136.
4   See also *Bristol DC v Clark* [1975] 1 WLR 1443 at 1448G-1449D.
5   Housing Act 1985, s 104(1).
6   Ante, p 733.
7   Ante, p 919.
8   Housing Act 1985, s 104(2). Variation of the terms of a tenancy agreement can be achieved only in the manner prescribed by Housing Act 1985, ss 102, 103, with the rider that the statutory variation notice required by these provisions has no relevance to variations of the rent or of payments in respect of services or facilities provided by the landlord or of payments in respect of rates (see Housing Act 1985, s 103(3)).

(1) Rent

In relation to secure tenants there exists no formal mechanism for the control of rent levels. An attempt was made in the Housing Finance Act 1972 to institute a 'fair rent' scheme to cover public sector tenants,[9] but since such a scheme would have had the effect in most cases of raising rent levels the scheme was abandoned in 1975.[10] Instead the present position is that a local housing authority may simply make 'such reasonable charges' as it may determine for the tenancy or occupation of its houses.[11] This power must be exercised by local authorities in conjunction with the statutory rent rebate scheme contained in the Social Security and Housing Benefits Act 1982.[12] The housing authority must from time to time review rents and 'make such changes, either of rents generally or of particular rents, as circumstances may require'.[13] Any unreasonable increase in the rent exacted may be challenged by proceedings for judicial review.[14]

(2) Assignment

The residential status conferred by a secure tenancy is essentially personal, non-commerciable and non-transmissible. The Housing Act 1985 thus incorporates a general prohibition of assignment in the case of most secure tenancies. A secure tenancy which is a periodic tenancy or a tenancy for a term certain granted on or after 5 November 1982 is incapable of being assigned except in three special cases.[15] These exceptional cases comprise the following circumstances.

(a) Assignment by way of exchange

It is a term of every secure tenancy that the tenant may, with the written consent of the landlord, assign his tenancy to another secure tenant who has likewise obtained his landlord's consent to the assignment of *his* tenancy either to the first secure tenant or to another similarly qualified tenant.[16] For this purpose the landlord's consent can be withheld only on one or other of the grounds laid down in Schedule 3 of the Housing Act 1985.[17] Thus, for instance, the landlord may decline to give his consent where either the assignor or the assignee is already obliged by court order to give up possession,[18] or where any

---

9   See Housing Finance Act 1972, s 49ff.
10 Housing Rents and Subsidies Act 1975, s 1(1).
11 Housing Act 1985, s 24(1). A 'fair rent' scheme operates in relation to quasi-public tenancies (such as those granted by the Housing Corporation, housing associations and housing trusts) in much the same manner as the 'fair rent' scheme which currently governs regulated tenancies under the Rent Act (see Rent Act 1977, s 86ff).
12 Social Security and Housing Benefits Act 1982, s 28ff.
13 Housing Act 1985, s 24(2). The authority may have reference to the relative means of different tenants in deciding rent increases for similar houses in the same area (see *Leeds Corpn v Jenkinson* [1935] 1 KB 168 at 175ff; but see also *Luby v Newcastle-under-Lyme Corpn* [1965] 1 QB 214 at 231A-B).
14 *Wandsworth LBC v Winder* [1985] AC 461 at 509D-510C.
15 Housing Act 1985, s 91(1). Even in these cases assignment is valid only if it is effected by deed or if there was sufficient writing to satisfy the rule in *Walsh v Lonsdale* (1882) 21 Ch D 9 (ante, p 471) or if there was part performance.
16 Housing Act 1985, s 92(1), (2). See [1985] Conv 76.
17 Housing Act 1985, s 92(3), as amended by Housing and Planning Act 1986, Sch 5, para 7.
18 Housing Act 1985, Sch 3, Ground 1.

of the first six grounds of Schedule 2 is satisfied,[19] or where the accommodation is substantially more extensive than is required by the proposed assignee[20] or is not reasonably suitable to the needs of such a person and his family.[1]

The net effect of these provisions is to confer on the secure tenant a 'right of exchange',[2] effectively injecting a limited element of transferability into the regime of the secure tenancy. However, any attempt to exact a premium as the price of such an exchange may expose the tenant to possession proceedings within Schedule 2 of the 1985 Act.[3]

(b) Assignment pursuant to a property transfer order

A secure tenancy constitutes transferable 'property' for the purpose of the court's jurisdiction to order transfers of property on or after the granting of divorce.[4] The court may thus order the transfer of a local authority tenancy from one spouse to another in exercise of the jurisdiction conferred by the Matrimonial Causes Act 1973.[5]

(c) Assignment to a potential successor

It is open to a secure tenant to accelerate the statutory devolution of his secure tenancy by assigning it to 'a person who would be qualified to succeed the tenant if the tenant died immediately before the assignment'.[6] Such an assignment may provide one means of resolving in advance a potential dispute between competing claimants to the statutory succession.

(3) Subletting

It is a term of every secure tenancy that the tenant has an unconditional right to allow any persons to reside as 'lodgers' in his dwelling-house.[7] The secure tenant may not, however, sublet or part with possession of *part* of the dwelling-house without the written consent of the landlord,[8] although such consent must not be unreasonably withheld.[9] The Housing Act 1985 effectively gives the secure tenant a qualified authority to sublet or part with possession, but this

---

19   Housing Act 1985, Sch 3, Ground 2.
20   Housing Act 1985, Sch 3, Ground 3.
 1   Housing Act 1985, Sch 3, Ground 4. Schedule 3 contains other grounds, related principally to 'special needs' accommodation.
 2   Housing Act 1985, s 91(3)(a).
 3   Housing Act 1985, Sch 2, Ground 6 (post, p 1056).
 4   See *Hale v Hale* [1975] 1 WLR 931 at 937E-H.
 5   Housing Act 1985, s 91(3)(b). See Matrimonial Causes Act 1973, s 24(1)(a); *Thompson v Thompson* [1976] Fam 25 at 29G; *Rodewald v Rodewald* [1977] Fam 192 at 196C-D. However, an even wider power of transfer of secure tenancies is conferred on the divorce court by the Matrimonial Homes Act 1983, Sch 1, Part I, para 1(1)(c) (ante, p 1004).
 6   Housing Act 1985, s 91(3)(c) (post, pp 1054, 1059). See, however, *Governors of the Peabody Donation Fund v Higgins* [1983] 1 WLR 1091.
 7   Housing Act 1985, s 93(1)(a). The term 'lodger' is not defined in the Housing Act 1985, and falls to be construed in accordance with the decision of the House of Lords in *Street v Mountford* [1985] AC 809 (ante, p 455).
 8   Housing Act 1985, s 93(1)(b).
 9   Housing Act 1985, s 94(2). If consent is withheld unreasonably, it is treated as if it had in fact been given.

privilege is limited to transactions relating to 'part' only of the dwelling-house. If the secure tenant sublets or parts with possession of the whole of the dwelling-house, the tenancy ceases to be a secure tenancy and cannot subsequently become a secure tenancy.[10]

The reasonableness of a withholding of consent may be measured in particular by whether the giving of consent would lead to statutory 'overcrowding' of the premises and by whether subletting is feasible in the light of any works which the landlord proposes to carry out on the dwelling-house or on the building of which it forms a part.[11] Consent cannot be given conditionally,[12] and if the tenant makes a written application for his landlord's consent to a subletting, the landlord must either give such consent or supply the tenant with a written statement of its reasons for refusing consent.[13]

(4) Maintenance and repair

The law relating to obligations of maintenance and repair under a secure tenancy has already been dealt with in Chapter 27.[14]

(5) Improvements

It is a statutorily implied term of every secure tenancy that the tenant will not make any improvement without the written consent of the landlord.[15] For this purpose an 'improvement' means 'any alteration in, or addition to, a dwelling-house',[16] and includes any change affecting landlord's fixtures and fittings or the provision of services to the dwelling-house,[17] the erection of a wireless or television aerial,[18] and the carrying out of external decoration.[19] However, the landlord must not unreasonably withhold its consent to any proposed improvement,[20] and its consent, if unreasonably withheld, is treated as having been duly given.[1]

(a) Reasonableness of consent

The reasonableness of a consent to a proposed improvement may be measured in particular by reference to whether the improvement would be likely to affect factors of safety, or would cause the landlord to incur otherwise avoidable

---

10 Housing Act 1985, s 93(2). This provision cannot be evaded by two or more sublettings, each of only a 'part' of the premises.
11 Housing Act 1985, s 94(3).
12 Housing Act 1985, s 94(5).
13 Housing Act 1985, s 94(6).
14 Ante, p 944.
15 Housing Act 1985, s 97(1).
16 Housing Act 1985, s 97(2).
17 Housing Act 1985, s 97(2)(a), (b).
18 Housing Act 1985, s 97(2)(c).
19 Housing Act 1985, s 97(2)(d).
20 The onus is on the landlord to show that any withholding of consent was not unreasonable (Housing Act 1985, s 98(1)). If the tenant makes a written application for his landlord's consent to a subletting, the landlord must either give such consent (whether conditionally or otherwise) or supply the tenant with a written statement of its reasons for refusing consent (Housing Act 1985, s 98(4)(a)).
1 Housing Act 1985, s 97(3). See also Housing Act 1985, s 98(4)(b).

expenditure, or would reduce either the open market price or the letting value of the property.[2] Consent may be given conditionally,[3] but a failure by a tenant to satisfy a reasonable condition imposed by his landlord is treated as a breach of an obligation of the tenancy and may lead to possession proceedings against the tenant.[4]

(b) Financial implications

Where, with the written consent of his landlord, a secure tenant has made an improvement which has materially added to the likely open market price or letting value of the property, the landlord has a discretionary power to reimburse the cost of the improvements at or after the end of his tenancy.[5] The amount which may be reimbursed to the tenant is such amount 'as the landlord considers to be appropriate',[6] and must not exceed the cost or likely cost of the improvement after deducting any improvement grant, repair grant or other grant available in respect of the relevant improvement.[7] The rent payable by an 'improving tenant' (or by his 'qualifying successor'[8]) is not to be increased on account of the improvements made except to the extent that the rent increase corresponds to a part of the cost of the improvement which was not borne by the tenant.[9]

4. SECURITY OF TENURE

Certain important provisions relating to security of tenure are conferred on public and quasi-public tenants by the Housing Act 1985. These provisions comprise, first, the scheme for statutory succession to the tenancy on the death of the secure tenant and, second, the more general protection afforded to the secure tenant against repossession of his home by the landlord.

(1) Statutory succession to a secure tenancy

The Housing Act 1985 contains a scheme of statutory succession modelled upon the Rent Act provisions for the devolution of private sector regulated tenancies. In essence the 1985 Act allows for one succession to a secure tenancy to occur on the death of the secure tenant,[10] with the result that the secure

---

2   Housing Act 1985, s 98(2).
3   Housing Act 1985, s 99(1). A landlord's consent which is subject to an unreasonable condition constitutes an unreasonable withholding of consent, provided that the tenant initially applied in writing for the relevant consent (Housing Act 1985, s 99(2)).
4   Housing Act 1985, s 99(4).
5   Housing Act 1985, s 100(1). This provision applies only to improvements begun on or after 3 October 1980.
6   Housing Act 1985, s 100(1).
7   Housing Act 1985, s 100(2). See Housing Act 1985, Part XV, as amended by Housing and Planning Act 1986, s 15, Sch 3.
8   See Housing Act 1985, s 101(3).
9   Housing Act 1985, s 101(2). The amount of any improvement, repair or other grant obtained by the tenant in connection with the carrying out of the improvement is deemed for this purpose to have been money provided by the tenant (Housing Act 1985, s 101(1)).
10   This one permissible succession is deemed to have been exhausted by the operation of survivorship between joint secure tenants (Housing Act 1985, s 88(1)(b)).

tenancy may pass either to the secure tenant's surviving spouse or to a member of his family. The operation of this scheme of statutory succession is dealt with in Chapter 31.[11]

(2) Protection against possession or termination

The Housing Act 1985 imposes strict limitations on the ways in which the public or quasi-public tenant may lose his status as a secure tenant. It is clear that a secure tenancy comes to an end if the tenant has sublet or parted with possession of the whole of his dwelling-house,[12] or has assigned it (other than in certain exceptional circumstances[13]). Likewise the secure tenant ceases to be a secure tenant if and when he exercises his statutory 'right to buy'[14] or his right to be granted a shared ownership lease.[15] In all other cases the loss of a secure tenancy must depend either on the making of a court order for possession or on the effluxion of time (in the case of a fixed-term tenancy).

(a) Alteration of traditional common law principles

The Housing Act 1985 (following the innovations contained in the Housing Act 1980), incorporates certain significant departures from the common law principles relating to the termination of contractual tenancies.[16]

(i) Effects of an expired fixed term The 1985 Act provides that where a secure tenancy for a fixed term comes to an end by the effluxion of time, there comes into existence a periodic tenancy of the same dwelling-house on the same terms as under the expired tenancy, the relevant period being ascertainable with reference to the rental periods under the former fixed-term tenancy.[17]

(ii) Termination of tenancy only by court order Although it is still open to the secure tenant to determine his tenancy by any of the traditional common law means (eg by notice to quit or surrender),[18] the landlord cannot terminate a secure tenancy otherwise than by obtaining a court order for possession or termination.[19] This restriction applies not only to periodic tenancies but also to any term certain which is subject to termination by the landlord.[20] Where the landlord does obtain an order for possession, the secure tenancy ends only on the date which is specified in that order for the delivery up of possession.[1] What is new about this provision is not that it makes a court order necessary before eviction can occur,[2] but rather that it makes a court order a requirement for the termination of the tenancy itself.

11 Post, p 1059.
12 Housing Act 1985, s 93(2) (ante, p 1053).
13 Housing Act 1985, s 91(2) (ante, p 1051).
14 Housing Act 1985, s 139(2).
15 Housing Act 1985, s 151(2).
16 See *Harrison v Hammersmith and Fulham LBC* [1981] 1 WLR 650 at 662A-C.
17 Housing Act 1985, s 86(1), (2).
18 Ante, pp 484, 486.
19 Housing Act 1985, s 82(1), (3).
20 Housing Act 1985, s 82(1).
1 Housing Act 1985, s 82(2).
2 This protection for the tenant is already available by virtue of Protection from Eviction Act 1977, ss 2, 3 (ante, p 954).

(b) Possession orders in respect of a secure tenancy

The circumstances in which the court may order possession—and thus simultaneously termination of the secure tenancy—are strictly defined by the Housing Act 1985. Where a dwelling-house is held on a secure tenancy, the court cannot entertain proceedings for possession or termination unless the landlord has first served on the tenant a notice in prescribed form specifying the ground on which the proceedings are being brought and giving particulars of that ground.[3] The court may not then make an order for possession of the dwelling-house except on one or more of the Grounds set out in Schedule 2 of the Housing Act 1985.[4] Even then the Court has an extended discretion (similar to that conferred by Rent Act 1977, s 100[5]) to adjourn proceedings, to stay or suspend the execution of a possession order, and to postpone the date of possession, in respect of the Grounds contained in Parts I and III of Schedule 2.[6]

The Grounds recited in Schedule 2 fall into three main categories.

(i) Grounds coupled with a requirement of reasonableness The court may make a possession order based on any one or more of Grounds 1 to 8 in Part I of Schedule 2, provided that the court 'considers it reasonable to make the order'.[7] These grounds in substance mirror many of the Cases for the recovery of possession contained in Part I of Schedule 15 of the Rent Act 1977.[8] The Grounds in Part I of Schedule 2 include such matters as the tenant's failure to pay rent or breach of other covenants,[9] the commission of nuisance or annoyance to neighbours,[10] neglect or default by the tenant which causes deterioration in the condition of the dwelling-house or the landlord's furniture,[11] or false statements by the tenant which induced the grant of the tenancy.[12]

(ii) Grounds coupled with a requirement of suitable alternative accommodation The court may make a possession order based on any one or more of Grounds 9 to 11 in Part II of Schedule 2, provided that the court is 'satisfied that suitable accommodation will be available for the tenant when the order takes effect'.[13] The suitability of accommodation is measured with reference to criteria which are detailed in Part IV of Schedule 2.[14] The Grounds in Part II of Schedule 2 include cases of statutory 'overcrowding',[15] demolition or the carrying out of other works on the premises,[16] and conflict with the objects of a charitable landlord.[17]

3   Housing Act 1985, s 83(1), (2). See *Torridge DC v Jones* (1985) 18 HLR 107 at 111ff.
4   Housing Act 1985, s 84(1).
5   Ante, p 1022.
6   Housing Act 1985, s 85(1), (2).
7   Housing Act 1985, s 84(2)(a). On the assessment of reasonableness, see *Woodspring DC v Taylor* (1982) 4 HLR 95 at 99.
8   Ante, p 1019.
9   Ground 1.
10   Ground 2.
11   Grounds 3 and 4.
12   Ground 5.
13   Housing Act 1985, s 84(2)(b). See eg *LB of Islington v Metcalfe and Peacock* (1983) LAG Bulletin 105; *Wandsworth LBC v Fadayomi* (1987) *Times*, 27 July.
14   Compare Rent Act 1977, s 98(1)(a), (4), Sch 15, Part IV (ante, p 1016).
15   Ground 9.
16   Ground 10.
17   Ground 11.

(iii) Grounds coupled with both requirements The court may make a possession order based on any one or more of Grounds 12 to 16 in Part III of Schedule 2, provided that the court *both* 'considers it reasonable to make the order' *and* is 'satisfied that suitable accommodation will be available for the tenant when the order takes effect'.[18] The Grounds in Part III of Schedule 2 relate in the main to circumstances in which the premises which are the subject of a secure tenancy have been used or adapted for some special purpose which is no longer relevant in relation to the current tenant. Such cases arise, for instance, where the dwelling-house was let to an employee and is now required for a new employee,[19] or where the premises have been adapted for disabled living, or have been used in order to further the purposes of some specialised housing association or trust, or were initially intended to provide sheltered or 'special needs' accommodation, and such needs no longer obtain in respect of the present tenant.[20]

A further Ground of recovery under Part III arises where, following the death of the secure tenant, the accommodation afforded by the dwelling-house is 'more extensive than is reasonably required' by his successor.[1] In *Enfield LBC v French*,[2] for instance, a successor tenant, on the death of his mother, had been left in possession of a two-bedroom flat with a garden attached. Although he was an extremely enthusiastic gardener, the Court of Appeal upheld an order for possession against him, even though the proffered alternative accommodation was without a garden. The tenant was a bachelor who lived alone and the Court clearly took the view that the exigency of the council's housing problems overrode the tenant's passionate interest in his hobby.[3]

(c) Recovery of possession of a determinable secure tenancy for a term certain

Special difficulties attend the recovery of possession of a dwelling-house held on a fixed-term secure tenancy which is subject to re-entry or forfeiture. In the event of a breach of covenant by the tenant, the court has no power to order possession in pursuance of the landlord's right of re-entry.[4] If, however, such an order would normally have been appropriate, the court must instead make an order 'terminating the tenancy on a date specified in the order',[5] at which point a periodic tenancy will automatically arise on the termination of the fixed term.[6] At this point the landlord may well take the view that the breach has now been sufficiently penalised by the tenant's loss of the rights and benefits associated with the fixed term. In such circumstances, having marked its

---

18 Housing Act 1985, s 84(2)(c).
19 Ground 12.
20 Grounds 13, 14, 15.
1 Ground 16.
2 (1985) 49 P & CR 223 at 229.
3 Goff LJ seemed to envisage that other kinds of 'need' might be given greater weight in this context, citing as an example the need of 'a lonely and immobile old lady [who] may have a cat to which she is devoted, and [who] may need a cat door with access to the outside world to enable it to get some exercise' ((1985) 49 P & CR 223 at 231).
4 Housing Act 1985, s 82(3).
5 Housing Act 1985, s 82(3). The provisions of section 146 of the Law of Property Act 1925 (ante, p 496) apply, with the exception of section 146(4) of that Act (see Housing Act 1985, s 82(4)).
6 Housing Act 1985, s 86(1) (ante, p 1055).

displeasure, the landlord may therefore be content to allow the periodic tenancy to continue in force unless or until there is any further breach by the tenant. Alternatively the landlord may seek both a termination of the fixed term and a simultaneous possession order in respect of the ensuing periodic tenancy, in which case the relationship of landlord and tenant has come conclusively to an end.

5. DISPOSAL TO THE PRIVATE SECTOR

The Housing and Planning Act 1986 contains provisions which authorise the relevant Secretary of State to give approval to the disposal of public sector housing into private ownership.[7] This 'privatisation' of council estates can be effected only after a process of consultation with the tenants who are affected by any particular act of disposal,[8] and the Secretary of State is prohibited from consenting to the disposal if it appears to him that a majority of those tenants do not wish the disposal to proceed.[9] If a disposal does proceed, the tenants in question clearly cease to be 'secure tenants' within the coverage of the Housing Act 1985, becoming instead regulated tenants having rights to protection under the Rent Act 1977. As such they enjoy the security of tenure appropriate to regulated tenants under the 1977 Act and may moreover apply for the registration of a 'fair rent'.

A public sector landlord which proposes to sell off its housing stock to a private landlord may, before doing so, apply to the rent officer for a certificate of 'fair rent', and this certificate is declaratory of the rent which will be deemed 'fair' after the disposal has been effected.[10] The rent level indicated in the certificate will predictably influence the decision of existing secure tenants either to support or to reject any proposed privatisation of their estate.

7   Housing Act 1985, Sch 3A, para 2, as supplied by Housing and Planning Act 1986, s 6, Sch 1.
8   Housing Act 1985, Sch 3A, para 3, as supplied by Housing and Planning Act 1986, s 6, Sch 1.
9   Housing Act 1985, Sch 3A, para 5(1), as supplied by Housing and Planning Act 1986, s 6, Sch 1.
10   Rent Act 1977, s 69(1A), as supplied by Housing and Planning Act 1986, s 7 (ante, p 1034).

CHAPTER 31

Statutory succession to tenancies

Certain kinds of tenancy are governed by provisions for statutory succession which enable a form of residential protection to devolve upon survivors of a deceased tenant. In this way the catastrophic event of death is not allowed to cause a precipitate destruction of the security of tenure otherwise enjoyed by members of that tenant's family. Such schemes of statutory devolution operate under the Housing Act 1985 in respect of public sector tenancies and under the Rent Act 1977 in respect of private sector tenancies.

1. PUBLIC SECTOR TENANCIES

The Housing Act 1985 provides for a limited form of statutory succession on the death of a 'secure tenant'.[1] This process of succession is modelled upon the analogy of tenancies regulated by the Rent Act 1977, but succession to a public sector tenancy is constrained by rather more exacting and less generous conditions than those which obtain in the private sector.

(1) The persons eligible as successors

Several conditions must be met before a person is qualified to succeed a deceased tenant under a secure tenancy.[2] First, the statutory succession is available only if the claimant 'occupies the dwelling-house as his only or principal home at the time of the tenant's death'.[3] Furthermore, the category of eligible successors is confined to two classes of person, the classifications here casting an interesting light on socially perceived boundaries of family relationship.

(a) Spouse of the deceased secure tenant

The secure tenant's spouse is an eligible successor,[4] and for the purpose of succession to a periodic tenancy is to be preferred to any other member of the tenant's family who is likewise eligible as a successor.[5] The surviving spouse is subject to no residence requirement other than that he or she should have occupied the relevant dwelling-house as an 'only or principal home' at the time

---

1 For the definition of 'secure tenancy', see Chapter 30 (ante, p 1045).
2 The burden is on the claimant to show that the preconditions of statutory succession have been satisfied (*Governors of the Peabody Donation Fund v Grant* (1982) 6 HLR 41 at 44).
3 Housing Act 1985, s 87.
4 Housing Act 1985, s 87(a).
5 Housing Act 1985, s 89(2)(a).

of the tenant's death.[6] The term 'spouse' refers only to a de iure spouse. A de facto partner qualifies as a successor only in his or her capacity as a 'member of the tenant's family',[7] and must therefore satisfy the residence requirement prescribed in relation to this class of successor.

(b) Other members of the secure tenant's family

The other class of eligible successor comprises any 'member of the tenant's family' who has 'resided with the tenant' during the twelve months immediately preceding his death.[8] This formulation only barely conceals a penumbra of uncertainty as to the meaning of residence and as to the meaning of family membership.

(i) Requirement of residence   The statutory reference to residence has been construed as requiring that there should be 'a sufficient measure of...factual community of family living and companionship' between the claimant and the now deceased secure tenant.[9] However, it has been held that a claimant may succeed to her father's secure tenancy even though she stayed in his flat only four nights a week during the last 18 months of his life.[10]

(ii) Definition of familial nexus   The criterion of family membership provides more difficulty, although the Housing Act 1985 offers an almost unprecedented definition of this concept. In the present context, section 113(1)(b) defines membership of the deceased tenant's family in terms which include the tenant's parent, grandparent, child,[11] grandchild, brother, sister, uncle, aunt, nephew and niece.[12] Also included is any person with whom the deceased tenant lived 'as husband and wife'.[13] This phrase is apt to catch relationships of heterosexual cohabitation,[14] but in *Harrogate BC v Simpson*[15] the Court of

---

6   There is, for instance, no requirement that the claimant spouse should have been living in the home with the deceased at the time of his death.

7   Parliament rejected a proposed amendment of the Housing Bill 1980 which would have resulted in an exact parity of treatment between the de iure and the de facto wife (see *Parliamentary Debates, House of Commons, Official Report* (Standing Committee F), Vol IX (Session 1979–80), Cols 675ff (28 February 1980)).

8   Housing Act 1985, s 87(b). Parliament rejected a qualification period of merely six months (which again would have produced parity with the law relating to Rent Act tenancies) for fear that relatives might be tempted to move in with elderly tenants precisely in order to qualify for succession to their tenancies (see *Parliamentary Debates, House of Commons, Official Report* (Standing Committee F), Vol IX (Session 1979–80), Cols 673ff (28 February 1980)).

9   *Governors of the Peabody Donation Fund v Grant* (1982) 6 HLR 41 at 45.

10   *Governors of the Peabody Donation Fund v Grant* (1982) 6 HLR 41 at 44f, 264 Estates Gazette 925.

11   See eg *Enfield LBC v French* (1984) 17 HLR 211 at 213.

12   For this purpose any relationship by marriage is treated as a relationship by blood, any relationship of the half blood as a relationship of the whole blood, any stepchild of a person as a child of that person, and any illegitimate person as the legitimate child of his mother and the reputed father (Housing Act 1985, s 113(2)). Foster children are regarded as members of the secure tenant's family, notwithstanding the absence of formal adoption, where they have always been treated as his natural children (*Reading BC v Ilsley* [1981] CLY 1323; (1981) LAG Bulletin 216).

13   Housing Act 1985, s 113(1)(a).

14   'The essential characteristic of living together as husband and wife...is that there should be a man and a woman and that they should be living together in the same household' (*Harrogate BC v Simpson* (1984) 17 HLR 205 at 210 per Ewbank J).

15   (1984) 17 HLR 205 at 210; [1985] Conv 355.

Appeal declined to accept that a homosexual or lesbian relationship is included within the ambit of the statutory language.[16] Although it could be argued quite strongly that this result discriminates unfairly between heterosexuals and homosexuals,[17] it is unlikely that such an extension of the concept of familial relationship could be recognised in the absence of some clearer statutory wording.[18] The European Commission on Human Rights has since declared inadmissible a complaint that the ruling in *Harrogate BC v Simpson* violated the surviving claimant's right to respect for her 'private and family life' and 'home'.[19]

(2) Operation of the statutory succession

The Housing Act 1985 allows the succession mechanism to operate only once in relation to a secure tenancy.[20] There is no possibility (as under the Rent Act 1977[1]) that there may be a second devolution of the secure tenancy upon a further generation of tenant. Moreover, the one permissible succession is deemed to be exhausted where survivorship operates between joint secure tenants,[2] but not where a tenant merely receives a secure tenancy by way of a court-ordered assignment on divorce (unless the assignor was himself a successor).[3]

16   Watkins LJ thought that it 'would be surprising in the extreme to learn that public opinion is such today that it would recognise a homosexual union as being akin to a state of living as husband and wife. The ordinary man and woman...would...not think even remotely of there being any true resemblance between those two very different states of affairs' ((1984) 17 HLR 205 at 210).
17   There was an unsuccessful attempt to insert in the Housing Bill 1980 a provision that membership of the tenant's family should include any 'cohabitant', a term which was defined as 'such person, man or woman, whom the tenant designates by declaration in writing to be his cohabitant.' The purpose of this proposed amendment (put down at the instance of the Campaign for Homosexual Equality) was to 'ensure that families should include cohabitees of the same sex.' The CHE had argued that homosexual couples contribute no less in financial terms to the costs of providing public housing and that it is therefore 'unjust that, while being obliged to finance the provision of housing services and having the same needs of them, they should be debarred by statute from enjoying equal rights with their fellow citizens' (see *Parliamentary Debates, House of Commons, Official Report* (Standing Committee F), Vol IX (Session 1979-80), Cols 675ff, (28 February 1980), 968 (6 March)).
18   The House of Lords subsequently refused leave to appeal, Lord Fraser of Tullybelton remarking that in effect the surviving partner was 'fighting for a social revolution, but that is more than the courts can do. It is a matter for Parliament' (*The Times*, 1 March 1985). Compare, however, the Government spokesman's statement during discussion of the Housing Bill 1980 that 'it is no part of the philosophy of this Bill to take a lead on an issue of social policy' (see *Parliamentary Debates, House of Commons, Official Report* (Standing Committee F), Vol IX (Session 1979-80), (28 February 1980)).
19   *Application No 11716/85 v* UK. The Commission took the view that a lesbian relationship is not protected by the family life aspect of Art 8 of the European Convention on Human Rights. Nor had the complainant suffered 'discrimination' within the terms of Art 14. Heterosexual cohabitation was viewed as 'meriting special protection in society', and the greater degree of protection afforded heterosexual family life under the Housing Act was considered to be 'objective and reasonable'. See (1986) 83 Law Soc Gaz 2320.
20   Housing Act 1985, s 87.
1   A proposal designed to produce parity with the private sector (post, p 1063) by allowing two statutory successions was defeated during the committee stage in the House of Commons' consideration of the Housing Bill 1980 (see *Parliamentary Debates, House of Commons, Official Report* (Standing Committee F), Vol IX (Session 1970-80), Cols 662ff (26 February 1980).
2   Housing Act 1985, s 88(1)(b).
3   Housing Act 1985, s 88(2). See Matrimonial Causes Act 1973, s 24(1)(a) (ante, p 1052).

Where two or more members of the family of a deceased secure tenant are eligible for succession to a periodic tenancy, the tenancy may be allocated to one or other by mutual agreement, and failing such an agreement the successor may be selected from their number by the landlord.[4]

2. PRIVATE SECTOR TENANCIES

It is likewise possible that a private sector tenancy governed by the Rent Act 1977 may devolve by statutory succession upon one or more members of the deceased tenant's family in turn. These successors then enjoy precisely the same protection under the Act as did the deceased tenant. This potential prolongation of a Rent Act tenancy is one of the most controversial features of the long-term security of tenure conferred upon the statutory tenant, since the effect may be to deprive the landlord of vacant possession of the rented property for up to three generations of tenant. From the tenant's point of view, however, the Rent Act has introduced a new and quite remarkable form of homestead property right designed to promote the interest of residential security.

(1) **Operation of statutory succession**

The operation of statutory succession under the Rent Act 1977 is somewhat more extensive and more complex than the equivalent provision under the Housing Act 1985.[5]

(a) *Spouse*

If the original tenant under a protected or statutory tenancy dies leaving a 'surviving spouse'[6] who was 'residing in the dwelling-house immediately before the death of the original tenant',[7] that spouse now becomes the statutory tenant by succession 'if and so long as he or she occupies the dwelling-house as his or her residence'.[8] The term 'surviving spouse' does not include a de facto spouse or a divorced spouse.

---

4   Housing Act 1985, s 89(2)(b).
5   The complexity will be accentuated with the coming into force of the Housing and Planning Act 1986. Under this enactment a 'preserved right to buy' pursuant to Housing Act 1985, s 171A, can be claimed by a number of persons if and when the relevant dwelling-house has been disposed of to a private landlord (ante, p 739). The 'preserved right to buy' may extend, on the death of the former secure tenant, to any of a number of 'qualifying successors', who include a surviving spouse of that tenant or a 'member' of his family (see Housing Act 1985, s 171B(4)(a), as supplied by Housing and Planning Act 1986, s 8(1)).
6   The term is now deliberately sex-neutral. See H.E. Markson, *Sex Discrimination and the Rent Acts*, (1977) 127 NLJ 485.
7   There is no requirement that the surviving spouse should have resided there for any specified period of time preceding the tenant's death.
8   Rent Act 1977, Sch 1, para 2 (as substituted by Housing Act 1980, s 76(1)). Section 2(3) of the Rent Act 1977 makes it clear that the requirement of continuity is to be governed by the same criteria as apply under section 2(1)(a) (ante, p 1007).

(b) Member of the tenant's family

If the deceased tenant is not survived by a spouse, then his Rent Act tenancy devolves upon any person who was 'a member of the original tenant's family'[9] and who was residing with the deceased at the time of, and for the period of six months immediately preceding, his death.[10] Such a person remains the statutory tenant by succession 'if and so long as he occupies the dwelling-house as his residence'.[11] If more than one person qualifies under this definition, the relevant parties may agree to allocate the tenancy to one of their number,[12] and failing such agreement the county court has a discretion to award the tenancy to one or other claimant.[13]

(c) Number of successions

The Rent Act 1977 allows for up to two statutory successions in respect of a relevant tenancy. The second succession may be claimed either by the surviving spouse of the first successor[14] or by a 'member of the first successor's family' who has resided with the first successor for at least six months immediately preceding his death.[15] These provisions open up the possibility that the process of statutory succession can span three entire generations, the tenancy enduring for the lifetime of the original tenant and passing on to his child (as first successor) and then his grandchild (as second successor).[16] It is even feasible that there may be three successions to the original tenancy, one at common law and two by statute. The original Rent Act tenancy, if held by joint tenants, is subject to survivorship on the death of one of those joint tenants,[17] and is thereafter potentially subject to the operation of two statutory successions.[18]

(2) Requirement of residence

In order to succeed to a Rent Act tenancy, all claimants (other than a spouse) must satisfy a condition of six months' residence with the former tenant

---

9   The term 'member' requires a singular construction, thus precluding any succession by a number of persons collectively as joint tenants enjoying as between themselves a right of survivorship. See *Dealex Properties Ltd v Brooks* [1966] 1 QB 542 at 551A-B, where Harman LJ pointed out the difficulty otherwise raised by a 'plurality of "members" who may agree together, and so have a sort of tontine which will last for so long as the survivor of them is in existence.'

10   Rent Act 1977, Sch 1, para 3.

11   Rent Act 1977, Sch 1, para 3. The requirement of continuity is governed by Rent Act 1977, s 2(1)(a), (3) (ante, p 1007).

12   Rent Act 1977, Sch 1, para 7. There is no requirement that the landlord should necessarily be a party to, or even be notified of, the agreement reached (*General Management Ltd v Locke* (1980) 255 Estates Gazette 155 at 157).

13   Rent Act 1977, Sch 1, para 7. Where the merits of the competing claimants are equally balanced, the wishes of the deceased tenant may be decisive (*Trayfoot v Lock* [1957] 1 WLR 351 at 353). See also *Williams v Williams* [1970] 1 WLR 1530 at 1533F-G.

14   Rent Act 1977, Sch 1, para 6 (as amended by Housing Act 1980, s 76(2)).

15   Rent Act 1977, Sch 1, para 7.

16   A person who becomes a statutory tenant by succession continues to be regarded as such even if he enters into a new contractual tenancy of the dwelling-house (Rent Act 1977, Sch 1, para 10).

17   Ante, p 296.

18   See *General Management Ltd v Locke* (1980) 255 Estates Gazette 155 at 157.

immediately preceding his death.[19] The clear purpose of this requirement is to preclude unmeritorious claims by relatives who choose to wait until the last moment to move in with a moribund tenant.

(a) Temporary absence

Merely temporary absence on the part of either the claimant or the now deceased tenant does not negative the statutory condition of residence,[20] although the prolonged confinement of the tenant in a hospital may preclude any claim of residence with that tenant during the closing months of his or her life.[1]

(b) The 'second home' problem

The claimant may still be held to have resided with the tenant even though he has another home or residence elsewhere,[2] but must be able to show that he had become in a true sense a part of the tenant's household. In *Swanbrae Ltd v Elliott*[3] the claimant had been accustomed over a period of several years to sleep three or four nights each week in the house of her gravely ill mother, while retaining another home for herself and her son nearby. The Court of Appeal refused to hold that she had succeeded to her mother's tenancy on the latter's death. In so far as the claimant had at all times had a 'settled abode' elsewhere and either intended ultimately to return to live there or at least had made no decision about the future, she could not be said to have been 'residing with' her mother at her death.[4]

(3) Definition of familial nexus

It has sometimes proved difficult to determine whether a given person can properly claim family membership in respect of a deceased tenant. The application of this criterion is heavily coloured by social and moral perceptions of the legitimacy of certain kinds of relationship, and the caselaw in this area discloses an interesting social history of the family over the last 50 years. The decisions reached by the courts are significant not least because they represent important conjectures as to the boundaries of kinship socially and legally recognised in the community.[5]

19   Rent Act 1977, Sch 1, paras 3, 7. The claimant must have 'shared for living purposes the whole of the premises to which he or she claims to have succeeded' (*Edmunds v Jones* [1957] 1 WLR 1118 at 1120).

20   *Greenway v Rawlings* (1952) 102 LJ News 360; *Kinlock v Harrigan* [1968] 3 NSWR 426 at 427. Compare *Carter v Carroll* [1968] 3 NSWR 542 at 547f. See (1981) 131 NLJ 1106 (P.F. Smith).

1   *Foreman v Beagley* [1969] 1 WLR 1387 at 1391C-H (mother in hospital for three years); *Gasking & Co Ltd v Evans, McGeachie and Proctor* (1981) 131 NLJ 903 (alleged de facto wife in hospital for last year of her life).

2   *Morgan v Murch* [1970] 1 WLR 778 at 782C; *Swanbrae Ltd v Elliott* (1986) *Times*, 6 December. The same approach has been applied to comparable provisions in the rented housing code of New York City. See New York City Rent and Eviction Regulations, s 56(d); *Doubledown Realty Corp v Harris*, 128 Misc 2d 403 (1985).

3   (1986) *Times*, 6 December.

4   Compare the more generous result achieved in the public sector in *Governors of the Peabody Donation Fund v Grant* (1982) 6 HLR 41 at 44f (ante, p 1060).

5   See A. Dickey, *The Notion of 'Family' in Law*, (1979-82) 14 U of Western Australia LR 417; A.A.S. Zuckerman, (1980) 96 LQR 248.

(a) The 'ordinary man' test

In view of the absence of any statutory definition of family membership in relation to Rent Act tenancies,[6] the courts have developed over the years a working definition of familial nexus. It seems that any definitional uncertainty must be resolved in accordance with the 'ordinary man' test initially formulated by Cohen LJ in *Brock v Wollams*.[7]

Under this test the court must determine whether 'an ordinary man' would conclude that a given postulant falls within the ambit of family relationship, the term 'family' being used here in a 'base, common and popular' sense.[8] The hypothetical 'ordinary man' must reach his conclusion not only in the terms of the semantic usage prevailing at the date of the tenant's death,[9] but also as if he were 'in possession of the evidence which the judge had before he gives his answer.'[10] The court must thus double-guess the thought-processes of the 'ordinary man' in order to determine whether in any given case he would have detected 'at least a broadly recognisable de facto familial nexus'.[11] However, the 'ordinary man' can speak only through the medium of the court and therefore, as Viscount Dilhorne observed in *Carega Properties SA v Sharratt*,[12] the 'ordinary man' test is not 'likely to extract any more than the judge's personal view'. In certain difficult or borderline cases the 'ordinary man' test does little more than provide respectable cover for subjective judicial pronouncements on the kinds of social grouping which qualify for recognition as a 'family'.[13]

(b) Relationships clearly within the ambit of familial nexus

It has been said that, in determining whether a person qualifies as a 'member' of the tenant's 'family', two elements require consideration—relationship and conduct.[14] The category of 'members' of a 'family' is not yet closed. Although the list of potential members has not so far been exhaustively defined, there is no doubt that the list includes many members of a de iure family,[15] together with relationships by marriage,[16] and relationships in loco parentis.[17]

---

6   Compare the rather comprehensive (but still unsatisfactory) definition of 'member of the family of a tenant' contained in the Republic of Ireland's Housing (Private Rented Dwellings) Act 1982, s 7(2).
7   [1949] 2 KB 388 at 395.
8   *Langdon v Horton* [1951] 1 KB 666 at 669 per Evershed MR, who for this purpose explicitly adopted the analogy of the description of the soldier in Shakespeare's *Henry V*, Act IV, Scene I.
9   That this is the effective date rather than the date of the relevant enactment or court hearing was confirmed in *Watson v Lucas* [1980] 1 WLR 1493 at 1497D per Stephenson LJ. For criticism of the necessarily fluctuating nature of such a statutory construction (first applied by the Court of Appeal in *Dyson Holdings Ltd v Fox* [1976] QB 503 at 509C, 511D), see *Helby v Rafferty* [1979] 1 WLR 13 at 16G-H, 23D-F, 25C-E. See also (1979) 95 LQR 161.
10   *Watson v Lucas* [1980] 1 WLR 1493 at 1497D.
11   *Ross v Collins* [1964] 1 WLR 425 at 432, approved in *Carega Properties SA v Sharratt* [1979] 1 WLR 928 at 931E-F per Lord Diplock.
12   [1979] 1 WLR 928 at 932D.
13   See B. Berkovits, *The Family and the Rent Acts: Reflections on Law and Policy*, [1981] JSWL 83.
14   *Ross v Collins* [1964] 1 WLR 425 at 430; *Joram Developments Ltd v Sharratt* [1979] 1 WLR 3 at 10H per Browne LJ.
15   *Price v Gould* (1930) 143 LT 333 at 334 (brother and sister); *Collier v Stoneman* [1957] 1 WLR 1108 at 1116 (grandchild).
16   *Jones v Whitehill* [1950] 2 KB 204 at 207 (niece by marriage); *Stewart v Higgins* [1951] EGD 353 (brother-in-law and sister-in-law).
17   *Brock v Wollams* [1949] 2 KB 388 at 394ff (informally adopted child).

However, the mere fact of relationship is not always sufficient to establish membership of a family for Rent Act purposes. The more remote the relationship, the more imperative it is that the familial nexus should be distinctively demonstrated in the conduct of the parties. In *Langdon v Horton*,[18] for instance, the Court of Appeal refused Rent Act protection to two elderly ladies who had for 30 years lived with their cousin in a house which she held on a statutory tenancy. Mere consanguinity was not enough to establish the required familial nexus where the cohabitation was motivated by nothing more than considerations of mutual convenience.[19]

(c) De facto relationships

More difficult questions arise in connection with de facto family relationships. In this context the caselaw discloses a distinct movement of opinion over time.

(i) The moralistic approach   It was thought during the 1950s that a de facto spouse could never claim to be a statutory successor, since any contrary view would 'presuppose an intention of Parliament to reward immorality with irremovability.'[20] In *Gammans v Ekins*,[1] for instance, the Court of Appeal invoked broad grounds of public policy in rejecting a claim to succession made by a male cohabitant on the death of his partner. Asquith LJ employed a double-edged argument to the effect that '[e]ither the relationship was platonic or it was not.'[2] If platonic, Asquith LJ could see no principle which would allow the court to recognise the cohabitants as members of the same family but which would not also require the court to concede the same status to 'two old cronies of the same sex innocently sharing a flat.' If on the other hand the relationship were not platonic, Asquith LJ thought it 'anomalous' that a person could acquire a status of irremovability 'by living or having lived in sin, even if the liaison has not been a mere casual encounter but protracted in time and conclusive in character.' He concluded that to say of 'two people masquerading...as husband and wife...that they were members of the same family, seems to be an abuse of the English language.' Evershed MR confessed to having experienced 'greater difficulty' in reaching the same conclusion, but was comforted by his belief that it 'may be no bad thing that by this decision it is shown that, in the Christian society in which we live, one, at any rate, of the privileges which may be derived from marriage is not equally enjoyed by those who are living together as man and wife but who are not married.'[3]

---

18   [1951] 1 KB 666 at 670ff.
19   In applying the equivalent statutory provision in New York (New York City Rent and Eviction Regulations, s 56(d)), it has been held that the claimant must show that he or she was 'an integral member of [the] tenant's family unit. Such relationships usually connote a fair degree of permanence and continuity' (*Goodhue House Co v Bernstein* (NYLJ, 12 December 1981, p 14)). Consanguinity, combined with a temporarily shared living arrangement, is insufficient to afford protection to a family member (see eg *829 Seventh Avenue Co v Reider*, 502 NYS.2d 715 at 717 (1986)).
20   *Watson v Lucas* [1980] 1 WLR 1493 at 1497E-F per Stephenson LJ.
1   [1950] 2 KB 328.
2   [1950] 2 KB 328 at 331.
3   [1950] 2 KB 328 at 334.

(ii) Relevance of children   In *Gammans v Ekins* the unmarried couple had no children, but the Court of Appeal left open the question whether the presence of children could bring a de facto spouse within the scope of the succession provisions of the Rent Act.[4] This question was finally answered in the affirmative in *Hawes v Evenden*,[5] and the attention of the more recent caselaw has been drawn to the status of childless de facto unions.

(iii) Changing social perceptions   In *Dyson Holdings Ltd v Fox*,[6] the claimant as statutory successor had lived with a protected tenant for 21 years before his death. The Court of Appeal ruled somewhat controversially that she could succeed to the deceased's tenancy. Lord Denning MR led the Court in overturning *Gammans v Ekins* on the ground that 'owing to the lapse of time, and the change in social conditions, the previous decision is not in accord with modern thinking.'[7] Bridge LJ was likewise of the opinion that 'between 1950 and 1975 there has been a complete revolution in society's attitude to unmarried partnerships', and that the social stigma which once attached to them 'has almost, if not entirely, disappeared.'[8]

(iv) Limits on liberalism   At this point it seemed as if the courts were becoming fairly amenable to the idea of treating most stable de facto relationships as coming within the ambit of the Rent Act. However, in *Dyson Holdings Ltd v Fox*[9] James LJ had been careful to state that 'relationships of a casual or intermittent character and those bearing indications of impermanence would not come within the popular concept of a family unit.' This note of caution was borne out in *Helby v Rafferty*,[10] where the Court of Appeal denied a tenancy by succession to a man who had lived with a statutory tenant for the last five years of her life. There was evidence in this case that the couple had deliberately remained unmarried and that the woman had been a lady of some independence who had not wished to assume the overt character of a wife in the conventional sense. The Court of Appeal held that the relationship lacked the permanence and stability necessary to justify the conclusion that the surviving cohabitee was a 'member of the original tenant's family' within the meaning of the Rent Act.[11]

In coming to this decision the Court of Appeal expressed grave disquiet as to the way in which the earlier and differently constituted Court of Appeal in

4   [1950] 2 KB 328 at 331ff.
5   [1953] 1 WLR 1169 at 1171.
6   [1976] QB 503. See D.C. Bradley, *Meaning of 'Family': Changing Morality and Changing Justice*, (1976) 39 MLR 222.
7   [1976] QB 503 at 509D.
8   [1976] QB 503 at 512G-H.
9   [1976] QB 503 at 511E.
10 [1979] 1 WLR 13 at 22G, 24B-C.
11 See also *Gasking & Co Ltd v Evans, McGeachie and Proctor* (1981) 131 NLJ 903, where Lord Denning MR led the Court of Appeal in rejecting a similar claim to succession based on colourable evidence of five or six years of cohabitation. An interesting comparison is found in the law of supplementary benefits, where extremely short-lived or partial cohabitation (even of a non-sexual nature) has been held to disqualify a claimant from benefit on the ground of cohabitation (Supplementary Benefits Act 1976, s 34(1), Sch 1, para 3). See *R v South West London SBAT, ex parte Barnett* (1973) SB 4; *Crake v Supplementary Benefits Commission* [1982] 1 All ER 498 at 508h-509a; *R(SB) 30/83*; *Campbell v Secretary of State for Social Services* (1983) 4 FLR 138 at 142.

Dyson Holdings Ltd v Fox had purported to overrule *Gammans v Ekins*.[12] It is now clear, however, that the Court of Appeal is not prepared, in the absence of definitive guidance from the House of Lords, to return to the construction adopted in *Gammans v Ekins*. In *Watson v Lucas*[13] Stephenson LJ indicated that a reversion to the approach taken in *Gammans v Ekins* would be 'to introduce impermanence and instability into our own decision.'

(v) The modern approach   In *Watson v Lucas* the Court of Appeal decided by a majority to uphold the devolution of a statutory tenancy upon a man who for almost 20 years had lived with a woman in a childless de facto union.[14] Throughout this entire period he had remained legally married to another woman who had left him several years before he began to cohabit with the now deceased statutory tenant. The majority in the Court considered that his subsisting marital status was not inconsistent with his having been a 'member' of someone else's 'family'. This conclusion was reached even though there was evidence that the parties had retained their separate names throughout the relationship and had not striven to hold themselves out as a married couple. Stephenson LJ felt 'bound to move with the times' and thus held that the social ethics underlying *Gammans v Ekins* had 'lost their relevance to the interpretation of this provision of the Rent Acts a quarter of a century later.'[15] In his opinion, the authority of *Dyson Holdings Ltd v Fox* constrained the court to find that a familial nexus was established wherever a de facto union 'looks like a marriage in the old and perhaps obsolete sense of a lifetime union, with nothing casual or temporary about it'.

All the members of the Court of Appeal in *Watson v Lucas*[16] expressed the firm view that the concept of familial nexus should not be extended beyond the boundaries indicated in *Dyson Holdings Ltd v Fox*. However, within those boundaries the Court of Appeal gave some indication of what may be a significant shift in the criteria to be applied by the courts in future. The majority took the position that the formal features of a relationship (such as subsisting marital status or the retention of a separate name) were significant only to the extent that they provided guidance as to the degree of mutual commitment present in the union. In *Watson v Lucas*, even these features could not override the fact that the relationship in question was 'a lasting, indeed a lifelong association, more permanent and stable than many marriages including [the man's] own.'[17]

In the final analysis the criteria of familial nexus for the purpose of Rent Act succession still appear to be related to the court's objective assessment of the degree of mutual commitment and permanence exhibited by the relationship under scrutiny. It is, however, interesting to note that the English approach to de facto relationships, while somewhat arbitrary and unsatisfactory, is more

12   The Court of Appeal made it clear (see [1979] 1 WLR 13 at 17A, 23H, 25F) that it was accepting, although distinguishing, *Dyson Holdings Ltd v Fox*, only on the ground that the Court of Appeal is (according to the better view) bound by its own previous decisions.
13   [1980] 1 WLR 1493 at 1498D. See (1980) LAG Bulletin 269 (A. Arden); [1981] Conv 78 (A. Sydenham).
14   See the strong dissent of Oliver LJ at [1980] 1 WLR 1493 at 1502ff.
15   [1980] 1 WLR 1493 at 1500F.
16   [1980] 1 WLR 1493 at 1501G, 1506G-H, 1507E.
17   [1980] 1 WLR 1493 at 1500D. The claimant here had refrained from seeking a divorce from his wife because he was a Roman Catholic.

liberal than the approach demonstrated by courts in comparable jurisdictions. In New York, for instance, the courts have in some respects accorded a broad application to the statutory transmission of tenants' rights.[18] Nevertheless the same courts have steadfastly refused to recognise that even a long-standing de facto liaison can entitle a surviving partner to succeed to the residential rights of a deceased tenant.[19]

(d) Other relationships

In *Gammans v Ekins*[20] Asquith LJ stated that a familial nexus would not exist, in the sense required by the Rent Act, between 'two old cronies of the same sex innocently sharing a flat.' Indeed Jenkins LJ went so far as to suggest that 'an alarming vista would...be opened up' if statutory succession were allowed to extend to such persons.[1] Likewise, in *Brock v Wollams*,[2] Cohen LJ indicated that it could not have been the intention of Parliament to provide Rent Act protection for such members of the original tenant's 'household' as his 'servants and lodgers'.[3]

(i) No artificial familial nexus

In *Ross v Collins*[4] the Court of Appeal was faced with a claim by a woman to be entitled to succeed to a statutory tenancy enjoyed by a man with whom she had lived for a substantial period of time. She had been nearly forty years younger than him and had looked after him dutifully, regarding him as 'a sort of elder relative, partly as...father, partly as...elder brother.' Although the conduct of the couple had clearly been of a familial nature, the Court of Appeal regarded the absence of kinship as precluding this platonic liaison from constituting the necessary familial nexus. Russell LJ ruled that 'two strangers cannot...ever establish artificially...a familial nexus by acting as brothers or as sisters, even if they call each other such and consider their relationship to be tantamount to that.' Nor, in Russell LJ's view, could 'an adult man and woman who establish a platonic relationship establish a familial nexus by acting as a devoted brother and sister or father and daughter would act, even if they address each other as such and regard their association as tantamount to such.'[5]

18 The New York courts have, for instance, extended a provision which expressly contemplates the transmission of residential rights on the tenant's *death* to cover the transmission of those same rights to de iure members of his family in the event of the tenant's *voluntary departure from the premises* (see *M & L Jacobs Inc v DelGrosso*, 490 NYS.2d 963 at 967f (1985), ante, p 1004).
19 See *L V Realty Co v Desommosy*, 462 NYS.2d 584 at 586f (1983); *Hudson View Properties v Weiss*, 463 NYS.2d 428 at 429 (1983); *Park South Associates v Daniels*, 469 NYS.2d 319 at 321 (1983). Compare *Zimmerman v Burton*, 434 NYS.2d 127 at 128f (1980), now probably no longer good law in the light of *Hudson View Properties v Weiss*.
20 [1950] 2 KB 328 at 331.
1 [1950] 2 KB 328 at 333.
2 [1949] 2 KB 388 at 394.
3 Compare *Bistany v Williams*, 372 NYS.2d 6 at 7 (1975), where in the same context the City Court in New York State was prepared to extend the concept of 'member of the deceased tenant's family' beyond the notion of 'immediate family' to cover the 'household' comprising 'not only the servants but also the head of the household and all persons in it related to him by blood or marriage.' See also *Waitzman v McGoldrick*, 121 NYS.2d 515 at 516 (1953).
4 [1964] 1 WLR 425.
5 [1964] 1 WLR 425 at 432.

(ii) Unorthodox social groupings   The restrictive ruling in *Ross v Collins* was later exposed to a strong challenge in *Carega Properties SA v Sharratt*,[6] where the House of Lords was confronted by a claim that the Rent Act should recognise the 'familial' quality of new or unconventional forms of social grouping.[7] Here an unrelated man and woman (separated in age by more than half a century) had lived together for 18 years in a platonic association which was 'wholly admirable and of the highest standard'.[8] The woman was the statutory tenant of the flat in which they lived. The couple referred to each other as 'Aunt Nora' and 'Bunny' respectively, and they shared a life of intellectual and cultural intimacy. The House of Lords decided that, when the statutory tenant eventually died at the age of 94, the tenancy could not devolve upon her faithful and much younger male companion. Following *Ross v Collins*, the House of Lords refused to recognise that changing social conditions had enlarged the meaning of the word 'family' so that it now signified 'household'.[9]

(e) Direction of future developments

It is clear that the courts, which are now being called upon with increasing frequency to reconsider the definition of family relationship, are placed in something of a dilemma. Ironically, if the term 'family' is confirmed in terms of the meaning which it bore under the social conditions of the 1920s,[10] this construction may in fact be closer to the notion of 'household' than to the modern concept of the nuclear family.[11] Alternatively, if the courts accept that the legal definition of 'family' fluctuates over time in response to changing moral and social perceptions, the implications may be both far-reaching and (for some) entirely unacceptable.

(i) Inadequacy of sex-based criteria   So far the courts, as in *Carega Properties SA v Sharratt*, have insisted that familial status involves something more than the mere performance of domestic functions. By attaching special significance to the sexual nature of a relationship, the courts have been gradually forced to concede that a permanent heterosexual union—notwithstanding its lack of

6   [1979] 1 WLR 928, on appeal from *Joram Developments Ltd v Sharratt* [1979] 1 WLR 3. See (1980) 43 MLR 77 (C.H. Sherrin).
7   Compare the recognition by the Supreme Court of New York in *In the Matter of Adult Anonymous II*, 452 NYS.2d 198 at 201 (1982), that '[t]he nuclear family arrangement is no longer the only mode of family life in America. The realities of present day urban life allow many different types of non-traditional families'.
8   [1979] 1 WLR 3 at 5D per Megaw LJ.
9   See also *Kavanagh v Lyroudias* [1985] 1 All ER 560 at 563d-f, where the Court of Appeal declined to hold that two unrelated males could constitute a 'family' for the purpose of determining the 'needs of the tenant and his family' in the slightly different context of 'suitable alternative accommodation' under the Rent Act (see Rent Act 1977, s 98(1)(a), Sch 15, Part IV, para 5(1), ante, p 1017).
10   The phrase 'member of the tenant's family' first appeared in statutory form in the Rent Restriction Act 1920, s 12(1)(g). There is a clear canon of statutory construction which requires that 'the words of an Act will generally be understood in the sense which they bore when it was passed' (see *Maxwell on Interpretation of Statutes* (12th edn, London 1969), p 85; *Helby v Rafferty* [1979] 1 WLR 13 at 25H-26A).
11   There is a further irony in the fact that the statutory tenant in *Carega Properties SA v Sharratt* was the widow of Salter J, a judge who had himself decided some of the earliest cases on the incipient Rent Acts. In *Salter v Lask* [1925] 1 KB 584 at 587, for instance, Salter J had been prepared to contemplate the possibility that the statutory reference to 'family' might well be 'equivalent to "household"...'

legal structure—may be constitutive of a 'family'. If this is so, it seems somewhat discriminatory to withhold the benefit of the Rent Act's succession provisions from the permanent homosexual relationship.[12] But then if homosexual partners constitute a familial nexus for Rent Act purposes, it in turn becomes exceedingly difficult to exclude the case of the 'two old cronies' who choose to live together for reasons of convenience. The law can scarcely deny platonic friends the facility of Rent Act succession merely on the ground that they have failed to include a sexual dimension in their relationship.[13]

(ii) The zoning analogy It may be that a better test of familial nexus is provided by focusing the courts' attention more clearly on the functional rather than purely sexual aspects of the unit or partnership under scrutiny. Such an approach has already been employed with some success in the resolution of a comparable problem arising in relation to the construction of local zoning ordinances in the United States which create residential zones in which habitation is confined to single 'families'.[14] In determining whether any particular social grouping comprises a 'family' for this purpose, the American courts have attached significance to the notion of a 'single non-profit-making housekeeping unit' rather than to any assessment of the affective or sexual bonds existing between the individuals involved.[15] In *City of White Plains v Ferraioli*[16] the Court of Appeals of New York considered it irrelevant whether 'a family be organised along ties of blood or formal adoptions, or be a similarly structured group sponsored by the State'. A zoning ordinance requiring 'family' habitation was fully satisfied provided 'the group home bears the generic character of a family unit as a relatively permanent household, and is not a framework for transients or transient living'.[17]

(iii) A functional approach In consequence American zoning law has proceeded on the basis of a broad willingness to allow the term 'family' to include any group 'whose lifestyle is...the functional equivalent of "family" life'.[18] Accordingly it has been held that the definition of a 'family' for this purpose

---

12 See, however, *Harrogate BC v Simpson* (1984) 17 HLR 205 at 210 (ante, p 1060), where the Court of Appeal baulked at this prospect in the parallel area of statutory succession to a public sector tenancy. Compare the willingness of the courts in New York to accept that homosexual partners are part of the tenant's 'immediate family' for the purpose of landlord and tenant law (see eg *420 East 80th Co v Chin*, 455 NYS.2d 42 at 44 (1982); *Avest Seventh Corp v Ringelheim*, 440 NYS.2d 159 (1981), revd 458 NYS.2d 903 (1982)). The irony is that the same courts refuse, for the same purpose, to accept that a heterosexual de facto partner constitutes 'immediate family' (see *Hudson View Properties v Weiss*, 463 NYS.2d 428 at 429 (1983)). It may be significant that in New York State it is possible for one homosexual legally to adopt his partner (see *In the Matter of Adult Anonymous II*, 452 NYS.2d 198 at 201 (1982)).

13 Compare *L V Realty Co v Desommosy*, 462 NYS.2d 584 at 586 (1983), where the Civil Court of the City of New York observed that [p]roperly the right to occupy an apartment should not be based on testimony as to whether the occupants sleep together or whether they in fact love each other...'

14 See J.A. Smith, 58 Cornell LR 138 (1972-73).

15 See *Brady v Superior Court*, 19 Cal Rptr 242 at 247, 250 (1962); *City of Des Plaines v Trottner*, 216 NE.2d 116 at 119 (1966); *Berger v State of New Jersey*, 364 A.2d 993 at 1003 (1976); *State of New Jersey v Baker*, 405 A.2d 368 at 372 (1979).

16 313 NE.2d 756 at 758 (1974) per Breitel CJ.

17 See also *Incorporated Village of Freeport v Association for the Help of Retarded Children*, 406 NYS.2d 221 at 223 (1977); *State of New Jersey v Baker*, 405 A.2d 368 at 372 (1979).

18 *Charter Township of Delta v Dinolfo*, 351 NW.2d 831 at 843 (1984). See also *Group House of Port Washington Inc v Board of Zoning, etc*, 408 NYS.2d 377 at 379f (1978).

cannot validly exclude such disparate social groupings as a household comprising two male students sharing accommodation,[19] community homes for disabled children[20] or retarded adults,[1] households consisting of surrogate parents and foster children,[2] and fundamentalist Christian communities sharing on New Testament principles.[3] It is therefore clear that a number of 'unrelated persons living together' may meet the 'indicia...set forth for the functional equivalent of a traditional family'.[4]

In perhaps the most important decision on this point, the Supreme Court of California acknowledged in *City of Santa Barbara v Adamson*[5] that many courts had 'redefined "family" to specify a concept more rationally and substantially related to the legitimate aim of maintaining a family style of living.' The Court held that so long as a group 'bears the generic character of a family unit as a relatively permanent household, it should be equally as entitled to occupy a single family dwelling as its biologically related neighbours.'[6] The Supreme Court thus decided by a majority of four to three to concede familial status for zoning purposes to the members of a communal living arrangement which described itself as an 'alternate family'. The commune consisted of 12 unrelated adults who claimed to have formed a 'close group with social, economic, and psychological commitments to each other'.[7] The members shared expenses, rotated chores and ate evening meals together, and the majority in the Supreme Court recognised that such a living arrangement 'does achieve many of the personal and practical needs served by traditional family living.'[8]

The English definition of familial nexus for the purpose of Rent Act succession is still fairly far removed from the liberal approach evident in the American zoning decisions. However, the concept of family relationship cannot and does not remain static in a multi-cultural and multi-racial community. The increasing incidence of lifestyles which deviate from the traditional Anglo-Saxon pattern may force a re-appraisal of non-traditional ideas of familial nexus, thereby confirming the drift already apparent in English law towards the fashioning of a new property law specific to household relationships.[9]

19   *Brady v Superior Court*, 19 Cal Rptr 242 at 250 (1962).
20   *State of Montana, ex rel Region II Child and Family Services Inc v District Court*, 609 P.2d 245 at 247f (1980).
1   *Costley v Caromin House Inc*, 313 NW.2d 21 at 25 (1981).
2   *City of White Plains v Ferraioli*, 313 NE.2d 756 at 758f (1974); *Hessling v City of Broomfield*, 563 P.2d 12 at 14 (1977); *Group House of Port Washington Inc v Board of Zoning, etc*, 408 NYS.2d 377 at 379f (1978).
3   *State of New Jersey v Baker*, 405 A.2d 368 at 375 (1979); *Charter Township of Delta v Dinolfo*, 351 NW.2d 831 at 842ff (1984)
4   *McMinn v Town of Oyster Bay*, 488 NE.2d 1240 at 1244 (1985).
5   610 P.2d 436 (1980).
6   610 P.2d 436 at 442 per Newman J.
7   610 P.2d 436 at 438.
8   610 P.2d 436 at 438. The dissenting opinion (given by Manuel J) disavowed any 'sort of dark animus against non-traditional living arrangements' and recognised that the commune-dwellers in the present case were 'unquestionably sincere in seeking to devise and test new life-styles'. However, the minority denied that the group shared many of the characteristics of a traditional family relationship, taking the view that such groups are 'voluntary, with fluctuating memberships who have no legal obligations of support or cohabitation. They are in no way subject to the State's vast body of domestic relations law. They do not have the biological links which characterise most families. Emotional ties between commune members may exist, but this is true of members of many groups' (610 P.2d 436 at 447).
9   Ante, p 817.

Index

Accidents in the home
liability of landlord. *see* LANDLORD
Accretion, 32-33
Actual occupation 185-189
family home, 188-189
garage, 189
notional, 187-189
physical fact, test of, 187
primarily factual criterion, 185-186
right of way, 189
symbolic, 187-189
Advancement
presumption of, *see* PRESUMPTION OF
ADVANCEMENT
Adverse possession, 740-759
acquisition of title by, 740 *et seq*
animus possidendi, 748-750
discontinuance of possession, 743-744
displaced residential occupier
meaning, 756
rights of entry, 756
dispossession of tenant by squatters, 742-
743
factual possession, 745-748
"fast possession action", 757-759
inception of "possession", 744-750
intention to possess, 748-750
Limitation Act 1980, 751-753
inchoate rights of squatter, 752-753
third parties, rights of, 752
limitation period, 741-743
accrual of right of action, 741-742
aggregation of periods, 742
necessity, no defence of, 753-754
overriding interest, as, 174
possessory title, registration, 751-752
RSC Ord 113, 757-759
rationale, 740-741
recovery of possession by paper owner, 753-
759
relativity of title, 64, 751-752
self-help, remedy of, 755-756
summons, remedy by, 757-759
surrender of dispossessed tenant's term, 743
tenancies, special rules in respect of, 742-
743
**Agreement for sale "subject to
contract", 206-209**
attempts to limit proviso, 206-208
estoppel doctrine, 208, 400
not legally binding, 206

**Agreement for sale "subject to
contract"**—*continued*
proposed reforms, 208-209
Airspace, 26-31
aerial surveillance, 30-31
civil immunity of overflying aircraft, 29-30
higher stratum, 28-29
invasion, 27
lower stratum, 27
vertical extent, 27
Alienability of land, 96-97
fragmentation of benefit, conflict with, 96
importance of, 96
restrictions on, 75-76
Annuities
registration, 112
Assault and battery, 959
Assignment
equitable, liability on covenants, 530
lease, of, 79, 463
legal, liability on covenants, 525 *et seq*
restrictive covenant in equity, of, 712 *et seq*
secure tenancy, of, 1051
sublease, of, 462
without consent, recovery of possession on
grounds of, 1020
Avulsion, 32-33
Bankruptcy, 875-887
adjustment of prior transactions at an
undervalue, 884-887
application for sale of family home, 876-
884
equity of exoneration, 883-884
homestead legislation, comparison with,
881-883
Insolvency Act 1986, 879-883
limited postponement of sale, 881
limited security of tenure for bankrupt's
spouse, 881
locus standi of trustee in bankruptcy, 876
statutory discretion, 876-879
co-owner of, power to realise assets, 861,
876 *et seq*
effects of, 875-887
rights to occupy matrimonial home
defeated by, 789, 881
Bare licence, 535-539
creation, 536-537
implied, 536-537
meaning, 535
revocation, 538-539

Bar licence—*continued*
revocation—*continued*
    effect, 538-539
    mode, 538
Building society
investigation of title by, 600
rate of interest, right to vary, 588-589
rules, 589
sale by, duty to obtain best price, 620
Buildings, 17-18
land, as, 17-18
Castle
"An Englishman's home is his castle', 537
Caveat Emptor,
tenancies, and, 902-903
Cestui que trust
enforcement of trust by
    creditors of trustee, against, 46
    donees of trustee, against, 46
    executors and administrators, against, 46
    purchasers from trustee, against, 46 *et seq*
    trustee, against, 45
meaning, 39
personal right against trustee, 45
proprietary rights, 50 *et seq*
relationship with trustee, 40
rights of
    equitable, 423, 555 *et seq*
    in personam, 49
    in rem, 49
Charges, 81
definition, 564
equitable, 577
Charging orders, 870-875
discretion of court, 872-875
    bankruptcy proceedings, relationship with, 875
    necessity for, 872
    property adjustment on divorce, relationship with, 873-875
effect, 870
enforcement, 870-875
function, 870
Law of Property Act 1925, s30 relationship with, 873
origin, 870
property on which imposed, 871
Coal
ownership of, 26
Common law
conflict with equity, 41
remedies, 42
Commonhold, 20, 945
Completion, 220-226
conveyancing practice, 224-225
equitable jurisdiction to set aside unconscionable bargains, 225-226
formalities, 221-224
reform of existing requirements for deed, 223-224
Conditions of sale
standard terms, 209-210

Constructive trust, 268-292, 811-818
bargain as basis of, 282-292
Canadian developments, 813-814
change of position, 275-280
    bargain, referable to, 278-280
    "detriment", 276, 277-278
    recognised forms, 276-277
    "sacrifice", 276, 277-278
common intention, 271-275
    origin of rights enforced, 274
    parties to agreement, 271
    recognised rights, 274
    subject matter of agreement, 273-274
    time-frame of agreement, 272
    unconventional rights, 274-275
component elements, 270-271
equitable fraud, 281-282
    attempted derogation from agreed entitlements, 281-282
    unconscientious use of legal title, 281
future developments, 817-818
general principle underlying, 269-270
intention, role of, 269
knowing reception of title held on trust, 292
"new model", 811-812
North American, 812
proprietary estoppel, relationship with, 419-421
remedial, 811-812
    property-based objections, 816-817
sphere of operation, 282-292
unfair prejudice to third party interests, 817
unjust enrichment, 334, 812-815
Consumer Credit Act 1974
protection of mortgagor under, 594 *et seq*
Contract
agreement for sale subject to, 206-209
breach of, remedies for, 216-217
closed, 209
completion, 220 *et seq*
destruction of property, effect of, 220
estate contract, registrable as, 135 *et seq*, 220
estate passes with, 217-218
exchange of contracts, 209-220
    conditional, 214
    deposits, 216
    postal, 215
    telephonic, 215
    written memorandum, 210-212
lease, to create, *see* LEASE
memorandum, 210–212
    contents, 210
    existing contract, recognition of, 211-212
    form, 210
    future reform, 212
    material terms, 210
    nature of document, 211
mortgage, to create, registrable land charge, as, 135

Contract—*continued*
open, 209
oral, unenforceability of, 210
part performance, 212 *et seq, see* PART
PERFORMANCE
race, 206
restricted, *see* RESTRICTED
CONTRACT
specific performance, *see* SPECIFIC
PERFORMANCE
standard term conditions of sale, 209-210
vendor as trustee, 217-220
Contractual licence, 541-559
cause and effect in characterisation of
property, 555
changing perceptions of "property", 558
disparate functions, 541-542
equitable approach, 547-548
equitable rights of property, meaning of,
555-559
family arrangements, *see* FAMILY
ARRANGEMENTS
implied term for quiet enjoyment, 543
implied term relating to fitness for purpose,
543
injunctive relief, 558
intellectual property, analogy of, 556-557
long-term functions, 542
medium-term functions, 542
priority of obligation, 555-556
property, meaning of, 555-559
"property right", hallmarks of, 557-559
property rights and personal rights, 558-
559
restrictive covenant, analogy of, 557
revocation, 545-549
"implied contract" theory, 546
injunctive relief, availability, 548-549
"licence coupled with an equity", 546
short-term functions, 541
terms, 543-545
third parties, effect on, 549-551
Denning doctrine, 550-551
actual occupation of contractual
licensee, 552-553
conveyance "subject to" rights of
contractual licence, 274-275, 553-
554
difficulties, 552-553
present position, 554-555
"licence coupled with an equity", 550
traditional rule, 549
modification, 549-550
transferability, 558
Conversion, doctrine of, 369-374
general theory, retreat from, 372-374
misapplication of theory, 370-371
present status, 373-374
reaction in context of family home, 372-373
"security claims", 372
supposed exceptions. 371

Conveyance
completion, *see* COMPLETION
deed, by, 221
formalities, 221 *et seq*
priority of interests after conveyance, 227-
229
registered land, of, 157
seal, necessity for, 222
solicitors' monopoly, 224
Conveyancing practice
agreement for sale 'subject to contract', 206
et seq
criticism, 224
dealings before exchange of contracts, 204-
209
ethos, 124, 225, 839-840
exchange of contracts, *see* CONTRACT
licensed conveyancers, 225
local authority searches, 206
preliminary enquiries, 204-205
Royal Commission report, 224
surveys, 205
Co-ownership, 293-343
bankruptcy, problems arising, 861,
876 *et seq*
beneficial interest
joint occupation as evidence, of, 838-839
concept, 293
concurrent interests in property legislation
of 1925, 337-341
co-ownership at law, 338-339
co-ownership in equity, 339-341
legal and equitable ownership, 337-338
coparcenary, 316
decision to deal with land, 375-385
joint tenancy, *see* JOINT TENANCY
movement from status to contract, 294
rent liability, 308 *et seq*
severance, *see* SEVERANCE
social context, 293-294
strict settlement, comparison with, 293-294
tenancy by entireties, *see* TENANCY BY
ENTIRETIES
tenancy in common, *see* TENANCY IN
COMMON
termination of, 341-343
conveyance to single third party, 343
partition, 341-342
union of property in one joint tenant,
342-343
trespass, 304-305
trust for sale, *see* TRUST FOR SALE
types of, 295 *et seq*
Coparcenary, 316
Corporeal hereditaments, 16-38
Covenants, 689-721
benefit of, 693-695
boundary between contract and property,
690-691
burden of, 695-697
contractual privity, 692

Covenants—*continued*
  equity, in, 697-721
    covenant must have been intended to
      run with covenantor's land, 704
    developments in caselaw, 698-700
    enforceable, characteristics of, 700-704
    restrictive or negative, must be, 700-701
    Tulk v *Moxhay*, 698-700
  function in planning of land use, 689-691
  law, at, 691-697
    transmission of benefit of, 693-695
    transmission of burden of, 695-697
  Law of Property Act 1925, s.56, 691-692
  leasehold covenants, *see* LEASE
  mutual benefit and burdens, 142
  negative, 690
  positive, 690
  private control of land use, 689-690
  reform of law, 720-721
  restrictive
    annexation, 707-712
      express, 707-709
      implied, 710
      statutory, 710-712
    assignment of benefit, 712-714
      annexation, relation with, 712-713
      preconditions, 713-714
    benefit, transmission of, 140-141, 706-707
    burden, transmission of, 140-141, 705-
      706
    compulsory purchase law, 720
    discharge, 720
    enforceability of, 704
    modification, 720
    planning law, 720
    remedies for breach, 719
    scheme of development, 715-719

Crown
  absolute landowner, 58
  letting by, not protected tenancy, 983
Cuius est solum eius est usque ad
  coelum et ad inferos, 16-17

Deed
  conveyance by, 221
  meaning, 221 *et seq*
  reform of requirements of formality, 223-
    224
  signed, sealed and delivered, 222-223

Deed of arrangement
  registration, 112

Disseisin
  novel, action of, 63

Distress, 510-513
  exemption for privileged goods, 512-513
  manner of, 511-512
  proposed abolition, 513
  restrictions on right, 510-511
  sale, 513
  time of, 511-512

Domestic violence
  co-ownership, and, 301
  homelessness, and, 763-764

Dominium
  meaning, 39

Easement, 8, 632-687
  benefit and burden, 646-647
  capability of forming subject matter of
    grant, 653-659
  capable grantee, 654
  capable grantor, 653
  covenant, relation with, 634-635
  creation of, 665-667
  definition, 632-633
  dominant and servient tenements, 644-648
    easement may run with both tenements,
      646-648
    registered land, 647-648
    unregistered land, 646-647
  dominant and servient tenements must be
    owned or occupied by different
    persons, 652-653
  examples, 80
  essential characteristics, 644-665
  exclusive occupation, 657-659
  exclusion of purely personal or commercial
    advantages, 648-649
  express grant, 667-668
  extinguishment, 686-687
  grant and reservation distinguished, 665-
    667
  grant of, 667-684
  implied grant, 668-678
    common intention, 671
    Law of Property Act 1925, s 62, 674-678
    neccessity, 668-671
    quasi-easements, 672-674
    Wheeldon v *Burrows*, rule in, 675-676
  informed creation, 665
  licences distinguished, 634
  local customary rights distinguished, 643-
    644
  must "accommodate" dominant tenement,
    648-652
  must not impose positive burden on
    servient owner, 657
  natural rights distinguished, 642-643
  nature of accommodation or benefit
    conferred, 650-652
    benefit to trade conducted on dominant
      tenement, 651
    enhancement of land value, 650
    exclusiveness of benefit not necessary,
      650
    integral aspects of commodious domestic
      living, 651
    purely recreational user, 651-652
  negative, reluctance to accept new, 655-656
  noise, to make, 656
  non-exclusiveness, 189, 648, 657 *et seq*
  novelty, 654-655
  prescription, 678-684
    common law prescription from long user,
      683

Easement—*continued*
  prescription—*continued*
    continuous user as of right, 679-680
    general principles, 679-682
    grounds, 683-684
    lost modern grant, 683-684
    Prescription Act 1832, 684
    proprietary estoppel, 684
    rationale, 679
    user in fee simple, 680-681
    user nec clam, 681
    user nec precario, 681
    user nec vi, 681
  propinquity, requirement of, 649-650
  public rights distinguished, 635-642
  quasi, 672-674
    conditions of operation, 673
    "continuous and apparent" user, 673-674
    contracts, application to, 674
    reasonable necessity, 674
    user at date of transfer, 674
  recognised, range of, 656
  release, 687
  requirements for legal character, 80
  reservation, 685-686
    express, 685
    implied, 685-686
  restrictive covenants distinguished, 634-635
  right must be sufficiently definite, 654
  unity of possession and ownership, 687
Educational institution
  letting by, not protected tenancy, 983
Entail
  barring of, 62
  meaning, 62
  statutory tenancy, and, 966, 1003
Entry
  conditional fee simple, ancillary to, right of, 73
  legal and equitable rights of, 82
  right of, equitable interest, as, 531-532
  right of, legal interest, as, 491, 529
Equitable charge, 577
Equitable easement, 141-143, *see also*
  LAND CHARGES
Equitable interests, 83
  analysis, 105, 108
  commercial, 96
  doctrine of notice, and, 85 *et seq*
  family, 96, 104, 108
  overreaching, trust for sale, in case of, 100 *et seq*, 355 *et seq*
  protection, 105 *et seq*
  registered land, in, 104, 108, 160
  squatter, binding on, 88
  strict settlement, under, overreaching, 100, 806
  successive, trust for sale, under, 345-346
Equity
  'clean hands', 414, 469-470

Equity—*continued*
  conflict with common law, 41-42
    in relation to leases, 471
  equitable rights of property, meaning, 423, 555 *et seq*
  'follows the law', 339, 360
  licence coupled with, *see* LICENCE
  mortgages, in relation to, 571 *et seq*, 580
    equity of redemption, 571-572
  relationship with law, 41-42
  remedies, 42
  See also TRUST
Equity of redemption, 571-572, 574
Estate contract
  meaning, 113, 135
  registrable land charge, as, 135 *et seq*
Estates, 55-65
  concept of, 58-60
  doctrine of, 58-65
  entailed interest, 62
  fee simple, 61, *see also* FEE SIMPLE
    infinite transferability, 61
    unrestricted alienability, 61
  formal creation, 79-80
  freehold, 60-62
  legal, *see* LEGAL ESTATES
  life interest, 62
  successive estates in land, 59-60
  time, division of, 59
  waste, doctrine of, 60
  words of limitation, 62-63
Eviction, unlawful, 954-960
  administrative remedies, 960
  civil remedies, 957-960
    assault and battery, 959
    breach of landlord's covenant for quiet enjoyment, 957-959
    nuisance, 959
    trespass, 959
    wrongful interference with goods, 960
  criminal sanctions, 955-957
  harassment, 956-957
Express trust, 235-242
  conclusive effect of declaration, 240-242
  formality, requirement of, 236-237
    exemptions, 237-240
  language, 236
  rectification, 242
  rescission for fraud or mistake, 242
  resulting trust, relationship with, 260
  subject matter, 236
Extortionate credit bargains, 594-597
  court's powers to reopen, 594
  "extortionate", meaning of, 594-595
  judicial treatment of interest rates, 595-597
  statutory criteria, 595
Fair rent, 1031-1038
  application for, 1031-1032
  assessment, 1034-1037
    capital return, 1034-1035
    comparable value, 1034-1035
    dwelling-house, condition of, 1035

Fair rent—*continued*
assessment—*continued*
furniture, condition of, 1036
general approach, 1034
inflation, relevance of, 1035
irrelevant factors, 1036-1037
lawful premiums, 1036
personal circumstances, 1036
reform, direction of, 1037-1038
relevant factors, 1035-1036
scarcity value, 1036
certificates, 1034
registration of, 1032-1033
appeal, 1033
effects, 1032-1033
variation, 1033
Family arrangements, 792-818
aliquot shares behind trust, 808-818
contributions towards acquisition or
retention, 809-811
Gissing, ruling, 810-811
improvements, 808-809
intention, role of, 808-811
"referability", requirement of, 809-810
analytical problems, 793-794
contractual classification, problems of, 793
contractual licence, 799
constructive trust, *see* CONSTRUCTIVE
TRUST
equitable licence, 800
informal origins, 792-793
irrevocable licence, 798-803
legally ineffective relationships, 794-796
"licence coupled with an equity", 798-799
life interest, *see* LIFE INTEREST
loan, 796-798
occupation lien pending repayment, 796
protection of lender, 796-798
non-commercial nature, 792
property classification, problems of, 794
property transfer order, 818
proprietary estoppel, *see* PROPRIETARY
ESTOPPEL
public policy, problems of, 794
residential, security in, 779 *et seq*
social credit, significance of, 792-793
Family home, 829-867
dealings with, 829-867
co-ownership of the legal title, 829
equitable effect of single trustee's
dealings, 833-850
actual occupation of family home, 845-
847
Boland's case, 843-845
significance of, 847-850
Class F land charge, 840-841
changing judicial outlook, 841-843
constructive notice, 837-839
conveyancing perspective 839-840
gender-discrimination, rejection of,
846-847

Family home—*continued*
dealings with—*continued*
modern approach to occupation rights,
840-843
mortgage perspective, 840
mortgage transaction, special
significance of, 834-835
range of parties involved, 833-834
registered land, 843-850
"shadow" theory, 846
unregistered land, 835-843
legal effect of single trustee's dealings,
831-833
methods of defeating undisclosed co-
ownership interests, 855-862
bankruptcy, 861-862
enquiry of vendor/mortgagor, 855-856
estoppel doctrine, 858-860
express consent from putative
beneficiaries, 856-857
insurance, 861
joint conveyance or mortgage, 860-861
strict proof of beneficial entitlement,
857-858
problems left in modern law, 850-862
range of relevant co-owners, 851-852
reform, proposals for, 862-868
automatic joint tenancy in equity, 863
criticisms of co-ownership scheme, 865
Land Registration and Law of
Property Bill 1985, 867-868
Law Commission's proposed reform of
overriding interests, 868
protection through registration, 863-
864
"registration requirement", 864-865
registered land, 832-833
relevant enquiry, range of, 852-855
solely owned family home, 829
statutory scheme of co-ownership, 862-
865
undisclosed equitable co-ownership, 830-
831
unregistered land, 831-832
decision to sell, 819-827
Law of Property Act 1925, s 30, 819-820
factual context, 820
primary rule, 820
trust for sale, collateral purpose of, 820-
827
breakdown of co-operative
relationships, 823
destruction of, 822-823
family-oriented approach, 824-827
minor children, needs of, 824
property-oriented approach, 823-824
relevance of public housing policy, 827
size of family home, 824
supervening divorce, 822
survival of, 821-822
wasting assets, 824

Fee simple, 71-78
absolute, meaning of, 71-72
alienation, restrictions on, 75-76
conditional fee simple, 72-74
ancillary "rights of entry", 73
distinguished from determinable, 73-74
legal quality of, 74
operation of, 74
determinable fee simple, 71-72
examples, 72
invalidity on grounds of public policy, 72
operation of, 74
subsequent impossibility, 72
discrimination, 77
judicial control over conditions and limitations, 74-75
marriage, restrictions on, 76
religious belief, restrictions on, 76-77
"in possession", meaning of, 77-78
estates "in remainder", 77-78
estates "in reversion", 78
Feoffment, 43, 64
fictitious feoffees, 43
uses, to, 43
Finders, rights of, 35-36
Fish, 35
Fishing
rights of, 31-32, 640
Fixtures, 20-25
chattels distinguished, 20-21
legal relevance, 23
contractual right to remove, 25
degree of annexation, 21-22
purpose of annexation, 21-22
removal by freehold owner, 23-24
rights of removal, 23
tenant for life, removal by, 25
tenant for years, removal by, 24
Flowers, 25-26
Flying freehold, 18-19
Foreclosure, 628-630
legal effects, 628
modern incidence of, 630
preconditions, 629
procedure, 629-630
Forfeiture of lease, 490-510
breach of tenant's repairing covenant, for, 500-502
capability of remedy, concept of, 498
effect of, 506-509
mortgagee, on, 508
squatter, on, 509
subtenant, on, 507-508
tenant, on, 506-507
irremediable breaches of covenant, 497-498
negative covenants, remediability of, 499-500
non-payment of rent, for, 493-496
court's general discretion to grant relief, 494-496

Forfeiture of lease—*continued*
non-payment of rent, for—*continued*
tenant's right to have possession proceedings stayed, 494
positive covenants, remediability of, 499
re-entry, right of, 491-493
reform, proposals for, 509-510
relief for breaches other than non-payment of rent, 502-504
remediable breaches of covenant, 497
section 146 notice, 496-502
waiver of breach, 504-506
Fraud
constructive trust, and, 281 *et seq*
equitable, 281
mortgagee's power of sale, on, 626
unravels everything, 123
Furnished house
fitness for habitation, implied condition of letting, 903 *et seq*
Gazumping
practice of, 206
Harassment
prohibition, 476, 956 *et seq*
Highway
ownership, 72
rights of passage along, 635-640
Holiday lettings
not protected tenancies, 983
Rent Act evasions, as, 1002
Homelessness, 760-779
conditions of eligibility, 761-774
constructive, 762
crisis accommodation, 762-763
definition, 762-766
denial of "homeless" status, 763
domestic violence, 763-764
exclusion orders, availability of, 764
general aim of legislation, 760-761
housing authority, duties of, 774-777
advice, 777
assistance, 777
further offers of accommodation, 776
inquiries, 774-775
notification, 773
reasonable consideration, 773
reasonable steps to secure that accommodation does not cease to be available, 776
securing accommodation available for occupation, 775-776
temporary accommodation, 776-777
intentional, 767-773
abandoned accommodation "available for occupation", 770-771
applicant must "cease" to occupy accommodation, 770
causal link between applicant's conduct and cessor of occupation, 772
changes in family status or living arrangements, 768-769
guilt by association, 769-770

1080   Index

Homelessness—*continued*
  intentional—*continued*
    indirect causal nexus, 768
    presumption of collective liability, 769
    "reasonable" for applicant to continue
        to occupy accommodation, 771-772
    relevant conduct, nature of, 767-768
    responsibility, nature of, 769-770
  local connection, definition of, 774
  priority needs, definition of, 766-767
  Puhlhofer ruling, 764-766
  qualitative test as to existing
      "accommodation", 764-766
  reasonableness of association, 764
  remedies, 777-778
  temporary accommodation, 762-763
Implied trust, 242-244
  classification, 243
  origin, 243-244
Incorporeal hereditaments, 38
Incumberances, 561 *et seq*
Industrial protest, 638-639
***Ius accrescendi*, 296-301**
Joint tenancy, 295-302
  absence of shareholding, 295-296
  advantages, 298 *et seq*
  at law, meaning of, 337-338
  distinguishing characteristics, 296-302
  express declaration of trust, created by, 241
  four unities, 301-302
  interest, unity of, 301-302
  ius accrescendi, 296 *et seq*
  mortgagees, position of, 340
  possession, unity of, 301, 303 *et seq*
  severance, *see* SEVERANCE
  survivorship, 296-301
  tenancy in common, distinguished from,
      303
  time, unity of, 302
  title, unity of, 302
  trustees, position of, 338
  undifferentiated form of co-ownership, 295
  union in one joint tenant, termination by,
      342
Killing, unlawful
  severance by, *see* SEVERANCE
Land, 16-38
  alienability of, *see* ALIENABILITY OF
      LAND
  corporeal hereditaments, 16-38, *see also*
      CORPOREAL HEREDITAMENTS
  distinctive features as property form, 6
  incorporeal hereditaments, 38
  legal definition, 16
Land certificate
  deposit until redemption of mortgage, 576-
      577, 605
  function, 149
Land charges, 113-125
  annuities, 112
  basic concept, 110

Land charges—*continued*
  basic flaw of registration system, 130-133
    partial remedy, 132
    practical precautions, 133
    statutory compensation, preconditions of,
        132-133
  categories, 133-143
  Class A, 133
  Class B, 133
  Class C, 134-138
  Class C(i), 134
  Class C (ii), 134
  Class C (iii), 134-135
  Class C (iv), 135-138
    accepted forms of estate contract, 135
    contracts for a lease, 469, 474-475
    contracts of agency, 137-138
    conveyancing function of estate contract,
        135
    rights of pre-emption, 136-137
  Class D, 138-143
  Class D (i), 138
  Class D (ii), 138-141
    enforcement of restrictive covenants,
        140-141, 705-706
    exclusions, 141
    function of restrictive covenant, 139
    proprietary status of restrictive covenant,
        139
    relevance of equitable doctrine of notice,
        139
    rule of registration, introduction of, 139-
        140, 705
  Class D (iii), 141-143
    estoppel-based easements, 141-143, 399,
        684
    uncertain coverage, 141
  Class E, 143
  Class F, 143
  integrity of registration system, 120-125
    "adequate" consideration, requirement
        of, 122
    different views of function of property
        law, 124
    "fraud unravels everything", 123
    "not fraud to take advantage of legal
        rights", 124-125
    purchase "for money or money's worth",
        whether, 121-122
    requirement of good faith in section 4(6)
        of Act, whether, 122-125
  deeds of arrangement, 112
  irrelevance of traditional doctrine of notice,
      116-120
    actual occupation, protection for, 118-
        119
    modification of doctrine of notice, 116
    moral criteria, attempts to reintroduce,
        118-119
    preference for certainty over justice, 116
    tension between certainty and justice,
        117-118

Land charges—*continued*
mode of entry in register, 113-114
negligent misstatement, 127
non-registration, effect of, 115-116
orders affecting land, 112
pending actions, 111
  matters registrable as, 111
  non-registration, effect of, 111
  registration, effect of, 111
registration, effect of, 114
search of register, 125-130
  consequence of discovering registered
    charge, 128
  defective registration, 128,129
  defective search, 129-130
  effect of, 126-128
    conclusive nature of certificate, 126-
      127
    policy preference in favour of official
      search, 127-128
    remedies in tort for damage caused by
      negligent misstatement, 127
  process of 126
  timing of, 125-126
"spite" registrations, 114
sub-purchaser, registration by, 113-114
writs 112

Land register
caution, entry of, 160-161
Charges Register, 149
details to be recorded in, 145
entry in, 94-95
error or omission in, indemnity, 199
minor interests, effects of failure to enter,
  162 *et seq*
official search, minor interests, for, 161-162
Property Register, 148
Proprietorship Register, 149
  restriction, entry in, 159
rectification, 193 *et seq*

Landlord
common law liability for personal injuries,
  946
crime, liability for, 950-954
  agents, 950
  employees, 950
  general duty to preserve tenant from crime,
    951-954
    implied contractual promise to preserve
      security, 953-954
    implied warranty of habitability, 952-
      953
    tort liability, extension of, 951-952
implied contractual duty of care, 946
negligence, 947-948
statutory liability for accidents, 949-950
  Defective Premises Act 1972, 949-950
  implied terms of tenancy, 949

Lease, 427-523, *see also* TENANCY,
  FORFEITURE OF LEASES
assignment, 463
chattel real, 427

Lease—*continued*
competent lessee, 431-432
competent lessor, 431
covenants, 475-484
  derogation from grant 476-477
  express obligations of landlord, 475
  implied obligations of landlord, 475-477
  quiet enjoyment, 476
  state of repair, 477
contract to create, 468-470
  anticipatory effect of equity, 470-471
  effect of, 472-475
  equitable lessee, position of, 474-475
  "privity of estate", and, 473
  specific performance, and, 473
creation, 464-466
determinable
  creation, 465
disclaimer, 489
enlargement, 490
equitable, 466
  implied covenants, 477
equitable, enforceability of covenants in,
  529-534
  liability as between landlord and tenant,
    529
  liability of assignees, 530-533
  liability of assignee to tenant, 530
  liability of sublessee to landlord or
    assignee, 533-534
  liability of tenant to assignee, 529-530
essential elements, 427 *et seq*
exclusive possession, 439-441
fixed maximum duration, 433-438
fixed term, 428-429
flexibility of arrangements, 462-464
forfeiture, 486, *see also* FORFEITURE OF
  LEASE
formalities, 464-475
frustration, 489-490
landlord's remedies for breach of covenant
  by tenant, 490-514
  action for arrears or rent, 514
  damages for breach of covenant, 513-514
  damages for waste, 514
  distress *see* DISTRESS
  forfeiture of lease, 490, 510, *see also*
    FORFEITURE OF LEASE
  injunction, 514
legal, enforceability of covenants in, 516-
  529
  assignment, and, 517, 520, 521-525
  forfeiture, remedy of, 529
  liability as between landlord and tenant,
    516-520
  liability of sublessee to landlord or
    assignee, 528-529
  liability based on "privity of estate",
    525-527
  liability of assignee to tenant, 523-525
  liability of tenant to assignee, 521

Lease—*continued*
legal, enforceability of covenants
   in—*continued*
    purely personal or collateral covenants,
     523
    restrictive covenants, enforcement of,
     528-529
    "touch and concern" requirement, 521-
     522
  lessor must retain reversionary interest, 433
  lessor, to, 433
  licence distinguished, 443-462
    accommodation based on friendship or
     generosity, 458-459
    ambivalent factors, 450-452
    "charity", accommodation based on,
     457-458
    competing criteria of exclusive possession
     and expressed intention, 445-449
    consideration of documents and
     circumstances, 452-454
    express exclusions from concept of
     "tenancy", 457-461
    expressed intention, relevance of, 448
    "gentleman's agreement, 459-460
    implied exclusions from concept of
     "tenancy", 454-456
    irrelevant factors, 450-452
    lodgers, 455-456
    "nature and quality" of occupancy, 449-
     454
    service occupancy, 460-461
    significance of distinction, 444-445
    Street v *Mountford*, decision in, 461-462
  life, for, 435-436
  marriage, until, 436
  maximum duration must be ascertainable,
   435
  merger, 489
  minor, to, 432
  must commence at "time certain", 433-434
  parties must be legally competent, 431-433
  periodic, 429-430
  perpetually renewable, 436
  privity of estate, 525-527, 528
  renewable
    creation, 465
  rent or other consideration, 441-443
    certainty of obligation, 442-443
    rent in kind, 443
  shared ownership, 738
  social and economic functions, 79
  statutory obligations of landlord, 477-479
    assignment by landlord, 478
    disclosure of information, 478
    identity of landlord, 478
    rent book, provision of, 478-479
    service charges, 479
  statutory obligations of tenant, 482
  sublease, 463-464
  surrender, 486-489
  tenant, express obligations of, 480

Lease—*continued*
  tenant, implied obligations of, 480-482
    "usual covenants" in equitable lease,
     481-482
  tenant's remedies for breach of covenant by
   landlord, 514-516
    disrepair, 514-515
    independence of covenants of landlord
     and tenant, 515
    proposals for reform, 515-516
  term may be of any length, 434-435
  termination, 484-490
    effluxion of time, 484
    notice to quit, 484-486
  time-share, 436
  types of, 428-431
  unlawful practices, 482-484
    discrimination, 482-483

Leasehold enfranchisement, 725-733
  eligible property, 727
  eligible tenancy, 727-729
  "human rights" challenge, 731-733
  legislative motivation, 726-727
  "long tenancy", 728
  "low rent", 728
  qualifying conditions, 727-729
  residence qualification, 728-729
  tenant's statutory rights, 729-731
    leasehold enfranchisement, 730-731
    leasehold extension, 730
    manner of exercise, 729-730
    price, 730-731

Leaseholds, 78-79, *see also* LEASE,
  TENANCY

Legal and equitable rights, 65-93
  distinction between, 65-71
    proper classification of rights in land, 70-
     71
    significance, 83-93
    statutory criterion, 70
  legal rights bind the world, 84-85

Legal estates, 71 *et seq*

Licences, 535-559
  bare, *see* BARE LICENCE
  contracting out of Rent Act, and, 998-1000
  contractual, *see* CONTRACTUAL
   LICENCE
  coupled with grant of interest, 539-540
    creation, 540
    revocation, 540
    types of "interest", 539-540
  easements distinguished, 634
  equitable
    family arrangements, and *see* FAMILY
     ARRANGEMENTS
  irrevocable *see* FAMILY
   ARRANGEMENTS
  lease distinguished, 443-462, *see also*
   LEASE

Licensed premises
dwelling-house comprising, not protected
tenancy, 983
Life interest, 803-808
Light, rights of, 663-665
Local authority
abatement notice, 935
allocation of secure tenancies, 1048-1050
dwelling-house unfit for human habitation,
powers as to, 927 *et seq*
homeless persons, duty to house, 775 *et seq*
letting by
not protected tenancy, 983
rent restriction, 1051
right to purchase reversion, 733 *et seq*
security of tenure, 1054 *et seq*
See also PUBLIC SECTOR TENANT
and SECURE TENANCY
multiple occupation, powers in connection
with, 938
statutory nuisance, powers in case of, 933 *et
seq*
vandalism, liability for, 950-951
Local authority searches, 206
Local land charges
general burdens, as, 202
registration, 112
Lost and hidden objects, 35-38
chattels found on ground, 36
"finders keepers", 36
objects found within ground, 35-36
treasure trove *see* TREASURE TROVE
trespassing finders, 36
Married woman
disabilities, 7
'object' of property, 11
Matrimonial home,
Act of 1967
automatic co-ownership, 790-791
future of, 789-791
mass invalidation of charges, 789-790
public awareness, 790
deserted wife's equity, 785-786
disadvantages, 785-786
rejection, 786
homestead legislation, 790, 881-882
improvements, 311, 809
rights of occupation enforceable against
persons outside family, 785-789
statutory rights of occupation, 782-785
beneficial co-owner, 784
cancellation of registration, 788
categories of spouse covered by, 783-784
entry in register, 787
judicial regulation of, 784-785
legal co-owner, 784
non-entitled spouse, 783-784
non-registration, consequence of, 789
process of registration, 786-788
property to which applicable, 784

Matrimonial home—*continued*
statutory rights of occupation—*continued*
registration, 786-789
registration for ulterior motives, 787-788
release of rights, 788
wife's common law right to occupy, 781-
782
Minerals, 26
Minor
lease to, 432
legal estate cannot be held by, 7, 366
Minor interests, 159-170
caution, 160-161
competing, 162
failure to protect by entry on register, 162-
170
acquiescence in exercise of unprotected
right, 169
collateral representation, 169
deliberate ploy to defeat unprotected
rights, 168-169
doctrine of notice, occasional re-
emergence of, 165-168
fraud and notice, historic dissociation of,
165
fraud, exception for, 164
fraud, recognised cases, 168-169
general irrelevance of notice, 163
mere knowledge of unprotected rights
not fraud, 165
orthodox rule, 163
rationale behind rule, 163-164
reform, proposals for, 169-170
transfer expressly "subject to"
unprotected rights, 169
inhibition, 161
notice, 160
overlap with overriding interests, 190-192
protection, 159-161
restriction, 159-160
search of register, 161-162
Mortgage, 563-631
action on mortgagor's personal covenant to
repay, 613
attempted exclusion of right to redeem,
582-583
attornment clause, 607-608
building society rules, 589
capital accumulation, 565
charge, distinguished from, 564
"clogs and fetters" doctrine, 581-582
"collateral advantages", rule against, 581-
582
commercial expansion, 566
contract to create, registrable land charge,
as, 135
definition, 563-564
deposit of title documents, 604-605
discharge of, 578
endowment mortgage, 564

Mortgage—*continued*
equitable, creation of, 575-577
  deposit of documents of title, 576-577
  equitable charge, 577
  equitable interest, 575
  informal mortgage of legal interest, 576
equitable mortgagee,
  right to possession, whether, 612-613
equity, intervention of, 571-572, 580
equity of redemption, 571-572, *see also*
  EQUITY OF REDEMPTION
exercise of mortgagee's right to possession,
  608-612
  brief emergence of remedial perspective,
    611
  factors inhibiting, 609-610
  mortgagee's strict liability to account,
    609-610
  right or access to remedy, whether, 610-
    612
  statutory control over residential
    property, 609
extortionate credit bargains, *see*
  EXTORTIONATE CREDIT
  BARGAINS
family finance, effect on, 565-566
foreclosure, *see* FORECLOSURE
harsh interest rates, 589-591
home ownership, 564-565
index linked interest rates, 591-593
  challenge based on equitable objections,
    592-593
  challenge based on grounds of public
    policy, 591-592
  potential impact of index-linking, 593
investigation of title by mortgagee, 600-604
  beneficial interests under trusts and
    settlements, 603
  equitable interests of beneficiaries behind
    trust for sale, 601-603
  loan moneys advanced to fraudulent
    trustee for sale, 602-603
  loan moneys advanced to sole trustee for
    sale, 601
  loan moneys advanced to two trustees for
    sale, 601-602
  tenancies by estoppel, 603-604
  unregistered contractual rights, 604
land certificate, deposit with Land
  Registry, 576-577, 605
legal, creation of, 571-575
  charge, by, 573
  freehold land, 573
  leasehold land, 573-574
  long demise by, 573
  long subdemise, by, 573-574
  mortgagor's equity of redemption, 571-
    572
  post-1925 modes, 572-574
  pre-1926 modes, 571

Mortgage—*continued*
life styles, effect on, 565
meaning, 81-82
mortgages, protection for, 600-605
mortgagee's recovery of possession, 888-897
  assertion of priority by beneficial owner,
    897
  court's inherent jurisdiction to grant
    relief to mortgager, 890-891
  court's statutory power to allay, 891-897
    limits of court's discretion, 896-897
    preconditions for, 892-893
    section 36, Administration of Justice
      Act 1970, effect of, 893-896
  right of mortgagor's spouse to tender
    payment of mortgage monies, 889
  supplementary benefit, and, 888-889
mortgagee's right to possession, 605-613
  attornment clauses, 607-608
  exclusion, 606-608
    express, 606
    implied, 606
    instalment mortgage, 606-607
  origin, 605-606
mortgagor, comparison with periodic
  tenant, 567-571
  mobility, 569-570
  "new feudalism", 569-570
  political manipulation of relative status,
    568
  security of tenure, 569
  "shared ownership" schemes, 570
  social status, 570-571
  utilities and obligations, 568-569
"oppressive and unconscionable" terms,
  judicial control of, 588-593
option for purchase incorporated in, 582-
  583
overall effect of 1925 legislation, 574-575
  "equity of redemption", 574
  legal title remains in borrower, 574
payment of interest by supplementary
  benefit, 888-889
penal interest rates, 593
personal covenant to repay, 613
political dimension, 566-567
postponement of date of redemption, 584-
  586
  exceptional intervention of equity, 584
  general approach, 584-586
power of sale, 614-627
  absence of statutory standard of fair
    dealing, 617
  duty of selling mortagee, 618-620
    arising, when, 614
    auction, sales by, 623-624
    damages for carelessness by
      mortgagee, 626
    "fraud on the power", 626
    fusion of subjective and objective
      criteria, 619-620

Mortgage—*continued*
  power of sale—*continued*
    duty of selling mortgagee—*continued*
      modalities of sale, 622-623
      objective criteria of reasonable
        behaviour, 619
      preliminaries of sale, 622-623
      reasonable care, 620-624
      sale price, 620-621
      sale to associated person, 625
      sale to mortgagee or representative,
        624-625
      subjective criteria of good faith, 618-
        619
      timing of sale, 621-622
    effect, 615-617
    exercisable, when, 614
    exercise of, 614-627
    mortgagee's duty in relation to
      application of proceeds, 617
    premature, 615
  public sector tenant's "right to buy", 567
  puisne, registrable land charge, as, 134, 605
  rate of interest
    increase, altered redemption date as
      compensation for, 589
    index-linking, 591, *et seq*
    right to vary, 589
    unconscionable, 590 *et seq*
  receiver, appointment of, *see* RECEIVER,
    627-628
  reform of law, 577-578
  registered charge, 193
  relaxation of rules prohibiting usury, 579-
    580
  remedies available to equitable mortgagee,
    630-631
  remedies available to legal mortgage, 613-
    630
  social significance, 564-571
  Solus agreements, 586-588
  tendancy towards preservation of status
    quo, 566-567
  undue influence, *see* UNDUE
    INFLUENCE
  upward mobility, 566
  variable interest rates, 588-589
Mutual benefit and burden, 142
National Trust
  leasehold enfranchisement, 728
  restrictive covenants, power to enforce, 703
Natural rights
  landowners, of
    easement, distinguished from, 642
    meaning, 642
    protection, 642-643
    support for land, 642
Navigable waters,
  rights of passage in, 640
Negligence
  landlord's liability in, 911-914 *see also*
    LANDLORD

Notice, doctrine of, 48, 85 *et seq*
  equitable rights governed by doctrine of
    notice, 85-93
    actual notice, 88-89
    constructive notice, 89-91
    imputed notice, 91-92
    bona fides, 87
    destructive effect of purchase for value
      without notice, 92-93
    purchase of legal estate, 87-88
    purchase for value, 88
Nuisance, 959
  landlord's liability for, 914-915
  public, 639-640
  recovery of possession on grounds of, 1019,
    1056
  statutory
    abatement notice, 935
    powers of local authority, 933 *et seq*
Occupation, rights of, 781-791
  family home, in *see* MATRIMONIAL
    HOME
  rights enforceable against other family
    members, 781-785
  statutory rights, *see* MATRIMONIAL
    HOME
  trust for sale, beneficiary of, 368-375
  wife's common law right to occupy, 781-
    782
Oil
  ownership, 26
Option
  registrable land charge, as, 136, 395, 524
  to purchase
    incorporated in mortgage, 582-583
    overriding interest, as, 179, 181
Overcrowding, 936-939
  ground for possession, 1031
  prohibition, 936 *et seq*
Overreaching *see* TRUST FOR SALE
Overriding interests, 170-192
  adverse possession, 174
  categories, 172-175
  conveyancing background, 171
  easements, 172-173, 647-648
  function of, 170-171
  overlap with minor interests, 190-192
  problematic nature, 171-172
  Section 70(1)*(g)*, Land Registration Act
    1925, 175 *et seq*
    "actual occupation" 185-189, *see also*
      ACTUAL OCCUPATION
    collateral contractual rights, 182-183
    continuing enforceability of overriding
      interest, 177
    contractual license, 182
    date on which overriding interest takes
      effect, 175-177
    derivative interests, protection of, 177-
      178
    enquiry under, 189-190
    Leasehold Reform Act 1967, notice
      under, 183

Overriding interests—*continued*
Section 70(1)*(g)*, Land Registration
    Act 1925—*continued*
    leases, 174-175
    matrimonial home, occupation of, 181-
      182
    nature of "rights" protected, 179-185
    operation of, 175-179
    "preserved right to buy", 183-184
    protection for commercial landlord, 178
    protection for persons in receipt of rents
      and profits, 178-179
    purpose of, 175
    reform, 192
    "registration gap", advantages of, 176-
      177
    "registration gap", disadvantages of, 176
    "rights" accepted within ambit of, 181
    rights excluded from scope of, 181
    "rights" must have been enforceable at
      date of transfer, 184-185
    "rights must subsist in reference to
      land", 179-180
    settled land beneficiaries, equitable
      rights of, 183
    statutory restrictions on range of, 183-
      184
Part performance, 212-214
    acts sufficient to constitute, 213
    conditions, 213
    easements, 665
    liability of landlord *see* LANDLORD
    mortgages, 576
    registration, 111
    trust, 238
Partnership
    tenancy in common in case of, 340
Plants, 25-26
Possession, exclusive, 439-441, 445-449
    exclusive occupation distinguished, 446
Preliminary enquiries, 204-205
Premiums, 428
    assignment, on, 1039
    payment by regulated tenant, 1038-1039
    restricted contracts, and, 1044
Presumption of advancement, 262-268
    husband's funds used for purchase in joint
      names, 267
    husband's funds used for purchase in name
      of wife, 266-267
    joint funds used for acquisition of legal
      title, 268
    mothers, applicability to, 264
    relationships which raise, 263
    spouses, applicability to, 264-266
    wife's funds used for purchase in joint
      names, 267
    wife's funds used for purchase in name of
      husband, 267
Profit à prendre, 632-637, *see also*
    EASEMENT
    creation of, 665-667
    definition, 633

Profit à prendre—*continued*
    easement distinguished, 633-634
    equitable, 665
    express grant, 667-668
    extinguishment, 686-687
    grant and reservation distinguished, 665-
      667
    grant of, 667-684
    "in gross", 633-634
    informal creation, 665
    prescription, 678-684
    release, 687
    scope of, 634
    unity of possession and ownership, 687
Property 1-15
    access rights replace exclusory rights, 14
    changing balance of family, work and
      government, 12-13
    changing concept, 11
    changing "objects" of, 11
    changing "subjects" of, 10
    contemporary redefinition, 13-14
    dependence, and, 7
    distinctive features of land as, 6
    infants, 7
    married woman, 7
    meaning of, 8-15
    'new property'
      agent of distributive justice, 14
      concept of, 11 *et seq*
      residential security, relation with, 13,
        372, 558
      rights of access as, 14
      social rights, 14-15, 966
    'objects' of, changing, 11
    personality, and, 7
    political dimension, 7
    potential multiplicity of competing users, 9
    'property rights', hallmarks of, 557-559
    property rights and personal rights, 558-
      559
    relationship as, 8 *et seq*
    Roman law, 39
    security of tenure as, 966-967, 1066-1067
    social view of property, 6
    social welfare rights, as, 11, 558
    'subjects' of, changing, 10
Property transfer order, 818
Proprietary estoppel, 386-426, 800-803
    assurance, 396-403
      manner of, 400-401
      state of mind of owner of land, 401-403
      source, 397-398
      subject matter, 398-400
    benefit of equity passing to third party, 424
    burden of equity passing to third party,
      424-426
      registered land, 426
      unregistered land, 425-426
    categories in caselaw, 388-396
    central concern, 386-387
    "common expectation" cases, 390-392

Proprietary estoppel—*continued*
constructive trust, relationship with, 419-
    421
detriment, 409-413
    bars to claim of unconscionable
        behaviour, 412-413
    unconscionability, criterion of, 410-412
doctrinal roots, 387-388
equity arising, when, 421-422
    concretised remedy, 422
    inchoate "equity", 421-422
equity comprising proprietary interest or
    interest in land, whether, 422-423
essential elements, 387
exceptional assistance in perfection of gift,
    388-389
extent of avoidable remedies, 420-421
extent of remedy, 413-419
    general principle, 413
    relevant criteria, 413-416
general theory, 387-388
grant of monetary compensation, 417-418
grant of right of occupation coupled with
    monetary compensation, 418
grant of right to occupy, 417
grant of unqualified estate or interest in
    land, 416
"imperfect gift" cases, 388-390
inhibitory effect of remedies, 418-419
misconduct, 414-415
money compensation, 801-802
nature of, 419-426
occupation rights, 800-801
onus of proof, 420
operation of, 396-413
"property right", meaning of, 423
range of possible remedies, 416-419
range of recognised contributions, 420
reliance, 403-409
    causal link between assurance and
        detriment, 403-404
    change of position, 404-407
    disadvantage unrelated to land, 405
    improvement of realty, 404-405
    personal effort and personal
        disadvantage, 405-407
    state of mind of claimant, 407-409
retreat from wide application, 802
"unilateral mistake" cases, 392-394
use as "sword" or "shield", 415-416
Protected tenancy, 970-982
"board or attendance" exemption, 985-987
    attendance, definition of, 986-987
    board, definition of, 985
    recent restrictions, 986
    sham provision, 986
business purposes, dwelling-house used for,
    982
dwelling-house, 971-972
dwelling-house let as separate dwelling,
    974-982
    capacity to sustain separate domestic
        existence, 979

Protected tenancy—*continued*
dwelling-house let as separate
    dwelling—*continued*
    fragmentation of domestic activity
        between different premises, 979-981
    joint tenants, letting to, 981-982
    letting to tenant who grants contractual
        licences, 982
    mixed user of premises, 982
    multiple lettings, 981
    "separate dwelling", nature of, 979-981
    sharing arrangements, 981-982
    "singular construction", 975-979
    unrestrictive aspects, 975-976
express exclusion from, 982-990
"holiday lettings" exemption, 983-984
    holiday, definition of, 984-985
fair rent, 1031 *et seq*
non-exclusive occupation agreements, 998-
    999
payments of money other than as "rent",
    973-974
performance of services, 973
premium, prohibition of, 1038 *et seq*
purpose of letting, 974-975
rent quantifiable in definite monetary
    terms, 972-974
"resident landlord" exception, 987-990
    joint residence in "purpose-built block of
        flats", 989
    "landlord", definition, 989
    landlord's residence in another part of
        same building, 989-990
    "part only of building", 988
    property to which tenancy relates, 988
    requirement of continuous residence by
        landlord, 990
    "residence", definition of, 990
shorthold, 1028 *et seq*
statutory tenancy after termination, 1007
Public nuisance, 639-640
Public rights
easement, relation with, 635
meaning, 635 *et seq*
Public sector housing
private sector, disposal to, 1058
Public sector tenancy, 1059-1062
assignment, restriction on, 1051-1052
lodgers, provision as to, 1052
persons eligible as successors, 1059-1061
recovery of possession, 1056 *et seq*
rent restriction, 1051
right to purchase reversion, 733 *et seq*
secure tenancy, concept of, 1045 *et seq*
security of tenure, 1054 *et seq*
statutory succession to, 1054-1055, 1059-
    1062
Public sector tenant, 733-739
right to buy, 733-739
    conditions, 734-735
    discounted price, 736
    nature of, 734
    "preserved", 739

Public sector tenant—*continued*
  right to buy—*continued*
    qualifying property, 734-735
    qualifying tenants, 735
    right to mortgage finance, 737
    shared ownership lease, 737-738
      principle, 738
      progressive purchase, 738
    terms and covenants affecting new title,
      737
    terms of purchase, 736-737
  statutory protection, 1045-1058
Purchasers of legal title
  protection of, 97-105
  free alienability of land titles, 97-98
  limited liability to pre-existing interests, 98-
    105
    categories of overreaching transaction,
      100-101
    consequences of overreaching, 101
    diminished role of traditional doctrine of
      notice, 102
    equitable rights in unregistered land, 100
    immunity of transferee, 104
    legal rights in unregistered land, 99
    "major interests", 103-104
    "minor interests", 103-104
    operation of overreaching, 101-102
    "overreaching", concept of, 100
    overriding interests, 104-105
    registered land, 102-103
  restriction of number of legal estates, 98
  restriction of number of owners of legal
    estate, 98
Quasi-easements, 672-674
Receiver,
  appointment by mortgagee, 627-628
    functions, 627
    liability for actions of, 627-628
    preconditions, 627
  appointment by tenant, 944-945
Recreational user,
  easement, as, 651-652
  public right, as, 641
  rights of, 641-642
Registered and unregistered land, 94-95
  geographical distinction, 94
  practical distinction, 94
Registered and unregistered title
  relationship between, 95
Registered charges, 193
Registered title
  essence of, 94-95
Registrable interests, 151-158
  absolute title, 154
  applicant with freehold estate, 154-155
  applicant with leasehold estate, 155
  compulsory registration, 151-154
  compulsory registration in non-compulsory
    areas, 153
  consequence of failure to effect first
    registration, 153-154

Registrable interests—*continued*
  easements, 153
  freehold estates, 152
  good leasehold title, 155-156
  leasehold estates, 152
  new statutory estate, whether, 157
  possessory title, 156
  possible grades of title, 154
  qualified title, 156
  subsequent transfers of registered estate,
    157-158
    consequences of non-registration of, 157-
      158
    effect of registration of, 158
    registration, requirement of, 157
  voluntary registration, 154
Registration of title, 144 *et seq*
  basic features, 145-147
  classification of interests, 151
  different system of land law, as, 147
  future reform, 201-203
    more equitable compensation for loss,
      202-203
    new guiding principles, 201
    restriction of overriding interests, 201
  land certificate, 149
  minor interests, 159-170, *see also* MINOR
    INTERESTS
  overriding interests, 170-192. *see also*
    OVERRIDING INTERESTS
  rectification, 193-200
    consent, 195
    default of title, 195-196
    double registrations, 195
    effect, 197-198
    fraud, entry obtained by, 195
    grounds, 194-197
    indemnity, 199-200
      incidence of claims, 200
      restrictions on, 200
    interest wrongly omitted or included in
      register, 194
    residual ground, 196-197
    restrictions on, 198-199
    subsisting overriding interest, 194
    wrongful registration of mortgage, 195
  Register, 147-150
    Charges Register, 149
    divisions of, 148-149
    Property Register, 148-149
    Proprietorship Register, 149
    public access to, 150
  registered and unregistered conveyancing
    distinguished, 144-145
  registered charges, 193
  registrable interests, 151-158. *see also*
    REGISTRABLE INTERESTS
  Registrar, functions of, 148
Rent
  action for arrears, 514
  advance payments, 1039
  book, duty to provide, 478-479

Rent—*continued*
certainty, 442-443
distress for, 510, *et seq*, *see* DISTRESS
failure to pay, recovery of possession on,
1019, 1056
fair, 1031 *et seq*
certificate of, 1034
determination of amount, 1034 *et seq*
registration, 1032
legal necessity in lease, 441
no protected tenancy without, 983
payment excessively in advance,
prohibition, 1039
register, 1031
restriction, *see* RESTRICTION OF
RENTS
public sector housing, in case of, 1051
restricted contract, in case of, 1043
Rent Acts, 961 *et seq*, 990 *et seq*
avoidance, 994
changing ideology of property, 966-970
contracting out of, 991-993
business tenancy, use of, 1002
"company let", 1001-1002
consent order, 993
courts' general approach to "shams",
995-996
evasive devices, 997-1002
"genuine transactions" and "shams"
994-997
identification of "sham", 996-997
licence, 998-1000
manipulations, 1002
options to purchase, 1001
rent-free tenancy coupled with
extortionate hire of furniture, 1000
rent-free tenancy coupled with
obligatory payment to third party,
1000
"rental purchase", 1001
contractual deviations from, 990-1002
contractual exchange of licence for
tenancy, 992-993
decline in private rented sector, 964
distributive justice, 967
evasion, 993-1002
false dichotomies, 967
history, 961-970
judicial concern, revival of, 965
net balance of, 964-965
origins of, 961-966
political influences, 963-964
property, shift in meaning of, 967-968
restriction of right to levy distress, 1039-
1040
return from contract to status, 969
social philosophy, 961-970
social rights of property, 966-967
"status of irremovability", 968-969
unlawful expropriation, 969-970

Rentcharge
extinguishment, 81
legal and equitable, distinguished, 81
meaning, 81
Residential security
forcible eviction, protection against, 954 *et
seq*
harassment, criminal offence, 956
increased emphasis on, 65, 372, 558, 966
matrimonial home, *see* MATRIMONIAL
HOME
mortgagors, of, 887 *et seq*
'new property', as, 13, 372, 558
Rent Act legislation, 966
Restraint of trade, 586
Restricted contract
definition, 1040-1041
express exclusion from scope of, 1041
grounds for possession, 1041 *et seq*
premium, prohibition, 1044
rent restriction, 1043
Restriction of rents, 1031-1038
"fair rent" *see* FAIR RENT
prohibition of unlawful payments by
regulated tenant, *see* PREMIUMS
Restrictive covenant, 138-141, *see also*
COVENANTS; LAND CHARGES
easements distinguished, 634-635
Resulting trust, 244-292
assumption of liability to repay loan of
money, 250
assumption of loan liability by another
beneficiary, 250-253
borrowed moneys, contribution of, 249-250
contribution of qualifying status or
eligibility, 253
contribution to initial deposit or legal
expenses, 253-254
direct contributions to cash price, 249
displacement of presumption, 260-262
gift, 261
legally ineffective relationships, 262
loan, 261-262
domestic endeavour, contribution of, 260
express trust, relationship with, 260
household expenses, contribution to, 256-
259
"common intention" judicial treatment
of, 258-259
response of traditional property lawyer,
257
"referability", requirement of, 257
ideology of, 245-246
joint contributions of money, effect of, 247-
248
mortgage instalments, contribution of, 254-
256
economic reality of instalment mortgage,
254-255
quantification of beneficial interests, 255-
256

Resulting trust—*continued*
referability, requirement of, 256
timing of relevant intention, 254
payment of periodic rent, 259-260
presumption of, 244-248
presumption of advancement, *see*
PRESUMPTION OF
ADVANCEMENT
"purchase money", 248-260
time-frame of relevant intentions, 246
Right to buy
right to purchase reversion, 733 *et seq*
Rights of entry, 82, 490
Rights of way, 660-663
Seal
deed, required in, 222, *see also* DEED
Secure tenancy, 1045-1048
assignment, 1051-1052
definition, 1045-1048
dwelling.house, 1047-1048
dwelling-house "let as separate dwelling",
1048
express exclusion from scope of, 1048
improvements, 1053-1054
landlord condition, 1046
local authority allocation, 1048-1050
maintenance, 1053
possession, protection against, 1055-1058
rent, 1051
repair, 1053, 1054
statutory succession to, 1054-1055
subletting, 1052-1053
tenancy or licence, 1047
tenant condition, 1046-1047
tenant must be "individual", 1046-1047
tenant must occupy dwelling-house as
"only or principal home", 1047
termination, protection against, 1055-1058
terms, 1050-1054
**Security of tenure under Rent Act, 1041-
1043**
discretionary grounds for possession, 1015-
1023
reasonableness of possession order, 1015-
1016
residual discretion of court, 1022-1023
suitable alternative accommodation,
1016-1019
needs and means of tenant, 1017-1019
proximity to place of work, 1017
mandatory grounds for possession, 1023-
1031
Case 11, 1024.1027
Case 12, 1027
Case 19, 1028-1030
protected shorthold, policy of, 1029-
1030
recovery of possession, 1028-1029
overcrowding, 1031
written notice, dispensing with
requirement of, 1027

**Security of tenure under Rent
Act**—*continued*
restricted contracts, and, 1041-1042
applications for registration of
"reasonable rent", 1042
court proceedings, necessity for, 1042
special ground of repossession, 1042
Seisin, 63-65
estate ownership, and, 63
feoffment with "livery of seisin", 63-64
modern importance of, 64-65
common law concept of "property" 64-
65
relativity of title, 64
residential security, protection of, 65
Severance, 296, 317-337
equitable intervention, by, 336-337
facility of, 317-318
law, at, abolition of, 318
merger of interests, by, 337
unlawful killing, and, 332-336
application of constructive trust
principle, 334
Forfeiture Act 1982, 335-336
general rule, 332
homicide as severing event, 333-334
unjust enrichment, 334
Williams v *Hensman* methods, 320-332
act of joint tenant "operating upon his
own share" 321-326
alienation by will, 324
alienation in equity, 323
alienation inter vivos, 321-322
commencement of litigation, 325
court order, 326
declaration of intention, 325
involuntary alienation, 324
mutual agreement, 326-328
mutual conduct, 329-332
examples, 329-331
general nature, 329
limitations on, 331-332
written notice, by, 318-320
advantages, 319
limitations, 319-320
Specific performance
contract for a lease, and, 469-470, 473
exchange of contracts, and, 217
remedy for disrepair in lease, as, 941-942
Squatting
action for possession, remedy by, 757
civil remedies, 755-759
criminal liability, 754-755
fast possession action, 757-759
inchoate rights of squatters, 752-753
relativity of title, 751-752
RSC Ord 113, 757-759
self-help, remedy of, 755-756
summons, remedy by, 757-759
See also ADVERSE POSSESSION,
TRESPASS and TRESPASSER

Statutory protection in the private sector, 961-1044
Statutory succession to tenancies, 1059-1072
familial nexus, definition of, 1064-1072
  artificial, 1069
  changing social perceptions, 1067
  children, relevance of, 1067
  de facto relationship, 1066
  functional approach, 1071-1072
  future developments, 1070-1072
  modern approach, 1068-1069
  moralistic approach, 1066
  "ordinary man" test, 1065
  relationships clearly within ambit of, 1065-1066
  unorthodox social groupings, 1070
  zoning analogy, 1071
member of tenant's family, 1063
number of successions, 1063
operation of, 1062-1063
private sector tenancies, 1062-1072
public sector tenancies, 1059-1062
Statutory tenancy, 1002-1014
compensation for compulsory purchase, right to, 1006
creation, 1002 *et seq*
death, succession on, 1062 *et seq*
destruction of dwelling-house, 1004
distress for rent, restriction of right to levy, 1039-1040
divorce, transmission on, 1004
fair rent, 1031 *et seq*
grounds for possession
  discretionary, 1015 *et seq*
  mandatory, 1023 *et seq*
irrelevance of strict property rules, 1005
nature, 1003 *et seq*
nominal tenant, 1014
non-transferability of statutory tenant's rights, 1004-1005
occupation of dwelling-house as residence, 1007-1014
  animus possidendi, 1009
  animus revertendi, 1009
  continued residence, 1008
  "continuity" problem, 1008-1009
  corpus possessionis, 1008-1009
  family members, by, 1011
  "second home" problem, 1011, 1014
  spouse, by, 1011
quasi-proprietary aspects, 1005-1007
rights and duties binding on third parties, 1006-1007
status of irremovability, 1003-1005
sublettings, right to grant, 1006
temporary absence of tenant, 1010
termination of protected tenancy, after, 1007
trespass, right to sue in, 1005-1006
vicarious residence by members of tenant's family, 1010-1011

Strata titles, 18-20
Australian model, 19-20
"flying freehold", 18-19
Strict settlement, 293-294
avoidance of, 806-808
Bannister, ruling, 804
conveyancing consequences, 805-806
  exercise of tenant for life's dispositive powers, 806
  vesting of legal estate in tenant for life, 805-806
life interests, application to, 804
meaning, 803
Subinfeudation, 57
Sublease
assignment, 462
creation, 463
destroyed by forfeiture of head lease, 507-508, 529
liability for covenants, 528-529, 533-534
Rent Act, and, 971
secure tenancy, of, 1052
without consent, recovery of possession on ground of, 1053
Supplementary benefit
payment of mortgage interest by, 888-889
Support for land, right to, 642-643
Surveys, 205
Survivorship, right of, 296-301
Tenancy, 427-533, *see also* LEASE
at sufferance, 431
at will, 430-431
breach of landlord's repairing covenants, 939-945
  damages, 939-941
  equitable set.off, 943
  right of recoupment from future rent, 942
  self-help, remedies of, 942-944
  specific performance, order for, 941-942
  statutory "right to repair", 944
caveat emptor, 902-903
creation, 464-466
environmental quality, 901-945
essential elements, 427 *et seq*
express exclusions from concept, 457-461
formalities, 464-475
implied condition of fitness for human habitation, 903-907
  content, 904
  limitations, 904
implied contractual duty of care, 907-910
  content, 907-908
  limitations, 909-910
implied exclusions from concept, 454-456
in common, *see* TENANCY IN COMMON
joint, *see* JOINT TENANCY
landlord's liability at common law, 903-916
licence, distinguished from, 443 *et seq*

Tenancy—*continued*
negligence, landlord's liability in, 911-914
defects arising after commencement of tenancy, 911-913
defects existing at commencement of tenancy, 913-914
nuisance, landlord's liability for, 914-915
periodic, 436-438, *see also* LEASE
creation of, 464-465
duration of term, 467
implied, legal quality of, 468
implied, terms of, 467-468
protected, *see* PROTECTED TENANCY
public sector, *see* PUBLIC SECTOR TENANCY and PRIVATE SECTOR TENANCY
quiet enjoyment, 910
Rylands v *Fletcher*, 915-916
service, 438
shorthold, 1028 *et seq*
statute, landlord's liability in, 916-939
control of noise pollution, 926
Defective Premises Act 1972, 923-925
fitness for human habitation, 916-918
Health and Safety at Work Act 1974, 925-926
improvement notice under Housing Act 1985, 931-933
overcrowding, 936-939
repair and maintenance, 918-923
repair notice under Housing Act 1985, 926-931
"state of disrepair", 927
local authority tenancies, 929-931
reasonableness of expenditure, 928-929
"unfit for human habitation", 927-930
"statutory nuisance", 933-936
statutory nuisance, 933-936
definition, 933-934
individual tenant, complaint made by, 935-936
local authority complaint, 934-935
termination, 484-490
types of, 428-431
Tenancy by entireties, 314-316
abortive revival of, 315-316
joint tenancy, conversion into, 315
Tenancy in common, 302-314
improvements, liability for, 311-314
equitable counterclaims, 313-314
in equity, meaning, 302 *et seq*
no right of survivorship, 303
occupation and use, 304-306
profit derived from industry of one tenant in common, 307-308
rent obligations as between tenants in common, 308-311
rents and profits received from stranger, 306-307
repairs, liability for, 311-314
equitable counterclaims, 313-314
trespass and ouster, 304-305
unity of possession, 303-314

Tenant for life
duality of interests, 805
legal estate, powers in relation to, 806
vesting of legal estate in, 805
Tenant's "right to buy", 725-739
Tenures, 55-65
classification, 56-57
doctrine of, 55-58
feudal pyramid, 57-58
free, 56
socage, 56
Statute Quia Emptores, 57-58
subinfuedation, 57
unfree, 56
virtual disappearance of concept, 58
Term of years absolute, 78-79
distinguishing characteristics, 79
Treasure trove, 37-38
compensation for finders, 38
scope, 37
trespasser, rights in relation to, 38
Trees, 25-26
Trespass
co-owner, by, 304-305
criminal, 754-755
landlord, by, 440, 959
tenant's rights in, 430, 440
Trespasser
acquisition of title by, 740 *et seq*
action for possession against, 757
fast possession action against, 757-759
right to eject, 755
summons for possession against, 757-759
treasure trove, rights in relation to, 38
Trust, 39-54, 233-292
active, 44-45
ascertainment of beneficial ownership, 233-235
bare, 44
cestui que trust, interest of, 49-54
fluctuating boundary between rights in rem and in personam, 50
nature of beneficial right, 51-54
rights in personam, 49
rights in rem, 49-50
classification, 234
constructive, *see* CONSTRUCTIVE TRUST
definition, 39
express *see* EXPRESS TRUST
function of, 40
historical significance, 44
implied, *see* IMPLIED TRUST
law and equity, relationship between, 41-42
conflict between jurisdictions, 41-42
development of jurisdiction of equity, 41
differences between remedies, 42
form and substance, distinction between, 41
medieval "use", 42-44
origin, 42-45
protective, 44